S0-ADH-552

THE COPELAND READER

AN ANTHOLOGY OF ENGLISH POETRY AND PROSE

CHOSEN AND EDITED
WITH AN INTRODUCTION BY

CHARLES TOWNSEND COPELAND

BOYLSTON PROFESSOR OF
RHETORIC AND ORATORY IN HARVARD UNIVERSITY

CHARLES SCRIBNER'S SONS

NEW YORK LONDON

MCMXXVI

Printed in the United States of America

To Mrs. Swan

MY OLDEST AND MY YOUNGEST FRIEND

WITH GREAT REGARD

ACKNOWLEDGMENTS

For the use of the copyrighted material in The Copeland Reader, all rights in which are reserved by the holders of the copyrights, permission has been obtained from the following publishers and authors:

Boni & Liveright, Inc.: "And in the Hanging Gardens" from "Priapus and the Pool" by Conrad Aiken; "An Occurrence at Owl Creek Bridge" from "In the Midst of Life" and "The Damned Thing" from "Can Such Things Be?" by Ambrose Bierce. Copyright 1918, 1925, by Boni & Liveright, Inc.

Dodd, Mead & Company: "The Great Lover" and "The Soldier" from "Poems" by Rupert Brooke; "Ethandune: The Last Charge" from "The Ballad of the White Horse" by Gilbert Keith Chesterton; "The Roman Road" and "The Burglars" from "The Golden Age" by Kenneth Grahame; "Madeline of the Movies" from "Further Foolishness" and "My Financial Career" from "Literary Lapses" by Stephen Leacock; "Wordsworth's Grave" from "Poems" by William Watson. Copyright 1892, 1893, 1911, 1916, by Dodd, Mead & Company.

Doubleday Page & Company: "Youth" by Joseph Conrad; "A Municipal Record" from "Strictly Business," "Calloway's Code" from "Whirligigs," "The Gift of the Magi" and "Memoirs of a Yellow Dog" from "The Four Million," "Roads of Destiny," and "Thimble, Thimble" from "Options," by O. Henry; "The Bell Buoy," "Chant-Pagan," "The 'Eathen," "The Last Chantey," "Mandalay" and "The Truce of the Bear" from "Rudyard Kipling's Verse, Inclusive Edition, 1885-1918" by Rudyard Kipling. Copyright 1903, 1906, 1909, 1910, 1911, 1926, by Doubleday Page & Company.

Duffield & Company: Chapter I from "Fern Seed" by Henry Milner Rideout. Copyright 1921 by Duffield & Company.

Harcourt, Brace & Company: "The Fifty-First Dragon" from "Seeing Things at Night" by Heywood Broun; "Into Battle" by Julian Grenfel, from "Some Soldier Poets" collected by Sturge Moore. Copyright 1920, 1921 by Harcourt, Brace & Company.

Harper & Brothers: "Wanted: an Income Taximeter" by Harper's Magazine, by Frederick Lewis Allen; Chapter I from "The Mayor of Casterbridge," and "The Darkling Thrush" from "Poems," by Thomas Hardy; "The Philosophy of Ceilings" from Harper's Magazine, by David Watson McCord; "A Daring Deed" and "A Pilot's Needs" from "Life on the Mississippi," "The Yankee's Fight with the Knights" from "A Connecticut Yankee at the Court of King Arthur," and "The Notorious Jumping Frog of Calaveras County," by Mark Twain; "A Village Singer," "A Kitchen Colonel" and "The Revolt of 'Mother'," from "A New England Nun and Other Stories" by Mary E. Wilkins Freeman. Copyright 1883, 1886, 1889, 1920, 1926 by Harper & Brothers.

Henry Holt & Company: "Christmas Afternoon" from "Of All things" by Robert Charles Benchley; "After Apple-Picking," "The Runaway" and "The Wood-Pile" from "North of Boston" by Robert Frost; "The Listeners," "The Sleeper" and "Winter Dusk" from "The Listeners" by Walter de la Mare. Copyright 1915, 1916, 1921 by Henry Holt & Company.

Houghton Mifflin Company: "Sargent's Portrait of Edwin Booth at 'The Players'" and "An Ode on the Unveiling of the Shaw Memorial on Boston Common" from "Poems" by Thomas Bailey Aldrich; "The Army of France" from "Zut and

Other Parisians" by Guy Wetmore Carryl; "Miggles," "Tennessee's Partner," "The Luck of Roaring Camp" and "The Outcasts of Poker Flat" from "The Luck of Roaring Camp and Other Tales" by Francis Bret Harte; "My Last Walk with the Schoolmistress" from "The Autocrat of the Breakfast Table," and "The Broomstick Train," "The Chambered Nautilus," and "The Last Leaf," from "Poetical Works" by Oliver Wendell Holmes; "The Town Poor" and "A Winter Courtship" by Sara Orne Jewett; "The High Woods" from "Admiral's Light" by Henry Milner Rideout. Copyright 1870, 1885, 1903, 1907, 1925 by Houghton Mifflin Company.

Alfred A. Knopf, Inc.: "The Burial in England" and "Gates of Damascus" from "Poems" by James Elroy Flecker.

Little, Brown & Company: "Harvard College in the War" from "Speeches" by Oliver Wendell Holmes II; "The Known Soldier," "The Sailor-Man" and "Spring on the Land" from "The Known Soldier" by Mark Anthony De Wolfe Howe. Copyright 1913 by Little, Brown & Company.

The Macmillan Company: "An Old Woman of the Roads" from "Wild Earth" by Padraic Colum; "Devil's Edge," "Flannan Isle" and "The Hare" from "Poems" by Wilfrid Wilson Gibson; "Eve" and "Time, you Old Gipsy Man" from "Poems" by Ralph Hodgson; "The Western Islands" from "A Mainsail Haul," "Cargoes" and "O little self, within whose smallness lies" from "Collected Poems," by John Masefield; "Old King Cole" from "Poems" by Edwin Arlington Robinson; "The Snare" from "Poems" by James Stephens; "Immortality" from "The Seven Ages of Washington" and "Lee's Surrender" from "Ulysses S. Grant" by Owen Wister; "The Lake Isle of Innisfree" from "Poems" and a part of the play: "Cathleen ni Hoolihan" by William Butler Yeats. Copyright 1900, 1905, 1907, 1913, 1916, 1917, 1921, 1922, by The Macmillan Company.

The Modern Library, Inc.: Chapter I from "American Literature" by John Macy. Copyright 1918 by The Modern Library, Inc.

The Neale Publishing Company: "An Occurrence at Owl Creek Bridge" from "In the Midst of Life" and "The Damned Thing" from "Can Such Things Be?" by Ambrose Bierce. Copyright 19[illegible]9 by The Neale Publishing Company.

G. P. Putnam's Sons: "Bernhardt" from "Enchanted Aisles" by Alexander Woollcott. Copyright 1924 by G. P. Putnam's Sons.

Small, Maynard & Company: "Mr. Booth off the Stage" from "Edwin Booth" by Charles Townsend Copeland; "On New Years' Resolutions," and "Rudyard Kipling" from "Mr. Dooley in the Hearts of His Countrymen" by Finley Peter Dunne. Copyright 1899, 190[illegible] by Small, Maynard & Company.

The Viking Press: "I'm a Fool" from "Horses and Men" by Sherwood Anderson. Copyright 1923 by The Viking Press.

William Stanley Braithwaite: "Sandy Star" and "Twenty Stars to Match His Face."

Mark Anthony De Wolfe Howe: "The Known Soldier," "The Sailor-Man" and "Spring on the Land" from "The Known Soldier."

Rudyard Kipling: "The Bell Buoy," "Chant-Pagan," "The 'Eathen," "The Last Chantey," "Mandalay," and "The Truce of the Bear" from "Rudyard Kipling's Verse, Inclusive Edition, 1885-1918." Copyright 1891, 1892, 1893, 1894, 1895, 1896, 1897, 1899, 1900, 1901, 1902, 1903, 1904, 1905, 1906, 1907, 1909, 1910, 1911, 1912, 1913, 1914, 1915, 1916, 1917, 1918, 1919 by Rudyard Kipling.

Gretchen Warren: "The Garden."

INTRODUCTION

The title of this anthology to a great degree expresses its composition and purpose. Wide as is its range, the selection includes only what I have read aloud during thirty-four years of teaching, lecturing, and reading.

Many of the pieces I have used with classes and audiences in Harvard University and Radcliffe College, many in excursions to other colleges and to schools, many with a surprising variety of clubs and societies,—chief among them the Harvard Club of New York, which for twenty-one years has made me thrice welcome and thrice grateful. I remember with particular pleasure two visits, professional and social, to Bowdoin College, the best college in my own state, one of the few best in all the states. My own bright and beautiful town, flouting the proverb, has often encouraged native talent to do its best. As for Christmas Eve, it won't seem like itself if Mrs. Lowell stops allowing me to bring my book, to add a bit to genial, truly hospitable parties. Each year these parties, for a "two hours traffic," make crowds of young men forget that they are away from home and kin.

As to many good schools, as to groups, coteries, the patient family circle, and single victims, all these must wait for their places in a big book of recollections and opinions, promised and some day to be written.

I shall soon take a year off, and after a rest, and with more leisure, I know I shall have the wish and I think I shall have the energy to write reminiscences. Let me set down here one memory of a single victim,—exquisite poet, renowned wit, and best of all talkers. I had been reading to him certain of his own poems when suddenly he exclaimed: "Come, Copeland, give us some of that fool woman's poetry." My friend used the word poetry with full intention, for much as he detested the lady's rhymes and the lack of them, not all his conservatism kept him from recognizing her genius. Why, by the way, did this wise American woman speak in a letter published many years after her death, of *red* as the most frequent color in New England wild flowers? How about yellow? Or even pink?

I had intended, following the good example of the editors of "The Golden Treasury," "The Golden Treasury of Modern Lyrics," and indeed of most anthologists, to make my introduction or preface very brief and purely explanatory. According to this intention it remains only to be stated that, although I do not always read the best literature—audiences are great choosers—I almost never, for any audience, choose either verse or prose that is not literature. So that, however the collection may be lacking in method, it will seldom be found to lack quality.

With this explanation I had thought to be done. But my invaluable colleague, Dr. Hood, my publisher, Mr. Maxwell Perkins of Scribners, and other friends whose advice is not to be gainsaid, have suggested that certain unpublished addresses and essays of mine would be welcome to many former students who remember them, and especially welcome to teachers. Although I have been cherishing these papers to make a volume, with additions, I gladly offer here some of the briefer and more appropriate. Teachers may like to use such material as I constantly use it, to introduce, explain, and praise authors from whom I am about to read.

"Bacon as an Essayist" was read at the Boston Public Library in observance of the three-hundred-and-fiftieth anniversary of the birth of Lord Bacon. Professor R. B. Perry, I remember, on "Bacon as a Philosopher," and Professor R. B. Merriman on "Bacon as an Historian," were among my fellow speakers and readers on a curiously interesting occasion. "Not 'Poor Charles Lamb'" is a fragment from an address in aid of the Radcliffe Fund three years ago. "Hawthorne's Inheritance and His Art" is a part of an anniversary discourse at Concord. "Dickens: His Best Book?" was written for the Harvard Club of New York. "Tennyson and Browning as Religious Poets" is taken from a college lecture, spoken, not written. "As to Margaret Ogilvy" is a bit from a lecture on Sir James Barrie to the Harvard Summer School. Here follow these addresses and other papers, in the order named.

BACON AS AN ESSAYIST

In Bacon's Essay, "Of Discourse," one of the brief original ten, printed in 1597, the author says: "To use too many circumstances ere one come to the matter, is wearisome; to use none at all is blunt." When a ten-minute speech is the matter in hand, one must be blunt. And so I abruptly inform the few unlettered persons in this great company that Bacon's Essays, like the lion in "A Midsummer Night's Dream," are not what they call themselves. They are not essays at all, in our acceptation of the word. The modern essay, from Addison to Stevenson, derives from Montaigne; the Baconian essay derives from the epigrammatic aphorism of antiquity. "The Tatler" and all its successors, even to this latest day, conform in general to Dr. Johnson's definition,—"A loose sally of the mind; an irregular, indigested piece." So, wherever and whenever we encounter the typical essayist, he is found to be a tatler, a spectator, a rambler, a lounger, and, in the best sense, a citizen of the world. But Bacon's intention, so richly fulfilled, was "to write certain brief notes, set down rather significantly than curiously, which I have called Essays; the word is late, but the thing is ancient. For Seneca's Epistles to Lucilius, if one mark them well, are but Essays,—that is, dispersed Meditations."

What Bacon intended, that he did. The final result is the wisest book of its size in the world, in its form much closer kin to Pascal than to Montaigne. By it and it alone is Bacon, mighty philosopher and man of science though he was, a part of existing literature. Whatever he may mean to scholars and men of letters, to the general mind of man he is bound up in this one weighty little volume. "Significantly" set down, indeed, are those rounded thoughts, these close-set maxims,—significantly, and far more "curiously" (that is, carefully) than the author was willing to admit. *Curiosa felicitas,* in truth, is the sign manual of Bacon's Essays, as it is of almost every enduring masterpiece in any art. I do not mean that Bacon's style is external, or niggling, or precious. No, it is the terse finality of a determination to say the thing he meant, and none other, in the fewest, most precise, and most expressive words. Nor is rhetorical intention absent. Bacon was too much the orator celebrated by Ben Jonson not to have his audience in mind; and even a tyro can see that his beginnings, to speak of those alone, were intended to waylay and grip the reader. "Revenge is a kind of wild justice," "men fear death as children fear to go in the dark," "he that hath wife and children hath given hostages to fortune,"—these and at least a dozen other openings of essays are famous wherever English is spoken. They deserve their fame. Can any man believe that they came by chance?

Thus arresting attention in the sixteenth century, Bacon holds it in the twentieth. That is why you and I are here tonight. The little book is still current. We quote from it, not always knowing whom we quote. And many a golden phrase of Bacon's coinage still rings and shines in our dull, common speech.

How much the priceless volume contains! How much it lacks! There is no moral enthusiasm in the Essays, no passion or emotion of any kind. No laughter; no tears. None of the humor of the age Bacon lived in; none of its strongly marked melancholy. In Bacon's essays there is no imagination, and no religion save that of formal reverence. He quotes scripture for his purpose, to be sure, with all the skill attributed to a certain powerful personage. And yet his purpose is not of hell any more than it is of heaven. His purpose and his teaching are of this immediate world. Although Bacon has been truly called Machiavellian, he is without the diabolism of Machiavelli. But in reading the Essays we never feel that "God is come into the camp."

Yet how much the great little book contains! The keenest wit, which is often more than wit, keeps us frequently from noting the absence of humor. Better for his aim than the imagination that the essayist lacks, is the inexhaustible fancy that wings his meaning with unforgetable analogies and startling contrasts, drawn often from the life that every man knows. Cool, tolerant, loving nature—especially in Gardens—admiring and envying youth, almost pitying age, searching his own time and the whole past for examples, Bacon urges his seeing mind among the motives, and hopes, and fears of men, with a triumphant skill that makes us suspect him of white magic. Black magic he deals in only at such half-repented moments as when, for extreme exigencies, he excuses simulation. Dissimulation is for him a virtue.

A thinker, Bacon is also the occasion of thought in others. And although the remark has probably been made—I should give you the authority if I knew it—I should like, in closing, to remind you that for most of us, only two men equal Bacon as breeders of thought. These two are Socrates and Emerson. Far nobler than Bacon, the essayist, they are less acute and not more homely or plain. His worldliness is a complement to their other-worldliness. The dignity of his manner is an education for any world. It is a piece of good fortune for ours that he still lives and teaches.

NOT "POOR CHARLES LAMB."

Carlyle speaks of Lamb's "proclivity to gin." People used to try to get away from it, smooth it over. It is wiser now to admit not only that he drank gin but a great many other things, and that he drank too much. Therefore many persons refer to him as "Poor Charles Lamb." Call Byron poor, if you will, who ruined his own happiness and that of many other people; call Keats poor, who died of consumption before he could do what his genius meant him to do; call Coleridge poor, stupefied and befogged as he was with opium, content to live on charity and have his family supported by his friends; but never call Lamb poor. To begin with, he saved two thousand pounds out of his small salary and innumerable benevolences, to take care of his sister after he should be gone. He helped everybody about him. Fielding's earliest biographer says that Fielding's table was always open to those who had been his friends in youth and had impaired their fortunes. Lamb's table during the later years in the Inner Temple and afterwards in other lodgings, was open to those who had impaired their fortunes, whether or not they had been his friends in youth.

He allowed fifty pounds a year for years to an old schoolmistress of his; he helped not only with money, of which he had little, but with care and thought and painstaking, of which you may find a hundred traces in his letters. You won't find in his letters more than necessary mention of the money he gave and lent. Therefore not poor Charles Lamb, but rich Charles Lamb, saint Charles Lamb, as Thackeray called him, and none the less a saint upon earth because he could not help drinking too much. The failing never kept him from his life-long duty. We may be sorry for it. We must be endlessly sorry because it grieved him and his sister for years. But to blame him were absurd; to pity were profane. Lamb himself resented even a hint of patronage. Coleridge called him "gentle-hearted," in print. Lamb wrote to him in one of the best passages in all his letters: "Substitute drunken-dog; ragged-head; seld-shaven; odd-eyed; stuttering; or any other epithet which truly and properly belongs to the gentleman in question."

But Lamb was important not merely to the needy. His letters, virtually an autobiography, are a record of great friendships and friendships with great men. The fame of his talk with them will never die. "No one," says Hazlitt, "ever stammered out such fine, piquant, deep, eloquent things in half a dozen half-sentences as he does. His jests scald like tears; and he probes a question with a play upon words."

Moreover, one cannot well condescend to a man who, although he was full of whims and pranks, of melancholy, and wild gaiety, was in essence as sensible as Ben Franklin. And his letters run the whole gamut.

HAWTHORNE'S INHERITANCE AND HIS ART

Honest, hearty, external romance is not for Hawthorne. His heart is not with Nathan Hale, or with Paul Revere on his ride, or with Wolfe taking the Heights of Abraham, and conquering the foe who courted death with the high chivalry of Sidney. Incident is not unimportant with Hawthorne, but it is important chiefly as the outward, bodily sign of the inward and moral drama. And if young readers (and all other readers) of Hawthorne would grasp this cardinal fact of his genius, they would cease demanding from him "action," in the conventional sense, and several other elements, to be noted anon, which, though in themselves admirable and to be desired, the author of "The Scarlet Letter" has not found indispensable to his unique endeavor.

In apparent contradiction to what has just been said, Hawthorne is often spoken of as if he were the historical novelist of New England, annalist-in-ordinary to "the old thirteen." In letter, nothing could be more false: in spirit, nothing more true. All that most of us know of the life of our ancestors resolves itself into a kind of tableau, intermittently present to the inward eye, and moralized by what we remember of "The Scarlet Letter," and "Legends of the Province House," and certain portions of "The House of the Seven Gables." Our not too graphic historians coöperate with the word of mouth, spoken on from generation to generation, to outline a sketch of the bleak past.

A few legends soberly color this sketch. Old portraits, old teaspoons, old chairs, and beautiful old brass candlesticks, document and certify the partial portrait; and even the average young New Englander, incurious of his country's past, is always able to draw aside the curtain from some such latent tableau or series of tableaux as this. He sees a long, narrow, wind-swept strip of land between forest and shore,—between the Indian and the deep sea. If it is muster day in any village of the strip, all the ancestors above sixteen years old are marching about in armor. The officers wear swords, the men carry "match-locks" or ten-foot pikes. If it is town-meeting, the ancestors, clad now in the small-clothes, jerkins, ruffs, and steeple-crown hats of peace, discuss even the least affairs with the patience of their constitutional breeding, and gravely cast the affirmative corn or the negative bean. If it is no day in particular, the young New Englander may look through the leaded panes of a log house and see the ancestor—*his* ancestor, perhaps—reading the Bible aloud, or dozing before a mighty fire, or making ready his guns against the Indian enemy who neither slumbered nor slept. Winter, Sunday, the little fortified meeting-house, and the rote of a few doleful hymns, probably appear often indeed to our contemporary's vision of those strenuous beginnings. If the conception he has, the conception most of us have, of the intellectual and moral life of the people is as grim as the physical conditions under which they thought, prayed, worked, and fought, Hawthorne is probably responsible for it. Those brave, intelligent fanatics—always brave, and always intelligent where superstition was not concerned—were no doubt morbidly sensitive in both religion and morals. The early government of Massachusetts has rightly been called a theocracy. Although the church-members probably felt themselves nearer the Unseen than any like body of modern men except the Scottish Covenanters, yet the gist of all their praying was, in the words of the hymn, "for a closer walk with God."

The truth of this general statement cannot be denied. But it is an imperfect statement, too often left without the obvious and needful supplement. In the Theocracy as such, in the preachings, prayings, and persecutions, we forget other quite as real aspects of these men. We forget them as soldiers and sailors; as law-makers, town-makers, and state-builders; as subjects of James and Charles and Cromwell, and Charles again. We lose sight of the secular man bound up with the consecrated man within the iron ribs of the Puritan. It is as if one should say that Franklin never lived because Jonathan Edwards was so much alive. And Hawthorne is to blame. Innocently, even unconsciously; yet still to blame. Other men have written about Puritans and their descendants; none other with Hawthorne's power, or with a tithe of his imagination.

People forget, too, how seldom that imagination exercises itself with simply historical subjects in dealing with New England life; and, although Hawthorne has unmistakably the historic consciousness, it might better be called the *frisson historique*. For, however he starts with a subject taken from history, in nine cases out of ten he either gives it an eerie twist, or makes it a mere point of departure into conscience-land, where, as an artist, he is forever pondering, in his inherited preoccupation with sin, grim, dusky problems of good and evil. The secular Puritan is nothing to him. The sinning good men, the persecutor and the persecuted, the bewitched, and the hag-ridden, are the Puritans for him. And this controlling bent of Hawthorne's mind, which shows itself first in tales of the early colonial time, still controls it in "The Blithedale Romance" and other stories of later New England life, as well as in "Rappacini's Daughter" and "Transformation."

At first, while Hawthorne was trying his hand at the external, the ethical preoccupation was probably unconscious. In "Mosses from an Old Manse" and in "Blithedale," where he is of course conscious enough of the habitual direction of his art, there are some admirable words of his own that are directly in point. "The Old Apple Dealer"—to be found in the "Mosses"—begins with the following sentence: "The lover of the moral picturesque may sometimes find what he seeks in a character which is nevertheless of too negative a description to be seized upon and represented to the imaginative vision by word painting." The inveterate "lover of the moral picturesque" causes Miles Coverdale to say: "I had never before experienced a mood that so robbed the actual world of its solidity. It nevertheless involved a charm, on which—a devoted epicure of my own emotions—I resolved to pause, and enjoy the moral sillabub until quite dissolved away." Coverdale, whatever his habitual relation to his creator, is evidently Hawthorne during that pause. Hawthorne himself is never more quintessentially Hawthorne than in a passage of the "Italian Note-Books," which, during some comment on the confessional, includes the pregnant remark:—"It must be very tedious to listen, day after day, to the minute and commonplace iniquities of the multitude of penitents, and it cannot be often that these are redeemed by the treasure-trove of a great sin." Hawthorne's provinciality, so far as he was provincial—and in some directions this quality carried him a good way—was important in circumscribing the field of his imagination. It was still more important to a writer whose professional treasure-trove was sin, or rather the sense of sin, that there were few or no outward distractions to beguile him from the main tendency of his genius. Hawthorne's heart was with New England, and his treasure was in the consecrated, Calvinistic part of the Puritan tradition.

But the Puritan, *redivivus,* would have thought this treasure ill-gotten gain, a fortune with a curse on it. The Reverend John Cotton, minister of "New Boston," being asked why in his later days he indulged *nocturnal studies* more than formerly, . . . pleasantly replied, "Because I love to sweeten my mouth with a piece of Calvin before I go to sleep." Now Mr. Cotton, were he still with us, might find many a piece of Calvin in the works of Hawthorne, but so flavored, sauced, and garnished as to be no better than witches' broth in the mouth of a Puritan divine. Mr. Henry James, who first expressed in precise terms the truth about Hawthorne's use of his material, thereby did an immense service to criticism in relieving the world of the impression, on the one hand, that he was the *romancier pessimiste* of Montégut's essay, and of the impression, on the other hand, that he was a kind of Neo-Puritanic teacher, with a moral and a purpose. Nothing in criticism is more subtle, and nothing, I am persuaded, more just, than Mr. James's pages concerning this matter. I risk injustice to him for the pleasure of quoting here a word or two of that remarkable exposition. "Nothing is more curious and interesting," says Mr. James, "than this almost exclusively *imported* character of the sense of sin in Hawthorne's mind; it seems to exist there merely for an artistic or literary purpose. He had ample cognizance of the Puritan conscience; it was his natural heritage; it was reproduced in him; looking into his soul he found it there. But his relation to it was only, as one may say, intellectual: it was not moral and theological. He played with it, and used it as a pigment; he treated it, as the metaphysicians say, objectively." In less dignified language, he found a great lump of Puritan black lead, which, by some process he never explained, arrived upon his palette as the varying hues of fancy. Hawthorne, indeed, was a psychoanalyst ahead of time.

DICKENS: HIS BEST BOOK?

Centenaries do two things, among others. They expose the community—in the case of Dickens a widest commonalty of race and speech—to a good deal of ill-regulated sentiment. And they breed much quiet and refreshing talk among friends. You, I doubt not, in corners of this great house of friendship, have lately been comparing notes about Charles Dickens. When you began to read him, and where; how much you read him now, and with how much pleasure; what are his best books, what even his best book—these are some of the recollections and opinions that engage all of us as the hundredth birthday draws nigh.

Where novelists are concerned, because with lyric poets novelists are the most personal of writers, the question of the best book is likely to be as alluring as it is ultimately futile. If "The Antiquary" and "Guy Mannering" and "The Heart of Midlothian" are to be placed at the head of Scott's list by reason of their sheer creative power, unaided by history, what then becomes of "Old Mortality" and the superbly constructed "Quentin Durward"? And if a man of taste, condemned to a desert island, were allowed to take with him just one Waverley novel, he would scarcely choose "The Abbot," or "Redgauntlet," or "Rob Roy," or even "Waverley." Yet are The Queen of Scots and the Young Chevalier, with all their inalienable charm, to be left behind on the never-to-be-revisited mainland?

Nor are the Janites without excellent divergences. The young and lively always prefer "Pride and Prejudice." As to those who are not so young as they have been, "Emma" is the book for them. A few amateurs of the pensive are all for "Persuasion." I have long since cast my vote for "Emma," and I know I shall never change it. But what a suffrage, that must exclude Elizabeth and Anne!

Thackeray is easy. On "the big four," everyone, I should suppose, is agreed—"Vanity Fair," "Pendennis," "Henry Esmond," and "The Newcomes," in order of composition. "Vanity Fair" is the greatest of the four; "Esmond" the most beautiful. But, with all its beauty and fire, with its English that lives in the memory like music, "Esmond" is yet a tour de force, conditioned by the manners and speech of a day long dead. However inferior in form "Vanity Fair" may be to "Henry Esmond," it yet has method enough to serve its high satirical purpose, and to liberate the characters that work out this purpose in a book whose height Thackeray never reached again.

As to Dickens's achievements, which most concern us just now, there is an extraordinary difference of opinion. There is still a multitude though a waning multitude, that, taking his novels in the gross, thanks its stars for all and each. God rest you merry, gentlemen, let nothing you dismay. A curious remnant, mainly devoid of humor, swear by Dickens's one humorless story, and maintain the primacy of "A Tale of Two Cities." By all academic standards, to be sure, its structure is uncommonly good, and gives it a notable place in that regard. For the rest, "A Tale of Two Cities" seems to most of us, in spite of some fine chapters, a fearsome blend of Carlyle's spirit and Dickens's least lovely mannerisms. Without humor, with few striking characters, this well-ordered tale is one of the author's very few least spontaneous productions. And spontaneity, like humor, is of his essence.

Another little committee, as the French say, are fondly attached to "Great Expectations," the title of which, by the way, like many another of Dickens's titles, is in itself a stroke of genius. The partisans of "Great Expectations" not only laud its construction, in which Dickens was uncommonly successful, but they hold that here the master is more constantly and consistently "real" than in any other of his novels. Well, reality—literal, not symbolic reality—is not Dickens's long suit. And, though the tone of this book is quieter than that of the others, Miss Havisham is of a ghastly artificiality, the melodrama is plentiful and dark and dour, and Joe Gargery and Trabb's boy save the book. Trabb's boy has all the bounce and salience of a social revolution. Joe is a triumph, and the best of all Dickens's workingmen.

To a far larger company, and with far more reason, "Martin Chuzzlewit" leads all the rest. Many of its pages are full of that dæmonic power, that hallucination more vivid than reality, which Dickens exercised in his early prime. And if half of "Chuzzlewit" were equal, or even half equal, to Mrs. Gamp, the great humorist's top achievement in humor, it would be such a book as the world has never seen. "Thou Manningtree ox, with the pudding in thy belly," send Quickly and Doll Tearsheet packing. Gamp is thy true helpmeet. She has not thy forgetive brain, thy wit or thy marvellous humor. All her humor resides in her creator. But she is thy soulmate, thine affinity. Take her, she is thine. Alas for "Chuzzlewit," Mrs. Gamp glorifies and immortalizes only a few of its chapters. Its form is invertebrate, it is choked with impossible characters, its total effect is bewildering.

Two books give "A Tale of Two Cities," "Great Expectations," and "Chuzzlewit" and all the others, a very long lead in popularity. In fact, "The Pickwick Papers" and "David Copperfield" probably divide the suffrages of the vast majority of those that read Dickens. "Copperfield" must always be viewed tenderly. To the degree that it is autobiography, it is enchanting. As with "Pendennis," "The Mill on the Floss," "Redgauntlet"—as always when a great writer looks back on his childhood and youth—there is a golden mist over the early days of Dickens transmuted into those of Copperfield. If only we could have those magical pages, and David, and the Micawbers, without Agnes or Dora—poor things—or Mr. Dick, or Rosa Dartle, or little Em'ly, or so many donkeys on the green! Micawber alone could furnish forth a volume.

You will be perceiving, as the Scotch minister said after eliminating all other fish in favor of the whale—you will be perceiving that "The Pickwick Papers" is the book most after my own heart. In that book Dickens attacks no abuses. There can be nothing but praise for the reforms he so nobly initiated in schools and courts and prisons. But for every reform his art suffered. In "Pickwick" there are no dark emotions, except in the incidental stories, which don't count; no love making, save as burlesque; no wallowing in pathos, and, happily, no plot to speak of. Whenever Dickens made a poor plot it hurt his book; whenever he made a good one it hurt him.

The very era of "Pickwick," "the year one thousand eight hundred and twenty-seven," was one of its good fortunes. Close to us in spirit, it is incredibly far from us in time. As regards the material and mechanical side of life Mr. Pickwick is aeons from us and almost synchronous with Julius Caesar. Railroads not having come to spoil whatever of "Merry England" was left by the Protestant Reformation, Mr. Pickwick moved about the island as Caesar did, with horses and wheels. Compare Carker's frantic railway trip with the flight of the Muggleton coach and you will see that Dickens himself was a man of stage coaches, not a man of railroads. Franklin had played a Yankee Prometheus on the cowshed, but electricity was still mainly confined to lightning rods. You cannot "call up" the Pickwickians at their club, or even telegraph to them. Telepathy is your only hope. Railroads won't bring you to Dingley Dell—there's no station within a thousand miles of it. Nor murder-wagons—"automobiles not allowed on this estate." Write first, and seal your letter (wafers are vulgar); then follow it in the coach, or in a postchaise, or in your own curricle.

In truth, in glad truth, "modern inventions" help us only by contrast to savor "The Pickwick Papers," where these things have no more place than in a fairy-tale. The book is, to be sure, a kind of cockney fairy-tale, strongly dashed with "Don Quixote." Not a few critics have called Mr. Pickwick a middle-class Don Quixote, and Sam Weller a cockney Sancho Panza. Though the comparison is inexact, especially concerning Sam, Mr. Pickwick, nevertheless—like Colonel Newcome, and Parson Adams, and My Uncle Toby, and Sir Roger de Coverley—is of the seed and lineage of the Don. "Quelle composition défectueuse," cried Flaubert, on finishing "Pickwick." Right, Brigadier; but, oddly enough, the defect of the composition is its quality. And so it is, of course, in the far greater work of Cervantes, in "Roderick Random," and in those other picaresque exemplars that young Copperfield-Dickens's father left for him in "the little room."

The naïve plan of "Pickwick" came clearly from the books in the little room. Worked in with it are much coaching and "posting," fantastic comedy, old English fun, broad humor and good humor, happiness and—this above all—the perpetual spirit of youth. The innocence of Mr. Pickwick helps to endear him to us. The least worldly of readers feel that they know a thing or two unknown to Mr. Pickwick. From this book you learn as little of sex as from "Robinson Crusoe" or Emerson's Essays. Without the sense of religion, without poetry, without psychology, without Swiveller and Micawber, and Gamp, "Pickwick" yet prevails by its score of old inns, its happy journeys, its sunlight and hearth-light and what Lamb called "punch-light." In its mirth and youthful jollity a tormented modern may forget Nietzsche, Mr. Bernard Shaw, and Mr. H. G. Wells. On the title-page of "Pickwick" belongs the famous motto for a sun-dial, "Horas non numero nisi serenas."

Gentlemen, the hundredth birthday of Charles Dickens falls on February seventh. If midnight of the sixth find you drinking a tankard of purl to his memory, you will see a brave and genial ghost.

TENNYSON AND BROWNING

AS RELIGIOUS POETS

When one comes to them as religious poets the difference is sharp indeed. Tennyson mirrors his time; he was brought up as a boy in the Church of England, and there is a loving, lingering touch in whatever he writes of the parish church or church-yard, or the rubrics, or any beautiful ceremony or observance,—such a love, almost, as you might imagine the later Romans would have had for all the rites of the temple in the literal truth of which they had ceased to believe. Because Tennyson went so far from the words "Our Father which art in Heaven" as to come to expressing faith in these lines which everyone remembers,—"One far-off divine event, To which the whole creation moves." He often mirrored doubt as to individual existence beyond the grave, but he did for the most part contrive to cling to the belief in it, as to which he made the extraordinary remark more than once that if he did not believe in personal immortality he should commit suicide. And so one has the feeling, as one has in those vehement lines of his against free-thinkers, that if his faith had been more complete, more spontaneous, less checkered by constantly recurring doubt, he would have been less insistent in his statements of it, and less perturbed by any attacks of the atheists and free-thinkers. Towards the end, in his old age, he came into a much more serene and undoubting mood.

How far, however, can we accept the latest utterances of an old man to be characteristic utterances of the man in his strength? The doubting faith of "In Memoriam" seems to me to represent the true Tennyson, the Tennyson for the greater part of his career, far more truly than the lovely lines of "Crossing the Bar," written in the last five years of his life. "And may there be no moaning of the bar, when I put out to sea." At the end he appeared to have a complete faith that there would be no moaning of the bar, and that he should see his Pilot face to face. But there were doubts many and grave in the earlier years, and the middle and later middle years of his career.

Browning, on the other hand, is an out and out personal believer, an exception to the greater number of the able writers of our time. As you would scarcely gather from most of Browning's poetry that there was such a country as England—Italy would appear to be the principal spot on the map in by far the greater part of Browning's poetry—so you would not gather from the greater number of his poems that there had been any such thing in the world as a discovery that had revolutionized human thought, that had turned it upside down as nothing had before since the beginning. These men were born into a world which everybody believed to be six thousand years old,—just about that,—they spent their manhood and died in a world which all persons whether intelligent or not knew, if they cared to know, must have existed for millions of years. They were born when everybody, almost everybody, believed that God made the world in six days, in a world which contemplated no God but a personal God, who dealt in special providences and special penalties, who exercised an intimate supervision over individual affairs; they passed their manhood and died in a world in which the leading intellectual spirits of the day were disposed to find no evidence of personal supervision whatever; a world whose operation was regulated as almost an infinitesimal part of the circling worlds about us. They think, the leading spirits of the time, that this small planet and all others, revolve in obedience to laws that proceed from we know not where or whom. You might read Browning and scarcely surmise what you are constantly reminded of in Tennyson,—all the time you are reminded in Tennyson of what the intellectual life of the time means to him, how it has interested him and disquieted him. And that very same personal feeling of Browning's, the old-fashioned feeling that the matter of life is between a man and God or a woman and God, that very feeling of Browning's keeps him from having much sympathy, or showing any sign of what is Tennyson's chief enthusiasm, that is order, patriotic order, and a patriotism that is ready some day to extend to the parliament of man, the federation of the world. Tennyson everywhere, when he doubts and when he believes, and he believes oftener than he doubts, is forever telling us of eternal process, of sublime order, and of the fact that is to him fact, that God fulfills himself in many ways through the new order as through the old. When his friend dies in early youth, Arthur Hallam, young as he was, Tennyson writes of him:

"The fame is quenched that I foresaw,
The head hath missed an earthly wreath;
I curse not nature, no, nor death;
For nothing is that errs from law."

And of this life and another he writes:

"Eternal process moving on,
From state to state the spirits walk;
And these are but the shattered stalk
Or ruin'd chrysalis of one."

The same enthusiasm for order and obedience to law, and desire for the ultimate well-being of the race is what lifts the ideal dreamer of "Locksley Hall" into such lines as these:

"Not in vain the distance beacons. Forward,
forward let us range,
Let the great world spin forever down the
ringing grooves of change."

"For all we thought and loved and did,
And hoped and suffer'd, is but seed
Of what in them is flower and fruit."

This is the crowning race to be:

"Whereof the man, that with me trod
This planet, was a noble type
Appearing ere the times were ripe,
That friend of mine who lives in God.

That God who ever lives and loves,
One God, one law, one element,
And one far-off divine event,
To which the whole creation moves."

All that is out of Browning; socially dynamic a good deal of his poetry is, if one went literally by it. Tennyson is an optimist, but as you may see, an optimist once removed; that is, the world as Tennyson sees it is very far indeed from pleasing him; the world Browning sees pleases him because the very imperfection delights him as the best earnest and proof that we are to go on and advance, each man for himself, if you please, not the race, but the individual; after his death the imperfection is to be made perfect. And with Browning apparently a conclusive proof of a life to come is that this life must be, for every man, in a way frustrated and imperfect; whereas in Tennyson the hope of immortality is a hope based on the justice, the beneficence of the law which rules it all.

AS TO "MARGARET OGILVY"

Perhaps not every one remembers what Stevenson wrote to Mr. Barrie from Vailima in December, 1892. "There are two of us now," he said, writing of the "Window," "that the Shirra might have patted on the head. And please do not think that when I thus seem to bracket myself with you I am wholly blinded with vanity. Jess is beyond my frontier line; I could not touch her skirt; I have no such glamour on my pen. I am a capable artist, but it begins to look to me as if you were a man of genius."

Whether Scott, the Shirra, would have patted Barrie on the head for "Margaret Ogilvy" must ever remain doubtful. Like Carlyle and like Barrie, he made for himself the discovery never made by most people, and first expressed by Gray in the year 1766, "that in one's whole life one can never have more than a single mother." Yet Scott's deepest testimony to this truth was not discovered till after he was gone. Although all know the passage, still I will read it. What emotion throbs under Lockhart's formal phrase:

> Perhaps the most touching evidence of the lasting tenderness of his early domestic feelings was exhibited to his executors when they opened his repositories in search of his testament the evening after his burial.
>
> On lifting up his desk we found arranged in careful order a series of little objects, which had obviously been placed there so that his eye might rest on them every morning before he began his tasks. These were the old-fashioned boxes that had garnished his mother's toilet, when he, a sickly child, slept in her dressing room—a silver taper stand which the young advocate had bought her with his first five-guinea fee—a row of small packets inscribed with her hand and containing the hair of her off-spring that had died before her—his father's snuff box and etui case—and more things of the like sort recalling the "old familiar faces."

Can "Margaret Ogilvy" say more? Yes, one thing more, at least. We—I mean the public—then first learned explicitly from Mr. Barrie how very poor and lowly had been his beginnings. Most self-made men either qualify—"everybody was poor in those days, you know"—or boast or hide. Barrie—but if you would know how he does it, you must recall or read "Margaret Ogilvy." At first reading one is likely to be shocked at the intimacy of the book, and to think that it never should have been written. At a second reading not only do we know that literature should not have been deprived of a masterpiece, but we realize as from no other volume the whole truth of Gray's famous discovery. Let no one who has not read the strange book be afraid of it. "Margaret Ogilvy" is almost as full of humor as of pathos. And its English is only less beautiful than its lowland Scotch.

So much for set pieces *before* any projected reading. Whatever such pieces may do by way of information and stimulus, all good teachers are aware that what comes *after* the reading is of more importance. Extemporaneous talks, question and answer, free discussion, are of the essence in all such affairs of the class-room, whether literature or composition be concerned. In the case of "The Critic," Sheridan's glorious farce, printed in The Copeland Reader, by the way, I have found that young people are vastly interested in the stage history of the time, old customs of the theatre, players of the early casts, Sheridan's other plays, and—of course—Sheridan himself. Best of all, after a few needful explanations, they are delighted and, as Lamb would say, much arrided by the trenchant, never-failing wit of the farce. Except for the inevitable, disinherited few that have no sense of humor, I have always found that young men and women understand and fully enjoy the splendid ridicule so cunningly directed against plays, play-actors, playwrights, stage-managers, critics, and audiences. They also understand the audacious digs at Shakespeare in the madness of Tilburina and the last combat of Don Ferolo Whiskerandos. In view of "The Critic" and all its implications, it is almost incredible yet after all natural enough that, in his own theatrical practice, Sheridan himself should have been an arch-conservative. Nothing shows his proverbial timidity better than the well-worn anecdote of Mrs. Siddons, Sheridan, and the sleep-walking scene. In that incident, the lady prevailed and was proved to be right, but most often Sheridan was "monstrous witty" yet also wise in his generation. Mrs. Fiske's highly original (and triumphant) conception of Mrs. Malaprop would have given Sheridan a very bad turn. Who can say how the public of his day would have decided?

Similarly introduced, Shakespeare will always go with any class or audience that is worth reading to. He that would precipitate a discussion in his class-room has only to read, after illuminating preface, the account of the death of Falstaff, from "King Henry V," and follow it with the death of Socrates from the "Phaedo." I have chosen both scenes for the collection, though the chronological order keeps them far apart. Dr. Furness, who was a capital reader, gave the whole Falstaff scene as broad farce, in which I venture to think he was almost entirely wrong. But here beginneth new matter—for the class-room. Certain portions of the Bible provoke fine differences of opinion. A few among many such I have found to be the Book of Ruth, the Book of Ecclesiastes, the story of the Prodigal Son, the story of Naaman and Elisha and Gehazi. "Are not Abana and Pharpar, rivers of Damascus, better than all the waters of Israel? May I not wash in them and be clean?"

Here is a good place to say that I should not like to have the Bible as much dramatized in church as I incline to dramatize it. The clergy should, however, be audible. Not all of them are. The clergy should give us the meaning. Not all of them do. The theological schools send out many of them not even emphasizing the negative in the Ten Commandments. How then can the laity be expected to be good?

But let us go back to College. Much as I have read with comment, I have favored and often practised a method praised in a recent article in the Boston *Herald*. "The head of the English department in a state university," this editorial piece begins, "recently said in discussing his work that he rated no influence that he was able to bring to bear upon students higher than that of reading aloud to them masterpieces, and accompanying the exercise with a minimum of critical discussion. . . . A member of the Yale faculty, whose department is not English, feels that one of the best things that he can do for selected groups of students is to stir their interest and appreciation of great literature in evenings of reading aloud and free discussion." These words bring to the minds of old Harvard men Child and the ballads, Palmer and his own translation of Homer. The few persons privileged to hear Mr. Palmer read Shelley and other modern verse today note with delight that the charm and the spell are quite what they so famously were in that distant time. There never sounded in the voices of those great professors the didactic, almost hectoring tone that often ruins the effect of literature made audible.

To conclude, without sequence but very heartily, Harvard undergraduates have become even better to teach and to read to in the last few years,—the years during which the tutorial system has begun to make itself felt. And further, in conclusion, among my few best audiences for more than a generation have been those assembled at Radcliffe College, in Sever Hall, at the Harvard Union, and at the Harvard clubs of Chicago and Boston. But all my audiences are good, and therefore I sha'n't blame them when they begin to give me a good-natured signal to stop lecturing and talking and reading.

C. T. Copeland.

Cambridge,
October, 1926.

CONTENTS

CONTENTS

III. AMERICAN SELECTIONS

CONTENTS

THE COPELAND READER

THE COPELAND READER

I. TRANSLATIONS

From The Bible (King James Version)

Judges, IV; V, 19-31

IV

And the children of Israel again did evil in the sight of the Lord,
when Ehud was dead.
2 And the Lord sold them into the hand of Jabin king of Canaan,
that reigned in Hazor; the captain of whose host *was* Sisera, which
dwelt in Harosheth of the Gentiles.
3 And the children of Israel cried unto the Lord; for he had nine
hundred chariots of iron; and twenty years he mightily oppressed the
children of Israel.
4 And Deborah a prophetess, the wife of Lapidoth, she judged Israel
at that time.
5 And she dwelt under the palm tree of Deborah, between Ramah
and Bethel in mount Ephraim; and the children of Israel came up to
her for judgment.
6 And she sent and called Barak, the son of Abinoam, out of
Kedesh-naphtali, and said unto him, Hath not the Lord God of Israel
commanded, *saying,* Go, and draw toward mount Tabor, and take with
thee ten thousand men of the children of Naphtali and of the children of
Zebulun?
7 And I will draw unto thee, to the river Kishon, Sisera, the captain
of Jabin's army, with his chariots and his multitude; and I will deliver
him into thine hand.
8 And Barak said unto her, If thou wilt go with me, then I will go;
but if thou wilt not go with me, *then* I will not go.
9 And she said, I will surely go with thee: notwithstanding the
journey that thou takest shall not be for thine honour; for the Lord

shall sell Sisera into the hand of a woman. And Deborah arose, and
went with Barak to Kedesh.

10 And Barak called Zebulun and Naphtali to Kedesh; and he went
up with ten thousand men at his feet: and Deborah went up with him.

11 Now Heber the Kenite, *which was* of the children of Hobab, the
father in law of Moses, had severed himself from the Kenites, and
pitched his tent unto the plain of Zaanaim, which *is* by Kedesh.

12 And they shewed Sisera that Barak the son of Abinoam was gone
up to mount Tabor.

13 And Sisera gathered together all his chariots, *even* nine hundred
chariots of iron, and all the people that *were* with him, from Harosheth
of the Gentiles unto the river of Kishon.

14 And Deborah said unto Barak, Up; for this *is* the day in which
the LORD hath delivered Sisera into thine hand: is not the LORD gone
out before thee? So Barak went down from mount Tabor, and ten
thousand men after him.

15 And the LORD discomfited Sisera, and all *his* chariots, and all *his*
host, with the edge of the sword, before Barak; so that Sisera lighted
down off *his* chariot, and fled away on his feet.

16 But Barak pursued after the chariots, and after the host, unto
Harosheth of the Gentiles: and all the host of Sisera fell upon the edge
of the sword; *and* there was not a man left.

17 Howbeit, Sisera fled away on his feet to the tent of Jael the wife
of Heber the Kenite: for *there was* peace between Jabin the king of
Hazor and the house of Heber the Kenite.

18 And Jael went out to meet Sisera, and said unto him, Turn in,
my lord, turn in to me; fear not: and when he had turned in unto her
into the tent, she covered him with a mantle.

19 And he said unto her, Give me, I pray thee, a little water to drink;
for I am thirsty: and she opened a bottle of milk, and gave him drink,
and covered him.

20 Again he said unto her, Stand in the door of the tent, and it shall
be, when any man doth come and inquire of thee, and say, Is there any
man here? that thou shalt say, No.

21 Then Jael, Heber's wife, took a nail of the tent, and took an
hammer in her hand, and went softly unto him, and smote the nail into
his temples, and fastened it into the ground; for he was fast asleep, and
weary: so he died.

22 And, behold, as Barak pursued Sisera, Jael came out to meet
him, and said unto him, Come, and I will shew thee the man whom thou

seekest. And when he came into her *tent,* behold, Sisera lay dead, and the nail *was* in his temples.

23 So God subdued on that day Jabin the king of Canaan before the children of Israel.

24 And the hand of the children of Israel prospered, and prevailed against Jabin the king of Canaan, until they had destroyed Jabin king of Canaan.

V

19 The kings came *and* fought; then fought the kings of Canaan in Taanach by the waters of Megiddo; they took no gain of money.

20 They fought from heaven; the stars in their courses fought against Sisera.

21 The river of Kishon swept them away, that ancient river, the river Kishon. O my soul, thou hast trodden down strength.

22 Then were the horsehoofs broken by the means of the pransings, the pransings of their mighty ones.

23 Curse ye Meroz, said the angel of the LORD; curse ye bitterly the inhabitants thereof; because they came not to the help of the LORD, to the help of the LORD against the mighty.

24 Blessed above women shall Jael the wife of Heber the Kenite be; blessed shall she be above women in the tent.

25 He asked water, *and* she gave *him* milk; she brought forth butter in a lordly dish.

26 She put her hand to the nail, and her right hand to the workmen's hammer; and with the hammer she smote Sisera; she smote off his head, when she had pierced and stricken through his temples.

27 At her feet he bowed, he fell, he lay down: at her feet he bowed, he fell; where he bowed there he fell down dead.

28 The mother of Sisera looked out at a window, and cried through the lattice, Why is his chariot *so* long in coming? why tarry the wheels of his chariots?

29 Her wise ladies answered her, yea, she returned answer to herself.

30 Have they not sped? have they *not* divided the prey; to every man a damsel *or* two? to Sisera a prey of divers colours, a prey of divers colours of needlework, of divers colours of needlework on both sides, *meet* for the necks of *them that take* the spoil?

31 So let all thine enemies perish, O LORD: but *let* them that love him *be* as the sun when he goeth forth in his might. And the land had rest forty years.

Ruth

I

Now it came to pass, in the days when the judges ruled, that there
was a famine in the land. And a certain man of Beth-lehem-judah went
to sojourn in the country of Moab, he, and his wife, and his two sons.

2 And the name of the man *was* Elimelech, and the name of his
wife Naomi, and the name of his two sons, Mahlon and Chilion, Ephra-
thites of Beth-lehem-judah. And they came into the country of Moab,
and continued there.

3 And Elimelech, Naomi's husband, died; and she was left, and her
two sons.

4 And they took them wives of the women of Moab; the name of
the one *was* Orpah, and the name of the other Ruth: and they dwelled
there about ten years.

5 And Mahlon and Chilion died also both of them; and the woman
was left of her two sons and her husband.

6 Then she arose, with her daughters in law, that she might return
from the country of Moab: for she had heard in the country of Moab
how that the LORD had visited his people in giving them bread.

7 Wherefore she went forth out of the place where she was, and her
two daughters in law with her: and they went on the way to return unto
the land of Judah.

8 And Naomi said unto her two daughters in law, Go, return each to
her mother's house: the LORD deal kindly with you, as ye have dealt with
the dead, and with me.

9 The LORD grant you that ye may find rest, each *of you* in the house
of her husband. Then she kissed them; and they lifted up their voice,
and wept.

10 And they said unto her, Surely we will return with thee unto thy
people.

11 And Naomi said, Turn again, my daughters, why will ye go with
me? *are* there yet *any more* sons in my womb, that they may be your
husbands?

12 Turn again, my daughters, go *your way;* for I am too old to
have an husband. If I should say, I have hope, *if* I should have an
husband also to night, and should also bear sons;

13 Would ye tarry for them till they were grown? would ye stay
for them from having husbands? nay, my daughters; for it grieveth me
much, for your sakes, that the hand of the LORD is gone out against me.

14 And they lifted up their voice, and wept again: and Orpah kissed
her mother in law, but Ruth clave unto her.
15 And she said, Behold, thy sister in law is gone back unto her
people, and unto her gods; return thou after thy sister in law.
16 And Ruth said, Entreat me not to leave thee, *or* to return from
following after thee: for whither thou goest, I will go; and where thou
lodgest, I will lodge: thy people *shall be* my people, and thy God my God:
17 Where thou diest will I die, and there will I be buried: the LORD
do so to me, and more also, *if ought* but death part thee and me.
18 When she saw that she was stedfastly minded to go with her,
then she left speaking unto her.
19 So they two went until they came to Beth-lehem. And it came
to pass, when they were come to Beth-lehem, that all the city was moved
about them, and they said, *Is* this Naomi?
20 And she said unto them, Call me not Naomi, call me Mara: for
the Almighty hath dealt very bitterly with me.
21 I went out full, and the LORD hath brought me home again
empty: why *then* call ye me Naomi, seeing the LORD hath testified against
me, and the Almighty hath afflicted me?
22 So Naomi returned, and Ruth the Moabitess, her daughter in
law, with her, which returned out of the country of Moab: and they
came to Beth-lehem in the beginning of barley harvest.

II

AND Naomi had a kinsman of her husband's, a mighty man of wealth
of the family of Elimelech; and his name *was* Boaz.
2 And Ruth the Moabitess said unto Naomi, Let me now go to the
field, and glean ears of corn after *him* in whose sight I shall find grace.
And she said unto her, Go, my daughter.
3 And she went, and came, and gleaned in the field after the reapers:
and her hap was to light on a part of the field *belonging* unto Boaz, who
was of the kindred of Elimelech.
4 And, behold, Boaz came from Beth-lehem, and said unto the reapers, The LORD *be* with you. And they answered him, The LORD bless
thee.
5 Then said Boaz unto his servant that was set over the reapers,
Whose damsel *is* this?
6 And the servant that was set over the reapers answered and said,
It *is* the Moabitish damsel that came back with Naomi out of the country
of Moab:

7 And she said, I pray you, let me glean and gather after the reapers
among the sheaves: so she came, and hath continued even from the morning until now, that she tarried a little in the house.

8 Then said Boaz unto Ruth, Hearest thou not, my daughter? Go
not to glean in another field, neither go from hence, but abide here fast
by my maidens:

9 *Let* thine eyes *be* on the field that they do reap, and go thou after
them: have I not charged the young men that they shall not touch thee?
and when thou art athirst, go unto the vessels, and drink of *that* which
the young men have drawn.

10 Then she fell on her face, and bowed herself to the ground, and
said unto him, Why have I found grace in thine eyes, that thou shouldest
take knowledge of me, seeing I *am* a stranger?

11 And Boaz answered and said unto her, It hath fully been shewed
me all that thou hast done unto thy mother in law since the death of thine
husband; and *how* thou hast left thy father and thy mother, and the land
of thy nativity, and art come unto a people which thou knewest not
heretofore.

12 The LORD recompense thy work, and a full reward be given thee
of the LORD God of Israel, under whose wings thou art come to trust.

13 Then she said, Let me find favour in thy sight, my lord; for that
thou hast comforted me, and for that thou hast spoken friendly unto
thine handmaid, though I be not like unto one of thine handmaidens.

14 And Boaz said unto her, At mealtime come thou hither, and eat
of the bread, and dip thy morsel in the vinegar. And she sat beside the
reapers: and he reached her parched *corn,* and she did eat, and was
sufficed, and left.

15 And when she was risen up to glean, Boaz commanded his young
men, saying, Let her glean even among the sheaves, and reproach her not:

16 And let fall also *some* of the handfuls of purpose for her, and
leave *them,* that she may glean *them,* and rebuke her not.

17 So she gleaned in the field until even, and beat out that she had
gleaned: and it was about an ephah of barley.

18 And she took *it* up, and went into the city; and her mother in law
saw what she had gleaned; and she brought forth, and gave to her that
she had reserved after she was sufficed.

19 And her mother in law said unto her, Where hast thou gleaned to
day? and where wroughtest thou? blessed be he that did take knowledge
of thee. And she shewed her mother in law with whom she had wrought,
and said, The man's name with whom I wrought to day *is* Boaz.

20 And Naomi said unto her daughter in law, Blessed *be* he of the

LORD, who hath not left off his kindness to the living and to the dead. And Naomi said unto her, The man *is* near of kin unto us, one of our next kinsmen.

21 And Ruth the Moabitess said, He said unto me also, Thou shalt keep fast by my young men, until they have ended all my harvest.

22 And Naomi said unto Ruth her daughter in law, *It is* good, my daughter, that thou go out with his maidens, that they meet thee not in any other field.

23 So she kept fast by the maidens of Boaz to glean unto the end of barley harvest, and of wheat harvest; and dwelt with her mother in law.

III

THEN Naomi her mother in law said unto her, My daughter, shall I not seek rest for thee, that it may be well with thee?

2 And now *is* not Boaz of our kindred, with whose maidens thou wast? Behold, he winnoweth barley to night in the threshingfloor.

3 Wash thyself, therefore, and anoint thee, and put thy raiment upon thee, and get thee down to the floor: *but* make not thyself known unto the man, until he shall have done eating and drinking.

4 And it shall be, when he lieth down, that thou shalt mark the place where he shall lie, and thou shalt go in, and uncover his feet, and lay thee down; and he will tell thee what thou shalt do.

5 And she said unto her, All that thou sayest unto me I will do.

6 And she went down unto the floor, and did according to all that her mother in law bade her.

7 And when Boaz had eaten and drunk, and his heart was merry, he went to lie down at the end of the heap of corn: and she came softly, and uncovered his feet, and laid her down.

8 And it came to pass at midnight, that the man was afraid, and turned himself; and, behold, a woman lay at his feet.

9 And he said, Who *art* thou? And she answered, I *am* Ruth thine handmaid; spread therefore thy skirt over thine handmaid; for thou *art* a near kinsman.

10 And he said, Blessed *be* thou of the Lord, my daughter; *for* thou hast shewed more kindness in the latter end than at the beginning, inasmuch as thou followest not young men, whether poor or rich.

11 And now, my daughter, fear not; I will do to thee all that thou requirest: for all the city of my people doth know that thou *art* a virtuous woman.

12 And now, it is true that I *am thy* near kinsman: howbeit, there is a kinsman nearer than I.

13 Tarry this night, and it shall be in the morning, *that* if he will perform unto thee the part of a kinsman, well; let him do the kinsman's part: but if he will not do the part of a kinsman to thee, then will I do the part of a kinsman to thee, *as* the Lord liveth: lie down until the morning.

14 And she lay at his feet until the morning; and she rose up before one could know another. And he said, Let it not be known that a woman came into the floor.

15 Also he said, Bring the vail that *thou hast* upon thee, and hold it. And when she held it, he measured six *measures* of barley, and laid *it* on her: and she went into the city.

16 And when she came to her mother in law, she said, Who *art* thou, my daughter? And she told her all that the man had done to her.

17 And she said, These six *measures* of barley gave he me: for he said to me, Go not empty unto thy mother in law.

18 Then said she, Sit still, my daughter, until thou know how the matter will fall: for the man will not be in rest, until he have finished the thing this day.

IV

THEN went Boaz up to the gate, and sat him down there: and, behold, the kinsman of whom Boaz spake, came by: unto whom he said, Ho, such a one! turn aside, sit down here. And he turned aside, and sat down.

2 And he took ten men of the elders of the city, and said, Sit ye down here. And they sat down.

3 And he said unto the kinsman, Naomi, that is come again out of the country of Moab, selleth a parcel of land, which *was* our brother Elimelech's:

4 And I thought to advertise thee, saying, Buy *it* before the inhabitants, and before the elders of my people. If thou wilt redeem *it,* redeem *it;* but if thou wilt not redeem *it, then* tell me, that I may know: for *there is* none to redeem *it* beside thee; and I *am* after thee. And he said, I will redeem *it.*

5 Then said Boaz, What day thou buyest the field of the hand of Naomi, thou must buy *it* also of Ruth the Moabitess, the wife of the dead, to raise up the name of the dead upon his inheritance.

6 And the kinsman said, I cannot redeem *it* for myself, lest I mar

mine own inheritance: redeem thou my right to thyself: for I cannot
redeem *it.*

7 Now this *was the manner* in former time in Israel, concerning
redeeming, and concerning changing, for to confirm all things; A man
plucked off his shoe, and gave *it* to his neighbour: and this *was* a testimony in Israel.

8 Therefore the kinsman said unto Boaz, Buy *it* for thee. So he
drew off his shoe.

9 And Boaz said unto the elders, and *unto* all the people, Ye *are*
witnesses this day, that I have bought all that *was* Elimelech's, and all
that *was* Chilion's and Mahlon's, of the hand of Naomi.

10 Moreover, Ruth the Moabitess, the wife of Mahlon, have I purchased to be my wife, to raise up the name of the dead upon his inheritance, that the name of the dead be not cut off from among his brethren
and from the gate of his place: ye *are* witnesses this day.

11 And all the people that *were* in the gate, and the elders, said,
We are witnesses. The LORD make the woman that is come into thine
house like Rachel and like Leah, which two did build the house of Israel:
and do thou worthily in Ephratah, and be famous in Beth-lehem:

12 And let thy house be like the house of Pharez, whom Tamar bare
unto Judah, of the seed which the LORD shall give thee of this young
woman.

13 So Boaz took Ruth, and she was his wife: and when he went in
unto her, the LORD gave her conception, and she bare a son.

14 And the women said unto Naomi, Blessed *be* the LORD, which
hath not left thee this day without a kinsman, that his name may be
famous in Israel.

15 And he shall be unto thee a restorer of *thy* life, and a nourisher
of thine old age: for thy daughter in law, which loveth thee, which is
better to thee than seven sons, hath born him.

16 And Naomi took the child, and laid it in her bosom, and became
nurse unto it.

17 And the women her neighbours gave it a name, saying, There
is a son born to Naomi; and they called his name Obed: he *is* the father
of Jesse, the father of David.

18 Now these *are* the generations of Pharez: Pharez begat Hezron,

19 And Hezron begat Ram, and Ram begat Amminadab,

20 And Amminadab begat Nahshon, and Nahshon begat Salmon.

21 And Salmon begat Boaz, and Boaz begat Obed,

22 And Obed begat Jesse, and Jesse begat David.

II. Samuel, XVIII, 1 —XIX, 4

XVIII

AND David numbered the people that *were* with him, and set captains of thousands and captains of hundreds over them.
2 And David sent forth a third part of the people under the hand
of Joab, and a third part under the hand of Abishai the son of Zeruiah,
Joab's brother, and a third part under the hand of Ittai the Gittite.
And the king said unto the people, I will surely go forth with you
myself also.
3 But the people answered, Thou shalt not go forth: for if we
flee away, they will not care for us; neither if half of us die, will they
care for us: but now *thou art* worth ten thousand of us: therefore now
it is better that thou succour us out of the city.
4 And the king said unto them, What seemeth you best I will do.
And the king stood by the gate side, and all the people came out by
hundreds and by thousands.
5 And the king commanded Joab and Abishai and Ittai, saying,
Deal gently for my sake with the young man, *even* with Absalom. And
all the people heard when the king gave all the captains charge concerning
Absalom.
6 So the people went out into the field against Israel: and the battle
was in the wood of Ephraim;
7 Where the people of Israel were slain before the servants of David;
and there was there a great slaughter that day of twenty thousand *men*.
8 For the battle was there scattered over the face of all the country:
and the wood devoured more people that day than the sword devoured.
9 And Absalom met the servants of David. And Absalom rode
upon a mule, and the mule went under the thick boughs of a great oak,
and his head caught hold of the oak, and he was taken up between the
heaven and the earth; and the mule that *was* under him went away.
10 And a certain man saw *it*, and told Joab, and said, Behold, I saw
Absalom hanged in an oak.
11 And Joab said unto the man that told him, And, behold, thou
sawest *him*, and why didst thou not smite him there to the ground?
and I would have given thee ten *shekels* of silver, and a girdle.
12 And the man said unto Joab, Though I should receive a thousand
shekels of silver in mine hand, *yet* would I not put forth mine hand
against the king's son: for in our hearing the king charged thee and

Abishai and Ittai, saying, Beware that none *touch* the young man Absalom.

13 Otherwise I should have wrought falsehood against mine own life: for there is no matter hid from the king, and thou thyself wouldest have set thyself against *me*.

14 Then said Joab, I may not tarry thus with thee. And he took three darts in his hand, and thrust them through the heart of Absalom, while he *was* yet alive in the midst of the oak.

15 And ten young men that bare Joab's armour compassed about and smote Absalom, and slew him.

16 And Joab blew the trumpet, and the people returned from pursuing after Israel: for Joab held back the people.

17 And they took Absalom, and cast him into a great pit in the wood, and laid a very great heap of stones upon him: and all Israel fled every one to his tent.

18 Now Absalom in his lifetime had taken and reared up for himself a pillar, which *is* in the king's dale: for he said, I have no son to keep my name in remembrance, and he called the pillar after his own name: and it is called unto this day, Absalom's place.

19 Then said Ahimaaz the son of Zadok, Let me now run, and bear the king tidings, how that the LORD hath avenged him of his enemies.

20 And Joab said unto him, Thou shalt not bear tidings this day, but thou shalt bear tidings another day; but this day thou shalt bear no tidings, because the king's son is dead.

21 Then said Joab to Cushi, Go tell the king what thou hast seen. And Cushi bowed himself unto Joab, and ran.

22 Then said Ahimaaz the son of Zadok yet again to Joab, but howsoever, let me, I pray thee, also run after Cushi. And Joab said, Wherefore wilt thou run, my son, seeing that thou hast no tidings ready?

23 But howsoever, *said he,* let me run. And he said unto him, Run. Then Ahimaaz ran by the way of the plain, and overran Cushi.

24 And David sat between the two gates: and the watchman went up to the roof over the gate unto the wall, and lifted up his eyes, and looked, and behold, a man running alone.

25 And the watchman cried, and told the king. And the king said, If he *be* alone, *there is* tidings in his mouth. And he came apace, and drew near.

26 And the watchman saw another man running, and the watchman called unto the porter, and said, Behold, *another* man running alone. And the king said, He also bringeth tidings.

27 And the watchman said, Me thinketh the running of the foremost is like the running of Ahimaaz the son of Zadok. And the king
said, He *is* a good man, and cometh with good tidings.
28 And Ahimaaz called, and said unto the king, All is well. And
he fell down to the earth upon his face before the king, and said, Blessed
be the LORD thy God, which hath delivered up the men that lifted up
their hand against my lord the king.
29 And the king said, Is the young man Absalom safe? And Ahimaaz answered, When Joab sent the king's servant, and *me* thy servant,
I saw a great tumult, but I knew not what *it was*.
30 And the king said *unto him*, Turn aside, *and* stand here. And
he turned aside, and stood still.
31 And, behold, Cushi came; and Cushi said, Tidings, my lord the
king: for the LORD hath avenged thee this day of all them that rose up
against thee.
32 And the king said unto Cushi, *Is* the young man Absalom safe?
And Cushi answered, The enemies of my lord the king, and all that
rise against thee to do *thee* hurt, be as *that* young man *is*.
33 And the king was much moved, and went up to the chamber over
the gate, and wept; and as he went, thus he said, O my son Absalom!
my son, my son Absalom! would God I had died for thee, O Absalom,
my son, my son!

XIX

AND it was told Joab, Behold, the king weepeth and mourneth for
Absalom.
2 And the victory that day was *turned* into mourning unto all the
people: for the people heard say that day how the king was grieved for
his son.
3 And the people gat them by stealth that day into the city, as people
being ashamed steal away when they flee in battle.
4 But the king covered his face, and the king cried with a loud voice,
O my son Absalom! O Absalom, my son, my son!

I. Kings, XVIII

AND it came to pass, *after* many days, that the word of the LORD
came to Elijah in the third year, saying, Go, shew thyself unto Ahab;
and I will send rain upon the earth.
2 And Elijah went to shew himself unto Ahab. And *there was* a
sore famine in Samaria.

3 And Ahab called Obadiah, which *was* the governor of *his* house.
(Now Obadiah feared the LORD greatly:
4 For it was *so,* when Jezebel cut off the prophets of the LORD,
that Obadiah took an hundred prophets, and hid them by fifty in a cave,
and fed them with bread and water.)
5 And Ahab said unto Obadiah, Go into the land, unto all fountains of water, and unto all brooks: peradventure we may find grass to
save the horses and mules alive, that we lose not all the beasts.
6 So they divided the land between them, to pass throughout it:
Ahab went one way by himself, and Obadiah went another way by himself.
7 And as Obadiah was in the way, behold, Elijah met him: and he
knew him, and fell on his face, and said, *Art* thou that my lord Elijah?
8 And he answered him, I *am:* go, tell thy lord, Behold, Elijah *is here.*
9 And he said, What have I sinned, that thou wouldest deliver thy
servant into the hand of Ahab, to slay me?
10 *As* the LORD thy God liveth, there is no nation or kingdom
whither my lord hath not sent to seek thee: and when they said, *He is*
not *there;* he took an oath of the kingdom and nation, that they found
thee not.
11 And now thou sayest, Go, tell thy lord, Behold, Elijah *is here.*
12 And it shall come to pass, *as soon as* I am gone from thee, that
the Spirit of the LORD shall carry thee whither I know not; and *so* when
I come and tell Ahab, and he cannot find thee, he shall slay me: but I
thy servant fear the LORD from my youth.
13 Was it not told my lord what I did when Jezebel slew the
prophets of the LORD, how I hid an hundred men of the LORD's prophets
by fifty in a cave, and fed them with bread and water?
14 And now thou sayest, Go, tell thy lord, Behold, Elijah *is here:*
and he shall slay me.
15 And Elijah said, *As* the LORD of hosts liveth, before whom I
stand, I will surely shew myself unto him to day.
16 So Obadiah went to meet Ahab, and told him: and Ahab went
to meet Elijah.
17 And it came to pass, when Ahab saw Elijah, that Ahab said
unto him, *Art* thou he that troubleth Israel?
18 And he answered, I have not troubled Israel; but thou and thy
father's house, in that ye have forsaken the commandments of the LORD,
and thou hast followed Baalim.
19 Now therefore send, *and* gather to me all Israel unto mount

Carmel, and the prophets of Baal four hundred and fifty, and the prophets of the groves four hundred, which eat at Jezebel's table.

20 So Ahab sent unto all the children of Israel, and gathered the prophets together unto mount Carmel.

21 And Elijah came unto all the people, and said, How long halt ye between two opinions? if the LORD *be* God, follow him: but if Baal, *then* follow him. And the people answered him not a word.

22 Then said Elijah unto the people, I, *even* I only, remain a prophet of the LORD; but Baal's prophets *are* four hundred and fifty men.

23 Let them therefore give us two bullocks; and let them choose one bullock for themselves, and cut it in pieces, and lay *it* on wood, and put no fire *under:* and I will dress the other bullock, and lay *it* on wood, and put no fire *under:*

24 And call ye on the name of your gods, and I will call on the name of the LORD: and the God that answereth by fire, let him be God. And all the people answered and said, It is well spoken.

25 And Elijah said unto the prophets of Baal, Choose you one bullock for yourselves, and dress *it* first; for ye *are* many: and call on the name of your gods, but put no fire *under.*

26 And they took the bullock which was given them, and they dressed *it,* and called on the name of Baal from morning even until noon, saying, O Baal, hear us. But *there was* no voice, nor any that answered. And they leaped upon the altar which was made.

27 And it came to pass at noon, that Elijah mocked them, and said, Cry aloud; for he *is* a god: either he is talking, or he is pursuing, or he is in a journey, *or* peradventure he sleepeth, and must be awaked.

28 And they cried aloud, and cut themselves, after their manner, with knives and lancets, till the blood gushed out upon them.

29 And it came to pass, when midday was past, and they prophesied until the *time* of the offering of the *evening* sacrifice, that *there was* neither voice, nor any to answer, nor any that regarded.

30 And Elijah said unto all the people, Come near unto me. And all the people came near unto him. And he repaired the altar of the LORD *that was* broken down.

31 And Elijah took twelve stones, according to the number of the tribes of the sons of Jacob, unto whom the word of the LORD came, saying, Israel shall be thy name:

32 And with the stones he built an altar in the name of the LORD: and he made a trench about the altar, as great as would contain two measures of seed.

33 And he put the wood in order, and cut the bullock in pieces,
and laid *him* on the wood, and said, Fill four barrels with water, and
pour *it* on the burnt sacrifice, and on the wood.

34 And he said, Do *it* the second time: and they did *it* the second
time. And he said, Do *it* the third time: and they did *it* the third time.

35 And the water ran round about the altar; and he filled the trench
also with water.

36 And it came to pass, at *the time of* the offering of the *evening's*
sacrifice, that Elijah the prophet came near, and said, LORD God of
Abraham, Isaac, and of Israel, let it be known this day that thou *art*
God in Israel, and *that* I *am* thy servant, and *that* I have done all these
things at thy word.

37 Hear me, O LORD, hear me; that this people may know that thou
art the LORD God, and *that* thou hast turned their heart back again.

38 Then the fire of the LORD fell, and consumed the burnt sacrifice,
and the wood, and the stones, and the dust, and licked up the water that
was in the trench.

39 And when all the people saw *it,* they fell on their faces: and
they said, The LORD, he *is* the God; the LORD, he *is* the God.

40 And Elijah said unto them, Take the prophets of Baal; let not
one of them escape. And they took them: and Elijah brought them
down to the brook Kishon, and slew them there.

41 And Elijah said unto Ahab, Get thee up, eat and drink; for
there is a sound of abundance of rain.

42 So Ahab went up to eat and to drink. And Elijah went up to
the top of Carmel; and he cast himself down upon the earth, and put
his face between his knees,

43 And said to his servant, Go up now, look toward the sea. And
he went up, and looked, and said, *There is* nothing. And he said, Go
again seven times.

44 And it came to pass at the seventh time, that he said, Behold,
there ariseth a little cloud out of the sea, like a man's hand. And he
said, Go up, say unto Ahab, Prepare *thy chariot,* and get thee down,
that the rain stop thee not.

45 And it came to pass in the mean while, that the heaven was black
with clouds and wind, and there was a great rain. And Ahab rode, and
went to Jezreel.

46 And the hand of the LORD was on Elijah: and he girded up his
loins, and ran before Ahab to the entrance of Jezreel.

II. Kings, V

Now Naaman, captain of the host of the king of Syria, was a great man with his master, and honourable, because by him the LORD had given deliverance unto Syria: he was also a mighty man in valour; *but he was* a leper.

2 And the Syrians had gone out by companies, and had brought away captive out of the land of Israel a little maid; and she waited on Naaman's wife.

3 And she said unto her mistress, Would God my lord *were* with the prophet that *is* in Samaria! for he would recover him of his leprosy.

4 And *one* went in, and told his lord, saying, Thus and thus said the maid that *is* of the land of Israel.

5 And the king of Syria said, Go to, go, and I will send a letter unto the king of Israel. And he departed, and took with him ten talents of silver, and six thousand *pieces* of gold, and ten changes of raiment.

6 And he brought the letter to the king of Israel, saying, Now, when this letter is come unto thee, behold, I have *therewith* sent Naaman my servant to thee, that thou mayest recover him of his leprosy.

7 And it came to pass, when the king of Israel had read the letter, that he rent his clothes, and said, *Am* I God, to kill and to make alive, that this man doth send unto me to recover a man of his leprosy? Wherefore consider, I pray you, and see how he seeketh a quarrel against me.

8 And it was *so,* when Elisha the man of God had heard that the king of Israel had rent his clothes, that he sent to the king, saying, Wherefore hast thou rent thy clothes? let him come now to me, and he shall know that there is a prophet in Israel.

9 So Naaman came with his horses and with his chariot, and stood at the door of the house of Elisha.

10 And Elisha sent a messenger unto him, saying, Go and wash in Jordan seven times, and thy flesh shall come again to thee, and thou shalt be clean.

11 But Naaman was wroth, and went away, and said, Behold, I thought, He will surely come out to me, and stand and call on the name of the LORD his God, and strike his hand over the place, and recover the leper.

12 *Are* not Abana and Pharpar, rivers of Damascus, better than all the waters of Israel? may I not wash in them, and be clean? So he turned, and went away in a rage.

13 And his servants came near, and spake unto him, and said, My father, *if* the prophet had bid thee *do some* great thing, wouldest thou

not have done *it?* how much rather then, when he saith to thee, Wash,
and be clean?
14 Then went he down, and dipped himself seven times in Jordan,
according to the saying of the man of God: and his flesh came again
like unto the flesh of a little child, and he was clean.
15 And he returned to the man of God, he and all his company,
and came and stood before him: and he said, Behold, now I know that
there is no God in all the earth, but in Israel: now therefore, I pray
thee, take a blessing of thy servant.
16 But he said, *As* the LORD liveth, before whom I stand, I will
receive none. And he urged him to take *it;* but he refused.
17 And Naaman said, Shall there not then, I pray thee, be given
to thy servant two mules' burden of earth? for thy servant will henceforth offer neither burnt offering nor sacrifice unto other gods, but unto
the LORD.
18 In this thing the LORD pardon thy servant, *that* when my master goeth into the house of Rimmon to worship there, and he leaneth
on my hand, and I bow myself in the house of Rimmon; when I bow
down myself in the house of Rimmon, the LORD pardon thy servant in
this thing.
19 And he said unto him, Go in peace. So he departed from him
a little way.
20 But Gehazi, the servant of Elisha the man of God, said, Behold,
my master hath spared Naaman this Syrian, in not receiving at his
hands that which he brought: but, *as* the LORD liveth, I will run after
him, and take somewhat of him.
21 So Gehazi followed after Naaman. And when Naaman saw
him running after him, he lighted down from the chariot to meet him,
and said, *Is* all well?
22 And he said, All *is* well. My master hath sent me, saying,
Behold, even now there be come to me from mount Ephraim two young
men of the sons of the prophets: give them, I pray thee, a talent of
silver, and two changes of garments.
23 And Naaman said, Be content, take two talents. And he urged
him, and bound two talents of silver in two bags, with two changes of
garments, and laid *them* upon two of his servants; and they bare *them*
before him.
24 And when he came to the tower, he took *them* from their hand,
and bestowed *them* in the house: and he let the men go, and they
departed.

25 But he went in, and stood before his master. And Elisha said unto him, Whence *comest thou,* Gehazi? And he said, Thy servant went no whither.

26 And he said unto him, Went not mine heart *with thee,* when the man turned again from his chariot to meet thee? *Is it* a time to receive money, and to receive garments, and oliveyards, and vineyards, and sheep, and oxen, and menservants, and maidservants?

27 The leprosy therefore of Naaman shall cleave unto thee, and unto thy seed for ever. And he went out from his presence a leper *as white* as snow.

Psalms, CXLVII; CXLVIII; CXLIX; CL

CXLVII

Praise ye the Lord: for *it is* good to sing praises unto our God; for *it is* pleasant; *and* praise is comely.

2 The Lord doth build up Jerusalem; he gathereth together the outcasts of Israel.

3 He healeth the broken in heart, and bindeth up their wounds.

4 He telleth the number of the stars; he calleth them all by *their* names.

5 Great *is* our Lord, and of great power: his understanding *is* infinite.

6 The Lord lifteth up the meek: he casteth the wicked down to the ground.

7 Sing unto the Lord with thanksgiving; sing praise upon the harp unto our God;

8 Who covereth the heaven with clouds, who prepareth rain for the earth, who maketh grass to grow upon the mountains.

9 He giveth to the beast his food, *and* to the young ravens which cry.

10 He delighteth not in the strength of the horse; he taketh not pleasure in the legs of a man.

11 The Lord taketh pleasure in them that fear him, in those that hope in his mercy.

12 Praise the Lord, O Jerusalem; praise thy God, O Zion.

13 For he hath strengthened the bars of thy gates; he hath blessed thy children within thee.

14 He maketh peace *in* thy borders, *and* filleth thee with the finest of the wheat.

15 He sendeth forth his commandment *upon* earth: his word runneth very swiftly.

16 He giveth snow like wool: he scattereth the hoarfrost like ashes.

17 He casteth forth his ice like morsels: who can stand before his
cold?
18 He sendeth out his word, and melteth them: he causeth his wind
to blow, *and* the waters flow.
19 He sheweth his word unto Jacob, his statutes and his judgments
unto Israel.
20 He hath not dealt so with any nation; and *as for his* judgments,
they have not known them. Praise ye the LORD.

CXLVIII

PRAISE ye the LORD. Praise ye the LORD from the heavens: praise
him in the heights.
2 Praise ye him, all his angels: praise ye him, all his hosts.
3 Praise ye him, sun and moon: praise him, all ye stars of light.
4 Praise him, ye heavens of heavens, and ye waters that *be* above
the heavens.
5 Let them praise the name of the LORD: for he commanded, and
they were created.
6 He hath also stablished them for ever and ever: he hath made
a decree which shall not pass.
7 Praise the LORD from the earth, ye dragons, and all deeps:
8 Fire, and hail; snow, and vapours; stormy wind fulfilling his word:
9 Mountains, and all hills; fruitful trees, and all cedars:
10 Beasts, and all cattle; creeping things, and flying fowl:
11 Kings of the earth, and all people; princes, and all judges of the
earth:
12 Both young men and maidens; old men and children:
13 Let them praise the name of the LORD: for his name alone is
excellent; his glory *is* above the earth and heaven.
14 He also exalteth the horn of his people, the praise of all his
saints, *even* of the children of Israel, a people near unto him. Praise
ye the LORD.

CXLIX

PRAISE ye the LORD. Sing unto the LORD a new song, *and* his
praise in the congregation of saints.
2 Let Israel rejoice in him that made him; let the children of Zion
be joyful in their King.
3 Let them praise his name in the dance: let them sing praises unto
him with the timbrel and harp.

4 For the LORD taketh pleasure in his people: he will beautify the meek with salvation.

5 Let the saints be joyful in glory: let them sing aloud upon their beds.

6 *Let* the high *praises* of God *be* in their mouth, and a two edged sword in their hand;

7 To execute vengeance upon the heathen, *and* punishments upon the people;

8 To bind their kings with chains, and their nobles with fetters of iron;

9 To execute upon them the judgment written: this honour have all his saints. Praise ye the LORD.

CL

PRAISE ye the LORD. Praise God in his sanctuary: praise him in the firmament of his power.

2 Praise him for his mighty acts: praise him according to his excellent greatness.

3 Praise him with the sound of the trumpet: praise him with the psaltery and harp.

4 Praise him with the timbrel and dance: praise him with stringed instruments and organs.

5 Praise him upon the loud cymbals: praise him upon the high sounding cymbals.

6 Let every thing that hath breath praise the LORD. Praise ye the LORD.

Ecclesiastes, III; IV; XI; XII

III

To every *thing there is* a season, and a time to every purpose under the heaven.

2 A time to be born, and a time to die: a time to plant, and a time to pluck up *that which is* planted:

3 A time to kill, and a time to heal: a time to break down, and a time to build up:

4 A time to weep, and a time to laugh: a time to mourn, and a time to dance:

5 A time to cast away stones, and a time to gather stones together: a time to embrace, and a time to refrain from embracing:

6 A time to get, and a time to lose: a time to keep, and a time to cast
away:
7 A time to rend, and a time to sew: a time to keep silence, and a
time to speak:
8 A time to love, and a time to hate: a time of war, and a time of
peace.
9 What profit hath he that worketh in that wherein he laboureth?
10 I have seen the travail, which God hath given to the sons of men
to be exercised in it.
11 He hath made every *thing* beautiful in his time: also he hath set
the world in their heart, so that no man can find out the work that God
maketh from the beginning to the end.
12 I know that *there is* no good in them, but for *a man* to rejoice,
and to do good in his life.
13 And also that every man should eat and drink, and enjoy the good
of all his labour, it *is* the gift of God.
14 I know that whatsoever God doeth, it shall be for ever: nothing
can be put to it, nor any thing taken from it: and God doeth *it* that *men*
should fear before him.
15 That which hath been is now; and that which is to be hath already
been; and God requireth that which is past.
16 And, moreover, I saw under the sun the place of judgment, *that*
wickedness *was* there; and the place of righteousness, *that* iniquity *was*
there.
17 I said in mine heart, God shall judge the righteous and the wicked:
for *there is* a time there for every purpose, and for every work.
18 I said in mine heart concerning the estate of the sons of men, that
God might manifest them, and that they might see that they themselves
are beasts.
19 For that which befalleth the sons of men befalleth beasts; even
one thing befalleth them: as the one dieth, so dieth the other; yea, they
have all one breath; so that a man hath no preeminence above a beast:
for all *is* vanity.
20 All go unto one place: all are of the dust, and all turn to dust again.
21 Who knoweth the spirit of man that goeth upward, and the spirit
of the beast that goeth downward to the earth?
22 Wherefore I perceive that *there is* nothing better, than that a man
should rejoice in his own works; for that *is* his portion: for who shall
bring him to see what shall be after him?

IV

So I returned, and considered all the oppressions that are done under the sun; and, behold, the tears of *such as were* oppressed, and they had no comforter; and on the side of their oppressors *there was* power; but they had no comforter.

2 Wherefore I praised the dead which are already dead, more than the living which are yet alive.

3 Yea, better *is he* than both they, which hath not yet been, who hath not seen the evil work that is done under the sun.

4 Again, I considered all travail, and every right work, that for this a man is envied of his neighbour. This *is* also vanity and vexation of spirit.

5 The fool foldeth his hands together, and eateth his own flesh.

6 Better *is* an handful *with* quietness, than both the hands full *with* travail and vexation of spirit.

7 Then I returned, and I saw vanity under the sun.

8 There is one *alone,* and *there* is not a second; yea, he hath neither child nor brother: yet *is there* no end of all his labour; neither is his eye satisfied with riches; neither *saith he,* For whom do I labour, and bereave my soul of good? This *is* also vanity, yea, it *is* a sore travail.

9 Two *are* better than one; because they have a good reward for their labour.

10 For if they fall, the one will lift up his fellow: but woe to him *that is* alone when he falleth; for *he hath* not another to help him up.

11 Again, if two lie together, then they have heat: but how can one be warm *alone?*

12 And if one prevail against him, two shall withstand him; and a threefold cord is not quickly broken.

13 Better *is* a poor and a wise child than an old and foolish king, who will no more be admonished.

14 For out of prison he cometh to reign; where also *he that is* born in his kingdom becometh poor.

15 I considered all the living which walk under the sun, with the second child that shall stand up in his stead.

16 *There is* no end of all the people, *even* of all that have been before them: they also that come after shall not rejoice in him. Surely this also *is* vanity and vexation of spirit.

XI

Cast thy bread upon the waters: for thou shalt find it after many days.

2 Give a portion to seven, and also to eight; for thou knowest not what evil shall be upon the earth.

3 If the clouds be full of rain, they empty *themselves* upon the earth: and if the tree fall toward the south or toward the north, in the place where the tree falleth, there it shall be.

4 He that observeth the wind, shall not sow; and he that regardeth the clouds, shall not reap.

5 As thou knowest not what *is* the way of the spirit, *nor* how the bones *do grow* in the womb of her that is with child; even so thou knowest not the works of God who maketh all.

6 In the morning sow thy seed, and in the evening withhold not thine hand: for thou knowest not whether shall prosper, either this or that, or whether they both *shall be* alike good.

7 Truly the light *is* sweet, and a pleasant *thing it is* for the eyes to behold the sun:

8 But if a man live many years, *and* rejoice in them all; yet let him remember the days of darkness; for they shall be many. All that cometh *is* vanity.

9 Rejoice, O young man, in thy youth, and let thy heart cheer thee in the days of thy youth, and walk in the ways of thine heart, and in the sight of thine eyes: but know thou, that for all these *things* God will bring thee into judgment.

10 Therefore remove sorrow from thy heart, and put away evil from thy flesh: for childhood and youth *are* vanity.

XII

Remember now thy Creator in the days of thy youth, while the evil days come not, nor the years draw nigh, when thou shalt say, I have no pleasure in them;

2 While the sun, or the light, or the moon, or the stars, be not darkened; nor the clouds return after the rain:

3 In the day when the keepers of the house shall tremble, and the strong men shall bow themselves, and the grinders cease because they are few, and those that look out of the windows be darkened,

4 And the doors shall be shut in the streets, when the sound of the

grinding is low, and he shall rise up at the voice of the bird, and all the
daughters of music shall be brought low:

5 Also *when* they shall be afraid of *that which is* high, and fears
shall be in the way, and the almond tree shall flourish, and the grasshopper
shall be a burden, and desire shall fail; because man goeth to his long
home, and the mourners go about the streets:

6 Or ever the silver cord be loosed, or the golden bowl be broken,
or the pitcher be broken at the fountain, or the wheel broken at the
cistern.

7 Then shall the dust return to the earth as it was; and the spirit
shall return unto God who gave it.

8 Vanity of vanities, saith the Preacher; all *is* vanity.

9 And, moreover, because the Preacher was wise, he still taught the
people knowledge; yea, he gave good heed, and sought out, *and* set in
order, many proverbs.

10 The Preacher sought to find out acceptable words: and *that which*
was written *was* upright, *even* words of truth.

11 The words of the wise *are* as goads, and as nails fastened *by* the
masters of assemblies, *which* are given from one shepherd.

12 And further, by these, my son, be admonished: of making many
books *there is* no end; and much study *is* a weariness of the flesh.

13 Let us hear the conclusion of the whole matter: Fear God, and
keep his commandments: for this *is* the whole *duty* of man.

14 For God shall bring every work into judgment, with every secret
thing, whether *it be* good, or whether *it be* evil.

Ezekiel, XXXVII, 1-14

THE hand of the LORD was upon me, and carried me out in the
spirit of the LORD, and set me down in the midst of the valley which *was*
full of bones,

2 And caused me to pass by them round about: and, behold, *there*
were very many in the open valley; and, lo, *they were* very dry.

3 And he said unto me, Son of man, can these bones live? And I
answered, O LORD GOD, thou knowest.

4 And he said unto me, Prophesy upon these bones, and say unto
them, O ye dry bones, hear the word of the LORD.

5 Thus saith the Lord GOD unto these bones, Behold, I will cause
breath to enter into you, and ye shall live:

6 And I will lay sinews upon you, and will bring up flesh upon you,

and cover you with skin, and put breath in you, and ye shall live; and ye
shall know that I *am* the LORD.

7 So I prophesied as I was commanded: and as I prophesied there was
a noise, and, behold, a shaking, and the bones came together, bone to
his bone.

8 And when I beheld, lo, the sinews and the flesh came up upon them,
and the skin covered them above; but *there was* no breath in them.

9 Then said he unto me, Prophesy unto the wind, prophesy, son of
man, and say to the wind, Thus saith the Lord GOD, Come from the four
winds, O breath, and breathe upon these slain, that they may live.

10 So I prophesied as he commanded me, and the breath came into
them, and they lived, and stood up upon their feet, an exceeding great
army.

11 Then he said unto me, Son of man, these bones are the whole
house of Israel: behold they say, Our bones are dried, and our hope is
lost; we are cut off for our parts.

12 Therefore prophesy, and say unto them, Thus saith the Lord GOD,
Behold, O my people, I will open your graves, and cause you to come up
out of your graves, and bring you into the land of Israel.

13 And ye shall know that I *am* the LORD, when I have opened your
graves, O my people, and brought you up out of your graves.

14 And shall put my spirit in you, and ye shall live; and I shall place
you in your own land: then shall ye know that I the LORD have spoken *it*,
and performed *it*, saith the LORD.

I. Esdras, III, 1 —IV, 42

III

Now when Darius reigned, he made a great feast unto all his subjects,
and unto all his household, and unto all the princes of Media and Persia.

2 And to all the governors and captains and lieutenants that were
under him, from India unto Ethiopia, of an hundred twenty and seven
provinces.

3 And when they had eaten and drunken, and being satisfied were
gone home, then Darius the king went into his bedchamber, and slept,
and soon after awaked.

4 Then three young men, that were of the guard that kept the king's
body, spake one to another;

5 Let every one of us speak a sentence: he that shall overcome, and

whose sentence shall seem wiser than the others, unto him shall the king
Darius give great gifts, and great things in token of victory:
6 As, to be clothed in purple, to drink in gold, and to sleep upon gold,
and a chariot with bridles of gold, and an headtire of fine linen, and a
chain about his neck:
7 And he shall sit next to Darius because of his wisdom, and shall
be called Darius his cousin.
8 And then every one wrote his sentence, sealed it, and laid it under
king Darius his pillow;
9 And said that, when the king is risen, some will give him the writings; and of whose side the king and the three princes of Persia shall
judge that his sentence is the wisest, to him shall the victory be given,
as was appointed.
10 The first wrote, Wine is the strongest.
11 The second wrote, The King is strongest.
12 The third wrote, Women are strongest: but above all things Truth
beareth away the victory.
13 ¶ Now when the king was risen up, they took their writings, and
delivered them unto him, and so he read them:
14 And sending forth he called all the princes of Persia and Media,
and the governors, and the captains, and the lieutenants, and the chief
officers;
15 And sat him down in the royal seat of judgment; and the writings
were read before them.
16 And he said, Call the young men, and they shall declare their own
sentences. So they were called, and came in.
17 And he said unto them, Declare unto us your mind concerning the
writings. Then began the first, who had spoken of the strength of wine;
18 And he said thus, O ye men, how exceeding strong is wine! it
causeth all men to err that drink it:
19 It maketh the mind of the king and of the fatherless child to be
all one; of the bondman and of the freeman, of the poor man and of the
rich:
20 It turneth also every thought into jollity and mirth, so that a man
remembereth neither sorrow nor debt:
21 And it maketh every heart rich, so that a man remembereth neither
king nor governor; and it maketh to speak all things by talents:
22 And when they are in their cups, they forget their love both to
friends and brethren, and a little after draw out swords:
23 But when they are from the wine, they remember not what they
have done.

24 O ye men, is not wine the strongest, that enforceth to do thus?
And when he had so spoken, he held his peace

IV

THEN the second, that had spoken of the strength of the king, began
to say,
2 O ye men, do not men excel in strength, that bear rule over sea and
land, and all things in them?
3 But yet the king is more mighty: for he is lord of all these things,
and hath dominion over them; and whatsoever he commandeth them
they do.
4 If he bid them make war the one against the other, they do it: if
he send them out against the enemies, they go, and break down mountains,
walls, and towers.
5 They slay and are slain, and transgress not the king's commandment: if they get the victory, they bring all to the king, as well the spoil,
as all things else.
6 Likewise for those that are no soldiers, and have not to do with
wars, but use husbandry, when they have reaped again that which they
had sown, they bring it to the king, and compel one another to pay tribute
unto the king.
7 And yet he is but one man: if he command to kill, they kill; if he
command to spare, they spare;
8 If he command to smite, they smite; if he command to make
desolate, they make desolate; if he command to build, they build;
If he command to cut down, they cut down; if he command to plant,
they plant.
10 So all his people and his armies obey him: furthermore he lieth
down, he eateth and drinketh, and taketh his rest:
11 And these keep watch round about him, neither may any one
depart, and do his own business, neither disobey they him in any thing.
12 O ye men, how should not the king be mightiest, when in such sort
he is obeyed? And he held his tongue.
13 ¶ Then the third, who had spoken of women, and of the truth,
(this was Zorobabel,) began to speak.
14 O ye men, it is not the great king, nor the multitude of men,
neither is it wine, that excelleth; who is it then that ruleth them, or hath
the lordship over them? are they not women?
15 Women have borne the king and all the people that bear rule by
sea and land.

16 Even of them came they: and they nourished them up that planted the vineyards, from whence the wine cometh.

17 These also make garments for men; these bring glory unto men; and without women cannot men be.

18 Yea, and if men have gathered together gold and silver, or any other goodly thing, do they not love a woman which is comely in favour and beauty?

19 And letting all those things go, do they not gape, and even with open mouth fix their eyes fast on her; and have not all men more desire unto her than unto silver or gold, or any goodly thing whatsoever?

20 A man leaveth his own father that brought him up, and his own country, and cleaveth unto his wife.

21 He sticketh not to spend his life with his wife, and remembereth neither father, nor mother, nor country.

22 By this also ye must know that women have dominion over you: do ye not labour and toil, and give and bring all to the woman?

23 Yea, a man taketh his sword, and goeth his way to rob and to steal, to sail upon the sea and upon rivers;

24 And looketh upon a lion, and goeth in the darkness; and when he hath stolen, spoiled, and robbed, he bringeth it to his love.

25 Wherefore a man loveth his wife better than father or mother.

26 Yea, many there be that have run out of their wits for women, and become servants for their sakes.

27 Many also have perished, have erred, and sinned, for women.

28 And now do ye not believe me? is not the king great in his power? do not all regions fear to touch him?

29 Yet did I see him and Apame the king's concubine, the daughter of the admirable Bartacus, sitting at the right hand of the king,

30 And taking the crown from the king's head, and setting it upon her own head; she also struck the king with her left hand.

31 And yet for all this the king gaped and gazed upon her with open mouth: if she laughed upon him, he laughed also: but if she took any displeasure at him, the king was fain to flatter, that she might be reconciled to him again.

32 O ye men, how can it be but women should be strong, seeing they do thus?

33 Then the king and the princes looked one upon another: so he began to speak of the truth.

34 O ye men, are not women strong? great is the earth, high is the heaven, swift is the sun in his course, for he compasseth the heavens round about, and fetcheth his course again to his own place in one day.

35 Is he not great that maketh these things? therefore great is the truth, and stronger than all things.

36 All the earth calleth upon the truth, and the heaven blesseth it: all works shake and tremble at it, and with it is no unrighteous thing.

37 Wine is wicked, the king is wicked, women are wicked, all the children of men are wicked, and such are all their wicked works; and there is no truth in them; in their unrighteousness also they shall perish.

38 As for the truth, it endureth, and is always strong; it liveth and conquereth for evermore.

39 With her there is no accepting of persons or rewards; but she doeth the things that are just, and refraineth from all unjust and wicked things; and all men do well like of her works.

40 Neither in her judgment is any unrighteousness; and she is the strength, kingdom, power, and majesty, of all ages. Blessed be the God of truth.

41 And with that he held his peace. And all the people then shouted, and said, Great is Truth, and mighty above all things.

42 Then said the king unto him, Ask what thou wilt more than is appointed in the writing, and we will give it thee, because thou art found wisest; and thou shalt sit next me, and shalt be called my cousin.

Ecclesiasticus, XXXVIII

Honour a physician with the honour due unto him for the uses which ye may have of him: for the lord hath created him.

2 For of the most High cometh healing, and he shall receive honour of the king.

3 The skill of the physician shall lift up his head: and in the sight of great men he shall be in admiration.

4 The lord hath created medicines out of the earth; and he that is wise will not abhor them.

5 Was not the water made sweet with wood, that the virtue thereof might be known?

6 And he hath given men skill, that he might be honoured in his marvellous works.

7 With such doth he heal [men,] and taketh away their pains.

8 Of such doth the apothecary make a confection; and of his works there is no end; and from him is peace over all the earth.

9 My son, in thy sickness be not negligent: but pray unto the lord, and he will make thee whole.

10 Leave off from sin, and order thine hands aright, and cleanse thy heart from all wickedness.

11 Give a sweet savour, and a memorial of fine flour; and make a fat offering, as not being.

12 Then give place to the physician, for the lord hath created him: let him not go from thee, for thou hast need of him.

13 There is a time when in their hands there is good success.

14 For they shall also pray unto the lord, that he would prosper that which they give for ease and remedy to prolong life.

15 He that sinneth before his Maker, let him fall into the hand of the physician.

16 My son, let tears fall down over the dead, and begin to lament, as if thou hadst suffered great harm thyself; and then cover his body according to the custom, and neglect not his burial.

17 Weep bitterly, and make great moan, and use lamentation, as he is worthy, and that a day or two, lest thou be evil spoken of: and then comfort thyself for thy heaviness.

18 For of heaviness cometh death, and the heaviness of the heart breaketh strength.

19 In affliction also sorrow remaineth: and the life of the poor is the curse of the heart.

20 Take no heaviness to heart: drive it away, and remember the last end.

21 Forget it not, for there is no turning again: thou shalt not do him good, but hurt thyself.

22 Remember my judgment: for thine also shall be so; yesterday for me, and to day for thee.

23 When the dead is at rest, let his remembrance rest; and be comforted for him, when his spirit is departed from him.

24 The wisdom of a learned man cometh by opportunity of leisure: and he that hath little business shall become wise.

25 How can he get wisdom that holdeth the plough, and that glorieth in the goad, that driveth oxen, and is occupied in their labours, and whose talk is of bullocks?

26 He giveth his mind to make furrows; and is diligent to give the kine fodder.

27 So every carpenter and workmaster, that laboureth night and day: and they that cut and grave seals, and are diligent to make great variety, and give themselves to counterfeit imagery, and watch to finish a work:

28 The smith also sitting by the anvil, and considering the iron work, the vapour of the fire wasteth his flesh, and he fighteth with the heat of the

furnace: the noise of the hammer and the anvil is ever in his ears, and his eyes look still upon the pattern of the thing that he maketh; he setteth his mind to finish his work, and watcheth to polish it perfectly:

29 So doth the potter sitting at his work, and turning the wheel about with his feet, who is always carefully set at his work, and maketh all his work by number;

30 He fashioneth the clay with his arm, and boweth down his strength before his feet; he applieth himself to lead it over; and he is diligent to make clean the furnace:

31 All these trust to their hands: and every one is wise in his work.

32 Without these cannot a city be inhabited: and they shall not dwell where they will, nor go up and down:

33 They shall not be sought for in publick counsel, nor sit high in the congregation: they shall not sit on the judges' seat, nor understand the sentence of judgment: they cannot declare justice and judgment; and they shall not be found where parables are spoken.

34 But they will maintain the state of the world, and [all] their desire is in the work of their craft.

Luke, XV

THEN drew near unto him all the publicans and sinners for to hear him.

2 And the Pharisees and scribes murmured, saying, This man receiveth sinners, and eateth with them.

3 And he spake this parable unto them, saying,

4 What man of you, having an hundred sheep, if he lose one of them, doth not leave the ninety and nine in the wilderness, and go after that which is lost, until he find it?

5 And when he hath found *it,* he layeth *it* on his shoulders, rejoicing.

6 And when he cometh home, he calleth together *his* friends and neighbours, saying unto them, Rejoice with me; for I have found my sheep which was lost.

7 I say unto you, that likewise joy shall be in heaven over one sinner that repenteth, more than over ninety and nine just persons, which need no repentance.

8 Either what woman having ten pieces of silver, if she lose one piece, doth not light a candle, and sweep the house, and seek diligently till she find *it?*

9 And when she hath found *it,* she calleth *her* friends and *her*

neighbours together, saying, Rejoice with me; for I have found the piece
which I had lost.

10 Likewise, I say unto you, there is joy in the presence of the angels
of God over one sinner that repenteth.

11 And he said, A certain man had two sons:

12 And the younger of them said to *his* father, Father, give me the
portion of goods that falleth *to me*. And he divided unto them *his* living.

13 And not many days after, the younger son gathered all together,
and took his journey into a far country, and there wasted his substance
with riotous living.

14 And when he had spent all, there arose a mighty famine in that
land; and he began to be in want.

15 And he went and joined himself to a citizen of that country;
and he sent him into his fields to feed swine.

16 And he would fain have filled his belly with the husks that the
swine did eat: and no man gave unto him.

17 And when he came to himself, he said, How many hired servants
of my father's have bread enough and to spare, and I perish with hunger!

18 I will arise and go to my father, and will say unto him, Father, I
have sinned against heaven, and before thee,

19 And am no more worthy to be called thy son: make me as one of
thy hired servants.

20 And he arose, and came to his father. But when he was yet a
great way off, his father saw him, and had compassion, and ran, and
fell on his neck, and kissed him.

21 And the son said unto him, Father, I have sinned against heaven,
and in thy sight, and am no more worthy to be called thy son.

22 But the father said to his servants, Bring forth the best robe, and
put *it* on him; and put a ring on his hand, and shoes on *his* feet:

23 And bring hither the fatted calf, and kill *it;* and let us eat, and be
merry:

24 For this my son was dead, and is alive again; he was lost, and is
found. And they began to be merry.

25 Now his elder son was in the field: and as he came and drew nigh
to the house, he heard music and dancing.

26 And he called one of the servants, and asked what these things
meant.

27 And he said unto him, Thy brother is come; and thy father hath
killed the fatted calf, because he hath received him safe and sound.

28 And he was angry, and would not go in: therefore came his father
out, and intreated him.

29 And he, answering, said to *his* father, Lo, these many years do I serve thee, neither transgressed I at any time thy commandment; and yet thou never gavest me a kid, that I might make merry with my friends:

30 But as soon as this thy son was come, which hath devoured thy living with harlots, thou hast killed for him the fatted calf.

31 And he said unto him, Son, thou art ever with me, and all that I have is thine.

32 It was meet that we should make merry, and be glad: for this thy brother was dead, and is alive again; and was lost, and is found.

General Epistle of James, III

My brethren, be not many masters, knowing that we shall receive the greater condemnation.

2 For in many things we offend all. If any man offend not in word, the same *is* a perfect man, *and* able also to bridle the whole body.

3 Behold, we put bits in the horses' mouths, that they may obey us; and we turn about their whole body.

4 Behold also the ships, which though *they be* so great, and *are* driven of fierce winds, yet are they turned about with a very small helm, whithersoever the governor listeth.

5 Even so the tongue is a little member, and boasteth great things. Behold, how great a matter a little fire kindleth!

6 And the tongue *is* a fire, a world of iniquity: so is the tongue among our members, that it defileth the whole body, and setteth on fire the course of nature; and it is set on fire of hell.

7 For every kind of beasts, and of birds, and of serpents, and of things in the sea, is tamed, and hath been tamed of mankind:

8 But the tongue can no man tame; *it is* an unruly evil, full of deadly poison.

9 Therewith bless we God, even the Father; and therewith curse we men, which are made after the similitude of God.

10 Out of the same mouth proceedeth blessing and cursing. My brethren, these things ought not so to be.

11 Doth a fountain send forth at the same place sweet *water* and bitter?

12 Can the fig tree, my brethren, bear olive berries? either a vine, figs? so *can* no fountain both yield salt water and fresh.

13 Who *is* a wise man and endued with knowledge among you? let him shew out of a good conversation his works with meekness of wisdom.

14 But if ye have bitter envying and strife in your hearts, glory not; and lie not against the truth.

15 This wisdom descendeth not from above, but *is* earthly, sensual, devilish.

16 For where envying and strife *is*, there *is* confusion and every evil work.

17 But the wisdom that is from above is first pure, then peaceable, gentle, *and* easy to be intreated, full of mercy and good fruits, without partiality, and without hypocrisy.

18 And the fruit of righteousness is sown in peace of them that make peace.

Revelation, VI; VII

VI

AND I saw when the Lamb opened one of the seals; and I heard, as it were the noise of thunder, one of the four beasts, saying, Come and see.

2 And I saw, and beheld a white horse: and he that sat on him had a bow; and a crown was given unto him: and he went forth conquering, and to conquer.

3 And when he had opened the second seal, I heard the second beast say, Come and see.

4 And there went out another horse *that was* red: and *power* was given to him that sat thereon to take peace from the earth, and that they should kill one another: and there was given unto him a great sword.

5 And when he had opened the third seal, I heard the third beast say, Come and see. And I beheld, and, lo, a black horse; and he that sat on him had a pair of balances in his hand.

6 And I heard a voice in the midst of the four beasts say, A measure of wheat for a penny, and three measures of barley for a penny; and *see* thou hurt not the oil and the wine.

7 And when he had opened the fourth seal, I heard the voice of the fourth beast say, Come and see.

8 And I looked, and behold a pale horse; and his name that sat on him was Death, and Hell followed with him. And power was given unto them over the fourth part of the earth, to kill with sword, and with hunger, and with death, and with the beasts of the earth.

9 And when he had opened the fifth seal, I saw under the altar the souls of them that were slain for the word of God, and for the testimony which they held:

10 And they cried with a loud voice, saying, How long, O Lord, holy
and true, dost thou not judge and avenge our blood on them that dwell
on the earth?

11 And white robes were given unto every one of them; and it was
said unto them, that they should rest yet for a little season, until their
fellowservants also and their brethren, that should be killed as they *were*,
should be fulfilled.

12 And I beheld when he had opened the sixth seal, and, lo, there was
a great earthquake; and the sun became black as sackcloth of hair, and
the moon became as blood;

13 And the stars of heaven fell unto the earth, even as a fig tree
casteth her untimely figs, when she is shaken of a mighty wind.

14 And the heaven departed as a scroll when it is rolled together;
and every mountain and island were moved out of their places.

15 And the kings of the earth, and the great men, and the rich men,
and the chief captains, and the mighty men, and every bondman, and every
free man, hid themselves in the dens and in the rocks of the mountains;

16 And said to the mountains and rocks, Fall on us, and hide us from
the face of him that sitteth on the throne, and from the wrath of the
Lamb:

17 For the great day of his wrath is come; and who shall be able to
stand?

VII

And after these things I saw four angels standing on the four corners
of the earth, holding the four winds of the earth, that the wind should
not blow on the earth, nor on the sea, nor on any tree.

2 And I saw another angel ascending from the east, having the seal
of the living God: and he cried with a loud voice to the four angels, to
whom it was given to hurt the earth and the sea,

3 Saying, Hurt not the earth, neither the sea, nor the trees, till we
have sealed the servants of our God in their foreheads.

4 And I heard the number of them which were sealed: *and there were*
sealed an hundred *and* forty *and* four thousand of all the tribes of the
children of Israel.

5 Of the tribe of Juda *were* sealed twelve thousand. Of the tribe of
Reuben *were* sealed twelve thousand. Of the tribe of Gad *were* sealed
twelve thousand.

6 Of the tribe of Aser *were* sealed twelve thousand. Of the tribe of
Nepthalim *were* sealed twelve thousand. Of the tribe of Manasses *were*
sealed twelve thousand.

7 Of the tribe of Simeon *were* sealed twelve thousand. Of the tribe of Levi *were* sealed twelve thousand. Of the tribe of Issachar *were* sealed twelve thousand.

8 Of the tribe of Zabulon *were* sealed twelve thousand. Of the tribe of Joseph *were* sealed twelve thousand. Of the tribe of Benjamin *were* sealed twelve thousand.

9 After this I beheld, and, lo, a great multitude, which no man could number, of all nations, and kindreds, and people, and tongues, stood before the throne, and before the Lamb, clothed with white robes, and palms in their hands;

10 And cried with a loud voice, saying, Salvation to our God which sitteth upon the throne, and unto the Lamb.

11 And all the angels stood round about the throne, and *about* the elders and the four beasts, and fell before the throne on their faces, and worshipped God.

12 Saying, Amen: Blessing, and glory, and wisdom, and thanksgiving, and honour, and power, and might, *be* unto our God for ever and ever. Amen.

13 And one of the elders answered, saying unto me, What are these which are arrayed in white robes? and whence came they?

14 And I said unto him, Sir, thou knowest. And he said to me, These are they which came out of great tribulation, and have washed their robes, and made them white in the blood of the Lamb.

15 Therefore are they before the throne of God, and serve him day and night in his temple: and he that sitteth on the throne shall dwell among them.

16 They shall hunger no more, neither thirst any more; neither shall the sun light on them, nor any heat.

17 For the Lamb, which is in the midst of the throne, shall feed them, and shall lead them unto living fountains of waters: and God shall wipe away all tears from their eyes.

From Homer's Iliad

The Grief of Achilles for the Slaying of Patroclus

(From Book XVIII; translated by George Chapman)

Angered against Agamemnon, the greatest king among the Achaeans besieging Troy, Achilles withdrew himself from battle. His mother Thetis secured from Zeus a pledge to honor her offended son at the expense of the Achaeans. With the Trojans gaining advantage, Agamemnon sent an embassage to Achilles, but Achilles denied him. The Trojans pressed hard upon the Achaeans, and broke within the wall that they had built to protect their ships. Patroclus, in the borrowed armor of Achilles, drove away the enemy from the ships; but he was slain at last by Hector. The grief of Achilles for the slaying of his comrade made him secure new armor from Hephaestus and go forth to battle. He wrought havoc among the men of Troy, driving them back within their gates, and finally slew Hector, and dragged his body to the ships.

They fought still like the rage of fire. And now Antilochus
Came to Æacides, whose mind was much solicitous
For that which, as he fear'd, was fall'n. He found him near the fleet
With upright sail-yards, uttering this to his heroic conceit:
"Ay me, why see the Greeks themselves, thus beaten from the field,
And routed headlong to their fleet? O let not heaven yield
Effect to what my sad soul fears, that, as I was foretold,
The strongest Myrmidon next me, when I should still behold
The sun's fair light, must part with it. Past doubt Menoetius' son
Is he on whom that fate is wrought. O wretch, to leave undone
What I commanded; that, the fleet once freed of hostile fire,
Not meeting Hector, instantly he should his powers retire."
As thus his troubled mind discoursed, Antilochus appear'd,
And told with tears the sad news thus: "My lord, that must be heard
Which would to heaven I might not tell; Menoetius' son lies dead,
And for his naked corse (his arms already forfeited,
And worn by Hector) the debate is now most vehement."
This said, grief darken'd all his powers. With both his hands he rent
The black mould from the forced earth, and pour'd it on his head,
Smear'd all his lovely face; his weeds, divinely fashioned,
All 'filed and mangled; and himself he threw upon the shore,
Lay, as laid out for funeral, then tumbled round, and tore
His gracious curls. His ecstasy he did so far extend,
That all the ladies won by him and his now slaughter'd friend,
Afflicted strangely for his plight, came shrieking from the tents,
And fell about him, beat their breasts, their tender lineaments
Dissolved with sorrow. And with them wept Nestor's warlike son,
Fell by him, holding his fair hands, in fear he would have done
His person violence; his heart, extremely straiten'd, burn'd
Beat, swell'd, and sigh'd as it would burst. So terribly he mourn'd,
That Thetis, sitting in the deeps of her old father's seas,
Heard, and lamented.

From Homer's Odyssey

Hermes in Calypso's Island

(From Book V; translated by George Chapman.)

Odysseus, on his homeward voyage after the destruction of Troy, to resume his throne in the island kingdom of Ithaca, was pursued by the wrath of Poseidon. After three years of wanderings and adventures, he came shipwrecked and alone to Calypso's island, where for seven years he was held, an unwilling guest. At the instance of the goddess Athene, Zeus sent the messenger Hermes to Calypso with orders of release. Hermes delivered the message, and Calypso unwillingly consented to the departure of Odysseus. Freed from the toils of Calypso, he built a raft and again set sail for home. On the eighteenth day of his voyage, he was discovered by Poseidon, who wrecked him on the island of Phaeacia. Naked and fainting, he struggled ashore, and fell asleep under some shrubs, in a bed of leaves. Book VI begins at this point. Nausicaä, daughter of King Alcinoüs, aided Odysseus. At a banquet, on hearing a song of Troy, Odysseus could not keep back his tears. He disclosed his name, and recounted the marvels and the hardships of his experience. The Phaeacians bore him in one of their marvelous ships to the coast of Ithaca. After revealing himself to his son Telemachus, he slew the insolent suitors who for years had beset his loyal wife Penelope, and took her to his heart again. Finally, going to the farm of his father Laërtes, he reveals himself to the aged man. There is an insurrection of the kinsmen of the suitors; but Athene, in the guise of Mentor, makes peace.

THUS charged he; nor Argicides denied,
But to his feet his fair wing'd shoes he tied,
Ambrosian, golden; that in his command
Put either sea, or the unmeasured land,
With pace as speedy as a puff of wind.
Then up his rod went, with which he declined
The eyes of any waker, when he pleased,
And any sleeper, when he wish'd, diseased.
This took, he stoop'd Pieria, and thence
Glid through the air, and Neptune's confluence
Kiss'd as he flew, and check'd the waves as light
As any sea-mew in her fishing flight
Her thick wings sousing in the savoury seas;
Like her, he pass'd a world of wilderness;
But when the far-off isle he touch'd, he went
Up from the blue sea to the continent,
And reach'd the ample cavern of the Queen,
Whom he within found; without seldom seen.
A sun-like fire upon the hearth did flame;
The matter precious, and divine the frame;
Of cedar cleft and incense was the pile,
That breathed an odour round about the isle.
Herself was seated in an inner room,
Whom sweetly sing he heard, and at her loom,
About a curious web, whose yarn she threw
In with a golden shittle. A grove grew
In endless spring about her cavern round,
With odorous cypress, pines, and poplars crown'd,
Where hawks, sea-owls, and long-tongued bittours bred,
And other birds their shady pinions spread;
All fowls maritimal; none roosted there,
But those whose labours in the waters were.
A vine did all the hollow cave embrace,
Still green, yet still ripe bunches gave it grace.
Four fountains, one against another, pour'd
Their silver streams; and meadows all enflower'd
With sweet balm-gentle, and blue violets hid,
That deck'd the soft breasts of each fragrant mead.
Should any one, though he immortal were,
Arrive and see the sacred objects there,
He would admire them, and be overjoy'd;
And so stood Hermes' ravish'd powers employ'd.
But having all admir'd, he enter'd on
The ample cave, nor could be seen unknown
Of great Calypso (for all Deities are
Prompt in each other's knowledge, though so far
Sever'd in dwellings) but he could not see
Ulysses there within; without was he
Set sad ashore, where 'twas his use to view
Th' unquiet sea, sigh'd, wept, and empty drew
His heart of comfort.

The Landing in Phaeacia (Book VI; translated by S. H. Butcher and A. Lang)

See the note prefixed to "Hermes in Calypso's Island," above.

So there he lay asleep, the steadfast goodly Odysseus, fordone with toil and drowsiness. Meanwhile Athene went to the land and the city of the Phæacians, who of old, upon a time, dwelt in spacious Hypereia; near the Cyclopes they dwelt, men exceeding proud, who harried them continually, being mightier than they. Thence the godlike Nausithous made them depart, and he carried them away, and planted them in Scheria, far off from men that live by bread. And he drew a wall around the town, and builded houses and made temples for the gods and meted out the fields. Howbeit ere this had he been stricken by fate, and had gone down to the house of Hades, and now Alcinous was reigning, with wisdom granted by the gods. To his house went the goddess, grey-eyed Athene, devising a return for the great-hearted Odysseus. She betook her to the rich-wrought bower, wherein was sleeping a maiden like to the gods in form and comeliness, Nausicaa, the daughter of Alcinous, high of heart. Beside her on either hand of the pillars of the door were two handmaids, dowered with beauty from the Graces, and the shining doors were shut.

But the goddess, fleet as the breath of the wind, swept towards the couch of the maiden, and stood above her head, and spake to her in the semblance of the daughter of a famous seafarer, Dymas, a girl of like age with Nausicaa, who had found grace in her sight. In her shape the grey-eyed Athene spake to the princess, saying:

"Nausicaa, how hath thy mother so heedless a maiden to her daughter? Lo, thou hast shining raiment that lies by thee uncared for, and thy marriage-day is near at hand, when thou thyself must needs go beautifully clad, and have garments to give to them who shall lead thee to the house of the bridegroom! And, behold, these are the things whence a good report goes abroad among men, wherein a father and lady mother take delight. But come, let us arise and go a-washing with the breaking of the day, and I will follow with thee to be thy mate in the toil, that without delay thou mayst get thee ready, since truly thou art not long to be a maiden. Lo, already they are wooing thee, the noblest youths of all the Phæacians, among that people whence thou thyself dost draw thy lineage. So come, beseech thy noble father betimes in the morning to furnish thee with mules and a wain to carry the men's raiment, and the robes, and the shining coverlets. Yea and for thyself it is seemlier far to go thus than on foot, for the places where we must wash are a great way off the town."

So spake the grey-eyed Athene, and departed to Olympus, where, as they say, is the seat of the gods that standeth fast for ever. Not by winds is it shaken, nor ever wet with rain, nor doth the snow come nigh thereto, but most clear air is spread about it cloudless, and the white light floats over it. Therein the blessed gods are glad for all their days, and thither Athene went when she had shown forth all to the maiden.

Anon came the throned Dawn, and awakened Nausicaa of the fair robes, who straightway marvelled on the dream, and went through the halls to tell her parents, her father dear and her mother. And she found them within, her mother sitting by the hearth with the women her handmaids, spinning yarn of sea-purple stain, but her father she met as he was going forth to the renowned kings in their council, whither the noble Phæacians called him. Standing close by her dear father she spake, saying: "Father, dear, couldst thou not lend me a high waggon with strong wheels, that I may take the goodly raiment to the river to wash, so much as I have lying soiled? Yea and it is seemly that thou thyself, when thou art with the princes in council, shouldest have fresh raiment to wear. Also, there are five dear sons of thine in the halls, two married, but three are lusty bachelors, and these are always eager for new-washen garments wherein to go to the dances; for all these things have I taken thought."

This she said, because she was ashamed to speak of glad marriage to her father; but he saw all and answered, saying:

"Neither the mules nor aught else do I grudge thee, my child. Go thy ways, and the thralls shall get thee ready a high waggon with good wheels, and fitted with an upper frame."

Therewith he called to his men, and they gave ear, and without the palace they made ready the smooth-running mule-wain, and led the mules beneath the yoke, and harnessed them under the car, while the maiden brought forth from her bower the shining raiment. This she stored in the polished car, and her mother filled a basket with all manner of food to the heart's desire, dainties too she set therein, and she poured wine into a goat-skin bottle, while Nausicaa climbed into the wain. And her mother gave her soft olive oil also in a golden cruse, that she and her maidens might anoint themselves after the bath. Then Nausicaa took the whip and the shining reins, and touched the mules to start them; then there was a clatter of hoofs, and on they strained without flagging, with their load of the raiment and the maiden. Not alone did she go, for her attendants followed with her.

Now when they were come to the beautiful stream of the river, where truly were the unfailing cisterns, and bright water welled up free from beneath, and flowed past, enough to wash the foulest garments clean, there the girls unharnessed the mules from under the chariot, and turning them loose they drove them along the banks of the eddying river to graze on the honey-sweet clover. Then they took the garments from the wain, in their hands, and bore them to the black water, and briskly trod them down in the trenches, in busy rivalry. Now when they had washed and cleansed all the stains, they spread all out in order along the shore of the deep, even where the sea, in beating on the coast, washed the pebbles clean. Then having bathed and anointed them well with olive oil, they took their mid-day meal on the river's banks, waiting till the clothes should dry in the brightness of the sun. Anon, when they were satisfied with food, the maidens and the princess, they fell to playing at ball, casting away their tires, and among them Nausicaa of the white arms began the song. And even as Artemis, the archer, moveth down the mountain, either along the ridges of lofty Taygetus or Erymanthus, taking her pastime in the chase of boars and swift deer, and with her the wild wood-nymphs disport them, the daughters of Zeus, lord of the ægis, and Leto is glad at heart, while high over all she rears her head and brows, and easily may she be known,—but all are fair; even so the girl unwed outshone her maiden company.

But when now she was about going homewards, after yoking the mules and folding up the goodly raiment, then grey-eyed Athene turned to other thoughts, that so Odysseus might awake, and see the lovely maiden, who should be his guide to the city of the Phæacian men. So then the princess threw the ball at one of her company; she missed the girl, and cast the ball into the deep eddying current, whereat they all raised a piercing cry. Then the goodly Odysseus awoke and sat up, pondering in his heart and spirit:

"Woe is me! to what men's land am I come now? say, are they froward, and wild, and unjust, or are they hospitable, and of God-fearing mind? How shrill a cry of maidens rings round me, of the nymphs that hold the steep hill-tops, and the river-springs, and the grassy water meadows! It must be, methinks, that I am near men of human speech. Go to, I myself will make trial and see."

Therewith the goodly Odysseus crept out from under the coppice, having broken with his strong hand a leafy bough from the thick wood, to hold athwart his body, that it might hide his nakedness withal. And forth he sallied like a lion mountain-bred, trusting in his strength, who fares out blown and rained upon, with flaming eyes; amid the kine he goes or amid the sheep or in the track of the wild deer; yea, his belly bids him go even to the good homestead to make assay upon the flocks. Even so Odysseus was fain to draw nigh to the fair-tressed maidens, all naked as he was, such need had come upon him. But he was terrible in their eyes, being marred with the salt sea foam, and they fled cowering here and there about the jutting spits of shore. And the daughter of Alcinous alone stood firm, for Athene gave her courage of heart, and took all trembling from her limbs. So she halted and stood over against him, and Odysseus considered whether he should clasp the knees of the lovely maiden, and so make his prayer, or should stand as he was, apart, and beseech her with smooth words, if haply she might show him the town, and give him raiment. And as he thought within himself, it seemed better to stand apart, and beseech her with smooth words, lest the maiden should be angered with him if he touched her knees: so straightway he spake a sweet and cunning word:

"I supplicate thee, O queen, whether thou art a goddess or a mortal! If indeed thou art a goddess of them that keep the wide heaven; to Artemis, then, the daughter of great Zeus, I mainly liken thee, for beauty and stature and shapeliness. But if thou art one of the daughters of men who dwell on earth, thrice blessed are thy father and thy lady mother, and thrice blessed thy brethren. Surely their souls ever glow with gladness for thy sake, each time they see thee entering the dance, so fair a flower of maidens. But he is of heart the most blessed beyond all other who shall prevail with gifts of wooing, and lead thee to his home. Never have mine eyes beheld such an one among mortals, neither man nor woman; great awe comes upon me as I look on thee. Yet in Delos once I saw as goodly a thing: a young sapling of a palm tree springing by the altar of Apollo. For thither too I went, and much people with me, on that path where my sore troubles were to be. Yea, and when I looked thereupon, long time I marvelled in spirit,—for never grew there yet so goodly a shoot from ground,—even in such wise as I wonder at thee, lady, and am astonied and do greatly fear to touch thy knees, though grievous sorrow is upon me. Yesterday, on the twentieth day, I escaped from the wine-dark deep, but all that time continually the wave bare me, and the vehement winds drave, from the isle Ogygia. And now some god has cast me on this shore, that here too, methinks, some evil may betide me; for I trow not that trouble will cease; the gods ere that time will yet bring many a thing to pass. But, queen, have pity on me, for after many trials and sore to thee first of all am I come, and of the other folk, who hold this city and land, I know no man. Nay show me the town, give me an old garment to cast about me, if thou hadst, when thou camest here, any wrap for the linen. And may the gods grant thee all thy heart's desire: a husband and a home, and a mind at one with his may they give—a good gift, for there is nothing mightier and nobler than when man and wife are of one heart and mind in a house, a grief to their foes, and to their friends great joy, but their own hearts know it best."

Then Nausicaa of the white arms answered him, and said: "Stranger, forasmuch as thou seemest no evil man nor foolish—and it is Olympian Zeus himself that giveth weal to men, to the good and to the evil, to each one as he will, and this thy lot doubtless is of him, and so thou must in anywise endure it:—and now, since thou hast come to our city and our land, thou shalt not lack raiment, nor aught else that is the due of a hapless suppliant, when he has met them who can befriend him. And I will show thee the town, and name the name of the people. The Phæacians hold this city and land, and I am the daughter of Alcinous, great of heart, on whom all the might and force of the Phæacians depend."

Thus she spake, and called to her maidens of the fair tresses: "Halt, my maidens, whither flee ye at the sight of a man? Ye surely do not take him for an enemy? That mortal breathes not, and never will be born, who shall come with war to the land of the Phæacians, for they are very dear to the gods. Far apart we live in the wash of the waves, the outermost of men, and no other mortals are conversant with us. Nay, but this man is some helpless one come hither in his wanderings, whom now we must kindly entreat, for all strangers and beggars are from Zeus, and a little gift is dear. So, my maidens, give the stranger meat and drink, and bathe him in the river, where withal is a shelter from the winds."

So she spake, but they had halted and called each to the other, and they brought Odysseus to the sheltered place, and made him sit down, as Nausicaa bade them, the daughter of Alcinous, high of heart. Beside him they laid a mantle, and doublet for raiment, and gave him soft olive oil in the golden cruse, and bade him wash in the streams of the river. Then goodly Odysseus spake among the maidens, saying: "I pray you stand thus apart, while I myself wash the brine from my shoulders, and anoint me with olive oil, for truly oil is long a stranger to my skin. But in your sight I will not bathe, for I am ashamed to make me naked in the company of fair-tressed maidens."

Then they went apart and told all to their lady. But with the river water the goodly Odysseus washed from his skin the salt scurf that covered his back and broad shoulders, and from his head he wiped the crusted brine of the barren sea. But when he had washed his whole body, and anointed him with olive oil, and had clad himself in the raiment that the unwedded maiden gave him, then Athene, the daughter of Zeus, made him greater and more mighty to behold, and from his head caused deep curling locks to flow, like the hyacinth flower. And as when some skillful man overlays gold upon silver—one that Hephæstus and Pallas Athene have taught all manner of craft, and full of grace is his handiwork—even so did Athene shed grace about his head and shoulders.

Then to the shore of the sea went Odysseus apart, and sat down, glowing in beauty and grace, and the princess marvelled at him, and spake among her fair-tressed maidens, saying:

"Listen, my white-armed maidens, and I will say somewhat. Not without the will of all the gods who hold Olympus hath this man come among the godlike Phæacians. Erewhile he seemed to me uncomely, but now he is like the gods that keep the wide heaven. Would that such an one might be called my husband, dwelling here, and that it might please him here to abide! But come, my maidens, give the stranger meat and drink."

Thus she spake, and they gave ready ear and hearkened, and set beside Odysseus meat and drink, and the steadfast goodly Odysseus did eat and drink eagerly, for it was long since he had tasted food.

Now Nausicaa of the white arms had another thought. She folded the raiment and stored it in the goodly wain, and yoked the mules strong of hoof, and herself climbed into the car. Then she called on Odysseus, and spake and hailed him: "Up now, stranger, and rouse thee to go to the city, that I may convey thee to the house of my wise father, where, I promise thee, thou shalt get knowledge of all the noblest of the Phæacians. But do thou even as I tell thee, and thou seemest a discreet man enough. So long as we are passing along the fields and farms of men, do thou fare quickly with the maidens behind the mules and the chariot, and I will lead the way. But when we set foot within the city, —whereby goes a high wall with towers; and there is a fair haven on either side of the town, and narrow is the entrance, and curved ships are drawn up on either hand of the mole, for all the folk have stations for their vessels, each man one for himself. And there is the place of assembly about the goodly temple of Poseidon, furnished with heavy stones, deep bedded in the earth. There men look to the gear of the black ships, hawsers and sails, and there they fine down the oars. For the Phæacians care not for bow nor quiver, but for masts, and oars of ships, and gallant barques, wherein rejoicing they cross the grey sea.

Their ungracious speech it is that I would avoid, lest some man afterward rebuke me, and there are but too many insolent folk among the people. And some one of the baser sort might meet me and say: "Who is this that goes with Nausicaa, this tall and goodly stranger? Where found she him? Her husband he will be, her very own. Either she has taken in some shipwrecked wanderer of strange men,—for no men dwell near us; or some god has come in answer to her instant prayer; from heaven has he descended, and will have her to wife for evermore. Better so, if herself she has ranged abroad and found a lord from a strange land, for verily she holds in no regard the Phæacians here in this country, the many men and noble who are her wooers." So will they speak, and this would turn to my reproach. Yea, and I myself would think it blame of another maiden who did such things in despite of her friends, her father and mother being still alive, and was conversant with men before the day of open wedlock. But, stranger, heed well what I say, that as soon as may be thou mayest gain at my father's hands an escort and a safe return. Thou shalt find a fair grove of Athene, a poplar grove near the road, and a spring wells forth therein, and a meadow lies all around. There is my father's demesne, and his fruitful close, within the sound of a man's shout from the city. Sit thee down there and wait until such time as we may have come into the city, and reached the house of my father. But when thou deemest that we are got to the palace, then go up to the city of the Phæacians, and ask for the house of my father Alcinous, high of heart. It is easily known, and a young child could be thy guide, for nowise like it are builded the houses of the Phæacians, so goodly is the palace of the hero Alcinous. But when thou art within the shadow of the halls and the court, pass quickly through the great chamber, till thou comest to my mother, who sits at the hearth in the light of the fire, weaving yarn of sea-purple stain, a wonder to behold. Her chair is leaned against a pillar, and her maidens sit behind her. And there my father's throne leans close to hers, wherein he sits and drinks his wine, like an immortal. Pass thou by him, and cast thy hands about my mother's knees, that thou mayest see quickly and with joy the day of thy returning, even if thou art from a very far country. If but her heart be kindly disposed toward thee, then is there hope that thou shalt see thy friends, and come to thy well-builded house, and to thine own country."

She spake, and smote the mules with the shining whip, and quickly they left behind them the streams of the river. And well they trotted and well they paced, and she took heed to drive in such wise that the maidens and Odysseus might follow on foot, and cunningly she plied the lash. Then the sun set, and they came to the famous grove, the sacred place of Athene; so there the goodly Odysseus sat him down. Then straightway he prayed to the daughter of mighty Zeus: "Listen to me, child of Zeus, lord of the ægis, unwearied maiden; hear me even now, since before thou heardest not when I was smitten on the sea, when the renowned Earth-shaker smote me. Grant me to come to the Phæacians as one dear, and worthy of pity."

So he spake in prayer, and Pallas Athene heard him; but she did not yet appear to him face to face, for she had regard unto her father's brother, who furiously raged against the godlike Odysseus, till he should come to his own country.

Odysseus Reveals Himself to His Father

(From Book XXIV; translated by George Chapman)

See the note prefixed to "The Landing in Phaeacia," above.

All this haste made not his staid faith so free
To trust his words; who said: "If you are he,
Approve it by some sign." "This scar then see,"
Replied Ulysses, "given me by the boar
Slain in Parnassus; I being sent before
By yours and by my honour'd mother's will,
To see your sire Autolycus fulfil
The gifts he vow'd at giving of my name.
I'll tell you, too, the trees, in goodly frame
Of this fair orchard, that I ask'd of you
Being yet a child, and follow'd for your show,
And name of every tree. You gave me then
Of fig-trees forty, apple-bearers ten,
Pear-trees thirteen, and fifty ranks of vine;
Each one of which a season did confine
For his best eating. Not a grape did grow
That grew not there, and had his heavy brow
When Jove's fair daughters, the all-ripening Hours,
Gave timely date to it." This charged the powers
Both of his knees and heart with such impression
Of sudden comfort, that it gave possession
Of all to trance; the signs were all so true;
And did the love that gave them so renew.
He cast his arms about his son and sunk,
The circle slipping to his feet; so shrunk
Were all his age's forces with the fire
Of his young love rekindled. The old sire
The son took up quite lifeless. But his breath
Again respiring, and his soul from death
His body's powers recovering, out he cried,
And said: "O Jupiter! I now have tried
That still there live in heaven remembering Gods
Of men that serve them; though the periods
They set on their appearances are long
In best men's sufferings, yet as sure as strong
They are in comforts; be their strange delays
Extended never so from days to days.
Yet see the short joys or the soon-fix'd fears

Of helps withheld by them so many years:
For if the wooers now have paid the pain
Due to their impious pleasures, now again
Extreme fear takes me, lest we straight shall see
The Ithacensians here in mutiny;
Their messengers dispatch'd to win to friend
The Cephallenian cities."

From PLATO'S PHAEDO

The Death of Socrates (Translated by Benjamin Jowett)

When Socrates drank the hemlock, in B. C. 399, he was in his seventieth year. His life had been spent in the effort to awaken moral consciousness and consideration of the eternal, in the minds of all who heard him. The charges of corrupting the youth and despising the gods, on which he had been condemned, had been dictated by political enemies. Though Socrates was allied to no party, these men hated him, as their predecessors in power had done, for his unsparing attacks on injustice and the false pretense of knowledge.

During the voyage of the sacred ship to Delos on the Theoric mission, which occupied thirty days, the execution was deferred. Socrates spent the time in daily conversations with a company of friends and disciples. At the beginning of the *Phædo,* the holy season is over, and the company come earlier than usual, to converse with him for the last time. Almost as soon as they enter the prison, Xanthippe and her children are sent home in the care of a servant of Crito's. The philosopher has just been released from chains. He explains why he welcomes death, and why he holds the immutable conviction that the soul is immortal. Then follows the last scene of all.

WHEN he had done speaking, Crito said: And have you any commands for us, Socrates—anything to say about your children, or any other matter in which we can serve you?

Nothing particular, Crito, he replied: only, as I have always told you, take care of yourselves; that is a service which you may be ever rendering to me and mine and to all of us, whether you promise to do so or not. But if you have no thought for yourselves, and care not to walk according to the rule which I have prescribed for you, not now for the first time, however much you may profess or promise at the moment, it will be of no avail.

We will do our best, said Crito: And in what way shall we bury you?

In any way that you like; but you must get hold of me, and take care that I do not run away from you. Then he turned to us, and added with a smile:—I cannot make Crito believe that I am the same Socrates who have been talking and conducting the argument; he fancies that I am the other Socrates whom he will soon see, a dead body—and he asks, How shall he bury me? And though I have spoken many words in the endeavour to show that when I have drunk the poison I shall leave you and go to the joys of the blessed,—these words of mine, with which I was comforting you and myself, have had, as I perceive, no effect upon Crito. And therefore I want you to be surety for me to him now, as at the trial he was surety to the judges for me: but let the promise be of another sort; for he was surety for me to the judges that I would remain, and you must be my surety to him that I shall not remain, but go away and depart; and then he will suffer less at my death, and not be grieved when he sees my body being burned or buried. I would not have him sorrow at my hard lot, or say at the burial, Thus we lay out Socrates, or, Thus we follow him to the grave or bury him; for false words are not only evil in themselves, but they infect the soul with evil. Be of good cheer then, my dear Crito, and say that you are burying my body only, and do with that whatever is usual, and what you think best.

When he had spoken these words, he arose and went into a chamber to bathe; Crito followed him and told us to wait. So we remained behind, talking and thinking of the subject of discourse, and also of the greatness of our sorrow; he was like a father of whom we were being bereaved, and we were about to pass the rest of our lives as orphans. When he had taken the bath his children were brought to him—(he had two young sons and an elder one); and the women of his family also came, and he talked to them and gave them a few directions in the presence of Crito; then he dismissed them and returned to us.

Now the hour of sunset was near, for a good deal of time had passed while he was within. When he came out, he sat down with us again after his bath, but not much was said. Soon the jailer, who was the servant of the Eleven, entered and stood by him, saying:—To you, Socrates, whom I know to be the noblest and gentlest and best of all who ever came to this place, I will not impute the angry feelings of other men, who rage and swear at me, when, in obedience to the authorities, I bid them drink the poison—indeed, I am sure that you will not be angry with me; for others, as you are aware, and not I, are to blame. And so fare you well, and try to bear lightly what must needs be—you know my errand. Then bursting into tears he turned away and went out.

Socrates looked at him and said: I return your good wishes, and will do as you bid. Then turning to us, he said, How charming the man is: since I have been in prison he has always been coming to see me, and at times he would talk to me, and was as good to me as could be, and now see how generously he sorrows on my account. We must do as he says, Crito; and therefore let the cup be brought, if the poison is prepared; if not, let the attendant prepare some.

Yet, said Crito, the sun is still upon the hill-tops, and I know that many a one has taken the draught late, and after the announcement has been made to him, he has eaten and drunk, and enjoyed the society of his beloved; do not hurry—there is time enough.

Socrates said: Yes, Crito, and they of whom you speak are right in so acting, for they think that they will be gainers by the delay; but I am right in not following their example, for I do not think that I should gain anything by drinking the poison a little later; I should only be ridiculous in my own eyes for sparing and saving a life which is already forfeit. Please then to do as I say, and not to refuse me.

Crito made a sign to the servant, who was standing by; and he went out, and having been absent for some time, returned with the jailer carrying the cup of poison. Socrates said: You, my good friend, who are experienced in these matters, shall give me directions how I am to proceed. The man answered: You have only to walk about until your legs are heavy, and then to lie down, and the poison will act. At the same time he handed the cup to Socrates, who in the easiest and gentlest manner, without the least fear or change of colour or feature, looking at the man with all his eyes, Echecrates, as his manner was, took the cup and said: What do you say about making a libation out of this cup to any god? May I, or not? The man answered: We only prepare, Socrates, just so much as we deem enough. I understand, he said: but I may and must ask the gods to prosper my journey from this to the other world—even so—and so be it according to my prayer. Then raising the cup to his lips, quite readily and cheerfully he drank off the poison. And hitherto most of us had been able to control our sorrow; but now when we saw him drinking, and saw too that he had finished the draught, we could no longer forbear, and in spite of myself my own tears were flowing fast; so that I covered my face and wept, not for him, but at the thought of my own calamity in having to part from such a friend. Nor was I the first; for Crito, when he found himself unable to restrain his tears, had got up, and I followed; and at that moment, Apollodorus, who had been weeping all the time, broke out in a loud and passionate cry which made cowards of us all. Socrates alone retained his calmness: What is this strange outcry? he said. I sent away the women mainly in order that they might not misbehave in this way, for I have been told that a man should die in peace. Be quiet then, and have patience. When we heard his words we were ashamed, and refrained our tears; and he walked about until, as he said, his legs began to fail, and then he lay on his back, according to the directions, and the man who gave him the poison now and then looked at his feet and legs; and after a while he pressed his foot hard, and asked him if he could feel; and he said, No; and then his leg, and so upwards and upwards, and showed us that he was cold and stiff. And he felt them himself, and said: When the poison reaches the heart, that will be the end. He was beginning to grow cold about the groin, when he uncovered his face, for he had covered himself up, and said—they were his last words—he said: Crito, I owe a cock to Æsculapius; will you remember to pay the debt? The debt shall be paid, said Crito; is there anything else? There was no answer to this question; but in a minute or two a movement was heard, and the attendants uncovered him; his eyes were set, and Crito closed his eyes and mouth.

Such was the end, Echecrates, of our friend; concerning whom I may truly say, that of all the men of his time whom I have known, he was the wisest and justest and best.

II. ENGLISH SELECTIONS

BALLADS

Sir Patrick Spens

THE king sits in Dumferling toune,
Drinking the blude-reid wine:
"O whar will I get guid sailor,
To sail this schip of mine?"

Up and spak an eldern knicht,
Sat at the kings richt kne:
"Sir Patrick Spence is the best sailor
That sails upon the se."

The king has written a braid letter,
And signd it wi his hand,
And sent it to Sir Patrick Spence,
Was walking on the sand.

The first line that Sir Patrick red,
A loud lauch lauched he;
The next line that Sir Patrick red,
The teir blinded his ee.

"O wha is this has don this deid,
This ill deid don to me,
To send me out this time o' the yeir,
To sail upon the se!

"Mak hast, mak haste, my mirry men all,
Our guid schip sails the morne:"
"O say na sae, my master deir,
For I feir a deadlie storme.

"Late late yestreen I saw the new moone,
Wi the auld moone in hir arme,
And I feir, I feir, my deir master,
That we will cum to harme."

O our Scots nobles wer richt laith
To weet their cork-heild schoone;
Bot lang owre a' the play wer playd,
Thair hats they swam aboone.

O lang, lang may their ladies sit,
Wi thair fans into their hand,
Or eir they se Sir Patrick Spence
Cum sailing to the land.

O lang, lang may the ladies stand,
Wi thair gold kems in their hair,
Waiting for thair ain deir lords,
For they'll se thame na mair.

Haf owre, haf owre to Aberdour,
It's fiftie fadom deip,
And thair lies guid Sir Patrick Spence,
Wi the Scots lords at his feit.

Clerk Saunders

Clark Sanders and May Margret
Walkt ower yon graveld green,
And sad and heavy was the love,
I wat, it fell this twa between.

"A bed, a bed," Clark Sanders said,
"A bed, a bed for you and I;"
"Fye no, fye no," the lady said
"Until the day we married be.

"For in it will come my seven brothers,
And a' their torches burning bright;
They'll say, We hae but ae sister,
And here her lying wi a knight."

"Ye'l take the sourde fray my scabbord,
And lowly, lowly lift the gin,
And you may say, your oth to save,
You never let Clark Sanders in.

"Yele take a napken in your hand,
And ye'l ty up baith your een,
And ye may say, your oth to save,
That ye saw na Sandy sen late yes-
treen.

"Yele take me in your armes twa,
 Yele carrey me ben into your bed,
And ye may say, your oth to save,
 In your bower-floor I never tread."

She has taen the sourde fray his scabbord,
 And lowly, lowly lifted the gin;
She was to swear, her oth to save,
 She never let Clerk Sanders in.

She has tain a napkin in her hand,
 And she ty'd up baith her eeen;
She was to swear, her oth to save,
 She say na him sene late yestreen.

She has taen him in her armes twa,
 And carried him ben into her bed;
She was to swear, her oth to save,
 He never in her bower-floor tread.

In and came her seven brothers,
 And all their torches burning bright;
Says thay, We hae but ae sister,
 And see there her lying wi a knight.

Out and speaks the first of them,
 "A wat they hay been lovers dear;"
Out an speaks the next of them,
 "They hay been in love this many a year."

Out an speaks the third of them,
 "It wear great sin this twa to twain;"
Out an speaks the fourth of them,
 "It wear a sin to kill a sleeping man."

Out an speaks the fifth of them,
 "A wat they'll near be twained by me;"
Out an speaks the sixt of them,
 "We'l tak our leave an gae our way."

Out an speaks the seventh of them,
 "Altho there wear no a man but me,
. . . .
 I bear the brand, I'le gar him die."

Out he has taen a bright long brand,
 And he has striped it throw the straw,
And throw and throw Clarke Sanders' body
 A wat he has gard cold iron gae.

Sanders he started, an Margret she lapt,
 Intill his arms whare she lay,
And well and wellsome was the night,
 A wat it was between these twa.

And they lay still, and sleeped sound,
 Untill the day began to daw;
And kindly till him she did say
 "It's time, trew-love, ye wear awa."

They lay still, and sleeped sound,
 Untill the sun began to shine;
She lookt between her and the wa,
 And dull and heavy was his eeen.

She thought it had been a loathsome sweat,
 A wat it had fallen this twa between;
But it was the blood of his fair body,
 A wat his life days wair na lang.

"O Sanders, I'le do for your sake
 What other ladys would na thoule;
When seven years is come and gone,
 There's near a shoe go on my sole.

"O Sanders, I'le do for your sake
 What other ladies would think mare;
When seven years is come an gone,
 Ther's nere a comb go in my hair.

"O Sanders, I'le do for your sake
 What other ladies would think lack;
When seven years is come an gone,
 I'le wear nought but dowy black."

The bells gaed clinking throw the towne,
 To carry the dead corps to the clay,
An sighing says her May Margret,
 "A wat I bide a doulfou day."

In an come her father dear,
 Stout steping on the floor;
. . . .
. . . .

"Hold your toung, my doughter dear,
 Let all your mourning a bee;
I'le carry the dead corps to the clay,
 An I'le come back an comfort thee."

"Comfort well your seven sons,
For comforted will I never bee;
For it was neither lord nor loune
That was in bower last night wi mee."

Johnie Armstrong

Is there never a man in all Scotland,
From the highest state to the lowest degree,
That can shew himself now before the king?
Scotland is so full of their traitery.

Yes, there is a man in Westmerland,
And John Armstrong some do him call;
He has no lands nor rents coming in,
Yet he keeps eightscore men within his hall.

He has horse and harness for them all,
And goodly steeds that be milk-white,
With their goodly belts about their necks,
With hats and feathers all alike.

The king he writ a lovely letter,
With his own hand so tenderly,
And has sent it unto John Armstrong,
To come and speak with him speedily.

When John he looked the letter upon,
Then, Lord! he was as blithe as a bird in a tree:
"I was never before no king in my life,
My father, my grandfather, nor none of us three.

"But seeing we must [go] before the king,
Lord! we will go most valiantly;
You shall every one have a velvet coat,
Laid down with golden laces three.

"And you shall every one have a scarlet cloak,
Laid down with silver laces five,
With your golden belts about your necks,
With hats [and] brave feathers all alike."

But when John he went from Guiltknock Hall!
The wind it blew hard, and full sore it did rain:
"Now fare you well, brave Guiltknock Hall!
I fear I shall never see thee again."

Now John he is to Edenborough gone,
And his eightscore men so gallantly,
And every one of them on a milk-white steed,
With their bucklers and swords hanging down to the knee.

But when John he came the king before,
With his eightscore men so gallant to see,
The king he moved his bonnet to him;
He thought he had been a king as well as he.

"O pardon, pardon, my soveraign leige,
Pardon for my eightscore men and me!
For my name it is John Armstrong,
And a subject of yours, my leige," said he.

"Away with thee, thou false traitor!
No pardon I will grant to thee,
But, to-morrow before eight of the clock,
I will hang thy eightscore men and thee."

O how John looked over his left shoulder!
And to his merry men thus said he:
I have asked grace of a graceless face,
No pardon here is for you nor me.

Then John pulld out a nut-brown sword,
And it was made of mettle so free;
Had not the king moved his foot as he did,
John had taken his head from his body.

"Come, follow me, my merry men all,
We will scorn one foot away to fly;

It never shall be said we were hung like doggs;
No, wee'l fight it out most manfully."

Then they fought on like champions bold—
For their hearts was sturdy, stout, and free—
Till they had killed all the kings good guard;
There was none left alive but onely three.

But then rise up all Edenborough,
They rise up by thousands three;
Then a cowardly Scot came John behind,
And run him thorow the fair body.

Said John, Fight on, my merry men all,
I am a little hurt, but I am not slain;
I will lay me down for to bleed a while,
Then I'le rise and fight with you again.

Then they fought on like mad men all,
Till many a man lay dead on the plain;
For they were resolved, before they would yield,
That every man would there be slain.

So there they fought couragiously,
'Till most of them lay dead there and slain,
But little Musgrave, that was his foot-page,
With his bonny grissell got away untain.

But when he came up to Guiltknock Hall,
The lady spyed him presently:
"What news, what news, thou little foot-page?
What news from thy master and his company?"

"My news is bad, lady," he said,
"Which I do bring, as you may see;
My master, John Armstrong, he is slain,
And all his gallant company.

"Yet thou are welcome home, my bonny grisel!
Full oft thou hast fed at the corn and hay,
But now thou shalt be fed with bread and wine,
And thy sides shall be spurred no more, I say."

O then bespoke his little son,
Ae he was set on his nurses knee:
"If ever I live for to be a man,
My fathers blood revenged shall be."

SIR THOMAS MALORY (Fifteenth Century)

From Le Morte d'Arthur

The Last Battle and the Passing of Arthur

Then were they condescended that King Arthur and Sir Mordred should meet betwixt both their hosts, and every each of them should bring fourteen persons; and they came with this word unto Arthur. Then said he: I am glad that this is done: and so he went into the field. And when Arthur should depart, he warned all his host that an they see any sword drawn: Look ye come on fiercely, and slay that traitor, Sir Mordred, for I in no wise trust him. In likewise Sir Mordred warned his host that: An ye see any sword drawn, look that ye come on fiercely, and so slay all that ever before you standeth; for in no wise I will not trust for this treaty, for I know well my father will be avenged on me. And so they met as their appointment was, and so they were agreed and accorded thoroughly; and wine was fetched, and they drank. Right soon came an adder out of a little heath bush, and it stung a knight on the foot. And when the knight felt him stung, he looked down and saw the adder, and then he drew his sword to slay the adder, and thought of none other harm. And when the host on both parties saw that sword drawn, then they blew beamous, trumpets, and horns, and shouted grimly. And so both hosts dressed them together. And King Arthur took his horse, and said: Alas this unhappy day! and so rode to his party. And Sir Mordred in likewise. And never was there seen a more dolefuller battle in no Christian land; for there was but rushing and riding, foining and striking, and many a grim word was there spoken either to other, and many a deadly stroke. But ever King Arthur rode throughout the battle of Sir Mordred many times, and did full nobly as a noble king should, and at all times he fainted never; and Sir Mordred that day put him in devoir, and in great peril. And thus they fought all the long day, and never stinted till the noble knights were laid to the cold earth; and ever they fought still till it was near night, and by that time was there an hundred thousand laid dead upon the down. Then was Arthur wood wroth out of measure, when he saw his people so slain from him. Then the king looked about him, and then was he ware, of all his host and of all his good knights, were left no more on live but two knights; that one was Sir Lucan the Butler, and his brother Sir Bedivere, and they were full sore wounded. Jesu mercy, said the king, where are all my noble knights become? Alas that ever I should see this doleful day, for now, said Arthur, I am come to mine end. But would to God that I wist where were that traitor Sir Mordred, that hath caused all this mischief. Then was King Arthur ware where Sir Mordred leaned upon his sword among a great heap of dead men. Now give me my spear, said Arthur unto Sir Lucan, for yonder I have espied the traitor that all this woe hath wrought. Sir, let him be, said Sir Lucan, for he is unhappy; and if ye pass this unhappy day ye shall be right well revenged upon him. Good lord, remember ye of your night's dream, and what the spirit of Sir Gawaine told you this night, yet God of his great goodness hath preserved you hitherto. Therefore, for God's sake, my lord, leave off by this, for blessed be God ye have won the field, for here we be three on live, and with Sir Mordred is none on live; and if ye leave off now this wicked day of destiny is past. Tide me death, betide me life, saith the king, now I see him yonder alone he shall never escape mine hands, for at a better avail shall I never have him. God speed you well, said Sir Bedivere. Then the king gat his spear in both his hands, and ran toward Sir Mordred, crying: Traitor, now is thy death day come. And when Sir Mordred heard Sir Arthur, he ran until him with his sword drawn in his hand. And there King Arthur smote Sir Mordred under the shield, with a foin of his spear, throughout the body, more than a fathom. And when Sir Mordred felt that he had his death wound he thrust himself with the might that he had up to the bur of King Arthur's spear. And right so he smote his father Arthur, with his sword holden in both his hands, on the side of the head, that the sword pierced the helmet and the brain pan, and therewithal Sir Mordred fell stark dead to the earth; and the noble Arthur fell in a swoon to the earth, and there he swooned ofttimes. And Sir Lucan the Butler and Sir Bedivere ofttimes heave him up. And so weakly they led him betwixt them both, to a little chapel not far from the seaside. And when the king was there he thought him well eased. Then heard they people cry in the field. Now go thou, Sir Lucan, said the king, and do me to wit what betokens that noise in the field. So Sir Lucan departed, for he was grievously wounded in many places. And so as he yede, he saw and hearkened by the moonlight, how that pillers and robbers were come into the field, to pill and to rob many a full noble knight of brooches, and beads, of many a good ring, and of many a rich jewel; and who that were not dead all out, there they slew them for their harness and their riches. When Sir Lucan understood this work, he came to the king as soon as he might, and told him all what he had heard and seen. Therefore by my rede, said Sir Lucan, it is best that we bring you to some town. I would it were so, said the king.

But I may not stand, mine head works so. Ah Sir Launcelot, said King Arthur, this day have I sore missed thee: alas, that ever I was against thee, for now have I my death, whereof Sir Gawaine me warned in my dream. Then Sir Lucan took up the king the one part, and Sir Bedivere the other part, and in the lifting the king swooned; and Sir Lucan fell in a swoon with the lift, that the part of his guts fell out of his body, and therewith the noble knight's heart brast. And when the king awoke, he beheld Sir Lucan, how he lay foaming at the mouth, and part of his guts lay at his feet. Alas, said the king, this is to me a full heavy sight, to see this noble duke so die for my sake, for he would have holpen me, that had more need of help than I. Alas, he would not complain him, his heart was so set to help me: now Jesu have mercy upon his soul! Then Sir Bedivere wept for the death of his brother. Leave this mourning and weeping, said the king, for all this will not avail me, for wit thou well an I might live myself, the death of Sir Lucan would grieve me evermore; but my time hieth fast, said the king. Therefore, said Arthur unto Sir Bedivere, take thou Excalibur, my good sword, and go with it to yonder water side, and when thou comest there I charge thee throw my sword in that water, and come again and tell me what thou there seest. My lord, said Bedivere, your commandment shall be done, and lightly bring you word again. So Sir Bedivere departed, and by the way he beheld that noble sword, that the pommel and the haft was all of precious stones; and then he said to himself: If I throw this rich sword in the water, thereof shall never come good, but harm and loss. And then Sir Bedivere hid Excalibur under a tree. And so, as soon as he might, he came again unto the king, and said he had been at the water, and had thrown the sword in the water. What saw thou there? said the king. Sir, he said, I saw nothing but waves and winds. That is untruly said of thee, said the king, therefore go thou lightly again, and do my commandment; as thou art to me lief and dear, spare not, but throw it in. Then Sir Bedivere returned again, and took the sword in his hand; and then him thought sin and shame to throw away that noble sword, and so efte he hid the sword, and returned again, and told to the king that he had been at the water, and done his commandment. What saw thou there? said the king. Sir, he said, I saw nothing but the waters wappe and waves wanne. Ah, traitor untrue, said King Arthur, now hast thou betrayed me twice. Who would have weened that, thou that has been to me so lief and dear? and thou art named a noble knight, and would betray me for the richness of the sword. But now go again lightly, for thy long tarrying putteth me in great jeopardy of my life, for I have taken cold. And but if thou do now as I bid thee, if ever I may see thee, I shall slay thee with mine own hands; for thou wouldst for my rich sword see me dead. Then Sir Bedivere departed, and went to the sword, and lightly took it up, and went to the water side; and there he bound the girdle about the hilts, and then he threw the sword as far into the water, as he might; and there came an arm and an hand above the water and met it, and caught it, and so shook it thrice and brandished, and then vanished away the hand with the sword in the water. So Sir Bedivere came again to the king, and told him what he saw. Alas, said the king, help me hence, for I dread me I have tarried over long. Then Sir Bedivere took the king upon his back, and so went with him to that water side. And when they were at the water side, even fast by the bank hoved a little barge with many fair ladies in it, and among them all was a queen, and all they had black hoods, and all they wept and shrieked when they saw

King Arthur. Now put me into the barge, said the king. And so he did softly; and there received him three queens with great mourning; and so they set them down, and in one of their laps King Arthur laid his head. And then that queen said: Ah, dear brother, why have ye tarried so long from me? alas, this wound on your head hath caught over-much cold. And so then they rowed from the land, and Sir Bedivere beheld all those ladies go from him. Then Sir Bedivere cried: Ah my lord Arthur, what shall become of me, now ye go from me and leave me here alone among mine enemies? Comfort thyself, said the king, and do as well as thou mayest, for in me is no trust for to trust in; for I will into the vale of Avilion to heal me of my grievous wound: and if thou hear never more of me, pray for my soul.

CHRISTOPHER MARLOWE
[1564-1593]

The Passionate Shepherd to his Love

COME live with me and be my Love,
And we will all the pleasures prove
That valleys, groves, hills and fields,
Woods or steepy mountain yields.

And we will sit upon the rocks
Seeing the shepherds feed their flocks,
By shallow rivers, to whose falls
Melodious birds sing madrigals.

And I will make thee beds of roses
And a thousand fragrant posies,
A cap of flowers, and a kirtle
Embroidered all with leaves of myrtle.

A gown made of the finest wool,
Which from our pretty lambs we pull,
Fair linèd slippers for the cold,
With buckles of the purest gold.

A belt of straw and ivy buds,
With coral clasps and amber studs:
And if these pleasures may thee move,
Come live with me and be my Love.

The shepherd swains shall dance and sing
For thy delight each May-morning:
If these delights thy mind may move,
Then live with me and be my Love.

SIR WALTER RALEIGH
[1552?-1618]

The Nymph's Reply to the Shepherd

IF all the world and love were young,
And truth in every shepherd's tongue,
These pretty pleasures might me move
To live with thee and be thy love.

But time drives flocks from field to fold,
When rivers rage and rocks grow cold;
And Philomel becometh dumb;
The rest complains of cares to come.

The flowers do fade, and wanton fields
To wayward winter reckoning yields:
A honey tongue, a heart of gall,
Is fancy's spring, but sorrow's fall.

Thy gowns, thy shoes, thy beds of roses,
Thy cap, thy kirtle, and thy posies,
Soon break, soon wither, soon forgotten,—
In folly ripe, in reason rotten.

Thy belt of straw and ivy buds,
Thy coral clasps and amber studs,—
All those in me no means can move
To come to thee and be thy love.

But could youth last, and love still breed;
Had joys no date, nor age no need;
Then those delights my mind might move
To live with thee and be thy love.

A Vision upon this Conceit of the Fairy Queen

This sonnet was appended to Spenser's *Faerie Queene,* Books i.-iii., published in 1590.

METHOUGHT I saw the grave where Laura lay,
Within that temple where the vestal flame
Was wont to burn: and, passing by that way,
To see that buried dust of living fame,
Whose tomb fair Love and fairer Virtue kept,
All suddenly I saw the Fairy Queen;
At whose approach the soul of Petrarch wept,
And from thenceforth those graces were not seen,
For they this Queen attended; in whose stead
Oblivion laid him down on Laura's hearse.
Hereat the hardest stones were seen to bleed,
And groans of buried ghosts the heavens did pierce:
 Where Homer's spright did tremble all for grief,
 And cursed the access of that celestial thief.

His Pilgrimage

GIVE me my scallop-shell of quiet,
 My staff of faith to walk upon,
My scrip of joy, immortal diet,
 My bottle of salvation,
My gown of glory, hope's true gage;
And thus I'll take my pilgrimage.

Blood must be my body's balmer;
 No other balm will there be given;
Whilst my soul, like quiet palmer,
 Travelleth towards the land of heaven;
Over the silver mountains,
Where spring the nectar fountains:
 There will I kiss
 The bowl of bliss;
And drink mine everlasting fill
Upon every milken hill.
My soul will be a-dry before;
But after, it will thirst no more.

Then by that happy blissful day,
 More peaceful pilgrims I shall see,
That have cast off their rags of clay,
 And walk apparell'd fresh like me.
 I'll take them first
 To quench their thirst
 And taste of nectar suckets,
 At those clear wells
 Where sweetness dwells,
 Drawn up by saints in crystal buckets.

And when our bottles and all we
Are fill'd with immortality,
Then the blessed paths we'll travel,
Strow'd with rubies thick as gravel;
Ceilings of diamonds, sapphire floors,
High walls of coral and pearly bowers.
From thence to heaven's bribeless hall,
Where no corrupted voices brawl;
No conscience molten into gold,
No forg'd accuser bought or sold,
No cause deferr'd, no vain-spent journey,
For there Christ is the king's Attorney,
Who pleads for all without degrees,
And He hath angels, but no fees.
And when the grand twelve-million jury
Of our sins, with direful fury,
Against our souls black verdicts give,
Christ pleads His death, and then we live.

 Be Thou my speaker, taintless pleader,
 Unblotted lawyer, true proceeder!
 Thou givest salvation even for alms;
 Not with a bribed lawyer's palms.
 And this is mine eternal plea
 To Him that made heaven, earth, and sea,

That, since my flesh must die so soon,
And want a head to dine next noon,
Just at the stroke, when my veins start and spread,
Set on my soul an everlasting head!
Then am I ready, like a palmer fit,
To tread those blest paths which before I writ.

Of death and judgment, heaven and hell,
Who oft doth think, must needs die well.

Verses found in his Bible in the Gate-House at Westminster

These verses were printed in *Reliquiae Wottonianae*, 1651, &c., with the title "Sir Walter Raleigh the night before his death." He was executed on October 29, 1618, in Old Palace Yard, Westminster.

Even such is time, that takes in trust
Our youth, our joys, our all we have,
And pays us but with earth and dust;
Who, in the dark and silent grave,
When we have wandered all our ways,
Shuts up the story of our days;
But from this earth, this grave, this dust,
My God shall raise me up, I trust!

From THE HISTORY OF THE WORLD

The Conqueror Death

These concluding paragraphs of Raleigh's *History of the World* suggest to readers acquainted with the facts of Raleigh's life and death a picture of the great courtier, poet, and warrior of earlier days, confined in the Bloody Tower under sentence of death for thirteen years, from 1603 to 1616. The *History* was written in the Tower, 1607-1614.

For the rest, if we seek a reason of the succession and continuance of this boundless ambition in mortal men, we may add to that which hath been already said, that the kings and princes of the world have always laid before them the actions, but not the ends, of those great ones which preceded them. They are always transported with the glory of the one, but they never mind the misery of the other, till they find the experience in themselves. They neglect the advice of God, while they enjoy life, or hope it; but they follow the counsel of Death upon his first approach. It is he that puts into man all the wisdom of the world, without speaking a word, which God, with all the words of his law, promises, or threats, doth not infuse. Death, which hateth and destroyeth man, is believed; God, which hath made him and loves him, is always deferred; *I have considered,* saith Solomon, *all the works that are under the sun, and, behold, all is vanity and vexation of spirit;* but who believes it, till Death tells it us? It was Death, which opening the conscience of Charles the Fifth, made him enjoin his son Philip to restore Navarre; and king Francis the First of France, to command that justice should be done upon the murderers of the protestants in Merindol and Cabrieres, which till then he neglected. It is therefore Death alone that can suddenly make a man to know himself. He tells the proud and insolent, that they are but abjects, and humbles them at the instant, makes them cry, complain, and repent, yea, even to hate their forepast happiness. He takes the account of the rich, and proves him a beggar, a naked beggar, which hath interest in nothing but in the gravel that fills his mouth. He holds a glass before the eyes of the most beautiful, and makes them see therein their deformity and rottenness, and they acknowledge it.

O eloquent, just, and mighty Death! whom none can advise, thou hast persuaded; what none hath dared, thou hast done; and whom all the world hath flattered, thou only hast cast out of the world and despised; thou hast drawn together all the far-stretched greatness, all the pride, cruelty, and ambition of man, and covered it all over with these two narrow words, *His jacet!*

From THE DISCOVERY OF GUIANA

Description of the Orinoco Country

I HAVE therefore laboured all my life, both according to my small power and persuasion, to advance all those attempts that might either promise return of profit to ourselves, or at least be a let and impeachment to the quiet course and plentiful trades of the Spanish nation; who, in my weak judgment, by such a war were as easily endangered and brought from his powerfulness as any prince in Europe, if it be considered from how many kingdoms and nations his revenues are gathered, and those so weak in their own beings and so far severed from mutual succour. But because such a preparation and resolution is not to be hoped for in haste, and that the time which our enemies embrace cannot be had again to advantage, I will hope that these provinces, and that empire now by me discovered, shall suffice to enable her Majesty and the whole kingdom with no less quantities of treasure than the king of Spain hath in all the Indies, East and West, which he possesseth; which if the same be considered and followed, ere the Spaniards enforce the same, and if her Majesty will undertake it, I will be contented to lose her Highness' favour and good opinion forever, and my life withal, if the same be not found to exceed than to equal whatsoever is in this discourse promised and declared.

. . . .

The empire of Guiana is directly east from Peru towards the sea, and lieth under the equinoctial line; and it hath more abundance of gold than any part of Peru, and as many or more great cities than ever Peru had when it flourished most. It is governed by the same laws, and the emperor and people observe the same religion, and the same form and policies in government as were used in Peru, not differing in any part. And I have been assured by such of the Spaniards as have seen Manoa, the imperial city of Guiana, which the Spaniards call El Dorado, that for the greatness, for the richness, and for the excellent seat, it far exceedeth any of the world, at least of so much of the world as is known to the Spanish nation. It is founded upon a lake of salt water of 200 leagues long, like unto Mare Caspium. And if we compare it to that of Peru, and but read the report of Francisco Lopez and others, it will seem more than credible; and because we may judge of the one by the other, I thought good to insert part of the 120. chapter of Lopez in his *General History of the Indies,* wherein he describeth the court and magnificence of Guayna Capac, ancestor to the emperor of Guiana, whose very words are these:

"All the vessels of his house, table, and kitchen, were of gold and silver, and the meanest of silver and copper for strength and hardness of metal. He had in his wardrobe hollow statues of gold which seemed giants, and the figures in proportion and bigness of all the beasts, birds, trees, and herbs, that the earth bringeth forth; and of all the fishes that the sea or waters of his kingdom breedeth. He had also ropes, budgets, chests, and troughs of gold and silver, heaps of billets of gold, that seemed wood marked out to burn. Finally, there was nothing in his country whereof he had not the counterfeit in gold. Yea, and they say, the Ingas had a garden of pleasure in an island near Puna, where they went to recreate themselves, when they would take the air of the sea, which had all kinds of garden-herbs, flowers, and trees of gold and silver; an invention and magnificence till then never seen. Besides all this, he had an infinite quantity of silver and gold unwrought in Cuzco, which was lost by the death of Guascar, for the Indians hid it, seeing that the Spaniards took it, and sent it into Spain."

. . . .

As we abode here awhile, our Indian pilot, called Ferdinando, would needs go ashore to their village to fetch some fruits and to drink of their artificial wines, and also to see the place and know the lord of it against another time, and took with him a brother of his which he had with him in the journey. When they came to the village of these people the lord of the islands offered to lay hands on them, purposing to have slain them both; yielding for reason that this Indian of ours had brought a strange nation into their territory to spoil and destroy them. But the pilot being quick and of a disposed body, slipt their fingers and ran into the woods, and his brother, being the better footman of the two, recovered the creek's mouth, where we stayed in our barge, crying out that his brother was slain. With that we set hands on one of them that was next us, a very old man, and brought him into the barge, assuring him that if we had not our pilot again we would presently cut off his head. This old man, being resolved that he should pay the loss of the other, cried out to those in the woods to save Ferdinando, our pilot; but they followed him notwithstanding, and hunted after him upon the foot with their deer-dogs, and with so main a cry that all the woods echoed with the shout they made. But at the last this poor chased Indian recovered the river side and got upon a tree, and, as we were coasting, leaped down and swam to the barge half dead with fear. But our good hap was that we kept the other old Indian, which we handfasted to redeem our pilot withal; for, being natural of those rivers, we assured ourselves that he knew the way better than any stranger could. And, indeed, but for this chance, I think we had never found the way either to Guiana or back to our ships; for Ferdinando after a few days knew nothing at all, nor which way to turn; yea, and many times the old man himself was in great doubt which river to take.

. . . .

On the banks of these rivers were divers sorts of fruits good to eat, flowers and trees of such variety as were sufficient to make ten volumes of *Herbals;* we relieved ourselves many times with the fruits of the country, and sometimes with fowl and fish. We saw birds of all colours, some carnation, some crimson, orange-tawny, purple, watchet, and of all other sorts, both simple and mixed, and it was unto us a great good-passing of the time to behold them, besides the relief we found by killing some store of them with our fowling-pieces; without which, having little or no bread, and less drink, but only the thick and troubled water of the river, we had been in a very hard case.

. . . .

When we were come to the tops of the first hills of the plains adjoining to the river, we beheld that wonderful breach of waters which ran down Caroli; and might from that mountain see the river how it ran in three parts, above twenty miles off, and there appeared some ten or twelve overfalls in sight, every one as high over the other as a church tower, which fell with that fury, that the rebound of water made it seem as if it had been all covered over with a great shower of rain; and in some places we took it at the first for a smoke that had risen over some great town. For mine own part I was well persuaded from thence to have returned, being a very ill footman; but the rest were all so desirous to go near the said strange thunder of waters, as they drew me on by little and little, till we came into the next valley, where we might better discern the same. I never saw a more beautiful country, nor more lively prospects; hills so raised here and there over the valleys; the river winding into divers branches; the plains adjoining without bush or stubble, all fair green grass; the ground of hard sand, easy to march on, either for horse or foot; the deer crossing in every path; the birds towards the evening singing on every tree with a thousand several tunes; cranes and herons of white, crimson, and carnation, perching in the river's side; the air fresh with a gentle easterly wind; and every stone that we stooped to take up promised either gold or silver by his complexion.

. . . . . .

Next unto Arui there are two rivers Atoica and Caura, and on that branch which is called Caura are a nation of people whose heads appear not above their shoulders; which though it may be thought a mere fable, yet for mine own part I am resolved it is true, because every child in the provinces of Aromaia and Canuri affirm the same. They are called Ewaipanoma; they are reported to have their eyes in their shoulders, and their mouths in the middle of their breasts, and that a long train of hair groweth backward between their shoulders. The son of Topiawari, which I brought with me into England, told me that they were the most mighty men of all the land, and use bows, arrows, and clubs twice as big as any of Guiana, or of the Orenoqueponi.

. . . . . .

When it grew towards sunset, we entered a branch of a river that fell into Orenoque, called Winicapora; where I was informed of the mountain of crystal, to which in truth for the length of the way, and the evil season of the year, I was not able to march, nor abide any longer upon the journey. We saw it afar off; and it appeared like a white church-tower of an exceeding height. There falleth over it a mighty river which toucheth no part of the side of the mountain, but rusheth over the top of it, and falleth to the ground with so terrible a noise and clamour, as if a thousand great bells were knocked one against another. I think there is not in the world so strange an overfall, nor so wonderful to behold. Berreo told me that there were diamonds and other precious stones on it, and that they shined very far off; but what it hath I know not, neither durst he or any of his men ascend to the top of the said mountain, those people adjoining being his enemies, as they were, and the way to it so impassable.

Dying Speech on the Scaffold

(*From Oldys*)

THE next morning, being Thursday, the 29th of October (1618), Sir Walter Ralegh was conducted, by the sheriffs of Middlesex, to the Old Palace Yard in Westminster, where there was a large scaffold erected before the parliament-house for his execution. He had on a wrought nightcap under his hat; a ruff band; a black wrought velvet nightgown over a hair-coloured satin doublet, and a black wrought waistcoat; a pair of black cut taffeta breeches, and ash-coloured silk stockings. He mounted the scaffold with a cheerful countenance, and saluted the lords, knights, and gentlemen of his acquaintance there present. Then proclamation being made by an officer for silence, he began his speech as follows:

"I thank God, that he has sent me to die in the light, and not in darkness. I likewise thank God that he has suffered me to die before such an assembly of honourable witnesses, and not obscurely in the Tower; where, for the space of thirteen years together, I have been oppressed with many miseries. And I return him thanks, that my fever hath not taken me at this time, as I prayed to him it might not, that I might clear myself of some accusations unjustly laid to my charge, and leave behind me the testimony of a true heart both to my king and country.

"There are two main points of suspicion that his Majesty hath conceived against me, and which, I conceive, have specially hastened my coming hither; therefore I desire to clear them to your lordships, and resolve you in the truth thereof. The first is, that his Majesty hath been informed, I have had some plot or confederacy with France, for which he had some reasons, though grounded upon a weak foundation. One was, that when I returned to Plymouth, I endeavoured to go to Rochel, which was because I would fain have made my peace before I returned to England. Another reason was, that again I would have bent my course to France, upon my last intended escape from London, being the place where I might have the best means of making such peace, and the best safeguard during that terror from above. These, joined with the coming of the French agent to my house here in London, only to confer about my said voyage, together with the report of my having a commission from the king of France, might occasion my being so suspected in this particular, and his Majesty to be so displeased with me. But this I say; for a man to call God to witness at any time to a falsehood, is a grievous sin. To call him as witness to a falsehood at the point of death, when there is no time for repentance, is a crime far more impious and desperate; therefore, for me to call that Majesty to witness an untruth, before whose tribunal I am instantly to appear, were beyond measure sinful, and without hope of pardon. I do yet call that great God to witness, that, as I hope to see him, to be saved by him, and live in the world to come, I never had any plot or intelligence with the French king; never had any commission from him, nor saw his hand or seal; that I never had any practice or combination with the French agent, nor ever knew or saw such a person, till I met him in my gallery unlooked for. If I speak not true, O Lord, let me never enter into thy kingdom.

"The second suspicion or imputation was, that his Majesty had been informed I had spoken disloyally of him. The only witness of this was a base Frenchman, a runagate, a chymical fellow, whom I soon knew to be perfidious; for being drawn by him into the action of freeing myself at Winchester, in which I confess my hand was touched, he, being sworn to secrecy overnight, revealed it the next morning. It is strange, that so mean a fellow could so far encroach himself into the favour of the lords; and, gaping after some great reward, could so falsely accuse me of seditious speeches against his Majesty, and be so credited. But this I here speak, it is no time for me to flatter or to fear princes, I, who am subject only unto death: and for me, who have now to do with God alone, to tell a lie to get the favour of the king were in vain: and yet, if ever I spake disloyally or dishonestly of the king, either to this Frenchman or any other; ever intimated the least thought hurtful or prejudicial of him, the Lord blot me out of the book of life.

"I confess, I did attempt to escape, and it was only to save my life. I likewise confess, that I feigned myself to be indisposed at Salisbury, but I hope it was no sin; for the prophet David did make himself a fool, and suffer spittal to fall upon his beard to escape from the hands of his enemies, and it was not imputed unto him as a sin: what I did was only to prolong time, till his Majesty came, in hopes of some commiseration from him.

"But I forgive that Frenchman, and likewise Sir Lewis Stucley the wrongs he hath done me, with all my heart; for I received the sacrament this morning of Mr. Dean, and I have forgiven all men; but, in charity to others, am bound to caution them against him, and such as he is. For Sir Lewis Stucley, my keeper and kinsman, hath affirmed, that I should tell him, my lord Carew and my lord of Doncaster here, did advise me to escape; but I protest before God I never told him any such thing; neither did these lords advise me to any such matter. It is not likely that I should acquaint two privy-counsellors of my escape; nor that I should tell him, my keeper, it was their advice; neither was there any reason to tell it him, or he to report it; for it is well known he left me six, eight, or ten days together alone, to go whither I listed, while he rode about the country. He further accused me, that I should shew him a letter, whereby I did signify that I would give him ten thousand pounds to escape; but God cast my soul into everlasting fire if ever I made such proffer of ten thousand pounds, or one thousand pounds; but indeed I shewed him a letter, that if he would go with me, there should be order taken for the discharge of his debts when he was gone; neither had I one thousand pounds, for, if I had, I could have made my peace better with it otherwise than by giving it Stucley. Further, he gave out, when I came to Sir Edward Parham's house, who had been a follower of mine, and gave me good entertainment, I had there received some dram of poison. When I answered, that I feared no such thing, for I was well-assured of those in the house; and therefore wished him to have no such thought. Now I will not only say, that God is the God of revenge, but also of mercy; and I desire God to forgive him, as I hope to be forgiven." Then casting his eye upon his note of remembrance, he went on thus:

"It was told the king, that I was brought perforce into England; and that I did not intend to return again: whereas Captain Charles Parker, Mr. Tresham, Mr. Leak, and divers others, that knew how I was dealt withal by the common soldiers, will witness to the contrary. They were an hundred and fifty of them who mutinied against me, and sent for me to come to them; for unto me they would not come. They kept me close prisoner in my cabin, and forced me to take an oath, that I would not go into England without their consent, otherwise they would have cast me into the sea. After I had taken this oath, I did, by wine, gifts, and fair words, so work upon the master-gunner, and ten or twelve of the faction, that I won them to desist from their purposes, and intended, when I returned home, to procure their pardon; in the mean while proposed, that I would dispose of some of them in Ireland; to which they agreed, and would have gone into the north parts, from which I dissuaded them, and told them, they were red-shanks who inhabited there, so drew them to the south; and the better to clear myself of them, was forced to get them a hundred and fifty pounds at Kingsale, otherwise I had never got from them.

"There was a report also, that I meant not to go to Guiana at all; and that I knew not of any mine, nor intended any such matter, but only to get my liberty, which I had not the wit to keep. But it was my full intent to go for gold, for the benefit of his Majesty, myself, and those who went with me, with the rest of my countrymen: though he that knew the head of the mine would not discover it when he saw my son was slain, but made himself away." Then turning to the earl of Arundel, he said, "My lord, you being in the gallery of my ship at my departure, I remember you took me by the hand, and said, you would request one thing of me; which was, whether I made a good voyage or a bad, that I would return again into England; which I then promised, and gave you my faith I would." "So you did," said his lordship; "it is true, and they were the last words I said to you." "Another slander was raised of me, that I should have gone away from them, and have left them at Guiana; but there were a great many worthy men, who accompanied me always, as my sergeant-major, and divers other (whom he named), that knew it was none of my intention. Also it hath been said, that I stinted them of fresh water; to which I answer, every one was, as they must be in a ship, furnished by measure, and not according to their appetites. This course all seamen know must be used among them, and to this strait were we driven. Another opinion was held, that I carried with me sixteen thousand pieces of gold; and that all the voyage I intended, was but to gain my liberty and this money into my hands: but, as I shall answer it before God, I had no more in all the world, directly or indirectly, than one hundred pounds; whereof I gave about forty-five pounds to my wife. But the ground of this false report was, that twenty thousand pounds being adventured, and but four thousand appearing in the surveyor's books, the rest had my hand to the bills for divers adventures; but, as I hope to be saved, I had not a penny more than one hundred pounds. These are the material points I thought good to speak of; I am at this instant to render my account to God, and I protest, as I shall appear before him, this that I have spoken is true.

"I will borrow but a little time more of Mr. Sheriff, that I may not detain him too long; and herein I shall speak of the imputation laid upon me through the jealousy of the people, that I had been a persecutor of my lord of Essex; that I rejoiced in his death, and stood in a window over-against him when he suffered, and puffed out tobacco in defiance of him; when as, God is my witness, that I shed tears for him when he died; and, as I hope to look God in the face hereafter, my lord of Essex did not see my face at the time of his death; for I was far off, in the armoury, where I saw him, but he saw not me. It is true, I was of a contrary faction; but I take the same God to witness, that I had no hand in his death, nor bear him any ill affection, but always believed it would be better for me that his life had been preserved; for after his fall, I got the hatred of those who wished me well before: and those who set me against him, set themselves afterwards against me, and were my greatest enemies: and my soul hath many times been grieved, that I was not nearer to him when he died; because, as I understood afterwards, he asked for me at his death, and desired to have been reconciled to me.

"And now I entreat, that you all will join with me in prayer to that great God of heaven whom I have grievously offended, being a man full of all vanity, who has lived a sinful life in such callings as have been most inducing to it; for I have been a soldier, a sailor, and a courtier, which are courses of wickedness and vice; that his almighty goodness will forgive me; that he will cast away my sins from me; and that he will receive me into everlasting life: so I take my leave of you all, making my peace with God."

Then proclamation being made, that all men should depart the scaffold, he prepared himself for death, giving away his hat and cap and money to some attendants who stood near him. When he took leave of the lords and other gentlemen, he entreated the lord Arundel to desire the king, that no scandalous writings to defame him might be published after his death; concluding, "I have a long journey to go, therefore must take my leave." Then having put off his gown and doublet, he called to the headsman to shew him the axe, which not being suddenly done, he said, "I prithee, let me see it. Dost thou think that I am afraid of it?" Having fingered the edge of it a little, he returned it, and said, smiling, to the sheriff, "This is a sharp medicine, but it is a sound cure for all diseases"; and having entreated the company to pray to God to assist and strengthen him, the executioner kneeled down and asked him forgiveness; which Ralegh, laying his hand upon his shoulder, granted. Then being asked which way he would lay himself on the block, he answered, "So the heart be right, it is no matter which way the head lies." As he stooped to lay himself along, and reclined his head, his face being towards the east, the headsman spread his own cloak under him. After a little pause, he gave the sign that he was ready for the stroke by lifting up his hand, and his head was struck off at two blows, his body never shrinking or moving. His head was shewed on each side of the scaffold, and then put into a red leather bag, and, with his velvet nightgown thrown over it, was afterwards conveyed away in a mourning coach of his lady's. His body, as we are told, was buried hard by, in the chancel of St. Margaret's church, near the altar; but his head was long preserved in a case by his widow, for she survived him twenty-nine years, as I have found by some anecdotes remaining in the family; and after her death it was kept also by her son Carew, with whom it is said to have been buried.

SIR PHILIP SIDNEY (1554-1586)

From ASTROPHEL AND STELLA

His Lady's Cruelty

(Sonnet XXXI. With how sad steps, O Moon, thou climb'st the skies!)

WITH how sad steps, O Moon, thou climb'st the skies!
How silently, and with how wan a face!
What! may it be that even in heavenly place
That busy archer his sharp arrows tries?
Sure, if that long-with-love-acquainted eyes
Can judge of love, thou feel'st a lover's case:
I read it in thy looks; thy languish'd grace

To me, that feel the like, thy state descries.
Then, even of fellowship, O Moon, tell me,
Is constant love deem'd there but want of wit?
Are beauties there as proud as here they be?
Do they above love to be loved, and yet
 Those lovers scorn whom that love doth possess?
 Do they call "virtue" there—ungratefulness?

Sleep

(Sonnet XXXIX. Come, Sleep; O Sleep! the certain knot of peace)

Come, Sleep; O Sleep! the certain knot of peace,
The baiting-place of wit, the balm of woe,
The poor man's wealth, the prisoner's release,
Th' indifferent judge between the high and low;
With shield of proof shield me from out the prease
Of those fierce darts Despair at me doth throw:
O make in me those civil wars to cease;
I will good tribute pay, if thou do so.
Take thou of me smooth pillows, sweetest bed,
A chamber deaf to noise and blind of light,
A rosy garland and a weary head;
And if these things, as being thine by right,
 Move not thy heavy grace, thou shalt in me,
 Livelier than elsewhere, Stella's image see.

Song. Absence

(Tenth Song)

O dear life, when shall it be
That mine eyes thine eyes shall see,
And in them thy mind discover
Whether absence have had force
Thy remembrance to divorce
From the image of thy lover?

Or if I myself find not,
After parting, aught forgot,
Nor debarred from Beauty's treasure,
Let not tongue aspire to tell
In what high joys I shall dwell;
Only thought aims at the pleasure.

Thought, therefore, I will send thee
To take up the place for me:
Long I will not after tarry,
There, unseen, thou mayst be bold,
Those fair wonders to behold,
Which in them my hopes do carry.

Thought, see thou no place forbear,
Enter bravely everywhere,
Seize on all to her belonging;
But if thou wouldst guarded be,
Fearing her beams, take with thee
Strength of liking, rage of longing.

Think of that most grateful time
When my leaping heart will climb,
In my lips to have his biding,
There those roses for to kiss,
Which do breathe a sugared bliss,
Opening rubies, pearls dividing.

* * * *

Think, think of those dallyings,
When with dove-like murmurings,
With glad moaning, passèd anguish,
We change eyes, and heart for heart,
Each to other do depart,
Joying till joy makes us languish.

O my thought, my thoughts surcease,
Thy delights my woes increase,
My life melts with too much thinking;
Think no more, but die in me,
Till thou shalt revivèd be,
At her lips my nectar drinking.

SIR FRANCIS BACON (1561-1626)

Of Friendship

It had been hard for him that spake it to have put more truth and untruth together in few words, than in that speech, *Whosoever is delighted in solitude is either a wild beast or a god.* For it is most true that a natural and secret hatred and aversation towards society in any man, hath somewhat of the savage beast; but it is most untrue that it should have any character at all of the divine nature; except it proceed, not out of a pleasure in solitude, but out of a love and desire to sequester a man's self for a higher conversation: such as is found to have been falsely and feignedly in some of the heathen; as Epimenides the Candian, Numa the Roman, Empedocles the Sicilian, and Apollonius of Tyana; and truly and really in divers of the ancient hermits and holy fathers of the church. But little do men perceive what solitude is, and how far it extendeth. For a crowd is not company; and faces are but a gallery of pictures; and talk but a tinkling cymbal, where there is no love. The Latin adage meeteth with it a little: *Magna civitas, magna solitudo,* because in a great town friends are scattered; so that there is not that fellowship, for the most part, which is in less neighbourhoods. But we may go further, and affirm most truly that it is a mere and miserable solitude to want true friends; without which the world is but a wilderness; and even in this sense also of solitude, whosoever in the frame of his nature and affections is unfit for friendship, he taketh it of the beast, and not from humanity.

A principal fruit of friendship is the ease and discharge of the fulness and swellings of the heart, which passions of all kinds do cause and induce. We know diseases of stoppings and suffocations are the most dangerous in the body; and it is not much otherwise in the mind; you may take sarza to open the liver, steel to open the spleen, flower of sulphur for the lungs, castoreum for the brain; but no receipt openeth the heart, but a true friend; to whom you may impart griefs, joys, fears, hopes, suspicions, counsels, and whatsoever lieth upon the heart to oppress it, in a kind of civil shrift or confession.

It is a strange thing to observe how high a rate great kings and monarchs do set upon this fruit of friendship whereof we speak: so great, as they purchase it many times at the hazard of their own safety and greatness. For princes, in regard of the distance of their fortune from that of their subjects and servants, cannot gather this fruit, except (to make themselves capable thereof) they raise some persons to be as it were companions and almost equals to themselves, which many times sorteth to inconvenience. The modern languages give unto such persons the name of favourites, or privadoes; as if it were matter of grace, or conversation. But the Roman name attaineth the true use and cause thereof, naming them *participes curarum;* for it is that which tieth the knot. And we see plainly that this hath been done, not by weak and passionate princes only, but by the wisest and most politic that ever reigned; who have oftentimes joined to themselves some of their servants; whom both themselves have called friends, and allowed others likewise to call them in the same manner; using the word which is received between private men.

L. Sylla, when he commanded Rome, raised Pompey (after surnamed the Great) to that height, that Pompey vaunted himself for Sylla's over-match. For when he had carried the consulship for a friend of his, against the pursuit of Sylla, and that Sylla did a little resent thereat, and began to speak great, Pompey turned upon him again, and in effect bade him be quiet; *for that more men adored the sun rising than the sun setting.* With Julius Cæsar, Decimus Brutus had obtained that interest, as he set him down in his testament for heir in remainder after his nephew. And this was the man that had power with him to draw him forth to his death. For when Cæsar would have discharged the senate, in regard of some ill presages, and specially a dream of Calpurnia; this man lifted him gently by the arm out of his chair, telling him he hoped he would not dismiss the senate till his wife had dreamt a better dream. And it seemeth his favour was so great, as Antonius, in a letter which is recited *verbatim* in one of Cicero's Philippics, calleth him *venefica, witch;* as if he had enchanted Cæsar. Augustus raised Agrippa (though of mean birth) to that height, as when he consulted with Mæcenas about the marriage of his daughter Julia, Mæcenas took the liberty to tell him, *that he must either marry his daughter to Agrippa, or take away his life: there was no third way, he had made him so great.* With Tiberius Cæsar, Sejanus had ascended to that height, as they two were termed and reckoned as a pair of friends. Tiberius in a letter to him saith, *hæc pro amicitiâ nostrâ non occultavi;* and the whole senate dedicated an altar to Friendship, as to a goddess, in respect of the great dearness of friendship between them two. The like or more was between Septimius Severus and Plautianus. For he forced his eldest son to marry the daughter of Plautianus; and would often maintain Plautianus in doing affronts to his son; and did write also in a letter to the senate, by these words: *I love the man so well, as I wish he may over-live me.* Now if these princes had been as a Trajan or a Marcus Aurelius, a man might have thought that this had proceeded of an abundant goodness of nature; but being men so wise, of such strength and severity of mind, and so extreme lovers of themselves, as all these were, it proveth most plainly that they found their own felicity (though as great as ever happened to mortal men) but as an half piece, except they mought have a friend to make it entire; and yet, which is more, they were princes that had wives, sons, nephews; and yet all these could not supply the comfort of friendship.

It is not to be forgotten what Comineus observeth of his first master, Duke Charles the Hardy; namely, that he would communicate his secrets with none; and least of all, those secrets which troubled him most. Whereupon he goeth on and saith that towards his latter time *that closeness did impair and a little perish his understanding.* Surely Comineus mought have made the same judgment also, if it had pleased him, of his second master Lewis the Eleventh, whose closeness was indeed his tormentor. That parable of Pythagoras is dark, but true; *Cor ne edito: Eat not the heart.* Certainly, if a man would give it a hard phrase, those that want friends to open themselves unto are cannibals of their own hearts. But one thing is most admirable (wherewith I will conclude this first fruit of friendship), which is, that this communicating of a man's self to his friend works two contrary effects; for it redoubleth joys, and cutteth griefs in halfs. For there is no man that imparteth his joys to his friend, but he joyeth the more: and no man that imparteth his griefs to his friend, but he grieveth the less. So that it is in truth of operation upon a man's mind, of like virtue as the alchymists use to attribute to their stone for man's body; that it worketh all contrary effects, but still to the good and benefit of nature. But yet without praying in aid of alchymists, there is a manifest image of this in the ordinary course of nature. For in bodies, union strengtheneth and cherisheth any natural action; and on the other side weakeneth and dulleth any violent impression: and even so it is of minds.

The second fruit of friendship is healthful and sovereign for the understanding, as the first is for the affections. For friendship maketh indeed a fair day in the affections, from storm and tempest; but it maketh daylight in the understanding, out of darkness and confusion of thoughts. Neither is this to be understood only of faithful counsel, which a man receiveth from his friend; but before you come to that, certain it is that whosoever hath his mind fraught with many thoughts, his wits and understanding do clarify and break up, in the communicating and discoursing with another; he tosseth his thoughts more easily; he marshalleth them more orderly; he seeth how they look when they are turned into words: finally, he waxeth wiser than himself; and that more by an hour's discourse than by a day's meditation. It was well said by Themistocles to the king of Persia, *That speech was like cloth of Arras, opened and put abroad; whereby the imagery doth appear in figure; whereas in thoughts they lie but as in packs.* Neither is the second fruit of friendship, in opening the understanding, restrained only to such friends as are able to give a man counsel; (they indeed are best;) but even without that, a man learneth of himself, and bringeth his own thoughts to light, and whetteth his wits as against a stone, which itself cuts not. In a word, a man were better relate himself to a statua or picture, than to suffer his thoughts to pass in smother.

Add now, to make this second fruit of friendship complete, that other point which lieth more open and falleth within vulgar observation; which is faithful counsel from a friend. Heraclitus saith well in one of his enigmas, *Dry light is ever the best.* And certain it is, that the light that a man receiveth by counsel from another, is drier and purer than that which cometh from his own understanding and judgment; which is ever infused and drenched in his affections and customs. So as there is as much difference between the counsel that a friend giveth, and that a man giveth himself, as there is between the counsel of a friend and of a flatterer. For there is no such flatterer as is a man's self; and there is no such remedy against flattery of a man's self, as the liberty of a friend. Counsel is of two sorts: the one concerning manners, the other concerning business. For the first, the best preservative to keep the mind in health is the faithful admonition of a friend. The calling of a man's self to a strict account is a medicine, sometime, too piercing and corrosive. Reading good books of morality is a little flat and dead. Observing our faults in others is sometimes improper for our case. But the best receipt (best, I say, to work, and best to take) is the admonition of a friend. It is a strange thing to behold what gross errors and extreme absurdities many (especially of the greater sort) do commit, for want of a friend to tell them of them; to the great damage both of their fame and fortune: for, as St. James saith, they are as men *that look sometimes into a glass, and presently forget their own shape and favour.* As for business, a man may think, if he will, that two eyes see no more than one; or that a gamester seeth always more than a looker-on; or that a man in anger is as wise as he that hath said over the four and twenty letters; or that a musket may be shot off as well upon the arm as upon a rest; and such other fond and high imaginations, to think himself all in all. But when all is done, the help of good counsel is that which setteth business straight. And if any man think that he will take counsel, but it shall be by pieces; asking counsel in one business of one man, and in another business of another man; it is well, (that is to say, better perhaps than if he asked none at all;) but he runneth two dangers: one, that he shall not be faithfully counselled; for it is a rare thing, except it be from a perfect and entire friend, to have counsel given, but such as shall be bowed and crooked to some ends which he hath that giveth it. The other, that he shall have counsel given, hurtful and unsafe, (though with good meaning,) and mixed partly of mischief and partly of remedy; even as if you would call a physician that is thought good for the cure of the disease you complain of, but is unacquainted with your body; and therefore may put you in way for a present cure, but overthroweth your health in some other kind; and so cure the disease and kill the patient. But a friend that is wholly acquainted with a man's estate will beware, by furthering any present business, how he dasheth upon other inconvenience. And therefore rest not upon scattered counsels; they will rather distract and mislead, than settle and direct.

After these two noble fruits of friendship, (peace in the affections, and support of the judgment,) followeth the last fruit; which is like the pomegranate, full of many kernels; I mean aid and bearing a part in all actions and occasions. Here the best way to represent to life the manifold use of friendship, is to cast and see how many things there are which a man cannot do himself; and then it will appear that it was a sparing speech of the ancients, to say, *that a friend is another himself;* for that a friend is far more than himself. Men have their time, and die many times in desire of some things which they principally take to heart; the bestowing of a child, the finishing of a work, or the like. If a man have a true friend, he may rest almost secure that the care of those things will continue after him. So that a man hath, as it were, two lives in his desires. A man hath a body, and that body is confined to a place; but where friendship is, all offices of life are as it were granted to him and his deputy. For he may exercise them by his friend. How many things are there which a man cannot, with any face or comeliness, say or do himself? A man can scarce allege his own merits with modesty, much less extol them; a man cannot sometimes brook to supplicate or beg; and a number of the like. But all these things are graceful in a friend's mouth, which are blushing in a man's own. So again, a man's person hath many proper relations which he cannot put off. A man cannot speak to his son but as a father; to his wife but as a husband; to his enemy but upon terms: whereas a friend may speak as the case requires, and not as it sorteth with the person. But to enumerate these things were endless; I have given the rule, where a man cannot fitly play his own part: if he have not a friend, he may quit the stage.

Of Studies

Studies serve for delight, for ornament, and for ability. Their chief use for delight, is in privateness and retiring; for ornament, is in discourse; and for ability, is in the judgment and disposition of business. For expert men can execute, and perhaps judge of particulars, one by one; but the general counsels, and the plots and marshalling of affairs, come best from those that are learned. To spend too much time in studies is sloth; to use them too much for ornament, is affectation; to make judgment wholly by their rules, is the humour of a scholar. They perfect nature, and are perfected by experience: for natural abilities are like natural plants, that need proyning by study; and studies themselves do give forth directions too much at large, except they be bounded in by experience. Crafty men contemn studies, simple men admire them, and wise men use them, for they teach not their own use; but that is a wisdom without them, and above them, won by observation. Read not to contradict and confute; nor to believe and take for granted; nor to find talk and discourse; but to weigh and consider. Some books are to be tasted, others to be swallowed, and some few to be chewed and digested; that is, some books are to be read only in parts; others to be read, but not curiously; and some few to be read wholly, and with diligence and attention. Some books also may be read by deputy, and extracts made of them by others; but that would be only in the less important arguments, and the meaner sort of books; else distilled books are like common distilled waters, flashy things. Reading maketh a full man; conference a ready man; and writing an exact man. And therefore, if a man write little, he had need have a great memory; if he confer little, he had need have a present wit: and if he read little, he had need have much cunning, to seem to know that he doth not. Histories make men wise; poets witty; the mathematics subtile; natural philosophy deep; moral grave; logic and rhetoric able to contend. *Abeunt studia in mores.* Nay there is no stond or impediment in the wit, but may be wrought out by fit studies: like as diseases of the body may have appropriate exercises. Bowling is good for the stone and reins; shooting for the lungs and breast; gentle walking for the stomach; riding for head; and the like. So if a man's wit be wandering, let him study the mathematics; for in demonstrations, if his wit be called away never so little, he must begin again. If his wit be not apt to distinguish or find differences, let him study the schoolmen; for they are *cymini sectores.* If he be not apt to beat over matters, and to call up one thing to prove and illustrate another, let him study the lawyer's cases. So every defect of the mind may have a special receipt.

MICHAEL DRAYTON
(1563-1632)

To the Cambro-Britons and their Harp, his Ballad of Agincourt

FAIR stood the wind for France,
When we our sails advance,
Nor now to prove our chance
Longer will tarry;
But putting to the main,
At Caux, the mouth of Seine,
With all his martial train,
Landed King Harry.

And taking many a fort,
Furnished in warlike sort,
Marcheth tow'rds Agincourt
In happy hour;
Skirmishing day by day,
With those that stopp'd his way,
Where the French gen'ral lay
With all his power.

Which in his height of pride,
King Henry to deride,
His ransom to provide,
To the king sending.
Which he neglects the while,
As from a nation vile,
Yet with an angry smile
Their fall portending.

And turning to his men,
Quoth our brave Henry then,
Though they to one be ten,
Be not amazed.
Yet have we well begun,
Battles so bravely won,
Have ever to the sun
By fame been raised.

And for myself (quoth he),
This my full rest shall be,
England ne'er mourn for me,
Nor more esteem me.
Victor I will remain,
Or on this earth lie slain,
Never shall she sustain
Loss to redeem me.

Poitiers and Cressy tell,
When most their pride did swell,
Under our swords they fell,
No less our skill is,
Than when our grandsire-great,
Claiming the regal seat,
By many a warlike feat
Lopp'd the French lilies.

The Duke of York so dread
The eager vaward led,
With the main, Henry sped,
Amongst his hench-men.
Exeter had the rear,
A braver man not there,
O Lord, how hot they were,
On the false Frenchmen!

They now to fight are gone,
Armour on armour shone,
Drum now to drum did groan,
To hear, was wonder;
That with the cries they make,
The very earth did shake,
Trumpet to trumpet spake,
Thunder to thunder.

Well it thine age became,
O noble Erpingham,
Which didst the signal aim
To our hid forces;
When from a meadow by,
Like a storm suddenly,
The English archery
Stuck the French horses.

With Spanish yew so strong,
Arrows a cloth-yard long,
That like to serpents stung,
Piercing the weather;
None from his fellow starts,
But playing manly parts,
And like true English hearts,
Stuck close together.

When down their bows they threw,
And forth their bilbos drew,
And on the French they flew,
Not one was tardy;

Arms were from shoulders sent,
Scalps to the teeth were rent,
Down the French peasants went,
  Our men were hardy.

This while our noble king,
His broad sword brandishing,
Down the French host did ding,
  As to o'erwhelm it,
And many a deep wound lent,
His arms with blood besprent,
And many a cruel dent
  Bruised his helmet.

Gloucester, that duke so good,
Next of the royal blood,
For famous England stood,
  With his brave brother;
Clarence, in steel so bright,
Though but a maiden knight,
Yet in that furious fight
  Scarce such another.

Warwick in blood did wade,
Oxford the foe invade,
And cruel slaughter made,
  Still as they ran up;
Suffolk his axe did ply,
Beaumont and Willoughby,
Bare them right doughtily,
  Ferrers and Fanhope.

Upon Saint Crispin's day
Fought was this noble fray,
Which fame did not delay
  To England to carry;
O when shall English men
With such acts fill a pen,
Or England breed again
  Such a King Harry?

WILLIAM SHAKESPEARE
(1564-1616)

Under the Greenwood Tree

UNDER the greenwood tree
Who loves to lie with me,
And turn his merry note
Unto the sweet bird's throat,
Come hither, come hither, come hither!
  Here shall he see
  No enemy
But winter and rough weather.

  Who doth ambition shun,
  And loves to live i' the sun,
  Seeking the food he eats,
  And pleased with what he gets,
Come hither, come hither, come hither!
  Here shall he see
  No enemy
But winter and rough weather.

  If it do come to pass
  That any man turn ass,
  Leaving his wealth and ease
  A stubborn will to please,
Ducdame, ducdame, ducdame!
  Here shall he see
  Gross fools as he,
An if he will come to me.

Hark, Hark! the Lark

HARK, hark! the lark at heaven's gate
  sings,
  And Phœbus gins arise
His steeds to water at those springs
  On chalic'd flowers that lies;
And winking Mary-buds begin
  To ope their golden eyes;
With every thing that pretty is,
  My lady sweet, arise,
  Arise, arise.

Full Fathom Five

FULL fathom five thy father lies;
  Of his bones are coral made;
Those are pearls that were his eyes:
  Nothing of him that doth fade
But doth suffer a sea-change
Into something rich and strange.
Sea-nymphs hourly ring his knell:
  Ding-dong.
  Hark! now I hear them,—ding-dong,
    bell.

Hamlet

Act II, Scene II

A room in the castle

Flourish. Enter KING, QUEEN, ROSENCRANTZ, GUILDENSTERN, *with others.*

King. Welcome, dear Rosencrantz and Guildenstern!
Moreover that we much did long to see you,
The need we have to use you did provoke
Our hasty sending. Something have you heard
Of Hamlet's transformation; so I call it,
Since not the exterior nor the inward man
Resembles that it was. What it should be,
More than his father's death, that thus hath put him
So much from the understanding of himself,
I cannot dream of. I entreat you both,
That, being of so young days brought up with him
And since so neighbour'd to his youth and humour,
That you vouchsafe your rest here in our court
Some little time; so by your companies
To draw him on to pleasures, and to gather
So much as from occasions you may glean,
[Whether aught, to us unknown, afflicts him thus,]
That, open'd, lies within our remedy.

Queen. Good gentlemen, he hath much talk'd of you;
And sure I am two men there are not living
To whom he more adheres. If it will please you
To show us so much gentry and good will
As to expend your time with us a while
For the supply and profit of our hope,
Your visitation shall receive such thanks
As fits a king's remembrance.

Ros. Both your Majesties
Might, by the sovereign power you have of us,
Put your dread pleasures more into command
Than to entreaty.

Guil. We both obey,
And here give up ourselves, in the full bent
To lay our services freely at your feet,
To be commanded.

King. Thanks, Rosencrantz and gentle Guildenstern.

Queen. Thanks, Guildenstern and gentle Rosencrantz,
And I beseech you instantly to visit
My too much changed son. Go, some of ye,
And bring the gentlemen where Hamlet is.

Guil. Heavens make our presence and our practices
Pleasant and helpful to him!

Queen. Amen!

[*Exeunt Rosencrantz, Guildenstern, and some Attendants*].

Enter POLONIUS.

Pol. The ambassadors from Norway, my good lord,
Are joyfully return'd.

King. Thou still hast been the father of good news.

Pol. Have I, my lord? Assure you, my good liege,
I hold my duty as I hold my soul,
Both to my God and to my gracious king.
And I do think, or else this brain of mine
Hunts not the trail of policy so sure
As it hath us'd to do, that I have found
The very cause of Hamlet's lunacy.

King. O, speak of that; that I do long to hear.

Pol. Give first admittance to the ambassadors.
My news shall be the fruit to that great feast.

King. Thyself do grace to them, and bring them in. [*Exit Polonius.*

He tells me, my sweet queen, that he hath found
The head and source of all your son's distemper.
Queen. I doubt it is no other but the main,
His father's death and our o'erhasty marriage.

Re-enter POLONIUS, *with* VOLTIMAND *and* CORNELIUS.

King. Well, we shall sift him.—Welcome, my good friends!
Say, Voltimand, what from our brother Norway?
Volt. Most fair return of greetings and desires.
Upon our first, he sent out to suppress
His nephew's levies, which to him appear'd
To be a preparation 'gainst the Polack,
But, better look'd into, he truly found
It was against your Highness. Whereat grieved,
That so his sickness, age, and impotence
Was falsely borne in hand, sends out arrests
On Fortinbras; which he, in brief, obeys,
Receives rebuke from Norway, and in fine
Makes vow before his uncle never more
To give the assay of arms against your Majesty.
Whereon old Norway, overcome with joy,
Gives him three thousand crowns in annual fee,
And his commission to employ those soldiers,
So levied as before, against the Polack;
With an entreaty, herein further shown, [*Giving a paper.*]
That it might please you to give quiet pass
Through your dominions for his enterprise,
On such regards of safety and allowance
As therein are set down.
King. It likes us well;
And at our more consider'd time we 'll read,
Answer, and think upon this business.
Meantime we thank you for your well-took labour.
Go to your rest; at night we 'll feast together.
Most welcome home!
[*Exeunt Voltimand and Cornelius.*]
Pol. This business is well ended.
My liege, and madam, to expostulate
What majesty should be, what duty is,
Why day is day, night night, and time is time,
Were nothing but to waste night, day, and time;
Therefore, since brevity is the soul of wit
And tediousness the limbs and outward flourishes,
I will be brief. Your noble son is mad.
Mad call I it; for, to define true madness,
What is 't but to be nothing else but mad?
But let that go.
Queen. More matter, with less art.
Pol. Madam, I swear I use no art at all.
That he is mad, 't is true; 't is true 't is pity,
And pity 't is 't is true. A foolish figure!
But farewell it, for I will use no art.
Mad let us grant him then; and now remains
That we find out the cause of this effect,
Or rather say, the cause of this defect,
For this effect defective comes by cause.
Thus it remains, and the remainder thus.
Perpend.
I have a daughter—have whilst she is mine—
Who, in her duty and obedience, mark,
Hath given me this. Now gather, and surmise.
[*Reads the letter.*]
"To the celestial and my soul's idol, the most beautified Ophelia,"—
That 's an ill phrase, a vile phrase; "beautified" is a vile phrase. But you shall hear. Thus:
"In her excellent white bosom, these."

Queen. Came this from Hamlet to her?

Pol. Good madam, stay a while. I will be faithful. [*Reads.*]

"Doubt thou the stars are fire,
Doubt that the sun doth move,
Doubt truth to be a liar,
But never doubt I love.

"O dear Ophelia, I am ill at these numbers. I have not art to reckon my groans; but that I love thee best, O most best, believe it. Adieu.

Thine evermore, most dear lady,
Whilst this machine is to him,
HAMLET."

This in obedience hath my daughter show'd me,
And more above, hath his solicitings,
As they fell out by time, by means, and place,
All given to mine ear.

King. But how hath she
Receiv'd his love?

Pol. What do you think of me?

King. As of a man faithful and honourable.

Pol. I would fain prove so. But what might you think,
When I had seen this hot love on the wing,—
As I perceiv'd it, I must tell you that,
Before my daughter told me,—what might you,
Or my dear Majesty your queen here, think,
If I had play'd the desk or table-book,
Or given my heart a winking, mute and dumb,
Or look'd upon this love with idle sight,
What might you think? No, I went round to work,
And my young mistress thus I did bespeak:
"Lord Hamlet is a prince, out of thy star.
This must not be;" and then I precepts gave her,
That she should lock herself from his resort,
Admit no messengers, receive no tokens.
Which done, she took the fruits of my advice;
And he, repulsed—a short tale to make—
Fell into a sadness, then into a fast,
Thence to a watch, thence into a weakness,
Thence to a lightness, and, by this declension,
Into the madness whereon now he raves,
And all we wail for.

King. Do you think 't is this?

Queen. It may be, very likely.

Pol. Hath there been such a time—I'd fain know that—
That I have positively said, " 'T is so,"
When it prov'd otherwise?

King. Not that I know.

Pol. Take this from this, if this be otherwise.
If circumstances lead me, I will find
Where truth is hid, though it were hid indeed
Within the centre.

King. How may we try it further?

Pol. You know, sometimes he walks four hours together
Here in the lobby.

Queen. So he has, indeed.

Pol. At such a time I 'll loose my daughter to him.
Be you and I behind an arras then;
Mark the encounter. If he love her not
And be not from his reason fallen thereon,
Let me be no assistant for a state,
But keep a farm and carters.

King. We will try it.

Enter HAMLET, *reading on a book.*

Queen. But look where sadly the poor wretch comes reading.

Pol. Away, I do beseech you, both away.
I 'll board him presently.

[*Exeunt King, Queen and Attendants.*]

O, give me leave,
How does my good Lord Hamlet?

Ham. Well, God-a-mercy.

Pol. Do you know me, my lord?

Ham. Excellent well; you are a fishmonger.

Pol. Not I, my lord.

Ham. Then I would you were so honest a man.

Pol. Honest, my lord!

Ham. Ay, sir. To be honest, as this world goes, is to be one man pick'd out of ten thousand.

Pol. That 's very true, my lord.

Ham. For if the sun breed maggots in a dead dog, being a good kissing carrion,—Have you a daughter?

Pol. I have, my lord.

Ham. Let her not walk i' the sun. Conception is a blessing, but not as your daughter may conceive. Friend, look to 't.

Pol. [*Aside.*] How say you by that? Still harping on my daughter. Yet he knew me not at first; he said I was a fishmonger. He is far gone, far gone. And truly in my youth I suff'red much extremity for love; very near this. I 'll speak to him again.—What do you read, my lord?

Ham. Words, words, words.

Pol. What is the matter, my lord?

Ham. Between who?

Pol. I mean, the matter you read, my lord.

Ham. Slanders, sir; for the satirical slave says here that old men have grey beards, that their faces are wrinkled, their eyes purging thick amber or plum-tree gum, and that they have a plentiful lack of wit, together with weak hams; all which, sir, though I most powerfully and potently believe, yet I hold it not honesty to have it thus set down; for you yourself, sir, should be old as I am, if like a crab you could go backward.

Pol. [*Aside.*] Though this be madness, yet there is method in 't.—Will you walk out of the air, my lord?

Ham. Into my grave?

Pol. Indeed, that is out o' the air. [*Aside.*] How pregnant sometimes his replies are! a happiness that often madness hits on, which reason and sanity could not so prosperously be deliver'd of. I will leave him, and suddenly contrive the means of meeting between him and my daughter.—My honourable lord, I will most humbly take my leave of you.

Ham. You cannot, sir, take from me anything that I will more willingly part withal,—[*Aside*] except my life, my life.

Pol. Fare you well, my lord.

Ham. These tedious old fools!

Enter ROSENCRANTZ *and* GUILDENSTERN.

Pol. You go to seek my Lord Hamlet? There he is.

Ros. [*To Polonius.*] God save you, sir!

[*Exit Polonius.*]

Guil. Mine honour'd lord!

Ros. My most dear lord!

Ham. My excellent good friends! How dost thou, Guildenstern? Oh, Rosencrantz! Good lads, how do ye both?

Ros. As the indifferent children of the earth.

Guil. Happy, in that we are not over-happy.
On Fortune's cap we are not the very button.

Ham. Nor the soles of her shoe?

Ros. Neither, my lord.

Ham. Then you live about her waist, or in the middle of her favour?

Guil. Faith, her privates we.

Ham. In the secret parts of Fortune? Oh, most true; she is a strumpet. What 's the news?

Ros. None, my lord, but that the world 's grown honest.

Ham. Then is doomsday near. But your news is not true. Let me question more in particular. What have you, my good friends, deserved at the hands of Fortune, that she sends you to prison hither?

Guil. Prison, my lord?

Ham. Denmark 's a prison.

Ros. Then is the world one.

Ham. A goodly one, in which there are many confines, wards, and dungeons, Denmark being one o' the worst.

Ros. We think not so, my lord.

Ham. Why, then, 't is none to you; for there is nothing either good or bad, but thinking makes it so. To me it is a prison.

Ros. Why, then, your ambition makes it one. 'T is too narrow for your mind.

Ham. O God, I could be bounded in a nutshell and count myself a king of infinite space, were it not that I have bad dreams.

Guil. Which dreams indeed are ambition, for the very substance of the ambitious is merely the shadow of a dream.

Ham. A dream itself is but a shadow.

Ros. Truly, and I hold ambition of so airy and light a quality that it is but a shadow's shadow.

Ham. Then are our beggars bodies, and our monarchs and outstretch'd heroes the beggars' shadows. Shall we to the court? for, by my fay, I cannot reason.

Ros., *Guil.* We 'll wait upon you.

Ham. No such matter. I will not sort you with the rest of my servants, for, to speak to you like an honest man, I am most dreadfully attended. But in the beaten way of friendship, what make you at Elsinore?

Ros. To visit you, my lord; no other occasion.

Ham. Beggar that I am, I am even poor in thanks, but I thank you; and sure, dear friends, my thanks are too dear a halfpenny. Were you not sent for? Is it your own inclining? Is it a free visitation? Come, deal justly with me. Come, come. Nay, speak.

Guil. What should we say, my lord?

Ham. Why, anything, but to the purpose. You were sent for; and there is a kind of confession in your looks which your modesties have not craft enough to colour. I know the good king and queen have sent for you.

Ros. To what end, my lord?

Ham. That you must teach me. But let me conjure you, by the rights of our fellowship, by the consonancy of our youth, by the obligation of our ever-preserved love, and by what more dear a better proposer could charge you withal, be even and direct with me, whether you were sent for or no!

Ros. [*Aside to Guil.*] What say you?

Ham. [*Aside.*] Nay, then, I have an eye of you.—If you love me, hold not off.

Guil. My lord, we were sent for.

Ham. I will tell you why; so shall my anticipation prevent your discovery, and your secrecy to the King and Queen moult no feather. I have of late—but wherefore I know not—lost all my mirth, forgone all custom of exercise; and indeed it goes so heavily with my disposition that this goodly frame, the earth, seems to me a sterile promontory, this most excellent canopy, the air, look you, this brave o'erhanging firmament, this majestical roof fretted with golden fire, why, it appears no other thing to me than a foul and pestilent congregation of vapours. What a piece of work is a man! How noble in reason! How infinite in faculty! In form and moving how express and admirable! In action how like an angel! In apprehension how like a god! The beauty of the world! The paragon of animals! And yet, to me, what is this quintessence of dust? Man delights not me,—no, nor woman neither, though by your smiling you seem to say so.

Ros. My lord, there was no such stuff in my thoughts.

Ham. Why did you laugh then, when I said, "Man delights not me"?

Ros. To think, my lord, if you delight not in man, what lenten entertainment the players shall receive from you. We coted them on the way, and hither are they coming to offer you service.

Ham. He that plays the king shall be welcome; his majesty shall have tribute of me; the adventurous knight shall use his foil and target; the lover shall not sigh gratis; the humorous man shall end his part in peace; the clown shall make those laugh whose lungs are tickle o' the sere; and the lady shall say her mind freely, or the blank verse shall halt for 't. What players are they?

Ros. Even those you were wont to take delight in, the tragedians of the city.

Ham. How chances it they travel? Their residence, both in reputation and profit, was better both ways.

Ros. I think their inhibition comes by the means of the late innovation.

Ham. Do they hold the same estimation they did when I was in the city? Are they so follow'd?

Ros. No, indeed, they are not.

Ham. How comes it? Do they grow rusty?

Ros. Nay, their endeavour keeps in the wonted pace; but there is, sir, an aery of children, little eyases, that cry out on the top of question, and are most tyrannically clapp'd for 't. These are now the fashion, and so berattle the common stages—so they call them—that many wearing rapiers are afraid of goose-quills and dare scarce come thither.

Ham. What, are they children? Who maintains 'em? How are they escoted? Will they pursue the quality no longer than they can sing? Will they not say afterwards, if they should grow themselves to common players,—as it is most like, if their means are no better—their writers do them wrong, to make them exclaim against their own succession?

Ros. Faith, there has been much to do on both sides, and the nation holds it no sin to tarre them to controversy. There was for a while no money bid for argument unless the poet and the player went to cuffs in the question.

Ham. Is 't possible?

Guil. O, there has been much throwing about of brains.

Ham. Do the boys carry it away?

Ros. Ay, that they do, my lord; Hercules and his load too.

Ham. It is not strange; for mine uncle is King of Denmark, and those that would make mows at him while my father lived, give twenty, forty, [fifty,] an hundred ducats apiece for his picture in little. ['Sblood,] there is something in this more than natural, if philosophy could find it out.

[*Flourish for the Players.*

Guil. There are the players.

Ham. Gentlemen, you are welcome to Elsinore. Your hands, come. The appurtenance of welcome is fashion and ceremony. Let me comply with you in the garb, lest my extent to the players, which, I tell you, must show fairly outward, should more appear like entertainment than yours. You are welcome; but my uncle-father and aunt-mother are deceiv'd.

Guil. In what, my dear lord?

Ham. I am but mad north-north-west. When the wind is southerly I know a hawk from a handsaw.

Enter Polonius.

Pol. Well be with you, gentlemen!

Ham. [*Aside to them.*] Hark you, Guildenstern, and you too, at each ear a hearer: that great baby you see there is not yet out of his swathing-clouts.

Ros. Happily he is the second time come to them, for they say an old man is twice a child.

Ham. I will prophesy he comes to tell me of the players; mark it. [*Aloud.*] You say right, sir; for o' Monday morning 't was so indeed.

Pol. My lord, I have news to tell you.

Ham. My lord, I have news to tell you. When Roscius was an actor in Rome,—

Pol. The actors are come hither, my lord.

Ham. Buzz, buzz!

Pol. Upon mine honour,—

Ham. "Then came each actor on his ass,"—

Pol. The best actors in the world, either for tragedy, comedy, history, pastoral, pastoral-comical, historical-pastoral, tragical-historical, tragical-comical-historical-pastoral, scene individable, or poem unlimited; Seneca cannot be too heavy, nor Plautus too light. For the law of writ and the liberty, these are the only men.

Ham. O Jephthah, judge of Israel, what a treasure hadst thou!

Pol. What a treasure had he, my lord?

Ham. Why,

"One fair daughter, and no more,
The which he loved passing well."

Pol. [*Aside.*] Still on my daughter.

Ham. Am I not i' the right, old Jephthah?

Pol. If you call me Jephthah, my lord, I have a daughter that I love passing well.

Ham. Nay, that follows not.

Pol. What follows, then, my lord?

Ham. Why.

"As by lot, God wot,"

and then, you know,

"It came to pass, as most like it was,"—The first row of the pious chanson will show you more, for look where my abridgements come.

Enter four or five PLAYERS.

You 're welcome, masters, welcome all. I am glad to see thee well. Welcome, good friends. O, my old friend! Thy face is valanc'd since I saw thee last; com'st thou to beard me in Denmark? What, my young lady and mistress! By 'r lady, your ladyship is nearer heaven than when I saw you last, by the altitude of a chopine. Pray God, your voice, like a piece of uncurrent gold, be not crack'd within the ring. Masters, you are all welcome. We 'll e'en to 't like French falconers—fly at anything we see; we 'll have a speech straight. Come, give us a taste of your quality; come, a passionate speech.

1. Play. What speech, my lord?

Ham. I heard thee speak me a speech once, but it was never acted; or, if it was, not above once. For the play, I remember, pleas'd not the million; 't was caviare to the general; but it was—as I receiv'd it, and others, whose judgment in such matters cried in the top of mine —an excellent play, well digested in the scenes, set down with as much modesty as cunning. I remember, one said there were no sallets in the lines to make the matter savoury, nor no matter in the phrase that might indict the author of affectation; but call'd it an honest method, [as wholesome as sweet, and by very much more handsome than fine.] One speech in it I chiefly lov'd; 't was Æneas' tale to Dido, and thereabout of it especially where he speaks of Priam's slaughter. If it live in your memory, begin at this line: let me see, let me see—

"The rugged Pyrrhus, like the Hyrcanian beast,"

—It is not so. It begins with Pyrrhus:—

"The rugged Pyrrhus, he whose sable arms,
Black as his purpose, did the night resemble
When he lay couched in the ominous horse,
Hath now this dread and black complexion smear'd
With heraldry more dismal. Head to foot
Now is he total gules, horribly trick'd
With blood of fathers, mothers, daughters, sons,
Bak'd and impasted with the parching streets,
That lend a tyrannous and damned light
To their vile murders. Roasted in wrath and fire,
And thus o'er-sized with coagulate gore,
With eyes like carbuncles, the hellish Pyrrhus

Old grandsire Priam seeks."
[So, proceed you.]

Pol. 'Fore God, my lord, well spoken, with good accent and good discretion.

1. Play. "Anon he finds him
Striking too short at Greeks. His antique sword,
Rebellious to his arm, lies where it falls,
Repugnant to command. Unequal match,
Pyrrhus at Priam drives, in rage strikes wide,
But with the whiff and wind of his fell sword
The unnerved father falls. Then senseless Ilium,
Seeming to feel his blow, with flaming top
Stoops to his base, and with a hideous crash
Takes prisoner Pyrrhus' ear; for, lo! his sword,
Which was declining on the milky head
Of reverend Priam, seem'd i' the air to stick.
So, as a painted tyrant, Pyrrhus stood
And like a neutral to his will and matter,
Did nothing.
But, as we often see, against some storm,
A silence in the heavens, the rack stand still,
The bold winds speechless and the orb below
As hush as death, anon the dreadful thunder
Doth rend the region; so, after Pyrrhus' pause,
Aroused vengeance sets him new a-work;
And never did the Cyclops' hammers fall
On Mars his armour forg'd for proof eterne
With less remorse than Pyrrhus' bleeding sword
Now falls on Priam.
Out, out, thou strumpet Fortune! All you gods,
In general synod take away her power!
Break all the spokes and fellies from her wheel,
And bowl the round nave down the hill of heaven
As low as to the fiends!"

Pol. This is too long.

Ham. It shall to the barber's, with your beard. Prithee, say on; he's for a jig or a tale of bawdry, or he sleeps. Say on; come to Hecuba.

1. Play. "But who, O, who had seen the mobled queen"—

Ham. "The mobled queen"?

Pol. That's good; "mobled queen" is good.

1. Play. "Run barefoot up and down, threat'ning the flame
With bisson rheum, a clout about that head
Where late the diadem stood, and for a robe,
About her lank and all o'er-teemed loins,
A blanket, in the alarm of fear caught up;—
Who this had seen, with tongue in venom steep'd,
'Gainst Fortune's state would treason have pronounc'd.
But if the gods themselves did see her then,
When she saw Pyrrhus make malicious sport
In mincing with his sword her husband's limbs,
The instant burst of clamour that she made,
Unless things mortal move them not at all,
Would have made milch the burning eyes of heaven,
And passion in the gods."

Pol. Look, whe'er he has not turn'd his colour and has tears in 's eyes. Pray you, no more.

Ham. 'Tis well; I'll have thee speak out the rest soon. Good my lord, will you see the players well bestow'd? Do ye hear? Let them be well us'd, for they are the abstracts and brief chronicles of the time; after your death you were better have a bad epitaph than their ill report while you lived.

Pol. My lord, I will use them according to their desert.

Ham. God's bodykins, man, better. Use every man after his desert, and who should scape whipping? Use them after your own honour and dignity. The less they deserve, the more merit is in your bounty. Take them in.

Pol. Come, sirs. [*Exit.*

Ham. Follow him, friends; we'll hear a play to-morrow. [*Exeunt all the Players but the First.*] Dost thou hear me, old friend? Can you play "The Murder of Gonzago"?

1. Play. Ay, my lord.

Ham. We'll ha 't to-morrow night. You could, for a need, study a speech of some dozen or sixteen lines, which I would set down and insert in 't, could ye not?

1. Play. Ay, my lord.

Ham. Very well. Follow that lord,—and look you mock him not. [*Exit 1. Player.*] My good friends, I'll leave you till night. You are welcome to Elsinore.

Ros. Good my lord!

[*Exeunt Rosencrantz and Guildenstern.*]

Ham. Ay, so, God buy ye.—Now I am alone.
O, what a rogue and peasant slave am I!
Is it not monstrous that this player here,
But in a fiction, in a dream of passion,
Could force his soul so to his own conceit
That from her working all his visage wann'd,
Tears in his eyes, distraction in 's aspect,
A broken voice, and his whole function suiting
With forms to his conceit? And all for nothing!
For Hecuba!
What's Hecuba to him, or he to Hecuba,
That he should weep for her? What would he do,
Had he the motive and the cue for passion
That I have? He would drown the stage with tears
And cleave the general ear with horrid speech,
Make mad the guilty and appall the free,
Confound the ignorant, and amaze indeed
The very faculty of eyes and ears.
Yet I,
A dull and muddy-mettled rascal, peak
Like John-a-dreams, unpregnant of my cause,
And can say nothing; no, not for a king,
Upon whose property and most dear life
A damn'd defeat was made. Am I a coward?
Who calls me villain, breaks my pate across,
Plucks off my beard and blows it in my face,
Tweaks me by the nose, gives me the lie i' the throat
As deep as to the lungs, who does me this?
Ha!
['Swounds,] I should take it; for it cannot be
But I am pigeon-liver'd and lack gall
To make oppression bitter, or ere this
I should have fatted all the region kites
With this slave's offal. Bloody, bawdy villain!
Remorseless, treacherous, lecherous, kindless villain!
O, vengeance!
Why, what an ass am I! Sure, this is most brave,
That I, the son of a dear father murdered,
Prompted to my revenge by heaven and hell,
Must, like a whore, unpack my heart with words,
And fall a-cursing, like a very drab,
A scullion!
Fie upon 't! Foh! About, my brain! I have heard
That guilty creatures sitting at a play
Have by the very cunning of the scene

Been struck so to the soul that presently
They have proclaim'd their malefactions;
For murder, though it have no tongue, will speak
With most miraculous organ. I'll have these players
Play something like the murder of my father
Before mine uncle. I'll observe his looks;
I'll tent him to the quick. If he but blench,
I know my course. The spirit that I have seen
May be the devil; and the devil hath power
To assume a pleasing shape; yea, and perhaps
Out of my weakness and my melancholy,
As he is very potent with such spirits,
Abuses me to damn me. I'll have grounds
More relative than this. The play's the thing
Wherein I'll catch the conscience of the King. [*Exit.*

Act III

Scene I. *A room in the castle.*

Enter King, Queen, Polonius, Ophelia, Rosencrantz, *and* Guildenstern.

King. And can you, by no drift of circumstance,
Get from him why he puts on this confusion,
Grating so harshly all his days of quiet
With turbulent and dangerous lunacy?

Ros. He does confess he feels himself distracted;
But from what cause he will by no means speak.

Guil. Nor do we find him forward to be sounded,
But, with a crafty madness, keeps aloof
When we would bring him on to some confession
Of his true state.

Queen. Did he receive you well?

Ros. Most like a gentleman.

Guil. But with much forcing of his disposition.

Ros. Niggard of question; but, of our demands,
Most free in his reply.

Queen. Did you assay him
To any pastime?

Ros. Madam, it so fell out, that certain players
We o'er-raught on the way; of these we told him,
And there did seem in him a kind of joy
To hear of it. They are about the court,
And, as I think, they have already order
This night to play before him.

Pol. 'T is most true.
And he beseech'd me to entreat your Majesties
To hear and see the matter.

King. With all my heart; and it doth much content me
To hear him so inclin'd.
Good gentlemen, give him a further edge,
And drive his purpose on to these delights.

Ros. We shall, my lord.

[*Exeunt Rosencrantz and Guildenstern.*]

King. Sweet Gertrude, leave us too,
For we have closely sent for Hamlet hither,
That he, as 't were by accident, may here
Affront Ophelia.
Her father and myself, lawful espials,
Will so bestow ourselves that, seeing unseen,
We may of their encounter frankly judge,
And gather by him, as he is behaved,
If 't be the affliction of his love or no
That thus he suffers for.

Queen. I shall obey you.
And for your part, Ophelia, I do wish
That your good beauties be the happy cause
Of Hamlet's wildness. So shall I hope your virtues

Will bring him to his wonted way again,
To both your honours.
Oph. Madam, I wish it may.
[*Exit Queen.*]
Pol. Ophelia, walk you here. Gracious, so please ye,
We will bestow ourselves. [*To Ophelia.*] Read on this book,
That show of such an exercise may colour
Your loneliness. We are oft to blame in this,—
'T is too much prov'd—that with devotion's visage
And pious action we do sugar o'er
The devil himself.
King. O, 't is true!
[*Aside.*] How smart a lash that speech doth give my conscience!
The harlot's cheek, beautied with plast'ring art,
Is not more ugly to the thing that helps it
Than is my deed to my most painted word.
O heavy burden!
Pol. I hear him coming. Let's withdraw, my lord. [*Exeunt King and Polonius*].

Enter HAMLET.

Ham. To be, or not to be: that is the question.
Whether 't is nobler in the mind to suffer
The slings and arrows of outrageous fortune,
Or to take arms against a sea of troubles,
And by opposing end them. To die; to sleep;
No more; and by a sleep to say we end
The heart-ache and the thousand natural shocks
That flesh is heir to. 'T is a consummation
Devoutly to be wish'd. To die; to sleep;—
To sleep? Perchance to dream! Ay, there's the rub;
For in that sleep of death what dreams may come,
When we have shuffl'd off this mortal coil,
Must give us pause. There's the respect
That makes calamity of so long life.
For who would bear the whips and scorns of time,
The oppressor's wrong, the proud man's contumely,
The pangs of dispriz'd love, the law's delay,
The insolence of office, and the spurns
That patient merit of the unworthy takes,
When he himself might his quietus make
With a bare bodkin? Who would fardels bear,
To grunt and sweat under a weary life,
But that the dread of something after death,
The undiscovered country from whose bourn
No traveller returns, puzzles the will
And makes us rather bear those ills we have
Than fly to others that we know not of?
Thus conscience does make cowards of us all;
And thus the native hue of resolution
Is sicklied o'er with the pale cast of thought,
And enterprises of great pith and moment
With this regard their currents turn awry,
And lose the name of action.—Soft you now!
The fair Ophelia! Nymph, in thy orisons
Be all my sins rememb'red.
Oph. Good my lord,
How does your honour for this many a day?
Ham. I humbly thank you, well, well, well.
Oph. My lord, I have remembrances of yours
That I have longed long to re-deliver.
I pray you, now receive them.
Ham. No, no;
I never gave you aught.

Oph. My honour'd lord, I know right well you did,
And, with them, words of so sweet breath compos'd
As made the things more rich. Their perfume lost,
Take these again; for to the noble mind
Rich gifts wax poor when givers prove unkind.
There, my lord.

Ham. Ha, ha! are you honest?

Oph. My lord!

Ham. Are you fair?

Oph. What means your lordship?

Ham. That if you be honest and fair, your honesty should admit no discourse to your beauty.

Oph. Could beauty, my lord, have better commerce than with honesty?

Ham. Ay, truly; for the power of beauty will sooner transform honesty from what it is to a bawd than the force of honesty can translate beauty into his likeness. This was sometime a paradox, but now the time gives it proof. I did love you once.

Oph. Indeed, my lord, you made me believe so.

Ham. You should not have believ'd me, for virtue cannot so inoculate our old stock but we shall relish of it. I loved you not.

Oph. I was the more deceived.

Ham. Get thee to a nunnery; why wouldst thou be a breeder of sinners? I am myself indifferent honest, but yet I could accuse me of such things that it were better my mother had not borne me. I am very proud, revengeful, ambitious, with more offences at my beck than I have thoughts to put them in, imagination to give them shape, or time to act them in. What should such fellows as I do crawling between heaven and earth? We are arrant knaves all; believe none of us. Go thy ways to a nunnery. Where's your father?

Oph. At home, my lord.

Ham. Let the doors be shut upon him, that he may play the fool nowhere but in 's own house. Farewell!

Oph. O, help him, you sweet heavens!

Ham. If thou dost marry, I 'll give thee this plague for thy dowry: be thou as chaste as ice, as pure as snow, thou shalt not escape calumny. Get thee to a nunnery, go. Farewell! Or, if thou wilt needs marry, marry a fool; for wise men know well enough what monsters you make of them. To a nunnery, go, and quickly too. Farewell!

Oph. O heavenly powers, restore him!

Ham. I have heard of your paintings too, well enough. God has given you one face, and you make yourselves another. You jig, you amble, and you lisp and nick-name God's creatures and make your wantonness your ignorance. Go to, I 'll no more on 't; it hath made me mad. I say, we will have no more marriages. Those that are married already, all but one, shall live; the rest shall keep as they are. To a nunnery, go. [*Exit.*

Oph. O, what a noble mind is here o'erthrown!
The courtier's, soldier's, scholar's, eye, tongue, sword;
The expectancy and rose of the fair state,
The glass of fashion and the mould of form,
The observ'd of all observers, quite, quite down!
And I, of ladies most deject and wretched,
That suck'd the honey of his music vows,
Now see that noble and most sovereign reason,
Like sweet bells jangled out of tune and harsh;
That unmatch'd form and feature of blown youth
Blasted with ecstasy. O, woe is me,
To have seen what I have seen, see what I see!

Re-enter King *and* Polonius.

King. Love! his affections do not that way tend;
Nor what he spake, though it lack'd form a little,
Was not like madness. There's something in his soul
O'er which his melancholy sits on brood,
And I do doubt the hatch and the disclose
Will be some danger; which for to prevent,
I have in quick determination
Thus set it down: he shall with speed to England
For the demand of our neglected tribute.
Haply the seas and countries different
With variable objects shall expel
This something-settled matter in his heart,
Whereon his brains still beating puts him thus
From fashion of himself. What think you on 't?
Pol. It shall do well; but yet do I believe
The origin and commencement of this grief
Sprung from neglected love. How now, Ophelia!
You need not tell us what Lord Hamlet said;
We heard it all. My lord, do as you please,
But, if you hold it fit, after the play
Let his queen mother all alone entreat him
To show his griefs. Let her be round with him,
And I'll be plac'd, so please you, in the ear
Of all their conference. If she find him not,
To England send him, or confine him where
Your wisdom best shall think.
King. It shall be so.
Madness in great ones must not unwatch'd go. [*Exeunt.*

Scene II. *A hall in the castle.*

Enter Hamlet *and* Players

Ham. Speak the speech, I pray you, as I pronounc'd it to you, trippingly on the tongue; but if you mouth it, as many of your players do, I had as lief the town-crier spoke my lines. Nor do not saw the air too much with your hand, thus, but use all gently; for in the very torrent, tempest, and, as I may say, the whirlwind of passion, you must acquire and beget a temperance that may give it smoothness. O, it offends me to the soul to see a robustious periwig-pated fellow tear a passion to tatters, to very rags, to split the ears of the groundlings, who for the most part are capable of nothing but inexplicable dumb-shows and noise. I could have such a fellow whipp'd for o'erdoing Termagant. It out-herods Herod. Pray you, avoid it.

1. Play. I warrant your honour.

Ham. Be not too tame neither, but let your own discretion be your tutor. Suit the action to the word, the word to the action; with this special observance, that you o'erstep not the modesty of nature. For anything so overdone is from the purpose of playing, whose end, both at the first and now, was and is, to hold, as 't were, the mirror up to nature; to show virtue her own feature, scorn her own image, and the very age and body of the time his form and pressure. Now this overdone, or come tardy off, though it make the unskilful laugh, cannot but make the judicious grieve; the censure of the which one must, in your allowance, o'erweigh a whole theatre of others. O, there be players that I have seen play, and heard others praise, and that highly, not to speak it profanely, that, neither having the accent of Christians nor the gait of Christian, pagan, nor man, have so strutted and bellowed that I have thought some of Nature's journeymen had made men and not made them well, they imitated humanity so abominably.

1. Play. I hope we have reform'd that indifferently with us, sir.

Ham. O, reform it altogether. And let those that play your clowns speak no more than is set down for them; for there be of them that will themselves laugh to set on some quantity of barren spectators to laugh too, though in the mean time some necessary question of the play be then to be considered. That's villainous, and shows a most pitiful ambition in the Fool that uses it. Go, make you ready. [*Exeunt Players.*

Enter POLONIUS, ROSENCRANTZ, *and* GUILDENSTERN.

How now, my Lord! Will the King hear this piece of work?

Pol. And the Queen too, and that presently.

Ham. Bid the players make haste.
[*Exit Polonius.*

Will you two help to hasten them?

Ros. }
Guil. } We will, my lord.

[*Exeunt Rosencrantz and Guildenstern.*

Ham. What ho! Horatio.

Enter HORATIO.

Hor. Here, sweet lord, at your service.

Ham. Horatio, thou art e'en as just a man
As e'er my conversation cop'd withal.

Hor. O, my dear lord,—

Ham. Nay, do not think I flatter,
For what advancement may I hope from thee
That no revenue hast but thy good spirits
To feed and clothe thee? Why should the poor be flatter'd?
No, let the candied tongue lick absurd pomp,
And crook the pregnant hinges of the knee
Where thrift may follow fawning. Dost thou hear?
Since my dear soul was mistress of my choice
And could of men distinguish, her election
Hath seal'd thee for herself; for thou hast been
As one, in suffering all, that suffers nothing,
A man that Fortune's buffets and rewards
Hath ta'en with equal thanks; and blest are those
Whose blood and judgement are so well commingled,
That they are not a pipe for Fortune's finger
To sound what stop she please. Give me that man
That is not passion's slave, and I will wear him
In my heart's core, ay, in my heart of heart,
As I do thee.—Something too much of this.—
There is a play to-night before the King.
One scene of it comes near the circumstance
Which I have told thee of my father's death.
I prithee, when thou seest that act a-foot,
Even with the very comment of thy soul
Observe mine uncle. If his occulted guilt
Do not itself unkennel in one speech,
It is a damned ghost that we have seen,
And my imaginations are as foul
As Vulcan's stithy. Give him heedful note;
For I mine eyes will rivet to his face,
And after we will both our judgements join
To censure of his seeming.

Hor. Well, my lord.
If he steal aught the whilst this play is playing,
And scape detecting, I will pay the theft.

Danish march. A flourish. Enter KING, QUEEN, POLONIUS, OPHELIA, ROSENCRANTZ, GUILDENSTERN, *and other Lords attendant, with the guard carrying torches.*

Ham. They are coming to the play;
I must be idle.
Get you a place.

King. How fares our cousin Hamlet?

Ham. Excellent, i' faith,—of the chameleon's dish. I eat the air, promise-cramm'd. You cannot feed capons so.

King. I have nothing with this answer, Hamlet; these words are not mine.

Ham. No, nor mine now. [*To Polonius.*] My lord, you play'd once i' the university, you say?

Pol. That I did, my lord, and was accounted a good actor.

Ham. And what did you enact?

Pol. I did enact Julius Cæsar. I was kill'd i' the Capitol; Brutus kill'd me.

Ham. It was a brute part of him to kill so capital a calf there. Be the players ready?

Ros. Ay, my lord, they stay upon your patience.

Queen. Come hither, my good Hamlet, sit by me.

Ham. No, good mother, here's metal more attractive.
[*Lying down at Ophelia's feet.*]

Pol. [*To the King.*] O, ho! do you mark that?

Ham. Lady, shall I lie in your lap?

Oph. No, my lord.

Ham. I mean, my head upon your lap?

Oph. Ay, my lord.

Ham. Do you think I meant country matters?

Oph. I think nothing, my lord.

Ham. That's a fair thought to lie between maid's legs.

Oph. What is, my lord?

Ham. Nothing.

Oph. You are merry, my lord.

Ham. Who, I?

Oph. Ay, my lord.

Ham. O God, your only jig-maker. What should a man do but be merry? For, look you, how cheerfully my mother looks, and my father died within 's two hours.

Oph. Nay, 't is twice two months, my lord.

Ham. So long? Nay then, let the devil wear black, for I 'll have a suit of sables. O heavens! die two months ago, and not forgotten yet? Then there's hope a great man's memory may outlive his life half a year; but, by 'r lady, he must build churches then, or else shall he suffer not thinking on, with the hobby-horse, whose epitaph is, "For, O, for, O, the hobby-horse is forgot."

Hautboys play. The dumb-show enters.

Enter a King and Queen very lovingly, the Queen embracing him. She kneels and makes show of protestation unto him. He takes her up and declines his head upon her neck; lays him down upon a bank of flowers. She, seeing him asleep, leaves him. Anon comes in a fellow, takes off his crown, kisses it, and pours poison in the King's ears, and exit. The Queen returns, finds the King dead, and makes passionate action. The poisoner, with some two or three Mutes, comes in again, seeming to lament with her. The dead body is carried away. The poisoner woos the Queen with gifts; she seems loath and unwilling a while, but in the end accepts his love. [*Exeunt.*

Oph. What means this, my lord?

Ham. Marry, this is miching mallecho; that means mischief.

Oph. Belike this show imports the argument of the play?

Enter PROLOGUE.

Ham. We shall know by this fellow. The players cannot keep counsel, they 'll tell all.

Oph. Will they tell us what this show meant?

Ham. Ay, or any show that you'll show him. Be not you asham'd to show, he 'll not shame to tell you what it means.

Oph. You are naught, you are naught. I 'll mark the play.

Pro. For us, and for our tragedy,
Here stooping to your clemency,
We beg your hearing patiently. [*Exit.*]

Ham. Is this a prologue, or the posy of a ring?

Oph. 'Tis brief, my lord.

Ham. As woman's love.

Enter [*two Players,*] KING *and his* QUEEN.

P. King. Full thirty times hath Phœbus' cart gone round
Neptune's salt wash and Tellus' orbed ground,
And thirty dozen moons with borrowed sheen
About the world have times twelve thirties been,
Since love our hearts and Hymen did our hands
Unite commutual in most sacred bands.

P. Queen. So many journeys may the sun and moon
Make us again count o'er ere love be done!
But, woe is me, you are so sick of late,
So far from cheer and from your former state,
That I distrust you. Yet, though I distrust,
Discomfort you, my lord, it nothing must;
For women's fear and love holds quantity,
In neither aught, or in extremity.
Now, what my love is, proof hath made you know;
And as my love is siz'd my fear is so.
[Where love is great, the littlest doubts are fear;
Where little fears grow great, great love grows there.]

P. King. Faith, I must leave thee, love, and shortly too.
My operant powers their functions leave to do;
And thou shalt live in this fair world behind,
Honour'd, belov'd; and haply one as kind
For husband shalt thou—

P. Queen. O, confound the rest!
Such love must needs be treason in my breast!
In second husband let me be accurst!
None wed the second but who kill'd the first.

Ham. [*Aside.*] Wormwood, wormwood!

P. Queen. The instances that second marriage move
Are base respects of thrift, but none of love.
A second time I kill my husband dead,
When second husband kisses me in bed.

P. King. I do believe you think what now you speak,
But what we do determine oft we break.
Purpose is but the slave to memory,
Of violent birth, but poor validity;
Which now, like fruit unripe, sticks on the tree,
But fall unshaken when they mellow be.
Most necessary 't is that we forget
To pay ourselves what to ourselves is debt.
What to ourselves in passion we propose,
The passion ending, doth the purpose lose.
The violence of either grief or joy
Their own enactures with themselves destroy.
Where joy most revels, grief doth most lament;
Grief joys, joy grieves, on slender accident.
This world is not for aye, nor 't is not strange
That even our loves should with our fortunes change,

For 't is a question left us yet to prove,
Whether love lead fortune, or else fortune love.
The great man down, you mark his favourite flies;
The poor advanc'd makes friends of enemies.
And hitherto doth love on fortune tend,
For who not needs shall never lack a friend;
And who in want a hollow friend doth try,
Directly seasons him his enemy.
But, orderly to end where I begun,
Our wills and fates do so contrary run
That our devices still are overthrown;
Our thoughts are ours, their ends none of our own.
So think thou wilt no second husband wed;
But die thy thoughts when thy first lord is dead.

P. Queen. Nor earth to me give food, nor heaven light!
Sport and repose lock from me day and night!
[To desperation turn my trust and hope!
An anchor's cheer in prison be my scope!]
Each opposite that blanks the face of joy
Meet what I would have well and it destroy!
Both here and hence pursue me lasting strife,
If, once a widow, ever I be wife!

Ham. If she should break it now!

P. King. 'T is deeply sworn. Sweet, leave me here a while.
My spirits grow dull, and fain I would beguile
The tedious day with sleep. [*Sleeps.*

P. Queen. Sleep rock thy brain,
And never come mischance between us twain! [*Exit.*

Ham. Madam, how like you this play?

Queen. The lady protests too much, methinks.

Ham. O, but she 'll keep her word.

King. Have you heard the argument? Is there no offence in 't?

Ham. No, no, they do but jest, poison in jest. No offence i' the world.

King. What do you call the play?

Ham. The Mouse-trap. Marry, how? Tropically. This play is the image of a murder done in Vienna. Gonzago is the duke's name; his wife, Baptista. You shall see anon. 'T is a knavish piece of work, but what o' that? Your Majesty and we that have free souls, it touches us not. Let the gall'd jade wince, our withers are unwrung.

Enter LUCIANUS.

This is one Lucianus, nephew to the king.

Oph. You are a good chorus, my lord.

Ham. I could interpret between you and your love, if I could see the puppets dallying.

Oph. You are keen, my lord, you are keen.

Ham. It would cost you a groaning to take off my edge.

Oph. Still better, and worse.

Ham. So you mistake your husbands. Begin, murderer; pox, leave thy damnable faces and begin. Come, "the croaking raven doth bellow for revenge."

Luc. Thoughts black, hands apt, drugs fit, and time agreeing;
Confederate season, else no creature seeing.
Thou mixture rank, of midnight weeds collected,
With Hecate's ban thrice blasted, thrice infected,
Thy natural magic and dire property
On wholesome life usurp immediately.
[*Pours the poison in* [*to the sleeper's*] *ears.*

Ham. He poisons him i' the garden for 's estate. His name's Gonzago; the story is extant, and writ in choice Italian. You shall see anon how the murderer gets the love of Gonzago's wife.

Oph. The King rises.

Ham. What, frighted with false fire?

Queen. How fares my lord?

Pol. Give o'er the play.

King. Give me some light. Away!

All. Lights, lights, lights!

[*Exeunt all but Hamlet and Horatio.*

Ham. Why, let the strucken deer go weep,
The hart ungalled play;
For some must watch, while some must sleep,—
So runs the world away.

Would not this, sir, and a forest of feathers—if the rest of my fortunes turn Turk with me—with two Provincial roses on my raz'd shoes, get me a fellowship in a cry of players, sir?

Hor. Half a share.

Ham. A whole one, I.
For thou dost know, O Damon dear,
This realm dismantled was
Of Jove himself; and now reigns here
A very, very—pajock.

Hor. You might have rhym'd.

Ham. O good Horatio, I'll take the ghost's word for a thousand pound. Didst perceive?

Hor. Very well, my lord.

Ham. Upon the talk of the poisoning?

Hor. I did very well note him.

Re-enter ROSENCRANTZ *and* GUILDENSTERN.

Ham. Ah, ha! Come, some music! Come, the recorders!
For if the King like not the comedy,
Why then, belike, he likes it not, perdy.
Come, some music!

Guil. Good my lord, vouchsafe me a word with you.

Ham. Sir, a whole history.

Guil. The King, sir,—

Ham. Ay, sir, what of him?

Guil. Is in his retirement marvellous distemper'd.

Ham. With drink, sir?

Guil. No, my lord, rather with choler.

Ham. Your wisdom should show itself more richer to signify this to his doctor; for, for me to put him to his purgation would perhaps plunge him into far more choler.

Guil. Good my lord, put your discourse into some frame, and start not so wildly from my affair.

Ham. I am tame, sir; pronounce.

Guil. The Queen, your mother, in most great affliction of spirit, hath sent me to you.

Ham. You are welcome.

Guil. Nay, good my lord, this courtesy is not of the right breed. If it shall please you to make me a wholesome answer I will do your mother's commandment; if not, your pardon and my return shall be the end of my business.

Ham. Sir, I cannot.

Guil. What, my lord?

Ham. Make you a wholesome answer. My wit 's diseas'd. But, sir, such answers as I can make, you shall command, or, rather, as you say, my mother. Therefore no more, but to the matter. My mother, you say,—

Ros. Then thus she says: your behaviour hath struck her into amazement and admiration.

Ham. O wonderful son, that can so astonish a mother! But is there no sequel at the heels of this mother's admiration? [Impart.]

Ros. She desires to speak with you in her closet ere you go to bed.

Ham. We shall obey, were she ten times our mother. Have you any further trade with us?

Ros. My lord, you once did love me.

Ham. So I do still, by these pickers and stealers.

Ros. Good my lord, what is your cause of distemper? You do surely bar the door upon your own liberty if you deny your griefs to your friend.

Ham. Sir, I lack advancement.

Ros. How can that be, when you have the voice of the King himself for your succession in Denmark?

Ham. Ay, but "While the grass grows,"—the proverb is something musty.

Re-enter one with a recorder.

O, the recorder! Let me see.—To withdraw with you:—why do you go about to recover the wind of me, as if you would drive me into a toil?

Guil. O, my lord, if my duty be too bold, my love is too unmannerly.

Ham. I do not well understand that. Will you play upon this pipe?

Guil. My lord, I cannot.

Ham. I pray you.

Guil. Believe me, I cannot.

Ham. I do beseech you.

Guil. I know no touch of it, my lord.

Ham. 'T is as easy as lying. Govern these ventages with your finger and thumb, give it breath with your mouth, and it will discourse most excellent music. Look you, these are the stops.

Guil. But these cannot I command to any utterance of harmony. I have not the skill.

Ham. Why, look you now, how unworthy a thing you make of me! You would play upon me, you would seem to know my stops, you would pluck out the heart of my mystery, you would sound me from my lowest note to the top of my compass; and there is much music, excellent voice, in this little organ, yet cannot you make it [speak. 'Sblood,] do you think that I am easier to be play'd on than a pipe? Call me what instrument you will, though you can fret me, you cannot play upon me.

Enter POLONIUS.

God bless you, sir.

Pol. My lord, the Queen would speak with you, and presently.

Ham. Do you see that cloud that 's almost in shape like a camel?

Pol. By the mass, and it 's like a camel, indeed.

Ham. Methinks it is like a weasel.

Pol. It is back'd like a weasel.

Ham. Or like a whale?

Pol. Very like a whale.

Ham. Then will I come to my mother by and by. [*Aside.*] They fool me to the top of my bent.—I will come by and by.

Pol. I will say so. [*Exit.*

Ham. "By and by" is easily said.
Leave me, friends.
[*Exeunt all but Hamlet.*]
'T is now the very witching time of night
When churchyards yawn and hell itself breathes out
Contagion to this world. Now could I drink hot blood,
And do such bitter business as the day
Would quake to look on. Soft! now to my mother.
O heart, lose not thy nature! Let not ever
The soul of Nero enter this firm bosom;
Let me be cruel, not unnatural.
I will speak daggers to her, but use none.
My tongue and soul in this be hypocrites;
How in my word soever she be shent
To give them seals never, my soul consent! [*Exit.*

SCENE III. *A room in the castle.*

Enter KING, ROSENCRANTZ, *and* GUILDENSTERN.

King. I like him not, nor stands it safe with us
To let his madness range. Therefore prepare you.
I your commission will forthwith dispatch,
And he to England shall along with you.
The terms of our estate may not endure
Hazard so dangerous as doth hourly grow
Out of his lunacies.

Guil. We will ourselves provide.
Most holy and religious fear it is
To keep those many many bodies safe
That live and feed upon your Majesty.

Ros. The single and peculiar life is bound
With all the strength and armour of the mind
To keep itself from noyance, but much more
That spirit upon whose weal depends and rests
The lives of many. The cease of majesty
Dies not alone, but, like a gulf, doth draw
What 's near it with it. It is a massy wheel,
Fixed on the summit of the highest mount,
To whose huge spokes ten thousand lesser things
Are mortis'd and adjoin'd; which, when it falls,
Each small annexment, petty consequence,
Attends the boisterous ruin. Never alone
Did the King sigh, but with a general groan.

King. Arm you, I pray you, to this speedy voyage,
For we will fetters put upon this fear,
Which now goes too free-footed.

Ros.
Guil. } We will haste us.

[*Exeunt Rosencrantz and Guildenstern.*

Enter POLONIUS.

Pol. My lord, he 's going to his mother's closet.
Behind the arras I 'll convey myself,
To hear the process. I 'll warrant she'll tax him home;
And, as you said, and wisely was it said,
'Tis meet that some more audience than a mother,
Since nature makes them partial, should o'erhear
The speech, of vantage. Fare you well, my liege.
I 'll call upon you ere you go to bed,
And tell you what I know.

King. Thanks, dear my lord.
[*Exit Polonius.*]

O, my offence is rank, it smells to heaven;
It hath the primal eldest curse upon 't,
A brother's murder. Pray can I not,
Though inclination be as sharp as will.
My stronger guilt defeats my strong intent,
And, like a man to double business bound,
I stand in pause where I shall first begin,
And both neglect. What if this cursed hand
Were thicker than itself with brother's blood,
Is there not rain enough in the sweet heavens
To wash it white as snow? Whereto serves mercy
But to confront the visage of offence?
And what 's in prayer but this twofold force,
To be forestalled ere we come to fall,
Or pardon'd being down? Then I'll look up;
My fault is past. But, O, what form of prayer
Can serve my turn? "Forgive me my foul murder"?
That cannot be; since I am still possess'd
Of those effects for which I did the murder,
My crown, mine own ambition, and my queen.
May one be pardon'd and retain the offence?
In the corrupted currents of this world
Offence's gilded hand may shove by justice,
And oft 't is seen the wicked prize itself
Buys out the law. But 't is not so above.
There is no shuffling, there the action lies
In his true nature; and we ourselves compell'd,
Even to the teeth and forehead of our faults,
To give in evidence. What then? What rests?
Try what repentance can. What can it not?

Yet what can it when one cannot repent?
O wretched state! O bosom black as death!
O limed soul, that, struggling to be free,
Art more engag'd! Help, angels! Make assay!
Bow, stubborn knees, and, heart with strings of steel,
Be soft as sinews of the new-born babe!
All may be well. [*Retires and kneels.*

Enter HAMLET.

Ham. Now might I do it pat, now he is praying.
And now I 'll do 't.—And so he goes to heaven;
And so am I reveng'd. That would be scann'd.
A villain kills my father, and for that,
I, his sole son, do this same villain send
To heaven.
Oh, this is hire and salary, not revenge.
He took my father grossly, full of bread,
With all his crimes broad blown, as flush as May;
And how his audit stands who knows save Heaven?
But in our circumstance and course of thought
'Tis heavy with him. And am I then reveng'd,
To take him in the purging of his soul,
When he is fit and season'd for his passage?
No!
Up, sword, and know thou a more horrid hent.
When he is drunk asleep, or in his rage,
Or in the incestuous pleasure of his bed,
At gaming, swearing, or about some act
That has no relish of salvation in 't,—
Then trip him, that his heels may kick at heaven,
And that his soul may be as damn'd and black
As hell, whereto it goes. My mother stays.
This physic but prolongs thy sickly days.
[*Exit.*

King. [*Rising.*] My words fly up, my thoughts remain below.
Words without thoughts never to heaven go. [*Exit.*

SCENE IV. *The Queen's closet.*

Enter QUEEN *and* POLONIUS.

Pol. He will come straight. Look you lay home to him.
Tell him his pranks have been too broad to bear with,
And that your Grace hath screen'd and stood between
Much heat and him. I 'll silence me e'en here.
Pray you, be round with him.

Ham. (*Within.*) Mother, mother, mother!

Queen. I 'll warrant you, fear me not.
Withdraw, I hear him coming.
[*Polonius hides behind the arras.*]

Enter HAMLET.

Ham. Now, mother, what's the matter?

Queen. Hamlet, thou hast thy father much offended.

Ham. Mother, you have my father much offended.

Queen. Come, come, you answer with an idle tongue.

Ham. Go, go, you question with a wicked tongue.

Queen. Why, how now, Hamlet!

Ham. What 's the matter now?

Queen. Have you forgot me?

Ham. No, by the rood, not so.
You are the Queen, your husband's brother's wife;
But would you were not so! You are my mother.

Queen. Nay, then, I 'll set those to you that can speak.

Ham. Come, come, and sit you down. You shall not budge.

You go not till I set you up a glass
Where you may see the inmost part of you.

Queen. What wilt thou do? Thou wilt not murder me?
Help, help, ho!

Pol. [*Behind.*] What, ho! help, help, help!

Ham. [*Drawing.*] How now! A rat? Dead, for a ducat, dead!
[*Kills Polonius through the arras.*]

Pol. [*Behind.*] O, I am slain!

Queen. O me, what hast thou done?

Ham. Nay, I know not.
Is it the King?

Queen. O, what a rash and bloody deed is this!

Ham. A bloody deed! Almost as bad, good mother,
As kill a king, and marry with his brother.

Queen. As kill a king!

Ham. Ay, lady, 't was my word.
[*Lifts up the arras and discovers Polonius.*]
Thou wretched, rash, intruding fool, farewell!
I took thee for thy better. Take thy fortune.
Thou find'st to be too busy is some danger.
—Leave wringing of your hands. Peace! Sit you down,
And let me wring your heart; for so I shall,
If it be made of penetrable stuff,
If damned custom have not braz'd it so
That it is proof and bulwark against sense.

Queen. What have I done, that thou dar'st wag thy tongue
In noise so rude against me?

Ham. Such an act
That blurs the grace and blush of modesty,
Calls virtue hypocrite, takes off the rose
From the fair forehead of an innocent love
And sets a blister there, makes marriage-vows
As false as dicers' oaths; O, such a deed
As from the body of contraction plucks
The very soul, and sweet religion makes
A rhapsody of words. Heaven's face doth glow,
Yea, this solidity and compound mass,
With tristful visage, as against the doom,
Is thought-sick at the act.

Queen. Ay me, what act,
That roars so loud and thunders in the index?

Ham. Look here, upon this picture, and on this,
The counterfeit presentment of two brothers.
See, what a grace was seated on this brow:
Hyperion's curls, the front of Jove himself,
An eye like Mars, to threaten or command,
A station like the herald Mercury
New-lighted on a heaven-kissing hill,
A combination and a form indeed,
Where every god did seem to set his seal,
To give the world assurance of a man.
This was your husband. Look you now what follows:
Here is your husband, like a mildew'd ear,
Blasting his wholesome brother. Have you eyes?
Could you on this fair mountain leave to feed,
And batten on this moor? Ha! have you eyes?
You cannot call it love, for at your age
The hey-day in the blood is tame, it 's humble,
And waits upon the judgement; and what judgement
Would step from this to this? [Sense sure you have,
Else could you not have motion; but sure, that sense
Is apoplex'd; for madness would not err,
Nor sense to ecstasy was ne'er so thrall'd

But it reserv'd some quantity of choice,
To serve in such a difference.] What devil was 't
That thus hath cozen'd you at hoodman-blind?
[Eyes without feeling, feeling without sight,
Ears without hands or eyes, smelling sans all,
Or but a sickly part of one true sense
Could not so mope.]
O shame! where is thy blush? Rebellious hell,
If thou canst mutine in a matron's bones,
To flaming youth let virtue be as wax,
And melt in her own fire. Proclaim no shame
When the compulsive ardour gives the charge,
Since frost itself as actively doth burn
And reason panders will.

Queen. O Hamlet, speak no more!
Thou turn'st mine eyes into my very soul,
And there I see such black and grained spots
As will not leave their tinct.

Ham. Nay, but to live
In the rank sweat of an enseamed bed,
Stew'd in corruption, honeying and making love
Over the nasty sty,—

Queen. O, speak to me no more!
These words like daggers enter in mine ears.
No more, sweet Hamlet!

Ham. A murderer and a villain!
A slave that is not twentieth part the tithe
Of your precedent lord! A vice of kings!
A cutpurse of the empire and the rule,
That from a shelf the precious diadem stole,
And put it in his pocket!

Queen. No more!

Enter Ghost.

Ham. A king of shreds and patches,—
Save me, and hover o'er me with your wings,
You heavenly guards! What would your gracious figure?

Queen. Alas, he 's mad!

Ham. Do you not come your tardy son to chide,
That, laps'd in time and passion, lets go by
The important acting of your dread command?
O, say!

Ghost. Do not forget! This visitation
Is but to whet thy almost blunted purpose.
But, look, amazement on thy mother sits.
O, step between her and her fighting soul.
Conceit in weakest bodies strongest works.
Speak to her, Hamlet.

Ham. How is it with you, lady?

Queen. Alas, how is 't with you,
That you do bend your eye on vacancy
And with the incorporal air do hold discourse?
Forth at your eyes your spirits wildly peep,
And, as the sleeping soldiers in the alarm,
Your bedded hair, like life in excrements,
Start up and stand on end. O gentle son,
Upon the heat and flame of thy distemper
Sprinkle cool patience. Whereon do you look?

Ham. On him, on him! Look you, how pale he glares!
His form and cause conjoin'd, preaching to stones,
Would make them capable. Do not look upon me,
Lest with this piteous action you convert
My stern effects; then what I have to do
Will want true colour, tears perchance for blood.

Queen. To whom do you speak this?

Ham. Do you see nothing there?

Queen. Nothing at all, yet all that is I see.

Ham. Nor did you nothing hear?

Queen. No, nothing but ourselves.

Ham. Why, look you there! Look, how it steals away!
My father, in his habit as he lived!
Look, where he goes, even now, out at the portal! [*Exit Ghost.*

Queen. This is the very coinage of your brain.
This bodiless creation ecstasy
Is very cunning in.

Ham. Ecstasy!
My pulse, as yours, doth temperately keep time,
And makes as healthful music. It is not madness
That I have uttered. Bring me to the test,
And I the matter will re-word, which madness
Would gambol from. Mother, for love of grace,
Lay not that flattering unction to your soul,
That not your trespass, but my madness speaks.
It will but skin and film the ulcerous place,
Whilst rank corruption, mining all within,
Infects unseen. Confess yourself to Heaven;
Repent what's past, avoid what is to come,
And do not spread the compost on the weeds,
To make them rank. Forgive me this my virtue
For in the fatness of these pursy times
Virtue itself of vice must pardon beg,
Yea, curb and woo for leave to do him good.

Queen. O Hamlet, thou hast cleft my heart in twain.

Ham. O, throw away the worser part of it,
And live the purer with the other half.
Good-night; but go not to mine uncle's bed.
Assume a virtue, if you have it not.
[That monster, custom, who all sense doth eat,
Of habits devil, is angel yet in this,
That to the use of actions fair and good
He likewise gives a frock or livery,
That aptly is put on.] Refrain to-night,
And that shall lend a kind of easiness
To the next abstinence; [the next more easy;
For use almost can change the stamp of nature,
And either master the devil or throw him out,
With wondrous potency.] Once more, good-night;
And when you are desirous to be blest,
I 'll blessing beg of you. For this same lord, [*Pointing to Polonius.*]
I do repent; but Heaven hath pleas'd it so,
To punish me with this and this with me,
That I must be their scourge and minister.
I will bestow him, and will answer well
The death I gave him. So, again, good-night.
I must be cruel, only to be kind.
Thus bad begins and worse remains behind.
[One word more, good lady.]

Queen. What shall I do?

Ham. Not this, by no means, that I bid you do:
Let the bloat king tempt you again to bed,
Pinch wanton on your cheek, call you his mouse,
And let him, for a pair of reechy kisses,
Or paddling in your neck with his damn'd fingers,
Make you to ravel all this matter out,
That I essentially am not in madness,
But mad in craft. 'T were good you let him know;
For who, that 's but a queen, fair, sober, wise,
Would from a paddock, from a bat, a gib,

Such dear concernings hide? Who would do so?
No, in despite of sense and secrecy,
Unpeg the basket on the house's top,
Let the birds fly, and like the famous ape,
To try conclusions, in the basket creep,
And break your own neck down.

Queen. Be thou assur'd, if words be made of breath,
And breath of life, I have no life to breathe
What thou hast said to me.

Ham. I must to England; you know that?

Queen. Alack,
I had forgot. 'T is so concluded on.

Ham. [There's letters sealed, and my two school-fellows,
Whom I will trust as I will adders fang'd,
They bear the mandate. They must sweep my way,
And marshal me to knavery. Let it work;
For 't is the sport to have the enginer
Hoist with his own petar; and 't shall go hard
But I will delve one yard below their mines,
And blow them at the moon. O, 't is most sweet,
When in one line two crafts directly meet.]
This man shall set me packing.
I 'll lug the guts into the neighbour room.
Mother, good-night. Indeed this counsellor
Is now most still, most secret, and most grave,
Who was in life a foolish prating knave.
Come, sir, to draw toward an end with you.
Good-night, mother.

[*Exeunt, severally, Hamlet tugging in Polonius.*

Henry V

ACT III, SCENE I.

France. Before Harfleur.

Alarm. Enter KING HENRY, EXETER, BEDFORD, GLOUCESTER, [and Soldiers, *with*] *scaling-ladders.*

K. *Hen.* Once more unto the breach, dear friends, once more,
Or close the wall up with our English dead.
In peace there 's nothing so becomes a man
As modest stillness and humility;
But when the blast of war blows in our ears,
Then imitate the action of the tiger;
Stiffen the sinews, summon up the blood,
Disguise fair nature with hard-favour'd rage;
Then lend the eye a terrible aspect;
Let it pry through the portage of the head
Like the brass cannon; let the brow o'erwhelm it
As fearfully as doth a galled rock
O'erhang and jutty his confounded base,
Swill'd with the wild and wasteful ocean.
Now set the teeth and stretch the nostril wide,
Hold hard the breath, and bend up every spirit
To his full height. On, on, you noblest English,
Whose blood is fet from fathers of war-proof!
Fathers that, like so many Alexanders,
Have in these parts from morn till even fought,
And sheath'd their swords for lack of argument.
Dishonour not your mothers; now attest
That those whom you call'd fathers did beget you.
Be copy now to men of grosser blood,
And teach them how to war. And you, good yeomen,

Whose limbs were made in England, show us here
The mettle of your pasture; let us swear
That you are worth your breeding, which I doubt not;
For there is none of you so mean and base,
That hath not noble lustre in your eyes.
I see you stand like greyhounds in the slips,
Straining upon the start. The game 's afoot!
Follow your spirit, and upon this charge
Cry, "God for Harry! England and Saint George!"

Act IV, Scene III.

The English camp.

Enter Gloucester, Bedford, Exeter, Erpingham, *with all his host:* Salisbury *and* Westmoreland.

Glou. Where is the King?

Bed. The King himself is rode to view their battle.

West. Of fighting men they have full three-score thousand.

Exe. There 's five to one; besides, they all are fresh.

Sal. God's arm strike with us! 't is a fearful odds.
God be wi' you, princes all; I 'll to my charge.
If we no more meet till we meet in heaven,
Then, joyfully, my noble Lord of Bedford,
My dear Lord Gloucester, and my good Lord Exeter,
And my kind kinsman, warriors all, adieu!

Bed. Farewell, good Salisbury, and good luck go with thee!

Exe. Farewell, kind lord; fight valiantly to-day!
And yet I do thee wrong to mind thee of it,
For thou art fram'd of the firm truth of valour. [*Exit Salisbury.*]

Bed. He is as full of valour as of kindness,
Princely in both.

Enter the King.

West. O that we now had here
But one ten thousand of those men in England
That do no work to-day!

K. Hen. What 's he that wishes so?
My cousin Westmoreland? No, my fair cousin.
If we are mark'd to die, we are enow
To do our country loss; and if to live,
The fewer men, the greater share of honour.
God's will! I pray thee, wish not one man more.
By Jove, I am not covetous for gold,
Nor care I who doth feed upon my cost;
It yearns me not if men my garments wear;
Such outward things dwell not in my desires;
But if it be a sin to covet honour,
I am the most offending soul alive.
No, faith, my coz, wish not a man from England.
God's peace! I would not lose so great an honour
As one man more, methinks, would share from me
For the best hope I have. O, do not wish one more!
Rather proclaim it, Westmoreland, through my host,
That he which hath no stomach to this fight,
Let him depart. His passport shall be made,
And crowns for convoy put into his purse.
We would not die in that man's company
That fears his fellowship to die with us.
This day is call'd the feast of Crispian.
He that outlives this day, and comes safe home,

Will stand a tip-toe when this day is named,
And rouse him at the name of Crispian.
He that shall live this day, and see old age,
Will yearly on the vigil feast his neighbours,
And say, "To-morrow is Saint Crispian."
Then will he strip his sleeve and show his scars,
And say, "These wounds I had on Crispin's day."
Old men forget; yet all shall be forgot,
But he 'll remember with advantages
What feats he did that day. Then shall our names,
Familiar in his mouth as household words,
Harry the King, Bedford, and Exeter,
Warwick and Talbot, Salisbury and Gloucester,
Be in their flowing cups freshly rememb'red.
This story shall the good man teach his son;
And Crispin Crispian shall ne'er go by,
From this day to the ending of the world,
But we in it shall be remembered,
We few, we happy few, we band of brothers.
For he to-day that sheds his blood with me
Shall be my brother; be he ne'er so vile,
This day shall gentle his condition;
And gentlemen in England now a-bed
Shall think themselves accurs'd they were not here,
And hold their manhoods cheap whiles any speaks
That fought with us upon Saint Crispin's day.

Re-enter SALISBURY.

Sal. My sovereign lord, bestow yourself with speed.
The French are bravely in their battles set,
And will with all expedience charge on us.

K. Hen. All things are ready, if our minds be so.

West. Perish the man whose mind is backward now!

K. Hen. Thou dost not wish more help from England, coz?

West. God's will! my liege, would you and I alone,
Without more help, could fight this royal battle!

K. Hen. Why, now thou hast unwish'd five thousand men,
Which likes me better than to wish us one.
You know your places. God be with you all!

Tucket. Enter MONTJOY.

Mont. Once more I come to know of thee, King Harry,
If for thy ransom thou wilt now compound,
Before thy most assured overthrow;
For certainly thou art so near the gulf,
Thou needs must be englutted. Besides, in mercy,
The Constable desires thee thou wilt mind
Thy followers of repentance; that their souls
May make a peaceful and a sweet retire
From off these fields, where, wretches, their poor bodies
Must lie and fester.

K. Hen. Who hath sent thee now?

Mont. The Constable of France.

K. Hen. I pray thee, bear my former answer back:
Bid them achieve me and then sell my bones.
Good God! why should they mock poor fellows thus?
The man that once did sell the lion's skin
While the beast liv'd, was kill'd with hunting him.
A many of our bodies shall no doubt
Find native graves, upon the which, I trust,

Shall witness live in brass of this day's work;
And those that leave their valiant bones in France,
Dying like men, though buried in your dung-hills,
They shall be fam'd; for there the sun shall greet them,
And draw their honours reeking up to heaven;
Leaving their earthly parts to choke your clime,
The smell whereof shall breed a plague in France.
Mark then abounding valour in our English,
That being dead, like to the bullet's grazing,
Break out into a second course of mischief,
Killing in relapse of mortality.
Let me speak proudly: tell the Constable
We are but warriors for the working-day.
Our gayness and our gilt are all besmirch'd
With rainy marching in the painful field;
There's not a piece of feather in our host—
Good argument, I hope, we will not fly—
And time hath worn us into slovenry;
But, by the mass, our hearts are in the trim;
And my poor soldiers tell me, yet ere night
They'll be in fresher robes, or they will pluck
The gay new coats o'er the French soldiers' heads
And turn them out of service. If they do this—
As, if God please, they shall,—my ransom then
Will soon be levied. Herald, save thou thy labour.
Come thou no more for ransom, gentle herald.
They shall have none, I swear, but these my joints;
Which if they have as I will leave 'em them,
Shall yield them little, tell the Constable.

Mont. I shall, King Harry. And so fare thee well;
Thou never shalt hear herald any more. [*Exit.*

K. Hen. I fear thou 'lt once more come again for ransom.

Enter YORK.

York. My lord, most humbly on my knee I beg
The leading of the vaward.

K. Hen. Take it, brave York. Now, soldiers, march away;
And how thou pleasest, God, dispose the day! [*Exeunt.*

Julius Cæsar

ACT IV.

SCENE I. *A house in Rome.*

ANTONY, OCTAVIUS, *and* LEPIDUS [*seated at a table*].

Ant. These many, then, shall die; their names are prick'd.

Oct. Your brother too must die; consent you, Lepidus?

Lep. I do consent,—

Oct. Prick him down, Antony.

Lep. Upon condition Publius shall not live,
Who is your sister's son, Mark Antony.

Ant. He shall not live; look, with a spot I damn him.
But, Lepidus, go you to Cæsar's house;
Fetch the will hither, and we shall determine
How to cut off some charge in legacies.

Lep. What, shall I find you here?

Oct. Or here, or at the Capitol. [*Exit Lepidus.*

Ant. This is a slight unmeritable man,

Meet to be sent on errands; is it fit,
The threefold world divided, he should stand
One of the three to share it?
Oct. So you thought him;
And took his voice who should be prick'd to die,
In our black sentence and proscription.
Ant. Octavius, I have seen more days than you;
And though we lay these honours on this man
To ease ourselves of divers slanderous loads,
He shall but bear them as the ass bears gold,
To groan and sweat under the business,
Either led or driven, as we point the way;
And having brought our treasure where we will,
Then take we down his load, and turn him off,
Like to the empty ass, to shake his ears
And graze in commons.
Oct. You may do your will;
But he's a tried and valiant soldier.
Ant. So is my horse, Octavius; and for that
I do appoint him store of provender.
It is a creature that I teach to fight,
To wind, to stop, to run directly on,
His corporal motion govern'd by my spirit.
And, in some taste, is Lepidus but so;
He must be taught and train'd and bid go forth;
A barren-spirited fellow; one that feeds
On abjects, orts, and imitations,
Which, out of use and stal'd by other men,
Begin his fashion. Do not talk of him
But as a property. And now, Octavius,
Listen great things. Brutus and Cassius
Are levying powers; we must straight make head;
Therefore let our alliance be combin'd,
Our best friends made, our means stretch'd;
And let us presently go sit in council
How covert matters may be best disclos'd
And open perils surest answered.
Oct. Let us do so; for we are at the stake,
And bay'd about with many enemies;
And some that smile have in their hearts, I fear,
Millions of mischiefs. [*Exeunt.*

SCENE II. *Camp near Sardis. Before Brutus's tent.*

Drum. Enter BRUTUS, LUCILIUS, [LUCIUS,] *and the army.* Titinius *and* PINDARUS *meet them.*

Bru. Stand, ho!
Lucil. Give the word, ho! and stand.
Bru. What now, Lucilius! is Cassius near?
Lucil. He is at hand; and Pindarus is come
To do you salutation from his master.
Bru. He greets me well. Your master, Pindarus,
In his own change, or by ill officers,
Hath given me some worthy cause to wish
Things done undone; but, if he be at hand,
I shall be satisfied.
Pin. I do not doubt
But that my noble master will appear
Such as he is, full of regard and honour.
Bru. He is not doubted. A word, Lucilius:
How he receiv'd you let me be resolv'd.
Lucil. With courtesy and with respect enough;
But not with such familiar instances,
Nor with such free and friendly conference,
As he hath us'd of old.
Bru. Thou hast describ'd
A hot friend cooling. Ever note, Lucilius,
When love begins to sicken and decay,
It useth an enforced ceremony.

There are no tricks in plain and simple faith;
But hollow men, like horses hot at hand,
Make gallant show and promise of their mettle; [*Low march within.*
But when they should endure the bloody spur
They fall their crests, and, like deceitful jades,
Sink in the trial. Comes his army on?
Lucil. They mean this night in Sardis to be quarter'd.
The greater part, the horse in general,
Are come with Cassius.

Enter CASSIUS *and his Powers.*

Bru. Hark! he is arriv'd.
March gently on to meet him.
Cas. Stand, ho!
Bru. Stand, ho! Speak the word along.
[*1. Sol.*] Stand!
[*2. Sol.*] Stand!
[*3. Sol.*] Stand!
Cas. Most noble brother, you have done me wrong.
Bru. Judge me, you gods! wrong I mine enemies?
And, if not so, how should I wrong a brother?
Cas. Brutus, this sober form of yours hides wrongs;
And when you do them—
Bru. Cassius, be content;
Speak your griefs softly; I do know you well.
Before the eyes of both our armies here,
Which should perceive nothing but love from us,
Let us not wrangle. Bid them move away;
Then in my tent, Cassius, enlarge your griefs,
And I will give you audience.
Cas. Pindarus,
Bid our commanders lead their charges off
A little from this ground.
Bru. [Lucius], do you the like; and let no man
Come to our tent till we have done our conference.
[Lucilius] and Titinius, guard our door. [*Exeunt.*

SCENE III. *Brutus's tent.*

[*Enter*] BRUTUS *and* CASSIUS.

Cas. That you have wrong'd me doth appear in this:
You have condemn'd and noted Lucius Pella
For taking bribes here of the Sardians;
Wherein my letters, praying on his side,
Because I knew the man was slighted off,—
Bru. You wrong'd yourself to write in such a case.
Cas. In such a time as this it is not meet
That every nice offence should bear his comment.
Bru. Let me tell you, Cassius, you yourself
Are much condemn'd to have an itching palm,
To sell and mart your offices for gold
To undeservers.
Cas. I an itching palm!
You know that you are Brutus that speaks this,
Or, by the gods, this speech were else your last.
Bru. The name of Cassius honours this corruption,
And chastisement doth therefore hide his head.
Cas. Chastisement!
Bru. Remember March, the ides of March remember:
Did not great Julius bleed for justice' sake?
What villain touch'd his body, that did stab
And not for justice? What, shall one of us,

That struck the foremost man of all this world
But for supporting robbers, shall we now
Contaminate our fingers with base bribes,
And sell the mighty space of our large honours
For so much trash as may be grasped thus?
I had rather be a dog, and bay the moon,
Than such a Roman.

Cas. Brutus, bait not me;
I 'll not endure it. You forget yourself
To hedge me in. I am a soldier, I,
Older in practice, abler than yourself
To make conditions.

Bru. Go to; you are not, Cassius.

Cas. I am.

Bru. I say you are not.

Cas. Urge me no more, I shall forget myself;
Have mind upon your health, tempt me no farther.

Bru. Away, slight man!

Cas. Is 't possible?

Bru. Hear me, for I will speak.
Must I give way and room to your rash choler?
Shall I be frighted when a madman stares?

Cas. O ye gods, ye gods! must I endure all this?

Bru. All this! ay, more. Fret till your proud heart break;
Go show your slaves how choleric you are,
And make your bondmen tremble. Must I budge?
Must I observe you? Must I stand and crouch
Under your testy humour? By the gods,
You shall digest the venom of your spleen,
Though it do split you; for, from this day forth,
I 'll use you for my mirth, yea, for my laughter,
When you are waspish.

Cas. Is it come to this?

Bru. You say you are a better soldier:
Let it appear so; make your vaunting true,
And it shall please me well. For mine own part,
I shall be glad to learn of noble men.

Cas. You wrong me every way; you wrong me, Brutus;
I said an elder soldier, not a better.
Did I say "better"?

Bru. If you did, I care not.

Cas. When Cæsar liv'd, he durst not thus have mov'd me.

Bru. Peace, peace! you durst not so have tempted him.

Cas. I durst not!

Bru. No.

Cas. What, durst not tempt him!

Bru. For your life you durst not.

Cas. Do not presume too much upon my love;
I may do that I shall be sorry for.

Bru. You have done that you should be sorry for.
There is no terror, Cassius, in your threats,
For I am arm'd so strong in honesty
That they pass by me as the idle wind,
Which I respect not. I did send to you
For certain sums of gold, which you deni'd me;
For I can raise no money by vile means.—
By heaven, I had rather coin my heart,
And drop my blood for drachmas, than to wring
From the hard hands of peasants their vile trash
By any indirection.—I did send
To you for gold to pay my legions,
Which you deni'd me. Was that done like Cassius?
Should I have answer'd Caius Cassius so?
When Marcus Brutus grows so covetous
To lock such rascal counters from his friends,

Be ready, gods, with all your thunder-bolts;
Dash him to pieces!
Cas. I deni'd you not.
Bru. You did.
Cas. I did not. He was but a fool that brought
My answer back. Brutus hath riv'd my heart.
A friend should bear his friend's infirmities,
But Brutus makes mine greater than they are.
Bru. I do not, till you practise them on me.
Cas. You love me not.
Bru. I do not like your faults.
Cas. A friendly eye could never see such faults.
Bru. A flatterer's would not, though they do appear
As huge as high Olympus.
Cas. Come, Antony, and young Octavius, come,
Revenge yourselves alone on Cassius,
For Cassius is aweary of the world;
Hated by one he loves; brav'd by his brother;
Check'd like a bondman; all his faults observ'd,
Set in a note-book, learn'd and conn'd by rote
To cast into my teeth. O, I could weep
My spirit from mine eyes! There is my dagger,
And here my naked breast; within, a heart
Dearer than Plutus' mine, richer than gold.
If that thou be'st a Roman, take it forth;
I, that deni'd thee gold, will give my heart.
Strike, as thou didst at Cæsar; for, I know,
When thou didst hate him worst, thou lov'dst him better
Than ever thou lov'dst Cassius.
Bru. Sheathe your dagger.
Be angry when you will, it shall have scope.
Do what you will, dishonour shall be humour.
O Cassius, you are yoked with a lamb
That carries anger as the flint bears fire;
Who, much enforced, shows a hasty spark,
And straight is cold again.
Cas. Hath Cassius liv'd
To be but mirth and laughter to his Brutus,
When grief and blood ill-temper'd vexeth him?
Bru. When I spoke that, I was ill-temper'd too.
Cas. Do you confess so much? Give me your hand.
Bru. And my heart too.
Cas. O Brutus!
Bru. What 's the matter?
Cas. Have not you love enough to bear with me,
When that rash humour which my mother gave me
Makes me forgetful?
Bru. Yes, Cassius; and, for henceforth,
When you are over earnest with your Brutus,
He 'll think your mother chides, and leave you so.
Poet. [*Within.*] Let me go in to see the generals;
There is some grudge between 'em, 't is not meet
They be alone.
Lucil. [*Within.*] You shall not come to them.
Poet. [*Within.*] Nothing but death shall stay me.

Enter POET [*followed by* LUCILIUS, TITINIUS, *and* LUCIUS].

Cas. How now! what 's the matter?
Poet. For shame, you generals! what do you mean?
Love, and be friends, as two such men should be;

For I have seen more years, I 'm sure, than ye.
Cas. Ha, ha! how vilely doth this cynic rhyme!
Bru. Get you hence, sirrah; saucy fellow, hence!
Cas. Bear with him, Brutus; 't is his fashion.
Bru. I 'll know his humour, when he knows his time.
What should the wars do with these jigging fools?
Companion, hence!
Cas. Away, away, be gone!
[*Exit Poet.*
Bru. Lucilius and Titinius, bid the commanders
Prepare to lodge their companies to-night.
Cas. And come yourselves, and bring Messala with you
Immediately to us.
[*Exeunt Lucilius and Titinius.*]
Bru. Lucius, a bowl of wine!
[*Exit Lucius.*]
Cas. I did not think you could have been so angry.
Bru. O Cassius, I am sick of many griefs.
Cas. Of your philosophy you make no use
If you give place to accidental evils.
Bru. No man bears sorrow better. Portia is dead.
Cas. Ha! Portia!
Bru. She is dead.
Cas. How scap'd I killing when I cross'd you so?
O insupportable and touching loss!
Upon what sickness?
Bru. Impatient of my absence,
And grief that young Octavius with Mark Antony
Have made themselves so strong,—for with her death
That tidings came,—with this she fell distract,
And, her attendants absent, swallow'd fire.
Cas. And died so?
Bru. Even so.
Cas. O ye immortal gods!

Re-enter Boy [Lucius], *with wine and tapers.*

Bru. Speak no more of her. Give me a bowl of wine.
In this I bury all unkindness, Cassius.
[*Drinks.*]
Cas. My heart is thirsty for that noble pledge.
Fill Lucius, till the wine o'erswell the cup;
I cannot drink too much of Brutus' love.
[*Drinks.*]

Re-enter TITINIUS, *with* MESSALA.

Bru. Come in, Titinius!
[*Exit Lucius.*]
Welcome, good Messala.
Now sit we close about this taper here,
And call in question our necessities.
Cas. Portia, art thou gone?
Bru. No more, I pray you.
Messala, I have here received letters
That young Octavius and Mark Antony
Come down upon us with a mighty power,
Bending their expedition toward Philippi.
Mes. Myself have letters of the selfsame tenour.
Bru. With what addition?
Mes. That by proscription and bills of outlawry,
Octavius, Antony, and Lepidus
Have put to death an hundred senators.
Bru. Therein our letters do not well agree;
Mine speak of seventy senators that died
By their proscriptions, Cicero being one.
Cas. Cicero one!
Mes. Cicero is dead,
And by that order of proscription.
Had you your letters from your wife, my lord?
Bru. No, Messala.
Mes. Nor nothing in your letters writ of her?

Bru. Nothing, Messala.
Mes. That, methinks, is strange.
Bru. Why ask you? Hear you aught of her in yours?
Mes. No, my lord.
Bru. Now, as you are a Roman, tell me true.
Mes. Then like a Roman bear the truth I tell:
For certain she is dead, and by strange manner.
Bru. Why, farewell, Portia. We must die, Messala.
With meditating that she must die once,
I have the patience to endure it now.
Mes. Even so great men great losses should endure.
Cas. I have as much of this in art as you,
But yet my nature could not bear it so.
Bru. Well, to our work alive. What do you think
Of marching to Philippi presently?
Cas. I do not think it good.
Bru. Your reason?
Cas. This it is:
'T is better that the enemy seek us.
So shall he waste his means, weary his soldiers,
Doing himself offence; whilst we, lying still,
Are full of rest, defence, and nimbleness.
Bru. Good reasons must, of force, give place to better.
The people 'twixt Philippi and this ground
Do stand but in a forc'd affection,
For they have grudg'd us contribution.
The enemy, marching along by them,
By them shall make a fuller number up,
Come on refresh'd, new-added, and encourag'd;
From which advantage shall we cut him off
If at Philippi we do face him there,
These people at our back.
Cas. Hear me, good brother.
Bru. Under your pardon. You must note beside,
That we have tried the utmost of our friends;
Our legions are brim-full, our cause is ripe.
The enemy increaseth every day;
We, at the height, are ready to decline.
There is a tide in the affairs of men,
Which, taken at the flood, leads on to fortune;
Omitted, all the voyage of their life
Is bound in shallows and in miseries.
On such a full sea are we now afloat;
And we must take the current when it serves,
Or lose our ventures.
Cas. Then, with your will, go on.
We 'll along ourselves, and meet them at Philippi.
Bru. The deep of night is crept upon our talk,
And nature must obey necessity;
Which we will niggard with a little rest.
There is no more to say?
Cas. No more. Good-night.
Early to-morrow will we rise, and hence.
Bru. Lucius! (*Re-enter Lucius.*)
My gown. [*Exit Lucius.*]
Farewell, good Messala!
Good-night, Titinius. Noble, noble Cassius,
Good-night, and good repose.
Cas. O my dear brother!
This was an ill beginning of the night.
Never come such division 'tween our souls!
Let it not, Brutus.

Re-enter LUCIUS, *with the gown.*

Bru. Everything is well.
Cas. Good-night, my lord.
Bru. Good-night, good brother.
Tit. Mes. Good-night, Lord Brutus.
Bru. Farewell, every one.
[*Exeunt all but Brutus and Lucius*].
Give me the gown. Where is thy instrument?
Luc. Here in the tent.
Bru. What, thou speak'st drowsily?

Poor knave, I blame thee not; thou art o'er-watch'd.
Call Claudius and some other of my men;
I 'll have them sleep on cushions in my tent.

Luc. Varro and Claudius!

Enter VARRO *and* CLAUDIUS.

Var. Calls my lord?

Bru. I pray you, sirs, lie in my tent and sleep;
It may be I shall raise you by and by
On business to my brother Cassius.

Var. So please you, we will stand and watch your pleasure.

Bru. I will not have it so: lie down, good sirs;
It may be I shall otherwise bethink me.
[*Varro and Claudius lie down.*]
Look, Lucius, here 's the book I sought for so;
I put it in the pocket of my gown.

Luc. I was sure your lordship did not give it me.

Bru. Bear with me, good boy, I am much forgetful.
Canst thou hold up thy heavy eyes a while,
And touch thy instrument a strain or two?

Luc. Ay, my lord, an 't please you.

Bru. It does, my boy.
I trouble thee too much, but thou art willing.

Luc. It is my duty, sir.

Bru. I should not urge thy duty past thy might;
I know young bloods look for a time of rest.

Luc. I have slept, my lord, already.

Bru. It was well done; and thou shalt sleep again;
I will not hold thee long. If I do live,
I will be good to thee.
[*Music, and a song.*
This is a sleepy tune. O murderous slumber,
Lay'st thou thy leaden mace upon my boy,
That plays thee music? Gentle knave, good-night;
I will not do thee so much wrong to wake thee.
If thou dost nod, thou break'st thy instrument.
I 'll take it from thee; and, good boy, good-night.
Let me see, let me see; is not the leaf turn'd down
Where I left reading? Here it is, I think.

Enter the GHOST *of Cæsar.*

How ill this taper burns! Ha! who comes here?
I think it is the weakness of mine eyes
That shapes this monstrous apparition.
It comes upon me. Art thou anything?
Art thou some god, some angel, or some devil,
That mak'st my blood cold and my hair to stare?
Speak to me what thou art.

Ghost. Thy evil spirit, Brutus.

Bru. Why com'st thou?

Ghost. To tell thee thou shalt see me at Philippi.

Bru. Well; then I shall see thee again?

Ghost. Ay, at Philippi.

Bru. Why, I will see thee at Philippi, then.
[*Exit Ghost.*]
Now I have taken heart thou vanishest.
Ill spirit, I would hold more talk with thee.
Boy, Lucius! Varro! Claudius! Sirs, awake!
Claudius!

Luc. The strings, my lord, are false.

Bru. He thinks he still is at his instrument.
Lucius, awake!

Luc. My lord?

Bru. Didst thou dream, Lucius, that thou so criedst out?

Luc. My lord, I do not know that I did cry.

Bru. Yes, that thou didst. Didst thou see anything?
Luc. Nothing, my lord.
Bru. Sleep again, Lucius. Sirrah Claudius!
Fellow thou, awake!
Var. My lord?
Clau. My lord?
Bru. Why did you so cry out, sirs, in your sleep?
Var. Clau. Did we, my lord?
Bru. Ay. Saw you anything?
Var. No, my lord, I saw nothing.
Clau. Nor I, my lord.
Bru. Go and commend me to my brother Cassius;
Bid him set on his powers betimes before,
And we will follow.
Var. Clau. It shall be done, my lord.
[*Exeunt.*

Macbeth

Act III, Scene IV

Hall in the palace.

A banquet prepar'd. Enter Macbeth, Lady Macbeth, Ross, Lennox, Lords, *and* Attendants.

Macb. You know your own degrees; sit down. At first
And last, the hearty welcome.
Lords. Thanks to your Majesty.
Macb. Ourself will mingle with society
And play the humble host.
Our hostess keeps her state, but in best time
We will require her welcome.
Lady M. Pronounce it for me, sir, to all our friends,
For my heart speaks they are welcome.
First Murderer [*appears at the door*].
Macb. See, they encounter thee with their hearts' thanks.
Both sides are even; here I 'll sit i' the midst.
Be large in mirth; anon we'll drink a measure
The table round. [*Approaching the door.*]—There 's blood upon thy face.
Mur. 'T is Banquo's then.
Macb. 'T is better thee without than he within.
Is he dispatch'd?
Mur. My lord, his throat is cut; that I did for him.
Macb. Thou art the best o' the cut-throats; yet he 's good
That did the like for Fleance. If thou didst it,
Thou art the nonpareil.
Mur. Most royal sir,
Fleance is scap'd.
Macb. Then comes my fit again. I had else been perfect,
Whole as the marble, founded as the rock,
As broad and general as the casing air;
But now I am cabin'd, cribb'd, confin'd, bound in
To saucy doubts and fears. But Banquo 's safe?
Mur. Ay, my good lord; safe in a ditch he bides,
With twenty trenched gashes on his head,
The least a death to nature.
Macb. Thanks, for that;
There the grown serpent lies. The worm that 's fled
Hath nature that in time will venom breed,
No teeth for the present. Get thee gone; to-morrow
We'll hear ourselves again.
[*Exit Murderer.*
Lady M. My royal lord,
You do not give the cheer. The feast is sold
That is not often vouch'd, while 't is a-making,
'T is given with welcome. To feed were best at home;

From thence, the sauce to meat is ceremony;
Meeting were bare without it.

Enter the Ghost *of Banquo, and sits in Macbeth's place.*

Macb. Sweet remembrancer!
Now, good digestion wait on appetite,
And health on both!

Len. May 't please your Highness sit.

Macb. Here had we now our country's honour roof'd,
Were the grac'd person of our Banquo present,
Who may I rather challenge for unkindness
Than pity for mischance.

Ross. His absence, sir,
Lays blame upon his promise. Please 't your Highness
To grace us with your royal company?

Macb. The table 's full.

Len. Here is a place reserv'd, sir.

Macb. Where?

Len. Here, my good lord. What is 't that moves your Highness?

Macb. Which of you have done this?

Lords. What, my good lord?

Macb. Thou canst not say I did it; never shake
Thy gory locks at me.

Ross. Gentlemen, rise: his Highness is not well.

Lady M. Sit, worthy friends; my lord is often thus,
And hath been from his youth. Pray you, keep seat;
The fit is momentary; upon a thought
He will again be well. If much you note him,
You shall offend him and extend his passion.
Feed, and regard him not. [*Aside to Macbeth.*] Are you a man?

Macb. Ay, and a bold one, that dare look on that
Which might appall the devil.

Lady M. [*Aside to Macbeth.*] O proper stuff!
This is the very painting of your fear;
This is the air-drawn dagger which, you said,
Led you to Duncan. O, these flaws and starts,
Impostors to true fear, would well become
A woman's story at a winter's fire,
Authoriz'd by her grandam. Shame itself!
Why do you make such faces? When all 's done,
You look but on a stool.

Macb. Prithee, see there! behold! look! lo! how say you?
Why, what care I? If thou canst nod, speak too.
If charnel-houses and our graves must send
Those that we bury back, our monuments
Shall be the maws of kites.

[*Ghost vanishes.*]

Lady M. [*Aside to Macbeth.*] What, quite unmann'd in folly?

Macb. If I stand here, I saw him.

Lady M. [*Aside to Macbeth.*] Fie, for shame!

Macb. Blood hath been shed ere now, i' the olden time,
Ere humane statute purg'd the gentle weal;
Ay, and since too, murders have been perform'd
Too terrible for the ear. The time has been,
That, when the brains were out, the man would die,
And there an end; but now they rise again,
With twenty mortal murders on their crowns,
And push us from our stools. This is more strange
Than such a murder is.

Lady M. My worthy lord,
Your noble friends do lack you.

Macb. I do forget.

Do not muse at me, my most worthy friends;
I have a strange infirmity, which is nothing
To those that know me. Come, love and health to all;
Then I 'll sit down. Give me some wine; fill full.

Re-enter Ghost.

I drink to the general joy o' the whole table,
And to our dear friend Banquo, whom we miss;
Would he were here! to all and him we thirst,
And all to all.

Lords. Our duties, and the pledge.

Macb. Avaunt! and quit my sight! let the earth hide thee!
Thy bones are marrowless, thy blood is cold;
Thou hast no speculation in those eyes
Which thou dost glare with!

Lady M. Think of this, good peers,
But as a thing of custom; 't is no other,
Only it spoils the pleasure of the time.

Macb. What man dare, I dare.
Approach thou like the rugged Russian bear,
The arm'd rhinoceros, or the Hyrcan tiger;
Take any shape but that, and my firm nerves
Shall never tremble. Or be alive again,
And dare me to the desert with thy sword;
If trembling I inhabit then, protest me
The baby of a girl. Hence, horrible shadow!
Unreal mockery, hence!

[*Ghost vanishes.*]

Why, so; being gone,
I am a man again. Pray you, sit still.

Lady M. You have displac'd the mirth, broke the good meeting,
With most admir'd disorder.

Macb. Can such things be,
And overcome us like a summer's cloud,
Without our special wonder? You make me strange
Even to the disposition that I owe,
When now I think you can behold such sights,
And keep the natural ruby of your cheeks,
When mine is blanch'd with fear.

Ross. What sights, my lord?

Lady M. I pray you, speak not; he grows worse and worse;
Question enrages him. At once, good-night.
Stand not upon the order of your going,
But go at once.

Len. Good-night; and better health
Attend his Majesty!

Lady M. A kind good-night to all!

[*Exeunt Lords.*

Macb. It will have blood, they say; blood will have blood.
Stones have been known to move and trees to speak;
Augures and understood relations have
By maggot-pies and choughs and rooks brought forth
The secret'st man of blood. What is the night?

Lady M. Almost at odds with morning, which is which.

Macb. How say'st thou, that Macduff denies his person
At our great bidding?

Lady M. Did you send to him, sir?

Macb. I hear it by the way; but I will send.
There 's not a one of them but in his house
I keep a servant fee'd. I will to-morrow,
And betimes I will, to the weird sisters.
More shall they speak; for now I am bent to know,
By the worst means, the worst. For mine own good
All causes shall give way. I am in blood
Stepp'd in so far that, should I wade no more,
Returning were as tedious as go o'er.
Strange things I have in head, that will to hand,

Which must be acted ere they may be
scann'd.

Lady M. You lack the season of all
natures, sleep.

Macb. Come, we 'll to sleep. My
strange and self-abuse
Is the initiate fear that wants hard use;
We are yet but young in deed. [*Exeunt.*

Act V, Scene I.

Dunsinane. Ante-room in the castle.

Enter a Doctor of Physic *and a* Waiting Gentlewoman.

Doct. I have two nights watch'd with you, but can perceive no truth in your report. When was it she last walk'd?

Gent. Since his Majesty went into the field, I have seen her rise from her bed, throw her nightgown upon her, unlock her closet, take forth paper, fold it, write upon 't, read it, afterwards seal it, and again return to bed; yet all this while in a most fast sleep.

Doct. A great perturbation in nature, to receive at once the benefit of sleep, and do the effects of watching! In this slumb'ry agitation, besides her walking and other actual performances, what, at any time, have you heard her say?

Gent. That, sir, which I will not report after her.

Doct. You may to me; and 't is most meet you should.

Gent. Neither to you nor any one; having no witness to confirm my speech.

Enter Lady Macbeth, *with a taper.*

Lo you, here she comes! This is her very guise; and, upon my life, fast asleep. Observe her; stand close.

Doct. How came she by that light?

Gent. Why, it stood by her. She has light by her continually; 't is her command.

Doct. You see, her eyes are open.

Gent. Ay, but their sense are shut.

Doct. What is it she does now? Look, how she rubs her hands.

Gent. It is an accustom'd action with her, to seem thus washing her hands. I have known her continue in this a quarter of an hour.

Lady M. Yet here 's a spot.

Doct. Hark! she speaks. I will set down what comes from her, to satisfy my remembrance the more strongly.

Lady M. Out, damned spot! out, I say!—One: two: why, then 't is time to do 't.—Hell is murky!—Fie, my lord, fie! a soldier, and afeard? What need we fear who knows it, when none can call our power to account?—Yet who would have thought the old man to have had so much blood in him?

Doct. Do you mark that?

Lady M. The thane of Fife had a wife; where is she now?—What, will these hands ne'er be clean?—No more o' that, my lord, no more o' that; you mar all with this starting.

Doct. Go to, go to; you have known what you should not.

Gent. She has spoke what she should not, I am sure of that; Heaven knows what she has known.

Lady M. Here 's the smell of the blood still; all the perfumes of Arabia will not sweeten this little hand. Oh, oh, oh!

Doct. What a sigh is there! The heart is sorely charg'd.

Gent. I would not have such a heart in my bosom for the dignity of the whole body.

Doct. Well, well, well,—

Gent. Pray God it be, sir.

Doct. This disease is beyond my practice; yet I have known those which have walk'd in their sleep who have died holily in their beds.

Lady M. Wash your hands, put on your nightgown; look not so pale.—I tell you yet again, Banquo 's buried; he cannot come out on 's grave.

Doct. Even so?

Lady M. To bed, to bed! there 's knocking at the gate. Come, come, come, come, give me your hand. What 's done cannot be undone.—To bed, to bed, to bed! [*Exit.*

Doct. Will she go now to bed?

Gent. Directly.

Doct. Foul whisp'rings are abroad; unnatural deeds
Do breed unnatural troubles; infected minds
To their deaf pillows will discharge their secrets.
More needs she the divine than the physician.
God, God, forgive us all! Look after her;
Remove from her the means of all annoyance,
And still keep eyes upon her. So, good-night!
My mind she has mated, and amaz'd my sight.
I think, but dare not speak.

Gent. Good-night, good doctor. [*Exeunt.*

SIR HENRY WOTTON
[1568-1639]

The Character of a Happy Life

How happy is he born and taught
  That serveth not another's will;
Whose armour is his honest thought,
  And simple truth his utmost skill;

Whose passions not his masters are;
  Whose soul is still prepared for death,
Untied unto the world by care
  Of public fame or private breath;

Who envies none that chance doth raise,
  Nor vice; who never understood
How deepest wounds are given by praise,
  Nor rules of state, but rules of good;

Who hath his life from rumours freed;
  Whose conscience is his strong retreat;
Whose state can neither flatterers feed,
  Nor ruin make oppressors great;

Who God doth late and early pray
  More of his grace than gifts to lend;
And entertains the harmless day
  With a religious book or friend—

This man is freed from servile bands
  Of hope to rise or fear to fall:
Lord of himself, though not of lands,
  And, having nothing, yet hath all.

On his Mistress the Queen of Bohemia

You meaner beauties of the night,
  That poorly satisfy our eyes
More by your number than your light,
  You common people of the skies;
What are you when the moon shall rise?

You curious chanters of the wood,
  That warble forth Dame Nature's lays,
Thinking your passions understood
  By your weak accents; what's your praise
When Philomel her voice shall raise?

You violets that first appear,
  By your pure purple mantles known
Like the proud virgins of the year,
  As if the spring were all your own;
What are you when the rose is blown?

So, when my mistress shall be seen
  In form and beauty of her mind,
By virtue first, then choice, a Queen,
  Tell me, if she were not design'd
Th' eclipse and glory of her kind.

GEORGE WITHER
[1588-1667]

A Christmas Carol

So now is come our joyfulst feast:
  Let every man be jolly,

Each room with ivy leaves is drest
  And every post with holly.
Though some churls at our mirth repine,
Round your foreheads garlands twine,
Drown sorrow in a cup of wine,
  And let us all be merry.

* * * * *

Now every lad is wondrous trim,
  And no man minds his labour;
Our lasses have provided them
  A bag-pipe and a tabor.
Young men and maids and girls and boys
Give life to one another's joys,
And you anon shall by their noise
  Perceive that they are merry.

Rank misers now do sparing shun,
  Their hall of music soundeth;
And dogs thence with whole shoulders run,
  So all things here aboundeth.
The country folk themselves advance,
For Crowdy-mutton's come out of France,
And Jack shall pipe, and Jill shall dance,
  And all the town be merry.

Ned Swash hath fetched his bands from pawn,
  And all his best apparel;
Brisk Nell hath bought a ruff of lawn
  With droppings of the barrel.
And those that hardly all the year
Had bread to eat or rags to wear,
Will have both clothes and dainty fare
  And all the day be merry.

* * * * *

The wenches with their wassail-bowls
  About the street are singing,
The boys are come to catch the owls,
  The wild-mare in is bringing.
Our kitchen-boy hath broke his box,
And to the dealing of the ox
Our honest neighbours come by flocks,
  And here they will be merry.

* * * * *

Then wherefore in these merry days
  Should we I pray be duller?
No, let us sing our roundelays
  To make our mirth the fuller;
And whilest thus inspired we sing
Let all the streets with echoes ring:
Woods, and hills, and every-thing
  Bear witness we are merry.

When we are upon the Seas

On those great waters now I am,
  Of which I have been told,
That whosoever thither came
  Should wonders there behold.
In this unsteady place of fear,
  Be present, Lord, with me;
For in these depths of water here
  I depths of danger see.

A stirring courser now I sit,
  A headstrong steed I ride,
That champs and foams upon the bit
  Which curbs his lofty pride.
The softest whistling of the winds
  Doth make him gallop fast;
And as their breath increased he finds
  The more he maketh haste.

Take Thou, oh Lord! the reins in hand,
  Assume our Master's room;
Vouchsafe Thou at our helm to stand,
  And pilot to become.
Trim Thou the sails, and let good speed
  Accompany our haste;
Sound Thou the channels at our need,
  And anchor for us cast.

A fit and favourable wind
  To further us provide;
And let it wait on us behind,
  Or lackey by our side.
From sudden gusts, from storms, from sands,
  And from the raging wave;
From shallows, rocks, and pirates' hands,
  Men, goods, and vessel save.

Preserve us from the wants, the fear,
  And sickness of the seas;
But chiefly from our sins, which are
  A danger worse than these.

Lord! let us also safe arrive
  Where we desire to be;
And for Thy mercies let us give
  Due thanks and praise to Thee.

The Prayer of Old Age

As this my carnal robe grows old,
Soil'd, rent, and worn by length of years,
Let me on that by faith lay hold
Which man in life immortal wears:
  So sanctify my days behind,
  So let my manners be refined,
That when my soul and flesh must part,
There lurk no terrors in my heart.

So shall my rest be safe and sweet
When I am lodgèd in my grave;
And when my soul and body meet,
A joyful meeting they shall have;
  Their essence then shall be divine,
  This muddy flesh shall starlike shine,
And God shall that fresh youth restore
Which will abide for evermore.

ROBERT HERRICK (1591-1674)

Corinna's Going a-Maying

GET up, get up for shame! The blooming morn
  Upon her wings presents the god unshorn.
  See how Aurora throws her fair
  Fresh-quilted colours through the air:
  Get up, sweet slug-a-bed, and see
  The dew bespangling herb and tree!
Each flower has wept and bow'd toward the east
Above an hour since, yet you not drest;
  Nay! not so much as out of bed?
  When all the birds have matins said
  And sung their thankful hymns, 'tis sin,
  Nay, profanation, to keep in,
Whereas a thousand virgins on this day
Spring sooner than the lark, to fetch in May.

Rise and put on your foliage, and be seen
To come forth, like the spring-time, fresh and green,
  And sweet as Flora. Take no care
  For jewels for your gown or hair:
  Fear not; the leaves will strew
  Gems in abundance upon you:
Besides, the childhood of the day has kept,
Against you come, some orient pearls unwept.
  Come, and receive them while the light
  Hangs on the dew-locks of the night:
  And Titan on the eastern hill
  Retires himself, or else stands still
Till you come forth! Wash, dress, be brief in praying:
Few beads are best when once we go a-Maying.

Come, my Corinna, come; and coming, mark
How each field turns a street, each street a park,
  Made green and trimm'd with trees! see how
  Devotion gives each house a bough
  Or branch! each porch, each door, ere this,
  An ark, a tabernacle is,
Made up of white-thorn neatly interwove,
As if here were those cooler shades of love.
  Can such delights be in the street
  And open fields, and we not see 't?
  Come, we'll abroad: and let 's obey
  The proclamation made for May,
And sin no more, as we have done, by staying;
But, my Corinna, come, let 's go a-Maying.

There's not a budding boy or girl this day
But is got up and gone to bring in May.
  A deal of youth ere this is come
  Back, and with white-thorn laden home.

Some have despatch'd their cakes and cream,
Before that we have left to dream:
And some have wept and woo'd, and plighted troth,
And chose their priest, ere we can cast off sloth:
Many a green-gown has been given,
Many a kiss, both odd and even:
Many a glance, too, has been sent
From out the eye, love's firmament:
Many a jest told of the keys betraying
This night, and locks pick'd: yet we're not a-Maying!

Come, let us go, while we are in our prime,
And take the harmless folly of the time!
We shall grow old apace, and die
Before we know our liberty.
Our life is short, and our days run
As fast away as does the sun.
And, as a vapour or a drop of rain,
Once lost, can ne'er be found again,
So when or you or I are made
A fable, song, or fleeting shade,
All love, all liking, all delight
Lies drown'd with us in endless night.
Then, while time serves, and we are but decaying,
Come, my Corinna, come, let 's go a-Maying.

The Night Piece

HER eyes the glow-worm lend thee,
The shooting stars attend thee;
And the elves also,
Whose little eyes glow
Like the sparks of fire, befriend thee.

No Will-o'-the-wisp mislight thee,
Nor snake or slow-worm bite thee;
But on, on thy way
Not making a stay,
Since ghost there 's none to affright thee.

Let not the dark thee cumber:
What though the moon does slumber?
The stars of the night
Will lend thee their light
Like tapers clear without number.

Then, Julia, let me woo thee,
Thus, thus to come unto me;
And when I shall meet
Thy silv'ry feet,
My soul I'll pour into thee.

To Daffodils

FAIR daffodils, we weep to see
You haste away so soon;
As yet the early-rising sun
Has not attain'd his noon.
Stay, stay
Until the hasting day
Has run
But to the evensong;
And, having pray'd together, we
Will go with you along.

We have short time to stay, as you,
We have as short a spring;
As quick a growth to meet decay,
As you, or anything.
We die
As your hours do, and dry
Away
Like to the summer's rain;
Or as the pearls of morning's dew,
Ne'er to be found again.

Upon Julia's Clothes

WHENAS in silks my Julia goes,
Then, then, methinks, how sweetly flows
The liquefaction of her clothes!

Next, when I cast mine eyes and see
That brave vibration each way free,
—O how that glittering taketh me!

To the Virgins, to make much of Time

GATHER ye rosebuds while ye may,
Old Time is still a-flying:

And this same flower that smiles to-day
  To-morrow will be dying.

The glorious lamp of heaven, the sun,
  The higher he 's a-getting,
The sooner will his race be run,
  And nearer he 's to setting.

That age is best which is the first,
  When youth and blood are warmer;
But being spent, the worse, and worst
  Times still succeed the former.

Then be not coy, but use your time,
  And while ye may, go marry:
For having lost but once your prime,
  You may for ever tarry.

THOMAS CAREW (1595?-1639?)

Epitaph on the Lady Mary Villiers

The Lady Mary Villiers lies
Under this stone; with weeping eyes
The parents that first gave her birth,
And their sad friends, laid her in earth.
If any of them, Reader, were
Known unto thee, shed a tear;
Or if thyself possess a gem
As dear to thee, as this to them,
Though a stranger to this place,
Bewail in theirs thine own hard case:
For thou perhaps at thy return
May'st find thy Darling in an urn.

JAMES SHIRLEY (1596-1666)

A Dirge

The glories of our blood and state
  Are shadows, not substantial things;
There is no armour against Fate;
  Death lays his icy hand on kings:
    Sceptre and Crown
    Must tumble down,
And in the dust be equal made
With the poor crookèd scythe and spade.

Some men with swords may reap the field,
  And plant fresh laurels where they kill:
But their strong nerves at last must yield;
  They tame but one another still:
    Early or late
    They stoop to fate,
And must give up their murmuring breath
When they, pale captives, creep to death.

The garlands wither on your brow;
  Then boast no more your mighty deeds!
Upon Death's purple altar now
  See where the victor-victim bleeds.
    Your heads must come
    To the cold tomb:
Only the actions of the just
Smell sweet and blossom in their dust.

SIR THOMAS BROWNE (1605-1682)

From Religio Medici

Faith in Mysteries

As for those wingy Mysteries in Divinity, and airy subtleties in Religion, which have unhing'd the brains of better heads, they never stretched the *Pia Mater* of mine. Methinks there be not impossibilities enough in Religion for an active faith; the deepest Mysteries ours contains have not only been illustrated, but maintained, by Syllogism and the rule of Reason. I love to lose my self in a mystery, to pursue my Reason to an *O altitudo!* 'Tis my solitary recreation to pose my apprehension with those involved Ænigmas and riddles of the Trinity, with Incarnation, and Resurrection. I can answer all the Objections of Satan and my rebellious reason with that odd resolution I learned of Tertullian, *Certum est, quia impossibile est.* I desire to exercise my faith in the difficultest point; for to credit ordinary and visible objects is not faith, but perswasion. Some believe the better for seeing CHRIST's Sepulchre; and, when they have seen the Red Sea, doubt not of the Miracle. Now, contrarily, I bless my self and am thankful that I lived not in the days of Miracles, that I never saw CHRIST nor His Disciples. I would not have been one of those Israelites that pass'd the Red Sea, nor one of CHRIST's patients on whom He wrought His wonders; then had my faith been thrust upon me, nor should I enjoy that greater blessing pronounced to all that believe and saw not. 'Tis an easie and necessary belief, to credit what our eye and sense hath examined. I believe He was dead, and buried, and rose again; and desire to see Him in His glory, rather than to contemplate Him in His Cenotaphe or Sepulchre. Nor is this much to believe; as we have reason, we owe this faith unto History: *they* only had the advantage of a bold and noble Faith, who lived before His coming, who upon obscure prophesies and mystical Types could raise a belief, and expect apparent impossibilities.

The Soul Illimitable

Now for my life, it is a miracle of thirty years, which to relate, were not a History, but a piece of Poetry, and would sound to common ears like a Fable. For the World, I count it not an Inn, but an Hospital; and a place not to live, but to dye in. The world that I regard is my self; it is the Microcosm of my own frame that I cast mine eye on; for the other, I use it but like my Globe, and turn it round sometimes for my recreation. Men that look upon my outside, perusing only my condition and Fortunes, do err in my Altitude; for I am above Atlas his shoulders. The earth is a point not only in respect of the Heavens above us, but of that heavenly and celestial part within us; that mass of Flesh that circumscribes me, limits not my mind: that surface that tells the Heavens it hath an end, cannot persuade me I have any: I take my circle to be above three hundred and sixty; though the number of the Ark do measure my body, it comprehendeth not my mind: whilst I study to find how I am a Microcosm, or little World, I find my self something more than the great. There is surely a piece of Divinity in us, something that was before the Elements, and owes no homage unto the Sun. Nature tells me

I am the Image of God, as well as Scripture: he that understands not thus much, hath not his introduction or first lesson, and is yet to begin the Alphabet of man. Let me not injure the felicity of others, if I say I am as happy as any: *Ruat cœlum, fiat voluntas Tua,* salveth all; so that whatsoever happens, it is but what our daily prayers desire. In brief, I am content; and what should Providence add more? Surely this is it we call Happiness, and this do I enjoy; with this I am happy in a dream, and as content to enjoy a happiness in a fancy, as others in a more apparent truth and realty. There is surely a neerer apprehension of any thing that delights us in our dreams, than in our waked senses: without this I were unhappy; for my awaked judgment discontents me, ever whispering unto me, that I am from my friend; but my friendly dreams in the night requite me, and make me think I am within his arms. I thank God for my happy dreams, as I do for my good rest; for there is a satisfaction in them unto reasonable desires, and such as can be content with a fit of happiness: and surely it is not a melancholy conceit to think we are all asleep in this World, and that the conceits of this life are as meer dreams to those of the next; as the Phantasms of the night, to the conceits of the day. There is an equal delusion in both, and the one doth but seem to be the embleme or picture of the other: we are somewhat more than our selves in our sleeps, and the slumber of the body seems to be but the waking of the soul. It is the ligation of sense, but the liberty of reason; and our waking conceptions do not match the Fancies of our sleeps. At my Nativity my Ascendant was the watery sign of Scorpius; I was born in the Planetary hour of Saturn, and I think I have a piece of that Leaden Planet in me. I am no way facetious, nor disposed for the mirth and galliardize of company; yet in one dream I can compose a whole Comedy, behold the action, apprehend the jests, and laugh my self awake at the conceits thereof. Were my memory as faithful as my reason is then fruitful, I would never study but in my dreams; and this time also would I chuse for my devotions: but our grosser memories have then so little hold of our abstracted understandings, that they forget the story, and can only relate to our awaked souls, a confused and broken tale of that that hath passed. Aristotle, who had written a singular Tract *Of Sleep,* hath not, methinks, throughly defined it; nor yet Galen, though he seem to have corrected it; for those Noctambuloes and night-walkers, though in their sleep, do yet injoy the action of their senses. We must therefore say that there is something in us that is not in the jurisdiction of Morpheus; and that those abstracted and ecstatick souls do walk about in their own corps, as spirits with the bodies they assume, wherein they seem to hear, see, and feel, though indeed the Organs are destitute of sense, and their natures of those faculties that should inform them. Thus it is observed, that men sometimes, upon the hour of their departure, do speak and reason above themselves; for then the soul, beginning to be freed from the ligaments of the body, begins to reason like her self, and to discourse in a strain above mortality.

From Hydriotaphia; or Urne Buriall

The Vanity of Ambition

Now since these dead bones have already out-lasted the living ones of *Methuselah,* and in a yard under ground, and thin walls of clay, out-worn all the strong and specious buildings above it; and quietly rested under the drums and tramplings of three conquests; what Prince can promise such diuturnity unto his Reliques, or might not gladly say,

Sic ego componi versus in ossa velim.

Time which antiquates Antiquities, and hath an art to make dust of all things, hath yet spared these *minor* Monuments.

In vain we hope to be known by open and visible conservatories, when to be unknown was the means of their continuation and obscurity their protection: If they dyed by violent hands, and were thrust into their Urnes, these bones become considerable, and some old Philosophers would honour them, whose souls they conceived most pure, which were thus snatched from their bodies; and to retain a stranger propension unto them: whereas they weariedly left a languishing corps, and with faint desires of reunion. If they fell by long and aged decay, yet wrapt up in the bundle of time, they fall into indistinction, and make but one blot with Infants. If we begin to die when we live, and long life be but a prolongation of death; our life is a sad composition; We live with death, and die not in a moment. How many pulses made up the life of *Methuselah,* were work for *Archimedes:* Common Counters summe up the life of *Moses* his man. Our dayes become considerable like petty sums by minute accumulations; where numerous fractions make up but small round numbers; and our dayes of a span long make not one little finger.

If the nearnesse of our last necessity, brought a nearer conformity into it, there were a happinesse in hoary hairs, and no calamity in half senses. But the long habit of living indisposeth us for dying; when Avarice makes us the sport of death; When even *David* grew politickly cruell; and *Solomon* could hardly be said to be the wisest of men. But many are too early old, and before the date of age. Adversity stretcheth our dayes, misery makes *Alcmenas* nights, and time hath no wings unto it. But the most tedious being is that which can unwish itself, content to be nothing, or never to have been, which was beyond the *male*content of *Job,* who cursed not the day of his life, but his Nativity: Content to have so farre been, as to have a Title to future being; Although he had lived here but in an hidden state of life, and as it were an abortion.

What Song the *Syrens* sang, or what name *Achilles* assumed when he hid himself among women, though puzling Questions, are not beyond all conjecture. What time the persons of these Ossuaries entred the famous Nations of the dead, and slept with Princes and Counsellours, might admit a wide solution. But who were the proprietaries of these bones, or what bodies these ashes made up, were a question above Antiquarism. Not to be resolved by man, nor easily perhaps by spirits, except we consult the Provinciall Guardians, or tutellary Observators. Had they made as good provision for their names, as they have done for their Reliques, they had not so grosly erred in the art of perpetuation. But to subsist in bones, and be but Pyramidally extant, is a fallacy in duration. Vain ashes, which in the oblivion of names, persons, times, and sexes, have found unto themselves, a fruitless continuation, and only arise unto late posterity, as Emblemes of mortall vanities; Antidotes against pride, vain-glory, and madding vices. Pagan vain-glories which thought the world might last for ever, had encouragement for ambition, and, finding no *Atropos* unto the immortality of their Names, were never dampt with the necessity of oblivion. Even old ambitions had the advantage of ours, in the attempts of their vain-glories, who acting early, and before the probable Meridian of time, have by this time found great accomplishment of their designes, whereby the ancient *Heroes* have already out-lasted their Monuments, and Mechanicall preservations. But in this latter Scene of time, we cannot expect such mummies unto our memories, when ambition may fear the Prophecy of *Elias,* and *Charles* the fifth can never hope to live within two *Methuselas* of *Hector.*

And therefore restlesse inquietude for the diuturnity of our memories unto present considerations, seems a vanity almost out of date, and superannuated peece of folly. We cannot hope to live so long in our names, as some have done in their persons, one face of *Janus* holds no proportion unto the other. 'Tis too late to be ambitious. The great mutations of the world are acted, or time may be too short for our designes. To extend our memories by Monuments, whose death we daily pray for, and whose duration we cannot hope, without injury to our expectations, in the advent of the last day, were a contradiction to our beliefs. We whose generations are ordained in this setting part of time, are providentially taken off from such imaginations; And being necessitated to eye the remaining particle of futurity, are naturally constituted unto thoughts of the next word, and cannot excusably decline the consideration of that duration, which maketh Pyramids pillars of snow, and all that's past a moment.

From The Garden of Cyrus

Sleep

But the quincunx of heaven runs low, and 'tis time to close the five ports of knowledge. We are unwilling to spin out our awaking thoughts into the phantasms of sleep, which often continueth precogitations; making cables of cobwebs, and wildernesses of handsome groves. Beside Hippocrates hath spoke so little, and the oneirocritical masters have left such frigid interpretations from plants, that there is little encouragement to dream of Paradise itself. Nor will the sweetest delight of gardens afford much comfort in sleep; wherein the dulness of that sense shakes hands with delectable odours; and though in the bed of Cleopatra, can hardly with any delight raise up the ghost of a rose.

Night, which Pagan theology could make the daughter of Chaos, affords no advantage to the description of order; although no lower than that mass can we derive its genealogy. All things began in order, so shall they end, and so shall they begin again; according to the ordainer of order and mystical mathematicks of the city of heaven.

Though Somnus in Homer be sent to rouse up Agamemnon, I find no such effects in these drowsy approaches of sleep. To keep our eyes open longer, were but to act our Antipodes. The huntsmen are up in America, and they are already past their first sleep in Persia. But who can be drowsy at that hour which freed us from everlasting sleep? or have slumbering thoughts at that time, when sleep itself must end, and, as some conjecture, all shall awake again?

EDMUND WALLER (1606-1687)

Go, lovely Rose

Go, lovely Rose!
Tell her that wastes her time and me,
That now she knows,
When I resemble her to thee
How sweet and fair she seems to be.

Tell her that's young,
And shuns to have her graces spied,
That had'st thou sprung
In deserts where no men abide,
Thou must have uncommended died.

Small is the worth
Of beauty from the light retired;
Bid her come forth!
Suffer herself to be desired,
And not blush so to be admired.

Then die: that she
The common fate of all things rare
May read in thee;
How small a part of time they share,
They are so wondrous sweet and fair.

On a Girdle

That which her slender waist confined,
Shall now my joyful temples bind;
No monarch but would give his crown
His arms might do what this has done.

It was my Heaven's extremest sphere,
The pale which held that lovely deer;
My joy, my grief, my hope, my love,
Did all within this circle move.

A narrow compass! and yet there
Dwelt all that's good, and all that's fair;
Give me but what this ribband bound,
Take all the rest the sun goes round.

JOHN MILTON (1608-1674)

On the Morning of Christ's Nativity

It was the Winter wilde,
While the Heav'n-born-childe,
All meanly wrapt in the rude manger lies;
Nature in aw to him
Had doff't her gawdy trim,
With her great Master so to sympathize:
It was no season then for her
To wanton with the Sun her lusty Paramour.

Only with speeches fair
She woo's the gentle Air
To hide her guilty front with innocent Snow,
And on her naked shame,
Pollute with sinfull blame,
The Saintly Vail of Maiden white to throw,
Confounded, that her Makers eyes
Should look so neer upon her foul deformities.

But he her fears to cease,
Sent down the meek-eyd Peace,
She crown'd with Olive green, came softly sliding
Down through the turning sphear
His ready Harbinger,
With Turtle wing the amorous clouds dividing,
And waving wide her mirtle wand,
She strikes a universall Peace through Sea and Land.

No War, or Battails sound
Was heard the World around,
The idle spear and shield were high up hung;
The hookèd Chariot stood
Unstain'd with hostile blood,
The Trumpet spake not to the armèd throng,

And Kings sate still with awfull eye,
As if they surely knew their sovran Lord
was by.

But peacefull was the night
Wherein the Prince of light
His raign of peace upon the earth
began:
The Windes with wonder whist,
Smoothly the waters kist,
Whispering new joyes to the milde
Ocean,
Who now hath quite forgot to rave,
While Birds of Calm sit brooding on the
charmèd wave.

The Stars with deep amaze
Stand fixt in stedfast gaze,
Bending one way their pretious in-
fluence,
And will not take their flight,
For all the morning light,
Or Lucifer that often warn'd them
thence;
But in their glimmering Orbs did glow,
Untill their Lord himself bespake, and
bid them go.

And though the shady gloom
Had given day her room,
The Sun himself with-held his wonted
speed,
And hid his head for shame,
As his inferiour flame,
The new enlightn'd world no more
should need;
He saw a greater Sun appear
Then his bright Throne, or burning
Axletree could bear.

The Shepherds on the Lawn,
Or ere the point of dawn,
Sate simply chatting in a rustick row;
Full little thought they than,
That the mighty Pan
Was kindly come to live with them
below;
Perhaps their loves, or els their sheep,
Was all that did their silly thoughts so
busie keep.

When such musick sweet
Their hearts and ears did greet,
As never was by mortall finger
strook,
Divinely-warbled voice
Answering the stringèd noise,
As all their souls in blisfull rapture
took
The Air such pleasure loth to lose,
With thousand echo's still prolongs each
heav'nly close.

Nature that heard such sound
Beneath the hollow round
Of Cynthia's seat, the Airy region
thrilling,
Now was almost won
To think her part was don,
And that her raign had here its last
fulfilling;
She knew such harmony alone
Could hold all Heav'n and Earth in
happier union.

At last surrounds their sight
A Globe of circular light,
That with long beams the shame-fac't
night array'd,
The helmèd Cherubim,
And sworded Seraphim,
Are seen in glittering ranks with wings
displaid,
Harping in loud and solemn quire,
With unexpressive notes to Heav'ns new-
born Heir.

Such musick (as 'tis said)
Before was never made,
But when of old the sons of morning
sung,
While the Creator Great
His constellations set,
And the well-ballanc't world on hinges
hung,
And cast the dark foundations deep,
And bid the weltring waves their oozy
channel keep.

Ring out ye Crystall sphears,
Once bless our human ears,
(If ye have power to touch our senses so)
And let your silver chime
Move in melodious time;
And let the Base of Heav'ns deep Organ blow
And with your ninefold harmony
Make up full consort to th'Angelike symphony.

For if such holy Song
Enwrap our fancy long,
Time will run back, and fetch the age of gold,
And speckl'd vanity
Will sicken soon and die,
And leprous sin will melt from earthly mould,
And Hell it self will pass away,
And leave her dolorous mansions to the peering day.

Yea Truth, and Justice then
Will down return to men,
Th'enameld Arras of the Rain-bow wearing,
And Mercy set between,
Thron'd in Celestiall sheen,
With radiant feet the tissued clouds down stearing,
And Heav'n as at som festivall,
Will open wide the Gates of her high Palace Hall.

But wisest Fate sayes no,
This must not yet be so,
The Babe lies yet in smiling Infancy,
That on the bitter cross
Must redeem our loss;
So both himself and us to glorifie:
Yet first to those ychain'd in sleep,
The wakefull trump of doom must thunder through the deep,

With such a horrid clang
As on mount Sinai rang
While the red fire, and smouldring clouds out brake:
The agèd Earth agast
With terrour of that blast,
Shall from the surface to the center shake;
When at the worlds last session,
The dreadfull Judge in middle Air shall spread his throne.

And then at last our bliss
Full and perfect is,
But now begins; for from this happy day
Th'old Dragon under ground
In straiter limits bound,
Not half so far casts his usurpèd sway,
And wrath to see his Kingdom fail,
Swindges the scaly Horrour of his foulded tail.

The Oracles are dumm,
No voice or hideous humm
Runs through the archèd roof in words deceiving.
Apollo from his shrine
Can no more divine,
With hollow shreik the steep of Delphos leaving.
No nightly trance, or breathèd spell,
Inspire's the pale-ey'd Priest from the prophetic cell.

The lonely mountains o're,
And the resounding shore,
A voice of weeping heard, and loud lament;
From haunted spring, and dale
Edg'd with poplar pale,
The parting Genius is with sighing sent,
With flowre-inwov'n tresses torn
The Nimphs in twilight shade of tangled thickets mourn.

In consecrated Earth,
And on the holy Hearth,
The Lars, and Lemures moan with midnight plaint,
In Urns, and Altars round,
A drear, and dying sound

Affrights the Flamins at their service quaint;
And the chill Marble seems to sweat,
While each peculiar power forgoes his wonted seat.

Peor, and Baalim,
Forsake their Temples dim,
With that twise-batter'd god of Palestine,
And moonèd Ashtaroth,
Heav'ns Queen and Mother both,
Now sits not girt with Tapers holy shine,
The Libyc Hammon shrinks his horn,
In vain the Tyrian Maids their wounded Thamuz mourn.

And sullen Moloch fled,
Hath left in shadows dred,
His burning Idol all of blackest hue,
In vain with Cymbals ring,
They call the grisly king,
In dismall dance about the furnace blue;
The brutish gods of Nile as fast,
Isis and Orus, and the Dog Anubis hast.

Nor is Osiris seen
In Memphian Grove, or Green,
Trampling the unshowr'd Grasse with lowings loud:
Nor can he be at rest
Within his sacred chest,
Naught but profoundest Hell can be his shroud,
In vain with Timbrel'd Anthems dark
The sable-stolèd Sorcerers bear his worshipt Ark.

He feels from Juda's Land
The dredded Infants hand,
The rayes of Bethlehem blind his dusky eyn;
Nor all the gods beside,
Longer dare abide,
Not Typhon huge ending in snaky twine:
Our Babe to shew his Godhead true,
Can in his swadling bands controul the damnèd crew.

So when the Sun in bed,
Curtain'd with cloudy red,
Pillows his chin upon an Orient wave,
The flocking shadows pale,
Troop to th'infernall jail,
Each fetter'd Ghost slips to his severall grave,
And the yellow-skirted Fayes,
Fly after the Night-steeds, leaving their Moon-lov'd maze.

But see the Virgin blest,
Hath laid her Babe to rest.
Time is our tedious Song should here have ending,
Heav'ns youngest teemèd Star,
Hath fixt her polisht Car,
Her sleeping Lord with Handmaid Lamp attending:
And all about the Courtly Stable,
Bright-harnest Angels sit in order serviceable.

L'Allegro

HENCE, loathèd Melancholy,
Of Cerberus and blackest Midnight born,
In Stygian cave forlorn
'Mongst horrid shapes, and shrieks, and sights unholy!
Find out some uncouth cell
Where brooding Darkness spreads his jealous wings
And the night-raven sings;
There under ebon shades, and low-browed rocks
As ragged as thy locks,
In dark Cimmerian desert ever dwell.

But come, thou Goddess fair and free,
In heaven ycleped Euphrosyne,
And by men, heart-easing Mirth,
Whom lovely Venus at a birth
With two sister Graces more

To ivy-crownèd Bacchus bore;
Or whether (as some sager sing)
The frolic wind that breathes the spring,
Zephyr, with Aurora playing,
As he met her once a-Maying,
There on beds of violets blue
And fresh-blown roses washt in dew
Filled her with thee, a daughter fair,
So buxom, blithe, and debonair.
Haste thee, Nymph, and bring with thee
Jest, and youthful jollity,
Quips, and cranks, and wanton wiles,
Nods, and becks, and wreathèd smiles
Such as hang on Hebe's cheek,
And love to live in dimple sleek;
Sport that wrinkled Care derides,
And Laughter holding both his sides.
Come, and trip it as ye go
On the light fantastic toe;
And in thy right hand lead with thee
The mountain Nymph, sweet Liberty;
And if I give thee honour due
Mirth, admit me of thy crew,
To live with her, and live with thee
In unreprovèd pleasures free;
To hear the lark begin his flight
And singing startle the dull night
From his watch-tower in the skies,
Till the dappled Dawn doth rise;
Then to come, in spite of sorrow,
And at my window bid good-morrow
Through the sweetbriar, or the vine,
Or the twisted eglantine:
While the cock with lively din
Scatters the rear of Darkness thin,
And to the stack, or the barn-door,
Stoutly struts his dames before:
Oft list'ning how the hounds and horn
Cheerly rouse the slumbring Morn,
From the side of some hoar hill,
Through the high wood echoing shrill:
Sometime walking, not unseen,
By hedge-row elms, on hillocks green,
Right against the eastern gate
Where the great Sun begins his state
Robed in flames and amber light,
The clouds in thousand liveries dight;
While the ploughman, near at hand,
Whistles o'er the furrowed land,
And the milkmaid singeth blithe,
And the mower whets his scythe,
And every shepherd tells his tale
Under the hawthorn in the dale.
Straight mine eye hath caught new pleasures
Whilst the lantskip round it measures:
Russet lawns, and fallows gray,
Where the nibbling flocks do stray;
Mountains, on whose barren breast
The labouring clouds do often rest;
Meadows trim with daisies pied,
Shallow brooks, and rivers wide;
Towers and battlements it sees
Bosomed high in tufted trees,
Where perhaps some Beauty lies,
The Cynosure of neighbouring eyes.
Hard by, a cottage chimney smokes
From betwixt two aged oaks,
Where Corydon and Thyrsis met
Are at their savoury dinner set
Of herbs and other country messes,
Which the neat-handed Phillis dresses;
And then in haste her bower she leaves
With Thestylis to bind the sheaves;
Or, if the earlier season lead,
To the tanned haycock in the mead.
Sometimes with secure delight
The upland hamlets will invite,
When the merry bells ring round,
And the jocund rebecks sound
To many a youth and many a maid,
Dancing in the chequered shade;
And young and old come forth to play
On a sun-shine holyday,
Till the live-long day-light fail:
Then to the spicy nut-brown ale,
With stories told of many a feat,
How fairy Mab the junkets eat:—
She was pincht and pulled, she said;
And he, by Friar's lantern led,
Tells how the drudging goblin sweat
To earn his cream-bowl duly set,
When in one night, ere glimpse of morn,
His shadowy flail hath threshed the corn
That ten day-labourers could not end;
Then lies him down, the lubbar fend,
And stretcht out all the chimney's length,

Basks at the fire his hairy strength,
And crop-full out of doors he flings,
Ere the first cock his matin rings.
Thus done the tales, to bed they creep,
By whispering winds soon lulled asleep.
Towered cities please us then,
And the busy hum of men,
Where throngs of knights and barons
bold,
In weeds of peace, high triumphs hold,
With store of ladies, whose bright eyes
Rain influence, and judge the prize
Of wit or arms, while both contend
To win her grace, whom all commend.
There let Hymen oft appear
In saffron robe, with taper clear,
And pomp, and feast, and revelry,
With mask and antique pageantry;
Such sights as youthful poets dream
On summer eves by haunted stream.
Then to the well-trod stage anon,
If Jonson's learnèd sock be on,
Or sweetest Shakspere, Fancy's child,
Warble his native wood-notes wild.
And ever against eating cares,
Lap me in soft Lydian airs,
Married to immortal verse,
Such as the meeting soul may pierce,
In notes with many a winding bout
Of linkèd sweetness long drawn out,
With wanton heed and giddy cunning,
The melting voice through mazes running,
Untwisting all the chains that tie
The hidden soul of harmony;
That Orpheus' self may heave his head
From golden slumber on a bed
Of heapt Elysian flowers, and hear
Such strains as would have won the ear
Of Pluto to have quite set free
His half-regained Eurydice.
These delights if thou canst give,
Mirth, with thee I mean to live.

Il Penseroso

HENCE, vain deluding Joys,
The brood of Folly without father
bred!
How little you bestead,
Or fill the fixèd mind with all your
toys!
Dwell in some idle brain,
And fancies fond with gaudy shapes
possess,
As thick and numberless
As the gay motes that people the sunbeams,
Or likest hovering dreams,
The fickle pensioners of Morpheus'
train.

But hail, thou Goddess sage and holy!
Hail, divinest Melancholy!
Whose saintly visage is too bright
To hit the sense of human sight,
And therefore to our weaker view
O'erlaid with black, staid Wisdom's hue;
Black, but such as in esteem
Prince Memnon's sister might beseem,
Or that starred Ethiop Queen that
strove
To set her beauty's praise above
The Sea-Nymphs, and their powers offended.
Yet thou art higher far descended:
Thee bright-haired Vesta, long of yore
To solitary Saturn bore;
His daughter she; in Saturn's reign
Such mixture was not held a stain.
Oft in glimmering bowers and glades
He met her, and in secret shades
Of woody Ida's inmost grove,
While yet there was no fear of Jove.
Come, pensive Nun, devout and pure,
Sober, steadfast, and demure,
All in a robe of darkest grain,
Flowing with majestic train,
And sable stole of cypress lawn
Over thy decent shoulders drawn.
Come; but keep thy wonted state,
With even step, and musing gait,
And looks commercing with the skies,
Thy rapt soul sitting in thine eyes:
There, held in holy passion still,
Forget thyself to marble, till
With a sad leaden downward cast
Thou fix them on the earth as fast.

And join with thee calm Peace, and Quiet,
Spare Fast, that oft with gods doth diet,
And hears the Muses in a ring
Aye round about Jove's altar sing;
And add to these retired Leisure,
That in trim gardens takes his pleasure;
But, first and chiefest, with thee bring
Him that yon soars on golden wing,
Guiding the fiery-wheelèd throne,
The Cherub Contemplation;
And the mute Silence hist along,
'Less Philomel will deign a song,
In her sweetest saddest plight,
Smoothing the rugged brow of Night,
While Cynthia checks her dragon yoke
Gently o'er th' accustomed oak.
—Sweet bird, that shunn'st the noise of folly,
Most musical, most melancholy!
Thee, Chauntress, oft the woods among
I woo, to hear thy even-song;
And, missing thee, I walk unseen
On the dry smooth-shaven green,
To behold the wandering Moon,
Riding near her highest noon,
Like one that had been led astray
Through the heaven's wide pathless way,
And oft, as if her head she bowed,
Stooping through a fleecy cloud.
Oft, on a plat of rising ground,
I hear the far-off curfew sound
Over some wide-watered shore,
Swinging slow with sullen roar;
Or, if the air will not permit,
Some still removèd place will fit,
Where glowing embers through the room
Teach light to counterfeit a gloom,
Far from all resort of mirth,
Save the cricket on the hearth,
Or the Bellman's drowsy charm
To bless the doors from nightly harm.
Or let my lamp, at midnight hour,
Be seen in some high lonely tower,
Where I may oft out-watch the Bear,
With thrice-great Hermes, or unsphere
The spirit of Plato, to unfold
What worlds or what vast regions hold
Th' immortal mind that hath forsook
Her mansion in this fleshly nook;
And of those Dæmons that are found
In fire, air, flood, or under ground,
Whose power hath a true consent
With planet or with element.
Sometime let gorgeous Tragedy
In sceptred pall come sweeping by,
Presenting Thebes, or Pelops' line,
Or the tale of Troy divine,
Or what (though rare) of later age
Ennobled hath the buskined stage.
But, O sad Virgin! that thy power
Might raise Musæus from his bower;
Or bid the soul of Orpheus sing
Such notes as, warbled to the string,
Drew iron tears down Pluto's cheek,
And made hell grant what Love did seek;
Or call up him that left half-told
The story of Cambuscan bold,
Of Camball, and of Algarsife,
And who had Canace to wife
That owned the virtuous ring and glass,
And of the wondrous horse of brass
On which the Tartar King did ride;
And if aught else great Bards beside
In sage and solemn tunes have sung
Of turneys, and of trophies hung,
Of forests, and enchantments drear,
Where more is meant than meets the ear.
Thus, Night oft see me in thy pale career,
Till civil-suited Morn appear,
Not tricked and frounced, as she was wont
With the Attic Boy to hunt,
But kerchieft in a comely cloud,
While rocking winds are piping loud,
Or ushered with a shower still,
When the gust hath blown his fill,
Ending on the rustling leaves,
With minute drops from off the eaves.
And, when the sun begins to fling
His flaring beams, me, Goddess, bring
To archèd walks of twilight groves,
And shadows brown, that Sylvan loves,
Or pine, or monumental oak,
Where the rude axe with heavèd stroke
Was never heard the Nymphs to daunt,

Or fright them from their hallowed
haunt.
There, in close covert, by some brook,
Where no profaner eye may look,
Hide me from Day's garish eye,
While the bee with honeyed thigh,
That at her flowery work doth sing,
And the waters murmuring,
With such consort as they keep,
Entice the dewy-feathered Sleep.
And let some strange mysterious dream,
Wave at his wings in airy stream,
Of lively portraiture displayed,
Softly on my eyelids laid.
And as I wake, sweet music breathe
Above, about, or underneath,
Sent by some Spirit to mortals good,
Or th' unseen Genius of the wood.
But let my due feet never fail
To walk the studious cloister's pale,
And love the high-embowèd roof,
With antic pillars massy proof,
And storied windows richly dight,
Casting a dim religious light.
There let the pealing organ blow,
To the full-voiced Quire below,
In service high and anthems clear,
As may with sweetness, through mine ear,
Dissolve me into ecstasies,
And bring all Heaven before mine eyes.
And may at last my weary age
Find out the peaceful hermitage,
The hairy gown and mossy cell,
Where I may sit and rightly spell,
Of every star that Heaven doth shew,
And every herb that sips the dew;
Till old experience do attain
To something like prophetic strain.
These pleasures, Melancholy, give,
And I with thee will choose to live.

Lycidas

YET once more, O ye Laurels, and once
more
Ye Myrtles brown, with ivy never sere,
I come to pluck your berries harsh and
crude,
And with forced fingers rude
Shatter your leaves before the mellowing
year.
Bitter constraint and sad occasion dear
Compels me to disturb your season due;
For Lycidas is dead, dead ere his prime,
Young Lycidas, and hath not left his
peer.
Who would not sing for Lycidas? he
knew
Himself to sing, and build the lofty
rhyme.
He must not float upon his watery bier
Unwept, and welter to the parching wind,
Without the meed of some melodious
tear.
Begin then, Sisters of the sacred well
That from beneath the seat of Jove doth
spring;
Begin, and somewhat loudly sweep the
string.
Hence with denial vain and coy excuse:
So may some gentle Muse
With lucky words favour *my* destined
urn,
And as he passes, turn
And bid fair peace be to my sable shroud!
For we were nursed upon the self-same
hill,
Fed the same flock, by fountain, shade,
and rill:
Together both, ere the high lawns ap-
peared
Under the opening eyelids of the Morn,
We drove a-field, and both together
heard
What time the grey-fly winds her sultry
horn,
Battening our flocks with the fresh dews
of night,
Oft till the star that rose at evening
bright
Toward heaven's descent had sloped his
westering wheel.
Meanwhile the rural ditties were not
mute;
Tempered to the oaten flute
Rough Satyrs danced, and Fauns with
cloven heel

From the glad sound would not be absent long;
And old Damœtas loved to hear our song.
But, oh! the heavy change, now thou art gone,
Now thou art gone and never must return!
Thee, Shepherd, thee the woods and desert caves
With wild thyme and the gadding vine o'er-grown,
And all their echoes, mourn.
The willows, and the hazel copses green,
Shall now no more be seen
Fanning their joyous leaves to thy soft lays.
As killing as the canker to the rose,
Or taint-worm to the weanling herds that graze,
Or frost to flowers that their gay wardrobe wear
When first the white-thorn blows;
Such, Lycidas, thy loss to shepherd's ear.
Where were ye, Nymphs, when the remorseless deep
Closed o'er the head of your loved Lycidas?
For neither were ye playing on the steep
Where your old bards, the famous Druids, lie,
Nor on the shaggy top of Mona high,
Nor yet where Deva spreads her wizard stream.
Ay me! I fondly dream
"Had ye been there" . . . For what could that have done?
What could the Muse herself that Orpheus bore,
The Muse herself, for her enchanting son,
Whom universal nature did lament,
When, by the rout that made the hideous roar,
His gory visage down the stream was sent,
Down the swift Hebrus to the Lesbian shore?
Alas! what boots it with uncessant care
To tend the homely, slighted, Shepherd's trade
And strictly meditate the thankless Muse?
Were it not better done, as others use,
To sport with Amaryllis in the shade,
Or with the tangles of Neæra's hair?
Fame is the spur that the clear spirit doth raise
(That last infirmity of noble mind)
To scorn delights, and live labourious days;
But the fair guerdon when we hope to find,
And think to burst out into sudden blaze,
Comes the blind Fury with the abhorrèd shears
And slits the thin-spun life. "But not the praise,"
Phœbus replied, and touched my trembling ears:
"Fame is no plant that grows on mortal soil,
Nor in the glistering foil
Set off to the world, nor in broad rumour lies,
But lives and spreads aloft by those pure eyes
And perfect witness of all-judging Jove;
As he pronounces lastly on each deed,
Of so much fame in heaven expect thy meed."
O fountain Arethuse, and thou honoured flood,
Smooth-sliding Mincius, crowned with vocal reeds,
That strain I heard was of a higher mood.
But now my oat proceeds,
And listens to the Herald of the Sea
That came in Neptune's plea.
He asked the waves, and asked the felon winds,
What hard mishap hath doomed this gentle swain?
And questioned every gust of rugged wings

That blows from off each beaked promontory.
They knew not of his story;
And sage Hippotades their answer brings,
That not a blast was from his dungeon strayed:
The air was calm, and on the level brine
Sleek Panope with all her sisters played.
It was that fatal and perfidious bark,
Built in th' eclipse, and rigged with curses dark,
That sunk so low that sacred head of thine.
Next Camus, reverend Sire, went footing slow,
His mantle hairy, and his bonnet sedge,
Inwrought with figures dim, and on the edge
Like to that sanguine flower inscribed with woe.
"Ah! who hath reft," quoth he, "my dearest pledge!"
Last came, and last did go,
The Pilot of the Galilean lake;
Two massy keys he bore of metals twain
(The golden opes, the iron shuts amain)
He shook his mitred locks, and stern bespake:—
"How well could I have spared for thee, young swain,
Enow of such, as for their bellies' sake
Creep, and intrude, and climb into the fold!
Of other care they little reck'ning make
Than how to scramble at the shearers' feast,
And shove away the worthy bidden guest.
Blind mouths! that scarce themselves know how to hold
A sheep-hook, or have learnèd aught else the least
That to the faithful herdsman's art belongs!
What recks it them? What need they? They are sped;
And, when they list, their lean and flashy songs
Grate on their scrannel pipes of wretched straw;
The hungry sheep look up, and are not fed,
But swoln with wind and the rank mist they draw
Rot inwardly, and foul contagion spread;
Besides what the grim wolf with privy paw
Daily devours apace, and nothing said.
—But that two-handed engine at the door
Stands ready to smite once, and smite no more."
Return, Alpheus; the dread voice is past
That shrunk thy streams; return, Sicilian Muse,
And call the vales, and bid them hither cast
Their bells and flowerets of a thousand hues.
Ye valleys low, where the mild whispers use
Of shades, and wanton winds, and gushing brooks,
On whose fresh lap the swart star sparely looks,
Throw hither all your quaint enamelled eyes,
That on the green turf suck the honeyed showers,
And purple all the ground with vernal flowers.
Bring the rathe primrose that forsaken dies,
The tufted crow-toe, and pale jessamine,
The white pink, and the pansy freaked with jet,
The glowing violet,
The musk-rose, and the well-attired woodbine,
With cowslips wan that hang the pensive head,
And every flower that sad embroidery wears.
Bid amaranthus all his beauty shed,
And daffodillies fill their cups with tears,
To strew the laureat hearse where Lycid lies.
For so, to interpose a little ease,

Let our frail thoughts dally with false surmise.
Ay me! whilst thee the shores and sounding seas
Wash far away, where'er thy bones are hurled;
Whether beyond the stormy Hebrides,
Where thou perhaps under the whelming tide
Visit'st the bottom of the monstrous world;
Or whether thou, to our moist vows denied,
Sleep'st by the fable of Bellerus old,
Where the great Vision of the guarded mount
Looks toward Namancos and Bayona's hold.
Look homeward, Angel, now, and melt with ruth:
And, O ye dolphins, waft the hapless youth!
 Weep no more, woeful shepherds, weep no more,
For Lycidas, your sorrow, is not dead,
Sunk though he be beneath the watery floor.
So sinks the day-star in the ocean-bed,
And yet anon repairs his drooping head
And tricks his beams, and with new-spangled ore
Flames in the forehead of the morning sky:
So Lycidas sunk low, but mounted high
Through the dear might of Him that walked the waves;
Where, other groves and other streams along,
With nectar pure his oozy locks he laves,
And hears the unexpressive nuptial song,
In the blest kingdoms meek of joy and love.
There entertain him all the Saints above
In solemn troops, and sweet societies,
That sing, and singing in their glory move,
And wipe the tears for ever from his eyes.
Now, Lycidas, the shepherds weep no more;
Henceforth thou art the Genius of the shore
In thy large recompense, and shalt be good
To all that wander in that perilous flood.
 Thus sang the uncouth swain to the oaks and rills,
While the still morn went out with sandals grey:
He touched the tender stops of various quills,
With eager thought warbling his Doric lay:
And now the sun had stretched out all the hills,
And now was dropt into the western bay.
At last he rose, and twitched his mantle blue:
To-morrow to fresh woods, and pastures new.

When the Assault was Intended to the City

Captain or Colonel, or Knight in Arms,
Whose chance on these defenceless doors may seize,
If deed of honour did thee ever please,
Guard them, and him within protect from harms.
He can requite thee; for he knows the charms
That call fame on such gentle acts as these,
And he can spread thy name o'er lands and seas,
Whatever clime the sun's bright circle warms.
Lift not thy spear against the Muses' bower:
The great Emathian conqueror bid spare
The house of Pindarus, when temple and tower
Went to the ground; and the repeated air
Of sad Electra's poet had the power
To save the Athenian walls from ruin bare.

On the Late Massacre in Piedmont

Avenge, O Lord! Thy slaughtered Saints, whose bones
Lie scattered on the Alpine mountains cold;
Even them who kept Thy truth so pure of old
When all our fathers worshiped stocks and stones,
Forget not: in Thy book record their groans
Who were Thy sheep, and in their ancient fold
Slain by the bloody Piemontese, that rolled
Mother with infant down the rocks. Their moans
The vales redoubled to the hills, and they
To Heaven. Their martyred blood and ashes sow
O'er all the Italian fields, where still doth sway
The triple Tyrant: that from these may grow
A hundred-fold, who, having learnt Thy way,
Early may fly the Babylonian woe.

On his Blindness

When I consider how my light is spent,
Ere half my days in this dark world and wide,
And that one Talent which is death to hide
Lodged with me useless, though my soul more bent
To serve therewith my Maker, and present
My true account, lest He returning chide,
"Doth God exact day-labour, light denied?"
I fondly ask. But patience, to prevent
That murmur, soon replies: "God doth not need
Either man's work, or His own gifts. Who best
Bear His mild yoke, they serve Him best. His state
Is kingly: thousands at His bidding speed
And post o'er land and ocean without rest.
They also serve who only stand and wait."

To Mr. Lawrence

Lawrence of virtuous Father virtuous Son,
Now that the Fields are dank, and ways are mire,
Where shall we sometimes meet, and by the fire
Help waste a sullen day; what may be won
From the hard Season gaining: time will run
On smoother, till Favonius re-inspire
The frozen earth; and clothe in fresh attire
The Lily and Rose, that neither sow'd nor spun.
What neat repast shall feast us, light and choice,
Of Attic taste with Wine, whence we may rise
To hear the Lute well toucht, or artfull voice
Warble immortal Notes and Tuscan Air?
He who of those delights can judge, and spare
To interpose them oft, is not unwise.

To Cyriack Skinner

Cyriack, whose grandsire on the royal bench
Of British Themis, with no mean applause,
Pronounced, and in his volumes taught, our laws,
Which others at their bar so often wrench,
To-day deep thoughts resolve with me to drench

In mirth that after no repenting draws;
Let Euclid rest, and Archimedes pause,
And what the Swede intend, and what the French.
To measure life learn thou betimes, and know
Toward solid good what leads the nearest way;
For other things mild Heaven a time ordains,
And disapproves that care, though wise in show,
That with superfluous burden loads the day,
And, when God sends a cheerful hour, refrains.

To the Same

Cyriack, this three years' day these eyes, though clear,
To outward view, of blemish or of spot,
Bereft of light, their seeing have forgot;
Nor to their idle orbs doth sight appear
Of sun, or moon, or star, throughout the year,
Or man, or woman. Yet I argue not
Against Heaven's hand or will, nor bate a jot
Of heart or hope, but still bear up and steer
Right onward. What supports me, dost thou ask?
The conscience, friend, to have lost them overplied
In Liberty's defence, my noble task,
Of which all Europe rings from side to side.
This thought might lead me through the world's vain mask
Content, though blind, had I no better guide.

On his Deceased Wife

Methought I saw my late espousèd Saint
Brought to me like Alcestis from the grave,
Whom Jove's great Son to her glad Husband gave,
Rescued from death by force though pale and faint.
Mine, as whom washt from spot of child-bed taint,
Purification in the old Law did save,
And such as yet once more I trust to have
Full sight of her in Heaven without restraint,
Came vested all in white, pure as her mind:
Her face was veiled, yet to my fancied sight,
Love, sweetness, goodness, in her person shined
So clear, as in no face with more delight.
But oh, as to embrace me she inclined
I waked, she fled, and day brought back my night.

EDWARD, EARL OF CLARENDON (1609-1674)

From The History of the Rebellion and Civil Wars in England

The Character of Lord Falkland

But I must here take leave a little longer to discontinue this narration; and if the celebrating the memory of eminent and extraordinary persons, and transmitting their great virtues, for the imitation of posterity, be one of the principal ends and duties of history, it will not be thought impertinent, in this place, to remember a loss which no time will suffer to be forgotten, and no success or good fortune could repair. In this unhappy battle was slain the Lord Viscount Falkland; a person of such prodigious parts of learning and knowledge, of that inimitable sweetness and delight in conversation, of so flowing and obliging a humanity and goodness to mankind, and of that primitive simplicity and integrity of life, that if there were no other brand upon this odious and accursed civil war, than that single loss, it must be most infamous and execrable to all posterity.

Turpe mori, post te, solo non posse dolore.

Before this parliament, his condition of life was so happy that it was hardly capable of improvement. Before he came to twenty years of age, he was master of a noble fortune, which descended to him by the gift of a grandfather, without passing through his father or mother, who were then both alive and not well enough contented to find themselves passed by in the descent. His education for some years had been in Ireland, where his father was lord deputy; so that, when he returned into England, to the possession of his fortune, he was unentangled with any acquaintance or friends, which usually grow up by the custom of conversation; and therefore was to make a pure election of his company; which he chose by other rules than were prescribed to the young nobility of that time. And it cannot be denied, though he admitted some few to his friendship for the agreeableness of their natures, and their undoubted affection to him, that his familiarity and friendship, for the most part, was with men of the most eminent and sublime parts, and of untouched reputation in point of integrity; and such men had a title to his bosom.

He was a great cherisher of wit and fancy and good parts in any man; and if he found them clouded with poverty or want, a most liberal and bountiful patron towards them, even above his fortune; of which, in those administrations, he was such a dispenser as if he had been trusted with it to such uses, and if there had been the least of vice in his expense he might have been thought too prodigal. He was constant and pertinacious in whatsoever he resolved to do, and not to be wearied by any pains that were necessary to that end. And therefore having once resolved not to see London, which he loved above all places, till he had perfectly learned the Greek tongue, he went to his own house in the country, and pursued it with that indefatigable industry, that it will not be believed in how short a time he was master of it, and accurately read all the Greek historians.

In this time, his house being within ten miles of Oxford, he contracted familiarity and friendship with the most polite and accurate men of that university; who found such an immenseness of wit, and such a solidity of judgment in him, so infinite a fancy, bound in by a most logical ratiocination, such a vast knowledge, that he was not ignorant in any thing, yet such an excessive humility, as if he had known nothing, that they frequently resorted, and dwelt with him, as in a college situated in a purer air; so that his house was a university bound in a less volume; whither they came not so much for repose as study, and to examine and refine those grosser propositions which laziness and consent made current in vulgar conversation.

Many attempts were made upon him by the instigation of his mother (who was a lady of another persuasion in religion, and of a most masculine understanding, allayed with the passion and infirmities of her own sex) to pervert him in his piety to the church of England, and to reconcile him to that of Rome; which they prosecuted with the more confidence, because he declined no opportunity or occasion of conference with those of that religion, whether priests or laics; having diligently studied the controversies and exactly read all or the choicest of the Greek and Latin fathers, and having a memory so stupendous, that he remembered on all occasions whatsoever he read. And he was so great an enemy to that passion and uncharitableness which he saw produced by difference of opinion in matters of religion, that in all those disputations with priests and others of the Roman church, he affected to manifest all possible civility to their persons, and estimation of their parts; which made them retain still some hope of his reduction; even when they had given over offering farther reasons to him to that purpose. But this charity towards them was much lessened, and any correspondence with them quite declined, when, by sinister arts, they had corrupted his two younger brothers, being both children, and stolen them from his house, and transported them beyond seas, and perverted his sisters: upon which occasion he writ two large discourses against the principal positions of that religion, with that sharpness of style, and full weight of reason, that the church is deprived of great jewels in the concealment of them, and that they are not published to the world.

He was superior to all those passions and affections which attend vulgar minds, and was guilty of no other ambition than of knowledge, and to be reputed a lover of all good men; and that made him too much a contemner of those arts which must be indulged to in the transaction of human affairs. In the last short parliament he was a burgess in the house of commons; and from the debates, which were then managed with all imaginable gravity and sobriety, he contracted such a reverence to parliaments, that he thought it really impossible that they could ever produce mischief or inconvenience to the kingdom, or that the kingdom could be tolerably happy in the intermission of them. And from the unhappy and unseasonable dissolution of that convention, he harboured, it may be, some jealousy and prejudice of the court, towards which he was not before immoderately inclined; his father having wasted a full fortune there, in those offices and employments by which other men use to obtain a greater. He was chosen again this parliament to serve in the same place, and, in the beginning of it, declared himself very sharply and severely against those exorbitancies which had been most grievous to the state; for he was so rigid an observer of established laws and rules, that he could not endure the least breach or deviation from them; and thought no mischief so intolerable as the presumption of ministers of state to break positive rules for reason[s] of state; or judges to transgress known laws, upon the title of conveniency or necessity; which made him so severe against the earl of Strafford and the lord Finch, contrary to his natural gentleness and temper: insomuch as they who did not know his composition to be as free from revenge as it was from pride, thought that the sharpness to the former might proceed from the memory of some unkindnesses, not without a mixture of injustice, from him towards his father. But without doubt he was free from those temptations, and was only misled by the authority of those who he believed understood the laws perfectly; of which himself was utterly ignorant; and if the assumption, which was scarce controverted, had been true, that an endeavour to overthrow the fundamental laws of the kingdom had been treason, a strict understanding might make reasonable conclusions to satisfy his own judgment, from the exorbitant parts of their several charges.

The great opinion he had of the uprightness and integrity of those persons who appeared most active, especially of Mr. Hambden, kept him longer from suspecting any design against the peace of the kingdom; and though he differed commonly from them in conclusions, he believed long their purposes were honest. When he grew better informed what was law, and discerned [in them] a desire to control that law by a vote of one or both houses, no man more opposed those attempts, and gave the adverse party more trouble by reason and argumentation; insomuch as he was, by degrees, looked upon as an advocate for the court, to which he contributed so little, that he declined those addresses, and even those invitations which he was obliged almost by civility to entertain. And he was so jealous of the least imagination that he should incline to preferment, that he affected even a morosity to the court and to the courtiers; and left nothing undone which might prevent and divert the king's or queen's favour towards him, but the deserving it. For when the king sent for him once or twice to speak with him, and to give him thanks for his excellent comportment in those councils, which his majesty graciously termed doing him service, his answers were more negligent and less satisfactory than might be expected; as if he cared only that his actions should be just, not that they should be acceptable, and that his majesty should think that they proceeded only from the impulsion of conscience, without any sympathy in his affections; which from a stoical and sullen nature might not have been misinterpreted; yet, from a person of so perfect a habit of generous and obsequious compliance with all good men, might very well have been interpreted by the king as more than an ordinary averseness to his service: so that he took more pains, and more forced his nature to actions unagreeable and unpleasant to it, that he might not be thought to incline to the court, than any man hath done to procure an office there. And if any thing but not doing his duty could have kept him from receiving a testimony of the king's grace and trust at that time, he had not been called to his council; not that he was in truth averse to the court or from receiving public employment; for he had a great devotion to the king's person, and had before used some small endeavour to be recommended to him for a foreign negociation, and had once a desire to be sent ambassador into France; but he abhorred an imagination or doubt should sink into the thoughts of any man, that, in the discharge of his trust and duty in parliament, he had any bias to the court, or that the king himself should apprehend that he looked for a reward for being honest.

For this reason, when he heard it first whispered that the king had a purpose to make him a counsellor, for which in the beginning there was no other ground but because he was known sufficient, (*haud semper errat fama, aliquando et eligit,*) he resolved to decline it; and at last suffered himself only to be overruled by the advice and persuasions of his friends to submit to it. Afterwards, when he found that the king intended to make him his secretary of state, he was positive to refuse it; declaring to his friends that he was most unfit for it, and that he must either do that which would be great disquiet to his own nature, or leave that undone which was most necessary to be done by one that was honoured with that place; for that the most just and honest men did every day that which he could not give himself leave to do. And indeed he was so exact and strict an observer of justice and truth, *ad amussim,* that he believed those necessary condescensions and applications to the weakness of other men, and those arts and insinuations which are necessary for discoveries and prevention of ill, would be in him a declension from the rule which he acknowledged fit, and absolutely necessary to be practised in those employments; and was, [in truth,] so precise in the practick principles he prescribed to himself, (to all others he was as indulgent,) as if he had lived *in republica Platonis, non in fæce Romuli.*

Two reasons prevailed with him to receive the seals, and but for those he had resolutely avoided them. The first, the consideration that it [his refusal] might bring some blemish upon the king's affairs, and that men would have believed that he had refused so great an honour and trust because he must have been with it obliged to do somewhat else not justifiable. And this he made matter of conscience, since he knew the king made choice of him before other men especially because he thought him more honest than other men. The other was, lest he might be thought to avoid it out of fear to do an ungracious thing to the house of commons, who were sorely troubled at the displacing sir Harry Vane, whom they looked upon as removed for having done them those offices they stood in need of; and the disdain of so popular an incumbrance wrought upon him next to the other. For as he had a full appetite of fame by just and generous actions, so he had an equal contempt of it by any servile expedients: and he so much the more consented to and approved the justice upon sir Harry Vane, in his own private judgment, by how much he surpassed most men in the religious observation of a trust, the violation whereof he would not admit of any excuse for.

For these reasons, he submitted to the king's command, and became his secretary, with as humble and devout an acknowledgment of the greatness of the obligation as could be expressed, and as true a sense of it in his heart. Yet two things he could never bring himself to whilst he continued in that office, that was to his death; for which he was contented to be reproached, as for omissions in a most necessary part of his place. The one, employing of spies, or giving any countenance or entertainment to them. I do not mean such emissaries as with danger would venture to view the enemy's camp, and bring intelligence of their number or quartering, or such generals as such an observation can comprehend; but those who, by communication of guilt, or dissimulation of manners, wound themselves into such trusts and secrets as enabled them to make discoveries for the benefit of the state. The other, the liberty of opening letters upon a suspicion that they might contain matter of dangerous consequence. For the first, he would say, such instruments must be void of all ingenuity and common honesty, before they could be of use; and afterwards they could never be fit to be credited: and that no single preservation could be worth so general a wound and corruption of human society, as the cherishing such persons would carry with it. The last, he thought such a violation of the law of nature, that no qualification by office could justify a single person in the trespass; and though he was convinced, by the necessity and iniquity of the time, that those advantages of information were not to be declined, and were necessarily to be practised, he found means to shift it from himself; when he confessed he needed excuse and pardon for the omission: so unwilling he was to resign any thing in his nature to an obligation in his office.

In all other particulars he filled his place plentifully, being sufficiently versed in languages to understand any that [are] used in business, and to make himself again understood. To speak of his integrity, and his high disdain of any bait that might seem to look towards corruption, *in tanto viro, injuria virtutum fuerit.* Some sharp expressions he used against the archbishop of Canterbury; and his concurring in the first bill to take away the votes of bishops in the house of peers, gave occasion to some to believe, and opportunity to others to conclude and publish, that he was no friend to the church, and the established government of it; and troubled his very friends much, who were more confident of the contrary than prepared to answer the allegations.

The truth is, he had unhappily contracted some prejudice to the archbishop; and having only known him enough to observe his passion, when, it may be, multiplicity of business or other indisposition had possessed him, did wish him less entangled and engaged in the business of the court or state: though, I speak it knowingly, he had a singular estimation and reverence of his great learning and confessed integrity; and really thought his letting himself to those expressions, which implied a disesteem of him, or at least an acknowledgment of his infirmities, would enable him to shelter him from part of the storm he saw raised for his destruction; which he abominated with his soul.

The giving his consent to the first bill for the displacing the bishops did proceed from two grounds: the first, his not understanding the original of their right and suffrage there: the other, an opinion, that the combination against the whole government of the church by bishops, was so violent and furious, that a less composition than the dispensing with their intermeddling in secular affairs would not preserve the order. And he was presuaded to this by the profession of many persons of honour, who declared, they did desire the one, and would then not press the other; which, in that particular, misled many men. But when his observation and experience made him discern more of their intentions than he before suspected, with great frankness he opposed the second bill that was preferred for that purpose; and had, without scruple, the order itself in perfect reference; and thought too great encouragement could not possibly be given to learning, nor too great rewards to learned men; and was never in the least degree swayed or moved by the objections which were made against that government, (holding them most ridiculous,) or affected to the other, which those men fancied to themselves.

He had a courage of the most clear and keen temper, and so far from fear, that he was not without appetite of danger; and therefore, upon any occasion of action, he always engaged his person in those troops which he thought, by the forwardness of the commanders, to be most like to be farthest engaged; and in all such encounters he had about him a strange cheerfulness and companiableness, without at all affecting the execution that was then principally to be attended, in which he took no delight, but took pains to prevent it, where it was not, by resistance, necessary: insomuch that at Edgehill, when the enemy was routed, he was like to have incurred great peril, by interposing to save those who had thrown away their arms, and against whom, it may be, others were more fierce for their having thrown them away: insomuch as a man might think, he came into the field only out of curiosity to see the face of danger, and charity to prevent the shedding of blood. Yet in his natural inclination he acknowledged he was addicted to the profession of a soldier; and shortly after he came to his fortune, and before he came to age, he went into the Low Countries with a resolution of procuring command, and to give himself up to it, from which he was converted by the complete inactivity of that summer: and so he returned into England, and shortly after entered upon that vehement course of study we mentioned before, till the first alarum from the north; and then again he made ready for the field, and though he received some repulse in the command of a troop of horse, of which he had a promise, he went a volunteer with the earl of Essex.

From the entrance into this unnatural war, his natural cheerfulness and vivacity grew clouded, and a kind of sadness and dejection of spirit stole upon him, which he had never been used to; yet being one of those who believed that one battle would end all differences, and that there would be so great a victory on one side, that the other would be compelled to submit to any conditions from the victor, (which supposition and conclusion generally sunk into the minds of most men, [and] prevented the looking after many advantages which might then have been laid hold of,) he resisted those indispositions, *et in luctu, bellum inter remedia erat.* But after the king's return from Brentford, and the furious resolution of the two houses not to admit any treaty for peace, those indispositions, which had before touched him, grew into a perfect habit of uncheerfulness; and he, who had been so exactly unreserved and affable to all men, that his face and countenance was always present and vacant to his company, and held any cloudiness and less pleasantness of the visage a kind of rudeness or incivility, became, on a sudden, less communicable; and thence, very sad, pale, and exceedingly affected with the spleen. In his clothes and habit, which he had intended before always with more neatness and industry and expense than is usual to so great a mind, he was not now only incurious, but too negligent; and in his reception of suitors, and the necessary or casual addresses to his place, so quick and sharp and severe, that there wanted not some men (who were strangers to his nature and disposition) who believed him proud and imperious, from which no mortal man was ever more free.

The truth is, that as he was of a most incomparable gentleness, application, and even a demissness and submission to good and worthy and entire men, so he was naturally (which could not but be more evident in his place, which objected him to another conversation and intermixture than his own election had done) *adversus malos injucundus;* and was so ill a dissembler of his dislike and disinclination to ill men, that it was not possible for such not to discern it. There was once in the house of commons such a declared acceptation of the good service an eminent member had done to them, and, as they said, to the whole kingdom, that it was moved, he being present, that the speaker might, in the name of the whole house, give him thanks; and then, that every member might, as a testimony of his particular acknowledgment, stir or move his hat towards him; the which (though not ordered) when very many did, the lord Falkland, (who believed the service itself not to be of that moment, and that an honourable and generous person could not have stooped to it for any recompense,) instead of moving his hat, stretched both his arms out, and clasped his hands together upon the crown of his hat, and held it close down to his head; that all men might see how odious that flattery was to him, and the very approbation of the person, though at that time most popular.

When there was any overture or hope of peace, he would be more erect and vigorous, and exceedingly solicitous to press any thing which he thought might promote it; and sitting amongst his friends, often, after a deep silence and frequent sighs, would, with a shrill and sad accent, ingeminate the word *Peace, Peace;* and would passionately profess, that the very agony of the war, and the view of the calamities and desolation of the kingdom did and must endure, took his sleep from him, and would shortly break his heart. This made some think, or pretend to think, that he was so much enamoured on peace, that he would have been glad the king should have bought it at any price; which was a most unreasonable calumny. As if a man, that was himself the most punctual and precise in every circumstance that might reflect upon conscience or honour, could have wished the king to have committed a trespass against either. And yet this senseless scandal made some impression upon him, or at least he used it for an excuse of the daringness of his spirit; for at the leaguer before Gloucester, when his friends passionately reprehended him for exposing his person unnecessarily to danger, (as he delighted to visit the trenches and nearest approaches, and to discover what the enemy did,) as being so much beside the duty of his place, that it might be understood against it, he would say merrily, that his office could not take away the privileges of his age; and that a secretary in war might be present at the greatest secret of danger; but withal alleged seriously, that it concerned him to be more active in enterprises of hazard than other men, that all might see that his impatiency for peace proceeded not from pusillanimity, or fear to adventure his own person.

In the morning before the battle, as always upon action, he was very cheerful, and put himself into the first rank of the lord Byron's regiment, who was then advancing upon the enemy, who had lined the hedges on both sides with musketeers; from whence he was shot with a musket in the lower part of the belly, and in the instant falling from his horse, his body was not found till the next morning; till when, there was some hope he might have been a prisoner; though his nearest friends, who knew his temper, received small comfort from that imagination. Thus fell that incomparable young man, in the four and thirtieth year of his age, having so much despatched the business of life, that the oldest rarely attain to that immense knowledge, and the youngest enter not into the world with more innocence: and whosoever leads such a life needs not care upon how short warning it be taken from him.

From THE LIFE OF EDWARD, EARL OF CLARENDON

The Stuart Family

THE truth is, it was the unhappy fate and constitution of that family, that they trusted naturally the judgments of those who were as much inferior to them in understanding as they were in quality, before their own, which was very good; and suffered even their natures, which disposed them to virtue and justice, to be prevailed upon and altered and corrupted by those who knew how to make use of some one infirmity that they discovered in them; and by complying with that, and cherishing and serving it, they by degrees wrought upon the mass, and sacrificed all the other good inclinations to that single vice. They were too much inclined to like men at first sight, and did not love the conversation of men of many more years than themselves, and thought age not only troublesome but impertinent. They did not love to deny, and less to strangers than to their friends; not out of bounty or generosity, which was a flower that did never grow naturally in the heart of either of the families, that of Stuart or the other of Bourbon, but out of an unskilfulness and defect in the countenance; and when they prevailed with themselves to make some pause rather than to deny, importunity removed all resolution, which they knew neither how to shut out nor to defend themselves against, even when it was evident enough that they had much rather not consent; which often made that which would have looked like bounty lose all its grace and lustre.

The Character of Charles I

To speak first of his private qualifications as a man, before the mention of his princely and royal virtues; he was, if ever any, the most worthy of the title of an honest man; so great a lover of justice, that no temptation could dispose him to a wrongful action, except it were so disguised to him that he believed it to be just. He had a tenderness and compassion of nature, which restrained him from ever doing a hard-hearted thing; and therefore he was so apt to grant pardon to malefactors, that his judges represented to him the damage and insecurity to the public that flowed from such his indulgence. And then he restrained himself from pardoning either murders or highway robberies, and quickly discerned the fruits of his severity by a wonderful reformation of those enormities. He was very punctual and regular in his devotions; so that he was never known to enter upon his recreations or sports, though never so early in the morning, before he had been at public prayers; so that on hunting days his chaplains were bound to a very early attendance. And he was likewise very strict in observing the hours of his private cabinet devotions; and was so severe an exactor of gravity and reverence in all mention of religion, that he could never endure any light or profane word, with what sharpness of wit soever it was covered: and though he was well pleased and delighted with reading verses made upon any occasion, no man durst bring before him any thing that was profane or unclean. That kind of wit had never any countenance then. He was so great an example of conjugal affection, that they who did not imitate him in that particular did not brag of their liberty: and he did not only permit, but direct his bishops to prosecute those scandalous vices, in the ecclesiastical courts, against persons of eminence and near relation to his service.

His kingly virtues had some mixture and allay, that hindered them from shining in full lustre, and from producing those fruits they should have been attended with. He was not in his nature bountiful, though he gave very much: which appeared more after the duke of Buckingham's death, after which those showers fell very rarely; and he paused too long in giving, which made those to whom he gave less sensible of the benefit. He kept state to the full, which made his court very orderly; no man presuming to be seen in a place where he had no pretence to be. He saw and observed men long, before he received any about his person, and did not love strangers, nor very confident men. He was a patient hearer of causes; which he frequently accustomed himself to at the council board; and judged very well, and was dexterous in the mediating part: so that he often put an end to causes by persuasion, which the stubbornness of men's humours made dilatory in courts of justice.

He was very fearless in his person, but not enterprising; and had an excellent understanding, but was not confident enough of it; which made him oftentimes change his own opinion for a worse, and follow the advice of a man that did not judge so well as himself. And this made him more irresolute than the conjuncture of his affairs would admit: if he had been of a rougher and more imperious nature, he would have found more respect and duty. And his not applying some severe cures to approaching evils proceeded from the lenity of his nature and the tenderness of his conscience, which, in all cases of blood, made him choose the softer way, and not hearken to severe counsels, how reasonably soever urged. This only restrained him from pursuing his advantage in the first Scottish expedition, when, humanly speaking, he might have reduced that nation to the most slavish obedience that could have been wished. But no man can say he had then many who advised him to it, but the contrary, by a wonderful indisposition all his council had to fighting, or any other fatigue. He was always an immoderate lover of the Scottish nation, having not only been born there, but educated by that people, and besieged by them always, having few English about him till he was king; and the major number of his servants being still of [that nation,] who he thought could never fail him. And then, no man had such an ascendant over him, by the lowest and humblest insinuations, as duke Hamilton had.

As he excelled in all other virtues, so in temperance he was so strict, that he abhorred all debauchery to that degree, that, at a great festival solemnity, where he once was, when very many of the nobility of the

English and Scots were entertained, [being] told by one who withdrew from thence, what vast draughts of wine they drank, and that there was one earl who had drank most of the rest down, and was not himself moved or altered, the king said that he deserved to be hanged; and that earl coming shortly [after] into the room where his majesty was, in some gayety, to shew how unhurt he was from that battle, the king sent one to bid him withdraw from his majesty's presence; nor did he in some days after appear before the king.

There were so many miraculous circumstances contributed to his ruin, that men might well think that heaven and earth conspired it, and that the stars designed it. Though he was, from the first declension of his power, so much betrayed by his own servants, that there were very few who remained faithful to him, yet that treachery proceeded not from any treasonable purpose to do him any harm, but from particular and personal animosities against other men. And, afterwards, the terror all men were under of the parliament, and the guilt they were conscious of themselves, made them watch all opportunities to make themselves gracious to those who could do them good; and so they became spies upon their master, and from one piece of knavery were hardened and confirmed to undertake another; till at last they had no hope of preservation but by the destruction of their master. And after all this, when a man might reasonably believe that less than a universal defection of three nations could not have reduced a great king to so ugly a fate, it is most certain, that in that very hour, when he was thus wickedly murdered in the sight of the sun, he had as great a share in the hearts and affections of his subjects in general, was as much beloved, esteemed, and longed for by the people in general of the three nations, as any of his predecessors had ever been. To conclude, he was the worthiest gentleman, the best master, the best friend, the best husband, the best father, and the best Christian, that the age in which he lived had produced. And if he were not the best king, if he [were] without some parts and qualities which have made some kings great and happy, no other prince was ever unhappy who was possessed of half his virtues and endowments, and so much without any kind of vice.

The Character of Cromwell

He was one of those men, *quos vituperare ne inimici quidem possunt, nisi ut simul laudent;* [whom his very enemies could not condemn without commending him at the same time:] for he could never have done half that mischief without great parts of courage and industry and judgment. And he must have had a wonderful understanding in the natures and humours of men, and as great a dexterity in the applying them, who from a private and obscure birth, (though of a good family,) without interest of estate, alliance or friendship, could raise himself to such a height, and compound and knead such opposite and contradictory tempers, humours, and interests into a consistence that contributed to his designs and to their own destruction; whilst himself grew insensibly powerful enough to cut off those by whom he had climbed, in the instant that they projected to demolish their own building. What Velleius Paterculus said of Cinna may very justly be said of him, *ausum eum, quæ nemo auderet bonus; perfecisse, quæ a nullo, nisi fortissimo, perfici possent:* [he attempted those things which no good man durst have ventured on; and achieved those in which none but a valiant and great man could have succeeded.] Without doubt, no man with more wickedness ever attempted any thing, or brought to pass what he desired more wickedly, more in the face and contempt of religion and moral honesty; yet wickedness as great as his could never have accomplished those trophies, without the assistance of a great spirit, an admirable circumspection and sagacity, and a most magnanimous resolution.

When he appeared first in the parliament, he seemed to have a person in no degree gracious, no ornament of discourse, none of those talents which use to reconcile the affections of the standers by: yet as he grew into place and authority, his parts seemed to be renewed, as if he had concealed faculties, till he had occasion to use them; and when he was to act the part of a great man, he did it without any indecency through the want of custom.

After he was confirmed and invested protector by *The humble petition and advice,* he consulted with very few upon any action of importance, nor communicated any enterprise he resolved upon with more than those who were to have principal parts in the execution of it; nor to them sooner than was absolutely necessary. What he once resolved, in which he was not rash, he would not be dissuaded from, nor endure any contradiction of his power and authority, but extorted obedience from them who were not willing to yield it.

When he had laid some very extraordinary tax upon the city, one Cony, an eminent fanatic, and one who had heretofore served him very notably, positively refused to pay his part, and loudly dissuaded others from submitting to it, as an imposition notoriously against the law and the propriety of the subject, which all honest men were bound to defend. Cromwell sent for him, and cajoled him with the memory of the old kindness and friendship that had been between them, and that of all men he did not expect this opposition from him, in a matter that was so necessary for the good of the commonwealth. But it was always his fortune to meet with the most rude and obstinate behaviour from those who had formerly been absolutely governed by him, and they commonly put him in mind of some expressions and sayings of his own in cases of the like nature; so this man remembered him how great an enemy he had expressed himself to such grievances, and declared that all who submitted to them, and paid illegal taxes, were more to blame, and greater enemies to their country, than they who imposed them, and that the tyranny of princes could never be grievous but by the tameness and stupidity of the people. When Cromwell saw that he could not convert him, he told him that he had a will as stubborn as his, and he would try, which of them two should be master. And thereupon, with some terms of reproach and contempt, he committed the man to prison; whose courage was nothing abated by it; but as soon as the term came, he brought his habeas corpus in the king's bench, which they then called the upper bench. Maynard, who was of council with the prisoner, demanded his liberty with great confidence, both upon the illegality of the commitment, and the illegality of the imposition, as being laid without any lawful authority. The judges could not maintain or defend either, but enough declared what their sentence would be; and therefore the protector's attorney required a farther day to answer what had been urged. Before that day, Maynard was committed to the Tower, for presuming to question or make doubt of his authority; and the judges were sent for, and severely reprehended for suffering that license; and when they with all humility mentioned the law and magna charta, Cromwell told them, their magna charta should not control his actions, which he knew were for the safety of the commonwealth. He asked them who made them judges; [whether] they had any authority to sit there but what he gave them; and that if his authority were at an end, they knew well enough what would become of themselves; and therefore advised them to be more tender of that which could only preserve them; and so dismissed them with caution, that they should not suffer the lawyers to prate what it would not become them to hear.

Thus he subdued a spirit that had been often troublesome to the most sovereign power, and made Westminster-hall as obedient and subservient to his commands as any of the rest of his quarters. In all other matters, which did not concern the life of his jurisdiction, he seemed to have great reverence for the law, and rarely interposed between party and party. And as he proceeded with this kind of indignation and haughtiness with those who were refractory, and dared to contend with his greatness, so towards those who complied with his good pleasure, and courted his protection, he used a wonderful civility, generosity, and bounty.

To reduce three nations, which perfectly hated him, to an entire obedience to all his dictates; to awe and govern those nations by an army that was indevoted to him, and wished his ruin, was an instance of a very prodigious address. But his greatness at home was but a shadow of the glory he had abroad. It was hard to discover which feared him most, France, Spain, or the Low Countries, where his friendship was current at the value he put upon it. And as they did all sacrifice their honour and their interest to his pleasure, so there is nothing he could have demanded, that either of them would have denied him. To manifest which, there need only two instances. The first is, when those of the valley of Lucerne had unwarily rebelled against the duke of Savoy, which gave occasion to the pope and the neighbour princes of Italy to call and solicit for their extirpation, which their prince positively resolved upon, Cromwell sent his agent to the duke of Savoy, a prince with whom he had no correspondence or commerce, and so engaged the cardinal, and even terrified the pope himself, without so much as doing any grace to the English [Roman] catholics, (nothing being more usual than his saying that his ships in the Mediterranean should visit Civita Vecchia, and that the sound of his cannon should be heard in Rome,) that the duke of Savoy thought it necessary to restore all that he had taken from them, and did renew all those privileges they had formerly enjoyed, and newly forfeited.

The other instance of his authority was yet greater, and more incredible. In the city of Nismes, which is one of the fairest in the province of Languedoc, and where those of the religion do most abound, there was a great faction at that season when the consuls (who are the chief magistrates) were to be chosen. Those of the [reformed] religion had the confidence to set up one of themselves for that magistracy; which they of the Roman religion resolved to oppose with all their power. The dissension between them made so much noise, that the intendant of the province, who is the supreme minister in all civil affairs throughout the whole province, went thither to prevent any disorder that might happen. When the day of the election came, those of the religion possessed themselves with many armed men of the town-house, where the election was to be made. The magistrates sent to know what their meaning was; to which they answered, they were there to give their voices for the choice of the new consuls, and to be sure that the election should be fairly made. The bishop of the city, the intendant of the province, with all the officers of the church, and the present magistrates of the town, went together in their robes to be present at the election, without any suspicion that there would be any force used. When they came near the gate of the town-house, which was shut, and they supposed would be opened when they came, they within poured out a volley of musket-shot upon them, by which the dean of the church, and two or three of the magistrates of the town were killed upon the place, and very many others wounded; whereof some died shortly after. In this confusion, the magistrates put themselves into as good a posture to defend themselves as they could, without any purpose of offending the other, till they should be better provided; in order to which they sent an express to the court with a plain relation of the whole matter of fact, and that there appeared to be no manner of combination with those of the religion in other places of the province; but that it was an insolence in those of the place, upon their presumption of their great numbers, which were little inferior to those of the catholics. The court was glad of the occasion, and resolved that this provocation, in which other places were not involved, and which nobody could excuse, should warrant all kind of severity in that city, even to the pulling down their temples, and expelling many of them for ever out of the city; which, with the execution and forfeiture of many of the principal persons, would be a general mortification to all of the religion in France; with whom they were heartily offended; and a part of the army was forthwith ordered to march towards Nismes, to see this executed with the utmost rigour.

Those of the religion in the town were quickly sensible into what condition they had brought themselves; and sent with all possible submission to the magistrates to excuse themselves, and to impute what had been done to the rashness of particular men, who had no order for what they did. The magistrates answered, that they were glad they were sensible of their miscarriage; but they could say nothing upon the subject till the king's pleasure should be known; to whom they had sent a full relation of all that had passed. The other very well knew what the king's pleasure would be, and forthwith sent an express, one Moulins a Scotchman, who had lived many years in that place and in Montpelier, to Cromwell, to desire his protection and interposition. The express made so much haste, and found so good a reception the first hour he came, that Cromwell, after he had received the whole account, bade him refresh himself after so long a journey, and he would take such care of his business, that by the time he came to Paris he should find it despatched; and that night, sent away another messenger to his ambassador Lockhart; who, by the time Moulins came thither, had so far prevailed with the cardinal, that orders were sent to stop the troops, which were upon their march towards Nismes; and within a few days after, Moulins returned with a full pardon and amnesty from the king, under the great seal of France, so fully confirmed with all circumstances, that there was never farther mention made of it, but all things passed as if there had never been any such thing. So that nobody can wonder that his memory remains still in those parts and with those people in great veneration.

He would never suffer himself to be denied any thing he ever asked of the cardinal, alleging that the people would not be otherwise satisfied; which he [the cardinal] bore very heavily, and complained of to those with whom he would be free. One day he visited madam Turenne, and when he took his leave of her, she, according to her custom, besought him to continue gracious to the churches. Whereupon the cardinal told her that he knew not how to behave himself; if he advised the king to punish and suppress their insolence, Cromwell threatened [him] to join with the Spaniard; and if he shewed any favour to them, at Rome they accounted him an heretic.

He was not a man of blood, and totally declined Machiavel's method, which prescribes, upon any alteration of a government, as a thing absolutely necessary, to cut off all the heads of those, and extirpate their families, who are friends to the old [one]. And it was confidently reported, that in the council of officers it was more than once proposed that there might be a general massacre of all the royal party, as the only expedient to secure the government; but Cromwell would never consent to it; it may be, out of too much contempt of his enemies. In a word, as he had all the wickednesses against which damnation is denounced, and for which hell-fire is prepared, so he had some virtues which have caused the memory of some men in all ages to be celebrated; and he will be looked upon by posterity as a brave bad man.

SIR JOHN SUCKLING (1609-1642)

A Ballad upon a Wedding

I TELL thee, Dick, where I have been,
Where I the rarest things have seen;
O, things without compare!
Such sights again cannot be found
In any place on English ground,
Be it at wake or fair.

At Charing-Cross, hard by the way,
Where we (thou know'st) do sell our hay,
There is a house with stairs;
And there did I see coming down
Such folk as are not in our town,
Forty at least, in pairs.

Amongst the rest, one pest'lent fine
(His beard no bigger though than thine)
Walked on before the rest:
Our landlord looks like nothing to him:
The King (God bless him) 'twould undo him,
Should he go still so drest.

At Course-a-Park, without all doubt,
He should have first been taken out
By all the maids i' th' town:

Though lusty Roger there had been,
Or little George upon the Green,
  Or Vincent of the Crown.

But wot you what? the youth was going
To make an end of all his wooing;
  The parson for him stay'd:
Yet by his leave (for all his haste)
He did not so much wish all past
  (Perchance), as did the maid.

The maid (and thereby hangs a tale),
For such a maid no Whitsun-ale
  Could ever yet produce:
No grape, that's kindly ripe, could be
So round, so plump, so soft as she,
  Nor half so full of juice.

Her finger was so small, the ring,
Would not stay on, which they did bring,
  It was too wide a peck:
And to say truth (for out it must)
It looked like the great collar (just)
  About our young colt's neck.

Her feet beneath her petticoat,
Like little mice, stole in and out,
  As if they fear'd the light:
But O she dances such a way!
No sun upon an Easter-day
  Is half so fine a sight.

Her cheeks so rare a white was on,
No daisy makes comparison,
  (Who sees them is undone),
For streaks of red were mingled there,
Such as are on a Catherine pear
  The side that's next the sun.

Her lips were red, and one was thin,
Compar'd to that was next her chin
  (Some bee had stung it newly);
But, Dick, her eyes so guard her face;
I durst no more upon them gaze
  Than on the sun in July.

Her mouth so small, when she does speak,
Thou'dst swear her teeth her words did break,
  That they might passage get;
But she so handled still the matter,
They came as good as ours, or better,
  And are not spent a whit.

Just in the nick the cook knocked thrice,
And all the waiters in a trice
  His summons did obey;
Each serving-man, with dish in hand,
Marched boldly up, like our trained band,
  Presented, and away.

When all the meat was on the table,
What man of knife or teeth was able
  To stay to be intreated?
And this the very reason was,
Before the parson could say grace,
  The company was seated.

The business of the kitchen's great,
For it is fit that men should eat;
  Nor was it there denied:
Passion o' me, how I run on!
There's that that would be thought upon
  (I trow) besides the bride.

Now hats fly off, and youths carouse;
Healths first go round, and then the house,
  The bride's came thick and thick:
And when 'twas nam'd another's health,
Perhaps he made it hers by stealth;
  And who could help it, Dick?

On the sudden up they rise and dance;
Then sit again and sigh, and glance:
  Then dance again and kiss:
Thus several ways the time did pass,
Whilst ev'ry woman wished her place,
  And every man wished his.

RICHARD LOVELACE [1618-1658]

To Althea from Prison

When love with unconfinèd wings
  Hovers within my gates,
And my divine Althea brings
  To whisper at the grates;
When I lie tangled in her hair,
  And fetter'd to her eye,

The birds that wanton in the air
  Know no such liberty.

When flowing cups run swiftly round
  With no allaying Thames,
Our careless heads with roses crown'd,
  Our hearts with loyal flames;
When thirsty grief in wine we steep,
  When healths and draughts go free—
Fishes that tipple in the deep
  Know no such liberty.

When, like committed linnets, I
  With shriller throat shall sing
The sweetness, mercy, majesty,
  And glories of my King;
When I shall voice aloud, how good
  He is, how great should be,
Enlargèd winds that curl the flood
  Know no such liberty.

Stone walls do not a prison make,
  Nor iron bars a cage;
Minds innocent and quiet take
  That for an hermitage;
If I have freedom in my love—
  And in my soul am free,
Angels alone, that soar above,
  Enjoy such liberty.

To Lucasta, on Going beyond Seas

If to be absent were to be
    Away from thee;
  Or that when I am gone
  You or I were alone;
Then, my Lucasta, might I crave
Pity from blustering wind, or swallowing wave.

But I'll not sigh one blast or gale
    To swell my sail,
  Or pay a tear to 'suage
  The foaming blue-god's rage;
For whether he will let me pass
Or no, I'm still as happy as I was.

Though seas and land betwixt us both,
    Our faith and troth,
  Like separated souls,
  All time and space controls:
Above the highest sphere we meet
Unseen, unknown, and greet as Angels greet.

So then we do anticipate
    Our after-fate,
  And are alive i' the skies,
  If thus our lips and eyes
Can speak like spirits unconfined
In Heaven, their earthy bodies left behind.

To Lucasta, on Going to the Wars

Tell me not, Sweet, I am unkind,
  That from the nunnery
Of thy chaste breast and quiet mind
  To war and arms I fly.

True, a new mistress now I chase,
  The first foe in the field;
And with a stronger faith embrace
  A sword, a horse, a shield.

Yet this inconstancy is such
  As you too shall adore—
I could not love thee, Dear, so much,
  Loved I not honour more.

ANDREW MARVELL [1621-1678]

Song of the Emigrants in Bermuda

Where the remote Bermudas ride
In th' ocean's bosom unespy'd,
From a small boat that row'd along
The list'ning winds received this song.
  "What should we do but sing His praise
That led us through the wat'ry maze
Unto an isle so long unknown,
And yet far kinder than our own?
Where He the huge sea-monsters wracks,
That lift the deep upon their backs;
He lands us on a grassy stage,
Safe from the storms, and prelate's rage:

He gave us this eternal Spring
Which here enamels everything,
And sends the fowls to us in care
On daily visits through the air.
He hangs in shades the orange bright
Like golden lamps in a green night,
And does in the pomegranates close
Jewels more rich than Ormus shows:
He makes the figs our mouths to meet
And throws the melons at our feet;
But apples, plants of such a price,
No tree could ever bear them twice.
With cedars chosen by His hand
From Lebanon He stores the land;
And makes the hollow seas that roar
Proclaim the ambergris on shore.
He cast (of which we rather boast)
The Gospel's pearl upon our coast;
And in these rocks for us did frame
A temple where to sound His name.
Oh! let our voice His praise exalt
Till it arrive at Heaven's vault,
Which thence (perhaps) rebounding may
Echo beyond the Mexique bay!"
—Thus sung they in the English boat
A holy and a cheerful note:
And all the way, to guide their chime,
With falling oars they kept the time.

Thoughts in a Garden

How vainly men themselves amaze
To win the palm, the oak, or bays,
And their uncessant labours see
Crown'd from some single herb or tree,
Whose short and narrow-vergèd shade
Does prudently their toils upbraid;
While all the flowers and trees do close
To weave the garlands of repose.

Fair Quiet, have I found thee here,
And Innocence thy sister dear!
Mistaken long, I sought you then
In busy companies of men:
Your sacred plants, if here below,
Only among the plants will grow:
Society is all but rude
To this delicious solitude.

No white nor red was ever seen
So am'rous as this lovely green.
Fond lovers, cruel as their flame,
Cut in these trees their mistress' name;
Little, alas, they know or heed
How far these beauties hers exceed!
Fair trees! wheres'e'er your barks I wound,
No name shall but your own be found.

When we have run our passions' heat
Love hither makes his best retreat:
The gods, who mortal beauty chase,
Still in a tree did end their race;
Apollo hunted Daphne so
Only that she might laurel grow;
And Pan did after Syrinx speed
Not as a nymph, but for a reed.

What wondrous life is this I lead!
Ripe apples drop about my head;
The luscious clusters of the vine
Upon my mouth do crush their wine;
The nectarine and curious peach
Into my hands themselves do reach;
Stumbling on melons, as I pass,
Ensnared with flowers, I fall on grass.

Meanwhile the mind, from pleasure less,
Withdraws into its happiness;
The mind, that ocean where each kind
Does straight its own resemblance find;
Yet it creates, transcending these,
Far other worlds, and other seas;
Annihilating all that's made
To a green thought in a green shade.

Here at the fountain's sliding foot
Or at some fruit-tree's mossy root,
Casting the body's vest aside
My soul into the boughs does glide;
There, like a bird, it sits and sings,
Then whets and claps its silver wings,
And, till prepared for longer flight,
Waves in its plumes the various light.

Such was that happy Garden-state
While man there walk'd without a mate:
After a place so pure and sweet,
What other help could yet be meet!

But 'twas beyond a mortal's share
To wander solitary there:
Two paradises 'twere in one
To live in Paradise alone.

How well the skilful gardner drew
Of flowers and herbs this dial new!
Where, from above, the milder sun
Does through a fragrant zodiac run:
And, as it works, th' industrious bee
Computes its time as well as we.
How could such sweet and wholesome hours
Be reckon'd, but with herbs and flowers!

JOHN BUNYAN (1628-1688)

From THE PILGRIM'S PROGRESS

Christian's Victory over Apollyon

The Pilgrim's Progress is the account of a dream, representing in allegorical narrative the life of a Christian, from his conversion to his death. In *Revelation*, IX, 11, Apollyon is mentioned as "the angel of the bottomless pit, whose name in the Hebrew tongue is Abaddon, but in the Greek hath his name Apollyon." The struggle of Christian with Apollyon, therefore, represents his struggle with the Evil One.

BUT now in this Valley of Humiliation poor Christian was hard put to it, for he had gone but a little way before he espied a foul fiend coming over the field to meet him; his name is Apollyon. Then did Christian begin to be afraid, and to cast in his mind whether to go back, or to stand his ground. But he considered again, that he had no armor for his back, and therefore thought that to turn the back to him, might give him greater advantage with ease to pierce him with his darts; therefore he resolved to venture, and stand his ground. For, thought he, had I no more in mine eye than the saving of my life, 'twould be the best way to stand.

So he went on, and Apollyon met him. Now the monster was hideous to behold: he was clothed with scales like a fish (and they are his pride); he had wings like a dragon, feet like a bear, and out of his belly came fire and smoke; and his mouth was as the mouth of a lion. When he was come up to Christian, he beheld him with a disdainful countenance, and thus began to question with him.

APOL. Whence come you? and whither are you bound?

CHR. I am come from the City of Destruction, which is the place of all evil, and am going to the City of Zion.

APOL. By this I perceive thou art one of my subjects, for all that country is mine; and I am the prince and god of it. How is it then that thou hast run away from thy king? Were it not that I hope thou mayest do me more service, I would strike thee now at one blow to the ground.

CHR. I was born indeed in your dominions, but your service was hard, and your wages such as a man could not live on, "for the wages of sin is death"; therefore when I was come to years, I did as other considerate persons do, look out, if perhaps I might mend myself.

APOL. There is no prince that will thus lightly lose his subjects, neither will I as yet lose thee: but since thou complainest of thy service and wages, be content to go back; what our country will afford, I do here promise to give thee.

CHR. But I have let myself to another, even to the King of princes, and how can I with fairness go back with thee?

APOL. Thou hast done in this, according to the proverb, changed a bad for a worse; but it is ordinary for those who have professed themselves his servants, after a while to give him the slip, and return again to me. Do thou so too, and all shall be well.

CHR. I have given him my faith, and sworn my allegiance to him; how then can I go back from this, and not be hanged as a traitor?

APOL. Thou didst the same to me, and yet I am willing to pass by all, if now thou wilt yet turn again and go back.

CHR. What I promised thee was in my nonage; and besides, I count that the Prince under whose banner now I stand, is able to absolve me; yea and to pardon also what I did as to my compliance with thee: and besides (O thou destroying Apollyon), to speak truth, I like his service, his wages, his servants, his government, his company, and country better than thine; and therefore leave off to persuade me further, I am his servant, and I will follow him.

APOL. Consider again when thou art in cold blood, what thou art like to meet with in the way that thou goest. Thou knowest that for the most part, his servants come to an ill end, because they are transgressors against me and my ways. How many of them have been put to shameful deaths! and besides, thou countest his service better than mine, whereas he never came yet from the place where he is, to deliver any that served him out of our hands; but as for me, how many times, as all the world very well knows, have I delivered, either by power or fraud, those that have faithfully served me, from him and his, though taken by them, and so I will deliver thee.

CHR. His forbearing at present to deliver them is on purpose to try their love, whether they will cleave to him to the end: and as for the ill end thou sayest they come to, that is most glorious in their account: For for present deliverance, they do not much expect it; for they stay for their glory, and then they shall have it, when their Prince comes in his, and the glory of the angels.

APOL. Thou hast already been unfaithful in thy service to him, and how dost thou think to receive wages of him?

CHR. Wherein, O Apollyon, have I been unfaithful to him?

APOL. Thou didst faint at first setting out, when thou wast almost choked in the Gulf of Despond; thou didst attempt wrong ways to be rid of thy burden, whereas thou shouldest have stayed till thy Prince had taken it off; thou didst sinfully sleep and lose thy choice thing; thou wast also almost persuaded to go back at the sight of the lions; and when thou talkest of thy journey, and of what thou hast heard and seen, thou art inwardly desirous of vainglory in all that thou sayest or doest.

CHR. All this is true, and much more, which thou hast left out; but the Prince whom I serve and honor is merciful, and ready to forgive; but besides, these infirmities possessed me in thy country, for there I sucked them in, and I have groaned under them, been sorry for them, and have obtained pardon of my Prince.

APOL. Then Apollyon broke out into a grievous rage, saying, I am an enemy to this Prince; I hate his person, his laws, and people; I am come out on purpose to withstand thee.

CHR. Apollyon, beware what you do, for I am in the King's highway, the way of holiness, therefore take heed to yourself.

APOL. Then Apollyon straddled quite over the whole breadth of the way, and said, I am void of fear in this matter, prepare thyself to die; for I swear by my infernal den thou shalt go no further; here will I spill thy soul.

And with that he threw a flaming dart at his breast, but Christian had a shield in his hand, with which he caught it, and so prevented the danger of that.

Then did Christian draw, for he saw 'twas time to bestir him; and Apollyon as fast made at him, throwing darts as thick as hail; by the which, notwithstanding all that Christian could do to avoid it, Apollyon wounded him in his head, his hand, and foot. This made Christian give a little back; Apollyon, therefore, followed his work amain, and Christian again took courage, and resisted as manfully as he could. This sore combat lasted for above half a day, even till Christian was almost quite spent. For you must know that Christian, by reason of his wounds, must needs grow weaker and weaker.

Then Apollyon, espying his opportunity, began to gather up close to Christian, and wrestling with him, gave him a dreadful fall; and with that Christian's sword flew out of his hand. Then said Apollyon, I am sure of thee now! and with that, he had almost pressed him to death, so that Christian began to despair of life. But as God would have it, while Apollyon was fetching of his last blow, thereby to make a full end of this good man, Christian nimbly reached out his hand for his sword, and caught it, saying, "Rejoice not against me, O mine enemy! when I fall, I shall arise"; and with that gave him a deadly thrust, which made him give back, as one that had received his mortal wound. Christian perceiving that, made at him again, saying, "Nay, in all these things we are more than conquerors." And with that Apollyon spread forth his dragon's wings, and sped him away, that Christian saw him no more.

JOHN DRYDEN (1631-1700)

From ANNUS MIRABILIS

The Fire of London

SUCH was the rise of this prodigious fire,
Which, in mean buildings first obscurely bred,
From thence did soon to open streets aspire,
And straight to palaces and temples spread.

The diligence of trades, and noiseful gain,
And luxury, more late, asleep were laid;
All was the Night's, and in her silent reign
No sound the rest of Nature did invade.

In this deep quiet, from what source unknown,
Those seeds of fire their fatal birth disclose;
And first few scattering sparks about were blown,
Big with the flames that to our ruin rose.

Then in some close-pent room it crept along,
And, smouldering as it went, in silence fed;
Till the infant monster, with devouring strong,
Walked boldly upright with exalted head.

Now, like some rich or mighty murderer,
Too great for prison which he breaks with gold,
Who fresher for new mischiefs does appear,
And dares the world to tax him with the old,

So scapes the insulting fire his narrow jail,
And makes small outlets into open air;
There the fierce winds his tender force assail,
And beat him downward to his first repair.

The winds, like crafty courtesans, withheld
His flames from burning but to blow them more:
And, every fresh attempt, he is repelled
With faint denials, weaker than before.

And now, no longer letted of his prey,
He leaps up at it with enraged desire,
O'erlooks the neighbours with a wide survey,
And nods at every house his threatening fire.

The ghosts of traitors from the Bridge descend,
With bold fanatic spectres to rejoice;
About the fire into a dance they bend,
And sing their sabbath notes with feeble voice.

Our guardian angel saw them where they sate,
Above the palace of our slumbering King;
He sighed, abandoning his charge to Fate,
And drooping oft looked back upon the wing.

At length the crackling noise and dreadful blaze
Called up some waking lover to the sight;
And long it was ere he the rest could raise,
Whose heavy eyelids yet were full of night.

The next to danger, hot pursued by fate,
Half-clothed, half-naked, hastily retire;
And frighted mothers strike their breasts too late
For helpless infants left amidst the fire.

Their cries soon waken all the dwellers near;
Now murmuring noises rise in every street;
The more remote run stumbling with their fear,
And in the dark men justle as they meet.

So weary bees in little cells repose;
But if night-robbers lift the well-stored hive,
An humming through their waxen city grows,
And out upon each other's wings they drive.

Now streets grow thronged and busy as by day;
Some run for buckets to the hallowed quire;
Some cut the pipes, and some the engines play,
And some more bold mount ladders to the fire.

In vain; for from the east a Belgian wind
His hostile breath through the dry rafters sent;
The flames impelled soon left their foes behind,
And forward with a wanton fury went.

A key of fire ran all along the shore,
And lightened all the river with a blaze;
The wakened tides began again to roar,
And wondering fish in shining waters gaze.

Old Father Thames raised up his reverend head,
But feared the fate of Simois would return;
Deep in his ooze he sought his sedgy bed,
And shrank his waters back into his urn.

The fire meantime walks in a broader gross;
To either hand his wings he opens wide;
He wades the streets, and straight he reaches 'cross
And plays his longing flames on the other side.

At first they warm, then scorch, and then they take;
Now with long necks from side to side they feed;
At length, grown strong, their mother-fire forsake,
And a new colony of flames succeed.

To every nobler portion of the town
The curling billows roll their restless tide;
In parties now they straggle up and down,
As armies unopposed for prey divide.

One mighty squadron, with a sidewind sped,
Through narrow lanes his cumbered fire does haste,

By powerful charms of gold and silver led
The Lombard bankers and the Change to waste.

Another backward to the Tower would go,
And slowly eats his way against the wind;
But the main body of the marching foe
Against the imperial palace is designed.

Now day appears; and with the day the King,
Whose early care had robbed him of his rest;
Far off the cracks of falling houses ring,
And shrieks of subjects pierce his tender breast.

Near as he draws, thick harbingers of smoke
With gloomy pillars cover all the place;
Whose little intervals of night are broke
By sparks that drive against his sacred face.

More than his guards his sorrows made him known,
And pious tears which down his cheeks did shower;
The wretched in his grief forgot their own;
So much the pity of a king has power.

He wept the flames of what he loved so well,
And what so well had merited his love;
For never prince in grace did more excel,
Or royal city more in duty strove.

From ABSALOM AND ACHITOPHEL,

Part I

Achitophel

Absalom and Achitophel (later known as Part I) appeared anonymously on November 17, 1681. At the moment, Charles II was exerting every effort to secure the Catholic succession in England. The opposition, led by the Earl of Shaftesbury, was equally intent upon securing the passage of the Exclusion Bill, which would have prevented Charles's brother from succeeding to the throne, and cleared the way for the eventual accession of the King's natural son, the Duke of Monmouth.

In the poem, Monmouth figures as Absalom, Shaftesbury as Achitophel, Charles as David, Cromwell as Saul, the Roman Catholics as Jebusites, the Dissenters as Levites. "The Plot" mentioned in the following selection is the so-called Popish Plot, of which Titus Oates (Corah in the poem) had accused the Catholics, in 1678. Shaftesbury had made great capital among the populace of the charge that the Catholics had plotted to kill King Charles and put at once on the throne his brother James, who was to bring about a return of England to the faith. The poem relates that Shaftesbury persuaded Monmouth to rebellion; that the King, after taking counsel, determined to draw the sword of "justice" against his foes; and that, with the consent of the Almighty, he succeeded. The strongest satiric elements appear in the descriptions of the leaders of the rebellion: Shaftesbury as Achitophel, and George Villiers, the second Duke of Buckingham, as Zimri. He had ridiculed Dryden as Bayes, in *The Rehearsal*.

OF these the false Achitophel was first,
A name to all succeeding ages curst:
For close designs and crooked counsels fit,
Sagacious, bold, and turbulent of wit,
Restless, unfixed in principles and place,
In power unpleased, impatient of disgrace;
A fiery soul which, working out its way,
Fretted the pigmy body to decay
And o'er-informed the tenement of clay.
A daring pilot in extremity,
Pleased with the danger, when the waves went high,
He sought the storms; but, for a calm unfit,
Would steer too nigh the sands to boast his wit.
Great wits are sure to madness near allied,
And thin partitions do their bounds divide;

Else, why should he, with wealth and honour blest,
Refuse his age the needful hours of rest?
Punish a body which he could not please,
Bankrupt of life, yet prodigal of ease?
And all to leave what with his toil he won
To that unfeathered two-legged thing, a son,
Got, while his soul did huddled notions try,
And born a shapeless lump, like anarchy.
In friendship false, implacable in hate,
Resolved to ruin or to rule the state;
To compass this the triple bond he broke,
The pillars of the public safety shook,
And fitted Israel for a foreign yoke;
Then, seized with fear, yet still affecting fame,
Usurped a patriot's all-atoning name.
So easy still it proves in factious times
With public zeal to cancel private crimes.
How safe is treason and how sacred ill,
Where none can sin against the people's will,
Where crowds can wink and no offence be known,
Since in another's guilt they find their own!
Yet fame deserved no enemy can grudge;
The statesman we abhor, but praise the judge.
In Israel's courts ne'er sat an Abbethdin
With more discerning eyes or hands more clean,
Unbribed, unsought, the wretched to redress,
Swift of despatch and easy of access.
Oh! had he been content to serve the crown
With virtues only proper to the gown,
Or had the rankness of the soil been freed
From cockle that oppressed the noble seed,
David for him his tuneful harp had strung
And Heaven had wanted one immortal song.
But wild ambition loves to slide, not stand,
And Fortune's ice prefers to Virtue's land.
Achitophel, grown weary to possess
A lawful fame and lazy happiness,
Disdained the golden fruit to gather free,
And lent the crowd his arm to shake the tree.
Now, manifest of crimes contrived long since,
He stood at bold defiance with his Prince,
Held up the buckler of the people's cause
Against the crown, and skulked behind the laws.
The wished occasion of the Plot he takes;
Some circumstances finds, but more he makes;
By buzzing emissaries fills the ears
Of listening crowds with jealousies and fears
Of arbitrary counsels brought to light,
And proves the King himself a Jebusite.
Weak arguments! which yet he knew full well
Were strong with people easy to rebel.
For, governed by the moon, the giddy Jews
Tread the same track when she the prime renews.
And once in twenty years their scribes record,
By natural instinct they change their lord.

From Absalom and Achitophel, Part II

The Malcontents. Zimri

See the note prefixed to "Achitophel," above. In this passage, the Levites are the Presbyterian leaders, and the Solymaean rout are the rabble of London dissenters.

To further this, Achitophel unites
The malcontents of all the Israelites,
Whose differing parties he could wisely join

For several ends to serve the same design;
The best, (and of the princes some were such,)
Who thought the power of monarchy too much;
Mistaken men and patriots in their hearts,
Not wicked, but seduced by impious arts;
By these the springs of property were bent
And wound so high they cracked the government.
The next for interest sought to embroil the state
To sell their duty at a dearer rate,
And make their Jewish markets of the throne,
Pretending public good to serve their own.
Others thought kings an useless heavy load,
Who cost too much and did too little good.
These were for laying honest David by
On principles of pure good husbandry.
With them joined all the haranguers of the throng
That thought to get preferment by the tongue.
Who follow next a double danger bring,
Not only hating David, but the King;
The Solymaean rout, well versed of old
In godly faction and in treason bold,
Cowering and quaking at a conqueror's sword,
But lofty to a lawful prince restored,
Saw with disdain an Ethnic plot begun
And scorned by Jebusites to be outdone.
Hot Levites headed these; who, pulled before
From the ark which in the Judges' days they bore,
Resumed their cant, and with a zealous cry
Pursued their old beloved theocracy,
Where Sanhedrin and priest enslaved the nation,
And justified their spoils by inspiration;
For who so fit for reign as Aaron's race,
If once dominion they could found in grace?
These led the pack; though not of surest scent,
Yet deepest mouthed against the government.
A numerous host of dreaming saints succeed
Of the true old enthusiastic breed:
'Gainst form and order they their power employ,
Nothing to build and all things to destroy.
But far more numerous was the herd of such
Who think too little and who talk too much.
These out of mere instínct, they knew not why,
Adored their fathers' God and property,
And by the same blind benefit of Fate
The Devil and the Jebusite did hate:
Born to be saved even in their own despite,
Because they could not help believing right.
Such were the tools; but a whole Hydra more
Remains of sprouting heads too long to score.
Some of their chiefs were princes of the land;
In the first rank of these did Zimri stand,
A man so various that he seemed to be
Not one, but all mankind's epitome:
Stiff in opinions, always in the wrong,
Was everything by starts and nothing long;
But in the course of one revolving moon
Was chymist, fiddler, statesman, and buffoon;
Then all for women, painting, rhyming, drinking,
Besides ten thousand freaks that died in thinking.
Blest madman, who could every hour employ

With something new to wish or to enjoy!
Railing and praising were his usual themes,
And both, to show his judgment, in extremes:
So over violent or over civil
That every man with him was God or Devil.
In squandering wealth was his peculiar art;
Nothing went unrewarded but desert.
Beggared by fools whom still he found too late,
He had his jest, and they had his estate.
He laughed himself from Court; then sought relief
By forming parties, but could ne'er be chief:
For spite of him, the weight of business fell
On Absalom and wise Achitophel;
Thus wicked but in will, of means bereft,
He left not faction, but of that was left.

A Song for St. Cecilia's Day

FROM harmony, from heavenly harmony
This universal frame began:
When Nature underneath a heap
Of jarring atoms lay
And could not heave her head,
The tuneful voice was heard from high,
"Arise, ye more than dead!"
Then cold, and hot, and moist, and dry,
In order to their stations leap,
And Music's power obey.
From harmony, from heavenly harmony
This universal frame began:
From harmony to harmony
Thro' all the compass of the notes it ran,
The diapason closing full in Man.

What passion cannot Music raise and quell!
When Jubal struck the chorded shell
His listening brethren stood around,
And, wondering, on their faces fell
To worship that celestial sound.
Less than a god they thought there could not dwell
Within the hollow of that shell
That spoke so sweetly and so well.
What passion cannot Music raise and quell!

The trumpet's loud clangor
Excites us to arms,
With shrill notes of anger
And mortal alarms.
The double double double beat
Of the thundering drum
Cries: "Hark! the foes come;
Charge, charge, 'tis too late to retreat!"

The soft complaining flute
In dying notes discovers
The woes of hopeless lovers,
Whose dirge is whisper'd by the warbling lute.

Sharp violins proclaim
Their jealous pangs and desperation,
Fury, frantic indignation,
Depth of pains, and height of passion
For the fair disdainful dame.

But oh! what art can teach,
What human voice can reach
The sacred organ's praise?
Notes inspiring holy love,
Notes that wing their heavenly ways
To mend the choirs above.

Orpheus could lead the savage race,
And trees unrooted left their place
Sequacious of the lyre:
But bright Cecilia raised the wonder higher:
When to her Organ vocal breath was given
An Angel heard, and straight appear'd—
Mistaking earth for heaven.

GRAND CHORUS

As from the power of sacred lays
The spheres began to move,

And sung the great Creator's praise
To all the blest above;
So when the last and dreadful hour
This crumbling pageant shall devour,
The trumpet shall be heard on high,
The dead shall live, the living die,
And Music shall untune the sky.

Alexander's Feast; or, The Power of Music

I

'Twas at the royal feast for Persia won
By Philip's warlike son:
Aloft in awful state
The godlike hero sate
On his imperial throne;
His valiant peers were placed around;
Their brows with roses and with myrtles bound:
(So should desert in arms be crown'd.)
The lovely Thais, by his side,
Sate like a blooming Eastern bride,
In flower of youth and beauty's pride.
Happy, happy, happy pair!
None but the brave,
None but the brave,
None but the brave deserves the fair.

CHORUS

Happy, happy, happy pair!
None but the brave,
None but the brave,
None but the brave deserves the fair.

II

Timotheus, placed on high
Amid the tuneful choir,
With flying fingers touch'd the lyre:
The trembling notes ascend the sky,
And heavenly joys inspire.
The song began from Jove,
Who left his blissful seats above,
(Such is the power of mighty love)
A dragon's fiery form belied the god:
Sublime on radiant spires he rode,
When he to fair Olympia press'd;
And while he sought her snowy breast:
Then, round her slender waist he curl'd,
And stamp'd an image of himself, a sovereign of the world.
The listening crowd admire the lofty sound,
"A present deity," they shout around;
"A present deity," the vaulted roofs rebound:
With ravished ears
The monarch hears,
Assumes the god,
Affects to nod,
And seems to shake the spheres.

Chorus: With ravished ears, etc.

III

The praise of Bacchus then the sweet musician sung,
Of Bacchus, ever fair and ever young.
The jolly god in triumph comes;
Sound the trumpets, beat the drums;
Flush'd with a purple grace
He shows his honest face:
Now give the hautboys breath; he comes, he comes.
Bacchus, ever fair and young,
Drinking joys did first ordain;
Bacchus' blessings are a treasure,
Drinking is the soldier's pleasure;
Rich the treasure,
Sweet the pleasure,
Sweet is pleasure after pain.

Chorus: Bacchus' blessings are a treasure, etc.

IV

Sooth'd with the sound, the king grew vain;
Fought all his battles o'er again;
And thrice he routed all his foes, and thrice he slew the slain.

The master saw the madness rise,
His glowing cheeks, his ardent eyes;
And while he heaven and earth defied,
Changed his hand, and check'd his pride.
He chose a mournful Muse,
Soft pity to infuse;
He sung Darius great and good,
By too severe a fate,
Fallen, fallen, fallen, fallen,
Fallen from his high estate,
And weltering in his blood;
Deserted at his utmost need
By those his former bounty fed;
On the bare earth exposed he lies,
With not a friend to close his eyes.
With downcast looks the joyless victor sate,
Revolving in his alter'd soul
The various turns of chance below:
And, now and then, a sigh he stole,
And tears began to flow.

CHORUS: Revolving in his alter'd soul, etc.

V

The mighty master smiled to see
That love was in the next degree;
'Twas but a kindred sound to move,
For pity melts the mind to love.
Softly sweet, in Lydian measures,
Soon he soothed his soul to pleasures.
"War," he sung, "is toil and trouble;
Honour but an empty bubble;
Never ending, still beginning,
Fighting still, and still destroying:
If the world be worth thy winning,
Think, O think it worth enjoying:
Lovely Thais sits beside thee,
Take the good the gods provide thee."
The many rend the skies with loud applause:
So Love was crown'd, but Music won the cause.
The prince, unable to conceal his pain,
Gazed on the fair
Who caused his care,
And sigh'd and look'd, sigh'd and look'd,
Sigh'd and look'd, and sigh'd again;
At length, with love and wine at once oppress'd,
The vanquish'd victor sunk upon her breast.

CHORUS: The prince, unable to conceal his pain, etc.

VI

Now strike the golden lyre again;
A louder yet, and yet a louder strain.
Break his bands of sleep asunder,
And rouse him, like a rattling peal of thunder.
Hark, hark, the horrid sound
Has raised up his head;
As awaked from the dead,
And, amazed, he stares around.
"Revenge, revenge!" Timotheus cries;
"See the Furies arise;
See the snakes that they rear,
How they hiss in their hair,
And the sparkles that flash from their eyes!
Behold a ghastly band,
Each a torch in his hand!
Those are Grecian ghosts, that in battle were slain,
And unburied remain
Inglorious on the plain:
Give the vengeance due
To the valiant crew.
Behold how they toss their torches on high,
How they point to the Persian abodes,
And glittering temples of their hostile gods."
The princes applaud with a furious joy;
And the king seized a flambeau with zeal to destroy;

Thais led the way,
To light him to his prey,
And, like another Helen, fired another Troy.

CHORUS: And the king seized a flambeau with zeal to destroy, etc.

VII

Thus, long ago,
Ere heaving bellows learned to blow,
While organs yet were mute,
Timotheus, to his breathing flute
And sounding lyre,
Could swell the soul to rage, or kindle soft desire.
At last divine Cecilia came,
Inventress of the vocal frame;
The sweet enthusiast, from her sacred store,
Enlarged the former narrow bounds,
And added length to solemn sounds,
With nature's mother wit, and arts unknown before.
Let old Timotheus yield the prize,
Or both divide the crown:
He raised a mortal to the skies;
She drew an angel down.

GRAND CHORUS

At last divine Cecilia came,
Inventress of the vocal frame;
The sweet enthusiast, from her sacred store,
Enlarged the former narrow bounds,
And added length to solemn sounds,
With nature's mother wit, and arts unknown before.
Let old Timotheus yield the prize,
Or both divide the crown:
He raised a mortal to the skies;
She drew an angel down.

DANIEL DEFOE (1659?-1731)

From ROBINSON CRUSOE, Part II

Friday and the Bear

BUT never was a fight managed so hardily, and in such a surprising manner, as that which followed between Friday and the bear, which gave us all, though at first we were surprised and afraid for him, the greatest diversion imaginable. As the bear is a heavy, clumsy creature, and does not gallop as the wolf does, who is swift and light, so he has two particular qualities, which generally are the rule of his actions: first, as to men, who are not his proper prey; I say, not his proper prey, because, though I cannot say what excessive hunger might do, which was now their case, the ground being all covered with snow; but as to men, he does not usually attempt them, unless they first attack him. On the contrary, if you meet him in the woods, if you don't meddle with him, he won't meddle with you; but then you must take care to be very civil to him, and give him the road, for he is a very nice gentleman. He won't go a step out of his way for a prince; nay, if you are really afraid, your best way is to look another way, and keep going on, for sometimes if you stop;

and stand still, and look steadily at him, he takes it for an affront; but if you throw or toss anything at him, and it hits him, though it were but a bit of a stick as big as your finger, he takes it for an affront, and sets all his other business aside to pursue his revenge; for he will have satisfaction in point of honour. That is his first quality; the next is, that if he be once affronted, he will never leave you, night or day, till he has his revenge, but follows, at a good round rate, till he overtakes you.

My man Friday had delivered our guide, and when we came up to him he was helping him off from his horse; for the man was both hurt and frighted, and indeed the last more than the first; when, on the sudden, we spied the bear come out of the wood, and a vast monstrous one it was, the biggest by far that ever I saw. We were all a little surprised when we saw him; but when Friday saw him, it was easy to see joy and courage in the fellow's countenance. "O! O! O!" says Friday, three times pointing to him. "O master! you give me te leave; me shakee te hand with him; me make you good laugh."

I was surprised to see the fellow so pleased. "You fool you," says I, "he will eat you up." "Eatee me up! eatee me up!" says Friday, twice over again; "me eatee him up; me make you good laugh; you all stay here, me show you good laugh." So down he sits, and gets his boots off in a moment, and put on a pair of pumps, as we call the flat shoes they wear, and which he had in his pocket, gives my other servant his horse, and with his gun away he flew, swift like the wind.

The bear was walking softly on, and offered to meddle with nobody till Friday, coming pretty near, calls to him, as if the bear could understand him, "Hark ye, hark ye," says Friday, "me speakee wit you." We followed at a distance; for now being come down on the Gascoign side of the mountains, we were entered a vast great forest, where the country was plain and pretty open, though many trees in it scattered here and there.

Friday, who had, as we say, the heels of the bear, came up with him quickly, and takes up a great stone and throws at him, and hit him just on the head, but did him no more harm than if he had thrown it against a wall. But it answered Friday's end, for the rogue was so void of fear, that he did it purely to make the bear follow him, and show us some laugh, as he called it.

As soon as the bear felt the stone, and saw him, he turns about, and comes after him, taking devilish long strides, and shuffling along at a strange rate, so as would have put a horse to a middling gallop. Away runs Friday, and takes his course as if he run towards us for help; so we all resolved to fire at once upon the bear, and deliver my man; though

I was angry at him heartily for bringing the bear back upon us, when he was going about his own business another way; and especially I was angry, that he had turned the bear upon us, and then run away; and I called out, "You dog," said I, "is this your making us laugh? Come away, and take your horse, that we may shoot the creature." He hears me, and cries out, "No shoot, no shoot; stand still, you get much laugh." And as the nimble creature run two feet for the beast's one, he turned on a sudden, on one side of us, and seeing a great oak tree fit for his purpose, he beckoned to us to follow; and doubling his pace, he gets nimbly up the tree, laying his gun down upon the ground, at about five or six yards from the bottom of the tree.

The bear soon came to the tree, and we followed at a distance. The first thing he did, he stopped at the gun, smelt to it, but let it lie, and up he scrambles into the tree, climbing like a cat, though so monstrously heavy. I was amazed at the folly, as I though it, of my man, and could not for my life see anything to laugh at yet, till seeing the bear get up the tree, we all rode nearer to him.

When we came to the tree, there was Friday got out to the small end of a large limb of the tree, and the bear got about half way to him. As soon as the bear got out to that part where the limb of the tree was weaker, "Ha!" says he to us, "now you see me teachee the bear dance." So he falls a-jumping and shaking the bough, at which the bear began to totter, but stood still, and began to look behind him, to see how he should get back. Then, indeed, we did laugh heartily. But Friday had not done with him by a great deal. When he sees him stand still, he calls out to him again, as if he had supposed the bear could speak English, "What, you no come farther? pray you come farther;" so he left jumping and shaking the tree; and the bear, just as if he had understood what he said, did come a little farther; then he fell a-jumping again, and the bear stopped again.

We thought now was a good time to knock him on the head, and I called to Friday to stand still, and we would shoot the bear; but he cried out earnestly, "O pray! O pray no shoot, me shoot by and then;" he would have said by-and-by. However, to shorten the story, Friday danced so much, and the bear stood so ticklish, that we had laughing enough indeed, but still could not imagine what the fellow would do: for first we thought he depended upon shaking the bear off; and we found the bear was too cunning for that too; for he would not go out far enough to be thrown down, but clings fast with his great broad claws and feet, so that we could not imagine what would be the end of it, and where the jest would be at last.

But Friday put us out of doubt quickly; for seeing the bear cling fast to the bough, and that he would not be persuaded to come any farther, "Well, well," says Friday, "you no come farther, me go, me go; you no come to me, me go come to you;" and upon this he goes out to the smallest end of the bough, where it would bend with his weight, and gently lets himself down by it, sliding down the bough till he came near enough to jump down on his feet and away he ran to his gun, takes it up, and stands still.

"Well," said I to him, "Friday, what will you do now? Why don't you shoot him?" "No shoot," says Friday, "no yet; me shoot now, me no kill; me stay, give you one more laugh." And indeed, so he did, as you will see presently; for when the bear sees his enemy gone, he comes back from the bough where he stood, but did it mighty leisurely, looking behind him every step, and coming backward till he got into the body of the tree; then with the same hinder end foremost he comes down the tree, grasping it with his claws, and moving one foot at a time, very leisurely. At this juncture, and just before he could set his hind feet upon the ground, Friday stepped up close to him, clapped the muzzle of his piece into his ear, and shot him dead as a stone.

Then the rogue turned about to see if we did not laugh; and when he saw we were pleased by our looks, he falls a-laughing himself very loud. "So we kill bear in my country," says Friday. "So you kill them?" says I; "why, you have no guns." "No," says he, "no gun, but shoot great much long arrow."

From A Journal of the Plague Year

The Story of the Piper

The full title of the work from which the following selection is taken, is "A Journal of the Plague Year: being observations or memorials of the most remarkable occurrences, as well public as private, which happened in London during the last visitation in 1665. Written by a Citizen who continued all the while in London. Never made public before." The book appeared in 1722, when the English public were alarmed at the outbreak of the plague in Marseilles in 1720-21. The *Journal* is, ostensibly, the work of a saddler, who lived, with a house-keeper, maid-servant, and two apprentices, "without Aldgate, about midway between Aldgate Church and Whitechapel Bars, on the left hand, or north side, of the street." Defoe himself was but six years of age at the time of the great plague; when he produced the *Journal,* however, he had accumulated much information from the reminiscences of survivors and from authoritative books written at the time. Its realism, at any rate, is unsurpassed.

It was under this John Hayward's care, and within his bounds, that the story of the piper, with which people have made themselves so merry, happened, and he assured me that it was true. It is said that it was a blind piper; but, as John told me, the fellow was not blind, but an ignorant, weak, poor man, and usually walked his rounds about ten o'clock at night and went piping along from door to door, and the people usually took him in at public-houses where they knew him, and would give him drink and victuals, and sometimes farthings; and he in return would pipe and sing and talk simply, which diverted the people; and thus he lived. It was but a very bad time for this diversion while things were as I have told, yet the poor fellow went about as usual, but was almost starved; and when anybody asked how he did he would answer, the dead cart had not taken him yet, but that they had promised to call for him next week.

It happened one night that this poor fellow, whether somebody had given him too much drink or no—John Hayward said he had not drink in his house, but that they had given him a little more victuals than ordinary at a public-house in Coleman Street—and the poor fellow, having not usually had a bellyful for perhaps not a good while, was laid all along upon the top of a bulk or stall, and fast asleep, at a door in the street near London Wall, towards Cripplegate, and that upon the same bulk or stall the people of some house, in the alley of which the house was a corner, hearing a bell, which they always rang before the cart came, had laid a body really dead of the plague just by him, thinking, too, that this poor fellow had been a dead body, as the other was, and laid there by some of the neighbours.

Accordingly, when John Hayward with his bell and the cart came along, finding two dead bodies lie upon the stall, they took them up with the instrument they used and threw them into the cart, and all this while the piper slept soundly.

From hence they passed along and took in other dead bodies, till, as honest John Hayward told me, they almost buried him alive in the cart; yet all this while he slept soundly. At length the cart came to the place where the bodies were to be thrown into the ground, which, as I do remember, was at Mount Mill; and as the cart usually stopped some time before they were ready to shoot out the melancholy load they had in it, as soon as the cart stopped the fellow awaked and struggled a little to get his head out from among the dead bodies, when, raising himself up in the cart, he called out, "Hey! where am I?" This frighted the fellow that attended about the work; but after some pause John Hayward, recovering himself, said, "Lord, bless us! There's somebody in the cart not quite dead!" So another called to him and said, "Who are you?" The fellow answered, "I am the poor piper. Where am I?" "Where are you?" says Hayward. "Why, you are in the dead-cart, and we are going to bury you." "But I an't dead though, am I?" says the piper, which made them laugh a little, though, as John said, they were heartily frighted at first: so they helped the poor fellow down, and he went about his business.

I know the story goes he set up his pipes in the cart and frighted the bearers and others so that they ran away; but John Hayward did not tell the story so, nor say anything of his piping at all; but that he was a poor piper, and that he was carried away as above I am fully satisfied of the truth of.

JONATHAN SWIFT (1667-1745)

From THE BATTLE OF THE BOOKS

The Spider and the Bee

The Battle of the Books appeared in 1704. It was suggested by a controversy that had originated in France, and had been carried on in England, about the relative merits of the Ancients and the Moderns. In Homeric style, it narrates "the terrible fight that happened on Friday last, between the ancient and modern books, in the king's library." The argument between the spider and the bee in St. James's library comes just before the actual commencement of hostilities. The spider, with his skill in fortification and mathematics, represents the excellences and other qualities of modern learning; the bee, with his wings and his voice, stands for the ancient. "Sweetness and light," the final words of the fable, provided the title of Matthew Arnold's famous essay on the Hebraic and Hellenistic elements of our spiritual inheritance.

THINGS were at this crisis, when a material accident fell out. For, upon the highest corner of a large window, there dwelt a certain spider, swollen up to the first magnitude by the destruction of infinite numbers of flies, whose spoils lay scattered before the gates of his palace, like human bones before the cave of some giant. The avenues to his castle were guarded with turnpikes and palisadoes, all after the modern way of fortification. After you had passed several courts, you came to the centre, wherein you might behold the constable himself in his own lodgings, which had windows fronting to each avenue, and ports to sally out, upon all occasions of prey or defence. In this mansion he had for some time dwelt in peace and plenty, without danger to his person by swallows from above, or to his palace, by brooms from below; when it was the pleasure of fortune to conduct thither a wandering bee, to whose curiosity a broken pane in the glass had discovered itself, and in he went; where, expatiating a while, he at last happened to alight upon one of the outward walls of the spider's citadel; which, yielding to the unequal weight, sunk down to the very foundation. Thrice he endeavoured to force his passage, and thrice the centre shook. The spider within, feeling the terrible convulsion, supposed at first that nature was approaching to her final dissolution; or else, that Beelzebub, with all his legions, was come to revenge the death of many thousands of his subjects, whom his enemy had slain and devoured. However, he at length valiantly resolved to issue forth, and meet his fate. Meanwhile the bee had acquitted himself of his toils, and, posted securely at some distance, was employed in cleansing his wings, and disengaging them from the ragged remnants of the cobweb. By this time the spider was adventured out, when, beholding the chasms, the ruins, and dilapidations of his fortress, he was very near at his wit's end; he stormed and swore like a madman, and swelled till he was ready to burst. At length, casting his eye upon the bee, and wisely gathering causes from events, (for they knew each other by sight): "A plague split you," said he, "for a giddy son of a . . . Is it you, with a vengeance, that have made this litter here? Could not you look before you, and be d—d? Do you think I have nothing else to do (in the devil's name) but to mend and repair after you . . .?"—"Good words, friend," said the bee, (having now pruned himself, and being disposed to droll,) "I'll give you my hand and word to come near your kennel no more; I was never in such a confounded pickle since I was born."—"Sirrah," replied the spider, "if it were not for breaking an old custom in our family, never to stir abroad against an enemy, I should come and teach you better manners."—"I pray have patience," said the bee, "or you'll spend your substance, and, for aught I see, you may stand in need of it all, toward the repair of your house."—"Rogue, rogue," replied the spider, "yet, methinks you should have more respect to a person, whom all the world allows to be so much your betters."—"By my troth," said the bee, "the comparison will amount to a very good jest, and you will do me a favour to let me know the reasons that all the world is pleased to use in so hopeful a dispute." At this the spider, having swelled himself into the size and posture of a disputant, began his argument in the true spirit of controversy, with resolution to be heartily scurrilous and angry, to urge on his own reasons, without the least regard to the answers or objections of his opposite, and fully predetermined in his mind against all conviction.

"Not to disparage myself," said he, "by the comparison with such a rascal, what art thou but a vagabond without house or home, without stock or inheritance? Born to no possession of your own, but a pair of wings and a drone-pipe. Your livelihood is a universal plunder upon nature; a freebooter over fields and gardens; and, for the sake of stealing, will rob a nettle as easily as a violet. Whereas I am a domestic animal, furnished with a native stock within myself. This large castle (to shew my improvements in the mathematics) is all built with my own hands, and the materials extracted altogether out of my own person."

"I am glad," answered the bee, "to hear you grant at least that I am come honestly by my wings and my voice; for then, it seems, I am obliged to Heaven alone for my flights and my music; and Providence would never have bestowed on me two such gifts, without designing them for the noblest ends. I visit indeed all the flowers and blossoms of the field and garden; but whatever I collect thence, enriches myself, without the least injury to their beauty, their smell, or their taste. Now, for you and your skill in architecture, and other mathematics, I have little to say: In that building of yours there might, for aught I know, have been labour and method enough; but, by woful experience for us both, it is plain, the materials are naught, and I hope you will henceforth take warning, and consider duration and matter, as well as method and art. You boast, indeed, of being obliged to no other creature, but of drawing and spinning out all from yourself; that is to say, if we may judge of the liquor in the vessel by what issues out, you possess a good plentiful store of dirt and poison in your breast; and, though I would by no means lessen or disparage your genuine stock of either, yet, I doubt you are somewhat obliged, for an increase of both, to a little foreign assistance. Your inherent portion of dirt does not fail of acquisitions, by sweepings exhaled from below; and one insect furnishes you with a share of poison to destroy another. So that, in short, the question comes all to this—Whether is the nobler being of the two, that which, by a lazy contemplation of four inches round, by an overweening pride, feeding and engendering on itself, turns all into excrement and venom, producing nothing at all, but flybane and a cobweb; or that which, by a universal range, with long search, much study, true judgment, and distinction of things, brings home honey and wax."

This dispute was managed with such eagerness, clamour, and warmth, that the two parties of books, in arms below, stood silent a while, waiting in suspense what would be the issue, which was not long undetermined: For the bee, grown impatient at so much loss of time, fled straight away to a bed of roses, without looking for a reply, and left the spider, like an orator, collected in himself, and just prepared to burst out.

It happened upon this emergency, that Æsop broke silence first. He had been of late most barbarously treated by a strange effect of the regent's humanity, who had tore off his title-page, sorely defaced one half of his leaves, and chained him fast among a shelf of Moderns. Where, soon discovering how high the quarrel was likely to proceed, he tried all his arts, and turned himself to a thousand forms. At length, in the borrowed shape of an ass, the regent mistook him for a Modern; by which means he had time and opportunity to escape to the Ancients, just when the spider and the bee were entering into their contest, to which he gave his attention with a world of pleasure; and when it was ended, swore in the loudest key, that in all his life he had never known two cases so parallel and adapt to each other, as that in the window, and this upon the shelves. "The disputants," said he, "have admirably managed the dispute between them, have taken in the full strength of all that is to be said on both sides, and exhausted the substance of every argument *pro* and *con*. It is but to adjust the reasonings of both to the present quarrel, then to compare and apply the labours and fruits of each, as the bee has learnedly deduced them, and we shall find the conclusion fall plain and close upon the Moderns and us. For, pray, gentlemen, was ever anything so modern as the spider in his air, his turns, and his paradoxes? He argues in the behalf of you his brethren and himself, with many boastings of his native stock and great genius; that he spins and spits wholly from himself, and scorns to own any obligation or assistance from without. Then he displays to you his great skill in architecture, and improvement in the mathematics. To all this the bee, as an advocate, retained by us the Ancients, thinks fit to answer—that, if one may judge of the great genius or inventions of the Moderns by what they have produced, you will hardly have countenance to bear you out, in boasting of either. Erect your schemes with as much method and skill as you please; yet if the materials be nothing but dirt, spun out of your own entrails (the guts of modern brains) the edifice will conclude at last in a cobweb, the duration of which, like that of other spiders' webs, may be imputed to their being forgotten, or neglected, or hid in a corner. For anything else of genuine that the Moderns may pretend to, I cannot recollect; unless it be a large vein of wrangling and satire, much of a nature and substance with the spider's poison; which, however they pretend to spit wholly out of themselves, is improved by the same arts, by feeding upon the insects and vermin of the age. As for us the Ancients, we are content, with the bee, to pretend to nothing of our own, beyond our wings and our voice, that is to say, our flights and our language. For the rest, whatever we have got, has been by infinite labour and search, and ranging through every corner of nature; the difference is, that, instead of dirt and poison, we have rather chosen to fill our hives with honey and wax, thus furnishing mankind with the two noblest of things, which are sweetness and light."

When I Come to be Old

Not to marry a young Woman,

Not to keep young Company unless they really desire it.

Not to be peevish or morose, or suspicious.

Not to scorn present Ways, or Wits, or Fashions, or Men, or War, &c.

Not to be fond of Children, *or let them come near me hardly.*

Not to tell the same story over and over to the same People.

Not to be covetous.

Not to neglect decency, or cleanliness, for fear of falling into Nastiness.

Not to be over severe with young People, but give Allowances for their youthful follies and weaknesses.

Not to be influenced by, or give ear to knavish tattling servants, or others.

Not to be too free of advise, nor trouble any but those that desire it.

To desire some good Friends to inform me which of these Resolutions I break, or neglect, and wherein; and reform accordingly.

Not to talk much, nor of myself.

Not to boast of my former beauty, or strength, or favor with Ladies, &c.

Not to hearken to Flatteries, nor conceive I can be beloved by a young woman, et eos qui hereditatem captant, odisse ac vitare.

Not to be positive or opiniative.

Not to set up for observing all these Rules; for fear I should observe none.

From The Journal to Stella

The Killing of Duke Hamilton

London, *Nov.* 15, 1712.

Before this comes to your hands you will have heard of the most terrible accident that hath almost ever happened. This morning at eight my man brought me word that Duke Hamilton had fought with Lord Mohun, and killed him, and was brought home wounded. I immediately sent him to the Duke's house, in St. James's Square; but the porter could hardly answer for tears, and a great rabble was about the house. In short, they fought at seven this morning. The dog Mohun was killed on the spot; and, while the Duke was over him, Mohun shortened his sword, stabbed him in at the shoulder to the heart. The Duke was helped toward the cakehouse by the ring in Hyde Park (where they fought), and died on the grass, before he could reach the house; and was brought home in his coach by eight, while the poor Duchess was asleep. Macartney and one Hamilton were the seconds, who fought likewise, and are both fled. I am told that a footman of Lord Mohun's stabbed Duke Hamilton, and some say Macartney did so too. Mohun gave the affront, and yet sent the challenge. I am infinitely concerned for the poor Duke, who was a frank, honest, good-natured man. I loved him very well, and I think he loved me better. He had the greatest mind in the world to have me go with him to France, but durst not tell it me; and those he did tell said

I could not be spared, which was true. They have removed the poor Duchess to a lodging in the neighbourhood, where I have been with her two hours, and am just come away. I never saw so melancholy a scene; for indeed all reasons for real grief belong to her; nor is it possible for anybody to be a greater loser in all regards. She has moved my very soul. The lodging was inconvenient, and they would have removed her to another; but I would not suffer it, because it had no room backward, and she must have been tortured with the noise of the Grub Street screamers mentioning her husband's murder in her ears.

From GULLIVER'S TRAVELS

Gulliver and the Lilliputians

WHAT became of my companions in the boat, as well as of those who escaped on the rock, or were left in the vessel, I cannot tell; but conclude they were all lost. For my own part, I swam as fortune directed me, and was pushed forward by wind and tide. I often let my legs drop, and could feel no bottom; but when I was almost gone, and able to struggle no longer, I found myself within my depth; and by this time the storm was much abated. The declivity was so small, that I walked near a mile before I got to the shore, which I conjectured was about eight o'clock in the evening. I then advanced forward near half a mile, but could not discover any sign of houses or inhabitants; at least I was in so weak a condition, that I did not observe them. I was extremely tired, and with that, and the heat of the weather, and about half a pint of brandy that I drank as I left the ship, I found myself much inclined to sleep. I lay down on the grass which was very short and soft, where I slept sounder than ever I remember to have done in my life, and, as I reckoned, about nine hours; for when I awaked, it was just day-light. I attempted to rise, but was not able to stir: for as I happened to lie on my back, I found my arms and legs were strongly fastened on each side to the ground; and my hair, which was long and thick, tied down in the same manner. I likewise felt several slender ligatures across my body, from my arm-pits to my thighs. I could only look upwards, the sun began to grow hot, and the light offended my eyes. I heard a confused noise about me, but in the posture I lay, could see nothing except the sky. In a little time I felt something alive moving on my left leg, which advanced gently forward over my breast, came almost up to my chin; when bending my eyes downwards as much as I could, I perceived it to be a human creature not six inches high, with a bow and arrow in his hands, and a quiver at his back.

In the mean time, I felt at least forty more of the same kind (as I conjectured) following the first. I was in the utmost astonishment, and roared so loud, that they all ran back in fright; and some of them, as I was afterwards told, were hurt with the falls they got by leaping from my sides upon the ground. However, they soon returned, and one of them, who ventured so far as to get a full sight of my face, lifting up his hands and eyes by way of admiration, cried out in a shrill, but distinct voice, *Hekinah degul:* the others repeated the same words several times, but then I knew not what they meant. I lay all this while, as the reader may believe, in great uneasiness: at length, struggling to get loose, I had the fortune to break the strings, and wrench out the pegs that fastened my left arm to the ground; for, by lifting it up to my face, I discovered the methods they had to bind me, and at the same time with a violent pull, which gave me excessive pain, I a little loosened the strings that tied down my hair on the left side, so that I was just able to turn my head about two inches. But the creatures ran off a second time, before I could seize them; whereupon there was a great shout in a very shrill accent, and after it ceased, I heard one of them cry aloud *Tolgo phonac;* when in an instant I felt above an hundred arrows discharged on my left hand, which pricked me like so many needles; and besides, they shot another flight into the air, as we do bombs in Europe, whereof many, I suppose, fell on my body, (though I felt them not) and some on my face, which I immediately covered with my left hand. When this shower of arrows was over, I fell agroaning with grief and pain, and then striving again to get loose, they discharged another volley larger than the first, and some of them attempted with spears to stick me in the sides; but, by good luck, I had on a buff jerkin, which they could not pierce. I thought it the most prudent method to lie still, and my design was to continue so till night, when, my left hand being already loose, I could easily free myself: and as for the inhabitants, I had reason to believe I might be a match for the greatest armies they could bring against me, if they were all of the same size with him that I saw. But fortune disposed otherwise of me. When the people observed I was quiet, they discharged no more arrows; but by the noise I heard, I knew their numbers increased; and about four yards from me, over against my right ear, I heard a knocking for above an hour, like that of people at work; when turning my head that way, as well as the pegs and strings would permit me, I saw a stage erected, about a foot and a half from the ground, capable of holding four of the inhabitants, with two or three ladders to mount it: from whence one of them, who seemed to be a person of quality, made me a long speech, whereof I understood not one syllable. But I should have mentioned, that before the principal person began his oration, he cried out three times, *Langro dehul san:* (these words and the former were afterwards repeated and explained to me). Whereupon immediately about fifty of the inhabitants came and cut the strings that fastened the left side of my head, which gave me the liberty of turning it to the right, and of observing the person and gesture of him that was to speak. He appeared to be of a middle age, and taller than any of the other three who attended him, whereof one was a page that held up his train, and seemed to be somewhat longer than my middle finger; the other two stood one on each side to support him. He acted every part of an orator, and I could observe many periods of threatenings, and others of promises, pity and kindness. I answered in a few words, but in the most submissive manner, lifting up my left hand, and both my eyes to the sun, as calling him for a witness; and being almost famished with hunger, having not eaten a morsel for some hours before I left the ship, I found the demands of nature so strong upon me, that I could not forbear showing my impatience (perhaps against the strict rules of decency) by putting my finger frequently on my mouth, to signify that I wanted food. The *Hurgo* (for so they call a great lord, as I afterwards learnt) understood me very well. He descended from the stage, and commanded that several ladders should be applied to my sides, on which above an hundred of the inhabitants mounted and walked towards my mouth, laden with baskets full of meat, which had been provided and sent thither by the King's orders, upon the first intelligence he received of me. I observed there was the flesh of several animals, but could not distinguish them by the taste. There were shoulders, legs, and loins, shaped like those of mutton, and very well dressed, but smaller than the wings of a lark. I eat them by two or three at a mouthful, and took three loaves at a time, about the bigness of musket bullets. They supplied me as fast as they could, showing a thousand marks of wonder and astonishment at my bulk and appetite. I then made another sign that I wanted a drink. They found by my eating, that a small quantity would not suffice me; and being a most ingenious people, they slung up with great dexterity one of their largest hogsheads, then rolled it towards my hand, and beat out the top; I drank it off at a draught, which I might well do, for it did not hold half a pint, and tasted like a small wine of Burgundy, but much more delicious. They brought me a second hogshead, which I drank in the same manner, and made signs for more, but they had none to give me. When I had performed these wonders, they shouted for joy, and danced upon my breast, repeating several times as they did at first, *Hekinah degul.* They made me a sign that I should throw down the two hogsheads, but first warning the people below to stand out of the way, crying aloud, *Borach mivola,* and when they saw the vessels in the air, there was an universal shout of *Hekinah degul.* I confess I was often tempted, while they were passing backwards and forwards on my body, to seize forty or fifty of the first that came in my reach, and dash them against the ground. But the remembrance of what I had felt, which probably might not be the worst they could do, and the promise of honour I made them, for so I interpreted my submissive behavior, soon drove out these imaginations. Besides, I now considered myself as bound by the laws of hospitality to a people who had treated me with so much expense and magnificence. However, in my thoughts, I could not sufficiently wonder at the intrepidity of these diminutive mortals, who durst venture to mount and walk upon my body, while one of my hands was at liberty, without trembling at the very sight of so prodigious a creature as I must appear to them. After some time, when they observed that I made no more demands for meat, there appeared before me a person of high rank from his Imperial Majesty. His Excellency, having mounted on the small of my right leg, advanced forwards up to my face, with about a dozen of his retinue. And producing his credentials under the Signet Royal, which he applied close to my eyes, spoke about ten minutes, without any signs of anger, but with a kind of determinate resolution; often pointing forwards, which, as I afterwards found, was towards the capital city, about half a mile distant, whither it was agreed by his Majesty in council that I must be conveyed. I answered in few words, but to no purpose, and made a sign with my hand that was loose, putting it to the other (but over his Excellency's head for fear of hurting him or his train) and then to my own head and body, to signify that I desired my liberty. It appeared that he understood me well enough, for he shook his head by way of disapprobation, and held his hand in a posture to show that I must be carried as a prisoner. However, he made other signs to let me understand that I should have meat and drink enough, and very good treatment. Whereupon I once more thought of attempting to break my bonds; but again, when I felt the smart of their arrows, upon my face and hands, which were all in blisters, and many of the darts still sticking in them, and observing likewise that the number of my enemies increased, I gave tokens to let them know that they might do with me what they pleased. Upon this, the *Hurgo* and his train withdrew, with much civility and cheerful countenances. Soon after I heard a general shout, with frequent repetitions of the words, *Peplom selan,* and I felt great numbers of people on my left side relaxing the cords to such a degree, that I was able to turn upon my right, and to ease myself. . . . But before this, they had daubed my face and both hands with a sort of ointment very pleasant to the smell, which in a few minutes removed all the smart of their arrows. These circumstances, added to the refreshment I had received by their victuals and drink, which were very nourishing, disposed me to sleep. I slept about eight hours, as I was afterwards assured; and it was no wonder, for the physicians, by the Emperor's order, had mingled a sleepy potion in the hogshead of wine.

It seems that upon the first moment I was discovered sleeping on the ground after my landing, the Emperor had early notice of it by an express; and determined in council that I should be tied in the manner I have related, (which was done in the night while I slept) that plenty of meat and drink should be sent to me, and a machine prepared to carry me to the capital city.

This resolution perhaps may appear very bold and dangerous, and I am confident would not be imitated by any prince in Europe on the like occasion; however, in my opinion, it was extremely prudent, as well as generous: for supposing these people had endeavoured to kill me with their spears and arrows while I was asleep, I should certainly have awaked with the first sense of smart, which might so far have roused my rage and strength, as to have enabled me to break the strings wherewith I was tied; after which, as they were not able to make resistance, so they could expect no mercy.

These people are most excellent mathematicians, and arrived to a great perfection in mechanics, by the countenance and encouragement of the Emperor, who is a renowned patron of learning. This prince hath several machines fixed on wheels, for the carriage of trees and other great weights. He often builds his largest men of war, whereof some are nine foot long, in the woods where the timber grows, and has them carried on these engines three or four hundred yards to the sea. Five hundred carpenters and engineers were immediately set at work to prepare the greatest engine they had. It was a frame of wood raised three inches from the ground, about seven foot long and four wide, moving upon twenty-two wheels. The shout I heard was upon the arrival of this engine, which it seems set out in four hours after my landing. It was brought parallel to me as I lay. But the principal difficulty was to raise and place me in this vehicle. Eighty poles, each of one foot high, were erected for this purpose, and very strong cords of the bigness of packthread were fastened by hooks to many bandages, which the workmen had girt round my neck, my hands, my body, and my legs. Nine hundred of the strongest men were employed to draw up these cords by many pulleys fastened on the poles, and thus, in less than three hours, I was raised and slung into the engine, and there tied fast. All this I was told, for, while the whole operation was performing, I lay in a profound sleep, by the force of that soporiferous medicine infused into my liquor. Fifteen hundred of the Emperor's largest horses, each about four inches and a half high, were employed to draw me towards the metropolis, which, as I said, was half a mile distant.

About four hours after we began our journey, I awaked by a very ridiculous accident; for the carriage being stopped a while to adjust something that was out of order, two or three of the young natives had the curiosity to see how I looked when I was asleep; they climbed up into the engine, and advancing very softly to my face, one of them, an officer in the guards, put the sharp of his half-spike a good way up into my left nostril, which tickled my nose like a straw, and made me sneeze violently: whereupon they stole off unperceived, and it was three weeks before I knew the cause of my awaking so suddenly. We made a long march the remaining part of that day, and rested at night with five hundred guards on each side of me, half with torches, and half with bows and arrows, ready to shoot me if I should offer to stir. The next morning at sunrise, we continued our march, and arrived within two hundred yards of the city gates about noon. The Emperor, and all his court, came to meet us; but his great officers would by no means suffer his Majesty to endanger his person by mounting on my body.

At the place where the carriage stopped, there stood an ancient temple, esteemed to be the largest in the whole kingdom; which having been polluted some years before by an unnatural murder, was, according to the zeal of those people, looked upon as profane, and therefore had been applied to common uses, and all the ornaments and furniture carried away. In this edifice it was determined I should lodge. The great gate fronting to the north was about four foot high, and almost two foot wide, through which I could easily creep. On each side of the gate was a small window not above six inches from the ground: into that on the left side, the King's smiths conveyed fourscore and eleven chains, like those that hang to a lady's watch in Europe, and almost as large, which were locked to my left leg with six and thirty padlocks. Over-against this temple, on t'other side of the great highway, at twenty foot distance, there was a turret at least five foot high. Here the Emperor ascended, with many principal lords of his court, to have an opportunity of viewing me, as I was told, for I could not see them. It was reckoned that above an hundred thousand inhabitants came out of the town upon the same errand; and, in spite of my guards, I believe there could not be fewer than ten thousand at several times, who mounted my body by the help of ladders. But a proclamation was soon issued to forbid it upon the pain of death. When the workmen found it was impossible for me to break loose, they cut all the strings that bound me; whereupon I rose up, with as melancholy a disposition as ever I had in my life. But the noise and astonishment of the people at seeing me rise and walk, are not to be expressed. The chains that held my left leg were about two yards long, and gave me not only the liberty of walking backwards and forwards in a semi-circle; but, being fixed within four inches of the gate, allowed me to creep in, and lie at my full length in the temple.

The Struldbrugs

One day in much good company I was asked by a person of quality, whether I had seen any of their *Struldbrugs,* or *Immortals.* I said I had not, and desired he would explain to me what he meant by such an appellation applied to a mortal creature. He told me, that sometimes, though very rarely, a child happened to be born in a family with a red circular spot in the forehead, directly over the left eyebrow, which was an infallible mark that it should never die. The spot, as he described it, was about the compass of a silver threepence, but in the course of time grew larger, and changed its colour; for at twelve years old it became green, so continued till five and twenty, then turned to a deep blue: at five and forty it grew coal black, and as large as an English shilling, but never admitted any further alteration. He said these births were so rare, that he did not believe there could be above eleven hundred *struldbrugs* of both sexes in the whole kingdom, of which he computed about fifty in the metropolis, and among the rest a young girl born about three years ago. That these productions were not peculiar to any family, but a mere effect of chance; and the children of the *struldbrugs* themselves, were equally mortal with the rest of the people.

After this preface, he gave me a particular account of the *struldbrugs* among them. He said they commonly acted like mortals, till about thirty years old, after which by degrees they grew melancholy and dejected, increasing in both till they came to fourscore. This he learned from their own confession: for otherwise there not being above two or three of that species born in an age, they were too few to form a general observation by. When they came to fourscore years, which is reckoned the extremity of living in this country, they had not only all the follies and infirmities of other old men, but many more which arose from the dreadful prospect of never dying. They were not only opinionative, peevish, covetous, morose, vain, talkative, but uncapable of friendship, and dead to all natural affection, which never descended below their grandchildren. Envy and impotent desires are their prevailing passions. But those objects against which their envy seems principally directed, are the vices of the younger sort, and the deaths of the old. By reflecting on the former, they find themselves cut off from all possibility of pleasure; and whenever they see a funeral, they lament and repine that others have gone to a harbour of rest, to which they themselves never can hope to arrive. They have no remembrance of anything but what they learned and observed in their youth and middle age, and even that is very imperfect. And for the truth or particulars of any fact, it is safer to depend on common traditions than upon their best recollections. The least miserable among them appear to be those who turn to dotage, and entirely lose their memories; these meet with more pity and assistance, because they want many bad qualities which abound in others.

If a *struldbrug* happen to marry one of his own kind, the marriage is dissolved of course by the courtesy of the kingdom, as soon as the younger of the two comes to be fourscore. For the law thinks it a reasonable indulgence, that those who are condemned without any fault of their own to a perpetual continuance in the world, should not have their misery doubled by the load of a wife.

As soon as they have completed the term of eighty years, they are looked on as dead in law; their heirs immediately succeed to their estates, only a small pittance is reserved for their support, and the poor ones are maintained at the public charge. After that period they are held incapable of any employment of trust or profit, they cannot purchase lands or take leases, neither are they allowed to be witnesses in any cause, either civil or criminal, not even for the decision of meers and bounds.

At ninety they lose their teeth and hair, they have at that age no distinction of taste, but eat and drink whatever they can get, without relish or appetite. The diseases they were subject to still continue without increasing or diminishing. In talking they forget the common appellation of things, and the names of persons, even of those who are their nearest friends and relations. For the same reason, they never can amuse themselves with reading, because their memory will not serve to carry them from the beginning of a sentence to the end; and by this defect they are deprived of the only entertainment whereof they might otherwise be capable.

The language of this country being always upon the flux, the *struldbrugs* of one age do not understand those of another, neither are they able after two hundred years to hold any conversation (farther than by a few general words) with their neighbours the mortals; and thus they lie under the disadvantage of living like foreigners in their own country.

This was the account given me of the *struldbrugs,* as near as I can remember. I afterwards saw five or six of different ages, the youngest not above two hundred years old, who were brought to me at several times by some of my friends; but although they were told that I was a great traveller, and had seen all the world, they had not the least curiosity to ask me a question; only desired I would give them *slumskudask,* or a token of remembrance, which is a modest way of begging, to avoid the law that strictly forbids it, because they are provided for by the public, although indeed with a very scanty allowance.

They are despised and hated by all sorts of people; when one of them is born, it is reckoned ominous, and their birth is recorded very particularly: so that you may know their age by consulting the registry, which however hath not been kept above a thousand years past, or at least hath been destroyed by time or public disturbances. But the usual way of computing how old they are, is by asking them what kings or great persons they can remember, and then consulting history, for infallibly the last prince in their mind did not begin his reign after they were fourscore years old.

They were the most mortifying sight I ever beheld, and the women more horrible than the men. Besides the usual deformities in extreme old age, they acquired an additional ghastliness in proportion to their number of years, which is not to be described; and among half a dozen, I soon distinguished which was the eldest, although there was not above a century or two between them.

SIR RICHARD STEELE (1672-1729)

The Tatler, No. 101, June 6, 1710: On Sorrow and Memory

—— Dies, ni fallor, adest, quem semper acerbum,
Semper honoratum, sic dii voluistis habebo.

THERE are those among mankind, who can enjoy no relish of their being, except the world is made acquainted with all that relates to them, and think everything lost that passes unobserved; but others find a solid delight in stealing by the crowd, and modeling their life after such a manner, as is as much above the approbation as the practice of the vulgar. Life being too short to give instances great enough of true friendship or good will, some sages have thought it pious to preserve a certain reverence for the *Manes* of their deceased friends; and have withdrawn themselves from the rest of the world at certain seasons, to commemorate in their own thoughts such of their acquaintance who have gone before them out of this life. And indeed, when we are advanced in years, there is not a more pleasing entertainment, than to recollect in a gloomy moment the many we have parted with, that have been dear and agreeable to us, and to cast a melancholy thought or two after those, with whom, perhaps, we have indulged ourselves in whole nights of mirth and jollity. With such inclinations in my heart I went to my closet yesterday in the evening, and resolved to be sorrowful; upon which occasion I could not but look with disdain upon myself, that though all the reasons which I had to lament the loss of many of my friends are now as forcible as at the moment of their departure, yet did not my heart swell with the same sorrow which I felt at that time; but I could, without tears, reflect upon many pleasing adventures I have had with some, who have long been blended with common earth.

Though it is by the benefit of nature, that length of time thus blots out the violence of afflictions; yet with tempers too much given to pleasure, it is almost necessary to revive the old places of grief in our memory; and ponder step by step on past life, to lead the mind into that sobriety of thought which poises the heart, and makes it beat with due time, without being quickened with desire, or retarded with despair, from its proper and equal motion. When we wind up a clock that is out of order, to make it go well for the future, we do not immediately set the hand to the present instant, but we make it strike the round of all its hours, before it can recover the regularity of its time. Such, thought I, shall be my method this evening; and since it is that day of the year which I dedicate to the memory of such in another life as I much delighted in when living, an hour or two shall be sacred to sorrow and their memory, while I run over all the melancholy circumstances of this kind which have occurred to me in my whole life. The first sense of sorrow I ever knew was upon the death of my father at which time I was not quite five years of age; but was rather amazed at what all the house meant, than possessed with a real understanding why nobody was willing to play with me. I remember I went into the room where his body lay, and my mother sat weeping alone by it. I had my battledore in my hand, and I fell a-beating the coffin, and calling papa; for, I know not how, I had some slight idea that he was locked up there. My mother catched me in her arms, and, transported beyond all patience of the silent grief she was before in, she almost smothered me in her embraces; and told me, in a flood of tears, "Papa could not hear me, and would play with me no more, for they were going to put him under ground, whence he could never come to us again." She was a very beautiful woman, of a noble spirit, and there was a dignity in her grief amidst all the wildness of her transport, which, methought, struck me with an instinct of sorrow, that, before I was sensible of what it was to grieve, seized my very soul, and has made pity the weakness of my heart ever since. The mind in infancy is, methinks, like the body in embryo, and receives impressions so forcible, that they are as hard to be removed by reason, as any mark, with which a child is born, is to be taken away by any future application. Hence it is, that good-nature in me is no merit; but having been so frequently overwhelmed with her tears before I knew the cause of any affliction, or could draw defenses from my own judgment. I imbibed commiseration, remorse, and an unmanly gentleness of mind, which has since ensnared me into ten thousand calamities; from whence I can reap no advantage, except it be, that, in such a humor as I am now in, I can the better indulge myself in the softnesses of humanity, and enjoy that sweet anxiety which arises from the memory of past afflictions.

We, that are very old, are better able to remember things which befel us in our distant youth, than the passages of later days. For this reason it is, that the companions of my strong and vigorous years present themselves more immediately to me in this office of sorrow. Untimely and unhappy deaths are what we are most apt to lament; so little are we able to make it indifferent when a thing happens, though we know it must happen. Thus we groan under life, and bewail those who are relieved from it. Every object that returns to our imagination raises different passions, according to the circumstances of their departure. Who can have lived in an army, and in a serious hour reflect upon the many gay and agreeable men that might long have flourished in the arts of peace, and not join with the imprecations of the fatherless and widow on the tyrant to whose ambition they fell sacrifices? But gallant men, who are cut off by the sword, move rather our veneration than our pity; and we gather relief enough from their own contempt of death, to make that no evil, which was approached with so much cheerfulness, and attended with so much honor. But when we turn our thoughts from the great parts of life on such occasions, and instead of lamenting those who stood ready to give death to those from whom they had the fortune to receive it; I say, when we let our thoughts wander from such noble objects, and consider the havoc which is made among the tender and the innocent, pity enters with an unmixed softness, and possesses all our souls at once.

Here (were there words to express such sentiments with proper tenderness) I should record the beauty, innocence and untimely death, of the first object my eyes ever beheld with love. The beauteous virgin!

how ignorantly did she charm, how carelessly excel! Oh Death! thou hast right to the bold, to the ambitious, to the high, and to the haughty; but why this cruelty to the humble, to the meek, to the undiscerning, to the thoughtless? Nor age, nor business, nor distress, can erase the dear image from my imagination. In the same week, I saw her dressed for a ball, and in a shroud. How ill did the habit of death become the pretty trifler? I still behold the smiling earth—— A large train of disasters were coming on to my memory, when my servant knocked at my closet door, and interrupted me with a letter, attended with a hamper of wine, of the same sort with that which is to be put to sale, on Thursday next, at Garraway's coffee-house. Upon the receipt of it, I sent for three of my friends. We are so intimate, that we can be company in whatever state of mind we meet, and can entertain each other without expecting always to rejoice. The wine we found to be generous and warming, but with such an heat as moved us rather to be cheerful than frolicsome. It revived the spirits, without firing the blood. We commended it until two of the clock this morning; and having to-day met a little before dinner, we found, that though we drank two bottles a man, we had much more reason to recollect than forget what had passed the night before.

The Spectator, No. 468, Wednesday, August 27, 1712: On the Death of Estcourt

Erat homo ingeniosus, acutus, acer, et qui plurimum et salis haberet et fellis, nec candoris minus.—Plin., Epist.

My paper is in a kind a letter of news, but it regards rather what passes in the world of conversation than that of business. I am very sorry that I have at present a circumstance before me which is of very great importance to all who have a relish for gaiety, wit, mirth, or humour. I mean the death of Dick Estcourt. I have been obliged to him for so many hours of jollity, that it is but a small recompense, though all I can give him, to pass a moment or two in sadness for the loss of so agreeable a man. Poor Estcourt! the last time I saw him, we were plotting to show the town his great capacity for acting in its full light, by introducing him as dictating to a set of young players, in what manner to speak this sentence, and utter t'other passion—he had so exquisite a discerning of what was defective in any object before him, that in an instant he could show you the ridiculous side of what would pass for beautiful and just, even to men of no ill judgment, before he had pointed at the failure. He was no less skilful in the knowledge of beauty;

and, I dare say, there is no one who knew him well but can repeat more well-turned compliments, as well as smart repartees, of Mr. Estcourt's than of any other man in England. This was easily to be observed in his inimitable faculty of telling a story, in which he would throw in natural and unexpected incidents, to make his court to one part, and rally the other part of the company. Then he would vary the usage he gave them, according as he saw them bear kind or sharp language. He had the knack to raise up a pensive temper, and mortify an impertinently gay one, with the most agreeable skill imaginable. There are a thousand things which crowd into my memory, which make me too much concerned to tell on about him. Hamlet, holding up the skull which the gravedigger threw to him with an account that it was the head of the king's jester, falls into very pleasing reflections, and cries out to his companion:—

"Alas, poor Yorick!—I knew him, Horatio: a fellow of infinite jest, of most excellent fancy: he hath borne me on his back a thousand times; and now, how abhorred in my imagination it is! my gorge rises at it. Here hung those lips, that I have kissed I know not how oft. Where be your gibes now? your gambols? your songs? your flashes of merriment, that were wont to set the table on a roar? Not one now, to mock your own grinning? quite chap-fallen? Now get you to my lady's chamber, and tell her, let her paint an inch thick, to this favour she must come; make her laugh at that."

It is an insolence natural to the wealthy to affix, as much as in them lies, the character of a man to his circumstances. Thus it is ordinary with them to praise faintly the good qualities of those below them, and say it is very extraordinary in such a man as he is, or the like, when they are forced to acknowledge the value of him whose lowness upbraids their exaltation. It is to this humour only that it is to be ascribed that a quick wit in conversation, a nice judgment upon any emergency that could arise, and a most blameless inoffensive behaviour, could not raise this man above being received only upon the foot of contributing to mirth and diversion. But he was as easy under that condition as a man of so excellent talents was capable; and since they would have it that to divert was his business, he did it with all the seeming alacrity imaginable, though it stung him to the heart that it was his business. Men of sense, who could taste his excellences, were well satisfied to let him lead the way in conversation, and play after his own manner; but fools, who provoked him to mimicry, found he had the indignation to let it be at their expense who called for it, and he would show the form of conceited heavy fellows as jests to the company at their own request, in revenge for interrupting him from being a companion to put on the character of a jester.

What was peculiarly excellent in this memorable companion was, that in the accounts he gave of persons and sentiments, he did not only hit the figure of their faces and manner of their gestures, but he would in his narration fall into their very way of thinking, and this when he recounted passages wherein men of the best wit were concerned, as well as such wherein were represented men of the lowest rank of understanding. It is certainly as great an instance of self-love to a weakness, to be impatient of being mimicked, as any can be imagined. There were none but the vain, the formal, the proud, or those who were incapable of amending their faults, that dreaded him; to others he was in the highest degree pleasing; and I do not know any satisfaction of any indifferent kind I ever tasted so much, as having got over an impatience of seeing myself in the air he could put me when I have displeased him. It is indeed to his exquisite talent this way, more than any philosophy I could read on the subject, that my person is very little of my care; and it is indifferent to me what is said of my shape, my air, my manner, my speech, or my address. It is to poor Estcourt I chiefly owe that I am arrived at the happiness of thinking nothing a diminution to me, but what argues a depravity of my will.

It has as much surprised me as anything in Nature to have it frequently said that he was not a good player: but that must be owing to a partiality for former actors in the parts in which he succeeded them, and judging by comparison of what was liked before, rather than by the nature of the thing. When a man of his wit and smartness could put on an utter absence of common sense in his face, as he did in the character of Bullfinch in the "Northern Lass," and an air of insipid cunning and vivacity in the character of Pounce in the "Tender Husband," it is folly to dispute his capacity and success, as he was an actor.

Poor Estcourt! let the vain and proud be at rest; they will no more disturb their admiration of their dear selves, and thou art no longer to drudge in raising the mirth of stupids, who know nothing of thy merit, for thy maintenance.

It is natural for the generality of mankind to run into reflections upon our mortality when disturbers of the world are laid at rest, but to take no notice when they who can please and divert are pulled from us: but for my part, I cannot but think the loss of such talents as the man of whom I am speaking was master of, a more melancholy instance of mortality than the dissolution of persons of never so high characters in the world, whose pretensions were that they were noisy and mischievous.

But I must grow more succinct, and, as a Spectator, give an account of this extraordinary man who, in his way, never had an equal in any age before him, or in that wherein he lived. I speak of him as a companion, and a man qualified for conversation. His fortune exposed him to an obsequiousness towards the worst sort of company, but his excellent qualities rendered him capable of making the best figure in the most refined. I have been present with him among men of the most delicate taste a whole night, and have known him (for he saw it was desired) keep the discourse to himself the most part of it, and maintain his good humour with a countenance, in a language so delightful, without offence to any person or thing upon earth, still preserving the distance his circumstances obliged him to; I say, I have seen him do all this in such a charming manner that I am sure none of those I hint at will read this without giving him some sorrow for their abundant mirth, and one gush of tears for so many bursts of laughter. I wish it were any honour to the pleasant creature's memory that my eyes are too much suffused to let me go on— T.

JOSEPH ADDISON (1672-1719)

The Spectator, No. 13, March 15, 1711: Signior Nicolini and his Lions

Dic mihi, si fueras tu leo, qualis eris?—Mart.

There is nothing that of late years has afforded matter of greater amusement to the town than Signior Nicolini's combat with a lion in the Haymarket, which has been very often exhibited to the general satisfaction of most of the nobility and gentry in the kingdom of Great Britain. Upon the first rumor of this intended combat, it was confidently affirmed, and is still believed by many in both galleries, that there would be a tame lion sent from the Tower every opera night, in order to be killed by Hydaspes; this report, though altogether groundless, so universally prevailed in the upper regions of the playhouse, that some of the most refined politicians in those parts of the audience gave it out in whisper, that the lion was a cousin-german of the tiger who made his appearance in King William's days, and that the stage would be supplied with lions at the public expense, during the whole session. Many likewise were the conjectures of the treatment which this lion was to meet with from the hands of Signior Nicolini; some supposed that he was to subdue him in recitativo, as Orpheus used to serve the wild beasts in his time, and afterwards to knock him on the head; some fancied that the lion would not pretend to lay his paws upon the hero, by reason of the received opinion, that a lion will not hurt a virgin: several, who pretended to have seen the opera in Italy, had informed their friends, that the lion was to act a part in High-Dutch, and roar twice or thrice to a thorough-base, before he fell at the feet of Hydaspes. To clear up a matter that was so variously reported, I have made it my business to examine whether this pretended lion is really the savage he appears to be, or only a counterfeit.

But before I communicate my discoveries, I must acquaint the reader, that upon my walking behind the scenes last winter, as I was thinking on something else, I accidentally justled against a monstrous animal that extremely startled me, and upon my nearer survey of it, appeared to be a lion rampant. The lion, seeing me very much surprised, told me, in a gentle voice, that I might come by him if I pleased: "for," (says he,) "I do not intend to hurt anybody." I thanked him very kindly, and passed by him. And in a little time after saw him leap upon the stage, and act his part with great applause. It has been observed by several, that the lion has changed his manner of acting twice or thrice since his first appearance; which will not seem strange, when I acquaint my reader that the lion has been changed upon the audience three several times. The first lion was a candle-snuffer, who being a fellow of a testy, choleric temper, overdid his part, and would not suffer himself to be killed so easily as he ought to have done; besides, it was observed of him, that he grew more surly every time he came out of the lion, and having dropt some words in ordinary conversation, as if he had not fought his best, and that he suffered himself to be thrown upon his back in the scuffle, and that he would wrestle with Mr. Nicolin for what he pleased, out of his lion's skin, it was thought proper to discard him: and it is verily believed, to this day, that had he been brought upon the stage another time, he could certainly have done mischief. Besides, it was objected against the first lion, that he reared himself so high upon his hinder paws, and walked in so erect a posture, that he looked more like an old man than a lion.

The second lion was a tailor by trade, who belonged to the playhouse, and had the character of a mild and peaceable man in his profession. If the former was too furious, this was too sheepish, for his part; insomuch that after a short modest walk upon the stage, he would fall at the first touch of Hydaspes, without grappling with him, and giving him an opporunity of showing his variety of Italian trips: it is said indeed, that he once gave him a rip in his flesh-colour doublet; but this was only to make work for himself, in his private character of a tailor. I must not omit that it was this second lion who treated me with so much humanity behind the scenes.

The acting lion at present is, as I am informed, a country gentleman, who does it for his diversion, but desires his name may be concealed. He says very handsomely in his own excuse, that he does not act for gain, that he indulges an innocent pleasure in it; and that it is better to pass away an evening in this manner, than in gaming and drinking: but at the same time says, with a very agreeable raillery upon himself, that if his name should be known, the ill-natured world might call him "The ass in the lion's skin." This gentleman's temper is made out of such a happy mixture of the mild and the choleric, that he outdoes both his predecessors, and has drawn together greater audiences than have been known in the memory of man.

I must not conclude my narrative, without taking notice of a groundless report that has been raised, to a gentleman's disadvantage of whom I must declare myself an admirer; namely, that Signior Nicolini and the lion have been seen sitting peaceably by one another, and smoking a pipe together, behind the scenes; by which their common enemies would insinuate, that it is but a sham combat which they represent upon the stage: but, upon inquiry I find, that if any such correspondence has passed between them, it was not till the combat was over, when the lion was to be looked upon as dead, according to the received rules of the drama. Besides, this is what is practised every day in Westminster hall, where nothing is more usual than to see a couple of lawyers, who have been tearing each other to pieces in the court, embracing one another as soon as they are out of it.

I would not be thought, in any part of this relation, to reflect upon Signior Nicolini, who in acting this part only complies with the wretched taste of his audience; he knows very well, that the lion has many more admirers than himself; as they say of the famous equestrian statue on the Pont-Neuf at Paris, that more people go to see the horse, than the king who sits upon it. On the contrary, it gives me a just indignation to see a person whose action gives new majesty to kings, resolution to heroes, and softness to lovers, thus sinking from the greatness of his behavior, and degraded into the character of the London Prentice. I have often wished that our tragedians would copy after this great master in action. Could they make the same use of their arms and legs, and inform their faces with as significant looks and passions, how glorious would an English tragedy appear with that action, which is capable of giving a dignity to the forced thoughts, cold conceits, and unnatural expressions of an Italian opera. In the mean time, I have related this combat of the lion, to show what are at present the reigning entertainments of the politer part of Great Britain.

Audiences have often been reproached by writers for the coarseness of their tastes; but our present grievance does not seem to be the want of a good taste, but of common sense.

The Spectator, No. 159, September 1, 1711: The Vision of Mirzah

—Omnem, quæ nunc obducta tuenti
Mortales hebetat visus tibi, et humida circum
Caligat, nubem eripiam—
—VIRG. Æn. ii. 604.

WHEN I was at Grand Cairo, I picked up several Oriental manuscripts, which I have still by me. Among others I met with one entitled The Visions of Mirza, which I have read over with great pleasure. I intend to give it to the public when I have no other entertainment for them; and shall begin with the first vision, which I have translated word for word as follows:—

"On the fifth day of the moon, which according to the custom of my forefathers I always keep holy, after having washed myself, and offered up my morning devotions, I ascended the high hills of Bagdad, in order to pass the rest of the day in meditation and prayer. As I was here airing myself on the tops of the mountains, I fell into a profound contemplation on the vanity of human life; and passing from one thought to another, 'Surely,' said I, 'man is but a shadow, and life a dream.' Whilst I was thus musing, I cast my eyes towards the summit of a rock that was not far from me, where I discovered one in the habit of a shepherd, with a musical instrument in his hand. As I looked upon him he applied it to his lips, and began to play upon it. The sound of it was exceedingly sweet, and wrought into a variety of tunes that were inexpressibly melodious, and altogether different from anything I had ever heard. They put me in mind of those heavenly airs that are played to the departed souls of good men upon their first arrival in Paradise, to wear out the impressions of their last agonies, and qualify them for the pleasures of that happy place. My heart melted away in secret raptures.

"I had been often told that the rock before me was the haunt of a Genius; and that several had been entertained with music who had passed by it, but never heard that the musician had before made himself visible. When he had raised my thoughts by those transporting airs which he played to taste the pleasures of his conversation, as I looked upon him like one astonished, he beckoned to me, and by the waving of his hand directed me to approach the place where he sat. I drew near with that reverence which is due to a superior nature; and as my heart was entirely subdued by the captivating strains I had heard, I fell down at his feet and wept. The Genius smiled upon me with a look of compassion and affability that familiarized him to my imagination, and at once dispelled all the fears and apprehensions with which I approached him. He lifted me from the ground, and taking me by the hand, 'Mirza,' said he, 'I have heard thee in thy soliloquies; follow me.'

"He then led me to the highest pinnacle of the rock, and placing me on the top of it, 'Cast thy eyes eastward,' said he, 'and tell me what thou seest.' 'I see,' said I, 'a huge valley, and a prodigious tide of water rolling through it.' 'The valley that thou seest,' said he, 'is the Vale of Misery, and the tide of water that thou seest is part of the great Tide of Eternity.' 'What is the reason,' said I, 'that the tide I see rises out of a thick mist at one end, and again loses itself in a thick mist at the other?' 'What thou seest,' said he, 'is that portion of eternity which is called time, measured out by the sun, and reaching from the beginning of the world to its consummation. Examine now,' said he, 'this sea that is bounded with darkness at both ends, and tell me what thou discoverest in it.' 'I see a bridge,' said I, 'standing in the midst of the tide.' 'The bridge thou seest,' said he, 'is Human Life: consider it attentively.' Upon a more leisurely survey of it, I found that it consisted of three score and ten entire arches, with several broken arches, which added to those that were entire, made up the number about a hundred. As I was counting the arches, the Genius told me that this bridge consisted at first of a thousand arches; but that a great flood swept away the rest, and left the bridge in the ruinous condition I now beheld it. 'But tell me farther,' said he, 'what thou discoverest on it.' 'I see multitudes of people passing over it,' said I, 'and a black cloud hanging on each end of it.' As I looked more attentively, I saw several of the passengers dropping through the bridge into the great tide that flowed underneath it; and upon farther examination, perceived there were innumerable trap-doors that lay concealed in the bridge, which the passengers no sooner trod upon, but they fell through them into the tide, and immediately disappeared. These hidden pitfalls were set very thick at the entrance of the bridge, so that throngs of people no sooner broke through the cloud, but many of them fell into them. They grew thinner towards the middle, but multiplied and lay closer together towards the end of the arches that were entire.

"There were indeed some persons, but their number was very small, that continued a kind of hobbling march on the broken arches, but fell through one after another, being quite tired and spent with so long a walk.

"I passed some time in the contemplation of this wonderful structure, and the great variety of objects which it presented. My heart was filled with a deep melancholy to see several dropping unexpectedly in the midst of mirth and jollity, and catching at everything that stood by them to save themselves. Some were looking up towards the heavens in a thoughtful posture, and in the midst of a speculation stumbled and fell out of sight. Multitudes were very busy in the pursuit of bubbles that glittered in their eyes and danced before them; but often when they thought themselves within the reach of them, their footing failed and down they sunk. In this confusion of objects, I observed some with scimitars in their hands, and others with urinals, who ran to and fro upon the bridge, thrusting several persons on trap-doors which did not seem to lie in their way, and which they might have escaped had they not been thus forced upon them.

"The Genius seeing me indulge myself on this melancholy prospect, told me I had dwelt long enough upon it. 'Take thine eyes off the bridge,' said he, 'and tell me if thou yet seest anything thou dost not comprehend.' Upon looking up, 'What mean,' said I, 'those great flights of birds that are perpetually hovering about the bridge, and settling upon it from time to time? I see vultures, harpies, ravens, cormorants, and among many other feathered creatures several little winged boys, that perch in great numbers upon the middle arches.' 'These,' said the Genius, 'are Envy, Avarice, Superstition, Despair, Love, with the like cares and passions that infest human life.'

"I here fetched a deep sigh. 'Alas,' said I, 'Man was made in vain! how is he given away to misery and mortality! tortured in life, and swallowed up in death!' The Genius being moved with compassion towards me, bid me quit so uncomfortable a prospect. 'Look no more,' said he, 'on man in the first stage of his existence, in his setting out for eternity; but cast thine eye on that thick mist into which the tide bears the several generations of mortals that fall into it.' I directed my sight as I was ordered, and (whether or no the good Genius strengthened it with any supernatural force, or dissipated part of the mist that was before too thick for the eye to penetrate) I saw the valley opening at the farther end, and spreading forth into an immense ocean, that had a huge rock of adamant running through the midst of it, and dividing it into two equal parts. The clouds still rested on one half of it, insomuch that I could discover nothing in it; but the other appeared to me a vast ocean planted with innumerable islands, that were covered with fruits and flowers, and interwoven with a thousand little shining seas that ran among them. I could see persons dressed in glorious habits with garlands upon their heads, passing among the trees, lying down by the sides of fountains, or resting on beds of flowers; and could hear a confused harmony of singing birds, falling waters, human voices, and musical instruments. Gladness grew in me upon the discovery of so delightful a scene. I wished for the wings of an eagle, that I might fly away to those happy seats; but the Genius told me there was no passage to them, except through the gates of death that I saw opening every moment upon the bridge. 'The islands,' said he, 'that lie so fresh and green before thee, and with which the whole face of the ocean appears spotted as far as thou canst see, are more in number than the sands on the seashore: there are myriads of islands behind those which thou here discoverest, reaching farther than thine eye, or even thine imagination can extend itself. These are the mansions of good men after death, who, according to the degree and kinds of virtue in which they excelled, are distributed among these several islands, which abound with pleasures of different kinds and degrees, suitable to the relishes and perfections of those who are settled in them: every island is a paradise accommodated to its respective inhabitants. Are not these, O Mirza, habitations worth contending for? Does life appear miserable that gives thee opportunities of earning such a reward? Is death to be feared that will convey thee to so happy an existence? Think not man was made in vain, who has such an eternity reserved for him.' I gazed with inexpressible pleasure on these happy islands. At length, said I, 'Show me now, I beseech thee, the secrets that lie hid under those dark clouds which cover the ocean on the other side of the rock of adamant.' The Genius making me no answer, I turned me about to address myself to him a second time, but I found that he had left me; I then turned again to the vision which I had been so long contemplating; but instead of the rolling tide, the arched bridge, and the happy islands, I saw nothing but the long hollow valley of Bagdad, with oxen, sheep, and camels grazing upon the sides of it."

C.

ALEXANDER POPE (1688-1744)

Ode on Solitude

Happy the man, whose wish and care
A few paternal acres bound,
Content to breathe his native air
In his own ground:

Whose herds with milk, whose fields with bread,
Whose flocks supply him with attire;
Whose trees in summer yield him shade,
In winter fire:

Blest, who can unconcern'dly find
Hours, days, and years slide soft away
In health of body, peace of mind,
Quiet by day:

Sound sleep by night; study and ease
Together mixt, sweet recreation,
And innocence, which most does please
With meditation.

Thus let me live, unseen, unknown;
Thus unlamented let me die;
Steal from the world, and not a stone
Tell where I lie.

From The Rape of the Lock

At the suggestion of Mr. John Caryll, a gentleman who was secretary to Queen Mary, wife of James II, Pope wrote the "heroi-comical poem," *The Rape of the Lock,* in order to put an end, by this sparkling satire, to a quarrel that had arisen between two noble families, on the occasion of Lord Petre's having cut off a lock of Miss Arabella Fermor's hair. The machinery of sylphs is based on the Rosicrucian ideas of spirits living in the elements.

For lo! the board with cups and spoons is crowned,
The berries crackle, and the mill turns round;
On shining altars of Japan they raise
The silver lamp; the fiery spirits blaze;
From silver spouts the grateful liquors glide,
While China's earth receives the smoking tide:
At once they gratify their scent and taste,
And frequent cups prolong the rich repast,
Straight hover round the fair her airy band;
Some, as she sipped, the fuming liquor fanned,
Some o'er her lap their careful plumes displayed,
Trembling, and conscious of the rich brocade.
Coffee (which makes the politician wise,
And see through all things with his half-shut eyes)
Sent up in vapours to the baron's brain
New stratagems the radiant lock to gain.
Ah, cease, rash youth! desist ere 'tis too late!
Fear the just gods, and think of Scylla's fate!
Changed to a bird, and sent to flit in air,
She dearly pays for Nisus' injured hair!
But when to mischief mortals bend their will,
How soon they find fit instruments of ill!
Just then Clarissa drew with tempting grace
A two-edged weapon from her shining case:
So ladies in romance assist their knight,
Present the spear, and arm him for the fight.
He takes the gift with reverence, and extends
The little engine on his fingers' ends;
This just behind Belinda's neck he spread,
As o'er the fragant steam she bends her head.
Swift to the lock a thousand sprites repair,
A thousand wings, by turns, blow back the hair;
And thrice they twitched the diamond in her ear;
Thrice she looked back, and thrice the foe drew near.
Just in that instant, anxious Ariel sought
The close recesses of the virgin's thought;
As on the nosegay in her breast reclined,

He watched th' ideas rising in her mind,
Sudden he viewed, in spite of all her art,
An earthly lover lurking at her heart.
Amazed, confused, he found his power expired,
Resigned to fate, and with a sigh retired.
The peer now spreads the glittering forfex wide,
T' inclose the lock; now joins it, to divide.
E'en then, before the fatal engine closed,
A wretched sylph too fondly interposed;
Fate urged the shears, and cut the sylph in twain,
(But airy substance soon unites again).
The meeting points the sacred hair dissever
From the fair head, forever, and forever!
Then flashed the living lightning from her eyes,
And screams of horror rend th' affrighted skies.
Not louder shrieks to pitying Heaven are cast,
When husbands, or when lap-dogs breathe their last;
Or when rich China vessels fallen from high,
In glittering dust and painted fragments lie!

HENRY FIELDING (1707-1754)

From TOM JONES

Partridge Sees Garrick's "Hamlet"

The party attending Garrick's performance of *Hamlet,* in the following selection, consists of Mrs. Miller, her younger daughter, Tom Jones, and Partridge. Partridge is Mr. Jones's attendant, faithful, observant, and not without shrewdness, but somewhat simple, and innocent of common sense. In his earlier days in the country, he had been a harmless failure as a schoolmaster and a husband; he had been a clerk also, and had had a sexton under him, as he informs us here.

In the first row then of the first gallery did Mr. Jones, Mrs. Miller, her youngest daughter, and Partridge, take their places. Partridge immediately declared that it was the finest place he had ever been in. When the first music was played, he said, "It was a wonder how so many fiddlers could play at one time, without putting one another out." While the fellow was lighting the upper candles, he cried out to Mrs. Miller, "Look, look, madam, the very picture of the man in the end of the common-prayer book before the gunpowder-treason service." Nor could he help observing, with a sigh, when all the candles were lighted, "That here were candles enough burnt in one night, to keep an honest poor family for a whole twelvemonth."

As soon as the play, which was Hamlet, Prince of Denmark, began, Partridge was all attention, nor did he break silence till the entrance of the ghost; upon which he asked Jones, "What man that was in the strange dress; something," said he, "like what I have seen in a picture? Sure it is not armour, is it?" Jones answered, "That is the ghost."

To which Partridge replied with a smile, "Persuade me to that, sir, if you can. Though I can't say I ever actually saw a ghost in my life, yet I am certain I should know one, if I saw him, better than that comes to. No, no, sir, ghosts don't appear in such dresses as that, neither." In this mistake, which caused much laughter in the neighbourhood of Partridge, he was suffered to continue, till the scene between the ghost and Hamlet, when Partridge gave that credit to Mr. Garrick, which he had denied to Jones, and fell into so violent a trembling, that his knees knocked against each other. Jones asked him what was the matter, and whether he was afraid of the warrior upon the stage? "O la! sir," said he, "I perceive now it is what you told me. I am not afraid of anything; for I know it is but a play. And if it was really a ghost, it could do one no harm at such a distance, and in so much company; and yet if I was frightened, I am not the only person." "Why, who," cries Jones, "dost thou take to be such a coward here besides thyself?" "Na, you may call me coward if you will; but if that little man there upon the stage is not frightened, I never saw any man frightened in my life. Ay, ay: go along with you: Ay, to be sure! Who's fool then? Will you? Lud have mercy upon such foolhardiness!—Whatever happens, it is good enough for you.——Follow you? I'd follow the devil as soon. Nay, perhaps it is the devil——for they say he can put on what likeness he pleases.—Oh! here he is again.——No farther! No, you have gone far enough already; farther than I'd have gone for all the king's dominions." Jones offered to speak, but Partridge cried, "Hush, hush! dear sir, don't you hear him?" And during the whole speech of the ghost, he sat with his eyes fixed partly on the ghost and partly on Hamlet, and with his mouth open; the same passions which succeeded each other in Hamlet, succeeding likewise in him.

When the scene was over, Jones said, "Why, Partridge, you exceed my expectations. You enjoy the play more than I conceived possible." "Nay, sir," answered Partridge, "if you are not afraid of the devil, I can't help it; but to be sure, it is natural to be surprised at such things, though I know there is nothing in them: not that it was the ghost that surprised me, neither; for I should have known that to have been only a man in a strange dress; but when I saw the little man so frightened himself, it was that which took hold of me." "And dost thou imagine, then, Partridge," cries Jones, "that he was really frightened?" "Nay, sir," said Partridge, "did not you yourself observe afterwards, when he found it was his own father's spirit, and how he was murdered in the garden, how his fear forsook him by degrees, and he was struck dumb with sorrow, as it were, just as I should have been, had it been my own case?—But hush! O la! what noise is that? There he is again.——Well to be certain, though I know there is nothing at all in it, I am glad I am not down yonder, where those men are." Then turning his eyes again upon Hamlet, "Ay, you may draw your sword; what signifies a sword against the power of the devil?"

During the second act, Partridge made very few remarks. He greatly admired the fineness of the dresses; nor could he help observing upon the king's countenance. "Well," said he, "how people may be deceived by faces! *Nulla fides fronti* is, I find, a true saying. Who would think, by looking in the king's face, that he had ever committed a murder?" He then inquired after the ghost; but Jones, who intended he should be surprised, gave him no other satisfaction, than, "that he might possibly see him again soon, and in a flash of fire."

Partridge sat in a fearful expectation of this; and now, when the ghost made his next appearance, Partridge cried out, "There, sir, now; what say you now? is he frightened now or no? As much frightened as you think me, and, to be sure, nobody can help some fears. I would not be in so bad a condition as what's his name, squire Hamlet, is there, for all the world. Bless me! what's become of the spirit? As I am a living soul, I thought I saw him sink into the earth." "Indeed, you saw right," answered Jones. "Well, well," cries Partridge, "I know it is only a play: and besides, if there was anything in all this, Madam Miller would not laugh so; for as to you, sir, you would not be afraid, I believe, if the devil was here in person.—There, there—Ay, no wonder you are in such a passion, shake the vile wicked wretch to pieces. If she was my own mother, I would serve her so. To be sure, all duty to a mother is forfeited by such wicked doings.——Ay, go about your business, I hate the sight of you."

Our critic was now pretty silent till the play, which Hamlet introduces before the king. This he did not at first understand, till Jones explained it to him; but he no sooner entered into the spirit of it, than he began to bless himself that he had never committed murder. Then turning to Mrs. Miller, he asked her, "If she did not imagine the king looked as if he was touched; though he is," said he, "a good actor, and doth all he can to hide it. Well, I would not have so much to answer for, as that wicked man there hath, to sit upon a much higher chair than he sits upon. No wonder he run away; for your sake I'll never trust an innocent face again."

The grave-digging scene next engaged the attention of Partridge, who expressed much surprise at the number of skulls thrown upon the stage. To which Jones answered, "That it was one of the most famous burial-places about town." "No wonder then," cries Partridge, "that the place is haunted. But I never saw in my life a worse grave-digger. I had a sexton, when I was clerk, that should have dug three graves while he is digging one. The fellow handles a spade as if it was the first time he had ever had one in his hand. Ay, ay, you may sing. You had rather sing than work, I believe."—Upon Hamlet's taking up the skull, he cried out, "Well! it is strange to see how fearless some men are: I never could bring myself to touch anything belonging to a dead man, on any account.—He seemed frightened enough too at the ghost, I thought. *Nemo omnibus horis sapit.*"

Little more worth remembering occurred during the play, at the end of which Jones asked him, "Which of the players he had liked best?" To this he answered, with some appearance of indignation at the question, "The king, without doubt." "Indeed, Mr. Partridge," says Mrs. Miller, "you are not of the same opinion with the town; for they are all agreed, that Hamlet is acted by the best player who ever was on the stage." "He is the best player!" cries Partridge, with a contemptuous sneer, "why, I could act as well as he myself. I am sure, if I had seen a ghost, I should have looked in the very same manner, and done just as he did. And then, to be sure, in that scene, as you called it, between him and his mother, where you told me he acted so fine, why, Lord help me, any man, that is, any good man, that had such a mother, would have done exactly the same. I know you are only joking with me; but indeed, madam, though I was never at a play in London, yet I have seen acting before in the country; and the king for my money; he speaks all his words distinctly, half as loud again as the other.—Anybody may see he is an actor."

Thus ended the adventure at the playhouse; where Partridge had afforded great mirth, not only to Jones and Mrs. Miller, but to all who sat within hearing, who were more attentive to what he said, than to anything that passed on the stage.

He durst not go to bed all that night, for fear of the ghost; and for many nights after sweated two or three hours before he went to sleep, with the same apprehensions, and waked several times in great horrors, crying out, "Lord have mercy upon us! there it is."

SAMUEL JOHNSON (1709-1784)

The Vanity of Human Wishes

Let observation with extensive view,
Survey mankind, from China to Peru;
Remark each anxious toil, each eager strife,
And watch the busy scenes of crowded life;
Then say how hope and fear, desire and hate,
O'erspread with snares the clouded maze of fate,
Where wav'ring man, betray'd by vent'rous pride,
To tread the dreary paths without a guide;
As treach'rous phantoms in the mist delude,
Shuns fancied ills, or chases airy good.
How rarely reason guides the stubborn choice,
Rules the bold hand, or prompts the suppliant voice;
How nations sink, by darling schemes oppress'd,
When vengeance listens to the fool's request.
Fate wings with ev'ry wish th' afflictive dart,
Each gift of nature, and each grace of art;
With fatal heat impetuous courage glows,
With fatal sweetness elocution flows;
Impeachment stops the speaker's pow'rful breath,
And restless fire precipitates on death.

But scarce observ'd, the knowing and the bold
Fall in the gen'ral massacre of gold;
Wide-wasting pest; that rages unconfin'd,
And crowds with crimes the records of mankind;
For gold his sword the hireling ruffian draws,
For gold the hireling judge distorts the laws;
Wealth heap'd on wealth, nor truth nor safety buys,
The dangers gather as the treasures rise.

Let hist'ry tell where rival kings command,
And dubious title shakes the madded land,
When statutes glean the refuse of the sword,
How much more safe the vassal than the lord,
Low skulks the hind beneath the rage of pow'r,
And leaves the wealthy traitor in the Tow'r,
Untouch'd his cottage, and his slumbers sound,
Tho' confiscation's vultures hover round.

The needy traveller, serene and gay,
Walks the wild heath, and sings his toil away.
Does envy seize thee? crush th' upbraiding joy,
Increase his riches, and his peace destroy;
New fears in dire vicissitude invade,
The rustling brake alarms, and quiv'ring shade;
Nor light nor darkness bring his pain relief,
One shews the plunder, and one hides the thief.

Yet still one gen'ral cry the skies assails,
And gain and grandeur load the tainted gales;
Few know the toiling statesman's fear or care,
Th' insidious rival and the gaping heir.

Once more, Democritus, arise on earth,
With cheerful wisdom and instructive mirth,
See motley life in modern trappings dress'd,
And feed with varied fools th' eternal jest:
Thou who couldst laugh where want enchain'd caprice,
Toil crush'd conceit, and man was of a piece;

Where wealth unlov'd without a mourner dy'd;
And scarce a sycophant was fed by pride;
Where ne'er was known the form of mock debate,
Or seen a new-made mayor's unwieldy state;
Where change of fav'rites made no change of laws,
And senates heard before they judg'd a cause;
How wouldst thou shake at Britain's modish tribe,
Dart the quick taunt, and edge the piercing gibe?
Attentive truth and nature to decry,
And pierce each scene with philosophic eye,
To thee were solemn toys or empty show,
The robes of pleasure and the veils of woe:
All aid the farce, and all thy mirth maintain,
Whose joys are causeless, or whose griefs are vain.

Such was the scorn that fill'd the sage's mind,
Renew'd at ev'ry glance on human kind;
How just that scorn ere yet thy voice declare,
Search every state, and canvass ev'ry pray'r.

Unnumber'd suppliants crowd Preferment's gate,
Athirst for wealth, and burning to be great;
Delusive Fortune hears th' incessant call,
They mount, they shine, evaporate, and fall.
On ev'ry stage the foes of peace attend,
Hate dogs their flight, and insult mocks their end.
Love ends with hope, the sinking statesman's door
Pours in the morning worshipper no more;
For growing names the weekly scribbler lies,
To growing wealth the dedicator flies;
From ev'ry room descends the painted face,
That hung the bright Palladium of the place,
And smok'd in kitchens, or in auctions sold,
To better features yields the frame of gold;
For now no more we trace in ev'ry line
Heroic worth, benevolence divine:
The form distorted justifies the fall,
And detestation rids th' indignant wall.

But will not Britain hear the last appeal,
Sign her foes' doom, or guard her fav'rites' zeal?
Thro' Freedom's sons no more remonstrance rings,
Degrading nobles and controlling kings;
Our supple tribes repress their patriot throats,
And ask no questions but the price of votes;
With weekly libels and septennial ale,
Their wish is full to riot and to rail.

In full-blown dignity, see Wolsey stand,
Law in his voice, and fortune in his hand:
To him the church, the realm, their pow'rs consign,
Thro' him the rays of regal bounty shine,
Still to new heights his restless wishes tow'r,
Claim leads to claim, and pow'r advances pow'r;
Till conquest unresisted ceas'd to please,
And rights submitted, left him none to seize.
At length his sovereign frowns—the train of state
Mark the keen glance, and watch the sign to hate.
Where'er he turns he meets a stranger's eye,
His suppliants scorn him, and his followers fly;
At once is lost the pride of awful state,
The golden canopy, the glitt'ring plate,
The regal palace, the luxurious board,

The liv'ried army, and the menial lord.
With age, with cares, with maladies oppress'd,
He seeks the refuge of monastic rest.
Grief aids disease, remember'd folly stings,
And his last sighs reproach the faith of kings.

Speak thou, whose thoughts at humble peace repine,
Shall Wolsey's wealth, with Wolsey's end, be thine?
Or liv'st thou now, with safer pride content,
The wisest justice on the banks of Trent?
For why did Wolsey near the steeps of fate,
On weak foundations raise th' enormous weight?
Why but to sink beneath misfortune's blow,
With louder ruin to the gulphs below?

What gave great Villiers to th' assassin's knife,
And fix'd disease on Harley's closing life?
What murder'd Wentworth, and what exil'd Hyde,
By kings protected, and to kings ally'd?
What but their wish indulg'd in courts to shine,
And pow'r too great to keep, or to resign?

When first the college rolls receive his name,
The young enthusiast quits his ease for fame;
Through all his veins the fever of renown
Spreads from the strong contagion of the gown;
O'er Bodley's dome his future labours spread,
And Bacon's mansion trembles o'er his head.
Are these thy views? proceed, illustrious youth,
And virtue guard thee to the throne of Truth!
Yet should thy soul indulge the gen'rous heat,
Till captive Science yields her last retreat;
Should Reason guide thee with her brightest ray,
And pour on misty Doubt resistless day;
Should no false Kindness lure to loose delight,
Nor Praise relax, nor Difficulty fright;
Should tempting Novelty thy cell refrain,
And Sloth effuse her opiate fumes in vain;
Should Beauty blunt on fops her fatal dart,
Nor claim the triumph of a letter'd heart;
Should no Disease thy torpid veins invade,
Nor Melancholy's phantoms haunt thy shade;
Yet hope not life from grief or danger free,
Nor think the doom of man revers'd for thee:
Deign on the passing world to turn thine eyes,
And pause awhile from letters, to be wise;
There mark what ills the scholar's life assail,
Toil, envy, want, the patron, and the jail.
See nations slowly wise, and meanly just,
To buried merit raise the tardy bust.
If dreams yet flatter, once again attend,
Hear Lydiat's life, and Galileo's end.

Nor deem, when Learning her last prize bestows,
The glitt'ring eminence exempt from woes;
See when the vulgar 'scape, despis'd or aw'd,
Rebellion's vengeful talons seize on Laud.
From meaner minds, tho' smaller fines content
The plunder'd palace or sequester'd rent;
Mark'd out by dang'rous parts he meets the shock,
And fatal learning leads him to the block:
Around his tomb let Art and Genius weep,

But hear his death, ye blockheads, hear and sleep.
The festal blazes, the triumphal show,
The ravish'd standard, and the captive foe,
The senate's thanks, the gazette's pompous tale,
With force resistless o'er the brave prevail.
Such bribes the rapid Greek o'er Asia whirl'd,
For such the steady Romans shook the world;
For such in distant lands the Britons shine,
And stain with blood the Danube or the Rhine;
This pow'r has praise, that virtue scarce can warm,
Till fame supplies the universal charm.
Yet Reason frowns on War's unequal game,
Where wasted nations raise a single name,
And mortgag'd states their grandsires' wreaths regret,
From age to age in everlasting debt;
Wreaths which at last the dear-bought right convey
To rust on medals, or on stones decay.
On what foundation stands the warrior's pride,
How just his hopes, let Swedish Charles decide;
A frame of adamant, a soul of fire,
No dangers fright him, and no labours tire;
O'er love, o'er fear, extends his wide domain,
Unconquer'd lord of pleasure and of pain;
No joys to him pacific sceptres yield,
War sounds the trump, he rushes to the field;
Behold surrounding kings their pow'rs combine,
And one capitulate, and one resign;
Peace courts his hand, but spreads her charms in vain;
"Think nothing gain'd," he cries, "till nought remain,
On Moscow's walls till Gothic standards fly,
And all be mine beneath the polar sky."
The march begins in military state,
And nations on his eye suspended wait;
Stern Famine guards the solitary coast,
And Winter barricades the realms of Frost;
He comes, nor want nor cold his course delay;—
Hide, blushing Glory, hide Pultowa's day:
The vanquish'd hero leaves his broken bands,
And shews his miseries in distant lands;
Condemn'd a needy supplicant to wait,
While ladies interpose, and slaves debate.
But did not Chance at length her error mend?
Did no subverted empire mark his end?
Did rival monarchs give the fatal wound?
Or hostile millions press him to the ground?
His fall was destin'd to a barren strand,
A petty fortress, and a dubious hand;
He left the name, at which the world grew pale,
To point a moral, or adorn a tale.
All times their scenes of pompous woes afford,
From Persia's tyrant, to Bavaria's lord.
In gay hostility, and barb'rous pride,
With half mankind embattled at his side,
Great Xerxes comes to seize the certain prey,
And starves exhausted regions in his way;
Attendant Flatt'ry counts his myriads o'er,
Till counted myriads soothe his pride no more;
Fresh praise is try'd till madness fires his mind,
The waves he lashes, and enchains the wind;
New pow'rs are claim'd, new pow'rs are still bestow'd,

Till rude resistance lops the spreading god;
The daring Greeks deride the martial show,
And heap their valleys with the gaudy foe;
Th' insulted sea with humbler thoughts he gains,
A single skiff to speed his flight remains;
Th' incumber'd oar scarce leaves the dreaded coast
Through purple billows and a floating host.

The bold Bavarian, in a luckless hour,
Tries the dread summits of Cæsarian pow'r,
With unexpected legions bursts away,
And sees defenceless realms receive his sway;
Short sway! fair Austria spreads her mournful charms,
The queen, the beauty, sets the world in arms;
From hill to hill the beacons' rousing blaze
Spreads wide the hope of plunder and of praise;
The fierce Croatian, and the wild Hussar,
And all the sons of ravage crowd the war;
The baffled prince in honour's flatt'ring bloom
Of hasty greatness finds the fatal doom,
His foes derision, and his subjects blame,
And steals to death from anguish and from shame.

Enlarge my life with multitude of days,
In health, in sickness, thus the suppliant prays;
Hides from himself his state, and shuns to know,
That life protracted, is protracted woe.
Time hovers o'er, impatient to destroy,
And shuts up all the passages of joy:
In vain their gifts the bounteous seasons pour,
The fruit autumnal, and the vernal flow'r,
With listless eyes the dotard views the store,
He views, and wonders that they please no more:
Now pall the tasteless meats, and joyless wines,
And Luxury with sighs her slave resigns.
Approach, ye minstrels, try the soothing strain,
And yield the tuneful lenitives of pain:
No sounds, alas, would touch th' impervious ear
Though dancing mountains witness'd Orpheus near,
Nor lute nor lyre his feeble pow'r attend,
Nor sweeter musick of a virtuous friend,
But everlasting dictates crowd his tongue,
Perversely grave or positively wrong.
The still returning tale, and ling'ring jest,
Perplex the fawning niece and pamper'd guest,
While growing hopes scarce awe the gath'ring sneer,
And scarce a legacy can bribe to hear;
The watchful guests still hint the last offence,
The daughter's petulance, the son's expence,
Improve his heady rage with treach'rous skill,
And mould his passions till they make his will.

Unnumber'd maladies his joints invade,
Lay siege to life, and press the dire blockade;
But unextinguish'd Av'rice still remains,
And dreaded losses aggravate his pains;
He turns, with anxious heart and crippled hands,
His bonds of debt, and mortgages of lands;
Or views his coffers with suspicious eyes,
Unlocks his gold, and counts it till he dies.

But grant, the virtues of a temp'rate prime
Bless with an age exempt from scorn or crime;

An age that melts in unperceiv'd decay,
And glides in modest innocence away;
Whose peaceful day Benevolence endears,
Whose night congratulating Conscience cheers;
The gen'ral fav'rite as the gen'ral friend:
Such age there is, and who could wish its end?
Yet ev'n on this her load Misfortune flings,
To press the weary minutes' flagging wings:
New sorrow rises as the day returns,
A sister sickens, or a daughter mourns.
Now kindred Merit fills the sable bier,
Now lacerated Friendship claims a tear.
Year chases year, decay pursues decay,
Still drops some joy from with'ring life away;
New forms arise, and diff'rent views engage,
Superfluous lags the vet'ran on the stage,
Till pitying Nature signs the last release,
And bids afflicted worth retire to peace.
But few there are whom hours like these await,
Who set unclouded in the gulphs of Fate.
From Lydia's monarch should the search descend,
By Solon caution'd to regard his end;
In life's last scene what prodigies surprise,
Fears of the brave, and follies of the wise?
From Marlb'rough's eyes the streams of dotage flow,
And Swift expires a driv'ler and a show.
The teeming mother, anxious for her race,
Begs for each birth the fortune of a face:
Yet Vane could tell what ills from beauty spring;
And Sedley curs'd the form that pleas'd a king.
Ye nymphs of rosy lips and radiant eyes,
Whom Pleasure keeps too busy to be wise,
Whom joys with soft varieties invite,
By day the frolick, and the dance by night,
Who frown with vanity, who smile with art,
And ask the latest fashion of the heart,
What care, what rules your heedless charms shall save,
Each nymph your rival, and each youth your slave?
Against your fame with fondness hate combines,
The rival batters, and the lover mines.
With distant voice neglected Virtue calls,
Less heard and less, the faint remonstrance falls;
Tir'd with contempt, she quits the slipp'ry reign,
And Pride and Prudence take her seat in vain.
In crowd at once, where none the pass defend,
The harmless Freedom, and the private Friend.
The guardians yield, by force superior ply'd;
To Int'rest, Prudence; and to Flatt'ry, Pride.
Now Beauty falls betray'd, despis'd, distress'd,
And hissing Infamy proclaims the rest.
Where then shall Hope and Fear their objects find?
Must dull Suspense corrupt the stagnant mind?
Must helpless man, in ignorance sedate,
Roll darkling down the torrent of his fate?
Must no dislike alarm, no wishes rise
No cries attempt the mercies of the skies?
Inquirer, cease, petitions yet remain,
Which heav'n may hear, nor deem religion vain.
Still raise for good the supplicating voice,
But leave to heav'n the measure and the choice.
Safe in his pow'r, whose eyes discern afar
The secret ambush of a specious pray'r;
Implore his aid, in his decisions rest,

Secure whate'er he gives, he gives the best.
Yet when the sense of sacred presence fires,
And strong devotion to the skies aspires,
Pour forth thy fervours for a healthful mind,
Obedient passions, and a will resign'd;
For love, which scarce collective man can fill;
For patience, sov'reign o'er transmuted ill;
For faith, that, panting for a happier seat,
Counts death kind Nature's signal of retreat:
These goods for man the laws of heav'n ordain,
These goods he grants, who grants the pow'r to gain;
With these celestial Wisdom calms the mind,
And makes the happiness she does not find.

On the Death of Dr. Robert Levett

Boswell informs us that Dr. Robert Levett was "an obscure practiser of physick amongst the lower people, his fees being sometimes very small sums, sometimes whatever provisions his patients could afford him; but of such extensive practice in that way, that Mrs. Williams has told me, his walk was from Houndsditch to Marybone." Dr. Levett for many years had lodging in Dr. Johnson's house, or his chambers, "and waited on Dr. Johnson every morning, through the whole course of his late and tedious breakfast." "He was of a strange grotesque appearance, stiff and formal in his manner, and seldom said a word while any company was present." He died in 1782. Boswell quotes the following memorandum by Johnson: "January 20, Sunday. Robert Levett was buried in the church-yard of Bridewell, between one and two in the afternoon. He died on Thursday 17, about seven in the morning, by an instantaneous death. He was an old and faithful friend; I have known him from about 46. *Commendavi.* May God have mercy on him. May he have mercy on me."

Condemn'd to Hope's delusive mine,
As on we toil from day to day,
By sudden blasts or slow decline
Our social comforts drop away.

Well tried through many a varying year,
See Levett to the grave descend,
Officious, innocent, sincere,
Of every friendless name the friend.

Yet still he fills affection's eye,
Obscurely wise and coarsely kind;
Nor, letter'd Arrogance, deny
Thy praise to merit unrefined.

When fainting nature call'd for aid,
And hov'ring death prepared the blow,
His vig'rous remedy display'd
The power of art without the show.

In Misery's darkest cavern known,
His useful care was ever nigh,
Where hopeless Anguish pour'd his groan,
And lonely Want retired to die.

No summons mock'd by chill delay,
No petty gain disdain'd by pride;
The modest wants of every day
The toil of every day supplied.

His virtues walk'd their narrow round,
Nor made a pause, nor left a void;
And sure th' Eternal Master found
The single talent well employ'd.

The busy day, the peaceful night,
Unfelt, uncounted, glided by;
His frame was firm—his powers were bright,
Though now his eightieth year was nigh.

Then with no fiery throbbing pain,
No cold gradations of decay,
Death broke at once the vital chain,
And freed his soul the nearest way.

Letter to Lord Chesterfield

In 1747, Dr. Johnson's difficult and highly important work, his *Dictionary of the English Language,* was announced to the world by the publication of its *Plan,* addressed to Philip Dormer, Earl of Chesterfield, then one of his Majesty's Principal Secretaries of State. Boswell describes the Earl as "a nobleman who was very ambitious of literary distinction, and who, upon being informed of the design, had expressed himself in terms very favourable to its success." Many years later, Johnson told Boswell, "Sir, the way in which the *Plan* of my *Dictionary* came to be inscribed to Lord Chesterfield was this: I had neglected to write it by the time appointed. Dodsley (one of the booksellers who had contracted with Johnson for the execution of the work) suggested a desire to have it addressed to Lord Chesterfield. I laid hold of this as a pretext for delay, that it might be better done, and let Dodsley have his desire. I said to my friend, Dr. Bathurst, 'Now if any good comes of my addressing to Lord Chesterfield, it will be ascribed to deep policy, when, in fact, it was only a casual excuse for laziness.'"

In 1754, the *Dictionary* was near publication. During the intervening years, Lord Chesterfield had behaved toward Johnson with coldness and neglect. Now, however, in the hope that Johnson would dedicate the work to him, he attempted to conciliate him by writing two papers in *The World,* commending the undertaking. Johnson then sent to Lord Chesterfield the following letter. It became famous through the peculiar circumstance that Lord Chesterfield, affecting unconcern, kept it lying on his table where anybody might see it, and even read it to Dodsley, with the remark that "this man has great powers." Johnson was reluctant to have the letter published. It was not until 1781 that Boswell, at great pains and after long delay on Johnson's part, secured a copy. He published it separately, in 1790, the year before his *Life of Johnson* came out, and six years after Johnson's death.

"To the Right Honourable the Earl of Chesterfield.

"February 7, 1755.

"My Lord, I have been lately informed, by the proprietor of *The World,* that two papers, in which my Dictionary is recommended to the publick, were written by your Lordship. To be so distinguished, is an honour, which, being very little accustomed to favours from the great, I know not well how to receive, or in what terms to acknowledge.

"When, upon some slight encouragement, I first visited your Lordship, I was overpowered, like the rest of mankind, by the enchantment of your address; and could not forbear to wish that I might boast myself *Le vainqueur du vainqueur de la terre;*—that I might obtain that regard for which I saw the world contending; but I found my attendance so little encouraged, that neither pride nor modesty would suffer me to continue it. When I had once addressed your Lordship in publick, I had exhausted all the art of pleasing which a retired and uncourtly scholar can possess. I had done all that I could; and no man is well pleased to have his all neglected, be it ever so little.

"Seven years, my Lord, have now past, since I waited in your outward rooms, or was repulsed from your door; during which time I have been pushing on my work through difficulties, of which it is useless to complain, and have brought it, at last, to the verge of publication, without one act of assistance, one word of encouragement, or one smile of favour. Such treatment I did not expect, for I never had a Patron before.

"The shepherd in Virgil grew at last acquainted with Love, and found him a native of the rocks.

"Is not a Patron, my Lord, one who looks with unconcern on a man struggling for life in the water, and, when he has reached ground, encumbers him with help? The notice which you have been pleased to take of my labours, had it been early, had been kind; but it has been delayed till I am indifferent, and cannot enjoy it; till I am solitary, and cannot impart it; till I am known, and do not want it. I hope it is no very cynical asperity not to confess obligations where no benefit has been received, or to be unwilling that the Publick should consider me as owing that to a Patron, which Providence has enabled me to do for myself.

"Having carried on my work thus far with so little obligation to any favourer of learning, I shall not be disappointed though I should conclude it, if less be possible, with less; for I have been long wakened from that dream of hope, in which I once boasted myself with so much exultation, my Lord, your Lordship's most humble, most obedient servant,

"Sam Johnson."

JAMES BOSWELL (1740-1795)

From The Life of Samuel Johnson, LL.D.

Johnson Dines with Jack Wilkes at Mr. Dilly's

At the close of the following account of the dinner at Mr. Dilly's, Boswell compliments himself on his successful negotiation of the meeting between Dr. Johnson and Mr. Wilkes, "two men, who though so widely different, had so many things in common—classical learning, modern literature, wit, and humour, and ready repartee—that it would have been much to be regretted if they had been for ever at a distance from each other." Johnson, a firm Tory, had written of Wilkes, in 1770, "Lampoon itself would disdain to speak ill of him, of whom no man speaks well." He called him "a retailer of sedition and obscenity"; and, in regard to the question of allowing Wilkes to take his seat in Parliament, after being twice expelled for seditious libel, said, "We are now disputing . . . whether Middlesex shall be represented, or not, by a criminal from a gaol." Wilkes, in his paper, *The North Briton,* had referred to Johnson, with very slight indirectness, as "a slave of state, hired by a stipend to obey his master." This fierce and formidable radical was, from all accounts, a most polished, urbane, charming person.

But I conceived an irresistible wish, if possible, to bring Dr. Johnson and Mr. Wilkes together. How to manage it, was a nice and difficult matter.

My worthy booksellers and friends, Messieurs Dilly in the Poultry, at whose hospitable and well-covered table I have seen a greater number of literary men, than at any other, except that of Sir Joshua Reynolds, had invited me to meet Mr. Wilkes and some more gentlemen on Wednesday, May 15. "Pray (said I,) let us have Dr. Johnson."—"What with Mr. Wilkes? not for the world, (said Mr. Edward Dilly:) Dr. Johnson would never forgive me."—"Come, (said I,) if you'll let me negociate for you, I will be answerable that all shall go well." DILLY. "Nay, if you will take it upon you, I am sure I shall be very happy to see them both here."

Notwithstanding the high veneration which I entertained for Dr. Johnson, I was sensible that he was sometimes a little actuated by the spirit of contradiction, and by means of that I hoped I should gain my point. I was persuaded that if I had come upon him with a direct proposal, "Sir, will you dine in company with Jack Wilkes?" he would have flown into a passion, and would probably have answered, "Dine with Jack Wilkes, Sir! I'd as soon dine with Jack Ketch." I therefore, while we were sitting quietly by ourselves at his house in an evening, took occasion to open my plan thus:—"Mr. Dilly, Sir, sends his respectful compliments to you, and would be happy if you would do him the honour to dine with him on Wednesday next along with me, as I must soon go to Scotland." JOHNSON. "Sir, I am obliged to Mr. Dilly. I will wait upon him—" BOSWELL. "Provided, Sir, I suppose, that the company which he is to have, is agreeable to you." JOHNSON. "What do you mean, Sir? What do you take me for? Do you think I am so ignorant of the world as to imagine that I am to prescribe to a gentleman what company he is to have at his table?" BOSWELL. "I beg your pardon, Sir, for wishing to prevent you from meeting people whom you might not like. Perhaps he may have some of what he calls his patriotick friends with him." JOHNSON. "Well, sir, and what then? What care *I* for his *patriotick friends?* Poh!" BOSWELL. "I should not be surprized to find Jack Wilkes there." JOHNSON. "And if Jack Wilkes *should* be there, what is that to *me,* Sir? My dear friend, let us have no more of this. I am sorry to be angry with you; but really it is treating me strangely to talk to me as if I could not meet any company whatever, occasionally." BOSWELL. "Pray forgive me, Sir: I meant well. But you shall meet whoever comes, for me." Thus I secured him, and told Dilly that he would find him very well pleased to be one of his guests on the day appointed.

Upon the much-expected Wednesday, I called on him about half an hour before dinner, as I often did when we were to dine out together, to see that he was ready in time, and to accompany him. I found him buffeting his books, as upon a former occasion, covered with dust, and making no preparation for going abroad. "How is this, Sir? (said I.) Don't you recollect that you are to dine at Mr. Dilly's?" JOHNSON. "Sir, I did not think of going to Dilly's: it went out of my head. I have ordered dinner at home with Mrs. Williams." BOSWELL. "But, my dear Sir, you know you were engaged to Mr. Dilly, and I told him so. He will expect you, and will be much disappointed if you don't come." JOHNSON. "You must talk to Mrs. Williams about this."

Here was a sad dilemma. I feared that what I was so confident I had secured would yet be frustrated. He had accustomed himself to shew Mrs. Williams such a degree of humane attention, as frequently imposed some restraint upon him; and I knew that if she should be obstinate, he would not stir. I hastened down stairs to the blind lady's room, and told her I was in great uneasiness, for Dr. Johnson had engaged to me to dine this day at Mr. Dilly's, but that he had told me he had forgotten his engagement, and had ordered dinner at home. "Yes, Sir, (said she, pretty peevishly,) Dr. Johnson is to dine at home."—"Madam, (said I,) his respect for you is such, that I know he will not leave you unless you absolutely desire it. But as you have so much of his company, I hope you will be good enough to forego it for a day; as Mr. Dilly is a very worthy man, has frequently had agreeable parties at his house for Dr. Johnson, and will be vexed if the Doctor neglects him to-day. And then, Madam, be pleased to consider my situation; I carried the message, and I assured Mr. Dilly that Dr. Johnson was to come, and no doubt he has made a dinner, and invited a company, and boasted of the honour he expected to have. I shall be quite disgraced if the Doctor is not there." She gradually softened to my solicitations, which were certainly as earnest as most entreaties to ladies upon any occasion, and was graciously pleased to empower me to tell Dr. Johnson, "That all things considered, she thought he should certainly go." I flew back to him, still in dust, and careless of what should be the event, "indifferent in his choice to go or stay"; but as soon as I had announced to him Mrs. Williams' consent, he roared, "Frank, a clean shirt," and was very soon drest. When I had him fairly seated in a hackney-coach with me, I exulted as much as a fortune-hunter who has got an heiress into a post-chaise with him to set out for Gretna-Green.

When we entered Mr. Dilly's drawing room, he found himself in the midst of a company he did not know. I kept myself snug and silent, watching how he would conduct himself. I observed him whispering to Mr. Dilly, "Who is that gentleman, Sir?"—"Mr. Arthur Lee."—JOHNSON. "Too, too, too," (under his breath,) which was one of his habitual mutterings. Mr. Arthur Lee could not but be very obnoxious to Johnson, for he was not only a *patriot* but an *American.* He was afterwards minister from the United States at the court of Madrid. "And who is the gentleman in lace?"—"Mr. Wilkes, Sir." This information confounded him still more; he had some difficulty to restrain himself, and taking up a book, sat down upon a window-seat and read, or at least kept his eye upon it intently for some time, till he composed himself. His feelings, I dare say, were awkward enough. But he no doubt recollected his having rated me for supposing that he could be at all disconcerted by any company, and he, therefore, resolutely set himself to behave quite as an easy man of the world, who could adapt himself at once to the disposition and manners of those whom he might chance to meet.

The cheering sound of "Dinner is upon the table," dissolved his reverie, and we *all* sat down without any symptom of ill humour. There were present, beside Mr. Wilkes, and Mr. Arthur Lee, who was an old companion of mine when he studied physick at Edinburgh, Mr. (now Sir John) Miller, Dr. Lettsom, and Mr. Slater the druggist. Mr. Wilkes placed himself next to Dr. Johnson, and behaved to him with so much attention and politeness, that he gained upon him insensibly. No man eat more heartily than Johnson, or loved better what was nice and delicate. Mr. Wilkes was very assiduous in helping him to some fine veal. "Pray give me leave, Sir:—It is better here—A little of the brown—Some fat, Sir—A little of the stuffing—Some gravy—Let me have the pleasure of giving you some butter—Allow me to recommend a squeeze of this orange;—or the lemon, perhaps, may have more zest."—"Sir, Sir, I am obliged to you, Sir," cried Johnson, bowing, and turning his head to him with a look for some time of "surly virtue," but, in a short while, of complacency.

Foote being mentioned, Johnson said, "He is not a good mimick." One of the company added, "A merry Andrew, a buffoon." JOHNSON. "But he has wit too, and is not deficient in ideas, or in fertility and variety of imagery and not empty of reading; he has knowledge enough to fill up his part. One species of wit he has in an eminent degree, that of escape. You drive him into a corner with both hands; but he's gone, Sir, when you think you have got him—like an animal that jumps over your head. Then he has a great range for wit; he never lets truth stand between him and a jest, and he is sometimes mighty coarse. Garrick is under many restraints from which Foote is free." WILKES. "Garrick's wit is more like Lord Chesterfield's." JOHNSON. "The first time I was in company with Foote was at Fitzherbert's. Having no good opinion of the fellow, I was resolved not to be pleased; and it is very difficult to please a man against his will. I went on eating my dinner pretty sullenly, affecting not to mind him. But the dog was so very comical, that I was obliged to lay down my knife and fork, throw myself back upon my chair, and fairly laugh it out. No, Sir, he was irresistible. He upon one occasion experienced, in an extraordinary degree, the efficacy of his powers of entertaining. Amongst the many and various modes which he tried of getting money, he became a partner with a small-beer brewer, and he was to have a share of the profits for procuring customers amongst his numerous acquaintance. Fitzherbert was one who took his small-beer; but it was so bad that the servants resolved not to drink it. They were at some loss how to notify their resolution, being afraid of offending their master, who they knew liked Foote much as a companion. At last they fixed upon a little black boy, who was rather a favourite, to be their deputy, and deliver their remonstrance; and having invested him with the whole authority of the kitchen, he was to inform Mr. Fitzherbert, in all their names, upon a certain day, that they would drink Foote's small-beer no longer. On that day Foote happened to dine at Fitzherbert's, and this boy served at table; he was so delighted with Foote's stories, and merriment, and grimace, that when he went down stairs, he told them, 'This is the finest man I have ever seen. I will not deliver your message. I will drink his small-beer.'"

Somebody observed that Garrick could not have done this. WILKES. "Garrick would have made the small-beer still smaller. He is now leaving the stage; but he will play *Scrub* all his life." I knew that Johnson would let nobody attack Garrick but himself, as Garrick once said to me, and I had heard him praise his liberality; so to bring out his commendation of his celebrated pupil, I said, loudly, "I have heard Garrick is liberal." JOHNSON. "Yes, Sir, I know that Garrick has given away more money than any man in England that I am acquainted with, and that not from ostentatious views. Garrick was very poor when he began life; so when he came to have money, he probably was very unskilful in giving away, and saved when he should not. But Garrick began to be liberal as soon as he could; and I am of opinion, the reputation of avarice which he has had, has been very lucky for him, and prevented his having many enemies. You despise a man for avarice, but do not hate him. Garrick might have been much better attacked for living with more splendour than is suitable to a player: if they had had the wit to have assaulted him in that quarter, they might have galled him more. But they have kept clamouring about his avarice, which has rescued him from much obloquy and envy."

Talking of the great difficulty of obtaining authentick information for biography, Johnson told us, "When I was a young fellow I wanted to write the *Life of Dryden*, and in order to get materials, I applied to the only two persons then alive who had seen him; these were old Swinney, and old Cibber. Swinney's information was no more than this, 'That at Will's coffee-house Dryden had a particular chair for himself, which was set by the fire in winter, and was then called his winter-chair; and that it was carried out for him to the balcony in summer, and was then called his summer-chair.' Cibber could tell no more but 'That he remembered him a decent old man, arbiter of critical disputes at Will's.' You are to consider that Cibber was then at a great distance from Dryden, had perhaps one leg only in the room, and durst not draw in the other." BOSWELL. "Yet Cibber was a man of observation?" JOHNSON. "I think not." BOSWELL. "You will allow his *Apology* to be well done." JOHNSON. "Very well done, to be sure, Sir. That book is a striking proof of the justice of Pope's remark:

"'Each might his several province well command
Would all but stoop to what they understand.'"

BOSWELL. "And his plays are good." JOHNSON. "Yes; but that was his trade; *l'esprit du corps:* he had been all his life among players and play-writers. I wondered that he had so little to say in conversation, for he had kept the best company, and learnt all that can be got by the ear. He abused Pindar to me, and then shewed me an Ode of his own, with an absurd couplet, making a linnet soar on an eagle's wing. I told him that when the ancients made a simile, they always made it like something real."

Mr. Wilkes remarked, that "among all the bold flights of Shakspeare's imagination, the boldest was making Birnam wood march to Dunsinane; creating a wood where there never was a shrub; a wood in Scotland! ha! ha! ha!" And he also observed, that "the clannish slavery of the Highlands of Scotland was the single exception to Milton's remark of 'The Mountain Nymph, sweet Liberty,' being worshipped in all hilly countries."—"When I was at Inverary (said he,) on a visit to my old friend, Archibald, Duke of Argyle, his dependents congratulated me on being such a favourite of his Grace. I said, 'It is then, gentlemen, truely lucky for me; for if I had displeased the Duke, and he had wished it, there is not a Campbell among you but would have been ready to bring John Wilkes's head to him in a charger. It would have been only

"'Off with his head! So much for Aylesbury.'

I was then member for Aylesbury."

Mr. Arthur Lee mentioned some Scotch who had taken possession of a barren part of America, and wondered why they should choose it. JOHNSON. "Why, Sir, all barrenness is comparative. The *Scotch* would not know it to be barren." BOSWELL. "Come, come, he is flattering the English. You have now been in Scotland, Sir, and say if you did not see meat and drink enough there." JOHNSON. "Why, yes, Sir; meat and drink enough to give the enhabitants sufficient strength to run away from home." All these quick and lively sallies were said sportively, quite in jest, and with a smile, which showed that he meant only wit. Upon this topick he and Mr. Wilkes could perfectly assimilate; here was a bond of union between them, and I was conscious that as both of them had visited Caledonia, both were fully satisfied of the strange narrow ignorance of those who imagine that it is a land of famine. But they amused themselves with persevering in the old jokes. When I claimed a superiority for Scotland over England in one respect, that no man can be arrested there for a debt merely because another swears it against him; but there must first be the judgement of a court of law ascertaining its justice; and that a seizure of the person, before judgement is obtained, can take place only, if his creditor should swear that he is about to fly from the country, or, as it is technically expressed, is *in meditatione fugæ:* WILKES. "That, I should think, may be safely sworn of all the Scotch nation." JOHNSON. (to Mr. Wilkes,) "You must know, Sir, I lately took my friend Boswell and shewed him genuine civilised life in an English provincial town. I turned him loose at Lichfield, my native city, that he might see for once real civility: for you know he lives among savages in Scotland, and among rakes in London." WILKES. "Except when he is with grave, sober, decent people like you and me." JOHNSON. (smiling,) "And we ashamed of him."

LAURENCE STERNE (1713-1768)

From TRISTRAM SHANDY

The Story of Le Fever

Lieutenant Le Fever is a poor officer, dying from want and sickness, one of the many recipients of kindness from good Uncle Toby, the central figure in *Tristram Shandy.*

It was to my uncle *Toby's* eternal honour,——though I tell it only for the sake of those, who, when coop'd in betwixt a natural and a positive law, know not, for their souls, which way in the world to turn themselves——That notwithstanding my uncle *Toby* was warmly engaged at that time in carrying on the siege of *Dendermond,* parallel with the allies, who pressed theirs on so vigorously, that they scarce allowed him time to get his dinner——that nevertheless he gave up *Dendermond,* though he had already made a lodgment upon the counterscarp;—and bent his whole thoughts towards the private distresses at the inn; and except that he ordered the garden gate to be bolted up, by which he might be said to have turned the siege of *Dendermond* into a blockade,——he left *Dendermond* to itself——to be relieved or not by the *French* king, as the *French* king thought good; and only considered how he himself should relieve the poor lieutenant and his son.

——That kind BEING, who is a friend to the friendless, shall recompence thee for this.

Thou hast left this matter short, said my uncle *Toby* to the corporal, as he was putting him to bed,——and I will tell thee in what, *Trim.*——In the first place, when thou madest an offer of my services to *Le Fever,* ——as sickness and travelling are both expensive, and thou knowest he was but a poor lieutenant, with a son to subsist as well as himself out of his pay,—that thou didst not make an offer to him of my purse; because, had he stood in need, thou knowest, *Trim,* he had been as welcome to it as myself.——Your honour knows, said the corporal, I had no orders;——True, quoth my uncle *Toby,*——thou didst very right, *Trim,* as a soldier,——but certainly very wrong as a man.

In the second place, for which, indeed, thou hast the same excuse, continued my uncle *Toby,*——when thou offeredst him whatever was in my house,——thou shouldst have offered him my house too:——A sick brother officer should have the best quarters, *Trim,* and if we had him with us,——we could tend and look to him:——Thou art an excellent nurse thyself, *Trim,*——and what with thy care of him, and the old woman's, and his boy's, and mine together, we might recruit him again at once, and set him upon his legs.——

——In a fortnight or three weeks, added my uncle *Toby,* smiling, ——he might march.——He will never march; an' please your honour, in this world, said the corporal:——He will march; said my uncle *Toby,* rising up, from the side of the bed, with one shoe off:——An' please your honour, said the corporal, he will never march but to his grave:—— He shall march, cried my uncle *Toby,* marching the foot which had a shoe on, though without advancing an inch,——he shall march to his regiment.——He cannot stand it, said the corporal;——He shall be supported, said my uncle *Toby;*——He'll drop at last, said the corporal, and what will become of his boy?——He shall not drop, said my uncle *Toby,* firmly.——A-well-o'-day,——do what we can for him, said *Trim,* maintaining his point,——the poor soul will die:——He shall not die, by G—, cried my uncle *Toby.*

——The ACCUSING SPIRIT, which flew up to heaven's chancery with the oath, blush'd as he gave it in;——and the RECORDING ANGEL, as he wrote it down, dropp'd a tear upon the word, and blotted it out for ever.

——My uncle *Toby* went to his bureau,——put his purse into his breeches pocket, and having ordered the corporal to go early in the morning for a physician,——he went to bed, and fell asleep.

The sun looked bright the morning after, to every eye in the village but *Le Fever's* and his afflicted son's; the hand of death press'd heavy upon his eye-lids,——and hardly could the wheel at the cistern turn round its circle,——when my uncle *Toby,* who had rose up an hour before his wonted time, entered the lieutenant's room, and without preface or apology, sat himself down upon the chair by the bed-side, and, independently of all modes and customs, opened the curtain in the manner an old friend and brother officer would have done it, and asked him how he did,——how he had rested in the night,——what was his complaint, ——where was his pain,——and what he could do to help him:——and without giving him time to answer any one of the enquiries, went on, and told him of the little plan which he had been concerting with the corporal the night before for him.——

——You shall go home directly, *Le Fever,* said my uncle *Toby,* to my house,——and we'll send for a doctor to see what's the matter,—— and we'll have an apothecary,——and the corporal shall be your nurse; ——and I'll be your servant, *Le Fever.*

There was a frankness in my uncle *Toby,*——not the *effect* of familiarity,——but the *cause* of it,——which let you at once into his soul, and shewed you the goodness of his nature; to this, there was something in his looks, and voice, and manner, superadded, which eternally beckoned to the unfortunate to come and take shelter under him; so that before my uncle *Toby* had half finished the kind offers he was making to the father, had the son insensibly pressed up close to his knees, and had taken hold of the breast of his coat, and was pulling it towards him.—— The blood and spirits of *Le Fever,* which were waxing cold and slow within him, and were retreating to their last citadel, the heart——rallied back,——the film forsook his eyes for a moment——he looked up wishfully in my uncle *Toby's* face,——then cast a look upon his boy,——and that *ligament,* fine as it was,——was never broken.——

Nature instantly ebb'd again,——the film returned to its place,——the pulse fluttered——stopp'd——went on——throbb'd——stopp'd again ——moved——stopp'd.

Tristram and the Ass

Tristram was setting forth from his inn at Lyons, to visit *"the tomb of the lovers,"* when he was stopped at the gate by the poor ass that figures in the following narration.

——'Twas by a poor ass, who had just turned in with a couple of large panniers upon his back, to collect eleemosynary turnip-tops and cabbage-leaves; and stood dubious, with his two fore-feet on the inside of the threshold, and with his two hinder feet towards the street, as not knowing very well whether he was to go in or no.

Now, 'tis an animal (be in what hurry I may) I cannot bear to strike ——there is a patient endurance of sufferings, wrote so unaffectedly in his looks and carriage, which pleads so mightily for him, that it always disarms me; and to that degree, that I do not like to speak unkindly to him: on the contrary, meet him where I will——whether in town or country——in cart or under panniers——whether in liberty or bondage——I have ever something civil to say to him on my part; and as one word begets another (if he has as little to do as I)——I generally fall into conversation with him; and surely never is my imagination so busy as in framing his responses from the etchings of his countenance——and where those carry me not deep enough——in flying from my own heart into his, and seeing what is natural for an ass to think——as well as a man, upon the occasion. In truth, it is the only creature of all the classes of beings below me, with whom I can do this: for parrots, jackdaws, &c. ——I never exchange a word with them——nor with the apes, &c., for pretty near the same reason; they act by rote, as the others speak by it, and equally make me silent: nay my dog and my cat, though I value them both——(and for my dog he would speak if he could)——yet somehow or other, they neither of them possess the talents for conversation——I can make nothing of a discourse with them, beyond the *proposition,* the *reply,* and *rejoinder,* which terminated my father's and my mother's conversations, in his beds of justice——and those utter'd——there's an end of the dialogue——

——But with an ass, I can commune forever.

Come, *Honesty!* said I,——seeing it was impracticable to pass betwixt him and the gate——art thou for coming in, or going out?

The ass twisted his head round to look up the street——

Well——replied I——we'll wait a minute for thy driver:

——He turned his head thoughtful about, and looked wistfully the opposite way——

I understand thee perfectly, answered I——If thou takest a wrong step in this affair, he will cudgel thee to death——Well! a minute is but a minute, and if it saves a fellow-creature a drubbing, it shall not be set down as ill spent.

He was eating the stem of an artichoke as this discourse went on, and in the little peevish contentions of nature betwixt hunger and unsavouriness, had dropt it out of his mouth half a dozen times, and pick'd it up again——God help thee, *Jack!* said I, thou hast a bitter breakfast on't——and many a bitter day's labour,——and many a bitter blow, I fear, for its wages——'tis all——all bitterness to thee, whatever life is to others.——And now thy mouth, if one knew the truth of it, is as bitter, I dare say, as soot——(for he had cast aside the stem) and thou hast not a friend perhaps in all this world, that will give thee a macaroon. ——In saying this, I pull'd out a paper of 'em, which I had just purchased, and gave him one——and at this moment that I am telling it, my heart smites me, that there was more of pleasantry in the conceit, of seeing *how* an ass would eat a macaroon——than of benevolence in giving him one, which presided in the act.

When the ass had eaten his macaroon, I press'd him to come in——the poor beast was heavy loaded——his legs seem'd to tremble under him——he hung rather backwards, and as I pull'd at his halter, it broke short in my hand——he look'd up pensive in my face——"Don't thrash me with it——but if you will, you may"——If I do, said, I, I'll be d——d.

The word was but one-half of it pronounced, like the abbess of *Andoüillets'*——(so there was no sin in it)——when a person coming in, let fall a thundering bastinado upon the poor devil's crupper, which put an end to the ceremony.

THOMAS GRAY (1716-1771)

The Progress of Poesy

Φωναντα συνετοῖσιν' ἐς
Δὲ τὸ παν ἑρμηνέων χατίζει
PINDAR, *Olymp.* II.

I. 1

AWAKE, Æolian lyre, awake
And give to rapture all thy trembling strings.
From Helicon's harmonious springs
A thousand rills their mazy progress take:
The laughing flowers, that round them blow,
Drink life and fragrance as they flow.
Now the rich stream of music winds along
Deep, majestic, smooth, and strong,
Thro' verdant vales, and Ceres' golden reign:
Now rolling down the steep amain,
Headlong, impetuous, see it pour:
The rocks and nodding groves rebellow to the roar.

I. 2

Oh! Sovereign of the willing soul,
Parent of sweet and solemn-breathing airs,
Enchanting shell! the sullen Cares,
And frantic Passions hear thy soft controul.
On Thracia's Hills the Lord of War
Has curb'd the fury of his car,
And drop'd his thirsty lance at thy command.
Perching on the scept'red hand
Of Jove, thy magic lulls the feather'd king
With ruffled plumes, and flagging wing:
Quench'd in dark clouds of slumber lie
The terror of his beak, and light'nings of his eye.

I. 3

Thee the voice, the dance, obey,
Temper'd to thy warbled lay.
O'er Idalia's velvet-green
The rosy-crownèd Loves are seen
On Cytherea's day
With antic sport, and blue-eyed Pleasures,
Frisking light in frolic measures;
Now pursuing, now retreating,
Now in circling troops they meet:
To brisk notes in cadence beating
Glance their many-twinkling feet.
Slow melting strains their Queen's approach declare:
Where'er she turns the Graces homage pay.
With arms sublime, that float upon the air,
In gliding state she wins her easy way:
O'er her warm cheek, and rising bosom, move
The bloom of young Desire and purple light of Love.

II. 1

Man's feeble race what ills await,
Labour, and penury, the racks of pain,
Disease, and sorrow's weeping train,
And death, sad refuge from the storms of fate!
The fond complaint, my song, disprove,
And justify the laws of Jove.
Say, has he given in vain the heavenly Muse?
Night, and all her sickly dews,
Her spectres wan, and birds of boding cry,
He gives to range the dreary sky:
Till down the eastern cliffs afar
Hyperion's march they spy, and glittering shafts of war.

II. 2

In climes beyond the solar road,
Where shaggy forms o'er ice-built mountains roam,
The Muse has broke the twilight-gloom
To cheer the shivering Native's dull abode.
And oft, beneath the odorous shade
Of Chili's boundless forests laid,
She deigns to hear the savage youth repeat

In loose numbers wildly sweet
Their feather-cinctur'd chiefs, and dusky loves.
Her track, where'er the Goddess roves,
Glory pursue, and generous shame,
Th' unconquerable mind, and freedom's holy flame.

II. 3

Woods, that wave o'er Delphi's steep,
Isles, that crown th' Ægean deep,
Fields, that cool Ilissus laves,
Or where Mæander's amber waves
In lingering labyrinths creep,
How do your tuneful echoes languish,
Mute, but to the voice of anguish!
Where each old poetic mountain
Inspiration breath'd around;
Ev'ry shade and hallow'd fountain
Murmur'd deep a solemn sound:
Till the sad Nine in Greece's evil hour
Left their Parnassus for the Latian plains.
Alike they scorn the pomp of tyrant-power,
And coward vice, that revels in her chains.
When Latium had her lofty spirit lost,
They sought, oh, Albion! next thy sea-encircled coast.

III. 1

Far from the sun and summer-gale,
In thy green lap was Nature's darling laid,
What time, where lucid Avon stray'd,
To him the mighty mother did unveil
Her awful face: The dauntless child
Stretch'd forth his little arms, and smil'd
This pencil take (she said) whose colours clear
Richly paint the vernal year:
Thine too these golden keys, immortal boy!
This can unlock the gates of Joy;
Of horror that, and thrilling fears,
Or ope the sacred source of sympathetic tears.

III. 2

Nor second He, that rode sublime
Upon the seraph-wings of extasy,
The secrets of th' abyss to spy.
He pass'd the flaming bounds of place and time:
The living throne, the sapphire-blaze,
Where Angels tremble, while they gaze,
He saw; but blasted with excess of light,
Clos'd his eyes in endless night.
Behold where Dryden's less presumptuous car,
Wide o'er the fields of glory bear
Two coursers of ethereal race,
With necks in thunder cloth'd, and long-resounding pace.

III. 3

Hark, his hands the lyre explore!
Bright-eyed Fancy hovering o'er
Scatters from her pictur'd urn
Thoughts that breathe, and words that burn.
But ah! 'tis heard no more——
Oh! Lyre divine, what daring Spirit
Wakes thee now? tho' he inherit
Nor the pride, nor ample pinion,
That the Theban Eagle bear
Sailing with supreme dominion
Thro' the azure deep of air:
Yet oft before his infant eyes would run
Such forms, as glitter in the Muse's ray
With orient hues, unborrow'd of the sun:
Yet shall he mount, and keep his distant way
Beyond the limits of a vulgar fate,
Beneath the good how far—but far above the great.

Elegy, Written in a Country Churchyard

The Curfew tolls the knell of parting day,
The lowing herd winds slowly o'er the lea,
The plowman homeward plods his weary way,

And leaves the world to darkness and
to me.

Now fades the glimmering landscape on
the sight,
And all the air a solemn stillness holds,
Save where the beetle wheels his droning
flight,
And drowsy tinklings lull the distant
folds;

Save that from yonder ivy-mantled tower
The moping owl does to the moon
complain
Of such, as wandering near her secret
bower,
Molest her ancient solitary reign.

Beneath those rugged elms, that yew-
tree's shade,
Where heaves the turf in many a
mouldering heap,
Each in his narrow cell for ever laid,
The rude Forefathers of the hamlet
sleep.

The breezy call of incense-breathing
Morn,
The swallow twittering from the
straw-built shed,
The cock's shrill clarion, or the echoing
horn,
No more shall rouse them from their
lowly bed.

For them no more the blazing hearth
shall burn,
Or busy housewife ply her evening
care:
No children run to lisp their sire's return,
Or climb his knees the envied kiss to
share.

Oft did the harvest to their sickle yield,
Their furrow oft the stubborn glebe
has broke;
How jocund did they drive their team
afield!
How bow'd the woods beneath their
sturdy stroke!

Let not Ambition mock their useful toil,
Their homely joys, and destiny obscure;
Nor Grandeur hear with a disdainful
smile,
The short and simple annals of the
poor.

The boast of heraldry, the pomp of
power,
And all that beauty, all that wealth
e'er gave,
Awaits alike th' inevitable hour.
The paths of glory lead but to the
grave.

Nor you, ye Proud, impute to These the
fault,
If Memory o'er their Tomb no Trophies raise,
Where through the long-drawn aisle and
fretted vault
The pealing anthem swells the note of
praise.

Can storied urn or animated bust
Back to its mansion call the fleeting
breath?
Can Honour's voice provoke the silent
dust,
Or Flattery sooth the dull cold ear of
Death?

Perhaps in this neglected spot is laid
Some heart once pregnant with celestial
fire;
Hands that the rod of empire might
have sway'd,
Or waked to ecstasy the living lyre.

But Knowledge to their eyes her ample
page
Rich with the spoils of time did ne'er
unroll;
Chill Penury repress'd their noble rage,
And froze the genial current of the
soul.

Full many a gem of purest ray serene,
The dark unfathom'd caves of ocean
bear:

Full many a flower is born to blush unseen,
And waste its sweetness on the desert air.

Some village Hampden, that with dauntless breast
The little Tyrant of his fields withstood;
Some mute inglorious Milton here may rest,
Some Cromwell guiltless of his country's blood.

Th' applause of listening senates to command,
The threats of pain and ruin to despise,
To scatter plenty o'er a smiling land,
And read their history in a nation's eyes,

Their lot forbade: nor circumscribed alone
Their growing virtues, but their crimes confin'd;
Forbade to wade through slaughter to a throne,
And shut the gates of mercy on mankind,

The struggling pangs of conscious truth to hide,
To quench the blushes of ingenuous shame,
Or heap the shrine of Luxury and Pride
With incense kindled at the Muse's flame.

Far from the madding crowd's ignoble strife,
Their sober wishes never learn'd to stray;
Along the cool sequester'd vale of life
They kept the noiseless tenor of their way.

Yet even these bones from insult to protect,
Some frail memorial still erected nigh,
With uncouth rhymes and shapeless sculpture deck't,
Implores the passing tribute of a sigh.

Their name, their years, spelt by th' unletter'd Muse,
The place of fame and elegy supply:
And many a holy text around she strews,
That teach the rustic moralist to die.

For who to dumb Forgetfulness a prey,
This pleasing anxious being e'er resign'd,
Left the warm precincts of the cheerful day,
Nor cast one longing lingering look behind?

On some fond breast the parting soul relies,
Some pious drops the closing eye requires;
Ev'n from the tomb the voice of Nature cries,
Ev'n in our Ashes live their wonted Fires.

For thee, who mindful of the unhonour'd Dead
Dost in these lines their artless tale relate,
If chance, by lonely Contemplation led,
Some kindred spirit shall inquire thy fate,

Haply some hoary-headed Swain may say,
"Oft have we seen him at the peep of dawn
Brushing with hasty steps the dews away
To meet the sun upon the upland lawn.

"Hard by yon wood, now smiling as in scorn,
Muttering his wayward fancies he would rove;
Now drooping, woeful-wan, like one forlorn,
Or crazed with care, or cross'd in hopeless love.

"One morn I miss'd him on the custom'd hill,
Along the heath, and near his favourite tree;
Another came; nor yet beside the rill,
Nor up the lawn, nor at the wood was he;

"The next with dirges due in sad array
Slow through the church-way path we saw him borne,—
Approach and read (for thou canst read) the lay
Graved on the stone beneath yon agèd thorn:"

THE EPITAPH

Here rests his head upon the lap of Earth
A youth, to Fortune and to Fame unknown;
Fair Science frown'd not on his humble birth
And Melancholy mark'd him for her own.

Large was his bounty, and his soul sincere;
Heaven did a recompense as largely send:
He gave to Misery (all he had) a tear,
He gain'd from Heaven ('twas all he wish'd) a friend.

No farther seek his merits to disclose,
Or draw his frailties from their dread abode
(There they alike in trembling hope repose)
The bosom of his Father and his God.

OLIVER GOLDSMITH (1728-1774)

The Haunch of Venison

THANKS, my lord, for your venison, for finer or fatter
Ne'er ranged in a forest, or smoked in a platter;
The haunch was a picture for painters to study,
The fat was so white, and the lean was so ruddy;
Though my stomach was sharp, I could scarce help regretting
To spoil such a delicate picture by eating:
I had thoughts, in my chamber, to place it in view,
To be shown to my friends as a piece of virtú:
As in some Irish houses, where things are so so,
One gammon of bacon hangs up for a show;
But, for eating a rasher of what they take pride in,
They'd as soon think of eating the pan it is fried in.
But hold—let me pause—don't I hear you pronounce
This tale of the bacon's a damnable bounce?
Well, suppose it a bounce—sure a poet may try,
By a bounce now and then, to get courage to fly.
But, my lord, it's no bounce: I protest in my turn,
It's a truth—and your lordship may ask Mr. Byrne.
To go on with my tale—as I gazed on the haunch,
I thought of a friend that was trusty and stanch;
So I cut it, and sent it to Reynolds undress'd,
To paint it, or eat it, just as he liked best:
Of the neck and the breast I had next to dispose;
'Twas a neck and a breast that might rival Monroe's:
But in parting with these I was puzzled again,
With the how, and the who, and the where, and the when.
There's Howard, and Coley, and Hogarth, and Hiff,

I think they love venison—I know they love beef.
There's my countryman Higgins—Oh! let him alone,
For making a blunder, or picking a bone.
But hang it—to poets who seldom can eat,
Your very good mutton's a very good treat;
Such dainties to them, their health it might hurt,
It's like sending them ruffles when wanting a shirt.
While thus I debated, in reverie centred,
An acquaintance, a friend as he call'd himself, enter'd:
An underbred, fine spoken fellow was he,
And he smiled as he look'd at the venison and me.
"What have we got here?—Why, this is good eating!
Your own, I suppose—or is it in waiting?"
"Why, whose should it be?" cried I with a flounce;
"I get these things often"—but this was a bounce:
"Some lords, my acquaintance, that settle the nation,
Are pleased to be kind—but I hate ostentation."
"If that be the case then," cried he, very gay,
"I'm glad to have taken this house in my way.
To-morrow you take a poor dinner with me;
No words—I insist on't—precisely at three:
We'll have Johnson, and Burke; all the wits will be there;
My acquaintance is slight, or I'd ask my lord Clare.
And, now that I think on't, as I am a sinner!
We wanted this venison to make out a dinner.
What say you?—a pasty, it shall, and it must,
And my wife, little Kitty, is famous for crust.
Here, porter—this venison with me to Mile-end;
No stirring, I beg—my dear friend—my dear friend!"
Thus snatching his hat, he brush'd off like the wind,
And the porter and eatables follow'd behind.
Left alone to reflect, having emptied my shelf,
And, "nobody with me at sea but myself";
Though I could not help thinking my gentleman hasty,
Yet Johnson, and Burke, and a good venison pasty
Were things that I never disliked in my life,
Though clogg'd with a coxcomb, and Kitty his wife.
So next day, in due splendour to make my approach,
I drove to his door in my own hackney-coach.
When come to the place where we were all to dine,
(A chair-lumber'd closet just twelve feet by nine),
My friend bade me welcome, but struck me quite dumb
With tidings that Johnson and Burke would not come;
"For I knew it," he cried, "both eternally fail,
The one with his speeches, and t'other with Thrale;
But no matter, I'll warrant we'll make up the party
With two full as clever, and ten times as hearty.
The one is a Scotchman, the other a Jew,
They're both of them merry, and authors like you;
The one writes the Snarler, the other the Scourge;
Some think he writes Cinna—he owns to Panurge."

While thus he described them by trade and by name,
They enter'd, and dinner was served as they came.
At the top a fried liver, and bacon were seen,
At the bottom was tripe in a swinging tureen;
At the sides there were spinach and pudding made hot;
In the middle a place where the pasty—was not.
Now, my lord, as for tripe, it's my utter aversion,
And your bacon I hate like a Turk or a Persian;
So there I sat stuck like a horse in a pound,
While the bacon and liver went merrily round:
But what vex'd me most was that d—d Scottish rogue,
With his long-winded speeches, his smiles, and his brogue,
And, "madam," quoth he, "may this bit be my poison,
A prettier dinner I never set eyes on;
Pray, a slice of your liver, though may I be cursed,
But I've eat of your tripe till I'm ready to burst."
"The tripe," quoth the Jew, with his chocolate cheek,
"I could dine on this tripe seven days in a week:
I like these here dinners so pretty and small,
But your friend there, the doctor, eats nothing at all."
"O—ho!" quoth my friend, "he'll come on in a trice,
He's keeping a corner for something that's nice;
There's a pasty"—"A pasty!" repeated the Jew;
"I don't care if I keep a corner for't too."
"What the de'il, mon, a pasty!" re-echoed the Scot;
"Though splitting, I'll still keep a corner for that."—
"We'll all keep a corner," the lady cried out;
"We'll all keep a corner," was echoed about.
While thus we resolved, and the pasty delay'd,
With looks that quite petrified, enter'd the maid;
A visage so sad, and so pale with affright,
Waked Priam, in drawing his curtains by night.
But we quickly found out (for who could mistake her?)
That she came with some terrible news from the baker:
And so it fell out, for that negligent sloven
Had shut out the pasty on shutting his oven.
Sad Philomel thus—but let similes drop—
And now that I think on't the story may stop.
To be plain, my good lord, it's but labour misplaced,
To send such good verses to one of your taste:
You've got an odd something—a kind of discerning—
A relish—a taste—sicken'd over by learning;
At least it's your temper, as very well known,
That you think very slightly of all that's your own:
So, perhaps, in your habits of thinking amiss,
You may make a mistake, and think slightly of this.

The Deserted Village

Sweet Auburn! loveliest village of the plain;
Where health and plenty cheered the labouring swain,
Where smiling spring its earliest visit paid,

And parting summer's lingering blooms delayed:
Dear lovely bowers of innocence and ease,
Seats of my youth, when every sport could please,
How often have I loitered o'er thy green,
Where humble happiness endeared each scene!
How often have I paused on every charm,
The sheltered cot, the cultivated farm,
The never-failing brook, the busy mill,
The decent church that topt the neighbouring hill,
The hawthorn bush, with seats beneath the shade
For talking age and whispering lovers made!
How often have I blest the coming day,
When toil remitting lent its turn to play,
And all the village train, from labour free,
Led up their sports beneath the spreading tree,
While many a pastime circled in the shade,
The young contending as the old surveyed;
And many a gambol frolicked o'er the ground,
And sleights of art and feats of strength went round.
And still, as each repeated pleasure tired,
Succeeding sports the mirthful band inspired;
The dancing pair that simply sought renown
By holding out to tire each other down;
The swain mistrustless of his smutted face,
While secret laughter tittered round the place;
The bashful virgin's side-long looks of love,
The matron's glance that would those looks reprove:
These were thy charms, sweet village! sports like these,
With sweet succession, taught even toil to please:
These round thy bowers their cheerful influence shed:
These were thy charms—but all these charms are fled.

Sweet smiling village, loveliest of the lawn,
Thy sports are fled, and all thy charms withdrawn.
Amidst thy bowers the tyrant's hand is seen,
And desolation saddens all thy green:
One only master grasps the whole domain,
And half a tillage stints thy smiling plain.
No more thy glassy brook reflects the day,
But, choked with sedges, works its weedy way;
Along the glades, a solitary guest,
The hollow sounding bittern guards its nest;
Amidst thy desert walks the lapwing flies,
And tires their echoes with unvaried cries;
Sunk are thy bowers in shapeless ruin all,
And the long grass o'ertops the mouldering wall;
And trembling, shrinking from the spoiler's hand,
Far, far away thy children leave the land.

Ill fares the land, to hastening ills a prey,
Where wealth accumulates, and men decay:
Princes and lords may flourish, or may fade;
A breath can make them, as a breath has made:
But a bold peasantry, their country's pride,
When once destroyed, can never be supplied.

A time there was, ere England's griefs began,
When every rood of ground maintained its man;

For him light labour spread her wholesome store,
Just gave what life required, but gave no more:
His best companions, innocence and health;
And his best riches, ignorance of wealth.
But times are altered; trade's unfeeling train
Usurp the land and dispossess the swain;
Along the lawn, where scattered hamlets rose,
Unwieldy wealth and cumbrous pomp repose,
And every want to opulence allied,
And every pang that folly pays to pride.
These gentle hours that plenty bade to bloom,
Those calm desires that asked but little room,
Those healthful sports that graced the peaceful scene,
Lived in each look, and brightened all the green;
These, far departing, seek a kinder shore,
And rural mirth and manners are no more.
Sweet Auburn! parent of the blissful hour,
Thy glades forlorn confess the tyrant's power,
Here, as I take my solitary rounds
Amidst thy tangling walks and ruined grounds,
And, many a year elapsed, return to view
Where once the cottage stood, the hawthorn grew,
Remembrance wakes with all her busy train,
Swells at my breast, and turns the past to pain.
In all my wanderings round this world of care,
In all my griefs—and God has given my share—
I still had hopes, my latest hours to crown,
Amidst these humble bowers to lay me down;
To husband out life's taper at the close,
And keep the flame from wasting by repose:
I still had hopes, for pride attends us still,
Amidst the swains to show my book-learned skill,
Around my fire an evening group to draw,
And tell of all I felt, and all I saw;
And, as an hare whom hounds and horns pursue
Pants to the place from whence at first she flew,
I still had hopes, my long vexations past,
Here to return—and die at home at last.
O blest retirement, friend to life's decline,
Retreats from care, that never must be mine,
How happy he who crowns in shades like these
A youth of labour with an age of ease;
Who quits a world where strong temptations try,
And, since 'tis hard to combat, learns to fly!
For him no wretches, born to work and weep,
Explore the mine, or tempt the dangerous deep;
No surly porter stands in guilty state,
To spurn imploring famine from the gate;
But on he moves to meet his latter end,
Angels around befriending Virtue's friend;
Bends to the grave with unperceived decay,
While resignation gently slopes the way;
And, all his prospects brightening to the last,
His heaven commences ere the world be past!
Sweet was the sound, when oft at evening's close
Up yonder hill the village murmur rose.
There, as I passed with careless steps and slow,

The mingling notes came softened from below;
The swain responsive as the milk-maid sung,
The sober herd that lowed to meet their young,
The noisy geese that gabbled o'er the pool,
The playful children just let loose from school,
The watch-dog's voice that bayed the whispering wind,
And the loud laugh that spoke the vacant mind;—
These all in sweet confusion sought the shade,
And filled each pause the nightingale had made.
But now the sounds of population fail,
No cheerful murmurs fluctuate in the gale,
No busy steps the grass-grown foot-way tread,
For all the bloomy flush of life is fled.
All but yon widowed, solitary thing,
That feebly bends beside the plashy spring:
She, wretched matron, forced in age, for bread,
To strip the brook with mantling cresses spread,
To pick her wintry faggot from the thorn,
To seek her nightly shed, and weep till morn;
She only left of all the harmless train,
The sad historian of the pensive plain.

Near yonder copse, where once the garden smiled,
And still where many a garden flower grows wild;
There, where a few torn shrubs the place disclose,
The village preacher's modest mansion rose.
A man he was to all the country dear,
And passing rich with forty pounds a year;
Remote from towns he ran his godly race,
Nor e'er had changed, nor wished to change his place;
Unpractised he to fawn, or seek for power,
By doctrines fashioned to the varying hour;
Far other aims his heart had learned to prize,
More skilled to raise the wretched than to rise.
His house was known to all the vagrant train;
He chid their wanderings but relieved their pain:
The long-remembered beggar was his guest,
Whose beard descending swept his aged breast;
The ruined spendthrift, now no longer proud,
Claimed kindred there, and had his claims allowed;
The broken soldier, kindly bade to stay,
Sat by the fire, and talked the night away,
Wept o'er his wounds, or, tales of sorrow done,
Shouldered his crutch and showed how fields were won.
Pleased with his guests, the good man learned to glow,
And quite forgot their vices in their woe;
Careless their merits or their faults to scan,
His pity gave ere charity began.

Thus to relieve the wretched was his pride,
And e'en his failings leaned to Virtue's side;
But in his duty prompt at every call,
He watched and wept, he prayed and felt for all;
And, as a bird each fond endearment tries
To tempt its new-fledged offspring to the skies,
He tried each art, reproved each dull delay,
Allured to brighter worlds, and led the way.

Beside the bed where parting life was laid,
And sorrow, guilt, and pain by turns dismayed,
The reverend champion stood. At his control
Despair and anguish fled the struggling soul;
Comfort came down the trembling wretch to raise,
And his last faltering accents whispered praise.

At church, with meek and unaffected grace,
His looks adorned the venerable place;
Truth from his lips prevailed with double sway,
And fools, who came to scoff, remained to pray.
The service past, around the pious man,
With steady zeal, each honest rustic ran;
Even children followed with endearing wile,
And plucked his gown to share the good man's smile.
His ready smile a parent's warmth exprest;
Their welfare pleased him, and their cares distrest:
To them his heart, his love, his griefs were given,
But all his serious thoughts had rest in heaven.
As some tall cliff that lifts its awful form,
Swells from the vale, and midway leaves the storm,
Tho' round its breast the rolling clouds are spread,
Eternal sunshine settles on its head.

Beside yon straggling fence that skirts the way,
With blossom'd furze unprofitably gay,
There, in his noisy mansion, skill'd to rule,
The village master taught his little school.
A man severe he was, and stern to view;
I knew him well, and every truant knew;
Well had the boding tremblers learned to trace
The day's disasters in his morning face;
Full well they laughed with counterfeited glee
At all his jokes, for many a joke had he;
Full well the busy whisper circling round
Conveyed the dismal tidings when he frowned.
Yet he was kind, or, if severe in aught,
The love he bore to learning was in fault;
The village all declared how much he knew:
'Twas certain he could write, and cipher too;
Lands he could measure, terms and tides presage,
And even the story ran that he could gauge;
In arguing, too, the parson owned his skill,
For, even tho' vanquished, he could argue still;
While words of learned length and thundering sound
Amazed the gazing rustics ranged around;
And still they gazed, and still the wonder grew,
That one small head could carry all he knew.

But past is all his fame. The very spot
Where many a time he triumphed is forgot.
Near yonder thorn, that lifts its head on high,
Where once the sign-post caught the passing eye,
Low lies that house where nut-brown draughts inspired,
Where graybeard mirth and smiling toil retired,
Where village statesmen talked with looks profound,
And news much older than their ale went round.
Imagination fondly stoops to trace

The parlour splendours of that festive place:
The white-washed wall, the nicely sanded floor,
The varnished clock that clicked behind the door:
The chest contrived a double debt to pay,
A bed by night, a chest of drawers by day;
The pictures placed for ornament and use,
The twelve good rules, the royal game of goose;
The hearth, except when winter chill'd the day,
With aspen boughs and flowers and fennel gay;
While broken tea-cups, wisely kept for show,
Ranged o'er the chimney, glistened in a row.

Vain transitory splendours! could not all
Reprieve the tottering mansion from its fall?
Obscure it sinks, nor shall it more impart
An hour's importance to the poor man's heart.
Thither no more the peasant shall repair
To sweet oblivion of his daily care;
No more the farmer's news, the barber's tale,
No more the woodman's ballad shall prevail;
No more the smith his dusky brow shall clear,
Relax his ponderous strength, and lean to hear;
The host himself no longer shall be found
Careful to see the mantling bliss go round;
Nor the coy maid, half willing to be prest,
Shall kiss the cup to pass it to the rest.

Yes! let the rich deride, the proud disdain,
These simple blessings of the lowly train;
To me more dear, congenial to my heart,
One native charm, than all the gloss of art.
Spontaneous joys, where Nature has its play,
The soul adopts, and owns their first born sway;
Lightly they frolic o'er the vacant mind,
Unenvied, unmolested, unconfined.
But the long pomp, the midnight masquerade,
With all the freaks of wanton wealth arrayed—
In these, ere triflers half their wish obtain,
The toiling pleasure sickens into pain;
And, e'en while fashion's brightest arts decoy,
The heart distrusting asks if this be joy.

Ye friends to truth, ye statesmen who survey
The rich man's joy increase, the poor's decay,
'Tis yours to judge, how wide the limits stand
Between a splendid and an happy land.
Proud swells the tide with loads of freighted ore,
And shouting Folly hails them from her shore;
Hoards e'en beyond the miser's wish abound,
And rich men flock from all the world around.
Yet count our gains! This wealth is but a name
That leaves our useful products still the same.
Not so the loss. The man of wealth and pride
Takes up a space that many poor supplied;
Space for his lake, his park's extended bounds,
Space for his horses, equipage, and hounds:
The robe that wraps his limbs in silken sloth
Has robbed the neighbouring fields of half their growth;

His seat, where solitary sports are seen,
Indignant spurns the cottage from the green:
Around the world each needful product flies,
For all the luxuries the world supplies;
While thus the land adorned for pleasure all
In barren splendour feebly waits the fall.
As some fair female unadorned and plain,
Secure to please while youth confirms her reign,
Slights every borrowed charm that dress supplies,
Nor shares with art the triumph of her eyes;
But when those charms are past, for charms are frail,
When time advances, and when lovers fail,
She then shines forth, solicitous to bless,
In all the glaring impotence of dress.
Thus fares the land by luxury betrayed:
In nature's simplest charms at first arrayed,
But verging to decline, its splendours rise,
Its vistas strike, its palaces surprise;
While, scourged by famine from the smiling land
The mournful peasant leads his humble band,
And while he sinks, without one arm to save,
The country blooms—a garden and a grave.
Where then, ah! where, shall poverty reside,
To 'scape the pressure of contiguous pride?
If to some common's fenceless limits strayed,
He drives his flock to pick the scanty blade,
Those fenceless fields the sons of wealth divide,
And even the bare-worn common is denied.

If to the city sped—what waits him there?
To see profusion that he must not share;
To see ten thousand baneful arts combined
To pamper luxury, and thin mankind;
To see those joys the sons of pleasure know
Extorted from his fellow-creature's woe.
Here while the courtier glitters in brocade,
There the pale artist plies the sickly trade;
Here while the proud their long-drawn pomps display,
There the black gibbet glooms beside the way.
The dome where pleasure holds her midnight reign
Here, richly deckt, admits the gorgeous train:
Tumultuous grandeur crowds the blazing square,
The rattling chariots clash, the torches glare.
Sure scenes like these no troubles e'er annoy!
Sure these denote one universal joy!
Are these thy serious thoughts?—Ah, turn thine eyes
Where the poor houseless shivering female lies.
She once, perhaps, in village plenty blest,
Has wept at tales of innocence distrest;
Her modest looks the cottage might adorn,
Sweet as the primrose peeps beneath the thorn:
Now lost to all; her friends, her virtue fled,
Near her betrayer's door she lays her head,
And, pinch'd with cold, and shrinking from the shower,
With heavy heart deplores that luckless hour,
When idly first, ambitious of the town,
She left her wheel and robes of country brown.

Do thine, sweet Auburn,—thine, the loveliest train,—
Do thy fair tribes participate her pain?
Even now, perhaps, by cold and hunger led,
At proud men's doors they ask a little bread!
Ah, no! To distant climes, a dreary scene,
Where half the convex world intrudes between,
Through torrid tracts with fainting steps they go,
Where wild Altama murmurs to their woe.
Far different there from all that charmed before
The various terrors of that horrid shore;
Those blazing suns that dart a downward ray,
And fiercely shed intolerable day;
Those matted woods, where birds forget to sing,
But silent bats in drowsy clusters cling;
Those poisonous fields with rank luxuriance crowned,
Where the dark scorpion gathers death around;
Where at each step the stranger fears to wake
The rattling terrors of the vengeful snake;
Where crouching tigers wait their hapless prey,
And savage men more murderous still than they;
While oft in whirls the mad tornado flies,
Mingling the ravaged landscape with the skies.
Far different these from every former scene,
The cooling brook, the grassy vested green,
The breezy covert of the warbling grove,
That only sheltered thefts of harmless love.
Good Heaven! what sorrows gloomed that parting day,
That called them from their native walks away;
When the poor exiles, every pleasure past,
Hung round the bowers, and fondly looked their last,
And took a long farewell, and wished in vain
For seats like these beyond the western main,
And shuddering still to face the distant deep,
Returned and wept, and still returned to weep.
The good old sire the first prepared to go
To new found worlds, and wept for others' woe;
But for himself, in conscious virtue brave,
He only wished for worlds beyond the grave.
His lovely daughter, lovelier in her tears,
The fond companion of his helpless years,
Silent went next, neglected of her charms,
And left a lover's for a father's arms.
With louder plaints the mother spoke her woes,
And blest the cot where every pleasure rose,
And kist her thoughtless babes with many a tear
And claspt them close, in sorrow doubly dear,
Whilst her fond husband strove to lend relief
In all the silent manliness of grief.
O luxury! thou curst by Heaven's decree,
How ill exchanged are things like these for thee!
How do thy potions, with insidious joy,
Diffuse their pleasure only to destroy!
Kingdoms by thee, to sickly greatness grown,
Boast of a florid vigour not their own.
At every draught more large and large they grow,
A bloated mass of rank unwieldy woe;
Till sapped their strength, and every part unsound,

Down, down, they sink, and spread a ruin round.
Even now the devastation is begun,
And half the business of destruction done;
Even now, methinks, as pondering here I stand,
I see the rural virtues leave the land.
Down where yon anchoring vessel spreads the sail,
That idly waiting flaps with every gale,
Downward they move, a melancholy band,
Pass from the shore, and darken all the strand.
Contented Toil, and hospitable Care,
And kind connubial tenderness, are there;
And piety with wishes placed above,
And steady loyalty, and faithful love.
And thou, sweet Poetry, thou loveliest maid,
Still first to fly where sensual joys invade;
Unfit in these degenerate times of shame
To catch the heart, or strike for honest fame;
Dear charming nymph, neglected and decried,
My shame in crowds, my solitary pride;
Thou source of all my bliss, and all my woe,
That found'st me poor at first, and keep'st me so;
Thou guide by which the nobler arts excel,
Thou nurse of every virtue, fare thee well!
Farewell, and oh! where'er thy voice be tried,
On Torno's cliffs, or Pambamarca's side,
Whether where equinoctial fervours glow,
Or winter wraps the polar world in snow,
Still let thy voice, prevailing over time,
Redress the rigours of the inclement clime;
Aid slighted truth with thy persuasive strain;
Teach erring man to spurn the rage of gain;
Teach him, that states of native strength possest,
Tho' very poor, may still be very blest;
That trade's proud empire hastes to swift decay,
As ocean sweeps the laboured mole away;
While self-dependent power can time defy,
As rocks resist the billows and the sky.

Retaliation

Garrick wrote the following account of the origin of this poem. "At a meeting of a company of gentlemen who were well known to each other, and diverting themselves among other things with the peculiar oddities of Dr. Goldsmith, who never would allow a superior in any art, from writing poetry down to dancing a hornpipe, the Doctor with great eagerness insisted upon trying his epigrammatic powers with Mr. Garrick, and each of them was to write the other's epitaph. Mr. Garrick immediately said that his epitaph was finished, and spoke the following distich extempore:

Here lies Nolly Goldsmith, for shortness call'd Noll,
Who wrote like an angel, but talk'd like poor Poll!

Goldsmith, upon the company's laughing very heartily, grew very thoughtful and either would not or could not write anything at that time: however, he set to work, and some weeks after produced the . . . poem called 'Retaliation,' which has been much admired and gone through several editions. The public in general have been mistaken in imagining that this poem was written in anger by the Doctor; it was just the contrary; the whole on all sides was done with the greatest good humour."

Other accounts have it that several members of the company, dining at the St. James's coffee-house, wrote epitaphs on Goldsmith, ridiculing his Irish accent, his person, and his unreadiness in speech. Garrick's was spoken at once; the others were read to Goldsmith when he next appeared at the St. James's coffee-house.

The complete poem was not produced at once—certainly not "at the next meeting." It was unfinished when Goldsmith died.

The persons mentioned as of the company were all good friends of the Doctor's.

"Our Burke" was Edmund Burke; "Garrick," David Garrick; "Reynolds," Sir Joshua Reynolds; and "Tommy Townshend," Mr. T. Townshend, member for Whitchurch. In the course of the poem, Goldsmith refers to the Rev. Dr. Dodd, hanged for forgery; Dr. Kenrick, who read lectures at the Devil Tavern, under the title of "The School of Shakespeare"; James Macpherson, who had lately published a translation of Homer; Hugh Kelly, a popular dramatist; and W. Woodfall, printer of the *Morning Chronicle.*

Of old, when Scarron his companions invited,
Each guest brought his dish, and the feast was united.
If our landlord supplies us with beef and with fish,
Let each guest bring himself, and he brings the best dish:
Our Dean shall be venison, just fresh from the plains,
Our Burke shall be tongue, with the garnish of brains,
Our Will shall be wild fowl, of excellent flavour,
And Dick with his pepper, shall heighten the savour:
Our Cumberland's sweetbread its place shall obtain,
And Douglas is pudding substantial and plain:
Our Garrick's a salad; for in him we see
Oil, vinegar, sugar, and saltness agree:
To make out the dinner full certain I am,
That Ridge is anchovy, and Reynolds is lamb;
That Hickey's a capon, and by the same rule,
Magnanimous Goldsmith a gooseberry fool.
At a dinner so various, at such a repast,
Who'd not be a glutton, and stick to the last?
Here, waiter, more wine, let me sit while I'm able,
Till all my companions sink under the table;
Then, with chaos and blunders encircling my head,
Let me ponder, and tell what I think of the dead.

Here lies the good Dean, reunited to earth,
Who mix'd reason with pleasure, and wisdom with mirth:
If he had any faults, he has left us in doubt,
At least, in six weeks I could not find them out;
Yet some have declared, and it can't be denied them,
That sly-boots was cursedly cunning to hide them.

Here lies our good Edmund, whose genius was such,
We scarcely can praise it, or blame it too much;
Who, born for the universe, narrow'd his mind,
And to party gave up what was meant for mankind:
Tho' fraught with all learning, yet straining his throat
To persuade Tommy Townshend to lend him a vote;
Who, too deep for his hearers, still went on refining,
And thought of convincing, while they thought of dining;
Though equal to all things, for all things unfit;
Too nice for a statesman, too proud for a wit;
For a patriot too cool; for a drudge disobedient;
And too fond of the *right* to pursue the *expedient*.
In short, 'twas his fate, unemploy'd, or in place, sir,
To eat mutton cold, and cut blocks with a razor.

Here lies honest William, whose heart was a mint,
While the owner ne'er knew half the good that was in't;
The pupil of impulse, it forced him along,

His conduct still right, with his argument wrong;
Still aiming at honour, yet fearing to roam,
The coachman was tipsy, the chariot drove home;
Would you ask for his merits? alas! he had none;
What was good was spontaneous, his faults were his own.

Here lies honest Richard whose fate I must sigh at;
Alas! that such frolic should now be so quiet!
What spirits were his! what wit and what whim!
Now breaking a jest, and now breaking a limb!
Now wrangling and grumbling to keep up the ball!
Now teasing and vexing, yet laughing at all!
In short, so provoking a devil was Dick,
That we wish'd him full ten times a day at Old Nick;
But, missing his mirth and agreeable vein,
As often we wish'd to have Dick back again.

Here Cumberland lies, having acted his parts,
The Terence of England, the mender of hearts;
A flattering painter, who made it his care
To draw men as they ought to be, not as they are.
His gallants are all faultless, his women divine,
And comedy wonders at being so fine:
Like a tragedy queen he has dizen'd her out,
Or rather like tragedy giving a rout.
His fools have their follies so lost in a crowd
Of virtues and feelings that folly grows proud;
And coxcombs, alike in their failings alone,
Adopting his portraits, are pleased with their own.
Say, where has our poet this malady caught?
Or wherefore his characters thus without fault?
Say, was it that vainly directing his view
To find out men's virtues, and finding them few,
Quite sick of pursuing each troublesome elf,
He grew lazy at last, and drew from himself.

Here Douglas retires from his toils to relax,
The scourge of impostors, the terror of quacks:
Come, all ye quack bards, and ye quacking divines,
Come, and dance on the spot where your tyrant reclines:
When satire and censure encircled his throne,
I fear'd for your safety, I fear'd for my own;
But now he is gone, and we want a detector,
Our Dodds shall be pious, our Kenricks shall lecture;
Macpherson write bombast, and call it a style;
Our Townshend make speeches, and I shall compile;
New Lauders and Bowers the Tweed shall cross over,
No countryman living their tricks to discover;
Detection her taper shall quench to a spark,
And Scotchman meet Scotchman, and cheat in the dark.

Here lies David Garrick, describe him who can,
An abridgment of all that was pleasant in man:
As an actor, confess'd without rival to shine;
As a wit, if not first, in the very first line:

Yet, with talents like these, and an excellent heart,
This man had his failings—a dupe to his art.
Like an ill judging beauty, his colours he spread,
And be-plaster'd with rouge his own natural red.
On the stage he was natural, simple, affecting;
'Twas only that when he was off he was acting.
With no reason on earth to go out of his way,
He turn'd and he varied full ten times a day:
Though secure of our hearts, yet confoundedly sick
If they were not his own by finessing and trick:
He cast off his friends, as a huntsman his pack,
For he knew when he pleased he could whistle them back.
Of praise a mere glutton, he swallow'd what came,
And the puff of a dunce he mistook it for fame;
Till his relish grown callous, almost to disease,
Who pepper'd the highest was surest to please.
But let us be candid, and speak out our mind,
If dunces applauded, he paid them in kind.
Ye Kenricks, ye Kellys, and Woodfalls so grave,
What a commerce was yours while you got and you gave!
How did Grub-street re-echo the shouts that you raised,
While he was be-Roscius'd, and you were be-praised!
But peace to his spirit, wherever it flies,
To act as an angel and mix with the skies:
Those poets, who owe their best fame to his skill,
Shall still be his flatterers, go where he will;
Old Shakespeare receive him with praise and with love,
And Beaumonts and Bens be his Kellys above.
Here Hickey reclines, a most blunt pleasant creature,
And slander itself must allow him good nature;
He cherish'd his friend, and he relish'd a bumper;
Yet one fault he had, and that was a thumper.
Perhaps you may ask if the man was a miser?
I answer, no, no, for he always was wiser:
Too courteous perhaps, or obligingly flat?
His very worst foe can't accuse him of that:
Perhaps he confided in men as they go,
And so was too foolishly honest? Ah no!
Then what was his failing? come, tell it, and burn ye,—
He was, could he help it? a special attorney.
Here Reynolds is laid, and, to tell you my mind,
He has not left a wiser or better behind:
His pencil was striking, resistless, and grand;
His manners were gentle, complying, and bland;
Still born to improve us in every part,
His pencil our faces, his manners our heart:
To coxcombs averse, yet most civilly steering,
When they judged without skill he was still hard of hearing;
When they talk'd of their Raphaels, Correggios, and stuff,
He shifted his trumpet, and only took snuff.
By flattery unspoiled. . .

WILLIAM COWPER (1731-1800)

The Diverting History of John Gilpin

Showing how he went farther than he intended, and came safe home again.

John Gilpin was a citizen
  Of credit and renown,
A train-band captain eke was he
  Of famous London town.

John Gilpin's spouse said to her dear—
  Though wedded we have been
These twice ten tedious years, yet we
  No holiday have seen.

To-morrow is our wedding-day,
  And we will then repair
Unto the Bell at Edmonton
  All in a chaise and pair.

My sister, and my sister's child,
  Myself, and children three,
Will fill the chaise; so you must ride
  On horseback after we.

He soon replied—I do admire
  Of womankind but one,
And you are she, my dearest dear,
  Therefore it shall be done.

I am a linen-draper bold,
  As all the world doth know,
And my good friend the calender
  Will lend his horse to go.

Quoth Mrs. Gilpin—That's well said;
  And, for that wine is dear,
We will be furnish'd with our own,
  Which is both bright and clear.

John Gilpin kiss'd his loving wife;
  O'erjoy'd was he to find
That, though on pleasure she was bent,
  She had a frugal mind.

The morning came, the chaise was brought,
  But yet was not allow'd
To drive up to the door, lest all
  Should say that she was proud.

So three doors off the chaise was stay'd,
  Where they did all get in;
Six precious souls, and all agog
  To dash through thick and thin!

Smack went the whip, round went the wheels,
  Were never folk so glad,
The stones did rattle underneath,
  As if Cheapside were mad.

John Gilpin at his horse's side
  Seiz'd fast the flowing mane,
And up he got, in haste to ride,
  But soon came down again;

For saddle-tree scarce reach'd had he,
  His journey to begin,
When, turning round his head, he saw
  Three customers come in.

So down he came; for loss of time,
  Although it griev'd him sore,
Yet loss of pence, full well he knew,
  Would trouble him much more.

'Twas long before the customers
  Were suited to their mind,
When Betty screaming came down stairs—
  "The wine is left behind!"

Good lack! quoth he—yet bring it me,
  My leathern belt likewise,
In which I bear my trusty sword
  When I do exercise.

Now mistress Gilpin (careful soul!)
  Had two stone bottles found,
To hold the liquor that she lov'd,
  And keep it safe and sound.

Each bottle had a curling ear,
  Through which the belt he drew,
And hung a bottle on each side,
  To make his balance true.

Then, over all, that he might be
Equipp'd from top to toe,
His long red cloak, well brush'd and neat,
He manfully did throw.

Now see him mounted once again
Upon his nimble steed,
Full slowly pacing o'er the stones,
With caution and good heed!

But, finding soon a smoother road
Beneath his well-shod feet,
The snorting beast began to trot,
Which gall'd him in his seat.

So, Fair and softly, John he cried,
But John he cried in vain;
That trot became a gallop soon,
In spite of curb and rein.

So stooping down, as needs he must
Who cannot sit upright,
He grasp'd the mane with both his hands,
And eke with all his might.

His horse, who never in that sort
Had handled been before,
What thing upon his back had got
Did wonder more and more.

Away went Gilpin, neck or nought;
Away went hat and wig!—
He little dreamt, when he set out,
Of running such a rig!

The wind did blow, the cloak did fly,
Like streamer long and gay,
Till, loop and button failing both,
At last it flew away.

Then might all people well discern
The bottles he had slung;
A bottle swinging at each side,
As hath been said or sung.

The dogs did bark, the children scream'd,
Up flew the windows all;
And ev'ry soul cried out—Well done!
As loud as he could bawl.

Away went Gilpin—who but he?
His fame soon spread around—
He carries weight! he rides a race!
'Tis for a thousand pound!

And still, as fast as he drew near,
'Twas wonderful to view
How in a trice the turnpike-men
Their gates wide open threw.

And now, as he went bowing down
His reeking head full low,
The bottles twain behind his back
Were shatter'd at a blow.

Down ran the wine into the road,
Most piteous to be seen,
Which made his horse's flanks to smoke
As they had basted been.

But still he seem'd to carry weight,
With leathern girdle brac'd;
For all might see the bottle-necks
Still dangling at his waist.

Thus all through merry Islington
These gambols he did play,
And till he came unto the Wash
Of Edmonton so gay.

And there he threw the wash about
On both sides of the way,
Just like unto a trundling mop,
Or a wild goose at play.

At Edmonton his loving wife
From the balcony spied
Her tender husband, wond'ring much
To see how he did ride.

Stop, stop, John Gilpin!—Here's the house—
They all at once did cry;
The dinner waits, and we are tir'd:
Said Gilpin—So am I!

But yet his horse was not a whit
Inclin'd to tarry there;
For why?—his owner had a house
Full ten miles off, at Ware.

So like an arrow swift he flew,
  Shot by an archer strong;
So did he fly—which brings me to
  The middle of my song.

Away went Gilpin, out of breath,
  And sore against his will,
Till at his friend the calender's
  His horse at last stood still.

The calender, amaz'd to see
  His neighbour in such trim,
Laid down his pipe, flew to the gate,
  And thus accosted him:—

What news? what news? your tidings tell;
  Tell me you must and shall—
Say why bare-headed you are come,
  Or why you come at all?

Now Gilpin had a pleasant wit,
  And lov'd a timely joke;
And thus unto the calender
  In merry guise he spoke:—

I came because your horse would come;
  And, if I well forebode,
My hat and wig will soon be here—
  They are upon the road.

The calender, right glad to find
  His friend in merry pin,
Return'd him not a single word,
  But to the house went in;

Whence straight he came with hat and wig;
  A wig that flow'd behind,
A hat not much the worse for wear,
  Each comely in its kind.

He held them up, and, in his turn,
  Thus show'd his ready wit—
My head is twice as big as yours,
  They therefore needs must fit.

But let me scrape the dirt away
  That hangs upon your face;
And stop and eat, for well you may
  Be in a hungry case.

Said John—It is my wedding-day,
  And all the world would stare,
If wife should dine at Edmonton
  And I should dine at Ware!

So, turning to his horse, he said—
  I am in haste to dine;
'Twas for your pleasure you came here,
  You shall go back for mine.

Ah, luckless speech, and bootless boast!
  For which he paid full dear;
For, while he spake, a braying ass
  Did sing most loud and clear;

Whereat his horse did snort, as he
  Had heard a lion roar,
And gallop'd off with all his might,
  As he had done before.

Away went Gilpin, and away
  Went Gilpin's hat and wig!
He lost them sooner than at first—
  For why?—they were too big!

Now, mistress Gilpin, when she saw
  Her husband posting down
Into the country far away,
  She pull'd out half a crown;

And thus unto the youth she said
  That drove them to the Bell—
This shall be yours when you bring back
  My husband safe and well.

The youth did ride, and soon did meet
  John coming back amain;
Whom in a trice he tried to stop,
  By catching at his rein;

But, not performing what he meant,
  And gladly would have done,
The frighted steed he frighted more,
  And made him faster run.

Away went Gilpin, and away
  Went post-boy at his heels!—
The post-boy's horse right glad to miss
  The lumb'ring of the wheels.

Six gentlemen upon the road,
  Thus seeing Gilpin fly,
With post-boy scamp'ring in the rear,
  They rais'd the hue and cry:

Stop thief! stop thief!—a highwayman!
  Not one of them was mute;
And all and each that pass'd that way
  Did join in the pursuit.

And now the turnpike gates again
  Flew open in short space;
The toll-men thinking, as before,
  That Gilpin rode a race.

And so he did—and won it too!—
  For he got first to town;
Nor stopp'd till where he had got up
  He did again get down.

Now let us sing—Long live the king,
  And Gilpin long live he;
And, when he next doth ride abroad,
  May I be there to see!

On the Loss of the Royal George

This poem commemorates the going down of the *Royal George,* in August, 1782, with Rear-Admiral Kempenfelt and all on board. The ship was refitting at Portsmouth, preparatory to proceeding with the fleet under Lord Howe to the relief of Gibraltar. She was careened, to permit the repairing of a leak below waterline. A large piece of her bottom fell out, and she went down at once, with the loss of at least eight hundred persons, for, besides the officers and men, there were many tradesmen and women and children aboard.

Toll for the Brave!
The brave that are no more!
All sunk beneath the wave
Fast by their native shore!

Eight hundred of the brave
Whose courage well was tried,
Had made the vessel heel
And laid her on her side.

A land-breeze shook the shrouds
And she was overset;
Down went the Royal George,
With all her crew complete.

Toll for the brave!
Brave Kempenfelt is gone;
His last sea-fight is fought,
His work of glory done.

It was not in the battle;
No tempest gave the shock;
She sprang no fatal leak,
She ran upon no rock.

His sword was in its sheath,
His fingers held the pen,
When Kempenfelt went down
With twice four hundred men.

—Weigh the vessel up
Once dreaded by our foes!
And mingle with our cup
The tears that England owes.

Her timbers yet are sound,
And she may float again
Full charged with England's thunder,
And plough the distant main:

But Kempenfelt is gone,
His victories are o'er;
And he and his eight hundred
Shall plough the wave no more.

The Poplar Field

The poplars are fell'd, farewell to the shade
And the whispering sound of the cool colonnade,
The winds play no longer, and sing in the leaves,
Nor Ouse on his bosom their image receives.

Twelve years have elaps'd since I first took a view
Of my favourite field and the bank where they grew,

And now in the grass behold they are
laid,
And the tree is my seat that once lent
me a shade.

The blackbird has fled to another retreat
Where the hazels afford him a screen
from the heat,
And the scene where his melody charm'd
me before,
Resounds with his sweet-flowing ditty no
more.

My fugitive years are all hasting away,
And I must ere long lie as lowly as they,
With a turf on my breast, and a stone
at my head,
Ere another such grove shall arise in its
stead.

'Tis a sight to engage me, if any thing
can,
To muse on the perishing pleasures of
man;
Though his life be a dream, his enjoyments, I see,
Have a being less durable even than he.

RICHARD BRINSLEY SHERIDAN (1751-1816)

The Critic; or, A Tragedy Rehearsed

A Dramatic Piece in Three Acts

To Mrs. Greville

Madam,—In requesting your permission to address the following pages to you, which, as they aim themselves to be critical, require every protection and allowance that approving taste or friendly prejudice can give them, I yet ventured to mention no other motive than the gratification of private friendship and esteem. Had I suggested a hope that your implied approbation would give a sanction to their defects, your particular reserve, and dislike to the reputation of critical taste, as well as of poetical talent, would have made you refuse the protection of your name to such a purpose. However, I am not so ungrateful as now to attempt to combat this disposition in you. I shall not here presume to argue that the present state of poetry claims and expects every assistance that taste and example can afford it; nor endeavour to prove that a fastidious concealment of the most elegant productions of judgment and fancy is an ill return for the possession of those endowments. Continue to deceive yourself in the idea that you are known only to be eminently admired and regarded for the valuable qualities that attach private friendships, and the graceful talents that adorn conversation. Enough of what you have written has stolen into full public notice to answer my purpose; and you will, perhaps, be the only person, conversant in elegant literature, who shall read this address and not perceive that by publishing your particular approbation of the following drama, I have a more interested object than to boast the true respect and regard with which I have the honour to be, Madam, your very sincere and obedient humble servant,

R. B. SHERIDAN.

DRAMATIS PERSONÆ

SIR FRETFUL PLAGIARY
PUFF
DANGLE
SNEER
SIGNOR PASTICCIO RITORNELLO
INTERPRETER
UNDER PROMPTER
MR. HOPKINS
MRS. DANGLE
SIGNORE PASTICCIO RITORNELLO

Scenemen, Musicians, *and* Servants.

CHARACTERS OF THE TRAGEDY

LORD BURLEIGH
GOVERNOR OF TILBURY FORT
EARL OF LEICESTER
SIR WALTER RALEIGH
SIR CHRISTOPHER HATTON
MASTER OF THE HORSE
DON FEROLO WHISKERANDOS
BEEFEATER
JUSTICE
SON
CONSTABLE
THAMES
TILBURINA
CONFIDANT
JUSTICE'S LADY
FIRST NIECE
SECOND NIECE

Knights, Guards, Constables, Sentinels, Servants, Chorus, Rivers, Attendants, &c., &c.

SCENE—LONDON: *in* DANGLE'S *House during the First Act, and throughout the rest of the Play in* DRURY LANE THEATRE.

PROLOGUE

BY THE HONOURABLE RICHARD FITZPATRICK

THE sister Muses, whom these realms obey,
Who o'er the drama hold divided sway,
Sometimes by evil counsellors, 'tis said,
Like earth-born potentates have been misled.
In those gay days of wickedness and wit,
When Villiers criticised what Dryden writ,
The tragic queen, to please a tasteless crowd,
Had learn'd to bellow, rant, and roar so loud,
That frighten'd Nature, her best friend before,
The blustering beldam's company foreswore;
Her comic sister, who had wit 'tis true,
With all her merits, had her failings too:
And would sometimes in mirthful moments use
A style too flippant for a well-bred muse;
Then female modesty abash'd began

To seek the friendly refuge of the fan,
Awhile behind that slight intrenchment stood,
Till driven from thence, she left the stage for good.
In our more pious, and far chaster times,
These sure no longer are the Muse's crimes!
But some complain that, former faults to shun,
The reformation to extremes has run.
The frantic hero's wild delirium past,
Now insipidity succeeds bombast:
So slow Melpomene's cold numbers creep,
Here dulness seems her drowsy court to keep,
And we are scarce awake, whilst you are fast asleep.
Thalia, once so ill-behaved and rude,
Reform'd, is now become an arrant prude;
Retailing nightly to the yawning pit
The purest morals, undefiled by wit!
Our author offers, in these motley scenes,
A slight remonstrance to the drama's queens:
Nor let the goddesses be over nice;
Free-spoken subjects give the best advice.
Although not quite a novice in his trade,
His cause to-night requires no common aid.
To this, a friendly, just, and powerful court,
I come ambassador to beg support.
Can he undaunted brave the critic's rage?
In civil broils with brother bards engage?
Hold forth their errors to the public eye,
Nay more, e'en newspapers themselves defy?
Say, must his single arm encounter all?
By number vanquish'd, e'en the brave may fall;
And though no leader should success distrust,
Whose troops are willing, and whose cause is just;
To bid such hosts of angry foes defiance,
His chief dependence must be, your alliance.

ACT I

Scene I.—*A Room in* Dangle's *House*

Mr. *and* Mrs. Dangle *discovered at breakfast, and reading newspapers*

Dang. [*Reading.*] *Brutus to Lord North.—Letter the second on the State of the Army*—Psha! *To the first L dash D of the A dash Y.—Genuine extract of a Letter from St. Kitt's.—Coxheath Intelligence.—It is now confidently asserted that Sir Charles Hardy*—Psha! nothing but about the fleet and the nation!—and I hate all politics but theatrical politics.—Where's the Morning Chronicle?

Mrs. Dang. Yes, that's your Gazette.

Dang. So, here we have it.—[*Reads.*] *Theatrical intelligence extraordinary.—We hear there is a new tragedy in rehearsal at Drury Lane Theatre, called the Spanish Armada, said to be written by Mr. Puff, a gentleman well known in the theatrical world. If we may allow ourselves to give credit to the report of the performers, who, truth to say, are in general but indifferent judges, this piece abounds with the most striking and received beauties of modern composition.*—So! I am very glad my friend Puff's tragedy is in such forwardness.—Mrs. Dangle, my dear, you will be very glad to hear that Puff's tragedy——

Mrs. Dang. Lord, Mr. Dangle, why will you plague me about such nonsense?—Now the plays are begun I shall have no peace.—Isn't it sufficient to make yourself ridiculous by your passion for the theatre, without continually teasing me to join you? Why can't you ride your hobby-horse without desiring to place me on a pillion behind you, Mr. Dangle?

Dang. Nay, my dear, I was only going to read——

Mrs. Dang. No, no; you will never read anything that's worth listening to. You hate to hear about your country; there are letters every day with Roman signatures, demonstrating the certainty of an invasion, and proving that the nation is utterly undone. But you never will read anything to entertain one.

Dang. What has a woman to do with politics, Mrs. Dangle?

Mrs. Dang. And what have you to do with the theatre, Mr. Dangle? Why should you affect the character of a critic? I have no patience with you!—haven't you made yourself the jest of all your acquaintance by your interference in matters where you have no business? Are you not called a theatrical Quidnunc, and a mock Mæcenas to second-hand authors?

Dang. True; my power with the managers is pretty notorious. But is it no credit to have applications from all quarters for my interest—from lords to recommend fiddlers, from ladies to get boxes, from authors to get answers, and from actors to get engagements?

Mrs. Dang. Yes, truly; you have contrived to get a share in all the plague and trouble of theatrical property, without the profit, or even the credit of the abuse that attends it.

Dang. I am sure, Mrs. Dangle, you are no loser by it, however; you have all the advantages of it. Mightn't you, last winter, have had the reading of the new pantomime a fortnight previous to its performance? And doesn't Mr. Fosbrook let you take places for a play before it is advertised, and set you down for a box for every new piece through the season? And didn't my friend, Mr. Smatter, dedicate his last farce to you at my particular request, Mrs. Dangle?

Mrs. Dang. Yes; but wasn't the farce damned, Mr. Dangle? And to be sure it is extremely pleasant to have one's house made the motley rendezvous of all the lackeys of literature; the very high 'Change of trading authors and jobbing critics!—Yes, my drawing-room is an absolute register-office for candidate actors, and poets without character.—Then to be continually alarmed with misses and ma'ams piping hysteric changes on Juliets and Dorindas, Pollys and Ophelias; and the very furniture trembling at the probationary starts and unprovoked rants of would-be Richards and Hamlets!—And what is worse than all, now that the manager has monopolized the Opera House, haven't we the signors and signoras calling here, sliding their smooth semibreves, and gargling glib divisions in their outlandish throats—with foreign emissaries and French spies, for aught I know, disguised like fiddlers and figure dancers?

Dang. Mercy! Mrs. Dangle!

Mrs. Dang. And to employ yourself so idly at such an alarming crisis as this too—when, if you had the least spirit, you would have been at the head of one of the Westminster associations—or trailing a volunteer pike in the Artillery Ground! But you—o' my conscience, I believe, if the French were landed to-morrow, your first inquiry would be, whether they had brought a theatrical troop with them.

Dang. Mrs. Dangle, it does not signify—I say the stage is *the mirror of Nature,* and the actors are *the Abstract and brief Chronicles of the Time:* and pray what can a man of sense study better?—Besides, you will not easily persuade me that there is no credit or importance in being at the head of a band of critics, who take upon them to decide for the whole town, whose opinion and patronage all writers solicit, and whose recommendation no manager dares refuse.

Mrs. Dang. Ridiculous!—Both managers and authors of the least merit laugh at your pretensions.—The public is their critic—without whose fair approbation they know no play can rest on the stage, and with whose applause they welcome such attacks as yours, and laugh at the malice of them, where they can't at the wit.

Dang. Very well, madam—very well!

Enter SERVANT

Ser. Mr. Sneer, sir, to wait on you.

Dang. Oh, show Mr. Sneer up.—[*Exit* SERVANT.]—Plague on't, now we must appear loving and affectionate, or Sneer will hitch us into a story.

Mrs. Dang. With all my heart; you can't be more ridiculous than you are.

Dang. You are enough to provoke—

Enter SNEER

Ha! my dear Sneer, I am vastly glad to see you.—My dear, here's Mr. Sneer.

Mrs. Dang. Good-morning to you, sir.

Dang. Mrs. Dangle and I have been diverting ourselves with the papers. Pray, Sneer, won't you go to Drury Lane Theatre the first night of Puff's tragedy?

Sneer. Yes; but I suppose one shan't be able to get in, for on the first night of a new piece they always fill the house with orders to support it. But here, Dangle, I have brought you two pieces, one of which you must exert yourself to make the managers accept, I can tell you that; for 'tis written by a person of consequence.

Dang. So! now my plagues are beginning.

Sneer. Ay, I am glad of it, for now you'll be happy. Why, my dear Dangle, it is a pleasure to see how you enjoy your volunteer fatigue, and your solicited solicitations.

Dang. It's a great trouble—yet, egad, it's pleasant too.—Why, sometimes of a morning I have a dozen people call on me at breakfast-time, whose faces I never saw before, nor ever desire to see again.

Sneer. That must be very pleasant indeed!

Dang. And not a week but I receive fifty letters, and not a line in them about any business of my own.

Sneer. An amusing correspondence!

Dang. [*Reading.*] *Bursts into tears and exit.*—What, is this a tragedy?

Sneer. No, that's a genteel comedy, not a translation—only taken from the French: it is written in a style which they have lately tried to run down; the true sentimental, and nothing ridiculous in it from the beginning to the end.

Mrs. Dang. Well, if they had kept to that, I should not have been such an enemy to the stage; there was some edification to be got from those pieces, Mr. Sneer!

Sneer. I am quite of your opinion, Mrs. Dangle: the theatre, in proper hands, might certainly be made the school of morality; but now, I am sorry to say it, people seem to go there principally for their entertainment!

Mrs. Dang. It would have been more to the credit of the managers to have kept it in the other line.

Sneer. Undoubtedly, madam; and hereafter perhaps to have had it recorded, that in the midst of a luxurious and dissipated age, they preserved two houses in the capital, where the conversation was always moral at least, if not entertaining!

Dang. Now, egad, I think the worst alteration is in the nicety of the audience!—No *double-entendre,* no smart innuendo admitted; even Vanbrugh and Congreve obliged to undergo a bungling reformation!

Sneer. Yes, and our prudery in this respect is just on a par with the artificial bashfulness of a courtesan, who increases the blush upon her cheek in an exact proportion to the diminution of her modesty.

Dang. Sneer can't even give the public a good word! But what have we here?—This seems a very odd——

Sneer. Oh, that's a comedy on a very new plan; replete with wit and mirth, yet of a most serious moral! You see it is called *The Reformed House-breaker;* where, by the mere force of humour, house-breaking is put in so ridiculous a light, that if the piece has its proper run, I have no doubt but that bolts and bars will be entirely useless by the end of the season.

Dang. Egad, this is new indeed!

Sneer. Yes; it is written by a particular friend of mine, who has discovered that the follies and foibles of society are subjects unworthy the notice of the comic muse, who should be taught to stoop only to the greater vices and blacker crimes of humanity—gibbeting capital offences in five acts, and pillorying petty larcenies in two.—In short, his idea is to dramatize the penal laws, and make the stage a court of ease to the Old Bailey.

DANG. It is truly moral.

Re-enter SERVANT

Ser. Sir Fretful Plagiary, sir.

Dang. Beg him to walk up.—[*Exit* SERVANT.] Now, Mrs. Dangle, Sir Fretful Plagiary is an author to your own taste.

Mrs. Dang. I confess he is a favourite of mine, because everybody else abuses him.

Sneer. Very much to the credit of your charity, madam, if not of your judgment.

Dang. But, egad, he allows no merit to any author but himself, that's the truth on't—though he's my friend.

Sneer. Never.—He is as envious as an old maid verging on the desperation of six and thirty; and then the insidious humility with which he seduces you to give a free opinion on any of his works, can be exceeded only by the petulant arrogance with which he is sure to reject your observations.

Dang. Very true, egad—though he's my friend.

Sneer. Then his affected contempt of all newspaper strictures; though, at the same time, he is the sorest man alive, and shrinks like scorched parchment from the fiery ordeal of true criticism: yet he is so covetous of popularity, that he had rather be abused than not mentioned at all.

Dang. There's no denying it—though he is my friend.

Sneer. You have read the tragedy he has just finished, haven't you?

Dang. Oh, yes; he sent it to me yesterday.

Sneer. Well, and you think it execrable, don't you?

Dang. Why, between ourselves, egad, I must own—though he is my friend—that it is one of the most——He's here—[*Aside.*]—finished and most admirable perform——

Sir Fret. [*Without.*] Mr. Sneer with him did you say?

Enter Sir Fretful Plagiary

Dang. Ah, my dear friend!—Egad, we were just speaking of your tragedy.—Admirable, Sir Fretful, admirable!

Sneer. You never did anything beyond it, Sir Fretful—never in your life.

Sir Fret. You make me extremely happy; for without a compliment, my dear Sneer, there isn't a man in the world whose judgment I value as I do yours and Mr. Dangle's.

Mrs. Dang. They are only laughing at you, Sir Fretful; for it was but just now that——

Dang. Mrs. Dangle!—Ah, Sir Fretful, you know Mrs. Dangle.—My friend Sneer was rallying just now:—he knows how she admires you, and——

Sir. Fret. O Lord, I am sure Mr. Sneer has more taste and sincerity than to——[*Aside.*] A damned double-faced fellow!

Dang. Yes, yes—Sneer will jest—but a better humoured——

Sir Fret. Oh, I know——

Dang. He has a ready turn for ridicule—his wit costs him nothing.

Sir Fret. No, egad—or I should wonder how he came by it. [*Aside.*

Mrs. Dang. Because his jest is always at the expense of his friend. [*Aside.*

Dang. But, Sir Fretful, have you sent your play to the managers yet?—or can I be of any service to you?

Sir Fret. No, no, I thank you: I believe the piece had sufficient recommendation with it.—I thank you though.—I sent it to the manager of Covent Garden Theatre this morning.

Sneer. I should have thought now, that it might have been cast (as the actors call it) better at Drury Lane.

Sir Fret. O Lud! no—never send a play there while I live—hark'ee! [*Whispers* SNEER.

Sneer. Writes himself!—I know he does.

Sir Fret. I say nothing—I take away from no man's merit—am hurt at no man's good fortune—I say nothing.—But this I will say—through all my knowledge of life, I have observed—that there is not a passion so strongly rooted in the human heart as envy.

Sneer. I believe you have reason for what you say, indeed.

Sir Fret. Besides—I can tell you it is not always so safe to leave a play in the hands of those who write themselves.

Sneer. What, they may steal from them, hey, my dear Plagiary?

Sir Fret. Steal!—to be sure they may; and, egad, serve your best thoughts as gypsies do stolen children, disfigure them to make 'em pass for their own.

Sneer. But your present work is a sacrifice to Melpomene, and he, you know, never——

Sir Fret. That's no security: a dexterous plagiarist may do anything. Why, sir, for aught I know, he might take out some of the best things in my tragedy, and put them into his own comedy.

Sneer. That might be done, I dare be sworn.

Sir Fret. And then, if such a person gives you the least hint or assistance, he is devilish apt to take the merit of the whole——

Dang. If it succeeds.

Sir Fret. Ay, but with regard to this piece, I think I can hit that gentleman, for I can safely swear he never read it.

Sneer. I'll tell you how you may hurt him more.

Sir Fret. How?

Sneer. Swear he wrote it.

Sir Fret. Plague on't now, Sneer, I shall take it ill!—I believe you want to take away my character as an author.

Sneer. Then I am sure you ought to be very much obliged to me.

Sir Fret. Hey!—sir!——

Dang. Oh, you know, he never means what he says.

Sir Fret. Sincerely then—do you like the piece?

Sneer. Wonderfully!

Sir Fret. But come, now, there must be something that you think might be mended, hey—Mr. Dangle, has nothing struck you?

Dang. Why, faith, it is but an ungracious thing for the most part, to——

Sir Fret. With most authors it is just so, indeed; they are in general strangely tenacious! But, for my part, I am never so well pleased as when a judicious critic points out any defect to me; for what is the purpose of showing a work to a friend, if you don't mean to profit by his opinion?

Sneer. Very true.—Why, then, though I seriously admire the piece upon the whole, yet there is one small objection; which, if you'll give me leave, I'll mention.

Sir Fret. Sir, you can't oblige me more.

Sneer. I think it wants incident.

Sir Fret. Good God! you surprise me!—wants incident!

Sneer. Yes; I own I think the incidents are too few.

Sir Fret. Good God! Believe me, Mr. Sneer, there is no person for whose judgment I have a more implicit deference. But I protest to you, Mr. Sneer, I am only apprehensive that the incidents are too crowded.—My dear Dangle, how does it strike you?

Dang. Really I can't agree with my friend Sneer. I think the plot quite sufficient; and the four first acts by many degrees the best I ever read or saw in my life. If I might venture to suggest anything, it is that the interest rather falls off in the fifth.

Sir Fret. Rises, I believe you mean, sir.

Dang. No, I don't upon my word.

Sir Fret. Yes, yes, you do, upon my soul!—it certainly don't fall off, I assure you.—No, no; it don't fall off.

Dang. Now, Mrs. Dangle, didn't you say it struck you in the same light?

Mrs. Dang. No, indeed, I did not.—I did not see a fault in any part of the play, from the beginning to the end.

Sir Fret. Upon my soul, the women are the best judges after all!

Mrs. Dang. Or, if I made any objection, I am sure it was to nothing in the piece; but that I was afraid it was on the whole, a little too long.

Sir Fret. Pray, madam, do you speak as to duration of time; or do you mean that the story is tediously spun out?

Mrs. Dang. O Lud! no.—I speak only with reference to the usual length of acting plays.

Sir Fret. Then I am very happy—very happy indeed—because the play is a short play, a remarkably short play. I should not venture to differ with a lady on a point of taste; but on these occasions, the watch, you know, is the critic.

Mrs. Dang. Then, I suppose it must have been Mr. Dangle's drawling manner of reading it to me.

Sir Fret. Oh, if Mr. Dangle read it, that's quite another affair!—But I assure you, Mrs. Dangle, the first evening you can spare me three hours and a half, I'll undertake to read you the whole, from beginning to end, with the prologue and epilogue, and allow time for the music between the acts.

Mrs. Dang. I hope to see it on the stage next.

Dang. Well, Sir Fretful, I wish you may be able to get rid as easily of the newspaper criticisms as you do of ours.

Sir Fret. The newspapers! Sir, they are the most villainous—licentious—abominable—infernal.—Not that I ever read them—no—I make it a rule never to look into a newspaper.

Dang. You are quite right; for it certainly must hurt an author of delicate feelings to see the liberties they take.

Sir Fret. No, quite the contrary! their abuse is, in fact, the best panegyric—I like it of all things. An author's reputation is only in danger from their support.

Sneer. Why, that's true—and that attack, now, on you the other day——

Sir Fret. What? where?

Dang. Ay, you mean in a paper of Thursday: it was completely ill-natured, to be sure.

Sir Fret. Oh so much the better.—Ha! ha! ha! I wouldn't have it otherwise.

Dang. Certainly it is only to be laughed at; for——

Sir Fret. You don't happen to recollect what the fellow said, do you?

Sneer. Pray, Dangle—Sir Fretful seems a little anxious——

Sir Fret. O Lud, no!—anxious!—not I—not the least.—I—but one may as well hear, you know.

Dang. Sneer, do you recollect?—[*Aside to* SNEER.] Make out something.

Sneer. [*Aside to* DANGLE.] I will.—[*Aloud.*] Yes, yes, I remember perfectly.

Sir Fret. Well, and pray now—not that it signifies—what might the gentleman say?

Sneer. Why, he roundly asserts that you have not the slightest invention or original genius whatever; though you are the greatest traducer of all other authors living.

Sir Fret. Ha! ha! ha!—very good!

Sneer. That as to comedy, you have not one idea of your own, he believes, even in your commonplace-book—where stray jokes and pilfered witticisms are kept with as much method as the ledger of the lost and stolen office.

Sir Fret. Ha! ha! ha!—very pleasant!

Sneer. Nay, that you are so unlucky as not to have the skill even to steal with taste:—but that you glean from the refuse of obscure volumes, where more judicious plagiarists have been before you; so that the body of your work is a composition of dregs and sentiments—like a bad tavern's worst wine.

Sir Fret. Ha! ha!

Sneer. In your more serious efforts, he says, your bombast would be less intolerable, if the thoughts were ever suited to the expression; but the homeliness of the sentiment stares through the fantastic encumbrance of its fine language, like a clown in one of the new uniforms!

Sir Fret. Ha! ha!

Sneer. That your occasional tropes and flowers suit the general coarseness of your style, as tambour sprigs would a ground of linsey-woolsey; while your imitations of Shakspeare resemble the mimicry of Falstaff's page, and are about as near the standard as the original.

Sir Fret. Ha!

Sneer. In short, that even the finest passages you steal are of no service to you; for the poverty of your own language prevents their assimilating; so that they lie on the surface like lumps of marl on a barren moor, encumbering what it is not in their power to fertilize!

Sir Fret. [*After great agitation.*] Now, another person would be vexed at this!

Sneer. Oh! but I wouldn't have told you—only to divert you.

Sir Fret. I know it—I am diverted.—Ha! ha! ha!—not the least invention!—Ha! ha! ha!—very good!—very good!

Sneer. Yes—no genius! ha! ha! ha!

Dang. A severe rogue! ha! ha! ha! But you are quite right, Sir Fretful, never to read such nonsense.

Sir Fret. To be sure—for if there is anything to one's praise, it is a foolish vanity to be gratified at it; and, if it is abuse—why one is always sure to hear of it from one damned good-natured friend or other!

Enter SERVANT

Ser. Sir, there is an Italian gentleman, with a French interpreter, and three young ladies, and a dozen musicians, who say they are sent by Lady Rondeau and Mrs. Fugue.

Dang. Gadso! they come by appointment!—Dear Mrs. Dangle, do let them know I'll see them directly.

Mrs. Dang. You know, Mr. Dangle, I shan't understand a word they say.

Dang. But you hear there's an interpreter.

Mrs. Dang. Well, I'll try to endure their complaisance till you come. [*Exit.*

Ser. And Mr. Puff, sir, has sent word that the last rehearsal is to be this morning, and that he'll call on you presently.

Dang. That's true—I shall certainly be at home.—[*Exit* SERVANT.] —Now, Sir Fretful, if you have a mind to have justice done you in the way of answer, egad, Mr. Puff's your man.

Sir Fret. Psha! sir, why should I wish to have it answered, when I tell you I am pleased at it?

Dang. True, I had forgot that. But I hope you are not fretted at what Mr. Sneer——

Sir Fret. Zounds! no, Mr. Dangle; don't I tell you these things never fret me in the least?

Dang. Nay, I only thought——

Sir Fret. And let me tell you, Mr. Dangle, 'tis damned affronting in you to suppose that I am hurt when I tell you I am not.

Sneer. But why so warm, Sir Fretful?

Sir Fret. Gad's life! Mr. Sneer, you are as absurd as Dangle: how often must I repeat it to you, that nothing can vex me but your supposing it possible for me to mind the damned nonsense you have been repeating to me!—and, let me tell you, if you continue to believe this, you must mean to insult me, gentlemen—and, then, your disrespect will affect me no more than the newspaper criticisms—and I shall treat it with exactly the same calm indifference and philosophic contempt—and so your servant. [*Exit.*

Sneer. Ha! ha! ha! poor Sir Fretful! Now will he go and vent his philosophy in anonymous abuse of all modern critics and authors.—But, Dangle, you must get your friend Puff to take me to the rehearsal of his tragedy.

Dang. I'll answer for't, he'll thank you for desiring it. But come and help me to judge of this musical family: they are recommended by people of consequence, I assure you.

Sneer. I am at your disposal the whole morning!—but I thought you had been a decided critic in music as well as in literature.

Dang. So I am—but I have a bad ear. I'faith, Sneer, though, I am afraid we were a little too severe on Sir Fretful—though he is my friend.

Sneer. Why, 'tis certain, that unnecessarily to mortify the vanity of any writer is a cruelty which mere dulness never can deserve; but where a base and personal malignity usurps the place of literary emulation, the aggressor deserves neither quarter nor pity.

Dang. That's true, egad!—though he's my friend!

SCENE II.—*A drawing-room in* DANGLE'S *House*

MRS. DANGLE, SIGNOR PASTICCIO RITORNELLO, SIGNORE PASTICCIO RITORNELLO, INTERPRETER, *and* MUSICIANS *discovered.*

Interp. Je dis, madame, j'ai l'honneur to introduce et de vous demander votre protection pour le Signor Pasticcio Ritornello et pour sa charmante famille.

Signor Past. Ah! vosignoria, noi vi preghiamo di favoritevi colla vostra protezione.

1 *Signora Past.* Vosignoria fatevi questi grazie.

2 *Signora Past.* Si, signora.

Interp. Madame—me interpret.—C'est à dire—in English—qu'ils vous prient de leur faire l'honneur——

Mrs. Dang. I say again, gentlemen, I don't understand a word you say.

Signor Past. Questo signore spiegheró——

Interp. Oui—me interpret.—Nous avons les lettres de recommendation pour Monsieur Dangle de——

Mrs. Dang. Upon my word, sir, I don't understand you.

Signor Past. La Contessa Rondeau è nostra padrona.

3 *Signora Past.* Si, padre, et Miladi Fugue.

Interp. O!—me interpret.—Madame, ils disent—in English—Qu'ils ont l'honneur d'être protégés de ces dames.—You understand?

Mrs. Dang. No, sir,—no understand!

Enter DANGLE *and* SNEER

Interp. Ah, voici, Monsieur Dangle!

All Italians. Ah! Signor Dangle!

Mrs. Dang. Mr. Dangle, here are two very civil gentlemen trying to make themselves understood, and I don't know which is the interpreter.

Dang. Eh, bien!

[*The* INTERPRETER *and* SIGNOR PASTICCIO *here speak at the same time.*]

Interp. Monsieur Dangle, le grand bruit de vos talens pour la critique, et de votre intérêt avec messieurs les directeurs à tous les théâtres——

Signor Past. Vosignoria siete si famoso par la vostra conoscenza, e vostra interessa colla le direttore da——

Dang. Egad, I think the interpreter is the hardest to be understood of the two!

Sneer. Why, I thought, Dangle, you had been an admirable linguist!

Dang. So I am, if they would not talk so damned fast.

Sneer. Well, I'll explain that—the less time we lose in hearing them the better—for that, I suppose, is what they are brought here for.

[*Speaks to* SIGNOR PASTICCIO—*they sing trios, &c.,* DANGLE *beating out of time.*]

Enter SERVANT *and whispers* DANGLE

Dang. Show him up.—[*Exit* SERVANT.] Bravo! admirable! bravissimo! admirablissimo!—Ah! Sneer! where will you find voices such as these in England?

Sneer. Not easily.

Dang. But Puff is coming.—Signor and little signoras obligatissimo! —Sposa Signora Danglena—Mrs. Dangle, shall I beg you to offer them some refreshments, and take their address in the next room.

[*Exit* MRS. DANGLE *with* SIGNOR PASTICCIO, SIGNORE PASTICCIO, MUSICIANS, *and* INTERPRETER, *ceremoniously.*]

Re-enter SERVANT

Ser. Mr. Puff, sir. [*Exit.*

Enter PUFF

Dang. My dear Puff!

Puff. My dear Dangle, how is it with you?

Dang. Mr. Sneer, give me leave to introduce Mr. Puff to you.

Puff. Mr. Sneer is this?—Sir, he is a gentleman whom I have long panted for the honour of knowing—a gentleman whose critical talents and transcendent judgment——

Sneer. Dear sir——

Dang. Nay, don't be modest, Sneer; my friend Puff only talks to you in the style of his profession.

Sneer. His profession.

Puff. Yes, sir; I make no secret of the trade I follow: among friends and brother authors, Dangle knows I love to be frank on the subject, and to advertise myself *vivâ voce.*—I am, sir, a practitioner in panegyric, or, to speak more plainly, a professor of the art of puffing, at your service—or anybody else's.

Sneer. Sir, you are very obliging!—I believe, Mr. Puff, I have often admired your talents in the daily prints.

Puff. Yes, sir, I flatter myself I do as much business in that way as any six of the fraternity in town.—Devilish hard work all the summer, friend Dangle,—never worked harder! But, hark'ee,—the winter managers were a little sore, I believe.

Dang. No; I believe they took it all in good part.

Puff. Ay! then that must have been affectation in them: for, egad, there were some of the attacks which there was no laughing at!

Sneer. Ay, the humorous ones.—But I should think, Mr. Puff, that authors would in general be able to do this sort of work for themselves.

Puff. Why, yes—but in a clumsy way. Besides, we look on that as an encroachment, and so take the opposite side. I dare say, now, you conceive half the very civil paragraphs and advertisements you see to be written by the parties concerned, or their friends? No such thing: nine out of ten manufactured by me in the way of business.

Sneer. Indeed!

Puff. Even the auctioneers now—the auctioneers, I say—though the rogues have lately got some credit for their language—not an article of the merit theirs: take them out of their pulpits, and they are as dull as catalogues!—No, sir; 'twas I first enriched their style—'twas I first taught them to crowd their advertisements with panegyrical superlatives, each epithet rising above the other, like the bidders in their own auction rooms! From me they learned to inlay their phraseology with variegated chips of exotic metaphor: by me too their inventive faculties were called forth:—yes, sir, by me they were instructed to clothe ideal walls with gratuitous fruits—to insinuate obsequious rivulets into visionary groves—to teach courteous shrubs to nod their approbation of the grateful soil; or on emergencies to raise upstart oaks, where there never had been an acorn; to create a delightful vicinage without the assistance of a neighbour; or fix the temple of Hygeia in the fens of Lincolnshire!

Dang. I am sure you have done them infinite service; for now, when a gentleman is ruined, he parts with his house with some credit.

Sneer. Service! if they had any gratitude, they would erect a statue to him; they would figure him as a presiding Mercury, the god of traffic and fiction, with a hammer in his hand instead of a caduceus.—But pray, Mr. Puff, what first put you on exercising your talents in this way?

Puff. Egad, sir, sheer necessity!—the proper parent of an art so nearly allied to invention. You must know, Mr. Sneer, that from the first time I tried my hand at an advertisement, my success was such, that for some time after I led a most extraordinary life indeed!

Sneer. How, pray?

Puff. Sir, I supported myself two years entirely by my misfortunes.

Sneer. By your misfortunes!

Puff. Yes, sir, assisted by long sickness, and other occasional disorders: and a very comfortable living I had of it.

Sneer. From sickness and misfortunes! You practised as a doctor and an attorney at once?

Puff. No, egad; both maladies and miseries were my own.

Sneer. Hey! what the plague!

Dang. 'Tis true, i'faith.

Puff. Hark'ee!—By advertisements—*To the charitable and humane!* and *To those whom Providence hath blessed with affluence!*

Sneer. Oh, I understand you.

Puff. And, in truth, I deserved what I got! for, I suppose never man went through such a series of calamities in the same space of time. Sir, I was five times made a bankrupt, and reduced from a state of affluence, by a train of unavoidable misfortunes: then, sir, though a very industrious tradesman, I was twice burned out, and lost my little all both times: I lived upon those fires a month. I soon after was confined by a most excruciating disorder, and lost the use of my limbs: that told very well; for I had the case strongly attested, and went about to collect the subscriptions myself.

Dang. Egad, I believe that was when you first called on me.

Puff. In November last?—O no; I was at that time a close prisoner in the Marshalsea, for a debt benevolently contracted to serve a friend. I was afterwards twice tapped for a dropsy, which declined into a very profitable consumption. I was then reduced to—O no—then, I became a widow with six helpless children, after having had eleven husbands pressed, and being left every time eight months gone with child, and without money to get me into an hospital!

Sneer. And you bore all with patience, I make no doubt?

Puff. Why yes; though I made some occasional attempts at *felo de se;* but as I did not find those rash actions answer, I left off killing myself very soon. Well, sir, at last, what with bankruptcies, fires, gout, dropsies, imprisonments and other valuable calamities, having got together a pretty handsome sum, I determined to quit a business which had always gone rather against my conscience, and in a more liberal way still to indulge my talents for fiction and embellishment, through my favourite channels of diurnal communication—and so, sir, you have my history.

Sneer. Most obligingly communicative indeed! and your confession, if published, might certainly serve the cause of true charity, by rescuing the most useful channels of appeal to benevolence from the cant of imposition. But surely, Mr. Puff, there is no great mystery in your present profession?

Puff. Mystery, sir! I will take upon me to say the matter was never scientifically treated nor reduced to rule before.

Sneer. Reduced to rule!

Puff. O Lud, sir, you are very ignorant, I am afraid!—Yes, sir, puffing is of various sorts; the principal are, the puff direct, the puff preliminary, the puff collateral, the puff collusive, and the puff oblique, or puff by implication. These all assume, as circumstances require, the various forms of Letter to the Editor, Occasional Anecdote, Impartial Critique, Observation from Correspondent, or Advertisement from the Party.

Sneer. The puff direct, I can conceive——

Puff. O yes, that's simple enough! For instance,—a new comedy or farce is to be produced at one of the theatres (though by-the-by they don't bring out half what they ought to do)—the author, suppose Mr. Smatter, or Mr. Dapper, or any particular friend of mine—very well; the day before it is to be performed, I write an account of the manner in which it was received; I have the plot from the author, and only add—"characters strongly drawn—highly coloured—hand of a master—fund of genuine humour—mine of invention—neat dialogue—Attic salt." Then for the performance—"Mr. Dodd was astonishingly great in the character of Sir Harry. That universal and judicious actor, Mr. Palmer, perhaps never appeared to more advantage than in the colonel;—but it is not in the power of language to do justice to Mr. King: indeed he more than merited those repeated bursts of applause which he drew from a most brilliant and judicious audience. As to the scenery—the miraculous powers of Mr. De Loutherbourg's pencil are universally acknowledged. In short, we are at a loss which to admire most, the unrivalled genius of the author, the great attention and liberality of the managers, the wonderful abilities of the painter, or the incredible exertions of all the performers."

Sneer. That's pretty well indeed, sir.

Puff. Oh, cool!—quite cool!—to what I sometimes do.

Sneer. And do you think there are any who are influenced by this?

Puff. O Lud, yes, sir! the number of those who undergo the fatigue of judging for themselves is very small indeed.

Sneer. Well, sir, the puff preliminary.

Puff. Oh, that, sir, does well in the form of a caution. In a matter of gallantry now—Sir Flimsy Gossamer wishes to be well with Lady Fanny Fete—he applies to me—I open trenches for him with a paragraph in the Morning Post.—"It is recommended to the beautiful and accomplished Lady F four stars F dash E to be on her guard against that dangerous character, Sir F dash G; who, however pleasing and insinuating his manners may be, is certainly not remarkable for the *constancy of his attachments!*"—in italics. Here, you see, Sir Flimsy Gossamer is introduced to the particular notice of Lady Fanny, who perhaps never thought of him before—she finds herself publicly cautioned to avoid him, which naturally makes her desirous of seeing him; the observation of their acquaintance causes a pretty kind of mutual embarrassment; this produces a sort of sympathy of interest, which if Sir Flimsy is unable to improve effectually, he at least gains the credit of having their names mentioned together, by a particular set, and in a particular way—which nine times out of ten is the full accomplishment of modern gallantry.

Dang. Egad, Sneer, you will be quite an adept in the business.

Puff. Now, Sir, the puff collateral is much used as an appendage to advertisements, and may take the form of anecdote.—"Yesterday, as the celebrated George Bonmot was sauntering down St. James's Street, he met the lively Lady Mary Myrtle coming out of the park:—'Good God, Lady Mary, I'm surprised to meet you in a white jacket,—for I expected never to have seen you, but in a full-trimmed uniform and a light horseman's cap!'—'Heavens, George, where could you have learned that?'—'Why,' replied the wit, 'I just saw a print of you, in a new publication called the Camp Magazine; which, by-the-by, is a devilish clever thing, and is sold at No. 3, on the right hand of the way, two doors from the printing-office, the corner of Ivy Lane, Paternoster Row, price only one shilling.' "

Sneer. Very ingenious indeed!

Puff. But the puff collusive is the newest of any; for it acts in the disguise of determined hostility. It is much used by bold booksellers and enterprising poets.—"An indignant correspondent observes, that the new poem called *Beelzebub's Cotillon, or Proserpine's Fête Champêtre,* is one of the most unjustifiable performances he ever read. The severity with which certain characters are handled is quite shocking: and as there are many descriptions in it too warmly coloured for female delicacy, the shameful avidity with which this piece is bought by all people of fashion is a reproach on the taste of the times, and a disgrace to the delicacy of the age." Here you see the two strongest inducements are held forth; first that nobody ought to read it; and secondly, that everybody buys it: on the strength of which the publisher boldly prints the tenth edition, before he had Sold ten of the first; and then establishes it by threatening himself with the pillory, or absolutely indicting himself for *scan. mag.*

Dang. Ha! ha! ha!—'gad, I know it is so.

Puff. As to the puff oblique, or puff by implication, it is too various and extensive to be illustrated by an instance: it attracts in titles and presumes in patents; it lurks in the limitation of a subscription, and invites in the assurance of crowd and incommodation at public places; it delights to draw forth concealed merit, with a most disinterested assiduity; and sometimes wears a countenance of smiling censure and tender reproach. It has a wonderful memory for parliamentary debates, and will often give the whole speech of a favoured member with the most flattering accuracy. But, above all, it is a great dealer in reports and suppositions. It has the earliest intelligence of intended preferments that will reflect honour on the patrons; and embryo promotions of modest gentlemen, who know nothing of the matter themselves. It can hint a ribbon for implied services in the air of a common report; and with the carelessness of a casual paragraph, suggest officers into commands, to which they have no pretension but their wishes. This, sir, is the last principal class of the art of puffing—an art which I hope you will now agree with me is of the highest dignity, yielding a tablature of benevolence and public spirit; befriending equally trade, gallantry, criticism, and politics: the applause of genius—the register of charity—the triumph of heroism—the self-defence of contractors—the fame of orators—and the gazette of ministers.

Sneer. Sir, I am completely a convert both to the importance and ingenuity of your profession; and now, sir, there is but one thing which can possibly increase my respect for you, and that is, your permitting me to be present this morning at the rehearsal of your new trage——

Puff. Hush, for heaven's sake!—*My* tragedy!—Egad, Dangle, I take this very ill: you know how apprehensive I am of being known to be the author.

Dang. I'faith I would not have told—but it's in the papers, and your name at length in the Morning Chronicle.

Puff. Ah! those damned editors never can keep a secret!—Well, Mr. Sneer, no doubt you will do me great honour—I shall be infinitely happy—highly flattered——

Dang. I believe it must be near the time—shall we go together?

Puff. No; it will not be yet this hour, for they are always late at that theatre: besides, I must meet you there, for I have some little matters here to send to the papers, and a few paragraphs to scribble before I go. —[*Looking at memorandums.*] Here is *A conscientious Baker, on the subject of the Army Bread; and a Detester of visible Brickwork, in favour of the new invented Stucco;* both in the style of Junius, and promised for to-morrow. The Thames navigation too is at a stand. Misomud or Anti-shoal must go to work again directly.—Here too are some political memorandums—I see; ay—*To take Paul Jones and get the Indiamen out of the Shannon—reinforce Byron—compel the Dutch to*—so!—I must do that in the evening papers, or reserve it for the Morning Herald; for I know that I have undertaken to-morrow, besides, to establish the unanimity of the fleet in the Public Advertiser, and to shoot Charles Fox in the Morning Post.—So, egad, I ha'n't a moment to lose.

Dang. Well, we'll meet in the Green Room.

[*Exeunt severally.*

ACT II

Scene I.—*The Theatre before the Curtain*

Enter Dangle, Puff, *and* Sneer

Puff. No, no, sir; what Shakespeare says of actors may be better applied to the purpose of plays; they ought to be *the abstract and brief chronicles of the time.* Therefore when history, and particularly the history of our own country, furnishes anything like a case in point, to the time in which an author writes, if he knows his own interest, he will take advantage of it; so, sir, I call my tragedy *The Spanish Armada;* and have laid the scene before Tilbury Fort.

Sneer. A most happy thought, certainly!

Dang. Egad it was—I told you so. But pray now, I don't understand how you have contrived to introduce any love into it.

Puff. Love! oh, nothing so easy! for it is a received point among poets, that where history gives you a good heroic outline for a play, you may fill up with a little love at your own discretion: in doing which, nine times out of ten, you only make up a deficiency in the private history of the times. Now, I rather think I have done this with some success.

Sneer. No scandal about Queen Elizabeth, I hope?

Puff. O Lud! no, no;—I only suppose the governor of Tilbury Fort's daughter to be in love with the son of the Spanish admiral.

Sneer. Oh, is that all!

Dang. Excellent, i'faith! I see at once. But won't this appear rather improbable?

Puff. To be sure it will—but what the plague! a play is not to show occurrences that happen every day, but things just so strange, that though they never did, they might happen.

Sneer. Certainly nothing is unnatural, that is not physically impossible.

Puff. Very true—and for that matter Don Ferolo Whiskerandos, for that's the lover's name, might have been over here in the train of the Spanish ambassador, or Tilburina, for that is the lady's name, might have been in love with him, from having heard his character, or seen his picture; or from knowing that he was the last man in the world she ought to be in love with—or for any other good female reason.—However, sir, the fact is, that though she is but a knight's daughter, egad! she is in love like any princess!

Dang. Poor young lady! I feel for her already! for I can conceive how great the conflict must be between her passion and her duty; her love for her country, and her love for Don Ferolo Whiskerandos!

Puff. Oh, amazing!—her poor susceptible heart is swayed to and fro by contending passions like——

Enter UNDER PROMPTER

Und. Promp. Sir, the scene is set, and everything is ready to begin, if you please.

Puff. Egad, then we'll lose no time.

Und. Promp. Though, I believe, sir, you will find it very short, for all the performers have profited by the kind permission you granted them.

Puff. Hey! what?

Und. Promp. You know, sir, you gave them leave to cut out or omit whatever they found heavy or unnecessary to the plot, and I must own they have taken very liberal advantage of your indulgence.

Puff. Well, well.—They are in general very good judges, and I know I am luxuriant.—Now, Mr. Hopkins, as soon as you please.

Und. Promp. [*To the* Orchestra.] Gentlemen, will you play a few bars of something, just to——

Puff. Ay, that's right; for as we have the scenes and dresses, egad, we'll go to't, as if it was the first night's performance;—but you need not mind stopping between the acts—[*Exit* UNDER PROMPTER.—Orchestra *play—then the bell rings.*] Soh! stand clear, gentlemen. Now you know there will be a cry of down! down!—Hats off!—Silence!—Then up curtain, and let us see what our painters have done for us.

[*Curtain rises.*

SCENE II.—*Tilbury Fort*

"*Two* SENTINELS *discovered asleep*"

Dang. Tilbury Fort!—very fine indeed!

Puff. Now, what do you think I open with?

Sneer. Faith, I can't guess——

Puff. A clock.—Hark!—[*Clock strikes.*] I open with a clock striking, to beget an awful attention in the audience: it also marks the time, which is four o'clock in the morning, and saves a description of the rising sun, and a great deal about gilding the eastern hemisphere.

Dang. But pray, are the sentinels to be asleep?

Puff. Fast as watchmen.

Sneer. Isn't that odd though at such an alarming crisis?

Puff. To be sure it is,—but smaller things must give way to a striking scene at the opening; that's a rule. And the case is, that two great men are coming to this very spot to begin the piece; now it is not to be supposed they would open their lips, if these fellows were watching them; so, egad, I must either have sent them off their posts, or set them asleep.

Sneer. Oh, that accounts for it. But tell us, who are these coming?

Puff. These are they—Sir Walter Raleigh, and Sir Christopher Hatton. You'll know Sir Christopher by his turning out his toes—famous, you know, for his dancing. I like to preserve all the little traits of character.—Now attend.

"*Enter* SIR WALTER RALEIGH *and* SIR CHRISTOPHER HATTON.

Sir Christ. True, gallant Raleigh!"

Dang. What, they had been talking before?

Puff. O yes; all the way as they came along.—[*To the* actors.] I beg pardon, gentlemen, but these are particular friends of mine, whose remarks may be of great service to us.—[*To* SNEER *and* DANGLE.] Don't mind interrupting them whenever anything strikes you.

"*Sir Christ.* True, gallant Raleigh!
But oh, thou champion of thy country's fame,
There is a question which I yet must ask:
A question which I never ask'd before—
What mean these mighty armaments?
This general muster? and this throng of chiefs?"

Sneer. Pray, Mr. Puff, how came Sir Christopher Hatton never to ask that question before?

Puff. What, before the play began?—how the plague could he?

Dang. That's true, i'faith!

Puff. But you will hear what he thinks of the matter.

"*Sir Christ.* Alas! my noble friend, when I behold
Yon tented plains in martial symmetry
Array'd; when I count o'er yon glittering lines
Of crested warriors, where the proud steeds' neigh,
And valour-breathing trumpet's shrill appeal,
Responsive vibrate on my listening ear;
When virgin majesty herself I view,
Like her protecting Pallas, veil'd in steel,
With graceful confidence exhort to arms!
When, briefly, all I hear or see bears stamp
Of martial vigilance and stern defence,
I cannot but surmise—forgive, my friend,
If the conjecture's rash—I cannot but
Surmise the state some danger apprehends!"

Sneer. A very cautious conjecture that.

Puff. Yes, that's his character; not to give an opinion but on secure grounds.—Now then.

"*Sir Walt.* O most accomplish'd Christopher!"——

Puff. He calls him by his Christian name, to show that they are on the most familiar terms.

"*Sir Walt.* O most accomplish'd Christopher! I find
Thy staunch sagacity still tracks the future,
In the fresh print of the o'ertaken past."

Puff. Figurative!

"*Sir Walt.* Thy fears are just.

Sir Christ. But where? whence? when? and what
The danger is,—methinks I fain would learn.

Sir Walt. You know, my friend, scarce two revolving suns,
And three revolving moons, have closed their course
Since haughty Philip, in despite of peace,
With hostile hand hath struck at England's trade.

Sir Christ. I know it well.

Sir Walt. Philip, you know, is proud Iberia's king!

Sir Christ. He is.

Sir Walt. His subjects in base bigotry
And Catholic oppression held;—while we,
You know, the Protestant persuasion hold.

Sir Christ. We do.

Sir Walt. You know, beside, his boasted armament,
The famed Armada, by the Pope baptized,
With purpose to invade these realms——

Sir Christ. Is sailed,
Our last advices so report.

Sir Walt. While the Iberian admiral's chief hope,
His darling son——

Sir Christ. Ferolo Whiskerandos hight—

Sir Walt. The same—by chance a prisoner hath been ta'en,
And in this fort of Tilbury——

Sir Christ. Is now
Confined—'tis true, and oft from yon tall turret's top
I've mark'd the youthful Spaniard's haughty mien—
Unconquer'd, though in chains.

Sir Walt. You also know"——

Dang. Mr. Puff, as he knows all this, why does Sir Walter go on telling him?

Puff. But the audience are not supposed to know anything of the matter, are they?

Sneer. True; but I think you manage ill: for there certainly appears no reason why Sir Walter should be so communicative.

Puff. 'Fore Gad, now, that is one of the most ungrateful observations I ever heard!—for the less inducement he has to tell all this, the more, I think, you ought to be obliged to him; for I am sure you'd know nothing of the matter without it.

Dang. That's very true, upon my word.

Puff. But you will find he was not going on.

"*Sir Christ.* Enough, enough—'tis plain—and I no more
Am in amazement lost!"——

Puff. Here, now you see, Sir Christopher did not in fact ask any one question for his own information.

Sneer. No, indeed: his has been a most disinterested curiosity!

Dang. Really, I find that we are very much obliged to them both.

Puff. To be sure you are. Now then for the commander-in-chief, the Earl of Leicester, who, you know, was no favourite but of the queen's. —We left off—*in amazement lost!*

"*Sir Christ.* Am in amazement lost.
But, see where noble Leicester comes! supreme
In honours and command.

Sir Walt. And yet, methinks,
At such a time, so perilous, so fear'd,
That staff might well become an abler grasp.

Sir Christ. And so, by Heaven! think I; but soft, he's here!"

Puff. Ay, they envy him!

Sneer. But who are these with him?

Puff. Oh! very valiant knights: one is the governor of the fort, the other the master of the horse. And now, I think, you shall hear some better language: I was obliged to be plain and intelligible in the first scene, because there was so much matter of fact in it; but now, i'faith, you have trope, figure, and metaphor, as plenty as noun-substantives.

"*Enter* EARL OF LEICESTER, GOVERNOR, MASTER OF THE HORSE, KNIGHTS, &c.

Leic. How's this, my friends! is't thus your new-fledged zeal,
And plumed valour moulds in roosted sloth?
Why dimly glimmers that heroic flame,
Whose reddening blaze, by patriot spirit fed,
Should be the beacon of a kindling realm?
Can the quick current of a patriot heart
Thus stagnate in a cold and weedy converse,
Or freeze in tideless inactivity?
No! rather let the fountain of your valour
Spring through each stream of enterprise,
Each petty channel of conducive daring,
Till the full torrent of your foaming wrath
O'erwhelm the flats of sunk hostility!"

Puff. There it is—followed up!

"*Sir Walt.* No more!—the freshening breath of thy rebuke
Hath fill'd the swelling canvas of our souls!
And thus, though fate should cut the cable of

[*All take hands.*

Our topmost hopes, in friendship's closing line
We'll grapple with despair, and if we fall,
We'll fall in glory's wake!

Leic. There spoke old England's genius!
Then, are we all resolved?

All. We are—all resolved.

Leic. To conquer—or be free?

All. To conquer, or be free.

Leic. All?

All. All."

Dang. *Nem. con.* egad!

Puff. O yes!—where they do agree on the stage, their unanimity is wonderful!

"*Leic.* Then let's embrace—and now—— [*Kneels.*"

Sneer. What the plague, is he going to pray?

Puff. Yes; hush!—in great emergencies, there is nothing like a prayer.

"Leic. O mighty Mars!"

Dang. But why should he pray to Mars?

Puff. Hush!

"Leic. If in thy homage bred,
Each point of discipline I've still observed;
Nor but by due promotion, and the right
Of service, to the rank of major-general
Have risen; assist thy votary now!
Gov. Yet do not rise—hear me! [*Kneels.*
Mast. And me! [*Kneels.*
Knight. And me! [*Kneels.*
Sir Walt. And me! [*Kneels.*"
Sir Christ. And me!

Puff. Now pray altogether.

"All. Behold thy votaries submissive beg,
That thou wilt deign to grant them all they ask;
Assist them to accomplish all their ends,
And sanctify whatever means they use
To gain them!"

Sneer. A very orthodox quintetto!

Puff. Vastly well, gentlemen!—Is that well managed or not? Have you such a prayer as that on the stage?

Sneer. Not exactly.

Leic. [*To* PUFF.] But, sir, you haven't settled how we are to get off here.

Puff. You could not go off kneeling, could you?

Sir Walt. [*To* PUFF.] O no, sir; impossible!

Puff. It would have a good effect i'faith, if you could exeunt praying!—Yes, and would vary the established mode of springing off with a glance at the pit.

Sneer. Oh, never mind, so as you get them off!—I'll answer for it, the audience won't care how.

Puff. Well, then, repeat the last line standing, and go off the old way.

"All. And sanctify whatever means we use
To gain them. [*Exeunt.*"

Dang. Bravo! a fine exit.

Sneer. Well, really, Mr. Puff——

Puff. Stay a moment!

"*The* SENTINELS *get up.*

1 *Sent.* All this shall to Lord Burleigh's ear.
2 *Sent.* 'Tis meet it should. [*Exeunt.*"

Dang. Hey!—why, I thought those fellows had been asleep?

Puff. Only a pretence; there's the art of it: they were spies of Lord Burleigh's.

Sneer. But isn't it odd they never were taken notice of, not even by the commander-in-chief?

Puff. O Lud, sir! if people who want to listen, or overhear, were not always connived at in a tragedy, there would be no carrying on any plot in the world.

Dang. That's certain.

Puff. But take care, my dear Dangle! the morning gun is going to fire. [*Cannon fires.*

Dang. Well, that will have a fine effect!

Puff. I think so, and helps to realize the scene.—[*Cannon twice.*] What the plague! three morning guns! there never is but one!—Ay, this is always the way at the theatre: give these fellows a good thing, and they never know when to have done with it.—You have no more cannon to fire?

Und. Promp. [*Within.*] No, sir.

Puff. Now, then, for soft music.

Sneer. Pray, what's that for?

Puff. It shows that Tilburina is coming!—nothing introduces you a heroine like soft music. Here she comes.

Dang. And her confidant, I suppose?

Puff. To be sure! Here they are—inconsolable to the minuet in Ariadne! [*Soft Music.*

"*Enter* TILBURINA *and* CONFIDANT.

Tilb. Now has the whispering breath of gentle morn
Bid Nature's voice and Nature's beauty rise;
While orient Phœbus, with unborrow'd hues,
Clothes the waked loveliness which all night slept
In heavenly drapery! Darkness is fled.
Now flowers unfold their beauties to the sun,
And, blushing, kiss the beam he sends to wake them—
The striped carnation, and the guarded rose,
The vulgar wallflower, and smart gillyflower,
The polyanthus mean—the dapper daisy,
Sweet-William, and sweet marjoram—and all
The tribe of single and of double pinks!
Now, too, the feather'd warblers tune their notes
Around, and charm the listening grove. The lark!

The linnet! chaffinch! bullfinch! goldfinch! greenfinch!
But O, to me no joy can they afford!
Nor rose, nor wallflower, nor smart gillyflower,
Nor polyanthus mean, nor dapper daisy,
Nor William sweet, nor marjoram—nor lark,
Linnet, nor all the finches of the grove!"

Puff. Your white handkerchief, madam!——

Tilb. I thought, sir, I wasn't to use that till *heart-rending woe.*

Puff. O yes, madam, at *the finches of the grove,* if you please.

"*Tilb.* Nor lark,
Linnet, nor all the finches of the grove! [*Weeps.*"

Puff. Vastly well, madam!

Dang. Vastly well, indeed!

"*Tilb.* For, O, too sure, heart-rending woe is now
The lot of wretched Tilburina!"

Dang. Oh!—it's too much.

Sneer. Oh!—it is indeed.

"*Con.* Be comforted, sweet lady; for who knows,
But Heaven has yet some milk-white day in store?

Tilb. Alas! my gentle Nora,
Thy tender youth as yet hath never mourn'd
Love's fatal dart. Else wouldst thou know, that when
The soul is sunk in comfortless despair,
It cannot taste of merriment."

Dang. That's certain.

"*Con.* But see where your stern father comes:
It is not meet that he should find you thus."

Puff. Hey, what the plague!—what a cut is here! Why, what is become of the description of her first meeting with Don Whiskerandos—his gallant behaviour in the sea-fight—and the simile of the canary-bird?

Tilb. Indeed, sir, you'll find they will not be missed.

Puff. Very well, very well!

Tilb. [*To* CONFIDANT.] The cue, ma'am, if you please.

"*Con.* It is not meet that he should find you thus.

Tilb. Thou counsel'st right; but 'tis no easy task
For barefaced grief to wear a mask of joy.

Enter GOVERNOR.

Gov. How's this!—in tears?—O Tilburina, shame!
Is this a time for maudling tenderness,
And Cupid's baby woes?—Hast thou not heard

That haughty Spain's pope-consecrated fleet
Advances to our shores, while England's fate,
Like a clipp'd guinea, trembles in the scale?

Tilb. Then is the crisis of my fate at hand!
I see the fleets approach—I see——"

Puff. Now, pray, gentlemen, mind. This is one of the most useful figures we tragedy writers have, by which a hero or heroine, in consideration of their being often obliged to overlook things that are on the stage, is allowed to hear and see a number of things that are not.

Sneer. Yes; a kind of poetical second-sight!

Puff. Yes.—Now then, madam.

"*Tilb.* I see their decks
Are clear'd!—I see the signal made!
The line is form'd!—a cable's length asunder!
I see the frigates station'd in the rear;
And now, I hear the thunder of the guns!
I hear the victor's shouts—I also hear
The vanquish'd groan!—and now 'tis smoke—and now
I see the loose sails shiver in the wind!
I see—I see—what soon you'll see——

Gov. Hold, daughter! peace! this love hath turn'd thy brain:
The Spanish fleet thou canst not see—because
—It is not yet in sight!"

Dang. Egad, though, the governor seems to make no allowance for this poetical figure you talk of.

Puff. No, a plain matter-of-fact man;—that's his character.

"*Tilb.* But will you then refuse his offer?
Gov. I must—I will—I can—I ought—I do.
Tilb. Think what a noble price.
Gov. No more—you urge in vain.
Tilb. His liberty is all he asks."

Sneer. All who asks, Mr. Puff? Who is——

Puff. Egad, sir, I can't tell! Here has been such cutting and slashing, I don't know where they have got to myself.

Tilb. Indeed, sir, you will find it will connect very well.

"—And your reward secure."

Puff. Oh, if they hadn't been so devilish free with their cutting here, you would have found that Don Whiskerandos has been tampering for his liberty, and has persuaded Tilburina to make this proposal to her father. And now, pray observe the conciseness with which the argument is conducted. Egad, the *pro* and *con* goes as smart as hits in a fencing match. It is indeed a sort of small-sword-logic, which we have borrowed from the French.

"*Tilb.* A retreat in Spain!
Gov. Outlawry here!
Tilb. Your daughter's prayer!
Gov. Your father's oath!
Tilb. My lover!
Gov. My country!
Tilb. Tilburina!
Gov. England!
Tilb. A title!
Gov. Honour!
Tilb. A pension!
Gov. Conscience!
Tilb. A thousand pounds!
Gov. Ha! thou hast touch'd me nearly!"

Puff. There you see—she threw in *Tilburina.* Quick, parry carte with *England!* Ha! thrust in tierce *a title!*—parried by *honour.* Ha! *a pension* over the arm!—put by by *conscience.* Then flankonade with *a thousand pounds*—and a palpable hit, egad!

"*Tilb.* Canst thou—
Reject the suppliant, and the daughter too?
Gov. No more; I would not hear thee plead in vain:
The father softens—but the governor
Is fix'd! [*Exit.*"

Dang. Ay, that antithesis of persons is a most established figure.

"*Tilb.* 'Tis well,—hence then, fond hopes,—fond passion hence;
Duty, behold I am all over thine——
Whisk. [*Without.*] Where is my love—my——
Tilb. Ha!

Enter DON FEROLO WHISKERANDOS.

Whisk. My beauteous enemy!——"

Puff. O dear, ma'am, you must start a great deal more than that! Consider, you had just determined in favour of duty—when, in a moment, the sound of his voice revives your passion—overthrows your resolution—destroys your obedience. If you don't express all that in your start, you do nothing at all.

Tilb. Well, we'll try again.

Dang. Speaking from within has always a fine effect.

Sneer. Very.

"*Whisk.* My conquering Tilburina! How! Is't thus
We meet? why are thy looks averse? what means
That falling tear—that frown of boding woe?
Ha! now indeed I am a prisoner!
Yes, now I feel the galling weight of these

Disgraceful chains—which, cruel Tilburina!
Thy doting captive gloried in before.—
But thou art false, and Whiskerandos is undone!
Tilb. O no! how little dost thou know thy Tilburina!
Whisk. Art thou then true?—Begone cares, doubts, and fears,
I make you all a present to the winds;
And if the winds reject you—try the waves."

Puff. The wind, you know, is the established receiver of all stolen sighs, and cast-off griefs and apprehensions.

"*Tilb.* Yet must we part!—stern duty seals our doom:
Though here I call yon conscious clouds to witness,
Could I pursue the bias of my soul,
All friends, all right of parents, I'd disclaim,
And thou, my Whiskerandos, shouldst be father
And mother, brother, cousin, uncle, aunt,
And friend to me!
Whisk. Oh, matchless excellence! and must we part?
Well, if—we must—we must—and in that case
The less is said the better."

Puff. Heyday! here's a cut!—What, are all the mutual protestations out?

Tilb. Now, pray, sir, don't interrupt us just here: you ruin our feelings.

Puff. Your feelings!—but, zounds, my feelings, ma'am!

Sneer. No, pray don't interrupt them.

"*Whisk.* One last embrace.
Tilb. Now,—farewell, for ever.
Whisk. For ever!
Tilb. Ay, for ever! [*Going.*"

Puff. 'Sdeath and fury!—Gad's life!—sir! madam! if you go out without the parting look, you might as well dance out. Here, here!

Con. But pray, sir, how am I to get off here?

Puff. You! pshaw! what the devil signifies how you get off! edge away at the top, or where you will—[*Pushes the* CONFIDANT *off.*] Now, ma'am, you see——

Tilb. We understand you, sir.

"Ay, for ever.
Both. Oh! [*Turning back, and exeunt.—Scene closes.*"

Dang. Oh, charming!

Puff. Hey!—'tis pretty well, I believe: you see I don't attempt to strike out anything new—but I take it I improve on the established modes.

Sneer. You do, indeed! But pray is not Queen Elizabeth to appear?

Puff. No, not once—but she is to be talked of for ever; so that, egad, you'll think a hundred times that she is on the point of coming in.

Sneer. Hang it, I think it's a pity to keep her in the green-room all the night.

Puff. O no, that always has a fine effect—it keeps up expectation.

Dang. But are we not to have a battle?

Puff. Yes, yes, you will have a battle at last: but, egad, it's not to be by land, but by sea—and that is the only quite new thing in the piece.

Dang. What, Drake at the Armada, hey?

Puff. Yes, i'faith—fire-ships and all; then we shall end with the procession. Hey, that will do, I think?

Sneer. No doubt on't.

Puff. Come, we must not lose time; so now for the under-plot.

Sneer. What the plague, have you another plot?

Puff. O Lord, yes; ever while you live have two plots to your tragedy. The grand point in managing them is only to let your under-plot have as little connection with your main-plot as possible.—I flatter myself nothing can be more distinct than mine; for as in my chief plot the characters are all great people, I have laid my under-plot in low life, and as the former is to end in deep distress, I make the other end as happy as a farce.—Now, Mr. Hopkins, as soon as you please.

Enter UNDER PROMPTER

Under Promp. Sir, the carpenter says it is impossible you can go to the park scene yet.

Puff. The park scene! no! I mean the description scene here, in the wood.

Under Promp. Sir, the performers have cut it out.

Puff. Cut it out!

Under Promp. Yes, sir.

Puff. What! the whole account of Queen Elizabeth?

Under Promp. Yes, sir.

Puff. And the description of her horse and side-saddle?

Under Promp. Yes, sir.

Puff. So, so; this is very fine indeed!—Mr. Hopkins, how the plague could you suffer this?

Mr. Hop. [*Within.*] Sir, indeed the pruning-knife——

Puff. The pruning-knife—zounds!—the axe! Why, here has been such lopping and topping, I shan't have the bare trunk of my play left presently!—Very well, sir—the performers must do as they please; but, upon my soul, I'll print it every word.

Sneer. That I would, indeed.

Puff. Very well, sir; then we must go on.—Zounds! I would not have parted with the description of the horse!—Well, sir, go on.—Sir, it was one of the finest and most laboured things.—Very well, sir; let them go on.—There you had him and his accoutrements, from the bit to the crupper.—Very well, sir; we must go to the park scene.

Under Promp. Sir, there is the point: the carpenters say, that unless there is some business put in here before the drop, they sha'n't have time to clear away the fort, or sink Gravesend and the river.

Puff. So! this is a pretty dilemma, truly!—Gentlemen, you must excuse me—these fellows will never be ready, unless I go and look after them myself.

Sneer. O dear, sir, these little things will happen.

Puff. To cut out this scene!—but I'll print it—egad, I'll print it every word! [*Exeunt.*

ACT III

SCENE I.—*The Theatre, before the curtain*

Enter PUFF, SNEER, *and* DANGLE

Puff. Well, we are ready; now then for the justices.

[*Curtain rises.*

"JUSTICES, CONSTABLES, &c., *discovered.*"

Sneer. This, I suppose, is a sort of senate scene.

Puff. To be sure; there has not been one yet.

Dang. It is the under-plot, isn't it?

Puff. Yes.—What, gentlemen, do you mean to go at once to the discovery scene?

Just. If you please, sir.

Puff. Oh, very well!—Hark'ee, I don't choose to say anything more; but, i'faith they have mangled my play in a most shocking manner.

Dang. It's a great pity!

Puff. Now, then, Mr. Justice, if you please.

"*Just.* Are all the volunteers without?
Const. They are.
Some ten in fetters, and some twenty drunk.
Just. Attends the youth, whose most opprobrious fame
And clear convicted crimes have stamp'd him soldier?
Const. He waits your pleasure; eager to repay
The best reprieve that sends him to the fields

Of glory, there to raise his branded hand
In honour's cause.

Just. 'Tis well—'tis justice arms him!
Oh! may he now defend his country's laws
With half the spirit he has broke them all!
If 'tis your worship's pleasure, bid him enter.

Const. I fly, the herald of your will. [*Exit.*"

Puff. Quick, sir.

Sneer. But, Mr. Puff, I think not only the Justice, but the clown seems to talk in as high a style as the first hero among them.

Puff. Heaven forbid they should not in a free country!—Sir, I am not for making slavish distinctions, and giving all the fine language to the upper sort of people.

Dang. That's very noble in you, indeed.

"*Enter* Justice's Lady."

Puff. Now, pray mark this scene.

"*Lady.* Forgive this interruption, good my love;
But as I just now pass'd a prisoner youth,
Whom rude hands hither lead, strange bodings seized
My fluttering heart, and to myself I said,
An' if our Tom had lived, he'd surely been
This stripling's height!

Just. Ha! sure some powerful sympathy directs
Us both—

Enter Constable *with* Son.

Son. What is thy name?
My name is Tom Jenkins—*alias* have I none—
Though orphan'd, and without a friend!

Just. Thy parents?

Son. My father dwelt in Rochester—and was,
As I have heard—a fishmonger—no more."

Puff. What, sir, do you leave out the account of your birth, parentage, and education?

Son They have settled it so, sir, here,

Puff. Oh! oh!

"*Lady.* How loudly nature whispers to my heart
Had he no other name?

Son. I've seen a bill
Of his sign'd Tomkins, creditor.

Just. This does indeed confirm each circumstance
The gypsy told!—Prepare!

Son. I do.

Just. No orphan, nor without a friend art thou—
I am thy father; here's thy mother; there
Thy uncle—this thy first cousin, and those
Are all your near relations!
Lady. O ecstasy of bliss!
Son. O most unlook'd for happiness!
Just. O wonderful event! [*They faint alternately in each others arms.*"

Puff. There, you see, relationship, like murder, will out.

"*Just.* Now let's revive—else were this joy too much!
But come—and we'll unfold the rest within;
And thou, my boy, must needs want rest and food.
Hence may each orphan hope, as chance directs,
To find a father—where he least expects! [*Exeunt.*"

Puff. What do you think of that?

Dang. One of the finest discovery-scenes I ever saw!—Why, this under-plot would have made a tragedy itself.

Sneer. Ay! or a comedy either.

Puff. And keeps quite clear you see of the other.

"*Enter* SCENEMEN, *taking away the seats.*"

Puff. The scene remains, does it?

Sceneman. Yes, sir.

Puff. You are to leave one chair, you know.—But it is always awkward in a tragedy, to have you fellows coming in in your play-house liveries to remove things.—I wish that could be managed better.—So now for my mysterious yeoman.

"*Enter* BEEFEATER.

Beef. Perdition catch my soul, but I do love thee."

Sneer. Haven't I heard that line before?

Puff. No, I fancy not.—Where, pray?

Dang. Yes, I think there is something like it in Othello.

Puff. Gad! now you put me in mind on't, I believe there is—but that's of no consequence; all that can be said is, that two people happened to hit upon the same thought—and Shakspeare made use of it first, that's all.

Sneer. Very true.

Puff. Now, sir, your soliloquy—but speak more to the pit, if you please—the soliloquy always to the pit, that's a rule.

"*Beef.* Though hopeless love finds comfort in despair,
It never can endure a rival's bliss!
But soft—I am observed. [*Exit.*"

Dang. That's a very short soliloquy.

Puff. Yes—but it would have been a great deal longer if he had not been observed.

Sneer. A most sentimental Beefeater that, Mr. Puff!

Puff. Hark'ee—I would not have you be too sure that he is a Beefeater.

Sneer. What, a hero in disguise?

Puff. No matter—I only give you a hint. But now for my principal character. Here he comes—Lord Burleigh in person! Pray, gentlemen, step this way—softly—I only hope the Lord High Treasurer is perfect—if he is but perfect!

"Enter LORD BURLEIGH, *goes slowly to a chair, and sits."*

Sneer. Mr. Puff!

Puff. Hush!—Vastly well, sir! vastly well! a most interesting gravity.

Dang. What, isn't he to speak at all?

Puff. Egad, I thought you'd ask me that!—Yes, it is a very likely thing—that a minister in his situation, with the whole affairs of the nation on his head, should have time to talk!—But hush! or you'll put him out.

Sneer. Put him out; how the plague can that be, if he's not going to say anything?

Puff. There's the reason! why, his part is to think; and how the plague do you imagine he can think if you keep talking?

Dang. That's very true, upon my word!

"LORD BURLEIGH *comes forward, shakes his head, and exit."*

Sneer. He is very perfect indeed! Now, pray what did he mean by that?

Puff. You don't take it?

Sneer. No, I don't, upon my soul.

Puff. Why, by that shake of the head, he gave you to understand that even though they had more justice in their cause, and wisdom in their measures—yet, if there was not a greater spirit shown on the part of the people, the country would at last fall a sacrifice to the hostile ambition of the Spanish monarchy.

Sneer. The devil! did he mean all that by shaking his head?

Puff. Every word of it—if he shook his head as I taught him.

Dang. Ah! there certainly is a vast deal to be done on the stage by dumb show and expressions of face; and a judicious author knows how much he may trust to it.

Sneer. Oh, here are some of our old acquaintance.

"Enter Sir Christopher *and* Sir Walter Raleigh.

Sir Christ. My niece and your niece too!
By Heaven! there's witchcraft in't.—He could not else
Have gain'd their hearts.—But see where they approach:
Some horrid purpose lowering on their brows!

Sir Walt. Let us withdraw and mark them. [*They withdraw."*

Sneer. What is all this?

Puff. Ah! here has been more pruning!—but the fact is, these two young ladies are also in love with Don Whiskerandos.—Now, gentlemen, this scene goes entirely for what we call situation and stage effect, by which the greatest applause may be obtained, without the assistance of language, sentiment, or character: pray mark!

"Enter the two Nieces.

1st Niece. Ellena here!
She is his scorn as much as I—that is
Some comfort still!"

Puff. O dear, madam, you are not to say that to her face!—Aside, ma'am, aside.—The whole scene is to be aside.

"*1st Niece.* She is his scorn as much as I—that is
Some comfort still! [*Aside.*

2nd Niece. I know he prizes not Pollina's love;
But Tilburina lords it o'er his heart. [*Aside.*

1st Niece. But see the proud destroyer of my peace.
Revenge is all the good I've left. [*Aside.*

2nd Niece. He comes, the false disturber of my quiet.
Now vengeance do thy worst. [*Aside.*

Enter Don Ferolo Whiskerandos.

Whisk. O hateful liberty—if thus in vain
I seek my Tilburina!

Both Nieces. And ever shalt!

Sir Christopher Hatton *and* Sir Walter Raleigh *come forward.*

Sir Christ. and Sir Walt. Hold! we will avenge you.

Whisk. Hold *you*—or see your nieces bleed!

[*The two* Nieces *draw their two daggers to strike* Whiskerandos: *the two* Uncles *at the instant, with their two swords drawn, catch their two* Nieces' *arms, and turn the points of their swords to* Whiskerandos, *who immediately draws two daggers, and holds them to the two* Nieces' *bosoms."*

Puff. There's situation for you! there's an heroic group!—You see the ladies can't stab Whiskerandos—he durst not strike them, for fear of their uncles—the uncles durst not kill him, because of their nieces.—

I have them all at a dead lock!—for every one of them is afraid to let go first.

Sneer. Why, then they must stand there for ever!

Puff. So they would, if I hadn't a very fine contrivance for't.—Now mind——

"*Enter* BEEFEATER, *with his halbert.*

Beef. In the queen's name I charge you all to drop
Your swords and daggers! [*They drop their swords and daggers.*"

Sneer. That is a contrivance indeed!

Puff. Ay—in the queen's name.

"*Sir Christ.* Come, niece!
Sir Walt. Come, niece! [*Exeunt with the two* NIECES.
Whisk. What's he, who bids us thus renounce our guard?
Beef. Thou must do more—renounce thy love!
Whisk. Thou liest—base Beefeater!
Beef. Ha! hell! the lie!
By Heaven thou'st roused the lion in my heart!
Off, yeoman's habit!—base disguise! off! off!

[*Discovers himself by throwing off his upper dress, and appearing in a very fine waistcoat.*

Am I a Beefeater now?
Or beams my crest as terrible as when
In Biscay's Bay I took thy captive sloop?"

Puff. There, egad! he comes out to be the very captain of the privateer who had taken Whiskerandos prisoner—and was himself an old lover of Tilburina's.

Dang. Admirably managed, indeed!

Puff. Now, stand out of their way.

"*Whisk.* I thank thee, Fortune, that hast thus bestowed
A weapon to chastise this insolent. [*Takes up one of the swords.*
Beef. I take thy challenge, Spaniard, and I thank thee,
Fortune, too! [*Takes up the other sword.*"

Dang. That's excellently contrived!—It seems as if the two uncles had left their swords on purpose for them.

Puff. No, egad, they could not help leaving them.

"*Whisk.* Vengeance and Tilburina!
Beef. Exactly so——

[*They fight—and after the usual number of wounds given,* WHISKERANDOS *falls.*

Whisk. O cursed parry!—that last thrust in tierce
Was fatal.—Captain, thou hast fenced well!
And Whiskerandos quits this bustling scene
For all eter——

Beef. ——nity—he would have added, but stern death
Cut short his being, and the noun at once!"

Puff. Oh, my dear sir, you are too slow: now mind me.—Sir, shall I trouble you to die again?

"*Whisk.* And Whiskerandos quits this bustling scene
For all eter——

Beef. ——nity—he would have added,——"

Puff. No, sir—that's not it—once more, if you please.

Whisk. I wish, sir, you would practise this without me—I can't stay dying here all night.

Puff. Very well; we'll go over it by-and-by.—[*Exit* WHISKERANDOS.] I must humour these gentlemen!

"*Beef.* Farewell, brave Spaniard! and when next——"

Puff. Dear sir, you needn't speak that speech, as the body has walked off.

Beef. That's true, sir—then I'll join the fleet.

Puff. If you please.—[*Exit* BEEFEATER.] Now, who comes on?

"*Enter* GOVERNOR, *with his hair properly disordered.*

Gov. A hemisphere of evil planets reign!
And every planet sheds contagious frenzy!
My Spanish prisoner is slain! my daughter,
Meeting the dead corse borne along, has gone
Distract! [*A loud flourish of trumpets.*
But hark! I am summoned to the fort:
Perhaps the fleets have met! amazing crisis!
O Tilburina! from thy aged father's beard
Thou'st pluck'd the few brown hairs which time had left! [*Exit.*"

Sneer. Poor gentleman!

Puff. Yes—and no one to blame but his daughter!

Dang. And the planets——

Puff. True.—Now enter Tilburina!

Sneer. Egad, the business comes on quick here.

Puff. Yes, sir—now she comes in stark mad in white satin.

Sneer. Why in white satin?

Puff. O Lord, sir—when a heroine goes mad, she always goes into white satin.—Don't she, Dangle?

Dang. Always—it's a rule.

Puff. Yes—here it is—[*Looking at the book.*] "Enter Tilburina stark mad in white satin, and her confidant stark mad in white linen."

"*Enter* TILBURINA *and* CONFIDANT, *mad, according to custom.*"

Sneer. But, what the deuce! is the confidant to be mad too?

Puff. To be sure she is: the confidant is always to do whatever her mistress does; weep when she weeps, smile when she smiles, go mad when she goes mad.—Now, Madam Confidant—but keep your madness in the background, if you please.

"*Tilb.* The wind whistles—the moon rises—see,
They have kill'd my squirrel in his cage:
Is this a grasshopper?—Ha! no; it is my
Whiskerandos—you shall not keep him—
I know you have him in your pocket—
An oyster may be cross'd in love!—who says
A whale's a bird?—Ha! did you call, my love?—
He's here! he's there!—He's everywhere!
Ah me! he's nowhere! [*Exit.*"

Puff. There, do you ever desire to see anybody madder than that?

Sneer. Never, while I live!

Puff. You observed how she mangled the metre?

Dang. Yes,—egad, it was the first thing made me suspect she was out of her senses!

Sneer. And pray what becomes of her?

Puff. She is gone to throw herself into the sea, to be sure—and that brings us at once to the scene of action, and so to my catastrophe—my sea-fight, I mean.

Sneer. What, you bring that in at last?

Puff. Yes, yes—you know my play is called *The Spanish Armada;* otherwise, egad, I have no occasion for the battle at all.—Now then for my magnificence!—my battle!—my noise!—and my procession!—You are all ready?

Und. Promp. [*Within.*] Yes, sir.

Puff. Is the Thames dressed?

"*Enter* THAMES *with two* ATTENDANTS."

Thames. Here I am, sir.

Puff. Very well, indeed!—See, gentlemen, there's a river for you!—This is blending a little of the masque with my tragedy—a new fancy, you know—and very useful in my case; for as there must be a procession, I suppose Thames, and all his tributary rivers, to compliment Britannia with a fête in honour of the victory.

Sneer. But pray, who are these gentlemen in green with him?

Puff. Those?—those are his banks.

Sneer. His banks?

Puff. Yes, one crowned with alders, and the other with a villa!—you take the allusions?—But hey! what the plague!—you have got both your banks on one side.—Here, sir, come round.—Ever while you live, Thames, go between your banks.—[*Bell rings.*] There, so! now for't! —Stand aside, my dear friends!—Away, Thames!

[*Exit* THAMES *between his banks.*

[*Flourish of drums, trumpets, cannon, &c., &c. Scene changes to the sea—the fleets engage—the music plays—"Britons strike home."—Spanish fleet destroyed by fire-ships, &c.—English fleet advances—music plays, "Rule Britannia."—The procession of all the English rivers, and their tributaries, with their emblems, &c., begins with Handel's water music, ends with a chorus to the march in Judas Maccabæus.—During this scene,* PUFF *directs and applauds everything—then*

Puff. Well, pretty well—but not quite perfect. So, ladies and gentlemen, if you please, we'll rehearse this piece again to-morrow.

[*Curtain drops.*

WILLIAM BLAKE (1757-1827)

Piping Down the Valleys Wild

PIPING down the valleys wild,
Piping songs of pleasant glee,
On a cloud I saw a child,
And he laughing said to me:

"Pipe a song about a Lamb!"
So I piped with merry cheer,
"Piper, pipe that song again;"
So I piped: he wept to hear.

"Drop thy pipe, thy happy pipe;
Sing thy songs of happy cheer!"
So I sung the same again,
While he wept with joy to hear.

"Piper, sit thee down and write
In a book that all may read."
So he vanish'd from my sight;
And I pluck'd a hollow reed,

And I made a rural pen,
And I stain'd the water clear,
And I wrote my happy songs
Every child may joy to hear.

The Lamb

LITTLE lamb, who made thee?
Dost thou know who made thee,
Gave thee life and bade thee feed
By the stream and o'er the mead;
Gave thee clothing of delight,
Softest clothing, woolly, bright;
Gave thee such a tender voice,
Making all the vales rejoice?
Little lamb, who made thee?
Dost thou know who made thee?

Little lamb, I'll tell thee;
Little lamb, I'll tell thee.
He is callèd by thy name,
For He calls himself a Lamb;
He is meek and He is mild,
He became a little child.
I a child and thou a lamb,
We are callèd by His name.
Little lamb, God bless thee!
Little lamb, God bless thee!

The Tiger

TIGER! Tiger! burning bright
In the forests of the night,
What immortal hand or eye
Could frame thy fearful symmetry?

In what distant deeps or skies
Burnt the fire of thine eyes?
On what wings dare he aspire?
What the hand dare seize the fire?

And what shoulder, and what art,
Could twist the sinews of thy heart?
And when thy heart began to beat,
What dread hand? and what dread feet?

What the hammer? what the chain?
In what furnace was thy brain?
What the anvil? what dread grasp
Dare its deadly terrors clasp?

When the stars threw down their spears,
And watered heaven with their tears,
Did he smile his work to see?
Did he who made the Lamb make thee?

Tiger! Tiger! burning bright
In the forests of the night,
What immortal hand or eye
Dare frame thy fearful symmetry?

Holy Thursday

'Twas on a Holy Thursday, their innocent faces clean,
Came children walking two and two, in red, and blue, and green;
Gray-headed beadles walked before, with wands as white as snow,
Till into the high dome of Paul's they like Thames waters flow.

Oh what a multitude they seemed, these flowers of London town!
Seated in companies they sit, with radiance all their own.
The hum of multitudes was there, but multitudes of lambs,
Thousands of little boys and girls raising their innocent hands.

Now like a mighty wind they raise to heaven the voice of song,
Or like harmonious thunderings the seats of heaven among:
Beneath them sit the agèd men, wise guardians of the poor.
Then cherish pity, lest you drive an angel from your door.

ROBERT BURNS (1759-1796)

John Anderson, my Jo

John Anderson my jo, John,
When we were first acquent,
Your locks were like the raven,
Your bonie brow was brent;
But now your brow is beld, John,
Your locks are like the snaw;
But blessings on your frosty pow,
John Anderson my jo!

John Anderson my jo, John,
We clamb the hill thegither;
And monie a cantie day, John,
We've had wi' ane anither:
Now we maun totter down, John,
But hand in hand we'll go,
And sleep thegither at the foot,
John Anderson my jo!

A Red, Red Rose

O, my luve is like a red, red rose,
That's newly sprung in June.
O, my luve is like the melodie
That's sweetly play'd in tune.

As fair art thou, my bonie lass,
So deep in luve am I,
And I will luve thee still, my dear,
Till a' the seas gang dry.

Till a' the seas gang dry, my dear,
And the rocks melt wi' the sun!
I will luve thee still, my dear,
While the sands o' life shall run.

And fare thee weel, my only luve,
And fare thee weel awhile!
And I will come again, my luve,
Tho' it were ten thousand mile.

SAMUEL ROGERS (1763-1855)

A Wish

Mine be a cot beside the hill;
A bee-hive's hum shall soothe my ear;

A willowy brook that turns a mill,
With many a fall shall linger near.

The swallow, oft, beneath my thatch
Shall twitter from her clay-built nest;
Oft shall the pilgrim lift the latch,
And share my meal, a welcome guest.

Around my ivied porch shall spring
Each fragrant flower that drinks the dew;
And Lucy, at her wheel, shall sing
In russet-gown and apron blue.

The village-church among the trees,
Where first our marriage-vows were given,
With merry peals shall swell the breeze
And point with taper spire to Heaven.

WILLIAM WORDSWORTH
(1770-1850)

Lines Written in Early Spring

I HEARD a thousand blended notes,
While in a grove I sate reclined,
In that sweet mood when pleasant thoughts
Bring sad thoughts to the mind.

To her fair works did Nature link
The human soul that through me ran;
And much it grieved my heart to think
What man has made of man.

Through primrose tufts, in that green bower,
The periwinkle trailed its wreaths;
And 'tis my faith that every flower
Enjoys the air it breathes.

The birds around me hopped and played,
Their thoughts I cannot measure:—
But the least motion which they made,
It seemed a thrill of pleasure.

The budding twigs spread out their fan,
To catch the breezy air;
And I must think, do all I can,
That there was pleasure there.

If this belief from heaven be sent,
If such be Nature's holy plan,
Have I not reason to lament
What man has made of man?

Lines composed a few miles above Tintern Abbey, on revisiting the Banks of the Wye during a Tour. July 13, 1789.

FIVE years have past; five summers, with the length
Of five long winters! and again I hear
These waters, rolling from their mountain-springs
With a soft inland murmur.—Once again
Do I behold these steep and lofty cliffs,
That on a wild secluded scene impress
Thoughts of more deep seclusion; and connect
The landscape with the quiet of the sky.
The day is come when I again repose
Here, under this dark sycamore, and view
These plots of cottage-ground, these orchard-tufts,
Which at this season, with their unripe fruits,
Are clad in one green hue, and lose themselves
'Mid groves and copses. Once again I see
These hedge-rows, hardly hedge-rows, little lines
Of sportive wood run wild: these pastoral farms,
Green to the very door; and wreaths of smoke
Sent up, in silence, from among the trees!
With some uncertain notice, as might seem
Of vagrant dwellers in the houseless woods,
Or of some Hermit's cave, where by his fire
The Hermit sits alone.

These beauteous forms,
Through a long absence, have not been to me
As is a landscape to a blind man's eye:
But oft, in lonely rooms, and 'mid the din
Of towns and cities, I have owed to them,
In hours of weariness, sensations sweet,
Felt in the blood, and felt along the heart;
And passing even into my purer mind,
With tranquil restoration:—feelings too
Of unremembered pleasure: such, perhaps,
As have no slight or trivial influence
On that best portion of a good man's life,
His little, nameless, unremembered, acts
Of kindness and of love. Nor less, I trust,
To them I may have owed another gift,
Of aspect more sublime; that blessed mood,
In which the burthen of the mystery,
In which the heavy and the weary weight
Of all this unintelligible world,
Is lightened:—that serene and blessed mood,
In which the affections gently lead us on,—
Until, the breath of this corporeal frame
And even the motion of our human blood
Almost suspended, we are laid asleep
In body, and become a living soul:
While with an eye made quiet by the power
Of harmony, and the deep power of joy,
We see into the life of things.

If this
Be but a vain belief, yet, oh! how oft—
In darkness and amid the many shapes
Of joyless daylight; when the fretful stir
Unprofitable, and the fever of the world,
Have hung upon the beatings of my heart—
How oft, in spirit, have I turned to thee,
O sylvan Wye! thou wanderer thro' the woods,
How often has my spirit turned to thee!
And now, with gleams of half-extinguished thought,
With many recognitions dim and faint,
And somewhat of a sad perplexity,
The picture of the mind revives again:
While here I stand, not only with the sense
Of present pleasure, but with pleasing thoughts
That in this moment there is life and food
For future years. And so I dare to hope,
Though changed, no doubt, from what I was when first
I came among these hills; when like a roe
I bounded o'er the mountains, by the sides
Of the deep rivers, and the lonely streams,
Wherever nature led: more like a man
Flying from something that he dreads than one
Who sought the thing he loved. For nature then
(The coarser pleasures of my boyish days,
And their glad animal movements all gone by)
To me was all in all.—I cannot paint
What then I was. The sounding cataract
Haunted me like a passion: the tall rock,
The mountain, and the deep and gloomy wood,
Their colours and their forms, were then to me
An appetite; a feeling and a love,
That had no need of a remoter charm,
By thought supplied, nor any interest
Unborrowed from the eye.—That time is past,
And all its aching joys are now no more,
And all its dizzy raptures. Not for this
Faint I, nor mourn nor murmur; other gifts
Have followed; for such loss, I would believe,
Abundant recompense. For I have learned
To look on nature, not as in the hour

Of thoughtless youth; but hearing oftentimes
The still, sad music of humanity,
Nor harsh nor grating, though of ample power
To chasten and subdue. And I have felt
A presence that disturbs me with the joy
Of elevated thoughts; a sense sublime
Of something far more deeply interfused,
Whose dwelling is the light of setting suns,
And the round ocean and the living air,
And the blue sky, and in the mind of man:
A motion and a spirit, that impels
All thinking things, all objects of all thought,
And rolls through all things. Therefore am I still
A lover of the meadows and the woods,
And mountains; and of all that we behold
From this green earth; of all the mighty world
Of eye, and ear,—both what they half create,
And what perceive; well pleased to recognise
In nature and the language of the sense
The anchor of my purest thoughts, the nurse,
The guide, the guardian of my heart, and soul
Of all my moral being.

Nor perchance,
If I were not thus taught, should I the more
Suffer my genial spirits to decay:
For thou art with me here upon the banks
Of this fair river; thou my dearest Friend,
My dear, dear Friend; and in thy voice I catch
The language of my former heart, and read
My former pleasures in the shooting lights
Of thy wild eyes. Oh! yet a little while
May I behold in thee what I was once,
My dear, dear Sister! and this prayer I make,
Knowing that Nature never did betray
The heart that loved her; 'tis her privilege,
Through all the years of this our life, to lead
From joy to joy: for she can so inform
The mind that is within us, so impress
With quietness and beauty, and so feed
With lofty thoughts, that neither evil tongues,
Rash judgments, nor the sneers of selfish men,
Nor greetings where no kindness is, nor all
The dreary intercourse of daily life,
Shall e'er prevail against us, or disturb
Our cheerful faith, that all which we behold
Is full of blessings. Therefore let the moon
Shine on thee in thy solitary walk;
And let the misty mountain-winds be free
To blow against thee: and, in after years,
When these wild ecstasies shall be matured
Into a sober pleasure; when thy mind
Shall be a mansion for all lovely forms,
Thy memory be as a dwelling-place
For all sweet sounds and harmonies; oh! then,
If solitude, or fear, or pain, or grief,
Should be thy portion, with what healing thoughts
Of tender joy wilt thou remember me,
And these my exhortations! Nor, perchance—
If I should be where I no more can hear
Thy voice, nor catch from thy wild eyes these gleams
Of past existence—wilt thou then forget
That on the banks of this delightful stream
We stood together; and that I, so long
A worshipper of Nature, hither came
Unwearied in that service: rather say

With warmer love—oh! with far deeper
 zeal
Of holier love. Nor wilt thou then
 forget
That after many wanderings, many years
Of absence, these steep woods and lofty
 cliffs,
And this green pastoral landscape, were
 to me
More dear, both for themselves and for
 thy sake!

Strange fits of passion have I known

STRANGE fits of passion have I known:
 And I will dare to tell,
But in the Lover's ear alone,
 What once to me befell.

When she I loved looked every day
 Fresh as a rose in June,
I to her cottage bent my way,
 Beneath an evening-moon.

Upon the moon I fixed my eye,
 All over the wide lea;
With quickening pace my horse drew nigh
 Those paths so dear to me.

And now we reached the orchard-plot;
 And, as we climbed the hill,
The sinking moon to Lucy's cot
 Came near, and nearer still.

In one of those sweet dreams I slept,
 Kind Nature's gentlest boon!
And all the while my eyes I kept
 On the descending moon.

My horse moved on; hoof after hoof
 He raised, and never stopped:
When down behind the cottage roof,
 At once, the bright moon dropped.

What fond and wayward thoughts will
 slide
 Into a Lover's head!
"O mercy!" to myself I cried,
 "If Lucy should be dead!"

She dwelt among the untrodden ways

SHE dwelt among the untrodden ways
 Beside the springs of Dove,
A Maid whom there were none to praise
 And very few to love:

A violet by a mossy stone
 Half hidden from the eye!
—Fair as a star, when only one
 Is shining in the sky.

She lived unknown, and few could know
 When Lucy ceased to be;
But she is in her grave, and, oh,
 The difference to me!

I travelled among unknown men

I TRAVELLED among unknown men,
 In lands beyond the sea;
Nor, England! did I know till then
 What love I bore to thee.

'Tis past, that melancholy dream!
 Nor will I quit thy shore
A second time; for still I seem
 To love thee more and more.

Among thy mountains did I feel
 The joy of my desire;
And she I cherished turned her wheel
 Beside an English fire.

Thy mornings showed, thy nights con-
 cealed,
 The bowers where Lucy played;
And thine too is the last green field
 That Lucy's eyes surveyed.

Three years she grew in sun and shower

THREE years she grew in sun and
 shower
Then Nature said, "A lovelier flower
On earth was never sown;

This Child I to myself will take;
She shall be mine, and I will make
A Lady of my own.

"Myself will to my darling be
Both law and impulse: and with me
The Girl, in rock and plain,
In earth and heaven, in glade and bower,
Shall feel an overseeing power
To kindle or restrain.

"She shall be sportive as the fawn
That wild with glee across the lawn
Or up the mountain springs;
And hers shall be the breathing balm,
And hers the silence and the calm
Of mute insensate things.

"The floating clouds their state shall lend
To her; for her the willow bend;
Nor shall she fail to see
Even in the motions of the Storm
Grace that shall mould the Maiden's form
By silent sympathy.

"The stars of midnight shall be dear
To her; and she shall lean her ear
In many a secret place
Where rivulets dance their wayward round,
And beauty born of murmuring sound
Shall pass into her face.

"And vital feelings of delight
Shall rear her form to stately height,
Her virgin bosom swell;
Such thoughts to Lucy I will give
While she and I together live
Here in this happy dell."

Thus Nature spake—The work was done—
How soon my Lucy's race was run!
She died, and left to me
This heath, this calm, and quiet scene;
The memory of what has been,
And never more will be.

A slumber did my spirit seal

A SLUMBER did my spirit seal;
I had no human fears:
She seemed a thing that could not feel
The touch of earthly years.

No motion has she now, no force;
She neither hears nor sees;
Rolled round in earth's diurnal course,
With rocks, and stones, and trees.

London, 1802

MILTON! thou shouldst be living at this hour:
England hath need of thee; she is a fen
Of stagnant waters: altar, sword, and pen,
Fireside, the heroic wealth of hall and bower,
Have forfeited their ancient English dower
Of inward happiness. We are selfish men;
Oh! raise us up, return to us again;
And give us manners, virtue, freedom, power.
Thy soul was like a Star, and dwelt apart:
Thou hadst a voice whose sound was like the sea:
Pure as the naked heavens, majestic, free,
So didst thou travel on life's common way,
In cheerful godliness; and yet thy heart
The lowliest duties on herself did lay.

It is not to be thought of that the flood

IT is not to be thought of that the flood
Of British freedom, which, to the open sea
Of the world's praise, from dark antiquity
Hath flow'd, "with pomp of waters, unwithstood,"—

Roused though it be full often to a mood
Which spurns the check of salutary bands,—
That this most famous stream in bogs and sands
Should perish; and to evil and to good
Be lost for ever. In our halls is hung
Armoury of the invincible Knights of old:
We must be free or die, who speak the tongue
That Shakespeare spake; the faith and morals hold
Which Milton held.—In everything we are sprung
Of Earth's first blood, have titles manifold.

Ode
Intimations of Immortality from Recollections of early Childhood

The Child is father of the Man;
And I could wish my days to be
Bound each to each by natural piety.

I

THERE was a time when meadow, grove, and stream,
The earth, and every common sight,
To me did seem
Apparelled in celestial light,
The glory and the freshness of a dream.
It is not now as it hath been of yore;—
Turn wheresoe'er I may,
By night or day,
The things which I have seen I now can see no more.

II

The Rainbow comes and goes,
And lovely is the Rose,
The Moon doth with delight
Look round her when the heavens are bare,
Waters on a starry night
Are beautiful and fair;
The sunshine is a glorious birth;
But yet I know, where'er I go,
That there hath past away a glory from the earth.

III

Now, while the birds thus sing a joyous song,
And while the young lambs bound
As to the tabor's sound,
To me alone there came a thought of grief:
A timely utterance gave that thought relief,
And I again am strong:
The cataracts blow their trumpets from the steep;
No more shall grief of mine the season wrong;
I hear the Echoes through the mountains throng.
The Winds come to me from the fields of sleep,
And all the earth is gay;
Land and sea
Give themselves up to jollity,
And with the heart of May
Doth every Beast keep holiday;—
Thou Child of Joy,
Shout round me, let me hear thy shouts, thou happy Shepherd-boy!

IV

Ye blessed Creatures, I have heard the call
Ye to each other make; I see
The heavens laugh with you in your jubilee;
My heart is at your festival,
My head hath its coronal,
The fulness of your bliss, I feel—I feel it all.
Oh evil day! if I were sullen
While Earth herself is adorning,
This sweet May-morning,
And the Children are culling
On every side,
In a thousand valleys far and wide,

Fresh flowers; while the sun shines warm,
And the Babe leaps up on his Mother's arm:—
I hear, I hear, with joy I hear!
—But there's a Tree, of many, one,
A single Field which I have looked upon,
Both of them speak of something that is gone:
The Pansy at my feet
Doth the same tale repeat:
Whither is fled the visionary gleam?
Where is it now, the glory and the dream?

V

Our birth is but a sleep and a forgetting:
The Soul that rises with us, our life's Star,
Hath had elsewhere its setting,
And cometh from afar:
Not in entire forgetfulness,
And not in utter nakedness,
But trailing clouds of glory do we come
From God, who is our home:
Heaven lies about us in our infancy!
Shades of the prison-house begin to close
Upon the growing Boy,
But he beholds the light, and whence it flows,
He sees it in his joy;
The Youth, who daily farther from the east
Must travel, still is Nature's Priest,
And by the vision splendid
Is on his way attended;
At length the Man perceives it die away,
And fade into the light of common day.

VI

Earth fills her lap with pleasures of her own;
Yearnings she hath in her own natural kind,
And, even with something of a Mother's mind,
And no unworthy aim,
The homely Nurse doth all she can
To make her Foster-child, her Inmate Man,
Forget the glories he hath known,
And that imperial palace whence he came.

VII

Behold the Child among his new-born blisses,
A six years' Darling of a pigmy size!
See, where 'mid work of his own hand he lies,
Fretted by sallies of his mother's kisses,
With light upon him from his father's eyes!
See, at his feet, some little plan or chart,
Some fragment from his dream of human life,
Shaped by himself with newly-learned art;
A wedding or a festival,
A mourning or a funeral;
And this hath now his heart,
And unto this he frames his song:
Then will he fit his tongue
To dialogues of business, love, or strife;
But it will not be long
Ere this be thrown aside,
And with new joy and pride
The little Actor cons another part;
Filling from time to time his "humorous stage"
With all the Persons, down to palsied Age,
That Life brings with her in her equipage;
As if his whole vocation
Were endless imitation.

VIII

Thou, whose exterior semblance doth belie
Thy Soul's immensity;
Thou best Philosopher, who yet dost keep
Thy heritage, thou Eye among the blind,
That, deaf and silent, read'st the eternal deep,
Haunted for ever by the eternal mind,—
Mighty Prophet! Seer blest!
On whom those truths do rest,

Which we are toiling all our lives to find,
In darkness lost, the darkness of the grave;
Thou, over whom thy Immortality
Broods like the Day, a Master o'er a Slave,
A Presence which is not to be put by;
Thou little Child, yet glorious in the might
Of heaven-born freedom on thy being's height,
Why with such earnest pains dost thou provoke
The years to bring the inevitable yoke,
Thus blindly with thy blessedness at strife?
Full soon thy Soul shall have her earthly freight,
And custom lie upon thee with a weight,
Heavy as frost, and deep almost as life!

IX

O joy! that in our embers
Is something that doth live,
That nature yet remembers
What was so fugitive!
The thought of our past years in me doth breed
Perpetual benediction: not indeed
For that which is most worthy to be blest;
Delight and liberty, the simple creed
Of Childhood, whether busy or at rest,
With new-fledged hope still fluttering in his breast:—
Not for these I raise
The song of thanks and praise;
But for those obstinate questionings
Of sense and outward things,
Fallings from us, vanishings;
Blank misgivings of a Creature
Moving about in worlds not realised,
High instincts before which our mortal Nature
Did tremble like a guilty Thing surprised:
But for those first affections,
Those shadowy recollections,
Which, be they what they may,
Are yet the fountain-light of all our day,
Are yet a master-light of all our seeing;
Uphold us, cherish, and have power to make
Our noisy years seem moments in the being
Of the eternal Silence: truths that wake,
To perish never:
Which neither listlessness, nor mad endeavour,
Nor Man nor Boy,
Nor all that is at enmity with joy,
Can utterly abolish or destroy!
Hence in a season of calm weather
Though inland far we be,
Our Souls have sight of that immortal sea
Which brought us hither,
Can in a moment travel thither,
And see the Children sport upon the shore,
And hear the mighty waters rolling evermore.

X

Then sing, ye Birds, sing, sing a joyous song!
And let the young Lambs bound
As to the tabor's sound!
We in thought will join your throng,
Ye that pipe and ye that play,
Ye that through your hearts today
Feel the gladness of the May!
What though the radiance which was once so bright
Be now for ever taken from my sight,
Though nothing can bring back the hour
Of splendour in the grass, of glory in the flower;
We will grieve not, rather find
Strength in what remains behind;
In the primal sympathy
Which having been must ever be;
In the soothing thoughts that spring
Out of human suffering;
In the faith that looks through death,
In years that bring the philosophic mind.

XI

And O, ye Fountains, Meadows, Hills, and Groves,
Forbode not any severing of our loves!
Yet in my heart of hearts I feel your might;
I only have relinquished one delight
To live beneath your more habitual sway.
I love the Brooks which down their channels fret,
Even more than when I tripped lightly as they;
The innocent brightness of a new-born Day
Is lovely yet;
The Clouds that gather round the setting sun
Do take a sober colouring from an eye
That hath kept watch o'er man's mortality;
Another race hath been, and other palms are won.
Thanks to the human heart by which we live,
Thanks to its tenderness, its joys, and fears,
To me the meanest flower that blows can give
Thoughts that do often lie too deep for tears.

To the Cuckoo

O Blithe New-comer! I have heard
I hear thee and rejoice.
O Cuckoo! shall I call thee Bird,
Or but a wandering Voice?

While I am lying on the grass
Thy twofold shout I hear;
From hill to hill it seems to pass
At once far off, and near.

Though babbling only to the Vale,
Of sunshine and of flowers,
Thou bringest unto me a tale
Of visionary hours.

Thrice welcome, darling of the Spring!
Even yet thou art to me
No bird, but an invisible thing,
A voice, a mystery;

The same whom in my schoolboy days
I listened to; that Cry
Which made me look a thousand ways
In bush, and tree, and sky.

To seek thee did I often rove
Through woods and on the green;
And thou wert still a hope, a love;
Still longed for, never seen.

And I can listen to thee yet;
Can lie upon the plain
And listen, till I do beget
That golden time again.

O blessèd Bird! the earth we pace
Again appears to be
An unsubstantial, faery place;
That is fit home for thee!

It is a beauteous evening, calm and free

It is a beauteous evening, calm and free,
The holy time is quiet as a Nun
Breathless with adoration; the broad sun
Is sinking down in its tranquillity;
The gentleness of heaven broods o'er the Sea:
Listen! the mighty Being is awake,
And doth with his eternal motion make
A sound like thunder—everlastingly.
Dear Child! dear Girl! that walkest with me here,
If thou appear untouched by solemn thought,
Thy nature is not therefore less divine:
Thou liest in Abraham's bosom all the year;
And worship'st at the Temple's inner shrine,
God being with thee when we know it not.

Composed upon Westminster Bridge, September 3, 1802

EARTH has not anything to show more fair:
Dull would he be of soul who could pass by
A sight so touching in its majesty:
This City now doth, like a garment, wear
The beauty of the morning; silent, bare,
Ships, towers, domes, theatres and temples lie
Open unto the fields, and to the sky;
All bright and glittering in the smokeless air.
Never did sun more beautifully steep
In his first splendour, valley, rock, or hill;
Ne'er saw I, never felt, a calm so deep!
The river glideth at his own sweet will:
Dear God! the very houses seem asleep;
And all that mighty heart is lying still!

The Solitary Reaper

BEHOLD her, single in the field,
Yon solitary Highland Lass!
Reaping and singing by herself;
Stop here, or gently pass!
Alone she cuts and binds the grain,
And sings a melancholy strain;
O listen! for the Vale profound
Is overflowing with the sound.

No Nightingale did ever chaunt
More welcome notes to weary bands
Of travellers in some shady haunt,
Among Arabian sands:
A voice so thrilling ne'er was heard
In spring-time from the Cuckoo-bird,
Breaking the silence of the seas
Among the farthest Hebrides.

Will no one tell me what she sings!—
Perhaps the plaintive numbers flow
For old, unhappy, far-off things,
And battles long ago:
Or is it some more humble lay,
Familiar matter of to-day?
Some natural sorrow, loss, or pain,
That has been, and may be again?

Whate'er the theme, the Maiden sang
As if her song could have no ending;
I saw her singing at her work,
And o'er the sickle bending;—
I listened, motionless and still;
And, as I mounted up the hill,
The music in my heart I bore,
Long after it was heard no more.

Stepping Westward

"What, you are stepping westward?"—
"Yea."
—'Twould be a *wildish* destiny,
If we, who thus together roam
In a strange Land, and far from home,
Were in this place the guests of Chance:
Yet who would stop, or fear to advance,
Though home or shelter he had none,
With such a sky to lead him on?

The dewy ground was dark and cold;
Behind, all gloomy to behold;
And stepping westward seemed to be
A kind of *heavenly* destiny:
I liked the greeting; 'twas a sound
Of something without place or bound;
And seemed to give me spiritual right
To travel through that region bright.

The voice was soft, and she who spake
Was walking by her native lake:
The salutation had to me
The very sound of courtesy:
Its power was felt; and while my eye
Was fixed upon the glowing Sky,
The echo of the voice enwrought
A human sweetness with the thought
Of travelling through the world that lay
Before me in my endless way.

I wandered lonely as a cloud

I WANDERED lonely as a cloud
That floats on high o'er vales and hills,
When all at once I saw a crowd,
A host, of golden daffodils;
Beside the lake, beneath the trees,
Fluttering and dancing in the breeze.

Continuous as the stars that shine
  And twinkle on the milky way,
They stretched in never-ending line
  Along the margin of a bay:
Ten thousand saw I at a glance,
Tossing their heads in sprightly dance.

The waves beside them danced; but they
  Out-did the sparkling waves in glee:
A poet could not but be gay,
  In such a jocund company:
I gazed—and gazed—but little thought
What wealth the show to me had brought:

For oft, when on my couch I lie
  In vacant or in pensive mood,
They flash upon that inward eye
  Which is the bliss of solitude;
And then my heart with pleasure fills,
And dances with the daffodils.

The world is too much with us, late and soon

THE world is too much with us; late and soon,
Getting and spending, we lay waste our powers:
Little we see in Nature that is ours;
We have given our hearts away, a sordid boon!
This Sea that bares her bosom to the moon;
The winds that will be howling at all hours,
And are up-gathered now like sleeping flowers;
For this, for everything, we are out of tune;
It moves us not.—Great God! I'd rather be
A Pagan suckled in a creed outworn;
So might I, standing on this pleasant lea,
Have glimpses that would make me less forlorn;
Have sight of Proteus rising from the sea;
Or hear old Triton blow his wreathèd horn.

To a Skylark

ETHEREAL minstrel! pilgrim of the sky!
Dost thou despise the earth where cares abound?
Or, while the wings aspire, are heart and eye
Both with thy nest upon the dewy ground?
Thy nest which thou canst drop into at will,
Those quivering wings composed, that music still!

Leave to the nightingale her shady wood;
A privacy of glorious light is thine;
Whence thou dost pour upon the world a flood
Of harmony, with instinct more divine;
Type of the wise who soar, but never roam;
True to the kindred points of Heaven and Home!

Yarrow Unvisited

FROM Stirling castle we had seen
  The mazy Forth unravelled;
Had trod the banks of Clyde, and Tay,
  And with the Tweed had travelled;
And when we came to Clovenford,
  Then said my *"winsome Marrow,"*
"Whate'er betide, we'll turn aside,
  And see the Braes of Yarrow."

"Let Yarrow folk, *frae* Selkirk town,
  Who have been buying, selling,
Go back to Yarrow, 'tis their own;
  Each maiden to her dwelling!
On Yarrow's banks let herons feed,
  Hares couch, and rabbits burrow!
But we will downward with the Tweed,
  Nor turn aside to Yarrow.

"There's Galla Water, Leader Haughs,
  Both lying right before us;
And Dryborough, where with chiming Tweed
  The lintwhites sing in chorus;

There's pleasant Tiviot-dale, a land
Made blithe with plough and harrow:
Why throw away a needful day
To go in search of Yarrow?

"What's Yarrow but a river bare,
That glides the dark hills under?
There are a thousand such elsewhere
As worthy of your wonder."
—Strange words they seemed of slight and scorn;
My True-love sighed for sorrow;
And looked me in the face, to think
I thus could speak of Yarrow!

"Oh, green," said I, "are Yarrow's holms,
And sweet is Yarrow flowing!
Fair hangs the apple frae the rock,
But we will leave it growing.
O'er hilly path, and open Strath,
We'll wander Scotland thorough;
But, though so near, we will not turn
Into the dale of Yarrow.

"Let beeves and home-bred kine partake
The sweets of Burn-mill meadow;
The swan on still St. Mary's Lake
Float double, swan and shadow!
We will not see them; will not go,
To-day, nor yet to-morrow;
Enough if in our hearts we know
There's such a place as Yarrow.

"Be Yarrow stream unseen, unknown!
It must, or we shall rue it:
We have a vision of our own;
Ah! why should we undo it?
The treasured dreams of times long past,
We'll keep them, winsome Marrow!
For when we're there, although 'tis fair,
'Twill be another Yarrow!

"If Care with freezing years should come,
And wandering seem but folly,—
Should we be loth to stir from home,
And yet be melancholy;
Should life be dull, and spirits low,
'Twill soothe us in our sorrow,
That earth hath something yet to show,
The bonny holms of Yarrow!"

Yarrow Visited, September, 1814

AND is this Yarrow?—*This* the Stream
Of which my fancy cherished,
So faithfully, a waking dream?
An image that hath perished!
O that some Minstrel's harp were near,
To utter notes of gladness,
And chase this silence from the air,
That fills my heart with sadness!

Yet why?—a silvery current flows
With uncontrolled meanderings;
Nor have these eyes by greener hills
Been soothed, in all my wanderings.
And, through her depths, Saint Mary's Lake
Is visibly delighted;
For not a feature of those hills
Is in the mirror slighted.

A blue sky bends o'er Yarrow vale,
Save where that pearly whiteness
Is round the rising sun diffused,
A tender hazy brightness;
Mild dawn of promise! that excludes
All profitless dejection;
Though not unwilling here to admit
A pensive recollection.

Where was it that the famous Flower
Of Yarrow Vale lay bleeding?
His bed perchance was yon smooth mound
On which the herd is feeding:
And haply from this crystal pool,
Now peaceful as the morning,
The water-wraith ascended thrice—
And gave his doleful warning.

Delicious is the Lay that sings
The haunts of happy Lovers,
The path that leads them to the grove,
The leafy grove that covers:
And Pity sanctifies the Verse
That paints, by strength of sorrow,
The unconquerable strength of love;
Bear witness, rueful Yarrow!

But thou, that didst appear so fair
To fond imagination,

Dost rival in the light of day
Her delicate creation:
Meek loveliness is round thee spread,
A softness still and holy;
The grace of forest charms decayed,
And pastoral melancholy.

That region left, the vale unfolds
Rich groves of lofty stature,
With Yarrow winding through the pomp
Of cultivated nature;
And, rising from those lofty groves,
Behold a Ruin hoary!
The shattered front of Newark's Towers,
Renowned in Border story.

Fair scenes for childhood's opening bloom,
For sportive youth to stray in;
For manhood to enjoy his strength;
And age to wear away in!
Yon cottage seems a bower of bliss,
A covert for protection
Of tender thoughts, that nestle there—
The brood of chaste affection.

How sweet, on this autumnal day,
The wild-wood fruits to gather,
And on my True-love's forehead plant
A crest of blooming heather!
And what if I enwreathed my own!
'Twere no offence to reason;
The sober Hills thus deck their brows
To meet the wintry season.

I see—but not by sight alone,
Loved Yarrow, have I won thee;
A ray of fancy still survives—
Her sunshine plays upon thee!
Thy ever-youthful waters keep
A course of lively pleasure;
And gladsome notes my lips can breathe
Accordant to the measure.

The vapours linger round the Heights,
They melt, and soon must vanish;
One hour is theirs, nor more is mine—
Sad thought, which I would banish,
But that I know, where'er I go,
Thy genuine image, Yarrow!
Will dwell with me—to heighten joy,
And cheer my mind in sorrow

Yarrow Revisited

The gallant Youth, who may have gained,
Or seeks, a "winsome Marrow,"
Was but an Infant in the lap
When first I looked on Yarrow;
Once more, by Newark's Castle-gate
Long left without a warder,
I stood, looked, listened, and with Thee
Great Minstrel of the Border!

Grave thoughts ruled wide on that sweet day,
Their dignity installing
In gentle bosoms, while sere leaves
Were on the bough, or falling;
But breezes played, and sunshine gleamed—
The forest to embolden;
Reddened the fiery hues, and shot
Transparence through the golden.

For busy thoughts the Stream flowed on
In foamy agitation;
And slept in many a crystal pool
For quiet contemplation:
No public and no private care
The freeborn mind enthralling,
We made a day of happy hours,
Our happy days recalling.

Brisk Youth appeared, the Morn of Youth,
With freaks of graceful folly,—
Life's temperate Noon, her sober Eve,
Her Night not melancholy;
Past, present, future, all appeared
In harmony united,
Like guests that meet, and some from far,
By cordial love invited.

And if, as Yarrow, through the woods
And down the meadow ranging,
Did meet us with unaltered face,
Though we were changed and changing;
If, *then,* some natural shadows spread
Our inward prospect over,
The soul's deep valley was not slow
Its brightness to recover.

Eternal blessings on the Muse,
  And her divine employment!
The blameless Muse, who trains her Sons
  For hope and calm enjoyment;
Albeit sickness, lingering yet,
  Has o'er their pillow brooded;
And Care waylays their steps—a Sprite
  Not easily eluded.

For thee, O Scott! compelled to change
  Green Eildon-hill and Cheviot
For warm Vesuvio's vine-clad slopes;
  And leave thy Tweed and Tiviot
For mild Sorrento's breezy waves;
  May classic Fancy, linking
With native Fancy her fresh aid,
  Preserve thy heart from sinking!

Oh! while they minister to thee,
  Each vying with the other,
May Health return to mellow Age,
  With Strength, her venturous brother;
And Tiber, and each brook and rill
  Renowned in song and story,
With unimagined beauty shine,
  Nor lose one ray of glory!

For Thou, upon a hundred streams,
  By tales of love and sorrow,
Of faithful love, undaunted truth,
  Hast shed the power of Yarrow;
And streams unknown, hills yet unseen,
  Wherever they invite Thee,
At parent Nature's grateful call,
  With gladness must requite Thee.

A gracious welcome shall be thine,
  Such looks of love and honour
As thy own Yarrow gave to me
  When first I gazed upon her;
Beheld what I had feared to see,
  Unwilling to surrender
Dreams treasured up from early days,
  The holy and the tender.

And what, for this frail world, were all
  That mortals do or suffer,
Did no responsive harp, no pen
  Memorial tribute offer?
Yea, what were mighty Nature's self?
  Her features, could they win us,
Unhelped by the poetic voice
  That hourly speaks within us?

Nor deem that localised Romance
  Plays false with our affections;
Unsanctifies our tears—made sport
  For fanciful dejections:
Ah, no! the visions of the past
  Sustain the heart in feeling
Life as she is—our changeful Life,
  With friends and kindred dealing.

Bear witness, Ye, whose thoughts that day
  In Yarrow's groves were centred;
Who through the silent portal arch
  Of mouldering Newark entered;
And clomb the winding stair that once
  Too timidly was mounted
By the "last Minstrel," (not the last!)
  Ere he his Tale recounted.

Flow on for ever, Yarrow Stream!
  Fulfil thy pensive duty,
Well pleased that future Bards should chant
  For simple hearts thy beauty;
To dream-light dear while yet unseen,
  Dear to the common sunshine,
And dearer still, as now I feel,
  To memory's shadowy moonshine!

Thought of a Briton on the Subjugation of Switzerland

Two Voices are there; one is of the sea,
One of the mountains; each a mighty Voice;
In both from age to age thou didst rejoice,
They were thy chosen music, Liberty!
There came a Tyrant, and with holy glee
Thou fought'st against him; but hast vainly striven:
Thou from thy Alpine holds at length art driven,
Where not a torrent murmurs heard by thee.

Of one deep bliss thine ear hath been bereft:
Then cleave, O cleave to that which still is left;
For, high-souled Maid, what sorrow would it be
That Mountain floods should thunder as before,
And Ocean bellow from his rocky shore,
And neither awful Voice be heard by thee!

JAMES KENNETH STEPHEN (1859-1892)

A Sonnet

This sonnet embodies in a form of verse with which Wordsworth had most conspicuous success, one of the chief points of criticism applicable to his work. It parodies in construction and in phrasing two very famous sonnets of Wordsworth's: "Thoughts of a Briton on the Subjugation of Switzerland," which begins with the line "Two voices are there; one is of the sea"; and another, which opens with the words "The world is too much with us." Both of these sonnets appear in this book, among the selections from Wordsworth. The reader familiar with the best and the worst of Wordsworth will recognize in single phrases in this parody, allusions to well-known elements and subjects in Wordsworth's poetry.

Two voices are there: one is of the deep;
It learns the storm cloud's thunderous melody,
Now roars, now murmurs with the changing sea,
Now birdlike pipes, now closes soft in sleep;
And one is of an old half-witted sheep
Which bleats articulate monotony,
And indicates that two and one are three,
That grass is green, lakes damp, and mountains steep:
And, Wordsworth, both are thine: at certain times,
Forth from the heart of thy melodious rhymes
The form and pressure of high thoughts will burst;
At other times—good Lord! I'd rather be
Quite unacquainted with the A, B, C,
Than write such hopeless rubbish as thy worst.

JAMES HOGG (1770-1835)

The Skylark

BIRD of the wilderness,
Blithesome and cumberless,
Sweet be thy matin o'er moorland and lea!
Emblem of happiness,
Blest is thy dwelling-place—
O to abide in the desert with thee!
Wild is thy lay and loud,
Far in the downy cloud,
Love gives it energy, love gave it birth,
Where, on thy dewy wing,
Where art thou journeying?
Thy lay is in heaven, thy love is on earth.
O'er fell and fountain sheen,
O'er moor and mountain green,
O'er the red streamer that heralds the day,
Over the cloudlet dim,
Over the rainbow's rim,
Musical cherub, soar, singing, away!
Then, when the gloaming comes,
Low in the heather blooms
Sweet will thy welcome and bed of love be!
Emblem of happiness,
Blest is thy dwelling-place—
O to abide in the desert with thee!

A Boy's Song

Where the pools are bright and deep,
Where the grey trout lies asleep,
Up the river and over the lea,
That's the way for Billy and me.

Where the blackbird sings the latest,
Where the hawthorn blooms the sweetest,
Where the nestlings chirp and flee,
That's the way for Billy and me.

Where the mowers mow the cleanest,
Where the hay lies thick and greenest,
There to track the homeward bee,
That's the way for Billy and me.

Where the hazel bank is steepest,
Where the shadow falls the deepest,
Where the clustering nuts fall free,
That's the way for Billy and me.

Why the boys should drive away
Little sweet maidens from the play,
Or love to banter and fight so well,
That's the thing I never could tell.

But this I know, I love to play
Through the meadow, among the hay;
Up the water and over the lea,
That's the way for Billy and me.

Kilmeny

Bonnie Kilmeny gaed up the glen;
But it wasna to meet Duneira's men,
Nor the rosy monk of the isle to see,
For Kilmeny was pure as pure could be.
It was only to hear the yorlin sing,
And pu' the cress-flower round the spring;
The scarlet hypp and the hindberrye,
And the nut that hung frae the hazel tree;
For Kilmeny was pure as pure could be.
But lang may her minny look o'er the wa',
And lang may she seek i' the green-wood shaw;
Lang the laird o' Duneira blame,
And lang, lang greet or Kilmeny come hame!

When many a day had come and fled,
When grief grew calm, and hope was dead,
When mess for Kilmeny's soul had been sung,
When the bedesman had pray'd and the dead bell rung,
Late, late in gloamin' when all was still,
When the fringe was red on the westlin hill,
The wood was sere, the moon i' the wane,
The reek o' the cot hung over the plain,
Like a little wee cloud in the world its lane;
When the ingle low'd wi' an eiry leme,
Late, late in the gloamin' Kilmeny came hame!

"Kilmeny, Kilmeny, where have you been?
Lang hae we sought baith holt and den;
By linn, by ford, and green-wood tree,
Yet you are halesome and fair to see.
Where gat you that joup o' the lily scheen?
That bonnie snood of the birk sae green?
And these roses, the fairest that ever were seen?
Kilmeny, Kilmeny, where have you been?"

Kilmeny look'd up with a lovely grace,
But nae smile was seen on Kilmeny's face;
As still was her look, and as still was her e'e,
As the stillness that lay on the emerant lea,
Or the mist that sleeps on a waveless sea.
For Kilmeny had been, she knew not where,
And Kilmeny had seen what she could not declare;
Kilmeny had been where the cock never crew,
Where the rain never fell, and the wind never blew.
But it seem'd as the harp of the sky had rung,
And the airs of heaven play'd round her tongue,
When she spake of the lovely forms she had seen,
And a land where sin had never been;
A land of love and a land of light,

Withouten sun, or moon, or night;
Where the river swa'd a living stream,
And the light a pure celestial beam;
The land of vision, it would seem,
A still, an everlasting dream.

In yon green-wood there is a waik,
And in that waik there is a wene,
And in that wene there is a maike,
That neither has flesh, blood, nor bane;
And down in yon green-wood he walks his lane.

In that green wene Kilmeny lay,
Her bosom happ'd wi' flowerets gay;
But the air was soft and the silence deep,
And bonnie Kilmeny fell sound asleep.
She kenn'd nae mair, nor open'd her e'e,
Till waked by the hymns of a far countrye.

She 'waken'd on a couch of the silk sae slim,
All striped wi' the bars of the rainbow's rim;
And lovely beings round were rife,
Who erst had travell'd mortal life;
And aye they smiled and 'gan to speer,
"What spirit has brought this mortal here?"—

"Lang have I journey'd, the world wide,"
A meek and reverend fere replied;
"Baith night and day I have watch'd the fair,
Eident a thousand years and mair.
Yes, I have watch'd o'er ilk degree,
Wherever blooms femenitye;
But sinless virgin, free of stain
In mind and body, fand I nane.
Never, since the banquet of time,
Found I a virgin in her prime,
Till late this bonnie maiden I saw
As spotless as the morning snaw:
Full twenty years she has lived as free
As the spirits that sojourn in this countrye:
I have brought her away frae the snares of men,
That sin or death she never may ken."—

They clasp'd her waist and her hands sae fair,
They kiss'd her cheek and they kemed her hair,
And round came many a blooming fere,
Saying, "Bonnie Kilmeny, ye're welcome here!
Women are freed of the littand scorn:
O blest be the day Kilmeny was born!
Now shall the land of the spirits see,
Now shall it ken what a woman may be!
Many a lang year, in sorrow and pain,
Many a lang year through the world we've gane,
Commission'd to watch fair womankind,
For it's they who nurice the immortal mind.
We have watch'd their steps as the dawning shone,
And deep in the green-wood walks alone;
By lily bower and silken bed,
The viewless tears have o'er them shed;
Have soothed their ardent minds to sleep,
Or left the couch of love to weep.
We have seen! we have seen! but the time must come,
And the angels will weep at the day of doom!

"O would the fairest of mortal kind
Aye keep the holy truths in mind,
That kindred spirits their motions see,
Who watch their ways with anxious e'e,
And grieve for the guilt of humanitye!
O, sweet to Heaven the maiden's prayer,
And the sigh that heaves a bosom sae fair!
And dear to Heaven the words of truth,
And the praise of virtue frae beauty's mouth!
And dear to the viewless forms of air,
The minds that kyth as the body fair!

"O bonnie Kilmeny! free frae stain,
If ever you seek the world again,
That world of sin, of sorrow and fear,
O tell of the joys that are waiting here;
And tell of the signs you shall shortly see;

Of the times that are now, and the times that shall be"—
They lifted Kilmeny, they led her away,
And she walk'd in the light of a sunless day;
The sky was a dome of crystal bright,
The fountain of vision, and fountain of light:
The emerald fields were of dazzling glow,
And the flowers of everlasting blow.
Then deep in the stream her body they laid,
That her youth and beauty never might fade;
And they smiled on heaven, when they saw her lie
In the stream of life that wander'd bye.
And she heard a song, she head it sung,
She kenn'd not where; but sae sweetly it rung,
It fell on the ear like a dream of the morn:
"O, blest be the day Kilmeny was born!
Now shall the land of the spirits see,
Now shall it ken what a woman may be!
The sun that shines on the world sae bright,
A borrow'd gleid frae the fountain of light;
And the moon that sleeks the sky sae dun,
Like a gouden bow, or a beamless sun,
Shall wear away, and be seen nae mair,
And the angels shall miss them travelling the air.
But lang, lang after baith night and day,
When the sun and the world have elyed away;
When the sinner has gane to his waesome doom,
Kilmeny shall smile in eternal bloom!"—

They bore her away, she wist not how,
For she felt not arm nor rest below;
But so swift they wain'd her through the light,
'Twas like the motion of sound or sight;
They seem'd to split the gales of air,
And yet nor gale nor breeze was there.
Unnumber'd groves below them grew,
They came, they pass'd, and backward flew,
Like floods of blossoms gliding on,
In moment seen, in moment gone.
O, never vales to mortal view
Appear'd like those o'er which they flew!
That land to human spirits given,
The lowermost vales of the storied heaven;
From thence they can view the world below,
And heaven's blue gates with sapphires glow,
More glory yet unmeet to know.

They bore her far to a mountain green,
To see what mortal never had seen;
And they seated her high on a purple sward,
And bade her heed what she saw and heard,
And note the changes the spirits wrought,
For now she lived in the land of thought.
She look'd, and she saw nor sun nor skies,
But a crystal dome of a thousand dyes:
She look'd, and she saw nae land aright,
But an endless whirl of glory and light:
And radiant beings went and came,
Far swifter than wind, or the linkèd flame.
She hid her e'en frae the dazzling view;
She look'd again, and the scene was new.

She saw a sun on a summer sky,
And clouds of amber sailing bye;
A lovely land beneath her lay,
And that land had glens and mountains gray;
And that land had valleys and hoary piles,
And marlèd seas, and a thousand isles.
Its fields were speckled, its forests green,
And its lakes were all of the dazzling sheen,
Like magic mirrors, where slumbering lay
The sun and the sky and the cloudlet gray;
Which heaved and trembled, and gently swung,

On every shore they seem'd to be hung;
For there they were seen on their downward plain
A thousand times and a thousand again;
In winding lake and placid firth,
Little peaceful heavens in the bosom of earth.

Kilmeny sigh'd and seem'd to grieve,
For she found her heart to that land did cleave;
She saw the corn wave on the vale,
She saw the deer run down the dale;
She saw the plaid and the broad claymore,
And the brows that the badge of freedom bore;
And she thought she had seen the land before.

She saw a lady sit on a throne,
The fairest that ever the sun shone on!
A lion lick'd her hand of milk,
And she held him in a leish of silk;
And a leifu' maiden stood at her knee,
With a silver wand and melting e'e;
Her sovereign shield till love stole in,
And poison'd all the fount within.

Then a gruff untoward bedesman came,
And hundit the lion on his dame;
And the guardian maid wi' the dauntless e'e,
She dropp'd a tear, and left her knee;
And she saw till the queen frae the lion fled,
Till the bonniest flower of the world lay dead;
A coffin was set on a distant plain,
And she saw the red blood fall like rain;
Then bonnie Kilmeny's heart grew sair,
And she turn'd away, and could look nae mair.

Then the gruff grim carle girn'd amain,
And they trampled him down, but he rose again;
And he baited the lion to deeds of weir,
Till he lapp'd the blood to the kingdom dear;
And weening his head was danger-preef,
When crown'd with the rose and clover leaf,
He gowl'd at the carle, and chased him away
To feed wi' the deer on the mountain gray.
He gowl'd at the carle, and geck'd at Heaven,
But his mark was set, and his arles given.
Kilmeny a while her e'en withdrew;
She look'd again, and the scene was new.

She saw before her fair unfurl'd
One half of all the glowing world,
Where oceans roll'd, and rivers ran,
To bound the aims of sinful man.
She saw a people, fierce and fell,
Burst frae their bounds like fiends of hell;
Their lilies grew, and the eagle flew;
And she herkèd on her ravening crew,
Till the cities and towers were wrapp'd in a blaze,
And the thunder it roar'd o'er the lands and the seas.
The widows they wail'd, and the red blood ran,
And she threaten'd an end to the race of man;
She never lened, nor stood in awe,
Till caught by the lion's deadly paw.
O, then the eagle swink'd for life,
And brainyell'd up a mortal strife;
But flew she north, or flew she south,
She met wi' the gowl o' the lion's mouth.

With a mooted wing and waefu' maen,
The eagle sought her eiry again;
But lang may she cower in her bloody nest,
And lang, lang sleek her wounded breast,
Before she sey another flight,
To play wi' the norland lion's might.

But to sing the sights Kilmeny saw,
So far surpassing nature's law,
The singer's voice wad sink away,
And the string of his harp wad cease to play.

But she saw till the sorrows of man were bye,
And all was love and harmony;
Till the stars of heaven fell calmly away,
Like flakes of snaw on a winter day.

Then Kilmeny begg'd again to see
The friends she had left in her own countrye;
To tell of the place where she had been,
And the glories that lay in the land unseen;
To warn the living maidens fair,
The loved of Heaven, the spirits' care,
That all whose minds unmeled remain
Shall bloom in beauty when time is gane.

With distant music, soft and deep,
They lull'd Kilmeny sound asleep;
And when she awaken'd, she lay her lane,
All happ'd with flowers, in the green-wood wene.
When seven lang years had come and fled,
When grief was calm, and hope was dead;
When scarce was remember'd Kilmeny's name,
Late, late in a gloamin' Kilmeny came hame!
And O, her beauty was fair to see,
But still and steadfast was her e'e!
Such beauty bard may never declare,
For there was no pride nor passion there;
And the soft desire of maiden's e'en
In that mild face could never be seen.
Her seymar was the lily flower,
And her cheek the moss-rose in the shower;
And her voice like the distant melodye,
That floats along the twilight sea.
But she loved to raike the lanely glen,
And keepèd afar frae the haunts of men;
Her holy hymns unheard to sing,
To suck the flowers, and drink the spring.
But wherever her peaceful form appear'd,
The wild beasts of the hill were cheer'd;
The wolf play'd blythly round the field,
The lordly byson low'd and kneel'd;
The dun deer woo'd with manner bland,
And cower'd aneath her lily hand.
And when at even the woodlands rung,
When hymns of other worlds she sung
In ecstasy of sweet devotion,
O, then the glen was all in motion!
The wild beasts of the forest came,
Broke from their bughts and faulds the tame,
And goved around, charm'd and amazed;
Even the dull cattle croon'd and gazed,
And murmur'd and look'd with anxious pain
For something the mystery to explain.
The buzzard came with the throstle-cock;
The corby left her houf in the rock;
The blackbird alang wi' the eagle flew;
The hind came tripping o'er the dew;
The wolf and the kid their raike began,
And the tod, and the lamb, and the leveret ran;
The hawk and the hern attour them hung,
And the merle and the mavis forhooy'd their young;
And all in a peaceful ring were hurl'd;
It was like an eve in a sinless world!

When a month and a day had come and gane,
Kilmeny sought the green-wood wene;
There laid her down on the leaves sae green,
And Kilmeny on earth was never mair seen.
But O, the words that fell from her mouth
Were words of wonder, and words of truth!
But all the land were in fear and dread,
For they kendna whether she was living or dead.
It wasna her hame, and she couldna remain;
She left this world of sorrow and pain,
And return'd to the land of thought again.

SIR WALTER SCOTT (1771-1832)

From The Abbot

Mary's Delirium

The fit of delirium here presented is apparently brought on by Lady Fleming's unfortunate reference to Sebastian. Catherine Seyton, attending Queen Mary, explains the circumstances to Roland Græme, the hero of the novel: "Know ye not that on the night of Henry Darnley's murder, and at the blowing up of the Kirk of Field, the Queen's absence was owing to her attending on a masque at Holyrood, given by her to grace the marriage of this same Sebastian, who, himself a favored servant, married one of her female attendants, who was near to her person?"

The historical background is familiar. Mary's first husband was Henry, Lord Darnley, son of Matthew Stuart, earl of Lennox. Within the second year after the marriage, some time in the night of February 9, 1567, Darnley was murdered, and the house in which he should have been sleeping was blown up, by agents of the unscrupulous and powerful Bothwell. On May 12, Bothwell was made Duke of Orkney and Shetland. On May 15, Mary and Bothwell were married. The Scotch lords in general, and the populace, regarded her as guiltily involved in the murder. On June 15, the confederate lords, with a well-disciplined force, met the army of the Queen and Bothwell at Carberry Hill, near Edinburgh. The royal army melted away, and at last it was agreed that the Queen should yield herself prisoner, and Bothwell retire in safety to Dunbar. The Queen was kept in the island castle of Lochleven until her escape, on the 2nd of May, 1568. She soon mustered an army of 6,000 men round Hamilton Palace, and revoked her abdication. With 4500 men, under leaders of high distinction, Murray, acting as regent for the infant son of Mary and Darnley, encountered the Queen's forces at the battle or rout of Langside, on the 13th of May, whence Mary fled, crossing the Solway three days later and landing at Workington in Cumberland.

Mary entered from her apartment, paler than usual, and apparently exhausted by a sleepless night, and by the painful thoughts which had ill supplied the place of repose; yet the languor of her looks was so far from impairing her beauty, that it only substituted the frail delicacy of the lovely woman for the majestic grace of the Queen. Contrary to her wont, her toilette had been very hastily dispatched, and her hair, which was usually dressed by Lady Fleming with great care, escaping from beneath the head-tire, which had been hastily adjusted, fell, in long and luxuriant tresses of Nature's own curling, over a neck and bosom which were somewhat less carefully veiled than usual.

As she stepped over the threshold of her apartment, Catherine, hastily drying her tears, ran to meet her royal mistress, and having first kneeled at her feet, and kissed her hand, instantly rose, and placing herself on the other side of the Queen, seemed anxious to divide with the Lady Fleming the honour of supporting and assisting her. The page, on his part, advanced and put in order the chair of state, which she usually occupied, and having placed the cushion and footstool for her accommodation, stepped back, and stood ready for service in the place usually occupied by his predecessor, the young Seneschal. Mary's eye rested an instant on him, and could not but remark the change of persons. Hers was not the female heart which could refuse compassion, at least, to a gallant youth who had suffered in her cause, although he had been guided in his enterprise by a too presumptuous passion; and the words "Poor Douglas!" escaped from her lips, perhaps unconsciously, as she leant herself back in her chair, and put the kerchief to her eyes.

"Yes, gracious madam," said Catherine, assuming a cheerful manner, in order to cheer her sovereign, "our gallant knight is indeed banished—the adventure was not reserved for him; but he has left behind him a youthful Esquire, as much devoted to your Grace's service, and who, by me, makes you tender of his hand and sword."

"If they may in aught avail your Grace," said Roland Græme, bowing profoundly.

"Alas!" said the Queen, "what needs this, Catherine?—why prepare new victims to be involved in, and overwhelmed by, my cruel fortune?—were we not better cease to struggle, and ourselves sink in the tide without further resistance, than thus drag into destruction with us every generous heart which makes an effort in our favour?—I have had but too much of plot and intrigue around me, since I was stretched an orphan child in my very cradle, while contending nobles strove which should rule in the name of the unconscious innocent. Surely time it were that all this busy and most dangerous coil should end. Let me call my prison a convent, and my seclusion a voluntary sequestration of myself from the world and its ways!"

"Speak not thus, madam, before your faithful servants," said Catherine, "to discourage their zeal at once, and to break their hearts. Daughter of kings, be not in this hour so unkingly—Come, Roland, and let us, the youngest of her followers, show ourselves worthy of her cause—let us kneel before her footstool, and implore her to be her own magnanimous self." And leading Roland Græme to the Queen's seat, they both kneeled down before her. Mary raised herself in her chair, and sat erect, while, extending one hand to be kissed by the page, she arranged with the other the clustering locks which shaded the bold yet lovely brow of the high-spirited Catherine.

"Alas! *mignonne*," she said, for so in fondness she often called her young attendant, "that you should thus desperately mix with my unhappy fate the fortune of your young lives!—Are they not a lovely couple, my Fleming? and is it not heartrending to think that I must be their ruin?"

"Not so," said Roland Græme, "it is we, gracious Sovereign, who will be your deliverers."

"Ex oribus parvulorum!" said the Queen, looking upward; "if it is by the mouth of these children that Heaven calls me to resume the stately thoughts which become my birth and my rights, thou wilt grant them thy protection, and to me the power of rewarding their zeal!"—Then turning to Fleming, she instantly added,—"Thou knowest, my friend, whether to make those who have served me happy, was not ever Mary's favourite pastime. When I have been rebuked by the stern preachers of the Calvinistic heresy—when I have seen the fierce countenances of my nobles averted from me, has it not been because I mixed in the harmless pleasures of the young and gay, and rather for the sake of their happiness than my own, have mingled in the masque, the song, or the dance, with the youth of my household? Well, I repent not of it—though Knox termed it sin, and Morton degradation—I was happy, because I saw happiness around me; and woe betide the wretched jealousy that can extract guilt out of the overflowings of an unguarded gaiety!—Fleming, if we are restored to our throne, shall we not have one blithesome day at a blithesome bridal, of which we must now name neither the bride nor the bridegroom? but that bridegroom shall have the barony of Blairgowrie, a fair gift even for a Queen to give, and that bride's chaplet shall be twined with the fairest pearls that ever were found in the depths of Lochlomond; and thou thyself, Mary Fleming, the best dresser of tires that ever busked the tresses of a Queen, and who would scorn to touch those of any woman of lower rank,—thou thyself shalt, for my love, twine them into the bride's tresses.—Look, my Fleming, suppose them such clustered locks as those of our Catherine, they would not put shame upon thy skill."

So saying, she passed her hand fondly over the head of her youthful favourite, while her more aged attendant replied despondently, "Alas! madam, your thoughts stray far from home."

"They do, my Fleming," said the Queen; "but is it well or kind in you to call them back?—God knows, they have kept the perch this night but too closely—Come, I will recall the gay vision, were it but to punish them. Yes, at that blithesome bridal, Mary herself shall forget the weight of sorrows, and the toil of state, and herself once more lead a measure.—At whose wedding was it that we last danced, my Fleming? I think care has troubled my memory—yet something of it I should remember—canst thou not aid me?—I know thou canst."

"Alas! madam," replied the lady——

"What!" said Mary, "wilt thou not help us so far? this is a peevish adherence to thine own graver opinion, which holds our talk as folly. But thou art court-bred, and wilt well understand me when I say, the Queen *commands* Lady Fleming to tell her where she led the last *branle*."

With a face deadly pale, and a mien as if she were about to sink into the earth, the court-bred dame, no longer daring to refuse obedience, faltered out—"Gracious Lady—if my memory err not—it was at the masque in Holyrood—at the marriage of Sebastian."

The unhappy Queen, who had hitherto listened with a melancholy smile, provoked by the reluctance with which the Lady Fleming brought out her story, at this ill-fated word interrupted her with a shriek so wild and loud that the vaulted apartment rang, and both Roland and Catherine sprung to their feet in the utmost terror and alarm. Meantime, Mary seemed, by the train of horrible ideas thus suddenly excited, surprised not only beyond self-command, but for the moment beyond the verge of reason.

"Traitress!" she said to the Lady Fleming, "thou wouldst slay thy sovereign—Call my French guards—*à moi! à moi! mes Français!*—I am beset with traitors in mine own palace—they have murdered my husband—Rescue! rescue! for the Queen of Scotland!" She started up from her chair—her features, late so exquisitely lovely in their paleness, now inflamed with the fury of frenzy, and resembling those of a Bellona. "We will take the field ourself," she said; "warn the city—warn Lothian and Fife—saddle our Spanish barb—and bid French Paris see our petronel be charged!—Better to die at the head of our brave Scotsmen, like our grandfather at Flodden, than of a broken heart, like our ill-starred father!"

"Be patient—be composed, dearest Sovereign!" said Catherine; and then addressing Lady Fleming angrily, she added, "How could you say aught that reminded her of her husband?"

The word reached the ear of the unhappy Princess, who caught it up, speaking with great rapidity. "Husband!—what husband?—Not his most Christian Majesty—he is ill at ease—he cannot mount on horseback.—Not him of the Lennox—but it was the Duke of Orkney thou wouldst say."

"For God's love, madam, be patient!" said the Lady Fleming.

But the Queen's excited imagination could by no entreaty be diverted from its course. "Bid him come hither to our aid," she said, "and bring with him his lambs, as he calls them—Bowton, Hay of Talla, Black Ormiston, and his kinsman Hob—Fie! how swart they are, and how they smell of sulphur! What! closeted with Morton? Nay, if the

Douglas and the Hepburn hatch the complot together, the bird, when it breaks the shell, will scare Scotland. Will it not, my Fleming?"

"She grows wilder and wilder," said Fleming; "we have too many hearers for these strange words."

"Roland," said Catherine, "in the name of God, begone! You cannot aid us here—Leave us to deal with her alone—Away—away."

She thrust him to the door of the anteroom; yet even when he had entered that apartment and shut the door, he could still hear the Queen talk in a loud and determined tone, as if giving forth orders, until at length the voice died away in a feeble and continued lamentation.

From THE HEART OF MIDLOTHIAN

The Plea of Jeanie Deans to Queen Caroline

Jeanie Deans is the elder daughter of David Deans, a stern, honest old Scotch Covenanter, who lives on his small farm near Edinburgh. Effie, his daughter by a second marriage, sent to service in Edinburgh, comes home unexpectedly, and is almost immediately arrested on a charge of child-murder, and imprisoned in the Tolbooth in Edinburgh (called by the natives "The Heart of Mid-Lothian"). Under the severe statute of William and Mary, still in force, the girl is convicted and sentenced to death. She has borne a child, the child has disappeared, and no one can testify that she communicated her situation beforehand. In a most pathetic scene at the trial, Jeanie refuses to tell aught but the truth, that Effie did not impart to her any information of her plight. As a matter of fact, Effie had been obliged to conceal the name of her lover, who was outlawed for his part in the Porteous riot, and her child had been taken from her by a villainous gypsy midwife, who she feared had done harm to it. She had had no opportunity to tell Jeanie these facts before her arrest. After the trial, Jeanie sets out on foot for London, to seek the aid of the Duke of Argyle in applying for a pardon for her sister.

BEFORE noon, a well-dressed gentleman entered Mrs. Glass's shop, and requested to see a young woman from Scotland.

"That will be my cousin, Jeanie Deans, Mr. Archibald," said Mrs. Glass, with a courtesy of recognizance. "Have you any message for her from his Grace the Duke of Argyle, Mr. Archibald? I will carry it to her in a moment."

"I believe I must give her the trouble of stepping down, Mrs. Glass."

"Jeanie—Jeanie Deans!" said Mrs. Glass, screaming at the bottom of the little staircase, which ascended from the corner of the shop to the higher regions. "Jeanie—Jeanie Deans, I say! come downstairs instantly; here is the Duke of Argyle's groom of the chambers desires to see you directly." This was announced in a voice so loud, as to make all who chanced to be within hearing aware of the important communication.

It may easily be supposed, that Jeanie did not tarry long in adjusting herself to attend the summons, yet her feet almost failed her as she came downstairs.

"I must ask the favor of your company a little way," said Archibald, with civility.

"I am quite ready, sir," said Jeanie.

"Is my cousin going out, Mr. Archibald? then I will hae to go wi' her, no doubt.—James Rasper—Look to the shop, James.—Mr. Archibald," pushing a jar toward him, "you take his Grace's mixture, I think. Please to fill your box, for old acquaintance' sake, while I get on my things."

Mr. Archibald transposed a modest parcel of snuff from the jar to his own mull, but said he was obliged to decline the pleasure of Mrs. Glass's company, as his message was particularly to the young person.

"Particularly to the young person?" said Mrs. Glass; "is not that uncommon, Mr. Archibald? But his Grace is the best judge; and you are a steady person, Mr. Archibald. It is not every one that comes from a great man's house I would trust my cousin with.—But, Jeanie, you must not go through the streets with Mr. Archibald with your tartan what d'ye call it there upon your shoulders, as if you had come up with a drove of Highland cattle. Wait till I bring down my silk cloak. Why, we'll have the mob after you!"

"I have a hackney-coach in waiting, madam," said Mr. Archibald, interrupting the officious old lady, from whom Jeanie might otherwise have found it difficult to escape, "and, I believe, I must not allow her time for any change of dress."

So saying, he hurried Jeanie into the coach, while she internally praised and wondered at the easy manner in which he shifted off Mrs. Glass's officious offers and inquiries, without mentioning his master's orders, or going into any explanation whatever.

On entering the coach, Mr. Archibald seated himself in the front seat, opposite to our heroine, and they drove on in silence. After they had proceeded nearly half-an-hour, without a word on either side, it occurred to Jeanie, that the distance and time did not correspond with that which had been occupied by her journey on the former occasion, to and from the residence of the Duke of Argyle. At length she could not help asking her taciturn companion, "Whilk way they were going?"

"My Lord Duke will inform you himself, madam," answered Archibald, with the same solemn courtesy which marked his whole demeanor. Almost as he spoke, the hackney-coach drew up, and the coachman dismounted and opened the door. Archibald got out, and assisted Jeanie to get down. She found herself in a large turnpike road, without the bounds of London, upon the other side of which road was drawn up a plain chariot and four horses, the panels without arms, and the servants without liveries.

"You have been punctual, I see, Jeanie," said the Duke of Argyle, as Archibald opened the carriage door. "You must be my companion for the rest of the way. Archibald will remain here with the hackney-coach till your return."

Ere Jeanie could make answer, she found herself, to her no small astonishment, seated by the side of a duke, in a carriage which rolled forward at a rapid yet smooth rate, very different in both particulars from the lumbering, jolting vehicle which she had just left; and which, lumbering and jolting as it was, conveyed to one who had seldom been in a coach before, a certain feeling of dignity and importance.

"Young woman," said the Duke, "after thinking as attentively on your sister's case as is in my power, I continue to be impressed with the belief that great injustice may be done by the execution of her sentence. So are one or two liberal and intelligent lawyers of both countries whom I have spoken with.—Nay, pray hear me out before you thank me.—I have already told you my personal conviction is of little consequence, unless I could impress the same upon others. Now I have done for you, what I would certainly not have done to serve any purpose of my own—I have asked an audience of a lady whose interest with the king is deservedly very high. It has been allowed me, and I am desirous that you should see her and speak for yourself. You have no occasion to be abashed; tell your story simply as you did to me."

"I am much obliged to your Grace," said Jeanie, remembering Mrs. Glass's charge; "and I am sure since I have had the courage to speak to your Grace, in poor Effie's cause, I have less reason to be shame-faced in speaking to a leddy. But, sir, I would like to ken what to ca' her, whether your grace, or your honor, or your leddyship, as we say to lairds and leddies in Scotland, and I will take care to mind it; for I ken leddies are full mair particular than gentlemen about their titles of honor."

"You have no occasion to call her anything but Madam. Just say what you think is likely to make the best impression—look at me from time to time—if I put my hand to my cravat so" (showing her the motion), "you will stop; but I shall only do this when you say anything that is not likely to please."

"But, sir, your Grace," said Jeanie, "if it wasna ower muckle trouble, wad it no be better to tell me what I should say, and I could get it by heart?"

"No, Jeanie, that would not have the same effect—that would be like reading a sermon, you know, which we good Presbyterians think has less unction than when spoken without book," replied the Duke. "Just speak as plainly and boldly to this lady, as you did to me the day before yesterday; and if you can gain her consent, I'll wad ye a plack, as we say in the north, that you get the pardon from the king."

As he spoke he took a pamphlet from his pocket, and began to read. Jeanie had good sense and tact, which constitute betwixt them that which is called natural good breeding. She interpreted the Duke's manœuvre as a hint that she was to ask no more questions, and she remained silent accordingly.

The carriage rolled rapidly onward through fertile meadows, ornamented with splendid old oaks, and catching occasionally a glance of the majestic mirror of a broad and placid river. After passing through a pleasant village, the equipage stopped on a commanding eminence, where the beauty of English landscape was displayed in its utmost luxuriance. Here the Duke alighted, and desired Jeanie to follow him. They paused for a moment on the brow of a hill, to gaze on the unrivalled landscape which it presented. A huge sea of verdure, with crossing and intersecting promontories of massive and tufted groves, was tenanted by numberless flocks and herds, which seemed to wander unrestrained and unbounded through the rich pastures. The Thames, here turreted with villas, and there garlanded with forests, moved on slowly and placidly, like the mighty monarch of the scene, to whom all its other beauties were but accessories, and bore on his bosom a hundred barques and skiffs, whose white sails and gaily fluttering pennons gave life to the whole.

The Duke of Argyle was, of course, familiar with this scene; but to a man of taste it must be always new. Yet, as he paused and looked on this inimitable landscape, with the feeling of delight which it must give to the bosom of every admirer of nature, his thoughts naturally reverted to his own more grand, and scarce less beautiful, domains of Inverary.—"This is a fine scene," he said to his companion, curious, perhaps, to draw out her sentiments; "we have nothing like it in Scotland."

"It's braw rich feeding for the cows, and they have a fine breed o' cattle here," replied Jeanie; "but I like just as weel to look at the craigs of Arthur's Seat, and the sea coming in ayont them, as at a' thae muckle trees."

The Duke smiled at a reply equally professional and national, and made a signal for the carriage to remain where it was. Then adopting an unfrequented footpath, he conducted Jeanie, through several complicated mazes, to a postern-door in a high brick wall. It was shut; but as the Duke tapped slightly at it, a person in waiting within, after reconnoitring through a small iron gate contrived for the purpose, unlocked the door, and admitted them. They entered, and it was immediately closed and fastened behind them. This was all done quickly, the door so instantly closing, and the person who opened it so suddenly disappearing, that Jeanie could not even catch a glimpse of his exterior.

They found themselves at the extremity of a deep and narrow alley, carpeted with the most verdant and close-shaven turf, which felt like velvet under their feet, and screened from the sun by the branches of the lofty elms which united over the path, and caused it to resemble, in the solemn obscurity of the light which they admitted, as well as from the range of columnar stems, and intricate union of their arched branches, one of the narrow side aisles in an ancient Gothic cathedral. Encouraged as she was by the courteous manners of her noble countryman, it was not without a feeling of something like terror that Jeanie felt herself in a place apparently so lonely, with a man of such high rank. That she should have been permitted to wait on the Duke in his own house, and have been there received to a private interview, was in itself an uncommon and distinguished event in the annals of a life so simple as hers; but to find herself his travelling companion in a journey, and then suddenly to be left alone with him in so secluded a situation, had something in it of awful mystery. A romantic heroine might have suspected and dreaded the power of her own charms; but Jeanie was too wise to let such a silly thought intrude on her mind. Still, however, she had a most eager desire to know where she now was, and to whom she was to be presented.

She remarked that the Duke's dress, though still such as indicated rank and fashion (for it was not the custom of men of quality at that time to dress themselves like their own coachmen or grooms), was nevertheless plainer than that in which she had seen him upon a former occasion, and was divested, in particular, of all those badges of external decoration which intimated superior consequence. In short, he was attired as plainly as any gentleman of fashion could appear in the streets of London in a morning; and this circumstance helped to shake an opinion which Jeanie began to entertain, that, perhaps, he intended she should plead her cause in the presence of royalty itself. "But, surely," said she to herself, "he wad hae putten on his braw star and garter, an he had thought o' coming before the face of Majesty—and after a', this is mair like a gentleman's policy than a royal palace."

There was some sense in Jeanie's reasoning; yet she was not sufficiently mistress either of the circumstances of etiquette, or the particular relations which existed betwixt the government and the Duke of Argyle, to form an accurate judgment. The Duke, as we have said, was at this time in open opposition to the administration of Sir Robert Walpole, and was understood to be out of favor with the royal family, to whom he had rendered such important services. But it was a maxim of Queen Caroline, to bear herself toward her political friends with such caution, as if there was a possibility of their one day being her enemies, and toward political opponents with the same degree of circumspection, as if they might again become friendly to her measures. Since Margaret of Anjou, no queen-consort had exercised such weight in the political affairs of England, and the personal address which she displayed on many occasions, had no small share in reclaiming from their political heresy many of those determined Tories, who, after the reign of the Stuarts had been extinguished in the person of Queen Anne, were disposed rather to transfer their allegiance to her brother the Chevalier de St. George, than to acquiesce in the settlement of the crown on the Hanover family. Her husband, whose most shining quality was courage in the field of battle, and who endured the office of King of England, without ever being able to acquire English habits, or any familiarity with English dispositions, found the utmost assistance from the address of his partner; and while he jealously affected to do everything according to his own will and pleasure, was in secret prudent enough to take and follow the advice of his more adroit consort. He entrusted to her the delicate office of determining the various degrees of favor necessary to attach the wavering, or to confirm such as were already friendly, or to regain those whose good-will had been lost.

With all the winning address of an elegant, and, according to the times, an accomplished woman, Queen Caroline possessed the masculine soul of the other sex. She was proud by nature, and even her policy could not always temper her expressions of displeasure, although few were more ready at repairing any false step of this kind, when her prudence came up to the aid of her passions. She loved the real possession of power, rather than the show of it, and whatever she did herself that was either wise or popular, she always desired that the king should have the full credit as well as the advantage of the measure, conscious that, by adding to his respectability, she was most likely to maintain her own. And so desirous was she to comply with all his tastes, that, when threatened with the gout, she had repeatedly had recourse to checking the fit, by the use of the cold bath, thereby endangering her life, that she might be able to attend the king in his walks.

It was a very consistent part of Queen Caroline's character, to keep up many private correspondences with those to whom in public she seemed unfavorable, or who, for various reasons, stood ill with the court. By this means she kept in her hands the thread of many a political intrigue, and, without pledging herself to anything, could often prevent discontent from becoming hatred, and opposition from exaggerating itself into rebellion. If by any accident her correspondence with such persons chanced to be observed or discovered, which she took all possible pains to prevent, it was represented as a mere intercourse of society, having no reference to politics; an answer with which even the prime minister, Sir Robert Walpole, was compelled to remain satisfied, when he discovered that the Queen had given a private audience to Pulteney, afterward Earl of Bath, his most formidable and most inveterate enemy.

In thus maintaining occasional intercourse with several persons who seemed most alienated from the crown, it may readily be supposed, that Queen Caroline had taken care not to break entirely with the Duke of Argyle. His high birth, his great talents, the estimation in which he was held in his own country, the great services which he had rendered the house of Brunswick in 1715, placed him high in that rank of persons who were not to be rashly neglected. He had, almost by his single and unassisted talents, stopped the irruption of the banded force of all the Highland chiefs; there was little doubt, that, with the slightest encouragement, he could put them all in motion, and renew the civil war; and it was well known that the most flattering overtures had been transmitted to the Duke from the court of St. Germains. The character and temper of Scotland were still little known, and it was considered as a volcano, which might, indeed, slumber for a series of years but was still liable, at a moment the least expected, to break out into a wasteful eruption. It was, therefore, of the highest importance to retain some hold over so important a personage as the Duke of Argyle, and Caroline preserved the power of doing so by means of a lady, with whom, as wife of George II., she might have been supposed to be on less intimate terms.

It was not the least instance of the Queens address, that she had contrived that one of her principal attendants, Lady Suffolk, should unite in her own person the two apparently inconsistent characters, of her husband's mistress, and her own very obsequious and complaisant confidant. By this dexterous management the Queen secured her power against the danger which might most have threatened it—the thwarting influence of an ambitious rival; and if she submitted to the mortification of being obliged to connive at her husband's infidelity, she was at least guarded against what she might think its most dangerous effects, and was besides at liberty, now and then, to bestow a few civil insults upon "her good Howard," whom, however, in general, she treated with great decorum. Lady Suffolk lay under strong obligations to the Duke of Argyle, for reasons which may be collected from Horace Walpole's Reminiscences of that reign, and through her means the Duke had some occasional correspondence with Queen Caroline, much interrupted, however, since the part he had taken in the debate concerning the Porteous mob, an affair which the Queen, though somewhat unreasonably, was disposed to resent, rather as an intended and premeditated insolence to her own person and authority, than as a sudden ebullition of popular vengeance. Still, however, the communication remained open betwixt them, though it had been of late disused on both sides. These remarks will be found necessary to understand the scene which is about to be presented to the reader.

From the narrow alley which they had traversed, the Duke turned into one of the same character, but broader and still longer. Here, for the first time since they had entered these gardens, Jeanie saw persons approaching them.

They were two ladies; one of whom walked a little behind the other, yet not so much as to prevent her from hearing and replying to whatever observation was addressed to her by the lady who walked foremost, and that without her having the trouble to turn her person. As they advanced very slowly, Jeanie had time to study their features and appearance. The Duke also slackened his pace, as if to give her time to collect herself, and repeatedly desired her not to be afraid. The lady who seemed the principal person had remarkably good features, though somewhat injured by the small-pox, that venomous scourge, which each village Esculapius (thanks to Jenner) can now tame as easily as their tutelary deity subdued the Python. The lady's eyes were brilliant, her teeth good, and her countenance formed to express at will either majesty or courtesy. Her form, though rather *embonpoint,* was nevertheless graceful; and the elasticity and firmness of her step gave no room to suspect, what was actually the case, that she suffered occasionally from a disorder the most unfavorable to pedestrian exercise. Her dress was rather rich than gay, and her manner commanding and noble.

Her companion was of lower stature, with light-brown hair and expressive blue eyes. Her features, without being absolutely regular, were perhaps more pleasing than if they had been critically handsome. A melancholy, or at least a pensive expression, for which her lot gave too much cause, predominated when she was silent, but gave way to a pleasing and good-humored smile when she spoke to anyone.

When they were within twelve or fifteen yards of these ladies, the

Duke made a sign that Jeanie should stand still, and stepping forward himself, with the grace which was natural to him, made a profound obeisance, which was formally, yet in a dignified manner, returned by the personage whom he approached.

"I hope," she said, with an affable and condescending smile, "that I see so great a stranger at court, as the Duke of Argyle has been of late, in as good health as his friends there and elsewhere could wish him to enjoy."

The Duke replied, "That he had been perfectly well"; and added, "that the necessity of attending to the public business before the House, as well as the time occupied by a late journey to Scotland, had rendered him less assiduous in paying his duty at the levee and drawing-room than he could have desired."

"When your Grace *can* find time for a duty so frivolous," replied the Queen, "you are aware of your title to be well received. I hope my readiness to comply with the wish which you expressed yesterday to Lady Suffolk, is a sufficient proof that one of the royal family, at least, has not forgotten ancient and important services, in resenting something which resembles recent neglect." This was said apparently with great good-humor, and in a tone which expressed a desire of conciliation.

The Duke replied, "That he would account himself the most unfortunate of men, if he could be supposed capable of neglecting his duty, in modes and circumstances when it was expected, and would have been agreeable. He was deeply gratified by the honor which her Majesty was now doing to him personally; and he trusted she would soon perceive that it was in a matter essential to his Majesty's interest, that he had the boldness to give her this trouble."

"You cannot oblige me more, my Lord Duke," replied the Queen, "than by giving me the advantage of your lights and experience on any point of the King's service. Your Grace is aware, that I can only be the medium through which the matter is subjected to his Majesty's superior wisdom; but if it is a suit which respects your Grace personally, it shall lose no support by being preferred through me."

"It is no suit of mine, madam," replied the Duke; "nor have I any to prefer for myself personally, although I feel in full force my obligation to your Majesty. It is a business which concerns his Majesty, as a lover of justice and of mercy, and which, I am convinced, may be highly useful in conciliating the unfortunate irritation which at present subsists among his Majesty's good subjects in Scotland."

There were two parts of this speech disagreeable to Caroline. In the first place, it removed the flattering notion she had adopted, that Argyle designed to use her personal intercession in making his peace with the administration, and recovering the employments of which he had been deprived; and next, she was displeased that he should talk of the discontents in Scotland as irritations to be conciliated, rather than suppressed.

Under the influence of these feelings, she answered hastily, "That his Majesty has good subjects in England, my Lord Duke, he is bound to thank God and the laws—that he has subjects in Scotland, I think he may thank God and his sword."

The Duke, though a courtier, colored slightly, and the Queen, instantly sensible of her error, added, without displaying the least change of countenance, and as if the words had been an original branch of the sentence—"And the swords of those real Scotchmen who are friends to the House of Brunswick, particularly that of His Grace of Argyle."

"My sword, madam," replied the Duke, "like that of my fathers, has been always at the command of my lawful king, and of my native country—I trust it is impossible to separate their real rights and interests. But the present is a matter of more private concern, and respects the person of an obscure individual."

"What is the affair, my lord?" said the Queen. "Let us find out what we are talking about, lest we should misconstrue and misunderstand each other."

"The matter, madam," answered the Duke of Argyle, "regards the fate of an unfortunate young woman in Scotland, now lying under sentence of death, for a crime of which I think it highly probable that she is innocent. And my humble petition to your Majesty is, to obtain your powerful intercession with the King for a pardon."

It was now the Queen's turn to color, and she did so over cheek and brow—neck and bosom. She paused a moment, as if unwilling to trust her voice with the first expression of her displeasure; and on assuming an air of dignity and an austere regard of control, she at length replied, "My Lord Duke, I will not ask your motives for addressing to me a request which circumstances have rendered such an extraordinary one. Your road to the King's closet, as a peer and a privy-councillor, entitled to request an audience, was open, without giving me the pain of this discussion. *I,* at least, have had enough of Scotch pardons."

The Duke was prepared for this burst of indignation, and he was not shaken by it. He did not attempt a reply while the Queen was in the first heat of displeasure, but remained in the same firm, yet respectful posture, which he had assumed during the interview. The Queen, trained from her situation to self-command, instantly perceived the advantage she might give against herself by yielding to passion; and added, in the same condescending and affable tone in which she had opened the interview, "You must allow me some of the privileges of the sex, my Lord; and do not judge uncharitably of me, though I am a little moved at the recollection of the gross insult and outrage done in your capital city to the royal authority, at the very time when it was vested in my unworthy person. Your Grace cannot be surprised that I should both have felt it at the time, and recollected it now."

"It is certainly a matter not speedily to be forgotten," answered the Duke. "My own poor thoughts of it have been long before your Majesty, and I must have expressed myself very ill if I did not convey my detestation of the murder which was committed under such extraordinary circumstances. I might, indeed, be so unfortunate as to differ with his Majesty's advisers on the degree in which it was either just or politic to punish the innocent instead of the guilty. But I trust your Majesty will permit me to be silent on a topic in which my sentiments have not the good fortune to coincide with those of more able men."

"We will not prosecute a topic on which we may probably differ," said the Queen. "One word, however, I may say in private—You know our good Lady Suffolk is a little deaf—the Duke of Argyle, when disposed to renew his acquaintance with his master and mistress, will hardly find many topics on which we should disagree."

"Let me hope," said the Duke, bowing profoundly to so flattering an intimation, "that I shall not be so unfortunate as to have found one on the present occasion."

"I must first impose on your Grace the duty of confession," said the Queen, "before I grant you absolution. What is your particular interest in this young woman? She does not seem" (and she scanned Jeanie, as she said this, with the eye of a connoisseur) "much qualified to alarm my friend the Duchess's jealousy."

"I think your Majesty," replied the Duke, smiling in his turn, "will allow my taste may be a pledge for me on that score."

"Then, though she has not much the air *d'une grande dame,* I suppose she is some thirtieth cousin in the terrible chapter of Scottish genealogy?"

"No, madam," said the Duke; "but I wish some of my nearer relations had half her worth, honesty, and affection."

"Her name must be Campbell, at least?" said Queen Caroline.

"No, madam; her name is not quite so distinguished, if I may be permitted to say so," answered the Duke.

"Ah! but she comes from Inverary or Argyleshire?" said the sovereign.

"She has never been farther north in her life than Edinburgh, madam."

"Then my conjectures are all ended," said the Queen, "and your Grace must yourself take the trouble to explain the affair of your protégée."

With that precision and easy brevity which is only acquired by habitually conversing in the higher ranks of society, and which is the diametrical opposite of that protracted style of disquisition,

Which squires call potter, and which men call prose,

the Duke explained the singular law under which Effie Deans had received sentence of death, and detailed the affectionate exertions which Jeanie had made in behalf of her sister, for whose sake she was willing to sacrifice all but truth and conscience.

Queen Caroline listened with attention; she was rather fond, it must be remembered, of an argument, and soon found matter in what the Duke told her for raising difficulties to his request.

"It appears to me, my Lord," she replied, "that this is a severe law. But still it is adopted upon good grounds, I am bound to suppose, as the law of the country, and the girl has been convicted under it. The very presumptions which the law construes into a positive proof of guilt exist in her case; and all that your Grace has said concerning the possibility of her innocence may be a very good argument for annulling the Act of Parliament, but cannot, while it stands good, be admitted in favor of any individual convicted upon the statute."

The Duke saw and avoided the snare; for he was conscious, that, by replying to the argument, he must have been inevitably led to a discussion, in the course of which the Queen was likely to be hardened in her own opinion, until she became obliged, out of mere respect to consistency, to let the criminal suffer. "If your Majesty," he said, "would condescend to hear my poor country-woman herself, perhaps she may find an advocate in your own heart, more able than I am, to combat the doubts suggested by your understanding."

The Queen seemed to acquiesce, and the Duke made a signal for Jeanie to advance from the spot where she had hitherto remained watching countenances, which were too long accustomed to suppress all apparent signs of emotion, to convey to her any interesting intelligence. Her Majesty could not help smiling at the awe-struck manner in which the quiet demure figure of the little Scotch-woman advanced toward her, and yet more at the first sound of her broad northern accent. But Jeanie had a voice low and sweetly toned, an admirable thing in woman, and eke besought "her Leddyship to have pity on a poor misguided young creature," in tones so affecting, that, like the notes of some of her native songs, provincial vulgarity was lost in pathos.

"Stand up, young woman," said the Queen, but in a kind tone, "and tell me what sort of a barbarous people your countryfolk are, where child-murder is become so common as to require the restraint of laws like yours?"

"If your Leddyship pleases," answered Jeanie, "there are mony places besides Scotland where mothers are unkind to their ain flesh and blood."

It must be observed, that the disputes between George the Second, and Frederick, Prince of Wales, were then at the highest, and that the good-natured part of the public laid the blame on the Queen. She colored highly, and darted a glance of a most penetrating character first at Jeanie, and then at the Duke. Both sustained it unmoved; Jeanie from total unconsciousness of the offence she had given, and the Duke from his habitual composure. But in his heart he thought, My unlucky protégée has, with this luckless answer, shot dead, by a kind of chance medley, her only hope of success.

Lady Suffolk, good-humoredly and skilfully, interposed in this awkward crisis. "You should tell this lady," she said to Jeanie, "the particular causes which render this crime common in your country."

"Some thinks it's the Kirk-Session—that is—it's the—it's the cutty-stool, if your Leddyship pleases," said Jeanie, looking down, and courtesying.

"The what?" said Lady Suffolk, to whom the phrase was new and who besides was rather deaf.

"That's the stool of repentance, madam, if it please your Leddyship," answered Jeanie, "for light life and conversation, and for breaking the seventh command." Here she raised her eyes to the Duke, saw his hand at his chin, and, totally unconscious of what she had said out of joint, gave double effect to the innuendo, by stopping short and looking embarrassed.

As for Lady Suffolk, she retired like a covering party, which, having interposed betwixt their retreating friends and the enemy, have suddenly drawn on themselves a fire unexpectedly severe.

The deuce take the lass, thought the Duke of Argyle to himself: there goes another shot—and she has hit with both barrels right and left!

Indeed the Duke had himself his share of the confusion, for, having acted as master of ceremonies to this innocent offender, he felt much in the circumstances of a country squire, who, having introduced his spaniel into a well-appointed drawing-room, is doomed to witness the disorder and damage which arises to china and to dress-gowns, in consequence of its untimely frolics. Jeanie's last chance hit, however, obliterated the ill impression which had arisen from the first; for her Majesty had not so lost the feelings of a wife in those of a Queen, but that she could enjoy a jest at the expense of "her good Suffolk." She turned toward the Duke of Argyle with a smile, which marked that she enjoyed the triumph, and observed, "the Scotch are a rigidly moral people." Then again applying herself to Jeanie, she asked, how she travelled up from Scotland.

"Upon my foot mostly, madam," was the reply.

"What, all that immense way upon foot?—How far can you walk in a day?"

"Five-and-twenty miles and a bittock."

"And a what?" said the Queen, looking toward the Duke of Argyle.

"And about five miles more," replied the Duke.

"I thought I was a good walker," said the Queen, "but this shames me sadly."

"May your Leddyship never hae sae weary a heart, that ye canna be sensible of the weariness of the limbs;" said Jeanie.

That came better off, thought the Duke; it's the first thing she has said to the purpose.

"And I didna just a'thegither walk the haill way neither, for I had whiles the cast of a cart; and I had the cast of a horse from Ferrybridge —and divers other easements," said Jeanie, cutting short her story, for she observed the Duke made the sign he had fixed upon.

"With all these accommodations," answered the Queen, "you must have had a very fatiguing journey, and, I fear, to little purpose; since, if the King were to pardon your sister, in all probability it would do her little good, for I suppose your people of Edinburgh would hang her out of spite."

She will sink herself now outright, thought the Duke.

But he was wrong. The shoals on which Jeanie had touched in this delicate conversation lay underground, and were unknown to her; this rock was above water, and she avoided it.

"She was confident," she said, "that baith town and country wad rejoice to see his Majesty taking compassion on a poor unfriended creature."

"His Majesty has not found it so in a late instance," said the Queen;

"but I suppose, my Lord Duke would advise him to be guided by the votes of the rabble themselves, who should be hanged and who spared?"

"No, madam," said the Duke; "but I would advise his Majesty to be guided by his own feelings, and those of his royal consort; and then, I am sure, punishment will only attach itself to guilt, and even then with cautious reluctance."

"Well, my Lord," said her Majesty, "all these fine speeches do not convince me of the propriety of so soon showing any mark of favor to your—I suppose I must not say rebellious?—but, at least, your very disaffected and intractable metropolis. Why, the whole nation is in a league to screen the savage and abominable murderers of that unhappy man; otherwise, how is it possible but that, of so many perpetrators, and engaged in so public an action for such a length of time, one at least must have been recognized? Even this wench, for aught I can tell, may be a depository of the secret.—Hark you, young woman, had you any friends engaged in the Porteous mob?"

"No, madam," answered Jeanie, happy that the question was so framed that she could, with a good conscience, answer it in the negative.

"But I suppose," continued the Queen, "if you were possessed of such a secret, you would hold it matter of conscience to keep it to yourself?"

"I would pray to be directed and guided what was the line of duty, madam," answered Jeanie.

"Yes, and take that which suited your own inclinations," replied her Majesty.

"If it like you, madam," said Jeanie, "I would hae gaen to the end of the earth to save the life of John Porteous, or any other unhappy man in his condition; but I might lawfully doubt how far I am called upon to be the avenger of his blood, though it may become the civil magistrate to do so. He is dead and gane to his place, and they that have slain him must answer for their ain act. But my sister, my puir sister Effie, still lives, though her days and hours are numbered!—She still lives, an a word of the King's mouth might restore her to a broken-hearted auld man, that never, in his daily and nightly exercise, forgot to pray that his Majesty might be blessed with a long and a prosperous reign, and that his throne, and the throne of his posterity, might be established in righteousness. Oh, madam, if ever ye kend what it was to sorrow for and with a sinning and a suffering creature, whose mind is sae tossed that she can be neither ca'd fit to live or die, have some compassion on our misery!—Save an honest house from dishonor, and an unhappy girl, not eighteen years of age, from an early and dreadful death! Alas! it is not when we sleep soft and wake merrily ourselves, that we think on other people's sufferings. Our hearts are waxed light within us then, and we are for righting our ain wrangs and fighting our ain battles. But when the hour of trouble comes to the mind or to the body—and seldom may it visit your Leddyship—and when the hour of death comes, that comes to high and low—lang and late may it be yours—Oh, my Leddy, then it isna what we hae dune for oursells, but what we hae dune for others, that we think on maist pleasantly. And the thoughts that ye hae intervened to spare the puir thing's life will be sweeter in that hour, come when it may, than if a word of your mouth could hang the haill Porteous mob at the tail of ae tow."

Tear followed tear down Jeanie's cheeks, as, her features glowing and quivering with emotion, she pleaded her sister's cause with a pathos which was at once simple and solemn.

"This is eloquence," said her Majesty to the Duke of Argyle. "Young woman," she continued, addressing herself to Jeanie, "*I* cannot grant a pardon to your sister—but you shall not want my warm intercession with his Majesty. Take this housewife case," she continued, putting a small embroidered needle-case into Jeanie's hands; "do not open it now, but at your leisure you will find something in it which will remind you that you have had an interview with Queen Caroline."

Jeanie, having her suspicions thus confirmed, dropped on her knees, and would have expanded herself in gratitude; but the Duke, who was upon thorns lest she should say more or less than just enough, touched his chin once more.

"Our business is, I think, ended for the present, my Lord Duke," said the Queen, "and, I trust, to your satisfaction. Hereafter I hope to see your Grace more frequently, both at Richmond and St. James's.—Come, Lady Suffolk, we must wish his Grace good morning."

They exchanged their parting reverences, and the Duke, so soon as the ladies had turned their backs, assisted Jeanie to rise from the ground, and conducted her back through the avenue, which she trode with the feeling of one who walks in her sleep.

From Waverley

The Trial of Fergus Mac-Ivor

Waverley is concerned with the Jacobite insurrection of 1745, led by Prince Charles Edward Stuart, grandson of King James II, who had escaped into exile in 1688. The Scotch Jacobites rallied to the banner of the prince, who in their eyes was the only rightful claimant to the throne of England. The powerful young highland chief, Fergus Mac-Ivor, or Vich Ian Vohr, after aiding the cause of the prince in the victory at Prestonpans and during the march into England, is taken in a skirmish at Clifton, brought to Carlisle, and put on trial for high treason. Evan Maccombich is the most conspicuous among the chieftain's host of loyal clansmen.

It was the third sitting of the court, and there were two men at the bar. The verdict of GUILTY was already pronounced. Edward just glanced at the bar during the momentous pause which ensued. There was no mistaking the stately form and noble features of Fergus Mac-Ivor, although his dress was squalid, and his countenance tinged with the sickly yellow hue of long and close imprisonment. By his side was Evan Maccombich. Edward felt sick and dizzy as he gazed on them; but he was recalled to himself as the Clerk of Arraigns pronounced the solemn words: "Fergus Mac-Ivor of Glennaquoich, otherwise called Vich Ian Vohr, and Evan Mac-Ivor, in the Dhu of Tarrascleugh, otherwise called Evan Dhu, otherwise called Evan Maccombich, or Evan Dhu Maccombich—you, and each of you, stand attainted of high treason. What have you to say for yourselves why the Court should not pronounce judgment against you, that you die according to law?"

Fergus, as the presiding Judge was putting on the fatal cap of judgment, placed his own bonnet upon his head, regarded him with a steadfast and stern look, and replied in a firm voice, "I cannot let this numerous audience suppose that to such an appeal I have no answer to make. But what I have to say, you would not bear to hear, for my defence would be your condemnation. Proceed, then, in the name of God, to do what is permitted to you. Yesterday, and the day before, you have condemned loyal and honourable blood to be poured forth like water. Spare not mine. Were that of all my ancestors in my veins, I would have peril'd it in this quarrel." He resumed his seat, and refused again to rise.

Evan Maccombich looked at him with great earnestness, and, rising up, seemed anxious to speak; but the confusion of the court, and the perplexity arising from thinking in a language different from that in which he was to express himself, kept him silent. There was a murmur of compassion among the spectators, from the idea that the poor fellow intended to plead the influence of his superior as an excuse for his crime. The Judge commanded silence, and encouraged Evan to proceed.

"I was only ganging to say, my lord," said Evan, in what he meant to be an insinuating manner, "that if your excellent honour, and the honourable Court, would let Vich Ian Vohr go free just this once, and let him gae back to France, and no to trouble King George's government again, that ony six o' the very best of his clan will be willing to be justified in his stead; and if you'll just let me gae down to Glennaquoich,

I'll fetch them up to ye mysell, to head or hang, and you may begin wi' me the very first man."

Notwithstanding the solemnity of the occasion, a sort of laugh was heard in the court at the extraordinary nature of the proposal. The Judge checked this indecency, and Evan, looking sternly around, when the murmur abated, "If the Saxon gentlemen are laughing," he said, "because a poor man, such as me, thinks my life, or the life of six of my degree, is worth that of Vich Ian Vohr, it's like enough they may be very right; but if they laugh because they think I would not keep my word, and come back to redeem him, I can tell them they ken neither the heart of a Hielandman, nor the honour of a gentleman."

From REDGAUNTLET

Charles Edward's Farewell to the Scottish Lords

Redgauntlet, like *Waverley,* is concerned with Prince Charles Edward Stuart, and an imaginary second attempt on his part to win the throne of England, an attempt which, Scott writes, "could scarcely have been more hopeless than his first." Edward Hugh Redgauntlet, a fanatical Jacobite of the older generation, is the centre of a plot to bring the Prince to Scotland, and foment a new uprising in his behalf. The Prince arrives, in disguise, accompanied by a woman against whose influence over him the Jacobite leaders have already protested. They are called together by Redgauntlet at a smuggler's tavern. The Prince is summoned to attend, but refuses to agree to dismiss the woman. His Jacobite adherents become disaffected; and are thrown into a frenzy of fear mixed with desperate loyalty by the appearance in their midst of "Black Colin Campbell," General of the British Army. The scene that follows ends the story.

AMID this scene of confusion, a gentleman, plainly dressed in a riding-habit, with a black cockade in his hat, but without any arms except a *couteau-de-chasse,* walked into the apartment without ceremony. He was a tall, thin, gentlemanly man, with a look and bearing decidedly military. He had passed through their guards, if in the confusion they now maintained any, without stop or question, and now stood, almost unarmed, among armed men, who, nevertheless, gazed on him as on the angel of destruction.

"You look coldly on me, gentlemen," he said. "Sir Richard Glendale—my Lord——, we were not always such strangers. Ha, Pate-in-Peril, how is it with you? and you, too, Ingoldsby—I must not call you by any other name—why do you receive an old friend so coldly? But you guess my errand."

"And are prepared for it, General," said Redgauntlet; "we are not men to be penned up like sheep for the slaughter."

"Pshaw! you take it too seriously—let me speak but one word with you."

"No words can shake our purpose," said Redgauntlet, "were your whole command, as I suppose is the case, drawn round the house."

"I am certainly not unsupported," said the General; "but if you would hear me——"

"Hear *me,* sir," said the Wanderer, stepping forward; "I suppose I am the mark you aim at—I surrender myself willingly, to save these gentlemen's danger—let this at least avail in their favour."

An exclamation of "Never, never!" broken from the little body of partisans, who threw themselves round the unfortunate Prince, and would have seized or struck down Campbell, had it not been that he remained with his arms folded, and a look, rather indicating impatience because they would not hear him, than the least apprehension of violence at their hand.

At length he obtained a moment's silence. "I do not," he said, "know this gentleman"—(making a profound bow to the unfortunate Prince)—"I do not wish to know him; it is a knowledge which would suit neither of us."

"Our ancestors, nevertheless, have been well acquainted," said Charles, unable to suppress, even in that hour of dread and danger, the painful recollections of fallen royalty.

"In one word, General Campbell," said Redgauntlet, "is it to be peace or war?—You are a man of honour, and we can trust you."

"I thank you, sir," said the General; "and I reply, that the answer to your question rests with yourself. Come, do not be fools, gentlemen; there was perhaps no great harm meant or intended by your gathering together in this obscure corner, for a bear-bait or a cock-fight, or whatever other amusement you may have intended; but it was a little imprudent, considering how you stand with government, and it has occasioned some anxiety. Exaggerated accounts of your purpose have been laid before government by the information of a traitor in your own counsels; and I was sent down post to take the command of a sufficient number of troops, in case these calumnies should be found to have any real foundation. I have come here, of course, sufficiently supported both with cavalry and infantry, to do whatever might be necessary; but my commands are—and I am sure they agree with my inclination—to make no arrests, nay, to make no farther enquiries of any kind, if this good assembly will consider their own interest so far as to give up their immediate purpose, and return quietly home to their own houses."

"What!—all?" exclaimed Sir Richard Glendale—"all, without exception?"

"All, without one single exception," said the General, "such are my orders. If you accept my terms, say so, and make haste; for things may happen to interfere with his Majesty's kind purposes towards you all."

"His Majesty's kind purposes?" said the Wanderer. "Do I hear you aright, sir?"

"I speak the King's very words, from his very lips," replied the General. "'I will,' said his Majesty, 'deserve the confidence of my subjects by reposing my security in the fidelity of the millions who acknowledge my title—in the good sense and prudence of the few who continue, from the errors of education, to disown it.'—His Majesty will not even believe that the most zealous Jacobites who yet remain can nourish a thought of exciting a civil war, which must be fatal to their families and themselves, besides spreading bloodshed and ruin through a peaceful land. He cannot even believe of his kinsman, that he would engage brave and generous, though mistaken men, in an attempt which must ruin all who have escaped former calamities; and he is convinced, that, did curiosity or any other motive lead that person to visit this country, he would soon see it was his wisest course to return to the continent; and his Majesty compassionates his situation too much to offer any obstacle to his doing so."

"Is this real?" said Redgauntlet. "Can you mean this?—Am I—are all, are any of these gentlemen at liberty, without interruption, to embark in yonder brig, which, I see, is now again approaching the shore?"

"You, sir—all—any of the gentlemen present," said the General,—"all whom the vessel can contain, are at liberty to embark uninterrupted by me; but I advise none to go off who have not powerful reasons, unconnected with the present meeting, for this will be remembered against no one."

"Then, gentlemen," said Redgauntlet, clasping his hands together as the words burst from him, "the cause is lost forever!"

General Campbell turned away to the window, as if to avoid hearing what they said. Their consultation was but momentary; for the door of escape which thus opened was as unexpected as the exigence was threatening.

"We have your word of honour for our protection," said Sir Richard Glendale, "if we dissolve our meeting in obedience to your summons?"

"You have, Sir Richard," answered the General.

"And I also have your promise," said Redgauntlet, "that I may go on board yonder vessel, with any friend whom I may choose to accompany me?"

"Not only that, Mr. Ingoldsby—or I *will* call you Redgauntlet once more—you may stay in the offing for a tide, until you are joined by any person who may remain at Fairladies. After that, there will be a sloop of war on the station, and I need not say your condition will then become perilous."

"Perilous it should not be, General Campbell," said Redgauntlet, "or more perilous to others than to us, if others thought as I do even in this extremity."

"You forget yourself, my friend," said the unhappy Adventurer; "you forget that the arrival of this gentleman only puts the cope-stone on our already adopted resolution to abandon our bull-fight, or by whatever other wild name this headlong enterprise may be termed. I bid you farewell, unfriendly friends—I bid *you* farewell," (bowing to the General,) "my friendly foe—I leave this strand as I landed upon it, alone, and to return no more!"

"Not alone," said Redgauntlet, "while there is blood in the veins of my father's son."

"Not alone," said the other gentlemen present, stung with feelings which almost overpowered the better reasons under which they had acted. "We will not disown our principles or see your person endangered."

"If it be only your purpose to see the gentleman to the beach," said General Campbell, "I will myself go with you. My presence among you, unarmed, and in your power, will be a pledge of my friendly intentions, and will overawe, should such be offered, any interruption on the part of officious persons."

"Be it so," said the Adventurer, with the air of a Prince to a subject; not of one who complied with the request of an enemy too powerful to be resisted.

They left the apartment—they left the house—an unauthenticated and dubious, but appalling, sensation of terror had already spread itself among the inferior retainers, who had so short time before strutted, and bustled, and thronged the doorway and the passages. A report had arisen, of which the origin could not be traced, of troops advancing towards the spot in considerable numbers; and men who, for one reason or other, were most of them amenable to the arm of power, had either shrunk into stables or corners, or fled the place entirely. There was solitude on the landscape, excepting the small party which now moved towards the rude pier, where a boat lay manned, agreeably to Redgauntlet's orders previously given.

The last heir of the Stewarts leant on Redgauntlet's arm as they walked towards the beach; for the ground was rough, and he no longer possessed the elasticity of limb and of spirit which had, twenty years before, carried him over many a Highland hill, as light as one of their native deer. His adherents followed, looking on the ground, their feelings struggling against the dictates of their reason.

General Campbell accompanied them with an air of apparent ease and indifference, but watching, at the same time, and no doubt with some anxiety, the changing features of those who acted in this extraordinary scene.

Darsie and his sister naturally followed their uncle, whose violence they no longer feared, while his character attracted their respect, and Alan Fairford accompanied them from interest in their fate, unnoticed in a party where all were too much occupied with their own thoughts and feelings, as well as with the impending crisis, to attend to his presence.

Half way betwixt the house and the beach, they saw the bodies of Nanty Ewart and Cristal Nixon blackening in the sun.

"That was your informer?" said Redgauntlet, looking back to General Campbell, who only nodded his assent.

"Caitiff wretch!" exclaimed Redgauntlet;—"and yet the name were better bestowed on the fool who could be misled by thee."

"That sound broadsword cut," said the General, "has saved us the shame of rewarding a traitor."

They arrived at the place of embarkation. The Prince stood a moment with folded arms, and looked around him in deep silence. A paper was then slipped into his hands—he looked at it, and said, "I find the two friends I have left at Fairladies are apprised of my destination, and propose to embark from Bowness. I presume this will not be an infringement on the conditions under which you have acted?"

"Certainly not," answered General Campbell; "they shall have all facility to join you."

"I wish, then," said Charles, "only another companion.—Redgauntlet, the air of this country is as hostile to you as it is to me. These gentlemen have made their peace, or rather they have done nothing to break it. But you—come you, and share my home where chance shall cast it. We shall never see these shores again; but we will talk of them, and of our disconcerted bull-fight."

"I follow you, Sire, through life," said Redgauntlet, "as I would have followed you to death. Permit me one moment."

The Prince then looked round, and seeing the abashed countenances of his other adherents bent upon the ground, he hastened to say, "Do not think that you, gentlemen, have obliged me less because your zeal was mingled with prudence, entertained, I am sure, more on my own account, and on that of your country, than from selfish apprehensions."

He stepped from one to another, and, amid sobs and bursting tears, received the adieus of the last remnant which had hitherto supported his lofty pretensions, and addressed them individually with accents of tenderness and affection.

The General drew a little aloof, and signed to Redgauntlet to speak with him while this scene proceeded. "It is now all over," he said, "and Jacobite will be henceforward no longer a party name. When you tire of foreign parts, and wish to make your peace, let me know. Your restless zeal alone has impeded your pardon hitherto."

"And now I shall not need it," said Redgauntlet. "I leave England for ever; but I am not displeased that you should hear my family adieus. —Nephew, come hither. In presence of General Campbell, I tell you, that though to breed you up in my own political opinions has been for many years my anxious wish, I am now glad that it could not be accomplished. You pass under the service of the reigning Monarch without the necessity of changing your allegiance—a change, however," he added, looking around him, "which sits more easy on honourable men than I could have anticipated; but some wear the badge of their loyalty on the sleeve, and others in the heart.—You will, from henceforth, be uncontrolled master of all the property of which forfeiture could not deprive your father—of all that belonged to him—excepting this, his good sword," (laying his hand on the weapon he wore,) "which shall never fight for the House of Hanover; and as my hand will never draw weapon more, I shall sink it forty fathoms deep in the wide ocean. Bless you, young man! If I have dealt harshly with you, forgive me. I had set my whole desires on one point,—God knows, with no selfish purpose; and I am justly punished by this final termination of my views, for having been too little scrupulous in the means by which I pursued them. Niece, farewell, and may God bless you also!"

"No, sir," said Lilias, seizing his hand eagerly. "You have been hitherto my protector,—you are now in sorrow, let me be your attendant and your comforter in exile."

"I thank you, my girl, for your unmerited affection; but it cannot and must not be. The curtain here falls between us. I go to the house of another—If I leave it before I quit the earth, it shall be only for the House of God. Once more, farewell both!—The fatal doom," he said, with a melancholy smile, "will, I trust, now depart from the House of Redgauntlet, since its present representative has adhered to the winning side. I am convinced he will not change it, should it in turn become the losing one."

The unfortunate Charles Edward had now given his last adieus to his downcast adherents. He made a sign with his hand to Redgauntlet, who came to assist him into the skiff. General Campbell also offered his assistance; the rest appearing too much affected by the scene which had taken place to prevent him.

"You are not sorry, General, to do me this last act of courtesy," said the Chevalier; "and, on my part, I thank you for it. You have taught me the principle on which men on the scaffold feel forgiveness and kindness even for their executioner.—Farewell!"

They were seated in the boat, which presently pulled off from the land. The Oxford divine broke out into a loud benediction, in terms which General Campbell was too generous to criticise at the time, or to remember afterwards;—nay, it is said that, Whig and Campbell as he was, he could not help joining in the universal Amen! which resounded from the shore.

From THE ANTIQUARY

The Escape of Sir Arthur Wardour and Isabella

The Antiquary deals with life in Scotland in 1795. The hero, Lovel, who later proves to be Major Neville, of the King's troops, and—what is more important to the happy ending of the story—the legitimate son of the Earl of Glenallan, and his heir, is at first decidedly out of favor with Sir Arthur Wardour's daughter Isabella. Jonathan Oldbuck, the antiquary, is host at dinner to Lovel, Isabella, and Sir Arthur. After dinner, Oldbuck and Sir Arthur grow heated in a discussion of antiquities and ancestors, and Sir Arthur leaves with Isabella. Lovel has slipped out unobserved, before them. They are intending to meet their carriage on the turnpike road; but at sight of Lovel, Isabella suggests taking another direction. Sir Arthur willingly consents. They turn down by the Mussel-craig, along the sands, wholly unaware of the unusual danger of a neap tide. Edie Ochiltree, who figures in the scene that follows, is a strange creature, a King's Bedesman, or Blue-Gown, a licensed mendicant, full of Scottish shrewdness and keen human philosophy. At various points in the story he appears, ever present, somehow, in time of need.

THE sun was now resting his huge disk upon the edge of the level ocean, and gilded the accumulation of towering clouds through which he had travelled the livelong day, and which now assembled on all sides, like misfortunes and disasters around a sinking empire and falling monarch.

Still, however, his dying splendour gave a sombre magnificence to the massive congregation of vapours, forming out of their unsubstantial gloom the show of pyramids and towers, some touched with gold, some with purple, some with a hue of deep and dark red. The distant sea, stretched beneath this varied and gorgeous canopy, lay almost portentously still, reflecting back the dazzling and level beams of the descending luminary, and the splendid colouring of the clouds amidst which he was setting. Nearer to the beach, the tide rippled onward in waves of sparkling silver, that imperceptibly, yet rapidly, gained upon the sand.

With a mind employed in admiration of the romantic scene, or perhaps on some more agitating topic, Miss Wardour advanced in silence by her father's side, whose recently offended dignity did not stoop to open any conversation. Following the windings of the beach, they passed one projecting point or headland of rock after another, and now found themselves under a huge and continued extent of the precipices by which that iron-bound coast is in most places defended. Long projecting reefs of rock, extending under water, and only evincing their existence by here and there a peak entirely bare, or by the breakers which foamed over those that were partially covered, rendered Knockwinnock bay dreaded by pilots and ship-masters. The crags which rose between the beach and the mainland, to the height of two or three hundred feet, afforded in their crevices shelter for unnumbered sea-fowls, in situations seemingly secured by their dizzy height from the rapacity of man. Many of these wild tribes, with the instinct which sends them to seek the land before a storm arises, were now winging towards their nests with the shrill and dissonant clang which announces disquietude and fear. The disk of the sun became almost totally obscured ere he had altogether sunk below the horizon, and an early and lurid shade of darkness blotted the serene twilight of a summer evening. The wind began next to arise; but its wild and moaning sound was heard for some time, and its effects became visible on the bosom of the sea, before the gale was felt on shore. The mass of waters, now dark and threatening, began to lift itself in larger ridges, and sink in deeper furrows, forming waves that rose high in foam upon the breakers, or burst upon the beach with a sound resembling distant thunder.

Appalled by this sudden change of weather, Miss Wardour drew close to her father, and held his arm fast. "I wish," at length she said, but almost in a whisper, as if ashamed to express her increasing apprehensions, "I wish we had kept the road we intended, or waited at Monkbarns for the carriage."

Sir Arthur looked round, but did not see, or would not acknowledge, any signs of an immediate storm. They would reach Knockwinnock, he said, long before the tempest began. But the speed with which he walked, and with which Isabella could hardly keep pace, indicated a feeling that some exertion was necessary to accomplish his consolatory prediction.

They were now near the centre of a deep but narrow bay, or recess, formed by two projecting capes of high and inaccessible rock, which shot out into the sea like the horns of a crescent; and neither durst communicate the apprehension which each began to entertain, that, from the unusually rapid advance of the tide, they might be deprived of the power of proceeding by doubling the promontory which lay before them, or of retreating by the road which brought them thither.

As they thus pressed forward, longing doubtless to exchange the easy curving line, which the sinuosities of the bay compelled them to adopt, for a straighter and more expeditious path, though less conformable to the line of beauty, Sir Arthur observed a human figure on the beach advancing to meet them. "Thank God," he exclaimed, "we shall get round Halket Head! that person must have passed it;" thus giving vent to the feeling of hope, though he had suppressed that of apprehension.

"Thank God indeed!" echoed his daughter, half audibly, half internally, as expressing the gratitude which she strongly felt.

The figure which advanced to meet them made many signs, which the haze of the atmosphere, now disturbed by wind and by a drizzling rain, prevented them from seeing or comprehending distinctly. Some time before they met, Sir Arthur could recognize the old blue-gowned beggar, Edie Ochiltree. It is said that even the brute creation lay aside their animosities and antipathies when pressed by an instant and common danger. The beach under Halket Head, rapidly diminishing in extent by the encroachments of a spring-tide and a northwest wind, was in like manner a neutral field, where even a justice of peace and a strolling mendicant might meet upon terms of mutual forbearance.

"Turn back! turn back!" exclaimed the vagrant; "why did ye not turn when I waved to you?"

"We thought," replied Sir Arthur, in great agitation, "we thought we could get round Halket Head."

"Halket Head! The tide will be running on Halket Head, by this time, like the Fall of Fyers! It was a' I could do to get round it twenty minutes since—it was coming in three feet abreast. We will maybe get back by Bally-burgh Ness Point yet. The Lord help us, it's our only chance. We can but try."

"My God, my child!"—"My father, my dear father!" exclaimed the parent and daughter, as, fear lending them strength and speed, they turned to retrace their steps, and endeavoured to double the point, the projection of which formed the southern extremity of the bay.

"I heard ye were here, frae the bit callant ye sent to meet your carriage," said the beggar, as he trudged stoutly on a step or two behind Miss Wardour, "and I couldna bide to think o' the dainty young leddy's peril, that has aye been kind to ilka forlorn heart that cam near her. Sae I lookit at the lift and the rin o' the tide, till I settled it that if I could get down time eneugh to gie you warning, we wad do weel yet. But I doubt, I doubt, I have been beguiled! for what mortal ee ever saw sic a race as the tide is rinning e'en now? See, yonder's the Ratton's Skerry—he aye held his neb abune the water in my day—but he's aneath it now."

Sir Arthur cast a look in the direction in which the old man pointed. A huge rock, which in general, even in spring-tides, displayed a hulk like the keel of a large vessel, was now quite under water, and its place only indicated by the boiling and breaking of the eddying waves which encountered its submarine resistance.

"Mak haste, mak haste, my bonny leddy," continued the old man, "mak haste, and we may do yet! Take haud o' my arm—an auld and frail arm it's now, but it's been in as sair stress as this is yet. Take haud o' my arm, my winsome leddy! D'ye see yon wee black speck amang the wallowing waves yonder? This morning it was as high as the mast o' a brig—it's sma' eneugh now—but, while I see as muckle black about it as the crown o' my hat, I winna believe but we'll get round the Ballyburgh Ness, for a' that's come and gane yet."

Isabella, in silence, accepted from the old man the assistance which Sir Arthur was less able to afford her. The waves had now encroached so much upon the beach, that the firm and smooth footing which they had hitherto had on the sand must be exchanged for a rougher path close to the foot of the precipice, and in some places even raised upon its lower ledges. It would have been utterly impossible for Sir Arthur Wardour, or his daughter, to have found their way along these shelves without the guidance and encouragement of the beggar, who had been there before in high tides, though never, he acknowledged, "in sae awsome a night as this."

It was indeed a dreadful evening. The howling of the storm mingled with the shrieks of the sea-fowl, and sounded like the dirge of the three devoted beings, who, pent between two of the most magnificent yet most dreadful objects of nature—a raging tide and an insurmountable precipice—toiled along their painful and dangerous path, often lashed by the spray of some giant billow, which threw itself higher on the beach than those that had preceded it. Each minute did their enemy gain ground perceptibly upon them! Still, however, loath to relinquish the last hopes of life, they bent their eyes on the black rock pointed out by Ochiltree. It was yet distinctly visible among the breakers, and continued to be so, until they came to a turn in their precarious path, where an intervening projection of rock hid it from their sight. Deprived of the view of the beacon on which they had relied, they now experienced the double agony of terror and suspense. They struggled forward, however; but, when they arrived at the point from which they ought to have seen the crag, it was no longer visible. The signal of safety was lost among a thousand white breakers, which, dashing upon the point of the promontory, rose in prodigious sheets of snowy foam, as high as the mast of a first-rate man-of-war, against the dark brow of the precipice.

The countenance of the old man fell. Isabella gave a faint shriek, and, "God have mercy upon us!" which her guide solemnly uttered, was piteously echoed by Sir Arthur—"My child! my child!—to die such a death!"

"My father! my dear father!" his daughter exclaimed, clinging to him—"and you too, who have lost your own life in endeavouring to save ours!"

"That's not worth the counting," said the old man. "I hae lived to be weary o' life; and here or yonder—at the back o' a dyke, in a wreath o' snaw, or in the wame o' a wave, what signifies how the auld gaberlunzie dies?"

"Good man," said Arthur, "can you think of nothing?—of no help? —I'll make you rich—I'll give you a farm—I'll——"

"Our riches will be soon equal," said the beggar, looking out upon the strife of the waters—"they are sae already; for I hae nae land, and you would give your fair bounds and barony for a square yard of rock that would be dry for twal hours."

While they exchanged these words, they paused upon the highest ledge of rock to which they could attain; for it seemed that any further attempt to move forward could only serve to anticipate their fate. Here, then, they were to await the sure though slow progress of the raging element, something in the situation of the martyrs of the early Church, who, exposed by heathen tyrants to be slain by wild beasts, were compelled for a time to witness the impatience and rage by which the animals were agitated, while awaiting the signal for undoing their grates, and letting them loose upon the victims.

Yet even this fearful pause gave Isabella time to collect the powers of a mind naturally strong and courageous, and which rallied itself at this terrible juncture. "Must we yield life," she said, "without a struggle? Is there no path, however dreadful, by which we could climb the crag, or at least attain some height above the tide, where we could remain till morning, or till help comes? They must be aware of our situation, and will raise the country to relieve us."

Sir Arthur, who heard, but scarcely comprehended, his daughter's question, turned, nevertheless, instinctively and eagerly, to the old man, as if their lives were in his gift. Ochiltree paused. "I was a bauld craigsman," he said, "ance in my life, and mony a kittywake's and lungie's nest hae I harried up amang thae very black rocks; but it's lang, lang syne, and nae mortal could speel them without a rope—and if I had ane, my ee-sight, and my footstep, and my hand-grip, hae a' failed mony a day sinsyne—and then how could I save *you?*—But there was a path here ance, though maybe, if we could see it, ye would rather bide where we are —His name be praised!" he ejaculated suddenly, "there's ane coming down the crag e'en now!"—Then, exalting his voice, he hilloa'd out to the daring adventurer such instructions as his former practice, and the remembrance of local circumstances, suddenly forced upon his mind:—"Ye're right—ye're right!—that gate, that gate!—fasten the rope weel round Crummie's Horn, that's the muckle black stane—cast twa plies round it—that's it!—now, weize yoursell a wee easel-ward—a wee mair yet to that ither stane—we ca'd it the Cat's Lug—there used to be the root o' an aik-tree there—that will do!—canny now, lad—canny now—tak tent and tak time—Lord bless ye, tak time.—Very weel!—Now ye maun get to Bessy's Apron, that's the muckle braid flat blue stane—and then, I think, wi' your help and the tow thegither, I'll win at ye, and then we'll be able to get up the young leddy and Sir Arthur."

The adventurer, following the directions of old Edie, flung him down the end of the rope, which he secured around Miss Wardour, wrapping her previously in his own blue gown, to preserve her as much as possible from injury. Then, availing himself of the rope, which was made fast at the other end, he began to ascend the face of the crag—a most precarious and dizzy undertaking, which, however, after one or two perilous escapes, placed him safe on the broad flat stone beside our friend Lovel. Their joint strength was able to raise Isabella to the place of safety which they had attained. Lovel then descended in order to assist Sir Arthur, around whom he adjusted the rope; and again mounting to their place of refuge, with the assistance of old Ochiltree, and such aid as Sir Arthur himself could afford, he raised himself beyond the reach of the billows.

The sense of reprieve from approaching and apparently inevitable death had its usual effect. The father and daughter threw themselves into each other's arms, kissed and wept for joy, although their escape was connected with the prospect of passing a tempestuous night on a precipitous ledge of rock, which scarcely afforded footing for the four shivering beings, who now, like the sea-fowl round them, clung there in hopes of some shelter from the devouring element which raged beneath. The spray of the billows, which attained in fearful succession the foot of the precipice, overflowing the beach on which they so lately stood, flew as high as their place of temporary refuge; and the stunning sound with which they dashed against the rocks beneath, seemed as if they still demanded the fugitives in accents of thunder as their destined prey. It was a summer night doubtless; yet the probability was slender, that a frame so delicate as that of Miss Wardour should survive till morning the drenching of the spray; and the dashing of the rain, which now burst in full violence, accompanied with deep and heavy gusts of wind, added to the constrained and perilous circumstances of their situation.

"The lassie, the puir sweet lassie," said the old man; "mony such a night have I weathered at hame and abroad; but, God guide us, how can she ever win through it!"

His apprehension was communicated in smothered accents to Lovel; for, with the sort of freemasonry by which bold and ready spirits correspond in moments of danger, and become almost instinctively known to each other, they had established a mutual confidence.—"I'll climb up the cliff again," said Lovel, "there's daylight enough left to see my footing; I'll climb up, and call for more assistance."

"Do so, do so, for heaven's sake!" said Sir Arthur eagerly.

"Are ye mad?" said the mendicant; "Francie o' Fowlsheugh, and he was the best craigsman that ever speel'd heugh (mair by token, he brake his neck upon the Dunbuy of Slaines), wadna hae ventured upon the Halket Head craigs after sundown—It's God's grace, and a great wonder besides, that ye are not in the middle o' that roaring sea wi what ye hae done already—I didna think there was the man left alive would hae come down the craigs as ye did. I question an I could hae done it mysell, at this hour and in this weather, in the youngest and yaldest of my strength—But to venture up again—it's a mere and clear tempting o' Providence."

"I have no fear," answered Lovel; "I marked all the stations perfectly as I came down, and there is still light enough left to see them quite well—I am sure I can do it with perfect safety. Stay here, my good friend, by Sir Arthur and the young lady."

"Deil be in my feet then," answered the bedesman sturdily; "if ye gang, I'll gang too; for between the twa o' us, we'll hae mair than wark eneugh to get to the tap o' the heugh."

"No, no—stay you here and attend to Miss Wardour—you see Sir Arthur is quite exhausted."

"Stay yourself then, and I'll gae," said the old man; "let death spare the green corn and take the ripe."

"Stay both of you, I charge you," said Isabella faintly; "I am well, and can spend the night very well here—I feel quite refreshed." So saying, her voice failed her—she sunk down, and would have fallen from the crag, had she not been supported by Lovel and Ochiltree, who placed her in a posture half sitting, half reclining, beside her father, who, exhausted by fatigue of body and mind so extreme and unusual, had already sat down on a stone in a sort of stupor.

"It is impossible to leave them," said Lovel. "What is to be done?—Hark! hark!—Did I not hear a halloo?"

"The skriegh of a Tammie Norie," answered Ochiltree, "I ken the skirl weel."

"No, by Heaven," replied Lovel, "it was a human voice."

A distant hail was repeated, the sound plainly distinguishable among the various elemental noises, and the clang of the sea-mews by which they were surrounded. The mendicant and Lovel exerted their voices in a loud halloo, the former waving Miss Wardour's handkerchief on the end of his staff to make them conspicuous from above. Though the shouts were repeated, it was some time before they were in exact response to their own, leaving the unfortunate sufferers uncertain whether, in the darkening twilight and increasing storm, they had made the persons, who apparently were traversing the verge of the precipice to bring them assistance, sensible of the place in which they had found refuge. At length their halloo was regularly and distinctly answered, and their courage confirmed, by the assurance that they were within hearing, if not within reach, of friendly assistance.

The Two Drovers

I SHALL never forget the charge of the venerable judge to the jury, although not at that time liable to be much affected either by that which was eloquent or pathetic.

"We have had," he said, "in the previous part of our duty" (alluding to some former trials) "to discuss crimes which infer disgust and abhorrence, while they call down the well-merited vengeance of the law. It is now our still more melancholy task to apply its salutary though severe enactments to a case of a very singular character, in which the crime (for a crime it is, and a deep one) arose less out of the malevolence of the heart than the error of the understanding—less from any idea of committing wrong than from an unhappily perverted notion of that which is right. Here we have two men, highly esteemed, it has been stated, in their rank of life, and attached, it seems, to each other as friends, one of whose lives has been already sacrificed to a punctilio, and the other is about to prove the vengeance of the offended laws; and yet both may claim our commiseration at least, as men acting in ignorance of each other's national prejudices, and unhappily misguided rather than voluntarily erring from the path of right conduct.

"In the original cause of the misunderstanding we must in justice give the right to the prisoner at the bar. He had acquired possession of the enclosure, which was the object of competition, by a legal contract with the proprietor, Mr. Ireby; and yet, when accosted with reproaches undeserved in themselves, and galling doubtless to a temper at least sufficiently susceptible of passion, he offered notwithstanding to yield up half his acquisition, for the sake of peace and good neighbourhood, and his amicable proposal was rejected with scorn. Then follows the scene at Mr. Heskett the publican's, and you will observe how the stranger was treated by the deceased, and, I am sorry to observe, by those around, who seem to have urged him in a manner which was aggravating in the highest degree. While he asked for peace and for composition, and offered submission to a magistrate, or to a mutual arbiter, the prisoner was insulted by the whole company, who seem on this occasion to have forgotten the national maxim of 'fair play'; and while attempting to escape from the place in peace, he was intercepted, struck down, and beaten to the effusion of his blood.

"Gentlemen of the Jury, it was with some impatience that I heard my learned brother, who opened the case for the crown, give an unfavourable turn to the prisoner's conduct on this occasion. He said the prisoner was afraid to encounter his antagonist in a fair fight, or to submit to the laws of the ring; and that therefore, like a cowardly Italian, he had recourse to his fatal stiletto, to murder the man whom he dared not meet in manly encounter. I observed the prisoner shrink from this part of the accusation with the abhorrence natural to a brave man; and as I would wish to make my words impressive, when I point his real crime, I must secure his opinion of my impartiality, by rebutting everything that seems to me a false accusation. There can be no doubt that the prisoner is a man of resolution—too much resolution—I wish to Heaven that he had less, or rather that he had had a better education to regulate it.

"Gentlemen, as to the laws my brother talks of, they may be known in the bull-ring, or the bear-garden, or the cockpit, but they are not known here. Or, if they should be so far admitted as furnishing a species of proof that no malice was intended in this sort of combat, from which fatal accidents do sometimes arise, it can only be so admitted when both parties are *in pari casu*, equally acquainted with, and equally willing to refer themselves to, that species of arbitrament. But will it be contended that a man of superior rank and education is to be subjected, or is obliged to subject himself, to this coarse and brutal strife, perhaps in opposition to a younger, stronger, or more skilful opponent? Certainly even the pugilistic code, if founded upon the fair play of Merry Old England, as my brother alleges it to be, can contain nothing so preposterous. And, gentlemen of the jury, if the laws would support an English gentleman, wearing, we will suppose, his sword, in defending himself by force against a violent personal aggression of the nature offered to this prisoner, they will not less protect a foreigner and a stranger, involved in the same unpleasing circumstances. If, therefore, gentlemen of the jury, when thus pressed by a *vis major*, the object of obloquy to a whole company, and of direct violence from one at least, and, as he might reasonably apprehend, from more, the panel had produced the weapon which his countrymen, as we are informed, generally carry about their persons, and the same unhappy circumstance had ensued which you have heard detailed in evidence, I could not in my conscience have asked from you a verdict of murder. The prisoner's personal defence might indeed, even in that case, have gone more or less beyond the *moderamen inculpatæ tutelæ,* spoken of by lawyers, but the punishment incurred would have been that of manslaughter, not of murder. I beg leave to add that I should have thought this milder species of charge was demanded in the case supposed, notwithstanding the statute of James I. cap. 8, which takes the case of slaughter by stabbing with a short weapon, even without malice prepense, out of the benefit of clergy. For this statute of stabbing, as it is termed, arose out of a temporary cause; and as the real guilt is the same, whether the slaughter be committed by the dagger or by sword or pistol, the benignity of the modern law places them all on the same, or nearly the same, footing.

"But, gentlemen of the jury, the pinch of the case lies in the interval of two hours interposed betwixt the reception of the injury and the fatal retaliation. In the heat of affray and *chaude mêlée*, law, compassionating the infirmities of humanity, makes allowance for the passions which rule such a stormy moment—for the sense of present pain, for the apprehension of further injury, for the difficulty of ascertaining with due accuracy the precise degree of violence which is necessary to protect the person of the individual, without annoying or injuring the assailant more than is absolutely necessary. But the time necessary to walk twelve miles, however speedily performed, was an interval sufficient for the prisoner to have recollected himself; and the violence with which he carried his purpose into effect, with so many circumstances of deliberate determination, could neither be induced by the passion of anger, nor that of fear. It was the purpose and the act of predetermined revenge, for which law neither can, will, nor ought to have sympathy or allowance.

"It is true, we may repeat to ourselves, in alleviation of this poor man's unhappy action, that his case is a very peculiar one. The country which he inhabits was, in the days of many now alive, inaccessible to the laws, not only of England, which have not even yet penetrated thither, but to those to which our neighbours of Scotland are subjected, and which must be supposed to be, and no doubt actually are, founded upon the general principles of justice and equity which pervade every civilised country. Amongst their mountains, as among the North American Indians, the various tribes were wont to make war upon each other, so that each man was obliged to go armed for his own protection. These men, from the ideas which they entertained of their own descent and of their own consequence, regarded themselves as so many cavaliers or men-at-arms, rather than as the peasantry of a peaceful country. Those laws of the ring, as my brother terms them, were unknown to the race of warlike mountaineers; that decision of quarrels by no other weapons than those which nature has given every man must to them have seemed as vulgar and as preposterous as to the noblesse of France. Revenge, on the other hand, must have been as familiar to their habits of society as to those of the Cherokees or Mohawks. It is indeed, as described by Bacon, at bottom a kind of wild untutored justice; for the fear of retaliation must withhold the hands of the oppressor where there is no regular law to check daring violence. But though all this may be granted, and though we may allow that, such having been the case of the Highlands in the days of the prisoner's fathers, many of the opinions and sentiments must still continue to influence the present generation, it cannot, and ought not, even in this most painful case, to alter the administration of the law, either in your hands, gentlemen of the jury, or in mine. The first object of civilisation is to place the general protection of the law, equally administered, in the room of that wild justice which every man cut and carved for himself according to the length of his sword and the strength of his arm. The law says to the subjects, with a voice only inferior to that of the Deity, 'Vengeance is mine.' The instant that there is time for passion to cool and reason to interpose, an injured party must become aware that the law assumes the exclusive cognizance of the right and wrong betwixt the parties, and opposes her inviolable buckler to every attempt of the private party to right himself. I repeat that this unhappy man ought personally to be the object rather of our pity than our abhorrence, for he failed in his ignorance, and from mistaken notions of honour. But his crime is not the less that of murder, gentlemen, and, in your high and important office, it is your duty so to find. Englishmen have their angry passions as well as Scots; and should this man's action remain unpunished, you may unsheath, under various pretences, a thousand daggers betwixt the Land's-end and the Orkneys."

The venerable judge ended what, to judge by his apparent emotion, and by the tears which filled his eyes, was really a painful task. The jury, according to his instructions, brought in a verdict of guilty; and Robin Oig M'Combich, *alias* M'Gregor, was sentenced to death, and left for execution, which took place accordingly. He met his fate with great firmness, and acknowledged the justice of his sentence. But he repelled indignantly the observations of those who accused him of attacking an unarmed man. "I give a life for the life I took," he said, "and what can I do more?"

The Violet

THE violet in her green-wood bower,
Where birchen boughs with hazels mingle,
May boast itself the fairest flower
In glen, or copse, or forest dingle.

Though fair her gems of azure hue,
Beneath the dew-drop's weight reclining;
I've seen an eye of lovelier blue,
More sweet through wat'ry lustre shining.

The summer sun that dew shall dry,
Ere yet the day be past its morrow;
Nor longer in my false love's eye
Remain'd the tear of parting sorrow.

Hunting Song

WAKEN, lords and ladies gay,
On the mountain dawns the day,
All the jolly chase is here,
With hawk, and horse, and hunting-spear!
Hounds are in their couples yelling,
Hawks are whistling, horns are knelling,
Merrily, merrily, mingle they,
"Waken, lords and ladies gay."

Waken, lords and ladies gay,
The mist has left the mountain grey,
Springlets in the dawn are steaming,
Diamonds on the brake are gleaming;
And foresters have busy been,
To track the buck in thicket green;
Now we come to chant our lay,
"Waken, lords and ladies gay."

Waken, lords and ladies gay,
To the green-wood haste away;
We can show you where he lies,
Fleet of foot, and tall of size;
We can show the marks he made,
When 'gainst the oak his antlers fray'd;

You shall see him brought to bay,
"Waken, lords and ladies gay."

Louder, louder chant the lay,
Waken, lords and ladies gay!
Tell them youth, and mirth, and glee,
Run a course as well as we;
Time, stern huntsman! who can baulk,
Stanch as hound, and fleet as hawk;
Think of this, and rise with day,
Gentle lords and ladies gay.

From Marmion

Lochinvar

Oh! young Lochinvar is come out of the west,
Through all the wide Border his steed was the best;
And save his good broadsword he weapons had none.
He rode all unarmed and he rode all alone.
So faithful in love and so dauntless in war,
There never was knight like the young Lochinvar.

He stayed not for brake and he stopped not for stone,
He swam the Eske river where ford there was none,
But ere he alighted at Netherby gate
The bride had consented, the gallant came late:
For a laggard in love and a dastard in war
Was to wed the fair Ellen of brave Lochinvar.

So boldly he entered the Netherby Hall,
Among bridesmen, and kinsmen, and brothers, and all:
Then spoke the bride's father, his hand on his sword,—
For the poor craven bridegroom said never a word,—
"Oh! come ye in peace here, or come ye in war,
Or to dance at our bridal, young Lord Lochinvar?"—

"I long wooed your daughter, my suit you denied;
Love swells like the Solway, but ebbs like its tide—
And now am I come, with this lost love of mine
To lead but one measure, drink one cup of wine.
There are maidens in Scotland more lovely by far,
That would gladly be bride to the young Lochinvar."

The bride kissed the goblet: the knight took it up,
He quaffed off the wine, and he threw down the cup.
She looked down to blush, and she looked up to sigh,
With a smile on her lips and a tear in her eye.
He took her soft hand ere her mother could bar,—
"Now tread we a measure!" said young Lochinvar.

So stately his form, and so lovely her face,
That never a hall such a galliard did grace;
While her mother did fret, and her father did fume,
And the bridegroom stood dangling his bonnet and plume;
And the bride-maidens whispered, "'Twere better by far
To have matched our fair cousin with young Lochinvar."

One touch to her hand and one word in her ear,
When they reached the hall-door, and the charger stood near;

So light to the croupe the fair lady he swung,
So light to the saddle before her he sprung!
"She is won! we are gone, over bank, bush, and scaur;
They'll have fleet steeds that follow," quoth young Lochinvar.

There was mounting 'mong Graemes of the Netherby clan;
Forsters, Fenwicks, and Musgraves, they rode and they ran:
There was racing and chasing on Cannobie Lee,
But the lost bride of Netherby ne'er did they see.
So daring in love and so dauntless in war,
Have ye e'er heard of gallant like young Lochinvar?

From The Lady of the Lake

Song: Soldier, rest! thy warfare o'er

Soldier, rest! thy warfare o'er,
Sleep the sleep that knows not breaking;
Dream of battled fields no more,
Days of danger, nights of waking.
In our isle's enchanted hall,
Hands unseen thy couch are strewing,
Fairy strains of music fall,
Every sense in slumber dewing.
Soldier, rest! thy warfare o'er,
Dream of fighting fields no more:
Sleep the sleep that knows not breaking,
Morn of toil, nor night of waking.

No rude sound shall reach thine ear,
Armour's clang, or war-steed champing,
Trump nor pibroch summon here
Mustering clan, or squadron tramping.
Yet the lark's shrill fife may come
At the day-break from the fallow,
And the bittern sound his drum,
Booming from the sedgy shallow.
Ruder sounds shall none be near
Guards nor warders challenge here,
Here's no war-steed's neigh and champing,
Shouting clans, or squadrons stamping.

Huntsman, rest! thy chase is done,
While our slumbrous spells assail ye,
Dream not, with the rising sun,
Bugles here shall sound reveillé.
Sleep! the deer is in his den;
Sleep! thy hounds are by thee lying;
Sleep! nor dream in yonder glen,
How thy gallant steed lay dying.
Huntsman, rest! thy chase is done,
Think not of the rising sun,
For at dawning to assail ye,
Here no bugles sound reveillé.

Coronach

He is gone on the mountain,
He is lost to the forest,
Like a summer-dried fountain,
When our need was the soarest.
The font, reappearing,
From the rain-drops shall borrow,
But to us comes no cheering,
To Duncan no morrow!
The hand of the reaper
Takes the ears that are hoary,
But the voice of the weeper
Wails manhood in glory.
The autumn winds rushing
Waft the leaves that are searest,
But our flower was in flushing,
When blighting was nearest.

Fleet foot on the correi,
Sage counsel in cumber,
Red hand in the foray,
How sound is thy slumber!
Like the dew on the mountain,
Like the foam on the river,
Like the bubble on the fountain,
Thou art gone, and for ever!

Battle of Beal' an Duine

THE Minstrel came once more to view
The eastern ridge of Benvenue,
For, ere he parted, he would say
Farewell to lovely Loch Achray—
Where shall he find, in foreign land,
So lone a lake, so sweet a strand!
There is no breeze upon the fern,
Nor ripple on the lake,
Upon her eyry nods the erne,
The deer has sought the brake;
The small birds will not sing aloud,
The springing trout lies still,
So darkly glooms yon thunder cloud,
That swathes, as with a purple shroud,
Benledi's distant hill.
Is it the thunder's solemn sound
That mutters deep and dread,
Or echoes from the groaning ground
The warrior's measured tread?
Is it the lightning's quivering glance
That on the thicket streams,
Or do they flash on spear and lance
The sun's retiring beams?
—I see the dagger-crest of Mar,
I see the Moray's silver star,
Wave o'er the cloud of Saxon war,
That up the lake comes winding far!
To hero bound for battle strife,
Or bard of martial lay,
'Twere worth ten years of peaceful life
One glance at their array!

Their light-arm'd archers far and near
Survey'd the tangled ground,
Their centre ranks, with pike and spear,
A twilight forest frown'd,
Their barbed horsemen, in the rear,
The stern battalia crown'd.
No cymbal clash'd, no clarion rang,
Still were the pipe and drum;
Save heavy tread, and armour's clang,
The sullen march was dumb.
There breathed no wind their crests to shake,
Or wave their flags abroad;
Scarce the frail aspen seem'd to quake,
That shadow'd o'er their road.
Their vaward scouts no tidings bring,
Can rouse no lurking foe,
Nor spy a trace of living thing,
Save when they stirr'd the roe;
The host moves, like a deep-sea wave,
Where rise no rocks its pride to brave,
High-swelling, dark, and slow.
The lake is pass'd, and now they gain
A narrow and a broken plain,
Before the Trosach's rugged jaws;
And here the horse and spearmen pause,
While, to explore the dangerous glen,
Dive through the pass the archer-men.

At once there rose so wild a yell
Within that dark and narrow dell,
As all the fiends, from heaven that fell,
Had peal'd the banner-cry of hell!
Forth from the pass in tumult driven,
Like chaff before the wind of heaven,
The archery appear;
For life! for life! their plight they ply—
And shriek, and shout, and battle-cry,
And plaids and bonnets waving high,
And broadswords flashing to the sky,
Are maddening in the rear.
Onward they drive, in dreadful race,
Pursuers and pursued;
Before that tide of flight and chase,
How shall it keep its rooted place,
The spearmen's twilight wood?—
"Down, down," cried Mar, "your lances down!
Bear back both friend and foe!"—
Like reeds before the tempest's frown,
That serried grove of lances brown
At once lay levell'd low;
And closely shouldering side to side,
The bristling ranks the onset bide.—
"We'll quell the savage mountaineer,
As their Tinchel cows the game!
They come as fleet as forest deer,
We'll drive them back as tame."—

Bearing before them, in their course,
The relics of the archer force,
Like wave with crest of sparkling foam,

Right onward did Clan-Alpine come.
  Above the tide, each broadsword bright
  Was brandishing like beam of light,
    Each targe was dark below;
  And with the ocean's mighty swing,
  When heaving to the tempest's wing,
    They hurl'd them on the foe.
I heard the lance's shivering crash,
As when the whirlwind rends the ash,
I heard the broadsword's deadly clang,
As if an hundred anvils rang!
But Moray wheel'd his rearward rank
Of horsemen on Clan-Alpine's flank,
  —"My banner-man, advance!
  I see," he cried, "their column shake.—
  Now, gallants! for your ladies' sake,
    Upon them with the lance!"—
  The horsemen dash'd among the rout,
    As deer break through the broom;
  Their steeds are stout, their swords are out,
    They soon make lightsome room.
  Clan-Alpine's best are backward borne—
    Where, where was Roderick then!
  One blast upon his bugle-horn
    Were worth a thousand men!
  And refluent through the pass of fear
    The battle's tide was pour'd;
  Vanish'd the Saxon's struggling spear,
    Vanish'd the mountain-sword.
  As Bracklinn's chasm, so black and steep,
    Receives her roaring linn,
  As the dark caverns of the deep
    Suck the wild whirlpool in,
So did the deep and darksome pass
Devour the battle's mingled mass:
None linger now upon the plain,
Save those who ne'er shall fight again.

From ROKEBY

O, Brignall banks are wild and fair

O, BRIGNALL banks are wild and fair,
  And Greta woods are green,
And you may gather garlands there,
  Would grace a summer queen.
And as I rode by Dalton-hall,
  Beneath the turrets high,
A Maiden on the castle wall
  Was singing merrily,—

Chorus

"O, Brignall banks are fresh and fair,
  And Greta woods are green;
I'd rather rove with Edmund there,
  Than reign our English queen."—

"If, Maiden, thou wouldst wend with me,
  To leave both tower and town,
Thou first must guess what life lead we,
  That dwell by dale and down!
And if thou canst that riddle read,
  As read full well you may,
Then to the greenwood shalt thou speed,
  As blithe as Queen of May."—

Chorus

Yet sung she, "Brignall banks are fair,
  And Greta woods are green;
I'd rather rove with Edmund there,
  Than reign our English queen.

"I read you, by your bugle-horn,
  And by your palfrey good,
I read you for a ranger sworn,
  To keep the king's greenwood."—
"A Ranger, lady, winds his horn,
  And 'tis at peep of light;
His blast is heard at merry morn,
  And mine at dead of night."—

Chorus

Yet sung she, "Brignall banks are fair,
  And Greta woods are gay;
I would I were with Edmund there,
  To reign his Queen of May!

"With burnish'd brand and musketoon,
  So gallantly you come,
I read you for a bold Dragoon,
  That lists the tuck of drum."—
"I list no more the tuck of drum,
  No more the trumpet hear;
But when the beetle sounds his hum,
  My comrades take the spear.

Chorus

"And, O! though Brignall banks be fair,
And Greta woods be gay,
Yet mickle must the maiden dare,
Would reign my Queen of May!

"Maiden! a nameless life I lead,
A nameless death I'll die!
The fiend, whose lantern lights the mead,
Were better mate than I!
And when I'm with my comrades met,
Beneath the greenwood bough,
What once we were we all forget,
Nor think what we are now.

Chorus

"Yet Brignall banks are fresh and fair,
And Greta woods are green,
And you may gather garlands there
Would grace a summer queen."

A weary lot is thine, fair maid

A WEARY lot is thine, fair maid,
A weary lot is thine!
To pull the thorn thy brow to braid,
And press the rue for wine!
A lightsome eye, a soldier's mien,
A feather of the blue,
A doublet of the Lincoln green,—
No more of me you knew,
My love!
No more of me you knew.

"This morn is merry June, I trow,
The rose is budding fain;
But she shall bloom in winter snow,
Ere we two meet again."
He turn'd his charger as he spake,
Upon the river shore,
He gave his bridle-reins a shake,
Said, "Adieu for evermore,
My love!
And adieu for evermore."—

Pibroch of Donuil Dhu

PIBROCH of Donuil Dhu,
Pibroch of Donuil,
Wake thy wild voice anew,
Summon Clan-Conuil.
Come away, come away,
Hark to the summons!
Come in your war array,
Gentles and commons.

Come from deep glen, and
From mountain so rocky,
The war-pipe and pennon
Are at Inverlochy.
Come every hill-plaid, and
True heart that wears one,
Come every steel blade, and
Strong hand that bears one.

Leave untended the herd,
The flock without shelter;
Leave the corpse uninterr'd,
The bride at the altar;
Leave the deer, leave the steer,
Leave nets and barges:
Come with your fighting gear,
Broadswords and targes.

Come as the winds come, when
Forests are rended,
Come as the waves come, when
Navies are stranded:
Faster come, faster come,
Faster and faster,
Chief, vassal, page and groom,
Tenant and master.

Fast they come, fast they come;
See how they gather!
Wide waves the eagle plume,
Blended with heather.
Cast your plaids, draw your blades,
Forward each man set!
Pibroch of Donuil Dhu,
Knell for the onset!

From MADGE WILDFIRE'S SONG

Proud Maisie is in the wood

PROUD Maisie is in the wood,
Walking so early;
Sweet Robin sits on the bush,
Singing so rarely.

"Tell me, thou bonny bird,
When shall I marry me?"—
"When six braw gentlemen
Kirkward shall carry ye."

"Who makes the bridal bed,
Birdie, say truly?"—
"The grey-headed sexton
That delves the grave duly.

"The glow-worm o'er grave and stone
Shall light thee steady.
The owl from the steeple sing,
'Welcome, proud lady.'"

Border Ballad

I. MARCH, march, Ettrick and Teviotdale,
Why the deil dinna ye march forward in order?
March, march, Eskdale and Liddesdale,
All the Blue Bonnets are bound for the Border.
Many a banner spread,
Flutters above your head,
Many a crest that is famous in story.
Mount and make ready then,
Sons of the mountain glen,
Fight for the Queen and our old Scottish glory.

II. Come from the hills where your hirsels are grazing,
Come from the glen of the buck and the roe;
Come to the crag where the beacon is blazing,
Come with the buckler, the lance, and the bow.
Trumpets are sounding,
War-steeds are bounding,
Stand to your arms, and march in good order,
England shall many a day
Tell of the bloody fray,
When the Blue Bonnets came over the Border.

Song: County Guy

AH! County Guy, the hour is nigh,
The sun has left the lea,
The orange flower perfumes the bower,
The breeze is on the sea.
The lark, his lay who thrill'd all day,
Sits hush'd his partner nigh;
Breeze, bird, and flower, confess the hour,
But where is County Guy?

The village maid steals through the shade,
Her shepherd's suit to hear;
To beauty shy, by lattice high,
Sings high-born Cavalier.
The star of Love, all stars above,
Now reigns o'er earth and sky;
And high and low the influence know—
But where is County Guy?

Song, to the Air of "The Bonnets of Bonny Dundee"

To the Lords of Convention 'twas Claver'se who spoke,
"Ere the King's crown shall fall there are crowns to be broke;
So let each Cavalier who loves honour and me,
Come follow the bonnet of Bonny Dundee.

"Come fill up my cup, come fill up my can,
Come saddle your horses, and call up your men;
Come open the West Port, and let me gang free,
And it's room for the bonnets of Bonny Dundee!"

Dundee he is mounted, he rides up the street,
The bells are rung backward, the drums they are beat;

But the Provost, douce man, said, "Just e'en let him be,
The Gude Town is weel quit of that Deil of Dundee."

As he rode down the sanctified bends of the Bow,
Ilk carline was flyting and shaking her pow;
But the young plants of grace they look'd couthie and slee,
Thinking, luck to thy bonnet, thou Bonny Dundee!

With sour-featured Whigs the Grass-market was cramm'd
As if half the West had set tryst to be hang'd;
There was spite in each look, there was fear in each e'e,
As they watch'd for the bonnets of Bonny Dundee.

These cowls of Kilmarnock had spits and had spears,
And lang-hafted gullies to kill Cavaliers;
But they shrunk to close-heads, and the causeway was free,
At the toss of the bonnet of Bonny Dundee.

He spurr'd to the foot of the proud Castle rock,
And with the gay Gordon he gallantly spoke;
"Let Mons Meg and her marrows speak twa words or three,
For the love of the bonnet of Bonny Dundee."

The Gordon demands of him which way he goes—
"Where'er shall direct me the shade of Montrose!
Your Grace in short space shall hear tidings of me,
Or that low lies the bonnet of Bonny Dundee.

"There are hills beyond Pentland, and lands beyond Forth,
If there's lords in the Lowlands, there's chiefs in the North;
There are wild Duniewassals three thousand times three,
Will cry *hoigh!* for the bonnet of Bonny Dundee.

"There's brass on the target of barken'd bull-hide;
There's steel in the scabbard that dangles beside;
The brass shall be burnish'd, the steel shall flash free,
At a toss of the bonnet of Bonny Dundee.

"Away to the hills, to the caves, to the rocks—
Ere I own an usurper, I'll couch with the fox;
And tremble, false Whigs, in the midst of your glee,
You have not seen the last of my bonnet and me!"

He waved his proud hand, and the trumpets were blown,
The kettle-drums clash'd, and the horsemen rode on,
Till on Ravelston's cliffs and on Clermiston's lee,
Died away the wild war-notes of Bonny Dundee.

Come fill up my cup, come fill up my can,
Come saddle the horses and call up the men,
Come open your gates, and let me gae free,
For it's up with the bonnets of Bonny Dundee!

JOHN GIBSON LOCKHART (1794-1854)

From The Life of Sir Walter Scott

"Vidi Tantum"

Lockhart quotes the following account of Scott's only meeting with Burns, from a letter addressed to him in 1827. The Latin phrase is Ovid's; Virgil died when Ovid was twenty-four; Ovid had "merely seen him."

"As for Burns," he writes, "I may truly say, *'Virgilium vidi tantum.'* I was a lad of fifteen in 1786-7, when he came first to Edinburgh, but had sense and feeling enough to be much interested in his poetry, and would have given the world to know him; but I had very little acquaintance with any literary people, and still less with the gentry of the west country,—the two sets that he most frequented. Mr. Thomas Grierson was at that time a clerk of my father's. He knew Burns, and promised to ask him to his lodgings to dinner, but had no opportunity to keep his word, otherwise I might have seen more of this distinguished man. As it was, I saw him one day at the late venerable Professor Fergusson's, where there were several gentlemen of literary reputation, among whom I remember the celebrated Mr. Dugald Stewart. Of course we youngsters sate silent, looked and listened. The only thing I remember which was remarkable in Burns' manner, was the effect produced upon him by a print of Bunbury's, representing a soldier lying dead on the snow, his dog sitting in misery on the one side, on the other his widow, with a child in her arms. These lines were written beneath,—

> "Cold on Canadian hills, or Minden's plain,
> Perhaps that parent wept her soldier slain:
> Bent o'er her babe, her eye dissolved in dew,
> The big drops, mingling with the milk he drew,
> Gave the sad presage of his future years,
> The child of misery baptised in tears."

Burns seemed much affected by the print, or rather the ideas which it suggested to his mind. He actually shed tears. He asked whose the lines were, and it chanced that nobody but myself remembered that they occur in a half-forgotten poem of Langhorne's, called by the unpromising title of 'The Justice of the Peace.' I whispered my information to a friend present, who mentioned it to Burns, who rewarded me with a look and a word, which, though of mere civility, I then received, and still recollect, with very great pleasure. . . . His conversation expressed perfect self-confidence, without the slightest presumption. Among the men who were the most learned of their time and country, he expressed himself with perfect firmness, but without the least intrusive forwardness; and when he differed in opinion, he did not hesitate to express it firmly, yet at the same time with modesty. I do not remember any part of his conversation distinctly enough to be quoted, nor did I ever see him again, except in the street, where he did not recognise me, as I could not expect he should."—*Letter to J. G. L.*, 1827.

Scott's Greatest Fright

The following reminiscence is quoted from a letter written in August, 1811, to Miss Joanna Baillie. It was inspired by her tragedy on the Passion of Fear, in a new volume of Tragedies which she had just sent him.

THE most dreadful fright I ever had in my life (being neither constitutionally timid, nor in the way of being exposed to real danger), was in returning from Hampstead the day which I spent so pleasantly with you. Although the evening was nearly closed, I foolishly chose to take the short cut through the fields, and in that enclosure, where the path leads close by a thick and high hedge—with several gaps in it, however—did I meet one of your very thorough-paced London ruffians, at least judging from the squalid and jail-bird appearance and blackguard expression of countenance. Like the man that met the devil, I had nothing to say to him, if he had nothing to say to me, but I could not help looking back to watch the movements of such a suspicious figure, and to my great uneasiness saw him creep through the hedge on my left hand. I instantly went to the first gap to watch his motions, and saw him stooping, as I thought, either to lift a bundle or to speak to some person who seemed lying in the ditch. Immediately after, he came cowering back up the opposite side of the hedge, as returning towards me under cover of it. I saw no weapons he had, except a stick, but as I moved on to gain the stile which was to let me into the free field—with the idea of a wretch springing upon me from the cover at every step I took—I assure you I would not wish the worst enemy I ever had to undergo such a feeling as I had for about five minutes; my fancy made him of that description which usually combines murder with plunder, and though I was well armed with a stout stick and a very formidable knife, which when opened becomes a sort of *skene-dhu*, or dagger, I confess my sensations, though those of a man much resolved not to die like a sheep, were vilely short of heroism; so much so, that when I jumped over the stile, a sliver of the wood ran a third of an inch between my nail and flesh, without my feeling the pain, or being sensible such a thing had happened.

However, I saw my man no more, and it is astonishing how my spirits rose when I got into the open field;—and when I reached the top of the little mount, and all the bells in London (for aught I know) began to jingle at once, I thought I had never heard anything so delightful in my life—so rapid are the alternations of our feelings. This foolish story,—for perhaps I had no rational ground for the horrible feeling which possessed my mind for a little while, came irresistibly to my pen when writing to you on the subject of terror.

The Hand

The following selection from Lockhart's *Life of Scott* comes between two letters from Scott to Mr. Morritt, in which appear statements about the writing of *Waverley*. In the letter which precedes, Scott writes: "I had written great part of the first volume, and sketched other passages, when I mislaid the MS., and only found it by the merest accident as I was rummaging the drawers of an old cabinet; and I took the fancy of finishing it, which I did so fast, that the last two volumes were written in three weeks." And in the letter which follows: "I will take care, in the next edition, to make the corrections you recommend. The second is, I believe, nearly through the press. It will hardly be printed faster than it was written; for though the first volume was begun long ago, and actually lost for a time, yet the other two were begun and finished between the 4th June and the 1st July, during all which I attended my duty in Court, and proceeded without loss of time or hindrance of business."

This statement as to the time occupied by the second and third volumes of Waverley, recalls to my memory a trifling anecdote, which, as connected with a dear friend of my youth, whom I have not seen for many years, and may very probably never see again in this world, I shall here set down, in the hope of affording him a momentary, though not an unmixed pleasure, when he may chance to read this compilation on a distant shore—and also in the hope that my humble record may impart to some active mind in the rising generation a shadow of the influence which the reality certainly exerted upon his. Happening to pass through Edinburgh in June, 1814, I dined one day with the gentleman in question (now the Honourable William Menzies, one of the Supreme Judges at the Cape of Good Hope), whose residence was then in George Street, situated very near to, and at right angles with, North Castle Street. It was a party of very young persons, most of them, like Menzies and myself, destined for the Bar of Scotland, all gay and thoughtless, enjoying the first flush of manhood, with little remembrance of the yesterday, or care of the morrow. When my companion's worthy father and uncle, after seeing two or three bottles go round, left the juveniles to themselves, the weather being hot, we adjourned to a library which had one large window looking northwards. After carousing here for an hour or more, I observed that a shade had come over the aspect of my friend, who happened to be placed immediately opposite to myself, and said something that intimated a fear of his being unwell. "No," said he, "I shall be well enough presently, if you will only let me sit where you are, and take my chair; for there is a confounded hand in sight of me here, which has often bothered me before, and now it won't let me fill my glass with a good will." I rose to change places with him accordingly, and he pointed out to me this hand which, like the writing on Belshazzar's wall, disturbed his hour of hilarity. "Since we sat down," he said, "I have been watching it—it fascinates my eye—it never stops—page after page is finished and thrown on that heap of MS., and still it goes on unwearied—and so it will be till candles are brought in, and God knows how long after that. It is the same every night—I can't stand a sight of it when I am not at my books."—"Some stupid, dogged, engrossing clerk, probably," exclaimed myself, or some other giddy youth in our society. "No, boys," said our host, "I well know what hand it is—'tis Walter Scott's." This was the hand that, in the evenings of three summer weeks, wrote the two last volumes of Waverley.

SAMUEL TAYLOR COLERIDGE
(1772-1834)

Dejection. An Ode

"Late, late yestreen I saw the new Moon,
With the old Moon in her arms;
And I fear, I fear, my Master dear!
We shall have a deadly storm."
Ballad of Sir Patrick Spence.

I

Well! if the Bard was weather-wise, who made
The grand old ballad of Sir Patrick Spence,
This night, so tranquil now, will not go hence
Unroused by winds, that ply a busier trade
Than those which mould yon clouds in lazy flakes.
Or the dull sobbing draft, that moans and rakes
Upon the strings of this Æolian lute,
Which better far were mute.
For lo! the New-moon winter-bright!
And overspread with phantom light,
(With swimming phantom light o'erspread
But rimmed and circled by a silver thread)
I see the old Moon in her lap, foretelling
The coming on of rain and squally blast.
And oh! that even now the gust were swelling,
And the slant night-shower driving loud and fast!
Those sounds which oft have raised me, whilst they awed,
And sent my soul abroad,
Might now perhaps their wonted impulse give,
Might startle this dull pain, and make it move and live!

II

A grief without a pang, void, dark, and drear,
A stifled, drowsy, unimpassioned grief,
Which finds no natural outlet, no relief,
In word, or sigh, or tear—

O Lady! in this wan and heartless mood,
To other thoughts by yonder throstle wooed,
All this long eve, so balmy and serene,
Have I been gazing on the western sky,
And its peculiar tint of yellow green:
And still I gaze—and with how blank an eye!
And those thin clouds above, in flakes and bars,
That give away their motion to the stars;
Those stars, that glide behind them or between,
Now sparkling, now bedimmed, but always seen;
Yon crescent Moon, as fixed as if it grew
In its own cloudless, starless lake of blue;
I see them all so excellently fair,
I *see*, not *feel* how beautiful they are!

III

My genial spirits fail;
And what can these avail,
To lift the smothering weight from off my breast?
It were a vain endeavour,
Though I should gaze for ever
On that green light that lingers in the west:
I may not hope from outward forms to win
The passion and the life, whose fountains are within.

IV

O Lady! we receive but what we give,
And in our life alone does nature live:
Ours is her wedding-garment, ours her shroud!
And would we aught behold, of higher worth,
Than that inanimate cold world allowed
To the poor loveless ever-anxious crowd,
Ah! from the soul itself must issue forth,
A light, a glory, a fair luminous cloud
Enveloping the Earth—
And from the soul itself must there be sent
A sweet and potent voice, of its own birth,
Of all sweet sounds the life and element.

V

O pure of heart! thou need'st not ask of me
What this strong music in the soul may be!
What, and wherein it doth exist,
This light, this glory, this fair luminous mist,
This beautiful, and beauty-making power.
Joy, virtuous Lady! Joy that ne'er was given,
Save to the pure, and in their purest hour,
Life, and Life's effluence, cloud at once and shower,
Joy, Lady! is the spirit and the power,
Which wedding Nature to us gives in dower
A new Earth and new Heaven,
Undreamt of by the sensual and the proud—
Joy is the sweet voice, Joy the luminous cloud—
We in ourselves rejoice!
And thence flows all that charms or ear or sight,
All melodies the echoes of that voice,
All colours a suffusion from that light.

VI

There was a time when, though my path was rough,
This joy within me dallied with distress,
And all misfortunes were but as the stuff
Whence Fancy made me dreams of happiness:
For hope grew round me, like the twining vine,
And fruits, and foliage, not my own, seemed mine.
But now afflictions bow me down to earth:

Nor care I that they rob me of my mirth,
But oh! each visitation
Suspends what nature gave me at my birth,
My shaping spirit of Imagination.
For not to think of what I needs must feel,
But to be still and patient, all I can;
And haply by abstruse research to steal
From my own nature all the natural man—
This was my sole resource, my only plan:
Till that which suits a part infects the whole,
And now is almost grown the habit of my soul.

VII

Hence, viper thoughts, that coil around my mind,
Reality's dark dream!
I turn from you, and listen to the wind,
Which long has raved unnoticed. What a scream
Of agony by torture lengthened out
That lute sent forth! Thou Wind, that ravest without,
Bare crag, or mountain-tairn, or blasted tree,
Or pine-grove whither woodman never clomb,
Or lonely house, long held the witches' home,
Methinks were fitter instruments for thee,
Mad Lutanist! who in this month of showers,
Of dark brown gardens, and of peeping flowers,
Mak'st Devils' yule, with worse than wintry song,
The blossoms, buds, and timorous leaves among.
Thou Actor, perfect in all tragic sounds!
Thou mighty Poet, e'en to frenzy bold!
What tell'st thou now about?
'Tis of the rushing of a host in rout,
With groans of trampled men, with smarting wounds—
At once they groan with pain, and shudder with the cold!
But hush! there is a pause of deepest silence!
And all that noise, as of a rushing crowd,
With groans and tremulous shudderings —all is over—
It tells another tale, with sounds less deep and loud!
A tale of less affright,
And tempered with delight,
As Otway's self had framed the tender lay—
'Tis of a little child
Upon a lonesome wild,
Not far from home, but she hath lost her way:
And now moans low in bitter grief and fear,
And now screams loud, and hopes to make her mother hear.

VIII

'Tis midnight, but small thoughts have I of sleep:
Full seldom may my friend such vigils keep!
Visit her, gentle Sleep! with wings of healing,
And may this storm be but a mountain-birth,
May all the stars hang bright above her dwelling,
Silent as though they watched the sleeping Earth!
With light heart may she rise,
Gay fancy, cheerful eyes,
Joy lift her spirit, Joy attune her voice:
To her may all things live, from pole to pole,
Their life the eddying of her living soul!
O simple spirit, guided from above,
Dear Lady! friend devoutest of my choice,
Thus mayst thou ever, evermore rejoice.

The Rime of the Ancient Mariner

Part I

An ancient Mariner meeteth three gallants bidden to a wedding feast, and detaineth one.

It is an ancient Mariner,
And he stoppeth one of three.
"By thy long grey beard and glittering eye,
Now wherefore stopp'st thou me?

The Bridegroom's doors are open'd wide,
And I am next of kin;
The guests are met, the feast is set:
May'st hear the merry din."

He holds him with his skinny hand,
"There was a ship," quoth he.
"Hold off! unhand me, grey-beard loon!"
Eftsoons his hand dropt he.

The Wedding-Guest is spellbound by the eye of the old seafaring man, and constrained to hear his tale.

He holds him with his glittering eye—
The Wedding-Guest stood still,
And listens like a three years' child:
The Mariner hath his will.

The Wedding-Guest sat on a stone:
He cannot choose but hear;
And thus spake on that ancient man,
The bright-eyed Mariner.

"The ship was cheer'd, the harbour clear'd,
Merrily did we drop
Below the kirk, below the hill,
Below the lighthouse top.

The Mariner tells how the ship sailed southward with a good wind and fair weather, till it reached the Line.

The Sun came up upon the left,
Out of the sea came he!
And he shone bright, and on the right
Went down into the sea.

Higher and higher every day,
Till over the mast at noon—"
The Wedding-Guest here beat his breast,
For he heard the loud bassoon.

The Wedding-Guest heareth the bridal music; but the Mariner continueth his tale.

The bride hath paced into the hall,
Red as a rose is she;
Nodding their heads before her goes
The merry minstrelsy.

The Wedding-Guest he beat his breast,
Yet he cannot choose but hear;
And thus spake on that ancient man,
The bright-eyed Mariner.

The ship drawn by a storm toward the South Pole.

"And now the Storm-blast came, and he
Was tyrannous and strong:
He struck with his o'ertaking wings,
And chased us south along.

With sloping masts and dipping prow,
As who pursued with yell and blow
Still treads the shadow of his foe,
And forward bends his head,
The ship drove fast, loud roar'd the blast,
And southward aye we fled.

And now there came both mist and snow,
And it grew wondrous cold:
And ice, mast-high, came floating by,
As green as emerald.

The land of ice, and of fearful sounds, where no living thing was to be seen.

And through the drifts the snowy clifts
Did send a dismal sheen:
Nor shapes of men nor beasts we ken—
The ice was all between.

The ice was here, the ice was there,
The ice was all around:
It crack'd and growl'd, and roar'd and howl'd,
Like noises in a swound!

Till a great sea-bird, called the Albatross, came through the snow-fog, and was received with great joy and hospitality

At length did cross an Albatross,
Thorough the fog it came;
As if it had been a Christian soul,
We hail'd it in God's name.

It ate the food it ne'er had eat,
And round and round it flew.
The ice did split with a thunder-fit;
The helmsman steer'd us through!

And lo! the Albatross proveth a bird of good omen, and followeth the ship as it returned northward through fog and floating ice.

And a good south wind sprung up behind;
The Albatross did follow,
And every day, for food or play,
Came to the mariners' hollo!

In mist or cloud, on mast or shroud,
It perch'd for vespers nine;
Whiles all the night, through fog-smoke white,
Glimmer'd the white moonshine."

The ancient Mariner inhospitably killeth the pious bird of good omen.

"God save thee, ancient Mariner,
From the fiends, that plague thee thus!—
Why look'st thou so?"—"With my crossbow
I shot the Albatross.

Part II

"The Sun now rose upon the right:
Out of the sea came he,
Still hid in mist, and on the left
Went down into the sea.

And the good south wind still blew behind,
But no sweet bird did follow,
Nor any day for food or play
Came to the mariners' hollo!

His shipmates cry out against the ancient Mariner for killing the bird of good luck.

And I had done a hellish thing,
And it would work 'em woe:
For all averr'd I had kill'd the bird
That made the breeze to blow.
Ah wretch! said they, the bird to slay,
That made the breeze to blow!

But when the fog cleared off, they justify the same, and thus make themselves accomplices in the crime.

Nor dim nor red, like God's own head,
The glorious Sun uprist,
Then all averr'd I had kill'd the bird
That brought the fog and mist.
'Twas right, said they, such birds to slay,
That bring the fog and mist.

The fair breeze continues; the ship enters the Pacific Ocean, and sails northward, even till it reaches the Line.

The fair breeze blew, the white foam flew,
The furrow follow'd free;
We were the first that ever burst
Into that silent sea.

The ship hath been suddenly becalmed.

Down dropt the breeze, the sails dropt down,
'Twas sad as sad could be;
And we did speak only to break
The silence of the sea!

All in a hot and copper sky,
The bloody Sun, at noon,
Right up above the mast did stand,
No bigger than the Moon.

Day after day, day after day,
We stuck, nor breath nor motion;
As idle as a painted ship
Upon a painted ocean.

And the Albatross begins to be avenged.

Water, water, everywhere,
And all the boards did shrink;
Water, water, everywhere,
Nor any drop to drink.

The very deep did rot: O Christ
That ever this should be!
Yea, slimy things did crawl with legs
Upon the slimy sea.

About, about, in reel and rout
The death-fires danced at night;
The water, like a witch's oils,
Burnt green, and blue, and white.

A Spirit had followed them; one of the invisible inhabitants of this planet, neither departed souls nor angels; concerning whom the learned Jew, Josephus, and the Platonic Constantinopolitan Michael Psellus may be consulted. They are very numerous, and there is no climate or element without one or more.

And some in dreams assurèd were
Of the Spirit that plagued us so;
Nine fathom deep he had follow'd us
From the land of mist and snow.

And every tongue, through utter drought,
Was wither'd at the root;
We could not speak, no more than if
We had been choked with soot.

The shipmates in their sore distress, would fain throw the whole guilt on the ancient Mariner: in sign whereof they hang the dead sea-bird round his neck.

Ah! well a-day! what evil looks
Had I from old and young!
Instead of the cross, the Albatross
About my neck was hung.

Part III

"There passed a weary time. Each throat
Was parch'd, and glazed each eye.
A weary time! a weary time!
How glazed each weary eye!

The ancient Mariner beholdeth a sign in the element afar off.

When looking westward, I beheld
A something in the sky.

At first it seem'd a little speck,
And then it seem'd a mist;
It moved and moved, and took at last
A certain shape, I wist.

A speck, a mist, a shape, I wist!
And still it near'd and near'd:
As if it dodged a water-sprite,
It plunged, and tack'd, and veer'd.

At its nearer approach, it seemeth him to be a ship; and at a dear ransom he freeth his speech from the bonds of thirst.

With throats unslaked, with black lips baked,
We could nor laugh nor wail;
Through utter drought all dumb we stood!
I bit my arm, I suck'd the blood,
And cried, A sail! a sail!

With throats unslaked, with black lips baked,
Agape they heard me call:

A flash of joy;

Gramercy! they for joy did grin,
And all at once their breath drew in,
As they were drinking all.

And horror follows. For can it be a ship that comes onward without wind or tide?

See! see! (I cried) she tacks no more!
Hither to work us weal—
Without a breeze, without a tide,
She steadies with upright keel!

The western wave was all aflame,
The day was wellnigh done!
Almost upon the western wave
Rested the broad, bright Sun;

When that strange shape drove suddenly
Betwixt us and the Sun.

It seemeth him but the skeleton of a ship.

And straight the Sun was fleck'd with bars
(Heaven's Mother send us grace!),
As if through a dungeon-grate he peer'd
With broad and burning face.

Alas! (thought I, and my heart beat loud)
How fast she nears and nears!
Are those her sails that glance in the Sun,
Like restless gossameres?

And its ribs are seen as bars on the face of the setting Sun. The Spectre-Woman and her Death-mate, and no other, on board the skeleton ship. Like vessel, like crew!

Are those her ribs through which the Sun
Did peer, as through a grate?
And is that Woman all her crew?
Is that a Death? and are there two?
Is Death that Woman's mate?

Her lips were red, her looks were free,
Her locks were yellow as gold:
Her skin was as white as leprosy,
The Nightmare Life-in-Death was she,
Who thicks man's blood with cold.

Death and Life-in-Death have diced for the ship's crew, and she (the latter) winneth the ancient Mariner.

The naked hulk alongside came,
And the twain were casting dice;
"The game is done! I've won! I've won!"
Quoth she, and whistles thrice.

No twilight within the courts of the Sun.

The Sun's rim dips; the stars rush out:
At one stride comes the dark;
With far-heard whisper, o'er the sea,
Off shot the spectre-bark.

We listen'd and look'd sideways up!
Fear at my heart, as at a cup,
My life-blood seem'd to sip!
The stars were dim, and thick the night,
The steersman's face by his lamp gleam'd white;
From the sails the dew did drip—

At the rising of the Moon,

Till clomb above the eastern bar
The hornèd Moon, with one bright star
Within the nether tip.

One after another,

One after one, by the star-dogg'd Moon,
Too quick for groan or sigh,
Each turn'd his face with a ghastly pang,
And cursed me with his eye.

His shipmates drop down dead.

Four times fifty living men
(And I heard nor sigh nor groan),
With heavy thump, a lifeless lump,
They dropp'd down one by one.

But Life-in-Death begins her work on the ancient Mariner.

The souls did from their bodies fly—
They fled to bliss or woe!
And every soul, it pass'd me by
Like the whizz of my cross-bow."

Part IV

The Wedding-Guest feareth that a spirit is talking to him.

"I fear thee, ancient Mariner!
I fear thy skinny hand!
And thou art long, and lank, and brown,
As is the ribb'd sea-sand.

I fear thee and thy glittering eye,
And thy skinny hand so brown."—

But the ancient Mariner assureth him of his bodily life, and proceedeth to relate his horrible penance.

"Fear not, fear not, thou Wedding-Guest!
This body dropt not down.

Alone, alone, all, all alone,
Alone on a wide, wide sea!
And never a saint took pity on
My soul in agony.

He despiseth the creatures of the calm.

The many men, so beautiful!
And they all dead did lie:
And a thousand thousand slimy things
Lived on; and so did I.

And envieth that they should live, and so many lie dead.

I look'd upon the rotting sea,
And drew my eyes away;
I look'd upon the rotting deck,
And there the dead men lay.

I look'd to heaven, and tried to pray;
But or ever a prayer had gusht,
A wicked whisper came, and made
My heart as dry as dust.

I closed my lids, and kept them close,
And the balls like pulses beat;
But the sky and the sea, and the sea and the sky,
Lay like a load on my weary eye,
And the dead were at my feet.

But the curse liveth for him in the eye of the dead men.

The cold sweat melted from their limbs,
Nor rot nor reek did they:
The look with which they look'd on me
Had never pass'd away.

An orphan's curse would drag to hell
A spirit from on high;
But oh! more horrible than that
Is the curse in a dead man's eye!
Seven days, seven nights, I saw that curse,
And yet I could not die.

In his loneliness and fixedness he yearneth towards the journeying Moon, and the stars that still sojourn, yet still move onward; and everywhere the blue sky belongs to them, and is their appointed rest and their native country and their own natural homes, which they enter unannounced, as lords that are certainly expected, and yet there is a silent joy at their arrival.

The moving Moon went up the sky,
And nowhere did abide;
Softly she was going up,
And a star or two beside—

Her beams bemock'd the sultry main,
Like April hoar-frost spread;
But where the ship's huge shadow lay,
The charmèd water burnt alway
A still and awful red.

By the light of the Moon he beholdeth God's creatures of the great calm.

Beyond the shadow of the ship,
I watch'd the water-snakes:
They moved in tracks of shining white,
And when they rear'd, the elfish light
Fell off in hoary flakes.

Within the shadow of the ship
I watch'd their rich attire:
Blue, glossy green, and velvet black,
They coil'd and swam; and every track
Was a flash of golden fire.

Their beauty and their happiness.

O happy living things! no tongue
Their beauty might declare:
A spring of love gush'd from my heart,

He blesseth them in his heart.

And I bless'd them unaware:
Sure my kind saint took pity
on me,
And I bless'd them unaware.

The spell begins to break.

The selfsame moment I could
pray;
And from my neck so free
The Albatross fell off, and
sank
Like lead into the sea.

PART V

"O sleep! it is a gentle thing,
Beloved from pole to pole!
To Mary Queen the praise be
given!
She sent the gentle sleep from
Heaven,
That slid into my soul.

By grace of the holy Mother, the ancient Mariner is refreshed with rain.

The silly buckets on the deck,
That had so long remain'd,
I dreamt that they were fill'd
with dew;
And when I awoke, it rain'd.

My lips were wet, my throat
was cold,
My garments all were dank;
Sure I had drunken in my
dreams,
And still my body drank.

I moved, and could not feel
my limbs:
I was so light—almost
I thought that I had died in
sleep,
And was a blessèd ghost.

He heareth sounds and seeth strange sights and commotions in the sky and the element.

And soon I heard a roaring
wind:
It did not come anear;
But with its sound it shook
the sails,
That were so thin and sere.

The upper air burst into life;
And a hundred fire-flags
sheen;
To and fro they were hurried
about!
And to and fro, and in and out,
The wan stars danced be-
tween.

And the coming wind did roar
more loud,
And the sails did sigh like
sedge;
And the rain pour'd down
from one black cloud;
The Moon was at its edge.

The thick black cloud was
cleft, and still
The Moon was at its side;
Like waters shot from some
high crag,
The lightning fell with never
a jag,
A river steep and wide.

The bodies of the ship's crew are inspired, and the ship moves on;

The loud wind never reach'd
the ship,
Yet now the ship moved on!
Beneath the lightning and the
Moon
The dead men gave a groan.

They groan'd, they stirr'd,
they all uprose,
Nor spake, nor moved their
eyes;
It had been strange, even in a
dream,
To have seen those dead men
rise.

The helmsman steer'd, the ship
moved on;
Yet never a breeze up-blew;
The mariners all 'gan work
the ropes,
Where they were wont to do;
They raised their limbs like
lifeless tools—
We were a ghastly crew.

The body of my brother's son
Stood by me, knee to knee:
The body and I pull'd at one rope,
But he said naught to me."

But not by the souls of the men, nor by demons of earth or middle air, but by a blessed troop of angelic spirits, sent down by the invocation of the guardian saint.

"I fear thee, ancient Mariner!"
"Be calm, thou Wedding-Guest:
'Twas not those souls that fled in pain,
Which to their corses came again,
But a troop of spirits blest:

For when it dawn'd—they dropp'd their arms,
And cluster'd round the mast;
Sweet sounds rose slowly through their mouths,
And from their bodies pass'd.

Around, around, flew each sweet sound,
Then darted to the Sun;
Slowly the sounds came back again,
Now mix'd, now one by one.

Sometimes a-dropping from the sky
I heard the skylark sing;
Sometimes all little birds that are,
How they seem'd to fill the sea and air
With their sweet jargoning!

And now 'twas like all instruments,
Now like a lonely flute;
And now it is an angel's song,
That makes the Heavens be mute.

It ceased; yet still the sails made on
A pleasant noise till noon,
A noise like of a hidden brook
In the leafy month of June,
That to the sleeping woods all night
Singeth a quiet tune.

Till noon we quietly sail'd on,
Yet never a breeze did breathe:
Slowly and smoothly went the ship,
Moved onward from beneath.

The lonesome Spirit from the South Pole carries on the ship as far as the Line, in obedience to the angelic troop, but still requireth vengeance.

Under the keel nine fathom deep,
From the land of mist and snow,
The Spirit slid: and it was he
That made the ship to go.
The sails at noon left off their tune,
And the ship stood still also.

The Sun, right up above the mast,
Had fix'd her to the ocean:
But in a minute she 'gan stir,
With a short uneasy motion—
Backwards and forwards half her length
With a short uneasy motion.

Then like a pawing horse let go,
She made a sudden bound:
It flung the blood into my head,
And I fell down in a swound.

The Polar Spirit's fellow-demons, the invisible inhabitants of the element, take part in his wrong; and two of them relate, one to the other, that penance long and heavy for the ancient Mariner hath been accorded to the Polar Spirit, who returneth southward.

How long in that same fit I lay,
I have not to declare;
But ere my living life return'd,
I heard, and in my soul discern'd
Two voices in the air.

'Is it he?' quoth one, 'is this the man?
By Him who died on cross,
With his cruel bow he laid full low
The harmless Albatross.

The Spirit who bideth by himself
In the land of mist and snow,
He loved the bird that loved the man
Who shot him with his bow.'

The other was a softer voice,
As soft as honey-dew:
Quoth he, 'The man hath penance done,
And penance more will do.'

PART VI

First Voice:

"'But tell me, tell me! speak again,
Thy soft response renewing—
What makes that ship drive on so fast?
What is the Ocean doing?'

Second Voice:

'Still as a slave before his lord,
The Ocean hath no blast;
His great bright eye most silently
Up to the Moon is cast—

If he may know which way to go;
For she guides him smooth or grim.
See, brother, see! how graciously
She looketh down on him.'

First Voice:

The Mariner hath been cast into a trance; for the angelic power causeth the vessel to drive northward faster than human life could endure.

'But why drives on that ship so fast,
Without or wave or wind?'

Second Voice:

'The air is cut away before,
And closes from behind.

Fly, brother, fly! more high, more high!
Or we shall be belated:
For slow and slow that ship will go,
When the Mariner's trance is abated.'

The supernatural motion is retarded; the Mariner awakes, and his penance begins anew.

I woke, and we were sailing on
As in a gentle weather:
'Twas night, calm night, the Moon was high;
The dead men stood together.

All stood together on the deck,
For a charnel-dungeon fitter:
All fix'd on me their stony eyes,
That in the Moon did glitter.

The pang, the curse, with which they died,
Had never pass'd away:
I could not draw my eyes from theirs,
Nor turn them up to pray.

The curse is finally expiated.

And now this spell was snapt: once more
I viewed the ocean green,
And look'd far forth, yet little saw
Of what had else been seen—

Like one that on a lonesome road
Doth walk in fear and dread,
And having once turn'd round, walks on,
And turns no more his head;
Because he knows a frightful fiend
Doth close behind him tread.

But soon there breathed a wind on me,
Nor sound nor motion made:
Its path was not upon the sea,
In ripple or in shade.

It raised my hair, it fann'd my cheek
Like a meadow-gale of spring—
It mingled strangely with my fears,
Yet it felt like a welcoming.

Swiftly, swiftly flew the ship,
Yet she sail'd softly too:
Sweetly, sweetly blew the breeze—
On me alone it blew.

And the ancient Mariner beholdeth his native country.

O dream of joy! is this indeed
The lighthouse top I see?
Is this the hill? is this the kirk?
Is this mine own countree?

We drifted o'er the harbour-bar,
And I with sobs did pray—
O let me be awake, my God!
Or let me sleep alway.

The harbour-bay was clear as glass,
So smoothly it was strewn!
And on the bay the moonlight lay,
And the shadow of the Moon.

The rock shone bright, the kirk no less
That stands above the rock:
The moonlight steep'd in silentness
The steady weathercock.

The angelic spirits leave the dead bodies,

And the bay was white with silent light
Till rising from the same,
Full many shapes, that shadows were,
In crimson colours came.

And appear in their own forms of light.

A little distance from the prow
Those crimson shadows were:
I turn'd my eyes upon the deck—
O Christ! what saw I there!

Each corse lay flat, lifeless and flat,
And, by the holy rood!
A man all light, a seraph-man,
On every corse there stood.

This seraph-band, each waved his hand:
It was a heavenly sight!
They stood as signals to the land,
Each one a lovely light;

This seraph-band, each waved his hand,
No voice did they impart—
No voice; but O, the silence sank
Like music on my heart.

But soon I heard the dash of oars,
I heard the Pilot's cheer;
My head was turn'd perforce away,
And I saw a boat appear.

The Pilot and the Pilot's boy,
I heard them coming fast:
Dear Lord in Heaven! it was a joy
The dead men could not blast.

I saw a third—I heard his voice:
It is the Hermit good!
He singeth loud his godly hymns
That he makes in the wood.
He'll shrieve my soul, he'll wash away
The Albatross's blood.

Part VII

The Hermit of the Wood.

"This hermit good lives in that wood
Which slopes down to the sea.
How loudly his sweet voice he rears!

He loves to talk with mar-
ineres
That come from a far countree.

He kneels at morn, and noon,
and eve—
He hath a cushion plump:
It is the moss that wholly hides
The rotted old oak-stump.

The skiff-boat near'd: I heard
them talk,
'Why, this is strange, I trow!
Where are those lights so
many and fair,
That signal made but now?'

Approach-eth the ship with wonder.

'Strange, by my faith!' the
Hermit said—
'And they answer'd not our
cheer!
The planks look warp'd! and
see those sails,
How thin they are and sere!
I never saw aught like to them,
Unless perchance it were

Brown skeletons of leaves that
lag
My forest-brook along;
When the ivy-tod is heavy with
snow,
And the owlet whoops to the
wolf below,
That eats the she-wolf's
young.'

'Dear Lord! it hath a fiendish
look—
(The Pilot made reply)
I am a-fear'd.'—'Push on,
push on!'
Said the Hermit cheerily.

The boat came closer to the
ship,
But I nor spake nor stirr'd;
The boat came close beneath
the ship,
And straight a sound was
heard.

The ship suddenly sinketh.

Under the water it rumbled on,
Still louder and more dread:
It reach'd the ship, it split the
bay;
The ship went down like lead.

The ancient Mariner is saved in the Pilot's boat

Stunn'd by that loud and
dreadful sound,
Which sky and ocean smote,
Like one that hath been seven
days drown'd
My body lay afloat;
But swift as dreams, myself I
found
Within the Pilot's boat.

Upon the whirl, where sank
the ship,
The boat spun round and
round;
And all was still, save that the
hill
Was telling of the sound.

I moved my lips—the Pilot
shriek'd
And fell down in a fit;
The holy Hermit raised his
eyes,
And pray'd where he did sit.

I took the oars: the Pilot's
boy,
Who now doth crazy go,
Laugh'd loud and long, and all
the while
His eyes went to and fro.
'Ha! ha!' quoth he, 'full plain
I see
The Devil knows how to row.'

And now, all in my own countree,
I stood on the firm land!

The Hermit stepp'd forth from the boat,
And scarcely he could stand.

The ancient Mariner earnestly entreateth the Hermit to shrieve him; and the penance of life falls on him.

'O shrieve me, shrieve me, holy man!'
The Hermit cross'd his brow.
'Say quick,' quoth he, 'I bid thee say—
What manner of man art thou?'

Forthwith this frame of mine was wrench'd
With a woful agony,
Which forced me to begin my tale;
And then it left me free.

And ever and anon throughout his future life an agony constraineth him to travel from land to land;

Since then, at an uncertain hour,
That agony returns:
And till my ghastly tale is told,
This heart within me burns.

I pass, like night, from land to land;
I have strange power of speech;
That moment that his face I see,
I know the man that must hear me:
To him my tale I teach.

What loud uproar bursts from that door!
The wedding-guests are there:
But in the garden-bower the bride
And bridemaids singing are:
And hark, the little vesper bell,
Which biddeth me to prayer!

O Wedding-Guest! this soul hath been
Alone on a wide, wide sea:
So lonely 'twas, that God Himself
Scarce seemed there to be.

O sweeter than the marriage-feast,
'Tis sweeter far to me,
To walk together to the kirk
With a goodly company!—

To walk together to the kirk,
And all together pray,
While each to his great Father bends,
Old men, and babes, and loving friends,
And youths and maidens gay!

And to teach, by his own example, love and reverence to all things that God made and loveth.

Farewell, farewell! but this I tell
To thee, thou Wedding-Guest!
He prayeth well, who loveth well
Both man and bird and beast.

He prayeth best, who loveth best
All things both great and small;
For the dear God who loveth us,
He made and loveth all."

The Mariner, whose eye is bright,
Whose beard with age is hoar,
Is gone: and now the Wedding-Guest
Turn'd from the bridegroom's door.

He went like one that hath been stunn'd,
And is of sense forlorn:
A sadder and a wiser man
He rose the morrow morn.

Kubla Khan

In Xanadu did Kubla Khan
A stately pleasure-dome decree:
Where Alph, the sacred river, ran
Through caverns measureless to man
Down to a sunless sea.

So twice five miles of fertile ground
With walls and towers were girdled round:
And there were gardens bright with sinuous rills
Where blossom'd many an incense-bearing tree;
And here were forests ancient as the hills,
Enfolding sunny spots of greenery.

But O, that deep romantic chasm which slanted
Down the green hill athwart a cedarn cover!
A savage place! as holy and enchanted
As e'er beneath a waning moon was haunted
By woman wailing for her demon-lover!
And from this chasm, with ceaseless turmoil seething,
As if this earth in fast thick pants were breathing,
A mighty fountain momently was forced;
Amid whose swift half-intermitted burst
Huge fragments vaulted like rebounding hail,
Or chaffy grain beneath the thresher's flail:
And 'mid these dancing rocks at once and ever
It flung up momently the sacred river.
Five miles meandering with a mazy motion
Through wood and dale the sacred river ran,
Then reach'd the caverns measureless to man,
And sank in tumult to a lifeless ocean:
And 'mid this tumult Kubla heard from far
Ancestral voices prophesying war!

The shadow of the dome of pleasure
Floated midway on the waves;
Where was heard the mingled measure
From the fountain and the caves.
It was a miracle of rare device,
A sunny pleasure-dome with caves of ice!

A damsel with a dulcimer
In a vision once I saw:
It was an Abyssinian maid,
And on her dulcimer she play'd,
Singing of Mount Abora.
Could I revive within me,
Her symphony and song,
To such a deep delight 'twould win me,
That with music loud and long,
I would build that dome in air,
That sunny dome! those caves of ice!
And all who heard should see them there.
And all should cry, Beware! Beware!
His flashing eyes, his floating hair!
Weave a circle round him thrice,
And close your eyes with holy dread,
For he on honey-dew hath fed,
And drunk the milk of Paradise.

WALTER SAVAGE LANDOR
(1775-1864)

Rose Aylmer

Ah what avails the sceptred race,
Ah what the form divine!
What every virtue, every grace!
Rose Aylmer, all were thine.

Rose Aylmer, whom these wakeful eyes
May weep, but never see,
A night of memories and of sighs
I consecrate to thee.

On his Seventy-Fifth Birthday

I strove with none; for none was worth my strife,
Nature I loved, and next to Nature, Art;
I warmed both hands before the fire of life,
It sinks, and I am ready to depart.

CHARLES LAMB (1775-1834)

The Old Familiar Faces

I HAVE had playmates, I have had companions,
In my days of childhood, in my joyful school-days,
All, all are gone, the old familiar faces.

I have been laughing, I have been carousing,
Drinking late, sitting late, with my bosom cronies,
All, all are gone, the old familiar faces.

I loved a love once, fairest among women;
Closed are her doors on me, I must not see her—
All, all are gone, the old familiar faces.

I have a friend, a kinder friend has no man;
Like an ingrate, I left my friend abruptly;
Left him, to muse on the old familiar faces.

Ghost-like, I paced round the haunts of my childhood.
Earth seemed a desert I was bound to traverse,
Seeking to find the old familiar faces.

Friend of my bosom, thou more than a brother,
Why wert not thou born in my father's dwelling?
So might we talk of the old familiar faces—

How some they have died, and some they have left me,
And some are taken from me; all are departed;
All, all are gone, the old familiar faces.

Hester

WHEN maidens such as Hester die,
Their place ye may not well supply,
Though ye among a thousand try,
With vain endeavour.

A month or more hath she been dead,
Yet cannot I by force be led
To think upon the wormy bed,
And her together.

A springy motion in her gait,
A rising step, did indicate
Of pride and joy no common rate,
That flush'd her spirit.

I know not by what name beside
I shall it call:—if 'twas not pride,
It was a joy to that allied,
She did inherit.

Her parents held the Quaker rule,
Which doth the human feeling cool,
But she was train'd in Nature's school,
Nature had blest her.

A waking eye, a prying mind,
A heart that stirs, is hard to bind,
A hawk's keen sight ye cannot blind,
Ye could not Hester.

My sprightly neighbour, gone before
To that unknown and silent shore,
Shall we not meet, as heretofore,
Some summer morning,

When from thy cheerful eyes a ray
Hath struck a bliss upon the day,
A bliss that would not go away,
A sweet forewarning?

Imperfect Sympathies

I am of a constitution so general, that it consorts and sympathiseth with all things; I have no antipathy, or rather idiosyncracy in anything. Those national repugnances do not touch me, nor do I behold with prejudice the French, Italian, Spaniard, or Dutch.—*Religio Medici.*

THAT the author of the Religio Medici, mounted upon the airy stilts of abstraction, conversant about notional and conjectural essences; in whose categories of Being the possible took the upper hand of the actual; should have overlooked the impertinent individualities of such poor concretions as mankind, is not much to be admired. It is rather to be wondered at, that in the genus of animals he should have condescended to distinguish that species at all. For myself—earth-bound and fettered to the scene of my activities,—

Standing on earth, not rapt above the sky,

I confess that I do feel the differences of mankind, national or individual, to an unhealthy excess. I can look with no indifferent eye upon things or persons. Whatever is, is to me a matter of taste or distaste; or when once it becomes indifferent, it begins to be disrelishing. I am, in plainer words, a bundle of prejudices—made up of likings and dislikings—the veriest thrall to sympathies, apathies, antipathies. In a certain sense, I hope it may be said of me that I am a lover of my species. I can feel for all indifferently, but I cannot feel towards all equally. The more purely-English word that expresses sympathy will better explain my meaning. I can be a friend to a worthy man, who upon another account cannot be my mate or *fellow*. I cannot *like* all people alike.[1]

[1] I would be understood as confining myself to the subject of *imperfect sympathies.* To nations or classes of men there can be no direct *antipathy.* There may be individuals born and constellated so opposite to another individual nature, that the same sphere cannot hold them. I have met with my moral antipodes, and can believe the story of two persons meeting (who never saw one another before in their lives) and instantly fighting.

——— We by proof find there should be
'Twixt man and man such an antipathy,
That though he can show no just reason why
For any former wrong or injury,
Can neither find a blemish in his fame,
Nor aught in face or feature justly blame,
Can challenge or accuse him of no evil,
Yet notwithstanding hates him as a devil.

The lines are from old Heywood's "Hierarchie of Angels," and he subjoins a curious story in confirmation, of a Spaniard who attempted to assassinate a King Ferdinand of Spain, and being put to the rack could give no other reason for the deed but an inveterate antipathy which he had taken to the first sight of the King.

——— The cause which to that act compell'd him
Was, he ne'er loved him since he first beheld him.

I have been trying all my life to like Scotchmen, and am obliged to desist from the experiment in despair. They cannot like me—and in truth, I never knew one of that nation who attempted to do it. There is something more plain and ingenuous in their mode of proceeding. We know one another at first sight. There is an order of imperfect intellects (under which mine must be content to rank) which in its constitution is essentially anti-Caledonian. The owners of the sort of faculties I allude to, have minds rather suggestive than comprehensive. They have no pretences to much clearness or precision in their ideas, or in their manner of expressing them. Their intellectual wardrobe (to confess fairly) has few whole pieces in it. They are content with fragments and scattered pieces of Truth. She presents no full front to them—a feature or side-face at the most. Hints and glimpses, germs and crude essays at a system, is the utmost they pretend to. They beat up a little game peradventure—and leave it to knottier heads, more robust constitutions, to run it down. The light that lights them is not steady and polar, but mutable and shifting; waxing, and again waning. Their conversation is accordingly. They will throw out a random word in or out of season, and be content to let it pass for what it is worth. They cannot speak always as if they were upon their oath—but must be understood, speaking or writing, with some abatement. They seldom wait to mature a proposition, but e'en bring it to market in the green ear. They delight to impart their defective discoveries as they arise, without waiting for their full development. They are no systematisers, and would but err more by attempting it. Their minds, as I said before, are suggestive merely. The brain of a true Caledonian (if I am not mistaken) is constituted upon quite a different plan. His Minerva is born in panoply. You are never admitted to see his ideas in their growth—if, indeed, they do grow, and are not rather put together upon principles of clockwork. You never catch his mind in an undress. He never hints or suggests any thing, but unlades his stock of ideas in perfect order and completeness. He brings his total wealth into company, and gravely unpacks it. His riches are always about him. He never stoops to catch a glittering something in your presence, to share it with you, before he quite knows whether it be true touch or not. You cannot cry *halves* to any thing that he finds. He does not find, but bring. You never witness his first apprehension of a thing. His understanding is always at its meridian—you never see the first dawn, the early streaks.—He has no faltering of self-suspicion. Surmises, guesses, misgivings, half-intuitions, semi-consciousnesses, partial illuminations, dim instincts, embryo conceptions, have no place in his brain, or vocabulary. The twilight of dubiety never falls upon him. Is he orthodox—he has no doubts. Is he an infidel—he has none either. Between the affirmative and the negative there is no border-land with him. You cannot hover with him upon the confines of truth, or wander in the maze of a probable argument. He always keeps the path. You cannot make excursions with him—for he sets you right. His taste never fluctuates. His morality never abates. He cannot compromise, or understand middle actions. There can be but a right and a wrong. His conversation is as a book. His affirmations have the sanctity of an oath. You must speak upon the square with him. He stops a metaphor like a suspected person in an enemy's country. "A healthy book!"—said one of his countrymen to me, who had ventured to give that appellation to John Buncle,—"did I catch rightly what you said? I have heard of a man in health, and of a healthy state of body, but I do not see how that epithet can be properly applied to a book." Above all, you must beware of indirect expressions before a Caledonian. Clap an extinguisher upon your irony, if you are unhappily blest with a vein of it. Remember you are upon your oath. I have a print of a graceful female after Leonardo da Vinci, which I was showing off to Mr. * * * *. After he had examined it minutely, I ventured to ask him how he liked MY BEAUTY (a foolish name it goes by among my friends)—when he very gravely assured me, that "he had considerable respect for my character and talents" (so he was pleased to say), "but had not given himself much thought about the degree of my personal pretensions." The misconception staggered me, but did not seem much to disconcert him.—Persons of this nation are particularly fond of affirming a truth—which nobody doubts. They do not so properly affirm as annunciate it. They do indeed appear to have such a love of truth (as if, like virtue, it were valuable for itself) that all truth becomes equally valuable, whether the proposition that contains it be new or old, disputed, or such as is impossible to become a subject of disputation. I was present not long since at a party of North Britons, where a son of Burns was expected; and happened to drop a silly expression (in my South British way), that I wished it were the father instead of the son—when four of them started up at once to inform me, that "that was impossible, because he was dead." An impracticable wish, it seems, was more than they could conceive. Swift has hit off this part of their character, namely their love of truth, in his biting way, but with an illiberality that necessarily confines the passage to the margin.[1] The tediousness of these people is certainly

[1] There are some people who think they sufficiently acquit themselves and entertain their company, with relating facts of no consequence, not at all out of the road of such common incidents as happen every day; and this I have observed more frequently among the Scots than any other nation, who are very careful not to omit the minutest circumstances of time or place; which kind of discourse, if it were not a little relieved

provoking. I wonder if they ever tire one another!—In my early life I had a passionate fondness for the poetry of Burns. I have sometimes foolishly hoped to ingratiate myself with his countrymen by expressing it. But I have always found that a true Scot resents your admiration of his compatriot, even more than he would your contempt of him. The latter he imputes to your "imperfect acquaintance with many of the words which he uses"; and the same objection makes it a presumption in you to suppose that you can admire him.—Thomson they seem to have forgotten. Smollett they have neither forgotten nor forgiven, for his delineation of Rory and his companion, upon their first introduction to our metropolis.—Speak of Smollett as a great genius, and they will retort upon you Hume's History compared with *his* Continuation of it. What if the historian had continued "Humphrey Clinker"?

I have, in the abstract, no disrespect for Jews. They are a piece of stubborn antiquity, compared with which Stonehenge is in its nonage. They date beyond the pyramids. But I should not care to be in habits of familiar intercourse with any of that nation. I confess that I have not the nerves to enter their synagogues. Old prejudices cling about me. I cannot shake off the story of Hugh of Lincoln. Centuries of injury, contempt, and hate, on the one side,—of cloaked revenge, dissimulation, and hate, on the other, between our and their fathers, must, and ought, to affect the blood of the children. I cannot believe it can run clear and kindly yet; or that a few fine words, such as candour, liberality, the light of a nineteenth century, can close up the breaches of so deadly a disunion. A Hebrew is nowhere congenial to me. He is least distasteful on 'Change—for the mercantile spirit levels all distinctions, as all are beauties in the dark. I boldly confess that I do not relish the approximation of Jew and Christian, which has become so fashionable. The reciprocal endearments have, to me, something hypocritical and unnatural in them. I do not like to see the Church and Synagogue kissing and congeeing in awkward postures of an affected civility. If *they* are converted, why do they not come over to us altogether? Why keep up a form of separation, when the life of it is fled? If they can sit with us at table, why do they keck at our cookery? I do not understand these half convertites. Jews christianising—Christians judaising—puzzle me. I like fish or flesh. A moderate Jew is a more confounding piece of anomaly than a wet Quaker. The spirit of the synagogue is essentially *separative*. B—— would have been more in keeping if he had abided by the faith of his forefathers. There is a fine scorn in his face, which nature meant to

by the uncouth terms and phrases, as well as accent and gesture peculiar to that country, would be hardly tolerable.—*Hints towards an Essay on Conversation.*

be of——Christians. The Hebrew spirit is strong in him, in spite of his proselytism. He cannot conquer the Shibboleth. How it breaks out, when he sings, "The Children of Israel passed through the Red Sea"! The auditors, for the moment, are as Egyptians to him, and he rides over our necks in triumph. There is no mistaking him.—B—— has a strong expression of sense in his countenance, and it is confirmed by his singing. The foundation of his vocal excellence is sense. He sings with understanding, as Kemble delivered dialogue. He would sing the Commandments, and give an appropriate character to each prohibition. His nation, in general, have not over-sensible countenances. How should they?—but you seldom see a silly expression among them. Gain, and the pursuit of gain, sharpen a man's visage. I never heard of an idiot being born among them.—Some admire the Jewish female physiognomy. I admire it—but with trembling. Jael had those full dark inscrutable eyes.

In the Negro countenance you will often meet with strong traits of benignity. I have felt yearnings of tenderness towards some of these faces—or rather masks—that have looked out kindly upon one in casual encounters in the streets and highways. I love what Fuller beautifully calls—these "images of God cut in ebony." But I should not like to associate with them, to share my meals and my good-nights with them—because they are black.

I love Quaker ways, and Quaker worship. I venerate the Quaker principles. It does me good for the rest of the day when I meet any of their people in my path. When I am ruffled or disturbed by any occurrence, the sight, or quiet voice of a Quaker, acts upon me as a ventilator, lightening the air, and taking off a load from the bosom. But I cannot like the Quakers (as Desdemona would say) "to live with them." I am all over sophisticated—with humours, fancies, craving hourly sympathy. I must have books, pictures, theatres, chit-chat, scandal, jokes, ambiguities, and a thousand whim-whams, which their simpler taste can do without. I should starve at their primitive banquet. My appetites are too high for the salads which (according to Evelyn) Eve dressed for the angel, my gusto too excited

> To sit a guest with Daniel at his pulse.

The indirect answers which Quakers are often found to return to a question put to them may be explained, I think, without the vulgar assumption, that they are more given to evasion and equivocating than other people. They naturally look to their words more carefully, and are more cautious of committing themselves. They have a peculiar character to keep up on this head. They stand in a manner upon their veracity. A Quaker is by law exempted from taking an oath. The custom of resorting to an oath in extreme cases, sanctified as it is by all religious antiquity, is apt (it must be confessed) to introduce into the laxer sort of minds the notion of two kinds of truth—the one applicable to the solemn affairs of justice, and the other to the common proceedings of daily intercourse. As truth bound upon the conscience by an oath can be but truth, so in the common affirmation of the shop and the market-place a latitude is expected, and conceded, upon questions wanting this solemn covenant. Something less than truth satisfies. It is common to hear a person say, "You do not expect me to speak as if I were upon my oath." Hence a great deal of incorrectness and inadvertency, short of falsehood, creeps into ordinary conversation; and a kind of secondary or laic-truth is tolerated, where clergy-truth—oath-truth, by the nature of the circumstances, is not required. A Quaker knows none of this distinction. His simple affirmation being received, upon the most sacred occasions, without any further test, stamps a value upon the words which he is to use upon the most indifferent topics of life. He looks to them, naturally, with more severity. You can have of him no more than his word. He knows, if he is caught tripping in a casual expression, he forfeits, for himself, at least, his claim to the invidious exemption. He knows that his syllables are weighed—and how far a consciousness of this particular watchfulness, exerted against a person, has a tendency to produce indirect answers, and a diverting of the question by honest means, might be illustrated, and the practice justified, by a more sacred example than is proper to be adduced upon this occasion. The admirable presence of mind, which is notorious in Quakers upon all contingencies, might be traced to this imposed self-watchfulness—if it did not seem rather an humble and secular scion of that old stock of religious constancy, which never bent or faltered, in the Primitive Friends, or gave way to the winds of persecution, to the violence of judge or accuser, under trials and racking examinations. "You will never be the wiser, if I sit here answering your questions till midnight," said one of those upright Justicers to Penn, who had been putting law-cases with a puzzling subtlety. "Thereafter as the answers may be," retorted the Quaker. The astonishing composure of this people is sometimes ludicrously displayed in lighter instances.—I was travelling in a stage coach with three male Quakers, buttoned up in the straitest nonconformity of their sect. We stopped to bait at Andover, where a meal, partly tea apparatus, partly supper, was set before us. My friends confined themselves to the tea-table. I in my way took supper. When the landlady brought in the bill, the eldest of my companions discovered that she had charged for both meals. This was resisted. Mine hostess was very clamorous and positive. Some mild arguments were used on the part of the Quakers, for which the heated mind of the good lady seemed by no means a fit recipient. The guard came in with his usual peremptory notice. The Quakers pulled out their money, and formally tendered it—so much for tea—I, in humble imitation, tendering mine—for the supper which I had taken. She would not relax in her demand. So they all three quietly put up their silver, as did myself, and marched out of the room, the eldest and gravest going first, with myself closing up the rear, who thought I could not do better than follow the example of such grave and warrantable personages. We got in. The steps went up. The coach drove off. The murmurs of mine hostess, not very indistinctly or ambiguously pronounced, became after a time inaudible—and now my conscience, which the whimsical scene had for a time suspended, beginning to give some twitches, I waited, in the hope that some justification would be offered by these serious persons for the seeming injustice of their conduct. To my great surprise, not a syllable was dropped on the subject. They sat as mute as at a meeting. At length the eldest of them broke silence, by inquiring of his next neighbour, "Hast thee heard how indigos go at the India House?" and the question operated as a soporific on my moral feeling as far as Exeter.

Dream-Children; A Reverie

Children love to listen to stories about their elders, when *they* were children; to stretch their imagination to the conception of a traditionary great-uncle or grandame, whom they never saw. It was in this spirit that my little ones crept about me the other evening to hear about their great-grandmother Field, who lived in a great house in Norfolk (a hundred times bigger than that in which they and papa lived) which had been the scene—so at least it was generally believed in that part of the country—of the tragic incidents which they had lately become familiar with from the ballad of the Children in the Wood. Certain it is that the whole story of the children and their cruel uncle was to be seen fairly carved out in wood upon the chimney-piece of the great hall, the whole story down to the Robin Redbreasts, till a foolish rich person pulled it down to set up a marble one of modern invention in its stead, with no story upon it. Here Alice put out one of her dear mother's looks, too tender to be called upbraiding. Then I went on to say, how religious and how good their great-grandmother Field was, how beloved and respected by everybody, though she was not indeed the mistress of this great house, but had only the charge of it (and yet in some respects she might be said to be the mistress of it too) committed to her by the owner, who preferred living in a newer and more fashionable mansion which he had purchased somewhere in the adjoining county; but still she lived in it in a manner as if it had been her own, and kept up the dignity of the great house in a sort while she lived, which afterwards came to decay, and was nearly pulled down, and all its old ornaments stripped and carried away to the owner's other house, where they were set up, and looked as awkward as if some one were to carry away the old tombs they had seen lately at the Abbey, and stick them up in Lady C.'s tawdry gilt drawing-room. Here John smiled, as much as to say, "that would be foolish indeed." And then I told how, when she came to die, her funeral was attended by a concourse of all the poor, and some of the gentry too, of the neighbourhood for many miles round, to show their respect for her memory, because she had been such a good and religious woman; so good indeed that she knew all the Psaltery by heart, ay, and a great part of the Testament besides. Here little Alice spread her hands. Then I told what a tall, upright, graceful person their great-grandmother Field once was; and how in her youth she was esteemed the best dancer—here Alice's little right foot played an involuntary movement, till upon my looking grave, it desisted—the best dancer, I was saying, in the county, till a cruel disease, called a cancer, came, and bowed her down with pain; but it could never bend her good spirits, or make them stoop, but they were still upright, because she was so good and religious. Then I told how she was used to sleep by herself in a lone chamber of the great lone house; and how she believed that an apparition of two infants was to be seen at midnight gliding up and down the great staircase near where she slept, but she said "those innocents would do her no harm"; and how frightened I used to be, though in those days I had my maid to sleep with me, because I was never half so good or religious as she—and yet I never saw the infants. Here John expanded all his eyebrows and tried to look courageous. Then I told how good she was to all her grand-children, having us to the great house in the holydays, where I in particular used to spend many hours by myself, in gazing upon the old busts of the Twelve Cæsars, that had been Emperors of Rome, till the old marble heads would seem to live again, or I to be turned into marble with them; how I never could be tired with roaming about that huge mansion, with its vast empty rooms, with their worn-out hangings, fluttering tapestry, and carved oaken panels, with the gilding almost rubbed out—sometimes in the spacious old-fashioned gardens, which I had almost to myself, unless when now and then a solitary gardening man would cross me—and how the nectarines and peaches hung upon the walls, without my ever offering to pluck them, because they were forbidden fruit, unless now and then,—and because I had more pleasure in strolling about among the old melancholy-looking yew trees, or the firs, and picking up the red berries, and the fir apples, which were good for nothing but to look at—or in lying about upon the fresh grass, with all the fine garden smells around me—or basking in the orangery, till I could almost fancy myself ripening too along with the oranges and the limes in that grateful warmth—or in watching the dace that darted to and fro in the fish-pond, at the bottom of the garden, with here and there a great sulky pike hanging midway down the water in silent state, as if it mocked at their impertinent friskings,—I had more pleasure in these busy-idle diversions than in all the sweet flavours of peaches, nectarines, oranges, and such like common baits of children. Here John slily deposited back upon the plate a bunch of grapes, which, not unobserved by Alice, he had meditated dividing with her, and both seemed willing to relinquish them for the present as irrelevant. Then in somewhat a more heightened tone, I told how, though their great-grandmother Field loved all her grandchildren, yet in an especial manner she might be said to love their uncle, John L——, because he was so handsome and spirited a youth, and a king to the rest of us; and, instead of moping about in solitary corners, like some of us, he would mount the most mettlesome horse he could get when but an imp no bigger than ourselves, and make it carry him half over the county in a morning, and join the hunters when there were any out—and yet he loved the old great house and gardens too, but had too much spirit to be always pent up within their boundaries—and how their uncle grew up to man's estate as brave as he was handsome, to the admiration of every body, but of their great-grandmother Field most especially; and how he used to carry me upon his back when I was a lame-footed boy—for he was a good bit older than me—many a mile when I could not walk for pain;—and how in after life he became lame-footed too, and I did not always (I fear) make allowances enough for him when he was impatient, and in pain, nor remember sufficiently how considerate he had been to me when I was lame-footed; and how when he died, though he had not been dead an hour, it seemed as if he had died a great while ago, such a distance there is betwixt life and death; and how I bore his death as I thought pretty well at first, but afterwards it haunted and haunted me; and though I did not cry or take it to heart as some do, and as I think he would have done if I had died, yet I missed him all day long, and knew not till then how much I had loved him. I missed his kindness, and I missed his crossness, and wished him to be alive again, to be quarrelling with him (for we quarrelled sometimes), rather than not have him again, and was as uneasy without him, as he their poor uncle must have been when the doctor took off his limb. Here the children fell a crying, and asked if their little mourning which they had on was not for uncle John, and they looked up, and prayed me not to go on about their uncle, but to tell them some stories about their pretty dead mother. Then I told how for seven long years, in hope sometimes, sometimes in despair, yet persisting ever, I courted the fair Alice W——n; and, as much as children could understand, I explained to them what coyness, and difficulty, and denial meant in maidens—when suddenly, turning to Alice, the soul of the first Alice looked out at her eyes with such a reality of re-presentment, that I became in doubt which of them stood there before me, or whose that bright hair was; and while I stood gazing, both the children gradually grew fainter to my view, receding, and still receding till nothing at last but two mournful features were seen in the uttermost distance, which, without speech, strangely impressed upon me the effects of speech; "We are not of Alice, nor of thee, nor are we children at all. The children of Alice call Bartrum father. We are nothing; less than nothing, and dreams. We are only what might have been, and must wait upon the tedious shores of Lethe millions of ages before we have existence, and a name"—and immediately awaking, I found myself quietly seated in my bachelor armchair, where I had fallen asleep, with the faithful Bridget unchanged by my side—but John L. (or James Elia) was gone for ever.

The Praise of Chimney-Sweepers

I LIKE to meet a sweep—understand me—not a grown sweeper—old chimney-sweepers are by no means attractive—but one of those tender novices, blooming through their first nigritude, the maternal washings not quite effaced from the cheek—such as come forth with the dawn, or somewhat earlier, with their little professional notes sounding like the *peep peep* of a young sparrow; or liker to the matin lark should I pronounce them, in their aerial ascents not seldom anticipating the sunrise?

I have a kindly yearning toward these dim specks—poor blots—innocent blacknesses—

I reverence these young Africans of our own growth—these almost clergy imps, who sport their cloth without assumption; and from their little pulpits (the tops of chimneys), in the nipping air of a December morning, preach a lesson of patience to mankind.

When a child, what a mysterious pleasure it was to witness their operation! to see a chit no bigger than one's self enter, one knew not by what process, into what seemed the *fauces Averni*—to pursue him in imagination, as he went sounding on through so many dark stifling caverns, horrid shades!—to shudder with the idea that "now, surely, he must be lost for ever!"—to revive at hearing his feeble shout of discovered daylight—and then (O fulness of delight) running out of doors, to come just in time to see the sable phenomenon emerge in safety, the brandished weapon of his art victorious like some flag waved over a conquered citadel! I seem to remember having been told, that a bad sweep was once left in a stack with his brush, to indicate which way the wind blew. It was an awful spectacle certainly; not much unlike the old stage direction in Macbeth, where the "Apparition of a child crowned with a tree in his hand rises."

Reader, if thou meetest one of these small gentry in thy early rambles, it is good to give him a penny. It is better to give him two-pence. If it be starving weather, and to the proper troubles of his hard occupation, a pair of kibed heels (no unusual accompaniment) be superadded, the demand on thy humanity will surely rise to a tester.

There is a composition, the ground-work of which I have understood to be the sweet wood 'yclept sassafras. This wood boiled down to a kind of tea, and tempered with an infusion of milk and sugar, hath to some tastes a delicacy beyond the China luxury. I know not how thy palate may relish it; for myself, with every deference to the judicious Mr. Read, who hath time out of mind kept open a shop (the only one he avers in London) for the vending of his "wholesome and pleasant beverage," on the south side of Fleet Street, as thou approachest Bridge Street—*the only Salopian house,*—I have never yet ventured to dip my own particular lip in a basin of his commended ingredients—a cautious premonition to the olfactories constantly whispering to me, that my stomach must infallibly, with all due courtesy, decline it. Yet I have seen palates, otherwise not uninstructed in dietetical elegances, sup it up with avidity.

I know not by what particular conformation of the organ it happens, but I have always found that this composition is surprisingly gratifying to the palate of a young chimney-sweeper—whether the oily particles (sassafras is slightly oleaginous) do attenuate and soften the fuliginous concretions, which are sometimes found (in dissections) to adhere to the roof of the mouth in these unfledged practitioners; or whether

Nature, sensible that she had mingled too much of bitter wood in the lot of these raw victims, caused to grow out of the earth her sassafras for a sweet lenitive—but so it is, that no possible taste or odour to the senses of a young chimney-sweeper can convey a delicate excitement comparable to this mixture. Being penniless, they will yet hang their black heads over the ascending steam, to gratify one sense if possible, seemingly no less pleased than those domestic animals—cats—when they purr over a new-found sprig of valerian. There is something more in these sympathies than philosophy can inculcate.

Now albeit Mr. Read boasteth, not without reason, that his is the *only Salopian house;* yet be it known to thee, reader—if thou art one who keepest what are called good hours, thou art haply ignorant of the fact—he hath a race of industrious imitators, who from stalls, and under open sky, dispense the same savoury mess to humbler customers, at that dead time of the dawn, when (as extremes meet) the rake, reeling home from his midnight cups, and the hard-handed artisan leaving his bed to resume the premature labours of the day, jostle, not unfrequently to the manifest disconcerting of the former, for the honours of the pavement. It is the time when, in summer, between the expired and the not yet relumined kitchen-fires, the kennels of our fair metropolis give forth their least satisfactory odours. The rake, who wisheth to dissipate his o'er-night vapours in more grateful coffee, curses the ungenial fume, as he passeth; but the artisan stops to taste, and blesses the fragrant breakfast.

This is *Saloop*—the precocious herb-woman's darling—the delight of the early gardener, who transports his smoking cabbages by break of day from Hammersmith to Covent Garden's famed piazzas—the delight, and, oh I fear, too often the envy of the unpennied sweep. Him shouldest thou haply encounter, with his dim visage pendent over the grateful steam, regale him with a sumptuous basin (it will cost thee but three halfpennies) and a slice of delicate bread and butter (an added halfpenny)—so may thy culinary fires, eased of the o'er-charged secretions from thy worse-placed hospitalities, curl up a lighter volume to the welkin—so may the descending soot never taint thy costly well-ingredienced soups—nor the odious cry, quick-reaching from street to street, of the *fired chimney,* invite the rattling engines from ten adjacent parishes, to disturb for a casual scintillation thy peace and pocket!

I am by nature extremely susceptible of street affronts; the jeers and taunts of the populace; the low-bred triumph they display over the casual trip, or splashed stocking, of a gentleman. Yet can I endure the jocularity of a young sweep with something more than forgiveness.—In the last winter but one, pacing along Cheapside with my accustomed precipitation when I walk westward, a treacherous slide brought me upon my back in an instant. I scrambled up with pain and shame enough—yet outwardly trying to face it down, as if nothing had happened—when the roguish grin of one of these young wits encountered me. There he stood, pointing me out with his dusky finger to the mob, and to a poor woman (I suppose his mother) in particular, till the tears for the exquisiteness of the fun (so he thought it) worked themselves out at the corners of his poor red eyes, red from many a previous weeping, and soot-inflamed, yet twinkling through all with such a joy, snatched out of desolation, that Hogarth——but Hogarth has got him already (how could he miss him?) in the March to Finchley, grinning at the pie-man——there he stood, as he stands in the picture, irremovable, as if the jest was to last for ever—with such a maximum of glee, and minimum of mischief, in his mirth—for the grin of a genuine sweep hath absolutely no malice in it—that I could have been content, if the honour of a gentleman might endure it, to have remained his butt and his mockery till midnight.

I am by theory obdurate to the seductiveness of what are called a fine set of teeth. Every pair of rosy lips (the ladies must pardon me) is a casket, presumably holding such jewels; but, methinks, they should take leave to "air" them as frugally as possible. The fine lady, or fine gentleman, who show me their teeth, show me bones. Yet must I confess, that from the mouth of a true sweep a display (even to ostentation) of those white and shining ossifications, strikes me as an agreeable anomaly in manners, and an allowable piece of foppery. It is, as when

> A sable cloud
> Turns forth her silver lining on the night.

It is like some remnant of gentry not quite extinct; a badge of better days; a hint of nobility:—and, doubtless, under the obscuring darkness and double night of their forlorn disguisement, oftentimes lurketh good blood, and gentle conditions, derived from lost ancestry, and a lapsed pedigree. The premature apprenticements of these tender victims give but too much encouragement, I fear, to clandestine, and almost infantile abductions; the seeds of civility and true courtesy, so often discernible in these young grafts (not otherwise to be accounted for), plainly hint at some forced adoptions; many noble Rachels mourning for their children, even in our days, countenance the fact; the tales of fairy-spiriting may shadow a lamentable verity, and the recovery of the young Montagu be but a solitary instance of good fortune, out of many irreparable and hopeless *defiliations*.

In one of the state beds at Arundel Castle, a few years since—under a ducal canopy—(that seat of the Howards is an object of curiosity to visitors, chiefly for its beds, in which the late duke was especially a connoisseur)—encircled with curtains of delicatest crimson, with starry coronets inwoven—folded between a pair of sheets whiter and softer than the lap where Venus lulled Ascanius—was discovered by chance, after all methods of search had failed, at noon-day, fast asleep, a lost chimney-sweeper. The little creature, having somehow confounded his passage among the intricacies of those lordly chimneys, by some unknown aperture had alighted upon this magnificent chamber; and, tired with his tedious explorations, was unable to resist the delicious invitement to repose, which he there saw exhibited; so, creeping between the sheets very quietly, laid his black head upon the pillow, and slept like a young Howard.

Such is the account given to the visitors at the Castle.—But I cannot help seeming to perceive a confirmation of what I have just hinted at in this story. A high instinct was at work in the case, or I am mistaken. Is it probable that a poor child of that description, with whatever weariness he might be visited, would have ventured, under such a penalty, as he would be taught to expect, to uncover the sheets of a Duke's bed, and deliberately to lay himself down between them, when the rug, or the carpet, presented an obvious couch, still far above his pretensions—is this probable, I would ask, if the great power of nature, which I contend for, had not been manifested within him, prompting to the adventure? Doubtless this young nobleman (for such my mind misgives me that he must be) was allured by some memory, not amounting to full consciousness, of his condition in infancy, when he was used to be lapt by his mother, or his nurse, in just such sheets as he there found, into which he was but now creeping back as into his proper *incunabula,* and resting-place.—By no other theory, than by this sentiment of a pre-existent state (as I may call it), can I explain a deed so venturous, and, indeed, upon any other system, so indecorous, in this tender, but unseasonable, sleeper.

My pleasant friend Jem White was so impressed with a belief of metamorphoses like this frequently taking place, that in some sort to reverse the wrongs of fortune in these poor changelings, he instituted an annual feast of chimney-sweepers, at which it was his pleasure to officiate as host and waiter. It was a solemn supper held in Smithfield, upon the yearly return of the fair of St. Bartholomew. Cards were issued a week before to the master-sweeps in and about the metropolis, confining the invitation to their younger fry. Now and then an elderly stripling would get in among us, and be good-naturedly winked at; but our main body were infantry. One unfortunate wight, indeed, who relying upon his dusky suit, had intruded himself into our party, but by tokens was providentially discovered in time to be no chimney-sweeper (all is not soot which looks so), was quoited out of the presence with universal indignation, as not having on the wedding garment; but in general the greatest harmony prevailed. The place chosen was a convenient spot among the pens, at the north side of the fair, not so far distant as to be impervious to the agreeable hubbub of that vanity; but remote enough not to be obvious to the interruption of every gaping spectator in it. The guests assembled about seven. In those little temporary parlours three tables were spread with napery, not so fine as substantial, and at every board a comely hostess presided with her pan of hissing sausages. The nostrils of the young rogues dilated at the savour. JAMES WHITE, as head waiter, had charge of the first table; and myself, with our trusty companion [1] BIGOD, ordinarily ministered to the other two. There was clambering and jostling, you may be sure, who should get at the first table—for Rochester in his maddest days could not have done the humours of the scene with more spirit than my friend. After some general expression of thanks for the honour the company had done him, his inaugural ceremony was to clasp the greasy waist of old dame Ursula (the fattest of the three), that stood frying and fretting, half-blessing, half-cursing "the gentleman," and imprint upon her chaste lips a tender salute, whereat the universal host would set up a shout that tore the concave, while hundreds of grinning teeth startled the night with their brightness. O it was a pleasure to see the sable younkers lick in the unctuous meat, with *his* more unctuous sayings—how he would fit the tit-bits to the puny mouths, reserving the lengthier links for the seniors—how he would intercept a morsel even in the jaws of some young desperado, declaring it "must to the pan again to be browned, for it was not fit for a gentleman's eating"—how he would recommend this slice of white bread, or that piece of kissing-crust, to a tender juvenile, advising them all to have a care of cracking their teeth, which were their best patrimony,—how genteelly he would deal about the small ale, as if it were wine, naming the brewer, and protesting, if it were not good he should lose their custom; with a special recommendation to wipe the lip before drinking. Then we had our toasts—"The King,"—the "Cloth,"—which, whether they understood or not, was equally diverting and flattering;—and for a crowning sentiment, which never failed, "May the Brush supersede the Laurel." All these, and fifty other fancies,

[1] John Fenwick.

which were rather felt than comprehended by his guests, would he utter, standing upon tables, and prefacing every sentiment with a "Gentlemen, give me leave to propose so and so," which was a prodigious comfort to those young orphans; every now and then stuffing into his mouth (for it did not do to be squeamish on these occasions) indiscriminate pieces of those reeking sausages, which pleased them mightily, and was the savouriest part, you may believe, of the entertainment.

Golden lads and lasses must,
As chimney-sweepers, come to dust—

James White is extinct, and with him these suppers have long ceased. He carried away with him half the fun of the world when he died—of my world at least. His old clients look for him among the pens; and, missing him, reproach the altered feast of St. Bartholomew, and the glory of Smithfield departed for ever.

The Gentle Giantess

The widow Blacket, of Oxford, is the largest female I ever had the pleasure of beholding. There may be her parallel upon the earth; but surely I never saw it. I take her to be lineally descended from the maid's aunt of Brainford, who caused Master Ford such uneasiness. She hath Atlantean shoulders; and, as she stoopeth in her gait,—with as few offences to answer for in her own particular as any one of Eve's daughters,—her back seems broad enough to bear the blame of all the peccadilloes that have been committed since Adam. She girdeth her waist—or what she is pleased to esteem as such—nearly up to her shoulders; from beneath which that huge dorsal expanse, in mountainous declivity, emergeth. Respect for her alone preventeth the idle boys, who follow her about in shoals, whenever she cometh abroad, from getting up and riding. But her presence infallibly commands a reverence. She is indeed, as the Americans would express it, something awful. Her person is a burthen to herself no less than to the ground which bears her. To her mighty bone, she had a pinguitude withal, which makes the depth of winter to her the most desirable season. Her distress in the warmer solstice is pitiable. During the months of July and August, she usually renteth a cool cellar, where ices are kept, whereinto she descendeth when Sirius rageth. She dates from a hot Thursday,—some twenty-five years ago. Her apartment in summer is pervious to the four winds. Two doors, in north and south direction, and two windows, fronting the rising and the setting sun, never closed, from every cardinal point catch the contributory breezes. She loves to enjoy what she calls a quadruple draught. That must be a shrewd zephyr that can escape her. I owe a painful face-ache, which oppresses me at this moment, to a cold caught, sitting by her, one day in last July, at this receipt of coolness. Her fan, in ordinary, resembleth a banner spread, which she keepeth continually on the alert to detect the least breeze. She possesseth an active and gadding mind, totally incommensurate with her person. No one delighteth more than herself in country exercises and pastimes. I have passed many an agreeable holiday with her in her favourite park at Woodstock. She performs her part in these delightful ambulatory excursions by the aid of a portable garden-chair. She setteth out with you at a fair foot-gallop, which she keepeth up till you are both well-breathed, and then reposeth she for a few seconds. Then she is up again for a hundred paces or so, and again resteth; her movements, on these sprightly occasions, being something between walking and flying. Her great weight seemeth to propel her forward, ostrich-fashion. In this kind of relieved marching, I have traversed with her many scores of acres on those well-wooded and well-watered domains. Her delight at Oxford is in the public walks and gardens, where, when the weather is not too oppressive, she passeth much of her valuable time. There is a bench at Maudlin, or rather situated between the frontiers of that and ———'s College (some litigation, latterly, about repairs, has vested the property of it finally in ———'s), where, at the hour of noon, she is ordinarily to be found sitting,—so she calls it by courtesy,—but, in fact, pressing and breaking of it down with her enormous settlement; as both those foundations,—who, however, are good-natured enough to wink at it,—have found, I believe, to their cost. Here she taketh the fresh air, principally at vacation-times, when the walks are freest from interruption of the younger fry of students. Here she passeth her idle hours, not idly, but generally accompanied with a book,—blessed if she can but intercept some resident Fellow (as usually there are some of that brood left behind at these periods), or stray Master of Arts (to most of them she is better known than their dinner bell), with whom she may confer upon any curious topic of literature. I have seen these shy gownsmen, who truly set but a very slight value upon female conversation, cast a hawk's eye upon her from the length of Maudlin Grove, and warily glide off into another walk,—true monks as they are; and urgently neglecting the delicacies of her polished converse for their own perverse and uncommunicating solitariness! Within-doors, her principal diversion is music, vocal and instrumental; in both which she is no mean professor. Her voice is wonderfully fine; but till I got used to it, I confess it staggered me. It is, for all the world, like that of a piping bullfinch; while, from her size and stature, you would expect notes to drown the deep organ. The shake, which most fine singers reserve for the close or cadence, by some unaccountable flexibility, or tremulousness of pipe, she carrieth quite through the composition; so that her time, to a common air or ballad, keeps double motion, like the earth,—running the primary circuit of the tune, and still revolving upon its own axis. The effect, as I said before, when you are used to it, is as agreeable as it is altogether new and surprising. The spacious apartment of her outward frame lodgeth a soul in all respects disproportionate. Of more than mortal make, she evinceth withal a trembling sensibility, a yielding infirmity of purpose, a quick susceptibility to reproach, and all the train of diffident and blushing virtues, which for their habitation usually seek out a feeble frame, an attenuated and meagre constitution. With more than man's bulk, her humours and occupations are eminently feminine. She sighs,—being six feet high. She languisheth,—being two feet wide. She worketh slender sprigs upon the delicate muslin,—her fingers being capable of moulding a Colossus. She sippeth her wine out of her glass daintily—her capacity being that of a tun of Heidelberg. She goeth mincingly with those feet of hers, whose solidity need not fear the black ox's pressure. Softest and largest of thy sex, adieu! By what parting attribute may I salute thee, last and best of the Titanesses,—Ogress, fed with milk instead of blood; not least, or least handsome, among Oxford's stately structures,—Oxford, who, in its deadest time of vacation, can never properly be said to be empty, having thee to fill it.

Poor Relations

A POOR Relation—is the most irrelevant thing in nature,—a piece of impertinent correspondency,—an odious approximation,—a haunting conscience,—a preposterous shadow, lengthening in the noontide of our prosperity,—an unwelcome remembrancer,—a perpetually recurring mortification,—a drain on your purse,—a more intolerable dun upon your pride,—a drawback upon success,—a rebuke to your rising,—a stain in your blood,—a blot on your 'scutcheon,—a rent in your garment,—a death's head at your banquet,—Agathocles' pot,—a Mordecai in your gate,—a Lazarus at your door,—a lion in your path,—a frog in your chamber,—a fly in your ointment,—a mote in your eye,—a triumph to your enemy, an apology to your friends,—the one thing not needful,—the hail in harvest,—the ounce of sour in a pound of sweet.

He is known by his knock. Your heart telleth you "That is Mr.

———." A rap, between familiarity and respect; that demands, and, at the same time, seems to despair of, entertainment. He entereth smiling and—embarrassed. He holdeth out his hand to you to shake, and draweth it back again. He casually looketh in about dinner-time—when the table is full. He offereth to go away, seeing you have company, but is induced to stay. He filleth a chair, and your visitor's two children are accommodated at a side table. He never cometh upon open days, when your wife says with some complacency, "My dear, perhaps Mr. ——— will drop in to-day." He remembereth birthdays—and professeth he is fortunate to have stumbled upon one. He declareth against fish, the turbot being small—yet suffereth himself to be importuned into a slice against his first resolution. He sticketh by the port—yet will be prevailed upon to empty the remainder glass of claret, if a stranger press it upon him. He is a puzzle to the servants, who are fearful of being too obsequious, or not civil enough, to him. The guests think "they have seen him before." Everyone speculateth upon his condition; and the most part take him to be—a tide waiter. He calleth you by your Christian name, to imply that his other is the same with your own. He is too familiar by half, yet you wish he had less diffidence. With half the familiarity he might pass for a casual dependent; with more boldness he would be in no danger of being taken for what he is. He is too humble for a friend, yet taketh on him more state than befits a client. He is a worse guest than a country tenant, inasmuch as he bringeth up no rent—yet 'tis odds, from his garb and demeanour, that your guests take him for one. He is asked to make one at the whist table; refuseth on the score of poverty, and—resents being left out. When the company break up he proffereth to go for a coach—and lets the servant go. He recollects your grandfather; and will thrust in some mean and quite unimportant anecdote of—the family. He knew it when it was not quite so flourishing as "he is blest in seeing it now." He reviveth past situations to institute what he calleth—favourable comparisons. With a reflecting sort of congratulation, he will inquire the price of your furniture: and insults you with a special commendation of your window-curtains. He is of opinion that the urn is the more elegant shape, but, after all, there was something more comfortable about the old tea-kettle—which you must remember. He dare say you must find a great convenience in having a carriage of your own, and appealeth to your lady if it is not so. Inquireth if you have had your arms done on vellum yet; and did not know, till lately, that such-and-such had been the crest of the family. His memory is unseasonable; his compliments perverse; his talk a trouble; his stay pertinacious; and when he goeth away, you dismiss his chair into a corner, as precipitately as possible, and feel fairly rid of two nuisances.

There is a worse evil under the sun, and that is—a female Poor Relation. You may do something with the other; you may pass him off tolerably well; but your indigent she-relative is hopeless. "He is an old humourist," you may say, "and affects to go threadbare. His circumstances are better than folks would take them to be. You are fond of having a Character at your table, and truly he is one." But in the indications of female poverty there can be no disguise. No woman dresses below herself from caprice. The truth must out without shuffling. "She is plainly related to the L——s; or what does she at their house?" She is, in all probability, your wife's cousin. Nine times out of ten, at least, this is the case. Her garb is something between a gentlewoman and a beggar, yet the former evidently predominates. She is most provokingly humble, and ostentatiously sensible to her inferiority. He may require to be repressed sometimes—*aliquando sufflaminandus erat*—but there is no raising her. You send her soup at dinner, and she begs to be helped—after the gentlemen. Mr. —— requests the honour of taking wine with her; she hesitates between Port and Madeira, and chooses the former—because he does. She calls the servant *Sir;* and insists on not troubling him to hold her plate. The housekeeper patronises her. The children's governess takes upon her to correct her, when she has mistaken the piano for a harpsichord.

Richard Amlet, Esq., in the play, is a noticeable instance of the disadvantages, to which this chimerical notion of *affinity constituting a claim to an acquaintance,* may subject the spirit of a gentleman. A little foolish blood is all that is betwixt him and a lady with a great estate. His stars are perpetually crossed by the malignant maternity of an old woman, who persists in calling him "her son Dick." But she has wherewithal in the end to recompense his indignities, and float him again upon the brilliant surface, under which it had been her seeming business and pleasure all along to sink him. All men, besides, are not of Dick's temperament. I knew an Amlet in real life, who wanting Dick's buoyancy, sank indeed. Poor W—— was of my own standing at Christ's, a fine classic, and a youth of promise. If he had a blemish, it was too much pride; but its quality was inoffensive; it was not of that sort which hardens the heart, and serves to keep inferiors at a distance; it only sought to ward off derogation from itself. It was the principle of self-respect carried as far as it could go, without infringing upon that respect, which he would have every one else equally maintain for himself. He would have you to think alike with him on this topic. Many a quarrel have I had with him, when we were rather older boys, and our tallness made us more obnoxious to observation in the blue clothes, because I would not thread the alleys and blind ways of the town with him to elude notice, when we have been out together on a holiday in the streets of this sneering and prying metropolis. W—— went, sore with these notions, to Oxford, where the dignity and sweetness of a scholar's life, meeting with the alloy of a humble introduction, wrought in him a passionate devotion to the place, with a profound aversion to the society. The servitor's gown (worse than his school array) clung to him with Nessian venom. He thought himself ridiculous in a garb, under which Latimer must have walked erect; and in which Hooker, in his young days, possibly flaunted in a vein of no discommendable vanity. In the depths of college shades, or in his lonely chamber, the poor student shrunk from observation. He found shelter among books, which insult not; and studies, that ask no questions of a youth's finances. He was lord of his library, and seldom cared for looking out beyond his domains. The healing influence of studious pursuits was upon him, to soothe and to abstract. He was almost a healthy man; when the waywardness of his fate broke out against him with a second and worse malignity. The father of W—— had hitherto exercised the humble profession of house-painter at N——, near Oxford. A supposed interest with some of the heads of colleges had now induced him to take up his abode in that city, with the hope of being employed upon some public works which were talked of. From that moment I read in the countenance of the young man, the determination which at length tore him from academical pursuits for ever. To a person unacquainted with our Universities, the distance between the gownsmen and the townsmen, as they are called—the trading part of the latter especially—is carried to an excess that would appear harsh and incredible. The temperament of W——'s father was diametrically the reverse of his own. Old W—— was a little, busy, cringing tradesman, who, with his son upon his arm, would stand bowing and scraping, cap in hand, to anything that wore the semblance of a gown—insensible to the winks and opener remonstrances of the young man, to whose chamber-fellow, or equal in standing, perhaps, he was thus obsequiously and gratuitously ducking. Such a state of things could not last. W—— must change the air of Oxford or be suffocated. He chose the former; and let the sturdy moralist, who strains the point of the filial duties as high as they can bear, censure the dereliction; he cannot estimate the struggle. I stood with W——, the last afternoon I ever saw him, under the eaves of his paternal dwelling. It was in the fine lane leading from the High Street to the back of **** college, where W—— kept his rooms. He seemed thoughtful and more reconciled. I ventured to rally him—finding him in a better mood—upon a representation of the Artist Evangelist, which the old man, whose affairs were beginning to flourish, had caused to be set up in a splendid sort of frame over his really handsome shop, either as a token of prosperity, or badge of gratitude to his saint. W—— looked up at the Luke, and, like Satan, "knew his mounted sign—and fled." A letter on his father's table the next morning, announced that he had accepted a commission in a regiment about to embark for Portugal. He was among the first who perished before the walls of St. Sebastian.

I do not know how, upon a subject which I began with treating half seriously, I should have fallen upon a recital so eminently painful; but this theme of poor relationship is replete with so much matter for tragic as well as comic associations, that it is difficult to keep the account distinct without blending. The earliest impressions which I received on this matter, are certainly not attended with anything painful, or very humiliating, in the recalling. At my father's table (no very splendid one) was to be found, every Saturday, the mysterious figure of an aged gentleman, clothed in neat black, of a sad yet comely appearance. His deportment was of the essence of gravity; his words few or none; and I was not to make a noise in his presence. I had little inclination to have done so—for my cue was to admire in silence. A particular elbow chair was appropriated to him, which was in no case to be violated. A peculiar sort of sweet pudding, which appeared on no other occasion, distinguished the days of his coming. I used to think him a prodigiously rich man. All I could make out of him was, that he and my father had been schoolfellows a world ago at Lincoln, and that he came from the Mint. The Mint I knew to be a place where all the money was coined—and I thought he was the owner of all that money. Awful ideas of the Tower twined themselves about his presence. He seemed above human infirmities and passions. A sort of melancholy grandeur invested him. From some inexplicable doom I fancied him obliged to go about in an eternal suit of mourning; a captive—a stately being, let out of the Tower on Saturdays. Often have I wondered at the temerity of my father, who, in spite of an habitual general respect which we all in common manifested towards him, would venture now and then to stand up against him in some argument, touching their youthful days. The houses of the ancient city of Lincoln are divided (as most of my readers know) between the dwellers on the hill, and in the valley. This marked distinction formed an obvious division between the boys who lived above (however brought together in a common school) and the boys whose paternal residence was on the plain; a sufficient cause of hostility in the code of these young Grotiuses. My father had been a leading Mountaineer; and would still maintain the general superiority, in skill and hardihood, of the *Above Boys* (his own faction) over the *Below Boys* (so were they called), of which party his contemporary had been a chieftain. Many and hot were the skirmishes on this topic—the only one upon which the old gentleman was ever brought out—and bad blood bred; even sometimes almost to the recommencement (so I expected) of actual hostilities. But my father, who scorned to insist upon advantages, generally contrived to turn the conversation upon some adroit by-commendation of the old Minster; in the general preference of which, before all other cathedrals in the island, the dweller on the hill, and the plain-born, could meet on a conciliating level, and lay down their less important differences. Once only I saw the old gentleman really ruffled, and I remembered with anguish the thought that came over me: "Perhaps he will never come here again." He had been pressed to take another plate of the viand, which I have already mentioned as the indispensable concomitant of his visits. He had refused with a resistance amounting to rigour—when my aunt, an old Lincolnian, but who had something of this in common with my cousin Bridget, that she would sometimes press civility out of season—uttered the following memorable application—"Do take another slice, Mr. Billet, for you do not get pudding every day." The old gentleman said nothing at the time—but he took occasion in the course of the evening, when some argument had intervened between them, to utter with an emphasis which chilled the company, and which chills me now as I write it—"Woman, you are superannuated." John Billet did not survive long, after the digesting of this affront; but he survived long enough to assure me that peace was actually restored! and, if I remember aright, another pudding was discreetly substituted in the place of that which had occasioned the offence. He died at the Mint (annò 1781) where he had long held, what he accounted, a comfortable independence; and with five pounds, fourteen shillings, and a penny, which were found in his escritoire after his decease, left the world, blessing God that he had enough to bury him, and that he had never been obliged to any man for a sixpence. This was—a Poor Relation.

Letter to Thomas Manning, December 27, 1800

At length George Dyer's phrenitis has come to a crisis; he is raging and furiously mad. I waited upon the Heathen, Thursday was a se'n-night. The first symptom which struck my eye, and gave me incontrovertible proof of the fatal truth, was a pair of nankeen pantaloons four times too big for him, which the said Heathen did pertinaciously affirm to be new.

They were absolutely ingrained with the accumulated dirt of ages; but he affirmed them to be clean. He was going to visit a lady that was nice about those things, and that's the reason he wore nankeen that day. And then he danced, and capered, and fidgeted, and pulled up his pantaloons, and hugged his intolerable flannel vestment closer about his poetic loins. Anon he gave it loose to the zephyrs which plentifully insinuate their tiny bodies through every crevice, door, window, or wainscot, expressly formed for the exclusion of such impertinents. Then he caught at a proof sheet, and catched up a laundress's bill instead—made a dart at Bloomfield's Poems, and threw them in agony aside. I could not bring him to one direct reply; he could not maintain his jumping mind in a right line for the tithe of a moment by Clifford's Inn clock. He must go to the printer's immediately: (the most unlucky accident!) he had struck off five hundred impressions of his Poems, which were ready for delivery to subscribers, and the Preface must all be expunged. There were eighty pages of Preface, and not till that morning had he discovered that in the very first page of said Preface he had set out with a principle of Criticism fundamentally wrong, which vitiated all his following reasoning. The Preface must be expunged, although it cost him £30, the lowest calculation, taking in paper and printing! In vain have his real friends remonstrated against this Midsummer madness. George is as obstinate as a Primitive Christian, and wards and parries off all our thrusts with one unanswerable fence:—"Sir, 'tis of great consequence that the *world* is not *misled*!"

As for the other Professor, he has actually begun to dive into Tavernier and Chardin's *Persian* Travels for a story, to form a new drama for the sweet tooth of this fastidious age. Hath not Bethlehem College a fair action for non-residents against such professors? Are poets so *few* in *this age,* that he must write poetry? *Is morals* a subject so exhausted, that he must quit that line? Is the metaphysic well (without a bottom) drained dry?

If I can guess at the wicked pride of the Professor's heart, I would take a shrewd wager that he disdains ever again to dip his pen in *Prose.* Adieu, ye splendid theories! Farewell, dreams of political justice! Lawsuits, where I was counsel for Archbishop Fénelon *versus* my own mother, in the famous fire cause!

Vanish from my mind, professors, one and all! I have metal more attractive on foot.

Man of many snipes,—I will sup with thee (Deo volente, et diabolo nolente,) on Monday night, the 5th of January, in the new year, and crush a cup to the infant century.

A word or two of my progress: Embark at six o'clock in the morning, with a fresh gale, on a Cambridge one-decker; very cold till eight at night; land at St. Mary's light-house, muffins and coffee upon table, (or any other curious production of Turkey, or both Indies,) snipes exactly at nine, punch to commence at ten, with *argument;* difference of opinion is expected to take place about eleven; perfect unanimity, with some haziness and dimness, before twelve.—N. B. My single affection is not so singly wedded to snipes; but the curious and epicurean eye would also take a pleasure in beholding a delicate and well-chosen assortment of teals, ortolans, the unctuous and palate-soothing flesh of geese, wild and tame, nightingales' brains, the sensorium of a young suckling pig, or any other Christmas dish, which I leave to the judgment of you and the cook of Gonville.

C. Lamb.

Letter to Mrs. William Wordsworth, February 18, 1818

East-India House, 18th Feb., 1818.

My dear Mrs. Wordsworth,—I have repeatedly taken pen in hand to answer your kind letter. My sister should more properly have done it, but she having failed, I consider myself answerable for her debts. I am now trying to do it in the midst of commercial noises, and with a quill which seems more ready to glide into arithmetical figures and names of gourds, cassia, cardamoms, aloes, ginger, or tea, than into kindly responses and friendly recollections. The reason why I cannot write letters at home, is, that I am never alone. Plato's—(I write to W. W. now)—Plato's double-animal parted never longed more to be reciprocally re-united in the system of its first creation than I sometimes do to be but for a moment single and separate. Except my morning's walk to the office, which is like treading on sands of gold for that reason, I am never so. I cannot walk home from office but some officious friend offers his unwelcome courtesies to accompany me. All the morning I am pestered. I could sit and gravely cast up sums in great books, or compare sum with sum, and write "paid" against this, and "unpaid" against t'other, and yet reserve in some corner of my mind "some darling thoughts all my own,"—faint memory of some passage in a book, or the tone of an absent friend's voice—a snatch of Miss Burrell's singing, or a gleam of Fanny Kelly's divine plain face. The two operations might be going on at the same time without thwarting, as the sun's two motions, (earth's I mean,) or as I sometimes turn round till I am giddy, in my back parlour, while my sister is walking longitudinally in the front; or as the shoulder of veal twists round with the spit, while the smoke wreathes up the chimney. But there are a set of amateurs of the Belles Lettres—the gay science—who come to me as a sort of rendezvous, putting questions of criticism, of British Institutions, Lalla Rookhs, &c.—what Coleridge said at the lecture last night—who have the form of reading men, but, for any possible use reading can be to them, but to talk of, might as well have been Ante-Cadmeans born, or have lain sucking out the sense of an Egyptian hieroglyph as long as the pyramids will last, before they should find it. These pests worrit me at business, and in all its intervals, perplexing my accounts, poisoning my little salutary warming-time at the fire, puzzling my paragraphs if I take a newspaper, cramming in between my own free thoughts and a column of figures, which had come to an amicable compromise but for them. Their noise ended, one of them, as I said, accompanies me home, lest I should be solitary for a moment; he at length takes his welcome leave at the door; up I go, mutton on table, hungry as hunter, hope to forget my cares, and bury them in the agreeable abstraction of mastication; knock at the door, in comes Mr. Hazlitt, or Mr. Martin Burney, or Morgan Demigorgon, or my brother, or somebody, to prevent my eating alone—a process absolutely necessary to my poor wretched digestion. O the pleasure of eating alone!—eating my dinner alone! let me think of it. But in they come, and make it absolutely necessary that I should open a bottle of orange; for my meat turns into stone when any one dines with me, if I have not wine. Wine can mollify stones; then *that* wine turns into acidity, acerbity, misanthropy, a hatred of my interrupters—(God bless 'em! I love some of 'em dearly), and with the hatred, a still greater aversion to their going away. Bad is the dead sea they bring upon me, choking and deadening, but worse is the deader dry sand they leave me on, if they go before bed-time. Come never, I would say to these spoilers of my dinner; but if you come, never go! The fact is, this interruption does not happen very often; but every time it comes by surprise, that present bane of my life, orange wine, with all its dreary stifling consequences, follows. Evening company I should always like had I any mornings, but I am saturated with human faces (*divine* forsooth!) and voices all the golden morning; and five evenings in a week would be as much as I should covet to be in company; but I assure you that is a wonderful week in which I can get two, or one to myself. I am never C. L., but always C. L. & Co. He who thought it not good for man to be alone, preserve me from the more prodigious monstrosity of being never by myself! I forget bed-time, but even there these sociable frogs clamber up to annoy me. Once a week, generally some singular evening that, being alone, I go to bed at the hour I ought always to be a-bed; just close to my bed-room window is the club-room of a public-house, where a set of singers, I take them to be chorus singers of the two theatres, (it must be *both of them,*) begin their orgies. They are a set of fellows (as I conceive) who, being limited by their talents to the burthen of the song at the play-houses, in revenge have got the common popular airs by Bishop, or some cheap composer, arranged for choruses; that is, to be sung all in chorus. At least I never can catch any of the text of the plain song, nothing but the Babylonish choral howl at the tail on't. "That fury being quenched"—the howl I mean—a burden succeeds of shouts and clapping, and knocking on the table. At length overtasked nature drops under it, and escapes for a few hours into the society of the sweet silent creatures of dreams, which go away with mocks and mows at cockcrow. And then I think of the words Christabel's father used (bless me, I have dipt in the wrong ink!) to say every morning by the way of variety when he awoke:

> "Every knell, the Baron saith,
> Wakes us up to a world of death"—

or something like it. All I mean by this senseless interrupted tale is, that by my central situation I am a little over-companied. Not that I have any animosity against the good creatures that are so anxious to drive away the harpy solitude from me. I like 'em, and cards, and a cheerful glass; but I mean merely to give you an idea, between office confinement and after-office society, how little time I can call my own. I mean only to draw a picture, not to make an inference. I would not that I know of have it otherwise. I only wish sometimes I could exchange some of my faces and voices for the faces and voices which a late visitation brought most welcome, and carried away, leaving regret, but more pleasure, even a kind of gratitude, at being so often favoured with that kind northern visitation. My London faces and noises don't hear me—I mean no disrespect, or I should explain myself, that instead of their return 220 times a year, and the return of W. W., &c., seven times in 104 weeks, some more equal distribution might be found. I have scarce room to put in Mary's kind love, and my poor name,

C. Lamb.

Letter to Samuel Taylor Coleridge, March 9, 1822

Dear Coleridge,—It gives me great satisfaction to hear that the pig turned out so well: they are interesting creatures at a certain age. What a pity such buds should blow out into the maturity of rank bacon! You had all some of the crackling and brain sauce. Did you remember to rub it with butter, and gently dredge it a little, just before the crisis? Did the eyes come away kindly with no Œdipean avulsion? Was the crackling the colour of the ripe pomegranate? Had you no complement of boiled neck of mutton before it, to blunt the edge of delicate desire? Did you flesh maiden teeth in it? Not that *I* sent the pig, or can form the remotest guess what part Owen could play in the business. I never knew him give any thing away in my life. He would not begin with strangers. I suspect the pig, after all, was meant for me; but at the unlucky juncture of time being absent, the present somehow went round to Highgate. To confess an honest truth, a pig is one of those things which I could never think of sending away. Teal, widgeon, snipes, barndoor fowls, ducks, geese—your tame villatic things—Welsh mutton, collars of brawn, sturgeon, fresh or pickled, your potted char, Swiss cheeses, French pies, early grapes, muscadines, I impart as freely unto my friends as to myself. They are but self-extended; but pardon me if I stop somewhere. Where the fine feeling of benevolence giveth a higher smack than the sensual rarity, there my friends (or any good man) may command me; but pigs are pigs, and I myself therein am nearest to myself. Nay, I should think it an affront, an undervaluing done to Nature who bestowed such a boon upon me, if in a churlish mood I parted with the precious gift. One of the bitterest pangs of remorse I ever felt was when a child—when my kind old aunt had strained her pocket-strings to bestow a sixpenny whole plumcake upon me. In my way home through the Borough I met a venerable old man, not a mendicant, but thereabouts; a look-beggar, not a verbal petitionist; and in the coxcombry of taught charity I gave away the cake to him. I walked on a little in all the pride of an Evangelical peacock, when of a sudden my old aunt's kindness crossed me; the sum it was to her; the pleasure she had a right to expect that I—not the old imposter—should take in eating her cake; the ingratitude by which, under the colour of a Christian virtue, I had frustrated her cherished purpose. I sobbed, wept, and took it to heart so grievously, that I think I never suffered the like; and I was right. It was a piece of unfeeling hypocrisy, and it proved a lesson to me ever after. The cake has long been masticated, consigned to the dung-hill with the ashes of that unseasonable pauper.

But when Providence, who is better to us all than our aunts, gives me a pig, remembering my temptation and my fall, I shall endeavour to act towards it more in the spirit of the donor's purpose.

Yours (short of pig) to command in every thing.

C. L.

Letter to Henry Crabbe Robinson, January 20, 1827

Colebrooke Row, Islington,
Saturday, 20th Jan., 1827.

DEAR ROBINSON,—I called upon you this morning, and found that you were gone to visit a dying friend. I had been upon a like errand. Poor Norris has been lying dying for now almost a week, such is the penalty we pay for having enjoyed a strong constitution! Whether he knew me or not, I know not; or whether he saw me through his poor glazed eyes; but the group I saw about him I shall not forget. Upon the bed, or about it, were assembled his wife and two daughters, and poor deaf Richard, his son, looking doubly stupified. There they were, and seem to have been sitting all the week. I could only reach out a hand to Mrs. Norris. Speaking was impossible in that mute chamber. By this time I hope it is all over with him. In him I have a loss the world cannot make up. He was my friend and my father's friend all the life I can remember. I seem to have made foolish friendships ever since. Those are friendships which outlive a second generation. Old as I am waxing, in his eyes I was still the child he first knew me. To the last he called me Charley. I have none to call me Charley now. He was the last link that bound me to the Temple. You are but of yesterday In him seem to have died the old plainness of manners and singleness of heart. Letters he knew nothing of, nor did his reading extend beyond the pages of the *Gentleman's Magazine.* Yet there was a pride of literature about him from being amongst books (he was librarian), and from some scraps of doubtful Latin which he had picked up in his office of entering students, that gave him very diverting airs of pedantry. Can I forget the erudite look with which, when he had been in vain trying to make out a black-letter text of Chaucer in the Temple Library, he laid it down and told me that—"in those old books, Charley, there is sometimes a deal of very indifferent spelling"; and seemed to console himself in the reflection! His jokes, for he had his jokes, are now ended· but they were old trusty perennials, staples that pleased after *decies repetita,* and were always as good as new. One song he had, which was reserved for the night of Christmas Day, which we always spent in the

Temple. It was an old thing, and spoke of the flat bottoms of our foes, and the possibility of their coming over in darkness, and alluded to threats of an invasion many years blown over; and when he came to the part—

> "We'll still make 'em run, and we'll still make 'em sweat,
> In spite of the Devil and *Brussels Gazette*,"

his eyes would sparkle as with the freshness of an impending event. And what is the *Brussels Gazette* now? I cry while I enumerate these trifles. "How shall we tell them in a stranger's ear?" His poor good girls will now have to receive their afflicted mother in an unsuccessful hovel in an obscure village in Herts, where they have been long struggling to make a school without effect; and poor deaf Richard, and the more helpless for being so, is thrown on the wide world.

My first motive in writing, and indeed in calling on you, was to ask if you were enough acquainted with any of the Benchers to lay a plain statement before them of the circumstances of the family. I almost fear not, for you are of another hall. But if you can oblige me and my poor friend, who is now insensible to any favours, pray exert yourself. You cannot say too much good of poor Norris and his poor wife.

Yours ever,

CHARLES LAMB.

BENJAMIN ROBERT HAYDON (1786-1846)

From THE AUTOBIOGRAPHY

An Evening with Charles Lamb

ON December 28th the immortal dinner came off in my painting-room, with Jerusalem towering up behind us as a background. Wordsworth was in fine cue, and we had a glorious set-to—on Homer, Shakespeare, Milton, and Virgil. Lamb got exceedingly merry, and exquisitely witty; and his fun, in the midst of Wordsworth's solemn intonations of oratory, was like the sarcasm and wit of the fool in the intervals of Lear's passion. He made a speech and voted me absent, and made them drink my health. "Now," said Lamb, "you old lake poet, you rascally poet, why do you call Voltaire dull?" We all defended Wordsworth, and affirmed there was a state of mind when Voltaire would be dull. "Well," said Lamb, "here's Voltaire—the Messiah of the French nation—and a very proper one too."

He then in a strain of humour beyond description abused me for putting Newton's head into my picture—"a fellow," said he, "who believed nothing unless it was as clear as the three sides of a triangle." And then he and Keats agreed that he had destroyed all the poetry of the rainbow, by reducing it to the prismatic colours. It was impossible to resist him, and we all drank "Newton's health, and confusion to mathematics." It was delightful to see the good humour of Wordsworth in giving in to all our frolics without affectation, and laughing as heartily as the best of us.

By this time other friends joined, amongst them poor Ritchie, who was going to penetrate by Fezzan to Timbuctoo. I introduced him to all as "a gentleman going to Africa." Lamb seemed to take no notice; but all of a sudden he roared out "Which is the gentleman we are going to lose?" We then drank the victim's health, in which Ritchie joined.

In the morning of this delightful day, a gentleman, a perfect stranger, had called on me. He said he knew my friends, had an enthusiasm for Wordsworth, and begged I would procure him the happiness of an introduction. He told me he was a Comptroller of Stamps, and often had correspondence with the poet. I thought it a liberty; but still, as he seemed a gentleman, I told him he might come.

When we retired to tea we found the Comptroller. In introducing him to Wordsworth I forgot to say who he was. After a little time the Comptroller looked down, looked up, and said to Wordsworth, "Don't you think, sir, Milton was a great genius?" Keats looked at me, Wordsworth looked at the Comptroller. Lamb, who was dozing by the fire, turned round and said, "Pray, sir, did you say Milton was a great genius?" "No, sir, I asked Mr. Wordsworth if he were not." "Oh," said Lamb, "then you are a silly fellow." "Charles! my dear Charles!" said Wordsworth; but Lamb, perfectly innocent of the confusion he had created, was off again by the fire.

After an awful pause the Comptroller said, "Don't you think Newton a great genius?" I could not stand it any longer. Keats put his head into my books. Ritchie squeezed in a laugh. Wordsworth seemed asking himself, "Who is this?" Lamb got up and taking a candle, said, "Sir, will you allow me to look at your phrenological development?" He then turned his back on the poor man, and at every question of the Comptroller he chanted—

"Diddle, diddle, dumpling, my son John
Went to bed with his breeches on."

The man in office finding Wordsworth did not know who he was, said in a spasmodic and half-chuckling anticipation of assured victory, "I have had the honour of some correspondence with you, Mr. Wordsworth." "With me, sir?" said Wordsworth, "not that I remember." "Don't you, sir? I am a Comptroller of Stamps." There was a dead silence; the Comptroller evidently thinking that was enough. While we were waiting for Wordsworth's reply, Lamb sung out—

"Hey diddle diddle,
The cat and the fiddle."

"My dear Charles!" said Wordsworth.

"Diddle, diddle, dumpling, my son John,"

chanted Lamb; and then rising, exclaimed, "Do let me have another look at that gentleman's organs." Keats and I hurried Lamb into the painting-room, shut the door, and gave way to inextinguishable laughter. Monkhouse followed and tried to get Lamb away. We went back, but the Comptroller was irreconcilable. We soothed and smiled, and asked him to supper. He stayed, though his dignity was sorely affected. However, being a good-natured man, we parted all in good humour, and no ill effects followed.

All the while, until Monkhouse succeeded, we could hear Lamb struggling in the painting-room and calling at intervals, "Who is that fellow? Allow me to see his organs once more."

JANE AUSTEN (1775-1817)

From Pride and Prejudice

An Eligible Newcomer

It is a truth universally acknowledged, that a single man in possession of a good fortune must be in want of a wife.

However little known the feelings or views of such a man may be on his first entering a neighborhood, this truth is so well fixed in the minds of the surrounding families, that he is considered as the rightful property of some one or other of their daughters.

"My dear Mr. Bennet," said his lady to him one day, "have you heard that Netherfield Park is let at last?"

Mr. Bennet replied that he had not.

"But it is," returned she; "for Mrs. Long has just been here and she told me all about it."

Mr. Bennet made no answer.

"Do not you want to know who has taken it?" cried his wife impatiently.

"*You* want to tell me and I have no objection to hearing it."

This was invitation enough.

"Why, my dear, you must know, Mrs. Long says that Netherfield is taken by a young man of large fortune from the north of England; that he came down on Monday in a chaise and four to see the place, and was so much delighted with it, that he agreed with Mr. Morris immediately; that he is to take possession before Michaelmas, and some of his servants are to be in the house by the end of next week."

"What is his name?"

"Bingley."

"Is he married or single?"

"Oh! single, my dear, to be sure! A single man of large fortune; four or five thousand a year. What a fine thing for our girls!"

"How so? how can it affect them?"

"My dear Mr. Bennet," replied his wife, "how can you be so tiresome! you must know that I am thinking of his marrying one of them."

"Is that his design in settling here?"

"Design! nonsense, how can you talk so! But it is very likely that he *may* fall in love with one of them, and therefore you must visit him as soon as he comes."

"I see no occasion for that. You and the girls may go, or you may send them by themselves, which perhaps will be still better, for as you are as handsome as any of them, Mr. Bingley might like you the best of the party."

"My dear, you flatter me. I certainly *have* had my share of beauty, but I do not pretend to be anything extraordinary now. When a woman has five grown-up daughters, she ought to give over thinking of her own beauty."

"In such cases, a woman has not often much beauty to think of."

"But, my dear, you must indeed go and see Mr. Bingley when he comes into the neighborhood."

"It is more than I engage for, I assure you."

"But consider your daughters. Only think what an establishment it would be for one of them. Sir William and Lady Lucas are determined to go, merely on that account, for in general, you know, they visit no newcomers. Indeed you must go, for it will be impossible for *us* to visit him if you do not."

"You are over-scrupulous, surely. I dare say Mr. Bingley will be very glad to see you; and I will send a few lines by you to assure him of my hearty consent to his marrying whichever he chooses of the girls: though I must throw in a good word for my little Lizzy."

"I desire you will do no such thing. Lizzy is not a bit better than the others; and I am sure she is not half so handsome as Jane, nor half so good-humored as Lydia. But you are always giving *her* the preference."

"They have none of them much to recommend them," replied he; "they are all silly and ignorant, like other girls; but Lizzy has something more of quickness than her sisters."

"Mr. Bennet, how can you abuse your own children in such a way! You take delight in vexing me. You have no compassion on my poor nerves."

"You mistake me, my dear. I have a high respect for your nerves. They are my old friends. I have heard you mention them with consideration these twenty years at least."

"Ah! you do not know what I suffer."

"But I hope you will get over it, and live to see many young men of four thousand a-year come into the neighborhood."

"It will be no use to us, if twenty such should come, since you will not visit them."

"Depend upon it, my dear, that when there are twenty, I will visit them all."

Mr. Bennet was so odd a mixture of quick parts, sarcastic humor, reserve, and caprice, that the experience of three-and-twenty years had been insufficient to make his wife understand his character. *Her* mind was less difficult to develop. She was a woman of mean understanding, little information, and uncertain temper. When she was discontented, she fancied herself nervous. The business of her life was to get her daughters married; its solace was visiting and news.

Mr. Bennet was among the earliest of those who waited on Mr. Bingley. He had always intended to visit him, though to the last always assuring his wife that he should not go; and till the evening after the visit was paid she had no knowledge of it. It was then disclosed in the following manner:—Observing his second daughter employed in trimming a hat, he suddenly addressed her with,

"I hope Mr. Bingley will like it, Lizzy."

"We are not in a way to know *what* Mr. Bingley likes," said her mother resentfully, "since we are not to visit."

"But you forget, mamma," said Elizabeth, "that we shall meet him at the assemblies, and that Mrs. Long has promised to introduce him."

"I do not believe Mrs. Long will do any such thing. She has two nieces of her own. She is a selfish, hypocritical woman, and I have no opinion of her."

"No more have I," said Mr. Bennett; "and I am glad to find that you do not depend on her serving you."

Mrs. Bennet deigned not to make any reply, but unable to contain herself, began scolding one of her daughters.

"Don't keep coughing so, Kitty, for Heaven's sake! Have a little compassion on my nerves. You tear them to pieces."

"Kitty has no discretion in her coughs," said her father; "she times them ill."

"I do not cough for my own amusement," replied Kitty fretfully. "When is your next ball to be, Lizzy?"

"To-morrow fortnight."

"Aye, so it is," cried her mother, "and Mrs. Long does not come back till the day before; so it will be impossible for her to introduce him, for she will not know him herself."

"Then, my dear, you may have the advantage of your friend, and introduce Mr. Bingley to *her.*"

"Impossible, Mr. Bennet, impossible, when I am not acquainted with him myself; how can you be so teasing?"

"I honor your circumspection. A fortnight's acquaintance is certainly very little. One cannot know what a man really is by the end of a fortnight. But if *we* do not venture somebody else will; and after all, Mrs. Long and her nieces must stand their chance; and, therefore, as she will think it an act of kindness, if you decline the offer, I will take it on myself."

The girls stared at their father. Mrs. Bennet said only, "Nonsense, nonsense!"

"What can be the meaning of that emphatic exclamation?" cried he. "Do you consider the forms of introduction, and the stress that is laid on them, as nonsense? I cannot quite agree with you *there.* What say you, Mary? for you are a young lady of deep reflection, I know, and read great books and make extracts."

Mary wished to say something very sensible, but knew not how.

"While Mary is adjusting her ideas," he continued, "let us return to Mr. Bingley."

"I am sick of Mr. Bingley," cried his wife.

"I am sorry to hear *that;* but why did not you tell me so before? If I had known as much this morning I certainly would not have called on him. It is very unlucky; but as I have actually paid the visit, we cannot escape the acquaintance now."

The astonishment of the ladies was just what he wished; that of Mrs. Bennet perhaps surpassing the rest; though, when the first tumult of joy was over, she began to declare that it was what she had expected all the while.

"How good it was in you, my dear Mr. Bennet! But I knew I should persuade you at last. I was sure you loved your girls too well to neglect such an acquaintance. Well, how pleased I am! and it is such a good joke, too, that you should have gone this morning and never said a word about it till now."

"Now, Kitty, you may cough as much as you choose," said Mr. Bennet; and, as he spoke, he left the room, fatigued with the raptures of his wife.

"What an excellent father you have, girls!" said she, when the door was shut. "I do not know how you will ever make him amends for his kindness; or me either, for that matter. At our time of life it is not so pleasant, I can tell you, to be making new acquaintance every day; but for your sakes, we would do anything. Lydia, my love, though you *are* the youngest, I dare say Mr. Bingley will dance with you at the next ball."

"Oh!" said Lydia stoutly, "I am not afraid; for though I *am* the youngest, I'm the tallest."

The rest of the evening was spent in conjecturing how soon he would return Mr. Bennet's visit, and determining when they should ask him to dinner.

An Offer of Marriage

Mr. Collins is a distant cousin who is to inherit the property, by entail of the Bennets. He has come to marry one of the Bennets and in that way soften the blow of inheriting the property which might otherwise go to the girls. He is a disagreeable compound of pompous pride and servility; about as unsuitable a match as possible for Elizabeth.

THE next day opened a new scene at Longbourn. Mr. Collins made his declaration in form. Having resolved to do it without loss of time, as his leave of absence extended only to the following Saturday, and having no feelings of diffidence to make it distressing to himself even at the moment, he set about it in a very orderly manner, with all the observances, which he supposed a regular part of the business. On finding Mrs. Bennet, Elizabeth, and one of the younger girls together, soon after breakfast, he addressed the mother in these words: "May

I hope, madam, for your interest with your fair daughter Elizabeth, when I solicit for the honor of a private audience with her in the course of this morning?"

Before Elizabeth had time for anything but a blush of surprise, Mrs. Bennet instantly answered, "Oh dear!—Yes—certainly. I am sure Lizzy will be very happy—I am sure she can have no objection. Come Kitty, I want you upstairs." And, gathering her work together, she was hastening away, when Elizabeth called out,

"Dear ma'am, do not go. I beg you will not go. Mr. Collins must excuse me. He can have nothing to say to me that anybody need not hear. I am going away myself."

"No, no, nonsense, Lizzy. I desire you will stay where you are." And upon Elizabeth's seeming really, with vexed and embarrassed looks, about to escape, she added, "Lizzy, I *insist* upon your staying and hearing Mr. Collins."

Elizabeth would not oppose such an injunction—and a moment's consideration making her also sensible that it would be wisest to get it over as soon and as quietly as possible, she sat down again, and tried to conceal, by incessant employment, the feelings which were divided between distress and diversion. Mrs. Bennet and Kitty walked off, and as soon as they were gone Mr. Collins began.

"Believe me, my dear Miss Elizabeth, that your modesty, so far from doing you any disservice, rather adds to your other perfections. You would have been less amiable in my eyes had there *not* been this little unwillingness; but allow me to assure you, that I have your respected mother's permission for this address. You can hardly doubt the purport of my discourse, however your natural delicacy may lead you to dissemble; my attentions have been too marked to be mistaken. Almost as soon as I entered the house, I singled you out as the companion of my future life. But before I am run away with by my feelings on this subject, perhaps it would be advisable for me to state my reasons for marrying—and, moreover, for coming into Hertfordshire with the design of selecting a wife, as I certainly did."

The idea of Mr. Collins, with all his solemn composure, being run away with by his feelings, made Elizabeth so near laughing, that she could not use the short pause he allowed in any attempt to stop him farther, and he continued:—

"My reasons for marrying are, first, that I think it a right thing for every clergyman in easy circumstances (like myself) to set the example of matrimony in his parish; secondly, that I am convinced it will add very greatly to my happiness! and thirdly—which perhaps I ought to have mentioned earlier, that it is the particular advice and recommendation of the very noble lady whom I have the honor of calling patroness. Twice has she condescended to give me her opinion (unasked too!) on this subject; and it was but the very Saturday night before I left Hunsford—between our pools at quadrille, while Mrs. Jenkinson was arranging Miss de Bourgh's footstool, that she said, 'Mr. Collins, you must marry. A clergyman like you must marry.—Choose properly, choose a gentlewoman for *my* sake; and for your *own,* let her be an active, useful sort of person, not brought up high, but able to make a small income go a good way. This is my advice. Find such a woman as soon as you can, bring her to Hunsford, and I will visit her.' Allow me, by the way, to observe, my fair cousin, that I do not reckon the notice and kindness of Lady Catherine de Bourgh as among the least of the advantages in my power to offer. You will find her manners beyond anything I can describe; and your wit and vivacity, I think, must be acceptable to her, especially when tempered with the silence and respect which her rank will inevitably excite. Thus much for my general intention in favor of matrimony; it remains to be told why my views were directed to Longbourn instead of my own neighborhood, where I assure you there are many amiable young women. But the fact is, that being, as I am, to inherit this estate after the death of your honored father (who, however, may live many years longer), I could not satisfy myself without resolving to choose a wife from among his daughters, that the loss to them might be as little as possible, when the melancholy event takes place—which, however, as I have already said, may not be for several years. This has been my motive, my fair cousin, and I flatter myself it will not sink me in your esteem. And now nothing remains for me but to assure you in the most animated language of the violence of my affection. To fortune I am perfectly indifferent, and shall make no demand of that nature on your father, since I am well aware that it could not be complied with; and that one thousand pounds in the 4 per cents., which will not be yours till after your mother's decease, is all that you may ever be entitled to. On that head, therefore, I shall be uniformly silent; and you may assure yourself that no ungenerous reproach shall ever pass my lips when we are married."

It was absolutely necessary to interrupt him now.

"You are too hasty, sir," she cried. "You forget that I have made no answer. Let me do it without further loss of time. Accept my thanks for the compliment you are paying me. I am very sensible of the honor of your proposals, but it is impossible for me to do otherwise than decline them."

"I am not now to learn," replied Mr. Collins, with a formal wave of the hand, "that it is usual with young ladies to reject the addresses of the man whom they secretly mean to accept, when he first applies for their favor; and that sometimes the refusal is repeated a second or even a third time. I am therefore by no means discouraged by what you have just said, and shall hope to lead you to the altar ere long."

"Upon my word, sir," cried Elizabeth, "your hope is rather an extraordinary one after my declaration. I do assure you that I am not one of those young ladies (if such young ladies there are) who are so daring as to risk their happiness on the chance of being asked a second time. I am perfectly serious in my refusal. You could not make *me* happy, and I am convinced that I am the last woman in the world who would make *you* so. Nay, were your friend Lady Catherine to know me, I am persuaded she would find me in every respect ill qualified for the situation."

"Were it certain that Lady Catherine would think so," said Mr. Collins very gravely—"but I cannot imagine that her ladyship would at all disapprove of you. And you may be certain that when I have the honor of seeing her again, I shall speak in the highest terms of your modesty, economy, and other amiable qualifications."

"Indeed, Mr. Collins, all praise of me will be unnecessary. You must give me leave to judge for myself, and pay me the compliment of believing what I say. I wish you very happy and very rich, and by refusing your hand, do all in my power to prevent your being otherwise. In making me the offer, you must have satisfied the delicacy of your feelings with regard to my family, and may take possession of Longbourn estate whenever it falls, without any self-reproach. This matter may be considered, therefore, as finally settled." And rising as she thus spoke, she would have quitted the room, had not Mr. Collins thus addressed her:

"When I do myself the honor of speaking to you next on the subject, I shall hope to receive a more favorable answer than you have now given me; though I am far from accusing you of cruelty at present, because I know it to be the established custom of your sex to reject a man on the first application, and perhaps you have even now said as much to encourage my suit as would be consistent with the true delicacy of the female character."

"Really, Mr. Collins," cried Elizabeth with some warmth, "you puzzle me exceedingly. If what I have hitherto said can appear to you in the form of encouragement, I know not how to express my refusal in such a way as may convince you of its being one."

"You must give me leave to flatter myself, my dear cousin, that your refusal of my addresses is merely words of course. My reasons for believing it are briefly these:—It does not appear to me that my hand is unworthy your acceptance, or that the establishment I can offer would be any other than highly desirable. My situation in life, my connections with the family of De Bourgh, and my relationship to your own, are circumstances highly in my favor; and you should take it into further consideration, that in spite of your manifold attractions, it is by no means certain that another offer of marriage may ever be made you. Your portion is unhappily so small, that it will in all likelihood undo the effects of your loveliness and amiable qualifications. As I must therefore conclude that you are not serious in your rejection of me, I shall choose to attribute it to your wish of increasing my love by suspense, according to the usual practice of elegant females."

"I do assure you, sir, that I have no pretensions whatever to that kind of elegance which consists in tormenting a respectable man. I would rather be paid the compliment of being believed sincere. I thank you again and again for the honor you have done me in your proposals, but to accept them is absolutely impossible. My feelings in every respect forbid it. Can I speak plainer? Do not consider me now as an elegant female, intending to plague you, but as a rational creature, speaking the truth from her heart."

"You are uniformly charming!" cried he, with an air of awkward gallantry; "and I am persuaded that when sanctioned by the express authority of both your excellent parents, my proposals will not fail of being acceptable."

To such perseverance in wilful self-deception Elizabeth would make no reply, and immediately and in silence withdrew; determined, that if he persisted in considering her repeated refusals as flattering encouragement, to apply to her father, whose negative might be uttered in such a manner as must be decisive, and whose behavior at least could not be mistaken for the affectation and coquetry of an elegant female.

Mr. Collins was not left long to the silent contemplation of his successful love; for Mrs. Bennet, having dawdled about in the vestibule to watch for the end of the conference, no sooner saw Elizabeth open the door and with quick step pass her towards the staircase, than she entered the breakfast-room, and congratulated both him and herself in warm terms on the happy prospect of their nearer connection. Mr. Collins received and returned these felicitations with equal pleasure, and then proceeded to relate the particulars of their interview, with the result of which he trusted he had every reason to be satisfied, since the refusal which his cousin had steadfastly given him would naturally flow from her bashful modesty and the genuine delicacy of her character.

This information, however, startled Mrs. Bennet;—she would have been glad to be equally satisfied that her daughter had meant to encourage him by protesting against his proposals, but she dared not believe it, and could not help saying so.

"But, depend upon it, Mr. Collins," she added, "that Lizzy shall be brought to reason. I will speak to her about it myself directly. She is a very headstrong, foolish girl, and does not know her own interest; but I will *make* her know it."

"Pardon me for interrupting you, madam," cried Mr. Collins; "but if she is really headstrong and foolish, I know not whether she would altogether be a very desirable wife to a man in my situation, who naturally looks for happiness in the marriage state. If therefore she actually persists in rejecting my suit, perhaps it were better not to force her into accepting me, because if liable to such defects of temper, she could not contribute much to my felicity."

"Sir, you quite misunderstand me," said Mrs. Bennet, alarmed. "Lizzy is only headstrong in such matters as these. In everything else she is as good-natured a girl as ever lived. I will go directly to Mr. Bennet, and we shall very soon settle it with her, I am sure."

She would not give him time to reply, but hurrying instantly to her husband, called out as she entered the library, "Oh! Mr. Bennet, you are wanted immediately; we are all in an uproar. You must come and make Lizzy marry Mr. Collins, for she vows she will not have him, and if you do not make haste he will change his mind and not have *her*."

Mr. Bennet raised his eyes from his book as she entered, and fixed them on her face with a calm unconcern which was not in the least altered by her communication.

"I have not the pleasure of understanding you," said he, when she had finished her speech. "Of what are you talking?"

"Of Mr. Collins and Lizzy. Lizzy declares she will not have Mr. Collins, and Mr. Collins begins to say that he will not have Lizzy."

"And what am I to do on the occasion?—It seems a hopeless business."

"Speak to Lizzy about it yourself. Tell her that you insist upon her marrying him."

"Let her be called down. She shall hear my opinion."

Mrs. Bennet rang the bell, and Miss Elizabeth was summoned to the library.

"Come here, child," cried her father as she appeared. "I have sent for you on an affair of importance. I understand that Mr. Collins has made you an offer of marriage. Is it true?"

Elizabeth replied that it was.

"Very well—and this offer of marriage you have refused?"

"I have, sir."

"Very well. We now come to the point. Your mother insists upon your accepting it. Is it not so, Mrs. Bennet?"

"Yes, or I will never see her again."

"An unhappy alternative is before you, Elizabeth. From this day you must be a stranger to one of your parents. Your mother will never see you again if you do *not* marry Mr. Collins, and I will never see you again if you *do*."

Elizabeth could not but smile at such a conclusion of such a beginning; but Mrs. Bennet, who had persuaded herself that her husband regarded the affair as she wished, was excessively disappointed.

"What do you mean, Mr. Bennet, by talking in this way? You promised me to *insist* upon her marrying him."

"My dear," replied her husband, "I have two small favors to request. First, that you will allow me the free use of my understanding on the present occasion; and secondly, of my room. I shall be glad to have the library to myself as soon as may be."

Not yet, however, in spite of her disappointment in her husband, did Mrs. Bennet give up the point. She talked to Elizabeth again and again; coaxed and threatened her by turns. She endeavored to secure Jane in her interest; but Jane, with all possible mildness, declined interfering; and Elizabeth, sometimes with real earnestness, and sometimes with playful gaiety, replied to her attacks. Though her manner varied, however, her determination never did.

Mr. Collins, meanwhile, was meditating in solitude on what had passed. He thought too well of himself to comprehend on what motive his cousin could refuse him; and though his pride was hurt, he suffered in no other way. His regard for her was quite imaginary; and the possibility of her deserving her mother's reproach prevented his feeling any regret.

WILLIAM HAZLITT (1778-1830)

From THE FIGHT

THE day, as I have said, was fine for a December morning. The grass was wet, and the ground miry, and ploughed up with multitudinous feet, except that, within the ring itself, there was a spot of virgin-green closed in and unprofaned by vulgar tread, that shone with dazzling brightness in the mid-day sun. For it was now noon, and we had an hour to wait. This is the trying time. It is then the heart sickens, as you think what the two champions are about, and how short a time will determine their fate. After the first blow is struck, there is no opportunity for nervous apprehensions; you are swallowed up in the immediate interest of the scene—but

> "Between the acting of a dreadful thing
> And the first motion, all the interim is
> Like a phantasma, or a hideous dream."

I found it so as I felt the sun's rays clinging to my back, and saw the white wintry clouds sink below the verge of the horizon. "So," I thought, "my fairest hopes have faded from my sight!—so will the Gas-man's glory, or that of his adversary, vanish in an hour." The *swells* were parading in their white box-coats, the outer ring was cleared with some bruises on the heads and shins of the rustic assembly (for the *cockneys* had been distanced by the sixty-six miles); the time drew near, I had got a good stand; a bustle, a buzz, ran through the crowd, and from the opposite side entered Neate, between his second and bottle-holder. He rolled along, swathed in his loose great coat, his knock-knees bending under his huge bulk; and, with a modest cheerful air, threw his hat into the ring. He then just looked round, and began quietly to undress; when from the other side there was a similar rush and an opening made, and the Gas-man came forward with a conscious air of anticipated triumph, too much like the cock-of-the-walk. He strutted about more than became a hero, sucked oranges with a supercilious air, and threw away the skin with a toss of his head, and went up and looked at Neate, which was an act of supererogation. The only sensible thing he did was, as he strode away from the modern Ajax, to fling out his arms, as if he wanted to try whether they would do their work that day. By this time they had stripped, and presented a strong contrast in appearance. If Neate was like Ajax, "with Atlantean shoulders, fit to bear" the pugilistic reputation of all Bristol, Hickman might be compared to Diomed, light, vigorous, elastic, and his back glistened in the sun, as he moved about, like a panther's hide. There was now a dead pause—attention was awe-struck. Who at that moment, big with a great event, did not draw his breath short—did not feel his heart throb? All was ready. They tossed up for the sun, and the Gas-man won. They were led up to the *scratch*—shook hands, and went at it.

In the first round every one thought it was all over. After making play a short time, the Gas-man flew at his adversary like a tiger, struck five blows in as many seconds, three first, and then following him as he staggered back, two more, right and left, and down he fell, a mighty ruin. There was a shout, and I said, "There is no standing this." Neate seemed like a lifeless lump of flesh and bone, round which the Gas-man's blows played with the rapidity of electricity or lightning, and you imagined he would only be lifted up to be knocked down again. It was as if Hickman held a sword or a fire in that right hand of his, and directed it against an unarmed body. They met again, and Neate seemed, not cowed, but particularly cautious. I saw his teeth clenched together and his brows knit close against the sun. He held out both his arms at full length straight before him, like two sledge-hammers, and raised his left an inch or two higher. The Gas-man could not get over this guard—they struck mutually and fell, but without advantage on either side. It was the same in the next round; but the balance of power was thus restored—the fate of the battle was suspended. No one could tell how it would end. This was the only moment in which opinion was divided; for, in the next, the Gas-man aiming a mortal blow at his adversary's neck, with his right hand, and failing from the length he had to reach, the other returned it with his left at full swing, planted a tremendous blow on his cheek-bone and eyebrow, and made a red ruin of that side of his face. The Gas-man went down, and there was another shout—a roar of triumph, as the waves of fortune rolled tumultuously from side to side. This was a settler. Hickman got up, and "grinned horrible a ghastly smile," yet he was evidently dashed in his opinion of himself; it was the first time he had ever been so punished; all one side of his face was perfect scarlet, and his right eye was closed in dingy blackness, as he advanced to the fight, less confident, but still determined. After one or two rounds, not receiving another such remembrancer, he rallied and went at it with his former impetuosity. But in vain. His strength had been weakened,—his blows could not tell at such a distance,—he was obliged to fling himself at his adversary, and could not strike from his feet; and almost as regularly as he flew at him with his right hand, Neate warded the blow, or drew back out of its reach, and felled him with the return of his left. There was little cautious sparring—no half-hits—no tapping and trifling, none of the *petit-maitreship* of the art—they were almost all knock-down blows:—the fight was a good stand-up fight. The wonder was the half-minute time. If there had been a minute or more allowed between each round, it would have been intelligible how they should by degrees recover strength and resolution; but to see two men smashed to the ground, smeared with gore, stunned, senseless, the breath beaten out of their bodies; and then, before you recover from the shock, to see them rise up with new strength and courage, stand ready to inflict or receive mortal offense, and rush upon each other "like two clouds over the Caspian"—this is the most astonishing thing of all:—this is the high and heroic state of man! From this time forward the event became more certain every round; and about the twelfth it seemed as if it must have been over. Hickman generally stood with his back to me; but in the scuffle, he had changed positions, and Neate just then made a tremendous lunge at him, and hit him full in the face. It was doubtful whether he would fall backwards or forwards; he hung suspended for a second or two, and then fell back, throwing his hands in the air, and with his face lifted up to the sky. I never saw any thing more terrific than his aspect just before he fell. All traces of life, of natural expression, were gone from him. His face was like a human skull, a death's head, spouting blood. The eyes were filled with blood, the nose streamed with blood, the mouth gaped blood. He was not like an actual man, but like a preternatural, spectral appearance, or like one of the figures in Dante's *Inferno.* Yet he fought on after this for several rounds, still striking the first desperate blow, and Neate standing on the defensive, and using the same cautious guard to the last, as if he had still all his work to do; and it was not till the Gas-man was so stunned in the seventeenth or eighteenth round, that his senses forsook him, and he could not come to time, that the battle was declared over. Ye who despise the Fancy, do something to shew as much *pluck,* or as much self-possession as this, before you assume a superiority which you have never given a single proof of by any one action in the whole course of your lives!—When the Gas-man came to himself, the first words he uttered were, "Where am I? What is the matter?" "Nothing is the matter, Tom,—you have lost the battle, but you are the bravest man alive." And Jackson whispered to him, "I am collecting a purse for you, Tom."—Vain sounds, and unheard at that moment! Neate instantly went up and shook him cordially by the hand, and seeing some old acquaintance, began to flourish with his fists, calling out, "Ah you always said I couldn't fight—What do you think now?" But all in good humour, and without any appearance of arrogance; only it was evident Bill Neate was pleased that he had won the fight. When it was over, I asked Cribb if he did not think it was a good one? He said, *"Pretty well!"* The carrier-pigeons now mounted into the air, and one of them flew with the news of her husband's victory to the bosom of Mrs. Neate. Alas, for Mrs. Hickman!

GEORGE GORDON NOEL, LORD BYRON (1788-1824)

She Walks in Beauty

SHE walks in beauty, like the night
  Of cloudless climes and starry skies;
And all that's best of dark and bright
  Meet in her aspect and her eyes:
Thus mellow'd to that tender light
  Which heaven to gaudy day denies.

One shade the more, one ray the less,
  Had half impair'd the nameless grace
Which waves in every raven tress,
  Or softly lightens o'er her face;
Where thoughts serenely sweet express
  How pure, how dear their dwelling-place.

And on that cheek, and o'er that brow,
  So soft, so calm, yet eloquent,
The smiles that win, the tints that glow,
  But tell of days in goodness spent,
A mind at peace with all below,
  A heart whose love is innocent!

From DON JUAN

The Shipwreck

'TWAS twilight, and the sunless day went down
  Over the waste of waters; like a veil,
Which, if withdrawn, would but disclose the frown
  Of one whose hate is mask'd but to assail.
Thus to their hopeless eyes the night was shown,
  And grimly darkled o'er the faces pale,
And the dim desolate deep: twelve days had Fear
Been their familiar, and now Death was here.

Some trial had been making at a raft,
  With little hope in such a rolling sea,
A sort of thing at which one would have laugh'd,
  If any laughter at such times could be,
Unless with people who too much have quaff'd,
  And have a kind of wild and horrid glee,
Half epileptical, and half hysterical:—
Their preservation would have been a miracle.

At half-past eight o'clock, booms, hen-coops, spars,
  And all things, for a chance, had been cast loose
That still could keep afloat the struggling tars,
  For yet they strove, although of no great use:
There was no light in heaven but a few stars,
  The boats put off o'ercrowded with their crews;
She gave a heel, and then a lurch to port,
And, going down head foremost—sunk, in short.

Then rose from sea to sky the wild farewell—
  Then shriek'd the timid, and stood still the brave—
Then some leap'd overboard with dreadful yell,
  As eager to anticipate their grave;
And the sea yawn'd around her like a hell,
  And down she suck'd with her the whirling wave,
Like one who grapples with his enemy,
And strives to strangle him before he die.

And first one universal shriek there rush'd,
  Louder than the loud ocean, like a crash
Of echoing thunder; and then all was hush'd,
  Save the wild wind and the remorseless dash
Of billows; but at intervals there gush'd,
  Accompanied with a convulsive splash,
A solitary shriek, the bubbling cry
Of some strong swimmer in his agony.

Haidée

How long in his damp trance young Juan lay
He knew not, for the earth was gone for him,
And time had nothing more of night nor day
For his congealing blood, and senses dim;
And how this heavy faintness pass'd away
He knew not, till each painful pulse and limb,
And tingling vein, seem'd throbbing back to life,
For Death, though vanquish'd, still retired with strife.

His eyes he open'd, shut, again unclosed,
For all was doubt and dizziness; he thought
He still was in the boat, and had but dozed,
And felt again with his despair o'erwrought,
And wish'd it death in which he had reposed,
And then once more his feelings back were brought,
And slowly by his swimming eyes was seen
A lovely female face of seventeen.

'Twas bending close o'er his, and the small mouth
Seem'd almost prying into his for breath;
And chafing him, the soft warm hand of youth
Recall'd his answering spirits back from death;
And, bathing his chill temples, tried to soothe
Each pulse to animation, till beneath
Its gentle touch and trembling care, a sigh
To these kind efforts made a low reply.

Then was the cordial pour'd, and mantle flung
Around his scarce-clad limbs; and the fair arm
Raised higher the faint head which o'er it hung;
And her transparent cheek, all pure and warm,
Pillow'd his death-like forehead; then she wrung
His dewy curls, long drench'd by every storm;
And watch'd with eagerness each throb that drew
A sigh from his heaved bosom—and hers, too,

And lifting him with care into the cave,
The gentle girl, and her attendant,—one
Young, yet her elder, and of brow less grave,
And more robust of figure—then begun
To kindle fire, and as the new flames gave
Light to the rocks that roof'd them, which the sun
Had never seen, the maid, or whatsoe'er
She was, appear'd distinct, and tall, and fair.

Her brow was overhung with coins of gold,
That sparkled o'er the auburn of her hair,
Her clustering hair, whose longer locks were roll'd
In braids behind; and though her stature were
Even of the highest for a female mould,
They nearly reach'd her heel; and in her air
There was a something which bespoke command,
As one who was a lady in the land.

Her hair, I said, was auburn; but her eyes
Were black as death, their lashes the same hue,

Of downcast length, in whose silk shadow lies
  Deepest attraction; for when to the view
Forth from its raven fringe the full glance flies,
  Ne'er with such force the swiftest arrow flew;
'Tis as the snake late coil'd, who pours his length,
And hurls at once his venom and his strength.

Her brow was white and low, her cheek's pure dye
  Like twilight rosy still with the set sun;
Short upper lip—sweet lips! that make us sigh
  Ever to have seen such; for she was one
Fit for the model of a statuary
  (A race of mere impostors, when all's done—
I've seen much finer women, ripe and real,
Than all the nonsense of their stone ideal).

Lambro's Return

He saw his white walls shining in the sun,
  His garden trees all shadowy and green;
He heard his rivulet's light bubbling run,
  The distant dog-bark; and perceived between
The umbrage of the wood so cool and dun,
  The moving figures, and the sparkling sheen
Of arms (in the East all arm)—and various dyes
Of colour'd garbs, as bright as butterflies.

And still more nearly to the place advancing,
  Descending rather quickly the declivity,
Through the waved branches, o'er the greensward glancing,
  'Midst other indications of festivity,
Seeing a troop of his domestics dancing
  Like dervises, who turn as on a pivot, he
Perceived it was the Pyrrhic dance so martial,
To which the Levantines are very partial.

And further on a group of Grecian girls,
  The first and tallest her white kerchief waving,
Were strung together like a row of pearls,
  Link'd hand in hand, and dancing: each too having
Down her white neck long floating auburn curls—
  (The least of which would set ten poets raving);
Their leader sang—and bounded to her song,
With choral step and voice, the virgin throng.

And here, assembled cross-legg'd round their trays,
  Small social parties just begun to dine;
Pilaus and meats of all sorts met the gaze,
  And flasks of Samian and of Chian wine,
And sherbet cooling in the porous vase;
  Above them their dessert grew on its vine,
The orange and pomegranate nodding o'er
Dropp'd in their laps, scarce pluck'd, their mellow store.

A band of children, round a snow-white ram,
  There wreathe his venerable horns with flowers;
While peaceful as if still an unwean'd lamb,
  The patriarch of the flock all gently cowers

His sober head, majestically tame,
  Or eats from out the palm, or playful lowers
His brow, as if in act to butt, and then
Yielding to their small hands, draws back again.

Their classical profiles, and glittering dresses,
  Their large black eyes, and soft seraphic cheeks
Crimson as cleft pomegranates, their long tresses,
  The gesture which enchants, the eye that speaks,
The innocence which happy childhood blesses,
  Made quite a picture of these little Greeks;
So that the philosophical beholder
Sigh'd for their sakes—that they should e'er grow older.

Afar, a dwarf buffoon stood telling tales
  To a sedate grey circle of old smokers,
Of secret treasures found in hidden vales,
  Of wonderful replies from Arab jokers,
Of charms to make good gold and cure bad ails,
  Of rocks bewitch'd that open to the knockers,
Of magic ladies who, by one sole act,
Transform'd their lords to beasts (but that's a fact).

Here was no lack of innocent diversion
  For the imagination or the senses,
Song, dance, wine, music, stories from the Persian,
  All pretty pastimes in which no offence is;
But Lambro saw all these things with aversion,
  Perceiving in his absence such expenses,
Dreading that climax of all human ills,
The inflammation of his weekly bills.

Ah! what is man? what perils still environ
  The happiest mortals even after dinner—
A day of gold from out an age of iron
  Is all that life allows the luckiest sinner;
Pleasure (whene'er she sings, at least) 's a siren,
  That lures, to flay alive, the young beginner;
Lambro's reception at his people's banquet
Was such as fire accords to a wet blanket.

He—being a man who seldom used a word
  Too much, and wishing gladly to surprise
(In general he surprised men with the sword)
  His daughter—had not sent before to advise
Of his arrival, so that no one stirr'd;
  And long he paused to reassure his eyes,
In fact much more astonish'd than delighted,
To find so much good company invited.

He did not know (alas! how men will lie)
  That a report (especially the Greeks)
Avouch'd his death (such people never die),
  And put his house in mourning several weeks,—
But now their eyes and also lips were dry;
  The bloom, too, had return'd to Haidée's cheeks.
Her tears, too, being return'd into their fount,
She now kept house upon her own account.

Hence all this rice, meat, dancing, wine, and fiddling,
  Which turn'd the isle into a place of pleasure;

The servants all were getting drunk or
idling,
A life which made them happy beyond
measure.
Her father's hospitality seem'd middling,
Compared with what Haidée did with
his treasure;
'Twas wonderful how things went on improving,
While she had not one hour to spare
from loving.

Perhaps you think, in stumbling on this
feast,
He flew into a passion, and in fact
There was no mighty reason to be
pleased;
Perhaps you prophesy some sudden act,
The whip, the rack, or dungeon at the
least,
To teach his people to be more exact,
And that, proceeding at a very high rate,
He show'd the royal *penchants* of a
pirate.

You're wrong.—He was the mildest man-
ner'd man
That ever scuttled ship or cut a throat,
With such true breeding of a gentleman,
You never could divine his real thought,
No courtier could, and scarcely woman
can
Gird more deceit within a petticoat:
Pity he loved adventurous life's variety,
He was so great a loss to good society.

Haidée Again

Of all the dresses I select Haidée's:
She wore two jelicks—one was of pale
yellow;
Of azure, pink, and white was her
chemise—
'Neath which her breast heaved like a
little billow;
With buttons form'd of pearls as large
as peas,
All gold and crimson shone her jelick's
fellow,
And the striped white gauze baracan that
bound her,
Like fleecy clouds about the moon, flow'd
round her.

One large gold bracelet clasp'd each
lovely arm,
Lockless—so pliable from the pure gold
That the hand stretch'd and shut it with-
out harm,
The limb which it adorn'd its only
mould;
So beautiful—its very shape would charm,
And clinging as if loath to lose its hold,
The purest ore enclosed the whitest skin
That e'er by precious metal was held in.

Around, as princess of her father's land,
A like gold bar above her instep roll'd
Announced her rank; twelve rings were
on her hand;
Her hair was starr'd with gems; her
veil's fine fold
Below her breast was fasten'd with a
band
Of lavish pearls, whose worth could
scarce be told;
Her orange silk full Turkish trousers
furl'd
About the prettiest ankle in the world.

Her hair's long auburn waves down to
her heel
Flow'd like an Alpine torrent which
the sun
Dyes with his morning light,—and would
conceal
Her person if allow'd at large to run,
And still they seem'd resentfully to feel
The silken fillet's curb, and sought to
shun
Their bonds whene'er some Zephyr caught
began
To offer his young pinion as her fan.

Round her she made an atmosphere of
life,
The very air seem'd lighted from her
eyes,

They were so soft and beautiful, and rife
  With all we can imagine of the skies,
And pure as Psyche ere she grew a wife—
  Too pure even for the purest human ties;
Her overpowering presence made you feel
  It would not be idolatry to kneel.

Her eyelashes, though dark as night, were tinged
  (It is the country's custom), but in vain;
For those large black eyes were so blackly fringed
  The glossy rebels mock'd the jetty stain,
And in their native beauty stood avenged:
  Her nails were touch'd with henna; but again
The power of art was turn'd to nothing, for
  They could not look more rosy than before.

Great Names

AND glory long has made the sages smile;
  'Tis something, nothing, words, illusion, wind—
Depending more upon the historian's style
  Than on the name a person leaves behind:
Troy owes to Homer what whist owes to Hoyle:
  The present century was growing blind
To the great Marlborough's skill in giving knocks,
  Until his late Life by Archdeacon Coxe.

Milton's the prince of poets—so we say;
  A little heavy, but no less divine:
An independent being in his day—
  Learn'd, pious, temperate in love and wine;
But his life falling into Johnson's way,
  We're told this great high priest of all the Nine
Was whipt at college—a harsh sire—odd spouse,
  For the first Mrs. Milton left his house.

All these are, *certes,* entertaining facts,
  Like Shakespeare's stealing deer, Lord Bacon's bribes;
Like Titus' youth, and Cæsar's earliest acts;
  Like Burns (whom Doctor Currie well describes);
Like Cromwell's pranks;—but although truth exacts
  These amiable descriptions from the scribes,
As most essential to their hero's story,
  They do not much contribute to his glory.

All are not moralists, like Southey, when
  He prated to the world of "Pantisocrasy;"
Or Wordsworth unexcised, unhired, who then
  Season'd his pedlar poems with democracy;
Or Coleridge, long before his flighty pen
  Let to the Morning Post its aristocracy;
When he and Southey, following the same path,
  Espoused two partners (milliners of Bath).

Such names at present cut a convict figure,
  The very Botany Bay in moral geography;
Their loyal treason, renegado rigour,
  Are good manure for their more bare biography;
Wordsworth's last quarto, by the way, is bigger
  Than any since the birthday of typography;
A drowsy frowzy poem, call'd the "Excursion,"
  Writ in a manner which is my aversion.

He there builds up a formidable dyke
  Between his own and others' intellect:
But Wordsworth's poem, and his followers, like
  Joanna Southcote's Shiloh, and her sect,

Are things which in this century don't strike
The public mind,—so few are the elect;
And the new births of both their stale virginities
Have proved but dropsies, taken for divinities.

We learn from Horace, "Homer sometimes sleeps;"
We feel without him, Wordsworth sometimes wakes,—
To show with what complacency he creeps,
With his dear *"Waggoners,"* around his lakes.
He wishes for "a boat" to sail the deeps—
Of ocean?—No, of air; and then he makes
Another outcry for "a little boat,"
And drivels seas to set it well afloat.

If he must fain sweep o'er the ethereal plain,
And Pegasus runs restive in his "Waggon,"
Could he not beg the loan of Charles's Wain?
Or pray Medea for a single dragon?
Or if, too classic for his vulgar brain,
He fear'd his neck to venture such a nag on,
And he must needs mount nearer to the moon,
Could not the blockhead ask for a balloon?

"Pedlars," and "Boats," and "Waggons!" Oh! ye shades
Of Pope and Dryden, are we come to this?
That trash of such sort not alone evades
Contempt, but from the bathos' vast abyss
Floats scumlike uppermost, and these Jack Cades
Of sense and song above your graves may hiss—
The "little boatman" and his "Peter Bell"
Can sneer at him who drew "Achitophel!"

London

THE sun went down, the smoke rose up, as from
A half-unquench'd volcano, o'er a space
Which well beseem'd the "Devil's drawing-room,"
As some have qualified that wondrous place:
But Juan felt, though not approaching *home,*
As one who, though he were not of the race,
Revered the soil, of those true sons the mother,
Who butcher'd half the earth, and bullied t'other.

A mighty mass of brick, and smoke, and shipping
Dirty and dusky, but as wide as eye
Could reach, with here and there a sail just skipping
In sight, then lost amidst the forestry
Of masts; a wilderness of steeples peeping
On tiptoe through their sea-coal canopy;
A huge, dun cupola, like a foolscap crown
On a fool's head—and there is London Town!

Aurora Raby

AND then there was—but why should I go on,
Unless the ladies should go off?—there was
Indeed a certain fair and fairy one,
Of the best class, and better than her class,—
Aurora Raby, a young star who shone
O'er life, too sweet an image for such glass,
A lovely being, scarcely form'd or moulded,
A rose with all its sweetest leaves yet folded;

Rich, noble, but an orphan; left an only
Child to the care of guardians good and kind;
But still her aspect had an air so lonely!
Blood is not water; and where shall we find
Feelings of youth like those which overthrown lie
By death, when we are left, alas! behind,
To feel, in friendless palaces, a home
Is wanting, and our best ties in the tomb?

Early in years, and yet more infantine
In figure, she had something of sublime
In eyes which sadly shone, as seraphs' shine.
All youth—but with an aspect beyond time;
Radiant and grave—as pitying man's decline;
Mournful—but mournful of another's crime;
She look'd as if she sat by Eden's door,
And grieved for those who could return no more.

She was a Catholic, too, sincere, austere,
As far as her own gentle heart allow'd,
And deem'd that fallen worship far more dear
Perhaps because 'twas fallen: her sires were proud
Of deeds and days when they had fill'd the ear
Of nations, and had never bent or bow'd
To novel power; and as she was the last,
She held their old faith and old feelings fast.

She gazed upon a world she scarcely knew,
As seeking not to know it; silent, lone,
As grows a flower, thus quietly she grew,
And kept her heart serene within its zone.
There was awe in the homage which she drew;
Her spirit seem'd as seated on a throne
Apart from the surrounding world, and strong
In its own strength—most strange in one so young!

Life

Between two worlds life hovers like a star,
'Twixt night and morn, upon the horizon's verge.
How little do we know that which we are!
How less what we may be! The eternal surge
Of time and tide rolls on, and bears afar
Our bubbles; as the old burst, new emerge,
Lash'd from the foam of ages; while the graves
Of empires heave but like some passing waves.

CHARLES WOLFE (1791-1823)

The Burial of Sir John Moore after Corunna

Not a drum was heard, not a funeral note,
As his corse to the rampart we hurried;
Not a soldier discharged his farewell shot
O'er the grave where our hero we buried.

We buried him darkly, at dead of night,
The sods with our bayonets turning;
By the struggling moonbeam's misty light,
And the lantern dimly burning.

No useless coffin enclosed his breast,
Not in sheet or in shroud we wound him,
But he lay like a warrior taking his rest,
With his martial cloak around him.

Few and short were the prayers we said,
And we spoke not a word of sorrow;
But we steadfastly gazed on the face that was dead,
And we bitterly thought of the morrow.

We thought, as we hollowed his narrow bed
And smoothed down his lonely pillow,
That the foe and stranger would tread o'er his head,
And we far away on the billow!

Lightly they'll talk of the spirit that's gone,
And o'er his cold ashes upbraid him;
But little he'll reck, if they let him sleep on
In the grave where a Briton has laid him.

But half of our weary task was done
When the clock struck the hour for retiring;
And we heard the distant and random gun
That the foe was sullenly firing.

Slowly and sadly we laid him down,
From the field of his fame fresh and gory;
We carved not a line, and we raised not a stone,
But we left him alone with his glory.

PERCY BYSSHE SHELLEY
(1792-1822)

Ozymandias

I MET a traveller from an antique land
Who said: Two vast and trunkless legs of stone
Stand in the desert. Near them, on the sand,
Half sunk, a shattered visage lies, whose frown,
And wrinkled lip, and sneer of cold command,
Tell that its sculptor well those passions read
Which yet survive, stamped on these lifeless things,
The hand that mocked them and the heart that fed:
And on the pedestal these words appear:
"My name is Ozymandias, king of kings:
Look on my works, ye Mighty, and despair!"
Nothing beside remains. Round the decay
Of that colossal wreck, boundless and bare
The lone and level sands stretch far away.

From PROMETHEUS UNBOUND

Asia's Song: My soul is an enchanted boat

MY soul is an enchanted boat,
Which, like a sleeping swan, doth float
Upon the silver waves of thy sweet singing;
And thine doth like an angel sit
Beside a helm conducting it,
Whilst all the winds with melody are ringing.
It seems to float ever, for ever,
Upon that many-winding river,
Between mountains, woods, abysses,
A paradise of wildernesses!
Till, like one in slumber bound,
Borne to the ocean, I float down, around,
Into a sea profound, of ever-spreading sound:

Meanwhile thy spirit lifts its pinions
In music's most serene dominions;
Catching the winds that fan that happy heaven.
And we sail on, away, afar,
Without a course, without a star,
But, by the instinct of sweet music driven;
Till through Elysian garden islets
By thee, most beautiful of pilots,
Where never mortal pinnace glided,
The boat of my desire is guided:
Realms where the air we breathe is love,

Which in the winds and on the waves
doth move,
Harmonizing this earth with what we
feel above.

We have passed Age's icy caves,
And Manhood's dark and tossing
waves,
And Youth's smooth ocean, smiling to
betray:
Beyond the glassy gulfs we flee
Of shadow-peopled Infancy,
Through Death and Birth, to a diviner
day;
A paradise of vaulted bowers,
Lit by downward-gazing flowers,
And watery paths that wind between
Wildernesses calm and green,
Peopled by shapes too bright to see,
And rest, having beheld; somewhat like
thee;
Which walk upon the sea, and chant
melodiously!

From THE CENCI

Song: False friend, wilt thou smile or weep

FALSE friend, wilt thou smile or
weep
When my life is laid asleep?
Little cares for a smile or a tear,
The clay-cold corpse upon the bier!
Farewell! Heigho!
What is this whispers low?
There is a snake in thy smile, my
dear;
And bitter poison within thy tear.

Sweet sleep, were death like to thee,
Or if thou couldst mortal be,
I would close these eyes of pain;
When to wake? Never again.
O World! Farewell!
Listen to the passing bell!
It says, thou and I must part,
With a light and a heavy heart.

The Cloud

I BRING fresh showers for the thirsting
flowers,
From the seas and the streams;
I bear light shade for the leaves when
laid
In their noonday dreams.
From my wings are shaken the dews that
waken
The sweet buds every one,
When rocked to rest on their mother's
breast,
As she dances about the sun.
I wield the flail of the lashing hail,
And whiten the green plains under,
And then again I dissolve it in rain,
And laugh as I pass in thunder.

I sift the snow on the mountains below,
And their great pines groan aghast,
And all the night 'tis my pillow white,
While I sleep in the arms of the
blast.
Sublime on the towers of my skiey
bowers,
Lightning, my pilot, sits,
In a cavern under is fettered the thunder,
It struggles and howls at fits;
Over earth and ocean, with gentle motion,
This pilot is guiding me,
Lured by the love of the genii that
move
In the depths of the purple sea;
Over the rills, and the crags, and the
hills,
Over the lakes and the plains,
Wherever he dream, under mountain or
stream,
The Spirit he loves remains;
And I all the while bask in heaven's blue
smile,
Whilst he is dissolving in rains.

The sanguine sunrise, with his meteor
eyes,
And his burning plumes outspread,
Leaps on the back of my sailing rack,
When the morning star shines dead,

As on the jag of a mountain crag,
Which an earthquake rocks and swings,
An eagle alit one moment may sit
In the light of its golden wings.
And when sunset may breathe, from the lit sea beneath,
Its ardours of rest and of love,
And the crimson pall of eve may fall
From the depth of heaven above,
With wings folded I rest, on mine airy nest,
As still as a brooding dove.

That orbèd maiden with white fire laden,
Whom mortals call the moon,
Glides glimmering o'er my fleece-like floor,
By the midnight breezes strewn;
And wherever the beat of her unseen feet,
Which only the angels hear,
May have broken the woof of my tent's thin roof,
The stars peep behind her and peer;
And I laugh to see them whirl and flee,
Like a swarm of golden bees,
When I widen the rent in my wind-built tent,
Till the calm rivers, lakes, and seas,
Like strips of the sky fallen through me on high,
Are each paved with the moon and these.

I bind the sun's throne with a burning zone,
And the moon's with a girdle of pearl;
The volcanoes are dim, and the stars reel and swim,
When the whirlwinds my banner unfurl.
From cape to cape, with a bridge-like shape,
Over a torrent sea,
Sunbeam-proof, I hang like a roof,
The mountains its columns be.
The triumphal arch through which I march
With hurricane, fire, and snow,
When the powers of the air are chained to my chair,
Is the million-coloured bow;
The sphere-fire above its soft colours wove,
While the moist earth was laughing below.

I am the daughter of earth and water,
And the nursling of the sky;
I pass through the pores of the ocean and shores;
I change, but I cannot die.
For after the rain, when with never a stain
The pavilion of heaven is bare,
And the winds and sunbeams, with their convex gleams,
Build up the blue dome of air,
I silently laugh at my own cenotaph.
And out of the caverns of rain,
Like a child from the womb, like a ghost from the tomb,
I arise and unbuild it again.

To a Skylark

HAIL to thee, blithe spirit!
Bird thou never wert,
That from heaven, or near it,
Pourest thy full heart
In profuse strain of unpremeditated art.

Higher still and higher
From the earth thou springest
Like a cloud of fire;
The blue deep thou wingest,
And singing still dost soar, and soaring ever singest.

In the golden lightning
Of the sunken sun,
O'er which clouds are brightning,
Thou dost float and run;
Like an unbodied joy whose race is just begun.

The pale purple even
Melts around thy flight;
Like a star of heaven,
In the broad daylight
Thou art unseen, but yet I hear thy shrill delight,

Keen as are the arrows
Of that silver sphere,
Whose intense lamp narrows
In the white dawn clear,
Until we hardly see, we feel that it is there.

All the earth and air
With thy voice is loud,
As, when night is bare,
From one lonely cloud
The moon rains out her beams, and heaven is overflowed.

What thou art we know not;
What is most like thee?
From rainbow clouds there flow not
Drops so bright to see,
As from thy presence showers a rain of melody.

Like a poet hidden
In the light of thought,
Singing hymns unbidden,
Till the world is wrought
To sympathy with hopes and fears it heeded not:

Like a high-born maiden
In a palace-tower,
Soothing her love-laden
Soul in secret hour
With music sweet as love, which overflows her bower:

Like a glow-worm golden
In a dell of dew,
Scattering unbeholden
Its aërial hue
Among the flowers and grass, which screen it from the view:

Like a rose embowered
In its own green leaves,
By warm winds deflowered,
Till the scent it gives
Makes faint with too much sweet these heavy-wingèd thieves:

Sound of vernal showers
On the twinkling grass,
Rain-awakened flowers,
All that ever was
Joyous, and clear, and fresh, thy music doth surpass:

Teach us, sprite or bird,
What sweet thoughts are thine:
I have never heard
Praise of love or wine
That panted forth a flood of rapture so divine.

Chorus Hymeneal,
Or triumphal chaunt,
Matched with thine would be all
But an empty vaunt,
A thing wherein we feel there is some hidden want.

What objects are the fountains
Of thy happy strain?
What fields, or waves, or mountains?
What shapes of sky or plain?
What love of thine own kind? what ignorance of pain?

With thy clear keen joyance
Languor cannot be:
Shadow of annoyance
Never came near thee:
Thou lovest; but ne'er knew love's sad satiety.

Waking or asleep,
Thou of death must deem
Things more true and deep
Than we mortals dream,
Or how could thy notes flow in such a crystal stream?

We look before and after,
And pine for what is not:
Our sincerest laughter
With some pain is fraught;
Our sweetest songs are those that tell of saddest thought.

Yet if we could scorn
Hate, and pride, and fear:
If we were things born
Not to shed a tear,
I know not how thy joy we ever should come near.

Better than all measures
Of delightful sound,
Better than all treasures
That in books are found,
Thy skill to poet were, thou scorner of the ground!

Teach me half the gladness
That thy brain must know,
Such harmonious madness
From my lips would flow,
The world should listen then, as I am listening now.

Ode to the West Wind

I

O WILD West Wind, thou breath of Autumn's being,
Thou, from whose unseen presence the leaves dead
Are driven, like ghosts from an enchanter fleeing,

Yellow, and black, and pale, and hectic red,
Pestilence-stricken multitudes: O thou,
Who chariotest to their dark wintry bed

The wingèd seeds, where they lie cold and low,
Each like a corpse within its grave, until
Thine azure sister of the spring shall blow

Her clarion o'er the dreaming earth, and fill
(Driving sweet buds like flocks to feed in air)
With living hues and odours plain and hill;

Wild Spirit, which art moving everywhere;
Destroyer and preserver; hear, Oh hear!

II

Thou on whose stream, 'mid the steep sky's commotion,
Loose clouds like earth's decaying leaves are shed,
Shook from the tangled boughs of Heaven and Ocean,

Angels of rain and lightning: there are spread
On the blue surface of thine airy surge,
Like the bright hair uplifted from the head

Of some fierce Mænad, even from the dim verge
Of the horizon to the zenith's height
The locks of the approaching storm. Thou dirge

Of the dying year, to which this closing night
Will be the dome of a vast sepulchre,
Vaulted with all thy congregated might

Of vapours, from whose solid atmosphere
Black rain, and fire, and hail will burst: Oh hear!

III

Thou who didst waken from his summer dreams
The blue Mediterranean, where he lay,
Lulled by the coil of his crystalline streams,

Beside a pumice isle in Baiæ's bay,
And saw in sleep old palaces and towers
Quivering within the wave's intenser day,

All overgrown with azure moss and flowers
So sweet, the sense faints picturing them! Thou
For whose path the Atlantic's level powers

Cleave themselves into chasms, while far below
The sea-blooms and the oozy woods which wear
The sapless foliage of the ocean, know

Thy voice, and suddenly grow gray with fear,
And tremble and despoil themselves: Oh hear!

IV

If I were a dead leaf thou mightest bear;
If I were a swift cloud to fly with thee;
A wave to pant beneath thy power, and share

The impulse of thy strength, only less free
Than thou, O uncontrollable! If even
I were as in my boyhood, and could be

The comrade of thy wanderings over heaven,
As then, when to outstrip thy skiey speed
Scarce seemed a vision; I would ne'er have striven

As thus with thee in prayer in my sore need.
Oh lift me as a wave, a leaf, a cloud!
I fall upon the thorns of life! I bleed!

A heavy weight of hours has chained and bowed
One too like thee: tameless, and swift, and proud.

V

Make me thy lyre, even as the forest is:
What if my leaves are falling like its own!
The tumult of thy mighty harmonies

Will take from both a deep, autumnal tone,
Sweet though in sadness. Be thou, spirit fierce,
My spirit! Be thou me, impetuous one!

Drive my dead thoughts over the universe
Like withered leaves to quicken a new birth!
And, by the incantation of this verse,

Scatter, as from an unextinguished hearth
Ashes and sparks, my words among mankind!
Be through my lips to unawakened earth

The trumpet of a prophecy! O, wind,
If Winter comes, can Spring be far behind?

The Sensitive Plant

PART FIRST

A SENSITIVE Plant in a garden grew,
And the young winds fed it with silver dew,
And it opened its fan-like leaves to the light,
And closed them beneath the kisses of Night.

And the Spring arose on the garden fair,
Like the Spirit of Love felt everywhere;
And each flower and herb on Earth's dark breast
Rose from the dreams of its wintry rest.

But none ever trembled and panted with bliss
In the garden, the field, or the wilderness,
Like a doe in the noontide with love's sweet want,
As the companionless Sensitive Plant.

The snowdrop, and then the violet,
Arose from the ground with warm rain wet,
And their breath was mixed with fresh odour, sent
From the turf, like the voice and the instrument.

Then the pied wind-flowers and the tulip tall,
And narcissi, the fairest among them all,

Who gaze on their eyes in the stream's recess,
Till they die of their own dear loveliness;

And the Naiad-like lily of the vale,
Whom youth makes so fair and passion so pale
That the light of its tremulous bells is seen
Through their pavilions of tender green;

And the hyacinth purple, and white, and blue,
Which flung from its bells a sweet peal anew
Of music so delicate, soft, and intense,
It was felt like an odour within the sense;

And the rose like a nymph to the bath addressed,
Which unveiled the depth of her glowing breast,
Till, fold after fold, to the fainting air
The soul of her beauty and love lay bare:

And the wand-like lily, which lifted up,
As a Mænad, its moonlight-coloured cup,
Till the fiery star, which is its eye,
Gazed through clear dew on the tender sky;

And the jessamine faint, and the sweet tuberose,
The sweetest flower for scent that blows:
And all rare blossoms from every clime
Grew in that garden in perfect prime.

And on the stream whose inconstant bosom
Was pranked, under boughs of embowering blossom,
With golden and green light, slanting through
Their heaven of many a tangled hue,
Broad water-lilies lay tremulously,
And starry river-buds glimmered by,
And around them the soft stream did glide and dance
With a motion of sweet sound and radiance.

And the sinuous paths of lawn and of moss,
Which led through the garden along and across,
Some open at once to the sun and the breeze,
Some lost among bowers of blossoming trees,

Were all paved with daisies and delicate bells
As fair as the fabulous asphodels,
And flow'rets which, drooping as day drooped too,
Fell into pavilions, white, purple, and blue,
To roof the glow-worm from the evening dew.

And from this undefilèd Paradise
The flowers (as an infant's awakening eyes
Smile on its mother, whose singing sweet
Can first lull, and at last must awaken it),

When Heaven's blithe winds had unfolded them,
As mine-lamps enkindle a hidden gem,
Shone smiling to Heaven, and every one
Shared joy in the light of the gentle sun;

For each one was interpenetrated
With the light and the odour its neighbour shed,
Like young lovers whom youth and love make dear
Wrapped and filled by their mutual atmosphere.

But the Sensitive Plant which could give small fruit
Of the love which it felt from the leaf to the root,

Received more than all, it loved more
than ever,
Where none wanted but it, could belong
to the giver,—

For the Sensitive Plant has no bright
flower;
Radiance and odour are not its dower;
It loves, even like Love, its deep heart is
full,
It desires what it has not, the Beautiful!

The light winds which from unsustaining
wings
Shed the music of many murmurings;
The beams which dart from many a star
Of the flowers whose hues they bear
afar;

The plumèd insects swift and free,
Like golden boats on a sunny sea,
Laden with light and odour, which pass
Over the gleam of the living grass;

The unseen clouds of the dew, which lie
Like fire in the flowers till the sun rides
high,
Then wander like spirits among the
spheres,
Each cloud faint with the fragrance it
bears;

The quivering vapours of dim noontide,
Which like a sea o'er the warm earth
glide,
In which every sound, and odour, and
beam,
Move, as reeds in a single stream;

Each and all like ministering angels were
For the Sensitive Plant sweet joy to
bear,
Whilst the lagging hours of the day went
by
Like windless clouds o'er a tender sky.

And when evening descended from
Heaven above,
And the Earth was all rest, and the air
was all love,

And delight, though less bright, was far
more deep,
And the day's veil fell from the world
of sleep,

And the beasts, and the birds, and the insects were drowned
In an ocean of dreams without a sound;
Whose waves never mark, though they
ever impress
The light sand which paves it, consciousness;

(Only overhead the sweet nightingale
Ever sang more sweet as the day might
fail,
And snatches of its Elysian chant
Were mixed with the dreams of the
Sensitive Plant);—

The Sensitive Plant was the earliest
Upgathered into the bosom of rest;
A sweet child weary of its delight,
The feeblest and yet the favourite,
Cradled within the embrace of Night.

Part Second

There was a Power in this sweet place,
An Eve in this Eden; a ruling Grace
Which to the flowers, did they waken or
dream,
Was as God is to the starry scheme.

A Lady, the wonder of her kind,
Whose form was upborne by a lovely
mind
Which, dilating, had moulded her mien
and motion
Like a sea-flower unfolded beneath the
ocean,

Tended the garden from morn to even:
And the meteors of that sublunar
Heaven,
Like the lamps of the air when Night
walks forth,
Laughed round her footsteps up from the
Earth!

She had no companion of mortal race,
But her tremulous breath and her flushing face
Told, whilst the morn kissed the sleep from her eyes,
That her dreams were less slumber than Paradise:

As if some bright Spirit for her sweet sake
Had deserted Heaven while the stars were awake,
As if yet around her he lingering were,
Though the veil of daylight concealed him from her.

Her step seemed to pity the grass it pressed;
You might hear by the heaving of her breast,
That the coming and going of the wind
Brought pleasure there and left passion behind.

And wherever her aëry footstep trod,
Her trailing hair from the grassy sod
Erased its light vestige, with shadowy sweep,
Like a sunny storm o'er the dark green deep.

I doubt not the flowers of that garden sweet
Rejoiced in the sound of her gentle feet;
I doubt not they felt the spirit that came
From her glowing fingers through all their frame.

She sprinkled bright water from the stream
On those that were faint with the sunny beam;
And out of the cups of the heavy flowers
She emptied the rain of the thunder-showers.

She lifted their heads with her tender hands,
And sustained them with rods and osier-bands;
If the flowers had been her own infants, she
Could never have nursed them more tenderly.

And all killing insects and gnawing worms,
And things of obscene and unlovely forms,
She bore, in a basket of Indian woof,
Into the rough woods far aloof,—

In a basket, of grasses and wild-flowers full,
The freshest her gentle hands could pull
For the poor banished insects, whose intent,
Although they did ill, was innocent.

But the bee and the beamlike ephemeris
Whose path is the lightning's, and soft moths that kiss
The sweet lips of the flowers, and harm not, did she
Make her attendant angels be.

And many an antenatal tomb,
Where butterflies dream of the life to come,
She left clinging round the smooth and dark
Edge of the odorous cedar bark.

This fairest creature from earliest Spring
Thus moved through the garden ministering
All the sweet season of Summertide,
And ere the first leaf looked brown—she died!

Part Third

Three days the flowers of the garden fair,
Like stars when the moon is awakened, were,
Or the waves of Baiæ, ere luminous
She floats up through the smoke of Vesuvius.

And on the fourth, the Sensitive Plant
Felt the sound of the funeral chant,
And the steps of the bearers, heavy and slow,
And the sobs of the mourners, deep and low;

The weary sound and the heavy breath,
And the silent motions of passing death,
And the smell, cold, oppressive and dank,
Sent through the pores of the coffin-plank;

The dark grass, and the flowers among the grass,
Were bright with tears as the crowd did pass;
From their sighs the wind caught a mournful tone,
And sate in the pines, and gave groan for groan.

The garden, once fair, became cold and foul,
Like the corpse of her who had been its soul,
Which at first was lovely as if in sleep,
Then slowly changed, till it grew a heap
To make men tremble who never weep.

Swift Summer into the Autumn flowed,
And frost in the mist of the morning rode,
Though the noonday sun looked clear and bright,
Mocking the spoil of the secret night.

The rose-leaves, like flakes of crimson snow,
Paved the turf and the moss below.
The lilies were drooping, and white, and wan,
Like the head and the skin of a dying man.

And Indian plants, of scent and hue
The sweetest that ever were fed on dew,
Leaf by leaf, day after day,
Were massed into the common clay.

And the leaves, brown, yellow, and gray, and red,
And white with the whiteness of what is dead,
Like troops of ghosts on the dry wind passed;
Their whistling noise made the birds aghast.

And the gusty winds waked the wingèd seeds,
Out of their birthplace of ugly weeds,
Till they clung round many a sweet flower's stem,
Which rotted into the earth with them.

The water-blooms under the rivulet
Fell from the stalks on which they were set;
And the eddies drove them here and there,
As the winds did those of the upper air.

Then the rain came down, and the broken stalks
Were bent and tangled across the walks;
And the leafless network of parasite bowers
Massed into ruin; and all sweet flowers.

Between the time of the wind and the snow
All loathliest weeds began to grow,
Whose coarse leaves were splashed with many a speck,
Like the water-snake's belly and the toad's back.

And thistles, and nettles, and darnels rank,
And the dock, and henbane, and hemlock dank,
Stretched out its long and hollow shank,
And stifled the air till the dead wind stank.

And plants, at whose names the verse feels loath,
Filled the place with a monstrous undergrowth,

Prickly, and pulpous, and blistering, and blue,
Livid, and starred with a lurid dew.

And agarics, and fungi, with mildew and mould
Started like mist from the wet ground cold;
Pale, fleshy, as if the decaying dead
With a spirit of growth had been animated!

Spawn, weeds, and filth, a leprous scum,
Made the running rivulet thick and dumb,
And at its outlet flags huge as stakes
Dammed it up with roots knotted like water-snakes.

And hour by hour, when the air was still,
The vapours arose which have strength to kill;
At morn they were seen, at noon they were felt,
At night they were darkness no star could melt.

And unctuous meteors from spray to spray
Crept and flitted in broad noonday
Unseen; every branch on which they alit
By a venomous blight was burned and bit.

The Sensitive Plant, like one forbid,
Wept, and the tears within each lid
Of its folded leaves, which together grew,
Were changed to a blight of frozen glue.

For the leaves soon fell, and the branches soon
By the heavy axe of the blast were hewn;
The sap shrank to the root through every pore
As blood to a heart that will beat no more.

For Winter came: the wind was his whip:
One choppy finger was on his lip:
He had torn the cataracts from the hills
And they clanked at his girdle like manacles;

His breath was a chain which without a sound
The earth, and the air, and the water bound;
He came, fiercely driven, in his chariot-throne
By the tenfold blasts of the Arctic zone.

Then the weeds which were forms of living death
Fled from the frost to the earth beneath.
Their decay and sudden flight from frost
Was but like the vanishing of a ghost!

And under the roots of the Sensitive Plant
The moles and the dormice died for want:
The birds dropped stiff from the frozen air
And were caught in the branches naked and bare.

First there came down a thawing rain
And its dull drops froze on the boughs again;
Then there steamed up a freezing dew
Which to the drops of the thaw-rain grew;

And a northern whirlwind, wandering about
Like a wolf that had smelt a dead child out,
Shook the boughs thus laden, and heavy, and stiff,
And snapped them off with his rigid griff.

When Winter had gone and Spring came back
The Sensitive Plant was a leafless wreck;
But the mandrakes, and toadstools, and docks, and darnels,
Rose like the dead from their ruined charnels.

CONCLUSION

Whether the Sensitive Plant, or that
Which within its boughs like a Spirit sat,
Ere its outward form had known decay,
Now felt this change, I cannot say.

Whether that Lady's gentle mind,
No longer with the form combined
Which scattered love, as stars do light,
Found sadness, where it left delight,

I dare not guess; but in this life
Of error, ignorance, and strife,
Where nothing is, but all things seem,
And we the shadows of the dream,

It is a modest creed, and yet
Pleasant if one considers it,
To own that death itself must be,
Like all the rest, a mockery.

That garden sweet, that lady fair,
And all sweet shapes and odours there,
In truth have never passed away:
'Tis we, 'tis ours, are changed; not they.

For love, and beauty, and delight,
There is no death nor change: their might
Exceeds our organs, which endure
No light, being themselves obscure.

Arethusa

I

ARETHUSA arose
From her couch of snows
In the Acroceraunian mountains,—
From cloud and from crag,
With many a jag,
Shepherding her bright fountains.
She leapt down the rocks,
With her rainbow locks
Streaming among the streams;—
Her steps paved with green
The downward ravine
Which slopes to the western gleams;
And gliding and springing
She went, ever singing,
In murmurs as soft as sleep;
The Earth seemed to love her,
And Heaven smiled above her,
As she lingered towards the deep.

II

Then Alpheus bold,
On his glacier cold,
With his trident the mountains strook;
And opened a chasm
In the rocks—with the spasm
All Erymanthus shook.
And the black south wind
It unsealed behind
The urns of the silent snow,
And earthquake and thunder
Did rend in sunder
The bars of the springs below.
And the beard and the hair
Of the River-god were
Seen through the torrent's sweep,
As he followed the light
Of the fleet nymph's flight
To the brink of the Dorian deep.

III

"Oh, save me! Oh, guide me!
And bid the deep hide me,
For he grasps me now by the hair!"
The loud Ocean heard,
To its blue depth stirred,
And divided at her prayer;
And under the water
The Earth's white daughter
Fled like a sunny beam;
Behind her descended
Her billows, unblended
With the brackish Dorian stream:—
Like a gloomy stain
On the emerald main
Alpheus rushed behind,—
As an eagle pursuing
A dove to its ruin
Down the streams of the cloudy wind.

IV

Under the bowers
Where the Ocean Powers
Sit on their pearlèd thrones;
Through the coral woods
Of the weltering floods,
Over heaps of unvalued stones;
Through the dim beams
Which amid the streams
Weave a network of coloured light;
And under the caves,
Where the shadowy waves
Are as green as the forest's night:—
Outspeeding the shark,
And the sword-fish dark,
Under the Ocean's foam,
And up through the rifts
Of the mountain clifts
They passed to their Dorian home.

V

And now from their fountains
In Enna's mountains,
Down one vale where the morning basks,
Like friends once parted
Grown single-hearted,
They ply their watery tasks.
At sunrise they leap
From their cradles steep
In the cave of the shelving hill;
At noontide they flow
Through the woods below
And the meadows of asphodel;
And at night they sleep
In the rocking deep
Beneath the Ortygian shore;—
Like spirits that lie
In the azure sky
When they love but live no more.

Hymn of Pan

From the forests and highlands
We come, we come;
From the river-girt islands,
Where loud waves are dumb,
Listening to my sweet pipings.
The wind in the reeds and the rushes,
The bees on the bells of thyme,
The birds on the myrtle bushes,
The cicale above in the lime,
And the lizards below in the grass,
Were as silent as ever old Tmolus was,
Listening to my sweet pipings.

Liquid Peneus was flowing,
And all dark Tempe lay
In Pelion's shadow, outgrowing
The light of the dying day,
Speeded by my sweet pipings.
The Sileni and Sylvans and Fauns,
And the Nymphs of the woods and waves,
To the edge of the moist river-lawns,
And the brink of the dewy caves,
And all that did then attend and follow,
Were silent with love, as you now, Apollo,
With envy of my sweet pipings.

I sang of the dancing stars,
I sang of the dædal earth,
And of heaven, and the giant wars,
And love, and death, and birth.
And then I changed my pipings—
Singing how down the vale of Mænalus
I pursued a maiden, and clasp'd a reed:
Gods and men, we are all deluded thus;
It breaks in our bosom, and then we bleed.
All wept—as I think both ye now would,
If envy or age had not frozen your blood—
At the sorrow of my sweet pipings.

To —— (One word is too often profaned)

One word is too often profaned
For me to profane it;
One feeling too falsely disdain'd
For thee to disdain it;

One hope is too like despair
For prudence to smother;
And pity from thee more dear
Than that from another.

I can give not what men call love:
But wilt thou accept not
The worship the heart lifts above
And the heavens reject not,
The desire of the moth for the star,
Of the night for the morrow,
The devotion to something afar
From the sphere of our sorrow?

Adonais

AN ELEGY ON THE DEATH OF JOHN KEATS

Αστὴρ πρὶν μὲν ἔλαμπες ἐνὶ ζωοῖσιν 'Εῷος.
Νῦν δε θανὼν λάμπεις Ἕσπερος ἐν φθιμένοις.
PLATO.

I WEEP for Adonais—he is dead!
Oh weep for Adonais! though our tears
Thaw not the frost which binds so dear a head!
And thou, sad Hour, selected from all years
To mourn our loss, rouse thy obscure compeers,
And teach them thine own sorrow! Say: "With me
Died Adonais; till the Future dares
Forget the Past, his fate and fame shall be
An echo and a light unto eternity!"

Where wert thou, mighty Mother, when he lay,
When thy Son lay, pierced by the shaft which flies
In darkness? where was lorn Urania
When Adonais died? With veilèd eyes,
'Mid listening Echoes, in her Paradise
She sate, while one, with soft enamoured breath,
Rekindled all the fading melodies
With which, like flowers that mock the corse beneath,
He had adorned and hid the coming bulk of death.

Oh weep for Adonais—he is dead!
Wake, melancholy Mother, wake and weep!
Yet wherefore? Quench within their burning bed
Thy fiery tears, and let thy lov'd heart keep,
Like his, a mute and uncomplaining sleep;
For he is gone, where all things wise and fair
Descend;—oh, dream not that the amorous Deep
Will yet restore him to the vital air;
Death feeds on his mute voice, and laughs at our despair.

Most musical of mourners, weep again
Lament anew, Urania!—He died,
Who was the Sire of an immortal strain,
Blind, old, and lonely, when his country's pride,
The priest, the slave, and the liberticide,
Trampled and mocked with many a loathed rite
Of lust and blood; he went, unterrified,
Into the gulf of death; but his clear Sprite
Yet reigns o'er earth; the third among the sons of light.

Most musical of mourners, weep anew!
Not all to that bright station dared to climb;
And happier they their happiness who knew,
Whose tapers yet burn through that night of time
In which suns perished; others more sublime,
Struck by the envious wrath of man or God,
Have sunk, extinct in their refulgent prime;
And some yet live, treading the thorny road,
Which leads, through toil and hate, to Fame's serene abode.

But now, thy youngest, dearest one has perished,
The nursling of thy widowhood, who grew,
Like a pale flower by some sad maiden cherished,
And fed with true love tears, instead of dew;
Most musical of mourners, weep anew!
Thy extreme hope, the loveliest and the last,
The bloom, whose petals nipt before they blew
Died on the promise of the fruit, is waste;
The broken lily lies—the storm is overpast.

To that high Capital, where kingly Death
Keeps his pale court in beauty and decay,
He came; and bought, with price of purest breath,
A grave among the eternal.—Come away!
Haste, while the vault of blue Italian day
Is yet his fitting charnel-roof! while still
He lies, as if in dewy sleep he lay;
Awake him not! surely he takes his fill
Of deep and liquid rest, forgetful of all ill.

He will awake no more, oh, never more!—
Within the twilight chamber spreads apace,
The shadow of white Death, and at the door
Invisible Corruption waits to trace
His extreme way to her dim dwelling-place;
The eternal Hunger sits, but pity and awe
Soothe her pale rage, nor dares she to deface
So fair a prey, till darkness, and the law
Of change shall o'er his sleep the mortal curtain draw.

Oh weep for Adonais!—The quick Dreams,
The passion-wingèd Ministers of thought,
Who were his flocks, whom near the living streams
Of his young spirit he fed, and whom he taught
The love which was its music, wander not,—
Wander no more, from kindling brain to brain,
But droop there, whence they sprung; and mourn their lot
Round the cold heart, where, after their sweet pain,
They ne'er will gather strength, or find a home again.

And one with trembling hands clasps his cold head,
And fans him with her moonlight wings, and cries;
"Our love, our hope, our sorrow, is not dead;
See, on the silken fringe of his faint eyes,
Like dew upon a sleeping flower, there lies
A tear some Dream has loosened from his brain."
Lost Angel of a ruined Paradise!
She knew not 'twas her own; as with no stain
She faded, like a cloud which had outwept its rain.

One from a lucid urn of starry dew
Washed his light limbs as if embalming them;
Another clipt her profuse locks, and threw
The wreath upon him, like an anadem,
Which frozen tears instead of pearls begem;
Another in her wilful grief would break
Her bow and wingèd reeds, as if to stem
A greater loss with one which was more weak;
And dull the barbèd fire against his frozen cheek.

Another Splendour on his mouth alit,
That mouth, whence it was wont to draw the breath
Which gave it strength to pierce the guarded wit,
And pass into the panting heart beneath
With lightning and with music: the damp death
Quenched its caress upon his icy lips;
And, as a dying meteor stains a wreath
Of moonlight vapour, which the cold night clips,
It flushed through his pale limbs, and passed to its eclipse.

And others came . . . Desires and Adorations,
Wingèd Persuasions and veilèd Destinies,
Splendours and Glooms, and glimmering Incarnations
Of hopes and fears, and twilight Phantasies;
And Sorrow, with her family of Sighs,
And Pleasure, blind with tears, led by the gleam
Of her own dying smile instead of eyes,
Came in slow pomp;—the moving pomp might seem
Like pageantry of mist on an autumnal stream.

All he had loved, and moulded into thought,
From shape, and hue, and odour, and sweet sound,
Lamented Adonais. Morning sought
Her eastern watch-tower, and her hair unbound,
Wet with the tears which should adorn the ground,
Dimmed the aërial eyes that kindle day;
Afar the melancholy thunder moaned,
Pale Ocean in unquiet slumber lay,
And the wild winds flew round, sobbing in their dismay.

Lost Echo sits amid the voiceless mountains,
And feeds her grief with his remembered lay,
And will no more reply to winds or fountains,
Or amorous birds perched on the young green spray,
Or herdsman's horn, or bell at closing day;
Since she can mimic not his lips, more dear
Than those for whose disdain she pined away
Into a shadow of all sounds:—a drear
Murmur, between their songs, is all the woodmen hear.

Grief made the young Spring wild, and she threw down
Her kindling buds, as if she Autumn were,
Or they dead leaves; since her delight is flown
For whom should she have waked the sullen year?
To Phœbus was not Hyacinth so dear
Nor to himself Narcissus, as to both
Thou Adonais: wan they stand and sere
Amid the faint companions of their youth,
With dew all turned to tears; odour, to sighing ruth.

Thy spirit's sister, the lorn nightingale,
Mourns not her mate with such melodious pain;
Not so the eagle, who like thee could scale
Heaven, and could nourish in the sun's domain
Her mighty youth with morning, doth complain,
Soaring and screaming round her empty nest,
As Albion wails for thee; the curse of Cain
Light on his head who pierced thy innocent breast
And scared the angel soul that was its earthly guest!

Ah woe is me! Winter is come and gone,
But grief returns with the revolving year;

The airs and streams renew their joyous tone:
The ants, the bees, the swallows reappear;
Fresh leaves and flowers deck the dead Season's bier;
The amorous birds now pair in every brake,
And build their mossy homes in field and brere;
And the green lizard, and the golden snake,
Like unimprisoned flames, out of their trance awake.

Through wood and stream and field and hill and Ocean
A quickening life from the Earth's heart has burst
As it has ever done, with change and motion,
From the great morning of the world when first
God dawned on Chaos; in its stream immersed
The lamps of Heaven flash with a softer light;
All baser things pant with life's sacred thirst;
Diffuse themselves; and spend in love's delight,
The beauty and the joy of their renewèd might.

The leprous corpse touched by this spirit tender
Exhales itself in flowers of gentle breath;
Like incarnations of the stars, when splendour
Is changed to fragrance, they illumine death
And mock the merry worm that wakes beneath;
Nought we know, dies. Shall that alone which knows
Be as a sword consumed before the sheath
By sightless lightning?—the intense atom glows
A moment, then is quenched in a most cold repose.

Alas! that all we loved of him should be
But for our grief, as if it had not been,
And grief itself be mortal! Woe is me!
Whence are we, and why are we? of what scene
The actors or spectators? Great and mean
Meet massed in death, who lends what life must borrow.
As long as skies are blue, and fields are green,
Evening must usher night, night urge the morrow,
Month follow month with woe, and year wake year to sorrow.

He will awake no more, oh, never more!
"Wake thou," cried Misery, "childless Mother, rise
Out of thy sleep, and slake, in thy heart's core,
A wound more fierce than his with tears and sighs."
And all the Dreams that watched Urania's eyes,
And all the Echoes whom their sister's song
Had held in holy silence, cried: "Arise!"
Swift as a Thought by the snake Memory stung,
From her ambrosial rest the fading Splendour sprung.

She rose like an autumnal Night, that springs
Out of the East, and follows wild and drear
The golden Day, which, on eternal wings,
Even as a ghost abandoning a bier,
Had left the Earth a corpse. Sorrow and fear
So struck, so roused, so rapt Urania;
So saddened round her like an atmosphere

Of stormy mist; so swept her on her way
Even to the mournful place where
Adonais lay.

Out of her secret Paradise she sped,
Through camps and cities rough with
stone, and steel,
And human hearts, which to her airy
tread
Yielding not, wounded the invisible
Palms of her tender feet where'er they
fell:
And barbèd tongues, and thoughts more
sharp than they
Rent the soft Form they never could
repel,
Whose sacred blood, like the young tears
of May,
Paved with eternal flowers that unde-
serving way.

In the death chamber for a moment
Death
Shamed by the presence of that living
Might
Blushed to annihilation, and the breath
Revisited those lips, and life's pale light
Flashed through those limbs, so late her
dear delight.
"Leave me not wild and drear and com-
fortless,
As silent lightning leaves the starless
night!
Leave me not!" cried Urania: her dis-
tress
Roused Death: Death rose and smiled,
and met her vain caress.

"Stay yet awhile! speak to me once
again;
Kiss me, so long but as a kiss may live;
And in my heartless breast and burning
brain
That word, that kiss, shall all thoughts
else survive,
With food of saddest memory kept
alive,
Now thou art dead, as if it were a part
Of thee, my Adonais! I would give
All that I am to be as thou now art!
But I am chained to Time, and cannot
thence depart!

"O gentle child, beautiful as thou wert,
Why didst thou leave the trodden paths
of men
Too soon, and with weak hands though
mighty heart
Dare the unpastured dragon in his den?
Defenceless as thou wert, oh where was
then
Wisdom, the mirrored shield, or scorn,
the spear?
Or hadst thou waited the full cycle, when
Thy spirit should have filled its crescent
sphere,
The monsters of life's waste had fled
from thee like deer.

"The herded wolves, bold only to pursue;
The obscene ravens, clamourous o'er the
dead;
The vultures to the conqueror's banner
true
Who feed where Desolation first has
fed,
And whose wings rain contagion;—how
they fled,
When like Apollo, from his golden bow,
The Pythian of the age one arrow sped
And smiled!—The spoilers tempt no sec-
ond blow,
They fawn on the proud feet that spurn
them lying low.

"The sun comes forth, and many reptiles
spawn;
He sets, and each ephemeral insect then
Is gathered into death without a dawn,
And the immortal stars awake again;
So is it in the world of living men:
A godlike mind soars forth, in its delight
Making earth bare and veiling heaven,
and when
It sinks, the swarms that dimmed or
shared its light
Leave to its kindred lamps the spirit's
awful night."

Thus ceased she: and the mountain shepherds came,
Their garlands sere, their magic mantles rent;
The Pilgrim of Eternity, whose fame
Over his living head like Heaven is bent,
An early but enduring monument,
Came, veiling all the lightnings of his song
In sorrow; from her wilds Ierne sent
The sweetest lyrist of her saddest wrong,
And love taught grief to fall like music from his tongue.

Midst others of less note, came one frail Form,
A phantom among men; companionless
As the last cloud of an expiring storm
Whose thunder is its knell; he, as I guess,
Had gazed on Nature's naked loveliness,
Actæon-like, and now he fled astray
With feeble steps o'er the world's wilderness,
And his own thoughts, along that rugged way,
Pursued, like raging hounds, their father and their prey.

A pardlike Spirit beautiful and swift—
A Love in desolation masked;—a Power
Girt round with weakness;—it can scarce uplift
The weight of the superincumbent hour;
It is a dying lamp, a falling shower,
A breaking billow;—even whilst we speak
Is it not broken? On the withering flower
The killing sun smiles brightly: on a cheek
The life can burn in blood, even while the heart may break.

His head was bound with pansies overblown,
And faded violets, white, and pied, and blue;
And a light spear topped with a cypress cone,
Round whose rude shaft dark ivy tresses grew
Yet dripping with the forest's noonday dew,
Vibrated, as the ever-beating heart
Shook the weak hand that grasped it; of that crew
He came the last, neglected and apart;
A herd-abandoned deer struck by the hunter's dart.

All stood aloof, and at his partial moan
Smiled through their tears; well knew that gentle band
Who in another's fate now wept his own;
As in the accents of an unknown land,
He sung new sorrow; sad Urania scanned
The Stranger's mien, and murmured: "Who art thou?"
He answered not, but with a sudden hand
Made bare his branded and ensanguined brow,
Which was like Cain's or Christ's—oh, that it should be so!

What softer voice is hushed over the dead?
Athwart what brow is that dark mantle thrown?
What form leans sadly o'er the white deathbed,
In mockery of monumental stone,
The heavy heart heaving without a moan?
If it be He, who, gentlest of the wise,
Taught, soothed, loved, honoured the departed one;
Let me not vex, with inharmonious sighs
The silence of that heart's accepted sacrifice.

Our Adonais has drunk poison—oh!
What deaf and viperous murderer could crown
Life's early cup with such a draught of woe?
The nameless worm would now itself disown:
It felt, yet could escape the magic tone

Whose prelude held all envy, hate, and wrong,
But what was howling in one breast alone,
Silent with expectation of the song,
Whose master's hand is cold, whose silver lyre unstrung.

Live thou, whose infamy is not thy fame!
Live! fear no heavier chastisement from me,
Thou noteless blot on a remembered name!
But be thyself, and know thyself to be!
And ever at thy season be thou free
To spill the venom when thy fangs o'erflow:
Remorse and Self-contempt shall cling to thee;
Hot Shame shall burn upon thy secret brow,
And like a beaten hound tremble thou shalt—as now.

Nor let us weep that our delight is fled
Far from these carrion kites that scream below;
He wakes or sleeps with the enduring dead;
Thou canst not soar where he is sitting now.—
Dust to the dust! but the pure spirit shall flow
Back to the burning fountain whence it came,
A portion of the Eternal, which must glow
Through time and change, unquenchably the same,
Whilst thy cold embers choke the sordid hearth of shame.

Peace, peace! he is not dead, he doth not sleep—
He hath awakened from the dream of life—
'Tis we, who lost in stormy visions, keep
With phantoms an unprofitable strife,
And in mad trance, strike with our spirit's knife
Invulnerable nothings.—*We* decay
Like corpses in a charnel; fear and grief
Convulse us and consume us day by day,
And cold hopes swarm like worms within our living clay.

He has outsoared the shadow of our night;
Envy and calumny and hate and pain,
And that unrest which men miscall delight,
Can touch him not and torture not again;
From the contagion of the world's slow stain
He is secure, and now can never mourn
A heart grown cold, a head grown gray in vain;
Nor, when the spirit's self has ceased to burn,
With sparkless ashes load an unlamented urn.

He lives, he wakes—'tis Death is dead, not he;
Mourn not for Adonais,—Thou young Dawn
Turn all thy dew to splendour, for from thee
The spirit thou lamentest is not gone;
Ye caverns and ye forests, cease to moan!
Cease ye faint flowers and fountains, and thou Air
Which like a mourning veil thy scarf hadst thrown
O'er the abandoned Earth, now leave it bare
Even to the joyous stars which smile on its despair!

He is made one with Nature: there is heard
His voice in all her music, from the moan
Of thunder to the song of night's sweet bird;
He is a presence to be felt and known
In darkness and in light, from herb and stone,
Spreading itself where'er that Power may move
Which has withdrawn his being to its own;

Which wields the world with never wearied love,
Sustains it from beneath, and kindles it above.

He is a portion of the loveliness
Which once he made more lovely: he doth bear
His part, while the one Spirit's plastic stress
Sweeps through the dull dense world, compelling there
All new successions to the forms they wear;
Torturing th' unwilling dross that checks its flight
To its own likeness, as each mass may bear;
And bursting in its beauty and its might
From trees and beasts and men into the Heaven's light.

The splendours of the firmament of time
May be eclipsed, but are extinguished not;
Like stars to their appointed height they climb
And death is a low mist which cannot blot
The brightness it may veil. When lofty thought
Lifts a young heart above its mortal lair,
And love and life contend in it, for what
Shall be its earthly doom, the dead live there
And move like winds of light on dark and stormy air.

The inheritors of unfulfilled renown
Rose from their thrones, built beyond mortal thought,
Far in the Unapparent. Chatterton
Rose pale, his solemn agony had not
Yet faded from him; Sidney, as he fought
And as he fell and as he lived and loved
Sublimely mild, a Spirit without spot,
Arose; and Lucan, by his death approved:
Oblivion as they rose shrank like a thing reproved.

And many more, whose names on Earth are dark
But whose transmitted effluence cannot die
So long as fire outlives the parent spark,
Rose, robed in dazzling immortality.
"Thou art become as one of us," they cry,
"It was for thee yon kingless sphere has long
Swung blind in unascended majesty,
Silent alone amid an Heaven of Song.
Assume thy wingèd throne, thou Vesper of our throng!"

Who mourns for Adonais? Oh come forth
Fond wretch! and know thyself and him aright.
Clasp with thy panting soul the pendulous Earth;
As from a centre, dart thy spirit's light
Beyond all worlds, until its spacious might
Satiate the void circumference: then shrink
Even to a point within our day and night;
And keep thy heart light lest it make thee sink
When hope has kindled hope, and lured thee to the brink.

Or go to Rome, which is the sepulchre
Oh! not of him, but of our joy: 'tis nought
That ages, empires, and religions there
Lie buried in the ravage they have wrought;
For such as he can lend,—they borrow not
Glory from those who made the world their prey;
And he is gathered to the kings of thought
Who waged contention with their time's decay,
And of the past are all that cannot pass away.

Go thou to Rome,—at once the Paradise,
The grave, the city, and the wilderness;
And where its wrecks like shattered mountains rise,
And flowering weeds, and fragrant copses dress
The bones of Desolation's nakedness,
Pass, till the Spirit of the spot shall lead
Thy footsteps to a slope of green access
Where, like an infant's smile, over the dead
A light of laughing flowers along the grass is spread.

And gray walls moulder round, on which dull Time
Feeds, like slow fire upon a hoary brand;
And one keen pyramid with wedge sublime,
Pavilioning the dust of him who planned
This refuge for his memory, doth stand
Like flame transformed to marble; and beneath,
A field is spread, on which a newer band
Have pitched in Heaven's smile their camp of death,
Welcoming him we lose with scarce extinguished breath.

Here pause: these graves are all too young as yet
To have outgrown the sorrow which consigned
Its charge to each; and if the seal is set,
Here, on one fountain of a mourning mind,
Break it not thou! too surely shalt thou find
Thine own well full, if thou returnest home,
Of tears and gall. From the world's bitter wind
Seek shelter in the shadow of the tomb.
What Adonais is, why fear we to become?

The One remains, the many change and pass;
Heaven's light forever shines, Earth's shadows fly;
Life, like a dome of many-coloured glass,
Stains the white radiance of Eternity,
Until Death tramples it to fragments.—Die,
If thou wouldst be with that which thou dost seek!
Follow where all is fled!—Rome's azure sky,
Flowers, ruins, statues, music, words, are weak
The glory they transfuse with fitting truth to speak.

Why linger, why turn back, why shrink, my Heart?
Thy hopes are gone before: from all things here
They have departed; thou shouldst now depart!
A light is past from the revolving year,
And man, and woman; and what still is dear
Attracts to crush, repels to make thee wither.
The soft sky smiles,—the low wind whispers near;
'Tis Adonais calls! oh, hasten thither,
No more let Life divide what Death can join together.

That Light whose smile kindles the Universe,
That Beauty in which all things work and move,
That Benediction which the eclipsing Curse
Of birth can quench not, that sustaining Love
Which through the web of being blindly wove
By man and beast and earth and air and sea,
Burns bright or dim, as each are mirrors of
The fire for which all thirst; now beams on me,
Consuming the last clouds of cold mortality.

The breath whose might I have invoked in song
Descends on me; my spirit's bark is driven,
Far from the shore, far from the trembling throng
Whose sails were never to the tempest given;
The massy earth and spherèd skies are riven!
I am borne darkly, fearfully, afar;
Whilst burning through the inmost veil of Heaven,
The soul of Adonais, like a star,
Beacons from the abode where the Eternal are.

From HELLAS

Chorus: The world's great age begins anew

THE world's great age begins anew,
The golden years return,
The earth doth like a snake renew
Her winter weeds outworn:
Heaven smiles, and faiths and empires gleam,
Like wrecks of a dissolving dream.

A brighter Hellas rears its mountains
From waves serener far;
A new Peneus rolls his fountains
Against the morning star.
Where fairer Tempes bloom, there sleep
Young Cyclads on a sunnier deep.

A loftier Argo cleaves the main,
Fraught with a later prize;
Another Orpheus sings again,
And loves, and weeps, and dies.
A new Ulysses leaves once more
Calypso for his native shore.

Oh, write no more the tale of Troy,
If earth Death's scroll must be!
Nor mix with Laian rage the joy
Which dawns upon the free:
Although a subtler Sphinx renew
Riddles of death Thebes never knew.

Another Athens shall arise,
And to remoter time
Bequeath, like sunset to the skies,
The splendour of its prime;
And leave, if nought so bright may live,
All earth can take or Heaven can give.

Saturn and Love their long repose
Shall burst, more bright and good
Than all who fell, than One who rose,
Than many unsubdued:
Not gold, not blood, their altar dowers,
But votive tears and symbol flowers.

Oh, cease! must hate and death return?
Cease! must men kill and die?
Cease! drain not to its dregs the urn
Of bitter prophecy.
The world is weary of the past,
Oh, might it die or rest at last!

The Indian Serenade

I ARISE from dreams of thee
In the first sweet sleep of night,
When the winds are breathing low,
And the stars are shining bright.
I arise from dreams of thee,
And a spirit in my feet
Hath led me—who knows how?
To thy chamber window, Sweet!

The wandering airs they faint
On the dark, the silent stream—
The champak's odours fail
Like sweet thoughts in a dream;
The nightingale's complaint,
It dies upon her heart,
As I must on thine,
O belovèd as thou art!

O lift me from the grass!
I die! I faint! I fail!
Let thy love in kisses rain
On my lips and eyelids pale.
My cheek is cold and white, alas!
My heart beats loud and fast:
O press it to thine own again,
Where it will break at last!

EDWARD JOHN TRELAWNY (1792-1881)

From RECOLLECTIONS OF THE LAST DAYS OF SHELLEY AND BYRON

The Burning of Shelley's Body

On July 8, 1822, Shelley and his friend Mr. Williams, and a sailor boy, Charles Vivian, were drowned in a sudden storm as they were sailing homeward in a small open boat from Leghorn toward Lerici, in the Gulf of Spezzia. The Italian laws forbade the transportation of the bodies, after they had been washed ashore. It was determined, however, "by those most interested, that Shelley's remains should be removed from where they lay, and conveyed to Rome, to be interred near the bodies of his child, and of his friend Keats, with a suitable monument, and that Williams's remains should be taken to England." It was therefore advisable to resort to the ancient custom of burning and reducing the bodies to ashes, "to obviate the obstacles offered by the quarantine laws." Trelawny took charge of the unusual procedure.

THE funereal pyre was now ready; I applied the fire, and the materials being dry and resinous the pine-wood burnt furiously, and drove us back. It was hot enough before, there was no breath of air, and the loose sand scorched our feet. As soon as the flames became clear, and allowed us to approach, we threw frankincense and salt into the furnace, and poured a flask of wine and oil over the body. The Greek oration was omitted, for we had lost our Hellenic bard. It was now so insufferably hot that the officers and soldiers were all seeking shade.

"Let us try the strength of these waters that drowned our friends," said Byron, with his usual audacity. "How far out do you think they were when their boat sank?"

"If you don't wish to be put into the furnace, you had better not try; you are not in condition."

He stripped, and went into the water, and so did I and my companion. Before we got a mile out, Byron was sick, and persuaded to return to the shore. My companion too, was seized with cramp, and reached the land by my aid. At four o'clock the funereal pyre burnt low, and when we uncovered the furnace, nothing remained in it but dark-coloured ashes, with fragments of the larger bones. Poles were now put under the red-hot furnace, and it was gradually cooled in the sea. I gathered together the human ashes, and placed them in a small oak-box, bearing an inscription on a brass plate, screwed it down, and placed it in Byron's carriage. He returned with Hunt to Pisa, promising to be with us on the following day at Via Reggio. I returned with my party in the same way we came, and supped and slept at the inn. On the following morning we went on board the same boats, with the same things and party, and rowed down the little river near Via Reggio to the sea, pulled along the coast towards Massa, then landed, and began our preparations as before.

Three white wands had been stuck in the sand to mark the Poet's grave, but as they were at some distance from each other, we had to cut a trench thirty yards in length, in the line of the sticks, to ascertain the exact spot, and it was nearly an hour before we came upon the grave.

In the meantime Byron and Leigh Hunt arrived in the carriage, attended by soldiers, and the Health Officer, as before. The lonely and grand scenery that surrounded us so exactly harmonised with Shelley's genius, that I could imagine his spirit soaring over us. The sea, with the islands of Gorgona, Capraji, and Elba, was before us; old battlemented watch-towers stretched along the coast, backed by the marble-crested Apennines glistening in the sun, picturesque from their diversified outlines, and not a human dwelling was in sight. As I thought of the delight Shelley felt in such scenes of loneliness and grandeur whilst living, I felt we were no better than a herd of wolves or a pack of wild dogs, in tearing out his battered and naked body from the pure yellow sand that lay so lightly over it, to drag him back to the light of day; but the dead have no voice, nor had I power to check the sacrilege—the work went on silently in the deep and unresisting sand, not a word was spoken, for the Italians have a touch of sentiment, and their feelings are easily excited into sympathy. Even Byron was silent and thoughtful. We were startled and drawn together by a dull hollow sound that followed the blow of a mattock; the iron had struck a skull, and the body was soon uncovered. Lime had been strewn on it; this, or decomposition, had the effect of staining it of a dark and ghastly indigo colour. Byron asked me to preserve the skull for him; but remembering that he had formerly used one as a drinking-cup, I was determined Shelley's should not be so profaned. The limbs did not separate from the trunk, as in the case of Williams's body, so that the corpse was removed entire into the furnace. I had taken the precaution of having more and larger pieces of timber, in consequence of my experience of the day before of the difficulty of consuming a corpse in the open air with our apparatus. After the fire was well kindled we repeated the ceremony of the previous day; and more wine was poured over Shelley's dead body than he had consumed during his life. This with the oil and salt made the yellow flames glisten and quiver. The heat from the sun and fire was so intense that the atmosphere was tremulous and wavy. The corpse fell open and the heart was laid bare. The frontal bone of the skull, where it had been struck with the mattock, fell off; and, as the back of the head rested on the red-hot bottom bars of the furnace, the brains literally seethed, bubbled, and boiled as in a cauldron, for a very long time.

Byron could not face this scene, he withdrew to the beach and swam off to the *Bolivar*. Leigh Hunt remained in the carriage. The fire was so fierce as to produce a white heat on the iron, and to reduce its contents to grey ashes. The only portions that were not consumed were some fragments of bones, the jaw, and the skull, but what surprised us all, was that the heart remained entire. In snatching this relic from the fiery furnace, my hand was severely burnt; and had any one seen me do the act I should have been put into quarantine.

JOHN KEATS (1795-1821)

On First Looking into Chapman's Homer

MUCH have I travell'd in the realms of gold,
And many goodly states and kingdoms seen;
Round many western islands have I been
Which bards in fealty to Apollo hold.
Oft of one wide expanse had I been told
That deep-browed Homer ruled as his demesne;
Yet did I never breathe its pure serene
Till I heard Chapman speak out loud and bold:
Then felt I like some watcher of the skies
When a new planet swims into his ken;
Or like stout Cortez when with eagle eyes
He star'd at the Pacific—and all his men
Look'd at each other with a wild surmise—
Silent, upon a peak in Darien.

On the Grasshopper and the Cricket

THE poetry of earth is never dead:
When all the birds are faint with the hot sun,
And hide in cooling trees, a voice will run
From hedge to hedge about the new-mown mead.
That is the grasshopper's—he takes the lead
In summer luxury,—he has never done
With his delights, for when tired out with fun,
He rests at ease beneath some pleasant weed.
The poetry of earth is ceasing never:
On a lone winter evening, when the frost
Has wrought a silence, from the stove there shrills
The Cricket's song, in warmth increasing ever,
And seems to one in drowsiness half-lost,
The Grasshopper's among some grassy hills.

The Eve of St. Agnes

ST. AGNES' Eve—Ah, bitter chill it was!
The owl, for all his feathers, was a-cold;
The hare limp'd trembling through the frozen grass,
And silent was the flock in woolly fold:
Numb were the Beadsman's fingers, while he told
His rosary, and while his frosted breath,
Like pious incense from a censer old,
Seem'd taking flight for heaven, without a death,
Past the sweet Virgin's picture, while his prayer he saith.

His prayer he saith, this patient, holy man
Then takes his lamp, and riseth from his knees,
And back returneth, meagre, barefoot, wan,
Along the chapel aisle by slow degrees:
The sculptur'd dead, on each side, seem to freeze,
Emprison'd in black, purgatorial rails:
Knights, ladies, praying in dumb orat'ries,
He passeth by; and his weak spirit fails
To think how they may ache in icy hoods and mails.

Northward he turneth through a little door,
And scarce three steps, ere Music's golden tongue
Flatter'd to tears this aged man and poor;
But no—already had his deathbell rung;
The joys of all his life were said and sung:
His was harsh penance on St. Agnes' Eve:
Another way he went, and soon among
Rough ashes sat he for his soul's reprieve,
And all night kept awake, for sinners' sake to grieve.

That ancient Beadsman heard the prelude soft;
And so it chanc'd, for many a door was wide,
From hurry to and fro. Soon, up aloft,
The silver, snarling trumpets 'gan to chide:
The level chambers, ready with their pride,
Were glowing to receive a thousand guests:
The carvèd angels, ever eager-eyed,
Star'd where upon their heads the cornice rests,
With hair blown back, and wings put cross-wise on their breasts.

At length burst in the argent revelry,
With plume, tiara, and all rich array,
Numerous as shadows haunting fairily
The brain, new stuff'd, in youth, with triumphs gay
Of old romance. These let us wish away,
And turn, sole-thoughted, to one Lady there,
Whose heart had brooded, all that wintry day,
On love, and wing'd St. Agnes' saintly care,
As she had heard old dames full many times declare.

They told her how, upon St. Agnes' Eve,
Young virgins might have visions of delight,
And soft adorings from their loves receive
Upon the honey'd middle of the night
If ceremonies due they did aright;
As, supperless to bed they must retire,
And couch supine their beauties, lily white;
Nor look behind, nor sideways, but require
Of Heaven with upward eyes for all that they desire.

Full of this whim was thoughtful Madeline;
The music, yearning like a God in pain,
She scarcely heard: her maiden eyes divine,
Fix'd on the floor, saw many a sweeping train
Pass by—she heeded not at all: in vain
Came many a tiptoe, amorous cavalier,
And back retir'd; not cool'd by high disdain,
But she saw not: her heart was otherwhere:
She sigh'd for Agnes' dreams, the sweetest of the year.

She danc'd along with vague, regardless eyes,
Anxious her lips, her breathing quick and short:

The hallow'd hour was near at hand: she sighs
Amid the timbrels, and the throng'd resort
Of whisperings in anger, or in sport;
'Mid looks of love, defiance, hate, and scorn,
Hoodwink'd with faery fancy; all amort,
Save to St. Agnes and her lambs unshorn,
And all the bliss to be before to-morrow morn.

So, purposing each moment to retire,
She linger'd still. Meantime, across the moors,
Had come young Porphyro, with heart on fire
For Madeline. Beside the portal doors,
Buttress'd from moonlight, stands he, and implores
All saints to give him sight of Madeline,
But for one moment in the tedious hours,
That he might gaze and worship all unseen;
Perchance speak, kneel, touch, kiss—in sooth such things have been.

He ventures in: let no buzz'd whisper tell:
All eyes be muffled, or a hundred swords
Will storm his heart, Love's fev'rous citadel:
For him, those chambers held barbarian hordes,
Hyena foemen, and hot-blooded lords,
Whose very dogs would execrations howl
Against his lineage: not one breast affords
Him any mercy, in that mansion foul,
Save one old beldame, weak in body and in soul.

Ah, happy chance! the aged creature came,
Shuffling along with ivory-headed wand,
To where he stood, hid from the torch's flame,
Behind a broad hall-pillar, far beyond
The sound of merriment and chorus bland.
He startled her; but soon she knew his face,
And grasp'd his fingers in her palsied hand,
Saying, "Mercy, Porphyro! hie thee from this place;
They are all here to-night, the whole blood-thirsty race!

"Get hence! get hence! there's dwarfish Hildebrand;
He had a fever late, and in the fit
He cursèd thee and thine, both house and land:
Then there's that old Lord Maurice, not a whit
More tame for his gray hairs—Alas me! flit!
Flit like a ghost away."—"Ah, Gossip dear,
We're safe enough; here in this arm-chair sit,
And tell me how"—"Good Saints! not here, not here;
Follow me, child, or else these stones will be thy bier."

He follow'd through a lowly archèd way,
Brushing the cobwebs with his lofty plume;
And as she mutter'd "Well-a—Well-a-day!"
He found him in a little moonlight room,
Pale, lattic'd, chill, and silent as a tomb.
"Now tell me where is Madeline," said he,
"O tell me, Angela, by the holy loom
Which none but secret sisterhood may see,
When they St. Agnes' wool are weaving piously."

"St. Agnes! Ah! it is St. Agnes' Eve—
Yet men will murder upon holy days:
Thou must hold water in a witch's sieve,
And be liege-lord of all the Elves and Fays,

To venture so: it fills me with amaze
To see thee, Porphyro!—St. Agnes' Eve!
God's help! my lady fair the conjurer plays
This very night; good angels her deceive!
But let me laugh awhile, I've mickle time to grieve."

Feebly she laugheth in the languid moon,
While Porphyro upon her face doth look,
Like puzzled urchin on an agèd crone
Who keepeth clos'd a wond'rous riddle-book,
As spectacled she sits in chimney nook.
But soon his eyes grew brilliant, when she told
His lady's purpose; and he scarce could brook
Tears, at the thought of those enchantments cold,
And Madeline asleep in lap of legends old.

Sudden a thought came like a full-blown rose,
Flushing his brow, and in his painèd heart
Made purple riot: then doth he propose
A stratagem, that makes the beldame start:
"A cruel man and impious thou art:
Sweet lady, let her pray, and sleep, and dream
Alone with her good angels, far apart
From wicked men like thee. Go, go!—I deem
Thou canst not surely be the same that thou didst seem."

"I will not harm her, by all saints I swear,"
Quoth Porphyro: "O may I ne'er find grace
When my weak voice shall whisper its last prayer,
If one of her soft ringlets I displace,
Or look with ruffian passion in her face:
Good Angela, believe me by these tears;
Or I will, even in a moment's space,
Awake, with horrid shout, my foemen's ears,
And beard them, though they be more fang'd than wolves and bears."

"Ah! why wilt thou affright a feeble soul?
A poor, weak, palsy-stricken church-yard thing,
Whose passing-bell may ere the midnight toll;
Whose prayers for thee, each morn and evening,
Were never miss'd." Thus plaining, doth she bring
A gentler speech from burning Porphyro;
So woful, and of such deep sorrowing,
That Angela gives promise she will do
Whatever he shall wish, betide her weal or woe.

Which was, to lead him, in close secrecy,
Even to Madeline's chamber, and there hide
Him in a closet, of such privacy
That he might see her beauty unespied,
And win perhaps that night a peerless bride,
While legion'd fairies pac'd the coverlet,
And pale enchantment held her sleepy-eyed.
Never on such a night have lovers met,
Since Merlin paid his Demon all the monstrous debt.

"It shall be as thou wishest," said the Dame:
"All cates and dainties shall be storèd there
Quickly on this feast-night: by the tambour frame
Her own lute thou wilt see: no time to spare,
For I am slow and feeble, and scarce dare
On such a catering trust my dizzy head.
Wait here, my child, with patience; kneel in prayer

The while: Ah! thou must needs the lady
wed,
Or may I never leave my grave among
the dead."

So saying, she hobbled off with busy fear.
The lover's endless minutes slowly
pass'd;
The dame return'd, and whisper'd in his
ear
To follow her; with agèd eyes aghast
From fright of dim espial. Safe at last,
Through many a dusky gallery, they gain
The maiden's chamber, silken, hush'd,
and chaste;
Where Porphyro took covert, pleas'd
amain.
His poor guide hurried back with agues
in her brain.

Her falt'ring hand upon the balustrade,
Old Angela was feeling for the stair,
When Madeline, St. Agnes' charmèd
maid,
Rose, like a mission'd spirit, unaware:
With silver taper's light, and pious care,
She turn'd, and down the agèd gossip led
To a safe level matting. Now prepare,
Young Porphyro, for gazing on that bed;
She comes, she comes again, like ring-
dove fray'd and fled.

Out went the taper as she hurried in;
Its little smoke, in pallid moonshine,
died:
She clos'd the door, she panted, all akin
To spirits of the air, and visions wide:
No uttered syllable, or, woe betide!
But to her heart, her heart was voluble,
Paining with eloquence her balmy side;
As though a tongueless nightingale should
swell
Her throat in vain, and die, heart-stifled,
in her dell.

A casement high and triple arch'd there
was,
All garlanded with carven imag'ries
Of fruits, and flowers, and bunches of
knot-grass.
And diamonded with panes of quaint de-
vice,
Innumerable of stains and splendid dyes,
As are the tiger-moth's deep-damask'd
wings;
And in the midst, 'mong thousand her-
aldries,
And twilight saints, and dim emblazon-
ings,
A shielded scutcheon blush'd with blood
of queens and kings.

Full on this casement shone the wintry
moon,
And threw warm gules on Madeline's
fair breast,
As down she knelt for heaven's grace
and boon;
Rose-bloom fell on her hands, together
prest,
And on her silver cross soft amethyst,
And on her hair a glory, like a saint:
She seem'd a splendid angel, newly drest,
Save wings, for heaven: Porphyro grew
faint:
She knelt, so pure a thing, so free from
mortal taint.

Anon his heart revives: her vespers done,
Of all its wreathed pearls her hair she
frees;
Unclasps her warmèd jewels one by one,
Loosens her fragrant bodice; by degrees
Her rich attire creeps rustling to her
knees;
Half-hidden, like a mermaid in seaweed,
Pensive awhile she dreams awake, and
sees,
In fancy, fair St. Agnes in her bed,
But dares not look behind, or all the
charm is fled.

Soon, trembling in her soft and chilly
nest,
In sort of wakeful swoon, perplex'd she
lay.
Until the poppied warmth of sleep oppress'd
Her soothèd limbs, and soul fatigued
away;

Flown, like a thought, until the morrow-
day;
Blissfully haven'd both from joy and
pain;
Clasp'd like a missal where swart Pay-
nims pray;
Blinded alike from sunshine and from
rain,
As though a rose should shut, and be a
bud again.

Stol'n to this paradise, and so entranced,
Porphyro gazed upon her empty dress,
And listen'd to her breathing, if it
chanced
To wake into a slumberous tenderness;
Which when he heard, that minute did he
bless,
And breath'd himself: then from the
closet crept,
Noiseless as fear in a wide wilderness,
And over the hush'd carpet, silent,
stepped,
And 'tween the curtains peep'd, where,
lo!—how fast she slept.

Then by the bedside, where the faded
moon
Made a dim, silver twilight, soft he set
A table, and, half-anguish'd, threw
thereon
A cloth of woven crimson, gold, and
jet:—
O for some drowsy Morphean amulet!
The boisterous, midnight, festive clarion,
The kettle-drum, and far-heard clarionet,
Affray his ears, though but in dying
tone:—
The hall door shuts again, and all the
noise is gone.

And still she slept an azure-lidded sleep,
In blanchèd linen, smooth, and laven-
der'd,
While he from forth the closet brought
a heap
Of candied apple, quince, and plum, and
gourd;
With jellies soother than the creamy
curd,
And lucent syrops, tinct with cinnamon;
Manna and dates, in argosy transferr'd
From Fez; and spicèd dainties, every one,
From silken Samarcand to cedar'd
Lebanon.

These delicates he heap'd with glowing
hand
On golden dishes and in baskets bright
Of wreathèd silver: sumptuous they
stand
In the retired quiet of the night,
Filling the chilly room with perfume
light.—
"And now, my love, my seraph fair,
awake!
Thou art my heaven, and I thine eremite:
Open thine eyes, for meek St. Agnes'
sake,
Or I shall drowse beside thee, so my soul
doth ache."

Thus whispering, his warm, unnervèd
arm
Sank in her pillow. Shaded was her
dream
By the dusk curtains:—'twas a midnight
charm
Impossible to melt as icèd stream:
The lustrous salvers in the moonlight
gleam:
Broad golden fringe upon the carpet lies:
It seem'd he never, never could redeem
From such a stedfast spell his lady's
eyes;
So mus'd awhile, entoil'd in woofèd
phantasies.

Awakening up, he took her hollow lute,—
Tumultuous,—and, in chords that ten-
derest be,
He play'd an ancient ditty, long since
mute,
In Provence call'd, "La belle dame sans
merci:"
Close to her ear touching the melody;
Wherewith disturb'd, she utter'd a soft
moan:
He ceased—she panted quick—and sud-
denly

Her blue affrayèd eyes wide open shone:
Upon his knees he sank, pale as smooth-
sculptured stone.

Her eyes were open, but she still beheld,
Now wide awake, the vision of her sleep:
There was a painful change, that nigh
expell'd
The blisses of her dream so pure and
deep
At which fair Madeline began to weep,
And moan forth witless words with many
a sigh;
While still her gaze on Porphyro would
keep;
Who knelt, with joinèd hands and piteous
eye,
Fearing to move or speak, she look'd so
dreamingly.

"Ah, Porphyro!" said she, "but even now
Thy voice was at sweet tremble in mine
ear,
Made tunable with every sweetest vow:
And those sad eyes were spiritual and
clear.
How chang'd thou art! how pallid, chill,
and drear!
Give me that voice again, my Porphyro,
Those looks immortal, those complain-
ings dear!
Oh leave me not in this eternal woe,
For if thou diest, my Love, I know not
where to go."

Beyond a mortal man impassion'd far
At these voluptuous accents, he arose,
Ethereal, flush'd, and like a throbbing
star
Seen mid the sapphire heaven's deep re-
pose;
Into her dream he melted, as the rose
Blendeth its odour with the violet,—
Solution sweet: meantime the frost wind
blows
Like Love's alarum pattering the sharp
sleet
Against the window-panes; St. Agnes'
moon hath set.

'Tis dark: quick pattereth the flaw-blown
sleet:
"This is no dream, my bride, my Made-
line!"
'Tis dark: the icèd gusts still rave and
beat:
"No dream, alas! alas! and woe is mine!
Porphyro will leave me here to fade and
pine.—
Cruel! what traitor could thee hither
bring?
I curse not, for my heart is lost in thine,
Though thou forsakest a deceivèd
thing;—
A dove forlorn and lost with sick un-
prunèd wing."

"My Madeline! sweet dreamer! lovely
bride!
Say, may I be for aye thy vassal blest?
The beauty's shield, heart-shap'd and ver-
meil dyed?
Ah, silver shrine, here will I take my
rest
After so many hours of toil and quest,
A famish'd pilgrim,—saved by miracle.
Though I have found, I will not rob thy
nest
Saving of thy sweet self; if thou think'st
well
To trust, fair Madeline, to no rude
infidel.

"Hark! 'tis an elfin-storm from faery
land,
Of haggard seeming, but a boon indeed:
Arise—arise! the morning is at hand;—
The bloated wassaillers will never
heed:—
Let us away, my love, with happy speed:
There are no ears to hear, or eyes to
see,—
Drown'd all in Rhenish and the sleepy
mead:
Awake! arise! my love, and fearless
be,
For o'er the southern moors I have a
home for thee."

She hurried at his words, beset with fears,
For there were sleeping dragons all around,
At glaring watch, perhaps, with ready spears—
Down the wide stairs a darkling way they found.—
In all the house was heard no human sound.
A chain-droop'd lamp was flickering by each door;
The arras, rich with horseman, hawk, and hound,
Flutter'd in the besieging wind's uproar;
And the long carpets rose along the gusty floor.

They glide, like phantoms, into the wide hall;
Like phantoms, to the iron porch, they glide;
Where lay the Porter, in uneasy sprawl,
With a huge empty flagon by his side:
The wakeful bloodhound rose, and shook his hide,
But his sagacious eye an inmate owns:
By one, and one, the bolts full easy slide:—
The chains lie silent on the footworn stones;—
The key turns, and the door upon its hinges groans.

And they are gone: ay, ages long ago
These lovers fled away into the storm.
That night the Baron dreamt of many a woe,
And all his warrior-guests, with shade and form
Of witch, and demon, and large coffin-worm,
Were long be-nightmar'd. Angela the old
Died palsy-twitch'd, with meagre face deform;
The Beadsman, after thousand aves told,
For aye unsought for slept among his ashes cold.

Ode to a Nightingale

My heart aches, and a drowsy numbness pains
My sense, as though of hemlock I had drunk,
Or emptied some dull opiate to the drains
One minute past, and Lethe-wards had sunk:
'Tis not through envy of thy happy lot,
But being too happy in thine happiness,—
That thou, light-wingèd Dryad of the trees,
In some melodious plot
Of beechen green, and shadows numberless,
Singest of summer in full-throated ease.

O, for a draught of vintage, that hath been
Cool'd a long age in the deep-delvèd earth,
Tasting of Flora and the country-green,
Dance, and Provençal song, and sunburnt mirth!
O for a beaker full of the warm South,
Full of the true, the blushful Hippocrene,
With beaded bubbles winking at the brim,
And purple-stainèd mouth;
That I might drink, and leave the world unseen,
And with thee fade away into the forest dim:

Fade far away, dissolve, and quite forget
What thou amongst the leaves hast never known,
The weariness, the fever, and the fret
Here, where men sit and hear each other groan;
Where palsy shakes a few, sad, last gray hairs,
Where youth grows pale, and spectre-thin, and dies;

Where but to think is to be full of sorrow
And leaden-eyed despairs,
Where Beauty cannot keep her lustrous eyes,
Or new Love pine at them beyond to-morrow.

Away! away! for I will fly to thee,
Not charioted by Bacchus and his pards,
But on the viewless wings of Poesy,
Though the dull brain perplexes and retards:
Already with thee! tender is the night,
And haply the Queen-Moon is on her throne,
Cluster'd around by all her starry Fays;
But here there is no light,
Save what from heaven is with the breezes blown
Through verdurous glooms and winding mossy ways.

I cannot see what flowers are at my feet,
Nor what soft incense hangs upon the boughs,
But, in embalmèd darkness, guess each sweet
Wherewith the seasonable month endows
The grass, the thicket, and the fruit-tree wild;
White hawthorn, and the pastoral eglantine;
Fast-fading violets cover'd up in leaves;
And mid-May's eldest child,
The coming musk-rose, full of dewy wine,
The murmurous haunt of flies on summer eves.

Darkling I listen; and, for many a time
I have been half in love with easeful Death,
Call'd him soft names in many a musèd rhyme,
To take into the air my quiet breath;
Now more than ever seems it rich to die,
To cease upon the midnight with no pain,
While thou art pouring forth thy soul abroad
In such an ecstasy!
Still wouldst thou sing, and I have ears in vain—
To thy high requiem become a sod.

Thou wast not born for death, immortal Bird!
No hungry generations tread thee down;
The voice I hear this passing night was heard
In ancient days by emperor and clown:
Perhaps the self-same song that found a path
Through the sad heart of Ruth, when, sick for home,
She stood in tears amid the alien corn;
The same that oft-times hath
Charm'd magic casements, opening on the foam
Of perilous seas, in faery lands forlorn.

Forlorn! the very word is like a bell
To toll me back from thee to my sole self!
Adieu! the fancy cannot cheat so well
As she is fam'd to do, deceiving elf.
Adieu! adieu! thy plaintive anthem fades
Past the near meadows, over the still stream,
Up the hill-side; and now 'tis buried deep
In the next valley-glades:
Was it a vision, or a waking dream?
Fled is that music:—Do I wake or sleep?

Ode on a Grecian Urn

THOU still unravish'd bride of quietness,
Thou foster-child of silence and slow time,

Sylvan historian, who canst thus express
  A flowery tale more sweetly than our rhyme:
What leaf-fring'd legend haunts about thy shape
  Of deities or mortals, or of both,
    In Tempe or the dales of Arcady?
What men or gods are these? What maidens loth?
  What mad pursuit? What struggle to escape?
    What pipes and timbrels? What wild ecstasy?

Heard melodies are sweet, but those unheard
  Are sweeter; therefore, ye soft pipes, play on;
Not to the sensual ear, but, more endear'd,
  Pipe to the spirit ditties of no tone:
Fair youth, beneath the trees, thou canst not leave
  Thy song, nor ever can those trees be bare;
    Bold Lover, never, never canst thou kiss
Though winning near the goal—yet, do not grieve;
  She cannot fade, though thou hast not thy bliss,
    For ever wilt thou love, and she be fair!

Ah, happy, happy boughs! that cannot shed
  Your leaves, nor ever bid the Spring adieu;
And, happy melodist, unweariè̀d,
  For ever piping songs for ever new;
More happy love! more happy, happy love!
  For ever warm and still to be enjoy'd,
    For ever panting, and for ever young;
All breathing human passion far above,
  That leaves a heart high-sorrowful and cloy'd,
    A burning forehead, and a parching tongue.

Who are these coming to the sacrifice?
  To what green altar, O mysterious priest,
Lead'st thou that heifer lowing at the skies,
  And all her silken flanks with garlands dressed?
What little town by river or sea-shore,
  Or mountain-built with peaceful citadel,
    Is emptied of this folk, this pious morn?
And, little town, thy streets for evermore
  Will silent be; and not a soul to tell
    Why thou art desolate, can e'er return.

O Attic shape! Fair attitude! with brede
  Of marble men and maidens overwrought,
With forest branches and the trodden weed;
  Thou, silent form, dost tease us out of thought
As doth eternity: Cold Pastoral!
  When old age shall this generation waste,
  Thou shalt remain, in midst of other woe
Than ours, a friend to man, to whom thou say'st,
  "Beauty is truth, truth beauty,"—that is all
    Ye know on earth, and all ye need to know.

Ode to Psyche

O GODDESS! hear these tuneless numbers, wrung
  By sweet enforcement and remembrance dear,
And pardon that thy secrets should be sung,
  Even into thine own soft-conchèd ear:
Surely I dreamt to-day, or did I see
  The wingèd Psyche with awaken'd eyes?

I wander'd in a forest thoughtlessly,
And, on the sudden, fainting with surprise,
Saw two fair creatures, couchèd side by side
In deepest grass, beneath the whispering roof
Of leaves and trembled blossoms, where there ran
A brooklet, scarce espied:
'Mid hush'd, cool-rooted flowers fragrant-eyed,
Blue, silver-white, and budded Tyrian,
They lay calm-breathing on the bedded grass;
Their arms embracèd, and their pinions too;
Their lips touch'd not, but had not bade adieu
As if disjoinèd by soft-handed slumber,
And ready still past kisses to outnumber
At tender eye-dawn of aurorean love:
The wingèd boy I knew;
But who wast thou, O happy, happy dove?
His Psyche true!

O latest-born and loveliest vision far
Of all Olympus' faded hierarchy!
Fairer than Phœbe's sapphire-region'd star,
Or Vesper, amorous glow-worm of the sky;
Fairer than these, though temple thou hast none,
Nor altar heap'd with flowers;
Nor Virgin-choir to make delicious moan
Upon the midnight hours;
No voice, no lute, no pipe, no incense sweet
From chain-swung censer teeming;
No shrine, no grove, no oracle, no heat
Of pale-mouth'd prophet dreaming.
O brightest! though too late for antique vows,
Too, too late for the fond believing lyre,
When holy were the haunted forest boughs,
Holy the air, the water, and the fire;
Yet even in these days so far retired
From happy pieties, thy lucent fans,
Fluttering among the faint Olympians,
I see, and sing, by my own eyes inspired.
So let me be thy choir, and make a moan
Upon the midnight hours!
Thy voice, thy lute, thy pipe, thy incense sweet
From swingèd censer teeming:
Thy shrine, thy grove, thy oracle, thy heat
Of pale-mouth'd prophet dreaming.

Yes, I will be thy priest, and build a fane
In some untrodden region of my mind,
Where branchèd thoughts, new-grown with pleasant pain,
Instead of pines shall murmur in the wind:
Far, far around shall those dark-cluster'd trees
Fledge the wild-ridgèd mountains steep by steep;
And there by zephyrs, streams, and birds, and bees,
The moss-lain Dryads shall be lull'd to sleep;
And in the midst of this wide quietness
A rosy sanctuary will I dress
With the wreath'd trellis of a working brain,
With buds, and bells, and stars without a name,
With all the gardener Fancy e'er could feign,
Who breeding flowers, will never breed the same:
And there shall be for thee all soft delight
That shadowy thought can win,
A bright torch, and a casement ope at night,
To let the warm Love in!

Lines on the Mermaid Tavern

Souls of poets dead and gone,
What Elysium have ye known,
Happy field or mossy cavern,
Choicer than the Mermaid Tavern?
Have ye tippled drink more fine
Than mine host's Canary wine?
Or are fruits of Paradise
Sweeter than those dainty pies
Of venison? O generous food!
Drest as though bold Robin Hood
Would, with his maid Marian,
Sup and bowse from horn and can.

I have heard that on a day
Mine host's sign-board flew away,
Nobody knew whither, till
An Astrologer's old quill
To a sheepskin gave the story,—
Said he saw you in your glory,
Underneath a new old-sign
Sipping beverage divine,
And pledging with contented smack
The Mermaid in the Zodiac.

Souls of poets dead and gone,
What Elysium have ye known,
Happy field or mossy cavern,
Choicer than the Mermaid Tavern?

Robin Hood

No! those days are gone away,
And their hours are old and gray,
And their minutes buried all
Under the down-trodden pall
Of the leaves of many years:
Many times have Winter's shears,
Frozen North, and chilling East,
Sounded tempests to the feast
Of the forest's whispering fleeces,
Since men knew nor rent nor leases.

No, the bugle sounds no more,
And the twanging bow no more;
Silent is the ivory shrill
Past the heath and up the hill;
There is no mid-forest laugh,
Where lone Echo gives the half
To some wight, amazed to hear
Jesting, deep in forest drear.

On the fairest time of June
You may go, with sun or moon,
Or the seven stars to light you,
Or the polar ray to right you;
But you never may behold
Little John, or Robin bold;
Never one, of all the clan,
Thrumming on an empty can
Some old hunting ditty, while
He doth his green way beguile
To fair hostess Merriment,
Down beside the pasture Trent;
For he left the merry tale,
Messenger for spicy ale.

Gone, the merry morris din;
Gone, the song of Gamelyn;
Gone, the tough-belted outlaw
Idling in the "grené shawe";
All are gone away and past!
And if Robin should be cast
Sudden from his tufted grave,
And if Marian should have
Once again her forest days,
She would weep, and he would craze;
He would swear, for all his oaks,
Fall'n beneath the dock-yard strokes,
Have rotted on the briny seas;
She would weep that her wild bees
Sang not to her—strange! that honey
Can't be got without hard money!

So it is; yet let us sing
Honour to the old bow-string!
Honour to the bugle-horn!
Honour to the woods unshorn!
Honour to the Lincoln green!
Honour to the archer keen!
Honour to tight Little John,
And the horse he rode upon!
Honour to bold Robin Hood,
Sleeping in the underwood:
Honour to Maid Marian,
And to all the Sherwood clan!
Though their days have hurried by
Let us two a burden try.

To Autumn

Season of mists and mellow fruitfulness,
Close bosom-friend of the maturing sun;
Conspiring with him how to load and bless
With fruit the vines that round the thatch-eaves run;
To bend with apples the mossed cottage-trees,
And fill all fruit with ripeness to the core;
To swell the gourd, and plump the hazel shells
With a sweet kernel; to set budding more,
And still more, later flowers for the bees,
Until they think warm days will never cease,
For Summer has o'er-brimmed their clammy cells.

Who hath not seen thee oft amid thy store?
Sometimes whoever seeks abroad may find
Thee sitting careless on a granary floor,
Thy hair soft-lifted by the winnowing wind;
Or on a half-reaped furrow sound asleep,
Drowsed with the fume of poppies, while thy hook
Spares the next swath and all its twinèd flowers:
And sometimes like a gleaner thou dost keep
Steady thy laden head across a brook;
Or by a cider-press, with patient look,
Thou watchest the last oozings hours by hours.

Where are the songs of Spring? Ay, where are they?
Think not of them, thou hast thy music too,—
While barrèd clouds bloom the soft-dying day,
And touch the stubble-plains with rosy hue;
Then in a wailful choir the small gnats mourn
Among the river sallows, borne aloft
Or sinking as the light wind lives or dies;
And full-grown lambs loud bleat from hilly bourn;
Hedge-crickets sing; and now with treble soft
The red-breast whistles from a garden-croft;
And gathering swallows twitter in the skies.

Ode on Melancholy

No, no! go not to Lethe, neither twist
Wolf's-bane, tight-rooted, for its poisonous wine;
Nor suffer thy pale forehead to be kiss'd
By nightshade, ruby grape of Proserpine;
Make not your rosary of yew-berries,
Nor let the beetle nor the death-moth be
Your mournful Psyche, nor the downy owl
A partner in your sorrow's mysteries;
For shade to shade will come too drowsily,
And drown the wakeful anguish of the soul.

But when the melancholy fit shall fall
Sudden from heaven like a weeping cloud,
That fosters the droop-headed flowers all,
And hides the green hill in an April shroud;
Then glut thy sorrow on a morning rose,
Or on the rainbow of the salt sand-wave,
Or on the wealth of globèd peonies;
Or if thy mistress some rich anger shows,

Emprison her soft hand, and let her rave,
And feed deep, deep upon her peerless eyes.

She dwells with Beauty—Beauty that must die;
And Joy, whose hand is ever at his lips
Bidding adieu; and aching Pleasure nigh,
Turning to poison while the bee-mouth sips:
Ay, in the very temple of Delight
Veil'd Melancholy has her sovran shrine,
Though seen of none save him whose strenuous tongue
Can burst Joy's grape against his palate fine:
His soul shall taste the sadness of her might,
And be among her cloudy trophies hung.

When I have fears that I may cease to be

When I have fears that I may cease to be
Before my pen has glean'd my teeming brain,
Before high-pilèd books, in charact'ry,
Hold like full garners the full-ripen'd grain;
When I behold, upon the night's starr'd face,
Huge cloudy symbols of a high romance,
And feel that I may never live to trace
Their shadows, with the magic hand of chance;
And when I feel, fair creature of an hour!
That I shall never look upon thee more,
Never have relish in the faery power
Of unreflecting love;—then on the shore
Of the wide world I stand alone, and think,
Till Love and Fame to nothingness do sink.

The Eve of St. Mark

Upon a Sabbath-day it fell;
Twice holy was the Sabbath-bell,
That call'd the folk to evening prayer;
The city streets were clean and fair
From wholesome drench of April rains;
And, on the western window panes,
The chilly sunset faintly told
Of unmatured green, vallies cold,
Of the green thorny bloomless hedge,
Of rivers new with spring-tide sedge,
Of primroses by shelter'd rills,
And daisies on the aguish hills.
Twice holy was the Sabbath-bell:
The silent streets were crowded well
With staid and pious companies,
Warm from their fire-side orat'ries;
And moving, with demurest air,
To even-song, and vesper prayer,
Each archèd porch, and entry low,
Was fill'd with patient folk and slow,
With whispers hush, and shuffling feet,
While play'd the organ loud and sweet.
The bells had ceased, the prayers begun,
And Bertha had not yet half done
A curious volume, patch'd and torn,
That all day long, from earliest morn,
Had taken captive her two eyes,
Among its golden broideries;
Perplex'd her with a thousand things,—
The stars of heaven, and angels' wings,
Martyrs in a fiery blaze,
Azure saints and silver rays,
Moses' breastplate, and the seven
Candlesticks John saw in heaven,
The wingèd Lion of Saint Mark,
And the Covenantal Ark,
With its many mysteries,
Cherubim and golden mice.

Bertha was a maiden fair,
Dwelling in th' old minster-square;
From her fire-side she could see,
Sidelong, its rich antiquity,
Far as the Bishop's garden-wall;
Where sycamores and elm-trees tall,
Full-leaved, the forest had outstript,
By no sharp north-wind ever nipt,

So shelter'd by the mighty pile.
Bertha arose, and read awhile,
With forehead 'gainst the window-pane.
Again she tried, and then again,
Until the dusk eve left her dark
Upon the legend of St. Mark.
From plaited lawn-frill, fine and thin,
She lifted up her soft warm chin,
With aching neck and swimming eyes,
And dazed with saintly imag'ries.

All was gloom, and silent all,
Save now and then the still foot-fall
Of one returning homewards late,
Past the echoing minster-gate.
The clamorous daws, that all the day
Above tree-tops and towers play,
Pair by pair had gone to rest,
Each in its ancient belfry-nest,
Where asleep they fall betimes,
To music and the drowsy chimes.
All was silent, all was gloom,
Abroad and in the homely room:
Down she sat, poor cheated soul!
And struck a lamp from the dismal coal;
Lean'd forward, with bright drooping hair
And slant book, full against the glare.
Her shadow, in uneasy guise,
Hover'd about, a giant size,
On ceiling-beam and old oak chair,
The parrot's cage, and panel square;
And the warm angled winter-screen,
On which were many monsters seen,
Call'd doves of Siam, Lima mice,
And legless birds of Paradise,
Macaw, and tender Av'davat,
And silken-furr'd Angora cat.
Untired she read, her shadow still
Glower'd about, as it would fill
The room with wildest forms and shades,
As though some ghostly queen of spades
Had come to mock behind her back,
And dance, and ruffle her garments black.
Untired she read the legend page,
Of holy Mark, from youth to age,
On land, on sea, in pagan chains,
Rejoicing for his many pains.
Sometimes the learnèd eremite,
With golden star, or dagger bright,
Referr'd to pious poesies
Written in smallest crow-quill size
Beneath the text; and thus the rhyme
Was parcell'd out from time to time:
——"Als writith he of swevenis,
Men han beforne they wake in bliss,
Whanne that hir friendes thinke him bound
In crimpèd shroude farre under grounde;
And how a litling child mote be
A saint er its nativitie,
Gif that the modre (God her blesse!)
Kepen in solitarinesse,
And kissen devoute the holy croce.
Of Goddes love, and Sathan's force,—
He writith; and thinges many mo
Of swiche thinges I may not shew.
Bot I must tellen verilie
Somdel of Saintè Cicilie,
And chieflie what he auctorethe
Of Saintè Markis life and dethe:"

At length her constant eyelids come
Upon the fervent martyrdom;
Then lastly to his holy shrine,
Exalt amid the tapers' shine
At Venice,—

La Belle Dame Sans Merci

O WHAT can ail thee, knight-at-arms,
Alone and palely loitering!
The sedge has wither'd from the lake,
And no birds sing.

O what can ail thee, knight-at-arms!
So haggard and so woe-begone?
The squirrel's granary is full,
And the harvest's done.

I see a lily on thy brow
With anguish moist and fever dew,
And on thy cheeks a fading rose
Fast withereth too.

I met a lady in the meads,
Full beautiful—a faery's child,
Her hair was long, her foot was light,
And her eyes were wild.

I made a garland for her head,
And bracelets too, and fragrant zone;
She look'd at me as she did love,
And made sweet moan.

I set her on my pacing steed,
And nothing else saw all day long.
For sidelong would she bend, and sing
A faery's song.

She found me roots of relish sweet,
And honey wild, and manna dew,
And sure in language strange she said—
"I love thee true."

She took me to her elfin grot,
And there she wept, and sigh'd full sore,
And there I shut her wild wild eyes
With kisses four.

And there she lullèd me asleep,
And there I dream'd—Ah! woe betide!
The latest dream I ever dream'd
On the cold hill's side.

I saw pale kings and princes too,
Pale warriors, death-pale were they all;
They cried—"La Belle Dame sans Merci
Hath thee in thrall!"

I saw their starv'd lips in the gloom,
With horrid warning gapèd wide,
And I awoke and found me here,
On the cold hill's side.

And this is why I sojourn here,
Alone and palely loitering,
Though the sedge is wither'd from the lake
And no birds sing.

Written on a Blank Page in Shakespeare's Poems, facing "A Lover's Complaint"

BRIGHT star! would I were steadfast as thou art—
Not in lone splendour hung aloft the night,
And watching, with eternal lids apart,
Like Nature's patient sleepless Eremite,
The moving waters at their priestlike task
Of pure ablution round earth's human shores,
Or gazing on the new soft-fallen mask
Of snow upon the mountains and the moors—
No—yet still steadfast, still unchangeable,
Pillow'd upon my fair love's ripening breast,
To feel for ever its soft fall and swell,
Awake for ever in a sweet unrest,
Still, still to hear her tender-taken breath,
And so live ever—or else swoon to death.

THOMAS CARLYLE (1795-1881)

From THE FRENCH REVOLUTION

The Fall of the Bastille

TO DESCRIBE this Siege of the Bastille (thought to be one of the most important in History) perhaps transcends the talent of mortals. Could one but, after infinite reading, get to understand so much as the plan of the building! But there is the open Esplanade, at the end of the Rue Saint-Antoine; there are such Forecourts, *Cour Avancée, Cour de l'Orme,* arched Gateway (where Louis Tournay now fights); then new drawbridges, dormant-bridges, rampart-bastions, and the grim Eight Towers; a labyrinthic Mass, high-frowning there, of all ages from twenty years to four hundred and twenty;—beleaguered, in this its last hour, as we said, by mere Chaos come again! Ordnance of all calibres; throats of all capacities; men of all plans, every man his own engineer: seldom since the war of Pygmies and Cranes was there seen so anomalous a thing. Half-pay Elie is home for a suit of regimentals; no one would heed him in coloured clothes; half-pay Hulin is haranguing Gardes Françaises in the Place de Grève. Frantic Patriots pick up the grapeshots; bear them, still hot (or seemingly so), to the Hôtel-de-Ville;—Paris, you perceive, is to be burnt! Flesselles is "pale to the very lips," for the roar of the multitude grows deep. Paris wholly has got to the acme of its frenzy; whirled, all ways, by panic madness. At every street-barricade, there whirls simmering a minor whirlpool,—strengthening the barricade, since God knows what is coming; and all minor whirlpools play distractedly into that grand Fire-Mahlstrom which is lashing round the Bastille.

And so it lashes and it roars. Cholat the wine-merchant has become an impromptu cannoneer. See Georget, of the Marine Service, fresh from Brest, ply the King of Siam's cannon. Singular (if we were not used to the like): Georget lay, last night, taking his ease at his inn; the King of Siam's cannon also lay, knowing nothing of *him,* for a hundred years. Yet now, at the right instant, they have got together, and discourse eloquent music. For, hearing what was toward, Georget sprang from the Brest Diligence, and ran. Gardes Françaises also will be here, with real artillery: were not the walls so thick!—Upwards from the Esplanade, horizontally from all neighbouring roofs and windows, flashes one irregular deluge of musketry, without effect. The Invalides lie flat, firing comparatively at their ease from behind stone; hardly through portholes, show the tip of a nose. We fall, shot; and make no impression!

Let conflagration rage; of whatsoever is combustible! Guard-rooms are burnt, Invalides mess-rooms. A distracted "Peruke-maker with two fiery torches" is for burning "the saltpetres of the Arsenal;"—had not a woman run screaming; had not a Patriot, with some tincture of Natural Philosophy, instantly struck the wind out of him (butt of musket on pit of stomach), overturned barrels, and stayed the devouring element. A young beautiful lady, seized escaping in these Outer Courts, and thought falsely to be De Launay's daughter, shall be burnt in De Launay's sight; she lies swooned on a paillasse: but again a Patriot, it is brave Aubin Bonnemère the old soldier, dashes in, and rescues her. Straw is burnt; three cartloads of it, hauled thither, go up in white smoke: almost to the choking of Patriotism itself; so that Elie had, with singed brows, to drag back one cart; and Réole the "gigantic haberdasher" another. Smoke as of Tophet; confusion as of Babel; noise as of the Crack of Doom!

Blood flows; the aliment of new madness. The wounded are carried into houses of the Rue Cerisaie; the dying leave their last mandate not to yield till the accursed Stronghold fall. And yet, alas, how fall? The walls are so thick! Deputations, three in number, arrive from the Hôtel-de-Ville; Abbé Fauchet (who was of one) can say, with what almost superhuman courage of benevolence. These wave their Town-flag in the arched Gateway; and stand, rolling their drum; but to no purpose. In such Crack of Doom, De Launay cannot hear them, dare not believe them: they return, with justified rage, the whew of lead still singing in their ears. What to do? The Firemen are here, squirting with their fire-pumps on the Invalides cannon, to wet the touchholes; they unfortunately cannot squirt so high; but produce only clouds of spray. Individuals of classical knowledge propose *catapults*. Santerre, the sonorous Brewer of the Suburb Saint-Antoine, advises rather that the place be fired, by a "mixture of phosphorus and oil-of-turpentine spouted up through forcing pumps:" O Spinola-Santerre, hast thou the mixture *ready?* Every man his own engineer! And still the fire-deluge abates not: even women are firing, and Turks; at least one woman (with her sweetheart), and one Turk. Gardes Françaises have come: real cannon, real cannoneers. Usher Maillard is busy; half-pay Elie, half-pay Hulin rage in the midst of thousands.

How the great Bastille Clock ticks (inaudible) in its Inner Court there, at its ease, hour after hour; as if nothing special, for it or the world, were passing! It tolled One when the firing began; and is now pointing towards Five, and still the firing slakes not.—Far down, in their vaults, the seven Prisoners hear muffled din as of earthquakes; their Turnkeys answer vaguely.

Wo to thee, De Launay, with thy poor hundred Invalides! Broglie is distant, and his ears heavy: Besenval hears, but can send no help. One poor troop of Hussars has crept, reconnoitering, cautiously along the Quais, as far as the Pont Neuf. "We are come to join you," said the Captain; for the crowd seems shoreless. A large-headed dwarfish individual of smoke-bleared aspect, shambles forward, opening his blue lips, for there is sense in him; and croaks: "Alight then, and give up your arms!" The Hussar-Captain is too happy to be escorted to the Barriers, and dismissed on parole. Who the squat individual was? Men answer, It is M. Marat, author of the excellent pacific *Avis au Peuple!* Great truly, O thou remarkable Dogleech, is this thy day of emergence and new-birth: and yet this same day come four years——!—But let the curtains of the Future hang.

What shall De Launay do? One thing only De Launay could have done: what he said he would do. Fancy him sitting, from the first, with lighted taper, within arm's length of the Powder-Magazine; motionless, like old Roman Senator, or Bronze Lamp-holder; coldly apprising Thuriot, and all men, by a slight motion of his eye, what his resolution was:—Harmless, he sat there, while unharmed; but the King's Fortress, meanwhile, could, might, would, or should, in nowise be surrendered, save to the King's Messenger: one old man's life is worthless, so it be lost with honour; but think, ye brawling *canaille,* how will it be when a whole Bastille springs skyward!—In such statuesque, taper-holding attitude, one fancies De Launay might have left Thuriot, the red Clerks of the Basoche, Curé of Saint Stephen and all the tag-rag-and-bobtail of the world, to work their will.

And yet, withal, he could not do it. Hast thou considered how each man's heart is so tremulously responsive to the hearts of all men; hast thou noted how omnipotent is the very sound of many men? How their shriek of indignation palsies the strong soul; their howl of contumely withers with unfelt pangs? The Ritter Gluck confessed that the ground-tone of the noblest passage, in one of his noblest Operas, was the voice of the Populace he had heard at Vienna, crying to their Kaiser: Bread! Bread! Great is the combined voice of men; the utterance of their *instincts,* which are truer than their *thoughts:* it is the greatest a man encounters, among the sounds and shadows which make up this World of Time. He who can resist that, has his footing somewhere *beyond* Time. De Launay could not do it. Distracted, he hovers between two; hopes in the middle of despair; surrenders not his Fortress; declares that he will blow it up, seizes torches to blow it up, and does not blow it. Unhappy old De Launay, it is the death-agony of thy Bastille and thee! Jail, Jailoring, and Jailor, all three, such as they may have been, must finish.

For four hours now has the World-Bedlam roared: call it the World-Chimæra, blowing fire! The poor Invalides have sunk under their battlements, or rise only with reversed muskets: they have made a white flag of napkins; go beating the *chamade,* or seeming to beat, for one can hear nothing. The very Swiss at the Portcullis look weary of firing; disheartened in the fire-deluge: a porthole at the drawbridge is opened, as by one that would speak. See Huissier Maillard, the shifty man! On his plank, swinging over the abyss of that stone Ditch; plank resting on parapet, balanced by weight of Patriots,—he hovers perilous: such a Dove towards such an Ark! Deftly, thou shifty Usher: one man already fell; and lies smashed, far down there, against the masonry; Usher Maillard falls not: deftly, unerring he walks, with outspread palm. The Swiss holds a paper through his porthole; the shifty Usher snatches it, and returns. Terms of surrender: Pardon, immunity to all! Are they accepted?—"*Foi d'officier,* On the word of an officer," answers half-pay Hulin,—or half-pay Elie, for men do not agree on it, "they are!" Sinks the drawbridge,—Usher Maillard bolting it when down; rushes-in the living deluge: the Bastille is fallen! *Victoire! La Bastille est prise!*

From Heroes and Hero-Worship

Samuel Johnson

As for Johnson, I have always considered him to be, by nature, one of our great English souls. A strong and noble man; so much left undeveloped in him to the last: in a kindlier element what might he not have been,—Poet, Priest, sovereign Ruler! On the whole, a man must not complain of his "element," of his "time," or the like; it is thriftless work doing so. His time is bad: well then, he is there to make it better!—Johnson's youth was poor, isolated, hopeless, very miserable. Indeed, it does not seem possible that, in any the favourablest outward circumstances, Johnson's life could have been other than a painful one. The world might have had more of profitable *work* out of him, or less; but his *effort* against the world's work could never have been a light one. Nature, in return for his nobleness, had said to him, Live in an element of diseased sorrow. Nay, perhaps the sorrow and the nobleness were intimately and even inseparably connected with each other. At all events, poor Johnson had to go about girt with continual hypochondria, physical and spiritual pain. Like a Hercules with the burning Nessus'-shirt on him, which shoots-in on him dull incurable misery: the Nessus'-shirt not to be stript-off, which is his own natural skin! In this manner *he* had to live. Figure him there, with his scrofulous diseases, with his great greedy heart, and unspeakable chaos of thoughts; stalking mournful as a stranger in this Earth; eagerly devouring what spiritual thing he could come at: school-languages and other merely grammatical stuff, if there were nothing better! The largest soul that was in all England; and provision made for it of "fourpence-halfpenny a day." Yet a giant invincible soul; a true man's. One remembers always that story of the shoes at Oxford: the rough, seamy-faced, rawboned College Servitor stalking about, in winter-season, with his shoes worn-out; how the charitable Gentleman Commoner secretly places a new pair at his door; and the rawboned Servitor, lifting them, looking at them near, with his dim eyes, with what thoughts,—pitches them out of window! Wet feet, mud, frost, hunger or what you will; but not beggary: we cannot stand beggary! Rude stubborn self-help here; a whole world of squalor, rudeness, confused misery and want, yet of nobleness and manfulness withal. It is a type of the man's life, this pitching-away of the shoes. An original man;—not a secondhand, borrowing or begging man. Let us stand on our own basis, at any rate! On such shoes as we ourselves can get. On frost and mud, if you will, but honestly on that;—on the reality and substance which Nature gives *us,* not on the semblance, on the thing she has given another than us!—

And yet with all this rugged pride of manhood and self-help was there ever soul more tenderly affectionate, loyally submissive to what was really higher than he? Great souls are always loyally submissive, reverent to what is over them; only small mean souls are otherwise. I could not find a better proof of what I said the other day, That the sincere man was by nature the obedient man; that only in a World of Heroes was there loyal Obedience to the Heroic. The essence of *originality* is not that it be *new:* Johnson believed altogether in the old; he found the old opinions credible for him, fit for him; and in a right heroic manner lived under them. He is well worth study in regard to that. For we are to say that Johnson was far other than a mere man of words and formulas; he was a man of truths and facts. He stood by the old formulas; the happier was it for him that he could so stand: but in all formulas that *he* could stand by, there needed to be a most genuine substance. Very curious how, in that poor Paper-age, so barren, artificial, thick-quilted with Pedantries, Hearsays, the great Fact of this Universe glared in, forever wonderful, indubitable, unspeakable, divine-infernal, upon this man too! How he harmonised his Formulas with it, how he managed at all under such circumstances: that is a thing worth seeing. A thing "to be looked at with reverence, with pity, with awe." That Church of St. Clement Danes, where Johnson still *worshipped* in the era of Voltaire, is to me a venerable place.

It was in virtue of his *sincerity,* of his speaking still in some sort from the heart of Nature, though in the current artificial dialect, that Johnson was a Prophet. Are not all dialects "artificial"? Artificial things are not all false;—nay every true Product of Nature will infallibly *shape* itself; we may say all artificial things are, at the starting of them, *true*. What we call "Formulas" are not in their origin bad; they are indispensably good. Formula is *method*, habitude; found wherever man is found. Formulas fashion themselves as Paths do, as beaten Highways, leading towards some sacred or high object, whither many men are bent. Consider it. One man, full of heartfelt earnest impulse, finds-out a way of doing somewhat,—were it of uttering his soul's reverence for the Highest, were it but of fitly saluting his fellow-man. An inventor was needed to do that, a *poet;* he has articulated the dim-struggling thought that dwelt in his own and many hearts. This is his way of doing that; these are his footsteps, the beginning of a "Path." And now see: the second man travels naturally in the footsteps of his foregoer, it is the *easiest* method. In the footsteps of his foregoer; yet with improvements, with changes where such seem good; at all events with enlargements, the Path ever *widening* itself as more travel it;—till at last there is a broad Highway whereon the whole world may travel and drive. While there remains a City or Shrine, or any Reality to drive to, at the farther end, the Highway shall be right welcome! When the City is gone, we will forsake the Highway. In this manner all Institutions, Practices, Regulated Things in the world have come into existence, and gone out of existence. Formulas all begin by being *full* of substance; you may call them the *skin*, the articulation into shape, into limbs and skin, of a substance that is already there: *they* had not been there otherwise. Idols, as we said, are not idolatrous till they become doubtful, empty for the worshipper's heart. Much as we talk against Formulas, I hope no one of us is ignorant withal of the high significance of *true* Formulas; that they were, and will ever be, the indispensablest furniture of our habitation in this world.—

Mark, too, how little Johnson boasts of his "sincerity." He has no suspicion of his being particularly sincere,—of his being particularly anything! A hard-struggling, weary-hearted man, or "scholar" as he calls himself, trying hard to get some honest livelihood in the world, not to starve, but to live—without stealing! A noble unconsciousness is in him. He does not "engrave *Truth* on his watch-seal;" no, but he stands by truth, speaks by it, works and lives by it. Thus it ever is. Think of it once more. The man whom Nature has appointed to do great things is, first of all, furnished with that openness to Nature which renders him incapable of being *in*sincere! To his large, open, deep-feeling heart Nature is a Fact: all hearsay is hearsay; the unspeakable greatness of this Mystery of Life, let him acknowledge it or not, nay even though he seem to forget it or deny it, is ever present to *him*,—

fearful and wonderful, on this hand and on that. He has a basis of sincerity; unrecognised, because never questioned or capable of question. Mirabeau, Mahomet, Cromwell, Napoleon: all the Great Men I ever heard-of have this as the primary material of them. Innumerable commonplace men are debating, are talking everywhere their commonplace doctrines, which they have learned by logic, by rote, at secondhand: to that kind of man all this is still nothing. He must have truth, truth which *he* feels to be true. How shall he stand otherwise? His whole soul, at all moments, in all ways, tells him that there is no standing. He is under the noble necessity of being true. Johnson's way of thinking about this world is not mine, any more than Mahomet's was: but I recognise the everlasting element of heart-*sincerity* in both; and see with pleasure how neither of them remains ineffectual. Neither of them is as *chaff* sown; in both of them is something which the seed-field will *grow*.

Johnson was a Prophet to his people; preached a Gospel to them,—as all like him always do. The highest Gospel he preached we may describe as a kind of Moral Prudence: "in a world where much is to be done, and little is to be known," see how you will *do* it! A thing well worth preaching. "A world where much is to be done, and little is to be known:" do not sink yourselves in boundless bottomless abysses of Doubt, of wretched god-forgetting Unbelief;—you were miserable then, powerless, mad: how could you *do* or work at all? Such Gospel Johnson preached and taught;—coupled, theoretically and practically, with this other great Gospel, "Clear your mind of Cant!" Have no trade with Cant: stand on the cold mud in the frosty weather, but let it be in your own *real* torn shoes: "that will be better for you," as Mahomet says! I call this, I call these two things *joined together*, a great Gospel, the greatest perhaps that was possible at that time.

Johnson's Writings, which once had such currency and celebrity, are now, as it were, disowned by the young generation. It is not wonderful; Johnson's opinions are fast becoming obsolete: but his style of thinking and of living, we may hope, will never become obsolete. I find in Johnson's Books the indisputablest traces of a great intellect and great heart:—ever welcome, under what obstructions and perversions soever. They are *sincere* words, those of his; he means things by them. A wondrous buckram style,—the best he could get to them; a measured grandiloquence, stepping or rather stalking along in a very solemn way, grown obsolete now; sometimes a tumid *size* of phraseology not in proportion to the contents of it: all this you will put-up with. For the phraseology, tumid or not, has always *something within it*. So many beautiful styles and books, with *nothing* in them;—a man is a *male*-factor to the world who writes such! *They* are the avoidable kind!—Had Johnson left nothing but his *Dictionary,* one might have traced there a great intellect, a genuine man. Looking to its clearness of definition, its general solidity, honesty, insight, and successful method, it may be called the best of all Dictionaries. There is in it a kind of architectural nobleness; it stands there like a great solid square-built edifice, finished, symmetrically complete: you judge that a true Builder did it.

One word, in spite of our haste, must be granted to poor Bozzy. He passes for a mean, inflated, gluttonous creature; and was so in many senses. Yet the fact of his reverence for Johnson will ever remain noteworthy. The foolish conceited Scotch Laird, the most conceited man of his time, approaching in such awestruck attitude the great dusty irascible Pedagogue in his mean garret there: it is a genuine reverence for Excellence; a *worship* for Heroes, at a time when neither Heroes nor worship were surmised to exist. Heroes, it would seem, exist always, and a certain worship of them! We will also take the liberty to deny altogether that of the witty Frenchman, that no man is a Hero to his valet-de-chambre. Or if so, it is not the Hero's blame, but the Valet's: that his soul, namely, is a mean *valet*-soul! He expects his Hero to advance in royal stage-trappings, with measured step, trains borne behind him, trumpets sounding before him. It should stand rather, No man can be a *Grand-Monarque* to his valet-de-chambre. Strip your Louis Quatorze of his king-gear, and there *is* left nothing but a poor forked radish with a head fantastically carved;—admirable to no valet. The Valet does not know a Hero when he sees him! Alas, no: it requires a kind of *Hero* to do that;—and one of the world's wants, in *this* as in other senses, is for the most part want of such.

On the whole, shall we not say, that Boswell's admiration was well bestowed; that he could have found no soul in all England so worthy of bending down before? Shall we not say, of this great mournful Johnson too, that he guided his difficult confused existence wisely; led it *well,* like a right-valiant man? That waste chaos of Authorship by trade; that waste chaos of Scepticism in religion and politics, in life-theory and life-practice; in his poverty, in his dust and dimness, with the sick body and the rusty coat: he made it do for him, like a brave man. Not wholly without a loadstar in the Eternal; he had still a loadstar, as the brave all need to have: with his eye set on that, he would change his course for nothing in these confused vortices of the lower sea of Time. "To the Spirit of Lies, bearing death and hunger, he would in no wise strike his flag." Brave old Samuel: *ultimus Romanorum!*

From Oliver Cromwell's Letters and Speeches

The Battle of Dunbar

And so the soldiers stand to their arms, or lie within instant reach of their arms, all night; being upon an engagement very difficult indeed. The night is wild and wet;—2nd of September means 12th by our calendar: the Harvest Moon wades deep among clouds of sleet and hail. Whoever has a heart for prayer, let him pray now, for the wrestle of death is at hand. Pray,—and withal keep his powder dry! And be ready for extremities, and quit himself like a man!—Thus they pass the night; making that Dunbar Peninsula and Brock Rivulet long memorable to me. We English have some tents; the Scots have none. The hoarse sea moans bodeful, swinging low and heavy against these whinstone bays; the sea and the tempests are abroad, all else asleep but we,—and there is One that rides on the wings of the wind.

Towards three in the morning the Scotch foot, by order of a Major-General say some, extinguish their matches, all but two in a company; cower under the corn-shocks, seeking some imperfect shelter and sleep. Be wakeful, ye English; watch, and pray, and keep your powder dry. About four o'clock comes order to my puddingheaded Yorkshire friend, that his regiment must mount and march straightway; his and various other regiments march, pouring swiftly to the left to Brocksmouth House, to the Pass over the Brock. With overpowering force let us storm the Scots' right wing there; beat that, and all is beaten. Major Hodgson riding along, heard, he says "a Cornet praying in the night"; a company of poor men, I think, making worship there, under the void Heaven, before battle joined: Major Hodgson, giving his charge to a brother Officer, turned aside to listen for a minute, and worship and pray along with them; haply his last prayer on this Earth, as it might prove to be. But no: this Cornet prayed with such effusion as was wonderful; and imparted strength to my Yorkshire friend, who strengthened his men by telling them of it. And the Heavens, in their mercy, I think, have opened us a way of deliverance!—The Moon gleams out, hard and blue, riding among hail-clouds; and over St. Abb's Head, a streak of dawn is rising.

And now is the hour when the attack should be, and no Lambert is yet here, he is ordering the line far to the right yet; and Oliver occasionally, in Hodgson's hearing, is impatient for him. The Scots too, on this wing, are awake: thinking to surprise us; there is their trumpet sounding, we heard it once; and Lambert, who was to lead the attack, is not here. The Lord General is impatient;—behold Lambert at last! The trumpets peal, shattering with fierce clangour Night's silence; the cannons awaken along all the Line: "The Lord of Hosts! The Lord of Hosts!" On, my brave ones, on!—

The dispute "on this right wing was hot and stiff, for three quarters of an hour." Plenty of fire, from fieldpieces, snaphances, matchlocks, entertains the Scotch main-battle across the Brock;—poor stiffened men, roused from the corn-shocks with their matches all out! But here on the right, their horse, "with lancers in the front rank," charge desperately; drive us back across the hollow of the Rivulet;—back a little; but the Lord gives us courage, and we storm home again, horse and foot, upon them, with a shock like tornado tempests; break them, beat them, drive them all adrift. "Some fled towards Copperspath, but most across their own foot." Their own poor foot, whose matches were hardly well alight yet! Poor men, it was a terrible awakening for them: fieldpieces and charge of foot across the Brocksburn; and now here is their own horse in mad panic trampling them to death. Above Three-thousand killed upon the place: "I never saw such a charge of foot and horse," says one; nor did I. Oliver was still near to Yorkshire Hodgson when the shock succeeded; Hodgson heard him say, "They run! I profess they run!" And over St. Abb's Head and the German Ocean, just then, bursts the first gleam of the level Sun upon us, "and I heard Nol say, in the words of the Psalmist, 'Let God arise, let His enemies be scattered.'"—or in Rous's metre,

Let God arise, and scattered
Let all his enemies be;
And let all those that do him hate
Before his presence flee!

Even so. The Scotch Army is shivered to utter ruin; rushes in tumultuous wreck, hither, thither; to Belhaven, or, in their distraction, even to Dunbar, the chase goes as far as Haddington; led by Hacker. "The Lord General made a halt," says Hodgson, "and sang the Hundred-and-seventeenth Psalm," till our horse could gather for the chase. Hundred-and-seventeenth Psalm, at the foot of the Doon Hill; there we uplift it, to the tune of Bangor, or some still higher score, and roll it strong and great against the sky:

O give ye praise unto the Lord,
All nati-ons that be;
Likewise ye people all, accord
His name to magnify!

For great to-us-ward ever are
His lovingkindnesses;
His truth endures forevermore:
The Lord O do ye bless!

And now, to the chase again.

The Prisoners are Ten-thousand,—all the foot in a mass. Many Dignitaries are taken; not a few are slain; of whom see Printed Lists,—full of blunders. Provost Jaffray of Aberdeen, Member of the Scots Parliament, one of the Committee of Estates, was very nearly slain: a trooper's sword was in the air to sever him, but one cried, He is a man of consequence; he can ransom himself!—and the trooper kept him prisoner. The first of the Scots Quakers, by and by; and an official person much reconciled to Oliver. Ministers also of the Kirk Committee were slain; two Ministers I find taken, poor Carstairs of Glasgow, poor Waugh of some other place,—of whom we shall transiently hear again.

General David Lesley, vigorous for flight as for other things, got to Edinburgh by nine o'clock; poor old Leven, not so light of movement, did not get till two. Tragical enough. What a change since January 1644, when we marched out of this same Dunbar up to the knees in snow! It was to help and save these very men that we then marched; with the Covenant in all our hearts. We have stood by the Letter of the Covenant; fought for our Covenanted Stuart King as we could;—they again, they stand by the substance of it, and have trampled us and the letter of it into this ruinous state!—Yes, my poor friends;—and now be wise, be taught! The Letter of your Covenant, in fact, will never rally again in this world. The spirit and substance of it, please God, will never die in this or in any world!

Such is Dunbar Battle; which might also be called Dunbar Drove, for it was a frightful rout. Brought on by miscalculation; misunderstanding of the difference between substances and semblances;—by mismanagement, and the chance of war. My Lord General's next Seven Letters, all written on the morrow, will now be intelligible to the reader. First, however, take the following

PROCLAMATION

Forasmuch as I understand there are several Soldiers of the Enemy's Army yet abiding in the Field, who by reason of their wounds could not march from thence:

These are therefore to give notice to the Inhabitants of this Nation That they may and hereby have free liberty to repair to the Field aforesaid, and, with their carts or "in" any other peaceable way, to carry away the said Soldiers to such places as they shall think fit:—provided they meddle not with, or take away, any the Arms there. And all Officers and Soldiers are to take notice that the same is permitted.

Given under my hand, at Dunbar, 4th September 1650.

OLIVER CROMWELL.

To be proclaimed by beat of drum.

From REMINISCENCES

Frank Dickson

FRANK was a notable kind of man, and one of the memorabilities, to Irving as well as me; a most quizzing, merry, entertaining, guileless, and unmalicious man; with very considerable logic, reading, contemptuous observation and intelligence, much real tenderness too, when not obstructed, and a mournful true affection especially for the friends he had lost by death! No mean impediment *there* any more (that was it), for Frank was very sensitive, easily moved to something of envy, and as if surprised when contempt was not possible; easy banter was what he habitually dwelt in; for the rest an honourable, bright, amiable man; alas, and his end was very tragic! I have hardly seen a man with more opulence of conversation, wit, fantastic bantering, ingenuity, and genial human sense of the ridiculous in men and things. Charles Buller, perhaps, but he was of far more refined, delicately managed, and less copious tone; finer by nature, I should say, as well as by culture, and had nothing of the fine *Annandale Rabelais* turn which had grown up, partly of will and at length by industry as well, in poor Frank Dickson in the valley of Dryfe amid his little stock of books and rustic phenomena. A slightly built man, nimble-looking and yet lazy-looking, our Annandale Rabelais; thin, neatly expressive aquiline face, grey genially laughing eyes, something sternly serious and resolute in the squarish fine brow, nose specially aquiline, thin and rather small. I well remember the play of point and nostrils there, while his wild home-grown *Gargantuisms* went on. He rocked rather, and negligently wriggled in walking or standing, something slightly twisted in the spine, I think; but he made so much small involuntary tossing and gesticulating while he spoke or listened, you never noticed the twist. What a childlike and yet half imp-like volume of laughter lay in Frank; how he would fling back his fine head, left cheek up, not himself laughing much or loud even, but showing you such continents of inward gleesome mirth and victorious mockery of the dear stupid ones who had crossed his sphere of observation. A wild roll of sombre eloquence lay in him too, and I have seen in his sermons sometimes that brow and aquiline face grow dark, sad, and thunderous like the eagle of Jove. I always liked poor Frank, and he me heartily. After having tried to banter me down and recognised the mistake, which he loyally did for himself and never repeated, we had much pleasant talk together first and last.

De Quincey

He was a pretty little creature, full of wire-drawn ingenuities, bankrupt enthusiasms, bankrupt pride, with the finest silver-toned low voice, and most elaborate gently-winding courtesies and ingenuities in conversation. "What wouldn't one give to have him in a box, and take him out to talk!" That was Her criticism of him, and it was right good. A bright, ready, and melodious talker, but in the end an inconclusive and long-winded. One of the smallest man figures I ever saw; shaped like a pair of tongs, and hardly above five feet in all. When he sate, you would have taken him, by candlelight, for the beautifullest little child; blue-eyed, sparkling face, had there not been a something, too, which said "*Eccovi*—this child has been in hell."

Wordsworth

During the last seven or ten years of his life, Wordsworth felt himself to be a recognised lion, in certain considerable London circles, and was in the habit of coming up to town with his wife for a month or two every season, to enjoy his quiet triumph and collect his bits of tribute *tales quales*. The places where I met him oftenest, were Marshall's (the great Leeds linen manufacturer, an excellent and very opulent man), Spring-Rice's (*i.e.*, Lord Monteagle's, who and whose house was strangely intermarried with this Marshall's), and the first Lord Stanley's of Alderly (who then, perhaps, was still Sir Thomas Stanley). Wordsworth took his bit of lionism very quietly, with a smile sardonic rather than triumphant, and certainly got no harm by it, if he got or expected little good. His wife, a small, withered, puckered, winking lady, who never spoke, seemed to be more in earnest about the affair, and was visibly and sometimes ridiculously assiduous to secure her proper place of precedence at table. One evening at Lord Monteagle's—Ah, who was it that then made me laugh as we went home together: Ah me! Wordsworth generally spoke a little with me on those occasions; sometimes, perhaps, we sat by one another; but there came from him nothing considerable, and happily at least nothing with an effort. "If you think me dull, be it just so!"—this seemed to a most respectable extent to be his inspiring humour. Hardly above once (perhaps at the Stanleys') do I faintly recollect something of the contrary on his part for a little while, which was not pleasant or successful while it lasted. The light was always afflictive to his eyes; he carried in his pocket something like a skeleton brass candlestick, in which, setting it on the dinner table, between him and the most afflictive or nearest of the chief lights, he touched a little spring, and there flirted out, at the top of his brass implement, a small vertical green circle which prettily enough threw his eyes into shade, and screened him from that sorrow. In proof of his equanimity as lion I remember, in connection with this green shade, one little glimpse which shall be given presently as finis. But first let me say that all these Wordsworth phenomena appear to have been indifferent to me, and have melted to steamy oblivion in a singular degree. Of his talk to others in my hearing I remember simply nothing, not even a word or gesture. To myself it seemed once or twice as if he bore suspicions, thinking I was not a real worshipper, which threw him into something of embarrassment, till I hastened to get them laid, by frank discourse on some suitable thing; nor, when we did talk, was there on his side or on mine the least utterance worth noting. The tone of his voice when I got him afloat on some Cumberland or other matter germane to him, had a braced rustic vivacity, willingness, and solid precision, which alone rings in my ear when all else is gone. Of some Druid-circle, for example, he prolonged his response to me with the addition, "And there is another some miles off, which the country people call Long Meg and her Daughters"; as to the now ownership of which "It" etc.; "and then it came into the hands of a Mr. Crackenthorpe;" the sound of those two phrases is still lively and present with me; meaning or sound of absolutely nothing more. Still more memorable is an ocular glimpse I had in one of these Wordsworthian lion-dinners, very symbolic to me of his general deportment there, and far clearer than the little feature of opposite sort, ambiguously given above (recollection of that viz. of unsuccessful exertion at a Stanley dinner being dubious and all but extinct, while this is still vivid to me as of yesternight). Dinner was large, luminous, sumptuous; I sat a long way from Wordsworth; dessert I think had come in, and certainly there reigned in all quarters a cackle as of Babel (only politer perhaps), which far up in Wordsworth's quarter (who was leftward on my side of the table) seemed to have taken a sententious, rather louder, logical and quasi-scientific turn, heartily unimportant to gods and men, so far as I could judge of it and of the other babble reigning. I look upwards, leftwards, the coast being luckily for a moment clear; then, far off, beautifully screened in the shadow of his vertical green circle, which was on the farther side of him, sate Wordsworth, silent, slowly but steadily gnawing some portion of what I judged to be raisins, with his eye and attention placidly fixed on these and these alone. The sight of whom, and of his rock-like indifference to the babble, quasi-scientific and other, with attention turned on the small practical alone, was comfortable and amusing to me, who felt like him but could not eat raisins. This little glimpse I could still paint, so clear and bright is it, and this shall be symbolical of all.

In a few years, I forget in how many and when, these Wordsworth appearances in London ceased; we heard, not of ill-health perhaps, but of increasing love of rest; at length of the long sleep's coming; and never saw Wordsworth more. One felt his death as the extinction of a public light, but not otherwise. The public itself found not much to say of him, and staggered on to meaner but more pressing objects.

THOMAS HOOD (1799-1845)

Ode to Autumn

I SAW old Autumn in the misty morn
Stand shadowless like Silence, listening
To silence, for no lonely bird would sing
Into his hollow ear from woods forlorn,
Nor lowly hedge nor solitary thorn;—
Shaking his languid locks all dewy bright
With tangled gossamer that fell by night,
Pearling his coronet of golden corn.

Where are the songs of Summer?—With the sun,
Oping the dusky eyelids of the south,
Till shade and silence waken up as one,
And Morning sings with a warm odorous mouth.
Where are the merry birds?—Away, away,
On panting wings through the inclement skies,
Lest owls should prey
Undazzled at noonday,
And tear with horny beak their lustrous eyes.

Where are the blooms of Summer?—In the west,
Blushing their last to the last sunny hours,
When the mild Eve by sudden Night is prest
Like tearful Proserpine, snatch'd from her flow'rs
To a most gloomy breast.
Where is the pride of Summer,—the green prime,
The many, many leaves all twinkling?—Three
On the moss'd elm; three on the naked lime
Trembling,—and one upon the old oak-tree!
Where is the Dryad's immortality?—
Gone into mournful cypress and dark yew,
Or wearing the long gloomy Winter through
In the smooth holly's green eternity.

The squirrel gloats on his accomplish'd hoard,
The ants have brimm'd their garners with ripe grain,
And honey bees have stored

The sweets of Summer in their luscious cells;
The swallows all have wing'd across the main;
But here the Autumn melancholy dwells,
And sighs her tearful spells
Amongst the sunless shadows of the plain.
Alone, alone,
Upon a mossy stone,
She sits and reckons up the dead and gone
With the last leaves for a love-rosary,
Whilst all the wither'd world looks drearily,
Like a dim picture of the drownèd past
In the hush'd mind's mysterious far away,
Doubtful what ghostly thing will steal the last
Into that distance, gray upon the gray.

O go and sit with her, and be o'ershaded
Under the languid downfall of her hair:
She wears a coronal of flowers faded
Upon her forehead, and a face of care;—
There is enough of wither'd everywhere
To make her bower,—and enough of gloom;
There is enough of sadness to invite,
If only for the rose that died, whose doom
Is Beauty's,—she that with the living bloom
Of conscious cheeks most beautifies the light:
There is enough of sorrowing, and quite
Enough of bitter fruits the earth doth bear,—
Enough of chilly droppings for her bowl;
Enough of fear and shadowy despair,
To frame her cloudy prison for the soul!

I Remember, I Remember

I

I REMEMBER, I remember,
The house where I was born,
The little window where the sun
Came peeping in at morn;
He never came a wink too soon,
Nor brought too long a day,
But now, I often wish the night
Had borne my breath away!

II

I remember, I remember,
The roses, red and white,
The vi'lets, and the lily-cups,
Those flowers made of light!
The lilacs where the robin built,
And where my brother set
The laburnum on his birthday,—
The tree is living yet!

III

I remember, I remember,
Where I was used to swing,
And thought the air must rush as fresh
To swallows on the wing;
My spirit flew in feathers then,
That is so heavy now,
And summer pools could hardly cool
The fever on my brow!

IV

I remember, I remember,
The fir trees dark and high;
I used to think their slender tops
Were close against the sky:
It was a childish ignorance,
But now 'tis little joy
To know I'm farther off from heav'n
Than when I was a boy.

THOMAS BABINGTON MACAULAY (1800-1859)

From THE HISTORY OF ENGLAND FROM THE ACCESSION OF JAMES THE SECOND

The Church

To this day the constitution, the doctrines, and the services of the Church, retain the visible marks of the compromise from which she sprang. She occupies a middle position between the Churches of Rome and Geneva. Her doctrinal confessions and discourses, composed by Protestants, set forth principles of theology in which Calvin or Knox would have found scarcely a word to disapprove. Her prayers and thanksgivings, derived from the ancient Breviaries, are very generally such that Cardinal Fisher or Cardinal Pole might have heartily joined in them. A controversialist who puts an Arminian sense on her Articles and Homilies will be pronounced by candid men to be as unreasonable as a controversialist who denies that the doctrine of baptismal regeneration can be discovered in her Liturgy.

The Church of Rome held that episcopacy was of divine institution, and that certain supernatural graces of a high order had been transmitted by the imposition of hands through fifty generations, from the Eleven who received their commission on the Galilean mount, to the bishops who met at Trent. A large body of Protestants, on the other hand, regarded prelacy as positively unlawful, and persuaded themselves that they found a very different form of ecclesiastical government prescribed in Scripture. The founders of the Anglican Church took a middle course. They retained episcopacy; but they did not declare it to be an institution essential to the welfare of a Christian society, or to the efficacy of the sacraments. Cranmer, indeed, on one important occasion, plainly avowed his conviction that, in the primitive times, there was no distinction between bishops and priests, and that the laying on of hands was altogether superfluous.

Among the Presbyterians, the conduct of public worship is, to a great extent, left to the minister. Their prayers, therefore, are not exactly the same in any two assemblies on the same day, or on any two days in the same assembly. In one parish they are fervent, eloquent, and full of meaning. In the next parish they may be languid or absurd. The priests of the Roman Catholic Church, on the other hand, have, during many generations, daily chaunted the same ancient confessions, supplications, and thanksgivings, in India and Lithuania, in Ireland and

Peru. The service, being in a dead language, is intelligible only to the learned; and the great majority of the congregation may be said to assist as spectators rather than as auditors. Here, again, the Church of England took a middle course. She copied the Roman Catholic forms of prayer, but translated them into the vulgar tongue, and invited the illiterate multitude to join its voice to that of the minister.

In every part of her system the same policy may be traced. Utterly rejecting the doctrine of transubstantiation, and condemning as idolatrous all adoration paid to the sacramental bread and wine, she yet, to the disgust of the Puritan, required her children to receive the memorials of divine love, meekly kneeling upon their knees. Discarding many rich vestments which surrounded the altars of the ancient faith, she yet retained, to the horror of weak minds, a robe of white linen, typical of the purity which belonged to her as the mystical spouse of Christ. Discarding a crowd of pantomimic gestures which, in the Roman Catholic worship, are substituted for intelligible words, she yet shocked many rigid Protestants by marking the infant just sprinkled from the font with the sign of the cross. The Roman Catholic addressed his prayers to a multitude of Saints, among whom were numbered many men of doubtful, and some of hateful, character. The Puritan refused the addition of Saint even to the apostle of the Gentiles, and to the disciple whom Jesus loved. The Church of England, though she asked for the intercession of no created being, still set apart days for the commemoration of some who had done and suffered great things for the faith. She retained confirmation and ordination as edifying rites; but she degraded them from the rank of sacraments. Shrift was no part of her system. Yet she gently invited the dying penitent to confess his sins to a divine, and empowered her ministers to soothe the departing soul by an absolution, which breathes the very spirit of the old religion. In general it may be said, that she appeals more to the understanding, and less to the senses and the imagination, than the Church of Rome, and that she appeals less to the understanding, and more to the senses and imagination, than the Protestant Churches of Scotland, France, and Switzerland.

The Extreme Puritans

While a section of the Anglican clergy quitted, in one direction, the position which they had originally occupied, a section of the Puritan body departed, in a direction diametrically opposite, from the principles and practices of their fathers. The persecution which the separatists had undergone had been severe enough to irritate, but not severe enough to destroy. They had not been tamed into submission, but baited into savageness and stubbornness. After the fashion of oppressed sects, they mistook their own vindictive feelings for emotions of piety, encouraged in themselves by reading and meditation a disposition to brood over their wrongs, and, when they had worked themselves up into hating their enemies, imagined that they were only hating the enemies of heaven. In the New Testament there was little indeed which, even when perverted by the most disingenuous exposition, could seem to countenance the indulgence of malevolent passions. But the Old Testament contained the history of a race selected by God to be witnesses of his unity and ministers of his vengeance, and specially commanded by him to do many things which, if done without his special command, would have been atrocious crimes. In such a history it was not difficult for fierce and gloomy spirits to find much that might be distorted to suit their wishes. The extreme Puritans therefore began to feel for the Old Testament a preference, which, perhaps, they did not distinctly avow even to themselves; but which showed itself in all their sentiments and habits. They paid to the Hebrew language a respect which they refused to that tongue in which the discourses of Jesus and the epistles of Paul have come down to us. They baptized their children by the names, not of Christian saints, but of Hebrew patriarchs and warriors. In defiance of the express and reiterated declarations of Luther and Calvin, they turned the weekly festival by which the Church had, from the primitive times, commemorated the resurrection of her Lord, into a Jewish Sabbath. They sought for principles of jurisprudence in the Mosaic law, and for precedents to guide their ordinary conduct in the books of Judges and Kings. Their thoughts and discourse ran much on acts which were assuredly not recorded as examples for our imitation. The prophet who hewed in pieces a captive king, the rebel general who gave the blood of a queen to the dogs, the matron who, in defiance of plighted faith, and of the laws of eastern hospitality, drove the nail into the brain of the fugitive ally who had just fed at her board, and who was sleeping under the shadow of her tent, were proposed as models to Christians suffering under the tyranny of princes and prelates. Morals and manners were subjected to a code resembling that of the synagogue, when the synagogue was in its worst state. The dress, the deportment, the language, the studies, the amusements of the rigid sect were regulated on principles resembling those of the Pharisees who, proud of their washed hands and broad phylacteries, taunted the Redeemer as a sabbath breaker and a wine bibber. It was a sin to hang garlands on a Maypole, to drink a friend's health, to fly a hawk, to hunt a stag, to play at chess, to wear lovelocks, to put starch into a ruff, to touch the virginals, to read the Fairy Queen. Rules such as these, rules which would have appeared insupportable to the free and joyous spirit of Luther, and contemptible to the serene and philosophical intellect of Zwingli, threw over all life a more than monastic gloom. The learning and eloquence by which the great reformers had been eminently distinguished, and to which they had been, in no small measure, indebted for their success, were regarded by the new school of Protestants with suspicion, if not with aversion. Some precisians had scruples about teaching the Latin grammar because the names of Mars, Bacchus, and Apollo occurred in it. The fine arts were all but proscribed. The solemn peal of the organ was superstitious. The light music of Ben Jonson's masques was dissolute. Half the fine paintings in England were idolatrous, and the other half indecent. The extreme Puritan was at once known from other men by his gait, his garb, his lank hair, the sour solemnity of his face, the upturned white of his eyes, the nasal twang with which he spoke, and, above all, by his peculiar dialect. He employed, on every occasion, the imagery and style of Scripture. Hebraisms violently introduced into the English language, and metaphors borrowed from the boldest lyric poetry of a remote age and country, and applied to the common concerns of English life, were the most striking peculiarities of this cant, which moved, not without cause, the derision both of prelatists and libertines.

The Character of Charles I

Just at this conjuncture James died. Charles the First succeeded to the throne. He had received from nature a far better understanding, a far stronger will, and a far keener and firmer temper than his father's. He had inherited his father's political theories, and was much more disposed than his father to carry them into practice. He was, like his father, a zealous episcopalian. He was, moreover, what his father had never been, a zealous Arminian, and, though no Papist, liked a Papist much better than a Puritan. It would be unjust to deny that Charles had some of the qualities of a good, and even of a great prince. He wrote and spoke, not, like his father, with the exactness of a professor, but after the fashion of intelligent and well educated gentlemen. His taste in literature and art was excellent, his manner dignified though not gracious, his domestic life without blemish. Faithlessness was the chief cause of his disasters, and is the chief stain on his memory. He was, in truth, impelled by an incurable propensity to dark and crooked ways. It may seem strange that his conscience, which, on occasions of little moment, was sufficiently sensitive, should never have reproached him with this great vice. But there is reason to believe that he was perfidious, not only from constitution and from habit, but also on principle. He seems to have learned from the theologians whom he most esteemed that between him and his subjects there could be nothing of the nature of mutual contract; that he could not, even if he would, divest himself of his despotic authority; and that, in every promise which he made, there was an implied reservation that such promise might be broken in case of necessity, and that of the necessity he was the sole judge.

The Relief of Londonderry

By this time July was far advanced; and the state of the city was, hour by hour, becoming more frightful. The number of the inhabitants had been thinned more by famine and disease than by the fire of the enemy. Yet that fire was sharper and more constant than ever. One of the gates was beaten in: one of the bastions was laid in ruins; but the breaches made by day were repaired by night with indefatigable activity. Every attack was still repelled. But the fighting men of the garrison were so much exhausted that they could scarcely keep their legs. Several of them, in the act of striking at the enemy, fell down from mere weakness. A very small quantity of grain remained, and was doled out by mouthfuls. The stock of salted hides was considerable, and by gnawing them the garrison appeased the rage of hunger. Dogs, fattened on the blood of the slain who lay unburied round the town, were luxuries which few could afford to purchase. The price of a whelp's paw was five shillings and sixpence. Nine horses were still alive, and but barely alive. They were so lean that little meat was likely to be found upon them. It was, however, determined to slaughter them for food. The people perished so fast that it was impossible for the survivors to perform the rites of sepulture. There was scarcely a cellar in which some corpse was not decaying. Such was the extremity of distress, that the rats who came to feast in those hideous dens were eagerly hunted and greedily devoured. A small fish, caught in the river, was not to be purchased with money. The only price for which such a treasure could be obtained was some handfuls of oatmeal. Leprosies, such as strange and unwholesome diet engenders, made existence a constant torment. The whole city was poisoned by the stench exhaled from the bodies of the dead and of the half dead. That there should be fits of discontent and insubordination among men enduring such misery was inevitable. At one moment it was suspected that Walker had laid up somewhere a secret store of food, and was revelling in private, while he exhorted others to suffer resolutely for the good cause. His house was strictly examined: his innocence was fully proved: he regained his popularity; and the garrison, with death in near prospect, thronged to the cathedral to hear him preach, drank in his earnest eloquence with delight, and went forth from the house of God with haggard faces and tottering steps, but with spirit still unsubdued. There were, indeed, some secret plottings. A very few obscure traitors opened communications with the enemy. But it was necessary that all such dealings should be carefully concealed. None dared to utter publicly any words save words of defiance and stubborn resolution. Even in that extremity the general cry was "No surrender." And there were not wanting voices which, in low tones, added, "First the horses and hides; and then the prisoners; and then each other." It was afterwards related, half in jest, yet not without a horrible mixture of earnest, that a corpulent citizen, whose bulk presented a strange contrast to the skeletons which surrounded him, thought it expedient to conceal himself from the numerous eyes which followed him with cannibal looks whenever he appeared in the streets.

It was no slight aggravation of the sufferings of the garrison that all this time the English ships were seen far off in Lough Foyle. Communication between the fleet and the city was almost impossible. One diver who had attempted to pass the boom was drowned. Another was hanged. The language of signals was hardly intelligible. On the thirteenth of July, however, a piece of paper sewed up in a cloth button came to Walker's hands. It was a letter from Kirke, and contained assurances of speedy relief. But more than a fortnight of intense misery had since elapsed; and the hearts of the most sanguine were sick with deferred hope. By no art could the provisions which were left be made to hold out two days more.

Just at this time Kirke received a despatch from England, which contained positive orders that Londonderry should be relieved. He accordingly determined to make an attempt which, as far as appears, he might have made, with at least an equally fair prospect of success, six weeks earlier.

Among the merchant ships which had come to Lough Foyle under his convoy was one called the Mountjoy. The master, Micaiah Browning, a native of Londonderry, had brought from England a large cargo of provisions. He had, it is said, repeatedly remonstrated against the inaction of the armament. He now eagerly volunteered to take the first risk of succouring his fellow citizens; and his offer was accepted. Andrew Douglas, master of the Phœnix, who had on board a great quantity of meal from Scotland, was willing to share the danger and the honour. The two merchantmen were to be escorted by the Dartmouth frigate of thirty-six guns, commanded by Captain John Leake, afterwards an admiral of great fame.

It was the thirtieth of July. The sun had just set: the evening sermon in the cathedral was over; and the heartbroken congregation had separated, when the sentinels on the tower saw the sails of three vessels coming up the Foyle. Soon there was a stir in the Irish camp. The besiegers were on the alert for miles along both shores. The ships were in extreme peril: for the river was low; and the only navigable channel ran very near to the left bank, where the head quarters of the enemy had been fixed, and where the batteries were most numerous. Leake performed his duty with a skill and spirit worthy of his noble profession, exposed his frigate to cover the merchantmen, and used his guns with great effect. At length the little squadron came to the place of peril. Then the Mountjoy took the lead, and went right at the boom. The huge barricade cracked and gave way: but the shock was such that the Mountjoy rebounded, and stuck in the mud. A yell of triumph rose from the banks: the Irish rushed to their boats, and were preparing to board; but the Dartmouth poured on them a well directed broadside, which threw them into disorder. Just then the Phœnix dashed at the breach which the Mountjoy had made, and was in a moment within the fence. Meantime the tide was rising fast. The Mountjoy began to move, and soon passed safe through the broken stakes and floating spars. But her brave master was no more. A shot from one of the batteries had struck him; and he died by the most enviable of all deaths, in sight of the city which was his birthplace, which was his home, and which had just been saved by his courage and self-devotion from the most frightful form of destruction. The night had closed in before the conflict at the boom began; but the flash of the guns was seen, and the noise heard, by the lean and ghastly multitude which covered the walls of the city. When the Mountjoy grounded, and when the shout of triumph rose from the Irish on both sides of the river, the hearts of the besieged died within them. One who endured the unutterable anguish of that moment has told us that they looked fearfully livid in each other's eyes. Even after the barricade had been passed, there was a terrible half hour of suspense. It was ten o'clock before the ships arrived at the quay. The whole population was there to welcome them. A screen made of casks filled with earth was hastily thrown up to protect the landing place from the batteries on the other side of the river; and then the work of unloading began. First were rolled on shore barrels containing six thousand bushels of meal. Then came great cheeses, casks of beef, flitches of bacon, kegs of butter, sacks of pease and biscuit, ankers of brandy. Not many hours before, half a pound of tallow and three quarters of a pound of salted hide had been weighed out with niggardly care to every fighting man. The ration which each now received was three pounds of flour, two pounds of beef, and a pint of pease. It is easy to imagine with what tears grace was said over the suppers of that evening. There was little sleep on either side of the wall. The bonfires shone bright along the whole circuit of the ramparts. The Irish guns continued to roar all night; and all night the bells of the rescued city made answer to the Irish guns with a peal of joyous defiance. Through the whole of the thirty-first of July the batteries of the enemy continued to play. But, soon after the sun had again gone down, flames were seen arising from the camp; and, when the first of August dawned, a line of smoking ruins marked the site lately occupied by the huts of the besiegers; and the citizens saw far off the long column of pikes and standards retreating up the left bank of the Foyle towards Strabane.

So ended this great siege, the most memorable in the annals of the British isles. It had lasted a hundred and five days. The garrison had been reduced from about seven thousand effective men to about three thousand. The loss of the besiegers cannot be precisely ascertained. Walker estimated it at eight thousand men. It is certain from the despatches of Avaux that the regiments which returned from the blockade had been so much thinned that many of them were not more than two hundred strong. Of thirty-six French gunners who had superintended the cannonading, thirty-one had been killed or disabled. The means both of attack and of defence had undoubtedly been such as would have moved the great warriors of the Continent to laughter; and this is the very circumstance which gives so peculiar an interest to the history of the contest. It was a contest, not between engineers, but between nations; and the victory remained with the nation which, though inferior in number, was superior in civilisation, in capacity for self-government, and in stubbornness of resolution.

JAMES CLARENCE MANGAN
(1803-1849)

Dark Rosaleen

O MY Dark Rosaleen,
  Do not sigh, do not weep!
The priests are on the ocean green,
  They march along the deep.
There's wine from the royal Pope,
  Upon the ocean green;
And Spanish ale shall give you hope,
  My Dark Rosaleen!
  My own Rosaleen!
Shall glad your heart, shall give you hope,
Shall give you health, and help, and hope,
  My Dark Rosaleen!

Over hills, and thro' dales,
  Have I roam'd for your sake;
All yesterday I sail'd with sails
  On river and on lake.
The Erne, at its highest flood,
  I dash'd across unseen,
For there was lightning in my blood,
  My Dark Rosaleen!
  My own Rosaleen!
O, there was lightning in my blood,
Red lightning lighten'd thro' my blood,
  My Dark Rosaleen!

All day long, in unrest,
  To and fro, do I move.
The very soul within my breast
  Is wasted for you, love!
The heart in my bosom faints
  To think of you, my Queen,
My life of life, my saint of saints,
  My Dark Rosaleen!
  My own Rosaleen!
To hear your sweet and sad complaints,
My life, my love, my saint of saints,
  My Dark Rosaleen!

Woe and pain, pain and woe,
  Are my lot, night and noon,
To see your bright face clouded so,
  Like to the mournful moon.
But yet will I rear your throne
  Again in golden sheen;
'Tis you shall reign, shall reign alone,
  My Dark Rosaleen!
  My own Rosaleen!
'Tis you shall have the golden throne,
'Tis you shall reign, and reign alone,
  My Dark Rosaleen!

Over dews, over sands,
  Will I fly, for your weal:
Your holy delicate white hands
  Shall girdle me with steel.
At home, in your emerald bowers,
  From morning's dawn till e'en,
You'll pray for me, my flower of flowers,
  My Dark Rosaleen!
  My fond Rosaleen!
You'll think of me through daylight hours,
My virgin flower, my flower of flowers,
  My Dark Rosaleen!

I could scale the blue air,
  I could plough the high hills,
O, I could kneel all night in prayer,
  To heal your many ills!
And one beamy smile from you
  Would float like light between
My toils and me, my own, my true,
  My Dark Rosaleen!
  My fond Rosaleen!
Would give me life and soul anew,
A second life, a soul anew,
  My Dark Rosaleen!

O, the Erne shall run red,
  With redundance of blood,
The earth shall rock beneath our tread,
  And flames wrap hill and wood,
And gun-peal and slogan-cry
  Wake many a glen serene,
Ere you shall fade, ere you shall die,
  My Dark Rosaleen!
  My own Rosaleen!
The Judgement Hour must first be nigh,
Ere you can fade, ere you can die,
  My Dark Rosaleen!

GEORGE BORROW (1803-1881)

From LAVENGRO

The Spirit of De Foe

I NOW took up the third book: it did not resemble the others, being longer and considerably thicker; the binding was of dingy calf-skin. I opened it, and as I did so another strange thrill of pleasure shot through my frame. The first object on which my eyes rested was a picture; it was exceedingly well executed, at least the scene which it represented made a vivid impression upon me, which would hardly have been the case had the artist not been faithful to nature. A wild scene it was—a heavy sea and rocky shore, with mountains in the background, above which the moon was peering. Not far from the shore, upon the water, was a boat with two figures in it, one of which stood at the bow, pointing with what I knew to be a gun at a dreadful shape in the water; fire was flashing from the muzzle of the gun, and the monster appeared to be transfixed. I almost thought I heard its cry. I remained motionless, gazing upon the picture, scarcely daring to draw my breath, lest the new and wondrous world should vanish of which I had now obtained a glimpse: "Who are those people, and what could have brought them into that strange situation?" I asked of myself; and now the seed of curiosity, which had so long lain dormant, began to expand, and I vowed to myself to become speedily acquainted with the whole history of the people in the boat. After looking on the picture till every mark and line in it were familiar to me, I turned over various leaves till I came to another engraving; a new source of wonder—a low sandy beach on which the furious sea was breaking in mountain-like billows; cloud and rack deformed the firmament, which wore a dull and leaden-like hue; gulls and other aquatic fowls were toppling upon the blast, or skimming over the tops of the maddening waves—"Mercy upon him! he must be drowned!" I exclaimed, as my eyes fell upon a poor wretch who appeared to be striving to reach the shore; he was upon his legs, but was evidently half smothered with the brine; high above his head curled a horrible billow, as if to engulf him for ever. "He must be drowned! he must be drowned!" I almost shrieked, and dropped the book. I soon snatched it up again, and now my eye lighted on a third picture; again a shore, but what a sweet and lovely one, and how I wished to be treading it; there were beautiful shells lying on the smooth white sand, some were empty like those I had occasionally seen on marble mantelpieces, but out of others peered the heads and bodies of wondrous crayfish; a wood of thick green trees skirted the beach and partly shaded it from the rays of the sun, which shone hot above, while blue waves slightly crested with foam were gently curling against it; there was a human figure upon the beach, wild and uncouth, clad in the skins of animals, with a huge cap on his head, a hatchet at his girdle, and in his hand a gun; his feet and legs were bare; he stood in an attitude of horror and surprise; his body was bent far back, and his eyes, which seemed starting out of his head, were fixed upon a mark on the sand—a large distinct mark—a human footprint!

Reader, is it necessary to name the book which now stood open in my hand, and whose very prints, feeble expounders of its wondrous lines, had produced within me emotions strange and novel? Scarcely, for it was a book which has exerted over the minds of Englishmen an influence certainly greater than any other of modern times, which has been in most people's hands, and with the contents of which even those who cannot read are to a certain extent acquainted; a book from which the most luxuriant and fertile of our modern prose writers have drunk inspiration; a book, moreover, to which, from the hardy deeds which it narrates, and the spirit of strange and romantic enterprise which it tends to awaken, England owes many of her astonishing discoveries both by sea and land, and no inconsiderable part of her naval glory.

Hail to thee, spirit of De Foe! What does not my own poor self owe to thee? England has better bards than either Greece or Rome, yet I could spare them easier far than De Foe, "unabashed De Foe," as the hunchbacked rhymer styled him.

Wind on the Heath

I NOW wandered along the heath, until I came to a place where, beside a thick furze, sat a man, his eyes fixed intently on the red ball of the setting sun.

"That's not you, Jasper?"

"Indeed, brother!"

"I've not seen you for years."

"How should you, brother?"

"What brings you here?"

"The fight, brother."

"Where are the tents?"

"On the old spot, brother."

"Any news since we parted?"

"Two deaths, brother."

"Who are dead, Jasper?"

"Father and mother, brother."

"Where did they die?"

"Where they were sent, brother."

"And Mrs. Herne?"

"She's alive, brother."

"Where is she now?"

"In Yorkshire, brother."

"What is your opinion of death, Mr. Petulengro?" said I, as I sat down beside him.

"My opinion of death, brother, is much the same as that in the old song of Pharaoh, which I have heard my grandam sing—

Canna marel o manus chivios andé puv,
Ta rovel pa leste o chavo ta romi.

When a man dies, he is cast into the earth, and his wife and child sorrow over him. If he has neither wife nor child, then his father and mother, I suppose; and if he is quite alone in the world, why, then, he is cast into the earth, and there is an end of the matter."

"And do you think that is the end of man?"

"There's an end of him, brother, more's the pity."

"Why do you say so?"

"Life is sweet, brother."

"Do you think so?"

"Think so!—There's night and day, brother, both sweet things; sun, moon, and stars, brother, all sweet things; there's likewise a wind on the heath. Life is very sweet, brother; who would wish to die?"

"I would wish to die——"

"You talk like a gorgio—which is the same as talking like a fool—were you a Rommany Chal you would talk wiser. Wish to die, indeed!—A Rommany Chal would wish to live for ever!"

"In sickness, Jasper?"

"There's the sun and the stars, brother."

"In blindness, Jasper?"

"There's the wind on the heath, brother; if I could only feel that, I would gladly live for ever. Dosta, we'll now go to the tents and put on the gloves; and I'll try to make you feel what a sweet thing it is to be alive, brother!"

On London Bridge

Slowly advancing along the bridge, I came to the highest point, and there stood still, close beside one of the stone bowers, in which, beside a fruitstall, sat an old woman, with a pan of charcoal at her feet, and a book in her hand, in which she appeared to be reading intently. There I stood, just above the principal arch, looking through the balustrade at the scene that presented itself—and such a scene! Towards the left bank of the river, a forest of masts, thick and close, as far as the eye could reach; spacious wharfs, surmounted with gigantic edifices; and, far away, Cæsar's Castle, with its White Tower. To the right, another forest of masts, and a maze of buildings, from which, here and there, shot up to the sky chimneys taller than Cleopatra's Needle, vomiting forth huge wreaths of that black smoke which forms the canopy—occasionally a gorgeous one—of the more than Babel city. Stretching before me, the troubled breast of the mighty river, and, immediately below, the main whirlpool of the Thames—the Maëlstrom of the bulwarks of the middle arch—a grisly pool, which, with its superabundance of horror, fascinated me. Who knows but I should have leapt into its depths?—I have heard of such things—but for a rather startling occurrence which broke the spell. As I stood upon the bridge, gazing into the jaws of the pool, a small boat shot suddenly through the arch beneath my feet. There were three persons in it; an oarsman in the middle, whilst a man and woman sat at the stern. I shall never forget the thrill of horror which went through me at this sudden apparition. What!—a boat—a small boat—passing beneath that arch into yonder roaring gulf! Yes, yes, down through that awful water-way, with more than the swiftness of an arrow, shot the boat, or skiff, right into the jaws of the pool. A monstrous breaker curls over the prow—there is no hope; the boat is swamped, and all drowned in that strangling vortex. No! the boat, which appeared to have the buoyancy of a feather, skipped over the threatening horror, and the next moment was out of danger, the boatman—a true boatman of Cockaigne, that—elevating one of his sculls in sign of triumph, the man hallooing, and the woman, a true Englishwoman that—of a certain class—waving her shawl. Whether any one observed them save myself, or whether the feat was a common one, I know not; but nobody appeared to take any notice of them. As for myself, I was so excited, that I strove to clamber up the balustrade of the bridge, in order to obtain a better view of the daring adventurers. Before I could accomplish my design, however, I felt myself seized by the body, and, turning my head, perceived the old fruit-woman, who was clinging to me.

"Nay, dear! don't—don't!" said she. "Don't fling yourself over—perhaps you may have better luck next time!"

"I was not going to fling myself over," said I, dropping from the balustrade; "how came you to think of such a thing?"

"Why, seeing you clamber up so fiercely, I thought you might have had ill luck, and that you wished to make away with yourself."

"Ill luck," said I, going into the stone bower and sitting down. "What do you mean? ill luck in what?"

"Why, no great harm, dear! cly-faking, perhaps."

"Are you coming over me with dialects," said I, "speaking unto me in fashions I wot nothing of?"

"Nay, dear! don't look so strange with those eyes of your'n, nor talk so strangely; I don't understand you."

"Nor I you; what do you mean by cly-faking?"

"Lor', dear! no harm; only taking a handkerchief now and then."

"Do you take me for a thief?"

"Nay, dear! don't make use of bad language; we never calls them thieves here, but prigs and fakers: to tell you the truth, dear, seeing you spring at that railing put me in mind of my own dear son, who is now at Bot'ny: when he had bad luck, he always used to talk of flinging himself over the bridge; and, sure enough, when the traps were after him, he did fling himself into the river, but that was off the bank; nevertheless, the traps pulled him out, and he is now suffering his sentence; so you see you may speak out, if you have done anything in the harmless line, for I am my son's own mother, I assure you."

"So you think there's no harm in stealing?"

"No harm in the world, dear! Do you think my own child would have been transported for it, if there had been any harm in it? and what's more, would the blessed woman in the book here have written her life as she has done, and given it to the world, if there had been any harm in faking? She, too, was what they call a thief and a cutpurse; ay, and was transported for it, like my dear son; and do you think she would have told the world so, if there had been any harm in the thing? Oh, it is a comfort to me that the blessed woman was transported, and came back—for come back she did, and rich too—for it is an assurance to me that my dear son, who was transported too, will come back like her."

"What was her name?"

"Her name, blessed Mary Flanders."

"Will you let me look at the book?"

"Yes, dear, that I will, if you promise me not to run away with it."

I took the book from her hand; a short, thick volume, at least a century old, bound with greasy black leather. I turned the yellow and dog's-eared pages, reading here and there a sentence. Yes, and no mistake! *His* pen, his style, his spirit might be observed in every line of the uncouth-looking old volume—the air, the style, the spirit of the writer of the book which first taught me to read. I covered my face with my hand, and thought of my childhood——

"This is a singular book," said I at last; "but it does not appear to have been written to prove that thieving is no harm, but rather to show the terrible consequences of crime: it contains a deep moral."

"A deep what, dear?"

"A—— but no matter, I will give you a crown for this volume."

"No, dear, I will not sell the volume for a crown."

"I am poor," said I; "but I will give you two silver crowns for your volume."

"No, dear, I will not sell my volume for two silver crowns; no, nor for the golden one in the king's tower down there; without my book I should mope and pine, and perhaps fling myself into the river; but I am glad you like it, which shows that I was right about you, after all; you are one of our party, and you have a flash about that eye of yours which puts me just in mind of my dear son. No, dear, I won't sell you my book; but, if you like, you may have a peep into it whenever you come this way. I shall be glad to see you; you are one of the right sort, for if you had been a common one, you would have run away with the thing; but you scorn such behaviour, and, as you are so flash of your money, though you say you are poor, you may give me a tanner to buy a little baccy with; I love baccy, dear, more by token that it comes from the plantations to which the blessed woman was sent."

"What's a tanner?" said I.

"Lor'! don't you know, dear? Why, a tanner is sixpence; and, as you were talking just now about crowns, it will be as well to tell you that those of our trade never calls them crowns, but bulls; but I am talking nonsense, just as if you did not know that already, as well as myself; you are only shamming—I'm no trap, dear, nor more was the blessed woman in the book. Thank you, dear—thank you for the tanner; if I don't spend it, I'll keep it in remembrance of your sweet face. What, you are going?—well, first let me whisper a word to you. If you have any clies to sell at any time, I'll buy them of you; all safe with me; I never 'peach, and scorns a trap; so now, dear, God bless you! and give you good luck. Thank you for your pleasant company, and thank you for the tanner."

The Funeral of Byron

One day, after a scene with the publisher similar to that which I have described above, I found myself about noon at the bottom of Oxford Street, where it forms a right angle with the road which leads or did lead to Tottenham Court. Happening to cast my eyes around, it suddenly occurred to me that something was expected; people were standing in groups on the pavement—the upstair windows of the houses were thronged with faces, especially those of women, and many of the shops were partly, and not a few entirely closed. What could be the reason of all this? All at once I bethought me that this street of Oxford was no other than the far-famed Tyburn way. Oh, oh, thought I, an execution; some handsome young robber is about to be executed at the farther end; just so, see how earnestly the women are peering; perhaps another Harry Simms—Gentleman Harry as they called him—is about to be carted along this street to Tyburn tree; but then I remembered that Tyburn tree had long since been cut down, and that criminals, whether young or old, good-looking or ugly, were executed before the big stone gaol, which I had looked at with a kind of shudder during my short rambles in the city. What could be the matter? Just then I heard various voices cry "There it comes!" and all heads were turned up Oxford Street, down which a hearse was slowly coming: nearer and nearer it drew; presently it was just opposite the place where I was standing, when, turning to the left, it proceeded slowly along Tottenham Road; immediately behind the hearse were three or four mourning coaches, full of people, some of which, from the partial glimpse which I caught of them, appeared to be foreigners; behind these came a very long train of splendid carriages, all of which, without one exception, were empty.

"Whose body is in that hearse?" said I to a dapper-looking individual, seemingly a shopkeeper, who stood beside me on the pavement, looking at the procession.

"The mortal relics of Lord Byron," said the dapper-looking individual, mouthing his words and smirking—"the illustrious poet, which have been just brought from Greece, and are being conveyed to the family vault in ——shire."

"An illustrious poet, was he?" said I.

"Beyond all criticism," said the dapper man; "all we of the rising generation are under incalculable obligation to Byron; I myself, in particular, have reason to say so; in all my correspondence my style is formed on the Byronic model."

I looked at the individual for a moment, who smiled and smirked to himself applause, and then I turned my eyes upon the hearse proceeding slowly up the almost endless street. This man, this Byron, had for many years past been the demigod of England, and his verses the daily food of those who read, from the peer to the draper's assistant; all were admirers, or rather worshippers, of Byron, and all doated on his verses; and then I thought of those who, with genius as high as his, or higher, had lived and died neglected. I thought of Milton abandoned to poverty and blindness; of witty and ingenious Butler consigned to the tender mercies of bailiffs; and starving Otway: they had lived, neglected and despised, and, when they died, a few poor mourners only had followed them to the grave; but this Byron had been made a half god of when living, and now that he was dead he was followed by worshipping crowds, and the very sun seemed to come out on purpose to grace his funeral. And, indeed, the sun, which for many days past had hidden its face in clouds, shone out that morning with wonderful brilliancy, flaming upon the black hearse and its tall ostrich plumes, the mourning coaches, and the long train of aristocratic carriages which followed behind.

"Great poet, sir," said the dapper-looking man, "great poet, but unhappy."

Unhappy? yes, I had heard that he had been unhappy; that he had roamed about a fevered, distempered man, taking pleasure in nothing—that I had heard; but was it true? was he really unhappy? was not this unhappiness assumed, with the view of increasing the interest which the world took in him? and yet who could say? He might be unhappy, and with reason. Was he a real poet, after all? might he not doubt himself? might he not have a lurking consciousness that he was undeserving of the homage which he was receiving? that it could not last? that he was rather at the top of fashion than of fame? He was a lordling, a glittering, gorgeous lordling: and he might have had a consciousness that he owed much of his celebrity to being so; he might have felt that he was rather at the top of fashion than of fame. Fashion soon changes, thought I, eagerly to myself—a time will come, and that speedily, when he will be no longer in the fashion; when this idiotic admirer of his, who is still grinning at my side, shall have ceased to mould his style on Byron's; and this aristocracy, squirearchy, and what not, who now send their empty carriages to pay respect to the fashionable corpse, shall have transferred their empty worship to some other animate or inanimate thing. Well, perhaps after all it was better to have been mighty Milton in his poverty and blindness—witty and ingenious Butler consigned to the tender mercies of bailiffs, and starving Otway; they might enjoy more real pleasure than this lordling; they must have been aware that the world would one day do them justice—fame after death is better than the top of fashion in life. They have left a fame behind them which shall never die, whilst this lordling—a time will come when he will be out of fashion and forgotten. And yet I don't know; didn't he write Childe Harold and that ode? Yes, he wrote Childe Harold and that ode. Then a time will scarcely come when he will be forgotten. Lords, squires, and cockneys may pass away, but a time will scarcely come when Childe Harold and that ode will be forgotten. He was a poet, after all, and he must have known it; a real poet, equal to—— to——what a destiny! Rank, beauty, fashion, immortality,—he could not be unhappy; what a difference in the fate of men—I wish I could think he was unhappy—

I turned away.

"Great poet, sir," said the dapper man, turning away too, "but unhappy—fate of genius, sir; I, too, am frequently unhappy."

Hurrying down a street to the right, I encountered Francis Ardry.

"What means the multitude yonder?" he demanded.

"They are looking after the hearse which is carrying the remains of Byron up Tottenham Road."

"I have seen the man," said my friend, as he turned back the way he had come, "so I can dispense with seeing the hearse—I saw the living man at Venice—ah, a great poet."

"Yes," said I, "a great poet, it must be so, everybody says so—what a destiny! What a difference in the fate of men; but 'tis said he was unhappy; you have seen him, how did he look?"

"Oh, beautiful!"

"But did he look happy?"

"Why, I can't say he looked very unhappy; I saw him with two—— very fair ladies."

The Apple-Woman

So I went to London Bridge, and again took my station on the spot by the booth where I had stood on the former occasion. The booth, however, was empty; neither the apple-woman nor her stall was to be seen. I looked over the balustrade upon the river; the tide was now, as before, rolling beneath the arch with frightful impetuosity. As I gazed upon the eddies of the whirlpool, I thought within myself how soon human life would become extinct there; a plunge, a convulsive flounder, and all would be over. When I last stood over that abyss I had felt a kind of impulse—a fascination; I had resisted it—I did not plunge into it. At present I felt a kind of impulse to plunge; but the impulse was of a different kind; it proceeded from a loathing of life. I looked wistfully at the eddies—what had I to live for?—what, indeed! I thought of Brandt and Struensee, and Yeoman Patch—should I yield to the impulse—why not? My eyes were fixed on the eddies. All of a sudden I shuddered; I thought I saw heads in the pool; human bodies wallowing confusedly; eyes turned up to heaven with hopeless horror; was that water, or——Where was the impulse now? I raised my eyes from the pool, I looked no more upon it—I looked forward, far down the stream in the far distance. "Ha! what is that?" I thought I saw a kind of Fata Morgana, green meadows, waving groves, a rustic home; but in the far distance—I stared—I stared—a Fata Morgana—it was gone——

I left the balustrade and walked to the farther end of the bridge, where I stood for some time contemplating the crowd; I then passed over to the other side with the intention of returning home; just half way over the bridge, in a booth immediately opposite to the one in which I had formerly beheld her, sat my friend, the old apple-woman, huddled up behind her stall.

"Well, mother," said I, "how are you?" The old woman lifted her head with a startled look.

"Don't you know me?" said I.

"Yes, I think I do. Ah, yes," said she, as her features beamed with recollection, "I know you, dear; you are the young lad that gave me the tanner. Well, child, got anything to sell?"

"Nothing at all," said I.

"Bad luck?"

"Yes," said I, "bad enough, and ill usage."

"Ah, I suppose they caught ye; well, child, never mind, better luck next time; I am glad to see you."

"Thank you," said I, sitting down on the stone bench; "I thought you had left the bridge—why have you changed your side?"

The old woman shook.

"What is the matter with you," said I, "are you ill?"

"No, child, no; only——"

"Only what? Any bad news of your son?"

"No, child, no; nothing about my son. Only low, child—every heart has its bitters."

"That's true," said I; "well, I don't want to know your sorrows; come, where's the book?"

The apple-woman shook more violently than before, bent herself down, and drew her cloak more closely about her than before. "Book, child, what book?"

"Why blessed Mary, to be sure."

"Oh, that; I ha'n't got it, child—I have lost it, have left it at home."

"Lost it," said I; "left it at home—what do you mean? Come, let me have it."

"I ha'n't got it, child."

"I believe you have got it under your cloak."

"Don't tell any one, dear; don't—don't," and the apple-woman burst into tears.

"What's the matter with you?" said I, staring at her.

"You want to take my book from me?"

"Not I, I care nothing about it; keep it, if you like, only tell me what's the matter?"

"Why, all about that book."

"The book?"

"Yes, they wanted to take it from me."

"Who did?"

"Why, some wicked boys. I'll tell you all about it. Eight or ten days ago, I sat behind my stall, reading my book; all of a sudden I felt it snatched from my hand; up I started, and see three rascals of boys grinning at me; one of them held the book in his hand. 'What book is this?' said he, grinning at it. 'What do you want with my book?' said I, clutching at it over my stall, 'give me my book.' 'What do you want a book for?' said he, holding it back; 'I have a good mind to fling it into the Thames.' 'Give me my book,' I shrieked; and, snatching at it, I fell over my stall, and all my fruit was scattered about. Off ran the boys—off ran the rascal with my book. Oh dear, I thought I should have died; up I got, however, and ran after them as well as I could; I thought of my fruit, but I thought more of my book. I left my fruit and ran after my book. 'My book! my book!' I shrieked, 'murder! theft! robbery!' I was near being crushed under the wheels of a cart; but I didn't care—I followed the rascals. 'Stop them! stop them!' I ran nearly as fast as they—they couldn't run very fast on account of the crowd. At last some one stopped the rascal, whereupon he turned round, and flinging the book at me, it fell into the mud; well, I picked it up and kissed it, all muddy as it was. 'Has he robbed you?' said the man. 'Robbed me, indeed; why, he had got my book.' 'Oh, your book,' said the man, and laughed, and let the rascal go. Ah, he might laugh, but——"

"Well, go on."

"My heart beats so. Well, I went back to my booth and picked up my stall and my fruits, what I could find of them. I couldn't keep my stall for two days I got such a fright, and when I got round I couldn't bide the booth where the thing had happened, so I came over to the other side. Oh, the rascals, if I could but see them hanged."

"For what?"

"Why, for stealing my book."

"I thought you didn't dislike stealing,—that you were ready to buy things—there was your son, you know——"

"Yes, to be sure."

"He took things."

"To be sure he did."

"But you don't like a thing of yours to be taken."

"No, that's quite a different thing; what's stealing handkerchiefs, and that kind of thing, to do with taking my book; there's a wide difference—don't you see?"

"Yes, I see."

"Do you, dear? well, bless your heart, I'm glad you do. Would you like to look at the book?"

"Well, I think I should."

"Honour bright?" said the apple-woman, looking me in the eyes.

"Honour bright," said I, looking the apple-woman in the eyes.

"Well then, dear, here it is," said she, taking it from under her cloak; "read it as long as you like, only get a little farther into the booth—— Don't sit so near the edge——you might——"

I went deep into the booth, and the apple-woman, bringing her chair round, almost confronted me. I commenced reading the book, and was soon engrossed by it; hours passed away, once or twice I lifted up my eyes, the apple-woman was still confronting me: at last my eyes began to ache, whereupon I returned the book to the apple-woman, and giving her another tanner, walked away.

The Fight with the Flaming Tinman

Two mornings after the period to which I have brought the reader in the preceding chapter, I sat by my fire at the bottom of the dingle; I had just breakfasted, and had finished the last morsel of food which I had brought with me to that solitude.

"What shall I now do?" said I, to myself; "shall I continue here, or decamp—this is a sad lonely spot—perhaps I had better quit it; but whither should I go? the wide world is before me, but what can I do therein? I have been in the world already without much success. No, I had better remain here; the place is lonely, it is true, but here I am free and independent, and can do what I please; but I can't remain here without food. Well, I will find my way to the nearest town, lay in a fresh supply of provision, and come back, turning my back upon the world, which has turned its back upon me. I don't see why I should not write a little sometimes; I have pens and an inkhorn, and for a writing-desk I can place the Bible on my knee. I shouldn't wonder if I could write a capital satire on the world on the back of that Bible; but first of all I must think of supplying myself with food."

I rose up from the stone on which I was seated, determining to go to the nearest town, with my little horse and cart, and procure what I wanted—the nearest town, according to my best calculation, lay about five miles distant; I had no doubt, however, that by using ordinary diligence, I should be back before evening. In order to go lighter, I determined to leave my tent standing as it was, and all the things which I had purchased of the tinker, just as they were. "I need not be apprehensive on their account," said I, to myself; "nobody will come here to meddle with them—the great recommendation of this place is its perfect solitude—I dare say that I could live here six months without seeing a single human visage. I will now harness my little gry and be off to the town."

At a whistle which I gave, the little gry, which was feeding on the bank near the uppermost part of the dingle, came running to me, for by this time he had become so accustomed to me, that he would obey my call for all the world as if he had been one of the canine species. "Now," said I to him, "we are going to the town to buy bread for myself, and oats for you—I am in a hurry to be back; therefore, I pray you to do your best, and to draw me and the cart to the town with all possible speed, and to bring us back; if you do your best, I promise you oats on your return. You know the meaning of oats, Ambrol?"

Ambrol whinnied as if to let me know that he understood me perfectly well, as indeed he well might, as I had never once fed him during the time he had been in my possession without saying the word in question to him. Now, Ambrol, in the Gypsy tongue, signifieth a pear.

So I caparisoned Ambrol, and then, going to the cart, I removed two or three things from out it into the tent; I then lifted up the shafts, and was just going to call to the pony to come and be fastened to them, when I thought I heard a noise.

I stood stock still supporting the shafts of the little cart in my hand,

and bending the right side of my face slightly towards the ground; but I could hear nothing; the noise which I thought I had heard was not one of those sounds which I was accustomed to hear in that solitude, the note of a bird, or the rustling of a bough; it was—there I heard it again, a sound very much resembling the grating of a wheel amongst gravel. Could it proceed from the road? Oh no, the road was too far distant for me to hear the noise of anything moving along it. Again I listened, and now I distinctly heard the sound of wheels, which seemed to be approaching the dingle; nearer and nearer they drew, and presently the sound of wheels was blended with the murmur of voices. Anon I heard a boisterous shout, which seemed to proceed from the entrance of the dingle. "Here are folks at hand," said I, letting the shaft of the cart fall to the ground, "is it possible that they can be coming here?"

My doubts on that point, if I entertained any, were soon dispelled; the wheels, which had ceased moving for a moment or two, were once again in motion, and were now evidently moving down the winding path which led to my retreat. Leaving my cart, I came forward and placed myself near the entrance of the open space, with my eyes fixed on the path down which my unexpected and I may say unwelcome visitors were coming. Presently I heard a stamping or sliding, as if of a horse in some difficulty; and then a loud curse, and the next moment appeared a man and a horse and cart; the former holding the head of the horse up to prevent him from falling, of which he was in danger, owing to the precipitous nature of the path. Whilst thus occupied, the head of the man was averted from me. When, however, he had reached the bottom of the descent, he turned his head, and perceiving me, as I stood bareheaded, without either coat or waistcoat, about two yards from him, he gave a sudden start, so violent, that the backward motion of his hand had nearly flung the horse upon his haunches.

"Why don't you move forward?" said a voice from behind, apparently that of a female, "you are stopping up the way, and we shall be all down upon one another;" and I saw the head of another horse overtopping the back of the cart.

"Why don't you move forward, Jack?" said another voice, also of a female, yet higher up the path.

The man stirred not, but remained staring at me in the posture which he had assumed on first perceiving me, his body very much drawn back, his left foot far in advance of his right, and with his right hand still grasping the halter of the horse, which gave way more and more, till it was clean down on its haunches.

"What is the matter?" said the voice which I had last heard.

"Get back with you, Belle, Moll," said the man, still staring at me, "here's something not over-canny or comfortable."

"What is it?" said the same voice; "let me pass, Moll, and I'll soon clear the way," and I heard a kind of rushing down the path.

"You need not be afraid," said I, addressing myself to the man, "I mean you no harm; I am a wanderer like yourself—come here to seek for shelter—you need not be afraid; I am a Rome chabo by matriculation—one of the right sort, and no mistake—Good day to ye, brother; I bids ye welcome."

The man eyed me suspiciously for a moment—then, turning to his horse with a loud curse, he pulled him up from his haunches, and led him and the cart farther down to one side of the dingle, muttering as he passed me, "Afraid. Hm!"

I do not remember ever to have seen a more ruffianly-looking fellow; he was about six feet high, with an immensely athletic frame; his face was black and bluff, and sported an immense pair of whiskers, but with here and there a grey hair, for his age could not be much under fifty. He wore a faded blue frock coat, corduroys, and highlows—on his black head was a kind of red nightcap, round his bull neck a Barcelona handkerchief—I did not like the look of the man at all.

"Afraid," growled the fellow, proceeding to unharness his horse; "that was the word, I think."

But other figures were now already upon the scene. Dashing past the other horse and cart, which by this time had reached the bottom of the pass, appeared an exceedingly tall woman, or rather girl, for she could scarcely have been above eighteen; she was dressed in a tight bodice and a blue stuff gown; hat, bonnet, or cap she had none, and her hair, which was flaxen, hung down on her shoulders unconfined; her complexion was fair, and her features handsome, with a determined but open expression—she was followed by another female, about forty, stout and vulgar-looking, at whom I scarcely glanced, my whole attention being absorbed by the tall girl.

"What's the matter, Jack?" said the latter, looking at the man.

"Only afraid, that's all," said the man, still proceeding with his work.

"Afraid of what—at that lad? why, he looks like a ghost—I would engage to thrash him with one hand."

"You might beat me with no hands at all," said I, "fair damsel, only by looking at me—I never saw such a face and figure, both regal—why, you look like Ingeborg, Queen of Norway; she had twelve brothers, you know, and could lick them all, though they were heroes—

" 'On Dovrefeld in Norway,
Were once together seen,
The twelve heroic brothers
Of Ingeborg the queen.' "

"None of your chaffing, young fellow," said the tall girl, "or I will give you what shall make you wipe your face; be civil, or you will rue it."

"Well, perhaps I was a peg too high," said I, "I ask your pardon—here's something a bit lower—

" 'As I was jawing to the gav yeck divvus
I met on the drom miro Rommany chi——' "

"None of your Rommany chies, young fellow," said the tall girl, looking more menacingly than before, and clenching her fist, "you had better be civil, I am none of your chies; and, though I keep company with gypsies, or, to speak more proper, half and halfs, I would have you to know that I come of Christian blood and parents, and was born in the great house of Long Melford."

"I have no doubt," said I, "that it was a great house; judging from your size, I shouldn't wonder if you were born in a church."

"Stay, Belle," said the man, putting himself before the young virago, who was about to rush upon me, "my turn is first—then, advancing to me in a menacing attitude, he said, with a look of deep malignity, " 'Afraid' was the word, wasn't it?"

"It was," said I, "but I think I wronged you; I should have said, aghast, you exhibited every symptom of one labouring under uncontrollable fear."

The fellow stared at me with a look of stupid ferocity, and appeared to be hesitating whether to strike or not: ere he could make up his mind, the tall girl stepped forward, crying, "He's chaffing; let me at him;" and, before I could put myself on my guard, she struck me a blow on the face which had nearly brought me to the ground.

"Enough," said I, putting my hand to my cheek; "you have now performed your promise, and made me wipe my face: now be pacified, and tell me fairly the ground of this quarrel."

"Grounds!" said the fellow; "didn't you say I was afraid; and if you hadn't, who gave you leave to camp on my ground?"

"Is it your ground?" said I.

"A pretty question," said the fellow; "as if all the world didn't know that. Do you know who I am?"

"I guess I do," said I; "unless I am much mistaken, you are he whom folks call the 'Flaming Tinman.' To tell you the truth, I'm glad we have met, for I wished to see you. These are your two wives, I suppose; I greet them. There's no harm done—there's room enough here for all of us—we shall soon be good friends, I dare say; and when we are a little better acquainted, I'll tell you my history."

"Well, if that doesn't beat all," said the fellow.

"I don't think he's chaffing now," said the girl, whose anger seemed to have subsided on a sudden; "the young man speaks civil enough."

"Civil," said the fellow, with an oath; "but that's just like you; with you it is a blow, and all over. Civil! I suppose you would have him stay here, and get into all my secrets, and hear all I may have to say to my two morts."

"Two morts," said the girl, kindling up, "where are they? Speak for one, and no more. I am no mort of yours, whatever some one else may be. I tell you one thing, Black John, or Anselo, for t'other an't your name, the same thing I told the young man here, be civil, or you will rue it."

The fellow looked at the girl furiously, but his glance soon quailed before hers; he withdrew his eyes, and cast them on my little horse, which was feeding amongst the trees. "What's this?" said he, rushing forward and seizing the animal. "Why, as I am alive, this is the horse of that mumping villain Slingsby."

"It's his no longer; I bought it and paid for it."

"It's mine now," said the fellow; "I swore I would seize it the next time I found it on my beat; ay, and beat the master too."

"I am not Slingsby."

"All's one for that."

"You don't say you will beat me?"

"Afraid was the word."

"I'm sick and feeble."

"Hold up your fists."

"Won't the horse satisfy you?"

"Horse nor bellows either."

"No mercy, then."

"Here's at you."

"Mind your eyes, Jack. There, you've got it. I thought so," shouted the girl, as the fellow staggered back from a sharp blow in the eye. "I thought he was chaffing at you all along."

"Never mind, Anselo. You know what to do—go in," said the vulgar woman, who had hitherto not spoken a word, but who now came forward with all the look of a fury; "go in apopli; you'll smash ten like he."

The Flaming Tinman took her advice, and came in bent on smashing, but stopped short on receiving a left-handed blow on the nose.

"You'll never beat the Flaming Tinman in that way," said the girl, looking at me doubtfully.

And so I began to think myself, when, in the twinkling of an eye, the Flaming Tinman, disengaging himself of his frock-coat, and dashing off his red night-cap, came rushing in more desperately than ever. To a flush hit which he received in the mouth he paid as little attention as a wild bull would have done; in a moment his arms were around me, and in another, he had hurled me down, falling heavily upon me. The fellow's strength appeared to be tremendous.

"Pay him off now," said the vulgar woman. The Flaming Tinman made no reply, but planting his knee on my breast, seized my throat with two huge horny hands. I gave myself up for dead, and probably should have been so in another minute but for the tall girl, who caught hold of the handkerchief which the fellow wore round his neck with a grasp nearly as powerful as that with which he pressed my throat.

"Do you call that fair play?" said she.

"Hands off, Belle," said the other woman; "do you call it fair play to interfere? hands off, or I'll be down upon you myself."

But Belle paid no heed to the injunction, and tugged so hard at the handkerchief, that the Flaming Tinman was nearly throttled; suddenly relinquishing his hold of me, he started on his feet, and aimed a blow at my fair preserver, who avoided it, but said coolly—

"Finish t'other business first, and then I'm your woman whenever you like; but finish it fairly—no foul play when I'm by—I'll be the boy's second, and Moll can pick up you when he happens to knock you down."

The battle during the next ten minutes raged with considerable fury, but it so happened that during this time I was never able to knock the Flaming Tinman down, but on the contrary received six knock-down blows myself. "I can never stand this," said I, as I sat on the knee of Belle, "I am afraid I must give in; the Flaming Tinman hits very hard," and I spat out a mouthful of blood.

"Sure enough you'll never beat the Flaming Tinman in the way you fight—it's of no use flipping at the Flaming Tinman with your left hand; why don't you use your right?"

"Because I'm not handy with it," said I; and then getting up, I once more confronted the Flaming Tinman, and struck him six blows for his one, but they were all left-handed blows, and the blow which the Flaming Tinman gave me knocked me off my legs.

"Now, will you use Long Melford?" said Belle, picking me up.

"I don't know what you mean by Long Melford," said I, gasping for breath.

"Why, this long right of yours," said Belle, feeling my right arm—"if you do, I shouldn't wonder if you yet stand a chance."

And now the Flaming Tinman was once more ready, much more ready than myself. I, however, rose from my second's knee as well as my weakness would permit me; on he came, striking left and right, appearing almost as fresh as to wind and spirit as when he first commenced the combat, though his eyes were considerably swelled, and his nether lip was cut in two; on he came, striking left and right, and I did not like his blows at all, or even the wind of them, which was anything but agreeable, and I gave way before him. At last he aimed a blow, which, had it taken full effect, would doubtless have ended the battle, but owing to his slipping, the fist only grazed my left shoulder, and came with terrific force against a tree, close to which I had been driven; before the tinman could recover himself, I collected all my strength, and struck him beneath the ear, and then fell to the ground completely exhausted, and it so happened that the blow which I struck the Tinker beneath the ear was a right-handed blow.

"Hurrah for Long Melford!" I heard Belle exclaim; "there is nothing like Long Melford for shortness all the world over."

At these words, I turned round my head as I lay, and perceived the Flaming Tinman stretched upon the ground apparently senseless. "He is dead," said the vulgar woman, as she vainly endeavoured to raise him up; "he is dead; the best man in all the north country, killed in this fashion, by a boy." Alarmed at these words, I made shift to get on my feet; and, with the assistance of the woman, placed my fallen adversary in a sitting posture. I put my hand to his heart, and felt a slight pulsation—"He's not dead," said I, "only stunned; if he were let blood, he would recover presently." I produced a penknife which I had in my pocket, and, baring the arm of the Tinman, was about to make the necessary incision, when the woman gave me a violent blow, and, pushing me aside, exclaimed, "I'll tear the eyes out of your head, if you offer to touch him. Do you want to complete your work, and murder him outright, now he's asleep? you have had enough of his blood already." "You are mad," said I, "I only seek to do him service. Well, if you won't let him be blooded, fetch some water and fling it into his face, you know where the pit is."

"A pretty manœuvre," said the woman; "leave my husband in the hands of you and that limmer, who has never been true to us; I should find him strangled or his throat cut when I came back." "Do you go," said I, to the tall girl, "take the can and fetch some water from the pit." "You had better go yourself," said the girl, wiping a tear as she looked on the yet senseless form of the tinker; "you had better go yourself, if you think water will do him good." I had by this time somewhat recovered my exhausted powers, and, taking the can, I bent my steps as fast as I could to the pit; arriving there, I lay down on the brink, took a long draught, and then plunged my head into the water; after which I filled the can, and bent my way back to the dingle. Before I could reach the path which led down into its depths, I had to pass some way along its side; I had arrived at a part immediately over the scene of the last encounter, where the bank, overgrown with trees, sloped precipitously down. Here I heard a loud sound of voices in the dingle; I stopped, and laying hold of a tree, leaned over the bank and listened. The two women appeared to be in hot dispute in the dingle. "It was all owing to you, you limmer," said the vulgar woman to the other; "had you not interfered, the old man would soon have settled the boy."

"I'm for fair play and Long Melford," said the other. "If your old man, as you call him, could have settled the boy fairly, he might, for all I should have cared, but no foul work for me; and as for sticking the boy with our gulleys when he comes back, as you proposed, I am not so fond of your old man or you that I should oblige you in it, to my soul's destruction." "Hold your tongue, or I'll—"; I listened no further, but hastened as fast as I could to the dingle. My adversary had just begun to show signs of animation; the vulgar woman was still supporting him, and occasionally cast glances of anger at the tall girl who was walking slowly up and down. I lost no time in dashing the greater part of the water into the Tinman's face, whereupon he sneezed, moved his hands, and presently looked round him. At first his looks were dull and heavy, and without any intelligence at all; he soon, however, began to recollect himself, and to be conscious of his situation; he cast a scowling glance at me, then one of the deepest malignity at the tall girl, who was still walking about without taking much notice of what was going forward. At last he looked at his right hand, which had evidently suffered from the blow against the tree, and a half-stifled curse escaped his lips. The vulgar woman now said something to him in a low tone, whereupon he looked at her for a moment, and then got upon his legs. Again the vulgar woman said something to him; her looks were furious, and she appeared to be urging him on to attempt something. I observed that she had a clasped knife in her hand. The fellow remained standing for some time as if hesitating what to do, at last he looked at his hand, and, shaking his head, said something to the woman which I did not understand. The tall girl, however, appeared to overhear him and, probably repeating his words, said, "No, it won't do; you are right there, and now hear what I have to say,—let bygones be bygones, and let us all shake hands, and camp here, as the young man was saying just now." The man looked at her, and then, without any reply, went to his horse, which was lying down among the trees, and kicking it up, led it to the cart, to which he forthwith began to harness it. The other cart and horse had remained standing motionless during the whole affair which I have been recounting, at the bottom of the pass. The woman now took the horse by the head, and leading it with the cart into the open part of the dingle turned both round, and then led them back, till the horse and cart had mounted a little way up the ascent; she then stood still and appeared to be expecting the man. During this proceeding Belle had stood looking on without saying anything; at last, perceiving that the man had harnessed his horse to the other cart, and that both he and the woman were about to take their departure, she said, "You are not going, are you?" Receiving no answer, she continued: "I tell you what, both of you, Black John, and you Moll, his mort, this is not treating me over civilly,—however, I am ready to put up with it, and go with you if you like, for I bear no malice. I'm sorry for what has happened, but you have only yourselves to thank for it. Now, shall I go with you, only tell me?" The man made no manner of reply, but flogged his horse. The woman, however, whose passions were probably under less control, replied, with a screeching tone, "Stay where you are, you jade, and may the curse of Judas cling to you,—stay with the bit of a mullo whom you helped, and my only hope is that he may gulley you before he comes to be—— Have you with us indeed! after what's past, no, nor nothing belonging to you. Fetch down your mailla go-cart and live here with your chabo." She then whipped on the horse, and ascended the pass, followed by the man. The carts were light, and they were not long in ascending the winding path. I followed to see that they took their departure. Arriving at the top, I found near the entrance a small donkey-cart, which I concluded belonged to the girl. The tinker and his mort were already at some distance; I stood looking after them for some little time, then taking the donkey by the reins I led it with the cart to the bottom of the dingle. Arrived there, I found Belle seated on the stone by the fireplace. Her hair was all dishevelled, and she was in tears.

"They were bad people," she said, "and I did not like them, but they were my only acquaintance in the wide world."

From The Romany Rye

Isopel's Refusal

I set out for the dingle alone. It was a dark night when I reached it, and descending I saw the glimmer of a fire from the depths of the dingle; my heart beat with fond anticipation of a welcome. "Isopel Berners is waiting for me," said I, "and the first words that I shall hear from her lips is that she has made up her mind. We shall go to America, and be so happy together." On reaching the bottom of the dingle, however, I saw seated near the fire, beside which stood the kettle simmering, not Isopel Berners, but a gypsy girl, who told me that Miss Berners when she went away had charged her to keep up the fire, and have the kettle boiling against my arrival. Startled at these words, I inquired at what hour Isopel had left, and whither she was gone, and was told that she had left the dingle, with her cart, about two hours after I departed; but where she was gone she, the girl, did not know. I then asked whether she had left no message, and the girl replied that she had left none, but had merely given directions about the kettle and fire, putting, at the same time, sixpence into her hand. "Very strange," thought I; then dismissing the gypsy girl I sat down by the fire. I had no wish for tea, but sat looking on the embers, wondering what could be the motive of the sudden departure of Isopel. "Does she mean to return?" thought I to myself. "Surely she means to return," Hope replied, "or she would not have gone away without leaving any message"—"and yet she could scarcely mean to return," muttered Foreboding, "or she assuredly would have left some message with the girl." I then thought to myself what a hard thing it would be, if, after having made up my mind to assume the yoke of matrimony, I should be disappointed of the woman of my choice. "Well, after all," thought I, "I can scarcely be disappointed; if such an ugly scoundrel as Sylvester had no difficulty in getting such a nice wife as Ursula, surely I, who am not a tenth part so ugly, cannot fail to obtain the hand of Isopel Berners, uncommonly fine damsel though she be. Husbands do not grow upon hedgerows; she is merely gone after a little business and will return to-morrow."

Comforted in some degree by these hopeful imaginings, I retired to my tent, and went to sleep.

Nothing occurred to me of any particular moment during the following day. Isopel Berners did not return; but Mr. Petulengro and his companions came home from the fair early in the morning. When I saw him, which was about midday, I found him with his face bruised and swelled. It appeared that, some time after I had left him, he himself perceived that the jockeys with whom he was playing cards were cheating him and his companion; a quarrel ensued, which terminated in a fight between Mr. Petulengro and one of the jockeys, which lasted some time, and in which Mr. Petulengro, though he eventually came off victor, was considerably beaten. His bruises, in conjunction with his pecuniary loss, which amounted to about seven pounds, were the cause of his being much out of humour; before night, however, he had returned to his usual philosophic frame of mind, and, coming up to me as I was walking about, apologized for his behaviour on the preceding day, and assured me that he was determined from that time forward, never to quarrel with a friend for giving him good advice.

Two more days passed, and still Isopel Berners did not return. Gloomy thoughts and forebodings filled my mind. During the day I wandered about the neighbouring roads in the hopes of catching an early glimpse of her and her returning vehicle; and at night lay awake, tossing about on my hard couch, listening to the rustle of every leaf, and occasionally thinking that I heard the sound of her wheels upon the distant road. Once at midnight, just as I was about to fall into unconsciousness, I suddenly started up, for I was convinced that I heard the sound of wheels. I listened most anxiously, and the sound of wheels striking against stones was certainly plain enough. "She comes at last," thought I, and for a few moments I felt as if a mountain had been removed from my breast;—"here she comes at last, now, how shall I receive her? Oh," thought I, "I will receive her rather coolly, just as if I was not particularly anxious about her—that's the way to manage these women." The next moment the sound became very loud, rather too loud, I thought, to proceed from her wheels, and then by degrees became fainter. Rushing out of my tent, I hurried up the path to the top of the dingle, where I heard the sound distinctly enough, but it was going from me, and evidently proceeded from something much larger than the cart of Isopel. I could, moreover, hear the stamping of a horse's hoof at a lumbering trot. Those only whose hopes have been wrought up to a high pitch, and then suddenly cast down, can imagine what I felt at that moment; and yet when I returned to my lonely tent, and lay down on my hard pallet, the voice of conscience told me that the misery I was then undergoing I had fully merited, for the unkind manner in which I had intended to receive her, when for a brief moment I supposed that she had returned.

It was on the morning after this affair, and the fourth, if I forget not, from the time of Isopel's departure, that, as I was seated on my stone at the bottom of the dingle, getting my breakfast, I heard an unknown voice from the path above—apparently that of a person descending—exclaim, "Here's a strange place to bring a letter to;" and presently an old woman, with a belt round her middle, to which was attached a leathern bag, made her appearance, and stood before me.

"Well, if I ever!" said she, as she looked about her. "My good gentlewoman," said I, "pray what may you please to want?" "Gentlewoman!" said the old dame, "please to want—well, I call that speaking civilly, at any rate. It is true, civil words cost nothing; nevertheless, we do not always get them. What I please to want is to deliver a letter to a young man in this place; perhaps you be he?" "What's the name on the letter?" said I, getting up, and going to her. "There's no name upon it," said she, taking a letter out of her scrip, and looking at it. "It is directed to the young man in Mumper's Dingle." "Then it is for me, I make no doubt," said I, stretching out my hand to take it. "Please to pay me ninepence first," said the old woman. "However," said she, after a moment's thought, "civility is civility, and, being rather a scarce article, should meet with some return. Here's the letter, young man, and I hope you will pay for it; for if you do not I must pay the postage myself." "You are the postwoman, I suppose," said I, as I took the letter. "I am the postman's mother," said the old woman; "but as he has a wide beat, I help him as much as I can, and I generally carry letters to places like this, to which he is afraid to come himself." "You say the postage is ninepence," said I, "here's a shilling." "Well, I call that honourable," said the old woman, taking the shilling, and putting it into her pocket—"here's your change, young man," said she, offering me threepence. "Pray keep that for yourself," said I; "you deserve it for your trouble." "Well, I call that genteel," said the old woman; "and as one good turn deserves another, since you look as if you couldn't read, I will read your letter for you. Let's see it; it's from some young woman or other, I dare say." "Thank you," said I, "but I can read." "All the better for you," said the old woman; "your being able to read will frequently save you a penny, for that's the charge I generally make for reading letters; though, as you behaved so genteelly to me, I should have charged you nothing. Well, if you can read, why don't you open the letter, instead of keeping it hanging between your finger and thumb?" "I am in no hurry to open it," said I, with a sigh. The old woman looked at me for a moment—"Well, young man," said she, "there are some—especially those who can read—who don't like to open their letters when anybody is by, more especially when they come from young women. Well, I won't intrude upon you, but leave you alone with your letter.

I wish it may contain something pleasant. God bless you," and with these words she departed.

I sat down on my stone, with my letter in my hand. I knew perfectly well that it could have come from no other person than Isopel Berners; but what did the letter contain? I guessed tolerably well what its purport was—an eternal farewell! yet I was afraid to open the letter, lest my expectation should be confirmed. There I sat with the letter, putting off the evil moment as long as possible. At length I glanced at the direction, which was written in a fine bold hand, and was directed, as the old woman had said, to the young man in "Mumpers' Dingle," with the addition, near ——, in the county of ——. Suddenly the idea occurred to me, that, after all, the letter might not contain an eternal farewell; and that Isopel might have written, requesting me to join her. Could it be so? "Alas! no," presently said Foreboding. At last I became ashamed of my weakness. The letter must be opened sooner or later. Why not at once? So as the bather who, for a considerable time, has stood shivering on the bank, afraid to take the decisive plunge, suddenly takes it, I tore open the letter almost before I was aware. I had no sooner done so than a paper fell out. I examined it; it contained a lock of bright flaxen hair. "This is no good sign," said I, as I thrust the lock and paper into my bosom, and proceeded to read the letter, which ran as follows:—

"TO THE YOUNG MAN IN MUMPERS' DINGLE.

"SIR,—I send these lines, with the hope and trust that they will find you well, even as I am myself at this moment, and in much better spirits, for my own are not such as I could wish they were, being sometimes rather hysterical and vapourish, and at other times, and most often, very low. I am at a sea-port, and am just going on shipboard; and when you get these I shall be on the salt waters, on my way to a distant country, and leaving my own behind me, which I do not expect ever to see again.

"And now, young man, I will, in the first place, say something about the manner in which I quitted you. It must have seemed somewhat singular to you that I went away without taking any leave, or giving you the slightest hint that I was going; but I did not do so without considerable reflection. I was afraid that I should not be able to support a leave-taking; and as you had said that you were determined to go wherever I did, I thought it best not to tell you at all; for I did not think it advisable that you should go with me, and I wished to have no dispute.

"In the second place, I wish to say something about an offer of wedlock which you made me; perhaps, young man, had you made it at the first period of our acquaintance, I should have accepted it, but you did not, and kept putting off and putting off, and behaving in a very strange manner, till I could stand your conduct no longer, but determined upon leaving you and Old England, which last step I had been long thinking about; so when you made your offer at last, everything was arranged—my cart and donkey engaged to be sold—and the greater part of my things disposed of. However, young man, when you did make it, I frankly tell you that I had half a mind to accept it; at last, however, after very much consideration, I thought it best to leave you for ever, because, for some time past, I had become almost convinced, that though with a wonderful deal of learning, and exceedingly shrewd in some things, you were—pray don't be offended—at the root mad! and though mad people, I have been told, sometimes make very good husbands, I was unwilling that your friends, if you had any, should say that Belle Berners, the workhouse girl, took advantage of your infirmity; for there is no concealing that I was born and bred up in a workhouse; notwithstanding that, my blood is better than your own, and as good as the best; you having yourself told me that my name is a noble name, and once, if I mistake not, that it was the same word as baron, which is the same thing as bear; and that to be called in old times a bear was considered a great compliment—the bear being a mighty strong animal, on which account our forefathers called all their great fighting-men barons, which is the same as bears.

"However, setting matters of blood and family entirely aside, many thanks to you, young man, from poor Belle, for the honour you did her in making that same offer; for, after all, it is an honour to receive an honourable offer, which she could see clearly yours was, with no floriness nor chaff in it; but, on the contrary, entire sincerity. She assures you that she shall always bear it and yourself in mind, whether on land or water; and as a proof of the good-will she bears to you, she sends you a lock of the hair which she wears on her head, which you were often looking at, and were pleased to call flax, which word she supposes you meant as a compliment, even as the old people meant to pass a compliment to their great folks, when they called them bears; though she cannot help thinking that they might have found an animal as strong as a bear, and somewhat less uncouth, to call their great folks after: even as she thinks yourself, amongst your great store of words, might have found something a little more genteel to call her hair after than flax, which, though strong and useful, is rather a coarse and common kind of article.

"And as another proof of the good-will she bears to you, she sends you, along with the lock, a piece of advice, which is worth all the hair in the world, to say nothing of the flax.

"*Fear God,* and take your own part. There's Bible in that, young man: see how Moses feared God, and how he took his own part against everybody who meddled with him. And see how David feared God, and took his own part against all the bloody enemies which surrounded him—so fear God, young man, and never give in! The world can bully, and is fond, provided it sees a man in a kind of difficulty, of getting about him, calling him coarse names, and even going so far as to hustle him: but the world, like all bullies, carries a white feather in its tail, and no sooner sees the man taking off his coat, and offering to fight its best, than it scatters here and there, and is always civil to him afterwards. So when folks are disposed to ill-treat you, young man, say, 'Lord have mercy upon me!' and then tip them to Long Melford, which, as the saying goes, there is nothing comparable for shortness all the world over; and these last words, young man, are the last you will ever have from her who is nevertheless,

"Your affectionate female servant,

"ISOPEL BERNERS."

After reading the letter I sat for some time motionless, holding it in my hand. The daydream in which I had been a little time before indulging, of marrying Isopel Berners, of going with her to America, and having by her a large progeny, who were to assist me in felling trees, cultivating the soil, and who would take care of me when I was old, was now thoroughly dispelled. Isopel had deserted me, and was gone to America by herself, where, perhaps, she would marry some other person, and would bear him a progeny, who would do for him what in my dream I had hoped my progeny by her would do for me. Then the thought came into my head that though she was gone, I might follow her to America, but then I thought that if I did I might not find her; America was a very large place, and I did not know the port to which she was bound; but I could follow her to the port from which she had sailed, and there possibly discover the port to which she was bound; but I did not even know the port from which she had set out, for Isopel had not dated her letter from any place. Suddenly it occurred to me that the post-mark on the letter would tell me from whence it came, so I forthwith looked at the back of the letter, and in the post-mark read the name of a well-known and not very distant sea-port. I then knew with tolerable certainty the port where she had embarked, and I almost determined to follow her, but I almost instantly determined to do no such thing. Isopel Berners had abandoned me, and I would not follow her; "Perhaps," whispered Pride, "if I overtook her, she would only despise me for running after her;" and it also told me pretty roundly, provided I ran after her, whether I overtook her or not, I should heartily despise myself. So I determined not to follow Isopel Berners; I took her lock of hair, and looked at it, then put it in her letter, which I folded up and carefully stowed away, resolved to keep both for ever, but I determined not to follow her. Two or three times, however, during the day, I wavered in my determination, and was again and again almost tempted to follow her, but every succeeding time the temptation was fainter. In the evening I left the dingle, and sat down with Mr. Petulengro and his family by the door of his tent; Mr. Petulengro soon began talking of the letter which I had received in the morning. "Is it not from Miss Berners, brother?" said he. I told him it was. "Is she coming back, brother?" "Never," said I; "she is gone to America, and has deserted me." "I always knew that you two were never destined for each other," said he. "How did you know that?" I inquired. "The dook told me so, brother; you are born to be a great traveller." "Well," said I, "if I had gone with her to America, as I was thinking of doing, I should have been a great traveller." "You are to travel in another direction, brother," said he. "I wish you would tell me all about my future wanderings," said I. "I can't, brother," said Mr. Petulengro, "there's a power of clouds before my eye." "You are a poor seer, after all," said I; and getting up, I retired to my dingle and my tent, where I betook myself to my bed, and there, knowing the worst, and being no longer agitated by apprehension, nor agonized by expectation, I was soon buried in a deep slumber, the first which I had fallen into for several nights.

ROBERT STEPHEN HAWKER
(1803-1874)

The Song of the Western Men

A good sword and a trusty hand!
  A merry heart and true!
King James's men shall understand
  What Cornish lads can do.

And have they fixed the where and when?
  And shall Trelawny die?
Here's twenty thousand Cornish men
  Will know the reason why!

Out spake their captain brave and bold,
  A merry wight was he:
"If London Tower were Michael's hold,
  We'll set Trelawny free!

We'll cross the Tamar, land to land,
  The Severn is no stay,
With 'one and all,' and hand in hand,
  And who shall bid us nay?

And when we come to London Wall,
  A pleasant sight to view,
Come forth! come forth! ye cowards all,
  Here's men as good as you.

Trelawny he's in keep and hold,
  Trelawny he may die:
But here's twenty thousand Cornish bold
  Will know the reason why!"

ALFRED, LORD TENNYSON
(1809-1892)

Song: A spirit haunts the year's last hours

I

A SPIRIT haunts the year's last hours
Dwelling amid these yellowing bowers:
To himself he talks;
For at eventide, listening earnestly,
At his work you may hear him sob and sigh
In the walks;
Earthward he boweth the heavy stalks
Of the mouldering flowers:
Heavily hangs the broad sunflower
Over its grave i' the earth so chilly;
Heavily hangs the hollyhock,
Heavily hangs the tiger-lily.

II

The air is damp, and hush'd, and close,
As a sick man's room when he taketh repose
An hour before death;
My very heart faints and my whole soul grieves
At the moist rich smell of the rotting leaves,
And the breath
Of the fading edges of box beneath,
And the year's last rose.
Heavily hangs the broad sunflower
Over its grave i' the earth so chilly;
Heavily hangs the hollyhock,
Heavily hangs the tiger-lily.

The Lady of Shalott

PART I

On either side the river lie
Long fields of barley and of rye,
That clothe the wold and meet the sky;
And thro' the field the road runs by
To many-tower'd Camelot;
And up and down the people go,
Gazing where the lilies blow
Round an island there below,
The island of Shalott.

Willows whiten, aspens quiver,
Little breezes dusk and shiver
Thro' the wave that runs for ever
By the island in the river
Flowing down to Camelot.
Four gray walls, and four gray towers,
Overlook a space of flowers.
And the silent isle imbowers
The Lady of Shalott.

By the margin, willow-veil'd,
Slide the heavy barges trail'd
By slow horses; and unhail'd
The shallop flitteth silken-sail'd
Skimming down to Camelot;
But who hath seen her wave her hand?
Or at the casement seen her stand?
Or is she known in all the land,
The Lady of Shalott?

Only reapers, reaping early
In among the bearded barley,
Hear a song that echoes cheerly
From the river winding clearly,
Down to tower'd Camelot;
And by the moon the reaper weary,
Piling sheaves in uplands airy,
Listening, whispers "'T is the fairy
Lady of Shalott."

PART II

There she weaves by night and day
A magic web with colours gay.
She has heard a whisper say,
A curse is on her if she stay
To look down to Camelot.
She knows not what the curse may be,
And so she weaveth steadily,
And little other care hath she,
The Lady of Shalott.

And moving thro' a mirror clear
That hangs before her all the year,

Shadows of the world appear.
There she sees the highway near
Winding down to Camelot;
There the river eddy whirls,
And there the surly village-churls,
And the red cloaks of market girls,
Pass onward from Shalott.

Sometimes a troop of damsels glad,
An abbot on an ambling pad,
Sometimes a curly shepherd-lad,
Or long-hair'd page in crimson clad,
Goes by to tower'd Camelot;
And sometimes thro' the mirror blue
The knights come riding two and two:
She hath no loyal knight and true,
The Lady of Shalott.

But in her web she still delights
To weave the mirror's magic sights,
For often thro' the silent nights
A funeral, with plumes and lights
And music, went to Camelot;
Or when the moon was overhead,
Came two young lovers lately wed:
"I am half sick of shadows," said
The Lady of Shalott.

PART III

A bow-shot from her bower-eaves,
He rode between the barley-sheaves,
The sun came dazzling thro' the leaves,
And flamed upon the brazen greaves
Of bold Sir Lancelot.
A red-cross knight for ever kneel'd
To a lady in his shield,
That sparkled on the yellow field,
Beside remote Shalott.

The gemmy bridle glitter'd free,
Like to some branch of stars we see
Hung in the golden Galaxy.
The bridle bells rang merrily
As he rode down to Camelot;
And from his blazon'd baldric slung
A mighty silver bugle hung,
And as he rode his armour rung,
Beside remote Shalott.

All in the blue unclouded weather
Thick-jewell'd shone the saddle-leather,
The helmet and the helmet-feather
Burn'd like one burning flame together,
As he rode down to Camelot;
As often thro' the purple night,
Below the starry clusters bright,
Some bearded meteor, trailing light,
Moves over still Shalott.

His broad clear brow in sunlight glow'd;
On burnish'd hooves his war-horse trode;
From underneath his helmet flow'd
His coal-black curls as on he rode,
As he rode down to Camelot.
From the bank and from the river
He flash'd into the crystal mirror,
"Tirra lirra," by the river
Sang Sir Lancelot.

She left the web, she left the loom,
She made three paces thro' the room,
She saw the water-lily bloom,
She saw the helmet and the plume,
She look'd down to Camelot.
Out flew the web and floated wide;
The mirror crack'd from side to side;
"The curse is come upon me," cried
The Lady of Shalott.

PART IV

In the stormy east-wind straining,
The pale yellow woods were waning,
The broad stream in his banks complaining,
Heavily the low sky raining
Over tower'd Camelot;
Down she came and found a boat
Beneath a willow left afloat,
And round about the prow she wrote
The Lady of Shalott.

And down the river's dim expanse
Like some bold seër in a trance,
Seeing all his own mischance—
With a glassy countenance
Did she look to Camelot.

And at the closing of the day
She loosed the chain, and down she lay;
The broad stream bore her far away,
The Lady of Shalott.

Lying, robed in snowy white
That loosely flew to left and right—
The leaves upon her falling light—
Thro' the noises of the night
She floated down to Camelot;
And as the boat-head wound along
The willowy hills and fields among,
They heard her singing her last song,
The Lady of Shalott.

Heard a carol, mournful, holy,
Chanted loudly, chanted lowly,
Till her blood was frozen slowly
And her eyes were darken'd wholly
Turn'd to tower'd Camelot.
For ere she reach'd upon the tide
The first house by the water-side,
Singing in her song she died,
The Lady of Shalott.

Under tower and balcony,
By garden-wall and gallery,
A gleaming shape she floated by,
Dead-pale between the houses high,
Silent into Camelot.
Out upon the wharfs they came,
Knight and burgher, lord and dame,
And round the prow they read her name,
The Lady of Shalott.

Who is this? and what is here?
And in the lighted palace near
Died the sound of royal cheer,
And they cross'd themselves for fear,
All the Knights at Camelot:
But Lancelot mused a little space;
He said, "She has a lovely face;
God in his mercy lend her grace,
The Lady of Shalott."

Œnone

THERE lies a vale in Ida, lovelier
Than all the valleys of Ionian hills.
The swimming vapour slopes athwart the glen,
Puts forth an arm, and creeps from pine to pine,
And loiters, slowly drawn. On either hand
The lawns and meadow-ledges midway down
Hang rich in flowers, and far below them roars
The long brook falling thro' the clov'n ravine
In cataract after cataract to the sea.
Behind the valley topmost Gargarus
Stands up and takes the morning: but in front
The gorges, opening wide apart, reveal
Troas, and Ilion's column'd citadel,
The crown of Troas.
Hither came at noon
Mournful Œnone, wandering forlorn
Of Paris, once her playmate on the hills.
Her cheek had lost the rose, and round her neck
Floated her hair or seem'd to float in rest.
She, leaning on a fragment twined with vine,
Sang to the stillness, till the mountain-shade
Sloped downward to her seat from the upper cliff.

"O mother Ida, many-fountain'd Ida,
Dear mother Ida, hearken ere I die.
For now the noonday quiet holds the hill:
The grasshopper is silent in the grass:
The lizard, with his shadow on the stone,
Rests like a shadow, and the cicala sleeps.
The purple flowers droop: the golden bee
Is lily-cradled: I alone awake.
My eyes are full of tears, my heart of love,
My heart is breaking, and my eyes are dim,
And I am all aweary of my life.

"O mother Ida, many-fountain'd Ida,
Dear mother Ida, hearken ere I die.

Hear me O Earth, hear me O Hills, O Caves
That house the cold crown'd snake! O mountain brooks,
I am the daughter of a River-God,
Hear me, for I will speak, and build up all
My sorrow with my song, as yonder walls
Rose slowly to a music slowly breathed,
A cloud that gather'd shape: for it may be
That, while I speak of it, a little while
My heart may wander from its deeper woe.

"O mother Ida, many-fountain'd Ida,
Dear mother Ida, hearken ere I die.
I waited underneath the dawning hills,
Aloft the mountain lawn was dewy-dark,
And dewy-dark aloft the mountain pine:
Beautiful Paris, evil-hearted Paris,
Leading a jet-black goat, white-horn'd, white-hooved,
Came up from reedy Simois all alone.

"O mother Ida, hearken ere I die.
Far-off the torrent call'd me from the cleft:
Far up the solitary morning smote
The streaks of virgin snow. With down-dropt eyes
I sat alone: white-breasted like a star
Fronting the dawn he moved; a leopard skin
Droop'd from his shoulder, but his sunny hair
Cluster'd about his temples like a God's;
And his cheek brighten'd as the foam-bow brightens
When the wind blows the foam, and all my heart
Went forth to embrace him coming ere he came.

"Dear mother Ida, hearken ere I die.
He smiled, and opening out his milk-white palm
Disclosed a fruit of pure Hesperian gold,
That smelt ambrosially, and while I look'd
And listen'd, the full-flowing river of speech
Came down upon my heart.

"'My own Œnone,
Beautiful-brow'd Œnone, my own soul,
Behold this fruit, whose gleaming rind ingrav'n
"For the most fair," would seem to award it thine,
As lovelier than whatever Oread haunt
The knolls of Ida, loveliest in all grace
Of movement, and the charm of married brows.'

"Dear mother Ida, hearken ere I die.
He prest the blossom of his lips to mine,
And added 'This was cast upon the board,
When all the full-faced presence of the Gods
Ranged in the halls of Peleus; whereupon
Rose feud, with question unto whom 'twere due:
But light-foot Iris brought it yester-eve,
Delivering, that to me, by common voice
Elected umpire, Herè comes to-day,
Pallas and Aphrodite, claiming each
This meed of fairest. Thou, within the cave
Behind yon whispering tuft of oldest pine,
Mayst well behold them unbeheld, unheard
Hear all, and see thy Paris judge of Gods.'

"Dear mother Ida, hearken ere I die.
It was the deep midnoon: one silvery cloud
Had lost his way between the piney sides
Of this long glen. Then to the bower they came,
Naked they came to that smooth-swarded bower,
And at their feet the crocus brake like fire,
Violet, amaracus, and asphodel,

Lotos and lilies: and a wind arose,
And overhead the wandering ivy and vine,
This way and that, in many a wild festoon
Ran riot, garlanding the gnarled boughs
With bunch and berry and flower thro' and thro'.

"O mother Ida, hearken ere I die.
On the tree-tops a crested peacock lit,
And o'er him flow'd a golden cloud, and lean'd
Upon him, slowly dropping fragrant dew.
Then first I heard the voice of her, to whom
Coming thro' Heaven, like a light that grows
Larger and clearer, with one mind the Gods
Rise up for reverence. She to Paris made
Proffer of royal power, ample rule
Unquestion'd, overflowing revenue
Wherewith to embellish state, 'from many a vale
And river-sunder'd champaign clothed with corn,
Or labour'd mines undrainable of ore.
Honour,' she said, 'and homage, tax and toll,
From many an inland town and haven large,
Mast-throng'd beneath her shadowing citadel
In glassy bays among her tallest towers.'

"O mother Ida, hearken ere I die.
Still she spake on and still she spake of power,
'Which in all action is the end of all;
Power fitted to the season; wisdom-bred
And throned of wisdom—from all neighbour crowns
Alliance and allegiance, till thy hand
Fail from the sceptre-staff. Such boon from me,
From me, Heaven's Queen, Paris, to thee king-born,
A shepherd all thy life but yet king-born,
Should come most welcome, seeing men, in power
Only, are likest gods, who have attain'd
Rest in a happy place and quiet seats
Above the thunder, with undying bliss
In knowledge of their own supremacy.'

"Dear mother Ida, hearken ere I die.
She ceased, and Paris held the costly fruit
Out at arm's-length, so much the thought of power
Flatter'd his spirit; but Pallas where she stood
Somewhat apart, her clear and barèd limbs
O'erthwarted with the brazen-headed spear
Upon her pearly shoulder leaning cold,
The while, above, her full and earnest eye
Over her snow-cold breast and angry cheek
Kept watch, waiting decision, made reply.

"'Self-reverence, self-knowledge, self-control,
These three alone lead life to sovereign power.
Yet not for power (power of herself
Would come uncall'd for), but to live by law,
Acting the law we live by without fear;
And, because right is right, to follow right
Were wisdom in the scorn of consequence.'

"Dear mother Ida, hearken ere I die.
Again she said: 'I woo thee not with gifts.
Sequel of guerdon could not alter me
To fairer. Judge thou me by what I am,
So shalt thou find me fairest.
Yet, indeed,
If gazing on divinity disrobed
Thy mortal eyes are frail to judge of fair,
Unbiass'd by self-profit, oh! rest thee sure

That I shall love thee well and cleave to thee,
So that my vigour, wedded to thy blood,
Shall strike within thy pulses, like a God's,
To push thee forward thro' a life of shocks,
Dangers, and deeds, until endurance grow
Sinew'd with action, and the full-grown will,
Circled thro' all experiences, pure law,
Commeasure perfect freedom.'
"Here she ceased,
And Paris ponder'd, and I cried, 'O Paris,
Give it to Pallas!' but he heard me not,
Or hearing would not hear me, woe is me!

"O mother Ida, many-fountain'd Ida,
Dear mother Ida, hearken ere I die.
Idalian Aphrodite beautiful,
Fresh as the foam, new-bathed in Paphian wells,
With rosy slender fingers backward drew
From her warm brows and bosom her deep hair
Ambrosial, golden round her lucid throat
And shoulder: from the violets her light foot
Shone rosy-white, and o'er her rounded form
Between the shadows of the vine-bunches
Floated the glowing sunlights, as she moved.

"Dear mother Ida, hearken ere I die.
She with a subtle smile in her mild eyes,
The herald of her triumph, drawing nigh
Half-whisper'd in his ear, 'I promise thee
The fairest and most loving wife in Greece,'
She spoke and laugh'd: I shut my sight for fear:
But when I look'd, Paris had raised his arm,
And I beheld great Herè's angry eyes,
As she withdrew into the golden cloud,
And I was left alone within the bower;
And from that time to this I am alone,
And I shall be alone until I die.

"Yet, mother Ida, hearken ere I die.
Fairest—why fairest wife? am I not fair?
My love hath told me so a thousand times.
Methinks I must be fair, for yesterday,
When I past by, a wild and wanton pard,
Eyed like the evening star, with playful tail
Crouch'd fawning in the weed. Most loving is she?
Ah me, my mountain shepherd, that my arms
Were wound about thee, and my hot lips prest
Close, close to thine in that quick-falling dew
Of fruitful kisses, thick as Autumn rains
Flash in the pools of whirling Simois.

"O mother, hear me yet before I die.
They came, they cut away my tallest pines,
My dark tall pines, that plumed the craggy ledge
High over the blue gorge, and all between
The snowy peak and snow-white cataract
Foster'd the callow eaglet—from beneath
Whose thick mysterious boughs in the dark morn
The panther's roar came muffled, while I sat
Low in the valley. Never, never more
Shall lone Œnone see the morning mist
Sweep thro' them; never see them overlaid
With narrow moon-lit slips of silver cloud,
Between the loud stream and the trembling stars.

"O mother, hear me yet before I die.
I wish that somewhere in the ruin'd folds,
Among the fragments tumbled from the glens,

Or the dry thickets, I could meet with her,
The Abominable, that uninvited came
Into the fair Peleïan banquet-hall,
And cast the golden fruit upon the board,
And bred this change; that I might speak my mind,
And tell her to her face how much I hate
Her presence, hated both of Gods and men.

"O mother, hear me yet before I die.
Hath he not sworn his love a thousand times,
In this green valley, under this green hill,
Ev'n on this hand, and sitting on this stone?
Seal'd it with kisses? water'd it with tears?
O happy tears, and how unlike to these!
O happy Heaven, how canst thou see my face?
O happy earth, how canst thou bear my weight?
O death, death, death, thou ever-floating cloud,
There are enough unhappy on this earth,
Pass by the happy souls, that love to live:
I pray thee, pass before my light of life,
And shadow all my soul, that I may die.
Thou weighest heavy on the heart within,
Weigh heavy on my eyelids: let me die.

"O mother, hear me yet before I die.
I will not die alone, for fiery thoughts
Do shape themselves within me, more and more,
Whereof I catch the issue, as I hear
Dead sounds at night come from the inmost hills,
Like footsteps upon wool. I dimly see
My far-off doubtful purpose, as a mother
Conjectures of the features of her child
Ere it is born: her child!—a shudder comes
Across me: never child be born of me,
Unblest, to vex me with his father's eyes!

"O mother, hear me yet before I die.
Hear me, O earth. I will not die alone,
Lest their shrill happy laughter come to me
Walking the cold and starless road of Death
Uncomforted, leaving my ancient love
With the Greek woman. I will rise and go
Down into Troy, and ere the stars come forth
Talk with the wild Cassandra, for she says
A fire dances before her, and a sound
Rings ever in her ears of armèd men.
What this may be I know not, but I know
That, wheresoe'er I am by night and day,
All earth and air seem only burning fire."

Of old sat Freedom on the heights

Of old sat Freedom on the heights,
The thunders breaking at her feet:
Above her shook the starry lights:
She heard the torrents meet.

There in her place she did rejoice,
Self-gather'd in her prophet-mind,
But fragments of her mighty voice
Came rolling on the wind.

Then stept she down thro' town and field
To mingle with the human race,
And part by part to men reveal'd
The fullness of her face—

Grave mother of majestic works,
From her isle-altar gazing down,
Who, God-like, grasps the triple forks,
And, King-like, wears the crown:

Her open eyes desire the truth.
The wisdom of a thousand years
Is in them. May perpetual youth
Keep dry their light from tears;

That her fair form may stand and shine,
Make bright our days and light our dreams,
Turning to scorn with lips divine
The falsehood of extremes!

Love thou thy land, with love far-brought

Love thou thy land, with love far-brought
From out the storied Past, and used
Within the Present, but transfused
Thro' future time by power of thought.

True love turn'd round on fixèd poles,
Love, that endures not sordid ends,
For English natures, freemen, friends,
Thy brothers and immortal souls.

But pamper not a hasty time,
Nor feed with crude imaginings
The herd, wild hearts and feeble wings,
That every sophister can lime.

Deliver not the tasks of might
To weakness, neither hide the ray
From those, not blind, who wait for day,
Tho' sitting girt with doubtful light.

Make knowledge circle with the winds;
But let her herald, Reverence, fly
Before her to whatever sky
Bear seed of men and growth of minds.

Watch what main-currents draw the years:
Cut Prejudice against the grain:
But gentle words are always gain:
Regard the weakness of thy peers:

Nor toil for title, place, or touch
Of pension, neither count on praise:
It grows to guerdon after-days:
Nor deal in watch-words overmuch;

Not clinging to some ancient saw;
Not master'd by some modern term;
Not swift nor slow to change, but firm
And in its season bring the law;

That from Discussion's lip may fall
With Life, that, working strongly, binds—
Set in all lights by many minds,
To close the interests of all.

For Nature also, cold and warm,
And moist and dry, devising long,
Thro' many agents making strong,
Matures the individual form.

Meet is it changes should control
Our being, lest we rust in ease.
We all are changed by still degrees,
All but the basis of the soul.

So let the change which comes be free
To ingroove itself with that which flies,
And work, a joint of state, that plies
Its office, moved with sympathy.

A saying, hard to shape in act;
For all the past of Time reveals
A bridal dawn of thunder-peals,
Wherever Thought hath wedded Fact.

Ev'n now we hear with inward strife
A motion toiling in the gloom—
The Spirit of the years to come
Yearning to mix himself with Life.

A slow-develop'd strength awaits
Completion in a painful school;
Phantoms of other forms of rule,
New Majesties of mighty States—

The warders of the growing hour,
But vague in vapour, hard to mark;
And round them sea and air are dark
With great contrivances of Power.

Of many changes, aptly join'd,
Is bodied forth the second whole.
Regard gradation, lest the soul
Of Discord race the rising wind;

A wind to puff your idol-fires,
And heap their ashes on the head;
To shame the boast so often made,
That we are wiser than our sires.

Oh yet, if Nature's evil star
Drive men in manhood, as in youth,
To follow flying steps of Truth
Across the brazen bridge of war—

If New and Old, disastrous feud,
Must ever shock, like armèd foes,
And this be true, till Time shall close,
That Principles are rain'd in blood;

Not yet the wise of heart would cease
To hold his hope thro' shame and guilt,
But with his hand against the hilt,
Would pace the troubled land, like Peace;

Not less, tho' dogs of Faction bay,
Would serve his kind in deed and word,
Certain, if knowledge bring the sword,
That knowledge takes the sword away—

Would love the gleams of good that broke
From either side, nor veil his eyes:
And if some dreadful need should rise
Would strike, and firmly, and one stroke:

To-morrow yet would reap to-day,
As we bear blossom of the dead;
Earn well the thrifty months, nor wed
Raw Haste, half-sister to Delay.

Morte d'Arthur

So all day long the noise of battle roll'd
Among the mountains by the winter sea;
Until King Arthur's table, man by man,
Had fall'n in Lyonnesse about their Lord,
King Arthur: then, because his wound was deep,
The bold Sir Bedivere uplifted him,
Sir Bedivere, the last of all his knights,
And bore him to a chapel nigh the field,
A broken chancel with a broken cross,
That stood on a dark strait of barren land.
On one side lay the Ocean, and on one
Lay a great water, and the moon was full.

Then spake King Arthur to Sir Bedivere:
"The sequel of to-day unsolders all
The goodliest fellowship of famous knights
Whereof this world holds record. Such a sleep
They sleep—the men I loved. I think that we
Shall never more, at any future time,
Delight our souls with talk of knightly deeds,
Walking about the gardens and the halls
Of Camelot, as in the days that were.
I perish by this people which I made,—
Tho' Merlin sware that I should come again
To rule once more—but let what will be, be,
I am so deeply smitten thro' the helm
That without help I cannot last till morn.
Thou therefore take my brand Excalibur,
Which was my pride: for thou rememberest how
In those old days, one summer noon, an arm
Rose up from out the bosom of the lake,
Clothed in white samite, mystic, wonderful,
Holding the sword—and how I row'd across
And took it, and have worn it, like a king:
And, wheresoever I am sung or told
In aftertime, this also shall be known:
But now delay not: take Excalibur,
And fling him far into the middle mere:
Watch what thou seëst, and lightly bring me word."

To him replied the bold Sir Bedivere:
"It is not meet, Sir King, to leave thee thus,
Aidless, alone, and smitten thro' the helm.
A little thing may harm a wounded man.
Yet I thy hest will all perform at full,
Watch what I see, and lightly bring thee word."

So saying, from the ruin'd shrine he stept

And in the moon athwart the place of tombs,
Where lay the mighty bones of ancient men,
Old knights, and over them the sea-wind sang
Shrill, chill, with flakes of foam. He, stepping down
By zig-zag paths, and juts of pointed rock,
Came on the shining levels of the lake.
  There drew he forth the brand Excalibur,
And o'er him, drawing it, the winter moon,
Brightening the skirts of a long cloud, ran forth
And sparkled keen with frost against the hilt:
For all the haft twinkled with diamond sparks,
Myriads of topaz-lights, and jacinth-work
Of subtlest jewellery. He gazed so long
That both his eyes were dazzled, as he stood,
This way and that dividing the swift mind,
In act to throw: but at the last it seem'd
Better to leave Excalibur conceal'd
There in the many-knotted waterflags,
That whistled stiff and dry about the marge.
So strode he back slow to the wounded King.
  Then spake King Arthur to Sir Bedivere:
"Hast thou perform'd my mission which I gave?
What is it thou hast seen? or what hast heard?"
  And answer made the bold Sir Bedivere:
"I heard the ripple washing in the reeds,
And the wild water lapping on the crag."
  To whom replied King Arthur, faint and pale:
"Thou hast betray'd thy nature and thy name,
Not rendering true answer, as beseem'd
Thy fealty, nor like a noble knight:
For surer sign had follow'd, either hand,
Or voice, or else a motion of the mere.
This is a shameful thing for men to lie.
Yet now, I charge thee, quickly go again
As thou art lief and dear, and do the thing
I bade thee, watch, and lightly bring me word."
  Then went Sir Bedivere the second time
Across the ridge, and paced beside the mere,
Counting the dewy pebbles, fix'd in thought;
But when he saw the wonder of the hilt,
How curiously and strangely chased, he smote
His palms together, and he cried aloud,
  "And if indeed I cast the brand away,
Surely a precious thing, one worthy note,
Should thus be lost for ever from the earth,
Which might have pleased the eyes of many men.
What good should follow this, if this were done?
What harm, undone? deep harm to disobey,
Seeing obedience is the bond of rule.
Were it well to obey then, if a king demand
An act unprofitable, against himself?
The King is sick, and knows not what he does.
What record, or what relic of my lord
Should be to aftertime, but empty breath
And rumours of a doubt? but were this kept,
Stored in some treasure-house of mighty kings,
Some one might show it at a joust of arms,
Saying, 'King Arthur's sword, Excalibur,
Wrought by the lonely maiden of the Lake.
Nine years she wrought it, sitting in the deeps

Upon the hidden bases of the hills.'
So might some old man speak in the aftertime
To all the people, winning reverence.
But now much honour and much fame were lost."
  So spake he, clouded with his own conceit,
And hid Excalibur the second time,
And so strode back slow to the wounded King.
  Then spoke King Arthur, breathing heavily:
"What is it thou hast seen? or what hast heard?"
  And answer made the bold Sir Bedivere:
"I heard the water lapping on the crag,
And the long ripple washing in the reeds."
  To whom replied King Arthur, much in wrath:
"Ah, miserable and unkind, untrue,
Unknightly, traitor-hearted! Woe is me!
Authority forgets a dying king,
Laid widow'd of the power in his eye
That bow'd the will. I see thee what thou art,
For thou, the latest-left of all my knights,
In whom should meet the offices of all,
Thou wouldst betray me for the precious hilt;
Either from lust of gold, or like a girl
Valuing the giddy pleasure of the eyes.
Yet, for a man may fail in duty twice,
And the third time may prosper, get thee hence:
But, if thou spare to fling Excalibur,
I will arise and slay thee with my hands."
  Then quickly rose Sir Bedivere, and ran,
And, leaping down the ridges lightly, plunged
Among the bulrush-beds, and clutch'd the sword,
And strongly wheel'd and threw it. The great brand
Made lightnings in the splendour of the moon,
And flashing round and round, and whirl'd in an arch,
Shot like a streamer of the northern morn,
Seen where the moving isles of winter shock
By night, with noises of the northern sea.
So flash'd and fell the brand Excalibur:
But ere he dipt the surface, rose an arm
Clothed in white samite, mystic, wonderful,
And caught him by the hilt, and brandish'd him
Three times, and drew him under in the mere.
And lightly went the other to the King.
  Then spoke King Arthur, drawing thicker breath:
"Now see I by thine eyes that this is done.
Speak out: what is it thou hast heard, or seen?"
  And answer made the bold Sir Bedivere:
"Sir King, I closed mine eyelids, lest the gems
Should blind my purpose, for I never saw,
Nor shall see, here or elsewhere, till I die,
Not tho' I live three lives of mortal men,
So great a miracle as yonder hilt.
Then with both hands I flung him, wheeling him;
But when I look'd again, behold an arm,
Clothed in white samite, mystic, wonderful,
That caught him by the hilt, and brandish'd him
Three times, and drew him under in the mere."
  And answer made King Arthur, breathing hard:
"My end draws nigh; 'tis time that I were gone.
Make broad thy shoulders to receive my weight,
And bear me to the margin; yet I fear
My wound hath taken cold, and I shall die."

So saying, from the pavement he half rose,
Slowly, with pain, reclining on his arm,
And looking wistfully with wide blue eyes
As in a picture. Him Sir Bedivere
Remorsefully regarded thro' his tears,
And would have spoken but he found not words,
Then took with care, and kneeling on one knee,
O'er both his shoulders drew the languid hands,
And rising bore him thro' the place of tombs.

But, as he walk'd, King Arthur panted hard,
Like one that feels a nightmare on his bed
When all the house is mute. So sigh'd the King,
Muttering and murmuring at his ear, "Quick, quick!
I fear it is too late, and I shall die."
But the other swiftly strode from ridge to ridge,
Clothed with his breath, and looking, as he walk'd,
Larger than human on the frozen hills.
He heard the deep behind him, and a cry
Before. His own thought drove him like a goad.
Dry clash'd his harness in the icy caves
And barren chasms, and all to left and right
The bare black cliff clang'd round him, as he based
His feet on juts of slippery crag that rang
Sharp-smitten with the dint of armèd heels—
And on a sudden, lo! the level lake,
And the long glories of the winter moon.

Then saw they how there hove a dusky barge,
Dark as a funeral scarf from stem to stern,
Beneath them; and descending they were ware
That all the decks were dense with stately forms
Black-stoled, black-hooded, like a dream—by these
Three Queens with crowns of gold—and from them rose
A cry that shiver'd to the tingling stars,
And, as it were one voice, an agony
Of lamentation, like a wind, that shrills
All night in a waste land, where no one comes,
Or hath come, since the making of the world.

Then murmur'd Arthur, "Place me in the barge,"
And to the barge they came. There those three Queens
Put forth their hands, and took the King, and wept.
But she, that rose the tallest of them all
And fairest, laid his head upon her lap,
And loosed the shatter'd casque, and chafed his hands,
And call'd him by his name, complaining loud,
And dropping bitter tears against his brow
Striped with dark blood: for all his face was white
And colourless, and like the wither'd moon
Smote by the fresh beam of the springing east;
And all his greaves and cuisses dash'd with drops
Of onset; and the light and lustrous curls—
That made his forehead like a rising sun
High from the dais-throne—were parch'd with dust;
Or, clotted into points and hanging loose,
Mix'd with the knightly growth that fringed his lips.
So like a shatter'd column lay the King;
Not like that Arthur who, with lance in rest,
From spur to plume a star of tournament,

Shot thro' the lists at Camelot, and charged
Before the eyes of ladies and of kings.
Then loudly cried the bold Sir Bedivere,
"Ah! my Lord Arthur, whither shall I go?
Where shall I hide my forehead and my eyes?
For now I see the true old times are dead,
When every morning brought a noble chance,
And every chance brought out a noble knight.
Such times have been not since the light that led
The holy Elders with the gift of myrrh.
But now the whole ROUND TABLE is dissolved
Which was an image of the mighty world;
And I, the last, go forth companionless,
And the days darken round me, and the years,
Among new men, strange faces, other minds."
And slowly answered Arthur from the barge:
"The old order changeth, yielding place to new,
And God fulfils Himself in many ways,
Lest one good custom should corrupt the world.
Comfort thyself: what comfort is in me?
I have lived my life, and that which I have done
May He within Himself make pure! but thou,
If thou shouldst never see my face again,
Pray for my soul. More things are wrought by prayer
Than this world dreams of. Wherefore, let thy voice
Rise like a fountain for me night and day.
For what are men better than sheep or goats
That nourish a blind life within the brain,
If, knowing God, they lift not hands of prayer
Both for themselves and those who call them friend?
For so the whole round earth is every way
Bound by gold chains about the feet of God.
But now farewell. I am going a long way
With these thou seëst—if indeed I go—
(For all my mind is clouded with a doubt)
To the island-valley of Avilion;
Where falls not hail, or rain, or any snow,
Nor ever wind blows loudly; but it lies
Deep-meadow'd, happy, fair with orchard-lawns
And bowery hollows crown'd with summer sea,
Where I will heal me of my grievous wound."
So said he, and the barge with oar and sail
Moved from the brink, like some full-breasted swan
That, fluting a wild carol ere her death,
Ruffles her pure cold plume, and takes the flood
With swarthy webs. Long stood Sir Bedivere
Revolving many memories, till the hull
Look'd one black dot against the verge of dawn,
And on the mere the wailing died away.

Here ended Hall, and our last light, that long
Had wink'd and threaten'd darkness, flared and fell:
At which the Parson, sent to sleep with sound,
And waked with silence, grunted "Good!" but we
Sat rapt: it was the tone with which he read—

Perhaps some modern touches here and there
Redeem'd it from the charge of nothingness—
Or else we loved the man and prized his work;
I know not: but we sitting, as I said,
The cock crew loud; as at that time of year
The lusty bird takes every hour for dawn:
Then Francis, muttering, like a man ill-used,
"There now—that's nothing!" drew a little back,
And drove his heel into the smoulder'd log,
That sent a blast of sparkles up the flue:
And so to bed; where yet in sleep I seem'd
To sail with Arthur under looming shores,
Point after point; till on to dawn, when dreams
Begin to feel the truth and stir of day,
To me, methought, who waited with a crowd,
There came a bark that, blowing forward, bore
King Arthur, like a modern gentleman
Of stateliest port; and all the people cried,
"Arthur is come again: he cannot die."
Then those that stood upon the hills behind
Repeated—"Come again, and thrice as fair;"
And, further inland, voices echoed—"Come
With all good things, and war shall be no more."
At this a hundred bells began to peal,
That with the sound I woke, and heard indeed
The clear church-bells ring in the Christmas morn.

Ulysses

It little profits that an idle king,
By this still hearth, among these barren crags,
Match'd with an agèd wife, I mete and dole
Unequal laws unto a savage race,
That hoard, and sleep, and feed, and know not me.
I cannot rest from travel: I will drink
Life to the lees: all times I have enjoy'd
Greatly, have suffer'd greatly, both with those
That loved me, and alone; on shore, and when
Thro' scudding drifts the rainy Hyades
Vex'd the dim sea; I am become a name;
For always roaming with a hungry heart
Much have I seen and known; cities of men,
And manners, climates, councils, governments,
Myself not least, but honour'd of them all;
And drunk delight of battle with my peers,
Far on the ringing plains of windy Troy.
I am a part of all that I have met.
Yet all experience is an arch where-thro'
Gleams that untravell'd world, whose margin fades
Forever and forever when I move.
How dull it is to pause, to make an end,
To rust unburnish'd, not to shine in use!
As tho' to breathe were life. Life piled on life
Were all too little, and of one to me
Little remains: but every hour is saved
From that eternal silence, something more,
A bringer of new things; and vile it were
For some three suns to store and hoard myself,
And this grey spirit yearning in desire
To follow knowledge like a sinking star,
Beyond the utmost bound of human thought.

This is my son, mine own Telemachus,
To whom I leave the sceptre and the isle—
Well-loved of me, discerning to fulfil
This labour, by slow prudence to make mild
A rugged people, and thro' soft degrees
Subdue them to the useful and the good.
Most blameless is he, centred in the sphere
Of common duties, decent not to fail
In offices of tenderness, and pay
Meet adoration to my household gods,
When I am gone. He works his work, I mine.
There lies the port; the vessel puffs her sail:
There gloom the dark broad seas. My mariners,
Souls that have toil'd, and wrought, and thought with me—
That ever with a frolic welcome took
The thunder and the sunshine, and opposed
Free hearts, free foreheads—you and I are old;
Old age hath his honour and his toil;
Death closes all: but something ere the end,
Some work of noble note, may yet be done,
Not unbecoming men that strove with Gods.
The lights begin to twinkle from the rocks:
The long day wanes: the slow moon climbs: the deep
Moans round with many voices. Come, my friends
'Tis not too late to seek a newer world.
Push off, and sitting well in order smite
The sounding furrows; for my purpose holds
To sail beyond the sunset, and the baths
Of all the western stars, until I die.
It may be that the gulfs will wash us down:
It may be we shall touch the Happy Isles,
And see the great Achilles, whom we knew.
Tho' much is taken, much abides; and tho'
We are not now that strength which in old days
Moved earth and heaven; that which we are, we are;
One equal temper of heroic hearts,
Made weak by time and fate, but strong in will
To strive, to seek, to find, and not to yield.

From IN MEMORIAM A. H. H.

The Danube to the Severn gave

THE Danube to the Severn gave
The darken'd heart that beat no more;
They laid him by the pleasant shore,
And in the hearing of the wave.

There twice a day the Severn fills;
The salt sea-water passes by,
And hushes half the babbling Wye,
And makes a silence in the hills.

The Wye is hush'd nor moved along,
And hush'd my deepest grief of all,
When fill'd with tears that cannot fall,
I brim with sorrow drowning song.

The tide flows down, the wave again
Is vocal in its wooded walls;
My deeper anguish also falls,
And I can speak a little then.

Yet if some voice that man could trust

YET if some voice that man could trust
Should murmur from the narrow house,
"The cheeks drop in; the body bows;
Man dies: nor is there hope in dust":
Might I not say: "Yet even here,
But for one hour, O Love, I strive
To keep so sweet a thing alive":
But I should turn mine eyes and hear

The moanings of the homeless sea,
The sound of streams that swift or slow
Draw down Æonian hills, and sow
The dust of continents to be;

And Love would answer with a sigh,
"The sound of that forgetful shore
Will change my sweetness more and more,
Half-dead to know that I shall die."

O me, what profits it to put
An idle case? If Death were seen
At first as Death, Love had not been,
Or been in narrowest working shut,

Mere fellowship of sluggish moods,
Or in his coarsest Satyr-shape
Had bruised the herb and crush'd the grape,
And bask'd and batten'd in the woods.

Oh yet we trust that somehow good

Oh yet we trust that somehow good
Will be the final goal of ill,
To pangs of nature, sins of will,
Defects of doubt, and taints of blood;

That nothing walks with aimless feet;
That not one life shall be destroy'd,
Or cast as rubbish to the void,
When God hath made the pile complete;

That not a worm is cloven in vain;
That not a moth with vain desire
Is shrivel'd in a fruitless fire,
Or but subserves another's gain.

Behold, we know not anything;
I can but trust that good shall fall
At last—far off—at last, to all,
And every winter change to spring.

So runs my dream: but what am I?
An infant crying in the night:
An infant crying for the light:
And with no language but a cry.

Heart-affluence in discursive talk

Heart affluence in discursive talk
From household fountains never dry;
The critic clearness of an eye,
That saw thro' all the Muses' walk;

Seraphic intellect and force
To seize and throw the doubts of man;
Impassion'd logic, which outran
The hearer in its fiery course;

High nature amorous of the good,
But touch'd with no ascetic gloom;
And passion pure in snowy bloom
Thro' all the years of April blood;

A love of freedom rarely felt,
Of freedom in her regal seat
Of England; not the schoolboy heat,
The blind hysterics of the Celt;

And manhood fused with female grace
In such a sort, the child would twine
A trustful hand, unask'd, in thine,
And find his comfort in thy face;

All these have been, and thee mine eyes
Have look'd on: if they look'd in vain,
My shame is greater who remain,
Nor let thy wisdom make me wise.

There rolls the deep where grew the tree

There rolls the deep where grew the tree.
O earth, what changes hast thou seen!
There where the long street roars, hath been
The stillness of the central sea.

The hills are shadows, and they flow
From form to form, and nothing stands;
They melt like mist, the solid lands,
Like clouds they shape themselves and go.

But in my spirit will I dwell,
And dream my dream, and hold it true;
For tho' my lips may breathe adieu,
I cannot think the thing farewell.

The Brook

"Here by this brook, we parted; I to the East
And he for Italy—too late—too late:
One whom the strong sons of the world despise;
For lucky rhymes to him were scrip and share,
And mellow metres more than cent for cent;
Nor could he understand how money breeds,
Thought it a dead thing; yet himself could make
The thing that is not as the thing that is.
O had he lived! In our schoolbooks we say,
Of those that held their heads above the crowd,
They flourish'd then or then; but life in him
Could scarce be said to flourish, only touch'd
On such a time as goes before the leaf,
When all the wood stands in a mist of green,
And nothing perfect: yet the brook he loved,
For which, in branding summers of Bengal,
Or ev'n the sweet half-English Neilgherry air
I panted, seems, as I re-listen to it,
Prattling the primrose fancies of the boy,
To me that loved him; for 'O brook,' he says,
'O babbling brook,' says Edmund in his rhyme,
'Whence come you?' and the brook, why not? replies.

I come from haunts of coot and hern,
I make a sudden sally
And sparkle out among the fern,
To bicker down a valley.

By thirty hills I hurry down,
Or slip between the ridges,
By twenty thorps, a little town,
And half a hundred bridges.

Till last by Philip's farm I flow
To join the brimming river,
For men may come and men may go,
But I go on for ever.

"Poor lad, he died at Florence, quite worn out,
Travelling to Naples. There is Darnley bridge,
It has more ivy; there the river; and there
Stands Philip's farm where brook and river meet.

I chatter over stony ways,
In little sharps and trebles,
I bubble into eddying bays,
I babble on the pebbles.

With many a curve my banks I fret
By many a field and fallow,
And many a fairy foreland set
With willow-weed and mallow.

I chatter, chatter as I flow
To join the brimming river,
For men may come and men may go,
But I go on for ever.

"But Philip chatter'd more than brook or bird;
Old Philip; all about the fields you caught
His weary daylong chirping, like the dry
High-elbow'd grigs that leap in summer grass.

I wind about, and in and out,
With here a blossom sailing,
And here and there a lusty trout,
And here and there a grayling,

And here and there a foamy flake
Upon me, as I travel
With many a silvery waterbreak
Above the golden gravel,

And draw them all along, and flow
To join the brimming river.
For men may come and men may go,
But I go on for ever.

"O darling Katie Willows, his one child!
A maiden of our century, yet most meek;
A daughter of our meadows, yet not coarse;
Straight, but as lissome as a hazel wand;
Her eyes a bashful azure, and her hair
In gloss and hue the chestnut, when the shell
Divides threefold to show the fruit within.

"Sweet Katie, once I did her a good turn,
Her and her far-off cousin and betrothed,
James Willows, of one name and heart with her.
For here I came, twenty years back—the week
Before I parted with poor Edmund; cross'd
By that old bridge which, half in ruins then,
Still makes a hoary eyebrow for the gleam
Beyond it, where the waters marry—cross'd,
Whistling a random bar of Bonny Doon,
And push'd at Philip's garden-gate. The gate,
Half-parted from a weak and scolding hinge,
Stuck; and he clamour'd from a casement, 'Run'
To Katie somewhere in the walks below,
'Run, Katie!' Katie never ran: she moved
To meet me, winding under woodbine bowers,
A little flutter'd, with her eyelids down,
Fresh apple-blossom, blushing for a boon.

"What was it? less of sentiment than sense
Had Katie; not illiterate; nor of those
Who dabbling in the fount of fictive tears,
And nursed by mealy-mouth'd philanthropies,
Divorce the Feeling from her mate the Deed.

"She told me. She and James had quarrell'd. Why?
What cause of quarrel? None, she said, no cause:
James had no cause: but when I prest the cause,
I learnt that James had flickering jealousies
Which anger'd her. Who anger'd James? I said.
But Katie snatch'd her eyes at once from mine,
And sketching with her slender pointed foot
Some figure like a wizard's pentagram
On garden gravel, let my query pass
Unclaim'd, in flushing silence, till I ask'd
If James were coming. 'Coming every day,'
She answer'd, 'ever longing to explain,
But evermore her father came across
With some long-winded tale, and broke him short;
And James departed vex'd with him and her.'
How could I help her? 'Would I—was it wrong?'
(Clasp'd hands and that petitionary grace
Of sweet seventeen subdued me ere she spoke)
'O would I take her father for one hour,
For one half-hour, and let him talk to me!'
And even while she spoke, I saw where James
Made toward us, like a wader in the surf,
Beyond the brook, waist-deep in meadow-sweet.

"O Katie, what I suffer'd for your sake!
For in I went, and call'd old Philip out
To show the farm: full willingly he rose:

He led me thro' the short sweet-smelling lanes
Of his wheat-suburb, babbling as he went.
He praised his land, his horses, his machines;
He praised his ploughs, his cows, his hogs, his dogs;
He praised his hens, his geese, his guinea-hens;
His pigeons, who in session on their roofs
Approved him, bowing at their own deserts:
Then from the plaintive mother's teat he took
Her blind and shuddering puppies, naming each,
And naming those, his friends, for whom they were:
Then cross'd the common into Darnley chase
To show Sir Arthur's deer. In copse and fern
Twinkled the innumerable ear and tail.
Then, seated on a serpent-rooted beech,
He pointed out a pasturing colt, and said:
'That was the four-year-old I sold the Squire.'
And there he told a long long-winded tale
Of how the Squire had seen the colt at grass,
And how it was the thing his daughter wish'd,
And how he sent the bailiff to the farm
To learn the price, and what the price he ask'd,
And how the bailiff swore that he was mad,
But he stood firm; and so the matter hung;
He gave them line: and five days after that
He met the bailiff at the Golden Fleece,
Who then and there had offer'd something more,
But he stood firm; and so the matter hung;
He knew the man; the colt would fetch its price;
He gave them line: and how by chance at last
(It may be May or April, he forgot,
The last of April or the first of May)
He found the bailiff riding by the farm,
And, talking from the point, he drew him in,
And there he mellow'd all his heart with ale,
Until they closed a bargain, hand in hand.

"Then, while I breathed in sight of haven, he,
Poor fellow, could he help it? recommenced,
And ran thro' all the coltish chronicle,
Wild Will, Black Bess, Tantivy, Tallyho,
Reform, White Rose, Bellerophon, the Jilt,
Arbaces, and Phenomenon, and the rest,
Till, not to die a listener, I arose,
And with me Philip, talking still; and so
We turn'd our foreheads from the falling sun,
And following our own shadows thrice as long
As when they follow'd us from Philip's door,
Arrived, and found the sun of sweet content
Re-risen in Katie's eyes, and all things well.

I steal by lawns and grassy plots,
I slide by hazel covers;
I move the sweet forget-me-nots
That grow for happy lovers.

I slip, I slide, I gloom, I glance
Among my skimming swallows,
I make the netted sunbeam dance
Against my sandy shallows.

I murmur under moon and stars
In brambly wildernesses;
I linger by my shingly bars;
I loiter round my cresses;

And out again I curve and flow
To join the brimming river,
For men may come and men may go,
But I go on for ever.

Yes, men may come and go; and these are gone,
All gone. My dearest brother, Edmund, sleeps,
Not by the well-known stream and rustic spire,
But unfamiliar Arno, and the dome
Of Brunelleschi; sleeps in peace: and he,
Poor Philip, of all his lavish waste of words
Remains the lean P. W. on his tomb:
I scraped the lichen from it: Katie walks
By the long wash of Australasian seas
Far off, and holds her head to other stars,
And breathes in converse seasons. All are gone."

So Lawrence Aylmer, seated on a stile
In the long hedge, and rolling in his mind
Old waifs of rhyme, and bowing o'er the brook
A tonsured head in middle age forlorn,
Mused, and was mute. On a sudden a low breath
Of tender air made tremble in the hedge
The fragile bindweed-bells and briony rings;
And he look'd up. There stood a maiden near,
Waiting to pass. In much amaze he stared
On eyes a bashful azure, and on hair
In gloss and hue the chestnut, when the shell
Divides threefold to show the fruit within:
Then, wondering, ask'd her "Are you from the farm?"
"Yes," answer'd she. "Pray stay a little: pardon me;
What do they call you?" "Katie." "That were strange.
What surname?" "Willows." "No!" "That is my name."
"Indeed!" and here he look'd so self-perplex'd
That Katie laugh'd, and laughing blush'd, till he
Laugh'd also, but as one before he wakes,
Who feels a glimmering strangeness in his dream.
Then looking at her; "Too happy, fresh and fair,
Too fresh and fair in our sad world's best bloom,
To be the ghost of one who bore your name
About these meadows, twenty years ago."

"Have you not heard?" said Katie, "we came back.
We bought the farm we tenanted before.
Am I so like her? so they said on board.
Sir, if you knew her in her English days,
My mother, as it seems you did, the days
That most she loves to talk of, come with me.
My brother James is in the harvest-field:
But she—you will be welcome—O, come in!"

Ode on the Death of the Duke of Wellington

Bury the Great Duke
With an empire's lamentation;
Let us bury the Great Duke
To the noise of the mourning of a mighty nation;
Mourning when their leaders fall,
Warriors carry the warrior's pall,
And sorrow darkens hamlet and hall.

Where shall we lay the man whom we deplore?
Here, in streaming London's central roar.
Let the sound of those he wrought for,
And the feet of those he fought for,
Echo around his bones for evermore.

Lead out the pageant: sad and slow,
As fits an universal woe,
Let the long, long procession go,
And let the sorrowing crowd about it grow,

And let the mournful martial music blow;
The last great Englishman is low.

Mourn, for to us he seems the last,
Remembering all his greatness in the past,
No more in soldier fashion will he greet
With lifted hand the gazer in the street.
O friends, our chief state-oracle is mute!
Mourn for the man of long-enduring blood,
The statesman-warrior, moderate, resolute,
Whole in himself, a common good.
Mourn for the man of amplest influence,
Yet clearest of ambitious crime,
Our greatest yet with least pretence,
Great in council and great in war,
Foremost captain of his time,
Rich in saving common-sense,
And, as the greatest only are,
In his simplicity sublime.
O good gray head which all men knew,
O voice from which their omens all men drew,
O iron nerve to true occasion true,
O fallen at length that tower of strength
Which stood four-square to all the winds that blew!
Such was he whom we deplore.
The long self-sacrifice of life is o'er.
The great World-victor's victor will be seen no more.

All is over and done,
Render thanks to the Giver,
England, for thy son.
Let the bell be toll'd.
Render thanks to the Giver,
And render him to the mould.
Under the cross of gold
That shines over city and river,
There he shall rest forever
Among the wise and the bold.
Let the bell be toll'd,
And a reverent people behold
The towering car, the sable steeds.
Bright let it be with its blazon'd deeds,
Dark in its funeral fold.
Let the bell be toll'd,
And a deeper knell in the heart be knoll'd;
And the sound of the sorrowing anthem roll'd
Thro' the dome of the golden cross;
And the volleying cannon thunder his loss;
He knew their voices of old.
For many a time in many a clime
His captain's-ear has heard them boom
Bellowing victory, bellowing doom.
When he with those deep voices wrought,
Guarding realms and kings from shame,
With those deep voices our dead captain taught
The tyrant, and asserts his claim
In that dread sound to the great name
Which he has worn so pure of blame,
In praise and in dispraise the same,
A man of well-attemper'd frame.
O civic muse, to such a name,
To such a name for ages long,
To such a name,
Preserve a broad approach of fame,
And ever-echoing avenues of song!

"Who is he that cometh, like an honour'd guest,
With banner and with music, with soldier and with priest,
With a nation weeping, and breaking on my rest?"—
Mighty Seaman, this is he
Was great by land as thou by sea.
Thine island loves thee well, thou famous man,
The greatest sailor since our world began.
Now, to the roll of muffled drums,
To thee the greatest soldier comes;
For this is he
Was great by land as thou by sea.
His foes were thine; he kept us free;
O, give him welcome, this is he
Worthy of our gorgeous rites,
And worthy to be laid by thee;
For this is England's greatest son,

He that gain'd a hundred fights,
Nor ever lost an English gun;
This is he that far away
Against the myriads of Assaye
Clash'd with his fiery few and won;
And underneath another sun,
Warring on a later day,
Round affrighted Lisbon drew
The treble works, the vast designs
Of his labour'd rampart-lines,
Where he greatly stood at bay,
Whence he issued forth anew,
And ever great and greater grew,
Beating from the wasted vines
Back to France her banded swarms,
Back to France with countless blows,
Till o'er the hills her eagles flew
Beyond the Pyrenean pines,
Follow'd up in valley and glen
With blare of bugle, clamour of men,
Roll of cannon and clash of arms,
And England pouring on her foes,
Such a war had such a close.
Again their ravening eagle rose
In anger, wheel'd on Europe-shadowing wings,
And barking for the throne of kings;
Till one that sought but Duty's iron crown
On that loud Sabbath shook the spoiler down;
A day of onsets of despair!
Dash'd on every rocky square,
Their surging charges foam'd themselves away;
Last, the Prussian trumpet blew;
Thro' the long-tormented air
Heaven flash'd a sudden jubilant ray,
And down we swept and charged and overthrew.
So great a soldier taught us there
What long-enduring hearts could do
In that world-earthquake, Waterloo!
Mighty Seaman, tender and true,
And pure as he from taint of craven guile,
O saviour of the silver-coasted isle,
O shaker of the Baltic and the Nile,
If aught of things that here befall
Touch a spirit among things divine,
If love of country move thee there at all,
Be glad, because his bones are laid by thine!
And thro' the centuries let a people's voice
In full acclaim,
A people's voice,
The proof and echo of all human fame,
A people's voice, when they rejoice
At civic revel and pomp and game,
Attest their great commander's claim
With honour, honour, honour, honour to him,
Eternal honour to his name.

A people's voice! we are a people yet.
Tho' all men else their nobler dreams forget,
Confused by brainless mobs and lawless Powers,
Thank Him who isled us here, and roughly set
His Briton in blown seas and storming showers,
We have a voice with which to pay the debt
Of boundless love and reverence and regret
To those great men who fought, and kept it ours.
And keep it ours, O God, from brute control!
O Statesmen, guard us, guard the eye, the soul
Of Europe, keep our noble England whole,
And save the one true seed of freedom sown
Betwixt a people and their ancient throne,
That sober freedom out of which there springs
Our loyal passion for our temperate kings!
For, saving that, ye help to save mankind
Till public wrong be crumbled into dust,
And drill the raw world for the march of mind,

Till crowds at length be sane and crowns
be just.
But wink no more in slothful overtrust.
Remember him who led your hosts;
He bade you guard the sacred coasts.
Your cannons moulder on the seaward
wall;
His voice is silent in your council-hall
For ever; and whatever tempests lour
For ever silent; even if they broke
In thunder, silent; yet remember all
He spoke among you, and the Man who
spoke;
Who never sold the truth to serve the
hour,
Nor palter'd with Eternal God for
power;
Who let the turbid streams of rumour
flow
Thro' either babbling world of high and
low;
Whose life was work, whose language
rife
With rugged maxims hewn from life;
Who never spoke against a foe;
Whose eighty winters freeze with one
rebuke
All great self-seekers trampling on the
right.
Truth-teller was our England's Alfred
named;
Truth-lover was our English Duke!
Whatever record leap to light
He never shall be shamed.

Lo! the leader in these glorious wars
Now to glorious burial slowly borne,
Follow'd by the brave of other lands,
He, on whom from both her open hands
Lavish Honour shower'd all her stars,
And affluent Fortune emptied all her
horn.
Yea, let all good things await
Him who cares not to be great
But as he saves or serves the state.
Not once or twice in our rough island-
story
The path of duty was the way to glory.
He that walks it, only thirsting
For the right, and learns to deaden
Love of self, before his journey closes,
He shall find the stubborn thistle burst-
ing
Into glossy purples, which out-redden
All voluptuous garden-roses.
Not once or twice in our fair island-story
The path of duty was the way to glory.
He, that ever following her commands,
On with toil of heart and knees and
hands,
Thro' the long gorge to the far light has
won
His path upward, and prevail'd,
Shall find the toppling crags of Duty
scaled
Are close upon the shining table-lands
To which our God Himself is moon and
sun.
Such was he: his work is done.
But while the races of mankind endure
Let his great example stand
Colossal, seen of every land,
And keep the soldier firm, the statesman
pure;
Till in all lands and thro' all human
story
The path of duty be the way to glory.
And let the land whose hearths he saved
from shame
For many and many an age proclaim
At civic revel and pomp and game,
And when the long-illumined cities flame,
Their ever-loyal iron leader's fame,
With honour, honour, honour, honour to
him,
Eternal honour to his name.

Peace, his triumph will be sung
By some yet unmoulded tongue
Far on in summers that we shall not see.
Peace, it is a day of pain
For one about whose patriarchal knee
Late the little children clung.
O peace, it is a day of pain
For one upon whose hand and heart and
brain
Once the weight and fate of Europe
hung.

Ours the pain, be his the gain!
More than is of man's degree
Must be with us, watching here
At this, our great solemnity.
Whom we see not we revere;
We revere, and we refrain
From talk of battles loud and vain,
And bawling memories all too free
For such a wise humility
As befits a solemn fane:
We revere, and while we hear
The tides of Music's golden sea
Setting toward eternity,
Uplifted high in heart and hope are we,
Until we doubt not that for one so true
There must be other nobler work to do
Than when he fought at Waterloo,
And victor he must ever be.
For tho' the Giant Ages heave the hill
And break the shore, and evermore
Make and break, and work their will,
Tho' world on world in myriad myriads roll
Round us, each with different powers,
And other forms of life than ours,
What know we greater than the soul?
On God and Godlike men we build our trust.
Hush, the Dead March wails in the people's ears;
The dark crowd moves, and there are sobs and tears;
The black earth yawns; the mortal disappears;
Ashes to ashes, dust to dust;
He is gone who seem'd so great.—
Gone, but nothing can bereave him
Of the force he made his own
Being here, and we believe him
Something far advanced in State,
And that he wears a truer crown
Than any wreath that man can weave him.
Speak no more of his renown,
Lay your earthly fancies down,
And in the vast cathedral leave him,
God accept him, Christ receive him!

The Charge of the Light Brigade

Half a league, half a league,
Half a league onward,
All in the valley of Death
  Rode the six hundred.
"Forward the Light Brigade!
Charge for the guns!" he said.
Into the valley of Death
  Rode the six hundred.

"Forward, the Light Brigade!"
Was there a man dismay'd?
Not tho' the soldier knew
  Some one had blunder'd.
Theirs not to make reply,
Theirs not to reason why,
Theirs but to do and die:
Into the valley of Death
  Rode the six hundred.

Cannon to right of them,
Cannon to left of them,
Cannon in front of them
  Volley'd and thunder'd;
Storm'd at with shot and shell,
Boldly they rode and well,
Into the jaws of Death,
Into the mouth of hell
  Rode the six hundred.

Flash'd all their sabres bare,
Flash'd as they turn'd in air
Sabring the gunners there,
Charging an army, while
  All the world wonder'd.
Plunged in the battery-smoke
Right thro' the line they broke;
Cossack and Russian
Reel'd from the sabre-stroke
  Shatter'd and sunder'd.
Then they rode back, but not—
  Not the six hundred.

Cannon to right of them,
Cannon to left of them,
Cannon behind them
  Volley'd and thunder'd;
Storm'd at with shot and shell,
While horse and hero fell,

They that had fought so well
Came thro' the jaws of Death,
Back from the mouth of Hell,
All that was left of them,
Left of six hundred.

When can their glory fade,
O the wild charge they made!
All the world wonder'd.
Honour the charge they made!
Honour the Light Brigade,
Noble six hundred!

The Revenge; A Ballad of the Fleet

At Flores in the Azores Sir Richard Grenville lay,
And a pinnace, like a fluttered bird, came flying from far away;
"Spanish ships of war at sea! we have sighted fifty-three!"
Then sware Lord Thomas Howard: "'Fore God I am no coward;
But I cannot meet them here, for my ships are out of gear,
And the half my men are sick. I must fly, but follow quick.
We are six ships of the line; can we fight with fifty-three?"

Then spake Sir Richard Grenville: "I know you are no coward;
You fly them for a moment to fight with them again.
But I've ninety men and more that are lying sick ashore.
I should count myself the coward if I left them, my Lord Howard,
To these Inquisition dogs and the devildoms of Spain."

So Lord Howard passed away with five ships of war that day,
Till he melted like a cloud in the silent summer heaven;
But Sir Richard bore in hand all his sick men from the land
Very carefully and slow,
Men of Bideford in Devon,
And we laid them on the ballast down below:
For we brought them all aboard,
And they blessed him in their pain, that they were not left to Spain,
To the thumb-screw and the stake, for the glory of the Lord.

He had only a hundred seamen to work the ship and to fight
And he sailed away from Flores till the Spaniard came in sight,
With his huge sea-castles heaving upon the weather bow.
"Shall we fight or shall we fly?
Good Sir Richard, tell us now,
For to fight is but to die!
There'll be little of us left by the time this sun be set."
And Sir Richard said again: "We be all good English men.
Let us bang these dogs of Seville, the children of the devil,
For I never turned my back upon Don or devil yet."

Sir Richard spoke and he laughed, and we roared a hurrah, and so
The little *Revenge* ran on sheer into the heart of the foe,
With her hundred fighters on deck, and her ninety sick below;
For half of their fleet to the right and half to the left were seen,
And the little *Revenge* ran on thro' the long sea-lane between.

Thousands of their soldiers looked down from their decks and laughed,
Thousands of their seamen made mock at the mad little craft
Running on and on, till delayed
By their mountain-like *San Philip* that, of fifteen hundred tons,
And up-shadowing high above us with her yawning tiers of guns,
Took the breath from our sails, and we stayed.

And while now the great *San Philip* hung above us like a cloud
Whence the thunderbolt will fall
Long and loud,
Four galleons drew away
From the Spanish fleet that day,
And two upon the larboard and two upon the starboard lay,
And the battle-thunder broke from them all.

But anon the great *San Philip*, she bethought herself and went,
Having that within her womb that had left her ill content;
And the rest they came aboard us, and they fought us hand to hand,
For a dozen times they came with their pikes and musqueteers,
And a dozen times we shook 'em off as a dog that shakes his ears
When he leaps from the water to the land.

And the sun went down, and the stars came out far over the summer sea,
But never a moment ceased the fight of the one and the fifty-three.
Ship after ship, the whole night long, their high-built galleons came,
Ship after ship, the whole night long, with her battle-thunder and flame:
Ship after ship, the whole night long, drew back with her dead and her shame.
For some were sunk and many were shattered, and so could fight us no more—
God of battles, was ever a battle like this in the world before?

For he said, "Fight on! fight on!"
Tho' his vessel was all but a wreck;
And it chanced that, when half of the short summer night was gone,
With a grisly wound to be dressed he had left the deck,
But a bullet struck him that was dressing it suddenly dead,
And himself he was wounded again in the side and the head,
And he said, "Fight on! fight on!"

And the night went down, and the sun smiled out far over the summer sea,
And the Spanish fleet with broken sides lay round us all in a ring;
But they dared not touch us again, for they feared that we still could sting,
So they watched what the end would be.
And we had not fought them in vain,
But in perilous plight were we,
Seeing forty of our poor hundred were slain,
And half of the rest of us maimed for life
In the crash of the cannonades and the desperate strife:
And the sick men down in the hold were most of them stark and cold,
And the pikes were all broken or bent, and the powder was all of it spent;
And the masts and the rigging were lying over the side;
But Sir Richard cried in his English pride:
"We have fought such a fight for a day and a night
As may never be fought again!
We have won great glory, my men!
And a day less or more
At sea or ashore,
We die—does it matter when?
Sink me the ship, Master Gunner—sink her, split her in twain!
Fall into the hands of God, not into the hands of Spain!"

And the gunner said, "Ay, ay," but the sea-men made reply:
"We have children, we have wives,
And the Lord hath spared our lives.
We will make the Spaniard promise, if we yield, to let us go;
We shall live to fight again and to strike another blow."
And the lion there lay dying, and they yielded to the foe.

And the stately Spanish men to their flagship bore him then,
Where they laid him by the mast, old Sir Richard caught at last,
And they praised him to his face with their courtly foreign grace;
But he rose upon their decks, and he cried:
"I have fought for Queen and Faith like a valiant man and true;
I have only done my duty as a man is bound to do.
With a joyful spirit I, Sir Richard Grenville, die!"
And he fell upon their decks, and he died.

And they stared at the dead that had been so valiant and true,
And had holden the power and glory of Spain so cheap
That he dared her with one little ship and his English few;
Was he devil or man? He was devil for aught they knew,
But they sank his body with honor down into the deep.
And they manned the *Revenge* with a swarthier alien crew,
And away she sailed with her loss, and longed for her own;
When a wind from the lands they had ruined awoke from sleep,
And the water began to heave and the weather to moan,
And or ever that evening ended a great gale blew,
And a wave like the wave that is raised by an earthquake grew,
Till it smote on their hulls and their sails and their masts and their flags,
And the whole sea plunged and fell on the shot-shattered navy of Spain,
And the little *Revenge* herself went down by the island crags
To be lost evermore in the main.

To Virgil

Roman Virgil, thou that singest
Ilion's lofty temples robed in fire,
Ilion falling, Rome arising,
wars, and filial faith, and Dido's pyre;

Landscape-lover, lord of language
more than he that sang the "Works and Days,"
All the chosen coin of fancy
flashing out from many a golden phrase;

Thou that singest wheat and woodland,
tilth and vineyard, hive and horse and herd;
All the charm of all the Muses
often flowering in a lonely word;

Poet of the happy Tityrus
piping underneath his beechen bowers;
Poet of the poet-satyr
whom the laughing shepherd bound with flowers;

Chanter of the Pollio, glorying
in the blissful years again to be,
Summers of the snakeless meadow,
unlaborious earth and oarless sea;

Thou that seest Universal
Nature moved by Universal Mind;
Thou majestic in thy sadness
at the doubtful doom of human kind;

Light among the vanish'd ages;
star that gildest yet this phantom shore;
Golden branch amid the shadows,
kings and realms that pass to rise no more;

Now thy Forum roars no longer,
fallen every purple Cæsar's dome—
Tho' thine ocean-roll of rhythm
sound forever of Imperial Rome—

Now the Rome of slaves hath perish'd,
and the Rome of freemen holds her
place,
I, from out the Northern Island
sunder'd once from all the human race,

I salute thee, Mantovano,
I that loved thee since my day began,
Wielder of the stateliest measure
ever moulded by the lips of man.

"Frater Ave Atque Vale"

Row us out from Desenzano, to your
Sirmione row!
So they row'd, and there we landed—
"O venusta Sirmio!"
There to me thro' all the groves of olive
in the summer glow,
There beneath the Roman ruin where the
purple flowers grow,
Came that "Ave atque Vale" of the
Poet's hopeless woe,
Tenderest of Roman poets nineteen hun-
dred years ago,
"Frater Ave atque Vale"—as we wan-
der'd to and fro
Gazing at the Lydian laughter of the
Garda Lake below
Sweet Catullus's all-but-island, olive-
silvery Sirmio!

Crossing the Bar

SUNSET and evening star,
And one clear call for me!
And may there be no moaning of the bar,
When I put out to sea,

But such a tide as moving seems asleep,
Too full for sound and foam,
When that which drew from out the
boundless deep
Turns again home.

Twilight and evening bell,
And after that the dark!
And may there be no sadness of farewell,
When I embark;

For tho' from out our bourne of Time
and Place
The flood may bear me far,
I hope to see my Pilot face to face
When I have cross'd the bar.

DR. JOHN BROWN (1810-1882)

Rab and His Friends

FOUR-AND-THIRTY years ago, Bob Ainslie and I were coming up Infirmary Street from the High School, our heads together, and our arms intertwisted, as only lovers and boys know how, or why.

When we got to the top of the street, and turned north, we espied a crowd at the Tron Church. "A dog-fight!" shouted Bob, and was off; and so was I, both of us all but praying that it might not be over before we got up! and is not this boy-nature? and human nature too? and don't we all wish a house on fire not to be out before we see it? Dogs like fighting; old Isaac says they "delight" in it, and for the best of all reasons; and boys are not cruel because they like to see the fight. They see three of the great cardinal virtues of dog or man—courage, endurance, and skill—in intense action. This is very different from a love of making dogs fight, and enjoying, and aggravating, and making gain by their pluck. A boy—be he ever so fond himself of fighting, if he be a good boy, hates and despises all this, but he would have run off with Bob and me fast enough: it is a natural, and a not wicked interest, that all boys and men have in witnessing intense energy in action.

Does any curious and finely-ignorant woman wish to know, how Bob's eye at a glance announced a dog-fight to his brain? He did not, he could not see the dogs fighting; it was a flash of an inference, a rapid induction. The crowd round a couple of dogs fighting, is a crowd, masculine mainly, with an occasional active, compassionate woman, fluttering wildly round the outside, and using her tongue and her hands freely upon the men, as so many "brutes;" it is a crowd annular, compact, and mobile; a crowd centripetal, having its eyes and its heads all bent downwards and inwards, to one common focus.

Well, Bob and I are up, and find it is not over: a small, thoroughbred, white bull-terrier, is busy throttling a large shepherd's dog, unaccustomed to war, but not to be trifled with. They are hard at it; the scientific little fellow doing his work in great style, his pastoral enemy fighting wildly, but with the sharpest of teeth and a great courage. Science and breeding, however, soon took their own; the Game Chicken, as the premature Bob called him, working his way up, took his final grip of poor Yarrow's throat,—and he lay gasping and done for. His master, a brown, handsome, big young shepherd from Tweedsmuir, would have liked to have knocked down any man, "drunk up Esil, or eaten a crocodile," for that part, if he had a chance: it was no use kicking the little dog; that would only make him hold the closer. Many were the means shouted out in mouthfuls, of the best possible ways of ending it. "Water!" but there was none near, and many shouted for it who might have got it from the well at Blackfriars Wynd. "Bite the tail!" and a large, vague, benevolent, middle-aged man, more anxious than wise, with some struggle got the bushy end of *Yarrow's* tail into his ample mouth, and bit it with all his might. This was more than enough for the much-enduring, much-perspiring shepherd, who, with a gleam of joy over his broad visage, delivered a terrific facer upon our large, vague, benevolent, middle-aged friend,—who went down like a shot.

Still the Chicken holds; death not far off. "Snuff! a pinch of snuff!" observed sharply a calm, highly-dressed young buck, with an eye-glass in his eye. "Snuff, indeed!" growled the angry crowd, affronted and glaring. "Snuff! a pinch of snuff!" again observes the buck, but with more urgency; whereon were produced several open boxes, and from a mull which may have been at Culloden, he took a pinch, knelt down, and presented it to the nose of the Chicken. The laws of physiology and of snuff take their course; the Chicken sneezes, and Yarrow is free!

The young pastoral giant stalks off with Yarrow in his arms,—comforting him.

But the Chicken's blood is up, and his soul unsatisfied; he grips the first dog he meets, but discovering she is not a dog, in Homeric phrase, he makes a brief sort of *amende,* and is off. The boys, with Bob and me at their head, are after him; down Niddry Street he goes, bent on mischief; up the Cowgate like an arrow—Bob and I, and our small men, panting behind.

There, under the large arch of the South Bridge, is a huge mastiff, sauntering down the middle of the causeway, as if with his hands in his pockets: he is old, grey, brindled; as big as a little Highland bull, and has the Shakesperian dewlaps shaking as he goes.

The Chicken makes straight at him, and fastens on his throat. To our astonishment, the great creature does nothing but stand still, hold himself up, and roar—yes, roar; a long, serious, remonstrative roar. How is this? Bob and I are up to them. *He is muzzled!* The bailies had proclaimed a general muzzling, and his master, studying strength and economy mainly, had encompassed his huge jaws in a home-made apparatus, constructed out of the leather of some ancient *breechin.* His mouth was open as far as it could; his lips curled up in rage—a sort of terrible grin; his teeth gleaming, ready, from out of the darkness; the strap across his mouth tense as a bowstring; his whole frame stiff with indignation and surprise; his roar asking us all round, "Did you ever see the like of this?" He looked a statue of anger and astonishment, done in Aberdeen granite.

We soon had a crowd: the Chicken held on. "A knife!" cried Bob; and a cobbler gave him his knife: you know the kind of knife, worn away obliquely to a point, and always keen. I put its edge to the tense leather; it ran before it; and then! one sudden jerk of that enormous head, a sort of dirty mist about his mouth, no noise,—and the bright and fierce little fellow is dropped, limp, and dead. A solemn pause; this was more than any of us had bargained for. I turned the little fellow over, and saw he was quite dead: the mastiff had taken him by the small of the back like a rat, and broken it.

He looked down at his victim appeased, ashamed, and amazed; snuffed him all over, stared at him, and taking a sudden thought, turned round and trotted off. Bob took the dead dog up, and said, "John, we'll bury him after tea." "Yes," said I; and was off after the mastiff. He made up the Cowgate at a rapid swing: he had forgotten some engagement. He turned up the Candlemaker Row, and stopped at the Harrow Inn.

There was a carrier's cart ready to start, and a keen, thin, impatient, black-a-vised little man, his hand at his grey horse's head, looking about angrily for something. "Rab, ye thief!" said he, aiming a kick at my great friend, who drew cringing up, and avoiding the heavy shoe with more agility than dignity, and watching his master's eye, slunk dismayed under the cart,—his ears down, and as much as he had of tail down too.

What a man this must be—thought I—to whom my tremendous hero turns tail! The carrier saw the muzzle hanging, cut and useless, from his neck, and I eagerly told him the story, which Bob and I always thought, and still think, Homer, or King David, or Sir Walter, alone were worthy to rehearse. The severe little man was mitigated, and condescended to say, "Rab, my man, puir Rabbie,"—whereupon the stump of a tail rose up, the ears were cocked, the eyes filled, and were comforted; the two friends were reconciled. "Hupp!" and a stroke of the whip were given to Jess; and off went the three.

Bob and I buried the Game Chicken that night (we hadn't much of a tea) in the back-green of his house, in Melville Street, No. 17, with considerable gravity and silence; and being at the time in the Iliad, and, like all boys, Trojans, we called him, of course, Hector.

Six years have passed,—a long time for a boy and a dog: Bob Ainslie is off to the wars; I am a medical student, and clerk at Minto House Hospital.

Rab I saw almost every week, on the Wednesday; and we had much pleasant intimacy. I found the way to his heart by frequent scratching of his huge head, and an occasional bone. When I did not notice him he would plant himself straight before me, and stand wagging that bud of a tail, and looking up, with his head a little to the one side. His master I occasionally saw; he used to call me "Maister John," but was laconic as any Spartan.

One fine October afternoon, I was leaving the hospital, when I saw the large gate open, and in walked Rab, with that great and easy saunter of his. He looked as if taking general possession of the place; like the Duke of Wellington entering a subdued city, satiated with victory and peace. After him came Jess, now white from age, with her cart; and in it a woman, carefully wrapped up,—the carrier leading the horse anxiously, and looking back. When he saw me, James (for his name was James Noble) made a curt and grotesque "boo," and said, "Maister John, this is the mistress; she's got a trouble in her breest—some kind o' an income we're thinkin'."

By this time I saw the woman's face; she was sitting on a sack filled with straw, her husband's plaid round her, and his big-coat, with its large white metal buttons, over her feet. I never saw a more unforgetable face—pale, serious, *lonely,*[1] delicate, sweet, without being what we call fine. She looked sixty, and had on a mutch, white as snow, with its black ribbon; her silvery smooth hair setting off her dark-grey eyes—eyes such as one sees only twice or thrice in a lifetime, full of suffering, but full also of the overcoming of it; her eye-brows black and delicate, and her mouth firm, patient, and contented, which few mouths ever are.

As I have said, I never saw a more beautiful countenance, or one more subdued to settled quiet. "Ailie," said James, "this is Maister John, the young doctor; Rab's freend, ye ken. We often speak aboot you, doctor." She smiled, and made a movement, but said nothing; and prepared to come down, putting her plaid aside and rising. Had Solomon, in all his glory, been handing down the Queen of Sheba at his palace gate, he could not have done it more daintily, more tenderly, more like a gentleman, than did James the Howgate carrier, when he lifted down Ailie, his wife. The contrast of his small, swarthy, weatherbeaten, keen, worldly face to hers—pale, subdued, and beautiful—was something wonderful. Rab looked on concerned and puzzled, but ready for anything that might turn up,—were it to strangle the nurse, the porter, or even me. Ailie and he seemed great friends.

"As I was sayin', she's got a kind o' trouble in her breest, doctor; wull ye tak' a look at it?" We walked into the consulting-room, all four; Rab grim and comic, willing to be happy and confidential if cause could be shown, willing also to be quite the reverse, on the same terms. Ailie sat down, undid her open gown and her lawn handkerchief round her neck, and, without a word, showed me her right breast. I looked at and examined it carefully,—she and James watching me, and Rab eyeing all three. What could I say? there it was, that had once been so soft, so shapely, so white, so gracious and bountiful, "so full of all blessed conditions,"—hard as a stone, a centre of horrid pain, making that pale face, with its grey, lucid, reasonable eyes, and its sweet resolved mouth, express the full measure of suffering overcome. Why was that gentle, modest, sweet woman, clean and lovable, condemned by God to bear such a burden?

I got her away to bed. "May Rab and me bide?" said James. "*You*

[1] It is not easy giving this look by one word; it was expressive of her being so much of her life alone.

may; and Rab, if he will behave himself." "I'se warrant he's do that, doctor;" and in slunk the faithful beast. I wish you could have seen him. There are no such dogs now: he belonged to a lost tribe. As I have said, he was brindled, and grey like Aberdeen granite; his hair short, hard, and close, like a lion's; his body thick set like a little bull—a sort of compressed Hercules of a dog. He must have been ninety pounds' weight, at the least; he had a large blunt head; his muzzle black as night; his mouth blacker than any night, a tooth or two—being all he had—gleaming out of his jaws of darkness. His head was scarred with the records of old wounds, a sort of series of fields of battle all over it; one eye out, one ear cropped as close as was Archbishop Leighton's father's—but for different reasons,—the remaining eye had the power of two; and above it, and in constant communication with it, was a tattered rag of an ear, which was for ever unfurling itself, like an old flag; and then that bud of a tail, about one inch long, if it could in any sense be said to be long, being as broad as long—the mobility, the instantaneousness of that bud was very funny and surprising, and its expressive twinklings and winkings, the intercommunications between the eye, the ear, and it, were of the subtlest and swiftest. Rab had the dignity and simplicity of great size; and having fought his way all along the road to absolute supremacy, he was as mighty in his own line as Julius Cæsar or the Duke of Wellington; and he had the gravity [1] of all great fighters.

You must have often observed the likeness of certain men to certain animals, and of certain dogs to men. Now, I never looked at Rab without thinking of the great Baptist preacher, Andrew Fuller.[2] The same large, heavy, menacing, combative, sombre, honest countenance, the same inevitable eye, the same look,—as of thunder asleep, but ready,—neither a dog nor a man to be trifled with.

Next day, my master, the surgeon, examined Ailie. There was no doubt it must kill her, and soon. It could be removed—it might never return—it would give her speedy relief—she should have it done. She curtsied, looked at James, and said, "When?" "Tomorrow," said the kind surgeon, a man of few words. She and James and Rab and I

[1] A Highland game-keeper, when asked why a certain terrier, of singular pluck, was so much graver than the other dogs, said, "Oh, Sir, life's full o' sairiousness to him—he just never can get enuff o' fechtin'."

[2] Fuller was in early life, when a farmer lad at Soham, famous as a boxer; not quarrelsome, but not without "the stern delight" a man of strength and courage feels in the exercise. Dr. Charles Stewart, of Dunearn, whose rare gifts and graces as a physician, a divine, a scholar, and a gentleman, live only in the memory of those few who knew and survive him, liked to tell how Mr. Fuller used to say, that when he was in the pulpit, and saw a buirdly man, he would instinctively draw himself up, measure his imaginary antagonist, and forecast how he would deal with him, his hands meanwhile condensing into fists. He must have been a hard hitter if he boxed as he preached—what "The Fancy" would call "an ugly customer."

retired. I noticed that he and she spoke little, but seemed to anticipate everything in each other. The following day, at noon, the students came in, hurrying up the great stair. At the first landing-place, on a small well-known black board, was a bit of paper fastened by wafers, and many remains of old wafers beside it. On the paper were the words, "An operation to-day. J. B. *Clerk.*"

Up ran the youths, eager to secure good places: in they crowded, full of interest and talk. "What's the case?" "Which side is it?"

Don't think them heartless; they are neither better nor worse than you or I: they get over their professional horrors, and into their proper work; and in them pity—as an *emotion,* ending in itself or at best in tears and a long-drawn breath, lessens, while pity as a *motive,* is quickened, and gains power and purpose. It is well for poor human nature that it is so.

The operating theatre is crowded; much talk and fun, and all the cordiality and stir of youth. The surgeon with his staff of assistants is there. In comes Ailie: one look at her quiets and abates the eager students. That beautiful old woman is too much for them; they sit down, and are dumb, and gaze at her. These rough boys feel the power of her presence. She walks in quickly, but without haste; dressed in her mutch, her neckerchief, her white dimity shortgown, her black bombazeen petticoat, showing her white worsted stockings and her carpet-shoes. Behind her was James, with Rab. James sat down in the distance, and took that huge and noble head between his knees. Rab looked perplexed and dangerous; for ever cocking his ear and dropping it as fast.

Ailie stepped up on a seat, and laid herself on the table, as her friend the surgeon told her; arranged herself, gave a rapid look at James, shut her eyes, rested herself on me, and took my hand. The operation was at once begun; it was necessarily slow; and chloroform—one of God's best gifts to his suffering children—was then unknown. The surgeon did his work. The pale face showed its pain, but was still and silent. Rab's soul was working within him; he saw that something strange was going on,—blood flowing from his mistress, and she suffering; his ragged ear was up, and importunate; he growled and gave now and then a sharp impatient yelp; he would have like to have done something to that man. But James had him firm, and gave him a glower from time to time, and an intimation of a possible kick;—all the better for James, it kept his eye and his mind off Ailie.

It is over: she is dressed, steps gently and decently down from the table, looks for James; then, turning to the surgeon and the students, she curtsies,—and in a low, clear voice, begs their pardon if she has behaved ill. The students—all of us—wept like children; the surgeon happed her up carefully,—and, resting on James and me, Ailie went to her room, Rab following. We put her to bed. James took off his heavy shoes, crammed with tackets, heel-capt and toe-capt, and put them carefully under the table, saying, "Maister John, I'm for nane o' yer strynge nurse bodies for Ailie. I'll be her nurse, and on my stockin' soles I'll gang about as canny as pussy." And so he did; and handy and clever, and swift and tender as any woman, was that horny-handed, snell, peremptory little man. Everything she got he gave her: he seldom slept; and often I saw his small, shrewd eyes out of the darkness, fixed on her. As before, they spoke little.

Rab behaved well, never moving, showing us how meek and gentle he could be, and occasionally, in his sleep, letting us know that he was demolishing some adversary. He took a walk with me every day, generally to the Candlemaker Row; but he was sombre and mild; declined doing battle, though some fit cases offered, and indeed submitted to sundry indignities; and was always very ready to turn, and came faster back, and trotted up the stair with much lightness, and went straight to *that* door.

Jess, the mare—now white—had been sent, with her weather-worn cart, to Howgate, and had doubtless her own dim and placid meditations and confusions, on the absence of her master and Rab, and her unnatural freedom from the road and her cart.

For some days Ailie did well. The wound healed "by the first intention;" as James said, "Oor Ailie's skin's ower clean to beil." The students came in quiet and anxious, and surrounded her bed. She said she liked to see their young, honest faces. The surgeon dressed her, and spoke to her in his own short kind way, pitying her through his eyes, Rab and James outside the circle,—Rab being now reconciled, and even cordial, and having made up his mind that as yet nobody required worrying, but, as you may suppose, *semper paratus.*

So far well: but, four days after the operation, my patient had a sudden and long shivering, a "groofin'," as she called it. I saw her soon after; her eyes were too bright, her cheek coloured; she was restless, and ashamed of being so; the balance was lost; mischief had begun. On looking at the wound, a blush of red told the secret: her pulse was rapid, her breathing anxious and quick, she wasn't herself, as she said, and was vexed at her restlessness. We tried what we could. James did everything, was everywhere; never in the way, never out of it; Rab subsided under the table into a dark place, and was motionless, all but his eye, which followed every one. Ailie got worse; began to wander in her mind, gently; was more demonstrative in her ways to James, rapid in her questions, and sharp at times. He was vexed, and said, "She was never that way afore; no, never." For a time she knew her head was wrong, and was always asking our pardon—the dear, gentle old woman: then delirium set in strong, without pause. Her brain gave way, and that terrible spectacle,

> "The intellectual power, through words and things,
> Went sounding on its dim and perilous way;"

she sang bits of old songs and Psalms, stopping suddenly, mingling the Psalms of David, and the diviner words of his Son and Lord, with homely odds and ends and scraps of ballads.

Nothing more touching, or in a sense more strangely beautiful, did I ever witness. Her tremulous, rapid, affectionate, eager Scotch voice,—the swift, aimless, bewildered mind, the baffled utterance, the bright and perilous eye; some wild words, some household cares, something for James, the names of the dead, Rab called rapidly and in a "fremyt" voice, and he starting up, surprised, and slinking off as if he were to blame somehow, or had been dreaming he heard. Many eager questions and beseechings which James and I could make nothing of, and on which she seemed to set her all and then sink back ununderstood. It was very sad, but better than many things that are not called sad. James hovered about, put out and miserable, but active and exact as ever; read to her, when there was a lull, short bits from the Psalms, prose and metre, chanting the latter in his own rude and serious way, showing great knowledge of the fit words, bearing up like a man, and doating over her as his "ain Ailie." "Ailie, ma woman!" "Ma ain bonnie wee dawtie!"

The end was drawing on: the golden bowl was breaking; the silver cord was fast being loosed—that *animula, blandula, vagula, hospes, comesque,* was about to flee. The body and the soul—companions for sixty years—were being sundered, and taking leave. She was walking, alone, through the valley of that shadow, into which one day we must all enter,—and yet she was not alone, for we know whose rod and staff were comforting her.

One night she had fallen quiet, and as we hoped, asleep; her eyes were shut. We put down the gas, and sat watching her. Suddenly she sat up in bed, and taking a bedgown which was lying on it rolled up, she held it eagerly to her breast,—to the right side. We could see her eyes bright with a surprising tenderness and joy, bending over this bundle of clothes. She held it as a woman holds her sucking child; opening out her nightgown impatiently, and holding it close, and brooding over it, and murmuring foolish little words, as over one whom his mother comforteth, and who is sucking, and being satisfied. It was pitiful and strange to see her wasted dying look, keen and yet vague—her immense love. "Preserve me!" groaned James, giving way. And then she rocked back and forward, as if to make it sleep, hushing it, and wasting on it her infinite fondness. "Wae's me, doctor; I declare she's thinkin' it's that bairn." "What bairn?" "The only bairn we ever had; our wee Mysie, and she's in the Kingdom, forty years and mair." It was plainly true: the pain in the breast, telling its urgent story to a bewildered, ruined brain; it was misread and mistaken; it suggested to her the uneasiness of a breast full of milk, and then the child; and so again once more they were together, and she had her ain wee Mysie in her bosom.

This was the close. She sunk rapidly; the delirium left her; but as she whispered, she was clean silly; it was the lightening before the final darkness. After having for some time lain still—her eyes shut, she said "James!" He came close to her, and lifting up her calm, clear, beautiful eyes, she gave him a long look, turned to me kindly but shortly, looked for Rab but could not see him, then turned to her husband again, as if she would never leave off looking, shut her eyes, and composed herself. She lay for some time breathing quick, and passed away so gently, that when we thought she was gone, James, in his old-fashioned way, held the mirror to her face. After a long pause, one small spot of dimness was breathed out; it vanished away, and never returned, leaving the blank clear darkness of the mirror without a stain. "What is our life? it is even a vapour, which appeareth for a little time, and then vanisheth away."

Rab all this time had been full awake and motionless: he came forward beside us: Ailie's hand, which James had held, was hanging down; it was soaked with his tears; Rab licked it all over carefully, looked at her, and returned to his place under the table.

James and I sat, I don't know how long, but for some time,—saying nothing: he started up abruptly, and with some noise went to the table, and putting his right fore and middle fingers each into a shoe, pulled them out, and put them on, breaking one of the leather latchets, and muttering in anger, "I never did the like o' that afore!"

I believe he never did; nor after either. "Rab!" he said roughly, and pointing with his thumb to the bottom of the bed. Rab leapt up, and settled himself; his head and eye to the dead face. "Maister John, ye'll wait for me," said the carrier; and disappeared in the darkness, thundering down stairs in his heavy shoes. I ran to a front window: there he was, already round the house, and out at the gate, fleeing like a shadow.

I was afraid about him, and yet not afraid; so I sat down beside Rab, and being wearied, fell asleep. I awoke from a sudden noise outside. It was November, and there had been a heavy fall of snow. Rab was in *statu quo;* he heard the noise too, and plainly knew it, but never moved. I looked out; and there, at the gate, in the dim morning—for the sun was not up, was Jess and the cart,—a cloud of steam rising from the old mare. I did not see James; he was already at the door, and came up the stairs, and met me. It was less than three hours since he left, and he must have posted out—who knows how?—to Howgate, full nine miles off; yoked Jess, and driven her astonished into town. He had an armful of blankets, and was streaming with perspiration. He nodded to me, spread out on the floor two pairs of old clean blankets, having at their corners, "A. G., 1794," in large letters in red worsted. These were the initials of Alison Græme, and James may have looked in at her from without—unseen but not unthought of—when he was "wat, wat, and weary," and had walked many a mile over the hills, and seen her sitting, while "a' the lave were sleepin';" and by the firelight putting her name on the blankets for her ain James's bed. He motioned Rab down, and taking his wife in his arms, laid her in the blankets, and happed her carefully and firmly up, leaving the face uncovered; and then lifting her, he nodded again sharply to me, and with a resolved but utterly miserable face, strode along the passage, and down stairs, followed by Rab. I also followed, with a light; but he didn't need it. I went out, holding stupidly the light in my hand in the frosty air; we were soon at the gate. I could have helped him, but I saw he was not to be meddled with, and he was strong, and did not need it. He laid her down as tenderly, as safely, as he had lifted her out ten days before—as tenderly as when he had her first in his arms when she was only "A. G.,"—sorted her, leaving that beautiful sealed face open to the heavens; and then taking Jess by the head, he moved away. He did not notice me, neither did Rab, who presided alone behind the cart.

I stood till they passed through the long shadow of the College, and turned up Nicolson Street. I heard the solitary cart sound through the streets, and die away and come again; and I returned, thinking of that company going up Libberton brae, then along Roslin muir, the morning light touching the Pentlands and making them like on-looking ghosts; then down the hill through Auchindinny woods, past "haunted Woodhouselee;" and as daybreak came sweeping up the bleak Lammermuirs, and fell on his own door, the company would stop, and James would take the key, and lift Ailie up again, laying her on her own bed, and, having put Jess up, would return with Rab and shut the door.

James buried his wife, with his neighbours mourning, Rab inspecting the solemnity from a distance. It was snow, and that black ragged hole would look strange in the midst of the swelling spotless cushion of white. James looked after everything; then rather suddenly fell ill, and took to bed; was insensible when the doctor came, and soon died. A sort of low fever was prevailing in the village, and his want of sleep, his exhaustion, and his misery, made him apt to take it. The grave was not difficult to re-open. A fresh fall of snow had again made all things white and smooth; Rab once more looked on, and slunk home to the stable.

And what of Rab? I asked for him next week at the new carrier's who got the goodwill of James's business, and was now master of Jess and her cart. "How's Rab?" He put me off, and said rather rudely, "What's *your* business wi' the dowg?" I was not to be so put off. "Where's Rab?" He, getting confused and red, and intermeddling with his hair, said, "'Deed, sir, Rab's deid." "Dead! what did he die of?" "Weel, sir," said he, getting redder, "he didna exactly die; he was killed. I had to brain him wi' a rack-pin; there was nae doin' wi' him. He lay in the treviss wi' the mear, and wadna come oot. I tempit him wi' kail and meat, but he wad tak' naething, and keepit me frae feedin' the beast, and he was aye gur gurrin', and grup gruppin' me by the legs. I was laith to mak' awa wi' the auld dowg, his like wasna atween this and Thornhill,—but 'deed, sir, I could do naething else." I believed him. Fit end for Rab, quick and complete. His teeth and his friends gone, why should he keep the peace and be civil?

MRS. GASKELL

From CRANFORD

A Visit to an Old Bachelor

Miss Matilda Jenkyns—Miss Matty—is the sole surviving member of her family. In her youth she had been in love with Mr. Thomas Holbrook, yeoman. Her father, the rector of the village of Cranford, and her sister Deborah had objected to the match; and Miss Matty had been dutifully obedient. When both she and Mr. Holbrook are old, they meet by chance in the village shop. Time has destroyed all vestiges of the barrier between them. In the following selection, the author tells of her visit to Mr. Holbrook with Miss Matty.

A FEW days after, a note came from Mr. Holbrook, asking us—impartially asking both of us—in a formal, old-fashioned style, to spend a day at his house—a long June day—for it was June now. He named that he had also invited his cousin, Miss Pole; so that we might join in a fly, which could be put up at his house.

I expected Miss Matty to jump at this invitation; but, no! Miss Pole and I had the greatest difficulty in persuading her to go. She thought it was improper; and was even half annoyed when we utterly ignored the idea of any impropriety in her going with two other ladies to see her old lover. Then came a more serious difficulty. She did not think Deborah would have liked her to go. This took us half a day's good hard talking to get over; but, at the first sentence of relenting, I seized the opportunity, and wrote and despatched an acceptance in her name—fixing day and hour, that all might be decided and done with.

The next morning she asked me if I would go down to the shop with her; and there, after much hesitation, we chose our three caps to be sent home and tried on, that the most becoming might be selected to take with us on Thursday.

She was in a state of silent agitation all the way to Woodley. She had evidently never been there before; and, although she little dreamt I knew anything of her early story, I could perceive she was in a tremor at the thought of seeing the place which might have been her home, and round which it is probable that many of her innocent girlish imaginations had clustered. It was a long drive there, through paved jolting lanes. Miss Matilda sat bolt upright, and looked wistfully out of the windows as we drew near the end of our journey. The aspect of the country was quiet and pastoral. Woodley stood among fields; and there was an old-fashioned garden where roses and currant-bushes touched each other, and where the feathery asparagus formed a pretty background to the pinks and gilly-flowers; there was no drive up to the door. We got out at a little gate, and walked up a straight box-edged path.

"My cousin might make a drive, I think," said Miss Pole, who was afraid of ear-ache, and had only her cap on.

"I think it is very pretty," said Miss Matty, with a soft plaintiveness in her voice, and almost in a whisper, for just then Mr. Holbrook appeared at the door, rubbing his hands in very effervescence of hospitality. He looked more like my idea of Don Quixote than ever, and yet the likeness was only external. His respectable housekeeper stood modestly at the door to bid us welcome; and, while she led the elder ladies upstairs to a bedroom, I begged to look about the garden. My request evidently pleased the old gentleman, who took me all round the place and showed me his six-and-twenty cows, named after the different letters of the alphabet. As we went along, he surprised me occasionally by repeating apt and beautiful quotations from the poets, ranging easily from Shakespeare and George Herbert to those of our own day. He did this as naturally as if he were thinking aloud, and their true and beautiful words were the best expression he could find for what he was thinking or feeling. To be sure he called Byron "my Lord Byrron," and pronounced the name of Goethe strictly in accordance with the English sound of the letters—"As Goethe says, 'Ye ever-verdant palaces,' " &c. Altogether, I never met with a man, before or since, who had spent so long a life in a secluded and not impressive country, with ever-increasing delight in the daily and yearly change of season and beauty.

When he and I went in, we found that dinner was nearly ready in the kitchen—for so I suppose the room ought to be called, as there were oak dressers and cupboards all round, all over by the side of the fireplace, and only a small Turkey carpet in the middle of the flag-floor. The room might have been easily made into a handsome dark oak dining-parlour by removing the oven and a few other appurtenances of a kitchen, which were evidently never used, the real cooking-place being at some distance. The room in which we were expected to sit was a stiffly-furnished, ugly apartment; but that in which we did sit was what Mr. Holbrook called the counting-house, where he paid his labourers their weekly wages at a great desk near the door. The rest of the pretty sitting-room—looking into the orchard, and all covered over with dancing tree-shadows—was filled with books. They lay on the ground, they covered the walls, they strewed the table. He was evidently half ashamed and half proud of his extravagence in this respect. They were of all kinds—poetry and wild weird tales prevailing. He evidently chose his books in accordance with his own tastes, not because such and such were classical or established favourites.

"Ah!" he said, "we farmers ought not to have much time for reading; yet somehow one can't help it."

"What a pretty room!" said Miss Matty, *sotto voce*.

"What a pleasant place!" said I, aloud, almost simultaneously.

"Nay! if you like it," replied he; "but can you sit on these great, black leather, three-cornered chairs? I like it better than the best parlour; but I thought ladies would take that for the smarter place."

It was the smarter place, but, like most smart things, not at all pretty, or pleasant, or home-like; so, while we were at dinner, the servant-girl dusted and scrubbed the counting-house chairs, and we sat there all the rest of the day.

We had pudding before meat; and I thought Mr. Holbrook was going to make some apology for his old-fashioned ways, for he began—

"I don't know whether you like new-fangled ways."

"Oh, not at all!" said Miss Matty.

"No more do I," said he. "My house-keeper *will* have these in her new fashion; or else I tell her that, when I was a young man, we used to keep strictly to my father's rule, 'No broth, no ball; no ball, no beef'; and always began dinner with broth. Then we had suet puddings, boiled in the broth with the beef: and then the meat itself. If we did not sup our broth, we had no ball, which we liked a deal better; and the beef came last of all, and only those had it who had done justice to the broth and the ball. Now folks begin with sweet things, and turn their dinners topsy-turvy."

When the ducks and green peas came, we looked at each other in dismay; we had only two-pronged, black-handled forks. It is true the steel was as bright as silver; but what were we to do? Miss Matty picked up her peas, one by one, on the point of the prongs, much as Aminé ate her grains of rice after her previous feast with the Ghoul. Miss Pole sighed over her delicate young peas as she left them on one side of her plate untasted, for they *would* drop between the prongs. I looked at my host: the peas were going wholesale into his capacious mouth, shovelled up by his large round-ended knife. I saw, I imitated, I survived! My friends, in spite of my precedent, could not muster up courage enough to do an ungenteel thing; and, if Mr. Holbrook had not been so heartily hungry, he would probably have seen that the good peas went away almost untouched.

After dinner, a clay pipe was brought in, and a spittoon; and, asking us to retire to another room, where he would soon join us, if we disliked tobacco-smoke, he presented his pipe to Miss Matty, and requested her to fill the bowl. This was a compliment to a lady in his youth; but it was rather inappropriate to propose it as an honour to Miss Matty, who had been trained by her sister to hold smoking of every kind in utter abhorrence. But if it was a shock to her refinement, it was also a gratification to her feelings to be thus selected; so she daintily stuffed the strong tobacco into the pipe, and then we withdrew.

"It is very pleasant dining with a bachelor," said Miss Matty softly, as we settled ourselves in the counting-house. "I only hope it is not improper; so many pleasant things are!"

"What a number of books he has!" said Miss Pole, looking round the room. "And how dusty they are!"

"I think it must be like one of the great Dr. Johnson's rooms," said Miss Matty. "What a superior man your cousin must be!"

"Yes!" said Miss Pole, "he's a great reader; but I am afraid he has got into very uncouth habits with living alone."

"Oh! uncouth is too hard a word. I should call him eccentric; very clever people always are!" replied Miss Matty.

When Mr. Holbrook returned, he proposed a walk in the fields; but the two elder ladies were afraid of damp, and dirt, and had only very unbecoming calashes to put on over their caps; so they declined, and I was again his companion in a turn which he said he was obliged to take to see after his men. He strode along, either wholly forgetting my existence, or soothed into silence by his pipe—and yet it was not silence exactly. He walked before me with a stooping gait, his hands clasped behind him; and, as some tree or cloud, or glimpse of distant upland pastures, struck him, he quoted poetry to himself, saying it out loud in a grand sonorous voice, with just the emphasis that true feeling and appreciation give. We came upon an old cedar tree, which stood at one end of the house—

"The cedar spreads his dark-green layers of shade."

"Capital term—'layers'! Wonderful man!" I did not know whether he was speaking to me or not; but I put in an assenting "wonderful," although I knew nothing about it, just because I was tired of being forgotten, and of being consequently silent.

He turned sharp round. "Ay! you may say 'wonderful.' Why, when I saw the review of his poems in *Blackwood,* I set off within an hour, and walked seven miles to Misselton (for the horses were not in the way) and ordered them. Now, what colour are ash-buds in March?"

Is the man going mad? thought I. He is very like Don Quixote.

"What colour are they, I say?" repeated he vehemently.

"I am sure I don't know, sir," said I, with the meekness of ignorance.

"I knew you didn't. No more did I—an old fool that I am!—till this young man comes and tells me. Black as ash-buds in March. And I've lived all my life in the country; more shame for me not to know. Black: they are jet-black, madam." And he went off again, swinging along to the music of some rhyme he had got hold of.

When we came back, nothing would serve him but he must read us the poems he had been speaking of; and Miss Pole encouraged him in his proposal, I thought, because she wished me to hear his beautiful reading, of which she had boasted; but she afterwards said it was because she had got to a difficult part of her crochet, and wanted to count her stitches without having to talk. Whatever he had proposed would have been right to Miss Matty; although she did fall sound asleep within five minutes after he had begun a long poem, called "Locksley Hall," and had a comfortable nap, unobserved, till he ended; when the cessation of his voice wakened her up, and she said, feeling that something was expected, and that Miss Pole was counting—

"What a pretty book!"

"Pretty, madam! it's beautiful! Pretty, indeed!"

"Oh yes! I meant beautiful!" said she, fluttered at his disapproval of her word. "It is so like that beautiful poem of Dr. Johnson's my sister used to read—I forget the name of it; what was it, my dear?" turning to me.

"Which do you mean, ma'am? What was it about?"

"I don't remember what it was about, and I've quite forgotten what the name of it was; but it was written by Dr. Johnson, and was very beautiful, and very like what Mr. Holbrook has just been reading."

"I don't remember it," said he reflectively. "But I don't know Dr. Johnson's poems well. I must read them."

As we were getting into the fly to return, I heard Mr. Holbrook say he should call on the ladies soon, and inquire how they got home; and this evidently pleased and fluttered Miss Matty at the time he said it; but after we had lost sight of the old house among the trees her sentiments towards the master of it were gradually absorbed into a distressing wonder as to whether Martha had broken her word, and seized on the opportunity of her mistress's absence to have a "follower." Martha looked good, and steady, and composed enough, as she came to help us out; she was always careful of Miss Matty, and to-night she made use of this unlucky speech—

"Eh! dear ma'am, to think of your going out in an evening in such a thin shawl! It's no better than muslin. At your age, ma'am, you should be careful."

"My age!" said Miss Matty, almost speaking crossly, for her, for she was usually gentle—"My age! Why, how old do you think I am, that you talk about my age?"

"Well, ma'am, I should say you were not far short of sixty: but folks' looks is often against them—and I'm sure I meant no harm."

"Martha, I'm not yet fifty-two!" said Miss Matty, with grave emphasis; for probably the remembrance of her youth had come very vividly before her this day, and she was annoyed at finding that golden time so far away in the past.

But she never spoke of any former and more intimate acquaintance with Mr. Holbrook. She had probably met with so little sympathy in her early love, that she had shut it up close in her heart; and it was only by a sort of watching, which I could hardly avoid since Miss Pole's confidence, that I saw how faithful her poor heart had been in its sorrow and its silence.

She gave me some good reason for wearing her best cap every day, and sat near the window, in spite of her rheumatism, in order to see, without being seen, down into the street.

He came. He put his open palms upon his knees, which were far apart, as he sat with his head bent down, whistling, after we had replied to his inquiries about our safe return. Suddenly he jumped up—

"Well, madam! have you any commands for Paris? I am going there in a week or two."

"To Paris!" we both exclaimed.

"Yes, madam! I've never been there, and always had a wish to go; and I think if I don't go soon, I mayn't go at all; so as soon as the hay is got in I shall go, before harvest time."

We were so much astonished that we had no commissions.

Just as he was going out of the room, he turned back, with his favourite exclamation—

"God bless my soul, madam! but I nearly forgot half my errand. Here are the poems for you you admired so much the other evening at my house." He tugged away at a parcel in his coat-pocket. "Good-bye, miss," said he; "good-bye, Matty! take care of yourself." And he was gone. But he had given her a book, and he had called her Matty, just as he used to do thirty years ago.

"I wish he would not go to Paris," said Miss Matilda anxiously. "I don't believe frogs will agree with him; he used to have to be very careful what he ate, which was curious in so strong-looking a young man."

Soon after this I took my leave, giving many an injunction to Martha to look after her mistress, and to let me know if she thought that Miss Matilda was not so well; in which case I would volunteer a visit to my old friend, without noticing Martha's intelligence to her.

Accordingly I received a line or two from Martha every now and then; and, about November, I had a note to say her mistress was "very low and sadly off her food"; and the account made me so uneasy that, although Martha did not decidedly summon me, I packed up my things and went.

I received a warm welcome, in spite of the little flurry produced by my impromptu visit, for I had only been able to give a day's notice. Miss Matilda looked miserably ill; and I prepared to comfort and cosset her.

I went down to have a private talk with Martha.

"How long has your mistress been so poorly?" I asked, as I stood by the kitchen fire.

"Well! I think it's better than a fortnight; it is, I know; it was one Tuesday, after Miss Pole had been, that she went into this moping way. I thought she was tired, and it would go off with a night's rest; but no! she has gone on and on ever since, till I thought it my duty to write to you, ma'am."

"You did quite right, Martha. It is a comfort to think she has so faithful a servant about her. And I hope you find your place comfortable?"

"Well, ma'am, missus is very kind, and there's plenty to eat and drink, and no more work but what I can do easily—but——" Martha hesitated.

"But what, Martha?"

"Why, it seems so hard of missus not to let me have any followers; there's such lots of young fellows in the town; and many a one has as much as offered to keep company with me; and I may never be in such a likely place again, and it's like wasting an opportunity. Many a girl as I know would have 'em unbeknownst to missus; but I've given my word, and I'll stick to it; or else this is just the house for missus never to be the wiser if they did come: and it's such a capable kitchen—there's such dark corners in it—I'd be bound to hide any one. I counted up last Sunday night—for I'll not deny I was crying because I had to shut the door in Jem Hearn's face, and he's a steady young man, fit for any girl; only I had given missus my word." Martha was all but crying again; and I had little comfort to give her, for I knew, from old experience, of the horror with which both the Miss Jenkynses looked upon "followers"; and in Miss Matty's present nervous state this dread was not likely to be lessened.

I went to see Miss Pole the next day, and took her completely by surprise, for she had not been to see Miss Matilda for two days.

"And now I must go back with you, my dear, for I promised to let her know how Thomas Holbrook went on; and, I'm sorry to say, his housekeeper has sent me word to-day that he hasn't long to live. Poor Thomas! that journey to Paris was quite too much for him. His housekeeper says he has hardly ever been round his fields since, but just sits with his hands on his knees in the counting-house, not reading or anything, but only saying what a wonderful city Paris was! Paris has much to answer for if it's killed my cousin Thomas, for a better man never lived."

"Does Miss Matilda know of his illness?" asked I—a new light as to the cause of her indisposition dawning upon me.

"Dear! to be sure, yes! Has not she told you? I let her know a fortnight ago, or more, when first I heard of it. How odd she shouldn't have told you!"

Not at all, I thought; but I did not say anything. I felt almost guilty of having spied too curiously into that tender heart, and I was not going to speak of its secrets—hidden, Miss Matty believed, from all the world. I ushered Miss Pole into Miss Matilda's little drawing-room, and then left them alone. But I was not surprised when Martha came to my bedroom door, to ask me to go down to dinner alone, for that missus had one of her bad headaches. She came into the drawing-room at tea-time, but it was evidently an effort to her; and, as if to make up for some reproachful feeling against her late sister, Miss Jenkyns, which had been troubling her all the afternoon, and for which she now felt penitent she kept telling me how good and how clever Deborah was in her youth; how she used to settle what gowns they were to wear at all the parties (faint, ghostly ideas of grim parties, far away in the distance, when Miss Matty and Miss Pole were young!); and how Deborah and her mother had started the benefit society for the poor, and taught girls cooking and plain sewing; and how Deborah had once danced with a lord; and how she used to visit at Sir Peter Arley's and tried to remodel the quiet rectory establishment on the plans of Arley Hall, where they kept thirty servants; and how she had nursed Miss Matty through a long, long illness, of which I had never heard before, but which I now dated in my own mind as following the dismissal of the suit of Mr. Holbrook. So we talked softly and quietly of old times through the long November evening.

The next day Miss Pole brought us word that Mr. Holbrook was dead. Miss Matty heard the news in silence; in fact, from the account of the previous day, it was only what we had to expect. Miss Pole kept calling upon us for some expression of regret, by asking if it was not sad that he was gone, and saying—

"To think of that pleasant day last June, when he seemed so well! And he might have lived this dozen years if he had not gone to that wicked Paris, where they are always having revolutions."

She paused for some demonstration on our part. I saw Miss Matty could not speak, she was trembling so nervously; so I said what I really felt; and after a call of some duration—all the time of which I have no doubt Miss Pole thought Miss Matty received the news very calmly—our visitor took her leave.

Miss Matty made a strong effort to conceal her feelings—a concealment she practised even with me, for she has never alluded to Mr. Holbrook again, although the book he gave her lies with her Bible on the little table by her bedside. She did not think I heard her when she asked the little milliner of Cranford to make her caps something like the Honourable Mrs. Jamieson's, or that I noticed the reply—

"But she wears widows' caps, ma'am!"

"Oh! I only meant something in that style; not widows', of course, but rather like Mrs. Jamieson's."

This effort at concealment was the beginning of the tremulous motion of head and hands which I have seen ever since in Miss Matty.

The evening of the day on which we heard of Mr. Holbrook's death, Miss Matilda was very silent and thoughtful; after prayers she called Martha back and then she stood uncertain what to say.

"Martha!" she said, at last, "you are young——" and then she made so long a pause that Martha, to remind her of her half-finished sentence, dropped a curtsey, and said—

"Yes, please, ma'am; two-and-twenty last third of October, please, ma'am."

"And, perhaps, Martha, you may some time meet with a young man you like, and who likes you. I did say you were not to have followers; but if you meet with such a young man, and tell me, and I find he is respectable, I have no objection to his coming to see you once a week. God forbid!" said she in a low voice, "that I should grieve any young hearts." She spoke as if she were providing for some distant contingency, and was rather startled when Martha made her ready eager answer—

"Please, ma'am, there's Jem Hearn, and he's a joiner making three-and-sixpence a-day, and six foot one in his stocking-feet, please, ma'am; and if you'll ask about him to-morrow morning, every one will give him a character for steadiness; and he'll be glad enough to come to-morrow night, I'll be bound."

Though Miss Matty was startled, she submitted to Fate and Love.

Poor Peter

After the death of Mr. Holbrook, Miss Matty, feeling that she might be about to die, set about destroying the family letters—her mother's and father's, then her sister's. Finally she came to those of Peter Jenkyns, her brother, and recalled his career, first at Shrewsbury School, and then subsequently, as here recounted.

Poor Peter's career lay before him rather pleasantly mapped out by kind friends, but *Bonus Bernardus non videt omnia,* in this map too.

He was to win honours at the Shrewsbury School, and carry them thick to Cambridge, and after that, a living awaited him, the gift of his godfather, Sir Peter Arley. Poor Peter! his lot in life was very different to what his friends had hoped and planned. Miss Matty told me all about it, and I think it was a relief when she had done so.

He was the darling of his mother, who seemed to dote on all her children, though she was, perhaps, a little afraid of Deborah's superior acquirements. Deborah was the favourite of her father, and when Peter disappointed him, she became his pride. The sole honour Peter brought away from Shrewsbury was the reputation of being the best good fellow that ever was, and of being the captain of the school in the art of practical joking. His father was disappointed, but set about remedying the matter in a manly way. He could not afford to send Peter to read with any tutor, but he could read with him himself; and Miss Matty told me much of the awful preparations in the way of dictionaries and lexicons that were made in her father's study the morning Peter began.

"My poor mother!" said she. "I remember how she used to stand in the hall, just near enough the study-door, to catch the tone of my father's voice. I could tell in a moment if all was going right, by her face. And it did go right for a long time."

"What went wrong at last?" said I. "That tiresome Latin, I dare say."

"No! it was not the Latin. Peter was in high favour with my father, for he worked up well for him. But he seemed to think that the Cranford people might be joked about, and made fun of, and they did not like it; nobody does. He was always hoaxing them; 'hoaxing' is not a pretty word, my dear, and I hope you won't tell your father I used it, for I should not like him to think that I was not choice in my language, after living with such a woman as Deborah. And be sure you never use it yourself. I don't know how it slipped out of my mouth, except it was that I was thinking of poor Peter and it was always his expression. But he was a very gentlemanly boy in many things. He was like dear Captain Brown in always being ready to help any old person or a child. Still, he did like joking and making fun; and he seemed to think the old ladies in Cranford would believe anything. There were many old ladies living here then; we are principally ladies now, I know, but we are not so old as the ladies used to be when I was a girl. I could laugh to think of some of Peter's jokes. No, my dear, I won't tell you of them, because they might not shock you as they ought to do, and they were very shocking. He even took in my father once, by dressing himself up as a lady that was passing through the town and wished to see the Rector of Cranford, 'who had published that admirable Assize Sermon.' Peter said he was awfully frightened himself when he saw how my father took it all in, and even offered to copy out all his Napoleon Buonaparte sermons for her—him, I mean—no, her, for Peter was a lady then. He told me he was more terrified than he ever was before, all the time my father was speaking. He did not think my father would have believed him; and yet if he had not, it would have been a sad thing for Peter. As it was, he was none so glad of it, for my father kept him hard at work copying out all those twelve Buonaparte sermons for the lady—that was for Peter himself, you know. He was the lady. And once when he wanted to go fishing, Peter said, 'Confound the woman!'—very bad language, my dear, but Peter was not always so guarded as he should have been; my father was so angry with him, it nearly frightened me out of my wits: and yet I could hardly keep from laughing at the little curtseys Peter kept making, quite slyly, whenever my father spoke of the lady's excellent taste and sound discrimination."

"Did Miss Jenkyns know of these tricks?" said I.

"Oh, no! Deborah would have been too much shocked. No, no one knew but me. I wish I had always known of Peter's plans; but sometimes he did not tell me. He used to say the old ladies in the town wanted something to talk about; but I don't think they did. They had the *St. James's Chronicle* three times a week, just as we have now, and we have plenty to say; and I remember the clacking noise there always was when some of the ladies got together. But, probably, schoolboys talk more than ladies. At last there was a terrible, sad thing happened." Miss Matty got up, went to the door, and opened it; no one was there. She rang the bell for Martha, and when Martha came, her mistress told her to go for eggs to a farm at the other end of the town.

"I will lock the door after you, Martha. You are not afraid to go, are you?"

"No, ma'am, not at all; Jem Hearn will be only too proud to go with me."

Miss Matty drew herself up, and as soon as we were alone, she wished that Martha had more maidenly reserve.

"We'll put out the candle, my dear. We can talk just as well by firelight, you know. There! Well, you see, Deborah had gone from home for a fortnight or so; it was a very still, quiet day, I remember, overhead; and the lilacs were all in flower, so I suppose it was spring. My father had gone out to see some sick people in the parish; I recollect seeing him leave the house with his wig and shovel-hat and cane. What possessed our poor Peter I don't know; he had the sweetest temper, and yet he always seemed to like to plague Deborah. She never laughed at his jokes, and thought him ungenteel, and not careful enough about improving his mind; and that vexed him.

"Well! he went to her room, it seems, and dressed himself in her old gown, and shawl, and bonnet; just the things she used to wear in Cranford, and was known by everywhere; and he made the pillow into a little—you are sure you locked the door, my dear, for I should not like anyone to hear—into—into a little baby, with white long clothes. It was only, as he told me afterwards, to make something to talk about in the town; he never thought of it as affecting Deborah. And he went and walked up and down in the Filbert walk—just half-hidden by the rails, and half-seen; and he cuddled his pillow, just like a baby, and talked to it all the nonsense people do. Oh dear! and my father came stepping stately up the street, as he always did; and what should he see but a little black crowd of people—I daresay as many as twenty—all peeping through his garden rails. So he thought, at first, they were only looking at a new rhododendron that was in full bloom, and that he was very proud of; and he walked slower, that they might have more time to admire. And he wondered if he could make out a sermon from the occasion, and thought, perhaps, there was some relation between the rhododendrons and the lilies of the field. My poor father! When he came nearer, he began to wonder that they did not see him; but their heads were all so close together, peeping and peeping! My father was amongst them, meaning, he said, to ask them to walk into the garden with him, and admire the beautiful vegetable production, when—oh, my dear, I tremble to think of it—he looked through the rails himself, and saw—I don't know what he thought he saw, but old Clare told me his face went quite grey-white with anger, and his eyes blazed out under his frowning black brows; and he spoke out—oh, so terribly!—and bade them all stop where they were—not one of them to go, not one of them to stir a step; and, swift as light, he was in at the garden door, and down the Filbert walk, and seized hold of poor Peter, and tore his clothes off his back—bonnet, shawl, gown, and all—and threw the pillow among the people over the railings: and then he was very, very angry indeed, and before all the people he lifted up his cane and flogged Peter!

"My dear, that boy's trick, on that sunny day, when all seemed going straight and well, broke my mother's heart, and changed my father for life. It did, indeed. Old Clare said, Peter looked as white as my father; and stood as still as a statue to be flogged; and my father struck hard! When my father stopped to take breath, Peter said, 'Have you done enough, sir?' quite hoarsely, and still standing quite quiet. I don't know what my father said—or if he said anything. But old Clare said, Peter turned to where the people outside the railing were, and made them a low bow, as grand and as grave as any gentleman; and then walked slowly into the house. I was in the store-room helping my mother to make cowslip wine. I cannot abide the wine now, nor the scent of the flowers; they turn me sick and faint, as they did that day, when Peter came in, looking as haughty as any man—indeed, looking like a man, not like a boy. 'Mother!' he said, 'I am come to say, God bless you for ever.' I saw his lips quiver as he spoke; and I think he durst not say anything more loving, for the purpose that was in his heart. She looked at him rather frightened, and wondering, and asked him what was to do. He did not smile or speak, but put his arms round her and kissed her as if he did not know how to leave off; and before she could speak again, he was gone. We talked it over, and could not understand it, and she bade me go and seek my father, and ask what it was all about. I found him walking up and down, looking very highly displeased.

"'Tell your mother I have flogged Peter, and that he richly deserved it.'

"I durst not ask any more questions. When I told my mother, she sat down, quite faint, for a minute. I remember, a few days after, I saw the poor, withered cowslip flowers thrown out to the leaf heap, to decay and die there. There was no making of cowslip wine that year at the rectory—nor, indeed, ever after.

"Presently my mother went to my father. I know I thought of Queen Esther and King Ahasuerus; for my mother was very pretty and delicate-looking, and my father looked as terrible as King Ahasuerus. Some time after they came out together; and then my mother told me what had happened, and that she was going up to Peter's room at my father's desire—though she was not to tell Peter this—to talk the matter over with him. But no Peter was there. We looked over the house; no Peter was there! Even my father, who had not liked to join in the search at first, helped us before long. The rectory was a very old house—steps up into a room, steps down into a room, all through. At first, my mother went calling low and soft, as if to reassure the poor boy, 'Peter! Peter, dear! it's only me;' but, by-and-by, as the servants came back from the errands my father had sent them, in different directions, to find where Peter was—as we found he was not in the garden, nor the hayloft, nor anywhere about—my mother's cry grew louder and wilder, 'Peter! Peter, my darling! where are you?' for then she felt and understood that that long kiss meant some sad kind of 'good-bye.' The afternoon went on—my mother never resting, but seeking again and again in every possible place that had been looked into twenty times before, nay, that she had looked into over and over again herself. My father sat with his head in his hands, not speaking except when his messengers came in, bringing no tidings; then he lifted up his face, so strong and sad, and told them to go again in some new direction. My mother kept passing from room to room, in and out of the house, moving noiselessly, but never ceasing. Neither she nor my father durst leave the house, which was the meeting-place for all the messengers. At last (and it was nearly dark), my father rose up. He took hold of my mother's arm as she came with wild, sad pace through one door, and quickly towards another. She started at the touch of his hand, for she had forgotten all in the world but Peter.

"'Molly!' said he, 'I did not think all this would happen.' He looked into her face for comfort—her poor face all wild and white; for neither she nor my father had dared to acknowledge—much less act upon—the terror that was in their hearts, lest Peter should have made away with himself. My father saw no conscious look in his wife's hot, dreary eyes, and he missed the sympathy that she had always been ready to give him—strong man as he was, and at the dumb despair in her face his tears began to flow. But when she saw this, a gentle sorrow came over her countenance, and she said, 'Dearest John! don't cry; come with me, and we'll find him,' almost as cheerfully as if she knew where he was. And she took my father's great hand in her little soft one, and led him along, the tears dropping as he walked on that same unceasing, weary walk, from room to room, through house and garden.

"Oh, how I wished for Deborah! I had no time for crying, for now all seemed to depend on me. I wrote for Deborah to come home. I sent a message privately to that same Mr. Holbrook's house—poor Mr. Holbrook;—you know who I mean. I don't mean I sent a message to him, but I sent one that I could trust to know if Peter was at his house. For at one time Mr. Holbrook was an occasional visitor at the rectory—you know he was Miss Pole's cousin—and he had been very kind to Peter, and taught him how to fish—he was very kind to everybody, and I thought Peter might have gone off there. But Mr. Holbrook was from home, and Peter had never been seen. It was night now; but the doors were all wide open, and my father and mother walked on and on; it was more than an hour since he had joined her, and I don't believe they had ever spoken all that time. I was getting the parlour fire lighted, and one of the servants was preparing tea, for I wanted them to have something to eat and drink and warm them, when old Clare asked to speak to me.

"'I have borrowed the nets from the weir, Miss Matty. Shall we drag the ponds to-night, or wait for the morning?'

"I remember staring in his face to gather his meaning; and when I did, I laughed out loud. The horror of that new thought—our bright, darling Peter, cold, and stark, and dead! I remember the ring of my own laugh now.

"The next day Deborah was at home before I was myself again. She would not have been so weak as to give way as I had done; but my screams (my horrible laughter had ended in crying) had roused my sweet dear mother, whose poor wandering wits were called back and collected as soon as a child needed her care. She and Deborah sat by my bedside; I knew by the looks of each that there had been no news of Peter—no awful, ghastly news, which was what I most had dreaded in my dull state between sleeping and waking.

"The same result of all the searching had brought something of the same relief to my mother, to whom, I am sure, the thought that Peter might even then be hanging dead in some of the familiar home places had caused that never-ending walk of yesterday. Her soft eyes never were the same again after that; they had always a restless, craving look, as if seeking for what they could not find. Oh! it was an awful time; coming down like a thunder-bolt on the still sunny day when the lilacs were all in bloom."

"Where was Mr. Peter?" said I.

"He had made his way to Liverpool; and there was war then; and some of the king's ships lay off the mouth of the Mersey; and they were only too glad to have a fine likely boy such as him (five foot nine he was), come to offer himself. The captain wrote to my father, and Peter wrote to my mother. Stay! those letters will be somewhere here."

We lighted the candle, and found the captain's letter and Peter's too. And we also found a little simple begging letter from Mrs. Jenkyns to Peter, addressed to him at the house of an old schoolfellow, whither she fancied he might have gone. They had returned it unopened; and unopened it had remained ever since, having been inadvertently put by among the other letters of that time. This is it:—

"My dearest Peter,—You did not think we should be so sorry as we are, I know, or you would never have gone away. You are too good. Your father sits and sighs till my heart aches to hear him. He cannot hold up his head for grief; and yet he only did what he thought was right. Perhaps he has been too severe, and perhaps I have not been kind enough; but God knows how we love you, my dear only boy. Don looks so sorry you are gone. Come back, and make us happy, who love you so much. I *know* you will come back."

But Peter did not come back. That spring day was the last time he ever saw his mother's face. The writer of the letter—the last—the only person who had ever seen what was written in it, was dead long ago; and I, a stranger, not born at the time when this occurrence took place, was the one to open it.

The captain's letter summoned the father and mother to Liverpool instantly, if they wished to see their boy; and, by some of the wild chances of life, the captain's letter had been detained somewhere, somehow.

Miss Matty went on, "And it was racetime, and all the post-horses at Cranford were gone to the races; but my father and mother set off in our own gig—and oh! my dear, they were too late—the ship was gone! And now read Peter's letter to my mother!"

It was full of love, and sorrow, and pride in his new profession, and a sore sense of his disgrace in the eyes of the people at Cranford; but ending with a passionate entreaty that she would come and see him before he left the Mersey: "Mother; we may go into battle. I hope we shall, and lick those French: but I must see you again before that time."

"And she was too late," said Miss Matty; "too late!"

We sat in silence, pondering on the full meaning of those sad, sad words. At length I asked Miss Matty to tell me how her mother bore it.

"Oh!" she said, "she was patience itself. She had never been strong, and this weakened her terribly. My father used to sit looking at her: far more sad than she was. He seemed as if he could look at nothing else when she was by; and he was so humble—so very gentle now. He would, perhaps, speak in his old way—laying down the law, as it were—and then, in a minute or two, he would come round and put his hand on our shoulders, and ask us in a low voice, if he had said anything to hurt us. I did not wonder at his speaking so to Deborah, for she was so clever; but I could not bear to hear him talking so to me.

"But, you see, he saw what we did not—that it was killing my mother. Yes! killing her (put out the candle, my dear; I can talk better in the dark), for she was but a frail woman, and ill-fitted to stand the fright and shock she had gone through; and she would smile at him and comfort him, not in words, but in her looks and tones, which were always cheerful when he was there. And she would speak of how she thought Peter stood a good chance of being admiral very soon—he was so brave and clever; and how she thought of seeing him in his navy uniform, and what sort of hats admirals wore; and how much more fit he was to be a sailor than a clergyman; and all in that way, just to make my father think she was quite glad of what came of that unlucky morning's work, and the flogging which was always in his mind, as we all knew. But oh, my dear! the bitter, bitter crying she had when she was alone; and at last, as she grew weaker, she could not keep her tears in when Deborah or me was by, and would give us message after message for Peter (his ship had gone to the Mediterranean, or somewhere down there, and then he was ordered off to India, and there was no overland route then); but she still said that no one knew where their death lay in wait, and that we were not to think hers was near. We did not think it, but we knew it, as we saw her fading away.

"Well, my dear, it's very foolish of me, I know, when in all likelihood I am so near seeing her again.

"And only think, love! the very day after her death—for she did not live quite a twelvemonth after Peter went away—the very day after—came a parcel for her from India—from her poor boy. It was a large, soft, white Indian shawl, with just a little narrow border all round; just what my mother would have liked.

"We thought it might rouse my father, for he had sat with her hand in his all night long; so Deborah took it in to him, and Peter's letter to her, and all. At first, he took no notice; and we tried to make a kind of light careless talk about the shawl, opening it out and admiring it. Then, suddenly, he got up, and spoke: 'She shall be buried in it,' he said; 'Peter shall have that comfort; and she would have liked it.'

"Well, perhaps it was not reasonable, but what could we do or say? One gives people in grief their own way. He took it up and felt it: 'It is just such a shawl as she wished for when she was married, and her mother did not give it her. I did not know of it till after, or she should have had it—she should; but she shall have it now.'

"My mother looked so lovely in her death! She was always pretty, and now she looked fair, and waxen, and young—younger than Deborah, as she stood trembling and shivering by her. We decked her in the long soft folds; she lay smiling, as if pleased; and people came—all Cranford came—to beg to see her, for they had loved her dearly, as well they might; and the countrywomen brought posies; old Clare's wife brought some white violets and begged they might lie on her breast.

"Deborah said to me, the day of my mother's funeral, that if she had a hundred offers she never would marry and leave my father. It was not very likely she would have so many—I don't know that she had one; but it was not less to her credit to say so. She was such a daughter to my father as I think there never was before or since. His eyes failed him, and she read book after book, and wrote, and copied, and was always at his service in any parish business. She could do many more things than my poor mother could; she even once wrote a letter to the bishop for my father. But he missed my mother sorely; the whole parish noticed it. Not that he was less active; I think he was more so, and more patient in helping every one. I did all I could to set Deborah at liberty to be with him; for I knew I was good for little, and that my best work in the world was to do odd jobs quietly, and set others at liberty. But my father was a changed man."

"Did Mr. Peter ever come home?"

"Yes, once. He came home a lieutenant; he did not get to be admiral. And he and my father were such friends! My father took him into every house in the parish, he was so proud of him. He never walked out without Peter's arm to lean upon. Deborah used to smile (I don't think we ever laughed again after my mother's death), and say she was quite put in a corner. Not but what my father always wanted her when there was letter-writing or reading to be done, or anything to be settled."

"And then?" said I, after a pause.

"Then Peter went to sea again; and, by-and-by, my father died, blessing us both, and thanking Deborah for all she had been to him; and, of course, our circumstances were changed; and, instead of living at the rectory, and keeping three maids and a man, we had to come to this small house, and be content with a servant-of-all-work; but, as Deborah used to say, we have always lived genteelly, even if circumstances have compelled us to simplicity. Poor Deborah!"

"And Mr. Peter?" asked I.

"Oh, there was some great war in India—I forget what they call it—and we have never heard of Peter since then. I believe he is dead myself; and it sometimes fidgets me that we have never put on mourning for him. And then again, when I sit by myself, and all the house is still, I think I hear his step coming up the street, and my heart begins to flutter and beat; but the sound always goes past—and Peter never comes.

"That's Martha back? No! *I'll* go, my dear; I can always find my way in the dark, you know. And a blow of fresh air at the door will do my head good, and it's rather got a trick of aching."

So she pattered off. I had lighted the candle, to give the room a cheerful appearance against her return.

"Was it Martha?" asked I.

"Yes. And I am rather uncomfortable, for I heard such a strange noise, just as I was opening the door."

"Where?" I asked, for her eyes were round with affright.

"In the street—just outside—it sounded like——"

"Talking?" I put in, as she hesitated a little.

"No! kissing——"

A Happy Return

In the failure of the Town and County Bank, Miss Matty lost her tiny fortune. With the aid of the ladies of Cranford, Mr. Smith, as Miss Matty's financial adviser, has managed to establish Miss Matty independently in her old home, selling tea. She lived on there, lodging with her former maid, Martha, now married to Jem Hearn. Among the great events in Cranford was reckoned the engagement of Mr. Hoggins, the doctor, to a charming Scotch widow, Lady Glenmire, who had come to Cranford to stay with her sister-in-law, the high and mighty Mrs. Jamieson. Mrs. Jamieson, herself the widow of a Baron's son, at first felt personally affronted at Lady Glenmire's defection from the ranks of the aristocracy. Another occurrence, of more consequence to the story, was the chance discovery by Mr. Smith's daughter that Poor Peter may still be alive in India. She wrote to him an account of Miss Matty's plight.

MARTHA was beginning to go about again, and I had already fixed a limit, not very far distant, to my visit, when one afternoon, as I was sitting in the shop-parlour with Miss Matty—I remember the weather was colder now than it had been in May, three weeks before, and we had a fire and kept the door fully closed—we saw a gentleman go slowly past the window, and then stand opposite to the door, as if looking out for the name which we had so carefully hidden. He took out a double eyeglass and peered about for some time before he could discover it. Then he came in. And, all on a sudden, it flashed across me that it was the Aga himself! For his clothes had an out-of-the-way foreign cut about them, and his face was deep brown, as if tanned and retanned by the sun. His complexion contrasted oddly with his plentiful snow-white hair, his eyes were dark and piercing, and he had an odd way of contracting them and puckering up his cheeks into innumerable wrinkles when he looked earnestly at objects. He did so to Miss Matty when he first came in. His glance had first caught and lingered a little upon me, but then turned, with the peculiar searching look I have described, to Miss Matty. She was a little fluttered and nervous, but no more so than she always was when any man came into her shop. She thought that he would probably have a note, or a sovereign at least, for which she would have to give change, which was an operation she very much disliked to perform. But the present customer stood opposite to her, without asking for anything, only looking fixedly at her as he drummed upon the table with his fingers, just for all the world as Miss Jenkyns used to do. Miss Matty was on the point of asking him what he wanted (as she told me afterwards), when he turned sharp to me: "Is your name Mary Smith?"

"Yes!" said I.

All my doubts as to his identity were set at rest, and I only wondered what he would say or do next, and how Miss Matty would stand the joyful shock of what he had to reveal. Apparently he was at a loss how to announce himself, for he looked round at last in search of something to buy, so as to gain time, and, as it happened, his eye caught on the almond-comfits, and he boldly asked for a pound of "those things." I doubt if Miss Matty had a whole pound in the shop, and, besides the unusual magnitude of the order, she was distressed with the idea of the indigestion they would produce, taken in such unlimited quantities. She looked up to remonstrate. Something of tender relaxation in his face struck home to her heart. She said, "It is—oh, sir! can you be Peter?" and trembled from head to foot. In a moment he was round the table and had her in his arms, sobbing the tearless cries of old age. I brought her a glass of wine, for indeed her colour had changed so as to alarm me and Mr. Peter too. He kept saying, "I have been too sudden for you, Matty—I have, my little girl."

I proposed that she should go at once up into the drawing-room and lie down on the sofa there. She looked wistfully at her brother, whose hand she had held tight, even when nearly fainting; but on his assuring her that he would not leave her, she allowed him to carry her upstairs.

I thought that the best I could do was to run and put the kettle on the fire for early tea, and then to attend to the shop, leaving the brother and sister to exchange some of the many thousand things they must have to say. I had also to break the news to Martha, who received it with a burst of tears which nearly infected me. She kept recovering herself to ask if I was sure it was indeed Miss Matty's brother, for I had mentioned that he had grey hair, and she had always heard that he was a very handsome young man. Something of the same kind perplexed Miss Matty at tea-time, when she was installed in the great easy chair opposite to Mr. Jenkyns in order to gaze her fill. She could hardly drink for looking at him, and as for eating, that was out of the question.

"I suppose hot climates age people very quickly," said she, almost to herself. "When you left Cranford you had not a grey hair in your head."

"But how many years ago is that?" said Mr. Peter, smiling.

"Ah, true! yes, I suppose you and I are getting old. But still I did not think we were so very old! But white hair is very becoming to you, Peter," she continued—a little afraid lest she had hurt him by revealing how his appearance had impressed her.

"I suppose I forget dates too, Matty, for what do you think I have brought for you from India? I have an Indian muslin gown and a pearl necklace for you somewhere in my chest at Portsmouth." He smiled as if amused at the idea of the incongruity of his presents with the appearance of his sister; but this did not strike her all at once, while the elegance of the articles did. I could see that for a moment her imagination dwelt complacently on the idea of herself thus attired; and instinctively she put her hand up to her throat—that little delicate throat which (as Miss Pole had told me) had been one of her youthful charms; but the hand met the touch of folds of soft muslin in which she was always swathed up to her chin, and the sensation recalled a sense of the unsuitableness of a pearl necklace to her age. She said, "I'm afraid I'm too old; but it was very kind of you to think of it. They are just what I should have liked years ago—when I was young."

"So I thought, my little Matty. I remembered your tastes; they were so like my dear mother's." At the mention of that name the brother and sister clasped each other's hands yet more fondly, and, although they were perfectly silent, I fancied they might have something to say if they were unchecked by my presence, and I got up to arrange my room for Mr. Peter's occupation that night, intending myself to share Miss Matty's bed. But at my movement, he started up. "I must go and settle about a room at the 'George.' My carpet-bag is there too."

"No!" said Miss Matty, in great distress—"you must not go; please, dear Peter—pray, Mary—oh! you must not go!"

She was so much agitated that we both promised everything she wished. Peter sat down again and gave her his hand, which for better security she held in both of hers, and I left the room to accomplish my arrangements.

Long, long into the night, far, far into the morning, did Miss Matty and I talk. She had much to tell me of her brother's life and adventures, which he had communicated to her as they had sat alone. She said all was thoroughly clear to her; but I never quite understood the whole story; and when in after days I lost my awe of Mr. Peter enough to question him myself, he laughed at my curiosity, and told me stories that sounded so very much like Baron Munchausen's, that I was sure he was making fun of me. What I heard from Miss Matty was that he had been a volunteer at the siege of Rangoon; had been taken prisoner by the Burmese; and somehow obtained favour and eventual freedom from knowing how to bleed the chief of the small tribe in some case of dangerous illness; that on his release from years of captivity he had had his letters returned from England with the ominous word "Dead" marked upon them; and, believing himself to be the last of his race, he had settled down as an indigo planter, and had proposed to spend the remainder of his life in the country to whose inhabitants and modes of life he had become habituated, when my letter had reached him; and, with the odd vehemence which characterised him in age as it had done in youth, he had sold his land and all his possessions to the first purchaser, and come home to the poor old sister, who was more glad and rich than any princess when she looked at him. She talked me to sleep at last, and then I was awakened by a slight sound at the door, for which she begged my pardon as she crept penitently into bed; but it seems that when I could no longer confirm her belief that the long-lost was really here—under the same roof—she had begun to fear lest it was only a waking dream of hers; that there never had been a Peter sitting by her all that blessed evening—but that the real Peter lay dead far away beneath some wild sea-wave, or under some strange eastern tree. And so strong had this nervous feeling of hers become, that she was fain to get up and go and convince herself that he was really there by listening through the door to his even, regular breathing—I don't like to call it snoring, but I heard it myself through two closed doors—and by-and-by it soothed Miss Matty to sleep.

I don't believe Mr. Peter came home from India as rich as a nabob; he even considered himself poor, but neither he nor Miss Matty cared much about that. At any rate, he had enough to live upon "very genteelly" at Cranford; he and Miss Matty together. And a day or two after his arrival, the shop was closed, while troops of little urchins gleefully awaited the shower of comfits and lozenges that came from time to time down upon their faces as they stood up-gazing at Miss Matty's drawing-room windows. Occasionally Miss Matty would say to them (half-hidden behind the curtains), "My dear children, don't make yourselves ill;" but a strong arm pulled her back, and a more rattling shower than ever succeeded. A part of the tea was sent in presents to the Cranford ladies; and some of it was distributed among the old people who remembered Mr. Peter in the days of his frolicsome youth. The Indian muslin gown was reserved for darling Flora Gordon (Miss Jessie

Brown's daughter). The Gordons had been on the Continent for the last few years, but were now expected to return very soon; and Miss Matty, in her sisterly pride, anticipated great delight in the joy of showing them Mr. Peter. The pearl necklace disappeared; and about that time many handsome and useful presents made their appearance in the households of Miss Pole and Mrs. Forrester; and some rare and delicate Indian ornaments graced the drawing-rooms of Mrs. Jamieson and Mrs. Fitz-Adam. I myself was not forgotten. Among other things, I had the handsomest-bound and best edition of Dr. Johnson's works that could be procured; and dear Miss Matty, with tears in her eyes, begged me to consider it as a present from her sister as well as herself. In short, no one was forgotten; and, what was more, every one, however insignificant, who had shown kindness to Miss Matty at any time, was sure of Mr. Peter's cordial regard.

WILLIAM MAKEPEACE THACKERAY (1811-1863)

The Ballad of Bouillabaisse

A STREET there is in Paris famous,
For which no rhyme our language yields,
Rue Neuve des Petits Champs its name is—
The New Street of the Little Fields.
And here's an inn, not rich and splendid,
But still in comfortable case;
The which in youth I oft attended,
To eat a bowl of Bouillabaisse.

This Bouillabaisse a noble dish is—
A sort of soup or broth, or brew,
Or hotchpotch of all sorts of fishes,
That Greenwich never could outdo;
Green herbs, red peppers, mussels, saffron,
Soles, onions, garlic, roach, and dace:
All these you eat at TERRÉ's tavern,
In that one dish of Bouillabaisse.

Indeed, a rich and savory stew 't is;
And true philosophers, methinks,
Who love all sorts of natural beauties,
Should love good victuals and good drinks.
And Cordelier or Benedictine
Might gladly, sure, his lot embrace,
Nor find a fast-day too afflicting,
Which served him up a Bouillabaisse.

I wonder if the house still there is?
Yes, here the lamp is, as before;
The smiling red-cheeked *écaillère* is
Still opening oysters at the door.
Is TERRÉ still alive and able?
I recollect his droll grimace:
He'd come and smile before your table,
And hoped you liked your Bouillabaisse.

We enter—nothing's changed or older.
"How's Monsieur TERRÉ, waiter, pray?"
The waiter stares and shrugs his shoulder—
"Monsieur is dead this many a day."
"It is the lot of saint and sinner,
So honest TERRÉ's run his race."
"What will Monsieur require for dinner?"
"Say, do you still cook Bouillabaisse?"

"Oh, oui, Monsieur," 's the waiter's answer;
"Quel vin Monsieur desire-t-il?"

"Tell me a good one."—"That I can, sir:
The Chambertin with yellow seal."
"So TERRÉ's gone," I say, and sink in
My old accustom'd corner-place;
"He's done with feasting and with drinking,
With Burgundy and Bouillabaisse."

My old accustom'd corner here is,
The table still is in the nook;
Ah! vanish'd many a busy year is
This well-known chair since last I took.
When first I saw ye, *cari luoghi,*
I'd scarce a beard upon my face,
And now a grizzled, grim old fogy,
I sit and wait for Bouillabaisse.

Where are you, old companions trusty
Of early days here met to dine?
Come, waiter! quick, a flagon crusty—
I'll pledge them in the good old wine.
The kind old voices and old faces
My memory can quick retrace;
Around the board they take their places,
And share the wine and Bouillabaisse.

There's JACK has made a wondrous marriage;
There's laughing TOM is laughing yet;
There's brave AUGUSTUS drives his carriage;
There's poor old FRED in the "Gazette";
On JAMES's head the grass is growing;
Good Lord! the world has wagged apace
Since here we set the Claret flowing,
And drank, and ate the Bouillabaisse.

Ah me! how quick the days are flitting!
I mind me of a time that's gone,
When here I'd sit, as now I'm sitting,
In this same place—but not alone.
A fair young form was nestled near me,
A dear, dear face looked fondly up,
And sweetly spoke and smiled to cheer me
—There's no one now to share my cup.

. . . .

I drink it as the Fates ordain it.
Come, fill it, and have done with rhymes:
Fill up the lonely glass, and drain it
In memory of dear old times.
Welcome the wine, whate'er the seal is;
And sit you down and say your grace
With thankful heart, whate'er the meal is,
—Here comes the smoking Bouillabaisse!

The Cane-Bottom'd Chair

IN tattered old slippers that toast at the bars,
And a ragged old jacket perfumed with cigars,
Away from the world and its toils and its cares,
I've a snug little kingdom up four pair of stairs.

To mount to this realm is a toil, to be sure,
But the fire there is bright and the air rather pure;
And the view I behold on a sunshiny day
Is grand through the chimney-pots over the way.

This snug little chamber is cramm'd in all nooks
With worthless old knick-knacks and silly old books,
And foolish old odds and foolish old ends,
Crack'd bargains from brokers, cheap keepsakes from friends.

Old armor, prints, pictures, pipes, china, (all crack'd),
Old rickety tables, and chairs broken-backed;
A twopenny treasury, wondrous to see;
What matter? 't is pleasant to you, friend, and me.

No better divan need the Sultan require,
Than the creaking old sofa that basks by the fire;
And 't is wonderful, surely, what music you get
From the rickety, ramshackle, wheezy spinet.

That praying-rug came from a Turcoman's camp;
By Tiber once twinkled that brazen old lamp;
A mameluke fierce yonder dagger has drawn:
'T is a murderous knife to toast muffins upon.

Long, long through the hours, and the night, and the chimes,
Here we talk of old books, and old friends, and old times,
As we sit in a fog made of rich Latakie.
This chamber is pleasant to you, friend, and me.

But of all the cheap treasures that garnish my nest,
There's one that I love and I cherish the best:
For the finest of couches that's padded with hair
I never would change thee, my cane-bottom'd chair.

'T is a bandy-legg'd, high-shoulder'd, worm-eaten seat,
With a creaking old back, and twisted old feet;
But since the fair morning when Fanny sat there,
I bless thee and love thee, old cane-bottom'd chair.

If chairs have but feeling, in holding such charms,
A thrill must have pass'd through your wither'd old arms!
I look'd, and I long'd, and I wish'd in despair;
I wish'd myself turn'd to a cane-bottom'd chair.

It was but a moment she sat in this place,
She'd a scarf on her neck, and a smile on her face!
A smile on her face, and a rose in her hair,
And she sat there, and bloom'd in my cane-bottom'd chair.

And so I have valued my chair ever since,
Like the shrine of a saint, or the throne of a prince;
Saint Fanny, my patroness sweet I declare,
The queen of my heart and my cane-bottom'd chair.

When the candles burn low, and the company's gone,
In the silence of night as I sit here alone—
I sit here alone, but we yet are a pair—
My Fanny I see in my cane-bottom'd chair.

She comes from the past and revisits my room;
She looks as she then did, all beauty and bloom;
So smiling and tender, so fresh and so fair,
And yonder she sits in my cane-bottom'd chair.

From VANITY FAIR

Cuff's Fight with Dobbin

It was perhaps the plain modesty of Dobbin (afterwards Captain and Colonel) that made Thackeray call *Vanity Fair* "a novel without a hero." In the following selection we learn of a boyish experience of Dobbin's in which appeared the same characteristics that marked him in later life. He remained the loyal friend of George Osborne. And ten years after the death of Captain George Osborne, he married Amelia, his widow.

CUFF'S fight with Dobbin, and the unexpected issue of that contest, will long be remembered by every man who was educated at Dr. Swishtail's famous school. The latter youth (who used to be called Heigh-ho Dobbin, Gee-ho Dobbin, and by many other names indicative of puerile contempt) was the quietest, the clumsiest, and, as it seemed, the dullest of all Dr. Swishtail's young gentlemen. His parent was a grocer in the city: and it was bruited abroad that he was admitted into Dr. Swishtail's academy upon what are called "mutual principles"—that is to say, the expenses of his board and schooling were defrayed by his father in goods, not money; and he stood there—almost at the bottom of the school—in his scraggy corduroys and jacket, through the seams of which his great big bones were bursting—as the representative of so many pounds of tea, candles, sugar, mottled-soap, plums (of which a very mild proportion was supplied for the puddings of the establishment), and other commodities. A dreadful day it was for young Dobbin when one of the youngsters of the school, having run into the town upon a poaching excursion for hardbake and polonies, espied the cart of Dobbin & Rudge, Grocers and Oilmen, Thames Street, London, at the Doctor's door, discharging a cargo of the wares in which the firm dealt.

Young Dobbin had no peace after that. The jokes were frightful, and merciless against him. "Hullo, Dobbin," one wag would say, "here's good news in the paper. Sugars is ris', my boy." Another would set a sum—"If a pound of mutton-candles cost sevenpence-halfpenny, how much must Dobbin cost?" and a roar would follow from all the circle of young knaves, usher and all, who rightly considered that the selling of goods by retail is a shameful and infamous practice, meriting the contempt and scorn of all real gentlemen.

"Your father's only a merchant, Osborne," Dobbin said in private to the little boy who had brought down the storm upon him. At which the latter replied haughtily, "My father's a gentleman, and keeps his carriage"; and Mr. William Dobbin retreated to a remote outhouse in the playground, where he passed a half-holiday in the bitterest sadness and woe. Who amongst us is there that does not recollect similar hours of bitter, bitter childish grief? Who feels injustice; who shrinks before a slight; who has a sense of wrong so acute, and so glowing a gratitude for kindness, as a generous boy? and how many of those gentle souls do you degrade, estrange, torture, for the sake of a little loose arithmetic, and miserable dog-latin?

Now, William Dobbin, from an incapacity to acquire the rudiments of the above language, as they are propounded in that wonderful book the Eton Latin Grammar, was compelled to remain among the very last of Doctor Swishtail's scholars, and was "taken down" continually by little fellows with pink faces and pinafores when he marched up with the lower form, a giant amongst them, with his downcast, stupefied look, his dog's-eared primer, and his tight corduroys. High and low, all made fun of him. They sewed up those corduroys, tight as they were. They cut his bed-strings. They upset buckets and benches, so that he might break his shins over them, which he never failed to do. They sent him parcels, which, when opened, were found to contain the paternal soap and candles. There was no little fellow but had his jeer and joke at Dobbin; and he bore everything quite patiently, and was entirely dumb and miserable.

Cuff, on the contrary, was the great chief and dandy of the Swishtail Seminary. He smuggled wine in. He fought the town-boys. Ponies used to come for him to ride home on Saturdays. He had his top-boots in his room, in which he used to hunt in the holidays. He had a gold repeater: and took snuff like the Doctor. He had been to the Opera, and knew the merits of the principal actors, preferring Mr. Kean to Mr. Kemble. He could knock you off forty Latin verses in an hour. He could make French poetry. What else didn't he know, or couldn't he do? They said even the Doctor himself was afraid of him.

Cuff, the unquestioned king of the school, ruled over his subjects, and bullied them, with splendid superiority. This one blacked his shoes: that toasted his bread, others would fag out, and give him balls at cricket during whole summer afternoons. "Figs" was the fellow whom he despised most, and with whom, though always abusing him, and sneering at him, he scarcely ever condescended to hold personal communication.

One day in private, the two young gentlemen had had a difference. Figs, alone in the school-room, was blundering over a home letter; when Cuff, entering, bade him go upon some message, of which tarts were probably the subject.

"I can't," says Dobbin; "I want to finish my letter."

"You *can't?*" says Mr. Cuff, laying hold of that document (in which many words were scratched out, many were misspelt, on which had been spent I don't know how much thought, and labor, and tears; for the poor fellow was writing to his mother, who was fond of him, although she was a grocer's wife, and lived in a back parlor in Thames Street). "You *can't?*" says Mr. Cuff: "I should like to know why, pray? Can't you write to old Mother Figs to-morrow?"

"Don't call names," Dobbin said, getting off the bench, very nervous.

"Well, sir, will you go?" crowed the cock of the school.

"Put down the letter," Dobbin replied; "no gentleman readth letterth."

"Well, *now* will you go?" says the other.

"No, I won't. Don't strike, or I'll *thmash* you," roars out Dobbin, springing to a leaden inkstand, and looking so wicked, that Mr. Cuff paused, turned down his coat sleeves again, put his hands into his pockets, and walked away with a sneer. But he never meddled personally with the grocer's boy after that; though we must do him the justice to say he always spoke of Mr. Dobbin with contempt behind his back.

Some time after this interview, it happened that Mr. Cuff, on a sunshiny afternoon, was in the neighborhood of poor William Dobbin, who was lying under a tree in the play-ground, spelling over a favorite copy of the *Arabian Nights* which he had—apart from the rest of the school, who were pursuing their various sports—quite lonely, and almost happy. If people would but leave children to themselves; if teachers would cease to bully them; if parents would not insist upon directing their thoughts, and dominating their feelings—those feelings and thoughts which are a mystery to all (for how much do you and I know of each other, of our children, of our fathers, of our neighbor, and how far more beautiful and sacred are the thoughts of the poor lad or girl whom you govern likely to be, than those of the dull and world-corrupted person who rules him?)—if, I say, parents and masters would leave their children alone a little more,—small harm would accrue, although a less quantity of *as in præsenti* might be acquired.

Well, William Dobbin had for once forgotten the world, and was away with Sindbad the Sailor in the Valley of Diamonds, or with Prince Ahmed and the Fairy Peribanou in that delightful cavern where the Prince found her, and whither we should all like to make a tour; when shrill cries, as of a little fellow weeping, woke up his pleasant reverie; and looking up, he saw Cuff before him, belaboring a little boy.

It was the lad who had peached upon him about the grocer's cart; but he bore little malice, not at least towards the young and small. "How dare you, sir, break the bottle?" says Cuff to the little urchin, swinging a yellow cricket-stump over him.

The boy had been instructed to get over the play-ground wall (at a selected spot where the broken glass had been removed from the top, and niches made convenient in the brick); to run a quarter of a mile; to purchase a pint of rum-shrub on credit; to brave all the Doctor's out-lying spies, and to clamber back into the play-ground again; during the performance of which feat, his foot had slipt, and the bottle was broken, and the shrub had been spilt, and his pantaloons had been damaged, and he appeared before his employer a perfectly guilty and trembling, though harmless, wretch.

"How dare you, sir, break it?" says Cuff; "you blundering little thief. You drank the shrub, and now you pretend to have broken the bottle. Hold out your hand, sir."

Down came the stump with a great heavy thump on the child's hand. A moan followed. Dobbin looked up. The Fairy Peribanou had fled into the inmost cavern with Prince Ahmed: the Roc had whisked away Sindbad the Sailor out of the Valley of Diamonds out of sight, far into the clouds: and there was every-day life before honest William; and a big boy beating a little one without cause.

"Hold out your other hand, sir," roars Cuff to his little school-fellow, whose face was distorted with pain. Dobbin quivered, and gathered himself up in his narrow old clothes.

"Take that, you little devil!" cried Mr. Cuff, and down came the wicket again on the child's hand.—Don't be horrified, ladies, every boy at a public school has done it. Your children will so do and be done by, in all probability. Down came the wicket again; and Dobbin started up.

I can't tell what his motive was. Torture in a public school is as much licensed as the knout in Russia. It would be ungentlemanlike (in a manner) to resist it. Perhaps Dobbin's foolish soul revolted against the exercise of tyranny; or perhaps he had a hankering feeling of revenge in his mind, and longed to measure himself against that splendid bully and tyrant, who had all the glory, pride, pomp, circumstance, banners flying, drums beating, guards saluting, in the place. Whatever may have been his incentive, however, up he sprang, and screamed out, "Hold off, Cuff; don't bully that child any more; or I'll—"

"Or you'll what?" Cuff asked in amazement at this interruption. "Hold out your hand, you little beast."

"I'll give you the worst thrashing you ever had in your life," Dobbin said, in reply to the first part of Cuff's sentence; and little Osborne, gasping and in tears, looked up with wonder and incredulity at seeing this amazing champion put up suddenly to defend him: while Cuff's astonishment was scarcely less. Fancy our late monarch George III. when he heard of the revolt of the North American colonies: fancy brazen Goliath when little David stepped forward and claimed a meeting; and you have the feelings of Mr. Reginald Cuff when this rencontre was proposed to him.

"After school," says he, of course; after a pause and a look, as much as to say, "Make your will, and communicate your last wishes to your friends between this time and that."

"As you please," Dobbin said. "You must be my bottle-holder, Osborne."

"Well, if you like," little Osborne replied; for you see his papa kept a carriage, and he was rather ashamed of his champion.

Yes, when the hour of battle came, he was almost ashamed to say, "Go it, Figs;" and not a single other boy in the place uttered that cry for the first two or three rounds of this famous combat; at the commencement of which the scientific Cuff, with a contemptuous smile on his face, and as light and as gay as if he was at a ball, planted his blows upon his adversary, and floored that unlucky champion three times running. At each fall there was a cheer; and everybody was anxious to have the honor of offering the conqueror a knee.

"What a licking I shall get when it's over," young Osborne thought, picking up his man. "You'd best give in," he said to Dobbin; "it's only a thrashing, Figs, and you know I'm used to it." But Figs, all whose limbs were in a quiver, and whose nostrils were breathing rage, put his little bottle-holder aside, and went in for a fourth time.

As he did not in the least know how to parry the blows that were aimed at himself, and Cuff had begun the attack on the three preceding occasions, without ever allowing his enemy to strike, Figs now determined that he would commence the engagement by a charge on his own part; and accordingly, being a left-handed man, brought that arm into action, and hit out a couple of times with all his might—once at Mr. Cuff's left eye, and once on his beautiful Roman nose.

Cuff went down this time, to the astonishment of the assembly. "Well hit, by Jove," says little Osborne, with the air of a connoisseur, clapping his man on the back. "Give it him with the left, Figs, my boy."

Figs's left made terrific play during all the rest of the combat. Cuff went down every time. At the sixth round, there were almost as many fellows shouting out, "Go it, Figs," as there were youths exclaiming, "Go it, Cuff." At the twelfth round the latter champion was all abroad, as the saying is, and had lost all presence of mind and power of attack or defence. Figs, on the contrary, was as calm as a quaker. His face being quite pale, his eyes shining open, and a great cut on his under lip bleeding profusely, gave this young fellow a fierce and ghastly air, which perhaps struck terror into many spectators. Nevertheless, his intrepid adversary prepared to close for the thirteenth time.

If I had the pen of a Napier, or a Bell's Life, I should like to describe this combat properly. It was the last charge of the Guard—(that is, *it would* have been, only Waterloo had not yet taken place)—it was Ney's column breasting the hill of La Haye Sainte, bristling with ten thousands bayonets, and crowned with twenty eagles—it was the shout of the beef-eating British, as leaping down the hill they rushed to hug the enemy in the savage arms of battle—in other words, Cuff coming up full of pluck, but quite reeling and groggy, the Fig-merchant put in his left as usual on his adversary's nose, and sent him down for the last time.

"I think *that* will do for him," Figs said, as his opponent dropped as neatly on the green as I have seen Jack Spot's ball plump into the pocket at billiards; and the fact is, when time was called, Mr. Reginald Cuff was not able, or did not choose, to stand up again.

And now all the boys set up such a shout for Figs as would have made you think he had been their darling champion through the whole battle; and as absolutely brought Dr. Swishtail out of his study, curious to know the cause of the uproar. He threatened to flog Figs violently, of course; but Cuff, who had come to himself by this time, and was washing his wounds, stood up and said, "It's my fault, sir—not Figs's—not Dobbin's. I was bullying a little boy; and he served me right." By which magnanimous speech he not only saved his conqueror a whipping, but got back all his ascendency over the boys which his defeat had nearly cost him.

Young Osborne wrote home to his parents an account of the transaction.

"SUGARCANE HOUSE, RICHMOND, March, 18—.

"DEAR MAMA,—I hope you are quite well. I should be much obliged to you to send me a cake and five shillings. There has been a fight here between Cuff & Dobbin. Cuff, you know, was the Cock of the School. They fought thirteen rounds, and Dobbin licked. So Cuff is now Only Second Cock. The fight was about me. Cuff was licking me for breaking a bottle of milk, and Figs wouldn't stand it. We call him Figs because his father is a Grocer—Figs & Rudge, Thames St., City—I think as he fought for me you ought to buy your Tea & Sugar at his father's. Cuff goes home every Saturday, but can't this, because he has 2 Black

Eyes. He has a white Pony to come and fetch him, and a groom in livery on a bay mare. I wish my Papa would let me have a Pony, and I am

"Your dutiful Son,

"George Sedley Osborne.

"P.S.—Give my love to little Emmy. I am cutting her out a Coach in card-board. Please not a seed-cake, but a plum-cake."

In consequence of Dobbin's victory, his character rose prodigiously in the estimation of all his schoolfellows, and the name of Figs, which had been a byword of reproach, became as respectable and popular a nickname as any other in use in the school. "After all, it's not his fault that his father's a grocer," George Osborne said, who, though a little chap, had a very high popularity among the Swishtail youth; and his opinion was received with great applause. It was voted low to sneer at Dobbin about this accident of birth. "Old Figs" grew to be a name of kindness and endearment; and the sneak of an usher jeered at him no longer.

A Rescue and a Catastrophe

At a party supervised by Lord Steyne, the too-triumphant star had been Becky, the wife of Colonel Rawdon Crawley. She had long been on suspiciously good terms with Lord Steyne, and her husband had been watching her closely for many days. After the party, he put her into her carriage, and accepted an invitation to walk with Wenham, a fellow guest. Suddenly and quite unexpectedly, he fell into the hands of the bailiffs and, unable to borrow the price of his freedom from Wenham, was imprisoned in the spunging-house of Mr. Moss, assistant officer to the Sheriff of Middlesex, at the suit of one Mr. Nathan for a debt of one hundred and thirty six, six, and eightpence.

Upon his first visit to Mr. Moss, the Colonel, then a bachelor, had been liberated by the generosity of his Aunt; on the second mishap, little Becky, with the greatest spirit and kindness, had borrowed a sum of money from Lord Southdown, and had coaxed her husband's creditor (who was her shawl, velvet-gown, lace pocket-handkerchief, trinket, and gimcrack purveyor, indeed) to take a portion of the sum claimed, and Rawdon's promissory note for the remainder: so on both these occasions the capture and release had been conducted with the utmost gallantry on all sides, and Moss and the Colonel were therefore on the very best of terms.

"You'll find your old bed, Colonel, and everything comfortable," that gentleman said, "as I may honestly say. You may be pretty sure it's kep' aired, and by the best of company, too. It was slep' in the night afore last by the Honorable Capting Famish, of the Fiftieth Dragoons, whose Mar took him out, after a fortnight, jest to punish him, she said.

But, Law bless you, I promise you, he punished my champagne, and had a party 'ere every night—reg'lar tip-top swells, down from the clubs and the West End—Capting Ragg, the Honorable Deuceace, who lives in the Temple, and some fellers as knows a good glass of wine, I warrant you. I've got a Doctor of Diwinity up stairs, five gents in the Coffee-room, and Mrs. Moss has a tably-dy-hoty at half-past five, and a little cards or music afterwards, when we shall be most happy to see you."

"I'll ring when I want anything," said Rawdon, and went quietly to his bed-room. He was an old soldier, we have said, and not to be disturbed by any little shocks of fate. A weaker man would have sent off a letter to his wife on the instant of his capture. "But what is the use of disturbing her night's rest?" thought Rawdon. "She won't know whether I am in my room or not. It will be time enough to write to her when she has had her sleep out, and I have had mine. It's only a hundred-and-seventy, and the deuce is in it if we can't raise that." And so, thinking about little Rawdon (whom he would not have know that he was in such a queer place), the Colonel turned into the bed lately occupied by Captain Famish, and fell asleep. It was ten o'clock when he woke up, and the ruddy-headed youth brought him, with conscious pride, a fine silver dressing-case, wherewith he might perform the operation of shaving. Indeed Mr. Moss's house, though somewhat dirty, was splendid throughout. There were dirty trays, and wine-coolers *en permanence* on the sideboard, huge dirty gilt cornices, with dingy yellow satin hangings to the barred windows which looked into Cursitor Street—vast and dirty gilt picture-frames surrounding pieces sporting and sacred, all of which works were by the greatest masters; and fetched the greatest prices, too, in the bill transactions, in the course of which they were sold and bought over and over again. The Colonel's breakfast was served to him in the same dingy and gorgeous plated ware. Miss Moss, a dark-eyed maid in curl papers, appeared with the teapot, and, smiling, asked the Colonel how he had slep'? and she brought him in the *Morning Post,* with the names of all the great people who had figured at Lord Steyne's entertainment the night before. It contained a brilliant account of the festivities, and of the beautiful and accomplished Mrs. Rawdon Crawley's admirable personifications.

After a lively chat with this lady (who sat on the edge of the breakfast table in an easy attitude displaying the drapery of her stocking and an ex-white satin shoe, which was down at heel), Colonel Crawley called for pens and ink, and paper; and being asked how many sheets, chose one which was brought to him between Miss Moss's own finger and thumb. Many a sheet had that dark-eyed damsel brought in; many a poor fellow had scrawled and blotted hurried lines of entreaty, and paced up and down that awful room until his messenger brought back the reply. Poor men always use messengers instead of the post. Who has not had their letters, with the wafers wet, and the announcement that a person is waiting in the hall?

Now on the score of his application, Rawdon had not many misgivings.

"DEAR BECKY," (Rawdon wrote,)

"I hope you slept well. Don't be *frightened* if I don't bring you in your *coffy.* Last night as I was coming home smoaking, I met with an *accadent.* I was *nabbed* by Moss of Cursitor Street—from whose *gilt and splendid parler* I write this—the same that had me this time two years. Miss Moss brought in my tea—she is grown very *fat,* and, as usual, had *her stockens down at heal.*

"It's Nathan's business—a hundred-and-fifty—with costs, hundred-and-seventy. Please send me my desk and some *cloths*—I'm in pumps and a white tye (something like Miss M.'s stockings—I've seventy in it. And as soon as you get this, Drive to Nathan's—offer him seventy-five down, and ask *him to renew*—say I'll take wine—we may as well have some dinner sherry; but not *picturs,* they're too dear.

"If he won't stand it. Take my ticker and such of your things as you can *spare,* and send them to Balls—we must, of course, have the sum to-night. It won't do to let it stand over, as to-morrow's Sunday; the beds here are not very *clean,* and there may be other things out against me—I'm glad it an't Rawdon's Saturday for coming home. God bless you.

"Yours in haste,

"P. S. Make haste and come." "R. C.

This letter, sealed with a wafer, was dispatched by one of the messengers who are always hanging about Mr. Moss's establishment; and Rawdon, having seen him depart, went out in the court-yard, and smoked his cigar with a tolerably easy mind—in spite of the bars overhead; for Mr. Moss's court-yard is railed in like a cage, lest the gentlemen who are boarding with him should take a fancy to escape from his hospitality.

Three hours, he calculated, would be the utmost time required, before Becky should arrive and open his prison doors: and he passed these pretty cheerfully in smoking, in reading the paper, and in the coffee-room with an acquaintance, Captain Walker, who happened to be there, and with whom he cut for sixpences for some hours, with pretty equal luck on either side.

But the day passed away and no messenger returned,—no Becky. Mr. Moss's tably-dy-hoty was served at the appointed hour of half-past five, when such of the gentlemen lodging in the house as could afford to pay for the banquet, came and partook of it in the splendid front parlour before described, and with which Mr. Crawley's temporary lodging communicated, when Miss M. (Miss Hem, as her papa called her,) appeared without the curl-papers of the morning, and Mrs. Hem did the honours of a prime boiled leg of mutton and turnips, of which the Colonel ate with a very faint appetite. Asked whether he would "stand" a bottle of champagne for the company, he consented, and the ladies drank to his 'ealth, and Mr. Moss, in the most polite manner, "looked towards him."

In the midst of this repast, however, the door-bell was heard,—young Moss of the ruddy hair, rose up with the keys and answered the summons, and coming back, told the Colonel that the messenger had returned with a bag, a desk and a letter, which he gave him. "No ceremony, Colonel, I beg," said Mrs. Moss with a wave of her hand, and he opened the letter rather tremulously.—It was a beautiful letter, highly scented, on a pink paper, and with a light green seal.

"MON PAUVRE CHER PETIT," (Mrs. Crawley wrote).

"I could not sleep *one wink* for thinking of what had become of *my odious old monstre:* and only got to rest in the morning after sending for Mr. Blench (for I was in a fever), who gave me a composing draught and left orders with Finette that I should be disturbed *on no account.* So that my poor old man's messenger, who had *bien mauvaise mine* Finette says, and *sentoit le Genièvre,* remained in the hall for some hours waiting my bell. You may fancy my state when I read your poor dear old ill-spelt letter.

"Ill as I was, I instantly called for the carriage, and as soon as I was dressed (though I couldn't drink a drop of chocolate—I assure you I couldn't without my *monstre* to bring it to me), I drove *ventre à terre* to Nathan's. I saw him—I wept—I cried—I fell at his odious knees. Nothing would mollify the horrid man. He would have all the money, he said, or keep my poor monstre in prison. I drove home with the intention of paying that *triste visite chez mon oncle* (when every trinket I have should be at your disposal though they would not fetch a hundred pounds, for some, you know, are with *ce cher oncle* already), and found Milor there with the Bulgarian old sheep-faced monster, who had come to compliment me upon last night's performances. Paddington came in, too, drawling and lisping and twiddling his hair; so did Champignac, and his chef—everybody with *foison* of compliments and pretty speeches—plaguing poor me, who longed to be rid of them, and was thinking *every moment of the time* of *mon pauvre prisonnier.*

"When they were gone, I went down on my knees to Milor; told him we were going to pawn everything, and begged and prayed him to give me two hundred pounds. He pish'd and psha'd in a fury—told me not to be such a fool as to pawn—and said he would see whether he could lend me the money. At last he went away, promising that he would send it me in the morning: when I will bring it to my poor old monster with a kiss from his affectionate

"BECKY.

"I am writing in bed. Oh I have such a headache and such a heartache!"

When Rawdon read over this letter, he turned so red and looked so savage, that the company at the table d'hôte easily perceived that bad news had reached him. All his suspicions, which he had been trying to banish, returned upon him. She could not even go out and sell her trinkets to free him. She could laugh and talk about compliments paid to her, whilst he was in prison. Who had put him there? Wenham had walked with him. Was there. . . . He could hardly bear to think of what he suspected. Leaving the room hurriedly, he ran into his own—opened his desk, wrote two hurried lines, which he directed to Sir Pitt or Lady Crawley, and bade the messenger carry them at once to Gaunt Street, bidding him to take a cab, and promising him a guinea if he was back in an hour.

In the note he besought his dear brother and sister, for the sake of God; for the sake of his dear child and his honour; to come to him and relieve him from his difficulty. He was in prison: he wanted a hundred pounds to set him free—he entreated them to come to him.

He went back to the dining-room after dispatching his messenger, and called for more wine. He laughed and talked with a strange boisterousness, as the people thought. Sometimes he laughed madly at his own fears, and went on drinking for an hour; listening all the while for the carriage which was to bring his fate back.

At the expiration of that time, wheels were heard whirling up to the gate—the young janitor went out with his gate-keys. It was a lady whom he let in at the bailiff's door.

"Colonel Crawley," she said, trembling very much. He, with a knowing look, locked the outer door upon her—then unlocked and opened the inner one, and calling out, "Colonel, you're wanted," led her into the back parlour, which he occupied.

Rawdon came in from the dining-parlour where all those people were carousing, into his back room; a flare of coarse light following him into the apartment where the lady stood, still very nervous.

"It is I, Rawdon," she said, in a timid voice, which she strove to render cheerful. "It is Jane." Rawdon was quite overcome by that kind voice and presence. He ran up to her—caught her in his arms—gasped out some inarticulate words of thanks, and fairly sobbed on her shoulder. She did not know the cause of his emotion.

The bills of Mr. Moss were quickly settled, perhaps to the disappointment of that gentleman, who had counted on having the Colonel as his guest over Sunday at least; and Jane, with beaming smiles and happiness in her eyes, carried away Rawdon from the bailiff's house, and they went homewards in the cab in which she had hastened to his release.

"Pitt was gone to a parliamentary dinner," she said, "when Rawdon's note came, and so, dear Rawdon, I—I came myself;" and she put her kind hand in his. Perhaps it was well for Rawdon Crawley that Pitt was away at that dinner. Rawdon thanked his sister a hundred times, and with an ardour of gratitude which touched and almost alarmed that soft-hearted woman. "Oh," said he, in his rude, artless way, "you—you don't know how I'm changed since I've known you, and—and little Rawdy. I—I'd like to change somehow. You see I want—I want—to be—."—He did not finish the sentence, but she could interpret it. And that night after he left her, and as she sate by her own little boy's bed, she prayed humbly for that poor wayworn sinner.

Rawdon left her and walked home rapidly. It was nine o'clock at night. He ran across the streets, and the great squares of Vanity Fair, and at length came up breathless opposite his own house. He started back and fell against the railings, trembling as he looked up. The drawing-room windows were blazing with light. She had said that she was in bed and ill. He stood there for some time, the light from the rooms on his pale face.

He took out his door-key and let himself into the house. He could hear laughter in the upper rooms. He was in the ball-dress in which he had been captured the night before. He went silently up the stairs; leaning against the banisters at the stair-head.—Nobody was stirring in the house besides—all the servants had been sent away. Rawdon heard laughter within—laughter and singing. Becky was singing a snatch of the song of the night before; a hoarse voice shouted "Brava! Brava!"—it was Lord Steyne's.

Rawdon opened the door and went in. A little table with a dinner was laid out—and wine and plate. Steyne was hanging over the sofa on which Becky sate. The wretched woman was in a brilliant full toilette, her arms and all her fingers sparkling with bracelets and rings; and the brilliants on her breast which Steyne had given her. He had her hand in his, and was bowing over it to kiss it, when Becky started up with a faint scream as she caught sight of Rawdon's white face. At the next instant she tried a smile, a horrid smile, as if to welcome her husband: and Steyne rose up, grinding his teeth, pale, and with fury in his looks.

He, too, attempted a laugh—and came forward holding out his hand. "What, come back! How d'ye do, Crawley?" he said, the nerves of his mouth twitching as he tried to grin at the intruder.

There was that in Rawdon's face which caused Becky to fling herself before him. "I am innocent, Rawdon," she said; "before God, I am innocent." She clung hold of his coat, of his hands; her own were all covered with serpents, and rings, and baubles. "I am innocent.—Say I am innocent," she said to Lord Steyne.

He thought a trap had been laid for him, and was as furious with the wife as with the husband. "You innocent! Damn you," he screamed out. "You innocent! Why every trinket you have on your body is paid for by me. I have given you thousands of pounds which this fellow has spent, and for which he has sold you. Innocent, by ——! You're as innocent as your mother, the ballet-girl, and your husband the bully. Don't think to frighten me as you have done others. Make way, sir, and let me pass;" and Lord Steyne seized up his hat, and, with flame in his eyes, and looking his enemy fiercely in the face, marched upon him, never for a moment doubting that the other would give way.

But Rawdon Crawley springing out, seized him by the neck-cloth, until Steyne, almost strangled, writhed, and bent under his arm. "You lie, you dog!" said Rawdon. "You lie, you coward and villain!" And he struck the Peer twice over the face with his open hand, and flung him bleeding to the ground. It was all done before Rebecca could interpose. She stood there trembling before him. She admired her husband, strong, brave, and victorious.

"Come here," he said.—She came up at once.

"Take off those things."—She began, trembling, pulling the jewels from her arms, and the rings from her shaking fingers, and held them all in a heap, quivering and looking up at him. "Throw them down," he said, and she dropped them. He tore the diamond ornament out of her breast, and flung it at Lord Steyne. It cut him on his bald forehead. Steyne wore the scar to his dying day.

"Come up stairs," Rawdon said to his wife. "Don't kill me, Rawdon," she said. He laughed savagely.—"I want to see if that man lies about the money as he has about me. Has he given you any?"

"No," said Rebecca, "that is—"

"Give me your keys," Rawdon answered, and they went out together.

Rebecca gave him all the keys but one: and she was in hopes that he would not have remarked the absence of that. It belonged to the little desk which Amelia had given her in early days, and which she kept in a secret place. But Rawdon flung open boxes and wardrobes, throwing the multifarious trumpery of their contents here and there, and at last he found the desk. The woman was forced to open it. It contained papers, love-letters many years old—all sorts of small trinkets and woman's memoranda. And it contained a pocket-book with bank notes. Some of these were dated ten years back, too, and one was quite a fresh one—a note for a thousand pounds which Lord Steyne had given her.

"Did he give you this?" Rawdon said.

"Yes," Rebecca answered.

"I'll send it to him to-day," Rawdon said (for day had dawned again, and many hours had passed in this search), "and I will pay Briggs, who was kind to the boy, and some of the debts. You will let me know where I shall send the rest to you. You might have spared me a hundred pounds, Becky, out of all this—I have always shared with you."

"I am innocent," said Becky. And he left her without another word.

The Arch of Death

THERE came a day when the round of decorous pleasures and solemn gayeties in which Mr. Jos Sedley's family indulged, was interrupted by an event which happens in most houses. As you ascend the staircase of your house from the drawing-room towards the bed-room floors, you may have remarked a little arch in the wall right before you, which at once gives light to the stair which leads from the second story to the third (where the nursery and servants' chambers commonly are) and serves for another purpose of utility, of which the undertaker's men can give you a notion. They rest the coffins upon that arch, or pass them through it so as not to disturb in any unseemly manner the cold tenant slumbering within the black arch.

That second-floor arch in a London house, looking up and down the well of the staircase, and commanding the main thoroughfare by which the inhabitants are passing; by which cook lurks down before daylight to scour her pots and pans in the kitchen; by which young master stealthily ascends, having left his boots in the hall, and let himself in after dawn from a jolly night at the Club; down which miss comes rustling in fresh ribbons and spreading muslins, brilliant and beautiful, and prepared for conquest and the ball; or master Tommy slides, preferring the banisters for a mode of conveyance, and disdaining danger and the stair; down which the mother is fondly carried smiling in her strong husband's arms, as he steps steadily step by step, and followed by the monthly nurse, on the day when the medical man has pronounced that the charming patient may go downstairs; up which John lurks to bed, yawning with a sputtering tallow-candle, and to gather up before sunrise the boots which are awaiting him in the passages;—that stair, up or down which babies are carried, old people are helped, guests are marshalled to the ball, the parson walks to the christening, the doctor to the sick room, and the undertaker's men to the upper floor—what a memento of Life, Death, and Vanity it is—that arch and stair—if you choose to consider it, and sit on the landing, looking up and down the well! The doctor will come up to us too for the last time there, my friend in motley. The nurse will look in at the curtains, and you take no notice—and then she will fling open the windows for a little, and let in the air. Then they will pull down all the front blinds of the house and live in the back rooms—then they will send for the lawyer and other men in black, etc.—Your comedy and mine will have been played then, and we shall be removed, O how far, from the trumpets, and the shouting, and the posture-making. If we are gentlefolks they will put hatchments over our late domicile, with gilt cherubim, and mottoes stating that there is "Quiet in Heaven." Your son will new furnish the house, or perhaps let it, and go into a more modern quarter; your name will be among the "Members Deceased," in the lists of your clubs next year. However much you may be mourned, your widow will like to have her weeds neatly made—the cook will send or come up to ask about dinner—the survivor will soon bear to look at your picture over the mantel-piece, which will presently be deposed from the place of honor, to make way for the portrait of the son who reigns.

Which of the dead are most tenderly and passionately deplored? Those who love the survivors the least, I believe. The death of a child occasions a passion of grief and frantic tears, such as your end, brother reader, will never inspire. The death of an infant which scarce knew you, which a week's absence from you would have caused to forget you, will strike you down more than the loss of your closest friend, or your first-born son—a man grown like yourself, with children of his own. We may be harsh and stern with Judah and Simeon—our love and pity gush out for Benjamin, the little one. And if you are old, as some reader of this may be or shall be—old and rich, or old and poor—you may one day be thinking for yourself—"These people are very good round about me; but they won't grieve too much when I am gone. I am very rich, and they want my inheritance—or very poor, and they are tired of supporting me."

From The Book of Snobs

On University Snobs (Ch. XV)

I should like to fill several volumes with accounts of various University Snobs, so fond are my reminiscences of them, and so numerous are they. I should like to speak, above all, of the wives and daughters of some of the Professor-Snobs—their amusements, habits, jealousies; their innocent artifices to entrap young men; their picnics, concerts, and evening parties. I wonder what has become of Emily Blades, daughter of Blades, the Professor of the Mandingo language? I remember her shoulders to this day, as she sat in the midst of a crowd of about seventy young gentlemen, from Corpus and Catherine Hall, entertaining them with ogles and French songs on the guitar. Are you married, fair Emily of the shoulders? What beautiful ringlets those were that used to dribble over them!—what a waist!—what a killing sea-green shot-silk gown!—what a cameo, the size of a muffin! There were thirty-six young men of the University in love at one time with Emily Blades; and no words are sufficient to describe the pity, the sorrow, the deep, deep commiseration—the rage, fury, and uncharitableness, in other words—with which the Miss Trumps (daughter of Trumps, the Professor of Phlebotomy) regarded her, because she *didn't* squint, and because she *wasn't* marked with the small-pox.

As for the young University Snobs, I am getting too old, now, to speak of such very familiarly. My recollections of them lie in the far, far past—almost as far back as Pelham's time.

We *then* used to consider Snobs raw-looking lads, who never missed chapel; who wore highlows and no straps; who walked two hours on the Trumpington road every day of their lives; who carried off the college scholarships, and who overrated themselves in hall. We were premature in pronouncing our verdict of youthful Snobbishness. The man without straps fulfilled his destiny and duty. He eased his old governor, the curate in Westmoreland, or helped his sister to set up the Ladies' School. He wrote a "Dictionary," or a "Treatise on Conic Sections," as his nature and genius prompted. He got a fellowship, and then took to himself a wife and a living. He presides over a parish now, and thinks it rather a dashing thing to belong to the "Oxford and Cambridge Club;" and his parishioners love him, and snore under his sermons. No, no; *he* is not a Snob. It is not straps that make the gentleman, or highlows that unmake him, be they ever so thick. My son, it is you who are the Snob if you lightly despise a man for doing his duty, and refuse to shake an honest man's hand because it wears a Berlin glove.

We then used to consider it not the least vulgar for a parcel of lads who had been whipped three months previous, and were not allowed more than three glasses of port at home, to sit down to pine-apples and ices at each other's rooms, and fuddle themselves with champagne and claret.

One looks back to what was called "a wine party" with a sort of wonder. Thirty lads round a table covered with bad sweetmeats, drinking bad wines, telling bad stories, singing bad songs over and over again. Milk punch—smoking—ghastly headache—frightful spectacle of dessert-table next morning, and smell of tobacco; your guardian, the clergyman, dropping in, in the midst of this, expecting to find you deep in Algebra, and discovering the Gyp administering soda-water.

There were young men who despised the lads who indulged in the coarse hospitalities of wine parties, who prided themselves in giving *récherché* little French dinners. Both wine-party-givers and dinner-givers were Snobs.

There were what used to be called "dressy" Snobs:—Jimmy, who might be seen at five o'clock elaborately rigged out, with a camelia in his button-hole, glazed boots, and fresh kid-gloves twice a day; Jessamy, who was conspicuous for his "jewellery"—a young donkey, glittering all over with chains, rings, and shirt-studs; Jacky, who rode every day solemnly on the Blenheim Road, in pumps and white silk stockings, with his hair curled;—all three of whom flattered themselves they gave laws to the University about dress—all three most odious varieties of Snobs.

Sporting Snobs of course there were, and are always—those happy beings in whom Nature has implanted a love of slang; who loitered about the horsekeeper's stables, and drove the London coaches—a stage in and out—and might be seen swaggering through the courts in pink of early mornings, and indulged in dice and blind-hookey at nights, and never missed a race or a boxing-match, and rode flat-races, and kept bull-terriers. Worse Snobs even than these were poor miserable wretches who did not like hunting at all, and could not afford it, and were in mortal fear at a two-foot ditch, but who hunted because Glenlivat and Cinqbars hunted. The Billiard Snob and the Boating Snob were varieties of these, and are to be found elsewhere than in Universities.

Then there were Philosophical Snobs, who used to ape statesmen at the spouting-clubs, and who believed as a fact that Government always had an eye on the University for the selection of orators for the House of Commons. There were audacious young freethinkers, who adored nobody or nothing, except perhaps Robespierre and the Koran, and panted for the day when the pale name of priest should shrink and dwindle away before the indignation of an enlightened world.

But the worst of all University Snobs are those unfortunates who go to rack and ruin from their desire to ape their betters. Smith becomes acquainted with great people at college, and is ashamed of his father the tradesman. Jones has fine acquaintances, and lives after their fashion like a gay free-hearted fellow as he is, and ruins his father, and robs his sister's portion, and cripples his younger brother's outset in life, for the pleasure of entertaining my lord, and riding by the side of Sir John. And though it may be very good fun for Robinson to fuddle himself at home as he does at College, and to be brought home by the policeman he has just been trying to knock down—think what fun it is for the poor old soul his mother!—the half-pay captain's widow, who has been pinching herself all her life long, in order that that jolly young fellow might have a University education.

A Visit to the Pontos

TIRED of the town, where the sight of the closed shutters of the nobility, my friends, makes my heart sick in my walks; afraid almost to sit in those vast Pall Mall solitudes, the Clubs, and of annoying the Club waiters, who might, I thought, be going to shoot in the country, but for me, I determined on a brief tour in the provinces, and paying some visits in the country which were long due.

My first visit was to my friend Major Ponto (H.P. of the Horse Marines), in Mangelwurzelshire. The Major, in his little phaeton, was in waiting to take me up at the station. The vehicle was not certainly splendid, but such a carriage as would accommodate a plain man (as Ponto said he was) and a numerous family. We drove by beautiful fresh fields and green hedges, through a cheerful English landscape; the high-road, as smooth and trim as the way in a nobleman's park, was charmingly chequered with cool shade and golden sunshine. Rustics in snowy smock-frocks jerked their hats off smiling as we passed. Children, with cheeks as red as the apples in the orchards, bobbed curtsies to us at the cottage-doors. Blue church spires rose here and there in the distance: and as the buxom gardener's wife opened the white gate at the Major's little ivy-covered lodge, and we drove through the neat plantations of firs and evergreens, up to the house, my bosom felt a joy and elation which I thought it was impossible to experience in the smoky atmosphere of a town. "Here," I mentally exclaimed, "is all peace, plenty, happiness. Here, I shall be rid of Snobs. There can be none in this charming Arcadian spot."

Stripes, the Major's man (formerly corporal in his gallant corps), received my portmanteau, and an elegant little present, which I had brought from town as a peace-offering to Mrs. Ponto; viz., a cod and oysters from Grove's, in a hamper about the size of a coffin.

Ponto's house ("The Evergreens" Mrs. P. has christened it) is a perfect paradise of a place. It is all over creepers, and bow windows, and verandahs. A wavy lawn tumbles up and down all round it, with flower-beds of wonderful shapes, and zigzag gravel walks, and beautiful but damp shrubberies of myrtles and glistening laurestines, which have procured it its change of name. It was called Little Bullock's Pound in old Doctor Ponto's time. I had a view of the pretty grounds, and the stable, and the adjoining village and church, and a great park beyond, from the windows of the bedroom whither Ponto conducted me. It was the yellow bedroom, the freshest and pleasantest of bed-chambers; the air was fragrant with a large bouquet that was placed on the writing-table; the linen was fragrant with the lavender in which it had been laid; the chintz hangings of the bed and the big sofa were, if not fragrant with flowers, at least painted all over with them; the pen-wiper on the table was the imitation of a double dahlia; and there was accommodation for my watch in a sun-flower on the mantelpiece. A scarlet-leafed creeper came curling over the windows, through which the setting sun was pouring a flood of golden light. It was all flowers and freshness. Oh, how unlike those black chimney-pots in St. Alban's Place, London, on which these weary eyes are accustomed to look!

"It must be all happiness here, Ponto," said I, flinging myself down into the snug *bergère,* and inhaling such a delicious draught of country air as all the *mille-fleurs* of Mr. Atkinson's shop cannot impart to any the most expensive pocket-handkerchief.

"Nice place, isn't it?" said Ponto. "Quiet and unpretending. I like everything quiet. You've not brought your valet with you? Stripes will arrange your dressing things;" and that functionary, entering at the same time, proceeded to gut my portmanteau, and to lay out the black kerseymeres, "the rich cut velvet Genoa waistcoat," the white choker, and other polite articles of evening costume, with great gravity and despatch. "A great dinner-party," thinks I to myself, seeing these preparations (and not, perhaps, displeased at the idea that some of the best people in the neighbourhood were coming to see me). "Hark, there's the first bell ringing!" said Ponto, moving away; and, in fact, a clamorous harbinger of victuals began clanging from the stable turret, and announced the agreeable fact that dinner would appear in half-an-hour. "If the dinner is as grand as the dinner-bell," thought I, "faith, I'm in good quarters!" and had leisure, during the half-hour's interval, not only to advance my own person to the utmost polish of elegance which it is capable of receiving, to admire the pedigree of the Pontos hanging over the chimney, and the Ponto crest and arms emblazoned on the wash-stand basin and jug, but to make a thousand reflections on the happiness of a country life—upon the innocent friendliness and cordiality of rustic intercourse; and to sigh for an opportunity of retiring, like Ponto, to my own fields, to my own vine and fig-tree, with a placens uxor in my domus, and a half-score of sweet young pledges of affection sporting round my paternal knee.

Clang! At the end of the thirty minutes, dinner-bell number two pealed from the adjacent turret. I hastened downstairs, expecting to find a score of healthy country folks in the drawing-room. There was only one person there; a tall and Roman-nosed lady, glistering over with bugles, in deep mourning. She rose, advanced two steps, made a majestic curtsey, during which all the bugles in her awful head-dress began to twiddle and quiver—and then said, "Mr. Snob, we are very happy to see you at the Evergreens," and heaved a great sigh.

This, then, was Mrs. Major Ponto; to whom making my very best bow, I replied, that I was very proud to make her acquaintance, as also that of so charming a place as the Evergreens.

Another sigh. "We are distantly related, Mr. Snob," said she, shaking her melancholy head. "Poor dear Lord Rubadub!"

"Oh!" said I; not knowing what the deuce Mrs. Major Ponto meant.

"Major Ponto told me that you were of the Leicestershire Snobs: a very old family, and related to Lord Snobbington, who married Laura Rubadub, who is a cousin of mine, as was her poor dear father, for whom we are mourning. What a seizure! only sixty-three, and apoplexy quite unknown until now in our family! In life we are in death, Mr. Snob. Does Lady Snobbington bear the deprivation well?"

"Why, really, ma'am, I—I don't know," I replied, more and more confused.

As she was speaking I heard a sort of *cloop,* by which well-known sound I was aware that somebody was opening a bottle of wine, and Ponto entered, in a huge white neckcloth, and a rather shabby black suit.

"My love," Mrs. Major Ponto said to her husband, "we were talking of our cousin—poor dear Lord Rubadub. His death has placed some of the first families in England in mourning. Does Lady Rubadub keep the house in Hill Street, do you know?"

I didn't know, but I said, "I believe she does," at a venture; and, looking down to the drawing-room table, saw the inevitable, abominable, maniacal, absurd, disgusting "Peerage" open on the table, interleaved with annotations, and open at the article "Snobbington."

"Dinner is served," says Stripes, flinging open the door; and I gave Mrs. Major Ponto my arm.

Of the dinner to which we now sat down, I am not going to be a severe critic. The mahogany I hold to be inviolable; but this I will say, that I prefer sherry to marsala when I can get it, and the latter was the wine of which I have no doubt I heard the "cloop" just before dinner. Nor was it particularly good of its kind; however, Mrs. Major Ponto did not evidently know the difference, for she called the liquor Amontillado during the whole of the repast, and drank but half a glass of it, leaving the rest for the Major and his guest.

Stripes was in the livery of the Ponto family—a thought shabby, but gorgeous in the extreme—lots of magnificent worsted lace, and livery buttons of a very notable size. The honest fellow's hands, I remarked, were very large and black; and a fine odour of the stable was wafted about the room as he moved to and fro in his ministration. I should have preferred a clean maidservant, but the sensations of Londoners are too acute perhaps on these subjects; and a faithful John, after all, *is* more genteel.

From the circumstance of the dinner being composed of pig's head mock-turtle soup, of pig's fry and roast ribs of pork, I am led to imagine that one of Ponto's black Hampshires had been sacrificed a short time previous to my visit. It was an excellent and comfortable repast; only there *was* rather a sameness in it, certainly. I made a similar remark the next day.

During the dinner Mrs. Ponto asked me many questions regarding the nobility, my relatives. "When Lady Angelina Skeggs would come out; and if the countess her mamma" (this was said with much archness and he-he-ing) "still wore that extraordinary purple hair-dye?" "Whether my Lord Guttlebury kept, besides his French chef, and an English cordon-bleu for the roasts, an Italian for the confectionery?" "Who attended at Lady Clapperclaw's conversazioni?" and "Whether Sir John Champignon's 'Thursday Mornings' were pleasant?" "Was it true that Lady Carabas, wanting to pawn her diamonds, found that they were paste, and that the Marquis had disposed of them beforehand?" "How was it that Snuffin, the great tobacco-merchant, broke off the marriage which was on the tapis between him and their second daughter; and was it true that a mulatto lady came over from the Havanna and forbade the match?"

"Upon my word, Madam," I had begun, and was going on to say that I didn't know one word about all these matters which seemed so to interest Mrs. Major Ponto, when the Major, giving me a tread or stamp with his large foot under the table, said—

"Come, come, Snob my boy, we are all tiled, you know. We *know* you're one of the fashionable people about town: *we* saw your name at

Lady Clapperclaw's *soirées,* and the Champignon breakfasts; and as for the Rubadubs, of course, as relations—"

"Oh, of course, I dine there twice a week," I said; and then I remembered that my cousin, Humphry Snob, of the Middle Temple, *is* a great frequenter of genteel societies, and to have seen his name in the *Morning Post* at the tag end of several party lists. So, taking the hint, I am ashamed to say I indulged Mrs. Major Ponto with a deal of information about the first families in England, such as would astonish those great personages if they knew it. I described to her most accurately the three reigning beauties of last season at Almack's: told her in confidence that his Grace the D—— of W—— was going to be married the day after his Statue was put up; that his Grace the D—— of D—— was also about to lead the fourth daughter of the Archduke Stephen to the hymeneal altar:—and talked to her, in a word, just in the style of Mrs. Gore's last fashionable novel.

Mrs. Major was quite fascinated by this brilliant conversation. She began to trot out scraps of French, just for all the world as they do in the novels; and kissed her hand to me quite graciously, telling me to come soon to caffy, *ung pu de Musick o salong*—with which she tripped off like an elderly fairy.

"Shall I open a bottle of port, or do you ever drink such a thing as Hollands and water?" says Ponto, looking ruefully at me. This was a very different style of thing to what I had been led to expect from him at our smoking-room at the Club: where he swaggers about his horses and his cellar: and slapping me on the shoulder used to say, "Come down to Mangelwurzelshire, Snob my boy, and I'll give you as good a day's shooting and as good a glass of claret as any in the county."—"Well," I said, "I liked Hollands much better than port, and gin even better than Hollands." This was lucky. It *was* gin; and Stripes brought in hot water on a splendid plated tray.

The jingling of a harp and piano soon announced that Mrs. Ponto's *ung pu de Musick* had commenced, and the smell of the stable again entering the dining-room, in the person of Stripes, summoned us to *caffy* and the little concert. She beckoned me with a winning smile to the sofa, on which she made room for me, and where we could command a fine view of the backs of the young ladies who were performing the musical entertainment. Very broad backs they were too, strictly according to the present mode, for crinoline or its substitutes is not an expensive luxury, and young people in the country can afford to be in the fashion at very trifling charges. Miss Emily Ponto at the piano, and her sister Maria at that somewhat exploded instrument, the harp, were in light blue dresses that looked all flounce, and spread out like Mr. Green's balloon when inflated.

"Brilliant touch Emily has—what a fine arm Maria's is," Mrs. Ponto remarked good-naturedly, pointing out the merits of her daughters, and waving her own arm in such a way as to show that she was not a little satisfied with the beauty of that member. I observed she had about nine bracelets and bangles, consisting of chains and padlocks, the Major's miniature, and a variety of brass serpents with fiery ruby or tender turquoise eyes, writhing up to her elbow almost, in the most profuse contortions.

"You recognize those polkas? They were played at Devonshire House on the 23rd of July, the day of the grande fête." So I said yes—I knew 'em quite intimately; and began wagging my head as if in acknowledgment of those old friends.

When the performance was concluded, I had the felicity of a presentation and conversation with the two tall and scraggy Miss Pontos; and Miss Wirt, the governess, sat down to entertain us with variations on "Sich a gettin' up Stairs." They were determined to be in the fashion.

For the performance of the "Gettin' up Stairs," I have no other name but that it was a *stunner*. First Miss Wirt, with great deliberation, played the original and beautiful melody, cutting it, as it were, out of the instrument, and firing off each note so loud, clear, and sharp, that I am sure Stripes must have heard it in the stable.

"What a finger!" says Mrs. Ponto; and indeed it *was* a finger, as knotted as a turkey's drumstick, and splaying all over the piano. When she had banged out the tune slowly, she began a different manner of "Gettin' up Stairs," and did so with a fury and swiftness quite incredible. She spun up stairs; she whirled up stairs: she galloped up stairs; she rattled up stairs; and then having got the tune to the top landing, as it were, she hurled it down again shrieking to the bottom floor, where it sank in a crash as if exhausted by the breathless rapidity of the descent. Then Miss Wirt played the "Gettin' up Stairs" with the most pathetic and ravishing solemnity: plaintive moans and sobs issued from the keys—you wept and trembled as you were gettin' up stairs. Miss Wirt's hands seemed to faint and wail and die in variations: again, and she went up with a savage clang and rush of trumpets, as if Miss Wirt was storming a breach; and although I knew nothing of music, as I sat and listened with my mouth open to this wonderful display, my *caffy* grew cold, and I wondered the windows did not crack and the chandelier start out of the beam at the sound of this earthquake of a piece of music.

"Glorious creature! Isn't she?" said Mrs. Ponto. "Squirtz's favourite pupil—inestimable to have such a creature. Lady Carabas would give her eyes for her! A prodigy of accomplishments! Thank you, Miss Wirt!"—and the young ladies gave a heave and a gasp of admiration—a deep-breathing gushing sound, such as you hear at church when the sermon comes to a full stop.

Miss Wirt put her two great double-knuckled hands round a waist of her two pupils, and said, "My dear children, I hope you will be able to play it soon as well as your poor little governess. When I lived with the Dunsinanes, it was the dear Duchess's favourite, and Lady Barbara and Lady Jane McBeth learned it. It was while hearing Jane play that, I remember, that dear Lord Castletoddy first fell in love with her; and though he is but an Irish Peer, with not more than fifteen thousand a year, I persuaded Jane to have him. Do you know Castletoddy, Mr. Snob?—round towers—sweet place—County Mayo. Old Lord Castletoddy (the present Lord was then Lord Inishowan) was a most eccentric old man—they say he was mad. I heard his Royal Highness the poor dear Duke of Sussex—(*such* a man, my dears, but alas! addicted to smoking!)—I heard his Royal Highness say to the Marquis of Anglesea, 'I am sure Castletoddy is mad!' but Inishowan wasn't in marrying my sweet Jane, though the dear child had but her ten thousand pounds *pour tout potage!*"

"Most invaluable person," whispered Mrs. Major Ponto to me. "Has lived in the very highest society:" and I, who have been accustomed to see governesses bullied in the world, was delighted to find this one ruling the roast, and to think that even the majestic Mrs. Ponto bent before her.

As for *my* pipe, so to speak, it went out at once. I hadn't a word to say against a woman who was intimate with every Duchess in the Red Book. She wasn't the rosebud, but she had been near it. She had rubbed shoulders with the great, and about these we talked all the evening incessantly, and about the fashions, and about the Court, until bed-time came.

"And are there Snobs in this Elysium?" I exclaimed, jumping into the lavender-perfumed bed. Ponto's snoring boomed from the neighbouring bed-room in reply.

From PENDENNIS

Pendennis in his Glory

ARTHUR'S own allowances were liberal all this time; indeed, much more so than those of the sons of far more wealthy men. Years before, the thrifty and affectionate John Pendennis, whose darling project it had ever been to give his son a university education, and those advantages of which his own father's extravagance had deprived him, had begun laying by a store of money which he called Arthur's Education Fund. Year after year in his book his executors found entries of sums vested as A.E.F., and during the period subsequent to her husband's decease and before Pen's entry at college, the widow had added sundry sums to this fund, so that when Arthur went up to Oxbridge it reached no inconsiderable amount. Let him be liberally allowanced, was Major Pendennis's maxim. Let him make his first *entrée* into the world as a gentleman, and take his place with men of good rank and station; after giving it to him, it will be his own duty to hold it. There is no such bad policy as stinting a boy—or putting him on a lower allowance than his fellows. Arthur will have to face the world and fight for himself presently. Meanwhile we shall have procured for him good friends, gentlemanly habits, and have him well backed and well trained against the time when the real struggle comes. And these liberal opinions the Major probably advanced both because they were just, and because he was not dealing with his own money.

Thus young Pen, the only son of an estated country gentleman, with a good allowance, and a gentlemanlike bearing and person, looked to be a lad of much more consequence than he was really; and was held by the Oxbridge authorities, tradesmen, and undergraduates, as quite a young buck and member of the aristocracy. His manner was frank, brave, and perhaps a little impertinent, as becomes a high-spirited youth. He was perfectly generous and free-handed with his money, which seemed pretty plentiful. He loved joviality, and had a good voice for a song. Boat-racing had not risen in Pen's time to the *fureur* which, as we are given to understand, it has since attained in the university; and riding and tandem-driving were the fashions of the ingenuous youth. Pen rode well to hounds, appeared in pink, as became a young buck, and not particularly extravagant in equestrian or any other amusement, yet managed to run up a fine bill at Nile's, the livery stable-keeper, and in a number of other quarters. In fact, this lucky young gentleman had almost every taste to a considerable degree. He was very fond of books of all sorts: Doctor

Portman had taught him to like rare editions, and his own taste led him to like beautiful bindings. It was marvellous what tall copies, and gilding, and marbling, and blind-tooling, the booksellers and binders put upon Pen's book-shelves. He had a very fair taste in matters of art, and a keen relish for prints of a high school—none of your French Opera-Dancers, or tawdry Racing Prints, such as had delighted the simple eyes of Mr. Spicer, his predecessor—but your Stranges, and Rembrandt etchings, and Wilkies before the letter, with which his apartments were furnished presently in the most perfect good taste, as was allowed in the university, where this young fellow got no small reputation. We have mentioned that he exhibited a certain partiality for rings, jewellery, and fine raiment of all sorts; and it must be owned that Mr. Pen, during his time at the university, was rather a dressy man, and loved to array himself in splendour. He and his polite friends would dress themselves out with as much care in order to go and dine at each other's rooms, as other folks would who were going to enslave a mistress. They said he used to wear rings over his kid gloves, which he always denies; but what follies will not youth perpetrate with its own admirable gravity and simplicity? That he took perfumed baths is a truth; and he used to say that he took them after meeting certain men of a very low set in hall.

In Pen's second year, when Miss Fotheringay made her chief hit in London, and scores of prints were published of her, Pen had one of these hung in his bedroom, and confided to the men of his set how awfully, how wildly, how madly, how passionately he had loved that woman. He showed them in confidence the verses that he had written to her, and his brow would darken, his eyes roll, his chest heave with emotion as he recalled that fatal period of his life, and described the woes and agonies which he had suffered. The verses were copied out, handed about, sneered at, admired, passed from coterie to coterie. There are few things which elevate a lad in the estimation of his brother boys, more than to have a character for a great and romantic passion. Perhaps there is something noble in it at all times—among very young men it is considered heroic—Pen was pronounced a tremendous fellow. They said he had almost committed suicide: that he had fought a duel with a baronet about her. Freshmen pointed him out to each other. As at the promenade time at two o'clock he swaggered out of college, surrounded by his cronies, he was famous to behold. He was elaborately attired. He would ogle the ladies who came to lionise the university, and passed before him on the arms of happy gownsmen, and give his opinion upon their personal charms, or their toilettes, with the gravity of a critic whose experience entitled him to speak with authority. Men used to say that they had been walking with Pendennis, and were as pleased to be seen in his company as some of us would be if we walked with a duke down Pall Mall. He and the Proctor capped each other as they met, as if they were rival powers, and the men hardly knew which was the greater.

In fact, in the course of his second year, Arthur Pendennis had become one of the men of fashion in the university. It is curious to watch that facile admiration, and simple fidelity of youth. They hang round a leader: and wonder at him, and love him, and imitate him. No generous boy ever lived, I suppose, that has not had some wonderment of admiration for another boy; and Monsieur Pen at Oxbridge had his school, his faithful band of friends, and his rivals. When the young men heard at the haberdashers's shops that Mr. Pendennis of Boniface had just ordered a crimson satin cravat, you would see a couple of dozen crimson satin cravats in Main Street in the course of the week—and Simon, the jeweller, was known to sell no less than two gross of Pendennis' pins, from a pattern which the young gentleman had selected in his shop.

From Henry Esmond

The Duke of Marlborough

And now, having seen a great military march through a friendly country; the pomps and festivities of more than one German court; the severe struggle of a hotly contested battle, and the triumph of victory, Mr. Esmond beheld another part of military duty: our troops entering the enemy's territory, and putting all around them to fire and sword; burning farms, wasted fields, shrieking women, slaughtered sons and fathers, and drunken soldiery, cursing and carousing in the midst of tears, terror, and murder. Why does the stately Muse of History, that delights in describing the valour of heroes and the grandeur of conquest, leave out these scenes, so brutal, mean, and degrading, that yet form by far the greater part of the drama of war? You, gentlemen of England, who live at home at ease, and compliment yourselves in the songs of triumph with which our chieftains are bepraised—you, pretty maidens, that come tumbling down the stairs when the fife and drum call you, and huzzah for the British Grenadiers—do you take account that these items go to make up the amount of the triumph you admire, and form part of the duties of the heroes you fondle? Our chief, whom England and all Europe, saving only the Frenchman, worshipped almost, had this of the godlike in him, that he was impassible before victory, before danger, before defeat. Before the greatest obstacle or the most trivial ceremony; before a hundred thousand men drawn in battalia, or a peasant slaughtered at the door of his burning hovel; before a carouse of drunken German lords, or a monarch's court, or a cottage table where his plans were laid, or an enemy's battery, vomiting flame and death, and strewing corpses round about him;—he was always cold, calm, resolute, like fate. He performed a treason or a court-bow, he told a falsehood as black as Styx, as easily as he paid a compliment or spoke about the weather. He took a mistress, and left her; he betrayed his benefactor, and supported him, or would have murdered him, with the same calmness always, and having no more remorse than Clotho when she weaves the thread, or Lachesis when she cuts it. In the hour of battle I have heard the Prince of Savoy's officers say, the Prince became possessed with a sort of warlike fury; his eyes lighted up; he rushed hither and thither, raging; he shrieked curses and encouragement, yelling and harking his bloody war-dogs on, and himself always at the first point of the hunt. Our Duke was as calm at the mouth of the cannon as at the door of a drawing-room. Perhaps he could not have been the great man he was, had he had a heart either for love or hatred, or pity or fear, or regret or remorse. He achieved the highest deed of daring, or deepest calculation of thought, as he performed the very meanest action of which a man is capable; told a lie, or cheated a fond woman, or robbed a poor beggar of a halfpenny, with a like awful serenity and equal capacity of the highest and lowest acts of our nature.

His qualities were pretty well known in the army, where there were parties of all politics, and of plenty of shrewdness and wit; but there existed such a perfect confidence in him, as the first captain of the world, and such a faith and admiration in his prodigious genius and fortune, that the very men whom he notoriously cheated of their pay, the chiefs whom he used and injured—for he used all men, great and small, that came near him, as his instruments alike, and took something of theirs, either some quality or some property—the blood of a soldier, it might be, or a jewelled hat, or a hundred thousand crowns from a king, or a portion out of a starving sentinel's three-farthings; or (when he was young) a kiss from a woman, and the gold chain off her neck, taking all he could from woman or man, and having, as I have said, this of the godlike in him, that he could see a hero perish or a sparrow fall, with the same amount of sympathy for either. Not that he had no tears: he could always order up this reserve at the proper moment to battle; he could draw upon tears or smiles alike, and whenever need was for using this cheap coin. He would cringe to a shoeblack, as he would flatter a minister or a monarch; be haughty, be humble, threaten, repent, weep, grasp your hand (or stab you whenever he saw occasion).—But yet those of the army, who knew him best and had suffered most from him, admired him most of all: and as he rode along the lines to battle or galloped up in the nick of time to a battalion reeling from before the enemy's charge or shot, the fainting men and officers got new courage as they saw the splendid calm of his face, and felt that his will made them irresistible.

After the great victory of Blenheim the enthusiasm of the army for the Duke, even of his bitterest personal enemies in it, amounted to a sort of rage—nay, the very officers who cursed him in their hearts were among the most frantic to cheer him. Who could refuse his meed of admiration to such a victory and such a victor? Not he who writes: a man may profess to be ever so much a philosopher; but he who fought on that day must feel a thrill of pride as he recalls it.

The Renunciation of Allegiance

Beatrix, daughter of Lady Castlewood, was a girl of marvelous beauty and most forceful character, but thoroughly designing and ambitious, striving to sell her charms for a profitable marriage. On the eve of her marriage to the Duke of Hamilton, he was slain in a duel by the same Mohun who had killed her father. Her next enterprise was to aid the secret landing of James, claimant to the throne of England. Into this project Henry Esmond, fondly in love with Beatrix, entered whole heartedly. The following selection recounts the end of his experience.

The Prince in *Esmond* is not at all like the James III of history. He may be a typical Stuart, but the actual James III was by no means the Frenchified house pet that Thackeray presents. He was, in fact, pious and serious, and rather dull. But fiction has full right to its own creations.

He went and tapped at the little window at the porter's lodge, gently, but repeatedly, until the man came to the bars.

"Who's there?" says he, looking out; it was the servant from Kensington.

"My Lord Castlewood and Colonel Esmond," we said, from below. "Open the gate and let us in without any noise."

"My Lord Castlewood?" says the other; "my lord's here, and in bed."

"Open, d—n you," says Castlewood, with a curse.

"I shall open to no one," says the man, shutting the glass window as Frank drew a pistol. He would have fired at the porter, but Esmond again held his hand.

"There are more ways than one," says he, "of entering such a great house as this." Frank grumbled that the west gate was half a mile round. "But I know of a way that's not a hundred yards off," says Mr. Esmond;

and leading his kinsman close along the wall, and by the shrubs which had now grown thick on what had been an old moat about the house, they came to the buttress, at the side of which the little window was, which was Father Holt's private door. Esmond climbed up to this easily, broke a pane that had been mended, and touched the spring inside, and the two gentlemen passed in that way, treading as lightly as they could; and so going through the passage into the court, over which the dawn was now reddening, and where the fountain plashed in the silence.

They sped instantly to the porter's lodge, where the fellow had not fastened his door that led into the court; and pistol in hand came upon the terrified wretch, and bade him be silent. Then they asked him (Esmond's head reeled, and he almost fell as he spoke) when Lord Castlewood had arrived? He said on the previous evening, about eight of the clock.—"And what then?"—His lordship supped with his sister.—"Did the man wait?" Yes, he and my lady's maid both waited: the other servants made the supper; and there was no wine, and they could give his lordship but milk, at which he grumbled; and—and Madam Beatrix kept Miss Lucy always in the room with her. And there being a bed across the court in the Chaplain's room, she had arranged my lord was to sleep there. Madam Beatrix had come down stairs laughing with the maids, and had locked herself in, and my lord had stood for a while talking to her through the door, and she laughing at him. And then he paced the court awhile, and she came again to the upper window; and my lord implored her to come down and walk in the room; but she would not, and laughed at him again, and shut the window; and so my lord, uttering what seemed curses, but in a foreign language, went to the Chaplain's room to bed.

"Was this all!"—"All," the man swore upon his honour; all as he hoped to be saved.—"Stop, there was one thing more. My lord, on arriving, and once or twice during supper, did kiss his sister, as was natural, and she kissed him." At this Esmond ground his teeth with rage, and well nigh throttled the amazed miscreant who was speaking, whereas Castlewood, seizing hold of his cousin's hand, burst into a great fit of laughter.

"If it amuses thee," says Esmond in French, "that your sister should be exchanging of kisses with a stranger, I fear poor Beatrix will give thee plenty of sport."—Esmond darkly thought, how Hamilton, Ashburnham, had before been masters of those roses that the young Prince's lips were now feeding on. He sickened at that notion. Her cheek was desecrated, her beauty tarnished; shame and honour stood between it and him. The love was dead within him; had she a crown to bring him with her love, he felt that both would degrade him.

But this wrath against Beatrix did not lessen the angry feelings of the Colonel against the man who had been the occasion if not the cause of the evil. Frank sat down on a stone bench in the courtyard, and fairly fell asleep, while Esmond paced up and down the court, debating what should ensue. What mattered how much or how little had passed between the Prince and the poor faithless girl? They were arrived in time perhaps to rescue her person, but not her mind; had she not instigated the young Prince to come to her; suborned servants, dismissed others, so that she might communicate with him? The treacherous heart within her had surrendered, though the place was safe; and it was to win this that he had given a life's struggle and devotion; this, that she was ready to give away for the bribe of a coronet or a wink of the Prince's eye.

When he had thought his thoughts out he shook up poor Frank from his sleep, who rose yawning, and said he had been dreaming of Clotilda. "You must back me," says Esmond, "in what I am going to do. I have been thinking that yonder scoundrel may have been instructed to tell that story, and that the whole of it may be a lie; if it be, we shall find it out from the gentleman who is asleep yonder. See if the door leading to my lady's rooms," (so we called the rooms at the north-west angle of the house,)—"see if the door is barred as he saith." We tried; it was indeed as the lacquey had said, closed within.

"It may have been opened and shut afterwards," says poor Esmond; "the foundress of our family let our ancestor in in that way."

"What will you do, Harry, if—if what that fellow saith should turn out untrue?" The young man looked scared and frightened into his kinsman's face; I dare say it wore no very pleasant expression.

"Let us first go see whether the two stories agree," says Esmond; and went in at the passage and opened the door into what had been his own chamber now for well nigh five-and-twenty years. A candle was still burning, and the Prince asleep dressed on the bed—Esmond did not care for making a noise. The Prince started up in his bed, seeing two men in his chamber: "Qui est là?" says he, and took a pistol from under his pillow.

"It is the Marquis of Esmond," says the Colonel, "come to welcome his Majesty to his house of Castlewood, and to report of what hath happened in London. Pursuant to the King's orders, I passed the night before last, after leaving his Majesty, in waiting upon the friends of the King. It is a pity that his Majesty's desire to see the country and to visit our poor house should have caused the King to quit London without notice yesterday, when the opportunity happened which in all human probability may not occur again; and had the King not chosen to ride to Castlewood, the Prince of Wales might have slept at St. James's."

"'Sdeath! gentlemen," says the Prince, starting off his bed, whereon he was lying in his clothes, "the Doctor was with me yesterday morning, and after watching by my sister all night, told me I might not hope to see the Queen."

"It would have been otherwise," says Esmond with another bow; "as, by this time, the Queen may be dead in spite of the Doctor. The Council was met, a new Treasurer was appointed, the troops were devoted to the King's cause; and fifty loyal gentlemen of the greatest names of this kingdom were assembled to accompany the Prince of Wales, who might have been the acknowledged heir of the throne, or the possessor of it, by this time, had your Majesty not chosen to take the air. We were ready; there was only one person that failed us, your Majesty's gracious—"

"Morbleu, Monsieur, you give me too much Majesty," said the Prince, who had now risen up and seemed to be looking to one of us to help him to his coat. But neither stirred.

"We shall take care," says Esmond, "not much oftener to offend in that particular."

"What mean you, my lord?" says the Prince, and muttered something about a *guet-à-pens,* which Esmond caught up.

"The snare, Sir," said he, "was not of our laying; it is not we that invited you. We came to avenge, and not to compass, the dishonour of our family."

"Dishonour! Morbleu, there has been no dishonour," says the Prince, turning scarlet, "only a little harmless playing."

"That was meant to end seriously."

"I swear," the Prince broke out impetuously, "upon the honour of a gentleman, my lords—"

"That we arrived in time. No wrong hath been done, Frank," says Colonel Esmond, turning round to young Castlewood, who stood at the door as the talk was going on. "See! here is a paper whereon his Majesty hath deigned to commence some verses in honour, or dishonour, of Beatrix. Here is 'Madame' and 'Flamme,' 'Cruelle' and 'Rebelle,' and 'Amour' and 'Jour,' in the Royal writing and spelling. Had the Gracious lover been happy, he had not passed his time in sighing." In fact, and actually as he was speaking, Esmond cast his eyes down towards the table, and saw a paper on which my young Prince had been scrawling a madrigal, that was to finish his charmer on the morrow.

"Sir," says the Prince, burning with rage (he had assumed his Royal coat unassisted by this time), "did I come here to receive insults?"

"To confer them, may it please your Majesty," says the Colonel, with a very low bow, "and the gentlemen of our family are come to thank you."

"Malédiction!" says the young man, tears starting into his eyes with helpless rage and mortification. "What will you with me, gentlemen?"

"If your Majesty will please to enter the next apartment," says Esmond, preserving his grave tone, "I have some papers there which I would gladly submit to you, and by your permission I will lead the way;" and, taking the taper up, and backing before the Prince with very great ceremony, Mr. Esmond passed into the little Chaplain's room, through which we had just entered into the house:—"Please to set a chair for his Majesty, Frank," says the Colonel to his companion, who wondered almost as much at this scene, and was as much puzzled by it, as the other actor in it. Then going to the crypt over the mantel-piece, the Colonel opened it, and drew thence the papers which so long had lain there.

"Here, may it please your Majesty," says he, "is the Patent of Marquis sent over by your Royal Father at St. Germains to Viscount Castlewood, my father: here is the witnessed certificate of my father's marriage to my mother, and of my birth and christening; I was christened of that religion of which your sainted sire gave all through life so shining example. These are my titles, dear Frank, and this what I do with them: here go Baptism and Marriage, and here the Marquisate and the August Sign-Manual, with which your predecessor was pleased to honour our race." And as Esmond spoke he set the papers burning in the brazier. "You will please, sir, to remember," he continued, "that our family hath ruined itself by fidelity to yours: that my grandfather spent his estate, and gave his blood and his son to die for your service; that my dear lord's grandfather (for lord you are now, Frank, by right and title too) died for the same cause; that my poor kinswoman, my father's second wife, after giving away her honour to your wicked perjured race, sent all her wealth to the King; and got in return that precious title that lies in ashes, and this inestimable yard of blue riband. I lay this at your feet and stamp upon it: I draw this sword, and break it and deny you; and, had you completed the wrong you designed us, by heaven I would have driven it through your heart, and no more pardoned you than your father pardoned Monmouth. Frank will do the same, won't you, cousin?"

Frank, who had been looking on with a stupid air at the papers, as they flamed in the old brazier, took out his sword and broke it, holding his head down:—"I go with my cousin," says he, giving Esmond a grasp of the hand. "Marquis or not, by ——, I stand by him any day. I beg your Majesty's pardon for swearing; that is—that is—I'm for the Elector of Hanover."

CHARLES DICKENS (1812-1870)

From THE POSTHUMOUS PAPERS OF THE PICKWICK CLUB

The first Day's Journey and the first Evening's Adventures; with their Consequences

THAT punctual servant of all work, the sun, had just risen, and begun to strike a light on the morning of the thirteenth of May, one thousand eight hundred and twenty-seven, when Mr. Samuel Pickwick burst like another sun from his slumbers, threw open his chamber window, and looked out upon the world beneath. Goswell street was at his feet, Goswell street was on his right hand—as far as the eye could reach, Goswell street extended on his left; and the opposite side of Goswell street was over the way. "Such," thought Mr. Pickwick, "are the narrow views of those philosophers who, content with examining the things that lie before them, look not to the truths which are hidden beyond. As well might I be content to gaze on Goswell street forever, without one effort to penetrate to the hidden countries which on every side surround it." And having given vent to this beautiful reflection, Mr. Pickwick proceeded to put himself into his clothes; and his clothes into his portmanteau. Great men are seldom over-scrupulous in the arrangement of their attire; the operation of shaving, dressing, and coffee-imbibing was soon performed: and, in another hour, Mr. Pickwick, with his portmanteau in his hand, his telescope in his great-coat pocket, and his note-book in his waistcoat, ready for the reception of any discoveries worthy of being noted down, had arrived at the coach stand in St. Martin's-le-Grand.

"Cab!" said Mr. Pickwick.

"Here you are, sir," shouted a strange specimen of the human race in a sackcloth coat, and apron of the same, who with a brass label and number round his neck, looked as if he were catalogued in some collection of rarities. This was the waterman. "Here you are, sir. Now, then, fust cab!" And the first cab having been fetched from the public-house, where he had been smoking his first pipe, Mr. Pickwick and his portmanteau were thrown into the vehicle.

"Golden Cross," said Mr. Pickwick.

"Only a bob's vorth, Tommy," cried the driver, sulkily, for the information of his friend the waterman, as the cab drove off.

"How old is that horse, my friend?" inquired Mr. Pickwick, rubbing his nose with the shilling he had reserved for the fare.

"Forty-two," replied the driver, eying him askant.

"What!" ejaculated Mr. Pickwick, laying his hand upon his note-book. The driver reiterated his former statement. Mr. Pickwick looked very hard at the man's face, but his features were immovable, so he noted down the fact forthwith.

"And how long do you keep him out at a time?" inquired Mr. Pickwick, searching for further information.

"Two or three veeks," replied the man.

"Weeks!" said Mr. Pickwick in astonishment—and out came the note-book again.

"He lives at Pentonwil when he's at home," observed the driver, coolly, "but we seldom takes him home, on account of his veakness."

"On account of his weakness," reiterated the perplexed Mr. Pickwick.

"He always falls down, when he's took out o' the cab," continued the driver, "but when he's in it we bears him up werry tight, and takes him in werry short, so as he can't werry well fall down, and we've got a pair o' precious large wheels on; so ven he *does* move, they run after him, and he must go on—he can't help it."

Mr. Pickwick entered every word of this statement in his note-book, with the view of communicating it to the club as a singular instance of the tenacity of life in horses, under trying circumstances. The entry was scarcely completed when they reached the Golden Cross. Down jumped the driver, and out got Mr. Pickwick. Mr. Tupman, Mr. Snodgrass, and Mr. Winkle, who had been anxiously waiting the arrival of their illustrious leader, crowded to welcome him.

"Here's your fare," said Mr. Pickwick, holding out the shilling to the driver.

What was the learned man's astonishment, when that unaccountable person flung the money on the pavement, and requested in figurative terms to be allowed the pleasure of fighting him (Mr. Pickwick) for the amount!

"You are mad," said Mr. Snodgrass.

"Or drunk," said Mr. Winkle.

"Or both," said Mr. Tupman.

"Come on," said the cab-driver, sparring away like clockwork. "Come on—all four on you."

"Here's a lark!" shouted half a dozen hackney coachmen. "Go to vork, Sam,"—and they crowded with great glee round the party.

"What's the row, Sam?" inquired one gentleman in black calico sleeves.

"Row!" replied the cabman, "what did he want my number for?"

"I didn't want your number," said the astonished Mr. Pickwick.

"What did you take it for, then?" inquired the cabman.

"I didn't take it," said Mr. Pickwick, indignantly.

"Would anybody believe," continued the cab-driver, appealing to the crowd,—"would anybody believe as an informer 'ud go about in a man's cab, not only takin' down his number, but ev'ry word he says into the bargain?" (a light flashed upon Mr. Pickwick—it was the note-book).

"Did he though?" inquired another cabman.

"Yes, did he," replied the first—"and then arter aggerawatin' me to assault him, gets three witnesses here to prove it. But I'll give it him, if I've six months for it. Come on," and the cabman dashed his hat upon the ground, with a reckless disregard of his own private property, and knocked Mr. Pickwick's spectacles off, and followed up the attack with a blow on Mr. Pickwick's nose, and another on Mr. Pickwick's chest, and a third in Mr. Snodgrass's eye, and a fourth, by way of variety, in Mr. Tupman's waistcoat, and then danced into the road, and then back again to the pavement, and finally dashed the whole temporary supply of breath out of Mr. Winkle's body; and all in half a dozen seconds.

"Where's an officer?" said Mr. Snodgrass.

"Put 'em under the pump," suggested a hot-pie man.

"You shall smart for this," gasped Mr. Pickwick.

"Informers," shouted the crowd.

"Come on," cried the cabman, who had been sparring without cessation the whole time.

The mob had hitherto been passive spectators of the scene, but as the intelligence of the Pickwickians being informers was spread among them, they began to canvass with considerable vivacity the propriety of enforcing the heated pastry-vender's proposition: and there is no saying what acts of personal aggression they might have committed, had not the affray been unexpectedly terminated by the interposition of a new-comer.

"What's the fun?" said a rather tall thin young man, in a green coat, emerging suddenly from the coach-yard.

"Informers!" shouted the crowd again.

"We are not," roared Mr. Pickwick, in a tone which, to any dispassionate listener, carried conviction with it.

"Ain't you, though,—ain't you?" said the young man, appealing to Mr. Pickwick, and making his way through the crowd, by the infallible process of elbowing the countenances of its component members.

That learned man in a few hurried words explained the real state of the case.

"Come along, then," said he of the green coat, lugging Mr. Pickwick after him by main force, and talking the whole way. "Here, No. 924, take your fare, and take yourself off—respectable gentleman,—know him well—none of your nonsense—this way, sir—where's your friends?—all a mistake, I see—never mind—accidents will happen—best regulated families—never say die—down upon your luck—pull him up—put that in his pipe—like the flavor—damned rascals." And with a lengthened string of similar broken sentences, delivered with extraordinary volubility, the stranger led the way to the travellers' waiting-room, whither he was closely followed by Mr. Pickwick and his disciples.

"Here, waiter," shouted the stranger, ringing the bell with tremendous violence, "glasses round,—brandy-and-water, hot and strong, and sweet, and plenty,—eye damaged, sir? Waiter; raw beef-steak for the gentleman's eye,—nothing like raw beef-steak for a bruise, sir; cold lamp-post very good, but lamp-post inconvenient—damned odd standing in the open street half an hour, with your eye against a lamp-post,—eh—very good—ha! ha!" And the stranger, without stopping to take breath, swallowed at a draught full half a pint of the reeking brandy-and-water, and flung himself into a chair with as much ease as if nothing uncommon had occurred.

While his three companions were busily engaged in proffering their thanks to their new acquaintance, Mr. Pickwick had leisure to examine his costume and appearance.

He was about the middle height, but the thinness of his body, and the length of his legs, gave him the appearance of being much taller. The green coat had been a smart dress garment in the days of swallow-tails, but had evidently in those times adorned a much shorter man than the stranger, for the soiled and faded sleeves scarcely reached to his wrists. It was buttoned closely up to his chin, at the imminent hazard of splitting the back; and an old stock, without a vestige of shirt collar, ornamented his neck. His scanty black trousers displayed here and there those shiny patches which bespeak long service, and were strapped very tightly over a pair of patched and mended shoes, as if to conceal the dirty white stockings, which were nevertheless distinctly visible. His long black hair escaped in negligent waves from beneath each side of his old pinched-up hat; and glimpses of his bare wrist might be observed, between the tops of his gloves, and the cuffs of his coat sleeves. His face was thin and haggard; but an indescribable air of jaunty impudence and perfect self-possession pervaded the whole man.

Such was the individual, on whom Mr. Pickwick gazed through his spectacles (which he had fortunately recovered), and to whom he proceeded, when his friends had exhausted themselves, to return, in chosen terms, his warmest thanks for his recent assistance.

"Never mind," said the stranger, cutting the address very short, "said enough,—no more; smart chap that cabman—handled his fives well; but if I'd been your friend in the green jemmy—damn me—punch his head—'cod I would,—pig's whisper,—pieman too,—no gammon."

This coherent speech was interrupted by the entrance of the Rochester coachman, to announce that "The Commodore" was on the point of starting.

"Commodore!" said the stranger, starting up, "my coach,—place booked,—one outside—leave you to pay for the brandy-and-water,—want change for a five,—bad silver—Brummagem buttons—won't do—no go—eh?" and he shook his head most knowingly.

Now it so happened that Mr. Pickwick and his three companions had resolved to make Rochester their first halting place too; and having intimated to their new-found acquaintance that they were journeying to the same city, they agreed to occupy the seat at the back of the coach, where they could all sit together.

"Up with you," said the stranger, assisting Mr. Pickwick on to the roof with so much precipitation, as to impair the gravity of that gentleman's deportment very materially.

"Any luggage, sir?" inquired the coachman.

"Who—I? Brown paper parcel here, that's all, other luggage gone by water,—packing cases, nailed up—big as houses—heavy, heavy, damned heavy," replied the stranger, as he forced into his pocket as much as he could of the brown paper parcel, which presented most suspicious indications of containing one shirt and a handkerchief.

"Heads, heads, take care of your heads," cried the loquacious stranger, as they came out under the low archway, which in those days formed the entrance to the coach-yard. "Terrible place—dangerous work—other day—five children—mother—tall lady, eating sandwiches—forgot the arch—crash—knock—children look round—mother's head off—sandwich in her hand—no mouth to put it in—head of a family off—shocking, shocking. Looking at Whitehall, sir,—fine place—little window—somebody else's head off there, eh, sir?—he didn't keep a sharp look-out enough either—eh, sir, eh?"

"I was ruminating," said Mr. Pickwick, "on the strange mutability of human affairs."

"Ah! I see—in at the palace door one day, out at the window the next. Philosopher, sir?"

"An observer of human nature, sir," said Mr. Pickwick.

"Ah, so am I. Most people are when they've little to do, and less to get. Poet, sir?"

"My friend Mr. Snodgrass has a strong poetic turn," said Mr. Pickwick.

"So have I," said the stranger. "Epic poem,—ten thousand lines—revolution of July—composed it on the spot—Mars by day, Apollo by night,—bang the field-piece, twang the lyre."

"You were present at that glorious scene, sir?" said Mr. Snodgrass.

"Present! think I was;[1] fired a musket,—fired with an idea,—rushed into wine shop—wrote it down—back again—whiz, bang—another idea—wine shop again—pen and ink—back again—cut and slash—noble time, sir. Sportsman, sir?" abruptly turning to Mr. Winkle.

"A little, sir," replied that gentleman.

"Fine pursuit, sir,—fine pursuit.—Dogs, sir?"

"Not just now," said Mr. Winkle.

"Ah! you should keep dogs—fine animals—sagacious creatures—dog of my own once—Pointer—surprising instinct—out shooting one day — entering enclosure — whistled — dog stopped — whistled again—Ponto—no go: stock-still—called him—Ponto, Ponto—wouldn't move—dog transfixed—staring at a board—looked up, saw an inscription—'Gamekeeper has orders to shoot all dogs found in this enclosure'—wouldn't pass it—wonderful dog—valuable dog that—very."

"Singular circumstance that," said Mr. Pickwick. "Will you allow me to make a note of it?"

"Certainly, sir, certainly—hundred more anecdotes of the same animal.—Fine girl, sir" (to Mr. Tracy Tupman, who had been bestowing sundry anti-Pickwickian glances on a young lady by the roadside).

"Very!" said Mr. Tupman.

"English girls not so fine as Spanish—noble creatures—jet hair—black eyes—lovely forms—sweet creatures—beautiful."

"You have been in Spain, sir?" said Mr. Tracy Tupman.

"Lived there—ages."

[1] A remarkable instance of the prophetic force of Mr. Jingle's imagination; this dialogue occurred in the year 1827: and the Revolution in 1830.

"Many conquests, sir?" inquired Mr. Tupman.

"Conquests! Thousands. Don Bolaro Fizzgig — Grande — only daughter—Donna Christina—splendid creature—loved me to distraction —jealous father—high-souled daughter—handsome Englishman—Donna Christina in despair—prussic acid—stomach pump in my portmanteau—operation performed—old Bolaro in ecstasies—consent to our union—join hands and floods of tears—romantic story—very."

"Is the lady in England now, sir?" inquired Mr. Tupman, on whom the description of her charms had produced a powerful impression.

"Dead, sir—dead," said the stranger, applying to his right eye the brief remnant of a very old cambric handkerchief. "Never recovered the stomach pump—undermined constitution—fell a victim."

"And her father?" inquired the poetic Snodgrass.

"Remorse and misery," replied the stranger. "Sudden disappearance —talk of the whole city—search made everywhere—without success—public fountain in the great square suddenly ceased playing—weeks elapsed—still a stoppage—workmen employed to clean it—water drawn off—father-in-law discovered sticking head first in the main pipe with a full confession in his right boot—took him out, and the fountain played away again, as well as ever."

"Will you allow me to note that little romance down, sir?" said Mr. Snodgrass, deeply affected.

"Certainly, sir, certainly,—fifty more if you like to hear 'em—strange life mine—rather curious history—not extraordinary, but singular."

In this strain, with an occasional glass of ale, by way of parenthesis, when the coach changed horses, did the stranger proceed, until they reached Rochester Bridge, by which time the note-books, both of Mr. Pickwick and Mr. Snodgrass, were completely filled with selections from his adventures.

"Magnificent ruin!" said Mr. Augustus Snodgrass, with all the poetic fervor that distinguished him, when they came in sight of the fine old castle.

"What a study for an antiquarian," were the very words which fell from Mr. Pickwick's mouth, as he applied his telescope to his eye.

"Ah! fine place," said the stranger, "glorious pile—frowning walls—tottering arches—dark nooks—crumbling staircases—old cathedral too —earthy smell—pilgrims' feet worn away the old steps—little Saxon doors—confessionals like money-takers' boxes at theatres—queer customers those monks—Popes, and Lord Treasurers, and all sorts of old fellows, with great red faces, and broken noses, turning up every day

—buff jerkins too—matchlocks—Sarcophagus—fine place—old legends too—strange stories: capital;" and the stranger continued to soliloquize until they reached the Bull Inn, in the High street, where the coach stopped.

"Do you remain here, sir?" inquired Mr. Nathaniel Winkle.

"Here—not I—but you'd better—good house—nice beds—Wright's next house, dear—very dear—half a crown in the bill, if you look at the waiter—charge you more if you dine at a friend's than they would if you dined in the coffee-room—rum fellows—very."

Mr. Winkle turned to Mr. Pickwick, and murmured a few words; a whisper passed from Mr. Pickwick to Mr. Snodgrass, from Mr. Snodgrass to Mr. Tupman, and nods of assent were exchanged. Mr. Pickwick addressed the stranger.

"You rendered us a very important service, this morning, sir," said he; "will you allow us to offer a slight mark of our gratitude by begging the favor of your company at dinner?"

"Great pleasure—not presume to dictate, but broiled fowl and mushrooms—capital thing! What time?"

"Let me see," replied Mr. Pickwick, referring to his watch. "It is now nearly three. Shall we say five?"

"Suit me excellently," said the stranger, "five precisely—till then—care of yourselves;" and lifting the pinched-up hat a few inches from his head, and carelessly replacing it very much on one side, the stranger, with half the brown paper parcel sticking out of his pocket, walked briskly up the yard, and turned into the High street.

"Evidently a traveller in many countries, and a close observer of men and things," said Mr. Pickwick.

"I should like to see his poem," said Mr. Snodgrass.

"I should like to have seen that dog," said Mr. Winkle.

Mr. Tupman said nothing; but he thought of Donna Christina, the stomach pump, and the fountain; and his eyes filled with tears.

A private sitting-room having been engaged, bedrooms inspected, and dinner ordered, the party walked out to view the city and adjoining neighborhood.

We do not find, from a careful perusal of Mr. Pickwick's notes on the four towns, Stroud, Rochester, Chatham, and Brompton, that his impressions of their appearance differ in any material point, from those of other travellers who have gone over the same ground. His general description is easily abridged.

"The principal productions of these towns," says Mr. Pickwick, "appear to be soldiers, sailors, Jews, chalk, shrimps, officers, and dock-yard men. The commodities chiefly exposed for sale in the public streets, are marine stores, hard-bake, apples, flat-fish and oysters. The streets present a lively and animated appearance, occasioned chiefly by the conviviality of the military. It is truly delightful to a philanthropic mind, to see these gallant men, staggering along under the influence of an overflow, both of animal and ardent spirits; more especially when we remember that the following them about, and jesting with them, affords a cheap and innocent amusement for the boy population. Nothing (adds Mr. Pickwick) can exceed their good humor. It was but the day before my arrival, that one of them had been most grossly insulted in the house of a publican. The barmaid had positively refused to draw him any more liquor; in return for which, he had (merely in playfulness) drawn his bayonet, and wounded the girl in the shoulder. And yet this fine fellow was the very first to go down to the house next morning, and express his readiness to overlook the matter, and forget what had occurred!

"The consumption of tobacco in these towns (continues Mr. Pickwick) must be very great: and the smell which pervades the streets must be exceedingly delicious to those who are extremely fond of smoking. A superficial traveller might object to the dirt which is their leading characteristic; but to those who view it as an indication of traffic, and commercial prosperity, it is truly gratifying."

Punctual to five o'clock came the stranger, and shortly afterwards the dinner. He had divested himself of his brown paper parcel, but had made no alteration in his attire; and was, if possible, more loquacious than ever.

"What's that?" he inquired, as the waiter removed one of the covers.

"Soles, sir."

"Soles—ah!—capital fish—all come from London—stage-coach proprietors get up political dinners—carriage of soles—dozens of baskets—cunning fellows. Glass of wine, sir?"

"With pleasure," said Mr. Pickwick—and the stranger took wine; first with him, and then with Mr. Snodgrass, and then with Mr. Tupman, and then with Mr. Winkle, and then with the whole party together, almost as rapidly as he talked.

"Devil of a mess on the staircase, waiter," said the stranger. "Forms going up—carpenters coming down—lamps, glasses, harps. What's going forward?"

"Ball, sir," said the waiter.

"Assembly—eh?"

"No, sir, not Assembly, sir. Ball for the benefit of a charity, sir."

"Many fine women in this town, do you know, sir?" inquired Mr. Tupman, with great interest.

"Splendid—capital. Kent, sir—everybody knows Kent—apples, cherries, hops, and women. Glass of wine, sir?"

"With great pleasure," replied Mr. Tupman. The stranger filled and emptied.

"I should very much like to go," said Mr. Tupman, resuming the subject of the ball, "very much."

"Tickets at the bar, sir," interposed the waiter, "half a guinea each, sir."

Mr. Tupman again expressed an earnest wish to be present at the festivity; but meeting with no response in the darkened eye of Mr. Snodgrass or the abstracted gaze of Mr. Pickwick, he applied himself with great interest to the port wine and dessert which had just been placed on the table. The waiter withdrew, and the party were left to enjoy the cosey couple of hours succeeding dinner.

"Beg your pardon, sir," said the stranger, "bottle stands—pass it round—way of the sun—through the button-hole—no heeltaps," and he emptied his glass, which he had filled about two minutes before; and poured out another, with the air of a man who was used to it.

The wine was passed, and a fresh supply ordered. The visitor talked, the Pickwickians listened. Mr. Tupman felt every moment more disposed for the ball. Mr. Pickwick's countenance glowed with an expression of universal philanthropy; and Mr. Winkle, and Mr. Snodgrass, fell fast asleep.

"They're beginning up-stairs," said the stranger—"hear the company—fiddles tuning—now the harp—there they go." The various sounds which found their way down-stairs, announced the commencement of the first quadrille.

"How I should like to go," said Mr. Tupman, again.

"So should I," said the stranger,—"confounded luggage—heavy smacks—nothing to go in—odd, ain't it?"

Now general benevolence was one of the leading features of the Pickwickian theory, and no one was more remarkable for the zealous manner in which he observed so noble a principle, than Mr. Tracy Tupman. The number of instances, recorded on the Transactions of the Society, in which that excellent man referred objects of charity to the houses of other members for left-off garments, or pecuniary relief, is almost incredible.

"I should be very happy to lend you a change of apparel for the purpose," said Mr. Tracy Tupman, "but you are rather slim, and I am"—

"Rather fat—grown-up Bacchus—cut the leaves—dismounted from the tub, and adopted kersey, eh?—not double distilled, but double milled—ha! ha!—pass the wine."

Whether Mr. Tupman was somewhat indignant at the peremptory tone in which he was desired to pass the wine which the stranger passed so quickly away; or whether he felt very properly scandalized, at an influential member of the Pickwick Club being ignominiously compared to a dismounted Bacchus, is a fact not yet completely ascertained. He passed the wine, coughed twice, and looked at the stranger for several seconds with a stern intensity; as that individual, however, appeared perfectly collected, and quite calm under his searching glance, he gradually relaxed, and reverted to the subject of the ball.

"I was about to observe, sir," he said, "that though my apparel would be too large, a suit of my friend Mr. Winkle's would, perhaps, fit you better."

The stranger took Mr. Winkle's measure with his eye; and that feature glistened with satisfaction as he said—"Just the thing!"

Mr. Tupman looked round him. The wine which had exerted its somniferous influence over Mr. Snodgrass, and Mr. Winkle, had stolen upon the senses of Mr. Pickwick. That gentleman had gradually passed through the various stages which precede the lethargy produced by dinner, and its consequences. He had undergone the ordinary transitions from the height of conviviality, to the depth of misery, and from the depth of misery to the height of conviviality. Like a gas lamp in the street, with the wind in the pipe, he had exhibited for a moment an unnatural brilliancy: then sunk so low as to be scarcely discernible: after a short interval, he had burst out again, to enlighten for a moment, then flickered with an uncertain, staggering sort of light, and then gone out altogether. His head was sunk upon his bosom; and perpetual snoring, with a partial choke, occasionally, were the only audible indications of the great man's presence.

The temptation to be present at the ball, and to form his first impressions of the beauty of the Kentish ladies, was strong upon Mr. Tupman. The temptation to take the stranger with him, was equally great. He was wholly unacquainted with the place, and its inhabitants; and the stranger seemed to possess as great a knowledge of both as if he had lived there from his infancy. Mr. Winkle was asleep, and Mr. Tupman had had sufficient experience in such matters to know, that the moment he awoke, he would, in the ordinary course of nature, roll heavily to bed. He was undecided. "Fill your glass, and pass the wine," said the indefatigable visitor.

Mr. Tupman did as he was requested; and the additional stimulus of the last glass settled his determination.

"Winkle's bedroom is inside mine," said Mr. Tupman; "I couldn't make him understand what I wanted, if I woke him now, but I know he has a dress suit, in a carpet bag; and supposing you wore it to the ball, and took it off when we returned, I could replace it without troubling him at all about the matter."

"Capital," said the stranger, "famous plan—damned odd situation—fourteen coats in the packing cases, and obliged to wear another man's—very good notion, that—very."

"We must purchase our tickets," said Mr. Tupman.

"Not worth while splitting a guinea," said the stranger, "toss who shall pay for both—I call; you spin—first time—woman—woman—bewitching woman," and down came the sovereign, with the Dragon (called by courtesy a woman) uppermost.

Mr. Tupman rang the bell, purchased the tickets, and ordered chamber candlesticks. In another quarter of an hour the stranger was completely arrayed in a full suit of Mr. Nathaniel Winkle's.

"It's a new coat," said Mr. Tupman, as the stranger surveyed himself with great complacency in a cheval glass. "The first that's been made with our club button,"—and he called his companion's attention to the large gilt button which displayed a bust of Mr. Pickwick in the centre, and the letters "P. C." on either side.

"P. C.," said the stranger,—"queer set out—old fellow's likeness, and 'P. C.'—What does 'P. C.' stand for—Peculiar Coat, eh?" Mr. Tupman, with rising indignation, and great importance, explained the mystic device.

"Rather short in the waist, ain't it?" said the stranger, screwing himself round, to catch a glimpse in the glass of the waist buttons which were half-way up his back. "Like a general postman's coat—queer coats those—made by contract—no measuring—mysterious dispensations of Providence—all the short men get long coats—all the long men short ones." Running on in this way, Mr. Tupman's new companion adjusted his dress, or rather the dress of Mr. Winkle; and accompanied by Mr. Tupman, ascended the staircase leading to the ball-room.

"What names, sir?" said the man at the door. Mr. Tracy Tupman was stepping forward to announce his own titles, when the stranger prevented him.

"No names at all,"—and then he whispered Mr. Tupman, "Names won't do—not known—very good names in their way, but not great ones—capital names for a small party, but won't make an impression in public assemblies—*incog.* the thing—Gentlemen from London—distinguished foreigners—anything." The door was thrown open; and Mr. Tracy Tupman and the stranger entered the ball-room.

It was a long room, with crimson-covered benches, and wax candles in glass chandeliers. The musicians were securely confined in an elevated den, and quadrilles were being systematically got through by two or three sets of dancers. Two card-tables were made up in the adjoining card-room, and two pairs of old ladies, and a corresponding number of stout gentlemen, were executing whist therein.

The finale concluded, the dancers promenaded the room, and Mr. Tupman and his companion stationed themselves in a corner, to observe the company.

"Charming women," said Mr. Tupman.

"Wait a minute," said the stranger, "fun presently—nobs not come yet—queer place—Dock-yard people of upper rank don't know Dock-yard people of lower rank—Dock-yard people of lower rank don't know small gentry—small gentry don't know tradespeople—Commissioner don't know anybody."

"Who's that little boy with the light hair and pink eyes, in a fancy dress?" inquired Mr. Tupman.

"Hush, pray—pink eyes—fancy dress—little boy—nonsense—Ensign Ninety-seventh—Honorable Wilmot Snipe—great family—Snipes—very."

"Sir Thomas Clubber, Lady Clubber, and the Miss Clubbers!" shouted the man at the door in a stentorian voice. A great sensation was created throughout the room, by the entrance of a tall gentleman in a blue coat and bright buttons, a large lady in blue satin, and two young ladies on a similar scale, in fashionably made dresses of the same hue.

"Commissioner—head of the yard—great man—remarkably great man," whispered the stranger in Mr. Tupman's ear, as the charitable committee ushered Sir Thomas Clubber and family to the top of the room. The Honorable Wilmot Snipe and other distinguished gentlemen crowded to render homage to the Miss Clubbers; and Sir Thomas Clubber stood bolt-upright, and looked majestically over his black neckerchief at the assembled company.

"Mr. Smithie, Mrs. Smithie, and the Misses Smithie," was the next announcement.

"What's Mr. Smithie?" inquired Mr. Tracy Tupman.

"Something in the yard," replied the stranger. Mr. Smithie bowed deferentially to Sir Thomas Clubber; and Sir Thomas Clubber acknowledged the salute with conscious condescension. Lady Clubber took a telescopic view of Mrs. Smithie and family through her eyeglass, and Mrs. Smithie stared, in her turn, at Mrs. Somebody else, whose husband was not in the dock-yard at all.

"Colonel Bulder, Mrs. Colonel Bulder, and Miss Bulder," were the next arrivals.

"Head of the garrison," said the stranger, in reply to Mr. Tupman's inquiring look.

Miss Bulder was warmly welcomed by the Miss Clubbers; the greeting between Mrs. Colonel Bulder and Lady Clubber was of the most affectionate description; Colonel Bulder and Sir Thomas Clubber exchanged snuff-boxes, and looked very much like a pair of Alexander Selkirks;—"Monarchs of all they surveyed."

While the aristocracy of the place—the Bulders, and Clubbers, and Snipes—were thus preserving their dignity at the upper end of the room, the other classes of society were imitating their example in other parts of it. The less aristocratic officers of the Ninety-seventh devoted themselves to the families of the less important functionaries from the dock-yard. The solicitors' wives, and the wine-merchant's wife, headed another grade (the brewer's wife visited the Bulders); and Mrs. Tomlinson, the postoffice keeper, seemed by mutual consent to have been chosen the leader of the trade party.

One of the most popular personages, in his own circle, present, was a little fat man, with a ring of upright black hair round his head, and an extensive bald plain on the top of it—Doctor Slammer, surgeon to the Ninety-seventh. The doctor took snuff with everybody, chatted with everybody, laughed, danced, made jokes, played whist, did everything, and was everywhere. To these pursuits, multifarious as they were, the little doctor added a more important one than any—he was indefatigable in paying the most unremitting and devoted attention to a little old widow whose rich dress and profusion of ornament bespoke her a most desirable addition to a limited income.

Upon the doctor and the widow, the eyes of both Mr. Tupman and his companion had been fixed for some time, when the stranger broke silence.

"Lots of money—old girl—pompous doctor—not a bad idea—good fun," were the intelligible sentences which issued from his lips. Mr. Tupman looked inquisitively in his face.

"I'll dance with the widow," said the stranger.

"Who is she?" inquired Mr. Tupman.

"Don't know—never saw her in all my life—cut out the doctor—

here goes." And the stranger forthwith crossed the room; and, leaning against a mantel-piece, commenced gazing with an air of respectful and melancholy admiration on the fat countenance of the little old lady. Mr. Tupman looked on, in mute astonishment. The stranger progressed rapidly, the little doctor danced with another lady—the widow dropped her fan; the stranger picked it up, and presented it,—a smile—a bow—a courtesy—a few words of conversation. The stranger walked boldly up to, and returned with, the master of the ceremonies; a little introductory pantomime; and the stranger and Mrs. Budger took their places in a quadrille.

The surprise of Mr. Tupman at this summary proceeding, great as it was, was immeasurably exceeded by the astonishment of the doctor. The stranger was young, and the widow was flattered. The doctor's attentions were unheeded by the widow; and the doctor's indignation was wholly lost on his imperturbable rival. Doctor Slammer was paralyzed. He, Doctor Slammer of the Ninety-seventh, to be extinguished in a moment, by a man whom nobody had ever seen before, and whom nobody knew even now! Doctor Slammer—Doctor Slammer of the Ninety-seventh rejected! Impossible! It could not be! Yes, it was; there they were. What! introducing his friend! Could he believe his eyes! He looked again, and was under the painful necessity of admitting the veracity of his optics; Mrs. Budger was dancing with Mr. Tracy Tupman, there was no mistaking the fact. There was the widow before him, bouncing bodily here and there, with unwonted vigor; and Mr. Tracy Tupman hopping about, with a face expressive of the most intense solemnity, dancing (as a good many people do) as if a quadrille were not a thing to be laughed at, but a severe trial to the feelings, which it requires inflexible resolution to encounter.

Silently and patiently did the doctor bear all this, and all the handings of negus, and watching for glasses, and darting for biscuits, and coquetting, that ensued; but, a few seconds after the stranger had disappeared to lead Mrs. Budger to her carriage, he darted swiftly from the room with every particle of his hitherto-bottled-up indignation effervescing from all parts of his countenance, in a perspiration of passion.

The stranger was returning, and Mr. Tupman was beside him. He spoke in a low tone, and laughed. The little doctor thirsted for his life. He was exulting. He had triumphed.

"Sir!" said the doctor in an awful voice, producing a card, and retiring into an angle of the passage, "my name is Slammer, Doctor Slammer, sir—Ninety-seventh regiment—Chatham Barracks—my card, sir, my card." He would have added more, but his indignation choked him.

"Ah!" replied the stranger, coolly, "Slammer—much obliged—polite attention—not ill now, Slammer—but when I am—knock you up."

"You—you're a shuffler, sir," gasped the furious doctor, "a poltroon —a coward—a liar—a—a—will nothing induce you to give me your card, sir?"

"Oh! I see," said the stranger, half aside, "negus too strong here —liberal landlord—very foolish—very—lemonade much better—hot rooms—elderly gentleman—suffer for it in the morning—cruel—cruel;" and he moved on a step or two.

"You are stopping in this house, sir," said the indignant little man; "you are intoxicated now, sir; you shall hear from me in the morning, sir. I shall find you out, sir; I shall find you out."

"Rather you found me out than found me at home," replied the unmoved stranger.

Doctor Slammer looked unutterable ferocity, as he fixed his hat on his head with an indignant knock: and the stranger and Mr. Tupman ascended to the bedroom of the latter to restore the borrowed plumage to the unconscious Winkle.

That gentleman was fast asleep; the restoration was soon made; the stranger was extremely jocose; and Mr. Tracy Tupman, being quite bewildered with wine, negus, lights, and ladies, thought the whole affair an exquisite joke. His new friend departed; and, after experiencing some slight difficulty in finding the orifice in his nightcap, originally intended for the reception of his head, and finally overturning his candlestick in his struggles to put it on, Mr. Tracy Tupman managed to get into bed, by a series of complicated evolutions, and shortly afterwards sank into repose.

Seven o'clock had hardly ceased striking on the following morning, when Mr. Pickwick's comprehensive mind was aroused from the state of unconsciousness, in which slumber had plunged it, by a loud knocking at his chamber door.

"Who's there?" said Mr. Pickwick, starting up in bed.

"Boots, sir."

"What do you want?"

"Please, sir, can you tell me which gentleman of your party wears a bright blue dress coat, with a gilt button with P. C. on it?"

"It's been given out to brush," thought Mr. Pickwick; "and the man has forgotten whom it belongs to—Mr. Winkle," he called out, "next room but two, on the right hand."

"Thank'ee, sir," said the Boots, and away he went.

"What's the matter?" cried Mr. Tupman, as a loud knocking at *his* door roused *him* from his oblivious repose.

"Can I speak to Mr. Winkle, sir?" replied the Boots, from the outside.

"Winkle—Winkle," shouted Mr. Tupman, calling into the inner room.

"Hallo!" replied a faint voice from within the bed-clothes.

"You're wanted—some one at the door—" and having exerted himself to articulate thus much, Mr. Tracy Tupman turned round and fell fast asleep again.

"Wanted!" said Mr. Winkle, hastily jumping out of bed, and putting on a few articles of clothing: "wanted! at this distance from town—who on earth can want me!"

"Gentleman in the coffee-room, sir," replied the Boots, as Mr. Winkle opened the door, and confronted him; "gentleman says he'll not detain you a moment, sir, but he can take no denial."

"Very odd!" said Mr. Winkle; "I'll be down directly."

He hurriedly wrapped himself in a travelling-shawl and dressing-gown, and proceeded down-stairs. An old woman and a couple of waiters were cleaning the coffee-room, and an officer in undress uniform was looking out of the window. He turned round as Mr. Winkle entered, and made a stiff inclination of the head. Having ordered the attendants to retire, and closed the door very carefully, he said, "Mr. Winkle, I presume?"

"My name *is* Winkle, sir."

"You will not be surprised, sir, when I inform you, that I have called here this morning on behalf of my friend, Dr. Slammer, of the Ninety-seventh."

"Doctor Slammer!" said Mr. Winkle.

"Doctor Slammer. He begged me to express his opinion that your conduct of last evening was of a description which no gentleman could endure: and (he added) which no one gentleman would pursue towards another."

Mr. Winkle's astonishment was too real, and too evident, to escape the observation of Doctor Slammer's friend; he therefore proceeded: "My friend, Doctor Slammer, requested me to add, that he is firmly persuaded you were intoxicated during a portion of the evening, and possibly unconscious of the extent of the insult you were guilty of. He commissioned me to say, that should this be pleaded as an excuse for your behavior, he will consent to accept a written apology, to be penned by you from my dictation."

"A written apology!" repeated Mr. Winkle, in the most emphatic tone of amazement possible.

"Of course you know the alternative," replied the visitor, coolly.

"Were you intrusted with this message to me, by name?" inquired Mr. Winkle, whose intellects were hopelessly confused by this extraordinary conversation.

"I was not present myself," replied the visitor, "and, in consequence of your firm refusal to give your card to Doctor Slammer, I was desired by that gentleman to identify the wearer of a very uncommon coat—a bright blue dress coat, with a gilt button, displaying a bust, and the letters 'P. C.' "

Mr. Winkle actually staggered with astonishment, as he heard his own costume thus minutely described. Doctor Slammer's friend proceeded:—

"From the inquiries I made at the bar, just now, I was convinced that the owner of the coat in question arrived here, with three gentlemen, yesterday afternoon. I immediately sent up to the gentleman who was described as appearing the head of the party; and he at once referred me to you."

If the principal tower of Rochester Castle had suddenly walked from its foundation, and stationed itself opposite the coffee-room window, Mr. Winkle's surprise would have been as nothing, compared with the profound astonishment with which he had heard this address. His first impression was, that his coat had been stolen. "Will you allow me to detain you one moment?" said he.

"Certainly," replied the unwelcome visitor.

Mr. Winkle ran hastily up-stairs, and, with a trembling hand, opened the bag. There was the coat in its usual place, but exhibiting, on a close inspection, evident tokens of having been worn on the preceding night.

"It must be so," said Mr. Winkle, letting the coat fall from his hands. "I took too much wine after dinner, and have a very vague recollection of walking about the streets, and smoking a cigar afterwards. The fact is, I was very drunk;—I must have changed my coat—gone somewhere—and insulted somebody—I have no doubt of it; and this message is the terrible consequence." Saying which, Mr. Winkle retraced his steps in the direction of the coffee-room, with the gloomy and dreadful resolve of accepting the challenge of the warlike Doctor Slammer, and abiding by the worst consequences that might ensue.

To this determination Mr. Winkle was urged by a variety of consideration, the first of which was, his reputation with the club. He had always been looked up to as a high authority on all matters of amusement and dexterity, whether offensive, defensive, or inoffensive; and if, on this very first occasion of being put to the test, he shrunk back from the trial, beneath his leader's eye, his name and standing were lost forever. Besides, he remembered to have heard it frequently surmised by the uninitiated in such matters, that by an understood arrangement between the seconds, the pistols were seldom loaded with ball; and, furthermore, he reflected that if he applied to Mr. Snodgrass to act as his second, and depicted the danger in glowing terms, that gentleman might possibly communicate the intelligence to Mr. Pickwick, who would certainly lose no time in transmitting it to the local authorities, and thus prevent the killing or maiming of his follower.

Such were his thoughts when he returned to the coffee-room, and intimated his intention of accepting the doctor's challenge.

"Will you refer me to a friend, to arrange the time and place of meeting?" said the officer.

"Quite unnecessary," replied Mr. Winkle; "name them to me, and I can procure the attendance of a friend afterwards."

"Shall we say—sunset this evening?" inquired the officer, in a careless tone.

"Very good," replied Mr. Winkle; thinking in his heart it was very bad.

"You know Fort Pitt?"

"Yes; I saw it yesterday."

"If you will take the trouble to turn into the field which borders the trench, take the foot-path to the left, when you arrive at an angle of the fortification; and keep straight on till you see me; I will precede you to a secluded place, where the affair can be conducted without fear of interruption."

"*Fear* of interruption!" thought Mr. Winkle.

"Nothing more to arrange, I think," said the officer.

"I am not aware of anything more," replied Mr. Winkle.

"Good-morning."

"Good-morning." And the officer whistled a lively air, as he strode away.

That morning's breakfast passed heavily off. Mr. Tupman was not in a condition to rise, after the unwonted dissipation of the previous night; Mr. Snodgrass appeared to labor under a poetical depression of spirits; and even Mr. Pickwick evinced an unusual attachment to silence and soda-water. Mr. Winkle eagerly watched his opportunity. It was not long wanting. Mr. Snodgrass proposed a visit to the castle, and as Mr. Winkle was the only other member of the party disposed to walk, they went out together.

"Snodgrass," said Mr. Winkle, when they had turned out of the public street; "Snodgrass, my dear fellow, can I rely upon your secrecy?" as he said this, he most devoutly and earnestly hoped he could not.

"You can," replied Mr. Snodgrass. "Hear me swear—"

"No, no," interrupted Winkle, terrified at the idea of his companion's unconsciously pledging himself not to give information; "don't swear, don't swear; it's quite unnecessary."

Mr. Snodgrass dropped the hand which he had, in the spirit of poesy, raised toward the clouds as he made the above appeal, and assumed an attitude of attention.

"I want your assistance, my dear fellow, in an affair of honor," said Mr. Winkle.

"You shall have it," replied Mr. Snodgrass, clasping his friend's hand.

"With a doctor—Doctor Slammer, of the Ninety-seventh," said Mr. Winkle, wishing to make the matter appear as solemn as possible; "an affair with an officer, seconded by another officer, at sunset this evening, in a lonely field beyond Fort Pitt."

"I will attend you," said Mr. Snodgrass.

He was astonished, but by no means dismayed. It is extraordinary how cool any party but the principal can be in such cases. Mr. Winkle had forgotten this. He had judged of his friend's feelings by his own.

"The consequences may be dreadful," said Mr. Winkle.

"I hope not," said Mr. Snodgrass.

"The doctor, I believe, is a very good shot," said Mr. Winkle.

"Most of these military men are," observed Mr. Snodgrass calmly, "but so are you, ain't you?"

Mr. Winkle replied in the affirmative; and perceiving that he had not alarmed his companion sufficiently, changed his ground.

"Snodgrass," he said, in a voice tremulous with emotion, "if I fall, you will find in a packet which I shall place in your hands a note for my—for my father."

This attack was a failure also. Mr. Snodgrass was affected, but he undertook the delivery of the note, as readily as if he had been a Twopenny Postman.

"If I fall," said Mr. Winkle, "or if the doctor falls, you, my dear friend, will be tried as an accessory before the fact. Shall I involve my friend in transportation—possibly for life!"

Mr. Snodgrass winced a little at this, but his heroism was invincible. "In the cause of friendship," he fervently exclaimed, "I would brave all dangers."

How Mr. Winkle cursed his companion's devoted friendship internally, as they walked silently along, side by side, for some minutes, each immersed in his own meditations! The morning was wearing away; he grew desperate.

"Snodgrass," he said, stopping suddenly, "do *not* let me be balked in this matter—do *not* give information to the local authorities—do *not* obtain the assistance of several peace officers, to take either me or Doctor Slammer, of the Ninety-seventh regiment, at present quartered in Chatham Barracks, into custody, and thus prevent this duel;—I say, do *not*."

Mr. Snodgrass seized his friend's hand warmly, as he enthusiastically replied, "Not for worlds!"

A thrill passed over Mr. Winkle's frame, as the conviction, that he had nothing to hope from his friend's fears, and that he was destined to become an animated target, rushed forcibly upon him.

The state of the case having been formally explained to Mr. Snodgrass, and a case of satisfaction pistols, with the satisfactory accompaniments of powder, ball and caps, having been hired from a manufacturer in Rochester, the two friends returned to their inn: Mr. Winkle, to ruminate on the approaching struggle; and Mr. Snodgrass, to arrange the weapons of war, and put them into proper order for immediate use.

It was a dull and heavy evening, when they again sallied forth on their awkward errand. Mr. Winkle was muffled up in a huge cloak to escape observation; and Mr. Snodgrass bore under his the instruments of destruction.

"Have you got everything?" said Mr. Winkle, in an agitated tone.

"Ev'rything," replied Mr. Snodgrass; "plenty of ammunition, in case the shots don't take effect. There's a quarter of a pound of powder in the case, and I have got two newspapers in my pocket, for the loadings."

These were instances of friendship, for which any man might reasonably feel most grateful. The presumption is, that the gratitude of Mr. Winkle was too powerful for utterance, as he said nothing, but continued to walk on—rather slowly.

"We are in excellent time," said Mr. Snodgrass, as they climbed the fence of the first field; "the sun is just going down." Mr. Winkle looked up at the declining orb, and painfully thought of the probability of his "going down" himself, before long.

"There's the officer," exclaimed Mr. Winkle, after a few minutes' walking.

"Where?" said Mr. Snodgrass.

"There;—the gentleman in the blue cloak." Mr. Snodgrass looked in the direction indicated by the forefinger of his friend, and observed a figure, muffled up, as he had described. The officer evinced his consciousness of their presence by slightly beckoning with his hand; and the two friends followed him, at a little distance, as he walked away.

The evening grew more dull every moment, and a melancholy wind sounded through the deserted fields, like a distant giant whistling for his house-dog. The sadness of the scene imparted a sombre tinge to the feelings of Mr. Winkle. He started, as they passed the angle of the trench—it looked like a colossal grave.

The officer turned suddenly from the path; and after climbing a paling, and scaling a hedge, entered a secluded field. Two gentlemen were waiting in it; one was a little fat man, with black hair; and the other—a portly personage in a braided surtout—was sitting with perfect equanimity on a camp-stool.

"The other party, and a surgeon, I suppose," said Mr. Snodgrass; "take a drop of brandy." Mr. Winkle seized the wicker bottle, which his friend proffered, and took a lengthened pull at the exhilarating liquid.

"My friend, sir, Mr. Snodgrass," said Mr. Winkle, as the officer approached. Doctor Slammer's friend bowed, and produced a case similar to that which Mr. Snodgrass carried.

"We have nothing further to say, sir, I think," he coldly remarked, as he opened the case; "an apology has been resolutely declined."

"Nothing, sir," said Mr. Snodgrass, who began to feel rather uncomfortable himself.

"Will you step forward?" said the officer.

"Certainly," replied Mr. Snodgrass. The ground was measured, and preliminaries arranged.

"You will find these better than your own," said the opposite second, producing his pistols. "You saw me load them. Do you object to use them?"

"Certainly not," replied Mr. Snodgrass. The offer relieved him from considerable embarrassment; for his previous notions of loading a pistol were rather vague and undefined.

"We may place our men, then, I think," observed the officer, with as much indifference as if the principals were chess-men, and the seconds players.

"I think we may," replied Mr. Snodgrass; who would have assented to any proposition, because he knew nothing about the matter. The officer crossed to Doctor Slammer, and Mr. Snodgrass went up to Mr. Winkle.

"It's all ready," he said, offering the pistol. "Give me your cloak."

"You have got the packet, my dear fellow," said poor Winkle.

"All right," said Mr. Snodgrass. "Be steady and wing him."

It occurred to Mr. Winkle that this advice was very like that which bystanders invariably give to the smallest boy in a street fight; namely, "Go in, and win:"—an admirable thing to recommend, if you only know how to do it. He took off his cloak, however, in silence—it always took a long time to undo that cloak—and accepted the pistol. The seconds retired, the gentleman on the camp-stool did the same, and the belligerents approached each other.

Mr. Winkle was always remarkable for extreme humanity. It is conjectured that his unwillingness to hurt a fellow-creature intentionally, was the cause of his shutting his eyes when he arrived at the fatal spot; and that the circumstance of his eyes being closed, prevented his observing the very extraordinary and unaccountable demeanor of Doctor Slammer. That gentleman started, stared, retreated, rubbed his eyes, stared again; and, finally, shouted "Stop, stop!"

"What's all this?" said Doctor Slammer, as his friend and Mr. Snodgrass came running up—"That's not the man."

"Not the man!" said Doctor Slammer's second.

"Not the man!" said Mr. Snodgrass.

"Not the man!" said the gentleman with the camp-stool in his hand.

"Certainly not," replied the little doctor. "That's not the person who insulted me last night."

"Very extraordinary!" exclaimed the officer.

"Very," said the gentleman with the camp-stool. "The only question is, whether the gentleman, being on the ground, must not be considered, as a matter of form, to be the individual who insulted our friend, Doctor Slammer, yesterday evening, whether he is really that individual or not." And having delivered this suggestion with a very sage and mysterious air, the man with the camp-stool took a large pinch of snuff, and looked profoundly round with the air of an authority in such matters.

Now Mr. Winkle had opened his eyes, and his ears too, when he heard his adversary call out for a cessation of hostilities; and perceiving by what he had afterward said, that there was beyond all question some mistake in the matter, he at once foresaw the increase of reputation he should inevitably acquire, by concealing the real motive of his coming out; he therefore stepped boldly forward, and said,—

"I am not the person. I know it."

"Then, that," said the man with the camp-stool, "is an affront to Doctor Slammer, and a sufficient reason for proceeding immediately."

"Pray be quiet, Payne," said the doctor's second. "Why did you not communicate this fact to me this morning, sir?"

"To be sure—to be sure," said the man with the camp-stool, indignantly.

"I entreat you to be quiet, Payne," said the other. "May I repeat my question, sir?"

"Because, sir," replied Mr. Winkle, who had had time to deliberate upon his answer—"because, sir, you described an intoxicated and ungentlemanly person as wearing a coat, which I have the honor, not only to wear, but to have invented—the proposed uniform, sir, of the Pickwick Club in London. The honor of that uniform I feel bound to maintain, and I therefore, without inquiry, accepted the challenge which you offered me."

"My dear sir," said the good-humored little doctor, advancing with extended hand, "I honor your gallantry. Permit me to say, sir, that I highly admire your conduct, and extremely regret having caused you the inconvenience of this meeting, to no purpose."

"I beg you won't mention it, sir," said Mr. Winkle.

"I shall feel proud of your acquaintance, sir," said the little doctor.

"It will afford me the greatest pleasure to know you, sir," replied Mr. Winkle. Thereupon the doctor and Mr. Winkle shook hands, and then Mr. Winkle and Lieutenant Tappleton (the doctor's second), and then Mr. Winkle and the man with the camp-stool, and finally, Mr. Winkle and Mr. Snodgrass: the last-named gentleman in an excess of admiration at the noble conduct of his heroic friend.

"I think we may adjourn," said Lieutenant Tappleton.

"Certainly," added the doctor.

"Unless," interposed the man with the camp-stool; "unless Mr. Winkle feels himself aggrieved by the challenge; in which case, I submit, he has a right to satisfaction."

Mr. Winkle, with great self-denial, expressed himself quite satisfied already.

"Or possibly," said the man with the camp-stool, "the gentleman's second may feel himself affronted with some observations which fell from me at an early period of this meeting: if so I shall be happy to give *him* satisfaction immediately."

Mr. Snodgrass hastily professed himself very much obliged with the handsome offer of the gentleman who had spoken last, which he was only induced to decline, by his entire contentment with the whole proceedings. The two seconds adjusted the cases, and the whole party left the ground in a much more lively manner than they had proceeded to it.

"Do you remain long here?" inquired Doctor Slammer of Mr. Winkle, as they walked on most amicably together.

"I think we shall leave here the day after to-morrow," was the reply.

"I trust I shall have the pleasure of seeing you and your friend at my rooms, and of spending a pleasant evening with you, after this awkward mistake," said the little doctor; "are you disengaged this evening?"

"We have some friends here," replied Mr. Winkle, "and I should not like to leave them to-night. Perhaps you and your friend will join us at the Bull."

"With great pleasure," said the little doctor; "will ten o'clock be too late to look in for half an hour?"

"Oh dear, no," said Mr. Winkle. "I shall be most happy to introduce you to my friends, Mr. Pickwick and Mr. Tupman."

"It will give me great pleasure, I am sure," replied Doctor Slammer, little suspecting who Mr. Tupman was.

"You will be sure to come?" said Mr. Snodgrass.

"Oh, certainly."

By this time they had reached the road. Cordial farewells were exchanged, and the party separated. Doctor Slammer and his friends repaired to the barracks, and Mr. Winkle, accompanied by his friend, Mr. Snodgrass, returned to their inn.

Mr. Pickwick on the Ice

"Now," said Wardle, after a substantial lunch, with the agreeable items of strong beer and cherry-brandy, had been done ample justice to, "what say you to an hour on the ice? We shall have plenty of time."

"Capital!" said Mr. Benjamin Allen.

"Prime!" ejaculated Mr. Bob Sawyer.

"You skate, of course, Winkle?" said Wardle.

"Ye—yes; oh, yes," replied Mr. Winkle. "I—I—am *rather* out of practice."

"Oh, *do* skate, Mr. Winkle," said Arabella. "I like to see it so much."

"Oh, it is *so* graceful," said another young lady.

A third young lady said it was elegant, and a fourth expressed her opinion that it was "swan-like."

"I should be very happy, I'm sure," said Mr. Winkle, reddening; "but I have no skates."

This objection was at once overruled. Trundle had a couple of pair, and the fat boy announced that there were half a dozen more downstairs; whereat Mr. Winkle expressed exquisite delight, and looked exquisitely uncomfortable.

Old Wardle led the way to a pretty large sheet of ice; and the fat boy and Mr. Weller, having shovelled and swept away the snow which had fallen on it during the night, Mr. Bob Sawyer adjusted his skates with a dexterity which to Mr. Winkle was perfectly marvellous, and described circles with his left leg, and cut figures of eight, and inscribed upon the ice, without once stopping for breath, a great many other pleasant and astonishing devices, to the excessive satisfaction of Mr. Pickwick, Mr. Tupman, and the ladies; which reached a pitch of positive enthusiasm, when old Wardle and Benjamin Allen, assisted by the aforesaid Bob Sawyer, performed some mystic evolutions, which they called a reel.

All this time, Mr. Winkle, with his face and hands blue with the cold, had been forcing a gimlet into the soles of his feet, and putting his skates on, with the points behind, and getting the straps into a very complicated and entangled state, with the assistance of Mr. Snodgrass, who knew rather less about skates than a Hindoo. At length, however, with the assistance of Mr. Weller, the unfortunate skates were firmly screwed and buckled on, and Mr. Winkle was raised to his feet.

"Now, then, sir," said Sam, in an encouraging tone; "off vith you, and show 'em how to do it."

"Stop, Sam, stop!" said Mr. Winkle, trembling violently, and clutching hold of Sam's arms with the grasp of a drowning man. "How slippery it is, Sam!"

"Not an uncommon thing upon ice, sir," replied Mr. Weller. "Hold up, sir!"

This last observation of Mr. Weller's bore reference to a demonstration Mr. Winkle made at the instant, of a frantic desire to throw his feet in the air, and dash the back of his head on the ice.

"These—these—are very awkward skates; ain't they, Sam?" inquired Mr. Winkle, staggering.

"I'm afeerd there's a orkard gen'l'm'n in 'em, sir," replied Sam.

"Now, Winkle," cried Mr. Pickwick, quite unconscious that there was anything the matter. "Come; the ladies are all anxiety."

"Yes, yes," replied Mr. Winkle, with a ghastly smile. "I'm coming."

"Just a-goin' to begin," said Sam, endeavouring to disengage himself. "Now, sir, start off!"

"Stop an instant, Sam," gasped Mr. Winkle, clinging most affectionately to Mr. Weller. "I find I've got a couple of coats at home that I don't want, Sam. You may have them, Sam."

"Thank'ee, sir," replied Mr. Weller.

"Never mind touching your hat, Sam," said Mr. Winkle hastily. "You needn't take your hand away to do that. I meant to have given you five shillings this morning for a Christmas box, Sam. I'll give it you this afternoon, Sam."

"You're wery good, sir," replied Mr. Weller.

"Just hold me at first, Sam! will you?" said Mr. Winkle. "There—that's right. I shall soon get in the way of it, Sam. Not too fast, Sam; not too fast."

Mr. Winkle, stooping forward, with his body half doubled up, was being assisted over the ice by Mr. Weller, in a very singular and unswan-like manner, when Mr. Pickwick most innocently shouted from the opposite bank—

"Sam!"

"Sir?"

"Here. I want you."

"Let go, sir," said Sam. "Don't you hear the governor a-callin'? Let go, sir."

With a violent effort, Mr. Weller disengaged himself from the grasp of the agonised Pickwickian, and, in so doing, administered a considerable impetus to the unhappy Mr. Winkle. With an accuracy which no degree of dexterity or practice could have insured, that unfortunate gentleman bore swiftly down into the centre of the reel, at the very moment when Mr. Bob Sawyer was performing a flourish of unparalleled beauty. Mr. Winkle struck wildly against him, and with a loud crash they both fell heavily down. Mr. Pickwick ran to the spot. Bob Sawyer had risen to his feet, but Mr. Winkle was far too wise to do anything of the kind, in skates. He was seated on the ice, making spasmodic efforts to smile; but anguish was depicted on every lineament of his countenance.

"Are you hurt?" inquired Mr. Benjamin Allen, with great anxiety.

"Not much," said Mr. Winkle, rubbing his back very hard.

"I wish you'd let me bleed you," said Mr. Benjamin, with great eagerness.

"No, thank you," replied Mr. Winkle hurriedly.

"I really think you had better," said Allen.

"Thank you," replied Mr. Winkle; "I'd rather not."

"What do *you* think, Mr. Pickwick?" inquired Bob Sawyer.

Mr. Pickwick was excited and indignant. He beckoned to Mr. Weller, and said in a stern voice, "Take his skates off."

"No; but really I had scarcely begun," remonstrated Mr. Winkle.

"Take his skates off," repeated Mr. Pickwick firmly.

The command was not to be resisted. Mr. Winkle allowed Sam to obey it, in silence.

"Lift him up," said Mr. Pickwick. Sam assisted him to rise.

Mr. Pickwick retired a few paces apart from the bystanders; and, beckoning his friend to approach, fixed a searching look upon him, and uttered in a low, but distinct and emphatic tone, these remarkable words—

"You're a humbug, sir."

"A what?" said Mr. Winkle, starting.

"A humbug, sir. I will speak plainer, if you wish it. An impostor, sir."

With these words, Mr. Pickwick turned slowly on his heel, and rejoined his friends.

While Mr. Pickwick was delivering himself of the sentiment just recorded, Mr. Weller and the fat boy, having by their joint endeavours cut out a slide, were exercising themselves thereupon, in a very masterly and brilliant manner. Sam Weller, in particular, was displaying that beautiful feat of fancy-sliding which is currently denominated "knocking at the cobbler's door," and which is achieved by skimming over the ice on one foot, and occasionally giving a postman's knock upon it with the other. It was a good long slide, and there was something in the motion which Mr. Pickwick, who was very cold with standing still, could not help envying.

"It looks a nice warm exercise that, doesn't it?" he inquired of Wardle, when that gentleman was thoroughly out of breath, by reason of the indefatigable manner in which he had converted his legs into a pair of compasses, and drawn complicated problems on the ice.

"Ah, it does, indeed," replied Wardle. "Do you slide?"

"I used to do so, on the gutters, when I was a boy," replied Mr. Pickwick.

"Try it now," said Wardle.

"Oh, do, please, Mr. Pickwick!" cried all the ladies.

"I should be very happy to afford you any amusement," replied Mr. Pickwick, "but I haven't done such a thing these thirty years."

"Pooh! pooh! Nonsense!" said Wardle, dragging off his skates with the impetuosity which characterised all his proceedings. "Here; I'll keep you company; come along!" And away went the good-tempered old fellow down the slide, with a rapidity which came very close upon Mr. Weller, and beat the fat boy all to nothing.

Mr. Pickwick paused, considered, pulled off his gloves and put them in his hat; took two or three short runs, balked himself as often, and at last took another run, and went slowly and gravely down the slide, with his feet about a yard and a quarter apart, amidst the gratified shouts of all the spectators.

"Keep the pot a-bilin', sir!" said Sam; and down went Wardle again, and then Mr. Pickwick, and then Sam, and then Mr. Winkle, and then Mr. Bob Sawyer, and then the fat boy, and then Mr. Snodgrass, following closely upon each other's heels, and running after each other with as much eagerness as if their future prospects in life depended on their expedition.

It was the most intensely interesting thing, to observe the manner in which Mr. Pickwick performed his share in the ceremony; to watch the torture of anxiety with which he viewed the person behind, gaining upon him at the imminent hazard of tripping him up; to see him gradually expend the painful force he had put on at first, and turn slowly round on the slide, with his face towards the point from which he had started; to contemplate the playful smile which mantled on his face when he had accomplished the distance, and the eagerness with which he turned round when he had done so, and ran after his predecessor, his black gaiters tripping pleasantly through the snow, and his eyes beaming cheerfulness and gladness through his spectacles. And when he was knocked down (which happened upon the average every third round), it was the most invigorating sight that can possibly be imagined, to behold him gather up his hat, gloves, and handkerchief, with a glowing countenance, and resume his station in the rank, with an ardour and enthusiasm that nothing could abate.

The sport was at its height, the sliding was at the quickest, the laughter was at the loudest, when a sharp smart crack was heard. There was a quick rush towards the bank, a wild scream from the ladies, and a shout from Mr. Tupman. A large mass of ice disappeared; the water bubbled up over it; Mr. Pickwick's hat, gloves, and handkerchief were floating on the surface; and this was all of Mr. Pickwick that anybody could see.

Dismay and anguish were depicted on every countenance; the males turned pale, and the females fainted; Mr. Snodgrass and Mr. Winkle grasped each other by the hand, and gazed at the spot where their leader had gone down, with frenzied eagerness; while Mr. Tupman, by way of rendering the promptest assistance, and at the same time conveying to any persons who might be within hearing, the clearest possible notion of the catastrophe, ran off across the country at his utmost speed, screaming "Fire!" with all his might.

It was at this moment, when old Wardle and Sam Weller were approaching the hole with cautious steps, and Mr. Benjamin Allen was holding a hurried consultation with Mr. Bob Sawyer on the advisability of bleeding the company generally, as an improving little bit of professional practice—it was at this very moment, that a face, head, and shoulders, emerged from beneath the water, and disclosed the features and spectacles of Mr. Pickwick.

"Keep yourself up for an instant—for only one instant!" bawled Mr. Snodgrass.

"Yes, do; let me implore you—for my sake!" roared Mr. Winkle, deeply affected. The adjuration was rather unnecessary; the probability being, that if Mr. Pickwick had declined to keep himself up for anybody else's sake, it would have occurred to him that he might as well do so, for his own.

"Do you feel the bottom there, old fellow?" said Wardle.

"Yes, certainly," replied Mr. Pickwick, wringing the water from his head and face, and gasping for breath. "I fell upon my back. I couldn't get on my feet at first."

The clay upon so much of Mr. Pickwick's coat as was yet visible, bore testimony to the accuracy of this statement; and as the fears of the spectators were still further relieved by the fat boy's suddenly recollecting that the water was nowhere more than five feet deep, prodigies of valour were performed to get him out. After a vast quantity of splashing, and cracking, and struggling, Mr. Pickwick was at length fairly extricated from his unpleasant position, and once more stood on dry land.

"Oh, he'll catch his death of cold," said Emily.

"Dear old thing!" said Arabella. "Let me wrap this shawl round you, Mr. Pickwick."

"Ah, that's the best thing you can do," said Wardle; "and when you've got it on, run home as fast as your legs can carry you, and jump into bed directly."

A dozen shawls were offered on the instant. Three or four of the thickest having been selected, Mr. Pickwick was wrapped up, and started off, under the guidance of Mr. Weller; presenting the singular phenomenon of an elderly gentleman, dripping wet, and without a hat, with his arms bound down to his sides, skimming over the ground, without any clearly-defined purpose, at the rate of six good English miles an hour.

But Mr. Pickwick cared not for appearances in such an extreme case, and urged on by Sam Weller, he kept at the very top of his speed until he reached the door of Manor Farm, where Mr. Tupman had arrived some five minutes before, and had frightened the old lady into palpitations of the heart by impressing her with the unalterable conviction that the kitchen chimney was on fire—a calamity which always presented itself in glowing colours to the old lady's mind, when anybody about her evinced the smallest agitation.

Mr. Pickwick paused not an instant until he was snug in bed. Sam Weller lighted a blazing fire in the room, and took up his dinner; a bowl of punch was carried up afterwards, and a grand carouse held in honour of his safety. Old Wardle would not hear of his rising, so they made the bed the chair, and Mr. Pickwick presided. A second and a third bowl were ordered in; and when Mr. Pickwick awoke next morning, there was not a symptom of rheumatism about him; which proves, as Mr. Bob Sawyer very justly observed, that there is nothing like hot punch in such cases; and that if ever hot punch did fail to act as a preventive, it was merely because the patient fell into the vulgar error of not taking enough of it.

Bob Sawyer's Party

MR. BOB SAWYER embellished one side of the fire, in his first-floor front, early on the evening for which he had invited Mr. Pickwick, and Mr. Ben Allen the other. The preparations for the reception of visitors appeared to be completed. The umbrellas in the passage had been heaped into the little corner outside the back-parlour door; the bonnet and shawl of the landlady's servant had been removed from the banisters; there were not more than two pairs of pattens on the street-door mat; and a kitchen candle, with a very long snuff, burned cheerfully on the ledge of the staircase window. Mr. Bob Sawyer had himself purchased the spirits at a wine vault in High Street, and had returned home preceding the bearer thereof, to preclude the possibility of their delivery at the wrong house. The punch was ready-made in a red pan in the bedroom; a little table, covered with a green baize cloth, had been borrowed from the parlour, to play at cards on; and the glasses of the establishment, together with those which had been borrowed for the occasion from the public-house, were all drawn up in a tray, which was deposited on the landing outside the door.

Notwithstanding the highly satisfactory nature of all these arrangements, there was a cloud on the countenance of Mr. Bob Sawyer, as he sat by the fireside. There was a sympathising expression, too, in the features of Mr. Ben Allen, as he gazed intently on the coals, and a tone of melancholy in his voice, as he said, after a long silence—

"Well, it *is* unlucky she should have taken it into her head to turn sour, just on this occasion. She might at least have waited till to-morrow."

"That's her malevolence—that's her malevolence," returned Mr. Bob Sawyer vehemently. "She says that if I can afford to give a party I ought to be able to pay her confounded 'little bill.'"

"How long has it been running?" inquired Mr. Ben Allen. A bill, by the bye, is the most extraordinary locomotive engine that the genius of man ever produced. It would keep on running during the longest lifetime, without ever once stopping of its own accord.

"Only a quarter, and a month or so," replied Mr. Bob Sawyer.

Ben Allen coughed hopelessly, and directed a searching look between the two top bars of the stove.

"It'll be a deuced unpleasant thing if she takes it into her head to let out, when those fellows are here, won't it?" said Mr. Ben Allen at length.

"Horrible," replied Bob Sawyer, "horrible."

A low tap was heard at the room door. Mr. Bob Sawyer looked expressively at his friend, and bade the tapper come in; whereupon a dirty, slipshod girl in black cotton stockings, who might have passed for the neglected daughter of a superannuated dustman in very reduced circumstances, thrust in her head, and said —

"Please, Mr. Sawyer, Mrs. Raddle wants to speak to *you.*"

Before Mr. Bob Sawyer could return any answer, the girl suddenly disappeared with a jerk, as if somebody had given her a violent pull behind; this mysterious exit was no sooner accomplished, than there was another tap at the door—a smart, pointed tap, which seemed to say, "Here I am, and in I'm coming."

Mr. Bob Sawyer glanced at his friend with a look of abject apprehension, and once more cried, "Come in."

The permission was not at all necessary, for, before Mr. Bob Sawyer had uttered the words, a little, fierce woman bounced into the room, all in a tremble with passion, and pale with rage.

"Now, Mr. Sawyer," said the little, fierce woman, trying to appear very calm, "if you'll have the kindness to settle that little bill of mine

I'll thank you, because I've got my rent to pay this afternoon, and my landlord's a-waiting below now." Here the little woman rubbed her hands, and looked steadily over Mr. Bob Sawyer's head, at the wall behind him.

"I am very sorry to put you to any inconvenience, Mrs. Raddle," said Bob Sawyer deferentially, "but——"

"Oh, it isn't any inconvenience," replied the little woman, with a shrill titter. "I didn't want it particular before to-day; leastways, as it has to go to my landlord directly, it was as well for you to keep it as me. You promised me this afternoon, Mr. Sawyer, and every gentleman as has ever lived here, has kept his word, sir, as of course anybody as calls himself a gentleman does." Mrs. Raddle tossed her head, bit her lips, rubbed her hands harder, and looked at the wall more steadily than ever. It was plain to see, as Mr. Bob Sawyer remarked in a style of Eastern allegory on a subsequent occasion, that she was "getting the steam up."

"I am very sorry, Mrs. Raddle," said Bob Sawyer, with all imaginable humility, "but the fact is, that I have been disappointed in the city to-day."—Extraordinary place that city. An astonishing number of men always *are* getting disappointed there.

"Well, Mr. Sawyer," said Mrs. Raddle, planting herself firmly on a purple cauliflower in the Kidderminster carpet, "and what's that to me, sir?"

"I—I—have no doubt, Mrs. Raddle," said Bob Sawyer, blinking this last question, "that before the middle of next week we shall be able to set ourselves quite square, and go on, on a better system, afterwards."

This was all Mrs. Raddle wanted. She had bustled up to the apartment of the unlucky Bob Sawyer, so bent upon going into a passion, that, in all probability, payment would have rather disappointed her than otherwise. She was in excellent order for a little relaxation of the kind, having just exchanged a few introductory compliments with Mr. R. in the front kitchen.

"Do you suppose, Mr. Sawyer," said Mrs. Raddle, elevating her voice for the information of the neighbours—"do you suppose that I'm a-going day after day to let a fellar occupy my lodgings as never thinks of paying his rent, nor even the very money laid out for the fresh butter and lump sugar that's bought for his breakfast, and the very milk that's took in, at the street door? Do you suppose a hard-working and industrious woman as has lived in this street for twenty year (ten year over the way, and nine year and three-quarters in this very house) has nothing else to do but to work herself to death after a parcel of lazy idle fellars, that are always smoking and drinking, and lounging, when they ought to be glad to turn their hands to anything that would help 'em to pay their bills? Do you——"

"My good soul," interposed Mr. Benjamin Allen soothingly.

"Have the goodness to keep your observashuns to yourself, sir, I beg," said Mrs. Raddle, suddenly arresting the rapid torrent of her speech, and addressing the third party with impressive slowness and solemnity. "I am not aweer, sir, that you have any right to address your conversation to me. I don't think I let these apartments to you, sir."

"No, you certainly did not," said Mr. Benjamin Allen.

"Very good, sir," responded Mrs. Raddle, with lofty politeness. "Then p'raps, sir, you'll confine yourself to breaking the arms and legs of the poor people in the hospitals, and keep yourself *to* yourself, sir, or there may be some persons here as will make you, sir."

"But you are such an unreasonable woman," remonstrated Mr. Benjamin Allen.

"I beg your parding, young man," said Mrs. Raddle, in a cold perspiration of anger. "But will you have the goodness just to call me that again, sir?"

"I didn't make use of the word in any invidious sense, ma'am," replied Mr. Benjamin Allen, growing somewhat uneasy on his own account.

"I beg your parding, young man," demanded Mrs. Raddle, in a louder and more imperative tone. "But who do you call a woman? Did you make that remark to me, sir?"

"Why, bless my heart!" said Mr. Benjamin Allen.

"Did you apply that name to me, I ask of you, sir?" interrupted Mrs. Raddle, with intense fierceness, throwing the door wide open.

"Why, of course I did," replied Mr. Benjamin Allen.

"Yes, of course you did," said Mrs. Raddle, backing gradually to the door, and raising her voice to its loudest pitch, for the special behoof of Mr. Raddle in the kitchen. "Yes, of course you did! And everybody knows that they may safely insult me in my own 'ouse while my husband sits sleeping downstairs, and taking no more notice than if I was a dog in the streets. He ought to be ashamed of himself (here Mrs. Raddle sobbed) to allow his wife to be treated in this way by a parcel of young cutters and carvers of live people's bodies, that disgraces the lodgings (another sob), and leaving her exposed to all manner of abuse; a base, faint-hearted, timorous wretch, that's afraid to come upstairs, and face the ruffinly creatures—that's afraid—that's afraid to come!" Mrs. Raddle paused to listen whether the repetition of the taunt had roused her better half; and finding that it had not been successful, proceeded to descend the stairs with sobs innumerable; when there came a loud double knock at the street door; whereupon she burst into an hysterical fit of weeping, accompanied with dismal moans, which was prolonged until the knock had been repeated six times, when, in an uncontrollable burst of mental agony, she threw down all the umbrellas, and disappeared into the back parlour, closing the door after her with an awful crash.

"Does Mr. Sawyer live here?" said Mr. Pickwick, when the door was opened.

"Yes," said the girl, "first floor. It's the door straight afore you, when you gets to the top of the stairs." Having given this instruction, the handmaid, who had been brought up among the aboriginal inhabitants of Southwark, disappeared, with the candle in her hand, down the kitchen stairs, perfectly satisfied that she had done everything that could possibly be required of her under the circumstances.

Mr. Snodgrass, who entered last, secured the street door, after several ineffectual efforts, by putting up the chain; and the friends stumbled upstairs, where they were received by Mr. Bob Sawyer, who had been afraid to go down, lest he should be waylaid by Mrs. Raddle.

"How are you?" said the discomfited student. "Glad to see you—take care of the glasses." This caution was addressed to Mr. Pickwick, who had put his hat in the tray.

"Dear me," said Mr. Pickwick, "I beg your pardon."

"Don't mention it, don't mention it," said Bob Sawyer. "I'm rather confined for room here, but you must put up with all that, when you come to see a young bachelor. Walk in. You've seen this gentleman before, I think?" Mr. Pickwick shook hands with Mr. Benjamin Allen, and his friends followed his example. They had scarcely taken their seats when there was another double knock.

"I hope that's Jack Hopkins!" said Mr. Bob Sawyer. "Hush. Yes, it is. Come up, Jack; come up."

A heavy footstep was heard upon the stairs, and Jack Hopkins presented himself. He wore a black velvet waistcoat, with thunder-and-lightning buttons; and a blue striped shirt, with a white false collar.

"You're late, Jack?" said Mr. Benjamin Allen.

"Been detained at Bartholomew's," replied Hopkins.

"Anything new?"

"No, nothing particular. Rather a good accident brought into the casualty ward."

"What was that, sir?" inquired Mr. Pickwick.

"Only a man fallen out of a four pair of stairs' window; but it's a very fair case indeed."

"Do you mean that the patient is in a fair way to recover?" inquired Mr. Pickwick.

"No," replied Mr. Hopkins carelessly. "No, I should rather say he wouldn't. There must be a splendid operation, though, to-morrow—magnificent sight if Slasher does it."

"You consider Mr. Slasher a good operator?" said Mr. Pickwick.

"Best alive," replied Hopkins. "Took a boy's leg out of the socket last week—boy ate five apples and a gingerbread cake—exactly two minutes after it was all over, boy said he wouldn't lie there to be made game of, and he'd tell his mother if they didn't begin."

"Dear me!" said Mr. Pickwick, astonished.

"Pooh! That's nothing, that ain't," said Jack Hopkins. "Is it, Bob?"

"Nothing at all," replied Mr. Bob Sawyer.

"By the bye, Bob," said Hopkins, with a scarcely perceptible glance at Mr. Pickwick's attentive face, "we had a curious accident last night. A child was brought in, who had swallowed a necklace."

"Swallowed what, sir?" interrupted Mr. Pickwick.

"A necklace," replied Jack Hopkins. "Not all at once, you know, that would be too much—*you* couldn't swallow that, if the child did—eh, Mr. Pickwick? ha, ha!" Mr. Hopkins appeared highly gratified with his own pleasantry, and continued—"No, the way was this. Child's parents were poor people who lived in a court. Child's eldest sister bought a necklace—common necklace, made of large black wooden beads. Child being fond of toys, cribbed the necklace, hid it, played with it, cut the string, and swallowed a bead. Child thought it capital fun, went back next day, and swallowed another bead."

"Bless my heart," said Mr. Pickwick, "what a dreadful thing! I beg your pardon, sir. Go on."

"Next day, child swallowed two beads; the day after that, he treated himself to three, and so on, till in a week's time he had got through the necklace—five-and-twenty beads in all. The sister, who was an industrious girl, and seldom treated herself to a bit of finery, cried her eyes out, at the loss of the necklace; looked high and low for it; but, I needn't say, didn't find it. A few days afterwards, the family were at dinner—baked shoulder of mutton, and potatoes under it—the child, who wasn't hungry, was playing about the room, when suddenly there was heard a devil of a noise, like a small hail-storm. 'Don't do that, my boy,' said the father. 'I ain't a-doin' nothing,' said the child. 'Well, don't do it again,' said the father. There was a short silence, and then the noise began again, worse than ever. 'If you don't mind what I say, my boy,' said the father, 'you'll find yourself in bed, in something less than a pig's whisper.' He gave the child a shake to make him obedient, and such a rattling ensued as nobody ever heard before. 'Why, damme, it's *in* the child!' said the father, 'he's got the croup in the wrong place!' 'No, I haven't, father,' said the child, beginning to cry, 'it's the necklace; I swallowed it, father.'—The father caught the child up, and ran with him to the hospital; the beads in the boy's stomach rattling all the way with the jolting; and the people looking up in the air, and down in the cellars, to see where the unusual sound came from. He's in the hospital now," said Jack Hopkins, "and he makes such a devil of a noise when he walks about, that they're obliged to muffle him in a watchman's coat, for fear he should wake the patients."

"That's the most extraordinary case I ever heard of," said Mr. Pickwick, with an emphatic blow on the table.

"Oh, that's nothing," said Jack Hopkins. "Is it, Bob?"

"Certainly not," replied Mr. Bob Sawyer.

"Very singular things occur in our profession, I can assure you, sir," said Hopkins.

"So I should be disposed to imagine," replied Mr. Pickwick.

Another knock at the door announced a large-headed young man in a black wig, who brought with him a scorbutic youth in a long stock. The next comer was a gentleman in a shirt emblazoned with pink anchors, who was closely followed by a pale youth with a plated watchguard. The arrival of a prim personage in clean linen and cloth boots rendered the party complete. The little table with the green baize cover was wheeled out; the first instalment of punch was brought in, in a white jug; and the succeeding three hours were devoted to *vingt-et-un* at sixpence a dozen, which was only once interrupted by a slight dispute between the scorbutic youth and the gentleman with the pink anchors; in the course of which, the scorbutic youth intimated a burning desire to pull the nose of the gentleman with the emblems of hope; in reply to which, that individual expressed his decided unwillingness to accept of any "sauce" on gratuitous terms, either from the irascible young gentleman with the scorbutic countenance, or any other person who was ornamented with a head.

When the last "natural" had been declared, and the profit and loss account of fish and sixpences adjusted, to the satisfaction of all parties, Mr. Bob Sawyer rang for supper, and the visitors squeezed themselves into corners while it was getting ready.

It was not so easily got ready as some people may imagine. First of all, it was necessary to awaken the girl, who had fallen asleep with her face on the kitchen table; this took a little time, and, even when she did answer the bell, another quarter of an hour was consumed in fruitless endeavours to impart to her a faint and distant glimmering of reason. The man to whom the order for the oysters had been sent, had not been told to open them; it is a very difficult thing to open an oyster with a limp knife and a two-pronged fork; and very little was done in this way. Very little of the beef was done either; and the ham (which was also from the German-sausage shop round the corner) was in a similar predicament. However, there was plenty of porter in a tin can; and the cheese went a great way, for it was very strong. So upon the whole, perhaps, the supper was quite as good as such matters usually are.

After supper, another jug of punch was put upon the table, together with a paper of cigars, and a couple of bottles of spirits. Then there was an awful pause; and this awful pause was occasioned by a very common occurrence in this sort of place, but a very embarrassing one notwithstanding.

The fact is, the girl was washing the glasses. The establishment boasted four: we do not record the circumstance as at all derogatory to Mrs. Raddle, for there never was a lodging-house yet, that was not short of glasses. The landlady's glasses were little, thin, blown-glass tumblers, and those which had been borrowed from the public-house were great, dropsical, bloated articles, each supported on a huge gouty leg. This would have been in itself sufficient to have possessed the company with the real state of affairs; but the young woman of all work had prevented the possibility of any misconception arising in the mind of any gentleman upon the subject, by forcibly dragging every man's glass away, long before he had finished his beer, and audibly stating, despite the winks and interruptions of Mr. Bob Sawyer, that it was to be conveyed downstairs, and washed forthwith.

It is a very ill wind that blows nobody any good. The prim man in the cloth boots, who had been unsuccessfully attempting to make a joke during the whole time the round game lasted, saw his opportunity, and availed himself of it. The instant the glasses disappeared, he commenced a long story about a great public character, whose name he had forgotten, making a particularly happy reply to another eminent and illustrious individual whom he had never been able to identify. He enlarged at some length and with great minuteness upon divers collateral circumstances, distantly connected with the anecdote in hand, but for the life of him he couldn't recollect at that precise moment what the anecdote was, although he had been in the habit of telling the story with great applause for the last ten years.

"Dear me," said the prim man in the cloth boots, "it is a very extraordinary circumstance."

"I am sorry you have forgotten it," said Mr. Bob Sawyer, glancing eagerly at the door, as he thought he heard the noise of glasses jingling; "very sorry."

"So am I," responded the prim man, "because I know it would have afforded so much amusement. Never mind; I dare say I shall manage to recollect it, in the course of half an hour or so."

The prim man arrived at this point just as the glasses came back, when Mr. Bob Sawyer, who had been absorbed in attention during the whole time, said he should very much like to hear the end of it, for, so far as it went, it was, without exception, the very best story he had ever heard.

The sight of the tumblers restored Bob Sawyer to a degree of equanimity which he had not possessed since his interview with his landlady. His face brightened up, and he began to feel quite convivial.

"Now, Betsy," said Mr. Bob Sawyer, with great suavity, and dispersing, at the same time, the tumultuous little mob of glasses the girl had collected in the centre of the table—"now, Betsy, the warm water; be brisk, there's a good girl."

"You can't have no warm water," replied Betsy.

"No warm water!" exclaimed Mr. Bob Sawyer.

"No," said the girl, with a shake of the head which expressed a more decided negative than the most copious language could have conveyed. "Mrs. Raddle said you warn't to have none."

The surprise depicted on the countenances of his guests imparted new courage to the host.

"Bring up the warm water instantly—instantly!" said Mr. Bob Sawyer, with desperate sternness.

"No. I can't," replied the girl, "Mrs. Raddle raked out the kitchen fire afore she went to bed, and locked up the kittle."

"Oh, never mind; never mind. Pray don't disturb yourself about such a trifle," said Mr. Pickwick, observing the conflict of Bob Sawyer's passions, as depicted in his countenance, "cold water will do very well."

"Oh, admirably," said Mr. Benjamin Allen.

"My landlady is subject to some slight attacks of mental derangement," remarked Bob Sawyer, with a ghastly smile; "I fear I must give her warning."

"No, don't," said Ben Allen.

"I fear I must," said Bob, with heroic firmness. "I'll pay her what I owe her, and give her warning to-morrow morning." Poor fellow! how devoutly he wished he could!

Mr. Bob Sawyer's heart-sickening attempts to rally under this last blow, communicated a dispiriting influence to the company, the greater part of whom, with the view of raising their spirits, attached themselves with extra cordiality to the cold brandy-and-water, the first perceptible effects of which were displayed in a renewal of hostilities between the scorbutic youth and the gentleman in the shirt. The belligerents vented their feelings of mutual contempt, for some time, in a variety of frownings and snortings, until at last the scorbutic youth felt it necessary to come to a more explicit understanding on the matter; when the following clear understanding took place.

"Sawyer," said the scorbutic youth, in a loud voice.

"Well, Noddy," replied Mr. Bob Sawyer.

"I should be very sorry, Sawyer," said Mr. Noddy, "to create any unpleasantness at any friend's table, and much less at yours, Sawyer—very; but I must take this opportunity of informing Mr. Gunter that he is no gentleman."

"And *I* should be very sorry, Sawyer, to create any disturbance in the street in which you reside," said Mr. Gunter, "but I'm afraid I shall be under the necessity of alarming the neighbours by throwing the person who has just spoken, out o' window."

"What do you mean by that, sir?" inquired Mr. Noddy.

"What I say, sir," replied Mr. Gunter.

"I should like to see you do it, sir," said Mr. Noddy.

"You shall *feel* me do it in half a minute, sir," replied Mr. Gunter.

"I request that you'll favour me with your card, sir," said Mr. Noddy.

"I'll do nothing of the kind, sir," replied Mr. Gunter.

"Why not, sir?" inquired Mr. Noddy.

"Because you'll stick it up over your chimney-piece, and delude your visitors into the false belief that a gentleman has been to see you, sir," replied Mr. Gunter.

"Sir, a friend of mine shall wait on you in the morning," said Mr. Noddy.

"Sir, I'm very much obliged to you for the caution, and I'll leave particular directions with the servant to lock up the spoons," replied Mr. Gunter.

At this point the remainder of the guests interposed, and remonstrated with both parties on the impropriety of their conduct; on which Mr. Noddy begged to state that his father was quite as respectable as Mr. Gunter's father; to which Mr. Gunter replied that his father was to the full as respectable as Mr. Noddy's father, and that his father's son was as good a man as Mr. Noddy, any day in the week. As this announcement seemed the prelude to a recommencement of the dispute, there was another interference on the part of the company; and a vast quantity of talking and clamouring ensued, in the course of which Mr. Noddy gradually allowed his feelings to overpower him, and professed that he had ever entertained a devoted personal attachment towards Mr. Gunter. To this Mr. Gunter replied that, upon the whole, he rather preferred Mr. Noddy to his own brother; on hearing which admission, Mr. Noddy magnanimously rose from his seat, and proffered his hand to Mr. Gunter. Mr. Gunter grasped it with affecting fervour; and everybody said that the whole dispute had been conducted in a manner which was highly honourable to both parties concerned.

"Now," said Jack Hopkins, "just to set us going again, Bob, I don't mind singing a song." And Hopkins, incited thereto by tumultuous applause, plunged himself at once into "The King, God bless him," which he sang as loud as he could, to a novel air, compounded of the "Bay of Biscay," and "A Frog he would." The chorus was the essence of the song; and, as each gentleman sang it to the tune he knew best, the effect was very striking indeed.

It was at the end of the chorus to the first verse, that Mr. Pickwick held up his hand in a listening attitude, and said, as soon as silence was restored—

"Hush! I beg your pardon. I thought I heard somebody calling from upstairs."

A profound silence immediately ensued; and Mr. Bob Sawyer was observed to turn pale.

"I think I hear it now," said Mr. Pickwick. "Have the goodness to open the door."

The door was no sooner opened than all doubt on the subject was removed.

"Mr. Sawyer! Mr. Sawyer!" screamed a voice from the two-pair landing.

"It's my landlady," said Bob Sawyer, looking round him with great dismay. "Yes, Mrs. Raddle."

"What do you mean by this, Mr. Sawyer?" replied the voice, with great shrillness and rapidity of utterance. "Ain't it enough to be swindled out of one's rent, and money lent out of pocket besides, and abused and insulted by your friends that dares to call themselves men, without having the house turned out of window, and noise enough made to bring the fire-engines here, at two o'clock in the morning?—Turn them wretches away."

"You ought to be ashamed of yourselves," said the voice of Mr. Raddle, which appeared to proceed from beneath some distant bed-clothes.

"Ashamed of themselves!" said Mrs. Raddle. "Why don't you go down and knock 'em every one downstairs? You would if you was a man."

"I should if I was a dozen men, my dear," replied Mr. Raddle pacifically, "but they have the advantage of me in numbers, my dear."

"Ugh, you coward!" replied Mrs. Raddle, with supreme contempt. "*Do* you mean to turn them wretches out, or not, Mr. Sawyer?"

"They're going, Mrs. Raddle, they're going," said the miserable Bob. "I am afraid you'd better go," said Mr. Bob Sawyer to his friends. "I *thought* you were making too much noise."

"It's a very unfortunate thing," said the prim man. "Just as we were getting so comfortable too!" The prim man was just beginning to have a dawning recollection of the story he had forgotten.

"It's hardly to be borne," said the prim man, looking round. "Hardly to be borne, is it?"

"Not to be endured," replied Jack Hopkins; "let's have the other verse, Bob. Come, here goes!"

"No, no, Jack, don't," interposed Bob Sawyer; "it's a capital song, but I am afraid we had better not have the other verse. They are very violent people, the people of the house."

"Shall I step upstairs, and pitch into the landlord?" inquired Hopkins, "or keep on ringing the bell, or go and groan on the staircase? You may command me, Bob."

"I am very much indebted to you for your friendship and good-nature, Hopkins," said the wretched Mr. Bob Sawyer, "but I think the best plan to avoid any further dispute is for us to break up at once."

"Now, Mr. Sawyer," screamed the shrill voice of Mrs. Raddle, "*are* them brutes going?"

"They're only looking for their hats, Mrs. Raddle," said Bob; "they are going directly."

"Going!" said Mrs. Raddle, thrusting her nightcap over the banisters just as Mr. Pickwick, followed by Mr. Tupman, emerged from the sitting-room. "Going! what did they ever come for?"

"My dear ma'am," remonstrated Mr. Pickwick, looking up.

"Get along with you, old wretch!" replied Mrs. Raddle, hastily withdrawing the nightcap. "Old enough to be his grandfather, you willin! You're worse than any of 'em."

Mr. Pickwick found it in vain to protest his innocence, so hurried downstairs into the street, whither he was closely followed by Mr. Tupman, Mr. Winkle, and Mr. Snodgrass. Mr. Ben Allen, who was dismally depressed with spirits and agitation, accompanied them as far as London Bridge, and in the course of the walk confided to Mr. Winkle, as an especially eligible person to intrust the secret to, that he was resolved to cut the throat of any gentleman, except Mr. Bob Sawyer, who should aspire to the affections of his sister Arabella. Having expressed his determination to perform this painful duty of a brother with proper firmness, he burst into tears, knocked his hat over his eyes, and, making the best of his way back, knocked double knocks at the door of the Borough Market office, and took short naps on the steps alternately, until daybreak, under the firm impression that he lived there, and had forgotten the key.

The visitors having all departed, in compliance with the rather pressing request of Mrs. Raddle, the luckless Mr. Bob Sawyer was left alone, to meditate on the probable events of to-morrow, and the pleasures of the evening.

From MARTIN CHUZZLEWIT

The first Appearance of Mrs. Gamp

MR. PECKSNIFF was in a hackney cabriolet, for Jonas Chuzzlewit had said "Spare no expense." Mankind is evil in its thoughts and in its base constructions, and Jonas was resolved it should not have an inch to stretch into an ell against him. It never should be charged upon his father's son that he had grudged the money for his father's funeral. Hence, until the obsequies should be concluded, Jonas had taken for his motto "Spend, and spare not!"

Mr. Pecksniff had been to the undertaker, and was now upon his way to another officer in the train of mourning: a female functionary, a nurse, and watcher, and performer of nameless offices about the persons of the dead: whom he had recommended. Her name, as Mr. Pecksniff gathered from a scrap of writing in his hand, was Gamp; her residence in Kingsgate Street, High Holborn. So Mr. Pecksniff, in a hackney cab, was rattling over Holborn stones, in quest of Mrs. Gamp.

This lady lodged at a bird-fancier's, next door but one to the celebrated mutton-pie shop, and directly opposite to the original cat's-meat warehouse; the renown of which establishments was duly heralded on their respective fronts. It was a little house, and this was the more convenient; for Mrs. Gamp being, in her highest walk of art, a monthly nurse, or, as her sign-board boldly had it, "Midwife," and lodging in the first-floor front, was easily assailable at night by pebbles, walking-sticks, and fragments of tobacco-pipe: all much more efficacious than the street-door knocker, which was so constructed as to wake the street with ease, and even spread alarms of fire in Holborn, without making the smallest impression on the premises to which it was addressed.

It chanced on this particular occasion, that Mrs. Gamp had been up all the previous night, in attendance upon a ceremony to which the usage of gossips has given that name which expresses, in two syllables, the curse pronounced on Adam. It chanced that Mrs. Gamp had not been regularly engaged, but had been called in at a crisis, in consequence of her great repute, to assist another professional lady with her advice; and thus it happened that, all points of interest in the case being over, Mrs. Gamp had come home again to the bird-fancier's, and gone to bed. So, when Mr. Pecksniff drove up in the hackney cab, Mrs. Gamp's curtains were drawn close, and Mrs. Gamp was fast asleep behind them.

If the bird-fancier had been at home, as he ought to have been, there would have been no great harm in this; but he was out, and his shop was closed. The shutters were down certainly; and in every pane of glass there was at least one tiny bird in a tiny bird-cage, twittering and hopping his little ballet of despair, and knocking his head against the roof: while one unhappy goldfinch who lived outside a red villa with his name on the door, drew the water for his own drinking, and mutely appealed to some good man to drop a farthing's worth of poison in it. Still, the door was shut. Mr. Pecksniff tried the latch, and shook it, causing a cracked bell inside to ring most mournfully; but no one came. The bird-fancier was an easy shaver also, and a fashionable hair-dresser also; and perhaps he had been sent for, express, from the court end of the town, to trim a lord, or cut and curl a lady; but however that might be, there, upon his own ground, he was not; nor was there any more distinct trace of him to assist the imagination of an inquirer, than a professional print or emblem of his calling (much favoured in the trade), representing a hair-dresser of easy manners curling a lady of distinguished fashion, in the presence of a patent upright grand pianoforte.

Noting these circumstances, Mr. Pecksniff, in the innocence of his heart, applied himself to the knocker; but at the first double knock, every window in the street became alive with female heads; and before he could repeat the performance, whole troops of married ladies (some about to trouble Mrs. Gamp themselves, very shortly) came flocking round the steps, all crying out with one accord, and with uncommon interest, "Knock at the winder, sir, knock at the winder. Lord bless you, don't lose no more time than you can help; knock at the winder!"

Acting upon this suggestion, and borrowing the driver's whip for the purpose, Mr. Pecksniff soon made a commotion among the first-floor flower-pots, and roused Mrs. Gamp, whose voice—to the great satisfaction of the matrons—was heard to say, "I'm coming."

"He's as pale as a muffin," said one lady, in allusion to Mr. Pecksniff.

"So he ought to be, if he's the feelings of a man," observed another.

A third lady (with her arms folded) said she wished he had chosen any other time for fetching Mrs. Gamp, but it always happened so with *her*.

It gave Mr. Pecksniff much uneasiness to find, from these remarks, that he was supposed to have come to Mrs. Gamp upon an errand touching—not the close of life, but the other end. Mrs. Gamp herself was under the same impression, for, throwing open the window, she cried behind the curtains, as she hastily attired herself:

"Is it Mrs. Perkins?"

"No!" returned Mr. Pecksniff, sharply. "Nothing of the sort."

"What, Mr. Whilks!" cried Mrs. Gamp. "Don't say it's you, Mr. Whilks, and that poor creetur Mrs. Whilks with not even a pincushion ready. Don't say it's you, Mr. Whilks!"

"It isn't Mr. Whilks," said Pecksniff. "I don't know the man. Nothing of the kind. A gentleman is dead; and some person being wanted in the house, you have been recommended by Mr. Mould the undertaker."

As she was by this time in a condition to appear, Mrs. Gamp, who had a face for all occasions, looked out of the window with her mourning countenance, and said she would be down directly. But the matrons took it very ill, that Mr. Pecksniff's mission was of so unimportant a kind; and the lady with her arms folded rated him in good round terms, signifying that she would be glad to know what he meant by terrifying delicate females "with his corpses;" and giving it as her opinion that he was quite ugly enough to know better. The other ladies were not at all behind-hand in expressing similar sentiments; and the children, of whom some scores had now collected, hooted and defied Mr. Pecksniff quite savagely. So, when Mrs. Gamp appeared, the unoffending gentleman was glad to hustle her with very little ceremony into the cabriolet, and drive off, overwhelmed with popular execration.

Mrs. Gamp had a large bundle with her, a pair of pattens, and a species of gig umbrella; the latter article in colour like a faded leaf, except where a circular patch of a lively blue had been dexterously let in at the top. She was much flurried by the haste she had made, and laboured under the most erroneous views of cabriolets, which she appeared to confound with mail-coaches or stage-waggons, inasmuch as she was constantly endeavouring for the first half mile to force her luggage through the little front window, and clamouring to the driver to "put it in the boot." When she was disabused of this idea, her whole being resolved itself into an absorbing anxiety about her pattens, with which she played innumerable games at quoits, on Mr. Pecksniff's legs. It was not until they were close upon the house of mourning that she had enough composure to observe:

"And so the gentleman's dead, sir! Ah! The more's the pity." She didn't even know his name. "But it's what we must all come to. It's as certain as being born, except that we can't make our calculations as exact. Ah! Poor dear!"

She was a fat old woman, this Mrs. Gamp, with a husky voice and a moist eye, which she had a remarkable power of turning up, and only showing the white of it. Having very little neck, it cost her some trouble to look over herself, if one may say so, at those to whom she talked. She wore a very rusty black gown, rather the worse for snuff, and a shawl and bonnet to correspond. In these dilapidated articles of dress she had, on principle, arrayed herself, time out of mind, on such occasions as the present; for this at once expressed a decent amount of veneration for the deceased, and invited the next of kin to present her with a fresher suit of weeds: an appeal so frequently successful, that the very fetch and ghost of Mrs. Gamp, bonnet and all, might be seen hanging up, any hour in the day, in at least a dozen of the second-hand clothes shops about Holborn. The face of Mrs. Gamp—the nose in particular—was somewhat red and swollen, and it was difficult to enjoy her society without becoming conscious of a smell of spirits. Like most persons who have attained to great eminence in their profession, she took to hers very kindly; insomuch, that setting aside her natural predilections as a woman, she went to a lying-in or a laying-out with equal zest and relish.

"Ah!" repeated Mrs. Gamp; for it was always a safe sentiment in cases of mourning. "Ah dear! When Gamp was summoned to his long home, and I see him a lying in Guy's Hospital with a penny-piece on each eye, and his wooden leg under his left arm, I thought I should have fainted away. But I bore up."

If certain whispers current in the Kingsgate Street circles had any truth in them, she had indeed borne up surprisingly; and had exerted such uncommon fortitude, as to dispose of Mr. Gamp's remains for the benefit of science. But it should be added, in fairness, that this had happened twenty years before; and that Mr. and Mrs. Gamp had long been separated, on the ground of incompatibility of temper in their drink.

"You have become indifferent since then, I suppose?" said Mr. Pecksniff. "Use is second nature, Mrs. Gamp."

"You may well say second nater, sir," returned that lady. "One's first ways is to find sich things a trial to the feelings, and so is one's lasting custom. If it wasn't for the nerve a little sip of liquor gives me (I never was able to do more than taste it), I never could go through with what I sometimes has to do. 'Mrs. Harris,' I says, at the very last case as ever I acted in, which it was but a young person, 'Mrs. Harris,' I says, 'leave the bottle on the chimley-piece, and don't ask me to take none, but let me put my lips to it when I am so dispoged, and then I will do what I'm engaged to do, according to the best of my ability.' 'Mrs. Gamp,' she says, in answer, 'if ever there was a sober creetur to be got at eighteen pence a day for working people, and three and six for gentlefolks—night watching,'" said Mrs. Gamp, with emphasis, "'being a extra charge—you are that inwallable person.' 'Mrs. Harris,' I says to her, 'don't name the charge, for if I could afford to lay all my feller creeturs out for nothink, I would gladly do it, sich is the love I bears 'em. But what I always says to them as has the management of matters, Mrs. Harris:'" here she kept her eye on Mr. Pecksniff: "'be they gents or be they ladies, is, don't ask me whether I won't take none, or whether I will, but leave the bottle on the chimley-piece, and let me put my lips to it when I am so dispoged.'"

From A Christmas Carol

The Cratchits' Dinner

Then up rose Mrs. Cratchit, Cratchit's wife, dressed out but poorly in a twice-turned gown, but brave in ribbons, which are cheap and make a goodly show for sixpence; and she laid the cloth, assisted by Belinda Cratchit, second of her daughters, also brave in ribbons; while Master Peter Cratchit plunged a fork into the saucepan of potatoes, and getting the corners of his monstrous shirt collar (Bob's private property, conferred upon his son and heir in honor of the day) into his mouth, rejoiced to find himself so gallantly attired, and yearned to show his linen in the fashionable Parks. And now two smaller Cratchits, boy and girl, came tearing in, screaming that outside the baker's they had smelt the goose, and known it for their own; and basking in luxurious thoughts of sage and onion, these young Cratchits danced about the table, and exalted Master Peter Cratchit to the skies, while he (not proud, although his collar near choked him) blew the fire, until the slow potatoes bubbling up, knocked loudly at the saucepan-lid to be let out and peeled.

"What has ever got your precious father then?" said Mrs. Cratchit. "And your brother, Tiny Tim! And Martha warn't as late last Christmas Day by half an hour!"

"Here's Martha, mother," said a girl appearing as she spoke.

"Here's Martha, mother!" cried the two young Cratchits. "Hurrah! There's *such* a goose, Martha!"

"Why, bless your heart alive, my dear, how late you are!" said Mrs. Cratchit, kissing her a dozen times, and taking off her shawl and bonnet for her with officious zeal.

"We'd a deal of work to finish up last night," replied the girl, "and had to clear away this morning, mother!"

"Well! never mind so long as you are come," said Mrs. Cratchit. "Sit ye down before the fire, my dear, and have a warm, Lord bless ye!"

"No no! There's father coming," cried the two young Cratchits, who were everywhere at once. "Hide, Martha, hide!"

So Martha hid herself, and in came little Bob, the father, with at least three feet of comforter exclusive of the fringe hanging down before him; and his threadbare clothes darned up and brushed, to look seasonable; and Tiny Tim upon his shoulder. Alas for Tiny Tim, he bore a little crutch, and had his limbs supported by an iron frame.

"Why, where's our Martha?" cried Bob Cratchit looking round.

"Not coming," said Mrs. Cratchit.

"Not coming!" said Bob, with a sudden declension in his high spirits; for he had been Tim's blood horse all the way from church, and had come home rampant. "Not coming upon Christmas Day!"

Martha didn't like to see him disappointed, if it were only a joke; so she came out prematurely from behind the closet door, and ran into his arms, while the two young Cratchits hustled Tiny Tim, and bore him off into the washhouse, that he might hear the pudding singing in the copper.

"And how did little Tim behave?" asked Mrs. Cratchit, when she had rallied Bob on his credulity, and Bob had hugged his daughter to his heart's content.

"As good as gold," said Bob, "and better. Somehow he gets thoughtful, sitting by himself so much, and thinks the strangest things you ever heard. He told me coming home, that he hoped the people saw him in the church, because he was a cripple, and it might be pleasant to them to remember upon Christmas Day, who made lame beggars walk and blind men see."

Bob's voice was tremulous when he told them this, and trembled more when he said that Tiny Tim was growing strong and hearty.

His active little crutch was heard upon the floor, and back came Tiny Tim before another word was spoken, escorted by his brother and sister to his stool beside the fire; and while Bob, turning up his cuffs—as if, poor fellow, they were capable of being made more shabby—compounded some hot mixture in a jug with gin and lemons, and stirred it round and round and put it on the hob to simmer; Master Peter and the two ubiquitous young Cratchits went to fetch the goose, with which they soon returned in high procession.

Such a bustle ensued that you might have thought a goose the rarest of all birds; a feathered phenomenon, to which a black swan was a matter of course—and in truth it was something very like it in that house. Mrs. Cratchit made the gravy (ready beforehand in a little saucepan) hissing hot: Master Peter mashed the potatoes with incredible vigor; Miss Belinda sweetened up the apple-sauce; Martha dusted the hot plates; Bob took Tiny Tim beside him in a tiny corner at the table; the two young Cratchits set chairs for everybody, not forgetting themselves, and mounting guard upon their posts, crammed spoons into their mouths, lest they should shriek for goose before their turn came to be helped. At last the dishes were set on, and grace was said. It was succeeded by a breathless pause, as Mrs. Cratchit, looking slowly all along the carving-knife, prepared to plunge it in the breast; but when she did, and when the long-expected gush of stuffing issued forth, one murmur of delight arose all round the board, and even Tiny Tim, excited by the two young Cratchits, beat on the table with the handle of his knife, and feebly cried Hurrah!

There never was such a goose. Bob said he didn't believe there ever was such a goose cooked. Its tenderness and flavor, size and cheapness, were the themes of universal admiration. Eked out by apple-sauce and mashed potatoes, it was a sufficient dinner for the whole family; indeed, as Mrs. Cratchit said with great delight (surveying one small atom of a bone upon the dish), they hadn't ate it all at last! Yet every one had had enough, and the youngest Cratchits in particular, were steeped in sage and onion to the eyebrows! But now the plates being changed by Miss Belinda, Mrs. Cratchit left the room alone—too nervous to bear witness—to take the pudding up, and bring it in.

Suppose it should not be done enough! Suppose it should break in turning out! Suppose somebody should have got over the wall of the backyard, and stolen it, while they were merry with the goose—a supposition at which the two young Cratchits became livid! All sorts of horrors were supposed.

Hallo! A great deal of steam! The pudding was out of the copper. A smell like a washing-day! That was the cloth. A smell like an eating-house and a pastrycook's next door to each other, with a laundress's next door to that! That was the pudding! In half a minute Mrs. Cratchit entered—flushed, but smiling proudly—with the pudding, like a speckled cannon-ball, so hard and firm, blazing in half of half a quartern of ignited brandy, and bedight with Christmas holly stuck into the top.

Oh, a wonderful pudding! Bob Cratchit said, and calmly too, that he regarded it as the greatest success achieved by Mrs. Cratchit since their marriage. Mrs. Cratchit said that now the weight was off her mind, she would confess she had her doubts about the quantity of flour. Everybody had something to say about it, but nobody said or thought it was at all a small pudding for a large family. It would have been flat heresy to do so. Any Cratchit would have blushed to hint at such a thing.

At last the dinner was all done, the cloth was cleared, the hearth swept, and the fire made up. The compound in the jug being tasted, and considered perfect, apples and oranges were put upon the table, and a shovel full of chestnuts on the fire. Then all the Cratchit family drew round the hearth, in what Bob Cratchit called a circle, meaning half a one; and at Bob Cratchit's elbow stood the family display of glass. Two tumblers and a custard-cup without a handle.

These held the hot stuff from the jug, however, as well as golden goblets would have done; and Bob served it out with beaming looks, while the chestnuts on the fire sputtered and cracked noisily. Then Bob proposed,—

"A Merry Christmas to us all, my dears. God bless us!"

Which all the family re-echoed.

"God bless us every one!" said Tiny Tim, the last of all.

From DAVID COPPERFIELD

My first Dissipation

Miss Betsey Trotwood, David Copperfield's great-aunt, wished him to become a proctor and, upon securing the young man's assent to her proposal, arranged at once to place him with Spenlow and Jorkins. He was to have a month's probation. Miss Trotwood secured bachelor's lodgings for him with Mrs. Crupp, in Buckingham Street in the Adelphi. The furniture had belonged to the last occupant, who, according to Mrs. Crupp, had died of drink and smoke. The young lady in the box is Agnes Wickfield, daughter of an attorney at Dover, in whose house David had lived while attending school. David had come to regard her as tenderly as a sister.

It was a wonderfully fine thing to have that lofty castle to myself, and to feel, when I shut my outer door, like Robinson Crusoe, when he had got into his fortification, and pulled his ladder up after him. It was a wonderfully fine thing to walk about town with the key of my house in my pocket, and to know that I could ask any fellow to come home, and make quite sure of its being inconvenient to nobody, if it were not so to me. It was a wonderfully fine thing to let myself in and out, and to come and go without a word to any one, and to ring Mrs. Crupp up, gasping, from the depths of the earth, when I wanted her—and when she was disposed to come. All this, I say, was wonderfully fine; but I must say, too, that there were times when it was very dreary.

It was fine in the morning, particularly in the fine mornings. It looked a very fresh, free life, by daylight: still fresher, and more free, by sunlight. But as the day declined, the life seemed to go down too. I don't know how it was; it seldom looked well by candle-light. I wanted somebody to talk to, then. I missed Agnes. I found a tremendous blank, in the place of that smiling repository of my confidence. Mrs. Crupp appeared to be a long way off. I thought about my predecessor, who had died of drink and smoke: and I could have wished he had been so good as to live, and not bother me with his decease.

After two days and nights, I felt as if I had lived there for a year, and yet I was not an hour older, but was quite as much tormented by my own youthfulness as ever.

Steerforth not yet appearing, which induced me to apprehend that he must be ill, I left the Commons early on the third day, and walked out to Highgate. Mrs. Steerforth was very glad to see me, and said that he had gone away with one of his Oxford friends to see another who lived near St. Alban's, but that she expected him to return tomorrow. I was so fond of him, that I felt quite jealous of his Oxford friends.

As she pressed me to stay to dinner, I remained, and I believe we talked about nothing but him all day. I told her how much the people liked him at Yarmouth, and what a delightful companion he had been. Miss Dartle was full of hints and mysterious questions, but took a great interest in all our proceedings there, and said, "was it really though?" and so forth, so often, that she got everything out of me she wanted to know. Her appearance was exactly what I have described it, when I first saw her; but the society of the two ladies was so agreeable, and came so natural to me, that I felt myself falling a little in love with her. I could not help thinking, several times in the course of the evening, and particularly when I walked home at night, what delightful company she would be in Buckingham Street.

I was taking my coffee and roll in the morning, before going to the Commons—and I may observe in this place that it is surprising how much coffee Mrs. Crupp used, and how weak it was, considering—when Steerforth himself walked in, to my unbounded joy.

"My dear Steerforth," cried I, "I began to think I should never see you again!"

"I was carried off, by force of arms," said Steerforth, "the very next morning after I got home. Why, Daisy, what a rare old bachelor you are here!"

I showed him over the establishment, not omitting the pantry, with no little pride, and he commended it highly. "I tell you what, old boy," he added, "I shall make quite a town-house of this place, unless you give me notice to quit."

This was a delightful hearing. I told him if he waited for that, he would have to wait till doomsday.

"But you shall have some breakfast!" said I, with my hand on the bell-rope, "and Mrs. Crupp shall make you some fresh coffee, and I'll toast you some bacon in a bachelor's Dutch-oven that I have got here."

"No, no!" said Steerforth. "Don't ring! I can't! I am going to breakfast with one of these fellows who is at the Piazza Hotel, in Covent Garden."

"But you'll come back to dinner?" said I.

"I can't, upon my life. There's nothing I should like better, but I *must* remain with these two fellows. We are all three off together to-morrow morning."

"Then bring them here to dinner," I returned. "Do you think they would come?"

"Oh! they would come fast enough," said Steerforth; "but we should inconvenience you. You had better come and dine with us somewhere."

I would not by any means consent to this, for it occurred to me that I really ought to have a little housewarming, and that there never could be a better opportunity. I had a new pride in my rooms after his approval of them, and burned with a desire to develop their utmost resources. I therefore made him promise positively in the names of his two friends, and we appointed six o'clock as the dinner-hour.

When he was gone, I rang for Mrs. Crupp, and acquainted her with my desperate design. Mrs. Crupp said, in the first place, of course it was well known she couldn't be expected to wait, but she knew a handy young man, who she thought could be prevailed upon to do it, and whose terms would be five shillings, and what I pleased. I said, certainly we would have him. Next, Mrs. Crupp said it was clear she couldn't be in two places at once (which I felt to be reasonable), and that "a young gal" stationed in the pantry with a bed-room candle, there never to desist from washing plates, would be indispensable. I said, what would be the expense of this young female, and Mrs. Crupp said she supposed eighteenpence would neither make me nor break me. I said I supposed not; and *that* was settled. Then Mrs. Crupp said, Now about the dinner.

It was a remarkable instance of want of forethought on the part of the ironmonger who had made Mrs. Crupp's kitchen fire-place, that it was capable of cooking nothing but chops and mashed potatoes. As to a fish-kittle, Mrs. Crupp said, well! would I only come and look at the range. She couldn't say fairer than that. Would I come and look at it? As I should not have been much the wiser if I *had* looked at it, I declined, and said, "Never mind fish." But Mrs. Crupp said, "Don't say that; oysters was in, and why not them?" So *that* was settled. Mrs. Crupp then said what she would recommend would be this. A pair of hot roast fowls—from the pastry-cook's; a dish of stewed beef, with vegetables—from the pastry-cook's; two little corner things, as a raised pie and a dish of kidneys—from the pastry-cook's; a tart, and (if I liked) a shape of jelly—from the pastry-cook's. This, Mrs. Crupp said, would leave her at full liberty to concentrate her mind on the potatoes, and to serve up the cheese and celery as she could wish to see it done.

I acted on Mrs. Crupp's opinion, and gave the order at the pastry-cook's myself. Walking along the Strand, afterwards, and observing a hard mottled substance in the window of a ham and beef shop, which resembled marble, but was labelled "Mock Turtle," I went in and bought a slab of it, which I have since seen reason to believe would have sufficed for fifteen people. This preparation, Mrs. Crupp, after some difficulty, consented to warm up; and it shrunk so much in a liquid state, that we found it what Steerforth called "rather a tight fit" for four.

These preparations happily completed, I bought a little dessert in Covent Garden Market, and gave a rather extensive order at a retail wine-merchant's in that vicinity. When I came home in the afternoon, and saw the bottles drawn up in a square on the pantry-floor, they looked so numerous (though there were two missing, which made Mrs. Crupp very uncomfortable), that I was absolutely frightened at them.

One of Steerforth's friends was named Grainger, and the other Markham. They were both very gay and lively fellows; Grainger, something older than Steerforth; Markham, youthful-looking, and I should say not more than twenty. I observed that the latter always spoke of himself indefinitely, as "a man," and seldom or never in the first person singular.

"A man might get on very well here, Mr. Copperfield," said Markham —meaning himself.

"It's not a bad situation," said I, "and the rooms are really commodious."

"I hope you have both brought appetites with you?" said Steerforth.

"Upon my honor," returned Markham, "town seems to sharpen a man's appetite. A man is hungry all day long. A man is perpetually eating."

Being a little embarrassed at first, and feeling much too young to preside, I made Steerforth take the head of the table when dinner was announced, and seated myself opposite to him. Everything was very good; we did not spare the wine; and he exerted himself so brilliantly to make the thing pass off well, that there was no pause in our festivity. I was not quite such good company during dinner, as I could have wished to be, for my chair was opposite the door, and my attention was distracted by observing that the handy young man went out of the room very often, and that his shadow always presented itself, immediately afterwards, on the wall of the entry, with a bottle at his mouth. The "young gal" likewise occasioned me some uneasiness: not so much by neglecting to wash the plates, as by breaking them. For being of an inquisitive disposition, and unable to confine herself (as her positive instructions were) to the pantry, she was constantly peering in at us, and constantly imagining herself detected; in which belief, she several times retired upon the plates (with which she had carefully paved the floor), and did a great deal of destruction.

These, however, were small drawbacks, and easily forgotten when the cloth was cleared, and the dessert put on the table; at which period of the entertainment the handy young man was discovered to be speechless. Giving him private directions to seek the society of Mrs. Crupp, and to remove the "young gal" to the basement also, I abandoned myself to enjoyment.

I began by being singularly cheerful and light-hearted; all sorts of half-forgotten things to talk about came rushing into my mind, and made me hold forth in a most unwonted manner. I laughed heartily at my own jokes, and everybody else's; called Steerforth to order for not passing the wine; made several engagements to go to Oxford; announced that I meant to have a dinner party exactly like that, once a week until further notice; and madly took so much snuff out of Grainger's box, that I was obliged to go into the pantry, and have a private fit of sneezing ten minutes long.

I went on, by passing the wine faster and faster yet, and continually starting up with a corkscrew to open more wine, long before any was needed. I proposed Steerforth's health. I said he was my dearest friend, the protector of my boyhood, and the companion of my prime. I said I was delighted to propose his health. I said I owed him more obligations than I could ever repay, and held him in a higher admiration than I could ever express. I finished by saying, "I'll give you Steerforth! God bless him! Hurrah!" We gave him three times three, and another, and a good one to finish with. I broke my glass in going round the table to shake hands with him, and I said (in two words) "Steerforth, you'retheguidingstarofmyexistence."

I went on, by finding suddenly that somebody was in the middle of a song. Markham was the singer, and he sang "When the heart of a man is depressed with care." He said, when he had sung it, he would give us "Woman!" I took objection to that, and I couldn't allow it. I said it was not a respectful way of proposing the toast, and I would never permit that toast to be drunk in my house otherwise than as "The Ladies!" I was very high with him, mainly I think because I saw Steerforth and Grainger laughing at me—or at him—or at both of us. He said a man was not to be dictated to. I said a man *was*. He said a man was not to be insulted, then. I said he was right there—never under my roof, where the Lares were sacred, and the laws of hospitality paramount. He said it was no derogation from a man's dignity to confess that I was a devilish good fellow. I instantly proposed his health.

Somebody was smoking. We were all smoking. *I* was smoking, and trying to suppress a rising tendency to shudder. Steerforth had made a speech about me, in the course of which I had been affected almost to tears. I returned thanks, and hoped the present company would dine with me to-morrow, and the day after—each day at five o'clock, that we might enjoy the pleasures of conversation and society through a long evening. I felt called upon to propose an individual. I would give them my aunt. Miss Betsey Trotwood, the best of her sex!

Somebody was leaning out of my bed-room window, refreshing his forehead against the cool stone of the parapet, and feeling the air upon his face. It was myself. I was addressing myself as "Copperfield," and saying, "Why did you try to smoke? You might have known you couldn't do it." Now, somebody was unsteadily contemplating his features in the looking-glass. That was I too. I was very pale in the looking-glass; my eyes had a vacant appearance; and my hair—only my hair, nothing else—looked drunk.

Somebody said to me, "Let us go to the theatre, Copperfield!" There was no bed-room before me, but again the jingling table covered with glasses; the lamp; Grainger on my right hand, Markham on my left, and Steerforth opposite—all sitting in a mist, and a long way off. The theatre? To be sure. The very thing. Come along! But they must excuse me if I saw everybody out first, and turned the lamp off—in case of fire.

Owing to some confusion in the dark, the door was gone. I was feeling for it in the window-curtains, when Steerforth laughing, took me by the arm and led me out. We went down stairs, one behind another. Near the bottom, somebody fell, and rolled down. Somebody else said it was Copperfield. I was angry at that false report, until, finding myself on my back in the passage, I began to think there might be some foundation for it.

A very foggy night, with great rings round the lamps in the streets! There was an indistinct talk of its being wet. *I* considered it frosty. Steerforth dusted me under a lamp-post, and put my hat into shape, which somebody produced from somewhere in a most extraordinary manner, for I hadn't had it on before. Steerforth then said, "You are all right, Copperfield, are you not?" and I told him, "Neverberrer."

A man, sitting in a pigeon-hole-place, looked out of the fog, and took money from somebody, inquiring if I was one of the gentlemen paid for, and appearing rather doubtful (as I remember in the glimpse I had of him) whether to take the money for me or not. Shortly afterwards, we were very high up in a very hot theatre, looking down into a large pit, that seemed to me to smoke; the people with whom it was crammed were so indistinct. There was a great stage, too, looking very clean and smooth after the streets; and there were people upon it, talking about something or other, but not at all intelligibly. There was an abundance of bright lights, and there was music, and there were ladies down in the boxes, and I don't know what more. The whole building looked to me, as if it were learning to swim; it conducted itself in such an unaccountable manner, when I tried to steady it.

On somebody's motion, we resolved to go down stairs to the dress-boxes, where the ladies were. A gentleman lounging, full dressed, on a sofa, with an opera-glass in his hand, passed before my view, and also my own figure at full length in a glass. Then I was being ushered into one of these boxes, and found myself saying something as I sat down, and people about me crying "Silence!" to somebody, and ladies casting indignant glances at me, and—what! yes!—Agnes, sitting on the seat before me, in the same box, with a lady and gentleman beside her whom I didn't know. I see her face now, better than I did then, I dare say, with its indelible look of regret and wonder turned upon me.

"Agnes!" I said, thickly, "Lorblessmer! Agnes!"

"Hush! Pray!" she answered, I could not conceive why. "You disturb the company. Look at the stage!"

I tried, on her injunction, to fix it, and to hear something of what was going on there, but quite in vain. I looked at her again by and by, and saw her shrink into her corner, and put her gloved hand to her forehead.

"Agnes!" I said. "I'mafraidyou'renorwell."

"Yes, yes. Do not mind me, Trotwood," she returned. "Listen! Are you going away soon?"

"Amigoarawaysoo?" I repeated.

"Yes."

I had a stupid intention of replying that I was going to wait, to hand her down stairs. I suppose I expressed it somehow; for after she had looked at me attentively for a little while, she appeared to understand, and replied in a low tone:

"I know you will do as I ask you, if I tell you I am very earnest in it. Go away now, Trotwood, for my sake, and ask your friends to take you home."

She had so far improved me, for the time, that though I was angry with her, I felt ashamed, and with a short "Goori!" (which I intended for "Good night!") got up and went away. They followed, and I stepped at once out of the box-door into my bed-room, where only Steerforth was with me, helping me to undress, and where I was by turns telling him that Agnes was my sister, and adjuring him to bring the corkscrew, that I might open another bottle of wine.

How somebody, lying in my bed, lay saying and doing all this over again, at cross purposes, in a feverish dream all night—the bed a rocking sea, that was never still! How, as that somebody slowly settled down into myself, did I begin to parch, and feel as if my outer covering of skin were a hard board; my tongue the bottom of an empty kettle, furred with long service, and burning up over a slow fire; the palms of my hands, hot plates of metal which no ice could cool!

But the agony of mind, the remorse and shame I felt, when I became conscious next day! My horror of having committed a thousand offences I had forgotten, and which nothing could ever expiate—my recollection of that indelible look which Agnes had given me—the torturing impossibility of communicating with her, not knowing, beast that I was, how she came to be in London, or where she stayed—my disgust of the very sight of the room where the revel had been held—my racking head—the smell of smoke, the sight of glasses, the impossibility of going out, or even getting up! Oh, what a day it was!

Oh, what an evening, when I sat down by my fire to a basin of mutton broth, dimpled all over with fat, and thought I was going the way of my predecessor, and should succeed to his dismal story as well as to his chambers, and had half a mind to rush express to Dover and reveal all! What an evening, when Mrs. Crupp, coming in to take away the broth-basin, produced one kidney on a cheese-plate as the entire remains of yesterday's feast, and I was really inclined to fall upon her nankeen breast, and say, in heartfelt penitence, "Oh, Mrs. Crupp, Mrs. Crupp, never mind the broken meats! I am very miserable!"—only that I doubted, even at that pass, if Mrs. Crupp were quite the sort of woman to confide in!

The Seven Poor Travellers

Strictly speaking, there were only six Poor Travellers, but, being a Traveller myself, though an idle one, and being withal as poor as I hope to be, I brought the number up to seven. This word of explanation is due at once, for what says the inscription over the quaint old door?

Richard Watts, Esq.
by his Will, dated 22 Aug. 1579,
founded this Charity
for Six poor Travellers,
who not being Rogues, or Proctors,
May receive gratis for one Night,
Lodging, Entertainment,
and Fourpence each.

It was in the ancient little city of Rochester in Kent, of all the good days in the year upon a Christmas-eve, that I stood reading this inscription over the quaint old door in question. I had been wandering about the neighboring Cathedral, and had seen the tomb of Richard Watts, with the effigy of worthy Master Richard starting out of it like a ship's figure-head; and I had felt that I could do no less, as I gave the Verger his fee, than inquire the way to Watts's Charity. The way being very short and very plain, I had come prosperously to the inscription and the quaint old door.

"Now," said I to myself, as I looked at the knocker, "I know *I* am not a Proctor; I wonder whether I am a Rogue!"

Upon the whole, though Conscience reproduced two or three pretty faces which might have had smaller attraction for a moral Goliath than they had had for me, who am but a Tom Thumb in that way, I came to the conclusion that I was not a Rogue. So, beginning to regard the establishment as in some sort my property, bequeathed to me and divers co-legatees, share and share alike, by the Worshipful Master Richard Watts, I stepped backward into the road to survey my inheritance.

I found it to be a clean white house, of a staid and venerable air, with the quaint old door already three times mentioned (an arched door), choice little long low lattice-windows, and a roof of three gables. The silent High-street of Rochester is full of gables, with old beams and timbers carved into strange faces. It is oddly garnished with a queer old clock that projects over the pavement out of a grave red-brick building, as if Time carried on business there, and hung out his sign. Sooth to say, he did an active stroke of work in Rochester, in the old days of the Romans, and the Saxons, and the Normans; and down to the times of King John, when the rugged castle—I will not undertake to say how many hundreds of years old then—was abandoned to the centuries of weather which have so defaced the dark apertures in its walls, that the ruin looks as if the rooks and daws had picked its eyes out.

I was very well pleased, both with my property and its situation. While I was yet surveying it with growing content, I espied, at one of the upper lattices which stood open, a decent body, of a wholesome matronly appearance, whose eyes I caught inquiringly addressed to mine. They said so plainly, "Do you wish to see the house?" that I answered aloud, "Yes, if you please." And within a minute the old door opened, and I bent my head, and went down two steps into the entry.

"This," said the matronly presence, ushering me into a low room on the right, "is where the Travellers sit by the fire, and cook what bits of suppers they buy with their fourpences."

"O! Then they have no Entertainment?" said I. For the inscription over the outer door was still running in my head, and I was mentally repeating, in a kind of tune, "Lodging, entertainment, and fourpence each."

"They have a fire provided for 'em," returned the matron,—a mighty civil person, not, as I could make out, overpaid; "and these cooking utensils. And this what's painted on a board is the rules for their behavior. They have their fourpences when they get their tickets from the steward over the way,—for I don't admit 'em myself, they must get their tickets first,—and sometimes one buys a rasher of bacon, and another a herring, and another a pound of potatoes, or what not. Sometimes two or three of 'em will club their fourpences together, and make a supper that way. But not much of anything is to be got for fourpence, at present, when provisions is so dear."

"True indeed," I remarked. I had been looking about the room, admiring its snug fireside at the upper end, its glimpse of the street through the low mullioned window, and its beams overhead. "It is very comfortable," said I.

"Ill-conwenient," observed the matronly presence.

I liked to hear her say so; for it showed a commendable anxiety to execute in no niggardly spirit the intentions of Master Richard Watts. But the room was really so well adapted to its purpose that I protested, quite enthusiastically, against her disparagement.

"Nay, ma'am," said I, "I am sure it is warm in winter and cool in summer. It has a look of homely welcome and soothing rest. It has a remarkably cosey fireside, the very blink of which, gleaming out into the street upon a winter night, is enough to warm all Rochester's heart. And as to the convenience of the six Poor Travellers—"

"I don't mean them," returned the presence. "I speak of its being an ill-conwenience to myself and my daughter, having no other room to sit in of a night."

This was true enough, but there was another quaint room of corresponding dimensions on the opposite side of the entry: so I stepped across to it, through the open doors of both rooms, and asked what this chamber was for.

"This," returned the presence, "is the Board Room. Where the gentlemen meet when they come here."

Let me see. I had counted from the street six upper windows besides these on the ground-story. Making a perplexed calculation in my mind, I rejoined, "Then the six Poor Travellers sleep up stairs?"

My new friend shook her head. "They sleep," she answered "in two little outer galleries at the back, where their beds has always been, ever since the Charity was founded. It being so very ill-conwenient to me as things is at present, the gentlemen are going to take off a bit of the back yard, and make a slip of a room for 'em there, to sit in before they go to bed."

"And then the six Poor Travellers," said I, "will be entirely out of the house?"

"Entirely out of the house," assented the presence, comfortably smoothing her hands. "Which is considered much better for all parties, and much more conwenient."

I had been a little startled, in the Cathedral, by the emphasis with which the effigy of Master Richard Watts was bursting out of his tomb; but I began to think, now, that it might be expected to come across the High-street some stormy night, and make a disturbance here.

Howbeit, I kept my thoughts to myself, and accompanied the presence to the little galleries at the back. I found them on a tiny scale, like the galleries in old inn-yards; and they were very clean. While I was looking at them, the matron gave me to understand that the prescribed number of Poor Travellers were forthcoming every night from year's end to year's end; and that the beds were always occupied. My questions upon this, and her replies, brought us back to the Board Room so essential to the dignity of "the gentlemen," where she showed me the printed accounts of the Charity hanging up by the window. From them I gathered that the greater part of the property bequeathed by the Worshipful Master Richard Watts for the maintenance of this foundation was, at the period of his death, mere marsh-land; but that, in course of time, it had been reclaimed and built upon, and was very considerably increased in value. I found, too, that about a thirtieth part of the annual revenue was now expended on the purposes commemorated in the inscription over the door; the rest being handsomely laid out in Chancery, law expenses, collectorship, receivership, poundage, and other appendages of management, highly complimentary to the importance of the six Poor Travellers. In short, I made the not entirely new discovery that it may be said of an establishment like this, in dear old England, as of the fat oyster in the American story, that it takes a good many men to swallow it whole.

"And pray, ma'am," said I, sensible that the blankness of my face began to brighten as a thought occurred to me, "could one see these Travellers?"

"Well!" she returned dubiously, "no!"

"Not to-night, for instance?" said I.

"Well!" she returned more positively, "no. Nobody ever asked to see them, and nobody ever did see them."

As I am not easily balked in a design when I am set upon it, I urged to the good lady that this was Christmas-eve; that Christmas comes but once a year,—which is unhappily too true, for when it begins to stay with us the whole year round we shall make this earth a very different place; that I was possessed by the desire to treat the Travellers to a supper and a temperate glass of hot Wassail; that the voice of Fame had been heard in that land, declaring my ability to make hot Wassail; that if I were permitted to hold the feast, I should be found conformable to reason, sobriety, and good hours; in a word, that I could be merry and wise myself, and had been even known at a pinch to keep others so, although I was decorated with no badge or medal, and was not a Brother, Orator, Apostle, Saint, or Prophet of any denomination whatever. In the end I prevailed, to my great joy. It was settled that at nine o'clock that night a Turkey and a piece of Roast Beef should smoke upon the board; and that I, faint and unworthy minister for once of Master Richard Watts, should preside as the Christmas-supper host of the six Poor Travellers.

I went back to my inn to give the necessary directions for the Turkey and Roast Beef, and, during the remainder of the day, could settle to nothing for thinking of the Poor Travellers. When the wind blew hard against the windows,—it was a cold day, with dark gusts of sleet alternating with periods of wild brightness, as if the year were dying fitfully,—I pictured them advancing towards their resting-place along various cold roads, and felt delighted to think how little they foresaw the supper that awaited them. I painted their portraits in my mind, and indulged in little heightening touches. I made them footsore; I made them weary; I made them carry packs and bundles; I made them stop by finger-posts and milestones, leaning on their bent sticks, and looking wistfully at what was written there; I made them lose their way, and filled their five wits with apprehensions of lying out all night, and being frozen to death. I took up my hat, and went out, climbed to the top of the Old Castle, and looked over the windy hills that slope down to the Medway, almost believing that I could descry some of my Travellers in the distance. After it fell dark, and the Cathedral bell was heard in the invisible steeple—quite a bower of frosty rime when I had last seen it—striking five, six, seven, I became so full of my Travellers that I could eat no dinner, and felt constrained to watch them still in the red coals of my fire. They were all arrived by this time, I thought, had got their tickets, and were gone in.—There my pleasure was dashed by the reflection that probably some Travellers had come too late and were shut out.

After the Cathedral bell had struck eight, I could smell a delicious savor of Turkey and Roast Beef rising to the window of my adjoining bed-room, which looked down into the inn-yard just where the lights of the kitchen reddened a massive fragment of the Castle Wall. It was high time to make the Wassail now; therefore I had up the materials (which, together with their proportions and combinations, I must decline to impart, as the only secret of my own I was ever known to keep), and made a glorious jorum. Not in a bowl; for a bowl anywhere but on a shelf is a low superstition, fraught with cooling and slopping; but in a brown earthenware pitcher, tenderly suffocated, when full, with a coarse cloth. It being now upon the stroke of nine, I set out for Watts's Charity, carrying my brown beauty in my arms. I would trust Ben, the waiter, with untold gold; but there are strings in the human heart which must never be sounded by another, and drinks that I make myself are those strings in mine.

The Travellers were all assembled, the cloth was laid, and Ben had brought a great billet of wood, and had laid it artfully on the top of the fire, so that a touch or two of the poker after supper should make a roaring blaze. Having deposited my brown beauty in a red nook of the hearth, inside the fender, where she soon began to sing like an ethereal cricket, diffusing at the same time odors as of ripe vineyards, spice forests, and orange groves—I say, having stationed my beauty in a place of security and improvement, I introduced myself to my guests by shaking hands all round, and giving them a hearty welcome.

I found the party to be thus composed. Firstly, myself. Secondly, a very decent man indeed, with his right arm in a sling, who had a certain clean agreeable smell of wood about him, from which I judged him to have something to do with ship-building. Thirdly, a little sailor-boy, a mere child, with a profusion of rich dark brown hair, and deep womanly-looking eyes. Fourthly, a shabby-genteel personage in a thread-bare black suit, and apparently in very bad circumstances, with a dry suspicious look; the absent buttons on his waistcoat eked out with red tape; and a bundle of extraordinarily tattered papers sticking out of an inner breast-pocket. Fifthly, a foreigner by birth, but an Englishman in speech, who carried his pipe in the band of his hat, and lost no time in telling me, in an easy, simple, engaging way, that he was a watch-maker from Geneva, and travelled all about the Continent, mostly on foot, working as a journeyman, and seeing new countries,—possibly (I thought) also smuggling a watch or so, now and then. Sixthly, a little widow, who had been very pretty and was still very young, but whose beauty had been wrecked in some great misfortune, and whose manner was remarkably timid, scared, and solitary. Seventhly and lastly, a Traveller of a kind familiar to my boyhood, but now almost obsolete,

—a Book-Pedler, who had a quantity of Pamphlets and Numbers with him, and who presently boasted that he could repeat more verses in an evening than he could sell in a twelvemonth.

All these I have mentioned in the order in which they sat at table. I presided, and the matronly presence faced me. We were not long in taking our places, for the supper had arrived with me, in the following procession:

Myself with the pitcher.
Ben with Beer.
Inattentive Boy with hot plates. Inattentive Boy with hot plates.
THE TURKEY.
Female carrying sauces to be heated on the spot.
THE BEEF.
Man with Tray on his head, containing Vegetables and Sundries.
Volunteer Hostler from Hotel, grinning,
And rendering no assistance.

As we passed along the High-street, comet-like, we left a long tail of fragrance behind us which caused the public to stop, sniffing in wonder. We had previously left at the corner of the inn-yard a wall-eyed young man connected with the Fly department, and well accustomed to the sound of a railway whistle which Ben always carries in his pocket, whose instructions were, so soon as he should hear the whistle blown, to dash into the kitchen, seize the hot plum-pudding and mince-pies, and speed with them to Watts's Charity, where they would be received (he was further instructed) by the sauce-female, who would be provided with brandy in a blue state of combustion.

All these arrangements were executed in the most exact and punctual manner. I never saw a finer turkey, finer beef, or greater prodigality of sauce and gravy; and my Travellers did wonderful justice to everything set before them. It made my heart rejoice to observe how their wind and frost hardened faces softened in the clatter of plates and knives and forks, and mellowed in the fire and supper heat. While their hats and caps and wrappers, hanging up, a few small bundles on the ground in a corner, and in another corner three or four old walking-sticks, worn down at the end to mere fringe, linked this snug interior with the bleak outside in a golden chain.

When supper was done, and my brown beauty had been elevated on the table, there was a general requisition to me to "take the corner"; which suggested to me comfortably enough how much my friends here made of a fire,—for when had *I* ever thought so highly of the corner, since the days when I connected it with Jack Horner? However, as I declined, Ben, whose touch on all convivial instruments is perfect, drew the table apart, and instructing my Travellers to open right and left on either side of me, and form round the fire, closed up the centre with myself and my chair, and preserved the order we had kept at table. He had already, in a tranquil manner, boxed the ears of the inattentive boys until they had been by imperceptible degrees boxed out of the room; and he now rapidly skirmished the sauce-female into the High-street, disappeared, and softly closed the door.

This was the time for bringing the poker to bear on the billet of wood. I tapped it three times, like an enchanted talisman, and a brilliant host of merry-makers burst out of it, and sported off by the chimney,—rushing up the middle in a fiery country dance, and never coming down again. Meanwhile, by their sparkling light, which threw our lamp into the shade, I filled the glasses, and gave my Travellers, CHRISTMAS!—CHRISTMAS-EVE, my friends, when the shepherds, who were Poor Travellers, too, in their way, heard the Angels sing, "On earth, peace. Good-will towards men!"

I don't know who was the first among us to think that we ought to take hands as we sat, in deference to the toast, or whether any of us anticipated the others, but at any rate we all did it. We then drank to the memory of the good Master Richard Watts. And I wish his Ghost may never have had worse usage under that roof than it had from us.

It was the witching time for Story-telling. "Our whole life, Travellers," said I, "is a story more or less intelligible,—generally less; but we shall read it by a clearer light when it is ended. I, for one, am so divided this night between fact and fiction, that I scarce know which is which. Shall I beguile the time by telling you a story as we sit here?"

They all answered, yes. I had little to tell them, but I was bound by my own proposal. Therefore, after looking for a while at the spiral column of smoke wreathing up from my brown beauty, through which I could have almost sworn I saw the effigy of Master Richard Watts less startled than usual, I fired away.

[The story was about a relative of the narrator's, named Richard. As a lad, he had given his sweetheart, Mary Marshall, cause to dismiss him. Assuming the name of Richard Doubledick, he enlisted in a regiment of the line, acting at first like the despicable, drunken scapegrace he was. Under the good influence of Captain Taunton, he changed from the worst of soldiers to the best, and in the course of the Peninsular War in India, rose to the rank of Ensign. Captain Taunton likewise rose, to the rank of Major; and the tattered colors of their regiment, carried by Ensign Doubledick, became the center of glorious legend throughout the British Army. Major Taunton was killed in action. Doubledick rose to the rank of Lieutenant, was severely wounded at the battle of Toulouse, and at Midsummer-time in 1814, was sent home invalided. To Taunton's mother, at her home in Somersetshire, he disclosed his story. Her little garden became the boundary of his home; and when, in the spring, he was able to rejoin his regiment, it was "the first time that he had ever turned his face toward the old colours with a woman's blessing."

At Waterloo, in June, he was wounded again. After many days of total unconsciousness, he awoke to find himself in a hospital in Brussels, with Mrs. Taunton ministering to him. Then one day he found another at his bedside—one whom he had last known, years before, as Mary Marshall. She is now Mrs. Captain Doubledick. While he was unconscious and expected momentarily to die, she had been married to him.

The story ends with his encountering in France the officer who had commanded the enemy under whose fire Captain Taunton had fallen. The man was now the host of Mrs. Taunton and of Doubledick's own family. And Doubledick discovered the Spirit of Forgiveness in time to make him feel that the memory of Major Taunton was the better for his letting the tragedies of war lie buried in the past. He never disclosed to any one, least of all to Mrs. Taunton, the identity of the kindly Frenchman, and renounced in fact and in spirit his long-cherished purpose of taking vengeance on the slayer of Major Taunton.]

My story being finished, and the Wassail too, we broke up as the Cathedral bell struck Twelve. I did not take leave of my Travellers that night; for it had come into my head to reappear, in conjunction with some hot coffee, at seven in the morning.

As I passed along the High-street, I heard the Waits at a distance, and struck off to find them. They were playing near one of the old gates of the City, at the corner of a wonderfully quaint row of red-brick tenements, which the clarionet obligingly informed me were inhabited by the Minor-Canons. They had odd little porches over the doors, like sounding-boards over old pulpits; and I thought I should like to see one of the Minor-Canons come out upon his top step, and favor us with a little Christmas discourse about the poor scholars of Rochester; taking for his text the words of his Master, relative to the devouring of Widows' houses.

The clarionet was so communicative, and my inclinations were (as they generally are) of so vagabond a tendency, that I accompanied the Waits across an open green called the Vines, and assisted—in the French sense—at the performance of two waltzes, two polkas, and three Irish melodies, before I thought of my inn any more. However, I returned to it then, and found a fiddle in the kitchen, and Ben, the wall-eyed young man, and two chamber-maids, circling round the great deal table with the utmost animation.

I had a very bad night. It cannot have been owing to the turkey or the beef,—and the Wassail is out of the question,—but in every endeavor that I made to get to sleep I failed most dismally. I was never asleep; and in whatsoever unreasonable direction my mind rambled, the effigy of Master Richard Watts perpetually embarrassed it.

In a word, I only got out of the Worshipful Master Richard Watts's way by getting out of bed in the dark at six o'clock, and tumbling, as my custom is, into all the cold water that could be accumulated for the purpose. The outer air was dull and cold enough in the street, when I came down there; and the one candle in our supper-room at Watts's Charity looked as pale in the burning as if it had had a bad night too. But my Travellers had all slept soundly, and they took to the hot coffee, and the piles of bread-and-butter, which Ben had arranged like deals in a timber-yard, as kindly as I could desire.

While it was yet scarcely daylight, we all came out into the street together, and there shook hands. The widow took the little sailor towards Chatham, where he was to find a steamboat for Sheerness; the lawyer, with an extremely knowing look, went his own way, without committing himself by announcing his intentions; two more struck off by the cathedral and old castle for Maidstone; and the book-pedler accompanied me over the bridge. As for me, I was going to walk by Cobham Woods, as far upon my way to London as I fancied.

When I came to the stile and footpath by which I was to diverge from the main road, I bade farewell to my last remaining Poor Traveller, and pursued my way alone. And now the mists began to rise in the most beautiful manner, and the sun to shine; and as I went on through the bracing air, seeing the hoar-frost sparkle everywhere, I felt as if all Nature shared in the joy of the great Birthday.

Going through the woods, the softness of my tread upon the mossy ground and among the brown leaves enhanced the Christmas sacredness by which I felt surrounded. As the whitened stems environed me, I thought how the Founder of the time had never raised his benignant hand, save to bless and heal, except in the case of one unconscious tree. By Cobham Hall, I came to the village, and the churchyard where the dead had been quietly buried, "in the sure and certain hope" which Christmas time inspired. What children could I see at play, and not be loving of, recalling who had loved them! No garden that I passed was out of unison with the day, for I remembered that the tomb was in a garden, and that "she supposing him to be the gardener," had said, "Sir, if thou have borne him hence, tell me where thou hast laid him, and I will take him away." In time, the distant river with the ships came full in view, and with it pictures of the poor fishermen, mending their nets, who arose and followed him,—of the teaching of the people from a ship pushed off a little way from shore, by reason of the multitude,—of a majestic figure walking on the water, in the loneliness of night. My very shadow on the ground was eloquent of Christmas; for did not the people lay their sick where the mere shadows of the men who had heard and seen him might fall as they passed along?

Thus Christmas begirt me, far and near, until I had come to Blackheath, and had walked down the long vista of gnarled old trees in Greenwich Park, and was being steam-rattled through the mists now closing in once more, towards the lights of London. Brightly they shone, but not so brightly as my own fire, and the brighter faces around it, when we came together to celebrate the day. And there I told of worthy Master Richard Watts, and of my supper with the Six Poor Travellers who were neither Rogues nor Proctors, and from that hour to this I have never seen one of them again.

From THE HOLLY-TREE

The Boots

The narrator of the following selection, a very bashful man, was snowed up in the Holly-Tree inn, somewhere on a Yorkshire moor, on the Great North Road. Installed in a very large and solitary sitting-room, screened in alone beside a blazing fire, he beguiled the hours with memories of inns he had known in many lands and of stories connected with them. But at length his memories ended. "A desperate idea came into my head. Under any other circumstances I should have rejected it; but, in the strait at which I was, I held it fast. Could I so far overcome the inherent bashfulness which withheld me from the landlord's table and the company which I might find there, as to call up the Boots, and ask him to take a chair,—and something in a liquid form,—and talk to me? I could. I would. I did."

WHERE had he been in his time? he repeated, when I asked him the question. Lord, he had been everywhere! And what had he been? Bless you, he had been everything you could mention a'most!

Seen a good deal? Why, of course he had. I should say so, he could assure me, if I only knew about a twentieth part of what had come in *his* way. Why, it would be easier for him, he expected, to tell what he hadn't seen than what he had. Ah! A deal, it would.

What was the curiousest thing he had seen? Well! He didn't know. He couldn't momently name what was the curiousest thing he had seen,—unless it was a Unicorn,—and he see *him* once at a Fair. But supposing a young gentleman not eight year old was to run away with a fine young woman of seven, might I think *that* a queer start? Certainly. Then that was a start as he himself had had his blessed eyes on, and he had cleaned the shoes they run away in—and they was so little that he couldn't get his hand into 'em.

Master Harry Walmer's father, you see, he lived at the Elmses, down away by Shooter's Hill there, six or seven miles from Lunnon. He was a gentleman of spirit, and good-looking, and held his head up when he walked, and had what you may call Fire about him. He wrote poetry, and he rode, and he ran, and he cricketed, and he danced, and he acted, and he done it all equally beautiful. He was uncommon proud of Master Harry as was his only child; but he didn't spoil him neither. He was a gentleman that had a will of his own and a eye of his own, and that would be minded. Consequently, though he made quite a companion of the fine bright boy, and was delighted to see him so fond of reading his fairy books, and was never tired of hearing him say my name in Norval, or hearing him sing his songs about Young May Moons is beaming love, and When he as adores thee has left but the name, and that; still he kept the command over the child, and the child *was* a child, and it's to be wished more of 'em was!

How did Boots happen to know all this? Why, through being under-gardener. Of course he couldn't be under-gardener, and be always about, in the summer-time, near the windows on the lawn, a mowing, and sweeping, and weeding, and pruning, and this and that, without getting acquainted with the ways of the family. Even supposing Master Harry hadn't come to him one morning early, and said, "Cobbs, how should you spell Norah, if you was asked?" and then began cutting it in print all over the fence.

He couldn't say he had taken particular notice of children before that; but really it was pretty to see them two mites a going about the place together, deep in love. And the courage of the boy! Bless your soul, he'd have throwed off his little hat, and tucked up his little sleeves, and gone in at a Lion, he would, if they had happened to meet one, and she had been frightened of him. One day he stops, along with her, where Boots was hoeing weeds in the gravel, and says, speaking up, "Cobbs," he says, "I like *you.*" "Do you, sir? I'm proud to hear it." "Yes, I do, Cobbs. Why do I like you, do you think, Cobbs?" "Don't know, Master Harry, I am sure." "Because Norah likes you, Cobbs." "Indeed, sir? That's very gratifying." "Gratifying, Cobbs? It's better than millions of the brightest diamonds to be liked by Norah." "Certainly, sir." "You're going away, ain't you, Cobbs?" "Yes, sir." "Would you like another situation, Cobbs?" "Well, sir, I shouldn't object, if it was a good 'un." "Then, Cobbs," says he, "you shall be our Head Gardener when we are married." And he tucks her, in her little sky-blue mantle, under his arm, and walks away.

Boots could assure me that it was better than a picter, and equal to a play, to see them babies, with their long, bright, curling hair, their sparkling eyes, and their beautiful light tread, a rambling about the garden, deep in love. Boots was of opinion that the birds believed they was birds, and kept up with 'em, singing to please 'em. Sometimes they would creep under the Tulip-tree, and would sit there with their arms round one another's necks, and their soft cheeks touching, a reading about the Prince and the Dragon, and the good and bad enchanters, and the king's fair daughter. Sometimes he would hear them planning about having a house in a forest, keeping bees and a cow, and living entirely on milk and honey. Once he came upon them by the pond, and heard Master Harry say, "Adorable Norah, kiss me, and say you love me to distraction, or I'll jump in head-foremost." And Boots made no question he would have done it if she hadn't complied. On the whole, Boots said it had a tendency to make him feel as if he was in love himself—only he didn't exactly know who with.

"Cobbs," said Master Harry, one evening, when Cobbs was watering the flowers, "I am going on a visit, this present Mid-summer, to my grandmamma's at York."

"Are you indeed, sir? I hope you'll have a pleasant time. I am going into Yorkshire, myself, when I leave here."

"Are you going to your grandmamma's, Cobbs?"

"No, sir. I haven't got such a thing."

"Not as a grandmamma, Cobbs?"

"No, sir."

The boy looked on at the watering of the flowers for a little while, and then said, "I shall be very glad indeed to go, Cobbs,—Norah's going."

"You'll be all right then, sir," says Cobbs, "with your beautiful sweetheart by your side."

"Cobbs," returned the boy, flushing, "I never let anybody joke about it, when I can prevent them."

"It wasn't a joke, sir," says Cobbs, with humility,—"wasn't so meant."

"I am glad of that, Cobbs, because I like you, you know, and you're going to live with us.—Cobbs!"

"Sir."

"What do you think my grandmamma gives me when I go down there?"

"I couldn't so much as make a guess, sir."

"A Bank of England five-pound note, Cobbs."

"Whew!" says Cobbs, "that's a spanking sum of money, Master Harry."

"A person could do a good deal with such a sum of money as that,—couldn't a person, Cobbs?"

"I believe you, sir!"

"Cobbs," said the boy, "I'll tell you a secret. At Norah's house, they have been joking her about me, and pretending to laugh at our being engaged,—pretending to make game of it, Cobbs!"

"Such, sir," said Cobbs, "is the depravity of human natur."

The boy, looking exactly like his father, stood for a few minutes with his glowing face towards the sunset, and then departed with, "Good night, Cobbs. I'm going in."

If I was to ask Boots how it happened that he was a going to leave that place just at that present time, well, he couldn't rightly answer me. He did suppose he might have stayed there till now if he had been anyways inclined. But, you see, he was younger then, and he wanted change. That's what he wanted,—change. Mr. Walmers, he said to him when he gave him notice of his intentions to leave, "Cobbs," he says, "have you anythink to complain of? I make the inquiry because if I find that any of my people really has anythink to complain of, I wish to make it right if I can." "No, sir," says Cobbs; "thanking you, sir, I find myself as well sitiwated here as I could hope to be anywheres. The truth is, sir, that I'm a going to seek my fortun." "O, indeed, Cobbs!" he says; "I hope you may find it." And Boots could assure me—which he did, touching his hair with his bootjack, as a salute in the way of his present calling—that he hadn't found it yet.

Well, sir! Boots left the Elmses when his time was up, and Master Harry, he went down to the old lady's at York, which old lady would have given that child the teeth out of her head (if she had had any), she was so wrapped up in him. What does that Infant do,—for Infant you may call him and be within the mark,—but cut away from that old lady's with his Norah, on a expedition to go to Gretna Green and be married!

Sir, Boots was at this identical Holly-Tree Inn (having left it several times since to better himself, but always come back through one thing or another), when, one summer afternoon, the coach drives up, and out of the coach gets them two children. The Guard says to our Governor, "I don't quite make out these little passengers, but the young gentleman's words was, that they was to be brought here." The young gentleman gets out; hands his lady out; gives the Guard something for himself; says to our Governor, "We're to stop here to-night, please. Sitting-room and two bedrooms will be required. Chops and cherry-pudding for two!" and tucks her, in her little sky-blue mantle, under his arm, and walks into the house much bolder than Brass.

Boots leaves me to judge what the amazement of that establishment was, when these two tiny creatures all alone by themselves was marched into the Angel,—much more so, when he, who had seen them without their seeing him, give the Governor his views of the expedition they was upon. "Cobbs," says the Governor, "if this is so, I must set off myself to York, and quiet their friends' minds. In which case you must keep your eye upon 'em, and humor 'em, till I come back. But before I take these measures, Cobbs, I should wish you to find from themselves whether your opinions is correct." "Sir, to you," says Cobbs, "that shall be done directly."

So Boots goes up stairs to the Angel, and there he finds Master Harry, on a e-normous sofa,—immense at any time, but looking like the Great Bed of Ware, compared with him,—a drying the eyes of Miss Norah with his pocket-hankercher. Their little legs was entirely off the ground, of course, and it really is not possible for Boots to express to me how small them children looked.

"It's Cobbs! It's Cobbs!" cries Master Harry, and comes running to him, and catching hold of his hand. Miss Norah comes running to him on t'other side and catching hold of his t'other hand, and they both jump for joy.

"I see you a getting out, sir," says Cobbs. "I thought it was you. I thought I couldn't be mistaken in your height and figure. What's the object of your journey, sir?—Matrimonial?"

"We are going to be married, Cobbs, at Gretna Green," returned the boy. "We have run away on purpose. Norah has been in rather low spirits, Cobbs; but she'll be happy, now we have found you to be our friend."

"Thank you, sir, and thank *you*, miss," says Cobbs, "for your good opinion. *Did* you bring any luggage with you, sir?"

If I will believe Boots when he gives me his word and honor upon it, the lady had got a parasol, a smelling-bottle, a round and a half of cold buttered toast, eight peppermint drops, and a hair-brush,—seemingly a doll's. The gentleman had got about half a dozen yards of string, a knife, three or four sheets of writing-paper folded up surprisingly small, an orange, and a Chaney mug with his name upon it.

"What may be the exact natur of your plans, sir?" says Cobbs.

"To go on," replied the boy,—which the courage of that boy was something wonderful!—"in the morning, and be married to-morrow."

"Just so, sir," says Cobbs. "Would it meet your views, sir, if I was to accompany you?"

When Cobbs said this, they both jumped for joy again, and cried out, "O yes, yes, Cobbs! Yes!"

"Well, sir," says Cobbs. "If you will excuse my having the freedom to give an opinion, what I should recommend would be this. I'm acquainted with a pony, sir, which, put in a pheayton that I could borrow, would take you and Mrs. Harry Walmers, Junior, (myself driving, if you approved,) to the end of your journey in a very short space of time. I am not altogether sure, sir, that this pony will be at liberty to-morrow, but even if you had to wait over to-morrow for him, it might be worth your while. As to the small account here, sir, in case you was to find yourself running at all short, that don't signify; because I'm a part proprietor of this inn, and it could stand over."

Boots assures me that when they clapped their hands, and jumped for joy again, and called him "Good Cobbs!" and "Dear Cobbs!" and bent across him to kiss one another in the delight of their confiding hearts, he felt himself the meanest rascal for deceiving 'em that ever was born.

"Is there anything you want just at present, sir?" says Cobbs, mortally ashamed of himself.

"We should like some cakes after dinner," answered Master Harry, folding his arms, putting out one leg, and looking straight at him, "and two apples,—and jam. With dinner we should like to have toast-and-water. But Norah has always been accustomed to half a glass of currant wine at dessert. And so have I."

"It shall be ordered at the bar, sir," says Cobbs; and away he went.

Boots has the feeling as fresh upon him at this minute of speaking as he had then, that he would far rather have had it out in half a dozen rounds with the Governor than have combined with him; and that he wished with all his heart there was any impossible place where those two babies could make an impossible marriage, and live impossibly happy ever afterwards. However, as it couldn't be, he went into the Governor's plans, and the Governor set off for York in half an hour.

The way in which the women of that house—without exception—every one of 'em—married *and* single—took to that boy when they heard the story, Boots considers surprising. It was as much as he could do to keep 'em from dashing into the room and kissing him. They climbed up all sorts of places, at the risk of their lives, to look at him through a pane of glass. They was seven deep at the keyhole. They was out of their minds about him and his bold spirit.

In the evening, Boots went into the room to see how the runaway couple was getting on. The gentleman was on the window-seat, supporting the lady in his arms. She had tears upon her face, and was lying, very tired and half asleep, with her head upon his shoulder.

"Mrs. Harry Walmers, Junior, fatigued, sir?" says Cobbs.

"Yes, she is tired, Cobbs; but she is not used to be away from home, and she has been in low spirits again. Cobbs, do you think you could bring a biffin, please?"

"I ask your pardon, sir," says Cobbs. "What was it you——?"

"I think a Norfolk biffin would rouse her, Cobbs. She is very fond of them."

Boots withdrew in search of the required restorative, and, when he brought it in, the gentleman handed it to the lady, and fed her with a spoon, and took a little himself; the lady being heavy with sleep, and rather cross. "What should you think, sir," says Cobbs, "of a chamber candlestick?" The gentleman approved; the chambermaid went first, up the great staircase; the lady, in her sky-blue mantle, followed, gallantly escorted by the gentleman; the gentleman embraced her at her door, and retired to his own apartment, where Boots softly locked him up.

Boots couldn't but feel with increased acuteness what a base deceiver he was, when they consulted him at breakfast (they had ordered sweet milk-and-water, and toast and currant jelly, over-night) about the pony. It really was as much as he could do, he don't mind confessing to me, to look them two young things in the face, and think what a wicked old father of lies he had grown up to be. Howsomever, he went on a lying like a Trojan about the pony. He told 'em that it did so unfort'nately happen that the pony was half clipped, you see, and that he couldn't be taken out in that state, for fear it should strike to his inside. But that he'd be finished clipping in the course of the day, and that to-morrow morning at eight o'clock the pheayton would be ready. Boots's view of the whole case, looking back on it in my room, is, that Mrs. Harry Walmers, Junior, was beginning to give in. She hadn't had her hair curled when she went to bed, and she didn't seem quite up to brushing it herself, and its getting in her eyes put her out. But nothing put out Master Harry. He sat behind his breakfast-cup, a tearing away at the jelly, as if he had been his own father.

After breakfast, Boots is inclined to consider that they drawed soldiers,—at least, he knows that many such was found in the fireplace, all on horseback. In the course of the morning, Master Harry rang the bell,—it was surprising how that there boy did carry on,—and said, in a sprightly way, "Cobbs, is there any good walks in this neighborhood?"

"Yes, sir," says Cobbs. "There's Love-lane."

"Get out with you, Cobbs!"—that was that there boy's expression,—"you're joking."

"Begging your pardon, sir," says Cobbs, "there really is Love-lane.

And a pleasant walk it is, and proud shall I be to show it to yourself and Mrs. Harry Walmers, Junior."

"Norah, dear," said Master Harry, "this is curious. We really ought to see Love-lane. Put on your bonnet, my sweetest darling, and we will go there with Cobbs."

Boots leaves me to judge what a Beast he felt himself to be, when that young pair told him, as they all three jogged along together, that they had made up their minds to give him two thousand guineas a year as head-gardener, on accounts of his being so true a friend to 'em. Boots could have wished at the moment that the earth would have opened and swallowed him up, he felt so mean, with their beaming eyes a looking at him, and believing him. Well, sir, he turned the conversation as well as he could, and he took 'em down Love-lane to the water-meadows, and there Master Harry would have drowned himself in half a moment more, a getting out a water-lily for her,—but nothing daunted that boy. Well, sir, they was tired out. All being so new and strange to 'em, they was tired as tired could be. And they laid down on a bank of daisies, like the children in the wood, leastways meadows, and fell asleep.

Boots don't know—perhaps I do,—but never mind, it don't signify either way—why it made a man fit to make a fool of himself to see them two pretty babies a lying there in the clear still sunny day, not dreaming half so hard when they was asleep as they done when they was awake. But, Lord! when you come to think of yourself, you know, and what a game you have been up to ever since you was in your own cradle, and what a poor sort of a chap you are, and how it's always either Yesterday with you, or else To-morrow, and never To-day, that's where it is!

Well, sir, they woke up at last, and then one thing was getting pretty clear to Boots, namely, that Mrs. Harry Walmers's, Junior's, temper was on the move. When Master Harry took her round the waist, she said he "teased her so;" and when he says, "Norah, my young May Moon, your Harry tease you?" she tells him, "Yes; and I want to go home!"

A biled fowl, and baked bread-and-butter pudding, brought Mrs. Walmers up a little; but Boots could have wished, he must privately own to me, to have seen her more sensible of the woice of love, and less abandoning of herself to currants. However, Master Harry, he kept up, and his noble heart was as fond as ever. Mrs. Walmers turned very sleepy about dusk, and began to cry. Therefore, Mrs. Walmers went off to bed as per yesterday; and Master Harry ditto repeated.

About eleven or twelve at night comes back the Governor in a chaise, along with Mr. Walmers and a elderly lady. Mr. Walmers looks amused and very serious, both at once, and says to our missis, "We are much indebted to you, ma'am, for your kind care of our little children, which we can never sufficiently acknowledge. Pray, ma'am, where is my boy?" Our missis says, "Cobbs has the dear child in charge, sir. Cobbs, show Forty!" Then he says to Cobbs, "Ah, Cobbs, I am glad to see *you!* I understood you was here!" And Cobbs says, "Yes, sir. Your most obedient, sir."

I may be surprised to hear Boots say it, perhaps; but Boots assures me that his heart beat like a hammer, going up stairs. "I beg your pardon, sir," says he, while unlocking the door; "I hope you are not angry with Master Harry. For Master Harry is a fine boy, sir, and will do you credit and honor." And Boots signifies to me, that, if the fine boy's father had contradicted him in the daring state of mind in which he then was, he thinks he should have "fetched him a crack," and taken the consequences.

But Mr. Walmers only says, "No, Cobbs. No, my good fellow. Thank you!" And, the door being opened, goes in.

Boots goes in too, holding the light, and he sees Mr. Walmers go up to the bedside, bend gently down, and kiss the little sleeping face. Then he stands looking at it for a minute, looking wonderfully like it (they do say he ran away with Mrs. Walmers); and then he gently shakes the little shoulder.

"Harry, my dear boy! Harry!"

Master Harry starts up and looks at him. Looks at Cobbs too. Such is the honor of that mite, that he looks at Cobbs, to see whether he has brought him into trouble.

"I am not angry, my child. I only want you to dress yourself and come home."

"Yes, pa."

Master Harry dresses himself quickly. His breast begins to swell when he has nearly finished, and it swells more and more as he stands, at last, a looking at his father: his father standing a looking at him, the quiet image of him.

"Please may I"—the spirit of that little creatur, and the way he kept his rising tears down!—"please, dear pa—may I—kiss Norah before I go?"

"You may, my child."

So he takes Master Harry in his hand, and Boots leads the way with the candle, and they come to that other bed-room, where the elder lady is seated by the bed, and poor little Mrs. Harry Walmers, Junior, is fast asleep. There the father lifts the child up to the pillow, and he lays his little face down for an instant by the little warm face of poor unconscious little Mrs. Harry Walmers, Junior, and gently draws it to him,—a sight so touching to the chambermaids who are peeping through the door, that one of them calls out, "It's a shame to part 'em!" But this chambermaid was always, as Boots informs me, a soft-hearted one. Not that there was any harm in that girl. Far from it.

Finally, Boots says, that's all about it. Mr. Walmers drove away in the chaise, having hold of Master Harry's hand. The elderly lady and Mrs. Harry Walmers, Junior, that was never to be (she married a Captain long afterwards, and died in India), went off next day. In conclusion, Boots put it to me whether I hold with him in two opinions: firstly, that there are not many couples on their way to be married who are half as innocent of guile as those two children; secondly, that it would be a jolly good thing for a great many couples on their way to be married, if they could only be stopped in time, and brought back separately.

From A Tale of Two Cities

The Last Scene

Sydney Carton, law student and idler, had led a dissipated, careless life; but he did many noble and courageous things. He remained loyal in his love for Lucy Manette, after she had married Charles Darnay. And later, in France, when Darnay, or St. Evrémonde, was caught in the toils of the Revolution of 1792, Sydney Carton came to the prison, obtained entrance by threatening to betray a turnkey whom he recognized as a spy, drugged Darnay, exchanged clothes with him, and effected Darnay's rescue by remaining to face La Guillotine in place of the young Frenchman, whom he strangely resembled. Dickens attributes to him a final thought—if he had chosen to express his thoughts—"It is a far, far better thing that I do, than I have ever done; it is a far, far better rest that I go to, than I have ever known."

Along the Paris streets, the death-carts rumble, hollow and harsh. Six tumbrils carry the day's wine to La Guillotine. All the devouring and insatiate Monsters imagined since imagination could record itself, are fused in the one realization, Guillotine. And yet there is not in France, with its rich variety of soil and climate, a blade, a leaf, a root, a sprig, a peppercorn which will grow to maturity under conditions more certain than those that have produced this horror. Crush humanity out of shape once more, under similar hammers, and it will twist itself into the same tortured forms. Sow the same seeds of rapacious license and oppression ever again, and it will surely yield the same fruit according to its kind.

Six tumbrils roll along the streets. Change these back again to what they were, thou powerful enchanter, Time, and they shall be seen to be the carriages of absolute monarchs, the equipages of feudal nobles, the toilets of flaring Jezebels, the churches that are not my father's house but dens of thieves, the huts of millions of starving peasants! No; the great magician who majestically works out the appointed order of the Creator, never reverses his transformations. "If thou be changed into this shape by the will of God," say the seers to the enchanted, in the wise Arabian stories, "then remain so! But, if thou wear this form through mere passing conjuration, then resume thy former aspect!" Changeless and hopeless, the tumbrils roll along.

As the sombre wheels of the six carts go round, they seem to plough up a long crooked furrow among the populace in the streets. Ridges of faces are thrown to this side and to that, and the ploughs go steadily onward. So used are the regular inhabitants of the houses to the spectacle, that in many windows there are no people, and in some the occupation of the hands is not so much as suspended, while the eyes survey the faces in the tumbrils. Here and there, the inmate has visitors to see the sight; then he points his finger, with something of the complacency of a curator or authorized exponent, to this cart and to this, and seems to tell who sat here yesterday, and who there the day before.

Of the riders in the tumbrils, some observe these things, and all things on their last roadside, with an impassive stare; others, with a lingering interest in the ways of life and men. Some, seated with drooping heads, are sunk in silent despair; again, there are some so heedful of their looks that they cast upon the multitude such glances as they have seen in theatres, and in pictures. Several close their eyes, and think, or try to get their straying thoughts together. Only one, and he a miserable creature of a crazed aspect, is so shattered and made drunk by horror that he sings, and tries to dance. Not one of the whole number appeals, by look or gesture, to the pity of the people.

There is a guard of sundry horsemen riding abreast of the tumbrils, and faces are often turned up to some of them and they are asked some question. It would seem to be always the same question, for, it is always followed by a press of people towards the third cart. The horsemen abreast of that cart, frequently point out one man in it with their swords. The leading curiosity is, to know which is he; he stands at the back of the tumbril with his head bent down, to converse with a mere girl who sits on the side of the cart, and holds his hand. He has no curiosity or care for the scene about him, and always speaks to the girl. Here and there in a long Street of St. Honoré, cries are raised against him. If they move him at all, it is only to a quiet smile, as he shakes his hair a little more loosely about his face. He cannot easily touch his face, his arms being bound.

On the steps of a church, awaiting the coming-up of the tumbrils, stands the Spy and prison-sheep. He looks into the first of them: not there. He looks into the second: not there. He already asks himself, "Has he sacrificed me?" when his face clears, as he looks into the third.

"Which is Evrémonde?" said a man behind him.

"That. At the back there."

"With his hand in the girl's?"

"Yes."

The man cries, "Down, Evrémonde! To the Guillotine all aristocrats! Down, Evrémonde!"

"Hush, hush!" the Spy entreats him, timidly.

"And why not, citizen?"

"He is going to pay the forfeit; it will be paid in five minutes more. Let him be at peace."

But, the man continuing to exclaim, "Down, Evrémonde!" the face of Evrémonde is for a moment turned towards him. Evrémonde then sees the Spy, and looks attentively at him, and goes his way.

The clocks are on the stroke of three, and the furrow ploughed among the populace is turning round, to come on into the place of execution, and end. The ridges thrown to this side and to that, now crumble in and close behind the last plough as it passes on, for all are following to the Guillotine. In front of it, seated in chairs as in a garden of public diversion, are a number of women, busily knitting. On one of the foremost chairs, stands The Vengeance, looking about for her friend.

"Thérèse!" she cries, in her shrill tones. "Who has seen her? Thérèse Defarge!"

"She never missed before," says a knitting-woman of the sisterhood.

"No; nor will she miss now," cries The Vengeance, petulantly. "Thérèse!"

"Louder," the woman recommends.

Ay! Louder, Vengeance, much louder, and still she will scarcely hear thee. Louder yet, Vengeance, with a little oath or so added, and yet it will hardly bring her. Send other women up and down to seek her, lingering somewhere; and yet, although the messengers have done dread deeds, it is questionable whether of their own wills they will go far enough to find her.

"Bad Fortune!" cries The Vengeance, stamping her foot in the chair, "and here are the tumbrils! And Evrémonde will be despatched in a wink, and she not here! See her knitting in my hand, and her empty chair ready for her. I cry with vexation and disappointment!"

As The Vengeance descends from her elevation to do it, the tumbrils begin to discharge their loads. The ministers of Sainte Guillotine are robed and ready. Crash!—A head is held up, and the knitting-women who scarcely lifted their eyes to look at it a moment ago when it could think and speak, count One.

The second tumbril empties and moves on; the third comes up. Crash!—And the knitting-women, never faltering or pausing in their work, count Two.

The supposed Evrémonde descends, and the seamstress is lifted out next after him. He has not relinquished her patient hand in getting out, but still holds it as he promised. He gently places her with her back to the crashing engine that constantly whirs up and falls, and she looks into his face and thanks him.

"But for you, dear stranger, I should not be so composed, for I am naturally a poor little thing, faint of heart; nor should I have been able to raise my thoughts to Him who was put to death, that we might have hope and comfort here to-day. I think you were sent to me by Heaven."

"Or you to me," says Sydney Carton. "Keep your eyes upon me, dear child, and mind no other object."

"I mind nothing while I hold your hand. I shall mind nothing when I let it go, if they are rapid."

"They will be rapid. Fear not!"

The two stand in the fast-thinning throng of victims, but they speak as if they were alone. Eye to eye, voice to voice, hand to hand, heart to heart, these two children of the Universal Mother, else so wide apart and differing, have come together on the dark highway, to repair home together and to rest in her bosom.

"Brave and generous friend, will you let me ask you one last question? I am very ignorant, and it troubles me—just a little."

"Tell me what it is."

"I have a cousin, an only relative and an orphan, like myself, whom I love very dearly. She is five years younger than I, and she lives in a farmer's house in the south country. Poverty parted us, and she knows nothing of my fate—for I cannot write—and if I could, how should I tell her! It is better as it is."

"Yes, yes: better as it is."

"What I have been thinking as we came along, and what I am still thinking now, as I look into your kind strong face which gives me so much support, is this:—If the Republic really does good to the poor, and they come to be less hungry, and in all ways to suffer less, she may live a long time; she may even live to be old."

"What then, my gentle sister?"

"Do you think:" the uncomplaining eyes in which there is so much endurance, fill with tears, and the lips part a little more and tremble: "that it will seem long to me, while I wait for her in the better land where I trust both you and I will be mercifully sheltered?"

"It cannot be, my child; there is no Time there, and no trouble there."

"You comfort me so much! I am so ignorant. Am I to kiss you now? Is the moment come?"

"Yes."

She kisses his lips; he kisses hers; they solemnly bless each other. The spare hand does not tremble as he releases it; nothing worse than a sweet, bright constancy is in the patient face. She goes next before him—is gone; the knitting-women count Twenty-Two.

"I am the Resurrection and the Life, saith the Lord: he that believeth in me, though he were dead, yet shall he live: and whosoever liveth and believeth in me, shall never die."

The murmuring of many voices, the upturning of many faces, the pressing on of many footsteps in the outskirts of the crowd, so that it swells forward in a mass, like one great heave of water, all flashes away. Twenty-Three.

From Great Expectations

Chapters I and III

CHAPTER I

My father's family name being Pirrip, and my christian name Philip, my infant tongue could make of both names nothing longer or more explicit than Pip. So, I called myself Pip, and came to be called Pip.

I give Pirrip as my father's family name, on the authority of his tombstone and my sister—Mrs. Joe Gargery, who married the blacksmith. As I never saw my father or my mother, and never saw any likeness of either of them (for their days were long before the days of photographs), my first fancies regarding what they were like, were unreasonably derived from their tombstones. The shape of the letters on my father's, gave me an odd idea that he was a square, stout, dark man, with curly black hair. From the character and turn of the inscription, *"Also Georgiana Wife of the Above,"* I drew a childish conclusion that my mother was freckled and sickly. To five little stone lozenges, each about a foot and a half long, which were arranged in a neat row beside their grave, and were sacred to the memory of five little brothers of mine—who gave up trying to get a living exceedingly early in that universal struggle—I am indebted for a belief I religiously entertained that they had all been born on their backs with their hands in their trousers-pockets, and had never taken them out in this state of existence.

Ours was the marsh country, down by the river, within, as the river wound, twenty miles of the sea. My first most vivid and broad impression of the identity of things, seems to me to have been gained on a memorable raw afternoon towards evening. At such a time I found out for certain, that this bleak place overgrown with nettles was the churchyard; and that Philip Pirrip, late of this parish, and also Georgiana wife of the above, were dead and buried; and that Alexander, Bartholomew, Abraham, Tobias, and Roger, infant children of the aforesaid, were also dead and buried; and that the dark flat wilderness beyond the churchyard, intersected with dykes and mounds and gates, with scattered cattle feeding on it, was the marshes; and that the low leaden line beyond, was the river: and that the distant savage lair from which the wind was rushing, was the sea; and that the small bundle of shivers growing afraid of it all and beginning to cry, was Pip.

"Hold your noise!" cried a terrible voice, as a man started up from among the graves at the side of the church porch. "Keep still, you little devil, or I'll cut your throat!"

A fearful man, all in coarse gray, with a great iron on his leg. A man with no hat, and with broken shoes, and with an old rag tied round his head. A man who had been soaked in water, and smothered in mud, and lamed by stones, and cut by flints, and stung by nettles, and torn by briars; who limped, and shivered, and glared and growled; and whose teeth chattered in his head as he seized me by the chin.

"O! Don't cut my throat, sir," I pleaded in terror. "Pray don't do it, sir."

"Tell us your name!" said the man. "Quick!"

"Pip, sir."

"Once more," said the man, staring at me. "Give it mouth!"

"Pip. Pip, sir."

"Show us where you live," said the man. "Pint out the place!"

I pointed to where our village lay, on the flat in-shore among the alder-trees and pollards, a mile or more from the church.

The man, after looking at me for a moment, turned me upside-down, and emptied my pockets. There was nothing in them but a piece of bread. When the church came to itself—for he was so sudden and strong that he made it go head-over-heels before me, and I saw the steeple under my feet—when the church came to itself, I say, I was seated on a high tombstone, trembling, while he ate the bread ravenously.

"You young dog," said the man, licking his lips, "what fat cheeks you ha' got."

I believe they were fat, though I was at that time under-sized for my years, and not strong.

"Darn me if I couldn't eat 'em," said the man, with a threatening shake of his head, "and if I han't half a mind to't!"

I earnestly expressed my hope that he wouldn't, and held tighter to the tombstone on which he had put me; partly, to keep myself upon it; partly, to keep myself from crying.

"Now lookee here!" said the man. "Where's your mother?"

"There, sir!" said I.

He started, made a short run, and stopped and looked over his shoulder.

"There, sir!" I timidly explained. "Also Georgiana. That's my mother."

"Oh!" said he, coming back. "And is that your father alonger your mother?"

"Yes, sir," said I; "him too; late of this parish."

"Ha!" he muttered then, considering. "Who d'ye live with—supposin' you're kindly let to live, which I han't made up my mind about?"

"My sister, sir—Mrs. Joe Gargery—wife of Joe Gargery, the blacksmith, sir."

"Blacksmith, eh?" said he. And looked down at his leg.

After darkly looking at his leg and at me several times, he came closer to my tombstone, took me by both arms, and tilted me back as far as he could hold me; so that his eyes looked most powerfully down into mine, and mine looked most helplessly up into his.

"Now lookee here," he said, "the question being whether you're to be let to live. You know what a file is?"

"Yes, sir."

"And you know what wittles is?"

"Yes, sir."

After each question he tilted me over a little more, so as to give me a greater sense of helplessness and danger.

"You get me a file." He tilted me again. "And you get me wittles." He tilted me again. "You bring 'em both to me." He tilted me again. "Or I'll have your heart and liver out." He tilted me again.

I was dreadfully frightened, and so giddy that I clung to him with both hands, and said, "If you would kindly please to let me keep upright, sir, perhaps I shouldn't be sick, and perhaps I could attend more."

He gave me a most tremendous dip and roll, so that the church jumped over its own weather-cock. Then, he held me by the arms, in an upright position on the top of the stone, and went on in these fearful terms:

"You bring me, to-morrow morning early, that file and them wittles. You bring the lot to me, at that old Battery over yonder. You do it, and you never dare to say a word or dare to make a sign concerning your having seen such a person as me, or any person sumever, and you shall be let to live. You fail, or you go from my words in any partickler, no matter how small it is, and your heart and your liver shall be tore out, roasted and ate. Now, I ain't alone, as you may think I am. There's a young man hid with me, in comparison with which young man I am a Angel. That young man hears the words I speak. That young man has a secret way pecooliar to himself, of getting at a boy, and at his heart, and at his liver. It is in wain for a boy to attempt to hide himself from that young man. A boy may lock his door, may be warm in bed, may tuck himself up, may draw the clothes over his head, may think himself comfortable and safe, but that young man will softly creep and creep his way to him and tear him open. I am a keeping that young man from harming of you at the present moment, with great difficulty. I find it wery hard to hold that young man off of your inside. Now, what do you say?"

I said that I would get him the file, and I would get him what broken bits of food I could, and I would come to him at the Battery, early in the morning.

"Say Lord strike you dead if you don't!" said the man.

I said so, and he took me down.

"Now," he pursued, "you remember what you've undertook, and you remember that young man, and you get home!"

"Goo-good night, sir," I faltered.

"Much of that!" said he, glancing about him over the cold wet flat. "I wish I was a frog. Or a eel!"

At the same time, he hugged his shuddering body in both his arms—

clasping himself, as if to hold himself together—and limped towards the low church wall. As I saw him go, picking his way among the nettles, and among the brambles that bound the green mounds, he looked in my young eyes as if he were eluding the hands of the dead people, stretching up cautiously out of their graves, to get a twist upon his ankle and pull him in.

When he came to the low church wall, he got over it, like a man whose legs were numbed and stiff, and then turned round to look for me. When I saw him turning, I set my face towards home, and made the best use of my legs. But presently I looked over my shoulder, and saw him going on again towards the river, still hugging himself in both arms, and picking his way with his sore feet among the great stones dropped into the marshes here and there, for stepping-places when the rains were heavy, or the tide was in.

The marshes were just a long black horizontal line then, as I stopped to look after him; and the river was just another horizontal line, not nearly so broad nor yet so black; and the sky was just a row of long angry red lines and dense black lines intermixed. On the edge of the river I could faintly make out the only two black things in all the prospect that seemed to be standing upright; one of these was the beacon by which the sailors steered—like an unhooped cask upon a pole—an ugly thing when you were near it; the other a gibbet, with some chains hanging to it which had once held a pirate. The man was limping on towards this latter, as if he were the pirate come to life, and come down, and going back to hook himself up again. It gave me a terrible turn when I thought so; and as I saw the cattle lifting their heads to gaze after him, I wondered whether they thought so too. I looked all round for the horrible young man, and could see no signs of him. But, now I was frightened again, and ran home without stopping.

[Pip spent a most wretched night, in childish terror at his plight. Very early in the morning, he raided Mrs. Joe Gargery's pantry, in fear and trembling, and stole a file from among Joe Gargery's tools, and ran for the misty meadows.]

CHAPTER III

It was a rimy morning, and very damp. I had seen the damp lying on the outside of my little window, as if some goblin had been crying there all night, and using the window for a pocket-handkerchief. Now I saw the damp lying on the bare hedges and spare grass, like a coarser sort of spiders' webs; hanging itself from twig to twig and blade to blade. On every rail and gate, wet lay clammy, and the marsh-mist was so thick, that the wooden finger on the post directing people to our village—a direction which they never accepted, for they never came there—was invisible to me until I was quite close under it. Then, as I looked up at it, while it dripped, it seemed to my oppressed conscience like a phantom devoting me to the Hulks.

The mist was heavier yet when I got out upon the marshes, so that instead of my running at everything, everything seemed to run at me. This was very disagreeable to a guilty mind. The gates and dykes and banks came bursting at me through the mist, as if they cried as plainly as could be, "A boy with Somebody-else's pork pie! Stop him!" The cattle came upon me with like suddenness, staring out of their eyes, and steaming out of their nostrils, "Holloa, young thief!" One black ox, with a white cravat on—who even had to my awakened conscience something of a clerical air—fixed me so obstinately with his eyes, and moved his blunt head round in such an accusatory manner as I moved round, that I blubbered out to him, "I couldn't help it, sir! It wasn't for myself I took it!" Upon which he put down his head, blew a cloud of smoke out of his nose, and vanished with a kick-up of his hind-legs and a flourish of his tail.

All this time, I was getting on towards the river; but however fast I went, I couldn't warm my feet, to which the damp cold seemed riveted, as the iron was riveted to the leg of the man I was running to meet. I knew my way to the Battery pretty straight, for I had been down there on a Sunday with Joe, and Joe, sitting on an old gun, had told me that when I was 'prentice to him, regularly bound, we would have such Larks there! However, in the confusion of the mist, I found myself at last too far to the right, and consequently had to try back along the river-side, on the bank of loose stones above the mud and the stakes that staked the tide out. Making my way along here with all despatch, I had just crossed a ditch which I knew to be very near the Battery, and had just scrambled up the mound beyond the ditch, when I saw the man sitting before me. His back was towards me, and he had his arms folded, and was nodding forward, heavy with sleep.

I thought he would be more glad if I came upon him with his breakfast, in that unexpected manner, so I went forward softly and touched him on the shoulder. He instantly jumped up, and it was not the same man but another man!

And yet this man was dressed in coarse gray, too, and had a great iron on his leg, and was lame, and hoarse, and cold, and was everything that the other man was; except that he had not the same face, and had a flat, broad-brimmed, low-crowned felt hat on. All this I saw in a moment, for I had only a moment to see it in: he swore an oath at me, made a hit at me—it was a round, weak blow that missed me and almost knocked himself down, for it made him stumble—and then he ran into the mist stumbling twice as he went, and I lost him.

"It's the young man!" I thought, feeling my heart shoot as I identified him. I dare say I should have felt a pain in my liver, too, if I had known where it was.

I was soon at the Battery, after that, and there was the right man—hugging himself and limping to and fro, as if he had never all night left off hugging and limping—waiting for me. He was awfully cold, to be sure. I half expected to see him drop down before my face and die of deadly cold. His eyes looked so awfully hungry, too, that when I handed him the file and he laid it down on the grass, it occurred to me he would have tried to eat it, if he had not seen my bundle. He did not turn me upside down, this time, to get at what I had, but left me right side upwards while I opened the bundle and emptied my pockets.

"What's in the bottle, boy?" said he.

"Brandy," said I.

He was already handing mincemeat down his throat in the most curious manner—more like a man who was putting it away somewhere in a violent hurry, than a man who was eating it—but he left off to take some of the liquor. He shivered all the while, so violently, that it was quite as much as he could do to keep the neck of the bottle between his teeth, without biting it off.

"I think you have got the ague," said I.

"I'm much of your opinion, boy," said he.

"It's bad about here," I told him. "You've been lying out on the meshes, and they're dreadful aguish. Rheumatic too."

"I'll eat my breakfast afore they're the death of me," said he, "I'd do that, if I was going to be strung up to that there gallows as there is over there, directly arterwards. I'll beat the shivers so far, *I'll* bet you."

He was gobbling mincemeat, meat-bone, bread, cheese, and pork pie, all at once: staring distrustfully while he did so at the mist all round us, and often stopping—even stopping his jaws—to listen. Some real or fancied sound, some clink upon the river or breathing of beast upon the marsh, now gave him a start, and he said, suddenly:

"You're not a deceiving imp? You brought no one with you?"

"No, sir! No!"

"Nor giv' no one the office to follow you?"

"No!"

"Well," said he, "I believe you. You'd be but a fierce young hound indeed, if at your time of life you could help to hunt a wretched warmint, hunted as near death and dunghill as this poor wretched warmint is!"

Something clicked in his throat as if he had works in him like a clock, and was going to strike. And he smeared his ragged rough sleeve over his eyes.

Pitying his desolation, and watching him as he gradually settled down upon the pie, I made bold to say, "I am glad you enjoy it."

"Did you speak?"

"I said I was glad you enjoyed it."

"Thankee, my boy. I do."

I had often watched a large dog of ours eating his food; and I now noticed a decided similarity between the dog's way of eating, and the man's. The man took strong, sharp, sudden bites, just like the dog. He swallowed, or rather snapped up, every mouthful, too soon and too fast; and he looked sideways here and there while he ate, as if he thought there was danger in every direction, of somebody's coming to take the pie away. He was altogether too unsettled in his mind over it, to appreciate it comfortably, I thought, or to have anybody to dine with him, without making a chop with his jaws at the visitor. In all of which particulars he was very like the dog.

"I am afraid you won't leave any of it for him," said I timidly; after a silence during which I had hesitated as to the politeness of making the remark. "There's no more to be got where that came from." It was the certainty of this fact that impelled me to offer the hint.

"Leave any for him? Who's him?" said my friend, stopping in his crunching of pie-crust.

"The young man. That you spoke of. That was hid with you."

"Oh ah!" he returned, with something like a gruff laugh. "Him? Yes, yes! *He* don't want no wittles."

"I thought he looked as if he did," said I.

The man stopped eating, and regarded me with the keenest scrutiny and the greatest surprise.

"Looked? When?"

"Just now."

"Where?"

"Yonder," said I, pointing; "over there, where I found him nodding asleep, and thought it was you."

He held me by the collar and stared at me so, that I began to think his first idea about cutting my throat had revived.

"Dressed like you, you know, only with a hat," I explained, trembling; "and—and"—I was very anxious to put this delicately—"and with—the same reason for wanting to borrow a file. Didn't you hear the cannon last night?"

"Then, there *was* firing!" he said to himself.

"I wonder you shouldn't have been sure of that," I returned, "for we heard it up at home, and that's further away, and we were shut in besides."

"Why, see now!" said he. "When a man's alone on these flats, with a light head and a light stomach, perishing of cold and want, he hears nothin' all night, but guns firing, and voices calling. Hears? He sees the soldiers, with their red coats lighted up by the torches carried afore, closing in round him. He hears his number called, hears himself challenged, hears the rattle of the muskets, hears the orders 'Make ready! Present! Cover him steady, men!' and is laid hands on—and there's nothin'! Why, if I see one pursuing party last night—coming up in order, Damn 'em, with their tramp, tramp—I see a hundred. And as to firing! Why, I see the mist shake with the cannon, arter it was broad day.—But this man;" he had said all the rest as if he had forgotten my being there; "did you notice anything in him?"

"He had a badly bruised face," said I, recalling what I hardly knew I knew.

"Not here?" exclaimed the man, striking his left cheek mercilessly, with the flat of his hand.

"Yes, there!"

"Where is he?" He crammed what little food was left, into the breast of his gray jacket. "Show me the way he went. I'll pull him down, like a bloodhound. Curse this iron on my sore leg! Give us hold of the file, boy."

I indicated in what direction the mist had shrouded the other man, and he looked up at it for an instant. But he was down on the rank wet grass, filing at his iron like a madman, and not minding me or minding his own leg, which had an old chafe upon it and was bloody, but which he handled as roughly as if it had no more feeling in it than the file. I was very much afraid of him again, now that he had worked himself into this fierce hurry, and I was likewise very much afraid of keeping away from home any longer. I told him I must go, but he took no notice, so I thought the best thing I could do was to slip off. The last I saw of him, his head was bent over his knee and he was working hard at his fetter, muttering impatient imprecations at it and at his leg. The last I heard of him, I stopped in the mist to listen, and the file was still going.

ROBERT BROWNING (1812-1889)

Cavalier Tunes

I. Marching Along

Kentish Sir Byng stood for his King,
Bidding the crop-headed Parliament swing:
And, pressing a troop unable to stoop
And see the rogues flourish and honest folk droop,
Marched them along, fifty-score strong,
Great-hearted gentlemen, singing this song.

God for King Charles! Pym and such carles
To the Devil that prompts 'em their treasonous parles!
Cavaliers, up! Lips from the cup,
Hands from the pastry, nor bite take nor sup
Till you're—
(*Chorus*) *Marching along, fifty-score strong,*
Great-hearted gentlemen, singing this song.

Hampden to Hell, and his obsequies' knell
Serve Hazelrig, Fiennes, and young Harry as well!
England, good cheer! Rupert is near!
Kentish and loyalists, keep we not here
(*Chorus*) *Marching along, fifty-score strong,*
Great-hearted gentlemen, singing this song?

Then, God for King Charles! Pym and his snarls
To the Devil that pricks on such pestilent carles!
Hold by the right, you double your might;
So, onward to Nottingham, fresh for the fight,
(*Chorus*) *March we along, fifty-score strong,*
Great-hearted gentlemen, singing this song!

II. Give a Rouse

King Charles, and who'll do him right now?
King Charles, and who's ripe for fight now?
Give a rouse: here's, in Hell's despite now,
King Charles!

Who gave me the goods that went since?
Who raised me the house that sank once?
Who helped me to gold I spent since?
Who found me in wine you drank once?
(*Chorus*) *King Charles, and who'll do him right now?*
King Charles, and who's ripe for fight now?
Give a rouse: here's, in Hell's despite now,
King Charles!

To whom used my boy George quaff else,
By the old fool's side that begot him?
For whom did he cheer and laugh else,
While Noll's damned troopers shot him?
(*Chorus*) *King Charles, and who'll do him right now?*
King Charles, and who's ripe for fight now?
Give a rouse: here's, in Hell's despite now,
King Charles!

III. Boot and Saddle

Boot, saddle, to horse, and away!
Rescue my Castle, before the hot day
Brightens to blue from its silvery grey,
(*Chorus*) *Boot, saddle, to horse, and away!*

Ride past the suburbs, asleep as you'd say;
Many's the friend there, will listen and pray
"God's luck to gallants that strike up the lay—
(*Chorus*) *Boot, saddle, to horse, and away!"*

Forty miles off, like a roebuck at bay,
Flouts Castle Brancepeth the Roundheads' array:
Who laughs, "Good fellows ere this, by my fay,
(*Chorus*) *Boot, saddle, to horse, and away?*"

Who? My wife Gertrude; that, honest and gay,
Laughs when you talk of surrendering, "Nay!
I've better counsellors; what counsel they?
(*Chorus*) *Boot, saddle, to horse, and away!*"

"How they brought the Good News from Ghent to Aix"

I SPRANG to the stirrup, and Joris, and he;
I galloped, Dirck galloped, we galloped all three;
"Good speed!" cried the watch, as the gate-bolts undrew;
"Speed!" echoed the wall to us galloping through;
Behind shut the postern, the lights sank to rest,
And into the midnight we galloped abreast.

Not a word to each other; we kept the great pace
Neck by neck, stride by stride, never changing our place;
I turned in my saddle and made its girths tight,
Then shortened each stirrup, and set the pique right,
Rebuckled the cheek-strap, chained slacker the bit,
Nor galloped less steadily Roland a whit.

'Twas moonset at starting; but while we drew near
Lokeren, the cocks crew and twilight dawned clear;
At Boom, a great yellow star came out to see;
At Düffeld, 'twas morning as plain as could be;
And from Mecheln church-steeple we heard the half-chime,
So Joris broke silence with, "Yet there is time!"

At Aershot, up leaped of a sudden the sun,
And against him the cattle stood black every one,
To stare through the mist at us galloping past,
And I saw my stout galloper Roland at last,
With resolute shoulders, each butting away
The haze, as some bluff river headland its spray:

And his low head and crest, just one sharp ear bent back
For my voice, and the other pricked out on his track;
And one eye's black intelligence,—ever that glance
O'er its white edge at me, his own master, askance!
And the thick heavy spume-flakes which aye and anon
His fierce lips shook upwards in galloping on.

By Hasselt, Dirck groaned; and cried Joris, "Stay, spur!
Your Roos galloped bravely, the fault's not in her.
We'll remember at Aix"—for one heard the quick wheeze
Of her chest, saw the stretched neck and staggering knees,
And sunk tail, and horrible heave of the flank,
As down on her haunches she shuddered and sank.

So, we were left galloping, Joris and I,
Past Looz and past Tongres, no cloud in the sky;
The broad sun above laughed a pitiless laugh,
'Neath our feet broke the brittle bright stubble like chaff;
Till over by Dalhem a dome-spire sprang white,
And "Gallop," gasped Joris, "for Aix is in sight!"

"How they'll greet us!"—and all in a moment his roan
Rolled neck and croup over, lay dead as a stone;
And there was my Roland to bear the whole weight
Of the news which alone could save Aix from her fate,
With his nostrils like pits full of blood to the brim,
And with circles of red for his eye-sockets' rim.

Then I cast loose my buffcoat, each holster let fall,
Shook off both my jack-boots, let go belt and all,
Stood up in the stirrup, leaned, patted his ear,
Called my Roland his pet-name, my horse without peer;
Clapped my hands, laughed and sang, any noise, bad or good,
Till at length into Aix Roland galloped and stood.

And all I remember is—friends flocking round
As I sat with his head 'twixt my knees on the ground;
And no voice but was praising this Roland of mine,
As I poured down his throat our last measure of wine,
Which (the burgesses voted by common consent)
Was no more than his due who brought good news from Ghent.

The Laboratory

[ANCIEN RÉGIME]

Now that I, tying thy glass mask tightly,
May gaze thro' these faint smokes curling whitely,
As thou pliest thy trade in this devil's-smithy—
Which is the poison to poison her, prithee?

He is with her; and they know that I know
Where they are, what they do: they believe my tears flow
While they laugh, laugh at me, at me fled to the drear
Empty church, to pray God in, for them!—I am here.

Grind away, moisten and mash up thy paste,
Pound at thy powder,—I am not in haste!
Better sit thus, and observe thy strange things,
Than go where men wait me and dance at the King's.

That in the mortar—you call it a gum?
Ah, the brave tree whence such gold oozings come!
And yonder soft phial, the exquisite blue,
Sure to taste sweetly,—is that poison too?

Had I but all of them, thee and thy treasures,
What a wild crowd of invisible pleasures!
To carry pure death in an earring, a casket,
A signet, a fan-mount, a filigree-basket!

Soon, at the King's, a mere lozenge to give
And Pauline should have just thirty minutes to live!

But to light a pastille, and Elise, with her head
And her breast and her arms and her hands, should drop dead!

Quick—is it finished? The colour's too grim!
Why not soft like the phial's, enticing and dim?
Let it brighten her drink, let her turn it and stir,
And try it and taste, ere she fix and prefer!

What a drop! She's not little, no minion like me—
That's why she ensnared him: this never will free
The soul from those masculine eyes,—say, "no!"
To that pulse's magnificent come-and-go.

For only last night, as they whispered, I brought
My own eyes to bear on her so, that I thought
Could I keep them one half minute fixed, she would fall,
Shrivelled; she fell not; yet this does it all!

Not that I bid you spare her the pain!
Let death be felt and the proof remain;
Brand, burn up, bite into its grace—
He is sure to remember her dying face!

Is it done? Take my mask off! Nay, be not morose;
It kills her, and this prevents seeing it close:
The delicate droplet, my whole fortune's fee—
If it hurts her, beside, can it ever hurt me?

Now, take all my jewels, gorge gold to your fill,
You may kiss me, old man, on my mouth if you will!
But brush this dust off me, lest horror it brings
Ere I know it—next moment I dance at the King's!

Up at a Villa—Down in the City

(As Distinguished by an Italian Person of Quality)

Had I but plenty of money, money enough and to spare,
The house for me, no doubt, were a house in the city-square;
Ah, such a life, such a life, as one leads at the window there!

Something to see, by Bacchus, something to hear, at least!
There, the whole day long, one's life is a perfect feast;
While up at a villa one lives, I maintain it, no more than a beast.

Well now, look at our villa! stuck like the horn of a bull
Just on a mountain-edge as bare as the creature's skull,
Save a mere shag of a bush with hardly a leaf to pull!
—I scratch my own, sometimes, to see if the hair's turned wool.

But the city, oh the city—the square with the houses! Why?
They are stone-faced, white as a curd, there's something to take the eye!
Houses in four straight lines, not a single front awry;
You watch who crosses and gossips, who saunters, who hurries by;
Green blinds, as a matter of course, to draw when the sun gets high;
And the shops with fanciful signs which are painted properly.

What of a villa? Though winter be over in March by rights,
'Tis May perhaps ere the snow shall have withered well off the heights:

You've the brown ploughed land before, where the oxen steam and wheeze,
And the hills over-smoked behind by the faint gray olive-trees.

Is it better in May, I ask you? You've summer all at once;
In a day he leaps complete with a few strong April suns.
'Mid the sharp short emerald wheat, scarce risen three fingers well,
The wild tulip, at end of its tube, blows out its great red bell
Like a thin clear bubble of blood, for the children to pick and sell.

Is it ever hot in the square? There's a fountain to spout and splash!
In the shade it sings and springs: in the shine such foambows flash
On the horses with curling fish-tails, that prance and paddle and pash
Round the lady atop in her conch—fifty gazers do not abash,
Though all that she wears is some weeds round her waist in a sort of sash.

All the year long at the villa, nothing to see though you linger,
Except yon cypress that points like death's lean lifted forefinger.
Some think fireflies pretty, when they mix i' the corn and mingle,
Or thrid the stinking hemp till the stalks of it seem a-tingle.
Late August or early September, the stunning cicala is shrill,
And the bees keep their tiresome whine round the resinous firs on the hill.
Enough of the seasons,—I spare you the months of the fever and chill.

Ere you open your eyes in the city, the blessed church-bells begin:
No sooner the bells leave off than the diligence rattles in:
You get the pick of the news, and it costs you never a pin.
By and by there's the travelling doctor gives pills, lets blood, draws teeth;
Or the Pulcinello-trumpet breaks up the market beneath.
At the post-office such a scene-picture—the new play, piping hot!
And a notice how, only this morning, three liberal thieves were shot.
Above it, behold the Archbishop's most fatherly of rebukes,
And beneath, with his crown and his lion, some little new law of the Duke's!
Or a sonnet with flowery marge, to the Reverend Don So-and-so,
Who is Dante, Boccaccio, Petrarca, Saint Jerome, and Cicero,
"And moreover" (the sonnet goes rhyming), "the skirts of Saint Paul has reached,
Having preached us those six Lent-lectures more unctuous than ever he preached."
Noon strikes,—here sweeps the procession! our Lady borne smiling and smart
With a pink gauze gown all spangles, and seven swords stuck in her heart!
Bang-whang-whang goes the drum, *tootle-te-tootle* the fife;
No keeping one's haunches still: it's the greatest pleasure in life.

But bless you, it's dear—it's dear! fowls, wine, at double the rate.
They have clapped a new tax upon salt, and what oil pays passing the gate
It's a horror to think of. And so, the villa for me, not the city!
Beggars can scarcely be choosers: but still—ah, the pity, the pity!
Look, two and two go the priests, then the monks with cowls and sandals,
And the penitents dressed in white shirts, a-holding the yellow candles;
One, he carries a flag up straight, and another a cross with handles,
And the Duke's guard brings up the rear, for the better prevention of scandals;

Bang-whang-whang goes the drum, *tootle-te-tootle* the fife.
Oh, a day in the city-square, there is no such pleasure in life!

A Toccata of Galuppi's

Oh Galuppi, Baldassare, this is very sad to find!
I can hardly misconceive you; it would prove me deaf and blind;
But although I take your meaning, 'tis with such a heavy mind!

Here you come with your old music, and here's all the good it brings.
What, they lived once thus at Venice where the merchants were the kings,
Where St. Mark's is, where the Doges used to wed the sea with rings?

Ay, because the sea's the street there; and 'tis arched by . . . what you call
. . . Shylock's bridge with houses on it, where they kept the carnival:
I was never out of England—it's as if I saw it all.

Did young people take their pleasure when the sea was warm in May?
Balls and masks begun at midnight, burning ever to mid-day,
When they made up fresh adventures for the morrow, do you say?

Was a lady such a lady, cheeks so round and lips so red,—
On her neck the small face buoyant, like a bell-flower on its bed,
O'er the breast's superb abundance where a man might base his head?

Well, and it was graceful of them—they'd break talk off and afford
—She, to bite her mask's black velvet—he, to finger on his sword,
While you sat and played Toccatas, stately at the clavichord?

What? Those lesser thirds so plaintive, sixths diminished, sigh on sigh,
Told them something? Those suspensions, those solutions—"Must we die?"
Those commiserating sevenths—"Life might last! we can but try!"

"Were you happy?"—"Yes."—"And are you still as happy?"—"Yes. And you?"
—"Then, more kisses!"—"Did *I* stop them, when a million seemed so few?"
Hark, the dominant's persistence till it must be answered to!

So, an octave struck the answer. Oh, they praised you, I dare say!
"Brave Galuppi! that was music! good alike at grave and gay!
I can always leave off talking when I hear a master play!"

Then they left you for their pleasure: till in due time, one by one,
Some with lives that came to nothing, some with deeds as well undone,
Death stepped tacitly and took them where they never see the sun.

But when I sit down to reason, think to take my stand nor swerve,
While I triumph o'er a secret wrung from nature's close reserve,
In you come with your cold music till I creep through every nerve.

Yes, you, like a ghostly cricket, creaking where a house was burned:
"Dust and ashes, dead and done with, Venice spent what Venice earned.
The soul, doubtless, is immortal—where a soul can be discerned.

"Yours for instance: you know physics, something of geology,
Mathematics are your pastime; souls shall rise in their degree;
Butterflies may dread extinction,—you'll not die, it cannot be!

"As for Venice and her people, merely born to bloom and drop,
Here on earth they bore their fruitage, mirth and folly were the crop:
What of soul was left, I wonder, when the kissing had to stop?

"Dust and ashes!" So you creak it, and I want the heart to scold.
Dear dead women, with such hair, too—what's become of all the gold
Used to hang and brush their bosoms? I feel chilly and grown old.

Home-Thoughts, from Abroad

Oh, to be in England
Now that April's there,
And whoever wakes in England
Sees, some morning, unaware,
That the lowest boughs and the brushwood sheaf
Round the elm-tree bole are in tiny leaf,
While the chaffinch sings on the orchard bough
In England—now!

And after April, when May follows,
And the whitethroat builds, and all the swallows!
Hark, where my blossomed pear-tree in the hedge
Leans to the field and scatters on the clover
Blossoms and dewdrops—at the bent spray's edge—
That's the wise thrush; he sings each song twice over,
Lest you should think he never could recapture
The first fine careless rapture!
And though the fields look rough with hoary dew,
All will be gay when noontide wakes anew
The buttercups, the little children's dower—
Far brighter than this gaudy melon-flower.

The Patriot

It was roses, roses, all the way,
With myrtle mixed in my path like mad:
The house-roofs seemed to heave and sway,
The church-spires flamed, such flags they had,
A year ago on this very day.

The air broke into a mist with bells,
The old walls rocked with the crowd and cries.
Had I said, "Good folk, mere noise repels—
But give me your sun from yonder skies!"
They had answered, "And afterward, what else?"

Alack, it was I who leaped at the sun
To give it my loving friends to keep!
Naught man could do, have I left undone:
And you see my harvest, what I reap
This very day, now a year is run.

There's nobody on the house-tops now—
Just a palsied few at the windows set;
For the best of the sight is, all allow,
At the Shambles' Gate—or, better yet,
By the very scaffold's foot, I trow.

I go in the rain, and, more than needs,
A rope cuts both my wrists behind;
And I think, by the feel, my forehead bleeds,
For they fling, whoever has a mind,
Stones at me for my year's misdeeds.

Thus I entered, and thus I go!
In triumphs, people have dropped down dead.
"Paid by the world, what dost thou owe
Me?"—God might question; now instead,
'Tis God shall repay: I am safer so.

My Last Duchess

FERRARA

THAT'S my last Duchess painted on the wall,
Looking as if she were alive. I call
That piece a wonder, now: Fra Pandolf's hands
Worked busily a day, and there she stands.
Will't please you sit and look at her? I said
"Fra Pandolf" by design, for never read
Strangers like you that pictured countenance,
The depth and passion of its earnest glance,
But to myself they turned (since none puts by
The curtain I have drawn for you, but I)
And seemed as they would ask me, if they durst,
How such a glance came there; so, not the first
Are you to turn and ask thus. Sir, 'twas not
Her husband's presence only, called that spot
Of joy into the Duchess' cheek: perhaps
Fra Pandolf chanced to say, "Her mantle laps
Over my lady's wrist too much," or "Paint
Must never hope to reproduce the faint
Half-flush that dies along her throat:" such stuff
Was courtesy, she thought, and cause enough
For calling up that spot of joy. She had
A heart—how shall I say?—too soon made glad,
Too easily impressed: she liked whate'er
She looked on, and her looks went everywhere.
Sir, 'twas all one! My favour at her breast,
The dropping of the daylight in the West,
The bough of cherries some officious fool
Broke in the orchard for her, the white mule
She rode with round the terrace—all and each
Would draw from her alike the approving speech,
Or blush, at least. She thanked men,—good! but thanked
Somehow—I know not how—as if she ranked
My gift of a nine-hundred-years-old name
With anybody's gift. Who'd stoop to blame
This sort of trifling? Even had you skill
In speech—(which I have not)—to make your will
Quite clear to such an one, and say, "Just this
Or that in you disgusts me; here you miss,
Or there exceed the mark"—and if she let
Herself be lessoned so, nor plainly set
Her wits to yours, forsooth, and made excuse,
—E'en then would be some stooping; and I choose
Never to stoop. Oh sir, she smiled, no doubt,
Whene'er I passed her; but who passed without
Much the same smile? This grew; I gave commands;
Then all smiles stopped together. There she stands
As if alive. Will't please you rise? We'll meet
The company below, then. I repeat,
The Count your master's known munificence
Is ample warrant that no just pretence
Of mine for dowry will be disallowed;
Though his fair daughter's self, as I avowed
At starting, is my object. Nay, we'll go
Together down, sir. Notice Neptune, though,
Taming a sea-horse, thought a rarity,
Which Claus of Innsbruck cast in bronze for me!

A Grammarian's Funeral, shortly after the Revival of Learning in Europe.

LET us begin and carry up this corpse,
Singing together.
Leave we the common crofts, the vulgar thorpes,
Each in its tether
Sleeping safe on the bosom of the plain,
Cared-for till cock-crow:
Look out if yonder be not day again
Rimming the rock-row!
That's the appropriate country; there, man's thought,
Rarer, intenser,
Self-gathered for an outbreak, as it ought,
Chafes in the censer!
Leave we the unlettered plain its herd and crop;
Seek we sepulture
On a tall mountain, citied to the top,
Crowded with culture!
All the peaks soar, but one the rest excels;
Clouds overcome it;
No, yonder sparkle is the citadel's
Circling its summit!
Thither our path lies; wind we up the heights:
Wait ye the warning?
Our low life was the level's and the night's;
He's for the morning!
Step to a tune, square chests, erect the head,
'Ware the beholders!
This is our master, famous, calm, and dead,
Borne on our shoulders.

Sleep, crop and herd! sleep, darkling thorpe and croft,
Safe from the weather!
He, whom we convoy to his grave aloft,
Singing together,
He was a man born with thy face and throat,
Lyric Apollo!
Long he lived nameless: how should spring take note
Winter would follow?
Till lo, the little touch, and youth was gone!
Cramped and diminished,
Moaned he, "New measures, other feet anon!
My dance is finished?"
No, that's the world's way! (keep the mountain-side,
Make for the city,)
He knew the signal, and stepped on with pride
Over men's pity;
Left play for work, and grappled with the world
Bent on escaping:
"What's in the scroll," quoth he, "thou keepest furled?
Show me their shaping,
Theirs, who most studied man, the bard and sage,—
Give!"—So he gowned him,
Straight got by heart that book to its last page:
Learned, we found him!
Yea, but we found him bald too—eyes like lead,
Accents uncertain:
"Time to taste life," another would have said,
"Up with the curtain!"—
This man said rather, "Actual life comes next?
Patience a moment!
Grant I have mastered learning's crabbed text,
Still, there's the comment.
Let me know all! Prate not of most or least,
Painful or easy:
Even to the crumbs I'd fain eat up the feast,
Ay, nor feel queasy!"
Oh, such a life as he resolved to live,
When he had learned it,
When he had gathered all books had to give!

Sooner, he spurned it.
Image the whole, then execute the parts—
Fancy the fabric
Quite, ere you build, ere steel strike fire from quartz,
Ere mortar dab brick!

(Here's the town-gate reached: there's the market-place
Gaping before us.)
Yea, this in him was the peculiar grace
(Hearten our chorus)
That before living he'd learn how to live—
No end to learning:
Earn the means first—God surely will contrive
Use for our earning.
Others mistrust and say—"But time escapes!
Live now or never!"
He said, "What's time? leave Now for dogs and apes!
Man has Forever."
Back to his book then: deeper drooped his head:
Calculus racked him:
Leaden before, his eyes grew dross of lead:
Tussis attacked him.
"Now, Master, take a little rest!"—not he!
(Caution redoubled!
Step two a-breast, the way winds narrowly)
Not a whit troubled,
Back to his studies, fresher than at first,
Fierce as a dragon
He (soul-hydroptic with a sacred thirst)
Sucked at the flagon.
Oh, if we draw a circle premature,
Heedless of far gain,
Greedy for quick returns of profit, sure,
Bad is our bargain!
Was it not great? did not he throw on God,
(He loves the burthen)—
God's task to make the heavenly period
Perfect the earthen?
Did not he magnify the mind, show clear
Just what it all meant?
He would not discount life, as fools do here,
Paid by instalment!
He ventured neck or nothing—Heaven's success
Found, or earth's failure:
"Wilt thou trust death or not?" He answered "Yes!
Hence with life's pale lure!"
That low man seeks a little thing to do,
Sees it and does it:
This high man, with a great thing to pursue,
Dies ere he knows it.
That low man goes on adding one to one,
His hundred's soon hit:
This high man, aiming at a million,
Misses an unit.
That, has the world here—should he need the next,
Let the world mind him!
This, throws himself on God, and unperplext
Seeking shall find Him,
So, with the throttling hands of Death at strife,
Ground he at grammar;
Still, thro' the rattle, parts of speech were rife:
While he could stammer
He settled *Hoti's* business—let it be!—
Properly based *Oun*—
Gave us the doctrine of the enclitic *De*,
Dead from the waist down.
Well, here's the platform, here's the proper place.
Hail to your purlieus,
All ye highfliers of the feathered race,
Swallows and curlews!
Here's the top-peak! the multitude below
Live, for they can, there.
This man decided not to Live but Know—
Bury this man there?
Here—here's his place, where meteors shoot, clouds form,
Lightnings are loosened,

Stars come and go! let joy break with the storm,
Peace let the dew send!
Lofty designs must close in like effects:
Loftily lying,
Leave him—still loftier than the world suspects,
Living and dying.

The Statue and the Bust

THERE'S a palace in Florence, the world knows well,
And a statue watches it from the square,
And this story of both do our townsmen tell.

Ages ago, a lady there,
At the farthest window facing the East
Asked, "Who rides by with the royal air?"

The brides-maids' prattle around her ceased;
She leaned forth, one on either hand;
They saw how the blush of the bride increased—

They felt by its beats her heart expand—
As one at each ear and both in a breath
Whispered, "The Great-Duke Ferdinand."

That selfsame instant, underneath,
The Duke rode past in his idle way,
Empty and fine like a swordless sheath.

Gay he rode, with a friend as gay,
Till he threw his head back—"Who is she?"
—"A bride the Riccardi brings home to-day."

Hair in heaps lay heavily
Over a pale brow spirit-pure—
Carved like the heart of the coal-black tree,

Crisped like a war-steed's encolure—
And vainly sought to dissemble her eyes
Of the blackest black our eyes endure.

And lo, a blade for a knight's emprise
Filled the fine empty sheath of a man,—
The Duke grew straightway brave and wise.

He looked at her, as a lover can;
She looked at him, as one who awakes,—
The past was a sleep, and her life began.

Now, love so ordered for both their sakes,
A feast was held that selfsame night
In the pile which the mighty shadow makes.

(For Via Larga is three-parts light,
But the palace overshadows one,
Because of a crime which may God requite!

To Florence and God the wrong was done,
Through the first republic's murder there
By Cosimo and his cursed son.)

The Duke (with the statue's face in the square)
Turned in the midst of his multitude
At the bright approach of the bridal pair.

Face to face the lovers stood
A single minute and no more,
While the bridegroom bent as a man subdued—

Bowed till his bonnet brushed the floor—
For the Duke on the lady a kiss conferred,
As the courtly custom was of yore.

In a minute can lovers exchange a word?
If a word did pass, which I do not think,
Only one out of the thousand heard.

That was the bridegroom. At day's brink
He and his bride were alone at last
In a bed-chamber by a taper's blink.

Calmly he said that her lot was cast,
That the door she had passed was shut on her
Till the final catafalque repassed.

The world meanwhile, its noise and stir,
Through a certain window facing the East
She could watch like a convent's chronicler.

Since passing the door might lead to a feast,
And a feast might lead to so much beside,
He, of many evils, chose the least.

"Freely I choose too," said the bride—
"Your window and its world suffice,"
Replied the tongue, while the heart replied—

"If I spend the night with that devil twice,
May his window serve as my loop of hell
Whence a damned soul looks on Paradise!

"I fly to the Duke who loves me well,
Sit by his side and laugh at sorrow
Ere I count another ave-bell.

" 'Tis only the coat of a page to borrow,
And tie my hair in a horse-boy's trim,
And I save my soul—but not tomorrow"—

(She checked herself and her eye grew dim)—
"My father tarries to bless my state:
I must keep it one day more for him.

"Is one day more so long to wait?
Moreover the Duke rides past, I know;
We shall see each other, sure as fate."

She turned on her side and slept. Just so!
So we resolve on a thing and sleep:
So did the lady, ages ago.

That night the Duke said, "Dear or cheap
As the cost of this cup of bliss may prove
To body or soul, I will drain it deep."

And on the morrow, bold with love,
He beckoned the bridegroom (close on call,
As his duty bade, by the Duke's alcove)

And smiled " 'Twas a very funeral,
Your lady will think, this feast of ours,—
A shame to efface, whate'er befall!

"What if we break from the Arno bowers,
And try if Petraja, cool and green,
Cure last night's fault with this morning's flowers?"

The bridegroom, not a thought to be seen
On his steady brow and quiet mouth,
Said, "Too much favour for me so mean!

"But, alas! my lady leaves the South;
Each wind that comes from the Apennine
Is a menace to her tender youth:

"Nor a way exists, the wise opine,
If she quits her palace twice this year,
To avert the flower of life's decline."

Quoth the Duke, "A sage and a kindly fear.
Moreover Petraja is cold this spring:
Be our feast to-night as usual here!"

And then to himself—"Which night shall bring
Thy bride to her lover's embraces, fool—
Or I am the fool, and thou art the king!

"Yet my passion must wait a night, nor cool—
For to-night the Envoy arrives from France,
Whose heart I unlock with thyself, my tool.

"I need thee still and might miss perchance.
To-day is not wholly lost, beside,
With its hope of my lady's countenance:

"For I ride—what should I do but ride?
And passing her palace, if I list,
May glance at its window—well betide!"

So said, so done: nor the lady missed
One ray that broke from the ardent brow,
Nor a curl of the lips where the spirit kissed.

Be sure that each renewed the vow,
No morrow's sun should arise and set
And leave them then as it left them now.

But next day passed, and next day yet,
With still fresh cause to wait one day more
Ere each leaped over the parapet.

And still, as love's brief morning wore,
With a gentle start, half smile, half sigh,
They found love not as it seemed before.

They thought it would work infallibly,
But not in despite of heaven and earth—
The rose would blow when the storm passed by.

Meantime they could profit in winter's dearth
By winter's fruits that supplant the rose:
The world and its ways have a certain worth!

And to press a point while these oppose
Were a simple policy; better wait:
We lose no friends and we gain no foes.

Meantime, worse fates than a lover's fate,
Who daily may ride and pass and look
Where his lady watches behind the grate!

And she—she watched the square like a book
Holding one picture and only one,
Which daily to find she undertook:

When the picture was reached the book was done,
And she turned from the picture at night to scheme
Of tearing it out for herself next sun.

So weeks grew months, years—gleam by gleam
The glory dropped from their youth and love,
And both perceived they had dreamed a dream;

Which hovered as dreams do, still above,—
But who can take a dream for a truth?
Oh, hide our eyes from the next remove!

One day as the lady saw her youth
Depart, and the silver thread that streaked
Her hair, and, worn by the serpent's tooth,

The brow so puckered, the chin so peaked,—
And wondered who the woman was,
Hollow-eyed and haggard-cheeked,

Fronting her silent in the glass—
"Summon here," she suddenly said,
"Before the rest of my old self pass,

"Him, the Carver, a hand to aid,
Who fashions the clay no love will change,
And fixes a beauty never to fade.

"Let Robbia's craft so apt and strange
Arrest the remains of young and fair,
And rivet them while the seasons range.

"Make me a face on the window there,
Waiting as ever, mute the while,
My love to pass below in the square!

"And let me think that it may beguile
Dreary days which the dead must spend
Down in their darkness under the aisle,

"To say, 'What matters it at the end?
I did no more while my heart was warm
Than does that image, my pale-faced friend.'

"Where is the use of the lip's red charm,
The heaven of hair, the pride of the brow,
And the blood that blues the inside arm—

"Unless we turn, as the soul knows how,
The earthly gift to an end divine?
A lady of clay is as good, I trow."

But long ere Robbia's cornice, fine
With flowers and fruits which leaves enlace,
Was set where now is the empty shrine—

(And, leaning out of a bright blue space,
As a ghost might lean from a chink of sky,
The passionate pale lady's face—

Eyeing ever with earnest eye
And quick-turned neck at its breathless stretch,
Some one who ever is passing by—)

The Duke had sighed like the simplest wretch
In Florence, "Youth—my dream escapes!
Will its record stay?" And he bade them fetch

Some subtle moulder of brazen shapes—
"Can the soul, the will, die out of a man
Ere his body find the grave that gapes?

"John of Douay shall effect my plan,
Set me on horseback here aloft,
Alive, as the crafty sculptor can,

"In the very square I have crossed so oft!
That men may admire, when future suns
Shall touch the eyes to a purpose soft,

"While the mouth and the brow stay brave in bronze—
Admire and say, 'When he was alive,
How he would take his pleasure once!'

"And it shall go hard but I contrive
To listen the while and laugh in my tomb
At idleness which aspires to strive."

So! while these wait the trump of doom,
How do their spirits pass, I wonder,
Nights and days in the narrow room?

Still, I suppose, they sit and ponder
What a gift life was, ages ago,
Six steps out of the chapel yonder.

Only they see not God, I know,
Nor all that chivalry of His,
The soldier-saints who, row on row,

Burn upward each to his point of bliss—
Since, the end of life being manifest,
He had burned his way thro' the world to this.

I hear you reproach, "But delay was best,
For their end was a crime."—Oh, a crime will do
As well, I reply, to serve for a test,

As a virtue golden through and through,
Sufficient to vindicate itself
And prove its worth at a moment's view!

Must a game be played for the sake of pelf?
Where a button goes, 'twere an epigram
To offer the stamp of the very Guelph.

The true has no value beyond the sham:
As well the counter as coin, I submit,
When your table's a hat, and your prize, a dram.

Stake your counter as boldly every whit,
Venture as truly, use the same skill,
Do your best, whether winning or losing it,

If you choose to play!—is my principle.
Let a man contend to the uttermost
For his life's set prize, be it what it will!

The counter our lovers staked was lost
As surely as if it were lawful coin:
And the sin I impute to each frustrate ghost

Is, the unlit lamp and the ungirt loin,
Though the end in sight was a vice, I say.
You of the virtue, (we issue join)
How strive you? *De te, fabula!*

"Childe Roland to the Dark Tower Came"

My first thought was, he lied in every word,
That hoary cripple, with malicious eye
Askance to watch the working of his lie
On mine, and mouth scarce able to afford
Suppression of the glee that pursed and scored
Its edge at one more victim gained thereby.

What else should he be set for, with his staff?
 What, save to waylay with his lies, ensnare
 All travellers that might find him posted there,
And ask the road? I guessed what skull-like laugh
Would break, what crutch 'gin write my epitaph
 For pastime in the dusty thoroughfare,

If at his counsel I should turn aside
 Into that ominous tract which, all agree,
 Hides the Dark Tower. Yet acquiescingly
I did turn as he pointed; neither pride
Nor hope rekindling at the end descried,
 So much as gladness that some end might be.

For, what with my whole world-wide wandering,
 What with my search drawn out through years, my hope
 Dwindled into a ghost not fit to cope
With that obstreperous joy success would bring,—
I hardly tried now to rebuke the spring
 My heart made, finding failure in its scope.

As when a sick man very near to death
 Seems dead indeed, and feels begin and end
 The tears and takes the farewell of each friend,
And hears one bid the other go, draw breath
Freelier outside, ("since all is o'er," he saith,
 "And the blow fallen no grieving can amend;")

While some discuss if near the other graves
 Be room enough for this, and when a day
 Suits best for carrying the corpse away,
With care about the banners, scarves and staves,—
And still the man hears all, and only craves
 He may not shame such tender love and stay.

Thus, I had so long suffered in this quest,
 Heard failure prophesied so oft, been writ
 So many times among "The Band"—to wit,
The knights who to the Dark Tower's search addressed
Their steps—that just to fail as they, seemed best,
 And all the doubt was now—should I be fit.

So, quiet as despair, I turned from him,
 That hateful cripple, out of his highway
 Into the path he pointed. All the day
Had been a dreary one at best, and dim
Was settling to its close, yet shot one grim
 Red leer to see the plain catch its estray.

For mark! no sooner was I fairly found
 Pledged to the plain, after a pace or two,
 Than, pausing to throw backward a last view
To the safe road, 'twas gone; grey plain all round:
Nothing but plain to the horizon's bound.
 I might go on; nought else remained to do.

So, on I went. I think I never saw
 Such starved ignoble nature; nothing throve;
 For flowers—as well expect a cedar grove!
But cockle, spurge, according to their law
Might propagate their kind, with none to awe,
 You'd think; a burr had been a treasure-trove.

No! penury, inertness and grimace,
In some strange sort, were the land's portion. "See
Or shut your eyes," said Nature peevishly,
"It nothing skills: I cannot help my case:
'Tis the Last Judgment's fire must cure this place,
Calcine its clods and set my prisoners free."

If there pushed any ragged thistle-stalk
Above its mates, the head was chopped—the bents
Were jealous else. What made those holes and rents
In the dock's harsh swarth leaves—bruised as to baulk
All hope of greenness? 'tis a brute must walk
Pashing their life out, with a brute's intents.

As for the grass, it grew as scant as hair
In leprosy; thin dry blades pricked the mud
Which underneath looked kneaded up with blood.
One stiff blind horse, his every bone a-stare,
Stood stupefied, however he came there:
Thrust out past service from the devil's stud!

Alive? he might be dead for aught I know,
With that red, gaunt and colloped neck a-strain,
And shut eyes underneath the rusty mane;
Seldom went such grotesqueness with such woe;
I never saw a brute I hated so;
He must be wicked to deserve such pain.

I shut my eyes and turned them on my heart.
As a man calls for wine before he fights,
I asked one draught of earlier, happier sights,
Ere fitly I could hope to play my part.
Think first, fight afterwards—the soldier's art:
One taste of the old time sets all to rights!

Not it! I fancied Cuthbert's reddening face
Beneath its garniture of curly gold,
Dear fellow, till I almost felt him fold
An arm in mine to fix me to the place,
That way he used. Alas, one night's disgrace!
Out went my heart's new fire and left it cold.

Giles, then, the soul of honour—there he stands
Frank as ten years ago when knighted first.
What honest men should dare (he said) he durst.
Good—but the scene shifts—faugh! what hangman's hands
Pin to his breast a parchment? his own bands
Read it. Poor traitor, spit upon and curst!

Better this present than a past like that;
Back therefore to my darkening path again.
No sound, no sight as far as eye could strain.
Will the night send a howlet or a bat?
I asked: when something on the dismal flat
Came to arrest my thoughts and change their train.

A sudden little river crossed my path
As unexpected as a serpent comes.
No sluggish tide congenial to the glooms—
This, as it frothed by, might have been a bath
For the fiend's glowing hoof—to see the wrath
Of its black eddy bespate with flakes and spumes.

So petty yet so spiteful! all along,
Low scrubby alders kneeled down over it;
Drenched willows flung them headlong in a fit
Of mute despair, a suicidal throng:
The river which had done them all the wrong,
Whate'er that was, rolled by, deterred no whit.

Which, while I forded,—good saints, how I feared
To set my foot upon a dead man's cheek,
Each step, or feel the spear I thrust to seek
For hollows, tangled in his hair or beard!
—It may have been a water-rat I speared,
But, ugh! it sounded like a baby's shriek.

Glad was I when I reached the other bank.
Now for a better country. Vain presage!
Who were the strugglers, what war did they wage
Whose savage trample thus could pad the dank
Soil to a plash? toads in a poisoned tank,
Or wild cats in a red-hot iron cage—

The fight must so have seemed in that fell cirque.
What penned them there, with all the plain to choose?
No foot-print leading to that horrid mews,
None out of it. Mad brewage set to work
Their brains, no doubt, like galley-slaves the Turk
Pits for his pastime, Christians against Jews.

And more than that—a furlong on—why, there!
What bad use was that engine for, that wheel,
Or brake, not wheel—that harrow fit to reel
Men's bodies out like silk? with all the air
Of Tophet's tool, on earth left unaware,
Or brought to sharpen its rusty teeth of steel.

Then came a bit of stubbed ground, once a wood,
Next a marsh, it would seem, and now mere earth
Desperate and done with; (so a fool finds mirth,
Makes a thing and then mars it, till his mood
Changes and off he goes!) within a rood—
Bog, clay and rubble, sand and stark black dearth.

Now blotches rankling, coloured gay and grim,
Now patches where some leanness of the soil's
Broke into moss or substances like boils;
Then came some palsied oak, a cleft in him
Like a distorted mouth that splits its rim
Gaping at death, and dies while it recoils.

And just as far as ever from the end!
Nought in the distance but the evening, nought
To point my footstep further! At the thought,
A great black bird, Apollyon's bosom-friend,
Sailed past, nor beat his wide wing dragon-penned
That brushed my cap—perchance the guide I sought.

For, looking up, aware I somehow grew,
'Spite of the dusk, the plain had given place
All round to mountains—with such name to grace

Mere ugly heights and heaps now stolen in view.
How thus they had surprised me,—solve it, you!
  How to get from them was no clearer case.

Yet half I seemed to recognise some trick
  Of mischief happened to me, God knows when—
  In a bad dream perhaps. Here ended, then,
Progress this way. When, in the very nick
Of giving up, one time more, came a click
  As when a trap shuts—you're inside the den!

Burningly it came on me all at once,
  This was the place! those two hills on the right,
  Crouched like two bulls locked horn in horn in fight;
While to the left, a tall scalped mountain . . . Dunce,
Fool, to be dozing at the very nonce,
  After a life spent training for the sight!

What in the midst lay but the Tower itself?
  The round squat turret, blind as the fool's heart,
  Built of brown stone, without a counterpart
In the whole world. The tempest's mocking elf
Points to the shipman thus the unseen shelf
  He strikes on, only when the timbers start.

Not see? because of night perhaps?—Why, day
  Came back again for that! before it left,
  The dying sunset kindled through a cleft:
The hills, like giants at a hunting, lay,
Chin upon hand, to see the game at bay,—
  "Now stab and end the creature—to the heft!"

Not hear? when noise was everywhere! it tolled
  Increasing like a bell. Names in my ears,
  Of all the lost adventurers my peers,—
How such a one was strong, and such was bold,
And such was fortunate, yet each of old
  Lost, lost! one moment knelled the woe of years.

There they stood, ranged along the hill-sides, met
  To view the last of me, a living frame
  For one more picture! in a sheet of flame
I saw them and I knew them all. And yet
Dauntless the slug-horn to my lips I set,
  And blew. *"Childe Roland to the Dark Tower came."*

An Epistle containing the Strange Medical Experience of Karshish, the Arab Physician

KARSHISH, the picker-up of learning's crumbs,
The not-incurious in God's handiwork
(This man's-flesh He hath admirably made,
Blown like a bubble, kneaded like a paste,
To coop up and keep down on earth a space
That puff of vapour from His mouth, man's soul)
—To Abib, all-sagacious in our art,
Breeder in me of what poor skill I boast,
Like me inquisitive how pricks and cracks
Befall the flesh through too much stress and strain,
Whereby the wily vapour fain would slip
Back and rejoin its source before the term,—
And aptest in contrivance, under God,

To baffle it by deftly stopping such:—
The vagrant Scholar to his Sage at home
Sends greeting (health and knowledge, fame with peace)
Three samples of true snake-stone—rarer still,
One of the other sort, the melon-shaped,
(But fitter, pounded fine, for charms than drugs)
And writeth now the twenty-second time.

My journeyings were brought to Jericho:
Thus I resume. Who studious in our art
Shall count a little labour unrepaid?
I have shed sweat enough, left flesh and bone
On many a flinty furlong of this land.
Also, the country-side is all on fire
With rumours of a marching hitherward:
Some say Vespasian cometh, some, his son.
A black lynx snarled and pricked a tufted ear;
Lust of my blood inflamed his yellow balls:
I cried and threw my staff and he was gone.
Twice have the robbers stripped and beaten me,
And once a town declared me for a spy,
But at the end, I reach Jerusalem,
Since this poor covert where I pass the night,
This Bethany, lies scarce the distance thence
A man with plague-sores at the third degree
Runs till he drops down dead. Thou laughest here!
'Sooth, it elates me, thus reposed and safe,
To void the stuffing of my travel-scrip
And share with thee whatever Jewry yields.
A viscid choler is observable
In tertians, I was nearly bold to say,
And falling-sickness hath a happier cure
Than our school wots of: there's a spider here
Weaves no web, watches on the ledge of tombs,
Sprinkled with mottles on an ash-grey back;
Take five and drop them . . . but who knows his mind,
The Syrian run-a-gate I trust this to?
His service payeth me a sublimate
Blown up his nose to help the ailing eye.
Best wait: I reach Jerusalem at morn,
There set in order my experiences,
Gather what most deserves, and give thee all—
Or I might add, Judæa's gum-tragacanth
Scales off in purer flakes, shines clearer-grained,
Cracks 'twixt the pestle and the porphyry,
In fine exceeds our produce. Scalp-disease
Confounds me, crossing so with leprosy—
Thou hadst admired one sort I gained at Zoar—
But zeal outruns discretion. Here I end.

Yet stay: my Syrian blinketh gratefully,
Protesteth his devotion is my price—
Suppose I write what harms not, though he steal?
I half resolve to tell thee, yet I blush,
What set me off a-writing first of all.
An itch I had, a sting to write, a tang
For, be it this town's barrenness—or else
The Man had something in the look of him—
His case has struck me far more than 'tis worth.
So, pardon if—(less presently I lose
In the great press of novelty at hand
The care and pains this somehow stole from me)
I bid thee take the thing while fresh in mind,
Almost in sight—for, wilt thou have the truth?
The very man is gone from me but now,
Whose ailment is the subject of discourse.
Thus then, and let thy better wit help all.

'Tis but a case of mania—subinduced
By epilepsy, at the turning-point
Of trance prolonged unduly some three days,
When, by the exhibition of some drug
Or spell, exorcization, stroke of art
Unknown to me and which 'twere well to know,
The evil thing out-breaking all at once
Left the man whole and sound of body indeed,—
But, flinging, so to speak, life's gates too wide,
Making a clear house of it too suddenly,
The first conceit that entered might inscribe
Whatever it was minded on the wall
So plainly at that vantage, as it were,
(First come, first served) that nothing subsequent
Attaineth to erase those fancy-scrawls
The just-returned and new-established soul
Hath gotten now so thoroughly by heart
That henceforth she will read or these or none.
And first—the man's own firm conviction rests
That he was dead (in fact they buried him)
—That he was dead and then restored to life
By a Nazarene physician of his tribe:
—'Sayeth, the same bade "Rise," and he did rise.
"Such cases are diurnal," thou wilt cry.
Not so this figment!—not, that such a fume,
Instead of giving way to time and health,
Should eat itself into the life of life,
As saffron tingeth flesh, blood, bones and all!
For see, how he takes up the after-life.
The man—it is one Lazarus a Jew,
Sanguine, proportioned, fifty years of age,
The body's habit wholly laudable,
As much, indeed, beyond the common health
As he were made and put aside to show.
Think, could we penetrate by any drug
And bathe the wearied soul and worried flesh,
And bring it clear and fair, by three days' sleep!
Whence has the man the balm that brightens all?
This grown man eyes the world now like a child.
Some elders of his tribe, I should premise,
Led in their friend, obedient as a sheep,
To bear my inquisition. While they spoke,
Now sharply, now with sorrow,—told the case,—
He listened not except I spoke to him,
But folded his two hands and let them talk,
Watching the flies that buzzed: and yet no fool.
And that's a sample how his years must go.
Look if a beggar, in fixed middle-life,
Should find a treasure, can he use the same
With straitened habits and with tastes starved small,
And take at once to his impoverished brain
The sudden element that changes things,
That sets the undreamed-of rapture at his hand,
And puts the cheap old joy in the scorned dust?
Is he not such an one as moves to mirth—
Warily parsimonious, when no need,
Wasteful as drunkenness at undue times?
All prudent counsel as to what befits
The golden mean, is lost on such an one:
The man's fantastic will is the man's law.
So here—we'll call the treasure knowledge, say,
Increased beyond the fleshly faculty—
Heaven opened to a soul while yet on earth,
Earth forced on a soul's use while seeing Heaven.
The man is witless of the size, the sum,
The value in proportion of all things,
Or whether it be little or be much.

Discourse to him of prodigious armaments
Assembled to besiege his city now,
And of the passing of a mule with gourds—
'Tis one! Then take it on the other side,
Speak of some trifling fact—he will gaze rapt
With stupor at its very littleness,
(Far as I see)—as if in that indeed
He caught prodigious import, whole results;
And so will turn to us the bystanders
In ever the same stupor (note this point)
That we too see not with his opened eyes.
Wonder and doubt come wrongly into play,
Preposterously, at cross purposes.
Should his child sicken unto death,—why, look
For scarce abatement of his cheerfulness,
Or pretermission of his daily craft—
While a word, gesture, glance, from that same child
At play or in the school or laid asleep,
Will startle him to an agony of fear,
Exasperation, just as like! demand
The reason why—" 'tis but a word," object—
"A gesture"—he regards thee as our lord
Who lived there in the pyramid alone,
Looked at us, dost thou mind?—when being young
We both would unadvisedly recite
Some charm's beginning, from that book of his,
Able to bid the sun throb wide and burst
All into stars, as suns grown old are wont.
Thou and the child have each a veil alike
Thrown o'er your heads, from under which ye both
Stretch your blind hands and trifle with a match
Over a mine of Greek fire, did ye know!
He holds on firmly to some thread of life—
(It is the life to lead perforcedly)
Which runs across some vast distracting orb
Of glory on either side that meagre thread,
Which, conscious of, he must not enter yet—
The spiritual life around the earthly life!
The law of that is known to him as this—
His heart and brain move there, his feet stay here.
So is the man perplext with impulses
Sudden to start off crosswise, not straight on,
Proclaiming what is right and wrong across,
And not along, this black thread through the blaze—
"It should be" balked by "here it cannot be"
And oft the man's soul springs into his face
As if he saw again and heard again
His sage that bade him "Rise" and he did rise.
Something, a word, a tick of the blood within
Admonishes—then back he sinks at once
To ashes, that was very fire before,
In sedulous recurrence to his trade
Whereby he earneth him the daily bread;
And studiously the humbler for that pride,
Professedly the faultier that he knows
God's secret, while he holds the thread of life.
Indeed the especial marking of the man
Is prone submission to the Heavenly will—
Seeing it, what it is, and why it is.
'Sayeth, he will wait patient to the last
For that same death which must restore his being
To equilibrium, body loosening soul
Divorced even now by premature full growth:
He will live, nay, it pleaseth him to live
So long as God please, and just how God please.
He even seeketh not to please God more
(Which meaneth, otherwise) than as God please.
Hence I perceive not he affects to preach

The doctrine of his sect whate'er it be,
Make proselytes as madmen thirst to do:
How can he give his neighbour the real ground,
His own conviction? ardent as he is—
Call his great truth a lie, why, still the old
"Be it as God please" reassureth him.
I probed the sore as thy disciple should—
"How, beast," said I, "this stolid carelessness
Sufficeth thee, when Rome is on her march
To stamp out like a little spark thy town,
Thy tribe, thy crazy tale and thee at once?"
He merely looked with his large eyes on me.
The man is apathetic, you deduce?
Contrariwise he loves both old and young,
Able and weak—affects the very brutes
And birds—how say I? flowers of the field—
As a wise workman recognises tools
In a master's workshop, loving what they make.
Thus is the man as harmless as a lamb:
Only impatient, let him do his best,
At ignorance and carelessness and sin—
An indignation which is promptly curbed:
As when in certain travels I have feigned
To be an ignoramus in our art
According to some preconceived design,
And happed to hear the land's practitioners
Steeped in conceit sublimed by ignorance,
Prattle fantastically on disease,
Its cause and cure—and I must hold my peace!

Thou wilt object—why have I not ere this
Sought out the sage himself, the Nazarene
Who wrought this cure, inquiring at the source,
Conferring with the frankness that befits?
Alas! it grieveth me, the learned leech
Perished in a tumult many years ago,
Accused,—our learning's fate,—of wizardry,
Rebellion, to the setting up a rule
And creed prodigious as described to me.
His death which happened when the earthquake fell
(Prefiguring, as soon appeared, the loss
To occult learning in our lord the sage
Who lived there in the pyramid alone)
Was wrought by the mad people—that's their wont—
On vain recourse, as I conjecture it,
To his tried virtue, for miraculous help—
How could he stop the earthquake? That's their way!
The other imputations must be lies:
But take one—though I loathe to give it thee,
In mere respect to any good man's fame!
(And after all, our patient Lazarus
Is stark mad; should we count on what he says?
Perhaps not: though in writing to a leech
'Tis well to keep back nothing of a case.)
This man so cured regards the curer then,
As—God forgive me—who but God himself,
Creator and Sustainer of the world,
That came and dwelt in flesh on it awhile!
—'Sayeth that such an One was born and lived,
Taught, healed the sick, broke bread at his own house,
Then died, with Lazarus by, for aught I know,
And yet was . . . what I said nor choose repeat,
And must have so avouched himself, in fact,
In hearing of this very Lazarus
Who saith—but why all this of what he saith?
Why write of trivial matters, things of price
Calling at every moment for remark?
I noticed on the margin of a pool
Blue-flowering borage, the Aleppo sort,
Aboundeth, very nitrous. It is strange!

Thy pardon for this long and tedious case,
Which, now that I review it, needs must seem
Unduly dwelt on, prolixly set forth!
Nor I myself discern in what is writ
Good cause for the peculiar interest
And awe indeed this man has touched me with.
Perhaps the journey's end, the weariness
Had wrought upon me first. I met him thus:
I crossed a ridge of short sharp broken hills
Like an old lion's cheek-teeth. Out there came
A moon made like a face with certain spots
Multiform, manifold and menacing:
Then a wind rose behind me. So we met
In this old sleepy town at unaware,
The man and I. I send thee what is writ.
Regard it as a chance, a matter risked
To this ambiguous Syrian—he may lose,
Or steal, or give it thee with equal good.
Jerusalem's repose shall make amends
For time this letter wastes, thy time and mine;
Till when, once more thy pardon and farewell!

The very God! think, Abib; dost thou think?
So, the All-Great, were the All-Loving too—
So, through the thunder comes a human voice
Saying, "O heart I made, a heart beats here!
Face, My hands fashioned, see it in Myself.
Thou hast no power nor may'st conceive of Mine,
But love I gave thee, with Myself to love,
And thou must love Me who have died for thee!"
The madman saith He said so: it is strange.

Fra Lippo Lippi

I AM poor brother Lippo, by your leave!
You need not clap your torches to my face.
Zooks, what's to blame? you think you see a monk!
What, it's past midnight, and you go the rounds,
And here you catch me at an alley's end
Where sportive ladies leave their doors ajar?
The Carmine's my cloister: hunt it up,
Do,—harry out, if you must show your zeal,
Whatever rat, there, haps on his wrong hole,
And nip each softling of a wee white mouse,
Weke, weke, that's crept to keep him company!
Aha, you know your betters? Then, you'll take
Your hand away that's fiddling on my throat,
And please to know me likewise. Who am I?
Why, one, sir, who is lodging with a friend
Three streets off—he's a certain . . . how d'ye call?
Master—a . . . Cosimo of the Medici,
In the house that caps the corner. Boh! you were best!
Remember and tell me, the day you're hanged,
How you affected such a gullet's-gripe!
But you, sir, it concerns you that your knaves
Pick up a manner nor discredit you.
Zooks, are we pilchards, that they sweep the streets
And count fair prize what comes into their net?
He's Judas to a tittle, that man is!
Just such a face! why, sir, you make amends.
Lord, I'm not angry! Bid your hang-dogs go

Drink out this quarter-florin to the health
Of the munificent House that harbours me
(And many more beside, lads! more beside!)
And all's come square again. I'd like his face—
His, elbowing on his comrade in the door
With the pike and lantern,—for the slave that holds
John Baptist's head a-dangle by the hair
With one hand ("look you, now," as who should say)
And his weapon in the other, yet unwiped!
It's not your chance to have a bit of chalk,
A wood-coal or the like? or you should see!
Yes, I'm the painter, since you style me so.
What, brother Lippo's doings, up and down,
You know them and they take you? like enough!
I saw the proper twinkle in your eye—
'Tell you, I liked your looks at very first.
Let's sit and set things straight now, hip to haunch.
Here's spring come, and the nights one makes up bands
To roam the town and sing out carnival,
And I've been three weeks shut within my mew,
A-painting for the great man, saints and saints
And saints again. I could not paint all night—
Ouf! I leaned out of window for fresh air.
There came a hurry of feet and little feet,
A sweep of lute-strings, laughs, and whifts of song,—
Flower o' the broom,
Take away love, and our earth is a tomb!
Flower o' the quince,
I let Lisa go, and what good's in life since?
Flower o' the thyme—and so on. Round they went.
Scarce had they turned the corner when a titter
Like the skipping of rabbits by moonlight,—three slim shapes—
And a face that looked up . . . zooks, sir, flesh and blood,
That's all I'm made of! Into shreds it went,
Curtain and counterpane and coverlet,
All the bed-furniture—a dozen knots,
There was a ladder! down I let myself,
Hands and feet, scrambling somehow, and so dropped,
And after them. I came up with the fun
Hard by Saint Laurence, hail fellow, well met,—
Flower o' the rose,
If I've been merry, what matter who knows?
And so as I was stealing back again
To get to bed and have a bit of sleep
Ere I rise up to-morrow and go work
On Jerome knocking at his poor old breast
With his great round stone to subdue the flesh,
You snap me of the sudden. Ah, I see!
Though your eye twinkles still, you shake your head—
Mine's shaved,—a monk, you say—the sting's in that!
If Master Cosimo announced himself,
Mum's the word naturally; but a monk!
Come, what am I a beast for? tell us, now!
I was a baby when my mother died
And father died and left me in the street.
I starved there, God knows how, a year or two
On fig skins, melon-parings, rinds and shucks,
Refuse and rubbish. One fine frosty day
My stomach being empty as your hat,
The wind doubled me up and down I went.
Old Aunt Lapaccia trussed me with one hand,
(Its fellow was a stinger as I knew)
And so along the wall, over the bridge,

By the straight cut to the convent. Six words, there,
While I stood munching my first bread that month:
"So, boy, you're minded," quoth the good fat father
Wiping his own mouth, 'twas refection-time,—
"To quit this very miserable world?
Will you renounce" . . . The mouthful of bread? thought I;
By no means! Brief, they made a monk of me;
I did renounce the world, its pride and greed,
Palace, farm, villa, shop and banking-house,
Trash, such as these poor devils of Medici
Have given their hearts to—all at eight years old.
Well, sir, I found in time, you may be sure,
'Twas not for nothing—the good bellyful,
The warm serge and the rope that goes all round,
And day-long blessed idleness beside!
"Let's see what the urchin's fit for"—that came next.
Not overmuch their way, I must confess.
Such a to-do! they tried me with their books.
Lord, they'd have taught me Latin in pure waste!
Flower o' the clove,
All the Latin I construe is, "amo" I love!
But, mind you, when a boy starves in the streets
Eight years together, as my fortune was,
Watching folk's faces to know who will fling
The bit of half-stripped grape-bunch he desires,
And who will curse or kick him for his pains—
Which gentleman processional and fine,
Holding a candle to the Sacrament
Will wink and let him lift a plate and catch
The droppings of the wax to sell again,
Or holla for the Eight and have him whipped,—
How say I?—nay, which dog bites, which lets drop
His bone from the heap of offal in the street,—
Why, soul and sense of him grow sharp alike,
He learns the look of things, and none the less
For admonitions from the hunger-pinch.
I had a store of such remarks, be sure,
Which, after I found leisure, turned to use:
I drew men's faces on my copy-books,
Scrawled them within the antiphonary's marge,
Joined legs and arms to the long music-notes,
Found nose and eyes and chin for A's and B's,
And made a string of pictures of the world
Betwixt the ins and outs of verb and noun,
On the wall, the bench, the door. The monks looked black.
"Nay," quoth the Prior, "turn him out, d'ye say?
In no wise. Lose a crow and catch a lark.
What if at last we get our man of parts,
We Carmelites, like those Camaldolese
And Preaching Friars, to do our church up fine
And put the front on it that ought to be!"
And hereupon they bade me daub away.
Thank you! my head being crammed, their walls a blank,
Never was such prompt disemburdening.
First, every sort of monk, the black and white,
I drew them, fat and lean: then, folks at church,
From good old gossips waiting to confess
Their cribs of barrel-droppings, candle-ends,—
To the breathless fellow at the altar-foot,
Fresh from his murder, safe and sitting there

With the little children round him in a row
Of admiration, half for his beard and half
For that white anger of his victim's son
Shaking a fist at him with one fierce arm,
Signing himself with the other because of Christ
(Whose sad face on the cross sees only this
After the passion of a thousand years)
Till some poor girl, her apron o'er her head
Which the intense eyes looked through, came at eve
On tip-toe, said a word, dropped in a loaf,
Her pair of earrings and a bunch of flowers
The brute took growling, prayed, and then was gone.
I painted all, then cried " 'tis ask and have—
Choose, for more's ready!"—laid the ladder flat,
And showed my covered bit of cloister-wall.
The monks closed in a circle and praised loud
Till checked,—taught what to see and not to see,
Being simple bodies,—"that's the very man!
Look at the boy who stoops to pat the dog!
That woman's like the Prior's niece who comes
To care about his asthma: it's the life!"
But there my triumph's straw-fire flared and funked—
Their betters took their turn to see and say:
The Prior and the learned pulled a face
And stopped all that in no time. "How? what's here?
Quite from the mark of painting, bless us all!
Faces, arms, legs and bodies like the true
As much as pea and pea! it's devil's-game!
Your business is not to catch men with show,
With homage to the perishable clay,
But lift them over it, ignore it all,
Make them forget there's such a thing as flesh.
Your business is to paint the souls of men—
Man's soul, and it's a fire, smoke . . . no it's not . . .
It's vapour done up like a new-born babe—
(In that shape when you die it leaves your mouth)
It's . . . well, what matters talking, it's the soul!
Give us no more of body than shows soul!
Here's Giotto, with his Saint a-praising God,
That sets you praising,—why not stop with him?
Why put all thoughts of praise out of our heads
With wonder at lines, colours, and what not?
Paint the soul, never mind the legs and arms!
Rub all out, try at it a second time.
Oh, that white smallish female with the breasts,
She's just my niece . . . Herodias, I would say,—
Who went and danced and got men's heads cut off—
Have it all out!" Now, is this sense, I ask?
A fine way to paint soul, by painting body
So ill, the eye can't stop there, must go further
And can't fare worse! Thus, yellow does for white
When what you put for yellow's simply black,
And any sort of meaning looks intense
When all beside itself means and looks naught.
Why can't a painter lift each foot in turn,
Left foot and right foot, go a double step,

Make his flesh liker and his soul more like,
Both in their order? Take the prettiest face,
The Prior's niece . . . patron-saint—is it so pretty
You can't discover if it means hope, fear,
Sorrow or joy? won't beauty go with these?
Suppose I've made her eyes all right and blue,
Can't I take breath and try to add life's flash,
And then add soul and heighten them threefold?
Or say there's beauty with no soul at all—
(I never saw it—put the case the same—)
If you get simple beauty and naught else,
You get about the best thing God invents,—
That's somewhat. And you'll find the soul you have missed,
Within yourself when you return Him thanks,
"Rub all out!" Well, well, there's my life, in short.
And so the thing has gone on ever since.
I'm grown a man no doubt, I've broken bounds—
You should not take a fellow eight years old
And make him swear to never kiss the girls.
I'm my own master, paint now as I please—
Having a friend, you see, in the Corner-house!
Lord, it's fast holding by the rings in front—
Those great rings serve more purposes than just
To plant a flag in, or tie up a horse!
And yet the old schooling sticks, the old grave eyes
Are peeping o'er my shoulder as I work,
The heads shake still—"It's art's decline, my son!
You're not of the true painters, great and old;
Brother Angelico's the man, you'll find;
Brother Lorenzo stands his single peer:
Fag on at flesh, you'll never make the third!"
Flower o' the pine,
You keep your mistr . . . manners, and I'll stick to mine!
I'm not the third, then: bless us, they must know!
Don't you think they're the likeliest to know,
They with their Latin? so, I swallow my rage,
Clench my teeth, suck my lips in tight, and paint
To please them—sometimes do, and sometimes don't,
For, doing most, there's pretty sure to come
A turn, some warm eve finds me at my saints—
A laugh, a cry, the business of the world—
(*Flower o' the peach,*
Death for us all, and his own life for each!)
And my whole soul revolves, the cup runs over,
The world and life's too big to pass for a dream,
And I do these wild things in sheer despite,
And play the fooleries you catch me at,
In pure rage! the old mill-horse, out at grass
After hard years, throws up his stiff heels so,
Although the miller does not preach to him
The only good of grass is to make chaff.
What would men have? Do they like grass or no—
May they or mayn't they? all I want's the thing
Settled for ever one way: as it is,
You tell too many lies and hurt yourself.

You don't like what you only like too much,
You do like what, if given you at your word,
You find abundantly detestable.
For me, I think I speak as I was taught—
I always see the garden and God there
A-making man's wife—and, my lesson learned,
The value and significance of flesh,
I can't unlearn ten minutes afterwards.

You understand me: I'm a beast, I know.
But see, now—why, I see as certainly
As that the morning-star's about to shine,
What will hap some day. We've a youngster here
Comes to our convent, studies what I do,
Slouches and stares and lets no atom drop—
His name is Guidi—he'll not mind the monks—
They call him Hulking Tom, he lets them talk—
He picks my practice up—he'll paint apace,
I hope so—though I never live so long,
I know what's sure to follow. You be judge!
You speak no Latin more than I, belike—
However, you're my man, you've seen the world
—The beauty and the wonder and the power,
The shapes of things, their colours, lights and shades,
Changes, surprises,—and God made it all!
—For what? do you feel thankful, ay or no,
For this fair town's face, yonder river's line,
The mountain round it and the sky above,
Much more the figures of man, woman, child,
These are the frame to? What's it all about?
To be passed over, despised? or dwelt upon,
Wondered at? oh, this last of course!—you say.
But why not do as well as say,—paint these
Just as they are, careless what comes of it?
God's works—paint any one, and count it crime
To let a truth slip. Don't object, "His works
Are here already—nature is complete:
Suppose you reproduce her—(which you can't)
There's no advantage! you must beat her, then."
For, don't you mark, we're made so that we love
First when we see them painted, things we have passed
Perhaps a hundred times nor cared to see;
And so they are better, painted—better to us,
Which is the same thing. Art was given for that—
God uses us to help each other so,
Lending our minds out. Have you noticed, now,
Your cullion's hanging face? A bit of chalk,
And trust me but you should, though! How much more,
If I drew higher things with the same truth!
That were to take the Prior's pulpit-place,
Interpret God to all of you! oh, oh,
It makes me mad to see what men shall do
And we in our graves! This world's no blot for us,
Nor blank—it means intensely, and means good:
To find its meaning is my meat and drink.
"Ay, but you don't so instigate to prayer!"
Strikes in the Prior: "when your meaning's plain
It does not say to folks—remember matins,

Or, mind you fast next Friday." Why, for this
What need of art at all? A skull and bones,
Two bits of stick nailed cross-wise, or, what's best,
A bell to chime the hour with, does as well.
I painted a Saint Laurence six months since
At Prato, splashed the fresco in fine style:
"How looks my painting, now the scaffold's down?"
I ask a brother: "Hugely," he returns—
"Already not one phiz of your three slaves
That turn the Deacon off his toasted side,
But's scratched and prodded to our heart's content,
The pious people have so eased their own
When coming to say prayers there in a rage:
We get on fast to see the bricks beneath.
Expect another job this time next year,
For pity and religion grow i' the crowd—
Your painting serves its purpose!" Hang the fools!

—That is—you'll not mistake an idle word
Spoke in a huff by a poor monk, God wot,
Tasting the air this spicy night which turns
The unaccustomed head like Chianti wine!
Oh, the church knows! don't misreport me, now!
It's natural a poor monk out of bounds
Should have his apt word to excuse himself:
And hearken how I plot to make amends.
I have bethought me: I shall paint a piece
. . . There's for you! Give me six months, then go, see
Something in Sant' Ambrogio's! Bless the nuns!
They want a cast of my office. I shall paint
God in the midst, Madonna and her babe,
Ringed by a bowery, flowery angel-brood,
Lilies and vestments and white faces, sweet
As puff on puff of grated orris-root
When ladies crowd to church at midsummer.
And then in the front, of course a saint or two—
Saint John, because he saves the Florentines,
Saint Ambrose, who puts down in black and white
The convent's friends and gives them a long day,
And Job, I must have him there past mistake,
The man of Uz, (and Us without the z,
Painters who need his patience.) Well, all these
Secured at their devotions, up shall come
Out of a corner when you least expect,
As one by a dark stair into a great light,
Music and talking, who but Lippo! I!—
Mazed, motionless and moon-struck—I'm the man!
Back I shrink—what is this I see and hear?
I, caught up with my monk's things by mistake,
My old serge gown and rope that goes all round,
I, in this presence, this pure company!
Where's a hole, where's a corner for escape?
Then steps a sweet angelic slip of a thing
Forward, puts out a soft palm—"Not so fast!"
—Addresses the celestial presence, "nay—
He made you and devised you, after all,
Though he's none of you! Could Saint John there, draw—
His camel-hair make up a painting-brush?
We come to brother Lippo for all that,
Iste perfecit opus!" So, all smile—
I shuffle sideways with my blushing face
Under the cover of a hundred wings
Thrown like a spread of kirtles when you're gay

And play hot cockles, all the doors being shut,
Till, wholly unexpected, in there pops
The hothead husband! Thus I scuttle off
To some safe bench behind, not letting go
The palm of her, the little lily thing
That spoke the good word for me in the nick,
Like the Prior's niece . . . Saint Lucy, I would say.
And so all's saved for me, and for the church
A pretty picture gained. Go, six months hence!
Your hand, sir, and good-bye: no lights, no lights!
The street's hushed, and I know my own way back,
Don't fear me! There's the grey beginning. Zooks!

The Bishop orders his Tomb at Saint Praxed's Church

[ROME, 15—.]

VANITY, saith the preacher, vanity!
Draw round my bed: is Anselm keeping back?
Nephews—sons mine . . . ah God, I know not! Well—
She, men would have to be your mother once,
Old Gandolf envied me, so fair she was!
What's done is done, and she is dead beside,
Dead long ago, and I am Bishop since,
And as she died so must we die ourselves,
And thence ye may perceive the world's a dream.
Life, how and what is it? As here I lie
In this state-chamber, dying by degrees,
Hours and long hours in the dead night, I ask
"Do I live, am I dead?" Peace, peace seems all.
Saint Praxed's ever was the church for peace;
And so, about this tomb of mine. I fought
With tooth and nail to save my niche, ye know:
—Old Gandolf cozened me, despite my care;
Shrewd was that snatch from out the corner South
He graced his carrion with, God curse the same!
Yet still my niche is not so cramped but thence
One sees the pulpit o' the epistle-side,
And somewhat of the choir, those silent seats,
And up into the aery dome where live
The angels, and a sunbeam's sure to lurk:
And I shall fill my slab of basalt there,
And 'neath my tabernacle take my rest,
With those nine columns round me, two and two,
The odd one at my feet where Anselm stands:
Peach-blossom marble all, the rare, the ripe
As fresh-poured red wine of a mighty pulse
—Old Gandolf with his paltry onion-stone,
Put me where I may look at him! True peach,
Rosy and flawless: how I earned the prize!
Draw close: that conflagration of my church
—What then? So much was saved if aught were missed!
My sons, ye would not be my death? Go dig
The white-grape vineyard where the oil-press stood,
Drop water gently till the surface sinks,
And if ye find . . . Ah, God I know not, I! . . .
Bedded in store of rotten figleaves soft,
And corded up in a tight olive-frail,
Some lump, ah God, of *lapis lazuli,*
Big as a Jew's head cut off at the nape,

Blue as a vein o'er the Madonna's breast . . .
Sons, all have I bequeathed you, villas, all,
That brave Frascati villa with its bath,
So, let the blue lump poise between my knees,
Like God the Father's globe on both His hands
Ye worship in the Jesu Church so gay,
For Gandolf shall not choose but see and burst!
Swift as a weaver's shuttle fleet our years:
Man goeth to the grave, and where is he?
Did I say basalt for my slab, sons? Black—
'Twas ever antique-black I meant! How else
Shall ye contrast my frieze to come beneath?
The bas-relief in bronze ye promised me,
Those Pans and Nymphs ye wot of, and perchance
Some tripod, thyrsus, with a vase or so,
The Saviour at his sermon on the mount,
Saint Praxed in a glory, and one Pan
Ready to twitch the Nymph's last garment off,
And Moses with the tables . . . but I know
Ye mark me not! What do they whisper thee,
Child of my bowels, Anselm? Ah, ye hope
To revel down my villas while I gasp
Bricked o'er with beggar's mouldy travertine
Which Gandolf from his tomb-top chuckles at!
Nay, boys, ye love me—all of jasper, then!
'Tis jasper ye stand pledged to, lest I grieve
My bath must needs be left behind, alas!
One block, pure green as a pistachio-nut,
There's plenty jasper somewhere in the world—
And have I not Saint Praxed's ear to pray
Horses for ye, and brown Greek manuscripts,
And mistresses with great smooth marbly limbs?
—That's if ye carve my epitaph aright,
Choice Latin, picked phrase, Tully's every word,
No gaudy ware like Gandolf's second line—
Tully, my masters? Ulpian serves his need!
And then how I shall lie through centuries,
And hear the blessed mutter of the mass,
And see God made and eaten all day long,
And feel the steady candle-flame, and taste
Good strong thick stupefying incense-smoke!
For as I lie here, hours of the dead night,
Dying in state and by such slow degrees,
I fold my arms as if they clasped a crook,
And stretch my feet forth straight as stone can point,
And let the bedclothes for a mortcloth drop
Into great laps and folds of sculptor's-work:
And as yon tapers dwindle, and strange thoughts
Grow, with a certain humming in my ears,
About the life before I lived this life,
And this life too, popes, cardinals and priests,
Saint Praxed at his sermon on the mount,
Your tall pale mother with her talking eyes,
And new-found agate urns as fresh as day,
And marble's language, Latin pure, discreet,
—Aha, ELUCESCEBAT quoth our friend?
No Tully, said I, Ulpian at the best!
Evil and brief hath been my pilgrimage.
All *lapis*, all, sons! Else I give the Pope
My villas: will ye ever eat my heart?
Ever your eyes were as a lizard's quick,
They glitter like your mother's for my soul,

Or ye would heighten my impoverished frieze,
Piece out its starved design, and fill my vase
With grapes, and add a vizor and a Term,
And to the tripod ye would tie a lynx
That in his struggle throws the thyrsus down,
To comfort me on my entablature
Whereon I am to lie till I must ask
"Do I live, am I dead?" There, leave me, there!
For ye have stabbed me with ingratitude
To death—ye wish it—God, ye wish it! Stone—
Gritstone, a-crumble! Clammy squares which sweat
As if the corpse they keep were oozing through—
And no more *lapis* to delight the world!
Well, go! I bless ye. Fewer tapers there,
But in a row: and, going, turn your backs
—Ay, like departing altar-ministrants,
And leave me in my church, the church for peace,
That I may watch at leisure if he leers—
Old Gandolf, at me, from his onion-stone,
As still he envied me, so fair she was!

Bishop Blougram's Apology

No more wine? then we'll push back chairs and talk.
A final glass for me, though: cool, i' faith!
We ought to have our Abbey back, you see.
It's different, preaching in basilicas,
And doing duty in some masterpiece
Like this of brother Pugin's, bless his heart!
I doubt if they're half baked, those chalk rosettes,
Ciphers and stucco-twiddlings everywhere;
It's just like breathing in a lime-kiln: eh?
These hot long ceremonies of our church
Cost us a little—oh, they pay the price,
You take me—amply pay it! Now, we'll talk.

So, you despise me, Mr. Gigadibs.
No deprecation,—nay, I beg you, sir!
Beside 'tis our engagement: don't you know,
I promised, if you'd watch a dinner out,
We'd see truth dawn together?—truth that peeps
Over the glass's edge when dinner's done,
And body gets its sop and holds its noise
And leaves soul free a little. Now's the time—
'Tis break of day! You do despise me then.
And if I say, "despise me,"—never fear—
I know you do not in a certain sense—
Not in my arm-chair for example: here,
I well imagine you respect my place
(Status, *entourage,* worldly circumstance)
Quite to its value—very much indeed
—Are up to the protesting eyes of you
In pride at being seated here for once—
You'll turn it to such capital account!
When somebody, through years and years to come,
Hints of the bishop,—names me—that's enough—
"Blougram? I knew him"—(into it you slide)
"Dined with him once, a Corpus Christi Day,
All alone, we two—he's a clever man—
And after dinner,—why, the wine you know,—
Oh, there was wine, and good!—what with the wine . . .
'Faith, we began upon all sorts of talk!
He's no bad fellow, Blougram—he had seen
Something of mine he relished—some review—
He's quite above their humbug in his heart,
Half-said as much, indeed—the thing's his trade—
I warrant, Blougram's sceptical at times—
How otherwise? I liked him, I confess!"

Che che, my dear sir, as we say at Rome,
Don't you protest now! It's fair give and take;
You have had your turn and spoken your home-truths:
The hand's mine now, and here you follow suit.

Thus much conceded, still the first fact stays—
You do despise me; your ideal of life
Is not the bishop's—you would not be I—
You would like better to be Goethe, now,
Or Buonaparte—or, bless me, lower still,
Count D'Orsay,—so you did what you preferred,
Spoke as you thought, and, as you cannot help,
Believed or disbelieved, no matter what,
So long as on that point, whate'er it was,
You loosed your mind, were whole and sole yourself.
—That, my ideal never can include,
Upon that element of truth and worth
Never be based! for say they make me Pope
(They can't—suppose it for our argument)
Why, there I'm at my tether's end—I've reached
My height, and not a height which pleases you.
An unbelieving Pope won't do, you say.
It's like those eerie stories nurses tell,
Of how some actor on a stage played Death,
With pasteboard crown, sham orb and tinselled dart,
And called himself the monarch of the world,
Then, going in the tire-room afterward
Because the play was done, to shift himself,
Got touched upon the sleeve familiarly
The moment he had shut the closet door
By Death himself. Thus God might touch a Pope
At unawares, ask what his baubles mean,
And whose part he presumed to play just now?
Best be yourself, imperial, plain and true!

So, drawing comfortable breath again,
You weigh and find, whatever more or less
I boast of my ideal realized
Is nothing in the balance when opposed
To your ideal, your grand simple life,
Of which you will not realize one jot.
I am much, you are nothing; you would be all,
I would be merely much—you beat me there.

No, friend, you do not beat me,—hearken why.
The common problem, yours, mine, every one's,
Is not to fancy what were fair in life
Provided it could be,—but, finding first
What may be, then find how to make it fair
Up to our means—a very different thing!
No abstract intellectual plan of life
Quite irrespective of life's plainest laws,
But one, a man, who is man and nothing more,
May lead within a world which (by your leave)
Is Rome or London—not Fool's-paradise.
Embellish Rome, idealize away,
Make paradise of London if you can,
You're welcome, nay, you're wise.

A simile!
We mortals cross the ocean of this world
Each in his average cabin of a life—
The best's not big, the worst yields elbow-room.
Now for our six months' voyage—how prepare?
You come on shipboard with a landsman's list
Of things he calls convenient—so they are!
An India screen is pretty furniture,

A piano-forte is a fine resource,
All Balzac's novels occupy one shelf,
The new edition fifty volumes long;
And little Greek books, with the funny type
They get up well at Leipsic, fill the next—
Go on! slabbed marble, what a bath it makes!
And Parma's pride, the Jerome, let us add!
'Twere pleasant could Correggio's fleeting glow
Hang full in face of one where'er one roams,
Since he more than the others brings with him
Italy's self,—the marvellous Modenese!—
Yet was not on your list before, perhaps.

—Alas! friend, here's the agent . . . is't the name?
The captain, or whoever's master here—
You see him screw his face up; what's his cry
Ere you set foot on shipboard? "Six feet square!"
If you won't understand what six feet mean,
Compute and purchase stores accordingly—
And if in pique because he overhauls
Your Jerome, piano, bath, you come on board
Bare—why, you cut a figure at the first
While sympathetic landsmen see you off;
Not afterwards, when, long ere half seas over,
You peep up from your utterly naked boards
Into some snug and well-appointed berth,
Like mine, for instance (try the cooler jug—
Put back the other, but don't jog the ice)
And mortified you mutter, "Well and good—
He sits enjoying his sea-furniture—
'Tis stout and proper, and there's store of it,
Though I've the better notion, all agree,
Of fitting rooms up! Hang the carpenter,
Neat ship-shape fixings and contrivances—
I would have brought my Jerome, frame and all!"
And meantime you bring nothing: never mind—
You've proved your artist-nature: what you don't,
You might bring, so despise me, as I say.

Now come, let's backward to the starting-place.
See my way: we're two college friends, suppose—
Prepare together for our voyage, then,
Each note and check the other in his work,—
Here's mine, a bishop's outfit; criticize!
What's wrong? why won't you be a bishop too?

Why, first, you don't believe, you don't and can't,
(Not statedly, that is, and fixedly
And absolutely and exclusively)
In any revelation called divine.
No dogmas nail your faith—and what remains
But say so, like the honest man you are?
First, therefore, overhaul theology!
Nay, I too, not a fool, you please to think,
Must find believing every whit as hard,
And if I do not frankly say as much,
The ugly consequence is clear enough.

Now, wait, my friend: well, I do not believe—
If you'll accept no faith that is not fixed,
Absolute and exclusive, as you say.
You're wrong—I mean to prove it in due time.
Meanwhile, I know where difficulties lie
I could not, cannot solve, nor ever shall,
So give up hope accordingly to solve—
(To you, and over the wine). Our dogmas then
With both of us, though in unlike degree,

Missing full credence—overboard with them!
I mean to meet you on your own premise—
Good, there go mine in company with yours!

And now what are we? unbelievers both,
Calm and complete, determinately fixed
To-day, to-morrow, and for ever, pray?
You'll guarantee me that? Not so, I think!
In no wise! all we've gained is, that belief,
As unbelief before, shakes us by fits,
Confounds us like its predecessor. Where's
The gain? how can we guard our unbelief,
Make it bear fruit to us?—the problem here.
Just when we are safest, there's a sunset-touch,
A fancy from a flower-bell, some one's death,
A chorus-ending from Euripides,—
And that's enough for fifty hopes and fears
As old and new at once as Nature's self,
To rap and knock and enter in our soul,
Take hands and dance there, a fantastic ring,
Round the ancient idol, on his base again,—
The grand Perhaps! We look on helplessly,—
There the old misgivings, crooked questions are—
This good God,—what he could do, if he would,
Would, if he could—then must have done long since:
If so, when, where, and how? some way must be,—
Once feel about, and soon or late you hit
Some sense, in which it might be, after all.
Why not, "The Way, the Truth, the Life?"

—That way
Over the mountain, which who stands upon
Is apt to doubt if it be indeed a road;
While if he views it from the waste itself,
Up goes the line there, plain from base to brow,
Not vague, mistakeable! what's a break or two
Seen from the unbroken desert either side?
And then (to bring in fresh philosophy)
What if the breaks themselves should prove at last
The most consummate of contrivances
To train a man's eye, teach him what is faith?
And so we stumble at truth's very test!
All we have gained then by our unbelief
Is a life of doubt diversified by faith,
For one of faith diversified by doubt:
We called the chess-board white,—we call it black.

"Well," you rejoin, "the end's no worse, at least;
We've reason for both colours on the board:
Why not confess, then, where I drop the faith
And you the doubt, that I'm as right as you?"

Because, friend, in the next place, this being so,
And both things even,—faith and unbelief
Left to a man's choice,—we'll proceed a step,
Returning to our image, which I like.

A man's choice, yes—but a cabin-passenger's—
The man made for the special life of the world—
Do you forget him? I remember though!
Consult our ship's conditions and you find
One and but one choice suitable to all,
The choice, that you unluckily prefer,

Turning things topsy-turvy—they or it
Going to the ground. Belief or unbelief
Bears upon life, determines its whole course,
Begins at its beginning. See the world
Such as it is,—you made it not, nor I;
I mean to take it as it is,—and you
Not so you'll take it,—though you get nought else.
I know the special kind of life I like,
What suits the most my idiosyncrasy,
Brings out the best of me and bears me fruit
In power, peace, pleasantness and length of days.
I find that positive belief does this
For me, and unbelief, no whit of this.
—For you, it does, however?—that we'll try!
'Tis clear, I cannot lead my life, at least,
Induce the world to let me peaceably,
Without declaring at the outset, "Friends,
I absolutely and peremptorily
Believe!"—I say, faith is my waking life.
One sleeps, indeed, and dreams at intervals,
We know, but waking's the main point with us,
And my provision's for life's waking part.
Accordingly, I use heart, head and hands
All day, I build, scheme, study and make friends;
And when night overtakes me, down I lie,
Sleep, dream a little, and get done with it,
The sooner the better, to begin afresh.
What's midnight's doubt before the day-spring's faith?
You, the philosopher, that disbelieve,
That recognize the night, give dreams their weight—
To be consistent you should keep your bed,
Abstain from healthy acts that prove you a man,
For fear you drowse perhaps at unawares!
And certainly at night you'll sleep and dream,
Live through the day and bustle as you please.
And so you live to sleep as I to wake,
To unbelieve as I to still believe?
Well, and the common sense o' the world calls you
Bed-ridden,—and its good things come to me.
Its estimation, which is half the fight,
That's the first cabin-comfort I secure—
The next . . . but you perceive with half an eye!
Come, come, it's best believing, if we may—
You can't but own that!

Next, concede again—
If once we choose belief, on all accounts
We can't be too decisive in our faith,
Conclusive and exclusive in its terms,
To suit the world which gives us the good things.
In every man's career are certain points
Whereon he dares not be indifferent;
The world detects him clearly, if he dare,
As baffled at the game, and losing life.
He may care little or he may care much
For riches, honour, pleasure, work, repose,
Since various theories of life and life's
Success are extant which might easily
Comport with either estimate of these;
And whoso chooses wealth or poverty,
Labour or quiet, is not judged a fool
Because his fellows would choose otherwise:
We let him choose upon his own account
So long as he's consistent with his choice.
But certain points, left wholly to himself,
When once a man has arbitrated on,
We say he must succeed there or go hang.
Thus, he should wed the woman he loves most
Or needs most, whatsoe'er the love or need—
For he can't wed twice. Then, he must avouch
Or follow, at the least, sufficiently,

The form of faith his conscience holds the best,
Whate'er the process of conviction was:
For nothing can compensate his mistake
On such a point, the man himself being judge—
He cannot wed twice, nor twice lose his soul.

Well now, there's one great form of Christian faith
I happened to be born in—which to teach
Was given me as I grew up, on all hands,
As best and readiest means of living by;
The same on examination being proved
The most pronounced moreover, fixed, precise
And absolute form of faith in the whole world—
Accordingly, most potent of all forms
For working on the world. Observe, my friend,
Such as you know me, I am free to say,
In these hard latter days which hamper one,
Myself, by no immoderate exercise
Of intellect and learning, and the tact
To let external forces work for me,
—Bid the street's stones be bread and they are bread,
Bid Peter's creed, or, rather, Hildebrand's,
Exalt me o'er my fellows in the world
And make my life an ease and joy and pride,
It does so,—which for me's a great point gained,
Who have a soul and body that exact
A comfortable care in many ways.
There's power in me and will to dominate
Which I must exercise, they hurt me else:
In many ways I need mankind's respect,
Obedience, and the love that's born of fear:
While at the same time, there's a taste I have,
A toy of soul, a titillating thing,
Refuses to digest these dainties crude.
The naked life is gross till clothed upon:
I must take what men offer, with a grace
As though I would not, could I help it, take!
An uniform I wear though over-rich—
Something imposed on me, no choice of mine;
No fancy-dress worn for pure fancy's sake
And despicable therefore! now folk kneel
And kiss my hand—of course the Church's hand.
Thus I am made, thus life is best for me,
And thus that it should be I have procured;
And thus it could not be another way,
I venture to imagine.

You'll reply,
So far my choice, no doubt, is a success;
But were I made of better elements,
With nobler instincts, purer tastes, like you,
I hardly would account the thing success
Though it did all for me I say.

But, friend,
We speak of what is—not of what might be,
And how 'twere better if 'twere otherwise.
I am the man you see here plain enough:
Grant I'm a beast, why, beasts must lead beasts' lives!
Suppose I own at once to tail and claws;
The tailless man exceeds me: but being tailed
I'll lash out lion-fashion, and leave apes
To dock their stump and dress their haunches up.
My business is not to remake myself,
But make the absolute best of what God made.
Or—our first simile—though you proved me doomed
To a viler berth still, to the steerage-hole,
The sheep-pen or the pig-sty, I should strive
To make what use of each were possible;

And as this cabin gets upholstery,
That hutch should rustle with sufficient
straw.

But, friend, I don't acknowledge quite
so fast
I fail of all your manhood's lofty tastes
Enumerated so complacently,
On the mere ground that you forsooth
can find
In this particular life I choose to lead
No fit provision for them. Can you not?
Say you, my fault is I address myself
To grosser estimators than should judge?
And that's no way of holding up the
soul—
Which, nobler, needs men's praise per-
haps, yet knows
One wise man's verdict outweighs all the
fools',—
Would like the two, but, forced to choose,
takes that.
I pine among my million imbeciles
(You think) aware some dozen men of
sense
Eye me and know me, whether I believe
In the last winking Virgin, as I vow,
And am a fool, or disbelieve in her
And am a knave,—approve in neither
case,
Withhold their voices though I look their
way:
Like Verdi when, at his worst opera's end
(The thing they gave at Florence,—
what's its name?)
While the mad houseful's plaudits near
out-bang
His orchestra of salt-box, tongs and
bones,
He looks through all the roaring and the
wreaths
Where sits Rossini patient in his stall.

Nay, friend, I meet you with an answer
here—
That even your prime men who appraise
their kind
Are men still, catch a wheel within a
wheel,
See more in a truth than the truth's sim-
ple self,
Confuse themselves. You see lads walk
the street
Sixty the minute; what's to note in that?
You see one lad o'erstride a chimney-
stack;
Him you must watch—he's sure to fall,
yet stands!
Our interest's on the dangerous edge of
things.
The honest thief, the tender murderer,
The superstitious atheist, demirep
That loves and saves her soul in new
French books—
We watch while these in equilibrium keep
The giddy line midway: one step aside,
They're classed and done with. I, then,
keep the line
Before your sages,—just the men to
shrink
From the gross weights, coarse scales, and
labels broad
You offer their refinement. Fool or
knave?
Why needs a bishop be a fool or knave
When there's a thousand diamond weights
between?
So I enlist them. Your picked twelve,
you'll find,
Profess themselves indignant, scandalized
At thus being held unable to explain
How a superior man who disbelieves
May not believe as well: that's Schel-
ling's way!
It's through my coming in the tail of time,
Nicking the minute with a happy tact.
Had I been born three hundred years
ago
They'd say, "What's strange? Blougram
of course believes;"
And, seventy years since, "disbelieves of
course."
But now, "He may believe; and yet, and
yet
How can he?"—All eyes turn with in-
terest.
Whereas, step off the line on either side—
You, for example, clever to a fault,

The rough and ready man who write apace,
Read somewhat seldomer, think perhaps even less—
You disbelieve! Who wonders and who cares?
Lord So-and-so—his coat bedropt with wax,
All Peter's chains about his waist, his back
Brave with the needlework of Noodledom,
Believes! Again, who wonders and who cares?
But I, the man of sense and learning too,
The able to think yet act, the this, the that,
I, to believe at this late time of day!
Enough; you see, I need not fear contempt.

—Except it's yours! admire me as these may,
You don't. But whom at least do you admire?
Present your own perfections, your ideal,
Your pattern man for a minute—oh, make haste!
Is it Napoleon you would have us grow?
Concede the means; allow his head and hand,
(A large concession, clever as you are)
Good!—In our common primal element
Of unbelief (we can't believe, you know—
We're still at that admission, recollect!)
Where do you find—apart from, towering o'er
The secondary temporary aims
Which satisfy the gross tastes you despise—
Where do you find his star?—his crazy trust
God knows through what or in what? it's alive
And shines and leads him and that's all we want.
Have we aught in our sober night shall point
Such ends as his were, and direct the means
Of working out our purpose straight as his,
Nor bring a moment's trouble on success
With after-care to justify the same?
—Be a Napoleon and yet disbelieve—
Why, the man's mad, friend, take his light away!
What's the vague good of the world for which you'd dare
With comfort to yourself blow millions up?
We neither of us see it! we do see
The blown-up millions—spatter of their brains
And writhing of their bowels and so forth,
In that bewildering entanglement
Of horrible eventualities
Past calculation to the end of time!
Can I mistake for some clear word of God
(Which were my ample warrant for it all)
His puff of hazy instincts, idle talk,
"The State, that's I," quack-nonsense about crowns,
And (when one beats the man to his last hold)
A vague idea of setting things to rights,
Policing people efficaciously,
More to their profit, most of all to his own;
The whole to end that dismallest of ends
By an Austrian marriage, cant to us the Church,
And resurrection of the old règime.
Would I, who hope to live a dozen years,
Fight Austerlitz for reasons such and such?
No: for, concede me but the merest chance
Doubt may be wrong—there's judgment, life to come!
With just that chance, I dare not. Doubt proves right?
This present life is all?—you offer me
Its dozen noisy years without a chance

That wedding an archduchess, wearing lace,
And getting called by divers new-coined names,
Will drive off ugly thoughts and let me dine,
Sleep, read and chat in quiet as I like!
Therefore, I will not.

Take another case;
Fit up the cabin yet another way.
What say you to the poets? shall we write
Hamlet, Othello—make the world our own,
Without a risk to run of either sort?
I can't!—to put the strongest reason first.
"But try," you urge, "the trying shall suffice;
The aim, if reached or not, makes great the life:
Try to be Shakespeare, leave the rest to fate!"
Spare my self-knowledge—there's no fooling me!
If I prefer remaining my poor self,
I say so not in self-dispraise but praise.
If I'm a Shakespeare, let the well alone—
Why should I try to be what now I am?
If I'm no Shakespeare, as too probable,—
His power and consciousness and self-delight
And all we want in common, shall I find—
Trying for ever? while on points of taste
Wherewith, to speak it humbly, he and I
Are dowered alike—I'll ask you, I or he,
Which in our two lives realizes most?
Much, he imagined—somewhat, I possess.
He had the imagination; stick to that!
Let him say "In the face of my soul's works
Your world is worthless and I touch it not
Lest I should wrong them"—I'll withdraw my plea.
But does he say so? look upon his life!
Himself, who only can, gives judgment there.
He leaves his towers and gorgeous palaces
To build the trimmest house in Stratford town;
Saves money, spends it, owns the worth of things,
Giulio Romano's pictures, Dowland's lute;
Enjoys a show, respects the puppets, too,
And none more, had he seen its entry once,
Than "Pandulph, of fair Milan cardinal."
Why then should I who play that personage,
The very Pandulph Shakespeare's fancy made,
Be told that had the poet chanced to start
From where I stand now (some degree like mine
Being just the goal he ran his race to reach)
He would have run the whole race back, forsooth,
And left being Pandulph, to begin write plays?
Ah, the earth's best can be but the earth's best!
Did Shakespeare live, he could but sit at home
And get himself in dreams the Vatican,
Greek busts, Venetian paintings, Roman walls,
And English books, none equal to his own,
Which I read, bound in gold, (he never did).
—Terni's fall Naples' bay and Gothard's top—
Eh, friend? I could not fancy one of these—
But, as I pour this claret, there they are—
I've gained them—crossed St. Gothards last July
With ten mules to the carriage and a bed
Slung inside; is my hap the worse for that?
We want the same things, Shakespeare and myself,
And what I want, I have: he, gifted more,
Could fancy he too had it when he liked,

But not so thoroughly that if fate allowed
He would not have it also in my sense.
We play one game. I send the ball aloft
No less adroitly that of fifty strokes
Scarce five go o'er the wall so wide and high
Which sends them back to me: I wish and get.
He struck balls higher and with better skill,
But at a poor fence level with his head,
And hit—his Stratford house, a coat of arms,
Successful dealings in his grain and wool,
While I receive heaven's incense in my nose
And style myself the cousin of Queen Bess.
Ask him, if this life's all, who wins the game?

Believe—and our whole argument breaks up.
Enthusiasm's the best thing, I repeat;
Only, we can't command it; fire and life
Are all, dead matter's nothing, we agree:
And be it a mad dream or God's very breath,
The fact's the same,—belief's fire once in us,
Makes of all else mere stuff to show itself:
We penetrate our life with such a glow
As fire lends wood and iron—this turns steel,
That burns to ash—all's one, fire proves its power
For good or ill, since men call flare success.
But paint a fire, it will not therefore burn.
Light one in me, I'll find it food enough!
Why, to be Luther—that's a life to lead,
Incomparably better than my own.
He comes, reclaims God's earth for God, he says,
Sets up God's rule again by simple means,
Re-opens a shut book, and all is done.
He flared out in the flaring of mankind;
Such Luther's luck was—how shall such be mine?
If he succeeded, nothing's left to do:
And if he did not altogether—well,
Strauss is the next advance. All Strauss should be
I might be also. But to what result?
He looks upon no Future: Luther did.
What can I gain on the denying side?
Ice makes no conflagration. State the facts,
Read the text right, emancipate the world—
The emancipated world enjoys itself
With scarce a thank-you—Blougram told it first
It could not owe a farthing,—not to him
More than Saint Paul! 'twould press its pay, you think?
Then add there's still that plaguy hundredth chance
Strauss may be wrong. And so a risk is run—
For what gain? not for Luther's, who secured
A real heaven in his heart throughout his life,
Supposing death a little altered things.

"Ay, but since really you lack faith," you cry,
"You run the same risk really on all sides,
In cool indifference as bold unbelief.
As well be Strauss as swing 'twixt Paul and him.
It's not worth having, such imperfect faith,
Nor more available to do faith's work
Than unbelief like mine. Whole faith, or none!"

Softly, my friend! I must dispute that point.
Once own the use of faith, I'll find you faith.
We're back on Christian ground. You call for faith:
I show you doubt, to prove that faith exists.

The more of doubt, the stronger faith, I say,
If faith o'ercomes doubt. How I know it does?
By life and man's free will, God gave for that!
To mould life as we choose it, shows our choice:
That's our one act, the previous work's His own.
You criticize the soil? it reared this tree—
This broad life and whatever fruit it bears!
What matter though I doubt at every pore,
Head-doubts, heart-doubts, doubts at my fingers' ends,
Doubts in the trivial work of every day,
Doubts at the very bases of my soul
In the grand moments when she probes herself—
If finally I have a life to show,
The thing I did, brought out in evidence
Against the thing done to me underground
By Hell and all its brood, for aught I know?
I say, whence sprang this? shows it faith or doubt?
All's doubt in me; where's break of faith in this?
It is the idea, the feeling and the love
God means mankind should strive for and show forth,
Whatever be the process to that end,—
And not historic knowledge, logic sound,
And metaphysical acumen, sure!
"What think ye of Christ," friend? when all's done and said,
Like you this Christianity or not?
It may be false, but will you wish it true?
Has it your vote to be so if it can?
Trust you an instinct silenced long ago
That will break silence and enjoin you love
What mortified philosophy is hoarse,
And all in vain, with bidding you despise?
If you desire faith—then you've faith enough:
What else seeks God—nay, what else seek ourselves?
You form a notion of me, we'll suppose,
On hearsay; it's a favourable one:
"But still," (you add) "there was no such good man,
Because of contradictions in the facts.
One proves, for instance, he was born in Rome,
This Blougram—yet throughout the tales of him
I see he figures as an Englishman."
Well, the two things are reconcilable.
But would I rather you discovered that,
Subjoining—"Still, what matter though they be?
Blougram concerns me nought, born here or there."

Pure faith indeed—you know not what you ask!
Naked belief in God the Omnipotent,
Omniscient, Omnipresent, sears too much
The sense of conscious creatures to be borne.
It were the seeing Him, no flesh shall dare.
Some think, Creation's meant to show Him forth:
I say, it's meant to hide Him all it can,
And that's what all the blessed evil's for.
Its use in Time is to environ us,
Our breath, our drop of dew, with shield enough
Against that sight till we can bear its stress.
Under a vertical sun, the exposed brain
And lidless eye and disemprisoned heart
Less certainly would wither up at once
Than mind, confronted with the truth of Him.
But time and earth case-harden us to live;
The feeblest sense is trusted most; the child
Feels God a moment, ichors o'er the place,
Plays on and grows to be a man like us.
With me, faith means perpetual unbelief

Kept quiet like the snake 'neath Michael's foot
Who stands calm just because he feels it writhe.
Or, if that's too ambitious,—here's my box—
I need the excitation of a pinch
Threatening the torpor of the inside-nose
Nigh on the imminent sneeze that never comes.
"Leave it in peace" advise the simple folk—
Make it aware of peace by itching-fits,
Say I—let doubt occasion still more faith!

You'll say, once all believed, man, woman, child,
In that dear middle-age these noodles praise.
How you'd exult if I could put you back
Six hundred years, blot out cosmogony,
Geology, ethnology, what not,
(Greek endings with the little passing-bell
That signifies some faith's about to die)
And set you square with Genesis again,—
When such a traveller told you his last news,
He saw the ark a-top of Ararat
But did not climb there since 'twas getting dusk
And robber-bands infest the mountain's foot!
How should you feel, I ask, in such an age,
How act? As other people felt and did;
With soul more blank than this decanter's knob,
Believe—and yet lie, kill, rob, fornicate
Full in belief's face, like the beast you'd be!

No, when the fight begins within himself,
A man's worth something. God stoops o'er his head,
Satan looks up between his feet—both tug—
He's left, himself, in the middle: the soul wakes
And grows. Prolong that battle through his life!
Never leave growing till the life to come!
Here, we've got callous to the Virgin's winks
That used to puzzle people wholesomely—
Men have outgrown the shame of being fools.
What are the laws of nature, not to bend
If the Church bid them?—brother Newman asks.
Up with the Immaculate Conception, then—
On to the rack with faith!—is my advice.
Will not that hurry us upon our knees,
Knocking our breasts, "It can't be—yet it shall!
Who am I, the worm, to argue with my Pope?
Low things confound the high things!" and so forth.
That's better than acquitting God with grace
As some folks do. He's tried—no case is proved,
Philosophy is lenient—He may go!

You'll say—the old system's not so obsolete
But men believe still: ay, but who and where?
King Bomba's lazzaroni foster yet
The sacred flame, so Antonelli writes;
But even of these, what ragamuffin-saint
Believes God watches him continually,
As he believes in fire that it will burn,
Or rain that it will drench him? Break fire's law,
Sin against rain, although the penalty
Be just a singe or soaking? "No," he smiles;
"Those laws are laws that can enforce themselves."

The sum of all is—yes, my doubt is great,
My faith's still greater—then my faith's enough,

I have read much, thought much, experienced much,
Yet would die rather than avow my fear
The Naples' liquefaction may be false,
When set to happen by the palace-clock
According to the clouds or dinner-time.
I hear you recommend, I might at least
Eliminate, decrassify my faith
Since I adopt it; keeping what I must
And leaving what I can—such points as this!
I won't—that is, I can't throw one away.
Supposing there's no truth in what I said
About the need of trials to man's faith,
Still, when you bid me purify the same,
To such a process I discern no end,
Clearing off one excrescence to see two;
There's ever a next in size, now grown as big,
That meets the knife—I cut and cut again!
First cut the Liquefaction, what comes last
But Fichte's clever cut at God Himself?
Experimentalize on sacred things!
I trust nor hand nor eye nor heart nor brain
To stop betimes: they all get drunk alike.
The first step, I am master not to take.

You'd find the cutting-process to your taste
As much as leaving growths of lies unpruned,
Nor see more danger in it, you retort.
Your taste's worth mine; but my taste proves more wise
When we consider that the steadfast hold
On the extreme end of the chain of faith
Gives all the advantage, makes the difference,
With the rough purblind mass we seek to rule.
We are their lords, or they are free of us
Just as we tighten or relax that hold.
So, other matters equal, we'll revert
To the first problem—which, if solved my way
And thrown into the balance, turns the scale—
How we may lead a comfortable life,
How suit our luggage to the cabin's size.

Of course you are remarking all this time
How narrowly and grossly I view life,
Respect the creature-comforts, care to rule
The masses, and regard complacently
"The cabin," in our old phrase! Well, I do.
I act for, talk for, live for this world now,
As this world calls for action, life and talk—
No prejudice to what next world may prove,
Whose new laws and requirements, my best pledge
To observe then, is that I observe these now,
Shall do hereafter what I do meanwhile.
Let us concede (gratuitously though)
Next life relieves the soul of body, yields
Pure spiritual enjoyments: well, my friend,
Why lose this life in the meantime, since its use
May be to make the next life more intense?

Do you know, I have often had a dream
(Work it up in your next month's article)
Of man's poor spirit in its progress still
Losing true life for ever and a day
Through ever trying to be and ever being
In the evolution of successive spheres,
Before its actual sphere and place of life,
Halfway into the next, which having reached,
It shoots with corresponding foolery
Halfway into the next still, on and off!
As when a traveller, bound from North to South,
Scouts fur in Russia—what's its use in France?
In France spurns flannel—where's its need in Spain?

In Spain drops cloth—too cumbrous for Algiers!
Linen goes next, and last the skin itself,
A superfluity at Timbuctoo.
When, through his journey, was the fool at ease?
I'm at ease now, friend—worldly in this world
I take and like its way of life; I think
My brothers who administer the means
Live better for my comfort—that's good too;
And God, if He pronounce upon it all,
Approves my service, which is better still.
If He keep silence,—why, for you or me
Or that brute-beast pulled-up in to-day's "Times,"
What odds is't, save to ourselves, what life we lead?

You meet me at this issue—you declare,
All special-pleading done with, truth is truth,
And justifies itself by undreamed ways.
You don't fear but it's better, if we doubt,
To say so, acting up to our truth perceived
However feebly. Do then,—act away!
'Tis there I'm on the watch for you! How one acts
Is, both of us agree, our chief concern:
And how you'll act is what I fain would see
If, like the candid person you appear,
You dare to make the most of your life's scheme
As I of mine, live up to its full law
Since there's no higher law that counterchecks.
Put natural religion to the test
You've just demolished the revealed with—quick,
Down to the root of all that checks your will,
All prohibition to lie, kill and thieve
Or even to be an atheistic priest!
Suppose a pricking to incontinence—
Philosophers deduce your chastity
Or shame, from just the fact that at the first
Whoso embraced a woman in the plain,
Threw club down, and forewent his brains beside,
So stood a ready victim in the reach
Of any brother-savage club in hand—
Hence saw the use of going out of sight
In wood or cave to prosecute his loves—
I read this in a French book t' other day.
Does law so analysed coerce you much?
Oh, men spin clouds of fuzz where matters end,
But you who reach where the first thread begins,
You'll soon cut that!—which means you can, but won't
Through certain instincts, blind, unreasoned-out,
You dare not set aside, you can't tell why,
But there they are, and so you let them rule.
Then, friend, you seem as much a slave as I,
A liar, conscious coward and hypocrite,
Without the good the slave expects to get,
Suppose he has a master after all!
You own your instincts—why, what else do I,
Who want, am made for, and must have a God
Ere I can be aught, do aught?—no mere name
Want, but the true thing with what proves its truth,
To wit, a relation from that thing to me,
Touching from head to foot—which touch I feel,
And with it take the rest, this life of ours!
I live my life here; yours you dare not live.

—Not as I state it, who (you please subjoin)
Disfigure such a life and call it names,
While, in your mind, remains another way
For simple men: knowledge and power have rights,

But ignorance and weakness have rights too.
There needs no crucial effort to find truth
If here or there or anywhere about—
We ought to turn each side, try hard and see,
And if we can't, be glad we've earned at least
The right, by one laborious proof the more,
To graze in peace earth's pleasant pasturage.
Men are not angels, neither are they brutes.
Something we may see, all we cannot see—
What need of lying? I say, I see all,
And swear to each detail the most minute
In what I think a Pan's face—you, mere cloud:
I swear I hear him speak and see him wink,
For fear, if once I drop the emphasis,
Mankind may doubt there's any cloud at all.
You take the simpler life—ready to see,
Willing to see—for no cloud's worth a face—
And leaving quiet what no strength can move,
And which, who bids you move? who has the right?
I bid you; but you are God's sheep, not mine—
"Pastor est tui Dominus." You find
In these the pleasant pastures of this life
Much you may eat without the least offence,
Much you don't eat because your maw objects,
Much you would eat but that your fellow-flock
Open great eyes at you and even butt,
And thereupon you like your mates so well
You cannot please yourself, offending them—
Though when they seem exorbitantly sheep,
You weigh your pleasure with their butts and bleats
And strike the balance. Sometimes certain fears
Restrain you—real checks since you find them so—
Sometimes you please yourself and nothing checks;
And thus you graze through life with not one lie,
And like it best.

But do you, in truth's name?
If so, you beat—which means, you are not I—
Who needs must make earth mine and feed my fill
Not simply unbutted at, unbickered with,
But motioned to the velvet of the sward
By those obsequious wethers' very selves.
Look at me, sir; my age is double yours:
At yours, I knew beforehand, so enjoyed,
What now I should be—as, permit the word,
I pretty well imagine your whole range
And stretch of tether twenty years to come.
We both have minds and bodies much alike.
In truth's name, don't you want my bishopric,
My daily bread, my influence and my state?
You're young, I'm old, you must be old one day;
Will you find then, as I do hour by hour,
Women their lovers kneel to, that cut curls
From your fat lap-dog's ears to grace a brooch—
Dukes, that petition just to kiss your ring—
With much beside you know or may conceive?
Suppose we die to-night: well, here am I,
Such were my gains, life bore this fruit to me,
While writing all the same my articles
On music, poetry, the fictile vase

Found at Albano, chess, or Anacreon's Greek.
But you—the highest honour in your life,
The thing you'll crown yourself with, all your days,
Is—dining here and drinking this last glass
I pour you out in sign of amity
Before we part for ever. Of your power
And social influence, worldly worth in short,
Judge what's my estimation by the fact,
I do not condescend to enjoin, beseech,
Hint secrecy on one of all these words!
You're shrewd and know that should you publish one
The world would brand the lie—my enemies first,
Who'd sneer—"the bishop's an arch-hypocrite,
And knave perhaps, but not so frank a fool."
Whereas I should not dare for both my ears
Breathe one such syllable, smile one such smile,
Before my chaplain who reflects myself—
My shade's so much more potent than your flesh.
What's your reward, self-abnegating friend?
Stood you confessed of those exceptional
And privileged great natures that dwarf mine—
A zealot with a mad ideal in reach,
A poet just about to print his ode,
A statesman with a scheme to stop this war,
An artist whose religion is his art,
I should have nothing to object! such men
Carry the fire, all things grow warm to them,
Their drugget's worth my purple, they beat me.
But you,—you're just as little those as I—
You, Gigadibs, who, thirty years of age,
Write statedly for Blackwood's Magazine,
Believe you see two points in Hamlet's soul
Unseized by the Germans yet—which view you'll print—
Meantime the best you have to show being still
That lively lightsome article we took
Almost for the true Dickens,—what's its name?
"The Slum and Cellar—or Whitechapel life
Limned after dark!" it made me laugh, I know,
And pleased a month and brought you in ten pounds.
—Success I recognize and compliment,
And therefore give you, if you choose, three words
(The card and pencil-scratch is quite enough)
Which whether here, in Dublin or New York,
Will get you, prompt as at my eyebrow's wink,
Such terms as never you aspired to get
In all our own reviews and some not ours.
Go write your lively sketches—be the first
"Blougram, or The Eccentric Confidence"—
Or better simply say, "The Outward-bound."
Why, men as soon would throw it in my teeth
As copy and quote the infamy chalked broad
About me on the church-door opposite.
You will not wait for that experience though,
I fancy, howsoever you decide,
To discontinue—not detesting, not
Defaming, but at least—despising me!

Over his wine so smiled and talked his hour
Sylvester Blougram, styled *in partibus*
Episcopus, nec non—(the deuce knows what
It's changed to by our novel hierarchy)

With Gigadibs the literary man,
Who played with spoons, explored his plate's design,
And ranged the olive-stones about its edge,
While the great bishop rolled him out a mind
Long crumpled, till creased consciousness lay smooth.

For Blougram, he believed, say, half he spoke.
The other portion, as he shaped it thus
For argumentatory purposes,
He felt his foe was foolish to dispute.
Some arbitrary accidental thoughts
That crossed his mind, amusing because new,
He chose to represent as fixtures there,
Invariable convictions (such they seemed
Beside his interlocutor's loose cards
Flung daily down, and not the same way twice)
While certain hell-deep instincts, man's weak tongue
Is never bold to utter in their truth
Because styled hell-deep ('tis an old mistake
To place hell at the bottom of the earth)
He ignored these,—not having in readiness
Their nomenclature and philosophy:
He said true things, but called them by wrong names.
"On the whole," he thought, "I justify myself
On every point where cavillers like this
Oppugn my life: he tries one kind of fence—
I close—he's worsted, that's enough for him;
He's on the ground! if the ground should break away
I take my stand on, there's a firmer yet
Beneath it, both of us may sink and reach.
His ground was over mine and broke the first:
So let him sit with me this many a year!"

He did not sit five minutes. Just a week
Sufficed his sudden healthy vehemence.
(Something had struck him in the "Outward-bound"
Another way than Blougram's purpose was)
And having bought, not cabin-furniture
But settler's-implements (enough for three)
And started for Australia—there, I hope,
By this time he has tested his first plough,
And studied his last chapter of St. John.

One Word More

TO E. B. B.

London, September, 1855

I

THERE they are, my fifty men and women
Naming me the fifty poems finished!
Take them, Love, the book and me together:
Where the heart lies, let the brain lie also.

II

Rafael made a century of sonnets,
Made and wrote them in a certain volume
Dinted with the silver-pointed pencil
Else he only used to draw Madonnas:
These, the world might view—but one, the volume.
Who that one, you ask? Your heart instructs you.
Did she live and love it all her lifetime?
Did she drop, his lady of the sonnets,
Die, and let it drop beside her pillow
Where it lay in place of Rafael's glory,
Rafael's cheek so duteous and so loving—
Cheek, the world was wont to hail a painter's,
Rafael's cheek, her love had turned a poet's?

III

You and I would rather read that volume,
(Taken to his beating bosom by it)
Lean and list the bosom-beats of Rafael,
Would we not? than wonder at Madonnas—
Her, San Sisto names, and Her, Foligno,
Her, that visits Florence in a vision,
Her, that's left with lilies in the Louvre—
Seen by us and all the world in circle.

IV

You and I will never read that volume.
Guido Reni, like his own eye's apple
Guarded long the treasure-book and loved it.
Guido Reni dying, all Bologna
Cried, and the world cried too, "Ours—the treasure!"
Suddenly, as rare things will, it vanished.

V

Dante once prepared to paint an angel:
Whom to please? You whisper "Beatrice."
While he mused and traced it and retraced it,
(Peradventure with a pen corroded
Still by drops of that hot ink he dipped for,
When, his left-hand i' the hair o' the wicked,
Back he held the brow and pricked its stigma,
Bit into the live man's flesh for parchment,
Loosed him, laughed to see the writing rankle,
Let the wretch go festering through Florence)—
Dante, who loved well because he hated,
Hated wickedness that hinders loving,
Dante standing, studying his angel,—
In there broke the folk of his Inferno.
Says he—"Certain people of importance"
(Such he gave his daily, dreadful line to)
"Entered and would seize, forsooth, the poet."
Says the poet—"Then I stopped my painting."

VI

You and I would rather see that angel,
Painted by the tenderness of Dante,
Would we not?—than read a fresh Inferno.

VII

You and I will never see that picture.
While he mused on love and Beatrice,
While he softened o'er his outlined angel,
In they broke, those "people of importance:"
We and Bice bear the loss for ever.

VIII

What of Rafael's sonnets, Dante's picture?
This: no artist lives and loves, that longs not
Once, and only once, and for one only,
(Ah, the prize!) to find his love a language
Fit and fair and simple and sufficient—
Using nature that's an art to others,
Not, this one time, art that's turned his nature.
Ay, of all the artists living, loving,
None but would forego his proper dowry,—
Does he paint? he fain would write a poem,—
Does he write? he fain would paint a picture,
Put to proof art alien to the artist's,
Once, and only once, and for one only,
So to be the man and leave the artist,
Gain the man's joy, miss the artist's sorrow.

IX

Wherefore? Heaven's gift takes earth's abatement!
He who smites the rock and spreads the water,

Bidding drink and live a crowd beneath him,
Even he, the minute makes immortal
Proves, perchance, his mortal in the minute,
Desecrates, belike, the deed in doing.
While he smites, how can he but remember,
So he smote before, in such a peril,
When they stood and mocked—"Shall smiting help us?"
When they drank and sneered—"A stroke is easy!"
When they wiped their mouths and went their journey,
Throwing him for thanks—"But drought was pleasant."
Thus old memories mar the actual triumph;
Thus the doing savours of disrelish;
Thus achievement lacks a gracious somewhat;
O'er-importuned brows becloud the mandate,
Carelessness or consciousness, the gesture.
For he bears an ancient wrong about him,
Sees and knows again those phalanxed faces,
Hears, yet one time more, the 'customed prelude—
"How shouldst thou, of all men, smite, and save us?"
Guesses what is like to prove the sequel—
"Egypt's flesh-pots—nay, the drought was better."

X

Oh, the crowd must have emphatic warrant!
Theirs, the Sinai-forehead's cloven brilliance,
Right-arm's rod-sweep, tongue's imperial fiat.
Never dares the man put off the prophet.

XI

Did he love one face from out the thousands,
(Were she Jethro's daughter, white and wifely,
Were she but the Æthiopian bond-slave,)
He would envy yon dumb patient camel,
Keeping a reserve of scanty water
Meant to save his own life in the desert;
Ready in the desert to deliver
(Kneeling down to let his breast be opened)
Hoard and life together for his mistress.

XII

I shall never, in the years remaining,
Paint you pictures, no, nor carve you statues,
Make you music that should all-express me;
So it seems: I stand on my attainment.
This of verse alone, one life allows me;
Verse and nothing else have I to give you.
Other heights in other lives, God willing—
All the gifts from all the heights, your own, Love!

XIII

Yet a semblance of resource avails us—
Shade so finely touched, love's sense must seize it.
Take these lines, look lovingly and nearly,
Lines I write the first time and the last time.
He who works in fresco, steals a hair-brush,
Curbs the liberal hand, subservient proudly,
Cramps his spirit, crowds its all in little,
Makes a strange art of an art familiar,
Fills his lady's missal-marge with flowerets.
He who blows through bronze, may breathe through silver,
Fitly serenade a slumbrous princess.
He who writes, may write for once, as I do.

XIV

Love, you saw me gather men and women,
Live or dead or fashioned by my fancy,
Enter each and all, and use their service,
Speak from every mouth,—the speech, a poem.
Hardly shall I tell my joys and sorrows,
Hopes and fears, belief and disbelieving:
I am mine and yours—the rest be all men's,
Karshook, Cleon, Norbert and the fifty.
Let me speak this once in my true person,
Not as Lippo, Roland or Andrea,
Though the fruit of speech be just this sentence—
Pray you, look on these my men and women,
Take and keep my fifty poems finished;
Where my heart lies, let my brain lie also!
Poor the speech; be how I speak, for all things.

XV

Not but that you know me! Lo, the moon's self!
Here in London, yonder late in Florence,
Still we find her face, the thrice-transfigured.
Curving on a sky imbrued with colour,
Drifted over Fiesole by twilight,
Came she, our new crescent of a hair's-breadth.
Full she flared it, lamping Samminiato,
Rounder 'twixt the cypresses and rounder,
Perfect till the nightingales applauded.
Now, a piece of her old self, impoverished,
Hard to greet, she traverses the house-roofs,
Hurries with unhandsome thrift of silver,
Goes dispiritedly, glad to finish.

XVI

What, there's nothing in the moon note-worthy?
Nay—for if that moon could love a mortal,
Use, to charm him (so to fit a fancy)
All her magic ('tis the old sweet mythos)
She would turn a new side to her mortal,
Side unseen of herdsman, huntsman, steersman—
Blank to Zoroaster on his terrace,
Blind to Galileo on his turret,
Dumb to Homer, dumb to Keats—him, even!
Think, the wonder of the moonstruck mortal—
When she turns round, comes again in heaven,
Opens out anew for worse or better?
Proves she like some portent of an iceberg
Swimming full upon the ship it founders,
Hungry with huge teeth of splintered crystals?
Proves she as the paved-work of a sapphire
Seen by Moses when he climbed the mountain?
Moses, Aaron, Nadab and Abihu
Climbed and saw the very God, the Highest,
Stand upon the paved-work of a sapphire.
Like the bodied heaven in his clearness
Shone the stone, the sapphire of that paved-work,
When they ate and drank and saw God also!

XVII

What were seen? None knows, none ever shall know.
Only this is sure—the sight were other,
Not the moon's same side, born late in Florence,
Dying now impoverished here in London.
God be thanked, the meanest of his creatures
Boasts two soul-sides, one to face the world with,
One to show a woman when he loves her.

XVIII

This I say of me, but think of you, Love!
This to you—yourself my moon of poets!
Ah, but that's the world's side, there's the wonder,

Thus they see you, praise you, think they know you.
There, in turn I stand with them and praise you,
Out of my own self, I dare to phrase it.
But the best is when I glide from out them,
Cross a step or two of dubious twilight,
Come out on the other side, the novel
Silent silver lights and darks undreamed of,
Where I hush and bless myself with silence.

XIX

Oh, their Rafael of the dear Madonnas,
Oh, their Dante of the dread Inferno,
Wrote one song—and in my brain I sing it,
Drew one angel—borne, see, on my bosom!

R. B.

Confessions

WHAT is he buzzing in my ears?
"Now that I come to die,
Do I view the world as a vale of tears?"
Ah, reverend sir, not I!

What I viewed there once, what I view again
Where the physic bottles stand
On the table's edge,—is a suburb lane,
With a wall to my bedside hand.

That lane sloped, much as the bottles do,
From a house you could descry
O'er the garden-wall: is the curtain blue
Or green to a healthy eye?

To mine, it serves for the old June weather
Blue above lane and wall;
And that farthest bottle labelled "Ether"
Is the house o'er-topping all.

At a terrace, somewhat near its stopper,
There watched for me, one June,
A girl: I know, sir, it's improper,
My poor mind's out of tune.

Only, there was a way . . . you crept
Close by the side, to dodge
Eyes in the house, two eyes except:
They styled their house "The Lodge."

What right had a lounger up their lane?
But, by creeping very close,
With the good wall's help,—their eyes might strain
And stretch themselves to Oes,

Yet never catch her and me together,
As she left the attic, there,
By the rim of the bottle labelled "Ether,"
And stole from stair to stair,

And stood by the rose-wreathed gate. Alas,
We loved, sir—used to meet:
How sad and bad and mad it was—
But then, how it was sweet!

Prospice

FEAR death?—to feel the fog in my throat,
The mist in my face,
When the snows begin, and the blasts denote
I am nearing the place,
The power of the night, the press of the storm,
The post of the foe;
Where he stands, the Arch Fear in a visible form,
Yet the strong man must go:
For the journey is done and the summit attained,
And the barriers fall,
Though a battle's to fight ere the guerdon be gained,
The reward of it all.
I was ever a fighter, so—one fight more,
The best and the last!
I would hate that death bandaged my eyes, and forbore,
And bade me creep past.
No! let me taste the whole of it, fare like my peers
The heroes of old,

Bear the brunt, in a minute pay glad life's arrears
Of pain, darkness and cold.
For sudden the worst turns the best to the brave,
The black minute's at end,
And the elements' rage, the fiend-voices that rave,
Shall dwindle, shall blend,
Shall change, shall become first a peace, then a joy,
Then a light, then thy breast,
O thou soul of my soul! I shall clasp thee again,
And with God be the rest!

The Householder

SHALL I sonnet-sing you about myself?
Do I live in a house you would like to see?
Is it scant of gear, has it store of pelf?
"Unlock my heart with a sonnet-key?"

Invite the world, as my betters have done?
"Take notice: this building remains on view,
Its suites of reception every one,
Its private apartment and bedroom too;

"For a ticket, apply to the Publisher."
No: thanking the public, I must decline.
A peep through my window, if folk prefer;
But, please you, no foot over threshold of mine!

I have mixed with a crowd and heard free talk
In a foreign land where an earthquake chanced
And a house stood gaping, naught to balk
Man's eye wherever he gazed or glanced.

The whole of the frontage shaven sheer,
The inside gaped: exposed to day,
Right and wrong and common and queer,
Bare, as the palm of your hand, it lay.

The owner? Oh, he had been crushed, no doubt!
"Odd tables and chairs for a man of wealth!
What a parcel of musty old books about!
He smoked,—no wonder he lost his health!

"I doubt if he bathed before he dressed.
A brasier?—the pagan, he burned perfumes!
You see it is proved, what the neighbors guessed:
His wife and himself had separate rooms."

Friends, the goodman of the house at least
Kept house to himself till an earthquake came:
'Tis the fall of its frontage permits you feast
On the inside arrangement you praise or blame.

Outside should suffice for evidence:
And whoso desires to penetrate
Deeper, must dive by the spirit-sense—
No optics like yours, at any rate!

"Hoity-toity! A street to explore,
Your house the exception! *'With this same key*
Shakespeare unlocked his heart,' once more!"
Did Shakespeare? If so, the less Shakespeare he!

Pheidippides

FIRST I salute this soil of the blessed, river and rock!
Gods of my birthplace, dæmons and heroes, honor to all!
Then I name thee, claim thee for our patron, co-equal in praise
—Ay, with Zeus the Defender, with Her of the ægis and spear!
Also, ye of the bow and the buskin, praised be your peer,
Now, henceforth and forever,—O latest to whom I upraise

Hand and heart and voice! For Athens, leave pasture and flock!
Present to help, potent to save, Pan—patron I call!

Archons of Athens, topped by the tettix, see, I return!
See, 'tis myself here standing alive, no spectre that speaks!
Crowned with the myrtle, did you command me, Athens and you,
"Run, Pheidippides, run and race, reach Sparta for aid!
Persia has come, we are here, where is She?" Your command I obeyed,
Ran and raced: like stubble, some field which a fire runs through,
Was the space between city and city: two days, two nights did I burn
Over the hills, under the dales, down pits and up peaks.

Into their midst I broke: breath served but for "Persia has come!
Persia bids Athens proffer slaves'-tribute, water and earth;
Razed to the ground is Eretria—but Athens, shall Athens sink,
Drop into dust and die—the flower of Hellas utterly die,
Die, with the wide world spitting at Sparta, the stupid, the stander-by?
Answer me quick, what help, what hand do you stretch o'er destruction's brink?
How,—when? No care for my limbs!—there's lightning in all and some—
Fresh and fit your message to bear, once lips give it birth!"

O my Athens—Sparta love thee? Did Sparta respond?
Every face of her leered in a furrow of envy, mistrust,
Malice,—each eye of her gave me its glitter of gratified hate!
Gravely they turned to take counsel, to cast for excuses. I stood
Quivering,—the limbs of me fretting as fire frets, an inch from dry wood:
"Persia has come, Athens asks aid, and still they debate?
Thunder, thou Zeus! Athene, are Spartans a quarry beyond
Swing of thy spear? Phoibos and Artemis, clang them 'Ye must'!"

No bolt launched from Olympus! Lo, their answer at last!
"Has Persia come,—does Athens ask aid,—may Sparta befriend?
Nowise precipitate judgment — too weighty the issue at stake!
Count we no time lost time which lags through respect to the gods!
Ponder that precept of old, 'No warfare, whatever the odds
In your favor, so long as the moon, half-orbed, is unable to take
Full-circle her state in the sky!' Already she rounds to it fast:
Athens must wait, patient as we—who judgment suspend."

Athens,—except for that sparkle,—thy name, I had mouldered to ash!
That sent a blaze through my blood; off, off and away was I back,
—Not one word to waste, one look to lose on the false and the vile!
Yet "O gods of my land!" I cried, as each hillock and plain,
Wood and stream, I knew, I named, rushing past them again,
"Have ye kept faith, proved mindful of honors we paid you erewhile?
Vain was the filleted victim, the fulsome libation! Too rash
Love in its choice, paid you so largely service so slack!

"Oak and olive and bay,—I bid you cease to enwreathe
Brows made bold by your leaf! Fade at the Persian's foot,
You that, our patrons were pledged, should never adorn a slave!

Rather I hail thee, Parnes,—trust to thy wild waste tract!
Treeless, herbless, lifeless mountain! What matter if slacked
My speed may hardly be, for homage to crag and to cave
No deity deigns to drape with verdure? at least I can breathe,
Fear in thee no fraud from the blind, no lie from the mute!"

Such my cry as, rapid, I ran over Parnes' ridge;
Gully and gap I clambered and cleared till, sudden, a bar
Jutted, a stoppage of stone against me, blocking the way.
Right! for I minded the hollow to traverse, the fissure across:
"Where I could enter, there I depart by! Night in the fosse?
Athens to aid? Though the dive were through Erebos, thus I obey—
Out of the day dive, into the day as bravely arise! No bridge
Better!"—when—ha! what was it I came on, of wonders that are?

There, in the cool of a cleft, sat he—majestical Pan!
Ivy drooped wanton, kissed his head, moss cushioned his hoof:
All the great god was good in the eyes grave-kindly—the curl
Carved on the bearded cheek, amused at a mortal's awe,
As, under the human trunk, the goat-thighs grand I saw.
"Halt, Pheidippides!"—halt I did, my brain of a whirl:
"Hither to me! Why pale in my presence?" he gracious began:
"How is it,—Athens, only in Hellas, holds me aloof?

"Athens, she only, rears me no fane, makes me no feast!
Wherefore? Than I what godship to Athens more helpful of old?
Go, bid Athens take heart, laugh Persia to scorn, have faith
In the temples and tombs! Go, say to Athens, 'The Goat-God saith:
When Persia—so much as strews not the soil—is cast in the sea,
Then praise Pan who fought in the ranks with your most and least,
Goat-thigh to greaved-thigh, made one cause with the free and the bold!'

"Say Pan saith: 'Let this, foreshowing the place, be the pledge!'"
(Gay, the liberal hand held out this herbage I bear
—Fennel—I grasped it a-tremble with dew—whatever it bode)
"While, as for thee" . . . But enough! He was gone. If I ran hitherto—
Be sure that, the rest of my journey, I ran no longer, but flew.
Parnes to Athens—earth no more, the air was my road:
Here am I back. Praise Pan, we stand no more on the razor's edge!
Pan for Athens, Pan for me! I too have a guerdon rare!

Then spoke Miltiades. "And thee, best runner of Greece,
Whose limbs did duty indeed,—what gift is promised thyself?
Tell it us straightway,—Athens the mother demands of her son!"
Rosily blushed the youth: he paused: but, lifting at length
His eyes from the ground, it seemed as he gathered the rest of his strength
Into the utterance—"Pan spoke thus: 'For what thou hast done
Count on a worthy reward! Henceforth be allowed thee release
From the racer's toil, no vulgar reward in praise or in pelf!'

"I am bold to believe, Pan means reward the most to my mind!
Fight I shall, with our foremost, wherever this fennel may grow,—

Pound—Pan helping us—Persia to dust, and, under the deep,
Whelm her away forever; and then,—no Athens to save,—
Marry a certain maid, I know keeps faith to the brave,—
Hie to my house and home: and, when my children shall creep
Close to my knees,—recount how the God was awful yet kind,
Promised their sire reward to the full—rewarding him—so!"

Unforeseeing one! Yes, he fought on the Marathon day:
So, when Persia was dust, all cried "To Akropolis!
Run, Pheidippides, one race more! the meed is thy due!
'Athens is saved, thank Pan,' go shout!" He flung down his shield,
Ran like fire once more: and the space 'twixt the Fennel-field
And Athens was stubble again, a field which a fire runs through,
Till in he broke: "Rejoice, we conquer!" Like wine through clay,
Joy in his blood bursting his heart, he died—the bliss!

So, to this day, when friend meets friend, the word of salute
Is still "Rejoice!"—his word which brought rejoicing indeed.
So is Pheidippides happy forever,—the noble strong man
Who could race like a god, bear the face of a god, whom a god loved so well;
He saw the land saved he had helped to save, and was suffered to tell
Such tidings, yet never decline, but, gloriously as he began,
So to end gloriously—once to shout, thereafter be mute:
"Athens is saved!"—Pheidippides dies in the shout for his meed.

From ASOLANDO: FANCIES AND FACTS

Epilogue

AT the midnight in the silence of the sleep-time,
When you set your fancies free,
Will they pass to where—by death, fools think, imprisoned—
Low he lies who once so loved you, whom you loved so,
—Pity me?

Oh to love so, be so loved, yet so mistaken!
What had I on earth to do
With the slothful, with the mawkish, the unmanly?
Like the aimless, helpless, hopeless did I drivel
—Being—who?

One who never turned his back but marched breast forward,
Never doubted clouds would break,
Never dreamed, though right were worsted, wrong would triumph,
Held we fall to rise, are baffled to fight better,
Sleep to wake.

No, at noonday in the bustle of man's work-time
Greet the unseen with a cheer!
Bid him forward, breast and back as either should be,
"Strive and thrive!" cry "Speed,—fight on, fare ever
There as here!"

EDWARD LEAR (1812-1888)

The Jumblies

I

THEY went to sea in a Sieve, they did,
In a Sieve they went to sea:
In spite of all their friends could say,
On a winter's morn, on a stormy day,
In a Sieve they went to sea!

And when the Sieve turned round and
round,
And every one cried, "You'll all be
drowned!"
They called aloud, "Our Sieve ain't big,
But we don't care a button! we don't
care a fig!
In a Sieve we'll go to sea!"
Far and few, far and few,
Are the lands where the Jumblies
live;
Their heads are green, and their
hands are blue,
And they went to sea in a Sieve.

II

They sailed away in a Sieve, they did,
In a Sieve they sailed so fast,
With only a beautiful pea-green veil
Tied with a riband by way of a sail,
To a small tobacco-pipe mast;
And every one said, who saw them go,
"O won't they be soon upset, you know!
For the sky is dark, and the voyage is
long,
And happen what may, it's extremely
wrong
In a Sieve to sail so fast!"
Far and few, far and few,
Are the lands where the Jumblies
live;
Their heads are green, and their
hands are blue,
And they went to sea in a Sieve.

III

The water it soon came in, it did,
The water it soon came in;
So to keep them dry, they wrapped their
feet
In a pinky paper all folded neat,
And they fastened it down with a pin.
And they passed the night in a crockery-
jar,
And each of them said, "How wise we
are!
Though the sky be dark, and the voyage
be long,
Yet we never can think we were rash or
wrong,
While round in our Sieve we spin!"
Far and few, far and few,
Are the lands where the Jumblies
live;
Their heads are green, and their
hands are blue,
And they went to sea in a Sieve.

IV

And all night long they sailed away;
And when the sun went down,
They whistled and warbled a moony song
To the echoing sound of a coppery gong,
In the shade of the mountains brown.
"O Timballo! How happy we are,
When we live in a sieve and a crockery-
jar,
And all night long in the moonlight pale,
We sail away with a pea-green sail,
In the shade of the mountains brown!"
Far and few, far and few,
Are the lands where the Jumblies
live;
Their heads are green, and their
hands are blue,
And they went to sea in a Sieve.

V

They sailed to the Western Sea, they did,
To a land all covered with trees,
And they bought an Owl, and a useful
Cart,
And a pound of Rice, and a Cranberry
Tart,
And a hive of silvery Bees.
And they bought a Pig, and some green
Jack-daws,
And a lovely Monkey with lollipop paws,
And forty bottles of Ring-Bo-Ree,
And no end of Stilton Cheese.
Far and few, far and few,
Are the lands where the Jumblies
live;
Their heads are green, and their
hands are blue,
And they went to sea in a Sieve.

VI

And in twenty years they all came back,
In twenty years or more,
And every one said, "How tall they've grown!
For they've been to the Lakes, and the Terrible Zone,
And the hills of the Chankly Bore;"
And they drank their health, and gave them a feast
Of dumplings made of beautiful yeast;
And every one said, "If we only live,
We too will go to sea in a Sieve,—
To the hills of the Chankly Bore!"
Far and few, far and few,
Are the lands where the Jumblies live;
Their heads are green, and their hands are blue,
And they went to sea in a Sieve.

The Pobble who has no Toes

I

THE Pobble who has no toes
Had once as many as we;
When they said, "Some day you may lose them all;"—
He replied,—"Fish fiddle de-dee!"
And his Aunt Jobiska made him drink
Lavender water tinged with pink,
For she said, "The World in general knows
"There's nothing so good for a Pobble's toes!"

II

The Pobble who has no toes,
Swam across the Bristol Channel;
But before he set out he wrapped his nose,
In a piece of scarlet flannel.
For his Aunt Jobiska said, "No harm
"Can come to his toes if his nose is warm;
"And it's perfectly known that a Pobble's toes
"Are safe,—provided he minds his nose."

III

The Pobble swam fast and well,
And when boats or ships came near him
He tinkledy-binkledy-winkled a bell,
So that all the world could hear him.
And all the Sailors and Admirals cried,
When they saw him nearing the further side,—
"He has gone to fish, for his Aunt Jobiska's
"Runcible Cat with crimson whiskers!"

IV

But before he touched the shore,
The shore of the Bristol Channel,
A sea-green Porpoise carried away
His wrapper of scarlet flannel.
And when he came to observe his feet,
Formerly garnished with toes so neat,
His face at once became forlorn
On perceiving that all his toes were gone!

V

And nobody ever knew
From that dark day to the present,
Whoso had taken the Pobble's toes,
In a manner so far from pleasant.
Whether the shrimps or crawfish gray,
Or crafty Mermaids stole them away—
Nobody knew; and nobody knows
How the Pobble was robbed of his twice five toes!

VI

The Pobble who has no toes
Was placed in a friendly Bark,
And they rowed him back, and carried him up,
To his Aunt Jobiska's Park.
And she made him a feast at his earnest wish
Of eggs and buttercups fried with fish;—
And she said,—"It's a fact the whole world knows,
"That Pobbles are happier without their toes."

JAMES ANTHONY FROUDE (1818-1894)

From THE HISTORY OF ENGLAND FROM THE FALL OF WOLSEY TO THE DEATH OF ELIZABETH

The Coronation of Anne Boleyn

IN anticipation of the timely close of the proceedings at Dunstable, notice had been given in the city early in May, that preparations should be made for the coronation on the first of the following month. Queen Anne was at Greenwich, but, according to custom, the few preceding days were to be spent at the Tower; and on the 19th of May she was conducted thither in state by the lord mayor and the city companies, with one of those splendid exhibitions upon the water which in the days when the silver Thames deserved its name, and the sun could shine down upon it out of the blue summer sky, were spectacles scarcely rivalled in gorgeousness by the world-famous wedding of the Adriatic. The river was crowded with boats; the banks and the ships in the pool swarmed with people; and fifty great barges formed the procession, all blazing with gold and banners. The queen herself was in her own barge, close to that of the lord mayor; and, in keeping with the fantastic genius of the time, she was preceded up the water by "a foyst or wafter full of ordnance, in which was a great dragon continually moving and casting wildfire, and round about the foyst stood terrible monsters and wild men, casting fire and making hideous noise." So, with trumpets blowing, cannon pealing, the Tower guns answering the guns of the ships, in a blaze of fireworks and splendour, Anne Boleyn was borne along to the great archway of the Tower, where the king was waiting on the stairs to receive her.

And now let us suppose eleven days to have elapsed, the welcome news to have arrived at length from Dunstable, and the fair summer morning of life dawning in treacherous beauty after the long night of expectation. No bridal ceremonial had been possible; the marriage had been huddled over like a stolen love-match, and the marriage feast had been eaten in vexation and disappointment. These past mortifications were to be atoned for by a coronation pageant which the art and the wealth of the richest city in Europe should be poured out in the most lavish profusion to adorn.

On the morning of the 31st of May, the families of the London citizens were stirring early in all houses. From Temple Bar to the Tower, the streets were fresh strewed with gravel, the footpaths were railed off along the whole distance, and occupied on one side by the guilds, their workmen, and apprentices, on the other by the city constables and officials in their gaudy uniforms, "with their staves in hand for to cause the people to keep good room and order." Cornhill and Gracechurch-street had dressed their fronts in scarlet and crimson, in arras and tapestry, and the rich carpet-work from Persia and the East. Cheapside, to outshine her rivals, was draped even more splendidly in cloth of gold, and tissue, and velvet. The sheriffs were pacing up and down on their great Flemish horses, hung with liveries, and all the windows were thronged with ladies crowding to see the procession pass. At length the Tower guns opened, the grim gates rolled back, and under the archway in the bright May sunshine, the long column began slowly to defile. Two states only permitted their representatives to grace the scene with their presence—Venice and France. It was, perhaps, to make the most of this isolated countenance, that the French ambassador's train formed the van of the cavalcade. Twelve French knights came riding foremost in surcoats of blue velvet with sleeves of yellow silk, their horses trapped in blue, with white crosses powdered on their hanging. After them followed a troop of English gentlemen, two and two, and then the Knights of the Bath, "in gowns of violet, with hoods purfled with miniver like doctors." Next, perhaps at a little interval, the abbots passed on, mitred in their robes; the barons followed in crimson velvet, the bishops then, and then the earls and marquises, the dresses of each order increasing in elaborate gorgeousness. All these rode on in pairs. Then came alone Audeley, lord-chancellor, and behind him the Venetian ambassador and the Archbishop of York; the Archbishop of Canterbury, and Du Bellay, Bishop of Bayonne and of Paris, not now with bugle and hunting-frock, but solemn with stole and crozier. Next, the lord mayor, with the city mace in hand, and Garter in his coat of arms; and then Lord William Howard—Belted Will Howard, of the Scottish Border, Marshal of England. The officers of the queen's household succeeded the marshal in scarlet and gold, and the van of the procession was closed by the Duke of Suffolk, as high constable, with his silver wand. It is no easy matter to picture to ourselves the blazing trail of splendour which in such a pageant must have drawn along the London streets,—those streets which now we know so black and smoke-grimed, themselves then radiant with masses of colour, gold, and crimson, and violet. Yet there it was, and there the sun could shine upon it, and tens of thousands of eyes were gazing on the scene out of the crowded lattices.

Glorious as the spectacle was, perhaps however, it passed unheeded.

Those eyes were watching all for another object, which now drew near. In an open space behind the constable there was seen approaching "a white chariot," drawn by two palfreys in white damask which swept the ground, a golden canopy borne above it making music with silver bells: and in the chariot sat the observed of all observers, the beautiful occasion of all this glittering homage; fortune's plaything of the hour, the Queen of England—queen at last—borne along upon the waves of this sea of glory, breathing the perfumed incense of greatness which she had risked her fair name, her delicacy, her honour, her self-respect, to win; and she had won it.

There she sate, dressed in white tissue robes, her fair hair flowing loose over her shoulders, and her temples circled with a light coronet of gold and diamonds—most beautiful—loveliest—most favoured perhaps, as she seemed at that hour, of all England's daughters. Alas! "within the hollow round" of that coronet—

Kept death his court, and there the antick sate,
Scoffing her state and grinning at her pomp.
Allowing her a little breath, a little scene
To monarchize, be feared, and kill with looks,
Infusing her with self and vain conceit,
As if the flesh which walled about her life
Were brass impregnable; and humoured thus,
Bored through her castle walls; and farewell, Queen.

Fatal gift of greatness! so dangerous ever! so more than dangerous in those tremendous times when the fountains are broken loose of the great deeps of thought; and nations are in the throes of revolution;—when ancient order and law and tradition are splitting in the social earthquake; and as the opposing forces wrestle to and fro, those unhappy ones who stand out above the crowd become the symbols of the struggle, and fall the victims of its alternating fortunes. And what if into an unsteady heart and brain, intoxicated with splendour, the outward chaos should find its way, converting the poor silly soul into an image of the same confusion,—if conscience should be deposed from her high place, and the Pandora box be broken loose of passions and sensualities and follies; and at length there be nothing left of all which man or woman ought to value, save hope of God's forgiveness.

Three short years have yet to pass, and again, on a summer morning, Queen Anne Boleyn will leave the Tower of London,—not radiant then with beauty on a gay errand of coronation, but a poor wandering ghost, on a sad tragic errand, from which she will never more return, passing away out of an earth where she may stay no longer, into a presence where, nevertheless, we know that all is well—for all of us—and therefore for her.

But let us not cloud her shortlived sunshine with the shadow of the future. She went on in her loveliness, the peeresses following in their carriages, with the royal guard in their rear. In Fenchurch-street she was met by the children of the city schools; and at the corner of Gracechurch-street a masterpiece had been prepared of the pseudo-classic art, then so fashionable, by the merchants of the Styllyard. A Mount Parnassus had been constructed, and a Helicon fountain upon it playing into a basin with four jets of Rhenish wine. On the top of the mountain sat Apollo with Calliope at his feet, and on either side the remaining Muses, holding lutes or harps, and singing each of them some "posy" or epigram in praise of the queen, which was presented, after it had been sung, written in letters of gold.

From Gracechurch-street the procession passed to Leadenhall, where there was a spectacle in better taste, of the old English Catholic kind, quaint perhaps and forced, but truly and even beautifully emblematic. There was again a "little mountain," which was hung with red and white roses; a gold ring was placed on the summit, on which, as the queen appeared, a white falcon was made to "descend as out of the sky,"—"and then incontinent came down an angel with great melody, and set a close crown of gold upon the falcon's head; and in the same pageant sat Saint Anne with all her issue beneath her; and Mary Cleophas with her four children, of the which children one made a goodly oration to the queen, of the fruitfulness of Saint Anne, trusting that like fruit should come of her."

With such "pretty conceits," at that time the honest tokens of an English welcome, the new queen was received by the citizens of London. These scenes must be multiplied by the number of the streets, where some fresh fancy met her at every turn. To preserve the festivities from flagging, every fountain and conduit within the walls ran all day with wine; the bells of every steeple were ringing; children lay in wait with songs, and ladies with posies, in which all the resources of fantastic extravagance were exhausted; and thus in an unbroken triumph—and to outward appearance received with the warmest affection—she passed under Temple Bar, down the Strand by Charing Cross to Westminster Hall. The king was not with her throughout the day; nor did he intend to be with her in any part of the ceremony. She was to reign without a rival, the undisputed sovereign of the hour.

Saturday being passed in showing herself to the people, she retired for the night to "the king's manour house at Westminster," where she slept. On the following morning, between eight and nine o'clock, she returned to the hall, where the lord mayor, the city council, and the peers were again assembled, and took her place on the high dais at the top of the stairs under the cloth of state; while the bishops, the abbots, and the monks of the abbey formed in the area. A railed way had been laid with carpets across Palace Yard and the Sanctuary to the abbey gates, and when all was ready, preceded by the peers in their robes of parliament, the Knights of the Garter in the dress of the order, she swept out under her canopy, the bishops and the monks "solemnly singing." The train was borne by the old Duchess of Norfolk her aunt, the Bishops of London and Winchester on either side "bearing up the lappets of her robe." The Earl of Oxford carried the crown on its cushion immediately before her. She was dressed in purple velvet furred with ermine, her hair escaping loose, as she usually wore it, under a wreath of diamonds.

On entering the abbey, she was led to the coronation chair, where she sat while the train fell into their places, and the preliminaries of the ceremonial were despatched. Then she was conducted up to the high altar, and anointed Queen of England, and she received from the hands of Cranmer, fresh come in haste from Dunstable, with the last words of his sentence upon Catherine scarcely silent upon his lips, the golden sceptre, and St. Edward's crown.

Did any twinge of remorse, any pang of painful recollection, pierce at that moment the incense of glory which she was inhaling? Did any vision flit across her of a sad mourning figure which once had stood where she was standing, now desolate, neglected, sinking into the darkening twilight of a life cut short by sorrow? Who can tell? At such a time, that figure would have weighed heavily upon a noble mind, and a wise mind would have been taught by the thought of it, that, although life be fleeting as a dream, it is long enough to experience strange vicissitudes of fortune. But Anne Boleyn was not noble and was not wise, —too probably she felt nothing but the delicious, all-absorbing, all-intoxicating present; and if that plain, suffering face presented itself to her memory at all, we may fear that it was rather as a foil to her own surpassing loveliness. Two years later she was able to exult over Catherine's death; she is not likely to have thought of her with gentler feelings in the first glow and flush of triumph.

The Execution of Mary, Queen of Scots

HER last night was a busy one. As she said herself there was much to be done and the time was short. A few lines to the King of France were dated two hours after midnight. They were to insist for the last time that she was innocent of the conspiracy, that she was dying for religion, and for having asserted her right to the crown; and to beg that out of the sum which he owed her, her servants' wages might be paid, and masses provided for her soul. After this she slept for three or four hours, and then rose and with the most elaborate care prepared to encounter the end.

At eight in the morning the Provost-marshal knocked at the outer door which communicated with her suite of apartments. It was locked and no one answered, and he went back in some trepidation lest the fears prove true which had been entertained the preceding evening. On his returning with the Sheriff, however, a few minutes later, the door was open, and they were confronted with the tall majestic figure of Mary Stuart standing before them in splendour. The plain grey dress had been exchanged for a robe of black satin; her jacket was of black satin also, looped and slashed and trimmed with velvet. Her false hair was arranged studiously with a coif, and over her head and falling down over her back was a white veil of delicate lawn. A crucifix of gold hung from her neck. In her hand she held a crucifix of ivory, and a number of jewelled Paternosters was attached to her girdle. Led by two of Paulet's gentlemen, the Sheriff walking before her, she passed to the chamber of presence in which she had been tried, where Shrewsbury, Kent, Paulet, Drury and others were waiting to receive her. Andrew Melville, Sir Robert's brother, who had been master of her household, was kneeling in tears. "Melville," she said, "you should rather rejoice than weep that the end of my troubles is come. Tell my friends I die a true Catholic. Commend me to my son. Tell him I have done nothing to prejudice his kingdom of Scotland, and so good Melville, farewell." She kissed him, and turning asked for her chaplain Du Preau. He was not present. There had been a fear of some religious melodrama which it was thought well to avoid. Her ladies, who had attempted to follow her, had been kept back also. She could not afford to leave the account of her death to be reported by enemies and Puritans, and she required assistance for the scene which she meditated. Missing them she asked the reason of their absence, and said she wished them to see her die. Kent said he feared they might scream or faint, or attempt perhaps to dip their handkerchiefs in her blood. She undertook that they should be quiet and obedient. "The Queen," she said, "would never deny her so slight a request;" and when Kent still hesitated, she added with tears, "You know I am cousin to your Queen, of the blood of Henry the Seventh, a married Queen of France, and anointed Queen of Scotland."

It was impossible to refuse. She was allowed to take six of her own people with her, and select them herself. She chose her physician Burgoyne, Andrew Melville, the apothecary Gorion, and her surgeon, with two ladies, Elizabeth Kennedy and Curle's young wife Barbara Mowbray, whose child she had baptised.

"Allons donc," she then said—"Let us go," and passing out attended by the Earls, and leaning on the arm of an officer of the guard, she descended the great staircase to the hall. The news had spread far through the country. Thousands of people were collected outside the walls. About three hundred knights and gentlemen of the country had been admitted to witness the execution. The tables and forms had been removed, and a great wood fire was blazing in the chimney. At the upper end of the hall, above the fire-place, but near it, stood the scaffold, twelve feet square and two feet and a half high. It was covered with black cloth; a low rail ran round it covered with black cloth also, and the Sheriff's guard of halberdiers were ranged on the floor below on the four sides to keep off the crowd. On the scaffold was the block, black like the rest; a square black cushion was placed behind it, and behind the cushion a black chair; on the right were two other chairs for the Earls. The axe leant against the rail, and two masked figures stood like mutes on either side at the back. The Queen of Scots as she swept in seemed as if coming to take a part in some solemn pageant. Not a muscle of her face could be seen to quiver; she ascended the scaffold with absolute composure, looked round her smiling, and sate down. Shrewsbury and Kent followed and took their places, the Sheriff stood at her left hand, and Beale then mounted a platform and read the warrant aloud.

In all the assembly Mary Stuart appeared the person least interested in the words which were consigning her to death.

"Madam," said Lord Shrewsbury to her, when the reading was ended, "you hear what we are commanded to do."

"You will do your duty," she answered, and rose as if to kneel and pray.

The Dean of Peterborough, Dr. Fletcher, approached the rail. "Madam," he began, with a low obeisance, "the Queen's most excellent Majesty;" "Madam, the Queen's most excellent Majesty"—thrice he commenced his sentence, wanting words to pursue it. When he repeated the words a fourth time, she cut him short.

"Mr. Dean," she said, "I am a Catholic, and must die a Catholic. It is useless to attempt to move me, and your prayers will avail me but little."

"Change your opinion, Madam," he cried, his tongue being loosed at last: "repent of your sins, settle your faith in Christ, by him to be saved."

"Trouble not yourself further, Mr. Dean," she answered; "I am settled in my own faith, for which I mean to shed my blood."

"I am sorry, Madam," said Shrewsbury, "to see you so addicted to Popery."

"That image of Christ you hold there," said Kent, "will not profit you if he be not engraved in your heart."

She did not reply, and turning her back on Fletcher knelt for her own devotions.

He had been evidently instructed to impair the Catholic complexion of the scene, and the Queen of Scots was determined that he should not succeed. When she knelt he commenced an extempore prayer in which the assembly joined. As his voice sounded out in the hall she raised her own, reciting with powerful deep-chested tones the penitential Psalms in Latin, introducing English sentences at intervals, that the audience might know what she was saying, and praying with especial distinctness for her holy father the Pope.

From time to time, with conspicuous vehemence, she struck the crucifix against her bosom, and then, as the Dean gave up the struggle, leaving her Latin, she prayed in English wholly, still clear and loud. She prayed for the Church which she had been ready to betray, for her son, whom she had disinherited, for the Queen whom she had endeavoured to murder. She prayed God to avert his wrath from England, that England which she had sent a last message to Philip to beseech him to invade. She forgave her enemies, whom she had invited Philip not to forget, and then, praying to the saints to intercede for her with Christ, and kissing the crucifix and crossing her own breast, "Even as thy arms, O Jesus," she cried, "were spread upon the cross, so receive me into thy mercy and forgive my sins."

With these words she rose; the black mutes stepped forward, and in the usual form begged her forgiveness.

"I forgive you," she said, "for now I hope you shall end all my troubles." They offered their help in arranging her dress. "Truly, my lords," she said with a smile to the Earls, "I never had such grooms waiting on me before." Her ladies were allowed to come up upon the scaffold to assist her; for the work to be done was considerable, and had been prepared with no common thought.

She laid her crucifix on her chair. The chief executioner took it as a perquisite, but was ordered instantly to lay it down. The lawn veil was lifted carefully off, not to disturb the hair, and was hung upon the rail. The black robe was next removed. Below it was a petticoat of crimson velvet. The black jacket followed, and under the jacket was a body of crimson satin. One of her ladies handed her a pair of crimson sleeves, with which she hastily covered her arms; and thus she stood on the black scaffold with the black figures all around her, blood-red from head to foot.

Her reasons for adopting so extraordinary a costume must be left to conjecture. It is only certain that it must have been carefully studied, and that the pictorial effect must have been appalling.

The women, whose firmness had hitherto borne the trial, began now to give way, spasmodic sobs bursting from them which they could not check. "Ne criez vous," she said, "j'ay promis pour vous." Struggling bravely, they crossed their breasts again and again, she crossing them in turn and bidding them pray for her. Then she knelt on the cushion. Barbara Mowbray bound her eyes with a handkerchief. "Adieu," she said, smiling for the last time and waving her hand to them, "Adieu, au revoir." They stepped back from off the scaffold and left her alone. On her knees she repeated the Psalm, In te, Domine, confido, "In thee, O Lord, have I put my trust." Her shoulders being exposed, two scars became visible, one on either side, and the Earls being now a little behind her, Kent pointed to them with his white wand and looked enquiringly at his companion. Shrewsbury whispered that they were the remains of two abscesses from which she had suffered while living with him at Sheffield.

When the psalm was finished she felt for the block, and laying down her head muttered: "In manus, Domine tuas, commendo animam meam." The hard wood seemed to hurt her, for she placed her hands under her neck. The executioners gently removed them, lest they should deaden the blow, and then one of them holding her slightly, the other raised the axe and struck. The scene had been too trying even for the practised headsman of the Tower. His arm wandered. The blow fell on the knot of the handkerchief, and scarcely broke the skin. She neither spoke nor moved. He struck again, this time effectively. The head hung by a shred of skin, which he divided without withdrawing the axe; and at once a metamorphosis was witnessed, strange as was ever wrought by wand of fabled enchanter. The coif fell off and the false plaits. The laboured illusion vanished. The lady who had knelt before the block was in the maturity of grace and loveliness. The executioner, when he raised the head, as usual, to shew it to the crowd, exposed the withered features of a grizzled, wrinkled old woman.

"So perish all enemies of the Queen," said the Dean of Peterborough. A loud Amen rose over the hall. "Such end," said the Earl of Kent, rising and standing over the body, "to the Queen's and the Gospel's enemies."

EMILY JANE BRONTE (1818-1848)

Stanzas: A little while, a little while

A LITTLE while, a little while,
The weary task is put away,
And I can sing and I can smile,
Alike, while I have holiday.

Where wilt thou go, my harassed heart—
What thought, what scene invites thee now?
What spot, or near or far apart,
Has rest for thee, my weary brow?

There is a spot, 'mid barren hills,
Where winter howls, and driving rain;
But, if the dreary tempest chills,
There is a light that warms again.

The house is old, the trees are bare,
Moonless above bends twilight's dome;
But what on earth is half so dear,
So longed for, as the hearth of home?

The mute bird sitting on the stone,
The dank moss dripping from the wall,
The thorn-trees gaunt, the walks o'er-grown,
I love them, how I love them all!

Still, as I mused, the naked room,
The alien firelight died away;
And from the midst of cheerless gloom,
I passed to bright, unclouded day.

A little and a lone green lane
That opened on a common wide;
A distant, dreamy, dim blue chain
Of mountains circling every side:

A heaven so clear, an earth so calm,
So sweet, so soft, so hushed an air;
And, deepening still the dream-like charm,
Wild moor-sheep feeding everywhere.

That was the scene, I knew it well;
I knew the turfy pathway's sweep,
That, winding o'er each billowy swell,
Marked out the tracks of wandering sheep.

Even as I stood with raptured eye,
Absorbed in bliss so deep and dear,
My hour of rest had fleeted by,
And back came labour, bondage, care.

Last Lines: No coward soul is mine

No coward soul is mine,
No trembler in the world's storm-troubled sphere.
I see Heaven's glories shine,
And faith shines equal, arming me from fear.

O God within my breast,
Almighty, ever-present Deity!
Life—that in me has rest,
As I—undying Life—have power in Thee!

Vain are the thousand creeds
That move men's hearts: unutterably vain;

Worthless as withered weeds,
Or idlest froth amid the boundless main,

To waken doubt in one
Holding so fast by Thine infinity;
So surely anchored on
The steadfast rock of immortality.

With wide embracing love
Thy Spirit animates eternal years,
Pervades and broods above,
Changes, sustains, dissolves, creates, and rears.

Though earth and man were gone
And suns and universes ceased to be,
And Thou were left alone,
Every existence would exist in Thee.

There is not room for Death,
Nor atom that his might could render void:
Thou—THOU art Being and Breath,
And what THOU art may never be destroyed.

ARTHUR HUGH CLOUGH (1819-1861)

Say not the struggle nought availeth

SAY not the struggle nought availeth,
The labour and the wounds are vain,
The enemy faints not, nor faileth,
And as things have been they remain.

If hopes were dupes, fears may be liars;
It may be, in yon smoke concealed,
Your comrades chase e'en now the fliers,
And, but for you, possess the field.

For while the tired waves, vainly breaking,
Seem here no painful inch to gain,
Far back, through creeks and inlets making,
Comes silent, flooding in, the main.

And not by eastern windows only,
When daylight comes, comes in the light,
In front, the sun climbs slow, how slowly,
But westward, look, the land is bright.

MATTHEW ARNOLD (1822-1888)

The Forsaken Merman

COME, dear children, let us away;
Down and away below.
Now my brothers call from the bay;
Now the great winds shoreward blow;
Now the salt tides seaward flow;
Now the wild white horses play,
Champ and chafe and toss in the spray.
Children dear, let us away.
This way, this way!

Call her once before you go.
Call once yet.
In a voice that she will know:
"Margaret! Margaret!"
Children's voices should be dear
(Call once more) to a mother's ear;
Children's voices, wild with pain.
Surely she will come again.
Call her once and come away.
This way, this way!
"Mother dear, we cannot stay."
The wild white horses foam and fret.
Margaret! Margaret!

Come, dear children, come away down.
Call no more.
One last look at the white-wall'd town,
And the little grey church on the windy shore.
Then come down.
She will not come though you call all day.
Come away, come away.

Children dear, was it yesterday
We heard the sweet bells over the bay?
In the caverns where we lay,
Through the surf and through the swell,

The far-off sound of a silver bell?
Sand-strewn caverns, cool and deep,
Where the winds are all asleep;
Where the spent lights quiver and
gleam;
Where the salt weed sways in the
stream;
Where the sea-beasts, ranged all round,
Feed in the ooze of their pasture-
ground;
Where the sea-snakes coil and twine,
Dry their mail, and bask in the brine;
Where great whales come sailing by,
Sail and sail, with unshut eye,
Round the world for ever and aye?
When did music come this way?
Children dear, was it yesterday?

Children dear, was it yesterday
(Call yet once) that she went away?
Once she sate with you and me,
On a red gold throne in the heart of the
sea,
And the youngest sate on her knee.
She comb'd its bright hair, and she tended
it well,
When down swung the sound of the far-
off bell.
She sigh'd, she look'd up through the clear
green sea.
She said, "I must go, for my kinsfolk pray
In the little grey church on the shore
to-day.
'Twill be Easter-time in the world—ah
me!
And I lose my poor soul, Merman, here
with thee."
I said, "Go up, dear heart, through the
waves.
Say thy prayer, and come back to the kind
sea-caves."
She smiled, she went up through the
surf in the bay.
Children dear, was it yesterday?

Children dear, were we long alone?
"The sea grows stormy, the little ones
moan.
Long prayers," I said, "in the world they
say.
Come," I said, and we rose through the
surf in the bay.
We went up the beach, by the sandy down
Where the sea-stocks bloom, to the white-
wall'd town.
Through the narrow paved streets, where
all was still,
To the little grey church on the windy
hill.
From the church came a murmur of folk
at their prayers,
But we stood without in the cold-blowing
airs.
We climb'd on the graves, on the stones
worn with rains,
And we gazed up the aisle through the
small leaded panes.
She sate by the pillar; we saw her
clear:
"Margaret, hist! come quick, we are
here.
Dear heart," I said, "we are long alone.
The sea grows stormy, the little ones
moan."
But, ah! she gave me never a look,
For her eyes were seal'd to the holy book.
Loud prays the priest; shut stands the
door.
Come away, children, call no more.
Come away, come down, call no
more.

Down, down, down;
Down to the depths of the sea.
She sits at her wheel in the humming
town,
Singing most joyfully.
Hark what she sings: "O joy, O joy,
For the humming street, and the child
with its toy.
For the priest, and the bell, and the holy
well.
For the wheel where I spun,
And the blessèd light of the sun."

And so she sings her fill,
Singing most joyfully,

Till the shuttle falls from her hand,
And the whizzing wheel stands still.
She steals to the window, and looks at the sand;
And over the sand at the sea;
And her eyes are set in a stare;
And anon there breaks a sigh,
And anon there drops a tear,
From a sorrow-clouded eye,
And a heart sorrow-laden,
A long, long sigh
For the cold strange eyes of a little Mermaiden,
And the gleam of her golden hair.

Come away, away, children.
Come children, come down.
The hoarse wind blows colder;
Lights shine in the town.
She will start from her slumber
When gusts shake the door;
She will hear the winds howling,
Will hear the waves roar.
We shall see, while above us
The waves roar and whirl,
A ceiling of amber,
A pavement of pearl.
Singing, "Here came a mortal,
But faithless was she:
And alone dwell for ever
The kings of the sea."

But, children, at midnight,
When soft the winds blow;
When clear falls the moonlight;
When spring-tides are low:
When sweet airs come seaward
From heaths starr'd with broom;
And high rocks throw mildly
On the blanch'd sands a gloom:
Up the still, glistening beaches,
Up the creeks we will hie;
Over banks of bright seaweed
The ebb-tide leaves dry.
We will gaze, from the sand-hills,
At the white, sleeping town;
At the church on the hill-side—
And then come back down.
Singing, "There dwells a loved one,
But cruel is she.
She left lonely for ever
The kings of the sea."

Memorial Verses. April, 1850

(William Wordsworth, 1770-1850)

Goethe in Weimar sleeps, and Greece,
Long since, saw Byron's struggle cease.
But one such death remained to come;
The last poetic voice is dumb—
We stand to-day by Wordsworth's tomb.

When Byron's eyes were shut in death,
We bowed our head and held our breath.
He taught us little; but our soul
Had *felt* him like the thunder's roll.
With shivering heart the strife we saw
Of passion with eternal law;
And yet with reverential awe
We watched the fount of fiery life
Which served for that Titanic strife.

When Goethe's death was told, we said
Sunk, then, is Europe's sagest head.
Physician of the iron age,
Goethe has done his pilgrimage.
He took the suffering human race,
He read each wound, each weakness clear:
And struck his finger on the place,
And said: *Thou ailest here, and here!*
He looked on Europe's dying hour
Of fitful dream and feverish power;
His eye plunged down the weltering strife,
The turmoil of expiring life—
He said: *The end is everywhere,*
Art still has truth, take refuge there!
And he was happy, if to know
Causes of things, and far below
His feet to see the lurid flow
Of terror, and insane distress,
And headlong fate, be happiness.

And Wordsworth!—Ah, pale ghosts, rejoice!
For never has such soothing voice

Been to your shadowy world conveyed,
Since erst, at morn, some wandering shade
Heard the clear song of Orpheus come
Through Hades, and the mournful gloom.
Wordsworth has gone from us—and ye,
Ah, may ye feel his voice as we!
He too upon a wintery clime
Had fallen—on this iron time
Of doubts, disputes, distractions, fears.
He found us when the age had bound
Our souls in its benumbing round;
He spoke, and loosed our hearts in tears.
He laid us as we lay at birth
On the cool flowery lap of earth,
Smiles broke from us, and we had ease;
The hills were round us, and the breeze
Went o'er the sun-lit fields again;
Our foreheads felt the wind and rain.
Our youth returned; for there was shed
On spirits that had long been dead,
Spirits dried up and closely furled,
The freshness of the early world.

Ah! since dark days still bring to light
Man's prudence and man's fiery might,
Time may restore us in his course
Goethe's sage mind and Byron's force;
But where will Europe's latter hour
Again find Wordsworth's healing power?
Others will teach us how to dare,
And against fear our breast to steel;
Others will strengthen us to bear—
But who, ah! who, will make us feel?
The cloud of mortal destiny,
Others will front it fearlessly—
But who, like him, will put it by?

Keep fresh the grass upon his grave,
O Rotha, with thy living wave!
Sing him thy best! for few or none
Hears thy voice right, now he is gone.

Requiescat

STREW on her roses, roses,
  And never a spray of yew!
In quiet she reposes;
  Ah, would that I did too!

Her mirth the world required;
  She bathed it in smiles of glee,
But her heart was tired, tired,
  And now they let her be.

Her life was turning, turning,
  In mazes of heat and sound.
But for peace her soul was yearning,
  And now peace laps her round.

Her cabin'd, ample spirit,
  It flutter'd and fail'd for breath.
To-night it doth inherit
  The vasty hall of death.

The Scholar Gipsy

Go, for they call you, Shepherd, from the hill;
  Go, Shepherd, and untie the wattled cotes:
    No longer leave thy wistful flock unfed,
  Nor let thy bawling fellows rack their throats,
    Nor the cropp'd grasses shoot another head.
      But when the fields are still,
  And the tired men and dogs all gone to rest,
    And only the white sheep are sometimes seen
  Cross and recross the strips of moon-blanch'd green;
Come, Shepherd, and again begin the quest.

Here, where the reaper was at work of late,
  In this high field's dark corner, where he leaves
    His coat, his basket, and his earthen cruse,
  And in the sun all morning binds the sheaves,
    Then here, at noon, comes back his stores to use;
      Here will I sit and wait,
  While to my ear from uplands far away

The bleating of the folded flocks is borne,
With distant cries of reapers in the corn—
All the live murmur of a summer's day.

Screen'd is this nook o'er the high, half-reap'd field,
And here till sundown, Shepherd, will I be.
Through the thick corn the scarlet poppies peep,
And round green roots and yellowing stalks I see
Pale blue convolvulus in tendrils creep:
And air-swept lindens yield
Their scent, and rustle down their perfumed showers
Of bloom on the bent grass where I am laid,
And bower me from the August sun with shade;
And the eye travels down to Oxford's towers:

And near me on the grass lies Glanvil's book—
Come, let me read the oft-read tale again:
The story of that Oxford scholar poor,
Of pregnant parts and quick inventive brain,
Who, tired of knocking at Preferment's door,
One summer morn forsook
His friends, and went to learn the Gipsy lore,
And roam'd the world with that wild brotherhood,
And came, as most men deem'd, to little good,
But came to Oxford and his friends no more.

But once, years after, in the country lanes,
Two scholars, whom at college erst he knew,
Met him, and of his way of life inquired.
Whereat he answer'd that the Gipsy crew,
His mates, had arts to rule as they desired
The workings of men's brains;
And they can bind them to what thoughts they will:
"And I," he said, "the secret of their art,
When fully learn'd, will to the world impart:
But it needs Heaven-sent moments for this skill!"

This said, he left them, and return'd no more,
But rumours hung about the country-side,
That the lost Scholar long was seen to stray,
Seen by rare glimpses, pensive and tongue-tied,
In hat of antique shape, and cloak of grey,
The same the Gipsies wore.
Shepherds had met him on the Hurst in spring;
At some lone alehouse in the Berkshire moors,
On the warm ingle-bench, the smock-frock'd boors
Had found him seated at their entering,

But, 'mid their drink and clatter, he would fly:
And I myself seem half to know thy looks,
And put the shepherds, Wanderer, on thy trace;
And boys who in lone wheatfields scare the rooks
I ask if thou hast pass'd their quiet place;
Or in my boat I lie
Moor'd to the cool bank in the summer heats,

'Mid wide grass meadows which the sunshine fills,
And watch the warm green-muffled Cumnor hills,
And wonder if thou haunt'st their shy retreats.

For most, I know, thou lov'st retirèd ground.
Thee, at the ferry, Oxford riders blithe,
Returning home on summer nights, have met
Crossing the stripling Thames at Bab-lock-hithe,
Trailing in the cool stream thy fingers wet,
As the slow punt swings round:
And leaning backwards in a pensive dream,
And fostering in thy lap a heap of flowers
Pluck'd in shy fields and distant Wychwood bowers,
And thine eyes resting on the moonlit stream:

And then they land, and thou art seen no more.
Maidens who from the distant hamlets come
To dance around the Fyfield elm in May,
Oft through the darkening fields have seen thee roam,
Or cross a stile into the public way.
Oft thou hast given them store
Of flowers—the frail-leaf'd, white anemone—
Dark bluebells drench'd with dews of summer eves,
And purple orchises with spotted leaves—
But none has words she can report of thee.

And, above Godstow Bridge, when hay-time's here
In June, and many a scythe in sunshine flames,
Men who through those wide fields of breezy grass
Where black-wing'd swallows haunt the glittering Thames,
To bathe in the abandon'd lasher pass,
Have often pass'd thee near
Sitting upon the river bank o'ergrown:
Mark'd thine outlandish garb, thy figure spare,
Thy dark vague eyes, and soft abstracted air;
But, when they came from bathing, thou wert gone.

At some lone homestead in the Cumnor hills,
Where at her open door the housewife darns,
Thou hast been seen, or hanging on a gate
To watch the threshers in the mossy barns.
Children, who early range these slopes and late
For cresses from the rills,
Have known thee watching, all an April day,
The springing pastures and the feeding kine;
And mark'd thee, when the stars come out and shine,
Through the long dewy grass move slow away.

In autumn, on the skirts of Bagley Wood,
Where most the Gipsies by the turf-edged way
Pitch their smoked tents, and every bush you see
With scarlet patches tagg'd and shreds of gray,
Above the forest-ground call'd Thessaly—
The blackbird picking food
Sees thee, nor stops his meal, nor fears at all;
So often has he known thee past him stray

Rapt, twirling in thy hand a wither'd spray,
And waiting for the spark from Heaven to fall.

And once, in winter, on the causeway chill
Where home through flooded fields foot-travellers go,
Have I not pass'd thee on the wooden bridge
Wrapt in thy cloak and battling with the snow,
Thy face towards Hinksey and its wintry ridge?
And thou hast climb'd the hill
And gain'd the white brow of the Cumnor range;
Turn'd once to watch, while thick the snowflakes fall,
The line of festal light in Christ Church hall—
Then sought thy straw in some sequester'd grange.

But what—I dream! Two hundred years are flown
Since first thy story ran through Oxford halls,
And the grave Glanvil did the tale inscribe
That thou wert wander'd from the studious walls
To learn strange arts, and join a Gipsy tribe:
And thou from earth art gone
Long since, and in some quiet churchyard laid;
Some country nook, where o'er thy unknown grave
Tall grasses and white flowering nettles wave—
Under a dark red-fruited yew-tree's shade.

—No, no, thou hast not felt the lapse of hours.
For what wears out the life of mortal men?
'Tis that from change to change their being rolls:
'Tis that repeated shocks, again, again,
Exhaust the energy of strongest souls,
And numb the elastic powers.
Till having used our nerves with bliss and teen,
And tired upon a thousand schemes our wit,
To the just-pausing Genius we remit
Our worn-out life, and are—what we have been.

Thou hast not lived, why shouldst thou perish, so?
Thou hadst *one* aim, *one* business, *one* desire:
Else wert thou long since number'd with the dead—
Else hadst thou spent, like other men, thy fire.
The generations of thy peers are fled,
And we ourselves shall go;
But thou possessest an immortal lot,
And we imagine thee exempt from age
And living as thou liv'st on Glanvil's page,
Because thou hadst—what we, alas, have not!

For early didst thou leave the world, with powers
Fresh, undiverted to the world without,
Firm to their mark, not spent on other things;
Free from the sick fatigue, the languid doubt,
Which much to have tried, in much been baffled, brings.
O Life unlike to ours!
Who fluctuate idly without term or scope,
Of whom each strives, nor knows for what he strives,
And each half-lives a hundred different lives;
Who wait like thee, but not, like thee, in hope.

Thou waitest for the spark from Heaven: and we,
Vague half-believers of our casual creeds,
Who never deeply felt, nor clearly will'd,
Whose insight never has borne fruit in deeds,
Whose weak resolves never have been fulfill'd;
For whom each year we see
Breeds new beginnings, disappointments new;
Who hesitate and falter life away,
And lose to-morrow the ground won to-day—
Ah, do not we, Wanderer, await it too?

Yes, we await it, but it still delays,
And then we suffer; and amongst us One,
Who most has suffer'd, takes dejectedly
His seat upon the intellectual throne;
And all his store of sad experience he
Lays bare of wretched days;
Tells us his misery's birth and growth and signs,
And how the dying spark of hope was fed,
And how the breast was soothed, and how the head,
And all his hourly varied anodynes.

This for our wisest: and we others pine,
And wish the long unhappy dream would end,
And waive all claim to bliss, and try to bear,
With close-lipp'd Patience for our only friend,
Sad Patience, too near neighbour to Despair:
But none has hope like thine.
Thou through the fields and through the woods dost stray,
Roaming the country-side, a truant boy,
Nursing thy project in unclouded joy,
And every doubt long blown by time away.

O born in days when wits were fresh and clear,
And life ran gaily as the sparkling Thames;
Before this strange disease of modern life,
With its sick hurry, its divided aims,
Its heads o'ertax'd, its palsied hearts, was rife—
Fly hence, our contact fear!
Still fly, plunge deeper in the bowering wood!
Averse, as Dido did with gesture stern
From her false friend's approach in Hades turn,
Wave us away, and keep thy solitude.

Still nursing the unconquerable hope,
Still clutching the inviolable shade,
With a free onward impulse brushing through,
By night, the silver'd branches of the glade—
Far on the forest-skirts, where none pursue,
On some mild pastoral slope
Emerge, and resting on the moonlit pales,
Freshen thy flowers, as in former years,
With dew, or listen with enchanted ears,
From the dark dingles, to the nightingales.

But fly our paths, our feverish contact fly!
For strong the infection of our mental strife,
Which, though it gives no bliss, yet spoils for rest;
And we should win thee from thy own fair life,.

Like us distracted, and like us unblest.
Soon, soon thy cheer would die,
Thy hopes grow timorous, and unfix'd thy powers,
And thy clear aims be cross and shifting made:
And then thy glad perennial youth would fade,
Fade, and grow old at last, and die like ours.

Then fly our greetings, fly our speech and smiles!
—As some grave Tyrian trader, from the sea,
Descried at sunrise an emerging prow
Lifting the cool-hair'd creepers stealthily,
The fringes of a southward-facing brow
Among the Ægean isles;
And saw the merry Grecian coaster come,
Freighted with amber grapes, and Chian wine,
Green bursting figs, and tunnies steep'd in brine;
And knew the intruders on his ancient home,

The young light-hearted Masters of the waves;
And snatch'd his rudder, and shook out more sail,
And day and night held on indignantly
O'er the blue Midland waters with the gale,
Betwixt the Syrtes and soft Sicily,
To where the Atlantic raves
Outside the Western Straits, and unbent sails
There, where down cloudy cliffs, through sheets of foam,
Shy traffickers, the dark Iberians come;
And on the beach undid his corded bales.

Rugby Chapel—November, 1857

Coldly, sadly descends
The autumn evening. The field
Strewn with its dank yellow drifts
Of withered leaves, and the elms,
Fade into dimness apace,
Silent;—hardly a shout
From a few boys late at their play!
The lights come out in the street,
In the schoolroom windows;—but cold,
Solemn, unlighted, austere,
Through the gathering darkness, arise
The chapel-walls, in whose bound
Thou, my father! art laid.

There thou dost lie, in the gloom
Of the autumn evening. But ah!
That word *gloom* to my mind
Brings thee back in the light
Of thy radiant vigor again.
In the gloom of November we passed
Days not dark at thy side;
Seasons impaired not the ray
Of thy buoyant cheerfulness clear.
Such thou wast! and I stand
In the autumn evening, and think
Of bygone autumns with thee.

Fifteen years have gone round
Since thou arosest to tread,
In the summer-morning, the road
Of death, at a call unforeseen,
Sudden. For fifteen years,
We who till then in thy shade
Rested as under the boughs
Of a mighty oak, have endured
Sunshine and rain as we might,
Bare, unshaded, alone,
Lacking the shelter of thee.

O strong soul, by what shore
Tarriest thou now? For that force,
Surely, has not been left vain!
Somewhere, surely, afar,
In the sounding labor-house vast
Of being, is practised that strength,
Zealous, beneficent, firm!

Yes, in some far-shining sphere,
Conscious or not of the past,
Still thou performest the word
Of the Spirit in whom thou dost live,
Prompt, unwearied, as here!
Still thou upraisest with zeal
The humble good from the ground,
Sternly repressest the bad;
Still, like a trumpet, dost rouse
Those who with half-open eyes
Tread the border-land dim
'Twixt vice and virtue; reviv'st,
Succorest. This was thy work,
This was thy life upon earth.

What is the course of the life
Of mortal men on the earth?
Most men eddy about
Here and there—eat and drink,
Chatter and love and hate,
Gather and squander, are raised
Aloft, are hurled in the dust,
Striving blindly, achieving
Nothing; and then they die,—
Perish; and no one asks
Who or what they have been,
More than he asks what waves,
In the moonlit solitudes mild
Of the midmost Ocean, have swelled,
Foamed for a moment, and gone.
And there are some whom a thirst
Ardent, unquenchable, fires,
Not with the crowd to be spent,
Not without aim to go round
In an eddy of purposeless dust,
Effort unmeaning and vain.
Ah yes! some of us strive
Not without action to die
Fruitless, but something to snatch
From dull oblivion, nor all
Glut the devouring grave.
We, we have chosen our path,—
Path to a clear-purposed goal,
Path of advance; but it leads
A long, steep journey, through sunk
Gorges, o'er mountains in snow.
Cheerful, with friends, we set forth:
Then, on the height, comes the storm.
Thunder crashes from rock
To rock; the cataracts reply;
Lightnings dazzle our eyes;
Roaring torrents have breached
The track; the stream-bed descends
In the place where the wayfarer once
Planted his footstep—the spray
Boils o'er its borders! aloft,
The unseen snow-beds dislodge
Their hanging ruin. Alas,
Havoc is made in our train!
Friends who set forth at our side
Falter, are lost in the storm.
We, we only are left!
With frowning foreheads, with lips
Sternly compressed, we strain on,
On—and at nightfall at last
Come to the end of our way,
To the lonely inn 'mid the rocks;
Where the gaunt and taciturn host
Stands on the threshold, the wind
Shaking his thin white hairs,
Holds his lantern to scan
Our storm-beat figures, and asks,—
Whom in our party we bring?
Whom we have left in the snow?

Sadly we answer, We bring
Only ourselves! we lost
Sight of the rest in the storm.
Hardly ourselves we fought through,
Stripped, without friends, as we are.
Friends, companions, and train,
The avalanche swept from our side.

But thou wouldst not *alone*
Be saved, my father! *alone*
Conquer and come to thy goal,
Leaving the rest in the wild.
We were weary, and we
Fearful, and we in our march
Fain to drop down and to die.
Still thou turnedst, and still
Beckonedst the trembler, and still
Gavest the weary thy hand.
If, in the paths of the world,
Stones might have wounded thy feet,
Toil or dejection have tried

Thy spirit, of that we saw
Nothing: to us thou wast still
Cheerful, and helpful, and firm!
Therefore to thee it was given
Many to save with thyself,
And, at the end of thy day,
O faithful shepherd, to come,
Bringing thy sheep in thy hand.

And through thee I believe
In the noble and great who are gone;
Pure souls honored and blest
By former ages, who else—
Such, so soulless, so poor,
Is the race of men whom I see—
Seemed but a dream of the heart,
Seemed but a cry of desire.
Yes! I believe that there lived
Others like thee in the past,
Not like the men of the crowd
Who all around me to-day
Bluster or cringe, and make life
Hideous and arid and vile;
But souls tempered with fire,
Fervent, heroic, and good,
Helpers and friends of mankind.

Servants of God!—or sons
Shall I not call you? because
Not as servants ye knew
Your Father's innermost mind,
His who unwillingly sees
One of his little ones lost,—
Yours is the praise, if mankind
Hath not as yet in its march
Fainted and fallen and died.

See! In the rocks of the world
Marches the host of mankind,
A feeble, wavering line.
Where are they tending? A God
Marshalled them, gave them their goal.
Ah, but the way is so long!
Years have they been in the wild:
Sore thirst plagues them; the rocks,
Rising all round, overawe;
Factions divide them; their host
Threatens to break, to dissolve.
—Ah! keep, keep them combined!
Else, of the myriads who fill
That army, not one shall arrive;
Sole they shall stray; in the rocks
Stagger forever in vain,
Die one by one in the waste.

Then, in such hour of need
Of your fainting, dispirited race,
Ye like angels appear,
Radiant with ardor divine.
Beacons of hope, ye appear!
Languor is not in your heart,
Weakness is not in your word,
Weariness not on your brow.
Ye alight in our van! at your voice,
Panic, despair, flee away.
Ye move through the ranks, recall
The stragglers, refresh the outworn,
Praise, re-inspire the brave.
Order, courage, return;
Eyes rekindling, and prayers,
Follow your steps as ye go.
Ye fill up the gaps in our files,
Strengthen the wavering line,
Stablish, continue our march,
On, to the bound of the waste,
On to the City of God.

Thyrsis

A MONODY, *to commemorate the author's friend,* ARTHUR HUGH CLOUGH, *who died at Florence,* 1861.

How changed is here each spot man makes or fills!
In the two Hinkseys nothing keeps the same;
The village street its haunted mansion lacks,
And from the sign is gone Sibylla's name,
And from the roofs the twisted chimney-stacks—
Are ye too changed, ye hills?
See, 'tis no foot of unfamiliar men
To-night from Oxford up your pathway strays!

Here came I often, often, in old days—
Thyrsis and I; we still had Thyrsis then.

Runs it not here, the track by Childsworth Farm,
Past the high wood, to where the elm-tree crowns
The hill behind whose ridge the sunset flames?
The signal-elm, that looks on Ilsley Downs,
The Vale, the three lone weirs, the youthful Thames?—
This winter-eve is warm,
Humid the air! leafless, yet soft as spring,
The tender purple spray on copse and briers!
And that sweet city with her dreaming spires,
She needs not June for beauty's heightening,

Lovely all times she lies, lovely to-night!—
Only, methinks, some loss of habit's power
Befalls me wandering through this upland dim.
Once pass'd I blindfold here, at any hour;
Now seldom come I, since I came with him.
That single elm-tree bright
Against the west—I miss it! is it gone?
We prized it dearly; while it stood, we said,
Our friend, the Gipsy Scholar, was not dead;
While the tree lived, he in these fields lived on.

Too rare, too rare, grow now my visits here,
But once I knew each field, each flower, each stick;
And with the country-folk acquaintance made
By barn in threshing-time, by new-built rick.
Here, too, our shepherd-pipes we first assay'd.
Ah me! this many a year
My pipe is lost, my shepherd's holiday!
Needs must I lose them, needs with heavy heart
Into the world and wave of men depart;
But Thyrsis of his own will went away.

It irk'd him to be here, he could not rest.
He loved each simple joy the country yields,
He loved his mates; but yet he could not keep,
For that a shadow lour'd on the fields,
Here with the shepherds and the silly sheep.
Some life of men unblest
He knew, which made him droop, and fill'd his head.
He went; his piping took a troubled sound
Of storms that rage outside our happy ground;
He could not wait their passing, he is dead.

So, some tempestuous morn in early June,
When the year's primal burst of bloom is o'er,
Before the roses and the longest day—
When garden-walks and all the grassy floor
With blossoms red and white of fallen May
And chestnut-flowers are strewn—
So have I heard the cuckoo's parting cry,
From the wet field, through the vext garden-trees,
Come with the volleying rain and tossing breeze:
The bloom is gone, and with the bloom go I!

Too quick despairer, wherefore wilt thou go?
Soon will the high Midsummer pomps come on.
Soon will the musk carnations break and swell,
Soon shall we have gold-dusted snapdragon,
Sweet-William with his homely cottage-smell,
And stocks in fragrant blow;
Roses that down the alleys shine afar,
And open, jasmine-muffled lattices,
And groups under the dreaming garden-trees,
And the full moon, and the white evening-star.

He hearkens not! light comer, he is flown!
What matters it? next year he will return,
And we shall have him in the sweet spring-days,
With whitening hedges, and uncrumpling fern,
And blue-bells trembling by the forest-ways,
And scent of hay new-mown.
But Thyrsis never more we swains shall see;
See him come back, and cut a smoother reed,
And blow a strain the world at last shall heed—
For Time, not Corydon, hath conquer'd thee!

Alack, for Corydon no rival now!—
But when Sicilian shepherds lost a mate,
Some good survivor with his flute would go,
Piping a ditty sad for Bion's fate;
And cross the unpermitted ferry's flow,
And relax Pluto's brow,
And make leap up with joy the beauteous head
Of Proserpine, among whose crownèd hair
Are flowers first open'd on Sicilian air,
And flute his friend, like Orpheus, from the dead.

O easy access to the hearer's grace
When Dorian shepherds sang to Proserpine!
For she herself had trod Sicilian fields,
She knew the Dorian water's gush divine,
She knew each lily white which Enna yields,
Each rose with blushing face;
She loved the Dorian pipe, the Dorian strain.
But ah, of our poor Thames she never heard!
Her foot the Cumner cowslips never stirr'd;
And we should tease her with our plaint in vain!

Well! wind-dispersed and vain the words will be,
Yet, Thyrsis, let me give my grief its hour
In the old haunt, and find our tree-topp'd hill!
Who, if not I, for questing here hath power?
I know the wood which hides the daffodil,
I know the Fyfield tree,
I know what white, what purple fritillaries
The grassy harvest of the river-fields,
Above by Ensham, down by Sandford, yields,
And what sedged brooks are Thames's tributaries;

I know these slopes; who knows them if not I?—
But many a dingle on the loved hill-side,
With thorns once studded, old, white-blossom'd trees,

Where thick the cowslips grew, and far descried
High tower'd the spikes of purple orchises,
Hath since our day put by
The coronals of that forgotten time;
Down each green bank hath gone the ploughboy's team,
And only in the hidden brookside gleam
Primroses, orphans of the flowery prime.

Where is the girl, who by the boatman's door,
Above the locks, above the boating throng,
Unmoor'd our skiff when through the Wytham flats,
Red loosestrife and blond meadow-sweet among
And darting swallows and light water-gnats,
We track'd the shy Thames shore?
Where are the mowers, who, as the tiny swell
Of our boat passing heaved the river-grass,
Stood with suspended scythe to see us pass?—
They all are gone, and thou art gone as well!

Yes, thou art gone! and round me too the night
In ever-nearing circle weaves her shade.
I see her veil draw soft across the day,
I feel her slowly chilling breath invade
The cheek grown thin, the brown hair sprent with grey;
I feel her finger light
Laid pausefully upon life's headlong train;—
The foot less prompt to meet the morning dew,
The heart less bounding at emotion new,
And hope, once crush'd, less quick to spring again.

And long the way appears, which seem'd so short
To the less practised eye of sanguine youth;
And high the mountain-tops, in cloudy air,
The mountain-tops where is the throne of Truth,
Tops in life's morning-sun so bright and bare!
Unbreachable the fort
Of the long-batter'd world uplifts its wall;
And strange and vain the earthly turmoil grows,
And near and real the charm of thy repose,
And night as welcome as a friend would fall.

But hush! the upland hath a sudden loss
Of quiet!—Look, adown the dusk hill-side,
A troop of Oxford hunters going home,
As in old days, jovial and talking, ride!
From hunting with the Berkshire hounds they come.
Quick! let me fly, and cross
Into yon farther field!—'Tis done; and see,
Back'd by the sunset, which doth glorify
The orange and pale violet evening-sky,
Bare on its lonely ridge, the Tree! the Tree!

I take the omen! Eve lets down her veil,
The white fog creeps from bush to bush about,
The west unflushes, the high stars grow bright,

And in the scatter'd farms the lights
come out.
I cannot reach the signal-tree to-
night,
Yet, happy omen, hail!
Hear it from thy broad lucent Arno-
vale
(For there thine earth-forgetting
eyelids keep
The morningless and unawakening
sleep
Under the flowery oleanders pale),

Hear it, O Thyrsis, still our tree is
there!—
Ah, vain! These English fields, this
upland dim,
These brambles pale with mist en-
garlanded,
That lone, sky-pointing tree, are not
for him;
To a boon southern country he is fled,
And now in happier air,
Wandering with the great Mother's
train divine
(And purer or more subtle soul than
thee,
I trow, the mighty Mother doth not
see)
Within a folding of the Apennine,

Thou hearest the immortal chants of
old!—
Putting his sickle to the perilous grain
In the hot cornfield of the Phrygian
king,
For thee the Lityerses-song again
Young Daphnis with his silver voice
doth sing;
Sings his Sicilian fold,
His sheep, his hapless love, his blinded
eyes—
And how a call celestial round him
rang,
And heavenward from the fountain-
brink he sprang,
And all the marvel of the golden skies.

There thou art gone, and me thou leavest
here
Sole in these fields! yet will I not
despair.
Despair I will not, while I yet descry
'Neath the mild canopy of English air
That lonely tree against the western
sky.
Still, still these slopes, 'tis clear,
Our Gipsy Scholar haunts, outliving
thee!
Fields where soft sheep from cages
pull the hay,
Woods with anemones in flower till
May,
Know him a wanderer still; then why
not me?

A fugitive and gracious light he seeks,
Shy to illumine; and I seek it too.
This does not come with houses or
with gold,
With place, with honour, and a flat-
tering crew;
'Tis not in the world's market bought
and sold—
But the smooth-slipping weeks
Drop by, and leave its seeker still un-
tired;
Out of the heed of mortals he is gone,
He wends unfollow'd, he must house
alone;
Yet on he fares, by his own heart in-
spired.

Thou too, O Thyrsis, on like quest wast
bound;
Thou wanderedst with me for a little
hour!
Men gave thee nothing; but this
happy quest,
If men esteem'd thee feeble, gave thee
power,
If men procured thee trouble, gave
thee rest.
And this rude Cumner ground,
Its fir-topped Hurst, its farms, its quiet
fields,

Here cam'st thou in thy jocund youthful time,
Here was thine height of strength, thy golden prime!
And still the haunt beloved a virtue yields.

What though the music of thy rustic flute
Kept not for long its happy, country tone;
Lost it too soon, and learnt a stormy note
Of men contention-tost, of men who groan,
Which task'd thy pipe too sore, and tired thy throat—
It fail'd, and thou wast mute!
Yet hadst thou alway visions of our light,
And long with men of care thou couldst not stay,
And soon thy foot resumed its wandering way,
Left human haunt, and on alone till night.

Too rare, too rare, grow now my visits here!
'Mid city-noise, not, as with thee of yore,
Thyrsis! in reach of sheep-bells is my home.
—Then through the great town's harsh, heart-wearying roar,
Let in thy voice a whisper often come,
To chase fatigue and fear:
Why faintest thou? I wander'd till I died.
Roam on! The light we sought is shining still.
Dost thou ask proof? Our tree yet crowns the hill,
Our Scholar travels yet the loved hill-side.

Dover Beach

THE sea is calm to-night,
The tide is full, the moon lies fair
Upon the straits;—on the French coast the light
Gleams and is gone; the cliffs of England stand,
Glimmering and vast, out in the tranquil bay.
Come to the window, sweet is the night-air!
Only, from the long line of spray
Where the sea meets the moon-blanch'd land,
Listen! you hear the grating roar
Of pebbles which the waves draw back, and fling,
At their return, up the high strand,
Begin, and cease, and then again begin,
With tremulous cadence slow, and bring
The eternal note of sadness in.

Sophocles long ago
Heard it on the Ægean, and it brought
Into his mind the turbid ebb and flow
Of human misery; we
Find also in the sound a thought,
Hearing it by this distant northern sea.

The Sea of Faith
Was once, too, at the full, and round earth's shore
Lay like the folds of a bright girdle furl'd.
But now I only hear
Its melancholy, long, withdrawing roar,
Retreating, to the breath
Of the night-wind, down the vast edges drear
And naked shingles of the world.

Ah, love, let us be true
To one another! for the world, which seems
To lie before us like a land of dreams,
So various, so beautiful, so new,
Hath really neither joy, nor love, nor light,
Nor certitude, nor peace, nor help for pain;
And we are here as on a darkling plain
Swept with confused alarms of struggle and flight,
Where ignorant armies clash by night.

DANTE GABRIEL ROSSETTI
(1828-1882)

The Blessed Damozel

The blessed damozel leaned out
From the gold bar of Heaven;
Her eyes were deeper than the depth
Of waters stilled at even;
She had three lilies in her hand,
And the stars in her hair were seven.

Her robe, ungirt from clasp to hem,
No wrought flowers did adorn,
But a white rose of Mary's gift,
For service meetly worn;
Her hair that lay along her back
Was yellow like ripe corn.

Her seemed she scarce had been a day
One of God's choristers;
The wonder was not yet quite gone
From that still look of hers;
Albeit, to them she left, her day
Had counted as ten years.

(To one, it is ten years of years.
. . . Yet now, and in this place,
Surely she leaned o'er me—her hair
Fell all about my face. . . .
Nothing: the autumn fall of leaves.
The whole year sets apace.)

It was the rampart of God's house
That she was standing on;
By God built over the sheer depth
The which is Space begun;
So high, that looking downward thence
She scarce could see the sun.

It lies in Heaven, across the flood
Of ether, as a bridge.
Beneath, the tides of day and night
With flame and darkness ridge
The void, as low as where this earth
Spins like a fretful midge.

Around her, lovers, newly met
'Mid deathless love's acclaims,
Spoke evermore among themselves
Their heart-remembered names;
And the souls mounting up to God
Went by her like thin flames.

And still she bowed herself and stooped
Out of the circling charm;
Until her bosom must have made
The bar she leaned on warm,
And the lilies lay as if asleep
Along her bended arm.

From the fixed place of Heaven she saw
Time like a pulse shake fierce
Through all the world. Her gaze still strove
Within the gulf to pierce
Its path; and now she spoke as when
The stars sang in their spheres.

The sun was gone now; the curled moon
Was like a little feather
Fluttering far down the gulf; and now
She spoke through the still weather.
Her voice was like the voice the stars
Had when they sang together.

(Ah sweet! Even now, in that bird's song,
Strove not her accents there,
Fain to be hearkened? When those bells
Possessed the mid-day air,
Strove not her steps to reach my side
Down all the echoing stair?)

"I wish that he were come to me,
For he will come," she said.
"Have I not prayed in Heaven?—on earth,
Lord, Lord, has he not pray'd?
Are not two prayers a perfect strength?
And shall I feel afraid?

"When round his head the aureole clings,
And he is clothed in white,
I'll take his hand and go with him
To the deep wells of light;
As unto a stream we will step down,
And bathe there in God's sight.

"We two will stand beside that shrine,
Occult, withheld, untrod,

Whose lamps are stirred continually
  With prayer sent up to God;
And see our old prayers, granted, melt
  Each like a little cloud.

"We two will lie i' the shadow of
  That living mystic tree
Within whose secret growth the Dove
  Is sometimes felt to be,
While every leaf that His plumes touch
  Saith His Name audibly.

"And I myself will teach to him,
  I myself, lying so,
The songs I sing here; which his voice
  Shall pause in, hushed and slow,
And find some knowledge at each pause,
  Or some new thing to know."

(Alas! We two, we two, thou say'st!
  Yea, one wast thou with me
That once of old. But shall God lift
  To endless unity
The soul whose likeness with thy soul
  Was but its love for thee?)

"We two," she said, "will seek the groves
  Where the lady Mary is,
With her five handmaidens, whose names
  Are five sweet symphonies,
Cecily, Gertrude, Magdalen,
  Margaret and Rosalys.

"Circlewise sit they, with bound locks
  And foreheads garlanded;
Into the fine cloth white like flame
  Weaving the golden thread,
To fashion the birth-robes for them
  Who are just born, being dead.

"He shall fear, haply, and be dumb:
  Then will I lay my cheek
To his, and tell about our love,
  Not once abashed or weak:
And the dear Mother will approve
  My pride, and let me speak.

"Herself shall bring us, hand in hand,
  To Him round whom all souls
Kneel, the clear-ranged unnumbered heads
  Bowed with their aureoles:
And angels meeting us shall sing
  To their citherns and citoles.

"There will I ask of Christ the Lord
  Thus much for him and me:—
Only to live as once on earth
  With Love, only to be,
As then awhile, forever now
  Together, I and he."

She gazed and listened and then said,
  Less sad of speech than mild,—
"All this is when he comes." She ceased.
  The light thrilled towards her, fill'd
With angels in strong level flight.
  Her eyes prayed, and she smil'd.

(I saw her smile.) But soon their path
  Was vague in distant spheres:
And then she cast her arms along
  The golden barriers,
And laid her face between her hands,
  And wept. (I heard her tears.)

Sister Helen

"WHY did you melt your waxed man,
  Sister Helen?
To-day is the third since you began."
"The time was long, yet the time ran,
  Little brother."
    (*O Mother, Mary Mother,*
Three days to-day, between Hell and Heaven!)

"But if you have done your work aright,
  Sister Helen,
You'll let me play, for you said I might."
"Be very still in your play to-night,
  Little brother."
    (*O Mother, Mary Mother,*
Third night, to-night, between Hell and Heaven!)

"You said it must melt ere vesper-bell,
  Sister Helen;
If now it be molten, all is well."

"Even so,—nay, peace! you cannot tell,
Little brother."
(*O Mother, Mary Mother,*
O what is this, between Hell and Heaven?)

"Oh the waxen knave was plump to-day,
Sister Helen;
How like dead folk he has dropped away!"
"Nay now, of the dead what can you say,
Little brother?"
(*O Mother, Mary Mother,*
What of the dead, between Hell and Heaven?)

"See, see, the sunken pile of wood,
Sister Helen,
Shines through the thinned wax red as blood!"
"Nay now, when looked you yet on blood,
Little brother?"
(*O Mother, Mary Mother,*
How pale she is, between Hell and Heaven!)

"Now close your eyes, for they're sick and sore,
Sister Helen,
And I'll play without the gallery door."
"Aye, let me rest,—I'll lie on the floor,
Little brother."
(*O Mother, Mary Mother,*
What rest to-night, between Hell and Heaven?)

"Here high up in the balcony,
Sister Helen,
The moon flies face to face with me."
"Aye, look and say whatever you see,
Little brother."
(*O Mother, Mary Mother,*
What sight to-night, between Hell and Heaven?)

"Outside it's merry in the wind's wake,
Sister Helen;
In the shaken trees the chill stars shake."
"Hush, heard you a horse-tread as you spake,
Little brother?"
(*O Mother, Mary Mother,*
What sound to-night, between Hell and Heaven?)

"I hear a horse-tread, and I see,
Sister Helen,
Three horsemen that ride terribly."
"Little brother, whence come the three,
Little brother?"
(*O Mother, Mary Mother,*
Whence should they come, between Hell and Heaven?)

"They come by the hill-verge from Boyne Bar,
Sister Helen,
And one draws nigh, but two are afar."
"Look, look, do you know them who they are,
Little brother?"
(*O Mother, Mary Mother,*
Who should they be, between Hell and Heaven?)

"Oh, it's Keith of Eastholm rides so fast,
Sister Helen,
For I know the white mane on the blast."
"The hour has come, has come at last,
Little brother!"
(*O Mother, Mary Mother,*
Her hour at last, between Hell and Heaven!)

"He has made a sign and called Halloo!
Sister Helen,
And he says that he would speak with you."
"Oh tell him I fear the frozen dew,
Little brother."
(*O Mother, Mary Mother,*
Why laughs she thus, between Hell and Heaven?)

"The wind is loud, but I hear him cry,
Sister Helen,
That Keith of Ewern's like to die."
"And he and thou, and thou and I,
Little brother."
(*O Mother, Mary Mother,*
And they and we, between Hell and Heaven!)

"For three days now he has lain abed,
Sister Helen,
And he prays in torment to be dead."
"The thing may chance, if he have prayed,
Little brother!"
(*O Mother, Mary Mother,*
If he have prayed, between Hell and
Heaven!)

"But he has not ceased to cry to-day,
Sister Helen,
That you should take your curse away."
"*My* prayer was heard,—he need but
pray,
Little brother!"
(*O Mother, Mary Mother,*
Shall God not hear, between Hell and
Heaven?)

"But he says, till you take back your ban,
Sister Helen,
His soul would pass, yet never can."
"Nay then, shall I slay a living man,
Little brother?"
(*O Mother, Mary Mother,*
A living soul, between Hell and Heaven!)

"But he calls for ever on your name,
Sister Helen,
And says that he melts before a flame."
"My heart for his pleasure fared the
same,
Little brother."
(*O Mother, Mary Mother,*
Fire at the heart, between Hell and
Heaven!)

"Here's Keith of Westholm riding fast,
Sister Helen,
For I know the white plume on the blast."
"The hour, the sweet hour I forecast,
Little brother!"
(*O Mother, Mary Mother,*
Is the hour sweet, between Hell and
Heaven?)

"He stops to speak, and he stills his horse,
Sister Helen;
But his words are drowned in the wind's
course."
"Nay hear, nay hear, you must hear per-
force,
Little brother!"
(*O Mother, Mary Mother,*
A word ill heard, between Hell and
Heaven!)

"Oh he says that Keith of Ewern's cry,
Sister Helen,
Is ever to see you ere he die."
"He sees me in earth, in moon and sky,
Little brother!"
(*O Mother, Mary Mother,*
Earth, moon and sky, between Hell and
Heaven!)

"He sends a ring and a broken coin,
Sister Helen,
And bids you mind the banks of Boyne."
"What else he broke will he ever join,
Little brother?"
(*O Mother, Mary Mother,*
Oh, never more, between Hell and
Heaven!)

"He yields you these and craves full fain,
Sister Helen,
You pardon him in his mortal pain."
"What else he took will he give again,
Little brother?"
(*O Mother, Mary Mother,*
No more, no more, between Hell and
Heaven!)

"He calls your name in an agony,
Sister Helen,
That even dead Love must weep to see."
"Hate, born of Love, is blind as he,
Little brother!"
(*O Mother, Mary Mother,*
Love turned to hate, between Hell and
Heaven!)

"Oh it's Keith of Keith now that rides
fast,
Sister Helen,
For I know the white hair on the blast."
"The short short hour will soon be past,
Little brother!"

(*O Mother, Mary Mother,*
Will soon be past, between Hell and Heaven!)

"He looks at me and he tries to speak,
Sister Helen,
But oh! his voice is sad and weak!"
"What here should the mighty Baron seek,
Little brother?"
(*O Mother, Mary Mother,*
Is this the end, between Hell and Heaven?)

"Oh his son still cries, if you forgive,
Sister Helen,
The body dies but the soul shall live."
"Fire shall forgive me as I forgive,
Little brother!"
(*O Mother, Mary Mother,*
As she forgives, between Hell and Heaven!)

"Oh he prays you, as his heart would rive,
Sister Helen,
To save his dear son's soul alive."
"Nay, flame cannot slay it, it shall thrive,
Little brother!"
(*O Mother, Mary Mother,*
Alas, alas, between Hell and Heaven!)

"He cries to you, kneeling in the road,
Sister Helen,
To go with him for the love of God!"
"The way is long to his son's abode,
Little brother."
(*O Mother, Mary Mother,*
The way is long, between Hell and Heaven!)

"O Sister Helen, you heard the bell,
Sister Helen!
More loud than the vesper-chime it fell."
"No vesper-chime, but a dying knell,
Little brother!"
(*O Mother, Mary Mother,*
His dying knell, between Hell and Heaven!)

"Alas! but I fear the heavy sound,
Sister Helen;
Is it in the sky or in the ground?"
"Say, have they turned their horses round,
Little brother?"
(*O Mother, Mary Mother,*
What would she more, between Hell and Heaven?)

"They have raised the old man from his knee,
Sister Helen,
And they ride in silence hastily."
"More fast the naked soul doth flee,
Little brother!"
(*O Mother, Mary Mother,*
The naked soul, between Hell and Heaven!)

"Oh the wind is sad in the iron chill,
Sister Helen,
And weary sad they look by the hill."
"But Keith of Ewern's sadder still,
Little brother!"
(*O Mother, Mary Mother,*
Most sad of all, between Hell and Heaven!)

"See, see, the wax has dropped from its place,
Sister Helen,
And the flames are winning up apace!"
"Yet here they burn but for a space,
Little brother!"
(*O Mother, Mary Mother,*
Here for a space, between Hell and Heaven!)

"Ah! what white thing at the door has cross'd,
Sister Helen?
Ah! what is this that sighs in the frost?"
"A soul that's lost as mine is lost,
Little brother!"
(*O Mother, Mary Mother,*
Lost, lost, all lost, between Hell and Heaven!)

GEORGE MEREDITH (1829-1882)

France. December, 1870

I

We look for her that sunlike stood
Upon the forehead of our day,
An orb of nations, radiating food
For body and for mind alway.
Where is the Shape of glad array;
The nervous hands, the front of steel,
The clarion tongue? Where is the bold
proud face?
We see a vacant place;
We hear an iron heel.

II

O she that made the brave appeal
For manhood when our time was dark,
And from our fetters drove the spark
Which was as lightning to reveal
New seasons, with the swifter play
Of pulses, and benigner day;
She that divinely shook the dead
From living man; that stretched ahead
Her resolute forefinger straight,
And marched toward the gloomy gate
Of earth's Untried, gave note, and in
The good name of Humanity
Called forth the daring vision! she,
She likewise half corrupt of sin,
Angel and Wanton! can it be?
Her star has foundered in eclipse,
The shriek of madness on her lips;
Shreds of her, and no more, we see.
There is horrible convulsion, smothered
din,
As of one that in a grave-cloth struggles
to be free.

III

Look not for spreading boughs
On the riven forest tree.
Look down where deep in blood and mire
Black thunder plants his feet and ploughs
The soil for ruin: that is France:
Still thrilling like a lyre,
Amazed to shivering discord from a fall
Sudden as that the lurid hosts recall
Who met in heaven the irreparable mis-
chance.
O that is France!
The brilliant eyes to kindle bliss,
The shrewd quick lips to laugh and kiss,
Breasts that a sighing world inspire,
And laughter-dimpled countenance
Where soul and senses caught desire!

IV

Ever invoking fire from heaven, the fire
Has grasped her, unconsumable, but
framed
For all the ecstasies of suffering dire.
Mother of Pride, her sanctuary shamed:
Mother of Delicacy, and made a mark
For outrage: Mother of Luxury, stripped
stark:
Mother of Heroes, bondsmen: through
the rains,
Across her boundaries, lo the league-long
chains!
Fond Mother of her martial youth; they
pass,
Are spectres in her sight, are mown as
grass!
Mother of Honour, and dishonoured:
Mother
Of Glory, she condemned to crown with
bays
Her victor, and be fountain of his praise.
Is there another curse? There is another:
Compassionate her madness: is she not
Mother of Reason? she that sees them
mown
Like grass, her young ones! Yea, in the
low groan
And under the fixed thunder of this hour
Which holds the animate world in one
foul blot
Tranced circumambient while relentless
Power
Breaks at her heart and claws her limbs
down-thrown,
She, with the plunging lightnings overshot,
With madness for an armour against
pain,

With milkless breasts for little ones athirst,
And round her all her noblest dying in vain,
Mother of Reason is she, trebly cursed,
To feel, to see, to justify the blow;
Chamber to chamber of her sequent brain
Gives answer of the cause of her great woe,
Inexorably echoing through the vaults,
"'Tis thus they reap in blood, in blood who sow:
This is the sum of self-absolvèd faults."
Doubt not that through her grief, with sight supreme,
Through her delirium and despair's last dream,
Through pride, through bright illusion and the brood
Bewildering of her various Motherhood,
The high strong light within her, though she bleeds,
Traces the letters of returned misdeeds.
She sees what seed long sown, ripened of late,
Bears this fierce crop; and she discerns her fate
From origin to agony, and on
As far as the wave washes long and wan
Off one disastrous impulse: for of waves
Our life is, and our deeds are pregnant graves
Blown rolling to the sunset from the dawn.

V

Ah, what a dawn of splendour, when her sowers
Went forth and bent the necks of populations,
And of their terrors and humiliations
Wove her the starry wreath that earthward lowers
Now in the figure of a burning yoke!
Her legions traversed North and South and East,
Of triumph they enjoyed the glutton's feast:
They grafted the green sprig, they lopped the oak.
They caught by the beard the tempests, by the scalp
The icy precipices, and clove sheer through
The heart of horror of the pinnacled Alp,
Emerging not as men whom mortals knew.
They were the earthquake and the hurricane,
The lightnings and the locusts, plagues of blight,
Plagues of the revel: they were Deluge rain,
And dreaded Conflagration; lawless Might.
Death writes a reeling line along the snows,
Where under frozen mists they may be tracked,
Who men and elements provoked to foes,
And Gods: they were of god and beast compact:
Abhorred of all. Yet, how they sucked the teats
Of Carnage, thirsty issue of their dam,
Whose eagles, angrier than their oriflamme,
Flushed the vext earth with blood, green earth forgets.
The gay young generations mask her grief;
Where bled her children hangs the loaded sheaf.
Forgetful is green earth; the Gods alone
Remember everlastingly: they strike
Remorselessly, and ever like for like.
By their great memories the Gods are known.

VI

They are with her now, and in her ears, and known.
'Tis they that cast her to the dust for Strength,
Their slave, to feed on her fair body's length,

That once the sweetest and the proudest shone;
Scoring for hideous dismemberment
Her limbs, as were the anguish-taking breath
Gone out of her in the insufferable descent
From her high chieftainship; as were she death,
Who hears a voice of justice, feels the knife
Of torture, drinks all ignominy of life.
They are with her, and the painful Gods might weep,
If ever rain of tears came out of heaven
To flatter Weakness and bid Conscience sleep,
Viewing the woe of this Immortal, driven
For the soul's life to drain the maddening cup
Of her own children's blood implacably:
Unsparing even as they to furrow up
The yellow land to likeness of a sea:
The bountiful fair land of vine and grain,
Of wit and grace and ardour, and strong roots,
Fruits perishable, imperishable fruits;
Furrowed to likeness of the dim grey main
Behind the black obliterating cyclone.

VII

Behold, the Gods are with her, and are known.
Whom they abandon misery persecutes
No more: them half-eyed apathy may loan
The happiness of pitiable brutes.
Whom the just Gods abandon have no light,
No ruthless light of introspective eyes
That in the midst of misery scrutinize
The heart and its iniquities outright.
They rest, they smile and rest; have earned perchance
Of ancient service quiet for a term;
Quiet of old men dropping to the worm;
And so goes out the soul. But not of France.
She cries for grief, and to the Gods she cries,
For fearfully their loosened hands chastize,
And icily they watch the rod's caress
Ravage her flesh from scourges merciless,
But she, inveterate of brain, discerns
That Pity has as little place as Joy
Among their roll of gifts; for Strength she yearns,
For Strength, her idol once, too long her toy.
Lo, Strength is of the plain root-Virtues born:
Strength shall ye gain by service, prove in scorn,
Train by endurance, by devotion shape.
Strength is not won by miracle or rape.
It is the offspring of the modest years,
The gift of sire to son, through those firm laws
Which we name Gods; which are the righteous cause,
The cause of man, and manhood's ministers.
Could France accept the fables of her priests,
Who blest her banners in this game of beasts,
And now bid hope that heaven will intercede
To violate its laws in her sore need,
She would find comfort in their opiates:
Mother of Reason! can she cheat the Fates?
Would she, the champion of the open mind,
The Omnipotent's prime gift—the gift of growth—
Consent even for a night-time to be blind,
And sink her soul on the delusive sloth,
For fruits ethereal and material, both,
In peril of her place among mankind?
The Mother of the many Laughters might

Call one poor shade of laughter in the light
Of her unwavering lamp to mark what things
The world puts faith in, careless of the truth:
What silly puppet-bodies danced on strings,
Attached by credence, we appear in sooth,
Demanding intercession, direct aid,
When the whole tragic tale hangs on a broken blade!

She swung the sword for centuries; in a day
It slipped her, like a stream cut off from source.
She struck a feeble hand, and tried to pray,
Clamoured of treachery, and had recourse
To drunken outcries in her dream that Force
Needed but hear her shouting to obey.
Was she not formed to conquer? The bright plumes
Of crested vanity shed graceful nods:
Transcendent in her foundries, Arts and looms,
Had France to fear the vengeance of the Gods?
Her faith was on her battle-roll of names
Sheathed in the records of old war; with dance
And song she thrilled her warriors and her dames,
Embracing her Dishonour: gave him France
From head to foot, France present and to come,
So she might hear the trumpet and the drum—
Bellona and Bacchante! rushing forth
On yon stout marching Schoolmen of the North.

Inveterate of brain, well knows she why
Strength failed her, faithful to himself the first:
Her dream is done, and she can read the sky,
And she can take into her heart the worst
Calamity to drug the shameful thought
Of days that made her as the man she served,
A name of terror, but a thing unnerved:
Buying the trickster, by the trickster bought,
She for dominion, he to patch a throne.

VIII

Henceforth of her the Gods are known,
Open to them her breast is laid.
Inveterate of brain, heart-valiant,
Never did fairer creature pant
Before the altar and the blade!

IX

Swift fall the blows, and men upbraid,
And friends give echo blunt and cold,
The echo of the forest to the axe.
Within her are the fires that wax
For resurrection from the mould.

X

She snatched at heaven's flame of old,
And kindled nations: she was weak:
Frail sister of her heroic prototype,
The Man; for sacrifice unripe,
She too must fill a Vulture's beak.
Deride the vanquished, and acclaim
The conqueror, who stains her fame,
Still the Gods love her, for that of high aim
Is this good France, the bleeding thing they stripe.

XI

She shall rise worthier of her prototype
Through her abasement deep; the pain that runs
From nerve to nerve some victory achieves.
They lie like circle-strewn soaked Autumn-leaves
Which stain the forest scarlet, her fair sons!

And of their death her life is: of their blood
From many streams now urging to a flood,
No more divided, France shall rise afresh.
Of them she learns the lesson of the flesh:—
The lesson writ in red since first Time ran
A hunter hunting down the beast in man:
That till the chasing out of its last vice,
The flesh was fashioned but for sacrifice.

Immortal Mother of a mortal host!
Thou suffering of the wounds that will not slay,
Wounds that bring death but take not life away!—
Stand fast and hearken while thy victors boast:
Hearken, and loathe that music evermore.
Slip loose thy garments woven of pride and shame:
The torture lurks in them, with them the blame
Shall pass to leave thee purer than before.
Undo thy jewels, thinking whence they came,
For what, and of the abominable name
Of her who in imperial beauty wore.

O Mother of a fated fleeting host
Conceived in the past days of sin, and born
Heirs of disease and arrogance and scorn,
Surrender, yield the weight of thy great ghost,
Like wings on air, to what the heavens proclaim
With trumpets from the multitudinous mounds
Where peace has filled the hearing of thy sons:
Albeit a pang of dissolution rounds
Each new discernment of the undying ones,
Do thou stoop to these graves here scattered wide
Along thy fields, as sunless billows roll;
These ashes have the lesson for the soul.
"Die to thy Vanity, and strain thy Pride,
Strip off thy Luxury: that thou may'st live,
Die to thyself," they say, "as we have died
From dear existence and the foe forgive,
Nor pray for aught save in our little space
To warn good seed to greet the fair earth's face."
O Mother! take their counsel, and so shall
The broader world breathe in on this thy home,
Light clear for thee the counter-changing dome,
Strength give thee, like an ocean's vast expanse
Off mountain cliffs, the generations all,
Not whirling in their narrow rings of foam,
But as a river forward. Soaring France!
Now is Humanity on trial in thee:
Now may'st thou gather humankind in fee:
Now prove that Reason is a quenchless scroll;
Make of calamity thine aureole,
And bleeding head us through the troubles of the sea.

CHRISTINA ROSSETTI (1830-1894)

Uphill

Does the road wind uphill all the way?
  Yes, to the very end.
Will the day's journey take the whole long day?
  From morn to night, my friend.

But is there for the night a resting-place?
  A roof for when the slow, dark hours begin.
May not the darkness hide it from my face?
  You cannot miss that inn.

Shall I meet other wayfarers at night?
  Those who have gone before.

Then must I knock, or call when just in sight?
They will not keep you waiting at that door.

Shall I find comfort, travel-sore and weak?
Of labour you shall find the sum.
Will there be beds for me and all who seek?
Yea, beds for all who come.

A Christmas Carol

THANK God, thank God, we do believe;
Thank God that this is Christmas Eve.
Even as we kneel upon this day,
Even so, the ancient legends say,
Nearly two thousand years ago
The stalled ox knelt, and even so
The ass knelt full of praise, which they
Could not express, while we can pray.
Thank God, thank God, for Christ was born
Ages ago, as on this morn.
In the snow-season undefiled
God came to earth a little child:
He put His ancient glory by
To live for us and then to die.

How shall we thank God? How shall we
Thank Him and praise Him worthily?
What will He have who loved us thus?
What presents will He take from us?
Will He take gold, or precious heap
Of gems? or shall we rather steep
The air with incense, or bring myrrh?
What man will be our messenger
To go to Him and ask His will?
Which having learned, we will fulfil
Though He choose all we most prefer:—
What man will be our messenger?

Thank God, thank God, the Man is found,
Sure-footed, knowing well the ground.
He knows the road, for this the way
He travelled once, as on this day.
He is our Messenger beside,
He is our door and path and Guide:
He also is our Offering:
He is the gift that we must bring.
Let us kneel down with one accord
And render thanks unto the Lord:
For unto us a Child is born
Upon this happy Christmas morn;
For unto us a Son is given,
Firstborn of God and Heir of Heaven.

LEWIS CARROLL (1832-1892)

From ALICE IN WONDERLAND

Down the Rabbit Hole

ALICE was beginning to get very tired of sitting by her sister on the bank, and of having nothing to do: once or twice she had peeped into the book her sister was reading, but it had no pictures or conversations in it, "and what is the use of a book," thought Alice, "without pictures or conversations?"

So she was considering, in her own mind (as well as she could, for the hot day made her feel very sleepy and stupid), whether the pleasure of making a daisy-chain would be worth the trouble of getting up and picking the daisies, when suddenly a White Rabbit with pink eyes ran close by her.

There was nothing so *very* remarkable in that; nor did Alice think it so *very* much out of the way to hear the Rabbit say to itself "Oh dear! Oh dear! I shall be too late!" (when she thought it over afterwards, it occurred to her that she ought to have wondered at this, but at the time it all seemed quite natural); but, when the Rabbit actually *took a watch out of its waistcoat-pocket,* and looked at it, and then hurried on, Alice started to her feet, for it flashed across her mind that she had never before seen a rabbit with either a waistcoat-pocket, or a watch to take out of it, and burning with curiosity, she ran across the field after it, and was just in time to see it pop down a large rabbit-hole under the hedge.

In another moment down went Alice after it, never once considering how in the world she was to get out again.

The rabbit-hole went straight on like a tunnel for some way, and then dipped suddenly down, so suddenly that Alice had not a moment to think about stopping herself before she found herself falling down what seemed to be a very deep well.

Either the well was very deep, or she fell very slowly, for she had plenty of time as she went down to look about her, and to wonder what was going to happen next. First, she tried to look down and make out what she was coming to, but it was too dark to see anything: then she looked at the sides of the well, and noticed that they were filled with cupboards and book-shelves: here and there she saw maps and pictures hung upon pegs. She took down a jar from one of the shelves as she passed: it was labeled "ORANGE MARMALADE," but to her great disappointment it was empty: she did not like to drop the jar, for fear of killing somebody underneath, so managed to put it into one of the cupboards as she fell past it.

"Well!" thought Alice to herself. "After such a fall as this, I shall think nothing of tumbling down-stairs! How brave they'll think me at home! Why, I wouldn't say anything about it, even if I fell off the top of the house!" (Which was very likely true.)

Down, down, down. Would the fall *never* come to an end? "I wonder how many miles I've fallen by this time?" she said aloud. "I must be getting somewhere near the centre of the earth. Let me see: that would be four thousand miles down, I think—" (for, you see, Alice had learnt several things of this sort in her lessons in the schoolroom, and though this was not a *very* good opportunity for showing off her knowledge, as there was no one to listen to her, still it was good practice to say it over) "—yes, that's about the right distance—but then I wonder what Latitude or Longitude I've got to?" (Alice had not the slightest idea what Latitude was, or Longitude either, but she thought they were nice grand words to say.)

Presently she began again. "I wonder if I shall fall right *through* the earth! How funny it'll seem to come out among the people that walk with their heads downwards! The antipathies, I think—" (she was rather glad there *was* no one listening, this time, as it didn't sound at all the right word) "—but I shall have to ask them what the name of the country is, you know. Please, Ma'am, is this New Zealand? Or Australia?" (and she tried to curtsey as she spoke—fancy, *curtseying* as you're falling through the air! Do you think you could manage it?) "And what an ignorant little girl she'll think me for asking! No, it'll never do to ask: perhaps I shall see it written up somewhere."

Down, down, down. There was nothing else to do, so Alice soon began talking again. "Dinah'll miss me very much to-night, I should think!" (Dinah was the cat.) "I hope they'll remember her saucer of milk at tea-time. Dinah, my dear! I wish you were down here with me! There are no mice in the air, I'm afraid, but you might catch a bat, and that's very like a mouse, you know. But do cats eat bats, I wonder?" And here Alice began to get rather sleepy, and went on saying to herself, in a dreamy sort of way, "Do cats eat bats? Do cats eat bats?" and sometimes "Do bats eat cats?", for, you see, as she couldn't answer either question, it didn't much matter which way she put it. She felt that she was dozing off, and had just begun to dream that she was walking hand in hand with Dinah, and was saying to her, very earnestly, "Now, Dinah, tell me the truth: did you ever eat a bat?", when suddenly, thump! thump! down she came upon a heap of sticks and dry leaves, and the fall was over.

Alice was not a bit hurt, and she jumped up on to her feet in a moment: she looked up, but it was all dark overhead: before her was another long passage, and the White Rabbit was still in sight, hurrying down it. There was not a moment to be lost: away went Alice like the wind, and was just in time to hear it say, as it turned a corner, "Oh my ears and whiskers, how late it's getting!" She was close behind it when she turned the corner, but the Rabbit was no longer to be seen: she found herself in a long, low hall, which was lit up by a row of lamps hanging from the roof.

There were doors all round the hall, but they were all locked; and when Alice had been all the way down one side and up the other, trying every door, she walked sadly down the middle, wondering how she was ever to get out again.

Suddenly she came upon a little three-legged table, all made of solid glass: there was nothing on it but a tiny golden key, and Alice's first idea was that this might belong to one of the doors of the hall; but, alas! either the locks were too large, or the key was too small, but at any rate it would not open any of them. However, on the second time round, she came upon a low curtain she had not noticed before, and behind it was a little door about fifteen inches high: she tried the little golden key in the lock, and to her great delight it fitted!

Alice opened the door and found that it led into a small passage, not much larger than a rat-hole: she knelt down and looked along the passage into the loveliest garden you ever saw. How she longed to get out of that dark hall, and wander about among those beds of bright flowers and those cool fountains, but she could not even get her head through the doorway; "and even if my head *would* go through," thought poor Alice, "it would be of very little use without my shoulders. Oh, how I wish I could shut up like a telescope! I think I could, if I only knew how to begin." For, you see, so many out-of-the-way things had happened lately, that Alice had begun to think that very few things indeed were really impossible.

There seemed to be no use in waiting by the little door, so she went back to the table, half hoping she might find another key on it, or at any rate a book of rules for shutting people up like telescopes: this time she found a little bottle on it ("which certainly was not here before," said Alice), and tied round the neck of the bottle was a paper label, with the words "DRINK ME" beautifully printed on it in large letters.

It was all very well to say "Drink me," but the wise little Alice was not going to do *that* in a hurry. "No, I'll look first," she said, "and see whether it's marked '*poison*' or not"; for she had read several nice little stories about children who had got burnt, and eaten up by wild beasts, and other unpleasant things, all because they *would* not remember the simple rules their friends had taught them: such as, that a red-hot poker will burn you if you hold it too long; and that, if you cut your finger *very* deeply with a knife, it usually bleeds; and she had never forgotten that, if you drink much from a bottle marked "poison," it is almost certain to disagree with you, sooner or later.

However, this bottle was *not* marked "poison," so Alice ventured to taste it, and, finding it very nice (it had, in fact, a sort of mixed flavour of cherry-tart, custard, pine-apple, roast turkey, toffy, and hot buttered toast), she very soon finished it off.

*   *   *   *   *   *
   *   *   *   *   *
*   *   *   *   *   *

"What a curious feeling!" said Alice. "I must be shutting up like a telescope!"

And so it was indeed: she was now only ten inches high, and her face brightened up at the thought that she was now the right size for going through the little door into that lovely garden. First, however, she waited for a few minutes to see if she was going to shrink any further: she felt a little nervous about this; "for it might end, you know," said Alice to herself, "in my going out altogether, like a candle. I wonder what I should be like then?" And she tried to fancy what the flame of a candle looks like after the candle is blown out, for she could not remember ever having seen such a thing.

After a while, finding that nothing more happened, she decided on going into the garden at once; but, alas for poor Alice! when she got to the door, she found she had forgotten the little golden key, and when she went back to the table for it, she found she could not possibly reach it: she could see it quite plainly through the glass, and she tried her best to climb up one of the legs of the table, but it was too slippery; and when she had tired herself out with trying, the poor little thing sat down and cried.

"Come, there's no use in crying like that!" said Alice to herself rather sharply. "I advise you to leave off this minute!" She generally gave herself very good advice (though she very seldom followed it), and sometimes she scolded herself so severely as to bring tears into her eyes; and once she remembered trying to box her own ears for having cheated herself in a game of croquet she was playing against herself, for this curious child was very fond of pretending to be two people. "But it's no use now," thought poor Alice, "to pretend to be two people! Why, there's hardly enough of me left to make *one* respectable person!"

Soon her eye fell on a little glass box that was lying under the table: she opened it, and found in it a very small cake, on which the words "EAT ME" were beautifully marked in currants. "Well, I'll eat it," said Alice, "and if it makes me grow longer, I can reach the key; and if it makes me grow smaller, I can creep under the door: so either way I'll get into the garden, and I don't care which happens!"

She ate a little bit, and said anxiously to herself "Which way? Which way?", holding her hand on the top of her head to feel which way it was growing; and she was quite surprised to find that she remained the same size. To be sure, this is what generally happens when one eats cake; but Alice had got so much into the way of expecting nothing but out-of-the-way things to happen, that it seemed quite dull and stupid for life to go on in the common way.

So she set to work, and very soon finished off the cake.

*   *   *   *   *   *
    *   *   *   *   *
*   *   *   *   *   *

The Pool of Tears

"CURIOUSER and curiouser!" cried Alice (she was so much surprised, that for the moment she quite forgot how to speak good English). "Now I'm opening out like the largest telescope that ever was! Good-bye, feet!" (for when she looked down at her feet, they seemed to be almost out of sight, they were getting so far off). "Oh, my poor little feet, I wonder who will put on your shoes and stockings for you now, dears? I'm sure *I* sha'n't be able! I shall be a great deal too far off to trouble myself about you: you must manage the best way you can—but I must be kind to them," thought Alice, "or perhaps they won't walk the way I want to go! Let me see. I'll give them a new pair of boots every Christmas."

And she went on planning to herself how she would manage it. "They must go by the carrier," she thought; "and how funny it'll seem, sending presents to one's own feet! And how odd the directions will look!

Alice's Right Foot, Esq.
Hearthrug,
near the Fender,
(with Alice's love).

Oh dear, what nonsense I'm talking!

Just at this moment her head struck against the roof of the hall: in fact she was now rather more than nine feet high, and she at once took up the little golden key and hurried off to the garden door.

Poor Alice! It was as much as she could do, lying down on one side, to look through into the garden with one eye; but to get through was more hopeless than ever: she sat down and began to cry again.

"You ought to be ashamed of yourself," said Alice, "a great girl like you," (she might well say this), "to go on crying in this way! Stop this moment, I tell you!" But she went on all the same, shedding gallons of tears, until there was a large pool all round her, about four inches deep, and reaching half down the hall.

After a time she heard a little pattering of feet in the distance, and she hastily dried her eyes to see what was coming. It was the White Rabbit returning, splendidly dressed, with a pair of white kid-gloves in one hand and a large fan in the other: he came trotting along in a great hurry, muttering to himself, as he came, "Oh! The Duchess, the Duchess! Oh! *Won't* she be savage if I've kept her waiting!" Alice felt so desperate that she was ready to ask help of any one: so, when the Rabbit came near her, she began, in a low, timid voice, "If you please, Sir——" The Rabbit started violently, dropped the white kid-gloves and the fan, and skurried away into the darkness as hard as he could go.

Alice took up the fan and gloves, and, as the hall was very hot, she kept fanning herself all the time she went on talking. "Dear, dear! How queer everything is to-day! And yesterday things went on just as usual. I wonder if I've been changed in the night? Let me think: *was* I the same when I got up this morning? I almost think I can remember feeling a little different. But if I'm not the same, the next question is 'Who in the world am I?' Ah, *that's* the great puzzle!" And she began thinking over all the children she knew that were of the same age as herself, to see if she could have been changed for any of them.

"I'm sure I'm not Ada," she said, "for her hair goes in such long ringlets, and mine doesn't go in ringlets at all; and I'm sure I can't be Mabel, for I know all sorts of things, and she, oh, she knows such a very little! Besides, *she's* she, and *I'm* I, and—oh dear, how puzzling it all is! I'll try if I know all the things I used to know. Let me see: four times five is twelve, and four times six is thirteen, and four times seven is—oh dear! I shall never get to twenty at that rate! However, the Multiplication-Table doesn't signify: let's try Geography. London is the capital of Paris, and Paris is the capital of Rome, and Rome—no, *that's* all wrong, I'm certain! I must have been changed for Mabel! I'll try and say '*How doth the little—*'," and she crossed her hands on her lap, as if she were saying lessons, and began to repeat it, but her voice sounded hoarse and strange, and the words did not come the same as they used to do:—

"How doth the little crocodile
Improve his shining tail,
And pour the waters of the Nile
On every golden scale!

"How cheerfully he seems to grin,
How neatly spreads his claws,
And welcomes little fishes in,
With gently smiling jaws!"

"I'm sure those are not the right words," said poor Alice, and her eyes filled with tears again as she went on, "I must be Mabel after all, and I shall have to go and live in that poky little house, and have next to no toys to play with, and oh, ever so many lessons to learn! No, I've made up my mind about it: if I'm Mabel, I'll stay down here! It'll be no use their putting their heads down and saying 'Come up again, dear!' I shall only look up and say 'Who am I, then? Tell me that first, and then, if I like being that person, I'll come up: if not, I'll stay down here till I'm somebody else'—but, oh dear!" cried Alice, with a sudden burst of tears, "I do wish they *would* put their heads down! I am so *very* tired of being all alone here!"

As she said this she looked down at her hands, and was surprised to see that she had put on one of the Rabbit's little white kid-gloves while she was talking. "How *can* I have done that?" she thought. "I must be growing small again." She got up and went to the table to measure herself by it, and found that, as nearly as she could guess, she was now about two feet high, and was going on shrinking rapidly: she soon found out that the cause of this was the fan she was holding, and she dropped it hastily, just in time to save herself from shrinking away altogether.

"That *was* a narrow escape!" said Alice, a good deal frightened at the sudden change, but very glad to find herself still in existence! "And now for the garden!" And she ran with all speed back to the little door; but, alas! the little door was shut again, and the little golden key was lying on the glass table as before, "and things are worse than ever," thought the poor child, "for I never was so small as this before, never! And I declare it's too bad, that it is!"

As she said these words, her foot slipped, and in another moment, splash! she was up to her chin in salt-water. Her first idea was that she had somehow fallen into the sea, "and in that case I can go back by railway," she said to herself. (Alice had been to the seaside once in her life, and had come to the general conclusion that, wherever you go to on the English coast, you find a number of bathing-machines in the sea, some children digging in the sand with wooden spades, then a row of lodging-houses, and behind them a railway-station.) However, she soon made out that she was in the pool of tears which she had wept when she was nine feet high.

"I wish I hadn't cried so much!" said Alice, as she swam about, trying to find her way out. "I shall be punished for it now, I suppose, by being drowned in my own tears! That *will* be a queer thing, to be sure! However, everything is queer to-day."

Just then she heard something splashing about in the pool a little way off, and she swam nearer to make out what it was: at first she thought it must be a walrus or hippopotamus, but then she remembered how small she was now, and she soon made out that it was only a mouse, that had slipped in like herself.

"Would it be of any use, now," thought Alice, "to speak to this mouse? Everything is so out-of-the-way down here, that I should think very likely it can talk: at any rate, there's no harm in trying." So she began: "O Mouse, do you know the way out of this pool? I am very tired of swimming about here, O Mouse!" (Alice thought this must be the right way of speaking to a mouse: she had never done such a thing before, but she remembered having seen, in her brother's Latin Grammar, "A mouse—of a mouse—to a mouse—a mouse—O mouse!" The mouse looked at her rather inquisitively, and seem to her to wink with one of its little eyes, but it said nothing.

"Perhaps it doesn't understand English," thought Alice. "I dare-say it's a French mouse, come over with William the Conqueror." (For, with all her knowledge of history, Alice had no very clear notion how long ago anything had happened.) So she began again: "Où est ma chatte?" which was the first sentence in her French lesson-book. The Mouse gave a sudden leap out of the water, and seemed to quiver all over with fright. "Oh, I beg your pardon!" cried Alice hastily, afraid that she had hurt the poor animal's feelings. "I quite forgot you didn't like cats."

"Not like cats!" cried the Mouse in a shrill, passionate voice. "Would *you* like cats, if you were me?"

"Well, perhaps not," said Alice in a soothing tone: "don't be angry about it. And yet I wish I could show you our cat Dinah. I think you'd take a fancy to cats, if you could only see her. She is such a dear quiet thing," Alice went on, half to herself, as she swam lazily about in the pool, "and she sits purring so nicely by the fire, licking her paws and washing her face—and she is such a nice soft thing to nurse—and she's such a capital one for catching mice—oh, I beg your pardon!" cried Alice again, for this time the Mouse was bristling all over, and she felt certain it must be really offended. "We won't talk about her any more, if you'd rather not."

"We, indeed!" cried the Mouse, who was trembling down to the end of its tail. "As if *I* would talk on such a subject! Our family always *hated* cats: nasty, low, vulgar things! Don't let me hear the name again!"

"I won't indeed!" said Alice, in a great hurry to change the subject of conversation. "Are you—are you fond—of—of dogs?" The Mouse did not answer, so Alice went on eagerly: "There is such a nice little dog, near the house, I should like to show you! A little bright-eyed terrier, you know, with oh, such long curly brown hair! And it'll fetch things when you throw them, and it'll sit up and beg for its dinner, and all sorts of things—I can't remember half of them—and it belongs to a farmer, you know, and he says it's so useful, it's worth a hundred pounds! He says it kills all the rats and—oh dear!" cried Alice in a sorrowful tone. "I'm afraid I've offended it again!" For the Mouse was swimming away from her as hard as it could go, and making quite a commotion in the pool as it went.

So she called softly after it, "Mouse dear! Do come back, and we won't talk about cats, or dogs either, if you don't like them!" When the Mouse heard this, it turned round and swam slowly back to her: its face was quite pale (with passion, Alice thought), and it said, in a low trembling voice, "Let us get to the shore, and then I'll tell you my history, and you'll understand why it is I hate cats and dogs."

It was high time to go, for the pool was getting quite crowded with the birds and animals that had fallen into it: there was a Duck and a Dodo, a Lory and an Eaglet, and several other curious creatures. Alice led the way, and the whole party swam to the shore.

Father William

"You are old, Father William," the young man said,
"And your hair has become very white;
And yet you incessantly stand on your head—
Do you think, at your age, it is right?"

"In my youth," Father William replied to his son,
"I feared it might injure the brain;
But, now that I'm perfectly sure I have none,
Why, I do it again and again."

"You are old," said the youth, "as I mentioned before,
And have grown most uncommonly fat;
Yet you turned a back-somersault in at the door—
Pray, what is the reason of that?"

"In my youth," said the sage, as he shook his grey locks,
"I kept all my limbs very supple
By the use of this ointment—one shilling the box—
Allow me to sell you a couple?"

"You are old," said the youth, "and your jaws are too weak
For anything tougher than suet;
Yet you finished the goose, with the bones and the beak—
Pray, how did you manage to do it?"

"In my youth," said his father, "I took to the law,
And argued each case with my wife;
And the muscular strength which it gave to my jaw
Has lasted the rest of my life."

"You are old," said the youth, "one would hardly suppose
That your eye was as steady as ever;

Yet you balanced an eel on the end of
your nose—
What made you so awfully clever?"
"I have answered three questions, and
that is enough,"
Said his father. "Don't give yourself
airs!
Do you think I can listen all day to such
stuff?
Be off, or I'll kick you down-stairs!"

The Whiting and the Snail

"WILL you walk a little faster?" said a
whiting to a snail,
"There's a porpoise close behind us, and
he's treading on my tail.
See how eagerly the lobsters and the
turtles all advance!
They are waiting on the shingle—will you
come and join the dance?
Will you, won't you, will you, won't
you, will you join the dance?
Will you, won't you, will you, won't
you, won't you join the dance?

"You can really have no notion how delightful it will be
When they take us up and throw us, with
the lobsters, out to sea!"
But the snail replied "Too far, too far!",
and gave a look askance—
Said he thanked the whiting kindly, but he
would not join the dance.
Would not, could not, would not, could
not, would not join the dance.
Would not, could not, would not, could
not, could not join the dance.

"What matters it how far we go?" his
scaly friend replied.
"There is another shore, you know, upon
the other side.
The further off from England the nearer
is to France—
Then turn not pale, beloved snail, but
come and join the dance.
Will you, won't you, will you, won't
you, will you join the dance?
Will you, won't you, will you, won't
you, won't you join the dance?"

From THROUGH THE LOOKING-GLASS

Jabberwocky

'TWAS brillig, and the slithy toves
Did gyre and gimble in the wabe:
All mimsy were the borogoves,
And the mome raths outgrabe.

"Beware the Jabberwock, my son!
The jaws that bite, the claws that
catch!
Beware the Jubjub bird, and shun
The frumious Bandersnatch!"

He took his vorpal sword in hand:
Long time the manxome foe he
sought—
So rested he by the Tumtum tree,
And stood awhile in thought.

And, as in uffish thought he stood,
The Jabberwock, with eyes of flame,
Came whiffling through the tulgey
wood,
And burbled as it came!

One, two! One, two! And through and
through
The vorpal blade went snicker-
snack!
He left it dead, and with its head
He went galumphing back.

"And hast thou slain the Jabberwock?
Come to my arms, my beamish boy!
O frabjous day! Callooh! Callay!"
He chortled in his joy.

'Twas brillig, and the slithy toves
Did gyre and gimble in the wabe:
All mimsy were the borogoves,
And the mome raths outgrabe.

The Walrus and the Carpenter

The sun was shining on the sea,
Shining with all his might:
He did his very best to make
The billows smooth and bright—
And this was odd, because it was
The middle of the night.

The moon was shining sulkily,
Because she thought the sun
Had got no business to be there
After the day was done—
"It's very rude of him," she said,
To come and spoil the fun!"

The sea was wet as wet could be,
The sands were dry as dry.
You could not see a cloud, because
No cloud was in the sky:
No birds were flying overhead—
There were no birds to fly.

The Walrus and the Carpenter
Were walking close at hand:
They wept like anything to see
Such quantities of sand:
"If this were only cleared away,"
They said, it *would* be grand!"

"If seven maids with seven mops
Swept it for half a year,
Do you suppose," the Walrus said,
"That they could get it clear?"
"I doubt it," said the Carpenter,
And shed a bitter tear.

"O Oysters, come and walk with us!"
The Walrus did beseech.
"A pleasant walk, a pleasant talk,
Along the briny beach:
We cannot do with more than four,
To give a hand to each."

The eldest Oyster looked at him,
But never a word he said:
The eldest Oyster winked his eye,
And shook his heavy head—
Meaning to say he did not choose
To leave the oyster-bed.

But four young Oysters hurried up,
All eager for the treat:
Their coats were brushed, their faces washed,
Their shoes were clean and neat—
And this was odd, because, you know,
They hadn't any feet.

Four other Oysters followed them,
And yet another four;
And thick and fast they came at last,
And more, and more, and more—
All hopping through the frothy waves,
And scrambling to the shore.

The Walrus and the Carpenter
Walked on a mile or so,
And then they rested on a rock
Conveniently low:
And all the little Oysters stood
And waited in a row.

"The time has come," the Walrus said
"To talk of many things:
Of shoes—and ships—and sealing-wax—
Of cabbages—and kings—
And why the sea is boiling hot—
And whether pigs have wings."

"But wait a bit," the Oysters cried,
Before we have our chat;
For some of us are out of breath,
And all of us are fat!"
"No hurry!" said the Carpenter.
They thanked him much for that.

"A loaf of bread," the Walrus said,
"Is what we chiefly need:
Pepper and vinegar besides
Are very good indeed—
Now, if you're ready, Oysters dear,
We can begin to feed."

"But not on us!" the Oysters cried,
Turning a little blue.
"After such kindness, that would be
A dismal thing to do!"
"The night is fine," the Walrus said.
"Do you admire the view?

"It was so kind of you to come!
And you are very nice!"
The Carpenter said nothing but
"Cut us another slice.
I wish you were not quite so deaf—
I've had to ask you twice!"

"It seems a shame," the Walrus said,
"To play them such a trick.
After we've brought them out so far,
And made them trot so quick!"
The Carpenter said nothing but
"The butter's spread too thick!"

"I weep for you," the Walrus said:
"I deeply sympathize."
With sobs and tears he sorted out
Those of the largest size,
Holding his pocket-handkerchief
Before his streaming eyes.

"O Oysters," said the Carpenter,
"You've had a pleasant run!
Shall we be trotting home again?"
But answer came there none—
And this was scarcely odd, because
They'd eaten every one.

RICHARD WATSON DIXON
(1833-1900)

Ode on Advancing Age

THOU goest more and more
To the silent things; thy hair is hoar,
Emptier thy weary face; like to the shore
Far-ruined, and the desolate billow white,
That recedes and leaves it waif-wrinkled, gap-rocked, weak.

The shore and the billow white
Groan, they cry and rest not; they would speak,
And call the eternal Night
To cease them for ever; bidding new things issue
From her cold tissue:
Night that is ever young, nor knows decay,
Though older by eternity than they.

Go down upon the shore.
The breakers dash, the smitten spray drops to the roar;
The spit upsprings, and drops again,
Where'er the white waves clash in the main.
Their sound is but one: 'tis the cry
That has risen from of old to the sky,
'Tis their silence!

Go now from the shore
Far-ruined: the grey shingly floor
To thy crashing step answers; the doteril cries,
And on dipping wings flies:
'Tis their silence!

And thou, oh thou
To that wild silence sinkest now.
No more remains to thee than the cry of silence, the cry
Of the waves, of the shore, of the bird to the sky.
The bald eyes 'neath as bald a brow
Ask but what nature gives
To the inarticulate cries
Of the waves, of the shore, of the bird.
Earth in earth thou art being interred:
No longer in thee lives
The lordly essence which was unlike all,
That was thy flower of soul, the imperial
Glory that separated thee
From all others that might be.

Thy dog hath died before.
Didst thou not mark him? did he not neglect
What roused his rapture once, but still loved thee?
Till, weaker grown, was he not fain reject
Thy pitying hand, thy meat and drink,
For all thou could'st implore?
Then, at the last, how mournfully
Did not his eyelids sink
With wearied sighs?
He sought at last that never-moving night
Which is the same in darkness, as in light,
The closing of the eyes.

So, Age, thou dealest us
To the elements: but no! Resume thy pride,

O man, that musest thus.
Be to the end what thou hast been before:
The ancient joy shall wrap thee still—the tide
Return upon the shore.

WILLIAM MORRIS (1834-1896)

Mother and Son

Now sleeps the land of houses,
and dead night holds the street,
And there thou liest, my baby,
and sleepest soft and sweet;
My man is away for awhile,
but safe and alone we lie,
And none heareth thy breath but thy mother,
and the moon looking down from the sky
On the weary waste of the town,
as it looked on the grass-edged road
Still warm with yesterday's sun,
when I left my old abode;
Hand in hand with my love,
that night of all nights in the year;
When the river of love o'erflowed
and drowned all doubt and fear,
And we two were alone in the world,
and once if never again,
We knew of the secret of earth
and the tale of its labour and pain.

Lo amidst London I lift thee,
and how little and light thou art,
And thou without hope or fear
thou fear and hope of my heart!
Lo here thy body beginning,
O son, and thy soul and thy life;
But how will it be if thou livest,
and enterest into the strife,
And in love we dwell together
when the man is grown in thee,
When thy sweet speech I shall hearken,
and yet 'twixt thee and me
Shall rise that wall of distance,
that round each one doth grow,
And maketh it hard and bitter
each other's thought to know?

Now, therefore, while yet thou art little
and hast no thought of thine own,
I will tell thee a word of the world;
of the hope whence thou hast grown;
Of the love that once begat thee,
of the sorrow that hath made
Thy little heart of hunger,
and thy hands on my bosom laid.
Then mayst thou remember hereafter
as whiles when people say
All this hath happened before
in the life of another day;
So mayst thou dimly remember
this tale of thy mother's voice,
As oft in the calm of dawning
I have heard the birds rejoice,
As oft I have heard the storm-wind
go moaning through the wood;
And I knew that earth was speaking,
and the mother's voice was good.

Now, to thee alone will I tell it
that thy mother's body is fair,
In the guise of the country maidens
who play with the sun and the air;
Who have stood in the row of the reapers
in the August afternoon,
Who have sat by the frozen water
in the high day of the moon,
When the lights of the Christmas feasting
were dead in the house on the hill,
And the wild geese gone to the salt-marsh
had left the winter still.
Yea, I am fair, my firstling;
if thou couldst but remember me!
The hair that thy small hand clutcheth
is a goodly sight to see;
I am true, but my face is a snare;
soft and deep are my eyes,
And they seem for men's beguiling
fulfilled with the dreams of the wise.
Kind are my lips, and they look
as though my soul had learned
Deep things I have never heard of,
my face and my hands are burned
By the lovely sun of the acres;
three months of London town

And thy birth-bed have bleached them indeed,
"But lo, where the edge of the gown"
(So said thy father) "is parting
the wrist that is white as the curd
From the brown of the hand that I love
bright as the wing of a bird."

Such is thy mother, O firstling,
yet strong as the maidens of old,
Whose spears and whose swords were the warders
of homestead, of field and of fold.
Oft were my feet on the highway,
often they wearied the grass;
From dusk unto dusk of the summer
three times in a week would I pass
To the downs from the house on the river
through the waves of the blossoming corn.
Fair then I lay down in the even,
and fresh I arose on the morn,
And scarce in the noon was I weary.
Ah, son, in the days of thy strife,
If thy soul could but harbour a dream
of the blossom of my life!
It would be as the sunlit meadows
beheld from a tossing sea,
And the soul should look on a vision
of the peace that is to be.

Yet, yet the tears on my cheek!
and what is this doth move
My heart to thy heart, beloved,
save the flood of yearning love?
For fair and fierce is thy father,
and soft and strange are his eyes
That look on the day that shall be
with the hope of the brave and the wise.
It was many a day that we laughed,
as over the meadows we walked,
And many a day I hearkened
and the pictures came as he talked;
It was many a day that we longed,
and we lingered late at eve
Ere speech from speech was sundered,
and my hand his hand could leave.
Then I wept when I was alone,
and I longed till the daylight came;
And down the stairs I stole,
and there was our housekeeping dame
(No mother of me, the foundling)
kindling the fire betimes
Ere the haymaking folk went forth
to the meadows down by the limes;
All things I saw at a glance;
the quickening fire-tongues leapt
Through the crackling heap of sticks,
and the sweet smoke up from it crept.
And close to the very hearth
the low sun flooded the floor,
And the cat and her kittens played
in the sun by the open door.
The garden was fair in the morning,
and there in the road he stood
Beyond the crimson daisies
and the bush of southernwood.
Then side by side together
through the grey-walled place we went,
And O the fear departed,
and the rest and sweet content!

Son, sorrow and wisdom he taught me,
and sore I grieved and learned
As we twain grew into one;
and the heart within me burned
With the very hopes of his heart.
Ah, son, it is piteous,
But never again in my life
shall I dare to speak to thee thus;
So may these lonely words
about thee creep and cling,
These words of the lonely night
in the days of our wayfaring.
Many a child of woman
to-night is born in the town,
The desert of folly and wrong;
and of what and whence are they grown?
Many and many an one
of wont and use is born;
For a husband is taken to bed
as a hat or a ribbon is worn.

Prudence begets her thousands;
"good is a housekeeper's life,
So shall I sell my body
that I may be matron and wife."
"And I shall endure foul wedlock
and bear the children of need."
Some are there born of hate,
many the children of greed.
"I, I too can be wedded,
though thou my love hast got."
"I am fair and hard of heart,
and riches shall be my lot."
And all these are the good and the happy,
on whom the world dawns fair.
O son, when wilt thou learn
of those that are born of despair,
As the fabled mud of the Nile
that quickens under the sun
With a growth of creeping things,
half dead when just begun?
E'en such is the care of Nature
that man should never die,
Though she breed of the fools of the earth,
and the dregs of the city sty.
But thou, O son, O son,
of very love wert born,
When our hope fulfilled bred hope,
and fear was a folly outworn.
On the eve of the toil and the battle
all sorrow and grief we weighed,
We hoped and we were not ashamed,
we knew and we were not afraid.

Now waneth the night and the moon;
ah, son, it is piteous
That never again in my life
shall I dare to speak to thee thus.
But sure from the wise and the simple
shall the mighty come to birth;
And fair were my fate, beloved,
if I be yet on the earth
When the world is awakened at last,
and from mouth to mouth they tell
Of thy love and thy deeds and thy valour,
and thy hope that nought can quell.

ALGERNON CHARLES SWINBURNE (1837-1909)

From ATALANTA IN CALYDON

The Youth of the Year

WHEN the hounds of spring are on winter's traces,
The mother of months in meadow or plain
Fills the shadows and windy places
With lisp of leaves and ripple of rain;
And the brown bright nightingale amourous
Is half assuaged for Itylus,
For the Thracian ships and the foreign faces,
The tongueless vigil, and all the pain.

Come with bows bent and with emptying of quivers,
Maiden most perfect, lady of light,
With a noise of winds and many rivers,
With a clamour of waters, and with might;
Bind on thy sandals, O thou most fleet,
Over the splendour and speed of thy feet,
For the faint east quickens, the wan west shivers,
Round the feet of the day and the feet of the night.

Where shall we find her, how shall we sing to her,
Fold our hands round her knees, and cling?
O that man's heart were as fire and could spring to her,
Fire, or the strength of the streams that spring!
For the stars and the winds are unto her
As raiment, as songs of the harp-player;
For the risen stars and the fallen cling to her,
And the southwest-wind and the west-wind sing.

For winter's rains and ruins are over,
And all the season of snows and sins;

The days dividing lover and lover,
The light that loses, the night that wins;
And time remembered is grief forgotten,
And frosts are slain and flowers begotten,
And in green underwood and cover
Blossom by blossom the spring begins.

The full streams feed on flower of rushes,
Ripe grasses trammel a travelling foot,
The faint fresh flame of the young year flushes
From leaf to flower and flower to fruit;
And fruit and leaf are as gold and fire,
And the oat is heard above the lyre,
And the hoofed heel of a satyr crushes
The chestnut-husk at the chestnut root.

And Pan by noon and Bacchus by night,
Fleeter of foot than the fleet-foot kid,
Follows with dancing and fills with delight
The Mænad and the Bassarid;
And soft as lips that laugh and hide,
The laughing leaves of the trees divide,
And screen from seeing and leave in sight
The god pursuing, the maiden hid.

The ivy falls with the Bacchanal's hair
Over her eyebrows hiding her eyes;
The wild vine slipping down leaves bare
Her bright breast shortening into sighs;
The wild vine slips with the weight of its leaves,
But the berried ivy catches and cleaves
To the limbs that glitter, the feet that scare
The wolf that follows, the fawn that flies.

A Forsaken Garden

In a coign of the cliff between lowland and highland,
At the sea-down's edge between windward and lee,
Walled round with rocks as an inland island,
The ghost of a garden fronts the sea.
A girdle of brushwood and thorn encloses
The steep square slope of the blossomless bed
Where the weeds that grew green from the graves of its roses
Now lie dead.

The fields fall southward, abrupt and broken,
To the low last edge of the long lone land.
If a step should sound or a word be spoken,
Would a ghost not rise at the strange guest's hand?
So long have the gray bare walks lain guestless,
Through branches and briars if a man make way,
He shall find no life but the sea-wind's, restless
Night and day.

The dense hard passage is blind and stifled
That crawls by a track none turn to climb
To the strait waste place that the years have rifled
Of all but the thorns that are touched not of time.
The thorns he spares when the rose is taken;
The rocks are left when he wastes the plain;
The wind that wanders, the weeds wind-shaken,
These remain.

Not a flower to be pressed of the foot that falls not;
As the heart of a dead man the seed-plots are dry;
From the thicket of thorns whence the nightingale calls not,
Could she call, there were never a rose to reply.

Over the meadows that blossom and wither,
  Rings but the note of a sea-bird's song.
Only the sun and the rain come hither
  All year long.

The sun burns sear, and the rain dishevels
  One gaunt bleak blossom of scentless breath.
Only the wind here hovers and revels
  In a round where life seems barren as death.
Here there was laughing of old, there was weeping,
  Haply, of lovers none ever will know,
Whose eyes went seaward a hundred sleeping
  Years ago.

Heart handfast in heart as they stood, "Look thither,"
  Did he whisper? "Look forth from the flowers to the sea;
For the foam-flowers endure when the rose-blossoms wither,
  And men that love lightly may die—But we?"
And the same wind sang, and the same waves whitened,
  And or ever the garden's last petals were shed,
In the lips that had whispered, the eyes that had lightened,
  Love was dead.

Or they loved their life through, and then went whither?
  And were one to the end—but what end who knows?
Love deep as the sea as a rose must wither,
  As the rose-red seaweed that mocks the rose.
Shall the dead take thought for the dead to love them?
  What love was ever as deep as a grave?
They are loveless now as the grass above them
  Or the wave.

All are at one now, roses and lovers,
  Not known of the cliffs and the fields and the sea.
Not a breath of the time that has been hovers
  In the air now soft with a summer to be.
Not a breath shall there sweeten the seasons hereafter
  Of the flowers or the lovers that laugh now or weep,
When, as they that are free now of weeping and laughter,
  We shall sleep.

Here death may deal not again forever;
  Here change may come not till all change end.
From the graves they have made they shall rise up never,
  Who have left naught living to ravage and rend.
Earth, stones, and thorns of the wild ground growing,
  When the sun and the rain live, these shall be;
Till a last wind's breath upon all these blowing
  Roll the sea.

Till the slow sea rise and the sheer cliff crumble,
  Till terrace and meadow the deep gulfs drink,
Till the strength of the waves of the high tides humble
  The fields that lessen, the rocks that shrink,
Here now in his triumph where all things falter,
  Stretched out on the spoils that his own hand spread,
As a god self-slain on his own strange altar,
  Death lies dead.

A Jacobite's Farewell

1716

THERE'S nae mair lands to tyne, my dear,
And nae mair lives to gie:
Though a man think sair to live nae mair,
There's but one day to die.

For a' things come and a' days gane,
What needs ye rend your hair?
But kiss me till the morn's morrow,
Then I'll kiss ye nae mair.

O lands are lost and life's losing,
And what were they to gie?
Fu' mony a man gives all he can,
But nae man else gives ye.

Our king wons ower the sea's water,
And I in prison sair:
But I'll win out the morn's morrow,
And ye'll see me nae mair.

A Jacobite's Exile

1746

THE weary day rins down and dies,
The weary night wears through:
And never an hour is fair wi' flower,
And never a flower wi' dew.

I would the day were night for me,
I would the night were day:
For then would I stand in my ain fair land,
As now in dreams I may.

O lordly flow the Loire and Seine,
And loud the dark Durance:
But bonnier shine the braes of Tyne
Than a' the fields of France;
And the waves of Till that speak sae still
Gleam goodlier where they glance.

O weel were they that fell fighting
On dark Drumossie's day:
They keep their hame ayont the faem,
And we die far away.

O sound they sleep, and saft, and deep,
But night and day wake we;
And ever between the sea-banks green
Sounds loud the sundering sea.

And ill we sleep, sae sair we weep,
But sweet and fast sleep they;
And the mool that haps them roun' and laps them
Is e'en their country's clay;
But the land we tread that are not dead
Is strange as night by day.

Strange as night in a strange man's sight,
Though fair as dawn it be:
For what is here that a stranger's cheer
Should yet wax blithe to see?

The hills stand steep, the dells lie deep,
The fields are green and gold:
The hill-streams sing, and the hill-sides ring,
As ours at home of old.

But hills and flowers are nane of ours,
And ours are oversea:
And the kind strange land whereon we stand,
It wotsna what were we
Or ever we came, wi' scathe and shame,
To try what end might be.

Scathe, and shame, and a waefu' name,
And a weary time and strange,
Have they that seeing a weird for dreeing
Can die, and cannot change.

Shame and scorn may we thole that mourn,
Though sair be they to dree:
But ill may we bide the thoughts we hide,
Mair keen than wind and sea.

Ill may we thole the night's watches,
And ill the weary day:
And the dreams that keep the gates of sleep,
A waefu' gift gie they;
For the sangs they sing us, the sights they bring us,
The morn blaws all away.

On Aikenshaw the sun blinks braw,
The burn rins blithe and fain:

There's nought wi' me I wadna gie
To look thereon again.

On Keilder-side the wind blaws wide;
There sounds nae hunting-horn
That rings sae sweet as the winds that beat
Round banks where Tyne is born.

The Wansbeck sings with all her springs,
The bents and braes give ear;
But the wood that rings wi' the sang she sings
I may not see nor hear;
For far and far thae blithe burns are,
And strange is a' thing near.

The light there lightens, the day there brightens,
The loud wind there lives free:
Nae light comes nigh me or wind blaws by me
That I wad hear or see.

But O gin I were there again,
Afar ayont the faem,
Cauld and dead in the sweet saft bed
That haps my sires at hame!

We'll see nae mair the sea-banks fair,
And the sweet grey gleaming sky,
And the lordly strand of Northumberland,
And the goodly towers thereby:
And none shall know but the winds that blow
The graves wherein we lie.

AUSTIN DOBSON (1840-1921)

A Gentleman of the Old School

He lived in that past Georgian day,
When men were less inclined to say
That "Time is Gold," and overlay
With toil their pleasure;
He held some land, and dwelt thereon,—
Where, I forget,—the house is gone;
His Christian name, I think, was John,—
His surname, Leisure.

Reynolds has painted him,—a face
Filled with a fine, old-fashioned grace,
Fresh-coloured, frank, with ne'er a trace
Of trouble shaded;
The eyes are blue, the hair is drest
In plainest way,—one hand is prest
Deep in a flapped canary vest,
With buds brocaded.

He wears a brown old Brunswick coat,
With silver buttons,—round his throat,
A soft cravat;—in all you note
An elder fashion,—
A strangeness, which, to us who shine
In shapely hats,—whose coats combine
All harmonies of hue and line,—
Inspires compassion.

He lived so long ago, you see!
Men were untravelled then, but we,
Like Ariel, post o'er land and sea
With careless parting;
He found it quite enough for him
To smoke his pipe in "garden trim,"
And watch, about the fish-tank's brim,
The swallows darting.

He liked the well-wheel's creaking tongue,—
He liked the thrush that fed her young,—
He liked the drone of flies among
His netted peaches;
He liked to watch the sunlight fall
Athwart his ivied orchard wall;
Or pause to catch the cuckoo's call
Beyond the beeches.

His were the times of Paint and Patch,
And yet no Ranelagh could match
The sober doves that round his thatch
Spread tails and sidled;
He liked their ruffling, puffed content,—
For him their drowsy wheelings meant
More than a Mall of Beaux that bent,
Or Belles that bridled.

Not that, in truth, when life began,
He shunned the flutter of the fan;
He too had maybe "pinked his man"
In Beauty's quarrel;

But now his "fervent youth" had flown
Where lost things go; and he was grown
As staid and slow-paced as his own
Old hunter, Sorrel.

Yet still he loved the chase, and held
That no composer's score excelled
The merry horn, when Sweetlip swelled
Its jovial riot;

But most his measured words of praise
Caressed the angler's easy ways,—
His idly meditative days,—
His rustic diet.

Not that his "meditating" rose
Beyond a sunny summer doze;
He never troubled his repose
With fruitless prying;

But held, as law for high and low,
What God withholds no man can know,
And smiled away inquiry so,
Without replying.

We read—alas, how much we read!
The jumbled strifes of creed and creed
With endless controversies feed
Our groaning tables;

His books—and they sufficed him—were
Cotton's "Montaigne," "The Grave" of Blair,
A "Walton"—much the worse for wear—
And "Æsop's Fables."

One more,—"The Bible." Not that he
Had searched its page as deep as we;
No sophistries could make him see
Its slender credit;

It may be that he could not count
The sires and sons to Jesse's fount,—
He liked the "Sermon on the Mount,"—
And more, he read it.

Once he had loved, but failed to wed,
A red-cheeked lass who long was dead;
His ways were far too slow, he said,
To quite forget her;

And still when time had turned him gray
The earliest hawthorn buds in May
Would find his lingering feet astray,
Where first he met her.

"In Cœlo Quies" heads the stone
On Leisure's grave,—now little known,
A tangle of wild-rose has grown
So thick across it;

The "Benefactions" still declare
He left the clerk an elbow-chair,
And "12 Pence Yearly to Prepare
A Christmas Posset."

Lie softly, Leisure! Doubtless you
With too serene a conscience drew
Your easy breath, and slumbered through
The gravest issue;

But we, to whom our age allows
Scarce space to wipe our weary brows,
Look down upon your narrow house,
Old friend, and miss you!

The Curé's Progress

Monsieur the Curé down the street
Comes with his kind old face,—
With his coat worn bare, and his straggling hair,
And his green umbrella-case.

You may see him pass by the little *"Grande Place,"*
And the tiny *"Hôtel-de-Ville"*;
He smiles, as he goes, to the *fleuriste* Rose,
And the *pompier* Théophile.

He turns, as a rule, through the *"Marché"* cool,
Where the noisy fish-wives call;
And his compliment pays to the *"Belle Thérèse,"*
As she knits in her dusky stall.

There's a letter to drop at the locksmith's shop,
And Toto, the locksmith's niece,
Has jubilant hopes, for the Curé gropes
In his tails for a *pain d'épice*.

There's a little dispute with a merchant of fruit,
Who is said to be heterodox,
That will ended be with a *"Ma foi, oui!"*
And a pinch from the Curé's box.

There is also a word that no one heard
To the furrier's daughter Lou;
And a pale cheek fed with a flickering red,
And a *"Bon Dieu garde M'sieu!"*

But a grander way for the *Sous-Préfet,*
And a bow for Ma'am'selle Anne;
And a mock "off-hat" to the Notary's cat,
And a nod to the Sacristan:—

For ever through life the Curé goes
With a smile on his kind old face—
With his coat worn bare, and his straggling hair,
And his green umbrella-case.

A Ballad of Heroes

BECAUSE you passed, and now are not,—
Because, in some remoter day,
Your sacred dust from doubtful spot
Was blown of ancient airs away,—
Because you perished,—must men say
Your deeds were naught, and so profane
Your lives with that cold burden? Nay
The deeds you wrought are not in vain!

Though, it may be, above the plot
That hid your once imperial clay,
No greener than o'er men forgot
The unregarding grasses sway;—
Though there no sweeter is the lay
From careless bird,—though you remain
Without distinction of decay,—
The deeds you wrought are not in vain!

No. For while yet in tower or cot
Your story stirs the pulses' play;
And men forget the sordid lot—
The sordid care, of cities gray;—
While yet, beset in homelier fray,
They learn from you the lesson plain
That Life may go, so Honour stay,—
The deeds you wrought are not in vain!

ENVOY

Heroes of old! I humbly lay
The laurel on your graves again;
Whatever men have done, men may,—
The deeds you wrought are not in vain.

The Ballad of Imitation

"C'est imiter quelqu'un que de planter des choux."—Alfred de Musset.

IF they hint, O Musician, the piece that you played
Is naught but a copy of Chopin or Spohr;
That the ballad you sing is but merely "conveyed"
From the stock of the Arnes and the Purcells of yore;
That there's nothing, in short, in the words or the score
That is not as out-worn as the "Wandering Jew,"
Make answer—Beethoven could scarcely do more—
That the man who plants cabbages imitates, too!

If they tell you, Sir Artist, your light and your shade
Are simply "adapted" from other men's lore;
That—plainly to speak of a "spade" as a "spade"—
You've "stolen" your grouping from three or from four;
That (however the writer the truth may deplore),
'Twas Gainsborough painted *your* "Little Boy Blue";
Smile only serenely—though cut to the core—
For the man who plants cabbages imitates, too!

And you too, my Poet, be never dismayed
If they whisper your Epic—"Sir Éperon d'Or"—
Is nothing but Tennyson thinly arrayed
In a tissue that's taken from Morris's store;

That no one, in fact, but a child could
ignore
That you "lift" or "accommodate" all
that you do;
Take heart—though your Pegasus'
withers be sore—
For the man who plants cabbages imitates,
too!

Postscriptum—And you, whom we all so
adore,
Dear Critics, whose verdicts are always
so new!—
One word in your ear. There were
Critics before . . .
And the man who plants cabbages imi-
tates, too!

THOMAS HARDY

From THE MAYOR OF CASTERBRIDGE

Chapter I

ONE evening of late summer, before the present century had reached its thirtieth year, a young man and woman, the latter carrying a child, were approaching the large village of Weydon-Priors, in Upper Wessex, on foot. They were plainly but not ill clad, though the thick hoar of dust which had accumulated on their shoes and garments from an obviously long journey lent a disadvantageous shabbiness to their appearance just now.

The man was of fine figure, swarthy, and stern in aspect; and he showed in profile a facial angle so slightly inclined as to be almost perpendicular. He wore a short jacket of brown corduroy, newer than the remainder of his suit, which was a fustian waistcoat with white horn buttons, breeches of the same, tanned leggings, and a straw hat overlaid with black glazed canvas. At his back he carried by a looped strap a rush basket, from which protruded at one end the crutch of a hay-knife, a wimble for hay-bonds being also visible in the aperture. His measured, springless walk was the walk of the skilled countryman as distinct from the desultory shamble of the general labourer; while in the turn and plant of each foot there was, further, a dogged and cynical indifference, personal to himself, showing its presence even in the regularly interchanging fustian folds, now in the left leg, now in the right, as he paced along.

What was really peculiar, however, in this couple's progress, and would have attracted the attention of any casual observer otherwise disposed to overlook them, was the perfect silence they preserved. They walked side by side in such a way as to suggest afar off the low, easy, confidential chat of people full of reciprocity; but on closer view it could be discerned that the man was reading, or pretending to read, a ballad sheet which he kept before his eyes with some difficulty by the hand that was passed through the basket strap. Whether this apparent cause were the real cause, or whether it were an assumed one to escape an intercourse that would have been irksome to him, nobody but himself could have said precisely; but his taciturnity was unbroken, and the woman enjoyed no society whatever from his presence. Virtually she walked the highway alone, save for the child she bore. Sometimes the man's bent elbow almost touched her shoulder, for she kept as close to his side as was possible without actual contact; but she seemed to have no idea of taking his arm, nor he of offering it; and far from exhibiting surprise at his ignoring silence, she appeared to receive it as a natural thing. If any word at all were uttered by the little group, it was an occasional whisper of the woman to the child—a tiny girl in short clothes and blue boots of knitted yarn—and the murmured babble of the child in reply.

The chief—almost the only—attraction of the young woman's face was its mobility. When she looked down sideways to the girl she became pretty, and even handsome, particularly that in the action her features caught slantwise the rays of the strongly coloured sun, which made transparencies of her eyelids and nostrils, and set fire on her lips. When she plodded on in the shade of the hedge, silently thinking, she had the hard, half-apathetic expression of one who deems anything possible at the hands of Time and Chance, except, perhaps, fair play. The first phase was the work of Nature, the second probably of civilization.

That the man and woman were husband and wife, and the parents of the girl in arms, there could be little doubt. No other than such relationship would have accounted for the atmosphere of stale familiarity which the trio carried along with them like a nimbus as they moved down the road.

The wife mostly kept her eyes fixed ahead, though with little interest —the scene for that matter being one that might have been matched at almost any spot in any county in England at this time of the year; a road neither straight nor crooked, neither level nor hilly, bordered by hedges, trees, and other vegetation, which had entered the blackened-green stage of colour that the doomed leaves pass through on their way to dingy and yellow, and red. The grassy margin of the bank, and the nearest hedgerow boughs, were powdered by the dust that had been stirred over them by hasty vehicles, the same dust as it lay on the road deadening their footfalls like a carpet; and this, with the aforesaid total absence of conversation, allowed every extraneous sound to be heard.

For a long time there was none, beyond the voice of a weak bird singing a trite old evening song that might doubtless have been heard on the hill at the same hour, and with the self-same trills, quavers, and breves, at any sunset of that season for centuries untold. But as they approached the village sundry distant shouts and rattles reached their ears from some elevated spot in that direction, as yet screened from view by foliage. When the outlying houses of Weydon-Priors could just be descried, the family group was met by a turnip-hoer with his hoe on his shoulder, and his dinner-bag suspended from it. The reader promptly glanced up.

"Any trade doing here?" he asked phlegmatically, designating the village in his van by a wave of the broadsheet. And thinking the labourer did not understand him, he added, "Anything in the hay-trussing line?"

The turnip-hoer had already begun shaking his head. "Why, save the man, what wisdom's in him that 'a should come to Weydon for a job of that sort this time o' year?"

"Then is there any house to let—a little small new cottage just a builded, or such like?" asked the other.

The pessimist still maintained a negative. "Pulling down is more the nater of Weydon. There were five houses cleared away last year, and three this; and the volk nowhere to go—no, not so much as a thatched hurdle; that's the way o' Weydon-Priors."

The hay-trusser, which he obviously was, nodded with some superciliousness. Looking towards the village, he continued, "There is something going on here, however, is there not?"

"Ay. 'Tis Fair Day. Though what you hear now is little more than the clatter and scurry of getting away the money o' children and fools, for the real business is done earlier than this. I've been working within sound o't all day, but I didn't go up—not I. 'Twas no business of mine."

The trusser and his family proceeded on their way, and soon entered the Fair-field, which showed standing-places and pens where many hundreds of horses and sheep had been exhibited and sold in the forenoon, but were now in great part taken away. At present, as their informant had observed, but little real business remained on hand, the chief being the sale by auction of a few inferior animals, that could not otherwise be disposed of, and had been absolutely refused by the better class of traders, who came and went early. Yet the crowd was denser now than during the morning hours, the frivolous contingent of visitors, including journeymen out for a holiday, a stray soldier or two home on furlough, village shopkeepers, and the like, having latterly flocked in; persons whose activities found a congenial field among the peep-shows, toy-stands, waxworks, inspired monsters, disinterested medical men who travelled for the public good, thimble-riggers, nick-nack vendors, and readers of Fate.

Neither of our pedestrians had much heart for these things, and they looked around for a refreshment tent among the many which dotted the down. Two, which stood nearest to them in the ochreous haze of expiring sunlight, seemed almost equally inviting. One was formed of new, milk-hued canvas, and bore red flags on its summit; it announced "Good Home-brewed Beer, Ale, and Cyder." The other was less new; a little iron stove-pipe came out of it at the back, and in front appeared the placard, "Good Furmity Sold Hear." The man mentally weighed the two inscriptions, and inclined to the former tent.

"No—no—the other one," said the woman. "I always like furmity; and so does Elizabeth-Jane; and so will you. It is nourishing after a long hard day."

"I've never tasted it," said the man. However, he gave way to her representations, and they entered the furmity booth forthwith.

A rather numerous company appeared within, seated at the long narrow tables that ran down the tent on each side. At the upper end stood a stove, containing a charcoal fire, over which hung a large three-legged crock, sufficiently polished round the rim to show that it was made of bell-metal. A haggish creature of about fifty presided, in a white apron, which, as it threw an air of respectability over her as far as it extended, was made so wide as to reach nearly round her waist. She slowly stirred the contents of the pot. The dull scrape of her large spoon was audible throughout the tent as she thus kept from burning the mixture of corn in the grain, milk, raisins, currants, and what not, that composed the antiquated slop in which she dealt. Vessels holding the separate ingredients stood on a white-clothed table of boards and trestles close by.

The young man and woman ordered a basin each of the mixture, steaming hot, and sat down to consume it at leisure. This was very well so far, for furmity, as the woman had said, was nourishing, and as proper a food as could be obtained within the four seas; though, to those not accustomed to it, the grains of wheat, swollen as large as lemon-pips, which floated on its surface, might have a deterrent effect at first.

But there was more in that tent than met the cursory glance; and the man, with the instinct of a perverse character, scented it quickly. After a mincing attack on his bowl, he watched the hag's proceedings from the corner of his eye, and saw the game she played. He winked to her, and passed up his basin in reply to her nod; when she took a bottle from under the table, slily measured out a quantity of its contents, and tipped the same into the man's furmity. The liquor poured in was rum. The man as slily sent back money in payment.

He found the concoction, thus strongly laced, much more to his satisfaction than it had been in its natural state. His wife had observed the proceeding with much uneasiness; but he persuaded her to have hers laced also, and she agreed to a milder allowance after some misgiving.

The man finished his basin, and called for another, the rum being signalled for in yet stronger proportion. The effect of it was soon apparent in his manner, and his wife but too sadly perceived that in strenuously steering off the rocks of the licensed liquor-tent she had only got into maelstrom depths here amongst the smugglers.

The child began to prattle impatiently, and the wife more than once said to her husband, "Michael, how about our lodging? You know we may have trouble in getting it if we don't go soon."

But he turned a deaf ear to those bird-like chirpings. He talked loud to the company. The child's black eyes, after slow, round, ruminating gazes at the candles when they were lighted, fell together; then they opened, then shut again, and she slept.

At the end of the first basin the man had risen to serenity; at the second he was jovial; at the third, argumentative; at the fourth, the qualities signified by the shape of his face, the occasional clench of his mouth, and the fiery spark of his dark eye, began to tell in his conduct; he was overbearing—even brilliantly quarrelsome.

The conversation took a high turn, as it often does on such occasions. The ruin of good men by bad wives, and more particularly, the frustration of many a promising youth's high aims and hopes, and the extinction of his energies, by an early imprudent marriage, was the theme.

"I did for myself that way thoroughly," said the trusser, with a contemplative bitterness that was well-nigh resentful. "I married at eighteen, like the fool that I was; and this is the consequence o't." He pointed at himself and family with a wave of the hand intended to bring out the penuriousness of the exhibition.

The young woman his wife, who seemed accustomed to such remarks, acted as if she did not hear them, and continued her intermittent private words on tender trifles to the sleeping and waking child, who was just big enough to be placed for a moment on the bench beside her when she wished to ease her arms. The man continued—

"I haven't more than fifteen shillings in the world, and yet I am a good experienced hand in my line. I'd challenge England to beat me in the fodder business; and if I were a free man again, I'd be worth a thousand pound before I'd done o't. But a fellow never knows these little things till all chance of acting upon 'em is past."

The auctioneer selling the old horses in the field outside could be heard saying, "Now this is the last lot—now who'll take the last lot for a song? Shall I say forty shillings? 'Tis a very promising brood-mare, a trifle over five years old, and nothing the matter with the hoss at all, except that she's a little holler in the back and had her left eye knocked out by the kick of another, her own sister, coming along the road."

"For my part I don't see why men who have got wives, and don't want 'em, shouldn't get rid of 'em as these gipsy fellows do their old horses," said the man in the tent. "Why shouldn't they put 'em up and sell 'em by auction to men who are in want of such articles? Hey? Why, begad, I'd sell mine this minute if anybody would buy her!"

"There's them that would do that," some of the guests replied, looking at the woman, who was by no means ill-favoured.

"True," said a smoking gentleman, whose coat had the fine polish about the collar, elbows, seams, and shoulder-blades that long-continued friction with grimy surfaces will produce, and which is usually more desired on furniture than on clothes. From his appearance he had possibly been in former time groom or coachman to some neighbouring county family. "I've had my breedings in as good circles, I may say, as any man," he added, "and I know true cultivation, or nobody do; and I can declare she's got it—in the bone, mind ye, I say—as much as any female in the fair—though it may want a little bringing out." Then, crossing his legs, he resumed his pipe with a nicely-adjusted gaze at a point in the air.

The fuddled young husband stared for a few seconds at this unexpected praise of his wife, half in doubt of the wisdom of his own attitude towards the possessor of such qualities. But he speedily lapsed into his former conviction, and said harshly—

"Well, then, now is your chance; I am open to an offer for this gem o' creation."

She turned to her husband and murmured, "Michael, you have talked this nonsense in public places before. A joke is a joke, but you may make it once too often, mind!"

"I know I've said it before; I meant it. All I want is a buyer."

At the moment a swallow, one among the last of the season, which had by chance found its way through an opening into the upper part of the tent, flew to and fro in quick curves above their heads, causing all eyes to follow it absently. In watching the bird till it made its escape the assembled company neglected to respond to the workman's offer, and the subject dropped.

But a quarter of an hour later the man, who had gone on lacing his furmity more and more heavily, though he was either so strong-minded or such an intrepid toper that he still appeared fairly sober, recurred to the old strain, as in a musical fantasy the instrument fetches up the original theme. "Here—I am waiting to know about this offer of mine. The woman is no good to me. Who'll have her?"

The company had by this time decidedly degenerated, and the renewed inquiry was received with a laugh of appreciation. The woman whispered; she was imploring and anxious: "Come, come, it is getting dark, and this nonsense won't do. If you don't come along, I shall go without you. Come!"

She waited and waited; yet he did not move. In ten minutes the man broke in upon the desultory conversation of the furmity drinkers with, "I asked this question, and nobody answered to 't. Will any Jack Rag or Tom Straw among ye buy my goods?"

The woman's manner changed, and her face assumed the grim shape and colour of which mention has been made.

"Mike, Mike," said she; "this is getting serious. Oh!—too serious!"

"Will anybody buy her?" said the man.

"I wish somebody would," said she firmly. "Her present owner is not at all to her liking!"

"Nor you to mine," said he. "So we are agreed about that. Gentlemen, you hear? It's an agreement to part. She shall take the girl if she wants to, and go her ways. I'll take my tools, and go my ways. 'Tis simple as Scripture history. Now then, stand up, Susan, and show yourself."

"Don't, my chiel," whispered a buxom staylace dealer in voluminous petticoats, who sat near the woman; "yer good man don't know what he's saying."

The woman, however, did stand up. "Now, who's auctioneer?" cried the hay-trusser.

"I be," promptly answered a short man, with a nose resembling a copper knob, a damp voice, and eyes like button-holes. "Who'll make an offer for this lady?"

The woman looked on the ground, as if she maintained her position by a supreme effort of will.

"Five shillings," said some one, at which there was a laugh.

"No insults," said the husband. "Who'll say a guinea?"

Nobody answered; and the female dealer in staylaces interposed.

"Behave yerself moral, good man, for Heaven's love! Ah, what a cruelty is the poor soul married to! Bed and board is dear at some figures, 'pon my 'vation 'tis!"

"Set it higher, auctioneer," said the trusser.

"Two guineas!" said the auctioneer; and no one replied.

"If they don't take her for that, in ten seconds they'll have to give more," said the husband. "Very well. Now, auctioneer, add another."

"Three guineas—going for three guineas!" said the rheumy man.

"No bid?" said the husband. "Good Lord, why she's cost me fifty times the money, if a penny. Go on."

"Four guineas!" cried the auctioneer.

"I'll tell ye what—I won't sell her for less than five," said the husband, bringing down his fist so that the basins danced. "I'll sell her for five guineas to any man that will pay me the money, and treat her well; and he shall have her for ever, and never hear aught o' me. But she shan't go for less. Now then—five guineas—and she's yours. Susan, you agree?"

She bowed her head with absolute indifference.

"Five guineas," said the auctioneer, "or she'll be withdrawn. Do anybody give it? The last time. Yes or no?"

"Yes," said a loud voice from the doorway.

All eyes were turned. Standing in the triangular opening which formed the door of the tent was a sailor, who, unobserved by the rest, had arrived there within the last two or three minutes. A dead silence followed his affirmation.

"You say you do?" asked the husband, staring at him.

"I say so," replied the sailor.

"Saying is one thing, and paying is another. Where's the money?"

The sailor hesitated a moment, looked anew at the woman, came in, unfolded five crisp pieces of paper, and threw them down upon the table-cloth. They were Bank-of-England notes for five pounds. Upon the face of this he chinked down the shillings severally—one, two, three, four, five.

The sight of real money in full amount, in answer to a challenge for the same till then deemed slightly hypothetical, had a great effect upon the spectators. Their eyes became riveted upon the faces of the chief actors, and then upon the notes as they lay, weighted by the shillings, on the table.

Up to this moment it could not positively have been asserted that the man, in spite of his tantalizing declaration, was really in earnest.

The spectators had indeed taken the proceedings throughout as a piece of mirthful irony carried to extremes; and had assumed that, being out of work, he was, as a consequence, out of temper with the world, and society, and his nearest kin. But with the demand and response of real cash the jovial frivolity of the scene departed. A lurid colour seemed to fill the tent, and change the aspect of all therein. The mirth-wrinkles left the listeners' faces, and they waited with parting lips.

"Now," said the woman, breaking the silence, so that her low dry voice sounded quite loud, "before you go further, Michael, listen to me. If you touch that money, I and this girl go with the man. Mind, it is a joke no longer."

"A joke? Of course it is not a joke!" shouted her husband, his resentment rising at her suggestion. "I take the money: the sailor takes you. That's plain enough. It has been done elsewhere—and why not here?"

"'Tis quite on the understanding that the young woman is willing," said the sailor blandly. "I wouldn't hurt her feelings for the world."

"Faith, nor I," said her husband. "But she is willing, provided she can have the child. She said so only the other day when I talked o't!"

"That you swear?" said the sailor to her.

"I do," said she, after glancing at her husband's face and seeing no repentance there.

"Very well, she shall have the child, and the bargain's complete," said the trusser. He took the sailor's notes and deliberately folded them, and put them with the shillings in a high remote pocket, with an air of finality.

The sailor looked at the woman and smiled. "Come along!" he said kindly. "The little one too—the more the merrier!" She paused for an instant, with a close glance at him. Then dropping her eyes again, and saying nothing, she took up the child and followed him as he made towards the door. On reaching it, she turned, and pulling off her wedding-ring, flung it across the booth in the hay-trusser's face.

"Mike," she said, "I've lived with thee a couple of years, and had nothing but temper! Now I'm no more to 'ee; I'll try my luck elsewhere. 'Twill be better for me and the child, both. So good-bye!"

Seizing the sailor's arm with her right hand, and mounting the little girl on her left, she went out of the tent sobbing bitterly.

A stolid look of concern filled the husband's face, as if, after all, he had not quite anticipated this ending; and some of the guests laughed.

"Is she gone?" he said.

"Faith, ay; she gone clane enough," said some rustics near the door.

He rose and walked to the entrance with the careful tread of one conscious of his alcoholic load. Some others followed, and they stood looking into the twilight. The difference between the peacefulness of inferior nature and the wilful hostilities of mankind was very apparent at this place. In contrast with the harshness of the act just ended within the tent was the sight of several horses crossing their necks and rubbing each other lovingly as they waited in patience to be harnessed for the homeward journey. Outside the fair, in the valleys and woods, all was quiet. The sun had recently set, and the west heaven was hung with rosy cloud, which seemed permanent, yet slowly changed. To watch it was like looking at some grand feat of stagery from a darkened auditorium. In presence of this scene, after the other, there was a natural instinct to abjure man as the blot on an otherwise kindly universe; till it was remembered that all terrestrial conditions were intermittent, and that mankind might some night be innocently sleeping when these quiet objects were raging loud.

"Where do the sailor live?" asked a spectator, when they had vainly gazed around.

"God knows that," replied the man who had seen high life. "He's without doubt a stranger here."

"He came in about five minutes ago," said the furmity woman, joining the rest with her hands on her hips. "And then 'a stepped back, and then 'a looked in again. I'm not a penny the better for him."

"Serves the husband well be-right," said the staylace vendor. "A comely respectable body like her—what can a man want more? I glory in the woman's sperrit. I'd ha' done it myself—od send if I wouldn't, if a husband had behaved so to me! I'd go, and 'a might call, and call, till his keacorn was raw; but I'd never come back—no, not till the great trumpet, would I!"

"Well, the woman will be better off," said another of a more deliberative turn. "For seafaring naters be very good shelter for shorn lambs, and the man do seem to have plenty of money, which is what she's not been used to lately, by all showings."

"Mark me—I'll not go after her!" said the trusser, returning doggedly to his seat. "Let her go! If she's up to such vagaries she must suffer for 'em. She'd no business to take the maid—'tis my maid; and if it were the doing again she shouldn't have her!"

Perhaps from some little sense of having countenanced an indefensible proceeding, perhaps because it was late, the customers thinned away from the tent shortly after this episode. The man stretched his elbows forward on the table, leant his face upon his arms, and soon began to snore. The furmity seller decided to close for the night, and after seeing the rum-bottles, milk, corn, raisins, &c., that remained on hand, loaded into the cart, came to where the man reclined. She shook him, but could not wake him. As the tent was not to be struck that night, the fair continuing for two or three days, she decided to let the sleeper, who was obviously no tramp, stay where he was, and his basket with him. Extinguishing the last candle, and lowering the flap of the tent, she left it, and drove away.

The Darkling Thrush

I LEANT upon a coppice gate
When Frost was spectre-gray,
And Winter's dregs made desolate
The weakening eye of day.
The tangled bine-stems scored the sky
Like strings of broken lyres,
And all mankind that haunted nigh
Had sought their household fires.

The land's sharp features seemed to be
The Century's corpse outleant,
His crypt the cloudy canopy,
The wind his death-lament.
The ancient pulse of germ and birth
Was shrunken hard and dry,
And every spirit upon earth
Seemed fervourless as I.

At once a voice arose among
The bleak twigs overhead
In a full-hearted evensong
Of joy illimited;
An aged thrush, frail, gaunt, and small,
In blast-beruffled plume,
Had chosen thus to fling his soul
Upon the growing gloom.

So little cause for carollings
Of such ecstatic sound
Was written on terrestrial things
Afar or nigh around,
That I could think there trembled through
His happy good-night air
Some blessed Hope, whereof he knew
And I was unaware.

ANDREW LANG (1844-1912)

From LETTERS TO DEAD AUTHORS

To Jane Austen

MADAM,—

If to the enjoyments of your present state be lacking a view of the minor infirmities or foibles of men, I cannot but think (were the thought permitted) that your pleasures are yet incomplete. Moreover, it is certain that a woman of parts who has once meddled with literature will never wholly lose her love for the discussion of that delicious topic, nor cease to relish what (in the cant of our new age) is styled "literary shop." For these reasons I attempt to convey to you some inkling of the present state of that agreeable art which you, madam, raised to its highest pitch of perfection.

As to your own works (immortal, as I believe), I have but little that is wholly cheering to tell one who, among women of letters, was almost alone in her freedom from a lettered vanity. You are not a very popular author: your volumes are not found in gaudy colors on every bookstall; or, if found, are not perused with avidity by the Emmas and Catherines of our generation. 'Tis not long since a blow was dealt (in the estimation of the unreasoning) at your character as an author by the publication of your familiar letters. The editor of these epistles, unfortunately, did not always take your witticisms, and he added others which were too unmistakably his own. While the injudicious were disappointed by the absence of your exquisite style and humor, the wiser sort were the more convinced of your wisdom. In your letters (knowing your correspondents) you gave but the small personal talk of the hour, for them sufficient; for your books you reserved matter and expression which are imperishable. Your admirers, if not very numerous, include all persons of taste, who, in your favor, are apt somewhat to abate the rule, or shake off the habit, which commonly confines them to but temperate laudation.

'Tis the fault of all art to seem antiquated and faded in the eyes of the succeeding generation. The manners of your age were not the manners of to-day, and young gentlemen and ladies who think Scott "slow," think Miss Austen "prim" and "dreary." Yet, even could you return among us, I scarcely believe that, speaking the language of the hour, as you might, and versed in its habits, you would win the general admiration. For how tame, madam, are your characters, especially your favorite heroines! how limited the life which you knew and described! how narrow the range of your incidents! how correct your grammar!

As heroines, for example, you chose ladies like Emma, and Elizabeth, and Catherine: women remarkable neither for the brilliance nor for the degradation of their birth; women wrapped up in their own and the parish's concerns, ignorant of evil, as it seems, and unacquainted with vain yearnings and interesting doubts. Who can engage his fancy with their match-makings and the conduct of their affections, when so many daring and dazzling heroines approach and solicit his regard?

Here are princesses dressed in white velvet stamped with golden fleurs-de-lys—ladies with hearts of ice and lips of fire, who count their rubles by the million, their lovers by the score, and even their husbands, very often, in figures of some arithmetical importance. With these are the immaculate daughters of itinerant Italian musicians, maids whose souls are unsoiled amidst the contaminations of our streets, and whose acquaintance with the art of Phidias and Praxiteles, of Dædalus and

Scopas, is the more admirable because entirely derived from loving study of the inexpensive collections vended by the plaster-of-Paris man round the corner. When such heroines are wooed by the nephews of dukes, where are your Emmas and Elizabeths? Your volumes neither excite nor satisfy the curiosities provoked by that modern and scientific fiction, which is greatly admired, I learn, in the United States as well as in France and at home.

You erred, it cannot be denied, with your eyes open. Knowing Lydia and Kitty so intimately as you did, why did you make of them almost insignificant characters? With Lydia for a heroine you might have gone far; and, had you devoted three volumes, and the chief of your time, to the passions of Kitty, you might have held your own, even now, in the circulating library. How Lyddy, perched on a corner of the roof, first beheld her Wickham; how, on her challenge, he climbed up by a ladder to her side; how they kissed, caressed, swung on gates together, met at odd seasons, in strange places, and finally eloped: all this might have been put in the mouth of a jealous elder sister, say Elizabeth, and you would not have been less popular than several favorites of our time. Had you cast the whole narrative into the present tense, and lingered lovingly over the thickness of Mary's legs, and the softness of Kitty's cheeks, and the blond fluffiness of Wickham's whiskers, you would have left a romance still dear to young ladies.

Or again, you might entrance your students still, had you concentrated your attention on Mrs. Rushworth, who eloped with Henry Crawford. These should have been the chief figures of "Mansfield Park." But you timidly decline to tackle Passion. "Let other pens," you write, "dwell on guilt and misery. I quit such odious subjects as soon as I can." Ah, *there* is the secret of your failure! Need I add that the vulgarity and narrowness of the social circles you describe impair your popularity? I scarce remember more than one lady of title, and but very few lords (and these unessential), in all your tales. Now, when we all wish to be in society, we demand plenty of titles in our novels, at any rate, and we get lords (and very queer lords) even from Republican authors, born in a country which in your time was not renowned for its literature. I have heard a critic remark, with a decided air of fashion, on the brevity of the notice which your characters give each other when they offer invitations to dinner. "An invitation to dinner next day was despatched," and this demonstrates that your acquaintance "went out" very little, and had but few engagements. How vulgar, too, is one of your heroines, who bids Mr. Darcy "keep his breath to cool his porridge." I blush for Elizabeth! It was superfluous to add that your characters are debased by being invariably mere members of the Church of England as by law established. The dissenting enthusiast, the open soul that glides from Esoteric Buddhism to the Salvation Army, and from the Higher Pantheism to the Higher Paganism, we look for in vain among your studies of character. Nay, the very words I employ are of unknown sound to you; so how can you help us in the stress of the soul's travailings?

You may say that the soul's travailings are no affair of yours; proving thereby that you have indeed but a lowly conception of the duty of the novelist. I only remember one reference, in all your works, to that controversy which occupies the chief of our attention—the great controversy on Creation or Evolution. Your Jane Bennet cries: "I have no idea of there being so much Design in the world as some persons imagine." Nor do you touch on our mighty social question, the Land Laws, save when Mrs. Bennet appears as a Land Reformer, and rails bitterly against the cruelty "of settling an estate away from a family of five daughters, in favor of a man whom nobody cared anything about." There, madam, in that cruelly unjust performance, what a text you had for a *Tendenz-Roman.* Nay, you can allow Kitty to report that a Private had been flogged, without introducing a chapter on Flogging in the Army. But you formally declined to stretch your matter out, here and there, "with solemn specious nonsense about something unconnected with the story." No "padding" for Miss Austen! In fact, madam, as you were born before Analysis came in, or Passion, or Realism, or Naturalism, or Irreverence, or Religious Open-mindedness, you really cannot hope to rival your literary sisters in the minds of a perplexed generation. Your heroines are not passionate, we do not see their red wet cheeks, and tresses dishevelled in the manner of our frank young Mænads. What says your best successor, a lady who adds fresh lustre to a name that in fiction equals yours? She says of Miss Austen: "Her heroines have a stamp of their own. They have *a certain gentle self-respect and humor and hardness of heart.* . . . Love with them does not mean a passion as much as an interest, deep and silent." I think one prefers them so, and that English-women should be more like Anne Elliot than Maggie Tulliver. "All the privilege I claim for my own sex is that of loving longest when existence or when hope is gone," said Anne; perhaps she insisted on a monopoly that neither sex has all to itself. Ah, madam, what a relief it is to come back to your witty volumes, and forget the follies of to-day in those of Mr. Collins and of Mrs. Bennet! How fine, nay, how noble is your art in its delicate reserve, never insisting, never forcing the note, never pushing the sketch into the caricature!

You worked without thinking of it, in the spirit of Greece, on a labor happily limited, and exquisitely organized. "Dear books," we say, with Miss Thackeray—"dear books, bright, sparkling with wit and animation, in which the homely heroines charm, the dull hours fly, and the very bores are enchanting."

To Sir Walter Scott, Bart.

Rodono, St. Mary's Loch:
Sept. 8, 1885.

Sir,—In your biography it is recorded that you not only won the favor of all men and women; but that a domestic fowl conceived an affection for you, and that a pig, by his will, had never been severed from your company. If some Circe had repeated in my case her favorite miracle of turning mortals into swine, and had given me a choice, into that fortunate pig, blessed among his race, would I have been converted! You, almost alone among men of letters, still, like a living friend, win and charm us out of the past; and if one might call up a poet, as the scholiast tried to call Homer, from the shades, who would not, out of all the rest, demand some hours of your society? Who that ever meddled with letters, what child of the irritable race, possessed even a tithe of your simple manliness, of the heart that never knew a touch of jealousy, that envied no man his laurels, that took honor and wealth as they came, but never would have deplored them had you missed both and remained but the Border sportsman and the Border antiquary?

Were the word "genial" not so much profaned, were it not misused, in easy good-nature, to extenuate lettered and sensual indolence, that worn old term might be applied, above all men, to "the Shirra." But perhaps we scarcely need a word (it would be seldom in use) for a character so rare, or rather so lonely, in its nobility and charm as that of Walter Scott. Here, in the heart of your own country, among your own gray round-shouldered hills (each so like the other that the shadow of one falling on its neighbor exactly outlines that neighbor's shape), it is of you and of your works that a native of the Forest is most frequently brought in mind. All the spirits of the river and the hill, all the dying refrains of ballad and the fading echoes of story, all the memory of the wild past, each legend of burn and loch, seem to have combined to inform your spirit, and to secure themselves an immortal life in your song. It is through you that we remember them; and in recalling them, as in treading each hillside in this land, we again remember you and bless you.

It is not "Sixty Years Since" the echo of the Tweed among his pebbles fell for the last time on your ear; not sixty years since, and how much is altered! But two generations have passed; the lad who used to ride from Edinburgh to Abbotsford, carrying new books for you, and old, is still vending, in George Street, old books and new. Of politics I have not the heart to speak. Little joy would you have had in most that has befallen since the Reform Bill was passed, to the chivalrous cry of "burke Sir Walter." We are still very Radical in the Forest, and you were taken away from many evils to come. How would the cheek of Walter Scott, or of Leyden, have blushed at the names of Majuba, The Soudan, Maiwand, and many others that recall political cowardice or military incapacity! On the other hand, who but you could have sung the dirge of Gordon, or wedded with immortal verse the names of Hamilton (who fell with Cavagnari), of the two Stewarts, of many another clansman, brave among the bravest! Only he who told how

> The stubborn spearmen still made good
> Their dark impenetrable wood

could have fitly rhymed a score of feats of arms in which, as at M'Neill's Zareeba and at Abu Klea,

> Groom fought like noble, squire like knight,
> As fearlessly and well.

Ah, Sir, the hearts of the rulers may wax faint, and the voting classes may forget that they are Britons; but when it comes to blows our fighting men might cry, with Leyden,

> My name is little Jock Elliot,
> And wha daur meddle wi' me!

Much is changed, in the country-side as well as in the country; but much remains. The little towns of your time are populous and excessively black with the smoke of factories—not, I fear, at present very flourishing. In Galashiels you still see the little change-house and the cluster of cottages round the Laird's lodge, like the clachan of Tully Veolan. But these plain remnants of the old Scotch towns are almost buried in a multitude of "smoky dwarf houses"—a living poet, Mr. Matthew Arnold, has found the fitting phrase for these dwellings, once for all. All over the Forest the waters are dirty and poisoned: I think they are filthiest below Hawick; but this may be mere local prejudice in a Selkirk man. To keep them clean costs money; and, though improvements are often promised, I cannot see much change for the better. Abbotsford, luckily, is above Galashiels, and only receives the dirt and dyes of Selkirk, Peebles,

Walkerburn, and Innerlethen. On the other hand, your ill-omened later dwelling, "the unhappy palace of your race," is overlooked by villas that prick a cockney ear among their larches, hotels of the future. Ah, Sir, Scotland is a strange place. Whiskey is exiled from some of our caravansaries, and they have banished Sir John Barleycorn. It seems as if the views of the excellent critic (who wrote your life lately, and said you had left no descendants, *le pauvre homme!*) were beginning to prevail. This pious biographer was greatly shocked by that capital story about the keg of whiskey that arrived at the Liddesdale farmer's during family prayers. Your Toryism also was an offence to him.

Among these vicissitudes of things and the overthrow of customs, let us be thankful that, beyond the reach of the manufacturers, the Border country remains as kind and homely as ever. I looked at Ashiestiel some days ago: the house seemed just as it may have been when you left it for Abbotsford, only there was a lawn-tennis net on the lawn, the hill on the opposite bank of the Tweed was covered to the crest with turnips, and the burn did not sing below the little bridge, for in this arid summer the burn was dry. But there was still a grilse that rose to a big March brown in the shrunken stream below Elibank. This may not interest you, who styled yourself

No fisher,
But a well-wisher
To the game!

Still, as when you were thinking over Marmion, a man might have "grand gallops among the hills"—those grave wastes of heather and bent that sever all the watercourses and roll their sheep-covered pastures from Dollar Law to White Combe, and from White Combe to the Three Brethren Cairn and the Windburg and Skelf-hill Pen. Yes, Teviotdale is pleasant still, and there is not a drop of dye in the water, *purior electro*, of Yarrow. St. Mary's Loch lies beneath me, smitten with wind and rain—the St. Mary's of North and of the Shepherd. Only the trout, that see a myriad of artificial flies, are shyer than of yore. The Shepherd could no longer fill a cart up Meggat with trout so much of a size that the country people took them for herrings.

The grave of Piers Cockburn is still not desecrated: hard by it lies, within a little wood; and beneath that slab of old sandstone, and the graven letters, and the sword and shield, sleep "Piers Cockburn and Marjory his wife." Not a hundred yards off was the castle-door where they hanged him; this is the tomb of the ballad, and the lady that buried him rests now with her wild lord.

Oh, wat ye no my heart was sair,
When I happit the mouls on his yellow hair;
Oh, wat ye no my heart was wae,
When I turned about and went my way!

Here too hearts have broken, and there is a sacredness in the shadow and beneath these clustering berries of the rowan-tree. That sacredness, that reverent memory of our old land, it is always and inextricably blended with our memories, with our thoughts, with our love of you. Scotchmen, methinks, who owe so much to you, owe you most for the example you gave of the beauty of a life of honor, showing them what, by Heaven's blessing, a Scotchman still might be.

Words, empty and unavailing—for what words of ours can speak our thoughts or interpret our affections! From you first, as we followed the deer with King James, or rode with William of Deloraine on his midnight errand, did we learn what Poetry means, and all the happiness that is in the gift of song. This, and more than may be told, you gave us, that are not forgetful, not ungrateful, though our praise be unequal to our gratitude. *Fungor inani munere!*

ROBERT LOUIS STEVENSON
(1845-1894)

From A Child's Garden of Verses

Whole Duty of Children

A child should always say what's true
And speak when he is spoken to,
And behave mannerly at table;
At least as far as he is able.

Foreign Lands

Up into the cherry tree
Who should climb but little me?
I held the trunk with both my hands
And looked abroad on foreign lands.

I saw the next door garden lie,
Adorned with flowers, before my eye,
And many pleasant places more
That I had never seen before.

I saw the dimpling river pass
And be the sky's blue looking-glass;
The dusty roads go up and down
With people tramping into town.

If I could find a higher tree
Farther and farther I should see,
To where the grown-up river slips
Into the sea among the ships,

To where the roads on either hand
Lead onward into fairy land,
Where all the children dine at five,
And all the playthings come alive.

The Land of Counterpane

When I was sick and lay a-bed,
I had two pillows at my head,
And all my toys beside me lay
To keep me happy all the day.

And sometimes for an hour or so
I watched my leaden soldiers go,
With different uniforms and drills,
Among the bed-clothes, through the hills;

And sometimes sent my ships in fleets
All up and down among the sheets;
Or brought my trees and houses out,
And planted cities all about.

I was the giant great and still
That sits upon the pillow-hill,
And sees before him, dale and plain,
The pleasant land of counterpane.

System

Every night my prayers I say,
And get my dinner every day;
And every day that I've been good,
I get an orange after food.

The child that is not clean and neat,
With lots of toys and things to eat,
He is a naughty child, I'm sure—
Or else his dear papa is poor.

Good and Bad Children

Children, you are very little,
And your bones are very brittle;
If you would grow great and stately,
You must try to walk sedately.

You must still be bright and quiet,
And content with simple diet;
And remain, through all bewild'ring,
Innocent and honest children.

Happy hearts and happy faces,
Happy play in grassy places—
That was how, in ancient ages,
Children grew to kings and sages.

But the unkind and the unruly,
And the sort who eat unduly,
They must never hope for glory—
Theirs is quite a different story!

Cruel children, crying babies,
All grow up as geese and gabies,
Hated, as their age increases,
By their nephews and their nieces.

The Unseen Playmate

When children are playing alone on the green
In comes the playmate that never was seen.
When children are happy and lonely and good,
The Friend of the Children comes out of the wood.

Nobody heard him and nobody saw,
His is a picture you never could draw,
But he's sure to be present, abroad or at home,
When children are happy and playing alone.

He lies in the laurels, he runs on the grass,
He sings when you tinkle the musical glass;
Whene'er you are happy and cannot tell why,
The Friend of the Children is sure to be by!

He loves to be little, he hates to be big,
'Tis he that inhabits the caves that you dig;
'Tis he when you play with your soldiers of tin
That sides with the Frenchmen and never can win.

'Tis he, when at night you go off to your bed,
Bids you go to your sleep and not trouble your head;
For wherever they're lying, in cupboard or shelf,
'Tis he will take care of your playthings himself!

From Underwoods

Requiem

Under the wide and starry sky,
Dig the grave and let me lie.
Glad did I live and gladly die,
And I laid me down with a will.

This be the verse you grave for me:
Here he lies where he longed to be;
Home is the sailor, home from sea,
And the hunter home from the hill.

The Celestial Surgeon

If I have faltered more or less
In my great task of happiness;
If I have moved among my race
And shown no glorious morning face;
If beams from happy human eyes
Have moved me not; if morning skies,
Books, and my food, and summer rain
Knocked on my sullen heart in vain:—
Lord, thy most pointed pleasure take
And stab my spirit broad awake;
Or, Lord, if too obdurate I,
Choose thou, before that spirit die,
A piercing pain, a killing sin,
And to my dead heart run them in!

Say not of me that weakly I declined

Say not of me that weakly I declined
The labours of my sires, and fled the sea,
The towers we founded and the lamps we lit,
To play at home with paper like a child.
But rather say: *In the afternoon of time*
A strenuous family dusted from its hands
The sand of granite, and beholding far
Along the sounding coast its pyramids
And tall memorials catch the dying sun,
Smiled well content, and to this childish task
Around the fire addressed its evening hours.

From The Manse

Probably Arboreal

Now I often wonder what I have inherited from this old minister. I must suppose, indeed, that he was fond of preaching sermons, and so am I, though I never heard it maintained that either of us loved to hear them. He sought health in his youth in the Isle of Wight, and I have sought it in both hemispheres; but whereas he found and kept it, I am still on the quest. He was a great lover of Shakespeare, whom he read aloud, I have been told, with taste; well, I love my Shakespeare also, and am persuaded I can read him well, though I own I never have been told so. He made embroidery, designing his own patterns; and in that kind of work I never made anything but a kettle-holder in Berlin wool, and an odd garter of knitting, which was as black as the chimney before I had done with it. He loved port, and nuts, and porter; and so do I, but they agreed better with my grandfather, which seems to me a breach of contract. He had chalk-stones in his fingers; and these, in good time, I may possibly inherit, but I would much rather have inherited his noble presence. Try as I please, I cannot join myself on with the reverend doctor; and all the while, no doubt, and even as I write the phrase, he moves in my blood, and whispers words to me, and sits efficient in the very knot and centre of my being. In his garden, as I played there, I learned the love of mills—or had I an ancestor a miller?—and a kindness for the neighborhood of graves, as homely things not without their poetry—or had I an ancestor a sexton? But what of the garden where he played himself?—for that, too, was a scene of my education. Some part of me played there in the eighteenth century, and ran races under the green avenue at Pilrig; some part of me trudged up Leith Walk, which was still a country place, and sat on the High School benches, and was thrashed, perhaps, by Dr. Adam. The house where I spent my youth was not yet thought upon; but we made holiday parties among the corn-fields on its site, and ate strawberries and cream near by at a gardener's. All this I had forgotten; only my grandfather remembered and once reminded me. I have forgotten, too, how we grew up, and took orders, and went to our first Ayrshire parish, and fell in love with and married a daughter of Burns's Dr. Smith—"Smith opens out his cauld harangues." I have forgotten, but I was there all the same, and heard stories of Burns at first hand.

And there is a thing stranger than all that; for this *homunculus* or part-man of mine that walked about the eighteenth century with Dr. Balfour in his youth, was in the way of meeting other *homunculos* or part-men, in the persons of my other ancestors. These were of a lower order, and doubtless we looked down upon them duly. But as I went to college with Dr. Balfour, I may have seen the lamp and oil man taking down the shutters from his shop beside the Tron;—we may have had a rabbit-hutch or a bookshelf made for us by a certain carpenter in I know not what wynd of the old, smoky city; or, upon some holiday excursion, we may have looked into the windows of a cottage in a flower-garden and seen a certain weaver plying his shuttle. And these were all kinsmen of mine upon the other side; and from the eyes of the lamp and oil man one-half of my unborn father, and one-quarter of myself, looked out upon us as we went by to college. Nothing of all this would cross the mind of the young student, as he posted up the Bridges with trim, stockinged legs, in that city of cocked hats and good Scotch still unadulterated. It would not cross his mind that he should have a daughter; and the lamp and oil man, just then beginning, by a not unnatural metastasis, to bloom into a lighthouse-engineer, should have a grandson; and that these two, in the fulness of time, should wed; and some portion of that student himself should survive yet a year or two longer in the person of their child.

But our ancestral adventures are beyond even the arithmetic of fancy; and it is the chief recommendation of long pedigrees, that we can follow backward the careers of our *homunculi* and be reminded of our antenatal lives. Our conscious years are but a moment in the history of the elements that build us. Are you a bank-clerk, and do you live at Peckham? It was not always so. And though to-day I am only a man of letters, either tradition errs or I was present when there landed at St. Andrews a French barber-surgeon, to tend the health and the beard of the great Cardinal Beaton; I have shaken a spear in the Debatable Land and shouted the slogan of the Elliots; I was present when a skipper, plying from Dundee, smuggled Jacobites to France after the '15; I was in a West India merchant's office, perhaps next door to Bailie Nichol Jarvie's, and managed the business of a plantation in St. Kitt's; I was with my engineer-grandfather (the son-in-law of the lamp and oil man) when he sailed north about Scotland on the famous cruise that gave us the *Pirate* and the *Lord of the Isles;* I was with him, too, on the Bell Rock, in the fog, when the *Smeaton* had drifted from her moorings, and the Aberdeen men, pick in hand, had seized upon the only boats, and he must stoop and lap sea-water before his tongue could utter audible words; and once more with him when the Bell Rock beacon took a "thrawe," and his workmen fled into the tower, then nearly finished, and he sat unmoved reading in his Bible—or affecting to read—till one after another slunk back with confusion of countenance to their engineer. Yes, parts of me have seen life, and met adventures, and sometimes met them well. And away in the still cloudier past, the threads that make me up can be traced by fancy into the bosoms of thousands and millions of ascendants: Picts who rallied round Macbeth and the old (and highly preferable) system of descent by females, fleërs from before the legions of Agricola, marchers in Pannonian morasses, star-gazers on Chaldæan plateaus; and, furthest of all, what face is this that fancy can see peering through the disparted branches? What sleeper in green tree-tops, what muncher of nuts, concludes my pedigree? Probably arboreal in his habits. . . .

And I know not which is the more strange, that I should carry about with me some fibres of my minister-grandfather; or that in him, as he sat in his cool study, grave, reverend, contented gentleman, there was an aboriginal frisking of the blood that was not his; tree-top memories, like undeveloped negatives, lay dormant in his mind; tree-top instincts awoke and were trod down; and Probably Arboreal (scarce to be distinguished from a monkey) gambolled and chattered in the brain of the old divine.

A Lodging for the Night

It was late in November, 1456. The snow fell over Paris with rigorous, relentless persistence; sometimes the wind made a sally and scattered it in flying vortices; sometimes there was a lull, and flake after flake descended out of the black night air, silent, circuitous, interminable. To poor people, looking up under moist eyebrows, it seemed a wonder where it all came from. Master Francis Villon had propounded an alternative that afternoon, at a tavern window: was it only Pagan Jupiter plucking geese upon Olympus? or were the holy angels moulting? He was only a poor Master of Arts, he went on; and as the question somewhat touched upon divinity, he durst not venture to conclude. A silly old priest from Montargis, who was among the company, treated the young rascal to a bottle of wine in honor of the jest and grimaces with which it was accompanied, and swore on his own white beard that he had been just such another irreverent dog when he was Villon's age.

The air was raw and pointed, but not far below freezing; and the flakes were large, damp, and adhesive. The whole city was sheeted up. An army might have marched from end to end and not a footfall given the alarm. If there were any belated birds in heaven, they saw the island like a large white patch, and the bridges like slim white spars, on the black ground of the river. High up overhead the snow settled among the tracery of the cathedral towers. Many a niche was drifted full; many a statue wore a long white bonnet on its grotesque or sainted head. The gargoyles had been transformed into great false noses, drooping towards the point. The crockets were like upright pillows swollen on one side. In the intervals of the wind, there was a dull sound of dripping about the precincts of the church.

The cemetery of St. John had taken its own share of the snow. All the graves were decently covered; tall white housetops stood around in grave array; worthy burghers were long ago in bed, benightcapped like their domiciles; there was no light in all the neighborhood but a little peep from a lamp that hung swinging in the church choir, and tossed the shadows to and fro in time to its oscillations. The clock was hard on ten when the patrol went by with halberds and a lantern, beating their hands; and they saw nothing suspicious about the cemetery of St. John.

Yet there was a small house, backed up against the cemetery wall, which was still awake, and awake to evil purpose, in that snoring district. There was not much to betray it from without; only a stream of warm vapor from the chimney-top, a patch where the snow melted on the roof, and a few half-obliterated footprints at the door. But within, behind the shuttered windows, Master Francis Villon the poet, and some of the thievish crew with whom he consorted, were keeping the night alive and passing round the bottle.

A great pile of living embers diffused a strong and ruddy glow from the arched chimney. Before this straddled Dom Nicolas, the Picardy monk, with his skirts picked up and his fat legs bared to the comfortable warmth. His dilated shadow cut the room in half; and the firelight only escaped on either side of his broad person, and in a little pool between his outspread feet. His face had the beery, bruised appearance of the continual drinker's; it was covered with a network of congested veins, purple in ordinary circumstances, but now pale violet, for even with his back to the fire the cold pinched him on the other side. His cowl had half fallen back, and made a strange excrescence on either side of his bull neck. So he straddled, grumbling, and cut the room in half with the shadow of his portly frame.

On the right, Villon and Guy Tabary were huddled together over a scrap of parchment; Villon making a ballade which he was to call the "Ballade of Roast Fish," and Tabary spluttering admiration at his shoulder. The poet was a rag of a man, dark, little, and lean, with hollow cheeks and thin black locks. He carried his four-and-twenty years with feverish animation. Greed had made folds about his eyes, evil smiles had puckered his mouth. The wolf and pig struggled together in his face. It was an eloquent, sharp, ugly, earthly countenance. His hands were small and prehensile, with fingers knotted like a cord; and they were continually flickering in front of him in violent and expressive pantomime. As for Tabary, a broad, complacent, admiring imbecility breathed from his squash nose and slobbering lips: he had become a thief, just as he might have become the most decent of burgesses, by the imperious chance that rules the lives of human geese and human donkeys.

At the monk's other hand, Montigny and Thevenin Pensete played a game of chance. About the first there clung some flavor of good birth and training, as about a fallen angel; something long, lithe, and courtly in the person; something aquiline and darkling in the face. Thevenin, poor soul, was in great feather: he had done a good stroke of knavery that afternoon in the Faubourg St. Jacques, and all night he had been gaining from Montigny. A flat smile illuminated his face; his bald head shone rosily in a garland of red curls; his little protuberant stomach shook with silent chucklings as he swept in his gains.

"Doubles or quits?" said Thevenin.

Montigny nodded grimly.

"Some men prefer to dine in state," wrote Villon, *"On bread and cheese on silver plate.* Or, or—help me out, Guido!"

Tabary giggled.

"Or parsley on a golden dish," scribbled the poet.

The wind was freshening without; it drove the snow before it, and sometimes raised its voice in a victorious whoop, and made sepulchral grumblings in the chimney. The cold was growing sharper as the night went on. Villon, protruding his lips, imitated the gust with something between a whistle and a groan. It was an eerie, uncomfortable talent of the poet's, much detested by the Picardy monk.

"Can't you hear it rattle in the gibbet?" said Villon. "They are all dancing the devil's jig on nothing, up there. You may dance, my gallants, you'll be none the warmer! Whew! what a gust! Down went somebody just now! A medlar the fewer on the three-legged medlar-tree!—I say, Dom Nicolas, it'll be cold to-night on the St. Denis Road?" he asked.

Dom Nicolas winked both his big eyes, and seemed to choke upon his Adam's apple. Montfaucon, the great grisly Paris gibbet, stood hard by the St. Denis Road, and the pleasantry touched him on the raw. As for Tabary, he laughed immoderately over the medlars; he had never heard anything more light-hearted; and he held his sides and crowed. Villon fetched him a fillip on the nose, which turned his mirth into an attack of coughing.

"Oh, stop that row," said Villon, "and think of rhymes to 'fish.'"

"Doubles or quits," said Montigny doggedly.

"With all my heart," quoth Thevenin.

"Is there any more in that bottle?" asked the monk.

"Open another," said Villon. "How do you ever hope to fill that big hogshead, your body, with little things like bottles? And how do you expect to get to heaven? How many angels, do you fancy, can be spared to carry up a single monk from Picardy? Or do you think yourself another Elias—and they'll send the coach for you?"

"Hominibus impossibile," replied the monk as he filled his glass.

Tabary was in ecstasies.

Villon filliped his nose again.

"Laugh at my jokes, if you like," he said.

"It was very good," objected Tabary.

Villon made a face at him. "Think of rhymes to 'fish,'" he said. "What have you to do with Latin? You'll wish you knew none of it at the great assizes, when the devil calls for Guido Tabary, clericus—the devil with the hump-back and red-hot finger-nails. Talking of the devil," he added in a whisper, "look at Montigny!"

All three peered covertly at the gamester. He did not seem to be enjoying his luck. His mouth was a little to a side; one nostril nearly shut, and the other much inflated. The black dog was on his back, as people say, in terrifying nursery metaphor; and he breathed hard under the gruesome burthen.

"He looks as if he could knife him," whispered Tabary, with round eyes.

The monk shuddered, and turned his face and spread his open hands to the red embers. It was the cold that thus affected Dom Nicolas, and not any excess of moral sensibility.

"Come now," said Villon—"about this ballade. How does it run so far?" And beating time with his hand, he read it aloud to Tabary.

They were interrupted at the fourth rhyme by a brief and fatal movement among the gamesters. The round was completed, and Thevenin was just opening his mouth to claim another victory, when Montigny leaped up, swift as an adder, and stabbed him to the heart. The blow took effect before he had time to utter a cry, before he had time to move. A tremor or two convulsed his frame; his hands opened and shut, his heels rattled on the floor; then his head rolled backward over one shoulder with the eyes wide open; and Thevenin Pensete's spirit had returned to Him who made it.

Every one sprang to his feet; but the business was over in two twos. The four living fellows looked at each other in rather a ghastly fashion; the dead man contemplating a corner of the roof with a singular and ugly leer.

"My God!" said Tabary; and he began to pray in Latin.

Villon broke out into hysterical laughter. He came a step forward and ducked a ridiculous bow at Thevenin, and laughed still louder. Then he sat down suddenly, all of a heap, upon a stool, and continued laughing bitterly, as though he would shake himself to pieces.

Montigny recovered his composure first.

"Let's see what he has about him," he remarked, and he picked the dead man's pockets with a practised hand, and divided the money into four equal portions on the table. "There's for you," he said.

The monk received his share with a deep sigh, and a single stealthy glance at the dead Thevenin, who was beginning to sink into himself and topple sideways off the chair.

"We're all in for it," cried Villon, swallowing his mirth. "It's a hanging job for every man jack of us that's here—not to speak of those who aren't." He made a shocking gesture in the air with his raised right hand, and put out his tongue and threw his head on one side, so as to counterfeit the appearance of one who has been hanged. Then he pocketed his share of the spoil, and executed a shuffle with his feet as if to restore the circulation.

Tabary was the last to help himself; he made a dash at the money, and retired to the other end of the apartment.

Montigny stuck Thevenin upright in the chair, and drew out the dagger, which was followed by a jet of blood.

"You fellows had better be moving," he said, as he wiped the blade on his victim's doublet.

"I think we had," returned Villon, with a gulp. "Damn his fat head!" he broke out. "It sticks in my throat like phlegm. What right has a man to have red hair when he is dead?" And he fell all of a heap again upon the stool, and fairly covered his face with his hands.

Montigny and Dom Nicolas laughed aloud, even Tabary feebly chiming in.

"Cry baby," said the monk.

"I always said he was a woman," added Montigny, with a sneer. "Sit up, can't you?" he went on, giving another shake to the murdered body. "Tread out that fire, Nick!"

But Nick was better employed; he was quietly taking Villon's purse, as the poet sat, limp and trembling, on the stool where he had been making a ballade not three minutes before. Montigny and Tabary dumbly demanded a share of the booty, which the monk silently promised as he passed the little bag into the bosom of his gown. In many ways an artistic nature unfits a man for practical existence.

No sooner had the theft been accomplished than Villon shook himself, jumped to his feet, and began helping to scatter and extinguish the embers. Meanwhile Montigny opened the door and cautiously peered into the street. The coast was clear; there was no meddlesome patrol in sight. Still it was judged wiser to slip out severally; and as Villon was himself in a hurry to escape from the neighborhood of the dead Thevenin, and the rest were in a still greater hurry to get rid of him before he should discover the loss of his money, he was the first by general consent to issue forth into the street.

The wind had triumphed and swept all the clouds from heaven. Only a few vapors, as thin as moonlight, fleeted rapidly across the stars. It was bitter cold; and by a common optical effect, things seemed almost more definite than in the broadest daylight. The sleeping city was absolutely still; a company of white hoods, a field full of little alps, below the twinkling stars. Villon cursed his fortune. Would it were still snowing! Now, wherever he went, he left an indelible trail behind him on the glittering streets; wherever he went he was still tethered to the house by the cemetery of St. John; wherever he went he must weave, with his own plodding feet, the rope that bound him to the crime and would bind him to the gallows. The leer of the dead man came back to him with a new significance. He snapped his fingers as if to pluck up his own spirits, and choosing a street at random, stepped boldly forward in the snow.

Two things preoccupied him as he went: the aspect of the gallows at Montfaucon in this bright, windy phase of the night's existence, for one; and for another, the look of the dead man with his bald head and garland of red curls. Both struck cold upon his heart, and he kept quickening his pace as if he could escape from unpleasant thoughts by mere fleetness of foot. Sometimes he looked back over his shoulder with a sudden nervous jerk; but he was the only moving thing in the white streets, except when the wind swooped round a corner and threw up the snow, which was beginning to freeze, in spouts of glittering dust.

Suddenly he saw, a long way before him, a black clump and a couple of lanterns. The clump was in motion, and the lanterns swung as though carried by men walking. It was a patrol. And though it was merely crossing his line of march he judged it wiser to get out of eyeshot as speedily as he could. He was not in the humor to be challenged, and he was conscious of making a very conspicuous mark upon the snow. Just on his left hand there stood a great hotel, with some turrets and a large porch before the door; it was half ruinous, he remembered, and had long stood empty; and so he made three steps of it, and jumped into the shelter of the porch. It was pretty dark inside, after the glimmer of the snowy streets, and he was groping forward with outspread hands, when he stumbled over some substance which offered an indescribable mixture of resistances, hard and soft, firm and loose. His heart gave a leap, and he sprang two steps back and stared dreadfully at the obstacle. Then he gave a little laugh of relief. It was only a woman, and she dead. He knelt beside her to make sure upon this latter point. She was freezing cold, and rigid like a stick. A little ragged finery fluttered in the wind about her hair, and her cheeks had been heavily rouged that same afternoon. Her pockets were quite empty; but in her stocking, underneath the garter, Villon found two of the small coins that went by the name of whites. It was little enough; but it was always something; and the poet was moved with a deep sense of pathos that she should have died before she had spent her money. That seemed to him a dark and pitiable mystery; and he looked from the coins in his hands to the dead woman, and back again to the coins, shaking his head over the riddle of man's life. Henry V. of England, dying at Vincennes just after he had conquered France, and this poor jade cut off by a cold draught in a great man's doorway, before she had time to spend her couple of whites—it seemed a cruel way to carry on the world. Two whites would have taken such a little while to squander; and yet it would have been one more good taste in the mouth, one more smack of the lips, before the devil got the soul, and the body was left to birds and vermin. He would like to use all his tallow before the light was blown out and the lantern broken.

While these thoughts were passing through his mind, he was feeling, half mechanically, for his purse. Suddenly his heart stopped beating; a feeling of cold scales passed up the back of his legs, and a cold blow seemed to fall upon his scalp. He stood petrified for a moment; then he felt again with one feverish movement; and then his loss burst upon him, and he was covered at once with perspiration. To spendthrifts money is so living and actual—it is such a thin veil between them and their pleasures! There is only one limit to their fortune—that of time; and a spendthrift with only a few crowns is the Emperor of Rome until they are spent. For such a person to lose his money is to suffer the most shocking reverse, and fall from heaven to hell, from all to nothing, in a breath. And all the more if he has put his head in the halter for it; if he may be hanged to-morrow for that same purse, so dearly earned, so foolishly departed! Villon stood and cursed; he threw the two whites into the street; he shook his fist at heaven; he stamped, and was not horrified to find himself trampling the poor corpse. Then he began rapidly to retrace his steps towards the house beside the cemetery. He had forgotten all fear of the patrol, which was long gone by at any rate, and had no idea but that of his lost purse. It was in vain that he looked right and left upon the snow: nothing was to be seen. He had not dropped it in the streets. Had it fallen in the house? He would have liked dearly to go in and see; but the idea of the grisly occupant unmanned him. And he saw besides, as he drew near, that their efforts to put out the fire had been unsuccessful; on the contrary, it had broken into a blaze, and a changeful light played in the chinks of door and window, and revived his terror for the authorities and Paris gibbet.

He returned to the hotel with the porch, and groped about upon the snow for the money he had thrown away in his childish passion. But he could only find one white; the other had probably struck sideways and sunk deeply in. With a single white in his pocket, all his projects for a rousing night in some wild tavern vanished utterly away. And it was not only pleasure that fled laughing from his grasp; positive discomfort, positive pain, attacked him as he stood ruefully before the porch. His perspiration had dried upon him; and although the wind had now fallen, a binding frost was setting in stronger with every hour, and he felt benumbed and sick at heart. What was to be done? Late as was the hour, improbable as was success, he would try the house of his adopted father, the chaplain of St. Benoît.

He ran there all the way, and knocked timidly. There was no answer. He knocked again and again, taking heart with every stroke; and at last steps were heard approaching from within. A barred wicket fell open in the iron-studded door, and emitted a gush of yellow light.

"Hold up your face to the wicket," said the chaplain from within.

"It's only me," whimpered Villon.

"Oh, it's only you, is it?" returned the chaplain; and he cursed him with foul unpriestly oaths for disturbing him at such an hour, and bade him be off to hell, where he came from.

"My hands are blue to the wrist," pleaded Villon; "my feet are dead and full of twinges; my nose aches with the sharp air; the cold lies at my heart. I may be dead before morning. Only this once, father, and before God, I will never ask again!"

"You should have come earlier," said the ecclesiastic coolly. "Young men require a lesson now and then." He shut the wicket and retired deliberately into the interior of the house.

Villon was beside himself; he beat upon the door with his hands and feet, and shouted hoarsely after the chaplain.

"Wormy old fox!" he cried. "If I had my hand under your twist, I would send you flying headlong into the bottomless pit."

A door shut in the interior, faintly audible to the poet down long passages. He passed his hand over his mouth with an oath. And then the humor of the situation struck him, and he laughed and looked lightly up to heaven, where the stars seemed to be winking over his discomfiture.

What was to be done? It looked very like a night in the frosty streets. The idea of the dead woman popped into his imagination, and gave him a hearty fright; what had happened to her in the early night might very well happen to him before morning. And he so young! and with such immense possibilities of disorderly amusement before him! He felt quite pathetic over the notion of his own fate, as if it had been some one else's, and made a little imaginative vignette of the scene in the morning when they should find his body.

He passed all his chances under review, turning the white between his thumb and forefinger. Unfortunately he was on bad terms with some old friends who would once have taken pity on him in such a plight. He had lampooned them in verses; he had beaten and cheated them; and yet now, when he was in so close a pinch, he thought there was at least one who might perhaps relent. It was a chance. It was worth trying at least, and he would go and see.

On the way, two little accidents happened to him which colored his musings in a very different manner. For, first he fell in with the track of a patrol, and walked in it for some hundred yards, although it lay out of his direction. And this spirited him up; at least he had confused his trail; for he was still possessed with the idea of people tracking him all about Paris over the snow, and collaring him next morning before he was awake. The other matter affected him quite differently. He passed a street corner, where, not so long before, a woman and her child had been devoured by wolves. This was just the kind of weather, he reflected, when wolves might take it into their heads to enter Paris again; and a lone man in these deserted streets would run the chance of something worse than a mere scare. He stopped and looked upon the place with an unpleasant interest—it was a centre where several lanes intersected each other; and he looked down them all, one after another, and held his breath to listen, lest he should detect some galloping black things on the snow or hear the sound of howling between him and the river. He remembered his mother telling him the story and pointing out the spot, while he was yet a child. His mother! If he only knew where she lived, he might make sure at least of shelter. He determined he would inquire upon the morrow; nay, he would go and see her too, poor old girl! So thinking, he arrived at his destination—his last hope for the night.

The house was quite dark, like its neighbors; and yet after a few taps, he heard a movement overhead, a door opening, and a cautious voice asking who was there. The poet named himself in a loud whisper, and waited, not without some trepidation, the result. Nor had he to wait long. A window was suddenly opened, and a pailful of slops splashed down upon the doorstep. Villon had not been unprepared for something of the sort, and had put himself as much in shelter as the nature of the porch admitted; but for all that, he was deplorably drenched below the waist. His hose began to freeze almost at once. Death from cold and exposure stared him in the face; he remembered he was of phthisical tendency, and began coughing tentatively. But the gravity of the danger steadied his nerves. He stopped a few hundred yards from the door where he had been so rudely used, and reflected with his finger to his nose. He could only see one way of getting a lodging, and that was to take it. He had noticed a house not far away, which looked as if it might be easily broken into, and thither he betook himself promptly, entertaining himself on the way with the idea of a room still hot, with a table still loaded with the remains of supper, where he might pass the rest of the black hours and whence he should issue, on the morrow, with an armful of valuable plate. He even considered on what viands and what wines he should prefer; and as he was calling the roll of his favorite dainties, roast fish presented itself to his mind with an odd mixture of amusement and horror.

"I shall never finish that ballade," he thought to himself; and then, with another shudder at the recollection, "Oh, damn his fat head!" he repeated fervently, and spat upon the snow.

The house in question looked dark at first sight; but as Villon made a preliminary inspection in search of the handiest point of attack, a little twinkle of light caught his eye from behind a curtained window.

"The devil!" he thought. "People awake! Some student or some saint, confound the crew! Can't they get drunk and lie in bed snoring like their neighbors? What's the good of curfew, and poor devils of bell-ringers jumping at a rope's end in bell-towers? What's the use of day, if people sit up all night? The gripes to them!" He grinned as he saw where his logic was leading him. "Every man to his business, after all," added he, "and if they're awake, by the Lord, I may come by a supper honestly for once, and cheat the devil."

He went boldly to the door and knocked with an assured hand. On both previous occasions, he had knocked timidly and with some dread of attracting notice; but now when he had just discarded the thought of a burglarious entry, knocking at a door seemed a mighty simple and innocent proceeding. The sound of his blows echoed through the house with thin, phantasmal reverberations, as though it were quite empty; but these had scarcely died away before a measured tread drew near, a couple of bolts were withdrawn, and one wing was opened broadly, as though no guile or fear of guile were known to those within. A tall figure of a man, muscular and spare, but a little bent, confronted Villon. The head was massive in bulk, but finely sculptured; the nose blunt at the bottom, but refining upward to where it joined a pair of strong and honest eyebrows; the mouth and eyes surrounded with delicate markings, and the whole face based upon a thick white beard, boldly and squarely trimmed. Seen as it was by the light of a flickering hand-lamp, it looked perhaps nobler than it had a right to do; but it was a fine face, honorable rather than intelligent, strong, simple, and righteous.

"You knock late, sir," said the old man in resonant, courteous tones.

Villon cringed and brought up many servile words of apology; at a crisis of this sort the beggar was uppermost in him, and the man of genius hid his head with confusion.

"You are cold," repeated the old man, "and hungry? Well, step in." And he ordered him into the house with a noble enough gesture.

"Some great seigneur," thought Villon, as his host, setting down the lamp on the flagged pavement of the entry, shot the bolts once more into their places.

"You will pardon me if I go in front," he said, when this was done; and he preceded the poet up-stairs into a large apartment, warmed with a pan of charcoal and lit by a great lamp hanging from the roof. It was very bare of furniture: only some gold plate on a sideboard; some folios; and a stand of armor between the windows. Some smart tapestry hung upon the walls, representing the crucifixion of our Lord in one piece, and in another a scene of shepherds and shepherdesses by a running stream. Over the chimney was a shield of arms.

"Will you seat yourself," said the old man, "and forgive me if I leave you? I am alone in my house to-night, and if you are to eat I must forage for you myself."

No sooner was his host gone than Villon leaped from the chair on which he had just seated himself, and began examining the room, with the stealth and passion of a cat. He weighed the gold flagons in his hand, opened all the folios, and investigated the arms upon the shield, and the stuff with which the seats were lined. He raised the window curtains, and saw that the windows were set with rich stained glass in figures, so far as he could see, of martial import. Then he stood in the middle of the room, drew a long breath, and retaining it with puffed cheeks, looked round and round him, turning on his heels, as if to impress every feature of the apartment on his memory.

"Seven pieces of plate," he said. "If there had been ten, I would have risked it. A fine house, and a fine old master, so help me all the saints!"

And just then, hearing the old man's tread returning along the corridor, he stole back to his chair, and began humbly toasting his wet legs before the charcoal pan.

His entertainer had a plate of meat in one hand and a jug of wine in the other. He set down the plate upon the table, motioning Villon to draw in his chair, and going to the sideboard, brought back two goblets which he filled.

"I drink your better fortune," he said, gravely touching Villon's cup with his own.

"To our better acquaintance," said the poet, growing bold. A mere man of the people would have been awed by the courtesy of the old seigneur, but Villon was hardened in that matter; he had made mirth for great lords before now, and found them as black rascals as himself. And so he devoted himself to the viands with a ravenous gusto, while the old man, leaning backward, watched him with steady, curious eyes.

"You have blood on your shoulder, my man," he said.

Montigny must have laid his wet right hand upon him as he left the house. He cursed Montigny in his heart.

"It was none of my shedding," he stammered.

"I had not supposed so," returned his host quietly. "A brawl?"

"Well, something of that sort," Villon admitted with a quaver.

"Perhaps a fellow murdered?"

"Oh, no, not murdered," said the poet, more and more confused. "It was all fair play—murdered by accident. I had no hand in it, God strike me dead!" he added fervently.

"One rogue the fewer, I dare say," observed the master of the house.

"You may dare to say that," agreed Villon, infinitely relieved. "As big a rogue as there is between here and Jerusalem. He turned up his toes like a lamb. But it was a nasty thing to look at. I dare say you've seen dead men in your time, my lord?" he added, glancing at the armor.

"Many," said the old man. "I have followed the wars, as you imagine."

Villon laid down his knife and fork, which he had just taken up again. "Were any of them bald?" he asked.

"Oh, yes, and with hair as white as mine."

"I don't think I should mind the white so much," said Villon. "His was red." And he had a return of his shuddering and tendency to laughter, which he drowned with a great draught of wine. "I'm a little put out when I think of it," he went on. "I knew him—damn him! And then the cold gives a man fancies—or the fancies give a man cold, I don't know which."

"Have you any money?" asked the old man.

"I have one white," returned the poet, laughing. "I got it out of a dead jade's stocking in a porch. She was as dead as Cæsar, poor wench, and as cold as a church, with bits of ribbon sticking in her hair. This is a hard world in winter for wolves and wenches and poor rogues like me."

"I," said the old man, "am Enguerrand de la Feuillée, seigneur de Brisetout, bailly du Patatrac. Who and what may you be?"

Villon rose and made a suitable reverence. "I am called Francis Villon," he said, "a poor Master of Arts of this university. I know some Latin, and a deal of vice. I can make chansons, ballades, lais, virelais, and roundels, and I am very fond of wine. I was born in a garret, and I shall not improbably die upon the gallows. I may add, my lord, that from this night forward I am your lordship's very obsequious servant to command."

"No servant of mine," said the knight; "my guest for this evening, and no more."

"A very grateful guest," said Villon politely, and he drank in dumb show to his entertainer.

"You are shrewd," began the old man, tapping his forehead, "very shrewd; you have learning; you are a clerk; and yet you take a small piece of money off a dead woman in the street. Is it not a kind of theft?"

"It is a kind of theft much practised in the wars, my lord."

"The wars are the field of honor," returned the old man proudly. "There a man plays his life upon the cast; he fights in the name of his lord the king, his Lord God, and all their lordships the holy saints and angels."

"Put it," said Villon, "that I were really a thief, should I not play my life also, and against heavier odds?"

"For gain but not for honor."

"Gain?" repeated Villon with a shrug. "Gain! The poor fellow wants supper, and takes it. So does the soldier in a campaign. Why, what are all these requisitions we hear so much about? If they are not gain to those who take them, they are loss enough to the others. The men-at-arms drink by a good fire, while the burgher bites his nails to buy them wine and wood. I have seen a good many ploughmen swinging on trees about the country; ay, I have seen thirty on one elm, and a very poor figure they made; and when I asked some one how all these came to be hanged, I was told it was because they could not scrape together enough crowns to satisfy the men-at-arms."

"These things are a necessity of war, which the low-born must endure with constancy. It is true that some captains drive overhard; there are spirits in every rank not easily moved by pity; and indeed many follow arms who are no better than brigands."

"You see," said the poet, "you cannot separate the soldier from the brigand; and what is a thief but an isolated brigand with circumspect manners? I steal a couple of mutton chops, without so much as disturbing people's sleep; the farmer grumbles a bit, but sups none the less wholesomely on what remains. You come up blowing gloriously on a trumpet, take away the whole sheep, and beat the farmer pitifully into the bargain. I have no trumpet; I am only Tom, Dick, or Harry; I am a rogue and a dog, and hanging's too good for me—with all my heart; but just ask the farmer which of us he prefers, just find out which of us he lies awake to curse on cold nights."

"Look at us two," said his lordship. "I am old, strong, and honored. If I were turned from my house to-morrow, hundreds would be proud to shelter me. Poor people would go out and pass the night in the streets with their children, if I merely hinted that I wished to be alone. And I find you up, wandering homeless, and picking farthings off dead women by the wayside! I fear no man and nothing; I have seen you tremble and lose countenance at a word. I wait God's summons contentedly in my own house, or, if it please the king to call me out again, upon the field of battle. You look for the gallows; a rough, swift death, without hope or honor. Is there no difference between these two?"

"As far as to the moon," Villon acquiesced. "But if I had been born lord of Brisetout, and you had been the poor scholar Francis, would the difference have been any the less? Should not I have been warming my knees at this charcoal pan, and would not you have been groping for farthings in the snow? Should not I have been the soldier, and you the thief?"

"A thief?" cried the old man. "I a thief! If you understood your words, you would repent them."

Villon turned out his hands with a gesture of inimitable impudence. "If your lordship had done me the honor to follow my argument!" he said.

"I do you too much honor in submitting to your presence," said the knight. "Learn to curb your tongue when you speak with old and honorable men, or some one hastier than I may reprove you in a sharper fashion." And he rose and paced the lower end of the apartment, struggling with anger and antipathy. Villon surreptitiously refilled his cup, and settled himself more comfortably in the chair, crossing his knees and leaning his head upon one hand and the elbow against the back of the chair. He was now replete and warm; and he was in nowise frightened for his host, having gauged him as justly as was possible between two such different characters. The night was far spent, and in a very comfortable fashion after all; and he felt morally certain of a safe departure on the morrow.

"Tell me one thing," said the old man, pausing in his walk. "Are you really a thief?"

"I claim the sacred rights of hospitality," returned the poet. "My lord, I am."

"You are very young," the knight continued.

"I should never have been so old," replied Villon, showing his fingers, "if I had not helped myself with these ten talents. They have been my nursing mothers and my nursing fathers."

"You may still repent and change."

"I repent daily," said the poet. "There are few people more given to repentance than poor Francis. As for change, let somebody change my circumstances. A man must continue to eat, if it were only that he may continue to repent."

"The change must begin in the heart," returned the old man solemnly.

"My dear lord," answered Villon, "do you really fancy that I steal for pleasure? I hate stealing, like any other piece of work or of danger. My teeth chatter when I see a gallows. But I must eat, I must drink, I must mix in society of some sort. What the devil! Man is not a solitary animal—*Cui Deus fœminam tradit*. Make me king's pantler—make me abbot of St. Denis; make me bailly of the Patatrac; and then I shall be changed indeed. But as long as you leave me the poor scholar Francis Villon, without a farthing, why, of course, I remain the same."

"The grace of God is all-powerful."

"I should be a heretic to question it," said Francis. "It has made you lord of Brisetout and bailly of the Patatrac; it has given me nothing but the quick wits under my hat and these ten toes upon my hands. May I help myself to wine? I thank you respectfully. By God's grace, you have a very superior vintage."

The lord of Brisetout walked to and fro with his hands behind his back. Perhaps he was not yet quite settled in his mind about the parallel between thieves and soldiers; perhaps Villon had interested him by some cross-thread of sympathy; perhaps his wits were simply muddled by so much unfamiliar reasoning; but whatever the cause, he somehow yearned to convert the young man to a better way of thinking, and could not make up his mind to drive him forth again into the street.

"There is something more than I can understand in this," he said at length. "Your mouth is full of subtleties, and the devil has led you very far astray; but the devil is only a very weak spirit before God's truth, and all his subtleties vanish at a word of true honor, like darkness at morning. Listen to me once more. I learned long ago that a gentleman should live chivalrously and lovingly to God, and the king, and his lady; and though I have seen many strange things done, I have still striven to command my ways upon that rule. It is not only written in all noble histories, but in every man's heart, if he will take care to read. You speak of food and wine, and I know very well that hunger is a difficult trial to endure; but you do not speak of other wants; you say nothing of honor, of faith to God and other men, of courtesy, of love without reproach. It may be that I am not very wise—and yet I think I am—but you seem to me like one who has lost his way and made a great error in life. You are attending to the little wants, and you have totally forgotten the great and only real ones, like a man who should be doctoring toothache on the Judgment Day. For such things as honor and love and faith are not only nobler than food and drink, but indeed I think we desire them more, and suffer more sharply for their absence. I speak to you as I think you will most easily understand me. Are you not, while careful to fill your belly, disregarding another appetite in your heart, which spoils the pleasure of your life and keeps you continually wretched?"

Villon was sensibly nettled under all this sermonising. "You think I have no sense of honor!" he cried. "I'm poor enough, God knows! It's hard to see rich people with their gloves, and you blowing in your hands. An empty belly is a bitter thing, although you speak so lightly of it. If you had had as many as I, perhaps you would change your tune. Anyway I'm a thief—make the most of that—but I'm not a devil from hell, God strike me dead. I would have you know I've an honor of my own, as good as yours, though I don't prate about it all day long, as if it was a God's miracle to have any. It seems quite natural to me; I keep it in its box till it's wanted. Why now, look you here, how long have I been in this room with you? Did you not tell me you were alone in the house? Look at your gold plate! You're strong, if you like, but you're old and unarmed, and I have my knife. What did I want but a jerk of the elbow and here would have been you with the cold steel in your bowels, and there would have been me, linking in the streets, with an armful of golden cups! Did you suppose I hadn't wit enough to see that? And I scorned the action. There are your damned goblets, as safe as in a church; there are you, with your heart ticking as good as new; and here am I, ready to go out again as poor as I came in, with my one white that you threw in my teeth! And you think I have no sense of honor—God strike me dead!"

The old man stretched out his right arm. "I will tell you what you are," he said. "You are a rogue, my man, an impudent and black-hearted rogue and vagabond. I have passed an hour with you. Oh! believe me, I feel myself disgraced! And you have eaten and drunk at my table. But now I am sick at your presence; the day has come, and the night-bird should be off to his roost. Will you go before, or after?"

"Which you please," returned the poet, rising. "I believe you to be strictly honorable." He thoughtfully emptied his cup. "I wish I could add you were intelligent," he went on, knocking on his head with his knuckles. "Age! age! the brains stiff and rheumatic."

The old man preceded him from a point of self-respect. Villon followed, whistling, with his thumbs in his girdle.

"God pity you," said the lord of Brisetout at the door.

"Good-bye, papa," returned Villon with a yawn. "Many thanks for the cold mutton."

The door closed behind him. The dawn was breaking over the white roofs. A chill, uncomfortable morning ushered in the day. Villon stood and heartily stretched himself in the middle of the road.

"A very dull old gentleman," he thought. "I wonder what his goblets may be worth."

Will o' the Mill

THE PLAIN AND THE STARS

THE Mill where Will lived with his adopted parents stood in a falling valley between pine-woods and great mountains. Above, hill after hill soared upwards until they soared out of the depth of the hardiest timber, and stood naked against the sky. Some way up, a long grey village lay like a seam or a rag of vapor on a wooded hillside; and when the wind was favorable, the sound of the church bells would drop down, thin and silvery, to Will. Below, the valley grew ever steeper and steeper, and at the same time widened out on either hand; and from an eminence beside the mill it was possible to see its whole length and away beyond it over a wide plain, where the river turned and shone, and moved on from city to city on its voyage towards the sea. It chanced that over this valley there lay a pass into a neighboring kingdom, so that, quiet and rural as it was, the road that ran along beside the river was a high thoroughfare between two splendid and powerful societies. All through the summer, travelling-carriages came crawling up, or went plunging briskly downwards past the mill; and as it happened that the other side was very much easier of ascent, the path was not much frequented, except by people going in one direction; and of all the carriages that Will saw go by, five-sixths were plunging briskly downwards and only one-sixth crawling up. Much more was this the case with foot-passengers. All the light-footed tourists, all the pedlers laden with strange wares, were tending downward like the river that accompanied their path. Nor was this all; for when Will was yet a child a disastrous war arose over a great part of the world. The newspapers were full of defeats and victories, the earth rang with cavalry hoofs, and often for days together and for miles around the coil of battle terrified good people from their labors in the field. Of all this, nothing was heard for a long time in the valley; but at last one of the commanders pushed an army over the pass by forced marches, and for three days horse and foot, cannon and tumbril, drum and standard, kept pouring downward past the mill. All day the child stood and watched them on their passage—the rhythmical stride, the pale, unshaven faces tanned about the eyes, the discolored regimentals and the tattered flags, filled him with a sense of weariness, pity, and wonder; and all night long, after he was in bed, he could hear the cannon pounding and the feet trampling, and the great armament sweeping onward and downward past the mill. No one in the valley ever heard the fate of the expedition, for they lay out of the way of gossip in those troublous times; but Will saw one thing plainly, that not a man returned. Whither had they all gone? Whither went all the tourists and pedlers with strange wares? whither all the brisk barouches with servants in the dicky? whither the water of the stream, ever coursing downward and ever renewed from above? Even the wind blew oftener down the valley, and carried the dead leaves along with it in the fall. It seemed like a great conspiracy of things animate and inanimate; they all went downward, fleetly and gaily downward, and only he, it seemed, remained behind, like a stock upon the wayside. It sometimes made him glad when he noticed how the fishes kept their heads up stream. They, at least, stood faithfully by him, while all else were posting downward to the unknown world.

One evening he asked the miller where the river went.

"It goes down the valley," answered he, "and turns a power of mills—six-score mills, they say, from here to Unterdeck—and it none the wearier after all. And then it goes out into the lowlands, and waters the great corn country, and runs through a sight of fine cities (so they say) where kings live all alone in great palaces, with a sentry walking up and down before the door. And it goes under bridges with stone men upon them, looking down and smiling so curious at the water, and living folks leaning their elbows on the wall and looking over too. And then it goes on and on, and down through marshes and sands, until at last it falls into the sea, where the ships are that bring parrots and tobacco from the Indies. Ay, it has a long trot before it as it goes singing over our weir, bless its heart!"

"And what is the sea?" asked Will.

"The sea!" cried the miller. "Lord help us all, it is the greatest thing God made! That is where all the water in the world runs down into a great salt lake. There it lies, as flat as my hand and as innocent-like as a child; but they do say when the wind blows it gets up into water-mountains bigger than any of ours, and swallows down great ships bigger than our mill, and makes such a roaring that you can hear it miles away upon the land. There are great fish in it five times bigger than a buli, and one old serpent as long as our river and as old as all the world, with whiskers like a man, and a crown of silver on her head."

Will thought he had never heard anything like this, and he kept on asking question after question about the world that lay away down the river, with all its perils and marvels, until the old miller became quite interested himself, and at last took him by the hand and led him to the hill-top that overlooks the valley and the plain. The sun was near setting, and hung low down in a cloudless sky. Everything was defined and glorified in golden light. Will had never seen so great an expanse of country in his life; he stood and gazed with all his eyes. He could see the cities, and the woods and fields, and the bright curves of the river, and far away to where the rim of the plain trenched along the shining heavens. An overmastering emotion seized upon the boy, soul and body; his heart beat so thickly that he could not breathe; the scene swam before his eyes; the sun seemed to wheel round and round, and throw off, as it turned, strange shapes which disappeared with the rapidity of thought, and were succeeded by others. Will covered his face with his hands, and burst into a violent fit of tears; and the poor miller, sadly disappointed and perplexed, saw nothing better for it than to take him up in his arms and carry him home in silence.

From that day forward Will was full of new hopes and longings. Something kept tugging at his heartstrings; the running water carried his desires along with it as he dreamed over its fleeting surface; the wind, as it ran over innumerable tree-tops, hailed him with encouraging words; branches beckoned downward; the open road, as it shouldered round the angles and went turning and vanishing faster and faster down the valley, tortured him with its solicitations. He spent long whiles on the eminence, looking down the river-shed and abroad on the flat lowlands, and watched the clouds that travelled forth upon the sluggish wind and trailed their purple shadows on the plain; or he would linger by the wayside, and follow the carriages with his eyes as they rattled downward by the river. It did not matter what it was; everything that went that way, were it cloud or carriage, bird or brown water in the stream, he felt his heart flow out after it in an ecstasy of longing.

We are told by men of science that all the ventures of mariners on the sea, all that countermarching of tribes and races that confounds old history with its dust and rumor, sprang from nothing more abstruse than the laws of supply and demand, and a certain natural instinct for cheap rations. To any one thinking deeply, this will seem a dull and pitiful explanation. The tribes that came swarming out of the North and East, if they were indeed pressed onward from behind by others, were drawn at the same time by the magnetic influence of the South and West. The fame of other lands had reached them; the name of the eternal city rang in their ears; they were not colonists, but pilgrims; they travelled towards wine and gold and sunshine, but their hearts were set on something higher. That divine unrest, that old stinging trouble of humanity that makes all high achievements and all miserable failure, the same that spread wings with Icarus, the same that sent Columbus into the desolate Atlantic, inspired and supported these barbarians on their perilous march. There is one legend which profoundly represents their spirit, of how a flying party of these wanderers encountered a very old man shod with iron. The old man asked them whither they were going; and they answered with one voice: "To the Eternal City!" He looked upon them gravely, "I have sought it," he said, "over the most part of the world. Three such pairs as I now carry on my feet have I worn out upon this pilgrimage, and now the fourth is growing slender underneath my steps. And all this while I have not found the city." And he turned and went his own way alone, leaving them astonished.

And yet this would scarcely parallel the intensity of Will's feeling for the plain. If he could only go far enough out there, he felt as if his eyesight would be purged and clarified, as if his hearing would grow more delicate, and his very breath would come and go with luxury. He was transplanted and withering where he was; he lay in a strange country and was sick for home. Bit by bit, he pieced together broken notions of the world below: of the river, ever moving and growing until it sailed forth into the majestic ocean; of the cities, full of brisk and beautiful people, playing fountains, bands of music and marble palaces, and lighted up at night from end to end with artificial stars of gold; of the great churches, wise universities, brave armies, and untold money lying stored in vaults; of the high-flying vice that moved in the sunshine, and the stealth and swiftness of midnight murder. I have said he was sick as if for home: the figure halts. He was like some one lying in twilit, formless pre-existence, and stretching out his hands lovingly towards many-colored, many-sounding life. It was no wonder he was unhappy, he would go and tell the fish: they were made for their life, wished for no more than worms and running water, and a hole below a falling bank; but he was differently designed, full of desires and aspirations, itching at the fingers, lusting with the eyes, whom the whole variegated world could not satisfy with aspects. The true life, the true bright sunshine, lay far out upon the plain. And O! to see this sunlight once before he died! to move with a jocund spirit in a golden land! to hear the trained singers and sweet church bells, and see the holiday gardens; "And O fish!" he would cry, "if you would only turn your noses down stream, you could swim so easily into the fabled waters and see the vast ships passing over your head like clouds, and hear the great water-hills making music over you all day long!" But the fish kept looking patiently in their own direction, until Will hardly knew whether to laugh or cry.

Hitherto the traffic on the road had passed by Will, like something seen in a picture: he had perhaps exchanged salutations with a tourist, or caught sight of an old gentleman in a travelling-cap at a carriage window; but for the most part it had been a mere symbol, which he contemplated from apart and with something of a superstitious feeling. A time came at last when this was to be changed. The miller, who was a greedy man in his way, and never forewent an opportunity of honest profit, turned the mill-house into a little wayside inn, and, several pieces of good fortune falling in opportunely, built stables and got the position of post master on the road. It now became Will's duty to wait upon people, as they sat to break their fasts in the little arbor at the top of the mill garden; and you may be sure that he kept his ears open, and learned many new things about the outside world as he brought the omelette or the wine. Nay, he would often get into conversation with single guests, and by adroit questions and polite attention, not only gratify his own curiosity, but win the good-will of the travellers. Many complimented the old couple on their serving-boy; and a professor was eager to take him away with him, and have him properly educated in the plain. The miller and his wife were mightily astonished and even more pleased. They thought it a very good thing that they should have opened their inn. "You see," the old man would remark, "he has a kind of talent for a publican; he never would have made anything else!" And so life wagged on in the valley, with high satisfaction to all concerned but Will. Every carriage that left the inn-door seemed to take a part of him away with it; and when people jestingly offered him a lift, he could with difficulty command his emotion. Night after night he would dream that he was awakened by flustered servants, and that a splendid equipage waited at the door to carry him down into the plain; night after night; until the dream, which had seemed all jollity to him at first, began to take on a color of gravity, and the nocturnal summons and waiting equipage occupied a place in his mind as something to be both feared and hoped for.

One day, when Will was about sixteen, a fat young man arrived at sunset to pass the night. He was a contented-looking fellow, with a jolly eye, and carried a knapsack. While dinner was preparing, he sat in the arbor to read a book; but as soon as he had begun to observe Will, the book was laid aside; he was plainly one of those who prefer living people to people made of ink and paper. Will, on his part, although he had not been much interested in the stranger at first sight, soon began to take a great deal of pleasure in his talk, which was full of good-nature and good-sense, and at last conceived a great respect for his character and wisdom. They sat far into the night; and about two in the morning Will opened his heart to the young man, and told him how he longed to leave the valley and what bright hopes he had connected with the cities of the plain. The young man whistled, and then broke into a smile.

"My young friend," he remarked, "you are a very curious little fellow, to be sure, and wish a great many things which you will never get. Why, you would feel quite ashamed if you knew how the little fellows in these fairy cities of yours are all after the same sort of nonsense, and keep breaking their hearts to get up into the mountains. And let me tell you, those who go down into the plains are a very short while there before they wish themselves heartily back again. The air is not so light nor so pure; nor is the sun any brighter. As for the beautiful men and women, you would see many of them in rags and many of them deformed with horrible disorders; and a city is so hard a place for people who are poor and sensitive that many choose to die by their own hand."

"You must think me very simple," answered Will. "Although I have never been out of this valley, believe me, I have used my eyes. I know how one thing lives on another; for instance, how the fish hangs in the eddy to catch his fellows; and the shepherd, who makes so pretty a picture carrying home the lamb, is only carrying it home for dinner. I do not expect to find all things right in your cities. That is not what troubles me; it might have been that once upon a time; but although I live here always, I have asked many questions and learned a great deal in these last years, and certainly enough to cure me of my old fancies. But you would not have me die like a dog and not see all that is to be seen, and do all that a man can do, let it be good or evil? you would not have me spend all my days between this road here and the river, and not so much as make a motion to be up and live my life?—I would rather die out of hand," he cried, "than linger on as I am doing."

"Thousands of people," said the young man, "live and die like you, and are none the less happy."

"Ah!" said Will, "if there are thousands who would like, why should not one of them have my place?"

It was quite dark; there was a hanging lamp in the arbor which lit up the table and the faces of the speakers; and along the arch, the leaves upon the trellis stood out illuminated against the night sky, a pattern of transparent green upon a dusky purple. The fat young man rose, and, taking Will by the arm, led him out under the open heavens.

"Did you ever look at the stars?" he asked, pointing upwards.

"Often and often," answered Will.

"And do you know what they are?"

"I have fancied many things."

"They are worlds like ours," said the young man. "Some of them less; many of them a million times greater; and some of the least sparkles that you see are not only worlds, but whole clusters of worlds turning about each other in the midst of space. We do not know what there may be in any of them; perhaps the answer to all our difficulties or the cure of all our sufferings: and yet we can never reach them; not all the skill of the craftiest of men can fit out a ship for the nearest of these our neighbors, nor would the life of the most aged suffice for such a journey. When a great battle has been lost or a dear friend is dead, when we are hipped or in high spirits, there they are unweariedly shining overhead. We may stand down here, a whole army of us together, and shout until we break our hearts, and not a whisper reaches them. We may climb the highest mountain, and we are no nearer them. All we can do is to stand down here in the garden and take off our hats; the starshine lights upon our heads, and where mine is a little bald, I dare say you can see it glisten in the darkness. The mountain and the mouse. That is like to be all we shall ever have to do with Arcturus or Aldebaran. Can you apply a parable?" he added, laying his hand upon Will's shoulder. "It is not the same thing as a reason, but usually vastly more convincing."

Will hung his head a little, and then raised it once more to heaven. The stars seemed to expand and emit a sharper brilliancy; and as he kept turning his eyes higher and higher, they seemed to increase in multitude under his gaze.

"I see," he said, turning to the young man. "We are in a rat-trap."

"Something of that size. Did you ever see a squirrel turning in a cage? and another squirrel sitting philosophically over his nuts? I needn't ask you which of them looked more of a fool."

THE PARSON'S MARJORY

After some years the old people died, both in one winter, very carefully tended by their adopted son, and very quietly mourned when they were gone. People who had heard of his roving fancies supposed he would hasten to sell the property, and go down the river to push his fortunes. But there was never any sign of such an intention on the part of Will. On the contrary, he had the inn set on a better footing, and hired a couple of servants to assist him in carrying it on; and there he settled down, a kind, talkative, inscrutable young man, six feet three in his stockings, with an iron constitution and a friendly voice. He soon began to take rank in the district as a bit of an oddity: it was not much to be wondered at from the first, for he was always full of notions, and kept calling the plainest common-sense in question; but what most raised the report upon him was the odd circumstance of his courtship with the parson's Marjory.

The parson's Marjory was a lass about nineteen, when Will would be about thirty; well enough looking, and much better educated than any other girl in that part of the country, as became her parentage. She held her head very high, and had already refused several offers of marriage with a grand air, which had got her hard names among the neighbors. For all that she was a good girl, and one that would have made any man well contented.

Will had never seen much of her; for although the church and parsonage were only two miles from his own door, he was never known to go there but on Sundays. It chanced, however, that the parsonage fell into disrepair, and had to be dismantled; and the parson and his daughter took lodgings for a month or so, on very much reduced terms, at Will's inn. Now, what with the inn, and the mill, and the old miller's savings, our friend was a man of substance; and besides that, he had a name for good temper and shrewdness, which make a capital portion in marriage; and so it was currently gossiped, among their ill-wishers, that the parson and his daughter had not chosen their temporary lodging with their eyes shut. Will was about the last man in the world to be cajoled or frightened into marriage. You had only to look into his eyes, limpid and still like pools of water, and yet with a sort of clear light that seemed to come from within, and you would understand at once that here was one who knew his own mind, and would stand to it immovably. Marjory herself was no weakling by her looks, with strong, steady eyes and a resolute and quiet bearing. It might be a question whether she was not Will's match in steadfastness, after all, or which of them would rule the roast in marriage. But Marjory had never given it a thought, and accompanied her father with the most unshaken innocence and unconcern.

The season was still so early that Will's customers were few and far between; but the lilacs were already flowering, and the weather was so mild that the party took dinner under the trellis, with the noise of the river in their ears and the woods ringing about them with the songs of birds. Will soon began to take a particular pleasure in these dinners. The parson was rather a dull companion, with a habit of dozing at table; but nothing rude or cruel ever fell from his lips. And as for the parson's daughter, she suited her surroundings with the best grace imaginable; and whatever she said seemed so pat and pretty that Will conceived a great idea of her talents. He could see her face, as she leaned forward, against a background of rising pine-woods; her eyes shone peaceably; the light lay around her hair like a kerchief; something that was hardly a smile rippled her pale cheeks, and Will could not contain himself from gazing on her in an agreeable dismay. She looked, even in her quietest moments, so complete in herself, and so quick with life down to her finger tips and the very skirts of her dress, that the remainder of created things became no more than a blot by comparison; and if Will glanced away from her to her surroundings, the trees looked inanimate and senseless, the clouds hung in heaven like dead things, and even the mountain tops were disenchanted. The whole valley could not compare in looks with this one girl.

Will was always observant in the society of his fellow-creatures; but his observation became almost painfully eager in the case of Marjory. He listened to all she uttered, and read her eyes, at the same time, for the unspoken commentary. Many kind, simple, and sincere speeches found an echo in his heart. He became conscious of a soul beautifully poised upon itself, nothing doubting, nothing desiring, clothed in peace. It was not possible to separate her thoughts from her appearance. The turn of her wrist, the still sound of her voice, the light in her eyes, the lines of her body, fell in tune with her grave and gentle words, like the accompaniment that sustains and harmonizes the voice of the singer. Her influence was one thing, not to be divided or discussed, only to be felt with gratitude and joy. To Will, her presence recalled something of his childhood, and the thought of her took its place in his mind beside that of dawn, of running water, and of the earliest violets and lilacs. It is the property of things seen for the first time, or for the first time after long, like the flowers in spring, to reawaken in us the sharp edge of sense and that impression of mystic strangeness which otherwise passes out of life with the coming of years; but the sight of a loved face is what renews a man's character from the fountain upwards.

One day after dinner Will took a stroll among the firs, a grave beatitude possessed him from top to toe, and he kept smiling to himself and the landscape as he went. The river ran between the stepping-stones with a pretty wimple; a bird sang loudly in the wood; the hill-tops looked immeasurably high, and as he glanced at them from time to time seemed to contemplate his movements with a beneficent but awful curiosity. His way took him to the eminence which overlooked the plain; and there he sat down upon a stone, and fell into deep and pleasant thought. The plain lay abroad with its cities and silver river; everything was asleep, except a great eddy of birds which kept rising and falling and going round and round in the blue air. He repeated Marjory's name aloud, and the sound of it gratified his ear. He shut his eyes, and her image sprang up before him, quietly luminous and attended with good thoughts. The river might run for ever; the birds fly higher and higher till they touched the stars. He saw it was empty bustle after all; for here, without stirring a foot, waiting patiently in his own narrow valley, he also had attained the better sunlight.

The next day Will made a sort of declaration across the dinner-table, while the parson was filling his pipe.

"Miss Marjory," he said, "I never knew any one I liked so well as you. I am mostly a cold, unkindly sort of man; not from want of heart, but out of strangeness in my way of thinking; and people seem far away from me. 'Tis as if there were a circle round me, which kept every one out but you; I can hear the others talking and laughing; but you come quite close. Maybe, this is disagreeable to you?" he asked.

Marjory made no answer.

"Speak up, girl," said the parson.

"Nay, now," returned Will, "I wouldn't press her, parson. I feel tongue-tied myself, who am not used to it; and she's a woman, and little more than a child, when all is said. But for my part, as far as I can understand what people mean by it, I fancy I must be what they call in love. I do not wish to be held as committing myself; for I may be wrong; but that is how I believe things are with me. And if Miss Marjory should feel any otherwise on her part, mayhap she would be so kind as shake her head."

Marjory was silent, and gave no sign that she had heard.

"How is that, parson?" asked Will.

"The girl must speak," replied the parson, laying down his pipe. "Here's our neighbor who says he loves you, Madge. Do you love him, ay or no?"

"I think I do," said Marjory, faintly.

"Well then, that's all that could be wished!" cried Will, heartily. And he took her hand across the table, and held it a moment in both of his with great satisfaction.

"You must marry," observed the parson, replacing his pipe in his mouth.

"Is that the right thing to do, think you?" demanded Will.

"It is indispensable," said the parson.

"Very well," replied the wooer.

Two or three days passed away with great delight to Will, although a bystander might scarce have found it out. He continued to take his meals opposite Marjory, and to talk with her and gaze upon her in her father's presence; but he made no attempt to see her alone, nor in any other way changed his conduct towards her from what it had been since the beginning. Perhaps the girl was a little disappointed, and perhaps not unjustly; and yet if it had been enough to be always in the thoughts of another person, and so pervade and alter his whole life, she might have been thoroughly contented. For she was never out of Will's mind for an instant. He sat over the stream, and watched the dust of the eddy, and the poised fish, and straining weeds; he wandered out alone into the purple even, with all the blackbirds piping round him in the wood; he rose early in the morning, and saw the sky turn from grey to gold, and the light leap upon the hill-tops; and all the while he kept wondering if he had never seen such things before, or how it was that they should look so different now. The sound of his own mill-wheel, or of the wind among the trees, confounded and charmed his heart. The most enchanting thoughts presented themselves unbidden in his mind. He was so happy that he could not sleep at night, and so restless that he could hardly sit still out of her company. And yet it seemed as if he avoided her rather than sought her out.

One day, as he was coming home from a ramble, Will found Marjory in the garden picking flowers, and as he came up with her, slackened his pace and continued walking by her side.

"You like flowers?" he said.

"Indeed I love them dearly," she replied. "Do you?"

"Why, no," said he, "not so much. They are a very small affair, when all is done. I can fancy people caring for them greatly, but not doing as you are just now."

"How?" she asked, pausing and looking up at him.

"Plucking them," said he. "They are a deal better off where they are, and look a deal prettier, if you go to that."

"I wish to have them for my own," she answered, "to carry them near my heart, and keep them in my room. They tempt me when they grow here; they seem to say, 'Come and do something with us;' but once I have cut them and put them by, the charm is laid, and I can look at them with quite an easy heart."

"You wish to possess them," replied Will, "in order to think no more about them. It's a bit like killing the goose with the golden eggs. It's a bit like what I wished to do when I was a boy. Because I had a fancy for looking out over the plain, I wished to go down there—where I couldn't look out over it any longer. Was not that fine reasoning? Dear, dear, if they only thought of it, all the world would do like me; and you would let your flowers alone, just as I stay up here in the mountains." Suddenly he broke off sharp. "By the Lord!" he cried. And when she asked him what was wrong, he turned the question off, and walked away into the house with rather a humorous expression of face.

He was silent at table; and after the night had fallen and the stars had come out overhead, he walked up and down for hours in the courtyard and garden with an uneven pace. There was still a light in the window of Marjory's room: one little oblong patch of orange in a world of dark blue hills and silver starlight. Will's mind ran a great deal on the window; but his thoughts were not very lover-like. "There she is in her room," he thought, "and there are the stars overhead:—a blessing upon both!" Both were good influences in his life; both soothed and braced him in his profound contentment with the world. And what more should he desire with either? The fat young man and his councils were so present to his mind, that he threw back his head, and, putting his hands before his mouth, shouted aloud to the populous heavens. Whether from the position of his head or the sudden strain of the exertion, he seemed to see a momentary shock among the stars, and a diffusion of frosty light pass from one to another along the sky. At the same instant, a corner of the blind was lifted up and lowered again at once. He laughed a loud ho-ho! "One and another!" thought Will, "The stars tremble, and the blind goes up. Why, before Heaven, what a great magician I must be! Now if I were only a fool, should not I be in a pretty way?" And he went off to bed, chuckling to himself: "If I were only a fool!"

The next morning, pretty early, he saw her once more in the garden, and sought her out.

"I have been thinking about getting married," he began abruptly; "and after having turned it all over, I have made up my mind it's not worth while."

She turned upon him for a single moment; but his radiant, kindly appearance would, under the circumstances, have disconcerted an angel, and she looked down again upon the ground in silence. He could see her tremble.

"I hope you don't mind," he went on, a little taken aback. "You ought not. I have turned it all over, and upon my soul there's nothing in it. We should never be one whit nearer than we are just now, and, if I am a wise man, nothing like so happy."

"It is unnecessary to go round about with me," she said. "I very well remember that you refused to commit yourself; and now that I see you were mistaken, and in reality have never cared for me, I can only feel sad that I have been so far misled."

"I ask your pardon," said Will stoutly; "you do not understand my meaning. As to whether I have ever loved you or not, I must leave that to others. But for one thing, my feeling is not changed; and for another, you may make it your boast that you have made my whole life and character something different from what they were. I mean what I say; no less. I do not think getting married is worth while. I would rather you went on living with your father, so that I could walk over and see you once, or maybe twice a week, as people go to church, and then we should both be all the happier between whiles. That's my notion. But I'll marry you if you will," he added.

"Do you know that you are insulting me?" she broke out.

"Not I, Marjory," said he; "if there is anything in a clear conscience, not I. I offer all my heart's best affections; you can take it or want it, though I suspect it's beyond either your power or mine to change what has once been done, and set me fancy-free. I'll marry you, if you like; but I tell you again and again, it's not worth while, and we had best stay friends. Though I am a quiet man I have noticed a heap of things in my life. Trust in me, and take things as I propose; or, if you don't like that, say the word, and I'll marry you out of hand."

There was a considerable pause, and Will, who began to feel uneasy, began to grow angry in consequence.

"It seems you are too proud to say your mind," he said. "Believe me that's a pity. A clean shrift makes simple living. Can a man be more downright or honorable to a woman than I have been? I have said my say, and given you your choice. Do you want me to marry you? or will you take my friendship, as I think best? or have you had enough of me for good? Speak out for the dear God's sake! You know your father told you a girl should speak her mind in these affairs."

She seemed to recover herself at that, turned without a word, walked rapidly through the garden, and disappeared into the house, leaving Will in some confusion as to the result. He walked up and down the garden, whistling softly to himself. Sometimes he stopped and contemplated the sky and hill-tops; sometimes he went down to the tail of the weir and sat there, looking foolishly in the water. All this dubiety and perturbation was so foreign to his nature and the life which he had resolutely chosen for himself, that he began to regret Marjory's arrival. "After all," he thought, "I was as happy as a man need be. I could come down here and watch my fishes all day long if I wanted: I was as settled and contented as my old mill."

Marjory came down to dinner, looking very trim and quiet; and no sooner were all three at table than she made her father a speech, with her eyes fixed upon her plate, but showing no other sign of embarrassment or distress.

"Father," she began, "Mr. Will and I have been talking things over. We see that we have each made a mistake about our feelings, and he has agreed, at my request, to give up all idea of marriage, and be no more than my very good friend, as in the past. You see, there is no shadow of a quarrel, and indeed I hope we shall see a great deal of him in the future, for his visits will always be welcome in our house. Of course, father, you will know best, but perhaps we should do better to leave Mr. Will's house for the present. I believe, after what has passed, we should hardly be agreeable inmates for some days."

Will, who had commanded himself with difficulty from the first, broke out upon this into an inarticulate noise, and raised one hand with an appearance of real dismay, as if he were about to interfere and contradict. But she checked him at once, looking up at him with a swift glance and an angry flush upon her cheek.

"You will perhaps have the good grace," she said, "to let me explain these matters for myself."

Will was put entirely out of countenance by her expression and the ring of her voice. He held his peace, concluding that there were some things about this girl beyond his comprehension, in which he was exactly right.

The poor parson was quite crestfallen. He tried to prove that this was no more than a true lovers' tiff, which would pass off before night; and when he was dislodged from that position, he went on to argue that where there was no quarrel there could be no call for a separation; for the good man liked both his entertainment and his host. It was curious to see how the girl managed them, saying little all the time, and that very quietly, and yet twisting them round her finger and insensibly leading them wherever she would by feminine tact and generalship. It scarcely seemed to have been her doing—it seemed as if things had merely so fallen out—that she and her father took their departure that same afternoon in a farm-cart, and went farther down the valley, to wait, until their own house was ready for them, in another hamlet.

But Will had been observing closely, and was well aware of her dexterity and resolution. When he found himself alone he had a great many curious matters to turn over in his mind. He was very sad and solitary, to begin with. All the interest had gone out of his life, and he might look up at the stars as long as he pleased, he somehow failed to find support or consolation. And then he was in such a turmoil of spirit about Marjory. He had been puzzled and irritated at her behavior, and yet he could not keep himself from admiring it. He thought he recognized a fine, perverse angel in that still soul which he had never hitherto suspected; and though he saw it was an influence that would fit but ill with his own life of artificial calm, he could not keep himself from ardently desiring to possess it. Like a man who has lived among shadows and now meets the sun, he was both pained and delighted.

As the days went forward he passed from one extreme to another; now pluming himself on the strength of his determination, now despising his timid and silly caution. The former was, perhaps, the true thought of his heart, and represented the regular tenor of the man's reflections; but the latter burst forth from time to time with an unruly violence, and then he would forget all consideration, and go up and down his house and garden or walk among the fir-woods like one who is beside himself with remorse. To equable, steady-minded Will this state of matters was intolerable; and he determined, at whatever cost, to bring it to an end. So, one warm summer afternoon he put on his best clothes, took a thorn switch in his hand, and set out down the valley by the river. As soon as he had taken his determination, he had regained at a bound his customary peace of heart, and he enjoyed the bright weather and the variety of the scene without any admixture of alarm or unpleasant eagerness. It was nearly the same to him how the matter turned out. If she accepted him he would have to marry her this time, which perhaps was all for the best. If she refused him, he would have done his utmost, and might follow his own way in the future with an untroubled conscience. He hoped, on the whole, she would refuse him; and then, again, as he saw the brown roof which sheltered her, peeping through some willows at an angle of the stream, he was half inclined to reverse the wish, and more than half ashamed of himself for this infirmity of purpose.

Marjory seemed glad to see him, and gave him her hand without affectation or delay.

"I have been thinking about this marriage," he began.

"So have I," she answered. "And I respect you more and more for a very wise man. You understood me better than I understood myself; and I am now quite certain that things are all for the best as they are."

"At the same time—" ventured Will.

"You must be tired," she interrupted. "Take a seat and let me fetch you a glass of wine. The afternoon is so warm; and I wish you not to be displeased with your visit. You must come quite often; once a week, if you can spare the time; I am always so glad to see my friends."

"O, very well," thought Will to himself. "It appears I was right after all." And he paid a very agreeable visit, walked home again in capital spirits, and gave himself no further concern about the matter.

For nearly three years Will and Marjory continued on these terms, seeing each other once or twice a week without any word of love between them; and for all that time I believe Will was nearly as happy as a man can be. He rather stinted himself the pleasure of seeing her; and he would often walk half-way over to the parsonage, and then back again, as if to whet his appetite. Indeed there was one corner of the road, whence he could see the church-spire wedged into a crevice of the valley between sloping fir-woods, with a triangular snatch of plain by way of background, which he greatly affected as a place to sit and moralize in before returning homewards; and the peasants got so much into the habit of finding him there in the twilight that they gave it the name of "Will o' the Mill's Corner."

At the end of three years Marjory played him a sad trick by suddenly marrying somebody else. Will kept his countenance bravely, and merely remarked that, for as little as he knew of women, he had acted very prudently in not marrying her himself three years before. She plainly knew very little of her own mind, and, in spite of a deceptive manner, was as fickle and flighty as the rest of them. He had to congratulate himself on an escape, he said, and would take a higher opinion of his own wisdom in consequence. But at heart, he was reasonably displeased, moped a good deal for a month or two, and fell away in flesh, to the astonishment of his serving-lads.

It was perhaps a year after this marriage that Will was awakened late one night by the sound of a horse galloping on the road, followed by precipitate knocking at the inn-door. He opened his window and saw a farm servant, mounted and holding a led horse by the bridle, who told him to make what haste he could and go along with him; for Marjory was dying, and had sent urgently to fetch him to her bedside. Will was no horseman, and made so little speed upon the way that the poor young wife was very near her end before he arrived. But they had some minutes' talk in private, and he was present and wept very bitterly while she breathed her last.

DEATH

Year after year went away into nothing, with great explosions and outcries in the cities on the plain: red revolt springing up and being suppressed in blood, battle swaying hither and thither, patient astronomers in observatory towers picking out and christening new stars, plays being performed in lighted theatres, people being carried into hospitals on stretchers, and all the usual turmoil and agitation of men's lives in crowded centres. Up in Will's valley only the winds and seasons made an epoch; the fish hung in the swift stream, the birds circled overhead, the pine-tops rustled underneath the stars, the tall hills stood over all; and Will went to and fro, minding his wayside inn, until the snow began to thicken on his head. His heart was young and vigorous; and if his pulses kept a sober time, they still beat strong and steady in his wrists. He carried a ruddy stain on either cheek, like a ripe apple; he stooped a little, but his step was still firm; and his sinewy hands were reached out to all men with a friendly pressure. His face was covered with those wrinkles which are got in open air, and which, rightly looked at, are no more than a sort of permanent sunburning; such wrinkles heighten the stupidity of stupid faces; but to a person like Will, with his clear eyes and smiling mouth, only give another charm by testifying to a simple and easy life. His talk was full of wise sayings. He had a taste for other people; and other people had a taste for him. When the valley was full of tourists in the season, there were merry nights in Will's arbor; and his views, which seemed whimsical to his neighbors, were often enough admired by learned people out of towns and colleges. Indeed, he had a very noble old age, and grew daily better known; so that his fame was heard of in the cities of the plain; and young men who had been summer travellers spoke together in *cafés* of Will o' the Mill and his rough philosophy. Many and many an invitation, you may be sure, he had; but nothing could tempt him from his upland valley. He would shake his head and smile over his tobacco-pipe with a deal of meaning. "You come too late," he would answer. "I am a dead man now: I have lived and died already. Fifty years ago you would have brought my heart into my mouth; and now you do not even tempt me. But that is the object of long living, that man should cease to care about life." And again: "There is only one difference between a long life and a good dinner: that, in the dinner, the sweets come last." Or once more: "When I was a boy, I was a bit puzzled, and hardly knew whether it was myself or the world that was curious and worth looking into. Now, I know it is myself, and stick to that."

He never showed any symptoms of frailty, but kept stalwart and firm to the last; but they say he grew less talkative towards the end, and would listen to other people by the hour in an amused and sympathetic silence. Only, when he did speak, it was more to the point and more charged with old experience. He drank a bottle of wine gladly; above all, at sunset on the hill-top or quite late at night under the stars in the arbor. The sight of something attractive and unattainable seasoned his enjoyment, he would say; and he professed he had lived long enough to admire a candle all the more when he could compare it with a planet.

One night, in his seventy-second year, he awoke in bed, in such uneasiness of body and mind that he arose and dressed himself and went out to meditate in the arbor. It was pitch dark, without a star; the river was swollen, and the wet woods and meadows loaded the air with perfume. It had thundered during the day, and it promised more thunder for the morrow. A murky, stifling night for a man of seventy-two! Whether it was the weather or the wakefulness, or some little touch of fever in his old limbs, Will's mind was besieged by tumultuous and crying memories. His boyhood, the night with the fat young man, the death of his adopted parents, the summer days with Marjory, and many of those small circumstances, which seem nothing to another, and are yet the very gist of a man's own life to himself—things seen, words heard, looks misconstrued—arose from their forgotten corners and usurped his attention. The dead themselves were with him, not merely taking part in this thin show of memory that defiled before his brain, but revisiting his bodily senses as they do in profound and vivid dreams. The fat young man leaned his elbows on the table opposite; Marjory came and went with an apronful of flowers between the garden and the arbor; he could hear the old parson knocking out his pipe or blowing his resonant nose. The tide of his consciousness ebbed and flowed: he was sometimes half asleep and drowned in his recollections of the past; and sometimes he was broad awake, wondering at himself. But about the middle of the night he was startled by the voice of the dead miller calling to him out of the house as he used to do on the arrival of custom. The hallucination was so perfect that Will sprang from his seat and stood listening for the summons to be repeated; and as he listened he became conscious of another noise besides the brawling of the river and the ringing in his feverish ears. It was like the stir of the horses and the creaking of harness, as though a carriage with an impatient team had been brought up upon the road before the courtyard gate. At such an hour, upon this rough and dangerous pass, the supposition was no better than absurd; and Will dismissed it from his mind, and resumed his seat upon the arbor chair; and sleep closed over him again like running water. He was once again awakened by the dead miller's call, thinner and more spectral than before; and once again he heard the noise of an equipage upon the road. And so thrice and four times, the same dream, or the same fancy, presented itself to his senses: until at length, smiling to himself as when one humors a nervous child, he proceeded towards the gate to set his uncertainty at rest.

From the arbor to the gate was no great distance, and yet it took Will some time; it seemed as if the dead thickened around him in the court, and crossed his path at every step. For, first, he was suddenly surprised by an overpowering sweetness of heliotropes; it was as if his garden had been planted with this flower from end to end, and the hot, damp night had drawn forth all their perfumes in a breath. Now the heliotrope had been Marjory's favorite flower, and since her death not one of them had ever been planted in Will's ground.

"I must be going crazy," he thought. "Poor Marjory and her heliotropes!"

And with that he raised his eyes towards the window that had once been hers. If he had been bewildered before, he was now almost terrified; for there was a light in the room; the window was an orange oblong as of yore; and the corner of the blind was lifted and let fall as on the night when he stood and shouted to the stars in his perplexity. The illusion only endured an instant; but it left him somewhat unmanned, rubbing his eyes and staring at the outline of the house and the black night behind it. While he thus stood, and it seemed as if he must have stood there quite a long time, there came a renewal of the noises on the road: and he turned in time to meet a stranger, who was advancing to meet him across the court. There was something like the outline of a great carriage discernible on the road behind the stranger, and, above that, a few black pine-tops, like so many plumes.

"Master Will?" asked the new-comer, in brief military fashion.

"That same, sir," answered Will. "Can I do anything to serve you?"

"I have heard you much spoken of, Master Will," returned the other; "much spoken of, and well. And though I have both hands full of business, I wish to drink a bottle of wine with you in your arbor. Before I go, I shall introduce myself."

Will led the way to the trellis, and got a lamp lighted and a bottle uncorked. He was not altogether unused to such complimentary interviews, and hoped little enough from this one, being schooled by many disappointments. A sort of cloud had settled on his wits and prevented him from remembering the strangeness of the hour. He moved like a person in his sleep; and it seemed as if the lamp caught fire and the bottle came uncorked with the facility of thought. Still, he had some curiosity about the appearance of his visitor, and tried in vain to turn the light into his face; either he handled the lamp clumsily, or there was a dimness over his eyes; but he could make out little more than a shadow at table with him. He stared and stared at this shadow, as he wiped out the glasses, and began to feel cold and strange about the heart. The silence weighed upon him, for he could hear nothing now, not even the river, but the drumming of his own arteries in his ears.

"Here's to you," said the stranger, roughly.

"Here is my service, sir," replied Will, sipping his wine, which somehow tasted oddly.

"I understand you are a very positive fellow," pursued the stranger.

Will made answer with a smile of some satisfaction and a little nod.

"So am I," continued the other; "and it is the delight of my heart to tramp on people's corns. I will have nobody positive but myself; not one. I have crossed the whims, in my time, of kings and generals and great artists. And what would you say," he went on, "if I had come up here on purpose to cross yours?"

Will had it on his tongue to make a sharp rejoinder; but the politeness of an old innkeeper prevailed; and he held his peace and made answer with a civil gesture of the hand.

"I have," said the stranger. "And if I did not hold you in a particular esteem, I should make no words about the matter. It appears you pride yourself on staying where you are. You mean to stick by your inn. Now I mean you shall come for a turn with me in my barouche; and before this bottle's empty, so you shall."

"That would be an odd thing, to be sure," replied Will, with a chuckle. "Why, sir, I have grown here like an old oak-tree; the Devil himself could hardly root me up: and for all I perceive you are a very entertaining old gentleman, I would wager you another bottle you lose your pains with me."

The dimness of Will's eyesight had been increasing all this while; but he was somehow conscious of a sharp and chilling scrutiny which irritated and yet overmastered him.

"You need not think," he broke out suddenly, in an explosive, febrile manner that startled and alarmed himself, "that I am a stay-at-home, because I fear anything under God. God knows I am tired enough of it all; and when the time comes for a longer journey than ever you dream of, I reckon I shall find myself prepared."

The stranger emptied his glass and pushed it away from him. He looked down for a little, and then, leaning over the table, tapped Will three times upon the forearm with a single finger. "The time has come!" he said solemnly.

An ugly thrill spread from the spot he touched. The tones of his voice were dull and startling, and echoed strangely in Will's heart.

"I beg your pardon," he said, with some discomposure. "What do you mean?"

"Look at me, and you will find your eyesight swim. Raise your hand; it is dead-heavy. This is your last bottle of wine, Master Will, and your last night upon the earth."

"You are a doctor?" quavered Will.

"The best that ever was," replied the other; "for I cure both mind and body with the same prescription. I take away all pain and I forgive all sins; and where my patients have gone wrong in life, I smooth out all complications and set them free again upon their feet."

"I have no need of you," said Will.

"A times comes for all men, Master Will," replied the doctor, "when the helm is taken out of their hands. For you, because you were prudent and quiet, it has been long of coming, and you have had long to discipline yourself for its reception. You have seen what is to be seen about your mill; you have sat close all your days like a hare in its form; but now that is at an end; and," added the doctor, getting on his feet, "you must arise and come with me."

"You are a strange physician," said Will, looking steadfastly upon his guest.

"I am a natural law," he replied, "and people call me Death."

"Why did you not tell me so at first?" cried Will. "I have been waiting for you these many years. Give me your hand, and welcome."

"Lean upon my arm," said the stranger, "for already your strength abates. Lean on me heavily as you need; for though I am old, I am very strong. It is but three steps to my carriage, and there all your trouble ends. Why, Will," he added, "I have been yearning for you as if you were my own son; and of all the men that ever I came for in my long days, I have come for you most gladly. I am caustic, and sometimes offend people at first sight; but I am a good friend at heart to such as you."

"Since Marjory was taken," returned Will, "I declare before God you were the only friend I had to look for."

So the pair went arm-in-arm across the courtyard.

One of the servants awoke about this time and heard the noise of horses pawing before he dropped asleep again; all down the valley that night there was a rushing as of a smooth and steady wind descending towards the plain; and when the world rose next morning, sure enough Will o' the Mill had gone at last upon his travels.

Markheim

"Yes," said the dealer, "our windfalls are of various kinds. Some customers are ignorant, and then I touch a dividend of my superior knowledge. Some are dishonest," and here he held up the candle, so that the light fell strongly on his visitor, "and in that case," he continued, "I profit by my virtue."

Markheim had but just entered from the daylight streets, and his eyes had not yet grown familiar with the mingled shine and darkness in the shop. At these pointed words, and before the near presence of the flame, he blinked painfully and looked aside.

The dealer chuckled. "You come to me on Christmas Day," he resumed, "when you know that I am alone in my house, put up my shutters, and make a point of refusing business. Well, you will have to pay for that; you will have to pay for my loss of time, when I should be balancing my books; you will have to pay, besides, for a kind of manner that I remark in you to-day very strongly. I am the essence of discretion, and ask no awkward questions; but when a customer cannot look me in the eyes, he has to pay for it." The dealer once more chuckled; and then, changing to his usual business voice, though still with a note of irony, "You can give, as usual, a clear account of how you came into the possession of the object?" he continued. "Still your uncle's cabinet? A remarkable collector, sir!"

And the little pale, round-shouldered dealer stood almost on tiptoe, looking over the top of his gold spectacles, and nodding his head with every mark of disbelief. Markheim returned his gaze with one of infinite pity, and a touch of horror.

"This time," said he, "you are in error. I have not come to sell, but to buy. I have no curios to dispose of; my uncle's cabinet is bare to the wainscot; even were it still intact, I have done well on the Stock Exchange, and should more likely add to it than otherwise, and my errand to-day is simplicity itself. I seek a Christmas present for a lady," he continued, waxing more fluent as he struck into the speech he had prepared; "and certainly I owe you every excuse for thus disturbing you upon so small a matter. But the thing was neglected yesterday; I must produce my little compliment at dinner; and, as you very well know, a rich marriage is not a thing to be neglected."

There followed a pause, during which the dealer seemed to weigh this statement incredulously. The ticking of many clocks among the curious lumber of the shop, and the faint rushing of the cabs in a near thoroughfare, filled up the interval of silence.

"Well, sir," said the dealer, "be it so. You are an old customer after all; and if, as you say, you have the chance of a good marriage, far be it from me to be an obstacle. Here is a nice thing for a lady now," he went on, "this hand glass—fifteenth century, warranted; comes from a good collection, too; but I reserve the name, in the interests of my customer, who was just like yourself, my dear sir, the nephew and sole heir of a remarkable collector."

The dealer, while he thus ran on in his dry and biting voice, had stooped to take the object from its place; and, as he had done so, a shock had passed through Markheim, a start both of hand and foot, a sudden leap of many tumultuous passions to the face. It passed as swiftly as it came, and left no trace beyond a certain trembling of the hand that now received the glass.

"A glass," he said hoarsely, and then paused, and repeated it more clearly. "A glass? For Christmas? Surely not?"

"And why not?" cried the dealer. "Why not a glass?"

Markheim was looking upon him with an indefinable expression. "You ask me why not?" he said. "Why, look here—look in it—look at yourself! Do you like to see it? No! nor I—nor any man."

The little man had jumped back when Markheim had so suddenly confronted him with the mirror; but now, perceiving there was nothing worse on hand, he chuckled. "Your future lady, sir, must be pretty hard favored," said he.

"I ask you," said Markheim, "for a Christmas present, and you give me this—this damned reminder of years, and sins and follies—this hand-conscience! Did you mean it? Had you a thought in your mind? Tell me. It will be better for you if you do. Come, tell me about yourself. I hazard a guess now, that you are in secret a very charitable man?"

The dealer looked closely at his companion. It was very odd, Markheim did not appear to be laughing; there was something in his face like an eager sparkle of hope, but nothing of mirth.

"What are you driving at?" the dealer asked.

"Not charitable?" returned the other, gloomily. "Not charitable; not pious; not scrupulous; unloving, unbeloved; a hand to get money, a safe to keep it. Is that all? Dear God, man, is that all?"

"I will tell you what it is," began the dealer, with some sharpness, and then broke off again into a chuckle. "But I see this is a love match of yours, and you have been drinking the lady's health."

"Ah!" cried Markheim, with a strange curiosity. "Ah, have you been in love? Tell me about that."

"I," cried the dealer. "I in love! I never had the time, nor have I the time to-day for all this nonsense. Will you take the glass?"

"Where is the hurry?" returned Markheim. "It is very pleasant to stand here talking; and life is so short and insecure that I would not hurry away from any pleasure—no, not even from so mild a one as this. We should rather cling, cling to what little we can get, like a man at a cliff's edge. Every second is a cliff, if you think upon it—a cliff a mile high—high enough, if we fall, to dash us out of every feature of humanity. Hence it is best to talk pleasantly. Let us talk of each other; why should we wear this mask? Let us be confidential. Who knows, we might become friends?"

"I have just one word to say to you," said the dealer. "Either make your purchase, or walk out of my shop."

"True, true," said Markheim. "Enough fooling. To business. Show me something else."

The dealer stooped once more, this time to replace the glass upon the shelf, his thin blond hair falling over his eyes as he did so. Markheim moved a little nearer, with one hand in the pocket of his great-coat; he drew himself up and filled his lungs; at the same time many different emotions were depicted together on his face—terror, horror, and resolve, fascination and a physical repulsion; and through a haggard lift of his upper lip, his teeth looked out.

"This, perhaps, may suit," observed the dealer; and then, as he began to re-arise, Markheim bounded from behind upon his victim. The long, skewer-like dagger flashed and fell. The dealer struggled like a hen, striking his temple on the shelf, and then tumbled on the floor in a heap.

Time had some score of small voices in that shop, some stately and slow as was becoming to their great age; others garrulous and hurried. All these told out the seconds in an intricate chorus of tickings. Then the passage of a lad's feet, heavily running on the pavement, broke in upon these smaller voices and startled Markheim into the consciousness of his surroundings. He looked about him awfully. The candle stood on the counter, its flame solemnly wagging in a draught; and by that inconsiderable movement, the whole room was filled with noiseless bustle and kept heaving like a sea: the tall shadows nodding, the gross blots of darkness swelling and dwindling as with respiration, the faces of the portraits and the china gods changing and wavering like images in water. The inner door stood ajar, and peered into that leaguer of shadows with a long slit of daylight like a pointing finger.

From these fear-stricken rovings, Markheim's eyes returned to the body of his victim, where it lay both humped and sprawling, incredibly small and strangely meaner than in life. In these poor, miserly clothes, in that ungainly attitude, the dealer lay like so much sawdust. Markheim had feared to see it, and, lo! it was nothing. And yet, as he gazed, this bundle of old clothes and pool of blood began to find eloquent voices. There it must lie; there was none to work the cunning hinges or direct the miracle of locomotion—there it must lie till it was found. Found! ay, and then? Then would this dead flesh lift up a cry that would ring over England, and fill the world with the echoes of pursuit. Ay, dead or not, this was still the enemy. "Time was, that when the brains were out," he thought; and the first word struck into his mind. Time, now that the deed was accomplished—time, which had closed for the victim, had become instant and momentous for the slayer.

The thought was yet in his mind, when, first one and then another, with every variety of pace and voice—one deep as the bell from a cathedral turret, another ringing on its treble notes the prelude of a waltz—the clocks began to strike the hour of three in the afternoon.

The sudden outbreak of so many tongues in that dumb chamber staggered him. He began to bestir himself, going to and fro with the candle, beleaguered by moving shadows, and startled to the soul by chance reflections. In many rich mirrors, some of home designs, some from Venice or Amsterdam, he saw his face repeated and repeated, as it were an army of spies; his own eyes met and detected him; and the sound of his own steps, lightly as they fell, vexed the surrounding quiet. And still as he continued to fill his pockets, his mind accused him, with a sickening iteration, of the thousand faults of his design. He should have chosen a more quiet hour; he should have prepared an alibi; he should not have used a knife; he should have been more cautious, and only bound and gagged the dealer, and not killed him; he should have been more bold, and killed the servant also; he should have done all things otherwise; poignant regrets, weary, incessant toiling of the mind to change what was unchangeable, to plan what was now useless, to be the architect of the irrevocable past. Meanwhile, and behind all this activity, brute terrors, like the scurrying of rats in a deserted attic, filled the more remote chambers of his brain with riot; the hand of the constable would fall heavy on his shoulder, and his nerves would jerk like a hooked fish; or he beheld, in galloping defile, the dock, the prison, the gallows, and the black coffin.

Terror of the people in the street sat down before his mind like a besieging army. It was impossible, he thought, but that some rumor of the struggle must have reached their ears and set on edge their curiosity; and now, in all the neighboring houses, he divined them sitting motionless and with uplifted ear—solitary people, condemned to spend Christmas dwelling alone on memories of the past, and now startlingly recalled from that tender exercise; happy family parties, struck into silence round the table, the mother still with raised finger: every degree and age and humor, but all, by their own hearts, prying and hearkening and weaving the rope that was to hang him. Sometimes it seemed to him he could not move too swiftly; the clink of the tall Bohemian goblets rang out loudly like a bell; and alarmed by the bigness of the ticking, he was tempted to stop the clocks. And then, again, with a swift transition of his terrors, the very silence of the place appeared a source of peril, and a thing to strike and freeze the passer-by; and he would step more boldly, and bustle aloud among the contents of the shop, and imitate, with elaborate bravado, the movements of a busy man at ease in his own house.

But he was now so pulled about by different alarms that, while one portion of his mind was still alert and cunning, another trembled on the brink of lunacy. One hallucination in particular took a strong hold on his credulity. The neighbor hearkening with white face beside his window, the passer-by arrested by a horrible surmise on the pavement—these could at worst suspect, they could not know; through the brick walls and shuttered windows only sounds could penetrate. But here, within the house, was he alone? He knew he was; he had watched the servant set forth sweet-hearting, in her poor best, "out for the day" written in every ribbon and smile. Yes, he was alone, of course; and yet, in the bulk of empty house above him, he could surely hear a stir of delicate footing—he was surely conscious, inexplicably conscious of some presence. Ay, surely; to every room and corner of the house his imagination followed it; and now it was a faceless thing, and yet had eyes to see with; and again it was a shadow of himself; and yet again behold the image of the dead dealer, reinspired with cunning and hatred.

At times, with a strong effort, he would glance at the open door which still seemed to repel his eyes. The house was tall, the skylight small and dirty, the day blind with fog; and the light that filtered down to the ground storey was exceedingly faint, and showed dimly on the threshold of the shop. And yet, in that strip of doubtful brightness, did there not hang wavering a shadow?

Suddenly, from the street outside, a very jovial gentleman began to beat with a staff on the shop-door, accompanying his blows with shouts and railleries in which the dealer was continually called upon by name. Markheim, smitten into ice, glanced at the dead man. But no! he lay quite still; he was fled away far beyond ear-shot of these blows and shoutings; he was sunk beneath seas of silence; and his name, which would once have caught his notice above the howling of a storm, had become an empty sound. And presently the jovial gentleman desisted from his knocking and departed.

Here was a broad hint to hurry what remained to be done, to get forth from this accusing neighborhood, to plunge into a bath of London multitudes, and to reach, on the other side of day, that haven of safety and apparent innocence—his bed. One visitor had come: at any moment another might follow and be more obstinate. To have done the deed, and yet not to reap the profit, would be too abhorrent a failure. The money, that was now Markheim's concern; and as a means to that, the keys.

He glanced over his shoulder at the open door, where the shadow was still lingering and shivering; and with no conscious repugnance of the mind, yet with a tremor of the belly, he drew near the body of his victim. The human character had quite departed. Like a suit half stuffed with bran, the limbs lay scattered, the trunk doubled, on the floor; and yet the thing repelled him. Although so dingy and inconsiderable to the eye, he feared it might have more significance to the touch. He took the body by the shoulders, and turned it on its back. It was strangely light and supple, and the limbs, as if they had been broken, fell into the oddest postures. The face was robbed of all expression; but it was pale as wax, and shockingly smeared with blood about one temple. That was, for Markheim, the one displeasing circumstance. It carried him back, upon the instant, to a certain fair day in a fishers' village: a grey day, a piping wind, a crowd upon the street, the blare of brasses, the booming of drums, the nasal voice of a ballad singer; and a boy going to and fro, buried over head in the crowd and divided between interest and fear, until, coming out upon the chief place of concourse, he beheld a booth and a great screen with pictures, dismally designed, garishly colored: Brownrigg with her apprentice; the Mannings with their murdered guest; We are in the death-grip of Thurtell; and a score besides of famous crimes. The thing was as clear as an illusion; he was once again that little boy; he was looking once again, and with the same sense of physical revolt, at these vile pictures; he was still stunned by the thumping of the drums. A bar of that day's music returned upon his memory; and at that, for the first time, a qualm came over him, a breath of nausea, a sudden weakness of the joints, which he must instantly resist and conquer.

He judged it more prudent to confront than to flee from these considerations; looking the more hardily in the dead face, bending his mind to realize the nature and greatness of his crime. So little a while ago that face had moved with every change of sentiment, that pale mouth had spoken, that body had been all on fire with governable energies; and now, and by his act, that piece of life had been arrested, as the horologist, with interjected finger, arrests the beating of the clock. So he reasoned in vain; he could rise to no more remorseful consciousness; the same heart which had shuddered before the painted effigies of crime, looked on its reality unmoved. At best, he felt a gleam of pity for one who had been endowed in vain with all those faculties that can make the world a garden of enchantment, one who had never lived and who was now dead. But of penitence, no, not a tremor.

With that, shaking himself clear of these considerations, he found the keys and advanced towards the open door of the shop. Outside, it had begun to rain smartly; and the sound of the shower upon the roof had banished silence. Like some dripping cavern, the chambers of the house were haunted by an incessant echoing, which filled the ear and mingled with the ticking of the clocks. And, as Markheim approached the door, he seemed to hear, in answer to his own cautious tread, the steps of another foot withdrawing up the stair. The shadow still palpitated loosely on the threshold. He threw a ton's weight of resolve upon his muscles, and drew back the door.

The faint, foggy daylight glimmered dimly on the bare floor and stairs; on the bright suit of armor posted, halbert in hand, upon the landing; and on the dark wood-carvings, and framed pictures that hung against the yellow panels of the wainscot. So loud was the beating of the rain through all the house that, in Markheim's ears, it began to be distinguished into many different sounds. Footsteps and sighs, the tread of regiments marching in the distance, the chink of money in the counting, and the creaking of doors held stealthily ajar, appeared to mingle with the patter of the drops upon the cupola and the gushing of the water in the pipes. The sense that he was not alone grew upon him to the verge of madness. On every side he was haunted and begirt by presences. He heard them moving in the upper chambers; from the shop, he heard the dead man getting to his legs; and as he began with a great effort to mount the stairs, feet fled quietly before him and followed stealthily behind. If he were but deaf, he thought, how tranquilly he would possess his soul! And then again, and hearkening with ever fresh attention, he blessed himself for that unresting sense which held the outposts and stood a trusty sentinel upon his life. His head turned continually on his neck; his eyes, which seemed starting from their orbits, scouted on every side, and on every side were half rewarded as with the tail of something nameless vanishing. The four-and-twenty steps to the first floor were four-and-twenty agonies.

On that first storey, the doors stood ajar, three of them like three ambushes, shaking his nerves like the throats of cannon. He could never again, he felt, be sufficiently immured and fortified from men's observing eyes; he longed to be home, girt in by walls, buried among bedclothes, and invisible to all but God. And at that thought he wondered a little, recollecting tales of other murderers and the fear they were said to entertain of heavenly avengers. It was not so, at least, with him. He feared the laws of nature, lest, in their callous and immutable procedure, they should preserve some damning evidence of his crime. He feared tenfold more, with a slavish, superstitious terror, some scission in the continuity of man's experience, some wilful illegality of nature. He played a game of skill, depending on the rules, calculating consequence from cause; and what if nature, as the defeated tyrant overthrew the chess-board, should break the mold of their succession? The like had befallen Napoleon (so writers said) when the winter changed the time of its appearance. The like might befall Markheim: the solid walls might become transparent and reveal his doings like those of bees in a glass hive; the stout planks might yield under his foot like quicksands and detain him in their clutch; ay, and there were soberer accidents that might destroy him: if, for instance, the house should fall and imprison him beside the body of his victim; or the house next door should fly on fire, and the firemen invade him from all sides. These things he feared; and, in a sense, these things might be called the hands of God reached forth against sin. But about God himself he was at ease; his act was doubtless exceptional, but so were his excuses, which God knew; it was there, and not among men, that he felt sure of justice.

When he had got safe into the drawing-room, and shut the door behind him, he was aware of a respite from alarms. The room was quite dismantled, uncarpeted besides, and strewn with packing-cases and incongruous furniture; several great pier-glasses, in which he beheld himself at various angles, like an actor on a stage; many pictures, framed and unframed, standing, with their faces to the wall; a fine Sheraton sideboard, a cabinet of marquetry, and a great old bed, with tapestry hangings. The windows opened to the floor; but by great good-fortune the lower part of the shutters had been closed, and this concealed him from the neighbors. Here, then, Markheim drew in a packing-case before the cabinet and began to search among the keys. It was a long business, for there were many; and it was irksome, besides; for after all, there might be nothing in the cabinet, and time was on the wing. But the closeness of the occupation sobered him. With the tail of his eye he saw the door—even glanced at it from time to time directly, like a besieged commander pleased to verify the good estate of his defences. But in truth he was at peace. The rain falling in the street sounded natural and pleasant. Presently, on the other side, the notes of a piano were wakened to the husic of a hymn, and the voices of many children took up the air and words. How stately, how comfortable was the melody! How fresh the youthful voices! Markheim gave ear to it smilingly, as he sorted out the keys; and his mind was thronged with answerable ideas and images; church-going children and the pealing of the high organ; children afield, bathers by the brookside, ramblers on the brambly common, kite-fliers in the windy and cloud-navigated sky; and then, at another cadence of the hymn, back again to church, and the somnolence of summer Sundays, and the high genteel voice of the parson (which he smiled a little to recall) and the painted Jacobean tombs, and the dim lettering of the Ten Commandments in the chancel.

And as he sat thus, at once busy and absent, he was startled to his feet. A flash of ice, a flash of fire, a bursting gush of blood, went over him, and then he stood transfixed and thrilling. A step mounted the stair slowly and steadily, and presently a hand was laid upon the knob, and the lock clicked, and the door opened.

Fear held Markheim in a vice. What to expect he knew not, whether the dead man walking, or the official ministers of human justice, or some chance witness blindly stumbling in to consign him to the gallows. But when a face was thrust into the aperture, glanced round the room, looked at him, nodded and smiled as if in friendly recognition, and then withdrew again, and the door closed behind it, his fear broke loose from his control in a hoarse cry. At the sound of this the visitant returned.

"Did you call me?" he asked, pleasantly, and with that he entered the room and closed the door behind him.

Markheim stood and gazed at him with all his eyes. Perhaps there was a film upon his sight, but the outlines of the new-comer seemed to change and waver like those of the idols in the wavering candle-light of the shop; and at times he thought he knew him; and at times he thought he bore a likeness to himself; and always, like a lump of living terror, there lay in his bosom the conviction that this thing was not of the earth and not of God.

And yet the creature had a strange air of the commonplace, as he stood looking on Markheim with a smile; and when he added: "You are looking for the money, I believe?" it was in the tones of every-day politeness.

Markheim made no answer.

"I should warn you," resumed the other, "that the maid has left her sweetheart earlier than usual and will soon be here. If Mr. Markheim be found in this house, I need not describe to him the consequences."

"You know me?" cried the murderer.

The visitor smiled. "You have long been a favorite of mine," he said; "and I have long observed and often sought to help you."

"What are you?" cried Markheim: "the devil?"

"What I may be," returned the other, "cannot affect the service I propose to render you."

"It can," cried Markheim; "it does! Be helped by you? No, never; not by you! You do not know me yet; thank God, you do not know me!"

"I know you," replied the visitant, with a sort of kind severity or rather firmness. "I know you to the soul."

"Know me!" cried Markheim. "Who can do so? My life is but a travesty and slander on myself. I have lived to belie my nature. All men do; all men are better than this disguise that grows about and stifles them. You see each dragged away by life, like one whom bravos have seized and muffled in a cloak. If they had their own control—if you could see their faces, they would be altogether different, they would shine out for heroes and saints! I am worse than most; my self is more overlaid; my excuse is known to me and God. But, had I the time, I could disclose myself."

"To me?" inquired the visitant.

"To you before all," returned the murderer. "I supposed you were intelligent. I thought—since you exist—you would prove a reader of the heart. And yet you would propose to judge me by my acts! Think of it; my acts! I was born and I have lived in a land of giants; giants have dragged me by the wrists since I was born out of my mother—the giants of circumstance. And you would judge me by my acts! But can you not look within? Can you not understand that evil is hateful to me? Can you not see within me the clear writing of conscience, never blurred by any wilful sophistry, although too often disregarded? Can you not read me for a thing that surely must be common as humanity—the unwilling sinner?"

"All this is very feelingly expressed," was the reply, "but it regards me not. These points of consistency are beyond my province, and I care not in the least by what compulsion you may have been dragged away, so as you are but carried in the right direction. But time flies; the servant delays, looking in the faces of the crowd and at the pictures on the hoardings, but still she keeps moving nearer; and remember, it is as if the gallows itself was striding towards you through the Christmas streets! Shall I help you; I, who know all? Shall I tell you where to find the money?"

"For what price?" asked Markheim.

"I offer you the service for a Christmas gift," returned the other.

Markheim could not refrain from smiling with a kind of bitter triumph. "No," said he, "I will take nothing at your hands; if I were dying of thirst, and it was your hand that put the pitcher to my lips, I should find the courage to refuse. It may be credulous, but I will do nothing to commit myself to evil."

"I have no objection to a death-bed repentance," observed the visitant.

"Because you disbelieve their efficacy!" Markheim cried.

"I do not say so," returned the other; "but I look on these things from a different side, and when the life is done my interest falls. The man has lived to serve me, to spread black looks under color of religion, or to sow tares in the wheat-field, as you do, in a course of weak compliance with desire. Now that he draws so near to his deliverance, he can add but one act of service—to repent, to die smiling, and thus to build up in confidence and hope the more timorous of my surviving followers. I am not so hard a master. Try me. Accept my help. Please yourself in life as you have done hitherto; please yourself more amply, spread your elbows at the board; and when the night begins to fall and the curtains to be drawn, I tell you, for your greater comfort, that you will find it even easy to compound your quarrel with your conscience, and to make a truckling peace with God. I came but now from such a death-bed, and the room was full of sincere mourners, listening to the man's last words: and when I looked into that face, which had been set as a flint against mercy, I found it smiling with hope."

"And do you, then, suppose me such a creature?" asked Markheim. "Do you think I have no more generous aspirations than to sin, and sin, and sin, and, at last, sneak into heaven? My heart rises at the thought. Is this, then, your experience of mankind? or is it because you find me with red hands that you presume such baseness? and is this crime of murder indeed so impious as to dry up the very springs of good?"

"Murder is to me no special category," replied the other. "All sins are murder, even as all life is war. I behold your race, like starving mariners on a raft, plucking crusts out of the hands of famine and feeding on each other's lives. I follow sins beyond the moment of their acting; I find in all that the last consequence is death; and to my eyes, the pretty maid who thwarts her mother with such taking graces on a question of a ball, drips no less visibly with human gore than such a murderer as yourself. Do I say that I follow sins? I follow virtues also; they differ not by the thickness of a nail, they are both scythes for the reaping angel of Death. Evil, for which I live, consists not in action but in character. The bad man is dear to me; not the bad act, whose fruits, if we could follow them far enough down the hurtling cataract of the ages, might yet be found more blessed than those of the rarest virtues. And it is not because you have killed a dealer, but because you are Markheim, that I offered to forward your escape."

"I will lay my heart open to you," answered Markheim. "This crime on which you find me is my last. On my way to it I have learned many lessons; itself is a lesson, a momentous lesson. Hitherto I have been driven with revolt to what I would not; I was a bond-slave to poverty, driven and scourged. There are robust virtues that can stand in these temptations; mine was not so: I had a thirst of pleasure. But to-day, and out of this deed, I pluck both warning and riches—both the power and a fresh resolve to be myself. I become in all things a free actor in the world; I begin to see myself all changed, these hands the agents of good, this heart at peace. Something comes over me out of the past; something of what I have dreamed on Sabbath evenings to the sound of the church organ, of what I forecast when I shed tears over noble books, or talked, an innocent child, with my mother. There lies my life; I have wandered a few years, but now I see once more my city of destination."

"You are to use this money on the Stock Exchange, I think?" remarked the visitor; "and there, if I mistake not, you have already lost some thousands?"

"Ah," said Markheim, "but this time I have a sure thing."

"This time, again, you will lose," replied the visitor quietly.

"Ah, but I keep back the half!" cried Markheim.

"That also you will lose," said the other.

The sweat started upon Markheim's brow. "Well, then, what matter?" he exclaimed. "Say it be lost, say I am plunged again in poverty, shall one part of me, and that the worst, continue until the end to override the better? Evil and good run strong in me, haling me both ways. I do not love the one thing, I love all. I can conceive great deeds, renunciations, martyrdoms; and though I be fallen to such a crime as murder, pity is no stranger to my thoughts. I pity the poor; who knows their trials better than myself? I pity and help them; I prize love, I love honest laughter; there is no good thing nor true thing on earth but I love it from my heart. And are my vices only to direct my life, and my virtues to lie without effect, like some passive lumber of the mind? Not so; good, also, is a spring of acts."

But the visitant raised his finger. "For six-and-thirty years that you have been in this world," said he, "through many changes of fortune and varieties of humor, I have watched you steadily fall. Fifteen years ago you would have started at a theft. Three years back you would have blenched at the name of murder. Is there any crime, is there any cruelty or meanness, from which you still recoil?—five years from now I shall detect you in the fact! Downward, downward, lies your way; nor can anything but death avail to stop you."

"It is true," Markheim said huskily, "I have in some degree complied with evil. But it is so with all: the very saints, in the mere exercise of living, grow less dainty, and take on the tone of their surroundings."

"I will propound to you one simple question," said the other; "and as you answer, I shall read to you your moral horoscope. You have grown in many things more lax; possibly you do right to be so; and at any account, it is the same with all men. But granting that, are you in any one particular, however trifling, more difficult to please with your own conduct, or do you go in all things with a looser rein?"

"In any one?" repeated Markheim, with an anguish of consideration. "No," he added, with despair, "in none! I have gone down in all."

"Then," said the visitor, "content yourself with what you are, for you will never change; and the words of your part on this stage are irrevocably written down."

Markheim stood for a long while silent, and indeed it was the visitor who first broke the silence. "That being so," he said, "shall I show you the money?"

"And grace?" cried Markheim.

"Have you not tried it?" returned the other. "Two or three years ago, did I not see you on the platform of revival meetings, and was not your voice the loudest in the hymn?"

"It is true," said Markheim; "and I see clearly what remains for me by way of duty. I thank you for these lessons from my soul; my eyes are opened, and I behold myself at last for what I am."

At this moment, the sharp note of the door-bell rang through the house; and the visitant, as though this were some concerted signal for which he had been waiting, changed at once in his demeanor.

"The maid!" he cried. "She has returned, as I forewarned you, and there is now before you one more difficult passage. Her master, you must say, is ill; you must let her in, with an assured but rather serious countenance—no smiles, no overacting, and I promise you success! Once the girl within, and the door closed, the same dexterity that has already rid you of the dealer will relieve you of this last danger in your path. Thenceforward you have the whole evening—the whole night, if needful—to ransack the treasures of the house and to make good your safety. This is help that comes to you with the mask of danger. Up!" he cried: "up, friend; your life hangs trembling in the scales: up, and act!"

Markheim steadily regarded his counsellor. "If I be condemned to evil acts," he said, "there is still one door of freedom open—I can cease from action. If my life be an ill thing, I can lay it down. Though I be, as you say truly, at the beck of every small temptation, I can yet, by one decisive gesture, place myself beyond the reach of all. My love of good is damned to barrenness; it may, and let it be! But I have still my hatred of evil; and from that, to your galling disappointment, you shall see that I can draw both energy and courage."

The features of the visitor began to undergo a wonderful and lovely change: they brightened and softened with a tender triumph; and, even as they brightened, faded and dislimned. But Markheim did not pause to watch or understand the transformation. He opened the door and went down-stairs very slowly, thinking to himself. His past went soberly before him; he beheld it as it was, ugly and strenuous like a dream, random as chance-medley—a scene of defeat. Life, as he thus reviewed it, tempted him no longer; but on the further side he perceived a quiet haven for his bark. He paused in the passage, and looked into the shop, where the candle still burned by the dead body. It was strangely silent. Thoughts of the dealer swarmed into his mind, as he stood gazing. And then the bell once more broke out into impatient clamor.

He confronted the maid upon the threshold with something like a smile.

"You had better go for the police," said he: "I have killed your master."

WILLIAM ERNEST HENLEY
(1849-1903)

From Hospital Sketches

Before

Behold me waiting—waiting for the knife.
A little while, and at a leap I storm
The thick, sweet mystery of chloroform,
The drunken dark, the little death-in-life.
The gods are good to me: I have no wife,
No innocent child, to think of as I near
The fateful minute; nothing all too dear
Unmans me for my bout of passive strife.
Yet I am tremulous and a trifle sick,
And, face to face with chance, I shrink a little:
My hopes are strong, my will is something weak.
Here comes the basket? Thank you. I am ready.
But, gentlemen my porters, life is brittle:
You carry Cæsar and his fortunes—steady!

Operation

You are carried in a basket,
Like a carcase from the shambles,
To the theatre, a cockpit
Where they stretch you on a table.

Then they bid you close your eyelids,
And they mask you with a napkin,
And the anæsthetic reaches
Hot and subtle through your being.

And you gasp and reel and shudder
In a rushing, swaying rapture,
While the voices at your elbow
Fade—receding—fainter—farther.

Lights about you shower and tumble,
And your blood seems crystallizing—
Edged and vibrant, yet within you
Racked and hurried back and forward.

Then the lights grow fast and furious,
And you hear a noise of waters,
And you wrestle, blind and dizzy,
In an agony of effort,

Till a sudden lull accepts you,
And you sound an utter darkness . . .
And awaken . . . with a struggle . . .
On a hushed, attentive audience.

Apparition

Thin-legged, thin-chested, slight unspeakably,
Neat-footed and weak-fingered: in his face—
Lean, large-boned, curved of beak, and touched with race,
Bold-lipped, rich-tinted, mutable as the sea,
The brown eyes radiant with vivacity—
There shines a brilliant and romantic grace,
A spirit intense and rare, with trace on trace
Of passion and impudence and energy.
Valiant in velvet, light in ragged luck,
Most vain, most generous, sternly critical,
Buffoon and poet, lover and sensualist:
A deal of Ariel, just a streak of Puck,
Much Antony, of Hamlet most of all,
And something of the Shorter-Catechist.

JOSEPH CONRAD (1857-1924)

Youth

THIS could have occurred nowhere but in England, where men and sea interpenetrate, so to speak—the sea entering into the life of most men, and the men knowing something or everything about the sea, in the way of amusement, of travel, or of bread-winning.

We were sitting round a mahogany table that reflected the bottle, the claret-glasses, and our faces as we leaned on our elbows. There was a director of companies, an accountant, a lawyer, Marlow, and myself. The director had been a *Conway* boy, the accountant had served four years at sea, the lawyer—a fine crusted Tory, High Churchman, the best of old fellows, the soul of honour—had been chief officer in the P. & O. service in the good old days when mail-boats were square-rigged at least on two masts, and used to come down the China Sea before a fair monsoon with stun'-sails set alow and aloft. We all began life in the merchant service. Between the five of us there was the strong bond of the sea, and also the fellowship of the craft, which no amount of enthusiasm for yachting, cruising, and so on can give, since one is only the amusement of life and the other is life itself.

Marlow (at least I think that is how he spelt his name) told the story, or rather the chronicle, of a voyage:—

"Yes, I have seen a little of the Eastern seas; but what I remember best is my first voyage there. You fellows know there are those voyages that seem ordered for the illustration of life, that might stand for a symbol of existence. You fight, work, sweat, nearly kill yourself, sometimes do kill yourself, trying to accomplish something—and you can't. Not from any fault of yours. You simply can do nothing, neither great nor little—not a thing in the world—not even marry an old maid, or get a wretched 600-ton cargo of coal to its port of destination.

"It was altogether a memorable affair. It was my first voyage to the East, and my first voyage as second mate; it was also my skipper's first command. You'll admit it was time. He was sixty if a day; a little man, with a broad, not very straight back, with bowed shoulders and one leg more bandy than the other, he had that queer twisted-about appearance you see so often in men who work in the fields. He had a nut-cracker face—chin and nose trying to come together over a sunken mouth—and it was framed in iron-gray fluffy hair, that looked like a chin-strap of cotton-wool sprinkled with coal-dust. And he had blue eyes in that old face of his, which were amazingly like a boy's, with that candid expression some quite common men preserve to the end of their days by a rare internal gift of simplicity of heart and rectitude of soul. What induced him to accept me was a wonder. I had come out of a crack Australian clipper, where I had been third officer, and he seemed to have a prejudice against crack clippers as aristocratic and high-toned. He said to me, 'You know, in this ship you will have to work.' I said I had to work in every ship I had ever been in. 'Ah, but this is different, and you gentlemen out of them big ships; . . . but there! I dare say you will do. Join to-morrow.'

"I joined to-morrow. It was twenty-two years ago; and I was just twenty. How time passes! It was one of the happiest days of my life. Fancy! Second mate for the first time—a really responsible officer! I wouldn't have thrown up my new billet for a fortune. The mate looked me over carefully. He was also an old chap, but of another stamp. He had a Roman nose, a snow-white, long beard, and his name was Mahon, but he insisted that it should be pronounced Mann. He was well connected; yet there was something wrong with his luck, and he had never got on.

"As to the captain, he had been for years in coasters, then in the Mediterranean, and last in the West Indian trade. He had never been round the Capes. He could just write a kind of sketchy hand, and didn't care for writing at all. Both were thorough good seamen of course, and between those two old chaps I felt like a small boy between two grandfathers.

"The ship also was old. Her name was the *Judea*. Queer name, isn't it? She belonged to a man Wilmer, Wilcox—some name like that; but he has been bankrupt and dead these twenty years or more, and his name don't matter. She had been laid up in Shadwell basin for ever so long. You may imagine her state. She was all rust, dust, grime—soot aloft, dirt on deck. To me it was like coming out of a palace into a ruined cottage. She was about 400 tons, had a primitive windlass, wooden latches to the doors, not a bit of brass about her, and a big square stern. There was on it, below her name in big letters, a lot of scrollwork, with the gilt off, and some sort of a coat of arms, with the motto 'Do or Die' underneath. I remember it took my fancy immensely. There was a touch of romance in it, something that made me love the old thing—something that appealed to my youth!

"We left London in ballast—sand ballast—to load a cargo of coal in a northern port for Bankok. Bankok! I thrilled. I had been six years at sea, but had only seen Melbourne and Sydney, very good places, charming places in their way—but Bankok!

"We worked out of the Thames under canvas, with a North Sea pilot on board. His name was Jermyn, and he dodged all day long about the galley drying his handkerchief before the stove. Apparently he never slept. He was a dismal man, with a perpetual tear sparkling at the end of his nose, who either had been in trouble, or was in trouble, or expected to be in trouble—couldn't be happy unless something went wrong. He mistrusted my youth, my common-sense, and my seamanship, and made a point of showing it in a hundred little ways. I dare say he was right. It seems to me I knew very little then, and I know not much more now; but I cherish a hate for that Jermyn to this day.

"We were a week working up as far as Yarmouth Roads, and then we got into a gale—the famous October gale of twenty-two years ago. It was wind, lightning, sleet, snow, and a terrific sea. We were flying light, and you may imagine how bad it was when I tell you we had smashed bulwarks and a flooded deck. On the second night she shifted her ballast into the lee bow, and by that time we had been blown off somewhere on the Dogger Bank. There was nothing for it but go below with shovels and try to right her, and there we were in that vast hold, gloomy like a cavern, the tallow dips stuck and flickering on the beams, the gale howling above, the ship tossing about like mad on her side; there we all were, Jermyn, the captain, every one, hardly able to keep our feet, engaged on that gravedigger's work, and trying to toss shovelfuls of wet sand up to windward. At every tumble of the ship you could see vaguely in the dim light men falling down with a great flourish of shovels. One of the ship's boys (we had two), impressed by the weirdness of the scene, wept as if his heart would break. We could hear him blubbering somewhere in the shadows.

"On the third day the gale died out, and by and by a north-country tug picked us up. We took sixteen days in all to get from London to the Tyne! When we got into dock we had lost our turn for loading, and they hauled us off to a tier where we remained for a month. Mrs. Beard (the captain's name was Beard) came from Colchester to see the old man. She lived on board. The crew of runners had left, and there remained only the officers, one boy and the steward, a mulatto who answered to the name of Abraham. Mrs. Beard was an old woman, with a face all wrinkled and ruddy like a winter apple, and the figure of a young girl. She caught sight of me once, sewing a button, and insisted on having my shirts to repair. This was something different from the captains' wives I had known on board crack clippers. When I brought her the shirts, she said: 'And the socks? They want mending, I am sure, and John's—Captain Beard's—things are all in order now. I would be glad of something to do.' Bless the old woman. She overhauled my outfit for me, and meantime I read for the first time *Sartor Resartus* and Burnaby's *Ride to Khiva.* I didn't understand much of the first then; but I remember I preferred the soldier to the philosopher at the time; a preference which life has only confirmed. One was a man, and the other was either more—or less. However, they are both dead and Mrs. Beard is dead, and youth, strength, genius, thoughts, achievements, simple hearts—all die. . . . No matter.

"They loaded us at last. We shipped a crew. Eight able seamen and two boys. We hauled off one evening to the buoys at the dock-gates, ready to go out, and with a fair prospect of beginning the voyage next day. Mrs. Beard was to start for home by a late train. When the ship was fast we went to tea. We sat rather silent through the meal—Mahon, the old couple, and I. I finished first, and slipped away for a smoke, my cabin being in a deck-house just against the poop. It was high water, blowing fresh with a drizzle; the double dock-gates were opened, and the steam-colliers were going in and out in the darkness with their lights burning bright, a great plashing of propellers, rattling of winches, and a lot of hailing on the pier-heads. I watched the procession of head-lights gliding high and of green lights gliding low in the night, when suddenly a red gleam flashed at me, vanished, came into view again, and remained. The fore-end of a steamer loomed up close. I shouted down the cabin, 'Come up, quick!' and then heard a startled voice saying afar in the dark, 'Stop her, sir.' A bell jingled. Another voice cried warningly, 'We are going right into that barque, sir.' The answer to this was a gruff 'All right' and the next thing was a heavy crash as the steamer struck a glancing blow with the bluff of her bow about our fore-rigging. There was a moment of confusion, yelling, and running about. Steam roared. Then somebody was heard saying, 'All clear, sir.' . . . 'Are you all right?' asked the gruff voice. I had jumped forward to see the damage, and hailed back, 'I think so.' 'Easy astern,' said the gruff voice. A bell jingled. 'What steamer is that?' screamed Mahon. By that time she was no more to us than a bulky shadow manœuvring a little way off. They shouted at us some name—a woman's name, Miranda or Melissa—or some such thing. 'This means another month in this beastly hole,' said Mahon to me, as we peered with lamps about the splintered bulwarks and broken braces. 'But where's the captain?'

"We had not heard or seen anything of him all that time. We went aft to look. A doleful voice arose hailing somewhere in the middle of the dock, '*Judea* ahoy!' . . . How the devil did he get there? . . . 'Hallo!' we shouted. 'I am adrift in our boat without oars,' he cried.

A belated water-man offered his services, and Mahon struck a bargain with him for half-a-crown to tow our skipper alongside; but it was Mrs. Beard that came up the ladder first. They had been floating about the dock in that mizzly cold rain for nearly an hour. I was never so surprised in my life.

"It appears that when he heard my shout 'Come up' he understood at once what was the matter, caught up his wife, ran on deck, and across, and down into our boat, which was fast to the ladder. Not bad for a sixty-year-old. Just imagine that old fellow saving heroically in his arms that old woman—the woman of his life. He set her down on a thwart, and was ready to climb back on board when the painter came adrift somehow, and away they went together. Of course in the confusion we did not hear him shouting. He looked abashed. She said cheerfully, 'I suppose it does not matter my losing the train now?' 'No, Jenny—you go below and get warm,' he growled. Then to us: 'A sailor has no business with a wife—I say. There I was, out of the ship. Well, no harm done this time. Let's go and look at what that fool of a steamer smashed.'

"It wasn't much, but it delayed us three weeks. At the end of that time, the captain being engaged with his agents, I carried Mrs. Beard's bag to the railway-station and put her all comfy into a third-class carriage. She lowered the window to say, 'You are a good young man. If you see John—Captain Beard—without his muffler at night, just remind him from me to keep his throat well wrapped up.' 'Certainly, Mrs. Beard,' I said. 'You are a good young man; I noticed how attentive you are to John—to Captain——' The train pulled out suddenly; I took my cap off to the old woman: I never saw her again. . . . Pass the bottle.

"We went to sea next day. When we made that start for Bankok we had been already three months out of London. We had expected to be a fortnight or so—at the outside.

"It was January, and the weather was beautiful—the beautiful sunny winter weather that has more charm than in the summer-time, because it is unexpected, and crisp, and you know it won't, it can't, last long. It's like a windfall, like a godsend, like an unexpected piece of luck.

"It lasted all down the North Sea, all down Channel; and it lasted till we were three hundred miles or so to the westward of the Lizards: then the wind went round to the sou'west and began to pipe up. In two days it blew a gale. The *Judea,* hove to, wallowed on the Atlantic like an old candle-box. It blew day after day: it blew with spite, without interval, without mercy, without rest. The world was nothing but an immensity of great foaming waves rushing at us, under a sky low enough to touch with the hand and dirty like a smoked ceiling. In the stormy space surrounding us there was as much flying spray as air. Day after day and night after night there was nothing round the ship but the howl of the wind, the tumult of the sea, the noise of water pouring over her deck. There was no rest for her and no rest for us. She tossed, she pitched, she stood on her head, she sat on her tail, she rolled, she groaned, and we had to hold on while on deck and cling to our bunks when below, in a constant effort of body and worry of mind.

"One night Mahon spoke through the small window of my berth. It opened right into my very bed, and I was lying there sleepless, in my boots, feeling as though I had not slept for years, and could not if I tried. He said excitedly—

" 'You got the sounding-rod in here, Marlow? I can't get the pumps to suck. By God! it's no child's play.'

"I gave him the sounding-rod and lay down again, trying to think of various things—but I thought only of the pumps. When I came on deck they were still at it, and my watch relieved at the pumps. By the light of the lantern brought on deck to examine the sounding-rod I caught a glimpse of their weary, serious faces. We pumped all the four hours. We pumped all night, all day, all the week—watch and watch. She was working herself loose, and leaked badly—not enough to drown us at once, but enough to kill us with the work at the pumps. And while we pumped the ship was going from us piecemeal: the bulwarks went, the stanchions were torn out, the ventilators smashed, the cabin-door burst in. There was not a dry spot in the ship. She was being gutted bit by bit. The long-boat changed, as if by magic, into matchwood where she stood in her gripes. I had lashed her myself, and was rather proud of my handiwork, which had withstood so long the malice of the sea. And we pumped. And there was no break in the weather. The sea was white like a sheet of foam, like a caldron of boiling milk; there was not a break in the clouds, no—not the size of a man's hand—no, not for so much as ten seconds. There was for us no sky, there were for us no stars, no sun, no universe—nothing but angry clouds and an infuriated sea. We pumped watch and watch, for dear life; and it seemed to last for months, for years, for all eternity, as though we had been dead and gone to a hell for sailors. We forgot the day of the week, the name of the month, what year it was, and whether we had ever been ashore. The sails blew away, she lay broadside on under a weather-cloth, the ocean poured over her, and we did not care. We turned those handles, and had the eyes of idiots. As soon as we had crawled on deck I used to take a round turn with a rope about the men, the pumps, and the mainmast, and we turned, we turned incessantly, with the water to our waists, to our necks, over our heads. It was all one. We had forgotten how it felt to be dry.

"And there was somewhere in me the thought: By Jove! this is the deuce of an adventure—something you read about; and it is my first voyage as second mate—and I am only twenty—and here I am lasting it out as well as any of these men, and keeping my chaps up to the mark. I was pleased. I would not have given up the experience for worlds. I had moments of exultation. Whenever the old dismantled craft pitched heavily with her counter high in the air, she seemed to me to throw up, like an appeal, like a defiance, like a cry to the clouds without mercy, the words written on her stern: '*Judea,* London. Do or Die.'

"O youth! The strength of it, the faith of it, the imagination of it! To me she was not an old rattletrap carting about the world a lot of coal for a freight—to me she was the endeavour, the test, the trial of life. I think of her with pleasure, with affection, with regret—as you would think of someone dead you have loved. I shall never forget her. . . . Pass the bottle.

"One night when tied to the mast, as I explained, we were pumping on, deafened with the wind, and without spirit enough in us to wish ourselves dead, a heavy sea crashed aboard and swept clean over us. As soon as I got my breath I shouted, as in duty bound, 'Keep on, boys!' when suddenly I felt something hard floating on deck strike the calf of my leg. I made a grab at it and missed. It was so dark we could not see each other's faces within a foot—you understand.

"After that thump the ship kept quiet for a while, and the thing, whatever it was, struck my leg again. This time I caught it—and it was a saucepan. At first, being stupid with fatigue and thinking of nothing but the pumps, I did not understand what I had in my hand. Suddenly it dawned upon me, and I shouted, 'Boys, the house on deck is gone. Leave this, and let's look for the cook.'

"There was a deck-house forward, which contained the galley, the cook's berth, and the quarters of the crew. As we had expected for days to see it swept away, the hands had been ordered to sleep in the cabin—the only safe place in the ship. The steward, Abraham, however, persisted in clinging to his berth, stupidly, like a mule—from sheer fright I believe, like an animal that won't leave a stable falling in an earthquake. So we went to look for him. It was chancing death, since once out of our lashings we were as exposed as if on a raft. But we went. The house was shattered as if a shell had exploded inside. Most of it had gone overboard—stove, men's quarters, and their property, all was gone;

but two posts, holding a portion of the bulkhead to which Abraham's bunk was attached, remained as if by a miracle. We groped in the ruins and came upon this, and there he was, sitting in his bunk, surrounded by foam and wreckage, jabbering cheerfully to himself. He was out of his mind; completely and for ever mad, with this sudden shock coming upon the fag-end of his endurance. We snatched him up, lugged him aft, and pitched him head-first down the cabin companion. You understand there was no time to carry him down with infinite precautions and wait to see how he got on. Those below would pick him up at the bottom of the stairs all right. We were in a hurry to go back to the pumps. That business could not wait. A bad leak is an inhuman thing.

"One would think that the sole purpose of that fiendish gale had been to make a lunatic of that poor devil of a mulatto. It eased before morning, and next day the sky cleared, and as the sea went down the leak took up. When it came to bending a fresh set of sails the crew demanded to put back—and really there was nothing else to do. Boats gone, decks swept clean, cabin gutted, men without a stitch but what they stood in, stores spoiled, ship strained. We put her head for home, and—would you believe it? The wind came east right in our teeth. It blew fresh, it blew continuously. We had to beat up every inch of the way, but she did not leak so badly, the water keeping comparatively smooth. Two hours' pumping in every four is no joke—but it kept her afloat as far as Falmouth.

"The good people there live on casualties of the sea, and no doubt were glad to see us. A hungry crowd of shipwrights sharpened their chisels at the sight of that carcass of a ship. And, by Jove! they had pretty pickings off us before they were done. I fancy the owner was already in a tight place. There were delays. Then it was decided to take part of the cargo out and caulk her topsides. This was done, the repairs finished, cargo reshipped; a new crew came on board, and we went out—for Bankok. At the end of a week we were back again. The crew said they weren't going to Bankok—a hundred and fifty days' passage—in a something hooker that wanted pumping eight hours out of the twenty-four; and the nautical papers inserted again the little paragraph: '*Judea*. Barque. Tyne to Bankok; coal; put back to Falmouth leaky and with crew refusing duty.'

"There were more delays—more tinkering. The owner came down for a day, and said she was as right as a little fiddle. Poor old Captain Beard looked like the ghost of a Geordie skipper—through the worry and humiliation of it. Remember he was sixty, and it was his first command. Mahon said it was a foolish business, and would end badly.

I loved the ship more than ever, and wanted awfully to get to Bankok. To Bankok! Magic name, blessed name. Mesopotamia wasn't a patch on it. Remember I was twenty, and it was my first second-mate's billet, and the East was waiting for me.

"We went out and anchored in the outer roads with a fresh crew—the third. She leaked worse than ever. It was as if those confounded shipwrights had actually made a hole in her. This time we did not even go outside. The crew simply refused to man the windlass.

"They towed us back to the inner harbour, and we became a fixture, a feature, an institution of the place. People pointed us out to visitors as 'That 'ere barque that's going to Bankok—has been here six months—put back three times.' On holidays the small boys pulling about in boats would hail, '*Judea,* ahoy!' and if a head showed above the rail shouted, 'Where you bound to?—Bankok?' and jeered. We were only three on board. The poor old skipper mooned in the cabin. Mahon undertook the cooking, and unexpectedly developed all a Frenchman's genius for preparing nice little messes. I looked languidly after the rigging. We became citizens of Falmouth. Every shopkeeper knew us. At the barber's or tobacconist's they asked familiarly, 'Do you think you will ever get to Bankok?' Meantime the owner, the underwriters, and the charterers squabbled amongst themselves in London, and our pay went on. . . . Pass the bottle.

"It was horrid. Morally it was worse than pumping for life. It seemed as though we had been forgotten by the world, belonged to nobody, would get nowhere; it seemed that, as if bewitched, we would have to live for ever and ever in that inner harbour, a derision and a byword to generations of long-shore loafers and dishonest boatmen. I obtained three months' pay and a five days' leave, and made a rush for London. It took me a day to get there and pretty well another to come back—but three months' pay went all the same. I don't know what I did with it. I went to a music-hall, I believe, lunched, dined, and supped in a swell place in Regent Street, and was back to time, with nothing but a complete set of Byron's works and a new railway rug to show for three months' work. The boat-man who pulled me off to the ship said: 'Hallo! I thought you had left the old thing. *She* will never get to Bankok.' 'That's all *you* know about it,' I said scornfully—but I didn't like that prophecy at all.

"Suddenly a man, some kind of agent to somebody, appeared with full powers. He had grog-blossoms all over his face, an indomitable energy, and was a jolly soul. We leaped into life again. A hulk came alongside, took our cargo, and then we went into dry dock to get our copper stripped. No wonder she leaked. The poor thing, strained beyond endurance by the gale, had, as if in disgust, spat out all the oakum of her lower seams. She was recaulked, new coppered and made as tight as a bottle. We went back to the hulk and reshipped our cargo.

"Then, on a fine moonlight night, all the rats left the ship.

"We had been infested with them. They had destroyed our sails, consumed more stores than the crew, affably shared our beds and our dangers, and now, when the ship was made seaworthy, concluded to clear out. I called Mahon to enjoy the spectacle. Rat after rat appeared on our rail, took a last look over his shoulder, and leaped with a hollow thud into the empty hulk. We tried to count them, but soon lost the tale. Mahon said: 'Well, well! don't talk to me about the intelligence of rats. They ought to have left before, when we had that narrow squeak from foundering. There you have the proof how silly is the superstition about them. They leave a good ship for an old rotten hulk, where there is nothing to eat, too, the fools! . . . I don't believe they know what is safe or what is good for them, any more than you or I.'

"And after some more talk we agreed that the wisdom of rats had been grossly overrated, being in fact no greater than that of men.

"The story of the ship was known, by this, all up the Channel from Land's End to the Forelands, and we could get no crew on the south coast. They sent us one all complete from Liverpool, and we left once more—for Bankok.

"We had fair breezes, smooth water right into the tropics, and the old *Judea* lumbered along in the sunshine. When she went eight knots everything cracked aloft, and we tied our caps to our heads; but mostly she strolled on at the rate of three miles an hour. What could you expect? She was tired—that old ship. Her youth was where mine is—where yours is—you fellows who listen to this yarn; and what friend would throw your years and your weariness in your face? We didn't grumble at her. To us aft, at least, it seemed as though we had been born in her, reared in her, had lived in her for ages, had never known any other ship. I would just as soon have abused the old village church at home for not being a cathedral.

"And for me there was also my youth to make me patient. There was all the East before me, and all life, and the thought that I had been tried in that ship and had come out pretty well. And I thought of men of old who, centuries ago, went that road in ships that sailed no better, to the land of palms, and spices, and yellow sands, and of brown nations ruled by kings more cruel than Nero the Roman, and more splendid than Solomon the Jew. The old bark lumbered on, heavy with her age and the burden of her cargo, while I lived the life of youth in ignorance and hope. She lumbered on through an interminable procession of days; and the fresh gilding flashed back at the setting sun, seemed to cry out over the darkening sea the words painted on her stern, '*Judea*, London. Do or Die.'

"Then we entered the Indian Ocean and steered northerly for Java Head. The winds were light. Weeks slipped by. She crawled on, do or die, and people at home began to think of posting us as overdue.

"One Saturday evening, I being off duty, the men asked me to give them an extra bucket of water or so—for washing clothes. As I did not wish to screw on the fresh-water pump so late, I went forward whistling, and with a key in my hand to unlock the forepeak scuttle, intending to serve the water out of a spare tank we kept there.

"The smell down below was as unexpected as it was frightful. One would have thought hundreds of paraffin-lamps had been flaring and smoking in that hole for days. I was glad to get out. The man with me coughed and said, 'Funny smell, sir.' I answered negligently, 'It's good for the health they say,' and walked aft.

"The first thing I did was to put my head down the square of the midship ventilator. As I lifted the lid a visible breath, something like a thin fog, a puff of faint haze, rose from the opening. The ascending air was hot, and had a heavy, sooty, paraffiny smell. I gave one sniff, and put down the lid gently. It was no use choking myself. The cargo was on fire.

"Next day she began to smoke in earnest. You see it was to be expected, for though the coal was of a safe kind, that cargo had been so handled, so broken up with handling, that it looked more like smithy coal than anything else. Then it had been wetted—more than once. It rained all the time we were taking it back from the hulk, and now with this long passage it got heated, and there was another case of spontaneous combustion.

"The captain called us into the cabin. He had a chart spread on the table, and looked unhappy. He said, 'The coast of West Australia is near, but I mean to proceed to our destination. It is the hurricane month, too; but we will just keep her head for Bankok, and fight the fire. No more putting back anywhere, if we all get roasted. We will try first to stifle this 'ere damned combustion by want of air.'

"We tried. We battened down everything, and still she smoked. The smoke kept coming out through imperceptible crevices; it forced itself through bulkheads and covers; it oozed here and there and everywhere in slender threads, in an invisible film, in an incomprehensible manner. It made its way into the cabin, into the forecastle; it poisoned the sheltered places on the deck, it could be sniffed as high as the mainyard. It was clear that if the smoke came out the air came in. This was disheartening. This combustion refused to be stifled.

"We resolved to try water, and took the hatches off. Enormous volumes of smoke, whitish, yellowish, thick, greasy, misty, choking, ascended as high as the trucks. All hands cleared out aft. Then the poisonous cloud blew away, and we went back to work in a smoke that was no thicker now than that of an ordinary factory chimney.

"We rigged the force-pump, got the hose along, and by and by it burst. Well, it was as old as the ship—a prehistoric hose, and past repair. Then we pumped with the feeble head-pump, drew water with buckets, and in this way managed in time to pour lots of Indian Ocean into the main hatch. The bright stream flashed in sunshine, fell into a layer of white crawling smoke, and vanished on the black surface of coal. Steam ascended mingling with the smoke. We poured salt water as into a barrel without a bottom. It was our fate to pump in that ship, to pump out of her, to pump into her; and after keeping water out of her to save ourselves from being drowned, we frantically poured water into her to save ourselves from being burnt.

"And she crawled on, do or die, in the serene weather. The sky was a miracle of purity, a miracle of azure. The sea was polished, was blue, was pellucid, was sparkling like a precious stone; extending on all sides, all round to the horizon—as if the whole terrestrial globe had been one jewel, one colossal sapphire, a single gem fashioned into a planet. And on the lustre of the great calm waters the *Judea* glided imperceptibly, enveloped in languid and unclean vapours, in a lazy cloud that drifted to leeward, light and slow; a pestiferous cloud defiling the splendour of sea and sky.

"All this time of course we saw no fire. The cargo smouldered at the bottom somewhere. Once Mahon, as we were working side by side, said to me with a queer smile: 'Now, if she only would spring a tidy leak—like that time when we first left the Channel—it would put a stopper on this fire. Wouldn't it?' I remarked irrelevantly, 'Do you remember the rats?'

"We fought the fire and sailed the ship too as carefully as though nothing had been the matter. The steward cooked and attended on us. Of the other twelve men, eight worked while four rested. Everyone took his turn, captain included. There was equality, and if not exactly fraternity, then a deal of good feeling. Sometimes a man, as he dashed a bucketful of water down the hatchway, would yell out, 'Hurrah for

Bankok!' and the rest laughed. But generally we were taciturn and serious—and thirsty. Oh! how thirsty! And we had to be careful with the water. Strict allowance. The ship smoked, the sun blazed. . . . Pass the bottle.

"We tried everything. We even made an attempt to dig down to the fire. No good, of course. No man could remain more than a minute below. Mahon, who went first, fainted there, and the man who went to fetch him out did likewise. We lugged them out on deck. Then I leaped down to show how easily it could be done. They had learned wisdom by that time, and contented themselves by fishing for me with a chainhook tied to a broom-handle, I believe. I did not offer to go and fetch up my shovel, which was left down below.

"Things began to look bad. We put the long-boat into the water. The second boat was ready to swing out. We had also another, a 14-foot thing, on davits aft, where it was quite safe.

"Then, behold, the smoke suddenly decreased. We redoubled our efforts to flood the bottom of the ship. In two days there was no smoke at all. Everybody was on the broad grin. This was on a Friday. On Saturday no work, but sailing the ship of course, was done. The men washed their clothes and their faces for the first time in a fortnight, and had a special dinner given them. They spoke of spontaneous combustion with contempt, and implied *they* were the boys to put out combustions. Somehow we all felt as though we each had inherited a large fortune. But a beastly smell of burning hung about the ship. Captain Beard had hollow eyes and sunken cheeks. I had never noticed so much before how twisted and bowed he was. He and Mahon prowled soberly about hatches and ventilators, sniffing. It struck me suddenly poor Mahon was a very, very old chap. As to me, I was as pleased and proud as though I had helped to win a great naval battle. O! Youth!

"The night was fine. In the morning a homeward-bound ship passed us hull down—the first we had seen for months; but we were nearing the land at last, Java Head being about 190 miles off, and nearly due north.

"Next day it was my watch on deck from eight to twelve. At breakfast the captain observed, 'It's wonderful how that smell hangs about the cabin.' About ten, the mate being on the poop, I stepped down on the main-deck for a moment. The carpenter's bench stood abaft the mainmast: I leaned against it sucking at my pipe, and the carpenter, a young chap, came to talk to me. He remarked, 'I think we have done very well, haven't we?' and then I perceived with annoyance the fool was trying to tilt the bench. I said curtly, 'Don't, Chips,' and immediately became aware of a queer sensation, of an absurd delusion,—I seemed somehow to be in the air. I heard all round me like a pent-up breath released—as if a thousand giants simultaneously had said Phoo!—and felt a dull concussion which made my ribs ache suddenly. No doubt about it—I was in the air, and my body was describing a short parabola. But short as it was, I had the time to think several thoughts in, as far as I can remember, the following order: 'This can't be the carpenter—What is it?—Some accident—Submarine volcano?—Coals, gas!—By Jove! we are being blown up—Everybody's dead—I am falling into the after-hatch—I see fire in it.'

"The coal-dust suspended in the air of the hold had glowed dull-red at the moment of the explosion. In the twinkling of an eye, in an infinitesimal fraction of a second since the first tilt of the bench, I was sprawling full length on the cargo. I picked myself up and scrambled out. It was quick like a rebound. The deck was a wilderness of smashed timber, lying crosswise like trees in a wood after a hurricane; an immense curtain of soiled rags waved gently before me—it was the mainsail blown to strips. I thought, The masts will be toppling over directly; and to get out of the way bolted on all-fours towards the poop-ladder. The first person I saw was Mahon, with eyes like saucers, his mouth open, and the long white hair standing straight on end round his head like a silver halo. He was just about to go down when the sight of the main-deck stirring, heaving up, and changing into splinters before his eyes, petrified him on the top step. I stared at him in unbelief, and he stared at me with a queer kind of shocked curiosity. I did not know that I had no hair, no eyebrows, no eyelashes, that my young moustache was burnt off, that my face was black, one cheek laid open, my nose cut, and my chin bleeding. I had lost my cap, one of my slippers, and my shirt was torn to rags. Of all this I was not aware. I was amazed to see the ship still afloat, the poop-deck whole—and, most of all, to see anybody alive. Also the peace of the sky and the serenity of the sea were distinctly surprising. I suppose I expected to see them convulsed with horror. . . . Pass the bottle.

"There was a voice hailing the ship from somewhere—in the air, in the sky—I couldn't tell. Presently I saw the captain—and he was mad. He asked me eagerly, 'Where's the cabin-table?' and to hear such a question was a frightful shock. I had just been blown up, you understand, and vibrated with that experience,—I wasn't quite sure whether I was alive. Mahon began to stamp with both feet and yelled at him, 'Good God! don't you see the deck's blown out of her?' I found my voice, and stammered out as if conscious of some gross neglect of duty, 'I don't know where the cabin-table is.' It was like an absurd dream.

"Do you know what he wanted next? Well, he wanted to trim the yards. Very placidly, and as if lost in thought, he insisted on having the foreyard squared. 'I don't know if there's anybody alive,' said Mahon, almost tearfully. 'Surely,' he said, gently, 'there will be enough left to square the foreyard.'

"The old chap, it seems, was in his own berth winding up the chronometers, when the shock sent him spinning. Immediately it occurred to him—as he said afterwards—that the ship had struck something, and he ran out into the cabin. There, he saw, the cabin-table had vanished somewhere. The deck being blown up, it had fallen down into the lazarette of course. Where we had our breakfast that morning he saw only a great hole in the floor. This appeared to him so awfully mysterious, and impressed him so immensely, that what he saw and heard after he got on deck were mere trifles in comparison. And, mark, he noticed directly the wheel deserted and his barque off her course—and his only thought was to get that miserable, stripped, undecked, smouldering shell of a ship back again with her head pointing at her port of destination. Bankok! That's what he was after. I tell you this quiet, bowed, bandy-legged, almost deformed little man was immense in the singleness of his idea and in his placid ignorance of our agitation. He motioned us forward with a commanding gesture, and went to take the wheel himself.

"Yes; that was the first thing we did—trim the yards of that wreck! No one was killed, or even disabled, but everyone was more or less hurt. You should have seen them! Some were in rags, with black faces, like coal-heavers, like sweeps, and had bullet heads that seemed closely cropped, but were in fact singed to the skin. Others, of the watch below, awakened by being shot out from their collapsing bunks, shivered incessantly, and kept on groaning even as we went about our work. But they all worked. That crew of Liverpool hard cases had in them the right stuff. It's my experience they always have. It is the sea that gives it—the vastness, the loneliness surrounding their dark stolid souls. Ah! Well! we stumbled, we crept, we fell, we barked our shins on the wreckage, we hauled. The masts stood, but we did not know how much they might be charred down below. It was nearly calm, but a long swell ran from the west and made her roll. They might go at any moment. We looked at them with apprehension. One could not foresee which way they would fall.

"Then we retreated aft and looked about us. The deck was a tangle of planks on edge, of planks on end, of splinters, of ruined woodwork. The masts rose from that chaos like big trees above a matted undergrowth. The interstices of that mass of wreckage were full of something whitish, sluggish, stirring—of something that was like a greasy fog. The smoke of the invisible fire was coming up again, was trailing, like a poisonous thick mist in some valley choked with dead wood. Already lazy wisps were beginning to curl upwards amongst the mass of splinters. Here and there a piece of timber, stuck upright, resembled a post. Half of a fife-rail had been shot through the foresail, and the sky made a patch of glorious blue in the ignobly soiled canvas. A portion of several boards holding together had fallen across the rail, and one end protruded overboard, like a gangway leading upon nothing, like a gangway leading over the deep sea, leading to death—as if inviting us to walk the plank at once and be done with our ridiculous troubles. And still the air, the sky—a ghost, something invisible was hailing the ship.

"Someone had the sense to look over, and there was the helmsman, who had impulsively jumped overboard, anxious to come back. He yelled and swam lustily like a merman, keeping up with the ship. We threw him a rope, and presently he stood amongst us streaming with water and very crestfallen. The captain had surrendered the wheel, and apart, elbow on rail and chin in hand, gazed at the sea wistfully. We asked ourselves, What next? I thought, Now, this is something like. This is great. I wonder what will happen. O youth!

"Suddenly Mahon sighted a steamer far astern. Captain Beard said, 'We may do something with her yet.' We hoisted two flags, which said in the international language of the sea, 'On fire. Want immediate assistance.' The steamer grew bigger rapidly, and by and by spoke with two flags on her foremast, 'I am coming to your assistance.'

"In half an hour she was abreast, to windward, within hail, and rolling slightly, with her engines stopped. We lost our composure, and yelled all together with excitement, 'We've been blown up'. A man in a white helmet, on the bridge, cried, 'Yes! All right! all right!' and he nodded his head, and smiled, and made soothing motions with his hand as though at a lot of frightened children. One of the boats dropped in the water, and walked towards us upon the sea with her long oars. Four Calashes pulled a swinging stroke. This was my first sight of Malay seamen. I've known them since, but what struck me then was their unconcern: they came alongside, and even the bowman standing up and holding to our main-chains with the book-hook did not deign to lift his head for a glance. I thought people who had been blown up deserved more attention.

"A little man, dry like a chip and agile like a monkey, clambered up. It was the mate of the steamer. He gave one look, and cried, 'O boys—you had better quit.'

"We were silent. He talked apart with the captain for a time,—seemed to argue with him. Then they went away together to the steamer.

"When our skipper came back we learned that the steamer was the *Somerville,* Captain Nash, from West Australia to Singapore *via* Batavia with mails, and that the agreement was she should tow us to Anjer or Batavia, if possible, where we could extinguish the fire by scuttling, and then proceed on our voyage—to Bankok! The old man seemed excited. 'We will do it yet,' he said to Mahon, fiercely. He shook his fist at the sky. Nobody else said a word.

"At noon the steamer began to tow. She went ahead slim and high, and what was left of the *Judea* followed at the end of seventy fathom of tow-rope,—followed her swiftly like a cloud of smoke with mast-heads protruding above. We went aloft to furl the sails. We coughed on the yards, and were careful about the bunts. Do you see the lot of us there, putting a neat furl on the sails of that ship doomed to arrive nowhere? There was not a man who didn't think that at any moment the masts would topple over. From aloft we could not see the ship for smoke, and they worked carefully, passing the gaskets with even turns. 'Harbour furl—aloft there!' cried Mahon from below.

"You understand this? I don't think one of those chaps expected to get down in the usual way. When we did I heard them saying to each other, 'Well, I thought we would come down overboard, in a lump—sticks and all—blame me if I didn't.' 'That's what I was thinking to myself,' would answer wearily another battered and bandaged scarecrow. And, mind, these were men without the drilled-in habit of obedience. To an onlooker they would be a lot of profane scallywags without a redeeming point. What made them do it—what made them obey me when I, thinking consciously how fine it was, made them drop the bunt of the foresail twice to try and do it better? What? They had no professional reputation—no examples, no praise. It wasn't a sense of duty; they all knew well enough how to shirk, and laze, and dodge—when they had a mind to it—and mostly they had. Was it the two pounds ten a-month that sent them there? They didn't think their pay half good enough. No, it was something in them, something inborn and subtle and everlasting. I don't say positively that the crew of a French or German merchantman wouldn't have done it, but I doubt whether it would have been done in the same way. There was a completeness in it, something solid like a principle, and masterful like an instinct—a disclosure of something secret—of that hidden something, that gift of good or evil that makes racial difference, that shapes the fate of nations.

"It was that night at ten that, for the first time since we had been fighting it, we saw the fire. The speed of the towing had fanned the smouldering destruction. A blue gleam appeared forward, shining below the wreck of the deck. It wavered in patches, it seemed to stir and creep like the light of a glowworm. I saw it first, and told Mahon. 'Then the game's up,' he said. 'We had better stop this towing, or she will burst out suddenly fore and aft before we can clear out.' We set up a yell; rang bells to attract their attention; they towed on. At last Mahon and I had to crawl forward and cut the rope with an axe. There was no time to cast off the lashings. Red tongues could be seen licking the wilderness of splinters under our feet as we made our way back to the poop.

"Of course they very soon found out in the steamer that the rope was gone. She gave a loud blast of her whistle, her lights were seen sweeping in a wide circle, she came up ranging close alongside, and stopped. We were all in a tight group on the poop looking at her. Every man had saved a little bundle or a bag. Suddenly a conical flame with a twisted top shot up forward and threw upon the black sea a circle of light, with the two vessels side by side and heaving gently in its centre. Captain Beard had been sitting on the gratings still and mute for hours, but now he rose slowly and advanced in front of us, to the mizzen-shrouds. Captain Nash hailed: 'Come along! Look sharp. I have mail-bags on board. I will take you and your boats to Singapore.'

"'Thank you! No!' said our skipper. 'We must see the last of the ship.'

"'I can't stand by any longer,' shouted the other. 'Mails—you know.'

"'Ay! ay! We are all right.'

"'Very well! I'll report you in Singapore. . . . Good-bye!'

"He waved his hand. Our men dropped their bundles quietly. The steamer moved ahead, and passing out of the circle of light, vanished at once from our sight, dazzled by the fire which burned fiercely. And then I knew that I would see the East first as commander of a small boat. I thought it fine; and the fidelity to the old ship was fine. We should see the last of her. Oh, the glamour of youth! Oh, the fire of it, more dazzling than the flames of the burning ship, throwing a magic light on the wide earth, leaping audaciously to the sky, presently to be quenched by time, more cruel, more pitiless, more bitter than the sea—and like the flames of the burning ship surrounded by an impenetrable night.

* * * * * * *

"The old man warned us in his gentle and inflexible way that it was part of our duty to save for the underwriters as much as we could of the ship's gear. Accordingly we went to work aft, while she blazed forward to give us plenty of light. We lugged out a lot of rubbish. What didn't we save? An old barometer fixed with an absurd quantity of screws nearly cost me my life: a sudden rush of smoke came upon me, and I just got away in time. There were various stores, bolts of canvas, coils of rope; the poop looked like a marine bazaar, and the boats were lumbered to the gunwales. One would have thought the old man wanted to take as much as he could of his first command with him. He was very, very quiet, but off his balance evidently. Would you believe it? He wanted to take a length of old stream-cable and a kedge-anchor with him in the long-boat. We said, 'Ay, ay, sir,' deferentially, and on the quiet let the things slip overboard. The heavy medicine-chest went that way, two bags of green coffee, tins of paint—fancy, paint!—a whole lot of things. Then I was ordered with two hands into the boats to make a stowage and get them ready against the time it would be proper for us to leave the ship.

"We put everything straight, stepped the long-boat's mast for our skipper, who was to take charge of her, and I was not sorry to sit down for a moment. My face felt raw, every limb ached as if broken, I was aware of all my ribs, and would have sworn to a twist in the backbone. The boats, fast astern, lay in a deep shadow, and all around I could see the circle of the sea lighted by the fire. A gigantic flame arose forward straight and clear. It flared fierce, with noises like the whirr of wings, with rumbles as of thunder. There were cracks, detonations, and from the cone of flame the sparks flew upwards, as man is born to trouble, to leaky ships, and to ships that burn.

"What bothered me was that the ship, lying broadside to the swell and to such a wind as there was—a mere breath—the boats would not keep astern where they were safe, but persisted, in a pig-headed way boats have, in getting under the counter and then swinging alongside. They were knocking about dangerously and coming near the flame, while the ship rolled on them, and, of course, there was always the danger of the masts going over the side at any moment. I and my two boat-keepers kept them off as best we could, with oars and boat-hooks; but to be constantly at it became exasperating, since there was no reason why we should not leave at once. We could not see those on board, nor could we imagine what caused the delay. The boat-keepers were swearing feebly, and I had not only my share of the work but also had to keep at it two men who showed a constant inclination to lay themselves down and let things slide.

"At last I hailed, 'On deck there,' and someone looked over. 'We're ready here,' I said. The head disappeared, and very soon popped up again. 'The captain says, All right, sir, and to keep the boats well clear of the ship.'

"Half an hour passed. Suddenly there was a frightful racket, rattle, clanking of chain, hiss of water, and millions of sparks flew up into the shivering column of smoke that stood leaning slightly above the ship. The cat-heads had burned away, and the two red-hot anchors had gone to the bottom, tearing out after them two hundred fathom of red-hot chain. The ship trembled, the mass of flame swayed as if ready to collapse, and the fore top-gallant-mast fell. It darted down like an arrow of fire, shot under, and instantly leaping up within an oar's-length of the boats, floated quietly, very black on the luminous sea. I hailed the deck again. After some time a man in an unexpectedly cheerful but also muffled tone, as though he had been trying to speak with his mouth shut, informed me, 'Coming directly, sir,' and vanished. For a long time I heard nothing but the whirr and roar of the fire. There were also whistling sounds. The boats jumped, tugged at the painters, ran at each other playfully, knocked their sides together, or, do what we would, swung in a bunch against the ship's side. I couldn't stand it any longer, and swarming up a rope, clambered aboard over the stern.

"It was as bright as day. Coming up like this, the sheet of fire facing me was a terrifying sight, and the heat seemed hardly bearable at first. On a settee cushion dragged out of the cabin Captain Beard, his legs drawn up and one arm under his head, slept with the light playing on him. Do you know what the rest were busy about? They were sitting on deck right aft, round an open case, eating bread and cheese and drinking bottled stout.

"On the background of flames twisting in fierce tongues above their heads they seemed at home like salamanders, and looked like a band of desperate pirates. The fire sparkled in the whites of their eyes, gleamed on patches of white skin seen through the torn shirts. Each had the marks as of a battle about him—bandaged heads, tied-up arms, a strip of dirty rag round a knee—and each man had a bottle between his legs and a chunk of cheese in his hand. Mahon got up. With his handsome and disreputable head, his hooked profile, his long white beard, and with an uncorked bottle in his hand, he resembled one of those reckless sea-robbers of old making merry amidst violence and disaster. 'The last meal on board,' he explained solemnly. 'We had nothing to eat all day, and it was no use leaving all this.' He flourished the bottle and indicated the sleeping skipper. 'He said he couldn't swallow anything, so I got him to lie down,' he went on; and as I stared, 'I don't know whether you are aware, young fellow, the man had no sleep to speak of for days—and there will be dam' little sleep in the boats.' 'There will be no boats by-and-by if you fool about much longer,' I said, indignantly. I walked up to the skipper and shook him by the shoulder. At last he opened his eyes, but did not move. 'Time to leave her, sir,' I said quietly.

"He got up painfully, looked at the flames, at the sea sparkling round the ship, and black, black as ink farther away; he looked at the stars shining dim through a thin veil of smoke in a sky black, black as Erebus.

"'Youngest first,' he said.

"And the ordinary seaman, wiping his mouth with the back of his hand, got up, clambered over the taffrail, and vanished. Others followed. One, on the point of going over, stopped short to drain his bottle, and with a great swing of his arm flung it at the fire. 'Take this!' he cried.

"The skipper lingered disconsolately, and we left him to commune alone for a while with his first command. Then I went up again and brought him away at last. It was time. The ironwork on the poop was hot to the touch.

"Then the painter of the long-boat was cut, and the three boats, tied together, drifted clear of the ship. It was just sixteen hours after the explosion when we abandoned her. Mahon had charge of the second boat, and I had the smallest—the 14-foot thing. The long-boat would have taken the lot of us; but the skipper said we must save as much property as we could—for the underwriters—and so I got my first command. I had two men with me, a bag of biscuits, a few tins of meat, and a breaker of water. I was ordered to keep close to the long-boat, that in case of bad weather we might be taken into her.

"And do you know what I thought? I thought I would part company as soon as I could. I wanted to have my first command all to myself. I wasn't going to sail in a squadron if there were a chance for independent cruising. I would make land by myself. I would beat the other boats. Youth! All youth! The silly, charming, beautiful youth.

"But we did not make a start at once. We must see the last of the ship. And so the boats drifted about that night, heaving and setting on the swell. The men dozed, waked, sighed, groaned. I looked at the burning ship.

"Between the darkness of earth and heaven she was burning fiercely upon a disc of purple sea shot by the blood-red play of gleams; upon a disc of water glittering and sinister. A high, clear flame, an immense and lonely flame, ascended from the ocean, and from its summit the black smoke poured continuously at the sky. She burned furiously; mournful and imposing like a funeral pile kindled in the night, surrounded by the sea, watched over by the stars. A magnificent death had come like a grace, like a gift, like a reward to that old ship at the end of her laborious days. The surrender of her weary ghost to the keeping of stars and sea was stirring like the sight of a glorious triumph. The masts fell just before daybreak, and for a moment there was a burst and turmoil of sparks that seemed to fill with flying fire the night patient and watchful, the vast night lying silent upon the sea. At daylight she was only a charred shell, floating still under a cloud of smoke and bearing a glowing mass of coal within.

"Then the oars were got out, and the boats forming in a line moved round her remains as if in procession—the long-boat leading. As we pulled across her stern a slim dart of fire shot out viciously at us, and suddenly she went down, head first, in a great hiss of steam. The unconsumed stern was the last to sink; but the paint had gone, had cracked, had peeled off, and there were no letters, there was no word, no stubborn device that was like her soul, to flash at the rising sun her creed and her name.

"We made our way north. A breeze sprang up, and about noon all the boats came together for the last time. I had no mast or sail in mine, but I made a mast out of a spare oar and hoisted a boat-awning for a sail, with a boat-hook for a yard. She was certainly over-masted, but I had the satisfaction of knowing that with the wind aft I could beat the other two. I had to wait for them. Then we all had a look at the captain's chart, and, after a sociable meal of hard bread and water, got our last instructions. These were simple: steer north, and keep together as much as possible. 'Be careful with that jury-rig, Marlow,' said the captain; and Mahon, as I sailed proudly past his boat, wrinkled his curved nose and hailed, 'You will sail that ship of yours under water, if you don't look out, young fellow.' He was a malicious old man—and may the deep sea where he sleeps now rock him gently, rock him tenderly to the end of time!

"Before sunset a thick rain-squall passed over the two boats, which were far astern, and that was the last I saw of them for a time. Next day I sat steering my cockle-shell—my first command—with nothing but water and sky around me. I did sight in the afternoon the upper sails of a ship far away, but said nothing, and my men did not notice her. You see I was afraid she might be homeward bound, and I had no mind to turn back from the portals of the East. I was steering for Java—another blessed name—like Bankok, you know. I steered many days.

"I need not tell you what it is to be knocking about in an open boat. I remember nights and days of calm, when we pulled, we pulled, and the boat seemed to stand still, as if bewitched within the circle of the sea horizon. I remember the heat, the deluge of rain-squalls that kept us baling for dear life (but filled our water-cask), and I remember sixteen hours on end with a mouth dry as a cinder and a steering-oar over the stern to keep my first command head on to a breaking sea. I did not know how good a man I was till then. I remember the drawn faces, the dejected figures of my two men, and I remember my youth and the feeling that will never come back any more—the feeling that I could last for ever, outlast the sea, the earth, and all men; the deceitful feeling that lures us on to joys, to perils, to love, to vain effort—to death; the triumphant conviction of strength, the heat of life in the handful of dust, the glow in the heart that with every year grows dim, grows cold, grows small, and expires—and expires, too soon, too soon—before life itself.

"And this is how I see the East. I have seen its secret places and have looked into its very soul; but now I see it always from a small boat, a high outline of mountains, blue and afar in the morning; like faint mist at noon; a jagged wall of purple at sunset. I have the feel of the oar in my hand, the vision of a scorching blue sea in my eyes. And I see a bay, a wide bay, smooth as glass and polished like ice, shimmering in the dark. A red light burns far off upon the gloom of the land, and the night is soft and warm. We drag at the oars with aching arms, and suddenly a puff of wind, a puff faint and tepid and laden with strange odours of blossoms, of aromatic wood, comes out of the still night—the first sigh of the East on my face. That I can never forget. It was impalpable and enslaving, like a charm, like a whispered promise of mysterious delight.

"We had been pulling this finishing spell for eleven hours. Two pulled, and he whose turn it was to rest sat at the tiller. We had made out the red light in that bay and steered for it, guessing it must mark some small coasting port. We passed two vessels, outlandish and high-sterned, sleeping at anchor, and, approaching the light, now very dim, ran the boat's nose against the end of a jutting wharf. We were blind with fatigue. My men dropped the oars and fell off the thwarts as if dead. I made fast to a pile. A current rippled softly. The scented obscurity of the shore was grouped into vast masses, a density of colossal clumps of vegetation, probably—mute and fantastic shapes. And at their foot the semicircle of a beach gleamed faintly, like an illusion. There was not a light, not a stir, not a sound. The mysterious East faced me, perfumed like a flower, silent like death, dark like a grave.

"And I sat weary beyond expression, exulting like a conqueror, sleepless and entranced as if before a profound, a fateful enigma.

"A splashing of oars, a measured dip reverberating on the level of water, intensified by the silence of the shore into loud claps, made me jump up. A boat, a European boat, was coming in. I invoked the name of the dead; I hailed: *Judea* ahoy! A thin shout answered.

"It was the captain. I had beaten the flagship by three hours, and I was glad to hear the old man's voice again, tremulous and tired. 'Is it you, Marlow?' 'Mind the end of that jetty, sir,' I cried.

"He approached cautiously, and brought up with the deep-sea lead-line which we had saved—for the underwriters. I eased my painter and fell alongside. He sat, a broken figure at the stern, wet with dew, his hands clasped in his lap. His men were asleep already. 'I had a terrible time of it,' he murmured. 'Mahon is behind—not very far.' We conversed in whispers, in low whispers, as if afraid to wake up the land. Guns, thunder, earthquakes would not have awakened the men just then.

"Looking round as we talked, I saw away at sea a bright light travelling in the night. 'There's a steamer passing the bay,' I said. She was not passing, she was entering, and she even came close and anchored. 'I wish,' said the old man, 'you would find out whether she is English. Perhaps they could give us a passage somewhere.' He seemed nervously anxious. So by dint of punching and kicking I started one of my men into a state of somnambulism, and giving him an oar, took another and pulled towards the lights of the steamer.

"There was a murmur of voices in her, metallic hollow clangs of the engine-room, footsteps on the deck. Her ports shone, round like dilated eyes. Shapes moved about, and there was a shadowy man high up on the bridge. He heard my oars.

"And then, before I could open my lips, the East spoke to me, but it was in a Western voice. A torrent of words was poured into the enigmatical, the fateful silence; outlandish, angry words, mixed with words and even whole sentences of good English, less strange but even more surprising. The voice swore and cursed violently; it riddled the solemn peace of the bay by a volley of abuse. It began by calling me Pig, and from that went crescendo into unmentionable adjectives—in English. The man up there raged aloud in two languages, and with a sincerity in his fury that almost convinced me I had, in some way, sinned against the harmony of the universe. I could hardly see him, but began to think he would work himself into a fit.

"Suddenly he ceased, and I could hear him snorting and blowing like a porpoise. I said—

" 'What steamer is this, pray?'

" 'Eh? What's this? And who are you?'

" 'Castaway crew of an English barque burnt at sea. We came here to-night. I am the second mate. The captain is in the long-boat, and wishes to know if you would give us a passage somewhere.'

" 'Oh, my goodness! I say. . . . This is the *Celestial* from Singapore on her return trip. I'll arrange with your captain in the morning, . . . and, . . . I say, . . . did you hear me just now?'

" 'I should think the whole bay heard you.'

" 'I thought you were a shore-boat. Now, look here—this infernal lazy scoundrel of a caretaker has gone to sleep again—curse him. The light is out, and I nearly ran foul of the end of this damned jetty. This is the third time he plays me this trick. Now, I ask you, can anybody stand this kind of thing? It's enough to drive a man out of his mind. I'll report him. . . . I'll get the Assistant Resident to give him the sack, by . . . ! See—there's no light. It's out, isn't it? I take you to witness the light's out. There should be a light, you know. A red light on the——'

" 'There was a light,' I said, mildly.

" 'But it's out, man! What's the use of talking like this? You can see for yourself it's out—don't you? If you had to take a valuable steamer along this God-forsaken coast you would want a light, too. I'll kick him from end to end of his miserable wharf. You'll see if I don't, I will——'

" 'So I may tell my captain you'll take us?' I broke in.

" 'Yes, I'll take you. Good-night,' he said, brusquely.

"I pulled back, made fast again to the jetty, and then went to sleep at last. I had faced the silence of the East. I had heard some of its language. But when I opened my eyes again the silence was as complete as though it had never been broken. I was lying in a flood of light, and the sky had never looked so far, so high, before. I opened my eyes and lay without moving.

"And then I saw the men of the East—they were looking at me. The whole length of the jetty was full of people. I saw brown, bronze, yellow faces, the black eyes, the glitter, the colour of an Eastern crowd. And all these beings stared without a murmur, without a sigh, without a movement. They stared down at the boats, at the sleeping men who at night had come to them from the sea. Nothing moved. The fronds of palms stood still against the sky. Not a branch stirred along the shore, and the brown roofs of hidden houses peeped through the green foliage, through the big leaves that hung shining and still like leaves forged of heavy metal. This was the East of the ancient navigators, so old, so mysterious, resplendent and sombre, living and unchanged, full of danger and promise. And these were the men. I sat up suddenly. A wave of movement passed through the crowd from end to end, passed along the heads, swayed the bodies, ran along the jetty like a ripple on the water, like a breath of wind on a field—and all was still again. I see it now—the wide sweep of the bay, the glittering sands, the wealth of green infinite and varied, the sea blue like the sea of a dream, the crowd of attentive faces, the blaze of vivid colour—the water reflecting it all, the curve of the shore, the jetty, the high-sterned outlandish craft floating still, and the three boats with the tired men from the West sleeping, unconscious of the land and the people and of the violence of sunshine. They slept thrown across the thwarts, curled on bottom-boards, in the careless attitudes of death. The head of the old skipper, leaning back in the stern of the long-boat, had fallen on his breast, and he looked as though he would never wake. Farther out old Mahon's face was upturned to the sky, with the long white beard spread out on his breast, as though he had been shot where he sat at the tiller; and a man, all in a heap in the bows of the boat, slept with both arms embracing the stem-head and with his cheek laid on the gunwale. The East looked at them without a sound.

"I have known its fascination since; I have seen the mysterious shores, the still water, the lands of brown nations, where a stealthy Nemesis lies in wait, pursues, overtakes so many of the conquering race, who are proud of their wisdom, of their knowledge, of their strength. But for me all the East is contained in that vision of my youth. It is all in that moment when I opened my young eyes on it. I came upon it from a tussle with the sea—and I was young—and I saw it looking at me. And this is all that is left of it! Only a moment; a moment of strength, of romance, of glamour—of youth! . . . A flick of sunshine upon a strange shore, the time to remember, the time for a sigh, and—good-bye!—Night—Good-bye . . . !"

He drank.

"Ah! The good old time—the good old time. Youth and the sea. Glamour and the sea! The good, strong sea, the salt, bitter sea, that could whisper to you and roar at you and knock your breath out of you."

He drank again.

"By all that's wonderful it is the sea, I believe, the sea itself—or is it youth alone? Who can tell? But you here—you all had something out of life: money, love—whatever one gets on shore—and, tell me, wasn't that the best time, that time when we were young at sea; young and had nothing, on the sea that gives nothing, except hard knocks—and sometimes a chance to feel your strength—that only—what you all regret?"

And we all nodded at him: the man of finance, the man of accounts, the man of law, we all nodded at him over the polished table that like a still sheet of brown water reflected our faces, lined, wrinkled; our faces marked by toil, by deceptions, by success, by love; our weary eyes looking still, looking always, looking anxiously for something out of life, that while it is expected is already gone—has passed unseen, in a sigh, in a flash—together with the youth, with the strength, with the romance of illusions.

SIR WILLIAM WATSON

Wordsworth's Grave

I

THE old rude church, with bare, bald tower, is here;
Beneath its shadow high-born Rotha flows;
Rotha, remembering well who slumbers near,
And with cool murmur lulling his repose.

Rotha, remembering well who slumbers near,
His hills, his lakes, his streams are with him yet.
Surely the heart that read her own heart clear
Nature forgets not soon: 'tis we forget.

We that with vagrant soul his fixity
Have slighted; faithless, done his deep faith wrong;
Left him for poorer loves, and bowed the knee
To misbegotten strange new gods of song.

Yet, led by hollow ghost or beckoning elf
Far from her homestead to the desert bourn,
The vagrant soul returning to herself,
Wearily wise, must needs to him return.

To him and to the powers that with him dwell:—
Inflowings that divulged not whence they came;
And that secluded Spirit unknowable,
The mystery we make darker with a name;

The Somewhat which we name but cannot know,
Ev'n as we name a star and only see
His quenchless flashings forth, which ever show
And ever hide him, and which are not he.

II

Poet who sleepest by this wandering wave!
When thou wast born, what birth-gift hadst thou then?
To thee what wealth was that the Immortals gave,
The wealth thou gavest in thy turn to men?

Not Milton's keen, translunar music thine;
Not Shakespeare's cloudless, boundless human view;

Not Shelley's flush of rose on peaks divine;
Nor yet the wizard twilight Coleridge knew.
What hadst thou that could make so large amends
For all thou hadst not and thy peers possessed,
Motion and fire, swift means to radiant ends?—
Thou hadst, for weary feet, the gift of rest.

From Shelley's dazzling glow or thunderous haze,
From Byron's tempest-anger, tempest-mirth,
Men turned to thee and found—not blast and blaze,
Tumult of tottering heavens, but peace on earth.

Nor peace that grows by Lethe, scentless flower,
There in white languors to decline and cease;
But peace whose names are also rapture, power,
Clear sight, and love: for these are parts of peace.

III

I hear it vouched the Muse is with us still;
If less divinely frenzied than of yore,
In lieu of feelings she has wondrous skill
To simulate emotion felt no more.

Not such the authentic Presence pure, that made
This valley vocal in the great days gone!—
In *his* great days, while yet the springtime played
About him, and the mighty morning shone.

No word-mosaic artificer, he sang
A lofty song of lowly weal and dole.
Right from the heart, right to the heart it sprang,
Or from the soul leapt instant to the soul.

He felt the charm of childhood, grace of youth,
Grandeur of age, insisting to be sung.
The impassioned argument was simple truth
Half-wondering at its own melodious tongue.

Impassioned? ay, to the song's ecstatic core!
But far removed were clangour, storm and feud;
For plenteous health was his, exceeding store
Of joy, and an impassioned quietude.

IV

A hundred years ere he to manhood came,
Song from celestial heights had wandered down,
Put off her robe of sunlight, dew and flame,
And donned a modish dress to charm the Town.

Thenceforth she but festooned the porch of things;
Apt at life's lore, incurious what life meant.
Dextrous of hand, she struck her lute's few strings;
Ignobly perfect, barrenly content.

Unflushed with ardour and unblanched with awe,
Her lips in profitless derision curled,
She saw with dull emotion—if she saw—
The vision of the glory of the world.

The human masque she watched, with dreamless eyes
In whose clear shallows lurked no trembling shade:

The stars, unkenned by her, might set and rise,
Unmarked by her, the daisies bloom and fade.

The age grew sated with her sterile wit.
Herself waxed weary on her loveless throne.
Men felt life's tide, the sweep and surge of it,
And craved a living voice, a natural tone.

For none the less, though song was but half true,
The world lay common, one abounding theme.
Man joyed and wept, and fate was ever new,
And love was sweet, life real, death no dream.

In sad, stern verse the rugged scholar-sage
Bemoaned his toil unvalued, youth uncheered.
His numbers wore the vesture of the age,
But, 'neath it beating, the great heart was heard.

From dewy pastures, uplands sweet with thyme,
A virgin breeze freshened the jaded day.
It wafted Collins' lonely vesper-chime,
It breathed abroad the frugal note of Gray.

It fluttered here and there, nor swept in vain
The dusty haunts where futile echoes dwell,—
Then, in a cadence soft as summer rain,
And sad from Auburn voiceless, drooped and fell.

It drooped and fell, and one 'neath northern skies,
With southern heart, who tilled his father's field,
Found Poesy a-dying, bade her rise
And touch quick Nature's hem and go forth healed.

On life's broad plain the ploughman's conquering share
Upturned the fallow lands of truth anew,
And o'er the formal garden's trim parterre
The peasant's team a ruthless furrow drew.

Bright was his going forth, but clouds ere long
Whelmed him; in gloom his radiance set, and those
Twin morning stars of the new century's song,
Those morning stars that sang together, rose.

In elvish speech the *Dreamer* told his tale
Of marvellous oceans swept by fateful wings.—
The *Seër* strayed not from earth's human pale,
But the mysterious face of common things

He mirrored as the moon in Rydal Mere
Is mirrored, when the breathless night hangs blue:
Strangely remote she seems and wondrous near,
And by some nameless difference born anew.

V

Peace—peace—and rest! Ah, how the lyre is loth,
Or powerless now, to give what all men seek!
Either it deadens with ignoble sloth
Or deafens with shrill tumult, loudly weak.

Where is the singer whose large notes and clear
Can heal, and arm, and plenish, and sustain?

Lo, one with empty music floods the ear,
And one, the heart refreshing, tires the brain.

And idly tuneful, the loquacious throng
Flutter and twitter, prodigal of time,
And little masters make a toy of song
Till grave men weary of the sound of rhyme.

And some go prankt in faded antique dress,
Abhorring to be hale and glad and free;
And some parade a conscious naturalness,
The scholar's not the child's simplicity.

Enough;—and wisest who from words forbear.
The gentle river rails not as it glides;
And suave and charitable, the winsome air
Chides not at all, or only him who chides.

VI

Nature! we storm thine ear with choric notes.
Thou answerest through the calm great nights and days,
"Laud me who will: not tuneless are your throats;
Yet if ye paused I should not miss the praise."

We falter, half-rebuked, and sing again.
We chant thy desertness and haggard gloom,
Or with thy splendid wrath inflate the strain,
Or touch it with thy colour and perfume.

One, his melodious blood aflame for thee,
Wooed with fierce lust, his hot heart world-defiled.
One, with the upward eye of infancy,
Looked in thy face, and felt himself thy child.

Thee he approached without distrust or dread—
Beheld thee throned, an awesome queen, above—
Climbed to thy lap and merely laid his head
Against thy warm wild heart of mother-love.

He heard that vast heart beating—thou didst press
Thy child so close, and lov'dst him unaware.
Thy beauty gladdened him; yet he scarce less
Had loved thee, had he never found thee fair!

For thou wast not as legendary lands
To which with curious eyes and ears we roam.
Nor wast thou as a fane 'mid solemn sands,
Where palmers halt at evening. Thou wast home.

And here, at home, still bides he; but he sleeps;
Not to be wakened even at thy word;
Though we, vague dreamers, dream he somewhere keeps
An ear still open to thy voice still heard,—

Thy voice, as heretofore, about him blown,
For ever blown about his silence now;
Thy voice, though deeper, yet so like his own
That almost, when he sang, we deemed 'twas thou!

VII

Behind Helm Crag and Silver Howe the sheen
Of the retreating day is less and less.
Soon will the lordlier summits, here unseen,
Gather the night about their nakedness.

The half-heard bleat of sheep comes from the hill.
Faint sounds of childish play are in the air.
The river murmurs past. All else is still.
The very graves seem stiller than they were.

Afar though nation be on nation hurled,
And life with toil and ancient pain depressed,
Here one may scarce believe the whole wide world
Is not at peace, and all man's heart at rest.

Rest! 'twas the gift *he* gave; and peace! the shade
He spread, for spirits fevered with the sun.
To him his bounties are come back—here laid
In rest, in peace, his labour nobly done.

KENNETH GRAHAME

From THE GOLDEN AGE

The Roman Road

ALL the roads of our neighbourhood were cheerful and friendly, having each of them pleasant qualities of their own; but this one seemed different from the others in its masterful suggestion of a serious purpose, speeding you along with a strange uplifting of the heart. The others tempted chiefly with their treasures of hedge and ditch; the rapt surprise of the first lords-and-ladies, the rustle of a field-mouse, the splash of a frog; while cool noses of brother-beasts were pushed at you through gate or gap. A loiterer you had need to be, did you choose one of them; so many were the tiny hands thrust out to detain you, from this side and that. But this one was of a sterner sort, and even in its shedding off of bank and hedgerow as it marched straight and full for the open downs, it seemed to declare its contempt for adventitious trappings to catch the shallow-pated. When the sense of injustice or disappointment was heavy on me, and things were very black within, as on this particular day, the road of character was my choice for that solitary ramble when I turned my back for an afternoon on a world that had unaccountably declared itself against me.

"The Knights' Road" we children had named it, from a sort of feeling that, if from any quarter at all, it would be down this track we might some day see Lancelot and his peers come pacing on their great war-horses; supposing that any of the stout band still survived, in nooks and unexplored places. Grown-up people sometimes spoke of it as the "Pilgrims' Way"; but I didn't know much about pilgrims—except Walter in the Horselberg story. Him I sometimes saw, breaking with haggard eyes out of yonder copse; and calling to the pilgrims as they hurried along on their desperate march to the Holy City, where peace and pardon were awaiting them. "All roads lead to Rome," I had once heard somebody say; and I had taken the remark very seriously, of course, and puzzled over it many days. There must have been some mistake, I concluded at last; but of one road at least I intuitively felt it to be true. And my belief was clinched by something that fell from Miss Smedley during a history-lesson, about a strange road that ran right down the middle of England till it reached the coast, and then began again in France, just opposite, and so on undeviating, through city and vineyard, right from the misty Highlands to the Eternal City. Uncorroborated, any statement of Miss Smedley's usually fell on incredulous ears; but here, with the road itself in evidence, she seemed, once in a way, to have strayed into truth.

Rome! It was fascinating to think that it lay at the other end of this white ribbon that rolled itself off from my feet over the distant downs. I was not quite so uninstructed as to imagine I could reach it that afternoon; but some day, I thought, if things went on being as unpleasant as they were now—some day, when Aunt Eliza had gone on a visit,—some day, we would see.

I tried to imagine what it would be like when I got there. The Coliseum I knew, of course, from a woodcut in the history-book: so to begin with I plumped that down in the middle. The rest had to be patched up from the little grey market-town where twice a year we went to have our hair cut; hence, in the result, Vespasian's amphitheatre was approached by muddy little streets, wherein the Red Lion and the Blue Boar, with Somebody's Entire along their front, and "Commercial Room" on their windows; the doctor's house, of substantial red-brick; and the façade of the New Wesleyan chapel, which we thought very fine, were the chief architectural ornaments: while the Roman populace pottered about in smocks and corduroys, twisting the tails of Roman calves and inviting each other to beer in musical Wessex. From Rome I drifted on to other cities, faintly heard of—Damascus, Brighton (Aunt Eliza's ideal), Athens, and Glasgow, whose glories the gardener sang; but there was a certain sameness in my conception of all of them: that Wesleyan chapel would keep cropping up everywhere. It was easier to go a-building among those dream-cities where no limitations were imposed, and one was sole architect, with a free hand. Down a delectable street of cloud-built palaces I was mentally pacing, when I happened upon the Artist.

He was seated at work by the roadside, at a point whence the cool large spaces of the downs, juniper-studded, swept grandly westwards.

His attributes proclaimed him of the artist tribe: besides, he wore knickerbockers like myself,—a garb confined, I was aware, to boys and artists. I knew I was not to bother him with questions, nor look over his shoulder and breathe in his ear—they didn't like it, this *genus irritabile*. But there was nothing about staring in my code of instructions, the point having somehow been overlooked: so, squatting down on the grass, I devoted myself to the passionate absorbing of every detail. At the end of five minutes there was not a button on him that I could not have passed an examination in; and the wearer himself of that homespun suit was probably less familiar with its pattern and texture than I was. Once he looked up, nodded, half held out his tobacco pouch, mechanically as it were, then, returning it to his pocket, resumed his work, and I my mental photography.

After another five minutes or so had passed, he remarked, without looking my way: "Fine afternoon we're having: going far to-day?"

"No, I'm not going any farther than this," I replied; "I *was* thinking of going on to Rome: but I've put it off."

"Pleasant place, Rome," he murmured: "you'll like it." It was some minutes later that he added: "But I wouldn't go just now, if I were you: too jolly hot."

"*You* haven't been to Rome, have you?" I inquired.

"Rather," he replied briefly. "I live there."

This was too much, and my jaw dropped as I struggled to grasp the fact that I was sitting there talking to a fellow who lived in Rome. Speech was out of the question: besides I had other things to do. Ten solid minutes had I already spent in an examination of him as a mere stranger and artist; and now the whole thing had to be done over again, from the changed point of view. So I began afresh, at the crown of his soft hat, and worked down to his solid British shoes, this time investing everything with the new Roman halo; and at last I managed to get out: "But you don't really live there, do you?" never doubting the fact, but wanting to hear it repeated.

"Well," he said, good-naturedly overlooking the slight rudeness of my query, "I live there as much as I live anywhere. About half the year sometimes. I've got a sort of shanty there. You must come and see it some day."

"But do you live anywhere else as well?" I went on, feeling the forbidden tide of questions surging up within me.

"O yes, all over the place," was his vague reply. "And I've got a diggings somewhere off Piccadilly."

"Where's that?" I inquired.

"Where's what?" said he. "O, Piccadilly! It's in London."

"Have you a large garden?" I asked; "and how many pigs have you got?"

"I've no garden at all," he replied sadly, "and they don't allow me to keep pigs, though I'd like to, awfully. It's very hard."

"But what do you do all day, then," I cried, "and where do you go and play, without any garden, or pigs, or things?"

"When I want to play," he said gravely, "I have to go and play in the street; but it's poor fun, I grant you. There's a goat, though, not far off, and sometimes I talk to him when I'm feeling lonely; but he's very proud."

"Goats *are* proud," I admitted. "There's one lives near here, and if you say anything to him at all, he hits you in the wind with his head. You know what it feels like when a fellow hits you in the wind?"

"I do, well," he replied, in a tone of proper melancholy, and painted on.

"And have you been to any other places," I began again presently, "besides Rome and Piccy-what's-his-name?"

"Heaps," he said. "I'm a sort of Ulysses—seen men and cities, you know. In fact, about the only place I never got to was the Fortunate Island."

I began to like this man. He answered your questions briefly and to the point, and never tried to be funny. I felt I could be confidential with him.

"Wouldn't you like," I inquired, "to find a city without any people in it at all?"

He looked puzzled. "I'm afraid I don't quite understand," said he.

"I mean," I went on eagerly, "a city where you walk in at the gates, and the shops are all full of beautiful things, and the houses furnished as grand as can be, and there isn't anybody there whatever! And you go into the shops, and take anything you want—chocolates and magic-lanterns and injirubber balls—and there's nothing to pay; and you choose your own house and live there and do just as you like, and never go to bed unless you want to!"

The artist laid down his brush. "That *would* be a nice city," he said. "Better than Rome. You can't do that sort of thing in Rome—or in Piccadilly either. But I fear it's one of the places I've never been to."

"And you'd ask your friends," I went on, warming to my subject; "only those you really like, of course; and they'd each have a house to themselves—there'd be lots of houses,—and there wouldn't be any relations at all, unless they promised they'd be pleasant; and if they weren't they'd have to go."

"So you wouldn't have any relations?" said the artist. "Well, perhaps you're right. We have tastes in common, I see."

"I'd have Harold," I said reflectively, "and Charlotte. They'd like it awfully. The others are getting too old. O, and Martha—I'd have Martha to cook and wash up and do things. You'd like Martha. She's ever so much nicer than Aunt Eliza. She's my idea of a real lady."

"Then I'm sure I should like her," he replied heartily, "and when I come to—what do you call this city of yours? Nephelo—something, did you say?"

"I—I don't know," I replied timidly. "I'm afraid it hasn't got a name—yet."

The artist gazed out over the downs. " 'The poet says, dear city of Cecrops,' " he said softly to himself, " 'and wilt not thou say, dear city of Zeus?' That's from Marcus Aurelius," he went on, turning again to his work. "You don't know him, I suppose; you will some day."

"Who's he?" I inquired.

"O, just another fellow who lived in Rome," he replied, dabbing away.

"O dear!" I cried disconsolately. "What a lot of people seem to live at Rome, and I've never even been there! But I think I'd like *my* city best."

"And so would I," he replied with unction. "But Marcus Aurelius wouldn't, you know."

"Then we won't invite him," I said; "will we?"

"*I* won't if you won't," said he. And that point being settled, we were silent for a while.

"Do you know," he said presently, "I've met one or two fellows from time to time, who have been to a city like yours—perhaps it was the same one. They won't talk much about it—only broken hints, now and then; but they've been there sure enough. They don't seem to care about anything in particular—and everything's the same to them, rough or smooth, and sooner or later they slip off and disappear; and you never see them again. Gone back, I suppose."

"Of course," said I. "Don't see what they ever came away for; *I* wouldn't. To be told you've broken things when you haven't, and stopped having tea with the servants in the kitchen, and not allowed to have a dog to sleep with you. But *I've* known people, too, who've gone there."

The artist stared, but without incivility.

"Well, there's Lancelot," I went on. "The book says he died, but it never seemed to read right, somehow. He just went away, like Arthur. And Crusoe, when he got tired of wearing clothes and being respectable. And all the nice men in the stories who don't marry the Princess, 'cos only one man ever gets married in a book, you know. They'll be there!"

"And the men who never come off," he said, "who try like the rest, but get knocked out, or somehow miss—or break down or get bowled over in the melée—and get no Princess, nor even a second-class kingdom—some of them'll be there, I hope?"

"Yes, if you like," I replied, not quite understanding him; "if they're friends of yours, we'll ask 'em, of course."

"What a time we shall have!" said the artist reflectively; "and how shocked old Marcus Aurelius will be!"

The shadows had lengthened uncannily, a tide of golden haze was flooding the grey-green surface of the downs, and the artist began to put his traps together, preparatory to a move. I felt very low: we would have to part, it seemed, just as we were getting on so well together. Then he stood up, and he was very straight and tall, and the sunset was in his hair and beard as he stood there, high over me. He took my hand like an equal. "I've enjoyed our conversation very much," he said. "That was an interesting subject you started, and we haven't half exhausted it. We shall meet again, I hope?"

"Of course we shall," I replied, surprised that there should be any doubt about it.

"In Rome perhaps?" said he.

"Yes, in Rome," I answered; "or Piccy-the-other-place, or somewhere."

"Or else," said he, "in that other city—when we've found the way there. And I'll look out for you, and you'll sing out as soon as you see me. And we'll go down the street arm-in-arm, and into all the shops, and then I'll choose my house, and you'll choose your house, and we'll live there like princes and good-fellows."

"O, but you'll stay in my house, won't you?" I cried; "I wouldn't ask everybody; but I'll ask *you.*"

He affected to consider a moment; then "Right!" he said: "I believe you mean it, and I *will* come and stay with you. I won't go to anybody else, if they ask me ever so much. And I'll stay quite a long time, too, and I won't be any trouble."

Upon this compact we parted, and I went down-heartedly from the man who understood me, back to the house where I never could do anything right. How was it that everything seemed natural and sensible to him, which these uncles, vicars, and other grown-up men took for the merest tomfoolery? Well, he would explain this, and many another thing, when we met again. The Knights' Road! How it always brought consolation! Was he possibly one of those vanished knights I had been looking for so long? Perhaps he would be in armour next time—why not? He would look well in armour, I thought. And I would take care to get there first, and see the sunlight flash and play on his helmet and shield, as he rode up the High Street of the Golden City.

Meantime, there only remained the finding it. An easy matter.

The Burglars

It was much too fine a night to think of going to bed at once, and so, although the witching hour of nine P. M. had struck, Edward and I were still leaning out of the open window in our nightshirts, watching the play of the cedar-branch shadows on the moonlit lawn, and planning schemes of fresh devilry for the sunshiny morrow. From below, strains of the jocund piano declared that the Olympians were enjoying themselves in their listless impotent way; for the new curate had been bidden to dinner that night, and was at the moment unclerically proclaiming to all the world that he feared no foe. His discordant vociferations doubtless started a train of thought in Edward's mind, for he presently remarked, *à propos* of nothing whatever that had been said before, "I believe the new curate's rather gone on Aunt Maria."

I scouted the notion; "Why, she's quite old," I said. (She must have seen some five-and-twenty summers.)

"Of course she is," replied Edward scornfully. "It's not her, it's her money he's after, you bet!"

"Didn't know she had any money," I observed timidly.

"Sure to have," said my brother with confidence. "Heaps and heaps."

Silence ensued, both our minds being busy with the new situation thus presented: mine, in wonderment at this flaw that so often declared itself in enviable natures of fullest endowment,—in a grown-up man and a good cricketer, for instance, even as this curate; Edward's (apparently) in the consideration of how such a state of things, supposing it existed, could be best turned to his own advantage.

"Bobby Ferris told me," began Edward in due course, "that there was a fellow spooning his sister once——"

"What's spooning?" I asked meekly.

"O *I* dunno," said Edward indifferently. "It's—it's—it's just a thing they do, you know. And he used to carry notes and messages and things between 'em, and he got a shilling almost every time."

"What, from each of 'em?" I innocently inquired.

Edward looked at me with scornful pity. "Girls never have any money," he briefly explained. "But she did his exercises, and got him out of rows, and told stories for him when he needed it—and much better ones than he could have made up for himself. Girls are useful in some ways. So he was living in clover, when unfortunately they went and quarrelled about something."

"Don't see what that's got to do with it," I said.

"Nor don't I," rejoined Edward. "But anyhow the notes and things stopped, and so did the shillings. Bobby was fairly cornered, for he had bought two ferrets on tick, and promised to pay a shilling a week, thinking the shillings were going on for ever, the silly young ass. So when the week was up, and he was being dunned for the shilling, he went off to the fellow and said: 'Your broken-hearted Bella implores you to meet her at sundown. By the hollow oak as of old, be it only for a moment. Do not fail!' He got all that out of some rotten book, of course. The fellow looked puzzled and said: "'What hollow oak? I don't know any hollow oak.'

"'Perhaps it was the Royal Oak?' said Bobby promptly, 'cos he saw he had made a slip, through trusting too much to the rotten book; but this didn't seem to make the fellow any happier."

"Should think not," I said, "the Royal Oak's an awful low sort of pub."

"I know," said Edward. "Well, at last the fellow said, 'I think I know what she means: the hollow tree in your father's paddock. It happens to be an elm, but she wouldn't know the difference. All right: say I'll be there.' Bobby hung about a bit, for he hadn't got his money. 'She was crying awfully,' he said. Then he got his shilling."

"And wasn't the fellow riled," I inquired, "when he got to the place and found nothing?"

"He found Bobby," said Edward indignantly. "Young Ferris was a gentleman, every inch of him. He brought the fellow another message from Bella: 'I dare not leave the house. My cruel parents immure me closely. If you only knew what I suffer. Your broken-hearted Bella.' Out of the same rotten book. This made the fellow a little suspicious, 'cos it was the old Ferrises who had been keen about the thing all through. The fellow, you see, had tin."

"But what's that got to——" I began again.

"O *I* dunno," said Edward impatiently. "I'm telling you just what Bobby told me. He got suspicious, anyhow, but he couldn't exactly call Bella's brother a liar, so Bobby escaped for the time. But when he was in a hole next week, over a stiff French exercise, and tried the same sort of game on his sister, she was too sharp for him, and he got caught out. Somehow women seem more mistrustful than men. They're so beastly suspicious by nature, you know."

"*I* know," said I. "But did the two—the fellow and the sister—make it up afterwards?"

"I don't remember about that," replied Edward indifferently; "but Bobby got packed off to school a whole year earlier than his people meant to send him. Which was just what he wanted. So you see it all came right in the end!"

I was trying to puzzle out the moral of this story—it was evidently meant to contain one somewhere—when a flood of golden lamplight mingled with the moon-rays on the lawn, and Aunt Maria and the new curate strolled out on the grass below us, and took the direction of a garden-seat which was backed by a dense laurel shrubbery reaching round in a half-circle to the house. Edward meditated moodily. "If we only knew what they were talking about," said he, "you'd soon see whether I was right or not. Look here! Let's send the kid down by the porch to reconnoitre!"

"Harold's asleep," I said; "it seems rather a shame——"

"O rot!" said my brother; "he's the youngest, and he's got to do as he's told!"

So the luckless Harold was hauled out of bed and given his sailing-orders. He was naturally rather vexed at being stood up suddenly on the cold floor, and the job had no particular interest for him; but he was both staunch and well disciplined. The means of exit were simple enough. A porch of iron trellis came up to within easy reach of the window, and was habitually used by all three of us, when modestly anxious to avoid public notice. Harold climbed deftly down the porch like a white rat, and his night-gown glimmered a moment on the gravel walk ere he was lost to sight in the darkness of the shrubbery. A brief interval of silence ensued; broken suddenly by a sound of scuffle, and then a shrill long-drawn squeal, as of metallic surfaces in friction. Our scout had fallen into the hands of the enemy!

Indolence alone had made us devolve the task of investigation on our younger brother. Now that danger had declared itself, there was no hesitation. In a second we were down the side of the porch, and crawling Cherokee-wise through the laurels to the back of the garden seat. Piteous was the sight that greeted us. Aunt Maria was on the seat, in a white evening frock, looking—for an aunt—really quite nice. On the lawn stood an incensed curate, grasping our small brother by a large ear, which—judging from the row he was making—seemed on the point of parting company with the head it completed and adorned. The gruesome noise he was emitting did not really affect us otherwise than æsthetically. To one who has tried both, the wail of genuine physical anguish is easily distinguishable from the pumped-up *ad misericordiam* blubber. Harold's could clearly be recognised as belonging to the latter class. "Now you young—" (whelp, *I* think it was, but Edward stoutly maintains it was devil), said the curate sternly; "tell us what you mean by it!"

"Well leggo of my ear then!" shrilled Harold, "and I'll tell you the solemn truth!"

"Very well," agreed the curate, releasing him, "now go ahead, and don't lie more than you can help."

We abode the promised disclosure without the least misgiving; but even we had hardly given Harold due credit for his fertility of resource and powers of imagination.

"I had just finished saying my prayers," began that young gentleman slowly, "when I happened to look out of the window, and on the lawn I saw a sight which froze the marrow in my veins! A burglar was approaching the house with snake-like tread! He had a scowl and a dark lantern, and he was armed to the teeth!"

We listened with interest. The style, though unlike Harold's native notes, seemed strangely familiar.

"Go on," said the curate grimly.

"Pausing in his stealthy career," continued Harold, "he gave a low whistle. Instantly the signal was responded to, and from the adjacent shadows two more figures glided forth. The miscreants were both armed to the teeth."

"Excellent," said the curate; "proceed."

"The robber chief," pursued Harold, warming to his work, "joined his nefarious comrades, and conversed with them in silent tones. His expression was truly ferocious, and I ought to have said that he was armed to the t——"

"There, never mind his teeth," interrupted the curate rudely; "there's too much jaw about you altogether. Hurry up and have done."

"I was in a frightful funk," continued the narrator, warily guarding his ear with his hand, "but just then the drawing-room window opened, and you and Aunt Maria came out—I mean emerged. The burglars vanished silently into the laurels, with horrid implications!"

The curate looked slightly puzzled. The tale was well sustained, and certainly circumstantial. After all, the boy might really have seen something. How was the poor man to know—though the chaste and lofty diction might have supplied a hint—that the whole yarn was a free adaptation from the last Penny Dreadful lent us by the knife-and-boot boy?

"Why did you not alarm the house?" he asked.

"'Cos I was afraid," said Harold sweetly, "that p'raps they mightn't believe me!"

"But how did you get down here, you naughty little boy?" put in Aunt Maria.

Harold was hard pressed—by his own flesh and blood, too!

At that moment Edward touched me on the shoulder and glided off through the laurels. When some ten yards away he gave a low whistle. I replied with another. The effect was magical. Aunt Maria started up with a shriek. Harold gave one startled glance around, and then fled like a hare, made straight for the back-door, burst in upon the servants at supper, and buried himself in the broad bosom of the cook, his special ally. The curate faced the laurels—hesitatingly. But Aunt Maria flung herself on him. "O Mr. Hodgitts!" I heard her cry, "you are brave! for my sake do not be rash!" He was not rash. When I peeped out a second later, the coast was entirely clear.

By this time there were sounds of a household timidly emerging; and Edward remarked to me that perhaps we had better be off. Retreat was an easy matter. A stunted laurel gave a leg-up on to the garden wall, which led in its turn to the roof of an out-house, up which, at a dubious angle, we could crawl to the window of the box-room. This overland route had been revealed to us one day by the domestic cat, when hard pressed in the course of an otter-hunt, in which the cat—somewhat unwillingly—was filling the title *rôle;* and it had proved distinctly useful on occasions like the present. We were snug in bed—minus some cuticle from knees and elbows—and Harold, sleepily chewing something sticky, had been carried up in the arms of the friendly cook, ere the clamour of the burglar-hunters had died away.

The curate's undaunted demeanour, as reported by Aunt Maria, was generally supposed to have terrified the burglars into flight, and much kudos accrued to him thereby. Some days later, however, when he had dropped in to afternoon tea, and was making a mild curatorial joke about the moral courage required for taking the last piece of bread-and-butter, I felt constrained to remark dreamily, and as it were to the universe at large: "Mr. Hodgitts! you are brave! for my sake, do not be rash!"

Fortunately for me, the vicar also was a caller on that day; and it was always a comparatively easy matter to dodge my long-coated friend in the open.

SIR JAMES MATTHEW BARRIE

From MY LADY NICOTINE

Matrimony and Smoking Compared

THE circumstances in which I gave up smoking were these.

I was a mere bachelor, drifting toward what I now see to be a tragic middle age. I had become so accustomed to smoke issuing from my mouth that I felt incomplete without it; indeed the time came when I could refrain from smoking if doing nothing else, but hardly during the hours of toil. To lay aside my pipe was to find myself soon afterwards wandering restlessly round my table. No blind beggar was ever more abjectly led by his dog, or more loth to cut the string.

I am much better without tobacco, and already have difficulty in sympathizing with the man I used to be. Even to call him up, as it were, and regard him without prejudice is a difficult task, for we forget the old selves on whom we have turned our backs as we forget a street that has been reconstructed. Does the freed slave always shiver at the crack of a whip? I fancy not, for I recall but dimly, and without acute suffering, the horrors of my smoking days. There were nights when I woke with a pain at my heart that made me hold my breath. I did not dare move. After perhaps ten minutes of dread, I would shift my position an inch at a time. Less frequently I felt this sting in the daytime, and believed I was dying while my friends were talking to me. I never mentioned these experiences to a human being; indeed, though a medical man was among my companions, I cunningly deceived him on the rare occasions when he questioned me about the amount of tobacco I was consuming weekly. Often in the dark I not only vowed to give up smoking, but wondered why I cared for it. Next morning I went straight from breakfast to my pipe, without the smallest struggle with myself. Latterly I knew, while resolving to break myself of the habit that I would be better employed trying to sleep. I had elaborate ways of cheating myself, for it became disagreeable to me to know how many ounces of tobacco I was smoking weekly. Often I smoked cigarettes to reduce the number of my cigars.

On the other hand, if these sharp pains be excepted, I felt quite well. My appetite was as good as it is now, and I worked as cheerfully and certainly harder. To some slight extent, I believe, I experienced the same pains in my boyhood, before I smoked, and I am not an absolute stranger to them yet. They were most frequent in my smoking days, but I have no other reason for charging them to tobacco. Possibly a doctor who smoked himself would have pooh-poohed them. Nevertheless, I have lit my pipe, and then, as I may say, hearkened for them. At the first intimation that they were coming I laid the pipe down and ceased to smoke—until they had passed.

I will not admit that, once sure it was doing me harm, I could not, unaided, have given up tobacco. But I was reluctant to make sure. I should like to say that I left off smoking because I considered it a mean form of slavery, to be condemned for moral as well as physical reasons; but though I see the folly of smoking clearly now, I was blind to it for some months after I had smoked my last pipe. I gave up my most delightful solace, as I regarded it, for no other reason than that the lady who was willing to fling herself away on me said that I must choose between it and her. This deferred our marriage for six months.

I have now come, as those who read will see, to look upon smoking with my wife's eyes. My old bachelor friends complain because I do not allow smoking in the house, but I am always ready to explain my position, and I have not an atom of pity for them. If I cannot smoke here neither shall they. When I visit them in the old Inn they take a poor revenge by blowing rings of smoke almost in my face. This ambition to blow rings is the most ignoble known to man. Once I was a member of a club for smokers, where we practised blowing rings. The most successful got a box of cigars as a prize at the end of the year. Those were days! Often I think wistfully of them. We met in a cosey room off the Strand. How well I can picture it still; time-tables lying everywhere, with which we could light our pipes. Some smoked clays, but for the Arcadia Mixture give me a briar. My briar was the sweetest ever known. It is strange now to recall a time when a pipe seemed to be my best friend.

My present state is so happy that I can only look back with wonder at my hesitation to enter upon it. Our house was taken while I was still arguing that it would be dangerous to break myself of smoking all at once. At that time my ideal of married life was not what it is now, and I remember Jimmy's persuading me to fix on this house because the large room upstairs with the three windows was a smoker's dream. He pictured himself and me there in the summer-time blowing rings, with our coats off and our feet out at the windows; and he said that the closet at the back, looking on to a blank wall, would make a charming drawing-room for my wife. For the moment his enthusiasm carried me away, but I see now how selfish it was, and I have before me the face of Jimmy when he paid us his first visit and found that the closet was not the drawing-room. Jimmy is a fair specimen of a man, not without parts, destroyed by devotion to his pipe. To this day he thinks that mantelpiece vases are meant for holding pipe-lights in. We are almost certain that when he stays with us he smokes in his bedroom—a detestable practice that I cannot permit.

Two cigars a day at ninepence apiece come to £27 7s. 6d. yearly, and four ounces of tobacco a week at nine shillings a pound come to £5 17s. yearly. That makes £33 4s. 6d. When we calculate the yearly expense of tobacco in this way we are naturally taken aback, and our extravagance shocks us the more after we have considered how much more satisfactorily the money might have been spent. With £33 4s. 6d. you can buy new Oriental rugs for the drawing-room, as well as a spring bonnet and a nice dress. These are things that give permanent pleasure, whereas you have no interest in a cigar after flinging away the stump. Judging by myself, I should say that it is want of thought rather than selfishness that makes heavy smokers of so many bachelors. Once a man marries his eyes are opened to many things that he was quite unaware of previously, among them being the delight of adding an article of furniture to the drawing-room every month and having a bedroom in pink and gold, the door of which is always kept locked. If men would only consider that every cigar they smoke would buy part of a new piano-stool in terra-cotta plush, and that for every pound tin of tobacco purchased away goes a vase for growing dead geraniums in, they would surely hesitate. They do not consider, however, until they marry, and then they are forced to it. For my own part, I fail to see why bachelors should be allowed to smoke as much as they like when we are debarred from it.

The very smell of tobacco is abominable, for one cannot get it out of the curtains, and there is little pleasure in existence unless the curtains are all right. As for a cigar after dinner, it only makes you dull and sleepy and disinclined for ladies' society. A far more delightful way of spending the evening is to go straight from dinner to the drawing-room and have a little music. It calms the mind to listen to your wife's niece singing "Oh, that we two were maying." Even if you are not musical, as is the case with me, there is a great deal in the drawing-room to refresh you. There are the Japanese fans on the wall, which are things of beauty, though your artistic taste may not be sufficiently educated to let you know it except by hearsay; and it is pleasant to feel that they were bought with money which, in the foolish old days, would have been squandered on a box of cigars. In like manner every pretty trifle in the room reminds you how much wiser you are now than you used to be. It is even gratifying to stand in summer at the drawing-room window and watch the very cabbies passing with cigars in their mouths. At the same time, if I had the making of the laws I would prohibit people's smoking in the street. If they are married men, they are smoking drawing-room fire-screens and mantelpiece borders for the pink and gold room. If they are bachelors, it is a scandal that bachelors should get the best of everything.

Nothing is more pitiable than the way some men of my acquaintance enslave themselves to tobacco. Nay, worse, they make an idol of some one particular tobacco. I know a man who considers a certain mixture so superior to all others that he will walk three miles for it. Surely every one will admit that this is lamentable. It is not even a good mixture, for I used to try it occasionally; and if there is one man in London who knows tobaccos, it is myself. There is only one mixture in London deserving the adjective superb. I will not say where it is to be got, for the result would certainly be that many foolish men would smoke more than ever; but I never knew anything to compare to it. It is deliciously mild yet of full fragrance, and it never burns the tongue. If you try it once you smoke it ever afterwards. It clears the brain and soothes the temper. When I went away for a holiday anywhere I took as much of that exquisite health-giving mixture as I thought would last me the whole time, but I always ran out of it. Then I telegraphed to London for more, and was miserable until it arrived. How I tore the lid off the canister! That is a tobacco to live for. But I am better without it.

Occasionally I feel a little depressed after dinner still, without being able to say why, and if my wife has left me I wander about the room restlessly, like one who misses something. Usually, however, she takes me with her to the drawing-room, and reads aloud her delightfully long home letters or plays soft music to me. If the music be sweet and sad it takes me away to a stair in an Inn, which I climb gaily and shake open a heavy door on the top floor, and turn up the gas. It is a little room I am in once again, and very dusty. A pile of papers and magazines stands as high as a table in the corner furthest from the door. The cane-chair shows the exact shape of Marriot's back. What is left (after lighting the fire) of a framed picture lies on the hearthrug. Gilray walks in uninvited. He has left word that his visitors are to be sent on to me. The room fills. My hand feels along the mantelpiece for a brown jar. The jar is between my knees, I fill my pipe. . . .

After a time the music ceases, and my wife puts her hand on my shoulder. Perhaps I start a little, and then she says I have been asleep. This is the book of my dreams.

My First Cigar

It was not in my chambers, but three hundred miles further north that I learned to smoke. I think I may say with confidence that a first cigar was never smoked in such circumstances before.

At that time I was a schoolboy, living with my brother who was a man. People mistook our relations, and thought I was his son. They would ask me how my father was, and when he heard of this he scowled at me. Even to this day I look so young that people who remember me as a boy, now think I must be that boy's younger brother. I shall tell presently of a strange mistake of this kind, but at present I am thinking of the evening when my brother's eldest daughter was born—perhaps the most trying evening he and I ever passed together. So far as I knew the affair was very sudden, and I felt sorry for my brother as well as for myself.

We sat together in the study, he on an armchair drawn near the fire and I on the couch. I cannot say now at what time I began to have an inkling that there was something wrong. It came upon me gradually and made me very uncomfortable, though of course I did not show this. I heard people going up and down stairs, but I was not at that time naturally suspicious. Comparatively early in the evening I felt that my brother had something on his mind. As a rule, when we were left together, he yawned or drummed with his fingers on the arm of his chair to show that he did not feel uncomfortable, or I made a pretence of being at ease by playing with the dog or saying that the room was close. Then one of us would rise, remark that he had left his book in the dining-room, and go away to look for it, taking care not to come back till the other had gone. In this crafty way we helped each other. On that occasion, however, he did not adopt any of the usual methods; and though I went up to my bedroom several times and listened through the wall, I heard nothing. At last some one told me not to go upstairs, and I returned to the study, feeling that I now knew the worst. He was still in the armchair, and I again took the couch. I could see by the way he looked at me over his pipe that he was wondering whether I knew anything. I don't think I ever liked my brother better than on that night; and I wanted him to understand that, whatever happened, it would make no difference between us. But the affair upstairs was too delicate to talk of, and all I could do was to try to keep his mind from brooding on it by making him tell me things about politics. This is the kind of man my brother is. He is an astonishing master of facts, and I suppose he never read a book yet, from a Blue Book to a volume of verse, without catching the author in error about something. He reads books for that purpose. As a rule, I avoided argument with him, because he was disappointed if I was right and stormed if I was wrong. It was therefore a dangerous thing to begin on politics, but I thought the circumstances warranted it. To my surprise he answered me in a rambling manner, occasionally breaking off in the middle of a sentence and seeming to listen for something. I tried him on history, and mentioned 1822 as the date of the Battle of Waterloo merely to give him his opportunity. But he let it pass. After that there was silence. By and by he rose from his chair, apparently to leave the room, and then sat down again, as if he had thought better of it. He did this several times, always eyeing me narrowly. Wondering how I could make it easier for him, I took up a book and pretended to read with deep attention, meaning to show him that he could go away if he liked without my noticing it. At last he jumped up, and, looking at me boldly, as if to show that the house was his and he could do what he liked in it, went heavily from the room. As soon as he was gone I laid down my book. I was now in a state of nervous excitement, though outwardly I was quite calm. I took a look at him as he went up the stairs, and noticed that he had slipped off his shoes on the bottom step. All haughtiness had left him now.

In a little while he came back. He found me reading. He lit his pipe and pretended to read too. I shall never forget that my book was "Anne Judge, Spinster," while his was a volume of "Blackwood." Every five minutes his pipe went out, and sometimes the book lay neglected on his knee as he stared at the fire. Then he would go out for five minutes and come back again. It was late now, and I felt that I should like to go to my bedroom and lock myself in. That, however, would have been selfish; so we sat on defiantly. At last he started from his chair, as some one knocked at the door. I heard several people talking, and then loud above their voices a younger one.

When I came to myself, the first thing I thought was that they would ask me to hold it. Then I remembered, with another sinking at the heart, that they might want to call it after me. These, of course, were selfish reflections; but my position was a trying one. The question was, what was the proper thing for me to do? I told myself that my brother might come back at any moment, and all I thought of after that was what I should say to him. I had an idea that I ought to congratulate him, but it seemed a brutal thing to do. I had not made up my mind when I heard him coming down. He was laughing and joking in what seemed to me a flippant kind of way, considering the circumstances. When his hand touched the door I snatched at my book and read as hard as I could. He was swaggering a little as he entered, but the swagger went out of him as soon as his eye fell on me. I fancy he had come down to tell me, and now he did not know how to begin. He walked up and down the room restlessly, looking at me as he walked the one way while I looked at him as he walked the other way. At length he sat down again and took up his book. He did not try to smoke. The silence was something terrible; nothing was to be heard but an occasional cinder falling from the grate. This lasted I should say for twenty minutes, and then he closed his book and flung it on the table. I saw that the game was up, and closed "Anne Judge, Spinster." Then he said, with affected jocularity, "Well, young man, do you know that you are an uncle?" There was silence again, for I was still trying to think out some appropriate remark. After a time I said, in a weak voice, "Boy or girl?" "Girl," he answered. Then I thought hard again, and all at once remembered something. "Both doing well?" I whispered. "Yes," he said, sternly. I felt that something great was expected of me, but I could not jump up and wring his hand. I was an uncle. I stretched out my arm toward the cigar-box, and firmly lit my first cigar.

The Arcadia Mixture

DARKNESS comes, and with it the porter to light our stair gas. He vanishes into his box. Already the Inn is so quiet that the tap of a pipe on a windowsill startles all the sparrows in the quadrangle. The men on my stair emerge from their holes. Scrymgeour, in a dressing-gown, pushes open the door of the boudoir on the first floor, and climbs lazily. The sentimental face and the clay with a crack in it are Marriot's. Gilray, who has been rehearsing his part in the new original comedy from the Icelandic, ceases muttering and feels his way along his dark lobby.

Jimmy pins a notice on his door "Called away on Business," and crosses to me. Soon we are all in the old room again, Jimmy on the hearthrug, Marriot in the cane-chair; the curtains are pinned together with a pen-nib, and the five of us are smoking the Arcadia Mixture.

Pettigrew will be welcomed if he comes, but he is a married man, and we seldom see him nowadays. Others will be regarded as intruders. If they are smoking common tobaccos, they must either be allowed to try ours or requested to withdraw. One need only put his head in at my door to realize that tobaccos are of two kinds, the Arcadia and others. No one who smokes the Arcadia would ever attempt to describe its delights, for his pipe would be certain to go out. When he was at school, Jimmy Moggridge smoked a cane-chair, and he has since said that from cane to ordinary mixtures was not so noticeable as the change from ordinary mixtures to the Arcadia. I ask no one to believe this, for the confirmed smoker in Arcadia detests arguing with anybody about anything. Were I anxious to prove Jimmy's statement, I would merely give you the only address at which the Arcadia is to be had. But that I will not do. It would be as rash as proposing a man with whom I am unacquainted for my club. You may not be worthy to smoke the Arcadia Mixture.

Even though I became attached to you, I might not like to take the responsibility of introducing you to the Arcadia. This mixture has an extraordinary effect upon character, and probably you want to remain as you are. Before I discovered the Arcadia, and communicated it to the other five—including Pettigrew—we had all distinct individualities, but now, except in appearance—and the Arcadia even tells on that—we are as like as holly-leaves. We have the same habits, the same ways of looking at things, the same satisfaction in each other. No doubt we are not yet absolutely alike, indeed I intend to prove this, but in given circumstances we would probably do the same thing, and, furthermore, it would be what other people would not do. Thus when we are together we are only to be distinguished by our pipes; but any one of us in the company of persons who smoke other tobaccos would be considered highly original. He would be a pigtail in Europe.

If you meet in company a man who has ideas and is not shy, yet refuses absolutely to be drawn into talk, you may set him down as one of us. Among the first effects of the Arcadia is to put an end to jabber. Gilray had at one time the reputation of being such a brilliant talker that Arcadians locked their doors on him, but now he is a man who can be invited anywhere. The Arcadia is entirely responsible for the change. Perhaps I myself am the most silent of our company, and hostesses usually think me shy. They ask ladies to draw me out, and when the ladies find me as hopeless as a sulky drawer they call me stupid. The charge may be true, but I do not resent it, for I smoke the Arcadia Mixture, and am consequently indifferent to abuse.

I willingly gibbet myself to show how reticent the Arcadia makes us. It happens that I have a connection with Nottingham, and whenever a man mentions Nottingham to me, with a certain gleam in his eye, I know that he wants to discuss the lace trade. But it is a curious fact that the aggressive talker constantly mixes up Nottingham and Northampton. "Oh, you know Nottingham," he says interestedly; "and how do you like Labouchere for a member?" Do you think I put him right? Do you imagine me thirsting to tell that Mr. Labouchere is the Christian member for Northampton? Do you suppose me swift to explain that Mr. Broadhurst is one of the Nottingham members and that the "Nottingham lambs" are notorious in the history of political elections? Do you fancy me explaining that he is quite right in saying that Nottingham has a large market-place? Do you see me drawn into half an hour's talk about Robin Hood? That is not my way. I merely reply that we like Mr. Labouchere pretty well. It may be said that I gain nothing by this; that the talker will be as curious about Northampton as he would have been about Nottingham, and that Bradlaugh and Labouchere and boots will serve his turn quite as well as Broadhurst and lace and Robin Hood. But that is not so. Beginning on Northampton in the most confident manner, it suddenly flashes across him that he has mistaken Northampton for Nottingham. "How foolish of me!" he says. I maintain a severe silence. He is annoyed. My experience of talkers tells me that nothing annoys them so much as a blunder of this kind. From the coldly polite way in which I have taken the talker's remarks he discovers the value I put upon them, and after that, if he has a neighbor on the other side, he leaves me alone.

Enough has been said to show that the Arcadian's golden rule is to be careful about what he says. This does not mean that he is to say nothing. As society is at present constituted you are bound to make an occasional remark. But you need not make it rashly. It has been said somewhere that it would be well for talkative persons to count twenty, or to go over the alphabet, before they let fall the observation that trembles on their lips. The non-talker has no taste for such an unintellectual exercise. At the same time he must not hesitate too long, for, of course, it is to his advantage to introduce the subject. He ought to think out a topic of which his neighbor will not be able to make very much. To begin on the fall of snow or the number of tons of turkeys consumed on Christmas Day as stated in the *Daily Telegraph,* is to deserve your fate. If you are at a dinner-party of men only, take your host aside, and in a few well-considered sentences find out from him what kind of men you are to sit between during dinner. Perhaps one of them is an African traveller. A knowledge of this prevents your playing into his hands by remarking that the papers are full of the relief of Emin Pasha. These private inquiries will also save you from talking about Mr. Chamberlain to a neighbor who turns out to be the son of a Birmingham elector. Allow that man his chance, and he will not only give you the Birmingham gossip, but what individual electors said about Mr. Chamberlain to the banker or the tailor, and what the grocer did the moment the poll was declared, with particulars about the antiquity of Birmingham and the fishing to be had in the neighborhood. What you ought to do is to talk about Emin Pasha to this man, and to the traveller about Mr. Chamberlain, taking care, of course, to speak in a low voice. In that way you may have comparative peace. Everything, however, depends on the calibre of your neighbors. If they agree to look upon you as an honorable antagonist, and so to fight fair, the victory will be to him who deserves it; that is to say, to the craftier man of the two. But talkers, as a rule, do not fight fair. They consider silent men their prey. It will thus be seen that I distinguish between talkers, admitting that some of them are worse than others. The lowest in the social scale is he who stabs you in the back, as it were, instead of crossing swords. If one of the gentlemen introduced to you is of that type, he will not be ashamed to say, "Speaking of Emin Pasha, I wonder if Mr. Chamberlain is interested in the relief expedition. I don't know if I told you that my father"—and there he is, fairly on horseback. It is seldom of any use to tempt him into other channels. Better turn to your traveller and let him describe the different routes to the Egyptian Equatorial Provinces, with his own views thereon. Allow him even to draw a map of Africa with a fork on the tablecloth. A talker of this kind is too full of his subject to insist upon your answering questions, so that he does not trouble you much. It is his own dinner that is spoilt rather than yours. Treat in the same way as the Chamberlain talker the man who sits down beside you and begins, "Remarkable man, Mr. Gladstone."

There was a ventilator in my room, which sometimes said "Crik-Crik!" reminding us that no one had spoken for half an hour. Occasionally, however, we had lapses of speech, when Gilray might tell over again—though not quite as I mean to tell it—the story of his first pipeful of the Arcadia, or Scrymgeour, the travelled man, would give us the list of famous places in Europe where he had smoked. But, as a rule, none of us paid much attention to what the others said, and after the last pipe, the room emptied—unless Marriot insisted on staying behind to bore me with his scruples—by first one and then another putting his pipe into his pocket and walking silently out of the room.

From SENTIMENTAL TOMMY

The Essay-Writing Contest

Hugh Blackadder, a Thrums man, had made his fortune in America, and bequeathed the interest of three hundred pounds to be competed for yearly by the youth of his native place. The prize was for the best essay in the Scots tongue.

Mr. Cathro, the dominie of the school in Thrums, had not intended to enter Master Thomas Sandys. Though he knew only too well Tommy's ability with the pen, he had thought that Tommy's failure in the bursary examinations ended the posssibility of Mr. McLean's aiding Tommy to go to the university. This obstacle, however, Grizel succeeded in removing; and Mr. Cathro was more than delighted to enter Tommy and thus, he was sure, avenge his pride on Mr. Ogilvy of the Glenquharity school, who for years had carried the Blackadder, and who this year had made by far the better showing with his boys in the bursary examinations.

The only competitor against Tommy was Laughlan McLaughlan of Mr. Ogilvy's school. The contest took place in the Thrums school. Besides some of Tommy's friends, outside, there were present, within, "the Rev. Mr. Duthie, the Rev. Mr. Dishart, the Rev. Mr. Gloag of Noran Side, the Rev. Mr. Lorrimer of Glenquharity (these on hair-bottomed chairs), and Mr. Cathro and Mr. Ogilvy (cane)." The subject assigned for the essay was "A Day in Church." Tommy began at once with a confident smirk that presently gave way to a most holy expression; while Laughlan gaped at him and at last got started also. Mr. Cathro sat smiling with the ministers, and Mr. Ogilvy dolefully paced the floor.

Before an hour had passed, the door of the little room in which the boys were writing was closed, to spare the feelings of Mr. Ogilvy, who had been unhappily peeping through at Tommy and poor Laughlan. But before the end of the two hours, Mr. Ogilvy, still hovering about the door, was quite unhappy. "'I'm an old fool,' the Dominie admitted, 'but I can't help being cast down. The fact is that—I have only heard the scrape of one pen for nearly an hour.'"

Presently Mr. Cathro winked at Mr. Ogilvy.

He winked a great deal more after a moment.

For after all—how to tell it! Tommy was ignominiously beaten, making such a beggarly show that the judges thought it unnecessary to take the essays home with them for leisurely consideration before pronouncing Mr. Lauchlan McLauchlan winner. There was quite a commotion in the school-room. At the end of the allotted time the two competitors had been told to hand in their essays, and how Mr. McLauchlan was sniggering is not worth recording, so dumfounded, confused and raging was Tommy. He clung to his papers, crying fiercely that the two hours could not be up yet, and Lauchlan having tried to keep the laugh in too long it exploded in his mouth, whereupon, said he, with a guffaw, "He hasna written a word for near an hour!"

"What! It was you I heard!" cried Mr. Ogilvy, gleaming, while the unhappy Cathro tore the essay from Tommy's hands. Essay! It was no more an essay than a twig is a tree, for the gowk had stuck in the middle of his second page. Yes, stuck is the right expression, as his chagrined teacher had to admit when the boy was cross-examined. He had not been "up to some of his tricks," he had stuck, and his explanations, as you will admit, merely emphasized his incapacity.

He had brought himself to public scorn for lack of a word. What word? they asked testily, but even now he could not tell. He had wanted a Scotch word that would signify how many people were in church, and it was on the tip of his tongue but would come no farther. Puckle was nearly the word, but it did not mean so many people as he meant. The hour had gone by just like winking; he had forgotten all about time while searching his mind for the word.

When Mr. Ogilvy heard this he seemed to be much impressed, repeatedly he nodded his head as some beat time to music, and he muttered to himself, "The right word—yes, that's everything," and "'the time went by like winking'—exactly, precisely," and he would have liked to examine Tommy's bumps, but did not, nor said a word aloud, for was he not there in McLauchlan's interest?

The other five were furious; even Mr. Lorrimer, though his man had won, could not smile in face of such imbecility. "You little tattie-doolie," Cathro roared, "were there not a dozen words to wile from if you had an ill-will to puckle? What ailed you at manzy, or——"

"I thought of manzy," replied Tommy woefully, for he was ashamed of himself, "but—but a manzy's a swarm. It would mean that the folk in the kirk were buzzing thegither like bees, instead of sitting still."

"Even if it does mean that," said Mr. Duthie, with impatience, "what was the need of being so particular? Surely the art of essay-writing consists in using the first word that comes and hurrying on."

"That's how I did," said the proud McLauchlan, who is now leader of a party in the church, and a figure in Edinburgh during the month of May.

"I see," interposed Mr. Gloag, "that McLauchlan speaks of there being a mask of people in the church. Mask is a fine Scotch word."

"Admirable," assented Mr. Dishart.

"I thought of mask," whimpered Tommy, "but that would mean the kirk was crammed, and I just meant it to be middling full."

"Flow would have done," suggested Mr. Lorrimer.

"Flow's but a handful," said Tommy.

"Curran, then, you jackanapes!"

"Curran's no enough."

Mr. Lorrimer flung up his hands in despair.

"I wanted something between curran and mask," said Tommy, dogged, yet almost at the crying.

Mr. Ogilvy, who had been hiding his admiration with difficulty, spread a net for him. "You said you wanted a word that meant middling full. Well, why did you not say middling full—or fell mask?"

"Yes, why not?" demanded the ministers, unconsciously caught in the net.

"I wanted one word," replied Tommy unconsciously avoiding it.

"You jewel!" muttered Mr. Ogilvy under his breath, but Mr. Cathro would have banged the boy's head had not the ministers interfered.

"It is so easy, too, to find the right word," said Mr. Gloag.

"It's no; it's as difficult as to hit a squirrel," cried Tommy, and again Mr. Ogilvy nodded approval.

But the ministers were only pained.

"The lad is merely a numskull," said Mr. Dishart, kindly.

"And no teacher could have turned him into anything else," said Mr. Duthie.

"And so, Cathro, you need not feel sore over your defeat," added Mr. Gloag; but nevertheless Cathro took Tommy by the neck and ran him out of the parish school of Thrums. When he returned to the others he found the ministers congratulating McLauchlan, whose nose was in the air, and complimenting Mr. Ogilvy, who listened to their formal phrases solemnly and accepted their hand-shakes with a dry chuckle.

"Ay, grin away, sir," the mortified dominie of Thrums said to him sourly, "the joke is on your side."

"You are right, sir," replied Mr. Ogilvy, mysteriously, "the joke is on my side, and the best of it is that not one of you knows what the joke is!"

And then an odd thing happened. As they were preparing to leave the school, the door opened a little and there appeared in the aperture the face of Tommy, tear-stained but excited. "I ken the word now," he cried, "it came to me a' at once; it is hantle!"

From MARGARET OGILVY

My Heroine

WHEN it was known that I had begun another story my mother might ask what it was to be about this time.

"Fine we can guess who it is about," my sister would say pointedly.

"Maybe you can guess, but it is beyond me," says my mother, with the meekness of one who knows that she is a dull person.

My sister scorned her at such times. "What woman is in all his books?" she would demand.

"I'm sure I canna say," replies my mother determinedly. "I thought the women were different every time."

"Mother, I wonder you can be so audacious! Fine you know what woman I mean."

"How can I know? What woman is it? You should bear in mind that I hinna your cleverness" (they were constantly giving each other little knocks).

"I won't give you the satisfaction of saying her name. But this I will say, it is high time he was keeping her out of his books."

And then as usual my mother would give herself away unconsciously.

"That is what I tell him," she says chuckling, "and he tries to keep me out, but he canna; it's more than he can do!"

On an evening after my mother had gone to bed, the first chapter would be brought upstairs, and I read, sitting at the foot of the bed, while my sister watched to make my mother behave herself, and my father cried H'sh! when there were interruptions. All would go well at the start, the reflections were accepted with a little nod of the head, the descriptions of scenery as ruts on the road that must be got over at a walking pace (my mother did not care for scenery, and that is why there is so little of it in my books). But now I am reading too quickly, a little apprehensively, because I know that the next paragraph begins with—let us say with, "Along this path came a woman": I had intended to rush on here in a loud bullying voice, but "Along this path came a woman" I read, and stop. Did I hear a faint sound from the other end of the bed? Perhaps I did not; I may only have been listening for it, but I falter and look up. My sister and I look sternly at my mother. She bites her under-lip and clutches the bed with both hands, really she is doing her best for me, but first comes a smothered gurgling sound, then her hold on herself relaxes and she shakes with mirth.

"That's a way to behave!" cries my sister.

"I cannot help it," my mother gasps.

"And there's nothing to laugh at."

"It's that woman," my mother explains unnecessarily.

"Maybe she's not the woman you think her," I say, crushed.

"Maybe not," says my mother doubtfully. "What was her name?"

"Her name," I answer with triumph, "was not Margaret"; but this makes her ripple again. "I have so many names nowadays," she mutters.

"H'sh!" says my father, and the reading is resumed.

Perhaps the woman who came along the path was of tall and majestic figure, which should have shown my mother that I had contrived to start my train without her this time. But it did not.

"What are you laughing at now?" says my sister severely. "Do you not hear that she was a tall, majestic woman?"

"It's the first time I ever heard it said of her," replies my mother.

"But she is."

"Ke fy, havers!"

"The book says it."

"There will be a many queer things in the book. What was she wearing?"

I have not described her clothes. "That's a mistake," says my mother. "When I come upon a woman in a book, the first thing I want to know about her is whether she was good-looking, and the second, how she was put on."

The woman on the path was eighteen years of age, and of remarkable beauty.

"That settles you," says my sister.

"I was no beauty at eighteen," my mother admits, but here my father interferes unexpectedly. "There wasna your like in this countryside at eighteen," says he stoutly.

"Pooh!" says she, well-pleased.

"Were you plain, then?" we ask.

"Sal," she replies briskly, "I was far from plain."

"H'sh!"

Perhaps in the next chapter this lady (or another) appears in a carriage.

"I assure you we're mounting in the world," I hear my mother murmur, but I hurry on without looking up. The lady lives in a house where there are footmen—but the footmen have come on the scene too hurriedly. "This is more than I can stand," gasps my mother, and just as she is getting the better of a fit of laughter, "Footman, give me a drink of water," she cries, and this sets her off again. Often the readings had to end abruptly because her mirth brought on violent fits of coughing.

Sometimes I read to my sister alone, and she assured me that she could not see my mother among the women this time. This she said to humor me. Presently she would slip upstairs to announce triumphantly, "You are in again!"

Or in the small hours I might make a confidant of my father, and when I had finished reading he would say thoughtfully, "That lassie is very natural. Some of the ways you say she had—your mother had them just the same. Did you ever notice what an extraordinary woman your mother is?"

Then would I seek my mother for comfort. She was the more ready to give it because of her profound conviction that if I was found out—that is, if readers discovered how frequently and in how many guises she appeared in my books—the affair would become a public scandal.

"You see Jess is not really you," I begin inquiringly.

"Oh, no, she is another kind of woman altogether," my mother says, and then spoils the compliment by adding naïvely, "She had but two rooms and I have six."

I sigh. "Without counting the pantry, and it's a great big pantry," she mutters.

This was not the sort of difference I could greatly plume myself upon, and honesty would force me to say, "As far as that goes, there was a time when you had but two rooms yourself——"

"That's long since," she breaks in. "I began with an up-the-stair, but I always had it in my mind—I never mentioned it, but there it was—to have the down-the-stair as well. Ay, and I've had it this many a year."

"Still, there is no denying that Jess had the same ambition."

"She had, but to her two-roomed house she had to stick all her born days. Was that like me?"

"No, but she wanted——"

"She wanted, and I wanted, but I got and she didna. That's the difference betwixt her and me."

"If that is all the difference, it is little credit I can claim for having created her."

My mother sees that I need soothing. "That is far from being all the difference," she would say eagerly. "There's my silk, for instance.

Though I say it mysel, there's not a better silk in the valley of Strathmore. Had Jess a silk of any kind—not to speak of a silk like that?"

"Well, she had no silk, but you remember how she got that cloak with beads."

"An eleven and a bit! Hoots, what was that to boast of! I tell you, every single yard of my silk cost——"

"Mother, that is the very way Jess spoke about her cloak!"

She lets this pass, perhaps without hearing it, for solicitude about her silk has hurried her to the wardrobe where it hangs.

"Ah, mother, I am afraid that was very like Jess!"

"How could it be like her when she didna even have a wardrobe? I tell you what, if there had been a real Jess and she had boasted to me about her cloak with beads, I would have said to her in a careless sort of voice, 'Step across with me, Jess, and I'll let you see something that is hanging in my wardrobe.' That would have lowered her pride!"

"I don't believe that is what you would have done, mother."

Then a sweeter expression would come into her face. "No," she would say reflectively, "it's not."

"What would you have done? I think I know."

"You canna know. But I'm thinking I would have called to mind that she was a poor woman, and ailing, and terrible windy about her cloak, and I would just have said it was a beauty and that I wished I had one like it."

"Yes, I am certain that is what you would have done. But oh, mother, that is just how Jess would have acted if some poorer woman than she had shown her a new shawl."

"Maybe, but though I hadna boasted about my silk I would have wanted to do it."

"Just as Jess would have been fidgeting to show off her eleven and a bit!"

It seems advisable to jump to another book; not to my first, because—well, as it was my first there would naturally be something of my mother in it, and not to the second, as it was my first novel and not much esteemed even in our family. (But the little touches of my mother in it are not so bad.) Let us try the story about the minister.

My mother's first remark is decidedly damping. "Many a time in my young days," she says, "I played about the Auld Licht manse, but I little thought I should live to be the mistress of it!"

"But Margaret is not you."

"N—no, oh no. She had a very different life from mine. I never let on to a soul that she is me!"

"She was not meant to be you when I began. Mother, what a way you have of coming creeping in!"

"You should keep better watch on yourself."

"Perhaps if I had called Margaret by some other name——"

"I should have seen through her just the same. As soon as I heard she was the mother I began to laugh. In some ways, though, she's no so very like me. She was long in finding out about Babbie. I'se uphaud I should have been quicker."

"Babbie, you see, kept close to the garden-wall."

"It's not the wall up at the manse that would have hidden her from me."

"She came out in the dark."

"I'm thinking she would have found me looking for her with a candle."

"And Gavin was secretive."

"That would have put me on my mettle."

"She never suspected anything."

"I wonder at her."

But my new heroine is to be a child. What has madam to say to that?

A child! Yes, she has something to say even to that. "This beats all!" are the words.

"Come, come, mother, I see what you are thinking, but I assure you that this time——"

"Of course not," she said soothingly, "oh, no, she canna be me"; but anon her real thoughts are revealed by the artless remark, "I doubt, though, this is a tough job you have on hand—it is so long since I was a bairn."

We came very close to each other in those talks. "It is a queer thing," she would say softly, "that near everything you write is about this bit place. You little expected that when you began. I mind well the time when it never entered your head, any more than mine, that you could write a page about our squares and wynds. I wonder how it has come about?"

There was a time when I could not have answered that question, but that time had long passed. "I suppose, mother, it was because you were most at home in your own town, and there was never much pleasure to me in writing of people who could not have known you, nor of squares and wynds you never passed through, nor of a countryside where you never carried your father's dinner in a flaggon. There is scarce a house in all my books where I have not seemed to see you a thousand times, bending over the fireplace or winding up the clock."

"And yet you used to be in such a quandary because you knew nobody you could make your women-folk out of! Do you mind that, and how we both laughed at the notion of your having to make them out of me?"

"I remember."

"And now you've gone back to my father's time. It's more than sixty years since I carried his dinner in a flaggon through the long parks of Kinnordy."

"I often go into the long parks, mother, and sit on the stile at the edge of the wood till I fancy I see a little girl coming toward me with a flaggon in her hand."

"Jumping the burn (I was once so proud of my jumps!) and swinging the flaggon round so quick that what was inside hadna time to fall out. I used to wear a magenta frock and a white pinafore. Did I ever tell you that?"

"Mother, the little girl in my story wears a magenta frock and a white pinafore."

"You minded that! But I'm thinking it wasna a lassie in a pinafore you saw in the long parks of Kinnordy, it was just a gey done auld woman."

"It was a lassie in a pinafore, mother, when she was far away, but when she came near it was a gey done auld woman."

"And a fell ugly one!"

"The most beautiful one I shall ever see."

"I wonder to hear you say it. Look at my wrinkled auld face."

"It is the sweetest face in all the world."

"See how the rings drop off my poor wasted finger."

"There will always be some one nigh, mother, to put them on again."

"Ay, will there! Well I know it. Do you mind how when you were but a bairn you used to say, 'Wait till I'm a man, and you'll never have a reason for greeting again'?"

I remember.

"You used to come running into the house to say, 'There's a proud dame going down the Marywellbrae in a cloak that is black on one side and white on the other; wait till I'm a man, and you'll have one the very same.' And when I lay on gey hard beds you said, 'When I'm a man you'll lie on feathers.' You saw nothing bonny, you never heard of my setting my heart on anything, but what you flung up your head and cried, 'Wait till I'm a man.' You fair shamed me before the neighbors, and yet I was windy, too. And now it has all come true like a dream. I can call to mind not one little thing I ettled for in my lusty days that hasna been put into my hands in my auld age; I sit here useless, surrounded by the gratification of all my wishes and all my ambitions, and at times I'm near terrified, for it's as if God had mista'en me for some other woman."

"Your hopes and ambitions were so simple," I would say, but she did not like that. "They werna that simple," she would answer, flushing.

I am reluctant to leave those happy days, but the end must be faced, and as I write I seem to see my mother growing smaller and her face more wistful, and still she lingers with us, as if God had said, "Child of mine, your time has come, be not afraid," and she was not afraid, but still she lingered, and He waited, smiling. I never read any of that last book to her; when it was finished she was too heavy with years to follow a story. To me this was as if my book must go out cold into the world (like all that may come after it from me), and my sister, who took more thought for others and less for herself than any other human being I have known, saw this, and by some means unfathomable to a man coaxed my mother into being once again the woman she had been. On a day but three weeks before she died my father and I were called softly upstairs. My mother was sitting bolt upright, as she loved to sit, in her old chair by the window, with a manuscript in her hands. But she was looking about her without much understanding. "Just to please him," my sister whispered, and then in a low, trembling voice my mother began to read. I looked at my sister. Tears of woe were stealing down her face. Soon the reading became very slow and stopped. After a pause, "There was something you were to say to him," my sister reminded her. "Luck," muttered a voice as from the dead, "luck." And then the old smile came running to her face like a lamp-lighter, and she said to me, "I am ower far gone to read, but I'm thinking I am in it again!" My father put her Testament in her hands, and it fell open—as it always does—at the Fourteenth of John. She made an effort to read but could not. Suddenly she stooped and kissed the broad page. "Will that do instead?" she asked.

R. L. S.

THESE familiar initials are, I suppose, the best beloved in recent literature, certainly they are the sweetest to me, but there was a time when my mother could not abide them. She said "That Stevenson man" with a sneer, and it was never easy to her to sneer. At thought of him her face would become almost hard, which seems incredible, and she would knit her lips and fold her arms, and reply with a stiff "oh" if you mentioned his aggravating name. In the novels we have a way of writing of our heroine, "she drew herself up haughtily," and when mine draw themselves up haughtily I see my mother thinking of Robert Louis Stevenson. He knew her opinion of him, and would write, "My ears tingled yesterday; I sair doubt she has been miscalling me again." But the more she miscalled him the more he delighted in her, and she was informed of this, and at once said "The scoundrel!" If you would know what was his unpardonable crime, it was this, he wrote better books than mine.

I remember the day she found it out, which was not, however, the day she admitted it. That day, when I should have been at my work, she came upon me in the kitchen, "The Master of Ballantrae" beside me, but I was not reading: my head lay heavy on the table and to her anxious eyes, I doubt not, I was the picture of woe. "Not writing!" I echoed, no, I was not writing, I saw no use in ever trying to write again. And down, I suppose, went my head once more. She misunderstood, and thought the blow had fallen; I had awakened to the discovery, always dreaded by her, that I had written myself dry; I was no better than an empty ink-bottle. She wrung her hands, but indignation came to her with my explanation, which was that while R. L. S. was at it we others were only 'prentices cutting our fingers on his tools. "I could never thole his books," said my mother immediately, and indeed vindictively.

"You have not read any of them," I reminded her.

"And never will," said she, with spirit.

And I have no doubt that she called him a dark character that very day. For weeks too, if not for months, she adhered to her determination not to read him, though I, having come to my senses and seen that there is a place for the 'prentice, was taking a pleasure, almost malicious, in putting "The Master of Ballantrae" in her way. I would place it on her table so that it said good-morning to her when she rose. She would frown, and carrying it downstairs, as if she had it in the tongs, replace it on its book-shelf. I would wrap it up in the cover she had made for the latest Carlyle: she would skin it contemptuously and again bring it down. I would hide her spectacles in it, and lay it on top of the clothes-basket and prop it up invitingly open against her tea-pot. And at last I got her, though I forget by which of many contrivances. What I recall vividly is a key-hole view, to which another member of the family invited me. Then I saw my mother wrapped up in "The Master of Ballantrae" and muttering the music to herself, nodding her head in approval, and taking a stealthy glance at the foot of each page before she began at the top. Nevertheless she had an ear for the door, for when I bounced in she had been too clever for me; there was no book to be seen, only an apron on her lap and she was gazing out at the window. Some such conversation as this followed:

"You have been sitting very quietly, mother."

"I always sit quietly, I never do anything, I'm just a finished stocking."

"Have you been reading?"

"Do I ever read at this time of day?"

"What is that in your lap?"

"Just my apron."

"Is that a book beneath the apron?"

"It might be a book."

"Let me see."

"Go away with you to your work."

But I lifted the apron. "Why, it's 'The Master of Ballantrae!'" I exclaimed, shocked.

"So it is!" said my mother, equally surprised. But I looked sternly at her, and perhaps she blushed.

"Well what do you think: not nearly equal to mine?" said I with humor.

"Nothing like them," she said determinedly.

"Not a bit," said I, though whether with a smile or a groan is immaterial; they would have meant the same thing. Should I put the book back on its shelf? I asked, and she replied that I could put it wherever I liked for all she cared, so long as I took it out of her sight (the implication was that it had stolen on to her lap while she was looking out at the window). My behavior may seem small, but I gave her a last chance, for I said that some people found it a book there was no putting down until they reached the last page.

"I'm no that kind," replied my mother.

Nevertheless our old game with the haver of a thing, as she called it, was continued, with this difference, that it was now she who carried the book covertly upstairs, and I who replaced it on the shelf, and several times we caught each other in the act, but not a word said either of us; we were grown self-conscious. Much of the play no doubt I forget, but one incident I remember clearly. She had come down to sit beside me while I wrote, and sometimes, when I looked up, her eye was not on me, but on the shelf where 'The Master of Ballantrae' stood inviting her. Mr. Stevenson's books are not for the shelf, they are for the hand;

even when you lay them down, let it be on the table for the next comer. Being the most sociable that man has penned in our time, they feel very lonely up there in a stately row. I think their eye is on you the moment you enter the room, and so you are drawn to look at them, and you take a volume down with the impulse that induces one to unchain the dog. And the result is not dissimilar, for in another moment you two are at play. Is there any other modern writer who gets round you in this way? Well, he had given my mother the look which in the ball-room means, "Ask me for this waltz," and she ettled to do it, but felt that her more dutiful course was to sit out the dance with this other less entertaining partner. I wrote on doggedly, but could hear the whispering.

"Am I to be a wall-flower?" asked James Durie reproachfully. (It must have been leap-year.)

"Speak lower," replied my mother, with an uneasy look at me.

"Pooh!" said James contemptuously, "that kail-runtle!"

"I winna have him miscalled," said my mother, frowning.

"I am done with him," said James (wiping his cane with his cambric handkerchief), and his sword clattered deliciously (I cannot think this was accidental), which made my mother sigh. Like the man he was, he followed up his advantage with a comparison that made me dip viciously.

"A prettier sound that," said he, clanking his sword again, "than the clack-clack of your young friend's shuttle."

"Whist!" cried my mother, who had seen me dip.

"Then give me your arm," said James, lowering his voice.

"I dare not," answered my mother. "He's so touchy about you."

"Come, come," he pressed her, "you are certain to do it sooner or later, so why not now?"

"Wait till he has gone for his walk," said my mother; "and, forby that, I'm ower old to dance with you."

"How old are you?" he inquired.

"You're gey an' pert!" cried my mother.

"Are you seventy?"

"Off and on," she admitted.

"Pooh!" he said, "a mere girl!"

She replied instantly, "I'm no to be catched with chaff"; but she smiled and rose as if he had stretched out his hand and got her by the finger-tip.

After that they whispered so low (which they could do as they were now much nearer each other) that I could catch only one remark. It came from James, and seems to show the tenor of their whisperings, for his words were, "Easily enough, if you slip me beneath your shawl."

That is what she did, and furthermore she left the room guiltily, muttering something about redding up the drawers. I suppose I smiled wanly to myself, or conscience must have been nibbling at my mother, for in less than five minutes she was back, carrying her accomplice openly, and she thrust him with positive viciousness into the place where my Stevenson had lost a tooth (as the writer whom he most resembled would have said). And then like a good mother she took up one of her son's books and read it most determinedly. It had become a touching incident to me, and I remember how we there and then agreed upon a compromise: she was to read the enticing thing just to convince herself of its inferiority.

"The Master of Ballantrae" is not the best. Conceive the glory, which was my mother's, of knowing from a trustworthy source that there are at least three better awaiting you on the same shelf. She did not know Alan Breck yet, and he was as anxious to step down as Mr. Bally himself. John Silver was there, getting into his leg, so that she should not have to wait a moment, and roaring, "I'll lay to that!" when she told me consolingly that she could not thole pirate stories. Not to know these gentlemen, what is it like? It is like never having been in love. But they are in the house! That is like knowing that you will fall in love to-morrow morning. With one word, by drawing one mournful face, I could have got my mother to adjure the jam-shelf—nay, I might have managed it by merely saying that she had enjoyed "The Master of Ballantrae." For you must remember that she only read it to persuade herself (and me) of its unworthiness, and that the reason she wanted to read the others was to get further proof. All this she made plain to me, eyeing me a little anxiously the while, and of course I accepted the explanation. Alan is the biggest child of them all, and I doubt not that she thought so, but curiously enough her views of him are among the things I have forgotten. But how enamored she was of "Treasure Island," and how faithful she tried to be to me all the time she was reading it! I had to put my hands over her eyes to let her know that I had entered the room, and even then she might try to read between my fingers, coming to herself presently, however, to say "It's a haver of a book."

"Those pirate stories are so uninteresting," I would reply without fear, for she was too engrossed to see through me. "Do you think you will finish this one?"

"I may as well go on with it since I have begun it," my mother says, so slily that my sister and I shake our heads at each other to imply, "Was there ever such a woman!"

"There are none of those one-legged scoundrels in my books," I say.

"Better without them," she replies promptly.

"I wonder, mother, what it is about the man that so infatuates the public?"

"He takes no hold of me," she insists. "I would a hantle rather read your books."

I offer obligingly to bring one of them to her, and now she looks at me suspiciously. "You surely believe I like yours best," she says with instant anxiety, and I soothe her by assurances, and retire advising her to read on, just to see if she can find out how he misleads the public. "Oh, I may take a look at it again by and by," she says indifferently, but nevertheless the probability is that as the door shuts the book opens, as if by some mechanical contrivance. I remember how she read "Treasure Island," holding it close to the ribs of the fire (because she could not spare a moment to rise and light the gas), and how, when bed-time came, and we coaxed, remonstrated, scolded, she said quite fiercely, clinging to the book, "I dinna lay my head on a pillow this night till I see how that laddie got out of the barrel."

After this, I think, he was as bewitching as the laddie in the barrel to her—Was he not always a laddie in the barrel himself, climbing in for apples while we all stood around, like gamins, waiting for a bite? He was the spirit of boyhood tugging at the skirts of this old world of ours and compelling it to come back and play. And I suppose my mother felt this, as so many have felt it: like others she was a little scared at first to find herself skipping again, with this masterful child at the rope, but soon she gave him her hand and set off with him for the meadow, not an apology between the two of them for the author left behind. But never to the end did she admit (in words) that he had a way with him which was beyond her son. "Silk and sacking, that is what we are," she was informed, to which she would reply obstinately, "Well, then, I prefer sacking."

"But if he had been your son?"

"But he is not!"

"You wish he were?"

"I dinna deny but what I could have found room for him."

And still at times she would smear him with the name of black (to his delight when he learned the reason). That was when some podgy red-sealed blue-crossed letter arrived from Vailima, inviting me to journey thither. (His directions were, "You take the boat at San Francisco, and then my place is the second to the left.") Even London seemed to her to carry me so far away that I often took a week to the journey (the first six days in getting her used to the idea), and these letters terrified her. It was not the finger of Jim Hawkins she now saw beckoning me across the seas, it was John Silver, waving a crutch. Seldom, I believe, did I read straight through one of these Vailima letters; when in the middle I suddenly remembered who was upstairs and what she was probably doing, and I ran to her, three steps at a jump, to find her, lips pursed, hands folded, a picture of gloom.

"I have a letter from——"

"So I have heard."

"Would you like to hear it?"

"No."

"Can you not abide him?"

"I canna thole him."

"Is he a black?"

"He is all that."

Well, Vailima was the one spot on earth I had any great craving to visit, but I think she always knew I would never leave her. Sometime, she said, she should like me to go, but not until she was laid away. "And how small I have grown this last winter. Look at my wrists. It canna be long now." No, I never thought of going, was never absent for a day from her without reluctance, and never walked so quickly as when I was going back. In the meantime that happened which put an end for ever to my scheme of travel. I shall never go up the Road of Loving Hearts now, on "a wonderful clear night of stars," to meet the man coming toward me on a horse. It is still a wonderful clear night of stars, but the road is empty. So I never saw the dear king of us all. But before he had written books he was in my part of the country with a fishing wand in his hand, and I like to think that I was the boy who met him that day by Queen Margaret's burn, where the rowans are, and busked a fly for him, and stood watching, while his lithe figure rose and fell as he cast and hinted back from the crystal waters of Noran-side.

From The Little White Bird

The Inconsiderate Waiter

They were the family of William, one of our club waiters who had been disappointing me grievously of late. Many a time have I deferred dining several minutes that I might have the attendance of this ingrate. His efforts to reserve the window-table for me were satisfactory, and I used to allow him privileges, as to suggest dishes; I have given him information, as that some one had startled me in the reading-room by slamming a door; I have shown him how I cut my finger with a piece of string. William was none of your assertive waiters. We could have plotted a murder safely before him. It was one member who said to him that Saucy Sarah would win the Derby and another who said that Saucy Sarah had no chance, but it was William who agreed with both. The excellent fellow (as I thought him) was like a cheroot which may be smoked from either end.

I date his lapse from one evening when I was dining by the window. I had to repeat my order "Devilled kidney," and instead of answering brightly, "Yes, sir," as if my selection of devilled kidney was a personal gratification to him, which is the manner one expects of a waiter, he gazed eagerly out at the window, and then, starting, asked, "Did you say devilled kidney, sir?" A few minutes afterward I became aware that some one was leaning over the back of my chair, and you may conceive my indignation on discovering that this rude person was William. Let me tell, in the measured words of one describing a past incident, what next took place. To get nearer the window he pressed heavily on my shoulder. "William," I said, "you are not attending to me!"

To be fair to him, he shook, but never shall I forget his audacious apology, "Beg pardon, sir, but I was thinking of something else."

And immediately his eyes resought the window, and this burst from him passionately, "For God's sake, sir, as we are man and man, tell me if you have seen a little girl looking up at the club-windows."

Man and man! But he had been a good waiter once, so I pointed out the girl to him. As soon as she saw William she ran into the middle of Pall Mall, regardless of hansoms (many of which seemed to pass over her), nodded her head significantly three times and then disappeared (probably on a stretcher). She was the tawdriest little Arab of about ten years, but seemed to have brought relief to William. "Thank God!" said he fervently, and in the worst taste.

I was as much horrified as if he had dropped a plate on my toes. "Bread, William," I said sharply.

"You are not vexed with me, sir?" he had the hardihood to whisper.

"It was a liberty," I said.

"I know, sir, but I was beside myself."

"That was a liberty again."

"It is my wife, sir, she—"

So William, whom I had favored in so many ways, was a married man. I felt that this was the greatest liberty of all.

I gathered that the troublesome woman was ailing, and as one who likes after dinner to believe that there is no distress in the world, I desired to be told by William that the signals meant her return to health. He answered inconsiderately, however, that the doctor feared the worst.

"Bah, the doctor," I said in a rage.

"Yes, sir," said William.

"What is her confounded ailment?"

"She was allus one of the delicate kind, but full of spirit, and you see, sir, she has had a baby-girl lately—"

"William, how dare you," I said, but in the same moment I saw that this father might be useful to me. "How does your baby sleep, William?" I asked in a low voice, "how does she wake up? what do you put in her bath?"

I saw surprise in his face, so I hurried on without waiting for an answer. "That little girl comes here with a message from your wife?"

"Yes, sir, every evening; she's my eldest, and three nods from her means that the missus is a little better."

"There were three nods to-day?"

"Yes, sir."

"I suppose you live in some low part, William?"

The impudent fellow looked as if he could have struck me. "Off Drury Lane," he said, flushing, "but it isn't low. And now," he groaned, "she's afeared she will die without my being there to hold her hand."

"She should not say such things."

"She never says them, sir. She allus pretends to be feeling stronger. But I knows what is in her mind when I am leaving the house in the morning, for then she looks at me from her bed, and I looks at her from the door—oh, my God, sir!"

"William!"

At last he saw that I was angry, and it was characteristic of him to beg my pardon and withdraw his wife as if she were some unsuccessful dish. I tried to forget his vulgar story in billiards, but he had spoiled my game, and next day to punish him I gave my orders through another waiter. As I had the window-seat, however, I could not but see that the little girl was late, and though this mattered nothing to me and I had finished my dinner, I lingered till she came. She not only nodded three times but waved her hat, and I arose, having now finished my dinner.

William came stealthily toward me. "Her temperature has gone down, sir," he said, rubbing his hands together.

"To whom are you referring?" I asked coldly, and retired to the billiard-room, where I played a capital game.

I took pains to show William that I had forgotten his maunderings, but I observed the girl nightly, and once, instead of nodding, she shook her head, and that evening I could not get into a pocket. Next evening there was no William in the dining-room, and I thought I knew what had happened. But, chancing to enter the library rather miserably, I was surprised to see him on a ladder dusting books. We had the room practically to ourselves, for though several members sat on chairs holding books in their hands they were all asleep, and William descended the ladder to tell me his blasting tale. He had sworn at a member!

"I hardly knew what I was doing all day, sir, for I had left her so weakly that——"

I stamped my foot.

"I beg your pardon for speaking of her," he had the grace to say. "But Irene had promised to come every two hours; and when she came about four o'clock and I saw she was crying, it sort of blinded me, sir, and I stumbled against a member, Mr. B——, and he said, 'Damn you!' Well, sir, I had but touched him after all, and I was so broken it sort of stung me to be treated so, and I lost my senses, and I said, 'Damn *you!*'"

His shamed head sank on his chest, and I think some of the readers shuddered in their sleep.

"I was turned out of the dining-room at once, and sent here until the committee have decided what to do with me. Oh, sir, I am willing to go on my knees to Mr. B——"

How could I but despise a fellow who would be thus abject for a pound a week?

"For if I have to tell her I have lost my place she will just fall back and die."

"I forbid your speaking to me of that woman," I cried wryly, "unless you can speak pleasantly," and I left him to his fate and went off to look for B——. "What is this story about your swearing at one of the waiters?" I asked him.

"You mean about his swearing at me," said B——, reddening.

"I am glad that was it," I said, "for I could not believe you guilty of such bad form. The version which reached me was that you swore at each other, and that he was to be dismissed and you reprimanded."

"Who told you that?" asked B——, who is a timid man.

"I am on the committee," I replied lightly, and proceeded to talk of other matters, but presently B——, who had been reflecting, said: "Do you know I fancy I was wrong in thinking that the waiter swore at me, and I shall withdraw the charge to-morrow."

I was pleased to find that William's troubles were near an end without my having to interfere in his behalf, and I then remembered that he would not be able to see the girl Irene from the library windows, which are at the back of the club. I was looking down at her, but she refrained from signalling because she could not see William, and irritated by her stupidity I went out and asked her how her mother was.

"My," she ejaculated after a long scrutiny of me, "I b'lieve you are one of them!" and she gazed at me with delighted awe. I suppose William tells them of our splendid doings.

The invalid, it appeared, was a bit better, and this annoying child wanted to inform William that she had took all the tapiocar. She was to indicate this by licking an imaginary plate in the middle of Pall Mall. I gave the little vulgarian a shilling, and returned to the club disgusted.

"By the way, William," I said, "Mr. B—— is to inform the committee that he was mistaken in thinking you used improper language to him, so you will doubtless be restored to the dining-room to-morrow."

I had to add immediately, "Remember your place, William."

"But Mr. B—— knows I swore," he insisted.

"A gentleman," I replied stiffly, "cannot remember for many hours what a waiter has said to him."

"No, sir, but—"

To stop him I had to say, "And—ah—William, your wife is decidedly better. She has eaten the tapioca—all of it."

"How can you know, sir?"

"By an accident."

"Irene signed to the window?"

"No."

"Then you saw her and went out and—"

"How dare you, William?"

"Oh, sir, to do that for me! May God bl—"

"William."

He was reinstated in the dining-room, but often when I looked at him I seemed to see a dying wife in his face, and so the relations between us were still strained. But I watched the girl, and her pantomime was so illuminating that I knew the sufferer had again cleaned the platter on Tuesday, had attempted a boiled egg on Wednesday (you should have seen Irene chipping it in Pall Mall, and putting in the salt), but was in a woful state of relapse on Thursday.

"Is your mother very ill to-day, Miss Irene?" I asked, as soon as I had drawn her out of range of the club-windows.

"My!" she exclaimed again, and I saw an ecstatic look pass between her and a still smaller girl with her, whom she referred to as a neighbor.

I waited coldly. William's wife, I was informed, had looked like nothing but a dead one till she got the brandy.

"Hush, child," I said, shocked. "You don't know how the dead look."

"Bless yer!" she replied.

Assisted by her friend, who was evidently enormously impressed by Irene's intimacy with me, she gave me a good deal of miscellaneous information, as that William's real name was Mr. Hicking, but that he was known in their street, because of the number of his shirts, as Toff Hicking. That the street held he should get away from the club before two in the morning, for his missus needed him more than the club needed him. That William replied (very sensibly) that if the club was short of waiters at supper-time some of the gentlemen might be kept waiting for their marrow-bone. That he sat up with his missus most of the night, and pretended to her that he got some nice long naps at the club. That what she talked to him about mostly was the kid. That the kid was in another part of London (in charge of a person called the old woman), because there was an epidemic in Irene's street.

"And what does the doctor say about your mother?"

"He sometimes says she would have a chance if she could get her kid back."

"Nonsense."

"And if she was took to the country."

"Then why does not William take her?"

"My! And if she drank porty wine."

"Doesn't she?"

"No. But father, he tells her 'bout how the gentlemen drinks it."

I turned from her with relief, but she came after me.

"Ain't yer going to do it this time?" she demanded with a falling face. "You done it last time. I tell her you done it"—she pointed to her friend who was looking wistfully at me—"ain't you to let her see you doing of it?"

For a moment I thought that her desire was another shilling, but by a piece of pantomime she showed that she wanted me to lift my hat to her. So I lifted it, and when I looked behind she had her head in the air and her neighbor was gazing at her awestruck. These little creatures are really not without merit.

About a week afterward I was in a hired landau, holding a newspaper before my face lest any one should see me in company of a waiter and his wife. William was taking her into Surrey to stay with an old nurse of mine, and Irene was with us, wearing the most outrageous bonnet.

I formed a mean opinion of Mrs. Hicking's intelligence from her pride in the baby, which was a very ordinary one. She created a regrettable scene when it was brought to her, because "she had been feared it would not know her again." I could have told her that they know no one for years had I not been in terror of Irene, who dandled the child on her knees and talked to it all the way. I have never known a bolder little hussy than this Irene. She asked the infant improper questions, such as "Oo know who gave me this bonnet?" and answered them herself. "It was the pretty gentleman there," and several times I had to affect sleep, because she announced, "Kiddy wants to kiss the pretty gentleman."

Irksome as all this necessarily was to a man of taste, I suffered still more acutely when we reached our destination, where disagreeable circumstances compelled me to drink tea with a waiter's family. William knew that I regarded thanks from persons of his class as an outrage, yet he looked them though he dared not speak them. Hardly had he sat down at the table by my orders than he remembered that I was a member of the club and jumped up. Nothing is in worse form than whispering, yet again and again he whispered to his poor, foolish wife, "How are you now? You don't feel faint?" and when she said she felt like another woman already, his face charged me with the change. I could not but conclude from the way she let the baby pound her that she was stronger than she pretended.

I remained longer than was necessary because I had something to say to William which I feared he would misunderstand, but when he announced that it was time for him to catch a train back to London, at which his wife paled, I delivered the message.

"William," I said, backing away from him, "the head-waiter asked me to say that you could take a fortnight's holiday. Your wages will be paid as usual."

Confound him.

"William," I cried furiously, "go away."

Then I saw his wife signing to him, and I knew she wanted to be left alone with me.

"William," I cried in a panic, "stay where you are."

But he was gone, and I was alone with a woman whose eyes were filmy. Her class are fond of scenes. "If you please, ma'am!" I said imploringly.

But she kissed my hand; she was like a little dog.

"It can be only the memory of some woman," said she, "that makes you so kind to me and mine."

Memory was the word she used, as if all my youth were fled. I suppose I really am quite elderly.

"I should like to know her name, sir," she said, "that I may mention her with loving respect in my prayers."

I raised the woman and told her the name. It was not Mary. "But she has a home," I said, "as you have, and I have none. Perhaps, ma'am, it would be better worth your while to mention me."

It was this woman, now in health, whom I intrusted with the purchase of the outfits, "one for a boy of six months," I explained to her, "and one for a boy of a year," for the painter had boasted to me of David's rapid growth. I think she was a little surprised to find that both outfits were for the same house; and she certainly betrayed an ignoble curiosity about the mother's Christian name, but she was much easier to brow-beat than a fine lady would have been, and I am sure she and her daughter enjoyed themselves hugely in the shops, from one of which I shall never forget Irene emerging proudly with a commissionaire, who conducted her under an umbrella to the cab where I was lying in wait. I think that was the most celestial walk of Irene's life.

I told Mrs. Hicking to give the articles a little active ill-treatment that they might not look quite new, at which she exclaimed, not being in my secret, and then to forward them to me. I then sent them to Mary and rejoiced in my devilish cunning all the evening, but chagrin came in the morning with a letter from her which showed she knew all, that I was her Mr. Anon, and that there never had been a Timothy. I think I was never so gravelled. Even now I don't know how she had contrived it.

Her cleverness raised such a demon in me that I locked away her letter at once and have seldom read it since. No married lady should have indited such an epistle to a single man. It said, with other things which I decline to repeat, that I was her good fairy. As a sample of the deliberate falsehoods in it, I may mention that she said David loved me already. She hoped that I would come in often to see her husband, who was very proud of my friendship, and suggested that I should pay him my first visit to-day at three o'clock, an hour at which, as I happened to know, he is always away giving a painting lesson. In short, she wanted first to meet me alone, so that she might draw the delicious, respectful romance out of me, and afterward repeat it to him, with sighs and little peeps at him over her pocket handkerchief.

She had dropped what were meant to look like two tears for me upon the paper, but I should not wonder though they were only artful drops of water.

I sent her a stiff and tart reply, declining to hold any communication with her.

FRANCIS THOMPSON (1860-1907)

Daisy

WHERE the thistle lifts a purple crown
Six foot out of the turf,
And the harebell shakes on the windy hill—
O breath of the distant surf!—

The hills look over on the South,
And southward dreams the sea;
And with the sea-breeze hand in hand
Came innocence and she.

Where 'mid the gorse the raspberry
Red for the gatherer springs,
Two children did we stray and talk
Wise, idle, childish things.

She listened with big-lipped surprise,
Breast-deep 'mid flower and spine:
Her skin was like a grape whose veins
Run snow instead of wine.

She knew not those sweet words she spake,
Nor knew her own sweet way;
But there's never a bird, so sweet a song
Thronged in whose throat that day.

Oh, there were flowers in Storrington
On the turf and on the spray;
But the sweetest flower on Sussex hills
Was the Daisy-flower that day!

Her beauty smoothed earth's furrowed face.
She gave me tokens three:—
A look, a word of her winsome mouth,
And a wild raspberry.

A berry red, a guileless look,
A still word,—strings of sand!
And yet they made my wild, wild heart
Fly down to her little hand.

For standing artless as the air,
And candid as the skies,
She took the berries with her hand,
And the love with her sweet eyes.

The fairest things have fleetest end,
Their scent survives their close:
But the rose's scent is bitterness
To him that loved the rose.

She looked a little wistfully,
Then went her sunshine way:—
The sea's eye had a mist on it,
And the leaves fell from the day.

She went her unremembering way,
She went and left in me
The pang of all the partings gone,
And partings yet to be.

She left me marvelling why my soul
Was sad that she was glad;
At all the sadness in the sweet,
The sweetness in the sad.

Still, still I seemed to see her, still
Look up with soft replies,
And take the berries with her hand,
And the love with her lovely eyes.

Nothing begins, and nothing ends,
That is not paid with moan;
For we are born in other's pain,
And perish in our own.

The Poppy

SUMMER set lip to earth's bosom bare,
And left the flushed print in a poppy there:
Like a yawn of fire from the grass it came,
And the fanning wind puffed it to flapping flame.

With burnt mouth, red like a lion's, it drank
The blood of the sun as he slaughtered sank,
And dipped its cup in the purpurate shine
When the Eastern conduits ran with wine.

Till it grew lethargied with fierce bliss,
And hot as a swinked gipsy is,
And drowsed in sleepy savageries,
With mouth wide a-pout for a sultry kiss.

A child and man paced side by side,
Treading the skirts of eventide;
But between the clasp of his hand and hers
Lay, felt not, twenty withered years.

She turned, with the rout of her dusk South hair,
And saw the sleeping gipsy there:
And snatched and snapped it in swift child's whim,
With—"Keep it, long as you live!"—to him.

And his smile, as nymphs from their laving meres,
Trembled up from a bath of tears;
And joy, like a mew sea-rocked apart,
Tossed on the waves of his troubled heart.

For *he* saw what she did not see,
That—as kindled by its own fervency—
The verge shrivelled inward smoulderingly:
And suddenly 'twixt his hand and hers
He knew the twenty withered years—
No flower, but twenty shrivelled years.

"Was never such thing until this hour,"
Low to his heart he said; "the flower
Of sleep brings wakening to me,
And of oblivion, memory."

"Was never this thing to me," he said,
"Though with bruisèd poppies my feet are red!"
And again to his own heart very low:
"Oh child! I love, for I love and know;

"But you, who love nor know at all
The diverse chambers in Love's guest-hall,
Where some rise early, few sit long:
In how differing accents hear the throng
His great Pentecostal tongue;

"Who know not love from amity,
Nor my reported self from me;
A fair fit gift is this, meseems,
You give—this withering flower of dreams.

"O frankly fickle, and fickly true,
Do you know what the days will do to you?
To your love and you what the days will do,
O frankly fickle, and fickly true?

"You have loved me, Fair, three lives—or days:
'Twill pass with the passing of my face.
But where *I* go, your face goes too,
To watch lest I play false to you.

"I am but, my sweet, your foster-lover,
Knowing well when certain years are over
You vanish from me to another;
Yet I know, and love, like the foster-mother.

"So, frankly fickle, and fickly true!
For my brief life-while I take from you
This token, fair and fit, meseems,
For me—this withering flower of dreams."

The sleep-flower sways in the wheat its head,
Heavy with dreams, as that with bread:
The goodly grain and the sun-flushed sleeper
The reaper reaps, and Time the reaper.

I hang 'mid men my needless head,
And my fruit is dreams, as theirs is bread:
The goodly men and the sun-hazed sleeper
Time shall reap, but after the reaper
The world shall glean of me, me the sleeper.

Love, love! your flower of withered dream
In leavèd rhyme lies safe, I deem,
Sheltered and shut in a nook of rhyme,
From the reaper man, and his reaper Time.

Love! *I* fall into the claws of Time:
But lasts within a leavèd rhyme
All that the world of me esteems—
My withered dreams, my withered dreams.

The Hound of Heaven

I FLED Him, down the nights and down the days;
I fled Him, down the arches of the years;
I fled Him, down the labyrinthine ways
Of my own mind; and in the mist of tears
I hid from Him, and under running laughter.
Up vistaed hopes I sped;
And shot, precipitated,
Adown Titanic glooms of chasmèd fears,
From those strong Feet that followed, followed after.
But with unhurrying chase,
And unperturbèd pace,
Deliberate speed, majestic instancy,
They beat—and a Voice beat
More instant than the Feet—
"All things betray thee, who betrayest Me."

I pleaded, outlaw-wise,
By many a hearted casement, curtained red,
Trellised with intertwining charities;
(For, though I knew His love Who followèd,
Yet was I sore adread
Lest, having Him, I must have naught beside.)
But, if one little casement parted wide,
The gust of His approach would clash it to:
Fear wist not to evade, as Love wist to pursue.
Across the margent of the world I fled,
And troubled the gold gateways of the stars,
Smiting for shelter on their clangèd bars;
Fretted to dulcet jars
And silvern chatter the pale ports o' the moon.
I said to Dawn: Be sudden—to Eve: Be soon;
With thy young skiey blossoms heap me over
From this tremendous Lover—
Float thy vague veil about me, lest He see!
I tempted all His servitors, but to find!
My own betrayal in their constancy,
In faith to Him their fickleness to me,
Their traitorous trueness, and their loyal deceit.
To all swift things for swiftness did I sue;
Clung to the whistling mane of every wind.
But whether they swept, smoothly fleet,
The long savannahs of the blue;
Or whether, Thunder-driven,
They clanged his chariot 'thwart a heaven,
Plashy with flying lightnings round the spurn o' their feet:—
Fear wist not to evade as Love wist to pursue.
Still with unhurrying chase,
And unperturbèd pace,
Deliberate speed, majestic instancy,
Came on the following Feet,
And a Voice above their beat—
"Naught shelters thee, who wilt not shelter Me."

I sought no more that after which I strayed
In face of man or maid;

But still within the little children's eyes
Seems something, something that replies,
They at least are for me, surely for me!
I turned me to them very wistfully;
But just as their young eyes grew sudden fair
With dawning answers there,
Their angel plucked them from me by the hair.
"Come then, ye other children, Nature's—share
With me" (said I) "your delicate fellowship;
Let me greet you lip to lip,
Let me twine with you caresses,
Wantoning
With our Lady-Mother's vagrant tresses,
Banqueting
With her in her wind-walled palace,
Underneath her azured daïs,
Quaffing, as your taintless way is,
From a chalice
Lucent-weeping out of the dayspring."
So it was done:
I in their delicate fellowship was one—
Drew the bolt of Nature's secrecies.
I knew all the swift importings
On the wilful face of skies;
I knew how the clouds arise
Spumèd of the wild sea-snortings;
All that's born or dies
Rose and drooped with; made them shapers
Of mine own moods, or wailful or divine;
With them joyed and was bereaven.
I was heavy with the even,
When she lit her glimmering tapers
Round the day's dead sanctities.
I laughed in the morning's eyes.
I triumphed and I saddened with all weather,
Heaven and I wept together,
And its sweet tears were salt with mortal mine;
Against the red throb of its sunset-heart
I laid my own to beat,
And share commingling heat;
But not by that, by that, was eased my human smart.
In vain my tears were wet on Heaven's grey cheek.
For ah! we know not what each other says,
These things and I; in sound *I* speak—
Their sound is but their stir, they speak by silences.
Nature, poor stepdame, cannot slake my drouth;
Let her, if she would owe me,
Drop yon blue bosom-veil of sky, and show me
The breasts o' her tenderness:
Never did any milk of hers once bless
My thirsting mouth.
Nigh and nigh draws the chase,
With unperturbèd pace,
Deliberate speed, majestic instancy;
And past those noisèd Feet
A voice comes yet more fleet—
"Lo! naught contents thee, who content'st not Me."

Naked I wait Thy love's uplifted stroke!
My harness piece by piece Thou hast hewn from me,
And smitten me to my knee;
I am defenceless utterly.
I slept, methinks, and woke,
And, slowly gazing, find me stripped in sleep.
In the rash lustihead of my young powers,
I shook the pillaring hours
And pulled my life upon me; grimed with smears,
I stand amid the dust o' the mounded years—
My mangled youth lies dead beneath the heap.
My days have crackled and gone up in smoke,
Have puffed and burst as sun-starts on a stream.
Yea, faileth now even dream
The dreamer, and the lute the lutanist;

Even the linked fantasies, in whose blossomy twist
I swung the earth a trinket at my wrist,
Are yielding; cords of all too weak account
For earth with heavy griefs so overplussed.
Ah! is Thy love indeed
A weed, albeit an amaranthine weed,
Suffering no flowers except its own to mount?
Ah! must—
Designer infinite!—
Ah! must Thou char the wood ere Thou canst limn with it?
My freshness spent its wavering shower i' the dust;
And now my heart is as a broken fount,
Wherein tear-drippings stagnate, spilt down ever
From the dank thoughts that shiver
Upon the sighful branches of my mind.
Such is; what is to be?
The pulp so bitter, how shall taste the rind?
I dimly guess what Time in mists confounds;
Yet ever and anon a trumpet sounds
From the hid battlements of Eternity;
Those shaken mists a space unsettle, then
Round the half-glimpsèd turrets slowly wash again.
But not ere him who summoneth
first have seen, enwound
With glooming robes purpureal, cypress-crowned;
His name I know, and what his trumpet saith.
Whether man's heart or life it be which yields
Thee harvest, must Thy harvest-fields
Be dunged with rotten death?

Now of that long pursuit
Comes on at hand the bruit;
That Voice is round me like a bursting sea:
"And is thy earth so marred,
Shattered in shard on shard?
Lo, all things fly thee, for thou fliest Me!
Strange, piteous, futile thing!
Wherefore should any set thee love apart?
Seeing none but I makes much of naught"
(He said),
"And human love needs human meriting:
How hast thou merited—
Of all man's clotted clay the dingiest clot?
Alack, thou knowest not
How little worthy of any love thou art!
Whom wilt thou find to love ignoble thee,
Save Me, save only Me?
All which I took from thee I did but take,
Not for thy harms,
But just that thou might'st seek it in My arms.
All which thy child's mistake
Fancies as lost, I have stored for thee at home:
Rise, clasp My hand, and come!"
Halts by me that footfall:
Is my gloom, after all,
Shade of His hand, outstretched caressingly?
"Ah, fondest, blindest, weakest,
I am He Whom thou seekest!
Thou dravest love from thee, who dravest Me."

WILLIAM BUTLER YEATS

The Lake Isle of Innisfree

I WILL arise and go now, and go to Innisfree,
And a small cabin build there, of clay and wattles made;
Nine bean rows will I have there, a hive for the honey bee,
And live alone in the bee-loud glade.

And I shall have some peace there, for peace comes dropping slow,
Dropping from the veils of the morning to where the cricket sings;
There midnight's all a glimmer, and noon a purple glow,
And evening full of the linnets' wings.

I will arise and go now, for always night and day
I hear lake water lapping with low sounds by the shore;
While I stand on the roadway, or on the pavements gray,
I hear it in the deep heart's core.

From CATHLEEN NI HOOLIHAN

One day in 1798, in a cottage close to Killala, Peter Gillane and his wife Bridget were busy with thoughts of the approaching wedding of their elder son Michael to Delia Cahel. The younger son, Patrick, a lad of twelve, saw an old woman wandering along the road, and watched her from the window. First she turned into the gap that went down to where Murteen and his sons were shearing their sheep. Patrick recalled a story of a strange woman that goes through the country whatever time there is war or trouble coming. Michael had just come in with Delia's marriage portion, a hundred pounds, and sent Patrick down to the town to see what might be causing the cheering they had heard, and Peter was glorying in the hundred pounds that Michael had brought home, when the poor old woman came to their own door.

PERSONS

PETER GILLANE
MICHAEL GILLANE.—*His son, going to be married*
PATRICK GILLANE.—*A lad of twelve,* MICHAEL'S *brother*
BRIDGET GILLANE.—*Peter's wife*
DELIA CAHEL.—*Engaged to* MICHAEL
THE POOR OLD WOMAN
NEIGHBOURS

SCENE: *Interior of a cottage close to Killala, in 1798.*

MICHAEL. They're not done cheering yet. [*He goes over to the door and stands there for a moment, putting up his hand to shade his eyes.*]

BRIDGET. Do you see anything?

MICHAEL. I see an old woman coming up the path.

BRIDGET. Who is it, I wonder?

MICHAEL. I don't think it's one of the neighbours, but she has her cloak over her face.

BRIDGET. Maybe it's the same woman Patrick saw a while ago. It might be some poor woman heard we were making ready for the wedding, and came to look for her share.

PETER. I may as well put the money out of sight. There's no use leaving it out for every stranger to look at. [*He goes over to a large box by the wall, opens it and puts the bag in, and fumbles with the lock.*]

MICHAEL. There she is, father! [*An* OLD WOMAN *passes the window slowly. She looks at* MICHAEL *as she passes.*] I'd sooner a stranger not to come to the house the night before the wedding.

BRIDGET. Open the door, Michael; don't keep the poor woman waiting. [*The* OLD WOMAN *comes in;* MICHAEL *stands aside to make way for her.*]

THE POOR OLD WOMAN. God save all here!

PETER. God save you kindly.

THE POOR OLD WOMAN. You have good shelter here.

PETER. You are welcome to whatever shelter we have.

BRIDGET. Sit down there by the fire and welcome.

THE POOR OLD WOMAN [*warming her hands*]. There's a hard wind outside.

MICHAEL *watches her curiously from the door.* PETER *comes over to the table.*

PETER. Have you travelled far to-day?

THE POOR OLD WOMAN. I have travelled far, very far; there are few have travelled so far as myself.

PETER. It is a pity, indeed, for any person to have no place of their own.

THE POOR OLD WOMAN. That is true for you indeed, and it is long I am on the road since I first went wandering. It is seldom I have any rest.

BRIDGET. It is a wonder you are not worn out with so much wandering.

THE POOR OLD WOMAN. Sometimes my feet are tired and my hands are quiet, but there is no quiet in my heart. When the people see me quiet, they think old age has come on me, and that all the stir has gone out of me.

BRIDGET. What was it put you astray?

THE POOR OLD WOMAN. Too many strangers in the house.

BRIDGET. Indeed you look as if you had had your share of trouble.

THE POOR OLD WOMAN. I have had trouble indeed.

BRIDGET. What was it put the trouble on you?

THE POOR OLD WOMAN. My land that was taken from me.

PETER. Was it much land they took from you?

THE POOR OLD WOMAN. My four beautiful green fields.

PETER. [*aside to* BRIDGET]. Do you think could she be the Widow Casey that was put out of her holding at Kilglas a while ago?

BRIDGET. She is not. I saw the Widow Casey one time at the market in Ballina, a stout, fresh woman.

PETER [*to* OLD WOMAN]. Did you hear a noise of cheering, and you coming up the hill?

THE POOR OLD WOMAN. I thought I heard the noise I used to hear when my friends came to visit me. [*She begins singing half to herself*]

I will go cry with the woman,
For yellow-haired Donough is dead;
With a hempen rope for a neckcloth
And a white cloth on his head.

MICHAEL [*coming from the door*]. What is that you are singing, ma'am?

THE POOR OLD WOMAN. Singing I am about a man I knew one time, yellow-haired Donough, that was hanged in Galway. [*She goes on singing much louder*]

I am come to cry with you, woman,
My hair is unwound and unbound;
I remember him ploughing his field,
Turning up the red side of the ground.

And building his barn on the hill
With the good mortared stone;
O! we'd have pulled down the gallows
Had it happened in Enniscrone!

MICHAEL. What was it brought him to his death?

THE POOR OLD WOMAN. He died for love of me; many a man has died for love of me.

PETER [*aside to* BRIDGET]. Her trouble has put her wits astray.

MICHAEL. Is it long since that song was made? Is it long since he got his death?

THE POOR OLD WOMAN. Not long, not long. But there were others that died for love of me a long time ago.

MICHAEL. Were they neighbours of your own, ma'am?

THE POOR OLD WOMAN. Come here beside me and I'll tell you about them. [MICHAEL *sits down beside her at the hearth.*] There was a red man of the O'Donells from the North, and a man of the O'Sullivans from the South, and there was one Brian that lost his life at Clontarf, by the sea, and there were a great many in the West, some that died hundreds of years ago, and there are some that will die to-morrow.

MICHAEL. Is it in the West that men will die to-morrow?

THE POOR OLD WOMAN. Come nearer, nearer to me.

BRIDGET. Is she right, do you think? or is she a woman from the North?

PETER. She doesn't know well what she's talking about, with the want and the trouble she has gone through.

BRIDGET. The poor thing, we should treat her well.

PETER. Give her a drink of milk and a bit of the oaten cake.

BRIDGET. Maybe we should give her something along with that to bring her on her way—a few pence, or a shilling itself, and we with so much money in the house.

PETER. Indeed, I'd not begrudge it to her if we had it to spare; but if we go running through what we have, we'll soon have to break the hundred pounds, and that would be a pity.

BRIDGET. Shame on you, Peter. Give her the shilling and your blessing with it, or our own luck will go from us.

PETER *goes to the box and takes out a shilling.*

BRIDGET [*to the* OLD WOMAN]. Will you have a drink of milk?

THE POOR OLD WOMAN. It is not food or drink that I want.

PETER [*offering the shilling*]. Here is something for you.

THE POOR OLD WOMAN. That is not what I want. It is not silver I want.

PETER. What is it you would be asking for?

THE POOR OLD WOMAN. If anyone would give me help he must give me himself, he must give me all. [PETER *goes over to the table, staring at the shilling in his hand in a bewildered way and stands whispering to* BRIDGET.]

MICHAEL. Have you no man of your own, ma'am?

THE POOR OLD WOMAN. I have not. With all the lovers that brought me their love, I never set out the bed for any.

MICHAEL. Are you lonely going the roads, ma'am?

THE POOR OLD WOMAN. I have my thoughts and I have my hopes.

MICHAEL. What hopes have you to hold to?

THE POOR OLD WOMAN. The hope of getting my beautiful fields back again; the hope of putting the strangers out of my house.

MICHAEL. What way will you do that, ma'am?

THE POOR OLD WOMAN. I have good friends that will help me. They are gathering to help me now. I am not afraid. If they are put down to-day, they will get the upper hand to-morrow. [*She gets up.*] I must be going to meet my friends. They are coming to help me, and I must be there to welcome them. I must call the neighbours together to welcome them.

MICHAEL. I will go with you.

BRIDGET. It is not her friends you have to go and welcome, Michael; it is the girl coming into the house you have to welcome. You have plenty to do; it is food and drink you have to bring to the house. The woman that is coming is not coming with empty hands; you would not have an empty house before her. [*To the* OLD WOMAN] Maybe you don't know, ma'am, that my son is going to be married to-morrow.

THE POOR OLD WOMAN. It is not a man going to his marriage that I look to for help.

PETER [*to* BRIDGET]. Who is she, do you think, at all?

BRIDGET. You did not tell us your name yet, ma'am.

THE POOR OLD WOMAN. Some call me the Poor Old Woman, and there are some that call me Cathleen the daughter of Hoolihan.

PETER. I think I knew some one of that name once. Who was it, I wonder? It must have been some one I knew when I was a boy. No, no, I remember I heard it in a song.

THE POOR OLD WOMAN [*who is standing in the doorway*]. They are wondering that there were songs made for me; there have been many songs made for me. I heard one on the wind this morning. [*She sings*]

Do not make a great keening
When the graves have been dug to-morrow.
Do not call the white-scarfed riders
To the burying that shall be to-morrow.
Do not spread food to call strangers
To the wakes that shall be to-morrow.
Do not give money for prayers
For the dead that shall die to-morrow.
They will have no need of prayers, they will
have no need of prayers.

MICHAEL. I do not know what that song means; but tell me something I can do for you.

PETER. Come over to me, Michael.

MICHAEL. Hush, father; listen to her.

THE POOR OLD WOMAN. It is a hard service they take that help me. Many that are red-cheeked now will be pale-cheeked; many that have been free to walk the hills and the bogs and the rushes will be sent to walk hard streets in far countries; many a good plan will be broken; many that have gathered money will not stay to spend it; many a child will be born and there will be no father at its christening to give it a name. They that had red cheeks will have pale cheeks for my sake; and for all that they will think they are well paid. [*She goes out. Her voice is heard outside singing*]

They shall be remembered for ever
They shall be alive for ever
They shall be speaking for ever
The people shall hear them for ever.

BRIDGET [*to* PETER]. Look at him, Peter; he has the look of a man that has got the touch. [*Raising her voice*] Look here, Michael, at the wedding clothes [*taking clothes from dresser*]. You have a right to fit them on now. It would be a pity to-morrow if they did not fit; the boys would be laughing at you. Take them, Michael, and go into the room and fit them on. [*She puts them on his arm.*]

MICHAEL. What wedding are you talking of? What clothes will I be wearing to-morrow?

BRIDGET. These are the clothes you are going to wear when you marry Delia Cahel to-morrow.

MICHAEL. I had forgotten that. [*He looks at the clothes and turns toward the inner room, but stops at the sound of cheering outside.*]

PETER. There is the shouting come to our own door. What is it has happened?

Neighbours come crowding in, PATRICK *and* DELIA *with them.*

PATRICK. There are ships in the bay; the French are landing at Killala.

PETER *takes his pipe from his mouth and his hat off and stands up. The clothes slip from* MICHAEL'S *arm.*

DELIA. Michael! [*He takes no notice.*] Michael! [*He turns towards her.*] Why do you look at me like a stranger? [*She drops his arm.* BRIDGET *goes over toward her.*]

PATRICK. The boys are all hurrying down the hillsides to meet the French.

DELIA. Michael won't be going to join the French.

BRIDGET [*to* PETER]. Tell him not to go, Peter.

PETER. It's no use. He doesn't hear a word we're saying.

BRIDGET. Try, Delia, and coax him over to the fire.

DELIA. Michael, Michael, you won't leave me! You won't join the French and we going to be married to-morrow! [*She puts her arms about him. He turns to her as if about to yield.*]

OLD WOMAN'S *voice outside*—

They shall be remembered for ever
The people shall hear them for ever.

MICHAEL *breaks away from* DELIA *and goes out.*

BRIDGET [*laying her hand on* PATRICK'S *arm*]. Did you see an old woman going down the path?

PATRICK. I did not, but I saw a young girl and she had the walk of a queen.

RUDYARD KIPLING

The Last Chantey

"And there was no more sea"

THUS said the Lord in the Vault above the Cherubim,
Calling to the Angels and the Souls in their degree:
"Lo! Earth has passed away
On the smoke of Judgment Day.
That Our word may be established shall We gather up the sea?"

Loud sang the souls of the jolly, jolly mariners:
"Plague upon the hurricane that made us furl and flee!
But the war is done between us,
In the deep the Lord hath seen us—
Our bones we'll leave the barracout', and God may sink the sea!"

Then said the soul of Judas that betrayèd Him:
"Lord, hast Thou forgotten Thy covenant with me?
How once a year I go
To cool me on the floe?
And Ye take my day of mercy if Ye take away the sea."

Then said the soul of the Angel of the Off-shore Wind:
(He that bits the thunder when the bull-mouthed breakers flee):
"I have watch and ward to keep
O'er Thy wonders on the deep,
And Ye take mine honour from me if Ye take away the sea!"

Loud sang the souls of the jolly, jolly mariners:
"Nay, but we were angry, and a hasty folk are we.
If we worked the ship together
Till she foundered in foul weather,
Are we babes that we should clamour for a vengeance on the sea?"

Then said the souls of the slaves that men threw overboard:
"Kennelled in the picaroon a weary band were we;
But Thy arm was strong to save,
And it touched us on the wave,
And we drowsed the long tides idle till Thy Trumpets tore the sea."

Then cried the soul of the stout Apostle Paul to God:
"Once we frapped a ship, and she laboured woundily.
There were fourteen score of these,
And they blessed Thee on their knees,
When they learned Thy Grace and Glory under Malta by the sea!"

Loud sang the souls of the jolly, jolly mariners,
Plucking at their harps, and they plucked unhandily:
"Our thumbs are rough and tarred,
And the tune is something hard—
May we lift a Deepsea Chantey such as seamen use at sea?"

Then said the souls of the gentlemen-adventurers—
Fettered wrist to bar all for red iniquity:
"Ho, we revel in our chains
O'er the sorrow that was Spain's;
Heave or sink it, leave or drink it, we were masters of the sea!"

Up spake the soul of a grey Gothavn 'speckshioner—
(He that led the flenching in the fleets of fair Dundee):
"Oh, the ice-blink white and near,
And the bowhead breaching clear!
Will Ye whelm them all for wantonness that wallow in the sea?"

Loud sang the souls of the jolly, jolly mariners,
Crying: "Under Heaven, here is neither lead nor lee!

Must we sing for evermore
On the windless, glassy floor?
Take back your golden fiddles and we'll beat to open sea!"

Then stooped the Lord, and He called the good sea up to Him,
And 'stablishèd its borders unto all eternity,
That such as have no pleasure
For to praise the Lord by measure,
They may enter into galleons and serve Him on the sea.

Sun, Wind, and Cloud shall fail not from the face of it,
Stinging, ringing spindrift, nor the fulmar flying free;
And the ships shall go abroad
To the Glory of the Lord
Who heard the silly sailor-folk and gave them back their sea!

The Truce of the Bear

Yearly, with tent and rifle, our careless white men go
By the pass called Muttianee, to shoot in the vale below.
Yearly by Muttianee he follows our white men in—
Matun, the old blind beggar, bandaged from brow to chin.

Eyeless, noseless, and lipless—toothless, broken of speech,
Seeking a dole at the doorway he mumbles his tale to each;
Over and over the story, ending as he began:
"Make ye no truce with Adam-zad—the Bear that walks like a Man!

"There was a flint in my musket—pricked and primed was the pan,
When I went hunting Adam-zad—the Bear that stands like a Man.
I looked my last on the timber, I looked my last on the snow,
When I went hunting Adam-zad fifty summers ago!

"I knew his times and his seasons, as he knew mine, that fed
By night in the ripened maizefield and robbed my house of bread.
I knew his strength and cunning, as he knew mine, that crept
At dawn to the crowded goat-pens and plundered while I slept.

"Up from his stony playground—down from his well-digged lair—
Out on the naked ridges ran Adam-zad the Bear;
Groaning, grunting, and roaring, heavy with stolen meals,
Two long marches to northward, and I was at his heels!

"Two long marches to northward, at the fall of the second night,
I came on mine enemy Adam-zad all panting from his flight.
There was a charge in the musket—pricked and primed was the pan—
My finger crooked on the trigger—when he reared up like a man.

"Horrible, hairy, human, with paws like hands in prayer,
Making his supplication rose Adam-zad the Bear!
I looked at the swaying shoulders, at the paunch's swag and swing,
And my heart was touched with pity for the monstrous, pleading thing.

"Touched with pity and wonder, I did not fire then . . .
I have looked no more on women—I have walked no more with men.
Nearer he tottered and nearer, with paws like hands that pray—
From brow to jaw that steel-shod paw, it ripped my face away!

"Sudden, silent, and savage, searing as flame the blow—
Faceless I fell before his feet, fifty summers ago.
I heard him grunt and chuckle—I heard him pass to his den.
He left me blind to the darkened years and the little mercy of men.

"Now ye go down in the morning with guns of the newer style,
That load (I have felt) in the middle and range (I have heard) a mile!
Luck to the white man's rifle, that shoots so fast and true,
But—pay, and I lift my bandage and show what the Bear can do!"

"(Flesh like slag in the furnace, knobbed and withered and grey—
Matun, the old blind beggar, he gives good worth for his pay.)
"Rouse him at noon in the bushes, follow and press him hard—
Not for his ragings and roarings flinch ye from Adam-zad.

"But (pay, and I put back the bandage) *this* is the time to fear,
When he stands up like a tired man, tottering near and near;
When he stands up as pleading, in wavering, man-brute guise,
When he veils the hate and cunning of his little, swinish eyes;

"When he shows as seeking quarter, with paws like hands in prayer,
That is the time of peril—the time of the Truce of the Bear!"

Eyeless, noseless, and lipless, asking a dole at the door,
Matun, the old blind beggar, he tells it o'er and o'er;
Fumbling and feeling the rifles, warming his hands at the flame,
Hearing our careless white men talk of the morrow's game;

Over and over the story, ending as he began:—
"There is no truce with Adam-zad, the Bear that looks like a Man!"

The Bell Buoy

THEY christened my brother of old—
And a saintly name he bears—
They gave him his place to hold
At the head of the belfry-stairs,
Where the minster-towers stand
And the breeding kestrels cry.
Would I change with my brother a league inland?
(*Shoal! 'Ware shoal!*) Not I!

In the flush of the hot June prime,
O'er sleek flood-tides afire,
I hear him hurry the chime
To the bidding of checked Desire;
Till the sweated ringers tire
And the wild bob-majors die.
Could I wait for my turn in the godly choir?
(*Shoal! 'Ware shoal!*) Not I!

When the smoking scud is blown—
When the greasy wind-rack lowers—
Apart and at peace and alone,
He counts the changeless hours.
He wars with darkling Powers
(I war with a darkling sea);
Would he stoop to my work in the gusty mirk?
(*Shoal! 'Ware shoal!*) Not he!

There was never a priest to pray,
There was never a hand to toll,
When they made me guard of the bay,
And moored me over the shoal.
I rock, I reel, and I roll—
My four great hammers ply—
Could I speak or be still at the Church's will?
(*Shoal! 'Ware shoal!*) Not I!

The landward marks have failed,
The fog-bank glides unguessed,

The seaward lights are veiled,
  The spent deep feigns her rest:
  But my ear is laid to her breast,
I lift to the swell—I cry!
  Could I wait in sloth on the Church's oath?
(*Shoal! 'Ware shoal!*) Not I!

At the careless end of night
  I thrill to the nearing screw;
I turn in the clearing light
  And I call to the drowsy crew;
  And the mud boils foul and blue
As the blind bow backs away.
  Will they give me their thanks if they clear the banks?
(*Shoal! 'Ware shoal!*) Not they!

The beach-pools cake and skim,
  The bursting spray-heads freeze,
I gather on crown and rim
  The grey, grained ice of the seas,
  Where, sheathed from bitt to trees,
The plunging colliers lie.
  Would I barter my place for the Church's grace?
(*Shoal! 'Ware shoal!*) Not I!

Through the blur of the whirling snow,
  Or the black of the inky sleet,
The lanterns gather and grow,
  And I look for the homeward fleet.
  Rattle of block and sheet—
"Ready about—stand by!"
  Shall I ask them a fee ere they fetch the quay?
(*Shoal! 'Ware shoal!*) Not I!

I dip and I surge and I swing
  In the rip of the racing tide,
By the gates of doom I sing,
  On the horns of death I ride.
  A ship-length overside,
Between the course and the sand,
  Fretted and bound I bide
    Peril whereof I cry.
  Would I change with my brother a league inland?
(*Shoal! 'Ware shoal!*) Not I!

Mandalay

By the old Moulmein Pagoda, lookin' eastward to the sea,
There's a Burma girl a-settin', and I know she thinks o' me;
For the wind is in the palm-trees, and the temple-bells they say:
"Come you back, you British soldier; come you back to Mandalay!"
  Come you back to Mandalay,
  Where the old Flotilla lay:
  Can't you 'ear their paddles chunkin' from Rangoon to Mandalay?
  On the road to Mandalay,
  Where the flyin'-fishes play,
  An' the dawn comes up like thunder outer China 'crost the Bay!

'Er petticoat was yaller an' 'er little cap was green,
An' 'er name was Supi-yaw-lat—jes' the same as Theebaw's Queen,
An' I seed her first a-smokin' of a whackin' white cheroot,
An' a-wastin' Christian kisses on an 'eathen idol's foot:
  Bloomin' idol made o' mud—
  Wot they called the Great Gawd Budd—
  Plucky lot she cared for idols when I kissed 'er where she stud!
  On the road to Mandalay . . .

When the mist was on the rice-fields an' the sun was droppin' slow,
She'd git 'er little banjo an' she'd sing "*Kulla-lo-lo!*"
With 'er arm upon my shoulder an' 'er cheek agin my cheek
We useter watch the steamers an' the *hathis* pilin' teak.
  Elephints a-pilin' teak
  In the sludgy, squdgy creek,
  Where the silence 'ung that 'eavy you was 'arf afraid to speak!
  On the road to Mandalay . . .

But that's all shove be'ind me—long ago an' fur away,
An' there ain't no 'busses runnin' from the Bank to Mandalay;
An' I'm learnin' 'ere in London what the ten-year soldier tells:
"If you've 'eard the East a-callin', you won't never 'eed naught else."
No! you won't 'eed nothin' else
But them spicy garlic smells,
An' the sunshine an' the palm-trees an' the tinkly temple-bells;
On the road to Mandalay . . .

I am sick o' wastin' leather on these gritty pavin'-stones,
An' the blasted Henglish drizzle wakes the fever in my bones;
'Tho' I walks with fifty 'ousemaids outer Chelsea to the Strand,
An' they talks a lot o' lovin', but wot do they understand?
Beefy face an' grubby 'and—
Law! wot do they understand?
I've a neater, sweeter maiden in a cleaner, greener land!
On the road to Mandalay . . .

Ship me somewheres east of Suez, where the best is like the worst,
Where there aren't no Ten Commandments an' a man can raise a thirst;
For the temple-bells are callin', an' it's there that I would be—
By the old Moulmein Pagoda, looking lazy at the sea;
On the road to Mandalay,
Where the old Flotilla lay,
With our sick beneath the awnings when we went to Mandalay!
O the road to Mandalay,
Where the flyin'-fishes play,
An' the dawn comes up like thunder outer China 'crost the Bay!

The 'Eathen

THE 'eathen in 'is blindness bows down to wood an' stone;
'E don't obey no orders unless they is 'is own;
'E keeps 'is side-arms awful: 'e leaves 'em all about,
An' then comes up the Regiment an' pokes the 'eathen out.

All along o' dirtiness, all along o' mess,
All along o' doin' things rather-more-or-less,
All along of abby-nay, kul, an' hazar-ho,
Mind you keep your rifle an' yourself jus' so!

The young recruit is 'aughty—'e draf's from Gawd knows where;
They bid 'im show 'is stockin's an' lay 'is mattress square;
'E calls it bloomin' nonsense—'e doesn't know, no more—
An' then up comes 'is Company an' kicks 'im round the floor!

The young recruit is 'ammered—'e takes it very hard;
'E 'angs 'is 'ead an' mutters—'e sulks about the yard;
'E talks o' "cruel tyrants" which 'e'll swing for by-an'-by,
An' the others 'ears an' mocks 'im, an' the boy goes orf to cry.

The young recruit is silly—'e thinks o' suicide;
'E's lost 'is gutter-devil; 'e 'asn't got 'is pride;
But day by day they kicks 'im, which 'elps 'im on a bit,
Till 'e finds 'isself one mornin' with a full an' proper kit.

Gettin' clear o' dirtiness, gettin' done with mess,
Gettin' shut o' doin' things rather-more-or-less;

Not so fond of abby-nay, kul, nor hazar-ho,
Learns to keep 'is rifle an' 'isself jus' so!

The young recruit is 'appy—'e throws a chest to suit;
You see 'im grow mustaches; you 'ear 'im slap 'is boot;
'E learns to drop the "bloodies" from every word 'e slings,
An' 'e shows an 'ealthy brisket when 'e strips for bars an' rings.

The cruel-tyrant-sergeants they watch 'im 'arf a year;
They watch 'im with 'is comrades, they watch 'im with 'is beer;
They watch 'im with the women at the regimental dance,
And the cruel-tyrant-sergeants send 'is name along for "Lance."

An' now 'e's 'arf o' nothin', an' all a private yet,
'Is room they up an' rags 'im to see what they will get.
They rags 'im low an' cunnin', each dirty trick they can,
But 'e learns to sweat 'is temper an' 'e learns to sweat 'is man.

An', last, a Colour-Sergeant, as such to be obeyed,
'E schools 'is men at cricket, 'e tells 'em on parade;
They sees 'im quick an' 'andy, uncommon set an' smart,
An' so 'e talks to orficers which 'ave the Core at 'eart.

'E learns to do 'is watchin' without it showin' plain;
'E learns to save a dummy, an' shove 'im straight again;
'E learns to check a ranker that's buyin' leave to shirk;
An' 'e learns to make men like 'im so they'll learn to like their work.

An' when it comes to marchin' he'll see their socks are right,
An' when it comes to action 'e shows 'em how to sight.
'E knows their ways of thinkin' and just what's in their mind;
'E knows when they are takin' on an' when they've fell be'ind.

'E knows each talkin' corpril that leads a squad astray;
'E feels 'is innards 'eavin', 'is bowels givin' way;
'E sees the blue-white faces all tryin' 'ard to grin,
An' 'e stands an' waits an' suffers till it's time to cap 'em in.

An' now the hugly bullets come peckin' through the dust,
An' no one wants to face 'em, but every beggar must;
So, like a man in irons, which isn't glad to go,
They moves 'em off by companies uncommon stiff an' slow.

Of all 'is five years' schoolin' they don't remember much
Excep' the not retreatin', the step an' keepin' touch.
It looks like teachin' wasted when they duck an' spread an' 'op—
But if 'e 'adn't learned 'em they'd be all about the shop.

An' now it's "'Oo goes backward?" an' now it's "'Oo comes on?"
An' now it's "Get the doolies, an' now the Captain's gone;
An' now it's bloody murder, but all the while they 'ear
'Is voice, the same as barrick-drill, a-shepherdin' the rear.

'E's just as sick as they are, 'is 'eart is like to split,
But 'e works 'em, works 'em, works 'em till he feels 'em take the bit;

The rest is 'oldin' steady till the watchful bugles play,
An' 'e lifts 'em, lifts 'em, lifts 'em through the charge that wins the day!

The 'eathen in 'is blindness bows down to wood an' stone;
'E don't obey no orders unless they is 'is own.
The 'eathen in 'is blindness must end where 'e began,
But the backbone of the Army is the Non-commissioned Man!

Keep away from dirtiness—keep away from mess,
Don't get into doin' things rather-more-or-less!
Let's ha' done with abby-nay, kul, and hazar-ho;
Mind you keep your rifle an' yourself jus' so!

Chant-Pagan

ME that 'ave been what I've been—
Me that 'ave gone where I've gone—
Me that 'ave seen what I've seen—
'Ow can I ever take on
With awful old England again,
An' 'ouses both sides of the street,
And 'edges two sides of the lane,
And the parson an' gentry between,
An' touchin' my 'at when we meet—
Me that 'ave been what I've been?

Me that 'ave watched 'arf a world
'Eave up all shiny with dew,
Kopje on kop to the sun,
An' as soon as the mist let 'em through
Our 'elios winkin' like fun—
Three sides of a ninety-mile square,
Over valleys as big as a shire—
Are ye there? Are ye there? Are ye there?
An' then the blind drum of our fire . . .
An' I'm rollin' 'is lawns for the Squire,
Me!

Me that 'ave rode through the dark
Forty mile, often, on end,
Along the Ma'ollisberg Range,
With only the stars for my mark
An' only the night for my friend,
An' things runnin' off as you pass,
An' things jumpin' up in the grass,
An' the silence, the shine an' the size
Of the 'igh, unexpressible skies—
I am takin' some letters almost
As much as a mile to the post,
An' "mind you come back with the change"!
Me!

Me that saw Barberton took
When we dropped through the clouds on their 'ead,
An' they 'ove the guns over and fled—
Me that was through Di'mond 'Ill,
An' Pieters an' Springs an' Belfast—
From Dundee to Vereeniging all—
Me that stuck out to the last
(An' five bloomin' bars on my chest)—
I am doin' my Sunday-school best,
By the 'elp of the Squire an' 'is wife
(Not to mention the 'ousemaid an' cook),
To come in an' 'ands up an' be still,
An' honestly work for my bread,
My livin' in that state of life
To which it shall please God to call
Me!

Me that 'ave followed my trade
In the place where the Lightnin's are made,
'Twixt the Rains and the Sun and the Moon—
Me that lay down an' got up
Three years with the sky for my roof—
That 'ave ridden my 'unger an' thirst
Six thousand raw mile on the hoof
With the Vaal and the Orange for cup,
An' the Brandwater Basin for dish,—
Oh! it's 'ard to be'ave as they wish
(Too 'ard, an' a little too soon),
I'll 'ave to think over it first—
Me!

I will arise an' get 'ence;—
I will trek South and make sure
If it's only my fancy or not
That the sunshine of England is pale,
And the breezes of England are stale,
An' there's somethin' gone small with the lot;
For *I* know of a sun an' a wind,
An' some plains and a mountain be'ind,
An' some graves by a barb-wire fence;
An' a Dutchman I've fought 'oo might give
Me a job were I ever inclined,
To look in an' offsaddle an' live
Where there's neither a road nor a tree—
But only my Maker an' me,
And I think it will kill me or cure,
So I think I will go there an' see.
Me!

LIONEL JOHNSON (1867-1902)

By the Statue of King Charles at Charing Cross

SOMBRE and rich, the skies;
Great glooms, and starry plains.
Gently the night wind sighs;
Else a vast silence reigns.

The splendid silence clings
Around me: and around
The saddest of all kings
Crowned, and again discrowned.

Comely and calm, he rides
Hard by his own Whitehall:
Only the night wind glides:
No crowds, nor rebels, brawl.

Gone, too, his Court; and yet,
The stars his courtiers are:
Stars in their stations set;
And every wandering star.

Alone he rides, alone,
The fair and fatal king:
Dark night is all his own,
That strange and solemn thing.

Which are more full of fate:
The stars; or those sad eyes?
Which are more still and great:
Those brows; or the dark skies?

Although his whole heart yearn
In passionate tragedy:
Never was face so stern
With sweet austerity.

Vanquished in life, his death
By beauty made amends:
The passing of his breath
Won his defeated ends.

Brief life, and hapless? Nay:
Through death, life grew sublime.
Speak after sentence? Yea:
And to the end of time.

Armoured he rides, his head
Bare to the stars of doom:
He triumphs now, the dead,
Beholding London's gloom.

Our wearier spirit faints,
Vexed in the world's employ:
His soul was of the saints;
And art to him was joy.

King, tried in fires of woe!
Men hunger for thy grace:
And through the night I go,
Loving thy mournful face.

Yet, when the city sleeps;
When all the cries are still:
The stars and heavenly deeps
Work out a perfect will.

JOHN GALSWORTHY

A Stoic

I

1 §

"Aequam memento rebus in arduis
Servare mentem."—HORACE.

IN the City of Liverpool, on a January day of 1905, the Boardroom of "The Island Navigation Company" rested, as it were, after the labors of the afternoon. The long table was still littered with the ink, pens, blotting-paper, and abandoned documents of six persons—a deserted battlefield of the brain. And, lonely, in his chairman's seat at the top end old Sylvanus Heythorp sat, with closed eyes, still and heavy as an image. One puffy, feeble hand, whose fingers quivered, rested on the arm of his chair; the thick white hair on his massive head glistened in the light from a green-shaded lamp. He was not asleep, for every now and then his sanguine cheeks filled, and a sound, half sigh, half grunt, escaped his thick lips between a white moustache and the tiny tuft of white hairs above his cleft chin. Sunk in the chair, that square thick trunk of a body in short black-braided coat seemed divested of all neck.

Young Gilbert Farney, secretary of "The Island Navigation Company," entering his hushed Board-room, stepped briskly to the table, gathered some papers, and stood looking at his chairman. Not more than thirty-five, with the bright hues of the optimist in his hair, beard, cheeks, and eyes, he had a nose and lips which curled ironically. For, in his view, he *was* the Company; and its Board did but exist to chequer his importance. Five days in the week for seven hours a day he wrote, and thought, and wove the threads of its business, and this lot came down once a week for two or three hours, and taught their grandmother to suck eggs. But watching that red-cheeked, white-haired, somnolent figure, his smile was not so contemptuous as might have been expected. For after all, the chairman was a wonderful old boy. A man of go and insight could not but respect him. Eighty! Half paralyzed, over head and ears in debt, having gone the pace all his life—or so they said!—till at last that mine in Ecuador had done for him—before the secretary's day, of course, but he had heard of it. The old chap had bought it up on spec'—*"de l'audace, toujours de l'audace,"* as he was so fond of saying—paid for it half in cash and half in promises, and then—the thing had turned out empty, and left him with £20,000 worth of the old shares unredeemed. The old boy had weathered it out without a bankruptcy so far. Indomitable old buffer; and never fussy like the rest of them! Young Farney, though a secretary, was capable of attachment; and his eyes expressed a pitying affection. The Board meeting had been long and "snaggy"—a final settling of that Pillin business. Rum go the chairman forcing it on them like this! And with quiet satisfaction the secretary thought: 'And he never would have got it through if I hadn't made up my mind that it really is good business!' For to expand the Company was to expand himself. Still, to buy four ships with the freight market so depressed was a bit startling, and there would be opposition at the general meeting. Never mind! He and the chairman could put it through—put it through. And suddenly he saw the old man looking at him.

Only from those eyes could one appreciate the strength of life yet flowing underground in that well-nigh helpless carcase—deep-colored little blue wells, tiny, jovial, round windows.

A sigh travelled up through layers of flesh, and he said almost inaudibly:

"Have they come, Mr. Farney?"

"Yes, sir. I've put them in the transfer office; said you'd be with them in a minute; but I wasn't going to wake you."

"Haven't been asleep. Help me up."

Grasping the edge of the table with his trembling hands, the old man pulled, and, with Farney heaving him behind, attained his feet. He stood about five feet ten, and weighed fully fourteen stone; not corpulent, but very thick all through; his round and massive head alone would have outweighed a baby. With eyes shut, he seemed to be trying to get the better of his own weight, then he moved with the slowness of a barnacle towards the door. The secretary, watching him, thought: 'Marvellous old chap! How he gets about by himself is a miracle! And he can't retire, they say—lives on his fees!'

But the chairman was through the green baize door. At his tortoise gait he traversed the inner office, where the youthful clerks suspended their figuring—to grin behind his back—and entered the transfer office, where eight gentlemen were sitting. Seven rose, and one did not. Old Heythorp raised a saluting hand to the level of his chest and moving to an arm-chair, lowered himself into it.

"Well, gentlemen?"

One of the eight gentlemen got up again.

"Mr. Heythorp, we've appointed Mr. Brownbee to voice our views. Mr. Brownbee!" And down he sat.

Mr. Brownbee rose—a stoutish man some seventy years of age, with little grey side whiskers, and one of those utterly steady faces only to be seen in England, faces which convey the sense of business from father to son for generations; faces which make wars, and passion, and free thought seem equally incredible; faces which inspire confidence, and awaken in one a desire to get up and leave the room. Mr. Brownbee rose, and said in a suave voice:

"Mr. Heythorp, we here represent about £14,000. When we had the pleasure of meeting you last July, you will recollect that you held out a prospect of some more satisfactory arrangement by Christmas. We are now in January, and I am bound to say we none of us get younger."

From the depths of old Heythorp a preliminary rumble came travelling, reached the surface, and materialized:

"Don't know about you—feel a boy, myself."

The eight gentlemen looked at him. Was he going to try and put them off again? Mr. Brownbee said with unruffled calm:

"I'm sure we're very glad to hear it. But to come to the point. We have felt, Mr. Heythorp, and I'm sure you won't think it unreasonable, that—er—bankruptcy would be the most satisfactory solution. We have waited a long time, and we want to know definitely where we stand; for, to be quite frank, we don't see any prospect of improvement; indeed, we fear the opposite."

"You think I'm going to join the majority."

This plumping out of what was at the back of their minds produced in Mr. Brownbee and his colleagues a sort of chemical disturbance. They coughed, moved their feet, and turned away their eyes, till the one who had not risen, a solicitor named Ventnor, said bluffly:

"Well, put it that way if you like."

Old Heythorp's little deep eyes twinkled.

"My grandfather lived to be a hundred; my father ninety-six—both of them rips. I'm only eighty, gentlemen; blameless life compared with theirs."

"Indeed," Mr. Brownbee said, "we hope you have many years of this life before you."

"More of this than of another." And a silence fell, till old Heythorp added: "You're getting a thousand a year out of my fees. Mistake to kill the goose that lays the golden eggs. I'll make it twelve hundred. If you force me to resign my directorships by bankruptcy, you won't get a rap, you know."

Mr. Brownbee cleared his throat:

"We think, Mr. Heythorp, you should make it at least fifteen hundred. In that case we might perhaps consider——"

Old Heythorp shook his head.

"We can hardly accept your assertion that we should get nothing in the event of bankruptcy. We fancy you greatly underrate the possibilities. Fifteen hundred a year is the least you can do for us."

"See you d——d first."

Another silence followed, then Ventnor, the solicitor, said irascibly:

"We know where we are, then."

Mr. Brownbee added almost nervously:

"Are we to understand that twelve hundred a year is your—your last word?"

Old Heythorp nodded. "Come again this day month, and I'll see what I can do for you;" and he shut his eyes.

Round Mr. Brownbee six of the gentlemen gathered, speaking in low voices; Mr. Ventnor nursed a leg and glowered at old Heythorp, who sat with his eyes closed. Mr. Brownbee went over and conferred with Mr. Ventnor, then clearing his throat, he said:

"Well, sir, we have considered your proposal; we agree to accept it for the moment. We will come again, as you suggest, in a month's time. We hope that you will by then have seen your way to something more substantial, with a view to avoiding what we should all regret, but which I fear will otherwise become inevitable."

Old Heythorp nodded. The eight gentlemen took their hats, and went out one by one, Mr. Brownbee courteously bringing up the rear.

The old man, who could not get up without assistance, stayed musing in his chair. He had diddled 'em for the moment into giving him another month, and when that month was up—he would diddle 'em again! A month ought to make the Pillin business safe, with all that hung on it. That poor funkey chap Joe Pillin! A gurgling chuckle escaped his red lips. What a shadow the fellow had looked, trotting in that evening just a month ago, behind his valet's announcement: "Mr. Pillin, sir."

What a parchmenty, precise, threadpaper of a chap, with his bird's claw of a hand, and his muffled-up throat, and his quavery:

"How do you do, Sylvanus? I'm afraid you're not——"

"First rate. Sit down. Have some port."

"Port! I never drink it. Poison to me! Poison!"

"Do you good!"

"Oh! I know, that's what you always say. You've a monstrous constitution, Sylvanus. If I drank port and smoked cigars and sat up till one o'clock, I should be in my grave to-morrow. I'm not the man I was. The fact is I've come to see if you can help me. I'm getting old; I'm growing nervous——"

"You always were as chickeny as an old hen, Joe."

"Well, my nature's not like yours. To come to the point, I want to sell my ships and retire. I need rest. Freights are very depressed. I've got my family to think of."

"Crack on, and go broke: buck you up like anything!"

"I'm quite serious, Sylvanus."

"Never knew you anything else, Joe."

A quavering cough, and out it had come:

"Now—in a word—won't your 'Island Navigation Company' buy my ships?"

A pause, a twinkle, a puff of smoke. "Make it worth my while!" He had said it in jest; and then, in a flash, the idea had come to him. Rosamund and her youngsters! What a chance to put something between them and destitution when he had joined the majority! And so he said: "We don't want your silly ships."

That claw of a hand waved in deprecation. "They're very good ships—all that. Doing quite well. It's only my wretched health. If I were a strong man I shouldn't dream——"

"What d'you want for 'em?" Good Lord! how he jumped if you asked him a plain question. The chap was as nervous as a guinea-fowl!

"Here are the figures—for the last four years. I think you'll agree that I couldn't ask less than seventy thousand."

Through the smoke of his cigar old Heythorp had digested those figures slowly, Joe Pillin feeling his teeth and sucking lozenges the while; then he said:

"Sixty thousand! And out of that you pay me ten per cent, if I get it through for you. Take it or leave it."

"My dear Sylvanus, that's almost—cynical."

"Too good a price—you'll never get it without me."

"But a—but a commission! You could never disclose it!"

"Arrange that all right. Think it over. Freights'll go lower yet. Have some port."

"No, no! Thank you. No! So you think freights will go lower?"

"Sure of it."

"Well, I'll be going. I'm sure I don't know. It's—it's—I must think."

"Think your hardest."

"Yes, yes. Good-bye. I can't imagine how you still go on smoking those things and drinking port."

"See you in your grave yet, Joe." What a feeble smile the poor fellow had! Laugh—he couldn't! And, alone again, he had browsed, developing the idea which had come to him.

Though, to dwell in the heart of shipping, Sylvanus Heythorp had lived at Liverpool twenty years, he was from the Eastern Counties, of a family so old that it professed to despise the Conquest. Each of its generations occupied nearly twice as long as those of less tenacious men. Traditionally of Danish origin, its men folk had as a rule bright reddish-brown hair, red cheeks, large round heads, excellent teeth and poor morals. They had done their best for the population of any county in which they had settled; their offshoots swarmed. Born in the early twenties of the nineteenth century, Sylvanus Heythorp, after an education broken by escapades both at school and college, had fetched up in that simple London of the late forties, where claret, opera, and eight per cent. for your money ruled a cheery roost. Made partner in his shipping firm well before he was thirty, he had sailed with a wet sheet and a flowing tide; dancers, claret, Clicquot, and piquet; a cab with a tiger; some travel—all that delicious early-Victorian consciousness of nothing save a golden time. It was all so full and mellow that he was forty before he had his only love affair of any depth—with the daughter of one of his own clerks, a *liaison* so awkward as to necessitate a sedulous concealment. The death of that girl, after three years, leaving him a natural son, had been the chief, perhaps the only real, sorrow of his life. Five years later he married. What for? God only knew! as he was in the habit of remarking. His wife had been a hard, worldly, well-connected woman, who presented him with two unnatural children, a girl and a boy, and grew harder, more worldly, less handsome, in the process. The migration to Liverpool, which took place when he was sixty and she forty-two, broke what she still had of heart, but she lingered on twelve years, finding solace in bridge, and being haughty towards Liverpool. Old Heythorp saw her to her rest without regret. He had felt no love for her whatever, and practically none for her two children—they were in his view colorless, pragmatical, very unexpected characters. His son Ernest—in the Admiralty—he thought a poor, careful stick. His daughter Adela, an excellent manager, delighting in spiritual conversation and the society of tame men, rarely failed to show him that she considered him a hopeless heathen. They saw as little as need be of each other. She was provided for under that settlement he had made on her mother fifteen years ago, well before the not altogether unexpected crisis in his affairs. Very different was the feeling he had bestowed on that son of his "under the rose." The boy, who had always gone by his mother's name of Larne, had on her death been sent to some relations of hers in Ireland, and there brought up. He had been called to the Dublin bar, and married, young, a girl half Cornish and half Irish; presently, having cost old Heythorp in all a pretty penny, he had died impecunious, leaving his fair Rosamund at thirty with a girl of eight and a boy of five. She had not spent six months of widowhood before coming over from Dublin to claim the old man's guardianship. A remarkably pretty woman, like a full-blown rose, with greenish hazel eyes, she had turned up one morning at the offices of "The Island Navigation Company," accompanied by her two children—for he had never divulged to them his private address. And since then they had always been more or less on his hands, occupying a small house in a suburb of Liverpool. He visited them there, but never asked them to the house in Sefton Park, which was in fact his daughter's; so that his proper family and friends were unaware of their existence.

Rosamund Larne was one of those precarious ladies who make uncertain incomes by writing full-bodied storyettes. In the most dismal circumstances she enjoyed a buoyancy bordering on the indecent, which always amused old Heythorp's cynicism. But of his grandchildren Phyllis and Jock (wild as colts) he had become fond. And this chance of getting six thousand pounds settled on them at a stroke had seemed to him nothing but heaven-sent. As things were, if he "went off"—and, of course, he might at any moment—there wouldn't be a penny for them; for he would "cut up" a good fifteen thousand to the bad. He was now giving them some three hundred a year out of his fees; and dead directors unfortunately earned no fees! Six thousand pounds at four and a half per cent., settled so that their mother couldn't "blue it," would give them a certain two hundred and fifty pounds a year—better than beggary. And the more he thought the better he liked it, if only that shaky chap, Joe Pillin, didn't shy off when he'd bitten his nails short over it!

Four evenings later, the "shaky chap" had again appeared at his house in Sefton Park.

"I've thought it over, Sylvanus. I don't like it."

"No; but you'll do it."

"It's a sacrifice. Fifty-four thousand for four ships—it means a considerable reduction in my income."

"It means security, my boy."

"Well, there is that; but you know, I really can't be party to a secret commission. If it came out, think of my name and goodness knows what."

"It won't come out."

"Yes, yes, so you say, but——"

"All you've got to do's to execute a settlement on some third parties that I'll name. I'm not going to take a penny of it myself. Get your own lawyer to draw it up and make him trustee. You can sign it when the purchase has gone through. I'll trust you, Joe. What stock have you got that gives four and a half per cent.?"

"Midland——"

"That'll do. You needn't sell."

"Yes, but who *are* these people?"

"Woman and her children I want to do a good turn to." What a face the fellow had made! "Afraid of being connected with a woman, Joe?"

"Yes, you may laugh—I *am* afraid of being connected with someone else's woman. I don't like it—I don't like it at all. I've not led your life, Sylvanus."

"Lucky for you; you'd have been dead long ago. Tell your lawyer it's an old flame of yours—you old dog!"

"Yes, there it is at once, you see. I might be subject to blackmail."

"Tell him to keep it dark, and just pay over the income, quarterly."

"I don't like it, Sylvanus—I don't like it."

"Then leave it, and be hanged to you. Have a cigar?"

"You know I never smoke. Is there no other way?"

"Yes. Sell stock in London, bank the proceeds there, and bring me six thousand pounds in notes. I'll hold 'em till after the general meeting. If the thing doesn't go through, I'll hand 'em back to you."

"No; I like that even less."

"Rather I trusted *you*, eh!"

"No, not at all, Sylvanus, not at all. But it's all playing round the law."

"There's no law to prevent you doing what you like with your money. What I do's nothing to you. And mind you, I'm taking nothing from it—not a mag. You assist the widowed and the fatherless—just your line, Joe!"

"What a fellow you are, Sylvanus; you don't seem capable of taking anything seriously."

"Care killed the cat!"

Left alone after this second interview he had thought: 'The beggar'll jump.'

And the beggar *had*. That settlement was drawn and only awaited signature. The Board to-day had decided on the purchase; and all that remained was to get it ratified at the general meeting. Let him but get that over, and this provision for his grandchildren made, and he would snap his fingers at Brownbee and his crew—the canting humbugs! "Hope you have many years of this life before you!" As if they cared for anything but his money—*their* money rather! And becoming conscious of the length of his reverie, he grasped the arms of his chair, heaved at his own bulk, in an effort to rise, growing redder and redder in face and neck. It was one of the hundred things his doctor had told him not to do for fear of apoplexy, the humbug! Why didn't Farney or one of those young fellows come and help him up? To call out was undignified. But was he to sit there all night? Three times he failed, and after each failure sat motionless again, crimson and exhausted; the fourth time he succeeded, and slowly made for the office. Passing through, he stopped and said in his extinct voice:

"You young gentlemen had forgotten me."

"Mr. Farney said you didn't wish to be disturbed, sir."

"Very good of him. Give me my hat and coat."

"Yes, sir."

"Thank you. What time is it?"

"Six o'clock, sir."

"Tell Mr. Farney to come and see me to-morrow at noon, about my speech for the general meeting."

"Yes, sir."

"Good-night to you."

"Good-night, sir."

At his tortoise gait he passed between the office stools to the door, opened it feebly, and slowly vanished.

Shutting the door behind him, a clerk said:

"Poor old chairman! He's on his last!"

Another answered:

"Gosh! He's a tough old hulk. He'll go down fightin'."

2 §

Issuing from the offices of "The Island Navigation Company," Sylvanus Heythorp moved towards the corner whence he always took tram to Sefton Park. The crowded street had all that prosperous air of catching or missing something which characterizes the town where London and New York and Dublin meet. Old Heythorp had to cross to the far side, and he sallied forth without regard to traffic. That snail-like passage had in it a touch of the sublime; the old man seemed saying: "Knock me down and be d——d to you—I'm not going to hurry." His life was saved perhaps ten times a day by the British character at large, compounded of phlegm and a liking to take something under its protection. The tram conductors on that line were especially used to him, never failing to catch him under the arms and heave him like a sack of coals, while with trembling hands he pulled hard at the rail and strap.

"All right, sir?"

"Thank you."

He moved into the body of the tram, where somebody would always get up from kindness and the fear that he might sit down on them; and there he stayed motionless, his little eyes tight closed. With his red face, tuft of white hairs above his square cleft block of shaven chin, and his big high-crowned bowler hat, which yet seemed too petty for his head with its thick hair—he looked like some kind of an idol dug up and decked out in gear a size too small.

One of those voices of young men from public schools and exchanges where things are bought and sold, said:

"How de do, Mr. Heythorp?"

Old Heythorp opened his eyes. That sleek cub, Joe Pillin's son! What a young pup—with his round eyes, and his round cheeks, and his little moustache, his fur coat, his spats, his diamond pin!

"How's your father?" he said.

"Thanks, rather below par, worryin' about his ships. Suppose you haven't any news for him, sir?"

Old Heythorp nodded. The young man was one of his pet abominations, embodying all the complacent, little-headed mediocrity of this new generation; natty fellows all turned out of the same mould, sippers and tasters, chaps without drive or capacity, without even vices; and he did not intend to gratify the cub's curiosity.

"Come to my house," he said; "I'll give you a note for him."

"Tha—anks; I'd like to cheer the old man up."

The old man! Cheeky brat! And closing his eyes he relapsed into immobility. The tram wound and ground its upward way, and he mused. When he was that cub's age—twenty-eight or whatever it might be—he had done most things; been up Vesuvius, driven four-in-hand, lost his last penny on the Derby and won it back on the Oaks, known all the dancers and operatic stars of the day, fought a duel with a Yankee at Dieppe and winged him for saying through his confounded nose that

Old England was played out; been a controlling voice already in his shipping firm; drunk five other of the best men in London under the table; broken his neck steeplechasing; shot a burglar in the legs; been nearly drowned, for a bet; killed snipe in Chelsea; been to Court for his sins; stared a ghost out of countenance; and travelled with a lady of Spain. If this young pup had done the last, it would be all he had; and yet, no doubt, he would call himself a "spark."

The conductor touched his arm.

"'Ere you are, sir."

"Thank you."

He lowered himself to the ground, and moved in the bluish darkness towards the gate of his daughter's house. Bob Pillin walked beside him, thinking: 'Poor old josser, he *is* gettin' a back number!' And he said: "I should have thought you ought to drive, sir. My old guv-nor would knock up at once if he went about at night like this."

The answer rumbled out into the misty air:

"Your father's got no chest; never had."

Bob Pillin gave vent to one of those fat cackles which come so readily from a certain type of man; and old Heythorp thought: 'Laughing at his father! Parrot!'

They had reached the porch.

A woman with dark hair and a thin, straight face and figure was arranging some flowers in the hall. She turned and said:

"You really ought not to be so late, Father! It's wicked at this time of year. Who is it—oh! Mr. Pillin, how do you do? Have you had tea? Won't you come to the drawing-room; or do you want to see my father?"

"Tha—anks! I believe your father——" And he thought: 'By Jove! the old chap *is* a caution!' For old Heythorp was crossing the hall without having paid the faintest attention to his daughter. Murmuring again:

"Tha—anks awfully; he wants to give me something," he followed. Miss Heythorp was not his style at all; he had a kind of dread of that thin woman who looked as if she could never be unbuttoned. They said she was a great churchgoer and all that sort of thing.

In his sanctum old Heythorp had moved to his writing-table, and was evidently anxious to sit down.

"Shall I give you a hand, sir?"

Receiving a shake of the head, Bob Pillin stood by the fire and watched. The old "sport" liked to paddle his own canoe. Fancy having to lower yourself into a chair like that! When an old Johnny got to such a state it was really a mercy when he snuffed out, and made way for younger men. How his Companies could go on putting up with such a fossil for chairman was a marvel! The fossil rumbled and said in that almost inaudible voice:

"I suppose you're beginning to look forward to your father's shoes?"

Bob Pillin's mouth opened. The voice went on:

"Dibs and no responsibility. Tell him from me to drink port—add five years to his life."

To this unwarranted attack Bob Pillin made no answer save a laugh; he perceived that a manservant had entered the room.

"A Mrs. Larne, sir. Will you see her?"

At this announcement the old man seemed to try and start; then he nodded, and held out the note he had written. Bob Pillin received it together with the impression of a murmur which sounded like: "Scratch a poll, Poll!" and passing the fine figure of a woman in a fur coat, who seemed to warm the air as she went by, he was in the hall again before he perceived that he had left his hat.

A young and pretty girl was standing on the bearskin before the fire, looking at him with round-eyed innocence. He thought: 'This is better; I mustn't disturb them for my hat'; and approaching the fire, he said:

"Jolly cold, isn't it?"

The girl smiled: "Yes—jolly."

He noticed that she had a large bunch of violets at her breast, a lot of fair hair, a short straight nose, and round blue-grey eyes very frank and open. "Er——" he said, "I've left my hat in there."

"What larks!" And at her little clear laugh something moved within Bob Pillin.

"You know this house well?"

She shook her head. "But it's rather scrummy, isn't it?"

Bob Pillin, who had never yet thought so, answered:

"Quite O.K."

The girl threw up her head to laugh again. "O.K.? What's that?"

Bob Pillin saw her white round throat, and thought: 'She *is* a ripper!' And he said with a certain desperation:

"My name's Pillin. Yours is Larne, isn't it? Are you a relation here?"

"He's our Guardy. Isn't he a chook?"

That rumbling whisper like "Scratch a poll, Poll!" recurring to Bob Pillin, he said with reservation:

"You know him better than I do."

"Oh! Aren't you his grandson, or something?"

Bob Pillin did not cross himself.

"Lord! No! My dad's an old friend of his; that's all."

"Is your dad like him?"

"Not much."

"What a pity! It would have been lovely if they'd been Tweedles."

Bob Pillin thought: 'This bit is something new. I wonder what her Christian name is.' And he said:

"What did your godfather and godmothers in your baptism——?"

The girl laughed; she seemed to laugh at everything.

"Phyllis."

Could he say: "Is my only joy"? Better keep it! But—for what? He wouldn't see her again if he didn't look out! And he said:

"I live at the last house in the park—the red one. D'you know it? Where do you?"

"Oh! a long way—23, Millicent Villas. It's a poky little house. I hate it. We have awful larks, though."

"Who are we?"

"Mother, and myself, and Jock—he's an awful boy. You can't conceive what an awful boy he is. He's got nearly red hair; I think he'll be just like Guardy when he gets old. He's *awful!*"

Bob Pillin murmured:

"I should like to see him."

"Would you? I'll ask mother if you can. You won't want to again; he goes off all the time like a squib." She threw back her head, and again Bob Pillin felt a little giddy. He collected himself, and drawled:

"Are you going in to see your Guardy?"

"No. Mother's got something special to say. We've never been here before, you see. Isn't he fun, though?"

"Fun!"

"I think he's the greatest lark: but he's awfully nice to me. Jock calls him the last of the Stoic'uns."

A voice called from old Heythorp's den:

"Phyllis!" It had a particular ring, that voice, as if coming from beautifully formed red lips, of which the lower one must curve the least bit over; it had, too, a caressing vitality, and a kind of warm falsity.

The girl threw a laughing look back over her shoulder, and vanished through the door into the room.

Bob Pillin remained with his back to the fire and his puppy round eyes fixed on the air that her figure had last occupied. He was experiencing a sensation never felt before. Those travels with a lady of Spain, charitably conceded him by old Heythorp, had so far satisfied the emotional side of this young man; they had stopped short at Brighton and Scarborough, and been preserved from even the slightest intrusion of love. A calculated and hygienic career had caused no anxiety either to himself or his father; and this sudden swoop of something more than admiration gave him an uncomfortable choky feeling just above his high round collar, and in the temples a sort of buzzing—those first symptoms of chivalry. A man of the world does not, however, succumb without a struggle; and if his hat had not been out of reach, who knows whether he would not have left the house hurriedly, saying to himself: "No, no, my boy; Millicent Villas is hardly your form, when your intentions are honorable"? For somehow that round and laughing face, bob of glistening hair, those wide-opened grey eyes, refused to awaken the beginnings of other intentions—such is the effect of youth and innocence on even the steadiest young men. With a kind of moral stammer, he was thinking: 'Can I—dare I offer to see them to their tram? Couldn't I even nip out and get the car round and send them home in it? No, I might miss them—better stick it out here! What a jolly laugh! What a ripping face—strawberries and cream, hay, and all that! Millicent Villas!' And he wrote it on his cuff.

The door was opening; he heard that warm vibrating voice: "Come along, Phyllis!"—the girl's laugh so high and fresh: "Right-o! Coming!" And with, perhaps, the first real tremor he had ever known, he crossed to the front door. All the more chivalrous to escort them to the tram without a hat! And suddenly he heard: "I've got your hat, young man!" And her mother's voice, warm, and simulating shock: "Phyllis, you awful gairl! Did you ever see such an awful gairl, Mr.——"

"Pillin, Mother."

And then—he did not quite know how—insulated from the January air by laughter and the scent of fur and violets, he was between them walking to their tram. It was like an experience out of the "Arabian Nights," or something of that sort, an intoxication which made one say one was going their way, though one would have to come all the way back in the same beastly tram. Nothing so warming had ever happened to him as sitting between them on that drive, so that he forgot the note in his pocket, and his desire to relieve the anxiety of the "old man," his father. At the tram's terminus they all got out. There issued a purr of invitation to come and see them some time; a clear: "Jock'll love to see you!" A low laugh: "You awful gairl!"

And a flash of cunning zigzagged across his brain. Taking off his hat, he said:

"Thanks awfully; rather!" and put his foot back on the step of the tram. Thus did he delicately expose the depths of his chivalry!

"Oh! you *said* you were going our way! What one-ers you do tell! Oh!" The words were as music; the sight of those eyes growing rounder, the most perfect he had ever seen; and Mrs. Larne's low laugh, so warm yet so preoccupied, and the tips of the girl's fingers waving back above her head. He heaved a sigh and knew no more till he was seated at his club before a bottle of champagne. Home! Not he! He wished to drink and dream. "The old man" would get his news all right to-morrow!

3 §

The words: "A Mrs. Larne to see you, sir," had been of a nature to astonish weaker nerves. What had brought her here? She knew she mustn't come! Old Heythorp had watched her entrance with cynical amusement. The way she whiffed herself at that young pup in passing, the way her eyes slid round! He had a very just appreciation of his son's widow; and a smile settled deep between his chin tuft and his moustache. She lifted his hand, kissed it, pressed it to her splendid bust, and said:

"So here I am at last, you see. Aren't you surprised?"

Old Heythorp shook his head.

"I really had to come and see you, Guardy; we haven't had a sight of you for such an age. And in this awful weather! How are you, dear old Guardy?"

"Never better." And, watching her green-grey eyes, he added: "Haven't a penny for you!"

Her face did not fall; she gave her feather-laugh.

"How dreadful of you to think I came for that! But I *am* in an awful fix, Guardy."

"Never knew you not to be."

"Just let me tell you, dear; it'll be some relief. I'm having the most terrible time."

She sank into a low chair, disengaging an overpowering scent of violets, while melancholy struggled to subdue her face and body.

"The most awful fix. I expect to be sold up any moment. We may be on the streets to-morrow. I daren't tell the children; they're so happy, poor darlings. I shall be obliged to take Jock away from school. And Phyllis will have to stop her piano and dancing; it's an absolute crisis. And all due to those Midland Syndicate people. I've been counting on at least two hundred for my new story, and the wretches have refused it."

With a tiny handkerchief she removed one tear from the corner of one eye. "It *is* hard, Guardy; I worked my brain silly over that story."

From old Heythorp came a mutter which sounded suspiciously like "Rats!"

Heaving a sigh, which conveyed nothing but the generosity of her breathing apparatus, Mrs. Larne went on:

"You couldn't, I suppose, let me have just one hundred?"

"Not a bob."

She sighed again, her eyes slid round the room; then in her warm voice she murmured:

"Guardy, you *were* my dear Philip's father, weren't you? I've never said anything; but *of course* you were. He was so like you, and so is Jock."

Nothing moved in old Heythorp's face. No pagan image consulted with flowers and song and sacrifice could have returned less answer. Her dear Philip! She had led him the devil of a life, or he was a Dutchman! And what the deuce made her suddenly trot out the skeleton like this? But Mrs. Larne's eyes were still wandering.

"What a lovely house! You know, I think you ought to help me, Guardy. Just imagine if your grandchildren were thrown out into the street!"

The old man grinned. He was not going to deny his relationship—it was her look-out, not his. But neither was he going to let her rush him.

"And they will be; you *couldn't* look on and see it. Do come to my rescue this once. You really might do something for them."

With a rumbling sigh he answered:

"Wait. Can't give you a penny now. Poor as a church mouse."

"Oh! Guardy!"

"Fact."

Mrs. Larne heaved one of her most buoyant sighs. She certainly did not believe him.

"Well!" she said; "you'll be sorry when we come round one night and sing for pennies under your window. Wouldn't you like to see Phyllis? I left her in the hall. She's growing such a sweet gairl. Guardy—just fifty!"

"Not a rap."

Mrs. Larne threw up her hands. "Well! You'll repent it. I'm at my last gasp." She sighed profoundly, and the perfume of violets escaped in a cloud. Then, getting up, she went to the door and called: "Phyllis!"

When the girl entered old Heythorp felt the nearest approach to a flutter of the heart for many years. She had put her hair up! She was like a spring day in January; such a relief from that scented humbug, her mother. Pleasant, the touch of her lips on his forehead, the sound of her clear voice, the sight of her slim movements, the feeling that she did him credit—clean-run stock, she and that young scamp Jock—better than the holy woman, his daughter Adela, would produce if anyone were ever fool enough to marry her, or that pragmatical fellow, his son Ernest.

And when they were gone he reflected with added zest on the six thousand pounds he was getting for them out of Joe Pillin and his ships. He would have to pitch it strong in his speech at the general meeting. With freights so low, there was bound to be opposition. No dash nowadays; nothing but flabby caution! They were a scrim-shanking lot on the Board—he had had to pull them round one by one—the deuce of a tug getting this thing through! And yet, the business was sound enough. Those ships would earn money, properly handled—good money!

His valet, coming in to prepare him for dinner, found him asleep. He had for the old man as much admiration as may be felt for one who cannot put his own trousers on. He would say to the housemaid Molly: "He's a game old blighter—must have been a rare one in his day. Cocks his hat at you, even now, I see!" To which the girl, Irish and pretty, would reply: "Well, an' sure I don't mind, if it gives um a pleasure. 'Tis better annyway than the sad eye I get from herself."

At dinner, old Heythorp always sat at one end of the rosewood table and his daughter at the other. It was the eminent moment of the day. With napkin tucked high into his waistcoat, he gave himself to the meal with passion. His palate was undimmed, his digestion unimpaired. He could still eat as much as two men, and drink more than one. And while he savored each mouthful he never spoke if he could help it. The holy woman had nothing to say that he cared to hear, and he nothing to say that she cared to listen to. She had a horror, too, of what she called "the pleasures of the table"—those lusts of the flesh! She was always longing to dock his grub, he knew. Would see her further first! What other pleasures were there at his age? Let her wait till *she* was eighty. But she never would be; too thin and holy!

This evening, however, with the advent of the partridge she *did* speak. "Who were your visitors, Father?"

Trust her for nosing anything out! Fixing his little blue eyes on her, he mumbled with a very full mouth: "Ladies."

"So I saw; what ladies?"

He had a longing to say: 'Part of one of my families under the rose.' As a fact it was the best part of the only one, but the temptation to multiply exceedingly was almost overpowering. He checked himself, however, and went on eating partridge, his secret irritation crimsoning his cheeks; and he watched her eyes, those cold precise and round grey eyes, noting it, and knew she was thinking: "He eats too much."

She said: "Sorry I'm not considered fit to be told. You ought not to be drinking hock."

Old Heythorp took up the long green glass, drained it, and repressing fumes and emotion went on with his partridge. His daughter pursed her lips, took a sip of water, and said:

"I know their name is Larne, but it conveyed nothing to me; perhaps it's just as well."

The old man, mastering a spasm, said with a grin:

"My daughter-in-law and my granddaughter."

"What! Ernest married—Oh! nonsense!"

He chuckled, and shook his head.

"Then do you mean to say, Father, that you were married before you married my mother?"

"No."

The expression on her face was as good as a play!

She said with a sort of disgust: "Not married! I see. I suppose those people are hanging round your neck, then; no wonder you're always in difficulties. Are there any more of them?"

Again the old man suppressed that spasm, and the veins in his neck and forehead swelled alarmingly. If he had spoken he would infallibly have choked. He ceased eating, and putting his hands on the table tried to raise himself. He could not, and subsiding in his chair sat glaring at the stiff, quiet figure of his daughter.

"Don't be silly, Father, and make a scene before Meller. Finish your dinner."

He did not answer. He was not going to sit there to be dragooned and insulted! His helplessness had never so weighed on him before. It was like a revelation. A log—that had to put up with anything! A log! And, waiting for his valet to return, he cunningly took up his fork.

In that saintly voice of hers she said:

"I suppose you don't realize that it's a shock to me. I don't know what Ernest will think——"

"Ernest be d——d."

"I do wish, Father, you wouldn't swear."

Old Heythorp's rage found vent in a sort of rumble. How the devil had he gone on all these years in the same house with that woman, dining with her day after day! But the servant had come back now, and putting down his fork he said:

"Help me up!"

The man paused, thunderstruck, with the *soufflé* balanced.

To leave dinner unfinished—it was a portent!

"Help me up!"

"Mr. Heythorp's not very well, Meller; take his other arm."

The old man shook off her hand.

"I'm very well. Help me up. Dine in my own room in future."

Raised to his feet, he walked slowly out; but in his sanctum he did not sit down, obsessed by this first overwhelming realization of his helplessness. He stood swaying a little, holding on to the table, till the servant, having finished serving dinner, brought in his port.

"Are you waiting to sit down, sir?"

He shook his head. Hang it, he could do that for himself, anyway. He must think of something to fortify his position against that woman. And he said:

"Send me Molly!"

"Yes, sir." The man put down the port and went.

Old Heythorp filled his glass, drank, and filled again. He took a cigar from the box and lighted it. The girl came in, a grey-eyed, dark-haired damsel, and stood with her hands folded, her head a little to one side, her lips a little parted. The old man said:

"You're a human being."

"I would hope so, sirr."

"I'm going to ask you something as a human being—not a servant—see?"

"No, sirr; but I will be glad to do annything you like."

"Then put your nose in here every now and then, to see if I want anything. Meller goes out sometimes. Don't say anything; just put your nose in."

"Oh! an' I will; 'tis a pleasure 'twill be to do ut."

He nodded, and when she had gone lowered himself into his chair with a sense of appeasement. Pretty girl! Comfort to see a pretty face—not a pale, peeky thing like Adela's. His anger burned up anew.

So she counted on his helplessness, had begun to count on that, had she? She should see that there was life in the old dog yet! And his sacrifice of the uneaten *soufflé,* the still less eaten mushrooms, the peppermint sweet with which he usually concluded dinner, seemed to consecrate that purpose. They all thought he was a hulk, without a shot left in the locker! He had seen a couple of them at the Board that afternoon shrugging at each other, as though saying: "Look at him!" And young Farney pitying him. Pity, forsooth! And that coarse-grained solicitor chap at the creditors' meeting curling his lips as much to say: "One foot in the grave!" He had seen the clerks dowsing the glim of their grins; and that young pup Bob Pillin screwing up his supercilious mug over his dog-collar. He knew that scented humbug Rosamund was getting scared that he'd drop off before she'd squeezed him dry. And his valet was always looking him up and down queerly. As to that holy woman——! Not quite so fast! Not quite so fast! And filling his glass for the fourth time, he slowly sucked down the dark red fluid, with the "old boots" flavor which his soul loved, and, drawing deep at his cigar, closed his eyes.

II

I §

The room in the hotel where the general meetings of "The Island Navigation Company" were held was nearly full when the secretary came through the door which as yet divided the shareholders from their directors. Having surveyed their empty chairs, their ink and papers, and nodded to a shareholder or two, he stood, watch in hand, contemplating the congregation. A thicker attendance than he had ever seen! Due, no doubt, to the lower dividend, and this Pillin business. And his tongue curled. For if he had a natural contempt for his Board, with the exception of the chairman, he had a still more natural contempt for his shareholders. Amusing spectacle when you come to think of it, a general meeting! Unique! Eighty or a hundred men, and five women, assembled through sheer devotion to their money. Was any other function in the world so single-hearted? Church was nothing to it—so many motives were mingled there with devotion to one's soul. A well-educated young man—reader of Anatole France, and other writers—he enjoyed ironic speculation. What earthly good did they think they got by coming here? Half-past two! He put his watch back into his pocket, and passed into the Board-room.

There, the fumes of lunch and of a short preliminary meeting made cosey the February atmosphere. By the fire four directors were conversing rather restlessly; the fifth was combing his beard; the chairman sat with eyes closed and red lips moving rhythmically in the sucking of a lozenge, the slips of his speech ready in his hand. The secretary said in his cheerful voice: "Time, sir."

Old Heythorp swallowed, lifted his arms, rose with help, and walked through to his place at the centre of the table. The five directors followed. And, standing at the chairman's right, the secretary read the minutes, forming the words precisely with his curling tongue. Then, assisting the chairman to his feet, he watched those rows of faces, and thought: 'Mistake to let them see he can't get up without help. He ought to have let me read his speech—I wrote it.'

The chairman began to speak:

"It is my duty and my pleasure, ladies and gentlemen, for the nineteenth consecutive year to present to you the directors' report and the accounts for the past twelve months. You will all have had special notice of a measure of policy on which your Board has decided, and to which you will be asked to-day to give your adherence—to that I shall come at the end of my remarks. . . ."

"Excuse me, sir; we can't hear a word down here."

'Ah!' thought the secretary, 'I was expecting that.'

The chairman went on, undisturbed. But several shareholders now rose, and the same speaker said testily: "We might as well go home. If the chairman's got no voice, can't somebody read for him?"

The chairman took a sip of water, and resumed. Almost all in the last six rows were now on their feet, and amid a hubbub of murmurs the chairman held out to the secretary the slips of his speech, and fell heavily back into his chair.

The secretary re-read from the beginning; and as each sentence fell from his tongue, he thought: 'How good that is!' 'That's very clear!' 'A neat touch!' 'This is getting them.' It seemed to him a pity they could not know it was all his composition. When at last he came to the Pillin sale he paused for a second.

"I come now to the measure of policy to which I made allusion at the beginning of my speech. Your Board has decided to expand your enterprise by purchasing the entire fleet of Pillin & Co., Ltd. By this transaction we become the owners of the four steamships *Smyrna, Damascus, Tyre,* and *Sidon,* vessels in prime condition with a total freight-carrying capacity of fifteen thousand tons, at the low inclusive price of sixty thousand pounds. Gentlemen, *'Vestigia nulla retrorsum!'* "—it was the chairman's phrase, his bit of the speech, and the secretary did it more than justice. "Times are bad, but your Board is emphatically of the opinion that they are touching bottom; and this, in their view, is the psychological moment for a forward stroke. They confidently recommend your adoption of their policy and the ratification of this purchase, which they believe will, in the not far distant future, substantially increase the profits of the Company." The secretary sat down with reluctance. The speech should have continued with a number of appealing sentences which he had carefully prepared, but the chairman had cut them out with the simple comment: "They ought to be glad of the chance." It was, in his view, an error.

The director who had combed his beard now rose—a man of presence, who might be trusted to say nothing long and suavely. While he was speaking the secretary was busy noting whence opposition was likely to come. The majority were sitting owl-like—a good sign; but some dozen were studying their copies of the report, and three at least were making notes—Westgate, for instance, who wanted to get on the Board, and was sure to make himself unpleasant—the time-honored method of vinegar; and Batterson, who also desired to come on, and might be trusted to support the Board—the time-honored method of oil; while, if one knew anything of human nature, the fellow who had complained that he might as well go home would have something uncomfortable to say. The director finished his remarks, combed his beard with his fingers, and sat down.

A momentary pause ensued. Then Messieurs Westgate and Batterson rose together. Seeing the chairman nod towards the latter, the secretary thought: 'Mistake! He should have humored Westgate by giving him precedence.' But that was the worst of the old man, he had no notion of the *suaviter in modo!* Mr. Batterson—thus unchained—would like, if he might be so allowed, to congratulate the Board on having piloted their ship so smoothly through the troublous waters of the past year. With their worthy chairman still at the helm, he had no doubt that in spite of the still low—he would not say falling—barometer, and the—er—unseasonable climacteric, they might rely on weathering the—er—he would not say storm. He would confess that the present dividend of four per cent. was not one which satisfied every aspiration ("Hear, hear!"), but speaking for himself, and he hoped for others—and here Mr. Batterson looked round—he recognized that in all the circumstances it was as much as they had the right—er—to expect. But following the bold but to *his* mind prudent development which the Board proposed to make, he thought that they might reasonably, if not sanguinely, anticipate a more golden future. ("No, no!") A shareholder said, "No, no!" That might seem to indicate a certain lack of confidence in the special proposal before the meeting. ("Yes!") From that lack of confidence he would like at once to dissociate himself. Their chairman, a man of foresight and acumen, and valor proved on many a field and—er—sea, would not have committed himself to this policy without good reason. In his opinion they were in safe hands, and he was glad to register his support of the measure proposed. The chairman had well said in his speech: *"Vestigia nulla retrorsum!"* Shareholders would agree with him that there could be no better motto for Englishmen. Ahem!

Mr. Batterson sat down. And Mr. Westgate rose: He wanted—he said—to know more, much more, about this proposition, which to his mind was of a very dubious wisdom . . . 'Ah!' thought the secretary, 'I told the old boy he must tell them more.' . . . To whom, for instance, had the proposal first been made? To him!—the chairman said. Good! But why were Pillins selling, if freights were to go up, as they were told?

"Matter of opinion."

"Quite so; and in my opinion they are going lower, and Pillins were right to sell. It follows that we are wrong to buy." ("Hear, hear!" "No, no!") "Pillins are shrewd people. What does the chairman say? Nerves! Does he mean to tell us that this sale was the result of nerves?"

The chairman nodded.

"That appears to me a somewhat fantastic theory; but I will leave that and confine myself to asking the grounds on which the chairman bases his confidence; in fact, what it is which is actuating the Board in pressing on us at such a time what I have no hesitation in stigmatizing as a rash proposal. In a word, I want light as well as leading in this matter."

Mr. Westgate sat down.

What would the chairman do now? The situation was distinctly awkward—seeing his helplessness and the luke-warmness of the Board behind him. And the secretary felt more strongly than ever the absurdity of his being an underling, he who in a few well-chosen words could so easily have twisted the meeting round his thumb. Suddenly he heard the long, rumbling sigh which preluded the chairman's speeches.

"Has any other gentleman anything to say before I move the adoption of the report?"

Phew! That would put their backs up. Yes, sure enough it had brought that fellow, who had said he might as well go home, to his feet! Now for something nasty!

"Mr. Westgate requires answering. I don't like this business. I don't impute anything to anybody; but it looks to me as if there were something behind it which the shareholders ought to be told. Not only that; but, to speak frankly, I'm not satisfied to be ridden over roughshod in this fashion by one who, whatever he may have been in the past, is obviously not now in the prime of his faculties."

With a gasp the secretary thought: "I knew that was a plain-spoken man!"

He heard again the rumbling beside him. The chairman had gone crimson, his mouth was pursed, his little eyes were very blue.

"Help me up," he said.

The secretary helped him, and waited, rather breathless.

The chairman took a sip of water, and his voice, unexpectedly loud, broke an ominous hush:

"Never been so insulted in my life. My best services have been at your disposal for nineteen years; you know what measure of success this Company has attained. I am the oldest man here, and my experience of shipping is, I hope, a little greater than that of the two gentlemen who spoke last. I have done my best for you, ladies and gentlemen, and we shall see whether you are going to endorse an indictment of my judgment and of my honour, if I am to take the last speaker seriously. This purchase is for your good. 'There is a tide in the affairs of men'—and I for one am not content, never have been, to stagnate. If that is what you want, however, by all means give your support to these gentlemen and have done with it. I tell you freights will go up before the end of the year; the purchase is a sound one, more than a sound one—I, at any rate, stand or fall by it. Refuse to ratify it, if you like; if you do, I shall resign."

He sank back into his seat. The secretary, stealing a glance, thought with a sort of enthusiasm: 'Bravo! Who'd have thought he could rally his voice like that? A good touch, too, about his honor! I believe he's knocked them. It's still dicky, though, if that fellow at the back gets up again; the old chap can't work that stop a second time.' Ah! here was 'old Applepie' on his hind legs. That was all right!

"I do not hesitate to say that I am an old friend of the chairman; we are, many of us, old friends of the chairman, and it has been painful to me, and I doubt not to others, to hear an attack made on him. If he is old in body, he is young in mental vigor and courage. I wish we were all as young. We ought to stand by him; I say, we ought to stand by him." ("Hear, hear! Hear, hear!") And the secretary thought: 'That's done it!' And he felt a sudden odd emotion, watching the chairman bobbing his body, like a wooden top, at old Appleby; and old Appleby bobbing back. Then, seeing a shareholder close to the door get up, thought: 'What's that? I know his face—Ah! yes; Ventnor, the solicitor—he's one of the chairman's creditors that are coming again this afternoon. What now?'

"I can't agree that we ought to let sentiment interfere with our judgment in this matter. The question is simply: How are our pockets going to be affected? I came here with some misgivings, but the attitude of the chairman has been such as to remove them; and I shall support the proposition." The secretary thought: 'That's all right—only, he said it rather queerly—rather queerly.'

Then, after a long silence, the chairman, without rising, said:

"I move the adoption of the report and accounts."

"I second that."

"Those in favor signify the same in the usual way. Contrary? Carried." The secretary noted the dissentients, six in number, and that Mr. Westgate did not vote.

A quarter of an hour later he stood in the body of the emptying room supplying names to one of the gentlemen of the Press.

The passionless fellow said: "Haythorp, with an 'a'; oh! an 'e'; he seems an old man. Thank you. I may have the slips? Would you like to see a proof? With an 'a' you said—oh! an 'e.' Good afternoon!" And the secretary thought: 'Those fellows, what *does* go on inside them? Fancy not knowing the old chairman by now!'. . .

2 §

Back in the proper office of "The Island Navigation Company" old Heythorp sat smoking a cigar and smiling like a purring cat. He was dreaming a little of his triumph, sifting with his old brain, still subtle, the wheat from the chaff of the demurrers: Westgate—nothing in that—professional discontent till they silenced him with a place on the Board—but not while *he* held the reins! That chap at the back—an ill-conditioned fellow: "Something behind!" Suspicious brute! There *was* something—but—hang it! they might think themselves lucky to get four ships at that price, and all due to him! It was on the last speaker that his mind dwelt with a doubt. That fellow Ventnor, to whom he owed money—there had been something just a little queer about his tone—as much as to say, "I smell a rat." Well! one would see that at the creditors' meeting in half an hour.

"Mr. Pillin, sir."

"Show him in!"

In a fur coat which seemed to extinguish his thin form, Joe Pillin entered. It was snowing, and the cold had nipped and yellowed his meagre face between its slight grey whiskering. He said thinly:

"How are you, Sylvanus? Aren't you perished in this cold?"

"Warm as toast. Sit down. Take off your coat."

"Oh! I should be lost without it. You must have a fire inside you. So—so it's gone through?"

Old Heythorp nodded; and Joe Pillin, wandering like a spirit, scrutinized the shut door. He came back to the table, and said in a low voice:

"It's a great sacrifice."

Old Heythorp smiled.

"Have you signed the deed poll?"

Producing a parchment from his pocket, Joe Pillin unfolded it with caution to disclose his signature, and said:

"I don't like it—it's irrevocable."

A chuckle escaped old Heythorp.

"As death."

Joe Pillin's voice passed up into the treble clef.

"I can't bear irrevocable things. I consider you stampeded me, playing on my nerves."

Examining the signatures old Heythorp murmured:

"Tell your lawyer to lock it up. He must think you a sad dog, Joe."

"Ah! Suppose on my death it comes to the knowledge of my wife!"

"She won't be able to make it hotter for you than you'll be already."

Joe Pillin replaced the deed within his coat, emitting a queer thin noise. He simply could not bear joking on such subjects.

"Well," he said, "you've got your way; you always do. Who is this Mrs. Larne? You oughtn't to keep me in the dark. It seems my boy met her at your house. You told me she didn't come there."

Old Heythorp said with relish:

"Her husband was my son by a woman I was fond of before I married; her children are my grandchildren. You've provided for them. Best thing you ever did."

"I don't know—I don't know. I'm sorry you told me. It makes it all the more doubtful. As soon as the transfer's complete, I shall get away abroad. This cold's killing me. I wish you'd give me your recipe for keeping warm."

"Get a new inside."

Joe Pillin regarded his old friend with a sort of yearning. "And yet," he said, "I suppose, with your full-blooded habit, your life hangs by a thread, doesn't it?"

"A stout one, my boy!"

"Well, good-bye, Sylvanus. You're a Job's comforter; I must be getting home." He put on his hat, and, lost in his fur coat, passed out into the corridor. On the stairs he met a man who said:

"How do you do, Mr. Pillin? I know your son. Been seeing the chairman? I see your sale's gone through all right. I hope that'll do us some good, but I suppose you think the other way?"

Peering at him from under his hat, Joe Pillin said:

"Mr. Ventnor, I think? Thank you! It's very cold, isn't it?" And, with that cautious remark, he passed on down.

Alone again, old Heythorp thought: 'By George! What a wavering, quavering, thread-paper of a fellow! What misery life must be to a chap like that! He walks in fear—he wallows in it. Poor devil!' And a curious feeling swelled his heart, of elation, of lightness such as he had not known for years. Those two young things were safe now from penury—safe! After dealing with those infernal creditors of his he would go round and have a look at the children. With a hundred and twenty a year the boy could go into the Army—best place for a young scamp like that. The girl would go off like hot cakes, of course, but she needn't take the first calf that came along. As for their mother, she must look after herself; nothing under two thousand a year would keep *her* out of debt. But trust her for wheedling and bluffing her way out of any scrape! Watching his cigar-smoke curl and disperse he was conscious of the strain he had been under these last six weeks, aware suddenly of how greatly he had balked at thought of to-day's general meeting. Yes! It might have turned out nasty. He knew well enough the forces on the Board, and off, who would be only too glad to shelve him. If he were shelved here his other two Companies would be sure to follow suit, and bang would go every penny of his income—he would be a pauper dependent on that holy woman. Well! Safe now for another year if he could stave off these sharks once more. It might be a harder job this time, but he was in luck—in luck, and it must hold. And taking a luxurious pull at his cigar, he rang the handbell.

"Bring 'em in here, Mr. Farney. And let me have a cup of China tea as strong as you can make it."

"Yes, sir. Will you see the proof of the press report, or will you leave it to me?"

"To you."

"Yes, sir. It was a good meeting, wasn't it?"

Old Heythorp nodded.

"Wonderful how your voice came back just at the right moment. I was afraid things were going to be difficult. The insult did it, I think, It was a monstrous thing to say. I could have punched his head."

Again old Heythorp nodded; and, looking into the secretary's fine blue eyes, he repeated: "Bring 'em in."

The lonely minute before the entrance of his creditors passed in the thought: 'So that's how it struck him! Short shrift I should get if it came out.'

The gentlemen, who numbered ten this time, bowed to their debtor, evidently wondering why the deuce they troubled to be polite to an old man who kept them out of their money. Then, the secretary reappearing with a cup of China tea, they watched while their debtor drank it. The feat was tremulous. Would he get through without spilling it all down his front, or choking? To those unaccustomed to his private life it was slightly miraculous. He put the cup down empty, tremblingly removed some yellow drops from the little white tuft below his lip, relit his cigar, and said:

"No use beating about the bush, gentlemen; I can offer you fourteen hundred a year so long as I live and hold my directorships, and not a penny more. If you can't accept that, you must make me bankrupt and get about sixpence in the pound. My qualifying shares will fetch a couple of thousand at market price. I own nothing else. The house I live in, and everything in it, barring my clothes, my wine, and my cigars, belong to my daughter under a settlement fifteen years old. My solicitors and bankers will give you every information. That's the position in a nutshell."

In spite of business habits the surprise of the ten gentlemen was only partially concealed. A man who owed them so much would naturally say he owned nothing, but would he refer them to his solicitors and bankers unless he were telling the truth? Then Mr. Ventnor said:

"Will you submit your pass books?"

"No, but I'll authorize my bankers to give you a full statement of my receipts for the last five years—longer, if you like."

The strategic stroke of placing the ten gentlemen round the Board table had made it impossible for them to consult freely without being overheard, but the low-voiced transference of thought travelling round was summed up at last by Mr. Brownbee.

"We think, Mr. Heythorp, that your fees and dividends should enable you to set aside for us a larger sum. Sixteen hundred, in fact, is what we think you should give us yearly. Representing, as we do, sixteen thousand pounds, the prospect is not cheering, but we hope you have some good years before you yet. We understand your income to be two thousand pounds."

Old Heythorp shook his head. "Nineteen hundred and thirty pounds in a good year. Must eat and drink; must have a man to look after me—not as active as I was. Can't do on less than five hundred pounds. Fourteen hundred's all I can give you, gentlemen; it's an advance of two hundred pounds. That's my last word."

The silence was broken by Mr. Ventnor.

"And it's my last word that I'm not satisfied. If these other gentleman accept your proposition I shall be forced to consider what I can do on my own account."

The old man stared at him, and answered:

"Oh! you will, sir; we shall see."

The others had risen and were gathered in a knot at the end of the table; old Heythorp and Mr. Ventnor alone remained seated. The old man's lower lip projected till the white hairs below stood out like bristles. 'You ugly dog,' he was thinking, 'you think you've got something up your sleeve. Well, do your worst!' The "ugly dog" rose abruptly and joined the others. And old Heythorp closed his eyes, sitting perfectly still, with his cigar, which had gone out, sticking up between his teeth. Mr. Brownbee turning to voice the decision come to, cleared his throat.

"Mr. Heythorp," he said, "if your bankers and solicitors bear out your statements, we shall accept your offer *faute de mieux,* in consideration of your——" but meeting the old man's eyes, which said so very plainly: "Blow your consideration!" he ended with a stammer. "Perhaps you will kindly furnish us with the authorization you spoke of?"

Old Heythorp nodded, and Mr. Brownbee, with a little bow, clasped his hat to his breast and moved towards the door. The nine gentlemen followed. Mr. Ventnor, bringing up the rear, turned and looked back. But the old man's eyes were already closed again.

The moment his creditors were gone, old Heythorp sounded the handbell.

"Help me up, Mr. Farney. That Ventnor—what's his holding?"

"Quite small. Only ten shares, I think."

"Ah! What time is it?"

"Quarter to four, sir."

"Get me a taxi."

After visiting his bank and his solicitors he struggled once more into his cab and caused it to be driven towards Millicent Villas. A kind of sleepy triumph permeated his whole being, bumped and shaken by the cab's rapid progress. So! He was free of those sharks now so long as he could hold on to his Companies; and he would still have a hundred a year or more to spare for Rosamund and her youngsters. He could live on four hundred, or even three-fifty, without losing his independence, for there would be no standing life in that holy woman's house unless he could pay his own scot! A good day's work! The best for many a long month!

The cab stopped before the villa.

3 §

There are rooms which refuse to give away their owners, and rooms which seem to say: 'They really are like this.' Of such was Rosamund Larne's—a sort of permanent confession, seeming to remark to anyone who entered: 'Her taste? Well, you can see—cheerful and exuberant; her habits—yes, she sits here all the morning in a dressing-gown, smoking cigarettes and dropping ink; kindly observe my carpet. Notice the piano—it has a look of coming and going, according to the exchequer. This very deep-cushioned sofa is permanent, however; the water-colors on the walls are safe, too—they're by herself. Mark the scent of mimosa—she likes flowers, and likes them strong. No clock, of course. Examine the bureau—she is obviously always ringing for "the drumstick," and saying: "Where's this, Ellen, and where's that? You naughty gairl, you've been tidying." Cast an eye on that pile of manuscript—she has evidently a genius for composition; it flows off her pen—like Shakespeare, she never blots a line. See how she's had the electric light put in, instead of that horrid gas; but try and turn either of them on—you can't; last quarter isn't paid, of course; and she uses an oil lamp, you can tell that by the ceiling. The dog over there, who will not answer to the name of "Carmen," a Pekinese spaniel like a little Djin, all prominent eyes rolling their blacks, and no nose between—yes, Carmen looks as if she didn't know what was coming next; she's right—it's a pet-and-slap-again life! Consider, too, the fittings of the tea-tray, rather soiled, though not quite tin, but I say unto you that no millionaire's in all its glory ever had a liqueur bottle on it.'

When old Heythorp entered this room, which extended from back to front of the little house, preceded by the announcement "Mr. Æsop," it was resonant with a very clatter-bodandigo of noises, from Phyllis playing the Machiche; from the boy Jock on the hearthrug, emitting at short intervals the most piercing notes from an ocarina; from Mrs. Larne on the sofa, talking with her trailing volubility to Bob Pillin; from Bob Pillin muttering: "Ye—es! Qui-ite! Ye—es!" and gazing at Phyllis over his collar. And, on the window-sill, as far as she could get from all this noise, the little dog Carmen was rolling her eyes. At sight of their visitor Jock blew one rending screech, and bolting behind the sofa, placed his chin on its top, so that nothing but his round pink unmoving face was visible, and the dog Carmen tried to climb the blind cord.

Encircled from behind by the arms of Phyllis, and preceded by the gracious perfumed bulk of Mrs. Larne, old Heythorp was escorted to the sofa. It was low, and when he had plumped down on to it, the boy Jock emitted a hollow groan. Bob Pillin was the first to break the silence.

"How are you, sir? I hope it's gone through."

Old Heythorp nodded. His eyes were fixed on the liqueur, and Mrs. Larne murmured:

"Guardy, you *must* try our new liqueur. Jock, you awful boy, get up and bring Guardy a glass."

The boy Jock approached the tea-table, took up a glass, put it to his eye and filled it rapidly.

"You horrible boy, you could see that glass has been used."

In a high round voice rather like an angel's, Jock answered:

"All right, Mother; I'll get rid of it," and rapidly swallowing the yellow liqueur, took up another glass.

Mrs. Larne laughed.

"What *am* I to do with him?"

A loud shriek prevented a response. Phyllis, who had taken her brother by the ear to lead him to the door, let him go to clasp her injured self. Bob Pillin went hastening towards her; and following the young man with her chin, Mrs. Larne said, smiling:

"Aren't those children awful? He's such a nice fellow. We like him so much, Guardy."

The old man grinned. So she was making up to that young pup! Rosamund Larne, watching him, murmured:

"Oh! Guardy, you're as bad as Jock. He takes after you terribly. Look at the shape of his head. Jock, come here!" The innocent boy approached; with his girlish complexion, his flowery blue eyes, his perfect mouth, he stood before his mother like a large cherub. And suddenly he blew his ocarina in a dreadful manner. Mrs. Larne launched a box at his ears, and receiving the wind of it he fell prone.

"That's the way he behaves. Be off with you, you awful boy. I want to talk to Guardy."

The boy withdrew on his stomach, and sat against the wall cross-legged, fixing his innocent round eyes on old Heythorp. Mrs. Larne sighed.

"Things are worse and worse, Guardy. I'm at my wit's end to tide over this quarter. You wouldn't advance me a hundred on my new story? I'm sure to get two for it in the end."

The old man shook his head.

"I've done something for you and the children," he said. "You'll get notice of it in a day or two; ask no questions."

"Oh! Guardy! Oh, you dear!" And her gaze rested on Bob Pillin, leaning over the piano, where Phyllis again sat.

Old Heythorp snorted. "What are you cultivating that young gaby for? She mustn't be grabbed up by any fool who comes along."

Mrs. Larne murmured at once:

"Of course, the dear gairl is *much* too young. Phyllis, come and talk to Guardy!"

When the girl was installed beside him on the sofa, and he had felt that little thrill of warmth the proximity of youth can bring, he said:

"Been a good girl?"

She shook her head.

"Can't when Jock's not at school. Mother can't pay for him this term."

Hearing his name, the boy Jock blew his ocarina till Mrs. Larne drove him from the room, and Phyllis went on:

"He's more awful than anything you can think of. Was my dad at all like him, Guardy? Mother's always so mysterious about him. I suppose you knew him well."

Old Heythorp, incapable of confusion, answered stolidly:

"Not very."

"Who was *his* father? I don't believe even mother knows."

"Man about town in my day."

"Oh! your day must have been jolly. Did you wear peg-top trousers, and dundrearies?"

Old Heythorp nodded.

"What larks! And I suppose you had lots of adventures with opera dancers and gambling. The young men are all so good now." Her eyes rested on Bob Pillin. "That young man's a perfect stick of goodness."

Old Heythorp grunted.

"You wouldn't know how good he was," Phyllis went on musingly, "unless you'd sat next him in a tunnel. The other day he had his waist squeezed and he simply sat still and did nothing. And then when the tunnel ended, it was Jock after all, not me. His face was—Oh! ah! ha! ha! Ah! ha!" She threw back her head, displaying all her white, round throat. Then edging near, she whispered:

"He likes to pretend, of course, that he's fearfully lively. He's promised to take mother and me to the theatre and supper afterwards. Won't it be scrummy! Only, I haven't anything to go in."

Old Heythorp said: "What do you want? Irish poplin?"

Her mouth opened wide: "Oh! Guardy! Soft white satin!"

"How many yards'll go round you?"

"I should think about twelve. We could make it ourselves. You *are* a chook!"

A scent of hair, like hay, enveloped him, her lips bobbed against his nose; and there came a feeling in his heart as when he rolled the first sip of a special wine against his palate. This little house was a rumpty-too affair, her mother was a humbug, the boy a cheeky young rascal, but there was a warmth here he never felt in that big house which had been his wife's and was now his holy daughter's. And once more he rejoiced at his day's work, and the success of his breach of trust, which put some little ground beneath these young feet, in a hard and unscrupulous world. Phyllis whispered in his ear:

"Guardy, do look; he *will* stare at me like that. Isn't it awful—like a boiled rabbit?"

Bob Pillin, attentive to Mrs. Larne, was gazing with all his might over her shoulder at the girl. The young man was moonstruck, that was clear! There was something almost touching in the stare of those puppy-dog's eyes. And he thought: 'Young beggar—wish I were his age!' The utter injustice of having an old and helpless body, when your desire for enjoyment was as great as ever! They said a man was as old as he felt Fools! A man was as old as his legs and arms, and not a day younger. He heard the girl beside him utter a discomfortable sound, and saw her face cloud as if tears were not far off; she jumped up, and going to the window, lifted the little dog and buried her face in its brown and white fur. Old Heythorp thought: 'She sees that her humbugging mother is using her as a decoy.' But she had come back, and the little dog, rolling its eyes horribly at the strange figure on the sofa, in a desperate effort to escape succeeded in reaching her shoulder, where it stayed perched like a cat, held by one paw and trying to back away into space. Old Heythorp said abruptly:

"Are you very fond of your mother?"

"Of course I am, Guardy. I adore her."

"H'm! Listen to me. When you come of age or marry, you'll have a hundred and twenty a year of your own that you can't get rid of. Don't ever be persuaded into doing what you don't want. And remember: Your mother's a sieve, no good giving her money; keep what you'll get for yourself—it's only a pittance, and you'll want it all—every penny."

Phyllis's eyes had opened very wide; so that he wondered if she had taken in his words.

"Oh! Isn't money horrible, Guardy?"

"The want of it."

"No, it's beastly altogether. If only we were like birds. Or if one could put out a plate overnight, and have just enough in the morning to use during the day."

Old Heythorp sighed.

"There's only one thing in life that matters—independence. Lose that, and you lose everything. That's the value of money. Help me up."

Phyllis stretched out her hands, and the little dog, running down her back, resumed its perch on the windowsill, close to the blind cord.

Once on his feet, old Heythorp said:

"Give me a kiss. You'll have your satin to-morrow."

Then looking at Bob Pillin, he remarked:

"Going my way? I'll give you a lift."

The young man, giving Phyllis one appealing look, answered dully: "Tha—anks!" and they went out together to the taxi. In that draughtless vehicle they sat, full of who knows what contempt of age for youth, and youth for age; the old man resenting this young pup's aspiration to his granddaughter; the young man annoyed that this old image had dragged him away before he wished to go. Old Heythorp said at last:

"Well?"

Thus expected to say something, Bob Pillin muttered:

"Glad your meetin' went off well, sir. You scored a triumph I should think."

"Why?"

"Oh! I don't know. I thought you had a good bit of opposition to contend with."

Old Heythorp looked at him.

"Your grandmother!" he said; then, with his habitual instinct of attack, added: "You make the most of your opportunities, I see."

At this rude assault Bob Pillin's red-cheeked face assumed a certain dignity. "I don't know what you mean, sir. Mrs. Larne is very kind to me."

"No doubt. But don't try to pick the flowers."

Thoroughly upset, Bob Pillin preserved a dogged silence. This fortnight, since he had first met Phyllis in old Heythorp's hall, had been the most singular of his existence up to now. He would never have believed that a fellow could be so quickly and completely bowled, could succumb without a kick, without even wanting to kick. To one with his philosophy of having a good time and never committing himself too far, it was in the nature of "a fair knock-out," and yet so pleasurable, except for the wear and tear about one's chances. If only he knew how far the old boy really counted in the matter! To say: "My intentions are strictly honorable" would be old-fashioned; besides—the old fellow might have no right to hear it. They called him Guardy, but without knowing more he did not want to admit the old curmudgeon's right to interfere.

"Are you a relation of theirs, sir?"

Old Heythorp nodded.

Bob Pillin went on with desperation:

"I should like to know what your objection to me is."

The old man turned his head so far as he was able; a grim smile bristled the hairs about his lips, and twinkled in his eyes. What did he object to? Why—everything! Object to! That sleek head, those puppy-dog eyes, fattish red cheeks, high collars, pearl pin, spats, and drawl—pah! the imbecility, the smugness of his mug; no go, no devil in any of his sort, in any of these fish-veined, coddled-up young bloods; nothing but playing for safety! And he wheezed out:

"Milk and water masquerading as port wine."

Bob Pillin frowned.

It was almost too much for the composure even of a man of the world. That this paralytic old fellow should express contempt for his virility was really the last thing in jests. Luckily he could not take it seriously. But suddenly he thought: 'What if he really has the power to stop my going there, and means to turn them against me!' And his heart quailed.

"Awfully sorry, sir," he said, "if you don't think I'm wild enough. Anything I can do for you in that line——"

The old man grunted; and realizing that he had been quite witty, Bob Pillin went on:

"I know I'm not in debt, no entanglements, got a decent income, pretty good expectations and all that; but I can soon put that all right if I'm not fit without."

It was perhaps his first attempt at irony, and he could not help thinking how good it was.

But old Heythorp preserved a deadly silence. He looked like a stuffed man, a regular Aunt Sally sitting there, with the fixed red in his cheeks, his stivered hair, square block of a body, and no neck that you could see—only wanting the pipe in his mouth! Could there really be danger from such an old idol? The idol spoke:

"I'll give you a word of advice. Don't hang around there, or you'll burn your fingers. Remember me to your father. Good-night!"

The taxi had stopped before the house in Sefton Park. An insensate impulse to remain seated and argue the point fought in Bob Pillin with an impulse to leap out, shake his fist in at the window, and walk off. He merely said, however:

"Thanks for the lift. Good-night!" And, getting out deliberately, he walked off.

Old Heythorp, waiting for the driver to help him up, thought:

"Fatter, but no more guts than his father!"

In his sanctum he sank at once into his chair. It was wonderfully still there every day at this hour; just the click of the coals, just the faintest ruffle from the wind in the trees of the park. And it was cosily warm, only the fire lightening the darkness. A drowsy beatitude pervaded the old man. A good day's work! A triumph—that young pup had said. Yes! Something of a triumph! He had held on, and won. And dinner to look forward to, yet. A nap—a nap! And soon, rhythmic, soft, sonorous, his breathing rose, with now and then that pathetic twitching of the old who dream.

III

1 §

When Bob Pillin emerged from the little front garden of 23, Millicent Villas ten days later, his sentiments were ravelled, and he could not get hold of an end to pull straight the stuff of his mind.

He had found Mrs. Larne and Phyllis in the sitting-room, and Phyllis had been crying; he was sure she had been crying; and that memory still infected the sentiments evoked by later happenings. Old Heythorp had said: "You'll burn your fingers." The process had begun. Having sent her daughter away on a pretext really a bit too thin, Mrs. Larne had installed him beside her scented bulk on the sofa, and poured into his ear such a tale of monetary woe and entanglement, such a mass of present difficulties and rosy prospects, that his brain still whirled, and only one thing emerged clearly—that she wanted fifty pounds, which she would repay him on quarter-day; for their Guardy had made a settlement by which, until the dear children came of age, she would have sixty pounds every quarter. It was only a question of a few weeks; he might ask Messrs. Scriven and Coles; they would tell him the security was quite safe. He certainly might ask Messrs. Scriven and Coles—they happened to be his father's solicitors; but it hardly seemed to touch the point. Bob Pillin had a certain shrewd caution, and the point was whether he was going to begin to lend money to a woman who, he could see, might borrow up to seventy times seven on the strength of his infatuation for her daughter. That was rather too strong! Yet, if he didn't—she might take a sudden dislike to him, and where would he be then? Besides, would not a loan make his position stronger? And then—such is the effect of love even on the younger generation—that thought seemed to him unworthy. If he lent at all, it would be from chivalry—ulterior motives might go hang! And the memory of the tear-marks on Phyllis's pretty pale-pink cheeks; and her petulantly mournful: "Oh! young man, isn't money beastly!" scraped his heart, and ravished his judgment. All the same, fifty pounds was fifty pounds, and goodness knew how much more; and what did he know of Mrs. Larne, after all, except that she was a relative of old Heythorp's, and wrote stories—told them too, if he was not mistaken? Perhaps it would be better to see Scrivens'. But again that absurd nobility assaulted him. Phyllis! Phyllis! Besides, were not settlements always drawn so that they refused to form security for anything? Thus, hampered and troubled, he hailed a cab. He was dining with the Ventnors on the Cheshire side, and would be late if he didn't get home sharp to dress.

Driving, white-tied and waistcoated, in his father's car, he thought with a certain contumely of the younger Ventnor girl, whom he had been wont to consider pretty before he knew Phyllis. And seated next her at dinner, he quite enjoyed his new sense of superiority to her charms, and the ease with which he could chaff and be agreeable. And all the time he suffered from the suppressed longing which scarcely ever left him now, to think and talk of Phyllis. Ventnor's fizz was good and plentiful, his old Madeira absolutely first chop, and the only other man present a teetotal curate, who withdrew with the ladies to talk his parish shop. Favored by these circumstances, and the perception that

Ventnor was an agreeable fellow, Bob Pillin yielded to his secret itch to get near the subject of his affections.

"Do you happen," he said airily, "to know a Mrs. Larne—relative of old Heythorp's—rather a handsome woman—she writes stories."

Mr. Ventnor shook his head. A closer scrutiny than Bob Pillin's would have seen that he also moved his ears.

"Of old Heythorp's? Didn't know he had any, except his daughter, and that son of his in the Admiralty."

Bob Pillin felt the glow of his secret hobby spreading within him. "She is, though—lives rather out of town; got a son and daughter. I thought you might know her stories—clever woman."

Mr. Ventnor smiled.

"Ah!" he said enigmatically, "these lady novelists! Does she make any money by them?"

Bob Pillin knew that to make money by writing meant success, but that not to make money by writing was artistic, and implied that you had private means, which perhaps was even more distinguished. And he said:

"Oh! she has private means, I know."

Mr. Ventnor reached for the Madeira.

"So she's a relative of old Heythorp's," he said. "He's a very old friend of your father's. He ought to go bankrupt, you know."

To Bob Pillin, glowing with passion and Madeira, the idea of bankruptcy seemed discreditable in connection with a relative of Phyllis. Besides, the old boy was far from that! Had he not just made this settlement on Mrs. Larne? And he said:

"I think you're mistaken. That's of the past."

Mr. Ventnor smiled.

"Will you bet?" he said.

Bob Pillin also smiled. "I should be bettin' on a certainty."

Mr. Ventnor passed his hand over his whiskered face. "Don't you believe it; he hasn't a mag to his name. Fill your glass."

Bob Pillin said, with a certain resentment:

"Well, I happen to know he's just made a settlement of five or six thousand pounds. Don't know if you call that being bankrupt."

"What! On this Mrs. Larne?"

Confused, uncertain whether he had said something derogatory or indiscreet, or something which added distinction to Phyllis, Bob Pillin hesitated, then gave a nod.

Mr. Ventnor rose and extended his short legs before the fire.

"No, my boy," he said. "No!"

Unaccustomed to flat contradiction, Bob Pillin reddened.

"I'll bet you a tenner. Ask Scrivens'."

Mr. Ventnor ejaculated:

"Scrivens'—but they're not——" then, staring rather hard he added: "I won't bet. You may be right. Scrivens' are your father's solicitors too, aren't they? Always been sorry he didn't come to me. Shall we join the ladies?" And to the drawing-room he preceded a young man more uncertain in his mind than on his feet. . . .

Charles Ventnor was not one to let you see that more was going on within than met the eye. But there was a good deal going on that evening, and after his conversation with young Bob he had occasion more than once to turn away and rub his hands together. When, after that second creditors' meeting, he had walked down the stairway which led to the offices of "The Island Navigation Company," he had been deep in thought. Short, squarely built, rather stout, with moustache and large mutton-chop whiskers of a red-brown, and a faint floridity in face and dress, he impressed at first sight only by a certain truly British vulgarity. One felt that here was a hail-fellow-well-met man who liked lunch and dinner, went to Scarborough for his summer holidays, sat on his wife, took his daughters out in a boat and was never sick. One felt that he went to church every Sunday morning, looked upwards as he moved through life, disliked the unsuccessful, and expanded with his second glass of wine. But then a clear look into his well-clothed face and red-brown eyes would give the feeling: 'There's something fulvous here; he might be a bit too foxy.' A third look brought the thought: 'He's certainly a bully.' He was not a large creditor of old Heythorp. With interest on the original, he calculated his claim at three hundred pounds—unredeemed shares in that old Ecuador mine. But he had waited for his money eight years, and could never imagine how it came about that he had been induced to wait so long. There had been, of course, for one who liked "big pots," a certain glamour about the personality of old Heythorp, still a bit of a swell in shipping circles, and a bit of an aristocrat in Liverpool. But during the last year Charles Ventnor had realized that the old chap's star had definitely set—when that happens, of course, there is no more glamour, and the time has come to get your money. Weakness in oneself and others is despicable! Besides, he had food for thought, and descending the stairs he chewed it. He smelt a rat—creatures for which both by nature and profession he had a nose. Through Bob Pillin, on whom he sometimes dwelt in connection with his younger daughter, he knew that old Pillin and old Heythorp had been friends for thirty years and more. That, to an astute mind, suggested something behind this sale. The thought had already occurred to him when he read his copy of the report. A commission would be a breach of trust, of course, but there were ways of doing things; the old chap was devilish hard pressed, and human nature was human nature! His lawyerish mind habitually put two and two together. The old fellow had deliberately appointed to meet his creditors again just after the general meeting which would decide the purchase—had said he might do something for them then. Had that no significance?

In these circumstances Charles Ventnor had come to the meeting with eyes wide open and mouth tight closed. And he had watched. It was certainly remarkable that such an old and feeble man with no neck at all, who looked indeed as if he might go off with apoplexy any moment, should actually say that he "stood or fell" by this purchase, knowing that if he fell he would be a beggar. Why should the old chap be so keen on getting it through? It would do him personally no good, unless—Exactly! He had left the meeting, therefore, secretly confident that old Heythorp had got something out of this transaction which would enable him to make a substantial proposal to his creditors. So that when the old man had declared that he was going to make none, something was turned sour in his heart, and he had said to himself: "All right, you old rascal! You don't know C. V." The cavalier manner of that beggarly old rip, the defiant look of his deep little eyes, had put a polish on the rancor of one who prided himself on letting no man get the better of him. All that evening, seated on one side of the fire, while Mrs. Ventnor sat on the other, and the younger daughter played Gounod's Serenade on the violin—he cogitated. And now and again he smiled, but not too much. He did not see his way as yet, but had little doubt that before long he would. It would not be hard to knock that chipped old idol off his perch. There was already a healthy feeling among the shareholders that he was past work and should be scrapped. The old chap should find that Charles V. was not to be defied; that when he got his teeth into a thing, he did not let it go. By hook or crook he would have the old man off his Boards, or his debt out of him as the price of leaving him alone. His life or his money—and the old fellow should determine which. With the memory of that defiance fresh within him, he almost hoped it might come to be the first, and turning to Mrs. Ventnor, he said abruptly:

"Have a little dinner Friday week, and ask young Pillin and the curate." He specified the curate, a teetotaller, because he had two daughters, and males and females must be paired, but he intended to pack him off after dinner to the drawing-room to discuss parish matters while he and Bob Pillin sat over their wine. What he expected to get out of the young man he did not as yet know.

On the day of the dinner, before departing for the office, he had gone to his cellar. Would three bottles of Perrier Jouet do the trick, or must he add one of the old Madeira? He decided to be on the safe side. A bottle or so of champagne went very little way with him personally, and young Pillin might be another.

The Madeira having done its work by turning the conversation into such an admirable channel, he had cut it short for fear young Pillin might drink the lot or get wind of the rat. And when his guests were gone, and his family had retired, he stood staring into the fire, putting together the pieces of the puzzle. Five or six thousand pounds—six would be ten per cent. on sixty! Exactly! Scrivens'—young Pillin had said! But Crow & Donkin, not Scriven & Coles, were old Heythorp's solicitors. What could that mean, save that the old man wanted to cover the tracks of a secret commission, and had handled the matter through solicitors who did not know the state of his affairs! But why Pillin's solicitors? With this sale just going through, it must look deuced fishy to them too. Was it all a mare's nest, after all? In such circumstances he himself would have taken the matter to a London firm who knew nothing of anybody. Puzzled, therefore, and rather disheartened, feeling too that touch of liver which was wont to follow his old Madeira, he went up to bed and woke his wife to ask her why the dickens they couldn't always have soup like that!

Next day he continued to brood over his puzzle, and no fresh light came; but having a matter on which his firm and Scrivens' were in touch, he decided to go over in person, and see if he could surprise something out of them. Feeling, from experience, that any really delicate matter would only be entrusted to the most responsible member of the firm, he had asked to see Scriven himself, and just as he had taken his hat to go, he said casually:

"By the way, you do some business for old Mr. Heythorp, don't you?"

Scriven, raising his eyebrows a little, muttered: "Er—no," in exactly the tone Mr. Ventnor himself used when he wished to imply that though he didn't as a fact do business, he probably soon would. He knew therefore that the answer was a true one. And nonplussed, he hazarded:

"Oh! I thought you did, in regard to a Mrs. Larne."

This time he had certainly drawn blood of sorts, for down came Scriven's eyebrows, and he said:

"Mrs. Larne—we know a Mrs. Larne, but not in that connection. Why?"

"Oh! Young Pillin told me——"

"Young Pillin! Why, it's his——!" A little pause, and then: "Old Mr. Heythorp's solicitors are Crow & Donkin, I believe."

Mr. Ventnor held out his hand. "Yes, yes," he said; "good-bye. Glad to have got that matter settled up," and out he went, and down the street, important, smiling. By George! He had got it! "It's his father"—Scriven had been going to say. What a plant! Exactly! Oh! neat! Old Pillin had made the settlement direct; and the solicitors were in the dark; that disposed of his difficulty about *them*. No money had passed between old Pillin and old Heythorp—not a penny. Oh! neat! But not neat enough for Charles Ventnor, who had that nose for rats. Then his smile died, and with a little chill he perceived that it was all based on supposition—not quite good enough to go on! What then? Somehow he must see this Mrs. Larne, or better—old Pillin himself. The point to ascertain was whether she had any connection of her own with Pillin. Clearly young Pillin didn't know of it; for, according to him, old Heythorp had made the settlement. By Jove! That old rascal was deep—all the more satisfaction in proving that he was not as deep as C. V. To unmask the old cheat was already beginning to seem in the nature of a public service. But on what pretext could he visit Pillin? A subscription to the Windeatt almshouses! That would make him talk in self-defence and he would take care to press the request to the actual point of getting a subscription. He caused himself to be driven to the Pillin residence in Sefton Park. Ushered into a room on the ground floor, heated in American fashion, Mr. Ventnor unbuttoned his coat. A man of sanguine constitution, he found this hot-house atmosphere a little trying. And having sympathetically obtained Joe Pillin's reluctant refusal—Quite so! One could not indefinitely extend one's subscriptions even for the best of causes!—he said gently:

"By the way, you know Mrs. Larne, don't you?"

The effect of that simple shot surpassed his highest hopes. Joe Pillin's face, never highly colored, turned a sort of grey; he opened his thin lips, shut them quickly, as birds do, and something seemed to pass with difficulty down his scraggy throat. The hollows, which nerve exhaustion delves in the cheeks of men whose cheek-bones are not high, increased alarmingly. For a moment he looked deathly; then, moistening his lips, he said:

"Larne—Larne? No, I don't seem——"

Mr. Ventnor, who had taken care to be drawing on his gloves, murmured:

"Oh! I thought—your son knows her; a relation of old Heythorp's," and he looked up.

Joe Pillin had his handkerchief to his mouth; he coughed feebly, then with more and more vigor:

"I'm in very poor health," he said, at last. "I'm getting abroad at once. This cold's killing me. What name did you say?" And he remained with his handkerchief against his teeth.

Mr. Ventnor repeated:

"Larne. Writes stories."

Joe Pillin muttered into his handkerchief:

"Ah! H'm! No—I—no! My son knows all sorts of people. I shall have to try Mentone. Are you going? Good-bye! Good-bye! I'm sorry; oh! ha! My cought—ah! ha h'h'm! Very distressing. Ye-hes! My cough—ah! ha h'h'm! Most distressing. Ye-hes!"

Out in the drive Mr. Ventnor took a deep breath of the frosty air. Not much doubt now! The two names had worked like charms. This weakly old fellow would make a pretty witness, would simply crumple under cross-examination. What a contrast to that hoary old sinner Heythorp, whose brazenness nothing could affect. The rat was as large as life! And the only point was how to make the best use of it. Then—for his experience was wide—the possibility dawned on him, that after all, this Mrs. Larne might only have been Old Pillin's mistress—or be his natural daughter, or have some other black-mailing hold on him. Any such connection would account for his agitation, for his denying her, for his son's ignorance. Only it wouldn't account for young Pillin's saying that old Heythorp had made the settlement. He could only have got that from the woman herself. Still, to make absolutely sure, he had better try and see her. But how? It would never do to ask Bob Pillin for an introduction, after this interview with his father. He would have to go on his own and chance it. Wrote stories did she? Perhaps a newspaper would know her address; or the Directory would give it—not a common name! And, hot on the scent, he drove to a post office. Yes, there it was, right enough! "Larne, Mrs. R.—23, Millicent Villas." And thinking to himself: 'No time like the present,' he turned in that direction. The job was delicate. He must be careful not to do anything which might compromise his power of making public use of his knowledge. Yes—ticklish! What he did now must have a proper legal bottom. Still, anyway you looked at it, he had a *right* to investigate a fraud on himself as a shareholder of "The Island Navigation Company," and a fraud on himself as a creditor of old Heythorp. Quite! But suppose this Mrs. Larne was really entangled with old Pillin, and the settlement a mere reward of virtue, easy or otherwise. Well! in that case there'd be no secret commission to make public, and he needn't go further. So that, in either event, he would be all right. Only—how to introduce himself? He might pretend he was a newspaper man wanting a story. No, that wouldn't do! He must not represent that he was what he was not, in case he had afterwards to justify his actions publicly, always a difficult thing, if you were not careful! At that moment there came into his mind a question Bob Pillin had asked the other night. "By the way, you can't borrow on a settlement, can you? Isn't there generally some clause against it?" Had this woman been trying to borrow from him on that settlement? But at this moment he reached the house, and got out of his cab still undecided as to how he was going to work the oracle. Impudence, constitutional and professional, sustained him in saying to the little maid:

"Mrs. Larne at home? Say Mr. Charles Ventnor, will you?"

His quick brown eyes took in the apparel of the passage which served for hall—the deep blue paper on the walls, lilac-patterned curtains over the doors, the well-known print of a nude young woman looking over her shoulder, and he thought: "H'm! Distinctly tasty!" They noted, too, a small brown-and-white dog cowering in terror at the very end of the passage, and he murmured affably: "Fluffy! Come here, Fluffy!" till Carmen's teeth chattered in her head.

"Will you come in, sir?"

Mr. Ventnor ran his hand over his whiskers, and, entering a room, was impressed at once by its air of domesticity. On a sofa a handsome woman and a pretty young girl were surrounded by sewing apparatus and some white material. The girl looked up, but the elder lady rose.

Mr. Ventnor said easily:

"You know my young friend, Mr. Robert Pillin, I think."

The lady, whose bulk and bloom struck him to the point of admiration, murmured in a full sweet drawl:

"Oh! Ye—es. Are you from Messrs. Scrivens'?"

With the swift reflection: 'As I thought!' Mr. Ventnor answered:

"Er—not exactly. I *am* a solicitor though; came just to ask about a certain settlement that Mr. Pillin tells me you're entitled under."

"Phyllis dear!"

Seeing the girl about to rise from underneath the white stuff, Mr. Ventnor said quickly:

"Pray don't disturb yourself—just a formality!" It had struck him at once that the lady would have to speak the truth in the presence of this third party, and he went on: "Quite recent, I think. This'll be your first interest—on six thousand pounds? Is that right?" And at the limpid assent of that rich, sweet voice, he thought: 'Fine woman; what eyes!'

Thank you; that's quite enough. I can go to Scrivens' for any detail. Nice young fellow, Bob Pillin, isn't he?" He saw the girl's chin tilt, and Mrs. Larne's full mouth curling in a smile.

"Delightful young man; we're very fond of him."

And he proceeded:

"I'm quite an old friend of his; have you known him long?"

"Oh! no. How long, Phyllis, since we met him at Guardy's? About a month. But he's so unaffected—quite at home with us. A *nice* fellow."

Mr. Ventnor murmured:

"Very different from his father, isn't he?"

"Is he! We don't know his father; he's a shipowner, I think."

Mr. Ventnor rubbed his hands: "Ye—es," he said, "just giving up—a warm man. Young Pillin's a lucky fellow—only son. So you met him at old Mr. Heythorp's. I know him too—relation of yours, I believe."

"Our dear Guardy—such a wonderful man."

Mr. Ventnor echoed: "Wonderful—regular old Roman."

"Oh! but he's so *kind!*" Mrs. Larne lifted the white stuff: "Look what he's given this naughty gairl!"

Mr. Ventnor murmured: "Charming! Charming! Bob Pillin said, I think, that Mr. Heythorp was your settlor."

One of those little clouds which visit the brows of women who have owed money in their time passed swiftly athwart Mrs. Larne's eyes. For a moment they seemed saying: 'Don't you want to know too much?' Then they slid from under it.

"Won't you sit down?" she said. "You must forgive our being at work."

Mr. Ventnor, who had need of sorting his impressions, shook his head.

"Thank you; I must be getting on. Then Messrs. Scriven can—a mere formality! Good-bye! Good-bye, Miss Larne. I'm sure the dress will be most becoming."

And with memories of a too clear look from the girl's eyes, of a warm firm pressure from the woman's hand, Mr. Ventnor backed towards the door and passed away just in time to avoid hearing in two voices:

"What a nice lawyer!"

"What a horrid man!"

Back in his cab, he continued to rub his hands. No, she *didn't* know old Pillin! That was certain; not from her words, but from her face. She wanted to know him, or about him, anyway. She was trying to hook young Bob for that sprig of a girl—it was clear as mud. H'm! it would astonish his young friend to hear that he had called. Well, let it! And a curious mixture of emotions beset Mr. Ventnor. He saw the whole thing now so plainly, and really could not refrain from a certain admiration. The law had been properly diddled! There was nothing to prevent a man from settling money on a woman he had never seen; and so old Pillin's settlement could probably not be upset. But old Heythorp could. It was neat, though, oh! neat! And that was a fine woman—remarkably! He had a sort of feeling that if only the settlement had been in danger, it might have been worth while to have made a bargain—a woman like that could have made it worth while! And he believed her quite capable of entertaining the proposition! Her eye! Pity—quite a pity! Mrs. Ventnor was not a wife who satisfied every aspiration. But alas! the settlement was safe. This baulking of the sentiment of love, whipped up, if anything, the longing for justice in Mr. Ventnor. That old chap should feel his teeth now. As a piece of investigation it was not so bad—not so bad at all! He had had a bit of luck, of course—no, not luck—just that knack of doing the right thing at the right moment which marks a real genius for affairs.

But getting into his train to return to Mrs. Ventnor, he thought: 'A woman like that would have been——!' And he sighed.

2 §

With a neatly written cheque for fifty pounds in his pocket Bob Pillin turned in at 23, Millicent Villas on the afternoon after Mr. Ventnor's visit. Chivalry had won the day. And he rang the bell with an elation which astonished him, for he knew he was doing a soft thing.

"Mrs. Larne is out, sir; Miss Phyllis is at home."

His heart leaped.

"Oh—h! I'm sorry. I wonder if she'd see me?"

The little maid answered:

"I think she's been washin' 'er 'air, sir, but it may be dry be now. I'll see."

Bob Pillin stood stock still beneath the young woman on the wall. He could scarcely breathe. If her hair were not dry—how awful! Suddenly he heard, floating down a clear but smothered: "Oh! Gefoozleme!" and other words which he could not catch. The little maid came running down.

"Miss Phyllis says, sir, she'll be with you in a jiffy. And I was to tell you that Master Jock is loose, sir."

Bob Pillin answered "Tha—anks," and passed into the drawing-room. He went to the bureau, took an envelope, enclosed the cheque, and addressing it: "Mrs. Larne," replaced it in his pocket. Then he crossed over to the mirror. Never till this last month had he really doubted his own face; but now he wanted for it things he had never wanted. It had too much flesh and color. It did not reflect his passion. This was a handicap. With a narrow white piping round his waistcoat opening, and a button-hole of tuberoses, he had tried to repair its deficiencies. But do what he would, he was never easy about himself nowadays, never up to that pitch which could make him confident in her presence. And until this month to lack confidence had never been his wont. A clear, high, mocking voice said:

"Oh—h! Conceited young man!"

And spinning round he saw Phyllis in the doorway. Her light brown hair was fluffed out on her shoulders, so that he felt a kind of fainting-sweet sensation, and murmured inarticulately:

"Oh! I say—how jolly!"

"Lawks! It's awful! Have you come to see mother?"

Balanced between fear and daring, conscious of a scent of hay and verbena and camomile, Bob Pillin stammered:

"Ye—es. I—I'm glad she's not in, though."

Her laugh seemed to him terribly unfeeling.

"Oh! oh! Don't be foolish. Sit down. Isn't washing one's head awful?"

Bob Pillin answered feebly:

"Of course, I haven't much experience."

Her mouth opened.

"Oh! You *are*—aren't you?"

And he thought desperately: "Dare I—oughtn't I—couldn't I somehow take her hand or put my arm round her, or something?" Instead, he sat very rigid at his end of the sofa, while she sat lax and lissom at the other, and one of those crises of paralysis which beset would-be lovers fixed him to the soul.

Sometimes during this last month memories of a past existence, when chaff and even kisses came readily to the lips, and girls were fair game, would make him think: 'Is she really such an innocent? Does she really want me to kiss her?" Alas! such intrusions lasted but a moment before a blast of awe and chivalry withered them, and a strange and tragic delicacy—like nothing he had ever known—resumed its sway. And suddenly he heard her say:

"Why do you know such awful men?"

"What? I don't know any *awful* men."

"Oh yes, you do; one came here yesterday; he had whiskers, and he was awful."

"Whiskers?" His soul revolted in disclaimer. "I believe I only know one man with whiskers—a lawyer."

"Yes—that was him; a perfectly horrid man. Mother didn't mind him, but *I* thought he was a beast."

"Ventnor! Came here? How d'you mean?"

"He did; about some business of yours, too." Her face had clouded over. Bob Pillin had of late been harassed by the still-born beginning of a poem:

> "I rode upon my way and saw
> A maid who watched me from the door."

It never grew longer, and was prompted by the feeling that her face was like an April day. The cloud which came on it now was like an April cloud, as if a bright shower of rain must follow. Brushing aside the two distressful lines, he said:

"Look here, Miss Larne—Phyllis—look here!"

"All right, I'm looking!"

"What does it mean—how did he come? What did he say?"

She shook her head, and her hair quivered; the scent of camomile, verbena, hay, was wafted; then looking at her lap, she muttered:

"I wish you wouldn't—I wish mother wouldn't—I hate it. Oh! Money! Beastly—beastly!" and a tearful sigh shivered itself into Bob Pillin's reddening ears.

"I say—don't! And do tell me, because——"

"Oh! you *know.*"

"I don't—I don't know anything at all. I never——"

Phyllis looked up at him. "Don't tell fibs; you know mother's borrowing money from you, and it's hateful!"

A desire to lie roundly, a sense of the cheque in his pocket, a feeling of injustice, the emotion of pity, and a confused and black astonishment about Ventnor, caused Bob Pillin to stammer:

"Well, I'm d——d!" and to miss the look which Phyllis gave him through her lashes—a look saying:

"Ah! that's better!"

"I *am* d——d! Look here! D'you mean to say that Ventnor came here about my lending money? I never said a word to him——"

"There you see—you *are* lending!"

He clutched his hair.

"We've got to have this out," he added.

"Not by the roots! Oh! you do look funny. I've never seen you with your hair untidy. Oh! oh!"

Bob Pillin rose and paced the room. In the midst of his emotion he could not help seeing himself sidelong in the mirror; and on pretext of holding his head in both his hands, tried earnestly to restore his hair. Then coming to a halt he said:

"Suppose I *am* lending money to your mother, what does it matter? It's only till quarter-day. Anybody might want money."

Phyllis did not raise her face.

"Why are you lending it?"

"Because—because—why shouldn't I?" and diving suddenly, he seized her hands.

She wrenched them free; and with the emotion of despair, Bob Pillin took out the envelope.

"If you like," he said, "I'll tear this up. I don't want to lend it, if you don't want me to; but I thought—I thought——" It was for her alone he had been going to lend this money!

Phyllis murmured through her hair:

"Yes! You thought that *I*—that's what's so hateful!"

Apprehension pierced his mind.

"Oh? I never—I swear I never——"

"Yes, you did; you thought I wanted you to lend it."

She jumped up, and brushed past him into the window.

So she thought she was being used as a decoy! That was awful—especially since it was true. He knew well enough that Mrs. Larne was working his admiration for her daughter for all that it was worth. And he said with simple fervor:

"What rot!" It produced no effect, and at his wits' end, he almost shouted: "Look, Phyllis! If you don't want me to—here goes!" Phyllis turned. Tearing the envelope across he threw the bits into the fire. "There it is," he said.

Her eyes grew round; she said in an awed voice: "Oh!"

In a sort of agony of honesty he said:

"It was only a cheque. Now you've got your way."

Staring at the fire she answered slowly:

"I expect you'd better go before mother comes."

Bob Pillin's mouth fell ajar; he secretly agreed, but the idea of sacrificing a moment alone with her was intolerable, and he said hardily:

"No, I shall stick it!"

Phyllis sneezed.

"My hair isn't a bit dry," and she sat down on the fender with her back to the fire.

A certain spirituality had come into Bob Pillin's face. If only he could get that wheeze off: "Phyllis is my only joy!" or even: "Phyllis—do you—won't you—mayn't I?" But nothing came—nothing.

And suddenly she said:

"Oh! don't breathe so loud; it's awful!"

"Breathe? I wasn't!"

"You were; just like Carmen when she's dreaming."

He had walked three steps towards the door, before he thought: 'What does it matter? I can stand anything from her'; and walked the three steps back again.

She said softly:

"Poor young man!"

He answered gloomily:

"I suppose you realize that this may be the last time you'll see me?"

"Why? I thought you were going to take us to the theatre."

"I don't know whether your mother will—after——"

Phyllis gave a little clear laugh.

"You don't know mother. Nothing makes any difference to her."

And Bob Pillin muttered:

"I see." He did not, but it was of no consequence. Then the thought of Ventnor again ousted all others. What on earth—how on earth! He searched his mind for what he could possibly have said the other night. Surely he had not asked him to do anything; certainly not given him their address. There was something very odd about it that had jolly well got to be cleared up! And he said:

"Are you sure the name of that johnny who came here yesterday was Ventnor?"

Phyllis nodded.

"And he was short, and had whiskers?"

"Yes; red, and red eyes."

He murmured reluctantly:

"It must be him. Jolly good cheek; I simply can't understand. I shall go and see him. How on earth did he know your address?"

"I expect you gave it him."

"I did not. I won't have you thinking me a squirt."

Phyllis jumped up. "Oh! Lawks! Here's mother!" Mrs. Larne was coming up the garden. Bob Pillin made for the door. "Good-bye," he said; "I'm going." But Mrs. Larne was already in the hall. Enveloping him in fur and her rich personality, she drew him with her into the drawing-room, where the back window was open and Phyllis gone.

"I hope," she said, "those naughty children have been making you comfortable. That nice lawyer of yours came yesterday. He seemed quite satisfied."

Very red above his collar, Bob Pillin stammered:

"I never told him to; he isn't my lawyer. I don't know what it means."

Mrs. Larne smiled. "My dear boy, it's all right. You needn't be so squeamish. I want it to be quite on a business footing."

Restraining a fearful inclination to blurt out: "It's not going to be on any footing!" Bob Pillin mumbled. "I must go; I'm late."

"And when will you be able——?"

"Oh! I'll—I'll send—I'll write. Good-bye!" And suddenly he found that Mrs. Larne had him by the lapel of his coat. The scent of violets and fur was overpowering, and the thought flashed through him: 'I believe she only wanted to take money off old Joseph in the Bible. I can't leave my coat in her hands; What shall I do?'

Mrs. Larne was murmuring:

"It would be *so* sweet of you if you could manage it to-day"; and her hand slid over his chest. "Oh! You *have* brought your cheque-book—what a nice boy!"

Bob Pillin took it out in desperation, and, sitting down at the bureau, wrote a cheque similar to that which he had torn and burned. A warm kiss lighted on his eyebrow, his head was pressed for a moment to a furry bosom; a hand took the cheque; a voice said: "How delightful!" and a sigh immersed him in a bath of perfume. Backing to the door, he gasped:

"Don't mention it; and—and *don't tell Phyllis, please*. Good-bye!"

Once through the garden gate, he thought: 'By gum! I've done it now. That Phyllis should know about it at all! That beast Ventnor!'

His face grew almost grim. He would go and see what that meant anyway!

3 §

Mr. Ventnor had not left his office when his young friend's card was brought to him. Tempted for a moment to deny his own presence, he thought: 'No! What's the good? Bound to see him sometime!' If he had not exactly courage, he had that particular blend of self-confidence and insensibility which must needs distinguish those who follow the law; nor did he ever forget that he was in the right.

"Show him in!" he said.

He would be quite bland, but young Pillin might whistle for an explanation; he was still tormented, too, by the memory of rich curves and moving lips, and the possibilities of better acquaintanceship.

While shaking the young man's hand his quick and fulvous eye detected at once the discomposure behind that mask of cheek and collar, and relapsing into one of those swivel chairs which give one an advantage over men more statically seated, he said:

"You look pretty bobbish. Anything I can do for you?"

Bob Pillin, in the fixed chair of the consulter, nursed his bowler on his knee.

"Well, yes, there is. I've just been to see Mrs. Larne."

Mr. Ventnor did not flinch.

"Ah! Nice woman; pretty daughter, too!" And into those words he put a certain meaning. He never waited to be bullied. Bob Pillin felt the pressure of his blood increasing.

"Look here, Ventnor," he said, "I want an explanation."

"What of?"

"Why, of your going there, and using my name, and God knows what."

Mr. Ventnor gave his chair two little twiddles before he said:

"Well, you won't get it."

Bob Pillin remained for a moment taken aback; then he muttered resolutely:

"It's not the conduct of a gentleman."

Every man has his illusions, and no man likes them disturbed. The gingery tint underlying Mr. Ventnor's coloring overlaid it; even the whites of his eyes grew red.

"Oh!" he said; "indeed. You mind your own business, will you?"

"It is my business—very much so. You made use of my name, and I don't choose——"

"The devil you don't! Now, I tell you what——" Mr. Ventnor

leaned forward—"you'd better hold your tongue, and not exasperate me. I'm a good-tempered man, but I won't stand your impudence."

Clenching his bowler hat, and only kept in his seat by that sense of something behind, Bob Pillin ejaculated:

"Impudence! That's good—after what you did! Look here, why did you? It's so extraordinary!"

Mr. Ventnor answered:

"Oh! is it? You wait a bit, my friend!"

Still more moved by the mystery of this affair, Bob Pillin could only mutter:

"I never gave you their address; we were only talking about old Heythorp."

And at the smile which spread between Mr. Ventnor's whiskers, he jumped up, crying:

"It's not the thing, and you're not going to put me off. I insist on an explanation."

Mr. Ventnor leaned back, crossing his stout legs, joining the tips of his thick fingers. In this attitude he was always self-possessed.

"You do—do you?"

"Yes. You must have had some reason."

Mr. Ventnor gazed up at him.

"I'll give you a piece of advice, young cock, and charge you nothing for it, too: Ask no questions, and you'll be told no lies. And here's another: Go away before you forget yourself again."

The natural stolidity of Bob Pillin's face was only just proof against this speech. He said thickly:

"If you go there again and use my name, I'll——. Well, it's lucky for you you're not my age. Anyway I'll relieve you of my acquaintanceship in future. Good-evening!" and he went to the door. Mr. Ventnor had risen.

"Very well," he said loudly. "Good riddance! You wait and see which boot the leg is on!"

But Bob Pillin was gone, leaving the lawyer with a very red face, a very angry heart, and a vague sense of disorder in his speech. Not only Bob Pillin, but his tender aspirations had all left him; he no longer dallied with the memory of Mrs. Larne, but like a man and a Briton thought only of how to get his own back and punish evildoers. The atrocious words of his young friend, "It's not the conduct of a gentleman," festered in the heart of one who was made gentle not merely by nature but by Act of Parliament, and he registered a solemn vow to wipe the insult out, if not with blood, with verjuice. It was his duty, and they should d——d well see him do it!

IV

1 §

Sylvanus Heythorp seldom went to bed before one or rose before eleven. The latter habit alone kept his valet from handling in the resignation which the former habit prompted almost every night.

Propped on his pillows in a crimson dressing-gown, and freshly shaved, he looked more Roman than he ever did, except in his bath. Having disposed of coffee, he was wont to read his letters, and *The Morning Post,* for he had always been a Tory, and could not stomach paying a halfpenny for his news. Not that there were many letters—when a man has reached the age of eighty, who should write to him, except to ask for money?

It was Valentine's Day. Through his bedroom window he could see the trees of the park, where the birds were in song, though he could not hear them. He had never been interested in Nature—full-blooded men with short necks seldom are.

This morning indeed there *were* two letters, and he opened that which smelt of something. Inside was a thing like a Christmas card, save that the naked babe had in his hands a bow and arrow, and words coming out of his mouth: "To be your Valentine." There was also a little pink note with one blue forget-me-not printed at the top. It ran:

"Dearest Guardy,—I'm sorry this is such a mangy little valentine; I couldn't go out to get it because I've got a beastly cold, so I asked Jock, and the pig bought this. The satin is simply scrumptious. If you don't come and see me in it some time soon, I shall come and show it to you. I wish I had a moustache, because my top lip feels just like a matchbox, but it's rather ripping having breakfast in bed. Mr. Pillin's taking us to the theatre the day after to-morrow evening. Isn't it nummy! I'm going to have rum and honey for my cold.

"Good-bye,

"Your Phyllis."

So this that quivered in his thick fingers, too insensitive to feel it, was a valentine for *him!* Forty years ago that young thing's grandmother had given him his last. It made him out a very old chap! Forty years ago! Had that been himself living then? And himself, who, as a youth, came on the town in 'forty-five? Not a thought, not a feeling the same! They said you changed your body every seven years. The mind with it, too, perhaps. Well, he had come to the last of his bodies, now! And that holy woman had been urging him to take it to Bath, with her face as long as a tea-tray, and some gammon from that doctor of his. Too full a habit—dock his port—no alcohol—might go off in a coma any night! Knock off—not he! Rather die any day than turn teetotaller! When a man had nothing left in life except his dinner, his bottle, his cigar, and the dreams they gave him—these doctors forsooth must want to cut them off! No, no! *Carpe diem!* while you lived, get something out of it. And now that he had made all the provision he could for those youngsters, his life was no good to anyone but himself; and the sooner he went off the better, if he ceased to enjoy what there was left, or lost the power to say: "I'll do this and that, and you be jiggered!" Keep a stiff lip until you crashed, and then go clean! He sounded the bell beside him twice—for Molly, not his man. And when the girl came in, and stood, pretty in her print frock, her fluffy overfine dark hair escaping from under her cap, he gazed at her in silence.

"Yes, sirr?"

"Want to look at you, that's all."

"Oh! an' I'm not tidy, sirr."

"Never mind. Had your valentine?"

"No, sirr; who would send me one, then?"

"Haven't you a young man?"

"Well, I might. But he's over in my country."

"What d'you think of this?"

He held out the little boy.

The girl took the card and scrutinized it reverently; she said in a detached voice:

"Indeed, an' ut's pretty, too."

"Would you like it?"

"Oh; if 'tis not taking ut from you."

Old Heythorp shook his head, and pointed to the dressing-table.

"Over there—you'll find a sovereign. Little present for a good girl."

She uttered a deep sigh. "Oh, sirr, 'tis too much; 'tis kingly."

"Take it."

She took it, and came back, her hands clasping the sovereign and the valentine, in an attitude as of prayer.

The old man's gaze rested on her with satisfaction.

"I like pretty faces—can't bear sour ones. Tell Meller to get my bath ready."

When she had gone he took up the other letter—some lawyer's writing—and opening it with the usual difficulty read:

"*February* 13*th*, 1905.

"SIR,—Certain facts having come to my knowledge, I deem it my duty to call a special meeting of the shareholders of 'The Island Navigation Coy.,' to consider circumstances in connection with the purchase of Mr. Joseph Pillin's fleet. And I give you notice that at this meeting your conduct will be called in question.

"I am, Sir,
"Yours faithfully,
"CHARLES VENTNOR.

"SYLVANUS HEYTHORP, Esq."

Having read this missive, old Heythorp remained some minutes without stirring. Ventnor! That solicitor chap who had made himself unpleasant at the creditors' meetings!

There are men whom a really bad bit of news at once stampedes out of all power of coherent thought and action, and men who at first simply do not take it in. Old Heythorp took it in fast enough; coming from a lawyer it was about as nasty as it could be. But, at once, with stoic wariness his old brain began casting round. What did this fellow really know? And what exactly could he do? One thing was certain; even if he knew everything, he couldn't upset that settlement. The youngsters were all right. The old man grasped the fact that only his own position was at stake. But this was enough in all conscience; a name which had been before the public fifty odd years—income, independence, more perhaps. It would take little, seeing his age and feebleness, to make his Companies throw him over. But what had the fellow got hold of? How decide whether or not to take notice; to let him do his worst, or to try and get into touch with him? And what was the fellow's motive? He held ten shares! That would never make a man take all this trouble, and over a purchase which was really first-rate business for the Company. Yes! His conscience was quite clean. He had not betrayed his Company—on the contrary, had done it a good turn, got them four sound ships at a low price—against much opposition. That he might have done the Company a better turn, and got the ships at fifty-four thousand, did not trouble him—the six thousand was a deuced sight better employed; and he had not pocketed a penny piece himself! But the fellow's motive? Spite? Looked like it. Spite, because he had been disappointed of his money, and defied into the bargain! H'm! If that were so, he might still be got to blow cold again. His eyes lighted on the pink note with the blue forget-me-not. It marked as it were the high-water mark of what was left to him of life; and this other letter in his hand—by Jove!—low-water mark! And with a deep and rumbling sigh he thought: 'No, I'm not going to be beaten by this fellow.'

"Your bath is ready, sir."

Crumpling the two letters into the pocket of his dressing-gown, he said:

"Help me up; and telephone to Mr. Farney to be good enough to come round." . . .

An hour later, when the secretary entered, his chairman was sitting by the fire perusing the articles of association. And, waiting for him to look up, watching the articles shaking in that thick, feeble hand, the secretary had one of those moments of philosophy not too frequent with his kind. Some said the only happy time of life was when you had no passions, nothing to hope and live for. But did you really ever reach such a stage? The old chairman, for instance, still had his passion for getting his own way, still had his prestige, and set a lot of store by it! And he said:

"Good-morning, sir; I hope you're all right in this east wind. The purchase is completed."

"Best thing the Company ever did. Have you heard from a shareholder called Ventnor? You know the man I mean."

"No, sir. I haven't."

"Well! You may get a letter that'll make you open your eyes. An impudent scoundrel! Just write at my dictation."

"February 14th, 1905.

"CHARLES VENTNOR, Esq.

"SIR,—I have your letter of yesterday's date, the contents of which I am at a loss to understand. My solicitors will be instructed to take the necessary measures."

'Phew! What's all this about?' the secretary thought.

"Yours truly . . . I'll sign."

And the shaky letters closed the page:

"SYLVANUS HEYTHORP."

"Post that as you go."

"Anything else I can do for you, sir?"

"Nothing, except to let me know if you hear from this fellow."

When the secretary had gone the old man thought: 'So! The

ruffian hasn't called the meeting yet. That'll bring him round here fast enough if it's his money he wants—blackmailing scoundrel!"

"Mr. Pillin, sir; and will you wait lunch, or will you have it in the dining-room?"

"In the dining-room."

At the sight of that death's-head of a fellow, old Heythorp felt a sort of pity. He looked bad enough already—and this news would make him look worse. Joe Pillin glanced round at the two closed doors.

"How are you, Sylvanus? I'm very poorly." He came closer, and lowered his voice: "Why did you get me to make that settlement? I must have been mad. I've had a man called Ventnor—I didn't like his manner. He asked me if I knew a Mrs. Larne."

"Ha! What did you say?"

"What could I say? I *don't* know her. But why did he ask?"

"Smells a rat."

Joe Pillin grasped the edge of the table with both hands.

"Oh!" he murmured. "Oh, don't say that!"

Old Heythorp held out to him the crumpled letter.

When he had read it Joe Pillin sat down abruptly before the fire.

"Pull yourself together, Joe; they can't touch you, and they can't upset either the purchase or the settlement. They can upset me, that's all."

Joe Pillin answered, with trembling lips:

"How you can sit there, and look the same as ever! Are you sure they can't touch me?"

Old Heythorp nodded grimly.

"They talk of an Act, but they haven't passed it yet. They might prove a breach of trust against me. But I'll diddle them. Keep your pecker up, and get off abroad."

"Yes, yes. I must. I'm very bad. I was going to-morrow. But I don't know, I'm sure, with this hanging over me. My son knowing her makes it worse. He knows this man Ventnor, too. And I daren't say anything to Bob. What are you thinking of, Sylvanus? You look very funny."

Old Heythorp seemed to rouse himself from a sort of coma.

"I want my lunch," he said. "Will you stop and have some?"

Joe Pillin stammered out:

"Lunch! I don't know when I shall eat again. What are you going to do, Sylvanus?"

"Bluff the beggar out of it."

"But suppose you can't?"

"Buy him off. He's one of my creditors."

Joe Pillin stared at him afresh. "You always had such nerve," he said yearningly. "Do you ever wake up between two and four? I do—and everything's black."

"Put a good stiff nightcap on, my boy, before going to bed."

"Yes; I sometimes wish I was less temperate. But I couldn't stand it. I'm told your doctor forbids you alcohol."

"He does. That's why I drink it."

Joe Pillin, brooding over the fire, said: "This meeting—d'you think they mean to have it? D'you think this man really knows? If my name gets into the newspapers——" but encountering his old friend's deep little eyes, he stopped. "So you advise me to get off to-morrow, then?"

Old Heythorp nodded.

"Your lunch is served, sir."

Joe Pillin started violently, and rose.

"Well, good-bye, Sylvanus—good-bye! I don't suppose I shall be back till the summer, if I ever come back!" He sank his voice: "I shall rely on you. You won't let them, will you?"

Old Heythorp lifted his hand, and Joe Pillin put into that swollen shaking paw his pale and spindly fingers. "I wish I had your pluck," he said sadly. "Good-bye, Sylvanus," and turning, he passed out.

Old Heythorp thought: 'Poor shaky chap. All to pieces at the first shot!' And, going to his lunch, ate more heavily than usual.

2 §

Mr. Ventnor, on reaching his office and opening his letters, found, as he had anticipated, one from "that old rascal." Its contents excited in him the need to know his own mind. Fortunately this was not complicated by a sense of dignity—he only had to consider the position with an eye on not being made to *look* a fool. The point was simply whether he set more store by his money than by his desire for—er—justice. If not, he had merely to convene the special meeting, and lay before it the plain fact that Mr. Joseph Pillin, selling his ships for sixty thousand pounds, had just made a settlement of six thousand pounds on a lady whom he did not know, a daughter, ward, or what-not—of the purchasing Company's chairman, who had said, moreover, at the general meeting, that he stood or fell by the transaction; he had merely to do this, and demand that an explanation be required from the old man of such a startling coincidence. Convinced that no explanation would hold water, he felt sure that his action would be at once followed by the collapse, if nothing more, of that old image, and the infliction of a nasty slur on old Pillin and his hopeful son. On the other hand, three hundred pounds was money; and if old Heythorp were to say to him: "What do you want to make this fuss for?—here's what I owe you!" could a man of business and the world let his sense of justice—however he might itch to have it satisfied—stand in the way of what was after all also his sense of justice?—for this money had been owing to him for the deuce of a long time. In this dilemma, the words: "My solicitors will be instructed" were of a notable service in helping him to form a decision, for he had a certain dislike of other solicitors, and an intimate knowledge of the law of libel and slander; if by any remote chance there should be a slip between the cup and the lip, Charles Ventnor might be in the soup—a position which he deprecated both by nature and profession. High thinking, therefore, decided him at last to answer thus:

"*February 15th*, 1905.

"SIR,—I have received your note. I think it may be fair, before taking further steps in this matter, to ask you for a personal explanation of the circumstances to which I alluded. I therefore propose with your permission to call on you at your private residence at five o'clock to-morrow afternoon.

"Yours faithfully,

"CHARLES VENTNOR.

"SYLVANUS HEYTHORP, Esq."

Having sent this missive, and arranged in his mind, the damning, if circumstantial, evidence he had accumulated, he awaited the hour with confidence, for his nature was not lacking in the cock-surety of a Briton. All the same, he dressed himself particularly well that morning, putting on a blue and white striped waistcoat which, with a cream-colored tie, set off his fulvous whiskers and full blue eyes; and he lunched, if anything, more fully than his wont, eating a stronger cheese and taking a glass of special Club ale. He took care to be late, too, to show the old fellow that his coming at all was in the nature of an act of grace. A strong scent of hyacinths greeted him in the hall; and Mr. Ventnor, who was an amateur of flowers, stopped to put his nose into a fine bloom and think uncontrollably of Mrs. Larne. Pity! The things one had to give up in life—fine women—one thing and another. Pity! The thought inspired in him a timely anger; and he followed the servant, intending to stand no nonsense from this paralytic old rascal.

The room he entered was lighted by a bright fire, and a single electric lamp with an orange shade on a table covered by a black satin cloth. There were heavily gleaming oil paintings on the walls, a heavy old brass chandelier without candles, heavy dark red curtains, and an indefinable scent of burnt acorns, coffee, cigars, and old man. He became conscious of a candescent spot on the far side of the hearth, where the light fell on old Heythorp's thick white hair.

"Mr. Ventnor, sir."

The candescent spot moved. A voice said: "Sit down."

Mr. Ventnor sat in an armchair on the opposite side of the fire, and, finding a kind of somnolence creeping over him, pinched himself. He wanted all his wits about him.

The old man was speaking in that extinct voice of his, and Mr. Ventnor said rather pettishly:

"Beg pardon, I don't get you."

Old Heythorp's voice swelled with sudden force:

"Your letters are Greek to me."

"Oh! indeed! I think we can soon make them into plain English!"

"Sooner the better."

Mr. Ventnor passed through a moment of indecision. Should he lay his cards on the table? It was not his habit, and the proceeding was sometimes attended with risk. The knowledge, however, that he could always take them up again, seeing there was no third person here to testify that he had laid them down, decided him, and he said:

"Well, Mr. Heythorp, the long and short of the matter is this: Our friend Mr. Pillin paid you a commission of ten per cent. on the sale of his ships. Oh! yes. He settled the money not on you, but on your relative Mrs. Larne and her children. This, as you know, is a breach of trust on your part."

The old man's voice: "Where did you get hold of that cock-and-bull story?" brought him to his feet before the fire.

"It won't do, Mr. Heythorp. My witnesses are Mr. Pillin, Mrs. Larne, and Mr. Scriven."

"What have you come here for, then—blackmail?"

Mr. Ventnor straightened his waistcoat; a rush of conscious virtue had dyed his face.

"Oh! you take that tone," he said, "do you? You think you can ride roughshod over everything? Well, you're very much mistaken. I advise you to keep a civil tongue and consider your position, or I'll make a beggar of you. I'm not sure this isn't a case for a prosecution!"

"Gammon!"

The choler in Charles Ventnor kept him silent for a moment; then he burst out:

"Neither gammon nor spinach. You owe me three hundred pounds, you've owed it me for years, and you have the impudence to take this attitude with me, have you? Now, I never bluster; I say what I mean. You just listen to me. Either you pay me what you owe at once, or I call this meeting and make what I know public. You'll very soon find out where you are. And a good thing, too, for a more unscrupulous—unscrupulous——" he paused for breath.

Occupied with his own emotion, he had not observed the change in old Heythorp's face. The imperial on that lower lip was bristling, the crimson of those cheeks had spread to the roots of his white hair. He grasped the arms of his chair, trying to rise; his swollen hands trembled; a little saliva escaped one corner of his lips. And the words came out as if shaken by his teeth:

"So—so—you—you bully me!"

Conscious that the interview had suddenly passed from the phase of negotiation, Mr. Ventnor looked hard at his opponent. He saw nothing but a decrepit, passionate, crimson-faced old man at bay, and all the instincts of one with everything on his side boiled up in him. The miserable old turkey-cock—the apoplectic image! And he said:

"And you'll do no good for yourself by getting into a passion. At your age, and in your condition, I recommend a little prudence. Now just take my terms quietly, or you know what'll happen. I'm not to be intimidated by any of your airs." And seeing that the old man's rage was such that he simply could not speak, he took the opportunity of going on: "I don't care two straws which you do—I'm out to show you who's master. If you think in your dotage you can domineer any longer—well, you'll find two can play at that game. Come, now, which are you going to do?"

The old man had sunk back in his chair, and only his little deep-blue eyes seemed living. Then he moved one hand, and Mr. Ventnor saw that he was fumbling to reach the button of an electric bell at the end of a cord. "I'll show him," he thought, and stepping forward, he put it out of reach.

Thus frustrated, the old man remained motionless, staring up. The word "blackmail" resumed its buzzing in Mr. Ventnor's ears. The impudence—the consummate impudence of it from this fraudulent old ruffian with one foot in bankruptcy and one foot in the grave, if not in the dock.

"Yes," he said, "it's never too late to learn; and for once you've come up against someone a leetle bit too much for you. Haven't you now? You'd better cry *'Peccavi.'* "

Then, in the deathly silence of the room, the moral force of his position, and the collapse as it seemed of his opponent, awakening a faint compunction, he took a turn over the Turkey carpet to readjust his mind.

"You're an old man, and I don't want to be too hard on you. I'm only showing you that you can't play fast and loose as if you were God Almighty any longer. You've had your own way too many years. And now you can't have it, see!" Then, as the old man again moved forward in his chair, he added: "Now, don't get into a passion again; calm yourself, because I warn you—this is your last chance. I'm a man of my word; and what I say, I do."

By a violent and unsuspected effort the old man jerked himself up and reached the bell. Mr. Ventnor heard it ring, and said sharply:

"Mind you, it's nothing to me which you do. I came for your own good. Please yourself. Well?"

He was answered by the click of the door and the old man's husky voice:

"Show this hound out! And then come back!"

Mr. Ventnor had presence of mind enough not to shake his fist. Muttering: "Very well, Mr. Heythorp! Ah! *Very* well!" he moved with dignity to the door. The careful shepherding of the servant renewed the fire of his anger. Hound! he had been called a hound!

3 §

After seeing Mr. Ventnor off the premises the man Meller returned to his master, whose face looked very odd—"all patchy-like," as he put it in the servants' hall, as though the blood driven to his head had mottled for good the snowy whiteness of the forehead. He received the unexpected order:

"Get me a hot bath ready, and put some pine stuff in it."

When the old man was seated there, the valet asked:

"How long shall I give you, sir?"

"Twenty minutes."

"Very good, sir."

Lying in that steaming brown fragrant liquid, old Heythorp heaved a stertorous sigh. By losing his temper with that ill-conditioned cur he had cooked his goose. It was done to a turn; and he was a ruined man. If only—oh! if only he could have seized the fellow by the neck and pitched him out of the room! To have lived to be so spoken to; to have been unable to lift hand or foot, hardly even his voice—he would sooner have been dead! Yes—sooner have been dead! A dumb and measureless commotion was still at work in the recesses of that thick old body, silver-brown in the dark water, whose steam he drew deep into his wheezing lungs, as though for spiritual relief. To be beaten by a cur like that! To have a common cad of a pettifogging lawyer drag him down and kick him about; tumble a name which had stood high, in the dust! The fellow had the power to make him a byword and a beggar! It was incredible! But it was a fact. And to-morrow he would begin to do it—perhaps had begun already. His tree had come down with a crash! Eighty years—eighty good years! He regretted none of them—regretted nothing; least of all this breach of trust which had provided for his grandchildren—one of the best things he had ever done. The fellow was a cowardly hound, too! The way he had snatched the bell-pull out of his reach—despicable cur! And a chap like that was to put "paid" to the account of Sylvanus Heythorp, to "scratch" him out of life—so near the end of everything, the very end. His hand raised above the surface fell back on his stomach through the dark water, and a bubble or two rose. Not so fast—not so fast! He had but to slip down a foot, let the water close over his head, and "Good-bye" to Master Ventnor's triumph! Dead men could not be kicked off the Boards of Companies. Dead men could not be beggared, deprived of their independence. He smiled and stirred a little in the bath till the water reached the white hairs on his lower lip. It smelt nice! And he took a long sniff. He had had a good life, a good life! And with the thought that he had it in his power at any moment to put Master Ventnor's nose out of joint—to beat the beggar after all, a sense of assuagement and well-being crept over him. His blood ran more evenly again. He closed his eyes. They talked about an after-life—people like that holy woman. Gammon! You went to sleep—a long sleep; no dreams. A nap after dinner! Dinner! His tongue sought his palate! Yes! he could eat a good dinner! That dog hadn't put him off his stroke! The best dinner he had ever eaten was the one he gave to Jack Herring, Chichester, Thornworthy, Nick Treffry and Jolyon Forsyte at Pole's. Good Lord! In 'sixty—yes—'sixty-five? Just before he fell in love with Alice Larne—ten years before he came to Liverpool. That *was* a dinner! Cost twenty-four pounds for the six of them—and Forsyte an absurdly moderate fellow. Only Nick Treffry and himself had been three-bottle men! Dead! Every jack man of them. And suddenly he thought: 'My name's a good one—I was never down before—never beaten!'

A voice above the steam said:

"The twenty minutes is up, sir."

"All right; I'll get out. Evening clothes."

And Meller, taking out dress suit and shirt, thought: 'Now, what does the old bloomer want dressin' up again for; why can't he go to bed and have his dinner there? When a man's like a baby, the cradle's the place for him.'

An hour later, at the scene of his encounter with Mr. Ventnor, where the table was already laid for dinner, old Heythorp stood and gazed. The curtains had been drawn back, the window thrown open to air the room, and he could see out there the shapes of the dark trees and a sky grape-colored, in the mild, moist night. It smelt good. A sensuous feeling stirred in him, warm from his bath, clothed from head to foot in fresh garments. Deuce of a time since he had dined in full fig! He would have liked a woman dining opposite—but not the holy woman; no, by George!—would have liked to see light falling on a woman's shoulders once again, and a pair of bright eyes! He crossed, snail-like, towards the fire. There that bullying fellow had stood with his back to it—confound his impudence!—as if the place belonged to him. And suddenly he had a vision of his three secretaries' faces—especially young Farney's—as they would look when the pack got him by the throat and pulled him down. His co-directors, too! Old Heythorp! How are the mighty fallen! And that hound jubilant!

His valet passed across the room to shut the window and draw the curtains. This chap too! The day he could no longer pay his wages, and had lost the power to say "Shan't want your services any more"—when he could no longer even pay his doctor for doing his best to kill him off! Power, interest, independence, all—gone! To be dressed and undressed, given pap, like a baby in arms, served as they chose to serve him, and wished out of the way—broken, dishonored! By money alone an old man had his being! Meat, drink, movement, breath! When all his money was gone the holy woman would let him know it fast enough. They would all let him know it; or if they didn't, it would be out of pity! He had never been pitied yet—thank God! And he said:

"Get me up a bottle of Perrier Jouet. What's the menu?"

"Germane soup, sir; filly de sole; sweetbread; cutler soubees, rum souffly."

"Tell her to give me a *hors d'œuvre*, and put on a savoury."

"Yes, sir."

When the man had gone, he thought: 'I should have liked an oyster—too late now!' and going over to his bureau he fumblingly pulled out the top drawer. There was little in it—just a few papers, business papers on his Companies, and a schedule of his debts; not even a copy of his will—he had not made one, nothing to leave! Letters he had never kept. Half a dozen bills, a few receipts, and the little pink note with the blue forget-me-not. That was the lot. An old tree gives up bearing leaves, and its roots dry up, before it comes down in a wind; an old man's world slowly falls away from him till he stands alone in the night. Looking at the pink note, he thought: 'Suppose I'd married Alice—a man never had a better mistress!' He fumbled the drawer to; but still he strayed feebly about the room, with a curious shrinking from sitting down, legacy from the quarter of an hour he had been compelled to sit while that hound worried at his throat. He was opposite one of the pictures now. It gleamed, dark and oily, limning a Scots Grey who had mounted a wounded Russian on his horse, and was bringing him back prisoner from the Balaclava charge. A very old friend—bought in 'fifty-nine. It had hung in his chambers in the Albany—hung with him ever since. With whom would it hang when he was gone? For that holy woman would scrap it, to a certainty, and stick up some Crucifixion or other, some newfangled high art thing! She could even do that now if she liked—for she owned it, owned every mortal stick in the room, to the very glass he would drink his champagne from; all made over under the settlement fifteen years ago, before his last big gamble went wrong. *"De l'audace, toujours de l'audace!"* The gamble which had brought him down till his throat at last was at the mercy of a bullying hound. The pitcher and the well! At the mercy——! The sound of a popping cork dragged him from reverie. He moved to his seat, back to the window, and sat down to his dinner. By George! They had got him an oyster! And he said:

"I've forgotten my teeth!"

While the man was gone for them, he swallowed the oysters, methodically touching them one by one with cayenne, Chili vinegar, and lemon. Ummm! Not quite what they used to be at Pimm's in the best days, but not bad—not bad! Then seeing the little blue bowl lying before him, he looked up and said:

"My compliments to cook on the oysters. Give me the champagne." And he lifted his trembling teeth. Thank God, he could still put 'em in for himself! The creaming goldenish fluid from the napkined bottle slowly reached the brim of his glass, which had a hollow stem; raising it to his lips, very red between the white hairs above and below, he drank with a gurgling noise, and put the glass down—empty. Nectar! And just cold enough!

"I frapped it the least bit, sir."

"Quite right. What's that smell of flowers?"

"It's from those 'yacinths on the sideboard, sir. They come from Mrs. Larne, this afternoon."

"Put 'em on the table. Where's my daughter?"

"She's had dinner, sir; goin' to a ball, I think."

"A ball!"

"Charity ball, I fancy, sir."

"Ummm! Give me a touch of the old sherry with the soup."

"Yes, sir. I shall have to open a bottle."

"Very well, then, do!"

On his way to the cellar the man confided to Molly, who was carrying the soup:

"The Gov'nor's going it to-night! What he'll be like to-morrow I dunno."

The girl answered softly:

"Poor old man, let um have his pleasure." And, in the hall, with the soup tureen against her bosom, she hummed above the steam, and thought of the ribbons on her new chemises, bought out of the sovereign he had given her.

And old Heythorp, digesting his oysters, snuffed the scent of the hyacinths, and thought of the St. Germain, his favorite soup. It wouldn't be first-rate, at this time of year—should be made with little young home-grown peas. Paris was the place for it. Ah! The French were the fellows for eating, and—looking things in the face! Not hypocrites—not ashamed of their reason or their senses!

The soup came in. He sipped it, bending forward as far as he could, his napkin tucked in over his shirt-front like a bib. He got the bouquet of that sherry to a T—his sense of smell was very keen to-night; rare old stuff it was—more than a year since he had tasted it—but no one drank sherry nowadays, hadn't the constitution for it! The fish came up, and went down; and with the sweetbread he took his second glass of champagne. Always the best, that second glass—the stomach well warmed, and the palate not yet dulled. Umm! So that fellow thought he had him beaten, did he? And he said suddenly:

"The fur coat in the wardrobe, I've no use for it. You can take it away to-night."

With tempered gratitude the valet answered:

"Thank you, sir; much obliged, I'm sure." So the old buffer had found out there was moth in it!

"Have I worried you much?"

"No, sir; not at all, sir—that is, no more than reason."

"Afraid I have. Very sorry—can't help it. You'll find that, when you get like me."

"Yes, sir; I've always admired your pluck, sir."

"Um! Very good of you to say so."

"Always think of you keepin' the flag flyin', sir."

Old Heythorp bent his body from the waist.

"Much obliged to you."

"Not at all, sir. Cook's done a little spinach in cream with the soubees."

"Ah! Tell her from me it's a capital dinner, so far."

"Thank you, sir."

Alone again, old Heythorp sat unmoving, his brain just narcotically touched. "The flag flyin'—the flag flyin'!" He raised his glass and sucked. He had an appetite now, and finished the three cutlets, and all the sauce and spinach. Pity! he could have managed a snipe—fresh shot! A desire to delay, to lengthen dinner, was strong upon him; there were but the *soufflé* and the savoury to come. He would have enjoyed, too, someone to talk to. He had always been fond of good company—been good company himself, or so they said—not that he had had a chance of late. Even at the Boards they avoided talking to him, he had noticed for a long time. Well! that wouldn't trouble him again—he had sat through his last Board, no doubt. They shouldn't kick him off, though; he wouldn't give them that pleasure—had seen the beggars hankering after his chairman's shoes too long. The *soufflé* was before him now, and lifting his glass, he said:

"Fill up."

"These are the special glasses, sir; only four to the bottle."

"Fill up."

The servant filled, screwing up his mouth.

Old Heythorp drank, and put the glass down empty with a sigh. He had been faithful to his principles, finished the bottle before touching the sweet—a good bottle—of a good brand! And now for the *soufflé!* Delicious, flipped down with the old sherry! So that holy woman was going to a ball, was she? How deuced funny! Who would dance with a dry stick like that, all eaten up with a piety which was just sexual disappointment? Ah! yes, lots of women like that—had often noticed 'em—pitied 'em too, until you had to do with them and they made you as unhappy as themselves, and were tyrants into the bargain. And he asked:

"What's the savoury?"

"Cheese remmykin, sir."

His favorite.

"I'll have my port with it—the 'sixty-eight."

The man stood gazing with evident stupefaction. He had not expected this. The old man's face was very flushed, but that might be the bath. He said feebly:

"Are you sure you ought, sir?"

"No, but I'm going to."

"Would you mind if I spoke to Miss Heythorp, sir?"

"If you do, you can leave my service."

"Well, sir, I don't accept the responsibility."

"Who asked you to?"

"No, sir."

"Well, get it, then; and don't be an ass."

"Yes, sir." If the old man were not humored he would have a fit, perhaps!

And the old man sat quietly staring at the hyacinths. He felt happy, his whole being lined and warmed and drowsed—and there was more to come! What had the holy folk to give you compared with the comfort of a good dinner? Could they make you dream, and see life rosy for a little? No, they could only give you promissory notes which would never be cashed. A man had nothing but his pluck—they only tried to undermine it, and make him squeal for help. He could see his precious doctor throwing up his hands: "Port after a bottle of champagne—you'll die of it!" And a very good death too—none better. A sound broke the silence of the closed-up room. Music. His daughter playing the piano overhead. Singing too! What a trickle of a voice! Jenny Lind! The Swedish nightingale—he had never missed the nights when she was singing—Jenny Lind!

"It's very hot, sir. Shall I take it out of the case?"

Ah. The ramequin!

"Touch of butter, and the cayenne!"

"Yes, sir."

He ate it slowly, savouring each mouthful; had never tasted a better. With cheese—port! He drank one glass, and said:

"Help me to my chair."

And settled there before the fire with decanter and glass and handbell on the little low table by his side, he murmured:

"Bring coffee, and my cigar, in twenty minutes."

To-night he would do justice to his wine, not smoking till he had finished. As old Horace said:

> "Aequam memento rebus in arduis
> Servare mentem."

And, raising his glass, he sipped slowly, spilling a drop or two, shutting his eyes.

The faint silvery squealing of the holy woman in the room above, the scent of hyacinths, the drowse of the fire, on which a cedar log had just been laid, the feeling of the port soaking down into the crannies of his being, made up a momentary Paradise. Then the music stopped; and no sound rose but the tiny groans of the log trying to resist the fire. Dreamily he thought: 'Life wears you out, wears you out. Logs on a fire!' And he filled his glass again. That fellow had been careless; there were dregs at the bottom of the decanter and he had got down to them! Then, as the last drop from his tilted glass trickled into the white hairs on his chin, he heard the coffee tray put down, and taking his cigar he put it to his ear, rolling it in his thick fingers. In prime condition! And drawing a first whiff, he said:

"Open that bottle of the old brandy in the sideboard."

"Brandy, sir? I really daren't, sir."

"Are you my servant or not?"

"Yes, sir, but——"

A minute of silence, then the man went hastily to the sideboard, took out the bottle, and drew the cork. The tide of crimson in the old man's face had frightened him.

"Leave it there."

The unfortunate valet placed the bottle on the little table. 'I'll have to tell her,' he thought; 'but if I take away the port decanter and the glass, it won't look so bad.' And, carrying them, he left the room.

Slowly the old man drank his coffee, and the liqueur of brandy. The whole gamut! And watching his cigar-smoke wreathing blue in the orange glow, he smiled. The last night to call his soul his own, the last night of his independence. Send in his resignations to-morrow—not wait to be kicked off! Not give that fellow a chance!

A voice which seemed to come from far off, said:

"Father! You're drinking brandy! How *can* you—you know it's simple poison to you!" A figure in white, scarcely actual, loomed up close. He took the bottle to fill up his liqueur glass, in defiance; but a hand in a long white glove, with another dangling from its wrist, pulled it away, shook it at him, and replaced it in the sideboard. And, just as when Mr. Ventnor stood there accusing him, a swelling and churning in his throat prevented him from speech; his lips moved, but only a little froth came forth.

His daughter had approached again. She stood quite close, in white satin, thin-faced, sallow, with eyebrows raised, and her dark hair frizzed—yes! frizzed—the holy woman! With all his might he tried to say: 'So you bully me, do you—you bully me *to-night!*' but only the word "so" and a sort of whispering came forth. He heard her speaking. "It's no good your getting angry, Father. After champagne—it's wicked!" Then her form receded in a sort of rustling white mist; she was gone; and he heard the spluttering and growling of her taxi, bearing her to the ball. So! She tryrannized and bullied, even before she had him at her mercy, did she? She should see! Anger had brightened his eyes; the room came clear again. And slowly raising himself he sounded the bell twice, for the girl, not for that fellow Meller, who was in the plot. As soon as her pretty black and white-aproned figure stood before him, he said:

"Help me up!"

Twice her soft pulling was not enough, and he sank back. The third time he struggled to his feet.

"Thank you! that'll do." Then, waiting till she was gone, he crossed the room, fumbled open the sideboard door, and took out the bottle. Reaching over the polished oak, he grasped a sherry glass; and holding the bottle with both hands, tipped the liquor into it, put it to his lips and sucked. Drop by drop it passed over his palate—mild, very old, old as himself, colored like sunlight, fragrant. To the last drop he drank it, then hugging the bottle to his shirt-front, he moved snail-like to his chair, and fell back into its depths.

For some minutes he remained there motionless, the bottle clasped to his chest, thinking: 'This is not the attitude of a gentleman. I must put it down on the table—on the table;' but a thick cloud was between him and everything. It was with his hands he would have to put the bottle on the table! But he could not find his hands, could not feel them. His mind see-sawed in strophe and antistrophe: "You can't move!"—"I will move!" "You're beaten"—"I'm not beat." "Give up"—"I won't." That struggle to find his hands seemed to last for ever—he *must* find them! After that—go down—all standing—after that! Everything round him was red. Then the red cloud cleared just a little, and he could hear the clock—"tick—tick—tick"; a faint sensation spread from his shoulders down to his wrists, down his palms; and yes—he could feel the bottle! He redoubled his struggle to get forward in his chair; to get forward and put the bottle down. It was not dignified like this! One arm he could move now; but he could not grip the bottle nearly tight enough to put it down. Working his whole body forward, inch by inch, he shifted himself up in the chair till he could lean sideways, and the bottle, slipping down his chest, dropped slanting to the edge of the low stool-table. Then with all his might he screwed his trunk and arms an inch further, and the bottle stood. He had done it—done it! His lips twitched into a smile; his body sagged back to its old position. He had done it! And he closed his eyes. . . .

At half-past eleven the girl Molly, opening the door, looked at him and said softly: "Sirr! there's some ladies, and a gentleman!" But he did not answer. And, still holding the door, she whispered out into the hall:

"He's asleep, miss."

A voice whispered back:

"Oh! Just let me go in, I won't wake him unless he does. But I do want to show him my dress."

The girl moved aside; and on tiptoe Phyllis passed in. She walked to where, between the lamp-glow and the fire-glow, she was lighted up. White satin—her first low-cut dress—the flush of her first supper party—a gardenia at her breast, another in her fingers! Oh! what a pity he was asleep! How red he looked! How funnily old men breathed! And mysteriously, as a child might, she whispered:

"Guardy!"

No answer! And pouting, she stood twiddling the gardenia. Then suddenly she thought: 'I'll put it in his buttonhole! When he wakes up and sees it, how he'll jump!'

And stealing close, she bent and slipped it in. Two faces looked at her from round the door; she heard Bob Pillin's smothered chuckle; her mother's rich and feathery laugh. Oh! How red his forehead was! She touched it with her lips; skipped back, twirled round, danced silently a second, blew a kiss, and like quicksilver was gone.

And the whispering, the chuckling, and one little outpealing laugh rose in the hall.

But the old man slept. Nor until Meller came at his usual hour of half-past twelve, was it known that he would never wake.

RALPH HODGSON

Time, you Old Gipsy Man

TIME, you old gipsy man,
Will you not stay,
Put up your caravan
Just for one day?

All things I'll give you
Will you be my guest,
Bells for your jennet
Of silver the best,
Goldsmiths shall beat you
A great golden ring,
Peacocks shall bow to you,
Little boys sing,
Oh, and sweet girls will
Festoon you with may.
Time, you old gipsy,
Why hasten away?

Last week in Babylon,
Last night in Rome,
Morning, and in the crush
Under Paul's dome;
Under Paul's dial
You tighten your rein—
Only a moment,
And off once again;
Off to some city
Now blind in the womb,
Off to another
Ere that's in the tomb.

Time, you old gipsy man,
Will you not stay,
Put up your caravan
Just for one day?

Eve

EVE, with her basket, was
Deep in the bells and grass,
Wading in bells and grass
Up to her knees,
Picking a dish of sweet
Berries and plums to eat,
Down in the bells and grass
Under the trees.

Mute as a mouse in a
Corner the cobra lay,
Curled round a bough of the
Cinnamon tall. . . .
Now to get even and
Humble proud heaven and
Now was the moment or
Never at all.

"Eva!" Each syllable
Light as a flower fell,
"Eva!" he whispered the
Wondering maid,
Soft as a bubble sung
Out of a linnet's lung,
Soft and most silverly
"Eva!" he said.

Picture that orchard sprite,
Eve, with her body white,
Supple and smooth to her
Slim finger tips,
Wondering, listening,
Listening, wondering,
Eve with a berry
Half-way to her lips.

Oh, had our simple Eve
Seen through the make-believe!
Had she but known the
Pretender he was!
Out of the boughs he came,
Whispering still her name,
Tumbling in twenty rings
Into the grass.

Here was the strangest pair
In the world anywhere,
Eve in the bells and grass
Kneeling, and he
Telling his story low. . . .
Singing birds saw them go
Down the dark path to
The Blasphemous Tree.

Oh, what a clatter when
Titmouse and Jenny Wren
Saw him successful and
Taking his leave!
How the birds rated him,

How they all hated him!
How they all pitied
Poor motherless Eve!

Picture her crying
Outside in the lane,
Eve, with no dish of sweet
Berries and plums to eat,
Haunting the gate of the
Orchard in vain. . . .
Picture the lewd delight
Under the hill to-night—
"Eva!" the toast goes round,
"Eva!" again.

WALTER DE LA MARE

The Sleeper

As Ann came in one summer's day,
She felt that she must creep,
So silent was the clear cool house,
It seemed a house of sleep.
And sure, when she pushed open the door,
Rapt in the stillness there,
Her mother sat, with stooping head,
Asleep upon a chair;
Fast—fast asleep; her two hands laid
Loose-folded on her knee,
So that her small unconscious face
Looked half unreal to be:
So calmly lit with sleep's pale light
Each feature was; so fair
Her forehead—every trouble was
Smoothed out beneath her hair.
But though her mind in dream now moved,
Still seemed her gaze to rest—
From out beneath her fast-sealed lids,
Above her moving breast—
On Ann; as quite, quite still she stood;
Yet slumber lay so deep
Even her hands upon her lap
Seemed saturate with sleep.
And as Ann peeped, a childlike dread
Stole over her, and then,
On stealthy, mouselike feet she trod,
And tiptoed out again.

Winter Dusk

Dark frost was in the air without,
The dusk was still with cold and gloom,
When less than even a shadow came
And stood within the room.

But of the three around the fire,
None turned a questioning head to look,
Still read a clear voice, on and on,
Still stoopèd they o'er their book.

The children watched their mother's eyes
Moving on softly line to line;
It seemed to listen too—that shade,
Yet made no outward sign.

The fire-flames crooned a tiny song,
No cold wind moved the wintry tree;
The children both in Faërie dreamed
Beside their mother's knee.

And nearer yet that spirit drew
Above that heedless one, intent
Only on what the simple words
Of her small story meant.

No voiceless sorrow grieved her mind,
No memory her bosom stirred,
Nor dreamed she, as she read to two,
'Twas surely three who heard.

Yet when, the story done, she smiled
From face to face, serene and clear,
A love, half dread, sprang up, as she
Leaned close and drew them near.

The Listeners

"Is there anybody there?" said the Traveller,
Knocking on the moonlit door;
And his horse in the silence champed the grasses
Of the forest's ferny floor:
And a bird flew up out of the turret,
Above the Traveller's head:
And he smote upon the door again a second time;
"Is there anybody there?" he said.
But no one descended to the Traveller;

No head from the leaf-fringed sill
Leaned over and looked into his grey
eyes,
Where he stood perplexed and still.
But only a host of phantom listeners
That dwelt in the lone house then
Stood listening in the quiet of the moonlight
To that voice from the world of men:
Stood thronging the faint moonbeams on
the dark stair,
That goes down to the empty hall,
Hearkening in an air stirred and shaken
By the lonely Traveller's call.
And he felt in his heart their strangeness,
Their stillness answering his cry,
While his horse moved, cropping the dark
turf,
'Neath the starred and leafy sky;
For he suddenly smote on the door, even
Louder, and lifted his head:—
"Tell them I came, and no one answered,
That I kept my word," he said.
Never the least stir made the listeners,
Though every word he spake
Fell echoing through the shadowiness of
the still house
From the one man left awake:
Ay, they heard his foot upon the stirrup,
And the sound of iron on stone,
And how the silence surged softly backward,
When the plunging hoofs were gone.

GILBERT KEITH CHESTERTON

From THE BALLAD OF THE WHITE HORSE

Book VII. Ethandune: The Last Charge

King Guthrun and his Northmen ravaged the land from Chester to the Humber, until they came to the heights of Wessex and the Hill of the Horse. Here, in the Battle of Ethandune, they were finally attacked by the hastily mustered forces of King Alfred and his Chiefs. In the first day's fighting the Chiefs—Saxon, Celt, Roman, and Norseman—all were slain, and Alfred was driven back, with a tiny remnant of his poor host.

AWAY in the waste of White Horse
Down
An idle child alone
Played some small game through hours
that pass
And patiently would pluck the grass,
Patiently push the stone.

On the lean, green edge for ever,
Where the blank chalk touched the
turf,
The child played on, alone, divine,
As a child plays on the last line
That sunders sand and surf.

For he dwelleth in high divisions
Too simple to understand,
Seeing on what morn of mystery
The Uncreated rent the sea
With roarings from the land.

Through the long infant hours like days
He built one tower in vain—
Piled up small stones to make a town,
And evermore the stones fell down,
And he piled them up again.

And crimson kings on battle-towers,
And saints on Gothic spires,
And hermits on their peaks of snow,
And heroes on their pyres,

And patriots riding royally
That rush the rocking town,
Stretch hands, and hunger and aspire,
Seeking to mount where high and higher,
The child whom Time can never tire,
Sings over White Horse Down.

And this was the might of Alfred
At the ending of the way;
That of such smiters wise or wild,
He was least distant from the child,
Piling stones all day.

For Eldred fought like a frank hunter,
That killeth and goeth home;

And Mark had fought because all arms
  Rang like the name of Rome.

And Colan fought with a double mind,
  Moody and madly gay;
But Alfred fought as gravely
  As a good child at play.

He saw wheels break and work run back,
  And all things as they were;
And his heart was orbed like victory,
  And simple like despair.

Therefore is Mark forgotten,
  That was wise with his tongue and brave;
And the cairn over Colan crumbled,
  And the cross on Eldred's grave.

Their great souls went on a wind away,
  And they have not tale or tomb;
And Alfred born in Wantage
  Rules England till the doom.

Because in the forest of all fears,
  Like a strange fresh gust from sea,
Struck him that ancient innocence
  That is more than mastery.

And as a child whose bricks fall down,
  Re-piles them o'er and o'er;
Came ruin and the rain that burns,
Returning as a wheel returns,
And crouching in the furze and ferns
  He began his life once more.

He took his ivory horn unslung
  And smiled, but not in scorn;
"Endeth the Battle of Ethandune
  With the blowing of a horn."

On a dark horse at the double way
  He saw great Guthrum ride;
Heard roar of brass and ring of steel,
The laughter and the trumpet peal,
  The pagan in his pride,

And Ogier's red and hated head
  Moved in some talk or task;
But the men seemed scattered in the brier,
And some of them had lit a fire,
  And one had broached a cask.

And waggons one or two stood up,
  Like tall ships in sight,
As if an outpost were encamped
  At the cloven ways for night.

And joyous of the sudden stay
  Of Alfred's routed few,
Sat one upon a stone to sigh;
And some slipped up the road to fly,
Till Alfred in the fern hard by
  Set horn to mouth and blew.

And they all abode like statues—
  One sitting on the stone,
One half-way through the thorn hedge tall,
One with a leg across a wall;
And one looked backwards, very small,
  Far up the road, alone.

Grey twilight and a yellow star
  Hung over thorn and hill.
Two spears and a cloven war-shield lay
Loose on the road as cast-away,
The horn died faint in the forests grey,
  And the fleeing men stood still.

"Brothers at arms," said Alfred,
  "On this side lies the foe;
Are slavery and starvation flowers
  That you should pluck them so?

"For whether is it better
  To be prodded with Danish poles,
Having hewn a chamber in a ditch,
And hounded like a howling witch,
  Or smoked to death in holes?

"Or that before the red cock crow,
  All we, a thousand strong,
Go down the dark road to God's house,
  Singing a Wessex song?

"To sweat a slave to a race of slaves,
  To drink up infamy?
No, brothers, by your leave, I think
Death is a better ale to drink;
And by all the stars of Christ that sink,
  The Danes shall drink with me.

"To grow old cowed in a conquered land,
With the sun itself discrowned,
To see trees crouch and cattle slink—
Death is a better ale to drink,
And by high Death on the fell brink,
That flagon shall go round.

"Though dead are all the paladins,
Whom Glory had in ken,
Though all your thunder-sworded thanes
With proud hearts died among the Danes,
While a man remains, great war remains;
Now is a war of men.

"The men that tear the furrows,
The men that fell the trees;
When all their lords be lost and dead,
The bondsmen of the earth shall tread
The tyrants of the seas.

"The wheel of the roaring stillness
Of all labours under the sun,
Speed the wild work as well at least,
As the whole world's work is done.

"Let Hildred hack the shield-wall,
Clean as he hacks the hedge;
Let Gurth the Fowler stand as cool
As he stands on the chasm's edge;

"Let Gorlias ride the sea-kings
As Gorlias rides the sea,
Then let all hell and Denmark drive,
Yelling to all its fiends alive,
And not a rag care we."

When Alfred's word was ended,
Stood firm that feeble line,
Each in his place with club or spear,
And fury deeper than deep fear,
And smiles as sour as brine.

And the King held up the horn and said,
"See ye my father's horn,
That Egbert blew in his empery,
Once, when he rode out commonly,
Twice when he rode for venery,
And thrice on the battle-morn.

"But heavier fates have fallen
The horn of the Wessex kings;
And I blew once, the riding sign,
To call you to the fighting line
And glory and all good things,

"And now two blasts, the hunting sign,
Because we turn to bay;
But I will not blow the three blasts,
Till we be lost or they.

"And now I blow the hunting sign,
Charge some, by rule and rod,
But when I blow the battle sign,
Charge all, and go to God."

Wild stared the Danes at the double ways
Where they loitered, all at large,
As that dark line for the last time
Doubled the knee to charge—

And caught their weapons clumsily,
And marvelled how and why—
In such degree, by rule and rod,
The people of the peace of God
Went roaring down to die.

And when the last arrow
Was fitted and was flown,
When the broken shield hung on the breast,
And the hopeless lance was laid in rest,
And the hopeless horn blown,

The King looked up, and what he saw
Was a great light like death,
For Our Lady stood on the standards rent,
As lonely and as innocent
As when between white walls she went
In the lilies of Nazareth.

One instant in a still light,
He saw Our Lady then,
Her dress was soft as western sky,
And she was a queen most womanly—
But she was a queen of men.

Over the iron forest
He saw Our Lady stand;

Her eyes were sad withouten art,
And seven swords were in her heart—
But one was in her hand.

Then the last charge went blindly,
And all too lost for fear;
The Danes closed round, a roaring ring,
And twenty clubs rose o'er the King,
Four Danes hewed at him, halloing,
And Ogier of the Stone and Sling
Drove at him with a spear.

But the Danes were wild with laughter,
And the great spear swung wide,
The point stuck to a straggling tree,
And either host cried suddenly,
As Alfred leapt aside.

Short time had shaggy Ogier
To pull his lance in line—
He knew King Alfred's axe on high,
He heard it rushing through the sky,

He cowered beneath it with a cry—
It split him to the spine;
And Alfred sprang over him dead,
And blew the battle sign.

Then bursting all and blasting,
Came Christendom like death,
Kicked from such catapults of will
The staves shiver, the barrels spill,
The waggons waver and crash and kill
The waggoners beneath.

Barriers go backwards, banners rend,
Great shields groan like a gong—
Horses like horns of nightmare
Neigh horribly and long.

Horses ramp high and rock and boil
And break their golden reins,
And slide on carnage clamorously,
Down where the bitter blood doth lie,
Where Ogier went on foot to die,
In the old way of the Danes.

"The high tide!" King Alfred cried;
"The high tide and the turn!
As a tide turns on the tall grey seas,
See how they waver in the trees,
How stray their spears, how knock their knees,
How wild their watchfires burn!

"The Mother of God goes over them,
Walking on wind and flame,
And the storm-cloud drifts from city and dale,
And the White Horse stamps in the White Horse Vale,
And we all shall yet drink Christian ale,
In the village of our name.

"The Mother of God goes over them,
On dreadful Cherubs borne;
And the psalm is roaring above the rune,
And the cross goes over the sun and moon;
Endeth the Battle of Ethandune,
With the blowing of the horn."

For back indeed disorderly
The Danes went clamouring,
Too worn to take anew the tale,
Or dazed with insolence and ale,
Or stunned of heaven, or stricken pale
Before the face of the King.

For dire was Alfred in his hour
The pale scribe witnesseth,
More mighty in defeat was he
Than all men else in victory;
And behind, his men came murderously,
Dry-throated, drinking death.

And Edgar of the Golden Ship
He broke with his own hand,
Took Ludwig from his lady's bower,
And smote down Harmer in his hour,
And vain and lonely stood the tower—
The tower in Guelderland.

And Torr out of his tiny boat,
Whose eyes beheld the Nile,
Wulf with his war cry on his lips,
And Hacro born in the eclipse,
Who blocked the Seine with battle-ships
Round Paris on the Isle.

And Hacon of the Harvest-song,
And Dirck from the Elbe he slew,

And Cnut that melted Durham bell,
And Fulk and fiery Oscar fell,
And Goderic and Sigael,
And Uriel of the Yew.

And highest sang the slaughter,
And fastest fell the slain,
When from the wood-road's blackening throat
A crowning and crashing wonder smote
The rear-guard of the Dane.

For the dregs of Colan's company—
Lost down the other road,
Had gathered and grown and heard the din,
And with wild yells came pouring in
Naked as their old British kin
And bright with blood for woad.

And bare and bloody and aloft
They bore before their band
The body of their mighty lord,
Colan of Caerleon, and the horde,
That bore King Alfred's battle-sword
Broken in his left hand.

And a strange music went with him,
Loud and yet strangely far;
The wild pipes of the western land,
Too keen for the ear to understand,
Sang high and deathly on each hand
When the dead man went to war.

Blocked between ghost and buccaneer,
Brave men have dropped and died,
And the wild sea-lords well might quail
As the ghastly war-pipes of the Gael
Called to the horns of White Horse Vale,
And all the horns replied.

And Hildred the poor hedger
Cut down four captains dead,
And Halfgar laid seven others low,
And the great earls wavered to and fro
For the living and the dead.

And Gorlias grasped the great flag,
The Raven of Odin, torn;
And the eyes of Guthrum altered,
For the first time since morn.

As a turn of the wheel of tempest
Tilts up the whole sky tall,
And cliffs of wan cloud luminous
Lean out like great walls over us,
As if the heavens might fall;

As such a tall and tilted sky
Sends certain snow or light,
So did the eyes of Guthrum change,
And the turn was more certain and more strange
Than a thousand men in flight.

For not till the floor of the skies is split
And hell-fire shines through the sea,
Or the stars look up through the rent earth's knees,
Cometh such rending of certainties,
As when one wise man truly sees
What is more wise than he.

He set his horse in the battle-breach
Even Guthrum of the Dane,
And as ever had fallen fell his brand,
A falling tower o'er many a land,
But Gurth the Fowler laid one hand
Upon this bridle rein.

King Guthrum was a great lord,
And higher than his gods—
He put the popes to laughter,
He chid the saints with rods.

He took this hollow world of ours
For a cup to hold his wine;
In the parting of the woodways
There came to him a sign.

In Wessex in the forest,
In the breaking of the spears,
We set a sign on Guthrum
To blaze a thousand years.

Where the high saddles jostle
And the horse-tails toss,
There rose to the birds flying
A roar of dead and dying;
In deafness and strong crying
We signed him with the cross.

Far out to the winding river
  The blood ran down for days,
When we put the cross on Guthrum
  In the parting of the ways.

JOHN MASEFIELD

Cargoes

Quinquireme of Nineveh from distant Ophir,
Rowing home to haven in sunny Palestine,
With a cargo of ivory,
And apes and peacocks,
Sandalwood, cedarwood, and sweet white wine.

Stately Spanish galleon coming from the Isthmus,
Dipping through the Tropics by the palm-green shores,
With a cargo of diamonds,
Emeralds, amethysts,
Topazes, and cinnamon, and gold moidores.

Dirty British coaster with a salt-caked smoke stack,
Butting through the Channel in the mad March days,
With a cargo of Tyne coal,
Road-rails, pig-lead,
Firewood, iron-ware, and cheap tin trays.

O little self, within whose smallness lies

O little self, within whose smallness lies
All that man was, and is, and will become,
Atom unseen that comprehends the skies
And tells the tracks by which the planets roam.
That, without moving, knows the joys of wings,
The tiger's strength, the eagle's secrecy,
And in the hovel can consort with kings,
Or clothe a god with his own mystery.
O with what darkness do we cloak thy light,
What dusty folly gather thee for food,
Thou who alone art knowledge and delight,
The heavenly bread, the beautiful, the good.
O living self, O god, O morning star,
Give us thy light, forgive us what we are.

The Western Islands

"Once there were two sailors; and one of them was Joe, and the other one was Jerry, and they were fishermen. And they'd a young apprentice-feller, and his name was Jim. And Joe was a great one for his pot, and Jerry was a wonder at his pipe; and Jim did all the work, and both of them banged him. So one time Joe and Jerry were in the beer-house, and there was a young parson there, telling the folks about foreign things, about plants and that. 'Ah,' he says, 'what wonders there are in the west.'

"'What sort of wonders, begging your pardon, sir,' says Joe. 'What sort of wonders might them be?'

"'Why, all sorts of wonders,' says the parson. 'Why, in the west,' he says, 'there's things you wouldn't believe. No, you wouldn't believe; not till you'd seen them,' he says. 'There's diamonds growing on the trees. And great, golden, glittering pearls as common as pea-straw. And there's islands in the west. Ah, I could tell you of them. Islands? I rather guess there's islands. None of your Isles of Man. None of your Alderney and Sark. Not in them seas.'

"'What sort of islands might they be, begging your pardon, sir?' says Jerry.

"'Why,' he says (the parson feller says), 'ISLANDS. Islands as big as Spain. Islands with rivers of rum and streams of sarsaparilla. And none of your roses. Rubies and ame-thynes is all the roses grows in them parts. With golden stalks to them, and big diamond sticks to them, and the taste of pork-crackling if you eat them. They're the sort of roses to have in your area,' he says.

"'And what else might there be in them parts, begging your pardon, sir?' says Joe.

"'Why,' he says, this parson says, 'there's wonders. There's not only wonders but miracles. And not only miracles, but sperrits.'

"'What sort of sperrits might they be, begging your pardon?' says Jerry. 'Are they rum and that?'

"'When I says sperrits,' says the parson feller, 'I mean ghosts.'

"'Of course ye do,' says Joe.

"'Yes, ghosts,' says the parson. 'And by ghosts I mean sperrits. And by sperrits I mean white things. And by white things I mean things as turn your hair white. And there's red devils there, and blue devils there, and a great gold queen a-waiting for a man to kiss her. And the first man as dares to kiss that queen, why he becomes king, and all her sacks of gold become his.'

"'Begging your pardon, sir,' said Jerry, 'but whereabouts might these here islands be?'

"'Why, in the west,' says the parson. 'In the west, where the sun sets.'

"'Ah,' said Joe and Jerry. 'What wonders there are in the world.'

* * * * *

"Now, after that, neither one of them could think of anything but these here western islands. So at last they take their smack, and off they go in search of them. And Joe had a barrel of beer in the bows, and Jerry had a box of twist in the waist, and pore little Jim stood and steered abaft all. And in the evenings Jerry and Joe would bang their pannikins together, and sing of the great times they meant to have when they were married to the queen. Then they would clump pore little Jim across the head, and tell him to watch out, and keep her to her course, or they'd ride him down like you would a main tack. And he'd better mind his eye, they told him, or they'd make him long to be boiled and salted. And he'd better put more sugar in the tea, they said, or they'd cut him up for cod-bait. And who was he, they asked, to be wanting meat for dinner, when there was that much weevilly biscuit in the bread-barge? And boys was going to the dogs, they said, when limbs the like of him had the heaven-born insolence to want to sleep. And a nice pass things was coming to, they said, when a lad as they'd done everything for, and saved, so to speak, from the workhouse, should go for to snivel when they hit him a clip. If they'd said a word, when they was hit, when they was boys, they told him, they'd have had their bloods drawed, and been stood in the wind to cool. But let him take heed, they said, and be a good lad, and do the work of five, and they wouldn't half wonder, they used to say, as he'd be a man before his mother. So the sun shone, and the stars came out golden, and all the sea was a sparkle of gold with them. Blue was the sea, and the wind blew, too, and it blew Joe and Jerry west as fast as a cat can eat sardines.

* * * * *

"And one fine morning the wind fell calm, and a pleasant smell came over the water, like nutmegs on a rum-milk-punch. Presently the dawn broke. And, lo and behold, a rousing great wonderful island, all scarlet with coral and with rubies. The surf that was beating on her sands went shattering into silver coins, into dimes, and pesetas, and francs, and fourpenny bits. And the flowers on the cliffs was all one gleam and glitter. And the beauty of that island was a beauty beyond the beauty of Sally Brown, the lady as kept the beer-house. And on the beach of that island, on a golden throne, like, sat a woman so lovely that to look at her was as good as a church-service for one.

" 'That's the party I got to kiss,' said Jerry. 'Steady, and beach her, Jim, boy,' he says. 'Run her ashore, lad. That's the party is to be my queen.'

" 'You've got a neck on you, all of a sudden,' said Joe. 'You ain't the admiral of this fleet. Not by a wide road you ain't. I'll do all the kissing as there's any call for. You keep clear, my son.'

"Here the boat ran her nose into the sand, and the voyagers went ashore.

" 'Keep clear, is it?' said Jerry. 'You tell me to keep clear? You tell me again, and I'll put a head on you—'ll make you sing like a kettle. Who are you to tell me to keep clear?'

" 'I tell you who I am,' said Joe. 'I'm a better man than you are. That's what I am. I'm Joe the Tank, from Limehouse Basin, and there's no tinker's donkey-boy'll make me stand from under. Who are you to go kissing queens? Who are you that talk so proud and so mighty? You've a face on you would make a Dago tired. You look like a sea-sick Kanaka that's boxed seven rounds with a buzz-saw. You've no more manners than a hog, and you've a lip on you would fetch the enamel off a cup.'

" 'If it comes to calling names,' said Jerry, 'you ain't the only pebble on the beach. Whatever you might think, I tell you you ain't. You're the round turn and two-half hitches of a figure of fun as makes the angels weep. That's what you are. And you're the right-hand strand, and the left-hand strand, and the centre strand, and the core, and the serving, and the marling, of a three-stranded, left-handed, poorly worked junk of a half begun and never finished odds and ends of a Port Mahon soldier. You look like a Portuguese drummer. You've a whelky red nose that shines like a port side-light. You've a face like a muddy field where they've been playing football in the rain. Your hair is an insult and a shame. I blush when I look at you. You give me a turn like the first day out to a first voyager. Kiss, will you? Kiss? Man, I tell you you'd paralyze a shark if you kissed him. Paralyze him, strike him cold. That's what a kiss of yours'd do.'

" 'You ought to 'a' been a parson,' said Joe, 'that's what you'd ought. There's many would 'a' paid you for talk like that. But for all your fine talk, and for all your dandy language, you'll not come the old soldier over me. No, nor ten of you. *You* talk of kissing, when there's a handsome young man, the likes of me, around. Neither you nor ten of you. To hear you talk one'd think you was a Emperor or a Admiral. One would think you was a Bishop or a King. One might mistake you for a General or a Member of Parliament. You might. Straight, you might. A General or a Bishop or a King. And what are you? What are you? I ask you plain. What are you?—I'll tell you what you are.

" 'You're him as hired himself out as a scarecrow, acos no one'd take you as a fo'c's'le hand. You're him as give the colic to a weather-cock. You're him as turned old Mother Bomby's beer. You're him as drowned the duck and stole the monkey. You're him as got the medal give him for having a face that made the bull tame. You're——'

" 'Now don't you cast no more to me,' said Jerry. 'For I won't take no lip from a twelve-a-shilling, cent-a-corner, the likes of you are. You're the clippings of old junk, what the Dagoes smoke in cigarettes. A swab, and a-wash-deck-broom, and the half of a pint of paint'd make a handsomer figger of a man than what you are. I've seen a coir whisk, what they grooms a mule with, as had a sweeter face than you got. So stand aside, before you're put aside. I'm the king of this here island. You can go chase yourself for another. Stand clear, I say, or I'll give you a jog'll make your bells ring.'

* * * * *

"Now, while they were argufying, young Jim, the young apprentice feller, he creeps up to the queen upon the throne. She was beautiful, she was, and she shone in the sun, and she looked straight ahead of her like a wax-work in a show. And in her hand she had a sack full of jewels, and at her feet she had a sack full of gold, and by her side was an empty throne ready for the king she married. But round her right hand there was a red snake, and round her left hand there was a blue snake, and the snakes hissed and twisted, and they showed their teeth full of poison. So Jim looked at the snakes, and he hit them a welt, right and left, and he kissed the lady.

"And immediately all the bells and the birds of the world burst out a-ringing and a-singing. The lady awoke from her sleep, and Jim's old clothes were changed to cloth of gold. And there he was, a king, on the throne beside the lady.

"But the red snake turned to a big red devil who took a-hold of Joe, and the blue snake turned to a big blue devil, who took a hold of Jerry. And 'Come you here, you brawling pugs,' they said, 'come and shovel sand.' And Joe and Jerry took the spades that were given to them. And 'Dig, now,' said the devils. 'Heave round. Let's see you dig. Dig, you scarecrows. And tell us when you've dug to London.' "

WILFRID WILSON GIBSON

Flannan Isle

"Though three men dwell on Flannan Isle
To keep the lamp alight,
As we steer'd under the lee, we caught
No glimmer through the night!"

A passing ship at dawn had brought
The news; and quickly we set sail,
To find out what strange thing might ail
The keepers of the deep-sea light.

The winter day broke blue and bright,
With glancing sun and glancing spray,
As o'er the swell our boat made way,
As gallant as a gull in flight.

But, as we near'd the lonely isle;
And look'd up at the naked height;
And saw the lighthouse towering while
With blinded lantern, that all night
Had never shot a spark
Of comfort through the dark,
So ghostly in the cold sunlight
It seem'd, that we were struck the while
With wonder all too dread for words.

And, as into the tiny creek
We stole beneath the hanging crag,
We saw three queer, black, ugly birds—
Too big, by far, in my belief,
For guillemot or shag—
Like seamen sitting bolt-upright
Upon a half-tide reef:

But, as we near'd, they plunged from sight
Without a sound, or spurt of white.

And still too mazed to speak,
We landed; and made fast the boat;
And climb'd the track in single file,
Each wishing he was safe afloat,
On any sea, however far,
So it be far from Flannan Isle:
And still we seem'd to climb, and climb,
As though we'd lost all count of time,
And so must climb for evermore.
Yet, all too soon, we reached the door—
The black, sun-blister'd lighthouse-door,
That gaped for us ajar.

As, on the threshold, for a spell,
We paused, we seem'd to breathe the smell
Of limewash and of tar,
Familiar as our daily breath,
As though 'twere some strange scent of death:
And so, yet wondering, side by side,
We stood a moment, still tongue-tied:
And each with black foreboding eyed
The door, ere we should fling it wide,
To leave the sunlight for the gloom:
Till, plucking courage up, at last,
Hard on each other's heels we pass'd
Into the living-room.

Yet, as we crowded through the door,
We only saw a table, spread
For dinner, meat and cheese and bread;
But all untouch'd; and no one there:
As though, when they sat down to eat,
Ere they could even taste,
Alarm had come; and they in haste
Had risen and left the bread and meat:
For at the table-head a chair
Lay tumbled on the floor.

We listen'd; but we only heard
The feeble cheeping of a bird
That starved upon its perch:
And, listening still, without a word,
We set about our hopeless search.

We hunted high, we hunted low,
And soon ransack'd the empty house;
Then o'er the Island, to and fro,
We ranged, to listen and to look
In every cranny, cleft or nook
That might have hid a bird or mouse:
But, though we search'd from shore to shore,
We found no sign in any place:
And soon again stood face to face
Before the gaping door:
And stole into the room once more
As frighten'd children steal.

Aye: though we hunted high and low,
And hunted everywhere,
Of the three men's fate we found no trace
Of any kind in any place,
But a door ajar, and an untouch'd meal,
And an overtoppled chair.

And, as we listen'd in the gloom
Of that forsaken living-room—
A chill clutch on our breath—
We thought how ill-chance came to all
Who kept the Flannan Light:
And how the rock had been the death
Of many a likely lad:
How six had come to a sudden end,
And three had gone stark mad:
And one whom we'd all known as friend
Had leapt from the lantern one still night,
And fallen dead by the lighthouse wall:
And long we thought
On the three we sought,
And of what might yet befall.

Like curs a glance has brought to heel,
We listen'd, flinching there:
And look'd, and look'd, on the untouch'd meal
And the overtoppled chair.

We seem'd to stand for an endless while,
Though still no word was said,
Three men alive on Flannan Isle,
Who thought on three men dead.

The Hare

My hands were hot upon a hare,
Half-strangled, struggling in a snare—
My knuckles at her warm wind-pipe—
When suddenly, her eyes shot back,
Big, fearful, staggering and black,
And ere I knew, my grip was slack;
And I was clutching empty air,
Half-mad, half-glad at my lost luck . . .
When I awoke beside the stack.

'Twas just the minute when the snipe
As though clock-wakened, every jack,
An hour ere dawn, dart in and out
The mist-wreaths filling syke and slack,
And flutter wheeling round about,
And drumming out the Summer night.
I lay star-gazing yet a bit;
Then, chilly-skinned, I sat upright,
To shrug the shivers from my back;
And, drawing out a straw to suck,
My teeth nipped through it at a bite . . .
The liveliest lad is out of pluck
An hour ere dawn—a tame cock-sparrow—
When cold stars shiver through his marrow,
And wet mist soaks his mother-wit.

But, as the snipe dropped, one by one;
And one by one the stars blinked out;
I knew 'twould only need the sun
To send the shudders right about:
And as the clear East faded white,
I watched and wearied for the sun—
The jolly, welcome, friendly sun—
The sleepy sluggard of a sun
That still kept snoozing out of sight,
Though well he knew the night was done . . .
And after all, he caught me dozing,
And leapt up, laughing, in the sky
Just as my lazy eyes were closing:
And it was good as gold to lie
Full-length among the straw, and feel
The day wax warmer every minute,
As, glowing glad, from head to heel,
I soaked, and rolled rejoicing in it . . .
When from the corner of my eye,
Upon a heathery knowe hard-by,
With long lugs cocked, and eyes astare,
Yet all serene, I saw a hare.

Upon my belly in the straw,
I lay, and watched her sleek her fur,
As, daintily, with well-licked paw,
She washed her face and neck and ears:
Then, clean and comely in the sun,
She kicked her heels up, full for fun,
As if she did not care a pin
Though she should jump out of her skin,
And leapt and lolloped, free of fears,
Until my heart frisked round with her.

"And yet, if I but lift my head,
You'll scamper off, young Puss," I said.
"Still, I can't lie, and watch you play,
Upon my belly half the day.
The Lord alone knows where I'm going:
But, I had best be getting there.
Last night I loosed you from the snare—
Asleep, or waking, who's for knowing!—
So, I shall thank you now for showing
Which art to take to bring me where
My luck awaits me. When you're ready
To start, I'll follow on your track.
Though slow of foot, I'm sure and steady . . ."
She pricked her ears, then set them back;
And like a shot was out of sight:
And, with a happy heart and light,
As quickly I was on my feet;
And following the way she went,
Keen as a lurcher on the scent,
Across the heather and the bent,
Across the quaking moss and peat.
Of course, I lost her soon enough,
For moorland tracks are steep and rough;
And hares are made of nimbler stuff
Than any lad of seventeen,
However lanky-legged and tough,
However kestrel-eyed and keen:
And I'd at last to stop and eat
The little bit of bread and meat
Left in my pocket overnight.
So, in a hollow, snug and green,

I sat beside a burn, and dipped
The dry bread in an icy pool;
And munched a breakfast fresh and cool . . .
And then sat gaping like a fool . . .
For, right before my very eyes,
With lugs acock and eyes astare,
I saw again the selfsame hare.

So, up I jumped, and off she slipped;
And I kept sight of her until
I stumbled in a hole, and tripped,
And came a heavy, headlong spill;
And she, ere I'd the wit to rise,
Was o'er the hill, and out of sight:
And, sore and shaken with the tumbling,
And sicker at my foot for stumbling,
I cursed my luck, and went on, grumbling,
The way her flying heels had fled.

The sky was cloudless overhead,
And just alive with larks asinging;
And in a twinkling I was swinging
Across the windy hills, lighthearted.
A kestrel at my footstep started,
Just pouncing on a frightened mouse,
And hung o'er head with wings a-hover;
Through rustling heath an adder darted:
A hundred rabbits bobbed to cover:
A weasel, sleek and rusty-red,
Popped out of sight as quick as winking:
I saw a grizzled vixen slinking
Behind a clucking brood of grouse
That rose and cackled at my coming:
And all about my way were flying
The peewit, with their slow wings creaking;
And little jack-snipe darted, drumming:
And now and then a golden plover
Or redshank piped with reedy whistle.
But never shaken bent or thistle
Betrayed the quarry I was seeking;
And not an instant, anywhere
Did I clap eyes upon a hare.

So, travelling still, the twilight caught me;
And as I stumbled on, I muttered:
"A deal of luck the hare has brought me!
The wind and I must spend together
A hungry night among the heather.
If I'd her here . . ." And as I uttered,
I tripped, and heard a frightened squeal;
And dropped my hands in time to feel
The hare just bolting 'twixt my feet.
She slipped my clutch: and I stood there
And cursed that devil-littered hare,
That left me stranded in the dark
In that wide waste of quaggy peat
Beneath black night without a spark:
When, looking up, I saw a flare
Upon a far-off hill, and said:
"By God, the heather is afire!
It's mischief at this time of year . . ."
And then, as one bright flame shot higher,
And booths and vans stood out quite clear,
My wits came back into my head;
And I remembered Brough Hill Fair.
And as I stumbled towards the glare
I knew the sudden kindling meant
The Fair was over for the day;
And all the cattle-folk away;
And gipsy folk and tinkers now
Were lighting supper-fires without
Each caravan and booth and tent.
And as I climbed the stiff hill-brow
I quite forgot my lucky hare.
I'd something else to think about:
For well I knew there's broken meat
For empty bellies after fair-time;
And looked to have a royal rare time
With something rich and prime to eat;
And then to lie and toast my feet
All night beside the biggest fire.

But, even as I neared the first,
A pleasant whiff of stewing burst
From out a smoking pot a-bubble:
And as I stopped behind the folk
Who sprawled around, and watched it seething,
A woman heard my eager breathing,
And, turning, caught my hungry eye:
And called out to me: "Draw in nigher,

Unless you find it too much trouble;
Or you've a nose for better fare,
And go to supper with the Squire . . .
You've got the hungry parson's air!".
And all looked up, and took the joke,
As I dropped gladly to the ground
Among them, when they all lay gazing
Upon the bubbling and the blazing.
My eyes were dazzled by the fire
At first; and then I glanced around;
And in those swarthy, fire-lit faces—
Though drowsing in the glare and heat
And snuffing the warm savour in,
Dead-certain of their fill of meat—
I felt the bit between the teeth,
The flying heels, the broken traces,
And heard the highroad ring beneath
The trampling hoofs; and knew them kin.
Then for the first time, standing there
Behind the woman who had hailed me,
I saw a girl with eyes astare
That looked in terror o'er my head;
And, all at once, my courage failed me . . .
For now again, and sore-adread,
My hands were hot upon a hare,
That struggled, strangling in the snare . . .
Then once more as the girl stood clear,
Before me—quaking cold with fear—
I saw the hare look from her eyes . . .

And when, at last, I turned to see
What held her scared, I saw a man—
A fat man with dull eyes aleer—
Within the shadow of the van;
And I was on the point to rise
To send him spinning 'mid the wheels
And stop his leering grin with mud . . .
And would have done it in a tick . . .
When, suddenly, alive with fright,
She started, with red, parted lips,
As though she guessed we'd come to grips,
And turned her black eyes full on me . . .
And as I looked into their light
My heart forgot the lust of fight,
And something shot me to the quick,
And ran like wildfire through my blood,
And tingled to my finger-tips . . .
And, in a dazzling flash, I knew
I'd never been alive before . . .
And she was mine for evermore.

While all the others slept asnore
In caravan and tent that night,
I lay alone beside the fire;
And stared into its blazing core,
With eyes that would not shut or tire,
Because the best of all was true,
And they looked still into the light
Of her eyes, burning ever bright
Within the brightest coal for me . . .
Once more, I saw her, as she started,
And glanced at me with red lips parted:
And as she looked, the frightened hare
Had fled her eyes; and merrily
She smiled, with fine teeth flashing white,
As though she, too, were happy-hearted . . .
Then she had trembled suddenly,
And dropped her eyes, as that fat man
Stepped from the shadow of the van,
And joined the circle, as the pot
Was lifted off, and, piping-hot,
The supper streamed in wooden bowls.
Yet, she had hardly touched a bite;
And had never raised her eyes all night
To mine again; but on the coals,
As I sat staring, she had stared—
The black curls, shining round her head
From under the red kerchief, tied
So nattily beneath her chin—
And she had stolen off to bed
Quite early, looking dazed and scared.
Then, all agape and sleepy-eyed,
Ere long the others had turned in:
And I was rid of that fat man,
Who slouched away to his own van.

And now, before her van, I lay,
With sleepless eyes, awaiting day;
And as I gazed upon the glare
I heard, behind, a gentle stir:
And, turning round, I looked on her
Where she stood on the little stair

Outside the van, with listening air—
And, in her eyes, the hunted hare . . .
And then, I saw her slip away,
A bundle underneath her arm,
Without a single glance at me.
I lay a moment wondering,
My heart a-thump like anything,
Then, fearing she should come to harm,
I rose, and followed speedily
Where she had vanished in the night.
And as she heard my step behind
She started, and stopt dead with fright;
Then blundered on as if struck blind:
And now as I caught up with her,
Just as she took the moorland track,
I saw the hare's eyes, big and black . . .
She'd made as though she'd double back . . .
But when she looked into my eyes,
She stood quite still and did not stir . . .
And picking up her fallen pack
I tucked it 'neath my arm; and she
Just took her luck quite quietly,
As she must take what chance might come,
And would not have it otherwise,
And walked into the night with me,
Without a word across the fells.

And all about us, through the night,
The mists were stealing, cold and white,
Down every rushy syke or slack:
But, soon the moon swung into sight;
And as we went my heart was light,
And singing like a burn in flood:
And in my ears were tinkling bells;
My body was a rattled drum:
And fifes were shrilling through my blood
That summer night, to think that she
Was walking through the world with me.

But when the air with dawn was chill,
As we were travelling down a hill,
She broke her silence with low-sobbing;
And told her tale, her bosom throbbing
As though her very heart were shaken
With fear she'd yet be overtaken . . .
She'd always lived in caravans—
Her father's, gay as any man's,
Grass-green, picked out with red and yellow
And glittering brave with burnished brass
That sparkled in the sun like flame,
And window curtains, white as snow . . .
But, they had died, ten years ago,
Her parents both, when fever came . . .
And they were buried, side by side,
Somewhere beneath the wayside grass . . .
In times of sickness, they kept wide
Of towns and busybodies, so
No parson's or policeman's tricks
Should bother them when in a fix . . .
Her father never could abide
A black coat or a blue, poor man . . .
And so, Long Dick, a kindly fellow,
When you could keep him from the can,
And Meg, his easy-going wife,
Had taken her into the van;
And kept her since her parents died . . .
And she had lived a happy life,
Until Fat Pete's young wife was taken . . .
But, ever since, he'd pestered her . . .
And she dared scarcely breathe or stir,
Lest she should see his eyes aleer . . .
And many a night she'd lain and shaken,
And very nearly died of fear—
Though safe enough within the van
With Mother Meg and her good-man—
For, since Fat Pete was Long Dick's friend,
And they were thick and sweet as honey,
And Dick owed Pete a lot of money,
She knew too well how it must end . . .
And she would rather lie stone dead
Beneath the wayside grass than wed
With leering Pete, and live the life,
And die the death, of his first wife . . .
And so, last night, clean-daft with dread,
She'd bundled up a pack and fled . . .

When all the sobbing tale was out,
She dried her eyes, and looked about,
As though she'd left all fear behind,
And out of sight were out of mind,

Then, when the dawn was burning red,
"I'm hungry as a hawk!" she said:
And from the bundle took out bread,
And at the happy end of night
We sat together by a burn:
And ate a thick slice, turn by turn;
And laughed and kissed between each
bite.

Then, up again, and on our way
We went; and tramped the livelong day
The moorland trackways, steep and
rough,
Though there was little fear enough
That they would follow on our flight.

And then again a shiny night
Among the honey-scented heather,
We wandered in the moonblaze bright,
Together through a land of light,
A lad and lass alone with life.
And merrily we laughed together,
When, starting up from sleep, we heard
The cock-grouse talking to his wife . . .
And "Old Fat Pete" she called the bird.

Six months and more have cantered by:
And, Winter past, we're out again—
We've left the fat and weatherwise
To keep their coops and reeking sties,
And eat their fill of oven-pies,
While we win free and out again
To take potluck beneath the sky
With sun and moon and wind and rain.
Six happy months . . . and yet, at night,
I've often wakened in affright,
And looked upon her lying there,
Beside me sleeping quietly,
Adread that when she waked, I'd see
The hunted hare within her eyes.

And only last night, as I slept
Beneath the shelter of a stack . . .
My hands were hot upon a hare,
Half-strangled, struggling in the snare,
When, suddenly, her eyes shot back,
Big, fearful, staggering and black;
And ere I knew, my grip was slack,
And I was clutching empty air . . .
Bolt-upright from my sleep I leapt . . .
Her place was empty in the straw . . .
And then, with quaking heart, I saw
That she was standing in the night,
A leveret cuddled to her breast . . .

I spoke no word; but as the light
Through banks of Eastern cloud was
breaking,
She turned, and saw that I was waking:
And told me how she could not rest;
And, rising in the night, she'd found
This baby-hare crouched on the ground;
And she had nursed it quite a while;
But, now, she'd better let it go . . .
Its mother would be fretting so . . .
A mother's heart . . .
I saw her smile
And look at me with tender eyes;
And as I looked into their light,
My foolish, fearful heart grew wise . . .
And now, I knew that never there
I'd see again the startled hare,
Or need to dread the dreams of night.

Devil's Edge

All night I lay on Devil's Edge,
Along an overhanging ledge
Between the sky and sea:
And as I rested 'waiting sleep,
The windless sky and soundless deep
In one dim, blue infinity
Of starry peace encompassed me.

And I remembered, drowsily,
How 'mid the hills last night I'd lain
Beside a singing moorland burn;
And waked at dawn, to feel the rain
Fall on my face, as on the fern
That drooped about my heather-bed;
And how by noon the wind had blown
The last grey shred from out the sky,
And blew my homespun jacket dry,
As I stood on the topmost stone
That crowns the cairn on Hawkshaw
Head,
And caught a gleam of far-off sea;
And heard the wind sing in the bent
Like those far waters calling me:
When, my heart answering to the call,

I followed down the seaward stream,
By silent pool and singing fall;
Till with a quiet, keen content,
I watched the sun, a crimson ball,
Shoot through grey seas a fiery gleam,
Then sink in opal deeps from sight.

And with the coming on of night,
The wind had dropped: and as I lay,
Retracing all the happy day,
And gazing long and dreamily
Across the dim, unsounding sea,
Over the far horizon came
A sudden sail of amber flame;
And soon the new moon rode on high
Through cloudless deeps of crystal sky.

Too holy seemed the night for sleep;
And yet, I must have slept, it seems;
For, suddenly, I woke to hear
A strange voice singing, shrill and clear,
Down in a gully black and deep
That cleft the beetling crag in twain.
It seemed the very voice of dreams
That drive hag-ridden souls in fear
Through echoing, unearthly vales,
To plunge in black, slow-crawling streams,
Seeking to drown that cry, in vain . . .
Or some sea creature's voice that wails
Through blind, white banks of fog unlifting
To God-forgotten sailors drifting
Rudderless to death . . .
And as I heard,
Though no wind stirred,
An icy breath
Was in my hair . . .
And clutched my heart with cold despair . . .
But, as the wild song died away,
There came a faltering break
That shivered to a sobbing fall;
And seemed half-human, after all . . .

And yet, what foot could find a track
In that deep gully, sheer and black . . .
And singing wildly in the night!
So, wondering, I lay awake,
Until the coming of the light
Brought day's familiar presence back.

Down by the harbour-mouth that day,
A fisher told the tale to me.
Three months before, while out at sea,
Young Philip Burn was lost, though how,
None knew, and none would ever know.
The boat becalmed at noonday lay . . .
And not a ripple on the sea . . .
And Philip standing in the bow,
When his six comrades went below
To sleep away an hour or so,
Dog-tired with working day and night,
While he kept watch . . . and not a sound
They heard, until, at set of sun
They woke; and coming up they found
The deck was empty, Philip gone . . .
Yet not another boat in sight . . .
And not a ripple on the sea.
How he had vanished, none could tell.
They only knew the lad was dead
They'd left but now, alive and well . . .
And he, poor fellow, newly-wed . . .
And when they broke the news to her,
She spoke no word to anyone:
But sat all day, and would not stir—
Just staring, staring in the fire,
With eyes that never seemed to tire;
Until, at last, the day was done,
And darkness came; when she would rise,
And seek the door with queer, wild eyes;
And wander singing all the night
Unearthly songs beside the sea:
But always the first blink of light
Would find her back at her own door.

'Twas Winter when I came once more
To that old village by the shore;
And as, at night, I climbed the street,
I heard a singing, low and sweet,
Within a cottage near at hand:
And I was glad awhile to stand
And listen by the glowing pane:
And as I hearkened, that sweet strain
Brought back the night when I had lain
Awake on Devil's Edge . . .
And now I knew the voice again,

So different, free of pain and fear—
Its terror turned to tenderness—
And yet the same voice none the less,
Though singing now so true and clear:
And drawing nigh the window-ledge,
I watched the mother sing to rest
The baby snuggling to her breast.

PADRAIC COLUM

An Old Woman of the Roads

O, TO have a little house!
To own the hearth and stool and all!
The heaped up sods upon the fire,
The pile of turf against the wall!

To have a clock with weights and chains
And pendulum swinging up and down!
A dresser filled with shining delph,
Speckled and white and blue and brown!

I could be busy all the day
Clearing and sweeping hearth and floor,
And fixing on their shelf again
My white and blue and speckled store!

I could be quiet there at night
Beside the fire and by myself,
Sure of a bed and loth to leave
The ticking clock and the shining delph!

Och! but I'm weary of mist and dark,
And roads where there's never a house
nor bush,
And tired I am of bog and road,
And the crying wind and the lonesome
hush!

And I am praying to God on high,
And I am praying Him night and day,
For a little house—a house of my own—
Out of the wind's and the rain's way.

JAMES STEPHENS

The Snare

I HEAR a sudden cry of pain!
There is a rabbit in a snare:
Now I hear the cry again,
But I cannot tell from where.

But I cannot tell from where
He is calling out for aid;
Crying on the frightened air,
Making everything afraid.

Making everything afraid,
Wrinkling up his little face,
As he cries again for aid;
And I cannot find the place!

And I cannot find the place
Where his paw is in the snare:
Little one! Oh, little one!
I am searching everywhere.

JAMES ELROY FLECKER
(1884-1915)

Gates of Damascus

FOUR great gates has the city of Damascus,
And four Grand Wardens, on their spears reclining,
All day long stand like tall stone men
And sleep on the towers when the moon is shining.

This is the song of the East Gate Warden
When he locks the great gate and smokes in his garden.

Postern of Fate, the Desert Gate, Disaster's Cavern, Fort of Fear,
The Portal of Bagdad am I, the Doorway of Diarbekir.

The Persian Dawn with new desires may net the flushing mountain spires:
But my gaunt buttress still rejects the suppliance of those mellow fires.

Pass not beneath, O Caravan, or pass not singing. Have you heard
That silence where the birds are dead yet something pipeth like a bird?

Pass not beneath! Men say there blows in stony deserts still a rose
But with no scarlet to her leaf—and from whose heart no perfume flows.

Wilt thou bloom red where she buds pale, thy sister rose? Wilt thou not fail
When noonday flashes like a flail? Leave nightingale the caravan!

Pass then, pass all! "Bagdad!" ye cry, and down the billows of blue sky
Ye beat the bell that beats to hell, and who shall thrust ye back? Not I.

The Sun who flashes through the head and paints the shadows green and red,—
The Sun shall eat thy fleshless dead, O Caravan, O Caravan!

And one who licks his lips for thirst with fevered eyes shall face in fear
The palms that wave, the streams that burst, his last mirage, O Caravan!

And one—the bird-voiced Singing-man—shall fall behind thee, Caravan!
And God shall meet him in the night, and he shall sing as best he can.

And one the Bedouin shall slay, and one, sand-stricken on the way,
Go dark and blind; and one shall say—"How lonely is the Caravan!"

Pass out beneath, O Caravan, Doom's Caravan, Death's Caravan!
I had not told ye, fools, so much, save that I heard your Singing-man.

This was sung by the West Gate's keeper
When heaven's hollow dome grew deeper.

I am the gate toward the sea: O sailor men, pass out from me!
I hear you high on Lebanon, singing the marvels of the sea.

The dragon-green, the luminous, the dark, the serpent-haunted sea,
The snow-besprinkled wine of earth, the white-and-blue-flower foaming sea.

Beyond the sea are towns with towers, carved with lions and lily flowers,
And not a soul in all those lonely streets to while away the hours.

Beyond the towns, an isle where, bound, a naked giant bites the ground:
The shadow of a monstrous wing looms on his back: and still no sound.

Beyond the isle a rock that screams like madmen shouting in their dreams,
From whose dark issues night and day blood crashes in a thousand streams.

Beyond the rock is Restful Bay, where no wind breathes or ripple stirs,
And there on Roman ships, they say, stand rows of metal mariners.

Beyond the bay in utmost West old Solomon the Jewish King
Sits with his beard upon his breast, and grips and guards his magic ring:

And when that ring is stolen, he will rise in outraged majesty,
And take the World upon his back, and fling the World beyond the sea.

This is the song of the North Gate's master,
Who singeth fast, but drinketh faster.

I am the gay Aleppo Gate: a dawn, a dawn and thou art there:
Eat not thy heart with fear and care, O brother of the beast we hate!

Thou hast not many miles to tread, nor other foes than fleas to dread;
Homs shall behold thy morning meal and Hama see thee safe in bed.

Take to Aleppo filigrane, and take them paste of apricots,
And coffee tables botched with pearl, and little beaten brassware pots:

And thou shalt sell thy wares for thrice the Damascene retailers' price,
And buy a fat Armenian slave who smelleth odorous and nice.

Some men of noble stock were made: some glory in the murder-blade:
Some praise a Science or an Art, but I like honourable Trade!

Sell them the rotten, buy the ripe! Their heads are weak; their pockets burn.
Aleppo men are mighty fools. Salaam Aleikum! Safe return!

This is the song of the South Gate Holder,
A silver man, but his song is older.

I am the Gate that fears no fall: the Mihrab of Damascus wall,
The bridge of booming Sinai: the Arch of Allah all in all.

O spiritual pilgrim rise: the night has grown her single horn:
The voices of the souls unborn are half adream with Paradise.

To Meccah thou hast turned in prayer with aching heart and eyes that burn:
Ah Hajji, whither wilt thou turn when thou art there, when thou art there?

God be thy guide from camp to camp: God be thy shade from well to well;
God grant beneath the desert stars thou hear the Prophet's camel bell.

And God shall make thy body pure, and give thee knowledge to endure
This ghost-life's piercing phantom-pain, and bring thee out to Life again.

And God shall make thy soul a Glass where eighteen thousand Æons pass,
And thou shalt see the gleaming Worlds as men see dew upon the grass.

And son of Islam, it may be that thou shalt learn at journey's end
Who walks thy garden eve on eve, and bows his head, and calls thee Friend.

The Burial in England

THESE then we honour: these in fragrant earth
Of their own country in great peace forget
Death's lion-roar and gust of nostril-flame
Breathing souls across to the Evening Shore.
Soon over these the flowers of our hill-sides
Shall wake and wave and nod beneath the bee
And whisper love to Zephyr year on year,
Till the red war gleam like a dim red rose
Lost in the garden of the Sons of Time.
But ah what thousands no such friendly doom
Awaits,—whom silent comrades in full night
Gazing right and left shall bury swiftly
By the cold flicker of an alien moon.
  Ye veilèd women, ye with folded hands,
Mourning those you half hoped for Death too dear,
I claim no heed of you. Broader than earth
Love stands eclipsing nations with his wings,
While Pain, his shadow, delves as black and deep
As he e'er flamed or flew. Citizens draw
Back from their dead awhile. Salute the flag!
  If this flag though royally always borne,
Deceived not dastard, ever served base gold;
If the dark children of the old Forest
Once feared it, or ill Sultans mocked it furled,
Yet now as on a thousand death-reaped days
It takes once more the unquestionable road.
O bright with blood of heroes, not a star
Of all the north shines purer on the sea!
  Our foes—the hardest men a state can forge,
An army wrenched and hammered like a blade
Toledo-wrought neither to break nor bend,

Dipped in that ice the pedantry of power,
And toughened with wry gospels of dismay;
Such are these who brake down the door of France,
Wolves worrying at the old World's honour,
Hunting Peace not to prison but her tomb.
But ever as some brown song-bird whose torn nest
Gapes robbery, darts on the hawk like fire,
So Peace hath answered, angry and in arms.
And from each grey hamlet and bright town of France
From where the apple or the olive grows
Or thin tall strings of poplars on the plains,
From the rough castle of the central hills,
From the three coasts—of mist and storm and sun,
And meadows of the four deep-rolling streams,
From every house whose windows hear God's bell
Crowding the twilight with the wings of prayer
And flash their answer in a golden haze,
Stream the young soldiers who are never tired.
For all the foul mists vanished when that land
Called clear, as in the sunny Alpine morn
The jodeler awakes the frosty slopes
To thunderous replies,—soon fading far
Among the vales like songs of dead children.
But the French guns' answer, ne'er to echoes weak
Diminished, bursts from the deep trenches yet;
And its least light vibration blew to dust
The weary factions,—priest's or guild's or king's,
And side by side troop up the old partisans,
The same laughing, invincible, tough men
Who gave Napoleon Europe like a loaf,
For slice and portion,—not so long ago!
Either to Alsace or loved lost Lorraine
They pass, or inexpugnable Verdun
Ceintured with steel, or stung with faith's old cry
Assume God's vengeance for his temple stones.
But you maybe best wish them for the north
Beside you 'neath low skies in loamèd fields,
Or where the great line hard on the duned shore
Ends and night leaps to England's sea-borne flame.
Never one drop of Lethe's stagnant cup
Dare dim the fountains of the Marne and Aisne
Since still the flowers and meadow-grass unmown
Lie broken with the imprint of those who fell,
Briton and Gaul—but fell immortal friends
And fell victorious and like tall trees fell.
  But young men, you who loiter in the town,
Need you be roused with overshouted words,
Country, Empire, Honour, Liége, Louvain?
Pay your own Youth the duty of her dreams.
For what sleep shall keep her from the thrill
Of War's star-smiting music, with its swell
Of shore and forest and horns high in the wind,
(Yet pierced with that too sharp piping which if man
Hear and not fear he shall face God unscathed)?
What, are you poets whose vain souls contrive

Sorties and sieges spun of the trickling moon
And such a rousing ghost-catastrophe
You need no concrete marvels to be saved?
Or live you here too lustily for change?
Sail you such pirate seas on such high quests,
Hunt you thick gold or striped and spotted beasts,
Or tread the lone ways of the swan-like mountains?
Excused. But if, as I think, breeched in blue,
Stalled at a counter, cramped upon a desk,
You drive a woman's pencraft—or a slave's,
What chain shall hold you when the trumpets play,
Calling from the blue hill behind your town,
Calling over the seas, calling for you!
"But"—do you murmur?—"we'd not be as those.
Death is a dour recruiting-sergeant: see,
These women weep, we celebrate the dead."
Boys, drink the cup of warning dry. Face square
That old grim hazard, "Glory-or-the-Grave."
Not we shall trick your pleasant years away,
Yet is not Death the great adventure still,
And is it all loss to set ship clean anew
When heart is young and life an eagle poised?
Choose, you're no cowards. After all, think some,
Since we are men and shrine immortal souls
Surely for us as for these nobly dead
The Kings of England lifting up their swords
Shall gather at the gate of Paradise.

RUPERT BROOKE (1887-1915)

The Great Lover

I HAVE been so great a lover: filled my days
So proudly with the splendour of Love's praise,
The pain, the calm, and the astonishment,
Desire illimitable, and still content,
And all dear names men use, to cheat despair,
For the perplexed and viewless streams that bear
Our hearts at random down the dark of life.
Now, ere the unthinking silence on that strife
Steals down, I would cheat drowsy Death so far,
My night shall be remembered for a star
That outshone all the suns of all men's days.
Shall I not crown them with immortal praise
Whom I have loved, who have given me, dared with me
High secrets, and in darkness knelt to see
The inenarrable godhead of delight?
Love is a flame;—we have beaconed the world's night.
A city:—and we have built it, these and I.
An emperor:—we have taught the world to die.
So, for their sakes I loved, ere I go hence,
And the high cause of Love's magnificence,
And to keep loyalties young, I'll write those names
Golden for ever, eagles, crying flames,
And set them as a banner, that men may know,
To dare the generations, burn, and blow
Out on the wind of Time, shining and streaming. . . .

These I have loved:
White plates and cups, clean-gleaming,
Ringed with blue lines; and feathery, faery dust;
Wet roofs, beneath the lamp-light; the strong crust
Of friendly bread; and many-tasting food;
Rainbows; and the blue bitter smoke of wood;
And radiant raindrops couching in cool flowers;
And flowers themselves, that sway through sunny hours,
Dreaming of moths that drink them under the moon;
Then, the cool kindliness of sheets, that soon
Smooth away trouble; and the rough male kiss
Of blankets; grainy wood; live hair that is
Shining and free; blue-massing clouds; the keen
Unpassioned beauty of a great machine;
The benison of hot water; furs to touch;
The good smell of old clothes; and other such—
The comfortable smell of friendly fingers,
Hair's fragrance, and the musty reek that lingers
About dead leaves and last year's ferns. . . .
Dear names,
And thousand other throng to me! Royal flames;
Sweet water's dimpling laugh from tap or spring;
Holes in the ground; and voices that do sing;
Voices in laughter, too; and body's pain,
Soon turned to peace; and the deep-panting train;
Firm sands; the little dulling edge of foam
That browns and dwindles as the wave goes home;
And washen stones, gay for an hour; the cold
Graveness of iron; moist black earthen mould;
Sleep; and high places; footprints in the dew;
And oaks; and brown horse-chestnuts, glossy-new;
And new-peeled sticks; and shining pools on grass;—
All these have been my loves. And these shall pass,
Whatever passes not, in the great hour,
Nor all my passion, all my prayers, have power
To hold them with me through the gate of Death.
They'll play deserter, turn with the traitor breath,
Break the high bond we made, and sell Love's trust
—Oh, never a doubt but, somewhere, I shall wake,
And give what's left of love again, and make
New friends, now strangers. . . .
But the best I've known,
Stays here, and changes, breaks, grows old, is blown
About the winds of the world, and fades from brains
Of living men, and dies.
Nothing remains.

O dear my loves, O faithless, once again
This one last gift I give: that after men
Shall know, and later lovers, far-removed,
Praise you, "All these were lovely"; say, "He loved."

The Soldier

If I should die, think only this of me:
That there's some corner of a foreign field
That is for ever England. There shall be

In that rich earth a richer dust concealed;
A dust whom England bore, shaped, made aware,
Gave, once, her flowers to love, her ways to roam,
A body of England's, breathing English air,
Washed by the rivers, blest by suns of home.

And think, this heart, all evil shed away,
A pulse in the eternal mind, no less
Gives somewhere back the thoughts by England given;
Her sights and sounds; dreams happy as her day;
And laughter, learnt of friends; and gentleness,
In hearts at peace, under an English heaven.

JULIAN GRENFEL (1888-1915)

Into Battle

THE naked earth is warm with Spring,
And with green grass and bursting trees
Leans to the sun's gaze glorying,
And quivers in the sunny breeze;

And life is Colour and Warmth and Light,
And a striving evermore for these;
And he is dead who will not fight,
And who dies fighting has increase.

The fighting man shall from the sun
Take warmth, and life from the glowing earth;
Speed with the light-foot winds to run
And with the trees to newer birth;
And find, when fighting shall be done,
Great rest, and fulness after dearth.

All the bright company of Heaven
Hold him in their high comradeship,
The Dog star, and the Sisters Seven,
Orion's belt and sworded hip:

The woodland trees that stand together,
They stand to him each one a friend;
They gently speak in the windy weather;
They guide to valley and ridge's end.

The kestrel hovering by day,
And the little owls that call by night,
Bid him be swift and keen as they,
As keen of ear, as swift of sight.

The blackbird sings to him: "Brother, brother,
If this be the last song you shall sing,
Sing well, for you may not sing another;
Brother, sing."

In dreary doubtful waiting hours,
Before the brazen frenzy starts,
The horses show him nobler powers;—
O patient eyes, courageous hearts!

And when the burning moment breaks
And all things else are out of mind,
And only joy of battle takes
Him by the throat and makes him blind,

Through joy and blindness he shall know,
Not caring much to know, that still
Nor lead nor steel shall reach him, so
That it be not the Destined Will.

The thundering line of battle stands,
And in the air Death moans and sings;
But Day shall clasp him with strong hands,
And Night shall fold him in soft wings.

III. AMERICAN SELECTIONS

BENJAMIN FRANKLIN (1706-1790)

From THE AUTOBIOGRAPHY

Franklin Arrives in Philadelphia

I WAS in my working dress, my best clothes being to come round by sea. I was dirty from my journey; my pockets were stuff'd out with shirts and stockings, and I knew no soul nor where to look for lodging. I was fatigued with travelling, rowing, and want of rest, I was very hungry; and my whole stock of cash consisted of a Dutch dollar, and about a shilling in copper. The latter I gave the people of the boat for my passage, who at first refus'd it, on account of my rowing; but I insisted on their taking it. A man being sometimes more generous when he has but a little money than when he has plenty, perhaps thro' fear of being thought to have but little.

Then I walked up the street, gazing about till near the market-house I met a boy with bread. I had made many a meal on bread, and, inquiring where he got it, I went immediately to the baker's he directed me to, in Second-street, and ask'd for bisket, intending such as we had in Boston; but they, it seems, were not made in Philadelphia. Then I asked for a three-penny loaf, and was told they had none such. So not considering or knowing the difference of money, and the greater cheapness nor the names of his bread, I bad him give me three-penny worth of any sort. He gave me, accordingly, three great puffy rolls. I was surpriz'd at the quantity, but took it, and, having no room in my pockets, walk'd off with a roll under each arm, and eating the other. Thus I went up Market-street as far as Fourth-street, passing by the door of Mr. Read, my future wife's father; when she, standing at the door, saw me, and thought I made, as I certainly did, a most awkward, ridiculous appearance. Then I turned and went down Chestnut-street and part of Walnut-street, eating my roll all the way, and, coming round, found myself again at Market-street wharf, near the boat I came in, to which I went for a draught of the river water; and, being filled with one of my rolls, gave the other two to a woman and her child that came down the river in the boat with us, and were waiting to go farther.

Thus refreshed, I walked again up the street, which by this time had many clean-dressed people in it, who were all walking the same way. I joined them, and thereby was led into the great meeting-house of the Quakers near the market. I sat down among them, and, after looking round awhile and hearing nothing said, being very drowsy thro' labor and want of rest the preceding night, I fell fast asleep, and continued so till the meeting broke up, when one was kind enough to rouse me. This was, therefore, the first house I was in, or slept in, in Philadelphia.

Walking down again toward the river, and, looking in the faces of people, I met a young Quaker man, whose countenance I lik'd, and, accosting him, requested he would tell me where a stranger could get lodging. We were then near the sign of the Three Mariners. "Here," says he, "is one place that entertains strangers, but it is not a reputable house; if thee wilt walk with me, I'll show thee a better." He brought me to the Crooked Billet in Water-street. Here I got a dinner; and, while I was eating it, several sly questions were asked me, as it seemed to be suspected from my youth and appearance, that I might be some runaway.

After dinner, my sleepiness return'd, and being shown to a bed, I lay down without undressing, and slept till six in the evening, was call'd to supper, went to bed again very early, and slept soundly till next morning. Then I made myself as tidy as I could, and went to Andrew Bradford the printer's. I found in the shop the old man his father, whom I had seen at New York, and who, travelling on horseback, had got to Philadelphia before me. He introduc'd me to his son, who receiv'd me civilly, gave me a breakfast, but told me he did not at present want a hand, being lately suppli'd with one; but there was another printer in town, lately set up, one Keimer, who, perhaps, might employ me; if not, I should be welcome to lodge at his house, and he would give me a little work to do now and then till fuller business should offer.

The old gentleman said he would go with me to the new printer; and when we found him, "Neighbor," says Bradford, "I have brought to see you a young man of your business; perhaps you may want such a one." He ask'd me a few questions, put a composing stick in my hand to see how I work'd, and then said he would employ me soon, though he had just then nothing for me to do; and, taking old Bradford, whom he had never seen before, to be one of the town's people that had a good will for him, enter'd into a conversation on his present undertaking and prospects; while Bradford, not discovering that he was the other printer's father, on Keimer's saying he expected soon to get the greatest part of the business into his own hands, drew him on by artful questions, and starting little doubts, to explain all his views, what interest he reli'd on, and in what manner he intended to proceed. I, who stood by and heard all, saw immediately that one of them was a crafty old sophister, and the other a mere novice. Bradford left me with Keimer, who was greatly surprised when I told him who the old man was.

Keimer's printing-house, I found, consisted of an old shatter'd press, and one small, worn-out font of English, which he was then using himself, composing an Elegy on Aquila Rose, before mentioned, an ingenious young man, of excellent character, much respected in the town, clerk of the Assembly, and a pretty poet. Keimer made verses too, but very indifferently. He could not be said to write them, for his manner was to compose them in the types directly out of his head. So there being no copy, but one pair of cases, and the Elegy likely to require all the letters no one could help him. I endeavor'd to put his press (which he had not yet us'd, and of which he understood nothing) into order fit to be work'd with; and, promising to come and print off his Elegy as soon as he should have got it ready, I return'd to Bradford's, who gave me a little job to do for the present, and there I lodged and dieted. A few days after, Keimer sent for me to print off the Elegy. And now he had got another pair of cases, and a pamphlet to reprint, on which he set me to work.

These two printers I found poorly qualified for their business. Bradford had not been bred to it, and was very illiterate; and Keimer, tho' something of a scholar, was a mere compositor, knowing nothing of presswork. He had been one of the French prophets, and could act their enthusiastic agitations. At this time he did not profess any particular religion, but something of all on occasion; was very ignorant of the world, and had, as I afterwards found, a good deal of the knave in his composition. He did not like my lodging at Bradford's while I work'd with him. He had a house, indeed, but without furniture, so he could not lodge me; but he got me a lodging at Mr. Read's, before mentioned, who was the owner of his house; and, my chest and clothes being come by this time, I made rather a more respectable appearance in the eyes of Miss Read than I had done when she first happen'd to see me eating my roll in the street.

Collins Refuses to Row

At New York I found my friend Collins, who had arriv'd there some time before me. We had been intimate from children, and had read the same books together; but he had the advantage of more time for reading and studying, and a wonderful genius for mathematical learning, in which he far outstript me. While I liv'd in Boston, most of my hours of leisure for conversation were spent with him, and he continu'd a sober as well as an industrious lad; was much respected for his learning by several of the clergy and other gentlemen, and seemed to promise making a good figure in life. But, during my absence, he had acquir'd a habit of sotting with brandy; and I found by his own account, and what I heard from others, that he had been drunk every day since his arrival at New York, and behav'd very oddly. He had gam'd, too, and lost his money, so that I was oblig'd to discharge his lodgings, and defray his expenses to and at Philadelphia, which prov'd extremely inconvenient to me.

The then governor of New York, Burnet (son of Bishop Burnet), hearing from the captain that a young man, one of his passengers, had a great many books, desir'd he would bring me to see him. I waited upon him accordingly, and should have taken Collins with me but that he was not sober. The gov'r. treated me with great civility, show'd me his library, which was a very large one, and we had a good deal of conversation about books and authors. This was the second governor who had done me the honor to take notice of me; which, to a poor boy like me, was very pleasing.

We proceeded to Philadelphia. I received on the way Vernon's money, without which we could hardly have finish'd our journey. Collins wished to be employ'd in some counting-house; but, whether they discover'd his dramming by his breath, or by his behavior, tho he had some recommendations, he met with no success in any application, and continu'd lodging and boarding at the same house with me, and at my expense. Knowing I had that money of Vernon's, he was continually borrowing of me, still promising repayment as soon as he should be in business. At length he had got so much of it that I was distress'd to think what I should do in case of being call'd on to remit it.

His drinking continu'd, about which we sometimes quarrell'd; for, when a little intoxicated, he was very fractious. Once, in a boat on the Delaware with some other young men, he refused to row in his turn. "I will be row'd home," says he. "We will not row you," says I. "You must, or stay all night on the water," says he, "just as you please." The others said, "Let us row; what signifies it?" But, my mind being soured with his other conduct, I continu'd to refuse. So he swore he would make me row, or throw me overboard; and coming along, stepping on the thwarts, toward me, when he came up and struck at me, I clapped my hand under his crutch, and, rising, pitched him head-foremost into the river. I knew he was a good swimmer, and so was under little concern about him; but before he could get round to lay hold of the boat, we had with a few strokes pull'd her out of his reach; and ever when he drew near the boat, we ask'd if he would row, striking a few strokes to slide her away from him. He was ready to die with vexation, and obstinately would not promise to row. However, seeing him at last beginning to tire, we lifted him in and brought him home dripping wet in the evening. We hardly exchang'd a civil word afterwards, and a West India captain, who had a commission to procure a tutor for the sons of a gentleman at Barbadoes, happening to meet with him, agreed to carry him thither. He left me then, promising to remit me the first money he should receive in order to discharge the debt; but I never heard of him after.

Mr. Whitefield's Preaching

In 1739 arrived among us from Ireland the Reverend Mr. Whitefield, who had made himself remarkable there as an itinerant preacher. He was at first permitted to preach in some of our churches; but the clergy, taking a dislike to him, soon refus'd him their pulpits, and he was oblig'd to preach in the fields. The multitudes of all sects and denominations that attended his sermons were enormous, and it was matter of speculation to me, who was one of the number, to observe the extraordinary influence of his oratory on his hearers, and how much they admir'd and respected him, notwithstanding his common abuse of them, by assuring them they were naturally *half beasts and half devils*. It was wonderful to see the change soon made in the manners of our inhabitants. From being thoughtless or indifferent about religion, it seem'd as if all the world were growing religious, so that one could not walk thro' the town in an evening without hearing psalms sung in different families of every street.

And it being found inconvenient to assemble in the open air, subject to its inclemencies, the building of a house to meet in was no sooner propos'd, and persons appointed to receive contributions, but sufficient sums were soon receiv'd to procure the ground and erect the building, which was one hundred feet long and seventy broad, about the size of Westminster Hall; and the work was carried on with such spirit as to be finished in a much shorter time than could have been expected. Both house and ground were vested in trustees, expressly for the use of any preacher of any religious persuasion who might desire to say something to the people at Philadelphia; the design in building not being to accommodate any particular sect, but the inhabitants in general; so that even if the Mufti of Constantinople were to send a missionary to preach Mohammedanism to us, he would find a pulpit at his service.

Mr. Whitefield, in leaving us, went preaching all the way thro' the colonies to Georgia. The settlement of that province had lately been begun, but, instead of being made with hardy, industrious husbandmen, accustomed to labor, the only people fit for such an enterprise, it was with families of broken shop-keepers and other insolvent debtors, many of indolent and idle habits, taken out of the jails, who, being set down in the woods, unqualified for clearing land, and unable to endure the hardships of a new settlement, perished in numbers, leaving many helpless children unprovided for. The sight of their miserable situation inspir'd the benevolent heart of Mr. Whitefield with the idea of building an Orphan House there, in which they might be supported and educated. Returning northward, he preach'd up this charity, and made large collections, for his eloquence had a wonderful power over the hearts and purses of his hearers, of which I myself was an instance.

I did not disapprove of the design, but, as Georgia was then destitute of materials and workmen, and it was proposed to send them from Philadelphia at a great expense, I thought it would have been better to have built the house here, and brought the children to it. This I advis'd; but he was resolute in his first project, rejected my counsel, and I therefore refus'd to contribute. I happened soon after to attend one of his sermons, in the course of which I perceived he intended to finish with a collection, and I silently resolved he should get nothing from me. I had in my pocket a handful of copper money, three or four silver dollars, and five pistoles in gold. As he proceeded I began to soften, and concluded to give the coppers. Another stroke of his oratory made me asham'd of that, and determin'd me to give the silver; and he finish'd so admirably, that I empty'd my pocket wholly into the collector's dish, gold and all. At this sermon there was also one of our club, who, being of my sentiments respecting the building in Georgia, and suspecting a collection might be intended, had, by precaution, emptied his pockets before he came from home. Towards the conclusion of the discourse, however, he felt a strong desire to give, and apply'd to a neighbour, who stood near him, to borrow some money for the purpose. The application was unfortunately [made] to perhaps the only man in the company who had the firmness not to be affected by the preacher. His answer was, *"At any other time, Friend Hopkinson, I would lend to thee freely; but not now, for thee seems to be out of thy right senses."*

Some of Mr. Whitefield's enemies affected to suppose that he would apply these collections to his own private emolument; but I, who was intimately acquainted with him (being employed in printing his Sermons and Journals, etc.), never had the least suspicion of his integrity, but am to this day decidedly of opinion that he was in all his conduct a perfectly *honest man;* and methinks my testimony in his favor ought to have the more weight, as we had no religious connection. He us'd, indeed, sometimes to pray for my conversion, but never had the satisfaction of believing that his prayers were heard. Ours was a mere civil friendship, sincere on both sides, and lasted to his death.

The following instance will show something of the terms on which we stood. Upon one of his arrivals from England at Boston, he wrote to me that he should come soon to Philadelphia, but knew not where he could lodge when there, as he understood his old friend and host, Mr. Benezet, was removed to Germantown. My answer was, "You know my house; if you can make shift with its scanty accommodations, you will be most heartily welcome." He reply'd, that if I made that kind offer for Christ's sake, I should not miss of a reward. And I returned, *"Don't let me be mistaken; it was not for Christ's sake, but for your sake."* One of our common acquaintance jocosely remark'd, that, knowing it to be the custom of the saints, when they received any favour, to shift the burden of the obligation from off their own shoulders, and place it in heaven, I had contriv'd to fix it on earth.

The last time I saw Mr. Whitefield was in London, when he consulted me about his Orphan House concern, and his purpose of appropriating it to the establishment of a college.

He had a loud and clear voice, and articulated his words and sentences so perfectly, that he might be heard and understood at a great distance, especially as his auditories, however numerous, observ'd the most exact silence. He preach'd one evening from the top of the Courthouse steps, which are in the middle of Market-street, and on the west side of Second-street, which crosses it at right angles. Both streets were fill'd with his hearers to a considerable distance. Being among the hindmost in Market-street, I had the curiosity to learn how far he could be heard, by retiring backwards down the street towards the river; and I found his voice distinct till I came near Front-street, when some noise in that street obscur'd it. Imagining then a semi-circle, of which my distance should be the radius, and that it were fill'd with auditors, to each of whom I allow'd two square feet, I computed that he might well be heard by more than thirty thousand. This reconcil'd me to the newspaper accounts of his having preach'd to twenty-five thousand people in the fields, and to the antient histories of generals haranguing whole armies, of which I had sometimes doubted.

WASHINGTON IRVING (1783-1859)

Rip Van Winkle

[The following Tale was found among the papers of the late Diedrich Knickerbocker, an old gentleman of New York, who was very curious in the Dutch history of the province, and the manners of the descendants from its primitive settlers. His historical researches, however, did not lie so much among books as among men; for the former are lamentably scanty on his favorite topics, whereas he found the old burghers, and still more their wives, rich in that legendary lore so invaluable to true history. Whenever, therefore, he happened upon a genuine Dutch family, snugly shut up in its low-roofed farmhouse, under a spreading sycamore, he looked upon it as a little clasped volume of black letter, and studied it with the zeal of a book-worm.

The result of all these researches was a history of the province during the reign of the Dutch governors, which he published some years since. There have been various opinions as to the literary character of his work, and, to tell the truth, it is not a whit better than it should be. Its chief merit is its scrupulous accuracy, which indeed was a little questioned on its first appearance, but has since been completely established; and it is now admitted into all historical collections as a book of unquestionable authority.

The old gentleman died shortly after the publication of his work, and now that he is dead and gone, it cannot do much harm to his memory to say, that his time might have been much better employed in weightier labors. He, however, was apt to ride his hobby his own way; and though it did now and then kick up the dust a little in the eyes of his neighbors, and grieve the spirit of some friends, for whom he felt the truest deference and affection; yet his errors and follies are remembered "more in sorrow than in anger," and it begins to be suspected that he never intended to injure or offend. But however his memory may be appreciated by critics, it is still held dear by many folk whose good opinion is well worth having, particularly by certain biscuit-bakers, who have gone so far as to imprint his likeness on their New-year cakes, and have thus given him a chance for immortality, almost equal to the being stamped on a Waterloo medal or a Queen Anne's farthing.]

RIP VAN WINKLE:

A POSTHUMOUS WRITING OF DIEDRICH KNICKERBOCKER

By Woden, God of Saxons,
From whence comes Wensday, that is Wodensday,
Truth is a thing that ever I will keep
Unto thylke day in which I creep into
My sepulchre—— Cartwright.

Whoever has made a voyage up the Hudson must remember the Kaatskill mountains. They are a dismembered branch of the great Appalachian family, and are seen away to the west of the river, swelling up to a noble height, and lording it over the surrounding country. Every change of season, every change of weather, indeed, every hour of the day, produces some change in the magical hues and shapes of these mountains, and they are regarded by all the good wives, far and near, as perfect barometers. When the weather is fair and settled, they are clothed in blue and purple, and print their bold outlines on the clear evening sky; but sometimes, when the rest of the landscape is cloudless, they will gather a hood of gray vapors about their summits, which, in the last rays of the setting sun, will glow and light up like a crown of glory.

At the foot of these fairy mountains, the voyager may have descried the light smoke curling up from a village, whose shingle-roofs gleam among the trees, just where the blue tints of the upland melt away into the fresh green of the nearer landscape. It is a little village, of great antiquity, having been founded by some of the Dutch colonists, in the early times of the province, just about the beginning of the government of the good Peter Stuyvesant (may he rest in peace!) and there were some of the houses of the original settlers standing within a few years, built of small yellow bricks brought from Holland, having latticed windows and gable fronts, surmounted with weathercocks.

In that same village and in one of these very houses (which, to tell the precise truth, was sadly time-worn and weather-beaten), there lived many years since, while the country was yet a province of Great Britain, a simple good-natured fellow, of the name of Rip Van Winkle. He was a descendant of the Van Winkles who figured so gallantly in the chivalrous days of Peter Stuyvesant, and accompanied him to the siege of Fort Christina. He inherited, however, but little of the martial character of his ancestors. I have observed that he was a simple good-natured man; he was, moreover, a kind neighbor, and an obedient henpecked husband. Indeed, to the latter circumstance might be owing that meekness of spirit which gained him such universal popularity; for those men are most apt to be obsequious and conciliating abroad, who are under the discipline of shrews at home. Their tempers, doubtless, are rendered pliant and malleable in the fiery furnace of domestic tribulation, and a curtain lecture is worth all the sermons in the world for teaching the virtues of patience and long-suffering. A termagant wife may, therefore, in some respects, be considered a tolerable blessing; and if so, Rip Van Winkle was thrice blessed.

Certain it is that he was a great favorite among all the good wives of the village, who, as usual with the amiable sex, took his part in all family squabbles; and never failed, whenever they talked those matters over in their evening gossipings, to lay all the blame on Dame Van Winkle. The children of the village, too, would shout with joy whenever he approached. He assisted at their sports, made their playthings, taught them to fly kites and shoot marbles, and told them long stories of ghosts, witches, and Indians. Whenever he went dodging about the village, he was surrounded by a troop of them hanging on his skirts, clambering on his back, and playing a thousand tricks on him with impunity; and not a dog would bark at him throughout the neighbourhood.

The great error in Rip's composition was an insuperable aversion to all kinds of profitable labour. It could not be from the want of assiduity or perseverance; for he would sit on a wet rock, with a rod as long and heavy as a Tartar's lance, and fish all day without a murmur, even though he should not be encouraged by a single nibble. He would carry a fowling-piece on his shoulder for hours together, trudging through woods and swamps, and up hill and down dale, to shoot a few squirrels or wild pigeons. He would never refuse to assist a neighbour even in the roughest toil, and was a foremost man at all country frolics for husking Indian corn, or building stone fences; the women of the village, too, used to employ him to run their errands, and to do such little odd jobs as their less obliging husbands would not do for them. In a word, Rip was ready to attend to anybody's business but his own; but as to doing family duty, and keeping his farm in order, he found it impossible.

In fact, he declared it was of no use to work on his farm; it was the most pestilent little piece of ground in the whole country; everything about it went wrong, and would go wrong, in spite of him. His fences were continually falling to pieces; his cow would either go astray, or get among the cabbages; weeds were sure to grow quicker in his fields than anywhere else; the rain always made a point of setting in just as he had some out-door work to do; so that though his patrimonial estate had dwindled away under his management, acre by acre, until there was little more left than a mere patch of Indian corn and potatoes, yet it was the worst conditioned farm in the neighbourhood.

His children, too, were as ragged and wild as if they belonged to nobody. His son Rip, an urchin begotten in his own likeness, promised to inherit the habits, with the old clothes of his father. He was generally seen trooping like a colt at his mother's heels, equipped in a pair of his father's cast-off galligaskins, which he had much ado to hold up with one hand, as a fine lady does her train in bad weather.

Rip Van Winkle, however, was one of those happy mortals, of foolish, well-oiled dispositions, who take the world easy, eat white bread or brown, whichever can be got with least thought or trouble, and would rather starve on a penny than work for a pound. If left to himself, he would have whistled life away in perfect contentment; but his wife kept continually dinning in his ears about his idleness, his carelessness, and the ruin he was bringing on his family. Morning, noon, and night, her tongue was incessantly going, and everything he said or did was sure to produce a torrent of household eloquence. Rip had but one way of replying to all lectures of the kind, and that, by frequent use, had grown into a habit. He shrugged his shoulders, shook his head, cast up his eyes, but said nothing. This, however, always provoked a fresh volley from his wife; so that he was fain to draw off his forces, and take to the outside of the house—the only side which, in truth, belongs to a hen-pecked husband.

Rip's sole domestic adherent was his dog Wolf, who was as much hen-pecked as his master; for Dame Van Winkle regarded them as companions in idleness, and even looked upon Wolf with an evil eye, as the cause of his master's going so often astray. True it is, in all points of spirit befitting an honourable dog, he was as courageous an animal as ever scoured the woods—but what courage can withstand the ever-during and all-besetting terrors of a woman's tongue? The moment Wolf entered the house, his crest fell, his tail drooped to the ground, or curled between his legs, he sneaked about with a gallows air, casting many a side-long glance at Dame Van Winkle, and at the least flourish of a broomstick or ladle, he would fly to the door with yelping precipitation.

Times grew worse and worse with Rip Van Winkle as years of matrimony rolled on; a tart temper never mellows with age, and a sharp tongue is the only edged tool that grows keener with constant use. For a long while he used to console himself, when driven from home, by frequenting a kind of perpetual club of the sages, philosophers, and other idle personages of the village; which held its sessions on a bench before a small inn, designated by a rubicund portrait of his Majesty George the Third. Here they used to sit in the shade through a long lazy summer's day, talking listlessly over village gossip, or telling endless sleepy stories about nothing. But it would have been worth any statesman's money to have heard the profound discussions that sometimes took place, when by chance an old newspaper fell into their hands from some passing traveller. How solemnly they would listen to the contents, as drawled out by Derrick Van Bummel, the schoolmaster, a dapper learned little man, who was not to be daunted by the most gigantic word in the dictionary; and how sagely they would deliberate upon public events some months after they had taken place.

The opinions of this junto were completely controlled by Nicholas Vedder, a patriarch of the village, and landlord of the inn, at the door of which he took his seat from morning till night, just moving sufficiently to avoid the sun and keep in the shade of a large tree; so that the neighbours could tell the hour by his movements as accurately as by a sundial. It is true he was rarely heard to speak, but smoked his pipe incessantly. His adherents, however (for every great man has his adherents), perfectly understood him, and knew how to gather his opinions. When anything that was read or related displeased him, he was observed to smoke his pipe vehemently, and to send forth short, frequent, and angry puffs, but when pleased he would inhale the smoke slowly and tranquilly, and emit it in light and placid clouds; and sometimes, taking the pipe from his mouth, and letting the fragrant vapor curl about his nose, would gravely nod his head in token of perfect approbation.

From even this stronghold the unlucky Rip was at length routed by his termagant wife, who would suddenly break in upon the tranquillity of the assemblage and call the members all to naught; nor was that august personage, Nicholas Vedder himself, sacred from the daring tongue of this terrible virago, who charged him outright with encouraging her husband in habits of idleness.

Poor Rip was at last reduced almost to despair; and his only alternative, to escape from the labor of the farm and clamor of his wife, was to take gun in hand and stroll away into the woods. Here he would sometimes seat himself at the foot of a tree, and share the contents of his wallet with Wolf, with whom he sympathized as a fellow-sufferer in persecution. "Poor Wolf," he would say, "thy mistress leads thee a dog's life of it; but never mind, my lad, whilst I live thou shalt never want a friend to stand by thee!" Wolf would wag his tail, look wistfully in his master's face, and if dogs can feel pity, I verily believe he reciprocated the sentiment with all his heart.

In a long ramble of the kind on a fine autumnal day, Rip had unconsciously scrambled to one of the highest parts of the Kaatskill mountains. He was after his favorite sport of squirrel-shooting, and the still solitudes had echoed and re-echoed with the reports of his gun. Panting and fatigued, he threw himself, late in the afternoon, on a green knoll, covered with mountain herbage, that crowned the brow of a precipice. From an opening between the trees he could overlook all the lower country for many a mile of rich woodland. He saw at a distance the lordly Hudson, far, far below him, moving on its silent but majestic course, with the reflection of a purple cloud, or the sail of a lagging bark, here and there sleeping on its glassy bosom, and at last losing itself in the blue highlands.

On the other side he looked down into a deep mountain glen, wild, lonely, and shagged, the bottom filled with fragments from the impending cliffs, and scarcely lighted by the reflected rays of the setting sun.

For some time Rip lay musing on this scene; evening was gradually advancing; the mountains began to throw their long blue shadows over the valleys; he saw that it would be dark long before he could reach the village, and he heaved a heavy sigh when he thought of encountering the terrors of Dame Van Winkle.

As he was about to descend, he heard a voice from a distance, hallooing, "Rip Van Winkle! Rip Van Winkle!" He looked round, but could see nothing but a crow winging its solitary flight across the mountain. He thought his fancy must have deceived him, and turned again to descend, when he heard the same cry ring through the still evening air: "Rip Van Winkle! Rip Van Winkle!"—at the same time Wolf bristled up his back, and, giving a loud growl, skulked to his master's side, looking fearfully down into the glen. Rip now felt a vague apprehension stealing over him; he looked anxiously in the same direction, and perceived a strange figure slowly toiling up the rocks, and bending under the weight of something he carried on his back. He was surprised to see any human being in this lonely and unfrequented place; but supposing it to be some one of the neighbourhood in need of his assistance, he hastened down to yield it.

On nearer approach he was still more surprised at the singularity of the stranger's appearance. He was a short, square-built old fellow, with thick bushy hair and a grizzled beard. His dress was of the antique Dutch fashion—a cloth jerkin, strapped round the waist—several pair of breeches, the outer one of ample volume, decorated with rows of buttons down the sides, and bunches at the knees. He bore on his shoulder a stout keg, that seemed full of liquor, and made signs for Rip to approach and assist him with the load. Though rather shy and distrustful of this new acquaintance, Rip complied with his usual alacrity; and mutually relieving each other, they clambered up a narrow gully, apparently the dry bed of a mountain torrent. As they ascended, Rip every now and then heard long rolling peals, like distant thunder, that seemed to issue out of a deep ravine, or rather cleft, between the lofty rocks, toward which their rugged path conducted. He paused for an instant, but supposing it to be the muttering of one of those transient thunder-showers which often take place in mountain heights, he proceeded. Passing through the ravine, they came to a hollow, like a small amphitheatre, surrounded by perpendicular precipices, over the brinks of which impending trees shot their branches, so that you only caught glimpses of the azure sky and the bright evening cloud. During the whole time Rip and his companion had labored on in silence, for though the former marvelled greatly what could be the object of carrying a keg of liquor up this wild mountain; yet there was something strange and incomprehensible about the unknown, that inspired awe and checked familiarity.

On entering the amphitheatre, new objects of wonder presented themselves. On a level spot in the centre was a company of odd-looking personages playing at nine-pins. They were dressed in a quaint outlandish fashion; some wore short doublets, others jerkins, with long knives in their belts, and most of them had enormous breeches, of similar style with that of the guide's. Their visages, too, were peculiar; one had a large head, broad face, and small piggish eyes; the face of another seemed to consist entirely of nose, and was surmounted by a white sugar-loaf hat, set off with a little red cock's tail. They all had beards, of various shapes and colors. There was one who seemed to be the commander. He was a stout old gentleman, with a weather-beaten countenance; he wore a laced doublet, broad belt and hanger, high-crowned hat and feather, red stockings, and high-heeled shoes, with roses in them. The whole group reminded Rip of the figures in an old Flemish painting, in the parlor of Dominie Van Shaick, the village parson, and which had been brought over from Holland at the time of the settlement.

What seemed particularly odd to Rip was, that though these folks were evidently amusing themselves, yet they maintained the gravest faces, the most mysterious silence, and were, withal, the most melancholy party of pleasure he had ever witnessed. Nothing interrupted the stillness of the scene but the noise of the balls, which, whenever they were rolled, echoed along the mountains like rumbling peals of thunder.

As Rip and his companion approached them, they suddenly desisted from their play, and stared at him with such fixed, statue-like gaze, and such strange, uncouth, lack-lustre countenances, that his heart turned within him, and his knees smote together. His companion now emptied the contents of the keg into large flagons, and made signs to him to wait upon the company. He obeyed with fear and trembling; they quaffed the liquor in profound silence, and then returned to their game.

By degrees Rip's awe and apprehension subsided. He even ventured, when no eye was fixed upon him, to taste the beverage, which he found had much of the flavor of excellent Hollands. He was naturally a thirsty soul, and was soon tempted to repeat the draught. One taste provoked another; and he reiterated his visits to the flagon so often, that at length his senses were overpowered, his eyes swam in his head, his head gradually declined, and he fell into a deep sleep.

On waking, he found himself on the green knoll whence he had first seen the old man of the glen. He rubbed his eyes—it was a bright sunny morning. The birds were hopping and twittering among the bushes, and the eagle was wheeling aloft, and breasting the pure mountain breeze. "Surely," thought Rip, "I have not slept here all night." He recalled the occurrences before he fell asleep. The strange man with a keg of liquor—the mountain ravine—the wild retreat among the rocks—the woe-begone party at nine-pins—the flagon—"Oh! that flagon! that wicked flagon!" thought Rip; "what excuse shall I make to Dame Van Winkle?"

He looked round for his gun, but in place of the clean well-oiled fowling-piece, he found an old firelock lying by him, the barrel incrusted with rust, the lock falling off, and the stock worm-eaten. He now suspected that the grave roysters of the mountain had put a trick upon him, and, having dosed him with liquor, had robbed him of his gun. Wolf, too, had disappeared, but he might have strayed away after a squirrel or partridge. He whistled after him, and shouted his name, but all in vain; the echoes repeated his whistle and shout, but no dog was to be seen.

He determined to revisit the scene of the last evening's gambol, and, if he met with any of the party, to demand his dog and gun. As he rose to walk he found himself stiff in the joints, and wanting in his usual activity. "These mountain beds do not agree with me," thought Rip; "and if this frolic should lay me up with a fit of the rheumatism, I shall have a blessed time with Dame Van Winkle." With some difficulty he got down into the glen: he found the gully up which he and his companion had ascended the preceding evening; but, to his astonishment, a mountain stream was now foaming down it—leaping from rock to rock, and filling the glen with babbling murmurs. He, however, made shift to scramble up its sides, working his toilsome way through thickets of birch, sassafras, and witch-hazel, and sometimes tripped up or entangled by the wild grape-vines that twisted their coils or tendrils from tree to tree, and spread a kind of network in his path.

At length he reached to where the ravine had opened through the cliffs to the amphitheatre; but no traces of such opening remained. The rocks presented a high impenetrable wall, over which the torrent came tumbling in a sheet of feathery foam, and fell into a broad, deep basin, black from the shadows of the surrounding forest. Here, then, poor Rip was brought to a stand. He again called and whistled after his dog; he was only answered by the cawing of a flock of idle crows, sporting high in air about a dry tree that overhung a sunny precipice; and who, secure in their elevation, seemed to look down and scoff at the poor man's perplexities. What was to be done?—the morning was passing away, and Rip felt famished for want of his breakfast. He grieved to give up his dog and his gun; he dreaded to meet his wife; but it would not do to starve among the mountains. He shook his head, shouldered the rusty firelock, and, with a heart full of trouble and anxiety, turned his steps homeward.

As he approached the village he met a number of people, but none whom he knew, which somewhat surprised him, for he had thought himself acquainted with everyone in the country round. Their dress, too, was of a different fashion from that to which he was accustomed. They all stared at him with equal marks of surprise, and, whenever they cast their eyes upon him, invariably stroked their chins. The constant recurrence of this gesture induced Rip, involuntarily, to do the same—when, to his astonishment, he found his beard had grown a foot long!

He had now entered the skirts of the village. A troop of strange children ran at his heels, hooting after him, and pointing at his gray beard. The dogs, too, not one of which he recognized for an old acquaintance, barked at him as he passed. The very village was altered; it was larger and more populous. There were rows of houses which he had never seen before, and those which had been his familiar haunts had disappeared. Strange names were over the doors—strange faces at the windows—everything was strange. His mind now misgave him; he began to doubt whether both he and the world around him were not bewitched. Surely this was his native village, which he had left but the day before. There stood the Kaatskill mountains—there ran the silver Hudson at a distance—there was every hill and dale precisely as it had always been. Rip was sorely perplexed. "That flagon last night," thought he, "has addled my poor head sadly!"

It was with some difficulty that he found the way to his own house, which he approached with silent awe, expecting every moment to hear the shrill voice of Dame Van Winkle. He found the house gone to decay—the roof fallen in, the windows shattered, and the doors off the hinges. A half-starved dog that looked like Wolf, was skulking about it. Rip called him by name, but the cur snarled, showed his teeth, and passed on. This was an unkind cut indeed—"My very dog," sighed poor Rip, "has forgotten me!"

He entered the house, which, to tell the truth, Dame Van Winkle had always kept in neat order. It was empty, forlorn, and apparently abandoned. The desolateness overcame all his connubial fears—he called loudly for his wife and children—the lonely chambers rang for a moment with his voice, and then all again was silence.

He now hurried forth, and hastened to his old resort, the village inn—but it too was gone. A large, rickety, wooden building stood in its place, with great gaping windows, some of them broken and mended with old hats and petticoats, and over the door was painted, "The Union Hotel, by Jonathan Doolittle." Instead of the great tree that used to shelter the quiet little Dutch inn of yore, there was now reared a tall naked pole, with something on the top that looked like a red nightcap, and from it was fluttering a flag, on which was a singular assemblage of stars and stripes—all this was strange and incomprehensible. He recognized on the sign, however, the ruby face of King George, under which he had smoked so many a peaceful pipe; but even this was singularly metamorphosed. The red coat was changed for one of blue and buff, a sword was held in the hand instead of a sceptre, the head was decorated with a cocked hat, and underneath was painted in large characters, GENERAL WASHINGTON.

There was, as usual, a crowd of folks about the door, but none that Rip recollected. The very character of the people seemed changed. There was a busy, bustling, disputatious tone about it, instead of the accustomed phlegm and drowsy tranquillity. He looked in vain for the sage Nicholas Vedder, with his broad face, double chin, and fair long pipe, uttering clouds of tobacco-smoke instead of idle speeches; or Van Bummel, the schoolmaster, doling forth the contents of an ancient newspaper. In place of these, a lean, bilious-looking fellow, with his pockets full of hand-bills, was haranguing vehemently about rights of citizens—elections—members of Congress—liberty—Bunker's Hill—heroes of seventy-six—and other words, which were a perfect Babylonish jargon to the bewildered Van Winkle.

The appearance of Rip, with his long grizzled beard, his rusty fowling-piece, his uncouth dress, and an army of women and children at his heels, soon attracted the attention of the tavern politicians. They crowded round him, eyeing him from head to foot with great curiosity. The orator bustled up to him, and, drawing him partly aside, inquired "on which side he voted?" Rip stared in vacant stupidity. Another short but busy little fellow pulled him by the arm, and, rising on tiptoe, inquired in his ear, "Whether he was Federal or Democrat?" Rip was equally at a loss to comprehend the question; when a knowing, self-important old gentleman, in a sharp cocked hat, made his way through the crowd, putting them to the right and left with his elbows as he passed, and planting himself before Van Winkle, with one arm akimbo, the other resting on his cane, his keen eyes and sharp hat penetrating, as it were, into his very soul, demanded in an austere tone, "What brought him to the election with a gun on his shoulder, and a mob at his heels, and whether he meant to breed a riot in the village?"—"Alas! gentlemen," cried Rip, somewhat dismayed, "I am a poor quiet man, a native of the place, and a loyal subject of the king, God bless him!"

Here a general shout burst from the bystanders—"A tory! a tory! a spy! a refugee! hustle him! away with him!" It was with great difficulty that the self-important man in the cocked hat restored order; and, having assumed a tenfold austerity of brow, demanded again of the unknown culprit, what he came there for, and whom he was seeking? The poor man humbly assured him that he meant no harm, but merely came there in search of some of his neighbors, who used to keep about the tavern.

"Well—who are they?—name them."

Rip bethought himself a moment, and inquired, "Where's Nicholas Vedder?"

There was a silence for a little while, when an old man replied in a thin piping voice, "Nicholas Vedder! why, he is dead and gone these eighteen years! There was a wooden tombstone in the churchyard that used to tell all about him, but that's rotten and gone too."

"Where's Brom Dutcher?"

"Oh, he went off to the army in the beginning of the war; some say he was killed at the storming of Stony Point—others say he was drowned in a squall at the foot of Antony's Nose. I don't know—he never came back again."

"Where's Van Bummell, the schoolmaster?"

"He went off to the wars too, was a great militia general, and is now in Congress."

Rip's heart died away at hearing of these sad changes in his home and friends, and finding himself thus alone in the world. Every answer puzzled him too, by treating of such enormous lapses of time, and of matters which he could not understand; war—Congress—Stony Point;—he had no courage to ask after any more friends, but cried out in despair, "Does anybody here know Rip Van Winkle?"

"Oh, Rip Van Winkle!" exclaimed two or three. "Oh, to be sure! that's Rip Van Winkle yonder, leaning against the tree."

Rip looked, and beheld a precise counterpart of himself, as he went up the mountain: apparently as lazy, and certainly as ragged. The poor fellow was now completely confounded. He doubted his own identity, and whether he was himself or another man. In the midst of his bewilderment, the man in the cocked hat demanded who he was, and what was his name?

"God knows," exclaimed he, at his wits' end; "I'm not myself—I'm somebody else—that's me yonder—no—that's somebody else got into my shoes—I was myself last night, but I fell asleep on the mountain, and they've changed my gun, and everything's changed, and I'm changed, and I can't tell what's my name, or who I am!"

The bystanders began now to look at each other, nod, wink significantly, and tap their fingers against their foreheads. There was a whisper, also, about securing the gun, and keeping the old fellow from doing mischief, at the very suggestion of which the self-important man in the cocked hat retired with some precipitation. At this critical moment a fresh, comely woman pressed through the throng to get a peep at the gray-bearded man. She had a chubby child in her arms, which, frightened at his looks, began to cry. "Hush, Rip," cried she, "hush, you little fool; the old man won't hurt you." The name of the child, the air of the mother, the tone of her voice, all awakened a train of recollections in his mind.

"What is your name, my good woman?" asked he.

"Judith Gardenier."

"And your father's name?"

"Ah, poor man, Rip Van Winkle was his name, but it's twenty years since he went away from home with his gun, and never has been heard of since—his dog came home without him; but whether he shot himself, or was carried away by the Indians, nobody can tell. I was then but a little girl."

Rip had but one question more to ask; but he put it with a faltering voice,—

"Where's your mother?"

"Oh, she too had died but a short time since; she broke a blood-vessel in a fit of passion at a New-England pedler."

There was a drop of comfort, at least, in this intelligence. The honest man could contain himself no longer. He caught his daughter and her child in his arms. "I am your father!" cried he—"Young Rip Van Winkle once—old Rip Van Winkle now!—Does nobody know poor Rip Van Winkle?"

All stood amazed, until an old woman, tottering out from among the crowd, put her hand to her brow, and peering under it in his face for a moment, exclaimed, "Sure enough! it is Rip Van Winkle—it is himself! Welcome home again, old neighbor—Why, where have you been these twenty long years?"

Rip's story was soon told, for the whole twenty years had been to him but as one night. The neighbors stared when they heard it; some were seen to wink at each other, and put their tongues in their cheeks: and the self-important man in the cocked hat, who, when the alarm was over, had returned to the field, screwed down the corners of his mouth, and shook his head—upon which there was a general shaking of the head throughout the assemblage.

It was determined, however, to take the opinion of old Peter Vanderdonk, who was seen slowly advancing up the road. He was a descendant of the historian of that name, who wrote one of the earliest accounts of the province. Peter was the most ancient inhabitant of the village, and well versed in all the wonderful events and traditions of the neighborhood. He recollected Rip at once, and corroborated his story in the most satisfactory manner. He assured the company that it was a fact, handed down from his ancestor the historian, that the Kaatskill mountains had always been haunted by strange beings. That it was affirmed that the great Hendrick Hudson, the first discoverer of the river and country, kept a kind of vigil there every twenty years, with his crew of the *Half-moon;* being permitted in this way to revisit the scenes of his enterprise, and keep a guardian eye upon the river, and the great city called by his name. That his father had once seen them in their old Dutch dresses playing at nine-pins in a hollow of the mountain; and that he himself had heard, one summer afternoon, the sound of their balls, like distant peals of thunder.

To make a long story short, the company broke up, and returned to the more important concerns of the election. Rip's daughter took him home to live with her; she had a snug, well-furnished house, and a stout cheery farmer for her husband, whom Rip recollected for one of the urchins that used to climb upon his back. As to Rip's son and heir, who was the ditto of himself, seen leaning against the tree, he was employed to work on the farm; but evinced an hereditary disposition to attend to anything else but his business.

Rip now resumed his old walks and habits; he soon found many of his former cronies, though all rather the worse for the wear and tear of time; and preferred making friends among the rising generation, with whom he soon grew into great favor.

Having nothing to do at home, and being arrived at that happy age when a man can be idle with impunity, he took his place once more on the bench at the inn door, and was reverenced as one of the patriarchs of the village, and a chronicle of the old times "before the war." It was some time before he could get into the regular track of gossip, or could be made to comprehend the strange events that had taken place during his torpor. How that there had been a revolutionary war—that the country had thrown off the yoke of Old England—and that, instead of being a subject of His Majesty George the Third, he was now a free citizen of the United States. Rip, in fact, was no politician; the changes of states and empires made but little impression on him; but there was one species of despotism under which he had long groaned, and that was—

petticoat government. Happily that was at an end; he had got his neck out of the yoke of matrimony, and could go in and out whenever he pleased without dreading the tyranny of Dame Van Winkle. Whenever her name was mentioned, however, he shook his head, shrugged his shoulders, and cast up his eyes; which might pass either for an expression of resignation to his fate, or joy at his deliverance.

He used to tell his story to every stranger that arrived at Mr. Doolittle's hotel. He was observed at first to vary on some points every time he told it, which was, doubtless, owing to his having so recently awaked. It at last settled down precisely to the tale I have related, and not a man, woman, or child in the neighborhood but knew it by heart. Some always pretended to doubt the reality of it, and insisted that Rip had been out of his head, and that this was one point on which he always remained flighty. The old Dutch inhabitants, however, almost universally gave it full credit. Even to this day they never hear a thunder-storm of a summer afternoon about the Kaatskill, but they say Hendrick Hudson and his crew are at their game of nine-pins; and it is a common wish of all henpecked husbands in the neighborhood, when life hangs heavy on their hands, that they might have a quieting draught out of Rip Van Winkle's flagon.

NOTE.—The foregoing tale, one would suspect, had been suggested to Mr. Knickerbocker by a little German superstition about the Emperor Frederick *der Rothbart,* and the Kypphaüser mountain; the subjoined note, however, which he had appended to the tale, shows that it is an absolute fact, narrated with his usual fidelity:—

"The story of Rip Van Winkle may seem incredible to many, but nevertheless I give it my full belief, for I know the vicinity of our old Dutch settlements to have been very subject to marvellous events and appearances. Indeed, I have heard many stranger stories than this in the villages along the Hudson, all of which were too well authenticated to admit of a doubt. I have even talked with Rip Van Winkle myself, who, when I last saw him, was a very venerable old man and so perfectly rational and consistent on every other point, that I think no conscientious person could refuse to take this into the bargain; nay, I have seen a certificate on the subject, taken before a country justice, and signed with a cross, in the justice's own handwriting. The story, therefore, is beyond the possibility of doubt.

D. K."

POSTSCRIPT.—The following are travelling notes from a memorandum-book of Mr. Knickerbocker:—

"The Kaatsberg, or Catskill Mountains, have always been a region full of fable. The Indians considered them the abode of spirits, who influenced the weather, spreading sunshine or clouds over the landscape, and sending good or bad hunting seasons. They were ruled by an old squaw spirit, said to be their mother. She dwelt on the highest peak of the Catskills, and had charge of the doors of day and night, to open and shut them at the proper hour. She hung up the new moons in the skies, and cut up the old ones into stars. In times of drought, if properly propitiated, she would spin light summer clouds out of cobwebs and morning dew, and send them off from the crest of the mountain, flake after flake, like flakes of carded cotton, to float in the air, until, dissolved by the heat of the sun, they would fall in gentle showers, causing the grass to spring, the fruits to ripen, and the corn to grow an inch an hour. If displeased, however, she would brew up clouds black as ink, sitting in the midst of them like a bottle-bellied spider in the midst of its web; and when these clouds broke, woe betide the valleys!

"In old times, say the Indian traditions, there was a kind of Manitou or Spirit, who kept about the wildest recesses of the Catskill Mountains, and took a mischievous pleasure in wreaking all kinds of evils and vexations upon the red men. Sometimes he would assume the form of a bear, a panther, or a deer, lead the bewildered hunter a weary chase through tangled forests and among ragged rocks, and then spring off with a loud ho! ho! leaving him aghast on the brink of a beetling precipice or raging torrent.

"The favorite abode of this Manitou is still shown. It is a great rock or cliff on the loneliest part of the mountains, and, from the flowering vines which clamber about it, and the wild flowers, which abound in its neighborhood, is known by the name of the Garden Rock. Near the foot of it is a small lake, the haunt of the solitary bittern, with water-snakes basking in the sun on the leaves of the pond-lilies which lie on the surface. This place was held in great awe by the Indians, insomuch that the boldest hunter would not pursue his game within its precincts. Once upon a time, however, a hunter who had lost his way penetrated to the Garden Rock, where he beheld a number of gourds placed in the crotches of trees. One of these he seized and made off with, but in the hurry of his retreat he let it fall among the rocks, when a great stream gushed forth, which washed him away and swept him down precipices, where he was dashed to pieces, and the stream made its way to the Hudson, and continues to flow to the present day, being the identical stream known by the name of the Kaaterskill."

WILLIAM CULLEN BRYANT
(1794-1878)

To a Waterfowl

WHITHER, midst falling dew,
While glow the heavens with the last steps of day,
Far, through their rosy depths, dost thou pursue
Thy solitary way?

Vainly the fowler's eye
Might mark thy distant flight to do thee wrong,
As, darkly seen against the crimson sky,
Thy figure floats along.

Seek'st thou the plashy brink
Of weedy lake, or marge of river wide,
Or where the rocking billows rise and sink
On the chafed ocean-side?

There is a Power whose care
Teaches thy way along that pathless coast—
The desert and illimitable air—
Lone wandering, but not lost.

All day thy wings have fanned,
At that far height, the cold, thin atmosphere,
Yet stoop not, weary, to the welcome land,
Though the dark night is near.

And soon that toil shall end;
Soon shalt thou find a summer home, and rest,
And scream among thy fellows; reeds shall bend,
Soon, o'er thy sheltered nest.

Thou'rt gone, the abyss of heaven
Hath swallowed up thy form; yet on my heart
Deeply hath sunk the lesson thou hast given,
And shall not soon depart:

He who, from zone to zone,
Guides through the boundless sky thy certain flight,
In the long way that I must tread alone,
Will lead my steps aright.

NATHANIEL HAWTHORNE (1804-1864)

The Great Stone Face

ONE afternoon, when the sun was going down, a mother and her little boy sat at the door of their cottage, talking about the Great Stone Face. They had but to lift their eyes, and there it was plainly to be seen, though miles away, with the sunshine brightening all its features.

And what was the Great Stone Face?

Embosomed amongst a family of lofty mountains, there was a valley so spacious that it contained many thousand inhabitants. Some of these good people dwelt in log-huts, with the black forest all around them, on the steep and difficult hill-sides. Others had their homes in comfortable farm-houses, and cultivated the rich soil on the gentle slopes or level surfaces of the valley. Others, again, were congregated into populous villages, where some wild, highland rivulet, tumbling down from its birthplace in the upper mountain region, had been caught and tamed by human cunning, and compelled to turn the machinery of cotton-factories. The inhabitants of this valley, in short, were numerous, and of many modes of life. But all of them, grown people and children, had a kind of familiarity with the Great Stone Face, although some possessed the gift of distinguishing this grand natural phenomenon more perfectly than many of their neighbors.

The Great Stone Face, then, was a work of Nature in her mood of majestic playfulness, formed on the perpendicular side of a mountain by some immense rocks, which had been thrown together in such a position as, when viewed at a proper distance, precisely to resemble the features of the human countenance. It seemed as if an enormous giant, or a Titan, had sculptured his own likeness on the precipice. There was the broad arch of the forehead, a hundred feet in height; the nose, with its long bridge; and the vast lips, which, if they could have spoken, would have rolled their thunder accents from one end of the valley to the other. True it is, that if the spectator approached too near, he lost the outline of the gigantic visage, and could discern only a heap of ponderous and gigantic rocks, piled in chaotic ruin one upon another. Retracing his steps, however, the wondrous features would again be seen; and the farther he withdrew from them, the more like a human face, with all its original divinity intact, did they appear; until, as it grew dim in the distance, with the clouds and glorified vapor of the mountains clustering about it, the Great Stone Face seemed positively to be alive.

It was a happy lot for children to grow up to manhood or womanhood with the Great Stone Face before their eyes, for all the features were noble, and the expression was at once grand and sweet, as if it were the glow of a vast, warm heart, that embraced all mankind in its affections, and had room for more. It was an education only to look at it. According to the belief of many people, the valley owed much of its fertility to this benign aspect that was continually beaming over it, illuminating the clouds, and infusing its tenderness into the sunshine.

As we began with saying, a mother and her little boy sat at their cottage-door, gazing at the Great Stone Face, and talking about it. The child's name was Ernest.

"Mother," said he, while the Titanic visage smiled on him, "I wish that it could speak, for it looks so very kindly that its voice must needs be pleasant. If I were to see a man with such a face, I should love him dearly."

"If an old prophecy should come to pass," answered his mother, "we may see a man, some time or other, with exactly such a face as that."

"What prophecy do you mean, dear mother?" eagerly inquired Ernest. "Pray tell me all about it!"

So his mother told him a story that her own mother had told to her, when she herself was younger than little Ernest; a story, not of things that were past, but of what was yet to come; a story, nevertheless, so very old, that even the Indians, who formerly inhabited this valley, had heard it from their forefathers, to whom, as they affirmed, it had been murmured by the mountain streams, and whispered by the wind among the tree-tops. The purport was, that, at some future day, a child should be born hereabouts, who was destined to become the greatest and noblest personage of his time, and whose countenance, in manhood, should bear an exact resemblance to the Great Stone Face. Not a few old-fashioned people, and young ones likewise, in the ardor of their hopes, still cherished an enduring faith in this old prophecy. But others, who had seen more of the world, had watched and waited till they were weary, and had beheld no man with such a face, nor any man that proved to be much greater or nobler than his neighbors, concluded it to be nothing but an idle tale. At all events, the great man of the prophecy had not yet appeared.

"O mother, dear mother!" cried Ernest, clapping his hands above his head, "I do hope that I shall live to see him!"

His mother was an affectionate and thoughtful woman, and felt that it was wisest not to discourage the generous hopes of her little boy. So she only said to him, "Perhaps you may."

And Ernest never forgot the story that his mother told him. It was always in his mind, whenever he looked upon the Great Stone Face. He spent his childhood in the log-cottage where he was born, and was dutiful to his mother, and helpful to her in many things, assisting her much with his little hands, and more with his loving heart. In this manner, from a happy yet often pensive child, he grew up to be a mild, quiet, unobtrusive boy, and sun-browned with labor in the fields, but with more intelligence brightening his aspect than is seen in many lads who have been taught at famous schools. Yet Ernest had had no teacher, save only that the great Stone Face became one to him. When the toil of the day was over, he would gaze at it for hours, until he began to imagine that those vast features recognized him, and gave him a smile of kindness and encouragement, responsive to his own look of veneration. We must not take upon us to affirm that this was a mistake, although the Face may have looked no more kindly at Ernest than at all the world besides. But the secret was that the boy's tender and confiding simplicity discerned what other people could not see; and thus the love, which was meant for all, became his peculiar portion.

About this time there went a rumor throughout the valley, that the great man, foretold from ages long ago, who was to bear a resemblance to the Great Stone Face, had appeared at last. It seems that, many years before, a young man had migrated from the valley and settled at a distant seaport, where, after getting together a little money, he had set up as a shopkeeper. His name—but I could never learn whether it was his real one, or a nickname that had grown out of his habits and success in life—was Gathergold. Being shrewd and active, and endowed by Providence with that inscrutable faculty which develops itself in what the world calls luck, he became an exceedingly rich merchant, and owner of a whole fleet of bulky-bottomed ships. All the countries of the globe appeared to join hands for the mere purpose of adding heap after heap to the mountainous accumulation of this one man's wealth. The cold regions of the north, almost within the gloom and shadow of the Arctic Circle, sent him their tribute in the shape of furs; hot Africa sifted for him the golden sands of her rivers, and gathered up the ivory tusks of her great elephants out of the forests; the East came bringing him the rich shawls, and spices, and teas, and the effulgence of diamonds, and the gleaming purity of large pearls. The ocean, not to be behindhand with the earth, yielded up her mighty whales, that Mr. Gathergold might sell their oil, and make a profit on it. Be the original commodity what it might, it was gold within his grasp. It might be said of him, as of Midas in the fable, that whatever he touched with his finger immediately glistened, and grew yellow, and was changed at once into sterling metal, or, which suited him still better, into piles of coin. And, when Mr. Gathergold had become so very rich that it would have taken him a hundred years only to count his wealth, he bethought himself of his native valley, and resolved to go back thither, and end his days where he was born. With this purpose in view, he sent a skilful architect to build him such a palace as should be fit for a man of his vast wealth to live in.

As I have said above, it had already been rumored in the valley that Mr. Gathergold had turned out to be the prophetic personage so long and vainly looked for, and that his visage was the perfect and undeniable similitude of the Great Stone Face. People were the more ready to believe that this must needs be the fact, when they beheld the splendid edifice that rose, as if by enchantment, on the site of his father's old weather-beaten farm-house. The exterior was of marble, so dazzlingly white that it seemed as though the whole structure might melt away in the sunshine, like those humbler ones which Mr. Gathergold, in his young play-days, before his fingers were gifted with the touch of transmutation, had been accustomed to build of snow. It had a richly ornamented portico, supported by tall pillars, beneath which was a lofty door, studded with silver knobs, and made of a kind of variegated wood that had been brought from beyond the sea. The windows, from the floor to the ceiling of each stately apartment, were composed, respectively, of but one enormous pane of glass, so transparently pure that it was said to be a finer medium than even the vacant atmosphere. Hardly anybody had been permitted to see the interior of this palace; but it was reported, and with good semblance of truth, to be far more gorgeous than the outside, insomuch that whatever was iron or brass in other houses was silver or gold in this; and Mr. Gathergold's bedchamber, especially, made such a glittering appearance that no ordinary man would have been able to close his eyes there. But, on the other hand, Mr. Gathergold was now so inured to wealth, that perhaps he could not have closed his eyes unless where the gleam of it was certain to find its way beneath his eyelids.

In due time, the mansion was finished; next came the upholsterers, with magnificent furniture; then, a whole troop of black and white servants, the harbingers of Mr. Gathergold, who, in his own majestic person, was expected to arrive at sunset. Our friend Ernest, meanwhile, had been deeply stirred by the idea that the great man, the noble man, the man of prophecy, after so many ages of delay, was at length to be made manifest to his native valley. He knew, boy as he was, that there were a thousand ways in which Mr. Gathergold, with his vast wealth, might transform himself into an angel of beneficence, and assume a control over human affairs as wide and benignant as the smile of the Great

Stone Face. Full of faith and hope, Ernest doubted not that what the people said was true, and that now he was to behold the living likeness of those wondrous features on the mountain-side. While the boy was still gazing up the valley, and fancying, as he always did, that the Great Stone Face returned his gaze and looked kindly at him, the rumbling of wheels was heard, approaching swiftly along the winding road.

"Here he comes!" cried a group of people who were assembled to witness the arrival. "Here comes the great Mr. Gathergold!"

A carriage, drawn by four horses, dashed round the turn of the road. Within it, thrust partly out of the window, appeared the physiognomy of the old man, with a skin as yellow as if his own Midas-hand had transmuted it. He had a low forehead, small, sharp eyes, puckered about with innumerable wrinkles, and very thin lips, which he made still thinner by pressing them forcibly together.

"The very image of the Great Stone Face!" shouted the people. "Sure enough, the old prophecy is true; and here we have the great man come, at last!"

And, what greatly perplexed Ernest, they seemed actually to believe that here was the likeness which they spoke of. By the roadside there chanced to be an old beggar-woman and two little beggar-children, stragglers from some far-off region, who, as the carriage rolled onward, held out their hands and lifted up their doleful voices, most piteously beseeching charity. A yellow claw—the very same that had clawed together so much wealth—poked itself out of the coach-window, and dropt some copper coins upon the ground; so that, though the great man's name seems to have been Gathergold, he might just as suitably have been nicknamed Scattercopper. Still, nevertheless, with an earnest shout, and evidently with as much good faith as ever, the people bellowed,—

"He is the very image of the Great Stone Face!"

But Ernest turned sadly from the wrinkled shrewdness of that sordid visage, and gazed up the valley, where, amid a gathering mist, gilded by the last sunbeams, he could still distinguish those glorious features which had impressed themselves into his soul. Their aspect cheered him. What did the benign lips seem to say?

"He will come! Fear not, Ernest; the man will come!"

The years went on, and Ernest ceased to be a boy. He had grown to be a young man now. He attracted little notice from the other inhabitants of the valley; for they saw nothing remarkable in his way of life, save that, when the labor of the day was over, he still loved to go apart and gaze and meditate upon the Great Stone Face. According to their idea of the matter, it was a folly, indeed, but pardonable, inasmuch as Ernest was industrious, kind, and neighborly, and neglected no duty for the sake of indulging this idle habit. They knew not that the Great Stone Face had become a teacher to him, and that the sentiment which was expressed in it would enlarge the young man's heart, and fill it with wider and deeper sympathies than other hearts. They knew not that thence would come a better wisdom than could be learned from books, and a better life than could be moulded on the defaced example of other human lives. Neither did Ernest know that the thoughts and affections which came to him so naturally, in the fields and at the fireside, and wherever he communed with himself, were of a higher tone than those which all men shared with him. A simple soul,—simple as when his mother first taught him the old prophecy,—he beheld the marvellous features beaming adown the valley, and still wondered that their human counterpart was so long in making his appearance.

By this time poor Mr. Gathergold was dead and buried; and the oddest part of the matter was, that his wealth, which was the body and spirit of his existence, had disappeared before his death, leaving nothing of him but a living skeleton, covered over with a wrinkled, yellow skin. Since the melting away of his gold, it had been very generally conceded that there was no such striking resemblance, after all, betwixt the ignoble features of the ruined merchant and that majestic face upon the mountain-side. So the people ceased to honor him during his lifetime, and quietly consigned him to forgetfulness after his decease. Once in a while, it is true, his memory was brought up in connection with the magnificent palace which he had built, and which had long ago been turned into a hotel for the accommodation of strangers, multitudes of whom came, every summer, to visit that famous natural curiosity, the Great Stone Face. Thus, Mr. Gathergold being discredited and thrown into the shade, the man of prophecy was yet to come.

It so happened that a native-born son of the valley, many years before, had enlisted as a soldier, and, after a great deal of hard fighting, had now become an illustrious commander. Whatever he may be called in history, he was known in camps and on the battle-field under the nickname of Old Blood-and-Thunder. This war-worn veteran, being now infirm with age and wounds, and weary of the turmoil of a military life, and of the roll of the drum and the clangor of the trumpet, that had so long been ringing in his ears, had lately signified a purpose of returning to his native valley, hoping to find repose where he remembered to have left it. The inhabitants, his old neighbors and their grown-up children, were resolved to welcome the renowned warrior with a salute of cannon and a public dinner; and all the more enthusiastically, it being affirmed that now, at last, the likeness of the Great Stone Face had actually appeared. An aide-de-camp of Old Blood-and-Thunder, travelling through the valley, was said to have been struck with the resemblance. Moreover the schoolmates and early acquaintances of the general were ready to testify, on oath, that, to the best of their recollection, the aforesaid general had been exceedingly like the majestic image, even when a boy, only that the idea had never occurred to them at that period. Great, therefore, was the excitement throughout the valley; and many people, who had never once thought of glancing at the Great Stone Face for years before, now spent their time in gazing at it, for the sake of knowing exactly how General Blood-and-Thunder looked.

On the day of the great festival, Ernest, with all the other people of the valley, left their work, and proceeded to the spot where the sylvan banquet was prepared. As he approached, the loud voice of the Rev. Dr. Battleblast was heard, beseeching a blessing on the good things set before them, and on the distinguished friend of peace in whose honor they were assembled. The tables were arranged in a cleared space of the woods, shut in by the surrounding trees, except where a vista opened eastward, and afforded a distant view of the Great Stone Face. Over the general's chair, which was a relic from the home of Washington, there was an arch of verdant boughs, with the laurel profusely intermixed, and surmounted by his country's banner, beneath which he had won his victories. Our friend Ernest raised himself on his tiptoes, in hopes to get a glimpse of the celebrated guest; but there was a mighty crowd about the tables anxious to hear the toasts and speeches, and to catch any word that might fall from the general in reply; and a volunteer company, doing duty as a guard, pricked ruthlessly with their bayonets at any particularly quiet person among the throng. So Ernest, being of an unobtrusive character, was thrust quite into the background, where he could see no more of Old Blood-and-Thunder's physiognomy than if it had been still blazing on the battle-field. To console himself, he turned towards the Great Stone Face, which, like a faithful and long-remembered friend, looked back and smiled upon him through the vista of the forest. Meantime, however, he could overhear the remarks of various individuals, who were comparing the features of the hero with the face on the distant mountain-side.

"'Tis the same face, to a hair!" cried one man, cutting a caper for joy.

"Wonderfully like, that's a fact!" responded another.

"Like! why, I call it Old Blood-and-Thunder himself, in a monstrous looking-glass!" cried a third. "And why not? He's the greatest man of this or any other age, beyond a doubt."

And then all three of the speakers gave a great shout, which communicated electricity to the crowd, and called forth a roar from a thousand voices, that went reverberating for miles among the mountains, until you might have supposed that the Great Stone Face had poured its thunder-breath into the cry. All these comments, and this vast enthusiasm, served the more to interest our friend; nor did he think of questioning that now, at length, the mountain-visage had found its human counterpart. It is true, Ernest had imagined that this long-looked-for personage would appear in the character of a man of peace, uttering wisdom, and doing good, and making people happy. But, taking an habitual breadth of view, with all his simplicity, he contended that Providence should choose its own method of blessing mankind, and could conceive that this great end might be effected even by a warrior and a bloody sword, should inscrutable wisdom see fit to order matters so.

"The general! the general!" was now the cry. "Hush! silence! Old Blood-and-Thunder's going to make a speech."

Even so; for, the cloth being removed, the general's health had been drunk, amid shouts of applause, and he now stood upon his feet to thank the company. Ernest saw him. There he was, over the shoulders of the crowd, from the two glittering epaulets and embroidered collar upward, beneath the arch of green boughs with intertwined laurel, and the banner drooping as if to shade his brow! And there, too, visible in the same glance, through the vista of the forest, appeared the Great Stone Face! And was there, indeed, such a resemblance as the crowd had testified? Alas, Ernest could not recognize it! He beheld a war-worn and weather-beaten countenance, full of energy, and expressive of an iron will; but the gentle wisdom, the deep, broad, tender sympathies, were altogether wanting in Old Blood-and-Thunder's visage; and even if the Great Stone Face had assumed his look of stern command, the milder traits would still have tempered it.

"This is not the man of prophecy," sighed Ernest to himself, as he made his way out of the throng. "And must the world wait longer yet?"

The mists had congregated about the distant mountain-side, and there were seen the grand and awful features of the Great Stone Face, awful but benignant, as if a mighty angel were sitting among the hills, and enrobing himself in a cloud-vesture of gold and purple. As he looked, Ernest could hardly believe but that a smile beamed over the whole visage, with a radiance still brightening, although without motion of the lips. It was probably the effect of the western sunshine, melting through the thinly diffused vapors that had swept between him and the object that he gazed at. But—as it always did—the aspect of his marvellous friend made Ernest as hopeful as if he had never hoped in vain.

"Fear not, Ernest," said his heart, even as if the Great Face were whispering him,—"fear not, Ernest; he will come."

More years sped swiftly and tranquilly away. Ernest still dwelt in his native valley, and was now a man of middle age. By imperceptible degrees, he had become known among the people. Now, as heretofore, he labored for his bread, and was the same simple-hearted man that he had always been. But he had thought and felt so much, he had given so many of the best hours of his life to unworldly hopes for some great good to mankind, that it seemed as though he had been talking with the angels, and had imbibed a portion of their wisdom unawares. It was visible in the calm and well-considered beneficence of his daily life, the quiet stream of which had made a wide green margin all along its course. Not a day passed by, that the world was not the better because this man, humble as he was, had lived. He never stepped aside from his own path, yet would always reach a blessing to his neighbor. Almost involuntarily, too, he had become a preacher. The pure and high simplicity of his thought, which, as one of its manifestations, took shape in the good deeds that dropped silently from his hand, flowed also forth in speech. He uttered truths that wrought upon and moulded the lives of those who heard him. His auditors, it may be, never suspected that Ernest, their own neighbor and familiar friend, was more than an ordinary man; least of all did Ernest himself suspect it; but, inevitably as the murmur of a rivulet, came thoughts out of his mouth that no other human lips had spoken.

When the people's minds had had a little time to cool, they were ready enough to acknowledge their mistake in imagining a similarity between General Blood-and-Thunder's truculent physiognomy and the benign visage on the mountain-side. But now, again, there were reports and many paragraphs in the newspapers, affirming that the likeness of the Great Stone Face had appeared upon the broad shoulders of a certain eminent statesman. He, like Mr. Gathergold and Old Blood-and-Thunder, was a native of the valley, but had left it in his early days, and taken up the trades of law and politics. Instead of the rich man's wealth and the warrior's sword, he had but a tongue, and it was mightier than both together. So wonderfully eloquent was he, that whatever he might choose to say, his auditors had no choice but to believe him; wrong looked like right, and right like wrong; for when it pleased him, he could make a kind of illuminated fog with his mere breath, and obscure the natural daylight with it. His tongue, indeed, was a magic instrument: sometimes it rumbled like the thunder; sometimes it warbled like the sweetest music. It was the blast of war,—the song of peace; and it seemed to have a heart in it, when there was no such matter. In good truth, he was a wondrous man; and when his tongue had acquired him all other imaginable success,—when it had been heard in halls of state, and in the courts of princes and potentates,—after it had made him known all over the world, even as a voice crying from shore to shore,—it finally persuaded his countrymen to select him for the Presidency. Before this time,—indeed, as soon as he began to grow celebrated,—his admirers had found out the resemblance between him and the Great Stone Face; and so much were they struck by it, that throughout the country this distinguished gentleman was known by the name of Old Stony Phiz. The phrase was considered as giving a highly favorable aspect to his political prospects; for, as is likewise the case with the Popedom, nobody ever becomes President without taking a name other than his own.

While his friends were doing their best to make him President, Old Stony Phiz, as he was called, set out on a visit to the valley where he was born. Of course, he had no other object than to shake hands with his fellow-citizens, and neither thought nor cared about any effect which his progress through the country might have upon the election. Magnificent preparations were made to receive the illustrious statesman; a cavalcade of horsemen set forth to meet him at the boundary line of the state, and all the people left their business and gathered along the wayside to see him pass. Among these was Ernest. Though more than once disappointed, as we have seen, he had such a hopeful and confiding nature, that he was always ready to believe in whatever seemed beautiful and good. He kept his heart continually open, and thus was sure to catch the blessing from on high when it should come. So now again, as buoyantly as ever, he went forth to behold the likeness of the Great Stone Face.

The cavalcade came prancing along the road, with a great clattering of hoofs and a mighty cloud of dust, which rose up so dense and high that the visage of the mountain-side was completely hidden from Ernest's eyes. All the great men of the neighborhood were there on horseback; militia officers, in uniform; the member of Congress; the sheriff of the county; the editors of newspapers; and many a farmer, too, had mounted his patient steed, with his Sunday coat upon his back. It really was a very brilliant spectacle, especially as there were numerous banners flaunting over the cavalcade, on some of which were gorgeous portraits of the illustrious statesman and the Great Stone Face, smiling familiarly at one another, like two brothers. If the pictures were to be trusted, the mutual resemblance, it must be confessed, was marvellous. We must not forget to mention that there was a band of music, which made the echoes of the mountains ring and reverberate with the loud triumph of its strains; so that airy and soul-thrilling melodies broke out among all the heights and hollows, as if every nook of his native valley had found a voice, to welcome the distinguished guest. But the grandest effect was when the far-off mountain precipice flung back the music; for then the Great Stone Face itself seemed to be swelling the triumphant chorus, in acknowledgment that, at length, the man of prophecy was come.

All this while the people were throwing up their hats and shouting, with enthusiasm so contagious that the heart of Ernest kindled up, and he likewise threw up his hat, and shouted, as loudly as the loudest, "Huzza for the great man! Huzza for Old Stony Phiz!" But as yet he had not seen him.

"Here he is, now!" cried those who stood near Ernest. "There! There! Look at Old Stony Phiz and then at the Old Man of the Mountain, and see if they are not as like as two twin-brothers!"

In the midst of all this gallant array came an open barouche, drawn by four white horses; and in the barouche, with his massive head uncovered, sat the illustrious statesman, Old Stony Phiz himself.

"Confess it," said one of Ernest's neighbors to him, "the Great Stone Face has met its match at last!"

Now, it must be owned that, at his first glimpse of the countenance which was bowing and smiling from the barouche, Ernest did fancy that there was a resemblance between it and the old familiar face upon the mountain-side. The brow, with its massive depth and loftiness, and all the other features, indeed, were boldly and strongly hewn, as if in emulation of a more than heroic, of a Titanic model. But the sublimity and stateliness, the grand expression of a divine sympathy, that illuminated the mountain visage and etherealized its ponderous granite substance into spirit, might here be sought in vain. Something had been originally left out, or had departed. And therefore the marvellously gifted statesman had always a weary gloom in the deep caverns of his eyes, as of a child that has outgrown its playthings or a man of mighty faculties and little aims, whose life, with all its high performances, was vague and empty, because no high purpose had endowed it with reality.

Still, Ernest's neighbor was thrusting his elbow into his side, and pressing him for an answer.

"Confess! confess! Is not he the very picture of your Old Man of the Mountain?"

"No!" said Ernest, bluntly, "I see little or no likeness."

"Then so much the worse for the Great Stone Face!" answered his neighbor; and again he set up a shout for Old Stony Phiz.

But Ernest turned away, melancholy, and almost despondent: for this was the saddest of his disappointments, to behold a man who might have fulfilled the prophecy, and had not willed to do so. Meantime, the cavalcade, the banners, the music, and the barouches swept past him, with the vociferous crowd in the rear, leaving the dust to settle down, and the Great Stone Face to be revealed again, with the grandeur that it had worn for untold centuries.

"Lo, here I am, Ernest!" the benign lips seemed to say. "I have waited longer than thou, and am not yet weary. Fear not; the man will come."

The years hurried onward, treading in their haste on one another's heels. And now they began to bring white hairs, and scatter them over the head of Ernest; they made reverend wrinkles across his forehead, and furrows in his cheeks. He was an aged man. But not in vain had he grown old: more than the white hairs on his head were the sage thoughts in his mind; his wrinkles and furrows were inscriptions that Time had graved, and in which he had written legends of wisdom that had been tested by the tenor of a life. And Ernest had ceased to be obscure. Unsought for, undesired, had come the fame which so many seek, and made him known in the great world, beyond the limits of the valley in which he had dwelt so quietly. College professors, and even the active men of cities, came from far to see and converse with Ernest; for the report had gone abroad that this simple husbandman had ideas unlike those of other men, not gained from books, but of a higher tone,—a tranquil and familiar majesty, as if he had been talking with the angels as his daily friends. Whether it were sage, statesman, or philanthropist, Ernest received these visitors with the gentle sincerity that had characterized him from boyhood, and spoke freely with them of whatever came uppermost, or lay deepest in his heart or their own. While they talked together, his face would kindle, unawares, and shine upon them, as with a mild evening light. Pensive with the fulness of such discourse, his guests took leave and went their way; and passing up the valley, paused to look at the Great Stone Face, imagining that they had seen its likeness in a human countenance, but could not remember where.

While Ernest had been growing up and growing old, a bountiful Providence had granted a new poet to this earth. He, likewise, was a native of the valley, but had spent the greater part of his life at a distance from that romantic region, pouring out his sweet music amid the bustle and din of cities. Often, however, did the mountains which had been familiar to him in his childhood lift their snowy peaks into the clear atmosphere of his poetry. Neither was the Great Stone Face forgotten, for the poet had celebrated it in an ode, which was grand enough to have been uttered by its own majestic lips. This man of genius, we may say, had come down from heaven with wonderful endowments. If he sang of a mountain, the eyes of all mankind beheld a mightier grandeur reposing on its breast, or soaring to its summit, than had before been seen there. If his theme were a lovely lake, a celestial smile had now been thrown over it, to gleam forever on its surface. If it were the vast old sea, even the deep immensity of its dread bosom seemed to swell the higher, as if moved by the emotions of the song. Thus the world assumed another and a better aspect from the hour that the poet blessed it with his happy eyes. The Creator had bestowed him, as the last best touch to his own handiwork. Creation was not finished till the poet came to interpret, and so complete it.

The effect was no less high and beautiful, when his human brethren were the subject of his verse. The man or woman, sordid with the common dust of life, who crossed his daily path, and the little child who played in it, were glorified if he beheld them in his mood of poetic faith. He showed the golden links of the great chain that intertwined them with an angelic kindred; he brought out the hidden traits of a celestial birth that made them worthy of such kin. Some, indeed, there were, who thought to show the soundness of their judgment by affirming that all the beauty and dignity of the natural world existed only in the poet's fancy. Let such men speak for themselves, who undoubtedly appear to have been spawned forth by Nature with a contemptuous bitterness; she having plastered them up out of her refuse stuff, after all the swine were made. As respects all things else, the poet's ideal was the truest truth.

The songs of this poet found their way to Ernest. He read them after his customary toil, seated on the bench before his cottage-door, where for such a length of time he had filled his repose with thought, by gazing at the Great Stone Face. And now as he read stanzas that caused the soul to thrill within him, he lifted his eyes to the vast countenance beaming on him so benignantly.

"O majestic friend," he murmured, addressing the Great Stone Face, "is not this man worthy to resemble thee?"

The Face seemed to smile, but answered not a word.

Now it happened that the poet, though he dwelt so far away, had not only heard of Ernest, but had meditated much upon his character, until he deemed nothing so desirable as to meet this man, whose untaught wisdom walked hand in hand with the noble simplicity of his life. One summer morning, therefore, he took passage by the railroad, and, in the decline of the afternoon, alighted from the cars at no great distance from Ernest's cottage. The great hotel, which had formerly been the palace of Mr. Gathergold, was close at hand, but the poet, with his carpet-bag on his arm, inquired at once where Ernest dwelt, and was resolved to be accepted as his guest.

Approaching the door, he there found the good old man, holding a volume in his hand, which alternately he read, and then, with a finger between the leaves, looked lovingly at the Great Stone Face.

"Good evening," said the poet. "Can you give a traveller a night's lodging?"

"Willingly," answered Ernest; and then he added, smiling, "Methinks I never saw the Great Stone Face look so hospitably at a stranger."

The poet sat down on the bench beside him, and he and Ernest talked together. Often had the poet held intercourse with the wittiest and the wisest, but never before with a man like Ernest, whose thoughts and feelings gushed up with such a natural freedom, and who made great truths so familiar by his simple utterance of them. Angels, as had been so often said, seemed to have wrought with him at his labor in the fields; angels seemed to have sat with him by the fireside; and, dwelling with angels as friend with friend, he had imbibed the sublimity of their ideas, and imbued it with the sweet and lowly charm of household words. So thought the poet. And Ernest, on the other hand, was moved and agitated by the living images which the poet flung out of his mind, and which peopled all the air about the cottage-door with shapes of beauty, both gay and pensive. The sympathies of these two men instructed them with a profounder sense than either could have attained alone. Their minds accorded into one strain, and made delightful music which neither of them could have claimed as all his own, nor distinguished his own share from the other's. They led one another, as it were, into a high pavilion of their thoughts, so remote, and hitherto so dim, that they had never entered it before, and so beautiful that they desired to be there always.

As Ernest listened to the poet, he imagined that the Great Stone Face was bending forward to listen too. He gazed earnestly into the poet's glowing eyes.

"Who are you, my strangly gifted guest?" he said.

The poet laid his finger on the volume that Ernest had been reading. "You have read these poems," said he. "You know me, then,—for I wrote them."

Again, and still more earnestly than before, Ernest examined the poet's features; then turned towards the Great Stone Face; then back, with an uncertain aspect, to his guest. But his countenance fell; he shook his head, and sighed.

"Wherefore are you sad?" inquired the poet.

"Because," replied Ernest, "all through life I have awaited the fulfilment of a prophecy; and, when I read these poems, I hoped that it might be fulfilled in you."

"You hoped," answered the poet, faintly smiling, "to find in me the likeness of the Great Stone Face. And you are disappointed, as formerly with Mr. Gathergold, and Old Blood-and-Thunder, and Old Stony Phiz. Yes Ernest, it is my doom. You must add my name to the illustrious three, and record another failure of your hopes. For—in shame and sadness do I speak it, Ernest—I am not worthy to be typified by yonder benign and majestic image."

"And why?" asked Ernest. He pointed to the volume. "Are not those thoughts divine?"

"They have a strain of the Divinity," replied the poet. "You can hear in them the far-off echo of a heavenly song. But my life, dear Ernest, has not corresponded with my thought. I have had grand dreams, but they have been only dreams, because I have lived—and that, too, by my own choice—among poor and mean realities. Sometimes even—shall I dare to say it?—I lack faith in the grandeur, the beauty, and the goodness, which my own works are said to have made more evident in nature and in human life. Why, then, pure seeker of the good and true, shouldst thou hope to find me, in yonder image of the divine?"

The poet spoke sadly, and his eyes were dim with tears. So, likewise, were those of Ernest.

At the hour of sunset, as had long been his frequent custom, Ernest was to discourse to an assemblage of the neighboring inhabitants in the open air. He and the poet, arm in arm, still talking together as they went along, proceeded to the spot. It was a small nook among the hills, with a gray precipice behind, the stern front of which was relieved by the pleasant foliage of many creeping plants that made a tapestry for the naked rock, by hanging their festoons from all its rugged angles. At a small elevation above the ground, set in a rich framework of verdure, there appeared a niche, spacious enough to admit a human figure, with freedom for such gestures as spontaneously accompany earnest thought and genuine emotion. Into this natural pulpit Ernest ascended, and threw a look of familiar kindness around upon his audience. They stood, or sat, or reclined upon the grass, as seemed good to each, with the departing sunshine falling obliquely over them, and mingling its subdued cheerfulness with the solemnity of a grove of ancient trees, beneath and amid the boughs of which the golden rays were constrained to pass. In another direction was seen the Great Stone Face, with the same cheer, combined with the same solemnity, in its benignant aspect.

Ernest began to speak, giving to the people of what was in his heart and mind. His words had power, because they accorded with his thoughts; and his thoughts had reality and depth, because they harmonized with the life which he had always lived. It was not mere breath that this preacher uttered; they were the words of life, because a life of good deeds and holy love was melted into them. Pearls, pure and rich, had been dissolved into this precious draught. The poet, as he listened, felt that the being and character of Ernest were a nobler strain of poetry than he had ever written. His eyes glistening with tears, he gazed reverentially at the venerable man, and said within himself that never was there an aspect so worthy of a prophet and a sage as that mild, sweet, thoughtful countenance, with the glory of white hair diffused about it. At a distance, but distinctly to be seen, high up in the golden light of the setting sun, appeared the Great Stone Face, with hoary mists around it, like the white hairs around the brow of Ernest. Its look of grand beneficence seemed to embrace the world.

At that moment, in sympathy with a thought which he was about to utter, the face of Ernest assumed a grandeur of expression, so imbued with benevolence, that the poet, by an irresistible impulse, threw his arms aloft, and shouted,—

"Behold! Behold! Ernest is himself the likeness of the Great Stone Face!"

Then all the people looked, and saw that what the deep-sighted poet said was true. The prophecy was fulfilled. But Ernest, having finished what he had to say, took the poet's arm, and walked slowly homeward, still hoping that some wiser and better man than himself would by and by appear, bearing a resemblance to the GREAT STONE FACE.

David Swan

WE can be but partially acquainted even with the events which actually influence our course through life, and our final destiny. There are innumerable other events, if such they may be called, which come close upon us, yet pass away without actual results, or even betraying their near approach, by the reflection of any light or shadow across our minds. Could we know all the vicissitudes of our fortunes, life would be too full of hope and fear, exultation or disappointment, to afford us a single hour of true serenity. This idea may be illustrated by a page from the secret of David Swan.

We have nothing to do with David until we find him, at the age of twenty, on the high road from his native place to the city of Boston, where his uncle, a small dealer in the grocery line, was to take him behind the counter. Be it enough to say, that he was a native of New Hampshire, born of respectable parents, and had received an ordinary school education, with a classic finish by a year at Gilmanton Academy. After journeying on foot from sunrise till nearly noon of a summer's day, his weariness and the increasing heat determined him to sit down in the first convenient shade, and await the coming up of the stagecoach. As if planted on purpose for him, there soon appeared a little tuft of maples, with a delightful recess in the midst, and such a fresh bubbling spring, that it seemed never to have sparkled for any wayfarer but David Swan. Virgin or not, he kissed it with his thirsty lips, and then flung himself along the brink, pillowing his head upon some shirts and a pair of pantaloons, tied up in a striped cotton handkerchief. The sunbeams could not reach him; the dust did not yet rise from the road, after the heavy rain of yesterday; and his grassy lair suited the young man better than a bed of down. The spring murmured drowsily beside him; the branches waved dreamily across the blue sky overhead; and a deep sleep, perchance hiding dreams within its depths, fell upon David Swan. But we are to relate events which he did not dream of.

While he lay sound asleep in the shade, other people were wide awake, and passed to and fro, afoot, on horseback, and in all sorts of vehicles, along the sunny road by his bed-chamber. Some looked neither to the right hand nor the left, and knew not that he was there; some merely glanced that way, without admitting the slumberer among their busy thoughts; some laughed to see how soundly he slept; and several, whose hearts were brimming full of scorn, ejected their venomous superfluity on David Swan. A middle-aged widow, when nobody else was near, thrust her head a little way into the recess, and vowed that the young fellow looked charming in his sleep. A temperance lecturer saw him, and wrought poor David into the texture of his evening's discourse, as an awful instance of dead drunkenness by the road-side. But censure, praise, merriment, scorn, and indifference, were all one, or rather all nothing, to David Swan.

He had slept only a few moments when a brown carriage, drawn by a handsome pair of horses, bowled easily along, and was brought to a standstill nearly in front of David's resting place. A linchpin had fallen out, and permitted one of the wheels to slide off. The damage was slight, and occasioned merely a momentary alarm to an elderly merchant and his wife, who were returning to Boston in the carriage. While the coachman and a servant were replacing the wheel, the lady and gentleman sheltered themselves beneath the maple-trees and there espied the bubbling fountain, and David Swan asleep beside it. Impressed with the awe which the humblest sleeper usually sheds around him, the merchant trod as lightly as the gout would allow; and his spouse took good heed not to rustle her silk gown, lest David should start up, all of a sudden.

"How soundly he sleeps!" whispered the old gentleman. "From what a depth he draws that easy breath! Such sleep as that, brought on without an opiate, would be worth more to me than half my income, for it would suppose health and an untroubled mind."

"And youth besides," said the lady. "Healthy and quiet age does not sleep thus. Our slumber is no more like his than our wakefulness."

The longer they looked the more did this elderly couple feel interested in the unknown youth, to whom the wayside and the maple shade was as a secret chamber, with the rich gloom of damask curtains brooding over him. Perceiving that a stray sunbeam glimmered down upon his face, the lady contrived to twist a branch aside, so as to intercept it. And having done this little act of kindness, she began to feel like a mother to him.

"Providence seems to have laid him here," whispered she to her husband, "and to have brought us hither to find him, after our disappointment in our cousin's son. Methinks I can see a likeness to our departed Henry. Shall we waken him?"

"To what purpose?" said the merchant, hesitating. "We know nothing of the youth's character."

"That open countenance!" replied his wife, in the same hushed voice, yet earnestly. "This innocent sleep!"

While these whispers were passing, the sleeper's heart did not throb, nor his breath become agitated, nor his features betray the least token of interest. Yet Fortune was bending over him, just ready to let fall a burthen of gold. The old merchant had lost his only son, and had no heir to his wealth, except a distant relative, with whose conduct he was dissatisfied. In such cases, people sometimes do stranger things than to act the magician, and awaken a young man to splendor, who fell asleep in poverty.

"Shall we not waken him?" repeated the lady, persuasively.

"The coach is ready, sir," said the servant, behind.

The old couple started, reddened, and hurried away, mutually wondering that they should ever have dreamed of doing anything so very ridiculous. The merchant threw himself back in the carriage, and occupied his mind with the plan of a magnificent asylum for unfortunate men of business. Meanwhile, David Swan enjoyed his nap.

The carriage could not have gone above a mile or two, when a pretty young girl came along with a tripping pace, which showed precisely how her little heart was dancing in her bosom. Perhaps it was this merry kind of motion that caused—is there any harm in saying it?—her garter to slip its knot. Conscious that the silken girth, if silk it were, was relaxing its hold, she turned aside into the shelter of the maple-trees, and there found a young man asleep by the spring! Blushing as red as any rose, that she should have intruded into a gentleman's bedchamber, and for such a purpose too, she was about to make her escape on tiptoe. But there was peril near the sleeper. A monster of a bee had been wandering overhead—buzz, buzz, buzz—now among the leaves, now flashing through the strips of sunshine, and now lost in the dark shade, till finally he appeared to be settling on the eyelid of David Swan. The sting of a bee is sometimes deadly. As free-hearted as she was innocent, the girl attacked the intruder with her handkerchief, brushed him soundly, and drove him from the maple shade. How sweet a picture! This good deed accomplished, with quickened breath, and a deeper blush, she stole a glance at the youthful stranger, for whom she had been battling with a dragon in the air.

"He is handsome!" thought she, and blushed redder yet.

How could it be that no dream of bliss grew so strong within him, that, shattered by its very strength, it should part asunder and allow him to perceive the girl among its phantoms? Why, at least, did no smile of welcome brighten upon his face? She was come, the maid whose soul, according to the old and beautiful idea, had been severed from his own, and whom, in all his vague but passionate desires, he yearned to meet. Her only could he love with a perfect love—him only could she receive into the depths of her heart—and now her image was faintly blushing in the fountain by his side; should it pass away, its happy lustre would never gleam upon his life again.

"How sound he sleeps!" murmured the girl.

She departed, but did not trip along the road so lightly as when she came.

Now, this girl's father was a thriving country merchant in the neighborhood, and happened, at that identical time, to be looking out for just such a young man as David Swan. Had David formed a wayside acquaintance with the daughter, he would have become the father's clerk, and all else in natural succession. So here, again, had good fortune—the best of fortunes—stolen so near that her garments brushed against him, and he knew nothing of the matter.

The girl was hardly out of sight when two men turned aside beneath the maple shade. Both had dark faces, set off by cloth caps, which were drawn down aslant over their brows. Their dresses were shabby, yet had a certain smartness. These were a couple of rascals, who got their living by whatever the devil sent them, and now, in the interim of other business, had staked the joint profits of their next piece of villainy on a game of cards, which was to have been decided here under the trees. But finding David asleep by the spring, one of the rogues whispered to his fellow—

"Hist!—Do you see that bundle under his head!"

The other villain nodded, winked, and leered.

"I'll bet you a horn of brandy," said the first, "that the chap has either a pocket-book or a snug little hoard of small change, stowed away amongst his shirts. And if not there, we shall find it in his pantaloons' pocket."

"But how if he wakes?" said the other.

His companion thrust aside his waistcoat, pointed to the handle of a dirk, and nodded.

"So be it!" muttered the second villain.

They approached the unconscious David, and, while one pointed the dagger towards his heart, the other began to search the bundle beneath his head. Their two faces, grim, wrinkled, and ghastly with guilt and fear, bent over their victim, looking horrible enough to be mistaken for fiends, should he suddenly awake. Nay, had the villains glanced aside into the spring, even they would hardly have known themselves, as reflected there. But David Swan had never worn a more tranquil aspect, even when asleep on his mother's breast.

"I must take away the bundle," whispered one.

"If he stirs, I'll strike," muttered the other.

But, at this moment, a dog, scenting along the ground, came in beneath the maple trees, and gazed alternately at each of these wicked men, and then at the quiet sleeper. He then lapped out of the fountain.

"Pshaw!" said one villain. "We can do nothing now. The dog's master must be close behind."

"Let's take a drink, and be off," said the other.

The man with the dagger thrust back the weapon into his bosom, and drew forth a pocket-pistol, but not of that kind which kills by a single discharge. It was a flask of liquor, with a block-tin tumbler screwed upon the mouth. Each drank a comfortable dram, and left the spot, with so many jests and such laughter at their unaccomplished wickedness that they might be said to have gone on their way rejoicing. In a few hours they had forgotten the whole affair, nor once imagined that the recording angel had written down the crime of murder against their souls in letters as durable as eternity. As for David Swan, he still slept quietly, neither conscious of the shadow of death when it hung over him, nor of the glow of renewed life when that shadow was withdrawn.

He slept, but no longer so quietly as at first. An hour's repose had snatched from his elastic frame the weariness with which many hours of toil had burthened it. Now he stirred—now moved his lips, without a sound—now talked in an inward tone to the noonday spectres of his dream. But a noise of wheels came rattling louder and louder along the road, until it dashed through the dispersing mist of David's slumber—and there was the stage-coach. He started up, with all his ideas about him.

"Halloo, driver!—Take a passenger?" shouted he.

"Room on top!" answered the driver.

Up mounted David, and bowled away merrily towards Boston, without so much as a parting glance at that fountain of dreamlike vicissitude. He knew not that a phantom of Wealth had thrown a golden hue upon its waters—nor that one of Love had sighed softly to their murmur—nor that one of Death had threatened to crimson them with his blood—all, in the brief hour since he lay down to sleep. Sleeping or waking, we hear not the airy footsteps of the strange things that almost happen. Does it not argue a superintending Providence, that, while viewless and unexpected events thrust themselves continually athwart our path, there should still be regularity enough in mortal life to render foresight even partially available?

From OUR OLD HOME

Dr. Johnson's Birthplace and the Site of the Penance

I WAS but little interested in the legends of the remote antiquity of Lichfield, being drawn thither partly to see its beautiful cathedral, and still more, I believe, because it was the birthplace of Dr. Johnson, with whose sturdy English character I became acquainted, at a very early period of my life, through the good offices of Mr. Boswell. In truth, he seems as familiar to my recollection, and almost as vivid in his personal aspect to my mind's eye, as the kindly figure of my own grandfather. It is only a solitary child,—left much to such wild modes of culture as he chooses for himself while yet ignorant what culture means, standing on tiptoe to pull down books from no very lofty shelf, and then shutting himself up, as it were, between the leaves, going astray through the volume at his own pleasure, and comprehending it rather by his sensibilities and affections than his intellect,—that child is the only student that ever gets the sort of intimacy which I am now thinking of, with a literary personage. I do not remember, indeed, ever caring much about any of the stalwart Doctor's grandiloquent productions, except his two stern and masculine poems, "London," and "The Vanity of Human Wishes"; it was as a man, a talker, and a humorist, that I knew and loved him, appreciating many of his qualities perhaps more thoroughly than I do now, though never seeking to put my instinctive perception of his character into language.

Beyond all question, I might have had a wiser friend than he. The atmosphere in which alone he breathed was dense; his awful dread of death showed how much muddy imperfection was to be cleansed out of him, before he could be capable of spiritual existence; he meddled only with the surface of life, and never cared to penetrate further than to ploughshare depth; his very sense and sagacity were but a one-eyed clear-sightedness. I laughed at him, sometimes, standing beside his knee. And yet, considering that my native propensities were towards Fairy Land, and also how much yeast is generally mixed up with the mental sustenance of a New-Englander, it may not have been altogether amiss, in those childish and boyish days, to keep pace with this heavy-footed traveller and feed on the gross diet that he carried in his knapsack. It is wholesome food even now. And, then, how English! Many of the latent sympathies that enabled me to enjoy the Old Country so well, and that so readily amalgamated themselves with the American ideas that seemed most adverse to them, may have been derived from, or fostered and kept alive by, the great English moralist. Never was a descriptive epithet more nicely appropriate than that! Dr. Johnson's morality was as English an article as a beefsteak.

Seeking for Johnson's birthplace, I found it in St. Mary's Square, which is not so much a square as the mere widening of a street. The house is tall and thin, of three stories, with a square front and a roof rising steep and high. On a side-view, the building looks as if it had been cut in two in the midst, there being no slope of the roof on that side. A ladder slanted against the wall, and a painter was giving a livelier hue to the plaster. In a corner-room of the basement, where old Michael Johnson may be supposed to have sold books, is now what we should call a dry-goods store, or, according to the English phrase, a mercer's and haberdasher's shop. The house has a private entrance on a cross-street, the door being accessible by several much-worn stone steps, which are bordered by an iron balustrade. I set my foot on the steps and laid my hand on the balustrade, where Johnson's hand and foot must many a time have been, and ascending to the door, I knocked once, and again, and again, and got no admittance. Going round to the shop-entrance, I tried to open it, but found it as fast bolted as the gate of Paradise. It is mortifying to be so balked in one's little enthusiasms; but looking round in quest of somebody to make inquiries of, I was a good deal consoled by the sight of Dr. Johnson himself, who happened, just at that moment, to be sitting at his ease nearly in the middle of St. Mary's Square, with his face turned towards his father's house.

Of course, it being almost fourscore years since the Doctor laid aside his weary bulk of flesh, together with the ponderous melancholy that had so long weighed him down, the intelligent reader will at once comprehend that he was marble in his substance, and seated in a marble chair, on an elevated stone pedestal. In short, it was a statue, sculptured by Lucas, and placed here in 1838, at the expense of Dr. Law, the reverend chancellor of the diocese.

The figure is colossal (though perhaps not much more so than the mountainous Doctor himself) and looks down upon the spectator from its pedestal of ten or twelve feet high, with a broad and heavy benignity of aspect, very like in feature to Sir Joshua Reynolds's portrait of Johnson, but calmer and sweeter in expression. Several big books are piled up beneath his chair, and, if I mistake not, he holds a volume in his hand, thus blinking forth at the world out of his learned abstraction, owl-like, yet benevolent at heart. The statue is immensely massive, a vast ponderosity of stone, not finely spiritualized, nor indeed, fully humanized, but rather resembling a great stone-bowlder than a man. You must look with the eyes of faith and sympathy, or, possibly, you might lose the human being altogether, and find only a big stone within your mental grasp. On the pedestal are three bas-reliefs. In the first, Johnson is represented as hardly more than a baby, bestriding an old man's shoulders, resting his chin on the bald head which he embraces with his little arms, and listening earnestly to the High-Church eloquence of Dr. Sacheverell. In the second tablet, he is seen riding to school on the shoulders of two of his comrades, while another boy supports him in the rear.

The third bas-relief possesses, to my mind, a great deal of pathos, to which my appreciative faculty is probably the more alive, because I have always been profoundly impressed by the incident here commemorated, and long ago tried to tell it for the behoof of childish readers. It shows Johnson in the market-place of Uttoxeter, doing penance for an act of disobedience to his father, committed fifty years before. He stands bareheaded, a venerable figure, and a countenance extremely sad and woe-begone, with the wind and rain driving hard against him, and thus helping to suggest to the spectator the gloom of his inward state. Some market-people and children gaze awe-stricken into his face, and an aged man and woman, with clasped and uplifted hands, seem to be praying for him. These latter personages (whose introduction by the artist is none the less effective, because, in queer proximity, there are some commodities of market-day in the shape of living ducks and dead poultry) I interpreted to represent the spirits of Johnson's father and mother, lending what aid they could to lighten his half-century's burden of remorse.

I had never heard of the above-described piece of sculpture before; it appears to have no reputation as a work of art, nor am I at all positive that it deserves any. For me, however, it did as much as sculpture could, under the circumstances, even if the artist of the Libyan Sibyl had wrought it, by reviving my interest in the sturdy old Englishman, and particularly by freshening my perception of a wonderful beauty and pathetic tenderness in the incident of the penance. So, the next day, I left Lichfield for Uttoxeter, on one of the few purely sentimental pilgrimages that I ever undertook, to see the very spot where Johnson had stood. Boswell, I think, speaks of the town (its name is pronounced Yuteoxeter) as being about nine miles off from Lichfield, but the county-map would indicate a greater distance; and by rail, passing from one line to another, it is as much as eighteen miles. I have always had an idea of old Michael Johnson sending his literary merchandise by carrier's wagon, journeying to Uttoxeter afoot on market-day morning, selling books through the busy hours, and returning to Lichfield at night. This could not possibly have been the case.

Arriving at the Uttoxeter station, the first objects that I saw, with a green field or two between them and me, were the tower and gray steeple of a church, rising among red-tiled roofs and a few scattered trees. A very short walk takes you from the station up into the town. It had been my previous impression that the market-place of Uttoxeter lay immediately roundabout the church; and, if I remember the narrative aright, Johnson, or Boswell in his behalf, describes his father's book-stall as standing in the market-place, close beside the sacred edifice. It is impossible for me to say what changes may have occurred in the topography of the town, during almost a century and a half since Michael

Johnson retired from business, and ninety years, at least, since his son's penance was performed. But the church has now merely a street of ordinary width passing around it, while the market-place, though near at hand, neither forms a part of it nor is really contiguous, nor would its throng and bustle be apt to overflow their boundaries and surge against the churchyard and the old gray tower. Nevertheless, a walk of a minute or two brings a person from the centre of the market-place to the church-door; and Michael Johnson might very conveniently have located his stall and laid out his literary ware in the corner at the tower's base; better there, indeed, than in the busy centre of an agricultural market. But the picturesque arrangement and full impressiveness of the story absolutely require that Johnson shall not have done his penance in a corner, ever so little retired, but shall have been the very nucleus of the crowd,—the midmost man of the market-place,—a central image of Memory and Remorse, contrasting with and overpowering the petty materialism around him. He himself, having the force to throw vitality and truth into what persons differently constituted might reckon a mere external ceremony, and an absurd one, could not have failed to see this necessity. I am resolved, therefore, that the true site of Dr. Johnson's penance was in the middle of the market-place.

That important portion of the town is a rather spacious and irregularly shaped vacuity, surrounded by houses and shops, some of them old, with red-tiled roofs, others wearing a pretence of newness, but probably as old in their inner substance as the rest. The people of Uttoxeter seemed very idle in the warm summer-day, and were scattered in little groups along the sidewalks, leisurely chatting with one another, and often turning about to take a deliberate stare at my humble self; insomuch that I felt as if my genuine sympathy for the illustrious penitent, and my many reflections about him, must have imbued me with some of his own singularity of mien. If their great-grandfathers were such redoubtable starers in the Doctor's day, his penance was no light one.

I stepped into one of the rustic hostelries and got my dinner,—bacon and greens, some mutton-chops, juicier and more delectable than all America could serve up at the President's table, and a gooseberry pudding; a sufficient meal for six yeomen, and good enough for a prince, besides a pitcher of foaming ale, the whole at the pitiful small charge of eighteen-pence! Dr. Johnson would have forgiven me, for nobody had a heartier faith in beef and mutton than himself.

Meanwhile I found myself still haunted by a desire to get a definite result out of my visit to Uttoxeter. The hospitable inn was called the Nag's Head, and standing beside the market-place, was as likely as any other to have entertained old Michael Johnson in the days when he used to come hither to sell books. He, perhaps, had dined on bacon and greens, and drunk his ale, and smoked his pipe, in the very room where I now sat, which was a low, ancient room, certainly much older than Queen Anne's time, with a red-brick floor, and a white-washed ceiling, traversed by bare, rough beams, the whole in the rudest fashion, but extremely neat. Neither did it lack ornament, the walls being hung with colored engravings of prize oxen and other pretty prints, and the mantel-piece adorned with earthen-ware figures of shepherdesses in the Arcadian taste of long ago. Michael Johnson's eyes might have rested on that selfsame earthen image, to examine which more closely I had just crossed the brick pavement of the room. And, sitting down again, still as I sipped my ale, I glanced through the open window into the sunny market-place, and wished that I could honestly fix on one spot rather than another, as likely to have been the holy site where Johnson stood to do his penance.

How strange and stupid it is that tradition should not have marked and kept in mind the very place! How shameful (nothing less than that) that there should be no local memorial of this incident, as beautiful and touching a passage as can be cited out of any human life! No inscription of it, almost as sacred as a verse of Scripture on the wall of the church! No statue of the venerable and illustrious penitent in the market-place to throw a wholesome awe over its earthliness, its frauds and petty wrongs of which the benumbed fingers of conscience can make no record, its selfish competition of each man with his brother or his neighbor, its traffic of soul-substance for a little worldly gain! Such a statue, if the piety of the people did not raise it, might almost have been expected to grow up out of the pavement of its own accord on the spot that had been watered by the rain that dripped from Johnson's garments, mingled with his remorseful tears.

Long after my visit to Uttoxeter, I was told that there were individuals in the town who could have shown me the exact, indubitable spot where Johnson performed his penance. I was assured, moreover, that sufficient interest was felt in the subject to have induced certain local discussions as to the expediency of erecting a memorial. With all deference to my polite informant, I surmise that there is a mistake, and decline, without further and precise evidence, giving credit to either of the above statements. The inhabitants know nothing, as a matter of general interest, about the penance, and care nothing for the scene of it. If the clergyman of the parish, for example, had ever heard of it, would he not have used the theme, time and again, wherewith to work tenderly and profoundly on the souls committed to his charge? If parents were familiar with it, would they not teach it to their young ones at the fireside, both to insure reverence to their own gray hairs, and to protect the children from such unavailing regrets as Johnson bore upon his heart for fifty years? If the site were ascertained, would not the pavement thereabouts be worn with reverential foot-steps? Would not every town-born child be able to direct the pilgrim thither? While waiting at the station, before my departure, I asked a boy who stood near me,—an intelligent and gentlemanly lad, twelve or thirteen years old, whom I should take to be a clergyman's son,—I asked him if he had ever heard the story of Dr. Johnson, how he stood an hour doing penance near that church, the spire of which rose before us. The boy stared and answered,—

"No!"

"Were you born in Uttoxeter?"

"Yes."

I inquired if no circumstance such as I had mentioned was known or talked about among the inhabitants.

"No," said the boy; "not that I ever heard of."

Just think of the absurd little town, knowing nothing of the only memorable incident which ever happened within its boundaries since the old Britons built it, this sad and lovely story, which consecrates the spot (for I found it holy to my contemplation, again, as soon as it lay behind me) in the heart of a stranger from three thousand miles over the sea!

HENRY WADSWORTH LONGFELLOW (1807-1881)

To the River Charles

River! that in silence windest
  Through the meadows, bright and free,
Till at length thy rest thou findest
  In the bosom of the sea!

Four long years of mingled feeling,
  Half in rest, and half in strife,
I have seen thy waters stealing
  Onward, like the stream of life.

Thou has taught me, Silent River!
  Many a lesson, deep and long;
Thou hast been a generous giver;
  I can give thee but a song.

Oft in sadness and in illness,
  I have watched thy current glide,
Till the beauty of its stillness
  Overflowed me, like a tide.

And in better hours and brighter,
  When I saw thy waters gleam,
I have felt my heart beat lighter,
  And leap onward with thy stream.

Not for this alone I love thee,
  Nor because thy waves of blue
From celestial seas above thee
  Take their own celestial hue.

Where yon shadowy woodlands hide thee,
  And thy waters disappear,
Friends I love have dwelt beside thee,
  And have made thy margin dear.

More than this;—thy name reminds me
Of three friends, all true and tried;
And that name, like magic, binds me
Closer, closer to thy side.

Friends my soul with joy remembers!
How like quivering flames they start,
When I fan the living embers
On the hearth-stone of my heart!

'Tis for this, thou Silent River!
That my spirit leans to thee;
Thou hast been a generous giver,
Take this idle song from me.

The Fire of Drift-Wood

We sat within the farmhouse old,
Whose windows, looking o'er the bay,
Gave to the sea-breeze, damp and cold,
An easy entrance, night and day.

Not far away we saw the port,—
The strange, old-fashioned, silent town,—
The lighthouse,—the dismantled fort,—
The wooden houses, quaint and brown.

We sat and talked until the night,
Descending, filled the little room;
Our faces faded from the sight,
Our voices only broke the gloom.

We spake of many a vanished scene,
Of what we once had thought and said,
Of what had been, and might have been,
And who was changed, and who was dead.

And all that fills the hearts of friends,
When first they feel, with secret pain,
Their lives thenceforth have separate ends,
And never can be one again;

The first slight swerving of the heart,
That words are powerless to express,
And leave it still unsaid in part,
Or say it in too great excess.

The very tones in which we spake
Had something strange, I could but mark;
The leaves of memory seemed to make
A mournful rustling in the dark.

Oft died the words upon our lips,
As suddenly, from out the fire
Built of the wreck of stranded ships,
The flames would leap and then expire.

And, as their splendor flashed and failed,
We thought of wrecks upon the main,—
Of ships dismasted, that were hailed
And sent no answer back again.

The windows, rattling in their frames,—
The ocean, roaring up the beach,—
The gusty blast,—the bickering flames,
All mingled vaguely in our speech;

Until they made themselves a part
Of fancies floating through the brain,
The long-lost ventures of the heart,
That send no answers back again.

O flames that glowed! O hearts that yearned!
They were indeed too much akin,
The drift-wood fire without that burned,
The thoughts that burned and glowed within.

My Lost Youth

Often I think of the beautiful town
That is seated by the sea;
Often in thought go up and down
The pleasant streets of that dear old town,
And my youth comes back to me.
And a verse of a Lapland song
Is haunting my memory still:
"A boy's will is the wind's will,
And the thoughts of youth are long, long thoughts."

I can see the shadowy lines of its trees,
And catch, in sudden gleams,
The sheen of the far-surrounding seas,
And islands that were the Hesperides
Of all my boyish dreams.
And the burden of that old song,
It murmurs and whispers still:
"A boy's will is the wind's will,
And the thoughts of youth are long, long thoughts."

I remember the black wharves and the slips,
And the sea-tides tossing free;
And the Spanish sailors with bearded lips,
And the beauty and mystery of the ships,
And the magic of the sea.
And the voice of that wayward song
Is singing and saying still:
"A boy's will is the wind's will,
And the thoughts of youth are long, long thoughts."

I remember the bulwarks by the shore,
And the fort upon the hill;
The sunrise gun, with its hollow roar,
The drum-beat repeated o'er and o'er,
And the bugle wild and shrill.
And the music of that old song
Throbs in my memory still:
"A boy's will is the wind's will,
And the thoughts of youth are long, long thoughts."

I remember the sea-fight far away,
How it thundered o'er the tide!
And the dead captains, as they lay
In their graves, o'erlooking the tranquil bay
Where they in battle died.
And the sound of that mournful song
Goes through me with a thrill:
"A boy's will is the wind's will,
And the thoughts of youth are long, long thoughts."

I can see the breezy dome of groves,
The shadows of Deering's Woods;
And the friendships old and the early loves
Come back with a Sabbath sound, as of doves
In quiet neighborhoods.
And the verse of that sweet old song,
It flutters and murmurs still:
"A boy's will is the wind's will,
And the thoughts of youth are long, long thoughts."

I remember the gleams and glooms that dart
Across the school-boy's brain;
The song and the silence in the heart,
That in part are prophecies, and in part
Are longings wild and vain.
And the voice of that fitful song
Sings on, and is never still:
"A boy's will is the wind's will,
And the thoughts of youth are long, long thoughts."

There are things of which I may not speak;
There are dreams that cannot die;
There are thoughts that make the strong heart weak,
And bring a pallor into the cheek
And a mist before the eye.
And the words of that fatal song
Come over me like a chill:
"A boy's will is the wind's will,
And the thoughts of youth are long, long thoughts."

Strange to me now are the forms I meet
When I visit the dear old town;
But the native air is pure and sweet,
And the trees that o'ershadow each well-known street,
As they balance up and down,
Are singing the beautiful song,
Are sighing and whispering still:
"A boy's will is the wind's will,
And the thoughts of youth are long, long thoughts."

And Deering's Woods are fresh and fair,
And with joy that is almost pain
My heart goes back to wander there,
And among the dreams of the days that were,
I find my lost youth again.
And the strange and beautiful song,
The groves are repeating it still:
"A boy's will is the wind's will,
And the thoughts of youth are long, long thoughts."

Paul Revere's Ride

LISTEN, my children, and you shall hear
Of the midnight ride of Paul Revere,
On the eighteenth of April, in Seventy-five;
Hardly a man is now alive
Who remembers that famous day and year.

He said to his friend, "If the British march
By land or sea from the town to-night,
Hang a lantern aloft in the belfry arch
Of the North Church tower as a signal light,—
One, if by land, and two, if by sea;
And I on the opposite shore will be,
Ready to ride and spread the alarm
Through every Middlesex village and farm,
For the country-folk to be up and to arm."

Then he said, "Good night!" and with muffled oar
Silently rowed to the Charlestown shore,
Just as the moon rose over the bay,
Where swinging wide at her moorings lay
The Somerset, British man-of-war;
A phantom ship, with each mast and spar
Across the moon like a prison bar,
And a huge black hulk, that was magnified
By its own reflection in the tide.

Meanwhile, his friend, through alley and street,
Wanders and watches with eager ears,
Till in silence around him he hears
The muster of men at the barrack door,
The sound of arms, and the tramp of feet,
And the measured tread of the grenadiers,
Marching down to their boats on the shore.

Then he climbed to the tower of the church,
Up the wooden stairs, with stealthy tread,
To the belfry-chamber overhead,
And startled the pigeons from their perch
On the sombre rafters, that round him made
Masses and moving shapes of shade—
Up the trembling ladder, steep and tall,
To the highest window in the wall,
Where he paused to listen and look down
A moment on the roofs of the town,
And the moonlight flowing over all.

Beneath, in the churchyard, lay the dead,
In their night-encampment on the hill,
Wrapped in silence so deep and still
That he could hear, like a sentinel's tread,
The watchful night-wind, as it went
Creeping along from tent to tent,
And seeming to whisper, "All is well!"
A moment only he feels the spell
Of the place and the hour, and the secret dread
Of the lonely belfry and the dead;
For suddenly all his thoughts are bent
On a shadowy something far away,
Where the river widens to meet the bay,—
A line of black that bends and floats
On the rising tide, like a bridge of boats.

Meanwhile, impatient to mount and ride,
Booted and spurred, with a heavy stride

On the opposite shore walked Paul Revere.
Now he patted his horse's side,
Now gazed at the landscape far and near,
Then, impetuous, stamped the earth,
And turned and tightened his saddle-girth;
But mostly he watched with eager search
The belfry-tower of the Old North Church,
As it rose above the graves on the hill,
Lonely and spectral and sombre and still.
And lo! as he looks, on the belfry's height
A glimmer, and then a gleam of light!
He springs to the saddle, the bridle he turns,
But lingers and gazes, till full on his sight
A second lamp in the belfry burns!

A hurry of hoofs in a village street,
A shape in the moonlight, a bulk in the dark,
And beneath, from the pebbles, in passing, a spark
Struck out by a steed flying fearless and fleet;
That was all! And yet, through the gloom and the light,
The fate of a nation was riding that night;
And the spark struck out by that steed, in his flight,
Kindled the land into flame with its heat.

He has left the village and mounted the steep,
And beneath him, tranquil and broad and deep,
Is the Mystic, meeting the ocean tides;
And under the alders, that skirt its edge,
Now soft on the sand, now loud on the ledge,
Is heard the tramp of his steed as he rides.

It was twelve by the village clock,
When he crossed the bridge into Medford town.
He heard the crowing of the cock,
And the barking of the farmer's dog,
And felt the damp of the river fog,
That rises after the sun goes down.

It was one by the village clock,
When he galloped into Lexington.
He saw the gilded weathercock
Swim in the moonlight as he passed,
And the meeting-house windows, blank and bare,
Gaze at him with spectral glare,
As if they already stood aghast
At the bloody work they would look upon.

It was two by the village clock,
When he came to the bridge in Concord town.
He heard the bleating of the flock,
And the twitter of birds among the trees,
And felt the breath of the morning breeze
Blowing over the meadows brown.
And one was safe and asleep in his bed
Who at the bridge would be first to fall,
Who that day would be lying dead,
Pierced by a British musket-ball.

You know the rest. In the books you have read,
How the British Regulars fired and fled,—
How the farmers gave them ball for ball,
From behind each fence and farmyard wall,
Chasing the red-coats down the lane,
Then crossing the fields to emerge again
Under the trees at the turn of the road,
And only pausing to fire and load.

So through the night rode Paul Revere;
And so through the night went his cry of alarm
To every Middlesex village and farm,—
A cry of defiance and not of fear,

A voice in the darkness, a knock at the door,
And a word that shall echo for evermore!
For, borne on the night-wind of the Past,
Through all our history, to the last,
In the hour of darkness and peril and need,
The people will waken and listen to hear
The hurrying hoof-beats of that steed,
And the midnight message of Paul Revere.

The Bells of Lynn

HEARD AT NAHANT

O CURFEW of the setting sun! O Bells of Lynn!
O requiem of the dying day! O Bells of Lynn!

From the dark belfries of yon cloud-cathedral wafted,
Your sounds aerial seem to float, O Bells of Lynn!

Borne on the evening wind across the crimson twilight,
O'er land and sea they rise and fall, O Bells of Lynn!

The fisherman in his boat, far out beyond the headland,
Listens, and leisurely rows ashore, O Bells of Lynn!

Over the shining sands the wandering cattle homeward
Follow each other at your call, O Bells of Lynn!

The distant lighthouse hears, and with his flaming signal
Answers you, passing the watch-word on, O Bells of Lynn!

And down the darkening coast run the tumultuous surges,
And clap their hands, and shout to you, O Bells of Lynn!

Till from the shuddering sea, with your wild incantations,
Ye summon up the spectral moon, O Bells of Lynn!

And startled at the sight, like the weird woman of Endor,
Ye cry aloud, and then are still, O Bells of Lynn!

JOHN GREENLEAF WHITTIER
(1807-1892)

Vesta

O CHRIST of God! whose life and death
Our own have reconciled,
Most quietly, most tenderly
Take home thy star-named child!

Thy grace is in her patient eyes,
Thy words are on her tongue;
The very silence round her seems
As if the angels sung.

Her smile is as a listening child's
Who hears its mother's call;
The lilies of Thy perfect peace
About her pillow fall.

She leans from out our clinging arms
To rest herself in Thine;
Alone to Thee, dear Lord, can we
Our well-beloved resign.

O, less for her than for ourselves
We bow our heads and pray;
Her setting star, like Bethlehem's,
To Thee shall point the way!

Barbara Frietchie

UP from the meadows rich with corn,
Clear in the cool September morn,

The clustered spires of Frederick stand
Green-walled by the hills of Maryland.

Round about them orchards sweep,
Apple and peach tree fruited deep,

Fair as the garden of the Lord
To the eyes of the famished rebel horde,

On that pleasant morn of the early fall
When Lee marched over the mountain wall;

Over the mountains winding down,
Horse and foot, into Frederick town.

Forty flags with their silver stars,
Forty flags with their crimson bars,

Flapped in the morning wind: the sun
Of noon looked down, and saw not one.

Up rose old Barbara Frietchie then,
Bowed with her fourscore years and ten;

Bravest of all in Frederick town,
She took up the flag the men hauled down.

In her attic window the staff she set,
To show that one heart was loyal yet.

Up the street came the rebel tread,
Stonewall Jackson riding ahead.

Under his slouched hat left and right
He glanced; the old flag met his sight.

"Halt!"—the dust-brown ranks stood fast.
"Fire!"—out blazed the rifle-blast.

It shivered the window, pane and sash;
It rent the banner with seam and gash.

Quick, as it fell, from the broken staff
Dame Barbara snatched the silken scarf.

She leaned far out on the window-sill,
And shook it forth with a royal will.

"Shoot, if you must, this old gray head,
But spare your country's flag," she said.

A shade of sadness, a blush of shame,
Over the face of the leader came;

The nobler nature within him stirred
To life at that woman's deed and word;

"Who touches a hair of yon gray head
Dies like a dog! March on!" he said.

All day long through Frederick street
Sounded the tread of marching feet:

All day long that free flag tossed
Over the heads of the rebel host.

Ever its torn folds rose and fell
On the loyal winds that loved it well;

And through the hill-gaps sunset light
Shone over it with a warm good-night.

Barbara Frietchie's work is o'er,
And the Rebel rides on his raids no more.

Honor to her! and let a tear
Fall, for her sake, on Stonewall's bier.

Over Barbara Frietchie's grave,
Flag of Freedom and Union, wave!

Peace and order and beauty draw
Round thy symbol of light and law;

And ever the stars above look down
On thy stars below in Frederick town!

Skipper Ireson's Ride

Of all the rides since the birth of time,
Told in story or sung in rhyme,—
On Apuleius's Golden Ass,
Or one-eyed Calender's horse of brass,
Witch astride of a human back,
Islam's prophet on Al-Borák,—
The strangest ride that ever was sped
Was Ireson's, out from Marblehead!
Old Floyd Ireson, for his hard heart,
Tarred and feathered and carried in a cart
By the women of Marblehead!

Body of turkey, head of owl,
Wings a-droop like a rained-on fowl,
Feathered and ruffled in every part,
Skipper Ireson stood in the cart.
Scores of women, old and young,
Strong of muscle, and glib of tongue,

Pushed and pulled up the rocky lane,
Shouting and singing the shrill refrain:
"Here's Flud Oirson, fur his horrd horrt
Torr'd an' futherr'd an' corr'd in a corrt
By the women o' Morble'ead!"

Wrinkled scolds with hands on hips,
Girls in bloom of cheek and lips,
Wild-eyed, free-limbed, such as chase
Bacchus round some antique vase,
Brief of skirt, with ankles bare,
Loose of kerchief and loose of hair,
With conch-shells blowing and fish-horns' twang,
Over and over the Mænads sang:
"Here's Flud Oirson, fur his horrd horrt,
Torr'd an' futherr'd an' corr'd in a corrt
By the women o' Morble'ead!"

Small pity for him!—He sailed away
From a leaking ship on Chaleur Bay,—
Sailed away from a sinking wreck,
With his own town's-people on her deck!
"Lay by! lay by!" they called to him.
Back he answered, "Sink or swim!
Brag of your catch of fish again!"
And off he sailed through the fog and rain!
Old Floyd Ireson, for his hard heart,
Tarred and feathered and carried in a cart
By the women of Marblehead!

Fathoms deep in dark Chaleur
That wreck shall lie forevermore.
Mother and sister, wife and maid,
Looked from the rocks of Marblehead
Over the moaning and rainy sea,—
Looked for the coming that might not be!
What did the winds and the sea-birds say
Of the cruel captain who sailed away?—
Old Floyd Ireson, for his hard heart,
Tarred and feathered and carried in a cart
By the women of Marblehead!

Through the street, on either side,
Up flew windows, doors swung wide;
Sharp-tongued spinsters, old wives gray,
Treble lent the fish-horn's bray.
Sea-worn grandsires, cripple-bound,
Hulks of old sailors run aground,
Shook head, and fist, and hat, and cane,
And cracked with curses the hoarse refrain:
"Here's Flud Oirson, fur his horrd horrt,
Torr'd an' futherr'd an' corr'd in a corrt
By the women o' Morble'ead!"

Sweetly along the Salem road
Bloom of orchard and lilac showed.
Little the wicked skipper knew
Of the fields so green and sky so blue.
Riding there in his sorry trim,
Like an Indian idol glum and grim,
Scarcely he seemed the sound to hear
Of voices shouting, far and near:
"Here's Flud Oirson, fur his horrd horrt,
Torr'd an' futherr'd an' corr'd in a corrt
By the women o' Morble'ead!"

"Hear me, neighbors!" at last he cried,—
"What to me is this noisy ride?
What is the shame that clothes the skin
To the nameless horror that lives within?
Waking or sleeping, I see a wreck,
And hear a cry from a reeling deck!
Hate me and curse me,—I only dread
The hand of God and the face of the dead!"
Said old Floyd Ireson, for his hard heart,
Tarred and feathered and carried in a cart
By the women of Marblehead!

Then the wife of the skipper lost at sea
Said, "God has touched him! why should we!"
Said an old wife mourning her only son,
"Cut the rogue's tether and let him run!"

So with soft relentings and rude excuse,
Half scorn, half pity, they cut him loose,
And gave him a cloak to hide him in,
And left him alone with his shame and sin.

Poor Floyd Ireson, for his hard heart,
Tarred and feathered and carried in a cart
By the women of Marblehead!

EDGAR ALLAN POE (1809-1849)

The City in the Sea

Lo! Death has reared himself a throne
In a strange city lying alone
Far down within the dim West,
Where the good and the bad and the worst and the best
Have gone to their eternal rest.
There shrines and palaces and towers
(Time-eaten towers that tremble not)
Resemble nothing that is ours.
Around, by lifting winds forgot,
Resignedly beneath the sky
The melancholy waters lie.

No rays from the holy heaven come down
On the long night-time of that town;
But light from out the lurid sea
Streams up the turrets silently,
Gleams up the pinnacles far and free:
Up domes, up spires, up kingly halls,
Up fanes, up Babylon-like walls,
Up shadowy long-forgotten bowers
Of sculptured ivy and stone flowers,
Up many and many a marvellous shrine
Whose wreathèd friezes intertwine
The viol, the violet, and the vine.

Resignedly beneath the sky
The melancholy waters lie.
So blend the turrets and shadows there
That all seem pendulous in air,
While from a proud tower in the town
Death looks gigantically down.

There open fanes and gaping graves
Yawn level with the luminous waves;
But not the riches there that lie
In each idol's diamond eye,—
Not the gayly-jewelled dead,
Tempt the waters from their bed;
For no ripples curl, alas,
Along that wilderness of glass;
No swellings tell that winds may be
Upon some far-off happier sea;
No heavings hint that winds have been
On seas less hideously serene!

But lo, a stir is in the air!
The wave—there is a movement there!
As if the towers had thrust aside,
In slightly sinking, the dull tide;
As if their tops had feebly given
A void within the filmy Heaven!
The waves have now a redder glow,
The hours are breathing faint and low;
And when, amid no earthly moans,
Down, down that town shall settle hence,
Hell, rising from a thousand thrones,
Shall do it reverence.

The Raven

ONCE upon a midnight dreary, while I pondered, weak and weary,
Over many a quaint and curious volume of forgotten lore,
While I nodded, nearly napping, suddenly there came a tapping,
As of some one gently rapping, rapping at my chamber door.
" 'Tis some visitor," I muttered, "tapping at my chamber door—
Only this and nothing more."

Ah, distinctly I remember it was in the bleak December,
And each separate dying ember wrought its ghost upon the floor.
Eagerly I wished the morrow; vainly I had sought to borrow
From my books surcease of sorrow—sorrow for the lost Lenore,
For the rare and radiant maiden whom the angels name Lenore—
Nameless *here* for evermore.

And the silken, sad, uncertain rustling of each purple curtain
Thrilled me—filled me with fantastic terrors never felt before;
So that now, to still the beating of my heart, I stood repeating,
" 'Tis some visitor entreating entrance at my chamber door—
Some late visitor entreating entrance at my chamber door—
This it is and nothing more."

Presently my soul grew stronger: hesitating then no longer,
"Sir," said I, "or Madam, truly your forgiveness I implore;
But the fact is I was napping, and so gently you came rapping,
And so faintly you came tapping, tapping at my chamber door,
That I scarce was sure I heard you"—here I opened wide the door—
Darkness there and nothing more.

Deep into that darkness peering, long I stood there, wondering, fearing,
Doubting, dreaming dreams no mortal ever dared to dream before;
But the silence was unbroken, and the stillness gave no token,
And the only word there spoken was the whispered word "Lenore!"
This I whispered, and an echo murmured back the word "Lenore!"
Merely this and nothing more.

Back into the chamber turning, all my soul within me burning,
Soon again I heard a tapping, somewhat louder than before.
"Surely," said I, "surely that is something at my window lattice;
Let me see, then, what thereat is, and this mystery explore,—
Let my heart be still a moment and this mystery explore—
'Tis the wind and nothing more."

Open here I flung the shutter, when, with many a flirt and flutter,
In there stepped a stately Raven of the saintly days of yore.
Not the least obeisance made he, not a minute stopped or stayed he,
But with mien of lord or lady perched above my chamber door—
Perched upon a bust of Pallas just above my chamber door—
Perched and sat, and nothing more.

Then, this ebony bird beguiling my sad fancy into smiling
By the grave and stern decorum of the countenance it wore,
"Though thy crest be shorn and shaven, thou," I said, "art sure no craven,
Ghastly, grim, and ancient Raven, wandering from the nightly shore:
Tell me what thy lordly name is on the night's Plutonian shore!"
Quoth the Raven, "Nevermore."

Much I marveled this ungainly fowl to hear discourse so plainly,
Though its answer little meaning, little relevancy bore;
For we cannot help agreeing that no living human being
Ever yet was blessed with seeing bird above his chamber door—
Bird or beast upon the sculptured bust above his chamber door—
With such name as "Nevermore."

But the Raven, sitting lonely on the placid bust, spoke only
That one word, as if his soul in that one word he did outpour.
Nothing farther then he uttered, not a feather then he fluttered;
Till I scarcely more than muttered, "Other friends have flown before;
On the morrow *he* will leave me, as my hopes have flown before."
Then the bird said, "Nevermore."

Startled at the stillness broken by reply so aptly spoken,
"Doubtless," said I, "what it utters is its only stock and store,
Caught from some unhappy master whom unmerciful Disaster
Followed fast and followed faster till his songs one burden bore,
Till the dirges of his hope that melancholy burden bore
Of 'Never—nevermore.' "

But the Raven still beguiling my sad fancy into smiling,
Straight I wheeled a cushioned seat in front of bird and bust and door;
Then, upon the velvet sinking, I betook myself to linking
Fancy unto fancy, thinking what this ominous bird of yore,
What this grim, ungainly, ghastly, gaunt, and ominous bird of yore
Meant in croaking "Nevermore."

Thus I sat engaged in guessing, but no syllable expressing
To the fowl whose fiery eyes now burned into my bosom's core;
This and more I sat divining, with my head at ease reclining
On the cushion's velvet lining that the lamp-light gloated o'er,
But whose velvet violet lining, with the lamp-light gloating o'er,
She shall press, ah, nevermore!

Then, methought, the air grew denser, perfumed from an unseen censer
Swung by seraphim whose footfalls tinkled on the tufted floor.
"Wretch!" I cried, "thy God hath lent thee,—by these angels he hath sent thee,
Respite—respite and nepenthe from thy memories of Lenore!
Quaff, oh quaff this kind nepenthe, and forget this lost Lenore!"
Quoth the Raven, "Nevermore."

"Prophet!" said I, "thing of evil, prophet still, if bird or devil!
Whether Tempter sent, or whether tempest tossed thee here ashore,
Desolate yet all undaunted, on this desert land enchanted—
On this home by horror haunted—tell me truly, I implore,
Is there—is there balm in Gilead?—tell me—tell me, I implore!"
Quoth the Raven, "Nevermore."

"Prophet!" said I, "thing of evil, prophet still, if bird or devil!
By that Heaven that bends above us—by that God we both adore—
Tell this soul with sorrow laden if, within the distant Aidenn,
It shall clasp a sainted maiden whom the angels name Lenore—
Clasp a rare and radiant maiden whom the angels name Lenore."
Quoth the Raven, "Nevermore."

"Be that word our sign of parting, bird or fiend!" I shrieked, up-starting;
"Get thee back into the tempest and the night's Plutonian shore!
Leave no black plume as a token of that lie thy soul hath spoken!
Leave my loneliness unbroken!—Quit the bust above my door!
Take thy beak from out my heart, and take thy form from off my door!"
Quoth the Raven, "Nevermore."

And the Raven, never flitting, still is sitting, still is sitting
On the pallid bust of Pallas just above my chamber door;
And his eyes have all the seeming of a demon's that is dreaming,
And the lamp-light o'er him streaming throws his shadow on the floor;
And my soul from out that shadow that lies floating on the floor
Shall be lifted—nevermore!

Ulalume

THE skies they were ashen and sober;
The leaves they were crispèd and sere,
The leaves they were withering and sere;
It was night in the lonesome October
Of my most immemorial year;
It was hard by the dim lake of Auber,
In the misty mid region of Weir:
It was down by the dank tarn of Auber,
In the ghoul-haunted woodland of Weir.

Here once, through an alley Titanic
Of cypress, I roamed with my Soul—
Of cypress, with Psyche, my Soul.
These were days when my heart was volcanic
As the scoriac rivers that roll,
As the lavas that restlessly roll
Their sulphurous currents down Yaanek
In the ultimate climes of the pole,
That groan as they roll down Mount Yaanek
In the realms of the boreal pole.

Our talk had been serious and sober,
But our thoughts they were palsied and sere,
Our memories were treacherous and sere,
For we knew not the month was October,
And we marked not the night of the year,
(Ah, night of all nights in the year!)
We noted not the dim lake of Auber
(Though once we had journeyed down here),
Remembered not the dank tarn of Auber
Nor the ghoul-haunted woodland of Weir.

And now, as the night was senescent
And star-dials pointed to morn,
As the star-dials hinted of morn,
At the end of our path a liquescent
And nebulous lustre was born,
Out of which a miraculous crescent
Arose with a duplicate horn,
Astarte's bediamonded crescent
Distinct with its duplicate horn.

And I said—"She is warmer than Dian:
She rolls through an ether of sighs,
She revels in a region of sighs:
She has seen that the tears are not dry on
These cheeks, where the worm never dies,
And has come past the stars of the Lion
To point us the path to the skies,
To the Lethean peace of the skies:
Come up, in despite of the Lion,
To shine on us with her bright eyes:
Come up through the lair of the Lion,
With love in her luminous eyes."

But Psyche, uplifting her finger,
Said—"Sadly this star I mistrust,
Her pallor I strangely mistrust:
Oh, hasten!—oh, let us not linger!
Oh, fly!—let us fly!—for we must."
In terror she spoke, letting sink her
Wings until they trailed in the dust;
In agony sobbed, letting sink her
Plumes till they trailed in the dust,
Till they sorrowfully trailed in the dust.

I replied—"This is nothing but dreaming:
Let us on by this tremulous light!
Let us bathe in this crystalline light!
Its sibyllic splendor is beaming
With hope and in beauty to-night:
See, it flickers up the sky through the night!
Ah, we safely may trust to its gleaming,
And be sure it will lead us aright:
We safely may trust to a gleaming
That cannot but guide us aright,
Since it flickers up to Heaven through the night."

Thus I pacified Psyche and kissed her,
And tempted her out of her gloom,
And conquered her scruples and gloom;

And we passed to the end of the vista,
But were stopped by the door of a tomb,
By the door of a legended tomb;
And I said—"What is written, sweet sister,
On the door of this legended tomb?"
She replied—"Ulalume—Ulalume—
'Tis the vault of thy lost Ulalume!"

Then my heart it grew ashen and sober
As the leaves that were crispèd and sere,
As the leaves that were withering and sere,
And I cried—"It was surely October
On this very night of last year
That I journeyed—I journeyed down here,
That I brought a dread burden down here:
On this night of all nights in the year,
Ah, what demon has tempted me here?
Well I know, now, this dim lake of Auber,
This misty mid region of Weir:
Well I know, now, this dank tarn of Auber,
This ghoul-haunted woodland of Weir."

To Helen

HELEN, thy beauty is to me
Like those Nicæan barks of yore
That gently, o'er a perfumed sea,
The weary way-worn wanderer bore
To his own native shore.

On desperate seas long wont to roam,
Thy hyacinth hair, thy classic face,
Thy Naiad airs have brought me home
To the glory that was Greece,
And the grandeur that was Rome.

Lo, in yon brilliant window-niche
How statue-like I see thee stand,
The agate lamp within thy hand,
Ah! Psyche, from the regions which
Are holy land!

For Annie

THANK Heaven! the crisis—
The danger is past,
And the lingering illness
Is over at last—
And the fever called "Living"
Is conquer'd at last.

Sadly, I know
I am shorn of my strength,
And no muscle I move
As I lie at full length:
But no matter—I feel
I am better at length.

And I rest so composedly
Now, in my bed,
That any beholder
Might fancy me dead—
Might start at beholding me,
Thinking me dead.

The moaning and groaning,
The sighing and sobbing,
Are quieted now,
With that horrible throbbing
At heart—ah, that horrible,
Horrible throbbing!

The sickness—the nausea—
The pitiless pain—
Have ceased, with the fever
That madden'd my brain—
With the fever called "Living"
That burn'd in my brain.

And O! of all tortures
That torture the worst
Has abated—the terrible
Torture of thirst
For the naphthaline river
Of Passion accurst—
I have drunk of a water
That quenches all thirst.

—Of a water that flows,
With a lullaby sound,
From a spring but a very few
Feet under ground—

From a cavern not very far
Down under ground.

And ah! let it never
Be foolishly said
That my room it is gloomy,
And narrow my bed;
For man never slept
In a different bed—
And, to *sleep,* you must slumber
In just such a bed.

My tantalized spirit
Here blandly reposes,
Forgetting, or never
Regretting its roses—
Its old agitations
Of myrtles and roses:

For now, while so quietly
Lying, it fancies
A holier odour
About it, of pansies—
A rosemary odour,
Commingled with pansies—
With rue and the beautiful
Puritan pansies.

And so it lies happily,
Bathing in many
A dream of the truth
And the beauty of Annie—
Drown'd in a bath
Of the tresses of Annie.

She tenderly kiss'd me,
She fondly caress'd,
And then I fell gently
To sleep on her breast—
Deeply to sleep
From the heaven of her breast.

When the light was extinguish'd,
She cover'd me warm,
And she pray'd to the angels
To keep me from harm—
To the queen of the angels
To shield me from harm.

And I lie so composedly,
Now, in my bed
(Knowing her love),
That you fancy me dead—
And I rest so contentedly,
Now, in my bed
(With her love at my breast),
That you fancy me dead—
That you shudder to look at me,
Thinking me dead.

But my heart it is brighter
Than all of the many
Stars in the sky,
For it sparkles with Annie—
It glows with the light
Of the love of my Annie—
With the thought of the light
Of the eyes of my Annie.

Annabel Lee

It was many and many a year ago,
In a kingdom by the sea,
That a maiden there lived whom you may know
By the name of Annabel Lee.
And this maiden she lived with no other thought
Than to love and be loved by me.

I was a child and she was a child
In this kingdom by the sea:
But we loved with a love that was more than love—
I and my Annabel Lee,
With a love that the wingèd seraphs of heaven
Coveted her and me.

And this was the reason that, long ago,
In this kingdom by the sea,
A wind blew out of a cloud, chilling
My beautiful Annabel Lee,
So that her high-born kinsmen came
And bore her away from me,
To shut her up in a sepulchre
In this kingdom by the sea.

The angels, not half so happy in heaven,
  Went envying her and me—
Yes! that was the reason (as all men know,
  In this kingdom by the sea)
That the wind came out of the cloud one night,
  Chilling and killing my Annabel Lee.
But our love it was stronger by far than the love
  Of those who were older than we—
  Of many far wiser than we—
And neither the angels in heaven above,
  Nor the demons down under the sea,
Can ever dissever my soul from the soul
  Of the beautiful Annabel Lee:

For the moon never beams without bringing me dreams
  Of the beautiful Annabel Lee;
And the stars never rise, but I feel the bright eyes
  Of the beautiful Annabel Lee;
And so, all the night-tide, I lie down by the side
  Of my darling—my darling—my life and my bride,
  In her sepulchre there by the sea,
  In her tomb by the sounding sea.

The Masque of the Red Death

(NORTHERN ITALY)

THE "Red Death" had long devastated the country. No pestilence had ever been so fatal, or so hideous. Blood was its avatar and its seal—the redness and the horror of blood. There were sharp pains, and sudden dizziness, and then profuse bleeding at the pores, with dissolution. The scarlet stains upon the body, and especially upon the face, of the victim were the pest ban which shut him out from the aid and from the sympathy of his fellow-men. And the whole seizure, progress, and termination of the disease were the incidents of half an hour.

But the Prince Prospero was happy and dauntless and sagacious. When his dominions were half depopulated, he summoned to his presence a thousand hale and light-hearted friends from among the knights and dames of his court, and with these retired to the deep seclusion of one of his castellated abbeys. This was an extensive and magnificent structure, the creation of the Prince's own eccentric yet august taste. A strong and lofty wall girdled it in. This wall had gates of iron. The courtiers, having entered, brought furnaces and massy hammers, and welded the bolts. They resolved to leave means neither of ingress or egress to the sudden impulses of despair or of frenzy from within. The abbey was amply provisioned. With such precautions the courtiers might bid defiance to contagion. The external world could take care of itself. In the mean time it was folly to grieve, or to think. The Prince had provided all the appliances of pleasure. There were buffoons, there were improvisatori, there were ballet-dancers, there were musicians, there was Beauty, there was wine. All these and security were within. Without was the "Red Death."

It was toward the close of the fifth or sixth month of his seclusion, and while the pestilence raged most furiously abroad, that the Prince Prospero entertained his thousand friends at a masked ball of the most unusual magnificence.

It was a voluptuous scene, that masquerade. But first let me tell of the rooms in which it was held. There were seven—an imperial suite. In many palaces, however, such suites form a long and straight vista, while the folding-doors slide back nearly to the walls on either hand, so that the view of the whole extent is scarcely impeded. Here the case was very different, as might have been expected from the Prince's love of the bizarre. The apartments were so irregularly disposed that the vision embraced but little more than one at a time. There was a sharp turn at every twenty or thirty yards, and at each turn a novel effect. To the right and left, in the middle of each wall, a tall and narrow Gothic window looked out upon a closed corridor which pursued the windings of the suite. These windows were of stained glass, whose color varied in accordance with the prevailing hue of the decorations of the chamber into which it opened. That at the eastern extremity was hung, for example, in blue—and vividly blue were its windows. The second chamber was purple in its ornaments and tapestries, and here the panes were purple. The third was green throughout, and so were the casements. The fourth was furnished and lighted with orange, the fifth with white, the sixth with violet. The seventh apartment was closely shrouded in black velvet tapestries that hung all over the ceiling and down the walls, falling in heavy folds upon a carpet of the same material and hue. But, in this chamber only, the color of the windows failed to correspond with the decorations. The panes here were scarlet—a deep blood-color. Now in no one of the seven apartments was there any lamp or candelabrum, amid the profusion of golden ornaments that lay scattered to and fro or depended from the roof. There was no light of any kind emanating from lamp or candle within the suite of chambers. But in the corridors that followed the suite there stood, opposite to each window, a heavy tripod, bearing a brazier of fire, that projected its rays through the tinted glass and so glaringly illumined the room. And thus were produced a multitude of gaudy and fantastic appearances. But in the western or black chamber the effect of the firelight that streamed upon the dark hangings through the blood-tinted panes was ghastly in the extreme, and produced so wild a look upon the countenances of those who entered that there were few of the company bold enough to set foot within its precincts at all.

It was in this apartment, also, that there stood against the western wall a gigantic clock of ebony. Its pendulum swung to and fro with a dull, heavy, monotonous clang; and when the minute-hand made the circuit of the face, and the hour was to be stricken, there came from the brazen lungs of the clock a sound which was clear and loud and deep and exceedingly musical, but of so peculiar a note and emphasis that, at each lapse of an hour, the musicians of the orchestra were constrained to pause, momentarily, in their performance, to hearken to the sound; and thus the waltzers perforce ceased their evolutions; and there was a brief disconcert of the whole gay company; and, while the chimes of the clock yet rang, it was observed that the giddiest grew pale, and the more aged and sedate passed their hands over their brows as if in confused revery or meditation. But when the echoes had fully ceased, a light laughter at once pervaded the assembly; the musicians looked at each other and smiled as if at their own nervousness and folly, and made whispering vows, each to the other, that the next chiming of the clock should produce in them no similar emotion; and then, after the lapse of sixty minutes (which embrace three thousand and six hundred seconds of the Time that flies) there came yet another chiming of the clock, and then were the same disconcert and tremulousness and meditation as before.

But, in spite of these things, it was a gay and magnificent revel. The tastes of the Prince were peculiar. He had a fine eye for colors and effects. He disregarded the *decora* of mere fashion. His plans were bold and fiery, and his conceptions glowed with barbaric lustre. There are some who would have thought him mad. His followers felt that he was not. It was necessary to hear and see and touch him to be *sure* that he was not.

He had directed, in great part, the movable embellishments of the seven chambers, upon occasion of this great *fête;* and it was his own guiding taste which had given character to the masqueraders. Be sure they were grotesque. There were much glare and glitter and piquancy and phantasm—much of what has been since seen in *Hernani*. There were arabesque figures with unsuited limbs and appointments. There were delirious fancies such as the madman fashions. There was much of the beautiful, much of the wanton, much of the bizarre, something of the terrible, and not a little of that which might have excited disgust. To and fro in the seven chambers there stalked, in fact, a multitude of dreams. And these—the dreams—writhed in and about, taking hue from the rooms, and causing the wild music of the orchestra to seem as the echo of their steps. And, anon, there strikes the ebony clock which stands in the hall of the velvet. And then, for a moment, all is still, and all is silent save the voice of the clock. The dreams are stiff-frozen as they stand. But the echoes of the chime die away—they have endured but an instant—and a light, half-subdued laughter floats after them as they depart. And now again the music swells, and the dreams live, and writhe to and fro more merrily than ever, taking hue from the many tinted windows through which stream the rays from the tripods. But to the chamber which lies most westwardly of the seven, there are now none of the maskers who venture; for the night is waning away, and there flows a ruddier light through the blood-colored panes; and the blackness of the sable drapery appalls; and to him whose foot falls upon the sable carpet, there comes from the near clock of ebony a muffled peal more solemnly emphatic than any which reaches *their* ears who indulge in the more remote gayeties of the other apartments.

But these other apartments were densely crowded, and in them beat feverishly the heart of life. And the revel went whirlingly on, until at length there commenced the sounding of midnight upon the clock. And then the music ceased, as I have told; and the evolutions of the waltzers were quieted; and there was an uneasy cessation of all things as before. But now there were twelve strokes to be sounded by the bell of the clock; and thus it happened, perhaps, that more of thought crept, with more of time, into the meditations of the thoughtful among those who revelled. And thus too it happened, perhaps, that before the last echoes of the last chime had utterly sunk into silence, there were many individuals in the crowd who had found leisure to become aware of the presence of a masked figure which had arrested the attention of no single individual before. And the rumor of this new presence having spread itself whisperingly around, there arose at length from the whole company a buzz, or murmur, expressive of disapprobation and surprise—then, finally, of terror, of horror, and of disgust.

In an assembly of phantasms such as I have painted, it may well be supposed that no ordinary appearance could have excited such sensation. In truth the masquerade license of the night was nearly unlimited; but the figure in question had out-Heroded Herod, and gone beyond the bounds of even the Prince's indefinite decorum. There are chords in the hearts of the most reckless which cannot be touched without emotion. Even with the utterly lost, to whom life and death are equally jests, there are matters of which no jest can be made. The whole company, indeed, seemed now deeply to feel that in the costume and bearing of the stranger neither wit nor propriety existed. The figure was tall and gaunt, shrouded from head to foot in the habiliments of the grave. The mask which concealed the visage was made so nearly to resemble the countenance of a stiffened corpse that the closest scrutiny must have had difficulty in detecting the cheat. And yet all this might have been endured, if not approved, by the mad revellers around. But the mummer had gone so far as to assume the type of the Red Death. His vesture was dabbled in *blood*—and his broad brow, with all the features of the face, was besprinkled with the scarlet horror.

When the eyes of Prince Prospero fell upon this spectral image (which with a slow and solemn movement, as if more fully to sustain its *rôle,* stalked to and fro among the waltzers) he was seen to be convulsed, in the first moment, with a strong shudder either of terror or distaste; but, in the next, his brow reddened with rage.

"Who dares?" he demanded hoarsely of the courtiers who stood near him—"who dares insult us with this blasphemous mockery? Seize him and unmask him—that we may know whom we have to hang at sunrise, from the battlements!"

It was in the eastern or blue chamber in which stood the Prince Prospero as he uttered these words. They rang throughout the seven rooms loudly and clearly—for the Prince was a bold and robust man, and the music had become hushed at the waving of his hand.

It was in the blue room where stood the Prince, with a group of pale courtiers by his side. At first, as he spoke, there was a slight rushing movement of this group in the direction of the intruder, who at the moment was also near at hand, and now, with deliberate and stately step, made closer approach to the speaker. But from a certain nameless awe with which the mad assumptions of the mummer had inspired the whole party, there were found none who put forth hand to seize him; so that, unimpeded, he passed within a yard of the Prince's person; and, while the vast assembly, as if with one impulse, shrank from the centres of the rooms to the walls, he made his way uninterruptedly, but with the same solemn and measured step which had distinguished him from the first, through the blue chamber to the purple—through the purple to the green—through the green to the orange—through this again to the white—and even thence to the violet, ere a decided movement had been made to arrest him. It was then, however, that the Prince Prospero, maddening with rage and the shame of his own momentary cowardice, rushed hurriedly through the six chambers, while none followed him on account of a deadly terror that had seized upon all. He bore aloft a drawn dagger, and had approached, in rapid impetuosity, to within three or four feet of the retreating figure, when the latter, having attained the extremity of the velvet apartment, turned suddenly and confronted his pursuer. There was a sharp cry—and the dagger dropped gleaming upon the sable carpet, upon which, instantly afterwards, fell prostrate in death the Prince Prospero. Then, summoning the wild courage of despair, a throng of the revellers at once threw themselves into the black apartment, and, seizing the mummer, whose tall figure stood erect and motionless within the shadow of the ebony clock, gasped in unutterable horror at finding the grave cerements and corpse-like mask, which they handled with so violent a rudeness, untenanted by any tangible form.

And now was acknowledged the presence of the Red Death. He had come like a thief in the night. And one by one dropped the revellers in the blood-bedewed halls of their revel, and died each in the despairing posture of his fall. And the life of the ebony clock went out with that of the last of the gay. And the flames of the tripods expired. And Darkness and Decay and the Red Death held illimitable dominion over all.

The Fall of the House of Usher

Son cœur est un luth suspendu;
Sitôt qu'on le touche il résonne.
Béranger.

During the whole of a dull, dark, and soundless day in the autumn of the year, when the clouds hung oppressively low in the heavens, I had been passing alone, on horseback, through a singularly dreary tract of country; and at length found myself, as the shades of the evening drew on, within view of the melancholy House of Usher. I know not how it was—but, with the first glimpse of the building, a sense of insufferable gloom pervaded my spirit. I say insufferable; for the feeling was unrelieved by any of that half-pleasurable, because poetic, sentiment with which the mind usually receives even the sternest natural images of the desolate or terrible. I looked upon the scene before me—upon the mere house, and the simple landscape features of the domain, upon the bleak walls, upon the vacant eye-like windows, upon a few rank sedges, and upon a few white trunks of decayed trees—with an utter depression of soul which I can compare to no earthly sensation more properly than to the after-dream of the reveller upon opium: the bitter lapse into everyday life, the hideous dropping off of the veil. There was an iciness, a sinking, a sickening of the heart, an unredeemed dreariness of thought which no goading of the imagination could torture into aught of the sublime. What was it—I paused to think—what was it that so unnerved me in the contemplation of the House of Usher? It was a mystery all insoluble; nor could I grapple with the shadowy fancies that crowded upon me as I pondered. I was forced to fall back upon the unsatisfactory conclusion, that while, beyond doubt, there *are* combinations of very simple natural objects which have the power of thus affecting us, still the analysis of this power lies among considerations beyond our depth. It was possible, I reflected, that a mere different arrangement of the particulars of the scene, of the details of the picture, would be sufficient to modify, or perhaps to annihilate, its capacity for sorrowful impression; and acting upon this idea, I reined my horse to the precipitous brink of a black and lurid tarn that lay in unruffled lustre by the dwelling, and gazed down—but with a shudder even more thrilling than before—upon the remodelled and inverted images of the gray sedge, and the ghastly tree-stems, and the vacant and eye-like windows.

Nevertheless, in this mansion of gloom I now proposed to myself a sojourn of some weeks. Its proprietor, Roderick Usher, had been one of my boon companions in boyhood; but many years had elapsed since our last meeting. A letter, however, had lately reached me in a distant part of the country—a letter from him—which in its wildly importunate nature had admitted of no other than a personal reply. The MS. gave evidence of nervous agitation. The writer spoke of acute bodily illness, of a mental disorder which oppressed him, and of an earnest desire to see me, as his best and indeed his only personal friend, with a view of attempting, by the cheerfulness of my society, some alleviation of his malady. It was the manner in which all this, and much more, was said—it was the apparent *heart* that went with his request—which allowed me no room for hesitation; and I accordingly obeyed forthwith what I still considered a very singular summons.

Although as boys we had been even intimate associates, yet I really knew little of my friend. His reserve had been always excessive and habitual. I was aware, however, that his very ancient family had been noted, time out of mind, for a peculiar sensibility of temperament, displaying itself, through long ages, in many works of exalted art, and manifested of late in repeated deeds of munificent yet unobtrusive charity, as well as in a passionate devotion to the intricacies, perhaps even more than to the orthodox and easily recognizable beauties, of musical science. I had learned, too, the very remarkable fact that the stem of the Usher race, all time-honored as it was, had put forth at no period any enduring branch; in other words, that the entire family lay in the direct line of descent, and had always, with very trifling and very temporary variation, so lain. It was this deficiency, I considered, while running over in thought the perfect keeping of the character of the premises with the accredited character of the people, and while speculating upon the possible influence which the one, in the long lapse of centuries, might have exercised upon the other—it was this deficiency perhaps, of collateral issue, and the consequent undeviating transmission from sire to son of the patrimony with the name, which had, at length, so identified the two as to merge the original title of the estate in the quaint and equivocal appellation of the "House of Usher"—an appellation which seemed to include, in the minds of the peasantry who used it, both the family and the family mansion.

I have said that the sole effect of my somewhat childish experiment, that of looking down within the tarn, had been to deepen the first singular impression. There can be no doubt that the consciousness of the rapid increase of my superstition—for why should I not so term it?—served mainly to accelerate the increase itself. Such, I have long known, is the paradoxical law of all sentiments having terror as a basis. And it might have been for this reason only, that, when I again uplifted my eyes to the house itself, from its image in the pool, there grew in my mind a strange fancy—a fancy so ridiculous, indeed, that I but mention it to show the vivid force of the sensations which oppressed me. I had so worked upon my imagination as really to believe that about the whole mansion and domain there hung an atmosphere peculiar to themselves and their immediate vicinity: an atmosphere which had no affinity with the air of heaven, but which had reeked up from the decayed trees, and the gray wall, and the silent tarn: a pestilent and mystic vapor, dull, sluggish, faintly discernible, and leaden-hued.

Shaking off from my spirit what *must* have been a dream, I scanned more narrowly the real aspect of the building. Its principal feature seemed to be that of an excessive antiquity. The discoloration of ages had been great. Minute fungi overspread the whole exterior, hanging in a fine tangled web-work from the eaves. Yet all this was apart from any extraordinary dilapidation. No portion of the masonry had fallen: and there appeared to be a wild inconsistency between its still perfect adaptation of parts and the crumbling condition of the individual stones. In this there was much that reminded me of the specious totality of old wood-work which has rotted for long years in some neglected vault, with no disturbance from the breath of the external air. Beyond this indication of extensive decay, however, the fabric gave little token of instability. Perhaps the eye of a scrutinizing observer might have discovered a barely perceptible fissure, which, extending from the roof of the building in front, made its way down the wall in a zigzag direction, until it became lost in the sullen waters of the tarn.

Noticing these things, I rode over a short causeway to the house. A servant in waiting took my horse, and I entered the Gothic archway of the hall. A valet, of stealthy step, thence conducted me, in silence, through many dark and intricate passages in my progress to the studio of his master. Much that I encountered on the way contributed, I know not how, to heighten the vague sentiments of which I have already spoken. While the objects around me—while the carvings of the ceilings, the sombre tapestries of the walls, the ebon blackness of the floors, and the phantasmagoric armorial trophies which rattled as I strode, were but matters to which, or to such as which, I had been accustomed from my infancy—while I hesitated not to acknowledge how familiar was all this—I still wondered to find how unfamiliar were the fancies which ordinary images were stirring up. On one of the staircases, I met the physician of the family. His countenance, I thought, wore a mingled expression of low cunning and perplexity. He accosted me with trepidation and passed on. The valet now threw open a door and ushered me into the presence of his master.

The room in which I found myself was very large and lofty. The windows were long, narrow, and pointed, and at so vast a distance from the black oaken floor as to be altogether inaccessible from within. Feeble gleams of encrimsoned light made their way through the trellised panes, and served to render sufficiently distinct the more prominent objects around; the eye, however, struggled in vain to reach the remoter angles of the chamber, or the recesses of the vaulted and fretted ceiling. Dark draperies hung upon the walls. The general furniture was profuse, comfortless, antique, and tattered. Many books and musical instruments lay scattered about, but failed to give any vitality to the scene. I felt that I breathed an atmosphere of sorrow. An air of stern, deep, and irredeemable gloom hung over all and pervaded all.

Upon my entrance, Usher arose from a sofa on which he had been lying at full length, and greeted me with a vivacious warmth which had much in it, I at first thought, of an overdone cordiality—of the constrained effort of the *ennuyé* man of the world. A glance, however, at his countenance, convinced me of his perfect sincerity. We sat down: and for some moments, while he spoke not, I gazed upon him with a feeling half of pity, half of awe. Surely man had never before so terribly altered, in so brief a period, as had Roderick Usher! It was with difficulty that I could bring myself to admit the identity of the wan being before me with the companion of my early boyhood. Yet the character of his face had been at all times remarkable. A cadaverousness of complexion; an eye large, liquid, and luminous beyond comparison; lips somewhat thin and very pallid, but of a surpassingly beautiful curve; a nose of a delicate Hebrew model, but with a breadth of nostril unusual in similar formations; a finely moulded chin, speaking, in its want of prominence, of a want of moral energy; hair of a more than web-like softness and tenuity; these features, with an inordinate expansion above the regions of the temple, made up altogether a countenance not easily to be forgotten. And now in the mere exaggeration of the prevailing character of these features, and of the expression they were wont to convey, lay so much of change that I doubted to whom I spoke. The now ghastly pallor of the skin, and the now miraculous lustre of the eye, above all things startled and even awed me. The silken hair, too, had been suffered to grow all unheeded, and as, in its wild gossamer texture, it floated rather than fell about the face, I could not, even with effort, connect its arabesque expression with any idea of simple humanity.

In the manner of my friend I was at once struck with an incoherence, an inconsistency; and I soon found this to arise from a series of feeble and futile struggles to overcome an habitual trepidancy, an excessive nervous agitation. For something of this nature I had indeed been prepared, no less by his letter than by reminiscences of certain boyish traits, and by conclusions deduced from his peculiar physical conformation and temperament. His action was alternately vivacious and sullen. His voice varied rapidly from a tremulous indecision (when the animal spirits seemed utterly in abeyance) to that species of energetic concision—that abrupt, weighty, unhurried, and hollow-sounding enunciation — that leaden, self-balanced and perfectly modulated guttural utterance—which may be observed in the lost drunkard, or the irreclaimable eater of opium, during the periods of his most intense excitement.

It was thus that he spoke of the object of my visit, of his earnest desire to see me, and of the solace he expected me to afford him. He entered, at some length, into what he conceived to be the nature of his malady. It was, he said, a constitutional and a family evil, and one for which he despaired to find a remedy—a mere nervous affection, he immediately added, which would undoubtedly soon pass off. It displayed itself in a host of unnatural sensations. Some of these, as he detailed them, interested and bewildered me; although, perhaps, the terms and the general manner of the narration had their weight. He suffered much from a morbid acuteness of the senses; the most insipid food was alone endurable; he could wear only garments of certain texture; the odors of all flowers were oppressive; his eyes were tortured by even a faint light; and there were but peculiar sounds, and these from stringed instruments, which did not inspire him with horror.

To an anomalous species of terror I found him a bounden slave. "I shall perish," said he, "I *must* perish in this deplorable folly. Thus, thus, and not otherwise, shall I be lost. I dread the events of the future, not in themselves, but in their results. I shudder at the thought of any, even the most trivial, incident, which may operate upon this intolerable agitation of soul. I have, indeed, no abhorrence of danger, except in its absolute effect—in terror. In this unnerved—in this pitiable condition, I feel that the period will sooner or later arrive when I must abandon life and reason together, in some struggle with the grim phantasm, FEAR."

I learned moreover at intervals, and through broken and equivocal hints, another singular feature of his mental condition. He was enchained by certain superstitious impressions in regard to the dwelling which he tenanted, and whence, for many years, he had never ventured forth—in regard to an influence whose supposititious force was conveyed in terms too shadowy here to be re-stated—an influence which some peculiarities in the mere form and substance of his family mansion, had by dint of long sufferance, he said, obtained over his spirit—an effect which the physique of the gray walls and turrets, and of the dim tarn into which they all looked down, had, at length, brought about upon the morale of his existence.

He admitted, however, although with hesitation, that much of the peculiar gloom which thus afflicted him could be traced to a more natural and far more palpable origin—to the severe and long-continued illness, indeed to the evidently approaching dissolution, of a tenderly beloved sister—his sole companion for long years, his last and only relative on earth. "Her decease," he said, with a bitterness which I can never forget, "would leave him (him the hopeless and the frail) the last of the ancient race of the Ushers." While he spoke, the lady Madeline (for so was she called) passed slowly through a remote portion of the apartment, and, without having noticed my presence, disappeared. I regarded her with an utter astonishment not unmingled with dread, and yet I found it impossible to account for such feelings. A sensation of stupor oppressed me, as my eyes followed her retreating steps. When a door, at length, closed upon her, my glance sought instinctively and eagerly the countenance of the brother; but he had buried his face in his hands, and I could only perceive that a far more than ordinary wanness had overspread the emaciated fingers through which trickled many passionate tears.

The disease of the lady Madeline had long baffled the skill of her physicians. A settled apathy, a gradual wasting away of the person, and frequent although transient affections of a partially cataleptical character, were the unusual diagnosis. Hitherto she had steadily borne up against the pressure of her malady, and had not betaken herself finally to bed; but, on the closing in of the evening of my arrival at the house, she succumbed (as her brother told me at night with inexpressible agitation) to the prostrating power of the destroyer; and I learned that the glimpse I had obtained of her person would thus probably be the last I should obtain—that the lady, at least while living, would be seen by me no more.

For several days ensuing, her name was unmentioned by either Usher or myself; and during this period I was busied in earnest endeavors to alleviate the melancholy of my friend. We painted and read together; or I listened, as if in a dream, to the wild improvisations of his speaking guitar. And thus, as a closer and still closer intimacy admitted me more unreservedly into the recesses of his spirit, the more bitterly did I perceive the futility of all attempt at cheering a mind from which darkness, as if an inherent positive quality, poured forth upon all objects of the moral and physical universe, in one unceasing radiation of gloom.

I shall ever bear about me a memory of the many solemn hours I thus spent alone with the master of the House of Usher. Yet I should fail in any attempt to convey an idea of the exact character of the studies, or of the occupations, in which he involved me, or led me the way. An excited and highly distempered ideality threw a sulphureous lustre over all. His long improvised dirges will ring forever in my ears. Among other things, I hold painfully in mind a certain singular perversion and amplification of the wild air of the last waltz of Von Weber. From the paintings over which his elaborate fancy brooded, and which grew, touch by touch, into vaguenesses at which I shuddered the more thrillingly because I shuddered knowing not why;—from these paintings (vivid as their images now are before me) I would in vain endeavor to educe more than a small portion which should lie within the compass of merely written words. By the utter simplicity, by the nakedness of his designs, he arrested and overawed attention. If ever mortal painted an idea, that mortal was Roderick Usher. For me at least, in the circumstances then surrounding me, there arose, out of the pure abstractions which the hypochondriac contrived to throw upon his canvas, an intensity of intolerable awe, no shadow of which felt I ever yet in the contemplation of the certainly glowing yet too concrete reveries of Fuseli.

One of the phantasmagoric conceptions of my friend, partaking not so rigidly of the spirit of abstraction, may be shadowed forth, although feebly, in words. A small picture presented the interior of an immensely long and rectangular vault or tunnel, with low walls, smooth, white, and without interruption or device. Certain accessory points of the design served well to convey the idea that this excavation lay at an exceeding depth below the surface of the earth. No outlet was observed in any portion of its vast extent, and no torch or other artificial source of light was discernible; yet a flood of intense rays rolled throughout, and bathed the whole in a ghastly and inappropriate splendor.

I have just spoken of that morbid condition of the auditory nerve which rendered all music intolerable to the sufferer, with the exception of certain effects of stringed instruments. It was, perhaps, the narrow limits to which he thus confined himself upon the guitar, which gave birth, in great measure, to the fantastic character of his performances. But the fervid *facility* of his impromptus could not be so accounted for. They must have been, and were, in the notes, as well as in the words of his wild fantasias (for he not unfrequently accompanied himself with rhymed verbal improvisations), the result of that intense mental collectedness and concentration to which I have previously alluded as observable only in particular moments of the highest artificial excitement. The words of one of these rhapsodies I have easily remembered. I was, perhaps, the more forcibly impressed with it, as he gave it, because, in the under or mystic current of its meaning, I fancied that I perceived, and for the first time, a full consciousness, on the part of Usher, of the tottering of his lofty reason upon her throne. The verses, which were entitled "The Haunted Palace," ran very nearly, if not accurately, thus:—

I

In the greenest of our valleys
  By good angels tenanted,
Once a fair and stately palace—
  Radiant palace—reared its head.
In the monarch Thought's dominion,
  It stood there;
Never seraph spread a pinion
  Over fabric half so fair.

II

Banners yellow, glorious, golden,
  On its roof did float and flow,
(This—all this—was in the olden
  Time long ago)

And every gentle air that dallied,
  In that sweet day,
Along the ramparts plumed and pallid,
  A wingèd odor went away.

III

Wanderers in that happy valley
  Through two luminous windows saw
Spirits moving musically
  To a lute's well-tunèd law,
Round about a throne where, sitting,
  Porphyrogene,
In state his glory well befitting,
  The ruler of the realm was seen.

IV

And all with pearl and ruby glowing
  Was the fair palace door,
Through which came flowing, flowing, flowing,
  And sparkling evermore,
A troop of Echoes whose sweet duty
  Was but to sing,
In voices of surpassing beauty,
  The wit and wisdom of their king.

V

But evil things, in robes of sorrow,
  Assailed the monarch's high estate;
(Ah, let us mourn, for never morrow
  Shall dawn upon him, desolate!)
And round about his home the glory
  That blushed and bloomed
Is but a dim-remembered story
  Of the old time entombed.

VI

And travellers now within that valley
  Through the red-litten windows see
Vast forms that move fantastically
  To a discordant melody;
While, like a ghastly rapid river,
  Through the pale door
A hideous throng rush out forever,
  And laugh—but smile no more.

I well remember that suggestions arising from this ballad led us into a train of thought, wherein there became manifest an opinion of

Usher's which I mention not so much on account of its novelty, (for other men have thought thus,) as on account of the pertinacity with which he maintained it. This opinion, in its general form, was that of the sentience of all vegetable things. But in his disordered fancy the idea had assumed a more daring character, and trespassed, under certain conditions, upon the kingdom of inorganization. I lack words to express the full extent, or the earnest *abandon* of his persuasion. The belief, however, was connected (as I have previously hinted) with the gray stones of the home of his forefathers. The conditions of the sentience had been here, he imagined, fulfilled in the method of collocation of these stones—in the order of their arrangement, as well as in that of the many fungi which overspread them, and of the decayed trees which stood around—above all, in the long undisturbed endurance of this arrangement, and in its reduplication in the still waters of the tarn. Its evidence—the evidence of the sentience—was to be seen, he said (and I here started as he spoke), in the gradual yet certain condensation of an atmosphere of their own about the waters and the walls. The result was discoverable, he added, in that silent, yet importunate and terrible influence which for centuries had moulded the destinies of his family, and which made *him* what I now saw him—what he was. Such opinions need no comment, and I will make none.

Our books—the books which, for years, had formed no small portion of the mental existence of the invalid—were, as might be supposed, in strict keeping with this character of phantasm. We pored together over such works as the Ververt and Chartreuse of Gresset; the Belphegor of Machiavelli; the Heaven and Hell of Swedenborg; the Subterranean Voyage of Nicholas Klimm by Holberg; the Chiromancy of Robert Flud, of Jean D'Indaginé, and of De la Chambre; the Journey into the Blue Distance of Tieck; and the City of the Sun of Campanella. One favorite volume was a small octavo edition of the *Directorium Inquisitorum,* by the Dominican Eymeric de Gironne; and there were passages in Pomponius Mela, about the old African Satyrs and Ægipans, over which Usher would sit dreaming for hours. His chief delight, however, was found in the perusal of an exceedingly rare and curious book in quarto Gothic—the manual of a forgotten church—the *Vigiliæ Mortuorum secundum Chorum Ecclesiæ Maguntinæ.*

I could not help thinking of the wild ritual of this work, and of its probable influence upon the hypochondriac, when one evening, having informed me abruptly that the lady Madeline was no more, he stated his intention of preserving her corpse for a fortnight, (previously to its final interment,) in one of the numerous vaults within the main walls of the building. The worldly reason, however, assigned for this singular proceeding, was one which I did not feel at liberty to dispute. The brother had been led to his resolution (so he told me) by consideration of the unusual character of the malady of the deceased, of certain obtrusive and eager inquiries on the part of her medical men, and of the remote and exposed situation of the burial-ground of the family. I will not deny that when I called to mind the sinister countenance of the person whom I met upon the staircase, on the day of my arrival at the house, I had no desire to oppose what I regarded as at best but a harmless, and by no means an unnatural, precaution.

At the request of Usher, I personally aided him in the arrangements for the temporary entombment. The body having been encoffined, we two alone bore it to its rest. The vault in which we placed it (and which had been so long unopened that our torches, half smothered in its oppressive atmosphere, gave us little opportunity for investigation) was small, damp, and entirely without means of admission for light; lying, at great depth, immediately beneath that portion of the building in which was my own sleeping apartment. It had been used, apparently, in remote feudal times, for the worst purposes of a donjon-keep, and in later days as a place of deposit for powder, or some other highly combustible substance, as a portion of its floor, and the whole interior of a long archway through which we reached it, were carefully sheathed with copper. The door, of massive iron, had been, also, similarly protected. Its immense weight caused an unusually sharp grating sound, as it moved upon its hinges.

Having deposited our mournful burden upon tressels within this region of horror, we partially turned aside the yet unscrewed lid of the coffin, and looked upon the face of the tenant. A striking similitude between the brother and sister now first arrested my attention; and Usher, divining, perhaps, my thoughts, murmured out some few words from which I learned that the deceased and himself had been twins, and that sympathies of a scarcely intelligible nature had always existed between them. Our glances, however, rested not long upon the dead—for we could not regard her unawed. The disease which had thus entombed the lady in the maturity of youth, had left, as usual in all maladies of a strictly cataleptical character, the mockery of a faint blush upon the bosom and the face, and that suspiciously lingering smile upon the lip which is so terrible in death. We replaced and screwed down the lid, and, having secured the door of iron, made our way, with toil, into the scarcely less gloomy apartments of the upper portion of the house.

And now, some days of bitter grief having elapsed, an observable change came over the features of the mental disorder of my friend. His ordinary manner had vanished. His ordinary occupations were neglected or forgotten. He roamed from chamber to chamber with hurried, unequal, and objectless step. The pallor of his countenance had assumed, if possible, a more ghastly hue—but the luminousness of his eye had utterly gone out. The once occasional huskiness of his tone was heard no more; and a tremulous quaver, as if of extreme terror, habitually characterized his utterance. There were times, indeed, when I thought his unceasingly agitated mind was laboring with some oppressive secret, to divulge which he struggled for the necessary courage. At times, again, I was obliged to resolve all into the mere inexplicable vagaries of madness, for I beheld him gazing upon vacancy for long hours, in an attitude of the profoundest attention, as if listening to some imaginary sound. It was no wonder that his condition terrified—that it infected me. I felt creeping upon me, by slow yet certain degrees, the wild influences of his own fantastic yet impressive superstitions.

It was, especially, upon retiring to bed late in the night of the seventh or eighth day after the placing of the lady Madeline within the donjon, that I experienced the full power of such feelings. Sleep came not near my couch, while the hours waned and waned away. I struggled to reason off the nervousness which had dominion over me. I endeavored to believe that much, if not all, of what I felt was due to the bewildering influence of the gloomy furniture of the room—of the dark and tattered draperies which, tortured into motion by the breath of a rising tempest, swayed fitfully to and fro upon the walls, and rustled uneasily about the decorations of the bed. But my efforts were fruitless. An irrepressible tremor gradually pervaded my frame; and at length there sat upon my very heart an incubus of utterly causeless alarm. Shaking this off with a gasp and a struggle, I uplifted myself upon the pillows, and, peering earnestly within the intense darkness of the chamber, hearkened—I know not why, except that an instinctive spirit prompted me—to certain low and indefinite sounds which came, through the pauses of the storm at long intervals, I knew not whence. Overpowered by an intense sentiment of horror, unaccountable yet unendurable, I threw on my clothes with haste, (for I felt that I should sleep no more during the night,) and endeavored to arouse myself from the pitiable condition into which I had fallen, by pacing rapidly to and fro through the apartment.

I had taken but few turns in this manner, when a light step on an adjoining staircase arrested my attention. I presently recognized it as that of Usher. In an instant afterward he rapped with a gentle touch at my door, and entered, bearing a lamp. His countenance was, as usual, cadaverously wan—but, moreover, there was a species of mad hilarity in his eyes—an evidently restrained hysteria in his whole demeanor. His air appalled me—but anything was preferable to the solitude which I had so long endured, and I even welcomed his presence as a relief.

"And you have not seen it?" he said abruptly, after having stared about him for some moments in silence—"you have not then seen it?—but, stay! you shall." Thus speaking, and having carefully shaded his lamp, he hurried to one of the casements, and threw it freely open to the storm.

The impetuous fury of the entering gust nearly lifted us from our feet. It was, indeed, a tempestuous yet sternly beautiful night, and one wildly singular in its terror and its beauty. A whirlwind had apparently collected its force in our vicinity; for there were frequent and violent alterations in the direction of the wind; and the exceeding density of the clouds (which hung so low as to press upon the turrets of the house) did not prevent our perceiving the life-like velocity with which they flew careering from all points against each other, without passing away into the distance. I say that even their exceeding density did not prevent our perceiving this; yet we had no glimpse of the moon or stars, nor was there any flashing forth of the lightning. But the under surfaces of the huge masses of agitated vapor, as well as all terrestrial objects immediately around us, were glowing in the unnatural light of a faintly luminous and distinctly visible gaseous exhalation which hung about and enshrouded the mansion.

"You must not—you shall not behold this!" said I, shudderingly, to Usher, as I led him with a gentle violence from the window to a seat. "These appearances, which bewilder you, are merely electrical phenomena not uncommon—or it may be that they have their ghastly origin in the rank miasma of the tarn. Let us close this casement; the air is chilling and dangerous to your frame. Here is one of your favorite romances. I will read, and you shall listen;—and so we will pass away this terrible night together."

The antique volume which I had taken up was the "Mad Trist" of Sir Launcelot Canning; but I had called it a favorite of Usher's more in sad jest than in earnest; for, in truth, there is little in its uncouth and unimaginative prolixity which could have had interest for the lofty and spiritual ideality of my friend. It was, however, the only book immediately at hand; and I indulged a vague hope that the excitement which now agitated the hypochondriac might find relief (for the history of mental disorder is full of similar anomalies) even in the extremeness of the folly which I should read. Could I have judged, indeed, by the wild overstrained air of vivacity with which he hearkened, or apparently hearkened, to the words of the tale, I might well have congratulated myself upon the success of my design.

I had arrived at that well-known portion of the story where Ethelred, the hero of the Trist, having sought in vain for peaceable admission into the dwelling of the hermit, proceeds to make good an entrance by force. Here, it will be remembered, the words of the narrative run thus:—

"And Ethelred, who was by nature of a doughty heart, and who was now mighty withal, on account of the powerfulness of the wine which he had drunken, waited no longer to hold parley with the hermit, who, in sooth, was of an obstinate and maliceful turn, but, feeling the rain upon his shoulders, and fearing the rising of the tempest, uplifted his mace outright, and with blows made quickly room in the plankings of the door for his gauntleted hand; and now pulling therewith sturdily, he so cracked, and ripped, and tore all asunder, that the noise of the dry and hollow-sounding wood alarumed and reverberated throughout the forest."

At the termination of this sentence I started, and for a moment paused; for it appeared to me (although I at once concluded that my excited fancy had deceived me)—it appeared to me that from some very remote portion of the mansion there came, indistinctly, to my ears, what might have been, in its exact similarity of character, the echo (but a stifled and dull one certainly) of the very cracking and ripping sound which Sir Launcelot had so particularly described. It was, beyond doubt, the coincidence alone which had arrested my attention; for, amid the rattling of the sashes of the casements, and the ordinary commingled noises of the still increasing storm, the sound, in itself, had nothing, surely, which would have interested or disturbed me. I continued the story:—

"But the good champion Ethelred, now entering within the door, was sore enraged and amazed to perceive no signal of the maliceful hermit; but, in the stead thereof, a dragon of a scaly and prodigious demeanor, and of a fiery tongue, which sate in guard before a palace of gold, with a floor of silver; and upon the wall there hung a shield of shining brass with this legend enwritten—

Who entereth herein, a conqueror hath bin;
Who slayeth the dragon, the shield he shall win.

And Ethelred uplifted his mace, and struck upon the head of the dragon, which fell before him, and gave up his pesty breath, with a shriek so horrid and harsh, and withal so piercing, that Ethelred had fain to close his ears with his hands against the dreadful noise of it, the like whereof was never before heard."

Here again I paused abruptly, and now with a feeling of wild amazement; for there could be no doubt whatever that, in this instance, I did actually hear (although from what direction it proceeded I found it impossible to say) a low and apparently distant, but harsh, protracted, and most unusual screaming or grating sound—the exact counterpart of what my fancy had already conjured up for the dragon's unnatural shriek as described by the romancer.

Oppressed, as I certainly was, upon the occurrence of this second and most extraordinary coincidence, by a thousand conflicting sensations, in which wonder and extreme terror were predominant, I still retained sufficient presence of mind to avoid exciting, by any observation, the sensitive nervousness of my companion. I was by no means certain that he had noticed the sounds in question; although, assuredly, a strange alteration had during the last few minutes taken place in his demeanor. From a position fronting my own, he had gradually brought round his chair, so as to sit with his face to the door of the chamber; and thus I could but partially perceive his features, although I saw that his lips trembled as if he were murmuring inaudibly. His head had dropped upon his breast—yet I knew that he was not asleep, from the wide and rigid opening of the eye as I caught a glance of it in profile. The motion of his body, too, was at variance with this idea—for he rocked from side to side with a gentle yet constant and uniform sway. Having rapidly taken notice of all this, I resumed the narrative of Sir Launcelot, which thus proceeded:—

"And now, the champion, having escaped from the terrible fury of the dragon, bethinking himself of the brazen shield, and of the breaking up of the enchantment which was upon it, removed the carcass from out of the way before him, and approached valorously over the silver pavement of the castle to where the shield was upon the wall; which in sooth tarried not for his full coming, but fell down at his feet upon the silver floor, with a mighty great and terrible ringing sound."

No sooner had these syllables passed my lips, than—as if a shield of brass had indeed, at the moment, fallen heavily upon a floor of silver—I became aware of a distinct, hollow, metallic and clangorous, yet apparently muffled reverberation. Completely unnerved, I leaped to my feet; but the measured rocking movement of Usher was undisturbed. I rushed to the chair in which he sat. His eyes were bent fixedly before him, and throughout his whole countenance there reigned a stony rigidity. But, as I placed my hand upon his shoulder, there came a strong shudder over his whole person; a sickly smile quivered about his lips; and I saw that he spoke in a low, hurried, and gibbering murmur, as if unconscious of my presence. Bending closely over him, I at length drank in the hideous import of his words.

"Not hear it?—yes, I hear it, and *have* heard it. Long—long—long—many minutes, many hours, many days, have I heard it—yet I dared not—oh, pity me, miserable wretch that I am!—I dared not—I *dared* not speak! *We have put her living in the tomb!* Said I not that my senses were acute? I *now* tell you that I heard her first feeble movements in the hollow coffin. I heard them—many, many days ago—yet I dared not—*I dared not speak!* And now—to-night—Ethelred—ha! ha!—the breaking of the hermit's door, and the death-cry of the dragon, and the clangor of the shield!—say, rather, the rending of her coffin, and the grating of the iron hinges of her prison, and her struggles within the coppered archway of the vault! Oh, whither shall I fly? Will she not be here anon? Is she not hurrying to upbraid me for my haste? Have I not heard her footstep on the stair? Do I not distinguish that heavy and horrible beating of her heart? Madman!"—here he sprang furiously to his feet, and shrieked out his syllables, as if in the effort he were giving up his soul—*"Madman! I tell you that she now stands without the door!"*

As if in the superhuman energy of his utterance there had been found the potency of a spell, the huge antique panels to which the speaker pointed threw slowly back, upon the instant, their ponderous and ebony jaws. It was the work of the rushing gust—but then without those doors there *did* stand the lofty and enshrouded figure of the lady Madeline of Usher. There was blood upon her white robes, and the evidence of some bitter struggle upon every portion of her emaciated frame. For a moment she remained trembling and reeling to and fro upon the threshold—then, with a low moaning cry, fell heavily inward upon the person of her brother, and, in her violent and now final death-agonies, bore him to the floor a corpse, and a victim to the terrors he had anticipated.

From that chamber, and from that mansion, I fled aghast. The storm was still abroad in all its wrath as I found myself crossing the old causeway. Suddenly there shot along the path a wild light, and I turned to see whence a gleam so unusual could have issued; for the vast house and its shadows were alone behind me. The radiance was that of the full, setting, and blood-red moon, which now shone vividly through that once barely discernible fissure, of which I have before spoken as extending from the roof of the building, in a zigzag direction, to the base. While I gazed, this fissure rapidly widened—there came a fierce breath of the whirlwind—the entire orb of the satellite burst at once upon my sight—my brain reeled as I saw the mighty walls rushing asunder—there was a long tumultuous shouting sound like the voice of a thousand waters—and the deep and dank tarn at my feet closed sullenly and silently over the fragments of the *"House of Usher."*

The Gold-Bug

What ho! what ho! this fellow is dancing mad!
He hath been bitten by the Tarantula.

All in the Wrong.

MANY years ago, I contracted an intimacy with a Mr. William Legrand. He was of an ancient Huguenot family, and had once been wealthy; but a series of misfortunes had reduced him to want. To avoid the mortification consequent upon his disasters, he left New Orleans, the city of his forefathers, and took up his residence at Sullivan's Island, near Charleston, South Carolina.

This island is a very singular one. It consists of little else than the sea sand, and is about three miles long. Its breadth at no point exceeds a quarter of a mile. It is separated from the main-land by a scarcely perceptible creek, oozing its way through a wilderness of reeds and slime, a favorite resort of the marsh-hen. The vegetation, as might be supposed, is scant, or at least dwarfish. No trees of any magnitude are to be seen. Near the western extremity, where Fort Moultrie stands, and where are some miserable frame buildings, tenanted during summer by the fugitives from Charleston dust and fever, may be found, indeed, the bristly palmetto; but the whole island, with the exception of this western point, and a line of hard white beach on the seacoast, is covered with a dense undergrowth of the sweet myrtle, so much prized by the horticulturists of England. The shrub here often attains the height of fifteen or twenty feet, and forms an almost impenetrable coppice, burdening the air with its fragrance.

In the utmost recesses of this coppice, not far from the eastern or more remote end of the island, Legrand had built himself a small hut, which he occupied when I first, by mere accident, made his acquaintance. This soon ripened into friendship—for there was much in the recluse to excite interest and esteem. I found him well educated, with unusual powers of mind, but infected with misanthropy, and subject to perverse moods of alternate enthusiasm and melancholy. He had with him many books, but rarely employed them. His chief amusements were gunning and fishing, or sauntering along the beach and through the myrtles, in quest of shells or entomological specimens;—his collection of the latter might have been envied by a Swammerdamm. In these excursions he was usually accompanied by an old negro, called Jupiter, who had been manumitted before the reverses of the family, but who could be induced, neither by threats nor by promises, to abandon what he considered his right of attendance upon the footsteps of his young "Massa Will." It is not improbable that the relatives of Legrand, conceiving him to be somewhat unsettled in intellect, had contrived to instil this obstinacy into Jupiter, with a view to the supervision and guardianship of the wanderer.

The winters in the latitude of Sullivan's Island are seldom very severe, and in the fall of the year it is a rare event indeed when a fire is considered necessary. About the middle of October, 18—, there occurred, however, a day of remarkable chilliness. Just before sunset I scrambled my way through the evergreens to the hut of my friend, whom I had not visited for several weeks—my residence being at that time in Charleston, a distance of nine miles from the island, while the facilities of passage and re-passage were very far behind those of the present day. Upon reaching the hut I rapped, as was my custom, and, getting no reply, sought for the key, where I knew it was secreted, unlocked the door and went in. A fine fire was blazing upon the hearth. It was a novelty, and by no means an ungrateful one. I threw off an overcoat, took an armchair by the crackling logs, and awaited patiently the arrival of my hosts.

Soon after dark they arrived, and gave me a most cordial welcome. Jupiter, grinning from ear to ear, bustled about to prepare some marsh-hens for supper. Legrand was in one of his fits—how else shall I term them?—of enthusiasm. He had found an unknown bivalve, forming a new genus, and, more than this, he had hunted down and secured, with Jupiter's assistance, a *scarabæus* which he believed to be totally new, but in respect to which he wished to have my opinion on the morrow.

"And why not to-night?" I asked, rubbing my hands over the blaze, and wishing the whole tribe of *scarabæi* at the devil.

"Ah, if I had only known you were here!" said Legrand, "but it's so long since I saw you; and how could I foresee that you would pay me a visit this very night of all others? As I was coming home I met Lieutenant G——, from the fort, and, very foolishly, I lent him the bug; so it will be impossible for you to see it until the morning. Stay here to-night, and I will send Jup down for it at sunrise. It is the loveliest thing in creation!"

"What?—sunrise?"

"Nonsense! no!—the bug. It is of a brilliant gold color—about the size of a large hickory-nut—with two jet black spots near one extremity of the back, and another, somewhat longer, at the other. The *antennæ* are—"

"Dey ain't *no* tin in him, Massa Will, I keep a tellin' on you," here interrupted Jupiter; "de bug is a goole-bug, solid, ebery bit of him, inside and all, 'sep him wing—neber feel half so hebby a bug in my life."

"Well, suppose it is, Jup," replied Legrand, somewhat more earnestly, it seemed to me, than the case demanded, "is that any reason for your letting the birds burn? The color"—here he turned to me—"is really almost enough to warrant Jupiter's idea. You never saw a more brilliant metallic lustre than the scales emit—but of this you cannot judge till to-morrow. In the mean time I can give you some idea of the shape." Saying this, he seated himself at a small table, on which were a pen and ink, but no paper. He looked for some in a drawer, but found none.

"Never mind," said he at length, "this will answer;" and he drew from his waistcoat pocket a scrap of what I took to be very dirty foolscap, and made upon it a rough drawing with the pen. While he did this, I retained my seat by the fire, for I was still chilly. When the design was complete, he handed it to me without rising. As I received it, a low growl was heard, succeeded by a scratching at the door. Jupiter opened it, and a large Newfoundland, belonging to Legrand, rushed in, leaped upon my shoulders, and loaded me with caresses; for I had shown him much attention during previous visits. When his gambols were over, I looked at the paper, and, to speak the truth, found myself not a little puzzled at what my friend had depicted.

"Well!" I said, after contemplating it for some minutes, "this *is* a strange *scarabæus*, I must confess; new to me: never saw anything like it before—unless it was a skull, or a death's-head, which it more nearly resembles than anything else that has come under *my* observation."

"A death's-head!" echoed Legrand—"Oh—yes—well, it has something of that appearance upon paper, no doubt. The two upper black spots look like eyes, eh? and the longer one at the bottom like a mouth—and then the shape of the whole is oval."

"Perhaps so," said I; "but, Legrand, I fear you are no artist. I must wait until I see the beetle itself, if I am to form any idea of its personal appearance."

"Well, I don't know," said he, a little nettled, "I draw tolerably—*should* do it at least—have had good masters, and flatter myself that I am not quite a blockhead."

"But, my dear fellow, you are joking then," said I, "this is a very passable *skull*,—indeed, I may say that it is a very *excellent* skull, according to the vulgar notions about such specimens of physiology—and your *scarabæus* must be the queerest *scarabæus* in the world if it resembles it. Why, we may get up a very thrilling bit of superstition upon this hint. I presume you will call the bug *scarabæus caput hominis,* or something of that kind—there are many similar titles in the Natural Histories. But where are the *antennæ* you spoke of?"

"The *antennæ!"* said Legrand, who seemed to be getting unaccountably warm upon the subject; "I am sure you must see the *antennæ.* I made them as distinct as they are in the original insect, and I presume that is sufficient."

"Well, well," I said, "perhaps you have—still I don't see them;" and I handed him the paper without additional remark, not wishing to ruffle his temper; but I was much surprised at the turn affairs had taken; his ill humor puzzled me—and, as for the drawing of the beetle, there were positively *no antennæ* visible, and the whole *did* bear a very close resemblance to the ordinary cuts of a death's-head.

He received the paper very peevishly, and was about to crumple it, apparently to throw it in the fire, when a casual glance at the design seemed suddenly to rivet his attention. In an instant his face grew violently red—in another as excessively pale. For some minutes he continued to scrutinize the drawing minutely where he sat. At length he arose, took a candle from the table, and proceeded to seat himself upon a sea-chest in the farthest corner of the room. Here again he made an anxious examination of the paper; turning it in all directions. He said nothing, however, and his conduct greatly astonished me; yet I thought it prudent not to exacerbate the growing moodiness of his temper by any comment. Presently he took from his coat pocket a wallet, placed the paper carefully in it, and deposited both in a writing-desk, which he locked. He now grew more composed in his demeanor; but his original air of enthusiasm had quite disappeared. Yet he seemed not so much sulky as abstracted. As the evening wore away he became more and more absorbed in revery, from which no sallies of mine could arouse him. It had been my intention to pass the night at the hut, as I had frequently done before, but, seeing my host in this mood, I deemed it proper to take leave. He did not press me to remain, but, as I departed, he shook my hand with even more than his usual cordiality.

It was about a month after this (and during the interval I had seen nothing of Legrand) when I received a visit, at Charleston, from his man, Jupiter. I had never seen the good old negro look so dispirited, and I feared that some serious disaster had befallen my friend.

"Well, Jup," said I, "what is the matter now?—how is your master?"

"Why, to speak de troof, massa, him not so berry well as mought be."

"Not well! I am truly sorry to hear it. What does he complain of?"

"Dar! dat's it!—him neber plain of notin'—but him berry sick for all dat."

"*Very* sick, Jupiter!—why didn't you say so at once? Is he confined to bed?"

"No, dat he ain't!—he ain't 'fined nowhar—dat's just whar de shoe pinch—my mind is got to be berry hebby 'bout poor Massa Will."

"Jupiter, I should like to understand what it is you are talking about. You say your master is sick. Hasn't he told you what ails him?"

"Why, massa, 'tain't worf while for to git mad 'bout de matter—Massa Will say noffin' at all ain't de matter wid him—but den what make him go about looking dis here way, wid he head down and he soldiers up, and as white as a gose? And den he keep a syphon all de time—"

"Keeps a what, Jupiter?"

"Keeps a syphon wid de figgurs on de slate—de queerest figgurs I ebber did see. I'se gittin' to be skeered, I tell you. Hab for to keep mighty tight eye 'pon him noovers. Todder day he gib me slip 'fore de sun up and was gone de whole ob de blessed day. I had a big stick ready cut for to gib him d——d good beating when he did come—but I'se sich a fool dat I hadn't de heart arter all—he look so berry poorly."

"Eh!—what?—ah yes!—upon the whole I think you had better not be too severe with the poor fellow—don't flog him, Jupiter—he can't very well stand it—but can you form no idea of what has occasioned this illness, or rather this change of conduct? Has anything unpleasant happened since I saw you?"

"No, massa, dey ain't bin noffin' onpleasant *since* den—'twas *'fore* den I'm feared—'twas de berry day you was dare."

"How? what do you mean?"

"Why, massa, I mean de bug—dare now."

"The what?"

"De bug—I'm berry sartain dat Massa Will bin bit somewhere 'bout de head by dat goole-bug."

"And what cause have you, Jupiter, for such a supposition?"

"Claws enuff, massa, and mouff too. I nebber did see sich a d——d bug—he kick and he bite ebery ting what cum near him. Massa Will cotch him fuss, but had for to let him go 'gin mighty quick, I tell you—den was de time he must ha' got de bite. I didn't like de look ob de bug mouff, myself, no how, so I wouldn't take hold ob him wid my finger, but I cotch him wid a piece ob paper dat I found. I wrap him up in de paper and stuff piece ob it in he mouff—dat was de way."

"And you think, then, that your master was really bitten by the beetle, and that the bite made him sick?"

"I don't tink noffin' about it—I nose it. What make him dream 'bout de goole so much, if 'tain't 'cause he bit by de goole-bug? I'se heerd 'bout dem goole-bugs 'fore dis."

"But how do you know he dreams about gold?"

"How I know? why 'cause he talk about it in he sleep—dat's how I nose."

"Well, Jup, perhaps you are right; but to what fortunate circumstance am I to attribute the honor of a visit from you to-day?"

"What de matter, massa?"

"Did you bring any message from Mr. Legrand?"

"No, massa, I bring dis here 'pissel;" and here Jupiter handed me a note which ran thus:

"MY DEAR ——, Why have I not seen you for so long a time? I hope you have not been so foolish as to take offence at any little *brusquerie* of mine; but no, that is improbable.

"Since I saw you I have had great cause for anxiety. I have something to tell you, yet scarcely know how to tell it, or whether I should tell it at all.

"I have not been quite well for some days past, and poor old Jup annoys me, almost beyond endurance, by his well-meant attentions. Would you believe it?—he had prepared a huge stick, the other day, with which to chastise me for giving him the slip, and spending the day, *solus,* among the hills on the mainland. I verily believe that my ill looks alone saved me a flogging.

"I have made no addition to my cabinet since we met.

"If you can, in any way, make it convenient, come over with Jupiter. *Do* come. I wish to see you *to-night,* upon business of importance. I assure you that it is of the *highest* importance.

"Ever yours,

"WILLIAM LEGRAND."

There was something in the tone of this note which gave me great uneasiness. Its whole style differed materially from that of Legrand. What could he be dreaming of? What new crotchet possessed his excitable brain? What "business of the highest importance" could *he* possibly have to transact? Jupiter's account of him boded no good. I dreaded lest the continued pressure of misfortune had, at length, fairly unsettled the reason of my friend. Without a moment's hesitation, therefore, I prepared to accompany the negro.

Upon reaching the wharf, I noticed a scythe and three spades, all apparently new, lying in the bottom of the boat in which we were to embark.

"What is the meaning of all this, Jup?" I inquired.

"Him syfe, massa, and spade."

"Very true; but what are they doing here?"

"Him de syfe and de spade what Massa Will 'sis 'pon my buying for him in de town, and de debbil's own lot of money I had to gib for 'em."

"But what, in the name of all that is mysterious, is your 'Massa Will' going to do with scythes and spades?"

"Dat's more dan *I* know, and debbil take me if I don't believe 'tis more dan he know, too. But it's all cum ob de bug."

Finding that no satisfaction was to be obtained of Jupiter, whose whole intellect seemed to be absorbed by "de bug," I now stepped into the boat and made sail. With a fair and strong breeze we soon ran into the little cove to the northward of Fort Moultrie, and a walk of some two miles brought us to the hut. It was about three in the afternoon when we arrived. Legrand had been awaiting us in eager expectation. He grasped my hand with a nervous *empressement,* which alarmed me and strengthened the suspicions already entertained. His countenance was pale even to ghastliness, and his deep-set eyes glared with unnatural lustre. After some inquiries respecting his health, I asked him, not knowing what better to say, if he had yet obtained the *scarabæus* from Lieutenant G——.

"Oh, yes," he replied, coloring violently, "I got it from him the next morning. Nothing should tempt me to part with that *scarabæus.* Do you know that Jupiter is quite right about it?"

"In what way?" I asked, with a sad foreboding at heart.

"In supposing it to be a bug of *real gold.*" He said this with an air of profound seriousness, and I felt inexpressibly shocked.

"This bug is to make my fortune," he continued, with a triumphant smile, "to reinstate me in my family possessions. Is it any wonder, then, that I prize it? Since Fortune has thought fit to bestow it upon me, I have only to use it properly and I shall arrive at the gold of which it is the index. Jupiter, bring me that *scarabæus!*"

"What! de bug, massa? I'd rudder not go fer trubble dat bug—you mus' git him for your own self." Hereupon Legrand arose, with a grave and stately air, and brought me the beetle from a glass case in which it was enclosed. It was a beautiful *scarabæus,* and, at that time, unknown to naturalists—of course a great prize in a scientific point of view. There were two round, black spots near one extremity of the back, and a long one near the other. The scales were exceedingly hard and glossy, with all the appearance of burnished gold. The weight of the insect was very remarkable, and, taking all things into consideration, I could hardly blame Jupiter for his opinion respecting it; but what to make of Legrand's agreement with that opinion, I could not, for the life of me, tell.

"I sent for you," said he, in a grandiloquent tone, when I had completed my examination of the beetle, "I sent for you, that I might have your counsel and assistance in furthering the views of Fate and of the bug"—

"My dear Legrand," I cried, interrupting him, "you are certainly unwell, and had better use some little precautions. You shall go to bed, and I will remain with you a few days, until you get over this. You are feverish and—"

"Feel my pulse," said he.

I felt it, and, to say the truth, found not the slightest indication of fever.

"But you may be ill, and yet have no fever. Allow me this once to prescribe for you. In the first place, go to bed. In the next—"

"You are mistaken," he interposed, "I am as well as I can expect to be under the excitement which I suffer. If you really wish me well, you will relieve this excitement."

"And how is this to be done?"

"Very easily. Jupiter and myself are going upon an expedition into the hills, upon the mainland, and, in this expedition, we shall need the aid of some person in whom we can confide. You are the only one we can trust. Whether we succeed or fail, the excitement which you now perceive in me will be equally allayed."

"I am anxious to oblige you in any way," I replied; "but do you mean to say that this infernal beetle has any connection with your expedition into the hills?"

"It has."

"Then, Legrand, I can become a party to no such absurd proceeding."

"I am sorry—very sorry—for we shall have to try it by ourselves."

"Try it by yourselves! The man is surely mad!—but stay—how long do you propose to be absent?"

"Probably all night. We shall start immediately, and be back, at all events, by sunrise."

"And will you promise me, upon your honor, that when this freak of yours is over, and the bug business (good God!) settled to your satisfaction, you will then return home and follow my advice implicitly, as that of your physician?"

"Yes; I promise; and now let us be off, for we have no time to lose."

With a heavy heart I accompanied my friend. We started about four o'clock—Legrand, Jupiter, the dog, and myself. Jupiter had with him the scythe and spades—the whole of which he insisted upon carrying, more through fear, it seemed to me, of trusting either of the implements within reach of his master, than from any excess of industry or complaisance. His demeanor was dogged in the extreme, and "dat d——d bug" were the sole words which escaped his lips during the journey. For my own part, I had charge of a couple of dark lanterns, while Legrand contented himself with the *scarabæus,* which he carried attached to the end of a bit of whip-cord; twirling it to and fro, with the air of a conjurer, as he went. When I observed this last, plain evidence of my friend's aberration of mind, I could scarcely refrain from tears. I thought it best, however, to humor his fancy, at least for the present, or until I could adopt some more energetic measures with a chance of success. In the meantime I endeavored, but all in vain, to sound him in regard to the object of the expedition. Having succeeded in inducing me to accompany him, he seemed unwilling to hold conversation upon any topic of minor importance, and to all my questions vouchsafed no other reply than "we shall see!"

We crossed the creek at the head of the island by means of a skiff, and, ascending the high grounds on the shore of the mainland, proceeded in a northwesterly direction, through a tract of country excessively wild and desolate, where no trace of a human footstep was to be seen. Legrand led the way with decision; pausing only for an instant, here and there, to consult what appeared to be certain landmarks of his own contrivance upon a former occasion.

In this manner we journeyed for about two hours, and the sun was just setting when we entered a region infinitely more dreary than any yet seen. It was a species of tableland, near the summit of an almost inaccessible hill, densely wooded from base to pinnacle, and interspersed with huge crags that appeared to lie loosely upon the soil, and in many cases were prevented from precipitating themselves into the valleys below merely by the support of the trees against which they reclined. Deep ravines, in various directions, gave an air of still sterner solemnity to the scene.

The natural platform to which we had clambered was thickly overgrown with brambles, through which we soon discovered that it would have been impossible to force our way but for the scythe; and Jupiter, by direction of his master, proceeded to clear for us a path to the foot of an enormously tall tulip-tree, which stood, with some eight or ten oaks, upon the level, and far surpassed them all, and all other trees which I had then ever seen, in the beauty of its foliage and form, in the wide spread of its branches, and in the general majesty of its appearance.

When we reached this tree, Legrand turned to Jupiter, and asked him if he thought he could climb it. The old man seemed a little staggered by the question, and for some moments made no reply. At length he approached the huge trunk, walked slowly around it, and examined it with minute attention. When he had completed his scrutiny, he merely said:

"Yes, massa, Jup climb any tree he ebber see in he life."

"Then up with you as soon as possible, for it will soon be too dark to see what we are about."

"How far mus' go up, massa?" inquired Jupiter.

"Get up the main trunk first, and then I will tell you which way to go—and here—stop! take this beetle with you."

"De bug, Massa Will!—de goole-bug!" cried the negro, drawing back in dismay—"what for mus' tote de bug way up de tree?—d—n if I do!"

"If you're afraid, Jup, a great big negro like you, to take hold of a harmless little dead beetle, why, you can carry it up by this string—but, if you do not take it up with you in some way, I shall be under the necessity of breaking your head with this shovel."

"What de matter now, massa?" said Jup, evidently shamed into compliance; "always want fur to raise fuss wid old nigger. Was only funnin' anyhow. *Me* feered de bug! what I keer for de bug?" Here he took cautiously hold of the extreme end of the string, and, maintaining the insect as far from his person as circumstances would permit, prepared to ascend the tree.

In youth, the tulip-tree, or *Liriodendron Tulipifera,* the most magnificent of American foresters, has a trunk peculiarly smooth, and often rises to a great height without lateral branches; but, in its riper age, the bark becomes gnarled and uneven, while many short limbs make their appearance on the stem. Thus the difficulty of ascension, in the present case, lay more in semblance than in reality. Embracing the huge cylinder, as closely as possible, with his arms and knees, seizing with his hands some projections, and resting his naked toes upon others, Jupiter, after one or two narrow escapes from falling, at length wriggled himself into the first great fork, and seemed to consider the whole business as virtually accomplished. The *risk* of the achievement was, in fact, now over, although the climber was some sixty or seventy feet from the ground.

"Which way mus' go now, Massa Will?" he asked.

"Keep up the largest branch,—the one on this side," said Legrand. The negro obeyed him promptly, and apparently with but little trouble, ascending higher and higher, until no glimpse of his squat figure could be obtained through the dense foliage which enveloped it. Presently his voice was heard in a sort of halloo.

"How much fudder is got for go?"

"How high up are you?" asked Legrand.

"Ebber so fur," replied the negro; "can see de sky fru de top ob de tree."

"Never mind the sky, but attend to what I say. Look down the trunk and count the limbs below you on this side. How many limbs have you passed?"

"One, two, three, four, fibe—I done pass fibe big limbs, massa, 'pon dis side."

"Then go one limb higher."

In a few minutes the voice was heard again, announcing that the seventh limb was attained.

"Now, Jup," cried Legrand, evidently much excited, "I want you to work your way out upon that limb as far as you can. If you see anything strange, let me know."

By this time what little doubt I might have entertained of my poor friend's insanity was put finally at rest. I had no alternative but to conclude him stricken with lunacy, and I became seriously anxious about getting him home. While I was pondering upon what was best to be done, Jupiter's voice was again heard.

"'Mos' feerd for to ventur 'pon dis limb berry far—'tis dead limb putty much all de way."

"Did you say it was a *dead* limb, Jupiter?" cried Legrand in a quavering voice.

"Yes, massa, him dead as de door-nail—done up for sartain—done departed dis here life."

"What in the name of heaven shall I do?" asked Legrand, seemingly in the greatest distress.

"Do!" said I, glad of an opportunity to interpose a word, "why come home and go to bed. Come now!—that's a fine fellow. It's getting late, and, besides, you remember your promise."

"Jupiter," cried he, without heeding me in the least, "do you hear me?"

"Yes, Massa Will, hear you ebber so plain."

"Try the wood well, then, with your knife, and see if you think it *very* rotten."

"Him rotten, massa, sure 'nuff," replied the negro in a few moments, "but not so berry rotten as mought be. Mought ventur out leetle way 'pon de limb by myself, dat's true."

"By yourself!—what do you mean?"

"Why, I mean de bug. 'Tis *berry* hebby bug. S'pose I drop him down fuss, and den de limb won't break wid just de weight ob one nigger."

"You infernal scoundrel!" cried Legrand, apparently much relieved, "what do you mean by telling me such nonsense as that? As sure as you let that beetle fall, I'll break your neck. Look here, Jupiter! do you hear me?"

"Yes, massa, needn't hollo at poor nigger dat style."

"Well! now listen!—if you will venture out on the limb as far as you think safe, and not let go the beetle, I'll make you a present of a silver dollar as soon as you get down."

"I'm gwine, Massa Will—'deed I is," replied the negro very promptly —"mos' out to the eend now."

"Out to the end!" here fairly screamed Legrand, "do you say you are out to the end of that limb?"

"Soon be to de eend, massa,—o-o-o-o-oh! Lor-gol-a-marcy! what *is* dis here 'pon de tree?"

"Well!" cried Legrand, highly delighted, "what is it?"

"Why 'tain't noffin' but a skull—somebody bin lef' him head up de tree, and de crows done gobble ebery bit ob de meat off."

"A skull, you say!—very well!—how is it fastened to the limb?—what holds it on?"

"Sure 'nuff, massa; mus' look. Why, dis berry curous sarcumstance, 'pon my word—dare's a great big nail in de skull, what fastens ob it on to de tree."

"Well now, Jupiter, do exactly as I tell you—do you hear?"

"Yes, massa."

"Pay attention, then!—find the left eye of the skull."

"Hum! hoo! dat's good! why, dar ain't no eye lef' at all."

"Curse your stupidity! do you know your right hand from your left?"

"Yes, I nose dat—nose all 'bout dat—'tis my lef' hand what I chops de wood wid."

"To be sure! you are left-handed; and your left eye is on the same side as your left hand. Now, I suppose, you can find the left eye of the skull, or the place where the left eye has been. Have you found it?"

Here was a long pause. At length the negro asked,

"Is de lef' eye of de skull 'pon de same side as de lef' hand of de skull, too?—'cause de skull ain't got not a bit ob hand at all—nebber mind! I got de lef' eye now—here de lef' eye! what mus' do wid it?"

"Let the beetle drop through it, as far as the string will reach—but be careful and not let go your hold of the string."

"All dat done, Massa Will; mighty easy ting for to put de bug fru de hole—look out for him dar below!"

During this colloquy no portion of Jupiter's person could be seen; but the beetle, which he had suffered to descend, was now visible at the end of the string, and glistened, like a globe of burnished gold, in the last rays of the setting sun, some of which still faintly illumined the eminence upon which we stood. The *scarabæus* hung quite clear of any branches, and, if allowed to fall, would have fallen at our feet. Legrand immediately took the scythe, and cleared with it a circular space, three or four yards in diameter, just beneath the insect, and, having accomplished this, ordered Jupiter to let go the string and come down from the tree.

Driving a peg, with great nicety, into the ground, at the precise spot where the beetle fell, my friend now produced from his pocket a tape-measure. Fastening one end of this at that point of the trunk of the tree which was nearest the peg, he unrolled it till it reached the peg, and thence farther unrolled it, in the direction already established by the two points of the tree and the peg, for the distance of fifty feet—Jupiter clearing away the brambles with the scythe. At the spot thus attained a second peg was driven, and about this, as a centre, a rude circle, about four feet in diameter, described. Taking now a spade himself, and giving one to Jupiter and one to me, Legrand begged us to set about digging as quickly as possible.

To speak the truth, I had no especial relish for such amusement at any time, and, at that particular moment, would most willingly have declined it; for the night was coming on, and I felt much fatigued with the exercise already taken; but I saw no mode of escape, and was fearful of disturbing my poor friend's equanimity by a refusal. Could I have depended, indeed, upon Jupiter's aid, I would have had no hesitation in attempting to get the lunatic home by force; but I was too well assured of the old negro's disposition to hope that he would assist me, under any circumstances, in a personal contest with his master. I made no doubt that the latter had been infected with some of the innumerable Southern superstitions about money buried, and that his fantasy had received confirmation by the finding of the *scarabæus,* or, perhaps, by Jupiter's obstinacy in maintaining it to be "a bug of real gold." A mind disposed to lunacy would readily be led away by such suggestions, especially if chiming in with favorite preconceived ideas; and then I called to mind the poor fellow's speech about the beetle's being "the index of his fortune." Upon the whole, I was sadly vexed and puzzled, but at length I concluded to make a virtue of necessity—to dig with a good will, and thus the sooner to convince the visionary, by ocular demonstration, of the fallacy of the opinions he entertained.

The lanterns having been lit, we all fell to work with a zeal worthy a more rational cause; and, as the glare fell upon our persons and implements, I could not help thinking how picturesque a group we composed, and how strange and suspicious our labors must have appeared to any interloper who, by chance, might have stumbled upon our whereabouts.

We dug very steadily for two hours. Little was said; and our chief embarrassment lay in the yelpings of the dog, who took exceeding interest in our proceedings. He, at length, became so obstreperous that we grew fearful of his giving the alarm to some stragglers in the vicinity; or, rather, this was the apprehension of Legrand; for myself, I should have rejoiced at any interruption which might have enabled me to get the wanderer home. The noise was, at length, very effectually silenced by Jupiter, who, getting out of the hole with a dogged air of deliberation, tied the brute's mouth up with one of his suspenders, and then returned, with a grave chuckle, to his task.

When the time mentioned had expired, we had reached a depth of five feet, and yet no signs of any treasure became manifest. A general pause ensued, and I began to hope that the farce was at an end. Legrand, however, although evidently much disconcerted, wiped his brow thoughtfully and recommenced. We had excavated the entire circle of four feet diameter, and now we slightly enlarged the limit, and went to the farther depth of two feet. Still nothing appeared. The gold-seeker, whom I sincerely pitied, at length clambered from the pit, with the bitterest disappointment imprinted upon every feature, and proceeded, slowly and reluctantly, to put on his coat, which he had thrown off at the beginning of his labor. In the mean time I made no remark. Jupiter, at a signal from his master, began to gather up his tools. This done, and the dog having been unmuzzled, we turned in profound silence towards home.

We had taken, perhaps, a dozen steps in this direction, when, with a loud oath, Legrand strode up to Jupiter, and seized him by the collar. The astonished negro opened his eyes and mouth to the fullest extent, let fall the spades, and fell upon his knees.

"You scoundrel," said Legrand, hissing out the syllables from between his clenched teeth—"you infernal black villain!—speak, I tell you!

—answer me this instant, without prevarication!—which—which is your left eye?"

"Oh, my golly, Massa Will! ain't dis here my lef' eye for sartain?" roared the terrified Jupiter, placing his hand upon his *right* organ of vision, and holding it there with a desperate pertinacity, as if in immediate dread of his master's attempt at a gouge.

"I thought so!—I knew it! hurrah!" vociferated Legrand, letting the negro go, and executing a series of curvets and caracoles, much to the astonishment of his valet, who, arising from his knees, looked mutely from his master to myself, and then from myself to his master.

"Come! we must go back," said the latter, "the game's not up yet;" and he again led the way to the tulip-tree.

"Jupiter," said he, when we reached its foot, "come here! was the skull nailed to the limb with the face outward, or with the face to the limb?"

"De face was out, massa, so dat de crows could get at de eyes good, widout any trouble."

"Well, then, was it this eye or that through which you dropped the beetle?"—here Legrand touched each of Jupiter's eyes.

"'Twas dis eye, massa—de lef' eye—jis' as you tell me," and here it was his right eye that the negro indicated.

"That will do—we must try it again."

Here my friend, about whose madness I now saw, or fancied that I saw, certain indications of method, removed the peg which marked the spot where the beetle fell, to a spot about three inches to the westward of its former position. Taking, now, the tape-measure from the nearest point of the trunk to the peg, as before, and continuing the extension in a straight line to the distance of fifty feet, a spot was indicated, removed by several yards, from the point at which we had been digging.

Around the new position a circle, somewhat larger than in the former instance, was now described, and we again set to work with the spades. I was dreadfully weary, but, scarcely understanding what had occasioned the change in my thoughts, I felt no longer any great aversion from the labor imposed. I had become most unaccountably interested—nay, even excited. Perhaps there was something, amid all the extravagant demeanor of Legrand—some air of forethought, or of deliberation—which impressed me. I dug eagerly, and now and then caught myself actually looking, with something that very much resembled expectation, for the fancied treasure, the vision of which had demented my unfortunate companion. At a period when such vagaries of thought most fully possessed me, and when we had been at work perhaps an hour and a half, we were again interrupted by the violent howlings of the dog. His uneasiness, in the first instance, had been evidently but the result of playfulness or caprice, but he now assumed a bitter and serious tone. Upon Jupiter's again attempting to muzzle him, he made furious resistance, and, leaping into the hole, tore up the mould frantically with his claws. In a few seconds he had uncovered a mass of human bones, forming two complete skeletons, intermingled with several buttons of metal, and what appeared to be the dust of decayed woollen. One or two strokes of a spade upturned the blade of a large Spanish knife, and, as we dug farther, three or four loose pieces of gold and silver coin came to light.

At sight of these the joy of Jupiter could scarcely be restrained, but the countenance of his master wore an air of extreme disappointment. He urged us, however, to continue our exertions, and the words were hardly uttered when I stumbled and fell forward, having caught the toe of my boot in a large ring of iron that lay half buried in the loose earth.

We now worked in earnest, and never did I pass ten minutes of more intense excitement. During this interval we had fairly unearthed an oblong chest of wood, which, from its perfect preservation and wonderful hardness, had plainly been subjected to some mineralizing process —perhaps that of the bichloride of mercury. This box was three feet and a half long, three feet broad, and two and a half feet deep. It was firmly secured by bands of wrought iron, riveted, and forming a kind of trellis-work over the whole. On each side of the chest, near the top, were three rings of iron—six in all—by means of which a firm hold could be obtained by six persons. Our utmost united endeavors served only to disturb the coffer very slightly in its bed. We at once saw the impossibility of removing so great a weight. Luckily, the sole fastenings of the lid consisted of two sliding bolts. These we drew back—trembling and panting with anxiety. In an instant, a treasure of incalculable value lay gleaming before us. As the rays of the lanterns fell within the pit, there flashed upwards, from a confused heap of gold and of jewels, a glow and a glare that absolutely dazzled our eyes.

I shall not pretend to describe the feelings with which I gazed. Amazement was, of course, predominant. Legrand appeared exhausted with excitement, and spoke very few words. Jupiter's countenance wore, for some minutes, as deadly a pallor as it is possible, in the nature of things, for any negro's visage to assume. He seemed stupefied—thunder-stricken. Presently he fell upon his knees in the pit, and, burying his naked arms up to the elbows in gold, let them there remain, as if enjoying the luxury of a bath. At length, with a deep sigh, he exclaimed, as if in a soliloquy:

"And dis all cum ob de goole-bug! de putty goole-bug! de poor little goole-bug, what I boosed in dat sabage kind ob style! Ain't you shamed ob yourself, nigger?—answer me dat!"

It became necessary, at last, that I should arouse both master and valet to the expediency of removing the treasure. It was growing late, and it behooved us to make exertion, that we might get everything housed before daylight. It was difficult to say what should be done, and much time was spent in deliberation—so confused were the ideas of all. We finally lightened the box by removing two-thirds of its contents, when we were enabled, with some trouble, to raise it from the hole. The articles taken out were deposited among the brambles, and the dog left to guard them, with strict orders from Jupiter neither, upon any pretence, to stir from the spot, nor to open his mouth until our return. We then hurriedly made for home with the chest; reaching the hut in safety, but after excessive toil, at one o'clock in the morning. Worn out as we were, it was not in human nature to do more just now. We rested until two, and had supper; starting for the hills immediately afterwards, armed with three stout sacks, which by good luck were upon the premises. A little before four we arrived at the pit, divided the remainder of the booty, as equally as might be, among us, and, leaving the holes unfilled, again set out for the hut, at which, for the second time, we deposited our golden burdens, just as the first streaks of the dawn gleamed from over the tree-tops in the East.

We were now thoroughly broken down; but the intense excitement of the time denied us repose. After an unquiet slumber of some three or four hours' duration, we arose, as if by preconcert, to make examination of our treasure.

The chest had been full to the brim, and we spent the whole day, and the greater part of the next night, in a scrutiny of its contents. There had been nothing like order or arrangement. Everything had been heaped in promiscuously. Having assorted all with care, we found ourselves possessed of even vaster wealth than we had at first supposed. In coin there was rather more than four hundred and fifty thousand dollars; estimating the value of the pieces, as accurately as we could, by the tables of the period. There was not a particle of silver. All was gold of antique date and of great variety: French, Spanish, and German money, with a few English guineas, and some counters, of which we had never seen specimens before. There were several very large and heavy coins, so worn that we could make nothing of their inscriptions. There was no American money. The value of the jewels we found more difficulty in estimating. There were diamonds—some of them exceedingly large and fine—a hundred and ten in all, and not one of them small; eighteen rubies of remarkable brilliancy; three hundred and ten emeralds, all very beautiful; and twenty-one sapphires, with an opal. These stones had all been broken from their settings and thrown loose in the chest. The settings themselves, which we picked out from among the other gold, appeared to have been beaten up with hammers, as if to prevent identification. Besides all this, there was a vast quantity of solid gold ornaments: nearly two hundred massive finger and ear rings; rich chains—thirty of these, if I remember; eighty-three very large and heavy crucifixes; five gold censers of great value; a prodigious golden punch-bowl, ornamented with richly chased vine-leaves and Bacchanalian figures; with two sword-handles exquisitely embossed, and many other smaller articles which I cannot recollect. The weight of these valuables exceeded three hundred and fifty pounds avoirdupois; and in this estimate I have not included one hundred and ninety-seven superb gold watches; three of the number being worth each five hundred dollars, if one. Many of them were very old, and as time-keepers valueless, the works having suffered more or less from corrosion; but all were richly jewelled and in cases of great worth. We estimated the entire contents of the chest, that night, at a million and a half dollars; and, upon the subsequent disposal of the trinkets and jewels (a few being retained for our own use), it was found that we had greatly undervalued the treasure.

When, at length, we had concluded our examination, and the intense excitement of the time had in some measure subsided, Legrand, who saw that I was dying with impatience for a solution of this most extraordinary riddle, entered into a full detail of all the circumstances connected with it.

"You remember," said he, "the night when I handed you the rough sketch I had made of the *scarabæus*. You recollect also, that I became quite vexed at you for insisting that my drawing resembled a death's-head. When you first made this assertion I thought you were jesting; but afterwards I called to mind the peculiar spots on the back of the insect, and admitted to myself that your remark had some little foundation in fact. Still, the sneer at my graphic powers irritated me—for I am considered a good artist—and, therefore, when you handed me the scrap of parchment, I was about to crumple it up and throw it angrily into the fire."

"The scrap of paper, you mean," said I.

"No: it had much of the appearance of paper, and at first I supposed it to be such, but when I came to draw upon it, I discovered it, at once, to be a piece of very thin parchment. It was quite dirty, you remember. Well, as I was in the very act of crumpling it up, my glance fell upon the sketch at which you had been looking, and you may imagine my astonishment when I perceived, in fact, the figure of a death's-head just where, it seemed to me, I had made the drawing of the beetle. For a moment I was too much amazed to think with accuracy. I knew that my design was very different in detail from this—although there was a certain similarity in general outline. Presently I took a candle and, seating myself at the other end of the room, proceeded to scrutinize the parchment more closely. Upon turning it over, I saw my own sketch upon the reverse, just as I had made it. My first idea, now, was mere surprise at the really remarkable similarity of outline—at the singular coincidence involved in the fact that, unknown to me, there should have been a skull upon the other side of the parchment, immediately beneath my figure of the *scarabæus,* and that this skull, not only in outline, but in size, should so closely resemble my drawing. I say the singularity of this coincidence absolutely stupefied me for a time. This is the usual effect of such coincidences. The mind struggles to establish a connection—a sequence of cause and effect—and, being unable to do so, suffers a species of temporary paralysis. But, when I recovered from this stupor, there dawned upon me gradually a conviction which startled me even far more than the coincidence. I began distinctly, positively, to remember that there had been *no* drawing on the parchment when I made my sketch of the *scarabæus.* I became perfectly certain of this; for I recollected turning up first one side and then the other, in search of the cleanest spot. Had the skull been then there, of course I could not have failed to notice it. Here was indeed a mystery which I felt it impossible to explain; but, even at that early moment, there seemed to glimmer, faintly, within the most remote and secret chambers of my intellect, a glow-worm-like conception of that truth which last night's adventure brought to so magnificent a demonstration. I arose at once, and, putting the parchment securely away, dismissed all farther reflection until I should be alone.

"When you had gone, and when Jupiter was fast asleep, I betook myself to a more methodical investigation of the affair. In the first place I considered the manner in which the parchment had come into my possession. The spot where we discovered the *scarabæus* was on the coast of the main-land, about a mile eastward of the island, and but a short distance above high-water mark. Upon my taking hold of it, it gave me a sharp bite, which caused me to let it drop. Jupiter, with his accustomed caution, before seizing the insect, which had flown towards him, looked about him for a leaf, or something of that nature, by which to take hold of it. It was at this moment that his eyes, and mine also, fell upon the scrap of parchment, which I then supposed to be paper. It was lying half-buried in the sand, a corner sticking up. Near the spot where we found it, I observed the remnants of the hull of what appeared to have been a ship's long boat. The wreck seemed to have been there for a very great while; for the resemblance to boat timbers could scarcely be traced.

"Well, Jupiter picked up the parchment, wrapped the beetle in it, and gave it to me. Soon afterwards we turned to go home, and on the way met Lieutenant G——. I showed him the insect, and he begged me to let him take it to the fort. On my consenting, he thrust it forthwith into his waistcoat pocket, without the parchment in which it had been wrapped, and which I had continued to hold in my hand during his inspection. Perhaps he dreaded my changing my mind, and thought it best to make sure of the prize at once—you know how enthusiastic he is on all subjects connected with Natural History. At the same time, without being conscious of it, I must have deposited the parchment in my own pocket.

"You remember that when I went to the table, for the purpose of making a sketch of the beetle, I found no paper where it was usually kept. I looked in the drawer, and found none there. I searched my pockets, hoping to find an old letter, and then my hand fell upon the parchment. I thus detail the precise mode in which it came into my possession; for the circumstances impressed me with peculiar force.

"No doubt you will think me fanciful—but I had already established a kind of *connection*. I had put together two links of a great chain. There was a boat lying on a seacoast, and not far from the boat was a parchment—*not a paper*—with a skull depicted on it. You will, of course, ask 'where is the connection?' I reply that the skull, or death's-head, is the well-known emblem of the pirate. The flag of the death's-head is hoisted in all engagements.

"I have said that the scrap was parchment, and not paper. Parchment is durable—almost imperishable. Matters of little moment are rarely consigned to parchment; since, for the mere ordinary purposes of drawing or writing, it is not nearly so well adapted as paper. This reflection suggested some meaning—some relevancy—in the death's-head. I did not fail to observe, also, the *form* of the parchment. Although one of its corners had been, by some accident, destroyed, it could be seen that the original form was oblong. It was just such a slip, indeed, as might have been chosen for a memorandum—for a record of something to be long remembered and carefully preserved."

"But," I interposed, "you say that the skull was *not* upon the parchment when you made the drawing of the beetle. How then do you trace any connection between the boat and the skull—since this latter, according to your own admission, must have been designed (God only knows how or by whom) at some period subsequent to your sketching the *scarabæus?*"

"Ah, hereupon turns the whole mystery; although the secret, at this point, I had comparatively little difficulty in solving. My steps were sure, and could afford but a single result. I reasoned, for example, thus: When I drew the *scarabæus,* there was no skull apparent on the parchment. When I had completed the drawing I gave it to you, and observed you narrowly until you returned it. *You,* therefore, did not design the skull, and no one else was present to do it. Then it was not done by human agency. And nevertheless it was done.

"At this stage of my reflections I endeavored to remember, and *did* remember, with entire distinctness, every incident which occurred about the period in question. The weather was chilly (O rare and happy accident!), and a fire was blazing on the hearth. I was heated with exercise and sat near the table. You, however, had drawn a chair close to the chimney. Just as I placed the parchment in your hand, and as you were in the act of inspecting it, Wolf, the Newfoundland, entered, and leaped upon your shoulders. With your left hand you caressed him and kept him off, while your right, holding the parchment, was permitted to fall listlessly between your knees, and in close proximity to the fire. At one moment I thought the blaze had caught it, and was about to caution you, but, before I could speak, you had withdrawn it, and were engaged in its examination. When I considered all these particulars, I doubted not for a moment that *heat* had been the agent in bringing to light, on the parchment, the skull which I saw designed on it. You are well aware that chemical preparations exist, and have existed time out of mind, by means of which it is possible to write on either paper or vellum, so that the characters shall become visible only when subjected to the action of fire. Zaffre, digested in *aqua regia,* and diluted with four times its weight of water, is sometimes employed; a green tint results. The regulus of cobalt, dissolved in spirit of nitre, gives a red. These colors disappear at longer or shorter intervals after the material written upon cools, but again become apparent upon the re-application of heat.

"I now scrutinized the death's-head with care. Its outer edges—

the edges of the drawing nearest the edge of the vellum—were far more *distinct* than the others. It was clear that the action of the caloric had been imperfect or unequal. I immediately kindled a fire, and subjected every portion of the parchment to a glowing heat. At first, the only effect was the strengthening of the faint lines in the skull: but, on persevering in the experiment, there became visible at the corner of the slip, diagonally opposite to the spot in which the death's-head was delineated, the figure of what I at first supposed to be a goat. A closer scrutiny, however, satisfied me that it was intended for a kid."

"Ha! ha!" said I, "to be sure I have no right to laugh at you—a million and a half of money is too serious a matter for mirth—but you are not about to establish a third link in your chain: you will not find any especial connection between your pirates and a goat; pirates, you know, have nothing to do with goats; they appertain to the farming interest."

"But I have just said that the figure was *not* that of a goat."

"Well, a kid, then—pretty much the same thing."

"Pretty much, but not altogether," said Legrand. "You may have heard of one *Captain* Kidd. I at once looked on the figure of the animal as a kind of punning or hieroglyphical signature. I say signature; because its position on the vellum suggested this idea. The death's-head at the corner diagonally opposite had, in the same manner, the air of a stamp, or seal. But I was sorely put out by the absence of all else—of the body to my imagined instrument—of the text for my context."

"I presume you expected to find a letter between the stamp and the signature."

"Something of that kind. The fact is, I felt irresistibly impressed with a presentiment of some vast good fortune impending. I can scarcely say why. Perhaps, after all, it was rather a desire than an actual belief;—but do you know that Jupiter's silly words, about the bug being of solid gold, had a remarkable effect on my fancy? And then the series of accidents and coincidences—these were so *very* extraordinary. Do you observe how mere an accident it was that these events should have occurred on the *sole* day of all the year in which it has been, or may be, sufficiently cool for fire, and that without the fire, or without the intervention of the dog at the precise moment in which he appeared, I should never have become aware of the death's-head, and so never the possessor of the treasure?"

"But proceed—I am all impatience."

"Well; you have heard, of course, the many stories current—the thousand vague rumors afloat about money buried, somewhere on the

Atlantic coast, by Kidd and his associates. These rumors must have had some foundation in fact. And that the rumors have existed so long and so continuously, could have resulted, it appeared to me, only from the circumstance of the buried treasure still *remaining* entombed. Had Kidd concealed his plunder for a time, and afterwards reclaimed it, the rumors would scarcely have reached us in their present unvarying form. You will observe that the stories told are all about money-seekers, not about money-finders. Had the pirate recovered his money, there the affair would have dropped. It seemed to me that some accident—say the loss of a memorandum indicating its locality—had deprived him of the means of recovering it, and that this accident had become known to his followers, who otherwise might never have heard that treasure had been concealed at all, and who, busying themselves in vain, because unguided, attempts to regain it, had given first birth, and then universal currency, to the reports which are now so common. Have you ever heard of any important treasure being unearthed along the coast?"

"Never."

"But that Kidd's accumulations were immense is well known. I took it for granted, therefore, that the earth still held them; and you will scarcely be surprised when I tell you that I felt a hope, nearly amounting to certainty, that the parchment so strangely found involved a lost record of the place of deposit."

"But how did you proceed?"

"I held the vellum again to the fire, after increasing the heat, but nothing appeared. I now thought it possible that the coating of dirt might have something to do with the failure; so I carefully rinsed the parchment by pouring warm water over it, and, having done this, I placed it in a tin pan, with the skull downwards, and put the pan upon a furnace of lighted charcoal. In a few minutes, the pan having become thoroughly heated, I removed the slip, and, to my inexpressible joy, found it spotted, in several places, with what appeared to be figures arranged in lines. Again I placed it in the pan, and suffered it to remain another minute. Upon taking it off, the whole was just as you see it now."

Here Legrand, having reheated the parchment, submitted it to my inspection. The following characters were rudely traced, in a red tint, between the death's-head and the goat:—

53‡‡†305))6*;4826)4‡.)4‡);806*;48†8¶60))85;;]8*:‡*8†83(88)5*†;46(;88*96*?;8)*‡(;485);5*†2:*‡(;4956*2(5*—4)8¶8*;4069285);)6†8)4‡‡;1(‡9;48081;8:8‡1;48†85;4)485†528806*81(‡9;48;(88;4(‡?34;48)4‡;161;:188;‡?;

"But," said I, returning him the slip, "I am as much in the dark as ever. Were all the jewels of Golconda awaiting me on my solution of this enigma, I am quite sure that I should be unable to earn them."

"And yet," said Legrand, "the solution is by no means so difficult as you might be led to imagine from the first hasty inspection of the characters. These characters, as any one might readily guess, form a cipher—that is to say, they convey a meaning; but then, from what is known of Kidd, I could not suppose him capable of constructing any of the more abstruse cryptographs. I made up my mind, at once, that this was of a simple species—such, however, as would appear, to the crude intellect of the sailor, absolutely insoluble without the key."

"And you really solved it?"

"Readily; I have solved others of an abstruseness ten thousand times greater. Circumstances, and a certain bias of mind, have led me to take interest in such riddles, and it may well be doubted whether human ingenuity can construct an enigma of the kind which human ingenuity may not, by proper application, resolve. In fact, having once established connected and legible characters, I scarcely gave a thought to the mere difficulty of developing their import.

"In the present case—indeed in all cases of secret writing—the first question regards the *language* of the cipher; for the principles of solution, so far, especially, as the more simple ciphers are concerned, depend on, and are varied by, the genius of the particular idiom. In general, there is no alternative but experiment (directed by probabilities) of every tongue known to him who attempts the solution, until the true one be attained. But, with the cipher now before us, all difficulty is removed by the signature. The pun upon the word 'Kidd' is appreciable in no other language than the English. But for this consideration I should have begun my attempts with the Spanish and French, as the tongues in which a secret of this kind would most naturally have been written by a pirate of the Spanish main. As it was, I assumed the cryptograph to be English.

"You observe there are no divisions between the words. Had there been divisions, the task would have been comparatively easy. In such case I should have commenced with a collation and analysis of the shorter words, and, had a word of a single letter occurred, as is most likely (*a* or *I*, for example), I should have considered the solution as assured. But, there being no division, my first step was to ascertain the predominant letters, as well as the least frequent. Counting all, I constructed a table, thus:

Of the character 8	there are	33
;	"	26
4	"	19
‡)	"	16
*	"	13
5	"	12
6	"	11
†1	"	8
0	"	6
92	"	5
:3	"	4
?	"	3
¶	"	2
]—.	"	1

"Now, in English, the letter which most frequently occurs is *e*. Afterwards the succession runs thus: *a o i d h n r s t u y c f g l m w b k p q x z*. *E* predominates, however, so remarkably that an individual sentence of any length is rarely seen, in which it is not the prevailing character.

"Here, then, we have, in the very beginning, the groundwork for something more than a mere guess. The general use which may be made of the table is obvious—but, in this particular cipher, we shall only very partially require its aid. As our predominant character is 8, we will commence by assuming it as the *e* of the natural alphabet. To verify the supposition, let us observe if the 8 be seen often in couples—for *e* is doubled with great frequency in English—in such words, for example, as 'meet,' 'fleet,' 'speed,' 'seen,' 'been,' 'agree,' &c. In the present instance we see it doubled no less than five times, although the cryptograph is brief.

"Let us assume 8, then, as *e*. Now, of all *words* in the language, 'the' is the most usual; let us see, therefore, whether there are not repetitions of any three characters, in the same order of collocation, the last of them being 8. If we discover repetitions of such letters, so arranged, they will most probably represent the word 'the.' On inspection, we find no less than seven such arrangements, the characters being ;48. We may, therefore, assume that the semicolon represents *t*, that 4 represents *h*, and that 8 represents *e*—the last being now well confirmed. Thus a great step has been taken.

"But, having established a single word, we are enabled to establish a vastly important point; that is to say, several commencements and terminations of other words. Let us refer, for example, to the last instance but one, in which the combination ;48 occurs—not far from the end of the cipher. We know that the semicolon immediately ensuing is the commencement of a word, and, of the six characters succeeding this 'the,' we are cognizant of no less than five. Let us set these characters down, thus, by the letters we know them to represent, leaving a space for the unknown—

t eeth.

"Here we are enabled, at once, to discard the *'th,'* as forming no portion of the word commencing with the first *t;* since, by experiment of the entire alphabet for a letter adapted to the vacancy, we perceive that no word can be formed of which this *th* can be a part. We are thus narrowed into

t ee,

and, going through the alphabet, if necessary, as before, we arrive at the word 'tree' as the sole possible reading. We thus gain another letter, *r,* represented by (, with the words 'the tree' in juxtaposition.

"Looking beyond these words, for a short distance, we again see the combination ;48, and employ it by way of *termination* to what immediately precedes. We have thus this arrangement:

the tree ;4(‡?34 the,

or, substituting the natural letters, where known, it reads thus:

the tree thr‡?3h the.

"Now, if, in place of the unknown characters, we leave blank spaces, or substitute dots, we read thus:

the tree thr . . . h the,

when the word 'through' makes itself evident at once. But this discovery gives us three new letters, *o, u,* and *g,* represented by ‡ ? and 3.

"Looking now, narrowly, through the cipher for combinations of known characters, we find, not very far from the beginning, this arrangement,

83(88, or egree,

which, plainly, is the conclusion of the word 'degree,' and gives us another letter, *d,* represented by †

"Four letters beyond the word 'degree,' we perceive the combination

;46(;88*

"Translating the known characters, and representing the unknown by dots, as before, we read thus:

th . rtee .

an arrangement immediately suggestive of the word 'thirteen,' and again furnishing us with two new characters, *i* and *n,* represented by 6 and *.

"Referring, now, to the beginning of the cryptograph, we find the combination,

53‡‡†.

"Translating, as before, we obtain

. good,

which assures us that the first letter is *A*, and that the first two words are 'A good.'

"To avoid confusion, it is now time that we arrange our key, as far as discovered, in a tabular form. It will stand thus:

5	represents	a
†	"	d
8	"	e
3	"	g
4	"	h
6	"	i
*	"	n
‡	"	o
(	"	r
;	"	t

"We have, therefore, no less than ten of the most important letters represented, and it will be unnecessary to proceed with the details of the solution. I have said enough to convince you that ciphers of this nature are readily soluble, and to give you some insight into the rationale of their development. But be assured that the specimen before us appertains to the very simplest species of cryptograph. It now only remains to give you the full translation of the characters upon the parchment, as unriddled. Here it is:

"'*A good glass in the bishop's hostel in the devil's seat twenty one degrees and thirteen minutes northeast and by north main branch seventh limb east side shoot from the left eye of the death's-head a bee line from the tree through the shot fifty feet out.*'"

"But," said I, "the enigma seems still in as bad a condition as ever. How is it possible to extort a meaning from all this jargon about 'devil's seats,' 'death's-heads,' and 'bishop's hotels'?"

"I confess," replied Legrand, "that the matter still wears a serious aspect, when regarded with a casual glance. My first endeavor was to divide the sentence into the natural division intended by the cryptographist."

"You mean, to punctuate it?"

"Something of that kind."

"But how was it possible to effect this?"

"I reflected that it had been a *point* with the writer to run his words together without division, so as to increase the difficulty of solution. Now, a not over-acute man, in pursuing such an object, would be nearly certain to overdo the matter. When, in the course of his composition, he arrived at a break in his subject which would naturally require a pause, or a point, he would be exceedingly apt to run his characters, at this place, more than usually close together. If you will observe the MS., in the present instance, you will easily detect five such cases of unusual crowding. Acting on this hint, I made the division thus:

" '*A good glass in the Bishop's hostel in the Devil's seat—twenty-one degrees and thirteen minutes—north-east and by north—main branch seventh limb east side—shoot from the left eye of the death's head—a bee-line from the tree through the shot fifty feet out.*' "

"Even this division," said I, "leaves me still in the dark."

"It left me also in the dark," replied Legrand, "for a few days; during which I made diligent inquiry, in the neighborhood of Sullivan's Island, for any building which went by the name of the 'Bishop's Hotel;' for, of course, I dropped the obsolete word 'hostel.' Gaining no information on the subject, I was on the point of extending my sphere of search, and proceeding in a more systematic manner, when one morning it entered into my head, quite suddenly, that this 'Bishop's Hostel' might have some reference to an old family, of the name of Bessop, which, time out of mind, had held possession of an ancient manor-house, about four miles to the northward of the island. I accordingly went over to the plantation, and reinstituted my inquiries among the older negroes of the place. At length one of the most aged of the women said that she had heard of such a place as *Bessop's Castle,* and thought that she could guide me to it, but that it was not a castle, nor a tavern, but a high rock.

"I offered to pay her well for her trouble, and, after some demur, she consented to accompany me to the spot. We found it without much difficulty, when, dismissing her, I proceeded to examine the place. The 'castle' consisted of an irregular assemblage of cliffs and rocks—one of the latter being quite remarkable for its height as well as for its insulated and artificial appearance. I clambered to its apex, and then felt much at a loss as to what should be next done.

"While I was busied in reflection, my eyes fell on a narrow ledge in the eastern face of the rock, perhaps a yard below the summit upon which I stood. This ledge projected about eighteen inches, and was not more than a foot wide, while a niche in the cliff just above it gave it a rude resemblance to one of the hollow-backed chairs used by our ancestors. I made no doubt that here was the 'devil's seat' alluded to in the MS., and now I seemed to grasp the full secret of the riddle.

"The 'good glass,' I knew, could have reference to nothing but a telescope; for the word 'glass' is rarely employed in any other sense by seamen. Now here, I at once saw, was a telescope to be used, and a definite point of view, *admitting no variation,* from which to use it. Nor did I hesitate to believe that the phrases, 'twenty-one degrees and thirteen minutes,' and 'north-east and by north,' were intended as directions for the levelling of the glass. Greatly excited by these discoveries, I hurried home, procured a telescope, and returned to the rock.

"I let myself down to the ledge, and found that it was impossible to retain a seat on it unless in one particular position. This fact confirmed my preconceived idea. I proceeded to use the glass. Of course, the 'twenty-one degrees and thirteen minutes' could allude to nothing but elevation above the visible horizon, since the horizontal direction was clearly indicated by the words, 'north-east and by north.' This latter direction I at once established by means of a pocket-compass; then, pointing the glass as nearly at an angle of twenty-one degrees of elevation as I could do it by guess, I moved it cautiously up or down, until my attention was arrested by a circular rift or opening in the foliage of a large tree that overtopped its fellows in the distance. In the centre of this rift I perceived a white spot, but could not, at first, distinguish what it was. Adjusting the focus of the telescope, I again looked, and now made it out to be a human skull.

"On this discovery I was so sanguine as to consider the enigma solved; for the phrase 'main branch, seventh limb, east side,' could refer only to the position of the skull on the tree, while 'shoot from the left eye of the death's-head' admitted, also, of but one interpretation, in regard to a search for buried treasure. I perceived that the design was to drop a bullet from the left eye of the skull, and that a bee-line, or, in other words, a straight line, drawn from the nearest point of the trunk through 'the shot' (or the spot where the bullet fell), and thence extended to a distance of fifty feet, would indicate a definite point—and beneath this point I thought it at least *possible* that a deposit of value lay concealed."

"All this," I said, "is exceedingly clear, and, although ingenious, still simple and explicit. When you left the Bishop's Hotel, what then?"

"Why, having carefully taken the bearings of the tree, I turned homewards. The instant that I left 'the devil's seat,' however, the circular rift vanished; nor could I get a glimpse of it afterwards, turn as I would. What seems to me the chief ingenuity in this whole business, is the fact (for repeated experiment has convinced me it *is* a fact) that the circular opening in question is visible from no other attainable point of view than that afforded by the narrow ledge on the face of the rock.

"In this expedition to the 'Bishop's Hotel' I had been attended by Jupiter, who had no doubt observed, for some weeks past, the abstraction of my demeanor, and took especial care not to leave me alone. But on the next day, getting up very early, I contrived to give him the slip, and went into the hills in search of the tree. After much toil I found it. When I came home at night my valet proposed to give me a flogging. With the rest of the adventure I believe you are as well acquainted as myself."

"I suppose," said I, "you missed the spot, in the first attempt at digging, through Jupiter's stupidity in letting the bug fall through the right instead of through the left eye of the skull."

"Precisely. This mistake made a difference of about two inches and a half in the 'shot'—that is to say, in the position of the peg nearest the tree; and had the treasure been *beneath* the 'shot,' the error would have been of little moment; but 'the shot,' together with the nearest point of the tree, were merely two points for the establishment of a line of direction; of course the error, however trivial in the beginning, increased as we proceeded with the line, and, by the time we had gone fifty feet, threw us quite off the scent. But for my deep-seated convictions that treasure was here somewhere actually buried, we might have had all our labor in vain."

"I presume the fancy of *the skull*—of letting fall a bullet through the skull's eye—was suggested to Kidd by the piratical flag. No doubt he felt a kind of poetical consistency in recovering his money through this ominous insignium."

"Perhaps so; still, I cannot help thinking that common-sense had quite as much to do with the matter as poetical consistency. To be visible from the Devil's seat, it was necessary that the object, if small, should be *white;* and there is nothing like your human skull for retaining and even increasing its whiteness under exposure to all vicissitudes of weather."

"But your grandiloquence, and your conduct in swinging the beetle—how excessively odd! I was sure you were mad. And why did you insist on letting fall the bug, instead of a bullet, from the skull?"

"Why, to be frank, I felt somewhat annoyed by your evident suspicions touching my sanity, and so resolved to punish you quietly, in my own way, by a little bit of sober mystification. For this reason I swung the beetle, and for this reason I let it fall from the tree. An observation of yours about its great weight suggested the latter idea."

"Yes, I perceive; and now there is only one point which puzzles me. What are we to make of the skeletons found in the hole?"

"That is a question I am no more able to answer than yourself. There seems, however, only one plausible way of accounting for them—and yet it is dreadful to believe in such atrocity as my suggestion would imply. It is clear that Kidd—if Kidd indeed secreted this treasure, which I doubt not—it is clear that he must have had assistance in the labor. But, the worst of this labor concluded, he may have thought it expedient to remove all participants in his secret. Perhaps a couple of blows with a mattock were sufficient, while his coadjutors were busy in the pit; perhaps it required a dozen—who shall tell?"

ABRAHAM LINCOLN (1809-1865)

First Inaugural Address

FELLOW-CITIZENS of the United States, In compliance with a custom as old as the government itself, I appear before you to address you briefly, and to take in your presence the oath prescribed by the Constitution of the United States to be taken by the President "before he enters on the execution of his office."

I do not consider it necessary at present for me to discuss those matters of administration about which there is no special anxiety or excitement.

Apprehension seems to exist among the people of the Southern States that by the accession of a Republican administration their property and their peace and personal security are to be endangered. There has never been any reasonable cause for such apprehension. Indeed, the most ample evidence to the contrary has all the while existed and been open to their inspection. It is found in nearly all the published speeches of him who now addresses you. I do but quote from one of those speeches when I declare that "I have no purpose, directly or indirectly, to interfere with the institution of slavery in the States where it exists. I believe I have no lawful right to do so, and I have no inclination to do so." Those who nominated and elected me did so with full knowledge that I had made this and many similar declarations, and had never recanted them. And, more than this, they placed in the platform for my acceptance, and as a law to themselves and to me, the clear and emphatic resolution which I now read:—

"*Resolved,* That the maintenance inviolate of the rights of the States, and especially the right of each State to order and control its own domestic institutions according to its own judgment exclusively, is essential to that balance of power on which the perfection and endurance of our political fabric depend, and we denounce the lawless invasion by armed force of the soil of any State or Territory, no matter under what pretext, as among the gravest of crimes."

I now reiterate these sentiments; and, in doing so, I only press upon the public attention the most conclusive evidence of which the case is susceptible, that the property, peace, and security of no section are to be in any wise endangered by the now incoming administration. I add, too, that all the protection which, consistently with the Constitution and the laws, can be given, will be cheerfully given to all the States when lawfully demanded, for whatever cause—as cheerfully to one section as to another.

There is much controversy about the delivering up of fugitives from service or labor. The clause I now read is as plainly written in the Constitution as any other of its provisions:—

"No person held to service or labour in one State, under the laws thereof, escaping into another, shall in consequence of any law or regulation therein be discharged from such service or labour, but shall be delivered up on claim of the party to whom such service or labour may be due."

It is scarcely questioned that this provision was intended by those who made it for the reclaiming of what we call fugitive slaves; and the intention of the lawgiver is the law. All members of Congress swear their support to the whole Constitution—to this provision as much as to any other. To the proposition, then, that slaves whose cases come within the terms of this clause "shall be delivered up," their oaths are unanimous. Now, if they would make the effort in good temper, could they not with nearly equal unanimity frame and pass a law by means of which to keep good that unanimous oath?

There is some difference of opinion whether this clause should be enforced by national or by State authority; but surely that difference is not a very material one. If the slave is to be surrendered, it can be of but little consequence to him or to others by which authority it is done. And should any one in any case be content that his oath shall go unkept on a merely unsubstantial controversy as to how it shall be kept?

Again, in any law upon this subject, ought not all the safeguards of liberty known in civilized and humane jurisprudence to be introduced, so that a free man be not, in any case, surrendered as a slave? And might it not be well at the same time to provide by law for the enforcement of that clause in the Constitution which guarantees that "the citizen of each State shall be entitled to all privileges and immunities of citizens in the several States"?

I take the official oath to-day with no mental reservations, and with no purpose to construe the Constitution or laws by any hypercritical rules. And while I do not choose now to specify particular acts of Congress as proper to be enforced, I do suggest that it will be much safer for all, both in official and private stations, to conform to and abide by all those acts which stand unrepealed, than to violate any of them, trusting to find impunity in having them held to be unconstitutional.

It is seventy-two years since the first inauguration of a President under our National Constitution. During that period fifteen different and greatly distinguished citizens have, in succession, administered the executive branch of the government. They have conducted it through many perils, and generally with great success. Yet, with all this scope of precedent, I now enter upon the same task for the brief constitutional term of four years under great and peculiar difficulty. A disruption of the Federal Union, heretofore only menaced, is now formidably attempted.

I hold that, in contemplation of universal law and of the Constitution, the Union of these States is perpetual. Perpetuity is implied, if not expressed, in the fundamental law of all national governments. It is safe to assert that no government proper ever had a provision in its organic law for its own termination. Continue to execute all the express provisions of our National Constitution, and the Union will endure for ever—it being impossible to destroy it except by some action not provided for in the instrument itself.

Again, if the United States be not a government proper, but an association of States in the nature of contract merely, can it, as a contract, be peaceably unmade by less than all the parties who made it? One party to a contract may violate it—break it, so to speak; but does it not require all to lawfully rescind it?

Descending from these general principles, we find the proposition that in legal contemplation the Union is perpetual confirmed by the history of the Union itself. The Union is much older than the Constitution. It was formed, in fact, by the Articles of Association in 1774.

It was matured and continued by the Declaration of Independence in 1776. It was further matured, and the faith of all the then thirteen States expressly plighted and engaged that it should be perpetual, by the Articles of Confederation in 1778. And, finally, in 1787 one of the declared objects for ordaining and establishing the Constitution was "to form a more perfect Union."

But if the destruction of the Union by one or by a part only of the States be lawfully possible, the Union is less perfect than before the Constitution, having lost the vital element of perpetuity.

It follows from these views that no State upon its own mere motion can lawfully get out of the Union; that resolves and ordinances to that effect are legally void; and that acts of violence, within any State or States, against the authority of the United States, are insurrectionary or revolutionary, according to circumstances.

I therefore consider that, in view of the Constitution and the laws, the Union is unbroken; and to the extent of my ability I shall take care, as the Constitution itself expressly enjoins upon me, that the laws of the Union be faithfully executed in all the States. Doing this I deem to be only a simple duty on my part; and I shall perform it so far as practicable, unless my rightful masters, the American people, shall withhold the requisite means, or in some authoritative manner direct the contrary. I trust this will not be regarded as a menace, but only as the declared purpose of the Union that it will constitutionally defend and maintain itself.

In doing this there needs to be no bloodshed or violence; and there shall be none, unless it be forced upon the national authority. The power confided to me will be used to hold, occupy, and possess the property and places belonging to the government, and to collect the duties and imposts; but beyond what may be necessary for these objects, there will be no invasion, no using of force against or among the people anywhere. Where hostility to the United States, in any interior locality, shall be so great and universal as to prevent competent resident citizens from holding the Federal offices, there will be no attempt to force obnoxious strangers among the people for that object. While the strict legal right may exist in the government to enforce the exercise of these offices, the attempt to do so would be so irritating, and so nearly impracticable withal, that I deem it better to forego for the time the uses of such offices.

The mails, unless repelled, will continue to be furnished in all parts of the Union. So far as possible, the people everywhere shall have that sense of perfect security which is most favourable to calm thought and reflection. The course here indicated will be followed unless current events and experience shall show a modification or change to be proper, and in every case and exigency my best discretion will be exercised according to circumstances actually existing, and with a view and a hope of a peaceful solution of the national troubles and the restoration of fraternal sympathies and affections.

That there are persons in one section or another who seek to destroy the Union at all events, and are glad of any pretext to do it, I will neither affirm nor deny; but if there be such, I need address no word to them. To those, however, who really love the Union may I not speak?

Before entering upon so grave a matter as the destruction of our national fabric, with all its benefits, its memories, and its hopes, would it not be wise to ascertain precisely why we do it? Will you hazard so desperate a step while there is any possibility that any portion of the ills you fly from have no real existence? Will you, while the certain ills you fly to are greater than all the real ones you fly from—will you risk the commission of so fearful a mistake?

All profess to be content in the Union if all constitutional rights can be maintained. Is it true, then, that any right, plainly written in the Constitution, has been denied? I think not. Happily the human mind is so constituted that no party can reach to the audacity of doing this. Think, if you can, of a single instance in which a plainly written provision of the Constitution has ever been denied. If by the mere force of numbers a majority should deprive a minority of any clearly written constitutional right, it might, in a moral point of view, justify revolution —certainly would if such a right were a vital one. But such is not our case. All the vital rights of minorities and of individuals are so plainly assured to them by affirmations and negations, guaranties and prohibitions, in the Constitution, that controversies never arise concerning them. But no organic law can ever be framed with a provision specifically applicable to every question which may occur in practical administration. No foresight can anticipate, nor any document of reasonable length contain, express provisions for all possible questions. Shall fugitives from labor be surrendered by national or by State authority? The Constitution does not expressly say. *May* Congress prohibit slavery in the Territories? The Constitution does not expressly say. *Must* Congress protect slavery in the Territories? The Constitution does not expressly say.

From questions of this class spring all our constitutional controversies, and we divide upon them into majorities and minorities. If the minority will not acquiesce, the majority must, or the government must cease.

There is no other alternative; for continuing the government is acquiescence on one side or the other.

If a minority in such case will secede rather than acquiesce, they make a precedent which in turn will divide and ruin them; for a minority of their own will secede from them whenever a majority refuses to be controlled by such minority. For instance, why may not any portion of a new confederacy a year or two hence arbitrarily secede again, precisely as portions of the present Union now claim to secede from it? All who cherish disunion sentiments are now being educated to the exact temper of doing this.

Is there such perfect identity of interests among the States to compose a new Union, as to produce harmony only, and prevent renewed secession?

Plainly, the central idea of secession is the essence of anarchy. A majority held in restraint by constitutional checks and limitations, and always changing easily with deliberate changes of popular opinions and sentiments, is the only true sovereign of a free people. Whoever rejects it does, of necessity, fly to anarchy or to despotism. Unanimity is impossible; the rule of a minority, as a permanent arrangement, is wholly inadmissible; so that, rejecting the majority principle, anarchy or despotism in some form is all that is left.

I do not forget the position, assumed by some, that constitutional questions are to be decided by the Supreme Court; nor do I deny that such decisions must be binding, in any case, upon the parties to a suit, as to the object of that suit, while they are also entitled to very high respect and consideration in all parallel cases by all other departments of the government. And while it is obviously possible that such decision may be erroneous in any given case, still the evil effect following it, being limited to that particular case, with the chance that it may be overruled and never become a precedent for other cases, can better be borne than could the evils of a different practice. At the same time, the candid citizen must confess that if the policy of the government, upon vital questions affecting the whole people, is to be irrevocably fixed by decisions of the Supreme Court, the instant they are made, in ordinary litigation between parties in personal actions, the people will have ceased to be their own rulers, having to that extent practically resigned their government into the hands of that eminent tribunal. Nor is there in this view any assault upon the court or the judges. It is a duty from which they may not shrink to decide cases properly brought before them, and it is no fault of theirs if others seek to turn their decisions to political purposes.

One section of our country believes slavery is right, and ought to be extended, while the other believes it is wrong, and ought not to be extended. This is the only substantial dispute. The fugitive-slave clause of the Constitution, and the law for the suppression of the foreign slave-trade, are each as well enforced, perhaps, as any law can ever be in a community where the moral sense of the people imperfectly supports the law itself. The great body of the people abide by the dry legal obligation in both cases, and a few break over in each. This, I think, cannot be perfectly cured; and it would be worse in both cases after the separation of the sections than before. The foreign slave-trade, now imperfectly suppressed, would be ultimately revived, without restrictions, in one section, while fugitive slaves, now only partially surrendered, would not be surrendered at all by the other.

Physically speaking, we cannot separate. We cannot remove our respective sections from each other, nor build an impassable wall between them. A husband and wife may be divorced, and go out of the presence and beyond the reach of each other; but the different parts of our country cannot do this. They cannot but remain face to face, and intercourse, either amicable or hostile, must continue between them. Is it possible, then, to make that intercourse more advantageous or more satisfactory after separation than before? Can aliens make treaties easier than friends can make laws? Can treaties be more faithfully enforced between aliens than laws can among friends? Suppose you go to war, you cannot fight always; and when, after much loss on both sides, and no gain on either, you cease fighting, the identical old questions as to terms of intercourse are again upon you.

This country, with its institutions, belongs to the people who inhabit it. Whenever they shall grow weary of the existing government, they can exercise their constitutional right of amending it, or their revolutionary right to dismember or overthrow it. I cannot be ignorant of the fact that many worthy and patriotic citizens are desirous of having the National Constitution amended. While I make no recommendation of amendments, I fully recognize the rightful authority of the people over the whole subject, to be exercised in either of the modes prescribed in the instrument itself; and I should, under existing circumstances, favor rather than oppose a fair opportunity being afforded to the people to act upon it. I will venture to add that to me the convention mode seems preferable, in that it allows amendments to originate with the people themselves, instead of only permitting them to take or reject propositions originated by others not especially chosen for the purpose, and which might not be precisely such as they would wish to either accept or refuse.

I understand a proposed amendment to the Constitution—which amendment, however, I have not seen—has passed Congress, to the effect that the Federal Government shall never interfere with the domestic institutions of the States, including that of persons held to service. To avoid misconstruction of what I have said, I depart from my purpose not to speak of particular amendments so far as to say that, holding such a provision to now be implied constitutional law, I have no objection to its being made express and irrevocable.

The chief magistrate derives all his authority from the people, and they have conferred none upon him to fix terms for the separation of the States. The people themselves can do this also if they choose; but the Executive, as such, has nothing to do with it. His duty is to administer the present government, as it came to his hands, and to transmit it, unimpaired by him, to his successor.

Why should there not be a patient confidence in the ultimate justice of the people? Is there any better or equal hope in the world? In our present differences, is either party without faith of being in the right? If the Almighty Ruler of Nations, with his eternal truth and justice, be on your side of the North, or on yours of the South, that truth and that justice will surely prevail by the judgment of this great tribunal of the American people.

By the frame of the government under which we live, this same people have wisely given their public servants but little power for mischief; and have, with equal wisdom, provided for the return of that little to their own hands at very short intervals. While the people retain their virtue and vigilance, no administration, by any extreme of wickedness or folly, can very seriously injure the government in the short space of four years.

My countrymen, one and all, think calmly and well upon this whole subject. Nothing valuable can be lost by taking time. If there be an object to hurry any of you in hot haste to a step which you would never take deliberately, that object will be frustrated by taking time; but no good object can be frustrated by it. Such of you as are now dissatisfied still have the old Constitution unimpaired, and, on the sensitive point, the laws of your own framing under it; while the new administration will have no immediate power, if it would, to change either. If it were admitted that you who are dissatisfied hold the right side in the dispute, there still is no single good reason for precipitate action. Intelligence, patriotism, Christianity, and a firm reliance on Him who has never yet forsaken this favored land, are still competent to adjust in the best way all our present difficulty.

In your hands, my dissatisfied fellow-countrymen, and not in mine, is the momentous issue of civil war. The government will not assail you. You can have no conflict without being yourselves the aggressors. You have no oath registered in heaven to destroy the government, while I shall have the most solemn one to "preserve, protect, and defend it."

I am loath to close. We are not enemies, but friends. We must not be enemies. Though passion may have strained, it must not break our bonds of affection. The mystic chords of memory, stretching from every battlefield and patriot grave to every living heart and hearthstone all over this broad land, will yet swell the chorus of the Union when again touched, as surely they will be, by the better angels of our nature.

Letter to Horace Greeley, August 22, 1862

I HAVE just read yours of the 19th instant, addressed to myself through the "New York Tribune."

If there be in it any statements or assumptions of fact which I may know to be erroneous, I do not now and here controvert them.

If there be in it any inferences which I may believe to be falsely drawn, I do not now and here argue against them.

If there be perceptible in it an impatient and dictatorial tone, I waive it, in deference to an old friend whose heart I have always supposed to be right.

As to the policy I "seem to be pursuing," as you say, I have not meant to leave any one in doubt. I would save the Union. I would save it in the shortest way under the Constitution.

The sooner the national authority can be restored, the nearer the Union will be,—the Union as it was.

If there be those who would not save the Union unless they could at the same time save slavery, I do not agree with them.

If there be those who would not save the Union unless they could at the same time destroy slavery, I do not agree with them.

My paramount object in this struggle is to save the Union, and not either to save or to destroy slavery.

If I could save the Union without freeing any slave, I would do it; if I could save it by freeing all the slaves, I would do it; and if I could save it by freeing some and leaving others alone, I would also do that.

What I do about slavery and the colored race, I do because I believe it helps to save the Union; and what I forbear, I forbear because I do not believe it would help to save the Union.

I shall do less whenever I shall believe that what I am doing hurts the cause; and I shall do more whenever I shall believe doing more will help the cause.

I shall try to correct errors where shown to be errors, and I shall adopt new views as fast as they shall appear to be true views.

I have here stated my purpose according to my views of official duty, and I intend no modification of my oft-expressed personal wish that all men everywhere could be free.

Letter to James C. Conkling, August 26, 1863

YOUR letter inviting me to attend a mass meeting of unconditional Union men, to be held at the capital of Illinois on the third day of September, has been received. It would be very agreeable to me to thus meet my old friends at my own home, but I cannot just now be absent from here so long as a visit there would require.

The meeting is to be of all those who maintain unconditional devotion to the Union; and I am sure my old political friends will thank me for tendering, as I do, the nation's gratitude to those and other noble men whom no partisan malice or partisan hope can make false to the nation's life.

There are those who are dissatisfied with me. To such I would say: You desire peace, and you blame me that we do not have it. But how can we attain it? There are but three conceivable ways. First, to suppress the rebellion by force of arms. This I am trying to do. Are you for it? If you are, so far we are agreed. If you are not for it, a second way is to give up the Union. I am against this. Are you for it? If you are, you should say so plainly. If you are not for force, nor yet for dissolution, there only remains some imaginable compromise. I do not believe any compromise embracing the maintenance of the Union is now possible. All I learn leads to a directly opposite belief. The strength of the rebellion is its military, its army. That army dominates all the country and all the people within its range. Any offer of terms made by any man or men within that range, in opposition to that army, is simply nothing for the present, because such man or men have no power whatever to enforce their side of a compromise, if one were made with them.

To illustrate: Suppose refugees from the South and peace men of the North get together in convention, and frame and proclaim a compromise embracing a restoration of the Union. In what way can that compromise be used to keep Lee's army out of Pennsylvania? Meade's army can keep Lee's out of Pennsylvania, and, I think, can ultimately drive it out of existence. But no paper compromise, to which the controllers of

Lee's army are not agreed, can at all affect that army. In an effort at such compromise we should waste time which the enemy would improve to our disadvantage; and that would be all. A compromise, to be effective, must be made either with those who control the rebel army, or with the people first liberated from the domination of that army by the success of our own army. Now, allow me to assure you that no word or intimation from that rebel army, or from any of the men controlling it, in relation to any peace compromise, has ever come to my knowledge or belief. All charges and insinuations to the contrary are deceptive and groundless. And I promise you that if any such proposition shall hereafter come, it shall not be rejected and kept a secret from you. I freely acknowledge myself the servant of the people, according to the bond of service,—the United States Constitution,—and that, as such, I am responsible to them.

But to be plain. You are dissatisfied with me about the negro. Quite likely there is a difference of opinion between you and myself upon that subject. I certainly wish that all men could be free, while I suppose you do not. Yet I have neither adopted nor proposed any measure which is not consistent with even your views, provided you are for the Union. I suggested compensated emancipation, to which you replied, you wished not to be taxed to buy negroes. But I had not asked you to be taxed to buy negroes, except in such way as to save you from greater taxation to save the Union exclusively by other means.

You dislike the Emancipation Proclamation, and perhaps would have it retracted. You say it is unconstitutional. I think differently. I think the Constitution invests its commander-in-chief with the law of war in time of war. The most that can be said—if so much—is that slaves are property. Is there, has there ever been, any question that, by the law of war, property, both of enemies and friends, may be taken when needed? And is it not needed whenever taking it helps us or hurts the enemy? Armies the world over destroy enemies' property when they cannot use it, and even destroy their own to keep it from the enemy. Civilized belligerents do all in their power to help themselves or hurt the enemy, except a few things regarded as barbarous or cruel. Among the exceptions are the massacre of vanquished foes and non-combatants, male and female.

But the proclamation, as law, either is valid or is not valid. If it is not valid, it needs no retraction. If it is valid, it cannot be retracted any more than the dead can be brought to life. Some of you profess to think its retraction would operate favorably for the Union. Why better after the retraction than before the issue? There was more than a year and a half of trial to suppress the rebellion before the proclamation issued, the last one hundred days of which passed under an explicit notice that it was coming, unless averted by those in revolt returning to their allegiance. The war has certainly progressed as favorably for us since the issue of the proclamation as before. I know, as fully as one can know the opinions of others, that some of the commanders of our armies in the field who have given us our most important successes, believe the emancipation policy and the use of colored troops constitute the heaviest blow yet dealt to the rebellion, and that at least one of these important successes could not have been achieved when it was but for the aid of black soldiers. Among the commanders holding these views are some who have never had any affinity with what is called Abolitionism or with Republican party politics, but who hold them purely as military opinions. I submit these opinions as being entitled to some weight against the objections often urged, that emancipation and arming the blacks are unwise as military measures, and were not adopted as such in good faith.

You say you will not fight to free negroes. Some of them seem willing to fight for you; but no matter. Fight you, then, exclusively to save the Union. I issued the proclamation on purpose to aid you in saving the Union. Whenever you shall have conquered all resistance to the Union, if I shall urge you to continue fighting, it will be an apt time then for you to declare you will not fight to free negroes.

I thought that in your struggle for the Union, to whatever extent the negroes should cease helping the enemy, to that extent it weakened the enemy in his resistance to you. Do you think differently? I thought that whatever negroes could be got to do as soldiers leaves just so much less for white soldiers to do in saving the Union. Does it appear otherwise to you? But negroes, like other people, act upon motives. Why should they do anything for us, if we will do nothing for them? If they stake their lives for us, they must be prompted by the strongest motive, even the promise of freedom. And the promise being made, must be kept.

The signs look better. The Father of Waters again goes unvexed to the sea. Thanks to the great Northwest for it. Nor yet wholly to them. Three hundred miles up they met New England, Empire, Keystone, and Jersey hewing their way right and left. The sunny South, too, in more colors than one, also lent a hand. On the spot, their part of the history was jotted down in black and white. The job was a great national one, and let none be banned who bore an honorable part in it. And while those who cleared the great river may well be proud, even that is not all. It is hard to say that anything has been more bravely and well done than at Antietam, Murfreesboro, Gettysburg, and on many fields of lesser note. Nor must Uncle Sam's web-feet be forgotten. At all the watery margins they have been present. Not only on the deep sea, the broad bay, and the rapid river, but also up the narrow, muddy bayou, and wherever the ground was a little damp, they have been and made their tracks. Thanks to all,—for the great Republic, for the principle it lives by and keeps alive, for man's vast future,—thanks to all.

Peace does not appear so distant as it did. I hope it will come soon, and come to stay; and so come as to be worth the keeping in all future time. It will then have been proved that among freemen there can be no successful appeal from the ballot to the bullet, and that they who take such appeal are sure to lose their case and pay the cost. And then there will be some black men who can remember that with silent tongue, and clenched teeth, and steady eye, and well-poised bayonet, they have helped mankind on to this great consummation, while I fear there will be some white ones unable to forget that with malignant heart and deceitful speech they strove to hinder it.

Still, let us not be over-sanguine of a speedy, final triumph. Let us be quite sober. Let us diligently apply the means, never doubting that a just God, in His own good time, will give us the rightful result.

Address at the Dedication of the National Cemetery at Gettysburg

Fourscore and seven years ago our fathers brought forth upon this continent a new nation, conceived in liberty, and dedicated to the proposition that all men are created equal.

Now we are engaged in a great civil war, testing whether that nation, or any nation so conceived and so dedicated, can long endure. We are met on a great battle-field of that war. We have come to dedicate a portion of that field as a final resting-place for those who here gave their lives that that nation might live. It is altogether fitting and proper that we should do this.

But in a larger sense we cannot dedicate, we cannot consecrate, we cannot hallow this ground. The brave men, living and dead, who struggled here, have consecrated it far above our power to add or detract. The world will little note nor long remember what we say here, but it can never forget what they did here. It is for us, the living, rather, to be dedicated here to the unfinished work which they who fought here have thus far so nobly advanced. It is rather for us to be here dedicated to the great task remaining before us; that from these honored dead we take increased devotion to that cause for which they gave the last full measure of devotion; that we here highly resolve that these dead shall not have died in vain; that this nation, under God, shall have a new birth of freedom; and that government of the people, by the people, and for the people, shall not perish from the earth.

Letter to Mrs. Bixby, of Boston, November 21, 1864

DEAR MADAM, I have been shown in the files of the War Department a statement of the Adjutant-General of Massachusetts that you are the mother of five sons who have died gloriously on the field of battle. I feel how weak and fruitless must be any words of mine which should attempt to beguile you from the grief of a loss so overwhelming. But I cannot refrain from tendering to you the consolation that may be found in the thanks of the Republic they died to save. I pray that our heavenly Father may assuage the anguish of your bereavement, and leave you only the cherished memory of the loved and lost, and the solemn pride that must be yours to have laid so costly a sacrifice upon the altar of freedom.

Yours very sincerely and respectfully,

ABRAHAM LINCOLN.

Second Inaugural Address

FELLOW-COUNTRYMEN, At this second appearance to take the oath of the Presidential office, there is less occasion for an extended address than there was at the first. Then a statement, somewhat in detail, of a course to be pursued, seemed fitting and proper. Now, at the expiration of four years, during which public declarations have been constantly called forth on every point and phase of the great contest which still absorbs the attention and engrosses the energies of the nation, little that is new could be presented. The progress of our arms, upon which all else chiefly depends, is as well known to the public as to myself; and it is, I trust, reasonably satisfactory and encouraging to all. With high hope for the future, no prediction in regard to it is ventured.

On the occasion corresponding to this four years ago, all thoughts were anxiously directed to an impending civil war. All dreaded it,—all sought to avert it. While the inaugural address was being delivered from this place, devoted altogether to saving the Union without war, insurgent agents were in the city seeking to destroy it without war,—seeking to dissolve the Union, and divide effects, by negotiation. Both parties deprecated war; but one of them would make war rather than let the nation survive, and the other would accept war rather than let it perish. And the war came.

One-eighth of the whole population were colored slaves, not distributed generally over the Union, but localized in the southern part of it. These slaves constituted a peculiar and powerful interest. All knew that this interest was, somehow, the cause of the war. To strengthen, perpetuate, and extend this interest was the object for which the insurgents would rend the Union, even by war; while the government claimed no right to do more than to restrict the territorial enlargement of it.

Neither party expected for the war the magnitude or the duration which it has already attained. Neither anticipated that the cause of the conflict might cease with, or even before, the conflict itself should cease. Each looked for an easier triumph and a result less fundamental and astounding. Both read the same Bible, and pray to the same God; and each invokes His aid against the other. It may seem strange that any men should dare to ask a just God's assistance in wringing their bread from the sweat of other men's faces; but let us judge not, that we be not judged. The prayers of both could not be answered—that of neither has been answered fully.

The Almighty has His own purposes. "Woe unto the world because of offences! for it must needs be that offences come; but woe to that man by whom the offence cometh." If we shall suppose that American slavery is one of those offences which, in the Providence of God, must needs come, but which having continued through His appointed time, He now wills to remove, and that He gives to both North and South this terrible war, as the woe due to those by whom the offence came, shall we discern therein any departure from those divine attributes which the believers in a living God always ascribe to Him? Fondly do we hope—fervently do we pray—that this mighty scourge of war may speedily pass away. Yet, if God wills that it continue until all the wealth piled up by the bondman's two hundred and fifty years of unrequited toil shall be sunk, and until every drop of blood drawn by the lash shall be paid by another drawn with the sword, as was said three thousand years ago, so still it must be said, "The judgments of the Lord are true and righteous altogether."

With malice toward none; with charity for all; with firmness in the right, as God gives us to see the right,—let us strive on to finish the work we are in: to bind up the nation's wounds; to care for him who shall have borne the battle, and for his widow and his orphan; to do all which may achieve and cherish a just and lasting peace among ourselves, and with all nations.

OLIVER WENDELL HOLMES
(1809-1894)

The Last Leaf

I SAW him once before,
As he passed by the door,
And again
The pavement stones resound,
As he totters o'er the ground
With his cane.

They say that in his prime,
Ere the pruning-knife of Time
Cut him down,
Not a better man was found
By the crier on his round
Through the town.

But now he walks the streets,
And he looks at all he meets
Sad and wan,
And he shakes his feeble head,
That it seems as if he said,
"They are gone."

The mossy marbles rest
On the lips that he has pressed
In their bloom,
And the names he loved to hear
Have been carved for many a year
On the tomb.

My grandmamma has said—
Poor old lady, she is dead
Long ago—
That he had a Roman nose,
And his cheek was like a rose
In the snow.

But now his nose is thin,
And it rests upon his chin
Like a staff,
And a crook is in his back,
And a melancholy crack
In his laugh.

I know it is a sin
For me to sit and grin
At him here;
But the old three-cornered hat,
And the breeches, and all that,
Are so queer!

And if I should live to be
The last leaf upon the tree
In the spring,
Let them smile, as I do now,
At the old, forsaken bough
Where I cling.

The Chambered Nautilus

THIS is the ship of pearl, which, poets feign,
Sails the unshadowed main,—
The venturous bark that flings
On the sweet summer wind its purpled wings
In gulfs enchanted, where the Siren sings,
And coral reefs lie bare,
Where the cold sea-maids rise to sun their streaming hair.

Its webs of living gauze no more unfurl;
Wrecked is the ship of pearl!
And every chambered cell,
Where its dim dreaming life was wont to dwell,
As the frail tenant shaped his growing shell,
Before thee lies revealed,—
Its irised ceiling rent, its sunless crypt unsealed!

Year after year beheld the silent toil
That spread his lustrous coil;
Still, as the spiral grew,
He left the past year's dwelling for the new,
Stole with soft step its shining archway through,
Built up its idle door,
Stretched in his last-found home, and knew the old no more.

Thanks for the heavenly message brought by thee,
Child of the wandering sea,
Cast from her lap, forlorn!
From thy dead lips a clearer note is born
Than ever Triton blew from wreathèd horn!
While on mine ear it rings,
Through the deep caves of thought I hear a voice that sings:

Build thee more stately mansions, O my soul,
As the swift seasons roll!
Leave thy low-vaulted past!
Let each new temple, nobler than the last,
Shut thee from heaven with a dome more vast,
Till thou at length art free,
Leaving thine outgrown shell by life's unresting sea!

The Broomstick Train

LOOK out! Look out, boys! Clear the track!
The witches are here! They've all come back!
They hanged them high,—No use! No use!
What cares a witch for a hangman's noose?
They buried them deep, but they wouldn't lie still,
For cats and witches are hard to kill;
They swore they shouldn't and wouldn't die,—
Books said they did, but they lie! they lie!
—A couple of hundred years, or so,
They had knocked about in the world below,
When an Essex Deacon dropped in to call,
And a homesick feeling seized them all;
For he came from a place they knew full well,
And many a tale he had to tell.
They long to visit the haunts of men,
To see the old dwellings they knew again,
And ride on their broomsticks all around
Their wide domain of unhallowed ground.

In Essex county there's many a roof
Well known to him of the cloven hoof;
The small square windows are full in view
Which the midnight hags went sailing through,
On their well-trained broomsticks mounted high,
Seen like shadows against the sky;
Crossing the track of owls and bats,
Hugging before them their coal-black cats.

Well did they know, those gray old wives,
The sights we see in our daily drives:
Shimmer of lake and shine of sea,
Brown's bare hill with its lonely tree,
(It wasn't then as we see it now,
With one scant scalp-lock to shade its brow;)
Dusky nooks in the Essex woods,
Dark, dim, Dante-like solitudes,
Where the tree-toad watches the sinuous snake
Glide through his forests of fern and brake;
Ipswich River; its old stone bridge;
Far off Andover's Indian Ridge,
And many a scene where history tells
Some shadow of bygone terror dwells,—
Of "Norman's Woe" with its tale of dread,
Of the Screeching Woman of Marblehead,
(The fearful story that turns men pale:
Don't bid me tell it,—my speech would fail.)

Who would not, will not, if he can,
Bathe in the breezes of fair Cape Ann,—
Rest in the bowers her bays enfold,
Loved by the sachems and squaws of old?

Home where the white magnolias bloom,
Sweet with the bayberry's chaste perfume,
Hugged by the woods and kissed by the sea!
Where is the Eden like to thee?

For that "couple of hundred years, or so,"
There had been no peace in the world below;
The witches still grumbling, "It isn't fair;
Come, give us a taste of the upper air!
We've had enough of your sulphur springs,
And the evil odor that round them clings;
We long for a drink that is cool and nice,—
Great buckets of water with Wenham ice;
We've served you well up-stairs, you know;
You're a good old—fellow—come, let us go!"

I don't feel sure of his being good,
But he happened to be in a pleasant mood,—
As fiends with their skins full sometimes are,—
(He'd been drinking with "roughs" at a Boston bar.)
So what does he do but up and shout
To a graybeard turnkey, "Let 'em out!"

To mind his orders was all he knew;
The gates swung open, and out they flew.
"Where are our broomsticks?" the beldams cried.
"Here are your broomsticks," an imp replied.
"They've been in—the place, you know—so long
They smell of brimstone uncommon strong;
But they've gained by being left alone,—
Just look, and you'll see how tall they've grown."
—"And where is my cat?" a vixen squalled.
"Yes, where are our cats?" the witches bawled,
And began to call them all by name:
As fast as they called the cats, they came:
There was bob-tailed Tommy and long-tailed Tim,
And wall-eyed Jacky and green-eyed Jim,
And splay-foot Benny and slim-legged Beau,
And Skinny and Squally, and Jerry and Joe,
And many another that came at call,—
It would take too long to count them all.
All black,—one could hardly tell which was which.
But every cat knew his own old witch;
And she knew hers as hers knew her,—
Ah, didn't they curl their tails and purr!

No sooner the withered hags were free
Than out they swarmed for a midnight spree;
I couldn't tell all they did in rhymes,
But the Essex people had dreadful times.
The Swampscott fishermen still relate
How a strange sea-monster stole their bait;
How their nets were tangled in loops and knots,
And they found dead crabs in their lobster-pots.
Poor Danvers grieved for her blasted crops,
And Wilmington mourned over mildewed hops.
A blight played havoc with Beverly beans,—
It was all the work of those hateful queans!
A dreadful panic began at "Pride's,"
Where the witches stopped in their midnight rides,
And there rose strange rumors and vague alarms
'Mid the peaceful dwellers at Beverly Farms.

Now when the Boss of the Beldams found
That without his leave they were ramping round,
He called,—they could hear him twenty miles,
From Chelsea beach to the Misery Isles;
The deafest old granny knew his tone
Without the trick of the telephone.
"Come here, you witches! Come here!" says he,—
"At your games of old, without asking me!
I'll give you a little job to do
That will keep you stirring, you godless crew!"

They came, of course, at their master's call,
The witches, the broomsticks, the cats, and all;
He led the hags to a railway train
The horses were trying to drag in vain.
"Now, then," says he, "you've had your fun,
And here are the cars you've got to run.
The driver may just unhitch his team,
We don't want horses, we don't want steam;
You may keep your old black cats to hug,
But the loaded train you've got to lug."

Since then on many a car you'll see
A broomstick plain as plain can be;
On every stick there's a witch astride,—
The string you see to her leg is tied.
She will do a mischief if she can,
But the string is held by a careful man,
And whenever the evil-minded witch
Would cut some caper, he gives a twitch.
As for the hag, you can't see her,
But hark! you can hear her black cat's purr,
And now and then, as a car goes by,
You may catch a gleam from her wicked eye.

Often you've looked on a rushing train,
But just what moved it was not so plain.
It couldn't be those wires above,
For they could neither pull nor shove;
Where was the motor that made it go
You couldn't guess, *but now you know.*

Remember my rhymes when you ride again
On the rattling rail by the broomstick train!

From The Autocrat of the Breakfast-Table

My Last Walk with the Schoolmistress

I can't say just how many walks she and I had taken together before this one. I found the effect of going out every morning was decidedly favorable on her health. Two pleasing dimples, the places for which were just marked when she came, played, shadowy, in her freshening cheeks when she smiled and nodded good-morning to me from the schoolhouse-steps.

I am afraid I did the greater part of the talking. At any rate, if I should try to report all that I said during the first-half dozen walks we took together, I fear that I might receive a gentle hint from my friends the publishers, that a separate volume, at my own risk and expense, would be the proper method of bringing them before the public.

—I would have a woman as true as Death. At the first real lie which works from the heart outward, she should be tenderly chloroformed into a better world, where she can have an angel for a governess, and feed on strange fruits which will make her all over again, even to her bones and marrow.—Whether gifted with the accident of beauty or not, she should have been moulded in the rose-red clay of Love, before the breath of life made a moving mortal of her. Love-capacity is a congenital endowment; and I think, after a while, one gets to know the warm-hued natures it belongs to from the pretty pipe-clay counterfeits of them.—Proud she may be, in the sense of respecting herself; but pride, in the sense of contemning others less gifted than herself, deserves the two lowest circles of a vulgar woman's Inferno, where the punishments are Smallpox and Bankruptcy.—She who nips off the end of a brittle courtesy, as one breaks the tip of an icicle, to bestow upon those whom she ought cordially and kindly to recognize, proclaims the fact that she comes not merely of low blood, but of bad blood. Consciousness of unquestioned position makes people gracious in proper measure to all; but if a woman put on airs with her real equals, she has something about herself or her family she is ashamed of, or ought to be. Middle, and more than middle-aged people, who know family histories, generally see through it. An official of standing was rude to me once. Oh, that is the maternal grandfather,—said a wise old friend to me,—he was a boor.—Better too few words, from the woman we love, than too many: while she is silent, Nature is working for her; while she talks, she is working for herself.—Love is sparingly soluble in the words of men; therefore they speak much of it; but one syllable of woman's speech can dissolve more of it than a man's heart can hold.

—Whether I said any or all of these things to the schoolmistress, or not,—whether I stole them out of Lord Bacon,—whether I cribbed them from Balzac,—whether I dipped them from the ocean of Tupperian wisdom,—or whether I have just found them in my head, laid there by that solemn fowl, Experience (who, according to my observation, cackles oftener than she drops real live eggs), I cannot say. Wise men have said more foolish things,—and foolish men, I don't doubt, have said as wise things. Anyhow, the schoolmistress and I had pleasant walks and long talks, all of which I do not feel bound to report.

—You are a stranger to me, Ma'am.—I don't doubt you would like to know all I said to the schoolmistress.—I sha'n't do it;—I had rather get the publishers to return the money you have invested in these pages.

Besides, I have forgotten a good deal of it. I shall tell only what I like of what I remember.

—My idea was, in the first place, to search out the picturesque spots which the city affords a sight of, to those who have eyes. I know a good many, and it was a pleasure to look at them in company with my young friend. There were the shrubs and flowers in the Franklin-Place front-yards or borders: Commerce is just putting his granite foot upon them. Then there are certain small seraglio-gardens, into which one can get a peep through the crevices of high fences,—one in Myrtle Street, or at the back of it,—here and there one at the North and South ends. Then the great elms in Essex Street. Then the stately horse-chestnuts in that vacant lot in Chambers Street, which hold their out-spread hands over your head (as I said in my poem the other day), and look as if they were whispering, "May grace, mercy, and peace be with you!"—and the rest of that benediction. Nay, there are certain patches of ground, which, having lain neglected for a time, Nature, who always has her pockets full of seeds, and holes in all her pockets, has covered with hungry plebeian growths, which fight for life with each other, until some of them get broad-leaved and succulent, and you have a coarse vegetable tapestry which Raphael would not have disdained to spread over the foreground of his masterpiece. The Professor pretends that he found such a one in Charles Street, which, in its dare-devil impudence of rough-and-tumble vegetation, beat the pretty-behaved flower-beds of the Public Garden as ignominiously as a group of young tatterdemalions playing pitch-and-toss beats a row of Sunday-school-boys with their teacher at their head.

But then the Professor has one of his burrows in that region, and puts everything in high colors relating to it. That is his way about everything.—I hold any man cheap,—he said,—of whom nothing stronger can be uttered than that all his geese are swans.—How is that, Professor?—said I;—I should have set you down for one of that sort. —Sir, said he,—I am proud to say, that Nature has so far enriched me, that I cannot own so much as a *duck* without seeing in it as pretty a swan as ever swam the basin in the garden of the Luxembourg. And the Professor showed the whites of his eyes devoutly, like one returning thanks after a dinner of many courses.

I don't know anything sweeter than this leaking in of Nature through all the cracks in the walls and floors of cities. You heap up a million tons of hewn rocks on a square mile or two of earth which was green once. The trees look down from the hill-sides and ask each other, as they stand on tiptoe,—"What are these people about?" And the small herbs at their feet look up and whisper back,—"We will go and see." So the small herbs pack themselves up in the least possible bundles, and wait until the wind steals to them at night and whispers,—"Come with me." Then they go softly with it into the great city,—one to a cleft in the pavement, one to a spout on the roof, one to a seam in the marbles over a rich gentleman's bones, and one to the grave without a stone where nothing but a man is buried,—and there they grow, looking down on the generations of men from mouldy roofs, looking up from between the less-trodden pavements, looking out through iron cemetery-railings. Listen to them, when there is only a light breath stirring, and you will hear them saying to each other,—"Wait awhile!" The words run along the telegraph of those narrow green lines that border the roads leading from the city, until they reach the slope of the hills, and the trees repeat in low murmurs to each other,—"Wait awhile!" By-and-by the flow of life in the streets ebbs, and the old leafy inhabitants—the smaller tribes always in front—saunter in, one by one, very careless seemingly, but very tenacious, until they swarm so that the great stones gape from each other with the crowding of their roots, and the feldspar begins to be picked out of the granite to find them food. At last the trees take up their solemn line of march, and never rest until they have encamped in the market-place. Wait long enough and you will find an old doting oak hugging a huge worn block in its yellow underground arms; that was the corner-stone of the State-House. Oh, so patient she is, this imperturbable Nature!

—Let us cry!—

But all this has nothing to do with my walks and talks with the schoolmistress. I did not say that I would not tell you something about them. Let me alone, and I shall talk to you more than I ought to, probably. We never tell our secrets to people that pump for them.

Books we talked about, and education. It was her duty to know something of these, and of course she did. Perhaps I was somewhat more learned than she, but I found that the difference between her reading and mine was like that of a man's and a woman's dusting a library. The man flaps about with a bunch of feathers; the woman goes to work softly with a cloth. She does not raise half the dust, nor fill her own eyes and mouth with it,—but she goes into all the corners and attends to the leaves as much as to the covers. Books are the *negative* pictures of thought, and the more sensitive the mind that receives their images, the more nicely the finest lines are reproduced. A woman (of the right kind), reading after a man, follows him as

Ruth followed the reapers of Boaz, and her gleanings are often the finest of the wheat.

But it was in talking of Life that we came most nearly together. I thought I knew something about that,—that I could speak or write about it somewhat to the purpose.

To take up this fluid earthly being of ours as a sponge sucks up water,—to be steeped and soaked in its realities as a hide fills its pores lying seven years in a tan-pit,—to have winnowed every wave of it as a mill-wheel works up the stream that runs through the flume upon its float-boards,—to have curled up in the keenest spasms and flattened out in the laxest languors of this breathing-sickness, which keeps certain parcels of matter uneasy for three or four score years,—to have fought all the devils and clasped all the angels of its delirium,—and then, just at the point when the white-hot passions have cooled down to cherry-red, plunge our experience into the ice-cold stream of some human language or other, one might think would end in a rhapsody with something of spring and temper in it. All this I thought my power and province.

The schoolmistress had tried life, too. Once in a while one meets with a single soul greater than all the living pageant which passes before it. As the pale astronomer sits in his study with sunken eyes and thin fingers, and weighs Uranus or Neptune as in a balance, so there are meek, slight women who have weighed all which this planetary life can offer, and hold it like a bauble in the palm of their slender hands. This was one of them. Fortune had left her, sorrow had baptized her; the routine of labor and the loneliness of almost friendless city-life were before her. Yet, as I looked upon her tranquil face, gradually regaining a cheerfulness which was often sprightly, as she became interested in the various matters we talked about and places we visited, I saw that eye and lip and every shifting lineament were made for love,—unconscious of their sweet office as yet, and meeting the cold aspect of Duty with the natural graces which were meant for the reward of nothing less than the Great Passion.

—I never addressed one word of love to the schoolmistress in the course of these pleasant walks. It seemed to me that we talked of everything but love on that particular morning. There was, perhaps, a little more timidity and hesitancy on my part than I have commonly shown among our people at the boarding-house. In fact, I considered myself the master at the breakfast-table; but, somehow, I could not command myself just then so well as usual. The truth is, I had secured a passage to Liverpool in the steamer which was to leave at noon,—

with the condition, however, of being released in case circumstances occurred to detain me. The schoolmistress knew nothing about all this, of course, as yet.

It was on the Common that we were walking. The *mall*, or boulevard of our Common, you know, has various branches leading from it in different directions. One of these runs down from opposite Joy Street southward across the whole length of the Common to Boylston Street. We called it the long path, and were fond of it.

I felt very weak indeed (though of a tolerably robust habit) as we came opposite the head of this path on that morning. I think I tried to speak twice without making myself distinctly audible. At last I got out the question,—Will you take the long path with me?—Certainly,—said the schoolmistress,—with much pleasure.—Think,—I said, —before you answer: if you take the long path with me now, I shall interpret it that we are to part no more!—The schoolmistress stepped back with a sudden movement, as if an arrow had struck her.

One of the long granite blocks used as seats was hard by,—the one you may still see close by the Gingko-tree.—Pray, sit down,—I said.—No, no, she answered, softly,—I will walk the *long path* with you! —The old gentleman who sits opposite met us walking, arm in arm, about the middle of the long path, and said, very charmingly,—"Good-morning, my dears!"

HENRY DAVID THOREAU (1817-1862)

From WALDEN OR, LIFE IN THE WOODS

I Went to the Woods

I WENT to the woods because I wished to live deliberately, to front only the essential facts of life, and see if I could not learn what it had to teach, and not, when I came to die, discover that I had not lived. I did not wish to live what was not life, living is so dear; nor did I wish to practice resignation, unless it was quite necessary. I wanted to live deep and suck out all the marrow of life, to live so sturdily and Spartan-like as to put to rout all that was not life, to cut a broad swath and shave close, to drive life into a corner, and reduce it to its lowest terms, and, if it proved to be mean, why then to get the whole and genuine meanness of it, and publish its meanness to the world; or if it were sublime, to know it by experience, and be able to give a true account of it in my next excursion. For most men, it appears to me, are in a strange uncertainty about it, whether it is of the devil or of God, and have *somewhat hastily* concluded that it is the chief end of man here to "glorify God and enjoy him forever."

Still we live meanly, like ants; though the fable tells us that we were long ago changed into men; like pygmies we fight with cranes; it is error upon error, and clout upon clout, and our best virtue has for its occasion a superfluous and evitable wretchedness. Our life is frittered away by detail. An honest man has hardly need to count more than his ten fingers, or in extreme cases he may add his ten toes, and lump the rest. Simplicity, simplicity, simplicity! I say, let your affairs be as two or three, and not a hundred or a thousand; instead of a million count half a dozen, and keep your accounts on your thumb nail. In the midst of this chopping sea of civilized life, such are the clouds and storms and quicksands and thousand-and-one items to be allowed for, that a man has to live, if he would not founder and go to the bottom and not make his port at all, by dead reckoning, and he must be a great calculator indeed who succeeds. Simplify, simplify. Instead of three meals a day, if it be necessary eat but one; instead of a hundred dishes, five; and reduce other things in proportion. Our life is like a German Confederacy, made up of petty states, with its boundary forever fluctuating, so that even a German cannot tell you how it is bounded at any moment. The nation itself, with all its so-called internal improvements, which, by the way are all external and superficial, is just such an unwieldy and overgrown establishment, cluttered with furniture and tripped up by its own traps, ruined by luxury and heedless expense, by want of calculation and a worthy aim, as the million households in the land; and the only cure for it as for them is in a rigid economy, a stern and more than Spartan simplicity of life and elevation of purpose. It lives too fast. Men think that it is essential that the *Nation* have commerce, and export ice, and talk through a telegraph, and ride thirty miles an hour, without a doubt, whether *they* do or not; but whether we should live like baboons or like men, is a little uncertain. If we do not get out sleepers, and forge rails, and devote days and nights to the work, but go to tinkering upon our *lives* to improve *them,* who will build railroads? And if railroads are not built, how shall we get to heaven in season? But if we stay at home and mind our business, who will want railroads? We do not ride on the railroad; it rides upon us. Did you ever think what those sleepers are that underlie the railroad? Each one is a man, an Irishman, or a Yankee man. The rails are laid on them, and they are covered with sand, and the cars run smoothly over them. They are sound sleepers, I assure you. And every few years a new lot is laid down and run over; so that, if some have the pleasure of riding on a rail, others have the misfortune to be ridden upon. And when they run over a man that is walking in his sleep, a supernumerary sleeper in the wrong position, and wake him up, they suddenly stop the cars, and make a hue and cry about it, as if this were an exception. I am glad to know that it takes a gang of men for every five miles to keep the sleepers down and level in their beds as it is, for this is a sign that they may sometime get up again.

Why should we live with such hurry and waste of life? We are determined to be starved before we are hungry. Men say that a stitch in time saves nine, and so they take a thousand stitches to-day to save nine to-morrow. As for *work,* we haven't any of any consequence. We have the Saint Vitus' dance, and cannot possibly keep our heads still. If I should only give a few pulls at the parish bell-rope, as for a fire, that is, without setting the bell, there is hardly a man on his farm in the outskirts of Concord, notwithstanding that press of engagements which was his excuse so many times this morning, nor a boy, nor a woman, I might almost say, but would forsake all and follow that sound, not mainly to save property from the flames, but, if we will confess the truth, much more to see it burn, since burn it must, and we, be it known, did not set it on fire,—or to see it put out, and have a hand in it, if that is done as handsomely; yes, even if it were the parish church itself. Hardly a man takes a half hour's nap after dinner, but when he wakes he holds up his head and asks, "What's the news?" as if the rest of mankind had stood his sentinels. Some give directions to be waked every half hour, doubtless for no other purpose; and then, to pay for it, they tell what they have dreamed. After a night's sleep the news is as indispensable as the breakfast. "Pray tell me anything new that has happened to a man anywhere on this globe,"—and he reads it over his coffee and rolls, that a man has had his eyes gouged out this morning on the Wachito River; never dreaming the while that he lives in the dark unfathomed mammoth cave of this world, and has but the rudiment of an eye himself.

JAMES RUSSELL LOWELL
(1819-1891)

The Courtin'

God makes sech nights, all white an' still
  Fur 'z you can look or listen;
Moonshine an' snow on field an' hill,
  All silence an' all glisten.

Zekle crep' up quite unbeknown
  An' peeked in thru the winder;
An' there sot Huldy all alone,
'Ith no one nigh to hinder.

A fireplace filled the room's one side
  With half a cord o' wood in—
There warn't no stoves (tell comfort died)
  To bake ye to a puddin'.

The wa'nut logs shot sparkles out
  Towards the pootiest, bless her,
An' leetle flames danced all about
  The chiny on the dresser.

Agin the chimbley crook-necks hung,
  An' in amongst 'em rusted
The ole queen's-arm thet gran'ther Young
  Fetched back from Concord busted.

The very room, coz she was in,
  Seemed warm from floor to ceilin',
An' she looked full ez rosy agin
  Ez the apples she was peelin'.

'Twas kin' o' kingdom-come to look
  On sech a blessed cretur;
A dogrose blushin' to a brook
  Ain't modester nor sweeter.

He was six foot o' man, A 1,
  Clean grit an' human natur';
None couldn't quicker pitch a ton
  Nor dror a furrer straighter.

He'd sparked it with full twenty gals,
  He'd squired 'em, danced 'em, druv 'em,
Fust this one, an' then thet, by spells—
  All is, he couldn't love 'em.

But long o' her his veins 'ould run
  All crinkly like curled maple;
The side she breshed felt full o' sun
  Ez a south slope in Ap'il.

She thought no v'ice hed sech a swing
  Ez hisn in the choir;
My! when he made Ole Hunderd ring,
  She *knowed* the Lord was nigher.

An' she'd blush scarlit, right in prayer,
  When her new meetin'-bunnet
Felt somehow thru its crown a pair
  O' blue eyes sot upon it.

Thet night, I tell ye, she looked some!
  She seemed to've gut a new soul,
For she felt sartin-sure he'd come,
  Down to her very shoe-sole.

She heered a foot, an' knowed it tu,
  A-raspin' on the scraper,—
All ways to once her feelin's flew
  Like sparks in burnt-up paper.

He kin' o' l'itered on the mat,
  Some doubtful o' the sekle;
His heart kep' goin' pity-pat,
  But hern went pity-Zekle.

An' yit she gin her cheer a jerk
  Ez though she wished him furder,
An' on her apples kep' to work,
  Parin' away like murder.

"You want to see my Pa, I s'pose?"
  "Wal—no—I come designin'"—
"To see my Ma? She's sprinklin' clo'es
  Again to-morrer's i'nin'."

To say why gals acts so or so,
  Or don't, 'ould be presumin';
Mebby to mean yes an' say no
  Comes nateral to women.

He stood a spell on one foot fust,
  Then stood a spell on t'other,
An' on which one he felt the wust
  He couldn't ha' told ye nuther.

Says he, "I'd better call agin";
  Says she, "Think likely, Mister"—
Thet last word pricked him like a pin,
  An'—wal he up an' kist her.

When Ma bimeby upon 'em slips,
  Huldy sot pale ez ashes,
All kin' o' smily roun' the lips
  An' teary roun' the lashes.

Fur she was jes' the quiet kind
  Whose naturs never vary,
Like streams that keep a summer mind
  Snow-hid in Jenooary.

The blood clost roun' her heart felt glued
  Too tight for all expressin',
Tell mother see how matters stood
  An' gin 'em both her blessin'.

Then her red come back like the tide
  Down to the Bay o' Fundy;
An' all I know is they was cried
  In meetin' come nex' Sunday.

Ode Recited at the Harvard Commemoration

I

  Weak-winged is song,
Nor aims at that clear-ethered height
Whither the brave deed climbs for light:
  We seem to do them wrong,
Bringing our robin's-leaf to deck their hearse
Who in warm life-blood wrote their nobler verse,
Our trivial song to honor those who come
With ears attuned to strenuous trump and drum,
And shaped in squadron-strophes their desire,
Live battle-odes whose lines were steel and fire:
  Yet sometimes feathered words are strong,
A gracious memory to buoy up and save
From Lethe's dreamless ooze, the common grave
  Of the unventurous throng.

II

To-day our Reverend Mother welcomes back
  Her wisest Scholars, those who understood
The deeper teaching of her mystic tome,
  And offered their fresh lives to make it good:
  No lore of Greece or Rome,
No science peddling with the names of things,
Or reading stars to find inglorious fates,
  Can lift our life with wings
Far from Death's idle gulf that for the many waits,
  And lengthen out our dates
With that clear fame whose memory sings
In manly hearts to come, and nerves them and dilates:

Nor such thy teaching, Mother of us all!
Not such the trumpet-call
Of thy diviner mood,
That could thy sons entice
From happy homes and toils, the fruitful nest
Of those half-virtues which the world calls best,
Into War's tumult rude;
But rather far that stern device
The sponsors chose that round thy cradle stood
In the dim, unventured wood,
The VERITAS that lurks beneath
The letter's unprolific sheath,
Life of whate'er makes life worth living,
Seed-grain of high emprise, immortal food,
One heavenly thing whereof earth hath the giving.

III

Many loved Truth, and lavished life's best oil
Amid the dust of books to find her,
Content at last, for guerdon of their toil,
With the cast mantle she hath left behind her.
Many in sad faith sought for her,
Many with crossed hands sighed for her;
But these, our brothers, fought for her,
At life's dear peril wrought for her,
So loved her that they died for her,
Tasting the raptured fleetness
Of her divine completeness:
Their higher instinct knew
Those love her best who to themselves are true,
And what they dare to dream of, dare to do;
They followed her and found her
Where all may hope to find,
Not in the ashes of the burnt-out mind,
But beautiful, with danger's sweetness round her.
Where faith made whole with deed
Breathes its awakening breath
Into the lifeless creed,
They saw her plumed and mailed,
With sweet, stern face unveiled,
And all-repaying eyes, look proud on them in death.

IV

Our slender life runs rippling by, and glides
Into the silent hollow of the past;
What is there that abides
To make the next age better for the last?
Is earth too poor to give us
Something to live for here that shall outlive us?
Some more substantial boon
Than such as flows and ebbs with Fortune's fickle moon?
The little that we see
From doubt is never free;
The little that we do
Is but half-nobly true;
With our laborious hiving
What men call treasure, and the gods call dross,
Life seems a jest of Fate's contriving,
Only secure in every one's conniving,
A long account of nothings paid with loss,
Where we poor puppets, jerked by unseen wires,
After our little hour of strut and rave,
With all our pasteboard passions and desires,
Loves, hates, ambitions, and immortal fires,
Are tossed pell-mell together in the grave.
But stay! no age was e'er degenerate,
Unless men held it at too cheap a rate,
For in our likeness still we shape our fate.
Ah, there is something here
Unfathomed by the cynic's sneer,

Something that gives our feeble light
A high immunity from Night,
Something that leaps life's narrow bars
To claim its birthright with the hosts of heaven;
A seed of sunshine that can leaven
Our earthy dulness with the beams of stars,
And glorify our clay
With light from fountains elder than the Day;
A conscience more divine than we,
A gladness fed with secret tears,
A vexing, forward-reaching sense
Of some more noble permanence;
A light across the sea,
Which haunts the soul and will not let it be,
Still beaconing from the heights of undegenerate years.

V

Whither leads the path
To ampler fates that leads?
Not down through flowery meads,
To reap an aftermath
Of youth's vainglorious weeds;
But up the steep, amid the wrath
And shock of deadly hostile creeds,
Where the world's best hope and stay
By battle's flashes gropes a desperate way,
And every turf the fierce foot clings to bleeds.
Peace hath her not ignoble wreath,
Ere yet the sharp, decisive word
Light the black lips of cannon, and the sword
Dreams in its easeful sheath;
But some day the live coal behind the thought,
Whether from Baäl's stone obscene,
Or from the shrine serene
Of God's pure altar brought,
Bursts up in flame; the war of tongue and pen
Learns with what deadly purpose it was fraught,
And, helpless in the fiery passion caught,
Shakes all the pillared state with shock of men:
Some day the soft Ideal that we wooed
Confronts us fiercely, foe-beset, pursued,
And cries reproachful: "Was it, then, my praise,
And not myself was loved? Prove now thy truth;
I claim of thee the promise of thy youth;
Give me thy life, or cower in empty phrase,
The victim of thy genius, not its mate!"
Life may be given in many ways,
And loyalty to Truth be sealed
As bravely in the closet as the field,
So bountiful is Fate;
But then to stand beside her,
When craven churls deride her,
To front a lie in arms and not to yield,
This shows, methinks, God's plan
And measure of a stalwart man,
Limbed like the old heroic breeds,
Who stands self-poised on manhood's solid earth,
Not forced to frame excuses for his birth,
Fed from within with all the strength he needs.

VI

Such was he, our Martyr-Chief,
Whom late the Nation he had led,
With ashes on her head,
Wept with the passion of an angry grief:
Forgive me, if from present things I turn
To speak what in my heart will beat and burn,
And hang my wreath on his world-honored urn.
Nature, they say, doth dote,
And cannot make a man
Save on some worn-out plan,
Repeating us by rote:
For him her Old-World moulds aside she threw,

And, choosing sweet clay from the breast
Of the unexhausted West,
With stuff untainted shaped a hero new,
Wise, steadfast in the strength of God, and true.
How beautiful to see
Once more a shepherd of mankind indeed,
Who loved his charge, but never loved to lead;
One whose meek flock the people joyed to be,
Not lured by any cheat of birth,
But by his clear-grained human worth,
And brave old wisdom of sincerity!
They knew that outward grace is dust;
They could not choose but trust
In that sure-footed mind's unfaltering skill,
And supple-tempered will
That bent like perfect steel to spring again and thrust.
His was no lonely mountain-peak of mind,
Thrusting to thin air o'er our cloudy bars,
A sea-mark now, now lost in vapors blind;
Broad prairie rather, genial, level-lined,
Fruitful and friendly for all human-kind,
Yet also nigh to heaven and loved of loftiest stars.
Nothing of Europe here,
Or, then, of Europe fronting morn-ward still,
Ere any names of Serf and Peer
Could Nature's equal scheme deface
And thwart her genial will;
Here was a type of the true elder race,
And one of Plutarch's men talked with us face to face.
I praise him not; it were too late;
And some innative weakness there must be
In him who condescends to victory
Such as the Present gives, and cannot wait,
Safe in himself as in a fate.
So always firmly he:
He knew to bide his time,
And can his fame abide,
Still patient in his simple faith sublime,
Till the wise years decide.
Great captains, with their guns and drums,
Disturb our judgment for the hour,
But at last silence comes;
These all are gone, and, standing like a tower,
Our children shall behold his fame,
The kindly-earnest, brave, foreseeing man,
Sagacious, patient, dreading praise, not blame,
New birth of our new soil, the first American.

VII

Long as man's hope insatiate can discern
Or only guess some more inspiring goal
Outside of Self, enduring as the pole,
Along whose course the flying axles burn
Of spirits bravely-pitched, earth's manlier brood;
Long as below we cannot find
The meed that stills the inexorable mind;
So long this faith to some ideal Good,
Under whatever mortal name it masks,
Freedom, Law, Country, this ethereal mood
That thanks the Fates for their severer tasks,
Feeling its challenged pulses leap,
While others skulk in subterfuges cheap,
And, set in Danger's van, has all the boon it asks,
Shall win man's praise and woman's love,
Shall be a wisdom that we set above

All other skills and gifts to culture dear,
A virtue round whose forehead we enwreathe
Laurels that with a living passion breathe
When other crowns grow, while we twine them, sear.
What brings us thronging these high rites to pay,
And seal these hours the noblest of our year,
Save that our brothers found this better way?

VIII

We sit here in the Promised Land
That flows with Freedom's honey and milk;
But 'twas they won it, sword in hand,
Making the nettle danger soft for us as silk.
We welcome back our bravest and our best;—
Ah me! not all! some come not with the rest,
Who went forth brave and bright as any here!
I strive to mix some gladness with my strain,
But the sad strings complain,
And will not please the ear:
I sweep them for a pæan, but they wane
Again and yet again
Into a dirge, and die away in pain.
In these brave ranks I only see the gaps,
Thinking of dear ones whom the dumb turf wraps,
Dark to the triumph which they died to gain:
Fitlier may others greet the living,
For me the past is unforgiving;
I with uncovered head
Salute the sacred dead,
Who went, and who return not.—Say not so!
'Tis not the grapes of Canaan that repay,
But the high faith that failed not by the way;
Virtue treads paths that end not in the grave;
No bar of endless night exiles the brave;
And to the saner mind
We rather seem the dead that stayed behind.
Blow, trumpets, all your exultations blow!
For never shall their aureoled presence lack:
I see them muster in a gleaming row,
With ever-youthful brows that nobler show;
We find in our dull road their shining track;
In every nobler mood
We feel the orient of their spirit glow,
Part of our life's unalterable good,
Of all our saintlier aspiration;
They come transfigured back,
Secure from change in their high-hearted ways,
Beautiful evermore, and with the rays
Of morn on their white Shields of Expectation!

IX

But is there hope to save
Even this ethereal essence from the grave?
What ever 'scaped Oblivion's subtle wrong
Save a few clarion names, or golden threads of song?
Before my musing eye
The mighty ones of old sweep by,
Disvoicèd now and insubstantial things,
As noisy once as we; poor ghosts of kings,
Shadows of empire wholly gone to dust,
And many races, nameless long ago,
To darkness driven by that imperious gust
Of ever-rushing Time that here doth blow:
O visionary world, condition strange,
Where naught abiding is but only Change,

Where the deep-bolted stars themselves still shift and range!
Shall we to more continuance make pretence?
Renown builds tombs; a life-estate is Wit;
And, bit by bit,
The cunning years steal all from us but woe:
Leaves are we, whose decays no harvest sow.
But, when we vanish hence,
Shall they lie forceless in the dark below,
Save to make green their little length of sods,
Or deepen pansies for a year or two,
Who now to us are shining-sweet as gods?
Was dying all they had the skill to do?
That were not fruitless: but the Soul resents
Such short-lived service, as if blind events
Ruled without her, or earth could so endure;
She claims a more divine investiture
Of longer tenure than Fame's airy rents;
Whate'er she touches doth her nature share;
Her inspiration haunts the ennobled air,
Gives eyes to mountains blind,
Ears to the deaf earth, voices to the wind,
And her clear trump sings succor everywhere
By lonely bivouacs to the wakeful mind;
For soul inherits all that soul could dare:
Yea, Manhood hath a wider span
And larger privilege of life than man.
The single deed, the private sacrifice,
So radiant now through proudly-hidden tears,
Is covered up ere long from mortal eyes
With thoughtless drift of the deciduous years;
But that high privilege that makes all men peers,
That leap of heart whereby a people rise
Up to a noble anger's height,
And, flamed on by the Fates, not shrink, but grow more bright,
That swift validity in noble veins,
Of choosing danger and disdaining shame,
Of being set on flame
By the pure fire that flies all contact base,
But wraps its chosen with angelic might,
These are imperishable gains,
Sure as the sun, medicinal as light,
These hold great futures in their lusty reins
And certify to earth a new imperial race.

X

Who now shall sneer?
Who dare again to say we trace
Our lines to a plebeian race?
Roundhead and Cavalier!
Dumb are those names erewhile in battle loud;
Dream-footed as the shadow of a cloud,
They flit across the ear:
That is best blood that hath most iron in't,
To edge resolve with, pouring without stint
For what makes manhood dear.
Tell us not of Plantagenets,
Hapsburgs, and Guelfs, whose thin bloods crawl
Down from some victor in a border-brawl!
How poor their outworn coronets,
Matched with one leaf of that plain civic wreath
Our brave for honor's blazon shall bequeath,
Through whose desert a rescued Nation sets

Her heel on treason, and the trumpet hears
Shout victory, tingling Europe's sullen ears
With vain resentments and more vain regrets!

XI

Not in anger, not in pride,
Pure from passion's mixture rude,
Ever to base earth allied,
But with far-heard gratitude,
Still with heart and voice renewed,
To heroes living and dear martyrs dead,
The strain should close that consecrates our brave.
Lift the heart and lift the head!
Lofty be its mood and grave,
Not without a martial ring,
Not without a prouder tread
And a peal of exultation:
Little right has he to sing
Through whose heart in such an hour
Beats no march of conscious power,
Sweeps no tumult of elation!
'Tis no Man we celebrate,
By his country's victories great,
A hero half, and half the whim of Fate,
But the pith and marrow of a Nation
Drawing force from all her men,
Highest, humblest, weakest, all,
For her time of need, and then
Pulsing it again through them,
Till the basest can no longer cower,
Feeling his soul spring up divinely tall,
Touched but in passing by her mantle-hem.
Come back, then, noble pride, for 'tis her dower!
How could poet ever tower,
If his passions, hopes, and fears,
If his triumphs and his tears,
Kept not measure with his people?
Boom, cannon, boom to all the winds and waves!
Clash out, glad bells, from every rocking steeple!
Banners, advance with triumph, bend your staves!
And from every mountain-peak
Let beacon-fire to answering beacon speak,
Katahdin tell Monadnock, Whiteface he,
And so leap on in light from sea to sea,
Till the glad news be sent
Across a kindling continent,
Making earth feel more firm and air breathe braver:
"Be proud! for she is saved, and all have helped to save her!
She that lifts up the manhood of the poor,
She of the open soul and open door,
With room about her hearth for all mankind!
The fire is dreadful in her eyes no more;
From her bold front the helm she doth unbind,
Sends all her handmaid armies back to spin,
And bids her navies, that so lately hurled
Their crashing battle, hold their thunders in,
Swimming like birds of calm along the unharmful shore.
No challenge sends she to the elder world,
That looked askance and hated; a light scorn
Plays o'er her mouth, as round her mighty knees
She calls her children back, and waits the morn
Of nobler day, enthroned between her subject seas."

XII

Bow down, dear Land, for thou hast found release!
Thy God, in these distempered days,

Hath taught thee the sure wisdom of His ways,
And through thine enemies hath wrought thy peace!
Bow down in prayer and praise!
No poorest in thy borders but may now
Lift to the juster skies a man's enfranchised brow.
O Beautiful! my Country! ours once more!
Smoothing thy gold of war-dishevelled hair
O'er such sweet brows as never other wore,
And letting thy set lips,
Freed from wrath's pale eclipse,
The rosy edges of their smile lay bare,
What words divine of lover or of poet
Could tell our love and make thee know it,
Among the Nations bright beyond compare?
What were our lives without thee?
What all our lives to save thee?
We reck not what we gave thee;
We will not dare to doubt thee,
But ask whatever else, and we will dare!

WALT WHITMAN (1819-1892)

Song of the Open Road

I

Afoot and light-hearted, I take to the open road,
Healthy, free, the world before me,
The long brown path before me, leading wherever I choose.

Henceforth I ask not good-fortune—I myself am good-fortune;
Henceforth I whimper no more, postpone no more, need nothing,
Strong and content, I travel the open road.

The earth—that is sufficient;
I do not want the constellations any nearer;
I know they are very well where they are;
I know they suffice for those who belong to them.

(Still here I carry my old delicious burdens;
I carry them, men and women—I carry them with me wherever I go;
I swear it is impossible for me to get rid of them;
I am fill'd with them, and I will fill them in return.)

2

You road I enter upon and look around!
I believe you are not all that is here;
I believe that much unseen is also here.

Here the profound lesson of reception, neither preference or denial;
The black with his woolly head, the felon, the diseas'd, the illiterate person, are not denied;
The birth, the hasting after the physician, the beggar's tramp, the drunkard's stagger, the laughing party of mechanics,
The escaped youth, the rich person's carriage, the fop, the eloping couple,
The early market-man, the hearse, the moving of furniture into the town, the return back from the town,
They pass—I also pass—anything passes—none can be interdicted;
None but are accepted—none but are dear to me.

3

You air that serves me with breath to speak!
You objects that call from diffusion my meanings, and give them shape!
You light that wraps me and all things in delicate equable showers!

You paths worn in the irregular hollows by the roadsides!
I think you are latent with unseen existences—you are so dear to me.

You flagg'd walks of the cities! you strong curbs at the edges!
You ferries! you planks and posts of wharves! you timber-lined sides! you distant ships!
You rows of houses! you window-pierced façades! you roofs!
You porches and entrances! you copings and iron guards!
You windows whose transparent shells might expose so much!
You doors and ascending steps! you arches!
You gray stones of interminable pavements! you trodden crossings!
From all that has been near you, I believe you have imparted to yourselves, and now would impart the same secretly to me;
From the living and the dead I think you have peopled your impassive surfaces, and the spirits thereof would be evident and amicable with me.

4

The earth expanding right hand and left hand,
The picture alive, every part in its best light,
The music falling in where it is wanted, and stopping where it is not wanted,
The cheerful voice of the public road—the gay fresh sentiment of the road.

O highway I travel! O public road! do you say to me, *Do not leave me?*
Do you say, *Venture not? If you leave me, you are lost?*
Do you say, *I am already prepared—I am well-beaten and undenied—adhere to me?*

O public road! I say back, I am not afraid to leave you—yet I love you;
You express me better than I can express myself;
You shall be more to me than my poem.

I think heroic deeds were all conceiv'd in the open air, and all great poems also;
I think I could stop here myself, and do miracles;
(My judgments, thoughts, I henceforth try by the open air, the road;)
I think whatever I shall meet on the road I shall like, and whoever beholds me shall like me;
I think whoever I see must be happy.

5

From this hour, freedom!
From this hour I ordain myself loos'd of limits and imaginary lines,
Going where I list, my own master, total and absolute,
Listening to others, and considering well what they say,
Pausing, searching, receiving, contemplating,
Gently, but with undeniable will, divesting myself of the holds that would hold me.

I inhale great draughts of space;
The east and the west are mine, and the north and the south are mine.

I am larger, better than I thought;
I did not know I held so much goodness.
All seems beautiful to me;
I can repeat over to men and women, You have done such good to me, I would do the same to you.

I will recruit for myself and you as I go;
I will scatter myself among men and women as I go;
I will toss the new gladness and roughness among them;

Whoever denies me, it shall not trouble me;
Whoever accepts me, he or she shall be blessed, and shall bless me.

6

Now if a thousand perfect men were to appear, it would not amaze me;
Now if a thousand beautiful forms of women appear'd, it would not astonish me.

Now I see the secret of the making of the best persons,
It is to grow in the open air, and to eat and sleep with the earth.

Here a great personal deed has room;
A great deed seizes upon the hearts of the whole race of men,
Its effusion of strength and will overwhelms law, and mocks all authority and all argument against it.

Here is the test of wisdom;
Wisdom is not finally tested in schools;
Wisdom cannot be pass'd from one having it, to another not having it;
Wisdom is of the Soul, is not susceptible of proof, is its own proof,
Applies to all stages and objects and qualities, and is content,
Is the certainty of the reality and immortality of things, and the excellence of things;
Something there is in the float of the sight of things that provokes it out of the Soul.

Now I reëxamine philosophies and religions,
They may prove well in lecture-rooms, yet not prove at all under the spacious clouds, and along the landscape and flowing currents.
Here is realization;
Here is a man tallied—he realizes here what he has in him;
The past, the future, majesty, love—if they are vacant of you, you are vacant of them.
Only the kernel of every object nourishes;
Where is he who tears off the husks for you and me?
Where is he that undoes stratagems and envelopes for you and me?

Here is adhesiveness—it is not previously fashion'd—it is apropos;
Do you know what it is, as you pass, to be loved by strangers?
Do you know the talk of those turning eye-balls?

7

Here is the efflux of the Soul;
The efflux of the Soul comes from within, through embower'd gates, ever provoking questions:
These yearnings, why are they? These thoughts in the darkness, why are they?
Why are there men and women that while they are nigh me, the sun-light expands my blood?
Why, when they leave me, do my pennants of joy sink flat and lank?
Why are there trees I never walk under, but large and melodious thoughts descend upon me?
(I think they hang there winter and summer on those trees, and always drop fruit as I pass;)
What is it I interchange so suddenly with strangers?
What with some driver, as I ride on the seat by his side?
What with some fisherman, drawing his seine by the shore, as I walk by, and pause?
What gives me to be free to a woman's or man's good-will? What gives them to be free to mine?

8

The efflux of the Soul is happiness—here is happiness;
I think it pervades the open air, waiting at all times;
Now it flows unto us—we are rightly charged.

Here rises the fluid and attaching character;
The fluid and attaching character is the freshness and sweetness of man and woman;
(The herbs of the morning sprout no fresher and sweeter every day out of the roots of themselves, than it sprouts fresh and sweet continually out of itself.)

Toward the fluid and attaching character exudes the sweat of the love of young and old;
From it falls distill'd the charm that mocks beauty and attainments;
Toward it heaves the shuddering longing ache of contact.

9

Allons! whoever you are, come travel with me!
Travelling with me, you find what never tires.

The earth never tires;
The earth is rude, silent, incomprehensible at first—Nature is rude and incomprehensible at first;
Be not discouraged—keep on—there are divine things, well envelop'd;
I swear to you there are divine things more beautiful than words can tell.

Allons! we must not stop here!
However sweet these laid-up stores—however convenient this dwelling, we cannot remain here;
However shelter'd this port, and however calm these waters, we must not anchor here;
However welcome the hospitality that surrounds us, we are permitted to receive it but a little while.

10

Allons! the inducements shall be greater;
We will sail pathless and wild seas;
We will go where winds blow, waves dash, and the Yankee clipper speeds by under full sail.

Allons! with power, liberty, the earth, the elements!
Health, defiance, gayety, self-esteem, curiosity;
Allons! from all formules!
From your formules, O bat-eyed and materialistic priests!

The stale cadaver blocks up the passage—the burial waits no longer.

Allons! yet take warning!
He travelling with me needs the best blood, thews, endurance;
None may come to the trial, till he or she brings courage and health.
Come not here if you have already spent the best of yourself;
Only those may come, who come in sweet and determin'd bodies;
No diseas'd person—no rum-drinker or venereal taint is permitted here.

I and mine do not convince by arguments, similes, rhymes;
We convince by our presence.

11

Listen! I will be honest with you;
I do not offer the old smooth prizes, but offer rough new prizes;
These are the days that must happen to you:
You shall not heap up what is call'd riches,

You shall scatter with lavish hand all that you earn or achieve,
You but arrive at the city to which you were destin'd—you hardly settle yourself to satisfaction, before you are call'd by an irresistible call to depart,
You shall be treated to the ironical smiles and mockings of those who remain behind you;
What beckonings of love you receive, you shall only answer with passionate kisses of parting,
You shall not allow the hold of those who spread their reach'd hands toward you.

12

Allons! after the GREAT COMPANIONS! and to belong to them!
They too are on the road! they are the swift and majestic men! they are the greatest women.
Over that which hinder'd them—over that which retarded—passing impediments large or small,
Committers of crimes, committers of many beautiful virtues.
Enjoyers of calms of seas, and storms of seas,
Sailors of many a ship, walkers of many a mile of land,
Habitués of many distant countries, habitués of far-distant dwellings,
Trusters of men and women, observers of cities, solitary toilers,
Pausers and contemplators of tufts, blossoms, shells of the shore,
Dancers at wedding-dances, kissers of brides, tender helpers of children, bearers of children,
Soldiers of revolts, standers by gaping graves, lowerers down of coffins,
Journeyers over consecutive seasons, over the years—the curious years, each emerging from that which preceded it,
Journeyers as with companions, namely, their own diverse phases,
Forth-steppers from the latent unrealized baby-days,
Journeyers gayly with their own youth—Journeyers with their bearded and well-grain'd manhood,
Journeyers with their womanhood, ample, unsurpass'd, content,
Journeyers with their own sublime old age of manhood or womanhood,
Old age, calm, expanded, broad with the haughty breadth of the universe,
Old age, flowing free with the delicious near-by freedom of death.

13

Allons! to that which is endless, as it was beginningless,
To undergo much, tramps of days, rests of nights,
To merge all in the travel they tend to, and the days and nights they tend to,
Again to merge them in the start of superior journeys;
To see nothing anywhere but what you may reach it and pass it,
To conceive no time, however distant, but what you may reach it and pass it,
To look up or down no road but it stretches and waits for you—however long, but it stretches and waits for you;
To see no being, not God's or any, but you also go thither,
To see no possession but you may possess it—enjoying all without labor or purchase—abstracting the feast, yet not abstracting one particle of it;
To take the best of the farmer's farm and the rich man's elegant villa, and the chaste blessings of the well-married couple, and the fruits of orchards and flowers of gardens,
To take to your use out of the compact cities as you pass through,
To carry buildings and streets with you afterward wherever you go,

To gather the minds of men out of their brains as you encounter them—to gather the love out of their hearts,
To take your lovers on the road with you, for all that you leave them behind you,
To know the universe itself as a road—as many roads—as roads for travelling souls.

14

The Soul travels;
The body does not travel as much as the soul;
The body has just as great a work as the soul, and parts away at last for the journeys of the soul.

All parts away for the progress of souls;
All religion, all solid things, arts, governments,—all that was or is apparent upon this globe or any globe, falls into niches and corners before the procession of Souls along the grand roads of the universe.

Of the progress of the souls of men and women along the grand roads of the universe, all other progress is the needed emblem and sustenance.

Forever alive, forever forward,
Stately, solemn, sad, withdrawn, baffled, mad, turbulent, feeble, dissatisfied,
Desperate, proud, fond, sick, accepted by men, rejected by men,
They go! they go! I know that they go, but I know not where they go;
But I know that they go toward the best—toward something great.

15

Allons! whoever you are! come forth!
You must not stay sleeping and dallying there in the house, though you built it, or though it has been built for you.

Allons! out of the dark confinement!
It is useless to protest—I know all, and expose it.

Behold, through you as bad as the rest,
Through the laughter, dancing, dining, supping, of people,
Inside of dresses and ornaments, inside of those wash'd and trimm'd faces,
Behold a secret silent loathing and despair.

No husband, no wife, no friend, trusted to hear the confession;
Another self, a duplicate of every one, skulking and hiding it goes,
Formless and wordless through the streets of the cities, polite and bland in the parlors,
In the cars of rail-roads, in steamboats, in the public assembly,
Home to the houses of men and women, at the table, in the bed-room, everywhere,
Smartly attired, countenance smiling, form upright, death under the breast-bones, hell under the skull-bones,
Under the broadcloth and gloves, under the ribbons and artificial flowers,
Keeping fair with the customs, speaking not a syllable of itself,
Speaking of anything else, but never of itself.

16

Allons! through struggles and wars!
The goal that was named cannot be countermanded.

Have the past struggles succeeded?
What has succeeded? yourself? your nation? nature?
Now understand me well—It is provided in the essence of things, that from any fruition of success, no matter what, shall come forth something to make a greater struggle necessary.

My call is the call of battle—I nourish active rebellion;
He going with me must go well arm'd;
He going with me goes often with spare diet, poverty, angry enemies, desertions.

17

Allons! the road is before us!
It is safe—I have tried it—my own feet have tried it well.

Allons! be not detain'd!
Let the paper remain on the desk unwritten, and the book on the shelf unopen'd!
Let the tools remain in the workshop! let the money remain unearn'd!
Let the school stand! mind not the cry of the teacher!
Let the preacher preach in his pulpit! let the lawyer plead in the court, and the judge expound the law.

Mon enfant! I give you my hand!
I give you my love, more precious than money,
I give you myself, before preaching or law;
Will you give me yourself? will you come travel with me?
Shall we stick by each other as long as we live?

Beat! Beat! Drums!

1

BEAT! beat! drums!—Blow! bugles! blow!
Through the windows—through doors—burst like a ruthless force,
Into the solemn church, and scatter the congregation;
Into the school where the scholar is studying;
Leave not the bridegroom quiet—no happiness must he have now with his bride;
Nor the peaceful farmer any peace, plowing his field or gathering his grain;
So fierce you whirr and pound, you drums—so shrill you bugles blow.

2

Beat! beat! drums!—Blow! bugles! blow!
Over the traffic of cities—over the rumble of wheels in the streets:
Are beds prepared for sleepers at night in the houses? No sleepers must sleep in those beds;
No bargainers' bargains by day—no brokers or speculators—Would they continue?
Would the talkers be talking? would the singer attempt to sing?
Would the lawyer rise in the court to state his case before the judge?
Then rattle quicker, heavier drums—you bugles wilder blow.

3

Beat! beat! drums!—Blow! bugles! blow!
Make no parley—stop for no expostulation;
Mind not the timid—mind not the weeper or prayer;
Mind not the old man beseeching the young man;
Let not the child's voice be heard, nor the mother's entreaties;
Make even the trestles to shake the dead, where they lie awaiting the hearses,
So strong you thump, O terrible drums—so loud you bugles blow.

A March in the Ranks Hard-Prest

A MARCH in the ranks hard-prest, and the road unknown;
A route through a heavy wood, with muffled steps in the darkness;
Our army foil'd with loss severe, and the sullen remnant retreating;

Till after midnight glimmer upon us, the lights of a dim-lighted building;
We come to an open space in the woods, and halt by the dim-lighted building;
'Tis a large old church at the crossing roads—'tis now an impromptu hospital;
—Entering but for a minute, I see a sight beyond all the pictures and poems ever made:
Shadows of deepest, deepest black, just lit by moving candles and lamps,
And by one great pitchy torch, stationary, with wild red flame, and clouds of smoke;
By these crowds, groups of forms, vaguely I see, on the floor, some in the pews laid down;
At my feet more distinctly, a soldier, a mere lad, in danger of bleeding to death, (he is shot in the abdomen;)
I staunch the blood temporarily, (the youngster's face is white as a lily;)
Then before I depart I sweep my eyes o'er the scene, fain to absorb it all;
Faces, varieties, postures beyond description, most in obscurity, some of them dead;
Surgeons operating, attendants holding lights, the smell of ether, the odor of blood;
The crowd, O the crowd of the bloody forms of soldiers—the yard outside also fill'd;
Some on the bare ground, some on planks or stretchers, some in the death-spasm sweating;
An occasional scream or cry, the doctor's shouted orders or calls;
The glisten of the little steel instruments catching the glint of the torches;
These I resume as I chant—I see again the forms, I smell the odor;
Then hear outside the orders given, *Fall in, my men, Fall in;*
But first I bend to the dying lad—his eyes open—a half-smile gives he me;
Then the eyes close, calmly close, and I speed forth to the darkness,
Resuming, marching, ever in darkness marching, on in the ranks,
The unknown road still marching.

When Lilacs Last in the Dooryard Bloom'd

1

WHEN lilacs last in the door-yard bloom'd,
And the great star early droop'd in the western sky in the night,
I mourn'd—and yet shall mourn with ever-returning spring.

O ever-returning spring! trinity sure to me you bring;
Lilac blooming perennial, and drooping star in the west,
And thought of him I love.

2

O powerful, western, fallen star!
O shades of night! O moody, tearful night!
O great star disappear'd! O the black murk that hides the star!
O cruel hands that hold me powerless! O helpless soul of me!
O harsh surrounding cloud, that will not free my soul!

3

In the door-yard fronting an old farm-house, near the whitewash'd palings,
Stands the lilac bush, tall-growing, with heart-shaped leaves of rich green,
With many a pointed blossom, rising, delicate, with the perfume strong I love,
With every leaf a miracle . . . and from this bush in the door-yard,
With delicate-color'd blossoms, and heart-shaped leaves of rich green,
A sprig, with its flower, I break.

4

In the swamp, in secluded recesses,
A shy and hidden bird is warbling a song.
Solitary, the thrush,
The hermit, withdrawn to himself, avoiding the settlements,
Sings by himself a song.
Song of the bleeding throat!
Death's outlet song of life—(for well, dear brother, I know
If thou wast not gifted to sing, thou would'st surely die.)

5

Over the breast of the spring, the land, amid cities,
Amid lanes, and through old woods, (where lately the violets peep'd from the ground, spotting the gray débris;)
Amid the grass in the fields each side of the lanes—passing the endless grass;
Passing the yellow-spear'd wheat, every grain from its shroud in the dark-brown fields uprising;
Passing the apple-tree blows of white and pink in the orchards;
Carrying a corpse to where it shall rest in the grave,
Night and day journeys a coffin.

6

Coffin that passes through lanes and streets,
Through day and night, with the great cloud darkening the land,
With the pomp of the inloop'd flags, with the cities draped in black,
With the show of the States themselves, as of crape-veil'd women, standing,
With processions long and winding, and the flambeaus of the night,
With the countless torches lit—with the silent sea of faces, and the unbared heads,
With the waiting depot, the arriving coffin, and the sombre faces,
With dirges through the night, with the thousand voices rising strong and solemn;
With all the mournful voices of the dirges, pour'd around the coffin,
The dim-lit churches and the shuddering organs—Where amid these you journey,
With the tolling, tolling bells' perpetual clang;
Here! coffin that slowly passes,
I give you my sprig of lilac.

7

(Nor for you, for one, alone;
Blossoms and branches green to coffins all I bring:
For fresh as the morning—thus would I carol a song for you, O sane and sacred death.

All over bouquets of roses,
O death! I cover you over with roses and early lilies;
But mostly and now the lilac that blooms the first,
Copious, I break, I break the sprigs from the bushes;
With loaded arms I come, pouring for you,
For you, and the coffins all of you, O death.)

8

O western orb, sailing the heaven!
Now I know what you must have meant, as a month since we walk'd,
As we walk'd up and down in the dark blue so mystic,
As we walk'd in silence the transparent shadowy night,
As I saw you had something to tell, as you bent to me night after night,
As you droop'd from the sky low down, as if to my side, (while the other stars all look'd on;)
As we wander'd together the solemn night, (for something, I know not what, kept me from sleep;)

As the night advanced, and I saw on the rim of the west, ere you went, how full you were of woe;
As I stood on the rising ground in the breeze, in the cold transparent night,
As I watch'd where you pass'd and was lost in the netherward black of the night,
As my soul, in its trouble, dissatisfied, sank, as where you, sad orb,
Concluded, dropt in the night, and was gone.

9

Sing on, there in the swamp!
O singer bashful and tender! I hear your notes—I hear your call;
I hear—I come presently—I understand you;
But a moment I linger—for the lustrous star has detain'd me;
The star, my departing comrade, holds and detains me.

10

O how shall I warble myself for the dead one there I loved?
And how shall I deck my song for the large sweet soul that has gone?
And what shall my perfume be, for the grave of him I love?

Sea-winds, blown from east and west,
Blown from the eastern sea, and blown from the western sea, till there on the prairies meeting:
These, and with these, and the breath of my chant,
I perfume the grave of him I love.

11

O what shall I hang on the chamber walls?
And what shall the pictures be that I hang on the walls,
To adorn the burial-house of him I love?

Pictures of growing spring, and farms, and homes,
With the Fourth-month eve at sundown, and the gray smoke lucid and bright,
With floods of the yellow gold of the gorgeous, indolent, sinking sun, burning, expanding the air;
With the fresh sweet herbage under foot, and the pale green leaves of the trees prolific;
In the distance the flowing glaze, the breast of the river, with a wind-dapple here and there;
With ranging hills on the banks, with many a line against the sky, and shadows;
And the city at hand, with dwellings so dense, and stacks of chimneys,
And all the scenes of life, and the workshops, and the workmen homeward returning.

12

Lo! body and soul! this land!
Mighty Manhattan, with spires, and the sparkling and hurrying tides, and the ships;
The varied and ample land—the South and the North in the light—Ohio's shores, and flashing Missouri,
And ever the far-spreading prairies, cover'd with grass and corn.

Lo! the most excellent sun, so calm and haughty;
The violet and purple morn, with just-felt breezes;
The gentle, soft-born, measureless light;
The miracle, spreading, bathing all—the fulfill'd noon;
The coming eve, delicious—the welcome night, and the stars,
Over my cities shining all, enveloping man and land.

13

Sing on! sing on, you gray-brown bird!
Sing from the swamps, the recesses—pour your chant from the bushes;
Limitless out of the dusk, out of the cedars and pines.

Sing on, dearest brother—warble your reedy song;
Loud human song, with voice of uttermost woe.

O liquid, and free, and tender!
O wild and loose to my soul! O wondrous singer!
You only I hear . . . yet the star holds me, (but will soon depart;)
Yet the lilac, with mastering odor, holds me.

14

Now while I sat in the day, and look'd forth,
In the close of the day, with its light, and the fields of spring, and the farmer preparing his crops,
In the large unconscious scenery of my land, with its lakes and forests,
In the heavenly aerial beauty, (after the perturb'd winds, and the storms;)
Under the arching heavens of the afternoon swift passing, and the voices of children and women,
The many-moving sea-tides,—and I saw the ships how they sail'd,
And the summer approaching with richness, and the fields all busy with labor,
And the infinite separate houses, how they all went on, each with its meals and minutia of daily usages;
And the streets, how their throbbings throbb'd, and the cities pent—lo! then and there,
Falling upon them all, and among them all, enveloping me with the rest,
Appear'd the cloud, appear'd the long black trail;
And I knew Death, its thought, and the sacred knowledge of death.

15

Then with the knowledge of death as walking one side of me,
And the thought of death close-walking the other side of me,
And I in the middle, as with companions, and as holding the hands of companions,
I fled forth to the hiding receiving night, that talks not,
Down to the shores of the water, the path by the swamp in the dimness,
To the solemn shadowy cedars, and ghostly pines so still.

And the singer so shy to the rest receiv'd me;
The gray-brown bird I know, receiv'd us comrades three;
And he sang what seem'd the carol of death, and a verse for him I love.

From deep secluded recesses,
From the fragrant cedars, and the ghostly pines so still,
Came the carol of the bird.

And the charm of the carol rapt me,
As I held, as if by their hands, my comrades in the night;
And the voice of my spirit tallied the song of the bird.

HERMAN MELVILLE (1819-1891)

From MOBY DICK; OR, THE WHITE WHALE

Captain Ahab, of the *Pequod,* cherished madly the one purpose in life or death of killing Moby Dick, the great white whale that, on a previous voyage, had taken off his leg. The *Pequod* sailed from Nantucket on the longest of voyages, round the Horn into the Pacific, to the Japanese whaling grounds and the South Seas. Captain Ahab swore the three mates, the three harpooners, and the crew to vengeance on Moby Dick. The killing of other whales did not in the least divert him from his maniacal purpose. Thoughts of home and of his young wife Mary and his boy, the child of his old age, could not deter him. Reports from other vessels of encounters with Moby Dick, and of the deaths thereby, only made him abandon sleep and remain on deck both night and day, driving the *Pequod* on in the hope of meeting the white monster. Fateful omens portended misfortune. A sea-hawk carried off his hat as he hung in a basket raised aloft, to scan the sea. Fedallah, a mysterious unsleeping Parsee of the crew, foretold that he should die, after the Parsee went and was seen again; but that neither hearse nor coffin could be his; that ere he could die two hearses must verily be seen by him on the sea, the first not made by mortal hands, and the visible wood of the last one grown in America; and that hemp alone could kill him. At last he sighted Moby Dick. The golden doubloon that had hung on the mast as a reward to the man who first saw the white whale was his own; but he left it where it was, for on that day Moby Dick destroyed with his jaws the small boat in which Captain Ahab set forth to harpoon him, and escaped, without harming the two other boats that had been lowered.

"Men," said Ahab, when he was brought back on board, "this gold is mine, for I earned it; but I shall let it abide here till the White Whale is dead; and then, whosoever of ye first raises him, upon the day he shall be killed, this gold is that man's; and if on that day I shall again raise him, then, ten times its sum shall be divided among all of ye!" With the sagacity of forty years' experience, Ahab drove his ship on in the wake of the whale through the night, and presently in the morning the lookouts at the mast-heads shouted "There she blows!—she blows!—she blows!—right ahead!" But the men in their headlong eagerness had mistaken some other thing for the whale-spout; for hardly had Ahab been raised again in his basket when "the triumphant halloo of thirty buckskin lungs was heard, as—much nearer to the ship than the place of the imaginary jet, less than a mile ahead—Moby Dick bodily burst into view! . . . 'There she breaches! there she breaches!' was the cry, as in his immeasurable bravadoes the White Whale tossed himself salmon-like to Heaven." This time from all three of the lowered boats irons went into Moby Dick; but he wrecked all three, and then dived down. The *Pequod* picked up her men—all but the Parsee—and the chase went on, through the second night.

The Chase—Third Day

THE morning of the third day dawned fair and fresh, and once more the solitary night-man at the fore-masthead was relieved by crowds of the daylight lookouts, who dotted every mast and almost every spar.

"D'ye see him?" cried Ahab; but the whale was not yet in sight.

"In his infallible wake, though; but follow that wake, that's all. Helm there; steady, as thou goest, and hast been going. What a lovely day again! were it a new-made world, and made for a summer-house to the angels, and this morning the first of its throwing open to them, a fairer day could not dawn upon that world. Here's food for thought, had Ahab time to think, but Ahab never thinks; he only feels, feels, feels, *that's* tingling enough for mortal man! to think's audacity. God only has that right and privilege. Thinking is, or ought to be, a coolness and a calmness; and our poor hearts throb, and our poor brains beat too much for that. And yet, I've sometimes thought my brain was very calm—frozen calm, this old skull cracks so, like a glass in which the contents turn to ice, and shiver it. And still this hair is growing now; this moment growing, and heat must breed it; but no, it's like that sort of common grass that will grow anywhere, between the earthly clefts of Greenland ice or in Vesuvius lava. How the wild winds blow it; they whip it about me as the torn shreds of split sails lash the tossed ship they cling to. A vile wind that has no doubt blown ere this through prison corridors and cells, and wards of hospitals, and ventilated them, and now comes blowing hither as innocent as fleeces. Out upon it!—it's tainted. Were I the wind, I'd blow no more on such a wicked, miserable world. I'd crawl somewhere to a cave, and slink there. And yet, 'tis a noble and heroic thing, the wind! who ever conquered it? In every fight it has the last and bitterest blow. Run tilting at it, and you but run through it. Ha! a coward wind that strikes stark naked men, but will not stand to receive a single blow. Even Ahab is a braver thing—a nobler thing than *that*. Would now the wind but had a body; but all the things that most exasperate and outrage mortal man, all these things are bodiless, but only bodiless as objects, not as agents. There's a most special, a most cunning, oh, a most malicious difference! And yet, I say again, and swear it now, that there's something all glorious and gracious in the wind. These warm Trade Winds, at least, that in the clear heavens blow straight on, in strong and steadfast, vigorous mildness; and veer not from their mark, however the baser currents of the sea may turn and tack, and mightiest Mississippis of the land shift and swerve about, uncertain where to go at last. And by the eternal Poles! these same Trades that so directly blow my good ship on; these Trades, or something like them—something so unchangeable, and full as strong, blow my keeled soul along! To it! Aloft there! What d'ye see?"

"Nothing, sir."

"Nothing! and noon at hand! The doubloon goes a-begging! See the sun! Aye, aye, it must be so. I've oversailed him. How, got the start? Aye, he's chasing *me* now; not I, *him*—that's bad; I might have known it, too. Fool! the lines—the harpoons he's towing. Aye,

aye, I have run him by last night. About! about! Come down, all of ye, but the regular lookouts! Man the braces!"

Steering as she had done, the wind had been somewhat on the *Pequod's* quarter, so that now being pointed in the reverse direction, the braced ship sailed hard upon the breeze as she rechurned the cream in her own white wake.

"Against the wind he now steers for the open jaw," murmured Starbuck to himself, as he coiled the new-hauled main-brace upon the rail. "God keep us, but already my bones feel damp within me, and from the inside wet my flesh. I misdoubt me that I disobey my God in obeying him!"

"Stand by to sway me up!" cried Ahab, advancing to the hempen basket. "We should meet him soon."

"Aye, aye, sir," and straightway Starbuck did Ahab's bidding, and once more Ahab swung on high.

A whole hour now passed; gold-beaten out to ages. Time itself now held long breaths with keen suspense. But at last, some three points off the weather-bow, Ahab descried the spout again, and instantly from the three mastheads three shrieks went up as if the tongues of fire had voiced it.

"Forehead to forehead I meet thee, this third time, Moby Dick! On deck there!—brace sharper up; crowd her into the wind's eye. He's too far off to lower yet, Mr. Starbuck. The sails shake! Stand over that helmsman with a topmaul! So, so; he travels fast, and I must down. But let me have one more good round look aloft here at the sea; there's time for that. An old, old sight, and yet somehow so young; aye, and not changed a wink since I first saw it, a boy, from the sand-hills of Nantucket! The same!—the same!—the same to Noah as to me. There's a soft shower to leeward. Such lovely leewardings! They must lead somewhere—to something else than common land, more palmy than the palms. Leeward! the white whale goes that way; look to windward, then; the better if the bitterer quarter. But good-bye, good-bye, old masthead! What's this?—green? aye, tiny mosses in these warped cracks. No such green weather stains on Ahab's head! There's the difference now between man's old age and matter's. But aye, old mast, we both grow old together; sound in our hulls, though, are we not, my ship? Aye, minus a leg, that's all. By heaven! this dead wood has the better of my live flesh every way. I can't compare with it; and I've known some ships made of dead trees outlast the lives of men made of the most vital stuff of vital fathers. What's that he said? he should still go before me, my pilot; and yet to be seen again? But where?

Shall I have eyes at the bottom of the sea, supposing I descend those endless stairs? and all night I've been sailing from him, wherever he did sink to. Aye, aye, like many more thou told'st direful truth as touching thyself, O Parsee; but, Ahab, there thy shot fell short. Good-bye, masthead—keep a good eye upon the whale, the while I'm gone. We'll talk to-morrow, nay, to-night, when the white whale lies down there, tied by head and tail."

He gave the word; and still gazing round him, was steadily lowered through the cloven blue air to the deck.

In due time the boats were lowered; but as standing in his shallop's stern, Ahab just hovered upon the point of the descent, he waved to the mate,—who held one of the tackle-ropes on deck—and bade him pause.

"Starbuck!"

"Sir?"

"For the third time my soul's ship starts upon this voyage, Starbuck."

"Aye, sir, thou wilt have it so."

"Some ships sail from their ports, and ever afterwards are missing, Starbuck!"

"Truth, sir: saddest truth."

"Some men die at ebb tide; some at low water; some at the full of the flood;—and I feel now like a billow that's all one crested comb, Starbuck. I am old;—shake hands with me, man."

Their hands met; their eyes fastened; Starbuck's tears the glue.

"Oh, my captain, my captain!—noble heart—go not—go not!—see, it's a brave man that weeps; how great the agony of the persuasion then!"

"Lower away!"—cried Ahab, tossing the mate's arm from him. "Stand by the crew!"

In an instant the boat was pulling round close under the stern.

"The sharks! the sharks!" cried a voice from the low cabin-window there; "O master, my master, come back!"

But Ahab heard nothing; for his own voice was high-lifted then; and the boat leaped on.

Yet the voice spake true; for scarce had he pushed from the ship, when numbers of sharks, seemingly rising from out the dark waters beneath the hull, maliciously snapped at the blades of the oars, every time they dipped in the water; and in this way accompanied the boat with their bites. It is a thing not uncommonly happening to the whale-boats in those swarming seas; the sharks at times apparently following them in the same prescient way that vultures hover over the banners of marching regiments in the east. But these were the first sharks that had been observed by the *Pequod* since the White Whale had been first descried; and whether it was that Ahab's crew were all such tiger-yellow barbarians, and therefore their flesh more musky to the senses of the sharks—a matter sometimes well known to affect them,—however it was, they seemed to follow that one boat without molesting the others.

"Heart of wrought steel!" murmured Starbuck, gazing over the side, and following with his eyes the receding boat—"canst thou yet ring boldly to that sight?—lowering thy keel among ravening sharks, and followed by them, open-mouthed, to the chase; and this the critical third day?—For when three days flow together in one continuous intense pursuit; be sure the first is the morning, the second the noon, and the third the evening and the end of that thing—be that end what it may. Oh! my God! what is this that shoots through me, and leaves me so deadly calm, yet expectant,—fixed at the top of a shudder! Future things swim before me, as in empty outlines and skeletons; all the past is somehow grown dim. Mary, girl! thou fadest in pale glories behind me; boy! I seem to see but thy eyes grown wondrous blue. Strangest problems of life seem clearing; but clouds sweep between—Is my journey's end coming? My legs feel faint; like his who has footed it all day. Feel thy heart,—beats it yet?—Stir thyself, Starbuck!—stave it off—move, move! speak aloud!—Masthead there! See ye my boy's hand on the hill?—Crazed;—aloft there!—keep thy keenest eye upon the boats:—mark well the whale!—Ho! again!—drive off that hawk! see! he pecks—he tears the vane"—pointing to the red flag flying at the main-truck—"Ha! he soars away with it!—Where's the old man now? sees't thou that sight, oh Ahab!—shudder, shudder!"

The boats had not gone very far, when by a signal from the mast-heads—a downward pointed arm, Ahab knew that the whale had sounded; but intending to be near him at the next rising, he held on his way a little sideways from the vessel; the becharmed crew maintaining the profoundest silence, as the head-beat waves hammered and hammered against the opposing bow.

"Drive, drive in your nails, oh ye waves! to their uttermost heads drive them in! ye but strike a thing without a lid; and no coffin and no hearse can be mine:—and hemp only can kill me! Ha! ha!"

Suddenly the waters around them slowly swelled in broad circles; then quickly upheaved, as if sideways sliding from a submerged berg of ice, swiftly rising to the surface. A low rumbling sound was heard; a subterraneous hum; and then all held their breaths; as bedraggled with trailing ropes, and harpoons, and lances, a vast form shot lengthwise, but obliquely from the sea. Shrouded in a thin drooping veil of mist, it hovered for a moment in the rainbowed air; and then fell swamping back into the deep. Crushed thirty feet upwards, the waters flashed for an instant like heaps of fountains, then brokenly sank in a shower of flakes, leaving the circling surface creamed like new milk round the marble trunk of the whale.

"Give way!" cried Ahab to the oarsmen, and the boats darted forward to the attack; but maddened by yesterday's fresh irons that corroded in him, Moby Dick seemed combinedly possessed by all the angels that fell from heaven. The wide tiers of welded tendons overspreading his broad white forehead, beneath the transparent skin, looked knitted together; as head on, he came churning his tail among the boats; and once more flailed them apart; spilling out the irons and lances from the two mates' boats, and dashing in one side of the upper part of their bows, but leaving Ahab's almost without a scar.

While Daggoo and Queequeg were stopping the strained planks; and as the whale swimming out from them, turned, and showed one entire flank as he shot by them again; at that moment a quick cry went up. Lashed round and round to the fish's back; pinioned in the turns upon turns in which, during the past night, the whale had reeled the involutions of the lines around him, the half torn body of the Parsee was seen; his sable raiment frayed to shreds; his distended eyes turned full upon old Ahab.

The harpoon dropped from his hand.

"Befooled, befooled!"—drawing in a long lean breath—"Aye, Parsee! I see thee again.—Aye, and thou goest before; and this, *this* then is the hearse that thou didst promise. But I hold thee to the last letter of thy word. Where is the second hearse? Away, mates, to the ship! those boats are useless now; repair them if ye can in time, and return to me; if not, Ahab is enough to die—Down, men! the first thing that but offers to jump from this boat I stand in, that thing I harpoon. Ye are not other men, but my arms and my legs; and so obey me.—Where's the whale? gone down again?"

But he looked too nigh the boat; for as if bent upon escaping with the corpse he bore, and as if the particular place of the last encounter had been but a stage in his leeward voyage, Moby Dick was now again steadily swimming forward; and had almost passed the ship,—which thus far had been sailing in the contrary direction to him, though for the present her headway had been stopped. He seemed swimming with his utmost velocity, and now only intent upon pursuing his own straight path in the sea.

"Oh! Ahab," cried Starbuck, "not too late is it, even now, the third day, to desist. See! Moby Dick seeks thee not. It is thou, thou, that madly seekest him!"

Setting sail to the rising wind, the lonely boat was swiftly impelled to leeward, by both oars and canvas. And at last when Ahab was sliding by the vessel, so near as plainly to distinguish Starbuck's face as he leaned over the rail, he hailed him to turn the vessel about, and follow him, not too swiftly, at a judicious interval. Glancing upwards, he saw Tashtego, Queequeg, and Daggoo, eagerly mounting to the three mast-heads; while the oarsmen were rocking in the two staved boats which had just been hoisted to the side, and were busily at work in repairing them. One after the other, through the port-holes, as he sped, he also caught flying glimpses of Stubb and Flask, busying themselves on deck among bundles of new irons and lances. As he saw all this; as he heard the hammers in the broken boats; far other hammers seemed driving a nail into his heart. But he rallied. And now marking that the vane or flag was gone from the main masthead, he shouted to Tashtego, who had just gained that perch, to descend again for another flag, and a hammer and nails, and so nail it to the mast.

Whether fagged by the three days' running chase, and the resistance to his swimming in the knotted hamper he bore; or whether it was some latent deceitfulness and malice in him: whichever was true, the White Whale's way now began to abate, as it seemed, from the boat so rapidly nearing him once more; though indeed the whale's last start had not been so long a one as before. And still as Ahab glided over the waves the unpitying sharks accompanied him; and so pertinaciously stuck to the boat; and so continually bit at the plying oars, that the blades became jagged and crunched, and left small splinters in the sea, at almost every dip.

"Heed them not! those teeth but give new rowlocks to your oars. Pull on! 'tis the better rest, the shark's jaw than the yielding water."

"But at every bite, sir, the thin blades grow smaller and smaller!"

"They will last long enough! pull on!—But who can tell"—he muttered—"whether these sharks swim to feast on a whale or on Ahab?—But pull on! Aye, all alive, now—we near him. The helm! take the helm; let me pass,"—and so saying, two of the oarsmen helped him forward to the bows of the still flying boat.

At length as the craft was cast to one side, and ran ranging along with the White Whale's flank, he seemed strangely oblivious of its advance—as the whale sometimes will—and Ahab was fairly within the smoky mountain mist, which, thrown off from the whale's spout, curled round his great, Monadnock hump. He was even thus close to him; when, with body arched back, and both arms lengthwise high-lifted to the poise, he darted his fierce iron, and his far fiercer curse into the hated whale. As both steel and curse sank to the socket, as if sucked into a morass, Moby Dick sideways writhed; spasmodically rolled his nigh flank against the bow, and, without staving a hole in it, so suddenly canted the boat over, that had it not been for the elevated part of the gunwale to which he then clung, Ahab would once more have been tossed into the sea. As it was, three of the oarsmen—who foreknew not the precise instant of the dart, and were therefore unprepared for its effects—these were flung out; but so fell, that, in an instant two of them clutched the gunwale again, and rising to its level on a combing wave, hurled themselves bodily inboard again; the third man helplessly drooping astern, but still afloat and swimming.

Almost simultaneously, with a mighty volition of ungraduated, instantaneous swiftness, the White Whale darted through the weltering sea. But when Ahab cried out to the steersman to take new turns with the line, and hold it so; and commanded the crew to turn round on their seats, and tow the boat up to the mark; the moment the treacherous line felt that double strain and tug, it snapped in the empty air!

"What breaks in me? Some sinew cracks!—'tis whole again; oars! oars! Burst in upon him!"

Hearing the tremendous rush of the sea-crashing boat, the whale wheeled round to present his blank forehead at bay; but in that evolution, catching sight of the nearing black hull of the ship; seemingly seeing in it the source of all his persecutions; bethinking it—it may be—a larger and nobler foe; of a sudden, he bore down upon its advancing prow, smiting his jaws amid fiery showers of foam.

Ahab staggered; his hand smote his forehead. "I grow blind; hands! stretch out before me that I may yet grope my way. Is't nigh?"

"The whale! The ship!" cried the cringing oarsmen.

"Oars! oars! Slope downwards to thy depths, O sea, that ere it be for ever too late, Ahab may slide this last, last time upon his mark! I see: the ship! the ship! Dash on, my men! Will ye not save my ship?"

But as the oarsmen violently forced their boat through the sledge-hammering seas, the before whale-smitten bow-ends of two planks burst through, and in an instant almost, the temporarily disabled boat lay nearly level with the waves; its half-wading, splashing crew trying hard to stop the gap and bale out the pouring water.

Meantime, for that one beholding instant, Tashtego's masthead hammer remained suspended in his hand; and the red flag, half-wrapping him as with a plaid, then streamed itself straight out from him, as his own forward-flowing heart; while Starbuck and Stubb, standing upon the bowsprit beneath, caught sight of the down-coming monster just as soon as he.

"The whale, the whale! Up helm, up helm! Oh, all ye sweet powers of air, now hug me close! Let not Starbuck die, if die he must, in a woman's fainting fit. Up helm, I say—ye fools, the jaw! the jaw! Is this the end of all my bursting prayers? all my life-long fidelities? Oh, Ahab, Ahab, lo, thy work. Steady! helmsman, steady. Nay, nay! Up helm again! He turns to meet us! Oh, his unappeasable brow drives on towards one, whose duty tells him he cannot depart. My God, stand by me now!

"Stand not by me, but stand under me, whoever you are that will now help Stubb; for Stubb, too, sticks here. I grin at thee, thou grinning whale! Whoever helped Stubb, or kept Stubb awake, but Stubb's own unwinking eye? And now poor Stubb goes to bed upon a mattress that is all too soft; would it were stuffed with brushwood! I grin at thee, thou grinning whale! Look ye, sun, moon and stars! I call ye assassins of as good a fellow as ever spouted up his ghost. For all that, I would yet ring glasses with ye, would ye but hand the cup! Oh, oh, oh, oh! thou grinning whale, but there'll be plenty of gulping soon! Why fly ye not, O Ahab? For me, off shoes and jacket to it, let Stubb die in his drawers! A most mouldy and over-salted death, though;—cherries! cherries! cherries! Oh, Flask, for one red cherry ere we die!"

"Cherries? I only wish that we were where they grow. Oh, Stubb, I hope my poor mother's drawn my part-pay ere this; if not, few coppers will come to her now, for the voyage is up."

From the ship's bows, nearly all the seamen now hung inactive; hammers, bits of plank, lances, and harpoons, mechanically retained in their hands, just as they had darted from their various employments; all their enchanted eyes intent upon the whale, which from side to side strangely vibrating his predestinating head, sent a broad band of overspreading semicircular foam before him as he rushed. Retribution, swift vengeance, eternal malice were in his whole aspect, and spite of all that mortal man could do, the solid white buttress of his forehead smote the ship's starboard bow, till men and timbers reeled. Some fell flat upon their faces. Like dislodged trucks, the heads of the harpooneers aloft shook on their bull-like necks. Through the breach, they heard the waters pour, as mountain torrents down a flume.

"The ship! The hearse!—the second hearse!" cried Ahab from the boat; "its wood could only be American!"

Diving beneath the settling ship, the Whale ran quivering along its keel; but turning under water, swiftly shot to the surface again, far off the other bow, but within a few yards of Ahab's boat, where, for a time, he lay quiescent.

"I turn my body from the sun. What ho, Tashtego! let me hear thy hammer. Oh! ye three unsurrendered spires of mine; thou uncracked keel; and only god-bullied hull; thou firm deck, and haughty helm, and Pole-pointed prow,—death-glorious ship! must ye then perish, and without me? Am I cut off from the last fond pride of the meanest shipwrecked captains? Oh, lonely death on lonely life! Oh, now I feel my topmost greatness lies in my topmost grief. Ho, ho! from all your furthest bounds, pour ye now in, ye bold billows of my whole foregone life, and top this one piled comber of my death! Towards thee I roll, thou all-destroying but unconquering whale; to the last I grapple with thee; from hell's heart I stab at thee; for hate's sake I spit my last breath at thee. Sink all coffins and all hearses to one common pool! and since neither can be mine let me then tow to pieces, while still chasing thee, though tied to thee, thou damned whale! *Thus,* I give up the spear!"

The harpoon was darted; the stricken whale flew forward! with igniting velocity the line ran through the groove; ran foul. Ahab stooped to clear it; he did clear it; but the flying turn caught him round the neck, and voicelessly as Turkish mutes bowstring their victim, he was shot out of the boat, ere the crew knew he was gone. Next instant, the heavy eyesplice in the rope's final end flew out of the stark-empty tub, knocked down an oarsman, and smiting the sea, disappeared in its depths.

For an instant, the tranced boat's crew stood still; then turned. "The ship? Great God, where is the ship?" Soon they through dim, bewildering mediums saw her sidelong fading phantom, as in the gaseous Fata Morgana; only the uppermost masts out of water; while fixed by infatuation, or fidelity, or fate, to their once lofty perches, the pagan harpooneers still maintained their sinking lookouts on the sea. And now, concentric circles seized the lone boat itself, and all its crew, and each floating oar, and every lance-pole, and spinning, animate and inanimate, all round and round in one vortex, carried the smallest chip of the *Pequod* out of sight.

But as the last whelmings intermixingly poured themselves over the sunken head of the Indian at the mainmast, leaving a few inches of the erect spar yet visible, together with long streaming yards of the flag, which calmly undulated, with ironical coincidings, over the destroying billows they almost touched;—at that instant, a red arm and a hammer hovered backwardly uplifted in the open air, in the act of nailing the flag faster and yet faster to the subsiding spar. A sky-hawk that tauntingly had followed the main-truck downwards from its natural home among the stars, pecking at the flag, and incommoding Tashtego there; this bird now chanced to intercept its broad fluttering wing between the hammer and the wood; and simultaneously feeling that ethereal thrill, the submerged savage beneath, in his death-gasp, kept his hammer frozen there; and so the bird of heaven, with unearthly shrieks, and his imperial beak thrust upwards, and his whole captive form folded in the flag of Ahab, went down with his ship, which, like Satan, would not sink to hell till she had dragged a living part of heaven along with her, and helmeted herself with it.

Now small fowls flew screaming over the yet yawning gulf; a sullen white surf beat against its steep sides; then all collapsed, and the great shroud of the sea rolled on as it rolled five thousand years ago.

EPILOGUE

"And I only am escaped alone to tell thee."—*Job.*

THE drama's done. Why then here does anyone step forth?—Because one did survive the wreck.

It so chanced, that after the Parsee's disappearance, I was he whom the Fates ordained to take the place of Ahab's bowsman, when that bowsman assumed the vacant post; the same, who, when on the last day the three men were tossed from out the rocky boat, was dropped astern. So, floating on the margin of the ensuing scene, and in full sight of it, when the half-spent suction of the sunk ship reached me, I was then, but slowly, drawn towards the closing vortex. When I reached it, it had subsided to a creamy pool. Round and round, then, and ever contracting towards the button-like black bubble at the axis of that slowly wheeling circle, like another Ixion I did revolve. Till, gaining that vital centre, the black bubble upward burst; and now, liberated by reason of its cunning spring, and, owing to its great buoyancy, rising with great force, the coffin life-buoy shot lengthwise from the sea, fell over, and floated by my side. Buoyed up by that coffin, for almost one whole day and night, I floated on a soft and dirge-like main. The unharming sharks, they glided by as if with padlocks on their mouths; the savage sea-hawks sailed with sheathed beaks. On the second day, a sail drew near, nearer, and picked me up at last. It was the devious-cruising *Rachel,* that in her retracing search after her missing children, only found another orphan.

EDWARD EVERETT HALE (1822-1909)

My Double, and How He Undid Me

It is not often that I trouble the readers of the *Atlantic Monthly.* I should not trouble them now, but for the importunities of my wife, who "feels to insist" that a duty to society is unfulfilled till I have told why I had to have a double, and how he undid me. She is sure, she says, that intelligent persons cannot understand that pressure upon public servants which alone drives any man into the employment of a double. And while I fear she thinks, at the bottom of her heart, that my fortunes will never be made, she has a faint hope that, as another Rasselas, I may teach a lesson to future publics, from which they may profit, though we die. Owing to the behavior of my double, or, if you please, to that public pressure which compelled me to employ him, I have plenty of leisure to write this communication.

I am, or rather was, a minister of the Sandemanian connection. I was settled in the active, wide-awake town of Naguadavick, on one of the finest water-powers in Maine. We used to call it a western town in the heart of the civilization of New England. A charming place it was and is. A spirited, brave young parish had I; and it seemed as if we might have all "the joy of eventful living" to our heart's content.

Alas! how little we knew on the day of my ordination, and in those halcyon moments of our first housekeeping. To be the confidential friend in a hundred families in the town,—cutting the social trifle, as my friend Haliburton says, "from the top of the whipped syllabub to the bottom of the sponge-cake, which is the foundation,"—to keep abreast of the thought of the age in one's study, and to do one's best on Sunday to interweave that thought with the active life of an active town, and to inspirit both and make both infinite by glimpses of the Eternal Glory, seemed such an exquisite forelook into one's life! Enough to do, and all so real and so grand! If this vision could only have lasted!

The truth is, that this vision was not in itself a delusion, nor, indeed, half bright enough. If one could only have been left to do his own business, the vision would have accomplished itself and brought out new paraheliacal visions, each as bright as the original. The misery was and is, as we found out, I and Polly, before long, that besides the vision, and besides the usual human and finite failures in life (such as breaking the old pitcher that came over in the *Mayflower,* and putting into the fire the alpenstock with which her father climbed Mont Blanc)—besides these, I say (imitating the style of *Robinson Crusoe*), there were pitchforked in on us a great rowen-heap of humbugs, handed down from some unknown seed-time, in which we were expected, and I chiefly, to fulfil certain public functions before the community, of the character of those fulfilled by the third row of supernumeraries who stand behind the Sepoys in the spectacle of the "Cataract of the Ganges." They were the duties, in a word, which one performs as member of one or another social class or subdivision, wholly distinct from what one does as A. by himself A. What invisible power put these functions on me it would be very hard to tell. But such power there was and is. And I had not been at work a year before I found I was living two lives, one real and one merely functional,—for two sets of people, one my parish, whom I loved, and the other a vague public, for whom I did not care two straws. All this was in a vague notion, which everybody had and has, that this second life would eventually bring out some great results, unknown at present, to somebody somewhere.

Crazed by this duality of life, I first read Dr. Wigan on the *Duality of the Brain,* hoping that I could train one side of my head to do these outside jobs, and the other to do my intimate and real duties. For Richard Greenough once told me, that, in studying for the statue of Franklin, he found that the left side of the great man's face was philosophic and reflective, and the right side funny and smiling. If you will go and look at the bronze statue you will find he has repeated this observation there for posterity. The eastern profile is the portrait of the statesman Franklin, the western of poor Richard. But Dr. Wigan does not go into these niceties of this subject, and I failed. It was then that, on my wife's suggestion, I resolved to look out for a double.

I was, at first, singularly successful. We happened to be recreating at Stafford Springs that summer. We rode out one day, for one of the relaxations of that watering-place, to the great Monson Poorhouse. We were passing through one of the large halls, when my destiny was fulfilled! I saw my man!

He was not shaven. He had on no spectacles. He was dressed in a green baize roundabout and faded blue overalls, worn sadly at the knee. But I saw at once that he was of my height, five feet four and a half. He had black hair, worn off by his hat. So have and have not I. He stooped in walking. So do I. His hands were large, and mine. And—choicest gift of Fate in all—he had, not "a strawberry mark on his left arm," but a cut from a juvenile brickbat over his right eye, slightly affecting the play of that eyebrow. Reader, so have I! My fate was sealed!

A word with Mr. Holley, one of the inspectors, settled the whole thing. It proved that this Dennis Shea was a harmless, amiable fellow, of the class known as shiftless, who had sealed his fate by marrying a dumb wife, who was at that moment ironing in the laundry. Before I left Stafford I had hired both for five years. We had applied to Judge Pynchon, then the probate judge at Springfield, to change the name of Dennis Shea to Frederic Ingham. We had explained to the Judge what was the precise truth, than an eccentric gentleman wished to adopt Dennis, under this new name, into his family. It never occurred to him that Dennis might be more than fourteen years old. And thus, to shorten this preface, when we returned at night to my parsonage at Naguadavick, there entered Mrs. Ingham, her new dumb laundress, myself, who am Mr. Frederic Ingham, and my double, who was Mr. Frederic Ingham by as good right as I.

Oh, the fun we had the next morning in shaving his beard to my pattern, cutting his hair to match mine, and teaching him how to wear and how to take off gold-bowed spectacles! Really, they were electroplate, and the glass was plain (for the poor fellow's eyes were excellent). Then in four successive afternoons I taught him four speeches. I had found these would be quite enough for the supernumerary-Sepoy line of life, and it was well for me they were; for though he was good-natured, he was very shiftless, and it was, as our national proverb says, "like pulling teeth" to teach him. But at the end of the next week he could say, with quite my easy and frisky air,—

1. "Very well, thank you. And you?" This for an answer to casual salutations.

2. "I am very glad you liked it."

3. "There has been so much said, and, on the whole, so well said, that I will not occupy the time."

4. "I agree, in general, with my friend the other side of the room."

At first I had a feeling that I was going to be at great cost for clothing him. But it proved, of course, at once, that, whenever he was out, I should be at home. And I went, during the bright period of his success, to so few of those awful pageants which require a black dress-coat and what the ungodly call, after Mr. Dickens, a white choker, that in the happy retreat of my own dressing-gowns and jackets my days went by as happily and cheaply as those of another Thalaba. And Polly declares there was never a year when the tailoring cost so little. He lived (Dennis, not Thalaba) in his wife's room over the kitchen. He had orders never to show himself at that window. When he appeared in the front of the house I retired to my sanctissimum and my dressing-gown. In short, the Dutchman and his wife, in the old weather-box, had not less to do with each other than he and I. He made the furnace-fire and split the wood before daylight; then he went to sleep again, and slept late; then came for orders, with a red silk bandanna tied round his head, with his overalls on, and his dresscoat and spectacles off. If we happened to be interrupted, no one guessed that he was Frederic Ingham as well as I; and, in the neighborhood, there grew up an impression that the minister's Irishman worked daytimes in the factory village at New Coventry. After I had given him his orders, I never saw him till the next day.

I launched him by sending him to a meeting of the Enlightenment Board. The Enlightenment Board consists of seventy-four members, of whom sixty-seven are necessary to form a quorum. One becomes a member under the regulations laid down in old Judge Dudley's will. I became one by being ordained pastor of a church in Naguadavick. You see you cannot help yourself if you would. At this particular time we had had four successive meetings, averaging four hours each,—wholly occupied in whipping in a quorum. At the first only eleven men were present; at the next, by force of three circulars, twenty-seven; at the third, thanks to two days' canvassing by Auchmuty and myself, begging men to come, we had sixty. Half the others were in Europe. But without a quorum we could do nothing. All the rest of us waited grimly for our four hours, and adjourned without any action. At the fourth meeting we had flagged, and only got fifty-nine together. But on the first appearance of my double—whom I sent on this fatal Monday to the fifth meeting—he was the *sixty-seventh* man who entered the room. He was greeted with a storm of applause! The poor fellow had missed his way—read the street signs ill through his spectacles (very ill, in fact, without them)—and had not dared to inquire. He entered the room, finding the president and secretary holding to their chairs two judges of the Supreme Court, who were also members *ex officio* and were begging leave to go away. On his entrance all was changed. *Presto,* the by-laws were amended, and the western property was given away. Nobody stopped to converse with him. He voted, as I had charged him to do, in every instance, with the minority. I won new laurels as a man of sense, though a little unpunctual—and Dennis, *alias* Ingham, returned to the parsonage, astonished to see with how little wisdom the world is governed. He cut a few of my parishioners in the street; but he had his glasses off, and I am known to be near-sighted. Eventually he recognized them more readily than I.

I "set him again" at the exhibition of the New Coventry Academy; and here he undertook a "speaking part"—as, in my boyish, worldly days, I remember the bills used to say of Mlle. Celeste. We are all trustees of the New Coventry Academy; and there has lately been "a good deal of feeling" because the Sandemanians are leaning toward Free-Will, and that we have, therefore, neglected these semi-annual exhibitions, while there is no doubt that Auchmuty last year went to Commencement at Waterville. Now the head master at New Coventry is a real good fellow, who knows a Sanskrit root when he sees it, and often cracks etymologies with me; so that, in strictness, I ought to go to their exhibitions. But think, reader, of sitting through three long July days in that Academy chapel, following the programme from

TUESDAY MORNING. *English Composition.* "SUNRISE." Miss Jones.

round to—

Trio on Three Pianos. Duel from the Opera of "Midshipman Easy." *Marryat.*

coming in at nine, Thursday evening! Think of this, reader, for men who know the world is trying to go backward, and who would give their lives if they could help it on! Well! The double had succeeded so well at the Board, that I sent him to the Academy. (Shade of Plato, pardon!) He arrived early on Tuesday, when, indeed, few but mothers and clergymen are generally expected, and returned in the evening to us, covered with honors. He had dined at the right hand of the chairman, and he spoke in high terms of the repast. The chairman had expressed his interest in the French conversation. "I am very glad you liked it," said Dennis; and the poor chairman, abashed, supposed the accent had been wrong. At the end of the day the gentlemen present had been called upon for speeches—the Rev. Frederic Ingham first, as it happened; upon which Dennis had risen, and had said: "There has been so much said, and, on the whole, so well said, that I will not occupy the time." The girls were delighted, because Dr. Dabney, the year before, had given them at this occasion a scolding on impropriety of behavior at lyceum lectures. They all declared Mr. Ingham was a love—and *so* handsome! (Dennis is good looking.) Three of them, with arms behind the others' waists, followed him up to the wagon he rode home in; and a little girl with a blue sash had been sent to give him a rosebud. After this *début* in speaking, he went to the exhibition for two days more, to the mutual satisfaction of all concerned. Indeed, Polly reported that he had pronounced the trustees' dinners of a higher grade than those of the parsonage. When the next term began I found six of the Academy girls had obtained permission to come across the river to attend our church. But this arrangement did not long continue.

After this he went to several Commencements for me, and ate the dinners provided. He sat through three of our Quarterly Conventions for me—always voting judiciously, by the simple rule mentioned above, of siding with the minority. And I, meanwhile, who had before been losing caste among my friends, as holding myself aloof from the associations of the body, began to rise in everybody's favor. "Ingham's a good fellow, always on hand;" "never talks much, but does the right thing at the right time;" "is not as unpunctual as he used to be—he comes early, and sits through to the end." "He has got over his old talkative habit, too. I spoke to a friend of his about it once; and I think Ingham took it kindly," etc., etc.

This voting power of Dennis was particularly valuable at the quarterly meetings of the proprietors of the Naguadavick Ferry. My wife inherited from her father some shares in that enterprise, which is not yet fully developed, though it doubtless will become a very valuable property. The law of Maine then forbade stockholders to appear by proxy at such meetings. Polly disliked to go, not being, in fact, a "hens'-rights hen," transferred her stock to me. I, after going once, disliked it more than she. But Dennis went to the next meeting, and liked it very much. He said the armchairs were good, the collation good, and the free rides to stockholders pleasant. He was a little frightened when they first took him upon one of the ferry-boats, but after two or three quarterly meetings he became quite brave.

Thus far I never had any difficulty with him. Indeed, being, as I implied, of that type which is called shiftless, he was only too happy to be told daily what to do, and to be charged not to be forthputting or in any way original in his discharge of that duty. He learned, however, to discriminate between the lines of his life, and very much preferred these stockholders' meetings and trustees' dinners and Commencement collations to another set of occasions, from which he used to beg off most piteously. Our excellent brother, Dr. Fillmore, had taken a notion at this time that our Sandemanian churches needed more expression of mutual sympathy. He insisted upon it that we were remiss. He said that if the bishop came to preach at Naguadavick all the Episcopal clergy of the neighborhood were present; if Dr. Pond came, all the Congregational clergymen turned out to hear him; if Dr. Nichols, all the Unitarians; and he thought we owed it to each other, that, whenever there was an occasional service at a Sandemanian church, the other brethren should all, if possible, attend. "It looked well," if nothing more. Now this really meant that I had not been to hear one of Dr. Fillmore's lectures on the Ethnology of Religion. He forgot that he did not hear one of my course on the "Sandemanianism of Anselm." But I felt badly when he said it; and afterwards I always made Dennis go to hear all the brethren preach, when I was not preaching myself. This was what he took exceptions to—the only thing, as I said, which he ever did except to. Now came the advantage of his long morning nap, and of the green tea with which Polly supplied the kitchen. But he would plead, so humbly, to be let off, only from one or two! I never excepted him, however. I knew the lectures were of value, and I thought it best he should be able to keep the connection.

Polly is more rash than I am, as the reader has observed in the outset of this memoir. She risked Dennis one night under the eyes of her own sex. Governor Gorges had always been very kind to us, and, when he gave his great annual party to the town, asked us. I confess I hated to go. I was deep in the new volume of Pfeiffer's "Mystics," which Haliburton had just sent me from Boston. "But how rude," said Polly, "not to return the Governor's civility and Mrs. Gorges', when they will be sure to ask why you are away!" Still I demurred, and at last she, with the wit of Eve and of Semiramis conjoined, let me off by saying that if I would go in with her, and sustain the initial conversations with the Governor and ladies staying there, we would risk Dennis for the rest of the evening. And that was just what we did. She took Dennis in training all that afternoon, instructed him in fashionable conversation, cautioned him against the temptations of the supper-table—and at nine in the evening he drove us all down in the carryall. I made the grand star *entrée* with Polly and the pretty Walton girls, who were staying with us. We had put Dennis into a great rough top-coat, without his glasses; and the girls never dreamed, in the darkness, of looking at him. He sat in the carriage, at the door, while we entered. I did the agreeable to Mrs. Gorges, was introduced to her niece, Miss Fernanda; I complimented Judge Jeffries on his decision in the great case of D'Aulnay *vs.* Laconia Mining Company; I stepped into the dressing-room for a moment, stepped out for another, walked home after a nod with Dennis and tying the horse to a pump;—and while I walked home, Mr. Frederic Ingham, my double, stepped in through the library into the Gorges' grand saloon.

Oh! Polly died of laughing as she told me of it at midnight! And even here, where I have to teach my hands to hew the beech for stakes to fence our cave, she dies of laughing as she recalls it, and says that single occasion was worth all we have paid for it. Gallant Eve that she is! She joined Dennis at the library-door, and in an instant presented him to Dr. Ochterlong, from Baltimore, who was on a visit in town, and was talking with her as Dennis came in. "Mr. Ingham would like to hear what you were telling us about your success among the German population." And Dennis bowed and said, in spite of a scowl from Polly, "I'm very glad you liked it." But Dr. Ochterlong did not observe, and plunged into the tide of explanation; Dennis listening like a prime minister, and bowing like a mandarin, which is, I suppose, the same thing. Polly declared it was just like Haliburton's Latin conversation with the Hungarian minister, of which he is very fond of telling. *"Quœne sit historia Reformationis in Ungaria?"* quoth Haliburton, after some thought. And his confrère replied gallantly, *"In seculo decimo tertio,"* etc., etc., etc.; and from *decimo tertio* to the nineteenth century and a half lasted till the oysters came. So was it that before Dr. Ochterlong came to the "success," or near it, Governor Gorges came to Dennis, and asked him to hand Mrs. Jeffries down to supper, a request which he heard with great joy.

Polly was skipping round the room, I guess, gay as a lark. Auchmuty came to her "in pity for poor Ingham," who was so bored by the stupid pundit; and Auchmuty could not understand why I stood so long. But when Dennis took Mrs. Jeffries down, Polly could not resist standing near them. He was a little flustered, till the sight of the eatables and drinkables gave him the same Mercian courage which it gave Diggory. A little excited then, he attempted one or two of his speeches to the judge's lady. But little he knew how hard it was to get in even a *promptu* there edgewise. "Very well, I thank you," said he, after the eating elements were adjusted; "and you?" And then did not he have to hear about the mumps, and the measles, and arnica, and belladonna, and camomile-flower, and dodecatheon, till she changed oysters for salad; and then about the old practice and the new, and what her sister said, and what her sister's friend said, and what the physician to her sister's friend said, and then what was said by the brother of the sister of the physician of the friend of her sister, exactly as if it had been in Ollendorff? There was a moment's pause, as she declined champagne. "I am very glad you liked it," said Dennis again, which he never should have said but to one who complimented a sermon. "Oh! you are so sharp, Mr. Ingham! No! I never drink any wine at all, except sometimes in summer a little currant shrub, from our own currants, you know. My own mother, that is, I call her my own mother, because, you know, I do not remember," etc., etc., etc.; till they came to the candied orange at the end of the feast, when Dennis, rather confused, thought he must say something, and tried No. 4,—"I agree, in general, with my friend the other side of the room,"—which he never should have said but at a public meeting. But Mrs. Jeffries, who never listens expecting to understand, caught him up instantly with "Well, I'm sure my husband returns the compliment; he always agrees with you, though we do worship with the Methodists; but you know, Mr. Ingham," etc., etc., etc., till the move upstairs; and as Dennis led her through the hall, he was scarcely understood by any but Polly, as he said, "There has been so much said, and, on the whole, so well said, that I will not occupy the time."

His great resource the rest of the evening was standing in the library, carrying on animated conversations with one and another in much the same way. Polly had initiated him in the mysteries of a discovery of mine, that it is not necessary to finish your sentences in a crowd, but by a sort of mumble, omitting sibilants and dentals. This, indeed, if your words fail you, answers even in public extempore speech, but better where other talking is going on. Thus: "We misssed you at the Natural History Society, Ingham." Ingham replied, "I am very gligloglum, that is, that you were mmmmmm." By gradually dropping the voice, the interlocutor is compelled to supply the answer. "Mrs. Ingham, I hope your friend Augusta is better." Augusta has not been ill. Polly cannot think of explaining, however, and answers, "Thank you, ma'am; she is very rearason wewahwewoh," in lower and lower tones. And Mrs. Throckmorton, who forgot the subject of which she spoke as soon as she asked the question, is quite satisfied. Dennis could see into the cardroom, and came to Polly to ask if he might not go and play all-fours. But, of course, she sternly refused. At midnight they came home delighted—Polly, as I said, wild to tell me the story of the victory; only both the pretty Walton girls said, "Cousin Frederic, you did not come near me all the evening."

We always called him Dennis at home, for convenience, though his real name was Frederic Ingham, as I have explained. When the election day came round, however, I found that by some accident there was only one Frederic Ingham's name on the voting list; and as I was quite busy that day in writing some foreign letters to Halle, I thought I would forego my privilege of suffrage, and stay quietly at home, telling Dennis that he might use the record on the voting-list, and vote. I gave him a ticket, which I told him he might use if he liked to. That was that very sharp election in Maine which the readers of the *Atlantic* so well remember, and it had been intimated in public that the ministers would do well not to appear at the polls. Of course, after that, we had to appear by self or proxy. Still, Naguadavick was not then a city, and this standing in a double queue at town-meeting several hours to vote was a bore of the first water; and so when I found that there was but one Frederic Ingham on the list, and that one of us must give up, I stayed at home and finished the letters (which, indeed, procured for Fothergill his coveted appointment of Professor of Astronomy at Leavenworth), and I gave Dennis, as we called him, the chance. Something in the matter gave a good deal of popularity to the Frederic Ingham name; and at the adjourned election, next week, Frederic Ingham was chosen to the legislature. Whether this was I or Dennis I never really knew. My friends seemed to think it was I; but I felt that as Dennis had done the popular thing, he was entitled to the honor: so I sent him to Augusta when the time came, and he took the oaths. And a very valuable member he made. They appointed him on the Committee on Parishes; but I wrote a letter for him, resigning, on the ground that he took an interest in our claim to the stumpage in the minister's sixteenths of Gore A, next to No. 7, in the 10th Range. He never made any speeches, and always voted with the minority, which was what he was sent to do. He made me and himself a great many good friends, some of whom I did not afterwards recognize as quickly as Dennis did my parishioners. On one or two occasions, when there was wood to saw at home, I kept him at home; but I took those occasions to go to Augusta myself. Finding myself often in his vacant seat at these times, I watched the proceedings with a great deal of care; and once was so much excited that I delivered my somewhat celebrated speech on the Central School-District question, a speech of which the *State of Maine* printed some extra copies. I believe there is no formal rule permitting strangers to speak; but no one objected.

Dennis himself, as I said, never spoke at all. But our experience this session led me to think that if, by some such "general understanding" as the reports speak of in legislation daily, every member of Congress might leave a double to sit through those deadly sessions and answer to roll-calls and do the legitimate party-voting, which appears stereotyped in the regular list of Ash, Bocock, Black, etc., we should gain decidedly in working-power. As things stand, the saddest state prison I ever visit is that Representatives' Chamber in Washington. If a man leaves for an hour, twenty "correspondents" may be howling, "Where was Mr. Prendergast when the Oregon bill passed?" And if poor Prendergast stays there! Certainly the worst use you can make of a man is to put him in prison!

I know, indeed, that public men of the highest rank have resorted to this expedient long ago. Dumas' novel of the "Iron Mask" turns on the brutal imprisonment of Louis the Fourteenth's double. There seems little doubt, in our own history, that it was the real General Pierce who shed tears when the delegate from Lawrence explained to him the sufferings of the people there, and only General Pierce's double who had given the orders for the assault on that town, which was invaded the next day. My charming friend, George Withers, has, I am almost sure, a double, who preaches his afternoon sermons for him. This is the reason that the theology often varies so from that of the forenoon. But the double is almost as charming as the original. Some of the most well-defined men, who stand out most prominently on the background of history, are in this way stereoscopic men, who owe their distinct relief to the slight differences between the doubles. All this I know. My present suggestion is simply the great extension of the system, so that all public machine work may be done by it.

But I see I loiter on my story, which is rushing to the plunge. Let me stop an instant more, however, to recall, were it only to myself, that charming year while all was yet well. After the double had become a matter of course, for nearly twelve months before he undid me, what a year it was! Full of active life, full of happy love, of the hardest work, of the sweetest sleep, and the fulfilment of so many of the fresh aspirations and dreams of boyhood! Dennis went to every school-committee meeting, and sat through all those late wranglings which used to keep me up till midnight and awake till morning. He attended all the lectures to which foreign exiles sent me tickets, begging me to come for the love of Heaven and of Bohemia. He accepted and used all the tickets for charity concerts which were sent to me. He appeared everywhere where it was specially desirable that "our denomination," or "our party," or "our class," or "our family," or "our street," or "our town," or "our country," or "our state," should be fully represented. And I fell back to that charming life which in boyhood one dreams of, when he supposes he shall do his own duty and make his own sacrifices, without being tied up with those of other people. My rusty Sanskrit, Arabic, Hebrew, Greek, Latin, French, Italian, Spanish, German, and English began to take polish. Heavens! how little I had done with them while I attended to my *public* duties! My calls on my parishioners became the friendly frequent, homelike sociabilities they were meant to be, instead of the hard work of a man goaded to desperation by the sight of his lists of arrears. And preaching! what a luxury preaching was when I had on Sunday the whole result of an individual, personal week, from which to speak to a people whom all that week I had been meeting as hand-to-hand friend;—I, never tired on Sunday, and in condition to leave the sermon at home, if I chose, and preach it extempore, as all men should do always. Indeed, I wonder, when I think that a sensible people, like ours—really more attached to their clergy than they were in the lost days, when the Mathers and Nortons were noblemen—should choose to neutralize so much of their ministers' lives, and destroy so much of their early training, by this undefined passion for seeing them in public. It springs from our balancing of sects. If a spirited Episcopalian takes an interest in the almshouse, and is put on the Poor Board, every other denomination must have a minister there, lest the poorhouse be changed into St. Paul's Cathedral. If a Sandemanian is chosen president of the Young Men's Library, there must be a Methodist vice-president and a Baptist secretary. And if a Universalist Sunday-School Convention collects five hundred delegates, the next Congregationalist Sabbath-School Conference must be as large "lest 'they'—whoever *they* may be—should think 'we'—whoever *we* may be—are going down."

Freed from these necessities, that happy year I began to know my wife by sight. We saw each other sometimes. In those long mornings, when Dennis was in the study explaining to map-peddlers that I had eleven maps of Jerusalem already, she and I were at work together, as in those old dreamy days, and in these of our log-cabin again. But all this could not last; and at length poor Dennis, my double, overtasked in turn, undid me.

It was thus it happened. There is an excellent fellow, once a minister, —I will call him Isaacs,—who deserves well of the world till he dies, and after, because he once, in a real exigency, did the right thing, in the right way, at the right time, as no other man could do it. In the world's great football match, the ball by chance found him loitering on the outside of the field; he closed with it, "camped" it, charged it home—yes, right through the other side—not disturbed, not frightened by his own success—and, breathless, found himself a great man, as the Great Delta rang applause. But he did not find himself a rich man; and the football has never come in his way again. From that moment to this moment he has been of no use, that one can see at all. Still, for that great act we speak of Isaacs gratefully and remember him kindly; and he forges on, hoping to meet the football somewhere again. In that vague hope he had arranged a "movement" for a general organization of the human family into Debating Clubs, County Societies, State Unions, etc., etc., with a view of inducing all children to take hold of the handles of their knives and forks, instead of the metal. Children have bad habits in that way. The movement, of course, was absurd; but we all did our best to forward, not it, but him. It came time for the annual county meeting on this subject to be held at Naguadavick. Isaacs came round, good fellow! to arrange for it—got the town-hall, got the Governor to preside (the saint! —he ought to have triplet doubles provided him by law), and then came to get me to speak. "No," I said, "I do not beleive in the enterprise. If I spoke it should be to say children should take hold of the prongs of the forks and the blades of the knives. I would subscribe ten dollars, but I would not speak a mill." So poor Isaacs went his way sadly, to coax Auchmuty to speak, and Delafield. I went out. Not long after he came back, and told Polly that they had promised to speak, the Governor would speak, and he himself would close with the quarterly report, and some interesting anecdotes regarding Miss Biffin's way of handling her knife and Mr. Nellis's way of footing his fork. "Now if Mr. Ingham will only come and sit on the platform, he need not say one word; but it will show well in the paper—it will show that the Sandemanians take as much interest in the movement as the Armenians or the Mesopotamians, and will be a great favor to me." Polly, good soul! was tempted, and she promised. She knew Mrs. Isaacs was starving, and the babies,—she knew Dennis was at home,—and she promised! Night came, and I returned. I heard her story. I was sorry. I doubted. But Polly had promised to beg me, and I dared all! I told Dennis to hold his peace, under all circumstances, and sent him down.

It was not half an hour more before he returned, wild with excitement,—in a perfect Irish fury,—which it was long before I understood. But I knew at once that he had undone me!

What happened was this. The audience got together, attracted by Governor Gorges' name. There were a thousand people. Poor Gorges was late from Augusta. They became impatient. He came in direct from the train at last, really ignorant of the object of the meeting. He opened it in the fewest possible words, and said other gentlemen were present who would entertain them better than he. The audience were disappointed, but waited. The Governor, prompted by Isaacs, said, "The Honorable Mr. Delafield will address you." Delafield! He had forgotten the knives and forks, and was playing the Ruy Lopez opening at the chess-club. "The Rev. Mr. Auchmuty will address you." Auchmuty had promised to speak late, and was at the school-committee. "I see Dr.

Stearns in the hall; perhaps he will say a word." Dr. Stearns said he had come to listen and not to speak. The Governor and Isaacs whispered. The Governor looked at Dennis, who was resplendent on the platform; but Isaacs, to give him his due, shook his head. But the look was enough. A miserable lad, ill-bred, who had once been in Boston, thought it would sound well to call for me, and peeped out, "Ingham!" A few more wretches cried, "Ingham! Ingham!" Still Isaacs was firm; but the Governor, anxious, indeed, to prevent a row, knew I would say something, and said, "Our friend Mr. Ingham is always prepared; and, though we had not relied upon him, he will say a word perhaps." Applause followed, which turned Dennis's head. He rose, fluttered, and tried No. 3. "There has been so much said, and, on the whole, so well said, that I will not occupy the time!" and sat down, looking for his hat; for things seemed squally. But the people cried, "Go on! go on!" and some applauded. Dennis, still confused, but flattered by the applause, to which neither he nor I are used, rose again, and this time tried No. 2: "I am very glad you liked it!" in a sonorous, clear delivery. My best friends stared. All the people who did not know me personally yelled with delight at the aspect of the evening; the Governor was beside himself, and poor Isaacs thought he was undone! Alas, it was I! A boy in the gallery cried in a loud tone, "It's all an infernal humbug," just as Dennis, waving his hand, commanded silence, and tried No. 4: "I agree, in general, with my friend the other side of the room." The poor Governor doubted his senses and crossed to stop him—not in time, however. The same gallery-boy shouted, "How's your mother?" and Dennis, now completely lost, tried, as his last shot, No. 1, vainly: "Very well, thank you. And you?"

I think I must have been undone already. But Dennis, like another Lockhard, chose "to make sicker." The audience rose in a whirl of amazement, rage, and sorrow. Some other impertinence, aimed at Dennis, broke all restraint, and, in pure Irish, he delivered himself of an address to the gallery, inviting any person who wished to fight to come down and do so—stating, that they were all dogs and cowards, and the sons of dogs and cowards—that he would take any five of them single-handed. "Shure, I have said all his Riverence and the Misthress bade me say," cried he, in defiance; and, seizing the Governor's cane from his hand, brandished it, quarter-staff fashion, above his head. He was, indeed, got from the hall only with the greatest difficulty by the Governor, the city marshal, who had been called in, and the superintendent of my Sunday-School.

The universal impression, of course, was that the Rev. Frederic Ingham had lost all command of himself in some of those haunts of intoxication which for fifteen years I have been laboring to destroy. Till this moment, indeed, that is the impression in Naguadavick. This number of the *Atlantic* will relieve from it a hundred friends of mine who have been sadly wounded by that notion now for years; but I shall not be likely ever to show my head there again.

No! My double has undone me.

We left town at seven the next morning. I came to No. 9 in the Third Range, and settled on the Minister's Lot. In the new towns of Maine, the first settled minister has a gift of a hundred acres of land. I am the first settled minister in No. 9. My wife and little Paulina are my parish. We raise corn enough to live on in summer. We kill bear's meat enough to carbonize it in winter. I work on steadily on my "Traces of Sandemanianism in the Sixth and Seventh Centuries," which I hope to persuade Phillips, Samson & Co. to publish next year. We are very happy, but the world thinks we are undone.

FRANK RICHARD STOCKTON (1834-1902)

The Lady, or the Tiger?

In the very olden time, there lived a semi-barbaric king, whose ideas, though somewhat polished and sharpened by the progressiveness of distant Latin neighbors, were still large, florid, and untrammelled, as became the half of him which was barbaric. He was a man of exuberant fancy, and, withal, of an authority so irresistible that, at his will, he turned his varied fancies into facts. He was greatly given to self-communing; and, when he and himself agreed upon anything, the thing was done. When every member of his domestic and political systems moved smoothly in its appointed course, his nature was bland and genial; but whenever there was a little hitch, and some of his orbs got out of their orbits, he was blander and more genial still, for nothing pleased him so much as to make the crooked straight, and crush down uneven places.

Among the borrowed notions by which his barbarism had become semified was that of the public arena, in which, by exhibitions of manly and beastly valor, the minds of his subjects were refined and cultured.

But even here the exuberant and barbaric fancy asserted itself. The arena of the king was built, not to give the people an opportunity of hearing the rhapsodies of dying gladiators, nor to enable them to view the inevitable conclusions of a conflict between religious opinions and hungry jaws, but for purposes far better adapted to widen and develop the mental energies of the people. This vast amphitheatre, with its encircling galleries, its mysterious vaults, and its unseen passages, was an agent of poetic justice, in which crime was punished, or virtue rewarded, by the decrees of an impartial and incorruptible chance.

When a subject was accused of a crime of sufficient importance to interest the king, public notice was given that on an appointed day the fate of the accused person would be decided in the king's arena,—a structure which well deserved its name; for, although its form and plan were borrowed from afar, its purpose emanated solely from the brain of this man, who, every barleycorn a king, knew no tradition to which he owed more allegiance than pleased his fancy, and who ingrafted on every adopted form of human thought and action the rich growth of his barbaric idealism.

When all the people had assembled in the galleries, and the king, surrounded by his court, sat high up on his throne of royal state on one side of the arena, he gave a signal, a door beneath him opened, and the accused subject stepped out into the amphitheatre. Directly opposite him, on the other side of the enclosed space, were two doors, exactly alike and side by side. It was the duty and the privilege of the person on trial, to walk directly to these doors and open one of them. He could open either door he pleased: he was subject to no guidance or influence but that of the aforementioned impartial and incorruptible chance. If he opened the one, there came out of it a hungry tiger, the fiercest and most cruel that could be procured, which immediately sprang upon him, and tore him to pieces, as a punishment for his guilt. The moment that the case of the criminal was thus decided, doleful iron bells were clanged, great wails went up from the hired mourners posted on the outer rim of the arena, and the vast audience, with bowed heads and downcast hearts, wended slowly their homeward way, mourning greatly that one so young and fair, or so old and respected, should have merited so dire a fate.

But, if the accused person opened the other door, there came forth from it a lady, the most suitable to his years and station that his majesty could select among his fair subjects; and to his lady he was immediately married, as a reward of his innocence. It mattered not that he might already possess a wife and family, or that his affections might be engaged upon an object of his own selection: the king allowed no such subordinate arrangements to interfere with his great scheme of retribution and reward. The exercises, as in the other instance, took place immediately, and in the arena. Another door opened beneath the king, and a priest, followed by a band of choristers, and dancing maidens blowing joyous airs on golden horns and treading an epithalamic measure, advanced to where the pair stood, side by side; and the wedding was promptly and cheerily solemnized. Then the gay brass bells rang forth their merry peals, the people shouted glad hurrahs, and the innocent man, preceded by children strewing flowers on his path, led his bride to his home.

This was the king's semi-barbaric method of administering justice. Its perfect fairness is obvious. The criminal could not know out of which door would come the lady: he opened either he pleased, without having the slightest idea whether, in the next instant, he was to be devoured or married. On some occasions the tiger came out of one door, and on some out of the other. The decisions of this tribunal were not only fair, they were positively determinate: the accused person was instantly punished if he found himself guilty; and, if innocent, he was rewarded on the spot, whether he liked it or not. There was no escape from the judgments of the king's arena.

The institution was a very popular one. When the people gathered together on one of the great trial days, they never knew whether they were to witness a bloody slaughter or a hilarious wedding. This element of uncertainty lent an interest to the occasion which it could not otherwise have attained. Thus, the masses were entertained and pleased, and the thinking part of the community could bring no charge of unfairness against this plan; for did not the accused person have the whole matter in his own hands?

This semi-barbaric king had a daughter as blooming as his most florid fancies, and with a soul as fervent and imperious as his own. As is usual in such cases, she was the apple of his eye, and was loved by him above all humanity. Among his courtiers was a young man of that fineness of blood and lowness of station common to the conventional heroes of romance who love royal maidens. This royal maiden was well satisfied with her lover, for he was handsome and brave to a degree unsurpassed in all this kingdom; and she loved him with an ardor that had enough of barbarism in it to make it exceedingly warm and strong. This love affair moved on happily for many months, until one day the king happened to discover its existence. He did not hesitate nor waver in regard to his duty in the premises. The youth was immediately cast into prison, and a day was appointed for his trial in the king's arena. This, of course, was an especially important occasion; and his majesty, as well as all the people, was greatly interested in the workings and development of this trial. Never before had such a case occurred; never before had a subject dared to love the daughter of a king. In after-years such things became commonplace enough; but then they were, in no slight degree, novel and startling.

The tiger-cages of the kingdom were searched for the most savage and relentless beasts, from which the fiercest monster might be selected for the arena; and the ranks of maiden youth and beauty throughout the land were carefully surveyed by competent judges, in order that the young man might have a fitting bride in case fate did not determine for him a different destiny. Of course, everybody knew that the deed with which the accused was charged had been done. He had loved the princess, and neither he, she, nor any one else thought of denying the fact; but the king would not think of allowing any fact of this kind to interfere with the workings of the tribunal, in which he took such great delight and satisfaction. No matter how the affair turned out, the youth would be disposed of; and the king would take an æsthetic pleasure in watching the course of events, which would determine whether or not the young man had done wrong in allowing himself to love the princess.

The appointed day arrived. From far and near the people gathered, and thronged the great galleries of the arena; and crowds, unable to gain admittance, massed themselves against its outside walls. The king and his court were in their places, opposite the twin doors,—those fateful portals, so terrible in their similarity.

All was ready. The signal was given. A door beneath the royal party opened, and the lover of the princess walked into the arena. Tall, beautiful, fair, his appearance was greeted with a low hum of admiration and anxiety. Half the audience had not known so grand a youth had lived among them. No wonder the princess loved him! What a terrible thing for him to be there!

As the youth advanced into the arena, he turned, as the custom was, to bow to the king: but he did not think at all of that royal personage; his eyes were fixed upon the princess, who sat to the right of her father. Had it not been for the moiety of barbarism in her nature, it is probable that lady would not have been there; but her intense and fervid soul would not allow her to be absent on an occasion in which she was so terribly interested. From the moment that the decree had gone forth, that her lover should decide his fate in the king's arena, she had thought of nothing, night or day, but this great event and the various subjects connected with it. Possessed of more power, influence, and force of character than any one who had ever before been interested in such a case, she had done what no other person had done,—she had possessed herself of the secret of the doors. She knew in which of the two rooms, that lay behind those doors, stood the cage of the tiger, with its open front, and in which waited the lady. Through these thick doors, heavily curtained with skins on the inside, it was impossible that any noise or suggestion should come from within to the person who should approach to raise the latch of one of them; but gold, and the power of a woman's will, had brought the secret to the princess.

And not only did she know in which room stood the lady ready to emerge, all blushing and radiant, should her door be opened, but she knew who the lady was. It was one of the fairest and loveliest of the damsels of the court who had been selected as the reward of the accused youth, should he be proved innocent of the crime of aspiring to one so far above him; and the princess hated her. Often had she seen, or imagined that she had seen, this fair creature throwing glances of admiration upon the person of her lover, and sometimes she thought these glances were perceived and even returned. Now and then she had seen them talking together; it was but for a moment or two, but much can be said in a brief space; it may have been on most unimportant topics, but how could she know that? The girl was lovely, but she had dared to raise her eyes to the loved one of the princess; and, with all the intensity of the savage blood transmitted to her through long lines of wholly barbaric ancestors, she hated the woman who blushed and trembled behind that silent door.

When her lover turned and looked at her, and his eye met hers as she sat there paler and whiter than any one in the vast ocean of anxious faces about her, he saw, by that power of quick perception which is given to those whose souls are one, that she knew behind which door crouched the tiger, and behind which stood the lady. He had expected her to know it. He understood her nature, and his soul was assured that she would never rest until she had made plain to herself this thing, hidden to all other lookers-on, even to the king. The only hope for the youth in which there was any element of certainty was based upon the success of the princess in discovering this mystery; and the moment he looked upon her, he saw she had succeeded, as in his soul he knew she would succeed.

Then it was that his quick and anxious glance asked the question: "Which?" It was as plain to her as if he shouted it from where he stood. There was not an instant to be lost. The question was asked in a flash; it must be answered in another.

Her right arm lay on the cushioned parapet before her. She raised her hand, and made a slight, quick movement toward the right. No one but her lover saw her. Every eye but his was fixed on the man in the arena.

He turned, and with a firm and rapid step he walked across the empty space. Every heart stopped beating, every breath was held, every eye was fixed immovably upon that man. Without the slightest hesitation, he went to the door on the right, and opened it.

Now, the point of the story is this: Did the tiger come out of that door, or did the lady?

The more we reflect upon this question, the harder it is to answer. It involves a study of the human heart which leads us through devious mazes of passion, out of which it is difficult to find our way. Think of it, fair reader, not as if the decision of the question depended upon yourself, but upon that hot-blooded, semi-barbaric princess, her soul at a white heat beneath the combined fires of despair and jealousy. She had lost him, but who should have him?

How often, in her waking hours and in her dreams, had she started in wild horror, and covered her face with her hands as she thought of her lover opening the door on the other side of which waited the cruel fangs of the tiger!

But how much oftener had she seen him at the other door! How in her grievous reveries had she gnashed her teeth, and torn her hair, when she saw his start of rapturous delight as he opened the door of the lady! How her soul had burned in agony when she had seen him rush to meet that woman, with her flushing cheek and sparkling eye of triumph; when she had seen him lead her forth, his whole frame kindled with the joy of recovered life; when she had heard the glad shouts from the multitude, and the wild ringing of the happy bells; when she had seen the priest, with his joyous followers, advance to the couple, and make them man and wife before her very eyes; and when she had seen them walk away together upon their path of flowers, followed by the tremendous shouts of the hilarious multitude, in which her one despairing shriek was lost and drowned!

Would it not be better for him to die at once, and go to wait for her in the blessed regions of semi-barbaric futurity?

And yet, that awful tiger, those shrieks, that blood!

Her decision had been indicated in an instant, but it had been made after days and nights of anguished deliberation. She had known she would be asked, she had decided what she would answer, and, without the slightest hesitation, she had moved her hand to the right.

The question of her decision is one not to be lightly considered, and it is not for me to presume to set myself up as the one person able to answer it. And so I leave it with all of you: Which came out of the opened door,—the lady, or the tiger?

MARK TWAIN (1835-1910)

The Notorious Jumping Frog of Calaveras County

In compliance with the request of a friend of mine, who wrote me from the East, I called on good-natured, garrulous old Simon Wheeler, and inquired after my friend's friend, Leonidas W. Smiley, as requested to do, and I hereunto append the result. I have a lurking suspicion that *Leonidas W.* Smiley is a myth; that my friend never knew such a personage; and that he only conjectured that if I asked Wheeler about him, it would remind him of his infamous *Jim* Smiley, and he would go to work and bore me to death with some exasperating reminiscence of him as long and as tedious as it should be useless to me. If that was the design, it succeeded.

I found Simon Wheeler dozing comfortably by the barroom stove of the dilapidated tavern in the decaying mining camp of Angel's, and I noticed that he was fat and bald-headed, and had an expression of winning gentleness and simplicity upon his tranquil countenance. He roused up, and gave me good-day. I told him a friend of mine had commissioned me to make some inquiries about a cherished companion of his boyhood named *Leonidas* W. Smiley—*Rev. Leonidas W.* Smiley, a young minister of the Gospel, who he had heard was at one time a resident of Angel's Camp. I added that if Mr. Wheeler could tell me anything about this Rev. Leonidas W. Smiley, I would feel under many obligations to him.

Simon Wheeler backed me into a corner and blockaded me there with his chair, and then sat down and reeled off the monotonous narrative which follows this paragraph. He never smiled, he never frowned, he never changed his voice from the gentle-flowing key to which he turned his initial sentence, he never betrayed the slightest suspicion of enthusiasm; but all through the interminable narrative there ran a vein of impressive earnestness and sincerity, which showed me plainly that, so far from his imagining that there was anything ridiculous or funny about his story, he regarded it as a really important matter, and admired its two heroes as men of transcendent genius in *finesse*. I let him go on in his own way, and never interrupted him once.

"Rev. Leonidas W. H'm, Reverend Le—well, there was a feller here once by the name of *Jim* Smiley, in the winter of '49—or maybe it was the spring of '50—I don't recollect exactly, somehow, though what makes me think it was one or the other is because I remember the big flume warn't finished when he first come to the camp; but anyway, he was the curiosest man about always betting on anything that turned up you ever see, if he could get anybody to bet on the other side; and if he couldn't he'd change sides. Any way that suited the other man would suit *him*—any way just so's he got a bet, *he* was satisfied. But still he was lucky, uncommon lucky; he most always came out winner. He was always ready and laying for a chance; there couldn't be no solit'ry thing mentioned but that feller'd offer to bet on it, and take ary side you please, as I was just telling you. If there was a horse-race, you'd find him flush or you'd find him busted at the end of it; if there was a dog-fight, he'd bet on it; if there was a cat-fight, he'd bet on it; if there was a chicken-fight, he'd bet on it; why, if there was two birds setting on a fence, he would bet you which one would fly first; or if there was a camp-meeting, he would be there reg'lar to bet on Parson Walker, which he judged to be the best exhorter about here, and so he was, too, and a good man. If he even see a straddle-bug start to go anywheres, he would bet you how long it would take him to get to—to wherever he was going to, and if you took him up, he would foller that straddle-bug to Mexico but what he would find out where he was bound for and how long he was on the road. Lots of the boys here has seen that Smiley, and can tell you about him. Why, it never made no difference to *him*—he'd bet on *any* thing—the dangdest feller. Parson Walker's wife laid very sick once, for a good while, and it seemed as if they warn't going to save her; but one morning he come in, and Smiley up and asked him how she was, and he said she was considerable better—thank the Lord for his inf'nite mercy—and coming on so smart that with the blessing of Prov'dence she'd get well yet; and Smiley, before he thought, says: 'Well, I'll resk two-and-a-half she don't anyway.'

"Thish-yer Smiley had a mare—the boys called her the fifteen-minute nag, but that was only in fun, you know, because, of course, she was faster than that—and he used to win money on that horse, for all she was so slow and always had the asthma, or the distemper, or the consumption, or something of that kind. They used to give her two or three hundred yards start, and then pass her under way; but always at the fag end of the race she'd get excited and desperate like, and come cavorting and straddling up, and scattering her legs around limber, sometimes in the air, and sometimes out to one side among the fences, and kicking up m-o-r-e dust and raising m-o-r-e racket with her coughing and sneezing and blowing her nose—and *always* fetch up at the stand just about a neck ahead, as near as you could cipher it down.

"And he had a little small bull-pup, that to look at him you'd think he warn't worth a cent but to set around and look ornery and lay for a chance to steal something. But as soon as money was up on him he was a different dog; his under-jaw'd begin to stick out like the fo'castle of a steamboat, and his teeth would uncover and shine like the furnaces. And a dog might tackle him and bully-rag him, and bite him, and throw him over his shoulder two or three times, and Andrew Jackson—which was the name of the pup—Andrew Jackson would never let on but what *he* was satisfied, and hadn't expected nothing else—and the bets being doubled and doubled on the other side all the time, till the money was all up; and then all of a sudden he would grab that other dog jest by the j'int of his hind leg and freeze to it—not chaw, you understand, but only just grip and hang on till they throwed up the sponge, if it was a year. Smiley always come out winner on that pup, till he harnessed a dog once that didn't have no hind legs, because they'd been sawed off in a circular saw, and when the thing had gone along far enough, and the money was all up, and he come to make a snatch for his pet holt, he see in a minute how he'd been imposed on, and how the other dog had him in the door, so to speak, and he 'peared surprised, and then he looked sorter discouraged-like and didn't try no more to win the fight, and so he got shucked out bad. He give Smiley a look, as much as to say his heart was broke, and it was *his* fault, for putting up a dog that hadn't no hind legs for him to take holt of, which was his main dependence in a fight, and then he limped off a piece and laid down and died. It was a good pup, was that Andrew Jackson, and would have made a name for hisself if he'd lived, for the stuff was in him and he had genius—I know it, because he hadn't no opportunities to speak of, and it don't stand to reason that a dog could make such a fight as he could under them circumstances if he hadn't no talent. It always makes me feel sorry when I think of that last fight of his'n, and the way it turned out.

"Well, thish-yer Smiley had rat-tarriers, and chicken cocks, and tomcats and all them kind of things, till you couldn't rest, and you couldn't fetch nothing for him to bet on but he'd match you. He ketched a frog one day, and took him home, and said he cal'lated to educate him; and so he never done nothing for three months but set in his back yard and learn that frog to jump. And you bet you he *did* learn him, too. He'd give him a little punch behind, and the next minute you'd see that frog whirling in the air like a doughnut—see him turn one summerset, or maybe a couple, if he got a good start, and come down flat-footed and all right, like a cat. He got him up so in the matter of ketching flies, and kep' him in practice so constant, that he'd nail a fly every time as fur as he could see him. Smiley said all a frog wanted was education, and he could do 'most anything—and I believe him. Why, I've seen him set Dan'l Webster down here on this floor—Dan'l Webster was the name of the frog—and sing out, "Flies, Dan'l, flies!" and quicker'n you could wink he'd spring straight up and snake a fly off'n the counter there, and flop down on the floor ag'in as solid as a gob of mud, and fall to scratching the side of his head with his hind foot as indifferent as if he hadn't no idea he'd been doin' any more'n any frog might do. You never see a frog so modest and straightfor'ard as he was, for all he was so gifted. And when it come to fair and square jumping on a dead level, he could get over more ground at one straddle than any animal of his breed you ever see. Jumping on a dead level was his strong suit, you understand; and when it come to that, Smiley would ante up money on him as long as he had a red. Smiley was monstrous proud of his frog, and well he might be, for fellers that had travelled and been everywheres all said he laid over any frog that ever *they* see.

"Well, Smiley kep' the beast in a little lattice box, and he used to fetch him down town sometimes and lay for a bet. One day a feller—a stranger in the camp, he was—come acrost him with his box, and says:

" 'What might it be that you've got in the box?'

"And Smiley says, sorter indifferent-like: 'It might be a parrot, or it might be a canary, maybe, but it ain't—it's only just a frog.'

"And the feller took it, and looked at it careful, and turned it round this way and that, and says: 'H'm—so 'tis. Well, what's *he* good for?'

" 'Well,' Smiley says, easy and careless, 'he's good enough for *one* thing, I should judge—he can out-jump any frog in Calaveras county.'

"The feller took the box again, and took another long, particular look, and give it back to Smiley, and says, very deliberate, 'Well,' he says, 'I don't see no p'ints about that frog that's any better'n any other frog.'

" 'Maybe you don't,' Smiley says. 'Maybe you understand frogs and maybe you don't understand 'em; maybe you've had experience, and maybe you ain't only a amature, as it were. Anyways, I've got *my* opinion, and I'll resk forty dollars that he can outjump any frog in Calaveras county.'

"And the feller studied a minute, and then says, kinder sad like, 'Well, I'm only a stranger here, and I ain't got no frog; but if I had a frog, I'd bet you.'

"And then Smiley says, 'That's all right—that's all right—if you'll hold my box a minute, I'll go and get you a frog.' And so the feller took the box, and put up his forty dollars along with Smiley's, and set down to wait.

"So he set there a good while thinking and thinking to hisself, and then he got the frog out and prized his mouth open and took a teaspoon and filled him full of quail-shot—filled him pretty near up to his chin—and set him on the floor. Smiley he went to the swamp and slopped around in the mud for a long time, and finally he ketched a frog, and fetched him in, and give him to this feller, and says:

" 'Now, if you're ready, set him alongside of Dan'l, with his forepaws just even with Dan'l's, and I'll give the word.' Then he says, 'One—two—three—*git!*' and him and the feller touched up the frogs from behind, and the new frog hopped off lively, but Dan'l give a heave, and hysted up his shoulders—so—like a Frenchman, but it warn't no use—he couldn't budge; he was planted as solid as a church, and he couldn't no more stir than if he was anchored out. Smiley was a good deal surprised, and he was disgusted too, but he didn't have no idea what the matter was, of course.

"The feller took the money and started away; and when he was going out at the door, he sorter jerked his thumb over his shoulder—so—at Dan'l, and says again, very deliberate, 'Well,' he says, '*I* don't see no p'ints about that frog that's any better'n any other frog.'

"Smiley he stood scratching his head and looking down at Dan'l a long time, and at last he says, 'I do wonder what in the nation that frog throw'd off for—I wonder if there ain't something the matter with him—he 'pears to look mighty baggy, somehow.' And he ketched Dan'l by the nap of the neck, and hefted him, and says, 'Why, blame my cats if he don't weigh five pound!' and turned him upside down and he belched out a double handful of shot. And then he see how it was, and he was the maddest man—he set the frog down and took out after that feller, but he never ketched him. And—"

[Here Simon Wheeler heard his name called from the front yard, and got up to see what was wanted.] And turning to me as he moved away, he said: "Just set where you are, stranger, and rest easy—I ain't going to be gone a second."

But, by your leave, I did not think that a continuation of the history of the enterprising vagabond *Jim* Smiley would be likely to afford me much information concerning the Rev. *Leonidas W.* Smiley, and so I started away.

At the door I met the sociable Wheeler returning, and he buttonholed me and re-commenced:

"Well, thish-yer Smiley had a yaller one-eyed cow that didn't have no tail, only just a short stump like a bannanner, and—"

However, lacking both time and inclination, I did not wait to hear about the afflicted cow, but took my leave.

From Life on the Mississippi

A Daring Deed

When I returned to the pilot-house St. Louis was gone, and I was lost. Here was a piece of river which was all down in my book, but I could make neither head nor tail of it: you understand, it was turned around. I had seen it when coming up-stream, but I had never faced about to see how it looked when it was behind me. My heart broke again, for it was plain that I had got to learn this troublesome river *both ways.*

The pilot-house was full of pilots, going down to "look at the river." What is called the "upper river" (the two hundred miles between St. Louis and Cairo, where the Ohio comes in) was low; and the Mississippi changes its channel so constantly that the pilots used to always find it necessary to run down to Cairo to take a fresh look, when their boats were to lie in port a week; that is, when the water was at a low stage. A deal of this "looking at the river" was done by poor fellows who seldom had a berth, and whose only hope of getting one lay in their being always freshly posted and therefore ready to drop into the shoes of some reputable pilot, for a single trip, on account of such pilot's sudden illness, or some other necessity. And a good many of them constantly ran up and down inspecting the river, not because they ever really hoped to get a berth, but because (they being guests of the boat) it was cheaper to "look at the river" than stay ashore and pay board. In time these fellows grew dainty in their tastes, and only infested boats that had an established reputation for setting good tables. All visiting pilots were useful, for they were always ready and willing, winter or summer, night or day, to go out in the yawl and help buoy the channel or assist the boat's pilots in any way they could. They were likewise welcomed because all pilots are tireless talkers, when gathered together, and as they talk only about the river they are always understood and are always interesting. Your true pilot cares nothing about anything on earth but the river, and his pride in his occupation surpasses the pride of kings.

We had a fine company of these river inspectors along this trip. There were eight or ten, and there was abundance of room for them in our great pilot-house. Two or three of them wore polished silk hats, elaborate shirt-fronts, diamond breastpins, kid gloves, and patent-leather boots. They were choice in their English, and bore themselves with a dignity proper to men of solid means and prodigious reputation as pilots. The others were more or less loosely clad, and wore upon their heads tall felt cones that were suggestive of the days of the Commonwealth.

I was a cipher in this august company, and felt subdued, not to say torpid. I was not even of sufficient consequence to assist at the wheel when it was necessary to put the tiller hard down in a hurry; the guest that stood nearest did that when occasion required—and this was pretty much all the time, because of the crookedness of the channel and the scant water. I stood in a corner; and the talk I listened to took the hope all out of me. One visitor said to another:

"Jim, how did you run Plum Point, coming up?"

"It was in the night, there, and I ran it the way one of the boys on the *Diana* told me; started out about fifty yards above the wood-pile on the false point, and held on the cabin under Plum Point till I raised the reef—quarter less twain—then straightened up for the middle bar till I got well abreast the old one-limbed cottonwood in the bend, then got my stern on the cottonwood, and head on the low place above the point, and came through a-booming—nine and a half."

"Pretty square crossing, an't it?"

"Yes, but the upper bar's working down fast."

Another pilot spoke up and said:

"I had better water than that, and ran it lower down; started out from the false point—mark twain—raised the second reef abreast the big snag in the bend, and had quarter less twain."

One of the gorgeous ones remarked:

"I don't want to find fault with your leadsmen, but that's a good deal of water for Plum Point, it seems to me."

There was an approving nod all around as this quiet snub dropped on the boaster and "settled" him. And so they went on talk-talk-talking. Meantime, the thing that was running in my mind was, "Now, if my ears hear aright, I have not only to get the names of all the towns and islands and bends, and so on, by heart, but I must even get up a warm personal acquaintanceship with every old snag and one-limbed cottonwood and obscure wood-pile that ornaments the banks of this river for twelve hundred miles; and more than that, I must actually know where these things are in the dark, unless these guests are gifted with eyes that can pierce through two miles of solid blackness. I wish the piloting business was in Jericho and I had never thought of it."

At dusk Mr. Bixby tapped the big bell three times (the signal to land), and the captain emerged from his drawing-room in the forward end of the "texas," and looked up inquiringly. Mr. Bixby said:

"We will lay up here all night, captain."

"Very well, sir."

That was all. The boat came to shore and was tied up for the night.

It seemed to me a fine thing that the pilot could do as he pleased, without asking so grand a captain's permission. I took my supper and went immediately to bed, discouraged by my day's observations and experiences. My late voyage's note-booking was but a confusion of meaningless names. It had tangled me all up in a knot every time I had looked at it in the daytime. I now hoped for respite in sleep; but no, it revelled all through my head till sunrise again, a frantic and tireless nightmare.

Next morning I felt pretty rusty and low-spirited. We went booming along, taking a good many chances, for we were anxious to "get out of the river" (as getting out to Cairo was called) before night should overtake us. But Mr. Bixby's partner, the other pilot, presently grounded the boat, and we lost so much time getting her off that it was plain the darkness would overtake us a good long way above the mouth. This was a great misfortune, especially to certain of our visiting pilots, whose boats would have to wait for their return, no matter how long that might be. It sobered the pilot-house talk a good deal. Coming up-stream, pilots did not mind low water or any kind of darkness; nothing stopped them but fog. But down-stream work was different; a boat was too nearly helpless, with a stiff current pushing behind her; so it was not customary to run down-stream at night in low water.

There seemed to be one small hope, however: if we could get through the intricate and dangerous Hat Island crossing before night, we could venture the rest, for we would have plainer sailing and better water. But it would be insanity to attempt Hat Island at night. So there was a deal of looking at watches all the rest of the day, and a constant ciphering upon the speed we were making; Hat Island was the eternal subject; sometimes hope was high and sometimes we were delayed in a bad crossing, and down it went again. For hours all hands lay under the burden of this suppressed excitement; it was even communicated to me, and I got to feeling so solicitous about Hat Island, and under such an awful pressure of responsibility, that I wished I might have five minutes on shore to draw a good, full, relieving breath, and start over again. We were standing no regular watches. Each of our pilots ran such portions of the river as he had run when coming up-stream, because of his greater familiarity with it; but both remained in the pilot-house constantly.

An hour before sunset Mr. Bixby took the wheel, and Mr. W. stepped aside. For the next thirty minutes every man held his watch in his hand and was restless, silent, and uneasy. At last somebody said, with a doomful sigh:

"Well, yonder's Hat Island—and we can't make it."

All the watches closed with a snap, everybody sighed and muttered something about its being "too bad, too bad—ah, if we could *only* have got here half an hour sooner!" and the place was thick with the atmosphere of disappointment. Some started to go out, but loitered, hearing no bell-tap to land. The sun dipped behind the horizon, the boat went on. Inquiring looks passed from one guest to another; and one who had his hand on the door-knob and had turned it, waited, then presently took away his hand and let the knob turn back again. We bore steadily down the bend. More looks were exchanged, and nods of surprised admiration—but no words. Insensibly the men drew together behind Mr. Bixby, as the sky darkened and one or two dim stars came out. The dead silence and sense of waiting became oppressive. Mr. Bixby pulled the cord, and two deep, mellow notes from the big bell floated off on the night. Then a pause, and one more note was struck. The watchman's voice followed, from the hurricane-deck:

"Labboard lead, there! Stabboard lead!"

The cries of the leadsmen began to rise out of the distance, and were gruffly repeated by the word-passers on the hurricane-deck.

"M-a-r-k three! M-a-r-k three! Quarter-less-three! Half twain! Quarter twain! M-a-r-k twain! Quarter-less—"

Mr. Bixby pulled two bell-ropes, and was answered by faint jinglings far below in the engine-room, and our speed slackened. The steam began to whistle through the gauge-cocks. The cries of the leadsmen went on—and it is a weird sound, always, in the night. Every pilot in the lot was watching now, with fixed eyes, and talking under his breath. Nobody was calm and easy but Mr. Bixby. He would put his wheel down and stand on a spoke, and as the steamer swung into her (to me) utterly invisible marks—for we seemed to be in the midst of a wide and gloomy sea—he would meet and fasten her there. Out of the murmur of half-audible talk, one caught a coherent sentence now and then—such as:

"There; she's over the first reef all right!"

After a pause, another subdued voice:

"Her stern's coming down just *exactly* right, by *George!*"

"Now she's in the marks; over she goes!"

Somebody else muttered:

"Oh, it was done beautiful—*beautiful!*"

Now the engines were stopped altogether, and we drifted with the current. Not that I could see the boat drift, for I could not, the stars being all gone by this time. This drifting was the dismalest work; it held one's heart still. Presently I discovered a blacker gloom than that which surrounded us. It was the head of the island. We were closing right down upon it. We entered its deeper shadow, and so imminent seemed the peril that I was likely to suffocate; and I had the strongest impulse to do *something,* anything, to save the vessel. But still Mr. Bixby stood by his wheel, silent, intent as a cat, and all the pilots stood shoulder to shoulder at his back.

"She'll not make it!" somebody whispered.

The water grew shoaler and shoaler, by the leadsman's cries, till it was down to:

"Eight-and-a-half! E-i-g-h-t feet! E-i-g-h-t feet! Seven-and—"

Mr. Bixby said warningly through his speaking-tube to the engineer:

"Stand by, now!"

"Ay, ay, sir!"

"Seven-and-a-half! Seven feet! *Six*-and—"

We touched bottom! Instantly Mr. Bixby set a lot of bells ringing, shouted through the tube, *"Now,* let her have it—every ounce you've got!" then to his partner, "Put her hard down! snatch her! snatch her!" The boat rasped and ground her way through the sand, hung upon the apex of disaster a single tremendous instant, and then over she went! And such a shout as went up at Mr. Bixby's back never loosened the roof of a pilot-house before!

There was no more trouble after that. Mr. Bixby was a hero that night; and it was some little time, too, before his exploit ceased to be talked about by river-men.

Fully to realize the marvelous precision required in laying the great steamer in her marks in that murky waste of water, one should know that not only must she pick her intricate way through snags and blind reefs, and then shave the head of the island so closely as to brush the overhanging foliage with her stern, but at one place she must pass almost within arm's reach of a sunken and invisible wreck that would snatch the hull timbers from under her if she should strike it, and destroy a quarter of a million dollars' worth of steamboat and cargo in five minutes, and maybe a hundred and fifty human lives into the bargain.

The last remark I heard that night was a compliment to Mr. Bixby, uttered in soliloquy and with unction by one of our guests. He said:

"By the Shadow of Death, but he's a lightning pilot!"

A Pilot's Needs

But I am wandering from what I was intending to do; that is, make plainer than perhaps appears in the previous chapters some of the peculiar requirements of the science of piloting. First of all, there is one faculty which a pilot must incessantly cultivate until he has brought it to absolute perfection. Nothing short of perfection will do. That faculty is memory. He cannot stop with merely thinking a thing is so and so; he must *know* it; for this is eminently one of the "exact" sciences. With what scorn a pilot was looked upon, in the old times, if he ever ventured to deal in that feeble phrase "I think," instead of the vigorous one, "I know!" One cannot easily realize what a tremendous thing it is to know every trivial detail of twelve hundred miles of river and know it with absolute exactness. If you will take the longest street in New York, and travel up and down it, conning its features patiently until you know every house and window and lamp-post and big and little sign by heart, and know them so accurately that you can instantly name the one you are abreast of when you are set down at random in that street in the middle of an inky black night, you will then have a tolerable notion of the amount and the exactness of a pilot's knowledge who carries the Mississippi River in his head. And then, if you will go on until you know every street-crossing, the character, size, and position of the crossing-stones, and the varying depth of mud in each of these numberless places, you will have some idea of what the pilot must know in order to keep a Mississippi steamer out of trouble. Next, if you will take half of the signs in that long street, and *change their places* once a month, and still manage to know their new positions accurately on dark nights, and keep up with these repeated changes without making any mistakes, you will understand what is required of a pilot's peerless memory by the fickle Mississippi.

I think a pilot's memory is about the most wonderful thing in the world. To know the Old and New Testaments by heart, and be able to recite them glibly, forward or backward, or begin at random anywhere in the book and recite both ways and never trip or make a mistake, is no extravagant mass of knowledge, and no marvelous facility, compared to a pilot's massed knowledge of the Mississippi and his marvelous facility in handling of it. I make this comparison deliberately, and believe I am not expanding the truth when I do it. Many will think my figure too strong, but pilots will not.

And how easily and comfortably the pilot's memory does its work; how placidly effortless is its way; how *unconsciously* it lays up its vast stores, hour by hour, day by day, and never loses or mislays a single valuable package of them all! Take an instance. Let a leadsman cry, "Half twain! half twain! half twain! half twain! half twain!" until it becomes as monotonous as the ticking of a clock; let conversation be going on all the time, and the pilot be doing his share of the talking, and no longer consciously listening to the leadsman; and in the midst of this endless string of half twains let a single "quarter twain!" be interjected, without emphasis, and then the half-twain cry go on again, just as before: two or three weeks later that pilot can describe with precision the boat's position in the river when that quarter twain was uttered, and give you such a lot of head-marks, stern-marks, and side-marks to guide you, that you ought to be able to take the boat there and put her in that same spot again yourself! The cry of "quarter twain" did not really take his mind from his talk, but his trained faculties instantly photographed the bearings, noted the change of depth, and laid up the important details for future reference without requiring any assistance from *him* in the matter. If you were walking and talking with a friend, and another friend at your side kept up a monotonous repetition of the vowel sound A, for a couple of blocks, and then in the midst interjected an R, thus, A, A, A, A, A, R, A, A, A, etc., and gave the R no emphasis, you would not be able to state, two or three weeks afterward, that the R had been put in, nor be able to tell what objects you were passing at the moment it was done. But you could if your memory had been patiently and laboriously trained to do that sort of thing mechanically.

Give a man a tolerably fair memory to start with, and piloting will develop it into a very colossus of capability. But *only in the matters it is daily drilled in.* A time would come when the man's faculties could not help noticing landmarks and soundings, and his memory could not help holding on to them with the grip of a vise; but if you asked that same man at noon what he had had for breakfast, it would be ten chances to one that he could not tell you. Astonishing things can be done with the human memory if you will devote it faithfully to one particular line of business.

At the time that wages soared so high on the Missouri River, my chief, Mr. Bixby, went up there and learned more than a thousand miles of that stream with an ease and rapidity that were astonishing. When he had seen each division *once* in the daytime and *once* at night, his education was so nearly complete that he took out a "daylight" license; a few trips later he took out a full license, and went to piloting day and night—and he ranked A 1, too.

Mr. Bixby placed me as steersman for a while under a pilot whose feats of memory were a constant marvel to me. However, his memory was born in him, I think, not built. For instance, somebody would mention a name. Instantly Mr. Brown would break in:

"Oh, I knew *him.* Sallow-faced, red-headed fellow, with a little scar on the side of his throat, like a splinter under the flesh. He was only in the Southern trade six months. That was thirteen years ago. I made a trip with him. There was five feet in the upper river then; the *Henry*

Blake grounded at the foot of Tower Island drawing four and a half; the *George Elliott* unshipped her rudder on the wreck of the *Sunflower*—"

"Why, the *Sunflower* didn't sink until—"

"*I* know when she sunk; it was three years before that, on the 2d of December; Asa Hardy was captain of her, and his brother John was first clerk; and it was his first trip in her, too; Tom Jones told me these things a week afterward in New Orleans; he was first mate of the *Sunflower*. Captain Hardy stuck a nail in his foot the 6th of July of the next year, and died of the lockjaw on the 15th. His brother John died two years after—3d of March—erysipelas. I never saw either of the Hardys—they were Alleghany River men—but people who knew them told me all these things. And they said Captain Hardy wore yarn socks winter and summer just the same, and his first wife's name was Jane Shook—she was from New England—and his second one died in a lunatic asylum. It was in the blood. She was from Lexington, Kentucky. Name was Horton before she was married."

And so on, by the hour, the man's tongue would go. He could *not* forget anything. It was simply impossible. The most trivial details remained as distinct and luminous in his head, after they had lain there for years, as the most memorable events. His was not simply a pilot's memory; its grasp was universal. If he were talking about a trifling letter he had received seven years before, he was pretty sure to deliver you the entire screed from memory. And then, without observing that he was departing from the true line of his talk, he was more than likely to hurl in a long-drawn parenthetical biography of the writer of that letter; and you were lucky indeed if he did not take up that writer's relatives, one by one, and give you their biographies, too.

Such a memory as that is a great misfortune. To it, all occurrences are of the same size. Its possessor cannot distinguish an interesting circumstance from an uninteresting one. As a talker, he is bound to clog his narrative with tiresome details and make himself an insufferable bore. Moreover, he cannot stick to his subject. . He picks up every little grain of memory he discerns in his way, and so is led aside. Mr. Brown would start out with the honest intention of telling you a vastly funny anecdote about a dog. He would be "so full of laugh" that he could hardly begin; then his memory would start with the dog's breed and personal appearance; drift into a history of his owner; of his owner's family, with descriptions of weddings and burials that had occurred in it, together with recitals of congratulatory verses and obituary poetry provoked by the same; then this memory would recollect that one of these events occurred during the celebrated "hard winter" of such-and-such a year, and a minute description of that winter would follow, along with the names of people who were frozen to death, and statistics showing the high figures which pork and hay went up to. Pork and hay would suggest corn and fodder; corn and fodder would suggest cows and horses; cows and horses would suggest the circus and certain celebrated bare-back riders; the transition from the circus to the menagerie was easy and natural; from the elephant to equatorial Africa was but a step; then of course the heathen savages would suggest religion; and at the end of three or four hours' tedious jaw, the watch would change, and Brown would go out of the pilot-house muttering extracts from sermons he had heard years before about the efficacy of prayer as a means of grace. And the original first mention would be all you had learned about that dog, after all this waiting and hungering.

A pilot must have a memory; but there are two higher qualities which he must also have. He must have good and quick judgment and decision, and a cool, calm courage that no peril can shake. Give a man the merest trifle of pluck to start with, and by the time he has become a pilot he cannot be unmanned by any danger a steamboat can get into; but one cannot quite say the same for judgment. Judgment is a matter of brains, and a man must *start* with a good stock of that article or he will never succeed as a pilot.

The growth of courage in the pilot-house is steady all the time, but it does not reach a high and satisfactory condition until some time after the young pilot has been "standing his own watch" alone and under the staggering weight of all the responsibilities connected with the position. When the apprentice has become pretty thoroughly acquainted with the river, he goes clattering along so fearlessly with his steamboat, night or day, that he presently begins to imagine that it is *his* courage that animates him; but the first time the pilot steps out and leaves him to his own devices he finds out it was the other man's. He discovers that the article has been left out of his own cargo altogether. The whole river is bristling with exigencies in a moment; he is not prepared for them; he does not know how to meet them; all his knowledge forsakes him; and within fifteen minutes he is as white as a sheet and scared almost to death. Therefore pilots wisely train these cubs by various strategic tricks to look danger in the face a little more calmly. A favorite way of theirs is to play a friendly swindle upon the candidate.

Mr. Bixby served me in this fashion once, and for years afterward I used to blush, even in my sleep, when I thought of it. I had become a good steersman; so good, indeed, that I had all the work to do on our watch, night and day. Mr. Bixby seldom made a suggestion to me; all he ever did was to take the wheel on particularly bad nights or in particularly bad crossings, land the boat when she needed to be landed, play gentleman of leisure nine-tenths of the watch, and collect the wages. The lower river was about bank-full, and if anybody had questioned my ability to run any crossing between Cairo and New Orleans without help or instruction, I should have felt irreparably hurt. The idea of being afraid of any crossing in the lot, in the *daytime,* was a thing too preposterous for contemplation. Well, one matchless summer's day I was bowling down the bend above Island 66, brimful of self-conceit and carrying my nose as high as a giraffe's, when Mr. Bixby said:

"I am going below awhile. I suppose you know the next crossing?"

This was almost an affront. It was about the plainest and simplest crossing in the whole river. One couldn't come to any harm, whether he ran it right or not; and as for depth, there never had been any bottom there. I knew all this, perfectly well.

"Know how to *run* it? Why, I can run it with my eyes shut."

"How much water is there in it?"

"Well, that is an odd question. I couldn't get bottom there with a church steeple."

"You think so, do you?"

The very tone of the question shook my confidence. That was what Mr. Bixby was expecting. He left, without saying anything more. I began to imagine all sorts of things. Mr. Bixby, unknown to me, of course, sent somebody down to the forecastle with some mysterious instructions to the leadsmen, another messenger was sent to whisper among the officers, and then Mr. Bixby went into hiding behind a smoke-stack where he could observe results. Presently the captain stepped out on the hurricane-deck; next the chief mate appeared; then a clerk. Every moment or two a straggler was added to my audience; and before I got to the head of the island I had fifteen or twenty people assembled down there under my nose. I began to wonder what the trouble was. As I started across, the captain glanced aloft at me and said, with a sham uneasiness in his voice:

"Where is Mr. Bixby?"

"Gone below, sir."

But that did the business for me. My imagination began to construct dangers out of nothing, and they multiplied faster than I could keep the run of them. All at once I imagined I saw shoal water ahead! The wave of coward agony that surged through me then came near dislocating every joint in me. All my confidence in that crossing vanished. I seized the bell-rope; dropped it, ashamed; seized it again; dropped it once more; clutched it tremblingly once again, and pulled it so feebly that I could hardly hear the stroke myself. Captain and mate sang out instantly, and both together:

"Starboard lead there! and quick about it!"

This was another shock. I began to climb the wheel like a squirrel; but I would hardly get the boat started to port before I would see new dangers on that side, and away I would spin to the other; only to find perils accumulating to starboard, and be crazy to get to port again. Then came the leadsman's sepulchral cry:

"D-e-e-p four!"

Deep four in a bottomless crossing! The terror of it took my breath away.

"M-a-r-k three! M-a-r-k three! Quarter-less-three! Half twain!"

This was frightful! I seized the bell-ropes and stopped the engines.

"Quarter twain! Quarter twain! *Mark* twain!"

I was helpless. I did not know what in the world to do. I was quaking from head to foot, and I could have hung my hat on my eyes, they stuck out so far.

"Quarter-*less*-twain! Nine-and-a-*half!*"

We were *drawing* nine! My hands were in a nerveless flutter. I could not ring a bell intelligibly with them. I flew to the speaking-tube and shouted to the engineer:

"Oh, Ben, if you love me, *back* her! Quick, Ben! Oh, back the immortal *soul* out of her!"

I heard the door close gently. I looked around, and there stood Mr. Bixby, smiling a bland, sweet smile. Then the audience on the hurricane-deck sent up a thundergust of humiliating laughter. I saw it all, now, and I felt meaner than the meanest man in human history. I laid in the lead, set the boat in her marks, came ahead on the engines, and said:

"It was a fine trick to play on an orphan, *wasn't* it? I suppose I'll never hear the last of how I was ass enough to heave the lead at the head of 66."

"Well, no, you won't, maybe. In fact I hope you won't; for I want you to learn something by that experience. Didn't you *know* there was no bottom in that crossing?"

"Yes, sir, I did."

"Very well, then. You shouldn't have allowed me or anybody else to shake your confidence in that knowledge. Try to remember that. And another thing: when you get into a dangerous place, don't turn coward. That isn't going to help matters any."

It was a good enough lesson, but pretty hardly learned. Yet about the hardest part of it was that for months I so often had to hear a phrase which I had conceived a particular distaste for. It was, "Oh, Ben, if you love me, back her!"

From A Connecticut Yankee at the Court of King Arthur

In 1879, Hank Morgan was superintendent of an arms factory in Hartford, in the state of Connecticut. Engaging in "a misunderstanding conducted with crowbars" with a workman known as Hercules, Hank was laid out "with a crusher alongside the head that made everything crack." He awoke under a tree near Camelot, the seat of King Arthur's court, in the year 528. He was captured and brought to Camelot by Sir Kay the Seneschal, and condemned to be burned at the stake. The execution was to take place at noon on the twenty-first of June, 528. In his former existence he had somehow learned that this was the exact day and hour of an eclipse. He therefore threatened to blot out the sun if he was harmed; and as the torch was about to be applied, the eclipse occurred, while he pretended to command it. Overcome, the King made the Yankee his minister, with the title of Sir Boss. The magician Merlin resented bitterly such success on the part of a rival, and endeavored by every means to destroy him. But through triumph after triumph, though often in the utmost danger, Sir Boss went on, introducing inventions and reforms. Not least interesting among the conflicts between him and the existing order was the tournament here related.

The Yankee's Fight with the Knights

Home again, at Camelot. A morning or two later I found the paper, damp from the press, by my plate at the breakfast-table. I turned to the advertising columns, knowing I should find something of personal interest to me there. It was this:

DE PAR LE ROI.

Know that the great lord and illustrious Kni8ht, SIR SAGRAMOR LE DESIROUS naving condescended to meet the King's Minister, Hank Morgan, the which is surnamed The Boss, for satisfgction of offence anciently given, these wilL engage in the lists by Camelot about the fourth hour of the morning of the sixteenth day of this next succeeding month. The battle will be à l outrance, sith the said offence was of a deadly sort, admitting of no comPosition.

DE PAR LE ROI

Clarence's editorial reference to this affair was to this effect:

thdrew.
work maintained
there since, soon
lastic have witq
oked interest
upon the ea-
ve been m d
by the an ns,
ent out ch y by
sterian *B* n, and
e some y ng men
of our under the
guidance of the
or aid in a known
the great enterprise
of making pure;
esent
movement had its
origin in preven-
has ever been a
sions id our
on the Mis-
other one
ospel,
by-
e
The
the same
to represent
ized thirty of
needs and hear-
which, years age!
design was osgan-
ing, the missions,
so that both had
to withdraw' and
much to their
grief,

It will be observed, by a gl7nce at our advertising columns, that the commu-nity is to be favored with a treat of un-usual interest in the tournament line. The n ames of the artists are warrant of good enterTamment. The box-office will be open at noon of the 13th; ad-mission 3 cents, reserve*d* seats 5; pro-ceeds to go to the hospital fund The royal pair and all tne Court will be pres-ent. With these exceptions, and the press and the clergy, the free list is strict-ly susTended. Parties are hereby warn-ed against buying tickets of speculators; they will not be good at the door. Everybody knows and likes The Boss, everybody knows and likes Sir Sag.; come, let us give tne lads a good send-off. ReMember, tne proceeds go to a great and free charity, and one whose broad begevolence stretches out its help-ing hand, warm with the blood of a lov-ing heart, to all that suffer, regardless of race, creed, condition or color—the only charity yet established in tne earth which has no politico-religious stop-cock on its compassion, but says Here flows the stream, let *all* come and drink! Turn out, all hands! fetch along your dou3hnuts and your gum drops and have a good time. Pie for sale on the grouna*s*, and rocks to crack it with; also CIRcus-lemonade—three drops of lime juice to a barrel of water.

N. B. *This is the first tournament under the new law, whidh allow each combatant to use any weapon he may pre-fer.* You want to make a note of that.

our disappoint
promptly and
two of their felo
eслain, and othe
ers have alread
spoken, you b
furnisned for
their use, m
make and
the kind
letters
of introd
duction whi
they are unin
ing friends to m
ried, and leave the
thot kind words
which you my joy-
hind; and it is a
home matter of b
it is our durp
direct them to
now under the
g fields as are
***T*nese youn3 men**
are warm-hearted.
azirl, regions bas
not to "build a
ond,', and the
der instructi
ons of our
another man
founhati's on.,
ociety, which
They go un-
say tqat "Mr
ionaries to mon
say sending mis

Up to the day set, there was no talk in all Britain of anything but this combat. All other topics sank into insignificance and passed out of men's thoughts and interest. It was not because a tournament was a great matter; it was not because Sir Sagramor had found the Holy Grail, for he had not, but had failed; it was not because the second (official) personage in the kingdom was one of the duelists; no, all these features were commonplace. Yet there was abundant reason for the extraordinary interest which this coming fight was creating. It was born of the fact that all the nation knew that this was not to be a duel between mere men, so to speak, but a duel between two mighty magicians; a duel not of muscle but of mind, not of human skill but of superhuman art and craft; a final struggle for supremacy between the two master enchanters of the age. It was realized that the most prodigious achievements of the most renowned knights could not be worthy of comparison with a spectacle like this; they could be but child's play, contrasted with this mysterious and awful battle of the gods. Yes, all the world knew it was going to be in reality a duel between Merlin and me, a measuring of his magic powers against mine. It was known that Merlin had been busy whole days and nights together, imbuing Sir Sagramor's arms and armor with supernal powers of offence and defence, and that he had procured for him from the spirits of the air a fleecy veil which would render the wearer invisible to his antagonist while still visible to other men. Against Sir Sagramor, so weaponed and protected, a thousand knights could accomplish nothing; against him no known enchantments could prevail. These facts were sure; regarding them there was no doubt, no reason for doubt. There was but one question: might there be still other enchantments, *unknown* to Merlin, which could render Sir Sagramor's veil transparent to me, and make his enchanted mail vulnerable to my weapons? This was the one thing to be decided in the lists. Until then the world must remain in suspense.

So the world thought there was a vast matter at stake here, and the world was right, but it was not the one they had in their minds. No a far vaster one was upon the cast of this die: *the life of knight-errantry.* I was entering the lists to either destroy knight-errantry or be its victim.
arts, I was the champion of hard unsentimental common sense and reason.
I was entering the lists to either destroy knight-errantry or be its victim.

Vast as the show-grounds were, there were no vacant spaces in them outside of the lists, at ten o'clock on the morning of the 16th. The mammoth grand-stand was clothed in flags, streamers, and rich tapestries, and packed with several acres of small-fry tributary kings, their suites, and the British aristocracy; with our own royal gang in the chief place, and each and every individual a flashing prism of gaudy silks and velvets —well, I never saw anything to begin with it but a fight between an Upper Mississippi sunset and the aurora borealis. The huge camp of beflagged and gay-colored tents at one end of the lists, with a stiff-standing sentinel at every door and a shining shield hanging by him for challenge, was another fine sight. You see, every knight was there who had any ambition or any caste feeling; for my feeling toward their order was not much of a secret, and so here was their chance. If I won my fight with Sir Sagramor, others would have the right to call me out as long as I might be willing to respond.

Down at our end there were but two tents; one for me, and another for my servants. At the appointed hour the king made a sign, and the heralds, in their tabards, appeared and made proclamation, naming the combatants and stating the cause of quarrel. There was a pause, then a ringing bugle-blast, which was the signal for us to come forth. All the multitude caught their breath, and an eager curiosity flashed into every face.

Out from his tent rode great Sir Sagramor, an imposing tower of iron, stately and rigid, his huge spear standing upright in its socket and grasped in his strong hand, his grand horse's face and breast cased in steel, his body clothed in rich trappings that almost dragged the ground —oh, a most noble picture. A great shout went up, of welcome and admiration.

And then out I came. But I didn't get any shout. There was a wondering and eloquent silence for a moment, then a great wave of laughter began to sweep along that human sea, but a warning bugle-blast cut its career short. I was in the simplest and comfortablest of gymnast costumes—flesh-colored tights from neck to heel, with blue silk puffings about my loins, and bareheaded. My horse was not above medium size, but he was alert, slender-limbed, muscled with watch-springs, and just a greyhound to go. He was a beauty, glossy as silk, and naked as he was when he was born, except for bridle and ranger-saddle.

The iron tower and the gorgeous bed-quilt came cumbrously but gracefully pirouetting down the lists, and we tripped lightly up to meet them. We halted; the tower saluted, I responded; then we wheeled and rode side by side to the grand-stand and faced our king and queen, to whom we made obeisance. The queen exclaimed:

"Alack, Sir Boss, wilt fight naked, and without lance or sword or—"

But the king checked her and made her understand, with a polite phrase or two, that this was none of her business. The bugles rang again; and we separated and rode to the ends of the lists, and took position. Now old Merlin stepped into view and cast a dainty web of gossamer threads over Sir Sagramor which turned him into Hamlet's ghost; the king made a sign, the bugles blew, Sir Sagramor laid his great lance in rest, and the next moment here he came thundering down the course with his veil flying out behind, and I went whistling through the air like an arrow to meet him—cocking my ear the while, as if noting the invisible knight's position and progress by hearing, not sight. A chorus of encouraging shouts burst out for him, and one brave voice flung out a heartening word for me—said:

"Go it, slim Jim!"

It was an even bet that Clarence had procured that favor for me —and furnished the language, too. When that formidable lance-point was within a yard and a half of my breast I twitched my horse aside without an effort, and the big knight swept by, scoring a blank. I got plenty of applause that time. We turned, braced up, and down we came again. Another blank for the knight, a roar of applause for me. The same thing was repeated once more; and it fetched such a whirlwind of applause that Sir Sagramor lost his temper, and at once changed his tactics and set himself the task of chasing me down. Why, he hadn't any show in the world at that; it was a game of tag, with all the advantage on my side; I whirled out of his path with ease whenever I chose, and once I slapped him on the back as I went to the rear. Finally I took the chase into my own hands; and after that, turn, or twist, or do what he would, he was never able to get behind me again; he found himself always in front at the end of his manœuver. So he gave up that business and retired to his end of the lists. His temper was clear gone now, and he forgot himself and flung an insult at me which disposed of mine. I slipped my lasso from the horn of my saddle, and grasped the coil in my right hand. This time you should have seen him come!—it was a business trip, sure; by his gait there was blood in his eye. I was sitting my horse at ease, and swinging the great loop of my lasso in wide circles about my head; the moment he was under way, I started for him; when the space between us had narrowed to forty feet, I sent the snaky spirals of the rope a-cleaving through the air, then darted aside and faced about and brought my trained animal to a halt with all his feet braced under him for a surge. The next moment the rope sprang taut and yanked Sir Sagramor out of the saddle! Great Scott, but there was a sensation!

Unquestionably, the popular thing in this world is novelty. These people had never seen anything of that cowboy business before, and it carried them clear off their feet with delight. From all around and everywhere, the shout went up:

"Encore! encore!"

I wondered where they got the word, but there was no time to cipher on philological matters, because the whole knight-errantry hive was just humming now, and my prospect for trade couldn't have been better. The moment my lasso was released and Sir Sagramor had been assisted to his tent, I hauled in the slack, took my station and began to swing my loop around my head again. I was sure to have use for it as soon as they could elect a successor for Sir Sagramor, and that couldn't take long where there were so many hungry candidates. Indeed, they elected one straight off—Sir Hervis de Revel.

Bzz! Here he came, like a house afire; I dodged: he passed like a flash, with my horse-hair coils settling around his neck; a second or so later, *fst!* his saddle was empty.

I got another encore; and another, and another, and still another. When I had snaked five men out, things began to look serious to the ironclads, and they stopped and consulted together. As a result, they decided that it was time to waive etiquette and send their greatest and best against me. To the astonishment of that little world, I lassoed Sir Lamorak de Galis, and after him Sir Galahad. So you see there was simply nothing to be done now, but play their right bower—bring out the superbest of the superb, the mightiest of the mighty, the great Sir Launcelot himself!

A proud moment for me? I should think so. Yonder was Arthur, King of Britain; yonder was Guinevere; yes, and whole tribes of little provincial kings and kinglets; and in the tented camp yonder, renowned knights from many lands; and likewise the selectest body known to chivalry, the Knights of the Table Round, the most illustrious in Christendom; and biggest fact of all, the very sun of their shining system was yonder couching his lance, the focal point of forty thousand adoring eyes; and all by myself, here was I laying for him. Across my mind flitted the dear image of a certain hello-girl of West Hartford, and I wished she could see me now. In that moment, down came the Invincible, with the rush of a whirlwind—the courtly world rose to its feet and bent forward—the fateful coils went circling through the air, and before you could wink I was towing Sir Launcelot across the field on his back, and kissing my hand to the storm of waving kerchiefs and the thunder-crash of applause that greeted me!

Said I to myself, as I coiled my lariat and hung it on my saddle-horn, and sat there drunk with glory, "The victory is perfect—no other will venture against me—knight-errantry is dead." Now imagine my astonishment—and everybody else's, too—to hear the peculiar bugle-call which announces that another competitor is about to enter the lists! There was a mystery here; I couldn't account for this thing. Next, I noticed Merlin gliding away from me; and then I noticed that my lasso was gone! The old sleight-of-hand expert had stolen it, sure, and slipped it under his robe.

The bugle blew again. I looked, and down came Sagramor riding again, with his dust brushed off and his veil nicely rearranged. I trotted up to meet him, and pretended to find him by the sound of his horse's hoofs. He said:

"Thou'rt quick of ear, but it will not save thee from this!" and he touched the hilt of his great sword. "An ye are not able to see it, because of the influence of the veil, know that it is no cumbrous lance, but a sword—and I ween ye will not be able to avoid it."

His visor was up; there was death in his smile. I should never be able to dodge his sword, that was plain. Somebody was going to die this time. If he got the drop on me, I could name the corpse. We rode forward together, and saluted the royalties. This time the king was disturbed. He said:

"Where is thy strange weapon?"

"It is stolen, sire."

"Hast another at hand?"

"No, sire, I brought only the one."

Then Merlin mixed in:

"He brought but the one because there was but the one to bring. There exists none other but that one. It belongeth to the king of the Demons of the Sea. This man is a pretender, and ignorant; else he had known that that weapon can be used in but eight bouts only, and then it vanisheth away to its home under the sea."

"Then is he weaponless," said the king. "Sir Sagramor, ye will grant him leave to borrow."

"And I will lend!" said Sir Launcelot, limping up. "He is as brave a knight of his hands as any that be on live, and he shall have mine."

He put his hand on his sword to draw it, but Sir Sagramor said: "Stay, it may not be. He shall fight with his own weapons; it was his privilege to choose them and bring them. If he has erred, on his head be it."

"Knight!" said the king. "Thou'rt overwrought with passion; it disorders thy mind. Wouldst kill a naked man?"

"An he do it, he shall answer it to me," said Sir Launcelot.

"I will answer it to any he that desireth!" retorted Sir Sagramor hotly.

Merlin broke in, rubbing his hands and smiling his low-downest smile of malicious gratification:

"'Tis well said, right well said! And 'tis enough of parleying, let my lord the king deliver the battle signal."

The king had to yield. The bugle made proclamation, and we turned apart and rode to our stations. There we stood, a hundred yards apart, facing each other, rigid and motionless, like horsed statues. And so we remained, in a soundless hush, as much as a full minute, everybody gazing, nobody stirring. It seemed as if the king could not take heart to give the signal. But at last he lifted his hand, the clear note of a bugle followed, Sir Sagramor's long blade described a flashing curve in the air, and it was superb to see him come. I sat still. On he came. I did not move. People got so excited that they shouted to me:

"Fly, fly! Save thyself! This is murther!"

I never budged so much as an inch till that thundering apparition had got within fifteen paces of me; then I snatched a dragoon revolver out of my holster, there was a flash and a roar, and the revolver was back in the holster before anybody could tell what had happened.

Here was a riderless horse plunging by, and yonder lay Sir Sagramor, stone dead.

The people that ran to him were stricken dumb to find that the life was actually gone out of the man and no reason for it visible, no hurt upon his body, nothing like a wound. There was a hole through the breast of his chain-mail, but they attached no importance to a little thing like that; and as a bullet-wound there produces but little blood, none came in sight because of the clothing and swaddlings under the armor. The body was dragged over to let the king and the swells look down upon it. They were stupefied with astonishment naturally. I was requested to come and explain the miracle. But I remained in my tracks, like a statue, and said:

"If it is a command, I will come, but my lord the king knows that I am where the laws of combat require me to remain while any desire to come against me."

I waited. Nobody challenged. Then I said:

"If there are any who doubt that this field is well and fairly won, I do not wait for them to challenge me, I challenge them."

"It is a gallant offer," said the king, "and well beseems you. Whom will you name first?"

"I name none, I challenge all! Here I stand, and dare the chivalry of England to come against me—not by individuals, but in mass!"

"What!" shouted a score of knights.

"You have heard the challenge. Take it, or I proclaim you recreant knights and vanquished, every one!"

It was a "bluff" you know. At such a time it is sound judgment to put on a bold face and play your hand for a hundred times what it is worth; forty-nine times out of fifty nobody dares to "call," and you rake in the chips. But just this once—well, things looked squally! In just no time, five hundred knights were scrambling into their saddles, and before you could wink a widely scattering drove were under way and clattering down upon me. I snatched both revolvers from the holsters and began to measure distances and calculate chances.

Bang! One saddle empty. Bang! another one. Bang—bang, and I bagged two. Well, it was nip and tuck with us, and I knew it. If I spent the eleventh shot without convincing these people, the twelfth man would kill me, sure. And so I never did feel so happy as I did when my ninth downed its man and I detected the wavering in the crowd which is premonitory of panic. An instant lost now could knock out my last chance. But I didn't lose it. I raised both revolvers and pointed them—the halted host stood their ground just about one good square moment, then broke and fled.

The day was mine. Knight-errantry was a doomed institution. The march of civilization was begun. How did I feel? Ah, you never could imagine it.

And Brer Merlin? His stock was flat again. Somehow, every time the magic of fol-de-rol tried conclusions with the magic of science, the magic of fol-de-rol got left.

THOMAS BAILEY ALDRICH
(1836-1907)

Sargent's Portrait of Edwin Booth at "The Players"

THAT face which no man ever saw
And from his memory banished quite,
With eyes in which are Hamlet's awe
And Cardinal Richelieu's subtle light
Looks from this frame. A master's hand
Has set the master-player here,
In the fair temple that he planned
Not for himself. To us most dear
This image of him! "It was thus
He looked; such pallor touched his cheek;
With that same grace he greeted us—
Nay, 'tis the man, could it but speak!"
Sad words that shall be said some day—
Far fall the day! O cruel Time,
Whose breath sweeps mortal things away,
Spare long this image of his prime,
That others standing in the place
Where, save as ghosts, we come no more,
May know what sweet majestic face
The gentle Prince of Players wore!

An Ode on the Unveiling of the Shaw Memorial on Boston Common

I

NOT with slow, funereal sound
Come we to this sacred ground;
Not with wailing fife and solemn muffled drum,
Bringing a cypress wreath
To lay, with bended knee,
On the cold brows of Death—
Not so, dear God, we come,
But with the trumpets' blare
And shot-torn battle-banners flung to air,
As for a victory!

Hark to the measured tread of martial feet,
The music and the murmurs of the street!
No bugle breathes this day
Disaster and retreat!—
Hark how the iron lips
Of the great battle-ships
Salute the City from her azure Bay!

II

Time was—time was, ah, unforgotten years!—
We paid our hero tribute of our tears.
But now let go
All sounds and signs and formulas of woe:
'Tis Life, not Death, we celebrate;
To Life, not Death, we dedicate
This storied bronze, whereon is wrought
The lithe immortal figure of our thought,
To show forever to men's eyes,
Our children's children's children's eyes,
How once he stood
In that heroic mood,
He and his dusky braves
So fain to glorious graves!—
One instant stood, and then
Drave through that cloud of purple steel and flame,
Which wrapt him, held him, gave him not again,
But in the trampled ashes left to Fame
An everlasting name!

III

That was indeed to live—
At one bold swoop to wrest
From darkling death the best
That death to life can give.
He fell as Roland fell
That day at Roncevaux,
With foot upon the ramparts of the foe!
A pæan, not a knell,
For heroes dying so!
No need for sorrow here,
No room for sigh or tear,
Save such rich tears as happy eyelids know.
See where he rides, our Knight!
Within his eyes the light
Of battle, and youth's gold about his brow;
Our Paladin, our Soldier of the Cross,
Not weighing gain with loss—
World-loser, that won all
Obeying duty's call!
Not his, at peril's frown,
A pulse of quicker beat;
Not his to hesitate
And parley hold with Fate,
But proudly to fling down
His gauntlet at her feet.
O soul of loyal valor and white truth,
Here, by this iron gate,
Thy serried ranks about thee as of yore,
Stand thou for evermore
In thy undying youth!

The tender heart, the eagle eye!
Oh, unto him belong
The homages of Song;
Our praises and the praise
Of coming days
To him belong—
To him, to him, the dead that shall not die!

ANNIE TRUMBULL SLOSSON

The Boy That was Scaret o' Dyin'

ONCE there was a boy that was dreadful scaret o' dyin'. Some folks is that way, you know; they ain't never done it to know how it feels, and they're scaret. And this boy was that way. He wa'n't very rugged, his health was sort o' slim, and mebbe that made him think about sech things more. 'T any 'rate, he was terr'ble scaret o' dyin'. 'Twas a long time ago this was,—the times when posies and creaturs could talk so's folks could know what they was sayin'.

And one day, as this boy, his name was Reuben,—I forget his other name,—as Reuben was settin' under a tree, an ellum tree, cryin', he heerd a little, little bit of a voice,—not squeaky, you know, but small and thin and soft like,—and he see 'twas a posy talkin'. 'Twas one o' them posies they call Benjamins, with three-cornered whitey blowths with a mite o' pink on 'em, and it talked in a kind o' pinky-white voice, and it say, "What you cryin' for, Reuben?" And he says, "'Cause I'm scaret o' dyin'," says he; "I'm dreadful scaret o' dyin'." Well, what do you think? That posy jest laughed,—the most cur'us little pinky-white laugh 'twas,—and it says, the Benjamin says: "Dyin'! Scaret o' dyin'? Why, I die myself every single year o' my life." "Die yourself!" says Reuben. "You're foolin'; you're alive this minute." "'Course I be," says the Benjamin; "but that's neither here nor there,—I've died every year sence I can remember." "Don't it hurt?" says the boy. "No, it don't," says the posy; "it's real nice. You see, you get kind o' tired a-holdin' up your head straight and lookin' peart and wide awake, and tired o' the sun shinin' so hot, and the winds blowin' you to pieces, and the bees a-takin' your honey. So it's nice to feel sleepy and kind o' hang your head down, and get sleepier and sleepier, and then find you're droppin' off. Then you wake up jest 't the nicest time o' year, and come up and look 'round, and—why, I like to die, I do." But someways that didn't help Reuben much as you'd think. "I ain't a posy," he think to himself, "and mebbe I wouldn't come up."

Well, another time he was settin' on a stone in the lower pastur', cryin' again, and he heerd another cur'us little voice. 'Twa'n't like the posy's voice, but 'twas a little, woolly, soft, fuzzy voice, and he see 'twas a caterpillar a-talkin' to him. And the caterpillar says, in his fuzzy little voice, he says, "What you cryin' for, Reuben?" And the boy, he says, "I'm powerful scaret o' dyin', that's why," he says. And that fuzzy caterpillar he laughed. "Dyin'!" he says. "I'm lottin' on dyin' myself. All my fam'ly," he says, "die every once in a while, and when they wake up they're jest splendid,—got wings, and fly about, and live on honey and things. Why, I wouldn't miss it for anything!" he says. "I'm lottin' on it." But somehow that didn't chirk up Reuben much. "I ain't a caterpillar," he says, "and mebbe I wouldn't wake up at all."

Well, there was lots o' other things talked to that boy, and tried to help him,—trees and posies and grass and crawlin' things, that was allers a-dyin' and livin', and livin' and dyin'. Reuben thought it didn't help him any, but I guess it did a little mite, for he couldn't help thinkin' o' what they every one on 'em said. But he was scaret all the same.

And one summer he begun to fail up faster and faster, and he got so tired he couldn't hardly hold his head up, but he was scaret all the same. And one day he was layin' on the bed, and lookin' out o' the east winder, and the sun kep' a-shinin' in his eyes till he shet 'em up, and he fell asleep. He had a real good nap, and when he woke up he went out to take a walk.

And he begun to think o' what the posies and trees and creaturs had said about dyin', and how they laughed at his bein' scaret at it, and he says to himself, "Why, someways I don't feel so scaret to-day, but I s'pose I be." And jest then what do you think he done? Why, he met a Angel. He'd never seed one afore, but he knowed it right off. And the Angel says, "Ain't you happy, little boy?" And Reuben says, "Well, I would be only I'm so dreadful scaret o' dyin'. It must be terr'ble cur'us," he says, "to be dead." And the Angel says, "Why, you be dead." And he was.

FRANCIS BRET HARTE (1839-1902)

The Luck of Roaring Camp

THERE was commotion in Roaring Camp. It could not have been a fight, for in 1850 that was not novel enough to have called together the entire settlement. The ditches and claims were not only deserted, but "Tuttle's grocery" had contributed its gamblers, who, it will be remembered, calmly continued their game the day that French Pete and Kanaka Joe shot each other to death over the bar in the front room. The whole camp was collected before a rude cabin on the outer edge of the clearing. Conversation was carried on in a low tone, but the name of a woman was frequently repeated. It was a name familiar enough in the camp,—"Cherokee Sal."

Perhaps the less said of her the better. She was a coarse and, it is to be feared, a very sinful woman. But at that time she was the only woman in Roaring Camp, and was just then lying in sore extremity, when she most needed the ministration of her own sex. Dissolute, abandoned, and irreclaimable, she was yet suffering a martyrdom hard enough to bear even when veiled by sympathizing womanhood, but now terrible in her loneliness. The primal curse had come to her in that original isolation which must have made the punishment of the first transgression so dreadful. It was, perhaps, part of the expiation of her sin that, at a moment when she most lacked her sex's intuitive tenderness and care, she met only the half-contemptuous faces of her masculine associates. Yet a few of the spectators were, I think, touched by her sufferings. Sandy Tipton thought it was "rough on Sal," and, in the contemplation of her condition, for a moment rose superior to the fact that he had an ace and two bowers in his sleeve.

It will be seen also that the situation was novel. Deaths were by no means uncommon in Roaring Camp, but a birth was a new thing. People had been dismissed the camp effectively, finally, and with no possibility of return; but this was the first time that anybody had been introduced *ab initio*. Hence the excitement.

"You go in there, Stumpy," said a prominent citizen known as "Kentuck," addressing one of the loungers. "Go in there, and see what you kin do. You've had experience in them things."

Perhaps there was a fitness in the selection. Stumpy, in other climes, had been the putative head of two families; in fact, it was owing to some legal informality in these proceedings that Roaring Camp—a city of refuge—was indebted to his company. The crowd approved the choice, and Stumpy was wise enough to bow to the majority. The door closed on the extempore surgeon and midwife, and Roaring Camp sat down outside, smoked its pipe, and awaited the issue.

The assemblage numbered about a hundred men. One or two of these were actual fugitives from justice, some were criminal, and all were reckless. Physically they exhibited no indication of their past lives and character. The greatest scamp had a Raphael face, with a profusion of blonde hair; Oakhurst, a gambler, had the melancholy air and intellectual abstraction of a Hamlet; the coolest and most courageous man was scarcely over five feet in height, with a soft voice and an embarrassed, timid manner. The term "roughs" applied to them was a distinction rather than a definition. Perhaps in the minor details of fingers, toes, ears, etc., the camp may have been deficient, but these slight omissions did not detract from their aggregate force. The strongest man had but three fingers on his right hand; the best shot had but one eye.

Such was the physical aspect of the men that were dispersed around the cabin. The camp lay in a triangular valley between two hills and a river. The only outlet was a steep trail over the summit of a hill that faced the cabin, now illuminated by the rising moon. The suffering woman might have seen it from the rude bunk whereon she lay,—seen it winding like a silver thread until it was lost in the stars above.

A fire of withered pine boughs added sociability to the gathering. By degrees the natural levity of Roaring Camp returned. Bets were freely offered and taken regarding the result. Three to five that "Sal would get through with it;" even that the child would survive; side bets as to the sex and complexion of the coming stranger. In the midst of an excited discussion an exclamation came from those nearest the door, and the camp stopped to listen. Above the swaying and moaning of the pines, the swift rush of the river, and the crackling of the fire rose a sharp, querulous cry,—a cry unlike anything heard before in the camp. The pines stopped moaning, the river ceased to rush, and the fire to crackle. It seemed as if Nature had stopped to listen too.

The camp rose to its feet as one man! It was proposed to explode a barrel of gunpowder; but in consideration of the situation of the mother, better counsels prevailed, and only a few revolvers were discharged; for whether owing to the rude surgery of the camp, or some other reason, Cherokee Sal was sinking fast. Within an hour she had climbed, as it were, that rugged road that led to the stars, and so passed out of Roaring Camp, its sin and shame, forever. I do not think that the announcement disturbed them much, except in speculation as to the fate of the child. "Can he live now?" was asked of Stumpy. The answer was doubtful. The only other being of Cherokee Sal's sex and maternal condition in the settlement was an ass. There was some conjecture as to fitness, but the experiment was tried. It was less problematical than the ancient treatment of Romulus and Remus, and apparently as successful.

When these details were completed, which exhausted another hour, the door was opened, and the anxious crowd of men, who had already formed themselves into a queue, entered in single file. Beside the low bunk or shelf, on which the figure of the mother was starkly outlined below the blankets, stood a pine table. On this a candle-box was placed, and within it, swathed in staring red flannel, lay the last arrival at Roaring Camp. Beside the candle-box was placed a hat. Its use was soon indicated. "Gentlemen," said Stumpy, with a singular mixture of authority and *ex officio* complacency,—"gentlemen will please pass in at the front door, round the table, and out at the back door. Them as wishes to contribute anything toward the orphan will find a hat handy." The first man entered with his hat on; he uncovered, however, as he looked about him, and so unconsciously set an example to the next. In such communities good and bad actions are catching. As the procession filed in comments were audible,—criticisms addressed perhaps rather to Stumpy in the character of showman: "Is that him?" "Mighty small specimen;" "Hasn't more'n got the color;" "Ain't bigger nor a derringer." The contributions were as characteristic: A silver tobacco box; a doubloon; a navy revolver, silver mounted; a gold specimen; a very beautifully embroidered lady's handkerchief (from Oakhurst the gambler); a diamond breastpin; a diamond ring (suggested by the pin, with the remark from the giver that he "saw that pin and went two diamonds better"); a slung-shot; a Bible (contributor not detected); a golden spur; a silver teaspoon (the initials, I regret to say, were not the giver's); a pair of surgeon's shears; a lancet; a Bank of England note for £5; and about $200 in loose gold and silver coin. During these proceedings Stumpy maintained a silence as impassive as the dead on his left, a gravity as inscrutable as that of the newly born on his right. Only one incident occurred to break the monotony of the curious procession. As Kentuck bent over the candle-box half curiously, the child turned, and, in a spasm of pain, caught at his groping finger, and held it fast for a moment. Kentuck looked foolish and embarrassed. Something like a blush tried to assert itself in his weather-beaten cheek. "The d—d little cuss!" he said, as he extricated his finger, with perhaps more tenderness and care than he might have been deemed capable of showing. He held that finger a little apart from its fellows as he went out, and examined it curiously. The examination provoked the same original remark in regard to the child. In fact, he seemed to enjoy repeating it. "He rastled with my finger," he remarked to Tipton, holding up the member, "the d—d little cuss!"

It was four o'clock before the camp sought repose. A light burnt in the cabin where the watchers sat, for Stumpy did not go to bed that night. Nor did Kentuck. He drank quite freely, and related with great gusto his experience, invariably ending with his characteristic condemnation of the newcomer. It seemed to relieve him of any unjust implication of sentiment, and Kentuck had the weakness of the nobler sex. When everybody else had gone to bed, he walked down to the river and whistled reflectively. Then he walked up the gulch past the cabin, still whistling with demonstrative unconcern. At a large redwood-tree he paused and retraced his steps, and again passed the cabin. Halfway down to the river's bank he again paused, and then returned and knocked at the door. It was opened by Stumpy. "How goes it?" said Kentuck, looking past Stumpy toward the candle-box. "All serene!" replied Stumpy. "Anything up?" "Nothing." There was a pause—an embarrassing one—Stumpy still holding the door. Then Kentuck had recourse to his finger, which he held up to Stumpy. "Rastled with it, —the d—d little cuss," he said, and retired.

The next day Cherokee Sal had such rude sepulture as Roaring Camp afforded. After her body had been committed to the hillside, there was a formal meeting of the camp to discuss what should be done with her infant. A resolution to adopt it was unanimous and enthusiastic. But an animated discussion in regard to the manner and feasibility of providing for its wants at once sprang up. It was remarkable that the argument partook of none of those fierce personalities with which discussions were usually conducted at Roaring Camp. Tipton proposed that they should send the child to Red Dog,—a distance of forty miles, —where female attention could be procured. But the unlucky suggestion met with fierce and unanimous opposition. It was evident that no plan which entailed parting from their new acquisition would for a moment be entertained. "Besides," said Tom Ryder, "them fellows at Red Dog would swap it, and ring in somebody else on us." A disbelief in the honesty of other camps prevailed at Roaring Camp, as in other places.

The introduction of a female nurse in the camp also met with objection. It was argued that no decent woman could be prevailed to accept Roaring Camp as her home, and the speaker urged that "they didn't want any more of the other kind." This unkind allusion to the defunct mother, harsh as it may seem, was the first spasm of propriety,—the first symptom of the camp's regeneration. Stumpy advanced nothing. Perhaps he felt a certain delicacy in interfering with the selection of a possible successor in office. But when questioned, he averred stoutly that he and "Jinny"—the mammal before alluded to—could manage to rear the child. There was something original, independent, and heroic about the plan that pleased the camp. Stumpy was retained. Certain articles were sent for to Sacramento. "Mind," said the treasurer, as he pressed a bag of gold-dust into the expressman's hand, "the best that can be got,—lace, you know, and filigree-work and frills,—d—n the cost!"

Strange to say, the child thrived. Perhaps the invigorating climate of the mountain camp was compensation for material deficiencies. Nature took the foundling to her broader breast. In that rare atmosphere of the Sierra foothills,—that air pungent with balsamic odor, that ethereal cordial at once bracing and exhilarating,—he may have found food and nourishment, or a subtle chemistry that transmuted ass's milk to lime and phosphorus. Stumpy inclined to the belief that it was the latter and good nursing. "Me and that ass," he would say, "has been father and mother to him! Don't you," he would add, apostrophizing the helpless bundle before him, "never go back on us."

By the time he was a month old the necessity of giving him a name became apparent. He had generally been known as "The Kid," "Stumpy's Boy," "The Coyote" (an allusion to his vocal powers), and even by Kentuck's endearing diminutive of "The d—d little cuss." But these were felt to be vague and unsatisfactory, and were at last dismissed under another influence. Gamblers and adventurers are generally superstitious, and Oakhurst one day declared that the baby had brought "the luck" to Roaring Camp. It was certain that of late they had been successful. "Luck" was the name agreed upon, with the prefix of Tommy for greater convenience. No allusion was made to the mother, and the father was unknown. "It's better," said the philosophical Oakhurst, "to take a fresh deal all round. Call him Luck, and start him fair." A day was accordingly set apart for the christening. What was meant by this ceremony the reader may imagine who has already gathered some idea of the reckless irreverence of Roaring Camp. The master of ceremonies was one "Boston," a noted wag, and the occasion seemed to promise the greatest facetiousness. This ingenious satirist had spent two days in preparing a burlesque of the Church service, with pointed local allusions. The choir was properly trained, and Sandy Tipton was to stand godfather. But after the procession had marched to the grove with music and banners, and the child had been deposited before a mock altar, Stumpy stepped before the expectant crowd. "It ain't my style to spoil fun, boys," said the little man, stoutly eyeing the faces around him, "but it strikes me that this thing ain't exactly on the squar. It's playing it pretty low down on this yer baby to ring in fun on him that he ain't goin' to understand. And ef there's goin' to be any godfathers round, I'd like to see who's got any better rights than me." A silence followed Stumpy's speech. To the credit of all humorists be it said that the first man to acknowledge its justice was the satirist thus stopped of his fun. "But," said Stumpy, quickly following up his advantage, "we're here for a christening, and we'll have it. I proclaim you Thomas Luck, according to the laws of the United States and the State of California, so help me God." It was the first time that the name of the Deity had been otherwise uttered than profanely in the camp. The form of christening was perhaps even more ludicrous than the satirist had conceived; but strangely enough, nobody saw it and nobody laughed. "Tommy" was christened as seriously as he would have been under a Christian roof, and cried and was comforted in as orthodox fashion.

And so the work of regeneration began in Roaring Camp. Almost imperceptibly a change came over the settlement. The cabin assigned to "Tommy Luck"—or "The Luck," as he was more frequently called—first showed signs of improvement. It was kept scrupulously clean and whitewashed. Then it was boarded, clothed, and papered. The rosewood cradle, packed eighty miles by mule, had in Stumpy's way of putting it, "sorter killed the rest of the furniture." So the rehabilitation of the cabin became a necessity. The men who were in the habit of lounging in at Stumpy's to see "how 'The Luck' got on" seemed to appreciate the change, and in self-defense the rival establishment of "Tuttle's grocery" bestirred itself and imported a carpet and mirrors. The reflections of the latter on the appearance of Roaring Camp tended to produce stricter habits of personal cleanliness. Again Stumpy imposed a kind of quarantine upon those who aspired to the honor and privilege of holding The Luck. It was a cruel mortification to Kentuck—who, in the carelessness of a large nature and the habits of frontier life, had begun to regard all garments as a second cuticle, which, like a snake's, only sloughed off through decay—to be debarred this privilege from certain prudential reasons. Yet such was the subtle influence of innovation that he thereafter appeared regularly every afternoon in a clean shirt and face still shining from his ablutions. Nor were moral and social sanitary laws neglected. "Tommy," who was supposed to spend his whole existence in a persistent attempt to repose, must not be disturbed by noise. The shouting and yelling, which had gained the camp its infelicitous title, were not permitted within hearing distance of Stumpy's. The men conversed in whispers or smoked with Indian gravity. Profanity was tacitly given up in these sacred precincts, [illegible]roughout the camp a popular form of expletive, known as "D—n [illegible] and "Curse the luck!" was abandoned, as having a new [illegible]ng. Vocal music was not interdicted, being supposed to [illegible] tranquilizing quality; and one song, sung by "Man-o'-[illegible]nglish sailor from her Majesty's Australian colonies, [illegible]s a lullaby. It was a lugubrious recital of the ex-[illegible]sa, Seventy-four," in a muffled minor, ending with [illegible]ll at the burden of each verse, "On b-oo-o-ard of [illegible] a fine sight to see Jack holding The Luck, rocking from side to side as if with the motion of a ship, and crooning forth this naval ditty. Either through the peculiar rocking of Jack or the length of his song,—it contained ninety stanzas, and was continued with conscientious deliberation to the bitter end,—the lullaby generally had the desired effect. At such times the men would lie at full length under the trees in the soft summer twilight, smoking their pipes and drinking in the melodious utterances. An indistinct idea that this was pastoral happiness pervaded the camp. "This 'ere kind o' think," said the Cockney Simmons, meditatively reclining on his elbow, "is 'evingly." It reminded him of Greenwich.

On the long summer days The Luck was usually carried to the gulch from whence the golden store of Roaring Camp was taken. There, on a blanket spread over pine boughs, he would lie while the men were working in the ditches below. Latterly there was a rude attempt to decorate this bower with flowers and sweet-smelling shrubs, and generally some one would bring him a cluster of wild honeysuckles, azaleas, or the painted blossoms of Las Mariposas. The men had suddenly awakened to the fact that there were beauty and significance in these trifles, which they had so long trodden carelessly beneath their feet. A flake of glittering mica, a fragment of variegated quartz, a bright pebble from the bed of the creek, became beautiful to eyes thus cleared and strengthened, and were invariably put aside for The Luck. It was wonderful how many treasures the woods and hillsides yielded that "would do for Tommy." Surrounded by playthings such as never child out of fairyland had before, it is to be hoped that Tommy was content. He appeared to be serenely happy, albeit there was an infantine gravity about him, a contemplative light in his round gray eyes, that sometimes worried Stumpy. He was always tractable and quiet, and it is recorded that once, having crept beyond his "corral,"—a hedge of tessellated pine boughs, which surrounded his bed,—he dropped over the bank on his head in the soft earth, and remained with his mottled legs in the air in that position for at least five minutes with unflinching gravity. He was extricated without a murmur. I hesitate to record the many oth[illegible] stances of his sagacity, which rest, unfortunately, upon th[illegible] of prejudiced friends. Some of them were not with[illegible] superstition. "I crep' up the bank just now," said K[illegible] in a breathless state of excitement, "and dern my [illegible] a-talking to a jaybird as was a-sittin' on his lap. T[illegible] as free and sociable as anything you please, a-jaw[illegible] like two cherrybums." Howbeit, whether creepin[illegible] or lying lazily on his back blinking at the leav[illegible] birds sang, the squirrels chattered, and the flowers bloomed. Nature was his nurse and playfellow. For him she would let slip between the leaves golden shafts of sunlight that fell just within his grasp; she would send wandering breezes to visit him with the balm of bay and resinous gum; to him the tall redwoods nodded familiarly and sleepily, the bumblebees buzzed, and the rooks cawed a slumbrous accompaniment.

Such was the golden summer of Roaring Camp. They were "flush times," and the luck was with them. The claims had yielded enormously. The camp was jealous of its privileges and looked suspiciously on strangers. No encouragement was given to immigration, and, to make their seclusion more perfect, the land on either side of the mountain wall that surrounded the camp they duly preëmpted. This, and a reputation for singular proficiency with the revolver, kept the reserve of Roaring Camp inviolate. The expressman—their only connecting link with the surrounding world—sometimes told wonderful stories of the camp. He would say, "They've a street up there in 'Roaring' that would lay over any street in Red Dog. They've got vines and flowers round their houses, and they wash themselves twice a day. But they're mighty rough on strangers, and they worship an Ingin baby."

With the prosperity of the camp came a desire for further improvement. It was proposed to build a hotel in the following spring, and to invite one or two decent families to reside there for the sake of The Luck, who might perhaps profit by female companionship. The sacrifice that this concession to the sex cost these men, who were fiercely skeptical in regard to its general virtue and usefulness, can only be accounted for by their affection for Tommy. A few still held out. But the resolve could not be carried into effect for three months, and the minority meekly yielded in the hope that something might turn up to prevent it. And it did.

The winter of 1851 will long be remembered in the foothills. The snow lay deep on the Sierras, and every mountain creek became a river, and every river a lake. Each gorge and gulch was transformed into a tumultuous watercourse that descended the hillsides, tearing down giant [illegible]attering its drift and débris along the plain. Red Dog had [illegible]nder water, and Roaring Camp had been forewarned. [illegible]gold into them gulches," said Stumpy. "It's been here [illegible]here again!" And that night the North Fork sud[illegible] banks and swept up the triangular valley of Roar-

[illegible]f rushing water, crashing trees, and crackling [illegible]ss which seemed to flow with the water and blot out the fair valley, but little could be done to collect the scattered camp. When the morning broke, the cabin of Stumpy, nearest the river-bank, was gone. Higher up the gulch they found the body of its unlucky owner; but the pride, the hope, the joy, The Luck, of Roaring Camp had disappeared. They were returning with sad hearts when a shout from the bank recalled them.

It was a relief-boat from down the river. They had picked up, they said, a man and an infant, nearly exhausted, about two miles below. Did anybody know them, and did they belong here?

It needed but a glance to show them Kentuck lying there, cruelly crushed and bruised, but still holding The Luck of Roaring Camp in his arms. As they bent over the strangely assorted pair, they saw that the child was cold and pulseless. "He is dead," said one. Kentuck opened his eyes. "Dead?" he repeated feebly. "Yes, my man, and you are dying too." A smile lit the eyes of the expiring Kentuck. "Dying!" he repeated; "he's a-taking me with him. Tell the boys I've got The Luck with me now;" and the strong man, clinging to the frail babe as a drowning man is said to cling to a straw, drifted away into the shadowy river that flows forever to the unknown sea.

The Outcasts of Poker Flat

As Mr. John Oakhurst, gambler, stepped into the main street of Poker Flat on the morning of the 23d of November, 1850, he was conscious of a change in its moral atmosphere since the preceding night. Two or three men, conversing earnestly together, ceased as he approached, and exchanged significant glances. There was a Sabbath lull in the air, which, in a settlement unused to Sabbath influences, looked ominous.

Mr. Oakhurst's calm, handsome face betrayed small concern in the indications. Whether he was conscious of any predisposing cause w another question. "I reckon they're after somebody," he reflected; "likely it's me." He returned to his pocket the handkerchief with which he had been whipping away the red dust of Poker Flat fr boots, and quietly discharged his mind of any further co

In point of fact, Poker Flat was "after somebody suffered the loss of several thousand dollars, two va a prominent citizen. It was experiencing a spasm quite as lawless and ungovernable as any of the a it. A secret committee had determined to rid th persons. This was done permanently in regard then hanging from the boughs of a sycamore in the gulch, and temporarily in the banishment of certain other objectionable characters. I regret to say that some of these were ladies. It is but due to the sex, however, to state that their impropriety was professional, and it was only in such easily established standards of evil that Poker Flat ventured to sit in judgment.

Mr. Oakhurst was right in supposing that he was included in this category. A few of the committee had urged hanging him as a possible example and a sure method of reimbursing themselves from his pockets of the sums he had won from them. "It's agin justice," said Jim Wheeler, "to let this yer young man from Roaring Camp—an entire stranger—carry away our money." But a crude sentiment of equity residing in the breasts of those who had been fortunate enough to win from Mr. Oakhurst overruled this narrower local prejudice.

Mr. Oakhurst received his sentence with philosophic calmness, none the less coolly that he was aware of the hesitation of his judges. He was too much of a gambler not to accept fate. With him life was at best an uncertain game, and he recognized the usual percentage in favor of the dealer.

A body of armed men accompanied the deported wickedness of Poker Flat to the outskirts of the settlement. Besides Mr. Oakhurst, who was known to be a coolly desperate man, and for whose intimidation the armed escort was intended, the expatriated party consisted of a young woman familiarly known as "The Duchess;" another who had won the title of "Mother Shipton;" and "Uncle Billy," a suspected sluice-robber and confirmed drunkard. The cavalcade provoked no comments from the spectators, nor was any word uttered by the escort. Only when the gulch which marked the uttermost limit of Poker Flat was reached, the leader spoke briefly and to the point. The exiles were forbidden to return at the peril of their lives.

As the escort disappeared, their pent-up feelings found vent in a few hysterical tears from the Duchess, some bad language from Mother Shipton, and a Parthian volley of expletives from Uncle Billy. The philosophic Oakhurst alone remained silent. He listened calmly to Mother Shipton's desire to cut somebody's heart out, to the repeated statements of the Duchess that she would die in the road, and to the alarming oaths that seemed to be bumped out of Uncle Billy as he rode forward. With the easy good humor characteristic of his class, he insisted upon exchanging his own riding-horse, "Five-Spot," for the sorry mule which the Duchess rode. But even this act did not draw the party into any closer sympathy. The young woman readjusted her somewhat draggled plumes with a feeble, faded coquetry; Mother Shipton eyed the possessor of "Five-Spot" with malevolence, and Uncle Billy included the whole party in one sweeping anathema.

The road to Sandy Bar—a camp that, not having as yet experienced the regenerating influences of Poker Flat, consequently seemed to offer some invitation to the emigrants—lay over a steep mountain range. It was distant a day's severe travel. In that advanced season the party soon passed out of the moist, temperate regions of the foothills into the dry, cold, bracing air of the Sierras. The trail was narrow and difficult. At noon the Duchess, rolling out of her saddle upon the ground, declared her intention of going no farther, and the party halted.

The spot was singularly wild and impressive. A wooded amphitheatre, surrounded on three sides by precipitous cliffs of naked granite, sloped gently toward the crest of another precipice that overlooked the valley. It was, undoubtedly, the most suitable spot for a camp, had camping been advisable. But Mr. Oakhurst knew that scarcely half the journey to Sandy Bar was accomplished, and the party were not equipped or provisioned for delay. This fact he pointed out to his companions curtly, with a philosophic commentary on the folly of "throwing up their hand before the game was played out." But they were furnished with liquor, which in this emergency stood them in place of food, fuel, rest, and prescience. In spite of his remonstrances, it was not long before they were more or less under its influence. Uncle Billy passed rapidly from a bellicose state into one of stupor, the Duchess became maudlin, and Mother Shipton snored. Mr. Oakhurst alone remained erect, leaning against a rock, calmly surveying them.

Mr. Oakhurst did not drink. It interfered with a profession which required coolness, impassiveness, and presence of mind, and, in his own language, he "couldn't afford it." As he gazed at his recumbent fellow exiles, the loneliness begotten of his pariah trade, his habits of life, his very vices, for the first time seriously oppressed him. He bestirred himself in dusting his black clothes, washing his hands and face, and other acts characteristic of his studiously neat habits, and for a moment forgot his annoyance. The thought of deserting his weaker and more pitiable companions never perhaps occurred to him. Yet he could not help feeling the want of that excitement which, singularly enough, was most conducive to that calm equanimity for which he was notorious. He looked at the gloomy walls that rose a thousand feet sheer above the circling pines around him, at the sky ominously clouded, at the valley below, already deepening into shadow; and, doing so, suddenly he heard his own name called.

A horseman slowly ascended the trail. In the fresh, open face of the newcomer Mr. Oakhurst recognized Tom Simson, otherwise known as "The Innocent," of Sandy Bar. He had met him some months before over a "little game," and had, with perfect equanimity, won the entire fortune—amounting to some forty dollars—of that guileless youth. After the game was finished, Mr. Oakhurst drew the youthful speculator behind the door and thus addressed him: "Tommy, you're a good little man, but you can't gamble worth a cent. Don't try it over again." He then handed him his money back, pushed him gently from the room, and so made a devoted slave of Tom Simson.

There was a remembrance of this in his boyish and enthusiastic greeting of Mr. Oakhurst. He had started, he said, to go to Poker Flat to seek his fortune. "Alone?" No, not exactly alone; in fact (a giggle), he had run away with Piney Woods. Didn't Mr. Oakhurst remember Piney? She that used to wait on the table at the Temperance House? They had been engaged a long time, but old Jake Woods had objected, and so they had run away, and were going to Poker Flat to be married, and here they were. And they were tired out, and how lucky it was they had found a place to camp, and company. All this the Innocent delivered rapidly, while Piney, a stout, comely damsel of fifteen, emerged from behind the pine tree, where she had been blushing unseen, and rode to the side of her lover.

Mr. Oakhurst seldom troubled himself with sentiment, still less with propriety; but he had a vague idea that the situation was not fortunate. He retained, however, his presence of mind sufficiently to kick Uncle Billy, who was about to say something, and Uncle Billy was sober enough to recognize in Mr. Oakhurst's kick a superior power that would not bear trifling. He then endeavored to dissuade Tom Simson from delaying further, but in vain. He even pointed out the fact that there was no provision, nor means of making a camp. But, unluckily, the Innocent met this objection by assuring the party that he was provided with an extra mule loaded with provisions, and by the discovery of a rude attempt at a log house near the trail. "Piney can stay with Mrs. Oakhurst," said the Innocent, pointing to the Duchess, "and I can shift for myself."

Nothing but Mr. Oakhurst's admonishing foot saved Uncle Billy from bursting into a roar of laughter. As it was, he felt compelled to retire up the cañon until he could recover his gravity. There he confided the joke to the tall pine-trees, with many slaps of his leg, contortions of his face, and the usual profanity. But when he returned to the party, he found them seated by a fire—for the air had grown strangely chill and the sky overcast—in apparently amicable conversation. Piney was actually talking in an impulsive girlish fashion to the Duchess, who was listening with an interest and animation she had not shown for many days. The Innocent was holding forth, apparently with equal effect, to Mr. Oakhurst and Mother Shipton, who was actually relaxing into amiability. "Is this yer a d—d picnic?" said Uncle Billy, with inward scorn, as he surveyed the sylvan group, the glancing firelight, and the tethered animals in the foreground. Suddenly an idea mingled with the alcoholic fumes that disturbed his brain. It was apparently of a jocular nature, for he felt impelled to slap his leg again and cram his fist into his mouth.

As the shadows crept slowly up the mountain, a slight breeze rocked the tops of the pine-trees and moaned through their long and gloomy aisles. The ruined cabin, patched and covered with pine boughs, was set apart for the ladies. As the lovers parted, they unaffectedly exchanged a kiss, so honest and sincere that it might have been heard above the swaying pines. The frail Duchess and the malevolent Mother Shipton were probably too stunned to remark upon this last evidence of simplicity, and so turned without a word to the hut. The fire was replenished, the men lay down before the door, and in a few minutes were asleep.

Mr. Oakhurst was a light sleeper. Toward morning he awoke benumbed and cold. As he stirred the dying fire, the wind, which was now blowing strongly, brought to his cheek that which caused the blood to leave it,—snow!

He started to his feet with the intention of awakening the sleepers, for there was no time to lose. But turning to where Uncle Billy had been lying, he found him gone. A suspicion leaped to his brain, and a curse to his lips. He ran to the spot where the mules had been tethered—they were no longer there. The tracks were already rapidly disappearing in the snow.

The momentary excitement brought Mr. Oakhurst back to the fire with his usual calm. He did not waken the sleepers. The Innocent slumbered peacefully, with a smile on his good-humored, freckled face; the virgin Piney slept beside her frailer sisters as sweetly as though attended by celestial guardians; and Mr. Oakhurst, drawing his blanket over his shoulders, stroked his mustaches and waited for the dawn. It came slowly in a whirling mist of snowflakes that dazzled and confused the eye. What could be seen of the landscape appeared magically changed. He looked over the valley, and summed up the present and future in two words, "Snowed in!"

A careful inventory of the provisions, which, fortunately for the party, had been stored within the hut, and so escaped the felonious fingers of Uncle Billy, disclosed the fact that with care and prudence they might last ten days longer. "That is," said Mr. Oakhurst *sotto voce* to the Innocent, "if you're willing to board us. If you ain't—and perhaps you'd better not—you can wait till Uncle Billy gets back with provisions." For some occult reason, Mr. Oakhurst could not bring himself to disclose Uncle Billy's rascality, and so offered the hypothesis that he had wandered from the camp and had accidentally stampeded the animals. He dropped a warning to the Duchess and Mother Shipton, who of course knew the facts of their associate's defection. "They'll find out the truth about us *all* when they find out anything," he added significantly, "and there's no good frightening them now."

Tom Simson not only put all his worldly store at the disposal of Mr. Oakhurst, but seemed to enjoy the prospect of their enforced seclusion. "We'll have a good camp for a week, and then the snow'll melt, and we'll all go back together." The cheerful gayety of the young man and Mr. Oakhurst's calm infected the others. The Innocent, with the aid of pine boughs, extemporized a thatch for the roofless cabin, and the Duchess directed Piney in the rearrangement of the interior with a taste and tact that opened the blue eyes of that provincial maiden to their fullest extent. "I reckon now you're used to fine things at Poker Flat," said Piney. The Duchess turned away sharply to conceal something that reddened her cheeks through their professional tint, and Mother Shipton requested Piney not to "chatter." But when Mr. Oakhurst returned from a weary search for the trail, he heard the sound of happy laughter echoed from the rocks. He stopped in some alarm, and his thoughts first naturally reverted to the whiskey, which he had prudently cachéd. "And yet it don't somehow sound like whiskey," said the gambler. It was not until he caught sight of the blazing fire through the still blinding storm, and the group around it, that he settled to the conviction that it was "square fun."

Whether Mr. Oakhurst had cachéd his cards with the whiskey as something debarred the free access of the community, I cannot say. It was certain that, in Mother Shipton's words, he "didn't say 'cards' once" during that evening. Haply the time was beguiled by an accordion, produced somewhat ostentatiously by Tom Simson from his pack. Notwithstanding some difficulties attending the manipulation of this instrument, Piney Woods managed to pluck several reluctant melodies from its keys, to an accompaniment by the Innocent on a pair of bone castanets. But the crowning festivity of the evening was reached in a rude camp-meeting hymn, which the lovers, joining hands, sang with great earnestness and vociferation. I fear that a certain defiant tone and Covenanter's swing to its chorus, rather than any devotional quality, caused it speedily to infect the others, who at last joined in the refrain:—

> "I'm proud to live in the service of the Lord,
> And I'm bound to die in His army."

The pines rocked, the storm eddied and whirled above the miserable group, and the flames of their altar leaped heavenward, as if in token of the vow.

At midnight the storm abated, the rolling clouds parted, and the stars glittered keenly above the sleeping camp. Mr. Oakhurst, whose professional habits had enabled him to live on the smallest possible amount of sleep, in dividing the watch with Tom Simson somehow managed to take upon himself the greater part of that duty. He excused himself to the Innocent by saying that he had "often been a week without sleep." "Doing what?" asked Tom. "Poker!" replied Oakhurst sententiously. "When a man gets a streak of luck,—nigger-luck,—he don't get tired. The luck gives in first. Luck," continued the gambler reflectively, "is a mighty queer thing. All you know about it for certain is that it's bound to change. And it's finding out when it's going to change that makes you. We've had a streak of bad luck since we left Poker Flat,—you come along, and slap you get into it, too. If you can hold your cards right along you're all right. For," added the gambler, with cheerful irrelevance—

> "'I'm proud to live in the service of the Lord,
> And I'm bound to die in His army.'"

The third day came, and the sun, looking through the white-curtained valley, saw the outcasts divide their slowly decreasing store of provisions for the morning meal. It was one of the peculiarities of that mountain climate that its rays diffused a kindly warmth over the wintry landscape, as if in regretful commiseration of the past. But it revealed drift on drift of snow piled high around the hut,—a hopeless, uncharted, trackless sea of white lying below the rocky shores to which the castaways still clung. Through the marvelously clear air the smoke of the pastoral village of Poker Flat rose miles away. Mother Shipton saw it, and from a remote pinnacle of her rocky fastness hurled in that direction a final malediction. It was her last vituperative attempt, and perhaps for that reason was invested with a certain degree of sublimity. It did her good, she privately informed the Duchess. "Just you go out there and cuss, and see." She then set herself to the task of amusing "the child," as she and the Duchess were pleased to call Piney. Piney was no chicken, but it was a soothing and original theory of the pair thus to account for the fact that she didn't swear and wasn't improper.

When night crept up again through the gorges, the reedy notes of the accordion rose and fell in fitful spasms and long-drawn gasps by the flickering campfire. But music failed to fill entirely the aching void left by insufficient food, and a new diversion was proposed by Piney,—story-telling. Neither Mr. Oakhurst nor his female companions caring to relate their personal experiences, this plan would have failed too, but for the Innocent. Some months before he had chanced upon a stray copy of Mr. Pope's ingenious translation of the Iliad. He now proposed to narrate the principal incidents of that poem—having thoroughly mastered the argument and fairly forgotten the words—in the current vernacular of Sandy Bar. And so for the rest of that night the Homeric demigods again walked the earth. Trojan bully and wily Greek wrestled in the winds, and the great pines in the cañon seemed to bow to the wrath of the son of Peleus. Mr. Oakhurst listened with quiet satisfaction. Most especially was he interested in the fate of "Ash-heels," as the Innocent persisted in denominating the "swift-footed Achilles."

So, with small food and much of Homer and the accordion, a week passed over the heads of the outcasts. The sun again forsook them, and again from leaden skies the snowflakes were sifted over the land. Day by day closer around them drew the snowy circle, until at last they looked from their prison over drifted walls of dazzling white, that towered twenty feet above their heads. It became more and more difficult to replenish their fires, even from the fallen trees beside them, now half hidden in the drifts. And yet no one complained. The lovers turned from the dreary prospect and looked into each other's eyes, and were happy. Mr. Oakhurst settled himself coolly to the losing game before him. The Duchess, more cheerful than she had been, assumed the care of Piney. Only Mother Shipton—once the strongest of the party—seemed to sicken and fade. At midnight on the tenth day she called Oakhurst to her side. "I'm going," she said, in a voice of querulous weakness, "but don't say anything about it. Don't waken the kids. Take the bundle from under my head, and open it." Mr. Oakhurst did so. It contained Mother Shipton's rations for the last week, untouched. "Give 'em to the child," she said, pointing to the sleeping Piney. "You've starved yourself," said the gambler. "That's what they call it," said the woman querulously, as she lay down again, and, turning her face to the wall, passed quietly away.

The accordion and the bones were put aside that day, and Homer was forgotten. When the body of Mother Shipton had been committed to the snow, Mr. Oakhurst took the Innocent aside, and showed him a pair of snowshoes, which he had fashioned from the old pack-saddle. "There's one chance in a hundred to save her yet," he said, pointing to Piney; "but it's there," he added, pointing toward Poker Flat. "If you can reach there in two days she's safe." "And you?" asked Tom Simson. "I'll stay here," was the curt reply.

The lovers parted with a long embrace. "You are not going, too?" said the Duchess, as she saw Mr. Oakhurst apparently waiting to accompany him. "As far as the cañon," he replied. He turned suddenly and kissed the Duchess, leaving her pallid face aflame, and her trembling limbs rigid with amazement.

Night came, but not Mr. Oakhurst. It brought the storm again and the whirling snow. Then the Duchess, feeding the fire, found that some one had quietly piled beside the hut enough fuel to last a few days longer. The tears rose to her eyes, but she hid them from Piney.

The women slept but little. In the morning, looking into each other's faces, they read their fate. Neither spoke, but Piney, accepting the position of the stronger, drew near and placed her arm around the Duchess's waist. They kept this attitude for the rest of the day. That night the storm reached its greatest fury, and, rending asunder the protecting vines, invaded the very hut.

Toward morning they found themselves unable to feed the fire, which gradually died away. As the embers slowly blackened, the Duchess crept closer to Piney, and broke the silence of many hours: "Piney, can you pray?" "No, dear," said Piney simply. The Duchess, without knowing exactly why, felt relieved, and, putting her head upon Piney's shoulder, spoke no more. And so reclining, the younger and purer pillowing the head of her soiled sister upon her virgin breast, they fell asleep.

The wind lulled as if it feared to waken them. Feathery drifts of snow, shaken from the long pine boughs, flew like white winged birds, and settled about them as they slept. The moon through the rifted clouds looked down upon what had been the camp. But all human stain, all trace of earthly travail, was hidden beneath the spotless mantle mercifully flung from above.

They slept all that day and the next, nor did they waken when voices and footsteps broke the silence of the camp. And when pitying fingers brushed the snow from their wan faces, you could scarcely have told from the equal peace that dwelt upon them which was she that had sinned. Even the law of Poker Flat recognized this, and turned away, leaving them still locked in each other's arms.

But at the head of the gulch, on one of the largest pine-trees, they found the deuce of clubs pinned to the bark with a bowie-knife. It bore the following, written in pencil in a firm hand:—

†
BENEATH THIS TREE
LIES THE BODY
OF
JOHN OAKHURST,
WHO STRUCK A STREAK OF BAD LUCK
ON THE 23D OF NOVEMBER 1850,
AND
HANDED IN HIS CHECKS
ON THE 7TH DECEMBER, 1850.
†

And pulseless and cold, with a Derringer by his side and a bullet in his heart, though still calm as in life, beneath the snow lay he who was at once the strongest and yet the weakest of the outcasts of Poker Flat.

Miggles

We were eight including the driver. We had not spoken during the passage of the last six miles, since the jolting of the heavy vehicle over the roughening road had spoiled the Judge's last poetical quotation. The tall man beside the Judge was asleep, his arm passed through the swaying strap and his head resting upon it,—altogether a limp, helpless looking object, as if he had hanged himself and been cut down too late. The French lady on the back seat was asleep too, yet in a half-conscious propriety of attitude, shown even in the disposition of the handkerchief which she held to her forehead and which partially veiled her face. The lady from Virginia City, traveling with her husband, had long since lost all individuality in a wild confusion of ribbons, veils, furs, and shawls. There was no sound but the rattling of wheels and the dash of rain upon the roof. Suddenly the stage stopped and we became dimly aware of voices. The driver was evidently in the midst of an exciting colloquy with some one in the road,—a colloquy of which such fragments as "bridge gone," "twenty feet of water," "can't pass," were occasionally distinguishable above the storm. Then came a lull, and a mysterious voice from the road shouted the parting adjuration—

"Try Miggles's."

We caught a glimpse of our leaders as the vehicle slowly turned, of a horseman vanishing through the rain, and we were evidently on our way to Miggles's.

Who and where was Miggles? The Judge, our authority, did not remember the name, and he knew the country thoroughly. The Washoe traveler thought Miggles must keep a hotel. We only knew that we were stopped by high water in front and rear, and that Miggles was our rock of refuge. A ten minutes' splashing through a tangled by-road, scarcely wide enough for the stage, and we drew up before a barred and boarded gate in a wide stone wall or fence about eight feet high. Evidently Miggles's, and evidently Miggles did not keep a hotel.

The driver got down and tried the gate. It was securely locked.

"Miggles! O Miggles!"

No answer.

"Migg-ells! You Miggles!" continued the driver, with rising wrath.

"Migglesy!" joined in the expressman persuasively. "O Miggy! Mig!"

But no reply came from the apparently insensate Miggles. The Judge, who had finally got the window down, put his head out and propounded a series of questions, which if answered categorically would have undoubtedly elucidated the whole mystery, but which the driver evaded by replying that "if we didn't want to sit in the coach all night we had better rise up and sing out for Miggles."

So we rose up and called on Miggles in chorus, then separately. And when we had finished, a Hibernian fellow passenger from the roof called for "Maygells!" whereat we all laughed. While we were laughing the driver cried, "Shoo!"

We listened. To our infinite amazement the chorus of "Miggles" was repeated from the other side of the wall, even to the final and supplemental "Maygells."

"Extraordinary echo!" said the Judge.

"Extraordinary d—d skunk!" roared the driver contemptuously. "Come out of that, Miggles, and show yourself! Be a man, Miggles! Don't hide in the dark; I wouldn't if I were you, Miggles," continued Yuba Bill, now dancing about in an excess of fury.

"Miggles!" continued the voice, "O Miggles!"

"My good man! Mr. Myghail!" said the Judge, softening the asperities of the name as much as possible. "Consider the inhospitality of refusing shelter from the inclemency of the weather to helpless females. Really, my dear sir"—But a succession of "Miggles," ending in a burst of laughter, drowned his voice.

Yuba Bill hesitated no longer. Taking a heavy stone from the road, he battered down the gate, and with the expressman entered the inclosure. We followed. Nobody was to be seen. In the gathering darkness all that we could distinguish was that we were in a garden—from the rose bushes that scattered over us a minute spray from their dripping leaves—and before a long, rambling wooden building.

"Do you know this Miggles?" asked the Judge of Yuba Bill.

"No, nor don't want to," said Bill shortly, who felt the Pioneer Stage Company insulted in his person by the contumacious Miggles.

"But, my dear sir," expostulated the Judge, as he thought of the barred gate.

"Lookee here," said Yuba Bill, with fine irony, "hadn't you better go back and sit in the coach till yer introduced? I'm going in," and he pushed open the door of the building.

A long room, lighted only by the embers of a fire that was dying on the large hearth at its farther extremity; the walls curiously papered, and the flickering firelight bringing out its grotesque pattern; somebody sitting in a large armchair by the fireplace. All this we saw as we crowded together into the room after the driver and expressman.

"Hello! be you Miggles?" said Yuba Bill to the solitary occupant.

The figure neither spoke nor stirred. Yuba Bill walked wrathfully toward it and turned the eye of his coach-lantern upon its face. It was a man's face, prematurely old and wrinkled, with very large eyes, in which there was that expression of perfectly gratuitous solemnity which I had sometimes seen in an owl's. The large eyes wandered from Bill's face to the lantern, and finally fixed their gaze on that luminous object without further recognition.

Bill restrained himself with an effort.

"Miggles! be you deaf? You ain't dumb anyhow, you know," and Yuba Bill shook the insensate figure by the shoulder.

To our great dismay, as Bill removed his hand, the venerable stranger apparently collapsed, sinking into half his size and an undistinguishable heap of clothing.

"Well, dern my skin," said Bill, looking appealingly at us, and hopelessly retiring from the contest.

The Judge now stepped forward, and we lifted the mysterious invertebrate back into his original position. Bill was dismissed with the lantern to reconnoitre outside, for it was evident that, from the helplessness of this solitary man, there must be attendants near at hand, and we all drew around the fire. The Judge, who had regained his authority, and had never lost his conversational amiability,—standing before us with his back to the hearth,—charged us, as an imaginary jury, as follows:—

"It is evident that either our distinguished friend here has reached that condition described by Shakespeare as 'the sere and yellow leaf,' or has suffered some premature abatement of his mental and physical faculties. Whether he is really the Miggles"—

Here he was interrupted by "Miggles! O Miggles! Migglesy! Mig!" and, in fact, the whole chorus of Miggles in very much the same key as it had once before been delivered unto us.

We gazed at each other for a moment in some alarm. The Judge, in particular, vacated his position quickly, as the voice seemed to come directly over his shoulder. The cause, however, was soon discovered in a large magpie who was perched upon a shelf over the fireplace, and who immediately relapsed into a sepulchral silence, which contrasted singularly with his previously volubility. It was, undoubtedly, his voice which we had heard in the road, and our friend in the chair was not responsible for the discourtesy. Yuba Bill, who reëntered the room after an unsuccessful search, was loth to accept the explanation, and still eyed the helpless sitter with suspicion. He had found a shed in which he had put up his horses, but he came back dripping and skeptical. "Thar ain't nobody but him within ten mile of the shanty, and that ar d—d old skeesicks knows it."

But the faith of the majority proved to be securely based. Bill had scarcely ceased growling before we heard a quick step upon the porch, the trailing of a wet skirt, the door was flung open, and with a flash of white teeth, a sparkle of dark eyes, and an utter absence of ceremony or diffidence, a young woman entered, shut the door, and, panting, leaned back against it.

"Oh, if you please, I'm Miggles!"

And this was Miggles! this bright-eyed, full-throated young woman, whose wet gown of coarse blue stuff could not hide the beauty of the feminine curves to which it clung; from the chestnut crown of whose head, topped by a man's oil-skin sou'wester, to the little feet and ankles, hidden somewhere in the recesses of her boy's brogans, all was grace,—this was Miggles, laughing at us, too, in the most airy, frank, off-hand manner imaginable.

"You see, boys," said she, quite out of breath, and holding one little hand against her side, quite unheeding the speechless discomfiture of our party or the complete demoralization of Yuba Bill, whose features had relaxed into an expression of gratuitous and imbecile cheerfulness,—"you see, boys, I was mor'n two miles away when you passed down the road.

I thought you might pull up here, and so I ran the whole way, knowing nobody was home but Jim,—and—and—I'm out of breath—and—that lets me out." And here Miggles caught her dripping oil-skin hat from her head, with a mischievous swirl that scattered a shower of raindrops over us; attempted to put back her hair; dropped two hairpins in the attempt; laughed, and sat down beside Yuba Bill, with her hands crossed lightly on her lap.

The Judge recovered himself first and essayed an extravagant compliment.

"I'll trouble you for that ha'rpin," said Miggles gravely. Half a dozen hands were eagerly stretched forward; the missing hairpin was restored to its fair owner; and Miggles, crossing the room, looked keenly in the face of the invalid. The solemn eyes looked back at hers with an expression we had never seen before. Life and intelligence seemed to struggle back into the rugged face. Miggles laughed again,—it was a singularly eloquent laugh,—and turned her black eyes and white teeth once more towards us.

"This afflicted person is"—hesitated the Judge.

"Jim!" said Miggles.

"Your father?"

"No!"

"Brother?"

"No!"

"Husband?"

Miggles darted a quick, half-defiant glance at the two lady passengers, who I had noticed did not participate in the general masculine admiration of Miggles, and said gravely, "No; it's Jim!"

There was an awkward pause. The lady passengers moved closer to each other; the Washoe husband looked abstractedly at the fire, and the tall man apparently turned his eyes inward for self-support at this emergency. But Miggles's laugh, which was very infectious, broke the silence.

"Come," she said briskly, "you must be hungry. Who'll bear a hand to help me get tea?"

She had no lack of volunteers. In a few moments Yuba Bill was engaged like Caliban in bearing logs for this Miranda; the expressman was grinding coffee on the veranda; to myself the arduous duty of slicing bacon was assigned; and the Judge lent each man his good-humored and voluble counsel. And when Miggles, assisted by the Judge and our Hibernian "deck-passenger," set the table with all the available crockery, we had become quite joyous, in spite of the rain that beat against the windows, the wind that whirled down the chimney, the two ladies who whispered together in the corner, or the magpie, who uttered a satirical and croaking commentary on their conversation from his perch above. In the now bright, blazing fire we could see that the walls were papered with illustrated journals, arranged with feminine taste and discrimination. The furniture was extemporized and adapted from candle-boxes and packing-cases, and covered with gay calico or the skin of some animal. The armchair of the helpless Jim was an ingenious variation of a flour-barrel. There was neatness, and even a taste for the picturesque, to be seen in the few details of the long, low room.

The meal was a culinary success. But more, it was a social triumph, —chiefly, I think, owing to the rare tact of Miggles in guiding the conversation, asking all the questions herself, yet bearing throughout a frankness that rejected the idea of any concealment on her own part, so that we talked of ourselves, of our prospects, of the journey, of the weather, of each other,—of everything but our host and hostess. It must be confessed that Miggles's conversation was never elegant, rarely grammatical, and that at times she employed expletives the use of which had generally been yielded to our sex. But they were delivered with such a lighting up of teeth and eyes, and were usually followed by a laugh—a laugh peculiar to Miggles—so frank and honest that it seemed to clear the moral atmosphere.

Once during the meal we heard a noise like the rubbing of a heavy body against the outer walls of the house. This was shortly followed by a scratching and sniffling at the door. "That's Joaquin," said Miggles, in reply to our questioning glances; "would you like to see him?" Before we could answer she had opened the door, and disclosed a half-grown grizzly, who instantly raised himself on his haunches, with his fore paws hanging down in the popular attitude of mendicancy, and looked admiringly at Miggles, with a very singular resemblance in his manner to Yuba Bill. "That's my watch-dog," said Miggles, in explanation. "Oh, he don't bite," she added, as the two lady passengers fluttered into a corner. "Does he, old Toppy?" (the latter remark being addressed directly to the sagacious Joaquin). "I tell you what, boys," continued Miggles, after she had fed and closed the door on Ursa Minor, "you were in big luck that Joaquin wasn't hanging round when you dropped in to-night."

"Where was he?" asked the Judge.

"With me," said Miggles. "Lord love you! he trots round with me nights like as if he was a man."

We were silent for a few moments, and listened to the wind. Perhaps we all had the same picture before us,—of Miggles walking through the rainy woods with her savage guardian at her side. The Judge, I remember, said something about Una and her lion; but Miggles received it, as she did other compliments, with quiet gravity. Whether she was altogether unconscious of the admiration she excited,—she could hardly have been oblivious of Yuba Bill's adoration,—I know not; but her very frankness suggested a perfect sexual equality that was cruelly humiliating to the younger members of our party.

The incident of the bear did not add anything in Miggles's favor to the opinions of those of her own sex who were present. In fact, the repast over, a chillness radiated from the two lady passengers that no pine boughs brought in by Yuba Bill and cast as a sacrifice upon the hearth could wholly overcome. Miggles felt it; and suddenly declaring that it was time to "turn in," offered to show the ladies to their bed in an adjoining room. "You, boys, will have to camp out here by the fire as well as you can," she added, "for thar ain't but the one room."

Our sex—by which, my dear sir, I allude of course to the stronger portion of humanity—has been generally relieved from the imputation of curiosity or a fondness for gossip. Yet I am constrained to say, that hardly had the door closed on Miggles than we crowded together, whispering, snickering, smiling, and exchanging suspicions, surmises, and a thousand speculations in regard to our pretty hostess and her singular companion. I fear that we even hustled that imbecile paralytic, who sat like a voiceless Memnon in our midst, gazing with the serene indifference of the Past in his passionless eyes upon our wordy counsels. In the midst of an exciting discussion the door opened again and Miggles reëntered.

But not, apparently, the same Miggles who a few hours before had flashed upon us. Her eyes were downcast, and as she hesitated for a moment on the threshold, with a blanket on her arm, she seemed to have left behind her the frank fearlessness which had charmed us a moment before. Coming into the room, she drew a low stool beside the paralytic's chair, sat down, drew the blanket over her shoulders, and saying, "If it's all the same to you, boys, as we're rather crowded, I'll stop here to-night," took the invalid's withered hand in her own, and turned her eyes upon the dying fire. An instinctive feeling that this was only premonitory to more confidential relations, and perhaps some shame at our previous curiosity, kept us silent. The rain still beat upon the roof, wandering gusts of wind stirred the embers into momentary brightness, until, in a lull of the elements, Miggles suddenly lifted up her head, and, throwing her hair over her shoulder, turned her face upon the group and asked,—

"Is there any of you that knows me?"

There was no reply.

"Think again! I lived at Marysville in '53. Everybody knew me there, and everybody had the right to know me. I kept the Polka Saloon until I came to live with Jim. That's six years ago. Perhaps I've changed some."

The absence of recognition may have disconcerted her. She turned her head to the fire again, and it was some seconds before she again spoke, and then more rapidly—

"Well, you see I thought some of you must have known me. There's no great harm done anyway. What I was going to say was this: Jim here"—she took his hand in both of hers as she spoke—"used to know me, if you didn't, and spent a heap of money upon me. I reckon he spent all he had. And one day—it's six years ago this winter—Jim came into my back room, sat down on my sofy, like as you see him in that chair, and never moved again without help. He was struck all of a heap, and never seemed to know what ailed him. The doctors came and said as how it was caused all along of his way of life,—for Jim was mighty free and wild-like,—and that he would never get better, and couldn't last long anyway. They advised me to send him to Frisco to the hospital, for he was no good to any one and would be a baby all his life. Perhaps it was something in Jim's eye, perhaps it was that I never had a baby, but I said 'No.' I was rich then, for I was popular with everybody,—gentlemen like yourself, sir, came to see me,—and I sold out my business and bought this yer place, because it was sort of out of the way of travel, you see, and I brought my baby here."

With a woman's intuitive tact and poetry, she had, as she spoke, slowly shifted her position so as to bring the mute figure of the ruined man between her and her audience, hiding in the shadow behind it, as if she offered it as a tacit apology for her actions. Silent and expressionless, it yet spoke for her; helpless, crushed, and smitten with the Divine thunderbolt, it still stretched an invisible arm around her.

Hidden in the darkness, but still holding his hand, she went on:—

"It was a long time before I could get the hang of things about yer, for I was used to company and excitement. I couldn't get any woman to help me, and a man I dursn't trust; but what with the Indians hereabout, who'd do odd jobs for me, and having everything sent from the North Fork, Jim and I managed to worry through. The Doctor would run up from Sacramento once in a while. He'd ask to see 'Miggles's baby,' as he called Jim, and when he'd go away, he'd say, 'Miggles, you're a trump,—God bless you,' and it didn't seem so lonely after that. But the last time he was here he said, as he opened the door to go, 'Do you know,

Miggles, your baby will grow up to be a man yet and an honor to his mother; but not here, Miggles, not here!' And I thought he went away sad,—and—and"—and here Miggles's voice and head were somehow both lost completely in the shadow.

"The folks about here are very kind," said Miggles, after a pause, coming a little into the light again. "The men from the Fork used to hang around here, until they found they wasn't wanted, and the women are kind, and don't call. I was pretty lonely until I picked up Joaquin in the woods yonder one day, when he wasn't so high, and taught him to beg for his dinner—and then thar's Polly—that's the magpie—she knows no end of tricks, and makes it quite sociable of evenings with her talk, and so I don't feel like as I was the only living being about the ranch. And Jim here," said Miggles, with her old laugh again, and coming out quite into the firelight,—"Jim—Why, boys, you would admire to see how much he knows for a man like him. Sometimes I bring him flowers, and he looks at 'em just as natural as if he knew 'em; and times, when we're sitting alone, I read him those things on the wall. Why, Lord!" said Miggles, with her frank laugh, "I've read him that whole side of the house this winter. There never was such a man for reading as Jim."

"Why," asked the Judge, "do you not marry this man to whom you have devoted your youthful life?"

"Well, you see," said Miggles, "it would be playing it rather low down on Jim to take advantage of his being so helpless. And then, too, if we were man and wife, now, we'd both know that I was *bound* to do what I do now of my own accord."

"But you are young yet and attractive"—

"It's getting late," said Miggles gravely, "and you'd better all turn in. Good-night, boys;" and throwing the blanket over her head, Miggles laid herself down beside Jim's chair, her head pillowed on the low stool that held his feet, and spoke no more. The fire slowly faded from the hearth; we each sought our blankets in silence; and presently there was no sound in the long room but the pattering of the rain upon the roof and the heavy breathing of the sleepers.

It was nearly morning when I awoke from a troubled dream. The storm had passed, the stars were shining, and through the shutterless window the full moon, lifting itself over the solemn pines without, looked into the room. It touched the lonely figure in the chair with an infinite compassion, and seemed to baptize with a shining flood the lowly head of the woman whose hair, as in the sweet old story, bathed the feet of him she loved. It even lent a kindly poetry to the rugged outline of Yuba Bill, half reclining on his elbow between them and his passengers, with savagely patient eyes keeping watch and ward. And then I fell asleep and only woke at broad day, with Yuba Bill standing over me, and "All aboard" ringing in my ears.

Coffee was waiting for us on the table, but Miggles was gone. We wandered about the house and lingered long after the horses were harnessed, but she did not return. It was evident that she wished to avoid a formal leave-taking, and had so left us to depart as we had come. After we had helped the ladies into the coach, we returned to the house and solemnly shook hands with the paralytic Jim, as solemnly setting him back into position after each handshake. Then we looked for the last time around the long low room, at the stool where Miggles had sat, and slowly took our seats in the waiting coach. The whip cracked, and we were off!

But as we reached the highroad, Bill's dexterous hand laid the six horses back on their haunches, and the stage stopped with a jerk. For there, on a little eminence beside the road, stood Miggles, her hair flying, her eyes sparkling, her white handkerchief waving, and her white teeth flashing a last "good-by." We waved our hats in return. And then Yuba Bill, as if fearful of further fascination, madly lashed his horses forward, and we sank back in our seats.

We exchanged not a word until we reached the North Fork and the stage drew up at the Independence House. Then, the Judge leading, we walked into the bar-room and took our places gravely at the bar.

"Are your glasses charged, gentlemen?" said the Judge, solemnly taking off his white hat.

They were.

"Well, then, here's to *Miggles*—GOD BLESS HER!"

Perhaps He had. Who knows?

Tennessee's Partner

I DO not think that we ever knew his real name. Our ignorance of it certainly never gave us any social inconvenience, for at Sandy Bar in 1854 most men were christened anew. Sometimes these appellatives were derived from some distinctiveness of dress, as in the case of "Dungaree Jack;" or from some peculiarity of habit, as shown in "Saleratus Bill," so called from an undue proportion of that chemical in his daily bread; or from some unlucky slip, as exhibited in "The Iron Pirate," a mild, inoffensive man, who earned that baleful title by his unfortunate mispronunciation of the term "iron pyrites." Perhaps this may have been the beginning of a rude heraldry; but I am constrained to think that it was because a man's real name in that day rested solely upon his own unsupported statement. "Call yourself Clifford, do you?" said Boston, addressing a timid newcomer with infinite scorn; "hell is full of such Cliffords!" He then introduced the unfortunate man, whose name happened to be really Clifford, as "Jaybird Charley,"—an unhallowed inspiration of the moment that clung to him ever after.

But to return to Tennessee's Partner, whom we never knew by any other than this relative title. That he had ever existed as a separate and distinct individuality we only learned later. It seems that in 1853 he left Poker Flat to go to San Francisco, ostensibly to procure a wife. He never got any farther than Stockton. At that place he was attracted by a young person who waited upon the table at the hotel where he took his meals. One morning he said something to her which caused her to smile not unkindly, to somewhat coquettishly break a plate of toast over his upturned, serious, simple face, and to retreat to the kitchen. He followed her, and emerged a few moments later, covered with more toast and victory. That day week they were married by a justice of the peace, and returned to Poker Flat. I am aware that something more might be made of this episode, but I prefer to tell it as it was current at Sandy Bar,—in the gulches and bar-rooms,—where all sentiment was modified by a strong sense of humor.

Of their married felicity but little is known, perhaps for the reason that Tennessee, then living with his partner, one day took occasion to say something to the bride on his own account, at which, it is said, she smiled not unkindly and chastely retreated,—this time as far as Marysville, where Tennessee followed her, and where they went to housekeeping without the aid of a justice of the peace. Tennessee's Partner took the loss of his wife simply and seriously, as was his fashion. But to everybody's surprise, when Tennessee one day returned from Marysville, without his partner's wife,—she having smiled and retreated with somebody else,—Tennessee's Partner was the first man to shake his hand and greet him with affection. The boys who had gathered in the cañon to see the shooting were naturally indignant. Their indignation might have found vent in sarcasm but for a certain look in Tennessee's Partner's eye that indicated a lack of humorous appreciation. In fact, he was a grave man, with a steady application to practical detail which was unpleasant in a difficulty.

Meanwhile a popular feeling against Tennessee had grown up on the Bar. He was known to be a gambler; he was suspected to be a thief. In these suspicions Tennessee's Partner was equally compromised; his continued intimacy with Tennessee after the affair above quoted could only be accounted for on the hypothesis of a co-partnership of crime. At last Tennessee's guilt became flagrant. One day he overtook a stranger on his way to Red Dog. The stranger afterward related that Tennessee beguiled the time with interesting anecdote and reminiscence, but illogically concluded the interview in the following words: "And now, young man, I'll trouble you for your knife, your pistols, and your money. You see your weppings might get you into trouble at Red Dog, and your money's a temptation to the evilly disposed. I think you said your address was San Francisco. I shall endeavor to call." It may be stated here that Tennessee had a fine flow of humor, which no business preoccupation could wholly subdue.

This exploit was his last. Red Dog and Sandy Bar made common cause against the highwayman. Tennessee was hunted in very much the same fashion as his prototype, the grizzly. As the toils closed around him, he made a desperate dash through the Bar, emptying his revolver at the crowd before the Arcade Saloon, and so on up Grizzly Cañon; but at its farther extremity he was stopped by a small man on a gray horse. The men looked at each other a moment in silence. Both were fearless, both self-possessed and independent, and both types of a civilization that in the seventeenth century would have been called heroic, but in the nineteenth simply "reckless."

"What have you got there?—I call," said Tennessee quietly.

"Two bowers and an ace," said the stranger as quietly, showing two revolvers and a bowie-knife.

"That takes me," returned Tennessee; and, with this gambler's epigram, he threw away his useless pistol and rode back with his captor.

It was a warm night. The cool breeze which usually sprang up with the going down of the sun behind the chaparral-crested mountain was that evening withheld from Sandy Bar. The little cañon was stifling with heated resinous odors, and the decaying driftwood on the Bar sent forth faint sickening exhalations. The feverishness of day and its fierce passions still filled the camp. Lights moved restlessly along the bank of the river, striking no answering reflection from its tawny current. Against the blackness of the pines the windows of the old loft above the express-office stood out staringly bright; and through their curtainless panes the loungers below could see the forms of those who were even then deciding the fate of Tennessee. And above all this, etched on the dark firmament, rose the Sierra, remote and passionless, crowned with remoter passionless stars.

The trial of Tennessee was conducted as fairly as was consistent with a judge and jury who felt themselves to some extent obliged to justify, in their verdict, the previous irregularities of arrest and indictment.

The law of Sandy Bar was implacable, but not vengeful. The excitement and personal feeling of the chase were over; with Tennessee safe in their hands, they were ready to listen patiently to any defense, which they were already satisfied was insufficient. There being no doubt in their own minds, they were willing to give the prisoner the benefit of any that might exist. Secure in the hypothesis that he ought to be hanged on general principles, they indulged him with more latitude of defense than his reckless hardihood seemed to ask. The Judge appeared to be more anxious than the prisoner, who, otherwise unconcerned, evidently took a grim pleasure in the responsibility he had created. "I don't take any hand in this yer game," had been his invariable but good-humored reply to all questions. The Judge—who was also his captor—for a moment vaguely regretted that he had not shot him "on sight" that morning, but presently dismissed this human weakness as unworthy of the judicial mind. Nevertheless, when there was a tap at the door, and it was said that Tennessee's Partner was there on behalf of the prisoner, he was admitted at once without question. Perhaps the younger members of the jury, to whom the proceedings were becoming irksomely thoughtful, hailed him as a relief.

For he was not, certainly, an imposing figure. Short and stout, with a square face, sunburned into a preternatural redness, clad in a loose duck "jumper" and trousers streaked and splashed with red soil, his aspect under any circumstances would have been quaint, and was now even ridiculous. As he stooped to deposit at his feet a heavy carpetbag he was carrying, it became obvious, from partially developed legends and inscriptions, that the material with which his trousers had been patched had been originally intended for a less ambitious covering. Yet he advanced with great gravity, and after shaking the hand of each person in the room with labored cordiality, he wiped his serious perplexed face on a red bandana handkerchief, a shade lighter than his complexion, laid his powerful hand upon the table to steady himself, and thus addressed the Judge:—

"I was passin' by," he began, by way of apology, "and I thought I'd just step in and see how things was gettin' on with Tennessee thar,—my pardner. It's a hot night. I disremember any sich weather before on the Bar."

He paused a moment, but nobody volunteering any other meteorological recollection, he again had recourse to his pocket-handkerchief, and for some moments mopped his face diligently.

"Have you anything to say on behalf of the prisoner?" said the Judge finally.

"Thet's it," said Tennessee's Partner, in a tone of relief. "I come yar as Tennessee's pardner,—knowing him nigh on four year, off and on, wet and dry, in luck and out o' luck. His ways ain't aller my ways, but thar ain't any p'ints in that young man, thar ain't any liveliness as he's been up to, as I don't know. And you sez to me, sez you,—confidential-like, and between man and man,—sez you, 'Do you know anything in his behalf?' and I sez to you, sez I,—confidential-like, as between man and man,—'What should a man know of his pardner?'"

"Is this all you have to say?" asked the Judge impatiently, feeling, perhaps, that a dangerous sympathy of humor was beginning to humanize the court.

"Thet's so," continued Tennessee's Partner. "It ain't for me to say anything agin' him. And now, what's the case? Here's Tennessee wants money, wants it bad, and doesn't like to ask it of his old pardner. Well, what does Tennessee do? He lays for a stranger, and he fetches that stranger; and you lays for *him,* and you fetches *him;* and the honors is easy. And I put it to you, bein' a fa'r-minded man, and to you, gentlemen all, as fa'r-minded men, ef this isn't so."

"Prisoner," said the Judge, interrupting, "have you any questions to ask this man?"

"No! no!" continued Tennessee's Partner hastily. "I play this yer hand alone. To come down to the bed-rock, it's just this: Tennessee, thar, has played it pretty rough and expensive-like on a stranger, and on this yer camp. And now, what's the fair thing? Some would say more, some would say less. Here's seventeen hundred dollars in coarse gold and a watch,—it's about all my pile,—and call it square!" And before a hand could be raised to prevent him, he had emptied the contents of the carpetbag upon the table.

For a moment his life was in jeopardy. One or two men sprang to their feet, several hands groped for hidden weapons, and a suggestion to "throw him from the window" was only overridden by a gesture from the Judge. Tennessee laughed. And apparently oblivious of the excitement, Tennessee's Partner improved the opportunity to mop his face again with his handkerchief.

When order was restored, and the man was made to understand, by the use of forcible figures and rhetoric, that Tennessee's offence could not be condoned by money, his face took a more serious and sanguinary hue, and those who were nearest to him noticed that his rough hand trembled slightly on the table. He hesitated a moment as he slowly returned the gold to the carpetbag, as if he had not yet entirely caught the elevated sense of justice which swayed the tribunal, and was perplexed with the belief that he had not offered enough. Then he turned to the Judge, and saying, "This yer is a lone hand, played alone, and without my pardner," he bowed to the jury and was about to withdraw, when the Judge called him back:—

"If you have anything to say to Tennessee, you had better say it now."

For the first time that evening the eyes of the prisoner and his strange advocate met. Tennessee smiled, showed his white teeth, and saying, "Euchred, old man!" held out his hand. Tennessee's Partner took it in his own, and saying, "I just dropped in as I was passin' to see how things was gettin' on," let the hand passively fall, and adding that "it was a warm night," again mopped his face with his handkerchief, and without another word withdrew.

The two men never again met each other alive. For the unparalleled insult of a bribe offered to Judge Lynch—who, whether bigoted, weak, or narrow, was at least incorruptible—firmly fixed in the mind of that mythical personage any wavering determination of Tennessee's fate; and at the break of day he was marched, closely guarded, to meet it at the top of Marley's Hill.

How he met it, how cool he was, how he refused to say anything, how perfect were the arrangements of the committee, were all duly reported, with the addition of a warning moral and example to all future evil-doers, in the "Red Dog Clarion," by its editor, who was present, and to whose vigorous English I cheerfully refer the reader. But the beauty of that midsummer morning, the blessed amity of earth and air and sky, the awakened life of the free woods and hills, the joyous renewal and promise of Nature, and above all, the infinite serenity that thrilled through each, was not reported, as not being a part of the social lesson. And yet, when the weak and foolish deed was done, and a life, with its possibilities and responsibilities, had passed out of the misshapen thing that dangled between earth and sky, the birds sang, the flowers bloomed, the sun shone, as cheerily as before; and possibly the "Red Dog Clarion" was right.

Tennessee's Partner was not in the group that surrounded the ominous tree. But as they turned to disperse, attention was drawn to the singular appearance of a motionless donkey-cart halted at the side of the road. As they approached, they at once recognized the venerable "jenny" and the two-wheeled cart as the property of Tennessee's Partner, used by him in carrying dirt from his claim; and a few paces distant the owner of the equipage himself, sitting under a buckeye-tree, wiping the perspiration from his glowing face. In answer to an inquiry, he said he had come for the body of the "diseased," "if it was all the same to the committee." He didn't wish to "hurry anything;" he could "wait." He was not working that day; and when the gentlemen were done with the "diseased," he would take him. "Ef thar is any present," he added, in his simple, serious way, "as would care to jine in the fun'l, they kin come." Perhaps it was from a sense of humor, which I have already intimated was a feature of Sandy Bar,—perhaps it was from something even better than that, but two thirds of the loungers accepted the invitation at once.

It was noon when the body of Tennessee was delivered into the hands of his partner. As the cart drew up to the fatal tree, we noticed that it contained a rough oblong box,—apparently made from a section of sluicing,—and half filled with bark and the tassels of pine. The cart was further decorated with slips of willow and made fragrant with buckeye-blossoms. When the body was deposited in the box, Tennessee's Partner drew over it a piece of tarred canvas, and gravely mounting the narrow seat in front, with his feet upon the shafts, urged the little donkey forward. The equipage moved slowly on, at that decorous pace which was habitual with Jenny even under less solemn circumstances. The men—half curiously, half jestingly, but all good-humoredly—strolled along beside the cart, some in advance, some a little in the rear of the homely catafalque. But whether from the narrowing of the road or some present sense of decorum, as the cart passed on, the company fell to the rear in couples, keeping step, and otherwise assuming the external show of a formal procession. Jack Folinsbee, who had at the outset played a funeral march in dumb show upon an imaginary trombone, desisted from a lack of sympathy and appreciation,—not having, perhaps, your true humorist's capacity to be content with the enjoyment of his own fun.

The way led through Grizzly Cañon, by this time clothed in funereal drapery and shadows. The redwoods, burying their moccasined feet in the red soil, stood in Indian file along the track, trailing an uncouth benediction from their bending boughs upon the passing bier. A hare, surprised into helpless inactivity, sat upright and pulsating in the ferns by the roadside as the cortége went by. Squirrels hastened to gain a secure outlook from higher boughs; and the blue-jays, spreading their wings, fluttered before them like outriders, until the outskirts of Sandy Bar were reached, and the solitary cabin of Tennessee's Partner.

Viewed under more favorable circumstances, it would not have been a cheerful place. The unpicturesque site, the rude and unlovely outlines, the unsavory details, which distinguish the nest-building of the California miner, were all here with the dreariness of decay superadded. A few paces from the cabin there was a rough inclosure, which, in the brief days of Tennessee's Partner's matrimonial felicity, had been used as a garden, but was now overgrown with fern. As we approached it, we were surprised to find that what we had taken for a recent attempt at cultivation was the broken soil about an open grave.

The cart was halted before the inclosure, and rejecting the offers of assistance with the same air of simple self-reliance he had displayed throughout, Tennessee's Partner lifted the rough coffin on his back, and deposited it unaided within the shallow grave. He then nailed down the board which served as a lid, and mounting the little mound of earth beside it, took off his hat and slowly mopped his face with his handkerchief. This the crowd felt was a preliminary to speech, and they disposed themselves variously on stumps and boulders, and sat expectant.

"When a man," began Tennessee's Partner slowly, "has been running free all day, what's the natural thing for him to do? Why, to come home. And if he ain't in a condition to go home, what can his best friend do? Why, bring him home. And here's Tennessee has been running free, and we brings him home from his wandering." He paused and picked up a fragment of quartz, rubbed it thoughtfully on his sleeve, and went on: "It ain't the first time that I've packed him on my back, as you see'd me now. It ain't the first time that I brought him to this yer cabin when he couldn't help himself; it ain't the first time that I and Jenny have waited for him on yon hill, and picked him up and so fetched him home, when he couldn't speak and didn't know me. And now that it's the last time, why"—he paused and rubbed the quartz gently on his sleeve—"you see it's sort of rough on his pardner. And now, gentlemen," he added abruptly, picking up his long-handled shovel, "the fun'l's over; and my thanks, and Tennessee's thanks, to you for your trouble."

Resisting any proffers of assistance, he began to fill in the grave, turning his back upon the crowd, that after a few moments' hesitation gradually withdrew. As they crossed the little ridge that hid Sandy Bar from view, some, looking back, thought they could see Tennessee's Partner, his work done, sitting upon the grave, his shovel between his knees, and his face buried in his red bandana handkerchief. But it was argued by others that you couldn't tell his face from his handkerchief at that distance, and this point remained undecided.

In the reaction that followed the feverish excitement of that day, Tennessee's Partner was not forgotten. A secret investigation had cleared him of any complicity in Tennessee's guilt, and left only a suspicion of his general sanity. Sandy Bar made a point of calling on him, and proffering various uncouth but well-meant kindnesses. But from that day his rude health and great strength seemed visibly to decline; and when the rainy season fairly set in, and the tiny grass-blades were beginning to peep from the rocky mound above Tennessee's grave, he took to his bed.

One night, when the pines beside the cabin were swaying in the storm and trailing their slender fingers over the roof, and the roar and rush of the swollen river were heard below, Tennessee's Partner lifted his head from the pillow, saying, "It is time to go for Tennessee; I must put Jinny in the cart;" and would have risen frim his bed but for the restraint of his attendant. Struggling, he still pursued his singular fancy: "There, now, steady, Jinny,—steady, old girl. How dark it is! Look out for the ruts,—and look out for him, too, old gal. Sometimes, you know, when he's blind drunk, he drops down right in the trail. Keep on straight up to the pine on the top of the hill. Thar! I told you so!—thar he is,—coming this way, too,—all by himself, sober, and his face a-shining. Tennessee! Pardner!"

And so they met.

OLIVER WENDELL HOLMES, JR.

Harvard College in the War

(Answer to a Toast at Harvard University Commencement, June 25, 1884.)

Mr. President and Gentlemen of the Alumni:—

Another day than this has been consecrated to the memories of the war. On that day we think not of the children of the University or the city, hardly even of the children whom the State has lost, but of a mighty brotherhood whose parent was our common country. To-day the College is the centre of all our feeling, and if we refer to the war it is in connection with the College, and not for its own sake, that we do so. What, then, did the College do to justify our speaking of the war now? She sent a few gentlemen into the field, who died there becomingly. I know of nothing more. The great forces which insured the North success would have been at work even if those men had been absent. Our means of raising money and troops would not have been less, I dare say. The great qualities of the race, too, would still have been there. The greatest qualities, after all, are those of a man, not those of a gentleman, and neither North nor South needed colleges to learn them. And yet—and yet I think we all feel that to us at least the war would seem less beautiful and inspiring if those few gentlemen had not died as they did. Look at yonder portrait and yonder bust, and tell me if stories such as they commemorate do not add a glory to the bare fact that the strongest legions prevailed. So it has been since wars began. After history has done its best to fix men's thoughts upon strategy and finance, their eyes have turned and rested on some single romantic figure,—some Sidney, some Falkland, some Wolfe, some Montcalm, some Shaw. This is that little touch of the superfluous which is necessary. Necessary as art is necessary, and knowledge which serves no mechanical end. Superfluous only as glory is superfluous, or a bit of red ribbon that a man would die to win.

It has been one merit of Harvard College that it has never quite sunk to believing that its only function was to carry a body of specialists through the first stage of their preparation. About these halls there has always been an aroma of high feeling, not to be found or lost in science or Greek,—not to be fixed, yet all-pervading. And the warrant of Harvard College for writing the names of its dead graduates upon its tablets is not in the mathematics, the chemistry, the political economy, which it taught them, but that in ways not to be discovered, by traditions not to be written down, it helped men of lofty natures to make good their faculties. I hope and I believe that it long will give such help to its children. I hope and I believe that, long after we and our tears for the dead have been forgotten, this monument to their memory still will give such help to generations to whom it is only a symbol,—a symbol of man's destiny and power for duty, but a symbol also of that something more by which duty is swallowed up in generosity, that something more which led men like Shaw to toss life and hope like a flower before the feet of their country and their cause.

AMBROSE BIERCE (1842-1913?)

The Damned Thing

I

ONE DOES NOT ALWAYS EAT WHAT IS ON THE TABLE

By the light of a tallow candle which had been placed on one end of a rough table a man was reading something written in a book. It was an old account book, greatly worn; and the writing was not, apparently, very legible, for the man sometimes held the page close to the flame of the candle to get a stronger light on it. The shadow of the book would then throw into obscurity a half of the room, darkening a number of faces and figures; for besides the reader, eight other men were present. Seven of them sat against the rough log walls, silent, motionless, and the room being small, not very far from the table. By extending an arm any one of them could have touched the eighth man, who lay on the table, face upward, partly covered by a sheet, his arms at his sides. He was dead.

The man with the book was not reading aloud, and no one spoke; all seemed to be waiting for something to occur; the dead man only was without expectation. From the blank darkness outside came in, through the aperture that served for a window, all the ever unfamiliar noises of night in the wilderness—the long nameless note of a distant coyote; the stilly pulsing thrill of tireless insects in trees; strange cries of night birds, so different from those of the birds of day; the drone of great blundering beetles, and all that mysterious chorus of small sounds that seem always to have been but half heard when they have suddenly ceased, as if conscious of an indiscretion. But nothing of all this was noted in that company; its members were not overmuch addicted to idle interest in matters of no practical importance; that was obvious in every line of their rugged faces—obvious even in the dim light of the single candle. They were evidently men of the vicinity—farmers and woodsmen.

The person reading was a trifle different; one would have said of him that he was of the world, worldly, albeit there was that in his attire which attested a certain fellowship with the organisms of his environment. His coat would hardly have passed muster in San Francisco; his foot-gear was not of urban origin, and the hat that lay by him on the floor (he was the only one uncovered) was such that if one had considered it as an article of mere personal adornment he would have missed its meaning. In countenance the man was rather prepossessing, with just a hint of sternness; though that he may have assumed or cultivated, as appropriate to one in authority. For he was a coroner. It was by virtue of his office that he had possession of the book in which he was reading; it had been found among the dead man's effects—in his cabin, where the inquest was now taking place.

When the coroner had finished reading he put the book into his breast pocket. At that moment the door was pushed open and a young man entered. He, clearly, was not of mountain birth and breeding: he was clad as those who dwell in cities. His clothing was dusty, however, as from travel. He had, in fact, been riding hard to attend the inquest.

The coroner nodded; no one else greeted him.

"We have waited for you," said the coroner. "It is necessary to have done with this business to-night."

The young man smiled. "I am sorry to have kept you," he said. "I went away, not to evade your summons, but to post to my newspaper an account of what I suppose I am called back to relate."

The coroner smiled.

"The account that you posted to your newspaper," he said, "differs, probably, from that which you will give here under oath."

"That," replied the other, rather hotly and with a visible flush, "is as you please. I used manifold paper and have a copy of what I sent. It was not written as news, for it is incredible, but as fiction. It may go as part of my testimony under oath."

"But you say it is incredible."

"That is nothing to you, sir, if I also swear that it is true."

The coroner was silent for a time, his eyes upon the floor. The men about the sides of the cabin talked in whispers, but seldom withdrew their gaze from the face of the corpse. Presently the coroner lifted his eyes and said: "We will resume the inquest."

The men removed their hats. The witness was sworn.

"What is your name?" the coroner asked.

"William Harker."

"Age?"

"Twenty-seven."

"You knew the deceased, Hugh Morgan?"

"Yes."

"You were with him when he died?"

"Near him."

"How did that happen—your presence, I mean?"

"I was visiting him at this place to shoot and fish. A part of my purpose, however, was to study him and his odd, solitary way of life. He seemed a good model for a character in fiction. I sometimes write stories."

"I sometimes read them."

"Thank you."

"Stories in general—not yours."

Some of the jurors laughed. Against a sombre background humor shows high lights. Soldiers in the intervals of battle laugh easily, and a jest in the death chamber conquers by surprise.

"Relate the circumstances of this man's death," said the coroner. "You may use any notes or memoranda that you please."

The witness understood. Pulling a manuscript from his breast pocket he held it near the candle and turning the leaves until he found the passage that he wanted began to read.

II

WHAT MAY HAPPEN IN A FIELD OF WILD OATS

". . . The sun had hardly risen when we left the house. We were looking for quail, each with a shotgun, but we had only one dog. Morgan said that our best ground was beyond a certain ridge that he pointed out, and we crossed it by a trail through the *chaparral*. On the other side was comparatively level ground, thickly covered with wild oats. As we emerged from the *chaparral* Morgan was but a few yards in advance. Suddenly we heard, at a little distance to our right and partly in front, a noise as of some animal thrashing about in the bushes, which we could see were violently agitated.

" 'We've started a deer,' I said. 'I wish we had brought a rifle.'

"Morgan, who had stopped and was intently watching the agitated *chaparral,* said nothing, but had cocked both barrels of his gun and was holding it in readiness to aim. I thought him a trifle excited, which surprised me, for he had a reputation for exceptional coolness, even in moments of sudden and imminent peril.

" 'O, come,' I said. 'You are not going to fill up a deer with quail-shot, are you?'

"Still he did not reply; but catching a sight of his face as he turned it slightly toward me I was struck by the intensity of his look. Then I understood that we had serious business in hand and my first conjecture was that we had 'jumped' a grizzly. I advanced to Morgan's side, cocking my piece as I moved.

"The bushes were now quiet and the sounds had ceased, but Morgan was as attentive to the place as before.

" 'What is it? What the devil is it?' I asked.

" 'That Damned Thing!' he replied, without turning his head. His voice was husky and unnatural. He trembled visibly.

"I was about to speak further, when I observed the wild oats near the place of the disturbance moving in the most inexplicable way. I can hardly describe it. It seemed as if stirred by a streak of wind, which not only bent it, but pressed it down—crushed it so that it did not rise; and this movement was slowly prolonging itself directly toward us.

"Nothing that I had ever seen had affected me so strangely as this unfamiliar and unaccountable phenomenon, yet I am unable to recall any sense of fear. I remember—and tell it here because, singularly enough, I recollected it then—that once in looking carelessly out of an open window I momentarily mistook a small tree close at hand for one of a group of larger trees at a little distance away. It looked the same size as the others, but being more distinctly and sharply defined in mass and detail seemed out of harmony with them. It was a mere falsification of the law of aërial perspective, but it startled, almost terrified me. We so rely upon the orderly operation of familiar natural laws that any seeming suspension of them is noted as a menace to our safety, a warning of unthinkable calamity. So now the apparently causeless movement of the herbage and the slow, undeviating approach of the line of disturbance were distinctly disquieting. My companion appeared actually frightened, and I could hardly credit my senses when I saw him suddenly throw his gun to his shoulder and fire both barrels at the agitated grain! Before the smoke of the discharge had cleared away I heard a loud savage cry—a scream like that of a wild animal—and flinging his gun upon the ground Morgan sprang away and ran swiftly from the spot. At the same instant I was thrown violently to the ground by the impact of something unseen in the smoke—some soft, heavy substance that seemed thrown against me with great force.

"Before I could get upon my feet and recover my gun, which seemed to have been struck from my hands, I heard Morgan crying out as if in mortal agony, and mingling with his cries were such hoarse, savage sounds as one hears from fighting dogs. Inexpressibly terrified, I struggled to my feet and looked in the direction of Morgan's retreat; and may Heaven in mercy spare me from another sight like that! At a distance of less than thirty yards was my friend, down upon one knee, his head thrown back at a frightful angle, hatless, his long hair in disorder and his whole body in violent movement from side to side, backward and forward. His right arm was lifted and seemed to lack the hand—at least, I could see none. The other arm was invisible. At times, as my memory now reports this extraordinary scene, I could discern but a part of his body; it was as if he had been partly blotted out—I cannot otherwise express it—then a shifting of his position would bring it all into view again.

"All this must have occurred within a few seconds, yet in that time Morgan assumed all the postures of a determined wrestler vanquished by superior weight and strength. I saw nothing but him, and him not always distinctly. During the entire incident his shouts and curses were heard, as if through an enveloping uproar of such sounds of rage and fury as I had never heard from the throat of man or brute!

"For a moment only I stood irresolute, then throwing down my gun I ran forward to my friend's assistance. I had a vague belief that he was suffering from a fit, or some form of convulsion. Before I could reach his side he was down and quiet. All sounds had ceased, but with a feeling of such terror as even these awful events had not inspired I now saw again the mysterious movement of the wild oats, prolonging itself from the trampled area about the prostrate man toward the edge of a wood. It was only when it had reached the wood that I was able to withdraw my eyes and look at my companion. He was dead."

III

A MAN THOUGH NAKED MAY BE IN RAGS

The coroner rose from his seat and stood beside the dead man. Lifting an edge of the sheet he pulled it away, exposing the entire body, altogether naked and showing in the candle-light a claylike yellow. It had, however, broad maculations of bluish black, obviously caused by extravasated blood from contusions. The chest and sides looked as if they had been beaten with a bludgeon. There were dreadful lacerations; the skin was torn in strips and shreds.

The coroner moved round to the end of the table and undid a silk handkerchief which had been passed under the chin and knotted on the top of the head. When the handkerchief was drawn away it exposed what had been the throat. Some of the jurors who had risen to get a better view repented their curiosity and turned away their faces. Witness Harker went to the open window and leaned out across the sill, faint and sick. Dropping the handkerchief upon the dead man's neck the coroner stepped to an angle of the room and from a pile of clothing produced one garment after another, each of which he held up a moment for inspection. All were torn, and stiff with blood. The jurors did not make a closer inspection. They seemed rather uninterested. They had, in truth, seen all this before; the only thing that was new to them being Harker's testimony.

"Gentlemen," the coroner said, "we have no more evidence, I think. Your duty has been already explained to you; if there is nothing you wish to ask you may go outside and consider your verdict."

The foreman rose—a tall, bearded man of sixty, coarsely clad.

"I should like to ask one question, Mr. Coroner," he said. "What asylum did this yer last witness escape from?"

"Mr. Harker," said the coroner, gravely and tranquilly, "from what asylum did you last escape?"

Harker flushed crimson again, but said nothing, and the seven jurors rose and solemnly filed out of the cabin.

"If you have done insulting me, sir," said Harker, as soon as he and the officer were left alone with the dead man, "I suppose I am at liberty to go?"

"Yes."

Harker started to leave, but paused, with his hand on the door latch. The habit of his profession was strong in him—stronger than his sense of personal dignity. He turned about and said:

"The book that you have there—I recognize it as Morgan's diary. You seemed greatly interested in it; you read in it while I was testifying. May I see it? The public would like——"

"The book will cut no figure in this matter," replied the official, slipping it into his coat pocket; "all the entries in it were made before the writer's death."

As Harker passed out of the house the jury reëntered and stood about the table, on which the now covered corpse showed under the sheet with sharp definition. The foreman seated himself near the candle, produced from his breast pocket a pencil and scrap of paper and wrote rather laboriously the following verdict, which with various degrees of effort all signed:

"We, the jury, do find that the remains come to their death at the hands of a mountain lion, but some of us thinks, all the same, they had fits."

IV

AN EXPLANATION FROM THE TOMB

In the diary of the late Hugh Morgan are certain interesting entries having, possibly, a scientific value as suggestions. At the inquest upon his body the book was not put in evidence; possibly the coroner thought it not worth while to confuse the jury. The date of the first of the entries mentioned cannot be ascertained; the upper part of the leaf is torn away; the part of the entry remaining follows:

". . . would run in a half-circle, keeping his head turned always toward the centre, and again he would stand still, barking furiously. At last he ran away into the brush as fast as he could go. I thought at first that he had gone mad, but on returning to the house found no other alteration in his manner than what was obviously due to fear of punishment.

"Can a dog see with his nose? Do odors impress some cerebral centre with images of the thing that emitted them? . . .

"Sept. 2.—Looking at the stars last night as they rose above the crest of the ridge east of the house, I observed them successively disappear—from left to right. Each was eclipsed but an instant, and only a few at the same time, but along the entire length of the ridge all that were within a degree or two of the crest were blotted out. It was as if something had passed along between me and them; but I could not see it, and the stars were not thick enough to define its outline. Ugh! I don't like this." . . .

Several weeks' entries are missing, three leaves being torn from the book.

"September 27.—It has been about here again—I find evidences of its presence every day. I watched again all last night in the same cover, gun in hand, double-charged with buckshot. In the morning the fresh footprints were there, as before. Yet I would have sworn that I did not sleep—indeed, I hardly sleep at all. It is terrible, insupportable! If these amazing experiences are real I shall go mad; if they are fanciful I am mad already.

"Oct. 3.—I shall not go—it shall not drive me away. No, this is *my* house, *my* land. God hates a coward. . . .

"Oct. 5.—I can stand it no longer; I have invited Harker to pass a few weeks with me—he has a level head. I can judge from his manner if he thinks me mad.

"Oct. 7.—I have the solution of the mystery; it came to me last night—suddenly, as by revelation. How simple—how terribly simple!

"There are sounds that we cannot hear. At either end of the scale are notes that stir no chord of that imperfect instrument, the human ear. They are too high or too grave. I have observed a flock of blackbirds occupying an entire tree-top—the tops of several trees—and all in full song. Suddenly—in a moment—at absolutely the same instant—all spring into the air and fly away. How? They could not all see one another—whole tree-tops intervened. At no point could a leader have been visible to all. There must have been a signal of warning or command, high and shrill above the din, but by me unheard. I have observed, too, the same simultaneous flight when all were silent, among not only blackbirds, but other birds—quail, for example, widely separated by bushes—even on opposite sides of a hill.

"It is known to seamen that a school of whales basking or sporting on the surface of the ocean, miles apart, with the convexity of the earth between, will sometimes dive at the same instant—all gone out of sight in a moment. The signal has been sounded—too grave for the ear of the sailor at the masthead and his comrades on deck—who nevertheless feel its vibrations in the ship as the stones of a cathedral are stirred by the bass of the organ.

"As with sounds, so with colors. At each end of the solar spectrum the chemist can detect the presence of what are known as 'actinic' rays. They represent colors—integral colors in the composition of light—which we are unable to discern. The human eye is an imperfect instrument; its range is but a few octaves of the real 'chromatic scale.' I am not mad; there are colors that we cannot see.

"And, God help me! the Damned Thing is of such a color!"

An Occurrence at Owl Creek Bridge

I

A MAN stood upon a railroad bridge in northern Alabama, looking down into the swift water twenty feet below. The man's hands were behind his back, the wrists bound with a cord. A rope closely encircled his neck. It was attached to a stout cross-timber above his head and the slack fell to the level of his knees. Some loose boards laid upon the sleepers supporting the metals of the railway supplied a footing for him and his executioners—two private soldiers of the Federal army, directed by a sergeant who in civil life may have been a deputy sheriff. At a short remove upon the same temporary platform was an officer in the uniform of his rank, armed. He was a captain. A sentinel at each end of the bridge stood with his rifle in the position known as "support," that is to say, vertical in front of the left shoulder, the hammer resting on the forearm thrown straight across the chest—a formal and unnatural position, enforcing an erect carriage of the body. It did not appear to be the duty of these two men to know what was occurring at the centre of the bridge; they merely blockaded the two ends of the foot planking that traversed it.

Beyond one of the sentinels nobody was in sight; the railroad ran straight away into a forest for a hundred yards, then, curving, was lost to view. Doubtless there was an outpost farther along. The other bank of the stream was open ground—a gentle acclivity topped with a stockade of vertical tree trunks, loop-holed for rifles, with a single embrasure through which protruded the muzzle of a brass cannon commanding the bridge. Midway of the slope between bridge and fort were the spectators—a single company of infantry in line, at "parade rest," the butts of the rifles on the ground, the barrels inclining slightly backward against the right shoulder, the hands crossed upon the stock. A lieutenant stood at the right of the line, the point of his sword upon the ground, his left hand resting upon his right. Excepting the group of four at the centre of the bridge, not a man moved. The company faced the bridge, staring stonily, motionless. The sentinels, facing the banks of the stream, might have been statues to adorn the bridge. The captain stood with folded arms, silent, observing the work of his subordinates, but making no sign. Death is a dignitary who when he comes announced is to be received with formal manifestations of respect, even by those most familiar with him. In the code of military etiquette silence and fixity are forms of deference.

The man who was engaged in being hanged was apparently about thirty-five years of age. He was a civilian, if one might judge from his habit, which was that of a planter. His features were good—a straight nose, firm mouth, broad forehead, from which his long dark hair was combed straight back, falling behind his ears to the collar of his well-fitting frock-coat. He wore a mustache and pointed beard, but no whiskers; his eyes were large and dark gray, and had a kindly expression which one would hardly have expected in one whose neck was in the hemp. Evidently this was no vulgar assassin. The liberal military code makes provision for hanging many kinds of persons, and gentlemen are not excluded.

The preparations being complete, the two private soldiers stepped aside and each drew away the plank upon which he had been standing. The sergeant turned to the captain, saluted and placed himself immediately behind that officer, who in turn moved apart one pace. These movements left the condemned man and the sergeant standing on the two ends of the same plank, which spanned three of the cross-ties of the bridge. The end upon which the civilian stood almost, but not quite, reached a fourth. This plank had been held in place by the weight of the captain; it was now held by that of the sergeant. At a signal from the former the latter would step aside, the plank would tilt and the condemned man go down between two ties. The arrangement commended itself to his judgment as simple and effective. His face had not been covered nor his eyes bandaged. He looked a moment at his "unsteadfast footing," then let his gaze wander to the swirling water of the stream racing madly beneath his feet. A piece of dancing driftwood caught his attention and his eyes followed it down the current. How slowly it appeared to move! What a sluggish stream!

He closed his eyes in order to fix his last thoughts upon his wife and children. The water, touched to gold by the early sun, the brooding mists under the banks at some distance down the stream, the fort, the soldiers, the piece of drift—all had distracted him. And now he became conscious of a new disturbance. Striking through the thought of his dear ones was a sound which he could neither ignore nor understand, a sharp, distinct, metallic percussion like the stroke of a blacksmith's hammer upon the anvil; it had the same ringing quality. He wondered what it was, and whether immeasurably distant or near by—it seemed both. Its recurrence was regular, but as slow as the tolling of a death knell. He awaited each stroke with impatience and—he knew not why—apprehension. The intervals of silence grew progressively longer; the delays became maddening. With their greater infrequency the sounds increased in strength and sharpness. They hurt his ear like the thrust of a knife; he feared he would shriek. What he heard was the ticking of his watch.

He unclosed his eyes and saw again the water below him. "If I could free my hands," he thought, "I might throw off the noose and spring into the stream. By diving I could evade the bullets and, swimming vigorously, reach the bank, take to the woods and get away home. My home, thank God, is as yet outside their lines; my wife and little ones are still beyond the invader's farthest advance."

As these thoughts, which have here to be set down in words, were flashed into the doomed man's brain rather than evolved from it the captain nodded to the sergeant. The sergeant stepped aside.

II

Peyton Farquhar was a well-to-do planter, of an old and highly respected Alabama family. Being a slave owner and like other slave owners a politician, he was naturally an original secessionist and ardently devoted to the Southern cause. Circumstances of an imperious nature, which it is unnecessary to relate here, had prevented him from taking service with the gallant army that had fought the disastrous campaigns ending with the fall of Corinth, and he chafed under the inglorious restraint, longing for the release of his energies, the larger life of the soldier, the opportunity for distinction. That opportunity, he felt, would come, as it comes to all in war time. Meanwhile he did what he could. No service was too humble for him to perform in aid of the South, no adventure too perilous for him to undertake if consistent with the character of a civilian who was at heart a soldier, and who in good faith and without too much qualification assented to at least a part of the frankly villainous dictum that all is fair in love and war.

One evening while Farquhar and his wife were sitting on a rustic bench near the entrance to his grounds, a gray-clad soldier rode up to the gate and asked for a drink of water. Mrs. Farquhar was only too happy to serve him with her own white hands. While she was fetching the water her husband approached the dusty horseman and inquired eagerly for news from the front.

"The Yanks are repairing the railroads," said the man, "and are getting ready for another advance. They have reached the Owl Creek bridge, put it in order and built a stockade on the north bank. The commandant has issued an order, which is posted everywhere, declaring that any civilian caught interfering with the railroad, its bridges, tunnels or trains will be summarily hanged. I saw the order."

"How far is it to the Owl Creek bridge?" Farquhar asked.

"About thirty miles."

"Is there no force on this side of the creek?"

"Only a picket post half a mile out, on the railroad, and a single sentinel at this end of the bridge."

"Suppose a man—a civilian and student of hanging—should elude the picket post and perhaps get the better of the sentinel," said Farquhar, smiling, "what could he accomplish?"

The soldier reflected. "I was there a month ago," he replied. "I observed that the flood of last winter had lodged a great quantity of driftwood against the wooden pier at this end of the bridge. It is now dry and would burn like tow."

The lady had now brought the water, which the soldier drank. He thanked her ceremoniously, bowed to her husband and rode away. An hour later, after nightfall, he repassed the plantation, going northward in the direction from which he had come. He was a Federal scout.

III

As Peyton Farquhar fell straight downward through the bridge he lost consciousness and was as one already dead. From this state he was awakened—ages later, it seemed to him—by the pain of a sharp pressure upon his throat, followed by a sense of suffocation. Keen, poignant agonies seemed to shoot from his neck downward through every fibre of his body and limbs. These pains appeared to flash along well-defined lines of ramification and to beat with an inconceivably rapid periodicity. They seemed like streams of pulsating fire heating him to an intolerable temperature. As to his head, he was conscious of nothing but a feeling of fulness—of congestion. These sensations were unaccompanied by thought. The intellectual part of his nature was already effaced; he had power only to feel, and feeling was torment. He was conscious of motion. Encompassed in a luminous cloud, of which he was now merely the fiery heart, without material substance, he swung through unthinkable arcs of oscillation, like a vast pendulum. Then all at once, with terrible suddenness, the light about him shot upward with the noise of a loud plash; a frightful roaring was in his ears, and all was cold and dark. The power of thought was restored; he knew that the rope had broken and he had fallen into the stream. There was no additional strangulation; the noose about his neck was already suffocating him and kept the water from his lungs. To die of hanging at the bottom of a river!—the idea seemed to him ludicrous. He opened his eyes in the darkness and saw above him a gleam of light, but how distant, how inaccessible! He was still sinking, for the light became fainter and fainter until it was a mere glimmer. Then it began to grow and brighten, and he knew that he was rising toward the surface—knew it with reluctance, for he was now very comfortable. "To be hanged and drowned," he thought, "that is not so bad; but I do not wish to be shot. No; I will not be shot; that is not fair."

He was not conscious of an effort, but a sharp pain in his wrist apprised him that he was trying to free his hands. He gave the struggle his attention, as an idler might observe the feat of a juggler, without interest in the outcome. What splendid effort!—what magnificent, what superhuman strength! Ah, that was a fine endeavor! Bravo! The cord fell away; his arms parted and floated upward, the hands dimly seen on each side in the growing light. He watched them with a new interest as first one and then the other pounced upon the noose at his neck. They tore it away and thrust it fiercely aside, its undulations resembling those of a water-snake. "Put it back, put it back!" He thought he shouted these words to his hands, for the undoing of the noose had been succeeded by the direst pang that he had yet experienced. His neck ached horribly; his brain was on fire; his heart, which had been fluttering faintly, gave a great leap, trying to force itself out at his mouth. His whole body was racked and wrenched with an insupportable anguish! But his disobedient hands gave no heed to the command. They beat the water vigorously with quick, downward strokes, forcing him to the surface. He felt his head emerge; his eyes were blinded by the sunlight; his chest expanded convulsively, and with a supreme and crowning agony his lungs engulfed a great draught of air, which instantly he expelled in a shriek!

He was now in full possession of his physical senses. They were, indeed, preternaturally keen and alert. Something in the awful disturbance of his organic system had so exalted and refined them that they made record of things never before perceived. He felt the ripples upon his face and heard their separate sounds as they struck. He looked at the forest on the bank of the stream, saw the individual trees, the leaves and the veining of each leaf—saw the very insects upon them: the locusts, the brilliant-bodied flies, the gray spiders stretching their webs from twig to twig. He noted the prismatic colors in all the dewdrops upon a million blades of grass. The humming of the gnats that danced above the eddies of the stream, the beating of the dragon-flies' wings, the strokes of the water-spiders' legs, like oars which had lifted their boat—all these made audible music. A fish slid along beneath his eyes and he heard the rush of its body parting the water.

He had come to the surface facing down the stream; in a moment the visible world seemed to wheel slowly round, himself the pivotal point, and he saw the bridge, the fort, the soldiers upon the bridge, the captain, the sergeant, the two privates, his executioners. They were in silhouette against the blue sky. They shouted and gesticulated, pointing at him. The captain had drawn his pistol, but did not fire; the others were unarmed. Their movements were grotesque and horrible, their forms gigantic.

Suddenly he heard a sharp report and something struck the water smartly within a few inches of his head, spattering his face with spray. He heard a second report, and saw one of the sentinels with his rifle at his shoulder, a light cloud of blue smoke rising from the muzzle. The man in the water saw the eye of the man on the bridge gazing into his own through the sights of the rifle. He observed that it was a gray eye and remembered having read that gray eyes were keenest, and that all famous marksmen had them. Nevertheless, this one had missed.

A counter-swirl had caught Farquhar and turned him half round; he was again looking into the forest on the bank opposite the fort. The sound of a clear, high voice in a monotonous singsong now rang out behind him and came across the water with a distinctness that pierced and subdued all other sounds, even the beating of the ripples in his ears. Although no soldier, he had frequented camps enough to know the dread significance of that deliberate, drawling, aspirated chant; the lieutenant on shore was taking a part in the morning's work. How coldly and pitilessly—with what an even, calm intonation, presaging, and enforcing tranquillity in the men—with what accurately measured intervals fell those cruel words:

"Attention, company! . . . Shoulder arms! . . . Ready! . . . Aim! . . . Fire!"

Farquhar dived—dived as deeply as he could. The water roared in his ears like the voice of Niagara, yet he heard the dulled thunder of the volley and, rising again toward the surface, met shining bits of metal, singularly flattened, oscillating slowly downward. Some of them touched him on the face and hands, then fell away, continuing their descent. One lodged between his collar and neck; it was uncomfortably warm and he snatched it out.

As he rose to the surface, gasping for breath, he saw that he had been a long time under water; he was perceptibly farther down stream—nearer to safety. The soldiers had almost finished reloading; the metal ramrods flashed all at once in the sunshine as they were drawn from the barrels, turned in the air, and thrust into their sockets. The two sentinels fired again, independently and ineffectually.

The hunted man saw all this over his shoulder; he was now swimming vigorously with the current. His brain was as energetic as his arms and legs; he thought with the rapidity of lightning.

"The officer," he reasoned, "will not make that martinet's error a second time. It is as easy to dodge a volley as a single shot. He has probably already given the command to fire at will. God help me, I cannot dodge them all!"

An appalling plash within two yards of him was followed by a loud, rushing sound, *diminuendo,* which seemed to travel back through the air to the fort and died in an explosion which stirred the very river to its deeps! A rising sheet of water curved over him, fell down upon him, blinded him, strangled him! The cannon had taken a hand in the game. As he shook his head free from the commotion of the smitten water he heard the deflected shot humming through the air ahead, and in an instant it was cracking and smashing the branches in the forest beyond.

"They will not do that again," he thought; "the next time they will use a charge of grape. I must keep my eye upon the gun; the smoke will apprise me—the report arrives too late; it lags behind the missile. That is a good gun."

Suddenly he felt himself whirled round and round—spinning like a top. The water, the banks, the forests, the now distant bridge, fort and men—all were commingled and blurred. Objects were represented by their colors only; circular horizontal streaks of color—that was all he saw. He had been caught in a vortex and was being whirled on with a velocity of advance and gyration that made him giddy and sick. In a few moments he was flung upon the gravel at the foot of the left bank of the stream—the southern bank—and behind a projecting point which concealed him from his enemies. The sudden arrest of his motion, the abrasion of one of his hands on the gravel, restored him, and he wept with delight. He dug his fingers into the sand, threw it over himself in handfuls and audibly blessed it. It looked like diamonds, rubies, emeralds; he could think of nothing beautiful which it did not resemble. The trees upon the bank were giant garden plants; he noted a definite order in their arrangement, inhaled the fragrance of their blooms. A strange, roseate light shone through the spaces among their trunks and the wind made in their branches the music of æolian harps. He had no wish to perfect his escape—was content to remain in that enchanting spot until retaken.

A whiz and rattle of grapeshot among the branches high above his head roused him from his dream. The baffled cannoneer had fired him a random farewell. He sprang to his feet, rushed up the sloping bank, and plunged into the forest.

All that day he travelled, laying his course by the rounding sun. The forest seemed interminable; nowhere did he discover a break in it, not even a woodman's road. He had not known that he lived in so wild a region. There was something uncanny in the revelation.

By nightfall he was fatigued, footsore, famishing. The thought of his wife and children urged him on. At last he found a road which led him in what he knew to be the right direction. It was as wide and straight as a city street, yet it seemed untravelled. No fields bordered it, no dwelling anywhere. Not so much as the barking of a dog suggested human habitation. The black bodies of the trees formed a straight wall on both sides, terminating on the horizon in a point, like a diagram in a lesson in perspective. Overhead, as he looked up through this rift in the wood, shone great golden stars looking unfamiliar and grouped in strange constellations. He was sure they were arranged in some order which had a secret and malign significance. The wood on either side was full of singular noises, among which—once, twice, and again—he distinctly heard whispers in an unknown tongue.

His neck was in pain, and lifting his hand to it he found it horribly swollen. He knew that it had a circle of black where the rope had bruised it. His eyes felt congested; he could no longer close them. His tongue was swollen with thirst; he relieved its fever by thrusting it forward from between his teeth into the cold air. How softly the turf had carpeted the untravelled avenue—he could no longer feel the roadway beneath his feet!

Doubtless, despite his suffering, he had fallen asleep while walking, for now he sees another scene—perhaps he has merely recovered from a delirium. He stands at the gate of his own home. All is as he left it, and all bright and beautiful in the morning sunshine. He must have travelled the entire night. As he pushes open the gate and passes up the wide white walk, he sees a flutter of female garments; his wife, looking fresh and cool and sweet, steps down from the veranda to meet him. At the bottom of the steps she stands waiting, with a smile of ineffable joy, an attitude of matchless grace and dignity. Ah, how beautiful she is! He springs forward with extended arms. As he is about to clasp her he feels a stunning blow upon the back of the neck; a blinding white light blazes all about him with a sound like the shock of a cannon—then all is darkness and silence!

Peyton Farquhar was dead; his body, with a broken neck, swung gently from side to side beneath the timbers of the Owl Creek bridge.

HENRY JAMES (1843-1916)

Four Meetings

I SAW her but four times, though I remember them vividly; she made her impression on me. I thought her very pretty and very interesting—a touching specimen of a type with which I had had other and perhaps less charming associations. I'm sorry to hear of her death, and yet when I think of it why *should* I be? The last time I saw her she was certainly not—! But it will be of interest to take our meetings in order.

I

The first was in the country, at a small tea-party, one snowy night of some seventeen years ago. My friend Latouche, going to spend Christmas with his mother, had insisted on my company, and the good lady had given in our honor the entertainment of which I speak. To me it was really full of savour—it had all the right marks: I had never been in the depths of New England at that season. It had been snowing all day and the drifts were knee-high. I wondered how the ladies had made their way to the house; but I inferred that just those general rigors rendered any assembly offering the attraction of two gentlemen from New York worth a desperate effort.

Mrs. Latouche in the course of the evening asked me if I "didn't want to" show the photographs to some of the young ladies. The photographs were in a couple of great portfolios, and had been brought home by her son, who, like myself, was lately returned from Europe. I looked round and was struck with the fact that most of the young ladies were provided with an object of interest more absorbing than the most vivid sun-picture. But there was a person alone near the mantel-shelf who looked round the room with a small vague smile, a discreet, a disguised yearning, which seemed somehow at odds with her isolation. I looked at her a moment and then chose. "I should like to show them to that young lady."

"Oh, yes," said Mrs. Latouche, "she's just the person. She doesn't care for flirting—I'll speak to her." I replied that if she didn't care for flirting she wasn't perhaps just the person; but Mrs. Latouche had already, with a few steps, appealed to her participation. "She's delighted," my hostess came back to report; "and she's just the person—so quiet and so bright." And she told me the young lady was by name Miss Caroline Spencer—with which she introduced me.

Miss Caroline Spencer was not quite a beauty, but was none the less, in her small odd way, formed to please. Close upon thirty, by every presumption, she was made almost like a little girl and had the complexion of a child. She had also the prettiest head, on which her hair was arranged as nearly as possible like the hair of a Greek bust, though indeed it was to be doubted if she had ever seen a Greek bust. She was "artistic," I suspected, so far as the polar influences of North Verona could allow for such yearnings or could minister to them. Her eyes were perhaps just too round and too inveterately surprised, but her lips had a certain mild decision and her teeth, when she showed them, were charming. About her neck she wore what ladies call, I believe, a "ruche" fastened with a very small pin of pink coral, and in her hand she carried a fan made of plaited straw and adorned with pink ribbon. She wore a scanty black silk dress. She spoke with slow soft neatness, even without smiles showing the prettiness of her teeth, and she seemed extremely pleased, in fact quite fluttered, at the prospect of my demonstrations. These went forward very smoothly after I had moved the portfolios out of their corner and placed a couple of chairs near a lamp. The photographs were usually things I knew—large views of Switzerland, Italy and Spain, landscapes, reproductions of famous buildings, pictures and statues. I said what I could for them, and my companion, looking at them as I held them up, sat perfectly still, her straw fan raised to her under-lip and gently, yet, as I could feel, almost excitedly, rubbing it. Occasionally, as I laid one of the pictures down, she said without confidence, which would have been too much: "Have you seen that place?" I usually answered that I had seen it several times—I had been a great traveller, though I was somehow particularly admonished not to swagger—and then I felt her look at me askance for a moment with her pretty eyes. I had asked her at the outset whether she had been to Europe; to this she had answered "No, no, no"—almost as much below her breath as if the image of such an event scarce, for solemnity, brooked phrasing. But after that, though she never took her eyes off the pictures, she said so little that I feared she was at last bored. Accordingly when we had finished one portfolio I offered, if she desired it, to desist. I rather guessed the exhibition really held her, but her reticence puzzled me and I wanted to make her speak. I turned round to judge better and then saw a faint flush in each of her cheeks. She kept waving her little fan to and fro. Instead of looking at me she fixed her eyes on the remainder of the collection, which leaned, in its receptacle, against the table.

"Won't you show me that?" she quavered, drawing the long breath of a person launched and afloat but conscious of rocking a little.

"With pleasure," I answered, "if you're really not tired."

"Oh I'm not tired a bit. I'm just fascinated." With which as I took up the other portfolio she laid her hand on it, rubbing it softly. "And have you been here too?"

On my opening the portfolio it appeared I had indeed been there. One of the first photographs was a large view of the Castle of Chillon by the Lake of Geneva. "Here," I said, "I've been many a time. Isn't it beautiful?" And I pointed to the perfect reflexion of the rugged rocks and pointed towers in the clear still water. She didn't say "Oh enchanting!" and push it away to see the next picture. She looked a while and then asked if it weren't where Bonnivard, about whom Byron wrote, had been confined. I assented, trying to quote Byron's verses, but not quite bringing it off.

She fanned herself a moment and then repeated the lines correctly, in a soft flat voice but with charming conviction. By the time she had finished, she was nevertheless blushing. I complimented her and assured her she was perfectly equipped for visiting Switzerland and Italy. She looked at me askance again, to see if I might be serious, and I added that if she wished to recognize Byron's descriptions she must go abroad speedily—Europe was getting sadly dis-Byronized. "How soon must I go?" she thereupon inquired.

"Oh I'll give you ten years."

"Well, I guess I can go in *that* time," she answered as if measuring her words.

"Then you'll enjoy it immensely," I said; "you'll find it of the highest interest." Just then I came upon a photograph of some nook in a foreign city which I had been very fond of and which recalled tender memories. I discoursed (as I suppose) with considerable spirit; my companion sat listening breathless.

"Have you been *very* long over there?" she asked some time after I had ceased.

"Well, it mounts up, put all the times together."

"And have you travelled everywhere?"

"I've travelled a good deal. I'm very fond of it and happily have been able."

Again she turned on me her slow shy scrutiny. "Do you know the foreign languages?"

"After a fashion."

"Is it hard to speak them?"

"I don't imagine you'd find it so," I gallantly answered.

"Oh I shouldn't want to speak—I should only want to listen." Then on a pause she added: "They say the French theatre's so beautiful."

"Ah the best in the world."

"Did you go there very often?"

"When I was first in Paris I went every night."

"Every night!" And she opened her clear eyes very wide. "That to me is"—and her expression hovered—"as if you tell me a fairy-tale." A few minutes later she put to me: "And which country do you prefer?"

"There's one I love beyond any. I think you'd do the same."

Her gaze rested as on a dim revelation and then she breathed "Italy?"

"Italy," I answered softly too; and for a moment we communed over it. She looked as pretty as if instead of showing her photographs I had been making love to her. To increase the resemblance she turned off blushing. It made a pause which she broke at last by saying: "That's the place which—in particular—I thought of going to."

"Oh that's the place—that's the place!" I laughed.

She looked at two or three more views in silence. "They say it's not very dear."

"As some other countries? Well, one gets back there one's money. That's not the least of the charms."

"But it's *all* very expensive, isn't it?"

"Europe, you mean?"

"Going there and travelling. That has been the trouble. I've very little money. I teach, you know," said Miss Caroline Spencer.

"Oh of course one must have money," I allowed; "but one can manage with a moderate amount judiciously spent."

"I think I should manage. I've saved and saved up, and I'm always adding a little to it. It's all for that." She paused a moment, and then went on with suppressed eagerness, as if telling me the story were a rare, but possibly an impure satisfaction. "You see it hasn't been only the money—it has been everything. Everything has acted against it. I've waited and waited. It has been my castle in the air. I'm almost afraid to talk about it. Two or three times it has come a little nearer, and then I've talked about it and it has melted away. I've talked about it too much," she said hypocritically—for I saw such talk was now a small tremulous ecstasy. "There's a lady who's a great friend of mine—she doesn't want to go, but I'm always at her about it. I think I must tire her dreadfully. She told me just the other day she didn't know what would become of me. She guessed I'd go crazy if I didn't sail, and yet certainly I'd go crazy if I did."

"Well," I laughed, "you haven't sailed up to now—so I suppose you *are* crazy."

She took everything with the same seriousness. "Well, I guess I must be. It seems as if I couldn't think of anything else—and I don't require photographs to work me up! I'm always right *on* it. It kills any interest in things nearer home—things I ought to attend to. That's a kind of craziness."

"Well then the cure for it's just to go," I smiled—"I mean the cure for this kind. Of course you may have the other kind worse," I added—"the kind you get over there."

"Well, I've a faith that I'll go *some* time all right!" she quite elatedly cried. "I've a relative right there on the spot," she went on, "and I guess he'll know how to control me." I expressed the hope that he would, and I forget whether we turned over more photographs; but when I asked her if she had always lived just where I found her, "Oh no sir," she quite eagerly replied; "I've spent twenty-two months and a half in Boston." I met it with the inevitable joke that in this case foreign lands might prove a disappointment to her, but I quite failed to alarm her. "I know more about them than you might think"—her earnestness resisted even that. "I mean by reading—for I've really read considerable. In fact I guess I've prepared my mind about as much as you *can*—in advance. I've not only read Byron—I've read histories and guide-books and articles and lots of things. I know I shall rave about everything."

"'Everything' is saying much, but I understand your case," I returned. "You've the great American disease, and you've got it 'bad'—the appetite, morbid and monstrous, for color and form, for the picturesque and the romantic at any price. I don't know whether we come into the world with it—with the germs implanted and antecedent to experience; rather perhaps we catch it early, almost before developed consciousness—we *feel,* as we look about, that we're going (to save our souls, or at least our senses) to be thrown back on it hard. We're like travellers in the desert—deprived of water and subject to the terrible mirage, the torment of illusion, of the thirst-fever. They hear the plash of fountains, they see green gardens and orchards that are hundreds of miles away. So we with *our* thirst—except that with us it's *more* wonderful: we have before us the beautiful old things we've never seen at all, and when we do at last see them—if we're lucky!—we simply recognize them. What experience does is merely to confirm and consecrate our confident dream."

She listened with her rounded eyes. "The way you express it's too lovely, and I'm sure it will be just like that. I've dreamt of everything—I'll know it all!"

"I'm afraid," I pretended for harmless comedy, "that you've wasted a great deal of time."

"Oh yes, that has been my great wickedness!" The people about us had begun to scatter; they were taking their leave. She got up and put out her hand to me, timidly, but as if quite shining and throbbing. "I'm going back there—one *has* to," I said as I shook hands with her. "I shall look out for you."

Yes, she fairly glittered with her fever of excited faith. "Well, I'll tell you if I'm disappointed." And she left me, fluttering all expressively her little straw fan.

II

A few months after this I crossed the sea eastward again and some three years elapsed. I had been living in Paris and, toward the end of October, went from that city to the Havre, to meet a pair of relatives who had written me they were about to arrive there. On reaching the Havre I found the steamer already docked—I was two or three hours late. I repaired directly to the hotel, where my travellers were duly established. My sister had gone to bed, exhausted and disabled by her voyage; she was the unsteadiest of sailors and her sufferings on this occasion had been extreme. She desired for the moment undisturbed rest and was able to see me but five minutes—long enough for us to agree to stop over, restoratively, till the morrow. My brother-in-law, anxious about his wife, was unwilling to leave her room; but she insisted on my taking him a walk for aid to recovery of his spirits and his land-legs.

The early autumn day was warm and charming, and our stroll through the bright-colored busy streets of the old French seaport beguiling enough. We walked along the sunny noisy quays and then turned into a wide pleasant street which lay half in sun and half in shade—a French provincial street that resembled an old water-color drawing: tall grey steep-roofed red-gabled many-storied houses; green shutters on windows and old scroll-work above them; flower-pots in balconies and white-capped women in doorways. We walked in the shade; all this stretched away on the sunny side of the vista and made a picture. We looked at it as we passed along; then suddenly my companion stopped—pressing my arm and staring. I followed his gaze and saw that we had paused just before reaching a café where, under an awning, several tables and chairs were disposed upon the pavement. The windows were open behind; half a dozen plants in tubs were ranged beside the door; the pavement was besprinkled with clean bran. It was a dear little quiet old-world café; inside, in the comparative dusk, I saw a stout handsome woman, who had pink ribbons in her cap, perched up with a mirror behind her back and smiling at some one placed out of sight. This, to be exact, I noted afterwards; what I first observed was a lady seated alone, outside, at one of the little marble-topped tables. My brother-in-law had stopped to look at her. Something had been put before her, but she only leaned back, motionless and with her hands folded, looking down the street and away from us. I saw her but in diminished profile; nevertheless I was sure I knew on the spot that we must already have met.

"The little lady of the steamer!" my companion cried.

"Was she on your steamer?" I asked with interest.

"From morning till night. She was never sick. She used to sit perpetually at the side of the vessel with her hands crossed that way, looking at the eastward horizon."

"And are you going to speak to her?"

"I don't know her. I never made acquaintance with her. I wasn't in form to make up to ladies. But I used to watch her and—I don't know why—to be interested in her. She's a dear little Yankee woman. I've an idea she's a school-mistress taking a holiday—for which her scholars have made up a purse."

She had now turned her face a little more into profile, looking at the steep grey house-fronts opposite. On this I decided. "I shall speak to her myself."

"I wouldn't—she's very shy," said my brother-in-law.

"My dear fellow, I know her. I once showed her photographs at a tea-party." With which I went up to her, making her, as she turned to look at me, leave me in no doubt of her identity. Miss Caroline Spencer had achieved her dream. But she was less quick to recognize me and showed a slight bewilderment. I pushed a chair to the table and sat down. "Well," I said, "I hope you're not disappointed!"

She stared, blushing a little—then gave a small jump and placed me. "It was you who showed me the photographs—at North Verona."

"Yes, it was I. This happens very charmingly, for isn't it quite for me to give you a formal reception here—the official welcome? I talked to you so much about Europe."

"You didn't say too much. I'm so intensely happy!" she declared.

Very happy indeed she looked. There was no sign of her being older; she was as gravely, decently, demurely pretty as before. If she had struck me then as a thin-stemmed mild-hued flower of Puritanism it may be imagined whether in her present situation this clear bloom was less appealing. Beside her an old gentleman was drinking absinthe; behind her the *dame de comptoir* in the pink ribbons called "Alcibiade, Alcibiade!" to the long-aproned waiter. I explained to Miss Spencer that the gentleman with me had lately been her shipmate, and my brother-in-law came up and was introduced to her. But she looked at him as if she had never so much as seen him, and I remembered he had told me her eyes were always fixed on the eastward horizon. She had evidently not noticed him, and, still timidly smiling, made no attempt whatever to pretend the contrary. I staid with her on the little terrace of the café while he went back to the hotel and to his wife. I remarked to my friend that this meeting of ours at the first hour of her landing partook, among all chances, of the miraculous, but that I was delighted to be there and receive her first impressions.

"Oh I can't tell you," she said—"I feel so much in a dream. I've been sitting here an hour and I don't want to move. Everything's so delicious and romantic. I don't know whether the coffee has gone to my head—it's *so* unlike the coffee of my dead past."

"Really," I made answer, "if you're so pleased with this poor prosaic

Havre you'll have no admiration left for better things. Don't spend your appreciation all the first day—remember it's your intellectual letter of credit. Remember all the beautiful places and things that are waiting for you. Remember that lovely Italy we talked about."

"I'm not afraid of running short," she said gaily, still looking at the opposite houses. "I could sit here all day—just saying to myself that here I am at last. It's so dark and strange—so old and different."

"By the way then," I asked, "how come you to be encamped in this odd place? Haven't you gone to one of the inns?" For I was half-amused, half-alarmed at the good conscience with which this delicately pretty woman had stationed herself in conspicuous isolation on the edge of the sidewalk.

"My cousin brought me here and—a little while ago—left me," she returned. "You know I told you I had a relation over here. He's still here—a real cousin. Well," she pursued with unclouded candor, "he met me at the steamer this morning."

It was absurd—and the case moreover none of my business; but I felt somehow disconcerted. "It was hardly worth his while to meet you if he was to desert you so soon."

"Oh he has only left me for half an hour," said Caroline Spencer. "He has gone to get my money."

I continued to wonder. "Where *is* your money?"

She appeared seldom to laugh, but she laughed for the joy of this. "It makes me feel very fine to tell you! It's in circular notes."

"And where are your circular notes?"

"In my cousin's pocket."

This statement was uttered with such clearness of candor that—I can hardly say why—it gave me a sensible chill. I couldn't at all at the moment have justified my lapse from ease, for I knew nothing of Miss Spencer's cousin. Since he stood in that relation to her—dear respectable little person—the presumption was in his favor. But I found myself wincing at the thought that half an hour after her landing her scanty funds should have passed into his hands. "Is he to travel with you?" I asked.

"Only as far as Paris. He's an art-student in Paris—I've always thought that so splendid. I wrote to him that I was coming, but I never expected him to come off to the ship. I supposed he'd only just meet me at the train in Paris. It's very kind of him. But he *is*," said Caroline Spencer, "very kind—and very bright."

I felt at once a strange eagerness to see this bright kind cousin who was an art-student. "He's gone to the banker's?" I inquired.

"Yes, to the banker's. He took me to an hotel—such a queer quaint cunning little place, with a court in the middle and a gallery all round, and a lovely landlady in such a beautifully fluted cap and such a perfectly fitting dress! After a while we came out to walk to the banker's, for I hadn't any French money. But I was very dizzy from the motion of the vessel and I thought I had better sit down. He found this place for me here—then he went off to the banker's himself. I'm to wait here till he comes back."

Her story was wholly lucid and my impression perfectly wanton, but it passed through my mind that the gentleman would never come back. I settled myself in a chair beside my friend and determined to await the event. She was lost in the vision and the imagination of everything near us and about us—she observed, she recognized and admired, with a touching intensity. She noticed everything that was brought before us by the movement of the street—the peculiarities of costume, the shapes of vehicles, the big Norman horses, the fat priests, the shaven poodles. We talked of these things, and there was something charming in her freshness of perception and the way her book-nourished fancy sallied forth for the revel.

"And when your cousin comes back what are you going to do?" I went on.

For this she had, a little oddly, to think. "We don't quite know."

"When do you go to Paris? If you go by the four o'clock train I may have the pleasure of making the journey with you."

"I don't think we shall do that." So far she was prepared. "My cousin thinks I had better stay here a few days."

"Oh!" said I—and for five minutes had nothing to add. I was wondering what our absentee was, in vulgar parlance, "up to." I looked up and down the street, but saw nothing that looked like a bright and kind American art-student. At last I took the liberty of observing that the Havre was hardly a place to choose as one of the æsthetic stations of a European tour. It was a place of convenience, nothing more; a place of transit, through which transit should be rapid. I recommended her to go to Paris by the afternoon train and meanwhile to amuse herself by driving to the ancient fortress at the mouth of the harbor—that remarkable circular structure which bore the name of Francis the First and figured a sort of small Castle of Saint Angelo. (I might really have foreknown that it was to be demolished.)

She listened with much interest—then for a moment looked grave. "My cousin told me that when he returned he should have something particular to say to me, and that we could do nothing or decide nothing till I should have heard it. But I'll make him tell me right off, and then we'll go to the ancient fortress. Francis the First, did you say? Why, that's lovely. There's no hurry to get to Paris; there's plenty of time."

She smiled with her softly severe little lips as she spoke those last words, yet, looking at her with a purpose, I made out in her eyes, I thought, a tiny gleam of apprehension. "Don't tell me," I said, "that this wretched man's going to give you bad news!"

She colored as if convicted of a hidden perversity, but she was soaring too high to drop. "Well, I guess it's a *little* bad, but I don't believe it's *very* bad. At any rate, I must listen to it."

I usurped an unscrupulous authority. "Look here; you didn't come to Europe to listen—you came to *see!*" But now I was sure her cousin would come back; since he had something disagreeable to say to her he'd infallibly turn up. We sat a while longer and I asked her about her plans of travel. She had them on her fingers' ends and told over the names as solemnly as a daughter of another faith might have told over the beads of a rosary: from Paris to Dijon and to Avignon, from Avignon to Marseilles and the Cornice road; thence to Genoa, to Spezia, to Pisa, to Florence, to Rome. It apparently had never occurred to her that there could be the least incommodity in her travelling alone; and since she was unprovided with a companion I of course civilly abstained from disturbing her sense of security.

At last her cousin came back. I saw him turn toward us out of a side-street, and from the moment my eyes rested on him I knew he could but be the bright, if not the kind, American art-student. He wore a slouch hat and a rusty black velvet jacket, such as I had often encountered in the Rue Bonaparte. His shirt-collar displayed a stretch of throat that at a distance wasn't strikingly statuesque. He was tall and lean, he had red hair and freckles. These items I had time to take in while he approached the café, staring at me with natural surprise from under his romantic brim. When he came up to us I immediately introduced myself as an old acquaintance of Miss Spencer's, a character she serenely permitted me to claim. He looked at me hard with a pair of small sharp eyes, then he gave me a solemn wave, in the "European" fashion, of his rather rusty sombrero.

"You weren't on the ship?" he asked.

"No, I wasn't on the ship. I've been in Europe these several years."

He bowed once more, portentously, and motioned me to be seated again. I sat down, but only for the purpose of observing him an instant—I saw it was time I should return to my sister. Miss Spencer's

European protector was, by my measure, a very queer quantity. Nature hadn't shaped him for a Raphaelesque or Byronic attire, and his velvet doublet and exhibited though not columnar throat weren't in harmony with his facial attributes. His hair was cropped close to his head; his ears were large and ill-adjusted to the same. He had a lackadaisical carriage and a sentimental droop which were peculiarly at variance with his keen conscious strange-colored eyes—of a brown that was almost red. Perhaps I was prejudiced, but I thought his eyes too shifty. He said nothing for some time; he leaned his hands on his stick and looked up and down the street. Then at last, slowly lifting the stick and pointing with it, "That's a very nice bit," he dropped with a certain flatness. He had his head to one side—he narrowed his ugly lids. I followed the direction of his stick; the object it indicated was a red cloth hung out of an old window. "Nice bit of color," he continued; and without moving his head transferred his half-closed gaze to me. "Composes well. Fine old tone. Make a nice thing." He spoke in a charmless vulgar voice.

"I see you've a great deal of eye," I replied. "Your cousin tells me you're studying art." He looked at me in the same way, without answering, and I went on with deliberate urbanity: "I suppose you're at the studio of one of those great men." Still on this he continued to fix me, and then he named one of the greatest of that day; which led me to ask him if he liked his master.

"Do you understand French?" he returned.

"Some kinds."

He kept his little eyes on me; with which he remarked: *"Je suis fou de la peinture!"*

"Oh I understand that kind!" I replied. Our companion laid her hand on his arm with a small pleased and fluttered movement; it was delightful to be among people who were on such easy terms with foreign tongues. I got up to take leave and asked her where, in Paris, I might have the honor of waiting on her. To what hotel would she go?

She turned to her cousin inquiringly and he favored me again with his little languid leer. "Do you know the Hôtel des Princes?"

"I know where it is."

"Well, that's the shop."

"I congratulate you," I said to Miss Spencer. "I believe it's the best inn in the world; but, in case I should still have a moment to call on you here, where are you lodged?"

"Oh it's such a pretty name," she returned gleefully. "A la Belle Normande."

"I guess I know my way round!" her kinsman threw in; and as I left them he gave me with his swaggering head-cover a great flourish that was like the wave of a banner over a conquered field.

III

My relative, as it proved, was not sufficiently restored to leave the place by the afternoon train; so that as the autumn dusk began to fall I found myself at liberty to call at the establishment named to me by my friends. I must confess that I had spent much of the interval in wondering what the disagreeable thing was that the less attractive of these had been telling the other. The *auberge* of the Belle Normande proved an hostelry in a shady by-street, where it gave me satisfaction to think Miss Spencer must have encountered local color in abundance. There was a crooked little court, where much of the hospitality of the house was carried on; there was a staircase climbing to bedrooms on the outer side of the wall; there was a small trickling fountain with a stucco statuette set in the midst of it; there was a little boy in a white cap and apron cleaning copper vessels at a conspicuous kitchen door; there was a chattering landlady, neatly laced, arranging apricots and grapes into an artistic pyramid upon a pink plate. I looked about, and on a green bench outside of an open door labelled Salle-à-Manger, I distinguished Caroline Spencer. No sooner had I looked at her than I was sure something had happened since the morning. Supported by the back of her bench, with her hands clasped in her lap, she kept her eyes on the other side of the court where the landlady manipulated the apricots.

But I saw that, poor dear, she wasn't thinking of apricots or even of landladies. She was staring absently, thoughtfully; on a nearer view I could have certified she had been crying. I had seated myself beside her before she was aware; then, when she had done so, she simply turned round without surprise and showed me her sad face. Something very bad indeed had happened; she was completely changed, and I immediately charged her with it. "Your cousin has been giving you bad news. You've had a horrid time."

For a moment she said nothing, and I supposed her afraïd to speak lest her tears should again rise. Then it came to me that even in the few hours since my leaving her she had shed them all—which made her now intensely, stoically composed. "My poor cousin has been having one," she replied at last. "He has had great worries. His news was bad." Then after a dismally conscious wait: "He was in dreadful want of money."

"In want of yours, you mean?"

"Of any he could get—honorably of course. Mine *is* all—well, that's available."

Ah it was as if I had been sure from the first! "And he has taken it from you?"

Again she hung fire, but her face meanwhile was pleading. "I gave him what I had."

I recall the accent of those words as the most angelic human sound I had ever listened to—which is exactly why I jumped up almost with a sense of personal outrage. "Gracious goodness, madam, do you call that his getting it 'honorably'?"

I had gone too far—she colored to her eyes. "We won't speak of it."

"We *must* speak of it," I declared as I dropped beside her again. "I'm your friend—upon my word I'm your protector; it seems to me you need one. What's the matter with this extraordinary person?"

She was perfectly able to say. "He's just badly in debt."

"No doubt he is! But what's the special propriety of your—in such tearing haste!—paying for that?"

"Well, he has told me all his story. I *feel* for him so much."

"So do I, if you come to that! But I hope," I roundly added, "he'll give you straight back your money."

As to this she was prompt. "Certainly he will—as soon as ever he can."

"And when the deuce will that be?"

Her lucidity maintained itself. "When he has finished his great picture."

It took me full in the face. "My dear young lady, damn his great picture! Where is this voracious man?"

It was as if she must let me feel a moment that I did push her!—though indeed, as appeared, he was just where he'd naturally be. "He's having his dinner."

I turned about and looked through the open door into the *salle-à-manger*. There, sure enough, alone at the end of a long table, was the object of my friend's compassion—the bright, the kind young art-student. He was dining too attentively to notice me at first, but in the act of setting down a well-emptied wine-glass he caught sight of my air of observation. He paused in his repast and, with his head on one side and his meagre jaws slowly moving, fixedly returned my gaze.

Then the landlady came brushing lightly by with her pyramid of apricots.

"And that nice little plate of fruit is for him?" I wailed.

Miss Spencer glanced at it tenderly. "They seem to arrange everything so nicely!" she simply sighed.

I felt helpless and irritated. "Come now, really," I said; "do you think it right, do you think it decent, that that long strong fellow should collar your funds?" She looked away from me—I was evidently giving her pain. The case was hopeless; the long strong fellow had "interested" her.

"Pardon me if I speak of him so unceremoniously," I said. "But you're really too generous, and he hasn't, clearly, the rudiments of delicacy. He made his debts himself—he ought to pay them himself."

"He has been foolish," she obstinately said—"of course I know that. He has told me everything. We had a long talk this morning—the poor fellow threw himself on my charity. He has signed notes to a large amount."

"The more fool he!"

"He's in real distress—and it's not only himself. It's his poor young wife."

"Ah he has a poor young wife?"

"I didn't know—but he made a clean breast of it. He married two years since—secretly."

"Why secretly?"

My informant took precautions as if she feared listeners. Then with low impressiveness: "She was a Countess!"

"Are you very sure of that?"

"She has written me the most beautiful letter."

"Asking you—whom she has never seen—for money?"

"Asking me for confidence and sympathy"—Miss Spencer spoke now with spirit. "She has been cruelly treated by her family—in consequence of what she has done for him. My cousin has told me every particular, and she appeals to me in her own lovely way in the letter, which I've here in my pocket. It's such a wonderful old-world romance," said my prodigious friend. "She was a beautiful young widow—her first husband was a Count, tremendously high-born, but really most wicked, with whom she hadn't been happy and whose death had left her ruined after he had deceived her in all sorts of ways. My poor cousin, meeting her in that situation and perhaps a little too recklessly pitying her and charmed with her, found her, don't you see?"—Caroline's appeal on this head was amazing!—"but too ready to trust a better man after all she had been through. Only when her 'people,' as he says—and I do like the word!—understood she *would* have him, poor gifted young American art-student though he simply was, because she just adored him, her great-aunt, the old Marquise, from whom she had expectations of wealth which she could yet sacrifice for her love, utterly cast her off and wouldn't so much as speak to her, much less to *him,* in their dreadful haughtiness and pride. They *can* be haughty over here, it seems," she ineffably developed—"there's no mistake about that! It's like something in some famous old book. The family, my cousin's wife's," she by this time almost complacently wound up, "are of the oldest Provençal noblesse."

I listened half-bewildered. The poor woman positively found it so interesting to be swindled by a flower of that stock—if stock or flower or solitary grain of truth was really concerned in the matter—as practically to have lost the sense of what the forfeiture of her hoard meant for her. "My dear young lady," I groaned, "you don't want to be stripped of every dollar for such a rigmarole!"

She asserted, at this, her dignity—much as a small pink shorn lamb might have done. "It isn't a rigmarole, and I shan't be stripped. I shan't live any worse than I *have* lived, don't you see? And I'll come back before long to stay with them. The Countess—he still gives her, he says, her title, as they do to noble widows, that is to 'dowagers,' don't you know? in England—insists on a visit from me *some* time. So I guess for *that* I can start afresh—and meanwhile I'll have recovered my money."

It was all too heart-breaking. "You're going home then at once?"

I felt the faint tremor of voice she heroically tried to stifle. "I've nothing left for a tour."

"You gave it *all* up?"

"I've kept enough to take me back."

I uttered, I think, a positive howl, and at this juncture the hero of the situation, the happy proprietor of my little friend's sacred savings and of the infatuated *grande dame* just sketched for me, reappeared with the clear consciousness of a repast bravely earned and consistently enjoyed. He stood on the threshold an instant, extracting the stone from a plump apricot he had fondly retained; then he put the apricot into his mouth and, while he let it gratefully dissolve there, stood looking at us with his long legs apart and his hands thrust into the pockets of his velvet coat. My companion got up, giving him a thin glance that I caught in its passage and which expressed at once resignation and fascination—the last dregs of her sacrifice and with it an anguish of upliftedness. Ugly vulgar pretentious dishonest as I thought him, and destitute of every grace of plausibility, he had yet appealed successfully to her eager and tender imagination. I was deeply disgusted, but I had no warrant to interfere, and at any rate felt that it would be vain. He waved his hand meanwhile with a breadth of appreciation. "Nice old court. Nice mellow old place. Nice crooked old staircase. Several pretty things."

Decidedly I couldn't stand it, and without responding I gave my hand to my friend. She looked at me an instant with her little white face and rounded eyes, and as she showed her pretty teeth I suppose she meant to smile. "Don't be sorry for me," she sublimely pleaded; "I'm very sure I shall see something of this dear old Europe yet."

I refused however to take literal leave of her—I should find a moment to come back next morning. Her awful kinsman, who had put on his sombrero again, flourished it off at me by way of a bow—on which I hurried away.

On the morrow early I did return, and in the court of the inn met the landlady, more loosely laced than in the evening. On my asking for Miss Spencer, *"Partie, monsieur,"* the good woman said. "She went away last night at ten o'clock, with her—her—not her husband, eh?—in fine her Monsieur. They went down to the American ship." I turned off—I felt the tears in my eyes. The poor girl had been some thirteen hours in Europe.

IV

I myself, more fortunate, continued to sacrifice to opportunity as I myself met it. During this period—of some five years—I lost my friend Latouche, who died of a malarious fever during a tour in the Levant. One of the first things I did on my return to America was to go up to North Verona on a consolatory visit to his poor mother. I found her in deep affliction and sat with her the whole of the morning that followed my arrival—I had come in late at night—listening to her tearful descant and singing the praises of my friend. We talked of nothing else, and our conversation ended only with the arrival of a quick little woman who drove herself up to the door in a "carry-all" and whom I saw toss the reins to the horse's back with the briskness of a startled sleeper throwing off the bed-clothes. She jumped out of the carry-all and she jumped into the room. She proved to be the minister's wife and the great town-gossip, and she had evidently, in the latter capacity, a choice morsel to communicate. I was as sure of this as I was that poor Mrs. Latouche was not absolutely too bereaved to listen to her. It seemed to me discreet to retire, and I described myself as anxious for a walk before dinner.

"And by the way," I added, "if you'll tell me where my old friend Miss Spencer lives I think I'll call on her."

The minister's wife immediately responded. Miss Spencer lived in the fourth house beyond the Baptist church; the Baptist church was the one on the right, with that queer green thing over the door; they called it a portico, but it looked more like an old-fashioned bedstead swung in the air. "Yes, do look up poor Caroline," Mrs. Latouche further enjoined. "It will refresh her to see a strange face."

"I should think she had had enough of strange faces!" cried the minister's wife.

"To see, I mean, a charming visitor"—Mrs. Latouche amended her phrase.

"I should think she had had enough of charming visitors!" her companion returned. "But *you* don't mean to stay ten years," she added with significant eyes on me.

"Has she a visitor of that sort?" I asked in my ignorance.

"You'll make out the sort!" said the minister's wife. "She's easily seen; she generally sits in the front yard. Only take care what you say to her, and be very sure you're polite."

"Ah she's so sensitive?"

The minister's wife jumped up and dropped me a curtsey—a most sarcastic curtsey. "That's what she is, if you please. 'Madame la Comtesse!'"

And pronouncing these titular words with the most scathing accent, the little woman seemed fairly to laugh in the face of the lady they designated. I stood staring, wondering, remembering.

"Oh I shall be very polite!" I cried; and, grasping my hat and stick, I went on my way.

I found Miss Spencer's residence without difficulty. The Baptist church was easily identified, and the small dwelling near it, of a rusty white, with a large central chimney-stack and a Virginia creeper, seemed naturally and properly the abode of a withdrawn old maid with a taste for striking effects inexpensively obtained. As I approached I slackened my pace, for I had heard that some one was always sitting in the front yard, and I wished to reconnoitre. I looked cautiously over the low white fence that separated the small garden-space from the unpaved street, but I descried nothing in the shape of a Comtesse. A small straight path led up to the crooked door-step, on either side of which was a little grass-plot fringed with currant-bushes. In the middle of the grass, right and left, was a large quince-tree, full of antiquity and contortions, and beneath one of the quince-trees were placed a small table and a couple of light chairs. On the table lay a piece of unfinished embroidery and two or three books in bright-colored paper covers. I went in at the gate and paused halfway along the path, scanning the place for some further token of its occupant, before whom—I could hardly have said why—I hesitated abruptly to present myself. Then I saw the poor little house to be of the shabbiest and felt a sudden doubt of my right to penetrate, since curiosity had been my motive and curiosity here failed of confidence. While I demurred a figure appeared in the open doorway and stood there looking at me. I immediately recognized Miss Spencer, but she faced me as if we had never met. Gently, but gravely and timidly, I advanced to the door-step, where I spoke with an attempt at friendly banter.

"I waited for you over there to come back, but you never came."

"Waited where, sir?" she quavered, her innocent eyes rounding themselves as of old. She was much older; she looked tired and wasted.

"Well," I said, "I waited at the old French port."

She stared harder, then recognized me, smiling, flushing, clasping her two hands together. "I remember you now—I remember that day." But she stood there, neither coming out nor asking me to come in. She was embarrassed.

I too felt a little awkward while I poked at the path with my stick. "I kept looking out for you year after year."

"You mean in Europe?" she ruefully breathed.

"In Europe of course! Here apparently you're easy enough to find."

She leaned her hand against the unpainted door-post and her head fell a little to one side. She looked at me thus without speaking, and I caught the expression visible in women's eyes when tears are rising. Suddenly she stepped out on the cracked slab of stone before her threshold and closed the door. Then her strained smile prevailed and I saw her teeth were as pretty as ever. But there had been tears too. "Have you been there ever since?" she lowered her voice to ask.

"Until three weeks ago. And you—you never came back?"

Still shining at me as she could, she put her hand behind her and reopened the door. "I'm not very polite," she said. "Won't you come in?"

"I'm afraid I incommode you."

"Oh no!"—she wouldn't hear of it now. And she pushed back the door with a sign that I should enter.

I followed her in. She led the way to a small room on the left of the narrow hall, which I supposed to be her parlor, though it was at the back of the house, and we passed the closed door of another apartment which apparently enjoyed a view of the quince-trees. This one looked out upon a small wood-shed and two clucking hens. But I thought it pretty until I saw its elegance to be of the most frugal kind; after which, presently, I thought it prettier still, for I had never seen faded chintz and old mezzotint engravings, framed in varnished autumn leaves, disposed with so touching a grace. Miss Spencer sat down on a very small section of the sofa, her hands tightly clasped in her lap. She looked ten years older, and I needn't now have felt called to insist on the facts of her person. But I still thought them interesting, and at any rate I was moved by them. She was peculiarly agitated. I tried to appear not to notice it; but suddenly, in the most inconsequent fashion—it was an irresistible echo of our concentrated passage in the old French port—I said to her: "I do incommode you. Again you're in distress."

She raised her two hands to her face and for a moment kept it buried in them. Then taking them away, "It's because you remind me," she said.

"I remind you, you mean, of that miserable day at the Havre?"

She wonderfully shook her head. "It wasn't miserable. It was delightful."

Ah was it? my manner of receiving this must have commented. "I never was so shocked as when, on going back to your inn the next morning, I found you had wretchedly retreated."

She waited an instant, after which she said: "Please let us not speak of that."

"Did you come straight back here?" I nevertheless went on.

"I was back here just thirty days after my first start."

"And here you've remained ever since?"

"Every minute of the time."

I took it in; I didn't know what to say, and what I presently said had almost the sound of mockery. "When then are you going to make that tour?" It might be practically aggressive; but there was something that irritated me in her depths of resignation, and I wished to extort from her some expression of impatience.

She attached her eyes a moment to a small sunspot on the carpet; then she got up and lowered the window-blind a little to obliterate it. I waited, watching her with interest—as if she had still something more to give me. Well, presently, in answer to my last question, she gave it. "Never!"

"I hope at least your cousin repaid you that money," I said.

At this again she looked away from me. "I don't care for it now."

"You don't care for your money?"

"For ever going to Europe."

"Do you mean you wouldn't go if you could?"

"I can't—I can't," said Caroline Spencer. "It's all over. Everything's different. I never think of it."

"The scoundrel never repaid you then!" I cried.

"Please, please—!" she began.

But she had stopped—she was looking toward the door. There had been a rustle and a sound of steps in the hall.

I also looked toward the door, which was open and now admitted another person—a lady who paused just within the threshold. Behind her came a young man. The lady looked at me with a good deal of fixedness—long enough for me to rise to a vivid impression of herself. Then she turned to Caroline Spencer and, with a smile and a strong foreign accent, *"Pardon, ma chère!* I didn't know you had company," she said. "The gentleman came in so quietly." With which she again gave me the benefit of her attention. She was very strange, yet I was at once sure I had seen her before. Afterwards I rather put it that I had only seen ladies remarkably like her. But I had seen them very far away from North Verona, and it was the oddest of all things to meet one of them in that frame. To what quite other scene did the sight of her transport me? To some dusky landing before a shabby Parisian *quatrième*—to an open door revealing a greasy ante-chamber and to Madame leaning over the banisters while she holds a faded wrapper together and bawls down to the portress to bring up her coffee. My friend's guest was a very large lady, of middle age, with a plump dead-white face and hair drawn back *à la chinoise*. She had a small penetrating eye and what is called in French *le sourire agréable*. She wore an old pink cashmere dressing-gown covered with white embroideries, and, like the figure in my momentary vision, she confined it in front with a bare and rounded arm and a plump and deeply-dimpled hand.

"It's only to spick about my *café,"* she said to her hostess with her *sourire agréable*. "I should like it served in the garden under the leetle tree."

The young man behind her had now stepped into the room, where he also stood revealed, though with rather less of a challenge. He was a gentleman of few inches but a vague importance. perhaps the leading man of the world of North Verona. He had a small pointed nose and a small pointed chin; also, as I observed, the most diminutive feet and a manner of no point at all. He looked at me foolishly and with his mouth open.

"You shall have your coffee," said Miss Spencer as if an army of cooks had been engaged in the preparation of it.

"C'est bien!" said her massive inmate. "Find your bouk"—and this personage turned to the gaping youth.

He gaped now at each quarter of the room. "My grammar, d'ye mean?"

The large lady however could but face her friend's visitor while persistently engaged with a certain laxity in the flow of her wrapper. "Find your bouk," she more absently repeated.

"My poetry, d'ye mean?" said the young man, who also couldn't take his eyes off me.

"Never mind your bouk"—his companion reconsidered. "To-day we'll just talk. We'll make some conversation. But we mustn't interrupt Mademoiselle's. Come, come"—and she moved off a step. "Under the leetle tree," she added for the benefit of Mademoiselle. After which she gave me a thin salutation, jerked a measured *"Monsieur!"* and swept away again with her swain following.

I looked at Miss Spencer, whose eyes never moved from the carpet, and I spoke, I fear, without grace. "Who in the world's that?"

"The Comtesse—that *was:* my *Cousine* as they call it in French."

"And who's the young man?"

"The Countess's pupil, Mr. Mixter." This description of the tie uniting the two persons who had just quitted us must certainly have upset my gravity; for I recall the marked increase of my friend's own as she continued to explain. "She gives lessons in French and music, the simpler sorts—"

"The simpler sorts of French?" I fear I broke in.

But she was still impenetrable, and in fact had now an intonation that put me vulgarly in the wrong. "She has had the worst reverses—with no one to look to. She's prepared for any exertion—and she takes her misfortunes with gaiety."

"Ah well," I returned—no doubt a little ruefully, "that's all I myself am pretending to do. If she's determined to be a burden to nobody, nothing could be more right and proper."

My hostess looked vaguely, though I thought quite wearily enough, about: she met this proposition in no other way. "I must go and get the coffee," she simply said.

"Has the lady many pupils?" I none the less persisted.

"She has only Mr. Mixter. She gives him all her time." It might have set me off again, but something in my whole impression of my friend's sensibility urged me to keep strictly decent. "He pays very well," she at all events inscrutably went on. "He's not very bright—as a pupil; but he's very rich and he's very kind. He has a buggy—with a back, and he takes the Countess to drive."

"For good long spells I hope," I couldn't help interjecting—even at the cost of her so taking it that she had still to avoid my eyes. "Well, the country's beautiful for miles," I went on. And then as she was turning away: "You're going for the Countess's coffee?"

"If you'll excuse me a few moments."

"Is there no one else to do it?"

She seemed to wonder who there should be. "I keep no servants."

"Then can't I help?" After which, as she but looked at me, I bettered it. "Can't she wait on herself?"

Miss Spencer had a slow headshake—as if that too had been a strange idea. "She isn't used to *manual* labor."

The discrimination was a treat, but I cultivated decorum. "I see—and you *are*." But at the same time I couldn't abjure curiosity. "Before you go, at any rate, please tell me this: who *is* this wonderful lady?"

"I told you just who in France—that extraordinary day. She's the wife of my cousin, whom you saw there."

"The lady disowned by her family in consequence of her marriage?"

"Yes; they've never seen her again. They've completely broken with her."

"And where's her husband?"

"My poor cousin's dead."

I pulled up, but only a moment. "And where's your money?"

The poor thing flinched—I kept her on the rack. "I don't know," she woefully said.

I scarce know what it didn't prompt me to—but I went step by step. "On her husband's death this lady at once came to you?"

It was as if she had had too often to describe it. "Yes, she arrived one day."

"How long ago?"

"Two years and four months."

"And has been here ever since?"

"Ever since."

I took it all in. "And how does she like it?"

"Well, not *very* much," said Miss Spencer divinely.

That too I took in. "And how do *you*—?"

She laid her face in her two hands an instant as she had done ten minutes before. Then, quickly, she went to get the Countess's coffee.

Left alone in the little parlor I found myself divided between the perfection of my disgust and a contrary wish to see, to learn more. At the end of a few minutes the young man in attendance on the lady in question reappeared as for a fresh gape at me. He was inordinately grave—to be dressed in such parti-colored flannels; and he produced with no great confidence on his own side the message with which he had been charged. "She wants to know if you won't come right out."

"Who wants to know?"

"The Countess. That French lady."

"She has asked you to bring me?"

"Yes sir," said the young man feebly—for I may claim to have surpassed him in stature and weight.

I went out with him, and we found his instructress seated under one of the small quince-trees in front of the house; where she was engaged in drawing a fine needle with a very fat hand through a piece of embroidery not remarkable for freshness. She pointed graciously to the chair beside her and I sat down. Mr. Mixter glanced about him and then accommodated himself on the grass at her feet; whence he gazed upward more gapingly than ever and as if convinced that between us something wonderful would now occur.

"I'm sure you spick French," said the Countess, whose eyes were singularly protuberant as she played over me her agreeable smile.

"I do, madam—*tant bien que mal,*" I replied, I fear, more dryly.

"Ah voilà!" she cried as with delight. "I knew it as soon as I looked at you. You've been in my poor dear country."

"A considerable time."

"You love it then, *mon pays de France?*"

"Oh it's an old affection." But I wasn't exuberant.

"And you know Paris well?"

"Yes, *sans me vanter,* madam, I think I really do." And with a certain conscious purpose I let my eyes meet her own.

She presently, hereupon, moved her own and glanced down at Mr. Mixter. "What are we talking about?" she demanded of her attentive pupil.

He pulled his knees up, plucked at the grass, stared, blushed a little. "You're talking French," said Mr. Mixter.

"La belle découverte!" mocked the Countess. "It's going on ten months," she explained to me, "since I took him in hand. Don't put yourself out not to say he's *la bêtise même,*" she added in fine style. "He won't in the least understand you."

A moment's consideration of Mr. Mixter, awkwardly sporting at our feet, quite assured me that he wouldn't. "I hope your other pupils do you more honor," I then remarked to my entertainer.

"I have no others. They don't know what French—or what anything else—is in this place; they don't want to know. You may therefore imagine the pleasure it is to me to meet a person who speaks it like yourself." I could but reply that my own pleasure wasn't less, and she continued to draw the stitches through her embroidery with an elegant curl of her little finger. Every few moments she put her eyes, near-sightedly, closer to her work—this as if for elegance too. She inspired me with no more confidence than her late husband, if husband he was, had done, years before, on the occasion with which this one so detestably matched: she was coarse, common, affected, dishonest—no more a Countess than I was a Caliph. She had an assurance—based clearly on experience; but this couldn't have been the experience of "race." Whatever it was indeed it did now, in a yearning fashion, flare out of her. "Talk to me of Paris, *mon beau Paris* that I'd give my eyes to see. The very name of it *me fait languir*. How long since you were there?"

"A couple of months ago."

"*Vous avez de la chance!* Tell me something about it. What were they doing? Oh for an hour of the Boulevard!"

"They were doing about what they're always doing—amusing themselves a good deal."

"At the theatres, *hein?*" sighed the Countess. "At the *cafés-concerts? sous ce beau ciel*—at the little tables before the doors? *Quelle existence!* You know I'm a Parisienne, monsieur," she added, "to my finger-tips."

"Miss Spencer was mistaken then," I ventured to return, "in telling me you're a Provençale."

She stared a moment, then put her nose to her embroidery, which struck me as having acquired even while we sat a dingier and more desultory air. "Ah, I'm a Provençale by birth, but a Parisienne by—inclination." After which she pursued: "And by the saddest events of my life—as well as by some of the happiest, *hélas!*"

"In other words by a varied experience!" I now at last smiled.

She questioned me over it with her hard little salient eyes. "Oh experience!—I could talk of that, no doubt, if I wished. *On en a de toutes les sortes*—and I never dreamed that mine, for example, would ever have *this* in store for me." And she indicated with her large bare elbow and with a jerk of her head all surrounding objects; the little white house, the pair of quince-trees, the rickety paling, even the rapt Mr. Mixter.

I took them all bravely in. "Ah if you mean you're decidedly in exile—!"

"You may imagine what it is. These two years of my *épreuve—elles m'en ont données, des heures, des heures!* One gets used to things"—and she raised her shoulders to the highest shrug ever accomplished at North Verona; "so that I sometimes think I've got used to this. But there are some things that are always beginning again. For example my coffee."

I so far again lent myself. "Do you always have coffee at this hour?"

Her eyebrows went up as high as her shoulders had done. "At what hour would you propose to me to have it? I must have my little cup after breakfast."

"Ah you breakfast at this hour?"

"At mid-day—*comme cela se fait*. Here they breakfast at a quarter past seven. That 'quarter past' is charming!"

"But you were telling me about your coffee," I observed sympathetically.

"My *cousine* can't believe in it; she can't understand it. *C'est une fille charmante,* but that little cup of black coffee with a drop of *'fine,'* served at this hour—they exceed her comprehension. So I have to break the ice each day, and it takes the coffee the time you see to arrive. And when it does arrive, *monsieur*—! If I don't press it on *you*—though *monsieur* here sometimes joins me!—it's because you've drunk it on the Boulevard."

I resented extremely so critical a view of my poor friend's exertions, but I said nothing at all—the only way to be sure of my civility. I dropped my eyes on Mr. Mixter, who, sitting cross-legged and nursing his knees, watched my companion's foreign graces with an interest that familiarity had apparently done little to restrict. She became aware, naturally, of my mystified view of him and faced the question with all her boldness. "He adores me, you know," she murmured with her nose again in her tapestry—"he dreams of becoming *mon amoureux*. Yes, *il me fait une cour acharnée*—such as you see him. That's what we've come to. He has read some French novel—it took him six months. But ever since that he has thought himself a hero and me—such as I am, *monsieur—je ne sais quelle dévergondée!*"

Mr. Mixter may have inferred that he was to that extent the object of our reference; but of the manner in which he was handled he must have had small suspicion—preoccupied as he was, as to my companion, with the ecstasy of contemplation. Our hostess moreover at this moment came out of the house, bearing a coffee-pot and three cups on a neat little tray. I took from her eyes, as she approached us, a brief but intense appeal—the mute expression, as I felt, conveyed in the hardest little look she had yet addressed me, of her longing to know what, as a man of the world in general and of the French world in particular, I thought of these allied forces now so encamped on the stricken field of her life. I could only "act" however, as they said at North Verona, quite impenetrably—only make no answering sign. I couldn't intimate, much less could I frankly utter, my inward sense of the Countess's probable past, with its measure of her virtue, value and accomplishments, and of the limits of the consideration to which she could properly pretend. I couldn't give my friend a hint of how I myself personally "saw" her interesting pensioner—whether as the runaway wife of a too-jealous hair-dresser or of a too-morose pastry-cook, say; whether as a very small *bourgeoise,* in fine, who had vitiated her case beyond patching up, or even as some character, of the nomadic sort, less edifying still. I couldn't let in, by the jog of a shutter, as it were, a hard informing ray and then, washing my hands of the business, turn my back for ever. I could on the contrary save the situation, my own at least, for the moment, by pulling myself together with a master hand and appearing to ignore everything but that the dreadful person between us *was* a *"grande dame."* This effort was possible indeed but as a retreat in good order and with all the forms of courtesy. If I couldn't speak, still less could I stay, and I think I must, in spite of everything, have turned black with disgust to see Caroline Spencer stand there like a waiting-maid. I therefore won't answer for the shade of success that may have attended my saying to the Countess, on my feet and as to leave her: "You expect to remain some time in these *parages?"*

What passed between us, as from face to face, while she looked up at me, *that* at least our companion may have caught, that at least may have sown, for the after-time, some seed of revelation. The Countess repeated her terrible shrug. "Who knows? I don't see my way—! It isn't an existence, but when one's in misery—! *Chère belle,"* she added as an appeal to Miss Spencer, "you've gone and forgotten the *'fine'!"*

I detained that lady as, after considering a moment in silence the small array, she was about to turn off in quest of this article. I held out my hand in silence—I had to go. Her wan set little face, severely mild and with the question of a moment before now quite cold in it, spoke of extreme fatigue, but also of something else strange and conceived—whether a desperate patience still, or at last some other desperation, being more than I can say. What was clearest on the whole was that she was glad I was going. Mr. Mixter had risen to his feet and was pouring out the Countess's coffee. As I went back past the Baptist church I could feel how right my poor friend had been in her conviction at the other, the still intenser, the now historic crisis, that she should still see something of that dear old Europe.

SARAH ORNE JEWETT (1849-1899)

The Town Poor

Mrs. William Trimble and Miss Rebecca Wright were driving along Hampden east road, one afternoon in early spring. Their progress was slow. Mrs. Trimble's sorrel horse was old and stiff, and the wheels were clogged by clay mud. The frost was not yet out of the ground, although the snow was nearly gone, except in a few places on the north side of the woods, or where it had drifted all winter against a length of fence.

"There must be a good deal o' snow to the nor'ard of us yet," said weather-wise Mrs. Trimble. "I feel it in the air; 'tis more than the ground-damp. We ain't goin' to have real nice weather till the up-country snow's all gone."

"I heard say yesterday that there was good sleddin' yet, all up through Parsley," responded Miss Wright. "I shouldn't like to live in them northern places. My cousin Ellen's husband was a Parsley man, an' he was obliged, as you may have heard, to go up north to his father's second wife's funeral; got back day before yesterday. 'Twas about twenty-one miles, an' they started on wheels; but when they'd gone nine or ten miles, they found 'twas no sort o' use, an' left their wagon an' took a sleigh. The man that owned it charged 'em four an' six, too. I shouldn't have thought he would; they told him they was goin' to a funeral; an' they had their own buffaloes an' everything."

"Well, I expect it's a good deal harder scratchin', up that way; they have to git money where they can; the farms is very poor as you go north," suggested Mrs. Trimble kindly. "'Tain't none too rich a country where we be, but I've always been grateful I wa'n't born up to Parsley."

The old horse plodded along, and the sun, coming out from the heavy spring clouds, sent a sudden shine of light along the muddy road.

Sister Wright drew her large veil forward over the high brim of her bonnet. She was not used to driving, or to being much in the open air; but Mrs. Trimble was an active business woman, and looked after her own affairs herself, in all weathers. The late Mr. Trimble had left her a good farm, but not much ready money, and it was often said that she was better off in the end than if he had lived. She regretted his loss deeply, however; it was impossible for her to speak of him, even to intimate friends, without emotion, and nobody had ever hinted that this emotion was insincere. She was most warm-hearted and generous, and in her limited way played the part of Lady Bountiful in the town of Hampden.

"Why, there's where the Bray girls lives, ain't it?" she exclaimed, as, beyond a thicket of witch-hazel and scrub-oak, they came in sight of a weather-beaten, solitary farmhouse. The barn was too far away for thrift or comfort, and they could see long lines of light between the shrunken boards as they came nearer. The fields looked both stony and sodden. Somehow, even Parsley itself could be hardly more forlorn.

"Yes'm," said Miss Wright, "that's where they live now, poor things. I know the place, though I ain't been up here for years. You don't suppose, Mis' Trimble—I ain't seen the girls out to meetin' all winter. I've re'lly been covetin' "—

"Why, yes, Rebecca, of course we could stop," answered Mrs. Trimble heartily. "The exercises was over earlier'n I expected, an' you're goin' to remain over night long o' me, you know. There won't be no tea till we git there, so we can't be late. I'm in the habit o' sendin' a basket to the Bray girls when any o' our folks is comin' this way, but I ain't been to see 'em since they moved up here. Why, it must be a good deal over a year ago. I know 'twas in the late winter they had to make the move. 'Twas cruel hard, I must say, an' if I hadn't been down with my pleurisy fever I'd have stirred round an' done somethin' about it. There was a good deal o' sickness at the time, an'—well, 'twas kind o' rushed through, breakin' of 'em up, an' lots o' folks blamed the selec'*men;* but when 'twas done, 'twas done, an' nobody took holt to undo it. Ann an' Mandy looked same's ever when they come to meetin', 'long in the summer,—kind o' wishful, perhaps. They've always sent me word they was gittin' on pretty comfortable."

"That would be their way," said Rebecca Wright. "They never was any hand to complain, though Mandy's less cheerful than Ann. If Mandy'd been spared such poor eyesight, an' Ann hadn't got her lame wrist that wa'n't set right, they'd kep' off the town fast enough. They both shed tears when they talked to me about havin' to break up, when

I went to see 'em before I went over to brother Asa's. You see we was brought up neighbors, an' we went to school together, the Brays an' me. 'Twas a special Providence brought us home this road, I've been so covetin' a chance to git to see 'em. My lameness hampers me."

"I'm glad we come this way, myself," said Mrs. Trimble.

"I'd like to see just how they fare," Miss Rebecca Wright continued. "They give their consent to goin' on the town because they knew they'd got to be dependent, an' so they felt 'twould come easier for all than for a few to help 'em. They acted real dignified an' right-minded, contrary to what most do in such cases, but they was dreadful anxious to see who would bid 'em off, town-meeting day; they did so hope 'twould be somebody right in the village. I just sat down an' cried good when I found Abel Janes's folks had got hold of 'em. They always had the name of bein' slack an' poor-spirited, an' they did it just for what they got out o' the town. The selectmen this last year ain't what we have had. I hope they've been considerate about the Bray girls."

"I should have be'n more considerate about fetchin' of you over," apologized Mrs. Trimble. "I've got my horse, an' you're lame-footed; 'tis too far for you to come. But time does slip away with busy folks, an' I forgit a good deal I ought to remember."

"There's nobody more considerate than you be," protested Miss Rebecca Wright.

Mrs. Trimble made no answer, but took out her whip and gently touched the sorrel horse, who walked considerably faster, but did not think it worth while to trot. It was a long, round-about way to the house, farther down the road and up a lane.

"I never had any opinion of the Bray girls' father, leavin' 'em as he did," said Mrs. Trimble.

"He was much praised in his time, though there was always some said his early life hadn't been up to the mark," explained her companion. "He was a great favorite of our then preacher, the Reverend Daniel Longbrother. They did a good deal for the parish, but they did it their own way. Deacon Bray was one that did his part in the repairs without urging. You know 'twas in his time the first repairs was made, when they got out the old soundin'-board an' them handsome square pews. It cost an awful sight o' money, too. They hadn't done payin' up that debt when they set to alter it again an' git the walls frescoed. My grandmother was one that always spoke her mind right out, an' she was dreadful opposed to breakin' up the square pews where she'd always set. They was countin' up what 'twould cost in parish meetin', an' she riz right up an' said 'twouldn't cost nothin' to let 'em stay, an' there wa'n't a house carpenter left in the parish that could do such nice work, an' time would come when the great-grandchildren would give their eye-teeth to have the old meetin'-house look just as it did then. But haul the inside to pieces they would and did."

"There come to be a real fight over it, didn't there?" agreed Mrs. Trimble soothingly. "Well, 'twa'n't good taste. I remember the old house well. I come here as a child to visit a cousin o' mother's, an' Mr. Trimble's folks was neighbors, an' we was drawed to each other then, young's we was. Mr. Trimble spoke of it many's the time,—that first time he ever see me, in a leghorn hat with a feather; 'twas one that mother had, an' pressed over."

"When I think of them old sermons that used to be preached in that old meetin'-house of all, I'm glad it's altered over, so's not to remind folks," said Miss Rebecca Wright, after a suitable pause. "Them old brimstone discourses, you know, Mis' Trimble. Preachers is far more reasonable, nowadays. Why, I set an' thought, last Sabbath, as I listened, that if old Mr. Longbrother an' Deacon Bray could hear the difference they'd crack the ground over 'em like pole beans, an' come right up 'long side their headstones."

Mrs. Trimble laughed heartily, and shook the reins three or four times by way of emphasis. "There's no gitting round you," she said, much pleased. "I should think Deacon Bray would want to rise, any way, if 'twas so he could, an' knew how his poor girls was farin'. A man ought to provide for his folks he's got to leave behind him, specially if they're women. To be sure, they had their little home; but we've seen how, with all their industrious ways, they hadn't means to keep it. I s'pose he thought he'd got time enough to lay by, when he give so generous in collections; but he didn't lay by, an' there they be. He might have took lessons from the squirrels: even them little wild creatur's makes them their winter hoards, an' men-folks ought to know enough if squirrels does. 'Be just before you are generous:' that's what was always set for the B's in the copybooks, when I was to school, and it often runs through my mind."

"'As for man, his days are as grass,'—that was for A; the two go well together," added Miss Rebecca Wright soberly. "My good gracious, ain't this a starved-lookin' place? It makes me ache to think them nice Bray girls has to brook it here."

The sorrel horse, though somewhat puzzled by an unexpected deviation from his homeward way, willingly came to a stand by the gnawed corner of the door-yard fence, which evidently served as hitching-place. Two or three ragged old hens were picking about the yard, and at last a face appeared at the kitchen window, tied up in a handkerchief, as if it were a case of toothache. By the time our friends reached the side door next this window, Mrs. Janes came disconsolately to open it for them, shutting it again as soon as possible, though the air felt more chilly inside the house.

"Take seats," said Mrs. Janes briefly. "You'll have to see me just as I be. I have been suffering these four days with the ague, and everything to do. Mr. Janes is to court, on the jury. 'Twas inconvenient to spare him. I should be pleased to have you lay off your things."

Comfortable Mrs. Trimble looked about the cheerless kitchen, and could not think of anything to say; so she smiled blandly and shook her head in answer to the invitation. "We'll just set a few minutes with you, to pass the time o' day, an' then we must go in an' have a word with the Miss Brays, bein' old acquaintance. It ain't been so we could git to call on 'em before. I don't know's you're acquainted with Miss R'becca Wright. She's been out of town a good deal."

"I heard she was stopping over to Plainfields with her brother's folks," replied Mrs. Janes, rocking herself with irregular motion, as she sat close to the stove. "Got back some time in the fall, I believe?"

"Yes'm," said Miss Rebecca, with an undue sense of guilt and conviction. "We've been to the installation over to the East Parish an' thought we'd stop in; we took this road home to see if 'twas any better. How is the Miss Brays gettin' on?"

"They're well's common," answered Mrs. Janes grudgingly. "I was put out with Mr. Janes for fetchin' of 'em here, with all I've got to do, an' I own I was kind o' surly to 'em 'long to the first of it. He gits the money from the town, an' it helps him out; but he bid 'em off for five dollars a month, an' we can't do much for 'em at no such price as that. I went an' dealt with the selec'men, an' made 'em promise to find their firewood an' some other things extra. They was glad to get rid o' the matter the fourth time I went, an' would ha' promised 'most anything. But Mr. Janes don't keep me half the time in oven-wood, he's off so much, an' we was cramped o' room, anyway. I have to store things up garrit a good deal, an' that keeps me trampin' right through their room. I do the best for 'em I can, Mis' Trimble, but 'tain't so easy for me as 'tis for you, with all your means to do with."

The poor woman looked pinched and miserable herself, though it was evident that she had no gift at house or home keeping. Mrs. Trimble's heart was wrung with pain, as she thought of the unwelcome inmates of such a place; but she held her peace bravely, while Miss Rebecca again gave some brief information in regard to the installation.

"You go right up them back stairs," the hostess directed at last. "I'm glad some o' you church folks has seen fit to come an' visit 'em. There ain't been nobody here this long spell, an' they've aged a sight since they come. They always send down a taste out of your baskets, Mis' Trimble, an' I relish it, I tell you. I'll shut the door after you, if you don't object. I feel every draught o' cold air."

"I've always heard she was a great hand to make a poor mouth. Wa'n't she from somewheres up Parsley way?" whispered Miss Rebecca, as they stumbled in the half-light.

"Poor meechin' body, wherever she come from," replied Mrs. Trimble, as she knocked at the door.

There was silence for a moment after this unusual sound; then one of the Bray sisters opened the door. The eager guests stared into a small, low room, brown with age, and gray, too, as if former dust and cobwebs could not be made wholly to disappear. The two elderly women who stood there looked like captives. Their withered faces wore a look of apprehension, and the room itself was more bare and plain than was fitting to their evident refinement of character and self-respect. There was an uncovered small table in the middle of the floor, with some crackers on a plate; and, for some reason or other, this added a great deal to the general desolation.

But Miss Ann Bray, the elder sister, who carried her right arm in a sling, with piteously drooping fingers, gazed at the visitors with radiant joy. She had not seen them arrive.

The one window gave only the view at the back of the house, across the fields, and their coming was indeed a surprise. The next minute she was laughing and crying together. "Oh, sister!" she said, "if here ain't our dear Mis' Trimble!—an' my heart o' goodness, 'tis 'Becca Wright, too! What dear good creatur's you be! I've felt all day as if something good was goin' to happen, an' was just sayin' to myself 'twas most sundown now, but I wouldn't let on to Mandany I'd give up hope quite yet. You see, the scissors stuck in the floor this very mornin' an' it's always a reliable sign. There, I've got to kiss ye both again!"

"I don't know where we can all set," lamented sister Mandana. "There ain't but the one chair an' the bed; t'other chair's too rickety; an' we've been promised another these ten days; but first they've forgot it, an' next Mis' Janes can't spare it,—one excuse an' another. I am goin' to git a stump o' wood an' nail a board on to it, when I can git outdoor again," said Mandana, in a plaintive voice. "There, I ain't goin' to complain o' nothin', now you've come," she added; and the guests sat down, Mrs. Trimble, as was proper, in the one chair.

"We've sat on the bed many's the time with you, 'Becca, an' talked over our girl nonsense, ain't we? You know where 'twas—in the little back bedroom we had when we was girls, an' used to peek out at our beaux through the strings o' mornin'-glories," laughed Ann Bray delightedly, her thin face shining more and more with joy. "I brought some o' them mornin'-glory seeds along when we come away, we'd raised 'em so many years; an' we got 'em started all right, but the hens found 'em out. I declare I chased them poor hens, foolish as 'twas; but the mornin'-glories I'd counted on a sight to remind me o' home. You see, our debts was so large, after my long sickness an' all, that we didn't feel 'twas right to keep back anything we could help from the auction."

It was impossible for any one to speak for a moment or two; the sisters felt their own uprooted condition afresh, and their guests for the first time really comprehended the piteous contrast between that neat little village house, which now seemed a palace of comfort, and this cold, unpainted upper room in the remote Janes farmhouse. It was an unwelcome thought to Mrs. Trimble that the well-to-do town of Hampden could provide no better for its poor than this, and her round face flushed with resentment and the shame of personal responsibility. "The girls shall be well settled in the village before another winter, if I pay their board myself," she made an inward resolution, and took another almost tearful look at the broken stove, the miserable bed, and the sisters' one hair-covered trunk, on which Mandana was sitting. But the poor place was filled with a golden spirit of hospitality.

Rebecca was again discoursing eloquently of the installation; it was so much easier to speak of general subjects, and the sisters had evidently been longing to hear some news. Since the late summer they had not been to church, and presently Mrs. Trimble asked the reason.

"Now, don't you go to pouring out our woes, Mandy!" begged little old Ann, looking shy and almost girlish, and as if she insisted upon playing that life was still all before them and all pleasure. "Don't you go to spoilin' their visit with our complaints! They know well's we do that changes must come, and we'd been so wonted to our home things that this come hard at first; but then they felt for us, I know just as well's can be. 'Twill soon be summer again, an' 'tis real pleasant right out in the fields here, when there ain't too hot a spell. I've got to know a sight o' singin' birds since we come."

"Give me the folks I've always known," sighed the younger sister, who looked older than Miss Ann, and less even-tempered. "You may have your birds, if you want 'em. I do re'lly long to go to meetin' an' see folks go by up the aisle. Now, I will speak of it, Ann, whatever you say. We need, each of us, a pair o' good stout shoes an' rubbers,—ours are all wore out; an' we've asked an' asked, an' they never think to bring 'em, an' "—

Poor old Mandana, on the trunk, covered her face with her arms and sobbed aloud. The elder sister stood over her, and patted her on the thin shoulder like a child, and tried to comfort her. It crossed Mrs. Trimble's mind that it was not the first time one had wept and the other had comforted. The sad scene must have been repeated many times in that long, drear winter. She would see them forever after in her mind as fixed as a picture, and her own tears fell fast.

"You didn't see Mis' Janes's cunning little boy, the next one to the baby, did you?" asked Ann Bray, turning round quickly at last, and going cheerfully on with the conversation. "Now, hush, Mandy, dear; they'll think you're childish! He's a dear, friendly little creatur', an' likes to stay with us a good deal, though we feel's if 'twas too cold for him, now we are waitin' to get us more wood."

"When I think of the acres o' woodland in this town!" groaned Rebecca Wright, "I believe I'm goin' to preach next Sunday, 'stead o' the minister, an' I'll make the sparks fly. I've always heard the saying, 'What's everybody's business is nobody's business,' an' I've come to believe it."

"Now, don't you, 'Becca. You've happened on a kind of a poor time with us, but we've got more belongings than you see here, an' a good large cluset, where we can store those things there ain't room to have about. You an' Miss Trimble have happened on a kind of poor day, you know. Soon's I git me some stout shoes an' rubbers, as Mandy says, I can fetch home plenty o' little dry boughs o' pine; you remember I was always a great hand to roam in the woods? If we could only have a front room, so 't we could look out on the road an' see passin', an' was shod for meetin', I don' know's we should complain. Now we're just goin' to give you what we've got, an' make out with a good welcome. We make more tea 'n we want in the mornin', an' then let the fire go down, since 't has been so mild. We've got a *good* cluset" (disappearing as she spoke), "an' I know this to be good tea, 'cause it's some o' yourn, Mis' Trimble. An' here's our sprigged chiny cups that R'becca knows by sight, if Mis' Trimble don't. We kep' out four of 'em, an' put the even half dozen with the rest of the auction stuff. I've often wondered who'd got 'em, but I never asked, for fear 'twould be somebody that would distress us. They was mother's, you know."

The four cups were poured, and the little table pushed to the bed, where Rebecca Wright still sat, and Mandana, wiping her eyes, came and joined her. Mrs. Trimble sat in her chair at the end, and Ann trotted about the room in pleased content for a while, and in and out of the closet, as if she still had much to do; then she came and stood opposite Mrs. Trimble. She was very short and small, and there was no painful sense of her being obliged to stand. The four cups were not quite full of cold tea, but there was a clean old tablecloth folded double, and a plate with three pairs of crackers neatly piled, and a small—it must be owned, a very small—piece of hard white cheese. Then, for a treat, in a glass dish, there was a little preserved peach, the last—Miss Rebecca knew it instinctively—of the household stores brought from their old home. It was very sugary, this bit of peach; and as she helped her guests and sister Mandy, Miss Ann Bray said, half unconsciously, as she often had said with less reason in the old days, "Our preserves ain't so good as usual this year; this is beginning to candy." Both the guests protested, while Rebecca added that the taste of it carried her back, and made her feel young again. The Brays had always managed to keep one or two peach-trees alive in their corner of a garden. "I've been keeping this preserve for a treat," said her friend. "I'm glad to have you eat some, 'Becca. Last summer I often wished you was home and could come an' see us, 'stead o' being away off to Plainfields."

The crackers did not taste too dry. Miss Ann took the last of the peach on her own cracker; there could not have been quite a small spoonful, after the others were helped, but she asked them first if they would not have some more. Then there was a silence, and in the silence a wave of tender feeling rose high in the hearts of the four elderly women. At this moment the setting sun flooded the poor plain room with light; the unpainted wood was all of a golden-brown, and Ann Bray, with her gray hair and aged face, stood at the head of the table in a kind of aureole. Mrs. Trimble's face was all a-quiver as she looked at her; she thought of the text about two or three being gathered together, and was half afraid.

"I believe we ought to 've asked Mis' Janes if she wouldn't come up," said Ann. "She's real good feelin', but she's had it very hard, an' gits discouraged. I can't find that she's ever had anything real pleasant to look back to, as we have. There, next time we'll make a good heartenin' time for her too."

The sorrel horse had taken a long nap by the gnawed fence-rail, and the cool air after sundown made him impatient to be gone. The two friends jolted homeward in the gathering darkness, through the stiffening mud, and neither Mrs. Trimble nor Rebecca Wright said a word until they were out of sight as well as out of sound of the Janes house. Time must elapse before they could reach a more familiar part of the road and resume conversation on its natural level.

"I consider myself to blame," insisted Mrs. Trimble at last. "I haven't no words of accusation for nobody else, an' I ain't one to take comfort in calling names to the board o' selec'*men*. I make no reproaches, an' I take it all on my own shoulders; but I'm goin' to stir about me, I tell you! I shall begin early to-morrow. They're goin' back to their own house,—it's been standin' empty all winter,—an' the town's goin' to give 'em the rent an' what firewood they need; it won't come to more than the board's payin' out now. An' you an' me'll take this same horse an' wagon, an' ride an' go afoot by turns, an' git means enough together to buy back their furniture an' whatever was sold at that plaguey auction; an' then we'll put it all back, an' tell 'em they've got to move to a new place, an' just carry 'em right back again where they come from. An' don't you never tell, R'becca, but here I be a widow woman, layin' up what I make from my farm for nobody knows who, an' I'm goin' to do for them Bray girls all I'm a mind to. I should be sca't to wake up in heaven, an' hear anybody there ask how the Bray girls was. Don't talk to me about the town o' Hampden, an' don't ever let me hear the name o' town poor! I'm ashamed to go home an' see what's set out for supper. I wish I'd brought 'em right along."

"I was goin' to ask if we couldn't git the new doctor to go up an' do somethin' for poor Ann's arm," said Miss Rebecca. "They say he's very smart. If she could get so's to braid straw or hook rugs again, she'd soon be earnin' a little somethin'. An' maybe he could do somethin' for Mandy's eyes. They did use to live so neat an' ladylike. Somehow I couldn't speak to tell 'em there that 'twas I bought them six best cups an' saucers, time of the auction; they went very low, as everything else did, an' I thought I could save it some other way. They shall have 'em back an' welcome. You're real whole-hearted, Mis' Trimble. I expect Ann'll be sayin' that her father's child'n wa'n't goin' to be left desolate, an' that all the bread he cast on the water's comin' back through you."

"I don't care what she says, dear creatur'!" exclaimed Mrs. Trimble. "I'm full o' regrets I took time for that installation, an' set there seepin' in a lot o' talk this whole day long, except for its kind of bringin' us to the Bray girls. I wish to my heart 'twas to-morrow mornin' a'ready, an' I a-startin' for the selec'*men.*"

A Winter Courtship

The passenger and mail transportation between the towns of North Kilby and Sanscrit Pond was carried on by Mr. Jefferson Briley, whose two-seated covered wagon was usually much too large for the demands of business. Both the Sanscrit Pond and North Kilby people were stayers-at-home, and Mr. Briley often made his seven-mile journey in entire solitude, except for the limp leather mail-bag, which he held firmly to the floor of the carriage with his heavily shod left foot. The mail-bag had almost a personality to him, born of long association. Mr. Briley was a meek and timid-looking body, but he held a warlike soul, and encouraged his fancies by reading awful tales of bloodshed and lawlessness in the far West. Mindful of stage robberies and train thieves, and of express messengers who died at their posts, he was prepared for anything; and although he had trusted to his own strength and bravery these many years, he carried a heavy pistol under his front-seat cushion for better defence. This awful weapon was familiar to all his regular passengers, and was usually shown to strangers by the time two of the seven miles of Mr. Briley's route had been passed. The pistol was not loaded. Nobody (at least not Mr. Briley himself) doubted that the mere sight of such a weapon would turn the boldest adventurer aside.

Protected by such a man and such a piece of armament, one gray Friday morning in the edge of winter, Mrs. Fanny Tobin was travelling from Sanscrit Pond to North Kilby. She was an elderly and feeble-looking woman, but with a shrewd twinkle in her eyes, and she felt very anxious about her numerous pieces of baggage and her own personal safety. She was enveloped in many shawls and smaller wrappings, but they were not securely fastened, and kept getting undone and flying loose, so that the bitter December cold seemed to be picking a lock now and then, and creeping in to steal away the little warmth she had. Mr. Briley was cold, too, and could only cheer himself by remembering the valor of those pony-express drivers of the pre-railroad days, who had to cross the Rocky Mountains on the great California route. He spoke at length of their perils to the suffering passenger, who felt none the warmer, and at last gave a groan of weariness.

"How fur did you say 'twas now?"

"I do' know's I said, Mis' Tobin," answered the driver, with a frosty laugh. "You see them big pines, and the side of a barn just this way, with them yellow circus bills? That's my three-mile mark."

"Be we got four more to make? Oh, my laws!" mourned Mrs. Tobin. "Urge the beast, can't ye, Jeff'son? I ain't used to bein' out in such bleak weather. Seems if I couldn't git my breath. I'm all pinched up and wigglin' with shivers now. 'Tain't no use lettin' the hoss go step-a-ty-step, this fashion."

"Landy me!" exclaimed the affronted driver. "I don't see why folks expects me to race with the cars. Everybody that gits in wants me to run the hoss to death on the road. I make a good average o' time, and that's all I *can* do. Ef you was to go back an' forth every day but Sabbath fur eighteen years, *you*'d want to ease it all you could, and let those thrash the spokes out o' their wheels that wanted to. North Kilby, Mondays, Wednesdays, and Fridays; Sanscrit Pond, Tuesdays, Thu's-days, an' Saturdays. Me an' the beast's done it eighteen years together, and the creatur' warn't, so to say, young when we begun it, nor I neither. I re'lly didn't know's she'd hold out till this time. There, git up, will ye, old mar'!" as the beast of burden stopped short in the road.

There was a story that Jefferson gave this faithful creature a rest three times a mile, and took four hours for the journey by himself, and longer whenever he had a passenger. But in pleasant weather the road was delightful, and full of people who drove their own conveyances, and liked to stop and talk. There were not many farms, and the third growth of white pines made a pleasant shade, though Jefferson liked to say that when he began to carry the mail his way lay through an open country of stumps and sparse underbrush, where the white pines nowadays completely arched the road.

They had passed the barn with circus posters, and felt colder than ever when they caught sight of the weather-beaten acrobats in their tights.

"My gorry!" exclaimed Widow Tobin, "them pore creatur's looks as cheerless as little birch-trees in snow-time. I hope they dresses 'em warmer this time o' year. Now, there! look at that one jumpin' through the little hoop, will ye?"

"He couldn't git himself through there with two pair o' pants on," answered Mr. Briley. "I expect they must have to keep limber as eels. I used to think, when I was a boy, that 'twas the only thing I could ever be reconciled to do for a livin'. I set out to run away an' follow a rovin' showman once, but mother needed me to home. There warn't nobody but me an' the little gals."

"You ain't the only one that's be'n disapp'inted o' their heart's desire," said Mrs. Tobin sadly. "'Twarn't so that I could be spared from home to learn the dressmaker's trade."

"'Twould 'a' come handy later on, I declare," answered the sympathetic driver, "bein' 's you went an' had such a passel o' gals to clothe an' feed. There, them that's livin' is all well off now, but it must ha' been some inconvenient for ye when they was small."

"Yes, Mr. Briley, but then I've had my mercies, too," said the widow somewhat grudgingly. "I take it master hard now, though, havin' to give up my own home and live round from place to place, if they be my own child'en. There was Ad'line and Susan Ellen fussin' an' bickerin' yesterday about who'd got to have me next; and, Lord be thanked, they both wanted me right off, but I hated to hear 'em talkin' of it over. I'd rather live to home, and do for myself."

"I've got consider'ble used to boardin'," said Jefferson, "sence ma'am died, but it made me ache 'long at the fust on 't, I tell ye. Bein' on the road's I be, I couldn't do no ways at keepin' house. I should want to keep right there and see to things."

"Course you would," replied Mrs. Tobin, with a sudden inspiration of opportunity which sent a welcome glow all over her. "Course you would, Jeff'son,"—she leaned toward the front seat; "that is to say, onless you had jest the right one to do it for ye."

And Jefferson felt a strange glow also, and a sense of unexpected interest and enjoyment.

"See here, Sister Tobin," he exclaimed with enthusiasm. "Why can't ye take the trouble to shift seats, and come front here 'long o' me? We could put one buff'lo top o' the other,—they're both wearin' thin,—and set close, and I do' know but we sh'd be more protected ag'inst the weather."

"Well, I couldn't be no colder if I was froze to death," answered the widow, with an amiable simper. "Don't ye let me delay you, nor put you out, Mr. Briley. I don't know's I'd set forth to-day if I'd known 'twas so cold; but I had all my bundles done up, and I ain't one that puts my hand to the plough an' looks back, 'cordin' to Scriptur'."

"You wouldn't wanted me to ride all them seven miles alone?" asked the gallant Briley sentimentally, as he lifted her down, and helped her up again to the front seat. She was a few years older than he, but they had been schoolmates, and Mrs. Tobin's youthful freshness was suddenly revived to his mind's eye. She had a little farm; there was nobody left at home now but herself, and so she had broken up housekeeping for the winter. Jefferson himself had savings of no mean amount.

They tucked themselves in, and felt better for the change, but there was a sudden awkwardness between them; they had not had time to prepare for an unexpected crisis.

"They say Elder Bickers, over to East Sanscrit, 's been and got married again to a gal that's four year younger than his oldest daughter," proclaimed Mrs. Tobin presently. "Seems to me 'twas fool's business."

"I view it so," said the stage-driver. "There's goin' to be a mild open winter for that fam'ly."

"What a joker you be for a man that's had so much responsibility!" smiled Mrs. Tobin, after they had done laughing. "Ain't you never 'fraid, carryin' mail matter and such valuable stuff, that you'll be set on an' robbed, 'specially by night?"

Jefferson braced his feet against the dasher under the worn buffalo skin. "It is kind o' scary, or would be for some folks, but I'd like to see anybody get the better o' me. I go armed, and I don't care who knows it. Some o' them drover men that comes from Canady looks as if they didn't care what they did, but I look 'em right in the eye every time."

"Men folks is brave by natur'," said the widow admiringly. "You know how Tobin would let his fist right out at anybody that ondertook to sass him. Town-meetin' days, if he got disappointed about the way things went, he'd lay 'em out in win'-rows; and ef he hadn't been a church-member he'd been a real fightin' character. I was always 'fraid to have him roused, for all he was so willin' and meechin' to home, and set round clever as anybody. My Susan Ellen used to boss him same's the kitten, when she was four year old."

"I've got a kind of a sideways cant to my nose, that Tobin give me when we was to school. I don't know's you ever noticed it," said Mr. Briley. "We was scufflin', as lads will. I never bore him no kind of a grudge. I pitied ye, when he was taken away. I re'lly did, now, Fanny. I liked Tobin first-rate, and I liked you. I used to say you was the han'somest girl to school."

"Lemme see your nose. 'Tis all straight, for what I know," said the widow gently, as with a trace of coyness she gave a hasty glance. "I don't know but what 'tis warped a little, but nothin' to speak of. You've got real nice features, like your marm's folks."

It was becoming a sentimental occasion, and Jefferson Briley felt that he was in for something more than he had bargained. He hurried the faltering sorrel horse, and began to talk of the weather. It certainly did look like snow, and he was tired of bumping over the frozen road.

"I shouldn't wonder if I hired a hand here another year, and went off out West myself to see the country."

"Why, how you talk!" answered the widow.

"Yes'm," pursued Jefferson. "'Tis tamer here than I like, and I was tellin' 'em yesterday I've got to know this road most too well. I'd like to go out an' ride in the mountains with some o' them great clipper coaches, where the driver don't know one minute but he'll be shot dead the next. They carry an awful sight o' gold down from the mines, I expect."

"I should be scairt to death," said Mrs. Tobin. "What creatur's men folks be to like such things! Well, I do declare."

"Yes," explained the mild little man. "There's sights of desp'radoes makes a han'some livin' out o' followin' them coaches, an' stoppin' an' robbin' 'em clean to the bone. Your money *or* your life!" and he flourished his stub of a whip over the sorrel mare.

"Landy me! you make me run all of a cold creep. Do tell somethin' heartenin', this cold day. I shall dream bad dreams all night."

"They put on black crape over their heads," said the driver mysteriously. "Nobody knows who most on 'em be, and like as not some o' them fellows come o' good families. They've got so they stop the cars, and go right through 'em bold as brass. I could make your hair stand on end, Mis' Tobin,—I could *so!*"

"I hope none on 'em 'll git round our way, I'm sure," said Fanny Tobin. "I don't want to see none on 'em in their crape bunnits comin' after me."

"I ain't goin' to let nobody touch a hair o' your head," and Mr. Briley moved a little nearer, and tucked in the buffaloes again.

"I feel considerable warm to what I did," observed the widow by way of reward.

"There, I used to have my fears," Mr. Briley resumed, with an inward feeling that he never would get to North Kilby depot a single man. "But you see I hadn't nobody but myself to think of. I've got cousins, as you know, but nothin' nearer, and what I've laid up would soon be parted out; and—well, I suppose some folks would think o' me if anything was to happen."

Mrs. Tobin was holding her cloud over her face,—the wind was sharp on that bit of open road,—but she gave an encouraging sound, between a groan and a chirp.

"'Twouldn't be like nothin' to me not to see you drivin' by," she said, after a minute. "I shouldn't know the days o' the week. I says to Susan Ellen last week I was sure 'twas Friday, and she said no, 'twas Thursday; but next minute you druv by and headin' toward North Kilby, so we found I was right."

"I've got to be a featur' of the landscape," said Mr. Briley plaintively. "This kind o' weather the old mare and me, we wish we was done with it, and could settle down kind o' comfortable. I've been lookin' this good while, as I drove the road, and I've picked me out a piece o' land two or three times. But I can't abide the thought o' buildin',—'t would plague me to death; and both Sister Peak to North Kilby and Mis' Deacon Ash to the Pond, they vie with one another to do well by me, fear I'll like the other stoppin'-place best."

"*I* shouldn't covet livin' 'long o' neither one o' them women," responded the passenger with some spirit. "I see some o' Mis' Peak's cookin' to a farmers' supper once, when I was visitin' Susan Ellen's folks, an' I says 'Deliver me from sech pale-complected baked beans as them!' and she give a kind of a quack. She was settin' jest at my left hand, and couldn't help hearin' of me. I wouldn't have spoken if I had known, but she needn't have let on they was hers an' make everything unpleasant. 'I guess them beans taste just as well as other folks',' says she, and she wouldn't never speak to me afterward."

"Do' know's I blame her," ventured Mr. Briley. "Women folks is dreadful pudjicky about their cookin'. I've always heard you was one o' the best o' cooks, Mis' Tobin. I know them doughnuts an' things you've give me in times past, when I was drivin' by. Wish I had some on 'em now. I never let on, but Mis' Ash's cookin's the best by a long chalk. Mis' Peak's handy about some things, and looks after mendin' of me up."

"It doos seem as if a man o' your years and your quiet make ought to have a home you could call your own," suggested the passenger. "I kind of hate to think o' your bangin' here and boardin' there, and one old woman mendin', and the other settin' ye down to meals that like 's not don't agree with ye."

"Lor', now, Mis' Tobin, le's not fuss round no longer," said Mr. Briley impatiently. "You know you covet me same's I do you."

"I don't nuther. Don't you go an' say fo'lish things you can't stand to."

"I've been tryin' to git a chance to put in a word with you ever sence— Well, I expected you'd want to get your feelin's kind o' calloused after losin' Tobin."

"There's nobody can fill his place," said the widow.

"I do' know but I can fight for ye town-meetin' days, on a pinch," urged Jefferson boldly.

"I never see the beat o' you men fur conceit," and Mrs. Tobin laughed. "I ain't goin' to bother with ye, gone half the time as you be, an' carryin' on with your Mis' Peaks and Mis' Ashes. I dare say you've promised yourself to both on 'em twenty times."

"I hope to gracious if I ever breathed a word to none on 'em!" protested the lover. "'Tain't for lack o' opportunities set afore me, nuther;" and then Mr. Briley craftily kept silence, as if he had made a fair proposal, and expected a definite reply.

The lady of his choice was, as she might have expressed it, much beat about. As she soberly thought, she was getting along in years, and must put up with Jefferson all the rest of the time. It was not likely she would ever have the chance of choosing again, though she was one who liked variety.

Jefferson wasn't much to look at, but he was pleasant and appeared boyish and young-feeling. "I do' know's I should do better," she said unconsciously and half aloud. "Well, yes, Jefferson, seein' it's you. But we're both on us kind of old to change our situation." Fanny Tobin gave a gentle sigh.

"Hooray!" said Jefferson. "I was scairt you meant to keep me sufferin' here a half an hour. I declare, I'm more pleased than I calc'lated on. An' I expected till lately to die a single man!"

"'Twould re'lly have been a shame; 'tain't natur'," said Mrs. Tobin, with confidence. "I don't see how you held out so long with bein' solitary."

"I'll hire a hand to drive for me, and we'll have a good comfortable winter, me an' you an' the old sorrel. I've been promisin' of her a rest this good while."

"Better keep her a steppin'," urged thrifty Mrs. Fanny. "She'll stiffen up faster, an' disapp'int ye, come spring."

"You'll have me, now, won't ye, sartin?" pleaded Jefferson, to make sure. "You ain't one o' them that plays with a man's feelin's. Say right out you'll have me."

"I s'pose I shall have to," said Mrs. Tobin somewhat mournfully. "I feel for Mis' Peak an' Mis' Ash, pore creatur's. I expect they'll be hardshipped. They've always been hard-worked, an' may have kind o' looked forward to a little ease. But one on 'em would be left lamentin', anyhow," and she gave a girlish laugh. An air of victory animated the frame of Mrs. Tobin. She felt but twenty-five years of age. In that moment she made plans for cutting her Briley's hair, and making him look smartened-up and ambitious. Then she wished that she knew for certain how much money he had in the bank; not that it would make any difference now. "He needn't bluster none before me," she thought gaily. "He's harmless as a fly."

"Who'd have thought we'd done such a piece of engineerin', when we started out?" inquired the dear one of Mr. Briley's heart, as he tenderly helped her to alight at Susan Ellen's door.

"Both on us, jest the least grain," answered the lover. "Gimme a good smack, now, you clever creatur';" and so they parted. Mr. Briley had been taken on the road in spite of his pistol.

HENRY CUYLER BUNNER (1855-1896)

The Love-Letters of Smith

WHEN the little seamstress had climbed to her room in the story over the top-story of the great brick tenement house in which she lived, she was quite tired out. If you do not understand what a story over a top-story is, you must remember that there are no limits to human greed, and hardly any to the height of tenement houses. When the man who owned that seven-story tenement found that he could rent another floor, he found no difficulty in persuading the guardians of our building laws to let him clap another story on the roof, like a cabin on the deck of a ship; and in the southeasterly of the four apartments on this floor the little seamstress lived. You could just see the top of her window from the street—the huge cornice that had capped the original front, and that served as her window-sill now, quite hid all the lower part of the story on top of the top-story.

The little seamstress was scarcely thirty years old, but she was such an old-fashioned little body in so many of her looks and ways that I had almost spelled her sempstress, after the fashion of our grandmothers. She had been a comely body, too; and would have been still, if she had not been thin and pale and anxious-eyed.

She was tired out to-night because she had been working hard all day for a lady who lived far up in the "New Wards" beyond Harlem River, and after the long journey home, she had to climb seven flights of tenement-house stairs. She was too tired, both in body and in mind, to cook the two little chops she had brought home. She would save them for breakfast, she thought. So she made herself a cup of tea on the miniature stove, and ate a slice of dry bread with it. It was too much trouble to make toast.

But after dinner she watered her flowers. She was never too tired for that; and the six pots of geraniums that caught the south sun on the top of the cornice did their best to repay her. Then she sat down in her rocking chair by the window and looked out. Her eyry was high above all the other buildings, and she could look across some low roofs opposite, and see the further end of Tompkins square, with its sparse Spring green showing faintly through the dusk. The eternal roar of the city floated up to her and vaguely troubled her. She was a country girl, and although she had lived for ten years in New York, she had never grown used to that ceaseless murmur. To-night she felt the languor of the new season as well as the heaviness of physical exhaustion. She was almost too tired to go to bed.

She thought of the hard day done and the hard day to be begun after the night spent on the hard little bed. She thought of the peaceful days in the country, when she taught school in the Massachusetts village where she was born. She thought of a hundred small slights that she had to bear from people better fed than bred. She thought of the sweet green fields that she rarely saw nowadays. She thought of the long journey forth and back that must begin and end her to-morrow's work, and she wondered if her employer would think to offer to pay her fare. Then she pulled herself together. She must think of more agreeable things, or she could not sleep. And as the only agreeable things she had to think about were her flowers, she looked at the garden on top of the cornice.

A peculiar gritting noise made her look down, and she saw a cylindrical object that glittered in the twilight, advancing in an irregular and uncertain manner toward her flower-pots. Looking closer, she saw that it was a pewter beer-mug, which somebody in the next apartment was pushing with a two-foot rule. On top of the beer-mug was a piece of paper, and on this paper was written, in a sprawling, half-formed hand:

porter
pleas excuse the libberty And
drink it

The seamstress started up in terror, and shut the window. She remembered that there was a man in the next apartment. She had seen him on the stairs, on Sundays. He seemed a grave, decent person; but—he must be drunk. She sat down on her bed, all a-tremble. Then she reasoned with herself. The man was drunk, that was all. He probably would not annoy her further. And if he did, she had only to retreat to Mrs. Mulvaney's apartment in the rear, and Mr. Mulvaney, who was a highly respectable man and worked in a boiler-shop, would protect her. So, being a poor woman who had already had occasion to excuse—and refuse—two or three "libberties" of like sort, she made up her mind to go to bed like a reasonable seamstress, and she did. She was rewarded, for when her light was out, she could see in the moonlight that the two-foot rule appeared again, with one joint bent back, hitched itself into the mug-handle, and withdrew the mug.

The next day was a hard one for the little seamstress, and she hardly thought of the affair of the night before until the same hour had come around again, and she sat once more by her window. Then she smiled at the remembrance. "Poor fellow," she said in her charitable heart, "I've no doubt he's *awfully* ashamed of it now. Perhaps he was never tipsy before. Perhaps he didn't know there was a lone woman in here to be frightened."

Just then she heard a gritting sound. She looked down. The pewter pot was in front of her, and the two-foot rule was slowly retiring. On the pot was a piece of paper, and on the paper was:

porter
good for the helth
it makes meet

This time the little seamstress shut her window with a bang of indignation. The color rose to her pale cheeks. She thought that she would go down to see the janitor at once. Then she remembered the seven flights of stairs; and she resolved to see the janitor in the morning. Then she went to bed and saw the mug drawn back just as it had been drawn back the night before.

The morning came, but, somehow, the seamstress did not care to complain to the janitor. She hated to make trouble—and the janitor might think—and—and—well, if the wretch did it again she would speak to him herself, and that would settle it.

And so, on the next night, which was a Thursday, the little seamstress sat down by her window, resolved to settle the matter. And she had not sat there long, rocking in the creaking little rocking-chair which she had brought with her from her old home, when the pewter pot hove in sight, with a piece of paper on the top.

This time the legend read:

Perhaps you are afrade i will
adress you
i am not that kind

The seamstress did not quite know whether to laugh or to cry. But she felt that the time had come for speech. She leaned out of her window and addressed the twilight heaven.

"Mr.—Mr.—sir—I—will you *please* put your head out of the window so that I can speak to you?"

The silence of the other room was undisturbed. The seamstress drew back, blushing. But before she could nerve herself for another attack, a piece of paper appeared on the end of the two-foot rule.

when i Say a thing i
mene it
i have Sed i would not
Adress you and i
Will not

What was the little seamstress to do? She stood by the window and thought hard about it. Should she complain to the janitor? But the creature was perfectly respectful. No doubt he meant to be kind. He certainly was kind, to waste these pots of porter on her. She remembered the last time—and the first—that she had drunk porter. It was at home, when she was a young girl, after she had had the diphtheria. She remembered how good it was, and how it had given her back her strength. And without one thought of what she was doing, she lifted the pot of porter and took one little reminiscent sip—two little reminiscent sips—and became aware of her utter fall and defeat. She blushed now as she had never blushed before, put the pot down, closed the window, and fled to her bed like a deer to the woods.

And when the porter arrived the next night, bearing the simple appeal:

Dont be afrade of it
drink it all

the little seamstress arose and grasped the pot firmly by the handle, and poured its contents over the earth around her largest geranium. She poured the contents out to the last drop, and then she dropped the pot, and ran back and sat on her bed and cried, with her face hid in her hands.

"Now," she said to herself, "you've done it! And you're just as nasty and hard-hearted and suspicious and mean as—as pusley!"

And she wept to think of her hardness of heart. "He will never give me a chance to say I am sorry," she thought. And, really, she might have spoken kindly to the poor man, and told him that she was much obliged to him, but that he really mustn't ask her to drink porter with him.

"But it's all over and done now," she said to herself as she sat at her window on Saturday night. And then she looked at the cornice, and saw the faithful little pewter pot travelling slowly toward her.

She was conquered. This act of Christian forbearance was too much for her kindly spirit. She read the inscription on the paper:

porter is good for Flours
but better for Fokes

and she lifted the pot to her lips, which were not half so red as her cheeks, and took a good, hearty, grateful draught.

She sipped in thoughtful silence after this first plunge, and presently she was surprised to find the bottom of the pot in full view.

On the table at her side a few pearl buttons were screwed up in a bit of white paper. She untwisted the paper and smoothed it out, and wrote in a tremulous hand—she *could* write a very neat hand—

Thanks.

This she laid on the top of the pot, and in a moment the bent two-foot rule appeared and drew the mail-carriage home. Then she sat still, enjoying the warm glow of the porter, which seemed to have permeated her entire being with a heat that was not at all like the unpleasant and oppressive heat of the atmosphere, an atmosphere heavy with the Spring damp. A gritting on the tin aroused her. A piece of paper lay under her eyes.

fine groing weather
Smith

it said.

Now it is unlikely that in the whole round and range of conversational commonplaces there was one other greeting that could have induced the seamstress to continue the exchange of communications. But this simple and homely phrase touched her country heart. What did "*groing weather*" matter to the toilers in this waste of brick and mortar? This stranger must be, like herself, a country-bred soul, longing for the new green and the upturned brown mould of the country fields. She took up the paper, and wrote under the first message:

Fine

But that seemed curt; *for* she added: "*for*" what? She did not know. At last in desperation she put down *potatos.* The piece of paper was withdrawn and came back with an addition:

Too mist for potatos.

And when the little seamstress had read this, and grasped the fact that *m-i-s-t* represented the writer's pronunciation of "moist," she laughed softly to herself. A man whose mind, at such a time, was seriously bent upon potatos, was not a man to be feared. She found a half-sheet of note-paper, and wrote:

I lived in a small village before I came to New York, but I am afraid I do not know much about farming. Are you a farmer?

The answer came:

have ben most Every thing
farmed a Spel in Maine
Smith

As she read this, the seamstress heard a church clock strike nine.

"Bless me, is it so late?" she cried, and she hurriedly penciled *Good Night,* thrust the paper out, and closed the window. But a few minutes later, passing by, she saw yet another bit of paper on the cornice, fluttering in the evening breeze. It said only *good nite,* and after a moment's hesitation, the little seamstress took it in and gave it shelter.

. . . . . .

After this, they were the best of friends. Every evening the pot appeared, and while the seamstress drank from it at her window, Mr. Smith drank from its twin at his; and notes were exchanged as rapidly as Mr. Smith's early education permitted. They told each other their histories, and Mr. Smith's was one of travel and variety, which he seemed to consider quite a matter of course. He had followed the sea, he had farmed, he had been a logger and a hunter in the Maine woods. Now he was foreman of an East River lumber yard, and he was prospering. In a year or two he would have enough laid by to go home to Bucksport and buy a share in a ship-building business. All this dribbled out in the course of a jerky but variegated correspondence, in which autobiographic details were mixed with reflections, moral and philosophical.

A few samples will give an idea of Mr. Smith's style:

i was one trip to van demens
land

To which the seamstress replied:

It must have been very interesting.

But Mr. Smith disposed of this subject very briefly:

it wornt

Further he vouchsafed:

i seen a chinese cook in
hong kong could cook flapjacks
like your Mother

a mishnery that sells Rum
is the menest of Gods crechers

a bulfite is not what it is
cract up to Be

the dagos are wussen the
brutes

i am 6 1 3/4
but my Father was 6 foot 4

The seamstress had taught school one Winter, and she could not refrain from making an attempt to reform Mr. Smith's orthography. One evening, in answer to this communication:

i killd a Bare in Maine 600
lbs waight

she wrote:

Isn't it generally spelled Bear?

but she gave up the attempt when he responded:

a bare is a mene animle any
way you spel him

The Spring wore on, and the Summer came, and still the evening drink and the evening correspondence brightened the close of each day for the little seamstress. And the draught of porter put her to sleep each night, giving her a calmer rest than she had ever known during her stay in the noisy city; and it began, moreover, to make a little *"meet"* for her. And then the thought that she was going to have an hour of pleasant companionship somehow gave her courage to cook and eat her little dinner, however tired she was. The seamstress's cheeks began to blossom with the June roses.

And all this time Mr. Smith kept his vow of silence unbroken, though the seamstress sometimes tempted him with little ejaculations and exclamations to which he might have responded. He was silent and invisible. Only the smoke of his pipe, and the clink of his mug as he set it down on the cornice, told her that a living, material Smith was her correspondent. They never met on the stairs, for their hours of coming and going did not coincide. Once or twice they passed each other in the street—but Mr. Smith looked straight ahead of him, about a foot over her head. The little seamstress thought he was a very fine-looking man, with his six feet one and three-quarters and his thick brown beard. Most people would have called him plain.

Once she spoke to him. She was coming home one Summer evening, and a gang of corner-loafers stopped her and demanded money to buy beer, as is their custom. Before she had time to be frightened, Mr. Smith appeared—whence, she knew not—scattered the gang like chaff, and, collaring two of the human hyenas, kicked them, with deliberate, ponderous, alternate kicks, until they writhed in ineffable agony. When he let them crawl away, she turned to him and thanked him warmly, looking very pretty now, with the color in her cheeks. But Mr. Smith answered no word. He stared over her head, grew red in the face, fidgeted nervously, but held his peace until his eyes fell on a rotund Teuton, passing by.

"Say, Dutchy!" he roared.

The German stood aghast.

"I ain't got nothing to write with!" thundered Mr. Smith, looking him in the eye. And then the man of his word passed on his way.

And so the Summer went on, and the two correspondents chatted silently from window to window, hid from sight of all the world below by the friendly cornice. And they looked out over the roof, and saw the green of Tompkins Square grow darker and dustier as the months went on.

Mr. Smith was given to Sunday trips into the suburbs, and he never came back without a bunch of daisies or black-eyed Susans or, later, asters or golden-rod for the little seamstress. Sometimes, with a sagacity rare in his sex, he brought her a whole plant, with fresh loam for potting.

He gave her also a reel in a bottle, which, he wrote, he had *"maid"* himself, and some coral, and a dried flying-fish, that was somewhat fearful to look upon, with its sword-like fins and its hollow eyes. At first, she could not go to sleep with that flying-fish hanging on the wall.

But he surprised the little seamstress very much one cool September evening, when he shoved this letter along the cornice:

Respected and Honored Madam: Having long and vainly sought an opportunity to convey to you the expression of my sentiments, I now avail myself of the privilege of epistolary communication to acquaint you with the fact that the Emotions, which you have raised in my breast, are those which should point to Connubial Love and Affection rather than to simple Friendship. In short, Madam, I have the Honor to approach you with a Proposal, the acceptance of which will fill me with ecstatic Gratitude, and enable me to extend to you those Protecting Cares, which the Matrimonial Bond makes at once the Duty and the Privilege of him, who would, at no distant date, lead to the Hymenal Altar one whose charms and virtues should suffice to kindle its Flames, without extraneous Aid

I remain, Dear Madam,

Your Humble Servant and

Ardent Adorer, J. Smith.

The little seamstress gazed at this letter a long time. Perhaps she was wondering in what Ready Letter-Writer of the last century Mr. Smith had found his form. Perhaps she was amazed at the results of his first attempt at punctuation. Perhaps she was thinking of something else, for there were tears in her eyes and a smile on her small mouth.

But it must have been a long time, and Mr. Smith must have grown nervous, for presently another communication came along the line where the top of the cornice was worn smooth. It read:

If not understood will you mary me?

The little seamstress seized a piece of paper and wrote:

If I say Yes, will you speak to me?

Then she rose and passed it out to him, leaning out of the window, and their faces met.

CHARLES TOWNSEND COPELAND

From EDWIN BOOTH

Mr. Booth off the Stage

OF Mr. Booth off the stage I can say only, *Tantum vidi Virgilium.* I saw him just once in his own person, within the next few years after his return from Germany. The precise year and month have escaped me, but the scene was Park Street in Boston; the time, a very cold and very bright winter morning. The street lay white under the sun, and the Common stretched white beyond. Doubtless there were other people about. I don't remember seeing any: I remember only that I caught sight of Booth at some distance, coming down the hill toward me. As he drew near, walking slow, I watched him intently; and even when we came face to face, it is to be feared that I still gazed. There was no harm—Mr. Booth must long before have formed the habit of being stared at! And it was a reverential stare. Such was my deep respect for him and all he had done, that, not knowing then the fate of Charles Lamb's "merry friend," Jem White, I came near taking off my hat to a gentleman I had never "met." It is a question whether, at that moment, Booth would have perceived even such an attack, for he seemed to be looking in, not out, with the curious, introverted gaze of his own *Hamlet*. Let no one suppose that his expression was subdued to a professional melancholy, or that he had the consciously unconscious air which so often marks the celebrity in his walks abroad. But as he came toward me on that glittering, bitter day—stepping lightly though not quickly, his head a little bent and his hands in his pockets—he looked like *Hamlet* in a greatcoat. I thought then that I had never seen so sad a face, and I have never yet beheld a sadder one.

Tribute to Dean Shaler

Professor Nathaniel Southgate Shaler, Dean of the Lawrence Scientific School of Harvard University, died in April, 1906. Many years before, he had founded the Summer School. In July, Professor Copeland, then lecturer on English Literature in the University, took occasion in the first of his general evening lectures to the Summer School to speak of Dean Shaler. He read a few pages from a book by Dean Shaler, entitled *The Individual,* in which the author condemned costly funerals and monuments, and suggested instead, as the best memorials, scholarships, charities, and such like, in the name of those who have gone before. Mr. Copeland said:

Good general counsel this, and for the common man, the best memorial is some beneficent thing or function that shall bear his name. But in the case of Professor Shaler we shall be content with no remembrance short of so much of himself as can be put into a book.

"It must not be one of those volumes ironically called 'lives' because they are so dead, but a true presentment of a man who was the very stuff of which biography is made. In the case of most men—even of most distinguished men—the record of their work is the record of them. When that is told, all is told; they have no overlapping personality. Not so with Mr. Shaler. Important, arduous and varied as was his work, what he was eclipsed what he did.

"And what he was expressed itself constantly in what he said as well as in what he did. 'Give us plenty of anecdote,' cried Dr. Johnson, to an intending biographer. Wherever Shaler went, he bred anecdote. No man of parts that ever spent an hour in his company is without some generous impression of him, some pungent reminiscence. Let our biographer but announce his intention, and his study table will be heaped with anecdotes, in the broad Johnsonian sense, from all parts of this country and from all other countries that contain pupils and friends of Mr. Shaler. Invaluable correspondence, also, will be placed at his disposal. The world of Shaler's friends will form a sort of corporate Boswell.

"Perhaps you do not all know how wide that world is. Statesmen, men of letters, eminent lawyers, doctors, farmers that he showed where to dig for water, miners that he told—in Bible phrase—where to dig for gold, sick men in hospitals where he has blown in like the west wind, changing foul weather to fair—with all of these he has brothered, and their minds are sown with memories of him. The biographer has but to reap and bind.

"Of course a sad deal is lost. Mr. Shaler's presence was magnetic and heartening; his speech was wine; his laugh a cordial. These may be suggested in writing; they cannot be recaptured. A man is always better than a book.

"Yet, though much is lost, consider how much remains—how much that must not be let perish. The true biographer—he must not be too old nor too young—will qualify his narrative in just proportions with Shaler's racy wit (not watering it down to placate the squeamish), with his unforced humor, his homely shrewdness, his persuasive wisdom, and the poetic feeling with which so much of what he said and wrote was tinctured. This true biographer will know men and be a master of language, for his task will be to transmit a personality, one of the most brilliant, winning, conquering personalities of our time.

"Greatheart is dead. The magnanimous teacher has been borne on the shoulders of his young men to the place where is no teaching, nor work, nor device, nor knowledge, nor wisdom; yet he will not all die—this friendly helper of the race, this minister to young men, settled forty years over the parish of Harvard—he will not die so long as there is a man alive that knew him. Let us in piety cherish the loyal hope that he may live for other generations in pages wisely planned and faithfully wrought."

OWEN WISTER

From The Seven Ages of Washington

Immortality

Go, when the day is fine, down the river to Mount Vernon. There, following the path up from the shore among the trees, you will slowly come to where his tomb is, the simple vault half up the hill, which vines partly cover, built according to his directions. From this you will still ascend among grass and trees, and pass up by old buildings, old barns, an old coach-house with the coach in it, and so come to the level green upon which the house gives with its connecting side offices at either flank. Inside the house, all through the rooms of bygone comfort so comfortable still, so mellowed with the long sense of home, you will feel the memory of his presence strangely, and how much his house is like him. He seems to come from his battles and his austere fame, and to be here by the fireplace. Here are some of his very books on the shelves, here the stairs he went up and down, here in the hall his swords, and the key of the Bastille that Lafayette sent to him. Upstairs is the room he died in, and the bed; still above this chamber, the little room where Martha Washington lived her last years after his death, with its window looking out upon the tomb where he was first laid. Everything, every object, every corner and step, seems to bring him close, not in the way of speaking of him or breathing of him, as some memorial places seem to speak and breathe their significance; a silence fills these passages and rooms, a particular motionlessness, that is not changed or disturbed by the constant moving back and forth of the visitors. What they do, their voices, their stopping and bending to look at this or that, does not seem to affect, or even to reach, the strange influence that surrounds them. It is an exquisite and friendly serenity which bathes one's sense, that brings him so near, that seems to be charged all through with some meaning of beneficence and reassurance, but nothing that could be put into words.

And then, not staying too long in the house, stroll out upon the grounds. Look away to the woods and fields, whence he rode home from hunting with Lord Fairfax, over which his maturer gaze roved as he watched his crops and his fences, and to which his majestic figure came back with pleasure and relief from the burdens and the admiration of the world. Turn into his garden and look at the walls and the walks he planned, the box hedges, the trees, the flower-beds, the great order and the great sweetness everywhere. And among all this, still the visitors are moving, looking, speaking, the men, women, and children from every corner of the country, some plain and rustic enough, some laughing and talking louder than need be, but all drawn here to see it, to remember it, to take it home with them, to be in their own ways and according to their several lights touched by it, and no more disturbing the lovely peace of it than they disturbed the house. For again, as in the house, only if possible more marvellously still, there comes from the trees, the box hedges, the glimpses of the river, that serenity with its message of beneficence and reassurance, that cannot be put into words. It seems to lay a hand upon all and make them, for a moment, one. You may spend an hour, you may spend a day, wandering, sitting, feeling this gentle power of the place; you may come back another time, it meets you, you cannot dispel it by familiarity.

Then go down the hill again, past the old buildings, past the tomb, among the trees to the shore. As you recede from the shore, you watch the place grow into the compactness of distance, and then it seems to speak: "I am still here, my countrymen, to do you what good I can." And as you think of this, and bless the devotion of those whose piety and care treasure the place, and keep it sacred and beautiful, you turn and look up the expanding river. From behind a wooded point, silent and far, the Nation's roof-tree, the dome of the Capitol, moves into sight. A turn of the river, and it moves behind the point again; but now, on the other side of the wide water distance, rises that shaft built to his memory, almost seeming to grow from the stream itself; presently, shaft and dome stand out against the sky, with the Federal City that he prophesied, Union's hearth-stone and high-seat, stretching between them.

From ULYSSES S. GRANT

Lee's Surrender

AT dark on April 5 word came from Sheridan to Grant: "I wish you were here. I see no escape for General Lee." Grant called for his horse, and rode through the night to Sheridan and Meade. And on the next day at Sailor's Creek the clouds sank lower round Lee. Again Grant's actions reveal his thoughts. On Friday, April 7, he wrote Lee: "The last week must convince you of the hopelessness of further resistance. I regard it as my duty to shift from myself the responsibility of any further effusion of blood by asking of you the surrender of the army of Northern Virginia." The unsuccessful battles, the dwindling regiments, the starvation, the retreat cut off,—all this was plainly the end; and it stared Lee in the face. But on such a sight Lee had not at first the moral strength to open his eyes. The pain was too blinding. In his youth he had taken an oath to support the government. That government had educated him to be a soldier. He had been against Secession. But, when the time came to choose between Secession and his oath, he chose (not without reluctance) to break his oath, and turn against the government the teaching it had given him. And now here he sat, with his lost cause like a broken idol in his hands. For a moment he shrank from the final pang of renunciation. "I have received your note," he replied to Grant on that same Friday. "Though not entertaining the opinion you express of the hopelessness of further resistance, I reciprocate your desire to avoid useless effusion of blood, and therefore ask the terms you will offer." And Grant on Saturday replied, "Peace being my great desire, there is but one condition—that the men and officers surrendered shall be disqualified for taking up arms until properly exchanged." And then follows a touch of his perfect consideration for the defeated opponent: "I will meet you or will designate officers to meet any officers you may name." So did Washington write to Cornwallis, as Horace Porter reminds us. But Lee would himself go through with whatever had to come. Only still he pushed the bitter cup away from him. "I cannot meet you with a view to surrender," he answered; "but, as far as your proposal may tend to the restoration of peace, I shall be pleased to meet you." And he named Sunday morning, on the old stage-road between the picket lines.

This disappointing word came to Grant in the heart of the night, where he lay sleepless from many hours of pain in his head. Hunger, fatigue, exposure, and strain had brought on such torments that he had allowed remedies to be tried, but without avail. He lay down again. In the early hours he was found walking up and down outside, holding his head with both hands. He now wrote a third time to Lee that he had no authority to treat of peace, but that peace could be had, and lives and property saved, by the South's laying down their arms. An urgency, almost an appeal, pervades this letter. He then declined advice to take an ambulance for the sake of his severe pain, and, mounting once more, proceeded toward Sheridan's front. It was near noon now; and, as he went, a despatch overtook him. Time and further mischances had brought Lee to the point. He requested an interview for the purpose of surrender according to the terms offered. As Grant read and understood that here in his hand at last lay peace, all pain left him. He dismounted, and by the roadside wrote his answer. While he was doing this, and hurrying forward to the meeting, Lee some six miles away lay waiting.

Stretched on a blanket under an apple-tree by the road, he contemplated the sunshine that bathed Virginia. Of his thoughts, also, only his actions reveal anything. When Grant's note reached him, he rose, and had soon ridden into Appomattox Court-house, and in a house there waited for Grant. In a little while Grant reached the grassy village street; and there, dismounted, stood Sheridan and others. No significant words were spoken in this hour. Silence is the only reference that men make to great events which they are in the midst of. The ordinary greetings of every day were briefly given. The house where General Lee waited was pointed out to Grant; and he went in, leaving most of the others upon the porch. There they sat, while General Lee's gray horse cropped the grass near them. Quietness was over the little village and the armies lying in the country round. The door opened, and two of those on the porch were signed to come in. They entered, it is said, treading as those do who steal into a sick-chamber, while the rest still sat on the porch. When the door next opened, they rose. For out of it General Lee came, splendid, tall, grey-bearded, immovable. They looked at him and his sword and spotless grey uniform. He stood absently on the step, gazing away across Virginia; and two or three times he struck one hand against the other. Then, having spoken no word, and noticing his grey horse that had been brought him, he mounted, and rode away. As he was going, Grant came through the door, saluted him in silence, and in silence also rode away. When Lee reached his army, the faithful men swarmed around him, cheering not their common misfortune, but the peace that he had made. They mingled their grief with his, grasping his hands; and then, almost overcome, he spoke: "Men, we have fought through the war together. I have done the best I could for you."

What Grant's features concealed on that day we know now from him: "What General Lee's feelings were I do not know. But my own, which had been quite jubilant on the receipt of his letter, were sad and depressed. I felt like anything rather than rejoicing at the downfall of a foe who had fought so long and valiantly, and had suffered so much for a cause, though that cause was, I believe, one of the worst for which a people ever fought, and one for which there was the least excuse."

But, inside the house, what had gone on between the two chiefs? The witnesses watched and moved always with the hush of a sick-room. And after the first greeting, when they sat down, it became Grant who shrank from the point. He talked to Lee about Mexico and old times, and how good peace was going to be now; and twice Lee had to remind him of the business they had to do. Then Grant wrote, as always, simple and clear words. In the middle, his eye fell upon Lee's beautiful sword;

and the chivalric act which it prompted has knighted his own spirit forever. "The surrender," he instantly wrote, "would not embrace the side-arms of the officers, nor their private horses or baggage." When Lee's eyes reached that sentence, his face changed for the first time; and he said, "This will have a very happy effect upon my army." He then told what was new to Grant, that the horses ridden by the men were their own. Again the conqueror's tenderness lifted him into a realm diviner than the renown of victory. He ordered that the men "take the animals home with them to work their little farms." To this nobility Lee's own responded. "This will have the best possible effect upon the men," he said. Moved to greater frankness, he told Grant of his army's hunger; and for this also Grant at once provided. These are the things which the conqueror had done when he came out of the house with unrelaxed countenance, and rode away. As he went, he heard firing from his lines. It was in honor of the news, already spreading. He stopped these salutes at once. "The war is over," he said. "The rebels are our countrymen again."

Thus, when his strength had quelled the four years' storm, did a rainbow rise from his great heart across the heavens of our native land.

LOUISE IMOGEN GUINEY (1861-1920)

The Precept of Peace

A CERTAIN sort of voluntary abstraction is the oldest and choicest of social attitudes. In France, where all esthetic discoveries are made, it was crowned long ago: *la sainte indifférence* is, or may be, a cult, and *le saint indifférent* an articled practitioner. For the Gallic mind, brought up at the knee of a consistent paradox, has found that not to appear concerned about a desired good is the only method to possess it; full happiness is given, in other words, to the very man who will never sue for it. This is a secret neat as that of the Sphinx: to "go softly" among events, yet domineer them. Without fear: not because we are brave, but because we are exempt; we bear so charmed a life that not even Baldur's mistletoe can touch us to harm us. Without solicitude: for the essential thing is trained, falcon-like, to light from above upon our wrists, and it has become with us an automatic motion to open the hand, and drop what appertains to us no longer. Be it renown or a new hat, the shorter stick of celery, or

"The friends to whom we had no natural right,
The homes that were not destined to be ours,"

it is all one: let it fall away! since only so, by depletions, can we buy serenity and a blithe mien. It is diverting to study, at the feet of Antisthenes and of Socrates his master, how many indispensables man can live without; or how many he can gather together, make over into luxuries, and so abrogate them. Thoreau somewhere expresses himself as full of divine pity for the "mover," who on May-Day clouds city streets with his melancholy household caravans: fatal impedimenta for an immortal. No: furniture is clearly a superstition. "I have little, I want nothing; all my treasure is in Minerva's tower." Not that the novice may not accumulate. Rather, let him collect beetles and Venetian interrogation-marks; if so be that he may distinguish what is truly extrinsic to him, and bestow these toys, eventually, on the children of Satan who clamor at the monastery gate. Of all his store, unconsciously increased, he can always part with sixteen-seventeenths, by way of concession to his individuality, and think the subtraction so much concealing marble chipped from the heroic figure of himself. He would be a donor from the beginning; before he can be seen to own, he will disencumber, and divide. Strange and fearful is his discovery, amid the bric-à-brac of the world, that this knowledge, or this material benefit, is for him alone. He would fain beg off from the acquisition, and shake the touch of the tangible from his imperious wings. It is not enough to cease to strive for personal favor; your true *indifférent* is Early Franciscan: caring not to have, he fears to hold. Things useful need never become to him things desirable. Towards all commonly-accounted sinecures, he bears the coldest front in Nature, like a magician walking a maze, and scornful of its flower-bordered detentions. "I enjoy life," says Seneca, "because I am ready to leave it." Meanwhile, they who act with too jealous respect for their morrow of civilized comfort, reap only indigestion, and crow's-foot traceries for their deluded eye-corners.

Now nothing is farther from *le saint indifférent* than cheap indifferentism, so-called: the sickness of sophomores. His business is to hide, not to display, his lack of interest in fripperies. It is not he who looks languid, and twiddles his thumbs for sick misplacedness, like Achilles among girls. On the contrary, he is a smiling industrious elf, monstrous attentive to the canons of polite society. In relation to others, he shows what passes for animation and enthusiasm; for at all times his character is founded on control of these qualities, not on the absence of them. It flatters his sense of superiority that he may thus pull wool about the ears of joint and several. He has so strong a will that it can be crossed and counter-crossed, as by himself, so by a dozen outsiders, without a break in his apparent phlegm. He has gone through volition, and come out at the other side of it; everything with him is a specific act: he has no habits. *Le saint indifférent* is a dramatic wight: he loves to refuse your proffered six per cent, when, by a little haggling, he may obtain three-and-a-half. For so he gets away with his own mental processes virgin: it is inconceivable to you that, being sane, he should so comport himself. Amiable, perhaps, only by painful propulsions and sore vigilance, let him appear the mere inheritor of easy good-nature. Unselfish out of sheer pride, and ever eager to claim the slippery side of the pavement, or the end cut of the roast (on the secret ground, be it understood, that he is not as Capuan men, who wince at trifles), let him have his ironic reward in passing for one whose physical connoisseurship is yet in the raw. That sympathy which his rule forbids his devoting to the usual objects, he expends, with some bravado, upon their opposites; for he would fain seem a decent partizan of some sort, not what he is, a bivalve intelligence, Tros Tyriusque. He is known here and there, for instance, as valorous in talk; yet he is by nature a solitary, and, for the most part, somewhat less communicative than

> "The wind that sings to himself as he makes stride,
> Lonely and terrible, on the Andean height."

Imagining nothing idler than words in the face of grave events, he condoles and congratulates with the genteelest air in the world. In short, while there is anything expected of him, while there are spectators to be fooled, the stratagems of the fellow prove inexhaustible. It is only when he is quite alone that he drops his jaw, and stretches his legs; then heigho! arises like a smoke, and envelopes him becomingly, the beautiful native well-bred torpidity of the gods, of poetic boredom, of "the Oxford manner."

"How weary, stale, flat, and unprofitable!" sighed Hamlet of this mortal outlook. As it came from him in the beginning, that plaint, in its sincerity, can come only from the man of culture, who feels about him vast mental spaces and depths, and to whom the face of creation is but comparative and symbolic. Nor will he breathe it in the common ear, where it may woo misapprehensions, and breed ignorant rebellion. The unlettered must ever love or hate what is nearest him, and, for lack of perspective, think his own fist the size of the sun. The social prizes, which, with mellowed observers, rank as twelfth or thirteenth in order of desirability, such as wealth and a foothold in affairs, seem to him first and sole; and to them he clings like a barnacle. But to our *indifférent*, nothing is so vulgar as close suction. He will never tighten his fingers on loaned opportunity; he is a gentleman, the hero of the habitually relaxed grasp. A light unprejudiced hold on his profits strikes him as decent and comely, though his true artistic pleasure is still in "fallings from us, vanishings." It costs him little to loose and to forego, to unlace his tentacles, and from the many who push hard behind, to retire, as it were, on a never-guessed-at competency, "richer than untempted kings." He would not be a life-prisoner, in ever so charming a bower. While the tranquil Sabine Farm is his delight, well he knows that on the dark trail ahead of him, even Sabine Farms are not sequacious. Thus he learns betimes to play the guest under his own cedars, and, with disciplinary intent, goes often from them; and, hearing his heart-strings snap the third night he is away, rejoices that he is again a freedman. Where his foot is planted (though it root not anywhere), he calls that spot home. No Unitarian in locality, it follows that he is the best of travellers, tangential merely, and pleased with each new vista of the human Past. He sometimes wishes his understanding less, that he might itch deliciously with a prejudice. With cosmic congruities, great and general forces, he keeps, all along, a tacit understanding, such as one has with beloved relatives at a distance; and his finger, airily inserted in his outer pocket, is really upon the pulse of eternity. His vocation, however, is to bury himself in·the minor and immediate task; and from his intent manner, he gets confounded, promptly and permanently, with the victims of commercial ambition.

The true use of the much-praised Lucius Cary, Viscount Falkland, has hardly been apprehended: he is simply the patron saint of *indifférents.* From first to last, almost alone in that discordant time, he seems to have heard far-off resolving harmonies, and to have been rapt away with foreknowledge. Battle, to which all knights were bred, was penitential to him. It was but a childish means: and to what end? He meanwhile —and no man carried his will in better abeyance to the scheme of the universe—wanted no diligence in camp or council. Cares sat handsomely on him who cared not at all, who won small comfort from the cause which his conscience finally espoused. He labored to be a doer, to stand well with observers; and none save his intimate friends read his agitation and profound weariness. "I am so much taken notice of," he writes, "for an impatient desire for peace, that it is necessary I should likewise make it appear how it is not out of fear for the utmost hazard of war." And so, driven from the ardor he had to the simulation of the ardor he lacked, loyally daring, a sacrifice to one of two transient opinions, and inly impartial as a star, Lord Falkland fell: the young never-to-be-forgotten martyr of Newburg field. The imminent deed he made a work of art; and the station of the moment the only post of honor.

Life and death may be all one to such a man: but he will at least take the noblest pains to discriminate between Tweedledum and Tweedledee, if he has to write a book about the variations of their antennæ. And like the Carolian exemplar is the disciple. The *indifférent* is a good thinker, or a good fighter. He is no "immartial minion," as dear old Chapman suffers Hector to call Tydides. Nevertheless, his sign-manual is content with humble and stagnant conditions. Talk of scaling the Himalayas of life affects him, very palpably, as "tall talk." He deals not with things, but with the impressions and analogies of things. The material counts for nothing with him: he has moulted it away. Not so sure of the identity of the higher course of action as he is of his consecrating dispositions, he feels that he may make heaven again, out of sundries, as he goes. Shall not a beggarly duty, discharged with perfect temper, land him in "the out-courts of Glory," quite as successfully as a grand Sunday-school excursion to front the cruel Paynim foe? He thinks so. Experts have thought so before him. Francis Drake, with the national alarum instant in his ears, desired first to win at bowls, on the Devon sward, "and afterwards to settle with the Don." No one will claim a buccaneering hero for an *indifférent,* however. The Jesuit novices were ball-playing almost at that very time, three hundred years ago, when some too speculative companion, figuring the end of the world in a few moments (with just leisure enough, between, to be shriven in chapel, according to his own thrifty mind), asked Louis of Gonzaga how he, on his part, should employ the precious interval. "I should go on with the game," said the most innocent and most ascetic youth among them. But to cite the behavior of any of the saints is to step over the playful line allotted. Indifference of the mundane brand is not to be confounded with their detachment, which is emancipation wrought in the soul, and the ineffable efflorescence of the Christian spirit. Like most supernatural virtues, it has a laic shadow; the counsel to abstain, and to be unsolicitous, is one not only of perfection, but also of polity. A very little nonadhesion to common affairs, a little reserve of unconcern, and the gay spirit of sacrifice, provide the moral immunity which is the only real estate. The *indifférent* believes in storms: since tales of shipwreck encompass him. But once among his own kind, he wonders that folk should be circumvented by merely extraneous powers! His favorite catch, woven in among escaped dangers, rises through the roughest weather, and daunts it:

> "Now strike your sailes, ye jolly mariners,
> For we be come into a quiet rode."

No slave to any vicissitude, his imagination is, on the contrary, the cheerful obstinate tyrant of all that is. He lives, as Keats once said of himself, "in a thousand worlds," withdrawing at will from one to another, often curtailing his circumference to enlarge his liberty. His universe is a universe of balls, like those which the cunning Oriental carvers make out of ivory; each entire surface perforated with the same delicate pattern, each moving prettily and inextricably within the other, and all but the outer one impossible to handle. In some such innermost asylum the right sort of dare-devil sits smiling, while men rage or weep.

MARY E. WILKINS FREEMAN

A Village Singer

THE trees were in full leaf, a heavy south wind was blowing, and there was a loud murmur among the new leaves. The people noticed it, for it was the first time that year that the trees had so murmured in the wind. The spring had come with a rush during the last few days.

The murmur of the trees sounded loud in the village church, where the people sat waiting for the service to begin. The windows were open; it was a very warm Sunday for May.

The church was already filled with this soft sylvan music—the tender harmony of the leaves and the south wind, and the sweet, desultory whistles of birds—when the choir arose and began to sing.

In the centre of the row of women singers stood Alma Way. All the people stared at her, and turned their ears critically. She was the new leading soprano. Candace Whitcomb, the old one, who had sung in the choir for forty years, had lately been given her dismissal. The audience considered that her voice had grown too cracked and uncertain on the upper notes. There had been much complaint, and after long deliberation the church-officers had made known their decision as mildly as possible to the old singer. She had sung for the last time the Sunday before, and Alma Way had been engaged to take her place. With the exception of the organist, the leading soprano was the only paid musician in the large choir. The salary was very modest, still the church people considered it large for a young woman. Alma was from the adjoining village of East Derby; she had quite a local reputation as a singer.

Now she fixed her large solemn blue eyes; her long, delicate face, which had been pretty, turned paler; the blue flowers on her bonnet trembled; her little thin gloved hands, clutching the singing-book, shook perceptibly; but she sang out bravely. That most formidable mountain-height of the world, self-distrust and timidity, arose before her, but her nerves were braced for its ascent. In the midst of the hymn she had a solo; her voice rang out piercingly sweet; the people nodded admiringly at each other; but suddenly there was a stir; all the faces turned toward the windows on the south side of the church. Above the din of the wind and the birds, above Alma Way's sweetly straining tones, arose another female voice, singing another hymn to another tune.

"It's her," the women whispered to each other; they were half aghast, half smiling.

Candace Whitcomb's cottage stood close to the south side of the church. She was playing on her parlor organ, and singing, to drown out the voice of her rival.

Alma caught her breath; she almost stopped; the hymn-book waved like a fan; then she went on. But the long husky drone of the parlor organ and the shrill clamor of the other voice seemed louder than anything else.

When the hymn was finished, Alma sat down. She felt faint; the woman next her slipped a peppermint into her hand. "It ain't worth minding," she whispered, vigorously. Alma tried to smile; down in the audience a young man was watching her with a kind of fierce pity.

In the last hymn Alma had another solo. Again the parlor organ droned above the carefully delicate accompaniment of the church organ, and again Candace Whitcomb's voice clamored forth in another tune.

After the benediction, the other singers pressed around Alma. She did not say much in return for their expressions of indignation and sympathy. She wiped her eyes furtively once or twice, and tried to smile. William Emmons, the choir leader, elderly, stout, and smooth-faced, stood over her, and raised his voice. He was the old musical dignitary of the village, the leader of the choral club and the singing-schools. "A most outrageous proceeding," he said. People had coupled his name with Candace Whitcomb's. The old bachelor tenor and old maiden soprano had been wont to walk together to her home next door after the Saturday night rehearsals, and they had sung duets to the parlor organ. People had watched sharply her old face, on which the blushes of youth sat pitifully, when William Emmons entered the singing-seats. They wondered if he would ever ask her to marry him.

And now he said further to Alma Way that Candace Whitcomb's voice had failed utterly of late, that she sang shockingly, and ought to have had sense enough to know it.

When Alma went down into the audience-room, in the midst of the chattering singers, who seemed to have descended, like birds, from song flights to chirps, the minister approached her. He had been waiting to speak to her. He was a steady-faced, fleshy old man, who had preached from that one pulpit over forty years. He told Alma, in his slow way, how much he regretted the annoyance to which she had been subjected, and intimated that he would endeavor to prevent a recurrence of it. "Miss Whitcomb—must be—reasoned with," said he; he had a slight hesitation of speech, not an impediment. It was as if his thoughts did not slide readily into his words, although both were present. He walked down the aisle with Alma, and bade her good-morning when he saw Wilson Ford waiting for her in the doorway. Everybody knew that Wilson Ford and Alma were lovers; they had been for the last ten years.

Alma colored softly, and made a little imperceptible motion with her head; her silk dress and the lace on her mantle fluttered, but she did not speak. Neither did Wilson, although they had not met before, that day. They did not look at each other's faces—they seemed to see each other without that—and they walked along side by side.

They reached the gate before Candace Whitcomb's little house. Wilson looked past the front yard, full of pink and white spikes on flowering bushes, at the lace-curtained windows; a thin white profile, stiffly inclined, apparently over a book, was visible at one of them. Wilson gave his head a shake. He was a stout man, with features so strong that they overcame his flesh. "I'm going up home with you, Alma," said he; "and then—I'm just coming back, to give Aunt Candace one blowing up."

"Oh, don't, Wilson."

"Yes, I shall. If you want to stand this kind of a thing you may; I sha'n't."

"There's no need of your talking to her. Mr. Pollard's going to."

"Did he say he was?"

"Yes. I think he's going in before the afternoon meeting, from what he said."

"Well, there's one thing about it, if she does that thing again this afternoon, I'll go in there and break that old organ up into kindling-wood." Wilson set his mouth hard, and shook his head again.

Alma gave little side glances up at him, her tone was deprecatory, but her face was full of soft smiles. "I suppose she does feel dreadfully about it," said she. "I can't help feeling kind of guilty, taking her place."

"I don't see how you're to blame. It's outrageous, her acting so."

"The choir gave her a photograph album last week, didn't they?"

"Yes. They went there last Thursday night, and gave her an album and a surprise-party. She ought to behave herself."

"Well, she's sung there so long, I suppose it must be dreadful hard for her to give it up."

Other people going home from church were very near Wilson and Alma. She spoke softly that they might not hear; he did not lower his voice in the least. Presently Alma stopped before a gate.

"What are you stopping here for?" asked Wilson.

"Minnie Lansing wanted me to come and stay with her this noon."

"You're going home with me."

"I'm afraid I'll put your mother out."

"Put mother out! I told her you were coming, this morning. She's got all ready for you. Come along; don't stand here."

He did not tell Alma of the pugnacious spirit with which his mother had received the announcement of her coming, and how she had stayed at home to prepare the dinner, and make a parade of her hard work and her injury.

Wilson's mother was the reason why he did not marry Alma. He would not take his wife home to live with her, and was unable to support separate establishments. Alma was willing enough to be married and put up with Wilson's mother, but she did not complain of his decision. Her delicate blond features grew sharper, and her blue eyes more hollow. She had had a certain fine prettiness, but now she was losing it, and beginning to look old, and there was a prim, angular, old maiden carriage about her narrow shoulders.

Wilson never noticed it, and never thought of Alma as not possessed of eternal youth, or capable of losing or regretting it.

"Come along, Alma," said he; and she followed meekly after him down the street.

Soon after they passed Candace Whitcomb's house, the minister went up the front walk and rang the bell. The pale profile at the window had never stirred as he opened the gate and came up the walk. However, the door was promptly opened, in response to his ring. "Good-morning, Miss Whitcomb," said the minister.

"*Good*-morning." Candace gave a sweeping toss of her head as she spoke. There was a fierce upward curl to her thin nostrils and her lips, as if she scented an adversary. Her black eyes had two tiny cold sparks of fury in them, like an enraged bird's. She did not ask the minister to enter, but he stepped lumberingly into the entry and she retreated rather than led the way into her little parlor. He settled into the great rocking-chair and wiped his face. Candace sat down again in her old place by the window. She was a tall woman, but very slender and full of pliable motions, like a blade of grass.

"It's a—very pleasant day," said the minister.

Candace made no reply. She sat still, with her head dropping. The wind stirred the looped lace-curtains; a tall rose-tree outside the window waved; soft shadows floated through the room. Candace's parlor organ stood in front of an open window that faced the church; on the corner was a pitcher with a bunch of white lilacs. The whole room was scented with them. Presently the minister looked over at them and sniffed pleasantly.

"You have—some beautiful—lilacs there."

Candace did not speak. Every line of her slender figure looked flexible, but it was a flexibility more resistant than rigor.

The minister looked at her. He filled up the great rocking-chair; his arms in his shiny black coat-sleeves rested squarely and comfortably upon the hair-cloth arms of the chair.

"Well, Miss Whitcomb, I suppose I—may as well come to—the point. There was—a little—matter I wished to speak to you about. I don't suppose you were—at least I can't suppose you were—aware of it, but—this morning, during the singing by the choir, you played and—sung a little too—loud. That is, with—the windows open. It—disturbed us—a little. I hope you won't feel hurt—my dear Miss Candace, but I knew you would rather I would speak of it, for I knew—you would be more disturbed than anybody else at the idea of such a thing."

Candace did not raise her eyes; she looked as if his words might sway her through the window. "I ain't disturbed at it," said she. "I did it on purpose; I meant to."

The minister looked at her.

"You needn't look at me. I know jest what I'm about. I sung the way I did on purpose, an' I'm goin' to do it again, an' I'd like to see you stop me. I guess I've got a right to set down to my own organ, an' sing a psalm tune on a Sabbath day, 'f I want to; an' there ain't no amount of talkin' an' palaverin' a-goin' to stop me. See there!" Candace swung aside her skirts a little. "Look at that!"

The minister looked. Candace's feet were resting on a large red-plush photograph album.

"Makes a nice footstool, don't it?" said she.

The minister looked at the album, then at her; there was a slowly gathering alarm in his face; he began to think she was losing her reason.

Candace had her eyes full upon him now, and her head up. She laughed, and her laugh was almost a snarl. "Yes; I thought it would make a beautiful footstool," said she. "I've been wantin' one for some time." Her tone was full of vicious irony.

"Why, miss—" began the minister; but she interrupted him:

"I know what you're a-goin' to say, Mr. Pollard, an' now I'm goin' to have my say; I'm a-goin' to speak. I want to know what you think of folks that pretend to be Christians treatin' anybody the way they've treated me? Here I've sung in those singin'-seats forty year. I 'ain't never missed a Sunday, except when I've been sick, an' I've gone an' sung a good many times when I'd better been in bed, an' now I'm turned out without a word of warnin'. My voice is jest as good as ever 'twas; there can't anybody say it ain't. It wa'n't ever quite so high-pitched as that Way girl's, mebbe; but she flats the whole durin' time. My voice is as good an' high to-day as it was twenty year ago; an' if it wa'n't, I'd like to know where the Christianity comes in. I'd like to know if it wouldn't be more to the credit of folks in a church to keep an old singer an' an old minister, if they didn't sing an' hold forth quite so smart as they used to, ruther than turn 'em off an' hurt their feelin's. I guess it would be full as much to the glory of God. S'pose the singin' an' the preachin' wa'n't quite so good, what difference would it make? Salvation don't hang on anybody's hittin' a high note, that I ever heard of. Folks are gettin' as high-steppin' an' fussy in a meetin'-house as they are in a tavern, nowadays. S'pose they should turn you off, Mr. Pollard, come an' give you a photograph album, an' tell you to clear out, how'd you like it? I ain't findin' any fault with your preachin'; it was always good enough to suit me; but it don't stand to reason folks'll be as took up with your sermons as when you was a young man. You can't expect it. S'pose they should turn you out in your old age, an' call in some young bob squirt, how'd you feel? There's William Emmons, too; he's three years older'n I am, if he does lead the choir an' run all the singin' in town. If my voice has gi'en out, it stan's to reason his has. It ain't, though. William Emmons sings jest as well as he ever did. Why don't they turn him out the way they have me, an' give him a photograph album? I dun know but it would be a good idea to send everybody, as soon as they get a little old an' gone by, an' young folks begin to push, onto some desert island, an' give 'em each a photograph album. Then they can sit down an' look at pictures the rest of their days. Mebbe government'll take it up.

"There they come here last week Thursday, all the choir, jest about eight o'clock in the evenin', an' pretended they'd come to give me a nice little surprise. Surprise! h'm! Brought cake an' oranges, an' was jest as nice as they could be, an' I was real tickled. I never had a surprise-party before in my life. Jenny Carr she played, an' they wanted me to sing alone, an' I never suspected a thing. I've been mad ever since to think what a fool I was, an' how they must have laughed in their sleeves.

"When they'd gone I found this photograph album on the table, all done up as nice as you please, an' directed to Miss Candace Whitcomb from her many friends, an' I opened it, an' there was the letter inside givin' me notice to quit.

"If they'd gone about it any decent way, told me right out honest that they'd got tired of me, an' wanted Alma Way to sing instead of me, I wouldn't minded so much; I should have been hurt 'nough, for I'd felt as if some that had pretended to be my friends wa'n't; but it wouldn't have been as bad as this. They said in the letter that they'd always set great value on my services, an' it wa'n't from any lack of appreciation that they turned me off, but they thought the duty was gettin' a little too arduous for me. H'm! I hadn't complained. If they'd turned me right out fair an' square, showed me the door, an' said, 'Here, you get out,' but to go an' spill molasses, as it were, all over the threshold, tryin' to make me think it's all nice an' sweet—

"I'd sent that photograph album back quick's I could pack it, but I didn't know who started it, so I've used it for a footstool. It's all it's good for, 'cordin' to my way of thinkin'. And I ain't been particular to get the dust off my shoes before I used it neither."

Mr. Pollard, the minister, sat staring. He did not look at Candace; his eyes were fastened upon a point straight ahead. He had a look of helpless solidity, like a block of granite. This country minister, with his steady, even temperament, treading with heavy precision his one track for over forty years, having nothing new in his life except the new sameness of the seasons, and desiring nothing new, was incapable of understanding a woman like this, who had lived as quietly as he, and all the time held within herself the elements of revolution. He could not account for such violence, such extremes, except in a loss of reason. He had a conviction that Candace was getting beyond herself. He himself was not a typical New-Englander; the national elements of character were not pronounced in him. He was aghast and bewildered at this outbreak, which was tropical, and more than tropical, for a New England nature has a floodgate, and the power which it releases is an accumulation. Candace Whitcomb had been a quiet woman, so delicately resolute that the quality had been scarcely noticed in her, and her ambition had been unsuspected. Now the resolution and the ambition appeared raging over her whole self.

She began to talk again. "I've made up my mind that I'm goin' to sing Sundays the way I did this mornin', an' I don't care what folks say," said she. "I've made up my mind that I'm goin' to take matters into my own hands. I'm goin' to let folks see that I ain't trod down quite flat, that there's a little rise left in me. I ain't goin' to give up beat yet a while; an' I'd like to see anybody stop me. If I ain't got a right to play a psalm tune on my organ an' sing, I'd like to know. If you don't like it, you can move the meetin'-house."

Candace had had an inborn reverence for clergymen. She had always treated Mr. Pollard with the utmost deference. Indeed, her manner toward all men had been marked by a certain delicate stiffness and dignity. Now she was talking to the old minister with the homely freedom with which she might have addressed a female gossip over the back fence. He could not say much in return. He did not feel competent to make headway against any such tide of passion; all he could do was to let it beat against him. He made a few expostulations, which increased Candace's vehemence; he expressed his regret over the whole affair, and suggested that they should kneel and ask the guidance of the Lord in the matter, that she might be led to see it all in a different light.

Candace refused flatly. "I don't see any use prayin' about it," said she. "I don't think the Lord's got much to do with it, anyhow."

It was almost time for the afternoon service when the minister left. He had missed his comfortable noontide rest, through this encounter with his revolutionary parishioner. After the minister had gone, Candace sat by the window and waited. The bell rang, and she watched the people file past. When her nephew Wilson Ford with Alma appeared, she grunted to herself. "She's thin as a rail," said she; "guess there won't be much left of her by the time Wilson gets her. Little soft-spoken nippin' thing, she wouldn't make him no kind of a wife, anyway. Guess it's jest as well."

When the bell had stopped tolling, and all the people entered the church, Candace went over to her organ and seated herself. She arranged a singing-book before her, and sat still, waiting. Her thin, colorless neck and temples were full of beating pulses; her black eyes were bright and eager; she leaned stiffly over toward the music-rack, to hear better. When the church organ sounded out she straightened herself; her long skinny fingers pressed her own organ-keys with nervous energy. She worked the pedals with all her strength; all her slender body was in motion. When the first notes of Alma's solo began, Candace sang. She had really possessed a fine voice, and it was wonderful how little she had lost it. Straining her throat with jealous fury, her notes were still for the main part true. Her voice filled the whole room;

she sang with wonderful fire and expression. That, at least, mild little Alma Way could never emulate. She was full of steadfastness and unquestioning constancy, but there were in her no smoldering fires of ambition and resolution. Music was not to her what it had been to her older rival. To this obscure woman, kept relentlessly by circumstances in a narrow track, singing in the village choir had been as much as Italy was to Napoleon—and now on her island of exile she was still showing fight.

After the church service was done, Candace left the organ and went over to her old chair by the window. Her knees felt weak, and shook under her. She sat down, and leaned back her head. There were red spots on her cheeks. Pretty soon she heard a quick slam of her gate, and an impetuous tread on the gravel-walk. She looked up, and there was her nephew Wilson Ford hurrying up to the door. She cringed a little, then she settled herself more firmly in her chair.

Wilson came into the room with a rush. He left the door open, and the wind slammed it to after him.

"Aunt Candace, where are you?" he called out, in a loud voice.

She made no reply. He looked around fiercely, and his eyes seemed to pounce upon her.

"Look here, Aunt Candace," said he, "are you crazy?" Candace said nothing. "Aunt Candace!" She did not seem to see him. "If you don't answer me," said Wilson, "I'll just go over there and pitch that old organ out of the window!"

"Wilson Ford!" said Candace, in a voice that was almost a scream.

"Well, what say! What have you got to say for yourself, acting the way you have? I tell you what 'tis, Aunt Candace, I won't stand it."

"I'd like to see you help yourself."

"I will help myself. I'll pitch that old organ out of the window, and then I'll board up the window on that side of your house. Then we'll see."

"It ain't your house, and it won't never be."

"Who said it was my house? You're my aunt, and I've got a little lookout for the credit of the family. Aunt Candace, what are you doing this way for?"

"It don't make no odds what I'm doin' so for. I ain't bound to give my reasons to a young fellar like you, if you do act so mighty toppin'. But I'll tell you one thing, Wilson Ford, after the way you've spoke to-day, you sha'n't never have one cent of my money, an' you can't never marry that Way girl if you don't have it. You can't never take her home to live with your mother, an' this house would have been mighty nice an' convenient for you some day. Now you won't get it. I'm goin' to make another will. I'd made one, if you did but know it. Now you won't get a cent of my money, you nor your mother neither. An' I ain't goin' to live a dreadful while longer, neither. Now I wish you'd go home; I want to lay down. I'm 'bout sick."

Wilson could not get another word from his aunt. His indignation had not in the least cooled. Her threat of disinheriting him did not cow him at all; he had too much rough independence, and indeed his aunt Candace's house had always been too much of an air-castle for him to contemplate seriously. Wilson, with his burly frame and his headlong common-sense, could have little to do with air-castles, had he been hard enough to build them over graves. Still, he had not admitted that he never could marry Alma. All his hopes were based upon a rise in his own fortunes, not by some sudden convulsion, but by his own long and steady labor. Some time, he thought, he should have saved enough for the two homes.

He went out of his aunt's house still storming. She arose after the door had shut behind him, and got out into the kitchen. She thought that she would start a fire and make a cup of tea. She had not eaten anything all day. She put some kindling-wood into the stove and touched a match to it; then she went back to the sitting-room, and settled down again into the chair by the window. The fire in the kitchen-stove roared, and the light wood was soon burned out. She thought no more about it. She had not put on the teakettle. Her head ached, and once in a while she shivered. She sat at the window while the afternoon waned and the dusk came on. At seven o'clock the meeting bell rang again, and the people flocked by. This time she did not stir. She had shut her parlor organ. She did not need to out-sing her rival this evening; there was only congregational singing at the Sunday-night prayer-meeting.

She sat still until it was nearly time for meeting to be done; her head ached harder and harder, and she shivered more. Finally she arose. "Guess I'll go to bed," she muttered. She went about the house, bent over and shaking, to lock the doors. She stood a minute in the back door, looking over the fields to the woods. There was a red light over there. "The woods are on fire," said Candace. She watched with a dull interest the flames roll up, withering and destroying the tender green spring foliage. The air was full of smoke, although the fire was half a mile away.

Candace locked the door and went in. The trees with their delicate garlands of new leaves, with the new nests of song birds, might fall, she was in the roar of an intenser fire; the growths of all her springs and the delicate wontedness of her whole life were going down in it. Candace went to bed in her little room off the parlor, but she could not sleep. She lay awake all night. In the morning she crawled to the door and hailed a little boy who was passing. She bade him go for the doctor as quickly as he could, then to Mrs. Ford's, and ask her to come over. She held on to the door while she was talking. The boy stood staring wonderingly at her. The spring wind fanned her face. She had drawn on a dress skirt and put her shawl over her shoulders, and her gray hair was blowing over her red cheeks.

She shut the door and went to her bed. She never arose from it again. The doctor and Mrs. Ford came and looked after her, and she lived a week. Nobody but herself thought until the very last that she would die; the doctor called her illness merely a light run of fever; she had her senses fully.

But Candace gave up at the first. "It's my last sickness," she said to Mrs. Ford that morning when she first entered; and Mrs. Ford had laughed at the notion; but the sick woman held to it. She did not seem to suffer much physical pain; she only grew weaker and weaker, but she was distressed mentally. She did not talk much, but her eyes followed everybody with an agonized expression.

On Wednesday William Emmons came to inquire for her. Candace heard him out in the parlor. She tried to raise herself on one elbow that she might listen better to his voice.

"William Emmons come in to ask how you was," Mrs. Ford said, after he was gone.

"I—heard him," replied Candace. Presently she spoke again. "Nancy," said she, "where's that photograph album?"

"On the table," replied her sister, hesitatingly.

"Mebbe—you'd better—brush it up a little."

"Well."

Sunday morning Candace wished that the minister should be asked to come in at the noon intermission. She had refused to see him before. He came and prayed with her, and she asked his forgiveness for the way she had spoken the Sunday before. "I—hadn't ought to —spoke so," said she. "I was—dreadful wrought up."

"Perhaps it was your sickness coming on," said the minister, soothingly.

Candace shook her head. "No—it wa'n't. I hope the Lord will—forigve me."

After the minister had gone, Candace still appeared unhappy. Her pitiful eyes followed her sister everywhere with the mechanical persistency of a portrait.

"What is it you want, Candace?" Mrs. Ford said at last. She had nursed her sister faithfully, but once in a while her impatience showed itself.

"Nancy!"

"What say?"

"I wish—you'd go out when—meetin's done, an'—head off Alma an' Wilson, an'—ask 'em to come in. I feel as if—I'd like to—hear her sing."

Mrs. Ford stared. "Well," said she.

The meeting was now in session. The windows were all open, for it was another warm Sunday. Candace lay listening to the music when it began, and a look of peace came over her face. Her sister had smoothed her hair back, and put on a clean cap. The white curtain in the bedroom window waved in the wind like a white sail. Candace almost felt as if she were better, but the thought of death seemed easy.

Mrs. Ford at the parlor window watched for the meeting to be out. When the people appeared, she ran down the walk and waited for Alma and Wilson. When they came she told them what Candace wanted, and they all went in together.

"Here's Alma an' Wilson, Candace," said Mrs. Ford, leading them to the bedroom door.

Candace smiled. "Come in," she said, feebly. And Alma and Wilson entered and stood beside the bed. Candace continued to look at them, the smile straining her lips.

"Wilson!"

"What is it, Aunt Candace?"

"I ain't altered that—will. You an' Alma can—come here an'—live—when I'm gone. Your mother won't mind livin' alone. Alma can have—all—my things."

"Don't, Aunt Candace." Tears were running over Wilson's cheeks, and Alma's delicate face was all of a quiver.

"I thought—maybe—Alma'd be willin' to—sing for me," said Candace.

"What do you want me to sing?" Alma asked, in a trembling voice.

"'Jesus, lover of my soul.'"

Alma, standing there beside Wilson, began to sing. At first she could hardly control her voice, then she sang sweetly and clearly.

Candace lay and listened. Her face had a holy and radiant expression. When Alma stopped singing it did not disappear, but she looked up and spoke, and it was like a secondary glimpse of the old shape of a forest tree through the smoke and flame of the transfiguring fire the instant before it falls. "You flatted a little on—soul," said Candace.

A Kitchen Colonel

BACK of the kitchen proper in the Lee house there was another shed-kitchen, unplastered and unpainted, that was used for rough work like soap-boiling and washing. Each kitchen had its own door opening directly into the green yard on the north side of the house.

Abel Lee sat in the door of the back kitchen cleaning dandelion greens. His long limbs in stiff blue cotton overalls sprawled down over the low wooden step into the grass. His white head showed out against the dark unpainted interior at his back. He had a tin pan full of dandelions between his knees, and he was scraping them assiduously with an old shoe-knife, and throwing them into another pan on the step beside him.

That morning the narrow green yard that stretched along the north side of the house had been all thickly set with yellow dandelion disks; now there were very few left, for Abel had dug them up for dinner.

It was early in May, and the air was full of sudden sweet calls of birds and delicate rustles of flowering boughs. In Ephraim Cole's next-door yard, on the other side of the gray picket-fence, stood three blossoming peach-trees. They were young and symmetrical trees, they stood in a line, and were in full pink bloom. Every time they stirred in the wind they gave out a stronger almond fragrance.

Abel, as he cleaned his dandelions, breathed it in without noticing. He had been out there all the morning, and had become accustomed to it, as it seems one would to the air of paradise. Moreover, he had seen seventy-eight seasons of blooming peach-trees, and a spring had become like an old and familiar picture on his wall; it had no new meaning for him. And, too, he was harnessed, as it were, with his head down, to dandelions.

Always as he sat there he could hear a heavy creaking step in the forward kitchen. Back and forth it went, and there were also loud rattling and clinking noises of dishes and iron kettles.

Suddenly, as he worked on the dandelions, the step and the noises ceased, and a voice took their place. It was a naturally soft and weak voice that had been strained into hard shrillness. "You mind you clean them dandelions thorough, father."

"I'm takin' all the pains I can with 'em," replied the old man. He examined one which he held in hand at the moment with great solicitude. He could not see the woman, but her eyes were upon him through the crack in the blind. She was at the window nearest the door.

"Well, you mind you do," she repeated. "How near done air they?"

The old man surveyed the pans with grave consideration. "'Bout half, I guess."

"Half! Good land! An' you've been quiddlin' out there all the mornin'."

"It's consider'ble work to dig 'em, mother."

"Work—talk about work! You dun know what work is. If you'd made the pies that I have since I got up from the breakfast-table you might think you'd done somethin'. If them greens ain't done in half an hour I can't get 'em boiled for dinner."

"I guess I can git 'em done in half an hour."

"Guess—there ain't no guess about it! You've got to if I git 'em done for dinner, an' I've got to have somethin' to eat with all them boarders. I want you to git them done, an' then wash up the breakfast dishes. I ain't had a minute. Now don't, for the land's sake, putter so long over that one; it's clean 'nough."

The voice ceased and the step began. Abel labored with diligence at his dandelion greens. After a while another old man came stiffly sauntering across the next-door yard, and took up a stand the other side of the picket-fence. He was small, with sharp features and a high forehead. He had very white hair and a long white beard, and he was smiling to himself. He stood between two of the blooming peach-trees, and looked smilingly at Abel, who toiled over his greens, and did not appear to see him.

"Well, Abel, how air ye?" said the old man finally. His smile deepened, his old blue eyes took on a hard twinkle, like blue beads, and stared straight into Abel's face.

"Well, I'm pooty fair, Ephraim. How air you?" Abel had not started when the other spoke; he merely glanced up from his greens with a friendly air.

"Well, I'm 'bout as usual, Abel." The old man paused for a second. When he spoke again it was more cautiously. He was near Abel, and also very near the kitchen window whence the sound of footsteps and dishes came. "Kitchen colonel this mornin', Abel?" he queried, in a soft and insinuating voice. His venerable white beard seemed to take quirks and curls like a satyr's; he gave a repressed chuckle.

"I dun' know what you call it," replied Abel, with a patient gravity. He took another dandelion out of the pan and examined it minutely.

"Goin' to the meetin' this arternoon?"

"What meetin'?"

"The town meetin': ain't ye heerd of it?"

"No, I ain't."

"It's a special town meetin' 'bout the waterworks they're talkin' 'bout puttin' in. There's notices up on all the trees down street. I should ha' thought you'd seen 'em, if you'd had eyes."

"Well, I ain't happened to somehow."

Ephraim cast a glance at the kitchen window, and again cautiously lowered his voice. "Been too busy in the kitchen, ain't ye?"

"Well, I dun' know 'bout that."

"I s'pose a kitchen colonel wouldn't git shot if he run for't; but he might git the pots an' kittles throwed at him." Ephraim doubled over the fence with merriment at his own humor.

Abel's face was imperturbable; he kept close at work on the greens.

"Well, I s'pose you'll go to the meetin'," continued Ephraim.

"I dun' know."

"I should think you'd want to go, if you was a man, an' have a leetle voice in things. Here they air talkin' 'bout puttin' in them waterworks, an' raisin' our taxes four per cent. to pay for't. I've got a good well, an' so've you, an' we don't want no waterworks."

"There's some that ain't got wells," observed Abel, shortly.

"Well, that ain't anything to us, is it? We've got 'em. Anyway, I should think you'd want to go to the meetin', an' see what *was* bein' done, if you was a man."

Abel said nothing. He began to gather up himself and his pans stiffly. The dandelions were all picked over. Ephraim, still smiling, leaned on the fence and watched him.

"What ye goin' to do now, Abel?"

Abel did not seem to hear. When he stood up, one could see how tall he was, although there was a stoop in his gaunt square shoulders. His spare face was pale, and his sharp handsome features had a severe downward cast, although their principal effect was gentle patience. He looked like a Roman senator turned begging friar as he stood there in his overalls holding his dandelion pans.

"Got the dishes washed, Abel?"

"No, I ain't yet," replied Abel, with a mixture of embarrassment and dignity in his tone. He turned on his heel, but Ephraim would not let him go.

"Stop a minute," said he. "Where's Fanny?"

"She's gone to school."

"Hm!" Ephraim, as he sniffed, cocked his head, and rolled his eyes towards the pink top of a peach-tree, as if in a spasm of contempt. "I rayther think *if* Fanny Lee was *my* granddaughter she'd quit school-teachin', an' stay to home an' help about the house-work, an' *I'd* quit bein' kitchen colonel; I rayther think I would."

Ephraim raised his voice incautiously; a woman's head appeared in the window.

"What's that?" she inquired, sharply.

"Oh, nothin'," replied Ephraim. "I was jest talkin' to Abel, Mis' Lee." Ephraim straightened himself from his lounge over the fence, and turned about with a deprecatory swiftness; but the woman's sharp old voice followed him up like a long-lashed whip.

"Well," said she, "if you ain't got anything better to do than to stan' leanin' on the fence talkin' nothin' to my husband all the forenoon, you had better come in here an' help me. I'll give you somethin' to do." Ephraim said nothing; he was in full retreat, and had passed the line of peach-trees. "You'd better go home an' help Mis' Coles carry in the water for her washin'," the woman's voice went on. "I see her carryin' in a pail jest now, an' she was bent over 'most double." Seeing that she could get no response, she stood looking after Ephraim with a comical expression that savored of malice and amusement. She turned around when Abel with the dandelions shuffled into the room. "Now, father, what air you bringin' that pan that you've put the scrapin's of the greens in in here for? Don't you know no better? I should think you'd knowed enough to took 'em down to the hens, many times as I've told ye. They're shut up now, an' they like green things."

"I'll take 'em down now."

"Take 'em down now! It does seem sometimes, father, as if you didn't have no sense at all. If I set you to doin' a piece of work, you're always takin' hold on't wrong end first. Take them greens down to the hens! I should think you'd know better, father."

Mrs. Lee was a small and frail-looking old woman, but she seemed always to have through her a strong quiver as of electric wires. It was as if she had an electric battery at the centre of her nervous system. Abel stood droopingly before her, his face full of mild dejection and bewilderment.

"Ain't I told you, father," she went on, "that them dandelion greens wouldn't get done for dinner if they wa'n't on? an' ain't they got to be washed? You know you ain't washed 'em, an' they ain't ready to put in the kittle, an' here you air talkin' 'bout goin' to the hen-coop! I ruther guess the hens can wait."

"I didn't know jest what you meant, mother."

"You don't act as if you knew what anything meant sometimes. It does seem to me as if you might have a leetle more sconce, father, with all I've got to do."

Abel set the pan of greens in the sink, and pumped water on them with vigor.

"Mind you git 'em clean," charged his wife. She was baking pies, and she moved about with such quickness that her motions seemed full of vibrations, and as if one could hear a hum, as with a bird. If she had about her any of the rustiness and clumsiness of age, she propelled herself with such energy that no hitches nor squeaks were apparent. She stepped heavily for so small a woman; it seemed impossible that her bodily weight could account for such heavy footsteps, and as if her character must add its own gravity to them. Mrs. Lee was but two years younger than her husband; but her light hair had not turned gray—it had only faded—and she did not wear a cap. She had been a very pretty woman, and there was still a suggestion of the prettiness in her face. She had withered complete, as some flowers do on their stalks, keeping all their original shapes, and fading into themselves, not scattering any of their graces abroad.

Everybody called Mrs. Abel Lee a very smart woman, and a very wonderful woman for one of her age. The house in which she lived had been left to her by her father. Abel had mortgaged it heavily, and she had taken boarders and nearly cleared it. Abel Lee had been a very unfortunate and unsuccessful man through his whole life. He had worked hard, and failed in everything that he had undertaken. Now he was an old man of seventy-eight, and his wife was taking boarders to support the family and clear the mortgage, and he was helping her about the housework. It seemed to be all that he could do.

The Lees had had one son, who had apparently inherited his father's ill-fortune. He had a sad life, and died without a dollar, leaving his daughter Fanny to the care of his old parents. Fanny was about eighteen now, and she taught school. Her school-house was a mile away, and she did not come home to dinner. However, Mrs. Lee's boarders all came, punctually at twelve o'clock. The boarders were four women, not very young, who worked in the shoe factory. When they got home, dingy and dull-faced, they always found dinner on the table—plenty of good food. Mrs. Lee was a splendid cook, after the village model. She did the helping with alacrity, and Abel had his portion after the boarders. He had a small allowance of greens to-day; they were the first of the season, and the boarders were hungry for them. The four women could not grasp many of the pleasures of life, and had to make the most of those that hung low enough for them. They took a deal of comfort in eating.

After dinner Abel hurried to clear off the table and wash the dishes. He was usually a long time about it, for he was hopelessly clumsy, although he was so faithful at such work. Abel at the dish-tub with one of his wife's aprons pinned around his waist was a piteous object. He bent to the task with a hopeless and dejected air, and mopped the plates with melancholy fussiness. But to-day he rattled the dishes quite like a woman. "Don't you rattle them plates round so; you'll nick 'em," his wife remarked once, and Abel obediently tempered his movements. Still, the dinner dishes were washed much sooner than usual. After they were set away, Abel took up a stand at the pantry door; he leaned against it, and regarded his wife with a hesitating air. Once in a while he opened his mouth as if to speak, then seemed to change his mind. Finally Mrs. Lee turned sharply on him. "Why don't you git the broom an' sweep up the kitchen, father," said she. "What air you standin' there for?"

Abel did not answer for a moment; he looked across the room at the broom on its nail, then at his wife—"I kinder thought—mebbe—I'd go to—that town meetin' this afternoon."

His wife faced about on him with a spoon in her hand. "What town meetin'?"

"The one they've 'p'inted about the water-works. I thought mebbe I'd better go an' kinder look into it a leetle."

"Look into it—a great difference it'll make your lookin' into it! I should think you'd got about all the town meetin' you could attend to to home, without goin' traipsin' off there. Here's the churnin' to be done, an' I ain't got no time nor strength for't. I shouldn't think you'd talk 'bout town meetin's, father."

"Well, I dun' know as I'd better go," said Abel, and went across for the broom. However, he swept with more dispatch than usual, and when he sat down to the churn it was with a forlorn hope that the butter might come in season for him to go to the town meeting. But the butter did not come until the meeting had been long dispersed, and not until Fanny came home from school. Abel was just lifting out the dasher when she appeared in the kitchen door with her dinner basket on her arm. "Well, grandpa, has the butter come?" said she.

"I guess you've brought it; it's been all the afternoon gittin' here." Abel surveyed her with adoration. Fanny was a pretty young girl. She looked at her grandparents and smiled radiantly, but evidently the smiles were about something that they did not understand.

"What air you lookin' so awful tickled about?" asked Mrs. Lee.

"Oh, nothing. Did you have any pudding left from dinner? I'm most starved."

"There's a saucer under the yellow bowl on the pantry shelf."

Fanny was still smiling when she sat down at the kitchen table with the pudding. "What does ail you?" Mrs. Lee asked again. She was at the other end of the table rolling out biscuits for tea.

"Oh, nothing, grandma. What makes you think there's anything?" Fanny ate her pudding with apparent unconcern, but all the time her eyes danced, and the corners of her mouth curved upward. "I didn't have to walk home to-night," she remarked, finally.

"Didn't have to walk home? Why not?"

"Well, Charley Page came along just about the time school was out, and—he brought me home in his buggy."

"Well, I never!" Mrs. Lee's sharp old face softened; she surveyed her granddaughter with admiring smiles. "That's the second time within a week, ain't it."

Fanny nodded, and bent lower over the pudding. She was blushing pink, and could not keep the smiles back. Abel, who was starting the fire, stook stock-still, and stared with delighted wonder at her and his wife. "That young Page is one of the smartest fellars in town," he volunteered; "an' his father's wuth a good deal of property."

Abel was so pleased that he paid little attention when, on carrying his basket around to the shed door for more light wood, Ephraim again hailed him from the fence. "Hullo, Abel!" he called; "I didn't see you to the town meetin'."

"No; I wa'n't there."

"Kitchen colonel again?"

Abel picked up wood vigorously. Ephraim surveyed him with a dissatisfied expression. "Who was that I see your Fanny a-ridin' home with?" he asked.

Abel straightened himself, and looked over at Ephraim. "That was the young Page fellar," he said, proudly.

"John Page's son?"

"Yes."

"H'm!"

In a moment Ephraim turned about and walked off. He had a daughter of his own who was about Fanny's age, and she was very plain-looking and unattractive, and was not liked by the young men.

Fanny was much sought for, she was so pretty, and she had such pleasant ways. She dressed nicely too; her grandmother encouraged her to spend her school money for clothes. Her grandparents had always petted her, and exacted very little from her. She did not help much about the house. To-night, after tea, she stood looking irresolutely at her pretty gray dress and her grandparents. "Don't you want me to take off my dress and help about the dishes?" said she.

"Land, no!" answered her grandmother. "Go 'long; it ain't wuth while to change your dress for this little passel of dishes. Father's goin' to wash 'em while I'm mixin' up the bread."

"Yes, you go right along an' set down in the parlor an' git rested, Fanny," chimed in Abel. "I ain't got a thing to do but the dishes, an' they ain't wuth talkin' about." Abel shuffled cheerfully around, gathering up the dishes from the tea-table.

Fanny went into the parlor as she was bidden; she had about her a sweet docility, and she would have changed her dress and washed the dishes just as readily. Fanny would always perform all the duties that she was told to, but probably not so very many others. She had little original directive power in the matter of duties, although she had a perfect willingness and sweetness in their execution.

She sat down at a parlor window with some fancy-work, and rocked to and fro comfortably. She could look out on the front yard full of green grass, with a blossoming cherry-tree, and a yellow-flowering bush down near the gate. The four women boarders were in the sitting-room, but she did not think of joining them, nor they her. Fanny's grandmother always insinuated her into the parlor when the boarders were in the sitting-room. In her heart she did not consider that these four dingy-handed shop-girls were fit associates for her granddaughter.

Fanny herself had no such feeling in the matter; she would have gone into the sitting-room and fraternized with the boarders, had her grandmother wished her to do so. But they rather repulsed her, and held themselves aloof with an awkward dignity, and Fanny was timid and easily rebuffed. They were quite acute enough to understand that Mrs. Lee did not consider them proper company for her granddaughter, and they felt injured and covertly resentful. They were also righteously indignant because Fanny was so petted by her grandparents, and did not help them more. To-night the four women in the sitting-room whispered together about Fanny; how she was sitting all dressed up in the parlor while her poor old grandparents were working in the kitchen. They thought that she ought to give up her school and stay at home and help. She was not earning much anyway, and it all went on to her back; she need not dress so fine.

While they whispered, Fanny, small and dainty, putting pretty stitches in her fancy-work, sat at the parlor window. When it was too dark for her to sew, she leaned her head against the window-casing and looked out. The yellow bush in the yard still showed out brightly in the dusk; the cherry-tree looked like a mist. Over in the east, beyond everything else, was a soft rise of shadow; that was Eagle Mountain.

It grew darker. After a while her grandmother came into the room, feeling her way. "Don't you want me to light a lamp, grandma?" asked Fanny, in a soft, absent voice.

"No; I don't want none. I'd jest as soon set down in the dark a few minutes; then I'm goin' to bed. Father's gone." The old woman fumbled into a chair at the other window. "Have you seen anything about your hat yet?" she asked Fanny, after they both had sat still a little while.

"Yes; I went into Miss Loring's on my way to school this morning."

"What you goin' to have?"

"That brown straw I've been talking about. I'm going to have it trimmed with some brown velvet and yellow daisies."

"It'll be real handsome. When you goin' to have it?"

"Next week—Friday. I've got to have it then, for I haven't a thing to wear if we go up to the mountain Saturday."

The old woman's face was invisible in the dusk, but her voice took on a pleased and significant tone, and she laughed softly. "I s'pose that Page fellar will be goin', won't he?"

"I don't know. He was invited." Fanny also laughed with pleased confusion. She had been climbing the mountain with young Page for the last hour in a dream, and she had worn the brown straw hat with the brown velvet and yellow daisies.

"Well, I guess he'll go, fast enough. I see his father down to the store the other day, an' he stopped an' shook hands an' asked how I was, and looked dreadful smilin' an' knowin'. I guess he's heerd how his son's been carryin' you home from school. Well, I guess he's a good, likely young fellar, an' that's wuth more'n his father's money." The old woman spoke the last words of her remark in a lagging and drowsy voice. The two were silent again. Presently there came a long heavy breath from the grandmother's corner.

"Grandma!" called Fanny.

"What?" the old woman responded, faintly.

"Wake up; you're goin' to sleep."

"Well, I dun' know but I be. I guess I'd better rouse up an' go to bed. I wouldn't set up much longer if I was you, Fanny."

"I ain't going to." But Fanny sat there and dreamed quite a while after her grandmother had fumbled out of the room.

That was on Thursday. It was the next day but one, Saturday, when old Ephraim Coles came to the fence and hailed Abel as he was paring potatoes at the kitchen door. "Hullo, Abel! how air ye?"

"'Bout as usual," answered Abel.

"Kitchen colonel this mornin'?"

"I dun' know what you call it." Abel was cutting the specks from the potatoes with clumsy pains. He sat on the door-step with the pan between his knees. Ephraim stood watching him. He had an important look, and his smile was different from his usual one.

Presently he leaned over the fence. "Abel!" said he, in a confidential whisper.

"What?"

"Come here a minute. Want to tell ye somethin'."

Abel hesitated; he peered uneasily around at the kitchen window. Then he set down the potatoes, arose, and slowly shuffled over to the fence. Ephraim reached over and caught him by the sleeve when he came near enough. "You know Maria an' me own two share in the railroad, don't ye?" he whispered. Abel nodded. "Well," continued Ephraim, "next Saturday there's a stockholder meetin' to Boston, an' Maria she don't care nothin' 'bout goin', 'cause she's goin' to have company, an' Abby she don't want to, an' so if you want to go on Maria's stock you *can*."

Abel stared at him in gentle bewilderment. "Go to Boston?"

"Of course—go to Boston for nothin'; 'twon't cost ye a cent. An' I'll stan' the dinner. We'll go in somewhere an' git somethin' to eat. An' we'll go round an' see the sights. What d'ye say to't?"

Ephraim looked at Abel with the air of an emperor tendering a royal bounty. He drew himself up, put his hands in his pockets, and smiled. Abel looked pleased and eager. "Thank ye," said he—"thank ye, Ephraim. I'd like to go fust-rate if—there ain't nothin' to hender."

"I'd like to know what there is to hender! I guess you can quit bein' kitchen colonel for one day. The meetin' comes a week from to-day, an' that's Saturday, an' Fanny she'll be home to help Mis' Lee."

"Yes, she will," assented Abel, thoughtfully. "Well, I must go an' finish them pertaters now, an' I'll see what mother says to it, an' let yer know."

Abel pared the potatoes with greater pains than ever; he washed them faithfully, and carried them into the kitchen, and tremblingly broached the subject of the Boston trip to his wife. To his great delight it was favorably received. Mrs. Lee said she did not see any reason why he could not go. She had entirely forgotten about Fanny's mountain party.

All the next week old Abel was in a tremor of delight. He had long conferences with Ephraim over the fence; delightful additions to the regular programme were planned; every day some new scheme was talked over. Abel had not had an outing for many years; he was like a child over this one. Still he did not neglect his household tasks; he worked with anxious zeal, he was so afraid that his wife might see so much to be done that she would veto the plan at the last moment. He was so anxious and nervous over it that he did not say much about it at home, for fear of having some damper cast upon him. Abel had not much shrewdness, but he had learned that a casual acceptance of a situation was much more likely than an eager one to make it lasting when his wife was concerned. Friday night at sunset both of the old men stood out in the yard with uplifted faces and scrutinized the heavens.

"It ain't goin' to be foul weather to-morrow," said Ephraim, judicially; "not if I know anything about signs."

"Ain't you afraid the wind ain't in jest the right quarter?" Abel asked, anxiously.

"H'm! I don't care nothin' about the wind. Everything p'ints square to fair weather, 'cordin' to my reck'nin'."

Ephraim was right. The next day was beautiful. Abel looked out of the window in the morning, and his face was like a boy's. Directly after breakfast he shaved himself at the kitchen glass and blacked his boots. Then he went into his bedroom to put on his Sunday clothes.

He was nearly ready—clean collar and the best stock and all—when he heard Fanny's voice and Ephraim's daughter Abby's out in the yard. He did not pay much attention at first; then he stood still and listened with a lengthening face. "No, I can't go any way in the world," Fanny was saying. Her voice was perfectly sweet and uncomplaining, but there was a sad inflection in it. "Grandma forgot all about it, and she says poor grandpa has been counting on going to Boston with your father for a whole week, and it would be real cruel to keep him at home; and it's baking-day, and she's got the sitting-room carpet to put down, and she can't get along alone. Of course I'm kind of sorry about it. I'd been counting on going; but I wouldn't keep grandpa at home for anything, and there isn't anything else for me to do but to stay myself."

"Well, I hope that pretty Rogers girl that's visiting up to Rhoda Emerson's won't cut you out with Charley Page. I saw him talking to her in the post-office last night," Abby said. Her voice was like her father's.

Abel unwound his stock, and painfully unbuttoned his stiff collar. Presently he appeared in the kitchen, and he had on his old clothes. His wife faced around on him. "For mercy's sakes, father, ain't you changed your clothes yet?"

"I ain't goin', after all, I guess."

"Ain't goin'! why not?"

Fanny was standing at the sink washing dishes, and she stopped and stared.

"Well," said Abel, "I've been thinkin' on't over, an' I've made up my mind I'd better not go, on several 'counts."

"I'd like to know what."

"Well, one thing is, it's kinder cheatin'. I've got to go as Maria Coles, an' I ain't Maria Coles. That's what it says in the stiffikit. I've got to show the conductor 'Maria Coles.' An' it ain't jest square, 'cordin' to my notions. I ain't thought 'twas all the time."

"Well, I think you air dreadful silly, father."

"Well, I don't think 'twould amount to much goin' anyhow, to tell the truth."

"I would go, grandpa," said Fanny.

But Abel stood fast in his position. His wife, and Fanny, who was anxious to acquit herself honorably in the matter, pleaded with him to no purpose. He was proof against even Ephraim's reproaches and sarcasms. "Well, stay to home, an' be a kitchen colonel all your life, if you want to," shouted Ephraim, as he strode out of the yard; "it's all you're fit for, 'cordin' to my way of thinkin'."

Abel went into the house and pushed Fanny away from the sink. "If there's anything else you want to do, Fanny," said he, "you'd better go an' do it. I ain't got another thing to set my hand to now."

Fanny looked at her grandmother.

"If he *ain't* goin', you might jest as well go an' get ready," said Mrs. Lee.

In a few minutes Abel heard Fanny's voice calling over to Abby: "Abby, Abby, wait for me! I'm goin', after all. It won't take me but a minute to get ready." And Fanny's voice sounded sweeter than a bird's to her grandfather at the kitchen sink.

Abel had a hard day of it. Putting down the sitting-room carpet was painful work for his old joints, and then there was churning to be done. When Fanny came home he sat in the old rocking-chair in the kitchen, with his head back, fast asleep. Presently his wife came out and aroused him. "Wake up, father," said she; "I want to tell you somethin'." Abel looked heavily up at her. "I—ruther guess Fanny an' that Page fellar have settled it betwixt 'em," whispered Mrs. Lee.

Abel's head was up in a minute, and he was looking at her, all alert. "You don't say so, mother!" Suddenly the old man put his hand up to his eyes and sobbed.

"Why, how silly you are, father!" said his wife. Then she went over to a window, with a brisk step, and stood there as if looking out. When she turned around her eyes were red. "I think you'd better go to bed, father, an' not set there dozin' in that chair any longer," said she, sharply; "you're all tuckered out."

The next day, when Abel had to stand a running fire, relative to the Boston trip, from Ephraim, he gave one counter-shot—the announcement of Fanny's engagement. He listened while Ephraim related the pleasures of his excursion and berated him; then he turned on him with an artfulness born of patience. "S'pose you've heard the news?" said he.

"What news?"

"Well, I s'pose our Fanny an' John Page's son have 'bout concluded to make a match on't."

"H'm!" Ephraim stood looking at him. "When they goin' to git married?"

"Well, I dun' know. Mother was saying she thought mebbe some time in the fall."

"H'm! Well, there's slips. Mebbe she won't git him, arter all. It's best not to be too sure 'bout it."

But Ephraim turned on his heel and went home across the yard, and left Abel to his Sunday peace.

Abel had to work harder than usual that summer. It was Fanny's vacation time, and she had been accustomed to assist some about the house-work, so Abel's labors had been lightened a little during hot weather. But this summer Fanny was sewing, getting ready to be married in the fall, and she could not do much else, so her grandfather got no respite in his kitchen work through the long hot days. He grew thinner and older, but he never complained even to himself. He was radiant over Fanny. She was going to make a match that would lift her out of all his own struggles and hardships. Poor old Abel, in the midst of his hard, pitiful little whirlpool, watched Fanny joyously making her way out of it, and no longer thought of himself.

Fanny was married in October. There was quite a large evening wedding, and Mrs. Lee had wedding-cake and pound-cake and tea and coffee passed around for refreshments. Fanny and her bridegroom were standing before the minister, who had already begun the ceremony. Fanny, all in white, bent her head delicately under her veil; her cheeks showed through it like roses. The bridegroom kept his handsome boyish face upon the minister with a brave and resolute air. Abel and his wife stood near with solemn and tearful faces. The four boarders stood together in a corner. The rooms were crowded with people in creaking silks and Sunday coats, and the air was heavy with cake and coffee and flowers.

Suddenly, in the midst of the ceremony, Mrs. Lee nudged Abel. "The milk is burnin', father," she whispered; "go out quick an' lift it off."

Abel looked at her. "Be quick," she whispered again; "the milk for the coffee is burnin'. Don't stan' there lookin', for mercy's sake!"

Abel tiptoed out solemnly, with his best boots creaking.

When he returned, Fanny was married, and the people were crowding around her. He felt a heavy poke in his side, and there was Ephraim. "Had to go out an' be kitchen colonel, didn't ye, Abel?" said he, quite loud.

The bridal couple drove away, and the guests dispersed gradually. Mrs. Lee had to stay in the parlor until the last of them disappeared; but as soon as Fanny and her husband had gone, Abel changed his clothes and went into the kitchen. Things needed to be set to rights a little before morning.

The happy bridal pair rode away through the October night, the wedding guests chattered merrily in the parlor and flocked gayly down the street, and the kitchen colonel fought faithfully in his humble field, where maybe he would some day win a homely glory all his own.

The Revolt of "Mother"

"FATHER!"

"What is it?"

"What are them men diggin' over there in the field for?"

There was a sudden dropping and enlarging of the lower part of the old man's face, as if some heavy weight had settled therein; he shut his mouth tight, and went on harnessing the great bay mare. He hustled the collar on to her neck with a jerk.

"Father!"

The old man slapped the saddle upon the mare's back.

"Look here, father, I want to know what them men are diggin' over in the field for, an' I'm goin' to know."

"I wish you'd go into the house, mother, an' 'tend to your own affairs," the old man said then. He ran his words together, and his speech was almost as inarticulate as a growl.

But the woman understood; it was her most native tongue. "I ain't goin' into the house till you tell me what them men are doin' over there in the field," said she.

Then she stood waiting. She was a small woman, short and straight-waisted like a child, in her brown cotton gown. Her forehead was mild and benevolent between the smooth curves of gray hair; there were meek downward lines about her nose and mouth; but her eyes, fixed upon the old man, looked as if the meekness had been the result of her own will, never of the will of another.

They were in the barn, standing before the wide open doors. The spring air, full of the smell of growing grass and unseen blossoms, came in their faces. The deep yard in front was littered with farm wagons and piles of wood; on the edges, close to the fence and the house, the grass was a vivid green, and there were some dandelions.

The old man glanced doggedly at his wife as he tightened the last buckles on the harness. She looked as immovable to him as one of the rocks in his pasture-land, bound to the earth with generations of blackberry vines. He slapped the reins over the horse, and started forth from the barn.

"Father!" said she.

The old man pulled up. "What is it?"

"I want to know what them men are diggin' over there in that field for."

"They're diggin' a cellar, I s'pose, if you've got to know."

"A cellar for what?"

"A barn."

"A barn? You ain't goin' to build a barn over there where we was goin' to have a house, father?"

The old man said not another word. He hurried the horse into the farm wagon, and clattered out of the yard, jouncing as sturdily on his seat as a boy.

The woman stood a moment looking after him, then she went out of the barn across a corner of the yard to the house. The house, standing at right angles with the great barn and a long reach of sheds and out-buildings, was infinitesimal compared with them. It was scarcely as commodious for people as the little boxes under the barn eaves were for doves.

A pretty girl's face, pink and delicate as a flower, was looking out of one of the house windows. She was watching three men who were digging over in the field which bounded the yard near the road line. She turned quietly when the woman entered.

"What are they digging for, mother?" said she. "Did he tell you?"

"They're diggin' for—a cellar for a new barn."

"Oh, mother, he ain't going to build another barn?"

"That's what he says."

A boy stood before the kitchen glass combing his hair. He combed slowly and painstakingly, arranging his brown hair in a smooth hillock over his forehead. He did not seem to pay any attention to the conversation.

"Sammy, did you know father was going to build a new barn?" asked the girl.

The boy combed assiduously.

"Sammy!"

He turned, and showed a face like his father's under his smooth crest of hair. "Yes, I s'pose I did," he said, reluctantly.

"How long have you known it?" asked his mother.

"'Bout three months, I guess."

"Why didn't you tell of it?"

"Didn't think 'twould do no good."

"I don't see what father wants another barn for," said the girl, in her sweet, slow voice. She turned again to the window, and stared out at the digging men in the field. Her tender, sweet face was full of a gentle distress. Her forehead was as bald and innocent as a baby's, with the light hair strained back from it in a row of curl-papers. She was quite large, but her soft curves did not look as if they covered muscles.

Her mother looked sternly at the boy. "Is he goin' to buy more cows?" said she.

The boy did not reply; he was tying his shoes.

"Sammy, I want you to tell me if he's goin' to buy more cows."

"I s'pose he is."

"How many?"

"Four, I guess."

His mother said nothing more. She went into the pantry, and there was a clatter of dishes. The boy got his cap from a nail behind the door, took an old arithmetic from the shelf, and started for school.

He was lightly built, but clumsy. He went out of the yard with a curious spring in the hips, that made his loose home-made jacket tilt up in the rear.

The girl went to the sink, and began to wash the dishes that were piled up there. Her mother came promptly out of the pantry, and shoved her aside. "You wipe 'em," said she; "I'll wash. There's a good many this mornin'."

The mother plunged her hands vigorously into the water, the girl wiped the plates slowly and dreamily. "Mother," said she, "don't you think it's too bad father's going to build that new barn, much as we need a decent house to live in?"

Her mother scrubbed a dish fiercely. "You ain't found out yet we're women-folks, Nanny Penn," said she. "You ain't seen enough of men-folks yet to. One of these days you'll find it out, an' then you'll know that we know only what men-folks think we do, so far as any use of it goes, an' how we'd ought to reckon men-folks in with Providence, an' not complain of what they do any more than we do of the weather."

"I don't care; I don't believe George is anything like that, anyhow," said Nanny. Her delicate face flushed pink, her lips pouted softly, as if she were going to cry.

"You wait an' see. I guess George Eastman ain't no better than other men. You hadn't ought to judge father, though. He can't help it, 'cause he don't look at things jest the way we do. An' we've been pretty comfortable here, after all. The roof don't leak—ain't never but once—that's one thing. Father's kept it shingled right up."

"I do wish we had a parlor."

"I guess it won't hurt George Eastman any to come to see you in a nice clean kitchen. I guess a good many girls don't have as good a place as this. Nobody's ever heard me complain."

"I ain't complained either, mother."

"Well, I don't think you'd better, a good father an' a good home as you've got. S'pose your father made you go out an' work for your livin'? Lots of girls have to that ain't no stronger an' better able to than you be."

Sarah Penn washed the frying-pan with a conclusive air. She scrubbed the outside of it as faithfully as the inside. She was a masterly keeper of her box of a house. Her one living-room never seemed to have in it any of the dust which the friction of life with inanimate matter produces. She swept, and there seemed to be no dirt to go before the broom; she cleaned, and one could see no difference. She was like an artist so perfect that he has apparently no art. To-day she got out a mixing bowl and a board, and rolled some pies, and there was no more flour upon her than upon her daughter who was doing finer work. Nanny was to be married in the fall, and she was sewing on some white cambric and embroidery. She sewed industriously while her mother cooked, her soft milk-white hands and wrists showed whiter than her delicate work.

"We must have the stove moved out in the shed before long," said Mrs. Penn. "Talk about not havin' things, it's been a real blessin' to be able to put a stove up in that shed in hot weather. Father did one good thing when he fixed that stove-pipe out there."

Sarah Penn's face as she rolled her pies had that expression of meek vigor which might have characterized one of the New Testament saints. She was making mince-pies. Her husband, Adoniram Penn, liked them better than any other kind. She baked twice a week. Adoniram often liked a piece of pie between meals. She hurried this morning. It had been later than usual when she began, and she wanted to have a pie baked for dinner. However deep a resentment she might be forced to hold against her husband, she would never fail in sedulous attention to his wants.

Nobility of character manifests itself at loop-holes when it is not provided with large doors. Sarah Penn's showed itself to-day in flaky dishes of pastry. So she made the pies faithfully, while across the table she could see, when she glanced up from her work, the sight that rankled in her patient and steadfast soul—the digging of the cellar of the new barn in the place where Adoniram forty years ago had promised her their new house should stand.

The pies were done for dinner. Adoniram and Sammy were home a few minutes after twelve o'clock. The dinner was eaten with serious haste. There was never much conversation at the table in the Penn family. Adoniram asked a blessing, and they ate promptly, then rose up and went about their work.

Sammy went back to school, taking soft sly lopes out of the yard like a rabbit. He wanted a game of marbles before school, and feared his father would give him some chores to do. Adoniram hastened to the door and called after him, but he was out of sight.

"I don't see what you let him go for, mother," said he. "I wanted him to help me unload that wood."

Adoniram went to work out in the yard unloading wood from the wagon. Sarah put away the dinner dishes, while Nanny took down her curl-papers and changed her dress. She was going down to the store to buy some more embroidery and thread.

When Nanny was gone, Mrs. Penn went to the door. "Father!" she called.

"Well, what is it!"

"I want to see you jest a minute, father."

"I can't leave this wood nohow. I've got to git it unloaded an' go for a load of gravel afore two o'clock. Sammy had ought to helped me. You hadn't ought to let him go to school so early."

"I want to see you jest a minute."

"I tell ye I can't, nohow, mother."

"Father, you come here." Sarah Penn stood in the door like a queen; she held her head as if it bore a crown; there was that patience which makes authority royal, in her voice. Adoniram went.

Mrs. Penn led the way into the kitchen, and pointed to a chair. "Sit down, father," said she; "I've got somethin' I want to say to you."

He sat down heavily; his face was quite stolid, but he looked at her with restive eyes. "Well, what is it, mother?"

"I want to know what you're buildin' that new barn for, father?"

"I ain't got nothin' to say about it."

"It can't be you think you need another barn?"

"I tell ye I ain't got nothin' to say about it, mother; an' I ain't goin' to say nothin'."

"Be you goin' to buy more cows?"

Adoniram did not reply; he shut his mouth tight.

"I know you be, as well as I want to. Now, father, look here"—Sarah Penn had not sat down; she stood before her husband in the humble fashion of a Scripture woman—"I'm goin' to talk real plain to you; I never have sence I married you, but I'm goin' to now. I ain't never complained, an' I ain't goin' to complain now, but I'm goin' to talk plain. You see this room here, father; you look at it well. You see there ain't no carpet on the floor, an' you see the paper is all dirty, an' droppin' off the walls. We ain't had no new paper on it for ten year, an' then I put it on myself, an' it didn't cost but ninepence a roll. You see this room, father; it's all the one I've had to work in an' eat in an' sit in sence we was married. There ain't another woman in the whole town whose husband ain't got half the means you have but what's got better. It's all the room Nanny's got to have her company in; an' there ain't one of her mates but what's got better, an' their fathers not so able as hers is. It's all the room she'll have to be married in. What would you have thought, father, if we had had our weddin' in a room no better than this? I was married in my mother's parlor, with a carpet on the floor, an' stuffed furniture, an' a mahogany card-table. An' this is all the room my daughter will have to be married in. Look here, father!"

Sarah Penn went across the room as though it were a tragic stage. She flung open a door and disclosed a tiny bedroom, only large enough for a bed and bureau, with a path between. "There, father," said she—"there's all the room I've had to sleep in forty year. All my children were born there—the two that died, an' the two that's livin'. I was sick with a fever there."

She stepped to another door and opened it. It led into the small, ill-lighted pantry. "Here," said she, "is all the buttery I've got—every place I've got for my dishes, to set away my victuals in, an' to keep my milk-pans in. Father, I've been takin' care of the milk of six cows in this place, an' now you're going to build a new barn, an' keep more cows, an' give me more to do in it."

She threw open another door. A narrow crooked flight of stairs wound upward from it. "There, father," said she, "I want you to look at the stairs that go up to them two unfinished chambers that are all the places our son an' daughter have had to sleep in all their lives. There ain't a prettier girl in town nor a more ladylike one than Nanny, an' that's the place she has to sleep in. It ain't so good as your horse's stall; it ain't so warm an' tight."

Sarah Penn went back and stood before her husband. "Now, father," said she, "I want to know if you think you're doin' right an' accordin' to what you profess. Here, when we was married, forty year ago, you promised me faithful that we should have a new house built in that lot over in the field before the year was out. You said you had money enough, an' you wouldn't ask me to live in no such place as this. It is forty year now, an' you've been makin' more money, an' I've been savin' of it for you ever since, an' you ain't built no house yet. You've built sheds an' cow-houses an' one new barn, an' now you're goin' to build another. Father, I want to know if you think it's right. You're lodgin' your dumb beasts better than you are your own flesh an' blood. I want to know if you think it's right."

"I ain't got nothin' to say."

"You can't say nothin' without ownin' it ain't right, father. An' there's another thing—I ain't complained; I've got along forty year, an' I s'pose I should forty more, if it wa'n't for that—if we don't have another house. Nanny she can't live with us after she's married. She'll have to go somewheres else to live away from us, an' it don't seem as if I could have it so, noways, father. She wa'n't ever strong. She's got considerable color, but there wa'n't never any backbone to her. I've always took the heft of everything off her, an' she ain't fit to keep house an' do everything herself. She'll be all worn out inside of a year. Think of her doin' all the washin' an' ironin' an' bakin' with them soft white hands an' arms, an' sweepin'! I can't have it so, noways, father."

Mrs. Penn's face was burning; her mild eyes gleamed. She had pleaded her little cause like a Webster; she had ranged from severity to pathos; but her opponent employed that obstinate silence which makes eloquence futile with mocking echoes. Adoniram arose clumsily.

"Father, ain't you got nothin' to say?" said Mrs. Penn.

"I've got to go off after that load of gravel. I can't stan' here talkin' all day."

"Father, won't you think it over, an' have a house built there instead of a barn?"

"I ain't got nothin' to say."

Adoniram shuffled out. Mrs. Penn went into her bedroom. When she came out, her eyes were red. She had a roll of unbleached cotton cloth. She spread it out on the kitchen table, and began cutting out some shirts for her husband. The men over in the field had a team to help them this afternoon; she could hear their halloos. She had a scanty pattern for the shirts; she had to plan and piece the sleeves.

Nanny came home with her embroidery, and sat down with her needlework. She had taken down her curl-papers, and there was a soft roll of fair hair like an aureole over her forehead; her face was as delicately fine and clear as porcelain. Suddenly she looked up, and the tender red flamed all over her face and neck. "Mother," said she.

"What say?"

"I've been thinking—I don't see how we're goin' to have any—wedding in this room. I'd be ashamed to have his folks come if we didn't have anybody else."

"Mebbe we can have some new paper before then; I can put it on. I guess you won't have no call to be ashamed of your belongin's."

"We might have the wedding in the new barn," said Nanny, with gentle pettishness. "Why, mother, what makes you look so?"

Mrs. Penn had started, and was staring at her with a curious expression. She turned again to her work, and spread out a pattern carefully on the cloth. "Nothin'," said she.

Presently Adoniram clattered out of the yard in his two-wheeled dump cart, standing as proudly upright as a Roman charioteer. Mrs. Penn opened the door and stood there a minute looking out; the halloos of the men sounded louder.

It seemed to her all through the spring months that she heard nothing but the halloos and the noises of saws and hammers. The new barn grew fast. It was a fine edifice for this little village. Men came on pleasant Sundays, in their meeting suits and clean shirt bosoms, and stood around it admiringly. Mrs. Penn did not speak of it, and Adoniram did not mention it to her, although sometimes, upon a return from inspecting it, he bore himself with injured dignity.

"It's a strange thing how your mother feels about the new barn," he said, confidentially, to Sammy one day.

Sammy only grunted after an odd fashion for a boy; he had learned it from his father.

The barn was all completed ready for use by the third week in July. Adoniram had planned to move his stock in on Wednesday; on Tuesday he received a letter which changed his plans. He came in with it early in the morning. "Sammy's been to the post-office," said he, "an' I've got a letter from Hiram." Hiram was Mrs. Penn's brother, who lived in Vermont.

"Well," said Mrs. Penn, "what does he say about the folks?"

"I guess they're all right. He says he thinks if I come up country right off there's a chance to buy jest the kind of a horse I want." He stared reflectively out of the window at the new barn.

Mrs. Penn was making pies. She went on clapping the rolling-pin into the crust, although she was very pale, and her heart beat loudly.

"I dun' know but what I'd better go," said Adoniram. "I hate to go off jest now, right in the midst of hayin', but the ten-acre lot's cut, an' I guess Rufus an' the others can git along without me three or four days. I can't get a horse round here to suit me, nohow, an' I've got to have another for all that wood-haulin' in the fall. I told Hiram to watch out, an' if he got wind of a good horse to let me know. I guess I'd better go."

"I'll get out your clean shirt an' collar," said Mrs. Penn calmly.

She laid out Adoniram's Sunday suit and his clean clothes on the bed in the little bedroom. She got his shaving-water and razor ready. At last she buttoned on his collar and fastened his black cravat.

Adoniram never wore his collar and cravat except on extra occasions. He held his head high, with a rasped dignity. When he was all ready, with his coat and hat brushed, and a lunch of pie and cheese in a paper bag, he hesitated on the threshold of the door. He looked at his wife, and his manner was defiantly apologetic. "*If* them cows come to-day, Sammy can drive 'em into the new barn," said he; "an' when they bring the hay up, they can pitch it in there."

"Well," replied Mrs. Penn.

Adoniram set his shaven face ahead and started. When he had cleared the door-step, he turned and looked back with a kind of nervous solemnity. "I shall be back by Saturday if nothin' happens," said he.

"Do be careful, father," returned his wife.

She stood in the door with Nanny at her elbow and watched him out of sight. Her eyes had a strange, doubtful expression in them; her peaceful forehead was contracted. She went in, and about her baking again. Nanny sat sewing. Her wedding-day was drawing nearer, and she was getting pale and thin with her steady sewing. Her mother kept glancing at her.

"Have you got that pain in your side this mornin'?" she asked.

"A little."

Mrs. Penn's face, as she worked, changed, her perplexed forehead smoothed, her eyes were steady, her lips firmly set. She formed a maxim for herself, although incoherently with her unlettered thoughts. "Unsolicited opportunities are the guide-posts of the Lord to the new roads of life," she repeated in effect, and she made up her mind to her course of action.

"S'posin' I *had* wrote to Hiram," she muttered once, when she was in the pantry—"s'posin' I had wrote, an' asked him if he knew of any horse? But I didn't, an' father's goin' wa'n't none of my doin'. It looks like a providence." Her voice rang out quite loud at the last.

"What you talkin' about, mother?" called Nanny.

"Nothin'."

Mrs. Penn hurried her baking; at eleven o'clock it was all done. The load of hay from the west field came slowly down the cart track, and drew up at the new barn. Mrs. Penn ran out. "Stop!" she screamed—"stop!"

The men stopped and looked; Sammy upreared from the top of the load, and stared at his mother.

"Stop!" she cried out again. "Don't you put the hay in that barn; put it in the old one."

"Why, he said to put it in here," returned one of the hay-makers, wonderingly. He was a young man, a neighbor's son, whom Adoniram hired by the year to help on the farm.

"Don't you put the hay in the new barn; there's room enough in the old one, ain't there?" said Mrs. Penn.

"Room enough," returned the hired man, in his thick, rustic tones. "Didn't need the new barn, nohow, far as room's concerned. Well, I s'pose he changed his mind." He took hold of the horses' bridles.

Mrs. Penn went back to the house. Soon the kitchen windows were darkened, and a fragrance like warm honey came into the room.

Nanny laid down her work. "I thought father wanted them to put the hay into the new barn?" she said, wonderingly.

"It's all right," replied her mother.

Sammy slid down from the load of hay, and came in to see if dinner was ready.

"I ain't goin' to get a regular dinner to-day, as long as father's gone," said his mother. "I've let the fire go out. You can have some bread an' milk an' pie. I thought we could get along." She set out some bowls of milk, some bread, and a pie on the kitchen table. "You'd better eat your dinner now," said she. "You might jest as well get through with it. I want you to help me afterward."

Nanny and Sammy stared at each other. There was something strange in their mother's manner. Mrs. Penn did not eat anything herself. She went into the pantry, and they heard her moving dishes while they ate. Presently she came out with a pile of plates. She got the clothes-basket out of the shed, and packed them in it. Nanny and Sammy watched. She brought out cups and saucers, and put them in with the plates.

"What you goin' to do, mother?" inquired Nanny, in a timid voice. A sense of something unusual made her tremble, as if it were a ghost. Sammy rolled his eyes over his pie.

"You'll see what I'm goin' to do," replied Mrs. Penn. "If you're through, Nanny, I want you to go up-stairs an' pack up your things; an' I want you, Sammy, to help me take down the bed in the bedroom."

"Oh, mother, what for?" gasped Nanny.

"You'll see."

During the next few hours a feat was performed by this simple, pious New England mother which was equal in its way to Wolfe's storming of the Heights of Abraham. It took no more genius and audacity of bravery for Wolfe to cheer his wondering soldiers up those steep precipices, under the sleeping eyes of the enemy, than for Sarah Penn, at the head of her children, to move all their little household goods into the new barn while her husband was away.

Nanny and Sammy followed their mother's instructions without a murmur; indeed, they were overawed. There is a certain uncanny and superhuman quality about all such purely original undertakings as their mother's was to them. Nanny went back and forth with her light loads, and Sammy tugged with sober energy.

At five o'clock in the afternoon the little house in which the Penns had lived for forty years had emptied itself into the new barn.

Every builder builds somewhat for unknown purposes, and is in a measure a prophet. The architect of Adoniram Penn's barn, while he designed it for the comfort of four-footed animals, had planned better than he knew for the comfort of humans. Sarah Penn saw at a glance its possibilities. Those great box-stalls, with quilts hung before them, would make better bedrooms than the one she had occupied for forty years, and there was a tight carriage-room. The harness-room, with its chimney and shelves, would make a kitchen of her dreams. . The great middle space would make a parlor, by-and-by, fit for a palace. Up stairs there was as much room as down. With partitions and windows, what a house would there be! Sarah looked at the row of stanchions before the allotted space for cows, and reflected that she would have her front entry there.

At six o'clock the stove was up in the harness-room, the kettle was boiling, and the table set for tea. It looked almost as home-like as the abandoned house across the yard had ever done. The young hired man milked, and Sarah directed him calmly to bring the milk to the new barn. He came gaping, dropping little blots of foam from the brimming pails on the grass. Before the next morning he had spread the story of Adoniram Penn's wife moving into the new barn all over the village. Men assembled in the store and talked it over, women with shawls over their heads scuttled into each other's houses before their work was done. Any deviation from the ordinary course of life in this quiet town was enough to stop all progress in it. Everybody paused to look at the staid, independent figure on the side track. There was a difference of opinion with regard to her. Some held her to be insane; some, of a lawless and rebellious spirit.

Friday the minister went to see her. It was in the forenoon, and she was at the barn door shelling peas for dinner. She looked up and returned his salutation with dignity, then she went on with her work. She did not invite him in. The saintly expression of her face remained fixed, but there was an angry flush over it.

The minister stood awkwardly before her, and talked. She handled the peas as if they were bullets. At last she looked up, and her eyes showed the spirit that her meek front had covered for a lifetime.

"There ain't no use talkin', Mr. Hersey," she said. "I've thought it all over an' over, an' I believe I'm doin' what's right. I've made it the subject of prayer, an' it's betwixt me an' the Lord an' Adoniram. There ain't no call for nobody else to worry about it."

"Well, of course, if you have brought it to the Lord in prayer, and feel satisfied that you are doing right, Mrs. Penn," said the minister, helplessly. His thin gray-bearded face was pathetic. He was a sickly man; his youthful confidence had cooled; he had to scourge himself up to some of his pastoral duties as relentlessly as a Catholic ascetic, and then he was prostrated by the smart.

"I think it's right jest as much as I think it was right for our forefathers to come over from the old country 'cause they didn't have what belonged to 'em," said Mrs. Penn. She arose. The barn threshold might have been Plymouth Rock from her bearing. "I don't doubt you mean well, Mr. Hersey," said she, "but there are things people hadn't ought to interfere with. I've been a member of the church for over forty year. I've got my own mind an' my own feet, an' I'm goin' to think my own thoughts an' go my own ways, an' nobody but the Lord is goin' to dictate to me unless I've a mind to have him. Won't you come in an' set down? How is Mis' Hersey?"

"She is well, I thank you," replied the minister. He added some more perplexed apologetic remarks; then he retreated.

He could expound the intricacies of every character study in the Scriptures, he was competent to grasp the Pilgrim Fathers and all historical innovators, but Sarah Penn was beyond him. He could deal with primal cases, but parallel ones worsted him. But, after all, although it was aside from his province, he wondered more how Adoniram Penn would deal with his wife than how the Lord would. Everybody shared the wonder. When Adoniram's four new cows arrived, Sarah ordered three to be put in the old barn, the other in the house shed where the cooking-stove had stood. That added to the excitement. It was whispered that all four cows were domiciled in the house.

Towards sunset on Saturday, when Adoniram was expected home, there was a knot of men in the road near the new barn. The hired man had milked, but he still hung around the premises. Sarah Penn had supper all ready. There were brown-bread and baked beans and a custard pie; it was the supper that Adoniram loved on a Saturday night. She had on a clean calico, and she bore herself imperturbably. Nanny and Sammy kept close at her heels. Their eyes were large, and Nanny was full of nervous tremors. Still there was to them more pleasant excitement than anything else. An inborn confidence in their mother over their father asserted itself.

Sammy looked out of the harness-room window. "There he is," he announced, in an awed whisper. He and Nanny peeped around the casing. Mrs. Penn kept on about her work. The children watched Adoniram leave the new horse standing in the drive while he went to the house door. It was fastened. Then he went around to the shed. That door was seldom locked, even when the family was away. The thought how her father would be confronted by the cow flashed upon Nanny. There was a hysterical sob in her throat. Adoniram emerged from the shed and stood looking about in a dazed fashion. His lips moved; he was saying something, but they could not hear what it was. The hired man was peeping around a corner of the old barn, but nobody saw him.

Adoniram took the new horse by the bridle and led him across the yard to the new barn. Nanny and Sammy slunk close to their mother. The barn doors rolled back, and there stood Adoniram, with the long mild face of the great Canadian farm horse looking over his shoulder.

Nanny kept behind her mother, but Sammy stepped suddenly forward, and stood in front of her.

Adoniram stared at the group. "What on airth you all down here for?" said he. "What's the matter over to the house?"

"We've come here to live, father," said Sammy. His shrill voice quavered out bravely.

"What"—Adoniram sniffed—"what is it smells like cookin'?" said he. He stepped forward and looked in the open door of the harness-room. Then he turned to his wife. His old bristling face was pale and frightened. "What on airth does this mean, mother?" he gasped.

"You come in here, father," said Sarah. She led the way into the harness-room and shut the door. "Now, father," said she, "you needn't be scared. I ain't crazy. There ain't nothin' to be upset over. But we've come here to live, an' we're goin' to live here. We've got jest as good a right here as new horses an' cows. The house wa'n't fit for us to live in any longer, an' I made up my mind I wa'n't goin' to stay there. I've done my duty by you forty year, an' I'm goin' to do it now; but I'm goin' to live here. You've got to put in some windows and partitions; an' you'll have to buy some furniture."

"Why, mother!" the old man gasped.

"You'd better take your coat off an' get washed—there's the wash-basin—an' then we'll have supper."

"Why, mother!"

Sammy went past the window, leading the new horse to the old barn. The old man saw him, and shook his head speechlessly. He tried to take off his coat, but his arms seemed to lack the power. His wife helped him. She poured some water into the tin basin, and put in a piece of soap. She got the comb and brush, and smoothed his thin gray hair after he had washed. Then she put the beans, hot bread, and tea on the table. Sammy came in, and the family drew up. Adoniram sat looking dazedly at his plate, and then waited.

"Ain't you goin' to ask a blessin', father?" said Sarah.

And the old man bent his head and mumbled.

All through the meal he stopped eating at intervals, and stared furtively at his wife; but he ate well. The home food tasted good to him, and his old frame was too sturdily healthy to be affected by his mind. But after supper he went out, and sat down on the step of the smaller door at the right of the barn, through which he had meant his Jerseys to pass in stately file, but which Sarah designed for her front house door, and he leaned his head on his hands.

After the supper dishes were cleared away and the milk-pans washed, Sarah went out to him. The twilight was deepening. There was a clear green glow in the sky. Before them stretched the smooth level of field; in the distance was a cluster of hay-stacks like the huts of a village; the air was very cool and calm and sweet. The landscape might have been an ideal one of peace.

Sarah bent over and touched her husband on one of his thin, sinewy shoulders. "Father!"

The old man's shoulders heaved: he was weeping.

"Why, don't do so, father," said Sarah.

"I'll—put up the—partitions, an'—everything you—want, mother."

Sarah put her apron up to her face; she was overcome by her own triumph.

Adoniram was like a fortress whose walls had no active resistance, and went down the instant the right besieging tools were used. "Why, mother," he said, hoarsely, "I hadn't no idee you was so set on't as all this comes to."

O. HENRY (1862-1910)

Thimble, Thimble

THESE are the directions for finding the office of Carteret & Carteret Mill Supplies and Leather Belting:

You follow the Broadway trail down until you pass the Crosstown Line, the Bread Line, and the Dead Line, and come to the Big Cañons of the Moneygrubber Tribe. Then you turn to the left, to the right, dodge a push-cart and the tongue of a two-ton, four-horse dray and hop, skip, and jump to a granite ledge on the side of a twenty-one-story synthetic mountain of stone and iron. In the twelfth story is the office of Carteret & Carteret. The factory where they make the mill supplies and leather belting is in Brooklyn. Those commodities—to say nothing of

Brooklyn—not being of interest to you, let us hold the incidents within the confines of a one-act, one-scene play, thereby lessening the toil of the reader and the expenditure of the publisher. So, if you have the courage to face four pages of type and Carteret & Carteret's office boy, Percival, you shall sit on a varnished chair in the inner office and peep at the little comedy of the Old Nigger Man, the Hunting-Case Watch, and the Open-Faced Question—mostly borrowed from the late Mr. Frank Stockton, as you will conclude.

First, biography (but pared to the quick) must intervene. I am for the inverted sugar-coated quinine pill—the bitter on the outside.

The Carterets were, or was (Columbia College professors please rule), an old Virginia family. Long time ago the gentlemen of the family had worn lace ruffles and carried tinless foils and owned plantations and had slaves to burn. But the war had greatly reduced their holdings. (Of course you can perceive at once that this flavor has been shoplifted from Mr. F. Hopkinson Smith, in spite of the "et" after "Carter.") Well, anyhow:

In digging up the Carteret history I shall not take you farther back than the year 1620. The two original American Carterets came over in that year, but by different means of transportation. One brother, named John, came in the *Mayflower* and became a Pilgrim Father. You've seen his picture on the covers of the Thanksgiving magazines, hunting turkeys in the deep snow with a blunderbuss. Blandford Carteret, the other brother, crossed the pond in his own brigantine, landed on the Virginia coast, and became an F.F.V. John became distinguished for piety and shrewdness in business; Blandford for his pride, juleps, marksmanship, and vast slave-cultivated plantations.

Then came the Civil War. (I must condense this historical interpolation.) Stonewall Jackson was shot; Lee surrendered; Grant toured the world; cotton went to nine cents; Old Crow whiskey and Jim Crow cars were invented; the Seventy-ninth Massachusetts Volunteers returned to the Ninety-seventh Alabama Zouaves the battle flag of Lundy's Lane which they bought at a second-hand store in Chelsea kept by a man named Skzchnzski; Georgia sent the President a sixty-pound watermelon—and that brings us up to the time when the story begins. My! but that was sparring for an opening! I really must brush up on my Aristotle.

The Yankee Carterets went into business in New York long before the war. Their house, as far as Leather Belting and Mill Supplies was concerned, was as musty and arrogant and solid as one of those old East India tea-importing concerns that you read about in Dickens. There were some rumors of a war, behind its counters, but not enough to affect the business.

During and after the war, Blandford Carteret, F.F.V., lost his plantations, juleps, marksmanship, and life. He bequeathed little more than his pride to his surviving family. So it came to pass that Blandford Carteret, the Fifth, aged fifteen, was invited by the leather-and-mill-supplies branch of that name to come North and learn business instead of hunting foxes and boasting of the glory of his fathers, on the reduced acres of his impoverished family. The boy jumped at the chance; and, at the age of twenty-five, sat in the office of the firm, equal partner with John, the Fifth, of the blunderbuss-and-turkey branch. Here the story begins again.

The young men were about the same age, smooth of face, alert, easy of manner, and with an air that promised mental and physical quickness. They were razored, blue-serged, straw-hatted, and pearl stick-pinned like other young New Yorkers who might be millionaires or bill clerks.

One afternoon at four o'clock, in the private office of the firm, Blandford Carteret opened a letter that a clerk had just brought to his desk. After reading it, he chuckled audibly for nearly a minute. John looked around from his desk inquiringly.

"It's from mother," said Blandford. "I'll read you the funny part of it. She tells me all the neighborhood news first, of course, and then cautions me against getting my feet wet and musical comedies. After that come vital statistics about calves and pigs and an estimate of the wheat crop. And now I'll quote some:

" 'And what do you think! Old Uncle Jake, who was seventy-six last Wednesday, must go travelling. Nothing would do but he must go to New York and see his "young Marster Blandford." Old as he is, he has a deal of common sense, so I've let him go. I couldn't refuse him—he seemed to have concentrated all his hopes and desires into this one adventure into the wide world. You know he was born on the plantation, and has never been ten miles away from it in his life. And he was your father's body servant during the war, and has been always a faithful vassal and servant of the family. He has often seen the gold watch—the watch that was your father's and your father's father's. I told him it was to be yours, and he begged me to allow him to take it to you and to put it into your hands himself.

" 'So he has it, carefully inclosed in a buckskin case, and is bringing it to you with all the pride and importance of a king's messenger. I gave him money for the round trip and for a two weeks' stay in the city. I wish you would see to it that he gets comfortable quarters—Jake won't need much looking after—he's able to take care of himself. But I have read in the papers that African bishops and colored potentates generally have much trouble in obtaining food and lodging in the Yankee metropolis. That may be all right; but I don't see why the best hotel there shouldn't take Jake in. Still, I suppose it's a rule.

" 'I gave him full directions about finding you, and packed his valise myself. You won't have to bother with him; but I do hope you'll see that he is made comfortable. Take the watch that he brings you—it's almost a decoration. It has been worn by true Carterets, and there isn't a stain upon it nor a false movement of the wheels. Bringing it to you is the crowning joy of old Jake's life. I wanted him to have that little outing and that happiness before it is too late. You have often heard us talk about how Jake, pretty badly wounded himself, crawled through the reddened grass at Chancellorsville to where your father lay with the bullet in his dear heart, and took the watch from his pocket to keep it from the "Yanks."

" 'So, my son, when the old man comes consider him as a frail but worthy messenger from the old-time life and home.

" 'You have been so long away from home and so long among the people that we have always regarded as aliens that I'm not sure that Jake will know you when he sees you. But Jake has a keen perception, and I rather believe that he will know a Virginia Carteret at sight. I can't conceive that even ten years in Yankee-land could change a boy of mine. Anyhow, I'm sure you will know Jake. I put eighteen collars in his valise. If he should have to buy others, he wears a number 15½. Please see that he gets the right ones. He will be no trouble to you at all.

" 'If you are not too busy, I'd like for you to find him a place to board where they have white-meal corn-bread, and try to keep him from taking his shoes off in your office or on the street. His right foot swells a little, and he likes to be comfortable.

" 'If you can spare the time, count his handkerchiefs when they come back from the wash. I bought him a dozen new ones before he left. He should be there about the time this letter reaches you. I told him to go straight to your office when he arrives.' "

As soon as Blandford had finished the reading of this, something happened (as there should happen in stories and must happen on the stage).

Percival, the office boy, with his air of despising the world's output of mill supplies and leather belting, came in to announce that a colored gentleman was outside to see Mr. Blandford Carteret.

"Bring him in," said Blandford, rising.

John Carteret swung around in his chair and said to Percival: "Ask him to wait a few minutes outside. We'll let you know when to bring him in."

Then he turned to his cousin with one of those broad, slow smiles that was an inheritance of all the Carterets, and said:

"Bland, I've always had a consuming curiosity to understand the differences that you haughty Southerners believe to exist between 'you all' and the people of the North. Of course, I know that you consider yourselves made out of finer clay and look upon Adam as only a collateral branch of your ancestry; but I don't know why. I never could understand the differences between us."

"Well, John," said Blandford, laughing, "what you don't understand about it is just the difference, of course. I suppose it was the feudal way in which we lived that gave us our lordly baronial airs and feeling of superiority."

"But you are not feudal, now," went on John. "Since we licked you and stole your cotton and mules you've had to go to work just as we 'damyankees,' as you call us, have always been doing. And you're just as proud and exclusive and upper-classy as you were before the war. So it wasn't your money that caused it."

"Maybe it was the climate," said Blandford, lightly, "or maybe our negroes spoiled us. I'll call old Jake in, now. I'll be glad to see the old villain again."

"Wait just a moment," said John. "I've got a little theory I want to test. You and I are pretty much alike in our general appearance. Old Jake hasn't seen you since you were fifteen. Let's have him in and play fair and see which of us gets the watch. The old darky surely ought to be able to pick out his 'young marster' without any trouble. The alleged aristocratic superiority of a 'reb' ought to be visible to him at once. He couldn't make the mistake of handing over the timepiece to a Yankee, of course. The loser buys the dinner this evening and two dozen 15½ collars for Jake. Is it a go?"

Blandford agreed heartily. Percival was summoned, and told to usher the "colored gentleman" in.

Uncle Jake stepped inside the private office cautiously. He was a little old man, as black as soot, wrinkled and bald except for a fringe of white wool, cut decorously short, that ran over his ears and around his head. There was nothing of the stage "uncle" about him: his black suit nearly fitted him; his shoes shone, and his straw hat was banded with a gaudy ribbon. In his right hand he carried something carefully concealed by his closed fingers.

Uncle Jake stopped a few steps from the door. Two young men sat in their revolving desk-chairs, ten feet apart, and looked at him in friendly silence. His gaze slowly shifted many times from one to the other. He felt sure that he was in the presence of one, at least, of the revered family among whose fortunes his life had begun and was to end.

One had the pleasing but haughty Carteret air; the other had the unmistakable straight, long family nose. Both had the keen black eyes, horizontal brows, and thin, smiling lips that had distinguished both the Carteret of the *Mayflower* and him of the brigantine. Old Jake had thought that he could have picked out his young master instantly from a thousand Northerners; but he found himself in difficulties. The best he could do was to use strategy.

"Howdy, Marse Blandford—howdy, suh?" he said, looking midway between the two young men.

"Howdy, Uncle Jake?" they both answered pleasantly and in unison. "Sit down. Have you brought the watch?"

Uncle Jake chose a hard-bottom chair at a respectful distance, sat on the edge of it, and laid his hat carefully on the floor. The watch in its buckskin case he gripped tightly. He had not risked his life on the battle-field to rescue that watch from his "old marster's" foes to hand it over again to the enemy without a struggle.

"Yes, suh; I got it in my hand, suh. I'm gwine give it to you right away in jus' a minute. Old Missus told me to put it in young Marse Blandford's hand and tell him to wear it for the family pride and honor. It was a mighty longsome trip for an old nigger man to make—ten thousand miles, it must be, back to old Vi'ginia, suh. You've growed mightily, young marster. I wouldn't have reconnized you but for yo' powerful resemblance to old marster."

With admirable diplomacy the old man kept his eyes roaming in the space between the two men. His words might have been addressed to either. Though neither wicked nor perverse, he was seeking for a sign.

Blandford and John exchanged winks.

"I reckon you done got you ma's letter," went on Uncle Jake. "She said she was gwine to write to you 'bout my comin' along up this er-way."

"Yes, yes, Uncle Jake," said John briskly. "My cousin and I have just been notified to expect you. We are both Carterets, you know."

"Although one of us," said Blandford, "was born and raised in the North."

"So if you will hand over the watch—" said John.

"My cousin and I—" said Blandford.

"Will then see to it—" said John.

"That comfortable quarters are found for you," said Blandford.

With creditable ingenuity, old Jake set up a cackling, high-pitched, protracted laugh. He beat his knee, picked up his hat and bent the brim in an apparent paroxysm of humorous appreciation. The seizure afforded him a mask behind which he could roll his eyes impartially between, above and beyond his two tormentors.

"I sees what!" he chuckled, after a while. "You gen'lemen is tryin' to have fun with the po' old nigger. But you can't fool old Jake. I knowed you, Marse Blandford, the minute I sot eyes on you. You was a po' skimpy little boy no mo' than about fo'teen when you lef' home to come No'th; but I knowed you the minute I sot eyes on you. You is the mawtal image of old marster. The other gen'leman resembles you mightily, suh; but you can't fool old Jake on a member of the old Vi'ginia family. No suh."

At exactly the same time both Carterets smiled and extended a hand for the watch.

Uncle Jake's wrinkled, black face lost the expression of amusement into which he had vainly twisted it. He knew that he was being teased, and that it made little real difference, as far as its safety went, into which of those outstretched hands he placed the family treasure. But it seemed to him that not only his own pride and loyalty but much of the Virginia Carterets' was at stake. He had heard down South during the war about that other branch of the family that lived in the North and fought on "the yuther side," and it had always grieved him. He had followed his "old marster's" fortunes from stately luxury through war to almost poverty. And now, with the last relic and reminder of him, blessed by "old missus," and intrusted implicitly to his care, he had come ten thousand miles (as it seemed) to deliver it into the hands of the one who was to wear it and wind it and cherish it and listen to it tick off the unsullied hours that marked the lives of the Carterets—of Virginia.

His experience and conception of the Yankees had been an impression of tyrants—"low-down, common trash"—in blue, laying waste with fire and sword. He had seen the smoke of many burning homesteads, almost as grand as Carteret Hall, ascending to the drowsy Southern skies. And now he was face to face with one of them—and he could not distinguish him from his "young marster" whom he had come to find and bestow upon him the emblem of his kingship—even as the arm "clothed in white samite, mystic, wonderful" laid Excalibur in the right hand of Arthur. He saw before him two young men, easy, kind, courteous, welcoming, either of whom might have been the one he sought. Troubled, bewildered, sorely grieved at his weakness of judgment, old Jake abandoned his loyal subterfuges. His right hand sweated against the buckskin cover of the watch. He was deeply humiliated and chastened. Seriously, now, his prominent, yellow-white eyes closely scanned the two young men. At the end of his scrutiny he was conscious of but one difference between them. One wore a narrow black tie with a white pearl stickpin. The other's "four-in-hand" was a narrow blue one pinned with a black pearl.

And then, to old Jake's relief, there came a sudden distraction. Drama knocked at the door with imperious knuckles, and forced Comedy to the wings, and Drama peeped with a smiling but set face over the footlights.

Percival, the hater of mill supplies, brought in a card, which he handed, with the manner of one bearing a cartel, to Blue-Tie.

" 'Olivia De Ormond,' " read Blue-Tie from the card. He looked inquiringly at his cousin.

"Why not have her in," said Black-Tie, "and bring matters to a conclusion?"

"Uncle Jake," said one of the young men, "would you mind taking that chair over there in the corner for a while? A lady is coming in—on some business. We'll take up your case afterward."

The lady whom Percival ushered in was young and petulantly, decidedly, freshly, consciously, and intentionally pretty. She was dressed with such expensive plainness that she made you consider lace and ruffles as mere tatters and rags. But one great ostrich plume that she wore would have marked her anywhere in the army of beauty as the wearer of the merry helmet of Navarre.

Miss De Ormond accepted the swivel chair at Blue-Tie's desk. Then the gentlemen drew leather-upholstered seats conveniently near, and spoke of the weather.

"Yes," said she, "I noticed it was warmer. But I mustn't take up too much of your time during business hours. That is," she continued, "unless we talk business."

She addressed her words to Blue-Tie, with a charming smile.

"Very well," said he. "You don't mind my cousin being present, do you? We are generally rather confidential with each other—especially in business matters."

"Oh no," caroled Miss De Ormond. "I'd rather he did hear. He knows all about it, anyhow. In fact, he's quite a material witness because he was present when you—when it happened. I thought you might want to talk things over before—well, before any action is taken, as I believe the lawyers say."

"Have you anything in the way of a proposition to make?" asked Black-Tie.

Miss De Ormond looked reflectively at the neat toe of one of her dull kid pumps.

"I had a proposal made to me," she said. "If the proposal sticks it cuts out the proposition. Let's have that settled first."

"Well, as far as—" began Blue-Tie.

"Excuse me, cousin," interrupted Black-Tie, "if you don't mind my cutting in." And then he turned, with a good-natured air, toward the lady.

"Now, let's recapitulate a bit," he said cheerfully. "All three of us, besides other mutual acquaintances, have been out on a good many larks together."

"I'm afraid I'll have to call the birds by another name," said Miss De Ormond.

"All right," responded Black-Tie, with unimpaired cheerfulness; "suppose we say 'squabs' when we talk about the 'proposal' and 'larks' when we discuss the 'proposition.' You have a quick mind, Miss De Ormond. Two months ago some half-dozen of us went in a motor-car for a day's run into the country. We stopped at a road-house for dinner. My cousin proposed marriage to you then and there. He was influenced to do so, of course, by the beauty and charm which no one can deny that you possess."

"I wish I had you for a press agent, Mr. Carteret," said the beauty, with a dazzling smile.

"You are on the stage, Miss De Ormond," went on Black-Tie. "You have had, doubtless, many admirers, and perhaps other proposals. You must remember, too, that we were a party of merrymakers on that occasion. There were a good many corks pulled. That the proposal of marriage was made to you by my cousin we cannot deny. But hasn't it been your experience that, by common consent, such things lose their seriousness when viewed in the next day's sunlight? Isn't there something of a 'code' among good 'sports'—I use the word in its best sense—that wipes out each day the follies of the evening previous?"

"Oh yes," said Miss De Ormond. "I know that very well. And I've always played up to it. But as you seem to be conducting the case—with the silent consent of the defendant—I'll tell you something more. I've got letters from him repeating the proposal. And they're signed, too."

"I understand," said Black-Tie gravely. "What's your price for the letters?"

"I'm not a cheap one," said Miss De Ormond. "But I had decided to make you a rate. You both belong to a swell family. Well, if I *am* on the stage nobody can say a word against me truthfully. And the money is only a secondary consideration. It isn't the money I was after. I—I believed him—and—and I liked him."

She cast a soft, entrancing glance at Blue-Tie from under her long eyelashes.

"And the price?" went on Black-Tie, inexorably.

"Ten thousand dollars," said the lady, sweetly.

"Or—"

"Or the fulfilment of the engagement to marry."

"I think it is time," interrupted Blue-Tie, "for me to be allowed to say a word or two. You and I, cousin, belong to a family that has held its head pretty high. You have been brought up in a section of the country very different from the one where our branch of the family lived. Yet both of us are Carterets, even if some of our ways and theories differ. You remember, it is a tradition of the family, that no Carteret ever failed in chivalry to a lady or failed to keep his word when it was given."

Then Blue-Tie, with frank decision showing on his countenance, turned to Miss De Ormond.

"Olivia," said he, "on what date will you marry me?"

Before she could answer, Black-Tie again interposed.

"It is a long journey," said he, "from Plymouth Rock to Norfolk Bay. Between the two points we find the changes that nearly three centuries have brought. In that time the old order has changed. We no longer burn witches or torture slaves. And to-day we neither spread our cloaks on the mud for ladies to walk over nor treat them to the ducking-stool. It is the age of common sense, adjustment, and proportion. All of us—ladies, gentlemen, women, men, Northerners, Southerners, lords, caitiffs, actors, hardware-drummers, senators, hod-carriers, and politicians—are coming to a better understanding. Chivalry is one of our words that changes its meaning every day. Family pride is a thing of many constructions—it may show itself by maintaining a moth-eaten arrogance in a cobwebbed Colonial mansion or by the prompt paying of one's debts.

"Now, I suppose you've had enough of my monologue. I've learned something of business and a little of life; and I somehow believe, cousin, that our great-great-grandfathers, the original Carterets, would indorse my view of this matter."

Black-Tie wheeled around to his desk, wrote in a check-book and tore out the check, the sharp rasp of the perforated leaf making the only sound in the room. He laid the check within easy reach of Miss De Ormond's hand.

"Business is business," said he. "We live in a business age. There is my personal check for $10,000. What do you say, Miss De Ormond—will it be orange blossoms or cash?"

Miss De Ormond picked up the check carelessly, folded it indifferently, and stuffed it into her glove.

"Oh, this'll do," she said, calmly. "I just thought I'd call and put it up to you. I guess you people are all right. But a girl has feelings, you know. I've heard one of you was a Southerner—I wonder which one of you it is?"

She arose, smiled sweetly, and walked to the door. There, with a flash of white teeth and a dip of the heavy plume, she disappeared.

Both of the cousins had forgotten Uncle Jake for the time. But now they heard the shuffling of his shoes as he came across the rug toward them from his seat in the corner.

"Young marster," he said, "take yo' watch."

And without hesitation he laid the ancient timepiece in the hand of its rightful owner.

A Municipal Report

The cities are full of pride.
Challenging each to each—
This from her mountainside,
That from her burthened beach.
R. Kipling.

Fancy a novel about Chicago or Buffalo, let us say, or Nashville, Tennessee! There are just three big cities in the United States that are "story cities"—New York, of course, New Orleans, and, best of the lot, San Francisco.—Frank Norris.

East is East, and West is San Francisco, according to Californians. Californians are a race of people; they are not merely inhabitants of a State. They are the Southerners of the West. Now, Chicagoans are no less loyal to their city; but when you ask them why, they stammer and speak of lake fish and the new Odd Fellows Building. But Californians go into detail.

Of course they have, in the climate, an argument that is good for half an hour while you are thinking of your coal bills and heavy underwear. But as soon as they come to mistake your silence for conviction, madness comes upon them, and they picture the city of the Golden Gate as the Bagdad of the New World. So far, as a matter of opinion, no refutation is necessary. But, dear cousins all (from Adam and Eve descended), it is a rash one who will lay his finger on the map and say: "In this town there can be no romance—what could happen here?" Yes, it is a bold and a rash deed to challenge in one sentence, history, romance, and Rand and McNally.

NASHVILLE.—A city, port of delivery, and the capital of the State of Tennessee, is on the Cumberland River and on the N. C. & St. L. and the L. & N. railroads. This city is regarded as the most important educational centre in the South.

I stepped off the train at 8 P. M. Having searched the thesaurus in vain for adjectives, I must, as a substitution, hie me to comparison in the form of a recipe.

Take of London fog 30 parts; malaria 10 parts; gas leaks 20 parts; dewdrops gathered in a brick yard at sunrise, 25 parts; odor of honeysuckle 15 parts. Mix.

The mixture will give you an approximate conception of a Nashville drizzle. It is not so fragrant as a moth-ball nor as thick as pea-soup; but 'tis enough—'twill serve.

I went to a hotel in a tumbril. It required strong self-suppression for me to keep from climbing to the top of it and giving an imitation of Sidney Carton. The vehicle was drawn by beasts of a bygone era and driven by something dark and emancipated.

I was sleepy and tired, so when I got to the hotel I hurriedly paid it the fifty cents it demanded (with approximate lagniappe, I assure you). I knew its habits; and I did not want to hear it prate about its old "marster" or anything that happened "befo' de wah."

The hotel was one of the kind described as "renovated." That means $20,000 worth of new marble pillars, tiling, electric lights and brass cuspidors in the lobby, and a new L. & N. time table and a lithograph of Lookout Mountain in each one of the great rooms above. The management was without reproach, the attention full of exquisite Southern courtesy, the service as slow as the progress of a snail and as good-humored as Rip Van Winkle. The food was worth travelling a thousand miles for. There is no other hotel in the world where you can get such chicken livers *en brochette*.

At dinner I asked a Negro waiter if there was anything doing in town. He pondered gravely for a minute, and then replied: "Well, boss, I don't really reckon there's anything at all doin' after sundown."

Sundown had been accomplished; it had been drowned in the drizzle long before. So that spectacle was denied me. But I went forth upon the streets in the drizzle to see what might be there.

It is built on undulating grounds; and the streets are lighted by electricity at a cost of $32,470 per annum.

As I left the hotel there was a race riot. Down upon me charged a company of freedmen, or Arabs, or Zulus, armed with—no, I saw with relief that they were not rifles, but whips. And I saw dimly a caravan of black, clumsy vehicles; and at the reassuring shouts, "Kyar you anywhere in the town, boss, fuh fifty cents," I reasoned that I was merely a "fare" instead of a victim.

I walked through long streets, all leading uphill. I wondered how those streets ever came down again. Perhaps they didn't until they were "graded." On a few of the "main streets" I saw lights in stores here and there; saw street cars go by conveying worthy burghers hither and yon; saw people pass engaged in the art of conversation, and heard a burst of semi-lively laughter issuing from a soda-water and ice-cream parlor. The streets other than "main" seemed to have enticed upon their borders houses consecrated to peace and domesticity. In many of them lights shone behind discreetly drawn window shades; in a few, pianos tinkled orderly and irreproachable music. There was, indeed, little "doing." I wished I had come before sundown. So I returned to my hotel.

In November, 1864, the Confederate General Hood advanced against Nashville, where he shut up a National force under General Thomas. The latter then sallied forth and defeated the Confederates in a terrible conflict.

All my life I have heard of, admired, and witnessed the fine marksmanship of the South in its peaceful conflicts in the tobacco-chewing regions. But in my hotel a surprise awaited me. There were twelve bright, new, imposing, capacious brass cuspidors in the great lobby, tall enough to be called urns and so wide-mouthed that the crack pitcher of a lady baseball team should have been able to throw a ball into one of them at five paces distant. But, although a terrible battle had raged and was still raging, the enemy had not suffered. Bright, new, imposing, capacious, untouched, they stood. But, shades of Jefferson Brick! the tile floor—the beautiful tile floor! I could not avoid thinking of the battle of Nashville, and trying to draw, as is my foolish habit, some deductions about hereditary marksmanship.

Here I first saw Major (by misplaced courtesy) Wentworth Caswell. I knew him for a type the moment my eyes suffered from the sight of him. A rat has no geographical habitat. My old friend, A. Tennyson, said, as he so well said almost everything:

"Prophet, curse me the blabbing lip,
And curse me the British vermin, the rat."

Let us regard the word "British" as interchangeable *ad lib.* A rat is a rat.

This man was hunting about the hotel lobby like a starved dog that had forgotten where he had buried a bone. He had a face of great acreage, red, pulpy, and with a kind of sleepy massiveness like that of Buddha. He possessed one single virtue—he was very smoothly shaven. The mark of the beast is not indelible upon a man until he goes about with a stubble. I think that if he had not used his razor that day I would have repulsed his advances, and the criminal calendar of the world would have been spared the addition of one murder.

I happened to be standing within five feet of a cuspidor when Major Caswell opened fire upon it. I had been observant enough to perceive that the attacking force was using Gatlings instead of squirrel rifles, so I side-stepped so promptly that the major seized the opportunity to apologize to a noncombatant. He had the blabbing lip. In four minutes he had become my friend and had dragged me to the bar.

I desire to interpolate here that I am a Southerner. But I am not one by profession or trade. I eschew the string tie, the slouch hat, the Prince Albert, the number of bales of cotton destroyed by Sherman, and plug chewing. When the orchestra plays Dixie I do not cheer. I slide a little lower on the leather-cornered seat and, well, order another Würzburger and wish that Longstreet had—but what's the use?

Major Caswell banged the bar with his fist, and the first gun at Fort Sumter re-echoed. When he fired the last one at Appomattox I began to hope. But then he began on family trees, and demonstrated that Adam was only a third cousin of a collateral branch of the Caswell family. Genealogy disposed of, he took up, to my distaste, his private family matters. He spoke of his wife, traced her descent back to Eve, and profanely denied any possible rumor that she may have had relations in the land of Nod.

By this time I began to suspect that he was trying to obscure by noise the fact that he had ordered the drinks, on the chance that I would be bewildered into paying for them. But when they were down he crashed a silver dollar loudly upon the bar. Then, of course, another serving was obligatory. And when I had paid for that I took leave of him brusquely; for I wanted no more of him. But before I had obtained my release he had prated loudly of an income that his wife received, and showed a handful of silver money.

When I got my key at the desk the clerk said to me courteously: "If that man Caswell has annoyed you, and if you would like to make a complaint, we will have him ejected. He is a nuisance, a loafer, and without any known means of support, although he seems to have some money most of the time. But we don't seem to be able to hit upon any means of throwing him out legally."

"Why, no," said I, after some reflection; "I don't see my way clear to making a complaint. But I would like to place myself on record as asserting that I do not care for his company. Your town," I continued, "seems to be a quiet one. What manner of entertainment, adventure, or excitement have you to offer to the stranger within your gates?"

"Well, sir," said the clerk, "there will be a show here next Thursday. It is—I'll look it up and have the announcement sent up to your room with the ice water. Good night."

After I went up to my room I looked out the window. It was only about ten o'clock, but I looked upon a silent town. The drizzle continued, spangled with dim lights, as far apart as currants in a cake sold at the Ladies' Exchange.

"A quiet place," I said to myself, as my first shoe struck the ceiling of the occupant of the room beneath mine. "Nothing of the life here that gives color and variety to the cities in the East and West. Just a good, ordinary, humdrum, business town."

Nashville occupies a foremost place among the manufacturing centres of the country. It is the fifth boot and shoe market in the United States, the largest candy and cracker manufacturing city in the South, and does an enormous wholesale drygoods, grocery, and drug business.

I must tell you how I came to be in Nashville, and I assure you the digression brings as much tedium to me as it does to you. I was travelling elsewhere on my own business, but I had a commission from a Northern literary magazine to stop over there and establish a personal connection between the publication and one of its contributors, Azalea Adair.

Adair (there was no clue to the personality except the handwriting) had sent in some essays (lost art!) and poems that had made the editors swear approvingly over their one o'clock luncheon. So they had commissioned me to round up said Adair and corner by contract his or her output at two cents a word before some other publisher offered her ten or twenty.

At nine o'clock the next morning, after my chicken livers *en brochette* (try them if you can find that hotel), I strayed out into the drizzle, which was still on for an unlimited run. At the first corner I came upon Uncle

Cæsar. He was a stalwart Negro, older than the pyramids, with gray wool and a face that reminded me of Brutus, and a second afterwards of the late King Cettiwayo. He wore the most remarkable coat that I ever had seen or expect to see. It reached to his ankles and had once been a Confederate gray in color. But rain and sun and age had so variegated it that Joseph's coat, beside it, would have faded to a pale monochrome. I must linger with that coat, for it has to do with the story—the story that is so long in coming, because you can hardly expect anything to happen in Nashville.

Once it must have been the military coat of an officer. The cape of it had vanished, but all adown its front it had been frogged and tasselled magnificently. But now the frogs and tassels were gone. In their stead had been patiently stitched (I surmised by some surviving "black mammy") new frogs made of cunningly twisted common hempen twine. This twine was frayed and dishevelled. It must have been added to the coat as a substitute for vanished splendors, with tasteless but painstaking devotion, for it followed faithfully the curves of the long-missing frogs. And, to complete the comedy and pathos of the garment, all its buttons were gone save one. The second button from the top alone remained. The coat was fastened by other twine strings tied through the button-holes and other holes rudely pierced in the opposite side. There was never such a weird garment so fantastically bedecked and of so many mottled hues. The lone button was the size of a half-dollar, made of yellow horn and sewed on with coarse twine.

This Negro stood by a carriage so old that Ham himself might have started a hack line with it after he left the ark with the two animals hitched to it. As I approached he threw open the door, drew out a feather duster, waved it without using it, and said in deep, rumbling tones:

"Step right in, suh; ain't a speck of dust in it—jus' got back from a funeral, suh."

I inferred that on such gala occasions carriages were given an extra cleaning. I looked up and down the street and perceived that there was little choice among the vehicles for hire that lined the curb. I looked in my memorandum book for the address of Azalea Adair.

"I want to go to 861 Jessamine Street," I said, and was about to step into the hack. But for an instant the thick, long, gorilla-like arm of the old Negro barred me. On his massive and saturnine face a look of sudden suspicion and enmity flashed for a moment. Then, with quickly returning conviction, he asked blandishingly: "What are you gwine there for, boss?"

"What is that to you?" I asked, a little sharply.

"Nothin', suh, jus' nothin'. Only it's a lonesome kind of part of town and few folks ever has business out there. Step right in. The seats is clean—jes' got back from a funeral, suh."

A mile and a half it must have been to our journey's end. I could hear nothing but the fearful rattle of the ancient hack over the uneven brick paving; I could smell nothing but the drizzle, now further flavored with coal smoke and something like a mixture of tar and oleander blossoms. All I could see through the streaming windows were two rows of dim houses.

The city has an area of 10 square miles; 181 miles of streets, of which 137 miles are paved; a system of waterworks that cost $2,000,000, with 77 miles of mains.

Eight-sixty-one Jessamine Street was a decayed mansion. Thirty yards back from the street it stood, outmerged in a splendid grove of trees and untrimmed shrubbery. A row of box bushes overflowed and almost hid the paling fence from sight; the gate was kept closed by a rope noose that encircled the gate post and the first paling of the gate. But when you got inside you saw that 861 was a shell, a shadow, a ghost of former grandeur and excellence. But in the story, I have not yet got inside.

When the hack had ceased from rattling and the weary quadrupeds came to a rest I handed my jehu his fifty cents with an additional quarter, feeling a glow of conscious generosity, as I did so. He refused it.

"It's two dollars, suh," he said.

"How's that?" I asked. "I plainly heard you call out at the hotel: 'Fifty cents to any part of the town.'"

"It's two dollars, suh," he repeated obstinately. "It's a long ways from the hotel."

"It is within the city limits and well within them," I argued. "Don't think that you have picked up a greenhorn Yankee. Do you see those hills over there?" I went on, pointing toward the east (I could not see them, myself, for the drizzle); "well, I was born and raised on their other side. You old fool nigger, can't you tell people from other people when you see 'em?"

The grim face of King Cettiwayo softened. "Is you from the South, suh? I reckon it was them shoes of yourn fooled me. They is somethin' sharp in the toes for a Southern gen'l'man to wear."

"Then the charge is fifty cents, I suppose?" said I inexorably.

His former expression, a mingling of cupidity and hostility, returned, remained ten seconds, and vanished.

"Boss," he said, "fifty cents is right; but I *needs* two dollars, suh; I'm *obleeged* to have two dollars. I ain't *demandin'* it now, suh; after I knows whar you's from; I'm jus' sayin' that I *has* to have two dollars to-night, and business is mighty po'."

Peace and confidence settled upon his heavy features. He had been luckier than he had hoped. Instead of having picked up a greenhorn, ignorant of rates, he had come upon an inheritance.

"You confounded old rascal," I said, reaching down to my pocket, "you ought to be turned over to the police."

For the first time I saw him smile. He knew; *he knew;* HE KNEW.

I gave him two one-dollar bills. As I handed them over I noticed that one of them had seen parlous times. Its upper right-hand corner was missing, and it had been torn through in the middle, but joined again. A strip of blue tissue paper, pasted over the split, preserved its negotiability.

Enough of the African bandit for the present: I left him happy, lifted the rope and opened the creaky gate.

The house, as I said, was a shell. A paint brush had not touched it in twenty years. I could not see why a strong wind should not have bowled it over like a house of cards until I looked again at the trees that hugged it close—the trees that saw the battle of Nashville and still drew their protecting branches around it against storm and enemy and cold.

Azalea Adair, fifty years old, white-haired, a descendant of the cavaliers, as thin and frail as the house she lived in, robed in the cheapest and cleanest dress I ever saw, with an air as simple as a queen's, received me.

The reception room seemed a mile square, because there was nothing in it except some rows of books, on unpainted white-pine bookshelves, a cracked marble-top table, a rag rug, a hairless horse-hair sofa and two or three chairs. Yes, there was a picture on the wall, a colored crayon drawing of a cluster of pansies. I looked around for the portrait of Andrew Jackson and the pine-cone hanging basket but they were not there.

Azalea Adair and I had conversation, a little of which will be repeated to you. She was a product of the old South, gently nurtured in the sheltered life. Her learning was not broad, but was deep and of splendid originality in its somewhat narrow scope. She had been educated at home, and her knowledge of the world was derived from inference and by inspiration. Of such is the precious, small group of essayists made. While she talked to me I kept brushing my fingers, trying, unconsciously, to rid them guiltily of the absent dust from the half-calf backs of Lamb,

Chaucer, Hazlitt, Marcus Aurelius, Montaigne and Hood. She was exquisite, she was a valuable discovery. Nearly everybody nowadays knows too much—oh, so much too much—of real life.

I could perceive clearly that Azalea Adair was very poor. A house and a dress she had, not much else, I fancied. So, divided between my duty to the magazine and my loyalty to the poets and essayists who fought Thomas in the valley of the Cumberland, I listened to her voice, which was like a harpsichord's, and found that I could not speak of contracts. In the presence of the nine Muses and the three Graces one hesitated to lower the topic to two cents. There would have to be another colloquy after I had regained my commercialism. But I spoke of my mission, and three o'clock of the next afternoon was set for the discussion of the business proposition.

"Your town," I said, as I began to make ready to depart (which is the time for smooth generalities), "seems to be a quiet, sedate place. A home town, I should say, where few things out of the ordinary ever happen."

It carries on an extensive trade in stoves and hollow ware with the West and South, and its flouring mills have a daily capacity of more than 2,000 barrels.

Azalea Adair seemed to reflect.

"I have never thought of it that way," she said, with a kind of sincere intensity that seemed to belong to her. "Isn't it in the still, quiet places that things do happen? I fancy that when God began to create the earth on the first Monday morning one could have leaned out one's window and heard the drops of mud splashing from His trowel as He built up the everlasting hills. What did the noisiest project in the world—I mean the building of the tower of Babel—result in finally? A page and a half of Esperanto in the *North American Review.*"

"Of course," said I platitudinously, "human nature is the same everywhere; but there is more color—er—more drama and movement and—er—romance in some cities than in others."

"On the surfaces," said Azalea Adair. "I have travelled many times around the world in a golden airship wafted on two wings—print and dreams. I have seen (on one of my imaginary tours) the Sultan of Turkey bowstring with his own hands one of his wives who had uncovered her face in public. I have seen a man in Nashville tear up his theatre tickets because his wife was going out with her face covered—with rice powder. In San Francisco's Chinatown I saw the slave girl Sing Yee dipped slowly, inch by inch, in boiling almond oil to make her swear she would never see her American lover again. She gave in when the boiling oil had reached three inches above her knee. At a euchre party in East Nashville the other night I saw Kitty Morgan cut dead by seven of her schoolmates and lifelong friends because she had married a house painter. The boiling oil was sizzling as high as her heart; but I wish you could have seen the fine little smile that she carried from table to table. Oh, yes, it is a humdrum town. Just a few miles of red brick houses and mud and stores and lumber yards."

Some one knocked hollowly at the back of the house. Azalea Adair breathed a soft apology and went to investigate the sound. She came back in three minutes with brightened eyes, a faint flush on her cheeks, and ten years lifted from her shoulders.

"You must have a cup of tea before you go," she said, "and a sugar cake."

She reached and shook a little iron bell. In shuffled a small Negro girl about twelve, barefoot, not very tidy, glowering at me with thumb in mouth and bulging eyes.

Azalea Adair opened a tiny, worn purse and drew out a dollar bill, a dollar bill with the upper right-hand corner missing, torn in two pieces and pasted together again with a strip of blue tissue paper. It was one of the bills I had given the piratical Negro—there was no doubt of it.

"Go up to Mr. Baker's store on the corner, Impy," she said, handing the girl the dollar bill, "and get a quarter of a pound of tea—the kind he always sends me—and ten cents worth of sugar cakes. Now, hurry. The supply of tea in the house happens to be exhausted," she explained to me.

Impy left by the back way. Before the scrape of her hard, bare feet had died away on the back porch, a wild shriek—I was sure it was hers—filled the hollow house. Then the deep, gruff tones of an angry man's voice mingled with the girl's further squeals and unintelligible words.

Azalea Adair rose without surprise or emotion and disappeared. For two minutes I heard the hoarse rumble of the man's voice; then something like an oath and a slight scuffle, and she returned calmly to her chair.

"This is a roomy house," she said, "and I have a tenant for part of it. I am sorry to have to rescind my invitation to tea. It was impossible to get the kind I always use, at the store. Perhaps to-morrow Mr. Baker will be able to supply me."

I was sure that Impy had not had time to leave the house. I inquired concerning street-car lines and took my leave. After I was well on my way I remembered that I had not learned Azalea Adair's name. But to-morrow would do.

That same day I started in on the course of iniquity that this uneventful city forced upon me. I was in the town only two days, but in that time I managed to lie shamelessly by telegraph, and to be an accomplice—after the fact, if that is the correct legal term—to a murder.

As I rounded the corner nearest my hotel the Afrite coachman of the polychromatic, nonpareil coat seized me, swung open the dungeony door of his peripatetic sarcophagus, flirted his feather duster and began his ritual: "Step right in, boss. Carriage is clean—jus' got back from a funeral. Fifty cents to any—"

And then he knew me and grinned broadly. "'Scuse me, boss; you is de gen'l'man what rid out with me dis mawnin'. Thank you kindly, suh."

"I am going out to 861 again to-morrow afternoon at three," said I, "and if you will be here, I'll let you drive me. So you know Miss Adair?" I concluded, thinking of my dollar bill.

"I belonged to her father, Judge Adair, suh," he replied.

"I judge that she is pretty poor," I said. "She hasn't much money to speak of, has she?"

For an instant I looked again at the fierce countenance of King Cettiwayo, and then he changed back to an extortionate old Negro hack driver.

"She ain't gwine to starve, suh," he said slowly. "She has reso'ces, suh; she has reso'ces."

"I shall pay you fifty cents for the trip," said I.

"Dat is puffeckly correct, suh," he answered humbly. "I jus' *had* to have dat two dollars dis mawnin', boss."

I went to the hotel and lied by electricity. I wired the magazine: "A. Adair holds out for eight cents a word."

The answer that came back was: "Give it to her quick, you duffer."

Just before dinner "Major" Wentworth Caswell bore down upon me with the greetings of a long-lost friend. I have seen few men whom I have so instantaneously hated, and of whom it was so difficult to be rid. I was standing at the bar when he invaded me; therefore I could not wave the white ribbon in his face. I would have paid gladly for the drinks, hoping, thereby, to escape another; but he was one of those despicable, roaring, advertising bibbers who must have brass bands and fireworks attend upon every cent that they waste in their follies.

With an air of producing millions he drew two one-dollar bills from a pocket and dashed one of them upon the bar. I looked once more at the dollar bill with the upper right-hand corner missing, torn through the middle, and patched with a strip of blue tissue paper. It was my dollar bill again. It could have been no other.

I went up to my room. The drizzle and the monotony of a dreary, eventless Southern town had made me tired and listless. I remember that just before I went to bed I mentally disposed of the mysterious dollar bill (which might have formed the clew to a tremendously fine detective story of San Francisco) by saying to myself sleepily: "Seems as if a lot of people here own stock in the Hack-Driver's Trust. Pays dividends promptly, too. Wonder if—" Then I fell asleep.

King Cettiwayo was at his post the next day, and rattled my bones over the stones out to 861. He was to wait and rattle me back again when I was ready.

Azalea Adair looked paler and cleaner and frailer than she had looked on the day before. After she had signed the contract at eight cents per word she grew still paler and began to slip out of her chair. Without much trouble I managed to get her up on the antediluvian horsehair sofa and then I ran out to the sidewalk and yelled to the coffee-colored Pirate to bring a doctor. With a wisdom that I had not suspected in him, he abandoned his team and struck off up the street afoot, realizing the value of speed. In ten minutes he returned with a grave, gray-haired and capable man of medicine. In a few words (worth much less than eight cents each) I explained to him my presence in the hollow house of mystery. He bowed with stately understanding, and turned to the old Negro.

"Uncle Cæsar," he said calmly, "run up to my house and ask Miss Lucy to give you a cream pitcher full of fresh milk and half a tumbler of port wine. And hurry back. Don't drive—run. I want you to get back sometime this week."

It occurred to me that Dr. Merriman also felt a distrust as to the speeding powers of the land-pirate's steeds. After Uncle Cæsar was gone, lumberingly, but swiftly, up the street, the doctor looked me over with great politeness and as much careful calculation until he had decided that I might do.

"It is only a case of insufficient nutrition," he said. "In other words, the result of poverty, pride, and starvation. Mrs. Caswell has many devoted friends who would be glad to aid her, but she will accept nothing except from that old Negro, Uncle Cæsar, who was once owned by her family."

"Mrs. Caswell!" said I, in surprise. And then I looked at the contract and saw that she had signed it "Azalea Adair Caswell."

"I thought she was Miss Adair," I said.

"Married to a drunken, worthless loafer, sir," said the doctor. "It is said that he robs her even of the small sums that her old servant contributes toward her support."

When the milk and wine had been brought the doctor soon revived Azalea Adair. She sat up and talked of the beauty of the autumn leaves that were then in season, and their height of color. She referred lightly to her fainting seizure as the outcome of an old palpitation of the heart. Impy fanned her as she lay on the sofa. The doctor was due elsewhere, and I followed him to the door. I told him that it was within my power and intentions to make a reasonable advance of money to Azalea Adair on future contributions to the magazine, and he seemed pleased.

"By the way," he said, "perhaps you would like to know that you have had royalty for a coachman. Old Cæsar's grandfather was a king in Congo. Cæsar himself has royal ways, as you may have observed."

As the doctor was moving off I heard Uncle Cæsar's voice inside: "Did he git bofe of dom two dollars from you, Mis' 'Zalea?"

"Yes, Cæsar," I heard Azalea Adair answer weakly. And then I went in and concluded business negotiations with our contributor. I assumed the responsibility of advancing fifty dollars, putting it as a necessary formality in binding our bargain. And then Uncle Cæsar drove me back to the hotel.

Here ends all of the story as far as I can testify as a witness. The rest must be only bare statements of facts.

At about six o'clock I went out for a stroll. Uncle Cæsar was at his corner. He threw open the door of his carriage, flourished his duster and began his depressing formula: "Step right in, suh. Fifty cents to anywhere in the city—hack's puffickly clean, suh—jus' got back from a funeral—"

And then he recognized me. I think his eyesight was getting bad. His coat had taken on a few more faded shades of color, the twine strings were more frayed and ragged, the last remaining button—the button of yellow horn—was gone. A motley descendant of kings was Uncle Cæsar!

About two hours later I saw an excited crowd besieging the front of a drug store. In a desert where nothing happens this was manna; so I wedged my way inside. On an extemporized couch of empty boxes and chairs was stretched the mortal corporeality of Major Wentworth Caswell. A doctor was testing him for the immortal ingredient. His decision was that it was conspicuous by its absence.

The erstwhile Major had been found dead on a dark street and brought by curious and ennuied citizens to the drug store. The late human being had been engaged in terrific battle—the details showed that. Loafer and reprobate though he had been, he had been also a warrior. But he had lost. His hands were yet clinched so tightly that his fingers would not be opened. The gentle citizens who had known him stood about and searched their vocabularies to find some good words, if it were possible, to speak of him. One kind-looking man said, after much thought: "When 'Cas' was about fo'teen he was one of the best spellers in school."

While I stood there the fingers of the right hand of "the man that was," which hung down the side of a white pine box, relaxed, and dropped something at my feet. I covered it with one foot quietly, and a little later on I picked it up and pocketed it. I reasoned that in his last struggle his hand must have seized that object unwittingly and held it in a death grip.

At the hotel that night the main topic of conversation, with the possible exceptions of politics and prohibition, was the demise of Major Caswell. I heard one man say to a group of listeners:

"In my opinion, gentlemen, Caswell was murdered by some of these no-account niggers for his money. He had fifty dollars this afternoon which he showed to several gentlemen in the hotel. When he was found the money was not on his person."

I left the city the next morning at nine, and as the train was crossing the bridge over the Cumberland River I took out of my pocket a yellow horn overcoat button the size of a fifty-cent piece, with frayed ends of coarse twine hanging from it, and cast it out of the window into the slow, muddy waters below.

I wonder what's doing in Buffalo!

Calloway's Code

THE New York *Enterprise* sent H. B. Calloway as special correspondent to the Russo-Japanese-Portsmouth war.

For two months Calloway hung about Yokohama and Tokio, shaking dice with the other correspondents for drinks of 'rickshaws—oh, no, that's something to ride in; anyhow, he wasn't earning the salary that his paper was paying him. But that was not Calloway's fault. The little brown men who held the strings of Fate between their fingers were not ready for the readers of the *Enterprise* to season their breakfast bacon and eggs with the battles of the descendants of the gods.

But soon the column of correspondents that were to go out with the First Army tightened their field-glass belts and went down to the Yalu with Kuroki. Calloway was one of these.

Now, this is no history of the battle of the Yalu River. That has been told in detail by the correspondents who gazed at the shrapnel smoke rings from a distance of three miles. But, for justice's sake, let it be understood that the Japanese commander prohibited a nearer view.

Calloway's feat was accomplished before the battle. What he did was to furnish the *Enterprise* with the biggest beat of the war. That paper published exclusively and in detail the news of the attack on the lines of the Russian General Zassulitch on the same day that it was made. No other paper printed a word about it for two days afterward, except a London paper, whose account was absolutely incorrect and untrue.

Calloway did this in face of the fact that General Kuroki was making his moves and laying his plans with the profoundest secrecy as far as the world outside his camps was concerned. The correspondents were forbidden to send out any news whatever of his plans; and every message that was allowed on the wires was censored with rigid severity.

The correspondent for the London paper handed in a cablegram describing Kuroki's plans; but as it was wrong from beginning to end the censor grinned and let it go through.

So, there they were—Kuroki on one side of the Yalu with forty-two thousand infantry, five thousand cavalry, and one hundred and twenty-four guns. On the other side, Zassulitch waited for him with only twenty-three thousand men, and with a long stretch of river to guard. And Calloway had got hold of some important inside information that he knew would bring the *Enterprise* staff around a cablegram as thick as flies around a Park Row lemonade stand. If he could only get that message past the censor—the new censor who had arrived and taken his post that day!

Calloway did the obviously proper thing. He lit his pipe and sat down on a gun carriage to think it over. And there we must leave him; for the rest of the story belongs to Vesey, a sixteen-dollar-a-week reporter on the *Enterprise.*

Calloway's cablegram was handed to the managing editor at four o'clock in the afternoon. He read it three times; and then drew a pocket mirror from a pigeon-hole in his desk, and looked at his reflection carefully. Then he went over to the desk of Boyd, his assistant (he usually called Boyd when he wanted him), and laid the cablegram before him.

"It's from Calloway," he said. "See what you make of it."

The message was dated at Wi-ju, and these were the words of it:

Foregone preconcerted rash witching. goes muffled rumour mine dark silent unfortunate richmond existing great hotly brute select mooted parlous beggars ye angel incontrovertible.

Boyd read it twice.

"It's either a cipher or a sunstroke," said he.

"Ever hear of anything like a code in the office—a secret code?" asked the m. e., who had held his desk for only two years. Managing editors come and go.

"None except the vernacular that the lady specials write in," said Boyd. "Couldn't be an acrostic, could it?"

"I thought of that," said the m. e., "but the beginning letters contain only four vowels. It must be a code of some sort."

"Try 'em in groups," suggested Boyd. "Let's see—'Rash witching goes'—not with me it doesn't. 'Muffled rumour mine'—must have an underground wire. 'Dark silent unfortunate richmond'—no reason why he should knock that town so hard. 'Existing great hotly'—no, it doesn't pan out. I'll call Scot."

The city editor came in a hurry, and tried his luck. A city editor must know something about everything; so Scott knew a little about cipher-writing.

"It may be what is called an inverted alphabet cipher," said he. "I'll try that. 'R' seems to be the oftenest used initial letter, with the exception of 'm.' Assuming 'r' to mean 'e', the most frequently used vowel, we transpose the letters—so."

Scott worked rapidly with his pencil for two minutes; and then showed the first word according to his reading—the word "Scejtzez."

"Great!" cried Boyd. "It's a charade. My first is a Russian general. Go on, Scott."

"No, that won't work," said the city editor. "It's undoubtedly a code. It's impossible to read it without the key. Has the office ever used a cipher code?"

"Just what I was asking," said the m. e. "Hustle everybody up that ought to know. We must get at it some way. Calloway has evidently got hold of something big, and the censor has put the screws on, or he wouldn't have cabled in a lot of chop suey like this."

Throughout the office of the *Enterprise* a drag-net was sent, hauling in such members of the staff as would be likely to know of a code, past or present, by reason of their wisdom, information, natural intelligence, or length of servitude. They got together in a group in the city room, with the m. e. in the centre. No one had heard of a code. All began to explain to the head investigator that newspapers never use a code, anyhow—that is, a cipher code. Of course the Associated Press stuff is a sort of code—an abbreviation, rather—but——

The m. e. knew all that, and said so. He asked each man how long he had worked on the paper. Not one of them had drawn pay from an *Enterprise* envelope for longer than six years. Calloway had been on the paper twelve years.

"Try old Heffelbauer," said the m. e. "He was here when Park Row was a potato patch."

Heffelbauer was an institution. He was half janitor, half handy-man about the office, and half watchman—thus becoming the peer of thirteen and one-half tailors. Sent for, he came, radiating his nationality.

"Heffelbauer," said the m. e., "did you ever hear of a code belonging to the office a long time ago—a private code? You know what a code is, don't you?"

"Yah," said Heffelbauer. "Sure I know vat a code is. Yah, apout dwelf or fifteen year ago der office had a code. Der reborters in der city-room haf it here."

"Ah!" said the m. e. "We're getting on the trail now. Where was it kept, Heffelbauer? What do you know about it?"

"Somedimes," said the retainer, "dey keep it in der little room behind der library room."

"Can you find it?" asked the m. e. eagerly. "Do you know where it is?"

"Mein Gott!" said Heffelbauer. "How long you dink a code live? Der reborters call him a maskeet. But von day he butt mit his head der editor, und——"

"Oh, he's talking about a goat," said Boyd. "Get out, Heffelbauer."

Again discomfited, the concerted wit and resource of the *Enterprise* huddled around Calloway's puzzle, considering its mysterious words in vain.

Then Vesey came in.

Vesey was the youngest reporter. He had a thirty-two-inch chest and wore a number fourteen collar; but his bright Scotch plaid suit gave him presence and conferred no obscurity upon his whereabouts. He wore his hat in such a position that people followed him about to see him take it off, convinced that it must be hung upon a peg driven into the back of his head. He was never without an immense, knotted, hard-wood cane with a German-silver tip on its crooked handle. Vesey was the best photograph hustler in the office. Scott said it was because no living human being could resist the personal triumph it was to hand his picture over to Vesey. Vesey always wrote his own news stories, except the big ones, which were sent to the rewrite men. Add to this fact that among all the inhabitants, temples, and groves of the earth nothing existed that could abash Vesey, and his dim sketch is concluded.

Vesey butted into the circle of cipher readers very much as Heffelbauer's "code" would have done, and asked what was up. Some one explained, with the touch of half-familiar condescension that they always used toward him. Vesey reached out and took the cablegram from the m. e.'s hand. Under the protection of some special Providence, he was always doing appalling things like that, and coming off unscathed.

"It's a code," said Vesey. "Anybody got the key?"

"The office has no code," said Boyd, reaching for the message. Vesey held to it.

"Then old Calloway expects us to read it, anyhow," said he. "He's up a tree, or something, and he's made this up so as to get it by the censor. It's up to us. Gee! I wish they had sent me, too. Say—we can't afford to fall down on our end of it. 'Foregone, preconcerted, rash, witching'—h'm."

Vesey sat down on a table corner and began to whistle softly, frowning at the cablegram.

"Let's have it, please," said the m. e. "We've got to get to work on it."

"I believe I've got a line on it," said Vesey. "Give me ten minutes."

He walked to his desk, threw his hat into a waste-basket, spread out flat on his chest like a gorgeous lizard, and started his pencil going. The wit and wisdom of the *Enterprise* remained in a loose group, and smiled at one another, nodding their heads toward Vesey. Then they began to exchange their theories about the cipher.

It took Vesey exactly fifteen minutes. He brought to the m. e. a pad with the code-key written on it.

"I felt the swing of it as soon as I saw it," said Vesey. "Hurrah for old Calloway! He's done the Japs and every paper in town that prints literature instead of news. Take a look at that."

Thus had Vesey set forth the reading of the code:

Foregone—conclusion
Preconcerted—arrangement
Rash—act

Witching—hour of midnight
Goes—without saying
Muffled—report
Rumour—hath it
Mine—host
Dark—horse
Silent—majority
Unfortunate—pedestrians *
Richmond—in the field
Existing—conditions
Great—White Way
Hotly—contested
Brute—force
Select—few
Mooted—question
Parlous—times
Beggars—description
Ye—correspondent
Angel—unawares
Incontrovertible—fact

"It's simply newspaper English," explained Vesey. "I've been reporting on the *Enterprise* long enough to know it by heart. Old Calloway gives us the cue word, and we use the word that naturally follows it just as we use 'em in the paper. Read it over, and you'll see how pat they drop into their places. Now, here's the message he intended us to get."

Vesey handed out another sheet of paper.

Concluded arrangement to act at hour of midnight without saying. Report hath it that a large body of cavalry and an overwhelming force of infantry will be thrown into the field. Conditions white. Way contested by only a small force. Question the *Times* description. Its correspondent is unaware of the facts.

"Great stuff!" cried Boyd excitedly. "Kuroki crosses the Yalu to-night and attacks. Oh, we won't do a thing to the sheets that make up with Addison's essays, real estate transfers, and bowling scores!"

"Mr. Vesey," said the m. e., with his jollying-which-you-should-regard-as-a-favor manner, "you have cast a serious reflection upon the literary standards of the paper that employs you. You have also assisted materially in giving us the biggest 'beat' of the year. I will let you know in a day or two whether you are to be discharged or retained at a larger salary. Somebody send Ames to me."

* Mr. Vesey afterward explained that the logical journalistic complement of the word "unfortunate" was once the word "victim." But, since the automobile became so popular, the correct following word is now "pedestrians." Of course, in Calloway's code it meant infantry.

Ames was the king-pin, the snowy-petalled marguerite, the star-bright looloo of the rewrite men. He saw attempted murder in the pains of green-apple colic, cyclones in the summer zephyr, lost children in every top-spinning urchin, an uprising of the down-trodden masses in every hurling of a derelict potato at a passing automobile. When not rewriting, Ames sat on the porch of his Brooklyn villa playing checkers with his ten-year-old son.

Ames and the "war editor" shut themselves in a room. There was a map in there stuck full of little pins that represented armies and divisions. Their fingers had been itching for days to move those pins along the crooked line of the Yalu. They did so now; and in words of fire Ames translated Calloway's brief message into a front page masterpiece that set the world talking. He told of the secret councils of the Japanese officers; gave Kuroki's flaming speeches in full; counted the cavalry and infantry to a man and a horse; described the quick and silent building of the bridge at Suikauchen, across which the Mikado's legions were hurled upon the surprised Zassulitch, whose troops were widely scattered along the river. And the battle!—well, you know what Ames can do with a battle if you give him just one smell of smoke for a foundation. And in the same story, with seemingly supernatural knowledge, he gleefully scored the most profound and ponderous paper in England for the false and misleading account of the intended movements of the Japanese First Army printed in its issue of *the same date.*

Only one error was made; and that was the fault of the cable operator at Wi-ju. Calloway pointed it out after he came back. The word "great" in his code should have been "gage" and its complemental words "of battle." But it went to Ames "conditions white," and of course he took that to mean snow. His description of the Japanese army struggling through the snow-storm, blinded by the whirling flakes, was thrillingly vivid. The artists turned out some effective illustrations that made a hit as pictures of the artillery dragging their guns through the drifts. But, as the attack was made on the first day of May, the "conditions white" excited some amusement. But it made no difference to the *Enterprise,* anyway.

It was wonderful. And Calloway was wonderful in having made the new censor believe that his jargon of words meant no more than a complaint of the dearth of news and a petition for more expense money. And Vesey was wonderful. And most wonderful of all are words, and how they make friends one with another, being oft associated, until not even obituary notices them do part.

On the second day following, the city editor halted at Vesey's desk where the reporter was writing the story of a man who had broken his leg by falling into a coal-hole—Ames having failed to find a murder motive in it.

"The old man says your salary is to be raised to twenty a week," said Scott.

"All right," said Vesey. "Every little helps. Say—Mr. Scott, which would you say—'We can state without fear of successful contradiction,' or, 'On the whole it can be safely asserted'?"

Roads of Destiny

I go to seek on many roads
What is to be.
True heart and strong, with love to light—
Will they not bear me in the fight
To order, shun or wield or mould
My Destiny?

Unpublished Poems of David Mignot.

THE song was over. The words were David's; the air, one of the countryside. The company about the inn table applauded heartily, for the young poet paid for the wine. Only the notary, M. Papineau, shook his head a little at the lines, for he was a man of books, and he had not drunk with the rest.

David went out into the village street, where the night air drove the wine vapor from his head. And then he remembered that he and Yvonne had quarrelled that day, and that he had resolved to leave his home that night to seek fame and honor in the great world outside.

"When my poems are on every man's tongue," he told himself, in a fine exhilaration, "she will, perhaps, think of the hard words she spoke this day."

Except the roysterers in the tavern, the village folk were abed. David crept softly into his room in the shed of his father's cottage and made a bundle of his small store of clothing. With this upon a staff, he set his face outward upon the road that ran from Vernoy.

He passed his father's herd of sheep huddled in their nightly pen—the sheep he herded daily, leaving them to scatter while he wrote verses on scraps of paper. He saw a light yet shining in Yvonne's window, and a weakness shook his purpose of a sudden. Perhaps that light meant that she rued, sleepless, her anger, and that morning might—But, no! His decision was made. Vernoy was no place for him. Not one soul there could share his thoughts. Out along that road lay his fate and his future.

Three leagues across the dim, moonlit champaign ran the road, straight as a ploughman's furrow. It was believed in the village that the road ran to Paris, at least; and this name the poet whispered often to himself as he walked. Never so far from Vernoy had David travelled before.

THE LEFT BRANCH

Three leagues, then, the road ran, and turned into a puzzle. It joined with another and a larger road at right angles. David stood, uncertain, for a while, and then took the road to the left.

Upon this more important highway were, imprinted in the dust, wheel tracks left by the recent passage of some vehicle. Some half an hour later these traces were verified by the sight of a ponderous carriage mired in a little brook at the bottom of a steep hill. The driver and postilions were shouting and tugging at the horses' bridles. On the road at one side stood a huge, black-clothed man and a slender lady wrapped in a long, light cloak.

David saw the lack of skill in the efforts of the servants. He quietly assumed control of the work. He directed the outriders to cease their clamor at the horses and to exercise their strength upon the wheels. The driver alone urged the animals with his familiar voice; David himself heaved a powerful shoulder at the rear of the carriage, and with one harmonious tug the great vehicle rolled up on solid ground. The outriders climbed to their places.

David stood for a moment upon one foot. The huge gentleman waved a hand. "You will enter the carriage," he said, in a voice large, like himself, but smoothed by art and habit. Obedience belonged in the path of such a voice. Brief as was the young poet's hesitation, it was cut shorter still by a renewal of the command. David's foot went to the step. In the darkness he perceived dimly the form of the lady upon the rear seat. He was about to seat himself opposite, when the voice again swayed him to its will. "You will sit at the lady's side."

The gentleman swung his great weight to the forward seat. The carriage proceeded up the hill. The lady was shrunk, silent, into her corner. David could not estimate whether she was old or young, but a delicate, mild perfume from her clothes stirred his poet's fancy to the belief that there was loveliness beneath the mystery. Here was an adventure such as he had often imagined. But as yet he held no key to it, for no word was spoken while he sat with his impenetrable companions.

In an hour's time David perceived through the window that the vehicle traversed the street of some town. Then it stopped in front of a closed and darkened house, and a postilion alighted to hammer impatiently upon the door. A latticed window above flew wide and a night-capped head popped out.

"Who are ye that disturb honest folk at this time of night? My house is closed. 'Tis too late for profitable travellers to be abroad. Cease knocking at my door, and be off."

"Open!" spluttered the postilion, loudly; "open for Monseigneur the Marquis de Beaupertuys."

"Ah!" cried the voice above. "Ten thousand pardons, my lord. I did not know—the hour is so late—at once shall the door be opened, and the house placed at my lord's disposal."

Inside was heard the clink of chain and bar, and the door was flung open. Shivering with chill and apprehension, the landlord of the Silver Flagon stood, half clad, candle in hand, upon the threshold.

David followed the marquis out of the carriage. "Assist the lady," he was ordered. The poet obeyed. He felt her small hand tremble as he guided her descent. "Into the house," was the next command.

The room was the long dining-hall of the tavern. A great oak table ran down its length. The huge gentleman seated himself in a chair at the nearer end. The lady sank into another against the wall, with an air of great weariness. David stood, considering how best he might now take his leave and continue upon his way.

"My lord," said the landlord, bowing to the floor, "h-ad I ex-expected this honor, entertainment would have been ready. T-t-there is wine and cold fowl and m-m-maybe—"

"Candles," said the marquis, spreading the fingers of one plump white hand in a gesture he had.

"Y-yes, my lord." He fetched half a dozen candles, lighted them, and set them upon the table.

"If monsieur would, perhaps, deign to taste a certain Burgundy—there is a cask—"

"Candles," said monsieur, spreading his fingers.

"Assuredly—quickly—I fly, my lord."

A dozen more lighted candles shone in the hall. The great bulk of the marquis overflowed his chair. He was dressed in fine black from head to foot save for the snowy ruffles at his wrist and throat. Even the hilt and scabbard of his sword were black. His expression was one of sneering pride. The ends of an upturned moustache reached nearly to his mocking eyes.

The lady sat motionless, and now David perceived that she was young, and possessed of pathetic and appealing beauty. He was startled from the contemplation of her forlorn loveliness by the booming voice of the marquis.

"What is your name and pursuit?"

"David Mignot. I am a poet."

The moustache of the marquis curled nearer to his eyes.

"How do you live?"

"I am also a shepherd; I guided my father's flock," David answered, with his head high, but a flush upon his cheek.

"Then listen, master shepherd and poet, to the fortune you have blundered upon to-night. This lady is my niece, Mademoiselle Lucie de Varennes. She is of noble descent and is possessed of ten thousand francs a year in her own right. As to her charms, you have but to observe for yourself. If the inventory pleases your shepherd's heart, she becomes your wife at a word. Do not interrupt me. To-night I conveyed her to the *château* of the Comte de Villemaur, to whom her hand had been promised. Guests were present; the priest was waiting; her marriage to one eligible in rank and fortune was ready to be accomplished. At the altar this demoiselle, so meek and dutiful, turned upon me like a leopardess, charged me with cruelty and crimes, and broke, before the gaping priest, the troth I had plighted for her. I swore there and then, by ten thousand devils, that she should marry the first man we met after leaving the *château,* be he prince, charcoal-burner, or thief. You, shepherd, are the first. Mademoiselle must be wed this night. If not you, then another. You have ten minutes in which to make your decision. Do not vex me with words or questions. Ten minutes, shepherd; and they are speeding."

The marquis drummed loudly with his white fingers upon the table. He sank into a veiled attitude of waiting. It was as if some great house had shut its doors and windows against approach. David would have spoken, but the huge man's bearing stopped his tongue. Instead, he stood by the lady's chair and bowed.

"Mademoiselle," he said, and he marvelled to find his words flowing easily before so much elegance and beauty. "You have heard me say I was a shepherd. I have also had the fancy, at times, that I am a poet. If it be the test of a poet to adore and cherish the beautiful, that fancy is now strengthened. Can I serve you in any way, mademoiselle?"

The young woman looked up at him with eyes dry and mournful.

His frank, glowing face, made serious by the gravity of the adventure, his strong, straight figure and the liquid sympathy in his blue eyes, perhaps, also, her imminent need of long-denied help and kindness, thawed her to sudden tears.

"Monsieur," she said, in low tones, "you look to be true and kind. He is my uncle, the brother of my father, and my only relative. He loved my mother, and he hates me because I am like her. He has made my life one long terror. I am afraid of his very looks, and never before dared to disobey him. But to-night he would have married me to a man three times my age. You will forgive me for bringing this vexation upon you, monsieur. You will, of course, decline this mad act he tries to force upon you. But let me thank you for your generous words, at least. I have had none spoken to me in so long."

There was now something more than generosity in the poet's eyes. Poet he must have been, for Yvonne was forgotten; this fine, new loveliness held him with its freshness and grace. The subtle perfume from her filled him with strange emotions. His tender look fell warmly upon her. She leaned to it, thirstily.

"Ten minutes," said David, "is given me in which to do what I would devote years to achieve. I will not say I pity you, mademoiselle; it would not be true—I love you. I cannot ask love from you yet, but let me rescue you from this cruel man, and, in time, love may come. I think I have a future, I will not always be a shepherd. For the present I will cherish you with all my heart and make your life less sad. Will you trust your fate to me, mademoiselle?"

"Ah, you would sacrifice yourself from pity!"

"From love. The time is almost up, mademoiselle."

"You will regret it, and despise me."

"I will live only to make you happy, and myself worthy of you."

Her fine small hand crept into his from beneath her cloak.

"I will trust you," she breathed, "with my life. And—and love—may not be so far off as you think. Tell him. Once away from the power of his eyes I may forget."

David went and stood before the marquis. The black figure stirred, and the mocking eyes glanced at the great hall clock.

"Two minutes to spare. A shepherd requires eight minutes to decide whether he will accept a bride of beauty and income! Speak up, shepherd, do you consent to become mademoiselle's husband?"

"Mademoiselle," said David, standing proudly, "has done me the honor to yield to my request that she become my wife."

"Well said!" said the marquis. "You have yet the making of a courtier in you, master shepherd. Mademoiselle could have drawn a worse prize, after all. And now to be done with the affair as quick as the Church and the devil will allow!"

He struck the table soundly with his sword hilt. The landlord came, knee-shaking, bringing more candles in the hope of anticipating the great lord's whims. "Fetch a priest," said the marquis, "a priest; do you understand? In ten minutes have a priest here, or—"

The landlord dropped his candles and flew.

The priest came, heavy-eyed and ruffled. He made David Mignot and Lucie de Varennes man and wife, pocketed a gold piece that the marquis tossed him, and shuffled out again into the night.

"Wine," ordered the marquis, spreading his ominous fingers at the host.

"Fill glasses," he said, when it was brought. He stood up at the head of the table in the candlelight, a black mountain of venom and conceit, with something like the memory of an old love, turned to poison, in his eye, as it fell upon his niece.

"Monsieur Mignot," he said, raising his wineglass, "drink after I say this to you: You have taken to be your wife one who will make your life a foul and wretched thing. The blood in her is an inheritance running black lies and red ruin. She will bring you shame and anxiety. The devil that descended to her is there in her eyes and skin and mouth that stoop even to beguile a peasant. There is your promise, monsieur poet, for a happy life. Drink your wine. At last, mademoiselle, I am rid of you."

The marquis drank. A little grievous cry, as if from a sudden wound, came from the girl's lips. David, with his glass in his hand, stepped forward three paces and faced the marquis. There was little of a shepherd in his bearing.

"Just now," he said, calmly, "you did me the honor to call me 'monsieur.' May I hope, therefore, that my marriage to mademoiselle has placed me somewhat nearer to you in—let us say, reflected rank—has given me the right to stand more as an equal to monseigneur in a certain little piece of business I have in my mind?"

"You may hope, shepherd," sneered the marquis.

"Then," said David, dashing his glass of wine into the contemptuous eyes that mocked him, "perhaps you will condescend to fight me."

The fury of the great lord outbroke in one sudden curse, like a blast from a horn. He tore his sword from its black sheath; he called to the hovering landlord: "A sword there, for this lout!" He turned to the lady, with a laugh that chilled her heart, and said: "You put much labor upon me, madame. It seems I must find you a husband and make you a widow in the same night."

"I know not sword-play," said David. He flushed to make the confession before his lady.

"'I know not sword-play,'" mimicked the marquis. "Shall we fight like peasants with oaken cudgels? *Hola!* François, my pistols!"

A postilion brought two shining great pistols ornamented with carven silver, from the carriage holsters. The marquis tossed one upon the table near David's hand. "To the other end of the table," he cried; "even a shepherd may pull a trigger. Few of them attain the honor to die by the weapon of a De Beaupertuys."

The shepherd and the marquis faced each other from the ends of the long table. The landlord, in an ague of terror, clutched the air and stammered: "M-M-Monseigneur, for the love of Christ! not in my house!—do not spill blood—it will ruin my custom—" The look of the marquis, threatening him, paralyzed his tongue.

"Coward," cried the lord of Beaupertuys, "cease chattering your teeth long enough to give the word for us, if you can."

Mine host's knees smote the floor. He was without a vocabulary. Even sounds were beyond him. Still, by gestures he seemed to beseech peace in the name of his house and custom.

"I will give the word," said the lady, in a clear voice. She went up to David and kissed him sweetly. Her eyes were sparkling bright, and color had come to her cheek. She stood against the wall, and the two men levelled their pistols for her count.

"Un—deux—trois!"

The two reports came so nearly together that the candles flickered but once. The marquis stood, smiling, the fingers of his left hand resting, outspread, upon the end of the table. David remained erect, and turned his head very slowly, searching for his wife with his eyes. Then, as a garment falls from where it is hung, he sank, crumpled, upon the floor.

With a little cry of terror and despair, the widowed maid ran and stooped above him. She found his wound, and then looked up with her old look of pale melancholy. "Through his heart," she whispered. "Oh, his heart!"

"Come," boomed the great voice of the marquis, "out with you to the carriage! Daybreak shall not find you on my hands. Wed you shall be again, and to a living husband, this night. The next we come upon, my lady, highwayman or peasant. If the road yields no other, then the churl that opens my gates. Out with you to the carriage!"

The marquis, implacable and huge, the lady wrapped again in the mystery of her cloak, the postilion bearing the weapons—all moved out to the waiting carriage. The sound of its ponderous wheels rolling away echoed through the slumbering village. In the hall of the Silver Flagon the distracted landlord wrung his hands above the slain poet's body, while the flames of the four and twenty candles danced and flickered on the table.

THE RIGHT BRANCH

Three leagues, then, the road ran, and turned into a puzzle. It joined with another and a larger road at right angles. David stood, uncertain, for a while, and then took the road to the right.

Whither it led he knew not, but he was resolved to leave Vernoy far behind that night. He travelled a league and then passed a large château which showed testimony of recent entertainment. Lights shone from every window; from the great stone gateway ran a tracery of wheel tracks drawn in the dust by the vehicles of the guests.

Three leagues farther and David was weary. He rested and slept for a while on a bed of pine boughs at the roadside. Then up and on again along the unknown way.

Thus for five days he travelled the great road, sleeping upon Nature's balsamic beds or in peasants' ricks, eating of their black, hospitable bread, drinking from streams or the willing cup of the goatherd.

At length he crossed a great bridge and set his foot within the smiling city that has crushed or crowned more poets than all the rest of the world. His breath came quickly as Paris sang to him in a little undertone her vital chant of greeting—the hum of voice and foot and wheel.

High up under the eaves of an old house in the Rue Conti, David paid for lodging, and set himself, in a wooden chair, to his poems. The street, once sheltering citizens of import and consequence, was now given over to those who ever follow in the wake of decline.

The houses were tall and still possessed of a ruined dignity, but many of them were empty save for dust and the spider. By night there was the clash of steel and the cries of brawlers straying restlessly from inn to inn. Where once gentility abode was now but a rancid and rude incontinence. But here David found housing commensurate to his scant purse. Daylight and candlelight found him at pen and paper.

One afternoon he was returning from a foraging trip to the lower world, with bread and curds and a bottle of thin wine. Halfway up his dark stairway he met—or rather came upon, for she rested on the stair—a young woman of a beauty that should balk even the justice of a poet's imagination. A loose, dark cloak, flung open, showed a rich gown beneath. Her eyes changed swiftly with every little shade of thought. Within one moment they would be round and artless like a child's, and long and cozening like a gipsy's. One hand raised her gown, undraping a little shoe, high-heeled, with its ribbons dangling, untied. So heavenly she was, so unfitted to stoop, so qualified to charm and command! Perhaps she had seen David coming, and had waited for his help there.

Ah, would monsieur pardon that she occupied the stairway, but the shoe!—the naughty shoe! Alas! it would not remain tied. Ah! if monsieur *would* be so gracious!

The poet's fingers trembled as he tied the contrary ribbons. Then he would have fled from the danger of her presence, but the eyes grew long and cozening, like a gipsy's, and held him. He leaned against the balustrade, clutching his bottle of sour wine.

"You have been so good," she said, smiling. "Does monsieur, perhaps, live in the house?"

"Yes, madame. I—I think so, madame."

"Perhaps in the third story, then?"

"No, madame; higher up."

The lady fluttered her fingers with the least possible gesture of impatience.

"Pardon. Certainly I am not discreet in asking. Monsieur will forgive me? It is surely not becoming that I should inquire where he lodges."

"Madame, do not say so. I live in the—"

"No, no, no; do not tell me. Now I see that I erred. But I cannot lose the interest I feel in this house and all that is in it. Once it was my home. Often I come here but to dream of those happy days again. Will you let that be my excuse?"

"Let me tell you, then, for you need no excuse," stammered the poet. "I live in the top floor—the small room where the stairs turn."

"In the front room?" asked the lady, turning her head sidewise.

"The rear, madame."

The lady sighed, as if with relief.

"I will detain you no longer, then, monsieur," she said, employing the round and artless eye. "Take good care of my house. Alas! only the memories of it are mine now. Adieu, and accept my thanks for your courtesy."

She was gone, leaving but a smile and a trace of sweet perfume. David climbed the stairs as one in slumber. But he awoke from it, and the smile and the perfume lingered with him and never afterward did either seem quite to leave him. This lady of whom he knew nothing drove him to lyrics of eyes, chansons of swiftly conceived love, odes to curling hair, and sonnets to slippers on slender feet.

Poet he must have been, for Yvonne was forgotten; this fine, new loveliness held him with its freshness and grace. The subtle perfume about her filled him with strange emotions.

On a certain night three persons were gathered about a table in a room on the third floor of the same house. Three chairs and the table and a lighted candle upon it was all the furniture. One of the persons was a huge man, dressed in black. His expression was one of sneering pride. The ends of his upturned moustache reached nearly to his mocking eyes. Another was a lady, young and beautiful, with eyes that could be round and artless, like a child's, or long and cozening, like a gipsy's, but were now keen and ambitious, like any other conspirator's. The third was a man of action, a combatant, a bold and impatient executive, breathing fire and steel. He was addressed by the others as Captain Desrolles.

This man struck the table with his fist, and said, with controlled violence:

"To-night. To-night as he goes to midnight mass. I am tired of the plotting that gets nowhere. I am sick of signals and ciphers and secret meetings and such *baragouin.* Let us be honest traitors. If France is to be rid of him, let us kill in the open, and not hunt with snares and traps. To-night, I say. I back my words. My hand will do the deed. To-night, as he goes to mass."

The lady turned upon him a cordial look. Woman, however wedded to plots, must ever thus bow to rash courage. The big man stroked his upturned moustache.

"Dear captain," he said, in a great voice, softened by habit, "this time I agree with you. Nothing is to be gained by waiting. Enough of the palace guards belong to us to make the endeavor a safe one."

"To-night," repeated Captain Desrolles, again striking the table. "You have heard me, marquis; my hand will do the deed."

"But now," said the huge man, softly, "comes a question. Word must be sent to our partisans in the palace, and a signal agreed upon. Our stanchest men must accompany the royal carriage. At this hour what messenger can penetrate so far as the south doorway? Ribout is stationed there; once a message is placed in his hands, all will go well."

"I will send the message," said the lady.

"You, countess?" said the marquis, raising his eyebrows. "Your devotion is great, we know, but—"

"Listen!" exclaimed the lady, rising and resting her hands upon the table; "in a garret of this house lives a youth from the provinces as guileless and tender as the lambs he tended there. I have met him twice or thrice upon the stairs. I questioned him, fearing that he might dwell too near the room in which we are accustomed to meet. He is mine, if I will. He writes poems in his garret, and I think he dreams of me. He will do what I say. He shall take the message to the palace."

The marquis rose from his chair and bowed. "You did not permit me to finish my sentence, countess," he said. "I would have said: 'Your devotion is great, but your wit and charm are infinitely greater.' "

While the conspirators were thus engaged, David was polishing some lines addressed to his *amourette d'escalier*. He heard a timorous knock at his door, and opened it, with a great throb, to behold her there, panting as one in straits, with eyes wide open and artless, like a child's.

"Monsieur," she breathed, "I come to you in distress. I believe you to be good and true, and I know of no other help. How I flew through the streets among the swaggering men! Monsieur, my mother is dying. My uncle is a captain of guards in the palace of the king. Some one must fly to bring him. May I hope—"

"Mademoiselle," interrupted David, his eyes shining with the desire to do her service, "your hopes shall be my wings. Tell me how I may reach him."

The lady thrust a sealed paper into his hand.

"Go to the south gate—the south gate, mind—and say to the guards there, 'The falcon has left his nest.' They will pass you, and you will go to the south entrance to the palace. Repeat the words, and give this letter to the man who will reply 'Let him strike when he will.' This is the password, monsieur, entrusted to me by my uncle, for now when the country is disturbed and men plot against the king's life, no one without it can gain entrance to the palace grounds after nightfall. If you will, monsieur, take him this letter so that my mother may see him before she closes her eyes."

"Give it me," said David, eagerly. "But shall I let you return home through the streets alone so late? I—"

"No, no—fly. Each moment is like a precious jewel. Some time," said the lady, with eyes long and cozening, like a gipsy's, "I will try to thank you for your goodness."

The poet thrust the letter into his breast, and bounded down the stairway. The lady, when he was gone, returned to the room below.

The eloquent eyebrows of the marquis interrogated her.

"He is gone," she said, "as fleet and stupid as one of his own sheep, to deliver it."

The table shook again from the batter of Captain Desrolles's fist.

"Sacred name!" he cried; "I have left my pistols behind! I can trust no others."

"Take this," said the marquis, drawing from beneath his cloak a shining, great weapon, ornamented with carven silver. "There are none truer. But guard it closely, for it bears my arms and crest, and already I am suspected. Me, I must put many leagues between myself and Paris this night. To-morrow must find me in my *château*. After you, dear countess."

The marquis puffed out the candle. The lady, well cloaked, and the two gentlemen softly descended the stairway and flowed into the crowd that roamed along the narrow pavements of the Rue Conti.

David sped. At the south gate of the king's residence a halberd was laid to his breast, but he turned its point with the words: "The falcon has left his nest."

"Pass, brother," said the guard, "and go quickly."

On the south steps of the palace they moved to seize him, but again the *mot de passe* charmed the watchers. One among them stepped forward and began: "Let him strike—" but a flurry among the guards told of a surprise. A man of keen look and soldierly stride suddenly pressed through them and seized the letter which David held in his hand. "Come with me," he said, and led him inside the great hall. Then he tore open the letter and read it. He beckoned to a man uniformed as an officer of musketeers, who was passing. "Captain Tetreau, you will have the guards at the south entrance and the south gate arrested and confined. Place men known to be loyal in their places." To David he said: "Come with me."

He conducted him through a corridor and an anteroom into a spacious chamber, where a melancholy man, sombrely dressed, sat brooding in a great, leather-covered chair. To that man he said:

"Sire, I have told you that the palace is as full of traitors and spies as a sewer is of rats. You have thought, sire, that it was my fancy. This man penetrated to your very door by their connivance. He bore a letter which I have intercepted. I have brought him here that your majesty may no longer think my zeal excessive."

"I will question him," said the king, stirring in his chair. He looked at David with heavy eyes dulled by an opaque film. The poet bent his knee.

"From where do you come?" asked the king.

"From the village of Vernoy, in the province of Eure-et-Loir, sire."

"What do you follow in Paris?"

"I—I would be a poet, sire."

"What did you in Vernoy?"

"I minded my father's flock of sheep."

The king stirred again, and the film lifted from his eyes.

"Ah! in the fields!"

"Yes, sire."

"You lived in the fields; you went out in the cool of the morning and lay among the hedges in the grass. The flock distributed itself upon the hillside; you drank of the living stream; you ate your sweet, brown bread in the shade, and you listened, doubtless, to blackbirds piping in the grove. Is not that so, shepherd?"

"It is, sire," answered David, with a sigh; "and to the bees at the flowers, and, maybe, to the grape gatherers singing on the hill."

"Yes, yes," said the king, impatiently; "maybe to them; but surely to the blackbirds. They whistled often, in the grove, did they not?"

"Nowhere, sire, so sweetly as in Eure-et-Loir. I have endeavored to express their song in some verses that I have written."

"Can you repeat those verses?" asked the king, eagerly. "A long time ago I listened to the blackbirds. It would be something better than a kingdom if one could rightly construe their song. And at night you drove the sheep to the fold and then sat, in peace and tranquillity, to your pleasant bread. Can you repeat those verses, shepherd?"

"They run this way, sire," said David, with respectful ardor:

"'Lazy shepherd, see your lambkins
Skip, ecstatic, on the mead;
See the firs dance in the breezes,
Hear Pan blowing at his reed.

"'Hear us calling from the tree-tops,
See us swoop upon your flock;
Yield us wool to make our nests warm
In the branches of the—'"

"If it please your majesty," interrupted a harsh voice, "I will ask a question or two of this rhymester. There is little time to spare. I crave pardon, sire, if my anxiety for your safety offends."

"The loyalty," said the king, "of the Duke d'Aumale is too well proven to give offence." He sank into his chair, and the film came again over his eyes.

"First," said the duke, "I will read you the letter he brought:

"'To-night is the anniversary of the dauphin's death. If he goes, as is his custom, to midnight mass to pray for the soul of his son, the falcon will strike, at the corner of the Rue Esplanade. If this be his intention, set a red light in the upper room at the southwest corner of the palace, that the falcon may take heed.'"

"Peasant," said the duke, sternly, "you have heard these words. Who gave you this message to bring?"

"My lord duke," said David, sincerely, "I will tell you. A lady gave it me. She said her mother was ill, and that this writing would fetch her uncle to her bedside. I do not know the meaning of the letter, but I will swear that she is beautiful and good."

"Describe the woman," commanded the duke, "and how you came to be her dupe."

"Describe her!" said David with a tender smile. "You would command words to perform miracles. Well, she is made of sunshine and deep shade. She is slender, like the alders, and moves with their grace. Her eyes change while you gaze into them; now round, and then half shut as the sun peeps between two clouds. When she comes, heaven is all about her; when she leaves, there is chaos and a scent of hawthorn blossoms. She came to me in the Rue Conti, number twenty-nine."

"It is the house," said the duke, turning to the king, "that we have been watching. Thanks to the poet's tongue, we have a picture of the infamous Countess Quebedaux."

"Sire and my lord duke," said David, earnestly, "I hope my poor words have done no injustice. I have looked into that lady's eyes. I will stake my life that she is an angel, letter or no letter."

The duke looked at him steadily. "I will put you to the proof," he said, slowly. "Dressed as the king, you shall, yourself, attend mass in his carriage at midnight. Do you accept the test?"

David smiled. "I have looked into her eyes," he said. "I had my proof there. Take yours how you will."

Half an hour before twelve the Duke d'Aumale, with his own hands, set a red lamp in a southwest window of the palace. At ten minutes to the hour, David, leaning on his arm, dressed as the king, from top to toe, with his head bowed in his cloak, walked slowly from the royal apartments to the waiting carriage. The duke assisted him inside and closed the door. The carriage whirled away along its route to the cathedral.

On the *qui vive* in a house at the corner of the Rue Esplanade was Captain Tetreau with twenty men, ready to pounce upon the conspirators when they should appear.

But it seemed that, for some reason, the plotters had slightly altered their plans. When the royal carriage had reached the Rue Christopher, one square nearer than the Rue Esplanade, forth from it burst Captain Desrolles, with his band of would-be regicides, and assailed the equipage. The guards upon the carriage, though surprised at the premature attack, descended and fought valiantly. The noise of conflict attracted the force of Captain Tetreau, and they came pelting down the street to the rescue. But, in the meantime, the desperate Desrolles had torn open the door of the King's carriage, thrust his weapon against the body of the dark figure inside, and fired.

Now, with loyal reinforcements at hand, the street rang with cries and the rasp of steel, but the frightened horses had dashed away. Upon the cushions lay the dead body of the poor mock king and poet, slain by a ball from the pistol of Monseigneur, the Marquis de Beaupertuys.

THE MAIN ROAD

Three leagues, then, the road ran, and turned into a puzzle. It joined with another and a larger road at right angles. David stood, uncertain, for a while, and then sat himself to rest upon its side.

Whither those roads led he knew not. Either way there seemed to lie a great world full of chance and peril. And then, sitting there, his eye fell upon a bright star, one that he and Yvonne had named for theirs. That set him thinking of Yvonne, and he wondered if he had not been too hasty. Why should he leave her and his home because a few hot words had come between them? Was love so brittle a thing that jealousy, the very proof of it, could break it? Mornings always brought a cure for the little heartaches of evening. There was yet time for him to return home without any one in the sweetly sleeping village of Vernoy being the wiser. His heart was Yvonne's; there where he had lived always he could write his poems and find his happiness.

David rose, and shook off his unrest and the wild mood that had tempted him. He set his face steadfastly back along the road he had come. By the time he had travelled the road to Vernoy, his desire to rove was gone. He passed the sheepfold, and the sheep scurried, with a drumming flutter, at his late footsteps, warming his heart by the homely sound. He crept without noise into his little room and lay there, thankful that his feet had escaped the distress of new roads that night.

How well he knew woman's heart! The next evening Yvonne was at the well in the road where the young congregated in order that the *curé* might have business. The corner of her eye was engaged in a search for David, albeit her set mouth seemed unrelenting. He saw the look; braved the mouth, drew from it a recantation and, later, a kiss as they walked homeward together.

Three months afterward they were married. David's father was shrewd and prosperous. He gave them a wedding that was heard of three leagues away. Both the young people were favorites in the village. There was a procession in the streets, a dance on the green; they had the marionettes and a tumbler out from Dreux to delight the guests.

Then a year, and David's father died. The sheep and the cottage descended to him. He already had the seemliest wife in the village. Yvonne's milk pails and her brass kettles were bright—*ouf!* they blinded you in the sun when you passed that way. But you must keep your eyes upon her yard, for her flower beds were so neat and gay they restored to you your sight. And you might hear her sing, aye, as far as the double chestnut tree above Père Gruneau's blacksmith forge.

But a day came when David drew out paper from a long-shut drawer, and began to bite the end of a pencil. Spring had come again and touched his heart. Poet he must have been, for now Yvonne was well-nigh forgotten. This fine new loveliness of earth held him with its witchery and grace. The perfume from her woods and meadows stirred him strangely. Daily had he gone forth with his flock, and brought it safe at night. But now he stretched himself under the hedge and pieced words together on his bits of paper. The sheep strayed, and the wolves, perceiving that difficult poems make easy mutton, ventured from the woods and stole his lambs.

David's stock of poems grew larger and his flock grew smaller. Yvonne's nose and temper waxed sharp and her talk blunt. Her pans and kettles grew dull, but her eyes had caught their flash. She pointed out to the poet that his neglect was reducing the flock and bringing woe upon the household. David hired a boy to guard the sheep, locked himself in the little room in the top of the cottage, and wrote more poems. The boy, being a poet by nature, but not furnished with an outlet in the way of writing, spent his time in slumber. The wolves lost no time in discovering that poetry and sleep are practically the same; so the flock steadily grew smaller. Yvonne's ill temper increased at an equal rate. Sometimes she would stand in the yard and rail at David through his high window. Then you could hear her as far as the double chestnut tree above Père Gruneau's blacksmith forge.

M. Papineau, the kind, wise, meddling old notary, saw this, as he saw everything at which his nose pointed. He went to David, fortified himself with a great pinch of snuff, and said:

"Friend Mignot, I affixed the seal upon the marriage certificate of your father. It would distress me to be obliged to attest a paper signifying the bankruptcy of his son. But that is what you are coming to. I speak as an old friend. Now, listen to what I have to say. You have your heart set, I perceive, upon poetry. At Dreux, I have a friend, one Monsieur Bril—Georges Bril. He lives in a little cleared space in a houseful of books. He is a learned man; he visits Paris each year; he himself has written books. He will tell you when the catacombs were made, how they found out the names of the stars, and why the plover has a long bill. The meaning and the form of poetry is to him as intelligent as the baa of a sheep is to you. I will give you a letter to him, and you shall take him your poems and let him read them. Then you will know if you shall write more, or give your attention to your wife and business."

"Write the letter," said David, "I am sorry you did not speak of this sooner."

At sunrise the next morning he was on the road to Dreux with the precious roll of poems under his arm. At noon he wiped the dust from his feet at the door of Monsieur Bril. That learned man broke the seal of M. Papineau's letter, and sucked up its contents through his gleaming spectacles as the sun draws water. He took David inside to his study and sat him down upon a little island beat upon by a sea of books.

Monsieur Bril had a conscience. He flinched not even at a mass of manuscript the thickness of a finger length and rolled to an incorrigible curve. He broke the back of the roll against his knee and began to read. He slighted nothing; he bored into the lump as a worm into a nut, seeking for a kernel.

Meanwhile, David sat, marooned, trembling in the spray of so much literature. It roared in his ears. He held no chart or compass for voyaging in that sea. Half the world, he thought, must be writing books.

Monsieur Bril bored to the last page of the poems. Then he took off his spectacles and wiped them with his handkerchief.

"My old friend, Papineau, is well?" he asked.

"In the best of health," said David.

"How many sheep have you, Monsieur Mignot?"

"Three hundred and nine, when I counted them yesterday. The flock has had ill fortune. To that number it has decreased from eight hundred and fifty."

"You have a wife and a home, and lived in comfort. The sheep brought you plenty. You went into the fields with them and lived in the keen air and ate the sweet bread of contentment. You had but to be vigilant and recline there upon nature's breast, listening to the whistle of the blackbirds in the grove. Am I right thus far?"

'It was so," said David.

"I have read all your verses," continued Monsieur Bril, his eyes wandering about his sea of books as if he conned the horizon for a sail. "Look yonder, through that window, Monsieur Mignot; tell me what you see in that tree."

"I see a crow," said David, looking.

"There is a bird," said Monsieur Bril, "that shall assist me where I am disposed to shirk a duty. You know that bird, Monsieur Mignot; he is the philosopher of the air. He is happy through submission to his lot. None so merry or full-crawed as he with his whimsical eye and rollicking step. The fields yield him what he desires. He never grieves that his plumage is not gay, like the oriole's. And you have heard, Monsieur Mignot, the notes that nature has given him? Is the nightingale any happier, do you think?"

David rose to his feet. The crow cawed harshly from his tree.

"I thank you, Monsieur Bril," he said, slowly. "There was not, then, one nightingale note among all those croaks?"

"I could not have missed it," said Monsieur Bril, with a sigh. "I read every word. Live your poetry, man; do not try to write it any more."

"I thank you," said David, again. "And now I will be going back to my sheep."

"If you would dine with me," said the man of books, "and overlook the smart of it, I will give you reasons at length."

"No," said the poet, "I must be back in the fields cawing at my sheep."

Back along the road to Vernoy he trudged with his poems under his arm. When he reached his village he turned into the shop of one Zeigler, a Jew out of Armenia, who sold anything that came to his hand.

"Friend," said David, "wolves from the forest harass my sheep on the hills. I must purchase firearms to protect them. What have you?"

"A bad day, this, for me, friend Mignot," said Zeigler, spreading his hands, "for I perceive that I must sell you a weapon that will not fetch a tenth of its value. Only last week I bought from a pedler a wagon full of goods that he procured at a sale by a *commissionaire* of the crown. The sale was of the *château* and belongings of a great lord—I know not his title—who has been banished for conspiracy against the king. There are some choice firearms in the lot. This pistol—oh, a weapon fit for a prince!—it shall be only forty francs to you, friend Mignot—if I lost ten by the sale. But perhaps an arquebuse—"

"This will do," said David, throwing the money on the counter. "Is it charged?"

"I will charge it," said Zeigler. "And, for ten francs more, add a store of powder and ball."

David laid his pistol under his coat and walked to his cottage. Yvonne was not there. Of late she had taken to gadding much among the neighbors. But a fire was glowing in the kitchen stove. David opened the door of it and thrust his poems in upon the coals. As they blazed up they made a singing, harsh sound in the flue.

"The song of the crow!" said the poet.

He went up to his attic room and closed the door. So quiet was the village that a score of people heard the roar of the great pistol. They flocked thither, and up the stairs where the smoke, issuing, drew their notice.

The men laid the body of the poet upon his bed, awkwardly arranging it to conceal the torn plumage of the poor black crow. The women chattered in a luxury of zealous pity. Some of them ran to tell Yvonne.

M. Papineau, whose nose had brought him there among the first, picked up the weapon and ran his eye over its silver mountings with a mingled air of connoisseurship and grief.

"The arms," he explained, aside, to the *curé*, "and crest of Monseigneur, the Marquis de Beaupertuys."

The Gift of the Magi

One dollar and eighty-seven cents. That was all. And sixty cents of it was in pennies. Pennies saved one and two at a time by bulldozing the grocer and the vegetable man and the butcher until one's cheeks burned with the silent imputation of parsimony that such close dealing implied. Three times Della counted it. One dollar and eighty-seven cents. And the next day would be Christmas.

There was clearly nothing to do but flop down on the shabby little couch and howl. So Della did it. Which instigates the moral reflection that life is made up of sobs, sniffles, and smiles, with sniffles predominating.

While the mistress of the home is gradually subsiding from the first stage to the second, take a look at the home. A furnished flat at

$8 per week. It did not exactly beggar description, but it certainly had that word on the lookout for the mendicancy squad.

In the vestibule below was a letter-box into which no letter would go, and an electric button from which no mortal finger could coax a ring. Also appertaining thereunto was a card bearing the name "Mr. James Dillingham Young."

The "Dillingham" had been flung to the breeze during a former period of prosperity when its possessor was being paid $30 per week. Now, when the income was shrunk to $20, the letters of "Dillingham" looked blurred, as though they were thinking seriously of contracting to a modest and unassuming D. But whenever Mr. James Dillingham Young came home and reached his flat above he was called "Jim" and greatly hugged by Mrs. James Dillingham Young, already introduced to you as Della. Which is all very good.

Della finished her cry and attended to her cheeks with the powder rag. She stood by the window and looked out dully at a gray cat walking a gray fence in a gray backyard. To-morrow would be Christmas Day, and she had only $1.87 with which to buy Jim a present. She had been saving every penny she could for months, with this result. Twenty dollars a week doesn't go far. Expenses had been greater than she had calculated. They always are. Only $1.87 to buy a present for Jim. Her Jim. Many a happy hour she had spent planning for something nice for him. Something fine and rare and sterling—something just a little bit near to being worthy of the honor of being owned by Jim.

There was a pier-glass between the windows of the room. Perhaps you have seen a pier-glass in an $8 flat. A very thin and very agile person may, by observing his reflection in a rapid sequence of longitudinal strips, obtain a fairly accurate conception of his looks. Della, being slender, had mastered the art.

Suddenly she whirled from the window and stood before the glass. Her eyes were shining brilliantly, but her face had lost its color within twenty seconds. Rapidly she pulled down her hair and let it fall to its full length.

Now, there were two possessions of the James Dillingham Youngs in which they both took a mighty pride. One was Jim's gold watch that had been his father's and his grandfather's. The other was Della's hair. Had the Queen of Sheba lived in the flat across the airshaft, Della would have let her hair hang out the window some day to dry, just to depreciate Her Majesty's jewels and gifts. Had King Solomon been the janitor, with all his treasures piled up in the basement, Jim would have pulled out his watch every time he passed, just to see him pluck at his beard from envy.

So now Della's beautiful hair fell about her, rippling and shining like a cascade of brown waters. It reached below her knee and made itself almost a garment for her. And then she did it up again nervously and quickly. Once she faltered for a minute and stood still while a tear or two splashed on the worn red carpet.

On went her old brown jacket; on went her old brown hat. With a whirl of skirts and with the brilliant sparkle still in her eyes, she fluttered out the door and down the stairs to the street.

Where she stopped the sign read: "Mme. Sofronie. Hair Goods of all Kinds." One flight up Della ran, and collected herself, panting. Madame, large, too white, chilly, hardly looked the "Sofronie."

"Will you buy my hair?" asked Della.

"I buy hair," said Madame. "Take yer hat off and let's have a sight at the looks of it."

Down rippled the brown cascade.

"Twenty dollars," said Madame, lifting the mass with a practised hand.

"Give it to me quick," said Della.

Oh, and the next two hours tripped by on rosy wings. Forget the hashed metaphor. She was ransacking the stores for Jim's present.

She found it at last. It surely had been made for Jim and no one else. There was no other like it in any of the stores, and she had turned all of them inside out. It was a platinum fob chain simple and chaste in design, properly proclaiming its value by substance alone and not by meretricious ornamentation—as all good things should do. It was even worthy of The Watch. As soon as she saw it she knew that it must be Jim's. It was like him. Quietness and value—the description applied to both. Twenty-one dollars they took from her for it, and she hurried home with the 87 cents. With that chain on his watch Jim might be properly anxious about the time in any company. Grand as the watch was, he sometimes looked at it on the sly on account of the old leather strap that he used in place of a chain.

When Della reached home her intoxication gave way a little to prudence and reason. She got out her curling irons and lighted the gas and went to work repairing the ravages made by generosity added to love. Which is always a tremendous task, dear friends—a mammoth task.

Within forty minutes her head was covered with tiny, close-lying curls that made her look wonderfully like a truant schoolboy. She looked at her reflection in the mirror long, carefully, and critically.

"If Jim doesn't kill me," she said to herself, "before he takes a second look at me, he'll say I look like a Coney Island chorus girl. But what could I do—oh! what could I do with a dollar and eighty-seven cents?"

At 7 o'clock the coffee was made and the frying-pan was on the back of the stove hot and ready to cook the chops.

Jim was never late. Della doubled the fob chain in her hand and sat on the corner of the table near the door that he always entered. Then she heard his step on the stair away down on the first flight, and she turned white for just a moment. She had a habit of saying little silent prayers about the simplest everyday things, and now she whispered: "Please God, make him think I am still pretty."

The door opened and Jim stepped in and closed it. He looked thin and very serious. Poor fellow, he was only twenty-two—and to be burdened with a family! He needed a new overcoat and he was without gloves.

Jim stopped inside the door, as immovable as a setter at the scent of quail. His eyes were fixed upon Della, and there was an expression in them that she could not read, and it terrified her. It was not anger, nor surprise, nor disapproval, nor horror, nor any of the sentiments that she had been prepared for. He simply stared at her fixedly with that peculiar expression on his face.

Della wriggled off the table and went for him.

"Jim, darling," she cried, "don't look at me that way. I had my hair cut off and sold it because I couldn't have lived through Christmas without giving you a present. It'll grow out again—you won't mind, will you? I just had to do it. My hair grows awfully fast. Say 'Merry Christmas!' Jim, and let's be happy. You don't know what a nice—what a beautiful, nice gift I've got for you."

"You've cut off your hair?" asked Jim, laboriously, as if he had not arrived at that patent fact yet even after the hardest mental labor.

"Cut it off and sold it," said Della. "Don't you like me just as well, anyhow? I'm me without my hair, ain't I?"

Jim looked about the room curiously.

"You say your hair is gone?" he said, with an air almost of idiocy.

"You needn't look for it," said Della. "It's sold, I tell you—sold and gone, too. It's Christmas Eve, boy. Be good to me, for it went for you. Maybe the hairs of my head were numbered," she went on with a sudden serious sweetness, "but nobody could ever count my love for you. Shall I put the chops on, Jim?"

Out of his trance Jim seemed quickly to wake. He enfolded his Della. For ten seconds let us regard with discreet scrutiny some inconsequential object in the other direction. Eight dollars a week or a million a year—what is the difference? A mathematician or a wit would give you the wrong answer. The magi brought valuable gifts, but that was not among them. This dark assertion will be illuminated later on.

Jim drew a package from his overcoat pocket and threw it upon the table.

"Don't make any mistake, Dell," he said, "about me. I don't think there's anything in the way of a haircut or a shave or a shampoo that could make me like my girl any less. But if you'll unwrap that package you may see why you had me going a while at first."

White fingers and nimble tore at the string and paper. And then an ecstatic scream of joy; and then, alas! a quick feminine change to hysterical tears and wails, necessitating the immediate employment of all the comforting powers of the lord of the flat.

For there lay The Combs—the set of combs, side and back, that Della had worshipped for long in a Broadway window. Beautiful combs, pure tortoise shell, with jewelled rims—just the shade to wear in the beautiful vanished hair.—They were expensive combs, she knew, and her heart had simply craved and yearned over them without the least hope of possession. And now, they were hers, but the tresses that should have adorned the coveted adornments were gone.

But she hugged them to her bosom, and at length she was able to look up with dim eyes and a smile and say: "My hair grows so fast, Jim!"

And then Della leaped up like a little singed cat and cried, "Oh, oh!"

Jim had not yet seen his beautiful present. She held it out to him eagerly upon her open palm. The dull precious metal seemed to flash with a reflection of her bright and ardent spirit.

"Isn't it a dandy, Jim? I hunted all over town to find it. You'll have to look at the time a hundred times a day now. Give me your watch. I want to see how it looks on it."

Instead of obeying, Jim tumbled down on the couch and put his hands under the back of his head and smiled.

"Dell," said he, "let's put our Christmas presents away and keep 'em a while. They're too nice to use just at present. I sold the watch to get the money to buy your combs. And now suppose you put the chops on."

The magi, as you know, were wise men—wonderfully wise men—who brought gifts to the Babe in the manger. They invented the art of giving Christmas presents. Being wise, their gifts were no doubt wise ones, possibly bearing the privilege of exchange in case of of duplication. And here I have lamely related to you the uneventful chronicle of two foolish children in a flat, who most unwisely sacrificed for each other the greatest treasures of their house. But in a last word to the wise of these days let it be said that of all who give gifts these two were the wisest. Of all who give and receive gifts, such as they are wisest. Everywhere they are wisest. They are the magi.

Memoirs of a Yellow Dog

I DON'T suppose it will knock any of you people off your perch to read a contribution from an animal. Mr. Kipling and a good many others have demonstrated the fact that animals can express themselves in remunerative English, and no magazine goes to press nowadays without an animal story in it, except the old-style monthlies that are still running pictures of Bryan and the Mont Pelée horror.

But you needn't look for any stuck-up literature in my piece, such as Bearoo, the bear, and Snakoo, the snake, and Tammanoo, the tiger, talk in the jungle books. A yellow dog that's spent most of his life in a cheap New York flat, sleeping in a corner on an old sateen underskirt (the one she spilled port wine on at the Lady 'Longshoremen's banquet), mustn't be expected to perform any tricks with the art of speech.

I was born a yellow pup; date, locality, pedigree and weight unknown. The first thing I can recollect, an old woman had me in a basket at Broadway and Twenty-third trying to sell me to a fat lady. Old Mother Hubbard was boosting me to beat the band as a genuine Pomeranian-Hambletonian-Red-Irish-Cochin-China-Stoke-Pogis fox terrier. The fat lady chased a V around among the samples of grosgrain flannelette in her shopping bag till she cornered it, and gave up. From that moment I was a pet—a mamma's own wootsey squidlums. Say, gentle reader, did you ever have a 200-pound woman, breathing a flavor of Camembert cheese and Peau d'Espagne, pick you up and wallop her nose all over you, remarking all the time in an Emma Eames tone of voice: "Oh, oo's um oodlum, doodlum, woodlum, toodlum, bitsy-witsy skoodlums?"

From pedigreed yellow pup I grew up to be an anonymous yellow cur looking like a cross between an Angora cat and a box of lemons. But my mistress never tumbled. She thought that the two primeval pups that Noah chased into the ark were but a collateral branch of my ancestors. It took two policemen to keep her from entering me at the Madison Square Garden for the Siberian bloodhound prize.

I'll tell you about that flat. The house was the ordinary thing in New York, paved with Parian marble in the entrance hall and cobblestones above the first floor. Our flat was three—well, not flights—climbs up. My mistress rented it unfurnished, and put in the regular things—1903 antique unholstered parlor set, oil chromo of geishas in a Harlem tea house, rubber plant and husband.

By Sirius! there was a biped I felt sorry for. He was a little man with sandy hair and whiskers a good deal like mine. Henpecked?—well, toucans and flamingoes and pelicans all had their bills in him. He wiped the dishes and listened to my mistress tell about the cheap, ragged things the lady with the squirrel-skin coat on the second floor hung out on her line to dry. And every evening while she was getting supper she made him take me out on the end of a string for a walk.

If men knew how women pass the time when they are alone they'd never marry. Laura Lean Jibbey, peanut brittle, a little almond cream on the neck muscles, dishes unwashed, half an hour's talk with the ice-man, reading a package of old letters, a couple of pickles and two bottles of malt extract, one hour peeking through a hole in the window shade into the flat across the air-shaft—that's about all there is to it. Twenty minutes before time for him to come home from work she straightens up the house, fixes her rat so it won't show, and gets out a lot of sewing for a ten-minute bluff.

I led a dog's life in that flat. 'Most all day I lay there in my corner watching that fat woman kill time. I slept sometimes and had pipe dreams about being out chasing cats into basements and growling at old ladies with black mittens, as a dog was intended to do. Then she would pounce upon me with a lot of that drivelling poodle palaver and kiss me on the nose—but what could I do? A dog can't chew cloves.

I began to feel sorry for Hubby, dog my cats if I didn't. We looked so much alike that people noticed it when we went out; so we shook the streets that Morgan's cab drives down, and took to climbing the piles of last December's snow on the streets where cheap people live.

One evening when we were thus promenading, and I was trying to look like a prize St. Bernard, and the old man was trying to look like he wouldn't have murdered the first organ-grinder he heard play Mendelssohn's wedding-march, I looked up at him and said, in my way:

"What are you looking so sour about, you oakum trimmed lobster? She don't kiss you. You don't have to sit on her lap and listen to talk that would make the book of a musical comedy sound like the maxims of Epictetus. You ought to be thankful you're not a dog. Brace up, Benedick, and bid the blues begone."

The matrimonial mishap looked down at me with almost canine intelligence in his face.

"Why, doggie," says he, "good doggie. You almost look like you could speak. What is it, doggie—Cats?"

Cats! Could speak!

But, of course, he couldn't understand. Humans were denied the speech of animals. The only common ground of communication upon which dogs and men can get together is in fiction.

In the flat across the hall from us lived a lady with a black-and-tan terrier. Her husband strung it and took it out every evening, but he always came home cheerful and whistling. One day I touched noses with the black-and-tan in the hall, and I struck him for an elucidation.

"See, here, Wiggle-and-Skip," I says, "you know that it ain't the nature of a real man to play dry nurse to a dog in public. I never saw one leashed to a bow-wow yet that didn't look like he'd like to lick every other man that looked at him. But your boss comes in every day as perky and set up as an amateur prestidigitator doing the egg trick. How does he do it? Don't tell me he likes it."

"Him?" says the black-and-tan. "Why, he uses Nature's Own Remedy. He gets spifflicated. At first when we go out he's as shy as the man on the steamer who would rather play pedro when they make 'em all jackpots. By the time we've been in eight saloons he don't care whether the thing on the end of his line is a dog or a catfish. I've lost two inches of my tail trying to sidestep those swinging doors."

The pointer I got from that terrier—vaudeville please copy—set me to thinking.

One evening about 6 o'clock my mistress ordered him to get busy and do the ozone act for Lovey. I have concealed it until now, but that is what she called me. The black-and-tan was called "Tweetness." I consider that I have the bulge on him as far as you could chase a rabbit. Still "Lovey" is something of a nomenclatural tin can on the tail of one's self respect.

At a quiet place on a safe street I tightened the line of my custodian in front of an attractive, refined saloon. I made a dead-ahead scramble for the doors, whining like a dog in the press despatches that lets the family know that little Alice is bogged while gathering lilies in the brook.

"Why, darn my eyes," says the old man, with a grin; "darn my eyes if the saffron-colored son of a seltzer lemonade ain't asking me in to take a drink. Lemme see—how long's it been since I saved shoe leather by keeping one foot on the foot-rest? I believe I'll—"

I knew I had him. Hot Scotches he took, sitting at a table. For an hour he kept the Campbells coming. I sat by his side rapping for the waiter with my tail, and eating free lunch such as mamma in her flat never equalled with her homemade truck bought at a delicatessen store eight minutes before papa comes home.

When the products of Scotland were all exhausted except the rye bread the old man unwound me from the table leg and played me outside like a fisherman plays a salmon. Out there he took off my collar and threw it into the street.

"Poor doggie," says he; "good doggie. She shan't kiss you any more. 'S a darned shame. Good doggie, go away and get run over by a street car and be happy."

I refused to leave. I leaped and frisked around the old man's legs happy as a pug on a rug.

"You old flea-headed woodchuck-chaser," I said to him—"you moon-baying, rabbit-pointing, egg-stealing old beagle, can't you see that I don't want to leave you? Can't you see that we're both Pups in the Wood and the missis is the cruel uncle after you with the dish towel and me with the flea liniment and a pink bow to tie on my tail. Why not cut that all out and be pards forever more?"

Maybe you'll say he didn't understand—maybe he didn't. But he kind of got a grip on the Hot Scotches, and stood still for a minute, thinking.

"Doggie," says he, finally, "we don't live more than a dozen lives on this earth, and very few of us live to be more than 300. If I ever see that flat any more I'm a flat, and if you do you're flatter; and that's no flattery. I'm offering 60 to 1 that Westward Ho wins out by the length of a dachshund."

There was no string, but I frolicked along with my master to the Twenty-third street ferry. And the cats on the route saw reason to give thanks that prehensile claws had been given them.

On the Jersey side my master said to a stranger who stood eating a currant bun:

"Me and my doggie, we are bound for the Rocky Mountains."

But what pleased me most was when my old man pulled both of my ears until I howled, and said:

"You common, monkey-headed, rat-tailed, sulphur-colored son of a door mat, do you know what I'm going to call you?"

I thought of "Lovey," and I whined dolefully.

"I'm going to call you 'Pete,'" says my master; and if I'd had five tails I couldn't have done enough wagging to do justice to the occasion.

RICHARD HARDING DAVIS (1864-1916)

Gallegher

We had had so many office-boys before Gallegher came among us that they had begun to lose the characteristics of individuals, and became merged in a composite photograph of small boys, to whom we applied the generic title of "Here, you"; or, "You, boy."

We had had sleepy boys, and lazy boys, and bright, "smart" boys, who became so familiar on so short an acquaintance that we were forced to part with them to save our own self-respect.

They generally graduated into district-messenger boys, and occasionally returned to us in blue coats with nickel-plated buttons, and patronized us.

But Gallegher was something different from anything we had experienced before. Gallegher was short and broad in build, with a solid, muscular broadness, and not a fat and dumpy shortness. He wore perpetually on his face a happy and knowing smile, as if you and the world in general were not impressing him as seriously as you thought you were, and his eyes, which were very black and very bright, snapped intelligently at you like those of a little black-and-tan terrier.

All Gallegher knew had been learnt on the streets; not a very good school in itself, but one that turns out very knowing scholars. And Gallegher had attended both morning and evening sessions. He could not tell you who the Pilgrim Fathers were, nor could he name the thirteen original States, but he knew all the officers of the twenty-second police district by name, and he could distinguish the clang of a fire-engine's gong from that of a patrol-wagon or an ambulance fully two blocks distant. It was Gallegher who rang the alarm when the Woolwich Mills caught fire, while the officer on the beat was asleep, and it was Gallegher who led the "Black Diamonds" against the "Wharf Rats," when they used to stone each other to their hearts' content on the coal-wharves of Richmond.

I am afraid, now that I see these facts written down, that Gallegher was not a reputable character; but he was so very young and so very old for his years that we all liked him very much nevertheless. He lived in the extreme northern part of Philadelphia, where the cotton- and woollen-mills run down to the river, and how he ever got home after leaving the *Press* building at two in the morning, was one of the mysteries of the office. Sometimes he caught a night car, and sometimes he walked all the way, arriving at the little house, where his mother and himself lived alone, at four in the morning. Occasionally he was given a ride on an early milk-cart, or on one of the newspaper delivery wagons, with its high piles of papers still damp and sticky from the press. He knew several drivers of "night hawks"—those cabs that prowl the streets at night looking for belated passengers—and when it was a very cold morning he would not go home at all, but would crawl into one of these cabs and sleep, curled up on the cushions, until daylight.

Besides being quick and cheerful, Gallegher possessed a power of amusing the *Press's* young men to a degree seldom attained by the ordinary mortal. His clog-dancing on the city editor's desk, when that gentleman was up-stairs fighting for two more columns of space, was always a source of innocent joy to us, and his imitations of the comedians of the variety halls delighted even the dramatic critic, from whom the comedians themselves failed to force a smile.

But Gallegher's chief characteristic was his love for that element of news generically classed as "crime."

Not that he ever did anything criminal himself. On the contrary, his was rather the work of the criminal specialist, and his morbid interest in the doings of all queer characters, his knowledge of their methods, their present whereabouts, and their past deeds of transgression often rendered him a valuable ally to our police reporter, whose daily feuilletons were the only portion of the paper Gallegher deigned to read.

In Gallegher the detective element was abnormally developed. He had shown this on several occasions, and to excellent purpose.

Once the paper had sent him into a Home for Destitute Orphans which was believed to be grievously mismanaged, and Gallegher while playing the part of a destitute orphan, kept his eyes open to what was going on around him so faithfully that the story he told of the treatment meted out to the real orphans was sufficient to rescue the unhappy little wretches from the individual who had them in charge, and to have the individual himself sent to jail.

Gallegher's knowledge of the aliases, terms of imprisonment, and various misdoings of the leading criminals in Philadelphia was almost as thorough as that of the chief of police himself, and he could tell to an hour when "Dutchy Mack" was to be let out of prison, and could identify at a glance "Dick Oxford, confidence man," as "Gentleman Dan, petty thief."

There were, at this time, only two pieces of news in any of the papers. The least important of the two was the big fight between the Champion of the United States and the Would-be Champion, arranged to take place near Philadelphia; the second was the Burrbank murder, which was filling space in newspapers all over the world, from New York to Bombay.

Richard F. Burrbank was one of the most prominent of New York's railroad lawyers; he was also, as a matter of course, an owner of much railroad stock, and a very wealthy man. He had been spoken of as a political possibility for many high offices, and, as the counsel for a great railroad, was known even further than the great railroad itself had stretched its system.

At six o'clock one morning he was found by his butler lying at the foot of the hall stairs with two pistol wounds above his heart. He was quite dead. His safe, to which only he and his secretary had the keys, was found open, and $200,000 in bonds, stocks, and money, which had been placed there only the night before, was found missing. The secretary was missing also. His name was Stephen S. Hade, and his name and his description had been telegraphed and cabled to all parts of the world. There was enough circumstantial evidence to show, beyond any question or possibility of mistake, that he was the murderer.

It made an enormous amount of talk, and unhappy individuals were being arrested all over the country, and sent on to New York for identification. Three had been arrested at Liverpool, and one man just as he landed at Sidney, Australia. But so far the murderer had escaped.

We were all talking about it one night, as everybody else was all over the country, in the local room, and the city editor said it was worth a fortune to any one who chanced to run against Hade and succeeded in handing him over to the police. Some of us thought Hade had taken passage from some one of the smaller seaports, and others were of the opinion that he had buried himself in some cheap lodging-house in New York, or in one of the smaller towns in New Jersey.

"I shouldn't be surprised to meet him out walking, right here in Philadelphia," said one of the staff. "He'll be disguised, of course, but you could always tell him by the absence of the trigger finger on his right hand. It's missing, you know; shot off when he was a boy."

"You want to look for a man dressed like a tough," said the city editor; "for as this fellow is to all appearances a gentleman, he will try to look as little like a gentleman as possible."

"No, he won't," said Gallegher, with that calm impertinence that made him dear to us. "He'll dress just like a gentleman. Toughs don't wear gloves, and you see he's got to wear 'em. The first thing he thought of after doing for Burrbank was of that gone finger, and how he was to hide it. He stuffed the finger of that glove with cotton so's to make it look like a whole finger, and the first time he takes off that glove they've got him—see, and he knows it. So what youse want to do is to look for a man with gloves on. I've been a doing it for two weeks now, and I can tell you it's hard work, for everybody wears gloves this kind of weather. But if you look long enough you'll find him. And when you think it's him, go up to him and hold out your hand in a friendly way, like a bunco-steerer, and shake his hand; and if you feel that his forefinger ain't real flesh, but just wadded cotton, then grip to it with your right and grab his throat with your left, and holler for help."

There was an appreciative pause.

"I see, gentlemen," said the city editor, dryly, "that Gallegher's reasoning has impressed you; and I also see that before the week is out all of my young men will be under bonds for assaulting innocent pedestrians whose only offence is that they wear gloves in midwinter."

* * * * * * *

It was about a week after this that Detective Hefflefinger, of Inspector Byrnes's staff, came over to Philadelphia after a burglar, of whose whereabouts he had been misinformed by telegraph. He brought the warrant, requisition, and other necessary papers for him, but the burglar had flown. One of our reporters had worked on a New York paper, and knew Hefflefinger, and the detective came to the office to see if he could help him in his so far unsuccessful search.

He gave Gallegher his card, and after Gallegher had read it, and had discovered who the visitor was, he became so demoralized that he was absolutely useless.

"One of Byrnes's men," was a much more awe-inspiring individual to Gallegher than a member of the Cabinet. He accordingly seized his hat and overcoat, and leaving his duties to be looked after by others, hastened out after the object of his admiration, who found his suggestions and knowledge of the city so valuable, and his company so entertaining, that they became very intimate, and spent the rest of the day together.

In the meanwhile the managing editor had instructed his subordinates to inform Gallegher, when he condescended to return, that his services were no longer needed. Gallegher had played truant once too often. Unconscious of this, he remained with his new friend until late the same evening, and started the next afternoon toward the *Press* office.

As I have said, Gallegher lived in the most distant part of the city, not many minutes' walk from the Kensington railroad station, where trains ran into the suburbs and on to New York.

It was in front of this station that a smoothly shaven, well-dressed man brushed past Gallegher and hurried up the steps to the ticket office.

He held a walking-stick in his right hand, and Gallegher, who now patiently scrutinized the hands of every one who wore gloves, saw that while three fingers of the man's hand were closed around the cane, the fourth stood out in almost a straight line with his palm.

Gallegher stopped with a gasp and with a trembling all over his little body, and his brain asked with a throb if it could be possible. But possibilities and probabilities were to be discovered later. Now was the time for action.

He was after the man in a moment, hanging at his heels and his eyes moist with excitement.

He heard the man ask for a ticket to Torresdale, a little station just outside of Philadelphia, and when he was out of hearing, but not out of sight, purchased one for the same place.

The stranger went into the smoking-car, and seated himself at one end toward the door. Gallegher took his place at the opposite end.

He was trembling all over, and suffered from a slight feeling of nausea. He guessed it came from fright, not of any bodily harm that might come to him, but at the probability of failure in his adventure and of its most momentous possibilities.

The stranger pulled his coat collar up around his ears, hiding the lower portion of his face, but not concealing the resemblance in his troubled eyes and close-shut lips to the likenesses of the murderer Hade.

They reached Torresdale in half an hour, and the stranger, alighting quickly, struck off at a rapid pace down the country road leading to the station.

Gallegher gave him a hundred yards' start, and then followed slowly after. The road ran between fields and past a few frame-houses set far from the road in kitchen gardens.

Once or twice the man looked back over his shoulder, but he saw only a dreary length of road with a small boy splashing through the slush in the midst of it and stopping every now and again to throw snowballs at belated sparrows.

After a ten minutes' walk the stranger turned into a side road which led to only one place, the Eagle Inn, an old roadside hostelry known now as the headquarters for pothunters from the Philadelphia game market and the battle-ground of many a cock-fight.

Gallegher knew the place well. He and his young companions had often stopped there when out chestnutting on holidays in the autumn.

The son of the man who kept it had often accompanied them on their excursions, and though the boys of the city considered him a dumb lout, they respected him somewhat owing to his inside knowledge of dog- and cock-fights.

The stranger entered the inn at a side door, and Gallegher, reaching it a few minutes later, let him go for the time being, and set about finding his occasional playmate, young Keppler.

Keppler's offspring was found in the woodshed.

" 'Tain't hard to guess what brings you out here," said the tavern-keeper's son, with a grin; "it's the fight."

"What fight?" asked Gallegher, unguardedly.

"What fight? Why, *the* fight," returned his companion, with the slow contempt of superior knowledge. "It's to come off here to-night. You knew that as well as me; anyway your sportin' editor knows it. He got the tip last night, but that won't help you any. You needn't think there's any chance of your getting a peep at it. Why, tickets is two hundred and fifty a piece!"

"Whew!" whistled Gallegher, "where's it to be?"

"In the barn," whispered Keppler. "I helped 'em fix the ropes this morning, I did."

"Gosh, but you're in luck," exclaimed Gallegher, with flattering envy. "Couldn't I jest get a peep at it?"

"Maybe," said the gratified Keppler. "There's a winder with a wooden shutter at the back of the barn. You can get in by it, if you have some one to boost you up to the sill."

"Sa-a-y," drawled Gallegher, as if something had but just that moment reminded him. "Who's that gent who come down the road just a bit ahead of me—him with the cape-coat! Has he got anything to do with the fight?"

"Him?" repeated Keppler in tones of sincere disgust. "No-oh, he ain't no sport. He's queer, Dad thinks. He come here one day last week about ten in the morning, said his doctor told him to go out 'en the country for his health. He's stuck up and citified, and wears gloves, and takes his meals private in his room, and all that sort of ruck. They was saying in the saloon last night that they thought he was hiding from something, and Dad, just to try him, asks him last night if he was coming to see the fight. He looked sort of scared, and said he didn't want to see no fight. And then Dad says, 'I guess you mean you don't want no fighters to see you.' Dad didn't mean no harm by it, just passed it as a joke; but Mr. Carleton, as he calls himself, got white as a ghost an' says, 'I'll go to the fight willing enough,' and begins to laugh and joke. And this morning he went right into the bar-room, where all the sports were setting, and said he was going into town to see some friends; and as he starts off he laughs an' says, 'This don't look as if I was afraid of seeing people, does it?' but Dad says it was just bluff that made him do it, and Dad thinks that if he hadn't said what he did, this Mr. Carleton wouldn't have left his room at all."

Gallegher had got all he wanted, and much more than he had hoped for—so much more that his walk back to the station was in the nature of a triumphal march.

He had twenty minutes to wait for the next train, and it seemed an hour. While waiting he sent a telegram to Hefflefinger at his hotel. It read: "Your man is near the Torresdale station, on Pennsylvania Railroad; take cab, and meet me at station. Wait until I come. GALLEGHER."

With the exception of one at midnight, no other train stopped at Torresdale that evening, hence the direction to take a cab.

The train to the city seemed to Gallegher to drag itself by inches. It stopped and backed at purposeless intervals, waited for an express to precede it, and dallied at stations, and when, at last, it reached the terminus, Gallegher was out before it had stopped and was in the cab and off on his way to the home of the sporting editor.

The sporting editor was at dinner and came out in the hall to see him, with his napkin in his hand. Gallegher explained breathlessly that he had located the murderer for whom the police of two continents were looking, and that he believed, in order to quiet the suspicions of the people with whom he was hiding, that he would be present at the fight that night.

The sporting editor led Gallegher into his library and shut the door. "Now," he said, "go over all that again."

Gallegher went over it again in detail, and added how he had sent for Hefflefinger to make the arrest in order that it might be kept from the knowledge of the local police and from the Philadelphia reporters.

"What I want Hefflefinger to do is to arrest Hade with the warrant he has for the burglar," explained Gallegher; "and to take him on to New York on the owl train that passes Torresdale at one. It don't get to Jersey City until four o'clock, one hour after the morning papers go to press. Of course, we must fix Hefflefinger so's he'll keep quiet and not tell who his prisoner really is."

The sporting editor reached his hand out to pat Gallegher on the head, but changed his mind and shook hands with him instead.

"My boy," he said, "you are an infant phenomenon. If I can pull the rest of this thing off to-night it will mean the $5000 reward and fame galore for you and the paper. Now, I'm going to write a note to the managing editor, and you can take it around to him and tell him what you've done and what I am going to do, and he'll take you back on the paper and raise your salary. Perhaps you didn't know you've been discharged?"

"Do you think you ain't a-going to take me with you?" demanded Gallegher.

"Why, certainly not. Why should I? It all lies with the detective and myself now. You've done your share, and done it well. If the man's caught, the reward's yours. But you'd only be in the way now. You'd better go to the office and make your peace with the chief."

"If the paper can get along without me, I can get along without the old paper," said Gallegher, hotly. "And if I ain't a-going with you, you ain't neither, for I know where Hefflefinger is to be, and you don't, and I won't tell you."

"Oh, very well, very well," replied the sporting editor, weakly capitulating. I'll send the note by a messenger; only mind, if you lose your place, don't blame me."

Gallegher wondered how this man could value a week's salary against the excitement of seeing a noted criminal run down, and of getting the news to the paper, and to that one paper alone.

From that moment the sporting editor sank in Gallegher's estimation.

Mr. Dwyer sat down at his desk and scribbled off the following note:

"I have received reliable information that Hade, the Burrbank murderer, will be present at the fight to-night. We have arranged it so that he will be arrested quietly and in such a manner that the fact may be kept from all other papers. I need not point out to you that this will be the most important piece of news in the country to-morrow.

"Yours, etc., MICHAEL E. DWYER."

The sporting editor stepped into the waiting cab, while Gallegher whispered the directions to the driver. He was told to go first to a district-messenger office, and from there up to the Ridge Avenue Road, out Broad Street, and on to the old Eagle Inn, near Torresdale.

It was a miserable night. The rain and snow were falling together, and freezing as they fell. The sporting editor got out to send his message to the *Press* office, and then lighting a cigar, and turning up the collar of his great-coat, curled up in the corner of the cab.

"Wake me when we get there, Gallegher," he said. He knew he had a long ride, and much rapid work before him, and he was preparing for the strain.

To Gallegher the idea of going to sleep seemed almost criminal. From the dark corner of the cab his eyes shone with excitement, and with the awful joy of anticipation. He glanced every now and then to where the sporting editor's cigar shone in the darkness, and watched it as it gradually burnt more dimly and went out. The lights in the shop windows threw a broad glare across the ice on the pavements, and the lights from the lamp-posts tossed the distorted shadow of the cab, and the horse, and the motionless driver, sometimes before and sometimes behind them.

After half an hour Gallegher slipped down to the bottom of the cab and dragged out a lap-robe, in which he wrapped himself. It was growing colder, and the damp, keen wind swept in through the cracks until the window-frames and woodwork were cold to the touch.

An hour passed, and the cab was still moving more slowly over the rough surface of partly paved streets, and by single rows of new houses standing at different angles to each other in fields covered with ash-heaps and brick-kilns. Here and there the gaudy lights of a drug-store, and the forerunner of suburban civilization, shone from the end of a new block of houses, and the rubber cape of an occasional policeman showed in the light of the lamp-post that he hugged for comfort.

Then even the houses disappeared, and the cab dragged its way between truck farms, with desolate-looking glass-covered beds, and pools of water, half-caked with ice, and bare trees, and interminable fences.

Once or twice the cab stopped altogether, and Gallegher could hear the driver swearing to himself, or at the horse, or the roads. At last they drew up before the station at Torresdale. It was quite deserted, and only a single light cut a swath in the darkness and showed a portion of the platform, the ties, and the rails glistening in the rain. They walked twice past the light before a figure stepped out of the shadow and greeted them cautiously.

"I am Mr. Dwyer, of the *Press,*" said the sporting editor, briskly. "You've heard of me, perhaps. Well, there shouldn't be any difficulty in our making a deal, should there? This boy here has found Hade, and we have reason to believe he will be among the spectators at the fight to-night. We want you to arrest him quietly, and as secretly as possible. You can do it with your papers and your badge easily enough. We want you to pretend that you believe he is this burglar you came over after. If you will do this, and take him away without any one so much as suspecting who he really is, and on the train that passes here at 1.20 for New York, we will give you $500 out of the $5000 reward. If, however, one other paper, either in New York or Philadelphia, or anywhere else, knows of the arrest, you won't get a cent. Now, what do you say?"

The detective had a great deal to say. He wasn't at all sure the man

Gallegher suspected was Hade; he feared he might get himself into trouble by making a false arrest, and if it should be the man, he was afraid the local police would interfere.

"We've no time to argue or debate this matter," said Dwyer, warmly. "We agree to point Hade out to you in the crowd. After the fight is over you arrest him as we have directed, and you get the money and the credit of the arrest. If you don't like this, I will arrest the man myself, and have him driven to town, with a pistol for a warrant."

Hefflefinger considered in silence and then agreed unconditionally. "As you say, Mr. Dwyer," he returned. "I've heard of you for a thoroughbred sport. I know you'll do what you say you'll do; and as for me I'll do what you say and just as you say, and it's a very pretty piece of work as it stands."

They all stepped back into the cab, and then it was that they were met by a fresh difficulty, how to get the detective into the barn where the fight was to take place, for neither of the two men had $250 to pay for his admittance.

But this was overcome when Gallegher remembered the window of which young Keppler had told him.

In the event of Hade's losing courage and not daring to show himself in the crowd around the ring, it was agreed that Dwyer should come to the barn and warn Hefflefinger; but if he should come, Dwyer was merely to keep near him and to signify by a prearranged gesture which one of the crowd he was.

They drew up before a great black shadow of a house, dark, forbidding, and apparently deserted. But at the sound of the wheels on the gravel the door opened, letting out a stream of warm, cheerful light, and a man's voice said, "Put out those lights. Don't youse know no better than that?" This was Keppler, and he welcomed Mr. Dwyer with effusive courtesy.

The two men showed in the stream of light, and the door closed on them, leaving the house as it was at first, black and silent, save for the dripping of the rain and snow from the eaves.

The detective and Gallegher put out the cab's lamps and led the horse toward a long, low shed in the rear of the yard, which they now noticed was almost filled with teams of many different makes, from the Hobson's choice of a livery stable to the brougham of the man about town.

"No," said Gallegher, as the cabman stopped to hitch the horse beside the others, "we want it nearest that lower gate. When we newspaper men leave this place we'll leave it in a hurry, and the man who is nearest town is likely to get there first. You won't be a-following of no hearse when you make your return trip."

Gallegher tied the horse to the very gate-post itself, leaving the gate open and allowing a clear road and a flying start for the prospective race to Newspaper Row.

The driver disappeared under the shelter of the porch, and Gallegher and the detective moved off cautiously to the rear of the barn. "This must be the window," said Hefflefinger, pointing to a broad wooden shutter some feet from the ground.

"Just you give me a boost once, and I'll get that open in a jiffy," said Gallegher.

The detective placed his hands on his knees, and Gallegher stood upon his shoulders, and with the blade of his knife lifted the wooden button that fastened the window on the inside, and pulled the shutter open.

Then he put one leg inside over the sill, and leaning down helped to draw his fellow-conspirator up to a level with the window. "I feel just like I was burglarizing a house," chuckled Gallegher, as he dropped noiselessly to the floor below and refastened the shutter. The barn was a large one, with a row of stalls on either side in which horses and cows were dozing. There was a hay-mow over each row of stalls, and at one end of the barn a number of fence-rails had been thrown across from one mow to the other. These rails were covered with hay.

In the middle of the floor was the ring. It was not really a ring, but a square, with wooden posts at its four corners through which ran a heavy rope. The space inclosed by the rope was covered with sawdust.

Gallegher could not resist stepping into the ring, and after stamping the sawdust once or twice, as if to assure himself that he was really there, began dancing around it, and indulging in such a remarkable series of fistic manœuvres with an imaginary adversary that the unimaginative detective precipitately backed into a corner of the barn.

"Now, then," said Gallegher, having apparently vanquished his foe, "you come with me." His companion followed quickly as Gallegher climbed to one of the hay-mows, and crawling carefully out on the fence-rail, stretched himself at full length, face downward. In this position, by moving the straw a little, he could look down, without being himself seen, upon the heads of whomsoever stood below. "This is better'n a private box, ain't it?" said Gallegher.

The boy from the newspaper office and the detective lay there in silence, biting at straws and tossing anxiously on their comfortable bed.

It seemed fully two hours before they came. Gallegher had listened without breathing, and with every muscle on a strain, at least a dozen times, when some movement in the yard had led him to believe that they were at the door.

And he had numerous doubts and fears. Sometimes it was that the police had learnt of the fight, and had raided Keppler's in his absence, and again it was that the fight had been postponed, or, worst of all, that it would be put off until so late that Mr. Dwyer could not get back in time for the last edition of the paper. Their coming, when at last they came, was heralded by an advance-guard of two sporting men, who stationed themselves at either side of the big door.

"Hurry up, now, gents," one of the men said with a shiver, "don't keep this door open no longer'n is needful."

It was not a very large crowd, but it was wonderfully well selected. It ran, in the majority of its component parts, to heavy white coats with pearl buttons. The white coats were shouldered by long blue coats with astrakhan fur trimmings, the wearers of which preserved a cliqueness not remarkable when one considers that they believed every one else present to be either a crook or a prize-fighter.

There were well-fed, well-groomed clubmen and brokers in the crowd, a politician or two, a popular comedian with his manager, amateur boxers from the athletic clubs, and quiet, close-mouthed sporting men from every city in the country. Their names if printed in the papers would have been as familiar as the types of the papers themselves.

And among these men, whose only thought was of the brutal sport to come, was Hade, with Dwyer standing at ease at his shoulder,—Hade, white, and visibly in deep anxiety, hiding his pale face beneath a cloth travelling-cap, and with his chin muffled in a woolen scarf. He had dared to come because he feared his danger from the already suspicious Keppler was less than if he stayed away. And so he was there, hovering restlessly on the border of the crowd, feeling his danger and sick with fear.

When Hefflefinger first saw him he started up on his hands and elbows and made a movement forward as if he would leap down then and there and carry off his prisoner single-handed.

"Lie down," growled Gallegher; "an officer of any sort wouldn't live three minutes in that crowd."

The detective drew back slowly and buried himself again in the straw, but never once through the long fight which followed did his eyes leave the person of the murderer. The newspaper men took their places in the foremost row close around the ring, and kept looking at their watches and begging the master of ceremonies to "shake it up, do."

There was a great deal of betting, and all of the men handled the great roll of bills they wagered with a flippant recklessness which could only be accounted for in Gallegher's mind by temporary mental derangement. Some one pulled a box out into the ring and the master of ceremonies mounted it, and pointed out in forcible language that as they were almost all already under bonds to keep the peace, it behooved all to curb their excitement and to maintain a severe silence, unless they wanted to bring the police upon them and have themselves "sent down" for a year or two.

Then two very disreputable-looking persons tossed their respective principals' high hats into the ring, and the crowd, recognizing this relic of the days when brave knights threw down their gauntlets in the lists as a sign that the fight was about to begin, cheered tumultuously.

This was followed by a sudden surging forward, and a mutter of admiration much more flattering than the cheers had been, when the principals followed their hats, and slipping out of their great-coats, stood forth in all the physical beauty of the perfect brute.

Their pink skin was as soft and healthy-looking as a baby's, and glowed in the lights of the lanterns like tinted ivory, and underneath this silken covering the great biceps and muscles moved in and out and looked like the coils of a snake around the branch of a tree.

Gentleman and blackguard shouldered each other for a nearer view; the coachmen, whose metal buttons were unpleasantly suggestive of police, put their hands, in the excitement of the moment, on the shoulders of their masters; the perspiration stood out in great drops on the foreheads of the backers, and the newspaper men bit somewhat nervously at the ends of their pencils.

And in the stalls the cows munched contentedly at their cuds and gazed with gentle curiosity at their two fellow-brutes, who stood waiting the signal to fall upon, and kill each other if need be, for the delectation of their brothers.

"Take your places," commanded the master of ceremonies.

In the moment in which the two men faced each other the crowd became so still that, save for the beating of the rain upon the shingled roof and the stamping of a horse in one of the stalls, the place was as silent as a church.

"Time," shouted the master of ceremonies.

The two men sprang into a posture of defence, which was lost as quickly as it was taken, one great arm shot out like a piston-rod; there was the sound of bare fists beating on naked flesh; there was an exultant indrawn gasp of savage pleasure and relief from the crowd, and the great fight had begun.

How the fortunes of war rose and fell, and changed and rechanged that night, is an old story to those who listen to such stories; and those who do not will be glad to be spared the telling of it. It was, they say, one of the bitterest fights between two men that this country has ever known.

But all that is of interest here is that after an hour of this desperate brutal business the champion ceased to be the favorite; the man whom he had taunted and bullied, and for whom the public had but little sympathy, was proving himself a likely winner, and under his cruel blows, as sharp and clean as those from a cutlass, his opponent was rapidly giving way.

The men about the ropes were past all control now; they drowned Keppler's petitions for silence with oaths and in inarticulate shouts of anger, as if the blows had fallen upon them, and in mad rejoicings. They swept from one end of the ring to the other, with every muscle leaping in unison with those of the man they favored, and when a New York correspondent muttered over his shoulder that this would be the biggest sporting surprise since the Heenan-Sayers fight, Mr. Dwyer nodded his head sympathetically in assent.

In the excitement and tumult it is doubtful if any heard the three quickly repeated blows that fell heavily from the outside upon the big doors of the barn. If they did, it was already too late to mend matters, for the door fell, torn from its hinges, and as it fell a captain of police sprang into the light from out of the storm, with his lieutenants and their men crowding close at his shoulder.

In the panic and stampede that followed, several of the men stood as helplessly immovable as though they had seen a ghost; others made a mad rush into the arms of the officers and were beaten back against the ropes of the ring; others dived headlong into the stalls, among the horses and cattle, and still others shoved the rolls of money they held into the hands of the police and begged like children to be allowed to escape.

The instant the door fell and the raid was declared Hefflefinger slipped over the cross rails on which he had been lying, hung for an instant by his hands, and then dropped into the centre of the fighting mob on the floor. He was out of it in an instant with the agility of a pickpocket, was across the room and at Hade's throat like a dog. The murderer, for the moment, was the calmer man of the two.

"Here," he panted, "hands off, now. There's no need for all this violence. There's no great harm in looking at a fight, is there? There's a hundred-dollar bill in my right hand; take it and let me slip out of this. No one is looking. Here."

But the detective only held him the closer.

"I want you for burglary," he whispered under his breath. "You've got to come with me now, and quick. The less fuss you make, the better for both of us. If you don't know who I am, you can feel my badge under my coat there. I've got the authority. It's all regular, and when we're out of this d—d row I'll show you the papers."

He took one hand from Hade's throat and pulled a pair of handcuffs from his pocket.

"It's a mistake. This is an outrage," gasped the murderer, white and trembling, but dreadfully alive and desperate for his liberty. "Let me go, I tell you! Take your hands off of me! Do I look like a burglar, you fool?"

"I know who you look like," whispered the detective, with his face close to the face of his prisoner. "Now, will you go easy as a burglar, or shall I tell these men who you are and what I *do* want you for? Shall I call out your real name or not? Shall I tell them? Quick, speak up; shall I?"

There was something so exultant—something so unnecessarily savage in the officer's face that the man he held saw that the detective knew him for what he really was, and the hands that had held his throat slipped down around his shoulders, or he would have fallen. The man's eyes opened and closed again, and he swayed weakly backward and forward, and choked as if his throat were dry and burning. Even to such a hardened connoisseur in crime as Gallegher, who stood closely by, drinking it in, there was something so abject in the man's terror that he regarded him with what was almost a touch of pity.

"For God's sake," Hade begged, "let me go. Come with me to my room and I'll give you half the money. I'll divide with you fairly. We can both get away. There's a fortune for both of us there. We both can get away. You'll be rich for life. Do you understand—for life!"

But the detective, to his credit, only shut his lips the tighter.

"That's enough," he whispered, in return. "That's more than I expected. You've sentenced yourself already. Come!"

Two officers in uniform barred their exit at the door, but Hefflefinger smiled easily and showed his badge.

"One of Byrnes's men," he said, in explanation; "came over expressly to take this chap. He's a burglar; 'Arlie' Lane, *alias* Carleton. I've shown the papers to the captain. It's all regular. I'm just going to get his traps at the hotel and walk him over to the station. I guess we'll push right on to New York to-night."

The officers nodded and smiled their admiration for the representative of what is, perhaps, the best detective force in the world, and let him pass.

Then Hefflefinger turned and spoke to Gallegher, who still stood as watchful as a dog at his side. "I'm going to his room to get the bonds and stuff," he whispered; "then I'll march him to the station and take that train. I've done my share; don't forget yours!"

"Oh, you'll get your money right enough," said Gallegher. "And, sa-ay," he added, with the appreciative nod of an expert, "do you know, you did it rather well."

Mr. Dwyer had been writing while the raid was settling down, as he had been writing while waiting for the fight to begin. Now he walked over to where the other correspondents stood in angry conclave.

The newspaper men had informed the officers who hemmed them in that they represented the principal papers of the country, and were expostulating vigorously with the captain, who had planned the raid, and who declared they were under arrest.

"Don't be an ass, Scott," said Mr. Dwyer, who was too excited to be polite or politic. "You know our being here isn't a matter of choice. We came here on business, as you did, and you've no right to hold us."

"If we don't get our stuff on the wire at once," protested a New York man, "we'll be too late for to-morrow's paper, and——"

Captain Scott said he did not care a profanely small amount for to-morrow's paper, and that all he knew was that to the station-house the newspaper men would go. There they would have a hearing, and if the magistrate chose to let them off, that was the magistrate's business, but that his duty was to take them into custody.

"But then it will be too late, don't you understand?" shouted Mr. Dwyer. "You've got to let us go *now,* at once."

"I can't do it, Mr. Dwyer," said the captain, "and that's all there is to it. Why, haven't I just sent the president of the Junior Republican Club to the patrol wagon, the man that put this coat on me, and do you think I can let you fellows go after that? You were all put under bonds to keep the peace not three days ago, and here you're at it—fighting like badgers. It's worth my place to let one of you off."

What Mr. Dwyer said next was so uncomplimentary to the gallant Captain Scott that that overwrought individual seized the sporting editor by the shoulder, and shoved him into the hands of two of his men.

This was more than the distinguished Mr. Dwyer could brook, and he excitedly raised his hand in resistance. But before he had time to do anything foolish his wrist was gripped by one strong, little hand, and he was conscious that another was picking the pocket of his great-coat.

He slapped his hands to his sides, and looking down, saw Gallegher standing close behind him and holding him by the wrist. Mr. Dwyer had forgotten the boy's existence, and would have spoken sharply if something in Gallegher's innocent eyes had not stopped him.

Gallegher's hand was still in that pocket, in which Mr. Dwyer had shoved his note-book filled with what he had written of Gallegher's work and Hade's final capture, and with a running descriptive account of the fight. With his eyes fixed on Mr. Dwyer, Gallegher drew it out, and with a quick movement shoved it inside his waistcoat. Mr. Dwyer gave a nod of comprehension. Then glancing at his two guardsmen, and finding that they were still interested in the wordy battle of the correspondents with their chief, and had seen nothing, he stooped and whispered to Gallegher: "The forms are locked at twenty minutes to three. If you don't get there by that time it will be of no use, but if you're on time you'll beat the town—and the country too."

Gallegher's eyes flashed significantly, and nodding his head to show he understood, he started boldly on a run toward the door. But the officers who guarded it brought him to an abrupt halt, and, much to Mr. Dwyer's astonishment, drew from him what was apparently a torrent of tears.

"Let me go to me father. I want me father," the boy shrieked, hysterically. "They've 'rested father. Oh, daddy, daddy. They're a-goin' to take you to prison."

"Who is your father, sonny?" asked one of the guardians of the gate.

"Keppler's me father," sobbed Gallegher. "They're a-goin' to lock him up, and I'll never see him no more."

"Oh, yes, you will," said the officer, good-naturedly; "he's there in that first patrol wagon. You can run over and say good night to him, and then you'd better get to bed. This ain't no place for kids of your age."

"Thank you, sir," sniffed Gallegher, tearfully, as the two officers raised their clubs, and let him pass out into the darkness.

The yard outside was in tumult, horses were stamping, and plunging, and backing the carriages into one another; lights were flashing from every window of what had been apparently an uninhabited house, and the voices of the prisoners were still raised in angry expostulation.

Three police patrol wagons were moving about the yard, filled with unwilling passengers, who sat or stood, packed together like sheep, and with no protection from the sleet and rain.

Gallegher stole off into a dark corner, and watched the scene until his eyesight became familiar with the position of the land.

Then with his eyes fixed fearfully on the swinging light of a lantern with which an officer was searching among the carriages, he groped his way between horses' hoofs and behind the wheels of carriages to the cab which he had himself placed at the furthermost gate. It was still there, and the horse, as he had left it, with its head turned toward the city. Gallegher opened the big gate noiselessly, and worked nervously at the hitching strap. The knot was covered with a thin coating of ice, and it was several minutes before he could loosen it. But his teeth finally pulled it apart, and with the reins in his hands he sprang upon the wheel. And as he stood so, a shock of fear ran down his back like an electric current, his breath left him, and he stood immovable, gazing with wide eyes into the darkness.

The officer with the lantern had suddenly loomed up from behind a carriage not fifty feet distant, and was standing perfectly still, with his lantern held over his head, peering so directly toward Gallegher that the boy felt that he must see him. Gallegher stood with one foot on the hub of the wheel and with the other on the box waiting to spring. It seemed a minute before either of them moved, and then the officer took a step forward, and demanded sternly, "Who is that? What are you doing there?"

There was no time for parley then. Gallegher felt that he had been taken in the act, and that his only chance lay in open flight. He leaped up on the box, pulling out the whip as he did so, and with a quick sweep lashed the horse across the head and back. The animal sprang forward with a snort, narrowly clearing the gate post, and plunged off into the darkness.

"Stop!" cried the officer.

So many of Gallegher's acquaintances among the 'longshoremen and mill hands had been challenged in so much the same manner that Gallegher knew what would probably follow if the challenge was disregarded. So he slipped from his seat to the footboard below, and ducked his head.

The three reports of a pistol, which rang out briskly from behind him, proved that his early training had given him a valuable fund of useful miscellaneous knowledge.

"Don't you be scared," he said, reassuringly, to the horse; "he's firing in the air."

The pistol-shots were answered by the impatient clangor of a patrol wagon's gong, and glancing over his shoulder Gallegher saw its red and green lanterns tossing from side to side and looking in the darkness like the side-lights of a yacht plunging forward in a storm.

"I hadn't bargained to race you against no patrol wagons," said Gallegher to his animal; "but if they want a race, we'll give them a tough tussle for it, won't we?"

Philadelphia, lying four miles to the south, sent up a faint yellow glow to the sky. It seemed very far away, and Gallegher's braggadocio grew cold within him at the loneliness of his adventure and the thought of the long ride before him.

It was still bitterly cold.

The rain and sleet beat through his clothes, and struck his skin with a sharp chilling touch that set him trembling.

Even the thought of the over-weighted patrol wagon probably sticking in the mud some safe distance in the rear, failed to cheer him, and the excitement that had so far made him callous to the cold died out and left him weaker and nervous.

But his horse was chilled with the long standing, and now leaped eagerly forward, only too willing to warm the half-frozen blood in its veins.

"You're a good beast," said Gallegher, plaintively. "You've got more nerve than me. Don't you go back on me now. Mr. Dwyer says we've got to beat the town." Gallegher had no idea what time it was as he rode through the night, but he knew he would be able to find out from a big clock over a manufactory at a point nearly three-quarters of the distance from Keppler's to the goal.

He was still in the open country and driving recklessly, for he knew the best part of his ride must be made outside the city limits.

He raced between desolate-looking cornfields with bare stalks and patches of muddy earth rising above the thin covering of snow. Truck farms and brick-yards fell behind him on either side. It was very lonely work, and once or twice the dogs ran yelping to the gates and barked after him.

Part of his way lay parallel with the railroad tracks, and he drove for some time beside long lines of freight and coal cars as they stood resting for the night. The fantastic Queen Anne suburban stations were dark and deserted, but in one or two of the block-towers he could see the operators writing at their desks, and the sight in some way comforted him.

Once he thought of stopping to get out the blanket in which he had wrapped himself on the first trip, but he feared to spare the time, and drove on with his teeth chattering and his shoulders shaking with the cold.

He welcomed the first solitary row of darkened houses with a faint cheer of recognition. The scattered lamp-posts lightened his spirits, and even the badly paved streets rang under the beats of his horse's feet like music. Great mills and manufactories, with only a night-watchman's light in the lowest of their many stories, began to take the place of the gloomy farm-houses and gaunt trees that had startled him with their grotesque shapes. He had been driving nearly an hour, he calculated, and in that time the rain had changed to a wet snow, that fell heavily and clung to whatever it touched. He passed block after block of trim workmen's houses, as still and silent as the sleepers within them, and at last he turned the horse's head into Broad Street, the city's great thoroughfare, that stretches from its one end to the other and cuts it evenly in two.

He was driving noiselessly over the snow and slush in the street, with his thoughts bent only on the clock-face he wished so much to see, when a hoarse voice challenged him from the sidewalk. "Hey, you, stop there, hold up!" said the voice.

Gallegher turned his head, and though he saw that the voice came from under a policeman's helmet, his only answer was to hit his horse sharply over the head with his whip and to urge it into a gallop.

This, on his part, was followed by a sharp, shrill whistle from the policeman. Another whistle answered it from a street-corner one block ahead of him. "Whoa," said Gallegher, pulling on the reins. "There's one too many of them," he added, in apologetic explanation. The horse stopped, and stood, breathing heavily, with great clouds of steam rising from its flanks.

"Why in hell didn't you stop when I told you to?" demanded the voice, now close at the cab's side.

"I didn't hear you," returned Gallegher, sweetly. "But I heard you whistle, and I heard your partner whistle, and I thought maybe it was me you wanted to speak to, so I just stopped."

"You heard me well enough. Why aren't your lights lit?" demanded the voice.

"Should I have 'em lit?" asked Gallegher, bending over and regarding them with sudden interest.

"You know you should, and if you don't, you've no right to be driving that cab. I don't believe you're the regular driver, anyway. Where'd you get it?"

"It ain't my cab, of course," said Gallegher, with an easy laugh. "It's Luke McGovern's. He left it outside Cronin's while he went in to get a drink, and he took too much, and me father told me to drive it round to the stable for him. I'm Cronin's son. McGovern ain't in no condition to drive. You can see yourself how he's been misusing the horse. He puts it up at Bachman's livery stable, and I was just going around there now."

Gallegher's knowledge of the local celebrities of the district confused the zealous officer of the peace. He surveyed the boy with a steady stare that would have distressed a less skilful liar, but Gallegher only shrugged his shoulders slightly, as if from the cold, and waited with apparent indifference to what the officer would say next.

In reality his heart was beating heavily against his side, and he felt that if he was kept on a strain much longer he would give way and break down. A second snow-covered form emerged suddenly from the shadow of the houses.

"What is it, Reeder?" it asked.

"Oh, nothing much," replied the first officer. "This kid hadn't any lamps lit, so I called to him to stop and he didn't do it, so I whistled to you. It's all right, though. He's just taking it round to Bachman's. Go ahead," he added, sulkily.

"Get up!" chirped Gallegher. "Good night," he added, over his shoulder.

Gallegher gave an hysterical little gasp of relief as he trotted away from the two policemen, and poured bitter maledictions on their heads for two meddling fools as he went.

"They might as well kill a man as scare him to death," he said, with an attempt to get back to his customary flippancy. But the effort was somewhat pitiful, and he felt guiltily conscious that a salt-warm tear was creeping slowly down his face, and that a lump that would not keep down was rising in his throat.

"'Tain't no fair thing for the whole police force to keep worrying at a little boy like me," he said, in shame-faced apology. "I'm not doing nothing wrong, and I'm half froze to death, and yet they keep a-nagging at me."

It was so cold that when the boy stamped his feet against the foot-board to keep them warm, sharp pains shot up through his body, and when he beat his arms about his shoulders, as he had seen real cabmen do, the blood in his finger-tips tingled so acutely that he cried aloud with the pain.

He had often been up that late before, but he had never felt so sleepy. It was as if some one was pressing a sponge heavy with chloroform near his face, and he could not fight off the drowsiness that laid hold of him.

He saw, dimly hanging above his head, a round disc of light that seemed like a great moon, and which he finally guessed to be the clock face for which he had been on the lookout. He had passed it before he realized this; but this fact stirred him into wakefulness again, and when his cab's wheels slipped around the City Hall corner, he remembered to look up at the other big clock face that keeps awake over the railroad station and measures out the night.

He gave a gasp of consternation when he saw that it was half-past two, and that there was but ten minutes left to him. This, and the many electric lights and the sight of the familiar pile of buildings, startled him into a semi-consciousness of where he was and how great was the necessity for haste.

He rose in his seat and called on the horse, and urged it into a reckless gallop over the slippery asphalt. He considered nothing else but speed, and looking neither to the left nor right dashed off down Broad Street into Chestnut, where his course lay straight away to the office, now only seven blocks distant.

Gallegher never knew how it began, but he was suddenly assaulted by shouts on either side, his horse was thrown back on its haunches, and he found two men in cabmen's livery hanging at its head, and patting its sides, and calling it by name. And the other cabmen who have their stand at the corner were swarming about the carriage, all of them talking and swearing at once, and gesticulating wildly with their whips.

They said they knew the cab was McGovern's, and they wanted to know where he was, and why he wasn't on it; they wanted to know where Gallegher had stolen it, and why he had been such a fool as to drive it into the arms of its owner's friends; they said that it was about time that a cab-driver could get off his box to take a drink without having his cab run away with, and some of them called loudly for a policeman to take the young thief in charge.

Gallegher felt as if he had been suddenly dragged into consciousness out of a bad dream, and stood for a second like a half-awakened somnambulist.

They had stopped the cab under an electric light, and its glare shone coldly down upon the trampled snow and the faces of the men around him.

Gallegher bent forward, and lashed savagely at the horse with his whip.

"Let me go," he shouted, as he tugged impotently at the reins. "Let me go, I tell you. I haven't stole no cab, and you've got no right to stop me. I only want to take it to the *Press* office," he begged. "They'll send it back to you all right. They'll pay you for the trip. I'm not running away with it. The driver's got the collar—he's 'rested—and I'm only a-going to the *Press* office. Do you hear me?" he cried, his voice rising and breaking in a shriek of passion and disappointment. "I tell you to let go those reins. Let me go, or I'll kill you. Do you hear me? I'll kill you." And leaning forward, the boy struck savagely with his long whip at the faces of the men about the horse's head.

Some one in the crowd reached up and caught him by the ankles, and with a quick jerk pulled him off the box, and threw him on to the street. But he was up on his knees in a moment, and caught at the man's head.

"Don't let them stop me, mister," he cried, "please let me go. I didn't steal the cab, sir. S'help me, I didn't. I'm telling you the truth. Take me to the *Press* office, and they'll prove it to you. They'll pay you anything you ask 'em. It's only such a little ways now, and I've come so far, sir. Please don't let them stop me," he sobbed, clasping the man about the knees. "For Heaven's sake, mister, let me go!"

* * * * * * *

The managing editor of the *Press* took up the india-rubber speaking-tube at his side, and answered, "Not yet" to an inquiry the night editor had already put to him five times within the last twenty minutes.

Then he snapped the metal top of the tube impatiently, and went up-stairs. As he passed the door of the local room, he noticed that the reporters had not gone home, but were sitting about on the tables and chairs, waiting. They looked up inquiringly as he passed, and the city editor asked, "Any news yet?" and the managing editor shook his head.

The compositors were standing idle in the composing-room, and their foreman was talking with the night editor.

"Well," said that gentleman, tentatively.

"Well," returned the managing editor, "I don't think we can wait; do you?"

"It's a half-hour after time now," said the night editor, "and we'll miss the suburban trains if we hold the paper back any longer. We can't afford to wait for a purely hypothetical story. The chances are all against the fight's having taken place or this Hade's having been arrested."

"But if we're beaten on it——" suggested the chief. "But I don't think that is possible. If there were any story to print, Dwyer would have had it here before now."

The managing editor looked steadily down at the floor.

"Very well," he said, slowly, "we won't wait any longer. Go ahead," he added, turning to the foreman with a sigh of reluctance. The foreman whirled himself about, and began to give his orders; but the two editors still looked at each other doubtfully.

As they stood so, there came a sudden shout and the sound of people running to and fro in the reportorial rooms below. There was the tramp of many footsteps on the stairs, and above the confusion they heard the voice of the city editor telling some one to "run to Madden's and get some brandy, quick."

No one in the composing-room said anything; but those compositors who had started to go home began slipping off their overcoats, and every one stood with his eyes fixed on the door.

It was kicked open from the outside, and in the doorway stood a cab-driver and the city editor, supporting between them a pitiful little figure of a boy, wet and miserable, and with the snow melting on his clothes and running in little pools to the floor. "Why, it's Gallegher," said the night editor, in a tone of the keenest disappointment.

Gallegher shook himself free from his supporters, and took an unsteady step forward, his fingers fumbling stiffly with the buttons of his waistcoat.

"Mr. Dwyer, sir," he began faintly, with his eyes fixed fearfully on the managing editor, "he got arrested—and I couldn't get here no sooner, 'cause they kept a-stopping me, and they took me cab from under me—but—" he pulled the notebook from his breast and held it out with its covers damp and limp from the rain, "but we got Hade, and here's Mr. Dwyer's copy."

And then he asked, with a queer note in his voice, partly of dread and partly of hope, "Am I in time, sir?"

The managing editor took the book, and tossed it to the foreman, who ripped out its leaves and dealt them out to his men as rapidly as a gambler deals out cards.

Then the managing editor stooped and picked Gallegher up in his arms, and, sitting down, began to unlace his wet and muddy shoes.

Gallegher made a faint effort to resist this degradation of the managerial dignity; but his protest was a very feeble one, and his head fell back heavily on the managing editor's shoulder.

To Gallegher the incandescent lights began to whirl about in circles, and to burn in different colors; the faces of the reporters kneeling before him and chafing his hands and feet grew dim and unfamiliar, and the roar and rumble of the great presses in the basement sounded far away, like the murmur of the sea.

And then the place and the circumstances of it came back to him again sharply and with sudden vividness.

Gallegher looked up, with a faint smile, into the managing editor's face. "You won't turn me off for running away, will you?" he whispered.

The managing editor did not answer immediately. His head was bent, and he was thinking, for some reason or other, of a little boy of his own, at home in bed. Then he said, quietly, "Not this time, Gallegher."

Gallegher's head sank back comfortably on the older man's shoulder, and he smiled comprehensively at the faces of the young men crowded around him. "You hadn't ought to," he said, with a touch of his old impudence, "'cause—I beat the town."

MARK ANTONY DE WOLFE HOWE

Spring on the Land

SPRING on the vineyards of Attica! Spring on the land,
All the dear land of the Hellenes loved of the sun!
The god Dionysus immortally breathes his command,
And the bars of the prison of winter dissolve, and are gone!

He hath slept—he awakes; he stirs on the hills—he is free,
And the blood at the bountiful heart of the earth throbs again;
Blue is the sky overhead and blue is the sea,
And green roll the billows on laughing valley and plain.

The sap, to the uttermost tendiils, is quick in the vine;
It shall creep, it shall mount, till the spheres of delight take form;
They shall blush, they shall swell—and their blood flowing red in the wine
Shall be one with the life-blood of men, all vibrant and warm.

Who but thee, Dionysus, hath guarded the vineyards at first?
Their fruit at the last shall be turned to thy kingly employ;
And cool at the lips of sorrowing mortals athirst
Flows ever thy chalice of kinship and freedom and joy.

The Known Soldier

(For the day of President Wilson's burial)

Now through the stifling air thick with the murk
Of self and pettiness—shame's perfect work—
A sense of greatness spreads from sea to sea;
For greatness was, when, bound in unity
Of generous aim, men of our blended race
Stood looking each into his neighbor's face
And said, "This towering thought, this cleaving word
Speaks for America"—and the world heard.
Then, with new vision of unwonted scope,
They lifted up their eyes to the hills of hope.
Today remembered greatness stirs again
The spirit that kindled once the hearts of men.
And out from smoldering embers starts a flame
Fanned by the whisper of a burning name.
Humblest and highest to that greatness thrill,
For the known soldier, dauntless of heart and will,
Mortally stricken in the long-drawn fray,
Reviling none, a wounded leader, lay,
And passed in silence to the eternal rest
Wherewith the soldier of the spirit is blest,
For all his weariness, his strength outpoured,
Blest even as the soldier of the sword.

Proud stands his country, bared and bowed of head,
While safe he sleeps among the deathless dead.

February 7, 1924.

The Sailor-Man

I LIKE the look of khaki and the cut of army wear,
And the men of mettle sporting it, at home and over there;
But there's something at the heartstrings that tautens when I meet
A blue-clad sailor-man adrift, on shore-leave from the fleet.

From flapping togs his sea-legs win some rhythm of old romance
That's proper to the keeper of the paths that lead to France;
For what were all the soldiers worth that ever tossed a gun
Without the ships and sailor-men to pit them 'gainst the Hun!

There's sunlight now and steady ground beneath the sailor's tread,
And every pleasure beckons him, and every snare is spread—
Speed well this visitor, whose home 'twixt heaving decks is set,
Whose playmates are the darkness, and the bitter cold, and wet!

His comrades these; his foe is ours, the foe of law and right,
The stealthy, murdering German "fish," that skulks from honest sight;
And none may sink him where he swims, flouting God's age-built plan,
None but the guardian of us all, the rolling sailor-man.

His hands are often cruel cold; his heart is oftener warm,
For in its depths he knows 'tis he that shields the world from harm;
Because I know it too, my heart beats warmer when I meet
A blue-clad sailor-man adrift, on shore-leave from the fleet.

December, 1917.

FINLEY PETER DUNNE

Rudyard Kipling

"I THINK," said Mr. Dooley, "th' finest pothry in th' wurruld is wrote be that frind iv young Hogan's, a man be th' name iv Roodyard Kipling. I see his pomes in th' pa-aper, Hinnissy; an' they're all right. They're all right, thim pomes. They was wan about scraggin' Danny Deever that done me a wurruld iv good. They was a la-ad I wanst knew be th' name iv Deever, an' like as not he was th' same man. He owed me money. Thin there was wan that I see mintioned in th' war news wanst in a while,—th' less we f'rget, th' more we raymimber. That was a hot pome an' a good wan. What I like about Kipling is that his pomes is right off th' bat, like me con-versations with you, me boy. He's a minyitman, a r-ready pote that sleeps like th' dhriver iv thruck 9, with his poetic pants in his boots beside his bed, an' him r-ready to jump out an' slide down th' pole th' minyit th' alarm sounds.

"He's not such a pote as Tim Scanlan, that hasn't done annything since th' siege iv Lim'rick; an' that was two hundherd year befure he was bor-rn. He's prisident iv th' Pome Supply Company,—fr-resh pothry delivered ivry day at ye'er dure. Is there an accident in a grain illyvator? Ye pick up ye'er mornin' pa-aper, an' they'se a pome about it be Roodyard Kipling. Do ye hear iv a manhole cover bein' blown up? Roodyard is there with his r-ready pen. ''Tis written iv Cashum-Cadi an' th' book iv th' gr-reat Gazelle that a manhole cover in anger is tin degrees worse thin hell.' He writes in all dialects an' anny language, plain an' fancy pothry, pothry f'r young an' old, pothry be weight or linyar measuremint, pothry f'r small parties iv eight or tin a specialty. What's the raysult, Hinnissy? Most potes I despise. But Roodyard Kipling's pothry is aisy. Ye can skip through it while ye're atin' breakfuss an' get a c'rrect idee iv th' current news iv th' day,—who won th' futball game, how Sharkey is thrainin' f'r th' fight, an' how manny votes th' pro-hybitionist got f'r gov'nor iv th' State iv Texas. No col' storage pothry f'r Kipling. Ivrything fr-resh an' up to date. All lays laïd this mornin'.

"Hogan was in to-day readin' Kipling's Fridah afthernoon pome, an' 'tis a good pome. He calls it 'Th' Thruce iv th' Bear.' This is th' way it happened: Roodyard Kipling had just finished his mornin' batch iv pothry f'r th' home-thrade, an' had et his dinner, an' was thinkin' iv r-runnin' out in th' counthry f'r a breath iv fr-resh air, whin in come a tillygram sayin' that th' Czar iv Rooshia had sint out a circular letther sayin' ivrybody in th' wurrld ought to get together an' stop makin' war an' live a quite an' dull life. Now Kipling don't like the czar. Him an' th' czar fell out about something, an' they don't speak. So says Roodyard Kipling to himsilf, he says: 'I'll take a crack at that fellow,' he says. 'I'll do him up,' he says. An' so he writes a pome to show that th' czar's letter's not on th' square. Kipling's like me, Hinnissy. When I want to say annything lib'lous, I stick it on to me Uncle Mike. So be Roodyard Kipling. He doesn't come r-right out, an' say, 'Nick, ye're a liar!' but he tells about what th' czar done to a man he knowed be th' name iv Muttons. Muttons, it seems, Hinnissy, was wanst a hunter; an' he wint out to take a shot at th' czar, who was dhressed up as a bear. Well, Muttons r-run him down, an' was about to plug him, whin th' czar says, 'Hol' on,' he says,—'hol' on there,' he says. 'Don't shoot,' he says. 'Let's talk this over,' he says. An' Muttons, bein' a foolish man, waited till th' czar come near him; an' thin th' czar feinted with his left, an' put in a right hook an' pulled off Mutton's face. I tell ye 'tis so. He jus' hauled it off th' way ye'd haul off a porous plasther,—raked off th' whole iv Muttons's fr-ront ilivation. 'I like ye'er face,' he says, an' took it. An' all this time, an' 'twas fifty year ago, Muttons hasn't had a face to shave. Ne'er a one. So he goes ar-round exhibitin' th' recent site, an' warnin' people that, whin they ar-re shootin' bears, they must see that their gun is kept loaded an' their face is nailed on securely. If ye iver see a bear that looks like a man, shoot him on th' spot, or, betther still, r-run up an alley. Ye must niver lose that face, Hinnissy.

"I showed th' pome to Father Kelly," continued Mr. Dooley.

"What did he say?" asked Mr. Hennessy.

"He said," Mr. Dooley replied, "that I cud write as good a wan mesilf; an' he took th' stub iv a pencil, an' wrote this. Lemme see— Ah! here it is:—

'Whin he shows as seekin' frindship with paws that're thrust in thine,
That is th' time iv pearl, that is th' thruce iv th' line.

'Collarless, coatless, hatless, askin' a dhrink at th' bar,
Me Uncle Mike, the Fenyan, he tells it near and far,

'Over an' over th' story: 'Beware iv th' gran' flimflam,
There is no thruce with Gazabo, th' line that looks like a lamb.'

"That's a good pome, too," said Mr. Dooley; "an' I'm goin' to sind it to th' nex' meetin' iv th' Anglo-Saxon 'liance."

On New Year's Resolutions

Mr. Hennessy looked out at the rain dripping down in Archey Road, and sighed, "A-ha, 'tis a bad spell iv weather we're havin'."

"Faith, it is," said Mr. Dooley, "or else we mind it more thin we did. I can't remimber wan day fr'm another. Whin I was young, I niver thought iv rain or snow, cold or heat. But now th' heat stings an' th' cold wrenches me bones; an', if I go out in th' rain with less on me thin a ton iv rubber, I'll pay dear f'r it in achin' j'ints, so I will. That's what old age means; an' now another year has been put on to what we had befure, an' we're expected to be gay. 'Ring out th' old,' says a guy at th' Brothers' School. 'Ring out th' old, ring in th' new,' he says. 'Ring out th' false, ring in th' thrue,' says he. It's a pretty sintimint, Hinnissy; but how ar-re we goin' to do it? Nawthin'd please me betther thin to turn me back on th' wicked an' ingloryous past, rayform me life, an' live at peace with th' wurruld to th' end iv me days. But how th' divvle can I do it? As th' fellow says, 'Can th' leopard change his spots,' or can't he?

"You know Dorsey, iv coorse, th' cross-eyed May-o man that come to this counthry about wan day in advance iv a warrant f'r sheep-stealin'? Ye know what he done to me, tellin' people I was caught in me cellar poorin' wather into a bar'l? Well, last night says I to mesilf, thinkin' iv Dorsey, I says: 'I swear that henceforth I'll keep me temper with me fellow-men. I'll not let anger or jealousy get th' betther iv me,' I says. 'I'll lave off all me old feuds; an' if I meet me inimy goin' down th' sthreet, I'll go up an' shake him be th' hand, if I'm sure he hasn't a brick in th' other hand.' Oh, I was mighty compliminthry to mesilf. I set be th' stove dhrinkin' hot wans, an' ivry wan I dhrunk made me more iv a pote. 'Tis th' way with th' stuff. Whin I'm in dhrink, I have manny a fine thought; an', if I wasn't too comfortable to go an' look f'r th' ink-bottle, I cud write pomes that'd make Shakespeare an' Mike Scanlan think they were wur-rkin' on a dredge. 'Why,' says I, 'carry into th' new year th' hathreds iv th' old?' I says. 'Let th' dead past bury its dead,' says I. 'Tur-rn ye'er lamps up to th' blue sky,' I says. (It was rainin' like th' divvle, an' th' hour was midnight; but I give no heed to that, bein' comfortable with th' hot wans.) An' I wint to th' dure, an', whin Mike Duffy come by on number wan hun-dherd an' five, ringin' th' gong iv th' ca-ar, I hollered to him: 'Ring out th' old, ring in th' new.' 'Go back into ye'er stall,' he says, 'an' wring ye'ersilf out,' he says. 'Ye'er wet through,' he says.

"Whin I woke up this mornin', th' pothry had all disappeared, an' I begun to think th' las' hot wan I took had somethin' wrong with it. Besides, th' lumbago was grippin' me till I cud hardly put wan foot befure th' other. But I remimbered me promises to mesilf, an' I wint out on th' sthreet, intindin' to wish ivry wan a 'Happy New Year,' an' hopin' in me hear-rt that th' first wan I wished it to'd tell me to go to th' divvle, so I cud hit him in th' eye. I hadn't gone half a block befure I spied Dorsey acrost th' sthreet. I picked up a half a brick an' put it in me pocket, an' Dorsey done th' same. Thin we wint up to each other. 'A Happy New Year,' says I. 'Th' same to you,' says he, 'an' manny iv thim,' he says. 'Ye have a brick in ye'er hand,' says I. 'I was thinkin' iv givin' ye a New Year's gift,' says he. 'Th' same to you, an' manny iv thim,' says I, fondlin' me own ammunition. ''Tis even all around,' says he. 'It is,' says I. 'I was thinkin' las' night I'd give up me gredge again ye,' says he. 'I had th' same thought mesilf,' says I. 'But, since I seen ye'er face,' he says, 'I've con-cluded that I'd be more comfortable hatin' ye thin havin' ye f'r a frind,' says he. 'Ye're a man iv taste,' says I. An' we backed away fr'm each other. He's a Tip, an' can throw a stone like a rifleman; an', Hinnissy, I'm some-thin' iv an amachoor shot with a half-brick mesilf.

"Well, I've been thinkin' it over, an' I've argied it out that life'd not be worth livin' if we didn't keep our inimies. I can have all th' frinds I need. Anny man can that keeps a liquor sthore. But a rale sthrong inimy, specially a May-o inimy,—wan that hates ye ha-ard, an' that ye'd take th' coat off yer back to do a bad tur-rn to,—is a luxury that I can't go without in me ol' days. Dorsey is th' right sort. I can't go by his house without bein' in fear he'll spill th' chimbly down on me head; an', whin he passes my place, he walks in th' middle iv th' sthreet, an' crosses himsilf. I'll swear off on annything but Dorsey. He's a good man, an' I despise him. Here's long life to him."

WILLIAM ALLEN WHITE

Mary White

THE Associated Press reports carrying the news of Mary White's death declared that it came as the result of a fall from a horse. How she would have hooted at that! She never fell from a horse in her life. Horses have fallen on her and with her—"I'm always trying to hold 'em in my lap," she used to say. But she was proud of few things, and one was that she could ride anything that had four legs and hair. Her death resulted not from a fall, but from a blow on the head which fractured her skull, and the blow came from the limb of an overhanging tree on the parking.

The last hour of her life was typical of its happiness. She came home from a day's work at school, topped off by a hard grind with the copy on the High School Annual, and felt that a ride would refresh her. She climbed into her khakis, chattering to her mother about the work she was doing, and hurried to get her horse and be out on the dirt roads for the country air and the radiant green fields of the spring. As she rode through the town on an easy gallop she kept waving at passers-by. She knew everyone in town. For a decade the little figure with the long pig-tail and the red hair-ribbon has been familiar on the streets of Emporia, and she got in the way of speaking to those who nodded at her. She passed the Kerrs, walking the horse, in front of the Normal Library, and waved at them; passed another friend a few hundred feet further on, and waved at her. The horse was walking and, as she turned into North Merchant Street she took off her cowboy hat, and the horse swung into a lope. She passed the Tripletts and waved her cowboy hat at them, still moving gaily north on Merchant Street. A *Gazette* carrier passed—a High School boy friend—and she waved at him, but with her bridle hand; the horse veered quickly, plunged into the parking where the low-hanging limb faced her, and, while she still looked back waving, the blow came. But she did not fall from the horse; she slipped off, dazed a bit, staggered and fell in a faint. She never quite recovered consciousness.

But she did not fall from the horse, neither was she riding fast. A year or so ago she used to go like the wind. But that habit was broken, and she used the horse to get into the open to get fresh, hard exercise, and to work off a certain surplus energy that welled up in her and needed a physical outlet. That need has been in her heart for years. It was back of the impulse that kept the dauntless, little brown-clad figure on the streets and country roads of this community and built into a strong, muscular body what had been a frail and sickly frame during the first years of her life. But the riding gave her more than a body. It released a gay and hardy soul. She was the happiest thing in the world. And she was happy because she was enlarging her horizon. She came to know all sorts and conditions of men; Charley O'Brien, the traffic cop, was one of her best friends. W. L. Holtz, the Latin teacher, was another. Tom O'Connor, farmer-politician, and Rev. J. H. J. Rice, preacher and police judge, and Frank Beach, music master, were her special friends, and all the girls, black and white, above the track and below the track, in Pepville and Stringtown, were among her acquaintances. And she brought home riotous stories of her adventures. She loved to rollick; persiflage was her natural expression at home. Her humor was a continual bubble of joy. She seemed to think in hyperbole and metaphor. She was mischievous without malice, as full of faults as an old shoe. No angel was Mary White, but an easy girl to live with, for she never nursed a grouch five minutes in her life.

With all her eagerness for the out-of-doors, she loved books. On her table when she left her room were a book by Conrad, one by Galsworthy, "Creative Chemistry," by E. E. Slosson, and a Kipling book. She read Mark Twain, Dickens and Kipling before she was ten—all of their writings. Wells and Arnold Bennett particularly amused and diverted her. She was entered as a student in Wellesley in 1922; was assistant editor of the High School Annual this year, and in line for election to the editorship of the Annual next year. She was a member of the executive committee of the High School Y. W. C. A.

Within the last two years she had begun to be moved by an ambition to draw. She began as most children do by scribbling in her school books, funny pictures. She bought cartoon magazines and took a course—rather casually, naturally, for she was, after all, a child with no strong purposes—and this year she tasted the first fruits of success by having her pictures accepted by the High School Annual. But the thrill of delight she got when Mr. Ecord, of the Normal Annual, asked her to do the cartooning for that book this spring, was too beautiful for words. She fell to her work with all her enthusiastic heart. Her drawings were accepted, and her pride—always repressed by a lively sense of the ridiculousness of the figure she was cutting—was a really gorgeous thing to see. No successful artist ever drank a deeper draught of satisfaction than she took from the little fame her work was getting among her schoolfellows. In her glory, she almost forgot her horse—but never her car.

For she used the car as a jitney bus. It was her social life. She never had a "party" in all her nearly seventeen years—wouldn't have one; but she never drove a block in the car in her life that she didn't begin to fill the car with pick-ups! Everybody rode with Mary White—white and black, old and young, rich and poor, men and women. She liked nothing better than to fill the car full of long-legged High School boys and an occasional girl, and parade the town. She never had a "date," nor went to a dance, except once with her brother, Bill, and the "boy proposition" didn't interest her—yet. But young people—great spring-breaking, varnish-cracking, fender-bending, door-sagging carloads of "kids" gave her great pleasure. Her zests were keen. But the most fun she ever had in her life was acting as chairman of the committee that got up the big turkey dinner for the poor folks at the county home; scores of pies, gallons of slaw; jam, cakes, preserves, oranges and a wilderness of turkey were loaded in the car and taken to the county home. And, being of a practical turn of mind, she risked her own Christmas dinner by staying to see that the poor folks actually got it all. Not that she was a cynic; she just disliked to tempt folks. While there she found a blind colored uncle, very old, who could do nothing but make rag rugs, and she rustled up from her school friends rags enough to keep him busy for a season. The last engagement she tried to make was to take the guests at the county home out for a car ride. And the last endeavor of her life was to try to get a rest room for colored girls in the High School. She found one girl reading in the toilet, because there was no better place for a colored girl to loaf, and it inflamed her sense of injustice and she became a nagging harpie to those who, she thought, could remedy the evil. The poor she had always with her, and was glad of it. She hungered and thirsted for righteousness; and was the most impious creature in the world. She joined the Congregational Church without consulting her parents; not particularly for her soul's good. She never had a thrill of piety in her life, and would have hooted at a "testimony." But even as a little child she felt the church was an agency for helping people to more of life's abundance, and she wanted to help. She never wanted help for herself. Clothes meant little to her. It was a fight to get a new rig on her; but eventually a harder fight to get it off. She never wore a jewel and had no ring but her High School class ring, and never asked for anything but a wrist watch. She refused to have her hair up; though she was nearly seventeen. "Mother," she protested, "you don't know how much I get by with, in my braided pigtails, that I could not with my hair up." Above every other passion of her life was her passion not to grow up, to be a child. The tomboy in her, which was big, seemed to loathe to be put away forever in skirts. She was a Peter Pan, who refused to grow up.

Her funeral yesterday at the Congregational Church was as she would have wished it; no singing, no flowers save the big bunch of red roses from her Brother Bill's Harvard classmen—Heavens, how proud that would have made her! and the red roses from the *Gazette* force—in vases at her head and feet. A short prayer, Paul's beautiful essay on "Love" from the Thirteenth Chapter of First Corinthians, some remarks about her democratic spirit by her friend, John H. J. Rice, pastor and police judge, which she would have deprecated if she could, a prayer sent down for her by her friend, Carl Nau, and opening the service the slow, poignant movement from Beethoven's Moonlight Sonata, which she loved, and closing the service a cutting from a joyously melancholy first movement of Tschaikowski's Pathetic Symphony, which she liked to hear in certain moods on the phonograph; then the Lord's Prayer by her friends in the High School.

That was all.

For her pall-bearers only her friends were chosen: her Latin teacher, W. L. Holtz; her High School principal, Rice Brown; her doctor, Frank Foncannon; her friend, W. W. Finney; her pal at the *Gazette* office, Walter Hughes; and her brother Bill. It would have made her smile to know that her friend, Charley O'Brien, the traffic cop, had been transferred from Sixth and Commercial to the corner near the church to direct her friends who came to bid her good-bye.

A rift in the clouds in a gray day threw a shaft of sunlight upon her coffin as her nervous, energetic little body sank to its last sleep. But the soul of her, the glowing, gorgeous, fervent soul of her, surely was flaming in eager joy upon some other dawn.

EDWIN ARLINGTON ROBINSON

Old King Cole

In Tilbury Town did Old King Cole
A wise old age anticipate,
Desiring, with his pipe and bowl,
No Khan's extravagant estate.
No crown annoyed his honest head,
No fiddlers three were called or needed;
For two disastrous heirs instead
Made music more than ever three did.

Bereft of her with whom his life
Was harmony without a flaw,
He took no other for a wife,
Nor sighed for any that he saw;
And if he doubted his two sons,
And heirs, Alexis and Evander,
He might have been as doubtful once
Of Robert Burns and Alexander.

Alexis, in his early youth,
Began to steal—from old and young.
Likewise Evander, and the truth
Was like a bad taste on his tongue.
Born thieves and liars, their affair
Seemed only to be tarred with evil—
The most insufferable pair
Of scamps that ever cheered the devil.

The world went on, their fame went on,
And they went on—from bad to worse;
Till, goaded hot with nothing done,
And each accoutred with a curse,
The friends of Old King Cole, by twos,
And fours, and sevens, and elevens,
Pronounced unalterable views
Of doings that were not of heaven's.

And having learned again whereby
Their baleful zeal had come about,
King Cole met many a wrathful eye
So kindly that its wrath went out—
Or partly out. Say what they would,
He seemed the more to court their candor;
But never told what kind of good
Was in Alexis and Evander.

And Old King Cole, with many a puff
That haloed his urbanity,
Would smoke till he had smoked enough,
And listen most attentively.
He beamed as with an inward light
That had the Lord's assurance in it;
And once a man was there all night,
Expecting something every minute.

But whether from too little thought,
Or too much fealty to the bowl,
A dim reward was all he got
For sitting up with Old King Cole.
"Though mine," the father mused aloud,
"Are not the sons I would have chosen,
Shall I, less evilly endowed,
By their infirmity be frozen?

"They'll have a bad end, I'll agree,
But I was never born to groan;
For I can see what I can see,
And I'm accordingly alone.
With open heart and open door,
I love my friends, I like my neighbors;
But if I try to tell you more,
Your doubts will overmatch my labors.

"This pipe would never make me calm,
This bowl my grief would never drown.
For grief like mine there is no balm
In Gilead, or in Tilbury Town.
And if I see what I can see,
I know not any way to blind it;
Nor more if any way may be
For you to grope or fly to find it.

"There may be room for ruin yet,
And ashes for a wasted love;
Or, like One whom you may forget,
I may have meat you know not of.
And if I'd rather live than weep
Meanwhile, do you find that surprising?
Why, bless my soul, the man's asleep!
That's good. The sun will soon be rising."

STEPHEN LEACOCK

My Financial Career

When I go into a bank I get rattled. The clerks rattle me; the wickets rattle me; the sight of the money rattles me; everything rattles me.

The moment I cross the threshold of a bank and attempt to transact business there, I become an irresponsible idiot.

I knew this beforehand, but my salary had been raised to fifty dollars a month and I felt that the bank was the only place for it.

So I shambled in and looked timidly round at the clerks. I had an idea that a person about to open an account must needs consult the manager.

I went up to a wicket marked "Accountant." The accountant was a tall, cool devil. The very sight of him rattled me. My voice was sepulchral.

"Can I see the manager?" I said, and added solemnly, "alone." I don't know why I said "alone."

"Certainly," said the accountant, and fetched him.

The manager was a grave, calm man. I held my fifty-six dollars clutched in a crumpled ball in my pocket.

"Are you the manager?" I said. God knows I didn't doubt it.

"Yes," he said.

"Can I see you," I asked, "alone?" I didn't want to say "alone" again, but without it the thing seemed self-evident.

The manager looked at me in some alarm. He felt that I had an awful secret to reveal.

"Come in here," he said, and led the way to a private room. He turned the key in the lock.

"We are safe from interruption here," he said; "sit down."

We both sat down and looked at each other. I found no voice to speak.

"You are one of Pinkerton's men, I presume," he said.

He had gathered from my mysterious manner that I was a detective. I knew what he was thinking, and it made me worse.

"No, not from Pinkerton's," I said, seeming to imply that I came from a rival agency.

"To tell the truth," I went on, as if I had been prompted to lie about it, "I am not a detective at all. I have come to open an account. I intend to keep all my money in this bank."

The manager looked relieved but still serious; he concluded now that I was a son of Baron Rothschild or a young Gould.

"A large account, I suppose," he said.

"Fairly large," I whispered. "I propose to deposit fifty-six dollars now and fifty dollars a month regularly."

The manager got up and opened the door. He called to the accountant.

"Mr. Montgomery," he said unkindly loud, "this gentleman is opening an account, he will deposit fifty-six dollars. Good morning."

I rose.

A big iron door stood open at the side of the room.

"Good morning," I said, and stepped into the safe.

"Come out," said the manager coldly, and showed me the other way.

I went up to the accountant's wicket and poked the ball of money at him with a quick convulsive movement as if I were doing a conjuring trick.

My face was ghastly pale.

"Here," I said, "deposit it." The tone of the words seemed to mean, "Let us do this painful thing while the fit is on us."

He took the money and gave it to another clerk.

He made me write the sum on a slip and sign my name in a book. I no longer knew what I was doing. The bank swam before my eyes.

"Is it deposited?" I asked in a hollow, vibrating voice.

"It is," said the accountant.

"Then I want to draw a cheque."

My idea was to draw out six dollars of it for present use. Some one gave me a cheque-book through a wicket and some one else began telling me how to write it out. The people in the bank had the impression that I was an invalid millionaire. I wrote something on the cheque and thrust it in at the clerk. He looked at it.

"What! Are you drawing it all out again?" he asked in surprise. Then I realized that I had written fifty-six instead of six. I was too far gone to reason now. I had a feeling that it was impossible to explain the thing. All the clerks had stopped writing to look at me.

Reckless with misery, I made a plunge.

"Yes, the whole thing."

"You withdraw your money from the bank?"

"Every cent of it."

"Are you not going to deposit any more?" said the clerk, astonished.

"Never."

An idiot hope struck me that they might think something had insulted me while I was writing the cheque and that I had changed my mind. I made a wretched attempt to look like a man with a fearfully quick temper.

The clerk prepared to pay the money.

"How will you have it?" he said.

"What?"

"How will you have it?"

"Oh"—I caught his meaning and answered without even trying to think—"in fifties."

He gave me a fifty-dollar bill.

"And the six?" he asked dryly.

"In sixes," I said.

He gave it me and I rushed out.

As the big door swung behind me I caught the echo of a roar of laughter that went up to the ceiling of the bank. Since then I bank no more. I keep my money in cash in my trousers pocket and my savings in silver dollars in a sock.

Madeline of the Movies

A Photoplay Done Back into the Words

(Explanatory Note.—In writing this I ought to explain that I am a tottering old man of forty-six. I was born too soon to understand moving pictures. They go too fast. I can't keep up. In my young days we used a magic lantern. It showed Robinson Crusoe in six scenes. It took all evening to show them. When it was done the hall was filled with black smoke and the audience quite unstrung with excitement. What I set down here represents my thoughts as I sit in front of a moving picture photoplay and interpret it as best I can.)

Flick, flick, flick . . . I guess it must be going to begin now, but it's queer the people don't stop talking: how can they expect to hear the pictures if they go on talking?

Now it's off. Passed by the Board of ——. Ah, this looks interesting—passed by the board of—wait till I adjust my spectacles and read what it——

It's gone. Never mind, here's something else, let me see—Cast of Characters—Oh, yes—let's see who they are—Madeline Meadowlark, a young something—Edward Dangerfield, a—a what? Ah, yes, a roo—at least, it's spelt r-o-u-e, that must be roo all right—But wait till I see what that is that's written across the top—MADELINE MEADOWLARK; OR, ALONE IN A GREAT CITY. I see, that's the title of it. I wonder which of the characters is alone. I guess not Madeline: she'd hardly be alone in a place like that. I imagine it's more likely Edward Dangerous the Roo. A roo would probably be alone a great deal, I should think. Let's see what the other characters are—JOHN HOLDFAST, a something; FARMER MEADOWLARK, MRS. MEADOWLARK, his something——

Pshaw, I missed the others, but never mind; flick, flick, it's beginning—What's this? A bedroom, eh! Looks like a girl's bedroom—pretty poor sort of place. I wish the picture would keep still a minute—in Robinson Crusoe it all stayed still and one could sit and look at it, the blue sea and the green palm trees and the black footprints in the yellow sand—but this blamed thing keeps rippling and flickering all the time— Ha! there's the girl herself—come into her bedroom. My! I hope she doesn't start to undress in it—that would be fearfully uncomfortable with all these people here. No, she's not undressing—she's gone and opened the cupboard. What's that she's doing—taking out a milk-jug and a glass—empty, eh? I guess it must be, because she seemed to hold it upside down. Now she's picked up a sugar bowl—empty, too, eh?—and a cake tin, and that's empty— What on earth does she take them all out for if they're empty? Why can't she speak? I think—hullo—who's this coming in? Pretty hard looking sort of woman—what's she got in her hand?—some sort of paper, I guess—she looks like a landlady, I shouldn't wonder if . . .

Flick, flick! Say! Look there on the screen:

YOU OWE ME THREE WEEKS' RENT.

Oh, I catch on! That's what the landlady says, eh? Say! that's a mighty smart way to indicate it, isn't it? I was on to that in a minute—flick, flick—hullo, the landlady's vanished—what's the girl doing now—say, she's praying! Look at her face! Doesn't she look religious, eh?

Flick, flick!

Oh, look, they've put her face, all by itself, on the screen. My! what a big face she's got when you see it like that.

She's in her room again—she's taking off her jacket—by Gee! She *is* going to bed! Here, stop the machine; it doesn't seem——Flick, flick!

Well, look at that! She's in bed, all in one flick, and fast asleep!

Something must have broken in the machine and missed out a chunk. There! she's asleep all right—looks as if she was dreaming. Now it's sort of fading. I wonder how they make it do that? I guess they turn the wick of the lamp down low: that was the way in Robinson Crusoe—— Flick, flick!

Hullo! where on earth is this—farmhouse, I guess—must be away upstate somewhere—who on earth are these people? Old man—white whiskers—old lady at a spinning-wheel—see it go, eh? Just like real! And a young man—that must be John Holdfast—and a girl with her hand in his. Why! Say! it's the girl, the same girl, Madeline—only what's she doing away off here at this farm—how did she get clean back from the bedroom to this farm? Flick, flick! What's this?

NO, JOHN, I CANNOT MARRY YOU.
I MUST DEVOTE MY LIFE
TO MY MUSIC.

Who says that? What music? Here, stop——

It's all gone. What's this new place? Flick, flick, looks like a street. Say! see the street-car coming along—well! say! isn't that great? A street-car! And here's Madeline. How on earth did she get back from the old farm all in a second? Got her street things on—that must be music under her arm—I wonder where—hullo—who's this man in a silk hat and swell coat? Gee! he's well dressed. See him roll his eyes at Madeline! He's lifting his hat—I guess he must be Edward Something, the Roo—only a roo could dress as well as he does—he's going to speak to her——

SIR, I DO NOT KNOW YOU. LET ME PASS.

Oh, I see! The Roo mistook her; he thought she was somebody that he knew! And she wasn't! I catch on! It gets easy to understand these pictures once you're on.

Flick, flick—— Oh, say, stop! I missed a piece—where is she? Outside a street door—she's pausing a moment outside—that was lucky her pausing like that—it just gave me time to read EMPLOYMENT BUREAU on the door. Gee! I read it quick.

Flick, flick! Where is it now?—oh, I see, she's gone in—she's in there—this must be the Bureau, eh? There's Madeline going up to a desk.

NO, WE HAVE TOLD YOU BEFORE WE HAVE NOTHING . . .

Pshaw! I read too slow—she's on the street again. Flick, flick!

No, she isn't—she's back in her room—cupboard still empty—no milk—no sugar——Flick, flick!

Kneeling down to pray—my! but she's religious—flick, flick—now she's on the street—got a letter in her hand—what's the address——Flick, flick!

Mr. Meadowlark
Meadow Farm
Meadow County
New York

Gee! They've put it right on the screen! The whole letter!

Flick, flick—here's Madeline again on the street with the letter still in her hand—she's gone to a letter box with it—why doesn't she post it? What's stopping her?

I CANNOT TELL THEM OF MY FAILURE. IT WOULD BREAK THEIR . . .

Break their what? They slide these things along altogether too quick—anyway, she won't post it—I see—she's torn it up—— Flick, flick!

Where is it now? Another street—seems like evening—that's a restaurant, I guess—say, it looks a swell place—see the people getting out of the motor and going in—and another lot right after them—there's Madeline—she's stopped outside the window—she's looking in—it's starting to snow! Hullo! here's a man coming along! Why, it's the Roo; he's stopping to talk to her, and pointing in at the restaurant—— Flick, flick!

LET ME TAKE YOU IN HERE TO DINNER.

Oh, I see! The Roo says that! My! I'm getting on to the scheme of these things—the Roo is going to buy her some dinner! That's decent of him. He must have heard about her being hungry up in her room—say, I'm glad he came along. Look, there's a waiter come out to the door to show them in—what! she won't go! Say! I don't understand! Didn't it say he offered to take her in? Flick, flick!

I WOULD RATHER DIE THAN EAT IT.

Gee! Why's that? What are all the audience applauding for? I must have missed something! Flick, flick!

Oh, blazes! I'm getting lost! Where is she now? Back in her room—flick, flick—praying—flick, flick! She's out on the street!—flick, flick!—in the employment bureau—flick, flick!—out of it—flick—darn the thing! It changes too much—where is it all? What is it all——? Flick, flick!

Now it's back at the old farm—I understand that all right, anyway! Same kitchen—same old man—same old woman—she's crying—who's this?—man in a sort of uniform—oh, I see, rural postal delivery—oh, yes, he brings them their letters—I see——

NO, MR. MEADOWLARK, I AM SORRY, I HAVE STILL NO LETTER FOR YOU . . .

Flick! It's gone! Flick, flick—it's Madeline's room again—what's she doing?—writing a letter?—no, she's quit writing—she's tearing it up——

I CANNOT WRITE. IT WOULD BREAK THEIR . . .

Flick—missed it again! Break their something or other—— Flick, flick!

Now it's the farm again—oh, yes, that's the young man John Holdfast—he's got a valise in his hand—he must be going away—they're shaking hands with him—he's saying something——

I WILL FIND HER FOR YOU IF I HAVE TO SEARCH ALL NEW YORK.

He's off—there he goes through the gate—they're waving good-bye—flick—it's a railway depot—flick—it's New York—say! That's the Grand Central Depot! See the people buying tickets! My! isn't it life-like?—and there's John—he's got here all right—I hope he finds her room——

The picture's changed—where is it now? Oh, yes, I see—Madeline and the Roo—outside a street entrance to some place—he's trying to get her to come in—what's that on the door? Oh, yes, DANCE HALL——Flick, flick!

Well, say, that must be the inside of the dance hall—they're dancing—see, look, look, there's one of the girls going to get up and dance on the table.

Flick! Darn it!—they've cut it off—it's outside again—it's Madeline and the Roo—she's saying something to him—my! doesn't she look proud——?

I WILL DIE RATHER THAN DANCE.

Isn't she splendid? Hear the audience applaud! Flick—it's changed—it's Madeline's room again—that's the landlady—doesn't she look hard, eh? What's this—— Flick!

IF YOU CANNOT PAY YOU MUST LEAVE TO-NIGHT.

Flick, flick—it's Madeline—she's out in the street—it's snowing—she's sat down on a doorstep—say, see her face, isn't it pathetic? There! they've put her face all by itself on the screen. See her eyes move! Flick, flick!

Who's this? Where is it? Oh, yes, I get it—it's John—at a police station—he's questioning them—how grave they look, eh? Flick, flick!

HAVE YOU SEEN A GIRL IN NEW YORK?

I guess that's what he asks them, eh? Flick, flick——

NO, WE HAVE NOT.

Too bad—flick—it's changed again—it's Madeline on the doorstep —she's fallen asleep—oh, say, look at that man coming near to her on tiptoes, and peeking at her—why, it's Edward, it's the Roo—but he doesn't waken her—what does it mean? What's he after? Flick, flick——

Hullo—what's this?—it's night—what's this huge dark thing all steel—with great ropes against the sky—it's Brooklyn Bridge—at midnight—there's a woman on it! It's Madeline—see! see! She's going to jump—stop her! Stop her! Flick, flick——

Hullo! she didn't jump after all—there she is again on the doorstep—asleep—how could she jump over Brooklyn Bridge and still be asleep?—I don't catch on—or, oh, yes, I do—she *dreamed* it—I see now, that's a great scheme, eh?—shows her *dream*——

The picture's changed—what's this place—a saloon, I guess—yes, there's the bartender, mixing drinks—men talking at little tables—aren't they a tough-looking lot?—see, that one's got a revolver—why, it's Edward the Roo—talking with two men—he's giving them money —what's this?——

GIVE US A HUNDRED APIECE AND WE'LL DO IT.

It's in the street again—Edward and one of the two toughs—they've got little black masks on—they're sneaking up to Madeline where she sleeps—they've got a big motor drawn up beside them—look, they've grabbed hold of Madeline—they're lifting her into the motor—help! Stop! Aren't there any police?—yes, yes, there's a man who sees it—by Gee! It's John, John Holdfast—grab them, John —pshaw! they've jumped into the motor, they're off!

Where is it now?—oh, yes—it's the police station again—that's John; he's telling them about it—he's all out of breath—look, that head man, the big fellow, he's giving orders——

INSPECTOR FORDYCE, TAKE YOUR BIGGEST CAR AND TEN MEN. IF YOU OVERTAKE THEM, SHOOT AND SHOOT TO KILL.

Hoorah! Isn't it great—hurry! don't lose a minute—see them all buckling on revolvers—get at it, boys, get at it! Don't lose a second——

Look, look—it's a motor—full speed down the street—look at the houses fly past—it's the motor with the thugs—there it goes round the corner—it's getting smaller, it's getting smaller, but look, here comes another—my! it's just flying—it's full of police—there's John in front—— Flick!

Now it's the first motor—it's going over a bridge—it's heading for the country—say, isn't that car just flying—— Flick, flick!

It's the second motor—it's crossing the bridge too—hurry, boys, make it go!—— Flick, flick!

Out in the country—a country road—early daylight—see the wind in the trees! Notice the branches waving? Isn't it natural?—whiz! Biff! There goes the motor—biff! There goes the other one—right after it—hoorah!

The open road again—the first motor flying along! Hullo, what's wrong? It's slackened, it stops—hoorah! it's broken down—there's Madeline inside—there's Edward the Roo! Say, isn't he pale and desperate!

Hoorah! the police! the police! all ten of them in their big car—see them jumping out—see them pile into the thugs! Down with them! Paste their heads off! Shoot them! Kill them! Isn't it great—isn't it educative—that's the Roo—Edward—with John at his throat! Choke him, John! Throttle him!

Hullo, it's changed—they're in the big motor—that's the Roo with the handcuffs on him.

That's Madeline—she's unbound and she's talking; say, isn't she just real pretty when she smiles?

YES, JOHN, I HAVE LEARNED THAT I WAS WRONG TO PUT MY ART BEFORE YOUR LOVE. I WILL MARRY YOU AS SOON AS YOU LIKE.

Flick, flick!

What pretty music! Ding! Dong! Ding! Dong! Isn't it soft and sweet!—like wedding bells. Oh, I see, the man in the orchestra's doing it with a little triangle and a stick—it's a little church up in the country—see all the people lined up—oh! there's Madeline! in a long white veil—isn't she just sweet!—and John——

Flick, flack, flick, flack.

BULGARIAN TROOPS ON THE MARCH.

What! Isn't it over? Do they all go to Bulgaria? I don't seem to understand. Anyway, I guess it's all right to go now. Other people are going.

GRETCHEN WARREN

The Garden

A MAN there was, of simple kind,
Who to the Lord gave all his mind.

For naught he cared, naught craved he,
Save his Lord's servant for to be,

And e'en his garden plot kept fair
Because, he said, the Lord walked there.

Of this his friends made many a jest,
Yet he toiled on with heart at rest.

The years went by. His head grown gray,
Still he believed Christ passed that way.

Then came a time when he was left
Of loving wife and child bereft.

"He will doubt now," the scoffers said,
"When wife and child and love are dead."

But all their words he heeded not,
And tended still the garden plot.

At last himself lay at death's door,
To love, believe and work no more.

His pitying friends stood by his bed,
And this is what to them he said:

"O bury me not in a church-yard mound
But lay me in my garden ground;

"From loving dust it needs must be
That flowers will spring more fair to see,

"And Christ will know, in my last sleep,
For Him I still the garden keep."

GUY WETMORE CARRYL

From LITTLE TAPIN

Little Jean-Marie-Michel Jumière had been drafted from the Breton village of Plougastel—away from home and from his Little Mother and his beloved Rosalie; not into the navy as he had hoped, but into the infantry. In the barracks at Paris he was unhappy. Learning to drum was no great hardship to Jean-Marie, or Little Tapin, as he was called. It was something at least to be in the open air. And he was the first to be assigned a place in the regimental band. "What cramped and crushed his tiny little heart, what clouded his queer, quizzical eyes, was nothing less than Paris, beautiful, careless Paris, that laughed, and danced, and sang about him, and had never a thought for Little Tapin, with his funny freckled face, and his ill-fitting uniform of red and blue, and his coarse boots, and his ineradicable Breton stare." He formed a plan to desert and return to Plougastel.

One day, for the third time since joining the regiment, Little Tapin was detailed as drummer to the guard at the Palace du Louvre. At seven o'clock he was ordered to go and drum the belated voyons out of the garden. Marching to the end of the garden, he stood for a moment, deep in his dream of Plougastel.

The Army of France

THE mid-August afternoon had been oppressively warm, and now a thin haze had risen from the wet wood pavement of the Place de la Concorde, and hovered low, pink in the light of the setting sun. Directly before Little Tapin the obelisk raised its warning finger, and beyond, the Champs Elysées, thickly dotted with carriages, and half veiled by great splotches of ruddy-yellow dust, swept away in a long, upward curve toward the distant Arc de l'Etoile.

But of all this Little Tapin saw nothing. He stood very still, with his back to the basin, where the fat goldfish went to and fro like lazy sentinels, on the watch for a possible belated little boy, with a pocket full of crumbs. He was still deep in his dream of Plougastel, so deep that he could almost smell the salt breeze rollicking in from the Goulet, and hear the chapel bell sending the Angelus out over the strawberry fields and the rock-dotted hillside.

After a minute, something—a teamster's shout, or the snap of a cocher's whip—roused him, and he glanced around with the same half-sensation of terror with which he had wakened in the night to hear the guards shouting "Le Mans!" and "Chartres!" Then the reality came back to him with a rush, and he grumbled to himself. Oh, it was all very well, the wonderful French army, all very well if one could have been a marshal or a general, or even a soldier of the line in time of war. There was a chance for glory, *bon sang!* But to be a drummer—a drummer one metre seventy in height, with flaming red hair and a freckled face—a drummer who was called Little Tapin; and to have, for one's most important duty, to drum the loungers out of a public garden! No, evidently he would desert.

"But why?" said a grave voice beside him.

Little Tapin was greatly startled. He had not thought he was saying the words aloud. And his fear increased when, on turning to see who had spoken, he found himself looking into the eyes of one who was evidently an officer, though his uniform was unfamiliar. He was plain-shaven and very short, almost as short, indeed, as Little Tapin himself, but about him there was a something of dignity and command which could not fail of its effect. He wore a great black hat like a gendarme's, but without trimming, and a blue coat with a white plastron, the tails lined with scarlet, and the sleeves ending in red and white cuffs. White breeches, and knee-boots carefully polished, completed the uniform, and from over his right shoulder a broad band of crimson silk was drawn tightly across his breast. A short sword hung straight at his hip, and on his left breast were three orders on red ribbons,—a great star, with an eagle in the centre, backed by a sunburst studded with brilliants; another eagle, this one of white enamel, pendant from a jeweled crown, and a smaller star of enameled white and green, similar to the large one.

Little Tapin had barely mastered these details when the other spoke again.

"Why art thou thinking to desert?" he said.

"Monsieur is an officer?" faltered the drummer,—"a general, perhaps. Pardon, but I do not know the uniform."

"A corporal, simply—a soldier of France, like thyself. Be not afraid, my little one. All thou sayest shall be held in confidence. Tell me thy difficulties."

His voice was very kind, the kindest Little Tapin had heard in three long months, and suddenly the barrier of his Breton reserve gave and broke. The nervous strain had been too great. He must have sympathy and advice—yes, even though it meant confiding in a stranger and the possible discovery and failure of his dearly cherished plans.

"A soldier of France!" he exclaimed, impulsively. "Ah, monsieur, there you have all my difficulty. What a thing it is to be a soldier of France! And not even that, but a drummer, a drummer who is called Little Tapin because he is the smallest and weakest in the corps. To be taken from home, from the country he loves, from Brittany, and made to serve among men who despise him, who laugh at him, who avoid him in the hours of leave, because he is not *bon camarade*. To wear a uniform that has been already worn. To sleep in a dormitory where there are *bêtes funestes*. To have no friends. To know that he is not to see Plougastel, and the sweetheart, and the Little Mother for three years. Never to fight, but, at best, to drum *voyous* out of a garden! That, monsieur, is what it is to be a soldier of France!"

There were tears in Little Tapin's eyes now, but he was more angry than sad. The silence of months was broken, and the hoarded resentment and despair of his long martyrdom, once given rein, were not to be checked a second time. He threw back his narrow shoulders defiantly, and said a hideous thing:—

"Conspuez l'armée française!"

There was an instant's pause, and then the other leaned forward, and with one white-gloved hand touched Little Tapin on the eyes.

. . . .

Before them a great plain, sloping very gradually upward in all directions, like a vast, shallow amphitheatre, spread away in a long series of low terraces to where, in the dim distance, the peaks of a range of purple hills nicked and notched a sky of palest turquoise. From where they stood, upon a slight elevation, the details of even the farthest slopes seemed singularly clean-cut and distinct,—the groups of grey willows; the poplars, standing stiffly in twos and threes; the short silver reaches of a little river, lying in the hollows where the land occasionally dipped; at long intervals, a whitewashed cottage, gleaming like a sail against this sea of green; even, on the most distant swell of all, a herd of ruddy cattle, moving slowly up toward the crest,—each and all of these, although in merest miniature, as clear and vivid in form and color as if they had been the careful creations of a Claude Lorrain.

Directly before the knoll upon which they were stationed, a wide road, dazzling white in the sunlight, swept in a superb full curve from left to right, and on its farther side the ground was covered with close-cropped turf, and completely empty for a distance of two hundred metres. But beyond! Beyond, every hectare of the great semicircle was occupied by dense masses of cavalry, infantry, and artillery, regiment upon regiment, division upon division, corps upon corps, an innumerable multitude, motionless, as if carved out of many-colored marbles!

In some curious, unaccountable fashion, Little Tapin seemed to know all these by name. There, to the left, were the *chasseurs à pied,* the huge bearskins flecked with red and green pompons, and their white cross-belts slashed like capital X's against the blue of their tunics; there, beside them, the foot artillery, a long row of metal collar plates, like dots of gold, and gold trappings against dark blue; to the right, the Garde Royale Hollandaise, in brilliant crimson and white; in the centre, the infantry of the Guard, with tall, straight pompons, red above white, and square black shakos, trimmed with scarlet cord.

Close at hand, surrounding Little Tapin and his companion, were the most brilliant figures of the scene, and these, too, he seemed to know by name. None was missing. Prince Murat, in a cream-white uniform blazing with gold embroidery, and with a scarlet ribbon across his breast; a group of marshals, Ney, Oudinot, Duroc, Macdonald, Augereau, and Soult, with their yellow sashes, and cocked hats laced with gold; a score of generals, Larouche, Durosnel, Marmont, Letort, Henrion, Chasteller, and the rest, with white instead of gold upon their hats,—clean-shaven, severe of brow and lip-line, they stood without movement, their gauntleted hands upon their sword-hilts, gazing straight before them.

Little Tapin drew a deep breath.

Suddenly from somewhere came a short, sharp bugle note, and instantly the air was full of the sound of hoofs, and the ring of scabbards and stirrup-irons, and the wide white road before them alive with flying cavalry. Squadron after squadron, they thundered by: mounted chasseurs, with pendants of orange-colored cloth fluttering from their shakos, and plaits of powdered hair bobbing at their cheeks; Polish light horse, with metal sunbursts gleaming on their square-topped helmets, and crimson and white pennons snapping in the wind at the points of their lances; Old Guard cavalry, with curving helmets like Roman legionaries; Mamelukes, with full red trousers, white and scarlet turbans, strange standards of horsehair surmounted by the imperial eagle, brazen stirrups singularly fashioned, and horse trappings of silver with flying crimson tassels; Horse Chasseurs of the Guard, in hussar tunics and yellow breeches, their *sabretaches* swinging as they rode; and Red Lancers, in gay uniforms of green and scarlet. Like a whirlwind they went past,—each squadron, in turn, wheeling to the left, and coming to a halt in the open space beyond the road, until the last lancer swept by.

A thick cloud of white dust, stirred into being by the flying horses, now hung between the army and the knoll, and through this one saw dimly the mounted band of the 20th Chasseurs, on gray stallions, occupying the centre of the line, and heard, what before had been drowned by the thunder of hoofs, the strains of "Partant pour la Syrie."

Slowly, slowly, the dust cloud thinned and lifted, so slowly that it seemed as if it would never wholly clear. But, on a sudden, a sharp puff of wind sent it whirling off in arabesques to the left, and the whole plain lay revealed.

"Bon Dieu!" said Little Tapin.

The first rank of cavalry was stationed within a metre of the farther border of the road, the line sweeping off to the left and right until details became indistinguishable. And beyond, reaching away in a solid mass, the vast host dwindled and dwindled, back to where the ascending slopes were broken by the distant willows and the reaches of the silver stream. With snowy white of breeches and plastrons, with lustre of scarlet velvet and gold lace, with sparkle of helmet and cuirass, and dull black of bearskin and smoothly groomed flanks, the army blazed and glowed in the golden sunlight like a mosaic of a hundred thousand jewels. Silent, expectant, the legions flashed crimson, emerald, and sapphire, rolling away in broad swells of light and color, motionless save for a long, slow heave, as of the ocean, lying, vividly iridescent, under the last rays of the setting sun. Then, without warning, as if the touch of a magician's wand had roused the multitude to life, a myriad sabres swept twinkling from their scabbards, and, by tens of thousands, the guns of the infantry snapped with a sharp click to a "present arms." The bugles sounded all along the line, the tricolors dipped until their golden fringes almost swept the ground, the troopers stood upright in their stirrups, their heads thrown back, their bronzed faces turned toward the knoll, their eyes blazing. And from the farthest slopes inward, like thunder that growls afar, and, coming nearer, swells into unbearable volume, a hoarse cry ran down the massed battalions and broke in a stupendous roar upon the shuddering air,—

"Vive l'empereur!"

. . . . . .

Little Tapin rubbed his eyes.

"I am ill," he murmured. "I have been faint. I seemed to see"—

"Thou hast seen," said the voice of his companion, very softly, very solemnly,—"thou hast seen simply what it is to be a soldier of France!"

His hand rested an instant on the drummer's shoulder, with the ghost of a caress.

"My little one," he added, tenderly, "forget not this. It matters nothing whether one is Emperor of the French or the smallest drummer of the corps, whom men call 'Little Tapin.' I, too, was called 'little'' in the time—'The Little Corporal' they called me, from Moscow to the Loire. But it is all the same. Chief of the army, drummer of the corps, on the field of battle, in the gardens of the Tuileries, routing the Prussians, or drumming out the *voyous,*—it is all the same, my little one, it is all the same. All that is necessary is to understand—to understand that it is all and always for *la belle France.* Empire or republic, in peace or war—what difference? It is still France, still the tricolor, still *l'armée française.*"

He lifted his hat, and looked steadily up at the sky, where the first stars were shouldering their way into view.

"Vive la France!" he added. And on his lips the phrase was like a prayer.

Through the Arc de l'Etoile the fading sunset looked back, as upon something it was loath to leave. Then Little Tapin flung back his head. There was a strange, new light in his eyes, and his breath came quickly, between parted lips. Without a word he swung upon his heels, slipped his drum into place, and marched steadily away, beating the long roll. Once, when he had gone a hundred metres, he looked back. The figure of the Little Corporal was still standing beside the basin, but now it was very thin and faint, like the dust clouds on the Champs Elysées. But, as the little drummer turned, it raised one hand to its forehead in salute.

Little Tapin stood motionless for an instant, and then he smiled, and, through the deepening twilight—

"Vive l'armée!" he shouted, shrilly. "Vive la France!"

ROBERT FROST

After Apple-Picking

My long two-pointed ladder's sticking through a tree
Toward heaven still,
And there's a barrel that I didn't fill
Beside it, and there may be two or three
Apples I didn't pick upon some bough.
But I am done with apple-picking now.
Essence of winter sleep is on the night,
The scent of apples: I am drowsing off.
I cannot rub the strangeness from my sight
I got from looking through a pane of glass
I skimmed this morning from the drinking trough
And held against the world of hoary grass.
It melted, and I let it fall and break.
But I was well
Upon my way to sleep before it fell,
And I could tell
What form my dreaming was about to take.
Magnified apples appear and disappear,
Stem end and blossom end,
And every fleck of russet showing clear.
My instep arch not only keeps the ache,
It keeps the pressure of a ladder-round.
I feel the ladder sway as the boughs bend.
And I keep hearing from the cellar bin
The rumbling sound
Of load on load of apples coming in.
For I have had too much
Of apple-picking: I am overtired
Of the great harvest I myself desired.
There were ten thousand thousand fruit to touch,
Cherish in hand, lift down, and not let fall.
For all
That struck the earth,
No matter if not bruised or spiked with stubble,
Went surely to the cider-apple heap
As of no worth.
One can see what will trouble
This sleep of mine, whatever sleep it is.
Were he not gone,
The woodchuck could say whether it's like his
Long sleep, as I describe its coming on,
Or just some human sleep.

The Wood-Pile

Out walking in the frozen swamp one grey day
I paused and said, "I will turn back from here.
No, I will go on farther—and we shall see."
The hard snow held me, save where now and then
One foot went down. The view was all in lines
Straight up and down of tall slim trees
Too much alike to mark or name a place by
So as to say for certain I was here
Or somewhere else: I was just far from home.
A small bird flew before me. He was careful
To put a tree between us when he lighted,
And say no word to tell me who he was
Who was so foolish as to think what *he* thought.
He thought that I was after him for a feather—
The white one in his tail; like one who takes
Everything said as personal to himself.
One flight out sideways would have undeceived him.
And then there was a pile of wood for which
I forgot him and let his little fear
Carry him off the way I might have gone,
Without so much as wishing him good-night.
He went behind it to make his last stand.
It was a cord of maple, cut and split

And piled—and measured, four by four by eight.
And not another like it could I see.
No runner tracks in this year's snow looped near it.
And it was older sure than this year's cutting,
Or even last year's or the year's before.
The wood was grey and the bark warping off it
And the pile somewhat sunken. Clematis
Had wound strings round and round it like a bundle.
What held it though on one side was a tree
Still growing, and on one a stake and prop,
These latter about to fall. I thought that only
Someone who lived in turning to fresh tasks
Could so forget his handiwork on which
He spent himself, the labor of his axe,
And leave it there far from a useful fireplace
To warm the frozen swamp as best it could
With the slow smokeless burning of decay.

The Runaway

ONCE when the sun of the year was beginning to fall
We stopped by a mountain pasture to say, "Whose colt?"
A little Morgan had one forefoot on the wall,
The other curled at his heart. He dipped his head
And snorted to us; and then he had to bolt.
We heard the muffled thunder when he fled
And we saw him or thought we saw him dim and grey
Like a shadow against the curtain of falling flakes.
We said, "The little fellow's afraid of the snow.
He isn't winter broken." "It isn't play
With the little fellow at all. He's running away.
I doubt if even his mother could tell him, 'Sakes,
It's only weather.' He'd think she didn't know.
Where is his mother? He can't be out alone."
And now he comes again with a clatter of stone
And mounts the wall again with whited eyes
And all his tail that isn't hair up straight.
He shudders his coat as if to throw off flies.
Whoever it is that leaves him out so late
When everything else has gone to stall and bin
Ought to be told to go and bring him in.

SHERWOOD ANDERSON

I'm a Fool

IT was a hard jolt for me, one of the most bitterest I ever had to face. And it all came about through my own foolishness, too. Even yet sometimes, when I think of it, I want to cry or swear or kick myself. Perhaps, even now, after all this time, there will be a kind of satisfaction in making myself look cheap by telling of it.

It began at three o'clock one October afternoon as I sat in the grand stand at the fall trotting and pacing meet at Sandusky, Ohio.

To tell the truth, I felt a little foolish that I should be sitting in the grand stand at all. During the summer before I had left my home town with Harry Whitehead and, with a nigger named Burt, had taken a job as swipe with one of the two horses Harry was campaigning through the fall race meets that year. Mother cried and my sister Mildred, who wanted to get a job as a school teacher in our town that fall, stormed and scolded about the house all during the week before I left. They both thought it something disgraceful that one of our family should take a place as a swipe with race horses. I've an idea Mildred thought my taking the place would stand in the way of her getting the job she'd been working so long for.

But after all I had to work, and there was no other work to be got. A big lumbering fellow of nineteen couldn't just hang around the house and I had got too big to mow people's lawns and sell newspapers. Little chaps who could get next to people's sympathies by their sizes were always getting jobs away from me. There was one fellow who kept saying to every one who wanted a lawn mowed or a cistern cleaned, that he was saving money to work his way through college, and I used to lay awake nights thinking up ways to injure him without being found out. I kept thinking of wagons running over him and bricks falling on his head as he walked along the street. But never mind him.

I got the place with Harry and I liked Burt fine. We got along splendid together. He was a big nigger with a lazy, sprawling body and soft, kind eyes, and when it came to a fight he could hit like Jack Johnson. He had Bucephalus, a big black pacing stallion that could do 2.09 or 2.10, if he had to, and I had a little gelding named Doctor Fritz that never lost a race all fall when Harry wanted him to win.

We set out from home late in July in a box car with the two horses and after that, until late November, we kept moving along to the race meets and the fairs. It was a peachy time for me, I'll say that. Sometimes now I think that boys who are raised regular in houses, and never have a fine nigger like Burt for best friend, and go to high schools and colleges, and never steal anything, or get drunk a little, or learn to swear from fellows who know how, or come walking up in front of a grand stand in their shirt sleeves and with dirty horsey pants on when the races are going on and the grand stand is full of people all dressed up— What's the use of talking about it? Such fellows don't know nothing at all. They've never had no opportunity.

But I did. Burt taught me how to rub down a horse and put the bandages on after a race and steam a horse out and a lot of valuable things for any man to know. He could wrap a bandage on a horse's leg so smooth that if it had been the same color you would think it was his skin, and I guess he'd have been a big driver, too, and got to the top like Murphy and Walter Cox and the others if he hadn't been black.

Gee whizz, it was fun. You got to a county seat town, maybe say on a Saturday or Sunday, and the fair began the next Tuesday and lasted until Friday afternoon. Doctor Fritz would be, say, in the 2.25 trot on Tuesday afternoon and on Thursday afternoon Bucephalus would knock 'em cold in the "free-for-all" pace. It left you a lot of time to hang around and listen to horse talk, and see Burt knock some yap cold that got too gay, and you'd find out about horses and men and pick up a lot of stuff you could use all the rest of your life, if you had some sense and salted down what you heard and felt and saw.

And then at the end of the week when the race meet was over, and Harry had run home to tend up to his livery stable business, you and Burt hitched the two horses to carts and drove slow and steady across the country, to the place for the next meeting, so as to not over-heat the horses, etc., etc., you know.

Gee whizz, Gosh a'mighty, the nice hickorynut and beechnut and oaks and other kinds of trees along the roads, all brown and red, and the good smells, and Burt singing a song that was called Deep River, and the country girls at the windows of houses and everything. You can stick your colleges up your nose for all me. I guess I know where I got my education.

Why, one of those little burgs of towns you come to on the way, say now on a Saturday afternoon, and Burt says, "let's lay up here." And you did.

And you took the horses to a livery stable and fed them, and you got your good clothes out of a box and put them on.

And the town was full of farmers gaping, because they could see you were race horse people, and the kids maybe never see a nigger before and was afraid and run away when the two of us walked down their main street.

And that was before prohibition and all that foolishness, and so you went into a saloon, the two of you, and all the yaps come and stood around, and there was always some one pretended he was horsey and knew things and spoke up and began asking questions, and all you did was to lie all you could about what horses you had, and I said I owned them, and then some fellow said "Will you have a drink of whiskey?" and Burt knocked his eye out the way he could say, off-hand like, "Oh well, all right, I'm agreeable to a little nip. I'll split a quart with you." Gee whizz.

But that isn't what I want to tell my story about. We got home late in November and I promised mother I'd quit the race horses for good. There's a lot of things you've got to promise a mother because she don't know any better.

And so, there not being any work in our town any more than when I left there to go to the races, I went off to Sandusky and got a pretty good place taking care of horses for a man who owned a teaming and delivery and storage and coal and real estate business there. It was a pretty good place with good eats, and a day off each week, and sleeping on a cot in a big barn, and mostly just shoveling in hay and oats to a lot of big good-enough skates of horses, that couldn't have trotted a race with a toad. I wasn't dissatisfied and I could send money home.

And then, as I started to tell you, the fall races come to Sandusky and I got the day off and I went. I left the job at noon and had on my good clothes and my new brown derby hat I'd just bought the Saturday before, and a stand-up collar.

First of all I went down-town and walked about with the dudes. I've always thought to myself, "put up a good front" and so I did it. I had forty dollars in my pocket and so I went into the West House, a big hotel, and walked up to the cigar stand. "Give me three twenty-five cent cigars," I said. There was a lot of horsemen and strangers and dressed-up people from other towns standing around in the lobby and in the bar, and I mingled amongst them. In the bar there was a fellow with a cane and a Windsor tie on, that it made me sick to look at him. I like a man to be a man and dress up, but not to go put on that kind of airs. So I pushed him aside, kind of rough, and had me a drink of whiskey. And then he looked at me, as though he thought maybe he'd get gay, but he changed his mind and didn't say anything. And then I had another drink of whiskey, just to show him something, and went out and had a hack out to the races, all to myself, and when I got there I bought myself the best seat I could get up in the grand stand, but didn't go in for any of these boxes. That's putting on too many airs.

And so there I was, sitting up in the grand stand as gay as you please and looking down on the swipes coming out with their horses, and with their dirty horsey pants on and the horse blankets swung over their shoulders, same as I had been doing all the year before. I liked one thing about the same as the other, sitting up there and feeling grand and being down there and looking up at the yaps and feeling grander and more important, too. One thing's about as good as another, if you take it just right. I've often said that.

Well, right in front of me, in the grand stand that day, there was a fellow with a couple of girls and they was about my age. The young fellow was a nice guy all right. He was the kind maybe that goes to college and then comes to be a lawyer or maybe a newspaper editor or something like that, but he wasn't stuck on himself. There are some of that kind are all right and he was one of the ones.

He had his sister with him and another girl and the sister looked around over his shoulder, accidental at first, not intending to start anything—she wasn't that kind—and her eyes and mine happened to meet.

You know how it is. Gee, she was a peach! She had on a soft dress, kind of a blue stuff and it looked carelessly made, but was well sewed and made and everything. I knew that much. I blushed when she looked right at me and so did she. She was the nicest girl I've ever seen in my life. She wasn't stuck on herself and she could talk proper grammar without being like a school teacher or something like that. What I mean is, she was O. K. I think maybe her father was well-to-do, but not rich enough to make her chesty because she was his daughter, as some are. Maybe he owned a drug store or a drygoods store in their home town, or something like that. She never told me and I never asked.

My own people are all O. K. too, when you come to that. My grandfather was Welsh and over in the old country in Wales he was— But never mind that.

The first heat of the first race come off and the young fellow setting there with the two girls left them and went down to make a bet. I knew what he was up to, but he didn't talk big and noisy and let every one around know he was a sport, as some do. He wasn't that kind. Well, he come back and I heard him tell the two girls what horse he'd bet on, and when the heat was trotted they all half got to their feet and acted in the excited, sweaty way people do when they've got money down on a race, and the horse they bet on is up there pretty close at the end, and they think maybe he'll come on with a rush, but he never does because he hasn't got the old juice in him, come right down to it.

And then, pretty soon, the horses came out for the 2.18 pace and there was a horse in it I knew. He was a horse Bob French had in his string but Bob didn't own him. He was a horse owned by a Mr. Mathers down at Marietta, Ohio.

This Mr. Mathers had a lot of money and owned some coal mines or something, and he had a swell place out in the country, and he was stuck on race horses, but was a Presbyterian or something, and I think more than likely his wife was one, too, maybe a stiffer one than himself. So he never raced his horses hisself, and the story round the Ohio race tracks was that when one of his horses got ready to go to the races he turned him over to Bob French and pretended to his wife he was sold.

So Bob had the horses and he did pretty much as he pleased and you can't blame Bob, at least, I never did. Sometimes he was out to win and sometimes he wasn't. I never cared much about that when I was swiping a horse. What I did want to know was that my horse had the speed and could go in front, if you wanted him to.

And, as I'm telling you, there was Bob in this race with one of Mr. Mathers' horses, named "About Ben Ahem" or something like that, and was fast as a streak. He was a gelding and had a mark of 2.21, but could step in .08 or .09.

Because when Burt and I were out, as I've told you, the year before, there was a nigger, Burt knew, worked for Mr. Mathers and we went out there one day when we didn't have no race on at the Marietta Fair and our boss Harry was gone home.

And so every one was gone to the fair but just this one nigger and he took us all through Mr. Mathers' swell house and he and Burt tapped a bottle of wine Mr. Mathers had hid in his bedroom, back in a closet, without his wife knowing, and he showed us this Ahem horse. Burt was always stuck on being a driver but didn't have much chance to get to the top, being a nigger, and he and the other nigger gulped that whole bottle of wine and Burt got a little lit up.

So the nigger let Burt take this About Ben Ahem and step him a mile in a track Mr. Mathers had all to himself, right there on the farm. And Mr. Mathers had one child, a daughter, kinda sick and not very good looking, and she came home and we had to hustle and get About Ben Ahem stuck back in the barn.

I'm only telling you to get everything straight. At Sandusky, that afternoon I was at the fair, this young fellow with the two girls was fussed, being with the girls and losing his bet. You know how a fellow is that way. One of them was his girl and the other his sister. I had figured that out.

"Gee whizz," I says to myself, "I'm going to give him the dope."

He was mighty nice when I touched him on the shoulder. He and the girls were nice to me right from the start and clear to the end. I'm not blaming them.

And so he leaned back and I gave him the dope on About Ben Ahem.

"Don't bet a cent on this first heat because he'll go like an oxen hitched to a plow, but when the first heat is over go right down and lay on your pile." That's what I told him.

Well, I never saw a fellow treat any one sweller. There was a fat man sitting beside the little girl, that had looked at me twice by this time, and I at her, and both blushing, and what did he do but have the nerve to turn and ask the fat man to get up and change places with me so I could set with his crowd.

Gee whizz, craps a'mighty. There I was. What a chump I was to go and get gay up there in the West House bar, and just because that dude was standing there with a cane and that kind of a necktie on, to go and get all balled up and drink that whiskey, just to show off.

Of course she would know, me sitting right beside her and letting her smell of my breath. I could have kicked myself right down out of that grand stand and all around that race track, and made a faster record than most of the skates of horses they had there that year.

Because that girl wasn't any mutt of a girl. What wouldn't I have give right then for a stick of chewing gum to chew, or a lozenger, or some liquorice, or most anything. I was glad I had those twenty-five cent cigars in my pocket and right away I gave that fellow one and lit one myself. Then that fat man got up and we changed places and there I was, plunked right down beside her.

They introduced themselves and the fellow's best girl he had with him was named Miss Elinor Woodbury, and her father was a manufacturer of barrels from a place called Tiffin, Ohio. And the fellow himself was named Wilbur Wessen and his sister was Miss Lucy Wessen.

I suppose it was their having such swell names got me off my trolley. A fellow, just because he has been a swipe with a race horse and works taking care of horses for a man in the teaming, delivery, and storage business, isn't any better or worse than any one else. I've often thought that, and said it too.

But you know how a fellow is. There's something in that kind of nice clothes, and the kind of nice eyes she had, and the way she had looked at me awhile before, over her brother's shoulder, and me looking back at her, and both of us blushing.

I couldn't show her up for a boob, could I?

I made a fool of myself, that's what I did. I said my name was Walter Mathers from Marietta, Ohio, and then I told all three of them the smashingest lie you ever heard. What I said was that my father owned the horse About Ben Ahem and that he had let him out to this Bob French for racing purposes, because our family was proud and had never gone into racing that way, in our own name, I mean. Then I had got started and they were all leaning over and listening, and Miss Lucy Wessen's eyes were shining, and I went the whole hog.

I told about our place down at Marietta, and about the big stables and the grand brick house we had on a hill, up above the Ohio River, but I knew enough not to do it in no bragging way. What I did was to start things and then let them drag the rest out of me. I acted just as reluctant to tell as I could. Our family hasn't got any barrel factory, and, since I've known us, we've always been pretty poor, but not asking anything of any one at that, and my grandfather, over in Wales—but never mind that.

We set there talking like we had known each other for years and years, and I went and told them that my father had been expecting maybe this Bob French wasn't on the square, and had sent me up to Sandusky on the sly to find out what I could.

And I bluffed it through I had found out all about the 2.18 pace, in which About Ben Ahem was to start.

I said he would lose the first heat by pacing like a lame cow and then he would come back and skin 'em alive after that. And to back up what I said I took thirty dollars out of my pocket and handed it to Mr. Wilbur Wessen and asked him, would he mind, after the first heat, to go down and place it on About Ben Ahem for whatever odds he could get. What I said was that I didn't want Bob French to see me and none of the swipes.

Sure enough the first heat come off and About Ben Ahem went off his stride, up the back stretch, and looked like a wooden horse or a sick one, and come in to be last. Then this Wilbur Wessen went down to the betting place under the grand stand and there I was with the two girls, and when that Miss Woodbury was looking the other way once, Lucy Wessen kinda, with her shoulder you know, kinda touched me. Not just tucking down, I don't mean. You know how a woman can do. They get close, but not getting gay either. You know what they do. Gee whizz.

And then they give me a jolt. What they had done, when I didn't know, was to get together, and they had decided Wilbur Wessen would bet fifty dollars, and the two girls had gone and put in ten dollars each of their own money, too. I was sick then, but I was sicker later.

About the gelding, About Ben Ahem, and their winning their money, I wasn't worried a lot about that. It come out O. K. Ahem stepped the next three heats like a bushel of spoiled eggs going to market before they could be found out, and Wilbur Wessen had got nine to two for the money. There was something else eating at me.

Because Wilbur come back, after he had bet the money, and after that he spent most of his time talking to that Miss Woodbury, and Lucy Wessen and I was left alone together like on a desert island. Gee, if I'd only been on the square or if there had been any way of getting myself on the square. There ain't any Walter Mathers, like I said to her and them, and there hasn't ever been one, but if there was, I bet I'd go to Marietta, Ohio, and shoot him to-morrow.

There I was, big boob that I am. Pretty soon the race was over, and Wilbur had gone down and collected our money, and we had a hack downtown, and he stood us a swell supper at the West House, and a bottle of champagne beside.

And I was with that girl and she wasn't saying much, and I wasn't saying much either. One thing I know. She wasn't stuck on me because of the lie about my father being rich and all that. There's a way you know. . . . Craps a'mighty. There's a kind of girl you see just once in your life, and if you don't get busy and make hay, then you're gone for good and all, and might as well go jump off a bridge. They give you a look from inside of them somewhere, and it ain't no vamping, and what it means is—you want that girl to be your wife, and you want nice things around her like flowers and swell clothes, and you want her to have the kids you're going to have, and you want good music played and no rag-time. Gee whizz.

There's a place over near Sandusky, across a kind of bay, and it's called Cedar Point. And after we had supper we went over to it in a launch, all by ourselves. Wilbur and Miss Lucy and that Miss Woodbury had to catch a ten o'clock train back to Tiffin, Ohio, because when you're out with girls like that you can't get careless and miss any trains and stay out all night, like you can with some kinds of Janes.

And Wilbur blowed himself to the launch and it cost him fifteen cold plunks, but I wouldn't never have knew if I hadn't listened. He wasn't no tin horn kind of a sport.

Over at the Cedar Point place, we didn't stay around where there was a gang of common kind of cattle at all.

There was big dance halls and dining places for yaps, and there was a beach you could walk along and get where it was dark, and we went there.

She didn't talk hardly at all and neither did I, and I was thinking how glad I was my mother was all right, and always made us kids learn to eat with a fork at table, and not swill soup, and not be noisy and rough like a gang you see around a race track that way.

Then Wilbur and his girl went away up the beach and Lucy and I sat down in a dark place, where there was some roots of old trees the water had washed up, and after that the time, till we had to go back in the launch and they had to catch their trains, wasn't nothing at all. It went like winking your eye.

Here's how it was. The place we were setting in was dark, like I said, and there was the roots from that old stump sticking up like arms, and there was a watery smell, and the night was like—as if you could put your hand out and feel it—so warm and soft and dark and sweet like an orange.

I most cried and I most swore and I most jumped up and danced, I was so mad and happy and sad.

When Wilbur come back from being alone with his girl, and she saw him coming, Lucy she says, "We got to go to the train now," and she was most crying too, but she never knew nothing I knew, and she couldn't be so all busted up. And then, before Wilbur and Miss Woodbury got up to where we was, she put her face up and kissed me quick and put her head up against me and she was all quivering and—Gee whizz.

Sometimes I hope I have cancer and die. I guess you know what I mean. We went in the launch across the bay to the train like that, and it was dark, too. She whispered and said it was like she and I could get out of the boat and walk on the water, and it sounded foolish, but I knew what she meant.

And then quick we were right at the depot, and there was a big gang of yaps, the kind that goes to the fairs, and crowded and milling around like cattle, and how could I tell her? "It won't be long because you'll write and I'll write to you." That's all she said.

I got a chance like a hay barn afire. A swell chance I got.

And maybe she would write me, down at Marietta that way, and the letter would come back, and stamped on the front of it by the U.S.A. "there ain't any such guy," or something like that, whatever they stamp on a letter that way.

And me trying to pass myself off for a bigbug and a swell—to her, as decent a little body as God ever made. Craps a'mighty—a swell chance I got!

And then the train come in, and she got on it, and Wilbur Wessen he come and shook hands with me, and that Miss Woodbury was nice too and bowed to me, and I at her, and the train went and I busted out and cried like a kid.

Gee, I could have run after that train and made Dan Patch look like a freight train after a wreck but, socks a'mighty, what was the use? Did you ever see such a fool?

I'll bet you what—if I had an arm broke right now or a train had run over my foot—I wouldn't go to no doctor at all. I'd go set down and let her hurt and hurt—that's what I'd do.

I'll bet you what—if I hadn't a drunk that booze I'd a never been such a boob as to go tell such a lie—that couldn't never be made straight to a lady like her.

I wish I had that fellow right here that had on a Windsor tie and carried a cane. I'd smash him for fair. Gosh darn his eyes. He's a big fool—that's what he is.

And if I'm not another you just go find me one and I'll quit working and be a bum and give him my job. I don't care nothing for working, and earning money, and saving it for no such boob as myself.

FRANK WILSON CHENEY HERSEY

The First Duel in Boston

The first duel in Boston was fought on the Common on the night of July 3, 1728, by Benjamin Woodbridge and Henry Phillips, two intimate friends. Phillips was of the class of 1724, Harvard College. Their ardent social nature led them to the gaming table, and gambling finally led to a fatal dispute. Woodbridge was slain; and Phillips fled to Rochelle, France, where, exactly one year after, he died of a broken heart.

"Here lyes interred the body of Mr. Benjamin Woodbridge, son of the Honourable Dudley Woodbridge Esq're, who dec'd July ye 3d, 1728, in ye 20th year of his age."

Granary Burying Ground.

THE dew bejewelled the greensward cold,
And the night-mist trailed from the marshes.
A spectral gleam where the river-tide rolled,
A lustre, pale as the succory's bloom,
On the mottled lawns and the leafy gloom,—
Lo, this was the sheen a midsummer sky
Had shed o'er the Common in Boston Town,
In the days when the province loved the crown.
The crickets chirped with a drowsy cry,
The frogs in the slime of their pond droned low,
And the sombre old town a sleep—like snow—
Had buried in silence deep as the tomb;
For good men dream when the black tides flow,
And the night-mist trails from the marshes.

Like phantoms gliding athwart their haunt,
Two striplings trod 'neath the shroud that hung
From the drooping limbs of the Great Elm gaunt,
Where gibbeted Quaker and witch had swung.

The twain stalked on through the shade
 of death,
With the lust of life agleam in their eyes;
Both waited the word that hate never
 saith,
Then hurled away cloaks and hats in a
 breath.
And whipped out their swords to clash
 and clink,
And flash in the gloom like fireflies;
While the echoes rang o'er the river-
 brink,
 And the night-mist trailed from the
 marshes.

Did the young hearts ache with remorse
 for the jeer
In the heat of the wine flung forth too
 free,
For the dicing in spite of the mother's
 tear?
Or throb with the maddening ecstasy
Of parry and thrust 'twixt peer and peer;
With the frantic hope and the deadly will
The blood that would quench their hate
 to spill,
 While the night-mist trailed from the
 marshes?

A twist of the arm, and a supple lunge,
A lithe recoil, and a clank of steel;
A dart of a blade like a snake in its
 plunge,
A moaning curse, a tottering reel,—
And a smooth white face lay bathed in
 dew;
While the blood and the hate ebbed away
 with the tide,
And the slayer of life wished himself
 had died
Where the shroud of the Elm drooped
 dimly blue,
 Where the night-mist trailed from the
 marshes.

GUY SCULL (1876-1920)

Men of Harvard

As it was in '61, so in the early spring of '98, in fewer numbers perhaps, because the need was less, but with just such a strong spirit as before, the men of Harvard University enlisted in the forming regiments for the front. Some went as commissioned officers, some as privates; some were in the infantry, others in the cavalry, others wore sewed to the sleeve of their shirts the red cross of the hospital corps; everywhere throughout the vast extent of armies, in Cuba, in Porto Rico, or left behind to sweat and toil in weariness, men we had known and men we had heard of, men they placed in command of companies, or in the third relief of the guard, were doing what ought to be done.

One man, a Senior, who enlisted as a private in the very beginning, was given a commission before there had been any fighting, and when the fighting began he was promoted. By a brave regiment he was called a brave man.

There are no more battles now. The men are returning, and we see them about the colleges as before, but of course not all who went in the spring; for the work that these men had set out to do would not permit of that. And to those whom we shall not see here, either this year or the next, who fought as their teaching had told them, and did it well, to them full honor is owing, and to them is given in sadness the great love of this University of Harvard. Hollister, Furness, Sanders, Crapo, Adsit, Lahman, Henshaw—they are the men who have gone. They died in service, and, when they were buried, United States troops stood at attention.

JOHN MACY

American Literature

AMERICAN literature is a branch of English literature, as truly as are English books written in Scotland or South Africa. Our literature lies almost entirely in the nineteenth century when the ideas and books of the western world were freely interchanged among the nations and became accessible to an increasing number of readers. In literature nationality is determined by language rather than by blood or geography. M. Maeterlinck, born a subject of King Leopold, belongs to French literature. Mr. Joseph Conrad, born in Poland, is already an English classic. Geography, much less important in the nineteenth century than before, was never, among modern European nations, so important as we sometimes are asked to believe. Of the ancestors of English literature "Beowulf" is scarcely more significant, and rather less graceful, than our tree-inhabiting forebears with prehensile toes; the true progenitors of English literature are Greek, Latin, Hebrew, Italian, and French.

American literature and English literature of the nineteenth century are parallel derivatives from preceding centuries of English literature. Literature is a succession of books from books. Artistic expression springs from life ultimately but not immediately. It may be likened to a river which is swollen throughout its course by new tributaries and by the seepages of its banks; it reflects the life through which it flows, taking color from the shores; the shores modify it, but its power and volume descend from distant headwaters and affluents far up stream. Or it may be likened to the race-life which our food nourishes or impoverishes, which our individual circumstances foster or damage, but which flows on through us, strangely impersonal and beyond our power to kill or create.

It is well for a writer to say: "Away with books! I will draw my inspiration from life!" For we have too many books that are simply better books diluted by John Smith. At the same time, literature is not born spontaneously out of life. Every book has its literary parentage, and students find it so easy to trace genealogies that much criticism reads like an Old Testament chapter of "begats." Every novel was suckled at the breasts of older novels, and great mothers are often prolific of anæmic offspring. The stock falls off and revives, goes a-wandering, and returns like a prodigal. The family records get blurred. But of the main fact of descent there is no doubt.

American literature is English literature made in this country. Its nineteenth-century characteristics are evident and can be analyzed and discussed with some degree of certainty. Its "American" characteristics —no critic that I know has ever given a good account of them. You can define certain peculiarities of American politics, American agriculture, American public schools, even American religion. But what is uniquely American in American literature? Poe is just as American as Mark Twain; Lanier is just as American as Whittier. The American spirit in literature is a myth, like American valor in war, which is precisely like the valor of Italians and Japanese. The American, deluded by a falsely idealized image which he calls America, can say that the purity of Longfellow represents the purity of American home life. An Irish Englishman, Mr. Bernard Shaw, with another falsely idealized image of America, surprised that a face does not fit his image, can ask: "What is Poe doing in that galley?" There is no answer. You never can tell. Poe could not help it. He was born in Boston, and lived in Richmond, New York, Baltimore, Philadelphia. Professor van Dyke says that Poe was a maker of "decidedly un-American cameos," but I do not understand what that means. Facts are uncomfortable consorts of prejudices and emotional generalities; they spoil domestic peace, and when there is a separation they sit solid at home while the other party goes. Irving, a shy, sensitive gentleman, who wrote with fastidious care, said: "It has been a matter of marvel, to European readers, that a man from the wilds of America should express himself in tolerable English." It is a matter of marvel, just as it is a marvel that Blake and Keats flowered in the brutal city of London a hundred years ago.

The literary mind is strengthened and nurtured, is influenced and mastered, by the accumulated riches of literature. In the last century the strongest thinkers in our language were Englishmen, and not only the traditional but the contemporary influences on our thinkers and artists were British. This may account for one negative characteristic of American literature—its lack of American quality. True, our records must reflect our life. Our poets, enamored of nightingales and Persian gardens, have not altogether forgotten the mocking-bird and the woods of Maine. Fiction, written by inhabitants of New York, Ohio, and Massachusetts, does tell us something of the ways of life in those mighty commonwealths, just as English fiction written by Lancashire men about Lancashire people is saturated with the dialect, the local habits and scenery of that country. But wherever an English-speaking man of imagination may dwell, in Dorset or Calcutta or Indianapolis, he is subject to the strong arm of the empire of English literature; he cannot escape it; it tears him out of his obscure bed and makes a happy slave of him. He is assigned to the department of the service for which his gifts qualify him, and his special education is undertaken by drill-masters and captains who hail from provinces far from his birthplace.

Dickens, who writes of London, influences Bret Harte, who writes of California, and Bret Harte influences Kipling, who writes of India. Each is intensely local in subject matter. The affinity between them is a matter of temperament, manifested, for example, in the swagger and exaggeration characteristic of all three. California did not "produce" Bret Harte; the power of Dickens was greater than that of the Sierras and the Golden Gate. Bret Harte created a California that never existed, and Indian gentlemen, Caucasian and Hindoo, tell us that Kipling invented an army and an empire unknown to geographers and war-officers.

The ideas at work among these English men of letters are world-encircling and fly between book and brain. The dominant power is on the British Islands, and the prevailing stream of influence flows west across the Atlantic. Sometimes it turns and runs the other way. Poe influenced Rossetti; Whitman influenced Henley. For a century Cooper has been in command of the British literary marine. Literature is reprehensibly unpatriotic, even though its votaries are, as individual citizens, afflicted with local prides and hostilities. It takes only a dramatic interest in the guns of Yorktown. Its philosophy was nobly uttered by Gaston Paris in the Collège de France in 1870, when the city was beleaguered by the German armies: "Common studies, pursued in the same spirit, in all civilized countries, form, beyond the restrictions of diverse and often hostile nationalities, a great country which no war profanes, no conqueror menaces, where souls find that refuge and unity which in former times was offered them by the city of God." The catholicity of English language and literature transcends the temporal boundaries of states.

What, then, of the "provincialism" of the American province of the empire of British literature? Is it an observable general characteristic, and is it a virtue or a vice? There is a sense in which American literature is not provincial enough. The most provincial of all literature is the Greek. The Greeks knew nothing outside of Greece and needed to know nothing. The Old Testament is tribal in its provinciality; its god is a local god, and its village police and sanitary regulations are erected into eternal laws. If this racial localism is not essential to the greatness of early literatures, it is inseparable from them; we find it there. It is not possible in our cosmopolitan age and there are few traces of it in American books. No American poet has sung of his neighborhood with naïve passion, as if it were all the world to him. Whitman is pugnaciously American, but his sympathies are universal, his vision is cosmic; when he seems to be standing in a city street looking at life, he is in a trance, and his spirit is racing with the winds.

The welcome that we gave Whitman betrays the lack of an admirable kind of provincialism; it shows us defective in local security of judgment. Some of us have been so anxiously abashed by high standards of European culture that we could not see a poet in our own back yard until European poets and critics told us he was there. This is queerly contradictory to a disposition found in some Americans to disregard world standards and proclaim a third-rate poet as the Milton of Oshkosh or the Shelley of San Francisco. The passage in Lowell's "Fable for Critics" about "The American Bulwers, Disraelis and Scotts" is a spoonful of salt in the mouth of that sort of gaping village reverence.

Of dignified and self-respecting provincialism, such as Professor Royce so eloquently advocates, there might well be more in American books. Our poets desert the domestic landscape to write pseudo-Elizabethan dramas and sonnets about Mont Blanc. They set up an artificial Tennyson park on the banks of the Hudson. Beside the shores of Lake Michigan they croon the love affairs of an Arab in the desert and his noble steed. This is not a very grave offence, for poets live among the stars, and it makes no difference from what point of the earth's surface they set forth on their aerial adventures. A Wisconsin poet may write very beautifully about nightingales, and a New England Unitarian may write beautifully about cathedrals; if it is beautiful, it is poetry, and all is well.

The novelists are the worst offenders. There have been few of them; they have not been adequate in numbers or in genius to the task of describing the sections of the country, the varied scenes and habits from New Orleans to the Portlands. And yet, small band as they are, with great domestic opportunities and responsibilities, they have devoted volumes to Paris, which has an able native corps of story-makers, and to Italy, where the home talent is first-rate. In this sense American literature is too globe-trotting, it has too little savor of the soil.

Of provincialism of the narrowest type American writers, like other men of imagination, are not guilty to any reprehensible degree. It is a vice sometimes imputed to them by provincial critics who view literature from the office of a London weekly review or from the lecture rooms of American colleges. Some American writers are parochial, for example, Whittier. Others, like Mr. Henry James, are provincial in outlook, but cosmopolitan in experience, and reveal their provinciality by a self-conscious internationalism. Probably English and French writers may be similarly classified as provincial or not. Mr. James says that Poe's collection of critical sketches "is probably the most complete and exquisite specimen of *provincialism* ever prepared for the edification of men." It is nothing like that. It is an example of what happens when a hack reviewer's work in local journals is collected into a volume because he turns out to be a genius. The list of Poe's victims is not more remarkable for the number of nonentities it includes than "The Lives of the Poets" by the great Doctor Johnson, who was hack for a bookseller, and "introduced" all the poets that the taste of the time encouraged the bookseller to print. Poe was cosmopolitan in spirit; his prejudices were personal and highly original, usually against the prejudices of his *moment* and *milieu.* Hawthorne is less provincial, in the derogatory sense, than his charming biographer, Mr. James, as will become evident if one compares Hawthorne's American notes on England, written in long ago days of national rancor, with Mr. James's British notes on America ("The American Scene"), written in our happy days of spacious vision.

Emerson's ensphering universality overspreads Carlyle like the sky above a volcanic island. Indeed Carlyle (who knew more about American life and about what other people ought to do than any other British writer earlier than Mr. Chesterton) justly complains that Emerson is not sufficiently local and concrete; Carlyle longs to see "some Event, Man's Life, American Forest, or piece of creation which this Emerson loves and wonders at, well *Emersonized.*" Longfellow would not stay at home and write more about the excellent village blacksmith; he made poetical tours of Europe and translated songs and legends from several languages for the delight of the villagers who remained behind. Lowell was so heartily cosmopolitan that American newspapers accused him of Anglomania—which proves their provincialism but acquits him. Mr. Howells has written a better book about Venice than about Ohio. Mark Twain lived in every part of America, from Connecticut to California, he wrote about every country under the sun (and about some countries beyond the sun), he is read by all sorts and conditions of men in the English-speaking world, and he is an adopted hero in Vienna. It is difficult to come to any conclusion about provincialism as a characteristic of American literature.

American literature is on the whole idealistic, sweet, delicate, nicely finished. There is little of it which might not have appeared in the

Youth's Companion. The notable exceptions are our most stalwart men of genius, Thoreau, Whitman, and Mark Twain. Any child can read American literature, and if it does not make a man of him, it at least will not lead him into forbidden realms. Indeed, American books too seldom come to grips with the problems of life, especially the books cast in artistic forms. The essayists, expounders, and preachers attack life vigorously and wrestle with the meaning of it. The poets are thin, moonshiny, meticulous in technique. Novelists are few and feeble, and dramatists are non-existent. These generalities, subject to exceptions, are confirmed by a reading of the first fifteen volumes of the *Atlantic Monthly,* which are a treasure-house of the richest period of American literary expression. In those volumes one finds a surprising number of vigorous, distinguished papers on politics, philosophy, science, even on literature and art. Many talented men and women, whose names are not well remembered, are clustered there about the half dozen salient men of genius; and the collection gives one a sense that the New England mind (aided by the outlying contributors) was, in its one Age of Thought, an abundant and diversified power. But the poetry is not memorable, except for some verses by the few standard poets. And the fiction is naïve. Edward Everett Hale's "The Man Without a Country" is almost the only story there that one comes on with a thrill either of recognition or of discovery.

It is hard to explain why the American, except in his exhortatory and passionately argumentative moods, has not struck deep into American life, why his stories and verses are, for the most part, only pretty things, nicely unimportant. Anthony Trollope had a theory that the absence of international copyright threw our market open too unrestrictedly to the British product, that the American novel was an unprotected infant industry; we printed Dickens and the rest without paying royalty and starved the domestic manufacturer. This theory does not explain. For there are many American novelists published, read, and probably paid for their work. The trouble is that they lacked genius; they dealt with trivial, slight aspects of life; they did not take the novel seriously in the right sense of the word, though no doubt they were in another sense serious enough about their poor productions. "Uncle Tom's Cabin" and "Huckleberry Finn" are colossal exceptions to the prevailing weakness and superficiality of American novels.

Why do American writers turn their backs on life, miss its intensities, its significance? The American Civil War was the most tremendous upheaval in the world after the Napoleonic period. The imaginative reaction on it consists of some fine essays, Lincoln's addresses, Whitman's war poetry, "Uncle Tom's Cabin" (which came before the war but is part of it), one or two passionate hymns by Whittier, the second series of the "Biglow Papers," Hale's "The Man Without a Country"—and what else? The novels laid in war-time are either sanguine melodrama or absurd idyls of maidens whose lovers are at the front—a tragic theme if tragically and not sentimentally conceived. Perhaps the bullet that killed Theodore Winthrop deprived us of our great novelist of the Civil War, for he was on the right road. In a general speculation such a might-have-been is not altogether futile; if Milton had died of whooping cough there would not have been any "Paradise Lost"; the reverse of this is that some geniuses whose works ought inevitably to have been produced by this or that national development may have died too soon. This suggestion, however, need not be gravely argued. The fact is that the American literary imagination after the Civil War was almost sterile. If no books had been written, the failure of that conflict to get itself embodied in some masterpieces would be less disconcerting. But thousands of books were written by people who knew the war at first hand and who had literary ambition and some skill, and from all these books none rises to distinction.

An example of what seems to be the American habit of writing about everything except American life is the work of General Lew Wallace. Wallace was one of the important secondary generals in the Civil War, distinguished at Fort Donelson and at Shiloh. After the war he wrote "Ben-Hur," a doubly abominable book, because it is not badly written and it shows a lively imagination. There is nothing in it so valuable, so dramatically significant as a week in Wallace's war experiences. "Ben-Hur," fit work for a country clergyman with a pretty literary gift, is a ridiculous inanity to come from a man who has seen the things that Wallace saw! It is understandable that the man of experience may not write at all, and, on the other hand, that the man of secluded life may have the imagination to make a military epic. But for a man crammed with experience of the most dramatic sort and discovering the ability and the ambition to write—for him to make spurious oriental romances which achieve an enormous popularity! The case is too grotesque to be typical, yet it is exceptional in degree rather than in kind. The American literary artist has written about everything under the skies except what matters most in his own life. General Grant's plain autobiography, not art and of course not attempting to be, is better literature than most of our books in artistic forms, because of its intellectual integrity and the profound importance of the subject-matter.

Our dreamers have dreamed about many wonderful things, but their faces have been averted from the mightier issues of life. They have been high-minded, fine-grained, eloquent in manner, in odd contrast to the real or reputed vigor and crudeness of the nation. In the hundred years from Irving's first romance to Mr. Howells's latest unromantic novel, most of our books are eminent for just those virtues which America is supposed to lack. Their physique is feminine; they are fanciful, dainty, reserved; they are literose, sophisticated in craftsmanship, but innocently unaware of the profound agitations of American life, of life everywhere. Those who strike the deeper notes of reality, Whitman, Thoreau, Mark Twain, Mrs. Stowe in her one great book, Whittier, Lowell and Emerson at their best, are a powerful minority. The rest, beautiful and fine in spirit, too seldom show that they are conscious of contemporaneous realities, too seldom vibrate with a tremendous sense of life.

The Jason of western exploration writes as if he had passed his life in a library. The Ulysses of great rivers and perilous seas is a connoisseur of Japanese prints. The warrior of 'Sixty-one rivals Miss Marie Corelli. The mining engineer carves cherry stones. He who is figured as gaunt, hardy and aggressive, conquering the desert with the steam locomotive, sings of a pretty little rose in a pretty little garden. The judge, haggard with experience, who presides over the most tragi-comic divorce court ever devised by man, writes love stories that would have made Jane Austen smile.

Mr. Arnold Bennett is reported to have said that if Balzac had seen Pittsburgh, he would have cried: "Give me a pen!" The truth is, the whole country is crying out for those who will record it, satirize it, chant it. As literary material, it is virgin land, ancient as life and fresh as a wilderness. American literature is one occupation which is not overcrowded, in which, indeed, there is all too little competition for the newcomer to meet. There are signs that some earnest young writers are discovering the fertility of a soil that has scarcely been scratched.

American fiction shows all sorts of merit, but the merits are not assembled, concentrated; the fine is weak, and the strong is crude. The stories of Poe, Hawthorne, Howells, James, Aldrich, Bret Harte are admirable in manner, but they are thin in substance, not of large vitality. On the other hand, some of the stronger American fictions fail in workmanship; for example, "Uncle Tom's Cabin," which is still vivid and moving long after its tractarian interest has faded; the novels of Frank Norris, a man of great vision and high purpose, who attempted to put national economics into something like an epic of daily bread; and Herman Melville's "Moby Dick," a madly eloquent romance of the sea. A few American novelists have felt the meaning of the life they knew and have tried sincerely to set it down, but have for various reasons failed to make first-rate novels; for example, Edward Eggleston, whose stories of early Indiana have the breath of actuality in them; Mr. E. W. Howe, author of "The Story of a Country Town"; Harold Frederic, a man of great ability, whose work was growing deeper, more significant when he died; George W. Cable, whose novels are unsteady and sentimental, but who gives a genuine impression of having portrayed a city and its people; and Stephen Crane, who, dead at thirty, had given in "The Red Badge of Courage" and "Maggie" the promise of better work. Of good short stories America has been prolific. Mrs. Wilkins-Freeman, Mrs. Annie Trumbull Slosson, Sarah Orne Jewett, Rowland Robinson, H. C. Bunner, Edward Everett Hale, Frank Stockton, Joel Chandler Harris, and "O. Henry" are some of those whose short stories are perfect in their several kinds. But the American novel, which multiplies past counting, remains an inferior production.

On a private shelf of contemporary fiction and drama in the English language are the works of ten British authors, Mr. Galsworthy, Mr. H. G. Wells, Mr. Arnold Bennett, Mr. Eden Phillpotts, Mr. George Moore, Mr. Leonard Merrick, Mr. J. C. Snaith, Miss May Sinclair, Mr. William De Morgan, Mr. Maurice Hewlett, Mr. Joseph Conrad, Mr. Bernard Shaw, yes, and Mr. Rudyard Kipling. Beside them I find but two Americans, Mrs. Edith Wharton and Mr. Theodore Dreiser. There may be others, for one cannot pretend to know all the living novelists and dramatists. Yet for every American that should be added, I would agree to add four to the British. However, a contemporary literature that includes Mrs. Wharton's "Ethan Frome" and Mr. Dreiser's "Jennie Gerhardt," both published last year, is not to be despaired of.

In the course of a century a few Americans have said in memorable words what life meant to them. Their performance, put together, is considerable, if not imposing. Any sense of dissatisfaction that one feels in contemplating it is due to this proportion between a limited expression and the multifarious immensity of the country. Our literature, judged by the great literatures contemporaneous with it, is insufficient to the opportunity and the need. The American Spirit may be figured as petitioning the Muses for twelve novelists, ten poets, and eight dramatists, to be delivered at the earliest possible moment.

HENRY MILNER RIDEOUT

From ADMIRAL'S LIGHT

The High Woods

THE road ran high and lonely over the ridges. Their eyes, dazzled with leagues of white glare, blurred with tears in the sweep of a freezing wind, gained power slowly to descry the milder gleam of the channel far beneath, and beyond this, the billowing of the Maine hills, softened by distance and the smoothing magic of the snow. Sometimes, dipping into a smothered hollow among firs, they suffered again a momentary blindness, in the obscurity of dark green and shadowed white; and again, yet once more dazed with wide brilliancy, climbed higher and farther from the river, up an immense and softly convex curve, toward the fugitive sky-line. Black evergreen tops, the distant relics of some grove, dotted the hills like ermine; or singly, and closer to hand, like feathered arrows that a giant might have shot straight downward. Rarely these, however; so free was the north wind, so shelterless and dry the snow, that by turns the sled groaned over frozen mud, and stuck fast in smoking drifts.

As the two men pushed and tugged to aid the horse, or slapped their aching hands, or stamped and kicked the sled, they exchanged few words. The slow jangling of the bells traveled in the void, a stray mote of cheerful sound.

To Miles, looking back down many a long slope, they chimed with vague but happy thoughts. He surveyed, in shining perspective from this eminence, not only his native valley, but the last fortnight of his life there. Ella was wrong, he had not moped; Tony was wrong, he had hardly considered their estrangement; here was the real truth: before that adventure in the fog, he had passed his days in a brown study, and after it, had been whirled into the glowing rout of life. A hundred dim things which had passed him by he now saw, heard, felt, and thrillingly understood.

Two regrets lingered: he had not seen again either the man or the girl of Alward's Cove; and from them he traveled farther at every shake of the bells. Yet all that was but temporary; and meanwhile, to his strange, new vision of the world, the simplest detail in this simple journey was a bit of exultation.

The woods at last received them into vast and crowded silence. The sorrel horse, with steaming haunches, plodded heavily through a dark lane of virgin whiteness, between puffy, undulating banks of buried underwood. Beyond or through these, in broken glimpses of depth, white and black trunks so lurked and interchanged in reciprocating movement as to create an illusion of presences—many, yet one—who dodged and spied and followed. There seemed no other life in all this stillness. Yet now and then, in sunny clearings, a line of tiny hollows, filled with shadowy blue, marked some late woodland errand; the straight trot of a fox, scored alongside with shallow scoops of his brush; the neat cuneiform written by partridge claws; the bunched all-fours of a leaping rabbit, or the beaten stream where his whole tribe had flowed over log and knoll into some green cavern. When drifts halted the sled, and brought the bells to silence or single notes, an invisible brook chuckled from among willows, its runnels gossiping under ice and snow.

At dusk the two men reached a dark little shanty in second-growth beeches.

"W'oa there, Gyasticus!" cried Hab. "Here y' are. Stand by to unlo'd dunnage!"

That night they spent in watches, turn about, sleeping and tending fire; and before daylight were out and away to distant groves of birch and maple. A week of happy, vigorous days fled by. Sometimes the two chopped side by side; sometimes they separated for whole mornings, each alone in the snowy wilderness, but for the ringing shock of the other's axe in frosty wood, half a mile away. The novice felled his trees, first with reluctance at such treachery to old friends, but later with a workman's pride. In the beginning they crashed through their neighbors' tops in a violent cloud of snow, dazzling as an explosion of diamond dust; but now they dropped, groaning, with one clean swing into their foreseen places.

At noon Miles met Habakkuk in the lee of a tall granite boulder, blackened with smoke, and crowned with the red spikes of sumac. Here, over a leaping fire, they boiled snow for their coffee, and thawed their frozen food; and here they lounged for a half hour of vernal warmth and drowsiness. Snow, melted by noonday sun above and flame beneath, dropped round them from the branches, in white bâtons that broke and dispersed in mid-air. A thin arc of pale green grass bordered the melting semicircle where they sat, with steaming moccasins, while Old-Hab growled some slow account of "getting out knees," of swamping, stumpage, the excellence of beech for "water-log work," and all the personal traits of Nasty Ellum, Old Popple, and Master Oak.

From FERN SEED

Chapter I

ONE evening in Santa Maria Novella he (Leonard Corsant) sat as long as he could sit with a dark, hushed, humped little crowd, looking out from mysterious gloom to where the altar floated in a haze of candle-light and of young voices singing. The contrast moved him, touched him within like an allegory of our poor humankind. He would have stayed there; but the mortal chill of the church had crept into his bones, and drove him away. As he went quietly out, through the vast empty rear of the darkness, a man, a shadow leaning on a pillar, turned to look at him. Leonard caught only a passing impression that the movement was quick and stiff. He thought no more of it.

"Well? To bed with the fleas again?" he asked himself, outdoors. "No, by gum. This is bad. A real go of the waggles!"

His body shook, his teeth chattered. Slapping himself like a teamster, he crossed the piazza by starlight, and hurried down a narrow street, to find some refuge, osteria, trattoria, wine-shop or eating-den, whatever might first appear. For some time he found nothing. The way was empty, dark, a rift among mediaeval shadows. When at last a pair of windows gave light, ahead, their panes all steamy with warmth inside, he turned toward them, opened the door between, and entered.

It was a dingy little old restaurant, a narrow room which in those days before the war ran through cat-a-corner from Sword Street to Sun Street. A dingy little old waiter leaned against the wall as though put there and abandoned like a worn-out umbrella. If alive, he was the only living creature to be seen. Leonard had chosen a table nearest the source of heat—a cavern-mouth that breathed out greasy kitchen odors—and had settled himself on a bench, before the old solitary moved or so much as blinked.

"Good evening," said Leonard. "Something hot, if you please."

The waiter slowly detached his back from the wall, and came forward mumbling excuses:

"The cook has gone home in rage, sir. A maledicted cook, who made asseverations . . ." Then, as he became aware that his guest sat shuddering, his aged eyes grew bright, shrewd, kindly. He stopped his apology, to cry one compassionate word: *"Freddo!"*

With that he darted into the kitchen, made a great clatter, and quickly burst again from the darkness, running with a tumbler, a black bottle, and a copper kettle that steamed.

"Prompt and intelligent cuss," quoth Leonard. In more polite phrases, he begged the man to get another tumbler and share his toddy.

"Oh, sir, you are too kind," was the reply. "I could not think of doing so."

The poor old chap was both surprised and frightened. Leonard had an easy way with him, however, and soon the pair were hobnobbing over Gorgonzola *verde* and a good round of loaf of bread. Chills vanished, likewise formality. The talk passed from weather and hard times to politics, then to warfare and memories; for this dried little ancient with his nut-cracker face and beady eyes had tramped as a boy soldier of Garibaldi's, and plainly a good one. With all the shop to themselves, they took their ease, found each other excellent company, and held a humble revel.

"You like that story, sir?"

"I do, I do!" cried Corsant, leaning back and wiping his eyes. "But it hurts to laugh so."

"Then, sir, I will tell you a yet more comical. At Orte were three sisters . . ."

Just then the Sword Street door quietly opened. A man came in.

The laughing veteran sprang up, drew away, and as though by a trick on the stage, faded shrivelling back into a sad old waiter.

He who caused this transformation paid it no heed, but stepped down into the room and looked about scornfully. He was a lusty blond young man, handsome after a fashion which, thought Leonard, was too professionally male. His English clothes fitted him too well, tighter than need be, and set off a muscular body powerful enough for an athlete's, but not loose enough.

"Good evening to you," he said in English.

Leonard returned the wish.

The stranger paused by Leonard's table. He was smiling, but his eyes remained too pale and cold.

"We always meet in odd places, don't we?" He spoke affably. His bass voice came from the throat and seemed to roughen it. "I shouldn't quite think you'd care for this, though. There are plenty of good beer-halls."

Corsant, when ruffled, had a sleepy way of looking at you. When angry—as a friend of his expressed it—his face died. Now he looked no more than sleepy.

"It does well enough, thanks," he said. "I can't recall any other places where we had the pleasure?"

"Oh, just as you like." The stranger laughed. Then, having turned to see that the servant was beyond ear-shot, he laughed again, and bent across the table. "I do not scrape friendship. But we're off duty, eh? One good turn deserves another, and I thought you might like to know that they are after you."

Leonard had forgotten all plagues of Egypt and all quarantine documents. Now he remembered. This warning seemed freely enough given, and probably true; still he did not like the giver, or the accompanying sneer of condescension.

"Oh. Much obliged," said he. "Let 'em come."

The light-colored eyes flashed down at him balefully.

"Good. We are even. I leave you to—your friend."

Removing his hat stiffly, the man swung round, marched rather than walked past the waiter—whom he ignored as from a height—and so went out by the other door into the darkness of Sun Street.

"Who was he, Gino?"

The waiter thawed, became human again, and flung off a most inimitable farewell with his hands.

"Ah, that brute! Ah, that white-eyed vassal! I never saw him before, sir."

"Nor I," said Leonard.

He was not so sure; that stiff wheel, and turn of the back all in a piece, reminded him how some one had watched him go out of church.

"For all his garments and his altitude," said Gino, grinning, "he behaved as one in a hurry. No repose. Why fluster so grandly? Why should one hurry, sir? The man cannot consume the time, no: the time consumes the man."

Corsant agreed.

"You speak like Horatius Flaccus. Have we any more hot water? If so, the evening is young. Come, sit down, and let us finish that yarn of the Three Sisters."

WILLIAM STANLEY BRAITHWAITE

Sandy Star

No more from out the sunset,
No more across the foam,
No more across the windy hills
Will Sandy Star come home.

He went away to search it
With a curse upon his tongue:
And in his hand the staff of life
Made music as it swung.

I wonder if he found it,
And knows the mystery now—
Our Sandy Star who went away,
With the secret on his brow?

Twenty Stars to Match His Face

TWENTY stars to match his face,
All the winds to blow his breath.
In the dark no eye can trace
Life or death.

The word came, and out he went,
Heard the unseen flutterings
Of wings that showed the dream he sent.
The song he sings.

Twenty stars to match his face,
The sea-foam, his permanence—
There is no wind can mark his place
Here, or hence.

KATHARINE FULLERTON GEROULD

Vain Oblations

As I was with Saxe during the four most desperate weeks of his life, I think I may say that I knew him better than any one else. Those were also the four most articulate weeks, for they were a period of terrible inaction, spent on the decks of ocean steamships. Saxe was not much given to talking, but there was nothing else to do. No book that has ever been written could have held his attention for two minutes. I was with him, for that matter, off and on, until the end. What I have to tell I got partly from my own observation, partly from a good little woman at the Mission, partly from Saxe's letters, largely from his own lips, and partly from natives. But if I recorded it as it came, unassimilated, unchronologized—one fact often limping into camp six months after its own result—the story would be as unintelligible as the *quipus* of the Incas. It has taken me three years of steady staring to see the thing whole. I know more about it now—including Saxe—than Saxe ever knew. In point of fact, one of the most significant pieces of evidence did not come in until after his death. (I wish it clearly understood, by the way, that Saxe did not commit suicide.) But, more than that, I have been thinking for three years about Mary Bradford. I could tell you as much about what she suffered—the subtlety and the brutality of her ordeal—as if she were one of my own heroines. God forbid that I should ever think of Mary Bradford as "material": that I should analyze her, or dramatize her, or look at her with the artist's squint. If I tell her story, it is because I think it right that we should know what things can be. For the most part, we keep to our own continents: the cruel nations are the insensitive nations, and the squeamish races are kind. But Mary Bradford was the finest flower of New England; ten home-keeping generations only lay between her and the Quest of 1620. It is chronic hyperæsthesia simply to *be* New English; and the pure-bred New Englander had best stick to the euphemisms, the approximations, the reticences, of his own extraordinary villages. But Mary Bradford encountered all the physical realities of life in their crudest form, alone, in the obscene heart of Africa, with black faces thrust always between her and the sky. Some cynic may put in his belittling word to the effect that the New Englander has always counted physical suffering less than spiritual discomfort. The mental torture was not lacking in Mary Bradford's case. For over a year, the temptation to suicide must have been like a terrible thirst, death—any death—luring her like a rippling spring. I told Saxe one night in mid-Atlantic, to comfort him, that she would of course have killed herself if she saw no chance of escape.

Saxe laughed dryly. "That's the most damnable thing about it," he said. "Mary would think it mortal sin to kill herself. She would stick on as long as God chose to keep the breath in her body."

"Sin?" I queried rather stupidly.

"Yes, sin," he answered. "You don't know anything about it: you were brought up in Europe."

"But Saxe," I cried, "rather than—" I did not finish.

"You don't know anything about New England," he said. "Damn your books! Missionaries face everything, and there's more than one kind of martyrdom. I hope she's dead. I rather think she is."

His voice was uneven, but with a meaningless unevenness like a boy's that is changing. There was no emotion in it. A week more of monotonous ploughing of the waves would just have broken him, I think; but he pulled himself together when he touched the soil of Africa. Something in him went out to meet the curse that hung low over the land in the tropic afternoon; and encountering the Antagonist, his eyes grew sane again. But with sanity came the reticence of battle. All that I know of Saxe's and Mary Bradford's early lives, I learned in those four weeks. I have made out some things about her, since then, that probably Saxe never knew. As I said, I have been thinking about Mary Bradford for three years, and it is no secret that to contemplate is, in the end, to know. The stigmata received by certain saints are, I take it, irrefutable proof of this. I do not pretend to carry upon me Mary Bradford's wounds; I do not even canonize her in my heart. But I seriously believe that she had, on the whole, the most bitter single experience ever undergone by woman; and much of the extraordinary horror of the adventure came from the very exquisiteness of the victim. I have often wondered if the Greek and Italian literatures that she knew so well offered her any mitigating memory of a woman more luckless than she. Except Jocasta, I positively cannot think of one; and Jocasta never lived. All of us have dreams of a market where we could sell our old lamps for new. How must not Mary Bradford have longed to change her humanities against mere foothold on the soil of America or Europe! But my preface is too long.

Now and then there is a story where all things work together for evil to the people involved; and these stories have, even for their protagonists, a horrible fascination. The story of Saxe and Mary Bradford is of this nature: a case, as it were, of double chicane. Everything happened precisely wrong. Almost anything happening differently would have given them a chance. If Mary Bradford had been born in Virginia, if her eyes had been blue instead of brown, if Ngawa had come back three hours sooner—Maupassant would have told it all from that point of view. But I am not trying to make literature out of it: it is as history that this story is important to me. Saxe had been engaged to Mary Bradford since her last year in college. Her mother had died when Mary was born, and the Reverend James Bradford had sailed, after his wife's death, for this little West African mission, leaving his child with a sister. Mary was brought up in America. When she was ten, her father came home for a year and took her back with him; but at twelve she was sent definitely home to be educated. James Bradford could not have conceived of depriving his child of Greek and trigonometry, and from school Mary went to college. She never, at any time, had any inclination to enter upon missionary work, though her religious faith was never at any moment in the smallest degree shaken. From her thirteenth year she had been an active and enthusiastic member of her father's denomination. She was a bit of a blue-stocking and occasionally somewhat ironic in speech. When I asked Saxe "if she had *no* faults," these were all he could think of. When she became engaged to Saxe, she stipulated that she should spend two winters with her father before marrying. The separation had never really parted Mary and her father; they had never lost the habit of each other. You see those sympathies sometimes between father and daughter: inarticulate, usually, like the speech of rock to rock, but absolutely indestructible. There was no question—I wish to emphasize this—about her love for Saxe. I had, for a time, her letters. It was a *grande passion*—to use the unhallowed historic phrase; twenty love stories of old Louisiana could have been melted up into it. Saxe, of course, consented to her going. During the second spring he was to go out, her father was to marry them at the Mission, and they were to return to America after a honeymoon in Italy. There is not one detail that does not, in the end, deepen the irony of it, if you look at it all long enough. Italy! All that romantic shimmer and tinkle against the savage fact that was. She went, and for six months seems to have busied herself happily enough with good little Mrs. Price at the Mission. She picked up a few dialects—she was always remarkably clever at languages. The Mission hangs above a tiny seaport—if you can call it a seaport, for there is a great reef a few miles out, and the infrequent steamships stop outside that and send passengers and letters in by boat. It is not one of the regular ports of call, and its chief significance lies in its position at the mouth of a largish river that winds inland for a few hundred miles, finishing no one knows exactly where. The natives for a hundred miles up-stream are fairly friendly and come down sometimes in big boats to trade; beyond that, the country runs into jungle and forest, and grows nastier and nastier. No one knows precisely about that region, and it lies just outside every one's sphere of influence; but there seems to be a network of unhealthy trails, a constant intertribal warfare, and an occasional raid by the precocious pupil of an Arab slave-trader. It is too far south for the big caravans, of course, but there is undoubtedly slave-stealing—though it is extremely difficult to learn anything definite about the country, as there are a dozen different tribes speaking entirely different languages, and each lying tortuously about all the rest. This is all that Saxe could tell me about that *hinterland* which he had never expected to be interested in.

In March, after Mary reached the Mission (she sailed in July, immediately after graduation), the chief of a small tribe some hundred miles up-stream descended in pomp to barter ivory for such treasure as oozes from European ships. Having seldom condescended to trade, he was disappointed at receiving so little for his ivory—a scanty lot of female tusks—and sought distraction and consolation within earshot of the Mission piano. He took especially kindly to the Reverend James Bradford, gravely inspected the school, and issued an invitation for Mr. Bradford to come up-stream and Christianize his tribe. The Mission had worked up and down the coast, as it could, but had never worked inland—more rumors than boats came down the waterway, which was not really a highroad and certainly led to nothing good.

They lacked money for such an enterprise, and workers; but, being missionaries, never forgot that the river, and all who dwelt on its banks, belonged to God. It did not occur to James Bradford to refuse the call, which he took quite simply, as from brother to brother; it did not occur to Mary Bradford to let him go alone, or to her father to protest against her accompanying him. The patriarchal tinge is still perceptible in the New English conception of the family. Let me say, here, that there is no evidence that Ngawa himself ever broke faith with his white protégés. He was, like them, a victim of circumstances.

They were to go for six months. That would bring them to September. In September, three new workers were to come out to the Mission, and James Bradford hoped that two could then be permanently spared for the new Mission up-stream, which he already foresaw and yearned over. In September, he and Mary would return to the port; in late April, Saxe was coming out to marry Mary. They departed under the escort of Ngawa himself. Mr. Price promised to get a boat up to them in May, or at least a runner with letters.

Such details of the final catastrophe as Saxe was acquainted with were brought to the Mission by a native boy in September, just before the boat was to start up-stream (taking Adams and Jenks, the new recruits) to bring the Bradfords down. All reports had hitherto been favorable, if not astonishingly so. Ngawa had listened, and his heart seemed to incline to Mr. Bradford's teachings. Mary had started a little school for the babies. But Ngawa had no intention of compelling his people to embrace Christianity: he simply courteously permitted it to exist in his dominion. As talk of war came on, he was preoccupied with the affairs of his thatched state. The populace—they seem to have been a gentle crowd enough—grew apathetic to their apostles and deposited the commanded tribute somewhat listlessly before their huts. The medicine-men, of course, were hostile from the first, and, as the war drums beat in the forest and the men of the village gathered to sharpen their tufted spears, wild talk had undoubtedly not been wanting. The end had really been a bitter accident. Ngawa absented himself for three days to do some last exhorting and recruiting in his other villages. The attack that had not been expected for a week, at least, was made a few hours before his return. It became a raid rather than a battle; the village resisted the siege only a short time, and the invaders did what they would in the monstrous tropic dusk. Many of the native women were stabbed quickly; but the youngest ones, and Mary Bradford, were dragged off as captives. Mr. Bradford was killed in the beginning—not by the enemy, who were busy despatching Ngawa's subjects, but by Ngawa's chief medicine-man, who stole out of the shadows, slit his throat twice across, caught the blood in a cup, and then slid back into the darkness. The boy who brought them the story averred that he had seen it all, having been present, though somehow left out of the *mêlée.* The enemy, afraid of Ngawa's return, did not stop for the half-grown children. The white girl tore away, the boy said, and started back to her father, but the warrior who held her hit her on the head, so that she dropped, and then carried her off. Oh yes, he had seen it all quite well: he had climbed into a tree. The huts were all burning, and it was lighter than day. Ngawa came back that night, and, later, they destroyed utterly the villages of the other tribe, but they got back no captives. These had been killed at once, probably, or sold. Ngawa had gone back to the medicine-men.

Ngawa's people must have been gentler than most of their color, for the boy answered all the questions of the stricken missionaries before he asked to hear the piano.

This was absolutely all that Saxe knew, when he stumbled into my rooms and asked me to go out to Africa with him. The first cablegrams had simply announced the massacre, and it was only on receipt of letters from the Prices that Saxe learned about Mary and her horrible, shadowy chance of life. The Prices promised to cable any news, but it was unlikely that they would have any more. The boy who had brought them this story drifted down the coast, and for some months few boats came down the stream. Ngawa, they heard vaguely, had died, and his son reigned in his stead, a bitter disciple of unclean rites. Young Adams, in the pity of his heart, had gone the hundred miles to the village, but the people had evidently nothing to tell. The white priest was dead, and the white girl was gone. Their own captives were gone, too, and if they had been able to recover them would they not have done it? Undoubtedly, they were killed, but their enemies had been punished. No: they were faithful to their own gods. What had the white god done for his priest, or for Ngawa, who had listened—and died? Doubtless Adams would have been killed, if they had been defeated in the war, but he profited by the magnanimity of triumph. It was astonishing how little impression, except on Ngawa and one old medicine-man, James Bradford had made. Save that he had achieved martyrdom for himself, he might as well have stayed peacefully at the Mission. It is all, from first to last, a story of vain oblations. The people were inclined to forget that he had ever been there, but they registered their opinion that his white brother had better go back at once. Saxe's face, as Adams gave him this last news, was tense. He gripped the hand of the one white man who had visited that bitter scene, as if he would never let it go.

If Saxe had been delayed in America, it was only in order to arrange his affairs so that he could stay away indefinitely. He intended to follow Mary Bradford down those dim and bloody trails until at least he should have seen some witness of her death. Saxe was not rich, and his arrangements took him a certain length of time. We sailed from New York in March, and caught the African liner at Plymouth.

I will not enter upon the details of Saxe's activity during the next months, nor of the results he gained. It was a case where governments were of no use: the jungle that had swallowed up Mary Bradford acknowledged no suzerain across the seas. Saxe visited Ngawa's village, of course—"I am steel proof," he said, and I think he believed it. The story of those months is a senseless story of perishing lights and clues of twisted sand. We spent three months in rescuing the yellow widow of a Portuguese pearl-fisher, who had been captured by coast pirates and sold inland. When Saxe stood face to face with the "white woman" he had worked blindly to deliver, he reeled before her. "Tell him that I will marry him," said the woman with a noble gesture. She was forty, fat, and hideous. I mention the incident—which turned me quite sick, and in which, to this day, I can see nothing humorous—simply to show the maddening nature of our task. Even I had believed that this mysterious white woman was Mary Bradford. In that land of rumor and superstition and ignorance and cunning—above all, of savage indifference—anything might be true, and anything might be false. Three days after we had started off to find the Portuguese hag, a real clue came into the Mission. Our three months had been quite lost, for the Prices could get no word to us on our knight-errant task. Poor Saxe!

In September, Saxe, following this clue, which seemed to bear some real relation to the events of the year before, travelled solemnly, accompanied by a few natives only, into the heart of that *hinterland* which stood, to all the coast above and below the Mission, for treachery, mystery, and death. In October, he reached the village of the chief in question—a sun-smitten kraal, caught between high blue mountains and the nasty bit of jungle that separated them from one of the big waterways of Africa. Politics are largely a matter of geography, and his position was one of enviable independence, though he was to the neighboring kings on the scale of Andorra to France and Spain. He was a greedy old man, and the sight of several pounds of beads made him very communicative. Half of his information was bound, by African code, to be false, and Saxe had no means of knowing which half; but he owned to having purchased, a few months before, from a wandering trader, a slave woman of white blood. She had come high, he affirmed, cocking his eye at Saxe. But she was not Saxe's slave—Saxe had put it in that way in order to be remotely intelligible to the savage mind. Oh, no! she was the daughter of a Mandingo woman and an Arab. The trader had told him that: he had known the mother. Oh, no! it could not be Saxe's slave. However, he was willing, for a really good price, to consider selling her. Saxe refused to be discouraged. The clue had seemed to him trustworthy; and the story about the Mandingo woman might be pure invention—bravado, to raise the price.

He asked to see her. Oh, certainly; before purchasing he should see her. But meanwhile there was the official cheer to taste—*kava,* above all, inimitably mixed—and she should be fetched. Where was she? A young slave girl suggested sardonically that she was probably at her toilet. Since she had heard of the white man's coming—Saxe had tactfully sent a runner ahead of him—she had been smearing herself meticulously with ochre and other precious pigments. This was said with a sidelong glance at the chief: obviously, he distributed those precious pigments only to his favorites. Saxe said that from that moment his heart misgave him. He had been somehow sure that this woman was Mary. Why his heart should have misgiven him, I do not know; or what devil of stupidity put it into his head that this was the trick of a half-breed slave to make herself irresistible to a white man. It sounded to him, he said, like the inspiration that would naturally occur to the daughter of an Arab by a Mendingo woman. It has never sounded to me in the least like that. He said that he still believed it was Mary; but I fancy he believed it after the fashion of the doubter who shouts his creed a little louder. Of course there was something preposterous in the idea of Mary Bradford's making herself barbarically *chic* with ochre to greet the lover who might be coming to rescue her. But was not the whole thing preposterous to the point of incredibility? And Mary Bradford was not an ordinary woman—not the yellow widow of a Portuguese pearl-fisher. It has always seemed to me that poor Saxe ought to have realized that.

Saxe consumed *kava* until he could consume no more. Then the slave girl announced that the woman had been found. Saxe rose to his feet. He was stifling in the great hut, where all the chief councillors had joined them at their feast, where the reek from greased bodies seemed to mount visibly into the twilight of the great conical roof. His head was reeling, and his heart was beating weakly, crazily, against his ribs—"as if it wanted to come out," he said. His hands were ice-cold. He had just presence of mind enough to drag the black interpreter out with him, and to leave one of his own men inside to watch the stuff with which he proposed to pay. The chief and most of his councillors remained within.

Outside the hut, her back to the setting sun, stood the woman. Saxe had of course known that Mary would be dressed like a native; but this figure staggered him. She was half naked, after the fashion of the tribe, a long petticoat being her only garment. Undoubtedly her skin had been originally fair, Saxe said; but it was tanned to a deep brown—virtually bronzed. For that matter, there was hardly an inch of her that was not tattooed or painted. Some great design, crudely smeared in with thick strokes of ochre, covered her throat, shoulders, and breast. Over it were hung rows and rows of shells, the longest rows reaching to the top of the petticoat. Her face was oddly marred—uncivilized, you might say—by a large nose-ring, and a metal disk that was set in the lower lip, distending it. Forehead and cheeks were streaked with paint, and her straight black hair was dressed after the tribal fashion: stiffened with grease, braided with shells, puffed out with wooden rolls to enormous size. Her eyelids were painted red. That was not a habit of the tribe, and might point to an Arab tradition. The painted eyelids and the streaks that seemed to elongate the eyes themselves were Saxe's despair—he had counted on meeting the eyes of Mary Bradford. To his consternation, the woman stood absolutely silent, her eyes bent on the ground, her face in shadow. Even Saxe, who had no psychology, seems to have seen that Mary Bradford would, in that plight—if it *was* she—wait for him to speak first. But I think he had expected her at least to faint. Saxe looked at her long without speaking. He was trying, he said, to penetrate her detestable disguise, to find some vulnerable point where he could strike at her very heart, and know. In the midst of his bewilderment, he grew cool—cold, even. He gave himself orders (he told me afterward) as a general might send them from the rear. His tongue, his hands, his feet were very far off, but they obeyed punctiliously. My own opinion is that Saxe never, from the moment when he saw the woman, believed it to be Mary.

Her back, as I have said, was against the light. As the purchaser of a slave, he might well wish to see her more fully revealed. He gave the order through the interpreter: "Turn to the light." As she turned obediently and stood in profile against the scarlet west, he saw that her form was unshapely. On her back were a few scars, long since healed.

That moment was undoubtedly Hell for Saxe, in spite of the doubt upon him. But what must it have been for the impassible creature before him? Saxe saw that he must play the game alone. "Mary," he said quietly in English, "I have come to take you home." In the circumstances, it was the stupidest thing he could have said; but the only thing he thought of was speaking in English. If it was Mary, those words, he thought, would reach her, would dispel her shame, or, if she were mad, pierce her madness.

She seemed not to have heard. "Bid her look me in the face," he said brutally to the interpreter. The order was repeated. She turned, raised her painted eyelids, and looked him straight in the eyes, with the apathetic look of the slave, the world over. "But were they Mary Bradford's eyes?" I cried to him, when he told me. "I don't know, damn you!" he said. "Mary had never looked at me like that—as if she didn't see me, and painted like a devil."

He seems to have felt—as far as I can define his feeling—that she was not Mary, but that perhaps he could bully her into being Mary. I do not know how else to explain his unconvinced but perfectly dogged insistence on her identity. He had, of course, been greatly shaken by the extraordinary appearance of the woman. Perhaps he was simply afraid it was she because it would be so terrible if it were, and was resolved not to shirk. Saxe, too, was a New Englander. At all events, he shouted his creed a little louder still. "You are treating me very badly, Mary. I am going in to buy you from the chief; and then you will listen to me."

The woman heard Saxe's voice and looked at the interpreter. Saxe, stupefied, repeated his speech to the negro, and the latter translated. At this, she threw up her arms and broke into guttural ejaculations. That painted form swayed grotesquely from side to side, Saxe said, and she tore the shells out of her hair, tearing the hair with them. Giving him one glance of devilish hatred, she ran to the chief's hut. Saxe followed. There was nothing else to do.

Then began, Saxe said, what for him was a horrible pantomime. He heard nothing of what was said, until afterward, for the interpreter could not keep up with the *prestissimo* of that scene; but one understood it without knowing. The woman grovelled at the chief's feet; she pointed to Saxe and wrung her hands. She was not Saxe's slave, and evidently did not wish to be. The other women drew near to listen, being, clearly, personally interested in the outcome. The chief was, as I have said, avaricious. He looked longingly at the shining heaps of beads, the bolts of scarlet cloth, above all, the Remington rifles. Yet it was clear that he had not wholly outgrown his sluggish *penchant* for the woman who clung to him. It does not often happen, for that matter, that a petty chief in the remote interior can count a white woman—even a half-breed—among his slaves; and the male savage has an instinct for mating above him. The woman saw whither the avaricious eye wandered. She rose from the ground, and stood between him and the treasures, she bent over him and murmured to him, she pointed to her own distorted form. . . . The little slave girl scowled, and the chief's eye gleamed. What at first had seemed a possible detriment, now showed as an advantage. "That was true!" he exclaimed. "Before long she would bring him a warrior son or a girl he could sell for many cows. Let the white man wait." Saxe stamped his foot. Not one day would he wait: the bargain should be completed then. He told me afterward that, after seeing her with the chief, he was absolutely convinced that the woman they were cheapening was the half-breed Arab they said she was; and the general in the rear of the battle wondered dully what he should do with her. But the woman had thrust herself cunningly beneath the chief's very feet, had twined her arms about his ankles, had welded herself to him like a footstool that he could not shake off. Over the chief's thick features, in the torch light (for night was falling outside), into his avaricious eyes, crept a swinish gleam. Let the white man wait until to-morrow. Night was falling; it was time to sleep. By the sunlight they could deal better. The woman panted heavily beneath his feet, never losing her hold. The young slave girl looked down at her with unconcealed malignity. Saxe found himself forced to retire from the royal hut—sleeping-chamber, banqueting-hall, audience-room in one. He said that all he thought of, as he stumbled out, was the idiotic figure he should make at the Mission as the owner of an Arab-Mandingo woman. It was worse than the yellow Portuguese.

He was conducted to his tent. The interpreter confirmed there all that Saxe had divined. Let it be said now that Saxe had one clear inspiration. Before leaving the hut, he had turned and spoken to the woman who was fawning on the wretched negro. "Mary," he said, "if you ask me to, I will shoot you straight through the heart." The woman had snarled unintelligibly at the sound of his voice, and had redoubled her caresses. Can you blame Saxe for having doubted? Remember that she had not for one moment given any sign of being Mary Bradford; remember that he had no proof that it was Mary Bradford. "Had you no intuition of her?" asked young Adams, later, at the Mission. "Intuition!" cried Saxe. "There wasn't a feature of Mary Bradford there: she was a loathsome horror." Let those who cannot believe in Saxe's failure to recognize her, reflect for an instant on all that is contained in that literal statement. Have you never failed, after a few years of separation, to recognize some one: some one whose face had not been subjected to barbaric decoration and disfigurement, not even to three years of the African sun; who, living all the while in the same quiet street, had merely passed for a time under the skilful transforming hands of sorrow? I have seen Mary Bradford's photograph, and was told at the same time that the not very striking face depended for its individuality on the expression of eyes and mouth. But painted eyes . . . and a lip-ring? She was undoubtedly, as Saxe said, "a loathsome horror"; and a loathsome horror who gave no sign. I firmly believe that she was not recognizable to the eye. Saxe's only chance would have lain in divination; in being able to say unerringly of the woman he loved: "Thus, or thus, in given circumstances, would she behave." Such knowledge of Mary Bradford could never have been easy to any man. In my opinion, no one can blame him for doubting. The magnificence of the performance was almost outside the realm of possibility. I asked Saxe once if Mary Bradford had been good at acting. He had never seen her do but one part: she had done that extremely well. And the part? Beatrice, in *Much Ado*. Beatrice!

The strain of it had told on Saxe, and he slept that night. But it is only fair to say that, before he slept, he had quite made up his mind that he was as far away from Mary Bradford as he had ever been. It is not to be wondered at. Only a man who had grasped Mary Bradford's idea—it has taken me three years to do that, entirely—could have believed that she would let Saxe go out baffled from the hut in which she deliberately chose to stay with her half-drunk, wholly vile captor. Women who could have done all the rest, would have turned at Saxe's offer of a kindly shot through the heart. But Mary Bradford was great. She was also infinitely wronged by Fate. It is all wanton, wanton—to the very last: all, that is, except her own part, which was sublimely reasoned.

Saxe slept, I say; and at dawn woke to his problem. The intelligence that works for us while we sleep waked him into the conviction that he must, at any cost, buy the woman. He said that, as he strode over to the chief's hut, he was thinking only of what price he ought to put on the child that would be such a fantastic mixture of breeds. He did not want the woman, but he felt that the purchase was inevitable. This, I am convinced, was only the New English leaven working him up to martyrdom. It would be unmitigatedly dreadful to have the woman on his hands, and therefore he ought probably to buy her.

The chief greeted him with temper, and soon Saxe learned why. The woman had left the hut before dawn, taking with her her master's largest knife. She was found later in her own little hovel, dead, with a clean stab to her heart. Suicide is virtually unknown among savages, and the village was astir. Saxe asked to see the body at once, but that, it seems, was not etiquette: he had to wait until it was prepared for burial. For an instant, he said, he thought of bargaining for the body, but forebore. He had a difficult return journey to make, and the point was, after all, to see it. When they permitted him to enter the hut, the face had been piously disfigured beyond recognition. He told me that he lifted the tattooed hand and kissed it: he did not know why. It was clear that if the woman had—preposterously—been Mary, she would not have wished it; and if she were the other, it was almost indecent. But he could not help it. This impulse of his seems to have been his only recognition of Mary Bradford. In life and in death, she suppressed every sign of herself with consummate art.

We were a fevered group that waited for Saxe day after day at the Mission; and he seemed to have been gone an intolerably long time. The broken leg that had kept me from going with him was almost well when he returned. Yet he had taken the shortest way back. It was also the unhealthiest. He said that he had heard war rumors that made him avoid the more frequented trail, but I fancy he rather hoped that the swamps he clung to would give him fever. In that sense—and in that sense only—Saxe could perhaps be said to have committed suicide. He stumbled into the Mission dining-room at noon one day. "And Mary?" we all cried, rising. "Oh, did you expect to see Mary?" he asked politely, but with evident astonishment.

We got him to bed at once. After the days of delirium were over, he told his story quite simply. It was pitifully short. The concrete facts seemed to be perfectly clear in his mind, and he gave them spontaneously; but what he himself had felt during that dramatic hour, I learned only by close questioning. He died suddenly, when he was apparently convalescent. The year he had been through had simply killed resiliency in him and he went down at the last as stupidly as a ninepin. I cannot imagine the source of the rumor that he had killed himself, unless it was some person who thought he ought to have done so. He started, at the end, to speak to me: "If Mary ever—" He never got beyond the three words; they showed sufficiently, however, that he was considering the possibility of Mary Bradford's being discovered after his death. He may have been wandering a little at the last; but, in my opinion, Saxe had never believed, even after the suicide, that the woman he had seen had been his betrothed.

Some weeks after Saxe's death, we received incontrovertible proof —if testimony is ever incontrovertible—that it had indeed been she. We had been surrounded for a year by a hideous jungle—blind, hostile, impenetrable. Now out of that jungle stalked a simple fact. One of the native girls who had been taken captive with Mary Bradford returned at length to her own tribe. She had shared Mary's fortunes, as it happened, almost to the last; then the chief who had bought them both sold her, and by the successive chance of purchase, raid, and battle she had reached her own people. It was hardly more than crawling home to die; but she managed to send word by one of her kinsmen to the white people down the river. Apparently she and Mary had promised each other to report if either should ever reach friends again. Her message was pitifully meagre: Mary had talked little in those wild months; and after she had seen that they were too well watched to escape, she had talked not at all. But the two had evidently clung together—an extraordinary tie, which was the last Mary Bradford was to know of friendship. The burden of the native's report was that the white girl was the favorite of a chief who gave her much finery. The dying woman seems to have thought it would set Mary Bradford's friends at rest—her kinsman, I remember, said that he had good news for us. The news was no news to me—I had been thinking; but I was glad that Saxe had died before he could hear it. Even the comfort of knowing that Mary was surely dead would never have made up to him for the ironic memory of the last hour he had spent with her. Besides, Saxe would never have understood.

I should probably never have touched this chapter of history with a public pen, if I had not heard a woman say, a few months since, that she thought Mary Bradford's conduct indelicate. Had the woman not said it to me directly, I should not have believed, even at my cynical age, that such a thing could be said. I greatly regret, myself, that the facts were ever told: they should have been buried in Africa with Saxe. But the Prices returned to America not long after it all happened, and apparently could not refrain from talking. Even so, I should have let Mary Bradford's legend alone, forever, had I not learned that she could be misjudged.

Consider dispassionately the elements of her situation; and tell me who has ever been so tortured. Physically unable to escape by flight, morally incapable, as you might say, of escaping by death—for there can be no doubt that, difficult as suicide would have been to a guarded captive, she could have found some poisonous root, courted the bite of some serpent, snatched for one instant some pointed weapon; and that she was deterred, as Saxe said, by the simple belief that to take one's life was the unpardonable sin against the Holy Ghost, the Comforter—she could but take what came. As a high-priced chattel, she was probably not, for the most part, ill-treated—save for the tattooing, which was not cruelly intended. The few scars that Saxe noted doubtless bore witness to her protest against the utmost bitterness of slavery, some sudden saint-like frenzy with which she opposed profanation. She may have wondered why God chose so to degrade her: her conduct with Saxe shows beyond a doubt how she rated her degradation. She made not one attempt to dignify or to defend her afflicted body. Her soul despised it: trampled it under foot.

What Mary Bradford suffered before Saxe came we cannot know, but the measure of it lies, I think, in the resolution she took (if we believe the jealous slave girl) when she heard of the white man's approach. She must have divined Saxe, leagues away, as he was unable to divine her, face to face. Her one intent was to deceive him, to steep herself in unrecognizable savagery. If Mary Bradford had conceived of any rôle possible for herself in her own world, she would not have created her great part. If she had felt herself fit even to care for lepers at Molokai, she would have washed away her paint and fallen at his feet. It is perfectly evident that she considered herself fit for nothing in life—hardly for death. Her hope was clearly that Saxe should not know her. I do not believe that it was pride. If there had been any pride left in Mary Bradford's heart, she could not have stood quietly ("apathetically," was his word!) before Saxe in the flare of the dying sun. It was not to save anything of hers that she went through her comedy, but only to save a little merciful blindness for Saxe himself. He undoubtedly made it as hard as possible for her. I am inclined to think that if he had gone away at once, she would be living still—mothering her half-breed child, teaching it secretly the fear of God. When she saw that all Saxe's bewilderment still left him with the firm determination to buy her—to take her away and study her at his leisure—she conceived her magnificent *chute de rideau.* When she went into the hut, she had decided, for Saxe's sake, to die. Mary Bradford grovelling at the feet of the drunken chief will always seem to me one of the most remarkable figures in history: I should never have mentioned Jocasta in the same breath with her. Only Christianity can give us tragedy like that. How must she not have longed, at Saxe's offer of a kindly shot through the heart, to turn, to fling herself at his feet, to cry out his name, once. She "redoubled her caresses," Saxe said! Has any man ever been so loved, do you think? For the sake of bestowing upon him that healing doubt, she let him go, she put off death, she spent her last night on earth not fifty yards from him, in the hut of a savage, that she might have, before dawn, the means of committing the unpardonable sin. Note that she did not commit suicide until she had made it perfectly plausible—from the point of view of the Arab-Mandingo woman. *She proved to him that it was not she.* She gauged Saxe perfectly. Nothing but some such evidence as later we received—perhaps not even that—would ever have made Saxe believe that Mary Bradford, with him by her side, had clung to that vile savage. Even Mary Bradford—whose soul must have been, by that time, far away from her body—a mere voice in her own ears, a remote counsellor to hands and feet—could not have done that, had she not intended to die. But remember that up to that day she had lived rather than rank herself with the "violenti contro se stessi." We can simply say that Mary Bradford chose the chance of Hell for the sake of sparing Saxe pain. The fact that you or I—I pass over the lady who thinks her indelicate; does she think, I wonder, that it would have been delicate for Mary Bradford to accompany Saxe back to civilization?—may believe her to be one of the saints, has nothing to do with what she thought. Mary Bradford came of a race that for many generations believed in predestination; but she herself believed in free will. Dreadful as it is to be foredamned, it is worse to have damned yourself. She had not even the cold comfort of Calvinism. I said that I understood Mary Bradford. I am not sure that it would not have taken a Spanish saint of the sixteenth century really to understand her. Sixteenth-century Spain is the only thing I know of that is in the least like New England.

I am not trying to make out a "case" for Mary Bradford; and I sincerely hope that the lady who thinks her indelicate will never read these pages. For most people, the facts will suffice, and I have no desire to interpret them for the others. You have only to meditate for a little on the ironic and tragic reflections of a hundred kinds that must have surged through Mary Bradford's brain, to be swept away, yourself, on the horrid current. Do I need, for example, to point out the difficulty—to use a word that I think the lady I have cited would approve—of merely meeting the man she adored, face to face? For never doubt that those souls who live least by the flesh feel themselves most defiled by its defilement. No, you have only to explore Mary Bradford's tragedy for yourself. It will take you three years, perhaps, as it has taken me, to penetrate the last recesses. And if you are tempted for a moment to think of her as mad, or *exaltée,* reflect on how completely she understood Saxe. I am only half a New Englander; and I confess that, though I reverence her heroism, I am even more humble before her intelligence. It is no blame to Saxe that he stumbled out of the chief's hut, completely her dupe. Poor Saxe! But the vivid vision of that scene leaves *Phèdre* tasteless to me. As I say, I am only half a New Englander. . .

RING W. LARDNER

Champion

MIDGE KELLY scored his first knockout when he was seventeen. The knockee was his brother Connie, three years his junior and a cripple. The purse was a half dollar given to the younger Kelly by a lady whose electric had just missed bumping his soul from his frail little body.

Connie did not know Midge was in the house, else he never would have risked laying the prize on the arm of the least comfortable chair in the room, the better to observe its shining beauty. As Midge entered from the kitchen, the crippled boy covered the coin with his hand, but the movement lacked the speed requisite to escape his brother's quick eye.

"Watcha got there?" demanded Midge.

"Nothin'," said Connie.

"You're a one-legged liar!" said Midge.

He strode over to his brother's chair and grasped the hand that concealed the coin.

"Let loose!" he ordered.

Connie began to cry.

"Let loose and shut up your noise," said the elder, and jerked his brother's hand from the chair arm.

The coin fell onto the bare floor. Midge pounced on it. His weak mouth widened into a triumphant smile.

"Nothin', huh?" he said. "All right, if it's nothin' you don't want it."

"Give that back," sobbed the younger.

"I'll give you a red nose, you little sneak! Where'd you steal it?"

"I didn't steal it. It's mine. A lady give it to me after she pretty near hit me with a car."

"It's a crime she missed you," said Midge.

Midge started for the front door. The cripple picked up his crutch, rose from his chair with difficulty, and, still sobbing, came toward Midge. The latter heard him and stopped.

"You better stay where you're at," he said.

"I want my money," cried the boy.

"I know what you want," said Midge.

Doubling up the fist that held the half dollar, he landed with all his strength on his brother's mouth. Connie fell to the floor with a thud, the crutch tumbling on top of him. Midge stood beside the prostrate form.

"Is that enough?" he said. "Or do you want this, too?"

And he kicked him in the crippled leg.

"I guess that'll hold you," he said.

There was no response from the boy on the floor. Midge looked at him a moment, then at the coin in his hand, and then went out into the street, whistling.

An hour later, when Mrs. Kelly came home from her day's work at Faulkner's Steam Laundry, she found Connie on the floor, moaning. Dropping on her knees beside him, she called him by name a score of times. Then she got up and, pale as a ghost, dashed from the house. Dr. Ryan left the Kelly abode about dusk and walked toward Halsted Street. Mrs. Dorgan spied him as he passed her gate.

"Who's sick, Doctor?" she called.

"Poor little Connie," he replied. "He had a bad fall."

"How did it happen?"

"I can't say for sure, Margaret, but I'd almost bet he was knocked down."

"Knocked down!" exclaimed Mrs. Dorgan. "Why, who—?"

"Have you seen the other one lately?"

"Michael? No, not since mornin'. You can't be thinkin'——"

"I wouldn't put it past him, Margaret," said the doctor gravely. "The lad's mouth is swollen and cut, and his poor, skinny little leg is bruised. He surely didn't do it to himself, and I think Helen suspects the other one."

"Lord save us!" said Mrs. Dorgan. "I'll run over and see if I can help."

"That's a good woman," said Doctor Ryan, and went on down the street.

Near midnight, when Midge came home, his mother was sitting at Connie's bedside. She did not look up.

"Well," said Midge, "what's the matter?"

She remained silent. Midge repeated his question.

"Michael, you know what's the matter," she said at length.

"I don't know nothin'," said Midge.

"Don't lie to me, Michael. What did you do to your brother?"

"Nothin'."

"You hit him."

"Well, then, I hit him. What of it? It ain't the first time."

Her lips pressed tightly together, her face like chalk, Ellen Kelly rose from her chair and made straight for him. Midge backed against the door.

"Lay off'n me, Ma. I don't want to fight no woman."

Still she came on breathing heavily.

"Stop where you're at, Ma," he warned.

There was a brief struggle and Midge's mother lay on the floor before him.

"You ain't hurt, Ma. You're lucky I didn't land good. And I told you to lay off'n me."

"God forgive you, Michael!"

Midge found Hap Collins in the showdown game at the Royal.

"Come on out a minute," he said.

Hap followed him out on the walk.

"I'm leavin' town for a w'ile," said Midge.

"What for?"

"Well, we had a little run-in up to the house. The kid stole a half buck off'n me, and when I went after it he cracked me with his crutch. So I nailed him. And the old lady came at me with a chair and I took it off'n her and she fell down."

"How is Connie hurt?"

"Not bad."

"What are you runnin' away for?"

"Who the hell said I was runnin' away? I'm sick and tired o' gettin' picked on; that's all. So I'm leavin' for a w'ile and I want a piece o' money."

"I ain't only got six bits," said Happy.

"You're in bad shape, ain't you? Well, come through with it."

Happy came through.

"You oughtn't to hit the kid," he said.

"I ain't astin' you who can I hit," snarled Midge. "You try to put somethin' over on me and you'll get the same dose. I'm goin' now."

"Go as far as you like," said Happy, but not until he was sure that Kelly was out of hearing.

Early the following morning, Midge boarded a train for Milwaukee.

He had no ticket, but no one knew the difference. The conductor remained in the caboose.

On a night six months later, Midge hurried out of the "stage door" of the Star Boxing Club and made for Duane's saloon, two blocks away. In his pocket were twelve dollars, his reward for having battered up one Demon Dempsey through the six rounds of the first preliminary.

It was Midge's first professional engagement in the manly art. Also it was the first time in weeks that he had earned twelve dollars.

On the way to Duane's he had to pass Niemann's. He pulled his cap over his eyes and increased his pace until he had gone by. Inside Niemann's stood a trusting bartender, who for ten days had staked Midge to drinks and allowed him to ravage the lunch on a promise to come in and settle the moment he was paid for the "prelim."

Midge strode into Duane's and aroused the napping bartender by slapping a silver dollar on the festive board.

"Gimme a shot," said Midge.

The shooting continued until the wind-up at the Star was over and part of the fight crowd joined Midge in front of Duane's bar. A youth in the early twenties, standing next to young Kelly, finally summoned sufficient courage to address him.

"Wasn't you in the first bout?" he ventured.

"Yeh," Midge replied.

"My name's Hersch," said the other.

Midge received the startling information in silence.

"I don't want to butt in," continued Mr. Hersch, "but I'd like to buy you a drink."

"All right," said Midge, "but don't overstrain yourself."

Mr. Hersch laughed uproariously and beckoned to the bartender.

"You certainly gave that wop a trimmin' to-night," said the buyer of the drink, when they had been served. "I thought you'd kill him."

"I would if I hadn't let up," Midge replied. "I'll kill 'em all."

"You got the wallop all right," the other said admiringly.

"Have I got the wallop?" said Midge. "Say, I can kick like a mule. Did you notice them muscles in my shoulders?"

"Notice 'em? I couldn't help from noticin' 'em," said Hersch. "I says to the fella settin' alongside o' me, I says: 'Look at them shoulders! No wonder he can hit,' I says to him."

"Just let me land and it's good-bye, baby," said Midge. "I'll kill 'em all."

The oral manslaughter continued until Duane's closed for the night.

At parting, Midge and his new friend shook hands and arranged for a meeting the following evening.

For nearly a week the two were together almost constantly. It was Hersch's pleasant rôle to listen to Midge's modest revelations concerning himself, and to buy every time Midge's glass was empty. But there came an evening when Hersch regretfully announced that he must go home to supper.

"I got a date for eight bells," he confided. "I could stick till then, only I must clean up and put on the Sunday clo'es, 'cause she's the prettiest little thing in Milwaukee."

"Can't you fix it for two?" asked Midge.

"I don't know who to get," Hersch replied. "Wait, though. I got a sister and if she ain't busy, it'll be O. K. She's no bum for looks herself."

So it came about that Midge and Emma Hersch and Emma's brother and the prettiest little thing in Milwaukee foregathered at Wall's and danced half the night away. And Midge and Emma danced every dance together, for though every little onestep seemed to induce a new thirst of its own, Lou Hersch stayed too sober to dance with his own sister.

The next day, penniless at last in spite of his phenomenal ability to make someone else settle, Midge Kelly sought out Doc Hammond, matchmaker for the Star, and asked to be booked for the next show.

"I could put you on with Tracy for the next bout," said Doc.

"What's they in it?" asked Midge.

"Twenty if you cop," Doc told him.

"Have a heart," protested Midge. "Didn't I look good the other night?"

"You looked all right. But you aren't Freddie Welsh yet by a consid'able margin."

"I ain't scared of Freddie Welsh or none of 'em," said Midge.

"Well, we don't pay our boxers by the size of their chests," Doc said. "I'm offerin' you this Tracy bout. Take it or leave it."

"All right; I'm on," said Midge, and he passed a pleasant afternoon at Duane's on the strength of his booking.

Young Tracy's manager came to Midge the night before the show.

"How do you feel about this go?" he asked.

"Me?" said Midge. "I feel all right. What you mean, how do I feel?"

"I mean," said Tracy's manager, "that we're mighty anxious to win, 'cause the boy's got a chanct in Philly if he cops this one."

"What's your proposition?" asked Midge.

"Fifty bucks," said Tracy's manager.

"What do you think I am, a crook? Me lay down for fifty bucks? Not me!"

"Seventy-five, then," said Tracy's manager.

The market closed on eighty and the details were agreed on in short order. And the next night Midge was stopped in the second round by a terrific slap on the forearm.

This time Midge passed up both Niemann's and Duane's, having a sizable account at each place, and sought his refreshment at Stein's farther down the street.

When the profits of his deal with Tracy were gone, he learned, by first-hand information from Doc Hammond and the matchmakers at the other "clubs," that he was no longer desired for even the cheapest of preliminaries. There was no danger of his starving or dying of thirst while Emma and Lou Hersch lived. But he made up his mind, four months after his defeat by Young Tracy, that Milwaukee was not the ideal place for him to live.

"I can lick the best of 'em," he reasoned, "but there ain't no more chanct for me here. I can maybe go east and get on somewheres. And besides——"

But just after Midge had purchased a ticket to Chicago with the money he had "borrowed" from Emma Hersch "to buy shoes," a heavy hand was laid on his shoulders and he turned to face two strangers.

"Where are you goin', Kelly?" inquired the owner of the heavy hand.

"Nowheres," said Midge. "What the hell do you care?"

The other stranger spoke:

"Kelly, I'm employed by Emma Hersch's mother to see that you do right by her. And we want you to stay here till you've done it."

"You won't get nothin' but the worst of it, monkeying with me," said Midge.

Nevertheless, he did not depart for Chicago that night. Two days later, Emma Hersch became Mrs. Kelly, and the gift of the groom, when once they were alone, was a crushing blow on the bride's pale cheek.

Next morning, Midge left Milwaukee as he had entered it—by fast freight.

"They's no use kiddin' ourself any more," said Tommy Haley. "He might get down to thirty-seven in a pinch, but if he done below that a mouse could stop him. He's a welter; that's what he is and he knows it as well as I do. He's growed like a weed in the last six mont's. I told him, I says, 'If you don't quit growin' they won't be nobody for you to box, only Willard and them.' He says, 'Well, I wouldn't run away from Willard if I weighed twenty pounds more.'"

"He must hate himself," said Tommy's brother.

"I never seen a good one that didn't," said Tommy. "And Midge is a good one; don't make no mistake about that. I wisht we could of got Welsh before the kid growed so big. But it's too late now. I won't make no holler, though, if we can match him up with the Dutchman."

"Who do you mean?"

"Young Goetz, the welter champ. We mightn't not get so much dough for the bout itself, but it'd roll in afterward. What a drawin' card we'd be, 'cause the people pays their money to see the fella with the wallop, and that's Midge. And we'd keep the title just as long as Midge could make the weight."

"Can't you land no match with Goetz?"

"Sure, 'cause he needs the money. But I've went careful with the kid so far and look at the results I got! So what's the use of takin' a chanct? The kid's comin' every minute and Goetz is goin' back faster'n big Johnson did. I think we could lick him now; I'd bet my life on it. But six mont's from now they won't be no risk. He'll of licked hisself before that time. Then all as we'll have to do is sign up with him and wait for the referee to stop it. But Midge is so crazy to get at him now that I can't hardly hold him back."

The brothers Haley were lunching in a Boston hotel. Dan had come down from Holyoke to visit with Tommy and to watch the latter's protégé go twelve rounds, or less, with Bud Cross. The bout promised little in the way of a contest, for Midge had twice stopped the Baltimore youth and Bud's reputation for gameness was all that had earned him the date. The fans were willing to pay the price to see Midge's hay-making left, but they wanted to see it used on an opponent who would not jump out of the ring the first time he felt its crushing force. But Cross was such an opponent, and his willingness to stop boxing-gloves with his eyes, ears, nose and throat had long enabled him to escape the horrors of honest labor. A game boy was Bud, and he showed it in his battered, swollen, discolored face.

"I should think," said Dan Haley, "that the kid'd do whatever you tell him after all you done for him."

"Well," said Tommy, "he's took my dope pretty straight so far, but he's so sure of hisself that he can't see no reason for waitin'. He'll do what I say, though; he'd be a sucker not to."

"You got a contrac' with him?"

"No, I don't need no contrac'. He knows it was me that drug him out o' the gutter and he ain't goin' to turn me down now, when he's got the dough and bound to get more. Where'd he of been at if I hadn't listened to him when he first come to me? That's pretty near two years ago now, but it seems like last week. I was settin' in the s'loon acrost from the Pleasant Club in Philly, waitin' for McCann to count the dough and come over, when this little bum blowed in and tried to stand the house off for a drink. They told him nothin' doin' and to beat it out o' there, and then he seen me and come over to where I was settin' and ast me wasn't I a boxin' man and I told him who I was. Then he ast me for money to buy a shot and I told him to set down and I'd buy it for him.

"Then we got talkin' things over and he told me his name and told me about fightin' a couple o' prelims out to Milwaukee. So I says, 'Well, boy, I don't know how good or how rotten you are, but you won't never get nowheres trainin' on that stuff.' So he says he'd cut it out if he could get on in a bout and I says I would give him a chanct if he played square with me and didn't touch no more to drink. So we shook hands and I took him up to the hotel with me and give him a bath and the next day I bought him some clo'es. And I staked him to eats and sleeps for over six weeks. He had a hard time breakin' away from the polish, but finally I thought he was fit and I give him his chanct. He went on with Smiley Sayer and stopped him so quick that Smiley thought sure he was poisoned.

"Well, you know what he's did since. The only beatin' in his record was by Tracy in Milwaukee before I got hold of him, and he's licked Tracy three times in the last year.

"I've gave him all the best of it in a money way and he's got seven thousand bucks in cold storage. How's that for a kid that was in the gutter two years ago? And he'd have still more yet if he wasn't so nuts over clo'es and got to stop at the good hotels and so forth."

"Where's his home at?"

"Well, he ain't really got no home. He came from Chicago and his mother canned him out o' the house for bein' no good. She give him a raw deal, I guess, and he says he won't have nothin' to do with her unlest she comes to him first. She's got a pile o' money, he says, so he ain't worryin' about her."

The gentleman under discussion entered the café and swaggered to Tommy's table, while the whole room turned to look.

Midge was the picture of health despite a slightly colored eye and an ear that seemed to have no opening. But perhaps it was not his healthiness that drew all eyes. His diamond horse-shoe tie pin, his purple cross-striped shirt, his orange shoes and his light blue suit fairly screamed for attention.

"Where you been?" he asked Tommy. "I been lookin' all over for you."

"Set down," said his manager.

"No time," said Midge. "I'm goin' down to the w'arf and see 'em unload the fish."

"Shake hands with my brother Dan," said Tommy.

Midge shook with the Holyoke Haley.

"If you're Tommy's brother, you're O. K. with me," said Midge, and the brothers beamed with pleasure.

Dan moistened his lips and murmured an embarrassed reply, but it was lost on the young gladiator.

"Leave me take twenty," Midge was saying. "I prob'ly won't need it, but I don't like to be caught short."

Tommy parted with a twenty dollar bill and recorded the transaction in a small black book the insurance company had given him for Christmas.

"But," he said, "it won't cost you no twenty to look at them fish. Want me to go along?"

"No," said Midge hastily. "You and your brother here prob'ly got a lot to say to each other."

"Well," said Tommy, "don't take no bad money and don't get lost. And you better be back at four o'clock and lay down a w'ile."

"I don't need no rest to beat this guy," said Midge. "He'll do enough layin' down for the both of us."

And laughing even more than the jest called for, he strode out through the fire of admiring and startled glances.

The corner of Boylston and Tremont was the nearest Midge got to the wharf, but the lady awaiting him was doubtless a more dazzling sight than the catch of the luckiest Massachusetts fisherman. She could talk, too—probably better than the fish.

"O you Kid!" she said, flashing a few silver teeth among the gold. "O you fighting man!"

Midge smiled up at her.

"We'll go somewheres and get a drink," he said. "One won't hurt."

In New Orleans, five months after he had rearranged the map of Bud Cross for the third time, Midge finished training for his championship bout with the Dutchman.

Back in his hotel after the final workout, Midge stopped to chat with some of the boys from up north, who had made the long trip to see a champion dethroned, for the result of this bout was so nearly a foregone conclusion that even the experts had guessed it.

Tommy Haley secured the key and the mail and ascended to the Kelly suite. He was bathing when Midge came in a half hour later.

"Any mail?" asked Midge.

"There on the bed," replied Tommy from the tub.

Midge picked up the stack of letters and postcards and glanced them over. From the pile he sorted out three letters and laid them on the table. The rest he tossed into the waste-basket. Then he picked up the three and sat for a few moments holding them, while his eyes gazed off into space. At length he looked again at the three unopened letters in his hand; then he put one in his pocket and tossed the other two at the basket. They missed their target and fell on the floor.

"Hell!" said Midge, and stooping over picked them up.

He opened one postmarked Milwaukee and read:

Dear Husband:

I have wrote to you so manny times and got no anser and I dont know if you ever got them, so I am writeing again in the hopes you will get this letter and anser. I dont like to bother you with my trubles and I would not only for the baby and I am not asking you should write to me but only send a little money and I am not asking for myself but the baby has not been well a day sence last Aug. and the dr. told me she cant live much longer unless I give her better food and thats impossible the way things are. Lou has not been working for a year and what I make dont hardley pay for the rent. I am not asking for you to give me any money, but only you should send what I loaned when convenient and I think it amts. to about $36.00. Please try and send that amt. and it will help me, but if you cant send the whole amt. try and send me something.

Your wife,

Emma.

Midge tore the letter into a hundred pieces and scattered them over the floor.

"Money, money, money!" he said. "They must think I'm made o' money. I s'pose the old woman's after it too."

He opened his mother's letter:

dear Michael Connie wonted me to rite and say you must beet the dutchman and he is sur you will and wonted me to say we wont you to rite and tell us about it, but I gess you havent no time to rite or we herd from you long beffore this but I wish you would rite jest a line or 2 boy becaus it wuld be better for Connie then a barl of medisin. It wuld help me to keep things going if you send me money now and then when you can spair it but if you cant send no money try and fine time to rite a letter onley a few lines and it will please Connie. jest think boy he hasent got out of bed in over 3 yrs. Connie says good luck.

Your Mother,

Ellen F. Kelly.

"I thought so," said Midge. "They're all alike."

The third letter was from New York. It read:

Hon:—This is the last letter you will get from me before your champ, but I will send you a telegram Saturday, but I can't say as much in a telegram as in a letter and I am writeing this to let you know I am thinking of you and praying for good luck.

Lick him good hon and don't wait no longer than you have to and don't forget to wire me as soon as its over. Give him that little old left of yours on the nose hon and don't be afraid of spoiling his good looks because he couldn't be no homlier than he is. But don't let him spoil my baby's pretty face. You won't will you hon.

Well hon I would give anything to be there and see it, but I guess you love Haley better than me or you wouldn't let him keep me away. But when your champ hon we can do as we please and tell Haley to go to the devil.

Well hon I will send you a telegram Saturday and I almost forgot to tell you I will need some more money, a couple hundred say and you will have to wire it to me as soon as you get this. You will won't you hon.

I will send you a telegram Saturday and remember hon I am pulling for you.

Well good-by sweetheart and good luck.

Grace.

"They're all alike," said Midge. "Money, money, money."

Tommy Haley, shining from his ablutions, came in from the adjoining room.

"Thought you'd be layin' down," he said.

"I'm goin' to," said Midge, unbuttoning his orange shoes.

"I'll call you at six and you can eat up here without no bugs to pester you. I got to go down and give them birds their tickets."

"Did you hear from Goldberg?" asked Midge.

"Didn't I tell you? Sure; fifteen weeks at five hundred, if we win. And we can get a guarantee o' twelve thousand, with privileges either in New York or Milwaukee."

"Who with?"

"Anybody that'll stand up in front of you. You don't care who it is, do you?"

"Not me. I'll make 'em all look like a monkey."

"Well, you better lay down aw'ile."

"Oh, say, wire two hundred to Grace for me, will you? Right away; the New York address."

"Two hundred! You just sent her three hundred last Sunday."

"Well, what the hell do you care?"

"All right, all right. Don't get sore about it. Anything else?"

"That's all," said Midge, and dropped onto the bed.

"And I want the deed done before I come back," said Grace as she rose from the table. "You won't fall down on me, will you, hon?"

"Leave it to me," said Midge. "And don't spend no more than you have to."

Grace smiled a farewell and left the café. Midge continued to sip his coffee and read his paper.

They were in Chicago and they were in the middle of Midge's first week in vaudeville. He had come straight north to reap the rewards of his glorious victory over the broken down Dutchman. A fortnight had been spent in learning his act, which consisted of a gymnastic exhibition and a ten minutes' monologue on the various excellences of Midge Kelly. And now he was twice daily turning 'em away from the Madison Theater.

His breakfast over and his paper read, Midge sauntered into the lobby and asked for his key. He then beckoned to a bell-boy, who had been hoping for that very honor.

"Find Haley, Tommy Haley," said Midge. "Tell him to come up to my room."

"Yes, sir, Mr. Kelly," said the boy, and proceeded to break all his former records for diligence.

Midge was looking out of his seventh-story window when Tommy answered the summons.

"What'll it be?" inquired his manager.

There was a pause before Midge replied.

"Haley," he said, "twenty-five per cent's a whole lot o' money."

"I guess I got it comin', ain't I?" said Tommy.

"I don't see how you figger it. I don't see where you're worth it to me."

"Well," said Tommy, "I didn't expect nothin' like this. I thought you was satisfied with the bargain. I don't want to beat nobody out o' nothin', but I don't see where you could have got anybody else that would of did all I done for you."

"Sure, that's all right," said the champion. "You done a lot for me in Philly. And you got good money for it, didn't you?"

"I ain't makin' no holler. Still and all, the big money's still ahead of us yet. And if it hadn't of been for me, you wouldn't of never got within grabbin' distance."

"Oh, I guess I could of went along all right," said Midge. "Who was it that hung that left on the Dutchman's jaw, me or you?"

"Yes, but you wouldn't been in the ring with the Dutchman if it wasn't for how I handled you."

"Well, this won't get us nowheres. The idear is that you ain't worth no twenty-five per cent now and it don't make no diff'rence what come off a year or two ago."

"Don't it?" said Tommy. "I'd say it made a whole lot of difference."

"Well, I say it don't and I guess that settles it."

"Look here, Midge," Tommy said, "I thought I was fair with you, but if you don't think so, I'm willin' to hear what you think is fair. I don't want nobody callin' me a Sherlock. Let's go down to business and sign up a contrac'. What's your figger?"

"I ain't namin' no figger," Midge replied. "I'm sayin' that twenty-five's too much. Now what are you willin' to take?"

"How about twenty?"

"Twenty's too much," said Kelly.

"What ain't too much?" asked Tommy.

"Well, Haley, I might as well give it to you straight. They ain't nothin' that ain't too much."

"You mean you don't want me at no figger?"

"That's the idear."

There was a minute's silence. Then Tommy Haley walked toward the door.

"Midge," he said, in a choking voice, "you're makin' a big mistake, boy. You can't throw down your best friends and get away with it. That damn woman will ruin you."

Midge sprang from his seat.

"You shut your mouth!" he stormed. "Get out o' here before they have to carry you out. You been spongin' off o' me long enough. Say one more word about the girl or about anything else and you'll get what the Dutchman got. Now get out!"

And Tommy Haley, having a very vivid memory of the Dutchman's face as he fell, got out.

Grace came in later, dropped her numerous bundles on the lounge and perched herself on the arm of Midge's chair.

"Well?" said she.

"Well," said Midge, "I got rid of him."

"Good boy!" said Grace. "And now I think you might give me that twenty-five per cent."

"Besides the seventy-five you're already gettin'?" said Midge.

"Don't be no grouch, hon. You don't look pretty when you're grouchy."

"It ain't my business to look pretty," Midge replied.

"Wait till you see how I look with the stuff I bought this mornin'!"

Midge glanced at the bundles on the lounge.

"There's Haley's twenty-five per cent," he said, "and then some."

The champion did not remain long without a manager. Haley's successor was none other than Jerome Harris, who saw in Midge a better meal ticket than his popular-priced musical show had been.

The contract, giving Mr. Harris twenty-five per cent of Midge's earnings, was signed in Detroit the week after Tommy Haley had heard his dismissal read. It had taken Midge just six days to learn that a popular actor cannot get on without the ministrations of a man who thinks, talks and means business. At first Grace objected to the new member of the firm, but when Mr. Harris had demanded and secured from the vaudeville people a one-hundred dollar increase in Midge's weekly stipend, she was convinced that the champion had acted for the best.

"You and my missus will have some great old times," Harris told Grace. "I'd of wired her to join us here, only I seen the Kid's bookin' takes us to Milwaukee next week, and that's where she is."

But when they were introduced in the Milwaukee hotel, Grace admitted to herself that her feeling for Mrs. Harris could hardly be called love at first sight. Midge, on the contrary, gave his new manager's wife the many times over and seemed loath to end the feast of his eyes.

"Some doll," he said to Grace when they were alone.

"Doll is right," the lady replied, "and sawdust where her brains ought to be."

"I'm li'ble to steal that baby," said Midge, and he smiled as he noted the effect of his words on his audience's face.

On Tuesday of the Milwaukee week the champion successfully defended his title in a bout that the newspapers never reported. Midge was alone in his room that morning when a visitor entered without knocking. The visitor was Lou Hersch.

Midge turned white at sight of him.

"What do you want?" he demanded.

"I guess you know," said Lou Hersch. "Your wife's starvin' to death and your baby's starvin' to death and I'm starvin' to death. And you're dirty with money."

"Listen," said Midge, "if it wasn't for you, I wouldn't never saw your sister. And, if you ain't man enough to hold a job, what's that to me? The best thing you can do is keep away from me."

"You give me a piece o' money and I'll go."

Midge's reply to the ultimatum was a straight right to his brother-in-law's narrow chest.

"Take that home to your sister."

And after Lou Hersch had picked himself up and slunk away, Midge thought: "It's lucky I didn't give him my left or I'd of croaked him. And if I'd hit him in the stomach, I'd of broke his spine."

There was a party after each evening performance during the Milwaukee engagement. The wine flowed freely and Midge had more of it than Tommy Haley ever would have permitted him. Mr. Harris offered no objection, which was possibly just as well for his own physical comfort.

In the dancing between drinks, Midge had his new manager's wife for a partner as often as Grace. The latter's face as she floundered round in the arms of the portly Harris, belied her frequent protestations that she was having the time of her life.

Several times that week, Midge thought Grace was on the point of starting the quarrel he hoped to have. But it was not until Friday night that she accommodated. He and Mrs. Harris had disappeared after the matinee and when Grace saw him again at the close of the night show, she came to the point at once.

"What are you tryin' to pull off?" she demanded.

"It's none o' your business, is it?" said Midge.

"You bet it's my business; mine and Harris's. You cut it short or you'll find out."

"Listen," said Midge, "have you got a mortgage on me or somethin'? You talk like we was married."

"We're goin' to be, too. And to-morrow's as good a time as any."

"Just about," Midge said. "You got as much chanct o' marryin' me to-morrow as the next day or next year and that ain't no chanct at all."

"We'll find out," said Grace.

"You're the one that's got somethin' to find out."

"What do you mean?"

"I mean I'm married already."

"You lie!"

"You think so, do you? Well, s'pose you go to this here address and get acquainted with my missus."

Midge scrawled a number on a piece of paper and handed it to her. She stared at it unseeingly.

"Well," said Midge, "I ain't kiddin' you. You go there and ask for Mrs. Michael Kelly, and if you don't find her, I'll marry you to-morrow before breakfast."

Still Grace stared at the scrap of paper. To Midge it seemed an age before she spoke again.

"You lied to me all this w'ile."

"You never ast me was I married. What's more, what the hell diff'rence did it make to you? You got a split, didn't you? Better'n fifty-fifty."

He started away.

"Where you goin'?"

"I'm goin' to meet Harris and his wife."

"I'm goin' with you. You're not goin' to shake me now."

"Yes, I am, too," said Midge quietly. "When I leave town to-morrow night, you're going to stay here. And if I see where you're goin' to make a fuss, I'll put you in a hospital where they'll keep you quiet. You can get your stuff to-morrow mornin' and I'll slip you a hundred bucks. And then I don't want to see no more o' you. And don't try and tag along now or I'll have to add another K. O. to the old record."

When Grace returned to the hotel that night, she discovered that Midge and the Harrises had moved to another. And when Midge left town the following night, he was again without a manager, and Mr. Harris was without a wife.

Three days prior to Midge Kelly's ten-round bout with Young Milton in New York City, the sporting editor of *The News* assigned Joe Morgan to write two or three thousand words about the champion to run with a picture lay-out for Sunday.

Joe Morgan dropped in at Midge's training quarters Friday afternoon. Midge, he learned, was doing road work, but Midge's manager, Wallie Adams, stood ready and willing to supply reams of dope about the greatest fighter of the age.

"Let's hear what you've got," said Joe, "and then I'll try to fix up something."

So Wallie stepped on the accelerator of his imagination and shot away.

"Just a kid; that's all he is; a regular boy. Get what I mean? Don't know the meanin' o' bad habits. Never tasted liquor in his life and would prob'bly get sick if he smelled it. Clean livin' put him up where he's at. Get what I mean? And modest and unassumin' as a school girl. He's so quiet you wouldn't never know he was round. And he'd go to jail before he'd talk about himself.

"No job at all to get him in shape, 'cause he's always that way. The only trouble we have with him is gettin' him to light into these poor bums they match him up with. He's scared he'll hurt somebody. Get what I mean? He's tickled to death over this match with Milton, 'cause everybody says Milton can stand the gaff. Midge'll maybe be able to cut loose a little this time. But the last two bouts he had, the guys hadn't no business in the ring with him, and he was holdin' back all the w'ile for the fear he'd kill somebody. Get what I mean?"

"Is he married?" inquired Joe.

"Say, you'd think he was married to hear him rave about them kiddies he's got. His fam'ly's up in Canada to their summer home and Midge is wild to get up there with 'em. He thinks more o' that wife and them kiddies than all the money in the world. Get what I mean?"

"How many children has he?"

"I don't know, four or five, I guess. All boys and every one of 'em a dead ringer for their dad."

"Is his father living?"

"No, the old man died when he was a kid. But he's got a grand old mother and a kid brother out in Chi. They're the first ones he thinks about after a match, them and his wife and kiddies. And he don't forget to send the old woman a thousand bucks after every bout. He's goin' to buy her a new home as soon as they pay him off for this match."

"How about his brother? Is he going to tackle the game?"

"Sure, and Midge says he'll be a champion before he's twenty years old. They're a fightin' fam'ly and all of 'em honest and straight as a die. Get what I mean? A fella that I can't tell you his name come to Midge in Milwaukee onct and wanted him to throw a fight and Midge give him such a trimmin' in the street that he couldn't go on that night. That's the kind he is. Get what I mean?"

Joe Morgan hung around the camp until Midge and his trainers returned.

"One o' the boys from *The News,*" said Wallie by way of introduction. "I been givin' him your fam'ly hist'ry."

"Did he give you good dope?" he inquired.

"He's some historian," said Joe.

"Don't call me no names," said Wallie smiling. "Call us up if they's anything more you want. And keep your eyes on us Monday night. Get what I mean?"

The story in Sunday's *News* was read by thousands of lovers of the manly art. It was well written and full of human interest. Its slight inaccuracies went unchallenged, though three readers, besides Wallie Adams and Midge Kelly, saw and recognized them. The three were Grace, Tommy Haley and Jerome Harris and the comments they made were not for publication.

Neither the Mrs. Kelly in Chicago nor the Mrs. Kelly in Milwaukee knew that there was such a paper as the New York *News.* And even if they had known of it and that it contained two columns of reading matter about Midge, neither mother nor wife could have bought it. For *The News* on Sunday is a nickel a copy.

Joe Morgan could have written more accurately, no doubt, if instead of Wallie Adams, he had interviewed Ellen Kelly and Connie Kelly and Emma Kelly and Lou Hersch and Grace and Jerome Harris and Tommy Haley and Hap Collins and two or three Milwaukee bartenders.

But a story built on their evidence would never have passed the sporting editor.

"Suppose you can prove it," that gentleman would have said, "it wouldn't get us anything but abuse to print it. The people don't want to see him knocked. He's champion."

Red Riding Hood

WELL, children, here is the story of little Red Riding Hood like I tell it to my little ones when they wake up in the morning with a headache after a tough night.

Well, one or two times they was a little gal that lived in the suburbs who they called her little Red Riding Hood because she always wore a red riding hood in the hopes that sometime a fresh guy in a high power roadster would pick her up and take her riding. But the rumor had spread the neighborhood that she was a perfectly nice gal, so she had to walk.

Red had a grandmother that lived over near the golf course and got in on most of the parties and one noon she got up and found that they wasn't no gin in the house for her breakfast so she called up her daughter and told her to send Red over with a bottle of gin as she was dying.

So Red starts out with a quart under her arm but had not went far when she met a police dog. A good many people has police dogs, and brags about them and how nice they are for children and etc. but personly I would just as leaf have my kids spend their week-end swimming in the State Shark Hatchery.

Well, this special police dog was like the most of them and hated everybody. When he seen Red he spoke to her and she answered him. Even a dog was better than nothing. She told him where she was going and he pertended like he wasn't paying no tension but no sooner had not she left him when he beat it up a alley and got to her grandmother's joint ahead of her.

Well the old lady heard him knock at the door and told him to come in, as she thought he must either be Red or a bootlegger. So he went in and the old lady was in bed with this hangover and the dog eat her alive.

Then he put on some pajamas and laid down in the bed and pertended like he was her, so pretty soon Red come along and knocked at the door and the dog told her to come in and she went up to the bed to hand him the quart. She thought of course it would be her grandmother laying in the bed and even when she seen the dog she still figured it was her grandmother and something she had drank the night before must of disagreed with her and made her look different.

"Well, grandmother," she says, "you must of hit the old hair tonic last night. Your arms looks like Luis Firpo."

"I will Firpo you in a minute," says the dog.

"But listen grandmother," says Red, "don't you think you ought to have your ears bobbed?"

"I will ear you in a minute," says the dog.

"But listen grandmother," says Red, "you are cock-eyed."

"Listen," says the dog, "if you had of had ½ of what I had last night you would of been stone blind."

"But listen grandmother," says Red, "where did you get the new store teeth?"

"I heard you was a tough egg," says the dog, "so I bought them to eat you with."

So then the dog jumped out of bed and went after Red and she screamed.

In the meanw'ile Red's father had been playing golf for a quarter a hole with a couple of guys that conceded themselfs all putts under 12 ft. and he was $.75 looser coming to the 10th. tee.

The 10th. hole is kind of tough as your drive has to have a carry of 50 yards or it will fall in a garbage incinerating plant. You can either lift out with a penalty of two strokes or else play it with a penalty of suffocation. Red's old man topped his drive and the ball rolled into the garbage. He elected to play it and made what looked like a beautiful shot, but when they got up on the green they found that he had hit a white radish instead of a golf ball.

A long argument followed during which the gallery went home to get his supper. The hole was finely conceded.

The 11th. hole on the course is probably the sportiest hole in golfdom. The tee and green are synonymous and the first shot is a putt, but the rules signify that the putt must be played off a high tee with a driver. Red's father was on in two and off in three more and finely sunk his approach for a birdie eight, squaring the match.

Thus the match was all square coming to the home hole which is right close to grandmother's cottage. Red's father hooked his drive through an open window in his mother-in-law's house and forced his caddy to lend him a niblick. He entered the cottage just as the dog was beginning to eat Red.

"What hole are you playing father?" asked Red.

"The eighteenth," says her father, "and it's a dog's leg."

Whereat he hit the police dog in the leg with his niblick and the dog was so surprised that he even give up the grandmother.

"I win, one up," says Red's father and he went out to tell the news to his two opponents. But they had quit and went home to dress for the Kiwanis Club dance.

ALEXANDER WOOLLCOTT

From Enchanted Aisles

Bernhardt

It was to "pauvre Rachel" that Bernhardt's thoughts flew as her boat pulled away from these shores after her first glittering tour more than forty years ago. A generation before that her forerunner in the French theater had, in a humiliating and grotesquely disastrous tour, found us a less hospitable, less civilized and less understanding land and had known the agony of playing her great scenes of tempest and woe to the whirr and rustle of a thousand turning pages, each head in the audience bent earnestly but disconcertingly over a translation of the play. "Pauvre Rachel" and the "Divine Sarah" are in the same company to-day—the illustrious company that lies in Père Lachaise, the sloping crowded cemetery, marooned now in a dreary part of Paris where elevated trains roar by and there is an unending rattle of trucks and trams on the streets all about.

It had been Bernhardt's plan to lie buried in a tomb cut deep into the seawashed rock of her own Belle Ile, that little, white-edged island which lies just off the ugly port of Saint Nazaire and which, in the morning sunlight, was the first glimpse of France that greeted the soldiers from America who sailed in the first contingent in the half-forgotten excitement of June, 1917. But, in the juggling of her moneys which distracted all her later years, she lost the island, so that, after all, it was to Père Lachaise that Paris carried her. She is in the company not only of Rachel, whose grave is in the older and leafier corner close to the twin tomb of Abélard and Héloise, but in the company, too, of others who, like herself, had had their day in the theater. Talma is there and Molière. Playwrights like De Musset, Beaumarchais, Oscar Wilde and Scribe; painters like Corot, Ingres, Daubigny, Gustave Doré and David. Dr. Hahnemann is there. So is August Comte and Balzac and Marshal Ney and La Fontaine. It is a great troupe—the company of Père Lachaise.

We saw her in her last June. There she sat in her little, cheerful sitting room up in the musty, frowsy, old house in the Boulevard

Pereire, which belongs, they say, to some South American government, but from which, since the day when an infatuated Minister had grandly placed it at her disposal, she had never been ousted. She was resplendent in a dressing gown of white satin with a saucy, fur-edged overjacket of blue Indian silk, and there were blazing rings on the ancient fingers which now and again adjusted the jacket so that there should always be a good view of the scarlet Legion of Honor badge on her breast. It had taken her so many years and so much trouble to get it. Her face was a white mask on which features were painted, but no craft of make-up could have wrought that dazzling smile which lighted the room. Just as in the glory of her early years, she had never suggested youth but seemed an ageless being from some other world, so now, in her seventy-eighth year, it was not easy to remember that she was old.

There she sat, mutilated, sick, bankrupt and, as always, more than a little raffish—a ruin, if you will, but one with a bit of gay bunting fluttering jauntily and defiant from the topmost battlement. There she sat, a gaudy old woman, if you will, with fainter and fainter memories of scandals, ovations, labors, rewards, intrigues, jealousies and heroisms, notoriety and fame, art and the circus. But there was no one in that room so young and so fresh that this great-grandmother did not make her seem colorless. She was nearly fourscore years of age and had just finished a long, harassing season. But she was in no mood to go off to the shore for her rest until she had adjusted her plans for this season. There were young playwrights to encourage with a pat on the head, there were scene designers and costumiers to be directed, there were artists to be interviewed and there was need of some sort of benign intervention in behalf of a new play struggling along in her own theater.

Above all, there were plays to be selected for the following season and, if none appeared, then there were playwrights to be lectured or cajoled into writing them for her. She had one hand on the younger Rostand, son of the finest imagination harnessed by the French theater in half a century, son of the Rostand who had written for her the very play that was halted at the Théâtre Sarah Bernhardt in the Place du Châtelet the night she died. This son of his, surely, could be depended on. And in case he couldn't she had her eye on the younger Guitry. Indeed, she had just had herself carried around to his house and had dazzled him all through luncheon for no other purpose. Out of this was born a project for a play about "Adam and Eve," which Sacha Guitry, reluctant but helpless, forthwith began to write. Bernhardt would play *Eve,* of course, and the elder Guitry, *Adam.* This prospect, at first encounter, seemed alarming and the author was questioned.

Surely, he was not thinking of writing for them the drama of Eden nor blandishing Bernhardt into thinking that she could suggest *Eve* before the Fall.

"I am not a fool," he replied, tartly. "When my play opens, *Eve* is 650 years old."

"And *Adam*?"

"*Adam* is 750 years old."

"But how did you know there was just that difference?"

"He read it," put in Guitry, *père, "dans la Gazette de Milton."*

ALAN SEEGER (1888-1916)

I Have a Rendezvous with Death

I HAVE a rendezvous with Death
At some disputed barricade,
When Spring comes back with rustling shade
And apple-blossoms fill the air—
I have a rendezvous with Death
When Spring brings back blue days and fair.

It may be he shall take my hand
And lead me into his dark land
And close my eyes and quench my breath—
It may be I shall pass him still.
I have a rendezvous with Death
On some scarred slope of battered hill,
When Spring comes round again this year
And the first meadow-flowers appear.

God knows 'twere better to be deep
Pillowed in silk and scented down,
Where Love throbs out in blissful sleep,
Pulse nigh to pulse, and breath to breath,
Where hushed awakenings are dear . . .
But I've a rendezvous with Death
At midnight in some flaming town,
When Spring trips north again this year,
And I to my pledged word am true;
I shall not fail that rendezvous.

HEYWOOD BROUN

The Fifty-First Dragon

OF all the pupils at the knight school Gawaine le Cœur-Hardy was among the least promising. He was tall and sturdy, but his instructors soon discovered that he lacked spirit. He would hide in the woods when the jousting class was called, although his companions and members of the faculty sought to appeal to his better nature by shouting to him to come out and break his neck like a man. Even when they told him that the lances were padded, the horses no more than ponies and the field unusually soft for late autumn, Gawaine refused to grow enthusiastic. The Headmaster and the Assistant Professor of Pleasaunce were discussing the case one spring afternoon and the Assistant Professor could see no remedy but expulsion.

"No," said the Headmaster, as he looked out at the purple hills which ringed the school, "I think I'll train him to slay dragons."

"He might be killed," objected the Assistant Professor.

"So he might," replied the Headmaster brightly, but he added, more soberly, "we must consider the greater good. We are responsible for the formation of this lad's character."

"Are the dragons particularly bad this year?" interrupted the Assistant Professor. This was characteristic. He always seemed restive when the head of the school began to talk ethics and the ideals of the institution.

"I've never known them worse," replied the Headmaster. "Up in the hills to the south last week they killed a number of peasants, two cows and a prize pig. And if this dry spell holds there's no telling when they may start a forest fire simply by breathing around indiscriminately."

"Would any refund on the tuition fee be necessary in case of an accident to young Cœur-Hardy?"

"No," the principal answered, judicially, "that's all covered in the contract. But as a matter of fact he won't be killed. Before I send him up in the hills I'm going to give him a magic word."

"That's a good idea," said the Professor. "Sometimes they work wonders."

From that day on Gawaine specialized in dragons. His course included both theory and practice. In the morning there were long lectures on the history, anatomy, manners and customs of dragons. Gawaine did not distinguish himself in these studies. He had a marvelously versatile gift for forgetting things. In the afternoon he showed to better advantage, for then he would go down to the South Meadow and practice with a battle-ax. In this exercise he was truly impressive, for he had enormous strength as well as speed and grace. He even developed a deceptive display of ferocity. Old alumni say that it was a thrilling sight to see Gawaine charging across the field toward the dummy paper dragon which had been set up for his practice. As he ran he would brandish his axe and shout "A murrain on thee!" or some other vivid bit of campus slang. It never took him more than one stroke to behead the dummy dragon.

Gradually his task was made more difficult. Paper gave way to papier-mâché and finally to wood, but even the toughest of these dummy dragons had no terrors for Gawaine. One sweep of the ax always did the business. There were those who said that when the practice was protracted until dusk and the dragons threw long, fantastic shadows across the meadow Gawaine did not charge so impetuously nor shout so loudly. It is possible there was malice in this charge. At any rate, the

Headmaster decided by the end of June that it was time for the test. Only the night before a dragon had come close to the school grounds and had eaten some of the lettuce from the garden. The faculty decided that Gawaine was ready. They gave him a diploma and a new battle-ax, and the Headmaster summoned him to a private conference.

"Sit down," said the Headmaster. "Have a cigarette."

Gawaine hesitated.

"Oh, I know it's against the rules," said the Headmaster. "But after all, you have received your preliminary degree. You are no longer a boy. You are a man. To-morrow you will go out into the world, the great world of achievement."

Gawaine took a cigarette. The Headmaster offered him a match, but he produced one of his own and began to puff away with a dexterity which quite amazed the principal.

"Here you have learned the theories of life," continued the Headmaster, resuming the thread of his discourse, "but after all, life is not a matter of theories. Life is a matter of facts. It calls on the young and the old alike to face these facts, even though they are hard and sometimes unpleasant. Your problem, for example, is to slay dragons."

"They say that those dragons down in the south wood are five hundred feet long," ventured Gawaine, timorously.

"Stuff and nonsense!" said the Headmaster. "The curate saw one last week from the top of Arthur's Hill. The dragon was sunning himself down in the valley. The curate didn't have an opportunity to look at him very long because he felt it was his duty to hurry back to make a report to me. He said the monster, or shall I say, the big lizard?—wasn't an inch over two hundred feet. But the size has nothing at all to do with it. You'll find the big ones even easier than the little ones. They're far slower on their feet and less aggressive, I'm told. Besides, before you go I'm going to equip you in such fashion that you need have no fear of all the dragons in the world."

"I'd like an enchanted cap," said Gawaine.

"What's that?" answered the Headmaster, testily.

"A cap to make me disappear," explained Gawaine.

The Headmaster laughed indulgently. "You mustn't believe all those old wives' stories," he said. "There isn't any such thing. A cap to make you disappear, indeed! What would you do with it? You haven't even appeared yet. Why, my boy, you could walk from here to London, and nobody would so much as look at you. You're nobody. You couldn't be more invisible than that."

Gawaine seemed dangerously close to a relapse into his old habit of whimpering. The Headmaster reassured him: "Don't worry; I'll give you something much better than an enchanted cap. I'm going to give you a magic word. All you have to do is to repeat this magic charm once and no dragon can possibly harm a hair of your head. You can cut off his head at your leisure."

He took a heavy book from the shelf behind his desk and began to run through it. "Sometimes," he said, "the charm is a whole phrase or even a sentence. I might, for instance, give you 'To make the'— No, that might not do. I think a single word would be best for dragons."

"A short word," suggested Gawaine.

"It can't be too short or it wouldn't be potent. There isn't so much hurry as all that. Here's a splendid magic word: 'Rumplesnitz.' Do you think you can learn that?"

Gawaine tried and in an hour or so he seemed to have the word well in hand. Again and again he interrupted the lesson to inquire, "And if I say 'Rumplesnitz' the dragon can't possibly hurt me?" And always the Headmaster replied, "If you only say 'Rumplesnitz,' you are perfectly safe."

Toward morning Gawaine seemed resigned to his career. At daybreak the Headmaster saw him to the edge of the forest and pointed him to the direction in which he should proceed. About a mile away to the southwest a cloud of steam hovered over an open meadow in the woods and the Headmaster assured Gawaine that under the steam he would find a dragon. Gawaine went forward slowly. He wondered whether it would be best to approach the dragon on the run as he did in his practice in the South Meadow or to walk slowly toward him, shouting "Rumplesnitz" all the way.

The problem was decided for him. No sooner had he come to the fringe of the meadow than the dragon spied him and began to charge. It was a large dragon and yet it seemed decidedly aggressive in spite of the Headmaster's statement to the contrary. As the dragon charged it released huge clouds of hissing steam through its nostrils. It was almost as if a gigantic teapot had gone mad. The dragon came forward so fast and Gawaine was so frightened that he had time to say "Rumplesnitz" only once. As he said it, he swung his battle-ax and off popped the head of the dragon. Gawaine had to admit that it was even easier to kill a real dragon than a wooden one if only you said "Rumplesnitz."

Gawaine brought the ears home and a small section of the tail. His schoolmates and the faculty made much of him, but the Headmaster wisely kept him from being spoiled by insisting that he go on with his work. Every clear day Gawaine rose at dawn and went out to kill dragons. The Headmaster kept him at home when it rained, because he said the woods were damp and unhealthy at such times and that he didn't want the boy to run needless risks. Few good days passed in which Gawaine failed to get a dragon. On one particularly fortunate day he killed three, a husband and wife and a visiting relative. Gradually he developed a technique. Pupils who sometimes watched him from the hilltops a long way off said that he often allowed the dragon to come within a few feet before he said "Rumplesnitz." He came to say it with a mocking sneer. Occasionally he did stunts. Once when an excursion party from London was watching him he went into action with his right hand tied behind his back. The dragon's head came off just as easily.

As Gawaine's record of killings mounted higher the Headmaster found it impossible to keep him completely in hand. He fell into the habit of stealing out at night and engaging in long drinking bouts at the village tavern. It was after such a debauch that he rose a little before dawn one fine August morning and started out after his fiftieth dragon. His head was heavy and his mind sluggish. He was heavy in other respects as well, for he had adopted the somewhat vulgar practice of wearing his medals, ribbons and all, when he went out dragon hunting. The decorations began on his chest and ran all the way down to his abdomen. They must have weighed at least eight pounds.

Gawaine found a dragon in the same meadow where he had killed the first one. It was a fair-sized dragon, but evidently an old one. Its face was wrinkled and Gawaine thought he had never seen so hideous a countenance. Much to the lad's disgust, the monster refused to charge and Gawaine was obliged to walk toward him. He whistled as he went. The dragon regarded him hopelessly, but craftily. Of course it had heard of Gawaine. Even when the lad raised his battle-ax the dragon made no move. It knew that there was no salvation in the quickest thrust of the head, for it had been informed that this hunter was protected by an enchantment. It merely waited, hoping something would turn up. Gawaine raised the battle-axe and suddenly lowered it again. He had grown very pale and he trembled violently. The dragon suspected a trick. "What's the matter?" it asked, with false solicitude.

"I've forgotten the magic word," stammered Gawaine.

"What a pity," said the dragon. "So that was the secret. It doesn't seem quite sporting to me, all this magic stuff, you know. Not cricket, as we used to say when I was a little dragon; but after all, that's a matter of opinion."

Gawaine was so helpless with terror that the dragon's confidence rose immeasurably and it could not resist the temptation to show off a bit.

"Could I possibly be of any assistance?" it asked. "What's the first letter of the magic word?"

"It begins with an 'r,' " said Gawaine weakly.

"Let's see," mused the dragon, "that doesn't tell us much, does it? What sort of a word is this? Is it an epithet, do you think?"

Gawaine could do no more than nod.

"Why, of course," exclaimed the dragon, "reactionary Republican."

Gawaine shook his head.

"Well, then," said the dragon, "we'd better get down to business. Will you surrender?"

With the suggestion of a compromise Gawaine mustered up enough courage to speak.

"What will you do if I surrender?" he asked.

"Why, I'll eat you," said the dragon.

"And if I don't surrender?"

"I'll eat you just the same."

"Then it doesn't mean any difference, does it?" moaned Gawaine.

"It does to me," said the dragon with a smile. "I'd rather you didn't surrender. You'd taste much better if you didn't."

The dragon waited for a long time for Gawaine to ask "Why?" but the boy was too frightened to speak. At last the dragon had to give the explanation without his cue line. "You see," he said, "if you don't surrender you'll taste better because you'll die game."

This was an old and ancient trick of the dragon's. By means of some such quip he was accustomed to paralyze his victims with laughter and then to destroy them. Gawaine was sufficiently paralyzed as it was, but laughter had no part in his helplessness. With the last word of the joke the dragon drew back his head and struck. In that second there flashed into the mind of Gawaine the magic word of "Rumplesnitz," but there was no time to say it. There was time only to strike and, without a word, Gawaine met the onrush of the dragon with a full swing. He put all his back and shoulders into it. The impact was terrific and the head of the dragon flew away almost a hundred yards and landed in a thicket.

Gawaine did not remain frightened very long after the death of the dragon. His mood was one of wonder. He was enormously puzzled. He cut off the ears of the monster almost in a trance. Again and again he thought to himself, "I didn't say 'Rumplesnitz'!" He was sure of that and yet there was no question that he had killed the dragon. In fact, he had never killed one so utterly. Never before had he driven a head for anything like the same distance. Twenty-five yards was perhaps his best previous record. All the way back to the knight school he kept rumbling about in his mind seeking an explanation for what had occurred. He went to the Headmaster immediately and after closing the door told him what had happened. "I didn't say 'Rumplesnitz,'" he explained with great earnestness.

The Headmaster laughed. "I'm glad you've found out," he said. "It makes you ever so much more of a hero. Don't you see that? Now you know that it was you who killed all these dragons and not that foolish little word 'Rumplesnitz.'"

Gawaine frowned. "Then it wasn't a magic word after all?" he asked.

"Of course not," said the Headmaster, "you ought to be too old for such foolishness. There isn't any such thing as a magic word."

"But you told me it was magic," protested Gawaine. "You said it was magic and now you say it isn't."

"It wasn't magic in a literal sense," answered the Headmaster, "but it was much more wonderful than that. The word gave you confidence. It took away your fears. If I hadn't told you that you might have been killed the very first time. It was your battle-ax did the trick."

Gawaine surprised the Headmaster by his attitude. He was obviously distressed by the explanation. He interrupted a long philosophic and ethical discourse by the Headmaster with, "If I hadn't of hit 'em all mighty hard and fast any one of 'em might have crushed me like a, like a—" He fumbled for a word.

"Egg shell," suggested the Headmaster.

"Like a egg shell," assented Gawaine, and he said it many times. All through the evening meal people who sat near him heard him muttering, "Like a egg shell, like a egg shell."

The next day was clear, but Gawaine did not get up at dawn. Indeed, it was almost noon when the Headmaster found him cowering in bed, with the clothes pulled over his head. The principal called the Assistant Professor of Pleasaunce, and together they dragged the boy toward the forest.

"He'll be all right as soon as he gets a couple more dragons under his belt," explained the Headmaster.

The Assistant Professor of Pleasaunce agreed. "It would be a shame to stop such a fine run," he said. "Why, counting that one yesterday, he's killed fifty dragons."

They pushed the boy into a thicket above which hung a meager cloud of steam. It was obviously quite a small dragon. But Gawaine did not come back that night or the next. In fact, he never came back. Some weeks afterward brave spirits from the school explored the thicket, but they could find nothing to remind them of Gawaine except the metal parts of his medals. Even the ribbons had been devoured.

The Headmaster and the Assistant Professor of Pleasaunce agreed that it would be just as well not to tell the school how Gawaine had achieved his record and still less how he came to die. They held that it might have a bad effect on school spirit. Accordingly, Gawaine has lived in the memory of the school as its greatest hero. No visitor succeeds in leaving the building to-day without seeing a great shield which hangs on the wall of the dining hall. Fifty pairs of dragons' ears are mounted upon the shield and underneath in gilt letters is "Gawaine le Cœur-Hardy," followed by the simple inscription, "He killed fifty dragons." The record has never been equalled.

CONRAD AIKEN

And in the Hanging Gardens

AND in the hanging gardens there is rain
From midnight until one, striking the leaves
And bells of flowers, and stroking boles of planes,
And drawing slow arpeggios over pools,
And stretching strings of sound from eaves to ferns.
The princess reads. The knave of diamonds sleeps.
The king is drunk, and flings a golden goblet
Down from the turret window (curtained with rain)
Into the lilacs.

And at one o'clock
The Vulcan under the garden wakes and beats
The gong upon his anvil. Then the rain
Ceases, but gently ceases, dripping still,
And sound of falling water fills the dark
As leaves grow bold and upright, and as eaves
Part with water. The princess turns the page
Beside the candle, and between two braids
Of golden hair. And reads: "From there I went
Northward a journey of four days, and came
To a wild village in the hills, where none
Was living save the vulture and the rat
And one old man who laughed but could not speak.
The roofs were fallen in, the well grown over
With weed. And it was here my father died.
Then eight days further, bearing slightly west,
The cold wind blowing sand against our faces,
The food tasting of sand. And as we stood
By the dry rock that marks the highest point
My brother said: 'Not too late is it yet
To turn, remembering home.' And we were silent
Thinking of home." The princess shuts her eyes
And feels the tears forming beneath her eyelids

And opens them, and tears fall on the page.
The knave of diamonds in the darkened room
Throws off his covers, sleeps, and snores again.
The king goes slowly down the turret stairs
To find the goblet.

And at two o'clock
The Vulcan in his smithy underground,
Under the hanging gardens, where the drip
Of rain among the clematis and ivy
Still falls from sipping flower to purple flower,
Smites twice his anvil, and the murmur comes
Among the roots and vines. The princess reads:
"As I am sick, and cannot write you more,
Nor have not long to live, I give this letter
To him, my brother, who will bear it south
And tell you how I died. Ask how it was,
There in the northern desert, where the grass
Was withered, and the horses, all but one,
Perished—" The princess drops her golden head
Upon the page between her two white arms
And golden braids. The knave of diamonds wakes
And at his window in the darkened room
Watches the lilacs tossing, where the king
Seeks for the goblet.

And at three o'clock
The moon inflames the lilac heads, and thrice
The Vulcan, in his root-bound smithy, clangs
His anvil; and the sounds creep softly up
Among the vines and walls. The moon is round,
Round as a shield above the turret top.
The princess blows her candle out, and weeps
In the pale room, where scent of lilacs comes,
Weeping, with hands across her eyelids, thinking
Of withered grass, withered by sandy wind.
The knave of diamonds, in his darkened room,
Holds in his hands a key, and softly steps
Along the corridor, and slides the key
Into the door that guards her. Meanwhile, slowly,
The king, with raindrops on his beard and hands,
And dripping sleeves, climbs up the turret stairs,
Holding the goblet upright in one hand;
And pauses on the midmost step, to taste
One drop of wine, wherewith wild rain has mixed.

ROBERT CHARLES BENCHLEY

Christmas Afternoon

Done in the Manner, if Not the Spirit, of Dickens

WHAT an afternoon! Mr. Gummidge said that, in his estimation, there never had *been* such an afternoon since the world began, a sentiment which was heartily endorsed by Mrs. Gummidge and all the little

Gummidges, not to mention the relatives who had come over from Jersey for the day.

In the first place, there was the *ennui*. And such *ennui* as it was! A heavy, overpowering *ennui,* such as results from a participation in eight courses of steaming, gravied food, topping off with salted nuts which the little old spinster Gummidge from Oak Hill said she never knew when to stop eating—and true enough she didn't—a dragging, devitalizing *ennui,* which left its victims strewn about the living-room in various attitudes of prostration suggestive of those of the petrified occupants in a newly unearthed Pompeiian dwelling; an *ennui* which carried with it a retinue of yawns, snarls and thinly veiled insults, and which ended in ruptures in the clan spirit serious enough to last throughout the glad new year.

Then there were the toys! Three and a quarter dozen toys to be divided among seven children. Surely enough, you or I might say, to satisfy the little tots. But that would be because we didn't know the tots. In came Baby Lester Gummidge, Lillian's boy, dragging an electric grain-elevator which happened to be the only toy in the entire collection which appealed to little Norman, five-year-old son of Luther, who lived in Rahway. In came curly-headed Effie in frantic and throaty disputation with Arthur, Jr., over the possession of an articulated zebra. In came Everett, bearing a mechanical negro which would no longer dance, owing to a previous forcible feeding, by the baby, of a marshmallow into its only available aperture. In came Fonlansbee, teeth buried in the hand of little Ormond, which bore a popular but battered remnant of what had once been the proud false-bosom of a hussar's uniform. In they all came, one after another, some crying, some snapping, some pulling, some pushing—all appealing to their respective parents for aid in their intra-mural warfare.

And the cigar smoke! Mrs. Gummidge said that she didn't mind the smoke from a good cigarette, but would they mind if she opened the windows for just a minute in order to clear the room of the heavy aroma of used cigars? Mr. Gummidge stoutly maintained that they were good cigars. His brother, George Gummidge, said that he, likewise, would say that they were. At which colloquial sally both the Gummidge brothers laughed testily, thereby breaking the laughter record for the afternoon.

Aunt Libbie, who lived with George, remarked from the dark corner of the room that it seemed just like Sunday to her. An amendment was offered to this statement by the cousin, who was in the insurance business, stating that it was worse than Sunday. Murmurings indicative of as hearty agreement with this sentiment as their lethargy would allow came from the other members of the family circle, causing Mr. Gummidge to suggest a walk in the air to settle their dinner.

And then arose such a chorus of protestations as has seldom been heard. It was too cloudy to walk. It was too raw. It looked like snow. It looked like rain. Luther Gummidge said that he must be starting along home soon, anyway, bringing forth the acid query from Mrs. Gummidge as to whether or not he was bored. Lillian said that she felt a cold coming on, and added that something they had had for dinner must have been undercooked. And so it went, back and forth, forth and back, up and down, and in and out, until Mr. Gummidge's suggestion of a walk in the air was reduced to a tattered impossibility and the entire company glowed with ill-feeling.

In the meantime, we must not forget the children. No one else could. Aunt Libbie said that she didn't think there was anything like children to make a Christmas; to which Uncle Ray, the one with the Masonic fob, said, "No, thank God!" Although Christmas is supposed to be the season of good cheer, you (or I, for that matter) couldn't have told, from listening to the little ones, but what it was the children's Armageddon season, when Nature had decreed that only the fittest should survive, in order that the race might be carried on by the strongest, the most predatory and those possessing the best protective coloring. Although there were constant admonitions to Fonlansbee to "Let Ormond have that whistle now; it's his," and to Arthur, Jr., not to be selfish, but to "give the kiddie-car to Effie; she's smaller than you are," the net result was always that Fonlansbee kept the whistle and Arthur, Jr., rode in permanent, albeit disputed, possession of the kiddie-car. Oh, that we mortals should set ourselves up against the inscrutable workings of Nature!

Hallo! A great deal of commotion! That was Uncle George stumbling over the electric train, which had early in the afternoon ceased to function and which had been left directly across the threshold. A great deal of crying! That was Arthur, Jr., bewailing the destruction of his already useless train, about which he had forgotten until the present moment. A great deal of recrimination! That was Arthur, Sr., and George fixing it up. And finally a great crashing! That was Baby Lester pulling over the tree on top of himself, necessitating the bringing to bear of all of Uncle Ray's knowledge of forestry to extricate him from the wreckage.

And finally Mrs. Gummidge passed the Christmas candy around. Mr. Gummidge afterward admitted that this was a tactical error on the part of his spouse. I no more believe that Mrs. Gummidge thought they wanted that Christmas candy than I believe that she thought they wanted the cold turkey which she later suggested. My opinion is that she wanted to drive them home. At any rate, that is what she succeeded in doing. Such cries as there were of "Ugh! Don't let me see another thing to eat!" and "Take it away!" Then came hurried scramblings in the coat-closet for overshoes. There were the rasping sounds made by cross parents when putting wraps on children. There were insincere exhortations to "come and see us soon" and to "get together for lunch some time." And, finally, there were slammings of doors and the silence of utter exhaustion, while Mrs. Gummidge went about picking up stray sheets of wrapping paper.

And, as Tiny Tim might say in speaking of Christmas afternoon as an institution, "God help us, every one."

FREDERICK LEWIS ALLEN

Wanted: An Income Taximeter

I SEE that Mr. Mellon and his friends in Washington are engaged in their annual sport of lowering the income taxes. This is all right so far as it goes; but if they want to make a real hit with a suffering public, why don't they invent an income-tax blank that can be filled out without the aid of slide-rule, a dictionary, and a staff of learned statisticians? I have just been taking the examination in higher mathematics known as Form 1040, and I speak from a full heart and an aching mind. The moment I saw the paper I knew I was going to flunk.

The beginning of it was comparatively easy, but I didn't let that fool me. In my college days I knew too many fellows who would come out of the examination room groaning that the first question was such a snap that they spent an hour and a half writing on it, and didn't even get to question 7b. So after printing my name and address in beautiful big letters, I started in concisely:

1. Are you a citizen or resident of the United States?

Answer: Both.

2. Is this a joint return of husband and wife?

Answer: I'm doing all the work myself, if that's what you mean.

3. Were you married and living with husband or wife on the last day of your taxable year?

Answer: Yes and no; wife, not husband.

I got this far and stopped. That last question kept running in my mind. *Were you married and living with husband or wife on the last day of your taxable year?* It had a sort of lyrical quality, although the scansion was not quite perfect. It faintly suggested the work of Alfred, Lord Tennyson on an off day. Would I be given extra credit if I caught the spirit of the thing and answered in verse? Perhaps the examiner expected something like this:

Was I married and living with husband or wife
On the last long day of my taxable year?
On the last long day when the old year tarried
I was living with someone to whom I was married

or possibly even this:

You must wake and call me early, call me early, Mellon dear,
To-morrow'll be the happiest time of all the taxable year,
Of all the taxable year, Mellon, the last and merriest day;
I'll be married and living with my wife, and it will certainly pay.

But with the next question came disillusionment. No longer did the bard of the Treasury strum his lyre. He descended from Parnassus to the somber levels of prose and asked, *How many dependent persons (other than husband or wife) under 18 years of age or incapable of self-support because mentally or physically defective were receiving their chief support from you on the last day of your taxable year?*

That fatal day again! Little, thought I, do we realize till long afterwards which are the really significant days. I looked at the instructions. Four hundred dollars apiece for dependents on that day, and I had let the chance slip! Next year I should be prepared. I took my engagement pad, turned to the page for December 30, 1926, and wrote firmly:

"To-morrow is the last day of my taxable year. Have guest room ready for mental and physical defectives."

It was while I was looking at the instructions that I began to realize why so many of our young men are unwilling to get married nowadays. Getting married (or, as the unromantic Mr. Mellon would put it, having a change of status) involves too much mathematics.

"Listen," I cried to my wife, who was reading in the next room, "aren't you glad our status didn't change during the year? I'll bet you can't understand this." And I read from the instructions:

"In case the status of a taxpayer changes during the taxable year, the personal exemption shall be the sum of an amount which bears the same ratio to $1000 as the number of months during which the taxpayer was single bears to 12 months, plus an amount which bears the same ratio to $2500 as the number of months during which the taxpayer was a married person living with husband or wife or was head of a family bears to 12 months."

"What are you reading?" said my wife sleepily. "A bear story? I thought you were figuring out your income tax."

"So I am," said I.

"All I could hear," said she, "was something about bears—singie bears and family bears. Didn't you say family bears to 12 months?"

I looked at the instructions again. "Yes, but—"

"Well," said the voice from the next room, "what do they think we're running—a zoo? Tell them we have no bears; tell them all our bears are more than 12 months old; tell them—Look here, do we get credit for bears or do we have to pay for them? It might come in handy to know in case we're offered one some time. 'A delightful pet,' we could say to our visitors, 'and we get a reduction on our income tax for him. In confidence I may add that he's a family bear, with defective dependents.'"

I gave her up as hopeless and turned swiftly to the section marked INCOME.

For some minutes I worked busily, and the figures flew. I consulted Schedule A, I consulted Instruction 18, I stated nature of income, I explained in Table on page 2. I was away down in Item 3a, trying to decide whether I had claimed exemption during the year, and if so, from what, when my wife wandered in and looked over my shoulder.

"Are you going to claim obsolescence?" said she.

"Why?" I asked.

She pointed to the instructions, and I read, "Enter on line 15 the amount claimed as depreciation by reason of exhaustion, wear and tear, obsolescence or depletion."

"I was thinking of your hat," she went on amiably. "You know—the gray one. That sentence sounds to me like a direct invitation to make a claim on that hat. Only if you do it, you seem to be letting yourself in for a good deal. The very next sentence says, 'If obsolescence is claimed, explain why useful life is less than actual life.' That would seem to call for a short metaphysical essay."

I looked long and hard at the instructions. *Useful life is less than actual life.* "I don't know just what that means," said I, "but I don't like it. It has a cynical sound. Do you think it proper for the Government to circulate a document like this, which may fall into the hands of the young? Think of the young men—minors having a net income of $1000 or $2500, according to the marital status, or a gross income of $5000—who may read this and go about saying hopelessly to one another, 'It's true, it's true, as we feared. There is no Santa Claus, and useful life is less than actual life.' Here is the Collector of Internal Revenue, who only a little while ago was writing poems about living with husband or wife, practically admitting that the whole thing is a miserable farce. 'Why go on with it any longer?' he seems to imply. 'Why not become a decedent, and let your executors or administrators make returns for you on Form 1040 or 1040A?'"

"Something ought to be done about it," agreed my wife. "You might write to Mr. Mellon. But meanwhile don't forget your hat."

It was days and days later in the taxable year when I finished my ordeal of additions, explanations, deductions, and computations and, sitting in the midst of a perfect snowdrift of scratch-paper, feebly set down the last item of all—BALANCE OF TAX. It wasn't very big, that last item; the newspapers will not itch to publish it; but by the time I reached it the words in the tax-return which had come to have the most vivid meaning to me were exhaustion and depletion. Oh, Mr. Mellon, why must you make things so complicated for us? Why don't you just ask us how much money we have made during the year and tell us what to divide it by, and ask us whether we had rather pay in advance or have it put on next month's bill?

JOHN GALLISHAW

Show Him Some Signs

THE cause, indirectly, was the kindliness of "Peter." That was the name we called him behind his back. He was the Headmaster, and in charge of the Sixth School at St. Patrick's Hall. We loved Peter, a tall, wiry Irishman in his early fifties. He was grey-haired, ascetic, and grimly sarcastic, yet so kindly that he always regretted his sarcasms the moment he uttered them, following them with a stricken, "God forgive me; my tongue ran away with me." I discovered his weakness early and played on his feelings; I could always avoid a beating at the hands of Peter by a torrent of weeping. At the first sign of tears, Peter would release me, saying, "He's so high-spirited that he can't bear to be punished; the rough side of my tongue will be punishment enough. God forgive me." I know not how many punishments I escaped thus—from Peter. But I aroused the envy of the less histrionically gifted, who whispered that I was "teacher's pet." The chastisement I escaped at the hands of the master I suffered at the hands of my fellow-pupils.

When I entered the Sixth School, I was a rather timid, sensitive boy of fourteen, much afraid of physical punishment. Although I could play a good game of hockey, or of "soccer" football, I usually chose the goaltender's position because that called for little actual tussling and physical struggle. I tried to avoid fist-fights; but no matter how much I tried, they were always forced upon me. Always, I was beaten. Because my heart was not in them, I submitted, took my punishment, and escaped. Yet the necessity for fighting always pursued me. All the boys I knew fought. We went in "crowds"; each neighborhood had its "crowd," formed as the adherents of some boy who had a redoubtable reputation as a fighter. This boy usually stimulated his followers to action; and when no better opportunity offered, fostered quarrels between members of his own crowd. The fights were nearly always begun with the same procedure. The bystanders, having stung the opposing boys to a willingness for action, placed a small stone or piece of wood on the shoulder of one, and said to his rival: "Knock it off." Once the stone was knocked off, the two opponents eyed each other, each striving by glares to intimidate his adversary. To one, the promoter of the fight said, "Say 'duff." This pregnant word being uttered, the promoter said to the other gladiator, "Give him a curly puff." The "curly puff" was a slight blow upon the chest or arm: never upon a vulnerable spot. It was a sort of sighting shot, a mere preliminary. Once the "curly puff" was delivered, the fighters were free to use such methods as they wished or could: kicking and biting were barred by the spectators; the object was for one boy to secure an arm hold around his adversary's neck with his left hand; then with his opponent's head in firm chancery, he "punched" with his right hand at the other's nose, stopping between each punch to ask, "Are you bet?" At the acknowledgment that a boy was "bet," he was released; the fight was over. When a newcomer came to the neighborhood, it was customary for him to establish himself by fighting some member of the crowd; usually I was selected. Every member of the "crowd" had at one time or another received my speedy acknowledgment that I was "bet."

When I was fourteen, however, I underwent a change. I grew up, as it were, over night, into a very tall, very wiry boy, with a smooth, girlish face which deceived many people as to my strength. I was very strong; and a good wrestler. Up till then I had submitted to defeat because I had no gusto for fighting, and no pride. Fighting bored me; and I didn't mind in the least being thought a poor fighter. I agreed with the verdict. But when I was fourteen, a new boy came into our crowd. It was in the winter-time; and we had been playing hockey on

Quidi Vidi Lake. The post-mortem laid the blame for our defeat upon me; the loudest in his denunciations being the newcomer. Ordinarily, I should have listened unmoved; but this new boy was the son of one of the newer pilots whom I had heard my father talk of rather disparagingly. Tribal pride rose in me; our family had been granted the original pilotage privilege for the port of St. John's, Newfoundland. For the first time I knew what real anger was. I challenged the new boy. He was shorter than I, but stockier. He said that he would fight me as soon as he took off his skates. My blood was up, and I retorted that I could fight him just as well on skates as off. There were no preliminaries; no chip on the shoulder; no "curly puff." I skated over; I struck him; he fell, rose to his feet, and we clinched. Locked in each other's arms we fought, rolling on the ice. I felt as a young bull must feel on finding unsuspected strength; fought with a passionate joy and with red hate. I had to be dragged away. A day or two later, we renewed the combat; again I won. Thereafter I actually liked fighting; joyed in it; sought it. I began with my own crowd, and went from them to the boys who at some time or another had beaten me.

I fought on the way to school; in school recess; on the way home from school; and often fought twice in the afternoon. I fought a redoubtable hero named "Brandy Nose," a great bully who had made my life miserable. In general, I have found that the common belief that all bullies are cowards has little foundation in fact. Between the roistering, swaggering, husky bully and the quiet little man in the corner, I prefer to take my chance with the quiet little man in the corner. "Brandy Nose" was certainly no coward. Although I conquered him, it was a near thing. I remember that we climbed the fence of the grounds surrounding Government House; and in a secluded spot where the snow had melted—it was just becoming Spring—we fought by rounds. We wore gloves; not boxing gloves, but regular winter gloves. A referee examined them solemnly, and although he appeared rather doubtful about the seams of my gloves, he at last pronounced them satisfactory. Each had his second; each had his group of adherents, who exhorted their champion to "show him some signs." They meant "science." I showed sufficient "signs" to win. "Brandy Nose" left his mark upon me; my face was cut; my nose was bleeding; I explained it at home by saying that in passing a furniture store on Water Street I had bumped into a chair which was hanging outside.

The formality of this fight was the reaction of boyhood to the great wave of interest in boxing that swept the island of Newfoundland that year. A local champion had arisen; had defeated opponent after opponent; and finally had been induced to meet the champion of the British North American Fleet at the Prince of Wales' Rink in St. John's. Every boy in St. John's wanted to go; every boy in St. John's was forbidden to go; every boy in St. John's determined to go, permission or no permission. To counteract the evil influence, Peter devised an entertainment: an operetta, which ran for three evenings, including the evening of the prize-fight. I was cast for a part: a waiting maid to the princess, in which I wore a white dress, white shoes and stockings, and a wreath. I made a very demure young maid; I had a few lines; they were fairly important. I have forgotten them now, but I remember that the house approved. The first night I received applause; the second night it was redoubled; for the news had spread that the part was being done by a boy. The third night was the night of the prize-fight. I came home early that afternoon, despondent; for I knew that most of the "crowd" were planning to go to the fight, starting from home, ostensibly for the operetta. I knew that, even if I had no conflicting engagement, I could not go, because I had only ten cents, whereas the admission to the fight was fifty cents. There was nobody at home; I wandered, disconsolate, over the house; and came at last to my mother's bedroom. On the dresser was a lacquered box, filled with small trinkets. For a moment I had a wild idea of selling these, as I had read that people did, in novels. But I knew of no place that would buy them. I figured them, looking them over curiously, lifting them from the box. Suddenly my curiosity changed to interest; at the bottom of the box lay some coins. I seized them, eagerly at first, later with a growing sense of disappointment; they were foreign coins, which my father had gathered on many voyages. Some there were, however, which I thought looked enough like our own coinage to pass for it; these I selected, replacing the rest.

That evening I went to the theatre, appeared in the dressing-room, said something about being very sick, disappeared, and ran, as fast as my legs could carry me, to the Prince's Rink. There was consternation, I was told later, when I did not appear; they flattered me by telling me that it spoiled the show. While they were searching, I was at the Rink, forcing piastres upon the man at the ticket window. A burly man came along while I was thus engaged, and recognized me. He took the foreign coins, and paid my way in. As I sat beside him, he questioned me. For a wonder, I did not lie; I confessed everything. He swore he would not tell my father; he returned the coins; we were great chums throughout the evening.

I shall never forget that first prize-fight: the great overhead lights glaring bluish-white upon the mob, close-packed on the benches, the odor of wet clothes steaming dry, of pine sawdust on the floor, of tobacco smoke from many loaded pipes, mingled in one heady aroma. Our man was Mike Shallow, a former boiler-maker; the navy man was "Gunner" Somebody. The fighters came into the ring, big men, white-fleshed; the Gunner wearing black trunks. The crowd gave a great roar of delight when Mike Shallow took off his dressing-gown, disclosing a silk belt of pink-white-and-green, the Newfoundland national colors. A brass band struck up the National Anthem. The burly man hummed it:

> The Pink the Rose of England shows,
> The Green, St. Patrick's emblem bright,
> Whilst in between, the spotless sheen
> Of Andrew's Cross, displays the White.
>
> Then hail the Pink, the White, the Green
> Our patriot flag, long may it stand;
> Long may it sway o'er bight and bay,
> Around the shores of Newfoundland!

There was a British warship in port. From the side of the rink opposite us, the navy men shouted encouragement: "Now, Gunner, put 'im across the road; show 'im wot for, Gunner"; to which our people retorted, "Knock his block off, Mike." The burly man beside me seemed a little disappointed at first, because Mike Shallow's legs were so thin; but he became reassured on observing the huge torso of the boiler-maker. When Mike Shallow squared off, and began sparring with his left hand, and using his right hand to guard, the burly man confided to me, "Nobody has ever felt the weight of his right hand; they tell me that he hit a bull once on the forehead with his right hand"—the burly man now leaned closer—"and *killed* the bull." Once, later, when the Gunner landed a smashing blow on our champion's face, the burly man leaned toward me, and said: "I hope that Gunner don't make Mike mad; because if he does, there's likely to be murder done, if Mike uses his right hand." Once Mike did use his right hand; the Gunner tottered; and the burly man beside me leaped to his feet, and shrieked, "Don't kill him, Mike." The crowd took up the cry, misinterpreting it; and shouted, "Kill him, Mike! Kill him, Mike!" The sailors encouraged their man; we encouraged Mike. Mike won; I think he was spurred to action by the shouts, "Show him some Science." The most enthusiastic of all his supporters was I, who shouted until I was hoarse, "Show him some signs, Mike; show him some signs!"

The burly man never told; I returned the piastres. In the dressing rooms at St. Patrick's Hall, people remembered that I had complained of feeling sick. I have never had much feeling of guilt. I lay the blame at the door of Peter's kindliness, which led me to fight in self-defense.

S. FOSTER DAMON

A Woman

HATED she lived, a house apart,
For in the window stood her heart,
A vase to hold whatever flower
Would please her for a single hour.

Always it held a rich bouquet
Of blossoms proud to meet the day;
And as each faded in the vase,
Gently she drew it from its place
To hide the petals in a book
Wherein no one might ever look.

At last the autumn came, but still
New blossoms graced her window-sill;
And she would pause beside her door
To gather proudly yet one more.

Until one dusk, as I passed by,
No square of lamplight met my eye,
While on the sill, the vase was crossed
With fragile patterns of the frost,
For she had moved from her stronghold.
The house surrendered to the cold.
But the chill vase yet held in bloom
Flowers which scented the still room,
With one bud, petals half astir
In memory of the traveller.

ROBERT SILLIMAN HILLYER

Nocturne

I FELT the wind on my cheek
And I awoke.
The night had come.
Out of the dark spoke
The flowing creek,—
All else was dumb.

My clothes were wet with dew,
My hands were caked with mud,
But the thought of you
Was a brazier to my blood.
And groping home
Through walls of black
I sang, "O never come,
Never come back!"

So long estranged, and now
So eloquently near
In the wind fanning my brow,
In the water singing clear,
Even in the vast black
And the valley lying dumb,—

O never come!
Never come back!

Moo!

SUMMER is over, the old cow said,
And they'll shut me up in a draughty shed
To milk me by lamplight in the cold,
But I won't give much, for I am old.
It's long ago that I came here
Gay and slim as a woodland deer;
It's long ago that I heard the roar
Of Smith's white bull by the sycamore.
And now there are bones where my flesh
should be;
My backbone sags like an old roof-tree,
And an apple snatched in a moment's
frolic
Is just so many days of colic.
I'm neither a Jersey nor Holstein now
But only a faded sort of cow.
My calves are veal and I had as lief
That I could lay me down as beef;
Somehow, they always kill by halves,—
Why not take me when they take my
calves?

Birch turns yellow and sumac red,
I've seen this all before, she said,
I'm tired of the field and tired of the shed.
There's no more grass, there's no more
clover;
Summer is over, summer is over.

GRANT HYDE CODE

Poppies and Lilies

SEVEN scarlet poppies
Like seven deadly pleasures
Clink their goblets.

Seven ballerinas
Stand in the green-room
Waiting for music.

Seven pretty girls
Shake with laughter.

Seven giddy ladies
Sway on pale green legs.

The prim yellow lilies
Like seven deadly virtues
Stand apart seriously
Without conversation.

Each sips the sunlight
In a thin yellow wineglass,
Pretending not to like it.

Each takes the sunlight
Just as a cordial
Against the spring dampness.

DAVID WATSON McCORD

The Philosophy of Ceilings

IT is about time that something was said on the general subject of ceilings. Hour after hour, as a child, I lay in quiet and profound contemplation of a number of them, for they were practically the only thing that I could view continually with any degree of composure. They never annoyed. Their uniform blankness was one with my state of mind. I cannot say now with any certainty how much those ancient plaster surfaces influenced my early life. A great deal, though, I expect.

I remember one in particular. It supplied the top to my nursery. Right above my crib appeared a curious combination of two or three cracks and a large water-stain dating back to a Saturday night when Delia overdid it in the bath on the floor above; a beautiful calcimine creation with four humps and prominent elbows, trekking across a fly-specked desert. It was a good thing, in its way, and diurnally came in for a bit of solid contemplation. To-day, no doubt, I should call it a camel, but at that period of my interesting life camels were wholly unknown. I had never been to Arabia or Ringling, nor was I permitted to indulge in the æsthetic and gastronomic delights of animal crackers. Practically speaking, I had no teeth.

Dimly associated with my yellowing friend is a less important stain. In the light of modern science I should suppose it to have been a spot of casual gravy, but at the time I accepted it as a part of the Eternal

Pattern of things, especially ceilings, and immediately adjusted it in my memory as a rather creditable if malicious face. I can still recall it. How dreadful it was! It used to leer at me over my bottle, and had a nasty habit of forming the basis of the most horrible nightmares whenever the old digestion decreed a slack day. It seems incredible that I should remember so much of a season when I was scarce a year old. But who can disprove me? When the memory is cross-examined for the real facts of our childhood there is a delicious backsliding and a fine conflux of years. I find it quite as easy to pull up recollections of the so-called bottle era as of the most ambitious college days. Easier in fact. . . . When I was three the ceiling was redone; and the presence, along with him of the several humps, passed damply away under the glistening swaths of the calcimine brush.

We pay a lot of attention to our hats. And yet they cover only one head at a time. A ceiling, on the other hand, simultaneously covers several (without imposing the least restriction on anybody), and often a lot of atrocious furniture as well. But who cares about it? A ceiling is no more to us than a necessary partition in space. Necessary to keep the feet of the fellow higher up from treading on our ears, and (once) a kind of buffer and free target for champagne corks. Who (I repeat), beyond babies, cares for ceilings? Not the artist. The nearer his picture comes to being skied the madder he is. Not the advertiser. Visually (but not otherwise) he will meet you on the level. And not you; and not I.

For my part, I have always felt that ceilings were made, more than anything else, to exhibit the strange capacity of the fly to walk upside down. Before there were any ceilings where did the common house-fly obtain that exquisite exercise which keeps him fit to dash round the rim of the cream pitcher and explore the difficult area of Uncle Arthur's whiskers? I confess I do not know. But as things stand now, ceilings are the proving ground of flies. Squads of them may be observed there any hot, June morning, manœuvring about in great solemnity; learning new tricks, I dare say, practicing approach shots for the jam pot, and the proper cadence for use on a bald head. The ceiling is also their refuge, and a wounded or disappointed fly will seek it quicker than the flypaper. He seems assured that none will pursue him there. And certainly I shall be the very last to do it. Almost anything in its proper place is an *ornament.* A bear in his den, a foot in a shoe, a fly on the ceiling, for example.

Of course, some ceilings are more attractive than others. Italian ceilings are situated somewhere up in the vicinity of the clouds, and by their mysterious isolation inveigle us into looking at them. I have often tried, but with only partial success. When the opportunity comes I shall visit an Italian villa I know, steal softly up the stairs, and saw a nice hole through the floor of the guest chamber. Then I shall stick my head through it and have a long look at an honest-to-glory Italian ceiling. I see no other way. Of course, too, there is "the vault of heaven," and "the canopy of stars," and all that sort of natural covering which the poets talk about. No one is fonder than I of a good, cheerful summer sky, if my hay fever isn't too bad and I can find a white duck hat round the house that will fit me; nor of a starry night, for that matter, if you'll stick to the main road. But I was speaking, rather, of the artificial ceiling, such as King Alfred sat under; the common sort, that has for centuries covered impartially emperor and clown. There's the one in the kitchen. Nobody in his right mind, to be sure, would look twice at that. But consider the one in the bathroom, which is no more than one-tenth the size. That is the one ceiling in the whole house with which I am quite familiar. Lying in a temperate bath, I have made a study of it. I have played (mentally) a game of chess on it; and once, when I was younger, I hit it with a wet sponge, trying to kill a mosquito. I missed him.

Public places have the decorative instinct toward ceilings. You have surely noticed it. The dome of the Grand Central Station in New York is simply littered with stars of various magnitudes and lively representations of the Olympus family in striking poses—all in all, one of the most satisfactory blue-prints of the heavens I have ever seen. The motive there is a simple one. It is the generous desire of the officials to make the traveller perfectly at home with the universe, so that a small journey in upper five (and porter, call me early!) to Chicago will seem like nothing at all. Or relatively nothing. And there are the hotels. I have seen hotel ceilings (in the dining rooms especially) so incrusted with cupids and cherubs and Rubens-like damsels reclining heavily on thin air that I have buried my face in the soup in sheer confusion. Not for the world, in some places I know, would I turn my eyes aloft. *"Look up, not down."* Poppycock. A good wall is enough for me. My crib days are over. If there is something to be seen, don't hang it over my head like a sword of Damocles. Put it where I can view it face to face. Even the Bible will bear me out in this. Belshazzar saw the writing on the wall, not on the ceiling. You don't want a stiff neck, do you? No? Well, neither do I.

INDEXES

INDEX OF AUTHORS

TRANSLATIONS AND ENGLISH SELECTIONS

INDEX OF FIRST LINES

TRANSLATIONS AND ENGLISH SELECTIONS

INDEX OF TITLES

TRANSLATIONS AND ENGLISH SELECTIONS

INDEX OF AUTHORS

AMERICAN SELECTIONS

INDEX OF FIRST LINES

AMERICAN SECTION

INDEX OF TITLES